TWELFTH EDITION

SCHROEDER'S
ANTIQUES
PRICE GUIDE

Edited by Sharon & Bob Huxford

COLLECTOR BOOKS
A Division of Schroeder Publishing Co., Inc.

The current values in this book should be used only as a guide. They are not intended to set prices, which vary from one section of the country to another. Auction prices as well as dealer prices vary greatly and are affected by condition as well as demand. Neither the Editors nor the Publisher assumes responsibility for any losses that might be incurred as a result of consulting this guide.

Searching For A Publisher?

We are always looking for knowledgable people considered experts within their fields. If you feel that there is a real need for a book on your collectible subject and have a large comprehensive collection, please contact us.

COLLECTOR BOOKS
P.O. Box 3009
Paducah, Kentucky 42002-3009

Introduction

As the editors and staff of *Schroeder's*, our goal is to compile the most useful, comprehensive, and accurate background and pricing information possible. Our guide encompasses nearly seven hundred categories, many of which you will not find in other price guides. Our sources are varied; we use auction results, dealer lists and trade paper ads, and we consult with national collectors' clubs, recognized authorities, researchers, and appraisers. We have by far the largest Advisory Board of any similar publication on the market. Each year we add several new advisors and now have nearly 350 who cover almost 500 categories. They go over our computer printouts line by line, deleting listings that are misleading or too vague to be of merit; they often send background information and photos. We appreciate their assistance very much. Only through their expertise and experience in their special fields are we able to offer with confidence what we feel are useful, accurate evaluations that provide a sound understanding of the dealings in the market place today. Correspondence with so large an advisory panel adds months of extra work to an already monumental task, but we feel that to a very large extent this is the foundation that makes *Schroeder's* the success that it has become.

Our Directory, which you will find in the back of the book, lists each contributor by state. These are people who have allowed us to photograph various examples of merchandise from their show booths, sent us pricing information, or in any way have contributed to this year's book. If you happen to be traveling, consult the Directory for shops along your way. We also list clubs who have worked with us and auction houses who have agreed to permit us the use of photographs from their catalogs.

Our Advisory Board lists only names and home states, so check the Directory for addresses and telephone numbers should you want to correspond with one of our experts. Remember, when you do, *always* enclose a self-addressed, stamped envelope (SASE). Thousands of people buy our guide, and hundreds contact our advisors. The only agreement we have with our advisors is that they edit their categories. They are in no way obligated to answer mail. Some are dealers who do many shows a month. The time they spend at home may be very limited, and they may not be open to contacts. There's no doubt that the reason behind the success of our book is their assistance. We regret seeing them becoming more and more burdened by phone and mail inquiries. We have lost some of our good advisors for this reason, and when we do, the book suffers, and, consequently so do our readers. Many of our listed reference sources report that they constantly receive long distance calls at all hours that are really valuation requests. If they are registered appraisers, they make their living at providing such information and expect a fee for their service and expertise.

If you find you need more information than *Schroeder's* provides, there are other sources available to you. Go to your local library; check their section on reference books. Museums are public facilities that are willing and able to help you establish the origin and possibly even the value of your particular treasure. Check the yellow pages of your phone book. Other cities' phone books are available from either your library or from the telephone company office. Look under the heading *Antique Dealers*. Those who are qualified appraisers will mention this credit in their advertisement. But remember that if you sell to a dealer, he will expect to buy your merchandise at a price low enough that he will be able to make an appreciable profit when he sells it. Once you decide to contact one of these appraisers, unless you intend to see them directly, you'll need to get photographs. Don't send photos that are under or over exposed, out of focus, or shot against a background that detracts from important details you want to emphasize. It is almost impossible for them to give you a value judgment on items they've not seen when your photos are of poor quality. Shoot the front, top, and the bottom; describe any marks and numbers (or send a pencil rubbing), explain how and when you acquired the article, and give accurate measurements and any further background information that may be helpful.

The auction houses listed in the Directory nearly all have a staff of appraisal experts. If the item you're attempting to research is of the calibre of material they deal with, they can offer extremely accurate evaluations. Of course, most have a fee. Be sure to send them only professional-quality photographs. Tell them if you expect to consign your item to their auction. If you disagree with the value they suggest, you are under no obligation to do so.

Nearly five hundred categories are included in our book. We have organized our topics alphabetically, following the most simple logic, usually either by manufacturer or by type of product. If you have difficulty in locating your subject, consult the index. Our guide is unique in that much more space has been allotted to background information than any other publication of this type, and it is easier to read due to the larger-than-average print. Our readers tell us that these are features they enjoy. To be able to do this, we have adopted a format of one-line listings wherein we describe the items to the fullest extent possible by using several common-sense abbreviations; they will be easy to read and understand if you will first take the time to quickly scan through them.

The Editors

Editorial Staff

Editors
Sharon and Bob Huxford

Research and Editorial Assistants
Michael Drollinger, Nancy Drollinger, Linda Holycross, Donna Newnum, Susie McCann, Loretta Woodrow

---

On the cover, clockwise from left:

Chocolate Pot, 9½", Mold 644, Winter portrait with blue highlights, heavy gold work on scrolled designs, glossy finish, $3,000.00-3,500.00. Courtesy of *Collector's Encyclopedia of R.S. Prussia, Third Series*, by Mary Frank Gaston.

Fire-King Philbe Cookie Jar w/cover, $950.00. Courtesy of *Collector's Encyclopedia of Depression Glass, 9th Edition*, by Gene Florence.

Judy Garland Doll, 21", body from Deanna Durbin, $500.00. Courtesy of *Ideal Dolls* by Judith Izen. Photo by Charles Backus.

Fancy Mirror, 6'3"x4', 1970s, not company authorized, decorator value. Courtesy of *Goldstein's Coca-Cola Collectibles* by Shelly Goldstein.

Compact, Houbigant – translucid face powder box, 3⅝"x1½", 1941, $45.00-60.00. Courtesy of *Collector's Encyclopedia of Compacts, Face Powder & Carryalls* by Laura Mueller.

Listing of Standard Abbreviations

The following is a list of abbreviations that have been used throughout this book in order to provide you with the most detailed descriptions possible in the limited space available. No periods are used after initials or abbreviations. When two dimensions are given, height is noted first. If only one dimension is listed, it will be height, except in the case of bowls, dishes, plates, or round platters, when it will be diameter. The standard two-letter state abbreviations apply.

For glassware, if no color is noted, the glass is clear. Hyphenated colors, for example blue-green, olive-amber, etc., describe a single color tone; colors divided by a slash mark indicate two or more colors, i.e. blue/white. A number following the last comma in a listing indicates how many items are included in the lot price. Teapots, sugar bowls, and butter dishes are assumed to be 'with cover.' Condition is extremely important in determining market value. Common sense suggests that art pottery, china, and glassware values would be given for examples in pristine, mint condition, while suggested prices for utility wares such as Redware, Mocha, and Blue and White Stoneware, for example, reflect the probability that since such items were subjected to everyday use in the home they may show minor wear (which is acceptable) but no notable damage. Values for other categories reflect the best average condition in which the particular collectible is apt to be offered for sale without the dealer feeling it necessary to mention wear or damage. For instance, advertising items are assumed to be in excellent condition since mint items are scarce enough that when one is offered for sale the dealer will most likely make mention of that fact. The same holds true for Toys, Banks, Coin-Operated Machines, and the like. A basic rule of thumb is that an item listed as VG (very good) will bring 40% to 60% of its mint price (a first-hand, personal evaluation will enable you to make the final judgment); EX (excellent) is a condition midway between mint and very good, and values would correspond.

Am ....American	dbl ....double	litho ....lithograph	rpl ....replaced
appl ....applied	dvtl ....dovetail	mahog ....mahogany	rstr ....restored
att ....attributed to	drw ....drawer	mk ....mark	rtcl ....reticulated
bbl ....barrel	emb ....embossed, embossing	MIG ....Made in Germany	rvpt ....reverse painted
bk ....back	embr ....embroidered	M ....mint	rnd ....round
bsk ....bisque	eng ...engraved, engraving	MIB ....mint in box	s&p ....salt and pepper
blk ....black	etch ....etched, etching	MOP ....mother-of-pearl	sgn ....signed
b3m ....blown 3-mold	EX ....excellent	mt, mtd ....mount, mounted	SP ....silverplated
bl ....blue	ft, ftd ....foot, feet, footed	mc ....multicolor	sz ....size
brn ....brown	fr ....frame, framed	NE ....New England	sq ....square
bulb ....bulbous	Fr ....French	NM ....near mint	std ....standard
can ....canister	G ....good	NP ....nickel plated	str ....straight
cb ....cardboard	grad ....graduated	opal ....opalescent	T'print ....Thumbprint
CI ....cast iron	grpt ....grain painted	orig ....original	trn ....turned, turning
C ....century	gr ....green	o/l ....overlay	turq ....turquoise
ca ....circa	HP ....hand painted	o/w ....otherwise	uphl ....upholstered
compo ....composition	hdl, hdld ....handle, handled	pnt ....paint	VG ....very good
c ....copyright	illus ....illustration, illustrated by	Pat ....patented	Vict ....Victorian
cr/sug ....creamer and sugar	imp ....impressed	ped ....pedestal	wht ....white
X, Xd ....cross, crossed	ind ....individual	pc ....piece	W ....width
c/s ....cup and saucer	int ....interior	pk ....pink	w/ ....with
cvd ....carved	irid ....iridescent	prof ....professional	w/o ....without
cvg ....carving	Invt ....Inverted	porc ....porcelain	yel ....yellow
dk ....dark	lav ....lavender	rfn ....refinished	(+) ....has been reproduced
dtd ....dated	ldgl ....leaded glass	re ....regarding	
decor ....decoration	L ....length, long	rpt ....repainted	
Dmn Quilt ..Diamond Quilted	lt ....light	rpr ....repaired	

A B C Plates

Children's plates featuring the alphabet as part of the design were popular from as early as 1820 until after the turn of the century. The earliest English creamware plates were decorated with embossed letters and prim moralistic verses; but the later Staffordshire products were conducive to a more relaxed mealtime atmosphere, often depicting playful animals and riddles or scenes of pleasant leisure-time activities. They were made around the turn of the century by American potters as well. All featured transfer prints, but color was sometimes brushed on by hand to add interest to the design. Braille plates were made for the blind, but these are rather scarce and, therefore, usually more valuable. You may also find an occasional bowl or mug.

Ceramic

At the Seaside, Roman numerals, ABC rim, bl transfer, 7½" 45.00
Blind Girl, bl transfer, Staffordshire, 6" 145.00
Boy & marbles, bl transfer, Staffordshire, 5½" 195.00
Boy in cart, red transfer, Staffordshire, 7" 150.00
Boy w/guitar, bird on fence, mc transfer, 7¾" 120.00

At the Seaside, Roman numerals around the rim, blue on white, 7½", $45.00.

Commander AH Foote, bl transfer, Staffordshire, 5⅛", EX 225.00
Couple working in fields, blk transfer w/mc, 5", EX 55.00
Cup & saucer, rooster & chicks, Germany 85.00
Experience Keeps a Dear School, beaded ABC rim, 5⅛" 125.00
For Age & Want Save While You May..., Staffordshire, 7½" 140.00
General Halleck, bl transfer, Staffordshire, 5⅛" 275.00
General Windfield Scott, bl transfer, Staffordshire, 6⅛" 395.00
Gleaners, bl transfer, Staffordshire, 6" 145.00
Harry Fishing & poem, bl transfer, Staffordshire, 6" 165.00
Keep Thy Shop & Thy Shop Will Keep Thee 75.00

Major General QA Gillmore, bl transfer, Staffordshire, 5⅛" 295.00
Major General US Grant, bl transfer, Staffordshire, 5⅛" 395.00
Mary Had a Little Lamb, 8" 130.00
Mother & Daughter, Dear to Each...., mc/blk transfer, 7" 135.00
Mug, Crusoe Teaching Friday, mc transfer 150.00
Now I Have a Cow, bead & ABC rim, Franklin Maxim, 5⅛" 110.00
Now I Have a Sheep, Franklin Proverb, 5¾" 150.00
Old man & child carry donkey across bridge, mc transfer, 7¼" 85.00
Old Mother Hubbard, brn transfer, mk Tunstall, 7⅜" 200.00
Rugby players, unmk 90.00
Sign language ABCs, tea party, red transfer, 6½", EX 165.00
Sign language in ABCs, bunnies in stylish dress, Ansley, 8" 135.00
Sioux Indian Chief, brn transfer, 7½" 135.00
These Children Trying Are You See, blk transfer, 5½", EX 45.00
Tulip & Butterfly, girl & boy, blk transfer/mc, Meakin, 5½" 85.00
Village Blacksmith, colored transfer on beige 75.00
Young Artist, Frolics of Youth series, ABC rim, 7¼" 100.00
3 cats, blk transfer, bl rim, 6", EX 90.00

Glass

ABC rim, souvenir Greenville OH, milk glass 125.00
Boy's portrait (also called Emma), bl, clear or amber, 6½" 28.00
Cane, basketweave center, 6" 30.00
Chicken in barnyard, brick wall background, ABC rim, 6" 75.00
Christmas Eve, Santa climbing down chimney, stippled rim, 6"..175.00
Dog's head, ABC rim, New Martinsville #532, 6½" (+) 28.00

Elephant with Howdah and Riders, 6", $70.00.

Flower bouquet, frosted flowers, 6" 50.00
Flying stork in center, marigold carnival 65.00
Garfield, ABC rim 95.00
Old Independence Hall, stippled ABCs, scalloped rim, 7" 95.00
Proud Dog, ABC rim 38.00
Quilted center, ABCs & numbers on stippled ground 95.00
Rabbit & alphabet, att Crystal Glass Co, 6" 50.00

Rabbit in grass, house behind 65.00
Stork, ABC rim, 6" 58.00
1000 Eye, clock center, amber, 6" 65.00

Tin

Cat playing w/yarn, sm 45.00
Cup, For a Good Boy, orig yel pnt 65.00
Hey Diddle Diddle, cow/cat/dog/fork/spoon, 8" 85.00
Jumbo, 5½" 100.00
Liberty, heads of children in center, 5½" 70.00
Mary Had a Little Lamb, 8" 125.00
Tom Thumb, 3¼" 65.00

Who Killed Cock Robin?, 7¾", EX, $85.00

Abingdon

From 1934 until 1950, the Abingdon Pottery Co. of Abingdon, Illinois, made a line of art pottery with a white vitrified body decorated with various types of glazes in many lovely colors. Novelties, cookie jars, utility ware, and lamps were made in addition to several lines of simple yet striking art ware. Fern Leaf, introduced in 1937, featured molded vertical feathering. La Fleur in 1939 consisted of flowerpots and flower-arranger bowls with rows of vertical ribbing. Classic, 1939-40, was a line of vases, many with evidence of Chinese influence. Several marks were used, most of which employed the company name. In 1950 the company reverted to the manufacture of sanitary ware that had been their mainstay before the Art Ware Division was formed.

Highly decorated examples and those with black, bronze, or red glaze usually command at least 25% higher prices.

Our advisors for Abingdon cookie jars are Joyce and Fred Roerig, authors of *The Collector's Encyclopedia of Cookie Jars*. Their address is in the Directory under South Carolina.

#101, vase, Alpha Classic 20.00
#102, vase, Beta, maroon, 10" 58.00
#104, vase, Delta Classic 28.00

#110, vase, Beta, bl, 6" 35.00
#116, vase, Classic, 10", from $18 up to 22.50
#126, candle holder, Classic, wht, 2", pr 38.00
#142, vase, Classic, bl, mini, 5½" 25.00
#200, pitcher, ice lip 30.00
#301, jar, Ming, turq 80.00
#305, bookend, sea gull, pr 60.00
#310, jar, Chang, wht matt, 1934-36, 10½" 245.00
#315, vase, Athena Classic, wht, 1934-36, 9" 38.00
#339, plate, salad; dk bl, sq 32.00
#351, vase, Capri, Regency gr 44.00
#363, bookend, colt, 5¾", pr 65.00
#375, wall pocket, dbl morning-glory, wht, 7¾" 45.00
#384, candle holder, sunflower, pr 35.00
#390, vase, morning-glory, turq, 1934-50, 10" 60.00
#3903, seated nude, minimum value 300.00
#3906, shepherdess & fawn, yel w/gold traces 95.00
#400, tea tile, geisha 80.00
#402, vase, Box 65.00
#408, bowl, leaf, beige, 1937, 6½" 65.00
#416, peacock, celadon gr, 7" 45.00
#420, vase, fern leaf, no decor, 7¼" 15.00
#429, vase/candle holder, Fern Leaf 25.00
#434, candle boat, Fern Leaf 27.50
#437, bowl (window box), Han Pansy 14.00
#442, vase, Laurel, turq matt, 1938-39, 5½" 33.00
#451, candle holder, dbl; aster, wht, 1934-38, 4½", pr 44.00
#460, bowl, Panel 40.00
#462, bowl, ribbon 12.00
#464, vase, medallion 30.00
#468, vase, gull, decor 35.00
#486, vase, acanthus, gray, 11" 42.00
#491, vase, flower holder; wht, 5" 25.00
#498, window box, Han, lg 25.00
#510, ashtray, donkey, blk, scarce, 5½" dia 95.00
#513, vase, swirl, med sz, from 15.00 up to 25.00
#517, vase, Arden, gr, 1934-50 ....24.00
#522, vase, Barre 23.00
#529, bowl, Ti Leaf 30.00
#540, bowl, flare 30.00
#543, bowl, bulb, rnd, sm 20.00
#544, bowl, Streamliner, sm 15.00
#550, vase, fluted 26.00
#565, cornucopia, blk, 1942-47, 7" 25.00
#568, mint compote, pk, ftd, 1942-47, 6" 28.00
#571, goose, wht, 5" 25.00
#574, heron 25.00
#584, vase, boot form 37.50
#593, vase, bow knot, bl, 9" 25.00
#599, vase, quilted, wht, 9" 30.00
#616, vase/bookend, cactus, ea 40.00
#645, bowl, Contour 22.00
#657, swordfish, decor 45.00
#661, swan, chartreuse, 3¾" 35.00
#668, planter, daffodil 20.00
#681/#682, sugar bowl & creamer, daisy 27.50
#700, bowl, pineapple 125.00
#709, bowl, irregular 15.00
#712, string holder, mouse 72.50
#716, candlestick, bamboo, decor, introduced 1939, pr 28.00
A-1, whatnot vase 75.00
Cookie jar, #471, Old Lady, plain or decor, 1942 ....210.00
Cookie jar, #471, Old Lady, rare gr 195.00

Cookie jar, #471D, Black Little Old Lady, $595.00.

Cookie jar, #495, Fat Boy	240.00
Cookie jar, #549, Hippo, decor, 1942	225.00
Cookie jar, #561, Baby, Blk decor	300.00
Cookie jar, #588, Money Bag, 1947	70.00
Cookie jar, #602, Hobby Horse	185.00
Cookie jar, #611, Jack-in-Box	255.00
Cookie jar, #622, Miss Muffet	205.00
Cookie jar, #651, Choo Choo (Locomotive)	150.00
Cookie jar, #653, Clock, 1949	85.00
Cookie jar, #662, Little Miss Muffet	205.00
Cookie jar, #663, Humpty Dumpty	250.00
Cookie jar, #664, Pineapple	60.00
Cookie jar, #665, Wigwam, minimum value	300.00
Cookie jar, #674, Pumpkin, 1949	310.00
Cookie jar, #677, Daisy, 1949	45.00
Cookie jar, #678, Windmill	185.00
Cookie jar, #692, Witch, minimum value	350.00
Cookie jar, #693, Little Girl	60.00
Cookie jar, #694, Bo Peep	240.00
Cookie jar, #695, Mother Goose	295.00
Cookie jar, #696, Three Bears	90.00
G-1, oil jar, tall	200.00
G-2, palm vase, squat	200.00
G-3, vase, floor; rope	180.00
P-7, jardiniere, 6"	24.00

Adams

Wm. Adams, whose potting skills were developed under the tutelage of Josiah Wedgwood, founded the Greengates Pottery at Tunstall, England, in 1769. Many types of wares including basalt, ironstone, parian, and jasper were produced, and various impressed or printed marks were employed. Until 1800 'Adams Co.' or 'Adams' impressed in block letters identified the company's earthenwares and a fine type of jasper similar in color and decoration to Wedgwood's. The latter mark was used again from 1845 to 1864 on parian figures. Most examples of their product found on today's market are transfer-printed dinnerwares with ornate backstamps which often include the pattern name and the initials 'W.A. & S.' This type of product was made from 1820 until about 1920. After 1890 the word 'England' was included in the mark; 'Tunstall' was added after 1896. From 1914 through 1940, a printed crown with 'Adams, Estbd 1657, England' identified their products. From 1900 to 1965, they produced souvenir plates with transfers of American scenes, many of which were marketed in this country by Roth

Importers of Peoria, Illinois. In 1965 the company affiliated with Wedgwood. Although there were other Adams potteries in Staffordshire, their marks incorporate either the first name initial or a partner's name and so are easily distinguished from those of this company. See also Spatter; Staffordshire; Adams Rose.

Pitcher, Jasperware, white figures on blue, tankard form, 6¼", $170.00.

Bowl, Cries of London, 10"	65.00
Plate, cut sponge, 4-color, floral, blk sponged rim, 8"	75.00
Plate, March (seasons), pk transfer, 9½"	55.00
Plate, soup; Blenheim Oxfordshire, dk bl transfer, 10⅛"	165.00
Plate, soup; Caledonia, red transfer, 11", EX	40.00
Plate, soup; cottage & children, dk bl transfer, 10"	185.00
Plate, soup; milkmaid & cows, dk bl transfer, 10", NM	130.00
Plate, Titian Ware, exotic bird/flowers, mc HP on cream, sq	25.00
Plate, 2 cupids, floral/bow border, med bl transfer, 10⅛"	95.00
Platter, bl feather edge, 15", VG	50.00
Tea bowl & saucer, gaudy floral, mk	45.00

Adams Rose, Early and Late

In the second quarter of the 19th century, the Adams and Son Pottery produced a line of hand-painted dinnerware decorated in large, red brush-stroke roses with green leaves on whiteware, which collectors call Adams Rose. Later, G. Jones and Son (and possibly others) made a similar ware with less brilliant colors on a gray-white surface.

Bowl, early, rare sz, 9", M	750.00
Bowl, vegetable; late, 10¾", M	125.00
Coffeepot, red/gr/bl, tall, rare	850.00
Creamer, early, 5¾", M	285.00
Pitcher, early, stains/minor flakes, 7"	205.00
Pitcher, late, 6¾", M	175.00
Plate, early, emb scalloped rim, 10½", EX	125.00
Plate, early, 9", M	190.00
Plate, late, 12", VG	125.00
Plate, late, 9½", M	110.00
Plate, soup; early, wear/minor stains/glaze flakes, 9"	80.00

Sugar bowl, w/lid, early, M 350.00
Sugar bowl, w/lid, late, M 175.00
Tea bowl & saucer, late, M 125.00
Tea bowl & saucer, scalloped rims, mk, early, EX 180.00
Teapot, early, dome lid, rpr, 11½" 750.00
Teapot, late, M 300.00

Advertising

The advertising world has always been a fiercely competitive field. In an effort to present their product to the customer, every imaginable gimmick was put into play. Colorful and artfully decorated signs and posters, thermometers, tape measures, fans, hand mirrors, and attractive tin containers (all with catchy slogans, familiar logos, and often-bogus claims) are only a few of the many examples of early advertising memorabilia that are of interest to today's collectors.

Porcelain signs were made as early as 1890 and are highly prized for their artistic portrayal of life as it was then . . . often allowing amusing insights into the tastes, humor, and way of life of a bygone era. As a general rule, older signs are made from a heavier gauge metal. Those with three or more fired-on colors are especially desirable.

Tin containers were used to package consumer goods ranging from crackers and coffee to tobacco and talcum. After 1880 can companies began to decorate their containers by the method of lithography. Though colors were still subdued, intricate designs were used to attract the eye of the consumer. False labeling and unfounded claims were curtailed by the Pure Food and Drug Administration in 1906, and the name of the manufacturer as well as the brand name of the product had to be printed on the label. By 1910 color was rampant with more than a dozen hues printed on the tin or on paper labels. The tins themselves were often designed with a second use in mind, such as canisters, lunch boxes, even toy trains. As a general rule, tobacco-related tins are the most desirable, though personal preference may direct the interest of the collector to peanut butter pails with illustrations of children, or talcum tins with irresistible babies or beautiful ladies. Coffee tins are popular, as are those made to contain a particularly successful or well-known product.

Perhaps the most visual of the early advertising gimmicks were the character logos, the Fairbank Company's Gold Dust Twins, the goose trademark of the Red Goose Shoe Company, Nabisco's ZuZu Clown and Uneeda Kid, the Campbell Kids, the RCA dog Nipper, and Mr. Peanut, to name only a few. Any example of these brings a high price on the market today.

Our listings are alphabetized by company name or, in lieu of that information, by word content or other pertinent description. When no condition is indicated, the items listed below are assumed to be in excellent condition, except glass and ceramic items, which are assumed mint. Remember that condition greatly affects value (especially true for tin items). For instance, a sign in excellent or mint condition may bring twice as much as the same one in only very good condition. On today's market, items in good to very good condition are slow to sell, unless they are extremely rare. Mint (or near-mint) examples are high.

As a general rule, beer tip trays in near-mint condition are worth $150 to $250. Spool cabinets (depending on condition) may be evaluated at $100 to $150 per drawer.

We have several advertising advisors; Allen Smith specializes in Buster Brown, Pepsi-Cola, Planters Peanuts, and Red Goose Shoes. He is listed in the Directory under Texas. Our Dr. Pepper advisor is Bill Ricketts, listed under North Carolina. Nearly all of the remaining topics and the general listings are under the advisement of Dennis O'Brien and George Goehring of Dennis and George Collectibles; they are listed in the Directory under Maryland. For further information, we recommend *Huxford's Collectible Advertising*, available at your local book-

store or from Collector Books. See also Advertising Dolls; Advertising Cards; Automobilia; Coca-Cola; Banks; Calendars; Cookbooks; Paperweights; Posters; Sewing Items.

Key:
cb — cardboard	ps — porcelain sign
cl — celluloid	sf — self-framed
lcs — litho on canvas sign	tc — tin container
pp — pre-prohibition	ts — tin sign

A-1 Beer, tip tray, coaster type, 3" dia, NM 12.00
ABC Bohemian Beer, tin sign, lion on mtn, fr, 31x43", EX 2,200.00
Acme Beer, cb sign, Wheel of Fortune, wood fr, 30x24", EX 60.00
Acorn Stoves & Ranges, zinc sign, 2-sided acorn, 48x48", EX ...3,850.00
AGFA Photos, canvas banner, orange & wht, 24x40", EX 75.00
Alaska Fur Co, cvd wood seal sign, hanging, 76x51", EX 17,600.00
Allen & Ginter, rvpt sgn, orig wood fr, 28x45", EX 575.00

Allen's Root Beer Extracts, paper sign, Donaldson Brothers litho, in frame, 14x20", NM, $650.00.

Am Liberty Beer, tip tray, Indian lady, pre-pro, 4", EX 175.00
Am Line, pocket mirror, ship, 2" dia, VG 20.00
Angeles Marshmallows, pocket mirror, cherubs, oval, EX 55.00
Anheuser-Busch, tin litho sign, Indians on raft, fr, 5x15", EX 125.00
Anheuser-Busch, tray, child, 1895-1901, 13½x16½", EX 425.00
Ansco Film, glass sign, 10x15", EX 45.00
Argonaut Beer, cb bottle display, miner & donkey, EX 48.00
Armour's Corn Flakes, sf tin sign, box & roses, 15x21", EX 140.00
Armour's Veribest Peanut Butter, tin-on-cb sign, 9x13", VG 250.00
Arrow Beer, electric clock, tin face/wood case, 15½" sq, EX 130.00
Atlantic Gasoline, porc sign, red & wht, 7x12", NM 80.00
Atlantic Motor Oil, cloth banner, 1940s, 36x50", EX 135.00
Atlas Beer, ceramic pitcher, eagle logo, master sz, EX 155.00

Bagdad Tobacco, pocket tin, short, EX 140.00
Bagley's Red Belt Tobacco, pocket tin, VG 60.00
Baker's Chocolate, tin sign, LaBell Chocolatiere, 44x32", G 450.00
Ballentine Ale, cl sign, lady w/wht hat, 1940s, 7x12", EX 80.00
Ballentine Beer, tip tray, wood grain w/3 rings, 5", EX 55.00
Bayuk Cigars, tc, emb letters, sq, 4½x5½", EX 32.00
Beech-Nut, tc, auto scene, Our Visit to..., 7x16x10", EX 77.00
Beech-Nut Tobacco, tin sign, John & Demi-John, 12x24", EX 88.00
Beich's Candy, emb glass jar w/lid, 13", G 35.00
Bell Roasted Coffee, pocket mirror, bell, 2", VG 20.00
Benson & Hedges Parliament Cigarettes, ts, mc, 12x14", EX 32.00
Bering Cigars, tin canister, paper label, portrait, EX 65.00
Berkeley Knit Ties, cb sign, man w/tie, 1925, 8x10", EX 27.50
Berry Bros Varnish, wood display, 10x33", EX 385.00
Bert & Harry Piels Beer, metal clock, electric, 13" sq, EX 125.00
Bickmore Gall Salve, cb sign, horses, 1940-50s, 22x34", EX 50.00
Big Ben Tobacco, pocket tin, horse, EX 48.00
Big Boy Hamburgers, glass ashtray, EX pnt, 4½" dia 25.00
Birely's Drink, tin sign, 4 emb bottles, 1940, 4x21", EX 110.00
Black Cat Shoe Dressing, match holder, Shoes/Stoves, VG 350.00
Blue Jay Corn Plasters, tin display, grandpa figural, 6", G 130.00
Bond Street Tobacco, cb canister, 1940s, EX 25.00
Bond Street Tobacco, pocket tin, 100 Years, NM 22.00
Borden's, brass belt buckle, Elsie figural, M 40.00
Borden's, cb sign, Elsie, 19½x16½", EX 99.00
Borden's, place mat, Elsie, Elmer, Beula, & Beuregard, 17x11" 12.50
Borden's, tumbler, juice; Celestine in brn, red stripe 35.00
Borden's Cottage Cheese, glass container/tin Elsie lid, 4", EX 25.00
Borden's Malted Milk Candy, jar, emb metal top, 9x5½", EX 100.00
Boston Herald, tin sign, wht on red, 12x23", G 80.00
Bower & Bartlett's Boston Bl Ribbon Brand Coffee, bin, 18" 120.00
Bowl of Roses Tobacco, pocket tin, short, NM 175.00
Breyer's Ice Cream, neon sign, 22x25", G 20.00
Broadway Brewing, bottle, emb letters, EX 22.00
Broadway Brewing, tip tray, hand w/hatchet, pre-pro, 4", EX 88.00
Buckingham Tobacco, pocket tin, sample sz, EX 120.00
Buffalo Rock Ginger Ale, tin easel-bk sign, 13x19", EX 170.00
Bull Brand Feeds, tin sign, cow, 1930s-40s, 36x72", VG 210.00
Bull Durham Tobacco, cb sign, corncob pipe, '30s, 10x25", EX .110.00
Busch Bavarian Beer, clock, modeled as a drum, 20th C, 13" 170.00

Buster Brown

Buster Brown was the creation of cartoonist Richard Felton; his comic strip first appeared in the *New York Herald* on May 4, 1902. Since then Buster and his dog Tige (short for Tiger) have adorned sundry commercial products but are probably best known as the trademark for the Brown Shoe Company established early in this century. Today hundreds of Buster Brown premiums, store articles, and advertising items bring substantial prices from many serious collectors.

Ad, clipped from magazine, mc, 1900s, 4¾x6½", EX 20.00
Bandana, mc print on linen, 1940s premium, EX 80.00
Bank, CI, horse & horseshoe, orig decal, Arcade, 4½", EX 245.00
Cigar, BB band, EX 10.00
Coat hook, orig 35.00
Coupon sheet, BB Guaranteed Stockings, 1900s, 2½x11", EX 65.00
Hatchet, BB logo, 13", EX 45.00
Lunar telephone, 1960s, M 25.00
Magic kit, 1920s-30s premium, complete, EX in cb mailer 90.00
Mask, BB Shoes, cb, NM 30.00
Mug, BB, girl, & Tige, china, 1900s, 2½", EX 75.00
Patch, felt, 1950s, EX 6.50
Periscope 22.50

Pin-bk, BB Blue Ribbon Shoes, BB & Tige, 1890s, 1", NM 75.00
Pin-bk, BB Hose Supporters, BB & Tige, mc, 1900s, ⅞", EX 35.00
Pitcher, cream; BB & girl, china, 1900s, 3", NM 85.00
Plate, BB & Tige, 4¾", NM 65.00
Picketknife, high-top shoe-form hdl, EX graphics, 3" 22.00
Poster, linen, BB & Tige, Outcault, Selchow, 17x24" 45.00
Ring, BB & Friends enameled on brass, 1940s, NM 80.00
Rug, BB & Tige, yel/bl/red, 48" dia, EX 200.00
Shoe brush, brn w/cream bristles, wooden hdl, 8½" 25.00
Shoe mirror, metal stand w/wood fr, 15x21½", VG 125.00
Shoehorn 40.00
Sign, paper, BB & Tige, US Litho, Morgan, 1904, 44x31", EX ..450.00
Stationery, BB letterhead, 1 sheet 2.50
Stick pin, BB enameled on brass, 1900s, 2½", NM 150.00

Stocking box, scarce, EX, $100.00.

String holder, BB/Tige/windmill top, CI base, 1900s, 15" 575.00
Valentine, BB & Tige, Tuck, 1904, 5½x3½", unused, EX 35.00
Whistle, tin litho, flat, EX 24.00
Wristwatch, BB Shoes, Ingersoll, 1930s, EX orig 300.00

C.D. Kenny

C.D. Kenny was determined to be a successful man, and he was. Between 1890 and 1934, he owned seventy-five groceries in fifteen states. He realized his success in two ways: fair business dealings and premium giveaways. These ranged from trade cards and advertising mirrors to tin commemorative plates and kitchen items. There were banks and toys, clocks and tins. Today's collectors are finding scores of these items, all carrying Kenny's name.

Calendar, 1919, Pennant 35.00
Coffee bag 6.50
Figurine, Hessian on horsebk, bsk, premium 20.00
Figurine, Indian in canoe, EX 20.00
Frame, Dutch motif 20.00
Funnel 22.00
Plaque, Geo. Washington, rnd, sm, EX+ 45.00
Plate, tin, child in snow scene 85.00
Plate, tin, Santa & sleeping child, 9½" 165.00
Plate, tin, Star Spangled Banner 40.00
Pocket mirror, folding, metal case, EX 40.00
Print, unfr, 1913, EX 22.00
Stamp holder, cl, Dutch waitresses 15.00
Strainer 45.00
Tape measure, retractable, NM 50.00
Tin, tea party, oval 150.00
Tip tray, lady in woods, flower border, M 110.00
Tip tray, raising flag 100.00

Tip tray, Thanksgiving, 1910, NM 155.00
Toothpick holder, bsk, gr glaze w/gold, EX 40.00

Cacao Droste Chocolate, cup & saucer, lady w/tray, 3" 55.00
Cadillac Eldorado, tin sign, wood fr, 1977, 24x18", NM 60.00
Calumet Baking Powder, wood thermometer, '30s, 22x6", EX 350.00
Camel Cigarettes, tin thermometer/sign, 1920-40s, 14x6", M 50.00
Camel Cigars, tin container, 5½", EX 50.00
Campbell's Soup, pottery bowl, 2¾x4", M 18.00
Campbell's Tomato Soup, electric can opener, can form, EX 50.00
Canada Dry, porc sign, logo, 4x20", NM 48.00
Canada Dry, tin sign, hand w/bottle, 1950s, 12" H, VG 25.00
Canada Dry, wooden stand-up sign, 1940s, 12x10", EX 45.00
Canadian Ace Beer & Ale, tip tray, coaster type, 3", EX 15.00
Canadian Club Whiskey, ceramic pitcher, EX 12.00
Cargray Gold Pump, porc sign, blk & gold, 1930s, 10" dia, M 210.00
Carlsburg Beer, cl sign, gold on blk, 3x10", M 12.50
Carnation Gum, sf tin sign,...Taste the Smell, 14" sq, EX 800.00
Carnation Malted Milk, display can, red/wht/gr, 8¾", EX 89.00
Carolina Gem Long Cut Tobacco, tin box, sq form, EX 30.00
Carson Pirie Scott Shoes, shoehorn, NM 10.00
Cascarettes, cb sign, sleeping hobo, 1900s, 16x22", EX 27.50
Cert-O-Lene Motor Oil, tc, silver, 1970s, 1-qt, NM 15.00

**Charms Co., tin litho pail, Hanzel and Gretel
scene, approximately 3", EX, $75.00.**

Chas E Higgins Soap, cb sign, Blk lady diecut, 5x12", NM 165.00
Chesterfield Cigarettes, cb sign, Ask for..., '40s, 24x24", EX 70.00
Chesterfield Cigarettes, tin sign, 1920-40s, 13x6", EX 50.00
Chocolate Shop Chocolates, wood box, bear finial, 8x18x4", EX ..330.00
Cinzano Vermouth, glass snifter, EX 10.00
Clark's Teaberry Gum, glass shelf, etched letters, 3x5", EX 150.00
Cognac Jacques, Fr stone litho sign, Bouchet, 62x47", EX 425.00
Colonial Club Cigars, tin flange sign, 2-sided, 9x19", VG 35.00
Colonial Dame Coffee, emb tin sign, 10x28", EX 30.00
Commando Rust Preventative, tc, men in combat, '40s, 6", EX ...50.00
Continental Cubes Tobacco, curved pocket tin, 2½x3½", VG ..200.00
Cook's Gold Blume Beer, tin sign, 2-sided, 14x28", M 115.00
Coors, pilsner glass, EX 4.00

Couch & Four Tobacco, pocket tin, NM 350.00
Craven Plain Cigarettes, tc, flat 50s, gr, Canada, VG 12.00
Crisco, porc sign, 2-tone bl on wht, pre-1900, 40x24", EX 2,900.00
Cyclone Twister Cigars, cb sign, ca 1928, 11¼x9", EX 80.00
Damascus Watch Springs, tc, Keller & Co, 2½x2½", NM 15.00
Danville Brewery, tip tray, Drink Hearty, pre-pro, 4", VG 50.00
Deines & Harris Drugs, mc wood sidewalk sign, 96x36", VG 360.00
DeLaval Separators, tin sign, cow diecut, Am Art, EX 100.00
DeLaval Separators, tin sign, maid/cow, 1915, 40x29", EX 1,350.00
DeLaval Separators, wood/tin cabinet, separator, 28", EX+ 600.00
Devoe Paints, porc-over-metal sign, 1930-40s, 29x19", EX 75.00
Diamond Dyes, cabinet, Evolution of Women, 30", EX 950.00
Diamond Dyes, cabinet, fairy/butterflies/parrot, 31", G 800.00
Diamond Dyes, cabinet, Maypole/mansion, 30", EX 1,200.00
Diamond Dyes, cabinet, Washer Woman, 30", VG 750.00
Dill's Best Cut Plug, tc, ½x2¼x3½", EX 28.00
Dill's Best Rubbed Cube Cut, tc, 3½x6½" dia, EX 40.00
Don Digo Cigars, glass change receiver, portrait, VG 25.00
Dr Brown's Sarsaparilla, wooden thermometer, 24x6", VG 170.00

Dr. Pepper

A young pharmacist, Charles C. Alderton, was hired by W.B. Morrison, owner of Morrison's Old Corner Drug Store in Waco, Texas around 1884. Alderton, an observant sort, noticed that the drugstore's patrons could never quite make up their minds as to which flavor of extract to order. He concocted a formula that combined many flavors, and Dr. Pepper was born. The name was chosen by Morrison in honor of a beautiful young girl with whom he had once been in love. The girl's father, a Virginia doctor by the name of Pepper, had discouraged the relationship due to their youth, but Morrison had never forgotten her. On December 1, 1885, a U.S. patent was issued to the creators of Dr. Pepper.

Bottle, clear, AM&B Co, circle A, EX 28.00
Bottle, seltzer, Cheerio-Memphis 165.00
Calendar, 1935, complete, EX 225.00
Calendar, 1950, girl w/half-mask, complete, NM 55.00
Calendar, 1951, 3-pg, 20x12", EX 35.00
Clock, bottle cap shape, EX 95.00
Clock, Mountain Herbs, sales presentation, 1982, M 375.00
Clock, Telechron, 14" 235.00
Dispenser, syrup; china w/metal legs, cylindrical, 18", EX 1,200.00
Door pull, metal, bottle form, EX 65.00
Fountain glass, Dr Pepper etched in wht rectangle, M 12.50
Pedal car, 1950s, EX 425.00
Pin-bk button, 10-2-4, blk & wht, ¾", EX 20.00
Plate, roses, Vienna Art 185.00
Postcard, 10¢ coupon, M 5.00
Push bar, button ea side, aluminum, EX 175.00
Sign, tin, cut-out cap, 28", NM 55.00
Street marker, Safety First, cast brass, early 70.00
Tray, roses, King of Beverages, Vienna 265.00
Truck, 1970s, NM 25.00
Watch fob, Billiken, brass, EX 120.00

Duffee's Laxative, emb tin sign, 9½x13⅝", VG 50.00
Dust Puff, tc, bl w/blk lid, 1915-25, 5¾x3¼", NM 80.00
Dutch Boy Paints, copper-clad display, boy figural, 20", EX 440.00
Dutch Boy Paints, plaster lamp, boy figural, EX 125.00
Dutch Boy Paints, 25-yr service charm on bracelet, 10k gold 45.00
Dutch Java Blend Coffee, cb sign, car/cattle diecut, 9x7", EX 120.00
Dwinell & Wright Boston Coffees, wooden box, 21x14x14", G ...55.00
Early Times Whiskey, plaster sign, wood fr, 23x29", NM 350.00

Edgeworth Smoking Tobacco, cardboard display, 33x42", EX, $125.00.

Eastside Old Tap Lager, cl sign, red/gold/blk, 9x20", NM 27.50
Edelweiss Beer, tray, Schoenhofen, 1913, 13½" dia, EX 250.00
Elgin Watches, decal litho-on-wood sign, 22x5", G 75.00
Empire Jewelry, plastic thimble, M 5.00
Epicure Tobacco, pocket tin, EX 295.00
Esso, silver-tone metal cuff links, flame man figural, pr 45.00
Eveready, playing cards, Reddy Kilowatt, EX in box 40.00
Fab, cl tape measure, sunset, EX 32.00
Fairbanks Scales, porc sign, minor chipping, 10x50", EX 150.00
Fairy's Soap, tray, child atop bar of soap, 13¾" dia, EX 40.00
Famous Dukes Tobacco, cb sign, midgets, 1920s, 18x13", EX 210.00
Farmwell Feeds, ceramic shakers, farmer figural, EX, pr 150.00
Fashion Cut Plug Tobacco, tc, touring car, 1900s, 4½", EX 170.00
Fatima Turkish Cigarettes, tin sign, girl, 1900s, 20x16", EX 200.00
Fehr's Brewing, tray, non-alcoholic Ambrosia, 13¼" dia, EX 155.00
Ferry's Seeds, tin litho sign, cherub, 1901, 34x25", M 220.00
Firestone Tire & Rubber, hose caddy, wood, Blk man cutout, 30" ...150.00
Fleischmann's Yeast, tin wall pocket, 8x6¼x3", EX 40.00
Flexible Flyer, paper sign, sled diecut, 3¼x6", VG 25.00
Flintstones Vitamins, mug, Dino the Dinosaur, F&F, NM 18.00
Fontana & Co CA Canned Fruits, tin sign, boy, 16x12", G 1,900.00
Forest & Stream, pocket tin, fisherman, EX 145.00
Forest & Stream, pocket tin, 2 men in canoe, EX 500.00
Four Roses, pocket tin, gr, NM 750.00
Four Roses, tin sign, cabin scene, 1910-30, 57x43", NM 800.00
Four Roses, tin sign, dead game scene, fr, 49x35", EX 825.00
Fox Head 400 Beer, tip tray, fox logo, 4x5", EX 37.50
Fram Auto Filter, tin thermometer, 39x8", EX 35.00
Freedom Motor Oil, tc, watchdog on bl, 1935-45, 1-qt, EX 55.00
Frisch's Big Boy, glass ashtray, orange on clear, 3¼" dia 28.00
Fritzmuth Smoking Tobacco, brass lamp, 16", EX 715.00
Frostie Root Beer, glass-front thermometer, 12" dia, EX 42.50
Gas & Oil, silk screened on galvanized metal, 36x14", EX 220.00
Gem Razor Blades, tin-fr mirror & dispenser, EX 215.00
Gem Safety Razors, cb box, 9x8" +6 unopened razors, EX 50.00
General Electric, light-up sign, 1930s-40s, 8½x14", EX 130.00
General Electric, pottery ashtray, fluorescent figural, M 48.00
General Electric, tape measure, vacuum figural, plastic, 3" 45.00
Githens, Rexamer & Co Coffee & Tea, cigar lighter, 12" 55.00
Glen-Lube Motor Oil, tc, red & bl, 1930s, 1-qt, EX 20.00
Goebel Beer, tip tray, Dutch girl, 4", NM 55.00
Goff's Best Braid, wooden display, 3-drw, 1900s, 11x17", VG 145.00

Goodyear Tires, cb standup, car/pedestrians diecut, 46x37", EX .150.00
Goodyear Tires, porc sign, shoe diecut, 1950-60, 64x21", EX 220.00
Gouldings Manures, clock, New Haven, 8-day, rvpt, 34", M 850.00
Grape Julep, tin sign, Grimm...Corp, 1940s, 8x20", VG 90.00
Great American Tea, slip-top canister, 7¾x4⅛", G 165.00
Green's Milk-Ice Cream, pottery creamer, EX 59.00
Greyhound Lines, porc sign, greyhound, 1940s, 21x36", EX 500.00
Hackerbrau Munchen Beer, porc mug, Germany, 5", EX   37.50

Hamilton Watch, tin sign, wood frame, 12x18", $500.00.

Harp Beer, glass mug, heavy, M 10.00
Harrison's Heart O' Orange, thermometer, porc face, 18" dia 125.00
Havoline Motor Oil, tc, Indian Oil..., 1935-45, 1-qt, EX 35.00
Hi Plane Tobacco, emb tin sign, 12x35", VG 55.00
Hi Plane Tobacco, pocket tin, 1-engine plane, EX 75.00
Hi Plane Tobacco, pocket tin, 2-engine plane, EX 85.00
Hickman Ebbert Wagons, sf tin sign, 26x38", EX 1,150.00
Hickory Brand Children's Garters, wood display, 13x10x6", EX ..315.00

Hires

Charles E. Hires, a drugstore owner in Philadelphia, became interested in natural teas. He began experimenting with roots and herbs and soon developed his own special formula. Hires introduced his product to his own patrons and soon began selling concentrated syrup to other soda fountains and grocery stores. Samples of his 'root beer' were offered for the public's approval at the 1876 Philadelphia Centennial. Today's collectors are often able to date their advertising items by observing the Hires boy on the logo. From 1891 to 1906, he wore a dress. From 1906 to 1914, he was shown in a bathrobe; and from 1915 until 1926, he was depicted in a dinner jacket. The apostrophe may or may not appear in the Hires name; this seems to have no bearing on dating an item.

Booklet, Merry Rhymes for Thirsty Times, NM 30.00
Buckle, belt; Drink Hires Root Beer, EX 6.50
Coaster, ceramic, Mettlach, rare, 4¾", EX 120.00
Dispenser, ceramic, orig pump, 14x7½" dia, EX 650.00
Mug, blk or gray stoneware, block letters, NM 50.00
Mug, ceramic, boy lifts mug, Mettlach, EX 165.00

Mug, stoneware, 6",
$100.00.

Opener, over-the-top, NM	15.00
Pocket mirror, Put Roses in Your Cheeks	185.00
Sign, emb tin, 9x27½", VG	135.00
Sign, paper, German peasant/Colonial man, 1890s, 18x21", EX	500.00
Sign, paper, lady in wicker chair, 10½x20", VG	110.00
Sign, sf tin, Hires boy, Say Hires, Beach, oval, 24", EX	3,500.00
Sign, window; paper, Thirsts...Suffocated, 7x11", M	85.00
Straw dispenser	765.00
Thermometer, tin, bottle form, EX	75.00
Tire cover, canvas, for spare, 29" dia, EX	225.00
Tray, girl on wood-grained background, 10½x13", EX	90.00
Tray, Just What the Doctor..., 1914, EX	425.00

Hitchner Biscuits, tin barrel, bl & red, 27x15", VG	25.00
Holeproof Hosiery, pocket mirror, 2½", EX	25.00
Holiday Tobacco, pocket tin, unopened, M	65.00
Horton Brewing, rvpt back-bar sign, hanging, 10x10", VG	65.00
Hubley Guns, metal display rack, 1950s, 17x22½", VG	10.00
Hudson River Day Line Ferry Boats, cb sign, 19x11", NM	30.00
Humble Oil, tin sign, Top Rated..., 1960s, 30x30", EX	120.00
Huntley & Palmer, biscuit tin, exotic bird, sq, oriental hdls	90.00
Huntley & Palmer, biscuit tin, farmhouse, NM	375.00
Huntley & Palmer, biscuit tin, library, stack of books, EX	155.00
Huntley & Palmer, biscuit tin, stack of plates, EX	220.00
Hyperial Tooth Preserve, paper sign, lady, 13x10", EX	425.00
Hyvis Motor Oil, tc, blk & wht, 1938, 1-qt, EX	30.00
Independent Motor Oil, tc, marching army, 1915-25, 1-gal, EX	130.00
Indian Motor Oil, tc, Indian on gr, 1915-30, 1-gal, EX	600.00
Invador Motor Oil, tc, knight in armor, ca 1965, 5½", M	30.00
Iroquois Refrigeration, mc wood sign, Indian diecut, 72"	990.00
Jackson's Best Chewing Tobacco Black, booklet, Donaldson, EX	45.00
Jacob Ruppert Beer & Ale, tin sign, 1940s, 12x24", VG	75.00
Jacquet & Co Cognac, cb sign, Fr, Champenois, 17x12", VG	20.00
Japan Air Lines, travel alarm clock, gold-tone case, 3", EX	27.50
Japp's Hair Rejuvenator, tin-on-cb sign, Beach, '10, 9x13", M	130.00
Jena Glass, porc-over-metal push plate, 1930s, 7¾", M	185.00
Jim Dandies Peanuts, tc, children play baseball, 10-lb, VG	330.00
Johnston Hot Fudge, dispenser, aluminum/pottery, electric, EX	125.00
Jubilee Hot Fudge, dispenser, aluminum/pottery, electric, EX	125.00
Juicy Fruit, CI & tin juice press, Schriver, 17x13" dia, VG	45.00
Jumbo Salted Peanuts, tc, 10-lb, 9½x8¼" dia, G	25.00
Just Suits Tobacco, porc sign, pipe form, 6½x16", VG	400.00
Kansas City Brewery, tip tray, crescent & star, pre-pro, 4", NM	115.00

Kaukauna Klub, stoneware butter crock, c 1933, 5x3¼", EX	25.00
KC Baking Powder, tin sign, 12x28", EX	45.00
Keene's Ice Cream, tray, Chinese youth, 13¼x10½", VG	45.00
Kellogg's, pottery shakers, Snap & Pop figural, pr, EX	75.00
Kelly Springfield Tires, convex tin sign, 1954, 22x36", EX	80.00
Kendall Oil, canvas banner, can on wht, 1930-40s, EX	100.00
Kentucky Fried Chicken, plastic shakers, Colonel figural, pr	165.00
King Bee Coffee, wood bin, stenciling, 32", EX	465.00
Kist Beverages, electric clock, ca 1931, 15½" sq, G	45.00
Knickerbocker Beer, tip tray, coaster type, 4" dia, NM	15.00
Kodacolor Film, cb display box, 4½x13½x4½", EX	15.00
Kodak Film, periscope, for Rose Bowl games, 22", EX	30.00
Kodak Film, porc sign, 2-sided, package on bl, 20x14", EX	425.00
Kwickwork Auto Enamel, cl-over-metal easel display, 11", VG	300.00
L&M Cigarettes, tin sign, Pack or Box, 1920-40s, 13x6", VG	35.00
Lancaster Salted Nuts, tc, Queen Quality Brand, 10-lb, EX	50.00
Leech-Lube Motor Oil, tc, yel on bl, 1935-45, 1-qt, NM	20.00
Licorice Lozenges, emb glass jar, metal top, 9½", EX	25.00
Lion of England Beer, ceramic mug, Japan, 7", EX	10.00

Log Cabin Syrup

Log Cabin Syrup tins have been made since the 1890s in variations of design that can be attributed to specific years of production. Until about 1914, they were made with paper labels. These are quite rare and highly prized by today's collectors. Tins with colored lithographed designs were made after 1914. When General Foods purchased the Towle Company in 1927, the letters 'GF' were added.

A cartoon series, illustrated with a mother flipping pancakes in the cabin window and various children and animals declaring their appreciation of the syrup in voice balloons, was introduced in the 1930s. A Frontier Village series followed in the late 1940s. A schoolhouse, jail, trading post, doctor's office, blacksmith shop, inn, and private homes were also available. Examples of either series today often command prices of $75.00 to $200.00 and up.

Bank, glass cabin figural, EX	32.00
Can opener, Towle's, metal	12.00
Container, plastic wigwam, yel letters, 1950, 2x2" dia	6.00
Syrup tin, bear in door, cartoon ends, Towle's, 5-lb	140.00
Syrup tin, blacksmith, 33-oz	135.00
Syrup tin, boy w/lasso, 1-lb	110.00

Syrup tin, child in
the door, 4¾",
$110.00.

Syrup tin, cartoon all sides, sm	110.00
Syrup tin, children, man by pump, Towle's, 33-oz	150.00
Syrup tin, children playing, Towle's, 33-oz, NM	135.00

Syrup tin, Dr RU Well, cartoon style, rare 250.00
Syrup tin, Express Office, coach, Towle's, 33-oz 150.00
Syrup tin, Frontier Inn, cowboys & horse, 5-lb 220.00
Syrup tin, Frontier Jail, 12-oz 150.00
Syrup tin, hand w/finger pointing on top, Towle's, med 165.00
Syrup tin, Home Sweet Home, 12-oz 150.00
Syrup tin, log cabin figural, Towle's, med, EX+ 55.00
Syrup tin, pancakes, VG 15.00
Syrup tin, paper label, sample sz, rare, 2x1½" 300.00
Syrup tin, red, 5-lb 50.00
Syrup tin, Stockade School, Towle's, 33-oz 150.00
Syrup tin, Wigwam, 1-lb, very rare, 4x3¼x3½" 500.00
Teaspoon 17.50

Los Angeles Brewery, tip tray, factory, pre-pro, 4" dia, NM 125.00
Lowenbrau Beer, coaster, from 1964 World's Fair, EX 3.00
Lowney's Breakfast Cocoa, paper sign, sexy lady, 6x10", EX 15.00
Lucky Spots, mustache cup, gambler's hand/4 aces, EX 75.00
Lucky Strike, sf porc-on-metal sign, 1900s, 39x38", VG 3,200.00
Lucky Strike Cut Plug, tc, ⅞x4½x2½", EX 38.00
Lucky Strike Roll Cut, pocket tin, sample sz, EX 135.00
Lucky Strike Roll Cut, pocket tin, 1910 stamp, EX 75.00
Maestro Cigars, cb sign, man smoking diecut, 17x15", EX 50.00
Mail Pouch Tobacco, porc thermometer, bl/wht/yel, 19½", EX ..275.00
Maltop Toddy Powdered Drink, tc, ca. 1925, 3½x4½", VG 10.00
Maryland Casualty, tin sign, blk & red, fr, 12x24", EX 45.00
Mason's Blacking, wooden box, EX labels, 5x11½x8", EX 140.00
Massey Harris, porc-on-metal sign, 1940s, 18x60", EX 330.00
Maxwell House Coffee, ceramic mug, M 8.00

Mayflower Women's Shoes, tin sign, self framed, 18x25", NM, $2,000.00.

Michelin Tires, porc sign, tire man, 1950s, 32x24", EX 160.00
Michelin Tires, porc sign, tire man on bike, 19x12", EX 800.00
Michelob, electric sign, 12x16", EX 25.00
Miller Genuine Draft, mirror, oak fr, 14x14", NM 25.00
Miller High Life, cb sign, CA 500 Raceway, 24x28", EX 27.50
Miller Lite Beer, Lucite tap knob, EX 10.00
Mission Orange, tin thermometer, 17x5", G 25.00
Mokaine Liqueur, sf tin sign, French, 14x9¾", G 25.00
Monkey Gas, tin sign, monkey diecut, 1930-50, 36x36", NM 325.00

Moxie

The Moxie Company was organized in 1884 by George Archer of Boston, Massachusetts. It was at first touted as a 'nerve food' to improve the appetite, promote restful sleep, and in general to make one 'feel better!' Emphasis was soon shifted, however, to the good taste of the brew, and extensive advertising campaigns rivaling those of such giant competitors as Hires and Coca-Cola resulted in successful marketing through the 1930s. Today the term Moxie has become synonymous with courage and audacity, traits displayed by the company who dared compete with such well-established rivals. For more information we recommend *The Book of Moxie* by Frank N. Potter, available at your local bookstore or from Collector Books.

Bottle, Moxie Nerve Food, Hutchinson type, aqua, 26-oz 15.00
Bottle, paper label, ca 1928, 16-oz 12.00
Bottle hanger, campfire scene, 2 7-oz bottles, M 17.50
Brochure, Making Money w/..., 1929, EX 55.00
Case, wooden, Crystal Lake Bottling, holds 24 7-oz bottles 17.50
Clicker, Moxie boy, rnd, NM 45.00
Clock, mantel; wooden, Moxie boy on face, EX 295.00
Fan, cb, Muriel Ostriche, 1916, 10" 27.50
Folder, President Roosevelt & Moxie, 4½x7", EX 78.00
Knife or fork, Milford Silver, ea 22.00
Label, Mad About...1884, 28-oz, late 1960s, NM 10.00
License plate, M 12.00
Photo, Essex Horsemobile, EX 45.00
Pin, lapel; Moxie boy, 1910, EX 110.00
Pin, Moxie girl, 1910, scarce 375.00
Plate, ceramic, Moxie boy, bird border, dinner sz 27.50
Pocket mirror, Zodiac, M 6.00
Postcard, Moxie barometer, EX 17.50
Sheet music, Moxie boy pointing on cover, 1921, EX 12.00

Sheet music, Moxie Fox Trot Song, full-color cover, 1930, EX, $22.00.

Sign, cb diecut, Moxie boy & girl, med sz, EX 225.00
Sign, cb diecut, Ted Williams, 3-D, 14" W, EX 125.00

Sign, stand-up; Moxie boy, cb, 1950 ....90.00
Sign, tin, bottle pouring, 19x54", EX 220.00
Sign, tin, Palmer Cox Brownies, Beach, 14x20", EX 1,300.00
Sign, tin diecut, Old Moxie-New Moxie, 19x27", NM 75.00
Smock, Moxie boy, EX 32.00
Spinner, Moxie boy, 2-sided metal diecut, 1911, EX 625.00
T-shirt, I've Got Moxie, orange w/red, early, M 6.00
Thermometer, Remember Those Days, orange, rnd, EX 45.00
Thermometer, tin, orange & gr, 25x10", EX 400.00
Thermometer, tin, 12x6", EX 85.00
Tip tray, I Just Love..., girl, 6" dia, EX 180.00
Token, bottle wagon, M 45.00
Tray, 100 Years 1884-1984, 11", M 27.50
Tumbler, clear glass, fluted base, flared top, 7-oz, M 17.50
Wooden nickel, M 2.50

My Own Cigars, clock, rvpt w/oak case, 40x17x5", EX 880.00
Nabisco Uneeda Bakers, emb cracker jar, 10" dia, EX 45.00
Nat'l Beer, tip tray, crown/coats of arms, 4x6", NM 12.00
Nature's Remedy, porc thermometer, Get It..., 27x5", EX 200.00
Nesbitt's Soft Drink, tin thermometer, professor, 27x5", EX 135.00
Nestle's Orig Toll House Cookies, pottery cookie jar, M 110.00
New Union Door Slides, wood/metal display, 1900s, 15x40", G ...75.00
Newberry...Store, rvpt mirror glass sign, 12x48", EX 385.00
Newport Cigarettes, tin sign, Blk couple, 16x22", NM 25.00
Nichol Cola, tin sign, lg bottle, 35½x12", EX 135.00
Nichol Cola, tin sign, Parker Metal, 1936, 36x12", VG 70.00
Nu-Grape, tin thermometer, emb & pnt, 1940s, 16", M 135.00
Nu-Grape, tray, lady in moonlight, Am Art, 13¼x10½", NM 160.00
Nu-Grape, tray, lady in moonlight, Am Art, 13¼x10½", VG 55.00
Numental Weatherstrips, wooden display, 1950s, 16x9", EX 80.00
Occident Flour, tin thermometer, 1920-40s, 17x5", VG 40.00
Old Colony Tobacco, pocket tin, silver, EX 95.00
Old Duck Handmade...Whiskey, rvpt sign, 17x20", EX 300.00
Old Gold Cigarettes, pocket tin, short, EX 20.00
Old Hill Side Cut Tobacco, fr paperboard sign, 1915, 26x22" 125.00
Old Overhold Rye, canvas sign, fisherman, fr, 36x42", EX 300.00
Oliver Chilled Plows, tin sign, men/store, fr, 36x27", VG 725.00
Onkin's Laundry, aluminum thimble, VG 3.00

Oscar Mayer Meats, tie tack, 50 Years in Meats, brass, EX 12.50
Ovum, porc sign, egg on red, Nothing Equals..., 32x23", VG 75.00
Pablum, cl tape measure, EX 30.00
Par-O-Vis Motor Oil, tc, yel on bl, 1960s, 1-qt, NM 10.00
Parkdale Beverages, bl glass seltzer bottle, w/label, VG 10.00
Parsley Brand Salmon, tip tray, 4" dia, EX 40.00
Patton's Sunproof Paints, tin cabinet, 15x16x11", VG 550.00
Peerless Motor Oil, tc, bl eagle on gray, 1935-45, ½-gal, EX 110.00
Penguin Motor Oil, tc, penguin on bl, 1935-45, 1-qt, EX 120.00
Penn Glenn Motor Oil, tc, propeller on red, 1935-45, 1-qt, EX .110.00
Pennzoil Motor Oil, tc, yel w/red bell, 1935-45, 1-qt, EX 30.00

Pepsi-Cola

Pepsi-Cola was first served in the early 1890s to customers of Caleb D. Bradham, a young pharmacist who touted his concoction to be medicinal as well as delicious. It was first called 'Brad's Drink' but was renamed Pepsi-Cola in 1898.

Bottle, amber, w/2 complete paper labels, 1930s, M 75.00
Bottle, clear emb throwaway type, 1950s, 12-oz 10.00
Bottle, clear w/paper label, 1950s, 24-oz, NM 55.00
Calendar, 1950, girl skater, 5-sheet, 22x13", EX 85.00
Calendar, 1955, cb, leggy girl, easel-bk, 12-sheet, 9x12", EX 70.00
Can, cone top, 1940s, 12-oz, NM 255.00
Can, pull tab, 1950s, 7-oz, M 6.00
Carrier, cb, Bigger Better, 6-pack, 1930s, 8x8", EX 35.00
Carrier, metal, 12-bottle, EX pnt, 1930s 120.00
Case, wooden, holds 24 bottles, 1930s, NM 55.00
Clock, electric, plexiglas face, Sessions, 14½x14½", G 50.00
Clock, glass front, lights up, 1940s, 15" dia, EX 115.00
Clock, glass front, wood fr, 1950s, 15" sq, EX 165.00
Clock, plastic, Please Pay Here, counter type, NM 55.00
Cooler, pnt metal, 1940s, 18x19x13", EX 120.00
Door push, tin plate w/Bakelite hdl, 1930s, 12x3", NM 135.00
Fan, cb, Pepsi Pete, 1930s, M 85.00
Menu board, cb w/tin fr, 1940s, 21x13", EX 165.00
Menu board, tin, Today's Specials, 1940s, 30x20", VG 1.30
Napkin holder, plastic, bottle form, 1960s, 9x3", NM 12.00
Opener, brass, 1940s, EX 70.00
Pen & pencil set, enameling on clips, MIB 50.00
Pencil, mechanical, 1950s, EX 32.00

Opia Cigar, tin sign, self framed, Shonk litho, 20x17", EX, $3,500.00.

Orange Crush, tin thermometer, bottle form, 28x7", EX 110.00
Orange-Julep, tray, bathing beauty w/parasol, 13¼x10½", VG 55.00

Push plate, tin, 1930s, 10x3", $200.00.

Pencil holder, ceramic, 3-compartment, 1930s, 3x5x1", EX 275.00
Radio, Bakelite, bottle form, 1940s, 28", EX 295.00
Ruler, wooden, Drink..., 1940s, 12", EX 32.00
Sign, cb, Bigger Better, hanging oval, 5x8", NM 135.00
Sign, cb, On the Lips of Millions, lady, 1930s, 11x28", EX 300.00
Sign, cl/tin, bottle cap, red/wht/bl, 1940s, 9" dia, NM 110.00
Sign, compo, Pour Your Own..., 1940s, 8x11", NM 135.00
Sign, plastic, 3-D cap, easel bk, EX 32.00
Sign, tin, Drive Slow..., boy w/Pepsi buckle, '70s, 40x16", NM ...90.00
Sign, tin, red & bl on cream, 11¼x23¾", NM 275.00
Spoon holder, ceramic, 1940s, 10x4" dia, NM 425.00
Straw holder, chrome, 1940s, 4x4x4", EX 250.00
String holder, tin, red/wht/bl, 1930s, 22x16", NM 425.00
Thermometer, tin, Any Weather's..., 1940s, 27x7", EX 150.00
Thermometer, tin, Say..., yel, 1950s, 27x7", NM 50.00
Thermometer, tin/cb, red/wht/bl, 1970s, 10x10", M 22.50
Tray, bottle over US map, Coast to Coast, 1930s, 11x14", NM .265.00
Tray, Hits the Spot, musical notes, 3-color, 1940s, 11x14", M ...125.00
Tray, red/wht/bl bottle cap, 1940s, 13" dia, EX 150.00
Watch fob, emb, 1900s, 2x2", EX 200.00

Pepsodent, Goldberg's puzzle, premium, EX 38.00
Peter Schuttler Wagons, cb sign, wagon train, fr, 25x31", EX 275.00
Peter's Weatherbird Shoes, mechanical pencil, EX 25.00
Peters Ammo, cb sign, hunter diecut, 1930s, fr, 52x38", M 600.00
Philadelphia Butcher's, tray, man w/bull, Beach, 14x17", VG 525.00
Picobac Tobacco, pocket tin, hand w/leaf, NM 65.00
Picobac Tobacco, pocket tin, lg leaf, EX 45.00
Piedmont Cigarettes, folding chair, porc bk, slant seat, EX 165.00
Pillsbury, paper sign, Young Cavalier, 1893, fr, 29x22", EX 235.00
Pippins 5 Cent Cigar, emb tin sign, 10x19½", G 25.00

Planters Peanuts

Mr. Peanut, the dashing peanut man with the top hat, spats, monocle, and cane, has represented the Planters Peanut Company from 1916 to 1961 when the company was purchased by Standard Brands. He promoted the company's product by appearing on premium giveaways, store displays, jars, scales, and in special promotional events. Among the favored treasures of collectors today are the glass display jars. They come in a variety of styles. Some are square, some hexagonal, some barrel-shaped, and others are round. The earliest, issued in 1926, was octagonal and is usually referred to as the 'pennant' jar. Although later reproduced, these are marked 'Made in Italy' on the bottom. The original is embossed on the back panel 'Sold Only in Printed Planters Red Pennant Bags.' In a second octagonal style, this embossed message was replaced with a paper label.

In 1930 a 'fishbowl' jar was introduced, and in 1932 a 'four-corner peanut' jar was issued. The rarest jar of all, the 'football' jar, was also used during the early 1930s. The Planters' square jar followed in the 1930s and was replaced by the 'barrel' jar. The six-sided jar with Mr. Peanut decals and the 'pickle' jar were later. All in all, more than fifteen different styles were developed.

In the late 1930s, premiums such as glass and metal figural paperweights, pens, and pencils were distributed. Post-war items were often made of plastic; Mr. Peanut salt and pepper shakers, mugs, and banks were popular. Today's collectors find a treasure trove of advertising memorabilia depicting that debonair gentleman, Mr. Peanut.

Bank, plastic, Mr Peanut 15.00
Bear, plush, Honey Bear from Planters, 8", M 18.00
Bic lighter, Mr Peanut, bl/yel, M 18.00
Bic razor, Mr Peanut 15.00

Cap, golf; Mr Peanut, M 18.00
Child's dinnerware, hard plastic, Mr Peanut, 3-pc 25.00
Color book, Am Ecology, Mr Peanut, 1972, NM 12.50
Color book, Presidents, 1977, EX 12.00
Cuff links, gold-tone metal, Mr Peanut figural, pr 75.00
Display, cb, Mr Peanut, 12" 10.00
Golf set, Mr Peanut, ball marker/tee/divet fixer, 3-pc 10.00
Iron-on, Mr Peanut, 8½" 5.00
Jar, Barrel, running Mr Peanut, paper label 275.00
Jar, chocolate-covered cashews, paper label, 1944, 4½-oz 25.00
Jar, Clipper, orig lid 150.00
Jar, Fish Bowl, rectangular label 150.00
Jar, Fish Bowl, sq paper label 150.00
Jar, Football, peanut finial 300.00
Jar, frosted label, big knob, rnd 45.00
Jar, Leap Year, orig lid 50.00
Jar, mixed nuts, paper label, orig lid, 1950s, 4½-oz 15.00
Jar, octagon, pennant 5¢, 7 sides emb 250.00
Jar, octagon, Pennant 5¢, 8 sides emb 300.00
Jar, peanut butter, early Mr Peanut on tin lid, scarce 25.00
Jar, Pennant 5¢, paper label 175.00
Jar, sq, peanut finial, Planters emb ea side 150.00
Jar, Streamline, tin lid 65.00
Jar, 4-corner, lg blown-out peanut ea corner, M 300.00
Jar, 6-sided, printed sq label 60.00
Lunch box, vinyl, Mr Peanut, bold colors, 5x8½x11", NM 30.00
Monogram, cloth, Mr Peanut, 2½" 3.00
Mug, pewter type, Breakin' the Noggin, Mr Peanut, 1978 ....38.00
Mug, pewter type, Mr Peanut, Wilton, dtd 1983, M 30.00
Note pad, Mr Peanut, cube type 18.00
Nut dish, plastic, Mr Peanut shape in bottom 12.00
Nut spoon, gold metal, Mr Peanut 18.00
Paint book, #2, 1919, NM 120.00
Paint book, Planters 50 States, 1968, EX 15.00
Pencil, mechanical; Mr Peanut figural, M in orig wrap 22.00

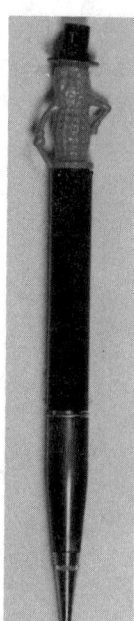

Mechanical pencil, $25.00.

Pin, 50th Anniversary, enamel 18.00
Pin-bk button, cl, Mr Peanut, old, EX 15.00
Plate, pewter type, Mr Peanut, ltd ed of 2000, 6", M 35.00
Plate, Planter's Snacks Super Bowl XIII, metal, 11", M 75.00

Playing cards, Tavern Nuts, complete deck, M in cl package **15.00**
Poster, History of Winter Olympics, 1980, 18x26", M **7.50**
Puzzle, Just Nuts About Mr Peanut, 18x23½", MIB **35.00**
Radio, can form, Mr Peanut, Cocktail Peanuts, MIB **45.00**
Radio, Mr Peanut figural, 10", MIB **75.00**
Raft, inflatable rubberized canvas, Mr Peanut, 72", M **95.00**
Refrigerator magnet, Mr Peanut figural **12.00**
Shakers, plastic, Mr Peanut figural, 3", pr **8.00**
Shirt, golf; Mr Peanut, M **45.00**
Ski cap, knit, Mr Peanut, 18" **18.00**
Sleeping bag, Salted Nuts, quilted, M **95.00**
Socks, Mr Peanut, pr **12.00**
Spoon, demitasse; gold-toned metal w/enamel Mr Peanut **22.00**
Spoon & fork, SP, Mr Peanut & peanuts on hdl **35.00**
Tag, luggage; Mr Peanut, yel & bl **15.00**
Tape measure/key chain, Mr Peanut **20.00**
Tie, Mr Peanut on maroon, MIB **45.00**
Tin, Salted Mixed Nuts, 7-oz **16.00**
Toothbrush, Mr Peanut figural, M **10.00**
Tray, dk gr plastic, Mr Peanut finial **35.00**
Tumbler, old fashioned; Cocktail Peanuts can, Mr Peanut **15.00**
Umbrella, gold; Mr Peanut, bl & yel, EX **45.00**
Whistle, lt bl plastic, Mr Peanut **3.00**
Windbreaker, nylon pullover, Mr Peanut, M **45.00**

Players Navy Cut Tobacco, tin sign, sailor, 29x20", VG **130.00**
Polarine Motor Oil, tc, full-color, 1-gal, VG **745.00**
Poll Parrot Shoes, cb sign, parrot, fr, 6x12", NM **75.00**
Pompeian Soap, panel, lady w/roses & ring, 1925, 33x13", EX **80.00**
Power Lube Motor Oil, porc sign, 2-sided, 1930s, 19x28", NM ..**750.00**
Pratt's Veterinary Remedies, oak cabinet, tin panel, 33", VG **775.00**
Prince Albert...Tobacco, tin charger, man smoking, 24", EX **675.00**
Prince Albert Tobacco, brass match safe, 2½x1¼" dia, VG **30.00**
Princess Prize Cigars, cigarette girl's box, w/strap, VG **160.00**
Purity Ice Cream, tray, girl in yel, 1913, 13¼" sq, EX **275.00**
Quaker Oats, cb display, Dionne Quints, 1936, 30x60", G **165.00**

RCA Victor

Nipper, the RCA Victor trademark, was the creation of Francis Barraud, an English artist. His pet's intent fascination with the music of the phonograph seemed to him a worthy subject for his canvas. Although he failed to find a publishing house who would buy his work, the Gramaphone Co. saw its potential and adopted Nipper to advertise their product. The company eventually became the Victor Talking Machine Co. and was purchased by RCA in 1929. Nipper's image appeared on packaged accessories and in ads and brochures. If you are very lucky you may find a life-size statue of him, but all are not old, they have been reproduced! Except for the years between 1971 and 1981, Nipper has seen active duty; and with his image spruced up only a bit for the present day, the ageless symbol for RCA still listens intently to 'His Master's Voice.'

Catalog, record; performers' photos, leatherette cover, 1917 ....**40.00**
Doll, RCA majorette, jtd wood, 1930s, EX **675.00**
Figure, Nipper, molded plastic, 36", EX **220.00**
Figure, Nipper, papier-mache, EX pnt, 1940s, 34", EX **925.00**
Figure, Nipper, papier-mache, glass eyes, early, 42", EX **1,500.00**
Figure, Nipper, papier-mache, 1930s, 13½" **200.00**
Needle tin, Nipper, 3-color, NM **28.00**
Pin-bk button, Little Nipper Club Member, 1930s, 1½", EX **65.00**
Postcard, hold-to-light, 1907 ....**12.00**
Puzzle, singers on record shape, 1908, M in pkg showing Nipper ..**95.00**

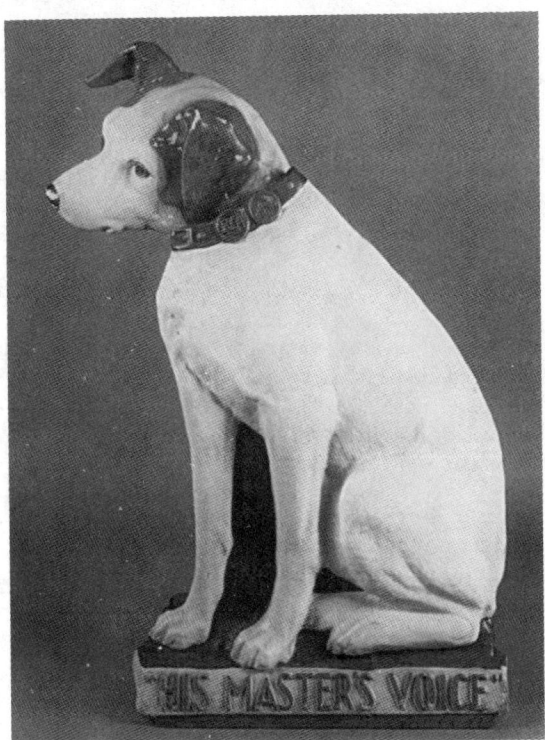

Figure, papier-mache, with movable head, fitted for sound in rear and at base, 40", $1,650.00.

Record brush, Nipper, 5½" L **30.00**
Sign, paper, His Master's Voice, textured, fr, 25x29", EX **675.00**
Sign, plastic/metal, ...Radio, lights up, 1940s, 15x37", EX **180.00**
Snow dome, Nipper **50.00**
Stick pin, Nipper **60.00**
Thermometer, porc, NM **485.00**
Watch fob, EX **25.00**

Raleigh Tobacco, dummy canister, 12x12x12", EX **45.00**
Ralston Purina, pottery ashtray, EX pnt, 6" dia, EX **35.00**
Ramon's Pills, wooden thermometer, 21", NM **275.00**
Ramsay's Biscuits, cb sign, matted in fr, rare, 24x36", EX **275.00**
Randolf Macon Cigars, sf ts, couple in reserve, 24x20", EX **575.00**
Ranier Beer, tray, Evelyn Nesbitt, 1901, 13¼" dia **450.00**
Reading Brewing, tin litho sign, factory, fr, 37x39", EX **3,080.00**

Red Goose Shoes

Realizing that his last name was difficult to pronounce, Herman Giesceke, a shoe company owner determined to give the public a modified, shortened version that would be better suited to the business world. The results suggested the use of the goose trademark with the last two letters, 'ke,' represented by the key that this early goose held in his mouth. Upon observing an employee casually coloring in the goose trademark with a red pencil, Giesceke saw new advertising potential and renamed the company Red Goose Shoes. Although the company has changed hands down through the years, the Red Goose emblem has remained. Collectors of this desirable fowl increase in number yearly, as do prices. Beware of reproductions; new chalkware figures are prevalent.

Address book, EX **6.00**
Bank, Save w/Shoes...Kid, tin, worn pnt, M-1585, 5⅝" **45.00**
Bell, Ring for Red Goose Shoes **25.00**

Blotter, cb, ...Circus Day, 1930s 12.00
Calendar, 1938, 10x17", EX 35.00
Clicker, yel, Red Goose logo, 1950s, M 12.50
Clock, papier-mache, Germany, 23", EX 1,200.00
Figure, goose, papier-mache, nodder, rpr, 24" 75.00
Figure, jtd compo goose, 1930s, 3", EX 200.00
Marbles, early logo, cb box of 5, EX 50.00
Pencil box, wood, sliding top, old, 2x9", EX 85.00
Shoe bench, seats 3 ....850.00
Shoe holder, wood, 18" 200.00
Shoehorn, pnt metal, 1930, 4½" 12.00
String holder, goose figural, CI, VG pnt 1,400.00
Tablet, school; Red Goose Rodeo, ca 1935, VG ..12.50
Thermometer, porc, EX 190.00
Watch fob, metal, oval, emb goose, rare, 2" 165.00
Whistle, tin; rectangular 15.00

Red Jacket Tobacco, cb sign, baseball scene, 28x22", EX 100.00
Regal Tobacco, pocket tin, flip lid, VG 150.00
Remington, oak & glass knife case, 20x15x10", VG 75.00
Revelation Tobacco, pocket tin, Phillip Morris, short, VG 20.00
Rheingold Extra Dry, neon tube sign, 15½x23", EX 75.00
Rislone Oil, metal thermometer, can, 24x10", EX 55.00
Rochelle Club Ginger Ale, cb sign, bottle form, 36", EX 37.50

Roly Poly

The Roly Poly tobacco tins were patented on November 5, 1912, by Washington Tuttle and produced by Tindeco of Baltimore, Maryland. There were six characters in all: Satisfied Customer, Storekeeper, Mammy, Dutchman, Singing Waiter, and Inspector. Four brands of tobacco were packaged in selected characters; some tins carry a printed tobacco box on the back to identify their contents. Mayo and Dixie Queen Tobacco were packed in all six; Red Indian and U.S. Marine Tobacco in only Mammy, Singing Waiter, and Storekeeper. Of the set, the Inspector is considered the rarest and in mint condition may fetch more than $1,100.00 on today's market.

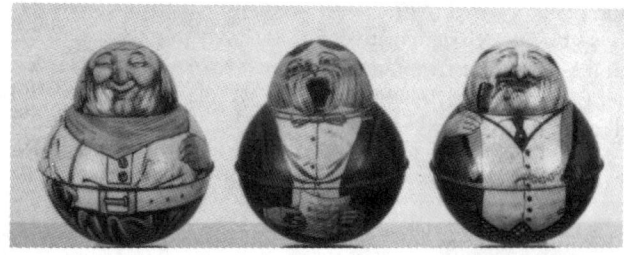

Dutchman, Mayo, EX, $500.00; Singing Waiter, Mayo, EX, $600.00; Satisfied Customer, Mayo, VG, $425.00.

Dutchman, Mayo, NM 550.00
Inspector from Scotland Yard, Mayo, EX 1,100.00
Mammy, EX 600.00
Singing Waiter, US Marine, VG 450.00
Storekeeper, Mayo, NM 695.00
Storekeeper, VG 365.00

Rose Leaf Tobacco, majolica plate, 3-D roses, 9", EX 225.00

Royal Crown Cola, metal thermometer, arrow, 27x10", EX 25.00
Royal Crown Cola, tin flange sign, 2-sided, 12x16", NM 135.00
Rumford Powder, tc, child & nurse, 4x2½", EX 110.00
Rumstaller Brewery, tip tray, lady w/dove, 5" dia, EX 130.00
Ruppert Beer, tip tray, comic dinner scene, 4" dia, NM 60.00
Ruppert Beer, tray, hands w/mugs, 13", dia, EX 70.00
Ruppert Beer & Ale, foam scraper holder, yel Catalin, EX 40.00
Rush Park Seeds, wooden box w/plaster vegetables, 21" W, EX ..415.00
Sanford's Ink, oak & glass cabinet, 3 decals, 11x16x14", EX 230.00
Sanford's Inks & Pastes, stoneware jar, no top, 7¾x7", EX 45.00
Sapolin Paint, CI stove on tin litho display, 9x12x5", VG 745.00
Sargent Paint, cb/tin/rvpt light, 1930s-40s, M 190.00
Sauer's Flavoring Extracts, wood thermometer, 48x9", EX 130.00
Schlitz, blotter, lady w/glass, EX 5.00
Schlitz, sf cb sign, couple at picnic, 1954, 35x43", EX 135.00
Schlitz, tray, touring car/blacksmith, 1900-10, 24" dia, VG 650.00
Schrader Tire Gauge, tin display, gauge diecut, 15", EX 175.00
Shawnee Mineral Water, dispenser, ice compartment, 46", EX ..330.00
Shoney's Big Boy Restaurant, glass tumbler, 3¾", M 25.00
Simon Pure Ale, tray, winged hops, 13" dia, EX 48.00
Simon Wallace Shoes, tip tray, lovely lady, 4" dia, EX 48.00
Sinclair Motor Oil, tc, dinosaur on red, 1936-45, 1-qt, EX 175.00
Singer Sewing Machines, porc sign, woman sewing, 24x36", G ..375.00
Slade's Epicurean Spices, lg tin w/6 tins inside, Ginna, EX 475.00
Smith's Potato Crisps, glass jar, aluminum top, 10x10x6", VG 45.00
Snowman Antifreeze, tc, snowman/cars, 1935-45, 2-gal, EX 100.00
Spidel Authorized Dealer, electric sign, 5x7x14", EX 40.00
Standard Electric Time, wall clock, brass finish, 17" dia, VG 35.00
Stanwix Ground Plug, pocket tin, bl, EX 325.00
Stegmaier Gold Medal Beer, tin-on-cb sign, 9x13", VG 25.00
Sun Insurance, porc sign, sun logo, English, 14x20", VG 100.00
Suncrest, tin thermometer, pnt & emb, 1940s, 15", EX 120.00
Sunoco, electric sign, hanging, 1988, 39x47½", NM 250.00
Sunoco, flanged porc sign, 2-sided, 1950-60s, 18x14", EX 80.00
Sunoco, hardbrd sign, Car Saver..., 1940s, 19x32", EX 100.00
Sunoco...Oil, porc rack w/bottles, w/light, 28x29x19", VG 465.00
Sunshine Beer, tray, Wholesome as Sunshine, 13" dia, EX 50.00
Sure Shot Brand, copper, display carton, 1950s, 3½x7", EX 40.00
Sweet Cuba Tobacco, tin bin, slant lid, 14x18x12", VG 100.00
Sweet Home, bread box, pnt wood, 33x23x24", VG 330.00
Talon Zippers, tin wind-up elephant, 5", EX 80.00
Tennyson Cigars, tin litho display/dispenser, 10x5x5", VG 265.00
Texaco, porc sign, No Smoking, 1940s, 23x4", M 185.00
Texaco Motor Oil, tc, Easy Pour, gr, 1923, ½-gal, EX 190.00
Texaco Motor Oil, tc, gr, 1927, ½-gal, 6½", NM 230.00
Texaco Oil, metal cart, rstr, 54x19x37", EX 360.00
Thos Wood Primrose Tea, wood crate, EX label, 13x25x16", EX 70.00
Three Feathers, pocket tin, EX 225.00
Tiger Chewing Tobacco, tc, tiger, 11½x8¾", G 80.00
Tom Keene Cigars, tc, paper label: Tom, 2½x4½x5½", EX 75.00
True Value Hardware, tin thermometer, 7x2½", EX 20.00
Turkey Red Cigarettes, sf cb sign, lady w/pack, 16x20", EX 365.00
Tuxedo Tobacco, pocket tin, man wearing hat, NM 25.00
Twin Oaks, pocket tin, sample sz, EX 150.00
Uncle Sam Peanuts, tin & glass warmer, 24x18x18", G 330.00
Uncle Sam Shoe Polish, tc, Uncle Sam, 1930s, 3½" dia, NM 35.00
Union Leader Tobacco, pocket tin, Uncle Sam, EX 88.00
Union Leader Tobacco, tin canister, Uncle Sam, knob top, EX 55.00
Universal Natural Milker System, tin sign, '20s, 11x36", EX 50.00
US Marine Tobacco, pocket tin, EX 300.00
Valley Forge Beer, tray, Washington's headquarters, 12" dia 40.00
Van Dole's Hot Chocolate, lustreware cup & saucer, Japan 65.00
Vat 69 Whiskey, ceramic pitcher, EX 12.00
Veedol Motor Oil, cb sign, Thomas litho, metal fr, 28x50", VG ...230.00

Veedol Motor Oil, porc sign, 2-sided, 1930s, 29x22", NM 360.00
Velvet Tobacco, porc sign, pack, 12x42", EX 500.00
Velvet Tobacco, tin canister, pipe, knob top, EX 35.00
Walter Baker, ceramic chocolate pot, brn & cream, 7", EX 175.00
Walter Baker, CI bookends, lady figural, 5x3", EX, pr 150.00
Walter Baker, cup & saucer, red & gold, Meissen, 4x5¼", EX 575.00
Walter Baker, glass cookie jar, lady in yel, 10", EX 145.00
Walter Baker, paper fan, chocolate lady, 9", VG 85.00
Walter Baker, porc plaque, lady, oval in ormolu fr, 7x5", EX 300.00
Walter Baker, porc plaque, lady serving, KPM, 9x7½", EX 770.00
Walter Baker, tip tray, EX color, 6" dia 150.00
Walter Baker, tray, tin litho, 14" dia, VG 175.00
Walter Baker, wooden box w/paper labels, 6x12x12", VG 120.00
Walter Baker Chocolate Bars, tin display, 5½" H, EX 200.00
Walter Baker Cocoa, ftd bombe tc, sporting scenes, 5", VG 110.00
Walter's Beer, tip tray, mountains, 4x6", NM 22.50
Welch's, decal, grape wreath, 12" dia, VG 10.00

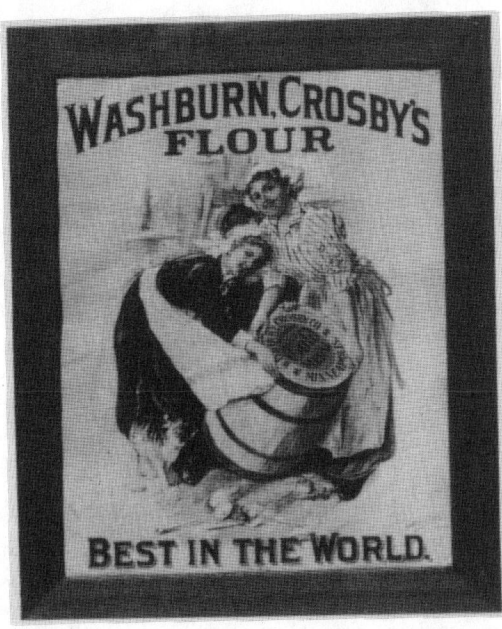

Washburn, Crosby's Flour, sign, Sentenne and Green, 28x22", $800.00.

West India Bananas, papier-mache display, bananas, 14x10x8" ..330.00
Westinghouse Electric Ranges, tile, commemorative, 1956, 4" 28.00
Whippet Motor Oil, tc, dog on wht, 1925-45, 2-gal, EX 210.00
Whistle Cola, tin sign, hand w/bottle, 1940s, 7x10", VG 235.00
White Rock Table Water, bottle, Psyche label, 1922, EX 12.50
Whittall Rugs, sign, rvpt w/wood fr, 1930s, 13x22", M 500.00
Will's Gold Flake Cigarettes, porc sign, 18" dia, EX 90.00
Willem II Cigars, pocket tin, portrait, flat, sm, EX 15.00
Willoughby Taylor Tobacco, pocket tin, royal bl, NM 30.00
Winchester Arms, envelope, illus, NM 48.00
WL Douglas Shoes, cb sign, gold portrait, 14x22", VG 200.00
WL Douglas Shoes, sf tin sign, 4-color, 1900s, 31x23", EX 150.00
Wrigley's Spearmint Gum, cb trolly sign, train, 11x21", EX 30.00
Wyandotte Clothing House, pocket mirror, lady, oval, EX 25.00
Yacht Club Tobacco, pocket tin, VG 125.00
Yellow Kid, pressed cb jackpot brd, 1940s, 13x14", EX 55.00
Zeppelin Motor Oil, tc, zeppelin, 1925-45, 2-gal, EX 375.00
666 Liquid, cb fan, Diana, EX 15.00

7-Up

Soda bottle, bicentennial, painted label, $4.00.

Lighter, aluminum, 2x1", EX 45.00
Playing cards, Fresh Up, NM in box 12.00
Push bar, porc, red/wht/blk/gr, 30x3", NM 32.00
Sign, cb, full color, 17x10", EX 12.50
Sign, tin, rainbow, pop-art style, 1974, 13x30", EX 30.00
Soda bottle, pnt glass, bicentennial, 11" 4.00
Thermometer, glass front, logo on red sq, 12" dia, EX 42.50
Thermometer, porc, 15x6", EX 40.00
Thermometer, tin, no bulb, 17x5", EX 26.00

Advertising Cards

Advertising trade cards enjoyed a heyday during the last quarter of the 19th century when the printing process known as chromolithography was refined and put into popular use. The purpose of the trade card was to acquaint the public with a place of business, a product, or a service. Most trade cards range in size from 2" x 3" to 3" x 5"; however, some are found in both smaller and larger sizes. Four categories of particular interest to collectors are:

Mechanical — those which achieve movement through the use of a pull tab, fold-out side, or rotating disk.

Metamorphic — cards that transform a person or a thing from a 'before' to an 'after' condition which, of course, represents a marked improvement immediately upon use of the featured product.

Hold-to-light — cards that reveal their design only when viewed before a strong light.

Diecuts — cards in figural forms such as the Heinz pickle series. Diecuts are usually in the shape of the advertised product or a theme-related object. For a more thorough study of the subject, we recommend *The Advertising Trade Card* by Kit Barry; his address can be found in the Directory under Vermont. When no condition is indicated, the items listed below are assumed to be in near-mint condition.

American Institute 55th Grand Expo, lady w/box 15.00
Andrews' Gem Holding Bed, woman at mirror 12.00
Armour & Co, 2 boys fight over product, others watch 12.00
Bixby's Best, man stands & receives shoe shine 10.00
Boston Baked Beans, man riding a pot pulled by fish 10.00
Boston Rubbers, bust of lady in hat 6.00

Buckeye Lawn Mower, boy w/hat, boy mowing below 10.00
Buckeye Lawn Mowers, child on flying bug 7.00
Buffalo Scale Co, inset of company & 5 sm vignettes 40.00
Bullard Hay Tedder, man driving horse-drawn tedder 25.00
Chas L Davis as Al Jolson, standing w/hoe by fence 8.00
Clipper Mower, girl mowing, croquet game in bkground 10.00
Congress Bitters, Capitol Building shown 15.00
Curtis & Son, blk & wht, gathering spruce gum 20.00
Deep Sea Mess Mackerel, fish in nets 8.00
Deering Twine Binder, inset of man using product 18.00
DS Morgan & Co, 8 farm machines shown 18.00
Dwight's Saleratus, picture of cow w/in fr 6.00
Enterprise Mfg Co, meat & food chopper 15.00
Enterprise Mfg Co, raisin seeder 15.00
Eureka Harness Oil, man showing harness to woman 8.00
French Laundry Soap, frog on rock 8.00
Gold Dust, diecut Twins in tub 25.00
Granite Iron Ware, The Little Housewife 8.00
Great Western & MI Central RR, Buffalo suspension bridge 12.00
Great Western & MI Central RW Line, Niagara Falls 12.00
Hecker's Flour, boy w/box over his head & girl's 8.00
Hiram Sibley & Co, waterfall scene inset 4.00
Huyler's, sm girl in chair w/cup & chocolate 12.00
Infallible Yeast Powder, 2 girls w/dog, 1 holds can 8.00
Japanese Soap, man w/parasol & soap 6.00
JS&M Peckham, Artisan stove 8.00
JS&M Peckham, Belfast stove 8.00
Kansas Salt Co, 2 views of single men dining 15.00
Kineo Stoves, 4 ice skaters, 1 fallen 5.00
Kumysgen, man milking cow w/child on his knee 8.00
Libby McNeill & Libby's, explorer w/dog 10.00
Major's Cement, childing handing rpr item to mother 8.00
Mechanical Bank, Speaking Dog 375.00
Mechanical Bank, Trick Pony 375.00
Merchant's Gargling Oil, 3 horses' heads at trough 8.00
Nestle's Milk Food, Little Miss Muffet 4.00
Nevius & Haviland, boy w/pointer dog & gun 15.00
Newark Machine Co, farm couple in field 8.00
Palmer's Perfumes, diecut flowers in vase 8.00
Pearl Shirts, woman showing new shirt to seated man 10.00
Philadelphia Lawn Mowers, boy mowing by fountain 15.00
Pike's Toothache Drops, woman in dentist's chair 25.00
Planet Jr, The; dbl-wheel hoe shown 20.00
Prov River Oyster Co, Blk man & dog tug at oyster 35.00
R&G Corsets, woman wearing corset looking in mirror 12.00
Reeves, Parvin & Co, lady (wearing hat) w/coffee cup 8.00
Royal Java, old lady w/kitten & child 5.00
Runkel Bros, Uncle Sam, Liberty, eagle 10.00
Scotts Emulsion, child in chair reaching for bottle 8.00
Sea Foam, bare-chested lady on shell 6.00
Sea Moss Farine, kitchen, boy & girl, girl on crate 15.00
Sedgwick Bros Co, farm fencing w/carriage at gate 15.00
Singer, sample card showing embroidery 10.00
Smith Organ & Piano, lady at piano, man w/violin 6.00
Sohmer Pianos, piano center w/known musicians pictured 12.00
Spaulding House, blk & wht, hotel w/carriages 25.00
Standard Sewing Machine Co, flag carried by soldiers 6.00
Studebaker Bros Mfg Co, blk & wht, factory shown 20.00
Sweet Peas, close-up of sweet peas, DM Ferry Co 8.00
Swift's Beef Extract, lady holding tray w/can on it 10.00
Tiger, The; man driving horse-drawn rake 25.00
Triumph Grain Drill & Seeder, 2 horses, man driving 25.00
Union Oyster Co, leaning lady holds flyer 15.00
United States Hotel Boston, blk & wht, Hotel shown 25.00

Thurber, Wayland & Co., strawberries, $6.00.

Van Houten's Cocoa, spider web puzzle 25.00
Vick's Choice Seeds, flowers & vegetables 12.00
Washburn & Crosby Co, 3 cows w/bags of flour 10.00
Wood's Acme Coffee, bearded man drinking Acme 8.00
Wood's May Queen Tea, box on table 15.00

Advertising Dolls

Whether your interest in ad dolls is fueled by nostalgia or strictly because of their amusing, often clever advertising impact, there are several points that should be considered before making your purchases. Condition is of utmost importance; never pay book price for dolls in poor condition, whether they are cloth or of another material. Restoring fabric dolls is usually unsatisfactory and involves a good deal of work. Seams must be opened, stuffing removed, the doll washed and dried, and then reassembled. Washing old fabrics may prove to be disastrous. Colors may fade or run, and most stains are totally resistant to washing. It's usually best to leave the fabric doll as it is.

Watch for new dolls as they become available. Save related advertising literature, extra coupons, etc., and keep these along with the doll to further enhance your collection. Old dolls with no marks are sometimes challenging to identify. While some products may use the same familiar trademark figures for a number of years (the Jolly Green Giant, Pillsbury's Poppin' Fresh, and the Keebler Elf, for example) others appear on the market for a short time only and may be difficult to trace. Most libraries have reference books with trademarks and logos that might provide a clue in tracking down your doll's identity. Children see advertising figures on Saturday morning cartoons that are often unfamiliar to adults, or other ad doll collectors may have the information you seek.

Some advertising dolls are still easy to find and relatively inexpensive, ranging in cost from $1.00 to $100.00. The hard plastic and early composition dolls are bringing the higher prices. Advertising dolls are popular with children as well as adults. For a more thorough study of the subject, we recommend *Advertising Dolls* by Joleen Robison and Kay Sellers. Joleen is our advisor; she is listed in the Directory under Kansas.

A&W Root Beer, Great Root Bear, hand puppet, 1976, 10", M 3.00
Adam's Gum, rabbit, cloth, 11", NM 140.00
Aim Toothpaste, Tweety Bird, M 8.00
Allied Van Lines, girl, cloth, 17", M 12.00
Beech-Nut Fruit Stripe Gum, man w/package-replica body, 7" 35.00
Big Boy Restaurant, boy, vinyl bank, 10", NM 7.50
Blue Ribbon Malt Extract, Lena, cloth, pre-1920s, 14", NM 150.00
Brach Candy, Bracho clown, cloth, litho ruffle, 17", NM 10.00
Budweiser, Bud Man, rubber, 18", M 50.00

C&H Sugar, Hawaiian boy & girl, cloth, 15", NM, ea 10.00
Campbell's, Campbell Kid, Horsman, orig clothes, 11", EX 300.00
Carnation Milk, Cry Baby, Horsman, 1962, 18", NM 35.00
Chesty Potato Chips, Chesty Boy, squeaker, 1950, 8", NM 85.00
Clark Candy Bars, boy, molded & pnt soft vinyl, 7", NM 45.00
Cox Gelatine, Scottish child, cloth, 1923, uncut 150.00
Curad, Taped Crusader, plastic bank, 1977, 8", M 45.00
Dodge Automobiles, Little Profit, nodder, 1960s, 6", NM 35.00
Downey's Honey-Butter, bee, yel plush, 10½", M 8.00
Esso, attendant, hard plastic bank, 5" 55.00
Fisk Tires, Fisk Boy, missing tire & candle, 4" 125.00

Fuller Brush Co., Thumbsy, cloth with removable jacket, 1962, 6", $18.00.

General Electric Radio, Bandy, jtd wood, 1919, 18", NM 450.00
Gerber, baby, rubber, orig clothes, 1954, 12", EX 25.00
Gold Medal Flour, girl, cloth, ca 1920s-30s, 7½", EX 60.00
Hawaiian Punch, Punchy, cloth, ca 1965, 13", NM 10.00
Honewell, Allergy Annie, cloth, NM 20.00
Hot Tamale Candies, Hot Tamale Kid, cloth, 18", NM 15.00
Jack Frost Sugar, Jack Frost, cloth, 20", NM 15.00
Keebler, elf, vinyl, Chase, 1974, 6½", M 15.00
Kellogg's, Cute 'n Cuddley Twins, vinyl, 1974, 9", pr 15.00
Kellogg's, Rice Krispie trio, cloth, 12½", ea 50.00
Kellogg's, Toucan Sam, cloth, 9x12", NM 15.00
Kitty Pan Litter, Glamour Kitty, vinyl, 1970s, 7½", NM 30.00
Long John Silver's, Long John Silver, cloth, 1972, 17", M 12.00
Lustre Creme Shampoo, Yorkie, furry fabric, 1967, 11", M 15.00
McDonald's Corp, Grimace, purple plush, M 10.00
Mr Turtle Candy, Mr Turtle, inflatable vinyl, 20", M 10.00
Nestle's, Little Hans, cloth, 1970, M 20.00
Nugget Casino, Nugget Sam, rubber, 1950s, 12½", EX 30.00
Old Crow Whiskey, Old Crow, hard plastic, 1950, 4½", NM 30.00
Peter Pan Ice Cream, Peter Pan, cloth, 1972, 18", M 15.00
Pillsbury, Doughboy, cloth, 1971, 16", NM 15.00
Planters, Mr Peanut, papier-mache nodder, 6½", NM 85.00
Purina Dog Chow, Shaggy DA dog, plush, 1977, 21", M 10.00

Puritan Flour, Puritan man, cloth, pre-1920, 15½", EX 150.00
RCA, Sellin' Fool, compo/wood, 1926, 15½", EX 400.00
Rexall Drugs, baby, vinyl, molded diaper, 7½", NM 30.00
Sambo Restaurants, tiger, rubber, 1972, 4¼", NM 10.00
Sunbeam Bread, Miss Sunbeam, vinyl/plastic, 1959, 17", M 65.00
Tastykake Bakeries, baker, cloth, 1974, 13", M 20.00
Texas Dairy Queen, cheerleader, cloth, 1979, M 10.00
Trailways, bus hostess, cloth, 1970s, 12½", M 10.00
Tru Test Paint, baby, compo head/cloth body, 1940s, 12", NM 25.00
Vermont Maid Syrup, Vermont Maid, vinyl, Uneeda, 15", M 60.00
Yukon Flour Mills, Peter Rabbit, cloth, 7", NM 55.00

African Art

African art does not consist of a single class of objects. Rather, these often-powerful sculptures are carved by many varying African tribes and groups across the central continent; each item represents specific cultural and spiritual functions and meanings. Many kinds of materials are used including wood, metal, fiber, ivory, and bone. Considerable numbers of these items are now being reproduced and sold to the tourist trade, but 'authentic' African art is generally considered to consist of objects which were used in cultural and religious activities. The items listed here are authentic, in good condition, and considered to be of average aesthetic quality. Scott Nelson, a collector of African art, is our advisor; his address is listed in the Directory under New Mexico.

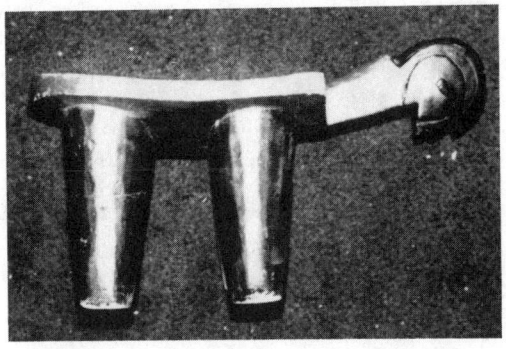

Stool, Hausa, plain legs, human head as handle, 8", $225.00.

Anklet, Ashanti, open wedge form, bronze, 6" 125.00
Basket, Zaire, open, cowrie shells, fiber, 15" dia 125.00
Beads, ceramic trade, string of 15 ....75.00
Bell, Yoruba, face, bronze, 4" 275.00
Cloth, Kuba, geometric decor, 18" sq 175.00
Comb, Chokwe, human head surmount, 5" 275.00
Divination board, Yoruba, figures, 16" dia 475.00
Doll, Ashanti, rnd head, simple design, 11" 275.00
Doll, Mossi, abstract human figure, leather covered, 10" 275.00
Door, Dogon, granary, 30 human figures, 2 turtles, 26" 1,250.00
Drum, Hemba, baboon head on side, 40" 600.00
Figure, Bamana, male standing figure, 24" 475.00
Figure, Baule, standing female, 20" 375.00
Figure, Dogon, male & female couple, 22" 1,250.00
Gold weight, Ashanti, bronze, bird, 3" 125.00
Hat, Kuba, fiber, decor 175.00
Headdress, Bamana, Tchi-wara (antelope), pr 1,500.00
Headrest, Luba, supporting human figure, 8" 375.00
Heddle pulley, Senufo, bird surmount, 7" 475.00
Ibejis, Yoruba, 9", pr 375.00
Knife, Kuba, throwing, str blade, 17" 125.00

Lock, Dogon, door, 2 human figural surmounts, 14" 675.00
Mask, Bamana, N'tomo, 14" 275.00
Mask, Bobo, antelope, polychrome, 24" 475.00
Mask, Chokwe, human face 375.00
Mask, Dan, human face, 16" 375.00
Mask, Dogon, Kanaga, 26" 800.00
Mask, Mende, helmet, female initiation, 12" 675.00
Mask, Pende, human face, 8" 375.00
Pendant, Songye, ivory human figure, ornate cvg, 4" ...600.00
Pipe, Makonde, human head bowl, 14" 275.00
Ring, Ashanti, bronze, horse/rider 150.00
Scepter, chief's; Yoruba, figural, 12" 475.00
Stool, Ashanti, crescent seat, 18" 325.00
Stool, Lega, human figural supports, 13" 375.00
Wisk, Tanzania, human figure, horsehair, 14" 200.00

Agata

Agata is New England peachblow (the factory called it 'Wild Rose') with an applied metallic stain which produces gold tracery and dark blue mottling. The stain is subject to wear, and the amount of remaining stain greatly affects the value. It is especially valuable (and rare) when found on peachblow of intense color. Caution! Be sure to use only gentle cleaning methods.

Currently rare types of art glass have been realizing erratic prices at auction; until they stablize, we can only suggest an average range of values. In the listings that follow, examples are glossy unless noted otherwise. Our advisors for this category are Betty and Clarence Maier; they are listed in the Directory under Pennsylvania. See also Green Opaque.

Bowl, 3-lobe rim, 5" dia 850.00
Creamer 1,200.00
Cruet, flared trefoil rim, EX mottling, appl hdl, 6" 1,625.00
Finger bowl, scalloped, EX mottling, 4½" dia 800.00
Punch cup, EX mottling, appl hdl, 2¾x3" 625.00
Salt shaker, rare 1,000.00
Spooner, mottled band w/gold border, 3¾x4⅛" 950.00
Toothpick holder, bulbous, ruffled rim, VG mottling 750.00
Toothpick holder, sq top, EX color & mottling 675.00
Tumbler, lemonade; tapered, curlique hdl, 5" 1,000.00
Tumbler, M mottling & gold, 3¾x2½" 795.00
Vase, baluster, EX coloring & mottling, 7¼" 1,450.00
Vase, lily; VG color & mottling, 5¾" 1,200.00
Vase, outstanding color, sq scalloped rim, 4½" 880.00

Akro Agate

The Akro Agate Co. founded in 1914 primarily as a marble maker, operated in Clarksburg, West Virginia, until 1951. Their popular wares included children's dishes, powder jars, flowerpots, and novelty items along with the famous 'Akro Aggies.' Much of their glass was produced in the distinctive marbleized colors they called Red Onyx, Blue Onyx, etc.; solid opaque and transparent colors were also produced. Most of the wares are marked with their trademark, a crow flying through the letter 'A' holding an Aggie in its beak and one in each claw. Other marks include 'J.P.' on children's pieces, 'J.V. Co., Inc,' 'Braun & Corwin,' 'N.Y.C. Vogue Merc Co. U.S.A.,' 'Hamilton Match Co.,' and 'Mexicali Pickwick Cosmetic Corp.' on novelty items. In 1936 Akro obtained the moulds from the Balmer-Westite Co. of Weston, West Virginia. Westite produced a similar line of products for several years. Their ware is drab in color when compared to Akro and is generally unmarked. The embossed Westite logo does appear occasionally on the

bottoms of some pieces. Westite is commonly accepted as a companion collectible of Akro.

For more information we recommend *The Collector's Encyclopedia of Children's Dishes* by Margaret and Kenn Whitmyer, available at your local bookstore. Our advisor for miscellaneous Akro Agate is Albert Morin; he is listed in the Directory under Massachusetts.

Chiquita

Chiquita, transparent cobalt, 12-piece set in original box, $100.00.

Creamer, gr opaque, 1½" 5.00
Cup, baked-on color, 1½" 7.00
Cup, cobalt, 1½" 10.00
Plate, gr opaque, 3¾" 3.00
Saucer, cobalt transparent, 3⅛" 4.00
Set, cobalt transparent, 22-pc, MIB 160.00
Set, gr opaque, 16-pc, MIB 67.50
Sugar bowl, baked-on color, 1½" 8.00
Sugar bowl, gr opaque, 1½" 5.00

Concentric Rib

Creamer, sm, gr or wht opaque, 1¼" 7.50
Plate, sm, gr or wht opaque, 3¼" 2.00
Set, sm, gr or wht opaque, 16-pc, MIB 70.00
Sugar bowl, sm, gr or wht opaque, 1¼" 7.50

Concentric Ring

Cereal, lg, any opaque color, 3⅜" 22.50
Creamer, sm, cobalt transparent, 1¼" 35.00
Cup, lg, any opaque color, 1⅜" 20.00
Cup, sm, cobalt transparent, 1¼" 30.00
Cup, sm, opaque colors other than gr or wht, 1¼" 7.50
Plate, sm, transparent cobalt, 3¼" 18.00
Saucer, sm, opaque colors other than gr or wht, 2¾" 4.50
Set, lg, any opaque color, 21-pc, MIB 365.00

Sugar bowl, lg, any opaque color, w/lid, 1⅜" 35.00
Sugar bowl, sm, cobalt transparent, 1¼" 35.00
Sugar bowl, sm, opaque colors other than gr or wht, 1¼" 10.00
Teapot, sm, opaque colors other than gr or wht, 2⅜" 17.50

Interior Panel, Marbleized

Cereal, lg, lemonade & oxblood, 3⅜" 30.00
Cereal, lg, red & wht, 3⅜" 27.50
Creamer, lg, azure bl, 1⅜" 30.00
Creamer, lg, bl & wht, 1⅜" 32.50
Creamer, lg, lemonade & oxblood, 1⅜" 35.00
Creamer, lg, pk lustre, 1⅜" 22.50
Creamer, lg, topaz transparent, 1⅜" 20.00
Creamer, sm, bl & wht, 1¼" 27.00
Creamer, sm, cobalt, 1¼" 25.00
Creamer, sm, gr & wht, 1¼" 25.00
Creamer, sm, jade lustre or pk lustre, 1¼" 25.00
Cup, lg, gr & wht, 1⅜" 20.00
Cup, lg, red & wht, 1⅜" 25.00
Cup, sm, azure bl or yel, 1¼" 22.00
Cup, sm, bl & wht, 1¼" 30.00
Cup, sm, red & wht, 1¼" 25.00
Cup, sm, topaz transparent, 1¼" 10.00
Pitcher, sm, topaz transparent, 2⅞" 15.00
Plate, lg, any solid color, 4¼" 10.00
Plate, lg, jade lustre, 4¼" 8.00
Plate, lg, lemonade & oxblood, 4¼" 15.00
Plate, sm, gr & wht, 3¼" 10.00
Plate, sm, gr and wht, 3¼" 7.50
Plate, sm, pk lustre, 3¼" 7.00
Plate, sm, red & wht, 3¼" 14.00
Plate, sm, topaz transparent, 3¼" 9.00
Saucer, sm, gr & wht, 2⅜" 6.00

Interior Panel, set, large, marbleized
blue and white, 21-piece set in VG
original box, $500.00.

Set, lg, lemonade & oxblood, 21-pc, MIB 525.00
Set, lg, red & wht, 21-pc, MIB 435.00
Set, lg, topaz transparent, 21-pc, MIB 280.00
Set, sm, any solid color, 16-pc, MIB 175.00
Set, sm, gr & wht, 16-pc, MIB 200.00

Sugar bowl, lg, bl & wht, w/lid, 1⅜" 40.00
Sugar bowl, lg, cobalt, w/wht lid, 1⅜" 40.00
Sugar bowl, lg, lemonade & oxblood, w/lid, 1⅜" 55.00
Sugar bowl, lg, red & wht, w/lid, 1⅜" 40.00
Sugar bowl, lg, topaz transparent, w/lid, 1⅜" 30.00
Sugar bowl, sm, bl & wht, 1¼" 27.00
Sugar bowl, sm, cobalt, 1¼" 25.00
Sugar bowl, sm, gr & wht, 1¼" 22.00
Sugar bowl, sm, jade lustre or pk lustre, 1¼" 25.00
Teapot, lg, bl & wht, 2⅝" 65.00
Teapot, lg, gr & wht, 2⅝" 45.00
Teapot, sm, azure bl or yel, 3⅜" 25.00
Teapot, sm, bl & wht, 2⅜" 40.00
Teapot, sm, jade lustre, 3⅜" 20.00
Teapot, sm, red & wht, 2⅜" 37.50
Teapot, sm, topaz transparent, 3⅜" 30.00
Tumbler, sm, topaz transparent, 2" 15.00

J.P. (Made for J. Pressman Company)

Cereal, lg, baked-on color, 3¼" 8.00
Creamer, lg, gr or brn transparent, 1½" 40.00
Cup, lg, bl transparent, 1½" 25.00
Plate, lg, baked-on colors, 4¼" 6.00
Plate, lg, brn or gr transparent, 4¼" 12.00
Saucer, lg, baked-on color, 3¼" 5.00
Set, lg, gr or brn transparent, 16-pc, MIB 300.00
Teapot, lg, bl transparent, w/lid, 2¾" 65.00

Miss America

Creamer, orange & wht 75.00
Creamer, wht 40.00
Cup, decal 45.00
Cup, gr 50.00
Plate, decal or gr 30.00
Plate, wht 20.00
Saucer, orange & wht 20.00
Saucer, wht 15.00
Set, decal, 17-pc, MIB 675.00
Set, gr, 12-pc, MIB 460.00
Sugar bowl, decal, w/lid 80.00
Sugar bowl, wht, w/lid 65.00
Teapot, decal 135.00
Teapot, wht 100.00

Octagonal

Cereal, lg, any opaque color, 5⅜" 11.00
Cereal, lg, lemonade & oxblood, 3⅜" 25.00
Creamer, lg, lemonade & oxblood, 1½" 30.00
Creamer, sm, any opaque color, open hdl, 1¼" 17.50
Cup, lg, any opaque color, open hdl, 1½" 15.00
Pitcher, sm, any opaque color, open hdl, 2⅞" 20.00
Plate, sm, any opaque color, 3⅜" 7.00
Set, lg, lemonade & oxblood, 21-pc, MIB 485.00
Sugar bowl, lg, any opaque color, closed hdl, w/lid, 1½" 17.00
Sugar bowl, lg, lemonade & oxblood, 1½" 40.00
Tumbler, sm, any opaque color, 2" 12.00

Raised Daisy

Creamer, sm, solid opaque, 1¼" 60.00
Cup, sm, solid opaque, 1¾" 20.00

Plate, sm, solid opaque, 3" 15.00
Saucer, sm, solid opaque, 2½" 10.00
Set, sm, solid opaque, 13-pc 235.00
Set, sm, solid opaque, 19-pc 495.00
Sugar bowl, sm, solid opaque, 1¼" 60.00
Teapot, sm, solid opaque, no lid, 2⅜" 35.00
Tumbler, sm, solid opaque, 2" 25.00

Stacked Disc

Creamer, sm, gr or wht solid, 1¼" 7.00
Cup, sm, any opaque color other than gr or wht, 1¼" 10.00
Cup, sm, pumpkin, 1¼" 25.00
Pitcher, sm, gr or wht solid, 2⅞" 10.00
Plate, sm, any opaque color other than gr or wht, 3¼" 5.00
Saucer, sm, any opaque color other than gr or wht, 2¾" 4.00
Set, sm, gr or wht opaque, 16-pc, MIB 80.00
Sugar bowl, sm, gr or wht opaque, 1¼" 7.00
Teapot, sm, any opaque color other than gr or wht, 2⅜" 14.00
Tumbler, sm, gr or wht opaque, 2" 6.00
Tumbler, sm, pk, 2" 8.00

Stacked Disc and Interior Panel

Cereal, lg, any solid color, 3⅜" 30.00
Cereal, lg, gr transparent, 3⅜" 20.00
Creamer, lg, cobalt transparent, 1⅜" 35.00
Creamer, sm, cobalt transparent, 1¼" 35.00
Creamer, sm, gr transparent, 1¼" 15.00
Cup, lg, gr transparent, 1⅜" 11.00
Cup, sm, azure bl, 1¼" 20.00
Cup, sm, pumpkin or cobalt, 1¼" 20.00
Pitcher, sm, cobalt transparent, 2⅞" 35.00
Pitcher, sm, gr transparent, 2⅞" 17.50
Plate, lg, any solid color, 4¼" 10.00
Plate, lg, gr transparent, 4¼" 8.00
Plate, sm, cobalt transparent, 3¼" 15.00
Set, lg, any solid color, 21-pc, MIB 410.00
Set, sm, any solid color, 16-pc, MIB 180.00
Set, sm, gr transparent, 16-pc, MIB 215.00
Sugar bowl, sm, cobalt, 1¼" 25.00
Sugar bowl, sm, gr transparent, 1¼" 30.00
Teapot, lg, cobalt transparent, 2⅝" 65.00
Teapot, lg, gr transparent, 2⅝" 45.00
Teapot, sm, cobalt transparent, 2⅜" 35.00
Tumbler, sm, any solid color, 2" 50.00
Tumbler, sm, gr transparent, 2" 10.00

Stippled Band

Creamer, lg, cobalt transparent, 1½" 35.00
Creamer, lg, gr transparent, 1½" 15.00
Creamer, sm, topaz transparent, 1¼" 25.00
Cup, sm, topaz transparent, 1¼" 7.00
Plate, lg, cobalt transparent, 4¼" 17.50
Plate, sm, topaz transparent, 3¼" 4.00
Set, sm, topaz transparent, 16-pc, MIB 125.00
Sugar bowl, lg, cobalt transparent, w/lid, 1½" 50.00
Sugar bowl, lg, gr transparent, w/lid, 1½" 25.00
Teapot, sm, topaz transparent, 2⅜" 18.00

Stippled Interior Panel

Creamer, lg, topaz transparent, 1½" 15.00

Creamer, sm, topaz transparent, 1¼" 30.00
Cup, sm, gr transparent, 1¼" 10.00
Cup, sm, topaz transparent, 1¼" 10.00
Pitcher, sm, topaz transparent, 2⅞" 15.00
Plate, sm, gr transparent, 3¼" 5.00
Plate, sm, topaz transparent, 3¼" 5.00
Set, lg, topaz transparent, 17-pc, MIB 180.00
Sugar bowl, lg, topaz transparent, w/lid, 1½" 25.00
Teapot, sm, gr transparent, 2⅜" 25.00
Teapot, sm, topaz transparent, 2⅜" 25.00

Miscellaneous

Ashtray, bl/wht, leaf 8.00
Ashtray, gr/wht, ellipsoid, 4¾" 20.00
Ashtray, Hotel Edison 45.00
Ashtray, Hotel Lincoln 45.00
Ashtray, Texas Centennial, 1836-1936 ....600.00
Basket, bl/wht, 2-hdl 35.00
Basket, orange/wht, 1-hdl 200.00
Bell, orange 165.00
Bell, wht 50.00
Bowl, bl, Stacked Disc 25.00
Bowl, blk, Graduated Darts, #320 ....35.00
Bowl, fruit; orange/wht, ftd 200.00
Candlestick, gr/wht, 3¼", pr 225.00
Candlestick, ivory, assembled lamp parts, pr 24.00
Candlestick, yel, 3¼", pr 250.00
Cornucopia, orange/wht, #765 ....6.00
Cornucopia, oxblood/wht, hand held, #766 ....18.00
Cup & saucer, demitasse; yel 24.00
Flowerpot, bl/wht, ribbed top, #292 ....6.00
Flowerpot, bl/wht, Stacked Disc, 4" 15.00
Flowerpot, blk, ribbed top, #294 ....25.00
Flowerpot, gr, Graduated Dart, fully sgn, 3" 28.00
Flowerpot, gr/wht, Stacked Disc, 5½" 20.00
Flowerpot, Graduated Dart, factory decor, #307 ....45.00

Flowerpot, Graduated Darts, royal blue, #308, $100.00.

Flowerpot, ivory, #1311, 4" 100.00
Flowerpot, ivory, Banded Dart, #300 ....20.00
Flowerpot, orange, #1307, 5¼" 200.00
Flowerpot, orange, Ribs & Flutes, #296 ....12.00
Flowerpot, orange/wht, Banded Dart, #301 ....35.00
Flowerpot, orange/wht, Ribbed & Dart, #295 ....125.00
Flowerpot, yel, Ribs & Flutes, #305 ....18.00

J Vivaudou, apothecary jar, blk 28.00
J Vivaudou, mortar & pestle, pk 24.00
J Vivaudou, powder box, orange/wht, rare 250.00
Knife, crystal, grid style, #739 ....35.00
Lamp, crystal, wall hanging 15.00
Lamp, milk wht, desk style 35.00
Marble box, Akro Moonies 600.00
Marble box, Game of Click 500.00
Marble box, Popeye set 600.00
Marble box, tin box #150 ....275.00
Marble box, 100 #0 assorted Royals 350.00
Pen holder, orange/wht, Goodrich Tires, tire form 60.00
Planter, bl/wht, rectangular, #656 ....10.00
Planter, rectangular, factory decor, #653 ....35.00
Powder jar, dk pk, Scotty dog form 50.00
Powder jar, ivory, apple form 400.00
Powder jar, orange, sawtooth, rare 250.00
Powder jar, transparent, Colonial lady form, rare 1,000.00
Vase, orange/wht, Graduated Dart, #312 ....65.00
Vase, royal bl, tab hdls, #317 ....30.00
Westite, ashtray, blk, hexagonal 15.00
Westite, candlestick, orange/beige, 8¼", pr 45.00
Westite, flowerpot, bl, #301 ....18.00
Westite, flowerpot, gr, #302 ....24.00
Westite, garden dish, brn/ivory, rnd, #600 ....65.00

Alexandrite

Alexandrite is a type of art glass introduced around the turn of the century by Thomas Webb and Sons of England. It is recognized by its characteristic shading, pale yellow to rose and blue. Although it was also produced by other companies, only examples made by Webb command premium prices. Amount and intensity of blue determines value. Our advisors for this category are Betty and Clarence Maier; they are listed in the Directory under Pennsylvania.

Finger bowl, fluted, w/underplate, 5" 900.00
Finger bowl, fluted rim, 2⅞x5" 650.00
Match holder, Dmn Quilt, sq top, 3x2½" 650.00
Toothpick holder, bulbous, collared sq top, 3x2½" 650.00
Tumbler, juice; Honeycomb, EX color, 3" 800.00
Vase, Honeycomb, corset waist, 3¼x2⅜" 595.00
Vase, 8-petal top, 8-panel amber std & base, 6½" 985.00
Wine, amber stem & ft, Webb, 4½x2⅜" 550.00
Wine, Optic, citron stemmed ft, rare, 4½x2⅜" 550.00

Almanacs

The earliest evidence indicates that almanacs were used as long ago as Ancient Egypt. Throughout the Dark Ages they were circulated in great volume and were referred to by more people than any other book except the Bible. *The Old Farmer's Almanac* first appeared in 1793 and has been issued annually since that time. Usually more of a pamphlet than a book (only a few have hard covers), the almanac provided planting and harvesting information to farmers, weather forecasts for seamen, medical advice, household hints, mathematical tutoring, postal rates, railroad schedules, weights and measures, 'receipts,' and jokes. Before 1800 the information was unscientific and based entirely on astrology and folklore. The first almanac in America was printed in 1639 by William Pierce Mariner; it contained data of this nature. One of the best-known editions, Ben Franklin's *Poor Richard's Almanac*, was introduced in 1732 and continued to be printed for twenty-five years.

By the 19th century, merchants saw the advertising potential in a publication so widely distributed, and the advertising almanac evolved. These were distributed free of charge by drug stores and mercantiles and were usually somewhat lacking in information, containing simply a calendar, a few jokes, and a variety of ads for quick remedies and quack cures.

Today their concept and informative, often amusing text make almanacs popular collectibles that may usually be had at reasonable prices. Because they were printed in such large numbers and often saved from year to year, their prices are still low. Most fall within a range of $4 to $15. Very common examples may be virtually worthless; those printed before 1860 are especially collectible. Quite rare and highly prized are the Kate Greenaway 'Almanacks,' printed in London from 1883 to 1897. These are illustrated with her drawings of children, one for each calendar month.

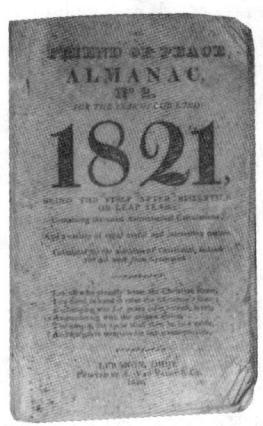

1821, Friend of Peace #2, astronomical calculations, 36 sewn pages, rare, G, $325.00.

1840, People's Almanac, EX 10.00
1846, German Almanac, Philadelphia pictured on front, EX 10.00
1850, New England Farmer's, EX 20.00
1858, German Almanac, EX 10.00
1861, Great Western Almanac, paddle wheeler front 15.00
1863, Webster's, woodcuts & stories, Albany NY, EX 6.50
1873, Centaur Liniment, EX 12.50
1873, Scovill & Co Farmer's & Mechanics 15.00
1880, Rush's Almanac & Guide to Health, Dr AH Flanders, G ...10.00
1883, Kate Greenaway, French, mini, EX 65.00
1884, Dr Harter's 8.00
1885, State Almanac, Burlington VT, EX 12.50
1888, Farmer's Almanac 10.00
1888, NY Almanac, colorful, EX 12.50
1890, Dr Ayer's American, EX 8.00
1894, Indianapolis News 12.00
1898, Dr Harter's, EX 12.00
1899, Peruna Drug Mfg, Columbus OH, EX 10.00
1905, Dr Herrick's, VG 6.00
1928, Dr Miles, VG 3.00
1931, Dr Pierce's Treasure Chest, NM 5.00
1933, Indiana Botanic Gardans, The Herbalist, VG 12.00
1936, Herb Medicine Co, G 7.50
1941, Goodrich Almanac, VG 8.00
1941, Illinois Herb Co, EX 12.00
1944, Flying Red Horse 6.00
1945, Goodrich Farmers' Handbook & Almanac, EX 12.00
1947, Indiana Botanic Gardens, The Herbalist, VG 10.00

Aluminum

Aluminum, though being the most abundant metal in the earth's crust, always occurs in combination with other elements. Before a practical method for its refinement was developed in the late 19th century, articles made of aluminum were very expensive. After the process for commercial smelting was perfected in 1916, it became profitable to adapt the ductile, non-tarnishing material to many uses.

By the late thirties, novelties, trays, pitchers, and many other tableware items were being produced. They were often handcrafted with elaborate decoration. Russel Wright designed a line of lovely pieces such as lamps, vases, and desk accessories that are becoming very collectible. Many who crafted the ware marked it with their company logo, and these signed pieces are attracting the most interest. Wendell August Forge (Grove City, PA) is a mark to watch for; this firm produced some particularly nice examples and upwardly mobile market values reflect their popularity with today's collectors. In general, 'spun' aluminum is from the thirties or early forties, and 'hammered' aluminum is from the fifties. Our advisor for this category is Ted Haun; he is listed in the Directory under Indiana. See also Russel Wright.

Bowl, chrysanthemum decor, Continental, 12" 14.00
Bowl, fruit; emb florals & fruit, hdls, 11" 17.50
Bowl, stylized deer, Kensington, 10" 22.50
Bracelet, hammered, foliage, Wendall August 65.00
Butter dish, Kent, ¼-lb 12.00
Butter tub, emb leaves, hammered 18.00
Candelabra, Buenilum, 3-lite, 12" 37.50
Candy dish, box shape, 3-section glass insert, 7½" dia 18.00
Casserole, Buenilum, hammered, w/lid 12.50
Clock, stepped sides w/emb florals, floral vase atop, 14" ...125.00
Coaster, emb florals, mk Everlast Forged Alum, set of 8, +tray 18.00
Garden ornament, rabbit, cast, 12" 75.00
Lazy susan, 7-part, inserts in 1950s colors, EX 28.00
Nut dish, rnd, unmk, 11" 8.50
Percolator, wood hdl, w/basket, 1-cup 17.50
Pitcher, water; Bascal, +6 tumblers in assorted colors 24.00
Pitcher, water; Buenilum, hand hammered 15.00
Shakers, hammered, pr 14.00
Silent butler, Buenilum 12.00

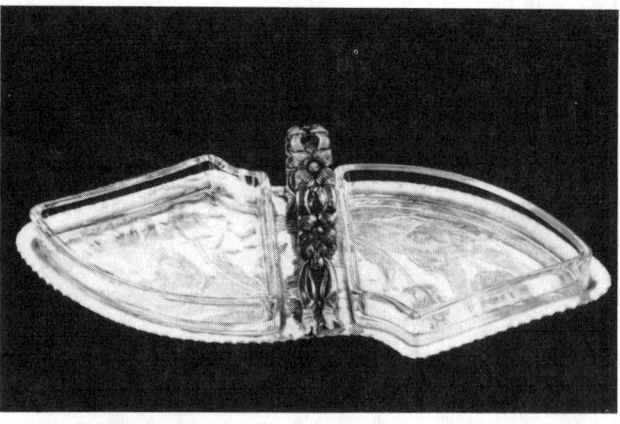

Relish tray, tulip motif, two glass inserts, signed Rodney Kent, $18.00.

Tray, Celleni-Craft, w/ceramic tile insert, 19x14" 135.00
Tray, dresser; hammered, w/2 glass powder-jar inserts, Kent 25.00
Tray, emb morning-glories, ceramic insert, Farberware, 11½" 15.00

Tray, emb tulips, fancy hdls, hammered, w/lid, Kent, #440 ....25.00
Tray, Palmer-Smith, Arts & Crafts decor, 22x15" 75.00
Tray, pineapple decor, Kensington, 12x6" 18.00
Tray, ship decor, Kensington, 11" sq 16.00
Tray, stag & doe decor, Continental, 18x11" 16.00
Tumbler, Buenilum, set of 8 ....20.00
Warming dish, hammered w/acorns, w/lid, Bakelite hdls 40.00

AMACO, American Art Clay Co

AMACO is the logo of the American Art Clay Co. Inc., founded in Indianapolis, Indiana in 1919 by Ted O. Philpot. They produced a line of art pottery from 1931 through 1938 that is today beginning to interest collectors. The company is still in business but now produces only supplies, implements, and tools for the ceramic trade.

Values for AMACO have risen sharply, especially those for figurals, items with Art Deco styling, and pieces with uncommon shapes.

Our advisor for this catgory is Virginia Heiss; she is listed in the Directory under Indiana.

Vase, #19, orange semi-matt, handles, four buttressed feet, 12", $350.00.

Vase, #186, bl gloss, scalloped cylinder form, 11½" 225.00
Vase, #22, gr matt, 2 sm hdls, 6" 45.00
Vase, #241, bl gloss, lg hdls, circular ridges, 4" 45.00
Vase, #242, bl gloss, Deco hdls, 4" 40.00
Vase, #246, bl gloss, 4" 35.00
Vase, #41, matt cream w/bl rim, 9½" 145.00
Vase, #44, gr matt, melon shape, 7½" 80.00
Vase, #48, matt gr w/Deco hdls, 9½" 110.00
Vase, #5, matt lt bl w/molded flowers, 4¼x5½" 110.00

Amberina

Amberina, one of the earliest types of art glass, was developed in 1883 by Joseph Locke, of the New England Glass Company. The trademark was registered by W.L. Libbey, who often signed his name in script within the pontil.

Amberina was made by adding gold powder to the batch, which produced glass in the basic amber hue. Part of the item, usually the top, was simply reheated to develop the characteristic deep red or fuchsia shading. Early amberina was mold-blown, but cut and pressed amberina was also produced. The rarest type is plated amberina, made by New England for a short time after 1886. It has been estimated that less than 2,000 pieces were ever produced. Other companies, among them Hobbs and Brockunier, Mt. Washington Glass Company, and Sowerby's Ellison Glassworks of England, made their own versions, being careful to change the name of their product to avoid infringing on Libbey's patent. Prices have been erratic at auction for several months; values given below are in the average range. See also Libbey.

Basket, gold flowers/fence, rigaree, wishbone ft, 15x6x9" 695.00
Bottle, raised arches pattern, emb Depose on base, 11x3⅜" 145.00
Bottle, wine; swirl, amber bubble stopper, 9½x3" 135.00
Bowl, amber wishbone ft & hdls, 6¼x10" 275.00
Bowl, flared rim, NE Glass, 3x5½" 365.00
Bowl, slightly ribbed, tricorner top, Mt WA, 2¼x5" 265.00
Bride's bowl, T'print, 9", Mt WA; in Pairpoint fr, 12" 885.00
Celery vase, Dmn Quilt w/scalloped sq top, NE Glass, 6½" 485.00
Celery vase, Invt T'print, fuchsia shaded, sq/scalloped, 6½" 515.00
Compote, swirl, amber cut finial on lid, 9¾x7" 265.00
Creamer, swirl ribs, rnd mouth, amber hdl, 4⅞x3½" 135.00
Cruet, Invt T'print, 3-petal top, amber ball stopper, 6¼" 295.00
Decanter, swirl, ped ft, rnd body w/dbl-loop hdl, 11x5½" 295.00
Dish, Daisy & Button, 5½" sq 120.00
Finger bowl, Dmn Quilt, trifold rim, NE Glass 195.00
Finger bowl, swirl, NE Glass, 2¼x4¼" 165.00
Pickle castor, Hobnail, Mt WA, 4½x3" 975.00
Pitcher, Invt T'print, reversed color, tankard, 5⅝x2¾" 145.00
Pitcher, Invt T'print, sq top, reed hdl, NE Glass, 4¼" 385.00
Pitcher, milk; Invt T'print, sq top, NE Glass, 6½x6" 465.00
Pitcher, swirl, appl hdl, 7½", +6 3¾" ftd tumblers 375.00
Plate, Invt T'print, NE Glass, 7" 145.00
Plate, ribbed, NE Glass, 8½" 300.00
Punch cup, Dmn Quilt, NE Glass, 2½x2¼" 125.00
Punch cup, Optic, appl reeded hdl, Mt WA, 2⅛" 250.00

Punch bowl, paneled sides, 15½" dia, with amber 17" underplate, $625.00.

Rose bowl, Baby Invt T'print, Mt WA, 3x3½" 425.00
Rose bowl, Dmn Quilt, ruffled, Mt WA, 4x4¼" 565.00
Shade, Dmn Quilt, bulbous, fits 6" ring, 5½" H 175.00
Shade, Dmn Quilt, Mt WA, 4¼x5" 585.00
Shakers, Invt T'print, pr in ftd/decor Wilcox-Meriden fr 350.00
Spooner, corset shape w/swirled ribs, polished pontil 245.00
Spooner, Dmn Quilt, scalloped sq top, NE Glass, 5⅛" 275.00

Toothpick holder, Daisy & Button 335.00
Tumbler, Dmn Quilt, NE Glass, 4x2⅝" 120.00
Tumbler, Herringbone, 4" 135.00
Tumbler, Invt T'print, 3¾x2⅝" 48.00
Tumbler, Swirl, 4" 175.00
Vase, appl crystal spiral trim, 8⅛x2⅝" 225.00
Vase, bud; swirled ribs, bottle shape, sgn Libbey, 9" 450.00
Vase, crimped top, 7½" 115.00
Vase, jack-in-the-pulpit; Invt T'print, pnt flowers, 12½" 375.00
Vase, jack-in-the-pulpit; lt ribbing, NE Glass, 6x3¼" 275.00
Vase, lily; ribbed, Mt WA, 10" 500.00
Vase, lily; ribbed, 15" 825.00
Vase, lily; ribbed, 5¾x3¼" 400.00
Vase, Optic Panels, cylindrical, NE Glass, 4" 195.00

Plated Amberina

Bowl, 5-lobe, 7½" 3,250.00
Butter dish, ribbed, SP base w/unicorn in center, 4¾" 3,400.00
Condiment, ribbed, 4" shakers in SP fr mk Toronto 2,000.00
Mug, ribbed, fine color, amber hdl 2,100.00
Pitcher, NE Glass, 7" 6,000.00
Pitcher, ribbed, EX color, amber hdl, tricorn, 4½" 4,750.00
Punch cup, EX ribbing & color 1,800.00
Tumbler, water; 3¾x2½" 1,800.00
Underplate, ribbed, ruffled, 6⅜" 1,150.00

American Encaustic Tiling Co.

A.E. Tile was organized in 1879 in Zanesville, Ohio. Until its closing in 1935, they produced beautiful ornamental and architectural tile equal to the best European imports. They also made vases, figurines, and novelty items with exceptionally fine modeling and glazes.

Advertising pc, maroon heart, 2" 65.00
Box, orange w/Oriental scene relief on lid, 3x9x6" 195.00
Inkwell, pk, 6x9" 95.00
Jar, temple; blk, w/lid, 9" 150.00
Lamp base, dk bl, 12" 125.00
Tile, bird, HP, wood fr, 10½x6¼", pr 350.00
Tile, Braham's portrait on gr, floral corners, 6" 65.00
Tile, dedication souvenir, bl, 4" 75.00
Tile, faience, peasant lady w/flowers, bl & wht, 6x6" 65.00
Tile, fish on waves, 4-color, 2x4" 65.00
Tile, HP on cream, sgn Rhead, fr, 6" 135.00
Tile, knight, mc, 10x14x1" 600.00

Tile, maid on bench, two children gathering grain, mauve gloss, signed H.M., crazing and edge chips, 12x18", $325.00.

Tile, maid on bench, 2 children harvest grain, 12x18", EX 325.00
Tile, Margery Daw, bright colors 65.00
Tile picture, woman in relief, bl gloss, fr, 3-pc, 18x5½" 185.00
Vase, lt gr, buttress-style arms, 8" 145.00

American Indian Art

That time when the American Indian was free to practice the crafts and culture that was his heritage has always held a fascination for many. They were a people who appreciated beauty of design and colorful decoration in their furnishings and clothing; and because instruction in their crafts was a routine part of their rearing, they were well accomplished. Several tribes developed areas in which they excelled. The Navajo were weavers and silversmiths, the Zuni lapidaries. Examples of their craftsmanship are very valuable. Today even the work of contemporary Indian artists — weavers, silversmiths, carvers, and others — is highly collectible. For a more thorough study we recommend *Arrowheads and Projectile Points* and *Indian Artifacts of the Midwest*, both by our advisor, Lar Hothem; you will find his address in the Directory under Ohio.

Key:
bw — beadwork
dmn — diamond
E — Eastern
NE — Northeastern

p-h — prehistoric
S — Southern
W — Western

Apparel and Accessories

Before the white traders brought the Indian women cloth from which to sew their garments and beads to use for decorating them, clothing was made from skins sewn together with sinew, usually made of buffalo tendon. Porcupine quills were dyed bright colors and woven into bags and armbands and used to decorate clothing and moccasins. Examples of early quillwork are scarce today and highly collectible.

Early in the 19th century, beads were being transported via pony pack trains. These 'pony' beads were irregular shapes of opaque glass imported from Venice. Nearly always blue or white, they were twice as large as the later 'seed' beads. By 1870 translucent beads in many sizes and colors had been made available, and Indian beadwork had become commercialized. Each tribe developed its own distinctive methods and preferred decorations, making it possible for collectors today to determine the origin of many items. Soon after the turn of the century, the craft of beadworking began to diminish.

Armband, Sioux, 4-color metallic bw, 12½" 95.00
Belt, Chippewa, bw on trade cloth, 5x34" 110.00
Blanket, wearing; Navajo child's, 5-color, 1900, 62x32" 450.00
Buffalo dance kilt, Jemez, pnt snakes, tin cones, MD Latoma 550.00
Cap, Sioux baby's, butterfly/Am flags, 5-color bw, 6", EX 975.00
Cuffs, Plains child's, 6-color bw, minor loss, 11", pr 575.00
Dress, N Plains girl's, wht doeskin w/6-color bw, 1925, 39" 250.00
Gauntlets, Cree, 6-color floral embr, 13", EX 350.00
Gauntlets, Plains, bw pictorials/foliage, wool lined, 16" 600.00
Hair suspension, Blackfeet, human hair drops/shells/bw/etc 500.00
Jacket, Sioux Reservation, geometric/figural bw, EX 600.00
Jacket, Woodlands, smoked hide w/embr, Hudson Bay buttons ..475.00
Leggings, Blackfoot, 5-color bw triangles/bands 900.00
Leggings, Plains, bw geometrics on wht, brass buttons, 16" 325.00
Moccasins, Plains, rose/pk/bl bw, sinew/thread sewing, 10" 425.00
Moccasins, Plains burial, allover bw/bw soles, velvet cuff 2,200.00
Moccasins, Sioux, faceted metallic bw on bl-wht, 1890, 11" 625.00
Moccasins, Sioux, yel-ochre stain/6-color bw, 11", EX 600.00

Sash, E Woodlands, finger-woven wool w/bw, fringe, 94", EX ..3,500.00
Shirt, Blackfoot, cloth w/dmn cutouts, fringe, early 850.00
Shirt, Plains, buckskin w/3-color pnt detail, 1800s, 26" 650.00
Shirt, Plains scout's, smoked hide w/bw at closure, fringe 1,200.00
Shirt/sash/pants, NE Woodlands, cloth w/bw & fringed hide 250.00
Vest, Sioux baby's, geometric/X/flags, 5-color bw, 1900 ....900.00

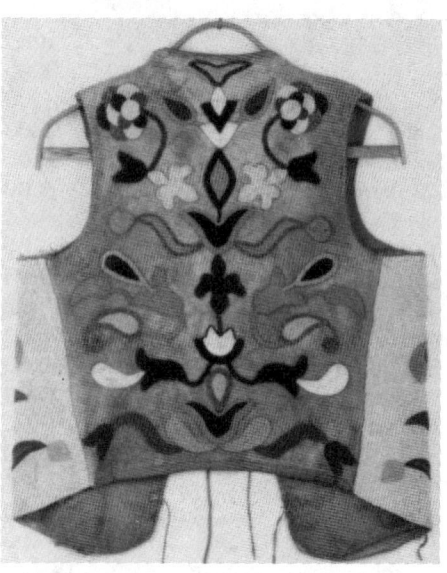

Vest, Plains, beadwork front and back, lined with trade cloth, 1800s, 21", $850.00.

War shirt, Gros Ventre, wide bw strips/panels, 1880s 35,000.00

Arrowheads and Points

Relics of this type usually display characteristics of a general area, time period, or a particular location. With study, those made by the Plains Indians are easily discerned from those of the West Coast. Because modern man has imitated the art of the Indian by reproducing these artifacts through modern means, use caution before investing your money in 'too good to be authentic' specimens.

Adena, MO, rose w/tan, classic, 5¼" 165.00
Baker's Creek, SE USA, lt brn, stemmed, 1⅞" 5.00
Beaver Lake, KY, tan, slightly fluted base, 3⅝" 135.00

Clovis point, early Paleo, ca 9500-9000 BC, found in Ohio, made of Upper Mercer (blue), fluted on both lower faces, 4x1⅛", $500.00+.

Dalton, AR, tan/red, 2", EX 25.00
Dalton, KY, brn, EX fluting, 1⅞" 35.00

Dalton, WI, brn sugar quartz, 4" **225.00**
Dalton-Hemphill, OH, tan flint, 2½" **30.00**
Dalton-Nuckolls, MS, tan flint, 2½" **22.00**
Desert birdpoint, AZ, red agate, made from flake, ⅝" **5.00**
Dickson, KS, lt brn, 2" **3.50**
Durst, KS, gray-brn, worn, 1½" **3.00**
Elam, TX, gray, 1¾" **8.00**
Greenbrier Dalton, IL, wht flint, fluted, well made, 1½" **28.50**
Greenville, TN, gray glossy chert, 2⅛" **6.00**
Hardaway, AR, tan, 2" **22.00**
Harrell, AR, wht flint, ⅞" **12.00**
Langtry, KY, lt tan, well made, 1⅛" **15.00**
Limestone, AL, gray-brn, shouldered/stemmed, 1½" **5.00**
Limestone, AL, gray/brn, left bevel, 1¾" **4.00**
Madison, AL, gray-brn, triangular, thin, 1⅞" **6.00**
Meserve, IL, exceptional, 3" **140.00**
Meserve, IL, off-wht, classic, 3¼" **165.00**
Nodena, AR, tan, 1⅛" **5.00**
Nolan, TX, beige, EX work, 2" **12.00**
Osceola, IL, red/tan, good example, 2" **20.00**
Paleo, TX, grays, steep bevels, basal grinding, thin, 3" **175.00**
Pedernales, TX, brn w/translucent edge, 4⅞" **285.00**
Refugio, MO, red, 2⅛" **6.00**
Scallorn, brn w/translucent edge, 1½", EX **3.00**
Searcy, OK, blk flint, 2¼" **28.50**
Stanley, AL, gray, shouldered/concave base, p-h, 1¾" **5.00**

Arts and Crafts

Blanket strip, Sioux, bw on hide, lines/disks/Xs, drops, 57" **1,980.00**
Bronze, Tasha/Seated Figure, rug-draped wood sq, Gorman, 25" ..**4,200.00**
Canoe model, NE Woodlands, peeled birchbark, foliage, 76" .**1,200.00**
Carving, NW Coast, eagle, dk patina w/blk traces, 10", EX **525.00**
Figure, NW Coast, cvd wood stylized male, pnt detail, 21" **1,200.00**
Gouache on brd, Going to Squaw Dance, Chee, 20x28" **1,100.00**
Gouache on paper, antelope dancers, Julian Martinez, 10x11" **1,200.00**
Gouache on paper, deer dancer, sgn Julian Martinez, 10x12" **825.00**
Gouache on paper, deer hunter, sgn Ma Pe Wi, 11x18" **2,200.00**
Gouache on paper, pueblo dancer, sgn Velino Shije, 12x24" ..**2,420.00**
Ledger drawing, Indian/soldier battle, 1800s, 8x5" **350.00**
Oil on canvas, Joe Black (Apache), G Perillo, 20x16" **450.00**
Tapestry, Navajo Germantown, Yei, bright mc on gray, 42x29" .**350.00**
Tapestry, Navajo Germantown, Yei, mc on rose, 52x36", EX **400.00**
Tapestry, Navajo Yei-bei-chai, sgn D Funston, 55x37" **2,050.00**
Tempera on blk art brd, heart line deer, R Montoya, 8x10" **220.00**
Tempera on paper, pipe ceremony, Mopope/'33, 10x8" **1,100.00**
Totem pole, NW Coast, cvd/pnt ea side, 21", EX **800.00**
Totem pole, NW Coast, figures ea side, 1910, 79" **2,000.00**
Totem pole, NW Coast, 2 dogs chase 3 bears, inlay, 32", EX ..**3,800.00**
Weaving, Navajo, Am flag, natural/aniline wool, 34x53" **1,100.00**
Weaving, Navajo, commercial 4-ply yarn, symbols, 48x25" **300.00**
Weaving, Navajo Germantown, 4-ply yarn, mc bars, 39x30" **550.00**

Bags and Cases

The Indians used bags for many purposes, and most display excellent form and workmanship. Of the types listed below, many collectors consider the pipe bag to be the most desirable form. Pipe bags were long, narrow, leather and bead or quillwork creations made to hold tobacco in a compartment at the bottom and the pipe with the bowl removed from the stem in the top. Long buckskin fringe was used as trim and complemented the quilled and beaded design to make the bag a masterpiece of Indian Art.

Apache, pouch, traditional X in bw, mc beaded fringe, 10x8" **500.00**
Blackfoot, knife sheath, mc bw 1 side, 12" **195.00**
Blackfoot, pipe, 4-color bw panels, bw heart drop, 24", EX **550.00**
Great Lakes, bandolier, 5-color floral/bird bw, 45", EX **1,250.00**
Great Lakes, lady's knife sheath, loom bw floral sqs, 11" **850.00**
Nez Perce, corn husk, aniline wool geometrics ea side, 8x7" **165.00**
Nez Perce, corn husk, geometric, bk: tree/floral, 14x18", EX **350.00**
Nez Perce/Plateau, mirror bag, turq w/5-color bw, hdls, 8" **325.00**
NW, pouch, net-beaded leather, mc bw, minor losses, 10x7" **45.00**
Parfleche, N Plains, worn geometrics att Crow, 26x13", EX **500.00**
Plains, awl case, bead-wrapped body, bw thongs/cones, 16" **495.00**
Plains, awl case, bw flap edge, tin cones/hide drops, 12" **350.00**
Plains, dr's, full bw, 1830, 4¾x5x10", VG **450.00**

Plains knife case, fully beaded parfleche (7 colors of beads), tin cones and wool suspensions, 10½", $3,950.00.

Plains, knife sheath, quilled, 20th C, w/Henkels knife **375.00**
Plains, parfleche, 3-color pnt geometrics, 11x9", VG **325.00**
Plains, pipe, quillwork/bw, tin cones/horsehair drops, 16" **1,300.00**
Plains, strike-a-lite, full bw w/triangles, cones/drops, 5" **1,430.00**
Plains, tobacco, 5-color bw, fringed bottom, 9x2½" **1,750.00**
Plains Sioux, quilled slats, tin/feather dangles, 6x4" **115.00**
S Plains, pouch, 2-color bw circles w/wht X, 7", EX **900.00**
Seminole, pouch, made from tanned crocodile ft, 8x5½" **150.00**
Sioux, mirror-style pouch, bw Am flags, loose beads, 6x4" **275.00**
Sioux, pipe, geometric 5-color bw, quill wrap, 33", VG **1,400.00**
Sioux, pipe, 6-color, quill-wrapped band (losses), 26" **875.00**
Sioux, pipe, 6-color bw, quilled/fringed, 1885, 32" **1,150.00**
Sioux, Xs in 5-color bw w/turq bw borders, fringe, 6x4" **250.00**

Baskets

In the following listings, examples are basket form and coiled unless noted otherwise.

Apache, bowl, star, martynia on willow, 2½x10" **425.00**
Apache, olla, dogs w/in dmns, positive/negative, 16x11" **6,600.00**
Apache, tray, arrow/zigzag, martynia/yucca root/willow, 13" **650.00**
Apache, tray, geometrics/stylized 4-leg bug, 1900, 18x21" **3,500.00**
CA Mission, bowl, serrated dmn band, blk/yel, 3x11" **935.00**

CA Mission, juncus/sumac, 1880s, wear/losses, 5x9", EX 400.00
CA Misson, bowl, expanding sun in juncus, 3½x12" dia, EX 650.00
E Woodlands, bl bands/curliques, w/lid, 13x16" dia, VG 200.00
Havasupai, tray, radiating swirls in martynia, 7" 130.00
Hopi, plaque, Orabi on 3rd mesa, t'bird on orange, 13" 125.00
Hopi, 2nd mesa, deer in soft colors on blk, #13, 9½" 65.00
Jacarilla Apache, fishing creel, anilined sumac, 7x16", EX 575.00
Karok, hat, geometrics, bear grass/fern/woodwardia, 1900 ....150.00
Klamath, bowl, tule grass in dmn design, wear/losses, 5x6" 45.00
Makah, faded bands of color on natural grass, w/lid, 3x5" 175.00
Mono, burden/pack, 3-color terraced bands, conical, 29" 1,650.00
Navajo, wedding, willow/martynia/sumac root, mc, 3x14" dia 150.00
Navajo, wedding tray, geometrics, wear/stitches missing, 12" 435.00
Nootka, whales on base (faded aniline), swirl on lid, 3x4" 170.00
Paiute, seed jar, willow, coil-wrap rim, lug hdls, 1895, 13" 550.00
Papago, martynia/yucca geometrics, w/lid, 4x8" 85.00
Pima, bowl, fine weave, martynia/willow fret design, 2½x4½" 50.00
Pima, olla, willow/martynia, braid rim, 1910, 7x9" 1,300.00
Pima/Papago, olla, step motif in martynia/willow, 6x8" 375.00
Pomo, geometrics, 13", VG 150.00
Pomo, gift bowl, sedge/bracken triangles, 1910, hole, 2½x5" 450.00
Pomo, gift type, quail topknot motif/feathered rim, 10" L 1,400.00
Tlinglit, bowl, cedar/bear grass banded design, 2¾x4¾" 75.00
Tlinglit, pottery vase w/twined basketry covering, 7" 250.00
Tlinglit, trinket, rust-brn aniline stepped motif, 1½x3" 230.00
Washo, bowl, dmns, redbud/fern root/willow, 1910, 6" 250.00
Yokuts, bowl, rattlesnake, redbud/bracken/sedge, 5x9", EX 2,100.00
Yokuts, bowl, 2 redbud bands on golden ground, 5x11" 1,100.00
Yurok, hat, stepped motif, fern/bear grass, 1910, lg, NM 450.00

Blankets, Navajo

Pueblo Indians first made blankets centuries ago, but today most are made by Navajo Indians. Pendleton and Hudson's Bay blankets became widely available in the 1800s; around the turn of the century, rugs were developed because tourists were more likely to buy them as floor coverings and wall-hangings. Rugs or blankets are made in various regional styles; an expert can usually identify the area where it was made, sometimes even the individual who made it. The colors of wool are natural (gray-white, brown-black), vegetal (from plant dyes), or artificial (aniline, from synthetic chemicals.) Value factors include size, tightness of weave, artistry of design, and condition. Examples by artists whose names are well known command the higher prices.

Chilkat, fringed ceremonial blanket, twined, woven with natural and native-dyed mountain goat wool, 4-color motif on cedar bark warp, fringe and suspensions, 54" long, $8,000.00.

Child's, salmon ravels w/homespun, bl/gr motif, late, 52x31" ..7,700.00
Germantown, rust, 5-color serrated dmns & arrows, 72x70" .12,000.00
Red w/5-color bars & bands, fringed corners, 58x34" 650.00
Saddle, brn w/4-color expanding dmn, natural/aniline, 42x36" ..300.00
Saddle, dbl, 3-color stripes, soil/wear, 63x36" 115.00
Saddle, dbl, 5-color stripes, stains, 51x34" 250.00
Saddle, Germantown pictorial w/prs of hands, 3-color on red .1,500.00
Saddle, Greek Key/stripes, 3-color, used/stained, 34x35" 125.00

Ceremonial Items

Dance bow, Hupa, fine red/wht/bl bw Am flags, no feathers 310.00
Dance head band, Hupa, basketry hoop, bw/buttons/tassels 550.00
Dance shield, SW Pueblo, pnt deer/circles on muslin, 1925 ....750.00
Dance stick, bead/leather-wrap wand w/deer hair, hoof end 75.00
Dance stick, Plains, cloth wrap, feather/hide drops, 36" 100.00
Drum, Cochiti Pueblo, pnt stripes on cottonwood, 20", EX 250.00
Headdress, Plains, buffalo horns, loom bw band, feathers 100.00
Horse dance stick, Sioux, wood w/pnt & horsehair, 19", VG 150.00
Mask, false face; Seneca, wood w/red ochre, horsehair, 8" 185.00
Mask, NW Coast, cvd, 5-color, ferocious expression, 10", EX 400.00
NW Coast, rattle, bear, wood, red/turq cvd details, 10" 3,100.00
NW Coast, totem pole, eagle/bear holding man, early, 14", EX .550.00
Rattle, duck form, wood, NW Coast, 6x13" 215.00

Totem model, Northwest Coast, carved ivory with yellow patina, 5½", $600.00.

Totem pole, NW Coast, 3-figure, primitive, 1920s, 13" 175.00

Dolls

Apache, fringed bw-trim hide attire, cones/shell/etc, 15" 2,900.00
Cheyenne, lady, wool/bw dress, bw hi-tops, buffalo hair, 14" ..1,100.00
Cree, male, arms move, wood, pnt/cvd features, dressed, 10" 90.00
Kachina, Cactus (male), att Tewaquaptewa, 9½", EX 2,600.00
Kachina, I-She, cottonwood root/mc pnt, early, 9", EX 900.00
Kachina, Kitten dancer, sgn Stancy Talahytewa, 10" 175.00
Kachina, Long Hair Mana dancer, sgn Bruce Aggiee, 10" 100.00
Kachina, Motsin dancer, sgn Virgil Namoki, 12½" 250.00
Kachina, Sun Towa social dancer, sgn Bakabi, EX cvg, 16" 70.00
Kachina, Tasaf figure, cottonwood root/mc pnt, early, 10" 950.00
Kachina, Wht Buffalo social dancer, sgn Bakabi, EX cvg, 15" 90.00
Kachina, Wolfman, sgn Chas Eagle Dawn, 18" 275.00
Kachina style, Eagle Dancer, feather costume, 28" 600.00

N Plains, male, buffalo hair braids, pnt leather attire, 15" 950.00
NE Woodlands, corn husk, bw cotton/wool dress, silk hair 900.00
Penobscot, fringed/beaded leather outfit, hair remnants, 12" 110.00
Plains, leather w/bead features, fringed outfit, '17, 11", VG 75.00
Sioux, lady, bw dress/boots, pnt hide face/buffalo hair, 11" 550.00
Skookum, woman in traditional blanket wrap, 1940s, 35" 300.00

Domestics

Baby carrier, Chippewa, cvd/pierced wood fr, cotton pad, 31" 750.00
Bottle, Yakima, bw geometrics/butterfly on glass bottle, 10" 125.00
Bowl, NE Woodlands, wood, turtle head hdl, 14" 650.00
Bucket, sugar; Algonquin, birch bark, spruce-root bound, 10" 450.00
Cradlebrd, Apache, wicker shade/bentwood fr, rag baby, 35" 450.00
Cradlebrd, Apache toy, wicker shade/bw, rag doll w/in, 13" 350.00

Cradle, Paiute, pony-beaded hide over bentwood and wicker-work frame, dated 1853 in pencil, 20" long, $1,500.00.

Dish, NW Coast, cvd beaver, abalone eyes/shell inlay, 15" 450.00
Fiddle, Apache, agave stalk w/HP, fringe, no string, VG 175.00
Ladle, E Woodlands, tiger maple, bird's head at hdl end, 9" 165.00
Ladle, Woodlands, curly maple, horse head w/brass eyes, 9½" .1,300.00
Spoon, E Woodlands, crooked hdl w/bird form surmount, 8" 325.00
Spoon, NW Coast, mtn sheep horn w/totemic cvgs, 12" 475.00

Jewelry and Adornments

As early as 500 A.D., Indians in the Southwest drilled turquoise nuggets and strung them on cords made of sinew or braided hair. The Spanish introduced them to coral, and it became a popular item of jewelry; abalone and clam shells were favored by the Coastal Indians. Not until the last half of the 19th century did the Indians learn to work with silver. Each tribe developed its own distinctive style and preferred design, which until about 1920 made it possible to determine tribal origin with some degree of accuracy. Since that time, because of modern means of communication and travel, motifs have become less distinct.

Quality Indian silver jewelry may be antique or contemporary. Age, though certainly to be considered, is not as important a factor as fine workmanship and good stones. Pre-1910 silver will show evidence of hammer marks, and designs are usually simple. Beads have sometimes been shaped from coins. Stones tend to be small; when silver wire was used, it is usually square. To insure your investment, choose a reputable dealer.

Bracelet, Navajo, stamped, 1 sq-cut turq, 1¼" W 165.00
Bracelet, Navajo, stamped cuff w/1 oval turq 325.00
Bracelet, Navajo, stamped cuff w/3 bezel-set turq, ¾" W 400.00
Bracelet, Navajo, 3-wire cuff w/15 lg bl gem turq 800.00
Bracelet, sand cast, openwork w/lg 'Bl Mine' turq, old pawn 190.00
Bracelet, Zuni, emb silver cuff w/lg turq-set oval 250.00
Breastpc, Plains, bone hair pipe/cowrie shells/beads, 38" 800.00
Breastplate, Plains, bone hair pipe/brass & mc beads, 45" 1,050.00
Concho belt, Navajo, 5 ovals+4 butterflies, turq cabs, 37" 1,300.00
Concho belt, Navajo, 7 ovals+5 butterflies, old pawn, 41" 500.00
Concho belt, Navajo, 7 star-emb 5x4" ovals, 1910 ....1,430.00
Concho belt, 11 1¾x2" conchos+buckle, ea w/sq-cut turq 900.00
Hair plate, Plains, silver w/cutouts & tooling, mk, 3½" 175.00
Necklace, Cherokee, silver rain, turq bear fetish, J Grant 140.00
Necklace, Plains, bone hair pipe/brass & gr beads, 24" 95.00

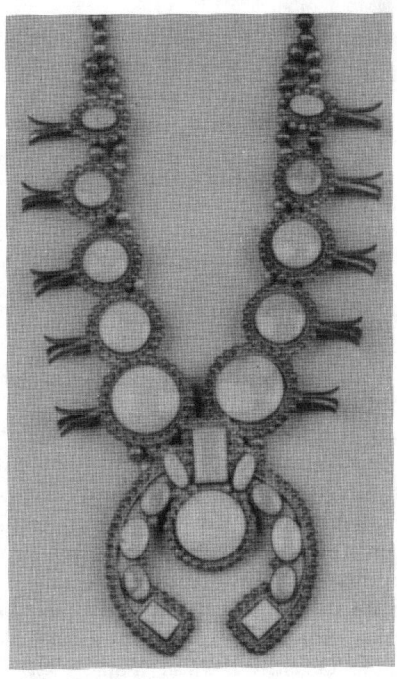

Necklace, Navajo, squash blossom, turquoise-set blossoms and naja, ca 1940, 14" long, $650.00.

Necklace, Santo Domingo, fetish, turq/shell/jet, t'bird drop 190.00
Necklace, squash blossom, fine turq pendant 180.00
Necklace, squash blossom, 1-strand, +1-stone turq naja 365.00
Necklace, SW Pueblo, 3-strand, coral/shell/turq, 1900, 18" 150.00
Necklace, turq nuggets, flat/mixed shapes & sizes, 2-strand 100.00
Necklace, Zuni, channel inlay turq, choker length 330.00
Necklace, Zuni, grad silver beads, 5 w/turq inlay 200.00
Ornament, Plains, German silver, scallops, 3 C-drops, 5½x6½" .175.00
Trade bead, TN, glass, Dutch, 1800s 7.50
Trade beads, faceted, lt bl, KS, 1800s, 1-strand 65.00
Trade beads, Russian bl, KS, 1800s, 4 for 9.00

Knives and Chipped Blades

The knife was an indispensable tool to the Indian whether he was in battle, hunting game, or doing chores at the campsite. Before the white man's metal blades, all were made of copper, obsidian, flint, or chert. Knife cases, fashioned of leather with intricate decorations of quilling or beadwork, were sometimes suspended from the neck, or they were attached to the belt.

Agate Basin, KY, brn, well made, 10" 475.00
Caddo Fulton, AR, serrated edges, 8" 1,200.00
Crooked, E Woodlands, scroll-cvd wood hdl w/brass wire wrap 45.00
Crooked, Eastern, bone hdl, tag: Hudson Bay Co from Senecas ...50.00

Dagger, Northwest Coast, native copper blade, whale bone wolf's head handle with abalone eyes and teeth, human hair insets, red patina, 19", $2,000.00.

Jack's Reef, TN, brn, classic, 7" 400.00
Paleo, AZ, lt gray quartzite, bazal grinding, thin, 3¾" 225.00
Plains, bone hdl w/brass tack motif, abalone in hdl end, 14" 300.00
Ramey, IL, dk red, 8" 1,200.00
Skinning, SC, off-wht, 3⅜" 17.50
Spear, Adena, MS, pk w/red top, classic, 4¾" 145.00
Spear, Adena, OH, lt tan, 6¾" 180.00
Spear, Afton, AL, lt pk chert, 4¼" 90.00
Spear, Agate Basin, IL, pk-tan, 4¼" 85.00
Spear, Agate Basin, IL, wht flint, EX chipping, 3⅛" 100.00
Spear, Benton, IN, off-wht, exceptional, 7⅝" 300.00
Spear, Clovis, IL, off-wht, shallow flutes, 4⅜" 285.00
Spear, Dalton, AR, tan, 4⅞" 165.00
Spear, Dalton, IL, off-wht, 4¼" 225.00
Spear, Etley, AR, tan flint, thin/well made, 6" 245.00
Spear, Godar, WI, tan sugar quartz, 2¾" 9.00
Spear, Smith, MO, off-wht, exceptional, 3" 135.00
Triangular, AL, off-wht, p-h, 2⅝" 7.50
Wadlow, MO, tan & gray, 7½" 225.00

Pipes

   Pipe bowls were usually carved from soft stone, such as catlinite or pipestone, an argilaceous sedimentary rock composed mainly of clay. Granite was also used. Some ceremonial pipes were simply styled, while others were intricately designed naturalistic figurals, sometimes in bird or frog forms called effigies. Their stems, made of wood and often covered with leather, were sometimes nearly a yard in length.

Catlinite, lead inlay, long stem w/bw & hair drops, 52" 125.00
Cherokee style, blk stone w/skeleton, raised head is bowl 325.00
NE Woodlands, elbow bowl w/bear astride, brn stone, 5" L 1,320.00
Pipe tomahawk, brass w/inlaid stem, heart-cutout blade, 18" 250.00
Pipe tomahawk, Plains, trade pipe bowl, bw/fringed drop 2,200.00
Plains, catlinite bowl cvd as horse w/eagle astride, 9", EX 1,500.00
Plains, catlinite elbow bowl, wood stem, 21" 300.00

Plains, catlinite stem w/steer heads & lines, 26", +T bowl 935.00
Plains, wood stem: sqd section w/ridge, quill wrap, 16" 700.00
SE style, blk elbow bowl w/cvd snake, 10" 250.00
Sioux, catlinite, blk w/red & lead inlay, bw stem, 22" 500.00
Sioux, catlinite bowl is figural woman, EX detail, 5" 375.00
Sioux, catlinite w/pewter inlay, orig wood stem, 11x23" 1,000.00
Tlingit, seal/raven/eagle/whale-cvd bowl, mc pnt, 2x3" 2,300.00

Pottery

   Indian pottery is nearly always decorated in such a manner as to indicate the tribe that produced it or the pueblo in which it was made. For instance, the designs of Cochiti potters were usually scattered forms from nature or sacred symbols. The Zuni preferred an ornate repetitive decoration of a closer configuration. They often used stylized deer and bird forms, sometimes in dimensional applications.

Acoma, jar, birds/geometrics/florals, 3-color, flat base, 9" 400.00
Acoma, olla, geometrics, red/blk on wht slip, rstr, 12" 2,300.00

Acoma, olla, white slip over white clay, black and orange devices, red painted bottom and inner lip, drill holes, 12½", $850.00.

Acoma, water jar, birds, orange/umber on wht, 1930s, 11x13" ..1,200.00
Acoma, wedding jar, avian motif, 2-color on cream, 6", VG 75.00
Casas Grandes, jar, mc w/tooled neck, D Gonzalez, 11x12" 200.00
Casas Grandes, jar, orange/blk on buff, contemporary, 8x10" 85.00
Casas Grandes, jar, 3-color 'wings' on buff, Oritz, 11x11" 150.00
Chaco, bowl, blk on wht, p-h, 7" 525.00
Cochiti, jar, relief frogs, pnt t'bird on wht, rpr, 11x13" 1,100.00
Cochiti, olla, foliate/geometric devices, 3-color, 10", EX 1,300.00
Hopi, canteen, stylized bird, mc, loom-woven band, 7x7" 250.00
Hopi, jar, Hano avian motif, 3-color, R Nampeyo, 9x11" 3,200.00
Hopi, jar, thunderbird, brn/red/orange, sgn Corn Woman, 10" ..530.00
Hopi, jar, X-hatched/geometric bands, 3-color, 5½" 300.00
Hopi, tile, kachina mask, 3-color, hexagonal, 6x4" 440.00
Santa Clara, blk-on-blk relief, Pablita Sta Clara, 8", NM 150.00
Santa Clara, vase, blkware, lg hdls, 7", NM 75.00
Santo Domingo, dbl-spout jar, 3-color, Silva, 1925, 14" 1,000.00
Santo Domingo, jar, birds/deer in mc, 9x8", NM 80.00
Santo Domingo, pot, blkware, deer track, MM Aguilar, 6x9" 100.00

Zia, jar, birds/geometrics, 3-color, 12x16" 1,000.00
Zia, jar, birds/plants, 4-color, 1880, glued rpr, 9" 1,800.00
Zia, water jar, ochre/umber motif on tan, 1800s, 10x12", EX ..1,000.00
Zuni, dough bowl, 2 deer, inset bl stones, 7x15", EX 2,500.00
Zuni, jar, deer/birds, 3-color, 1885, 9", EX 1,700.00
Zuni, jar, umber/red ochre motif on wht slip, 1890s, 9x12" 2,350.00

Pottery, San Ildefonso

The pottery of the San Ildefonso pueblo is especially sought after by collectors today. Under the leadership of Maria Martinez and her husband Julian, experiments began about 1918 which led to the development of the 'black-on-black' design achieved through exacting methods of firing the ware. They discovered that by smothering the fire at a specified temperature, the carbon in the smoke that ensued caused the pottery to blacken. Maria signed her work (often 'Marie') from the late teens to the 1960s; she died in 1980. Today a piece with her signature may bring prices in the $500 to $4,500 range.

Bowl, blkware, band motif, sgn Marie, 2⅜x7½" 950.00
Bowl, blkware, feathered rim band, Blue Corn, 2½x6½" 365.00
Bowl, blkware, feathers, sgn Florence & Joe, 4x8" 150.00
Bowl, blkware, frieze of stepped motif, sgn Marie, 2¾" H 875.00
Bowl, blkware, incurvate rim, sgn Marie, 1½x4¾" 325.00
Bowl, blkware, sgn Lupita Martinez, ca 1957, 4½" 150.00
Bowl, blkware, worn, unsgn, 3¾x7½" 200.00
Bowl vase, blkware, water serpent motif, Blue Corn, 4" 935.00
Dish, blkware, bird form, Marie & Julian, 6" L 465.00
Jar, blkware, att Maria, 1¾x2" 225.00
Jar, blkware, band of stylized wings, Maria/Popovi, 3½" 875.00

Jar, black-on-black butterflies and linear devices, signed Marie & Julian, 7x9", $2,200.00.

Jar, blkware, flaring sides, sgn Lucy Martinez, 2½x4" 200.00
Jar, blkware, hooked/stepped frieze, wide body, Tonita, 7½" 700.00
Jar, blkware, Marie & Julian, 1935, 3¾x4½" 650.00
Jar, wht slip top band on polished red, Susana, 1940, 5x10" 1,500.00
Olla, red/blk motif on gray slip, blk rim, 1920, 9x11", EX 900.00
Plate, blkware, sgn Marie & Julian, some wear, 5" 325.00

Rugs, Navajo

Bordered rectangle w/geometrics, 4-color, 1925, 92x71", EX 590.00
Brn w/boxed 3-color geometrics, natural/aniline, 137x89" 7,100.00
Chief's blanket type, 5-color 4th-phase block/stripe, 54x46" 450.00
Crystal, ivory w/whirling logs in red blocks on tan, 90x62" 2,300.00
Dmn stripes, 6-color, 47x44", EX 100.00
Ganado, gr warp/true red/dk brn/carded tan, natural, 81x42" 250.00
Ganado, lg geometric central medallion, 4-color, 84x65", EX 500.00
Ganado, serrated dmns, 4-color, ca 1915, rpr, 60x48" 550.00
Ganado, serrated/Saltillo designs, triangular border, 78x48" 435.00
Ganado area, St Andrew's X/stripe ends, 3-color, 38x15", EX 245.00

Gray w/4-color Vallero stars, blk/wht border, 71x48" 600.00
Ivory w/blk & gray serrated dmns, natural/aniline, 90x52" 495.00
Red w/3-color concentric Xs, natural/aniline, 63x60" 1,300.00
Red w/5-color geometrics & pictorials, faded, 53x30" 350.00
Saltillo design, red/brn/carded brn on wht, 36x17" 150.00
Storm pattern, fine weave, 3-color+Gando red, 46x36" 350.00
Storm pattern, hand carded/natural/commercial yarns, 59x36" ..400.00
Storm pattern, spun/carded, 4-color, 66x42" 600.00
Terraced dmns, 4-color, wear/slight bleeding, 64x42" 250.00
Traditional, Ganado red/gold/rust/gray/wht/brn, 106x52" 900.00
Transitional Eye Dazzler, 4-color on red, 90x62" 1,400.00
W Reservation Storm, gray/blk/natural, 1930s, 68x37", EX 1,000.00
Wht w/4-color boxed geometrics, natural/aniline, 52x35" 365.00
Wide Ruins, feather/stripes, natural colors on brn, 40x37" 300.00
Wide Ruins, serrated stripes, earth tones, modern, 62x46" 400.00
Yei, turq/red/natural/gray/blk, minor bleeding, 50x45" 450.00
2 Gray Hills, 5-color geometric, hand carded, 1950, 60x47" 650.00
2nd Phase Chief's, 5-color, natural/aniline homespun, 76x56" ..2,000.00

Stone Artifacts

Discoidal, AR, hardstone, dbl-cupped, 3" dia 375.00
Discoidal, MO, biscuit form, 2" 65.00
Discoidal, 1¾" dia 115.00
Gorget, AR, jasper, 2-hole, oval w/sqd-off ends, 2½" 85.00
Plummet, IL, hardstone, ridge at top, 3½" 145.00

Tools

Axe, AR, full-grooved, 4" 17.50
Axe, dbl-bitted; AR, flaked, 4½" 22.00
Axe, IL, gray, ¾-grooved, 6" 175.00
Axe, MO, greenstone, ¾-grooved, 6" 225.00
Axe, MO, lt tan granite, ¾-grooved, well shaped, 4½" 165.00
Celt, AR, jasper, chipped/polished, 4½" 12.00
Celt, AR, yel jasper, 5½" 28.00
Celt, OH, gray sandstone, 3½" 12.00
Celt, OH, slate, very thin, 3" 18.00
Chisel, AL, gray stone, rectangular oval, 2¾" 6.00
Drill, AL, dk gray, slightly shouldered, 1⅝" 10.00
Drill, CO, T-style, brn, 1" 12.50
Flaking tool, AR, made from antler, 5¾" 25.00
Hide scraper, AR, brn flint, 2" 6.00
Hide scraper, AR, tan, 3" 12.00
Hide scraper, MS, tan stone, sq bk, 2½" 6.00
Hoe, AR, flaked, 5½" 20.00
Hook, halibut; Tlingit, yew/cedar raven head, rpr, 10" 200.00
Pipe drill, beveled, brn, scraper on opposite end, 2" 15.00
Scraper, Plains, hide thong-secured iron blade, 13" 200.00

Weapons

Axe, Cheyenne, full bw hdl, 1880, rare sz, 13x3" 150.00
Bow, Woodlands, sinew bkd, horn tips, 1850, 75x1" 400.00
Club, ball head w/set-in iron barb, human face cvg ea end 8,000.00
Skull cracker, Plains, sinew sewn, w/hdl attachments, 36" 675.00
Spear point, Texas, prehistoric, 8" 30.00
Tomahawk, Iroquois, drop forged, wagon wheel spoke hdl 85.00

Miscellaneous

Badge, US Bureau of...Affairs Police, silver shield, 2½" 145.00
Box, E Woodlands, bark w/stitched rim, 5x18" L, EX 125.00
Log bin, NE Woodlands, birchbark/peeled decor, sgn/'03, 22" ..1,875.00

Orotone, Canon del Muerto, ES Curtis, 10x8" 5,200.00
Orotone, Rush Gatherer, ES Curtis, 8x10" 4,500.00
Orotone, Signal Fire to Mtn God, ES Curtis, 13x11" 2,200.00
Peace medal, John Adams 1797, SP bronze, 2 drilled holes, 3" ...100.00
Peace medal, silver, eng eagle/Treaty of Greenville 1795, 4" 295.00
Photogravure, Arikara Medicine Ceremony..., Curtis, 6x7" 165.00
Photogravure, Mono Home, ES Curtis, 12x15" 440.00
Playing cards, Am Indian Souvenir, 1900, Lazarus/Melzer, VG ..1,500.00
Quirt, leather & braided horsehair, 4-color, 18"+ends, VG 75.00
Saddle blanket, Plains, trade cloth w/bw stripes & fringe 2,300.00
Snowshoes, NE Woodlands, 1-pc bentwood fr, red wool tassels .165.00
Trade axe, iron, stamped RO in cartouch, 5½" 60.00
Trade axe head, hand forged 'steeled' type w/eye, 5" 65.00
Trade silver, NE Woodlands, pipe, appl beaver, eng Indians ...2,100.00
Trade silver, NE Woodlands, pipe, appl beavers, sgn, 23" 1,400.00

Amphora

The Amphora Porcelain Works in the Teplitz-Turn area of Bohemia produced Art Nouveau-styled vases and figurines during the late 1800s through the first few decades of the 20th century. They marked their wares with various stamps, some incorporating the name and location of the pottery with a crown or a shield. Because Bohemia was part of the Austro-Hungarian empire prior to WWI, some examples are marked Austria; items marked with the Czechoslovakia designation were made after the war. Our advisor for this category is Jack Gunsaulus; he is listed in the Directory under Michigan.

Vase, portrait of a lady, three bands: one scenic, one with florals, and the bottom third 'jeweled,' marked, 8½", $2,500.00.

Basket, Cupid on side w/lilac garland, 7½x5" 325.00
Basket, turq w/appl wht floral, Imperial mk, 11", NM 300.00
Bowl, molded as 3 children w/baskets, brns/grs, 9" 600.00
Centerpiece, boy w/2 hunting dogs in forest, 1925, 11½" H 450.00
Compote, appl blkberries, lg dbl hdls, gilt-spotted gr, 6" 350.00
Ewer, cat's head bosses top & base of gourd form, 15" 1,100.00
Ewer, emb Egyptian motif on bl w/cobalt details, 5½" 145.00
Ewer, emb florals, mc on bl jug form, 7¾x5½" 90.00
Ewer, emb minstrel on horse, pressed mk, ca 1891, 14" 350.00
Ewer, emb robed figures on gray mottled, cobalt rim, 8x3½" 125.00

Ewer, leaves, gr/gilt on bl, curving stems form hdls, 15" 500.00
Figurine, boy by pot, matt finish, 8x8" 200.00
Jug, profile of wise man, HP, 5½" 350.00
Vase, appl draped nude, jewels, sgn Ries, Imperial mk, 11" 1,295.00
Vase, appl roses on bowl top, 4 stems enclose ped, 9½" 600.00
Vase, emb pk florals w/gr leaves/gold, hdls, 10½", pr 195.00
Vase, emb poppies at shoulder, spiders in webs, 1900, 17" 1,100.00
Vase, floral, cobalt/bl/gold on wht, cobalt rim, RSK, 8¼" 250.00
Vase, floral w/emb bird, triangles at neck, cobalt rim, 10½" 180.00
Vase, gilt/appl/jeweled circles etc on cream, ftd ovoid, 10" 950.00
Vase, grapes/foliage in high relief, long neck, 20" 500.00
Vase, Greek figures on wide textured band, #2122-64, 14x8" 450.00
Vase, lady stands on wide base, rtcl/jeweled floral, 11" 800.00
Vase, lg leaves/buckeyes appl to base, cvd florals, 11x5" 800.00
Vase, lg winged dragon coiled on gr matt, Stellmacher, 17" 1,700.00
Vase, neck w/granulated texture, vertical ribbed leaves, 12" 900.00
Vase, octopus coils about slim cylinder, crab at base, 19" 2,000.00
Vase, pnt/emb florals, Deco style, mk, 9¼x6½" 195.00
Vase, serpent hdls, 10" 295.00
Vase, 2 lg emb leaves, tips curve out/form neck hdls, 16" 600.00
Vase, 4 sections, 3 w/mc medallions, cylindrical, 14½" 250.00

Animal Dishes with Covers

Covered animal dishes have been produced for nearly two centuries and are as varied as their manufacturers. They were made in many types of glass (slag, colored, clear, and milk glass) as well as china and pottery. On bases of nests and baskets, you will find animals and birds of every sort. The most common was the hen.

Some of the smaller versions made by McKee, Indiana Tumbler and Goblet Company, and Westmoreland Glass of Pittsburgh, Pennsylvania were sold to food-processing companies who filled them with prepared mustard, baking powder, etc. Occasionally one will be found with the paper label identifying the product and processing company still intact.

Many of the glass versions produced during the late 19th century have been recently reproduced. As late as the 1960s, the Kemple Glass Company made the rooster, fox, lion, cat, lamb, hen, horse, turkey, duck, dove, and rabbit on split-ribbed or basketweave bases. They were made in amethyst, blue, amber, and milk glass, as well as a variegated slag. It is sometimes necessary to compare items in question to verified examples of older glass in order to recognize reproductions.

For more information, we recommend *Covered Animal Dishes* by our advisor, Everett Grist, whose address is in the Directory under Illinois. In the listings below, when only one dimension is given, it is length.

Bird on rnd basketweave base, milk glass, Vallerysthal, 6½" 95.00

Boar's head, milk glass, dated May 29, 1888, 9½", $975.00.

Cat, milk glass head, bl body & base, Westmoreland, 5¼" 120.00
Chick emerging from horizontal egg, milk glass, unmk 95.00
Chick in vertical egg, milk glass, sm, 3¾" 125.00
Chicks in oblong basket, milk glass, unmk, 2¼x4¼" 325.00
Dog, Pekingese; milk glass, att Sandwich, 4¾" 425.00
Dolphin w/sawtooth rim, milk glass, reproduction 65.00
Dove, milk glass, mk Mckee (both pcs), 5½" oval base 275.00
Duck, Atterbury; milk glass, 'Patent Apld for' on base, 11" 275.00
Duck, Dominecker; fired-on pnt, 8" 150.00
Duck, Swimming; yel opaque, Vallerysthal, 5" 120.00
Eagle, Mother; milk glass, Westmoreland 75.00
Elephant, milk glass, mk McKee, 5½" oval base 1,500.00
Fish, Entwined; milk glass, lacy base 200.00
Fish (flat) on ribbed base, milk glass, att Fostoria, 8½" 100.00
Fish on skiff, milk glass, unmk, 7½" 75.00
Fox, Ribbed; on ribbed base, milk glass, dtd 175.00
Hand & dove, milk glass, mk WG base 95.00
Hen, Little; milk glass, mk Hazel Atlas 15.00
Hen, milk glass, Fenton, 8" 150.00
Hen, milk glass, Vallerysthal, 2" 35.00
Hen, milk glass head, bl body & base, Westmoreland, 5¼" 85.00
Hen (str head), clear w/pnt comb, Indiana, lg 10.00
Hen on cattail base, milk glass, unmk, 5½" 65.00
Hen on lacy base, bl transparent head, Atterbury 275.00
Hen on lacy base, bl w/marbled bk, Atterbury 300.00
Hen on wide-rib base, carnival/milk glass mottle, Degenhart 25.00
Hen w/chicks, milk glass, unmk McKee, 5½" oval base 165.00
Horse, milk glass, reproduction (att St Clair), 5½" 75.00
Lion on picket base, milk glass, Westmoreland 85.00
Quail on scroll base, milk glass, unmk, 5½" 65.00
Rabbit, Atterbury; bl opaque, Imperial reproduction, 6" 65.00
Rabbit, Atterbury; milk glass, Aug 6 1889, 9" 195.00
Rabbit, clear, mk Vallerysthal 95.00
Rabbit, Domed; milk glass, 5½" 75.00
Rabbit, Mule Eared; on picket base, milk glass, Westmoreland 70.00
Rabbit on egg, any color, Vallerysthal, sm or lg 225.00
Robin on ped base, bl opaque, mk Vallerysthal 125.00
Rooster, goofus glass, milk glass base, unmk 65.00
Rooster, Large; on basketweave base, bl opaque, Westmoreland ...125.00
Rooster, milk glass w/bl head, Westmoreland, 5¼" 125.00
Rooster on basketweave, milk glass, Challinor, Taylor & Co 125.00
Rooster on wide-rib base, milk glass, Westmoreland, 5¼" 85.00
Squirrel finial on fancy dish, milk glass, unmk 95.00
Swan, Block; clear frosted, Challinor, Taylor & Co, 7" 145.00
Swan, Block; gr variegated, Challinor, Taylor & Co, 7" 650.00
Swan, clear frosted, Vallerysthal, 5½" 95.00
Swan, Raised-Wing; milk glass, molded eyes, Westmoreland 75.00
Turkey, clear frost, unmk, lg 150.00
Turtle, amber, unmk, lg 100.00
Water buffalo (resting), milk glass, unmk 350.00

Anna Pottery

Founded in 1859 near a town in Illinois by the same name, the Anna Pottery operated for about thirty-five years, producing stoneware items and small animal figures as well as brick and tile from the native clay. They are best known for their whimsey jugs decorated with writhing snakes and flasks modeled as pigs. Examples are rare and expensive today.

Flask, Blk girl (exposed genitalia) hugs shoulder, 6½" 9,000.00
Jug, 13 appl snakes (4 heads now gone), unmk, 11" 650.00
Jug, 4 snakes' heads & man's lower torso, sgn, dtd 1881, 9" 2,750.00

Appliances, Electric

Electric appliances have been very collectible for quite some time with almost every type being sought. Even larger appliances such as early washing machines and refrigerators add a finishing touch to remodeled period rooms. Smaller appliances such as toasters, coffee makers, waffle irons, fans, and other table-top items should be in working order. Check for safety before using. (Beware: old refrigerators are dangerous if their cooling units start leaking; the fluids in them are poisonous.)

Prices listed below are for appliances in very good to excellent condition and in working order. Our advisor for this category is Jim Barker; he is listed in the Directory under Pennsylvania.

Broiler, Farberware, chrome, 3-prong plug, 1920s 22.50
Chafing dish, Manning-Bowman, Deco chrome, 1930s 45.00
Coffeepot, Manning-Bowman, Bakelite & chrome 125.00
Coffeepot, Westinghouse #CM-81, nickel w/Bakelite hdls, 14" 25.00
Drinkmaster, Hamilton Beach, blk porc, EX 95.00
Egg cooker, Hankscraft #599, china base, 1920s 35.00
Hot plate, Universal Thermax, wooden hdl, 1920s 24.00
Luminair/fan, cast metal, Victor, 59" H, VG 550.00
Mixer, Gilbert Polar Cub, gray pnt metal, 10", EX 60.00
Mixer, Hamilton Beach, 10-speed deluxe, milk glass bowl, old 25.00
Mixer, Hamilton Beach G, Bakelite hdl, 1930s, EX 38.00
Percolator, Manning-Bowman, aluminum, 3-part, 1920s, 12½" ...38.00
Percolator, Manning-Bowman #391 ....45.00
Popcorn popper, Berstead #302, chrome w/glass lid, EX 50.00
Popcorn popper, US Mfg #1, red & silver, wooden legs 22.00
Space heater, Saint-Gobain, glass, Deco style, 19x16" 175.00
Stove, table top; Universal New & Improved #E-988, 1922 ....85.00
Teakettle, Mirro, internal heating element, 1930s, 4-qt 22.00
Toaster, #169T26, EX 90.00
Toaster, Edison #214-T-5, nickel body, 1910s 50.00
Toaster, Electro Weld, EX 150.00
Toaster, General Mills #GM 5 A, Bakelite hdls, 1940s 45.00
Toaster, Hotpoint #125T22, EX 45.00
Toaster, Kenmore, chrome, 2-slice, 1940s 25.00
Toaster, Knapp Monarch #21-501, chrome, Bakelite hdls, 1930s .22.50
Toaster, L&H Electrics #202, EX 75.00
Toaster, L&H Electrics #204, EX 65.00
Toaster, Meteor #1231, EX 35.00
Toaster, Montgomery Ward & Co #94-KW 2298-B, 1930s 20.00
Toaster, PA Aircraft Works Co #68, aluminum, pop-down type ..150.00
Toaster, Toast O Lator, Model H, EX 175.00
Toaster, Universal E-944, flip-down sides, Bakelite hdls 55.00
Toaster, Westinghouse #284032, EX 95.00
Toaster, Westinghouse #TT-23, EX 50.00
Toaster/hot plate, Breakfaster, Calkins #T-2, 1930s 45.00
Vacuum, Fairfax, wet/dry, chrome, Deco design, +attachments 50.00
Waffle iron, Berstead, chrome w/Bakelite hdls & ft, 1930s 35.00
Waffle iron, Dominion, 2 wells, chrome, wooden hdls, 1940s 35.00
Waffle iron, Knapp-Monarch, nickel w/wooden hdl, 1930s, sm 25.00
Waffle iron, Manning-Bowman Twin-O-Matic, Bakelite stand 75.00
Whipper, Knapp Monarch, chrome-housed motor, 1930s, 7" 22.00

Arequipa

The Arequipa Pottery operated from 1911 until 1918 at a sanitorium near Fairfax, California. Its purpose was two-fold: therapy for the patients and financial support for the institution. Frederick H. Rhead was the originator and director. The ware, made from local clays, was often hand thrown, simply styled and decorated. Marks were varied but always incorporated the name of the pottery and the state. A circular arrangement encompassing the negative image of a vase beside a tree is most common.

Bowl, leaves cvd on brn & bl high glaze, 2¾x4½" 550.00
Bowl, striated brn clay, low, hairline, 4" 195.00
Vase, hydrangeas emb on plum, mk GG 256 MS111, 8" 1,150.00

Vase, incised leaves, 6", $750.00.

Vase, Nouveau floral, cvd/lav-pnt on dk brn, #301/16, 6" 650.00
Vase, stylized vine at shoulder, gr/pk on bl, 8½x4" 1,600.00
Vase, wisteria, emb/rtcl, gr irid, unmk, 11x5" 1,800.00

Argy-Rousseau, G.

Gabriel Argy-Rousseau produced both fine art glass and quality commercial ware in Paris, France, in 1918. He favored Art Nouveau as well as Art Deco and in the twenties produced a line of vases in the Egyptian manner, made popular by the discovery of King Tut's tomb. One of the most important types of glass he made was pate-de-verre. Most of his work is signed. Items listed below are pate-de-verre unless noted otherwise.

Vase, molded with dancing figures, yellow, orange, and black on yellow mottle, signed, 6", $20,000.00.

Bowl, anemones, red/blk/wht on taupe, 4½" **4,180.00**
Box, allover relief flowers, compressed sphere, 4" dia **5,500.00**
Vase, berry clusters/leaves, pk/rust/gr on lt gray, rnd, 2½" **2,420.00**
Vase, cherry branches on lt ground, bulbous, 5¾" **7,700.00**
Vase, chile plant, yel/lav on lt mottle, ovoid, 5" **5,280.00**
Vase, daisies, violet/bl on lt mottle, tapered cylinder, 6" **7,050.00**
Vase, floral band, red/brn on lt mottle, gourd form, 4½" **1,870.00**
Vase, overlapping triangles, bl/gr, ftd cylinder, 8½" **2,900.00**
Vase, row of long-stemmed poppies, red on mauve, 7x5½" ...**12,100.00**
Vase, row of masks in red/purple band on streaky gray, 10" **7,700.00**
Vase, sq panels w/bl & blk florals on gray, cylindrical, 9" **7,000.00**
Vase, 3 figures/foliage on brn band on streaky gray, 9" **16,500.00**
Veilleuse, dome shade w/moths & flower, iron base, 5½" **13,000.00**

Art Deco

To the uninformed observer, 'Art Deco' evokes images of chrome and glass, streamlined curves and aerodynamic shapes, mirrored prints of pink flamingos, and statues of slender nudes and greyhound dogs. Though the Deco movement began in 1925 at the Paris International Exposition and lasted to some extent into the 1950s, within that period of time the evolution of fashion and taste continued as it always has, resulting in subtle variations.

The French Deco look was one of opulence — exotic inlaid woods, rich material, lush fur, and leather. Lines tended toward symmetrical curves. American designers adapted the concept to cover every aspect of fashion and home furnishings from small inexpensive picture frames, cigarette lighters, and costume jewelry to high-fashion designer clothing and exquisite massive furniture with squared or circular lines. Vinyl was a popular covering, and chrome-plated brass was used for chairs, cocktail shakers, lamps, and tables. Dinnerware, glassware, theaters, and train stations were designed to reflect the new 'Modernism.'

The Deco movement made itself apparent into the fifties in wrought iron lamps with stepped pink plastic shades and Venetian blinds. The sheer volume of production during those twenty-five years provides collectors today with fine examples of the period that can be bought for as little as $10 or $20 up to the thousands. Chrome items signed 'Chase' are prized by collectors, and blue glass radios and tables with blue glass tops are high on the list of desirability in many areas.

Those interested in learning more about this subject will want to read *Collector's Guide to Art Deco* by our advisor, Mary Frank Gaston. She is listed in the Directory under Texas. See also Bronzes; Chase; Frankart; Furniture; Jewelry; Lalique; Radios; etc.

Ashtray, bl glass base w/chrome sailboat at side, FDCo, 5" **55.00**
Ashtray, nude (gold-pnt metal) w/amber glass tray, Nu Art **115.00**
Bowl, onyx base & bowl, cast metal lady support, 8½" **135.00**
Box, enameled metal, nude w/harp, Mergier, 4½" dia **650.00**
Candelabra, chrome, 3 joined rings/cups on std, Hagenauer, pr .**495.00**
Candelabrum, cast aluminum athlete, blk glass/wood base, 8" **300.00**
Cigarette case, Bakelite & pigskin, sliding top, Rolinx **75.00**
Cigarette case, blk lacquer, ivory/lacquer/gilt on 2 corners **550.00**
Cigarette holder, blk plastic w/narrow gold band, 5" **27.50**
Cigarette lighter/paperweight, elephant figural, chrome **165.00**
Clock, brass w/stepped chrome & glass sides, Weber, 13" **935.00**
Clock, chrome hand supports clock face, Hagenauer, 12" **2,000.00**
Cocktail shaker, penguin, SP, Napier, 12" **1,200.00**
Coffee urn, NP, +cr/sug & tray, Universal, M **40.00**
Compact, gr celluloid w/rhinestones, w/hdl & tassel **140.00**
Compact, mc rhinestones allover, 2" sq **30.00**
Compact, wood inlay, metal Scotties on top, EX **35.00**
Decanter, enameled nude/foliage, 10", +8 glasses, Czech **3,300.00**

Ewer, pewter, tilted oval w/tall 3-side collar, Peltro, 15" **1,100.00**
Figurine, dancer w/cape, bronze/ivory/marble, Lorenzl, 10½" ..**3,750.00**
Figurine, flapper dancer, bronze, mc pnt, Marcuse, 11½" **3,250.00**
Figurine, Isadora Duncan, bronze, marble base, Chiparus, 22" ..**6,000.00**
Figurine, lady reclines, greyhound at side, plaster, sgn, 25" **1,100.00**
Figurine, lady/goat sit on bridge, bronzed metal, 15x31" **550.00**
Figurine, Spanish dancer, bronze, mc pnt, Barner, 10½" **2,750.00**
Figurine, wolfhound pr, mtd on marble base, French, 30" L **850.00**
Grate, wrought iron, abstract geometrics & florals, 39x24" **200.00**
Incense burner, ceramic, Egyptian lady figural, Lisne, 6½" **375.00**

Sapphire blue basket with embossed diamonds, dark blue thorn handle, 7½", $265.00.

Lamp, crackled glass globe, two dancing girls on base, $90.00.

Lamp, heavy floral enamel on glass, Fr, 8" **2,500.00**
Lamp, 12" lighthouse, cobalt/chrome, boat on stepped base **170.00**
Manicure kit, Bakelite, complete, EX **35.00**
Mannequin head, plaster, gold finish, 10" **165.00**
Mirror, chrome fr: lady's arms, head atop, Hagenauer, 24" **4,400.00**
Paperweight, brass sea gull on quartz base, sgn **22.50**
Paperweight, silver, recumbent deer, #d, Denmark, 4" **100.00**
Pitcher, penguin form, silver finish w/blk eyes, Tess, 7" **330.00**
Pocket lighter, tortoise shell, chrome trim, Ronson **70.00**
Powder box, ceramic, nude w/drape finial, Germany **85.00**
Tray, horse figural, chrome, Hagenauer, 22", w/2 cordials **990.00**
Vase, enamell on copper, geometrics, C Faure Limoges, 12" ...**1,650.00**
Vase, enamel on copper, arcs/circles, Faure Limoges, 6" **1,900.00**
Vase, enamel on copper, chevrons/checks, Faure Limoges, 11" ...**4,400.00**
Vase, enamel on copper, overlapping leaves, Sarlandie, 9" **1,980.00**
Vase, frosted glass, cascading circles, Hunebelle, 13" **600.00**
Wash bowl & pitcher, Rose Marie, Keller & Guerin, 12½" dia ..**225.00**

Art Glass Baskets

A popular novelty and gift item during the Victorian era, these one-of-a-kind works of art were produced in just about any type of art glass in use at that time. They were never marked, since these were not true production pieces but 'whimsies' made by glassworkers to relieve the tedium of the long work day. Some were made as special gifts. The more decorative and imaginative the design, the more valuable the basket.

Apple gr opaque satin, fluted, clear hdl, 7x7⅜x8¼" **175.00**

Bl o/l w/sapphire bl thorn hdl, ruffled, 5¼x5¼x6" **165.00**
Bl shaded o/l, clear thorn hdl, ruffled, 9x8½x9¾" **245.00**
Cream o/l, appl vaseline leaves/red berries, 8x6¾" **265.00**
Cream opaque, appl spatter flowers, vaseline hdl/ft, 7½" **195.00**
Dk pk w/wht ext, ribbed/ruffled, camphor twist hdl, 10" L **400.00**
Dk rose o/l, emb swirl, Hobnail edge, sqd/ruffled rim, 5x7" **225.00**
Emerald gr, emb swirl & medallions, clear hdl, 6½x4¾" **110.00**
Gold & pk spatter, clear thorn hdl, 7¾x5" **145.00**
Gr opal w/pk & wht spatter flower, 8-crimp, 6x4" **135.00**
Gr opaque satin, Hobnail rim, amber hdl, 8¾x8¼x9⅛" **450.00**
Mc spatter w/wht int, clear shells on rim, thorn hdl, 7x5" **175.00**
Pk & wht spatter w/emb dmns, clear ruffle & hdl, 7x5½" **125.00**
Pk o/l w/mica, ruffled, clear thorn hdl, 7½x4⅛" **165.00**
Pk opal w/pk appl flower, clear hdl, 6¾x5¼" **145.00**
Pk satin, ruffled Hobnail edge, vaseline hdl, 6½x7½x9" **295.00**
Pk stripe swirl o/l, clear twisted thorn hdl, 7½x4¾" **165.00**
Pk w/wht stripe o/l, emb florals, clear hdl, 7½x7¾" **175.00**
Pk/brn/wht spatter, wht int, clear thorn hdl, 6x4¾" **165.00**
Rose o/l, HP flowers, clear ruffle & hdl, 6¾x4x7" **245.00**
Rose o/l, twisted amber hdl, amber ruffle, 8x6½" **165.00**
Rose spangle, lg mica flakes, rnd/ruffled, clear hdl, 8" **175.00**
Rubena opal, Dmn Quilt, ruffled, tab hdls, 4¾x7¾x11" **245.00**
Vaseline opal, Dmn Quilt, sq, pk appl flowers, 7¼x5x6" **210.00**
Wht MOP satin, bl int, Herringbone, satin hdl, 5¾" **320.00**
Yel & wht spatter, emb basketweave, clear hdl, 5¾x4½" **95.00**

Art Nouveau

From the famous 'L'Art Nouveau' shop in the rue de Provence in Paris, 'New Art' spread across the continent and belatedly arrived in America in time to add its curvilineal elements and asymmetrical ornamentations to the ostentatious remains of the Rococo revival of the 1800s. Nouveau manifested itself in every facet of decorative art. In glassware Tiffany turned the concept into a commercial success that lasted well into the second decade of this century and created a style that inspired other American glassmakers for decades. Furniture, lamps, bronzes, jewelry, and automobiles were designed within the realm of its dictates. Today's market abounds with lovely examples of Art Nouveau, allowing the collector to choose one or several areas that hold a special interest. Our advisor for this category is Steven Whipel; he is listed in the Directory under Arkansas. See also Bronzes; Jewelry; Tiffany; Silver; specific manufacturers; etc.

Buckle, for lady's sash, SP over brass, lady's head, 4" 65.00
Bust, ceramic, maid weaves flowers into hair, #388, 23" 1,400.00
Candlestick, gilt over brass, lady figural, 12" 90.00
Candlestick, Imperial SP, female std, 2-lite, #269, 11½" 1,100.00
Chalice, Posen, silver, 3-ribbon & poppy std, #800, '05, 13" 935.00
Chandelier, wrought metal, bell harp w/leaves & 3-D monkey ..650.00
Clock, gilt over wht metal, lady's head, Ansonia, 9" 400.00
Compote, Wahliss, tall nude holds lily pad behind her, 17" 900.00
Eyeglasses case, sterling, emb lady w/flowing hair 125.00
Fr, metal, nude full length of side, floral on other, 10x7" 600.00
Inkwell, gilt bronze, nude kneels between 2 wells, 9" L 825.00
Inkwell, Korschann, bronze, nymph/flower on dmn-form, 11" 1,300.00
Inkwell, SP over brass, stylized vines & leaves, 6" 125.00
Letter opener, brass, stylized flower, 7" 45.00
Magnifying glass, lady w/flowing hair hdl, rpl glass 250.00
Mirror, gilt bronze, nymph/foliage scrolls ea side, 11x15" 900.00

Mirror, E. Jonchery, titled 'Tete Byzantine,' four lights, $1,800.00.

Pitcher, gr glass w/gold floral, concave style, +6 tumblers 420.00
Plaque, Wahliss, couple holds musical score, #244, 21x18" 2,400.00
Screen, 3-part w/shaped top, wood w/HP maidens, 78x72" 3,800.00
Tray, cast copper, semi-nude lady w/flowing hair, 5" 90.00
Tray, Geschutzt, bronze, bust of lady as hdls, florals, 16" 990.00
Vase, brass, appl iris/foliage, waisted cylinder, 14" 300.00
Vase, pottery, winged lizard coils gr-blk bottle form, 12" 400.00

Arts and Crafts

The Arts and Crafts movement began in England during the last quarter of the 19th century, and its influence was soon felt in this country. Among its proponents in America were Elbert Hubbard (see Roycroft) and Gustav Stickley (see Stickley). They rebelled against the mechanized mass production of the Industrial Revolution and against the cumulative influence of hundreds of years of man's changing taste. They subscribed to the theory of purification of the styles: that designs be geared strictly to necessity. At the same time they sought to elevate these basic ideals to the level of accepted 'art.' Simplicity was their virtue; to their critics it was a fault.

The type of furniture they promoted was squarely built, usually of heavy oak, and so simple was its appearance that as a result many began to copy the style which became known as 'Mission.' Soon factories had geared production toward making cheap copies of their designs. In 1915 Stickley's own operation failed, forced into bankruptcy by the machinery he so despised. Hubbard lost his life that same year on the ill-fated *Lusitania*. Within the decade the style had lost its popularity.

Metal ware was produced by numerous crafts people, from experts such as Dirk Van Erp and Albert Berry to unknown novices. Prices for Arts and Crafts accessories rose dramatically in 1988, but by the beginning of 1991 leveled off and (in some cases) dropped. Metal items or hardware should not be scrubbed or scoured; to do so could remove or damage the rich, dark patina typical of this period. Our advisor for this category is Bruce Austin; he is listed in the Directory under New York. See also Furniture; Roycroft; Silver; Furniture; Stickley; and specific manufacturers.

Andirons, Cahill, wrought iron, top-curled strap on arch ft 400.00
Andirons, patinated brass/iron, geometric finial, 25" 250.00
Ashtray, Oscar Bach, brass, 4 rams as ft, aurene tray, 5x9" 250.00
Book, Craftsman, leather-bound, Vols 1 & 2, worn, 10x7" 275.00
Bowl, C Sorensen, bronze, wide flat rim, #1194, 2x12", EX 250.00
Bowl, Jarvie, hammered copper, orig patina, imp mk, 4x6" 550.00
Bowl vase, D Van Erp, hammered copper, red-brn patina, 5¾" 1,100.00
Box, ET Hurley, bronze, sea horses/waves on lid, 2x5", EX 650.00

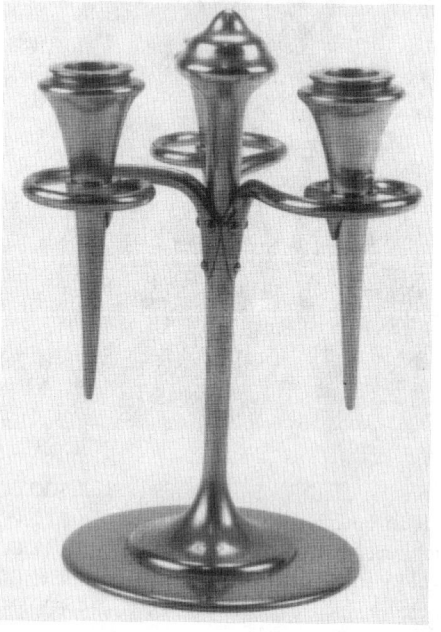

Candelabra, Jarvie, brass, lightly polished, 11", EX, $6,500.00.

Candlestick, C Rohlfs, oak/copper 2-tier X, EX patina 125.00
Candlestick, C Rohlfs, 4 wood pencil posts, copper cup, 7" 850.00
Candlestick, ET Hurley, sea horse std, orig patina, 13", pr 1,500.00
Candlestick, ET Hurley, sea horse std, unmk, 7x5", EX 500.00
Candlestick, Jarvie, bronze, Beta, mk B, 13", pr 2,900.00
Candlestick, Jarvie, bronze, sgn, orig patina, 14" 3,700.00
Candlestick, Liberty & Co, silver, appl stems/leaves, 8" 3,300.00
Candlestick Old Mission Kopper Kraft, twist std, unmk, 10" 300.00
Catalog, Chas Limbert, furniture book #117, color illus, VG 495.00
Chamberstick, Chas Rohlfs, mahog/copper, 3-sided/ftd, varnish ..350.00
Clock, mantel; Liberty & Co, pnt/pewter, stylized trees, 13" ...2,600.00
Clock, tall case; oak, ldgl door, brass #s/dial, rfn, 76" 935.00
Creamer, K Kipp, hammered copper, band w/flower, 4", VG 260.00
Footstool, oak w/spring seat, corbel supports, 23" L 300.00
Humidor, copper/brass, 6 framed panels on rnd base, 8" 135.00
Inkwell, Marshall Field, brass, scarab/floral emb, pyramid 130.00
Jardiniere, mk AF, copper w/flower band at rim, 7x10" 400.00
Lamp, Al Berry, seashells in copper mushroom shade, 19x14" .1,300.00
Lamp, D Van Erp, flared base, cone shade w/mica panels, 20" ..5,500.00
Lamp, D Van Erp, riveted gourd base, mica shade, 24x20" 8,800.00
Lamp, Limbert, 4-panel mica & o/l shade, 2-ped std, 20x24" ..2,300.00
Letter rack, K Kipp, copper, 3-panel, orig patina, 6x5" 300.00

Mail box, hammered copper, 12" 110.00
Pedestal, Limbert #246 rnd top/shelf/base, label, rfn, 43" 1,100.00
Pitcher, D Van Erp, hammered SP copper, sqd, mk, 8x8" 1,100.00
Plate, Karl Kipp, hammered copper w/sm emb floral, mk, 9¾" ...375.00
Poster, daisies, from Craftsman 1916 exhibition, 32x24" 240.00
Rug, Drugget, bl/gold zigzag border on ivory, 36x72", EX 160.00
Rug, Drugget, flowers in oatmeal/brn/ivory wool, 60x40", G 150.00
Rug, Drugget tag, geometric flowers, 7-color, 136x115", EX 600.00
Rug, Kazak, 4-color geometric wool, 1900s, 117x61", EX 750.00
Tablecloth, foliate motif embroidered on linen, fringe, 44" 195.00
Torchere, bronze w/2 mica-lined shades, leaf base, 18", pr 1,400.00
Tray, D Van Erp, hammered copper, closed hdls, repatina, 13" ..400.00
Vase, hammered copper, silver band, orb mk, heavy, 6x3", M ..1,400.00
Woodblock, Bertha Lum, river/plants/cartouches, fr, 12x10" 500.00
Woodblock, Wm Rice, Old Oaken Bucket, sgn, orig fr, 12x9" 750.00
Woodblock print, Marblehead Harbor, sgn Butler, 10x12" 275.00

Attwell, Mabel Lucie

Born in London in 1879, Mabel Lucie Attwell put her talent in illustration and design toward many outlets. Merchandise ranging from children's books and dinnerware, postcards, advertising, dolls, calendars, and greeting cards were marketed under her direction. She also designed a line of china called Nursery ware for the Shelley China Company (See also Shelley). Our advisor for this category is David Ehrhard; he is listed in the Directory under California.

Boo Boo creamer, $150.00; Sarah (by Wade), $65.00; Oval baby's plate with verse, Shelley, 8", $100.00; Mug, Shelley, $75.00; Celluloid doll 'Diddums,' 6", $35.00 (8", $55.00; 10", $75.00); Crawford biscuit tin, $350.00.

Book, Children's Stories by Lucie Attwell, Whitman 40.00
Book, Lucie Attwell's Pop-Up Book of Rhymes, Dean, 1973 ....60.00
Cake plate, If I Had a Fairy, Shelley Nursery Ware 85.00
Calendar, Never Forget if the World Goes Wry..., 5x7" 35.00
Figurine, Boo Boo on a puppy, Shelley, 4" 300.00
Figurine, Bride, Shelley, 8" 600.00
Figurine, Diddums, Shelley, 8" 400.00
Figurine, Toddler, girl w/doll in hand, Shelley 500.00
Handkerchief set, Lucie Attwell's Picture Hankys, M 60.00
Plaque, This Is a Home Not an Ashtray, 4x10" 40.00
Plate, Bobby Bear Went to Moon..., Shelley Nursery Ware, 5" 60.00
Plate, If I had a Fairy..., Shelley Nursery Ware, 5" 85.00
Print, Fairies Are Mischiefing Dorothy Dell, 4x6" 40.00
Print, Where's Daddy's Twosers?, 8x10" 35.00
Print, Working of the Act, 8x10" 45.00
Saucer, Oh! Mr Rabbit Do Put Up..., Shelley Nursery Ware 45.00

Tea set, mushroom house pot/toadstool sugar/Boo Boo creamer ..500.00
Teapot, flying plane scene & verse, Shelley Nursery Ware 150.00
Tin container, Huntley Palmers, Little Friends, 1 of 6, 5"dia 25.00
Tray, for Wright's Biscuits, Mischief, 15x20" 85.00

Austrian Glass

Many examples of fine art glass were produced in Austria during the time of Loetz and Moser that cannot be attributed to any glasshouse in particular, though much of it bears striking similarities to the products of both artists.

Vase, floriform; dk bl-gr irid, flattened fan form, 12" 1,100.00
Vase, gr-gold irid w/purple waves, ruffled trumpet form, 25" ...1,200.00
Vase, gr/purple irid w/bl waves, dimpled rose jar form, 7" 550.00
Vase, opal-cased gr w/trailings, dimpled base, 13" 550.00
Vase, red lustre w/wht steaks, twisted, att Pallme-Konig, 12" 220.00
Vase, silver o/l florals on bl/gr swirled irid, 5" 935.00
Vase, silver o/l vines/blossoms on purple baluster form, 6" 880.00

Austrian Ware

From the late 1800s until the beginning of WWI, several companies were located in the area known at the turn of the century as Bohemia. They produced hard-paste porcelain dinnerware and decorative items primarily for the American trade. Today examples bearing the marks of these firms are usually referred to by collectors as Austrian ware, indicating simply the country of their origin. Of those various companies, these marks are best known: M.Z. Austria; Victoria, Carlsbad, Austria (Schmidt and Company); and O. & E.G. (Royal) Austria.

Though most of the decorations were transfer designs which were sometimes signed by the original artist, pieces marked Royal Austria were often hand painted and so indicated alongside the backstamp.

Of these three companies, Victoria, Carlsbad, Austria, is the most highly valued. Collectors should note that in our listings transfer decorations showing 'signatures' (sgn), such as 'Wagner,' 'Kauffmann,' 'LeBrun,' etc., were not actually painted by those artists but were merely based on their original paintings.

Ewer, floral on tan, gold hdl/spout, sgn MBS, crown mk, 5" 95.00
Humidor, cherub/women, sgn Kauffmann, pewter lid w/pipe 285.00
Jug, rum; floral medallions on pearlized ground, much gold 95.00
Plate, Constance portrait, bl beehive mk, 9¼" 110.00
Plate, dog portrait, gold rococo edge, 13" 225.00
Plate, lady's portrait on gr, sgn Carlson, Carlsbad, 10" 85.00
Plate, 2 birds in Baroque reserve, Xd V mk, 10", in gold fr 125.00
Vase, Bohemian girl, ornate gold hdls, Victoria, 12x5½" 275.00
Vase, Cupid/clouds, coiled snake hdl, split top, Victoria, 8" 150.00
Vase, floral w/gold trim, sgn Hanke, gold floral hdls, 17" 225.00
Vase, girl in bl stone-set jewelry, gold hdls, Crown W, 12" 150.00
Vase, HP fuchsias on cobalt, hdls, 14½" 365.00

Autographs

Autograph collecting, also known as 'philography' or 'love of writing,' used to be a hobby shared by a few thousand dedicated collectors. But in recent years, autograph collecting has become a serious pursuit for more than 2,000,000 collectors worldwide. And in the past decade, more investors are adding rare and valuable autograph portfolios to their traditional investments. One reason for this sudden interest in autograph investing relates to the simple economic law of supply and demand. Rare autographs have a 'fixed' supply, meaning that unlike diamonds, gold, silver, stock certificates, etc., no more are being produced. There are only so many Abraham Lincoln, Marilyn Monroe, and Charles Lindbergh autographs available. In the meantime, it's estimated that more than 20,000 new collectors enter the market each year, thus creating an ever-increasing demand. Hence, the rare autographs generally rise steadily in value each year. Because of this scarcity, a serious collector will pay over $10,000 for a photograph signed by both Wilbur and Orville Wright, or as much as $25,000 for a handwritten letter of George Washington.

But by far, the majority of autograph collectors in the country do it for the love of the hobby. A polite letter and self-addressed, stamped envelope sent to a famous person will often bring the desired result. And occasionally one receives not only an autograph but a nice handwritten letter thanking the fan as well!

In terms of value, there are five general types of autographs: 1) mere signatures on an album page or card; 2) signed photographs; 3) signed documents; 4) typed letters signed; and 5) handwritten letters. The signatures are the least valuable, and handwritten letters the most valuable. The reasoning here is simple: with a handwritten letter, not only do you get an autograph but the handwritten message of the person as well. And this content can sometimes increase the value many times over. A handwritten letter of Babe Ruth thanking a fan for a gift might fetch a few thousand dollars. But if the letter were to mention Ruth's feelings on the day he retired, it could easily sell for $10,000 or more.

There are several major autograph collector organizations where members can exchange celebrity addresses or buy, sell, and trade their autographed wares. Philography can be a fun and rewarding hobby. And who knows! In ten or twenty years, those autographs you got for free could be worth a small fortune!

In the listings below, photos are assumed black and white unless noted color. Our advisor for autographs is Tim Anderson; he is listed in the Directory under Utah.

Key:

ADS — handwritten document signed	ins — inscription
ALS — handwritten letter signed	ISP — inscribed signed photo
	LH — letterhead
ANS — handwritten note signed	LS — signed letter, typed or written by someone else
AQS — autograph quotation signed	PLH — personal letterhead
	sig — signature
CS — counter signed	SP — signed photo
DS — document signed	

Adams, Ansel; bold sig on Photography magazine cover, 1978 ..125.00
Albert, Eddie; ISP, blk/wht, 8x10" 22.00
Alcott, Louisa May; ALS, story for newspaper, 3-pg 715.00
Arthur, Chester; ALS, as Collector of Customs in NY, 1871 .....450.00
Astaire, Fred; & Rogers, Ginger; SP, dancing, 8x10" 250.00
Bacall, Lauren; SP, full-length portrait, 1940s 10.00
Banks, Nathaniel P; sig on carte de visite, EX 450.00
Bardot, Brigitte; SP, sexy pose in bed 55.00
Bassinger, Kim; SP, full-length sexy beach portrait 48.00
Bernhardt, Sarah; ANS, dtd 1913 by her 165.00
Bernstein, Leonard; SP, blk/wht, 6x8" 165.00
Berra, Yogi; SP, color, 8x10" 37.50
Blanc, Mel; ISP, color, 8x10" 125.00
Bolton, Sarah; ALS, re use of poem, 1892, 1-pg 22.50
Brice, Fanny; sig on program cover 65.00
Bridges, Jeff; SP, color still from Starman, 1984 ....12.50
Bridges, Robert; ALS, meeting arrangements, 2-pg 40.00
Buck, Pearl; LS, sending autograph, 1959, 1-pg 37.50
Burr, Aaron; ALS, declines land offer, 1793, 1-pg, EX 650.00

Burton, Richard; ISP, blk/wht, 8x10" 175.00
Calhoun, John C; ALS, thanks for pamphlet, as Vice President ..155.00
Carmichael, Hoagy; SP, blk/wht, 8x10" 78.00
Cather, Willa; LS, to friend w/travel news, 1911, 2-pg 450.00
Chambers, Marilyn; SP, blk/wht 22.00
Chaney, Lon Jr; ISP, blk/wht, 7x5", EX 130.00
Clemens, Samuel H; ALS, thank-you note, 1890, 1-pg 1,600.00
Clemente, Roberto; sig in bl ink on sm wht paper, EX 280.00
Cleveland, Grover; sig on 1882 City of Buffalo beer license 165.00
Cohan, George M; ins & bold sig on 3x2" card 65.00
Coolidge, Calvin; DS, appointment for RI postmaster, 1926 ......140.00
Cooper, James Fenimore; ALS, in French, 1831, 1-pg 325.00
Costello, Lou; ISP, fine & dk sig, 10x8" 250.00
Crawford, Joan; ISP, sentimental, lg sz 55.00
Daly, Augustin; ALS, on theatre stationery, 1888, 1-pg 40.00
Davis, Bette; SP, blk/wht, 8x10" 75.00
Davis Jr, Sammy; SP, blk/wht, 8x10" 75.00
Dean, Dizzy; sig w/4 other Cub players on album pg, 1938 ....125.00
DeBakey, Michael; SP, bold sig, blk/wht, 5x7" 45.00
Dempsey, Jack; SP, color, 8x10" 135.00
Dewey, Thomas E; sig on NY governor's card 55.00
Dickinson, Anna; ALS, cancelling engagement, 1868, 2-pg 22.00
Dietrich, Marlene; bold sig below sm photo 22.00
DiMaggio, Joe; SP, blk/wht, 8x10" 115.00
Downey, Senator Sheridan; SP, blk/wht, 8x10" 25.00
Dumas, Alexander; LS, as general during 1830 revolution, 2-pg ...550.00
Earhart, Amelia; sig on 5x3" paper 375.00
Eastwood, Clint; SP, color, as Rowdy Yates, NM 20.00
Einstein, Albert; LS, contribution to book, 1948, 1-pg 1,500.00
Eisenhower, Dwight D; ISP, in uniform, 8x10" 300.00
Enola Gay Crew (Tibbets, Ferebee, Van Kirk), SP w/plane 37.50
Fairbanks, Douglas Sr; mtd newspaper photo sgn on mt, EX 110.00
Fiske, John; ALS, information re Benedict Arnold, 1889, 2-pg 27.50
Fleming; Rhonda; SP, 1955 ....18.00
Fremont, John C; ALS, re organic studies from OR, 2-pg 1,400.00

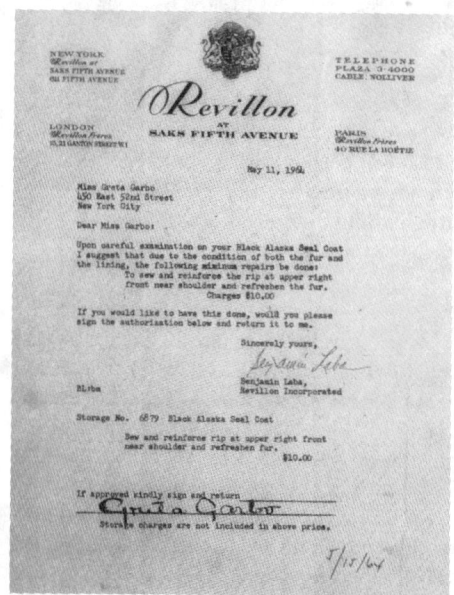

Greta Garbo, autograph on letter from Saks Fifth Avenue asking for endorsement to proposed repair of fur, 1964, $1,800.00.

Gehrig, Lou; sig in blk ink on yellowed paper, EX 300.00
Gibson, Bob; sig (bold) on sm wht paper, M 85.00
Hancock, John; DS, military appointment, 1874, EX 4,200.00
Harrison, Caroline Scott; sig on Executive Mansion card 265.00
Hemingway, Ernest; sig on menu 550.00

Henry, Patrick; DS, bold sig, dtd 1784 ....600.00
Hoover, J Edgar; LS, discusses FBI, 1963, EX 45.00
Hopkins, Anthony; SP, as Hannibal Lechter 55.00
Hurst, Frannie; LS, photo concerns, 1941, 1-pg 35.00
Jefferson, Thomas; DS, military appointment, 1809, EX 1,900.00
Kelly, John; ISP, blk/wht, 8x10" 17.50
Lamarr, Hedy; SP, 1940s, rare 42.00
Landon, Alfred M; LS, re collectible campaign materials, 1978 ...32.00
Lauper, Cyndi; ISP, color, 8x10" 45.00
Leonard, Sugar Ray; SP, color, 8x10" 45.00
Levenson, Boris; 5-line ANS on photo bk, 1942 ....36.00
Liberace, SP, at piano, blk/wht, 8x10" 150.00

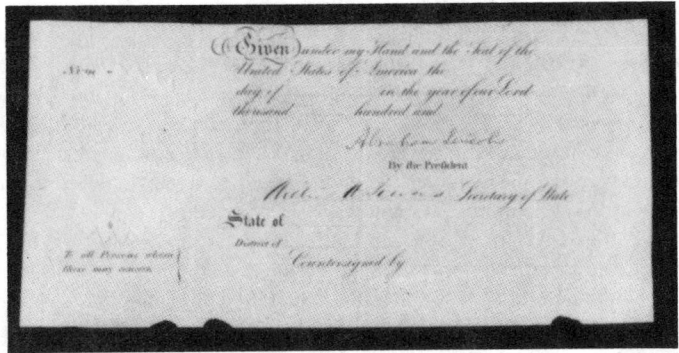

Abraham Lincoln, signature on portion of (not complete) undated printed military commission, countersigned by Wm Seward, creased, discolored, $2,090.00. If complete and undamaged, $5,000.00.

Marks, Johnny; ISP, w/2 bars of music, 8x10" 175.00
Mays, Willie; sig (bold, bl marker) on sm paper, M 85.00
McCarthy, Joe; LS, birth of daughter, 1957 ....65.00
Monroe, James; DS as Secretary of State, 3-pg, EX 800.00
Morris, Robert H; lg bold clipped sig 65.00
Munch, Charles; sig on program cover, 1949, EX 20.00
Page, Geraldine; ALS, thank you, 1-pg 55.00
Page, Geraldine; sig on greeting card 22.00
Pershing, John J; newspaper photo as General, sgn mt, 4x5" 185.00
Rather, Dan; SP, blk/wht, 8x10" 15.00
Rhea, Jona; sig on Paterson lottery ticket, printed by Wood 140.00
Robinson, Edwin Arlington; ANS on postcard, 1932 ....27.50
Robinson, Jackie; sig on magazine cover, EX 325.00
Rogers, Roy; SP, Back in the Saddle Again 18.00
Roosevelt, Theodore; sig on eng invitation, dtd 1905 ....300.00
Ruth, Babe; sig in blk ink on wht paper, NM 500.00
Salk, Jonas; SP, 5x7" 75.00
Scotte, Winfield; sig on mt of carte de visite by Anthony 900.00
Sinclair, Upton; ANS, initial sig, 1-pg 55.00
Starr, Kay; ISP, blk/wht, 5x7" 22.50
Tierney, Gene; SP, from Rings on Her Fingers, 1942 ....17.50
Truman, Harry S; LS, thanks for birthday wishes, 1972, 1-pg 185.00
Warhol, Andy; sig in his book America 235.00
Washington, Booker T; LS, activities of Tuskegee Normal, 1902 .55.00
Wayne, John; ISP, blk/wht, 8x10" 320.00
Wilkes, Charles; sig on mt of carte de visite, EX 420.00
Yamagata, Prince Aritomo; bold sig on card, English/Japanese ...115.00

Automobilia

While some automobilia buffs are primarily concerned with restor-

ing vintage cars, others concentrate on only one area of collecting. For instance, hood ornaments were often quite spectacular. Made of chrome or nickel plate on brass or bronze, they were designed to represent the 'winged maiden' Victory, flying bats, sleek greyhounds, soaring eagles, and a host of other creatures. Today they often bring prices in the $75 to $200 range. R. Lalique glass ornaments go much higher!

Horns, radios, clocks, gear shift knobs, and key chains with company emblems are other areas of interest. Generally, items pertaining to the classics of the thirties are most in demand. Paper advertising material, manuals, and catalogs in excellent condition are also collectible.

License plate collectors search for the early porcelain-on-cast-iron examples. First year plates (e.g., Massachusetts, 1903; Wisconsin, 1905; Indiana, 1913) are especially valuable. The last of the states to issue regulation plates were South Carolina and Texas in 1917, and Florida in 1918. While many northeastern states had registered hundreds of thousands of vehicles by the 1920s making these plates relatively common, those from the southern and western states of that period are considered rare. Naturally, condition is important. While a pair in mint condition might sell for as much as $100 to $125, a pair with chipped or otherwise damaged porcelain may sometimes be had for as little as $25 to $30. Our advisors for this category are Dennis O'Brien and George Goehring of Dennis and George Collectibles; they are listed in the Directory under Maryland. See also Gas Globes and Panels.

Almanac, Ford Farm, 1936, 48-pg, EX 12.00
Ashtray, Dodge-Plymouth logos on glass, 4½" sq 22.00
Ashtray, Ford crest on glass, 4" sq 15.00
Ashtray, Graham Motor Cars emb on aluminum, helmet logo, EX ...48.00
Badge, chauffeur; MI, 1909 ....200.00
Badge, chauffeur; NY, 1926 ....15.00
Badge, employee; Studebaker, shaped like 1920s radiator, EX 145.00
Badge, hat; Kaiser-Willys Guard, chrome-plated shield, EX 37.50
Blotter, Socony Motor Oil, 1922 auto in winter scene, 6x3" 4.50
Book, Body by Fisher, 1967, lg, NM 26.00
Brochure, De Lorean, scarce, M 15.00
Brush, upholstery; Atlantic Gasoline, emb brass top, 1920s 27.50
Catalog, Cadillac Motor Cars, mc 46-pg, 1927, EX 195.00
Catalog, Oldsmobile dealer's, hardbound, 1951-52, 14x10", VG ..60.00
Coaster, Ford Twin Cities plant, metal, 1950s, rare 40.00
Crank hdl, for early Model-T Ford, aluminum, EX 35.00
Envelope, Hupmobile, pictures open touring car, 4x2½", NM 3.50
Figure, Pontiac Indian, plaster/wood, 1940s, 92", EX 3,500.00
Foldout, 1946 Chrysler Town & Country car models, EX 27.50
Gearshift knob, Ford Rotunda, blk plastic, chrome insert, NM ...350.00
Gearshift knob, simulated ivory w/Rotary Internat'l logo 45.00
Hat visor, Chevrolet bl & wht bow tie logo, cb, EX 5.00
Hood ornament, bulldog, CI, from Mac truck, EX 35.00
Hood ornament, Pontiac, Indian w/headdress, metal, 1920s, 3½" ...10.00
Hubcap, Hupmobile, 1929, aluminum, for wooden wheel, EX 32.50
Key, ignition; Willy's Overland script, EX 6.50
Key chain medallion, Buick script, celluloid, early 25.00
Key chain medallion, Cadillac Standard of the World, 1⅛" 40.00
Key holder, impressed 1936 Chevy on leather 14.00
Lamp, brass, carbide, w/hooks, Springfield IL, 4" 20.00
Lapel pin, Studebaker, birds & crowns logo, mc enamel, ⅞", NM 25.00
Letter opener, GMC Trucks logo, mc on plastic, 8½", NM 32.00
Letter opener, Keystone Spring Works Golden Anniv...Est 1870 .35.00
Letter opener, Pontiac emblem on hammered brass, 1930s, 9" ...100.00
License plate, CA, 1914, porc, EX 78.00
License plate, CA, 1929, VG 12.00
License plate, IL, 1918, no pnt 14.00
License plate, MA, 1908, porc, EX 150.00
License plate, NJ, 1909, porc, EX 165.00
License plate, OH, 1913, EX 55.00

License plate, UT, 1928, EX **35.00**
License plate attachment, Tydol Oil & Gasoline figure, 1930s **60.00**
License plate attachment, 48-star US flag, full color **22.50**
Magazine, Vehicle Monthly, auto news, Nov 1921, 10x13", EX **7.50**
Manual, Nash Rambler owner's, 1958, 40-pg, 4x6", EX **9.00**
Map, Sinclair, pictures cars/Sinclair Minstrels/etc, 1933 ....**40.00**
Nameplate, Hudson, letters under plastic cover, ca 1950 ....**12.00**
Oil change reminder button, Ford script, 1½", EX **32.00**
Paperweight, Ford 50th Anniversary, bronze, 1953 ....**75.00**
Pencil, mechanical; Chevrolet bow tie logo, NM **8.50**
Pencil, mechanical; Ford script in blk oval, EX **20.00**
Pin-back button, Buick Best in Class, 3-shield logo, NM **35.00**
Program, Indianapolis 500, 1959, 100-pg, EX **20.00**

Promotional car, 1957 Chevy, wind-up, Delco, 12", M in VG box, $295.00.

Promotional, Rolls-Royce, bronze winged female, Gorham, 6" ..**650.00**
Radiator cap, Chevrolet Eagle, chrome plated, 1931-32, EX **88.00**
Radiator medallion, Chrysler across center, 1920s **12.50**
Radiator medallion, Hupmobile, lg H w/red enameling, 1930s **12.50**
Radiator medallion, whippet dog, 4", NM **68.00**
Ruler, Studebaker, wooden, folder, 12", EX **50.00**
Spark plug, Automat, spring-loaded valve atop porc, NM **65.00**
Spoon, demitasse; Cadillac in block letters on hdl, SP **25.00**
Stick pin, Buick, gold enamel on bl & wht **45.00**
Tape measure, DeSoto, celluloid, ca 1930s, EX **80.00**
Thermometer, Hash Airflytes logo, blk & wht fiberboard, 6" **22.00**
Tie clip, GM Chevrolet Genuine Parts, M **15.00**
Token, Free Winter Inspection, bow tie logo, brass, EX **6.50**
Watch fob, Chrysler, wreath w/lightning bolts, mc on gold **45.00**

Autumn Leaf

In 1933 the Hall China Company designed a line of dinnerware for the Jewel Tea Company, who offered it to their customers as premiums. Although you may hear the ware referred to as 'Jewel Tea,' it was officially named 'Autumn Leaf' in the 1940s. In addition to the dinnerware, frosted Libbey glass tumblers, stemware, and a melmac service with the orange and gold bittersweet pod were available over the years, as were tablecloths, plastic covers for bowls and mixers, and metal items such as cake safes, hot pads, coasters, wastebaskets, and canisters. Even shelf paper and playing cards were made to coordinate. In 1958 the International Silver Company designed silverplated flatware in a pattern called 'Autumn' which was to be used with dishes in the Autumn Leaf pattern. A year later, a line of stainless flatware was introduced. These accessory lines are prized by collectors today.

One of the most fascinating aspects of collecting the Autumn Leaf pattern has been the wonderful discoveries of previously unlisted pieces.

Among these items are two different bud-ray lid one-pound butter dishes; most recently a one-pound butter dish in the 'Zephyr' or 'Bingo' style; a miniature set of the 'Casper' salt and pepper shakers; coffee, tea, and sugar canisters; a pair of candlesticks; an experimental condiment jar; and a covered candy dish. All of these china pieces are attributed to the Hall China Company. Other unusual items have turned up in the accessory lines as well and include a Libbey frosted tumbler in a pilsner shape, a wooden serving bowl, and an apron made from the oilcloth (plastic) material that was used in the 1950s tablecloth. These latter items appear to be professionally done, and we can only speculate as to their origin. Collectors believe that the Hall items were sample pieces that were never meant to be distributed.

Hall discontinued the Autumn Leaf line in 1978. At that time the date was added to the backstamp to mark ware still in stock in the Jewel warehouse. A special promotion by Jewel saw the reintroduction of basic dinnerware and serving pieces with the 1978 backstamp. These pieces have made their way into many collections. Additionally, in 1979 Jewel released a line of enamel-clad cookware and a Vellux blanket made by Martex which were decorated with the Autumn Leaf pattern. They continued to offer these items for a few years only, then all distribution of Autumn Leaf items was discontinued.

It should be noted that the Hall China Company has produced several limited edition items for the National Autumn Leaf Collectors Club (NALCC): a New York-style teapot (1984); a vase (1987, different than the original shape); candlesticks (1988); a Philadelphia-style teapot, creamer and sugar set (1990); a sugar packet holder (1990); a tea-for-two set and a Solo tea set (1991), a donut jug, and a large oval casserole. New items for the NALCC: small ball jug, 1-cup French teapot, and a set of four chocolate mugs. The NALCC has also given their club members special items over the past few years made for them by Hall China: a sugar packet holder, a chamberstick, and an oyster cocktail. Other items are scheduled for production. All of these are plainly marked as having been made for the NALCC and are appropriately dated. A few other pieces have been made by Hall as limited editions for an Ohio company, but these are easily identified: the Airflow teapot and the Norris refrigerator pitcher (neither of which was previously decorated with the Autumn Leaf decal), a square-handled beverage mug, and the new-style Irish mug. A production problem with the square-handled mugs halted their production. The company then issued a regular conic-style mug with a round handle. Additional items available now are a covered onion soup, tall bud vase, china kitchen memo board, and egg drop-style salt and pepper shakers with a mustard pot. They have also issued a deck of playing cards and Libbey tumblers.

Ball jug #3, $28.00.

Baker, oval, Fort Pitt **90.00**
Batter bowl, Saf-Hdl **2,500.00**

Bean pot, 1-hdl	500.00
Bean pot, 2-hdl, 2¼-qt	135.00
Bowl, cereal; 6"	10.00
Bowl, coupe soup	12.00
Bowl, cream soup; 2-hdl	18.00
Bowl, fruit; 5½"	4.00
Bowl, metal, enamelware, set of 3	200.00
Bowl, mixing; set of 3: 6¼", 7½", 9"	100.00
Bowl, Royal Glas-Bake, set of 4	45.00
Bowl, salad	14.00
Bowl, stackette; set of 3: 18-oz, 24-oz, 34-oz, w/lid	75.00
Bowl, vegetable; divided, 10½"	75.00
Bowl, vegetable; oval, w/lid, 10"	35.00
Bowl, vegetable; oval, 10½"	15.00
Bowl, vegetable; rnd, 9"	75.00
Bowl cover set, plastic, 8-pc: 7 assorted covers in pouch	50.00
Bread box, metal	225.00
Butter dish, 1-lb	325.00
Butter dish, ¼-lb	150.00
Butter dish, ¼-lb, Square Top	500.00
Butter dish, ¼-lb, Wings	750.00
Cake plate, 9½"	12.00
Cake safe, metal, motif on top & sides, 5"	35.00
Cake safe, metal, side decor only, 4½x10½"	30.00
Cake stand, metal base, orig box	150.00
Candy dish	350.00
Canister, metal, rnd, w/coppertone lid, set of 4	175.00
Canister, metal, rnd, w/ivory plastic lid	10.00
Canister, metal, rnd, w/matching lid, 6"	15.00
Canister, metal, rnd, w/matching lid, 7"	25.00
Canister, metal, rnd, w/matching lid, 8¼"	35.00
Canister, metal, sq, set of 4: 8½" & 4½"	175.00

Casserole, 2-qt, 9" dia, $28.00.

Casserole, Royal Glas-Bake, deep, w/clear glass lid	25.00
Casserole, Royal Glas-Bake, shallow, w/clear glass lid	20.00
Casserole, Tootsie-hdl, w/lid	22.00
Casserole/souffle, swirl, 3-pt	15.00
Casserole/souffle, 10-oz	10.00
Casserole/souffle, 2-pt	85.00
Cleanser can, metal, sq, 6", M	500.00
Clock, orig works	400.00
Coaster, metal, 3⅛"	4.00
Coffee dispenser/canister, metal, wall type, 10½x19" dia	175.00
Coffee maker, 5-cup, all china, w/china insert	250.00
Coffee maker, 9-cup, w/metal dripper, 8"	35.00
Coffee percolator, electric, all china	225.00

Coffee percolator/carafe, Douglas, w/warmer base, MIB	250.00
Cookie jar, Tootsie	165.00
Creamer, New Style	8.00
Creamer, Old Style, 4¼"	15.00
Cup & saucer	8.00
Cup & saucer, St Denis	22.00
Custard cup	4.00
Flatware, silverplate, ea	15.00
Flatware, stainless, ea	10.00
Fruit cake tin, metal	10.00
Golden Ray base, to use w/candy dish or cake plate, pr	50.00
Gravy boat	18.00
Hot pad, metal, red or gr felt-like bking, rnd	15.00
Hot pad, oval	12.00
Hurricane lamp, Douglas, w/metal base, pr	400.00
Kitchen utility chair, metal	450.00
Marmalade jar, 3-pc	55.00
Mixer cover, Mary Dunbar, plastic	25.00
Mug, beverage	55.00
Mug, Irish coffee	95.00
Mustard jar, 3½"	55.00
Napkin, ecru muslin	25.00
Pickle dish or gravy liner, oval, 9"	18.00
Picnic thermos, metal	250.00
Pie baker, 9½"	18.00
Pitcher, utility; 2½-pt, 6"	15.00
Place mat, paper, scalloped	25.00
Place mat, set of 8, M in orig package	195.00
Plate, 10"	12.00
Plate, 6" or 7", ea	4.00
Plate, 8"	8.00
Plate, 9"	10.00
Platter, 11½"	15.00
Platter, 13½"	18.00
Playing cards, regular or Pinochle	125.00
Range set, shakers & covered drippings jar	35.00
Sauce dish, serving; Douglas, Bakelite hdl	125.00
Shakers, Casper, pr	18.00
Shakers, range, hdl, pr	18.00
Sugar bowl, New Style	12.00
Sugar bowl, Old Style, 3½"	18.00
Tablecloth, cotton sailcloth w/gold stripe, 54x54"	75.00
Tablecloth, cotton sailcloth w/gold stripe, 54x72"	85.00
Tablecloth, ecru muslin, 56x81"	150.00
Tablecloth, plastic	150.00
Teakettle, metal enamelware	150.00
Teapot, Aladdin	38.00
Teapot, long spout, 7"	45.00
Teapot, Newport	145.00
Teapot, Newport, dtd 1978	125.00
Toaster cover, plastic, fits 2-slice toaster	25.00
Towel, dish; pattern & clock motif	45.00
Towel, tea; cotton, 16x33"	35.00
Trash can, metal, red	100.00
Tray, glass, wood hdl, 19½x11¼"	95.00
Tray, metal, oval	55.00
Tray, red w/allover red & yel design, red border	65.00
Tray, tidbit; 2-tier	35.00
Tray, tidbit; 3-tier	55.00
Tumbler, Brockway, 13-oz	18.00
Tumbler, Brockway, 16-oz	20.00
Tumbler, Brockway, 9-oz	16.00
Tumbler, frosted, 14-oz, 5½"	12.00
Tumbler, frosted, 9-oz, 3¾"	18.00

Tumbler, gold frost etched, flat, 10-oz 30.00
Tumbler, gold frost etched, flat, 15-oz 45.00
Tumbler, gold frost etched, ftd, 10-oz 45.00
Tumbler, gold frost etched, ftd, 6½-oz 45.00
Vase, bud; 6" 175.00
Warmer base, oval 150.00
Warmer base, rnd 110.00
Warmer base, rnd, w/4 orig candles, orig mk box 125.00

Aviation

Aviation buffs are interested in any phase of flying, from early developments with gliders, balloons, airships and flying machines to more modern innovations. Books, catalogs, photos, patents, lithographs, ad cards, and posters are among the paper ephemera they treasure alongside models of unlikely flying contraptions, propellers and rudders, insignia and equipment from WWI and WWII, and memorabilia from the flights of the Wright Brothers, Lindbergh, Earhart, and the Zeppelins. See also Militaria. Our advisor for this category is John R. Joiner; he is listed in the Directory under Georgia.

Tippco model of the Hindenburg, tinplate, key wind, ca 1936, 11", in original box, $3,250.00.

Award, Bulova Am Airline, million miles, to captain, 1958 ......125.00
Ballpoint pen, Western Airlines, New Non-stop to San Diego, M .10.00
Book, Story of the Airship, hard-bk, 6th edition, 1931, EX 60.00
Bookends, Lindbergh figural, 8½", pr 65.00
Booklet, Am Airlines, maps & schedules, 1946, EX 22.00
Charm, Columbia space shuttle, pewter-like replica, 1980s 18.00
Coin, Lucky Lindbergh, brass, Lindy/plane/horseshoe/clover, NM ...25.00
Knife, American Airlines, DC-3 hdl 30.00
Knife, fork, & spoon, TWA, SP, arrow through TWA on hdl 40.00
Label, baggage; TWA DC-3, The Lindbergh Line 15.00
Magazine, Bill Barnes Air Trails, color cover, Oct 1936, EX 20.00
Magazine, Famous First Flights, many photos, 1929, EX 25.00
Manual, Aviation Pocket-Book, 1918, 362-pg, 4½x7", EX 60.00
Model, Spirit of St Louis, plastic, 1950s, MIB 20.00
Money clip, Flying Tiger 30.00
Pass, Nat'l Air Races, Chicago, 1930 ....25.00
Pin, Apollo 11 Anniv Commemorative, 5-color, 1¼" dia 15.00
Pin-bk button, Alaska Airlines, wht on bl, 1960s, 2¼" 15.00
Pin-bk button, Captain Charles A Lindbergh photo, 1¼" 35.00
Pin-bk button, Welcome Corrigan, blk/wht portrait, 1¾", EX 35.00
Plate, Pan-Am Clipper 45.00
Postcard, Lindbergh tour, blk/wht photo, unused 20.00
Scarf, vest, & long-sleeve sweater, Nat'l Airlines, 3-pc set 40.00
Ticket, air show; Mitchell Trophy Race...MI, 1938, EX 30.00
Tumbler, juice; Eastern Airlines etched logo, early 25.00

Tumbler, Mercury Spacecraft Cape Canaveral, 1960s, 5½" 50.00
Wings, United Airlines stewardess, sterling 110.00

Avon

The California Perfume Company, the parent of the Avon Co., was founded in 1886. Although an 'Avon' line was introduced by the company in the mid-twenties, not until 1939 did it become known as Avon Products, Inc. Collectible Avon items include not only figural bottles and jars but jewelry, awards, product samples, magazine ads, and catalogs as well. Our advisor for this category is Tammy Rodrick; she is listed in the Directory under Illinois. For more information concerning the Avon Collectors Club, see the Clubs, Newsletters, and Catalogs section of the Directory. See also California Perfume Company.

In the listings that follow, unless noted MIB, prices are for bottles only.

Albee Better Way Award, W Germany Dresdner Art, 1969 ....350.00
Bath Urn, Nile Blue, Skin So Soft oil, 1972, 6-oz 8.00
Chessman, Smart Move, 2 fragrances, 1971, MIB 12.00
Delft Blue Pitcher & Bowl, Skin So Soft bath oil, 1972, 5-oz 10.00
Extra Special Male, Jeep, 2 fragrances, 1977, 3-oz 5.00
Fostoria Egg Soap Dish, soap, 1977, 6-oz 15.00
Globe Bank Bubble Bath, 1966, 10-oz 15.00
Indian TePee, 2 fragrances, 1974, 4-oz 5.00
Jeweled Owl Pin Perfume Glace, 10 fragrances, 1968 ....10.00
Kitchen crock candle, milk glass w/flower border, 1974 ....5.00
La Bell Telephone, 3 fragrances, 1974, 1-oz 8.00
Merry Christmas Tree Hostess Set, 1979 ....35.00
NFL Decanter, 3 fragrances, choice of 28 emblems, 6-oz, '76 ....5.00
Old 99 Train Engine Soap, 1958, MIB 40.00
Packard Roadster, 2 fragrances, 1970, 6-oz 10.00
Rapture Talc Tin, 1965, 2 ¾-oz 5.00

Ring-Around- Rosie, 1966, MIB, $25.00.

Shaving Soap, 2 cakes, brn box, 1936 ....50.00
Travel Kit, lady's, 6-pc, pk plastic bag, 1957 ....75.00
Travel Kit, men's, 4-pc, blk gold-lined case, 1931 ....150.00
Young Hearts Set, cologne, talc, bubble bath, 1953, MIB 100.00

Baccarat

The Baccarat Glass company was founded in 1765 near Luneville, France, and continues to this day to produce quality crystal tableware, vases, perfume bottles, and figurines. The firm became famous for the high-quality millefiori and caned paperweights produced there from 1845 until about 1860. Examples of these range from $300 to as much as several thousand. Since 1953 they have resumed the production of paperweights on a limited edition basis. Our advisors for this category are Randall Monsen and Rod Baer; their address is listed in the Directory under Virginia. See also Paperweights.

Bottle, scent; clear, faceted, orig box from Crystal Baccarat 88.00
Bottle, scent; Deco-style cut geometrics, w/stopper, 8" 120.00
Bottle, scent; It's You, Elizabeth Arden, clear/frosted hand 3,300.00
Bottle, scent; It's You, Elizabeth Arden, crystal hand 1,540.00
Bottle, scent; Miss Dior, C Dior, red/clear amphora shape 935.00
Bottle, scent; paneled/bulbous, hollow stopper, sgn, 4½" 135.00
Bottle, scent; Rose Tiente Swirl, swirl stopper, 5½" 70.00
Bottle, scent; Subtitle, Houbigant, Buddha shape, gold ring 412.00
Bust, lady w/flowing hair, clear/frosted, octagonal base 200.00
Candelabra, Rose Tiente, 2-arm baluster w/prisms, 24", pr 1,200.00
Candelabra, 2-light, prisms, HP hurricane shades, 27", pr 1,500.00
Cruet, gold pansies on lt bl, clear faceted stopper 245.00
Cruet, lilies of the valley on lt gr opal, faceted stopper 215.00
Decanter, chipped ice w/gilt swags, ftd, 11", +2 cordials 585.00
Epergne, ribbed, clear/frosted, 1 lily in compote, 19" 725.00
Jar, Swirl, sapphire bl, 6x3" dia 85.00
Lamp, fairy; Rose Tiente Swirl, saucer base, 4x5⅝" 250.00
Lamp, fairy; Sunburst on clear, saucer base, mk, 3⅞x5¾" 165.00
Sculpture, Skyscraper, 4 joined prismatic blocks, 9½" 385.00

Sweetmeat stand with three lattice-work dishes and bouquet holder, ca 1860, 22", $1,300.00.

Toothpick holder, cameo cut, cranberry to wht frost, 2¼" 180.00
Toothpick holder, Rose Tiente Swirl 75.00
Vase, cameo trees/butterflies, amber on frost, fan form, 5" 415.00
Vase, frosted w/HP purple violets, gilt, sq cylinder, 8" 565.00
Vase, iris in red cut back to textured lt gr, gilt, sqd, 8" 500.00
Vase, octagonal, sharply waisted, very heavy, 12" 600.00
Vase, opal, serpent coiled on stem, bug at rim, rock base, 8" ...2,150.00
Watch holder, clear & frosted figure ea side, 4¾" 175.00
Wine, D'Assass pattern, clear 55.00

Badges

The breast badge came into general usage in this country about 1840. Since most are not marked and styles have changed very little to the present day, they are often difficult to date. The most reliable clue is the pin and catch. One of the earliest types, used primarily before the turn of the century, involved a 't-pin' and a 'shell' catch. In a second style, the pin was hinged with a small square of sheet metal, and the clasp was cylindrical. From the late 1800s until about 1940, the pin and clasp were made from one continuous piece of thin metal wire. The same type with the addition of a flat back plate was used a little later. There are exceptions to these findings, and other types of clasps were

also used. Hallmarks and inscriptions may also help pinpoint an approximate age.

Badges have been made from a variety of materials, usually brass or nickel silver; but even solid silver and gold were used for special orders. They are found in many basic shapes and variations — stars with five to seven points, shields, disks, ovals, and octagonals being most often encountered. Of prime importance to collectors, however, is that the title and/or location appear on the badge. Those with designations of positions no longer existing (City Constable, for example) and names of early western states and towns are most valuable.

Badges are among the most commonly-reproduced (and faked) types of antiques on the market. At any flea market, ten fakes can be found for every authentic example. Genuine law badges start at $30.00 to $40.00 for recent examples (1950-1970); earlier pieces (1910-1930) usually bring $50.00 to $90.00. Pre-1900 badges often sell for more than $100.00. Authentic gold badges are usually priced at a minimum of scrap value (karat, weight, spot price for gold); fine gold badges from before 1900 can sell for $400.00 to $800.00, and a few will bring even more. A fire badge is usually valued at about half the price of a law badge from the same circa and material. Our advisor for this category is Gene Matzke; he is listed in the Directory under Wisconsin.

Boston Press, gold-plated, eng florals, oval, 1890s, 2x1", EX 35.00
Central Truck Lines, arrowhead shape, orange/blk enamel 35.00
Chief Am Protection League Secret Service, blk on chrome 100.00
Chief of Police Thompson CT, eagle atop rnd shield, EX 55.00
County Detective Lycoming Co PA, star w/in shield, EX 40.00
Deputy Sheriff Bronx Co NY 1922-25, enamel, #d bk 75.00
Deputy Sheriff Juneau Co, gold-plated metal, 1940s, 2½" 40.00
Deputy Sheriff Worcester Co Mass, 8-sided shield, sm 30.00
Detective Sergeant Chicago, star, presentation, '20s, EX in box ..150.00
Patrolman Grafton WV Police, eagle atop shield, lt wear 40.00
Police Amherst OH, eagle atop shield, SP, EX 40.00
Police Detective Sergeant Chicago, 6-point star, Capone era 100.00
Sergeant Police Atlantic Coast Line, SP shield 75.00
Sheriff Middlesex Co, 2-pc hollow shield, EX 85.00
Special Police, SP brass star w/blk enamel, 1930s, 2½" 42.50

Toledo Newsboys Asso'n, 1912, $20.00.

Town Constable, eagle atop RI seal center, wht metal, 1920s 40.00
Trenton Police, SP brass shield w/blk lettering, 1930s, 2¼" 40.00
US Police Officer (Federal), bl letters, 2-pc, hollow 150.00

Banks

This year the continuing impact of auctions shows in the listings. Again, condition, condition, condition is what is driving the market. In addition, some banks with outstanding provenances were available, and they brought prices that reflect their individual value to a specific collector but distort the real market value of similar banks. The spread between a bank in good condition and an excellent or original condition example continues to widen. It is imperative that you realize the importance of paint and the completeness of a bank. Also some banks have a wide margin of value based on color variations. It becomes more and more important that you attend as many shows and auctions as possible. Direct contact with collectors and knowledgeable dealers is the only way you can get a feel for prices and the desirability of banks, both mechanical and still. Banks continue to hold their value. However, it is becoming extremely important for collectors to understand the market.

Let's take a look at the price variations possible on an Uncle Sam mechanical bank. If you find one with considerable paint missing but with some good color showing, the price would be around $1,000.00. If it has repairs or restoration, the value would drop to something like $800.00 or less. If you had another example, and it had two thirds of its original paint and no repairs, it would be priced around $1,800.00. One with minor nicks and 90% of the original paint could go as high as $3,500.00. Or if you find one that is in near-original paint and has no repairs, $5,000.00 would not be out of line. In the listing this year, you will find one that sold for $8,000.00. Why? It was a near-perfect bank with a provenance that made it extremely desirable to the buyer. This should help you see what causes price variations. After considering all of these factors, remember the final price is always determined by what a willing buyer and seller agree on for a specific bank.

Still banks are found in nearly every shape and size, and many types of material have been used in their making. Exactly how many styles were made is unknown; but about three thousand have been identified, and there are thousands more that are unlisted in any book. Cast iron examples are the most popular, but there is increasing interest in early tin and pottery banks made in the United States.

The category of mechanical banks is unique. Along with cast iron bell toys, they are among the most outstanding products of the Industrial Revolution and are recognized as some of the most successful of the mass-produced products of the 19th century. The earliest mechanicals were made of wood or lead but when John Hall introduced Hall's Excelsior, a cast iron mechanical bank, it was an immediate success. J. & E. Stevens produced the bank for Hall and soon began to make their own designs. Several companies followed suit, most of which were already in the hardware business. They used newly developed iron-molding techniques to produce these novelty savings devices for the emerging toy market. Mechanical banks reflect the social and political attitudes of the times, racial prejudices, the excitement of the circus, and humorous everyday events. Their designers made the most of simple mechanics to produce banks with captivating actions that served not only to amuse but to promote the concept of thrift to the children. The quality of detail in the castings are truly fine examples of industrial art. The most collectible examples were made during the period of 1870 to 1900; however, they continued to be made until the early days of World War II. J. & E. Stevens, Shepard Hardware, and Kyser and Rex are some of the more well-known manufacturers; most made still banks as well.

Still banks are widely collected, and you can literally choose from thousands of banks. No one knows exactly how many different banks were made, but at least three thousand have been identified in the various books published on the subject. Cast iron examples still dominate the market, but the lead banks from Europe are growing in value. Tin and early pottery banks are drawing more interest as well. American pottery banks which were primarily collected by Americana collectors are becoming more important in the still bank field. This market has not been as volatile as the mechanical banks, but the number of collectors is growing. The auction market on still banks is not as extensive as with the mechanicals, but some nice examples do turn up. Collectors and dealers are still the best source.

While the cast iron banks dominate the market, there are examples made from many other materials. Combinations of tin and cardboard and banks made from tin alone are very collectible. Some of the

European tin banks are quite rare; England made some fine cast iron mechanicals and many aluminum examples. The popularity of old mechanicals has created a market for reproductions and fakes. Reproductions may have minor value as such, but not as true collectibles. A few of the fakes have attained collectible status but are still not regarded as true mechanical banks.

As both value and interest continue on the increase, it becomes even more important to educate one's self to the fullest extent possible. We recommend these books for your library: *The Dictionary of Still Banks* by Long and Pitman, *The Penny Bank Book* by Moore, and *The Bank Book* by Norman. If you are primarily interested in mechanicals, *Penny Lane*, a book by Davidson, is considered the most complete reference available. It contains a cross-reference listing of numbers from all other publications on mechanical banks.

In the listings that follow, banks are identified by L for Long, G for Griffith, M for Moore, N for Norman, D for Davidson, and W for Whiting.

Key:
CI — cast iron   NPCI — nickel-plated cast iron
EPCI — electroplated cast iron

Advertising

Acorn Stoves Will Save...Money, pottery acorn, gr, 3" **50.00**
Chaufette Oven, oven, French, NPCI, hinged top, 3½", VG **130.00**
Cities Service, cb **20.00**
Coke machine, tin litho, minor scratches, 3⅞", VG **75.00**
Commercial Travelers, pottery, man w/coin head, 6", M **125.00**
Countryside Farms Milk, jug, tin litho, scratches, 4⅛", G **25.00**
Economy Foundry & Machine, pig, Compliments of, pnt CI, G ...**135.00**
Electrolux, refrigerator shape, lead, 4", G **15.00**
Electrolux, vacuum cleaner shape, NM **50.00**
Emerson, radio shape, M **40.00**
Esso, Flame Man figural, EX **85.00**
Esso, service station man figural, plastic, 5", EX **65.00**
Eveready Battery, plastic cat figural, 1981, EX **25.00**
Frigidaire, Nat'l Products, pot metal, EX wht pnt, 4x2" **38.00**
Gem Stove, M-1364, pnt CI, 4¾", G **65.00**
Heinz, molded & pnt plastic, 5¾", VG **125.00**
Hershey's Syrup, can shape, pottery, M **28.00**
Kelvinator, M-1338, refrigerator shape, door opens, 4", G **50.00**
King Edward VII's Railway Saloon, M-1475, tin litho, G **45.00**
Kodak Bank, M-875, pnt CI, 4¼", VG **170.00**
Lion & Healey's, M-840, piano, 5⅛", G **90.00**
Loft's Candies, truck, tin litho, friction, key lock, 10", G **25.00**
Magic Chef, M-1339, stove shape, wht metal, 3½", G **60.00**
Majestic Ice Box, M-1332, CI & sheet metal **250.00**
Marshall Stove, M-1362, stove shape, pnt CI, 3⅞", VG **140.00**
Maytag Dryer, wht metal, 3¼", G **35.00**
Mellow Stove, M-1363, stove shape, pnt CI, 3¾", G **55.00**
Pet Stoves, stove shape, Turnpin, pnt CI, 2¼", VG **90.00**
Red Goose Shoes, M-610, goose figural, pnt CI, 3¾", VG **150.00**
Republic Pig Iron, M-331, pig, Bank on..., pnt CI, 7", VG **25.00**
Sinclair Power X, EX **12.00**
Unico Freezer, tin freezer, blk/bl on wht, 4", EX **35.00**
Viking Coffee, tin, 4" **18.00**
York Stove, M-1351, stove shape, pnt CI, 4", G **120.00**

Mechanical

Always Did 'Spise a Mule, N-2940B, Stevens, yel, NM **2,700.00**
Always Did 'Spise a Mule, N-2950A, jockey, Stevens, NM **3,700.00**
Beehive, D-32, Northside Building Loan, pnt CI, 6¾", VG **250.00**
Boy on Trapeze, D-50, pnt CI, 9⅛", G **2,000.00**

Bulldog, D-69, standing, CI, worn pnt, 3½" 400.00
Cabin, D-93, pnt CI, 3⅝", VG 300.00
Camera, N-1670B, Wrightsville, CI, NM pnt, rpl hdl 7,500.00
Cat & Mouse, N-1700B, Stevens, gray pnt, CI, M 5,000.00
Chandlers, N-1720, Nat'l Brass Works, pnt CI, NM 500.00
Chief Big Moon, N-1740C, Stevens, CI, red variant, M 6,000.00
Chinaman, N-4830A, reclining, J&E Stevens, yel pants, EX ..11,500.00
Columbian Magic, N-1960A, Introduction, pnt CI, ca 1892, M ..500.00
Creedmoor, D-137, J&E Stevens, pnt CI, lt wear, 10", EX 2,300.00
Creedmoor, N-2000A, J&E Stevens, pnt CI, Pat 1877, M 1,700.00
Cross-Leg Minstrel, N-2020A, w/verse, Levey, Pat 1909, M ...1,700.00
Devil, M-32, 2-faced, pnt CI, 4¼", VG 600.00
Dinah, D-153, long sleeves, pnt CI, 6½", VG 370.00
Dinah, N-2150A, Harper, short sleeves, pnt CI, 1911, NM 1,700.00
Dog on Turntable, D-159, CI, copper finish, 4¾", G 165.00
Dog on Turntable, N-2170A, Judd, pnt CI, ca 1870s, M 1,900.00
Eagle & Eaglets, D-165, J&E Stevens, pnt CI, no trap, 8", EX ...715.00
Electric Safe, N-2240A, Louis, pnt CI, Pat 1904, M 450.00
Elephant, N-2280A, man pops up, Enterprise, pnt CI, 1884, M ...2,300.00
Feed the Goose, N-2400D, bronze, Pat 1927, EX 450.00
Fowler, N-2480B, J&E Stevens, pnt CI, red base, M 55,000.00
Freedman's Bureau, N-2500, pnt CI, M 1,100.00
Frog, D-200, pnt CI, 4¼", G 650.00
Frog, D-203, on rock, Kilgore, pnt CI, minor wear, 2¾" 700.00
Frog, N-2530, on base, J&E Stevens, pnt CI, Pat 1872, EX 1,200.00
Hall's Excelsior, D-228, pnt CI, rpl figure, 5¼", G 65.00
Hall's Excelsior, N-2710C, J&E Stevens, pnt CI, rpl arms 650.00
Hall's Lilliput, N-2730C, Stevens, no tray, Pat 1877, NM 2,000.00
Hen & Chick, D-236, pnt CI, sluggish, 9⅞", G 2,000.00
Home, N-2850, w/dormers, Stevens, pnt CI, M 4,500.00
Hoop-La Bank, N-2870, Harper, pnt CI, Reg...1895, EX 2,200.00
Horse Race, N-2880, Stevens, pnt CI, 1870, NM 12,000.00
Humpty Dumpty, D-248, pnt CI, 7½", G 275.00
Indian Shooting Bear, D-257, Stevens, pnt CI, 10¼", EX 2,100.00
Initiating 2nd Degree, N-3010, Mechanical Novelty, CI, NM ..9,000.00
Jennings Trick Money Box, N-3440, pnt CI, NM 600.00
Jolly Joe Clown, N-3070A, w/verse, pnt CI, 1920s, EX 900.00
Jolly Nigger, N-3270, Starkies, pnt CI, Pat 1920, M 900.00
Jolly Nigger, N-3410, unknown English mfg, pnt CI, EX 375.00
Leap Frog, G-147, Shepard Hardware, pnt CI, 7½", EX 3,300.00
Lion & Monkeys, N-3650B, Kyser & Rex, pnt CI, 1883, EX ..2,700.00
Little Joe, N-3690, att John Harper, pnt CI, ca 1910, NM 700.00
Magic Bank, N-3730A, J&E Stevens, pnt CI, Pat 1875, EX ...3,200.00
Magic Safe, N-3740A, Germany, pnt CI, ca 1930, EX 550.00
Mama Katzenjammer, D-317, pnt CI, 5⅞", G 550.00
Milking Cow, Book of Knowledge repro, 9⅝" 65.00
Minstrel Bank, N-2020A, w/verse, Germany, Pat 1902, EX 850.00

Mason, D-312, Shepard Hardware, cast iron, EX, $6,600.00.

Monkey & Parrot, N-3950, att Selheimer & Strauss, pnt CI, M ...800.00
Monkey w/Tray, N-4000A, Germany, pnt CI, ca 1910, NM 350.00
Mosque Patterns, N-4010, Judd, brass roof, ca 1875, M 700.00
Mule Entering Barn, N-4030B, Stevens, gr variant, M 2,200.00
Nat'l Bank, N-4180A, J&E Stevens, pnt CI, NM 24,000.00
New Creedmoor, N-4220, J&E Stevens, pnt CI, ca 1891, NM ..2,400.00
Novelty, N-4260B, Stevens, yel variant, 1873, NM 2,300.00
Octagonal Fort, N-4280, unknown mfg, pnt CI, 1890s, M 6,000.00
Organ Bank, N-4320A, cat/dog, Kyser & Rex, red coat, EX ...1,900.00
Organ Grinder & Bear, N-4350A, Kyser & Rex, pnt CI, NM .9,000.00
Owl, D-375, turns head, pnt CI, yel eyes, 7¼", VG 300.00
Owl, N-4380A, J&E Stevens, pnt CI, Pat 1880, NM 2,500.00
Paddy & the Pig, N-4400B, J&E Stevens, gr coat, EX 3,700.00
Peg-Leg Beggar, D-380, Judd, pnt CI, 5½", EX 2,500.00
Pig in Highchair, N-4570, J&E Stevens, pnt CI, M 1,800.00
Popeye Knockout, N-4620, Straits, pnt CI, ca 1935, M 3,700.00
Presto Bank, N-4650, Kyser & Rex, pnt CI, ca 1894, NM 1,100.00

Punch and Judy, D-404, Shepard Hardware, cast iron with excellent paint, small letters, $2,500.00.

Quarter Century, Reynolds, complete w/ingots, NM 550.00
Rooster, D-419, Kyser & Rex, pnt CI, 6½", EX 550.00
Rooster, N-4920, Kyser & Rex, pnt CI, 1880s, M 2,500.00
Sailor, N-4980A, saluting, Germany, pnt CI, ca 1925, M 1,600.00
Savo, N-5020, circular, pnt CI, Pat 1930, M 300.00
Scotchman, N-5070B, Selheimer & Strauss, pnt CI, M 1,600.00
Squirrel & Tree Stump, N-5270, Mechanical Novelty, EX 3,500.00
Stollwerk Postman, N-5290, Stollwerk Bros, 1920s, EX 550.00
Stollwerk Victoria, N-5350B, Stollwerk Bros, 1920s, EX 800.00
Stump Speaker, D-453, Shepard, pnt CI, 9½", EX 2,100.00
Stump Speaker, N-5370, Shepard, pnt CI, 1886, M 4,200.00
Tammany, D-455, pnt CI, 5¾", VG 125.00
Teddy & the Bear, D-459, CI, worn pnt, 7½", VG 1,300.00
Telephone, D-462, J&E Stevens, NPCI, minor rust, 6½" 700.00
Thrifty's Tom Jigger, N-5510, Strauss, 1910, EX 1,900.00
Toad on Stump, N-5570A, J&E Stevens, dk gr, 1880s, M 3,000.00
Tommy, N-5590, Harper, pnt CI, Pat 1914, EX 5,000.00
Trick Dog, N-5610, Hubley, pnt CI, rstr, EX 1,900.00
Trick Dog, N-5630B, Hubley, solid base, yel & brn, EX 2,500.00
Trick Pony, N-5640B, Shepard, red base, Pat 1885, EX 2,900.00
Uncle Sam, N-5740, Shepard, pnt CI, M, extreme price 8,000.00
Uncle Tom, N-5760F, lapels w/star, Kyser & Rex, 1882, EX ...1,600.00

Uncle Tom, N-5780D, no stars, Kyser & Rex, yel coat, EX 1,100.00
US Bank, N-5810, J&E Stevens, pnt CI, 1870s, EX 6,000.00
Victorian Money Box, N-5839, English mfg, wooden, EX 2,100.00
Weedens Plantation Darkey, D-562, emb tin, 5½", G 350.00
William Tell, D-565, pnt CI, 10¾" L, G 325.00
Wireless, N-5980, Hugo, Pat 1913-26, orig battery, M 1,000.00
World's Fair, D-573, J&E Stevens, CI, partial rpt, 8", EX 825.00
Zoo, N-6070, Kyser & Rex, pnt CI, ca 1894, EX 2,600.00

Registering

White painted metal, quarter registering, 7½", $35.00.

Bed Post 5¢ register, M-1305 ....70.00
Beehive 10¢ register, M-681, Am Mfg, pnt CI, lt wear, 5½" 440.00
Gem 10¢ register, emb eagle, EX 20.00
NY World's Fair 1¢ register, M-1566, tin, M on card 55.00
Snow White 185.00
Trunk, Phoenix 10¢ register, M-947, NPCI, worn blk pnt, 5" 95.00
Uncle Sam's 3-Coin, Durable Toy & Novelty, pnt tin, EX 38.00

Still

Angry Bear, M-704, pnt lead, padlock, 3", G 165.00
Auto, M-1483, Model-T Ford, pnt CI, 6⅜" L, VG 675.00
Auto, M-1487, CI, worn mc pnt, 6¾", VG 375.00
Baseball & 3 Bats, M-1608 (variant), pnt CI, 5⅛", EX 475.00
Battleship Maine, M-1439, pnt CI, minor wear, 10¼" 395.00
Bear, M-697, arms folded, pnt lead, 3¼", VG 185.00
Bear Stealing Honey, M-1308, pnt CI, 7", VG 160.00
Billiken, M-73, on throne, CI, gold pnt, 6⅜", EX 115.00
Billy Bounce, M-14, Wing, pnt CI, 4¾", EX 650.00
Black Boy, M-83, 2-faced, pnt CI, 4⅛", G 100.00
Boston Bull Terrier, M-421, pnt CI, 5¼", VG 100.00
Boy w/Large Football, M-10, CI, worn pnt, 5⅛" 1,600.00
Brink's Truck, M-1500, pnt metal, 8¼" L, VG 85.00
Buick Fireball Eight, tin litho, key lock, 4⅜", VG 65.00
Bungalow, M-999, pnt CI, 3¾", VG 295.00
Buster Brown & Tige, M-242, pnt CI, 5½", G 150.00
Canadian Beaver, M-750, CI, worn pnt, rare, 2½" 3,400.00
Capitolist, M-5, pnt CI, 5", EX 1,300.00
Captain Kidd, M-38, pnt CI, 5⅝", G 250.00
Cat, W-248, seated, CI, pnt traces 195.00
Chanticleer, M-214, pnt CI, 4⅝", EX 3,400.00
Charlie McCarthy, M-207, Crown, compo, EX 310.00
Chimney Sweep, M-6, lead, 4¼", EX 1,600.00
City Bank, M-1095, w/crown, pnt CI, 5½", EX 750.00

Clown, M-210, crooked hat, pnt CI, 6¾", VG 1,525.00
College Hat, M-1391, pnt tin, 4⅛", G 55.00
County Bank, M-1110, brass, 4¼", EX 135.00
Crosley Radio, M-819, Kenton, pnt CI, 5⅛", NM 800.00
Crosley Radio, M-820, Kenton, pnt CI, 4¼", EX 210.00
Derby, Pass Round the Hat, CI, worn pnt, 3⅛" 365.00
Dime Bullet, M-1407, brass, conversion, 7¼", G 80.00
Dog, M-359, on tub, CI, worn pnt, 4⅛" 145.00
Dolphin, M-33, Grey Iron, pnt CI, 4½", EX 450.00
Donkey, M-500, pnt CI, minor wear, 7" 265.00
Drum, Remember Pearl Harbor, tin litho, 2¼", VG 45.00
Dutch Boy, M-17, Grey Iron, CI, worn pnt, 6¾" 575.00
Dutch Boy, M-180, pnt CI, minor wear, 5½" 75.00
Eggman, M-108, Arcade, CI, pnt traces, rare, 4⅛" 2,000.00
Eiffel Tower, M-1075, CI, EX pnt, 10⅜" 925.00
Elephant, M-445, seated, CI, worn pnt, 4¼", EX 650.00
Elephant, M-479, w/chariot, Hubley, pnt CI, 4¾", EX 2,700.00
Elephant, M-487, w/blanket, Kenton, pnt CI, 3⅛", NM 725.00
English Throne, M-1327, aluminum, gold pnt, 3⅜", VG 15.00
Flatiron Building, M-1159, Kenton, pnt CI, 8¼", EX 1,250.00
Flower Girl, M-1650, lead, lt pnt wear, 4¾" 755.00
Football Player, M-11, Williams, CI, no pnt, 5⅞" 325.00
Foxy Grandpa, M-320, Hubley, pnt CI, 5½", EX 450.00
General Butler, M-54, J&E Stevens, pnt CI, ca 1884, NM 3,400.00
Gingerbread House, M-1029, pnt CI, 3⅞", VG 575.00
Globe on Wire Arc, M-785, Arcade, pnt CI, 4⅝", NM 300.00
Globe Savings, M-1199, pnt CI, 7⅛", EX 2,200.00
Golliwog, M-85, pnt CI, 6¼", VG 300.00

Graf Zeppelin, M-1428, cast iron with silver paint, 7", EX, $250.00.

Great Northern Goat, M-588, lead, EX pnt, 3½" 575.00
High Rise, M-1216, Kenton, pnt CI, 7", VG 600.00
Home, M-1019, pnt CI, 4", NM 750.00
Hoover/Curtis Elephant, M-463, CI, worn pnt, 3⅜" 1,475.00
Horse, Saddle; M-507, Grey Iron, CI, worn pnt, 4⅜" 400.00
House, M-1212, bay window, pnt CI, 4", VG 650.00
Ideola Juke Box, M-1580, plastic, music box, 6¼", G 25.00
Indian, M-215, 2-faced, pnt CI, 4¼", EX 2,100.00
Indian Bust, M-221, full headdress, lead, 3½", VG 55.00
Iron Master's House, M-1027, Kyser & Rex, pnt CI, 4¼", NM ..975.00
Jarmulowsky Building, M-1086, Stevens, CI, EX pnt, 7¾" 1,500.00
Jiminy Cricket, M-284, Crown, compo, EX pnt, 5⅞" 110.00
John Bull, M-1655, lead, VG pnt, 4½" 275.00
Kewpie, M-301, glass, pnt traces, tin lid, 3¼" 50.00
King Midas, M-13, Hubley, pnt CI, 4½", VG 2,300.00
Liliput, M-967, CI, worn pnt, 4½" 900.00
Lion, M-747, on tub, CI, worn pnt, 4⅛" 140.00
Mammy, M-175, w/basket, wht metal, 5¼", EX 275.00
Man on Cotton Bale, M-37, CI, worn pnt, 4⅞" 2,500.00

Mascot, M-3, Hubley, pnt CI, 1914, 5¾", EX 1,800.00
Masonic Temple, M-1061, brass, 5" 525.00
Mermaid, M-34, Grey Iron, CI, worn pnt, 4¾" 500.00
Metropolitan, M-904, pnt CI, lock broken, 5⅞", G 185.00
Mickey Mouse, M-202, compo, movable head, EX pnt 225.00
Mickey Mouse Chest, M-204, vinyl & tin, 2¾", EX 180.00
Mulligan, M-177, policeman, pnt CI, 5¾", G 55.00
Noah's Ark, brass, 5⅛", VG 100.00
Officer, M-8, Hubley, pnt CI, 1905-15, 5¾", EX 325.00
Old South Church, M-991, pnt CI, rare, 13", NM 7,275.00
Oregon Gunboat, M-1463, pnt CI, 5¼" w/masts, EX 975.00
Parrot, M-554, wht wings, lead, worn pnt, 5½", G 225.00
Pickaninny, M-171, pnt CI, 5⅛", VG 300.00
Policeman, M-182, Arcade, pnt CI, 5½", NM 900.00
Possum, M-561, pnt CI, 2⅜", G 400.00
Punch & Judy, M-1298, tin, 2⅞", EX 150.00
Quilted Lion, M-758, CI, worn gold pnt, 5" 245.00
Rabbit in Cabbage, N-4790, pnt CI, EX 625.00
Recording Bank, M-1062, NPCI, worn finish, 6⅝" 195.00
Rhino, M-721, Arcade, pnt CI, 2⅝", EX 525.00
Rhino, M-721, pnt CI, 2⅝", VG 300.00
Roosevelt (New Deal), M-148, pnt CI, 5", EX 450.00
Safe, M-884, geometric designs, pnt CI, 5⅜", G 275.00
Santa, M-59, Wing/Hubley, CI, worn pnt, 5⅞" 425.00
Santa, M-61, w/tree, Hubley, CI, lt pnt wear, 5⅞" 515.00
Scottie, M-432, Deco style, NP lead, 4½", EX 165.00
Scotties (6) in Basket, M-427, wht metal, 4½", VG 55.00
Sharecropper, M-173, pnt CI, minor wear, 5½" 185.00
Snowman, M-92, w/broom, Reynolds, aluminum, 4⅝", NM 70.00
Soccer Player, M-276, lead, worn pnt, 4½" 485.00
Spaniel, M-361, begging, lead, EX pnt, 4⅜" 300.00
Spaniel, wht metal, partial World's Fair label, 4⅝", G 25.00
Spirit of Saving, aluminum, key lock, sm puncture, 7½" L, G 300.00
Spitz, M-409, CI, pnt traces, lt rust, 4", VG 175.00
Stop Sign, M-1479, Dent, pnt CI, 4½", EX 290.00
Tank Bank USA 1918, M-1435, pnt CI, 3", VG 275.00

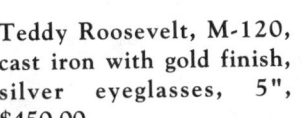

Teddy Roosevelt, M-120, cast iron with gold finish, silver eyeglasses, 5", $450.00.

Templetone Radio, M-826, Kenton, pnt CI, 4¼", EX 360.00
Terrier, wht metal, trap missing, 5½", VG 100.00
Three Little Pigs, tin litho, corner crease, 3", G 100.00
Turkey, M-587, pnt CI, 3⅜", EX 160.00
US Letter Box, M-860, tin, VG pnt, 9¾" 500.00
US Mail, M-849, w/eagle, CI, worn pnt, 4⅛" 200.00
Villa, M-959, Kyser & Rex, CI, worn pnt, 5½" 400.00

Washington Momument, M-1049, CI, worn pnt, 7½" 275.00
West Point Mule, M-501, lead, EX pnt, 4⅞" 225.00
White City Safe #10, M-913, pnt CI, 4⅝", EX 200.00
Wirehaired Terrier, M-422, pnt CI, 4⅝", EX 150.00
Wisconsin War Eagle, M-678, pnt CI, 2⅞", EX 1,250.00
Woolworth Building, M-1041, CI, gold pnt, 8", EX 95.00
Yellow Cab, M-1493, pnt CI, steel wheels, 8" L, G 650.00

Miscellaneous

Child's head, pottery, amber glaze, 3½" 55.00
Comic policeman's head, pottery, bl glaze, 3¼" 235.00
Dog, seated, redware w/brn spots, worn/flaked, 4" 85.00
House, Rockingham, 2 chimneys, 4⅛" 65.00
Pear, pottery, realistic yel-gr w/pk blush, 4" 95.00
Pig, pottery, brn/bl sponging on cream, 5¾", NM 85.00
Pig, pottery, 2-tone marbleized brn/bl on cream, 5" L, EX 45.00

Barber Shop Collectibles

Even for the stranger in town, the local barber shop was easy to find, its location vividly marked with the traditional red and white striped barber pole that for centuries identified such establishments. As far back as the 12th century, the barber has had a place in recorded history. At one time he not only groomed the beards and cut the hair of his gentlemen clients but was known as the 'blood-letter' as well, hence the red stripe for blood and the white for the bandages. Many early barbers even pulled teeth! Later, laws were enacted that divided the practices of barbering and surgery.

The Victorian barber shop reflected the charm of that era with fancy barber chairs upholstered in rich wine-colored velvet; rows of bottles made from colored art glass held hair tonics and shaving lotion. Backbars of richly carved oak with beveled mirrors lined the wall behind the barber's station. During the late 19th century, the barber pole with a blue stripe added to the standard red and white as a patriotic gesture came into vogue.

Today the barber shop has all but disappeared from the American scene, replaced by modern unisex salons. Collectors search for the barber poles, the fancy chairs, and the tonic bottles of an era gone but not forgotten. See also Bottles; Razors; Shaving Mugs.

Blade bank, frog figural, porc, Listerine, EX 37.50
Blade sharpener, Steel Strop, MIB 15.00
Blade sharpener, Twinplex, MIB 17.50
Brush, shaving lather; SP, ornate design, NM 27.50
Brush, shaving lather; sterling hdl, lt wear 45.00

Catalog, embossed on front in gold: Barber Shop & Beauty Parlor Equipment, Emil J. Paidar Co., Chicago USA, 25 color plates, 125-pg, ca 1920-30, 10x13", VG, $175.00.

Case, razor; Boker, glass w/wood fr, 15" W, NM 125.00
Case, 3 glass shelves, Dill Co...PA, 1910s, 17x13x9", EX 100.00
Certificate, State of IN...1939, 5½x6½", EX 75.00
Chair, Archer, simple style w/orig red uphl, early, EX 650.00
Chair, child's, adult's style w/NP trim, leather uphl, EX 475.00
Chair, Hollstegge-Bauman, oak/CI, 42", EX 575.00
Chair, Melchior Imperial, oak/leather/CI, 50", EX 1,980.00
Chair, oak/iron w/velvet upholstery, Pat 1890, child's, EX 600.00
Chair, shoeshine; bent wire/CI, w/drw, 52", EX 440.00
Hone, Hibbard, Spencer, Bartlett & Co, EX in tin litho box 27.50
Jar, Barbaso, 8-sided, NM 10.00
Jar, glass, Barbicide, holds combs, EX 27.50
Mirror, oak, beveled side mirrors, swivels, 80x95", EX 935.00
Neck duster, cherry wood hdl, EX 27.50
Photo, view of shop interior, ca 1900, EX 32.00
Pole, laminated wood w/3-color rpt & 'Joe's,' 65" 175.00
Pole, neon, 1930s, working, EX 3,000.00
Pole, porc over metal, 4-color, ca 1920, rstr, 77" 1,100.00
Pole, trn wood, blk & silver stripes, 74", VG 150.00
Pole, trn wood, gold/red/bl/wht, weathered, 26" 235.00
Pole, trn wood, red/wht/bl pnt, ca 1890s, 96", EX 2,300.00
Pole, trn wood, red/wht/bl/gold pnt, 45x7½", EX 550.00
Pole, trn wood, wht w/blk over red stripes, early, 45", G 130.00
Rack, shaving mug; oak, cvd details, 40 compartments, 48", EX ..525.00
Rack, shaving mug; oak, simple, holds 35 mugs, 45x28x5½" 65.00
Razor kit, Valet Autostrop, metal case, complete 17.50
Shaving mug & tray, Waldorf system, milk glass/brass, EX 165.00
Shaving stand, SP, beveled mirror & accessories, 1910s 250.00
Sign, Barber Shop, mc, porc over steel, 12x24", EX 85.00
Sign, Look Better Feel Better, porc over metal, 48x48", M 100.00
Sign, Modern Service, curved porc on metal, 1900s, 48x48", G ...90.00
Station, oak, turnings/moldings, 77x47", EX 825.00
Station, oak w/brass ft, marble tops, Koken, 3-pc, EX 1,320.00
Sterilizer cabinet, glass w/metal door, wire racks, Koch, EX 42.50
Strop, horsehide, NM 16.50
Strop, Kriss-Kross, EX 25.00
Towel steamer, NP copper, Ideal Metal Works, 61" 425.00
Towel steamer, NP copper body w/porc-over-steel base, EX 525.00

Barometers

Barometers are instruments designed to measure the weight or pressure of the atmosphere in order to anticipate approaching weather changes. Those made around the turn of the century (earlier in England and on the continent) were beautifully housed in period cases of mahogany, rosewood, walnut, or cherry, often with brass trim. These quality pieces bring high prices on today's market.

A Buseya, Preston, mahog veneer w/inlay, banjo form, 39" 600.00
Chas Wilder, rosewood grpt case, 1860s, rpr, 38", VG 500.00
D Gugeri, mahog veneer Hplwht w/inlay sunbursts etc, 38" 900.00
Gauge & Instrument Mfr Co 12/35, aneroid, 9½" 200.00
Short & Mason, brass, pocket type, 2" dia, EX 95.00
W Norton, stick type, 1850s, 37" 350.00
Watkins-Hill, mahog stick type, molded cornice, temp, 37" ...1,300.00
Woodruff's Pat June 5 1860, rosewood veneer, 38" 400.00

Baskets

Basket weaving is a craft as old as ancient history. Baskets have been used to harvest crops, for domestic chores, and to contain the catch of fishermen. Materials at hand were utilized, and baskets from a specific region are often distinguishable simply by analyzing the natural fibers used in their construction. Early Indian baskets were made of corn husks or woven grasses. Willow splint, straw, rope, and paper were also used. Until the invention of the veneering machine in the late 1800s, splint was made by water-soaking a split log until the fibers were softened and flexible. Long strips were pulled out by hand and, while still wet and pliable, woven into baskets in either a cross-hatch or hexagonal weave.

Most handcrafted baskets on the market today were made between 1860 and the early 1900s. Factory baskets with a thick, wide splint cut by machine are of little interest to collectors. The more popular baskets are those designed for a specific purpose, rather than the more commonly-found utility baskets that had multiple uses. Among the most costly forms are the Nantucket Lighthouse baskets, which were basically copied from those made there for centuries by aboriginal Indians. They were designed in the style of whale oil barrels and named for the South Shoal Nantucket Lightship where many were made during the last half of the 19th century. Cheese baskets (used to separate curds from whey), herb-gathering baskets, and finely woven Shaker miniatures are other highly-prized examples of the basket weaver's art.

In the listings that follow, assume that each has a center bentwood handle (unless handles of another type are noted) that is not included in the height. Unless another type of material is indicated, assume that each is made of splint. See also American Indian; Eskimo; Sewing; Shaker.

Buttocks, boat shaped, minor damage, 7x11x12" 55.00
Buttocks, EX color, minor damage, 7½x12½x15" 130.00
Buttocks, EX detail, minor damage, 7x14" 185.00
Buttocks, fine weave, well made, 7x13x14" 300.00
Buttocks, iron riveted hdl, well made, 8x13x13" 225.00
Buttocks, minor breaks, 4¾x8x9" 125.00
Buttocks, old varnish, 6x11x11" 125.00
Buttocks, well made, 6x11x12" 175.00
Cheese, openweave, hexagonal, minor damage, 12" 200.00
Gathering, 4½x12½x14" 175.00
Herb drying, wide splint, 2x16x24" 135.00
Laundry, rim hdls, minor damage, 12½x20x28" 85.00
Loom, wall hanging, wide splint, minor damage, 13x12" 100.00
Loom, 2-part, wide splint, traces of yel pnt, wear, 17" 375.00

Miniature Nantucket basket, finely woven, swing handle, some breaks, 3x3", 1,900.00.

Miniature, buttocks, EX patina, minor damage, 2¾x4½x5" 250.00
Miniature, buttocks, some age, 4¾x5¾" 225.00
Miniature, buttocks, 1-egg sz, 3x3½" 350.00
Miniature, buttocks, 2-tone splint, 4½x4x6", EX 250.00

Miniature, splint, lt bl pnt, 2x3" dia 175.00
Nantucket, label: AD Wms, w/lid, 9x9", EX 1,200.00
Nantucket, swing hdl, brass fasteners, 5x6½", NM 1,400.00
Nantucket, swivel hdl, trn base, wear/damage, 4x9" dia 275.00
Potato print, red design alternates w/yel, lid, 17", EX 250.00
Potato prints in blk, varnish, tall sides, 6½x4", NM 325.00
Rye straw, hanging loop, wear/dk patina, 3½x11¾" 45.00
Splint, bowl shape, dk gr pnt, 1860, 9x13" 135.00
Splint, curlique band, 6¾x13" dia 155.00
Splint, dk patina, minor damage, 6x10" dia 160.00
Splint, faded red band, oblong, 8x14x20" 90.00
Splint, fine weave, 6½x12½x16" 135.00
Splint, hdl sgn Haver, well made, 4½x7" dia 250.00
Splint, old gr pnt, 8½" dia 225.00
Splint, radiating ribs, 6x12x15" 115.00
Splint, rim hdls, rectangular, 14" L 115.00
Splint, 2-tone, oblong, 8½x13x20" 150.00
Splint, 6 lg scallops in rim, minor damage, 4x10" dia 250.00
Storage, goose feather; w/lid, side hdls, 24x16" 95.00
Swing hdl, mustard yel pnt, minor damage, 9x17x18" 1,300.00
Swing hdl, some damage, 6x12" 150.00
Swing hdl, well made, not early, old red pnt, 10x14" 175.00
Tray, gathering; gr pnt, 9½" dia 145.00

Batchelder

Ernest A. Batchelder was a leading exponent of the Arts and Crafts movement in the United States. His influential book, *Design in Theory and Practice*, was originally published in 1910. He is best known, however, for his artistic tiles which he first produced in Pasadena, California, from 1909 to 1916. In 1906 the business was relocated to Los Angeles where it continued until 1932 and closed because of the Depression.

In 1938 Batchelder resumed production in Pasadena under the name of 'Kinneola Kiln.' Output of the new pottery consisted of delicately cast bowls and vases in an Oriental style. This business closed in 1951. Tiles carry a die-stamped mark; vases and bowls are hand incised.

Our advisor for this category is Jack Chipman, author of *Collector's Encyclopedia of California Pottery*; he is listed in the Directory under California.

Bookend, 2¾" tiles set in Potter Studio brass mts, pr 250.00
Bowl, bl, flared rim, incised mk, 3¼x7½" 80.00
Bowl, dk teal, rose int, Pasadena mk, 3x7" 75.00
Bowl, rose, oval, Pasadena mk, 4x12x7" 135.00
Tile, advertising, unglazed, hexagonal, 3½" 150.00
Tile, Hispanic decor, satin matt, imp mk, 1928, 6" sq 65.00
Tile, La Mayan, terra cotta, 3½" sq 85.00
Tile, medieval landscape, unglazed, imp mk, 4" sq 85.00
Tile, peacocks in high relief, bl wash, mk, 12" 200.00

Tile, medieval hunt, marked, ca 1928, 4", $85.00.

Vase, gray, cylindrical, 9½" 175.00
Vase, yel, flared rim, 6" 110.00
Vase, yel, sq shape, 7" 100.00

Battersea

Battersea is a term that refers to enameling on copper or other metal. Though originally produced at Battersea, England, in the mid-18th century, the craft was later practiced throughout the Staffordshire district. Boxes are the most common examples. Some are figurals, and many bear an inscription. Values are given for examples with only minimal damage, which is normal. Our advisor for this category is John Harrigan; he is listed in the Directory under Minnesota.

Box, Admiral Lord Nelson on lid, 1¾" dia, EX 400.00
Box, bluebird in foliage, hinged lid, 1½" 285.00
Box, florals on bl w/gold, rectangular, 2¼x3¼" 275.00
Box, maid/lamb, bk: cherubs & lady w/fan, 1¾" dia 500.00
Box, patch; lady's torso form, head figural lid, 3" 1,600.00
Box, patch; Peace & Plenty, wht doves & cobalt, 1780s 700.00
Box, 2 boxers/10 spectators on lid, cobalt base, ¾x2x1½" 375.00

Candlesticks, polychrome decoration, England, 1760s, 12", $1,650.00 for the pair.

Candlestick, floral, scalloped drip pans, 9", pr 1,250.00
Locket, ship, bk: clock face, EX 265.00
Mirror holder, eagle/E Pluribus Unum, mc, rpr, 2", pr, VG 450.00
Mirror holder, Gen Washington, mc w/pk banner, 2", pr 1,225.00
Needle case, flowers on bl w/in gold fr, 2½" 600.00
Opera glasses, children hunting & fishing, 4" W, in case 425.00

Bauer

Originally founded in Paducah, Kentucky, in 1885, the J.A. Bauer Company moved to Los Angeles where it was re-established in 1909. Until the 1920s, their major products were terra cotta gardenware, flowerpots, and stoneware and yellowware bowls. During prohibition they produced crocks for home use. A more artful form of product began to develop with the addition of designer Louis Ipsen to the staff in 1915. Some of his work, a line of molded vases, flowerpots, bowls, etc., was awarded a bronze medal at the Pacific International Exposition the following year.

In 1930 the first of many dinnerware lines was tested on the market. Their initial pattern, Plain Ware, was well accepted and led the way to the introduction of the most popular dinnerware in their history and with today's collectors, Ring Ware. It was produced from 1932 into the early 1960s in solid colors of jade green, royal blue, Chinese yellow, light blue, orange-red, and (in very limited quantities) black or white. Its simple pattern was a design of closely-spaced concentric ribs, either convex or concave. Over the years, more than one hundred shapes were available. Some were made in limited quantities, resulting in rare items to whet the appetites of Bauer buffs today. Other patterns were La Linda, produced during the 1940s and 1950s, and Monterey Moderne, introduced in 1948 and remaining popular into the 1950s (made in pink, black, gray, brown, and green.)

After WWII a flood of foreign imports drastically curtailed their sales, and the pottery began a steady decline that ended in failure in 1962. Prices listed below reflect the California market. For more information, we recommend *The Collector's Encyclopedia of California Pottery* by Jack Chipman, our advisor for this category. Mr Chipman's address may be found in the Directory under California.

Ashtray, Monterey, wht, rare 150.00
Ashtray, Ring, blk, 3" 50.00

Artware vases handmade by Mat Carlton: 9½", $200.00; 17", $450.00; 7½", $125.00.

Bean pot, plain, all colors but blk, no hdl, 1-pt 35.00
Beverage server/storage, Monterey, all colors 85.00
Bowl, batter; Ring, blk, 1-qt 175.00
Bowl, dessert; Monterey Modern, blk, 5" 22.50
Bowl, fruit; Monterey, wht, 12" 200.00
Bowl, fruit; Monterey Moderne, all colors but blk, 4¼" 12.50
Bowl, fruit/dessert; Al Fresco, speckled, gr, or gray, 5" 5.00
Bowl, mixing; La Linda, gr, yel, or turq, #36, 1-pt 12.00
Bowl, mixing; plain, all colors but blk, 1½-gal 145.00
Bowl, mixing; Ring, lt bl, chartreuse, or red-brn, #24, 1-qt ...20.00
Bowl, ramekin; La Linda, burgundy or dk brn 10.00
Bowl, salad; Ring, blk, 9" 100.00
Bowl, serving; Monterey, all colors, 9½" 37.50

Bowl, vegetable; Al Fresco, coffee brn or Dubonnet, 9¼" 18.00
Bowl, vegetable; Contempo, all colors, 9½" 15.00
Bowl, vegetable; Monterey Modern, blk, oval, 9" 50.00
Butter dish, Ring, dk bl, burgundy, or wht, oblong 125.00
Candlestick, Ring, orange-red, dk bl, or burgundy, 2½" 45.00
Canister, grease; Al Fresco, coffee brn or Dubonnet 12.00
Casserole, French; Contempo, all colors, w/lid, ind 15.00
Casserole, Ring, dk bl, ivory, or wht, w/lid, ind 45.00
Coffee server, Monterey, wht, 8-cup 45.00
Coffeepot, Ring, orange-red, burgundy, or wht, 8-cup 200.00
Creamer, La Linda, burgundy or dk brn, new shape 20.00
Creamer, Ring, chartreuse, olive, or turq, 12-oz 20.00
Cup & saucer, Al Fresco, coffee brn or Dubonnet 12.00
Cup & saucer, Monterey, all colors 26.00
Cup & saucer, Ring, orange-red, dk bl, or ivory, tea sz 30.00

Fish set, marked Z.S. & Co., 13-piece, $400.00.

Flowerpot, Ring & Gardenware, blk, rolled rim, 6" 45.00
Gravy boat, Al Fresco, coffee brn or Dubonnet 12.50
Gravy boat, Contempo, all colors 8.00
Gravy bowl, Ring, blk 145.00
Hostess tray & cup, Al Fresco, speckled, gr, or gray 12.00
Jardiniere, Ring, orange-red, dk bl, or wht, 10" 95.00
Mug, plain, blk, 8-oz 65.00
Oil jar, all colors but blk, #129, 20" 750.00
Pickle dish, Ring, all colors but blk 35.00
Pitcher, La Linda, gr, yel, or turq, ice lip, 2-qt 45.00
Plate, Al Fresco, coffee brn or Dubonnet, 10" 10.00
Plate, Contempo, all colors, 10" 8.00
Plate, El Chico, all colors, 9" 25.00
Plate, grill; Monterey Moderne, blk, sq, rare 50.00
Plate, Monterey, all colors, 6" 8.50
Plate, Monterey Moderne, all colors but blk, 10½" 18.00
Plate, plain, blk, 9" 50.00
Platter, La Linda, lt brn, pk, or gray, 12" 18.00
Platter, Monterey Moderne, all colors but blk, oval, 12" 18.00
Platter, plain, all colors but blk, oval, 12" 25.00
Platter, Ring, dk bl, burgundy, or wht, oval, 12" 30.00
Relish plate, Monterey, all colors but wht, oval, 10½" 45.00
Shakers, Ring, orange-red, ivory, or wht, bbl form, pr 30.00
Souffle dish, Ring, yel, olive, or gray 125.00
Soup plate, Ring, yel, jade gr, or turq, 7½" 45.00
Stein, Ring, blk, cylindrical, 5" 200.00
Sugar bowl, Monterey, wht, w/lid 30.00
Teapot, Contempo, all colors, 6-cup 20.00
Teapot, La Linda, lt brn, ivory, or olive gr, 6-cup 35.00
Teapot, plain, all colors but blk, 6-cup 100.00
Tumbler, Monterey, all colors but wht, 8-oz 15.00
Tumbler, Ring, blk, no hdl, 6-oz 45.00
Tumbler, Ring, lt bl or olive, raffia-wrapped hdl, 6-oz 35.00
Vase, Ring & Gardenware, dk bl or ivory, florist stock, 12" 75.00

Bavaria

Bavaria, Germany was long the center of that country's pottery industry; in the 1800s, many firms operated in and around the area. Chinaware vases, novelties, and table accessories were decorated with transfer prints as well as by hand by artists who sometimes signed their work. The examples here are marked with 'Bavaria' and the logos of some of the various companies which were located there.

Chocolate pot, floral, gold trim & hdl	95.00
Cookie jar, roses, pk on gr shaded w/gold, mk, 7½x5½"	110.00
Jam jar, HP florals on pastel, sgn Hall, 5x3⅝"	70.00
Pitcher, Grecian ladies, gold tracing, mk, 6x4"	100.00
Plate, floral, wht on gr, sgn Phillips, Sevres Bavaria, 8"	65.00
Plate, peonies, sgn Phillips, mk Sevres, Hortensia, 7½"	65.00
Plate, pheasant & brood, 14"	125.00
Plate, quail, sgn Mignon ZS&Co, 7½"	25.00
Shelf sitter, boy fishing, gr hat, orange pants	50.00
Tray, poppies, orange on cream w/gold, mk, 11½x8½"	65.00

Beer Cans

When the flat-top can was first introduced in 1934, it came with printed instructions on how to use the triangular punch opener. Cone-top cans, which are rare today, were patented in 1935 by the Continental Can Company. By the 1960s, aluminum cans with pull tabs had made both types obsolete.

The hobby of collecting beer cans has been rapidly gaining momentum over the past ten years. Series types, such as South African Brewery, Lion, and the Cities Series by Schmit and Tucker, are especially popular.

Condition is an important consideration when evaluating market price. Grade 1 must be in like-new condition with no rust. However, the triangular punch hole is acceptable. Grade 2 cans may have slight scratches or dimples but must be free of rust. For Grade 3, light rust, minor scratching, and some fading may be acceptable. When these defects are more pronounced, a can is defaulted to Grade 4. Those in less-than-excellent condition devaluate sharply. In the listings that follow, cans are arranged alphabetically by brand name, not by brewery. Unless noted otherwise, values are for cans in Grade 1 condition.

Acme, wht label, flat top, 12-oz	45.00
Altas Beer, Atlas, Detroit, cone top, 12-oz	55.00
Atlas, Chicago, red & wht, flat top, 12-oz	20.00
Atlas Prager, red & wht, flat top, 12-oz	12.00
Ballantine's Ale, cone top, 1-qt	75.00
Ballantine's Export Light, gold & blk, cone top, 32-oz	75.00
Beckers, red/wht/bl, flat top, 12-oz	28.00
BOH Bohemian, Enterprise, flat top, 12-oz	5.00
Bull Dog Malt Liquor, red/wht/bl/gold, flat top, 12-oz	10.00
Busch Bavarian, Anheuser Busch, pull top, 10-oz	2.00
Butte Special, cone top, 12-oz	75.00
Cascade, bl & gold on wht, pull top, 15-oz	5.00
Champagne Velvet, Heileman, pull top, 11-oz	1.00
Clear Lake, mtn & lake scene, flat top, 12-oz	120.00
Colt 45 Malt Liquor, Nat'l, pull top, 8-oz	2.00
Duke, portrait on wht, pull top, 12-oz	3.00
Edelweiss Light Beer, pull top, 16-oz	7.50
Erin Brew, Standard, flat top, 12-oz	32.00
Falls City, red/wht/gold, flat top, 12-oz	7.50
Fallstaff, gold & blk on wht, pull top, 16-oz	1.50
Fort Pitt Special, cone top, 12-oz	48.00

Fox DeLuxe, cone top, 1-qt	95.00
Golden Crown, General, pull top, 12-oz	2.50
Heileman's Lager, bl & wht mtn scene, flat top, 12-oz	25.00
Highlander, red & wht on gold, cone top, 12-oz	145.00
Iron City, red on wht, pull top, 16-oz	3.50
Jax, red/wht/gold, Jackson, flat top, 12-oz	18.00
Koehler, bl/wht/silver, Erie, pull top, 12-oz	2.00
Lucky Lager, flat top, 7-oz	10.00
Manhattan, cone top, 1-qt	120.00
Mickey's Malt Liquor, Sterling, flat top, 8-oz	45.00
Mile Hi, red/wht/bl, Tivoli, flat top, 12-oz	40.00
Miller, red/wht/blk on gold, pull top, 16-oz	2.75
Narrangansett, red/bl/gold/wht, pull top, 16-oz	2.00
Nat'l Bohemian, blk & wht on red, cone top, 12-oz	70.00
Nat'l Bohemian, red on wht, pull top, 8-oz	7.50
Norvic, DuBois, pull top, 12-oz	17.50
Old German Premium Lager, Queen City, flat top, 12-oz	5.00
Old Vienna, yel & red on wht, Maier, pull top, 12-oz	35.00
Olympia Light, yel & wht, pull top, 16-oz	3.00
Orig Old German Brand, red/wht/bl/yel, cone top, 16-oz	9.00
Pabst Blue Ribbon, red/wht/bl, flat top, 12-oz	6.50
Point, red & wht on bl, Stevens Point, pull top, 12-oz	2.00
Prima Ale, red & wht on bl, cone top, 12-oz	135.00
Regency, red & wht on yel, Maier, flat top, 12-oz	32.00
Rheingold, pull top, 7-oz	2.00
Schmidt's City Club, red/wht/yel, flat top, 12-oz	32.00
Sheridan, red & blk on yel, flat top, 12-oz	30.00
Special Export Malt Liquor, Heileman, flat top, 8-oz	38.00
Tuborg, Carling, pull top, 10-oz	7.50
Valley Forge, red & wht on gold, pull top, 12-oz	2.50
Walter, 1-gal	265.00
Weber, red & wht on gr, flat top, 12-oz	42.50

Bellaire, Marc

A contemporary of Sasha Brastoff, Marc Bellaire worked in California during the fifties and sixties, producing high-quality ceramics often decorated with Jamaican or Polynesian figures. His work had a distinctive ultra-modern flair; shapes were free-forms and his figures stylized. Some of his studio pieces depict Picasso-like females. One of his best-known lines is Mardi Gras, decorated with slim Mardi Gras dancers on spattered colors of pink and black. The ware is signed on the decorated surface as well as on the back. Our advisor for this category is Judy Potter; she is listed in the Directory under Iowa.

Plate, Polynesian dancer in black on coral, gold tracing, 9", $175.00.

Ashtray, Mardi Gras, figures on pk/blk, 4-ftd, 10" 125.00
Box, Mardi Gras, free-form, figures on pk/blk, 8" L 175.00
Candle holder, Mardi Gras, figures on pk/blk, 10½", pr 300.00
Charger, Picasso-type female, hand thrown, 12½" 800.00
Figure, Mardi Gras, reclining man, very slim, 24" 1,600.00
Figure, Mardi Gras, standing man, very slim, 36" 1,600.00
Figure, Polynesian man w/horn, 12", minimum value 800.00
Plate, Polynesian man w/musical instrument, gold trim, 9" 175.00
Tray, abstracts in 2 tan bands on blk matt, uptrn sides, 8" 250.00
Tray, Mardi Gras, 2 joined ovals, figures on pk/blk, 9x10" 125.00
Tray, yel ovals w/blk figures & gr leaves on brn/wht, 13" 135.00
Vase, Mardi Gras, oval base/rim, str sides, 7½x9" 225.00

Belleek, American

From 1883 until 1930, several American potteries located in New Jersey and Ohio manufactured a type of china similar to the famous Irish Belleek soft-paste porcelain. The American manufacturers identified their porcelain by using 'Belleek' or 'Beleek' in their marks. American Belleek is considered the highest achievement of the American porcelain industry. Production centered around artistic cabinet pieces and luxury tablewares. Many examples emulated Irish shapes and decor with marine themes and other naturalistic styles. While all are highly collectible, some companies' products are rarer than others. The best-known manufacturers are Ott and Brewer, Willets, The Ceramic Art Company (CAC), and Lenox. You will find more detailed information in those specific categories. For a more thorough study of the subject, we recommend you refer to *American Belleek* by our advisor Mary Frank Gaston; you will find her address in the Directory under Texas.

Key:
AAC — American Art China   CAP — Columbian Art Pottery
AB C — American Beleek   Works
      Company

Cream soup, Bouquet, Coxon, w/underplate 175.00
Creamer, floral band, gold trim, ornate rim & hdl, AAC, 4" 350.00
Cup, demitasse; gold non-factory decor, Beleek mk, 2¼" 75.00
Cup & saucer, demitasse; Tridacna, worn gold trim, CAP 100.00
Cup & saucer, morning-glories, Morgan 150.00
Salt cellar, sponged gold on scalloped rim & base, AAC, 2½" 125.00
Shell dish, pink lustre int, ABC mk, 4x5" 150.00
Teapot, dragon form, gold paste leaves, CAP, 7½x9" 1,000.00
Tumbler, Souvenir David's Society...1899, CAP, 4¼" 300.00

Belleek, Irish

Belleek is a very thin translucent porcelain that takes its name from the village in Ireland where it originated in 1857. The glaze is a creamy ivory color with a pearl-like lustre. Tablewares, baskets, figurines, and vases have been produced; Shamrock, Tridacna, Echinus, and Lotus are but a few of the many patterns.

It is possible to date an example to within twenty to thirty years of manufacture by the mark. Pieces with an early stamp often bring prices nearly triple that of a similar but current item. With some variation, the marks have always incorporated the wolfhound, round tower, harp, and shamrock. The first three marks (usually in black) were used from 1863 to 1946. A series of green marks has been in use since 1946; the seventh mark, introduced in 1980 and discontinued in December, 1992, was gold. In the listings below, numbers designated with the prefix 'D' relate to the book *Belleek, The Complete Collector's Guide and Illustrated Reference, Second Edition* (due to be released in the fall of 1993) —Wallace–Homestead Book Company, One Chilton Way, Radnor, PA 19089-0230. Our advisor for Belleek is Richard K. Degenhardt; he is listed in the Directory under North Carolina.

Key:
A — pearl/plain   I — 1863-1890
B — cob lustre   II — 1891-1926
C — hand tinted   III — 1926-1946
D — hand painted   IV — 1946-1955
E — hand-painted shamrocks   V — 1955-1965
F — hand gilted   VI — 1965-3/31/1980
G — hand tinted and gilted   VII — 4/1/1980-12/22/1992
H — hand-painted shamrocks
      and gilted
I — hand painted and gilted

Aberdeen, vase, floral, D55-II, A, lg 850.00
Aberdeen, vase, floral (gobal), D58-IV, D, med sz 300.00
Basket, oval, D118, 4-strand, D, 12" 1,350.00
Basket, oval, floral, D1270, 4-strand, D, 6¾" 600.00
Basket, oval w/lid, D113, 4-strand, D, lg 4,500.00
Bust of Clytie, D14-I, A, 9" 3,200.00
Bust of Joy, D1129-IV, A, 11" 700.00
Bust of Sorrow, D1132-II, 10" 3,000.00
Calawite, candle extinguisher & stand, D1507-I, A, 3½" 850.00
Celtic Tea Ware, plate, D1435-III, I, 6½" 150.00
Celtic Tea Ware, teacup & saucer, D1437-III/D1438-III, I 175.00
Chinese Tea Ware, creamer, D486-I, D...................................400.00
Chinese Tea Ware, sugar bowl, D485-I, D, 3" 350.00
Chinese Tea Ware, tea urn, D482-I, D, lg 1,200.00
Clearly, creamer, D249 (CR)-VI, B 30.00
Clearly, spill, D193-VI, A 35.00
Double Shell, creamer & sugar bowl, D288-VI/D1301-VI, B.........55.00
Echinus Tea Ware, mustache cup, D664 (C)-I, F, 2½" 350.00
Egg frame & cups (6), D621-VI, G 350.00
Erne, vase, D83-II, C, 7"...650.00
Erne Tea Ware, creamer, D447-II, B, 2¾" 135.00
Erne Tea Ware, teacup & saucer, D445-II, D............................150.00
Feather, vase, D155-V, B, sm 40.00
Figurine, boy & girl basket bearers, D17-III/D19-III, A, pr..........750.00
Figurine, boy and candlestick, pierced, D19-I, A, 9" 1,750.00
Figurine, girl basket bearer, D17-I, D, 9" 1,750.00
Figurine, leprechaun, D1142-III, A, 5½" 300.00
Figurine, Meditation, D20-II, A, 14½" 2,200.00
Figurine, pig, D231-II, B, lg...225.00
Figurine spaniel on cushion, D1555-VI, A, 3"...........................100.00
Fish, spill, D184-I, B, 7" 750.00
Five O 'Clock Tea Ware, teapot, D1420-II, C, 4½" 600.00
Florence, jug, D1288-VII, G, sm 85.00
Forget-Me-Not, trinket box, D111, D, 3" 750.00
Grass Tea Ware, honey pot on stand, D755-I, I, 6½", EX...............800.00
Harp Shamrock Tea Ware, teapot, D525-VI, E, 4½" 225.00
Henshall, basket, D121, 4-strand, D, 6½" 1,000.00
Hexagon Tea Ware, coffee cup & saucer, D397-II, G.....................175.00
Hexagon Tea Ware, dejeuner tray, D395-II, D 1,200.00
Hexagon Tea Ware, teacup & saucer, D391-II, A.........................135.00
Indian Corn, spill vase, D190-I, A, 6¼" 300.00
Ivy, creamer, D240-III, B, med sz 100.00
Lattice, ashtray, D1581-VI, B, 4" dia 25.00
Lifford, creamer, D301-I, B, 3¼" 200.00
Limpet Tea Ware, teapot, D565-III, B....................................300.00
Lithophane, Girl at Wall, D1538-III, A, 8x6½" 3,000.00
Lithophane, Girl w/Goat, D1537-III, A, 8½x6¾" 3,000.00
Lyre, wall bracket, D1546-I, A, 8½" 1,600.00

Mask Tea Ware, creamer, tall shape, D1483-II, A, lg 140.00
Mask Tea Ware, creamer, tall shape, D1484-III, A, sm 100.00
Mask Tea Ware, plate, D1491-III, B, 6¼" 100.00
Nautilus on coral, D131-I, C, 9" 850.00
Neptune Tea Ware, teapot, D415-II, C, 5" 400.00

Neptune Tea Ware, green trim, second black mark, 18" tray, teapot, creamer and sugar bowl, and four cups and saucers, $2,250.00.

Plaque, Praise Ye the Lord, earthenware, D1582-I, D, 8x9" 650.00
Ribbon, creamer, D243 (CR)-III, B, 3½" 75.00
Sea Horse & Shell, flower holder, D129-I, 4½" 1,050.00
Shamrock Ware, basket, D 109, 3-strand, A, 5" 750.00
Shamrock Ware, coffee cup & saucer, D372-II, E 135.00
Shamrock Ware, dresser tray, D1583-III, E, 10¼"x5" 225.00
Shamrock Ware, teapot, D367-III, E, med sz....................275.00
Shamrock Ware, teapot, D384-III, E, lg 325.00
Shamrock Ware, trinket box, D604-III, B, E, 4" 200.00
Shamrock Ware, trinket box, oval, D604-II, H, 4" 275.00
Shell, biscuit jar, D599-II, C, 8" 950.00
Shell, comport, D27-I, A, 3¾x9¾" 450.00
Shell Tea Ware, creamer, D590-II, B............................150.00
Shell Tea Ware, teacup & saucer, D587-II, A..................160.00
Sydenham, basket, D108, 4-strand, A, 10" 1,500.00
Table centre, D56-VI, D.....................................1,200.00
Tridacna Tea Ware, coffee cup & saucer, D462-II, B.............110.00
Tridacna Tea Ware, mustard, D1348-III, B, 2½".................60.00
Tridacna Tea Ware, teacup & saucer, D454-II, A...............110.00
Tridacna Tea Ware, teacup & saucer, D454-IV, B...............45.00
Tridacna Tea Ware, teapot, D475-II, B, lg....................375.00
Undine, creamer, D305-VI, B, 5" dia..........................40.00
Vase, dbl fish, D 1204-I, D, 12¾" 3,300.00

Bells

Some areas of interest represented in the study of bells are history, religion, and geography. Since Biblical times, bells have announced morning church services, vespers, deaths, christenings, school hours, fires, and community events. Countries have used them en masse to peal out the good news of Christmas, New Year's, and the endings of World Wars I and II. They've been rung in times of great sorrow, such as the death of Abraham Lincoln.

Our advisor, Dorothy Malone Anthony, is the author of a series of nine books entitled *World of Bells*. All have over two hundred colored pictures covering many bell categories. Her address is in the directory under Kansas. See also Schoolhouse Collectibles.

Bell metal, CI yoke/clapper, GW Coffin Cincinnati, 21" 225.00
Brass, Becky Sharp from Vanity Fair figural, 5¼" 75.00
Bronze, Civil War mule, 3¾" 60.00

Bronze, El Camino Real light post, 9" 35.00
Bronze, iron maiden torture device shape, 4" 60.00

Bronze bell, Robin Hood as handle, by Ballantyne, 6½", $200.00.

Ceramic, Little Red Riding Hood, 1950s, 4½" 30.00
Ceramic, Toby figure, 3" 20.00
Glass, custard, souvenir, 6½" 95.00
Glass, Dmn Daisy, pressed, 1800s, 5¾" 80.00
Glass, gold washed, jeweled flowers, Hungary, 6¼" 75.00
Glass, pressed butter dish lid w/openwork around base, 8" 150.00
Glass, 1893 Columbian Exposition, Libbey, 5" 135.00
Iron, blk wrought Wells Fargo figural hdl, 7" 30.00
Mechanical, Toledo Ware turtle, head or tail rings bell, 6" 200.00
Oriental, ivory Immortal hdl on enamel-on-copper bell, 4½" 160.00
Oriental, many-headed cobra atop tall hdl on bronze bell, 7" 75.00

Bennett, John

Bringing with him the knowledge and experience he had gained at the Doulton (Lambeth) Pottery in England, John Bennett opened a studio in New York City around 1877, where he continued his methods of decorating faience under the glaze. Early wares utilized imported English biscuit, though subsequently local clays (both white and cream-colored) were also used. His first kiln was on Lexington Avenue; he built another on East Twenty-Fourth Street. Pieces are usually signed 'J. Bennett, N.Y.,' often with the street address and date. Later examples may be marked 'West Orange, N.J.,' where he retired. The pottery was in operation approximately six years in New York. Pieces signed with other initials are usually worth less. Our advisor for this category is Robert Tuggle; he is listed in the Directory under New York.

Vase, maroon flowers on yel, w/lid, GR, 7¼" 750.00
Vase, sm yel flowers w/lg gr leaves on celadon, MDB, 10x7" ...1,500.00
Vase, wine roses/gr leaves on ivory, slim neck, WAA, 10" 800.00

Bennington

Although the term has become a generic one for the mottled brown ware produced there, Bennington is not a type of pottery, but rather a town in Vermont where two important potteries were located.

The Norton Company, founded in 1793, produced mainly redware and salt-glazed stoneware; only during a brief partnership with Fenton (1845-47) was any Rockingham attempted. The Norton Company endured until 1894, operated by succeeding generations of the Norton family. Fenton organized his own pottery in 1847. There he manufactured not only redware and stoneware, but more artistic types as well — graniteware, scroddled ware, flint enamel, a fine parian, and vast amounts of their famous Rockingham. Though from an esthetic standpoint his work rated highly among the country's finest ceramic achievements, he was economically unsuccessful. His pottery closed in 1858.

It is estimated that only one in five Fenton pieces were marked; and although it has become a common practice to link any fine piece of Rockingham to this area, careful study is vital in order to be able to distinguish Bennington's from the similar wares of many other American and Staffordshire potteries. Although the practice was without the permission of the proprietor, it was nevertheless a common occurrence for a potter to take his molds with him when moving from one pottery to the next, so particularly well-received designs were often reproduced at several locations. Of eight known Fenton marks, four are variations of the '1849' impressed stamp: 'Lyman Fenton Co., Fenton's Enamel Patented 1849, Bennington, Vermont.' These are generally found on examples of Rockingham and flint enamel. A raised, rectangular scroll with 'Fenton's Works, Bennington, Vermont,' was used on early examples of porcelain. From 1852 to 1858, the company operated under the title of the United States Pottery Company. Three marks — the ribbon mark with the initials USP, the oval with a scrollwork border and the name in full, and the plain oval with the name in full — were used during that period.

Among the more sought-after examples are the bird and animal figurines, novelty pitchers, figural bottles, and all of the more finely modeled items. Recumbent deer, cows, standing lions with one forepaw on a ball, and opposing pairs of poodles with baskets in their mouths and 'coleslaw' fur were made in Rockingham, flint enamel, and occasionally in parian. Numbers in the listings below refer to the book *Bennington Pottery and Porcelain* by Barret. Our advisors for Bennington (except for parian and stoneware) are Barbara and Charles Adams; they are listed in the Directory under Massachusetts.

Key:
c/s — cobalt on salt glaze

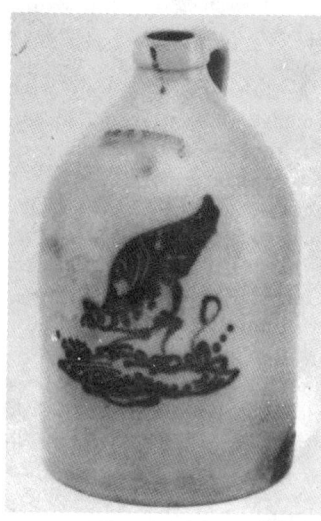

Jar, pecking chicken on mass of foliage, cobalt on salt glaze, marked J.&E. Norton, 13¼", NM, $1,500.00.

Book flask, Bennington Companion, flint enamel, 4-qt, M 3,000.00
Book flask, Hermit's Companion, flint enamel, mk, pt, EX 1,100.00
Bowl, flint enamel, 1⅝x3¾" 275.00

Bowl, mixing; flint enamel, 1849 mk, B 149-A, 10" dia, NM 800.00
Cake mold, Rockingham, 4½x10" 220.00
Candlestick, flint enamel, B 198, 8" 600.00
Candlestick, flint enamel w/bl flecks, B 198-A, 9½", pr 1,500.00
Candlestick, Rockingham, B 197-C, 8", M 550.00
Chamber pot, flint enamel, 1849 mk, 8¾" dia, EX 250.00
Chamberstick, Rockingham, yel-brn mottle, B 195-A, 3x4½" ...2,500.00
Coachman, Rockingham, 1849 mk, B 419-B, M 850.00
Cuspidor, Rockingham, lady's sz, 6¾" dia 60.00
Cuspidor, scroddled ware, scalloped ribs, 9" dia 1,200.00
Cuspidor, Shell, 2 side vents, 8½" 150.00
Foot bath, flint enamel, Creased Rib, 1849 mk, 20" 1,800.00
Foot warmer, Rockingham, 4 concave sides, 8½" 300.00
Goblet, Rockingham, w/hdl, 4½", M 595.00
Lamp, fluid; flint enamel std/base, prisms missing, 15", M 3,500.00
Picture frame, Rockingham, oval, 8", NM 800.00
Pie pan, Rockingham, 9", NM 150.00
Pitcher, flint enamel, Tulip & Heart, 1849 mk, 6½", EX 750.00
Pitcher, smear glaze, Leaf & Flower, Fenton Works mk, 9" 400.00
Snuff jar, Rockingham, orig lid, B 418-B, NM 850.00
Snuff jar, toby, non-flint, 4½" 850.00
Snuff jar, toby, Rockingham, orig lid, B 418-B, NM 850.00
Teapot, Rockingham, squat pear form, att, 4" 425.00
Tile, flint enamel, lattice design, 1849 mk, 8½x7", EX 600.00
Vase, flint enamel, heron 575.00
Vase, tulip; flint enamel, 10", NM 1,200.00
Wash bowl, flint enamel, mk, rare sm sz, B 169, 13½" 900.00

Stoneware

Crock, bird on branch, quilled, c/s, FB Norton Sons, 10" 325.00
Crock, chicken pecking corn, c/s, J Norton, 2-gal 800.00
Crock, floral (delicate), c/s, Norton & Fenton, 11", EX 250.00
Crock, floral (stylized), c/s, E&LP, 10" 325.00
Jar, bird on branch, c/s, J&E, sm chips, 10" 450.00

Pitcher, flint enamel, Alternate Rib, with impressed 1849 mark, 10", $1,250.00.

Jug, bird in brn brushed slip, L Norton & Son, 11", EX 2,700.00
Jug, bird on branch, quilled/blurred, c/s, J&E, 11" 350.00
Jug, bird on dotted leafy branch, c/s, E&LP, 4-gal, M 1,500.00
Jug, floral, brushed, c/s, Norton & Fenton, 13" 350.00

Big Little Books

The first Big Little Book was published in 1933 and copyrighted in 1932 by the Whitman Publishing Company of Racine, Wisconsin. Its hero was Dick Tracy. The concept was so well accepted that others soon followed Whitman's example; and though the 'Big Little Book' phrase became a trademark of the Whitman Company, the formats of his competitors (Saalfield, Goldsmith, Van Wiseman, Lynn, and World Syndicate) were exact copies. Today's Big Little Book buffs collect them all.

These hand-sized sagas of adventure were illustrated with full-page cartoons on the right-hand page and the story narration on the left. Colorful cardboard covers contained hundreds of pages, usually totaling over an inch in thickness. Big Little Books originally sold for 10¢ at the dime store; as late as the mid-1950s when the popularity of comic books caused sales to decline signaling an end to production, their price had risen to a mere 20¢. Their appeal was directed toward the pre-teens who bought, traded, and hoarded Big Little Books. Because so many were stored in attics and closets, many have survived. Among the super heroes are G-Men, Flash Gordon, Tarzan, the Lone Ranger, and Red Ryder; in a lighter vein, you'll find such lovable characters as Blondie and Dagwood, Mickey Mouse, Little Orphan Annie, and Felix the Cat.

In the early to mid-'30s, Whitman published several Big Little Books as advertising premiums for the Coco Malt Company, who packed them in boxes of their cereal. These are highly prized by today's collectors, as are Disney stories and super-hero adventures. Our advisor for this category is Ron Donnelly; he is listed in the Directory under Florida.

Airfighters of America, Whitman, 1941, NM 35.00
Allen Pike of Parachute Squad USA, Whitman, 1941, EX 28.00
Alley Oop & Dinny in Jungle of Moo, Whitman, 1938, VG 22.00
Andy Panda & Mad Dog Mystery, Whitman, 1947, G 8.50
Andy Panda & Mad Dog Mystery, Whitman, 1947, NM 35.00
Andy Panda's Vacation, Whitman, 1946, VG 28.00
Apple Mary & Dennie Foil Swindlers, Whitman, 1936, NM 45.00
Arizona Kid on Bandit Trail, Whitman, 1936, EX 20.00
Barney Baxter in the Air w/Eagle Squadron, Whitman, 1938, G .12.00
Believe It or Not, Whitman, 1933, G 12.00
Big Chief Wahoo & Lost Pioneers, Whitman, 1942, EX 30.00
Billy the Kid, Whitman, 1934, G 12.00
Black Silver & His Pirate Crew, Whitman, 1937, EX 22.00
Blondie, Baby Dumpling & All; Whitman, 1941, G 20.00
Blondie, Count Cookie in Too!; Whitman, 1947, G 16.00
Blondie, Who's Boss?; Whitman, 1942, VG 25.00
Blondie & Dagwood in Hot Water, Whitman, 1946, VG 32.00
Blondie or Life Among the Bumsteads, Whitman, 1944, VG 22.00
Bob Stone the Young Detective, Whitman, 1937, VG 22.00
Buck Jones & Killers of Crooked Butte, Whitman, 1940, EX 35.00
Buck Rogers & Depth Men of Jupiter, Whitman, 1935, EX 100.00
Buffalo Bill, World Syndicate, 1934, G 8.00
Camels Are Coming, movie version, Saalfield, 1935, G 18.00
Captain Easy Behind Enemy Lines, Whitman, 1943, EX 40.00
Captain Midnight & Secret Squadron, Whitman, 1941, VG 38.00
Chester Gump in Pole to Pole Flight, Whitman, 1937, VG 27.50
Clyde Beatty Lions & Tigers, photos, Whitman, 1934, VG 17.50
Cowboy Millionaire, movie version, Saalfield, 1935, VG 30.00
Dan Dunn Secret Operative 48, Crime Never Pays, 1934, G 20.00
Danger Trails in Africa, Whitman, 1935, NM 38.00

Daniel Boone, World Syndicate, 1934, G 12.00
David Copperfield, movie version, Whitman, 1934, EX 45.00
Detective Higgins of the Racket Squad, Whitman, 1938, VG 15.00
Dick Tracy & Tiger Lily Gang, Whitman, 1949, VG 27.50
Dick Tracy Solves the Penfield Mystery, Whitman, 1934, EX 60.00
Dickie Moore in Little Red Schoolhouse, Whitman, 1936, G 18.00
Doomed To Die, Saalfield, 1938, VG 17.50
Erik Noble & the Forty-Niners, Whitman, 1934, NM 40.00
Flame Boy & Indians' Secret, Whitman, 1938, VG 27.50
Foreign Spies-Dr Doom & Ghost Submarine, Whitman, '39, VG ..32.00
G-Man & Gun Runners, Whitman, 1940, EX 18.00
Gang Busters in Action, Whitman, 1938, G 12.00
Gene Autry Cowboy Detective, Whitman, 1940, EX 35.00
George O'Brien in Gun Law, movie version, Whitman, '35, NM .58.00
Hall of Fame of the Air, Whitman, VG 17.50
Hoosier Schoolmaster, Five Star Library, 1935, G 18.00
Inspector Wade of Scotland Yard, Saalfield, 1940, VG 15.00
Invisible Scarlet O'Neil Vs King of Slums, Whitman, 1946, G 12.50
Jack Swift & His Rocket Ship, Whitman, 1934, VG 30.00
Jerry Parker...& Candid Camera Club, Whitman, 1942, NM 25.00
Joe Penner's Duck Farm, Goldsmith, 1935, G 7.50
Just Kids, Whitman, 1937, VG 32.00
Kazan in Revenge of the North, Whitman, 1937, VG 17.50
Law of the Wild, color cover, Saalfield, EX 16.00

Little Annie Rooney on the Highway Adventure, G, $10.00.

Little Annie Rooney & Orphan House, Whitman, 1936, G 12.00
Little Mary Mix Up & Grocery Robberies, Saalfield, 1940, VG ...30.00
Little Men, movie version, Whitman, 1934, EX 30.00
Lone Star Martin of the Texas Rangers, Whitman, 1939, VG 15.00
Mandrake the Magician & Midnight Monster, Whitman, '39, EX 45.00
Mary Lee & Mystery of Indian Beads, Whitman, 1937, EX 20.00
Mickey Mouse & Dude Ranch Bandit, Whitman, 1943, EX 50.00
Mickey Mouse Mail Pilot, Whitman, 1933, EX 75.00
Mickey Mouse Sails for Treasure Island, Whitman, 1935, EX 90.00
Mr District Attorney on the Job, Whitman, 1941, NM 30.00
Myra North Special Nurse & Foreign Spies, Whitman, '38, VG ..28.00
Nancy Has Fun, comic strips, Whitman, 1944, EX 32.00
Ned Brandt Adventure Bound, Saalfield, 1940, VG 18.00
Pete Rice Up Dead Horse Canyon, Saalfield, 1940, NM 12.50

ug, floral, quilled, c/s, J&E, lip chip/base flake 250.00
ug, parrot on branch, c/s J Norton, 11" 600.00
Pitcher, Albany slip, E&LP, 1½-gal 300.00

Peter Pan, Whitman, Wee Little Book, 1934, G 5.00
Pilot Pete Dive Bomber, Whitman, 1941, VG 25.00
Plainsman, movie version, Whitman, 1939, G 10.00
Popeye in Puddleburg, Saalfield, 1934, G 22.00
Porky Pig & His Gang, Whitman, 1946, VG 40.00
Prairie Bill & Covered Wagon, Whitman, 1934, EX 30.00
Radio Patrol & Big Dan's Mobsters, Whitman, 1940, EX 24.00
Riders of Lone Trails, Whitman, 1937, VG 20.00
Rio Raiders, Saalfield, 1938, EX 18.00
Shooting Sheriffs of the Wild West, Whitman, 1936, EX 32.00
Sir Lancelot, Whitman, 1958, NM 12.00
Smilin' Jack in Wings Over the Pacific, Whitman, 1939, VG 27.50
Smitty in Going Native, Whitman, 1938, EX 28.00
Smokey Stover Foolish Foo Fighter, Whitman, 1945, EX 35.00
Stan Kent Freshman Fullback, Saalfield, 1936, VG 12.50
Story of Donald Duck, Whitman, 1938, VG 28.00
Superman in the Phantom Zone Connection, Whitman, 1980, M .8.00
Tailspin Tommy & Sky Bandits, Whitman, 1938, EX 45.00
Tailspin Tommy Air Racer, H Forest, Saalfield, 1940, EX 32.00

Tarzan Escapes, VG, $45.00.

Tarzan in Mark of Red Hyena, Whitman, 1967, VG 8.00
Tarzan Lord of the Jungle, Whitman, 1946, EX 45.00
Tim Tyler, Adventures of; Whitman, 1935, VG 32.00
Tom Mix & Stranger from the South, Whitman, 1936, NM 42.00
Tom Mix in the Range War, Whitman, 1937, VG 24.00
Tommy of Troop Six, Saalfield, 1937, EX 22.00
Treasure Island, movie version, Whitman, 1934, EX 50.00
Uncle Don's Strange Adventures, Whitman, 1936, VG 18.00
Union Pacific, movie version, Whitman, 1939, VG 27.50
Windy Wayne & His Flying Wing, Whitman, 1942, VG 22.50
Wyatt Earp, Hugh O'Brian, Whitman, 1958, NM 18.00

Bing and Grondahl

In 1853 brothers M.H. and J.H. Bing formed a partnership with Frederick Vilhelm Grondahl in Copenhagen, Denmark. Their early wares were porcelain plaques and figurines designed by the noted sculptor Thorvaldsen of Denmark. Dinnerware production began in 1863, and by 1889 their underglaze color 'Copenhagen Blue' had earned them

worldwide acclaim. They are perhaps most famous today for their Christmas plates, the first of which was made in 1895. See also Limited Edition Plates.

Figurine, beagle, standing puppy, #12564, 4½" 195.00
Figurine, boy standing w/dog, #1747 ....135.00
Figurine, boy stirs pot, cat at side, #2305 ....185.00
Figurine, boy wearing cape, holding book, #170 ....165.00
Figurine, Buttoning My Shoe, #2317 ....175.00
Figurine, cat, spotted, #2466, 4¾" 95.00
Figurine, children reading, #1567 ....170.00
Figurine, clown, #2511 ....50.00
Figurine, cocker spaniel, #12172, 3¼" 98.00
Figurine, Come to Mom, #2324, 4½" 165.00
Figurine, dachshund, #1755 ....85.00
Figurine, First Book, #2247 ....135.00
Figurine, German Shepherd, recumbent, #11765, 8½" 395.00
Figurine, girl & 2 sheep, #2010HH, 11" 310.00
Figurine, girl reaching for dog held by lady, #2202 ....155.00
Figurine, girl tennis player, #2364 ....165.00
Figurine, girl w/ball, #1982 ....135.00
Figurine, goat, licking, #1700, 4" 135.00
Figurine, Good Morning, #1624 ....95.00
Figurine, Goose Girl, mold mk under skirt, c 1946, #527, 9" 265.00
Figurine, lady feeding chickens, #2220, 9½" 220.00
Figurine, Little Match Girl, #1655 ....180.00
Figurine, Little Mother, #1779 ....145.00
Figurine, mandolinist on stool, #1500, 11" 335.00
Figurine, Marianne, #2373 ....195.00
Figurine, Milkmaid, sgn, #899, 1955, 11½" 515.00
Figurine, Miss Charming, #2387 ....140.00
Figurine, nude child, wht, #2230, 6½" 55.00
Figurine, Nurse, #2379, 9" 235.00
Figurine, Ole, matt finish, #1747 ....165.00
Figurine, penguin, #417, 10½" 355.00
Figurine, Sandman, #2055 ....180.00
Figurine, Shepherdess, #2010, 10½" 475.00
Figurine, starling, #1880, 7½" 185.00
Figurine, Two Friends, boy w/dog, #1790, 4" 235.00
Figurine, Vagabond, hands in pockets, #2473, 8½" 330.00
Figurine, Who Is Calling?, #2251 ....145.00
Figurine, 18th-Century Mala cellist, #2032 ....650.00

Bisque

Bisque is a term referring to unglazed earthenware or porcelain that has been fired only once. During the Victorian era, bisque figurines became very popular. Most were highly decorated in pastels and gilt and demonstrated a fine degree of workmanship in the quality of their modeling. Few were marked. See also Heubach; Nodders; Dolls; Piano Babies.

Blk boy w/spilled dish in lap, spoon in hand, Germany, 5½" 375.00
Boy w/book, pack on bk, #d, 9" 100.00
Boy w/fish, girl w/shells, on floral ped, Fr, 14", pr 400.00
Bust, gent in flowered bib, high collar, fancy hat, Fr, 11" 295.00
Bust, girl in bl hat, boy in feathered hat, Fr, 11", pr 325.00
Conch shell boat w/boy w/oar (& girl in pk/bl), Fr, 8", pr 375.00
Dancing couple, EX pnt & details, 6" 150.00
Edwardian man, tan coat/pk jacket, she in bl, Fr, 21", pr 1,150.00
Frog standing next to trunk, mc pnt, Germany, 8" 245.00
Girl w/dog in apron, boy w/feeding dish, mc, 13x4", pr 395.00
Girl w/fruit basket, EX pnt w/gold trim, Germany, 7" 115.00
Girl w/spoon (1 w/bugle), pastels, English, no mk, 10", pr 285.00

Goddess in flower-decor chariot pulled by cherubs, 15" L 350.00
Musicians, mc pnt, Germany, 5", 6-pc set 120.00
Warrior, swan atop helmet, embraces maid, ornate base, 18" ..1,100.00

Couple in country-style clothing, hands shielding eyes, 24", $1,200.00 for the pair.

Black Americana

Black memorabilia is without a doubt a field that encompasses the most widely exploited ethnic group in our history. But within this field there are many levels of interest: arts and achievements such as folk music and literature, caricatures in advertising, souvenirs, toys, fine art, and legitimate research into the days of their enslavement and enduring struggle for equality. The list is endless.

In the listings below are some with a derogatory connotation. Thankfully, these are from a bygone era and represent the mores of a culture that existed nearly a century ago. They are included only to convey the fact that they are a part of this growing area of collecting interest.

Our advisor for this category is Linda Rothe; she is listed in the Directory under Washington. Black Americana catalogs featuring a wide variety of items for sale are available; see the Directory under Clubs, Newsletters, and Catalogs for more information. See also Postcards; Posters; Sheet Music.

Apron, Aunt Jemima Pancake Jamboree, 1960s, EX 80.00
Ashtray, boy w/donkey pulling toilet-shaped cart, ceramic 25.00
Ashtray, boys push & pull cart made of dice, ceramic, NM 35.00
Ashtray, Coon Chicken Inn, smiling face on clear glass 35.00
Ashtray, head figural, protruding lip rest, ceramic, 4", EX 45.00
Ashtray, Mammy w/breast in wringer, chalkware, 5x3½" 75.00
Ashtray, sm child, For Old Butts..., Japan, 1940s, 3x3½" 37.50
Bank, nude child on alligator nodder, compo, worn pnt 37.50
Bell, Chef figural, mc pnt, Occupied Japan, 4", NM 135.00
Book, Afro-Am Folk Songs, Krehbiel, 1971, 3rd printing, EX 12.50
Book, Am Negro Songs & Spirituals, Bonanza, 1940, EX 15.00
Book, Little Missy, Lindsay, Boston, 1922, 1st ed, VG 15.00
Book, Mammy's White Folks, Sampson, 1919, 1st ed, G 22.50
Book, Old Folks at Home, Foster, London, 1888, VG 45.00
Book, Pickaninny Twins, Perkins, Houghton Mifflin, 1931, VG ..30.00
Book, Strange Tale of 10 Little Nigger Boys, fabric, 1890s, EX ..275.00
Bookends, Mammy, heavy plaster, EX pnt, 5¾x5½x4", pr 48.00
Bowl, cereal; Golliwog, Robertson, Staffordshire, 6¾" 89.00

Bowl, cereal; Little Black Sambo, Schramberg Germany, 1920s .125.00
Bowl, soup; Coon Chicken Inn 195.00
Box, take-out; Coon Chicken Inn, bright logo, 3x7x4", EX 75.00
Candle holder, Mammy, yel, ceramic 90.00
Cookbook, Aunt Jemima, ca 1906, EX 175.00
Cookbook, Fine Old Dixie Recipes, wooden cover, 1959, EX 60.00
Cookie jar, Mammy, F&F, pnt touch up, EX 385.00
Creamer & sugar bowl, boy & girl, ceramic, 2½", pr 75.00
Cruets, Mammy & Mose, ceramic, EX pnt, 6½", pr 125.00
Cup, measuring; minstrel figural, cold-pnt pottery, set of 4 ....50.00
Doll, Aunt Jemima, stuffed oilcloth, EX 75.00
Doll, Mammy, stuffed cloth, wire in limbs, 1940s, 9", EX 30.00
Doll, topsy-turvy, compo, minor pnt wear, 1920s, 7", EX 245.00
Figurine, boy w/watermelon slice, chalkware, worn pnt, 4" 25.00
Figurine, boy w/watermelon slice on potty, bsk, 4" 95.00
Figurine, Chef, cast metal, EX pnt, Barclay, 1940s, 3¼" 50.00
Figurine, Fat Albert, hard rubber, 3", M 10.00
Figurine, girl reclining, ceramic, HP, Japan, '30s, 5½" L 30.00
Figurine, Red Cap, cast metal, EX pnt, 1940s, 3¼", EX 40.00
Figurine, 3 boys in band, ceramic, Japan, 2x2", M 37.50
Game, darts, Sambo target, heavy, stand on bk, old, NM 125.00
Hat, chef's; Aunt Jemima's Pancake Days, EX 45.00
Humidor, barefoot boy in sailor suit, Austria, 5½x5", EX 185.00
Label, Lucky Man & Woman Liniment, couple, '30s, 3½x1½" 10.00
Label, Sweet Georgia Brown Talcum Powder, Deco lady, 3x5½" .10.00
Letter opener, metal, man in alligator's mouth 48.00
Marionette, molded compo boy, cloth attire, straw hat, 14" 225.00
Mask, Aunt Jemima cb diecut, cutouts for nose & eyes, 12", M 200.00
Mask, man w/exaggerated features, papier-mache, 9½", EX 50.00
Match book, Coon Chicken Inn, M 47.50
Match holder, Coon Chicken Inn, metal 295.00
Memo board, Mammy, We Needs, NM 75.00
Memo pad holder, Mammy, red plastic, M 85.00
Menu, child's; Coon Chicken Inn, EX 175.00
Menu, lunch; Coon Chicken Inn, EX 150.00
Mold, pancake; Aunt Jemima, NM 155.00
Newspaper, Times Picayune, complete w/color comics, 1916, EX ..15.00
Pan, cornbread; Aunt Jemima form, scarce 150.00
Paperweight, boy on potty, CI w/worn pnt, St Louis, 1904 ....60.00
Pencil, mechanical; alligator & man figural, celluloid, '30s 90.00
Pie bird, Mammy, glazed pottery, brn/pk/wht, 4½", EX 60.00
Pin tray, baby in relief, EX color, ceramic, 1940s, 4¼x3" 45.00
Pin-bk button, Black Power, 1960s, NM 5.00
Place mat, Aunt Jemima, paper, M 15.00
Planter, boy w/melon slice beside melon, ceramic, 6" 40.00
Planter, head (open), gold earrings, red lips, ceramic, 6" 75.00
Planter, Mammy, porc, mc pnt, 1930s, 4½", M 125.00
Plate, Aunt Jemima, paper, M 45.00

Plate, Topsy's, 'Eat With Your Fingers,' marked Inca Ware, Shenango, rare, 7¼", $450.00.

Plate, Aunt Jemima's face, old style, ceramic 165.00
Plate, Coon Chicken Inn, lg Blk face in center, 9½", 4 for 900.00
Poster, Dixie Boy Firecrackers, boy melon & pole, '40s, 19x29" ...22.00
Poster, Uncle Wabash Cupcakes, man w/banjo, '24, 14x11", EX ..60.00
Potholder caddy, Chef, wood diecut, EX pnt, 1930s, 5½" 45.00
Potholder caddy, children w/watermelon slice, chalk, 5" 32.00
Print, Mammy in rocker w/crystal ball, H Roseland, 9½x8" 85.00
Puzzle, Aunt Jemima, ca 1902, EX 150.00
Puzzle, Little Black Sambo, color litho, 1920s, 7x8½", EX 55.00
Receipt for chicken dinner, Coon Chicken Inn, M 27.50
Sack, cornmeal; Aunt Jemima, 10-lb, M 18.00
Saucer, Coon Chicken Inn 135.00
Shaker, pancake; Aunt Jemima, yel bottom, ceramic, 8½", EX 65.00
Shakers, Aunt Jemima & Uncle Mose, F&F, 5", pr 65.00
Shakers, babies in basket, ceramic, 3½" in 4" basket, pr 88.00
Shakers, boy w/watermelon shakers, ceramic, 3-pc set 80.00
Shakers, boys on lettuce, red shorts, ceramic, Japan, EX, pr 37.50
Shakers, Chef w/jugs (holding shakers), 5" 65.00
Shakers, children in basket, Japan, M, pr 125.00
Shakers, clown (salt) on drum (pepper), ceramic, pr, M 60.00
Shakers, head & watermelon slice, M, pr 48.00
Shakers, Jonah & whale, 2" boy & 4" L fish, interlocking, pr 45.00
Shakers, Mammy, gr skirt, Luzianne, F&F Dieworks, 5¼", pr 175.00
Shakers, Mammy, pnt wood, 3¼", M, pr 22.50
Shakers, Mammy, yel, Brayton Laguna, pr 125.00
Shakers, Mammy, yoke holds shakers, ceramic, 4½", pr 70.00
Shakers, Mammy & Butler, ceramic, 4¾", pr 145.00
Shakers, Peppy & Salty, Pearl China, lg, M, pr 285.00
Shakers, Rastus & Liza, wood, 1940s, pr 45.00
Shakers, teapot, face on side, yel hat, red clay, Japan, pr 45.00
Shakers, Valentine couple, ceramic, Japan, 1950s, M, pr 145.00
Sheet music, Ain't Dat a Shame?, Queen/Wilson, 1901, G 20.00
Sheet music, Cabin Near Mississippi Shore, Wise, 1895, VG 10.00
Sheet music, Dusty Rose, Allen, Boston, 1905, G 17.50
Sheet music, Good Bye Eliza Jane, Tilzer, 1903, VG 25.00
Sheet music, Mammy's Little Pumpkin Colored Coons, 1897, VG ..32.50
Sign, Colored Waiting Room, minor aging, 6½x18", EX 25.00
Sign, We Serve Colored Carry Out Only, 1930s, 5x12", EX 20.00
Smoking stand, bellhop, wood w/mc pnt, 34" 195.00
Spice rack, metal, Aunt Jemima, 6 F&F spices, scarce, NM 525.00
Spice set, Mammy & Chef, ceramic, 3¼", 4-pc 65.00
Spoon rest, Mammy's face, ceramic, wall hanger, M 145.00
String holder, Chef, NAPCO, 1949, EX 275.00
String holder, girl holding flowers, chalkware, worn pnt 195.00
String holder, Mammy, Aunt's Dinah's String, wood diecut, M ...90.00
String holder, Mammy, ceramic, Japan 195.00
String holder, Mammy (young), ceramic, Japan 225.00
String holder, Mammy face, ceramic, 1940s, rare 275.00
String holder, Red Cap, Fredericksburg Art Pottery 295.00
Teapot, boy on camel figural, ceramic, 5½x9", NM 88.00
Teapot, Chef figural, EX color, ceramic, 4¼" 275.00
Toothpick holder, man in tuxedo, ceramic 47.50
Towel, kitchen; Mammy serving pie, EX 45.00
Towel, kitchen; tap-dancing children, M 50.00
Tumbler, iced tea; cannibal in jungle scene, 7", 4 for 35.00
Valentine, mechanical, banjo-playing minstrel, 1930s, 4¼" 25.00
Valentine, mechanical, child rolls eyes, 1930s, 4¾", NM 20.00
Watch, Little Rascals, Buckwheat on band, 1986, MIB 125.00

Black Cats

Made in Japan during the fifties, these novelty cats may be found bearing the labels of several different importers, all with their own partic-

ular characteristics. The best known and most collectible of these cats are from the Shafford line. Even when unmarked, they are easily identified by their red bows, green eyes, white whiskers, eyeliners, and eyebrows. Relco/Royal Sealy cats are tall and slender, and their bow ties are gold with red dots. Wales is a wonderful line with yellow eyes and gold detailing; Enesco cats have blue eyes, and there are other lines as well. When evaluating your black cats, be sure to inspect their paint and judge them accordingly. 50% paint should relate to 50% of our suggested values, which are given for cats in mint (or nearly mint) paint.

Ashtray, face only, flat, gr eyes, Shafford, 4½" 20.00
Ashtray, full figure, flat, 'Ashes' in body, 2½x3¾" 7.50
Ashtray, head shape w/open mouth, Shafford, 3" 18.00

Cigarette lighter, Shafford, 5½", $125.00.

Condiment set, 2 heads, J&M bows w/spoons, Shafford, 4" 50.00
Cookie jar, cat head, Shafford 85.00
Creamer & sugar bowl, cat-head lids are shakers, 5⅜" 40.00
Cruets, he w/O eyes, she w/V eyes & hair bow, Shafford, pr 50.00
Decanter, sq, upright, head stopper, 6 shots on bk, 11⅜" 50.00
Egg cup, cat face on bowl, ped ft, Shafford 25.00
Grease jar, sm cat head, Shafford 50.00
Measuring cups, 4 on wood rack w/cat face, Shafford 125.00
Pincushion, cushion on bk, tongue measure 22.50
Pitcher, milk; upright, Shafford 75.00
Pot holder caddy, 'teapot' cat, 3-hook, Shafford 65.00
Shakers, range; Shafford, 5", pr 40.00
Shakers, seated, bl eyes, Enesco label, 5¾", pr 15.00
Spice set, 6 shakers w/faces, bow tie pulls, Shafford, +rack 125.00
Strainer, w/cat face, long wood hdl, Shafford 50.00
Sugar bowl, seated, red bow, gr eyes, Shafford, 4⅞" 18.00
Teapot, bulbous body, head lid, gr eyes, Shafford, 6½" 45.00
Teapot, crouched, scarf/gold disk, spout through mouth, 3¾" 20.00
Teapot, w/creamer & sugar bowl, stacking 50.00
Wall pocket, gr eyes, red bow, sq pocket at bk, 5½" 65.00
Wine, emb cat's face, gr eyes, Shafford, sm 20.00

Black Glass

Black glass is a type of colored glass that when held to strong light usually appears deep purple, though since each glasshouse had its own formula, tones may vary. It was sometimes etched or given a satin finish; and occasionally it was decorated with silver, gold, enamel, coralene, or any of these in combination. The decoration was done either by the glasshouse or by firms that specialized in decorating glassware. Crystal, jade, colored glass, or milk glass was sometimes used with the black as an accent. Black glass has been made by many companies since the 17th century. Contemporary glasshouses produced black glass during the Depression, seldom signing their product. It is still being made today.

To learn more about the subject, we recommend *A Collector's Guide to Black Glass*, written by our advisor, Marlena Toohey; she is listed in the Directory under Colorado. Look for her newly updated value guide. See also Tiffin, L.E. Smith, and other specific manufacturers.

Bottle, scent; HP florals w/gold, tulip stopper, 9¼" 110.00
Bowl, flared, unknown mfg, 1920s, 10" 15.00
Bowl, silver flowers & scrolls, 3-ftd, 3x12½" 65.00

Bowl, Mt. Pleasant, L.E. Smith Glass Co., 8", $25.00.

Candlestick, Ellen, unknown mfg, pr 25.00
Candlestick, hexagonal std, rnd base, 7", pr 55.00
Candy dish, cloverleaf, rtcl finial, silver trim, 7" 22.00
Celery tray, Greensburg, #681, ca 1930 ....32.50
Compote, paneled, flared rim, ftd, unknown mfg, 6x8¾" 40.00
Cordial, clear w/blk ft, unknown mfg, 1-oz 22.50
Creamer, Cloverleaf, Hazel-Atlas 12.50
Creamer & sugar bowl, Octagon Scroll, US Glass, 1930s 20.00
Creamer & sugar bowl, Ovide, silver decor, Hazel-Atlas 25.00
Egg cup, unknown mfg, 6-oz 12.00
Goblet, clear bowl, blk ft, unknown mfg, 8-oz 16.00
Jug, cream; European, ca 1870-90, 4" 45.00
Ladle, mayonnaise; unknown mfg, 1920s 20.00
Paper-cup holder, unknown mfg, 2½" 10.00
Pitcher, cylinder form, unknown mfg, 1920s, 1-pt 18.00
Plate, maple leaf form, unknown mfg 35.00
Salver, Shaggy Daisy, 3-ftd, US Glass, 1930, 10" 40.00
Tumbler, clear w/blk scalloped ft, att Seneca, 8-oz 15.00
Vase, bottle form, unknown mfg, 10½" 18.00
Vase, bulbous, scalloped rim, unknown mfg, 4½" 15.00
Vase, classic form, att Sinclaire, 9" 35.00
Vase, slim w/wide flared rim, unknown mfg, 10½" 40.00
Wall vase, Crackle, US Glass, 1920s, 5¾" 45.00

Blown Glass

Blown glass is rather difficult to date; 18th and 19th century examples vary little as to technique or style; it ranges from the primitive to the sophisticated. But the metallic content of very early glass

caused tiny imperfections that are obvious upon examination, and these are often indicative of age.

In America, Stiegel introduced the English technique of using a patterned, part-size mold, a practice which was generally followed by many glasshouses after the Revolution. From 1820 to about 1850, glass was blown into full-size 3-part molds. In the listings below, glass is assumed clear unless color is mentioned. Numbers refer to a standard reference book, *American Glass*, by Helen McKearin. See also Bottles and specific manufacturers. Our advisor for this category is Mark Vuono; he is listed in the Directory under Connecticut.

Key:
ps — pontil scar

Bowl, amethyst, expanded dmn, appl ft, 3½" H 325.00
Bowl, aqua, folded rim, ps, 1820-50, 2x4½" 105.00
Bowl, cut starbursts, boat shaped, ftd, 1790s, 10x13½" 715.00
Bowl, sapphire bl, appl blown ft/stem, ps, 4" 220.00
Bowl, sapphire bl, solid appl ft, ca 1900, 2¾x4½" 105.00
Compote, folded rim, stemmed ft, ps, 3⅝x6½" 125.00
Creamer, aqua, tooled lip, incised ring at neck, 5⅝" 225.00
Creamer, bright bl, sheared rim, ps, 4", EX 100.00
Creamer, bright bl, 16 swirled ribs, appl hdl/ft, 4¼" 330.00
Creamer, cobalt, cylindrical w/appl hdl/rigaree, 3¼" 425.00
Creamer, fiery opal, appl ft, crimped hdl, tooled lip, 4½" 135.00
Decanter, eng florals, thin, ps, 1820-40, 8¾" 175.00
Flask, 26 honeycomb cells over 25 flutes, sheared lip, 5⅛" 250.00
Goblet, clear w/cotton twist latticinio stem, ribbed, 5½" 75.00
Inkwell, fountain; C-1307, NE Glass, 1870s, 4" 300.00
Jar, aqua, folded-over rim, tooled hollow ft, 8" 175.00
Jar, bright gr, sheared mouth, ps, 1800-60, 4⅜" 170.00
Lamp, sparking; clear, waisted form, sheared rim, 4⅜" 85.00
Milk pan, aqua, folded, pouring spout, 1850s, 5x18" 275.00
Pan, amber, folded rim, 7" 425.00
Paperweight, swan figural, aqua, solid, 2¾x2⅝" 50.00
Pitcher, aqua, 11 bands of threading at lip, appl hdl, 6¼" 235.00
Pitcher, aqua, 12 bands at neck, appl hdl w/3 ribs, 7½" 385.00
Pitcher, bl, dbl incised rim, appl ft/hdl, 1840-50, 6¾" 415.00
Pitcher, bl, 8 lg panels on lower body, 1840s, 6" 500.00
Pitcher, dmn pattern, folded-over lip, Emil Larson, 9½" 100.00
Pitcher, med bl, crimped ft, Whitney, 1850s, 6¾" 3,200.00
Pitcher, 12 threaded bands at neck, HP florals, 1830s, 9¾" 1,980.00
Pitcher, 2 bands of broken chains, T Cains type, 6¾" 255.00
Salt cellar, bl, 18-dmn pattern, dbl-ogee form, 1780s, 3" 85.00
Snuff bottle, olive amber, collared mouth, rectangular, 6¼" 90.00
Snuff bottle, olive amber, sq w/beveled corners, 5" 130.00
Snuff bowl, egg form, label: RR Mills...Scotch Snuff, 6¼" 165.00
Storage container, med aqua, str-sided cylinder, 11⅛" 155.00

Sugar bowl, clear flint with hand cutting, European (att), ca 1850s, 6¾", $450.00.

Sugar bowl, aqua, galleried rim, lid w/folded rim, 5¾" **2,300.00**
Sugar bowl, bright bl, galleried rim, appl ft, 1820-40, 6⅜" **200.00**
Sugar bowl, bright bl, galleried rim, appl ft/knop finial, 6" **330.00**
Sugar bowl, bright bl, galleried rim, blown ft, 6¼" **880.00**
Sugar bowl, dk bl, galleried rim, appl solid ft, w/lid, 6" **330.00**
Sugar bowl, galleried rim, appl ft, knop finial, 8½" **715.00**
Sugar bowl, 12-petal pattern on base, lid w/folded rim, 6¼" **1,320.00**
Tankard, aqua w/wht loopings, appl solid hdl, 1850s, 7" **425.00**
Twine holder, clear w/bl lip & bottom edge, 1850s, 4" **265.00**
Vase, med bl w/wht loopings, knop stem w/1842 dime, 9¾" **600.00**
Wall pocket (for holy water), med aqua, folded rim, 1890s **125.00**
Whimsey, bellows bottle, cobalt, quilled rigaree, 7½" **235.00**
Whimsey, hat, olive gr, ps, 1800-30, 2" **375.00**
Whimsey, powder horn, amber, 28 ribs, 1790-1830, 6½" **1,320.00**
Wine, dbl-knopped stem, red & wht spirals, lt haze, 6¼" **285.00**
Wine, knop stem w/wht spirals, waisted bell bowl, 7" **525.00**
Wine, wht opaque twist, eng vintage, corkscrew ft, 6¼" **255.00**

Blown Three-Mold Glass

A popular collectible in the 1920s, '30s, and '40s, blown three-mold glass has again gained the attention of many. Produced from approximately 1815 to 1840 in various New York, New England, and Midwestern glasshouses, it was a cheaper alternative to the expensive imported Irish cut glass.

Distinguishing features of blown three-mold glass are the three distinct mold marks and the concave-convex appearance of the glass. For every indentation on the inner surface of the ware, there will be a corresponding protuberance on the outside. Blown three-mold glass is most often clear with the exception of inkwells and a few known decanters. Any colored three-mold glass commands a premium price.

The numbers in the listings that follow refer to the book *American Glass* by George and Helen McKearin. Our advisor for this category is Mark Vuono; he is listed in the Directory under Connecticut.

Sugar bowl, GII-18, clear with faint bluish tint, applied foot and knob finial, Sandwich, 6½", $2,700.00.

Bowl, GII-22, folded rim, att Sandwich, 1¼x5¾" **70.00**
Bowl, GIII-18, folded rim, pontil scar, 1⅜x5⅞" **150.00**
Bowl, GIII-20, inwardly folded rim, att Keene, 1½x6¼" **90.00**
Bowl, GIII-21, flared sides, folded rim, 2½x5" **138.00**
Castor set, GI-13, 4 bottles in pewter fr, 8½" **190.00**
Creamer, GV-14, solid crimped hdl (sm crack), 4¼" **165.00**

Decanter, GII-18, 2 dbl bands of quilled rigaree, ½-pt **198.00**
Decanter, GIII-2-2, 'Brandy' emb, 1825-40, 1-qt **275.00**
Decanter, GV-8, lt haze, #10 stopper, 1825-40, 1-qt **165.00**
Flip glass, GII-22, pale amethyst, sheared rim, 5⅞x4⅝" **110.00**
Pitcher, GII-18, hollow hdl w/crimping, 1825-40, 5¼", EX **245.00**
Pitcher, GII-33, bulbous w/appl hdl & rigaree, 6½x5⅜" **600.00**
Plate, GII-19, folded rim, pontil scar, sm stain, 6⅞" **110.00**
Salt cellar, GIII-4, pontil scar, 1825-40, 2½" **175.00**
Tumbler, GII-18, bbl shape, pontil scar, 1825-40, 5¾" **120.00**
Tumbler, GII-18, bbl shaped, pontil scar, 1825-40, 3½" **95.00**
Tumbler, GII-18, pontil scar, 1825-40, 2½" **88.00**
Tumbler, GII-18, str sides, pontil scar, 1825-40, 4¾" **110.00**
Tumbler, GIII-20, str sided, pontil scar, 1825-40, 3½" **165.00**
Tumbler, GIV-2, sheared rim, pontil scar, 3⅛x2⅞" **375.00**
Whimsey, hat, GII-18, folded rim, pontil scar, 2" **135.00**

Blue and White Stoneware

Blue and white stoneware, much of which was decorated with such in-mold designs as grazing cows and Dutch children, was made by practically every American pottery from the turn of the century until the mid-1930s. Crocks, pitchers, wash sets, rolling pins, and canisters are only a few of the items that may be found in this type of 'country' pottery that has become one of today's popular collectibles.

Roseville, Brush-McCoy, Uhl Co., and Burley Winter were among those who produced it; but very few pieces were ever signed. Naturally, condition must be a prime consideration, especially if one is buying for resale; pieces with good, strong color and fully molded patterns bring premium prices. Normal wear and signs of age are to be expected since this was utility ware and received heavy use in busy households. In the listings that follow, crocks and jars are assumed without lids unless noted otherwise. For further information we recommend *Blue and White Stoneware* by Kathryn McNerny. See also specific manufacturers.

Batter jar, Wildflower, thick appl hdl, 8x7" **195.00**
Bean pot, Boston Baked Beans, Swirl, heavy diffused pattern **300.00**
Bedpan, Diffused Bl, 12x12" **120.00**
Beer cooler, Elves, brass spigot, 18x14" **850.00**
Berry crock, Fluted, 3x4" **95.00**
Bowl, Apricot, 9½" **85.00**
Bowl, berry; Diffused Bl, 2½x4½" **75.00**
Bowl, Daisy on Waffle, 10¾" **95.00**
Bowl, Gadroon Arches (Feather Panels), 4½x9½" **150.00**
Bowl, mixing; Flying Bird, 4x7½" **225.00**
Bowl, plain, 11" **65.00**
Bowl, Reverse Pyramids w/Reverse Picket Fence, 2½x4½" **150.00**
Butter crock, Butterfly, orig lid & bail, 6½" **175.00**
Butter crock, Daisy & Trellis, orig lid & bail, 4½" **175.00**
Butter crock, Eagle, orig lid & bail, M **450.00**
Butter crock, Grapes & Leaves, dbl ring around rim, 3x6½" **175.00**
Butter crock, Printed Cows, no lid, 5x6½" **110.00**
Canister, Snowflake, rpl lid, 6½x5¾" **150.00**
Chamberpot, Wildflower, stenciled pattern, 6x11" **135.00**
Coffeepot, Oval, Diffused Bl, bl-tipped knob, str sides, 11x4" **250.00**
Coffeepot, Swirl, 'spurs' on hdl, acorn finial, 11½x6" **450.00**
Cookie jar, Brickers, flat button finial, 8x8" **325.00**
Cookie jar, Turkey Eye color drip, Diffused Bl bands, 9x8" **250.00**
Cup, Bow Tie, bird transfer, 3¾x3½" **95.00**
Cup, Wildflower w/emb Ribbon & Bow, 4½x2½" **85.00**
Custard cup, Fishscale, 5x2½" **75.00**
Egg storage crock, Barrel Staves, bail hdl, 5½x6" **185.00**
Foot warmer, Diffused Bl, A Warm Friend, 12½x6½" **275.00**
Ice crock, Barrel Staves, rope/tongs/ice block emb, 4½x6" **225.00**

Iced tea cooler, Bl Band, flat lid, complete, 13x11" 295.00
Measuring cup, Spearpoint & Flower Panels, 6x6¾" 120.00
Milk crock, Daisy & Lattice, 4x8", NM 125.00
Milk crock, Lovebird, rstr bail & handgrip, 5½x9" 145.00
Mug, beer; advertising, Diffused Bl, sqd hdl 150.00
Mug, Cattails 125.00
Mug, Flying Bird, 5x3" 200.00
Mug, plain 65.00
Mug, Windy City (Fannie Flagg), Robinson Clay Products 200.00
Pickle crock, Bl Band, advertising, recessed lid, 12x9" 225.00
Pickle crock, Heart Band, advertising, rolled rim, 8x8" 225.00
Pie plate, Bl Walled Brick-Edge, star emb base, 10½" 100.00
Pitcher, Acorns, stenciled, 8x6½" 135.00
Pitcher, American Beauty Rose, 10" 275.00
Pitcher, Apricot, 8" 165.00
Pitcher, Avenue of Trees, allover bl, 9x7" 200.00
Pitcher, Barrel, +6 mugs 395.00
Pitcher, Basketweave & Flower, 9" 225.00
Pitcher, Bl Band, plain 80.00
Pitcher, Bl Band Scroll 160.00
Pitcher, Bl Sawtooth, Wht Hall 95.00
Pitcher, Bluebird, 9x7" 250.00
Pitcher, Bow Tie 135.00
Pitcher, Butterfly, 4¾" 245.00
Pitcher, Butterfly, 9x7" 250.00
Pitcher, Castle & Fishscale, 8" 195.00
Pitcher, Cattails, 7½" 150.00
Pitcher, Cattails, 9" 185.00
Pitcher, Cattails & Butterfly 150.00
Pitcher, Cherries & Leaves, w/printing, 9½" 350.00
Pitcher, Cherry Cluster, 7½" 195.00
Pitcher, Cherry Cluster & Basketweave, 10" 175.00
Pitcher, Cosmos 195.00
Pitcher, Cow, 8½" 225.00
Pitcher, Diffused Bl, 8¾", M 100.00
Pitcher, Doe & Fawn, sparce bl, 8½" 185.00
Pitcher, Dutch Boy & Girl by Windmill, 9" 225.00
Pitcher, Dutch Landscape, stenciled, tall 175.00

Pitcher, Indian Head in War Bonnet, waffled body, 9" 275.00
Pitcher, Iris, 9" 175.00
Pitcher, Leaping Deer, 8½" 165.00
Pitcher, Lincoln w/Log Cabin 450.00
Pitcher, Lovebird, arc bands, deep color, 8½" 400.00
Pitcher, Lovebird, pale color, 8½", EX 300.00
Pitcher, Morning-Glory 225.00
Pitcher, Peacock, 7¾x6½" 450.00
Pitcher, Pine Cone, 9½" 200.00
Pitcher, Poinsettia, 6½" 250.00
Pitcher, Rose & Fishscale, 6" 165.00
Pitcher, Rose on Trellis 165.00
Pitcher, Scroll & Leaf, advertising, 8" 250.00
Pitcher, Stag & Pine Trees, 9" 295.00
Pitcher, Swan, long beak, arched neck, deep color, 8½" 275.00
Pitcher, Swan, lt bl, 8½" 295.00
Pitcher, tavern scene, Flemish Jugs...Kinney & Levan, 9" 165.00
Pitcher, Tulip, 8x4" 225.00
Pitcher, Wild Rose, sponged bands, 9" 295.00
Pitcher, Wild Rose, 9x6" 185.00
Pitcher, Wildflower, stenciled 200.00
Pitcher, Windmill & Bush, 9" 225.00
Pitcher, Windy City (Fannie Flagg), Robinson Clay, 8½" 450.00
Pitcher, 2 old men w/canes, dog's-head spout, Germany, 11" 200.00
Roaster, Diffused Bl, appl hdls, flat finial, 9x19" 225.00
Roaster, Wildflower, domed lid, 8½x12" 195.00
Rolling pin, Swirl, orig wooden hdls, 13" 475.00
Rolling pin, Wildflower & Bl Band 250.00
Salt crock, Apricot, orig lid 145.00
Salt crock, Bl Band, printed letters, 6x5" 135.00
Salt crock, Butterfly, orig lid 185.00
Salt crock, Daisy on Snowflakes, orig lid, 6½x6" 220.00
Salt crock, Flying Bird, orig lid, 9" 350.00
Salt crock, Grapevine on Fence, pale bl, orig lid, 6½x6¾" 225.00
Soap dish, Beaded Rose 135.00
Soap dish, cat's head 165.00
Soap dish, Indian in War Bonnet 195.00
Syrup dispenser, Pep-So, rpl lid, 12x9" 325.00
Teapot, Swirl, dbl wire bail hdl, ball shape, 9x6½" 450.00
Toothbrush holder, Bow Tie, stenciled flower 50.00

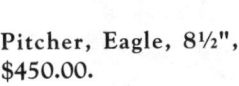
**Pitcher, Eagle, 8½",
$450.00.**

**Toothbrush holder, Beaded Ribs
with Open Rose, 5", $78.00.**

Pitcher, Eagle w/Shield & Arrows, rare 500.00
Pitcher, Edelweiss, metal thumb rest, 9x5" 300.00
Pitcher, Fishscale & Wild Rose, 10" 160.00
Pitcher, Flowers, stenciled 100.00
Pitcher, Flying Bird, 9" 550.00
Pitcher, Grape Cluster in Shield, 8x6" 225.00
Pitcher, Grape Cluster on Trellis, allover bl, 7x7" 200.00
Pitcher, Hunting Scene, rare, 7x8" 400.00
Pitcher, Indian Boy & Girl, 6" 300.00

Vase, Swirl, cone shape 300.00
Vinegar/cider crock, Brushed Leaves, stippled ground, 19x16" ...175.00
Wash set, Rose on Trellis, 2-pc 300.00
Water cooler, Apple Blossom, brass spigot, 17x15" 700.00
Water cooler, Bl Band, orig lid 175.00
Water cooler, Cupid, brass spigot, patterned lid, 15x12" 700.00

Water cooler, Polar Bear, brass NP spigot, 17x15" 700.00
Water jug, Diffused Bl, cork affixed to stopper, 7x7" 195.00

Bluebird China

Made from 1910 to 1934, Bluebird china is lovely ware decorated with bluebirds flying among pink flowering branches. It was inexpensive dinnerware and reached the height of its popularity in the second decade of this century. Several potteries produced it; shapes differ from one manufacturer to another, but the decal remains basically the same. Among the backstamps you'll find W.S. George, Cleveland, Carrolton, Homer Laughlin, Limoges China of Sebring, Ohio; and there are others.

Bowl, fruit; Homer Laughlin, 4x5½" 13.50
Bowl, gravy; w/saucer, Hopewell China 50.00
Bowl, rnd, Homer Laughlin, 8x6" 32.50
Bowl, sauce; SP Co, 4½" 12.50
Bowl, soup; WS George, 8½" 28.00
Casserole, Royal China Internat'l, 7x11½" 120.00

Footed chocolate cup, 3½", $35.00; Syrup pitcher, 4¼", $35.00.

Plate, Homer Laughlin, 8½" 15.00
Plate, PMC China, 7¼" 12.50
Plate, Steubenville China, 9" 15.00
Platter, Homer Laughlin, 10½x15½" 85.00
Platter, Homer Laughlin, 6x8" 35.00
Platter, Hopewell, 10x13" 65.00
Platter, Steubenville China, 9½x12½" 65.00
Sauce ladle, gold scrolling 40.00
Syrup, unmk, 4" 35.00
Teapot, ELP Co, 8½x8½" 125.00

Blue Ridge

Blue Ridge dinnerware was produced by Southern Potteries of Erwin, Tennessee from the late 1930s until 1956 in eight basic styles and eight hundred different patterns, all of which were hand decorated under the glaze. Vivid colors lit up floral arrangements of seemingly endless variation, fruit of every sort from simple clusters to lush assortments, barnyard fowl, peasant figures, and unpretentious textured patterns. Although it is these dinnerware lines for which they are best known, collectors prize the artist-signed plates from the forties and the limited line of character jugs made during the fifties most highly. Examples of the French Peasant pattern are valued at double the prices listed below; very simple patterns will bring 25% to 50% less.

Our advisors, Betty and Bill Newbound, have compiled a lovely book, *Blue Ridge Dinnerware, Revised Third Edition*, with beautiful color illustrations and current market values. They are listed in the Directory under Michigan. For information concerning the National Blue Ridge Newsletter, see the Clubs, Newsletters, and Catalogs section of the Directory.

Ashtray, advertising, w/rest 55.00
Ashtray, individual 13.00
Bonbon, divided, center hdls, china 85.00
Bowl, cereal/soup; 6" 9.00
Bowl, divided, 8" 25.00
Bowl, fruit; 5" 4.00
Bowl, mixing; 8½" 28.00
Bowl, rnd, 8" 13.00
Bowl, salad; 10½" 45.00
Bowl, soup; flat, 8" 15.00
Bowl, vegetable; divided, oval, 9" 22.50
Bowl, vegetable; oval, 9" 20.00
Box, candy; rnd w/lid 95.00
Box, cigarette 65.00
Box, cigarette; w/4 trays 120.00
Box, Mallard 400.00
Box, raised or sculptured designs 90.00
Box, Sherman Lily 600.00
Breakfast set 450.00
Butter dish, ¼-lb, w/lid 40.00
Butter pat/coaster 20.00
Cake lifter 22.50
Carafe, w/lid 60.00
Casserole, w/lid 40.00
Celery, leaf shape, china 30.00
Celery, Skyline shape 25.00
Child's cereal bowl 28.00
Child's feeding dish, deep 30.00
Child's feeding dish, divided 28.00
Child's mug 20.00
Child's plate 28.00
Child's play set 275.00
Chocolate pot, pedestal, china 175.00
Coffeepot 100.00

Coffeepot, Ovoid shape, $100.00.

Creamer, china 45.00
Creamer, demitasse 50.00
Creamer, regular 8.00
Cup & saucer, demitasse; china 30.00

Cup & saucer, regular	13.00
Dish, baking; 13x8"	27.50
Egg cup, dbl	25.00
Egg dish, deviled	32.50
Gravy boat	17.00
Gravy tray	17.00
Jug, batter; w/lid	70.00
Jug, character; china	500.00
Jug, syrup; w/lid	80.00
Lamp, china	110.00
Lazy susan	550.00
Pie baker	25.00
Pitcher, fancy, china	95.00
Plate, aluminum edge, 12"	19.00
Plate, artist sgn, china	500.00
Plate, cake; 10½"	30.00
Plate, Christmas or Turkey	65.00
Plate, dinner; 10"	17.00
Plate, dinner; 9½"	10.00

Plate, French Peasant, 9½", $50.00.

Plate, party; w/cup well & cup	22.50
Plate, salad; bird decor, 8½"	55.00
Plate, salad; 8½"	7.00
Plate, snack; 3-compartment	17.00
Plate, sq, 7½"	9.00
Plate, 11½"	28.00
Plate, 6"	3.00
Platter, artist sgn, 17½"	770.00
Platter, Thanksgiving Turkey	195.00
Platter, Turkey w/Acorns	195.00
Platter, 11"	11.00
Platter, 12½"	17.00
Platter, 13"	17.00
Platter, 15"	22.00
Ramekin, w/lid, 5"	20.00
Ramekin, w/lid, 7½"	25.00
Relish, deep shell, china	50.00
Relish, heart shape, sm	45.00
Relish, loop hdl, china	70.00
Relish, Maple Leaf, china	55.00
Relish, Martha, 3-compartment, china	90.00
Relish, T-hdl, china	40.00
Salad fork	30.00
Salad spoon	30.00
Server, center hdl	28.00
Shakers, Apple, pr	14.00
Shakers, Blossom Top, pr	32.50

Shakers, Bud Top, pr	32.50
Shakers, chickens, pr	90.00
Shakers, ftd, china, tall, pr	45.00
Shakers, mallards, pr	150.00
Shakers, Palisades, pr	28.00
Shakers, range; pr	32.50
Shakers, regular, short, pr	20.00
Sugar bowl, demitasse	28.00
Sugar bowl, ped or flare, china	45.00
Sugar bowl, regular, w/lid	13.00
Tea tile, rnd or sq	32.50
Teapot, china	90.00
Teapot, demitasse; china	100.00
Teapot, earthenware	80.00
Tidbit, 2-tier	30.00
Tidbit, 3-tier	32.50
Toast, covered	100.00
Tray, for chocolate pot; china	400.00
Tray, demitasse	90.00
Tray, flat shell, china	80.00
Vase, boot, 8"	70.00
Vase, bud	85.00
Vase, hdls, china, 7¼"	70.00
Vase, rnd, china, 5½"	65.00
Vase, ruffled top, 9¼"	90.00
Vase, tapered	90.00

Boch Freres

Founded in the early 1840s in La Louviere, Boch Freres Keramis became the foremost producer of art pottery in Belgium. Primarily they served a localized market, but in 1844 they earned worldwide recognition for some of their sculptural works on display at the International Exposition in Paris.

In 1907 Charles Catteau of France was appointed head of the art department. Before that time, the firm had concentrated on developing glazes and perfecting elegant forms. The style they pursued was traditional, favoring the re-creation of established 18th-century ceramics. Catteau brought with him to Boch Freres the New Wave (or Art Nouveau) influence in form and decoration. His designs won him international acclaim at the Exhibition d'Art Decoratif in Paris in 1925, and it is for his work that Boch Freres is so highly regarded today. He occasionally signed his work as well as that of others who under his direct supervision carried out his preconceived designs. He was associated with the company until 1950 and lived the remainder of his life in Nice, France, where he died in 1966. The Boch Freres Keramis factory continues to operate today, producing bathroom fixtures and other utilitarian wares. A variety of marks have been used, most incorporating some combination of 'Boch Freres,' 'Keramis,' 'BFK,' or 'Ch Catteau.' A shield topped by a crown and flanked by a 'B' and an 'F' was used as well. Our advisor for this category is Wayne B. Kielsmeier; he is listed in the Directory under Arizona.

Compote, dmn motif, bl/aqua on wht, hex base/bowl, 8"	250.00
Jardiniere, lg deer eating leaves, Catteau, #943, 8" H	1,100.00
Lamp, arcs/elongated Deco designs on lt gr crackle, 14"	350.00
Lamp, parade of penguins, wood base, bulbous, 11"	770.00
Lamp, stylized floral, cvd/mc pnt on gr, ca 1930s, 20"	210.00
Vase, floral clusters & swags on ivory, Catteau, #901, 10"	990.00
Vase, floral clusters on vertical stripes, Catteau, 13x9"	2,100.00
Vase, Jacobean floral, mc on ivory, Catteau, pear form, 11"	825.00
Vase, lg deer eating leaves on cream, ovoid, 6½"	350.00
Vase, stripes/waves/dots, turq on crazed cream, 11"	660.00

Vase, stylized flowers in yellow, blue and green on cream crazed ground, marked Keramis, 13½", $900.00.

Vase, stylized clouds, ivory/yel/bl on brn, ovoid, #721, 9" **990.00**
Vase, stylized deer/trees, blk/gold/bl, att Chevalier, 20" **4,000.00**
Vase, stylized parrots/jungle foliage, ovoid, #961B K, 20" **1,300.00**
Vase, stylized repeating floral, brn/blk/yel on gray, 12" **935.00**
Vase, vertical bands/waves/ovals, cvd/mc on cream, 12" **650.00**
Vase, 5 panels w/birds, brn on tan, folded rim, Catteau, 11" ...**1,200.00**

Boehm

Boehm sculptures were the creation of Edward Marshall Boehm, a ceramic artist who coupled his love of the art with his love of nature to produce figurines of birds, animals, and flowers in lovely background settings accurate to the smallest detail. Sculptures of historical figures and those representing the fine arts were also made and along with many of the bird figurines, have established secondary-market values many times their original prices. His first pieces were made in the very early 1950s in Trenton, New Jersey under the name of Osso Ceramics. Mr. Boehm died in 1969, and the firm has since been managed by his wife. Today known as Edward Marshall Boehm, Inc., the private family-held corporation produces not only porcelain sculptures but collector plates as well. Both limited and non-limited editions of their works have been issued. Examples are marked with various backstamps, all of which have incorporated the Boehm name since 1951. 'Osso Ceramics' in upper case lettering was used in 1950 and 1951.

American Eagle, lg **1,000.00**
Black-Capped Chickadee, #d **310.00**
Blue Grosbeak **1,450.00**
Bust of Madonna, wht bsk, mk USA, 6x5½" **200.00**
Cape May Warbler **875.00**
Cardinals, 1955 ....**3,200.00**
Catbird **1,500.00**
European Goldfinch **1,250.00**
Fledgling Magpie **145.00**
Flicker **2,400.00**

Indigo Bunting, #d **200.00**
Lapwing **2,900.00**
Least Tern, 1979 ....**2,150.00**
Meadow Lark, 1957 ....**2,500.00**
Mountain Bluebirds **5,750.00**
Nonpareil Buntings **875.00**
Parula Warblers, 1965 ....**2,500.00**
Roadrunner **2,600.00**
Screech Owl **2,600.00**
Sculpture, Pope Pius XII **1,000.00**
Song Thrushes **3,200.00**
Western Bluebirds **6,250.00**
Yellowhammers **4,000.00**
Young American Eagle, 1969 ....**1,250.00**

Bohemian Glass

The term 'Bohemian glass' has come to refer to a type of glass developed in Bohemia in the late 16th century at the Imperial Court of Rudolf II, the Hapsburg Emperor. The popular artistic pursuit of the day was stone carving, and it naturally followed to transfer familiar procedures to the glassmaking industry. During the next century, a formula was discovered that produced a glass with a fine crystal appearance which lent itself well to deep, intricate engraving, and the art was further advanced.

Although many other kinds of art glass were made there, collectors today use the term 'Bohemian glass' to most often indicate clear glass overlaid with color through which a design is cut or etched. (Unless otherwise described, the items in the listing that follows are of this type.) Red or yellow on crystal is common, but other colors may also be found. Another type of Bohemian glass involves cutting through and exposing two layers of color in patterns that are often very intricate. Items such as these are sometimes further decorated with enamel and/or gilt work. Our advisor for this category is Thomas P. Bradshaw; he is listed in the Directory under California.

Beaker, amber, snake/cornucopia/etc, 1836, 5½" **275.00**

Beaker, red, cut with trees and animals in forest scene, 4¾", $100.00.

Candy dish, red, grapes, 3-toed, lg, w/lid **125.00**
Cordial, red, scrolls & birds, 3½" **25.00**
Decanter, red, castle/deer/stork, ball form, 8", +6 cordials **185.00**
Decanter, red, grapevine mid-band/stoppers, 9", pr **150.00**

Goblet, red, stag/doe/trees, 6½" 175.00
Goblet, wine; red, deer & castle, 5⅛" 40.00
Stein, red, castle by lake, glass top, pewter mts, 5½" ...295.00
Vase, amber, grapes/mitres/X-cuts, narrow fluted neck, 6x5" 90.00
Vase, red, birds & trees, 12" 150.00
Vase, red, deer/birds/castle, ornate, 5¼" 100.00
Vase, red, deer & castle, bulbous, 3" 35.00
Vase, red, deer & castle, flared, 5" 60.00

Bookends

Though a few were produced before 1880, bookends became a necessary library accessory and a popular commodity after the printing industry was revolutionized by Mergenthaler's invention, the linotype. Books became abundantly available at such affordable prices that almost every home suddenly had need for bookends. They were carved from wood, cast in iron, bronze, or brass, or cut from stone. Today's collectors may find such designs as ships, animals, flowers, and children. Patriotic themes, art reproductions, and those with Art Nouveau and Art Deco styling provide a basis for a diverse and interesting collection.

Abraham Lincoln, seated, cast lead w/bronze finish, 6½" 65.00
Amish man (lady) seated, CI, 4¾x4¾" 125.00
Aviator, bronzed metal 45.00
Baseball player in action, pnt CI, 5" 385.00
Batter in action, plated wht metal, mk WB, 6½" 195.00
Batter in relief, cast bronze, c 1905-10, 6", EX 275.00
Boy in armchair, Nu Art 75.00
Bust of Deco lady, Frankart 165.00
Daffodil silhouette, bronze, G Thew, 1928, mk, 6" 200.00

Deco-style nude with hoop in foliage, painted cast iron, 9", $75.00.

Dutch boy & girl, Frankart, pr 125.00
End of Trail, man & horse, bronze finish on metal 45.00
Fish, Deco, bright & satin-finish nickel plate, 6" 100.00
Flower basket, pnt CI, pr 40.00
Hartford Fire Insurance, bronze, 1935 ....80.00
Horse & foal, metal on wooden base 65.00
Horse head, stylized, Frankart 120.00
Horse rearing, bronzed finish, Frankart 75.00
Indian head, pnt CI, NM 125.00
Jester on stepped plinth, bronze w/brn patina, Zach, 6" ...1,100.00
Lincoln bust, bronze flashed, 1909 Centennial, 4x6" 50.00
Lindbergh bust 125.00
Nude, bronzed cast metal, Deco style, 8½" 175.00
Nude, CI, Nouveau style 75.00
Pirate w/parrot, copper clad, mk Verona 45.00
Pitcher & batter, plated wht metal, mk WB, 8", EX 575.00

Scottie dog, Frankart 145.00
Spaniel, wht metal w/ebonized & bronze finish, 4" 75.00
Sunbonnet Girl, pnt CI 125.00

Bootjacks and Bootscrapers

Bootjacks were made from metal or wood. Some were fancy figural shapes, others strictly business! Their purpose was to facilitate the otherwise awkward process of removing one's boots. Bootscrapers were handy gadgets that provided an effective way to clean the soles of mud and such.

Bootjacks

Am Bull Dog, CI, pistol shaped, folding, blk pnt, 8" 75.00
Beetle, orig worn pnt, Reading PA, 4x11x3", EX 115.00
Boss emb on shaft, lacy CI, 15" L 135.00

Cast iron with black paint, openwork between hexagonal supports, 6" long, $65.00.

Cricket, Webster Bros & Co, Reading PA, 11" 55.00
Fish (stylized), cvd wood, worn finish, 22" L 115.00
Heart figural, scalloped sides, CI, 13" L 130.00
Lever action, wood & CI, EX 100.00
Naughty Nellie, CI, mc pnt, 11x5x2½", EX 200.00
Naughty Nellie, CI, pnt traces, 9" 85.00
Pine w/sq nails, lg, early 150.00
Try Me, CI, openwork, no pnt, ca 1890s, 12x4x1¾" 70.00
V-shape, ornate CI, VG 45.00

Bootscrapers

Aunt Jemima figure atop, CI, rpt, 14½" 250.00
CI, on pan w/griffins, worn pnt, 13x17½" 215.00
Dachshund, CI, old worn wht pnt, 1900s, 7x22x5" 225.00
Deco fox/hare, hammered wrought iron, Dieterich, 7x14" ...1,300.00
Duck, full bodied, scraper on bk, CI, 14½" L 350.00
Pointer on 'bridge,' brushes in base at 1 time, CI/rpt, 16" 330.00
Wrought iron, ram's horn scrolls, in marble block 135.00
Wrought iron, simple uprights w/scooped blade set in stone 150.00
Wrought iron, spiral coiled finials, in sandstone block, 12" 300.00
2 quail ea end, CI, rectangular pan, pnt traces, 7x16" 275.00

Boru, Sorcha

Sorcha Boru was the professional name used by California ceramist

Claire Stewart. She was a founding member of the Allied Arts Guild of Menlo Park (California) where she maintained a studio from 1932 to 1938. From 1938 until 1955, she operated Sorcha Boru Ceramics, a production studio in San Carlos. Her highly acclaimed output consisted of colorful, slip-decorated figurines, salt and pepper shakers, vases, wall pockets, and flower bowls. Most production work was incised 'S.B.C.' by hand.

Bowl, maroon, appl peony on lid, 6" 65.00
Bowl, pussy willows on beige, 10" 55.00
Cup, 3 dinosaur hdls 45.00
Figurine, angel w/Christmas tree, 6" 75.00
Figurine, bluebird, 5x10" 95.00
Figurine, little Blk girl, 6" 275.00
Figurine, 2 girls dancing, hands clasped 145.00
Pitcher, pk lustre florals w/gold centers, beading, 6½" 65.00
Planter, appl flowers, pr 125.00
Shakers, fawns, turq, sm, pr 45.00
Shakers, sailor boy & girl, pr 65.00
Sugar shaker, lady figural, 6" 85.00

Bottle Openers

Around the turn of the century, manufacturers began to seal bottles with a metal cap that required a new type of bottle opener. Now the screw cap and the flip top have made bottle openers nearly obsolete. There are many variations, some in combination with other tools. Many openers were used as means of advertising a product. Various materials were used, including silver and brass.

A figural bottle opener is defined as a figure designed for the sole purpose of lifting a bottle cap. The actual opener must be an integral part of the figure itself. A base-plate opener is one where the lifter is a separate metal piece attached to the underside of the figure. The major producers of iron figurals were Wilton Products, John Wright Inc., Gadzik Sales, and L & L Favors. Openers may be free-standing and three-dimensional, wall hung, or flat. They can be made of cast iron (often painted), brass, bronze, or aluminum.

Numbers within the listings refer to *Figural Bottle Openers* by the FBOC (Figural Bottle Opener Collectors) organization. Those seeking additional information are encouraged to contact FBOC, whose address can be found in the Directory under Clubs, Newsletters, and Catalogs.

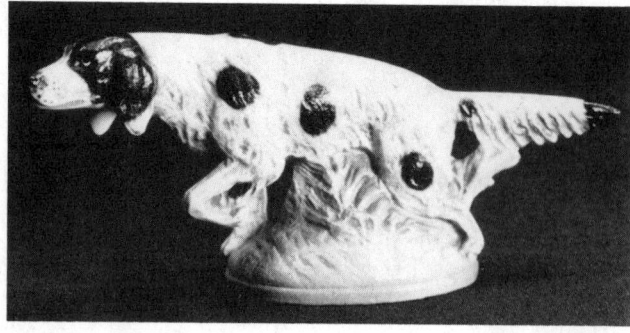

**Hunting dog, painted cast iron, marked Rubal, New York, 3",
$45.00.**

Alligator & boy, CI, J Wright, F-133 ....200.00
Auto jack, chrome, mk Duff Norton, F-211 ....30.00
Bear head, CI, J Wright, F-426, VG pnt 65.00
Billy goat, CI, J Wright, F-74 ....150.00
Canada goose, CI, Wilton Pdts, F-105 ....65.00

Clown head, CI, J Wright, F-417 ....95.00
Cockatoo, CI, J Wright, F-121, 1947, VG 180.00
Cowboy & signpost, CI, J Wright, F-14 ....125.00
Cowboy w/guitar, CI, J Wright, F-27, VG 80.00
Cowboy w/guitar & cactus, HBM, F-28, 4⅝" 350.00
Dachshund, brass, F-83 ....30.00
Deco parrot w/corkscrew, chrome, F-117 ....15.00
Dinky Dan, CI, Gadzik Sales, F-42 ....375.00
Donkey, CI, J Wright, F-61, EX 35.00
False teeth, CI, Wilton Pdts, F-420 ....65.00
Flamingo, HBM, Wilton Pdts, F-120 ....95.00
Foundryman, CI, J Wright, F-29, EX 100.00
Goat, Wilton Pdts, F-71 ....40.00
Hanging drunk, Wilton Pdts, F-415 ....75.00
Iroquois Indian, aluminum, F-197, EX 20.00
Mallard, Wilton Pdts, F-106 ....60.00
Miss 4-Eyes, CI, Wilton Pdts, F-408, VG 50.00
Monkey, blk & wht, J Wright, F-89 ....130.00
Nude, standing w/wreath above head, brass, EX details, F-172 .....25.00
Palm tree, Wilton Pdts, F-21 ....140.00
Parrot, long bl tail, J Wright, F-108, 5¼" 30.00
Parrot, Wilton Pdts, F-112, sm 40.00
Pelican, J Wright, F-130, M 125.00
Pretzel, aluminum, F-230, EX pnt 40.00
Rooster, pot metal, wht, hollow, F-98, VG 65.00
Sailor, CI, J Wright, F-17, EX 40.00
Setter dog, CI, blk/wht, J Wright, F-79, 1947, EX 55.00
Skunk, CI, J Wright, F-92, 1947, EX 140.00
Squirrel, J Wright, F-91 ....80.00
4-eyed lady, CI, J Wright, F-407 ....50.00
4-eyed man, CI, J Wright, F-413, EX 55.00

Bottles and Flasks

As far back as the 1st century B.C., the Romans preferred blown glass containers for their pills and potions. Though you're not apt to find many of those, you will find bottles of every size, shape, and color made to hold perfume, ink, medicine, soda, spirits, vinegar, and many other liquids. American business firms preferred glass bottles in which to package their commercial products and used them extensively from the late 18th century on. Bitters bottles contained 'medicine' (actually herb-flavored alcohol) and, judging from the number of these found today, their contents found favor with many! Because of a heavy tax imposed on the sale of liquor in 17th-century England by King George, who hoped to curtail alcohol abuse among his subjects, bottlers simply added 'curative' herbs to their brew and thus avoided taxation. Since gin was taxed in America as well, the practice continued in this country. Scores of brands were sold; among the most popular were Dr. H.S. Flint & Co. Quaker Bitters, Dr. Kaufman's Anti-Cholera Bitters, and Dr. J. Hostetter's Stomach Bitters. Most bitters bottles were made in shades of amber, brown, and aquamarine. Clear glass was used to a lesser extent, as were green tones. Blue, amethyst, red-brown, and milk glass examples are rare. (Please note that color is a strong factor when pricing bottles. For example, an amber Hostetter's Bitters sells for $25.00 or less, but a green variant can bring hundreds of dollars. An aqua scroll flask may bring $50.00, but a cobalt blue variation will command over $1,000.00.)

Perfume or scent bottles were produced abroad by companies all over Europe from the late 16th century on. Perfume making became such a prolific trade that as a result beautifully decorated bottles were fashionable. In America they were produced in great quantities by Stiegel in 1770 and by Boston and Sandwich in the early 19th century. Cologne bottles were first made in about 1830 and toilet-water bottles in the 1880s. Rene Lalique produced fine scent bottles from as early as the turn of the century. The first were one-of-a-kind creations with silver casings. He later designed bottles for the Coty Perfume Company with a different style for each Coty fragrance. Prices for commercial perfumes vary according to condition, whether it is sealed and full, and if it has the original label and most of the original packaging or box. Deluxe versions bring premium prices. Example: blue flat Dans La Nuit cologne by Rene Lalique, value for 6" size, $250.00. Dans La Nuit, enameled with stars by Rene Lalique, 3" round ball, $900.00.

Spirit flasks from the 19th century were blown in specially designed molds with varied motifs including political subjects, railroad trains, and symbolic devices. The most commonly used colors were amber, dark brown, and green.

From the 20th century, early pop and beer bottles are very collectible, as is nearly every extinct commercial container. Dairy bottles are a relatively new area of interest; look for round bottles in good condition with both city and state as well as a nice graphic relating to the farm or the dairy.

Bottles may be dated by the methods used in their production. For instance, a rough pontil indicates a date before 1845. After the bottle was blown, a pontil rod was attached to the bottom, a glob of molten glass acting as the 'glue.' This allowed the glassblower to continue to manipulate the extremely hot bottle until it was finished. From about 1845 until approximately 1860, the molten glass 'glue' was omitted. The rod was simply heated to a temperature high enough to cause it to afix itself to the bottle. When the rod was snapped off, a metallic residue was left on the base of the bottle; this is called an 'iron pontil'. A seam that reaches from base to lip marks a machine-made bottle from after 1903, while an applied or hand-finished lip points to an early mold-blown bottle. The Industrial Revolution saw keen competition between manufacturers, and as a result, scores of patents were issued. Many concentrated on various types of closures; the crown bottle cap, for instance, was patented in 1892. If a manufacturer's name is present, consulting a book on marks may help you date your bottle.

Among our advisors for this category are Madeleine France (see the Directory under Florida), Mark Vuono (Connecticut), Steve Ketcham (Minnesota), Monsen and Baer (Virginia), and John Tutton (Virginia). In the listings that follow (most of which have been taken from auction catalogs), glass is assumed to be clear unless color is indicated. Numbers refer to a standard reference book, *American Glass*, by George and Helen McKearin. See also Advertising, various companies; Avon; Barber Shop Collectibles; Blown Glass; Blown Three-Mold Glass; California Perfume Company; Czechoslovakia; De Vilbiss; Firefighting; Lalique; Medical Collectibles; Steuben.

Key:
am — applied mouth	GW — Glass Works
bbl — barrel	ip — iron pontil
bt — blob top	ps — pontil scar
b3m — blown 3-mold	rm — rolled mouth
cm — collared mouth	sb — smooth base
fm — flared mouth	sl — sloping
gm — ground mouth	sm — sheared mouth
gp — graphite pontil	tm — tooled mouth
grd — ground pontil	

Barber Bottles

Amethyst, HP wht floral, orange & wht beads	65.00
Amethyst, Mary Gregory type, wht cottage, 8½"	325.00
Clambroth, porc stopper, 'Water' label, 7½x3½", EX	40.00
Clear opal w/stripes, rm, 7"	65.00
Clear w/silver HP geometrics, sm, 1925-35, 7"	40.00

Cobalt, Mary Gregory-type boy, tm/ps, bulbous, 8"	260.00
Cobalt cut to clear, floral-cut base, w/orig stopper, 6"	110.00
Coin Spot, cranberry, bulbous, 7"	80.00
Emerald gr, Mary Gregory-type man w/net in hand, lg	150.00
Emerald gr, mc florals, waisted cylinder, tm/ps, 7½"	110.00
Hobnail, clear opal, ground base, 7½"	120.00
Hobnail, cranberry opal, 4 neck rings, 7½"	50.00
Milk glass, 'Cologne' & HP floral, 9"	95.00
Milk glass, 'Hair Tonic' w/mc flowers, rm, 9"	125.00
Milk glass, HP decor, cylindrical, 11"	120.00
Red Fox, hair oil, 1940s, M w/contents	15.00
Royal bl, gold leaf & wht enameling, lg	95.00
Spanish Lace, cranberry opal, sq ground base, 8½"	195.00

Bitters Bottles

E. Dexter Loveridge/Wahoo Bitters – DWD – 1863 – XXX – Patd., L-126, deep amber, smooth base, applied mouth, inside stain, 9¾", $250.00.

Alpine, bright yel-gr, globular ribbed form, 5½x6½"	110.00
AMS 2/1864 Constitution..., dk amethyst, ribs, am, 9¼"	1,650.00
Atwood's Vegetable Syspeptic, aqua, am/ip, 6½"	120.00
Bakers Orange Grove, olive-amber, 2 full labels, stain, 9½"	375.00
Bakers Orange Grove, yel, sq w/roped corners, am, 9½"	725.00
Barto's/Great Gun..., amber, am/sb, cannon, 11"	3,150.00
Ben-Hur Celebrated Stomach New Orleans, gold-amber, 9"	50.00
Bitter Witch, amber, witch emb, oval, dbl cm/sb, 8"	175.00
Brown's Celebrated Indian Herb Pat 1867, aqua, 12⅛"	6,875.00
Brown's Celebrated Indian Herb Pat 1867, gold-amber, 12", EX	145.00
Brown's Celebrated Indian Herb Pat 1867, med gold-amber, 12"	325.00
Brown's Celebrated Indian Herb Pat 1867, yel, 12¼"	3,000.00
Brown's Celebrated Indian Herb Pat 1868, chocolate-amber, 12"	300.00
Brown's Celebrated Indian Herb Pat 1868, yel-gr, 12"	2,950.00
Canteen Bitters For All Disorders..., dk bl-gr, am/sb, 9¾"	900.00
Catawba Wine, yel-emerald gr, emb grapes, am/sb, 9½"	1,700.00
Clarke's Vegetable Sherry Wine Sharon MA, aqua, cm/sb, 14"	275.00
Curtis Cordial Calisaya..., olive-yel, sb/am, 11½"	3,550.00
David Andrews/Vegetable..., aqua, am/ps, tombstone, 8"	675.00
Dingens' Napoleon Cocktail..., gold-amber, am/ip, 9½"	4,000.00
Dingens' Napoleon Cocktail..., med olive-amber, ped ft, 10"	2,500.00

Doyle's Hop 1872, citron, branch emb, am/sb, 1880s, 9¾" 1,500.00
Dr Beach's, med yel-amber, am/sb, semi-cabin, 9¾" 2,150.00
Dr Birmingham's Anti Billious..., med emerald gr, 8¾" 7,000.00
Dr CW Roback's Stomach, deep olive gr, am/sb, bbl, 9⅝" 2,700.00
Dr CW Roback's Stomach Cincinnati O, apricot-yel, bbl, 10" ..2,800.00
Dr CW Roback's Stomach Cincinnati O, apricot-yel, bbl, 9½" ..900.00
Dr J Hostetter's Stomach, amber, open bubble, 9" 20.00
Dr Stephen Jewett's Celebrated Health..., olive-amber, 7⅛" ...1,400.00
Dr Stephen Jewett's Celebrated Health..., yel-amber, cm, 7½" ...850.00
Dr Stoughten's Nat'l Hamburg PA, med amber, am/sb, 10" 1,700.00
Dr Wonser's...Indian Root, med to dk root-beer amber, 11" ...2,200.00
Dr XX Lovegood's Family, amber, am/sb, sq cabin, 11" 1,850.00
Favorite Powell & Stutenroth Pat Appl For, amber, bbl, 9" 7,650.00
Globe Mfg Only By Byrne Bros...NY, yel-amber, cannon, 10¾" .575.00
Great Tonic Caldwells Herb, gold-amber, triangular, 12¼" 300.00
Greeley's Bourbon, G-101, pk-amber, cm/sb, bbl, 9¼" 355.00
Greeley's Bourbon, med olive gr, cm/sb, bbl, 9⅜" 1,600.00
Greeley's Bourbon Whiskey, med copper-puce, am/sb, 9¼" 350.00
Hall's, med amber w/hint of puce, sb/am, bbl, 9½" 2,350.00
Holtzermann's Pat Stomach, gold-amber, 4-roof cabin, 10" 180.00
Holtzermann's Pat Stomach, honey-amber, 2-roof cabin, 9" 2,500.00
HP Herb Wild Cherry, bright gr, cherry tree emb, cabin, 8¾" 3,800.00
HP Herb Wild Cherry, med amber, sl cm/sb, orig foil, 10" 230.00
Julius Jungbluth, med gold-amber, 12-sided, 10⅜" 90.00
Kelly's Old Cabin Patd 1863, apricot-yel, am/sb, cabin, 9¼" ...1,450.00
Kelly's Old Cabin Patd 1863, dk olive gr, cabin, 9⅛" 4,350.00
Kelly's Old Cabin Patd 1863, yel-amber, cabin, 9⅛" 975.00
Keystone, med gold-amber, am/sb, bbl, 9¾" 600.00
Kimball's Jaundice, honey olive-amber, am/ip, 7" 350.00
Kimball's Jaundice, olive-amber, am/ip, 7" 475.00
Litthauer Stomach Invented 1864..., milk glass, am/sb, 9⅜" 155.00
McKeevers Army Bitters, M-58, amber, sl cm/sb, drum, 10½" ...1,980.00
Nat'l, med pk-puce, am/sb, ear of corn, 12¼" 1,100.00
Nat'l Pat 1867, gold-amber, am/sb, ear of corn, lt haze, 12" 220.00
Nat'l Pat 1867, yel, am/sb, ear of corn, 12⅜" 500.00
Old Homestead Wild Cherry Pat, gold-amber, cabin, 9½" 125.00
Old Homestead Wild Cherry Pat, med gold-amber, cabin, 9¾" ..400.00
Old Sachem & Wigwam Tonic, bright amber, am/ip, bbl, 9⅜" ..200.00
Old Sachem & Wigwam Tonic, dk red-puce, cm/sb, bbl, 9" 245.00
Old Sachem & Wigwam Tonic, med gasoline-copper, bbl, 9½" .600.00
Only 75 Cts Clarke's Vegetable Sherry Wine..., aqua, am, 12" ...160.00
Queen Louise German Brand..., olive gr, mc label, 11½" 75.00
Reinhardt's German Vegetable Elixer, aqua, rm, 3¾" 220.00
Russ St Domingo NY, bright yel-olive gr, am/sb, sq, 10" 450.00
Russian Imperial Tonic, aqua, sq w/roped corners, 9½" 725.00
Simons Centennial Trade Mark, aqua, Washington bust, 10" 475.00
ST Drakes 1860 Plant'n X Pat 1862, celery gr, 6-log, 9⅝" 2,500.00
ST Drakes 1860 Plant'n X Pat 1862, champagne-yel, 6-log, 10" ...725.00
ST Drakes 1860 Plant'n X Pat 1862, dk strawberry-puce, 10" 125.00
ST Drakes 1860 Plant'n X Pat 1862, gold-amber, 6-log, 9⅞" 145.00
ST Drakes 1860 Plant'n X Pat 1862, honey-amber, 4-log 145.00
ST Drakes 1860 Plant'n X Pat 1862, med bl-gr, 6-log, 10" 3,450.00
ST Drakes 1860 Plant'n X Pat 1862, olive-yel, 6-log, 10" 600.00
ST Drakes 1860 Plant'n X Pat 1862, puce, 6-log, 10" 130.00
ST Drakes 1860 Plant'n X Pat 1862, strawberry-puce, 6-log, 10" ..300.00
Staudingers NY, olive gr, am/sb, lady's leg, 9¼" 250.00
Thos A Hurley's Stomach Louisville Ky, med yel-amber, 10½" ..650.00
Walker's Tonic, med yel-amber, lady's leg neck, 11½" 775.00
Wm Allen's Congress, emerald gr, sb/am, 10¼" 525.00

Blown Glass Bottles and Flasks

Chestnut flask, bright olive gr, am/ps, 1780-1830, 5⅝" 145.00
Chestnut flask, bright olive-amber, am/ps, 1780-1830, 5⅝" 130.00

Chestnut flask, dk forest gr, am/ps, 8⅜" 135.00
Chestnut flask, gold-amber, am/ps, 1820-50, 11¼" 150.00
Chestnut flask, gold-amber w/olive tones, 24-rib, sm/ps, 5¼" 385.00
Chestnut flask, med olive-amber, flattened teardrop, 5⅜" 180.00
Chestnut flask, olive gr, free-blown, am/ps, 1780-1830, 8⅜" 110.00
Chestnut flask, olive gr, sl cm/ps, 1780-1830, 8½" 120.00
Chestnut flask, olive-amber, am w/bevel, ps, flake, 11" 145.00
Chestnut flask, sapphire bl, spiral threaded neck, am/ps, 4" 525.00
Decanter, b3m, 'Rum' emb, ps, 1-qt 330.00
Decanter, GI-29, b3m, ps, #21 stopper, ½-pt 120.00
Decanter, GI-29, b3m, ps, ribbed tam-o'-shanter stopper 660.00
Decanter, GII-10, gray-aqua, b3m, fm, period stopper, 1-qt 60.00
Decanter, GII-18, b3m, rare sqd-off shape, ½-pt 175.00
Decanter, GII-18, b3m, 3 quilled neck bands, ps, 1-pt 145.00
Decanter, GII-22, b3m, 3 dbl rigaree bands, ps, 1-qt 175.00
Decanter, GII-27 (similar), b3m, fm, w/stopper, 1-pt 160.00
Decanter, GIII-15, b3m, fm/ps, period stopper, 1-qt, EX 80.00
Decanter, GIII-16, olive-amber, b3m, sm/ps, Keene, 1-pt 330.00
Decanter, GIII-20, b3m, ps, #22 stopper, 1825-40, 1-pt 200.00
Decanter, GIII-26, b3m, ps, 1925-40, 1-pt 110.00
Decanter, GIII-6, b3m, fm/ps, no stopper, 1-pt 140.00
Decanter, GIII-6, b3m, ps, #2 stopper, ½-pt 190.00
Decanter, GIII-6, pale gray, snake threading on neck, 1-pt 800.00
Decanter, GIII-9, b3m, fm/ps, 1820-40, 1-pt 170.00
Decanter, GIV-5, b3m, ps, scratched, #26 stopper, 1-qt 135.00
Decanter, GIV-7, 'Brandy,' b3m, ps, broken bubble, 1-qt 190.00
Decanter, GIV-7, 'Gin' emb, sm/ps, w/period stopper, 1-pt 335.00
Decanter, GV-12, b3m, fm/ps, period stopper, 1-qt, EX 90.00
Decanter, GV-13, b3m, fm/ps, 1820-40, 1-qt 100.00
Decanter, GV-8, b3m, fm/ps, 1820-40, 1-qt 120.00
Decanter, med aqua, free-blown, 3 quilled neck rings, 1-qt 145.00
Flask, GII-24, bright yel-gr, from ½-pt decanter form 19,000.00
Gin type, yel-gr, sq tapered form, am/ps, 1780-1830, 10" 95.00
Globular, med olive-yel, rm/ps, w/o flattened sides, 5¼" 150.00
Nursing, filler hole mid body, appl nipple, fm, 1830s, 9¾" 150.00
Pitkin flask, bright med gr, 19 broken rib swirl, sm/ps, 6" 525.00
Pitkin flask, bright yel-gr, sm/ps, 1820-60, wear, ½-pt 150.00
Pitkin flask, cobalt, 18 vertical ribs, sm/ps, flake, ½-pt 440.00
Pitkin flask, dk olive gr, 36 broken rib swirl, ca 1800, 7" 495.00
Pitkin flask, dk to med gold-amber, 36 broken rib swirl, ½-pt 500.00
Pitkin flask, gr, 16-rib swirl, sm/ps, 1800-30, 5¾" 350.00
Pitkin flask, med olive gr, 36 broken rib swirl, sm/ps, 6½" 300.00
Pitkin flask, med yel-gr, 32 broken rib swirl, 6½" 325.00
Pitkin flask, yel-olive, 38-rib swirl, sm/ps, 6⅞" 260.00
Pocket flask, olive gr, am/ps, flattened oval, 4½" 55.00
Snuff, yel-amber, flared tm/ps, flake, 4" 130.00
Toilet water, GI-3-2, cobalt, b3m, fm/ps, w/stopper, 6⅜" 190.00
Toilet water, GI-3-2, deep sapphire bl, b3m, fm/ps 165.00
Toilet water, GI-7-4, deep sapphire bl, b3m, fm/ps, 6" 165.00
Toilet water, GI-7-4, sapphire bl, b3m, fm/ps, 6¾", EX 120.00
Utility, dk yel-olive, dip mold, cylindrical, cm/ps, 9½" 80.00
Utility, olive gr, appl sl cm, ps, 1840-60, 7⅞x3¾" 120.00
Utility, yel-lime gr, rectangular, cm/ps, 1840-60, 5½" 175.00

Cologne, Perfume, and Toilet Water Bottles

Amethyst, 10-sided, corset waist, tm/sb, New England, 6½" 300.00
Amethyst, 12-sided, sb/am, New England, 4¾" 120.00
Amethyst, 22-sided, am/sb, New England, lt haze, 6½" 105.00
Aventurine, mc w/gold spangles, lays down, hinged lid 255.00
Blown, doughnut form, w/cut design, 2" 55.00
Blown, swirled ribs, coiled tail, 3", NM 65.00
French enamel, garden scene w/man or lady, 4¼", pr 285.00
Peacock bl, 8-sided, waisted, wide front/bk, 4¾" 360.00

Pressed glass with gold diagonal, 14k gold top, Dutch hallmarks, 4", in original fitted case, $275.00.

Pressed, canary, waisted/elipse pattern, teardrop stopper, 8" 420.00
Sea horse, lt aqua, wht loopings, appl rigaree, 3½" 165.00
Yel-gr w/silver o/l, fm, bulbous, ca 1900, 3¼x2⅛" 240.00

Commercial Perfume Bottles

#49, Hattie Carnegie, gold woman's head & shoulders, 4" 500.00
Belle de Jour, D'Orsay, wht satin glass, molded ribbon, 5½" 415.00
Caravan de France, Aubusson, clear flat oval, 2¾", MIB 35.00
Cassandra, Weil, column form, gold label, 3½", sealed 90.00
Chu Chin Chow, Bryenne, cobalt, wht opal overcap, 2⅜" 750.00
Cie, Shulton Cosmetics, gemstone-like stopper, 3⅜", +box 75.00
Collage, Adele Simpson, clear urn shape w/ped base, empty, 6" ...50.00
Danger, Ciro, stacked rectangles, blk Bakelite cap, 3" 60.00
Detchema, Revillon, snifter form, label on stopper, 2", +box 88.00
Essence Rare, Houbigant, polyhedron shape, gold cap, 3⅞" 115.00
Evening in Paris, Bourjois, cobalt, w/atomizer, 2", +box 105.00
Forever Amber, Kathryn, woman's torso, abstract stopper, 9¼" 95.00
Gamin, Fragonard, gold covered urn form, 2⅜" 88.00
Golden Shadows, Evyan, bell shape, gold label, 3¼", sealed 55.00
HIS, House for Men, tuxedo form, face-shaped stopper, 6¼" 145.00
Intoxication, D'Orsay, star-shaped stopper, 6", sealed, MIB 95.00
Invitation, Jean Patou, faceted sides, front label, 3" 85.00
L'Aimant, Coty, flask, gr cap, front label, 4", +box 22.00
L'Heur Intime, Vigny, molded sqs, front label, 4" 50.00
Le Narcisse Noir, Caron, clear w/blk stopper, 2¼", 3½", pr 150.00
Mystikum, Scherk, front label, 3", sealed, M in yel box 88.00
New Horizons, Ciro, bl enameling, eagle figural cap, 2¾" 45.00
On Dit, Elizabeth Arden, women whispering, frosted, 3¾" 415.00
Perfidia, Saravel, front label, blk stopper, 2¾", +box 650.00
Sequoia, Pierre Dune, 4¼" w/3¼" stopper, 1920s, M 525.00
Slumber Song, Helena Rubenstein, angel form, 6½", +box 660.00
Snob, Le Galion, column shape, gold labels, 2", +box 22.00
Stradivari, Matchabelli, crown shape, gr/gold, 2¼" 110.00
Strategy, Mary Chess, knight chesspc form, enameling, 4¼" 85.00
Tabu, Dana, front label, frosted stopper, 6¾", sealed 55.00
Taglio, Lucien Lelong, rectangular w/medallion, 2⅜", +box 105.00
Tornade, Revillon, scalloped side, gold label, 2¾", MIB 45.00
Tourjours Fidele, D'Orsay, dog on pillow stopper, 3½" 400.00

Vivons, Merle Norman, rectangular, 4", empty in box 45.00
Voeu de Noel, Caron, emb florals on wht opal, 3½" 525.00
Votre Charm, Celares, gold enameling on clear, 3¼", +box 38.50

Dairy

Allentown Dairy Co Inc emb, 1-pt 4.50
Alta Crest Farms, Spencer Mass, gr, w/paper cap, NM 900.00

Alta Crest Farms milk bottle, green with paper seat cap, Alta Crest top cover, light case wear, $700.00.

Chewton Dairy, Wampum, PA, Abe Lincoln, red pyro, 1-qt 35.00
Deary Brothers, DB in dmn, red pyro, 1-qt 12.50
English Dairy, Salem NJ, pyro, ½-pt 5.00
Gardner Dairy, amber, sq, 1-qt 12.00
Green's Dairy, Ashland Penna, gr pyro, baby top, 1-qt 80.00
HC Hall's Willow Spring Dairy emb, 1-pt 3.00
JH Brokhoff, Pottsville PA emb, cream top, 1-pt 15.00
Mackenzie Guernsey Milk...Keene NH, calf, orange, 1-qt 20.00
Maine Condensed Milk Co, Boston, tin top emb Am 1890, ½-pt ..50.00
Melrose Diary, Ormond Fla, bl pyro, 1-qt 15.00
Modern Dairy, Berlin PA, red pyro, cream top, 1-qt 35.00
People's Milk Co emb, amber, 1-qt, EX 65.00
PM Bupp York PA emb, 1-qt 12.00
Royal Dairy, Hanover PA emb, 1-pt 6.00
Seward Dairy Milk, Seward Alaska, red pyro, 1-qt 75.00
Spencer Milk Co, Sydney NY emb, ¼-pt 15.00
Superior Creamery, Superior Wis emblem emb, 1-qt 12.00
Twilley's Dairy, Cambridge MD, red pyro, 1-qt 15.00
Walker's Creamery, Warren PA, red pyro, 1-gal 25.00

Figural Bottles

Bear, dk gr, cm/sb, w/full label, Russia, 1860-90, 11⅜" 125.00
Boot, T Parker Deptford Stone Pottery, emb star, 8¼" 200.00
Coachman, pottery, toby form, cobalt/salt glaze, 8", EX 65.00
Dog, appl ft & head, ps, early, ca 1750s, 4¼x7" 285.00
Flintlock pistol, pottery, brn, mk S Green England, 9" 150.00
Flintlock pistol, pottery, lt brn, England, 1840-60, 9½" 260.00
Pig, Berkshire Amann & Co Cincinnati O, amber, 10½" 1,600.00
Pig, Berkshire Bitters, amber, am/sb, 1860-80, 4x10⅛" 1,300.00
Pig, Suffolk Bitters, amber, rnd cm w/bevel, 10½" 550.00
Pig, Suffolk Bitters, yel-amber, dbl cm, lt wear, 10" 385.00
Pineapple, JFL Capitol Bitters, bright med gold-amber, 9¼" ...1,350.00
Pineapple, Patd Oct 1st 1870 By AL Lacraix, aqua, 9⅛" 950.00

Pineapple, W&Co NY, amber, am/ps, 8¼" 180.00
Pineapple, W&Co NY, med bl-gr, am/ps, 8⅜" 2,750.00
Pineapple, W&Co NY, olive gr, am/ps, 8⅜" 1,000.00
Pineapple, W&Co NY, olive-yel, dbl cm/ps, 8½" 990.00
Pineapple, yel-amber, dbl cm, ps, att Whitney, 8½" 275.00
Revolver, ceramic, steel bl/blk, England, 1900s, 4¼x7⅜" 50.00

Flasks

Adams/Jefferson, GI-114, gold-amber, sm/ps, 1830-50, ½-pt 120.00
Baltimore Monument/Liberty & Union, GVI-3, aqua, cm/ps, 1-pt..200.00
Baltimore Monument/Sloop, GVI-2, bright yel-gr, sm/ps, ½-pt ..325.00
Beaded Eagle/Sunburst, GII-7, lt emerald gr, sm, 1-pt 4,000.00
Charter Oak/Eagle, GII-60, med gold-amber, lt stain, ½-pt 1,000.00
Clasped Hands/Eagle, GXII-18, pale gr-aqua, am/sb, 1-pt 60.00
Clasped Hands/Eagle, GXII-2, aqua, dbl cm/ip, 1845-60, 1-qt 150.00
Columbia/Eagle, GI-117, aqua, sm/ps, sm chip, 1-pt 300.00
Columbia/Eagle, GI-121, aqua, sm/ps, 1830-50, 1-pt 190.00
Columbus, GI-127, gm w/threading, sb, ½-pt 150.00
Concentric Ring Eagle, GII-76, sea gr, sm/ps, crack, 1-qt 650.00
Corn for the World, GVI-4, olive gr, flattened cm, 1-qt 880.00
Cornucopia/Cornucopia, GIII-2, aqua, sm/ps, ½-pt 80.00
Cornucopia/Urn, GIII-12, bright olive-amber, sm/ps, ½-pt 110.00
Cornucopia/Urn, GIII-14, emerald gr, sm/ps, ½-pt 255.00
Cornucopia/Urn, GIII-16, dk aqua, sm/ps, open bubble, 1-pt 200.00
Cornucopia/Urn, GIII-17, bright bl-gr, sm/ps, 1-pt 140.00
Cornucopia/Urn, GIII-17, teal gr, sm/ps, open bubble, 1-pt 80.00
Dbl Eagle, GII-103, brilliant bl, am/sb, 1-qt 160.00
Dbl Eagle, GII-24, lt turq, sm/ps, 1850s, 1-pt 155.00

Double Eagle, GII-24, sapphire blue, sheared lip, pontil scar, Kentucky Glassworks, pint, $3,500.00.

Dbl Eagle, GII-3 variant, aqua, sm/ps, 1-pt 225.00
Dbl Eagle, GII-31, dk aqua, rnd cm/ps, 1855-65, 1-qt 2,200.00
Dbl Eagle, GII-70, bright olive gr, sm/ps, 1820-48, 1-pt 155.00
Dbl Eagle, GII-70, dk olive gr, sm/ps, 1830-48, 1-pt 140.00
Dbl Eagle, GII-71, yel-olive, sm/ps, ½-pt 150.00
Dbl Eagle, GII-78, olive-amber, sm/ps, lt wear, 1-qt 240.00
Dbl Eagle, GII-88, bright olive-amber, sm/ps, ½-pt 75.00
Eagle/Cornucopia, GII-11, lt gr-aqua, sm/ps, flakes, ½-pt 110.00
Eagle/Cornucopia, GII-73, yel-olive, expanded mouth, 1-pt ...9,000.00
Eagle/Flag, GII-53, aqua, rm/ps, 1836-47, 1-pt 100.00
Eagle/Grapes, GII-56, yel, sm/ps, prof rpr, ½-pt 325.00
Eagle/Liberty, GII-60, aqua, sm/ps, ½-pt 175.00
Eagle/Stag, GII-49, aqua, sm/ps, 1836-47, 1-pt 190.00

Eagle/Tree, GII-60, dk gold-amber, sm/ps, 1820s, ½-pt 1,200.00
Eagle/Willington Glass Co, GII-62, emerald gr, cm/sb, 1-pt 600.00
Eagle/Willington Glass Co, GII-63, bright yel-gr, ½-pt 285.00
Eagle/Willington Glass Co, GII-64, dk forest gr, 1-pt 145.00
Early Eagle/Cornucopia, GII-16, dk aqua, sm, 1820s, ½-pt 280.00
Emil Larson type, amethyst, invt swirled dmn, sm/ps, 5⅝" 110.00
For Pike's Peak/Eagle, GII-21, lt bl-gr, am/sb, 1-pt 275.00
For Pike's Peak/Eagle, GXI-22, aqua, sm/sb, 1860-80, 1-pt 60.00
Franklin/Dyott, GI-94, aqua, sm/ps, 1820-40, 1-pt 125.00
Franklin/Dyott, GI-96, aqua, sm/ps, 1820-40, 1-qt 150.00
General Lafayette/Eagle, GI-90, aqua, sm/ps, 1820-40, 1-pt 110.00
Good Game Stag/Willow Tree, GX-1, aqua, sm/ps, 1836-47, 1-pt ..90.00
Hero of Manila/Admiral Dewey, oval, gm/sb, 1900, ½-pt 90.00
Horse & Cart/Eagle, GV-9, olive-amber, sm/ps, 1-pt 165.00
Hunter/Fisherman, GXIII-4, gold-amber, sl cm/ip, calabash 145.00
Jenny Lind Lyre, GI-108, aqua, sm/ps, 1-pt 825.00
Jenny Lind/Glass Factory, GI-103, aqua, sl cm/ps, 1-qt 75.00
JR & Son, GIX-43, bl-aqua, waisted scroll, sm/ps, 1-pt 450.00
Kossuth/Frigate, GI-112, aqua, rnd cm/ps, 1-qt 120.00
Kossuth/Tree, GI-113, olive-yel, sl cm w/bevel, ps, calabash 330.00
Lafayette/DeWitt Clinton, GI-80, olive-amber, sm/ps, 1-pt 415.00
Lafayette/Eagle, GI-91 variant, aqua, sm/ps, 1820s, 1-pt 385.00
Lafayette/Liberty Cap, GI-85, olive-amber, sm/ps, 1-pt 450.00
Lafayette/Liberty Cap, GI-86, gold-amber, sm/ps, ½-pt 450.00
Lafayette/Liberty Cap, GI-86, yel olive-amber, sm/ps, ½-pt 450.00
Liberty/Sheaf of Wheat/Star, aqua, sm/ps, 1840-60, 1-pt 475.00
Liberty/Willington Glass Co, GII-64, med amber-gr, 1-pt 210.00
Lowell RR/Eagle, GV-10, gold-amber w/olive tone, sm, ½-pt 200.00
Masonic/Eagle, GIV-1, bright lt bl-gr, sm/ps, Keene, 1-pt 185.00
Masonic/Eagle, GIV-14, olive gr, long neck, bruise, ½-pt 3,500.00
Masonic/Eagle, GIV-2, lt gr, sm/ps, Keene, 1815-30, 1-pt 250.00
Masonic/Eagle, GIV-24, bright yel-olive, sm/ps, Keene, ½-pt 160.00
Masonic/Eagle, GIV-24, dk olive gr, sm/ps, 1820s, ½-pt 145.00
Masonic/Frigate, GIV-34, aqua, sm/ps, 1820-40, 1-pt 150.00
Masonic/Masonic, peacock gr, tm/ps, 1815-30, ½-pt 475.00
North Bend/Tippecanoe, GVII-1, dk forest gr, cabin, 1-pt 17,000.00
Ravenna Glass Works/Star, GXIII-83, lt citron, am/sb, 1-pt 900.00
RR Lowell Horse & Cart/Eagle, GV-10, dk gr, sm/ps, ½-pt 265.00
S M'Kee, GIX-26, aqua, scroll, sm/ps, 1840-60, 1-pt 775.00
Scroll, GIX-10, dk gold-amber, am/ip, 1840-60, 1-pt 245.00
Scroll, GIX-14, lt ice bl, sm/ps, 1840-60, 1-pt 130.00
Scroll, GIX-30a, aqua, fleur-de-lis emb, 1800s, 2-qt 235.00
Seeing Eye/Masonic, GIV-43, gold-amber, sm/ps, 1846-60, 1-pt ..125.00
Sheaf of Grain w/Star/Westford..., GXIII-36, olive gr, 1-pt 140.00
Sheaf of Grain/Westford...Conn, GXIII-35, olive-amber, 1-pt ...170.00
Sheaf of Wheat/Star, GXIII-43, bright lt citron, cm/ps, 1-pt 225.00
Sheaf of Wheat/Star, GXIII-45, amber, hdl, calabash 300.00
Shield & Clasped Hands/Eagle, GXII-24 (similar), citron, 1-pt .360.00
Sloop/Star, GX-9, lt gr, sm/ps, 1840-60, ½-pt 300.00
Success to the RR, GII-3, dk gr, sm/ps, Keene, stain, 1-pt 200.00
Success to the RR, GV-1b, bright aqua, sm/ps, 1849-60, 1-pt 375.00
Success to the RR, GV-4, dk forest gr, sm/ps, Keene, 1-pt 200.00
Success to the RR, GV-5, dk gr, sm/ps, 1820s, 1-pt 220.00
Success to the RR/Eagle, GV-8, olive-amber, sm/ps, 1-pt 185.00
Sunburst, GVIII-10 variant, olive gr, sm/ps, Keene, ½-pt 425.00
Sunburst, GVIII-12, dk olive-amber, sm/ps, Keene, 1-pt, EX ..3,700.00
Sunburst, GVIII-16, lt yel-olive, sm/ps, 1815-30, ½-pt 300.00
Sunburst, GVIII-16, med forest gr, sm/ps, ½-pt 375.00
Sunburst, GVIII-18, gold-amber, sm/ps, 1820-30, ½-pt 350.00
Sunburst, GVIII-2, gr-aqua, sm/ps, sm chip, att Keene, 1-pt 190.00
Sunburst, GVIII-20, copper-amber, sm, lt wear, 1-pt 2,100.00
Sunburst, GVIII-25, copper-puce, oval, sm, ½-pt 4,500.00
Sunburst, GVIII-25, med apricot-puce, sm/ps, ½-pt 5,225.00
Sunburst, GVIII-26, bright yel-gr, sm/ps, 1820-30, 1-pt 1,000.00

Sunburst, GVIII-29, bl-gr, elliptical, sm, 1820s, 1-pt 180.00
Sunburst, GVIII-29, lt bl-gr, tm/ps, 1820-30, ½-pt 160.00
Sunburst, GVIII-29, tm/ps, 1820-30, 1-pt 375.00
Sunburst, GVIII-3, bright olive-amber, sm/ps, 1-pt 420.00
Sunburst, GVIII-3, lt gr-olive, sm/ps, sm crack, 1-pt 145.00
Sunburst, GVIII-3, lt olive-amber, sm/ps, flakes, 1-pt 275.00
Sunburst, GVIII-8, dk forest gr, sm/ps, Keene, 1-pt 300.00
Sunburst, GVIII-9, bright gold-amber, sm/ps, Keene, ½-pt 275.00
Sunburst, GVIII-9, dk gr, sm/ps, Keene, 1822-30, ½-pt 275.00
Sunburst, GVIII-9, olive-amber, sm/ps, Keene, ½-pt 250.00
Traveler's Companion/Ravenna Glass Co, GXIV-2, bl-aqua, 1-pt 90.00
Tree w/Bird/Sheaf of Rye, GXIII-47, dk yel-gr, 1-qt 450.00
Washington/Classical Bust, GI-25, bright med gr, sm/ps, 1-qt 700.00
Washington/Eagle, GI-14, aqua, sm/ps, 1820-38, 1-pt 375.00
Washington/Eagle 'TWD,' GI-115, aqua, sm/ps, 1-pt 155.00
Washington/Historical Bust, GI-25, aqua, sm/ps, 1-qt 85.00
Washington/Jackson, GI-31, bright yel-amber, Keene, 1-pt 130.00
Washington/Jackson, GI-32, olive-amber, sm/ps, 1830-50, 1-pt .130.00
Washington/Jackson, GI-33, olive-amber, sm/ps, 1-pt 100.00
Washington/Jackson, GI-34, olive-amber, sm/ps, 1830-48, ½-pt .175.00
Washington/Jackson, GI-34, yel-olive, sm/ps, 1830-48, ½-pt 90.00
Washington/Sheaf of Grain, GI-59, bright bl, sm/ps, ½-pt 1,430.00
Washington/Taylor, GI-24, bright bl-gr, sm/ps, 1-pt 600.00
Washington/Taylor, GI-37, bright bl-gr, sm/ps, 1-qt 140.00
Washington/Taylor, GI-39, dk emerald gr, sm/ps, 1840s, 1-qt 880.00
Washington/Taylor, GI-42, bright med gr-bl, cm/ps, 1-qt 200.00
Washington/Taylor, GI-51, med sapphire bl, sm chip, 1-qt 900.00
Washington/Taylor, GI-54, gr-aqua, appl sl cm, ps, 1-qt 50.00
Washington/Taylor Bridgeton NJ, GI-24, gold-amber, 1-pt 670.00

Food Bottles and Jars

Cathedral pickle bottles: Light green with yellowish tint, iron pontil, rolled lip, 11½", $525.00; Deep aqua, iron pontil, rolled lip, unusual design, 11½", $185.00.

Catsup, Flaccus Bros Steer Head...VA, tm/sb, stain, 9" 350.00
Coffee, Coffee & Spices Trade Mills Montreal, aqua, drum, 6½" 110.00

Mustard, F Ientz Phila Factory, aqua, branch emb, 5⅛x2⅜" 100.00
Mustard, NW Opermann Factory, aqua, branch emb, 4¾" 110.00
Mustard, W Braunewell, aqua, tm/ps, 4¼" 50.00
Mustard, W Diedz A Co Factory, aqua, cylindrical, rm/ps, 5" 50.00
Peppersauce, emerald gr, 6-sided cathedral, 1850s, 8¾" 130.00
Peppersauce, olive yel-gr, 8-sided, ring neck, 1840, 8⅝" 2,100.00
Pickle, aqua, cathedral, sq w/4 oval panels, 11" 130.00
Pickle, gr-aqua, cathedral w/3 X-hatched panels, rm/sb, 14" 185.00
Pickle, lt gr, Gothic Arch, appl lip, 12" 250.00
Pickle, med bl-gr, cathedral, rm/sb, sq, 1860-80, stain, 13" 270.00

Ink Bottles

Bread loaf, blk, emb D at neck, fm/ps, ca 1820, 2⅛" 130.00
Butler/Cin, aqua, rm/ps, sq, 2⅜x1¼" 175.00

Carter, cathedral master, cobalt, smooth base, automatic bottle machine lip, 50% label, scarce size, 6¼", $190.00.

Cylinder, deep emerald gr, sl cm/ps, Am, 5¼" 85.00
Fountain, Morgan's Pat July 16 1867, pewter cap 105.00
Fountain, snail form, gm/sb, France, 1870-90, 1½x2¾" 175.00
J Underwood & Co NY, cream-colored glaze, 1860-90, 3½x1¾" ..100.00
Jones No 1, aqua, fm/ps, minor int stain, 2⅞x1½" 275.00
Joy's, cobalt, cylindrical, fm/sb, 2⅜x2¾" 385.00
Snail, milk glass, in CI wheelbarrow stand, 7¾" L 260.00
Teakettle, amethyst-purple, 6-sided, s & gm/sb, 2x2⅜" 700.00
Teakettle, cobalt, brass collar & cap, 4½x2¾", EX 800.00
Teakettle, cobalt, gm w/metal cap, sb, 1830-60, 2¼x3⅛" 1,025.00
Teakettle, deep bl, gm w/metal band, France, 1820s, 2x3½" 250.00
Teakettle, puce-amethyst, 8-sided, gm/sb, 2x2⅛" 350.00
Teakettle, sapphire bl, 8-sided, 1¾x2¼", +brass cap 495.00
Umbrella, bright olive-gr, 8-sided, rm/ps, 2½x2¾" 750.00
Umbrella, dk cherry red, 8-sided, sm/ps, 2½x2⅜", EX 660.00
Umbrella, olive-amber, 8-sided, sm/ps, 1830-50, 2¼x2⅜" 120.00
12-sided w/spout, olive gr, sl cm/ip, haze, 8¾x3¾" 935.00

Medicine Bottles

Cook's Balm of Life, lt med bl, strapped sides, oval, cm, 8" 210.00
Dr Davis's Depurative Phila, med gr, am/ip, sq, 9⅝" 700.00
Dr Kilmer's Swamp Root Kidney Liver..., olive-yel, 8" 100.00
Dr Magnin's Lucina Cordial..., am/ps, 6" 185.00
Dr Tebbett's...Hair Regenerator, gold-amber, tm/sb, 7½" 40.00

Dr Tebbett's...Hair Regenerator, plum-amethyst, cm/sb, 7½" **125.00**
Dr Tebbett's...Hair Regenerator, wine-amethyst, am/sb, 7½" **170.00**
Dr Warren's Tonic Cordial Cinci & NY, aqua, full label, 9" **300.00**
EC Allen Concentrated Electric Past(e)..., bl-gr, rm/ps, 3" **500.00**
Little's White Oil Scottsville VA, aqua, am/ps, 6⅝" **240.00**
Mackensie's Tonic Febrifuge, aqua, am/ps, indented panel, 5⅜" ..**250.00**
Morse's Celebrated Syrup Prov RI, dk aqua, cm/ps, 9¼" **70.00**
Myers Rock Rose New Haven, med emerald gr, ip, 1860, 9¼" ..**1,250.00**
NY Pharmacal Association, cobalt, tm/sb, sq, 8⅛" **80.00**
Oldridge's Balm of Columbia..., aqua, rectangular, am, 5⅝" **95.00**
Phelp's Arcanum Worcester MA, dk yel-olive, cm/ps, 8¾" **1,000.00**
Rheumatic Syrup...1882...NY, gold-amber, tree emb, 9¾" **400.00**
Sanford's Extract of Hamamelis..., med sapphire bl, 9¼" **150.00**
Shaker Hair Restorer, honey-amber, tm/sb, lt haze, 7¾" **650.00**
Shecut's Southern Balm for Coughs..., aqua, am, 6⅛" **250.00**
Swaim's Panacea Phila, bright sea gr, sl cm/sb, 8⅛" **300.00**
Swaim's Panacea Phila, yel-olive, sl cm/ps, 1840-60, 7¾" **175.00**
Swift's Syphilitic Specific, deep bl, oval, am/sb, 9⅛" **240.00**
The Craig Kidney Cure Co, med gold-amber, am/sb, 1880, 9½" **140.00**
Trafton's Tuckthorn Syrup..., aqua, am, 1850s, 6⅝" **280.00**
USA Hosp Dept, gr-yel, cylindrical, am/sb, 1870s, 9½" **425.00**
Wilson's Hair Colorer, bright bl-aqua, rectangular, rm, 5" **135.00**

Mineral Water and Soda Bottles

B&G San Francisco Superior, med bl, mug base, ip, 6¾" **230.00**
Bolen Waack & Co NY, dk copper-amber, burst bubble, 1-pt **475.00**
Cas AH Umbach...Savanna GA, emerald gr, eagle emb, bt, 7½" **260.00**
Congress & Empire...Mineral Water, gold amber, sl cm/sb, 1-pt **200.00**
Dr Townsend's Sarsaparilla, olive gr, sl cm/ps, 1800-30, 9½" **110.00**
Eagle w/arrows & olive branches emb, med yel-gr, bt/ip, 7" **110.00**
Fields Superior Charleston SC, bright bl, am/ip, stain, 8" **375.00**
From the...Spring of CE Franklin..., gold-amber, 1-qt **650.00**

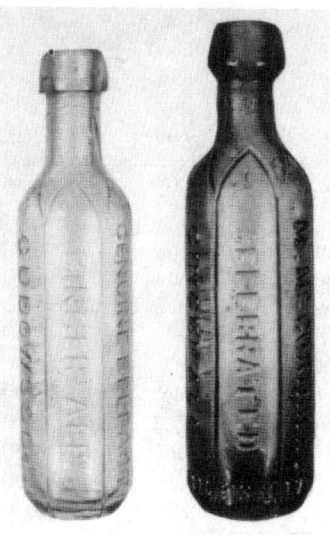

Genuine Belfast Ginger Ale - G.D. Dows & Co. Boston, aqua, round bottom, smooth base, applied mouth, light stain, $15.00; M. McCormack's Celebrated Ginger Ale, Nashville, Tenn. - This Bottle Is Never Sold, medium cobalt, round bottom, smooth base, applied mouth, light wear, $200.00.

Geo Gemenden Savannah Geo, dk bl-gr, eagle emb, bt, 7½" **220.00**
Geo Gemenden Savannah Geo, med bl-gr, eagle emb, bt, 7⅜" ..**190.00**
Henry Kneeble 458 4th St NY, med bl, 8-sided, bt, bruise, 7" **130.00**
Highrock Congress Spring 1767...NY, deep amber, cm/sb, 1-qt ..**130.00**
Hygea, dk olive gr, woman emb, am/sb, 1880-1900, 11⅝" **75.00**
J Boardman & Co NY, peachy gasoline, am/ip, 1845-60, 7½" **250.00**
John Ryan Philada XX Porter & Ale, cherry-purple, ip, 6⅜" **300.00**
Meinchke & Ebberwein 1882 Savannah..., gold-amber, bt, 8⅜" **70.00**
RC Worthendyke Agent Superior, cobalt, octagonal, ½-pt **325.00**
Superior, bright med bl, eagle emb, am/ip, 7¾" **450.00**

Taylor Never Surrenders/Union GW..., med bl, am/ip **1,050.00**
W Heiss Jr's Superior No 213..., yel-gr, eagle emb, 7" **1,500.00**

Poison Bottles

Flask, bright med bl-gr, hobnailed, tm/ps, 1840-60, 5¾" **500.00**
JG Godding Apothecaries Boston MA, cobalt, hexagonal, 5⅝" .**150.00**
Owl emb on cobalt, tm/sb, 1890s, 7⅞" **750.00**
Poison emb on skull form, cobalt, tm/sb, 1880-1900, 2¾" **1,650.00**
Poison emb on skull form, cobalt, tm/sb, 1880-1900, 3½" **1,350.00**
Triloids Wm R Warner & Co NY-St Louis on label, cobalt, 3½" .**35.00**
WTCo USA, cobalt, owl standing on mortar trademk, 9½" **425.00**

Poison, Norwich, 4A on base, amber coffin shape, smooth base tooled lip, rare, 5", $1,450.00; Poison, Pat Appl'd For, Pat June, 26th, 1894, cobalt figural skull, repaired at the nose, small potstone crack, 3½", $950.00.

Sarsaparilla Bottles

Dr Townsend's, dk gr, sl cm/ip, sq, 9½" **200.00**
Dr Townsend's, med bl-gr, sl cm/ip, sq, 10" **245.00**
Dr Townsend's, yel-olive, cm/ps, 9½" **300.00**
Dr Townsend's Albany NY, emerald gr, am/ip, 9⅜" **250.00**
Dr Townsend's Albany NY, emerald gr, am/sb, 9¼" **120.00**
Dr Townsend's Albany/NY, olive gr, rare '/' before NY, 9¼" **260.00**
Gooch's, cornflower bl, tm, 9" **85.00**
John Bull Extract of..., dk aqua, am/ps, 9" **145.00**
Old Dr Townsend's, cornflower bl/ice bl, bt/ip, 9¼" **700.00**

Spirits Bottles

AM Bininger & Co, amber, dbl cm/ps, bbl, 1855-65, 8" **415.00**
AM Bininger & Co...NY, bright yel-gr, hdld jug, 8" **500.00**
AM Bininger...Old KY Bourbon 1849..., gold-amber, bbl, 8" **200.00**
Bladder form, dk olive-amber, am/ps, 1750-80, wear, 9⅛" **120.00**
Cosmopoliet JJ Melcherswz Schiedham (gin), olive-amber, 10⅜" ..**80.00**
Creme D' Italie, milk glass, sm/sb, hdl, orig label, 8" **40.00**
Cylindrical w/sl shoulders, olive gr, am/ps, 1750-70, 10" **350.00**
DJM 1841/Mtn Dew, cobalt, vintage eng, dbl ring am, 12⅞" ..**1,900.00**
Drink While It Lasts From..., amethystine, hog form, 6½" **165.00**
Forest Lawn JVH, bright forest gr, sl cm/ip, 7½x4½" **225.00**
Free-blown, bright yel-olive, sm w/appl ring, ps, 1750s, 7" **100.00**
Free-blown, dk forest gr, squat cylinder, sm/ps, 1710-30, 7¼" **110.00**
Free-blown, olive-amber, squat cylinder, sm/ps, 1720-40, 8" **70.00**
Geo Bieler Sons Bourbon, pottery, gr/yel, pear form, 6¾" **60.00**
Gin type, yel-gr, crude am/sb, tapered sq, 12¼" **220.00**
H Pharazyn Phila...Secured, med honey-amber, Indian, 12" ..**1,000.00**

Philantrop Only Imported By Luicipsaila Demerara, olive, 11" ..125.00
Rum type, olive gr, squat cylinder, am/ps, 1770, 9⅛" 200.00
Timo Horsfield 1771, dk olive gr, appl seal, sm/ps, 9¾" 350.00
Turner Brothers NY, amber w/chocolate tone, bbl, 1870, 10" 170.00
WI Johnson Kentucky, gold-amber, hdld pear form, 8¼" 175.00

Boxes

Boxes have been used by civilized man since ancient Egypt and Rome. Down through the centuries, specifically designed containers have been made from every conceivable material. Precious metals, papier-mache, battersea, Oriental lacquer, and wood have held riches from the treasuries of kings, snuff for the fashionable set of the last century, China tea, and countless other commodities. See also Toleware; specific manufacturers.

Wallpaper-covered hat box, paper depicts 'Clayton's Ascension,' S.M. Hurlbert's Paste Board Band Box Manufactory No. 25, 17" long, $1,300.00.

Band, wallpaper w/bldgs & trees on bentwood, 19", EX 400.00
Band, wallpaper w/bldgs & trees on cardboard, 16", VG 500.00
Bentwood, dk bl pnt, 7¾" dia 275.00
Bentwood, floral decor, 3-color on brn, 11½", VG 325.00
Bentwood, gray rpt, initialed, 8¾" dia, EX 175.00
Bentwood, gray-bl pnt, edge damage, 5" dia 75.00
Bentwood, olive gr w/red rpt, branded Murdock, 6½" dia 225.00
Bentwood, pine w/gr-blk rpt, John Beck stamped inside, 15" 225.00
Bentwood, red pnt, edge damage/old tin rpr, 7½x12" 400.00
Bentwood, red pnt w/floral, minor damage, 3¾" L 135.00
Bentwood, varnished, 6½" dia 95.00
Bentwood, worn yel varnish, 9½" dia 190.00
Bentwood, yel pnt over orig bl, minor age cracks, 12" 325.00
Bentwood, 1-finger, iron tacks, red, handwritten label, 5" 200.00
Book shape, walnut w/emb paper in gr-gilt/red, 12", EX 200.00
Burl veneer, 1910, 14" 175.00
Candle, pine w/dk red finish, sliding lid, 13" 350.00
Candle, poplar w/red pnt, sliding lid, 15" 175.00
Candle, walnut, sq pegged, sliding peaked lid, 10" 150.00
Curly maple & cherry w/red wash, dvtl, moldings, 12" 500.00
Hanging, maple/pine, pierced front brd w/cvd medallion, 15" .1,700.00
Hanging, poplar w/worn pnt, 2-compartment, 18x11x5½" 350.00
Knife, curly maple, trn hdl on divider, rprs, 10x14" 150.00
Knife, mahog Geo III, slant lid, brass escutcheon, 12½" 240.00

Knife, pine w/worn dk red grpt, worn int, 9½x12½" 145.00
Knife, poplar w/yel striping, florals, name, 8½x13" 200.00
Knife, walnut, cut-out finger holes, 13" 135.00
Lehnware, red w/4-color stripes, oval portrait, trn ft, 10" 850.00
Pantry, wood w/gr-gray pnt, wire hdl w/wood grip, 1800s, 7x12" ..185.00
Pine, dvtl, rfn, 25" L 250.00
Pnt, bl w/mc border & vintage, sgn, 14", EX 225.00
Pnt bird on branch on yel, striping, dtd 1858, 2½x8x9" 700.00
Poplar, 2 drws w/porc pulls, yel-brn grpt, 19" 195.00
Poplar w/brn vinegar grpt, iron hdls+emb brass hdl, 20" 350.00
Poplar w/gr pnt & blk striping, mk Boston Mass, 12", EX 175.00
Poplar w/red grpt, dvtl, brass bail hdl, rpl hinges, 14" 150.00
Poplar w/red pnt, blk/yel dots, dome top, 14" 825.00
Poplar w/red pnt & foliage, dome top, 21", EX 500.00
Strong box, iron, dmn panels, blk pnt w/gold stripes, 14" 130.00
Tulipwood, grpt as exotic wood w/inlay, 11" 100.00
Walnut, brass corners, fruitwood int, Biedermeier, 19" L 4,400.00
Wood, allover chip cvg, sliding lid, 3½" 100.00
Writing, pine w/re-grpt, slant top, fitted int, 10x20x20" 225.00
Writing, rosewood w/brass mts, Victorian, on later stand 365.00

Boyd Crystal Art Glass

Boyd Crystal Art Glass is a small but productive glass factory located in Cambridge, Ohio. It was established in 1978 when the Boyd family bought out the Degenhart factory. Over the years Boyd has produced more than 200 molds; while many were their own design, they acquired others from glasshouses no longer in business. All the Boyd pieces are marked with a distinct logo of a 'B' in diamond. Further dating is possible because a line was added under the diamond in 1983, and an additional line was added above the diamond in 1988. Boyd's glass is prized because of the colors they formulated and the fact that once a piece is produced in a particular color it will not be produced in that color again, even if that color is brought back years later. All pieces are hand pressed from glass that is from a single-day tank. Colors are made for about six weeks or less, thus, limiting the number of pieces that can be produced in that color. More than 225 different colors have been used and developed by the Boyds. Much like Degenhart glass, the colors can be confusing and difficult to identify. Exceptional slags and hand-painted pieces can command up to 50% higher prices. Satin glass variations are priced 10% to 30% higher when they can be found.

In the following listings, (N) indicates a mold that was new in 1992-93. (R) indicates a yearly special edition of a retired piece. Our advisor for this category is Joyce Pringle; she is listed in the Directory under Texas.

Airplane, Cobalt (N) 17.50
Artie the Penguin, Classic Black (N) 9.00
Beaded Oval Toothpick, Classic Black 7.50
Bow Slipper, Cardinal Red 8.50
Bow Slipper, Delphinium 20.00
Bow Slipper, Primrose (yel) 7.50
Bow Slipper, Ruby 22.50
Brian Bunny, Skytop Blue 18.00
Bull Dog Head, Majic Marble 10.00
Bunny Salt, Buckeye 6.00
Bunny Salt, Cardinal Red (R) 9.00
Bunny Salt, Thistlebloom 25.00
Cat Slipper, Chocolate 15.00
Cat Slipper, Classic Black Slag 10.00
Chick Salt, Bermuda, 1" 16.00
Chick Salt, Pebble Beige, 1" 6.00
Chick Salt, Ruby Gold, 1" 100.00

Chicken Covered Dish, Cardinal Red, 3" 11.50
Chuckles Clown, Confetti, 4" 11.50
Elephant Head Toothpick, Champagne Pink 20.00
Elizabeth Doll, Lime Carnival, 2" 25.00
Elizabeth Doll, Teal, 2" 8.00
Forget-Me-Not Toothpick, Avocado/Red 7.00
Forget-Me-Not Toothpick, Elizabeth Slag #4 ....20.00
Forget-Me-Not Toothpick, John's Surprise 22.50
Forget-Me-Not Toothpick, Vaseline 7.00
Freddie the Clown, Alexandrite, 3" 8.00
Fuzzy Bear, Cashmire Pink (R) 11.00
Fuzzy Bear, Ritz Blue 17.50
Gypsy Pot Toothpick, Marigold 20.00
Hand Dish, Leprechaun 20.00
Hand Dish, Primrose 5.00
Hand Dish, Snow 15.00
Heart Jewel Box, Cardinal Red 11.50
Heart Jewel Box, Opaline Blue Swirl 35.00
Heart Toothpick, Frosty Blue 15.00
Heart Toothpick, Vaseline 8.00
Hen Covered Dish, Furr Green, 5" 20.00
Hen Covered Dish, Winter Swirl, 5" 40.00
JB Scottie Dog, Azure Blue 35.00
JB Scottie Dog, Cashmire Pink (R) 10.00
JB Scottie Dog, Cornsilk 12.50
Joey the Horse, Candy Swirl 22.50
Kitten on a Pillow, Frosty Blue 15.00
Kitten on a Pillow, Sandpiper 13.50
Lucky the Unicorn, Bermuda Slag 16.50
Mini Vase, Flame, HP 20.00
Mini Vase, Smoke 6.00
Mini Vase, Sunburst 30.00
Miss Cotton (the kitten), Heather Gray 7.00
Owl, Cardinal Red 10.00
Owl, Firefly 22.50
Owl, Peridot Satin 18.00
Owl Bell, Snow 10.00
Skate Boot, Cardinal Red Carnival 10.00
Skate Boot, Snow Slag 35.00
Sugar & Creamer, Heather 22.50
Tall Boot, Heather Gray 9.00
Tall Boot, Persimmon 20.00
Tucker (car), Grape Parfait 12.50
Zak the Elephant, Cardinal Red Carnival 17.50

Zak the Elephant, Lemonade 35.00
Zak the Elephant, Mardi Gras 20.00
Zak the Elephant, Mulberry Mist 60.00
Zak the Elephant, Sandpiper 15.00

Bradley and Hubbard

The Bradley and Hubbard Mfg. Company was a firm which produced metal accessories for the home. They operated from about 1860 until the early part of this century, and their products reflected both the Arts and Crafts and Art Nouveau influence. Their logo was a device with a triangular arrangement of the company name containing a smaller triangle and an Aladdin lamp. Our advisor for this category is Daniel Batchelor; he is listed in the Directory under New York.

Lamps

Table lamp, octagonal 18" shade of green and gold-amber glass panels in gilt-metal frame creating tropical island scene, metallic finish on base is worn, 24", $1,200.00.

Banquet, HP globe w/flowers; cast base, sgn, 37" 425.00
Paneled 18" shade w/metal floral o/l; base w/glass panels 800.00
Piano, frosted beaded drape 10" shade, brass/wrought iron 550.00
Slag glass 18" 6-sided shade w/palm tree o/l; mk metal std 525.00
Table, paneled 15" gr/wht slag shade w/red border; mk std 425.00
Table, stylized filigree on 22" slag glass shade; sq base 1,300.00

Miscellaneous

Andirons, CI w/sun face, #9150, rust pitting on ft, 17", pr 800.00
Andirons, CI winged griffin form, #9537, 20½" 2,500.00
Andirons, wrought iron inverted Y-form w/ball finial, 16" 300.00
Bookends, brass, Colonial lady & driver w/coach, 6½", pr 95.00
Candlestick, brass, std flares to wide base, mk, 12x6", pr 650.00
Cigar stand, brass, tray w/3 etched cups & cutter, 30" 225.00
Mirror, brass easel bk w/openwork & mythological mask, 12" 225.00

Zak the Elephant, flame, $45.00.

Brass

Brass is an alloy consisting essentially of copper and zinc in variable proportions. It is a medium that has been used for both utilitarian items and objects of artistic merit. Today, with the inflated price of copper and the popular use of plastics, almost anything made of brass is collectible. Our advisor, Mary Frank Gaston, has compiled a lovely book, *Antique Brass and Copper*, with full-color photos; you will find her address in the Directory under Texas. See also Candlesticks.

Box, tobacco; eng Adam & Eve, 1700s, oval, Dutch 200.00
Box, tobacco; town eng on lid, octagonal, Dutch 230.00
Candle holder, baluster w/push-ups, 1850s, 8½", pr 135.00
Chamberstick, heart shape, England, 7¼" L 215.00
Curtain tie-bk, Art Deco design, pr 40.00
Dust pan, emb florals & wreaths, England, 8½x8" 55.00
Figure, rooster, EX detail, mc pnt, 4" 300.00
Fire dogs, ball finial, sgn Hunneman Boston, 11", EX 400.00
Kettle, gooseneck copper spout, English, 10x12" 260.00
Kettle, spun, iron bail hdl, dents, 12x18" 75.00
Lamp, kerosene; mk Rayo, late 1800s, rpl shade, 20" 175.00
Lamp, table; slag glass inserts in fringed shade, electric 250.00
Lock box, +key/keeper/doorknob, dent/rpr, 8" L 175.00
Mold, for pewter spoons, 17" wrought iron hinged hdl 400.00
Mortar, goblet shape, 6½", w/pestle 175.00
Pail, spun, iron bail hdl, Hayden's Pat, 11x17" 150.00
Pan, 8", w/10" wrought iron hdl 45.00
Statuette, fighting cocks, EX detail, 1900s, 11" W, pr 225.00

Sundial with engraved face dated 1689, 8", $750.00.

Taster, 3" bowl, hanger (bent), w/11" wrought iron hdl 175.00
Teakettle, gooseneck spout, trn hdl, handmade, polished, 8" 65.00
Wall sconce, emb bird scenic, England, 19x15" 350.00
Watering can, hinged lid, European, 8x11", EX 65.00

Brastoff, Sascha

The son of immigrant parents, Sascha Brastoff was encouraged to develop his artistic talents to the fullest, encouragement that was well taken, as his achievements aptly attest. Though at various times he has been a dancer, sculptor, Hollywood costume designer, jeweler, and painter, it is his ceramics that are today becoming highly regarded collectibles.

Sascha began his career in the United States in the late 1940s. In a beautiful studio built for him by his friend and mentor, Winthrop Rockefeller, he designed innovative wares that even then were among the most expensive on the market. All designing was done personally by Brastoff; he also supervised the staff which at the height of production numbered approximately 150. Wares signed with his full signature (not merely backstamped 'Sascha Brastoff') were personally crafted by him and are valued much more highly than those signed 'Sascha B.,' indicating work done under his supervision. Sascha Brastoff still resides in Los Angeles, California producing 'Sascha Holograms,' which are distributed by the Hummelwerk Company.

Another medium he used in his work was resin, and such pieces are also very collectible, though extremely scarce. In the listings below, all items are signed 'Sascha B.' unless otherwise indicated (full signature).

Our advisor for this category is Jack Chipman, author of *Collector's Encyclopedia of California Pottery*; Mr. Chipman is listed in the Directory under California.

Ashtray, abstract enameling on copper, 4" 22.50
Ashtray, enamel ware, artichoke shape, 5½" 22.00
Ashtray, free-form, cvd leaves, 8½" 20.00
Bowl, lav marbleized, 'Surf Ballet' line, 10" 85.00
Bowl, Star Steed (horse), turq/pk, ftd 42.50
Cigarette box, horse decor 48.00
Cigarette holder & lighter, turq, 2-pc set 45.00
Figure, horse, platinum on pk matt, ca 1957, 10½" 150.00
Figure, poodle, satin matt crackle, 7x9" 125.00
Lighter, bl w/gold base 15.00
Plate, dinner; Winrock, porc, 11" 25.00
Sculpture, horse head, satin matt crackle, 7½" 225.00
Sculpture, resin, seal, red 225.00

Teapot, porcelain, green and blue fans with gold trim on white, 9", $150.00.

Tray, circus elephant, mc on gray mottle, sq, 8" 45.00
Vase, abstract linear design, 12" 75.00
Vase, houses, full signature, 10" 185.00
Vase, husky dog, slender form, 'Alaska' line, 20" 95.00
Vase, resin, grapes on amber, cylindrical, 10" 80.00
Wall mask, native, blk & gold, 9½" 125.00

Brayton, Laguna

Durlin E. Brayton made hand-crafted vases, lamps, and dinnerware in a small kiln at his Laguna Beach, California, home in 1927. He soon married; and with his wife, Ellen Webster Grieve, as his partner, the small business became a successful commercial venture. They are most famous for their amusing, well-detailed figurines, some of which were commissioned by Walt Disney Studios. Though very successful even through the Depression years, with the influx of imported novelties that deluged the country after WWII, business began to decline. By 1968 the pottery was closed. For more information on this as well as many other potteries in the state, we recommend *The Collectors Encyclopedia of California Pottery* by Jack Chipman; he is listed in the Directory under California.

Cookie jar, Circus Tent	175.00
Cookie jar, Gingham Dog, unmk	195.00
Cookie jar, Goose Woman, mk	145.00
Cookie jar, Grandma	225.00
Cookie jar, Lady, mk	200.00
Cookie jar, Mammy	395.00
Creamer, cat figural	45.00
Creamer & sugar bowl, Provincial	70.00
Figurine, panther, red, 13" L	95.00
Figurine, peacock, 17"	85.00
Flower holder, Sally	30.00

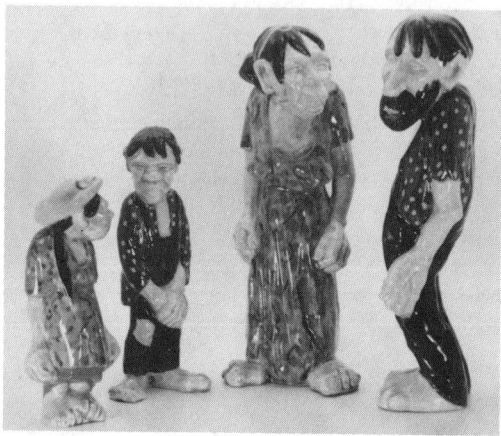

Hillbilly Family, 8½", 11½", 4-piece set, $400.00.

Planter, Mandy	45.00
Shakers, boy & girl, flowered skirt & shirt, pr	50.00
Shakers, Mammy & Chef, pr	75.00
Toothpick holder, Gingham Dog	75.00

Bread Plates and Trays

Bread plates and trays have been produced not only in many types of glass but in metal and pottery as well. Those considered most collectible were made during the last quarter of the 19th century from pressed glass with well-detailed embossed designs, many of them portraying a particularly significant historical event. A great number of these plates were sold at the 1876 Philadelphia Centennial Exposition by various glass manufacturers who exhibited their wares on the grounds. Among the themes depicted are the Declaration of Independence, the Constitution, McKinley's memorial 'It Is God's Way,' Rememberance of Three Presidents, the Purchase of Alaska, and various presidential campaigns, to mention only a few.

'L' numbers correspond with a reference book by Lindsey; 'S' refers to a book by Stuart. Our advisor for this category is Darlene Yohe; she is listed in the Directory under Arkansas.

Actress, Miss Nelson, 13x9"	90.00
American Flag, notched border, L-51	195.00

Bates, L-375	65.00
Beehive, Be Industrious, deer border	75.00
Bible, L-200	55.00
Bishop, L-201	200.00
Black Builders of Bicentennial, 1775-1976	35.00
Bunker Hill Monument, L-44, 13¼x9"	100.00
California Bear, 1894 Expo, L-104	140.00
Columbia, L-54	115.00
Constitution, L-43	70.00
Continental Hall, hand hdls, 12¾" L	75.00
Dewdrop w/Sheaf of Wheat, Give Us This Day, S-7, 11"	50.00
Diagonal Band	28.00
Egyptian, Cleopatra center, 13" L	50.00
Egyptian, 10"	55.00
Frosted Lion, Give Us This Day, 12"	175.00
Frosted Stork	50.00
Frosted Stork w/101 border, 11½x8"	55.00
Garden of Eden, Give Us This Day, 12½x9"	35.00
Garfield Drape, We Mourn Our Nation's Loss, L-303, 11½"	55.00
Garfield Memorial, L-302, 10" L	65.00
Good Luck, 12"	65.00
Grant, L-291, 10" sq	115.00
Grant, Let Us Have Peace, amber, L-289, 10½"	75.00
Grant Memorial, L-288	65.00
Heroes of Bunker Hill	70.00
It Is Pleasant To Labor for Those We Love, hdls, 12½"	55.00
Jewel Band	25.00
Kansas, motto	48.00
Knights of Labor, L-513	135.00
Liberty & Freedom, w/eagle, 12" L	75.00
Liberty Bell, John Hancock, oval, 13"	50.00
Liberty Bell, Signers, oval, 13½"	85.00
Lotus & Serpent	30.00
Maple Leaf, vaseline, oval, 13x9½"	45.00
McKinley, Gold Standard, 10½"	250.00
McKinley, Protection, L-333	45.00
Memorial Hall	60.00
Mormon Temple, w/eye & beehive	300.00
Nelly Bly, L-136, 12" L	200.00
Niagara Falls, milk glass, 2 American flags	55.00
Old State House Philadelphia, bl, L-32	110.00
Polar Bear, ship, L-486, 16"	165.00
Prescott Stark, Heroes of Bunker Hill, 13" L	100.00

Reaper, 13", $50.00.

Retriever, milk glass	80.00
Rock of Ages, milk glass, oval	165.00

Ruth the Gleaner, Gillinder 140.00
Scroll w/Flowers, 12" dia 35.00
Star Rosetted, Good Mother 35.00
Stippled Cherry, Our Daily Bread, 9½" 25.00
Teddy Roosevelt, dancing bears, L-357, 10" L 140.00
Three Graces, Faith, Hope & Charity 45.00
Three Presidents in Remembrance, 12½x10" 95.00
Union Pacific Railroad 80.00
Warrior 150.00
Washington Centennial 1876, frosted, L-27 ....130.00
Wildflower, sq 28.00
William J Bryan, milk glass 42.00

Bride's Baskets and Bowls

Victorian brides were showered with gifts, as brides have always been; one of the most popular gift items was the bride's basket. Art glass inserts from both European and American glasshouses, some in lovely transparent hues with dainty enameled florals, others of Peachblow, Vasa Murrhina, satin or cased glass, were cradled in complementary silverplated holders. While many of these holders were simply engraved or delicately embossed, others such as those from Pairpoint and Wilcox were wonderfully ornate, often with figurals of cherubs or animals. The bride's basket was no longer in fashion after the turn of the century.

Watch for 'marriages' of bowls and frames. To warrant the best price, the two pieces should be the original pairing. If you can't be certain of this, at least check to see that the bowl fits snugly into the frame. Beware of later-made bowls (such as Fenton's) in Victorian holders.

In the listings that follow, if no frame is described, the price is for a bowl only.

Amberina, T'print, Mt WA, 9"; in Pairpoint fr, 12" 885.00
Bl o/l, HP daisies, ruffled rim, 5x10" 265.00
Bl o/l satin, HP florals w/gold, 6½x13½" 325.00
Cranberry opal Hobnail, fluted rim; orig SP fr, 10" 295.00
Invt T'print, cranberry w/bl florals; SP Homan fr, 11¾x7¾" 550.00
Lime Coinspot MOP, bl ruffled edge; ormolu ft, 9x9x14" 695.00
Peach Herringbone MOP, bl int, floral; Meriden fr w/2 lions ..1,900.00
Peach shaded satin o/l, HP florals, handkerchief edge, 4" 245.00

Pink Mother-of-Pearl with hand-painted floral sprigs, Diamond Quilted, gold-decorated crimped edge, 7x7x4", $650.00.

Pk cased w/clear ruffle; ornate rstr Tufts fr w/3-D fruit 595.00
Pk Dmn Quilt MOP; rstr Manhattan SP fr, 11x7x12" 795.00
Pk o/l, HP florals, serrated leaf edge, 3⅜x11⅜" 195.00
Pk o/l satin, HP florals; mk Aurora SP fr, 7x9⅛x10" 295.00
Pk w/sm wht flowers, clear ruffle, wht cased, 11"; ftd SP fr 225.00
Purple o/l satin, HP floral; SP fr, 8½x12¼" 295.00
Rubena w/etched floral, ruffled; Tufts SP fr 250.00

Bristol Glass

Bristol is a type of semi-opaque opaline glass whose name was derived from the area in England where it was first produced. Similar glass was made in France, Germany, and Italy. In this country, it was made by the New England Glass Company and to a lesser extent by its contemporaries. During the 18th and 19th centuries, Bristol glass was imported in large amounts and sold cheaply, thereby contributing to the demise of the earlier glasshouses here in America. It is very difficult to distinguish the English Bristol from other opaline types. Style, design, and decoration serve as clues to its origin; but often only those well versed in the field can spot these subtle variations.

Biscuit jar, turq, HP floral, brass trim, 7x5" 175.00
Biscuit jar, turq, HP herons/trees, SP trim, 7x5" 195.00
Bottle, scent; bl, HP floral, matching stopper, 8¼x3" ...120.00
Bottle, scent; bl, HP floral, w/stopper, 5⅜x2¼" 110.00
Bottle, scent; bl, HP floral & scrolls, 5¼x1⅞" 75.00
Bottle, scent; gr, gold trim, tulip stopper, 9½" 100.00
Bottle, scent; pk, HP floral, teardrop stopper, 8¾" 120.00
Bottle, scent; wht, HP floral, tulip stopper, 11¼" 110.00
Mustard pot, gr, HP floral, SP hinged top, 3⅛" 40.00
Vase, turq, HP bird & floral, ped ft, 12x4" 125.00
Vase, turq, HP floral w/gold, melon ribs, ped ft, 9⅜" 75.00
Vase, wht, HP roses w/gold beading, scalloped, 8", pr ...85.00
Vase, wht w/bl ft, HP coach & horses reserve, gilt, 14" ...150.00

British Royalty Commemoratives

Royalty commemoratives have been issued for royal events from Edward VI's 1547 coronation up to the present time. This makes it possible to start collecting at any period of history. Many collectors begin with Queen Victoria's reign, collecting examples for each succeeding monarch, and continuing on through. While some identify with a particular royal personage and so limit their collecting, others look to the future, expanding their collections to include the heir apparents Prince Charles/Princess Diana and their first-born son, Prince William. Royalty commemorative collecting is often further refined around a particular type of collectible. Nearly any item with room for a portrait and a description has been manufactured as a souvenir. Ranging from glassware, ceramics, metals, plastics, and fabric items, there's something for everyone at a level they can afford — expensive limited edition ceramics down to souvenir key chains, puzzles, matchbooks, etc.

Many recent royalty headline events have been commemorated. At moderate issue prices, these souvenirs have excellent investment potential. For further study we recommend *British Royal Commemoratives* by our advisor for this category, Audrey Zeder; she is listed in the Directory under California.

Key:
anniv — anniversary   inscr — inscribed
chr — christening   jub — jubilee
com — commemorative   LE — limited edition
cor — coronation   mem — memorial
ILN — Illustrated London News   wed — wedding

Beaker, Charles/Di betrothal w/mc portrait, Caverswall 100.00
Beaker, Geo V cor w/gr portrait, ships of war, Whitley 125.00
Beaker, Geo VI cor w/mc portraits, Official Design 50.00
Bell, Charles/Di wed w/mc portrait, Royal Grafton, 7" 40.00
Bookmark, Elizabeth II 1977 jub, blk leather 15.00
Bust, Charles/Di, Royal Staffordshire, LE 500, 4½", pr 150.00

Bust, Geo V & Mary, parian, G details, 5½", pr 250.00
Bust, Queen Mother, Royal Staffordshire, LE 500, 4½" 75.00
Bust, William, inscr Jan 1 1831 by Sam Parker, metal, blk 425.00
Calendar, Princess Elizabeth, 1949, 4¾x8½" 40.00
Cup & saucer, Charles/Di wed w/mc portraits, china 45.00
Cup & saucer, Elizabeth II 60th birthday, mc portrait, Coalport ...65.00
Cup & saucer, Geo V cor, mc portrait, fluted shape 150.00
Cup & saucer, Victoria/Albert portraits on pk lustre, 1851 .....250.00
Cup plate, Charles/Di 1992 separation, 3½" 20.00
Cup plate, Elizabeth II, gr glass, 3½" 20.00
Cup plate, Elizabeth II, 40 yrs on throne, amethyst glass, 3½" 20.00
Cup plate, Queen Mother 85th birthday, bl glass, 3½" 25.00
Cup plate, Queen Mother 90th birthday, lav glass, 3¾" 20.00
Cup plate, Victoria 1837 cor, clear pressed glass, 3½" 190.00
Doll, Charles/Di in wed outfits, Goldberger, 11", pr 100.00
Egg cup, Elizabeth II/Philip, mc portrait, Bavarian style 25.00
Egg cup, Geo V 1911 cor, mc portrait, ftd 45.00
Egg cup, Queen Mother 90th birthday, mc portrait, ftd 25.00
Ephemera, Anne, Illustrated magazine, 1950 .....25.00
Ephemera, Charles 1969 Investiture, Official Program 25.00
Ephemera, Charles/Di wed, Country Life magazine 25.00
Ephemera, Charles/Di wed, ILN magazine 20.00
Ephemera, Diana, paper dolls, Golden, 1985 .....10.00
Ephemera, Edward VII March, sheet music 50.00
Ephemera, Elizabeth cor, Everybody's magazine 25.00
Ephemera, Elizabeth 60th birthday, Radio Times magazine 20.00
Ephemera, Geo V, fabric label, color/gold 25.00
Ephemera, Geo V 1935 jub, ILN magazine 35.00
Ephemera, Geo VI cor, booklet w/cor procession TV info 20.00
Ephemera, Margaret wed, ILN magazine, 1950 .....45.00
Ephemera, Margaret wed, Official Program, 1950 .....35.00
Ephemera, Victoria, fabric label, color/gold 25.00
Ephemera, Victoria, Sunkist orange crate label 20.00
Figural, Prince of Wales 1862 w/dog, Staffordshire, 14½" 1,200.00
Gin bottle, Victoria cor, Tipstaff stoneware, S Greene 70.00
Glass, Charles/Di wed, pin dish, bl w/gold portrait, 4½" 25.00
Glass, Edward VII 1902 cor, tumbler w/etched portrait, 4½" 50.00
Glass, Elizabeth, 1959 Canada visit, tumbler, portraits 25.00
Glass, Elizabeth jub, pin dish, cobalt w/restaurant jub menu 45.00
Glass, Victoria, humidor, w/Victoria bust lid, milk glass 290.00
Glass, Victoria 1887, bowl, clear, pressed/cut, 7½x10" 250.00
Glass, Victoria 1887, pitcher, elaborate design, 4½" 150.00
Glass, Victoria 1897, beaker, relief beaded decor, 4½" 175.00
Medal, Prince of Wales 1886 exhibition, bronze, 2" 75.00
Medal, Princess Charlotte 1820 memorial, ¾" 50.00
Medal, Victoria 1887 w/photo on triangles, brass, 1¾" 60.00
Medal, Victoria 1897 jug w/portrait head, copper, 2¼" 190.00
Mug, Charles/Di 1992 separation, mc portraits 30.00
Mug, Elizabeth cor, gold coat of arms, mc enameling, Myott 35.00
Mug, Elizabeth cor, sepia protrait, mc flags 35.00
Mug, Elizabeth 1992 'Annus Horribulus' w/events, mc portrait 25.00
Mug, Elizabeth 40 years on throne, octagonal 35.00
Newspaper, Victoria 1901 death, w/pictures & narrative 45.00
Novelty, Charles/Di wed, Royal State Landau w/Queen, Corgi ..275.00
Novelty, Elizabeth Ruby Anniversary, Lledo car w/inscr 25.00
Novelty, Victoria, buckle clasp, relief/cut-out design 30.00
Novelty, Victoria, stickpin, rope bezel w/shilling 45.00
Novelty, Victoria 1887, whiskey decanter, w/portrait 295.00
Novelty, Victoria 1901, unused oval soap bar, w/inscr 45.00
Paperweight, Elizabeth 40 yrs on throne, crystal w/postage stamp ...35.00
Photograph, Elizabeth, jug w/her & Philip, blk/wht, 6x8" 20.00
Photograph, Elizabeth II cor, family on balcony, blk/wht 25.00
Photograph, 1861 Princess Beatrice, 2½x4" 30.00
Pin, Elizabeth II cor, portrait on gold-tone, w/orig card 25.00
Pin-bk, Geo VI cor, family group picture, 1¼" 35.00
Pin-bk, Geo VI cor, mc portraits of king & queen, 1¼" 25.00
Plaque, Eliz/Queen Mother/Anne/Diana/Sara, mc portrait, 6x8" .20.00
Plaque, Elizabeth II, parian head on bl velvet 75.00
Plaque, Elizabeth II/Philip, mc portrait on blk, 6x8" 20.00
Plaque, Victoria 1889, emb portrait/details, bronze, 7x10" 375.00
Plate, Charles/Di wed, mc wed portrait, 10½" 250.00
Plate, Diana, 3 portrait versions, LE, Royal Doulton, 10½" 175.00
Plate, Duke & Duchess of Cornwall 1901 Canada visit, 8½" 175.00
Plate, Edward VIII 1937 cor, Deco-style w/portrait, 6½" 50.00
Plate, Elizabeth cor, official design, 6½" 40.00
Plate, Geo VI cor, bl emb portrait, Wedgwood, pr 300.00
Plate, Queen Mother's 90th birthday, mc portrait, inscr, 8" 35.00
Plate, Victoria 1897 jub, brn transfer, Wagstaff & Brunt 250.00
Plate, 3 royal ladies 1990 birthday, mc portrait, 10" 100.00
Postcard, Charles/Di 1991 Canada visit 5.00
Postcard, Edward VII, in uniform, mc Oilette by Tuck 20.00
Postcard, Geo V cor, Dunbar, Delhi, blk/wht 20.00
Postcard, Lady Helen Windsor 1992 marriage, LE 50 .....10.00
Postcard, Princess Diana 30th birthday, LE 500 .....10.00
Postcard, Queen Elizabeth 60th birthday, blk/wht 6.00
Postcard, Queen Mother 90th birthday, LE, Enterprise 5.00
Pot lid, Victoria portrait, advertising Cherry Toothpaste 110.00
Print, Princess Charlotte, blk/wht, 19th C, 4½x7" 25.00
Print, Victoria on throne wearing blk, 19th C, 12x17" 25.00
Puzzle, Charles/Di wed w/engagement picture 35.00
Puzzle, Charles/Di 1992 separation, mc portraits, 4x6" 10.00
Puzzle, Elizabeth II collage of 1953 cor tins, 11x14" 25.00
Puzzle, Queen Mother 90th birthday, 6" dia 10.00
Spoon, Elizabeth II cor, relief portrait, SP 25.00
Spoon, Prince William 1982 birth, relief design, SP 15.00
Spoon, Princess Eugenie birth, relief design, SP 15.00
Sticker album, royal family as of 1984 .....35.00
Tea set, Charles/Di, mc portraits, child's, 12-pc 75.00
Tea set, Charles/Di, mc portraits, mini, 7" teapot 60.00
Teapot, Charles/Di, mc portraits, 2-cup 50.00
Teapot, Geo V 1911 cor, mc portrait & design, 2-cup 225.00
Teapot, 3 royal ladies Aug 1990 birthday, mc portraits 75.00
Teapot stand, Elizabeth II jub, emb portrait on chrome 25.00
Textile, Charles/Di, towel, linen, portrait, mc design 25.00
Textile, Edward VII, silk, woven, oval, fr, 6x5" 150.00
Textile, Elizabeth II, Nottingham lace w/her & Buckingham 25.00
Textile, Elizabeth II 1977 jub, linen towel 20.00
Textile, Elizabeth II 40 yrs on throne, linen towl 12.00
Textile, Victoria 1887 jub, bookmark, woven, in fr 175.00
Textile, Victoria 1897 jub, 4 generation, 28x28" 200.00
Thimble, Charles/Di wed, mc portrait in wed clothes 15.00
Thimble, Charles/Di 1983 visit to Australia, china 25.00

Tin, King George VI and Queen Elizabeth, souvenir from 1937, 6" long, $40.00.

Tin, Charles/Di wed, mc portrait on plaid, Walkers 30.00
Tin, Edward VII cor, mc portrait, Rowntree, 5x2¼x¼" 65.00
Tin, Prince William birth, mc portrait, hinged lid 35.00
Tin, Princesses Elizabeth & Margaret, sepia, Rileys, 1½x5" dia 50.00
Tin, Victoria & Generals, basketweave bkground 175.00
Toby mug, Charles/Di, 2-sided Spitting Image satire 150.00
Toby mug, Elizabeth II on throne w/Corgi, HP, LE, K Francis ...250.00
Toby mug, Queen Mother 90th birthday, HP, LE, K Francis 250.00
Tray, Charles/Di wed, mc engagement portrait, mc rim, 6x7" 25.00
Tray, Elizabeth cor, mc Elizabeth/Philip, faux wood sides, 13" dia ..45.00
Tray, Geo V 1935 jub, SP, emb portrait/design, 12" dia 75.00
Vehicle, Elizabeth II 40 yrs on throne, Thornycroft van, 5x2½" ...40.00

Broadmoor

In October of 1933, the Broadmoor Art Pottery was formed and space rented at 217 East Pikes Peak Avenue, Colorado Springs, Colorado. Most of the pottery produced would not be considered elaborate and only a handful was decorated. Many pieces were signed by P.H. Genter, J.B. Hunt, Eric Hellman, and Cecil Jones. It is reported that this plant closed in 1936, and Genter moved his operations to Denver.

Broadmoor pottery is marked in several ways: a Greek or Egyptian-type label depicting two potters (one at the wheel and one at a tile-pressing machine) and the word Broadmoor; an ink-stamped 'Broadmoor Pottery, Colorado Springs (or Denver), Colorado;' and an incised version of the latter.

The bottoms of all pieces are always white and can be either glazed or unglazed. Glaze colors are turquoise, green, yellow, cobalt blue, light blue, white, pink, pink with blue, maroon red, black, and a copper lustre. Both matt and high gloss finishes were used.

The company produced many advertising tiles, novelty items, coasters, ashtrays, and vases for local establishments around Denver and as far away as Wyoming. An Indian head was incised into many of the advertising items, which also often bear a company or a product name. A series of small animals (horses, dogs, elephants, lamb, squirrels, a toucan bird, and a hippo), each about 2" high, are easily recognized by the style of their modeling and glaze treatments, though all are unmarked. Our advisors for this category are Carol and Jim Carlton; they are listed in the Directory under Colorado.

Animal figurine, ea **45.00**
Ashtray/match holder, Lincoln Zephyr advertising, 1938 ....**38.00**
Bowl/ashtray, maroon, ruffled **25.00**
Cigarette urn, wht tulip cup, 5", on 5" turq leafy pad **25.00**
Paperweight, beetle **35.00**
Tile, HP mc parrot, orange border, sgn CJ Jones, mk, 6" **135.00**
Toothpick holder **20.00**
Vase, blk gloss, bulbous, orig label, 7½" **65.00**
Vase, bud; maroon, 8" **45.00**
Vase, cobalt, ovoid w/vertical ribbing, orig label, 16" **150.00**
Vase, maroon, Indian portrait emb, mk Plains Hotel/1935, 17" .**500.00**
Vase, maroon, rings & hdls, 5" **65.00**
Vase, maroon, urn form, hdls, 7½" **70.00**
Vase, turq, shouldered cylinder, 7" **25.00**

Broadsides

Webster defines a broadside as simply a large sheet of paper printed on one side. During the 1880s, they were the most practical means of mass-communication. By the middle of the century, they had become elaborate and lengthy with information, illustrations, portraits, and fancy border designs. Those printed on coated stock are usually worth more.

Boston town meeting Dec. 1773, sgn Samuel Adams/etc, EX ..**2,500.00**
Committee of correspondence...Boston...Mar 1773, 19x13" **700.00**
Emancipation Proclamation, vignettes, Dimmick, 1864, fr, EX ..**800.00**
House of Representatives, raising men for Army, Sept 1776 ....**300.00**
Lincoln's Farewell Address, speech/portrait/dates, 19x14", EX ...**800.00**
MA Bay proclamation to form government, 1776, 17x14", EX ...**5,500.00**
Mass Bay Colony list of colonists for war, 1776, 1-pg, EX **4,200.00**
McKinley assassination news, dtd, 1-pg, sm **400.00**
Names of those convicted/shot to death by Jackson, 1828, EX ..**1,400.00**
News of Lincoln's Death, 3-column text, fold lines, EX **400.00**
Thanksgiving proclamation, sgn Wm McKinney, 1897, 8x13" **15.00**
To the Laboring Men of NY...Stand by the Law, 1863, 19x12" ..**100.00**
Victory! Last of Confederacy, Lee's surrender, mtd, EX **500.00**
1st Continental Congress votes on trade, Oct 1774, EX **800.00**

Bronzes

Thomas Ball, George Bessell, and Leonard Volk were some of the earliest American sculptors who produced figures in bronze for home decor during the 1840s. Pieces of historical significance were the most popular, but by the 1880s a more fanciful type of artwork took hold. Some of the fine sculptors of the day were Daniel Chester French, Augustus St. Gaudens, and John Quincy Adams Ward. Bronzes reached the height of their popularity at the turn of the century. The American West was portrayed to its fullest by Remington, Russell, James Frazier, Hermon MacNeil, and Solon Borglum. Animals of every species were modeled by A.P. Proctor, Paul Bartlett, and Albert Laellele, to name but a few.

Art Nouveau and Art Deco influenced the medium during the twenties, evidenced by the works of Allen Clark, Harriet Frismuth, E.F. Sanford, and Bessie P. Vonnoh.

Be aware that recasts abound. While often esthetically satisfactory, they are not original and should be priced accordingly. In much the same manner as prints are evaluated, the original castings made under the direction of the artist are the most valuable. Later castings from the original mold are worth less. A recast is not made from the original mold. Instead, a rubber-like substance is applied to the bronze, peeled away, and filled with wax. Then, using the same 'lost wax' procedure as the artist uses on completion of his original wax model, a clay-like substance is formed around the wax figure and the whole fired to vitrify the clay. The wax, of course, melts away, hence the term 'lost wax.' Recast bronzes lose detail and are somewhat smaller than the original due to the shrinkage of the clay mold. For further study we recommend *Huxford's Fine Art Value Guide*, available at your local bookstore or from Collector Books.

A. Hutsmann, Nude on Horseback, on marble plinth, 20th Century, 16", $2,200.00.

Alonzo, D; semi-nude on rock, windblown gown, gilded, 11" .3,000.00
Ancilloti, T; bust: medieval soldier, marble plinth, 24" 950.00
Aouard, HA; Souviens Toi, father scolds son, 29" 3,600.00
Austrian, bronco buster, rearing horse, cold pnt, 1900s, 8" 500.00
Austrian, golfer having just swung, cold pnt, 12½" 1,900.00
Austrian, heron, no base, cold pnt, 4" 300.00
Austrian, semi-nude dancer, cold pnt, 13" 2,000.00
Austrian, setter w/game bird in mouth, cold pnt, 5½" 250.00
Austrian, 2 Muslims at prayer on prayer rug, cold pnt, 3" 600.00
Austrian, 3 Egyptian children dance, 4th w/flute, 5" L 1,000.00
Austrian, 3 elephants under lg palm tree, 18" 1,400.00
Barye, A; African lion, 11x17" 2,450.00
Bergmann, F; Turk, astonished posture, cold pnt, 13" 1,000.00
Bitter, Ary; elephant pr, gilt patina, Susse Freres, 6½" 660.00
Boese, J; nude hold baby aloft, gold patina, 21" 1,700.00
Bouraine, bust of young girl, cire perdue Etling Paris, 18" 1,650.00
Bouraine, dancer, skirt swirled before her, gilt, 1925, 15" 1,400.00
Bouraine, nude w/hat & fan, rose in her teeth, 27" 1,850.00
Bureau, L; flying hawk, orig gilt, 14" 900.00
Calot, H, after; snake charmer, gilt patina, 25" 550.00
Calot, H; roller skater, marble base, gilt patina, 21" 600.00
Carnier, E; boy sits on stump/examines sword, 25" 500.00
Chalon, L; equestrienne Valkyrie w/spear, parcel gilt, 20" 2,750.00
Chalon, L; Nouveau maid w/flowers in hair, 21" 1,900.00
Chiparus, dancer, stands/holds mirror, marble base, 17" 5,500.00
Chiparus, Syrian dancer, base w/plaque of 2nd dancer, 14" 1,650.00
Colinet, Claire Jeanne Roberte; dancer, arm upraised, 24" 3,300.00
Collet, maid w/star as crown, brn/blk patina, 1900, 18" 1,500.00
Coudray, G; Fille d'Assouan, water carrier, onyx base, 14" 750.00
Darsont, J; Heinze & Barth, nude w/panther, 19" 1,000.00
de Haen, V; 2 nudes recline in grapes, dk gr patina, 19" 2,750.00
Descomps, Joe; dancer, breasts exposed, on 1 ft, 18" 1,500.00
Descomps, Joe; maid w/staff followed by goat, 28" 1,800.00
Drouot, E; man plows w/oxen, marble base, 24" 1,200.00
Dubucand, A, after; hound at point, 6" L 150.00
Erte, Arctic Sea, 1988, 29" 4,000.00
Erte, Beauty & Beast, 1980, 16½" 6,600.00
Erte, La Jalousie, parcel gilt, 1980, 14" 2,400.00
Erte, maid, bl robe w/stars, Fine Art Aquisitions, '85, 18" 3,300.00
Ferri, kneeling Indian maid, gold-brn patina, #936, 14" 935.00
Galatea, lamp: nymph supported by 3 branches for bulbs, 33" .1,300.00
Geo Recipon, nude drives spike into horseshoe, 5" 990.00
Guilbert, E; semi-nude, mirror in left hand, blk patina, 31" 1,300.00
Guirande, TD; dancer in pleated gown waves garland, 25" ...10,980.00
Gurschner, kneeling nude ea side of basin, Austria, 11" 900.00
Hagenauer, horse's head, mk Made in Austria, 9" 600.00
Hanak, Anton (att); standing nude, sq wood base, 1916, 32" .1,100.00
Hottot, L; Arab woman w/jar, Arab man w/gun, mc, 20", pr ...5,500.00
Hottot, L; bas-relief, warrior (Arab woman), 16x25", pr 850.00
Houdon, The Kiss, busts of 2 lovers in embrace, brn, 19" 1,500.00
Humlik, J; seated birdman, 5½" 440.00
Hutsmann, A; nude sits on grazing horse, marble base, 16" 2,200.00
Japanese, pheasant, mc patina, cvd wood base, 1850s, 28" L ...4,200.00
Kauba, C; St George slays dragon, gilt/marble base, 7½" 850.00
Kawalczewski, maid smiles at frog prince, brn patina, 10" 1,400.00
Kelety, Alex; man w/oar, reclining nude, in gondola, 35" L 3,000.00
Lanceray, 3 Cossack/horses, snowy ground (marble), 16x21" ..5,600.00
Laporte, E; juggler balancing balls, wht onyx base, 13" 1,500.00
Laurel, P; high-stepping maid w/grapes, 1925, 13" 1,650.00
Levasseur, H, after; Aurore, draped nude w/crescent, 37" 2,700.00
Lorenzl, dancer, ivory head/hands, pnt costume, 1925, 16" ...13,200.00
Lorenzl, dancer w/fan, Pierrot kneeling beside, 9" 825.00
Maignan, M; En Peril, fisherman in perilous storm, 17" 2,200.00
Maindron, EH; Velleda, classical maid leans on tree, 18" 1,200.00

Marcy, G, after; Rape of Orithea by Boreas, dk brn, 36" 9,000.00
Marquet, R; bk-to-bk dancing nudes, gilt patina, 15" 2,500.00
Mayer, N; Le Matin, bust of awakening Nouveau maid, 22" ...2,400.00
Mayer, N; Le Matin, 22" bust of lady, on columnar ped, 48" ...2,850.00
McKee, woman kneels before satyr, sgn/1930, Valsuani, 10" ...1,200.00
Menconi, D; bust: Geo Washington, dtd 1862, 26", +plinth ...4,300.00
Mene, PJ; 4 dogs attack wild boar, oval plinth, 18" 2,700.00
Moigniez, J; cock phesant, 23" 2,000.00
Moreau, A; Nouveau maid, flowing dress/hair, 29" 2,000.00
Moreau, A; Venus disarming Cupid, 35" 4,500.00
Mucha, after; Tetes Byzantines, plaque, 8", pr 1,950.00
Pautrot, F; seated hound w/duck, 12" 875.00
Philippe, P; nude, stretching, blk marble base, 1925, 12" 550.00
Pilz, O; maid rides leaping gazelle, dk brn patina, 14" 770.00
Pompom, Francis; dove on rectangular base, blk patina, 10" ...2,400.00
Remington, after; bust of Indian, 10" 150.00
Remington, after; Horse Thief, 11" 150.00
Reter, V; 2 bear cubs wrestling, 5" 750.00
Richter, F; nude dancer, right arm raised, marble base, 8" 375.00
Russell, CM, after; Indian on horsebk shoots buffalo, 17" L 375.00
Schotz, Benno; child's head, on 2¼" wood base, 9" 400.00
Siegel, C; Bacchante, nude w/grapes & wine cup, 19" 800.00
Silvestre, Leda & Swan, Susse Fes Edts Paris, 32x14" 2,200.00
Stoll, F; nude before stylized tree, parcel gilt, 33" 9,500.00
Trouillard, G; satyr pursues nymph, 1800s, 20" 1,800.00
Unmk, bust of Beethoven, marble socket, 1870s, 20" 900.00

Vienna bulldog, 3", $650.00.

Viennese, lamp: Arab kneels in hut, fish beside him, 9", EX 495.00
Viennese, owl stands on book, EX detail, 6½" 600.00
Viennese, parrot, cold pnt, 1800s, 14" L 500.00
Villanis, E; Sapho, draped lady w/harp, gold-brn, 17" 1,200.00

Brouwer

Theophlis A. Brouwer, recognized as an accomplished artist even before his interests turned to the medium of pottery, started a small one-man operation in 1894 in East Hampton, New York. Two years later he relocated in Westhampton where he perfected the technique of fire-painting, learning to control the effects of the kiln to produce the best-possible results. In 1925 he founded the Ceramic Flame Company in New York, but it is for his earlier work that he is best known. Brouwer died in 1932.

Vase, dk brn metallic w/some copper, gr & purple irid, 5x6" 800.00

Vase, gr/orange/yel/brn fire-pnt mottle, can neck/hdls, 7" **1,200.00**

Brownies by Palmer Cox

Created by Palmer Cox in 1883, the Brownies charmed children through the pages of books and magazines, as dolls, on their dinnerware, in advertising material, and on souvenirs. Each had his own personality, among them The Bellhop, The London Bobby, The Chairman, and Uncle Sam. But the oversized, triangular face with the startled expression, the protruding tummy, and the spindlelegs were characteristics of them all. They were inspired by the Scottish legends related to Cox as a child by his parents, who were of English descent. His introduction of the Brownies to the world was accomplished by a poem called *The Brownies Ride*. Books followed in rapid succession, thirteen in the series, all written as well as illustrated by Palmer Cox.

By the late 1890s, the Brownies were active in advertising. They promoted such products as games, coffee, toys, patent medicines, and rubber boots. 'Greenies' were the Brownies' first cousins, created by Cox to charm and to woo through the pages of the advertising almanacs of the G.G. Green Company of New Jersey. Perhaps the best-known endorsement in the Brownies' career was for the Kodak Brownie, which became so popular and sold in such volume that their name became synonymous with this type of camera. Our advisor for this category is Faye Pisello; she is listed in the Directory under New York.

Ashtray, RS Germany, 1913 ....**45.00**
Basket, SP, Brownies w/chocolate advertising, Tufts **140.00**
Book, Brownie Clown of Brownietown, Century, 1908, EX **200.00**
Book, Brownies' Kind Deed, WB Conkey, Chicago, 1903, VG **25.00**
Book, Funny Stories About Funny People, 1905, EX **35.00**
Book, Queer People, Palmer Cox illus, 1894, EX **45.00**
Box, Log Cabin Brownies, cabin form, Nat'l Biscuit Co, 1920s ..**125.00**
Brownie Portrait Cubes, McLoughlin Bros, c Palmer Cox 1892 .**300.00**
Candlestick, Uncle Sam, majolica, 7½" **235.00**
Candy dish, 15 Brownies, Tufts SP, ball ft, 7x5½" **195.00**
Cigar holder/ashtray, full-figure Brownie, Pairpoint SP **335.00**
Cloth, 6 printed dolls to stuff, uncut, NM **600.00**
Comic sheet, 1907, lg, EX **25.00**
Creamer, Little Boy Blue verse & 4 Brownies, gold trim, china.....**75.00**
Cup & saucer, 4 full-figure Brownies on cup, 5 on saucer **75.00**
Dish, child's, SP, 19 Brownies, 8½" **125.00**
Doll, Brownie, Palmer Cox, orig clothes & top hat, 37", EX **300.00**
Figurine, any character, majolica, 9" **300.00**
Game, Brownie Horseshoes, early, complete in box **50.00**
Humidor, Bobby head figural, majolica, 6" **165.00**

Inkwell, majolica **95.00**
Napkin ring, SP, Brownie climbs up side **165.00**
Needle book, Brownies, 1892 World's Fair, rare **35.00**
Paperweight, Brownie figural, SP **110.00**
Paperweight, 3 intaglio-cut Brownies in glass base, gold pnt, 3" .**135.00**
Pin box, SP, 6 Brownies on lid **75.00**
Pitcher, Brownies playing golf on tan, china, 6" **100.00**
Plate, head in center, china 7" **50.00**
Plate, 10 action Brownies on rim, china 10" **50.00**
Plate, 5 Brownies wrapped in tattered Am flag, china 7½" **50.00**
Puzzle, Brownies skating, 20-pc, early, fr, 10½x12½" **95.00**
Rubber stamp, set of 12 ....**100.00**
Sheet music, Dance of the Brownies **25.00**
Spoon, 3 action brownies, Compliments of Wonderland, SP **25.00**
Table set, brass, emb Brownies, 3-pc (knife/fork/spoon) **70.00**
Tea tile, 6 dancing Brownies, 6¼" dia **95.00**
Toothpick, satin glass, 3 Brownies, Mt WA **400.00**
Tray, 2 fencing Brownies, self hdls, china 6¼x4½" **75.00**

Brush

George Brush began his career in the pottery industry in 1901 working for the J.B. Owens Pottery Co. in Zanesville, Ohio. He left the company in 1907 to go into business for himself, only to have fire completely destroy his pottery less than one year after it was founded. Brush became associated with J.W. McCoy in 1909 and for many years served in capacities ranging from General Manager to President. (From 1911 until 1925, the firm was known as The Brush-McCoy Pottery Co.; see that section for information.) After McCoy died, the family withdrew their interests, and in 1925 the name of the firm was changed to The Brush Pottery. The era of hand-decorated art pottery had passed for the most part and would soon be completely replaced by the production of commercial lines. Of all the wares bearing the later Brush script mark, their figural cookie jars are the most collectible.

For additional information on Brush cookie jars, we recommend *The Encyclopedia of Cookie Jars* by our cookie jar advisors, Joyce and Fred Roerig; they are listed in the Directory under South Carolina. See also Brush-McCoy.

Cookie Jars

Antique Touring Car, minimum value **375.00**
Boy w/Balloons, minimum value **500.00**
Cherry Jar, H5 ....**45.00**
Chick in Nest **385.00**
Cinderella Pumpkin **165.00**
Circus Horse, gr, minimum value **500.00**
Circus Horse, pk, minimum value **750.00**
Clown, yel pants **185.00**
Clown Bust **225.00**
Cookie House **65.00**
Covered Wagon **585.00**
Cow w/Cat on Bk, brn **110.00**
Cow w/Cat on Bk, purple, minimum value **500.00**
Davy Crockett, gold trim **385.00**
Davy Crockett, no gold **200.00**
Dog w/Basket **325.00**
Donkey w/Cart, #23, brn **285.00**
Donkey w/Cart, #33, gray **350.00**
Elephant w/Baby Bonnet & Ice Cream Cone, wht **375.00**
Elephant w/Monkey on Bk, minimum value **1,000.00**
Fish **475.00**
Formal Pig, yel hat & coat **285.00**

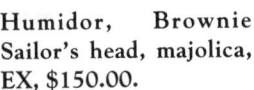
Humidor, Brownie Sailor's head, majolica, EX, $150.00.

Granny, pk apron, bl dots on skirt 225.00
Granny, plain skirt 360.00
Happy Bunny, wht 210.00
Hen on Basket 110.00
Hillbilly Frog, minimum value 3,000.00
Hobby Horse, minimum value 500.00
Humpty Dumpty, w/beanie & bow tie 235.00
Humpty Dumpty, w/peaked brn hat & shoes 200.00
Lantern, brn/cream, mk K1 ....65.00
Laughing Hippo 635.00
Little Angel, minimum value 775.00
Little Boy Blue, gold trim, K25 USA, sm, minimum value 650.00
Little Boy Blue, K24 Brush USA, lg 750.00
Little Boy Blue, no gold, sm 650.00
Little Girl 285.00
Little Red Riding Hood, gold trim, mk, lg, minimum value 700.00
Little Red Riding Hood, no gold, K24 USA, sm 465.00
Nite Owl 95.00
Old Clock 185.00
Old Shoe 85.00
Panda 240.00
Peter Pan, gold trim, lg 800.00
Peter Pan, sm 465.00
Pumpkin w/Lock on Door, W24 ....325.00
Puppy Police 525.00
Raggedy Ann 465.00
Sitting Hippo 465.00
Sitting Pig 465.00
Smiling Bear 465.00
Squirrel on Log 85.00
Squirrel w/Top Hat, blk coat & hat 235.00
Squirrel w/Top Hat, gr coat 220.00
Stylized Owl 425.00
Stylized Siamese 460.00
Teddy Bear, feet apart 250.00
Teddy Bear, feet together 150.00
Treasure Chest 160.00

Miscellaneous

Basket, wht w/emb daisies & bow, #632, 8x7" 30.00
Carafe, Coppertone, brn irid w/drip glaze, 8-cup 40.00
Figurine, rooster, beige w/red comb, #136, 14", minimum value .350.00
Figurine, squirrel holding nut to mouth, #482, 8½" 125.00
Jardiniere, Cameo, wht swags on yel, #273, 11" 150.00
Planter, elephant, cartoon-like extra-lg head, #136, 8x8" 40.00
Planter, rabbit sits atop log section, #209, 6" L 20.00
Vase, gray-bl w/pk pagoda, sqd form, #225, 7½" 35.00

Vase, Blue Onyx, late 1920s, #112, 9½", $95.00.

Vase, lime gr drip glaze, concave w/ribbed waist, hdls, 12" 40.00
Vase, pk, long S-shape hdls join body at middle, #211, 12" 40.00
Vase, Southern bell figural, #218 ....40.00
Vase, swan figural, #631, 6x9½" 30.00
Vase, V form w/emb eagle, 8" 65.00
Vase, wht w/diagonal emb floral band, snail hdls, #632, 7x8" 35.00

Brush-McCoy

The Brush-McCoy Pottery was formed in 1911 in Zanesville, Ohio, an alliance between George Brush and J.W. McCoy. Brush's original pottery had been destroyed by fire in 1907; McCoy had operated his own business there since 1899. After the merger, the company expanded and produced not only their staple commercial wares, but also fine artware. Lines such as Navarre, Venetian, Oriental, and Sylvan were of fine quality equal to that of their larger competitors. Because very little of the ware was marked, it is often mistaken for Weller, Roseville, or Peters and Reed.

In 1918 after a fire in Zanesville had destroyed the manufacturing portion of that plant, all production was contained in their Roseville, Ohio plant #2. A stoneware type of clay was used there; as a result, the artware lines of Jewel, Zuniart, King Tut, Florastone, Jetwood, Krakle-Kraft, and Panelart are so distinctive that they are more easily recognizable. Examples of these lines are unique and very beautiful, also quite rare and highly prized!

The Brush-McCoy Pottery operated under that name until after 1925 when it became the Brush Pottery. The Brush-Barnett family retained their interest in the pottery until 1981 when it was purchased by the Dearborn Company. For more information we recommend *The Guide to Brush-McCoy Pottery*, written by Martha and Steve Stanford and edited by David P. Stanford, our advisors for this category. They are listed in the Directory under California. See also Brush.

Bowl, gr matt, #01, 5" 75.00
Candlestick, Cleo, #020, 1914, pr 375.00
Cookie jar, Kolorkraft, #344, 8½" 175.00
Decanter, Bl Onyx, pinch bottle w/music box, 10" 175.00
Jardiniere, Blue-bird, #222, 9" 550.00
Jardiniere, Egyptian, 3 scenes, 1912, 10½" 600.00
Jardiniere, Roman, gladiator holding lion, 1914 ....700.00
Jardiniere, Vogue, #213, 8½" 250.00
Jardiniere & pedestal, Oriental, #2210, 1913 ....2,400.00
Pitcher, New Rock, #331, 1926, 4-pt, 7½" 175.00
Stein, Woodland, #133, 16-oz 125.00
Tankard, Corn Line, #50, 1912, 11" 325.00
Umbrella stand, Oakwood, #81, 23" 725.00
Urn, Gr Onyx, #699, 11½" 225.00
Vase, Florastone, #077, 6" 550.00
Vase, Jetwood, type 1, #045, 11" 750.00
Vase, Jewel, #040, 6" 275.00
Vase, King Tut, scarab design, #050, 1923, 6" 1,000.00
Vase, King Tut, walking figures, #050, 6" 1,200.00
Vase, Kolorkraft, #0162, 12" 200.00
Vase, Krackle-Kraft, #064, 8" 750.00
Vase, Panelart, #076, 1924, 7" 1,100.00
Vase, Red Onyx, #049, 7" 95.00
Vase, Zuniart #051, 4" 225.00

Buffalo Pottery

The founding of the Buffalo Pottery in Buffalo, New York, in 1901 was a direct result of the success achieved by John Larkin through his innovative methods of marketing 'Sweet Home Soap.' Choosing to omit 'middle-man' profits, Larkin preferred to deal directly with the consumer and offered premiums as an enticement for sales. The pottery soon proved a success in its own right and began producing advertising and commemorative items for other companies, as well as commercial tableware. In 1905 they introduced their Blue Willow line after extensive experimentation resulted in the development of the first successful underglaze cobalt achieved by an American company. Between 1905 and 1909, a line of pitchers and jugs were hand decorated in historical, literary, floral, and outdoor themes. Twenty-nine styles are known to have been made. These have been found in a wide array of color variations.

Their most famous line was Deldare Ware, the bulk of which was made from 1908 to 1909. It was hand decorated after illustrations by Cecil Aldin. Views of English life were portrayed in detail through unusual use of color against the natural olive green cast of the body. Today the 'Fallowfield Hunt' scenes are more difficult to locate than 'Scenes of Village Life in Ye Olden Days.' A Deldare calendar plate was made in 1910. These are very rare and are highly valued by collectors. The line was revived in 1923 and dropped again in 1925. Every piece was marked 'Made at Ye Buffalo Pottery, Deldare Ware Underglaze.' Most are dated, though date has no bearing on the value. Emerald Deldare, made with the same olive body and on standard Deldare Ware shapes, featured historical scenes and Art Nouveau decorations. Most pieces are found with a 1911 date stamp. Production was very limited due to the intricate, time-consuming detail. Needless to say, it is very rare and extremely desirable.

Abino Ware, most of which was made in 1912, also used standard Deldare shapes, but its colors were earthy and the decorations more delicately applied. Sailboats, windmills, and country scenes were favored motifs. These designs were achieved by overpainting transfer prints and were often signed by the artist. The ware is marked 'Abino' in hand-printed block letters. Production was limited; as a result, examples of this line are scarce today. Prices only slightly trail those of Emerald Deldare Ware.

The many uncataloged items that have been found over the years indicate that Buffalo Pottery decorators were free to use their own ideas and talents to create many beautiful one-of-a-kind pieces.

Our advisors for this category are Lila and Fred Shrader; they are listed in the Directory under California. See also Willow Ware.

Abino

Bowl, sauce; windmills, 5½"	450.00
Candlestick, sailing scene, 9½"	575.00
Creamer, sailing scene, 4¼"	485.00
Plate, sailing ships, 10¼"	625.00
Plate, scene, 'Portland, Maine,' 8½"	525.00
Tankard, meadow & stream, 10"	1,200.00
Teapot, sailing scene, w/lid	975.00
Tray, mill pond scene, 12x9"	1,150.00
Vase, windmill & pond, 7"	875.00

Deldare

Ashtray/matchbox holder, Ye Olden Days	525.00
Bowl, Fallowfield Hunt, Breakfast, 12"	900.00
Bowl, fruit; Ye Olden Days, 9"	485.00
Candle holder/matchbox holder, w/finger ring	500.00
Candlestick, Emerald, 9"	950.00
Candlestick, shield-bk, 7"	950.00
Chocolate pot, Dr Syntax Reading..., w/lid	1,975.00
Creamer, Fallowfield Hunt	285.00
Creamer & sugar bowl, Scenes of Village Life, w/lid	400.00
Cup & saucer, chocolate; Ye Olden Days	410.00

Cup & saucer, demitasse; Ye Olden Days	350.00
Hair receiver, Ye Village Street	365.00
Humidor, Fallowfield Hunt	750.00
Humidor, Ye Lion Inn	600.00
Matchbox holder, Emerald, evening scene	725.00
Mug, Emerald, American Indian, colorfully dressed	700.00
Mug, Fallowfield Hunt, Breaking Cover, 3½"	325.00
Mug, Fallowfield Hunt, untitled, 4½"	360.00
Mug, Ye Lion Inn, 3½"	275.00
Mug, Ye Lion Inn, 4½"	300.00
Pin tray, Emerald, 6½x3½"	525.00
Pitcher, Emerald, Dr Syntax Hunting..., 10"	1,050.00
Pitcher, Fallowfield Hunt, The Return, 8"	625.00
Pitcher, Fallowfield Hunt, The Start, 9"	675.00
Pitcher, Ye Village Scenes, Annual Rent, 8"	550.00
Pitcher, Ye Village Scenes, Their Manner..., 6"	500.00
Pitcher, Ye Village Scenes, Ye Lion Inn, 10"	750.00
Plaque, Fallowfield Hunt, Breakfast at 3 Pigeons, 12"	590.00
Plaque, Ye Lion Inn, 12"	500.00
Plate, calendar; 1910, 9½"	1,650.00
Plate, chop; Ye Lion Inn, 14"	625.00
Plate, Deldare Ware, salesman's sample, 7"	1,025.00
Plate, Emerald, Dr Syntax Making a Discovery, 10"	875.00
Plate, Emerald, Dr Syntax Star Gazing, 9½"	750.00
Plate, Fallowfield Hunt, Breaking Cover, 10"	285.00
Plate, Fallowfield Hunt, The Start, 9¼"	220.00
Plate, Ye Olden Times, 9½"	185.00
Plate, Ye Village Street, 7¼"	125.00
Powder jar, Ye Village Street, w/lid	365.00
Punch bowl, Fallowfield Hunt, 14½"	5,100.00
Relish dish, Ye Olden Times, 12x6"	450.00
Shakers, Emerald, artist sgn, pr	550.00
Sugar bowl, Fallowfield Hunt, 6-sided	285.00
Tankard, Fallowfield Hunt, 12"	950.00
Tankard, Ye Lion Inn, 12"	900.00
Tankard, Ye Lion Inn, 7"	825.00
Tea tile, Emerald, Dr Syntax, 6"	550.00
Tea tile, Traveling in Ye Olden Days, 6"	300.00
Teapot, Fallowfield Hunt	435.00
Toothpick holder, Emerald, 2¼"	395.00
Tray, calling card; Emerald, Dr Syntax, 7"	570.00
Tray, calling card; Fallowfield Hunt, Breakfast, 7¾"	395.00

Tray, Dancing Ye Minuet, 9x12", $595.00.

Tray, tea; Heirlooms, 14½x10"	695.00
Vase, Emerald, Art Nouveau geometric design, 8"	1,050.00
Vase, Fallowfield, horse decor at shoulder, 7"	855.00

Vase, untitled scenes of fashionable people, 8" 925.00

Miscellaneous

Ashtray, Sea Cave Restaurant, Multifleure Lamelle 45.00
Bowl, Japan pattern, 7" 75.00
Bowl, Vienna pattern, oval, 9" 75.00
Butter pat, Blue Willow 18.00
Butter pat, Bluebird 12.50
Creamer, Roosevelt Bears, 2¾" 85.00
Creamer, Roycroft, Inn, 3" 38.00
Fish set, platter+6 9" plates 450.00
Game set, 15x11" platter+6 9" plates 450.00
Gravy boat, Blue Willow, w/underplate 85.00
Mug, Tom & Jerry, Colorido ware 50.00
Mug, Vacation, 4½" 110.00
Pitcher, Blue Willow, 7½" 235.00
Pitcher, Buffalo Hunt scenes, 6" 385.00
Pitcher, Chrysanthemum, 7½" 65.00
Pitcher, Dr Syntax, blue design w/floral border 350.00
Pitcher, Gaudy Willow, 7½" 400.00
Pitcher, Geranium, mc, 3½" 95.00
Pitcher, Holland, 6" 450.00
Pitcher, Roosevelt Bears, 8" 1,300.00
Pitcher, Vienna pattern, 6½" 165.00
Plate, Christmas; 1950-1960, ea 50.00
Plate, commemorative; Faneuil Hall, bl, 10½" 65.00
Plate, commemorative; Mt Vernon, 7½" 65.00
Plate, Davenport's, 1929, 9½" 38.50
Plate, Forest Service, US Dept of Ag, 9½" 45.00
Plate, Gaudy Willow, 10½" 155.00
Plate, Globe Dairy Lunch, LA, Cal, 8" 45.00
Plate, Roosevelt Bears, 7¼" 250.00
Platter, Fallowfield Hunt scenes on Colorido body 350.00
Teapot, ivory body w/platinum decor, w/orig teaball 175.00
Teapot, Princess, ornate hdl 150.00
Vase, Geranium, teal, 4" 75.00

Burmese

Burmese glass was patented in 1885 by the Mount Washington Glass Co. It is typically shaded from canary yellow to a rosy salmon color. The yellow is produced by the addition of uranium oxide to the mix. The salmon color comes from the addition of gold salts and is achieved by reheating the object (partially) in the furnace. Thus, it is called 'heat sensitive' glass. Thomas Webb of England was licensed to produce Burmese and often added more gold, giving an almost fuchsia tinge to the salmon in some cases. They called their glass 'Queen's Burmese,' and this is sometimes etched on the base of the object. This is not to be confused with Mount Washington's 'Queen's Design,' which refers to the design painted on the object. Both companies added decoration to many pieces. Mount Washington-Pairpoint produced some Burmese in the late 1920s and Gunderson and Bryden in the '50s and '70s, but the color and shapes are different. Our advisors for this category are Dolli and Wilfred Cohen; they are listed in the Directory under California. In the listings that follow, examples are assumed to have the satin finish unless noted shiny.

Bottle, scent; floral, sterling top, Webb, 3½" 615.00
Bowl, berries, collared 6-sided top, Webb, 3¼x4" 325.00
Bowl, floral, appl lobed rim, Webb, 3¾x6" 1,100.00
Bowl, folded-over star-shaped top, unmk Webb, 2¼x3⅞" 210.00
Bowl, lav 5-petal floral, collared 6-sided top, 3x4" 310.00

Creamer, Mt WA, 3¾" 350.00
Cruet, melon ribs, Mt WA, 6½" 1,065.00
Cruet set, ribbed, 2 w/pr cylinder shakers in SP fr, Mt WA 2,250.00
Fairy lamp, ruffled base, mk Clarke cup, 5¼x7" 650.00
Jam dish, appl yel shell band as fitter, SP basket fr, 7x7" 295.00
Mustard, sm coral/wht flowers, ribbed, SP top, 3¼" 385.00
Pitcher, gold mums, bk: wht mums, sq lip, Mt WA, 4¾x3½" 650.00
Pitcher, lemonade; bulbous, sqd hdl, Webb, 7" 850.00
Pitcher, pine cones & needles, unmk Webb, 3⅛x2½" 595.00
Pitcher, tapering cylinder, 6½" 300.00
Punch cup, Mt WA, 2¾x2½" 395.00
Rose bowl, floral, 6-crimp, Webb, 2¼x2⅜" 295.00
Rose bowl, no decor, 8-crimp, unmk Webb, 3¼x3⅛" 225.00
Rose bowl, 5-petal floral, lav/gr/brn, 8-crimp, Webb, 3" 395.00
Sugar shaker, egg form, HP florals, unfired, Mt WA 495.00
Sweetmeat, appl shell trim, Webb, SP basket fr, 7½x6½" 295.00
Toothpick holder, collared 6-sided top, unmk Webb, 2⅝" 275.00
Tumbler, water; 3¾x2¾" 245.00
Vase, acorns & leaves, gold & gr, unmk Webb, 4¼x3" 325.00
Vase, acorns & leaves, ruffled, unmk Webb, 3¾x2½" 300.00
Vase, berries, lt ribbing, ftd trumpet form, Webb, 3¾" 275.00
Vase, berries, star-shape top, Webb, Queen's, 3¼x2¼" 335.00
Vase, berries & leaves, hexagonal top, Webb, 3¼x4" 300.00
Vase, berries & leaves, red/gr, petal top, Webb, 3x2⅞" 325.00
Vase, Dmn Quilt, floral, tricorner folded-in rim, 2" 300.00
Vase, floral, bl/gr/brn, dimpled w/long neck, unmk Webb, 8" 495.00
Vase, floral, bulbous w/collared 6-sided top, Webb, 3⅛" 295.00
Vase, floral, ruffled top, Webb, 4¼x2⅝" 325.00
Vase, floral, Webb, Queen's, 7⅜x4⅛" 695.00
Vase, flowering vines/2 birds, Webb, 12x5¼", pr 4,230.00
Vase, folded-over star-shaped top, unmk Webb, 3x3⅜" 225.00
Vase, ivy, bulbous w/long slim neck, Webb, 10x5½" 995.00
Vase, ivy, pinched-in sides, shield-shape top, Webb, 3⅛" 325.00
Vase, jack-in-pulpit; crimped/folded, 12" 725.00
Vase, lily; Mt WA, 10x4¼" 375.00
Vase, lily; sm floral, coral rims, blush w/in throat, 8" 995.00
Vase, lily; 14" 550.00
Vase, overall 3-color coralene branches, Mt WA, 8x6" 1,500.00
Vase, shiny, flared/scalloped cylinder, rnd mk, 8½" 440.00
Vase, waisted neck, fluted rim, att Mt WA, 13x4½" 475.00
Vase, yel ribs, flared scalloped top, unmk Webb, 3½x2⅝" 225.00
Vase, 4 birds, incurvate top, Mt WA label dtd 1885, 9", pr 3,300.00

Butter Molds and Stamps

The art of decorating butter began in Europe during the reign of Charles II. This practice was continued in America by the farmer's wife who sold her homemade butter at the weekly market to earn extra money during hard times. A mold or stamp with a special design, hand carved either by her husband or a local craftsman, not only made her product more attractive but also helped identify it as hers. The pattern became the trademark of Mrs. Smith, and all who saw it knew that this was her butter. It was usually the rule that no two farms used the same mold within a certain area, thus the many variations and patterns available to the collector today. The most valuable are those which have animals, birds, or odd shapes. The most sought-after motifs are the eagle, cow, fish, and rooster. These works of early folk art are quickly disappearing from the market.

Molds

Compote of fruit & vegetables, EX detail, rpl ft, 4x5" 250.00
Cornflower, EX cvg, rnd case w/plunger, 4¾" dia 90.00

Fish, cracked case, scrubbed, 3¾" dia 350.00
Geometric, deep cvg, cherry, 4½x7", EX 100.00
Roses & cherries, age cracks, rectangular, 2-part, 4x7" 95.00
Sheaf of wheat, dbl, 2½x3¾" L 75.00
Strawberries/leaves, Pat 1866, 6" L 135.00
Strawberry, staved hexagonal case w/pewter bands, 4", VG 125.00

Stamps

Butter stamps: Large berry with two leaves, EX, 4¼", $125.00; Sheaf of wheat with rosettes and foliage, 5½", $275.00.

Berry & leaves, deep cvg, lg, EX 185.00
Cow, sm image, trn threaded hdl, scrubbed, 4" 125.00
Cow w/fence & grain, cvd edge, trn hdl, 4¾" dia 325.00
Double, floral ea side, deeply cvd, edge damage, 4½" dia 250.00
Double, pineapple in ea of 2 parts, rectangular, 2¾x5" 100.00
Eagle & foliage, banner: R Richardson, age cracks, 3¾" dia 250.00
Eagle w/foliage & starflowers, trn hdl, 4" dia 175.00
Floral, stylized, w/cvd lines, age cracks, 4" dia 65.00
Floral, stylized, 1-pc trn hdl, edge damage, 5" dia 75.00
Heart w/edge design, lollipop type 395.00
Leaves (3), 1-pc trn hdl, minor age cracks, 3½" dia 65.00
Lollipop, floral, chip-cvd edge, initials, 6½" 325.00
Lollipop, stylized design w/stars, scrubbed, 9½" 125.00
Lollipop, stylized floral w/hearts, 8" 300.00
Peacock & branch, trn threaded hdl, 4¾" dia 725.00
Pineapple, EX cvg, 1850s, 3¼x4⅛" dia 80.00
Pineapple, semicircular w/trn inserted hdl, 3⅜x7" 200.00
Pineapple w/X-hatched center, knob hdl, 1-pc, 1800s, 3½" 135.00
Pinwheel, deep cvg, trn inserted hdl, scrubbed, 4⅜" dia 300.00
Rose & thistle, 1-pc trn hdl, scrubbed, 4" 125.00
Sheaf & foliage, semicircular, scrubbed/edge wear, 3½x7" 150.00
Sheaf of wheat, 1-pc trn hdl, age cracks, 4½" 80.00
Starflower, stylized, worn, 3¾" dia 40.00
Starflower/Star of David, cvd bk/hdl, 6", EX 300.00
Starwflower variant, deep cvg, serrated border, 2½x4" 95.00
Sunflower & pineapple, X-hatching, EX patina, 3x4" 95.00
Tulip, EX cvg, contained atop V-bk, 6¾" L 400.00
Tulip, EX detail, deep cvg, trn hdl, 5" dia, EX 180.00
Tulip, primitive, 4¾" dia 100.00
Tulip, rectangular, dk stains, 3½x5" 250.00

Buttonhooks

Buttonhooks were made from around the mid-1800s when high-button shoes made of stiff leather became fashionable and continued to be used to some extent until 1935. They were made of bone, brass, iron, or silver — simple utilitarian no-nonsense styles, fold-up styles with jeweled gold handles, and combination styles with built-in gadgets — all designed to ease the struggle of buttoning high-top shoes, long kid gloves, and stiffly starched collars. While most do have a hook end, some were made with a wire loop instead. Study the construction; quality workmanship is an important worth-assesing factor in addition to the more obvious elements of material and design.

Brass, repousse, folding type, 2 hooks 27.00
Celluloid, 7" 9.00
Glove, gold-washed metal, 1" pearl hdl, 2½" 22.50
Ivory hdl, 2½" 25.00
Lead, lady's leg 40.00
Mother-of-pearl hdl, 3½" 18.00
Pilque-a-jour, HP floral, gold on silver, Shiebler, 3¼" 165.00
SP, repousse, hollow hdl, 7¼" 26.00
Sterling, floral, Reed & Barton, 8" 40.00
Sterling, orange/dk gr stones, Scotland, 1900, 2½" 65.00

Calendar Plates

Calendar plates were advertising giveaways most popular from about 1906 until the late twenties. They were decorated with colorful underglaze decals of lovely ladies, flowers, animals, birds and, of course, the twelve months of the year of their issue. During the late thirties they came into vogue again, but never to the extent they were originally. Those with exceptional detailing, or those with scenes of a particular activity are most desirable, so are any from before 1906.

1908, lady, Detroit MI 38.00
1908, Merry Christmas, 4 lg cat faces 45.00
1909, dog's head, Compliments of John S Stewart..., 9" 40.00
1910, Betsy Ross making flag, 9¼" 38.00
1910, horseshoe encircles hunter w/gun 40.00
1910, Newfoundland dog w/pole, EX 30.00
1910, Washington's Old Home at Mt Vernon, roses & ribbons 35.00
1911, hunter w/dog & quail 40.00
1911, lg rose, calendar on horseshoe w/ribbons, 8½" 25.00
1912, biplane, Cincinnati grocery 65.00
1912, El Capitan Yosemite Valley, CA, 8½" 25.00
1912, flowers & cherubs, 8½" 25.00
1912, Indian maiden sits by fire & husks corn 40.00
1912, owl, Augusta IL 35.00
1913, boy in rags under arch, 8" 24.00
1914, Sandpiper, sgn RK Beck, 9½" 45.00
1914, 3 plums & 1 pear, 7¼" 25.00
1915, buck deer at edge of woods, people in canoe, 7" 27.50
1915, Panama Canal, w/Am flag, 6" 50.00

1915, Panama Canal, 7", $50.00.

1918, violets & 21 clocks from cities around the world, 9¼" 28.00
1919, flag center, Lubbers Co...MI 35.00
1921, dove & 5 Allied flags, 7½" 37.50
1924, flowers, holly berries & leaves around calendar, 9" 30.00

Calendars

Calendars are collected for their colorful prints, often attributed to a well-recognized artist of the period. Advertising calendars from the turn of the century often have a double appeal when representing a company whose tins, signs, store displays, etc. are also collectible. See also Parrish, Maxfield.

1881, Brooks & Co Varnishes, Blk comic scenes, 25x26", EX 350.00
1890, Dubuque Fire & Marine Insurance, complete, EX 75.00
1892, Hood's Sarsaparilla, Sewing Circle, complete pad 35.00
1895, Royal Fire Insurance, full pad 25.00
1897, Berlin Iron Bridge Co, bridges & factory, 14x11", VG 80.00
1898, Rock Spring Brewery, girl on phone, full pad, 20x14", EX ..900.00
1899, Commercial Cable Co, mtd on heavy cb, 22x14", G 25.00
1900, Hood's Sarsaparilla, proverbs, girls diecut, 6¼", EX 32.00

1900, United States Fidelity and Guaranty Co., naval officer vignettes, framed, 14x20", EX, $425.00.

1901, Du Pont Smokeless Powder, EH Osthaus, 28x14", EX ...1,400.00
1903, A&P Tea, shopkeeper & products, full pad, 19x15", EX ...180.00
1904, Christian Herald, children's heads in butterflies, NM 350.00
1904, De Laval, children in field, 18x12", VG 250.00
1906, Frank Coe's Fertilizer, full pad, 13x9", EX 70.00
1908, Bemis Brothers Bag Co, 1st 12 presidents, 14x10", VG 90.00
1909, Columbus Brewing, emb diecut, boy & girl 750.00
1911, Pratt's Veterinary Remedies, lady & horse, 16x10", NM ..225.00
1911, Springfield Breweries, lady in blk, 31x23", EX 400.00
1912, Hubbard Fertilizer, 18x24", EX 50.00
1912, Sharples, EX+ 300.00
1913, Bartel's Brewing, girl in profile, full pad, 25x16", VG 450.00
1914, Springfield Breweries, Traver illus, 34x23", VG 425.00
1915, Hood's Sarsaparilla, School Days, complete, EX 45.00
1915, Magic Yeast, boy w/yeast & stick, 18x10", VG 225.00
1916, Dinner Calender, Fannie Merritt Farmer, 56-pg, EX 35.00
1917, De Laval, girl/dog, full pad, 24x12", EX 275.00
1919, Cream City Sash & Door, Santa's elves/factory, 16", EX ..500.00
1919, De Laval, boy w/fish, top only 75.00
1920, Globe Feeds, children & chickens, EX 110.00
1924, Doe-Wah Jack Peaceful Counsel emb, 1924, EX 65.00

1925, Peters Cartridge Co, mallards, 33x18", EX 350.00
1927, Lesson on Thrift, Commercial State Bank, EX 75.00
1936, Burnham Boilers, man in rocker by furnace, 32x21", NM ...35.00
1936, Christener Trucking, die-cut stock truck, EX 150.00
1937, Centennial Beer, man points to ad on wall, 31x19", EX ...350.00
1946, Vargas girls, complete, 12x18" 70.00

Caliente

Caliente was a line of colored dinnerware made by the Paden City Pottery Company in Paden City, West Virginia. It was produced during the 1930s and 1940s in tangerine, yellow, blue, green, and cobalt blue.

Bowl, salad; 10" 25.00
Bowl, 9" 20.00
Candle holder 15.00
Creamer 14.00
Cup & saucer, cobalt 15.00
Plate, 6" 7.50
Plate, 9½" 10.00
Platter, 14" 25.00
Shakers, pr 25.00
Sugar bowl, w/lid 18.00
Teapot 45.00

California Faience

California Faience was the trade name used by William V. Bragdon and Chauncy R. Thomas on vases, bowls, and other artware produced at their pottery known as 'The Tile Shop' in Berkeley, California from 1920 to 1930. Faience tile was the principal product of the business during these years and is the favorite with today's collectors. Items in a glossy glaze are rare and, therefore, more valuable. Tiles were marked 'California Faience' with a die stamp.

Candle holders & curved bowl, bl gloss, 3-pc set 150.00
Flower frog, bsk, 3 high-relief crabs, 2x5" 85.00
Flower holder, Oriental lady washing clothes, 6-color, 6" 85.00
Tile, florals, octagonal 275.00
Tile, flower, red w/gr leaves on sky bl, mk, 5½" dia 250.00
Tile, gr, for corner, sq w/rnd corner, 4½x4½" 25.00
Tile, mc flowers in basket, mk Evans, 5¼" dia 295.00
Tile, trees/tower, 4-color on gr gloss, 5" dia 250.00
Vase, blk matt ext, yel gloss int, flared, 9x6" 180.00
Vase, red gloss, stylized leaves, 6½" 175.00
Vase, rose gloss, mk, 7" 195.00

California Perfume Company

D.H. McConnell, Sr, founded the California Perfume Company (C.P. Company; C.P.C.) in 1886 in New York City. He had previously been a salesman for a book company, which he later purchased. His door-to-door sales usually involved the lady of the house, to whom he presented a complimentary bottle of inexpensive perfume. Upon determining his perfume to be more popular than his books, he decided that the manufacture of perfume might be more lucrative. He bottled toiletries under the name 'California Perfume Company' and a line of household products called 'Perfection.' In 1928 the name 'Avon' appeared on the label, and in 1939 the C.P.C. name was entirely removed from the product. The success of the company is attributed to the door-to-door sales approach and 'money back' guarantee offered by his first 'Depot Agent,' Mrs. P.F.E. Albee, known today as the 'Avon Lady.'

The company's containers are quite collectible today, especially the older, hard-to-find items. Advanced collectors seek bottles and other items labeled Goetting & Co., New York; Goetting's; or Savoi Et Cie, Paris. Such examples date from 1871 to 1896. The Goetting Company was purchased by D.H. McConnell; Savoi Et Cie was a line which they imported to sell through department stores. Also of special interest are packaging and advertising with the Ambrosia or Hinze Ambrosia Company label. This was a subsidiary company whose objective seems to have been to produce a line of face creams, etc., for sale through drugstores and other such commercial outlets. They operated in New York from about 1875 until 1954. Because very little is known about these companies and since only a few examples of their product containers and advertising material have been found, market values for such items have not yet been established. Other items sought by the collector include products marked Gertrude Recordon; Marvel Electric Silver Cleaner; Easy Day Automatic Clothes Washer; pre-1930 catalogs; and California Perfume Company 1909 and 1910 calendars.

There are hundreds of local Avon Collector Clubs throughout the world that also have C.P.C. collectors in their membership. If you are interested in joining, locating, or starting a new club, contact the National Association of Avon Collectors, Inc., listed in the Directory under Clubs, Newsletters, and Catalogs. Those wanting a National Newsletter Club or price guides may contact Avon Times or Avon Collectors' Club Western World listed in the same section. Inquiries concerning California Perfume Company items should be directed toward our advisor, Dick Pardini, whose address is given under California. (Please send a large SASE; not interested in Avons, 'Perfection' marked C.P.C.'s, or Anniversary Keepsakes.)

Natoma Rose Talcum, triangular tin container, 1914, 4-oz, M, $120.00.

American Ideal Box 'C' Set, perfume+powder sachet, 1911, M .300.00
Army & Navy Kit, 6 grooming items, 1918, MIB 200.00
Atomizer Set, atomizer+3 perfumes, ca 1900, M 350.00
Baby Set, oil+powder+soap+boric acid, 1925, M in yel box 300.00
Baking Powder 'California,' 16-oz, 1-lb or 5-lb szs, M, ea 75.00
Bay Rum, came in 4-, 8- & 16-oz, 1890s, M, ea 150.00
Daphne Set, 1-oz perfume, face powder, rouge, 1918, M 200.00
Easy Day/Simplex Automatic Clothes Washer, 1918, MIB 100.00
Flavoring Extract Set, 20 1-oz bottles in blk case, 1912, M 1,100.00
Gentleman's Shaving Set, 7 items, 1923, MIB 300.00
Gertrude Recordons Facial Treatment Set, 4-pc, 1929, MIB 250.00
Gift Box Set #1, ½-oz perfume+powder sachet, 1915, MIB 175.00
Holly Set, pr ½-oz perfumes, 1912, M in Holly-pattern box 250.00
Little Folks Set, 4 sm perfumes, 1915, MIB 300.00
Manicure Set, holds 8 different items, 1912, M 250.00
Marvel Electric Silver Cleaner, 1918, MIB 100.00
Memories That Linger Set, 3 different perfumes, 1913, M 300.00

Mission Garden Perfume, Bavarian glass, 1½-oz, MIB 200.00
Natoma Rose Talcum, triangular tin conainer, 4-oz, 1914, M 120.00
Shoe White, 5-oz sack of powder, 1915, MIB 75.00
Supreme Huile D'Olive Oil, 1-pt or 1-qt can, 1923, M, ea 50.00
Trailing Arbutus Gift Box 'T,' 3-pc, 1915, M in mc box 300.00
Vernafleur Threesom Gift Set, 3-pc, 1928, MIB 200.00
Violet Gift Set 'H,' 1-oz perfume+talc+sachet+atomizer, M 325.00

Calling Cards, Cases, and Receivers

The practice of announcing one's arrival with a calling card borne by the maid to the mistress of the house was a social grace of the Victorian era. Different messages (condolences, a personal visit, or a good-by) were related by turning down one corner or another. The custom was forgotten by WWI. Fashionable ladies and gents carried their personally engraved cards in elaborate cases made of such materials as embossed silver, mother-of-pearl with intricate inlay, tortoise shell, and ivory. Card receivers held cards left by visitors who called while the mistress was out or 'not receiving.' Calling cards with fringe, die-cut flaps that cover the name, or an unusual decoration are worth about $3.00 to $4.00, while plain cards usually sell for around $1.00.

Cases

Calling cards, about $2.00 each.

Ivory, cvd birds & flowers, Oriental, 3¾" L 185.00
MOP, cvd cameo & monogram, 3⅝" 85.00
MOP, Dmn Quilt pattern, blk silk int, 3¾" L 85.00
Silver, emb flower & fruit, bk: eagle, mk L&W, Japan 250.00
Sterling, chinoiserie relief, grapevines, 3¾" 215.00
Sterling, Deco design & initial, w/link chain 75.00
Sterling, envelope form w/postage & address, Shiebler, 3" 385.00
Tortoise shell, fishing scene, canted corners, 4" L 82.50
Tortoise shell, ivory mts, English, 1800s 85.00
Tortoise shell w/ivory & MOP inlays, 3⅝" 125.00

Receivers

Brass, Nouveau nude on shell, Lo-Mar Works 45.00
Pewter, lady w/harp beside tray, Archibald Knox, EX 315.00
Pewter-like metal, lady w/flowing hair, 4½x7" 85.00

Porcelain, bust of armored knight, Derby, 3¾x5" **70.00**
Sterling, allover diapering w/monogram, ftd, Schultz, 6" **120.00**
Sterling, repousse floral border, claw ft, Dominick & Haff **325.00**

Camark

The Camden Art and Tile Company (commonly known as Camark) of Camden, Arkansas was organized in the Fall of 1926 by Samuel J. 'Jack' Carnes. Using clays from Arkansas, John Lessell, who had been hired as Art Director by Carnes, produced the initial lustre and iridescent Lessell wares for Camark ('CAM'den, 'ARK'ansas) before his death in December 1926. Before the plant opened in the Spring of 1927, Carnes brought John's wife Jeanne and step-daughter Billie to oversee the art department's manufacture of Le-Camark. Production by the Lessell family included variations of J.B. Owens' Soudanese and Opalesce and Weller's Marengo and Lamar. Camark's version of Marengo was called Old English. They also made wares identical to Weller's LaSa. Pieces made by John Lessell back in Ohio were signed 'Lessell,' while those made by Jeanne and Billie in Arkansas during 1927 were signed 'Le-Camark.' By 1928 Camark's production centered on traditional glazes. Drip glazes similar to Muncie Pottery were produced, in particular the green drip over pink. In the 1930s commercial castware with simple glossy and matt finishes became the primary focus and would continue so until Camark closed in the early 1960s. Between the 1960s and 1980s, the company operated mainly as a retail store selling existing inventory, but some limited production occurred. In 1986 the company was purchased by the Ashcraft family of Camden, but no pottery has yet been made at the factory.

Our advisor for this category is David Edwin Gifford. He is listed in the Directory under Arkansas. Mr. Gifford is starting an Arkansas Pottery Collector's Society (Camark, Niloak, and others) and seeks those who are interested in joining to write him.

Figurine, cat, blk gloss, climbing, 12" **35.00**
Figurine, cat, wht gloss, beside fishbowl, 8" **30.00**
Jug, mini whiskey, golden brn gloss, 'Pure Corn,' 5" **30.00**
Jug, orange & gr, ball form, clay stopper, 6½" **38.00**
Novelty, cotton dispenser, rabbit, orange, 3" **12.00**
Novelty, dogs, Pointer & Setter, pr **18.00**
Pitcher, parrot hdl, bl gloss, 6½" **65.00**
Planter, swans, blk, dbl neck, 8" **15.00**
Shakers, letters S&P, bl, pr **10.00**
Sign, state of Arkansas, gr, 6½" **60.00**

Vase, fish form, orange
and brown mottle, 8",
$45.00.

Vase, crackle finish, wht, gold mk, 8" **125.00**
Vase, gold lustre palm trees on bronze, sgn Lessell, 12" **500.00**
Vase, gr over pk, horizontally ribbed & fluted, 6¼" **30.00**

Vase, Old English, plum & cream, sgn LeCamark, 8½" **350.00**
Vase, orange & gr, fluted, 5" **25.00**
Wall pocket, flour scoop, pk, 8" **12.00**

Cambridge Glass

The Cambridge Glass Company began operations in 1901 in Cambridge, Ohio. Primarily they made crystal dinnerware and well-designed accessory pieces until the 1920s when they introduced the concept of color that was to become so popular on the American dinnerware market. Always maintaining high standards of quality and elegance, they produced many lines that became best-sellers; through the twenties and thirties they were recognized as the largest manufacturer of this type of glassware in the world.

Of the various marks the company used, the 'C in triangle' is the most familiar. Production stopped in 1958. For a more thorough study of the subject, we recommend *Colors in Cambridge Glass* by the National Cambridge Collectors, Inc.; their address may be found in the Directory under Clubs. *Glass Animals and Figural Flower Frogs from the Depression Era* by Lee Garmon and Dick Spencer is a wonderful source for an in-depth view of this particular aspect of glass collecting. They are both listed in the Directory under Illinois. See also Carnival Glass; Glass Animals.

Apple Blossom, crystal; bowl, cereal; 6" **12.00**
Apple Blossom, crystal; comport, fruit cocktail; 4" **12.50**
Apple Blossom, crystal; pitcher, ball form, 80-oz **115.00**
Apple Blossom, crystal; stem, cordial; #3130, 1-oz **55.00**
Apple Blossom, crystal; tumbler, #3130, ftd, 8-oz **12.00**
Apple Blossom, pk or gr; bowl, relish; 4-part, 12" **60.00**
Apple Blossom, pk or gr; pitcher, #3130, 64-oz **250.00**
Apple Blossom, pk or gr; plate, grill; 10" **50.00**
Apple Blossom, pk or gr; shakers, pr **90.00**
Apple Blossom, pk or gr; sugar bowl, ftd **20.00**
Apple Blossom, pk or gr; vase, 2 styles, 8" **85.00**
Apple Blossom, yel or amber; bowl, pickle; 9" **30.00**
Apple Blossom, yel or amber; butter dish, w/lid, 5½" **200.00**
Apple Blossom, yel or amber; cup **22.00**
Apple Blossom, yel or amber; plate, salad; sq **12.00**
Apple Blossom, yel or amber; plate, 8½" **20.00**
Apple Blossom, yel or amber; stem, cocktail; #3135, 3-oz **22.00**
Apple Blossom, yel or amber; tumbler, #3135, ftd, 8-oz **25.00**
Caprice, bl or pk; bonbon, #155, ftd, oval, 6" **40.00**
Caprice, bl or pk; bowl, #62, belled, 4-ftd, 13" **70.00**
Caprice, bl or pk; bowl, pickle; #102, 9" **50.00**
Caprice, bl or pk; candlestick, #646, 2-light, keyhole, 5" **50.00**
Caprice, bl or pk; cigarette box, #207, w/lid, 3½x2¼" **45.00**
Caprice, bl or pk; cracker jar, #202, w/lid **600.00**
Caprice, bl or pk; finger bowl, #16, w/liner **85.00**
Caprice, bl or pk; oil, #100, w/stopper, 5-oz **175.00**
Caprice, bl or pk; plate, bread & butter; #21, 6½" **20.00**
Caprice, bl or pk; plate, cabaret; #32, 4-ftd, 11" **55.00**
Caprice, bl or pk; saucer, #17 ....**5.50**
Caprice, bl or pk; shakers, #91, ball form, pr **100.00**
Caprice, bl or pk; stem, cocktail; #300, blown, 3-oz **42.50**
Caprice, bl or pk; stem, sherbet; #300, blown, low, 6-oz **15.00**
Caprice, bl or pk; stem, wine; #6, 3-oz **100.00**
Caprice, bl or pk; sugar bowl, #41, lg **15.00**
Caprice, bl or pk; tumbler, #12, ftd, 3-oz **45.00**
Caprice, bl or pk; tumbler, whiskey; #300, 2½-oz **200.00**
Caprice, bl or pk; vase, #344, crimped, 4½" **165.00**
Caprice, crystal; ashtray, #214, 3" **6.00**
Caprice, crystal; bowl, #49, 4-ftd, 8" **30.00**

Caprice, crystal; bowl, #53, crimped, 4-ftd, 10½" 30.00
Caprice, crystal; bowl, #66, crimped, 4-ftd, 13" 32.50
Caprice, crystal; butter dish, #52, ¼-lb 209.00
Caprice, crystal; candy dish, #165, w/lid, 3-ftd, 6" 42.50
Caprice, crystal; comport, #136, 7" 35.00
Caprice, crystal; creamer, #41, lg 10.00
Caprice, crystal; marmalade, #89, w/lid, 6-oz 45.00
Caprice, crystal; pitcher, #183, ball form, 80-oz 90.00
Caprice, crystal; plate, #22, 8½" 14.00
Caprice, crystal; plate, cabaret; #33, 4-ftd, 14" 27.50
Caprice, crystal; punch bowl, ftd 2,000.00
Caprice, crystal; shakers, #92, flat, ind, pr 30.00
Caprice, crystal; stem, claret; #300, blown, 4½-oz 50.00
Caprice, crystal; stem, claret; #5, 4½-oz 35.00
Caprice, crystal; tray, #42, oval, 9" 18.00
Caprice, crystal; tumbler, #11, ftd, 5-oz 20.00
Caprice, crystal; tumbler, juice; #300, ftd, 5-oz 18.00
Caprice, crystal; vase, ivy bowl; #232, 5" 40.00
Chantilly, bowl, flared, 4-ftd, 10" 35.00
Chantilly, bowl, relish/pickle; 2-part, 7" 18.00
Chantilly, bowl, 4-ftd, oval, 12" 35.00
Chantilly, candlestick, 3-light, 6" 37.50
Chantilly, candy box, w/lid, ftd 125.00
Chantilly, cocktail icer, 2-pc 55.00
Chantilly, creamer 14.50
Chantilly, hat, lg 200.00
Chantilly, hurricane lamp, candlestick base 110.00
Chantilly, marmalade, w/lid 55.00
Chantilly, mayonnaise, w/lid & ladle 37.50
Chantilly, pitcher, upright 175.00
Chantilly, plate, cake; tab hdld, 13½" 32.50
Chantilly, plate, dinner; 10½" 55.00
Chantilly, plate, salad; 8" 12.50
Chantilly, salad dressing bottle 75.00
Chantilly, shakers, ftd, pr 30.00
Chantilly, stem, cocktail; #3600, 2½" 24.00
Chantilly, stem, oyster cocktail; #3775, 4½" 15.00
Chantilly, stem, sherbet; #3600, tall, 7-oz 30.00
Chantilly, stem, water; #3779, 9-oz 20.00
Chantilly, stem, wine; #3600, 2½-oz 30.00
Chantilly, sugar bowl, #3900, scalloped edge, ind 11.00
Chantilly, tumbler, juice; #3600, ftd, 5-oz 15.00
Chantilly, tumbler, juice; #3625, ftd, 5-oz 14.00
Chantilly, tumbler, water; #3625, ftd, 10-oz 17.50
Chantilly, vase, bud; 10" 30.00
Cleo, all colors but bl; bowl, cereal; Decagon, 6" 40.00
Cleo, all colors but bl; bowl, console; 12" 35.00
Cleo, all colors but bl; bowl, cranberry; 6½" 37.50
Cleo, all colors but bl; bowl, vegetable; w/lid, 9" 125.00
Cleo, all colors but bl; candy dish, w/lid, tall 75.00
Cleo, all colors but bl; ice tub 45.00
Cleo, all colors but bl; pitcher, #804, w/lid, 60-oz 225.00
Cleo, all colors but bl; pitcher, #937, w/lid, 68-oz 275.00
Cleo, all colors but bl; platter, 15" 175.00
Cleo, all colors but bl; salt cellar, 1½" 65.00
Cleo, all colors but bl; stem, cocktail; #3115, 3½-oz 25.00
Cleo, all colors but bl; stem, sherbet; #3077, low, 6-oz 15.00
Cleo, all colors but bl; syrup pitcher, w/glass lid 165.00
Cleo, all colors but bl; tray, hdld, 12" 150.00
Cleo, all colors but bl; tumbler, #3077, ftd, 8-oz 25.00
Cleo, all colors but bl; tumbler, #3155, ftd, 2½-oz 45.00
Cleo, all colors but bl; tumbler, #3225, ftd, 10-oz 37.50
Cleo, all colors but bl; vase, 11" 125.00
Cleo, all colors but bl; vase, 5¼" 65.00

Cleo, all colors but bl; wafer tray 195.00
Cleo, bl; bowl, pickle; Decagon, 9" 125.00
Cleo, bl; bowl, relish; 2-part 40.00
Cleo, bl; candlestick, 2-light 75.00
Cleo, bl; creamer, Decagon 27.50
Cleo, bl; mayonnaise, ftd 45.00
Cleo, bl; plate, dinner; Decagon, 9½" 85.00
Cleo, bl; saucer, Decagon 5.00
Cleo, bl; sugar bowl, Decagon 25.00
Cleo, bl; tumbler, #3077, ftd, 2½-oz 85.00
Crown Tuscan, ball jug, #3400/114, 64-oz 310.00
Crown Tuscan, candlestick, #1307, 3-light, gold decor, pr 170.00
Crown Tuscan, candlestick, nude stem 110.00
Crown Tuscan, cigarette holder, #1337, Ebony ashtray ft 125.00
Crown Tuscan, compote, seashell, floral decor, 7" 125.00

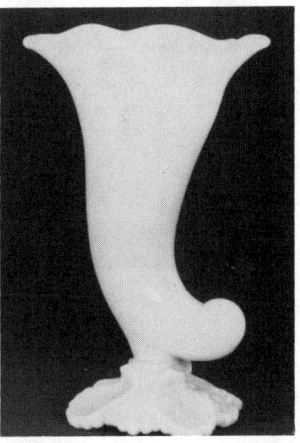

Crown Tuscan, cornucopia vase, 10", $75.00.

Crown Tuscan, decanter, #1321, 28-oz, +2 2-oz sherries 370.00
Crown Tuscan, epergne, #2355 ....70.00
Crown Tuscan, flower block, #2899, 3" 35.00
Crown Tuscan, globe vase, #3400/102, gold decor, 5" 140.00
Crown Tuscan, mannequin head, 18" 1,400.00
Crown Tuscan, vase, #1253, emb florals, 12" 210.00
Crown Tuscan, vase, #1300, Rose Point in gold, 8" 100.00
Crown Tuscan, vase, centerpc; shell, ftd, 8" 88.00
Crown Tuscan, vase, cornucopia; #3900/575, 10" 55.00
Decagon, pastels; bowl, cereal; flat rim, 5¾" 10.00
Decagon, pastels; bowl, cream soup; w/liner 10.00
Decagon, pastels; bowl, fruit; belled, 5½" 5.50
Decagon, pastels; bowl, relish; 2-part, 9" 9.00
Decagon, pastels; comport, 5¾" 12.50
Decagon, pastels; creamer, scalloped edge 8.00
Decagon, pastels; ice bucket 35.00
Decagon, pastels; plate, bread & butter; 6¼" 3.00
Decagon, pastels; plate, service; 12½" 9.00
Decagon, pastels; sauce boat & plate 45.00
Decagon, pastels; stem, cocktail; 3½-oz 12.00
Decagon, pastels; stem, sherbet; high, 6-oz 10.00
Decagon, pastels; tray, pickle; 9" 10.00
Decagon, pastels; tray, service; 12" 10.00
Decagon, pastels; tumbler, ftd, 12-oz 20.00
Decagon, pastels; tumbler, ftd, 5-oz 10.00
Decagon, red or bl; bowl, berry; 10" 20.00
Decagon, red or bl; bowl, cereal; belled, 6" 15.00
Decagon, red or bl; bowl, cranberry; belled, 3½" 17.50
Decagon, red or bl; bowl, vegetable; rnd, 9" 24.00
Decagon, red or bl; creamer, ftd 20.00
Decagon, red or bl; cup 10.00

Decagon, red or bl; ice tub **45.00**
Decagon, red or bl; plate, dinner; 9½" **30.00**
Decagon, red or bl; salt cellar, ftd, 1½" **20.00**
Decagon, red or bl; saucer **2.50**
Decagon, red or bl; server, center hdl **20.00**
Decagon, red or bl; stem, sherbet; low, 6-oz **15.00**
Decagon, red or bl; sugar bowl, ftd **20.00**
Decagon, red or bl; tray, celery; 11" **20.00**
Decagon, red or bl; tumbler, ftd, 10-oz **25.00**
Decagon, red or bl; tumbler, ftd, 2½-oz **22.00**
Diane, basket, ftd, hdls; 6" **16.00**

Diane, bowl, 4-footed, 12", $75.00.

Diane, bowl, celery or relish; 3-part, 9" **30.00**
Diane, bowl, cereal; 6" **25.00**
Diane, bowl, cream soup; #3400, w/liner **27.50**
Diane, candelabrum, 3-light, keyhole **32.50**
Diane, candlestick, 5" **17.50**
Diane, cocktail shaker, w/glass top **125.00**
Diane, creamer **14.00**
Diane, cup **20.00**
Diane, decanter, ball form **175.00**
Diane, hurricane lamp, candlestick base **110.00**
Diane, mayonnaise, w/liner & ladle **35.00**
Diane, pitcher, martini **750.00**
Diane, plate, bread & butter; sq, 6" **5.00**
Diane, plate, dinner; 10½" **60.00**
Diane, plate, salad; 8" **10.00**
Diane, platter, 13½" **65.00**
Diane, shakers, flat, pr **28.00**
Diane, stem, cocktail; #1066, 3-oz **16.00**
Diane, stem, water; #1066, 11-oz **20.00**
Diane, stem, water; #3122, 9-oz **20.00**
Diane, tumbler, iced tea; #1066, 12-oz **20.00**
Diane, tumbler, juice; #1066, 5-oz **12.50**
Diane, tumbler, juice; #3122, 5-oz **13.00**
Diane, tumbler, sham bottom, 2½-oz **35.00**
Diane, vase, bud; 10" **35.00**
Diane, vase, flower; 13" **85.00**
Elaine, bowl, flared, 3-ftd, 10" **30.00**
Elaine, bowl, relish; 2-part, 6" **16.00**
Elaine, candlestick, 2-light, 6" **27.50**
Elaine, comport, 5½" **30.00**
Elaine, cup **20.00**
Elaine, mayonnaise, w/liner & ladle **30.00**
Elaine, plate, dinner; 10½" **60.00**
Elaine, plate, service; 4-ftd, 12" **25.00**
Elaine, shakers, flat, pr **27.50**

Elaine, stem, cocktail; #1402, 3½-oz **20.00**
Elaine, stem, cordial; #1402, 1-oz **55.00**
Elaine, stem, sherbet; #3104, tall, 7-oz **50.00**
Elaine, stem, sherry; #3104, 2-oz **90.00**
Elaine, stem, water; #3121, 10-oz **21.00**
Elaine, tumbler, iced tea; #1402, 12-oz **25.00**
Elaine, tumbler, juice; #3500, ftd, 5-oz **18.00**
Elaine, vase, keyhole, ftd, 9" **45.00**
Flower frog, Bashful Charlotte, bl frost, 11" **495.00**
Flower frog, Bashful Charlotte, crystal, 11" **155.00**
Flower frog, Bashful Charlotte, crystal, 6½" **70.00**
Flower frog, Bashful Charlotte, gr, 11" **250.00**
Flower frog, Bashful Charlotte, gr, 6½" **145.00**
Flower frog, Bashful Charlotte, pk frost, 11" **195.00**
Flower frog, Draped Lady, crystal, 13" **160.00**
Flower frog, Draped lady, crystal, 8½" **97.00**
Flower frog, Draped Lady, dk amber, 13" **290.00**
Flower frog, Draped Lady, dk amber, 8½" **195.00**

Flower frog, Draped Lady, green, 8½", $120.00.

Flower frog, Draped Lady, gr frost, 8½" **125.00**
Flower frog, Draped Lady, lt amber, 8½" **165.00**
Flower frog, Draped Lady, lt pk frost, 13" **175.00**
Flower frog, Draped Lady, med pk, 8½" **100.00**
Flower frog, Draped Lady, moonlight bl, 8½" **325.00**
Flower frog, Draped Lady, pk frost, 8½" **125.00**
Flower frog, Draped Lady, ½ frost & ½ lt pk, 13" **165.00**
Flower frog, Mandolin Lady, crystal **195.00**
Flower frog, Mandolin Lady, gr **295.00**
Flower frog, Rose Lady, crystal, tall base, 9½" **155.00**
Flower frog, Rose Lady, dk amber, tall base, 9½" **245.00**
Flower frog, Rose Lady, dk pk, 8½" **190.00**
Flower frog, Rose Lady, gr, 8½" **245.00**
Flower frog, Two Kids, crystal **150.00**
Gloria, colors; bowl, cream soup; w/rnd liner **35.00**
Gloria, colors; bowl, fruit; 5½" **15.00**
Gloria, colors; comport, fruit cocktail; 4" **20.00**
Gloria, colors; cup, 4-ftd, sq **60.00**
Gloria, colors; plate, bread & butter; 6" **9.00**
Gloria, colors; plate, salad; sq **12.00**
Gloria, colors; saucer, after dinner; rnd **10.00**
Gloria, colors; sugar bowl, ftd, tall **19.00**
Gloria, colors; tumbler, juice; #3115, ftd, 5-oz **20.00**

Gloria, colors; tumbler, juice; #3135, 5-oz 20.00
Gloria, colors; vase, 11" 95.00
Gloria, crystal; bowl, cranberry; 4-ftd, 3½" 17.50
Gloria, crystal; bowl, fruit; hdls, 11" 30.00
Gloria, crystal; candlestick, 6" 17.50
Gloria, crystal; creamer, ftd 11.00
Gloria, crystal; pitcher, ball form, 80-oz 135.00
Gloria, crystal; plate, dinner; 9½" 50.00
Gloria, crystal; shakers, w/glass top, tall, pr 27.50
Gloria, crystal; stem, cocktail; #3035, 3-oz 17.50
Gloria, crystal; tray, sandwich; center hdld, 11" 20.00
Gloria, crystal; tumbler, #3120, ftd, 10-oz 12.00
Gloria, crystal; tumbler, iced tea; #3135, 12-oz 17.00
Imperial Hunt Scene, colors; bowl, 8" 60.00
Imperial Hunt Scene, colors; comport, #3085, 5½" 30.00
Imperial Hunt Scene, colors; finger bowl, #3085, 63-oz 35.00
Imperial Hunt Scene, colors; stem, parfait; #3085, 5½-oz 60.00
Imperial Hunt Scene, colors; tumbler, #3085, ftd, 8-oz 25.00
Imperial Hunt Scene, crystal; cup 45.00
Imperial Hunt Scene, crystal; pitcher, #711, w/lid, 76-oz 150.00
Imperial Hunt Scene, crystal; stem, sherbet; #1420, 10-oz 40.00
Imperial Hunt Scene, crystal; tumbler, #1420, flat, 5-oz 20.00
Mt Vernon, amber or crystal; ashtray, #63, 3½" 8.00
Mt Vernon, amber or crystal; bonbon, #10, ftd, 7" 12.50
Mt Vernon, amber or crystal; bowl, #128, belled, 11½" 30.00
Mt Vernon, amber or crystal; bowl, cereal; #32, 6" 12.50
Mt Vernon, amber or crystal; bowl, pickle; #78, hdl, 6" 12.00
Mt Vernon, amber or crystal; bowl, preserve; #76 ....12.00
Mt Vernon, amber or crystal; bowl, relish; #103, 3-part, 8" 20.00
Mt Vernon, amber or crystal; box, #17, w/lid, sq, 4" 30.00
Mt Vernon, amber or crystal; cake stand, #150, ftd, 10½" 35.00
Mt Vernon, amber or crystal; candlestick, #35, 8" 25.00
Mt Vernon, amber or crystal; celery, #79, 10½" 15.00
Mt Vernon, amber or crystal; comport, #96, belled, 6½" 27.50
Mt Vernon, amber or crystal; creamer, #4, ind 10.00
Mt Vernon, amber or crystal; decanter, #52, w/stopper, 40-oz 70.00
Mt Vernon, amber or crystal; ice bucket, #92, w/tongs 35.00
Mt Vernon, amber or crystal; plate, bread & butter; #4, 6" 3.00
Mt Vernon, amber or crystal; plate, dinner; #40, 10½" 27.50
Mt Vernon, amber or crystal; shakers, #89, tall, pr 25.00
Mt Vernon, amber or crystal; stem, claret; #25, 4½-oz 13.50
Mt Vernon, amber or crystal; stem, water; #1, 10-oz 15.00
Mt Vernon, amber or crystal; sugar bowl, #4, ind 12.00
Mt Vernon, amber or crystal; tumbler, #56, 5-oz 12.00
Mt Vernon, amber or crystal; tumbler, #59, tall, 14-oz 17.00
Mt Vernon, amber or crystal; tumbler, cordial; #87, ftd, 1-oz ...22.00
Mt Vernon, amber or crystal; vase, #119, crimped, 6" 20.00
Nude stem, amber; brandy 100.00
Nude stem, amber; champagne 125.00
Nude stem, amber; cigarette holder, oval 650.00
Nude stem, amber; cocktail 90.00
Nude stem, amber; comport 175.00
Nude stem, amber; cordial 650.00
Nude stem, amber; vase, bud 650.00
Nude stem, amethyst; claret 100.00
Nude stem, amethyst; cocktail 90.00
Nude stem, amethyst; goblet, water 115.00
Nude stem, amethyst; mint dish 375.00
Nude stem, carmen; brandy 120.00
Nude stem, carmen; comport, cupped 130.00
Nude stem, carmen; goblet, water 120.00
Nude stem, cobalt; ashtray 450.00
Nude stem, cobalt; candlestick 950.00
Nude stem, cobalt; cigarette box, short 350.00

Nude stem, cobalt; cigarette box, tall 850.00
Nude stem, cobalt; cocktail, tulip 450.00
Nude stem, cobalt; comport, flared 350.00
Nude stem, cobalt; cordial 750.00
Nude stem, cobalt; mint dish 850.00
Nude stem, cobalt; vase, bud 850.00
Nude stem, cobalt/frosted stem; ivy ball 325.00
Nude stem, Crown Tuscan; candlestick 135.00
Nude stem, Crystal Optic; brandy 115.00
Nude stem, crystal; compote, cupped, Apple Blossom etch 675.00
Nude stem, crystal; compote, Gloria etch 1,200.00
Nude stem, crystal/blk stem; cocktail 140.00
Nude stem, dk emerald gr; comport, flared, Gloria etch 975.00
Nude stem, dk gr; brandy 85.00
Nude stem, dk gr; claret 100.00
Nude stem, dk gr; cocktail 90.00
Nude stem, dk gr; goblet, water 125.00
Nude stem, Gold Krystol; brandy 100.00
Nude stem, Gold Krystol; cocktail 100.00
Nude stem, mocha; cocktail 125.00
Nude stem, moonlight bl; cocktail 135.00
Nude stem, pistaschio; ashtray 600.00
Nude stem, pk; ashtray 495.00
Nude stem, pk; cocktail 140.00
Nude stem, red; candlestick, bobeche & prisms 650.00
Nude stem, red; cocktail, tulip 545.00
Nude stem, red; cordial 750.00
Nude stem, royal bl; ashtray 295.00
Nude stem, royal bl; vase, bud 750.00
Nude stem, smoke crackle; cocktail 650.00
Nude stem, smoke; ashtray 475.00
Portia, basket, hdl, 7" 195.00
Portia, bowl, celery or relish; 5-part, 12" 37.50
Portia, bowl, cranberry; sq, 3½" 20.00
Portia, bowl, flared, 4-ftd, 10" 35.00
Portia, bowl, grapefruit or oyster; 6" 17.00
Portia, bowl, pickle or relish; 7" 22.00
Portia, bowl, relish; 2-part, 6" 16.00
Portia, candlestick, 3-light, 6" 45.00
Portia, candlestick, 5" 20.00
Portia, candy box, w/lid, rnd 65.00
Portia, cigarette holder, urn form 55.00
Portia, cocktail icer, 2-part 60.00
Portia, comport, 5½" 27.50
Portia, creamer, ball form, hdld 25.00
Portia, hurricane lamp, w/candlestick base 145.00
Portia, ice bucket, w/chrome hdl 65.00
Portia, mayonnaise, w/liner & ladle 65.00
Portia, plate, bread & butter; 6½" 7.50
Portia, plate, dinner; 10½" 60.00
Portia, plate, torte; 14" 35.00
Portia, saucer, sq or rnd 3.00
Portia, shakers, flat, pr 25.00
Portia, stem, cocktail; #3121, 3-oz 20.00
Portia, stem, cordial; #3121, 1-oz 55.00
Portia, stem, goblet; #3121, 10-oz 22.50
Portia, stem, goblet; #3126, 9-oz 20.00
Portia, stem, oyster cocktail; #3121, 4½" 15.00
Portia, stem, wine; #3121, 3-oz 27.50
Portia, sugar bowl, ball form, hdld, ftd 22.50
Portia, tray, celery; 11" 27.50
Portia, tumbler, iced tea; #3121, ftd, 12-oz 25.00
Portia, tumbler, iced tea; #3130, 12-oz 22.00
Portia, tumbler, juice; #3121, ftd, 5-oz 16.00

Portia, tumbler, juice; #3124, 5-oz 12.50
Portia, tumbler, juice; #3126, 5-oz 14.00
Portia, tumbler, water; #3124, 10-oz 15.00
Portia, vase, bud; 10" 40.00
Portia, vase, ftd, 6" 40.00
Rosalie, amber; bowl, cream soup 18.00
Rosalie, amber; bowl, fruit; 5½" 10.00
Rosalie, amber; bowl, relish; 2-part, 11" 20.00
Rosalie, amber; bowl, 10" 25.00
Rosalie, amber; celery, 11" 20.00
Rosalie, amber; comport, almond; ftd, 6" 25.00
Rosalie, amber; cup 25.00
Rosalie, amber; marmalade 75.00
Rosalie, amber; plate, bread & butter; 6¾" 5.00
Rosalie, amber; plate, dinner; 9½" 30.00
Rosalie, amber; saucer 4.00
Rosalie, amber; sherbet, #3077, high, 6-oz 14.00
Rosalie, amber; tray, center hdl, 11" 20.00
Rosalie, amber; tumbler, #3077, ftd, 10-oz 20.00
Rosalie, bl, pk, or gr; bowl, console; 13" 50.00
Rosalie, bl, pk, or gr; bowl, cranberry; 3½" 25.00
Rosalie, bl, pk, or gr; bowl, soup; 8½" 40.00
Rosalie, bl, pk, or gr; bowl, 11" 40.00
Rosalie, bl, pk, or gr; candy dish, w/lid, 6" 95.00
Rosalie, bl, pk, or gr; comport, 5¾" 30.00
Rosalie, bl, pk, or gr; creamer, ftd 17.00
Rosalie, bl, pk, or gr; ice tub 60.00
Rosalie, bl, pk, or gr; nut, ftd, 2½" 55.00
Rosalie, bl, pk, or gr; plate, salad; 7½" 10.00
Rosalie, bl, pk, or gr; salt cellar, ftd, 1½" 45.00
Rosalie, bl, pk, or gr; vase, 6" 55.00
Rose Point, ashtray, stack set on metal pole; #1715 .....195.00
Rose Point, basket, #119, hdld, 7" 365.00
Rose Point, bowl, #221, 3-part, 8½" 140.00
Rose Point, bowl, #3400/160, fancy rim, 4-ftd, oblong, 12" 77.50
Rose Point, bowl, #3500/115, hdld, ftd, 9½" 120.00
Rose Point, bowl, #3500/19, fancy edge, ftd, 11" 120.00
Rose Point, bowl, cereal; #3400/53, 6" 57.50
Rose Point, bowl, cranberry; #3400/70, 3½" 80.00
Rose Point, bowl, cream soup; #3400, w/liner 135.00
Rose Point, bowl, fruit; #3400/10, 5" 42.50
Rose Point, bowl, fruit; #3400/1199, 11" 80.00
Rose Point, bowl, nappy; #3400/56, 5½" 42.50
Rose Point, bowl, nut; #3400/71, 4-ftd, 3" 67.50
Rose Point, bowl, salad; Pristine #427 ....125.00
Rose Point, butter dish, #506, w/lid, rnd 175.00
Rose Point, candelabrum, #3500/94, 2-light 90.00
Rose Point, candle holder, #3500/90, torchere, cup ft 165.00
Rose Point, candlestick, #1700/501, sq base & lights 150.00
Rose Point, candlestick, #3121, 7" 70.00
Rose Point, candlestick, #3400/646, keyhole, 1-light, 5" 30.00
Rose Point, candy box, #3121/3, w/lid, tall stem, 5⅜" 135.00
Rose Point, candy box, #3500/57, w/lid, 3-part, 8" 72.50
Rose Point, celery, #3400/652, 12" 57.50
Rose Point, celery & relish, #3900/126, 3-part, 12" 57.50
Rose Point, cheese dish, #980, w/lid, 5" 400.00
Rose Point, cigarette box, #747, w/lid 150.00
Rose Point, coaster, #1628, 3½" 50.00
Rose Point, cocktail icer, #3600, 2-pc 70.00
Rose Point, cocktail shaker, #98, w/metal top, 12-oz ...135.00
Rose Point, comport, #3900/135, 5" 40.00
Rose Point, comport, #3900/136, scalloped edge, 5½" 52.50
Rose Point, creamer, #137, flat 110.00
Rose Point, creamer, #3900/40, scalloped edge, ind 20.00

Rose Point, cup, after dinner; #3400/69 ....225.00
Rose Point, cup, punch; #488, 5-oz 37.50
Rose Point, decanter, #1321, w/stopper, 28-oz 275.00
Rose Point, dressing bottle, #1263, flat 265.00
Rose Point, hat, #1703 ....400.00
Rose Point, honey dish, #3500/139, w/lid 265.00
Rose Point, hurricane lamp, #1617, candlestick base ...175.00
Rose Point, ice bucket, #1402/52 ....185.00
Rose Point, marmalade, #147, 8-oz 130.00
Rose Point, mustard, #151, 3-oz 130.00
Rose Point, oil, #3400/99, ball form, w/stopper, 6-oz ...110.00
Rose Point, pitcher, #3400/152, w/ice lip, 76-oz 275.00
Rose Point, pitcher, martini; #1408, 60-oz 1,750.00
Rose Point, plate, bread & butter; #3400/60, 6" 13.50
Rose Point, plate, breakfast; #3400/62, 8½" 20.00
Rose Point, plate, canape; #693, 6⅛" 150.00
Rose Point, plate, crescent salad; #485, 9½" 225.00
Rose Point, plate, dinner; #3900/24, 10½" 125.00
Rose Point, plate, torte; #3400/65, 14" 120.00
Rose Point, relish, #3400/90, 2-part, 6" 32.50
Rose Point, relish, #3500/85, hdld, 10" 70.00
Rose Point, shakers, #1471, w/glass base, rnd, lg, pr 80.00
Rose Point, stem, brandy; #3106, ¾-oz 100.00
Rose Point, stem, brandy; #3121, 1-oz 110.00
Rose Point, stem, claret; #3121, 4½" 85.00
Rose Point, stem, cocktail; #37801, 4-oz 45.00
Rose Point, stem, oyster cocktail; #3106, 5-oz 30.00
Rose Point, stem, sherry; #3106, 2-oz 40.00
Rose Point, stem, water; #3121, 10-oz 30.00
Rose Point, sugar bowl, #3500/15, pie crust edge, ind ...22.50
Rose Point, sugar bowl, #944, flat 130.00
Rose Point, tray, sandwich; center hdl, #3400/10, 11" ...135.00
Rose Point, tray, service; #3500/99, hdls, oval, 12" 195.00

Rose Point, 3-part divided relish tray, 12", $55.00.

Rose Point, tumbler, #3400/115, 13-oz 45.00
Rose Point, tumbler, #498, str sides, 5-oz 45.00
Rose Point, tumbler, iced tea; #3500, ftd, tall, 12-oz 32.50
Rose Point, tumbler, juice; #3121, ftd, low, 5-oz 32.50
Rose Point, tumbler, water; #3121, ftd, low, 10-oz 27.50
Rose Point, vase, #1242, 10" 115.00
Rose Point, vase, #3400/102, globe form, 5" 70.00
Rose Point, vase, #797, flat, flared, 8" 120.00
Rose Point, vase, sweet pea; #629 ....225.00
Valencia, ashtray, #3500/128, rnd, 4½" 18.00
Valencia, bowl, #1402/88, 11" 35.00
Valencia, bowl, cereal; #3500/37, 6" 20.00

Valencia, comport, #3500/37, 7" 40.00
Valencia, creamer, #3500/15, ind 17.50
Valencia, cup, #3500/1 ....17.50
Valencia, decanter, #3400/119, ball form, 12-oz 85.00
Valencia, honey dish, #3500/139, w/lid 95.00
Valencia, mayonnaise, #3500/59, 3-pc 40.00
Valencia, plate, breakfast; #3500/5, 8½" 12.00
Valencia, plate, torte; #3500/38, 13" 25.00
Valencia, shakers, #3400/18 ....50.00
Valencia, stem, cocktail; #1402 ....20.00
Valencia, stem, cordial; #1402 ....65.00
Valencia, stem, oyster cocktail; #3500, 4½" 15.00
Valencia, sugar basket, #3500/13 ....75.00
Valencia, tumbler, #3500, ftd, 13-oz 17.50
Valencia, tumbler, #3500, ftd, 3-oz 14.00
Wildflower, basket, #3400/1182, hdls, 6" 25.00
Wildflower, bowl, #3900/54, flared, 4-ftd, 10" 35.00
Wildflower, bowl, bonbon; #3900/130, hdls, 7" 20.00
Wildflower, bowl, relish; 2-part, 6" 17.50
Wildflower, butter dish, #3900/52, ¼-lb 165.00
Wildflower, candlestick, #3400/646, 5" 25.00
Wildflower, candy box, #3900/165, w/lid, rnd 50.00
Wildflower, cocktail shaker, #3400/175 ....75.00
Wildflower, creamer, #3900/41 ....12.50
Wildflower, hurricane lamp, #1617, w/candlestick base 135.00
Wildflower, oil, #3900/100, w/stopper, 6-oz 75.00
Wildflower, pitcher, #3900/115, 76-oz 150.00
Wildflower, plate, dinner; #3900/24, 10½" 65.00
Wildflower, plate, torte; #3900/65, 14" 32.50
Wildflower, shakers, #3400/77, pr 35.00
Wildflower, stem, claret; #3121, 4½-oz 38.00
Wildflower, stem, cordial; #3121, 1-oz 55.00
Wildflower, tray, for creamer & sugar bowl, #3900/40 ....15.00
Wildflower, tumbler, iced tea; #3121, 12-oz 22.00
Wildflower, vase, #1238, ftd, keyhole, 12" 65.00
Wildflower, vase, flower; #6004, ftd, 8" 35.00

Cameo

The technique of glass carving was perfected 2,000 years ago in ancient Rome and Greece. The most famous ancient example of cameo glass is the Portland Vase, made in Rome around 100 A.D. After glass blowing was developed, glassmakers devised a method of casing several layers of colored glass together, often with a light color over a darker base, to enhance the design. Skilled carvers meticulously worked the fragile glass to produce incredibly detailed classic scenes. In the 18th and 19th centuries Oriental and Near-Eastern artisans used the technique more extensively. European glassmakers revived the art during the last quarter of the 19th century. In France, Galle and Daum produced some of the finest examples of modern times, using as many as five layers of glass to develop their designs, usually scenics or subjects from nature. Hand carving was supplemented by the use of a copper engraving wheel, and acid was used to cut away the layers more quickly.

In England, Thomas Webb and Sons used modern machinery and technology to eliminate many of the problems that plagued early glass carvers. One of Webb's best-known carvers, George Woodall, is credited with producing over four hundred pieces. Woodall was trained in the art by John Northwood, famous for reproducing the Portland Vase in 1876. Cameo glass became very popular during the late 1800s, resulting in a market that demanded more than could be produced, due to the tedious procedures involved. In an effort to produce greater volume, less elaborate pieces with simple floral or geometric designs were made, often entirely acid etched with little or no hand carving. While very

little cameo glass was made in this country, a few pieces were produced by James Gillender, Tiffany, and the Libbey Glass Company. Though some continued to be made on a limited scale into the 1900s, (and until about 1920 in France) for the most part, inferior products caused a marked reduction in its manufacture by the turn of the century. See also specific manufacturers.

Beware of new 'French' cameo glass from Romania and Taiwan. Some of it is very good and may be signed with 'old' signatures. Watch for stencil-cut designs that are 'disconnected' and segmented. Know your dealer! Our advisor for this category is Don Williams; he is listed in the Directory under Missouri.

English

Bottle, scent; morning-glories/gold vines on bl, 1¾x1½" 950.00
Epergne, mirrored, morning-glories, wht on red, 10½" 4,000.00
Perfume, lay down; floral, wht on bl, 3¾x2" 1,500.00
Sweetmeat, fancy leaves, wht on sapphire, silver lid, 6" 1,800.00
Vase, floral, bl on wht, cvd top band, 3x4½" 800.00
Vase, floral, bl on wht, wht bands at top & base, 4¾" 995.00
Vase, floral, wht on citron, 3¾x2¾" 750.00
Vase, floral band on Dmn Quilt MOP, wht on apricot, 5x5" ..3,000.00
Vase, jasmine, bl-wht on turq, elongated bottle form, 8¾" 2,400.00
Vase, sm insect/passion flowers, wht on yel, gourd form, 9" 2,500.00
Vase, tiny flowers/thorny limbs, wht on rose, ovoid, 4¾" 1,200.00
Vase, 3-leaf flower, wht & clear on wht-cased red, 2½" 850.00

French

Vase, butterflies, tan on yel, metal 3-leaf mt, Ovirit, 11" 1,100.00
Vase, concentric arcs in sqs, lt/dk bl on clear, Degue, 15" 1,200.00
Vase, floral, amber on bl to clear, Fritz Heckert, 5½" 275.00
Vase, floral on shaded yel, Verrerie D'Art, BS&C, 4x2½" 275.00

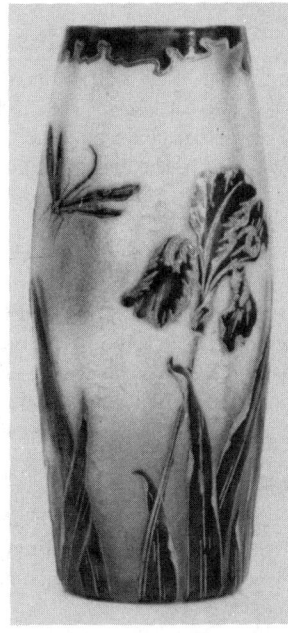

Vase, floral in red and gold on textured crystal frost, St. Denis, 12", $1,250.00.

Vase, fuchsia, bl on bl-streaked opal, Pantin, slim, 16" 825.00
Vase, hydrangeas, dbl o/l, Arsall, 12x5½" 800.00
Vase, irises, lime/bl on opaque clear, St Louis, 18" 2,000.00
Vase, lily pads/lilies, gray/olive on gray/yel, Arsall, 10" 825.00
Vase, long stem flowers, red/bl on gray/yel, Degue, 9½" 1,100.00
Vase, marquetry, butterfly/orchids, Verrerie D'Art, 5x3" 4,500.00

Vase, marquetry, orchids on purple, Verrerie D'Art, 6½x4" **2,500.00**
Vase, morning-glories, martele, gilt, Burgun & Schverer, 4½" ...**4,500.00**
Vase, mums, lav to cobalt on pk/gray opal, Degue, 18x10" **1,650.00**
Vase, poppies, etched/pnt on yel/wht, Degue, 7x7½" **600.00**
Vase, sailing ship/bk: lighthouse, bl on rust, Michel, 10" **1,800.00**
Vase, scenic, bl dk gr on pk-streaked gray, Raspilleu, 12" **875.00**
Vase, stylized floral, bl/purple on bright pk, Degue, 13" **985.00**
Vase, stylized leaves, orange/bl on frost, Degue, 1925, 9" **750.00**
Vase, thistles etc, turq on opal w/bl & yel, Pantin, 15" **2,100.00**
Vase, wisteria, lav on amethyst/frost/purple, Verriere, 14" **1,050.00**

Canary Lustre

Canary lustre was produced from the late 1700s until about the mid-19th century in the Staffordshire district of England. The body of the ware was of yellow clay with a yellow overglaze; more often than not, copper or silver lustre trim was added. Decorations were usually black-printed transfers, though occasionally hand-painted polychrome designs were also used.

Creamer, bl/gray stripes, emb ribs, hairline/wear, 3" **125.00**
Cup & saucer, gr foliage band, brn/blk bands, brn stars, NM **340.00**
Cup plate, blk transfer of fat child eating, emb rim, Wood **350.00**
Mug, child's, blk transfer sunburst w/M, silver rim, 2" **375.00**
Mug, child's, Boys Balancing, brn transfer, leaf hdl, NM **225.00**
Mug, child's, children play, blk transfer, 2⅝", EX **235.00**
Mug, child's, Remember Me, child/dog, purple lustre trim **310.00**
Mug, HP florals at rim, 1810s, prof rpr, 4x4" **325.00**
Mug, landscape, blk transfer, silver resist trim, 3⅝", NM **250.00**
Pitcher, satyr face mold, HP face/silver sprigwork, 6" **600.00**
Plate, mc floral, molded rim design, 7½", set of 4 ....**600.00**
Plate, single flower on stem, rust linear border, rpr, 6¼" **275.00**

Candle Holders

The earliest type of candlestick, called a pricket, was constructed with a sharp point on which the candle was impaled. The socket type, first used in the 16th century, consisted of the socket and a short stem with a wide drip pan and base. These were made from sheets of silver or other metal; not until late in the 17th century were candlesticks made by casting. By the 1700s, styles began to vary from the traditional fluted column or baluster form and became more elaborate. A Rococo style with scrolls, shellwork, and naturalistic leaves and flowers came into vogue that afforded the individual silversmith the opportunity to exhibit his skill and artistry. The last half of the 18th century brought a return to fluted columns with neoclassic motifs. Because they were made of thin sheet silver, weighted bases were used to add stability. The Rococo styles of the Regency period were heavily encrusted with applied figures and flowers. Candelabra with six to nine branches became popular. By the Victorian era when lamps came into general use, there was less innovation and more adaptation of the earlier styles. See also Silver; specific manufacturers.

Key: QA — Queen Anne

Brass, capstan, early, somewhat battered, 5" **415.00**
Brass, chamberstick, deep base, push-up, rpr, 5", EX **60.00**
Brass, fluted column on rnd acanthus base, 1800s, 9½", pr **325.00**
Brass, QA, base initialed/dtd 1772, 6", VG, pr **600.00**
Brass, screw-in stems, 9½", pr **150.00**
Brass, trn std, wide rnd base w/sm heart-like ft, 5½" **125.00**

Brass, Victorian, w/push-up, 8", pr **170.00**
Brass, w/push-up, 6¾", pr **130.00**
CI, sticking tommy, dmns/crosses decor, refined hook, 1700s **395.00**
Glass, canary, hexagonal, 8", pr, EX **180.00**
Glass, clambroth, dolphin std, sq base, NE, 10½", EX, pr **625.00**
Glass, flint, hexagonal base, petal sockets, 8½", NM, pr **150.00**
Iron, hogscraper, w/push-up mk Shaw, lip hanger, 7", EX **125.00**
Iron, hogscraper, w/push-up mk Shaw, no lip hanger, 8" **70.00**
Iron & brass, hogscraper, 1800s, miniature, 5" **700.00**
Sheet brass, chamberstick, oval, 7¾" **125.00**
Silverplate, EX detail, 12", pr **200.00**
Tin, hogscraper, w/push-up & lip hanger, 5" **95.00**
Tin, tinder lighter base has damper/flint/steel, 3½x4" dia **350.00**
Tin cup moves along 6 wires embedded in wood base, 8¾" **295.00**
Wrought iron, adjustable push-up, 3 scroll legs, 11", pr **600.00**
Wrought iron, hogscraper, w/push-up & lip hanger, 6" **150.00**
Wrought iron, long twisted hanging rod, 14½" **125.00**
Wrought iron, primitive, 3 tall ft, pitted, 14" **425.00**
Wrought iron, spiral push-up, lip hanger, wood base, 7" **220.00**
Wrought iron, sticking tommy, 11" **105.00**
Wrought iron, sticking tommy, 8", EX **140.00**
Wrought iron chandelier, 3-arm, 2-part twisted hanger, 11½" ...**600.00**
Wrought steel, spiral push-up, wood base, 7" **200.00**

Candlewick

Candlewick crystal was made by the Imperial Glass Corporation, a division of Lenox Inc., Bellaire, Ohio. It was introduced in 1936; though never marked except for paper labels, it is easily recognized by the beaded crystal rims, stems, and handles inspired by the tufted needlework called candlewicking, practiced by our pioneer women. During its production, more than 741 items were designed and produced. In September 1982 when Imperial closed its doors, thirty-four pieces were still being made.

Identification numbers and mold numbers used by the company help collectors recognize the various styles and shapes. Most of the pieces are from the #400 series, though other series numbers were also used. Stemware was made in eight styles — five from the #400 series made from 1941 to 1962, one from #3400 series made in 1937, another from #3800 series made in 1941, and the eighth style from the #4000 series made in 1947. In the listings that follow, some #400 items lack the mold number because that information was not found in the company files.

A few pieces have been made in color or with a gold wash. At least two lines, Valley Lily and Floral, utilized Candlewick with floral patterns cut into the crystal. These are scarce today. Other rare items include gifts such as the desk calendar made by the company for its employees and customers; the dresser set comprised of a mirror, clock, puff jar, and cologne; and the chip and dip set.

Ashtray, #1776/1, eagle form, 6½" **50.00**
Ashtray, #400/133, rnd, 5" **8.00**
Ashtray, #400/134/1, oblong, 4½" **6.00**
Ashtray, #400/172, heart form, 5½" **11.00**
Basket, #400/40/0, hdld, 6½" **27.50**
Bell, #400/108, 5" **75.00**
Bottle, bitters; #400/117, w/tube, 4-oz **55.00**
Bowl, #400/53H, heart form, 5½" **17.50**
Bowl, banana; #400/103E, 10" **1,250.00**
Bowl, butter/jam; #400/262, 3-part, 10½" **70.00**
Bowl, celery boat; #400/46, oval, 11" **55.00**
Bowl, cottage cheese; #400/85, 6" **25.00**
Bowl, cream soup; #400/50, 5" **40.00**

Bowl, finger; #3800 ....25.00
Bowl, fruit; #400/3F, 6" 11.00
Bowl, mint; #400/51F, hdl, 6" 18.00
Bowl, pickle/celery; #400/57, 7½" 25.00
Bowl, pickle/celery; #400/58, 8½" 20.00
Bowl, relish; #400/234, divided, sq, 7" 100.00
Bowl, relish; #400/268, 2-part, 8" 20.00
Bowl, relish; #400/84, 2-part, 6½" 22.00
Butter & jam set, #400/204, 5-pc 225.00
Cake stand, #400/103D, high, 11" 65.00
Calendar, desk; #1947 ....150.00
Candle holder, #400/280, flat, 3½" 20.00
Candle holder, #400/40HC, heart form, 5" 40.00
Candle holder, flower; #400/40C, 5" 27.50
Candle holder, mushroom; #400/86 ....22.00
Candy box, #400/140, w/lid, beaded ft 200.00
Candy box, #400/259, w/lid, 7" 125.00
Cigarette box, #400/134, w/lid 30.00
Clock, rnd, 4" 250.00
Coaster, #400/226, w/spoon rest 13.00
Cocktail, seafood; #400/190, w/bead ft 50.00
Compote, fruit; #40/103C, ftd, crimped, 10" 110.00

Pewter, octagonal standard and bobeche, rubbed touchmark, ca 1675, provenance, 8½", EX, $7,000.00.

Creamer, #400/126, flat, bead hdl 30.00
Creamer, #400/18, domed ft 110.00
Cruet, #400/279, hdl, bulbous bottom, 6-oz 75.00
Cup, punch; #400/211 ....7.50
Cup, tea; #400/35 ....8.00
Decanter, #400/18, w/stopper, 18-oz 350.00
Deviled egg server, #400/154, center hdl, 12" 95.00
Egg cup, #400/19, bead ft 45.00
Fork & spoon set, #400/75 ....35.00
Hurricane lamp, #400/79, 2-pc, candle base 110.00
Ice tub, #400/63, 5½" deep, 8" dia 80.00
Icer, seafood/fruit cocktail; #400/53/3, 2-pc 95.00
Jar, tower; #400/655, 3-part 250.00

Knife, butter; #4000 ....200.00
Ladle, marmalade; #400/130, 3-bead stem 10.00
Mayonnaise set, #400/52/3, tray w/hdl, bowl & ladle, 3-pc 45.00
Mirror, standing, rnd, 4½" 85.00
Mustard jar, #400/156, w/spoon 30.00
Pitcher, #400/18, beaded ft, 80-oz 200.00
Pitcher, #400/330, short/rnd, 14-oz 100.00
Pitcher, #400/424, plain, 80-oz 55.00
Pitcher, juice/cocktail; #400/19, 40-oz 165.00
Plate, bread/butter; #400/1D, 6" 8.00
Plate, crescent salad; #400/120, 8¼" 42.50
Plate, dinner; #400/10D, 10" 35.00
Plate, luncheon; #400/7D, 9" 12.50
Plate, salad; #400/3D, 7" 8.00
Plate, salad; #400/5D, 8" 9.00
Platter, #400/124D, 13" 90.00
Punch ladle, #400/91 ....22.50
Salt cellar, #400/61, 2" 9.00
Sauce boat, #400/169 ....95.00
Saucer, after dinner; #400/77AD 5.00
Saucer, tea or coffee; #400/35 or #400/37 ....2.50
Snack jar, #400/139/1, w/lid, bead ft 400.00
Stem, brandy; #3800 ....25.00
Stem, oyster cocktail; #3400, 4-oz 14.00
Stem, sherbet; #400/190, 6-oz 14.00
Stem, water goblet; #3800, 9-oz 25.00
Strawberry set, #400/83, 2-pc 50.00
Sugar bowl, #400/126, flat, bead hdl 27.50
Sugar bowl, #400/30, bead hdl, 6-oz 6.50
Tidbit server, #400/2701, cupped, 2-tier 45.00
Toast, #400/123, w/lid, 7¾" 225.00
Tumbler, juice; #3800, 5-oz 25.00
Tumbler, juice; #400/18, 5-oz 35.00
Tumbler, old fashioned; #400/10, 7-oz 30.00
Tumbler, sherbet, #400/19, low, 5-oz 14.00
Tumbler, tea; #400/19, 14-oz 20.00
Tumbler, water; #400/18, 9-oz 35.00

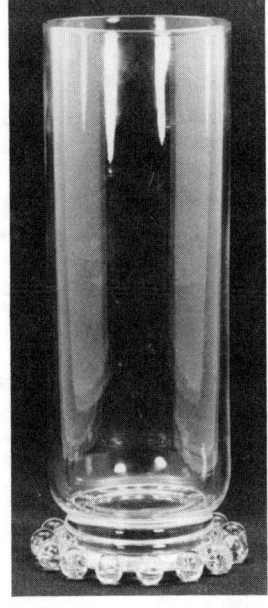

Vase, bead feet, straight sides, $140.00.

Vase, #400/193, ftd, 10" 150.00
Vase, #400/198, 6" dia 175.00

Vase, ivy bowl, #400/74J, 7" 50.00
Vase, mini bud; #400/107, bead ft, 5¾" 40.00
Vase, rose bowl; #400/132, ftd, 7½" 150.00

Candy Containers

Figural glass candy containers were first created in 1876 when ingenious candy manufacturers began to use them to package their products. Two of the first containers, the Liberty Bell and Independence Hall, were distributed for our country's centennial celebration. Children found these toys appealing, and an industry was launched that lasted into the mid-1960s.

Figural candy containers include animals, comic characters, guns, telephones, transportation vehicles, household appliances, and many other intriguing designs. The oldest (those made prior to 1920) were usually hand painted and often contained extra metal parts in addition to the metal strip or screw closures. During the 1950s these metal parts were replaced with plastic, a practice that continued until candy containers met their demise in the 1960s. While predominately clear, they are found in nearly all colors of glass including milk glass, green, amber, pink, emerald, cobalt, ruby flashed, and light blue. Usually the color was intentional, but leftover glass was used as well and resulted in unplanned colors. Various examples are found in light or ice blue, and new finds are always being discovered. Production of the glass portion of candy containers was centered around the western Pennsylvania city of Jeannette. Major producers include Westmoreland Glass, West Bros., Victory Glass, J.H. Millstein, J.C. Crosetti, L.E. Smith, Jack Stough, and T.H. Stough. While 90% of all glass candies were made in the Jeannette area, other companies such as Eagle Glass, Play Toy, and Geo. Borgfeldt Co. have a few to their credit as well.

Buyer beware! Many candy containers have been reproduced. Some, including the Camera and the Rabbit Pushing Wheelbarrow, come already painted from distributors. Others may have a slick or oily feel to the touch. The following list may also alert you to possible reproductions:

    #12 Chicken on Nest
    #24 Dog (clear and cobalt)
    #38 Mule and Waterwagon (original marked Jeannette, PA)
    #47 Rabbit Pushing Wheelbarrow (eggs are speckled on the repro; solid on the original)
    #55 Peter Rabbit
    #58 Rocking Horse (original in clear only)
    #76 Independence Hall (original is rectangular; repro has offset base with red felt-lined closure)
    #89 Happifats on Drum (no notches on repro for closure to hook into)
    #90 Jackie Coogan (marked inside 'B')
    #91 Kewpie (must have Geo. Borgfeldt on base to be original)
    #94 Naked Child
    #103 Santa (original has plastic head; repro is all glass and opens at bottom)
    #114 Mantel Clock
    #144 Amber Pistol (first sold full in the 1970s)
    #168 Uncle Sam's Hat
    #233 Santa's Boot
    #242 Carpet Sweeper
    #243 Carpet Sweeper
    #246 Display Case
    #254 Mailbox
    #255 Drum Mug
    #268 Safe
    #289 Piano (original in only clear and milk glass, both painted)
    #352 Auto
    #377 Auto

    #378 Station Wagon
    #386 Fire Engine
    Others are possible.

Our advisor for this category is Jeff Bradfield; he is listed in the Directory under Virginia. You may contact him with questions, if you will include an SASE. See Clubs, Newsletters, and Catalogs for the address of the Candy Container Collectors of America. A bimonthly newsletter offers insight into new finds, reproductions, updates, and articles from over four hundred collectors and members, including all authors of books on candy containers.

'L' numbers used in this guide refer to a standard reference series, *An Album of Candy Containers*, Vols 1 and 2, by Jennie Long. 'E&A' numbers correlate with *The Compleat American Glass Candy Containers Handbook* by Eikelberner and Agadjanian, revised by Adele Bowden. Values are given for undamaged examples with original paint and metal parts when applicable or unless noted otherwise. Repaired pieces (often repainted) are worth only a small fraction of one that is perfect. The symbol (+) at the end of some of the following lines was used to indicate items that have been reproduced. See also Christmas; Easter; Halloween.

Airplane, Passenger; L #323 (E&A #7) 275.00
Airplane, Stough's, musical, L #331 or #333 (E&A #1 or #3), ea .25.00
Amos & Andy, L #77 (E&A #21), EX pnt 450.00
Auto, rear trunk, L #367 (E&A #38), G pnt 140.00
Auto w/Tassels #1, L #360 (E&A #64) 185.00
Barney Google on Pedestal, L #78 (E&A #72) 220.00
Basket, flower design, L #224 (E&A #81) 35.00
Basket, ruby flashed, L #225 ....35.00
Battleship on Waves, L #335 (E&A #96) 165.00
Bear on Circus Tub, orig blades, L #1 (E&A #83) 350.00
Bell, Hand; wood hdl, L #494 ....175.00
Bird Cage, L #230 (E&A #94) 225.00
Black Cat for Luck, L #4 (E&A #136-1) 1,200.00
Black Cat Sitting, L #5 ....1,000.00
Bottle, Rnd Nurser; L #70 (E&A #549) 20.00
Bucket, domed lid, L #235 ....35.00
Bucket, Kid Kandy, L #508 ....515.00
Buddy Bank, L #449 ....400.00
Bugle or Megaphone, L #278 ....22.00
Bureau, L #125 (E&A #112) 145.00
Bus, Jitney; closure, L #340 (E&A #114) 350.00
Bus, Rapid Transit; G pnt, L #345 (E&A #116) 550.00
Candy Cane, Mercury Glass; L #613 ....80.00
Cannon, cobalt bbl, rpl carriage, L #534 (E&A #122) 300.00
Cannon, Quick Firer; orig carriage, L #537 ....1,000.00
Cannon #2, 2 wheels, 6 spokes, L #138 (E&A #123) 350.00
Car, Electric Coupe; Long Hood #1, L #357 (E&A #50-B) 150.00
Car, Long Hood Coupe #3; L #359 (E&A #51) 110.00
Car, Ribbed-Top Sedan; closure, L #376 (E&A #32) 25.00
Cash Register, fancy scrolls, L #614 ....520.00
Charlie Chaplin by Barrel, Borgfeldt, closure, L #83 (E&A #137) .150.00
Chicken, fancy closure, L #9 ....500.00
Chicken in Sagging Basket, L #8 (E&A #148) 65.00
Chicken on Rnd Base, L #11 (E&A #146) 225.00
Clock, Mantel; #2, paper face, L #116 (E&A #164), NM 140.00
Decorettes, L #655 ....70.00
Defense Field Gun, orig gun, L #142 (E&A #128) 300.00
Dirigible, Los Angeles; L #322 (E&A #176) 175.00
Dog, Mutt, L #20 (E&A #194) 50.00
Dog w/Glass Hat, L #22 (E&A #181), lg 25.00
Dog w/Top Hat, L #480 (E&A #194-2) 25.00
Don't Park Here, L #314 (E&A #196) 185.00
Duckling, L #30 (E&A #197) 115.00

Esther Coach, all orig, L #397 (E&A #165) 400.00
Express Wagon, L #440 (E&A #821) 475.00
Fanny Farmer (Uncle Sam), L #529 ....125.00
Felix by Barrel, G pnt, L #85 (E&A #211) 600.00
Fire Engine, bl glass, L #381 (E&A #218-1) 100.00
Fire Engine, Little Boiler, L #383 (E&A #217) 75.00

Fire Engine, Victory Glass, 5¼" long, #386,
$15.00.

Flossie Fisher Bed, L #127 (E&A #234) 900.00
Flossie Fisher Chair, L #128 (E&A #232) 300.00
Gas Pump, L #316 (E&A #240) 225.00
Glass House, top closure, L #512 ....150.00
Gun, cork closure, L #540 ....25.00
Gun, metal, L #157 ....75.00
Happifats on Drum, orig pnt & closure, #89 (E&A #208)(+) 275.00
Horn, Millsteins, L #282 (E&A #311) 20.00
Horn, 3-valve, w/mouthpc, L #281 (E&A #312) 175.00
Hot Doggie, clear w/pnt, L #14 (E&A #320) 450.00
Ice Truck, all orig, L #458 (E&A #784) 650.00
Jack-O'-Lantern, blk cat, L #158 (E&A #349-1) 450.00
Jackie Coogan, #1, G pnt, L #90 (E&A #345) 1,150.00
Kiddies' Band, complete, L #277 (E&A #314) 175.00
Kiddies' Breakfast Bell, L #18 (E&A #192) 25.00
Lamp, Valentine; L #556, all orig 450.00
Lantern, barn type #2, L #178 (E&A #427-B) 75.00
Lantern, beaded globe, L #560 (E&A #449) 35.00
Lantern, Japanese paper type, L #572 (E&A #389) 300.00
Lantern, oval panels, L #570 ....30.00
Lantern, Victory Glass #1, L #191 (E&A #443)(+ by Avon) 20.00
Laundry Truck, L #606 (E&A #785) 650.00
Library Lamp, L #207 (E&A #372) 500.00
Limousine, Westmoreland Specialty, L #351 (E&A #45) 175.00
Locomotive, dbl sq windows, orig closure, L #414 (E&A #497) .110.00
Locomotive, dbl sq windows, repro closure, L #414 (E&A #497) .50.00
Locomotive, no wheels, L #395 (E&A #485) 50.00
Locomotive, screw cap, L #411 (E&A #493-1) 110.00
Locomotive, 888; single window, w/closure, E&A #481 .....25.00
Lucky Lindy Candy Air Mail, L #666 ....450.00
Mailbox, silver pnt, L #254 (E&A #521)(+) 115.00
Maud Muller Milk Carrier, L #69 ....175.00
Military Hat, L #170 (E&A #131), orig closure 35.00
Model Cruiser, L #339 (E&A #98), orig closure 22.00
Mr Rabbit w/Hat, L #39 (E&A #610), worn pnt 1,500.00
Mug, Child's Tumbler, L #256 (E&A #541), orig closure 200.00
Mule Pulling Barrel, L #38 (E&A #539) 70.00
Naked Child w/Derby, L #95 (E&A #544) 45.00
Nurser Bottle, Waisted; L #71 (E&A #548) 25.00
Pencil, L #263 (E&A #567) 57.50
Peter Rabbit, L #55 (E&A #618) 25.00
Pocket Watch, 'Jeannette' on paper face, L #457 (E&A #825) ..450.00
Poodle Dog, glass head, L #471 ....30.00

Pumpkin Head Witch, L #265 (E&A #594) 550.00
Rabbit, aluminum ears, L #487 ....115.00
Rabbit, Stough's, closure, L #54 (E&A #617)(+) 20.00
Rabbit Crouching, L #41 (E&A #615), EX pnt 105.00

Rabbit in Eggshell, gold paint,
#48, 5½", $75.00.

Rabbit Nibbling Carrot, L #53 (E&A #609) 35.00
Rabbit Running on Log, gold pnt, L #42 (E&A #603) 200.00
Rocking Horse #1, L #58 (E&A #651)(+) 350.00
Rooster Crowing, orig pnt, L #56 (E&A #151), EX 225.00
Santa Claus, banded coat, L #97 (E&A #669) 200.00
Scottie Dog, L #17 (E&A #184) 12.00
Seltzer Bottle, L #505 ....350.00
Swan, L #492 ....125.00
Telephone, Redlich's No 3, L #294 (E&A #752) 400.00
Telephone, Stough's #3, L #308 (E&A #751) 40.00
Telephone, Victory Glass #1, L #298 (E&A #746-1) 200.00
Telescope, L #270 (E&A #764) 625.00
Toonerville Trolly, L #111 (E&A #767) 700.00
Village Buildings, no glass inserts, L #76, set of 8, ea 25.00
Volkswagon, L #373 (E&A #58) 35.00
Wheelbarrow, w/closure, L #273 (E&A #832) 80.00
Willy's Jeep Scout Car, L #391 (E&A #350) 30.00
Windmill, pewter top, L #443 (E&A #840) 400.00
Windmill, shaker top, orig blades, L #445 (E&A #842) 250.00

Papier-Mache, Composition

Boar, gr flocked, wire tail, 4½x7½", EX 165.00
Chinaman sits on log, Germany, 4" 155.00
Dog, wht w/glass eyes, 4x4½", EX 175.00
Duck, wht rabbit fur, glass eyes, head removes, 9x8½" 335.00
George Washington on horse, bsk face, 11x9", EX 750.00
Gnome, compo face, cotton clothes, Germany, 3¾" 135.00
Pig, gr w/blk hat & coat, gr pants, 6x6", EX 215.00
Rabbit, brn w/celluloid face, 5", EX 135.00
Rabbit, upright, flocked tan coat, glass eyes, 8", EX 145.00
Rabbit, upright, wht plaster ext, glass eyes, red tie, 8" 135.00
Rabbit, walking, wht plaster coat, glass beaded finish, 7" ..165.00
Rabbit pulling wooden cart w/cb wheels, 8½" L, NM 185.00
Snow White & 7 Dwarfs, mica on cb, 6" 225.00

Stump w/cherries, leaves, & hatchet, 4¾", VG 95.00
Turkey, blk/gr/wht/red/gold, Germany, 5½", M 185.00
Turkey, compo, hair wattle, head removes, Germany, 7½" 235.00
Turkey, metal ft, EX details, Germany, 6" 195.00

Canes

Fancy canes and walking sticks were once the mark of a gentleman. Hand-carved examples are collected and admired as folk art from the past. The glass canes that never could have been practical are unique whimseys of the glass-blower's profession. Gadget and container sticks, which were produced in a wide variety, are highly desirable. Character, political, and novelty types are also sought after as are those with handles made of precious metals. Our advisor for this category is Bruce Thalberg.

Ash, cvd head of bearded man w/cap (lg/detailed) 800.00
Ash, spiraling snake, blk & red ink-drawn scales, 36", EX 165.00
Bamboo, floral-cvd bone hdl w/bird, pewter band, rpr, 34" 135.00
Bamboo, floral-cvd ivory hdl, ferrule damaged, 37" 100.00
Bamboo, ivory hdl w/sterling silver trim, 36" 185.00
Bamboo, sterling trim, clock mk Brevete in knob end, 33" 325.00
Birch, intarsia floral & leaves inlay hdl, 36" 35.00
Blown glass, amber w/appl wht spiral, Am, 1840-1880, 37" 170.00
Blown glass, aquamarine, appl mc spirals, baton, 1860s, 44" 250.00
Blown glass, blk/bl/wht spiral threads in clear, 35" 100.00
Blown glass, cranberry & wht twists on clear, 50" 150.00
Blown glass, cranberry cased w/clear, swirled int ribs, 32" 150.00
Blown glass, gold/red/wht/yel stripes, 1870s, 17" 120.00
Blown glass, red clambroth/lt bl/med bl twists, 52" 175.00
Blown glass, wht/yel/mahog looping in clear, 59" 150.00
Bone, ivory fist hdl, horn segment divider, 35" 575.00
Bronze, cast Blk man's head, rosewood shaft 450.00

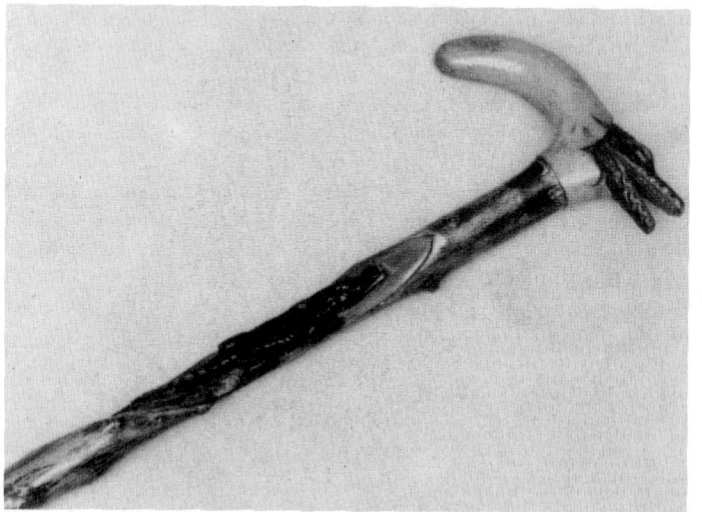

Carved wood, alligators on shaft and handle, $100.00.

Ebonized wood & bone, rope-trn, 1850s 220.00
Ebony, cvd smiling man's head ivory hdl, Japan, 36" 525.00
Ebony, ivory sphinx hdl, ivory tip, 37½" 415.00
Gadget type, drinking (flask & glass inside) 200.00
Gadget type, 1939 World's Fair, map inside 250.00
Gambler's stick, wooden hdl opens to reveal chips & dice 660.00
Gutta percha, dolphin hdl, ebony shaft, horn tip, 36" 110.00

Mahogany, ivory tip, paneled bulbous knob, 33" 275.00
Malacca, cvd lady's leg hdl, 35" 135.00
Ram's horn, horse's head hdl, walnut shaft, horn tip, 36" 200.00
Rhinoceros horn, 5½" inset of ivory under hdl, horn tip, 36" 350.00
Rosewood, cat's eye hdl, sterling ferrule, crown bezel, 35" 200.00
Scrimshaw, spiral cvd, herringbone cvd knob, 1870s, 35" 1,250.00
Scrimshaw newhal tusk, mahog tip, 1850s, 32", EX 1,400.00
Tiffany & Co, sterling repousse knob, ivory miniature inset ...1,200.00
Unger Bros, floral repousse sterling knob, rosewood shaft 465.00
Walnut, cvd man's head (detailed), coral forked tongue 210.00
Walrus ivory Turk's head on MOP & ivory-inlay ebony base, VG .700.00
Whalebone, ebony separator, trn ivory knob hdl, 36", EX 300.00
Wood, bird hdl, dragon on shaft highlighted in blk, 37", EX 185.00
Wood, bird's head hdl w/glass eyes, ivory beak, horn tip 185.00
Wood, cvd bulldog, glass eyes, silver o/l trim, 38" 275.00
Wood, cvd Indian head hdl w/mc pnt, 1900s, 37", EX 125.00
Wood, cvd parrot's head hdl w/polychrome, Brazil, 36" 135.00
Wood, cvd vines & Xmas 1898, varnished, 33½", EX 125.00
Wood, Dartmouth Sr Class Indian Head HP, names on shaft 220.00
Wood, grip: hand w/Odd Fellows insignia, rope-cvd shaft 85.00
Wood, mc bas-relief cvg of eagle/snake/turtle/lizard, 36" 145.00
Wood, turk's head knot hdl, rope-cvd shaft, 36", EX 165.00
Wood, 2 snakes cvd in relief twist along shaft, 1890s, 36" 225.00

Canton

Canton is a blue and white porcelain that was first exported in the 1790s by clipper ships from China to the United States, a practice that continued into the 1920s. Canton became very popular along the East coast where the major ports were located. Its popularity was due to several factors: it was readily available, inexpensive, and (due to the fact that it came in many different forms) appealing to the housewife.

The porcelain's blue and white color and simple motif (teahouse, trees, bridge, and a rain-cloud border) have made it a favorite of people who collect early American furniture and accessories. Buyers of Canton should shop at large outdoor shows and up-scale antique shows. Collections are regularly sold at auction. Collectors usually prefer a rich, deep tone rather than a lighter blue. Cracks, large chips, and major repairs will substantially affect values. Prices of Canton have escalated sharply over the last twenty years, and rare forms are highly sought after by advanced collectors. Our advisor for this category is Hobart D. Van Deusen; he is listed in the Directory under Connecticut.

Pitcher, 1850s, 8", EX, $750.00; Covered sweetmeat, 1800s, 5" dia, NM, $475.00; Scalloped bowl, 1850s, 10½", NM, $500.00; Creamer, helmet, 1800s, 4", EX, $400.00; Ewer, early 1800s, 8", EX, $1,300.00.

Bowl, almond shape, sm chips, 10½" L 300.00
Bowl, berry finial, minor flakes, 6" L 400.00

Bowl, salad; shaped rim w/4 opposing notches, 9½" **975.00**
Bowl, scalloped, 4½x9½x9¾" **750.00**
Bowl, shallow, deeply scalloped, sm chips, 9¾" **500.00**
Bowl, vegetable; shallow, sq, 3x8¾x8¾" **350.00**
Bowl, 6-scallop rim, pattern w/in, minor rim chips, 9½" **700.00**
Butter dish, w/liner, 4x7" dia **800.00**
Chop plate, 14" **600.00**
Creamer, helmet shape, 4¼" **400.00**
Dish, sq w/canted corners, pattern on lid, shallow, 8x10" **385.00**
Dish, vegetable; rectangular, w/lid, pineapple finial, 8" **350.00**
Fruit basket, rtcl, 8" L **650.00**
Hot water dish, minor glaze wear, 9" **330.00**
Platter, mk China, 14" **350.00**
Platter, octagonal, orange peel glaze, sm flake, 13" **300.00**
Platter, octagonal, orange peel glaze, 16" **375.00**
Platter, orange peel glaze, hairlines, 20" **550.00**
Platter, well & tree, chips, 17x20" **880.00**
Syllabub, twist hdls, berry finial, 4", EX **150.00**
Teapot, curved spout, str sides, sm flakes, 5" **400.00**
Teapot, EX color, 8" **700.00**
Teapot, fruit finial, str sides/spout, 6" **400.00**
Trencher, octagonal, 4" L, pr **875.00**
Tureen, gravy, boar's head hdls, 7¾", EX, +undertray **425.00**
Tureen, soup; boar's head hdls, w/lid, 11¾", EX **1,000.00**

Capo-Di-Monte

Established in 1743 near Naples and sponsored by Charles II, who was King of Naples at that time, Capo-Di-Monte produced soft-paste porcelain figurines and dinnerware usually marked with a 'crown over N' device, though a fleur-de-lis was used on occasion. The factory was closed throughout the 1760s but reopened in 1771 in the city of Naples. There both hard- and soft-paste porcelains were made, sometimes decorated with applied florals in high relief. Their technique as well as their marks were blatantly copied. As a result, this type of encrusted decoration is often referred to today as Capo-Di-Monte. The original factory closed in 1821. Some of their molds were purchased by the Docceia Porcelain factory in Florence which continues to operate to the present time. Most examples on the market today are of fairly recent manufacture. Capo-Di-Monte type wares have been made in Hungary and Germany as well as France and Italy. Many of these pieces continue to bear the 'crown over N' gold stamp. As more collectors recognize and appreciate the quality of the older ware, buyer demand drives prices higher.

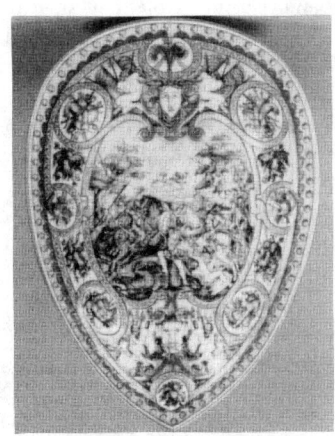

Shield, relief battle scene, 23" long, $900.00.

Bowl, figural-emb shaped border, crest/floral sprays, 15" **1,250.00**

Box, cherubs ride goat in landscape, quatrefoil shape, 4" **125.00**
Box, jewel; roses, red/yel on brn & ivory, 4-ftd, 9x8" **80.00**
Box, lid w/Venus & Cupid in landscape, shaped, ormolu, 9" **290.00**
Box, mythological figures on lid, masks etc on base, 9" L **350.00**
Box, nymphs/figures, floral arabesques, gilt mts, 9" L **375.00**
Box, Venus & putti on lid, floral-decor int, oval, 10" L **425.00**
Candelabra, 5-light, 4 arms on std w/female masks, 12", pr **950.00**
Ewer, 2 figures on hdl, cherub under rim/on shoulder, 12" **400.00**
Figurine, Buccaneer, gr pants, red cape, sgn Cole, 12x6" **225.00**
Figurine, girl stands by tree, 1 w/dog, 1 w/parasol, 10", pr **250.00**
Figurine, man holds bag w/shell & pearl, Bonalberti, 10x8" **250.00**
Lamp, cherubs & satyrs emb on ewer form, 15", pr **400.00**
Plate, crest in center, molded border, 7½", set of 12 ....**900.00**
Platter, floral sprays in center, emb figural border, 17" **850.00**
Stein, nymphs/cherubs in high relief, female as hdl, 15" **800.00**
Tazza, shaped rim, crest, mermaids as support, 5", pr **650.00**
Tray, floral sprays in center, scroll/floral rim, 14", pr **425.00**
Tureen, winged maid hdls, putti surmount, 13" L, +tray **1,200.00**
Urn, cherubs, gold hdls, cherub w/wreath finial, 4-ftd, 21" **550.00**
Urn, reclining nymphs, dragon hdls, bulbous w/rnd ft, 9½" **200.00**

Carlton

Carlton Ware was the product of Wiltshaw and Robinson, who operated in the Staffordshire district of England from about 1890. During the 1920s, they produced ornamental ware with enameled and gilded decorations such as flowers and birds, often on a black background. In 1958 the firm was renamed Carlton Ware Ltd. Their trademark was a crown over a circular stamp with 'W & R, Stoke on Trent' surrounding a swallow. 'Carlton Ware' was sometimes added by hand.

Vase, fantasy garden and butterflies on dark blue, gold handles, #1689G on bottom, 6", $175.00.

Bookends, ladies w/shields & serpents, pr **185.00**
Bowl, Rouge Royale, HP spider web & dragonfly, oval, 12" **120.00**
Bowl, Rouge Royale w/gold Deco trim, 10½" **110.00**
Ginger jar, birds & flowers w/gold on cobalt **95.00**
Jar, mahog w/gold trim, HP flowers, bulbous, mk, 5" **65.00**
Sugar shaker, tree figural, mc, mk, 4⅝x2⅞" **55.00**

Vase, gr & blk w/gold trim, ewer form, 3" 15.00

Carnival Collectibles

Carnival items from the early part of this century represent the lighter side of an America that was alternately prospering and sophisticated or devastated by war and domestic conflict. But whatever the country's condition, the carnival's thrilling rides and shooting galleries were a sure way of letting it all go by — at least for an evening.

For further information on chalkware figures, we recommend *The Carnival Chalk Prize* by our advisor Thomas G. Morris, who is listed in the Directory under Oregon. Our advisors for shooting gallery targets are Richard and Valerie Tucker; their address is listed in the Directory under Texas.

Chalkware figure, Bell Hop, HP, mk 1934, 11½" 40.00
Chalkware figure, Boy & Horse, unmk, 1935-45, 11½" 20.00

Chalkware figure, flapper girl, pink chalk, mohair wig, crepe paper dress and ribbon, ca 1919, 11½", $110.00.

Chalkware figure, Ferdinand the Bull, mk Liza, 1940s, 8½" 30.00
Chalkware figure, Hollywood Star, JY Jenkins, 1933, 9" 40.00
Chalkware figure, I Love Me Girl, HP, mohair wig, 11¼" 85.00
Chalkware figure, Indian Boy, unmk Jenkins style, 8½" 20.00
Chalkware figure, Kewpie-type Devil, unmk, 6½" 45.00
Chalkware figure, Lone Ranger & Silver, 1938-50, 10½" 45.00
Chalkware figure, Mae West, c Rainwater, 10½" 65.00
Chalkware figure, Maggie & Jiggs, 9½", 8½", pr 185.00
Chalkware figure, Majorette, JT Gittins, 1941, 10½" 30.00
Chalkware figure, Mexican Girl, HP, JY Jenkins, 1925, 14½" 115.00
Chalkware figure, Miss America, mk on base, 15¾" 40.00
Chalkware figure, Popeye, King Features, 1929-50, 18" 120.00
Chalkware figure, Uncle Sam, unmk, 1935-45, 15" 50.00
Shooting gallery target, convict, pnt wood & tin, 1930s, 12" 325.00
Shooting gallery target, dbl, bird & lg star, lt rust, 8" 95.00
Shooting gallery target, dmn card suit shape, self standing 40.00
Shooting gallery target, ducks, floating, 9x8x2", EX 110.00
Shooting gallery target, Hitler head, pnt CI, 10½" 225.00
Shooting gallery target, man smoking pipe, old pnt, 6x2x1¼" 30.00
Shooting gallery target, man-in-moon profile, CI, 6", EX 135.00
Shooting gallery target, rabbit, jumping, CI, worn pnt, 6x8" 65.00
Shooting gallery target, shore bird, long support leg, 5½" 65.00
Shooting gallery target, spinning 6-pointed star, 8x2¼x1" 65.00

Shooting gallery target, squirrel, running, 10", EX 85.00
Shooting gallery target, tom turkey, mk Evans, 7" 165.00

Carnival Glass

Carnival glass is pressed glass that has been coated with a sodium solution and fired to give it an exterior lustre. First made in America in 1905, it was produced until the late 1920s and had great popularity in the average American household; for unlike the costly art glass produced by Tiffany, carnival glass could be mass-produced at a small cost. Colors most found are marigold, green, blue, and purple; but others exist in lesser quantities and include white, clear, red, aqua opalescent, peach opalescent, ice blue, ice green, amber, lavender, and smoke.

Companies mainly responsible for its production in America include the Fenton Art Glass Company, Williamstown, West Virginia; the Northwood Glass Company, Wheeling, West Virginia; the Imperial Glass Company, Bellaire, Ohio; the Millersburg Glass Company, Millersburg, Ohio; and the Dugan Glass Company (Diamond Glass), Indiana, Pennsylvania. In addition to these major manufacturers, lesser producers included the U.S. Glass Company, the Cambridge Glass Company, the Westmoreland Glass Company, and the McKee Glass Company.

Carnival glass has been highly collectible since the 1950s and has been reproduced for the last twenty-five years. Several national and state collectors' organizations exist, and many fine books are available on old carnival glass, including *The Standard Encyclopedia of Carnival Glass* by Bill Edwards.

Acanthus (Imperial), plate, marigold, 10" 275.00
Acorn (Fenton), bowl, peach opal, 7" or 8½" 290.00
Acorn Burrs (Northwood), bowl, pastel, flat, 5" 170.00
Acorn Burrs (Northwood), tumbler, gr 85.00
Age Herold (Fenton), bowl, amethyst, rare, 9¼" 1,085.00
Apple & Pear Intaglio (Northwood), bowl, marigold, 5" 30.00
Apple Blossom Twigs (Dugan), bowl, peach opal 165.00
Apple Blossoms (Dugan), plate, marigold, 8¼" 195.00
Apple Panels (English), sugar bowl (open), marigold 30.00
Apple Tree (Fenton), tumbler, marigold 44.00
Arcadia Baskets, plate, marigold, 8" 50.00
Arcs (Imperial), bowl, amethyst, 8½" 42.00
Asters, bowl, marigold, 6" 58.00
Autumn Acorns (Fenton), bowl, pastel, 8¾" 100.00
Aztec (McKee), creamer 200.00
Ball & Swirl, mug, marigold 90.00
Balloons (Imperial), cake plate, marigold 60.00
Bambi, powder jar, marigold, w/lid 25.00
Band (Dugan), violet hat, amethyst 38.00
Banded Diamonds (Crystal), bowl, amethyst, 10" 110.00
Banded Grape (Fenton), tumbler, bl 45.00
Banded Panels (Crystal), sugar bowl (open), marigold 35.00
Basketweave (Fenton), vase whimsey, marigold, rare 650.00
Basketweave & Cable (Westmoreland), creamer, gr 85.00
Beaded Acanthus (Imperial), milk pitcher, marigold 75.00
Beaded Bullseye (Imperial), vase, gr, 8" or 14" 45.00
Beaded Cable (Northwood), rose bowl, marigold 60.00
Beaded Hearts (Northwood), bowl, amethyst 60.00
Beaded Panels (Westmoreland), compote, marigold 40.00
Beaded Shell (Dugan), mug, marigold 200.00
Beaded Shell (Dugan), mug whimsey, amethyst 400.00
Beaded Spears (Crystal), pitcher, marigold, rare 175.00
Beaded Stars (Fenton), bowl, peach opal 75.00
Beaded Stars (Fenton), rose bowl, marigold 45.00
Beaded Swirl (English), compote, bl 55.00
Beaded Swirl (English), sugar bowl, marigold 40.00

Beads (Northwood), bowl, amethyst, 8½" 55.00
Bells & Beads (Dugan), bowl, peach opal, 7½" 60.00
Bells & Beads (Dugan), nappy, amethyst 65.00
Big Basketweave (Dugan), basket, marigold, sm 35.00
Big Basketweave (Dugan), vase, aqua opal, 6" or 14" 180.00
Big Fish (Millersburg), banana bowl, gr, rare 1,800.00
Big Fish (Millersburg), bowl, marigold, sq, very rare 700.00
Bird of Paradise (Northwood), bowl, advertising; amethyst 195.00
Birds & Cherries (Fenton), bonbon, marigold 40.00
Birds & Cherries (Fenton), bowl, marigold, rare, 9½" 200.00
Birds & Cherries (Fenton), compote, bl 60.00
Blackberry (Fenton), hat, red, open edge 480.00
Blackberry (Fenton), plate, marigold, rare 775.00
Blackberry (Fenton), spittoon whimsey, marigold, rare 2,600.00
Blackberry (Northwood), bowl, amethyst, ftd, 9" 60.00

Blackberry (Fenton), vase whimsey, marigold, rare, $250.00.

Blackberry (Northwood), compote, marigold 52.00
Blackberry Banded (Fenton), hat shape, peach opal 85.00
Blackberry Block (Fenton), pitcher, vaseline pastel 5,000.00
Blackberry Block (Fenton), tumbler, wht pastel 200.00
Blackberry Bramble (Fenton), compote, bl 50.00
Blackberry Spray (Fenton), bonbon, marigold 30.00
Blackberry Spray (Fenton), hat shape, red 440.00
Blackberry Wreath (Millersburg), bowl, gr, 5" 65.00
Blocks & Arches (Crystal), pitcher, marigold, rare 150.00
Blocks & Arches (Crystal), tumbler, amethyst, rare 85.00
Blossom & Spears, plate, marigold, 8" 45.00
Blossoms & Band (Imperial), bowl, amethyst, 5" 28.00
Blossoms & Band (Imperial), bowl, marigold, 10" 35.00
Blossomtime (Northwood), compote, amethyst 180.00
Blueberry (Fenton), pitcher, bl, scarce 850.00
Blueberry (Fenton), tumbler, wht pastel, scarce 140.00
Border Plants (Dugan), bowl, amethyst, flat, 8½" 60.00
Bouquet, toothpick holder, marigold 65.00
Bouquet (Fenton), tumbler, wht pastel 85.00
Boutonniere (Millersburg), compote, amethyst 200.00
Bow & English Hob (English), nut bowl, bl 55.00
Briar Patch, hat shape, marigold 36.00
Brocaded Acorns (Fostoria), bonbon, pastel 62.00
Brocaded Daffodils, cake tray 90.00
Brocaded Palms, ice bucket, pastel 90.00
Brocaded Roses, rose bowl, pastel 90.00

Broken Arches (Imperial), punch bowl & base, marigold 350.00
Broken Arches (Imperial), punch cup, amethyst 30.00
Brooklyn, bottle, marigold, w/stopper 70.00
Bull Dog, paperweight, marigold 250.00
Bull's Eye & Leaves (Northwood), bowl, amethyst, 8½" 50.00
Bull's Eye & Loop (Millersburg), vase, gr, rare, 7" or 11" 400.00
Butterflies (Fenton), card tray, marigold 35.00
Butterflies & Bells (Crystal), compote, marigold 90.00
Butterfly, pin tray, marigold 35.00
Butterfly (Fenton), ornament, bl, rare 200.00
Butterfly (Northwood), bonbon, gr, regular 70.00
Butterfly & Berry (Fenton), bowl, gr, ftd, 10" 240.00
Butterfly & Berry (Fenton), vase, pastel, rare 400.00
Butterfly & Fern (Fenton), pitcher, gr 575.00
Butterfly & Fern (Fenton), tumbler, bl 50.00
Butterfly & Tulip (Dugan), bowl, marigold, ftd, scarce, 10½" 475.00
Butterfly & Tulip (Dugan), bowl, marigold, whimsey, rare 1,250.00
Butterfly Bower (Crystal), compote, amethyst 115.00
Butterfly Bush (Crystal), compote, marigold, lg 110.00
Buttermilk (Fenton), goblet, amethyst, plain 65.00
Buzz Saw (Cambridge), cruet, gr, rare, 6" 400.00
Canada Dry, bottle, wht pastel 28.00
Cane (Imperial), compote, marigold 70.00
Cane (Imperial), pickle dish, pastel 45.00
Cane & Scroll (Sea Thistle, English), rose bowl, marigold 55.00
Cannonball Vt, pitcher, wht pastel 400.00
Cannonball Vt, tumbler, wht pastel 85.00
Capitol (Westmoreland), bowl, amethyst, ftd, sm 65.00
Captive Rose (Fenton), bonbon, bl 55.00
Captive Rose (Fenton), compote, bl 48.00
Captive Rose (Fenton), plate, marigold, 7" 80.00
Carnival Honeycomb (Imperial), bonbon, marigold 35.00
Carnival Honeycomb (Imperial), creamer, marigold 28.00
Carnival Honeycomb (Imperial), sugar bowl, marigold 28.00
Carolina Dogwood (Westmoreland), bowl, marigold, 8½" 65.00
Caroline (Dugan), bowl, peach opal, 7" or 10" 185.00
Cathedral (Curved Star, Sweden), chalice, bl, 7" 115.00
Cathedral (Curved Star, Sweden), compote, marigold 40.00
Cathedral (Curved Star, Sweden), creamer, marigold, ftd 45.00
Chatelaine (Imperial), tumbler, amethyst, rare 460.00
Checkerboard (Westmoreland), goblet, marigold, rare 260.00
Checkerboard (Westmoreland), tumbler, amethyst, rare 450.00
Checkers, ashtray, marigold 30.00
Checkers, bowl, marigold, 4" 18.00
Cherry (Dugan), bowl, amethyst, flat, 5" 40.00
Cherry (Dugan), bowl, amethyst, flat, 8" 60.00
Cherry (Dugan), bowl, amethyst, ftd, 8½" 275.00
Cherry (Dugan), plate, amethyst, 6" 125.00
Cherry (Millersburg), bowl, amethyst, scarce, 9" 95.00
Cherry (Millersburg), bowl, bl, Hobnail exterior, rare, 5" 750.00
Cherry (Millersburg), bowl, ice cream; bl, 10" 600.00
Cherry (Millersburg), compote, gr, rare, lg 1,100.00
Cherry & Cable (Northwood), bowl, marigold, scarce, 9" 95.00
Cherry & Daisies (Fenton), banana boat, bl 960.00
Cherry Chain (Fenton), bonbon, wht pastel 80.00
Cherry Chain (Fenton), compote, wht pastel 115.00
Cherry Smash (US Glass), bowl, marigold, 8" 50.00
Chippendale Souvenir, creamer or sugar bowl, marigold 65.00
Chrysanthemum (Fenton), bowl, gr, flat, 9" 85.00
Chrysanthemum (Fenton), bowl, red, ftd, 10" 1,175.00
Circle Scroll (Dugan), bowl, amethyst, 10" 75.00
Circle Scroll (Dugan), creamer or spooner, marigold 150.00
Circle Scroll (Dugan), tumbler, amethyst, rare 525.00
Classic Arts (Czech), powder jar, marigold 475.00

Cleveland Memorial (Millersburg), ashtray, marigold, rare 2,450.00
Cobblestones (Dugan), bowl, marigold, 9" 55.00
Cobblestones (Imperial), bonbon, gr 55.00
Cobblestones (Imperial), bowl, gr, 5" 45.00
Cobblestones (Imperial), bowl, marigold, 8½" 50.00
Coin Dot (Fenton), pitcher, amethyst, rare 425.00
Coin Dot (Fenton), rose bowl, gr 75.00
Coin Dot Vt (Westmoreland), bowl, gr 65.00
Coin Dot Vt (Westmoreland), compote, aqua opal 225.00
Coin Spot (Dugan), compote, peach opal 190.00
Colonial (Imperial), sugar bowl (open) gr 45.00
Colonial (Imperial), toothpick holder, gr 85.00
Colonial (Imperial), vase, marigold 38.00
Columbia (Imperial), compote, gr 57.00

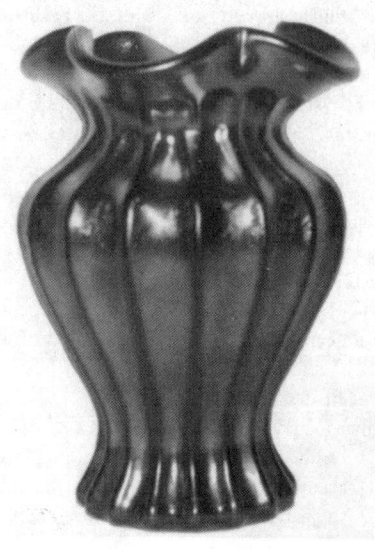

Colonial Lady (Imperial), vase, marigold, rare, $900.00.

Columbia (Imperial), vase, amethyst 48.00
Concave Diamonds (Dugan), coaster, pastel, not iridized 20.00
Concave Flute (Westmoreland), rose bowl, marigold 50.00
Concord (Fenton), bowl, bl, scarce, 9" 195.00
Concord (Fenton), plate, marigold, rare, 10" 400.00
Constellation (Dugan), compote, amethyst 55.00
Coral (Fenton), bowl, bl, 9" 95.00
Coral (Fenton), compote, marigold, rare 265.00
Corinth (Dugan), banana dish, peach opal 280.00
Corinth (Dugan), bowl, amethyst, 9" 50.00
Corinth (Westmoreland), vase, amethyst 45.00
Cornucopia (Fenton), vase, wht pastel, 5" 100.00
Cosmos & Cane, bowl, marigold, 10" 58.00
Cosmos & Cane, butter dish, marigold, w/lid 175.00
Cosmos & Cane, rose bowl, amethyst 150.00
Cosmos Vt (Fenton), bowl, amethyst, 9" or 10" 35.00
Cosmos Vt (Fenton), plate, marigold, rare, 10" 85.00
Country Kitchen (Millersburg), creamer, amethyst 325.00
Crab Claw (Imperial), tumbler, marigold, scarce 95.00
Crackle (Imperial), auto vase, amethyst 35.00
Crackle (Imperial), bowl, gr, 5" 15.00
Crackle (Imperial), pitcher, gr, dome base 140.00
Cut Arcs (Fenton), bowl, marigold, 7½" or 10" 32.00
Cut Arcs (Fenton), compote, bl 45.00
Cut Ovals (Fenton), bowl, marigold, 7" or 10" 50.00
Cut Ovals (Fenton), candlestick, marigold, pr 165.00
Dahlia (Dugan), bowl, amethyst, ftd, 10" 130.00
Dahlia (Dugan), tumbler, marigold, rare 75.00

Daisy (Fenton), bonbon, bl, scarce 195.00
Daisy & Plume (Northwood), candy dish, peach opal 100.00
Daisy & Plume (Northwood), rose bowl, pastel 500.00
Daisy Squares, rose bowl, amethyst 400.00
Daisy Web (Dugan), hat, amethyst, rare 95.00
Dandelion (Northwood), mug, aqua opal 485.00
Dandelion (Northwood), tumbler, bl 90.00
De Vilbiss, perfumer, marigold 40.00
Deep Grape (Millersburg), compote, gr, rare 1,300.00
Diamond & Daisy Cut (US Glass), compote, bl 60.00
Diamond & File, banana bowl, marigold 55.00
Diamond & Rib (Fenton), funeral vase, bl, 17" or 22" 975.00
Diamond & Rib (Fenton), vase, gr, 7" or 12" 32.00
Diamond & Sunburst (Imperial), bowl, gr, 8" 48.00
Diamond & Sunburst (Imperial), decanter, amethyst 140.00
Diamond Band (Crystal), float set, marigold 250.00
Diamond Band (Crystal), sugar bowl (open), amethyst 45.00
Diamond Checkerboard, bowl, marigold, 5" 25.00
Diamond Checkerboard, butter dish, marigold 70.00
Diamond Lace (Imperial), bowl, marigold, 10" or 11" 45.00
Diamond Lace (Imperial), pitcher, amethyst 285.00
Diamond Ovals (English), creamer, marigold 35.00
Diamond Point, basket, amethyst, rare 850.00
Diamond Point Columns (Imperial), vase, gr 40.00
Diamond Points (Northwood), vase, aqua opal, 7" or 14" 490.00
Diamond Ring (Imperial), bowl, marigold, 9" 37.00
Diamond Ring (Imperial), fruit bowl, pastel, 9½" 57.00
Diamond Star, mug, marigold 85.00
Diamond Star, vase, marigold, 8" 60.00
Diamonds (Millersburg), pitcher, amethyst 285.00
Diving Dolphins (English), bowl, gr, ftd, 7" 275.00
Dogwood Sprays (Dugan), bowl, marigold, 9" 37.00
Dolphins (Millersburg), compote, bl, rare 4,200.00
Double Dolphins (Fenton), compote, pastel 60.00
Double Dutch (Imperial), bowl, amethyst, ftd, 9" 60.00
Double Loop (Northwood), creamer, gr 70.00
Double Loop (Northwood), sugar bowl, bl 100.00
Double Scroll (Imperial), candlestick, marigold, pr 50.00
Double Star (Cambridge), pitcher, marigold, scarce 600.00
Double Star (Cambridge), tumbler, gr, scarce 50.00
Double Stem Rose (Dugan), bowl, bl, w/dome base, 8½" 55.00
Dragon & Lotus (Fenton), bowl, aqua opal, flat, 9" 860.00
Dragon & Lotus (Fenton), plate, peach opal, rare, 9½" 1,100.00
Dragon & Strawberry (Fenton), bowl, bl, flat, scarce, 9" 475.00
Drapery (Northwood), rose bowl, amethyst 75.00
Drapery (Northwood), vase, bl 48.00
Dugan Fan (Dugan), gravy boat, pastel, ftd 90.00
Dugan Fan (Dugan), sauce dish, marigold, 5" 38.00
Dutch Mill, ashtray, marigold 35.00
Elks (Fenton), Atlantic City plate, gr, rare 1,150.00
Elks (Fenton), Detroit bowl, gr, scarce 350.00
Elks (Millersburg), paperweight, amethyst, rare 1,200.00
Embroidered Mums (Northwood), bowl, aqua opal, 9" 1,175.00
Emu (Crystal), bowl, marigold, rare, 10" 180.00
Enamelled Grape (Northwood), tumbler, bl 40.00
English Hob & Button (English), bowl, amethyst, 7" or 10" 75.00
Engraved Grapes (Fenton), candy jar, marigold, w/lid 45.00
Engraved Grapes (Fenton), pitcher, marigold, squat 80.00
Engraved Grapes (Fenton), pitcher, marigold, tall 85.00
Engraved Grapes (Fenton), tumbler, marigold 20.00
Estate (Westmoreland), creamer or sugar bowl, marigold 48.00
Fanciful (Dugan), bowl, peach opal, 8½" 275.00
Fanciful (Dugan), plate, amethyst, 9" 225.00
Fancy Flowers (Imperial), compote, marigold 95.00

Fantail (Fenton), bowl, bl, ftd, 9" 135.00
Fantail (Fenton), compote, bl 160.00
Farmyard (Dugan), bowl, peach opal, 10" 9,600.00
Fashion (Imperial), bride's basket, marigold 100.00
Feather & Heart (Millersburg), pitcher, amethyst, scarce 700.00
Feather & Heart (Millersburg), tumbler, gr, scarce 105.00
Feather Stitch (Fenton), bowl, marigold, gr, 8½" or 10" 68.00
Feathered Serpent (Fenton), bowl, amethyst, 10" 70.00
Feathers (Northwood), vase, gr, 7" or 12" 45.00
Feldman Brothers (Northwood), bowl, amethyst 250.00
Fenton's Arched Flute (Fenton), toothpick holder, marigold 75.00
Fentonia, bowl, bl, ftd, 9½" 70.00
Fentonia, butter dish, marigold 110.00
Fentonia Fruit (Fenton), pitcher, marigold, rare 475.00
Fentonia Fruit (Fenton), tumbler, bl, rare 150.00
Fern (Northwood), bowl, gr, 6½" or 9" 50.00
Fern (Northwood), hat, marigold 52.00
Field Flower (Imperial), pitcher, gr, scarce 365.00
Field Flower (Imperial), tumbler, bl, scarce 150.00
Field Thistle (US Glass), butter dish, marigold, rare 125.00
Field Thistle (US Glass), vase, marigold 60.00
File (Imperial & English), pitcher, marigold, rare 265.00
Fine Cut & Roses (Northwood), rose bowl, amethyst, ftd 66.00
Fine Cut Rings (English), sugar bowl, marigold, stemmed 45.00
Fine Cut Rings (English), vase, marigold 50.00
Fine Rib (Northwood, Fenton & Dugan), plate, marigold, 9" 70.00
Fish Net (Dugan), epergne, amethyst 585.00
Fishscale & Beads (Dugan), bowl, pastel, 6" or 8" 50.00
Five Hearts (Dugan), bowl, amethyst, w/dome base, 8¾" 52.00
Flannel Flower, cake stand, amethyst 175.00
Fleur-De-Lis (Millersburg), bowl, gr, flat, 8½" 275.00
Floral & Optic (Imperial), bowl, red, ftd, 8" or 10" 420.00
Floral & Optic (Imperial), cake plate, peach opal, ftd 180.00
Floral Optic (Imperial), cake plate, peach opal, ftd 180.00

Floral & Wheat (US Glass), bonbon, peach opal, stemmed, $155.00.

Floral Oval (Hig-Bee), bowl, marigold, 8" 45.00
Florentine (Fenton & Norwood), candlestick, bl, pr 115.00
Flower & Beads, plate, marigold, 6-sided, 7½" 95.00
Flowering Dill (Fenton), hat, bl 40.00
Flowers & Frames (Dugan), bowl, peach opal, 8" or 10" 300.00
Flute (Millersburg), bowl, marigold, 10" 65.00
Flute (Northwood), creamer or sugar bowl, amethyst 85.00
Flute & Cane (Imperial), pitcher, milk; marigold 120.00
Flute #3 (Imperial), tumbler, amethyst 180.00
Flying Bat, hatpin, amethyst, scarce 55.00
Folding Fan (Dugan), compote, peach opal 120.00

Footed Prism Panels (English), vase, gr 75.00
Footed Rib (Northwood), vase, bl 70.00
Forget-Me-Not (Fenton), pitcher, bl 385.00
Formal (Dugan), hatpin holder, marigold, rare 175.00
Four Flowers, bowl, bl, 10" 90.00
Four Flowers, plate, gr, 6½" 75.00
Four Flowers Vt, plate, gr, rare, 10½" 650.00
French Knots (Fenton), hat, gr 50.00
Frosted Block (Imperial), bowl, marigold, 6½" or 7½" 26.00
Frosted Block (Imperial), celery tray, marigold 40.00
Frosted Block (Imperial), pickle dish, marigold, hdl, rare 40.00
Fruit & Berries (English), bean pot, marigold, w/lid, rare 250.00
Fruit & Flowers (Northwood), bonbon, bl, stemmed 65.00
Fruit & Flowers (Northwood), bowl, gr, 9" 70.00
Fruit Salad (Westmoreland), cup, marigold, rare 30.00
Fruit Salad (Westmoreland), punch bowl, amethyst, rare 885.00
Garden Mums (Northwood), bowl, bl, 8½" or 10" 85.00
Garden Path (Dugan), fruit bowl, marigold, 10" 85.00

Garden Path Vt (Dugan), plate, amethyst, rare, 11" $3,000.00.

Garland (Fenton), rose bowl, bl, ftd 65.00
Gay 90s (Millersburg), pitcher, amethyst, rare 8,500.00
Gay 90s (Millersburg), tumbler, amethyst, rare 1,150.00
God & Home (Dugan), tumbler, bl, rare 285.00
Goddess of Harvest (Fenton), bowl, marigold, rare, 9½" 4,300.00
Golden Harvest (US Glass), decanter, marigold, w/stopper 137.00
Golden Honeycomb (Imperial), compote, marigold 47.00
Golden Honeycomb (Imperial), creamer, marigold 32.00
Good Luck (Northwood), bowl, gr, 8¼" 265.00
Gooseberry Spray, compote, amethyst, rare 110.00
Gothic Arches, vase, gr, rare, 8" or 12" 70.00
Grape, Heavy (Dugan), bowl, amethyst, 10" 265.00
Grape, Heavy (Imperial), bowl, pastel, 9" 60.00
Grape, Heavy (Imperial), plate, gr, 6" 65.00
Grape (Fenton's Grape & Cable), orange bowl, bl, ftd 175.00
Grape (Imperial), basket, gr, hdl, rare 85.00
Grape (Imperial), cup & saucer, marigold 80.00
Grape (Imperial), goblet, gr, rare 65.00
Grape (Imperial), plate, bl, 7" or 12" 160.00
Grape (Northwood's Grape & Cable), bowl, bl, flat, 9" or 10" 75.00
Grape (Northwood's Grape & Cable), nappy, gr 65.00
Grape (Northwood's Grape & Cable), tumbler, gr, jumbo 200.00
Grape & Cherry (English), bowl, marigold, rare, 8½" 65.00
Grape & Gothic Arches (Northwood), tumbler, gr 90.00
Grape Arbor (Dugan), bowl, amethyst, ftd, 9½" or 11" 75.00
Grape Delight (Dugan), nut bowl, bl, ftd, 6" 180.00
Grape Leaves (Northwood), bowl, gr, 8¾" 75.00

Grape Wreath (Millersburg), bowl, amethyst, 7½" or 9" 65.00
Grapevine Lattice (Dugan), bowl, bl, 8½" 60.00
Grapevine Lattice (Fenton), pitcher, bl, rare 625.00
Greek Key (Northwood), plate, marigold, rare, 9" or 11" 685.00
Greek Key Vt, hatpin, amethyst 28.00
Harvest Flower (Dugan), tumbler, marigold 120.00
Harvest Poppy, compote, pastel 70.00
Hattie (Imperial), plate, gr, rare 530.00
Hawaiian Lei (Higbee), creamer or sugar bowl, marigold 65.00
Headdress, bowl, gr, 9" 45.00
Heart & Trees (Fenton), bowl, bl, 8¾" 175.00
Heart Band Souvenir (McKee), mug, gr, sm 95.00
Hearts & Flowers (Northwood), plate, gr, rare, 9" 1,625.00
Heavy Diamond (Imperial), compote, marigold 45.00
Heavy Diamond (Imperial), creamer, marigold 28.00
Heavy Prisms, celery vase, bl, 6" 85.00
Heavy Vine, atomizer, marigold 65.00
Heisey #357, water bottle, marigold 75.00
Heisey Set, creamer & tray, marigold 75.00
Heron (Dugan), mug, amethyst, rare 265.00
Hobnail (Millersburg), butter dish, gr, rare 650.00
Hobnail (Millersburg), pitcher, gr, rare 2,150.00
Hobnail Soda Gold (Imperial), spittoon, gr, lg 65.00
Hobstar (Imperial), bowl, berry; pastel, 5" 45.00
Hobstar (Imperial), butter dish, amethyst 195.00
Hobstar & Arches (Imperial), bowl, gr, 9" 57.00
Hobstar & Cut Triangles (English), rose bowl, gr 70.00
Hobstar & Feather (Millersburg), creamer, amethyst, rare 800.00
Hobstar & Fruit (Westmoreland), bowl, peach opal, rare, 6" 90.00
Hobstar Band (Imperial), compote, marigold, rare 90.00
Hobstar Flower (Northwood), compote, gr, scarce 70.00
Hobstar Panels (English), sugar bowl, marigold, stemmed 45.00
Hobstar Reversed (English), spooner, marigold 45.00
Hobstar Whirl (Whirligig), compote, bl, 4½" 60.00
Holly, Panelled (Northwood), bonbon, gr, ftd 80.00
Holly (Fenton), goblet, amethyst 36.00
Holly & Berry (Dugan), bowl, peach opal, 7" or 9" 60.00
Holly Sprig or Whirl (Millersburg), compote, marigold, rare 450.00
Holly Sprig Vt (Millersburg), bowl, marigold, scarce 190.00
Honeycomb & Hobstar (Millersburg), vase, bl, rare, 8¼" 6,100.00
Honeycomb Ornament, hatpin, amethyst 70.00
Horses Heads (Fenton), bowl, wht pastel, flat, 7½" 210.00
Horses Heads (Fenton), plate, gr, 6½" or 8½" 210.00
Ice Crystals, bowl, pastel, ftd 85.00
Ice Crystals, salt shaker, pastel, ftd 65.00
Idyll (Fenton), vase, amethyst, rare 675.00
Illusion (Fenton), bonbon, marigold 47.00
Imperial #5 (Imperial), bowl, marigold, 8" 40.00
Inca, vase, amethyst, rare, 7" 900.00
Indiana Statehouse (Fenton), plate, marigold, rare 2,850.00
Intaglio Daisy (English), bowl, marigold, 7½" 48.00
Intaglio Ovals (US Glass), plate, aqua opal, 7½" 80.00
Inverted Coin Dot (Northwood-Fenton), pitcher, amethyst 450.00
Inverted Feather (Cambridge), cracker jar, gr, w/lid 585.00
Inverted Feather (Cambridge), spooner, marigold, rare 390.00
Inverted Feather (Cambridge), wine, marigold, rare 190.00
Inverted Strawberry, bowl, gr, 9" or 10½" 285.00
Inverted Strawberry, compote, marigold, rare, sm 400.00
Inverted Strawberry, pitcher, gr, rare 2,800.00
Inverted Thistle (Cambridge), pitcher, marigold, rare 3,700.00
Inverted Thistle (Cambridge), pitcher, milk; amethyst, rare ...2,600.00
Iris (Heavy, Dugan), pitcher, peach opal 1,250.00
Jack-In-The-Pulpit (Dugan), vase, bl 80.00
Jacobean Ranger (Czech & English), tumbler, marigold 75.00

Jeweled Heart (Dugan), bowl, amethyst, 10" 95.00
Jeweled Heart (Dugan), tumbler, marigold, rare 100.00
Jewels (Imperial), candlestick, red, pr 310.00
Jewels (Imperial), vase, marigold 90.00
Kangaroo (Australian), bowl, amethyst, 9½" 200.00
Kittens (Fenton), cup & saucer, marigold, scarce 252.00
Kittens (Fenton), spooner, bl, rare, 2½" 265.00
Kiwi (Australian), bowl, amethyst, rare, 10" 300.00
Knotted Beads (Fenton), vase, bl, 4" or 12" 37.00
Kokomo (English), rose bowl, gr, ftd 60.00
Kookaburra & Vts (Australian), bowl, amethyst, 5" 48.00
Lacy Dewdrop (Westmoreland), compote, pastel, w/lid 285.00
Large Kangaroo (Australian), bowl, amethyst, 5" 52.00
Lattice (Dugan), bowl, amethyst, various sizes 65.00
Lattice & Daisy (Dugan), bowl, marigold, 5" 30.00
Lattice & Daisy (Dugan), pitcher, marigold 235.00
Lattice & Grape (Fenton), pitcher, bl 410.00
Lattice & Grape (Fenton), spittoon whimsey, marigold, rare ..2,350.00
Lattice & Leaves, vase, bl, 9½" 67.00
Lattice & Points, vase, marigold 35.00
Lattice Heart (English), bowl, bl, 10" 70.00
Laurel Leaves (Imperial), plate, marigold 47.00
Lea & Vt (English), bowl, marigold, ftd 38.00
Lea & Vt (English), creamer, amethyst, ftd 52.00
Leaf & Beads (Northwood-Dugan), bowl, amethyst, 9" 80.00
Leaf & Beads (Northwood-Dugan), candy dish, peach opal, ftd .290.00
Leaf & Beads (Northwood-Dugan), rose bowl, bl, ftd 75.00
Leaf Chain (Fenton), bowl, aqua opal, 7" or 9" 1,200.00
Leaf Column (Northwood), vase, peach opal 155.00
Leaf Swirl (Westmoreland), compote, amethyst 55.00
Leaf Tiers (Fenton), bowl, marigold, ftd, 5" 30.00
Lily of the Valley (Fenton), tumbler, marigold, rare 600.00
Lined Lattice (Dugan), vase, gr, 7" or 14" 45.00
Lion (Fenton), bowl, marigold, scarce, 7" 85.00
Little Beads, bowl, marigold, 8" 18.00
Little Beads, compote, aqua opal, sm 85.00
Little Daisies (Fenton), bowl, marigold, rare, 8" or 9½" 290.00
Little Fishes (Fenton), bowl, bl, flat or ftd, 10" 265.00
Little Fishes (Fenton), plate, wht pastel, rare, 10½" 950.00
Little Flowers (Fenton), plate, marigold, rare, 10" 750.00
Little Stars (Millersburg), bowl, amethyst, rare, 10½" 700.00
Little Stars (Millersburg), bowl, gr, scarce, 7" 90.00
Loganberry (Imperial), vase, gr, scarce 375.00
Long Hobstar, bowl, marigold, 10½" 56.00

Long Hobstar, punch bowl, marigold, with base, $125.00.

Long Thumbprint (Dugan), creamer or sugar bowl, marigold 38.00
Long Thumbprint (Dugan), vase, bl, 7" or 11" 38.00
Lotus & Grape (Fenton), bonbon, bl 42.00
Lotus & Grape (Fenton), bowl, amethyst, ftd, 7" 50.00
Lotus & Grape (Fenton), plate, gr, rare, 9½" 625.00
Louisa (Westmoreland), rose bowl, bl 65.00
Lustre & Clear (Imperial), butter dish, marigold 65.00
Lustre & Clear (Imperial), creamer or sugar bowl, amethyst 65.00
Lustre & Clear (Lightolier), shade, marigold 40.00
Lustre Flute (Northwood), cup, gr 20.00
Lustre Flute (Northwood), hat, amethyst 40.00
Lustre Rose (Imperial), ferner, amethyst 60.00
Lustre Rose (Imperial), pitcher, marigold 85.00
Magnolia Drape, tumbler, marigold 50.00
Magpie (Australian), bowl, marigold, 6" or 10" 45.00
Malaga (Dugan), bowl, amethyst, scarce, 9" 90.00
Many Fruits (Dugan), cup, bl 40.00
Many Fruits (Dugan), punch bowl, amethyst, w/base 450.00
Many Stars (Millersburg), bowl, gr, ruffled, scarce, 9" 460.00
Maple Leaf (Dugan), bowl, bl, stemmed, 4½" 30.00
Marilyn (Millersburg), pitcher, amethyst, rare 975.00
Mary Ann (Dugan), vase, marigold, 7" 35.00
Mayflower, bowl, peach opal, 7½" 155.00
Mayflower, hat, pastel 60.00
Maypole, vase, gr, 6¼" 56.00
Melon Rib (Imperial), pitcher, marigold 60.00
Melon Rib (Imperial), powder jar, marigold, w/lid 35.00
Memphis (Northwood), cup, amethyst 38.00
Memphis (Northwood), fruit bowl, bl, w/base 2,250.00
Mikado (Fenton), compote, gr, lg 645.00
Milady (Fenton), pitcher, bl 500.00
Milady (Fenton), tumbler, gr 120.00
Mirrored Lotus (Fenton), bowl, gr, 7" or 8½" 58.00
Mirrored Lotus (Fenton), plate, bl, rare, 7½" 185.00
Mitered Diamond & Pleats (English), bowl, marigold, 4½" 20.00
Mitered Ovals (Millersburg), vase, marigold, rare 5,000.00
Moonprint (English), sugar bowl, marigold, stemmed 50.00
Morning-Glory (Millersburg), pitcher, amethyst, rare 8,500.00
Morning-Glory (Millersburg), tumbler, gr, rare 1,000.00
Multi-Fruits & Flowers (Millersburg), tumbler, gr, rare 850.00
My Lady, powder jar, marigold, w/lid 87.00
Narcissus & Ribbon (Fenton), wine bottle, marigold, rare 885.00
Nautilus (Dugan-Northwood), vase whimsey, marigold, rare ..1,600.00
Nesting Swan (Millersburg), bowl, bl, ruffled, scarce, 10" 2,800.00
Night Stars (Millersburg), bonbon, amethyst, rare 650.00
Nippon (Northwood), bowl, aqua opal, 8½" 745.00
Northern Star (Fenton), bowl, marigold, 6" or 7" 28.00
Northwood Jack-In-The-Pulpit, vase, pastel, all sizes 75.00
Northwood Jester's Cap, vase, aqua opal 215.00
Northwood's Nearcut, compote, amethyst 130.00
Northwood's Poppy, tray, bl, oval, rare 225.00
Nu-Art (Imperial), plate, bl, scarce 1,095.00
Nu-Art Chrysanthemum (Imperial), plate, gr, rare 1,000.00
Number 2351 (Cambridge), punch cup, gr 65.00
Number 270 (Westmoreland), compote, peach opal 85.00
Number 4 (Imperial), bowl, marigold, ftd 26.00
Octagon (Imperial), bowl, gr, 4½" 28.00
Octagon (Imperial), creamer or spooner, marigold 48.00
Octagon (Imperial), pitcher, milk; amethyst, scarce 210.00
Octet (Northwood), bowl, amethyst, 8½" 60.00
Oklahoma (Mexican), tumble-up, marigold, complete 175.00
Olympus, shade, marigold 50.00
Open Flower (Dugan), bowl, gr, flat or ftd, 7" 38.00
Open Rose (Imperial), fruit bowl, amethyst, 7" or 10" 65.00

Open Rose (Imperial), plate, gr, 9" 185.00
Optic (Imperial), bowl, amethyst, 6" 47.00
Optic & Buttons (Imperial), bowl, marigold, hdls, 12" 42.00
Optic & Buttons (Imperial), plate, marigold, 10½" 70.00
Optic Flute (Imperial), bowl, amethyst, 5" 40.00
Orange Tree (Fenton), butter dish, marigold 235.00
Orange Tree (Fenton), creamer or spooner, marigold 45.00
Orange Tree (Fenton), plate, bl, 8" or 9½" 210.00
Orange Tree & Scroll (Fenton), pitcher, bl 585.00
Orange Tree Orchard (Fenton), tumbler, marigold 45.00

Orange Tree Orchard (Fenton), pitcher, marigold, $420.00.

Oriental Poppy (Northwood), pitcher, bl 2,500.00
Ostrich (Australian), compote, amethyst, rare, lg 160.00
Oval & Round (Imperial), bowl, amethyst, 9" 45.00
Oval Star & Fan (Jenkins), rose bowl, amethyst 57.00
Palm Beach (US Glass), bowl, marigold, 9" 50.00
Palm Beach (US Glass), plate, pastel, rare, 9" 225.00
Panelled Dandelion (Fenton), pitcher, bl 600.00
Panelled Hobnail (Dugan), vase, peach opal, 5" or 10" 75.00
Panelled Tree Trunk (Dugan), vase, gr, rare, 7" or 12" 110.00
Pansy (Imperial), bowl, amethyst, 8¾" 48.00
Pansy (Imperial), plate, amethyst, ruffled, rare 90.00
Panther (Fenton), bowl, gr, ftd, 10" 375.00
Pastel Panels (Imperial), tumbler, pastel 70.00
Peach (Northwood), bowl, wht pastel, 9" 210.00
Peach & Pear (Dugan), banana bowl, amethyst 95.00
Peach Blossom, bowl, marigold, 7½" 55.00
Peacock, Fluffy (Fenton), pitcher, bl 850.00
Peacock (Millersburg), plate, amethyst, rare, 6" 775.00
Peacock & Dahlia (Fenton), bowl, gr, 7½" 125.00
Peacock & Grape (Fenton), plate, amethyst, 9" 400.00
Peacock & Urn (Fenton), bowl, peach opal, 8½" 1,600.00
Peacock & Urn (Northwood), plate, amethyst, rare, 11" 750.00
Peacock at the Fountain (Northwood), bowl, bl, 9" 98.00
Peacock at the Fountain (Northwood), tumbler, gr 475.00
Peacock Strutting (Westmoreland), creamer, gr, w/lid 60.00

Peacock Tail (Fenton), bonbon, bl 40.00
Peacock Tail & Daisy, bowl, marigold, very rare 1,000.00
Peacock Tail Vt (Millersburg), compote, gr, scarce 90.00
Persian Garden (Dugan), bowl, berry; amethyst, 10" 250.00
Persian Garden (Dugan), plate, marigold, rare, 6" 90.00
Persian Medallion (Fenton), compote, gr 54.00
Persian Medallion (Fenton), punch bowl, gr, w/base 390.00
Persian Medallion (Fenton), rose bowl, pastel 90.00
Petal & Fan (Dugan), bowl, pastel, 10" 120.00
Petal & Fan (Dugan), plate, amethyst, ruffled, 6" 95.00
Petals (Dugan), compote, marigold 45.00
Peter Rabbit (Fenton), plate, bl, rare, 10" 2,000.00
Pillow & Sunburst (Westmoreland), bowl, amethyst, 7½" 54.00
Pin-Ups (Australian), bowl, marigold, rare, 8¾" 90.00
Pine Cone (Fenton), plate, gr, 6½" 58.00
Pineapple (English), creamer, marigold 40.00
Pinwheel (Dugan), bowl, marigold, 6" 38.00
Pinwheel (Dugan), plate, marigold, 6½" 58.00
Pinwheel (English), vase, amethyst, 6½" 200.00
Plaid (Fenton), bowl, gr, 8¾" 265.00
Plain Jane, paperweight, marigold 80.00
Plume Panels, vase, red, 7" or 12" 490.00
Poinsettia (Imperial), pitcher, milk; amethyst 850.00
Poinsettia (Northwood), bowl, gr, flat or ftd, 8½" 480.00
Pond Lily (Fenton), bonbon, bl 52.00
Pony (Dugan), bowl, amethyst, 8½" 120.00
Poppy (Millersburg), compote, amethyst, scarce 550.00
Poppy & Fish Net (Imperial), vase, red, rare, 6" 500.00
Poppy Show (Imperial), hurricane whimsey, amethyst 2,000.00
Portland (US Glass), bowl, pastel, 8½" 150.00
Premium (Imperial), underplate, red, 14" 130.00
Pretty Panels (Fenton), tumbler, red, hdl 70.00
Pretty Panels (Northwood), pitcher, marigold 120.00
Primrose (Millersburg), bowl, gr, ruffled, 8¾" 150.00
Prism, shakers, marigold, pr 60.00
Prism & Cane (English), bowl, amethyst, rare, 5" 65.00
Prism Band (Fenton), pitcher, bl, w/decor 385.00
Prisms (Westmoreland), compote, amethyst, scarce, 5" 110.00
Propeller (Imperial), bowl, marigold, rare, 9½" 80.00
Propeller (Imperial), vase, marigold, stemmed, rare 75.00
Pulled Loop (Dugan), vase, peach opal 50.00
Puzzle (Dugan), bonbon, gr, stemmed 54.00
Puzzle (Dugan), compote, white pastel 60.00
Quartered Block, sugar bowl, marigold 50.00
Question Marks (Dugan), bonbon, peach opal 70.00
Quill (Dugan), pitcher, amethyst, rare 2,700.00
Ragged Robin (Fenton), bowl, bl, scarce, 8¾" 80.00
Rainbow (Northwood), compote, amethyst 110.00
Raindrops (Dugan), pitcher, gr 260.00
Ranger (Mexican), creamer, marigold 40.00
Rasberry (Northwood), bowl, amethyst, 9" 56.00
Rasberry (Northwood), compote, gr 58.00
Rays (Dugan), bowl, amethyst or gr, 9" 90.00
Rays & Ribbons (Millersburg), bowl, gr, ruffled, 8½" 90.00
Ribbed Swirl, tumbler, marigold 56.00
Ribbon Tie (Fenton), bowl, red, 8¾" 1,600.00
Ripple (Imperial), vase, pastel, various sizes 50.00
Rising Sun (US Glass), creamer, marigold 75.00
Rising Sun (US Glass), tumbler, marigold, rare 400.00
Rock Crystal (McKee), cup, amethyst 45.00
Rococo (Imperial), bowl, marigold, 5" 30.00
Rosalind (Millersburg), bowl, amethyst, scarce, 10" 260.00
Rosalind (Millersburg), compote, jelly; amethyst, rare, 9" 1,800.00
Rose Column (Millersburg), vase, gr, rare 1,150.00

Rose Garden (Sweden), bowl, bl, 8¾" 60.00
Rose Panels (Australian), compote, marigold, lg 120.00
Rose Pinwheel, bowl, marigold, rare 1,700.00
Rose Show (Northwood), bowl, aqua opal, 8¾" 900.00
Rose Show Variant (Northwood), plate, peach opal, 9" 875.00
Rose Tree (Fenton), bowl, marigold, rare, 10" 350.00
Roses & Fruit (Millersburg), bonbon, bl, ftd, rare 1,000.00
Rosettes (Northwood), bowl, amethyst, w/dome base, 9" 85.00
Round-Up (Dugan), bowl, wht pastel, 8¾" 140.00
Round-Up (Dugan), plate, bl, rare, 9" 175.00
Royalty (Imperial), cup, marigold, rare, 9" 128.00
Ruffled Rib (Northwood), vase, marigold, 7" or 14" 60.00
Rustic (Fenton), vase, funeral; bl, 15" or 20" 185.00
S-Band (Australian), compote, marigold 50.00
S-Repeat (Dugan), cup, amethyst, rare 110.00
Sailboats (Fenton), bowl, red, 6" 350.00
Sailboats (Fenton), plate, pastel 295.00
Sailing Ship, plate, marigold, 8" 40.00
Satin Swirl, atomizer, clear pastel 65.00
Scale Band (Fenton), bowl, peach opal, 6" 40.00
Scale Band (Fenton), pitcher, bl 210.00
Scales (Westmoreland), bowl, peach opal, 7" or 10" 70.00
Scales (Westmoreland), plate, amethyst, 9" 95.00
Scarab, hatpin, amethyst 35.00
Scottie, paperweight, marigold, rare 200.00

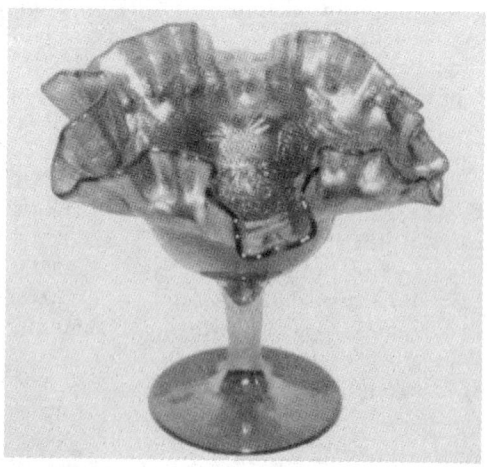

Scotch Thistle (Fenton), blue, compote, $45.00.

Scroll (Westmoreland), pin tray, marigold 45.00
Scroll Embossed (Imperial), compote, gr, sm 60.00
Scroll Embossed (Imperial), plate, amethyst, 9" 97.00
Scroll Embossed Vt (English), plate, marigold, 7" 150.00
Seaweed (Millersburg), bowl, gr, ruffled, scarce, 10½" 295.00
Seaweed (Millersburg), bowl, marigold, rare, 5" 400.00
Shell (Imperial), bowl, amethyst, 7" or 9" 46.00
Shell & Jewel (Westmoreland), creamer, gr, w/lid 60.00
Sheraton (US Glass), creamer or spooner, pastel 65.00
Sheraton (US Glass), tumbler, pastel 48.00
Shrine (US Glass), toothpick holder, clear pastel 175.00
Silver & Gold, pitcher, marigold 100.00
Silver Queen, tumbler, marigold 45.00
Singing Birds (Northwood), creamer or spooner, amethyst 100.00
Singing Birds (Northwood), tumbler, gr 58.00
Single Flower (Dugan), basket whimsey, marigold, hdld, rare 225.00
Single Flower (Dugan), bowl, gr, 8" 38.00
Single Flower Framed (Dugan), bowl, amethyst, 8¾" 90.00
Six Petals (Dugan), plate, peach opal, rare 190.00
Six-Sided (Imperial), candlestick, gr, ea 275.00

Ski-Star (Dugan), basket, peach opal, hdld, rare 500.00
Small Blackberry (Northwood), compote, marigold 45.00
Small Rib (Dugan), compote, amethyst 40.00
Small Thumbprint, toothpick holder, marigold 50.00
Smooth Panels (Imperial), vase, peach opal 65.00
Smooth Rays (Northwood-Dugan), plate, peach opal, 7" or 9" 80.00
Smooth Rays (Northwood-Dugan), rose bowl, marigold 40.00

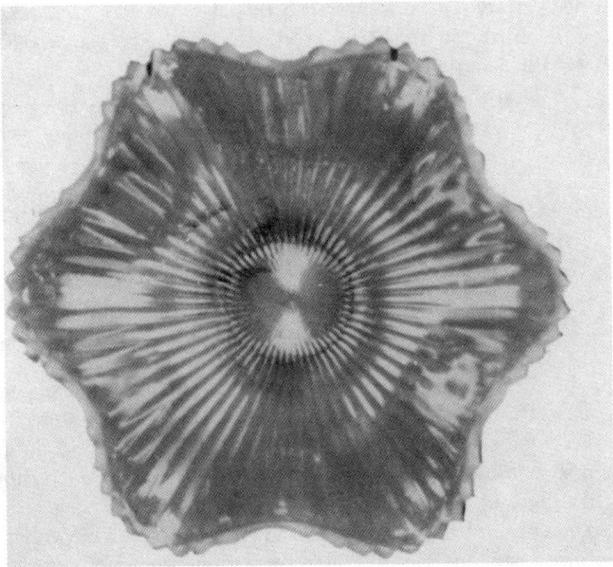

Smooth Rays (Westmoreland), bowl, green, flat, 7" or 9",
$47.00.

Soda Gold (Imperial), bowl, marigold, 9" 45.00
Soda Gold (Imperial), tumbler, marigold 40.00
Soda Gold Spears (Dugan), bowl, marigold, 4½" 26.00
Soldiers & Sailors (Fenton), plate, bl, Illinois, rare 1,000.00
Soutache (Dugan), plate, peach opal, rare, 10½" 365.00
Spiderweb (Northwood-Dugan), vase, pastel, 8" 75.00
Spiral (Imperial), candlestick, amethyst, ea 70.00
Spiralex (English), vase, bl, various sizes 50.00
Split Diamond (English), sugar bowl (open), marigold 40.00
Spokes (Fostoria), bowl, pastel, 10" 95.00
Spring Basket (Imperial), basket, smoke pastel, hdld, 5" 48.00
Springtime (Northwood), bowl, marigold, 5" 40.00
Springtime (Northwood), creamer or spooner, marigold 320.00
Square Daisy & Button (Imperial), toothpick holder, pastel 120.00
Stag & Holly, plate, amethyst, ftd, 9" 900.00
Stag & Holly (Fenton), rose bowl, bl, ftd 1,000.00
Star & Fan, vase, marigold, rare, 9½" 250.00
Star & File (Imperial), bonbon, marigold 30.00
Star & File (Imperial), pitcher, marigold 185.00
Star & File (Imperial), vase, marigold, hdld 50.00
Star Center (Imperial), bowl, pastel, 8½" 42.00
Star Medallion (Imperial), bowl, marigold, 7" or 9" 28.00
Star Medallion (Imperial), pickle dish, marigold 40.00
Star of David (Imperial), bowl, gr, scarce, 8¾" 80.00
Star of David & Bows (Northwood), bowl, gr, 8½" 70.00
Star Spray (Imperial), bowl, marigold, 7" 28.00
Star Spray (Imperial), plate, marigold, scarce, 7½" 50.00
Starbright, vase, amethyst, 6½" 42.00
Starfish (Dugan), compote, peach opal 90.00
Starflower, pitcher, marigold, rare 2,600.00
Stars & Stripes (Old Glory), plate, marigold, rare, 7½" 125.00
Stippled Acorns, candy dish, bl, ftd, w/lid 90.00

Stippled Diamond Swag (English), compote, bl 56.00
Stippled Petals (Dugan), bowl, amethyst, 9" 80.00
Stippled Rambler Rose (Dugan), bowl, nut; marigold, ftd 60.00
Stippled Rays (Fenton), plate, gr, 7" 45.00
Stippled Rays (Imperial), creamer, gr, stemmed 46.00
Stippled Rays (Northwood), compote, amethyst 58.00
Stippled Strawberry (Jenkins), creamer, marigold 30.00
Stork & Rushes (Dugan), creamer or spooner, amethyst, rare 100.00
Stork & Rushes (Dugan), tumbler, bl 70.00
Strawberry (Dugan), epergne, amethyst 900.00
Strawberry (Fenton), bonbon, red 450.00
Strawberry (Millersburg), bowl, gr, tricornered, 9½" 400.00
Strawberry (Northwood), bowl, aqua opal, 8" or 10" 1,850.00
Strawberry (Northwood), plate, marigold, handgrip, 7" 175.00
Strawberry Intaglio (Northwood), bowl, marigold, 5½" 25.00
Strawberry Scroll (Fenton), pitcher, bl, rare 2,000.00
Strawberry Scroll (Fenton), tumbler, marigold, rare 150.00
Stream of Hearts (Fenton), compote, marigold, rare 90.00
Studs (Imperial), tumbler, juice; marigold 30.00
Sunflower (Millersburg), pin tray, gr, rare 300.00
Sunk Diamond Band (US Glass), pitcher, marigold, rare 145.00
Sunken Daisy (English), sugar bowl, bl 36.00
Superb Drape (Northwood), vase, aqua opal, rare 2,500.00
Sweetheart (Cambridge), cookie jar, marigold w/lid, rare 1,300.00
Swirl (Northwood), tumbler, gr 65.00
Swirl Hobnail (Millersburg), rose bowl, gr, rare 585.00
Swirl Variant (Imperial), epergne, gr 170.00
Swirled Flute (Fenton), vase, wht pastel, 7" or 12" 60.00
Swirled Ribs (Northwood), tumbler, marigold 60.00
Sword & Circle, tumbler, marigold, rare 85.00
Taffeta Lustre (Fostoria), candlestick, gr, rare, pr 300.00
Target (Fenton), vase, gr, 7" or 11" 48.00
Ten Mums (Fenton), bowl, gr, 8" or 11" 110.00
Texas, tumbler, bl, giant 185.00
Thin Rib & Drape (Fenton), vase, marigold, 8" or 14" 36.00
Thin Rib & Vts (Northwood), vase, aqua opal, 6" or 11" 190.00
Thistle, shade, marigold 40.00
Thistle (Fenton), plate, amethyst, rare, 9" 1,400.00
Thistle & Lotus (Fenton), bowl, bl, 7" 60.00
Thistle & Thorn (English), bowl, marigold, ftd, 6" 46.00
Thistle & Thorn (English), plate, marigold, ftd, 8½" 130.00
Three Diamonds (Dugan), vase, peach opal, 6" or 10" 75.00
Three Fruits (Northwood), bowl, pastel, 9" 90.00
Three Fruits (Northwood), plate, bl, rnd, 9" 135.00
Three Fruits Vt (Dugan), plate, gr, 12-sided 200.00
Three Row (Imperial), vase, marigold, rare 800.00
Three-In-One (Imperial), bowl, gr, 8¾" 36.00
Thumbprint & Oval (Imperial), vase, amethyst, rare, 5½" 600.00
Thumbprint & Spears, creamer, gr 56.00
Tiger Lily (Imperial), pitcher, gr 300.00
Tornado (Northwood), vase, bl, plain 900.00
Tracery (Millersburg), bonbon, amethyst, rare 650.00
Tree Bark (Imperial), candlestick, marigold, 4½", pr 30.00
Tree Bark (Imperial), pitcher, marigold, w/lid 70.00
Tree of Life (Imperial), basket, marigold, hdld 30.00
Tree of Life (Imperial), tumbler, marigold 22.00
Tree Trunk (Northwood), jardiniere whimsey, marigold, rare 290.00
Triands (English), butter dish, marigold 60.00
Triplets (Dugan), bowl, gr, 6" or 8" 42.00
Trout & Fly (Millersburg), bowl, gr, various shapes, 8¾" 595.00
Tulip (Millersburg), compote, amethyst, rare, 9" 700.00
Tulip & Cane (Imperial), goblet, marigold, rare, 8-oz 75.00
Tulip Scroll (Millersburg), vase, gr, rare, 6" or 12" 350.00
Twins (Imperial), bowl, pastel, 9" 42.00

Two Flowers (Fenton), plate, marigold, rare, 13" 695.00
Two Flowers (Fenton), rose bowl, gr, rare 140.00
Two Fruits (Fenton), bowl, bl, divided, scarce, 5½" 85.00
Two Fruits (Northwood), spooner, bl, rare 450.00
Umbrella Prisms, hatpin, amethyst, sm 26.00
Valentine (Northwood), bowl, marigold, rare, 5" 95.00
Venetian (Cambridge), butter dish, marigold, rare 600.00
Venetian (Cambridge), creamer, marigold, rare 400.00
Victorian, bowl, amethyst, rare, 10" or 12" 350.00
Vineyard (Dugan), pitcher, peach opal 800.00
Vining Leaf & Vt (English), vase, marigold, rare 250.00
Vintage (Fenton), bowl, gr or bl, 10" 60.00
Vintage (Fenton), cup, amethyst 30.00
Vintage (Millersburg), bowl, bl, rare, 5" 800.00
Vintage Banded (Dugan), pitcher, marigold 200.00
Virginia Blackberry (US Glass), pitcher, bl, rare, sm 225.00
Waffle Block (Imperial), bowl, marigold, 7" or 9" 36.00
Waffle Block (Imperial), cup, marigold 18.00
Waffle Block (Imperial), shakers, marigold, pr 75.00
Water Lily (Fenton), bonbon, bl 45.00
Water Lily & Cattails (Fenton), bowl, bl, 5" 50.00
Water Lily & Cattails (Northwood), tumbler, amethyst 165.00
Wavy Satin, hatpin, amethyst 25.00
Weeping Cherry, bowl, amethyst, flat base 75.00
Western Daisy (Westmoreland), bowl, amethyst 52.00
Wheat (Northwood), sweetmeat, amethyst, w/lid, rare 2,350.00
Whirling Hobstar (US Glass), pitcher, marigold 250.00
Whirling Star (Imperial), compote, marigold 55.00
White Oak, tumbler, marigold, rare 300.00
Wide Panel (Northwood-Fenton-Imperial), bowl, marigold, 9" ...40.00
Wide Panel (Westmoreland), bowl, amber pastel, 8¼" 62.00
Wide Rib (Dugan), vase, bl 46.00
Wild Blackberry (Fenton), bowl, amethyst, scarce, 8½" 65.00
Wild Fern (Australian), compote, amethyst 165.00

Wild Rose, syrup, marigold, rare, $595.00.

Wild Strawberry (Dugan), bowl, amethyst, 9" or 10½" 135.00
Wildflower (Millersburg), compote, jelly; amethyst, rare 1,600.00
Windflower (Dugan), plate, marigold, 9" 130.00
Windmill (Imperial), bowl, amethyst or gr, 9" 37.00
Windmill (Imperial), pitcher, marigold 70.00
Wine & Roses (Fenton), wine, bl 90.00
Wishbone (Imperial), flower arranger, marigold 85.00
Wishbone (Northwood), bowl, amethyst or gr, flat, 8" or 10" 100.00
Wishbone (Northwood), plate, amethyst, flat, rare, 10" 490.00

Wishbone & Spades (Dugan), bowl, peach opal, 8½" 140.00
Wishbone & Spades (Dugan), plate, amethyst, rare, 10½" 1,000.00
Wisteria (Northwood), bank whimsey, wht pastel, rare 1,000.00
Woodpecker (Dugan), wall vase, marigold 38.00
Wreath of Roses (Fenton), compote, bl 42.00
Wreath of Roses (Fenton), cup, peach opal 300.00
Wreath of Roses Vt (Dugan), compote, gr or bl 60.00
Wreathed Bleeding Hearts (Dugan), vase, marigold, 5¼" 90.00
Wreathed Cherry (Dugan), bowl, peach opal, oval, 10½" 375.00
Zig Zag (Fenton), pitcher, bl, w/decor, rare 400.00
Zig Zag (Millersburg), card tray, gr, rare 750.00
Zipper Vt (English), sugar bowl, marigold, w/lid 47.00
Zippered Heart, bowl, amethyst, 5" 48.00
474 (Imperial), cordial, marigold, rare 90.00
474 (Imperial), tumbler, gr, scarce 65.00
474 (Imperial), vase, red, rare, 7" 2,500.00
49'er (Imperial), tumbler, marigold 75.00

Cartoon Art

Collectors of cartoon art are interested in many forms of original art — animation cels, sports, political or editorial cartoons, syndicated comic strip panels, and caricature. To produce even a short animated cartoon strip, hundreds of original drawings are required, each showing the characters in slightly advancing positions. Called 'cels' because those made prior to the 1950s were made from a celluloid material, collectors often pay hundreds of dollars for a frame from a favorite movie. Prices of Disney cels with backgrounds vary widely. Background paintings, model sheets, storyboards, and preliminary sketches are also collectible — so are comic book drawings executed in India ink and signed by the artist. Daily 'funnies' originals, especially the earlier ones portraying super heroes, and Sunday comic strips, the early as well as the later ones, are collected. Cartoon art has become recognized and valued as a novel yet valid form of contemporary art.

Animation Cel, Full Color

Autocat, driving car, HP track bkground 295.00
Casey Bats Again, Casey's daughter on floor, full sz 750.00
Den, Den making love to Kath, heavy metal bkground 385.00

Fantasia, blue centaurette, gouache on celluloid, Courvoisier background stamped WDP and labeled, 1940, 5½x5½", $900.00.

Flintstones, Barney holding Pebbles, dbl matted, fr 110.00
Mickey Mouse, later-style figure, hands in pockets, 6" image ..1,250.00
Mighty Mouse, Mike in working clothes, bright colors 195.00
Olympic Pink, Pink Panther in empty stadium, full cel 165.00
Pecos Bill, Slue Foot Sue, hand inked, 1947, full cel 975.00
Popeye w/arm out, lg close-up, early, 7½x7½" 195.00
Popeye's nephews, gr towels & toys, matted & fr 350.00
Robin Hood, Little John in disguise, full cel 385.00
Sleeping Beauty, Aurora w/basket, 1959, 9½x8" 755.00
Snow White & 7 Dwarfs, pleased Grumpy, 1939, 8¼x6¼" 1,600.00
Space Ghost, in flight on HP ground, matted & fr 300.00
Taarna, full figure, walking, frontal view 185.00
Working for Peanuts, Donald Duck & elephant, 1953, full cel ...975.00

Animation Drawing

Black Cauldron, Creeper, bl/blk pencil, scarce 285.00
Black Cauldron, soldier close-up, bl/blk pencil, lg 175.00
Christmas Carol, Morley w/gold, pants falling, pencil, lg 235.00
Clock Cleaners, Goofy on ground w/lg turning wheel, graphite ..500.00
Dude Duck, Donald Duck, close-up half-figure, 1951 ....195.00
Fox & Hound, Tod exhausted, red pencil, lg 190.00
Lady & Tramp, Jack in puddle, blk/red pencil, lg 450.00
Mickey's Man Friday, Mickey swimming, ca 1935, 6x6" 600.00
Modern Inventions, Donald Duck, 1937, 10x12" 195.00
Mr Bumble, Hoppity w/arms around Mr Bumble, red pencil 215.00
Northwest Hounded Police, wolf in prison, red/blk pencil, '46 ..200.00
Reginald the Fox, fox w/telephones to ear, 1949 ....195.00
Tom & Jerry, girl cat, bl pencil shading on eyes, early 235.00

Daily Newspaper Comic Strip

Bobo Whopper, sgn Riley Thompson, set of 3, ea: 4½x22" 450.00
Dick Tracy, sgn Chester Gould, 12/1/59, 5x16" 350.00
Donald Duck, Walt Disney Productions, 7/18/57, 6x19" 175.00
Family Circus, sgn Bill Keane, 6/26/82, 10x8" 150.00
Peanuts, Charlie & Lucy, sgn C Schultz, 1/21/86, 5x21" 600.00
Ripley's Believe It or Not, King Features, 9/23/59, 14x11" 150.00
Sam's Strip, sgn Dumas, 9/15/62, 6x20" 150.00

Model Sheets

Aladdin & His Wonderful Lamp, Olive in costume, 4 images 195.00
Autograph Hound, Studio Cop, Donald & waiter 300.00
Clock Cleaners, Mickey Mouse & stork, 1937 ....300.00
Donald Gets Drafted, Peg Leg Pete & Donald Duck, WWII 300.00
Flying Squirrel, Donald Duck & squirrel, 1954 ....200.00
Paul Bunyon, Babe, clean-up sheet, fine-line renderings 200.00
Snow White, Snow White & dwarfs, blk/wht, 11x14" 475.00
Suzie the Coupe, Suzie & other cars, sgn Bill Peet 395.00

Sunday Newspaper Comics

BC, sgn Johnny Hart, 2/17/85, 11x16" 300.00
Beetle Bailey, hand colored, sgn Mort Walker, 3/14/83, 10x15" .300.00
Blondie, sgn Chic Young, 4/7/40, 14x17" 575.00
Buck Rogers, color, 1935 strip, EX 175.00
Captain & the Kids, sgn Rudolph Dirks, 5/31/42, 14½x22½" 300.00
For Better or Worse, sgn Lynn Johnston, 8/24/86, 9x13" 275.00
Hagar the Horrible, sgn Dik Browne, 2/6/83, 10x15" 275.00
Judge Rummy, sgn Tad Dorgan, 3/4/17, 14x20" 325.00
Little Jimmy, sgn James Swinnerton, 2/13/09, 18½x14½" 500.00
Little Jimmy, sgn James Swinnerton, 4/10/46, 11x15" 275.00
Little King, sgn Otto Soglow, 10/24/60, 13x19" 275.00

Mickey Mouse, Walt Disney Productions, 9/2/84, 10x15" 235.00
Reg'lar Fellers, sgn Gene Byrnes, 2 sections, 12½x17½" 300.00
Superman, Phila Inquirer, 1929, 1st color strip 225.00

Cartoon Books

'Books of cartoons' were printed during the first decade of the 20th century and remained popular until the advent of the modern comic book in the late thirties. Cartoon books, printed in both color and black and white, were merely reprints of current newspaper comic strips. The books, ranging from thirty to seventy pages and in sizes from 3½" x 8" up to 11" x 17", were usually bound with cardboard covers and were often distributed as premiums in exchange for coupons saved from the daily paper. One of the largest of the companies who printed these books was Cupples and Leon, producer of nearly half of the two hundred titles on record. Among the most popular sellers were *Mutt and Jeff*, *Bringing Up Father*, and *Little Orphan Annie*.

Bringing Up Father, #1, Cupples & Leon, NM 195.00
Bringing Up Father, #11, Cupples & Leon, scarce, EX+ 70.00
Bringing Up Father, #3, Cupples & Leon, EX 60.00

Bringing Up Father, #7, Cupples & Leon, EX, $45.00.

Charlie Chaplin Comic Capers, #1, Donohue, 1917, NM 150.00
Charlie Chaplin Up in the Air, #1, EX 70.00
Charlie Chaplin's Funny Stunts, MA Donohue, 1917 ....55.00
Funny Larks of Hans & Fritz, Dirks, Saalfield, 1929, EX 80.00
Little Orphan Annie in Cosmic City, Cupples & Leon, NM 70.00
Little Orphan Annie in the Circus, Cupples & Leon, EX 40.00
Little Orphan Annie Shipwrecked, Cupples & Leon, EX 38.00
Mutt & Jeff, Bud Fisher, 1911, EX 150.00
Percy & Ferdie, MacGill, Cupples & Leon, 1921, EX 48.00
Skeezix & the Circus, Reilly & Lee, 1926, VG 32.00
Skeezix & Uncle Walt, Frank King, 1st edition, c 1924, NM 135.00
Winnie Winkle, #2, Cupples & Leon, NM 50.00

Cash Registers

By 1970, antique cash registers had risen to become blue chip collectibles, joining the ranks of fine paintings, bronzes, firearms, clocks, and other categories having permanent established worth. Some extremely scarce and elegant cash registers will command up to $20,000.

Register prices are determined by make, model, size, desirability of pattern, accessories such as add-on clocks, topsigns and personalized nameplates, which may be cast as topsigns or 'lid ovals' but on occasion, cast into the register's front or back plates. Of immense consideration is the register's condition.

This column uses 'mint' condition (M) to indicate registers which have been cleaned, oiled, polished, and lacquered by a professional and have perfect glass, keytops, and indicators. Some restorers will replace the velvet underneath the lid (where applicable), which is an added touch of elegance. 'Very good' condition (VG) describes unrestored, unpolished registers which are complete and operating. Their values are usually about half of the restored model's value. All prices may vary as much as 20%, depending on geography and demand.

For further information, we recommend the highly informative books *Antique Cash Registers 1880-1920* by Bartsch and Sanchez (Mr. Bartsch's address may be found in our Directory under Oregon); and *The Incorruptible Cashier* Vols. I & II, currently available from our other advisor, John Apple, listed in our Directory under Wisconsin.

National Cash Register Co., brass and marble, serial #5400363K1054, M, $1,200.00; VG, $650.00.

NCR #1000 class, autographic box attachment, 1910, M	**1,200.00**
NCR #1000 class, autographic box attachment, 1910, VG	**650.00**
NCR #130, M	**1,500.00**
NCR #130, VG	**850.00**
NCR #215, brass, VG	**800.00**
NCR #250, brass, VG	**900.00**
NCR #312 or #313, dolphin pattern, 1908-16, M, ea	**1,200.00**
NCR #312 or #313, dolphin pattern, 1908-16, VG, ea	**750.00**
NCR #317, M	**1,250.00**
NCR #323, marble on 3 sides, extended base, sm, M	**1,800.00**
NCR #327, brass, VG	**900.00**

NCR #332 or #333, brass top, sgn, M	**1,100.00**
NCR #332 or #333, brass top, sgn, VG	**500.00**
NCR #442-452, M	**1,500.00**
NCR #442-452, VG	**750.00**
NCR #442E to #452E, M	**2,000.00**
NCR #442E to #452E, VG	**900.00**
NCR #47, mahog w/inlay, up to $5, 18x18x16", VG	**2,000.00**
NCR #50, brass, Renaissance pattern, VG	**1,000.00**
NCR #500 series, floor model, M	**4,500.00**
NCR #500 series, floor model, VG	**2,000.00**
NCR #522 class, 2-drw, requires electricity, 1906, M	**2,400.00**
NCR #522 class, 2-drw, requires electricity, 1906, VG	**1,500.00**
NCR #711 to #717, factory pnt mahog grain finish on steel, M	**250.00**
NCR #711 to #717, factory pnt oak grain finish on steel, M	**350.00**
NCR #8, VG	**700.00**
St Louis #38, Cheesecutter, factory pnt oak grain on steel, M	**400.00**

Cast Iron

In the mid-1800s, the cast iron industry was raging in the United States. It was recognized as a medium extremely adaptable for uses ranging from ornamental architectural filigree to actual building construction. It could be cast from a mold into any conceivable design that could be reproduced over and over at a relatively small cost. It could be painted to give an entirely versatile appearance. Furniture with open-work designs of grapevines, leaves, and intricate lacy scrollwork was cast for gardens as well as inside use. Figural doorstops of every sort, bootjacks, trivets, and a host of other useful and decorative items were made before the 'ferromania' had run its course. Our advisor for this category is J.M. Ellwood; he is listed in the Directory under Arizona. See also Kitchen, Cast Iron Bakers and Kettles; and other specific categories.

Ashtray, fly form, EX detail, blk pnt, Simpson, 4½"	**140.00**
Ashtray, lion's head emb center, pear shape, 1890s, 5½x6"	**120.00**
Bench, fern motif, Kramer Bros, rpt, 59"	**950.00**
Bench, scrolling leafy vines, spandrels under seat, 38"	**675.00**
Bench, 3-part bk w/scrolls & ornate crests, rpt, 44"	**495.00**
Birdhouse, Victorian style, octagonal, Pat 1868, 14", VG	**1,850.00**
Birdhouse, Victorian style, raised metal base, 6x7x10", EX	**1,980.00**
Birdhouse, Victorian style, raised spire, gold pnt, 12", EX	**1,870.00**
Birdhouse, Victorian style w/side porches, 15", VG	**1,750.00**
Box lock, eagle (high relief), porc knob, Eagle Lock, 5", pr	**130.00**
Candlestick, gargoyle shape	**55.00**
Cuspidor, turtle form	**950.00**
Dog, mk Hines, pnt traces, 1¾"	**35.00**
Eagle on stepped octagonal plinth, blk rpt, 33"	**750.00**
Eagle w/open wings, gold pnt, 4½x10x1½", EX	**125.00**
Finial, pineapple form, worn gray rpt, 21", pr	**450.00**
Frog, gr pnt, yel eyes, 1880s, 2x7x7½"	**220.00**
Frog, old pnt/lt rust, 5"	**35.00**
Gate, sheep under tree casting, 1856, 28x43", EX	**250.00**
Greyhound, lying down, alert, rpt, welded rpr, 37"	**800.00**
Hitching post, Blk boy w/open shirt & baggy pants, rpr, 46"	**750.00**
Hitching post, Blk jockey, mc rpt, lt rust, 37"	**350.00**
Hitching post, horse head, spiral/emb vasiform/etc, 64"	**2,450.00**
Hitching post, horse's head atop cylinder plinth, 14"	**85.00**
Hitching post, whip form, end coiled about shaft, 40"	**275.00**
Kettle shelf, rtcl top, 10x11x17"	**65.00**
Lion, tail curled above bk, lt rust, 8½" L	**150.00**
Mailbox holder, Uncle Sam figural, orig pnt, 57", EX	**550.00**
Model, fire hydrant, EX pnt, 17"	**250.00**
Mortar, emb 'icicles,' att S Jersey foundry, 7", +pestle	**60.00**
Ornament, eagle, mc pnt, 1900, 24" wingspan	**600.00**

Paperweight, bird, solid cast, blk rpt, 4¾" 65.00
Paperweight, puppy 35.00
Paperweight, spreadwing eagle, bronze finish, 8½" W 85.00
Paperweight, spreadwing eagle on stepped plinth, 7½" 45.00
Pitcher pump, Red Jacket Pumps, red pnt, 19x8x9", EX 90.00
Rabbit, full-bodied, pnt traces, welded seams, 12" 225.00
Rabbit, full-bodied, worn/rusted wht pnt, 11" 245.00
Rack, pie; wall type, folding, Pat Dec 14, 1880 ....175.00
Safe, decorative door detail, pnt w/decals, worn, 9¾" 150.00
Settee, rtcl grapevine motif, wht pnt, 40" L, pr 625.00
Shelf, scalloped gallery, ornate brackets, 36" L 75.00
Shelf, stove pipe; Woman's Friend, half rnd, 10½x20" ea side 150.00
Shutter dog, w/3-D girl's head, anchor mk, Brevete SGDG, 9" 75.00
Sign, Speed Limit-Horses at Walk...., 1910, 16x31", VG 475.00
Snowbird, spreadwing eagle, 5", pr 130.00
Spittoon, orig gray & wht pnt, corset form, 1880s, 6x8½" 48.00
Sugar devil, wood hdl, 16" 40.00
Sugar nippers 125.00
Tie rod decoration, fleur-de-lis design, CI, no pnt, 10x9x1½" 60.00
Top hat, enameled band/ribbon/size label w/in, 7" 195.00
Umbrella stand, dog & canes, mc pnt, 25", EX 2,000.00
Umbrella stand, Jack & the Beanstalk, mc pnt, 33", EX 1,750.00
Umbrella stand, Red Riding Hood figural, mc pnt, 37", EX 3,300.00

Urn, relief classical figures, loop handles, English, 1800s, 31", $650.00.

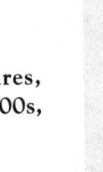

Urn, goblet shape, rpt, 19x16"+anchor rod 180.00
Urn, simple casting, wht rpt, 16" 125.00
Wafer iron, circular design, wrought iron hdls, 33" 85.00
Wall pocket, half-rnd, arched hanging crest, 7x11" 55.00

Castor Sets

Castor sets became popular during the early years of the 18th century and continued to be used through the late Victorian era. Their purpose was to hold various condiments for table use. The most common type was a circular arrangement with a center handle on a revolving pedestal base that held three, four, five, or six bottles. Some had extras; a few were equipped with a bell for calling the servant. Frames were made of silverplate, glass, or pewter. Though most bottles were of pressed glass, some of the designs were cut; and occasionally colored glass with enameled decorations was used. To maintain authenticity and value, castor sets should have matching bottles. Prices listed below are for those with matching bottles and in frames with plating that is in excellent condition (unless noted otherwise).

Watch for new frames and bottles in both clear and colored glass; these have recently been appearing on the market.

Key: D&B — Daisy and Button

3-bottle, blown, Gothic Arch, orig stoppers; pewter fr 95.00
3-bottle, cranberry, cut, SP tops; ornate SP fr, 5½x3¾" 200.00
3-bottle, rubena, cut dmns; SP fr, 5½x4" 175.00
4-bottle, clear, paneled; pewter fr revolves, fancy bail, mini 150.00
4-bottle, cut glass; SP Walker & Hall fr, Sheffield 125.00
4-bottle, D&B (colors), orig stoppers; pressed glass fr 225.00
4-bottle, Jacob's Ladder; orig SP fr 115.00
4-bottle, King's Crown, ruby stained; orig glass stand 335.00
5-bottle, Button Band; orig SP fr 175.00
5-bottle, etched amberina, cut amberina stoppers; gilt fr, EX ..2,000.00
5-bottle, gray cut/polished dots; rstr Tufts fr, fancy bail 165.00
5-bottle, opaque, HP floral, att Mt WA; rstr Middleton fr 395.00

Six-bottle, pressed, in silver-plated frame, 17", $125.00.

6-bottle, cut vintage; SP Rogers Smith & Co fr 235.00
6-bottle, cut; SP pewter mechanical-door housing, Gleason ...1,500.00
6-bottle, D&B, clear; ornate rstr bowl & Wilcox fr, revolves 350.00
6-bottle, etched wreath; lg Reed & Barton fr w/cupid 350.00
6-bottle, etched; rstr ornate fr w/call bell sgn Meriden 395.00
6-bottle, pressed; 18" Simpson-Hall-Miller fr w/VG SP 125.00
6-bottle, Sawtooth; ornate Meriden fr, call bell, dtd 1888, EX ...425.00
7-bottle, cut crystal; gadrooned/shell-border Geo III fr 465.00

Catalina Island

Catalina Island pottery was made on the island of the same name, which is about twenty-six miles off the coast of Los Angeles. The pottery was started in 1927 at Pebbly Beach by Wm. Wrigley, Jr., who was instrumental in developing and using the native clays. Its principal products were brick and tile to be used for construction on the island. Garden pieces were first produced, then vases, bookends, lamps, ashtrays, novelty items, and finally dinnerware. The ware became very popular and was soon being shipped to the mainland as well.

Some of the pottery was hand thrown; some was made in molds. Most pieces are marked Catalina Island or Catalina with a printed incised stamp, or handwritten with a pointed tool. Cast items were sometimes marked in the mold; a few have an ink stamp, and a paper label was also used.

The color of the clay can help to identify approximately when a piece was made: 1927 to 1932, brown to red clay; 1931 to 1932, an experimental period with various colors; 1932 to 1937, mainly white clay, but tan to brown were also used on occasion.

Items marked Catalina Pottery are listed in Gladding McBean. For further information we recommend *The Collector's Encyclopedia of California Pottery* by our advisor, Jack Chipman; he is listed in the Directory under California.

Dinnerware

Catalina Island, bowl, berry 25.00
Catalina Island, bowl, cereal 45.00
Catalina Island, candle holder, low 75.00
Catalina Island, creamer 35.00
Catalina Island, cup, coffee/tea 45.00
Catalina Island, custard cup 25.00
Catalina Island, pitcher, squat base 75.00
Catalina Island, plate, dinner; wide rim, 10½" 35.00
Catalina Island, plate, rolled rim, 12½" 75.00
Catalina Island, sugar bowl, w/lid 45.00
Catalina Island, teapot, traditional English style 250.00
Catalina Island, wine cup, hdld 22.50

Rope Edge: Sugar bowl, $45.00; Teapot, $125.00; Creamer, $35.00.

Rope Edge, casserole, w/lid 50.00
Rope Edge, cup & saucer 35.00
Rope Edge, plate, dinner; 10½" 25.00

Miscellaneous

Ashtray, goat figural, bl, souvenir, 4" 225.00
Bookends, monk design, matt gr, pr 750.00
Candelabrum, 3-hole, half-circle 175.00
Flowerpot, Ring style, 6" 55.00
Plate, HP Mexican scene, mk, ca 1932, 11½" 500.00
Shakers, tulip, pr 65.00
Tile, Spanish, mc, 6x6" 100.00
Tray, turq, rolled edge, 14½", w/forged iron hdl 95.00
Vase, bl, gourd form, hdls, early 1930s, 8½" 275.00
Vase, bl, ped ft, 4-corner scalloped rim, 8", NM 265.00
Vase, flared top, 7½" 185.00
Vase, Monterey Brn, flowerpot form, old mk, 5½" 60.00
Vase, Toyon red, bulbous base, 6" 175.00
Wall pocket, basketweave, 9" 200.00
Wall pocket, seashell form, turq, incised mk 150.00

Catalogs

Catalogs are not only intriguing to collect on their own merit, but for the collector with a specific interest, they are often the only remain-

ing source of background information available, and as such they offer a wealth of otherwise unrecorded data. The mail-order industry can be traced as far back as the mid-1800s. Even before Aaron Montgomery Ward began his career in 1872, Laacke and Joys of Wisconsin and the Orvis Company of Vermont, both dealers in sporting goods, had been well established for many years. The E.C. Allen Company sold household necessities and novelties by mail on a broad scale in the 1870s. By the end of the Civil War, sewing machines, garden seed, musical instruments, even medicine, were available from catalogs. In the 1880s, Macy's of New York issued a 127-page catalog; Sears and Spiegel followed suit in about 1890. Craft and art supply catalogs were first available about 1880 and covered such varied fields as china painting, stenciling, wood burning, brass embossing, hair weaving, and shellcraft. Today some collectors confine their interests not only to craft catalogs in general but often to one subject only. There are several factors besides rarity which make a catalog valuable: age, condition, profuse illustrations, how collectible the field is that it deals with, the amount of color used in its printing, its size (format and number of pages), and whether it is a manufacturer's catalog verses a jobber's catalog (the former being the most desirable).

Alden's Christmas, 1946, 1970-pg, EX 45.00
Anchor Electric, Boston, telephone supplies, 1897, 25-pg 40.00
Bauer & Black Medical Supplies, color illus, 1929, 95-pg, EX 48.00
Bausch & Lomb Lab Microscopes, 1941, EX 15.00
Bellas Hess Fashions, EX illus, 1915, 276-pg, EX 35.00
Best & Co Lilliputian Bazaar, children's things, 1935, 48-pg 20.00
Breck's Christmas, Howdy Doody cover, 1951, 38-pg 18.00
Bright Hardware, kitchenware, pnt, etc, 1921, 500-pg, EX 85.00
California Perfume Co, ca 1905, 63-pg, VG 38.00
Carson, Pirie, Scott; notions, 1915, 172-pg 65.00
Chicago Cottage Organs, ca 1900, 24-pg, 7x10" 35.00
Chittenden & Eastman, furniture, 1940, 650-pg, EX 80.00
Clay, barn equipment, 1936, 144-pg, EX 8.00
Colson Wheelchairs & Cripple Machines, 1920, 48-pg 15.00
De La Rue, miscellaneous items, color illus, 1916, EX 45.00
Dean Foster, soda counter goods, 1908, EX 48.00
Delco, lighting fixtures, early 1900s, 65-pg, EX 65.00
EC Atkins & Co Saws, 1906, 238-pg, EX 25.00
Electric Storage Battery Co, 1912, 260-pg 18.00
Fairbanks Scales, 1928, EX 11.00
FAO Schwarz Christmas, 1956, EX 45.00
FE Myers & Bros Pumps, Hay Rakes & Hardware, 1920, 406-pg ..35.00
Flyer & Silver Wing Bicycles, 1931, EX 85.00
Franz Builders, hardware, 1925, 120-pg 11.00
Friedrich Violins, 1924, 100-pg, EX 50.00
Frigidaire, 3 from new series, 1948, 16-pg, EX 9.00
Funsten Furs, 1920s, EX 20.00
General Electric Fans, 1940, 32-pg, EX 12.50
Gertz Christmas, lg toy section, 1964, 90-pg 22.00
Hartford Contractors Supply Co, 1920, lg, EX 75.00
HH Ayers, Phila, lady's clothes, 20-pg, 1907-08, 20-pg 20.00
HJ Caulkins Dental Supplies, 1915, 982-pg 69.00
Hohner Accordeona, 1926, 72-pg, EX 65.00
Human Hair Goods, color illus, 1896, 24-pg, EX 65.00
Independent Silos, 1920s, EX 35.00
Jamesway Book, farm equipment, illus, EX 40.00
John Deere Hay Tools, 1940, lg pgs 40.00
Kittinger Furniture, 1939, 100-pg, EX 27.50
Kraus Farm Cultivators, 1911, 62-pg 20.00
Lenox Furniture, 1929, 100-pg, EX 32.50
Lockwoven Hosiery, lingerie, 1930, 20-pg, +sample sheets 45.00
Loomis Electric Engines, Motors & Lathes, 1920, EX 10.00
Mac-Beth Evans Shades & Globes, 1912, 106-pg 90.00

McCall's Patterns, lg format, 1904, 48-pg 38.00
Melotte Cream Separators, 1925, EX 7.50
Meteorological instruments, detailed illus, 1917, 58-pc, EX 48.00
Miller-Stockman, Western wear, 1948, 70-pc 35.00
Mills Bros Ice Cream Equipment, early, EX 30.00
Montgomery Ward, 1881, EX 200.00
Montgomery Ward Supplement, 1913, 200-pg, EX 30.00
National Casket Co, color illus, price lists, 1922, 260-pg 150.00
National Cloak & Suit Co, EX illus, 1911, 224-pg 45.00
NF Dubois Co, plumbing fixtures, hardbk, 1904, 578-pg, EX 60.00
Perfection Milkers, 1930s, EX 5.00
Pitkin Laboratories, toiletries/remedies, salesman's, 1909 ....120.00
QRS Recordo Reproducing Player Rolls, 1927, 175-pg 27.50
Republican Kitchen Ware, tin/enamel/granite/etc, 1911, 394-pg .85.00
Royal Stoves & Ranges, blk/wht illus, 1901, EX 50.00
Sears, band instruments, 1910, 75-pg, EX 37.50
Sears, cameras, optical goods, 1918, EX 32.00
Sears, Rockwell cover, 1932, EX 65.00
Sears Christmas, 1958, EX 50.00
Sears Christmas, 1960, 481-pg, EX 45.00
Sefton Specialty Boxes, 1905, 94-pg, EX 30.00
Simples Sampling Assoc, cloth samples, 1925, 62-pg 125.00
Southern New England Electric Co, 1931, 656-pg, EX 90.00
Spiegel Christmas, lg doll & toy section, 1947, EX 45.00
Spirella Corsets, 1924, 128-pg, EX 35.00
Stanley Tools, #34, 1958, 224-pg, EX 30.00
Starrett Tools, 1938, 275-pg, EX 15.00
Steuben Glass, 1940, EX 40.00

Structo Toys, 1956, EX, $25.00.

Thomas Plant Co, leather covers, 1921, 60-pg, EX 35.00
True Value Christmas, 1976, 24-pg 13.50
Universal Millwork, hardbound, 1920s, 400-pg, EX 75.00
Ward's Christmas, many toys, 1933, EX 45.00
Wilcox Crittenden & Co, marine hardware, illus, 1941, 172-pg ..40.00

Caughley Ware

The Caughley Coalport Porcelain Manufactory operated from about 1775 until 1799 in Caughley, near Salop, Shropshire, in England. The owner was Thomas Turner, who gained his potting experience from his association with the Worcester Pottery Company. The wares he manufactured in Caughley are referred to as 'Salopian.' He is most famous for his blue-printed earthenwares, particularly the Blue Willow

pattern, designed for him by Thomas Minton. For a more detailed history, see Coalport.

Bowl, scene w/lamb & sheep, brn transfer, scalloped, 5" 90.00
Cake bowl, deer, mc on blk transfer, bl rim, mk S, 1¾x7½" 700.00
Coffeepot, scene w/lamb & sheep, brn transfer, 10½" 200.00
Creamer, cottage w/man fishing, mc/blk, sqd hdl, 4½", VG 85.00
Creamer, scene w/lamb & sheep, brn transfer, 4" 85.00
Cup & saucer, cottage & men w/flock, w/hdl, rosette mk, EX 140.00
Cup & saucer, deer, mc on blk transfer, w/hdl, mk C, EX 150.00
Cup plate, cottage/shepherds/flock, scalloped, 4½", NM 100.00
Plate, cottage/shepherds/flock, blk transfer, scalloped, 7" 525.00
Plate, toddy; castle ruins, blk transfer, 5" 85.00
Sugar bowl, Oriental design, acorn knob, rnd body, 4½", NM 130.00
Tea bowl & saucer, bl chinoiserie, mk C 175.00
Tea bowl & saucer, Oriental design, brn transfer, bl rim 40.00
Tea bowl & saucer, river & pagoda, mc/blk transfer, S mk, EX ..220.00

Ceramic Art Company

Jonathan Coxon, Sr., and Walter Scott Lenox established the Ceramic Art Company in 1889 in Trenton, New Jersey, where they produced fine belleek porcelain. Both were experienced in its production, having previously worked for Ott and Brewer. They hired artists to hand paint their wares with portraits, scenes, and lovely florals. Today artist-signed examples bring the highest prices. Several marks were used, three of which contain the 'CAC' monogram. A green wreath surrounding the company name in full was used on special-order wares, but these are not often encountered. Coxon eventually left the company, and it was later reorganized under the Lenox name. See also Lenox. Our advisor for this category is Mary Frank Gaston; she is listed in the Directory under Texas.

Box, trinket; lav Delft-style scene, artist sgn, mk, 5¼" 195.00
Candlesticks, cream w/gold, palette mk, 8½", pr 110.00
Cup & saucer, demi; gr, flower garland int, in sterling fr, mk 150.00
Jar, perfume; lily of the valley, factory decor, lav mk 195.00
Jug, wine; cavalier portrait, toast on bk, artist sgn, 5½" 395.00
Mug, HP apples on orange, not factory decor, 6" 135.00
Mug, monk holds open box on brn, gr mk, 5¾" 85.00
Pitcher, cider; grapes, 3-color, palette mk 165.00
Pitcher, tankard; monk/leaves, factory decor, purple mk, 14" 395.00
Sherbet, gold paste florals, ped ft, mk, 3¼" 130.00
Stein, monk scene, silver trim on lid, brn mk, 7½" 675.00
Vase, floral, factory decor, 1895, 10½" 450.00
Vase, lady's portrait in medallion w/gold, mk, 11½" 245.00
Vase, portrait, blossoms, & gold trim, palette mk, 10" 325.00
Vase, spider mums, mc on shaded, bulbous, mk, ca 1889, 10" 245.00

Ceramic Arts Studio, Madison

The Ceramic Arts Studio Company began operations sometime prior to the 1940s, but it was about then that Betty Harrington started marketing her goods through this company. Betty Harrington is the designer primarily responsible for creating the line of figurines and knick-knacks that has become so popular with collectors. There were two others — Ulli Rebus, who not only designed several of the animals and various other pieces but taught Betty the art of mold-making as well; and Ruth Planter, who's work may have been very limited. About 65% of these items are marked, but even unmarked items become easily recognizable after only a brief study of their distinctive styling and glaze colors. At least seven different marks were used, among them the black ink stamp and the incised mark: 'Ceramic Arts Studio, Madison, Wisc.' A paper sticker was used in the early years.

After the 1955 demise of the company in Madison, the owner (Ruben Sand) went to Japan where he continued production under the same name using many of the same molds. After a short time, the old molds were retired, and new and quite different items were produced. Most of the Japan pieces can be found with a Ceramic Arts Studio backstamp. The Japan identification was on a paper label and is often missing. Japan pieces are never marked 'Madison, Wisc.,' but not all Madison pieces are either. Red or blue backstamps are exclusively Japanese.

Another company that also produced figurines operated at about the same time as the Madison studio. It was called Ceramic Art (no 's') Studio; do not confuse the two.

A second and larger building in the C.A.S. complex in Madison was for the exclusive production of metal accessories. The creator and designer of this related line was Zona Liberace, Liberace's stepmother, who was Art Director for the line of figurines as well. These pieces are rising fast in value and because they weren't marked can sometimes be found at bargain prices. They were so popular that other ceramic companies bought them to complement their lines as well, so they may also be found with ceramic figures other than C.A.S.'s.

For those seeking additional information, video tapes (Series 1 and 2) are available from the author, BA Wellman, whose address can be found under Massachusetts. 1992-93 price guides are available. Mr. Wellman encourages collectors to write him with any new information concerning company history and/or production. He sends Vera a 'thank you' for helping us with this year's updates.

Bank, Paisley pig, 3"	75.00
Bell, Lillibelle, 6½"	60.00
Bell, Summer Belle, peach & bl trim, 5¼"	52.00
Bell, Winter Belle, 5¼"	52.00
Bowl, any Pixie series, shield shape, 5" W	45.00
Bowl, shallow, rectangular, 2¼"	25.00
Candle holders, Bedtime boy & girl, 4¾", pr	55.00

Candle holders, See No Evil, Hear No Evil, 5", pr, $65.00.

Figurine, angel, singing, 3½"	32.00
Figurine, Archibald the Dragon, 8"	165.00
Figurine, Bali Gong, 5½"	45.00
Figurine, Balinese dance couple, 9½", pr	165.00
Figurine, bass viol boy, 4¾"	42.00
Figurine, bride & groom, 4¾", 5", pr	65.00
Figurine, Bright Eyes cat, 3"	22.00
Figurine, chipmunk, 2"	24.00
Figurine, Cocker Spaniel, standing/sitting, 2¾", 2½", pr	55.00
Figurine, colonial boy & girl, 5¼", 5", pr	55.00

Figurine, drummer girl, 4¼"	35.00
Figurine, Dutch Love boy & girl, 5", pr	45.00
Figurine, Egyptian man & woman, 9½", pr	285.00
Figurine, Elsie elephant, 5"	45.00
Figurine, farm boy, fishing, no pole, 4¾"	45.00
Figurine, Fifi & Fufu, 3", 2½", pr	42.00
Figurine, French boy & girl, 3", pr	35.00
Figurine, Frisky lamb, garland around neck, 2¾"	18.00
Figurine, Gay '90s couple (Harry & Lillibeth redesigned), pr	58.00
Figurine, Hiawatha, 3½"	65.00

Figurine, hunter 'Al' with rifle, $40.00. (Made to go with hunting dog 'Kirby.')

Figurine, Inkey skunk, 2"	22.00
Figurine, Jim & June, 4¾", 4", pr	38.00
Figurine, kitten washing paw, 2"	16.00
Figurine, Little Bo Peep & Little Boy Blue, 4½", 5½", pr	40.00
Figurine, Little Miss Muffet, 4½"	30.00
Figurine, Lu-Tang & Wing-Sang, pr	45.00
Figurine, Madonna, gold halo, 9½"	68.00
Figurine, Modern Dance Man/Woman, 9½", pr	125.00
Figurine, Mr Monk monkey, 4"	28.00
Figurine, Mr Skunky, 3"	32.00
Figurine, Our Lady of Fatima, 9¼"	62.00
Figurine, Pensive & Blythe, 6", 6½", pr	115.00
Figurine, Peter Pan & Wendy, 5¼", pr	95.00
Figurine, Petrov & Petrushka, 5¼", 5", pr	38.00
Figurine, Pioneer Sam & Suzie, w/broom, 5½", 5", pr	50.00
Figurine, Polish boy & girl, 6¾", 6", pr	38.00
Figurine, pomeranian, sitting/standing, 2¼", 2¾", pr	38.00
Figurine, Squeaky squirrel, 3¼"	20.00
Figurine, St George on charger, 8½"	145.00
Figurine, Summer Sally, 3½"	38.00
Figurine, Temple dancers, 6¾", pr	185.00
Figurine, turtle w/cane, 3¼"	28.00
Figurine, Winter Willy, 4"	35.00
Jug, Adam & Eve, twig hdl, 3½"	35.00
Jug, Diana the Huntress, 3"	28.00
Jug, Miss Forward, 4"	65.00
Lamp, Bali Hi & Bali Lao, rotating disk	245.00
Planter, Bonnie, 7"	45.00
Planter, Lotus & Manchu, 7¾", 7½", pr	125.00

Planter, Svea & Sven, 6", 6½", pr 84.00
Plaque, Attitude & Arabesque, 9½", pr 68.00
Plaque, Chinese lantern man & woman, 8", pr 125.00
Plaque, Cockatoo, pr 75.00
Plaque, Harlequin & Columbine, 8", pr 140.00
Plaque, Neptune, rare, 6" 125.00
Plaque, Water Sprite, fish w/head down, 4¼" 48.00
Shakers, chick in nest, 2¾" overall, pr 65.00
Shakers, chihuahua & doghouse, 1¾" overall, pr 38.00
Shakers, Dutch boy & girl, bl, 4", pr 26.00
Shakers, elephant & native boy, 5", 2¾", pr 165.00
Shakers, fighting cocks, red & gr, 3¾", pr 30.00
Shakers, fish, up on tail, 4", pr 45.00
Shakers, French boy & girl, 3", pr 28.00
Shakers, frog & toadstool, 2", 3", pr 35.00
Shakers, horse head, 3½", pr 32.00
Shakers, Indian boy & girl, 3", pr 32.00
Shakers, Little Black Sambo & tiger, 3½", 5" L, pr 195.00
Shakers, Mr & Mrs Penguin, 3¾", pr 36.00
Shakers, Paul Bunyan & tree, 4½", 2½", pr 65.00
Shakers, snuggle kitten & cream pitcher, 2½", pr 38.00
Shakers, snuggle mother & baby bear, blk, 4¼", pr 125.00
Shakers, snuggle mother & baby bear, wht, 4¼", pr 45.00
Shakers, snuggle mother & baby kangaroo, 4¾", pr 42.00
Shakers, snuggle Suzette on pillow, 3", pr 55.00
Shelf sitter, Chinese boy & girl, 4", pr 35.00
Shelf sitter, Fluffy cat, 4¾" 45.00
Shelf sitter, Maurice & Michelle, 7", pr 68.00
Shelf sitter, Mexican boy & girl, pr 58.00
Shelf sitter, Pierrot & Pierette, gr, 6½", pr 185.00
Vase, bud; Lu-Tang on bamboo, wht w/gr trim, 7" 42.00
Vase, modern, sq, 2" 22.00
Vase, rose motif, rnd, 2¼" 22.00

Metal Accessories

Arched window, for Madonna w/child 38.00
Artist palette, left & right, 12", pr 65.00
Artist palette w/shelves, left & right, 12", pr 68.00
Beanstalk for Jack, rare 95.00
Birdcage w/perch, 14" 45.00
Diamond shadow box, for Attitude & Arabesque 45.00
Free-form, left & right, pr 48.00
Free-form w/shelf, left & right, pr 52.00
Pyramid shelves, ea 35.00
Shadow box, w/wood, sq, 13" 30.00
Sofa, for Maurice & Michele 32.00
Star, holds any 1 of angel trio, 9" 20.00
Triple ring shelves, ea 32.00

Chalkware

Chalkware figures were a popular commodity from approximately 1860 until 1890. They were made from gypsum or plaster of Paris formed in a mold and then hand painted in oils or watercolors. Items such as animals and birds, figures, banks, toys, and religious ornaments modeled after more expensive Staffordshire wares were often sold door to door. Their origin is attributed to Italian immigrants. Today regarded as a form of folk art, 19th century American pieces bring prices in the hundreds of dollars. Carnival chalkware from this century is also collectible, especially figures that are personality related. See Carnival Collectibles.

Cat, seated, blk pnt, EX patina, 8½" 200.00

Cat, seated, pipe in mouth, worn mc pnt, 10" 235.00
Dog, standing, worn red & blk pnt, 7" 165.00
Garniture, fruit compote, EX detail & color, 12½" 900.00
Girl reading, seated/Xd legs, wearing hat, 1800s, 19" ...550.00
Lovebird, leaves on base, orig pnt, 1 w/base crack, 11", pr 750.00
Parrot on plinth, worn mc pnt, 8" 350.00
Rabbit, sitting on haunches, gr/red/blk, 5½" 1,350.00
Ram, recumbent, orig red/blk pnt, rpr horn, 4¼" L 225.00
Rooster, worn mc pnt, sm hole, 7" 800.00
Rooster, yel/blk/red/gr, minor wear, EX color, 6½" 550.00
Squirrel, acorn in mouth, worn mc pnt, rprs, 6" 300.00

Champleve

Champleve, enameling on brass, differs from cloisonne in that the design is depressed or incised into the metal, rather than being built up with wire dividers as in the cloisonne procedure. The cells, or depressions, are filled in with color, and the piece is then fired.

Ash stand, knobbed shaft, Oriental, 29" 300.00
Candlestick, passion flowers, pricket type, 11½" 100.00
Incense burner, pierced cloud top, dragon hdls, ftd, 6½" 85.00
Inkwell, in form of Louis XVI bureau, ormolu mts, 6" 800.00

Inkwell, sea horse mounts, on undertray, $300.00.

Jardiniere, mums/scrolls, bud hdls, 3 short ft, 10" dia 250.00
Mantel clock, Rococo style, French, 1880s, 14" 1,000.00
Mirror, foliate band, flower crest, cherub ft, 18x14" ...2,000.00
Teapot, dragon form w/3 monkey ft, monkey finial, rpr, 12" 400.00
Urn, florals/scrolls, 3-color, ormolu hdls, onyx base, 11" 200.00
Urn, gilt bronze w/scroll-cast hdls, champleve base/lid, 9" 250.00
Vase, porc w/HP cherub, champleve socle, onyx base, 8", pr 700.00
Vase, set w/sardonyx etc, ring/mask hdls, 1800s, 9½" 250.00

Chase Brass & Copper Company

Americans were shocked in 1923 when an invitation to stage an exhibit at the first major postwar fair, *The 1925 Exposition des Arts Decoratifs et Industriels*, was declined by the American government, because the U.S. could not comply with the exposition's requirement that only original work would be exhibited. Even though American industry produced a vast quantity of varied goods, there was very little 'original American' to show, since most design ideas were brought in from Europe.

This blow to American prestige and the uproar that resulted prompted a dispatch of designers (among them Donald Deskey, Walter Dorwin Teague, and Russel Wright) to the Paris exhibition. They were to determine what steps would be necessary in order for U.S. designs to compete with European standards. They returned championing the new modernist style. By the mid-1930s, products were being designed and marketed that were attractive to the reluctant consumer insistent upon buying a streamline style that was uniquely American. During the decade of the thirties, the Chase Brass & Copper Company offered lamps, smoking acessories, and housewares similar to those Americans were seeing on the Hollywood screen at prices the average buyer could afford. These products are highly valued today not only because of their superior quality but also because of those who created them. Walter von Nessen, Gerth & Gerth, Rockwell Kent, Russel Wright, Laurelle Guild, and Dr. A. Reimann were some of Chases' well-known designers. Emily Post, who served as spokesperson for Chase, promoted a trend away from expensive silver and toward chromium serving pieces.

Besides chromium, Chase manufactured many products in brass, copper, nickel plate, or a combination of these metals; all are equally collectible. Some items had glass inserts which collectors also seek.

Nearly all Chase products were marked, either on the item itself or on a screw or rivet. On sets containing several pieces, the trademark may appear on only one. Be cautious. Check unmarked items to make sure they measure up to Chase's standard of quality, and lighting fixtures that are unmarked may be compared with pictures of verified examples. For safety's sake, replace both cords and internal wiring before attempting to use any electrical product. Not only will you be protected against possible loss from fire, but you will enhance the value of your collectible as well.

For more thorough study we recommend *Art Deco Chrome, The Chase Era*, and *Art Deco Chrome, Book 2, A Collector's Guide, Industrial Design in the Chase Era*. Both are authored by Richard J. Kilbride; Mrs. Kilbride is listed in the Directory under Connecticut. In the listings that follow, examples are polished unless noted satin. Prices are an average of values reported by members of the Chase Collector's Society. See Directory, Clubs and Newsletters.

Cigarette box, patinated metal, designed by Rockwell Kent with Bacchus and goats in relief, ca 1930, 6½" long, $1,650.00.

Ash receiver, Ribbed, crystal/chrome, #879, 4½"	120.00
Ash receiver, Summer Rose, chrome, #28010, 4¼"	50.00
Ashtray, Golfers, chrome w/golf club rests, #890, 4"	60.00
Ashtray, Nob-Top, chrome w/red knob on ped, #810, 6½"	70.00
Ashtray, Snuffer, chrome w/blk fish center, #845, 6½"	70.00
Ashtray, Wing, chrome & blk, #854, 5¼"	85.00
Bank, oval hdl, chrome, no advertising, #405004, 2x4x2"	80.00
Bell, Cuckoo, chrome w/blk nickel bird hdl, #13004, 2½"	85.00

Bookends, Arch, satin brass/copper, #17020, 5½x4", pr	385.00
Bookends, Horse, satin nickel/blk, #17044, 6¼x4", pr	530.00
Bookends, Ring, satin brass/copper, #17019, 5x5", pr	300.00
Bowl, confection; chrome w/blk glass insert, #90027, 4"	90.00
Bowl, jelly; Duplex, chrome basket w/glass insert, 5½"	40.00
Bowl, mint & nut; chrome, twin bowls, loop hdl, #29003	40.00
Bowl, nut; chrome & walnut, #90084, 10x6¾", +4 picks	95.00
Bowl, sauce; Lotus, chrome w/blk hdl, #17045, w/ladle & tray	60.00
Bud holder, 4-tube, chrome, #11230, 9"	40.00
Buffet warming oven, chrome & walnut, #90096, 10¼x7⅛"	150.00
Candlestick, Bubble, chrome/bl glass, #17063, 2½", pr	105.00
Candlestick, Diana, chrome/walnut, #24009, 1⅞x3½", pr	50.00
Candlestick, Disc, chrome, 2-candle, 4¾x8½", ea	270.00
Candlestick, Fiesta, chrome/blk base, #29001, 8⅜x8", pr	175.00
Candy dish, brass w/fruited knob on lid, glass insert, 7"	35.00
Cheese knife, chrome w/reeded hdl, #17062, 7"	90.00
Cheese server, chrome w/cutting board, #09009, 3-pc set, 14"	155.00
Cigarette box, Connoisseur, satin copper, #842, 7" L	90.00
Cigarette box, Cosmopolitan, chrome w/wht plastic, 5" L	85.00
Cigarette server, Ball, chrome & red, #853, 3⅝"	55.00
Cigarette server, Cube, 2-compartment, red/wht, #17070	170.00
Cocktail ball, chrome w/red rubber base, #90071, 3⅜"	40.00
Cocktail shaker, Bl Moon, chrome w/bl top, #90066	100.00
Cocktail shaker, Gaiety, chrome w/blk rings, #90034	45.00
Coffee service, Diplomat, chrome, #17029, 4-pc set+tray	635.00
Cruet, chrome, ribbed glass, #26009, 8x6½", pr	150.00
Cup, Bl Moon Cocktail, chrome w/bl glass, #90067, 3½"	35.00
Cup, Cocktail, chrome hemisphere, #26002, 2¾"	9.00
Cup, iced drink; chrome w/leaf-hdl stirrer, 5¼"	35.00
Cup, old-fashioned cocktail; chrome w/muddler, 2⅞"	40.00
Doorstop, stylized cat figural, copper & brass, #90035	260.00
Flower bowl, Fiesta, chrome w/blk wood base, #29002, 8"	115.00
Lamp, desk; chrome, C-shape w/rpl shade, 14½"	85.00
Mixer, cocktail; chrome, #17049, 8¾", w/spoon	135.00
Pitcher, Tavern, copper w/brass hdl, #17026, 10¼"	460.00
Pitcher, water; Sparta, chrome, wht plastic hdl, #90055, 8"	85.00
Plate, Trojan, chrome w/integral hdls, #09004, 12"	105.00
Saucer, Olympia, chrome, 390072, 6⅜"	35.00
Shakers, Sphere, chrome, #28004, 1¾", 1⅛", pr	65.00
Silent butler, chrome w/wht plastic hdl, #17111	60.00
Smoke stand, Lazy Boy, chrome & red, #17031, 27"	445.00
Smoke stand, Stratosphere, chrome & blk, #17076, 26"	390.00
Sugar shaker, Sphere, #90078, 2⅝"	60.00
Table butler, chrome/wht plastic w/o dish, #17093, 8⅞"	120.00
Teapot, chrome w/wht hdl, spherical, non-electric, #17082	100.00
Tray, Cocktail, chrome, #09013, 15⅞x5⅜"	50.00
Tray, Meridian, chrome w/wht hdls, #17078, 7⅞"	50.00
Tray, Ring, chrome, etch circular design, #0058, 12"	70.00
Tray, serving; Four-in-Hand, chrome, wht hdl, 10¼"	110.00
Tray, Tiffin, chrome w/blk hdls, #17027, 18x12"	185.00
Tray, Triple, chrome (all metal), folding, #09001	55.00
Watering can, Sunshine, brass & copper, 8½" L	95.00
Wine cooler, chrome, Rockwell Kent, #27015, 9¼"	815.00

Chelsea

The Chelsea Porcelain Works operated in London from the middle of the 18th century, making porcelain of the finest quality. In 1770 it was purchased by the owner of the Derby Pottery and for about twenty years operated as a decorating shop. Production periods are indicated by trademarks: 1745-1750 — incised triangle, sometimes with 'Chelsea' and the year added; early 1750s — raised anchor mark on oval pad; 1752-1756 — small painted red anchor, only rarely found in blue underglaze; 1756-1769 — gold anchor; 1769-84 — Chelsea Derby mark with the script 'D' containing a horizontal anchor. Many reproductions have been made; be suspicious of any anchor mark larger than ¼".

Bowl, floral bouquets, fluted/scalloped, 1756, oval, 9½", EX 750.00
Figurine, Milton by column stacked w/books, gold mk, 12" 650.00
Figurine, Shakespeare rests elbow on stack of books, 12" 700.00
Plate, honeysuckle/floral sprig, 1759, 8", EX 1,650.00
Teabowl, prunus tree/bamboo in mc, octagonal, 1750, 3¼" 875.00
Tureen, cauliflower mold, 1774, 4½x4½", EX 2,500.00
Vase, lg bird/snail etc, 1756, w/lid, 9", VG 1,750.00

Chelsea Dinnerware

Made from about 1830 to 1880 in the Staffordshire district of England, this white dinnerware is decorated with lustre embossings in the grape, thistle, sprig, or fruit and cornucopia patterns. The relief designs vary from lavender to blue, and the body of the ware may be porcelain, ironstone, or earthenware. Because it was not produced in Chelsea as the name would suggest, dealers often prefer to call it 'Grandmother's Ware.'

Thistle, plate, 7", $15.00.

Grape, bowl, sauce; 6" 8.00
Grape, bowl, 8" 30.00
Grape, coffeepot, 2-cup, stick hdl, 7" 65.00
Grape, creamer 35.00
Grape, cup & saucer 25.00
Grape, egg cup 25.00
Grape, pitcher, milk; 40-oz 50.00
Grape, plate, 6" 12.00
Grape, plate, 7" 18.00
Grape, plate, 8" 20.00
Grape, sauce boat 30.00
Grape, sugar bowl, w/lid 40.00
Grape, teacup 25.00
Grape, teapot, 2-cup 65.00
Grape, waste bowl 40.00
Sprig, cup & saucer 40.00
Sprig, pitcher, milk 45.00

Sprig, plate, cake; 9" 40.00
Sprig, plate, dinner 25.00
Sprig, plate, 7" 18.00
Thistle, butter pat 15.00
Thistle, cup & saucer 35.00
Thistle, plate, 7" 15.00

Chelsea Keramic Art Works

Established in 1872 in Chelsea, Massachusetts, by several members of the Robertson family who later formed the Dedham Pottery, this firm is most noted for its experiments in attempting to re-create the ancient Oriental oxblood-red glaze. They succeeded in this in 1885 and also developed several other outstanding glazes as a result of their perseverance. One was their Oriental crackle glaze which they ultimately used in the manufacture of the very successful Dedham dinnerware. Though their very early artware utilized a redware body, by the late 1870s it was replaced with yellow- or buff-burning clay. A line called Bourgla-Reine (underglaze slip-decorated ware with primarily blue and green backgrounds) was produced, though not to any great extent. Other pieces were designed in imitation of metalware, even to the extent that surfaces were 'hammered' to further enhance the effect. Occasionally live flora was pressed into the damp vessel walls to leave a decorative impression. The pottery closed in 1889. Early wares were not marked; those made from 1875 to 1880 were marked with either two or three lines containing 'Chelsea Keramic Art Works, Robertson and Son,' the 'C-KA-W' cipher, or 'CPUS' in a 4-leaf clover. These were used up to 1889. A paper label was used for a short time on the crackleware. Our advisor for this category is Wayne B. Kielsmeier; he is listed in the Directory under Arizona. See also Dedham.

Vase, fans and flowers in relief on blue gloss, signed GWF, marked CKAW, 7¾", $1,200.00; Pilgrim flask, relief floral on redware, signed with Robertson's early co-joined monogram, marked, 9½", $2,500.00.

Bowl, brn streaks on bl gloss, scalloped, CKAW, 3¾x7", EX 100.00
Flask, floral on textured conforming circle, redware, 9½" 2,500.00
Flask, striated gr/brn, flat rnd body, 4 ball ft, 9", EX 375.00
Pitcher, gr glossy, bulbous, mk CKAW, 5¾" 200.00

Plate, Rabbit, bl on wht crackle, CPUS, 8½" **245.00**
Shoe, emb clovers, yel gloss, curled toe/sq heel, mk, 6" **300.00**
Slipper, olive gr/brn mottle, turned-up toe, CKAW, 6" L, NM ..**300.00**
Tile, vase in relief, golden-brn gloss, 12x6", EX **160.00**
Vase, bl, pillow form/sm loop hdls, glaze loss at hdls, 13" **165.00**
Vase, oxblood, long neck on slender ovoid, CKAW, 8" **950.00**
Vase, relief bands w/stylized fans etc, bl gloss, CWF, 8" **1,200.00**

Chicago Crucible

For only a few years during the 1920s, the Chicago (IL) Crucible Company made a limited amount of decorative pottery in addition to their regular line of architectural wares. Examples are very scarce today; they carry a variety of marks, all with the company name and location.

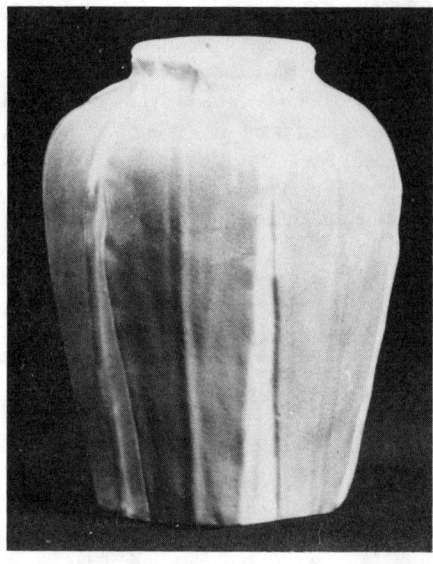

Vase, upright leaves in relief on blue and white, 7", $275.00.

Vase, dappled lt/dk gr w/brn, 5 openings, hdls, 9" **600.00**
Vase, gr matt, swirled leaves/stems, bulbous shoulder, 9x5½" **650.00**
Vase, gr/brn mottled flambe, bulbous w/long neck, mk, 11x6" ...**375.00**
Vase, leaves on brn gloss, shouldered ovoid, 6½" **400.00**
Vase/lamp base, frothy gr/brn flambe, akimbo hdls, 7x5" **225.00**

Children's Books

Children's books, especially those from the Victorian era, are charming collectibles. Colorful lithographic illustrations that once delighted little boys in long curls and tiny girls in long stockings and lots of ribbons and lace have lost none of their appeal. Some collectors limit themselves to a specific subject, while others may be far more interested in the illustrations. First editions are more valuable than later issues, and condition and rarity are very important factors to consider before making your purchase.

Ann of Avonlea, Montgomery, Thrushwood, dust jacket, VG **7.50**
Balaster Boys, Channing, Wild, 1902, VG **7.50**
Beasts from a Brush, Kepes, NY, 1st edition, 1955, NM **50.00**
Birches, Frost, Young illus, Holt, 1st edition, 1988, NM **18.00**
Bouncing Betsy, Lathrop, Macmillan, 1st edition, 1936, EX **48.00**
Bumble, Eldon, Scribner's, worn dust jacket, 1951, EX **24.00**
Camp Fire Girls on Farm, Stewart, Saalfield, 1914, EX **5.00**
Captured by Arabs, Foster, Saalfield, dust jacket, 1933, VG **5.00**
Cherry Ames Boarding School Nurse, Wells, picture cover, EX **5.00**

Covered Bridge, Meigs, Di Angeli illus, 1936, VG **12.50**
Daring Wings, Dean, Goldsmith, dust jacket, 1931, VG **6.50**
Dixie School Girl, Jackson, Donohue, 1913, VG **6.50**
Down-Adown-Derry, de la Mare, Holt, 1922, EX **62.50**
Early in the Morning, Causley, Viking, 1st edition, 1986, NM **20.00**
Edward Lear's ABC, Lear, Pike illus, 1st edition, 1986, NM **18.00**
Emerald City of Oz, Baum, Reilly & Lee, 1940s, 298-pg, VG **40.00**
Eskimo Stories, Smith, Rand McNally, 1902, 175-pg, EX **24.00**
Fairies & Chimneys, Fyleman, Doubleday, 1952 reprint, VG **18.00**
Five Little Starrs, LE Roy, Burt, dust jacket, 1912, VG **10.00**
Foxy Grandpa, Donohue, 1905, EX **75.00**
Gem from Mother Goose, McLoughlin Bros, 1898, EX **45.00**
Gilbert the Trapper, Ashley, McKay, 1900, VG **5.00**
Glittering Festival, Harrison, McClurg, 1st edition, 1911, EX **50.00**
Happy Surprises, de Segur, Whitman, 2nd printing, 1930, VG **18.00**
Haunted Hangar, Van Powell, Saalfield, 1932, VG **6.50**
Haunted Lagoon, Keen, picture cover, 1959, EX **15.00**
I Love Spring, Lewis, Boston, 1st edition, 1965, EX **18.00**
Interference, Sherman, Goldsmith, dust jacket, 1932, EX **5.00**
Jabberwocky, Carroll, Zalben illus, 1st Am edition, 1977, NM **35.00**
Johnny Crow's Garden, Leslie, Warne, 1967 reprint, EX **37.50**
Land of Dreams, Blake, Bianco illus, Macmillan, 1928, VG **32.00**
Little Auto, Lenski, Oxford University Press, 12th printing, EX ..**12.50**
Little Hill, Behn, Harcourt Brace, 1st edition, 1949, EX **35.00**
Little Lame Prince, Mulock, Whitman, 4th printing, 1937, EX **17.50**
Little Witch, Preussler, Abelard-Schuman, 1961, EX **12.50**
Lulu Meets Peter, Steiner, Doubleday, Doran, 1942, VG **10.00**
Madeline, Bemelmens, Simon & Schuster, 1929, EX **48.00**
Marjorie Dean College Freshman, Lester, Burt, 1922, EX **10.00**
My Skyscraper City, Hamond, photo illus, Doubleday, '63, NM ..**22.50**
Near the Window Tree, Kuskin, Harper & Row, 1975, EX **32.00**
New Adventures of Tarzan, pop-up, Bl Ribbon, Burroughs, '35 .**575.00**
New Book of Days, Farjeon, Walck, 1st Am edition, 1961, EX **32.50**
Night & the Cat, Coatsworth, Foujita illus, Macmillan, '50, NM .**32.50**
Once Upon a Rhyme, Corrin, 1st edition, London, 1982, EX **18.00**
Peep Show, Blake, Macmillan, 1st edition, 1973, VG **14.00**
Penny Fiddle, Graves, Doubleday, 1st Am edition, 1960, NM **50.00**
Real Mother Goose, 1941 edition, EX **25.00**
Rosie Posie Book, Anderson, color illus, VG **60.00**
Season Songs, Hughes, London, 1st edition, 1975, EX **22.50**
Secret of Moon Castle, Blyton, Blackwell, dust jacket, '53, VG **8.00**
Secret of Skull Mountain, Dixon, dust jacket, 1948, VG **9.00**
Seventeen To Sing, Adshead & Shapiro, 1st edition, 1946, EX ...**18.00**
Sing a Song of Popcorn, DeRegniers, 1st edition, 1988, NM **22.50**
Skin Spinners, Aiken, Viking, 1st edition, dust jacket, EX **20.00**
Songs from Shakespeare, Harold, Barnes, 1961, 39-pg, EX **32.00**
Story of a Bold Tin Soldier, Hope, Smith illus, 1920, VG **6.50**
Strange Teepee, Hart, Saalfied, dust jacket, 1932, VG **5.50**
Stubb's Brother, Otis, Harper, 1910, VG **7.50**
Tale of John Barleycorn, Azarian, Boston, 1st edition, 1982, NM .**25.00**
Teapots & Quails, Lear, Harvard Univ, 1st edition, 1953, EX **40.00**
Trailer Trio, Jacobs, Winston, w/dust jacket, 1942, VG **22.00**
Trixie Beldon & Secret of Mansion, Campbell, Whitman, VG **7.50**
Trouble for Jerry, Gates, Viking, 1st edition, 1944, VG **20.00**
What Katy Did, Coolidge, Roberts, 1892, VG **7.50**
Who Is It?, Gay, Viking, 1st edition, 1955, EX **42.50**
Wind Has Wings, Downie, Cleaver illus, Walck, 1968, EX **14.00**
Wonder Why, Harnden, Houghton Mifflin, 1st print, 1971, EX ..**22.50**

Children's Things

Nearly every item devised for adult furnishings has been reduced to child's size — furniture, dishes, sporting goods, even some tools. All are very collectible. During the late 17th and early 18th centuries, miniature china dinnerware sets were made both in China and in England. They were not intended primarily as children's playthings, but instead were made to furnish miniature rooms and cabinets that provided a popular diversion for the adults of that period. By the 19th century, the emphasis had shifted, and most of the small-scaled dinnerware and tea sets were made for children's play.

Late in the 19th century and well into the 20th, toy pressed glass dishes were made, many in the same pattern as full-scale glassware. Today these toy dishes often fetch prices in the same range as those for the 'grown-ups'!

Authorities Margaret and Kenn Whitmyer have compiled a lovely book, *The Collector's Encyclopedia of Children's Dishes*, with full-color photos and current market values; you will find their address in the Directory under Ohio. We also recommend *Children's Glass Dishes, China, and Furniture* by Doris Anderson Lechler, available at your local bookstore or public library. See also A B C Plates; Canary Lustre; Willow Ware.

Key:
ds — doll size   Emp – Empire
Fr – French

China

Box, Blue Onion, Mehl, Germany, 4¼"	125.00
Cake plate, floral, Japan, 4⅜"	5.00
Candelabrum, 3-branch, 2½"	35.00
Casserole, Blue Willow, Japan, w/lid	22.50
Casserole, floral medallions in bl band, Noritake, w/lid, 6"	15.00
Casserole, floral on tan lustre, oval, Japan, 1⅝"	12.00
Creamer, Butterfly, Japan, 2¼"	6.50
Creamer, Dutch figures, Edwin M Knowles, 2⅛"	8.00
Creamer, Polka Dots, red on ivory, 2½"	7.50
Creamer, Roman Chariots, Cauldon England, 2"	30.00
Creamer & sugar bowl, hunt scene, pk lustre, Germany, w/lid	50.00
Cup, Blue Willow, Japan, 1½"	7.00
Cup & saucer, floral band, Nippon, 1½", 4¼"	10.00
Cup & saucer, Floral Medallion, Japan, 1¾", 3⅛"	4.00
Cup & saucer, Kate Greenaway, Cleve-ron China USA	30.00
Cup & saucer, Mickey Mouse, Occupied Japan	12.00
Cup & saucer, Punch & Judy, 1⅞", 4¼"	38.00
Dishes, bl & gold trim on wht porc, Germany, 4-place, ds, MIB	165.00
Plate, Blue Willow, Japan, 4⅜"	12.00
Plate, Old Curiosity Shop, Ridgway's, 4½"	12.50
Plate, Otter, Noritake, 4¼"	17.50
Plate, Those Who Dainties Love..., blk transfer/mc, 5"	50.00
Plate, Who Saw Me Mt Rocking Horse..., bl on pearlware, 6"	195.00
Platter, Bears, Japan, 6¼"	7.50
Platter, Bluebird, Noritake, 7⅛"	15.00
Platter, Little Bo Peep, Godey Prints	9.00
Sugar bowl, Bluebird, Japan, w/lid, 2¼"	6.00
Sugar bowl, floral, Occupied Japan, w/lid	7.50
Sugar bowl, Floral Medallion, Japan, w/lid, 2½"	3.50
Sugar bowl, Mickey Mouse, Japan, w/lid, 2¾"	12.00
Tea set, Blue Willow, 6-place, ds, MIB	175.00
Tea set, boy & girl transfer on wht porc, Japan, 1950s, 4-place	78.00
Tea set, Deco cube decor on lustre, 23-pc, 6-place, MIB	195.00
Tea set, floral on tan lustre, Japan, 2-place	27.50
Tea set, gold leaves on wht porc, Germany, 16-pc, MIB	240.00
Tea set, gold lustre w/floral inset, 1930s, M in Christmas box	145.00
Tea set, HP porc, bird-shaped hdls, ds, M in VG box	235.00
Tea set, lemon lustre w/Nile gr & blk trim, 1920, 4-place, MIB	200.00
Tea set, marigold lustre, plum blossoms, 4-place, 1930s	125.00

Tea set, Mieto, wht w/gold trim, Japan, 4-place	40.00
Tea set, Moss Rose, Morimura Bros, 1917, 6-place, MIB	235.00
Tea set, pk roses on wht porc, 1930s, 4-place, MIB	125.00
Tea set, Snow White, W Disney Enterprises, Japan, 4-place	88.00

Teapot, Blossom Children, England, ca 1880, 5¾", $90.00.

Teapot, Blue Onion, ironstone	20.00
Teapot, Circus, Edwin M Knowles, 4½"	25.00
Teapot, Dutch Children, tan lustre, Japan	12.00
Teapot, Dutch figures, Japan	7.50
Teapot, Nursery Scenes, Germany, 4½"	35.00
Teapot, Silhouette, Japan, 4⅛"	10.00
Teapot, Silhouette Children, 3⅝"	17.50
Teapot, tan lustre, Occupied Japan	10.00
Tureen, Little Orphan Annie, Japan, 4½"	20.00
Waste bowl, waterfront scene, bl on wht	12.50

Furniture

Examples with no dimensions given are child size unless noted doll size.

Bed, curly maple, scrolled head/ft brds, pencil posts, EX	1,550.00
Bed, rope; ball & bell trn post, wood stain, 12x20x15"	200.00
Cabinet, Hoosier; gr pnt w/decal on top rail, complete, 17¼"	2,250.00
Chair, arrow-bk side; worn red/blk grpt & wht stripes, 28"	460.00
Chair, ladder-bk side; rabbit-ear posts, paper seat, 25"	45.00
Chair, side; Windsor cage-bk, pnt traces, 25"	150.00
Chair, Windsor bow-bk arm, 1920s repro, VG	75.00
Chest, cherry & walnut Empire, 3-drw, scrolled front ft, 13"	850.00
Chest, cherry-finish pine, 5-drw, heart-cutout crest, 14"	350.00
Chest, Hplwht mahog, 12½x11x7½"	650.00
Chest, pine, 5-drw, sq nails, minor damage, 19x15"	400.00
Chest, pine Co Empire, 4-drw, curving stiles, 22x18"	475.00
Clock, tall case; English, 56"	1,500.00
Cradle, Co Windsor, worn gr pnt, bentwood ends, rpr, 36"	250.00
Cradle, pine/poplar, sq nails, rpr scrolled edges, 19"	85.00
Cradle, poplar w/orig blk pnt & mc florals, rprs/damage, ds	125.00
Cradle, poplar w/orig 2-color pnt, dtd 1880, scalloped, 16"	150.00
Cradle, 2-color grpt, cut-out rockers, ball finials, 42"	350.00
Cupboard, corner; cherry, 2 panel doors, wire nails, 32x13"	350.00
Cupboard, pnt wood, 4 flat panel doors, stencil, 45"	800.00
Desk, Governor Winthrop, bracket ft, 2-drw, 1810, 12x10x1½"	750.00
Desk, lap; suitcase style, England, 6¼x8⅛x4"	450.00
Desk, roll top; oak & chestnut, 15x18x9"	775.00

Desk, side cylinder bookshelf, English, 1700s, 8x12½x12" **1,750.00**
Dresser, serpentine top drw, tilt mirror, brass pulls, 26" **500.00**
Dresser, walnut, marble top, 55x27x14" **2,400.00**
Dry sink, pine, dk stain, 1-door, 7½x8" **650.00**
Highchair, arrow-bk, rabbit-ear crests, curly maple legs **500.00**
Highchair, Windsor, bamboo trn, rabbit-ear posts, rpt, 34" **700.00**
Highchair, Windsor, bamboo trn, step-down crest, rpt, 36" **400.00**
Ice box, oak; 3-door, nickeled brass hardware, 16½x12x6" **775.00**
Ladder, CI, gr pnt, Kilgore, ds, EX **40.00**
Murphy bed, chestnut, wardrobe/bed combination, 15x10½x6" .**325.00**
Playground slide, pnt CI, Kilgore, ds **50.00**
Rocker, emb kitten on headrest **200.00**
Rocker, late spindle construction, splint seat, rpt, 28" **125.00**
Rocker, 5-spindle, orig pnt/stenciling, very worn, 27" **125.00**
Secretary, Dutch marquetry, shaped front, bun ft, 1840s, 33" ..**7,000.00**
Sofa, Empire, horsehair, CT, 1840s, 20x40x12" **1,500.00**
Table, drop leaf; walnut, drw in end, 8x12x12" w/leaves up **475.00**
Table, pine Hplwht w/pnt, rpl dvtl drw, 19x16x21" **175.00**
Table, walnut, burl octagonal top, ornate base, 4½x5" **315.00**
Washstand, tiger maple, 3 drws w/6 wooden knobs, 6" **575.00**

Painted and decorated settee, roses and pinstriping on light green, ca 1840, wear and repairs, 24" long, $1,300.00.

Glassware

Acorn, creamer 120.00
Acorn, sugar bowl, w/lid 175.00
Amazon, creamer 40.00
Amazon, spooner 32.00
Arrowhead-in-Ovals, butter dish 42.50
Arrowhead-in-Ovals, cake stand, 3½x6¼" 40.00
Arrowhead-in-Ovals, creamer 24.00
Baby Flute, bowl, 20-point base ray 90.00
Bead & Scroll, spooner 55.00
Bead & Scroll, sugar bowl, w/lid 135.00
Beaded Swirl Variation, butter dish 35.00
Braided Belt, butter dish, milk glass 225.00
Bucket, creamer 50.00
Butterfly & Log, mug 65.00
Button Arches, sugar bowl 75.00
Button Panel, spooner 67.50
Christmas Eve, plate 135.00
Clear & Dmn Panels, butter dish, lg 78.00
Clear & Dmn Panels, sugar bowl, w/lid 35.00
Cloud Band, butter dish, milk glass 175.00
Cupid & Venus, mug 35.00

Diamond Ridge, creamer 75.00
Divided Block w/Sunburst, mug 30.00
Dog Medallion, cup & saucer 135.00
Doyle #500, sugar bowl, w/lid 60.00
Doyle #500, tray 40.00
Drape, castor set 135.00
Drum, butter dish 150.00
Drum, creamer 60.00
Drum, sugar bowl, w/lid 110.00
Dutch Boudoir, bowl, gr 250.00
Dutch Boudoir, pitcher, milk glass 110.00
Fine Cut Star & Fan, butter dish 35.00
Fine Cut Star & Fan, sugar bowl, w/lid 28.00
Flattened Diamond (Thumbelina), butter dish 35.00
Garden of Eden, mug 40.00
Grapevine w/Ovals, creamer 60.00
Grapevine w/Ovals, sugar bowl, w/lid 85.00
Hawaiian Lei, sugar bowl, w/lid 32.50
Heart & Vines, mug 30.00
Hickman, tray 50.00
HMS Pinafore Little Buttercup, mug 85.00
Hobnail w/T'print, butter dish, bl 100.00
Hobnail w/T'print, tray, bl 50.00
Horizontal Threads, creamer 30.00
Horizontal Threads, spooner 40.00
Inv't Strawberry, punch bowl 50.00
Lamb, butter dish 185.00
Lamb, creamer, milk glass 150.00
Large Block, spooner, amber 125.00
Large Block, sugar bowl, bl or bl opaque 165.00
Liberty Bell, butter dish 235.00
Lion, butter dish 135.00
Lion, creamer 60.00
Lion, cup & saucer, frosted 90.00
Little Bo Peep, mug 125.00
Loops & Ropes, cup & saucer 25.00
Menagerie, spooner, bl 140.00
Michigan, butter dish, w/flashing 150.00
Michigan, pitcher, gold trim 35.00
Michigan, pitcher, water 30.00
Michigan, sugar bowl, gold trim, w/lid 90.00
Michigan, sweetmeat 50.00
Nursery Rhyme, bowl, berry 20.00
Nursery Rhyme, butter dish 65.00
Nursery Rhyme, creamer 40.00
Nursery Rhyme, pitcher 110.00
Nursery Rhyme, punch bowl, +6 cups 250.00
Nursery Rhyme, punch bowl, bl opaque, +6 cups 600.00
Nursery Rhyme, punch bowl, milk glass, +6 cups 300.00
Nursery Rhyme, spooner 75.00
Nursery Rhyme, tumbler 25.00
Oval Star, pitcher, water 65.00
Oval Star, punch bowl 55.00
Oval Star, tumbler 10.00
Pattee Cross, pitcher 75.00
Pattee Cross, tumbler 12.00
Pennsylvania, sugar bowl, gr w/gold, w/lid, 4" 225.00
Petite Hobnail Square, pitcher, red flashed 105.00
Portland, pitcher 35.00
Portland, pitcher, water 30.00
Rex (Fancy Cut), creamer 25.00
Rex (Fancy Cut), pitcher 65.00
Rex (Fancy Cut), punch bowl 125.00
Rexford/Euclid, butter dish 40.00

Ribbon Candy, cake stand, gr 80.00
Rooster, creamer 135.00
Rooster, plate 70.00
Rooster, sugar bowl, w/lid 200.00
Sawtooth, butter dish 50.00
Sawtooth, creamer 40.00
Sherwood, castor set 165.00
Standing Lamb, sugar bowl, dog finial, clear or frosted 800.00
Stippled Diamond, butter dish, amber or bl 170.00
Stippled Diamond, sugar bowl, w/lid 90.00
Stippled Forget-Me-Not, sugar bowl, w/lid 85.00
Stippled Vine & Beads, creamer 70.00
Sunbeam (Twin Snowshoes), butter dish 175.00
Swan, mug 20.00
Tappan, butter dish 32.50
Tulip & Honeycomb, butter dish, lg 42.50
Tumble-up, amethyst, plain, 5⅜" 255.00
Tumble-up, bl pitcher w/etching & yel hdl, 5" ...375.00
Tumble-up, Bohemian, deer in wood, 5" 365.00
Tumble-up, Bohemian type, flashing on clear, 4⅞" ...250.00
Tumble-up, cobalt, Mary Gregory style, 1½" 300.00
Tumble-up, ruby, wooded scenes, 4¼" 365.00
Twist, sugar bowl 45.00
Two Band, butter dish 50.00
Wee Branches, butter dish 140.00
Wee Branches, creamer 50.00
Wheat Sheaf, bowl, berry; sm 10.00
Wheat Sheaf, punch bowl 35.00
Whirligig (Buzz Star), butter dish 25.00
Wild Rose, butter dish, clear opal 65.00
Wild Rose, butter dish, milk glass 75.00
Wild Rose, candlestick, ea 165.00
Wild Rose, creamer, milk glass 55.00
Wild Rose, punch bowl, clear opal 90.00

Miscellaneous

Bake set, aluminum, 1940s-50s, M in Campbell Kid illus box 48.00
Chamber, boy w/dogs, children w/hoops, mc/gray transfer, EIL ..350.00
Cook set, aluminum, Like Mother's, Mirro, 1940s, 16-pc, MIB ..450.00
Cook set, stove/pots/spoons, Wonderland Toy, 1950s, 8-pc, MIB ..40.00
Doll carriage, wood w/orig decor, leather top, 28x32" 400.00

**Electric stove, 7½x8",
$80.00.**

Kaleidoscope, Am Indian trade beads, tin cylinder, 1820s, 7" 220.00
Percolator set, TootsieToy, 1930s, MIB 80.00
Rattle, celluloid, Porky Pig, EX 12.50
Rattle, celluloid, stork w/baby figural, USA 65.00

Rattle, celluloid, Tom Thumb w/pig, EX color 95.00
Rattle, wood lattice cage, red/gr pnt, EX trn/cvg, 7", EX 100.00
Rattle, 4 1" crotal bells on looped leather strap, wood hdl ..65.00
Roller skates, ball bearing, Torrington CT, w/key, 1930s, MIB 50.00
Sled, bentwood runners & braces, steel seat guard, rpt, 33" 275.00
Sled, wood/steel, orig mc pnt/AW Davis, 39" 425.00
Sleigh, bentwood/scrolled steel runners, orig decor, 39" 900.00

Chocolate Glass

Jacob Rosenthal developed chocolate glass, a rich shaded opaque brown sometimes referred to as caramel slag, in 1900 at the Indiana Tumbler and Goblet Company of Greentown, Indiana. Later, other companies produced similar ware. Only the latter is listed here. See also Greentown. Our advisors for this category are Jerry and Sandi Garrett; they are listed in the Directory under Indiana.

Bottle, scent; Venetian, w/stopper 600.00
Bowl, Aldine, oval, w/lid 1,500.00
Bowl, File, 8" 550.00
Bowl, Geneva, oval, 10½" 425.00
Bowl, sauce; File 300.00
Bowl, sauce; Waffle 400.00
Bowl, Shield w/Daisy & Button, 8⅜" 1,250.00
Butter dish, Chrysanthemum Leaf 1,300.00
Butter dish, Wild Rose w/Bow Knot 450.00
Compote, jelly; Majestic 750.00
Compote, Melrose, 6" 225.00
Creamer, Chrysanthemum Leaf 600.00
Creamer, Rose Garland 1,200.00
Creamer, Strigal, tankard form 150.00
Cuff box, rnd, 4½" H 485.00
Mug, Swirl 540.00
Nappy, Beaded Triangle, hdls 315.00
Pitcher, Feather, milk sz 1,250.00
Pitcher, Geneva 900.00
Salt cellar, Honeycomb, 3½" dia 575.00
Shaker, Chrysanthemum Leaf 500.00

Tray, Wild Rose and Bow Knot, McKee & Brothers, Pittsburgh, PA, 10½x8", $375.00.

Tumbler, Chrysanthemum Leaf 550.00
Tumbler, Geneva 150.00
Tumbler, Wild Rose w/Bow Knot 135.00
Vase, Beaded Triangle, 6¼" 200.00

Christmas Collectibles

Christmas past . . . lovely mementos from long ago attest to the ostentatious Victorian celebrations of the season.

St. Nicholas, better known as Santa, has changed much since 300 A.D. when the good Bishop Nicholas showered needy children with gifts and kindnesses. During the early 18th century, Santa was portrayed as the kind gift-giver to well-behaved children and the stern switch-bearing disciplinarian to those who were bad. In 1822 Clement Clark Moore, a New York poet, wrote his famous *Night Before Christmas*, and the Santa he described was jolly and jovial — a lovable old elf who was stern with no one. Early Santas wore robes of yellow, brown, blue, green, red, white, or even purple. But Thomas Nast, who worked as an illustrator for Harper's Weekly, was the first to depict Santa in a red suit instead of the traditional robe and to locate him the entire year at the North Pole headquarters.

Today's collectors prize early Santa figures, especially those in robes of fur or mohair or those dressed in an unusual color. Some early examples of Christmas memorabilia are the pre-1870 ornaments from Dresden, Germany. These cardboard figures — angels, gondolas, umbrellas, dirigibles, and countless others — sparkled with gold and silver trim. Late in the 1870s, blown glass ornaments were imported from Germany. There were over 6,000 recorded designs, all painted inside with silvery colors. From 1890 through 1910, blown glass spheres were often decorated with beads, tassels, and tinsel rope.

Christmas lights, made by Sandwich and some of their contemporaries, were either pressed or mold-blown glass shaped into a form similar to a water tumbler. They were filled with water and then hung from the tree by a wire handle; oil floating on the surface of the water served as fuel for the lighted wick.

Kugels are glass ornaments that were made as early as 1820 and as late as 1890. Ball-shaped examples are more common than the fruit and vegetable forms and have been found in sizes ranging from 1" to 14" in diameter. They were made of thick glass with heavy brass caps, in cobalt, green, gold, silver, red, and occasionally in amethyst.

Although experiments involving the use of electric lightbulbs for the Christmas tree occurred before 1900, it was 1903 before the first manufactured socket set was marketed. These were very expensive and often proved a safety hazard. In 1921 safety regulations were established, and products were guaranteed safety approved. The early bulbs were smaller replicas of Edison's household bulb. By 1910 G.E. bulbs were rounded with a pointed end, and until 1919 all bulbs were hand blown. The first figural bulbs were made around 1910 in Austria. Japan soon followed, but their product was never of the high quality of the Austrian wares. American manufacturers produced their first machine-made figurals after 1919. Today, figural bulbs (especially character-related examples) are very popular collectibles. Bubble lights were popular from about 1945 to 1960 when miniature lights were introduced. These tiny lamps dampened the public's enthusiasm for the bubblers, and manufacturers stopped providing replacement bulbs.

Feather trees were made from 1850 to 1950. All are collectible. Watch for newly-manufactured feather trees that have lately been reintroduced.

For further information concerning Christmas collectibles, we recommend two highly informative books, *Christmas Collectibles* by Margaret & Kenn Whitmyer and *Christmas Ornaments, Lights, & Decorations, a Collector's Identification & Value Guide*, by George Johnson. Both books are available from Collector Books or your local bookstore.

Bulbs

Acorn, mc pnt, clear glass, EX 32.00
Andy Gump, mc pnt, milk glass, NM 95.00

Apricot, yel w/orange pnt, clear glass, EX 17.50
Baby in red stocking, milk glass, EX 45.00
Bear in pajamas, pk, celluloid, EX 75.00
Bell w/3 Santa faces, mc pnt, milk glass, 3", EX 35.00
Betty Boop, mc pnt, milk glass, EX 85.00
Boy in hip boots, worn pnt, milk glass 35.00
Candy cane, red & wht pnt, milk glass, 3", NM 38.00
Cat, bright colors, milk glass, 4" 45.00
Choir girl, worn pnt, milk glass, EX 45.00
Clown head, 2-faced, pointed cap, mc pnt, milk glass, EX 50.00
Cottage, mc pnt, milk glass, 2½", EX 12.50
Cross, pk pnt, milk glass, 3" 32.00
Darla, girl in pk dress, orange hair, milk glass, NM 135.00
Dick Tracy, EX pnt, milk glass, 3" 150.00
Dismal Desmond, polka-dots, mc pnt, milk glass, M 55.00
Dog, brn & red pnt, milk glass, 4" 55.00
Donald Duck, mc pnt, clear glass 45.00
Drummer boy, mc pnt, milk glass, EX 55.00
Duckling, mc pnt, milk glass, NM 55.00
Dunce head, EX pnt, milk glass 65.00
Ear of corn, mc pnt, milk glass, 3" 65.00
Father Christmas w/tree, red robe/gold staff, Hungary, NM 145.00
Grapes, mc w/gr leaves, milk glass, 3¼" 25.00
Hayseed Farmer, EX pnt, milk glass 95.00
Jack-o'-Lantern, EX pnt, milk glass 65.00
Kayo, squatting, milk glass, 1935, EX 65.00
Lady w/cross, mc pnt, milk glass, 3½", EX 42.50
Lantern, molded swirls, mc pnt, clear glass, Germany, NM 55.00
Lantern, VG pnt, milk glass, Japan, sm 22.00
Lemon, worn pnt, clear glass, VG 25.00
Little Orphan Annie, mc pnt, milk glass, c 1935, 3⅛" 110.00
Lucky Lindy, mc pnt on milk glass, NM 55.00
Matchless star, bl w/amber center, 2" 35.00
Moon Mullins, mc pnt, milk glass, rare, VG 135.00
Owl, mc pnt, clear glass, Germany 75.00
Pear, red pnt, brass base, ivory insulator, EX 25.00
Pig in chimney, yel & pk pnt, milk glass, EX 75.00
Rabbit, sitting, mc pnt, milk glass, NM 115.00
Rose bud, pk pnt, milk glass, sm 28.00
Sandy, mc pnt, milk glass, 3", EX 110.00

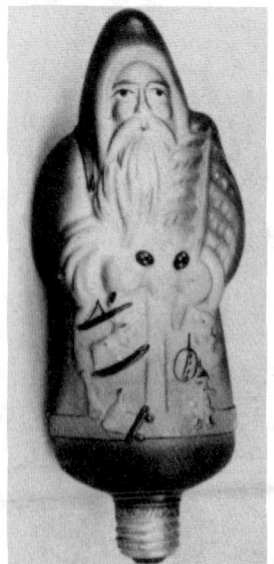

Santa Claus, 1940, 8¾", $150.00.

Santa, full figure w/pack, mc pnt, milk glass, EX 45.00
Santa atop chimney, mc pnt, milk glass, EX 75.00

Santa in oval, mc pnt, milk glass, 3¾", NM 65.00
Seashell w/roses, tan & bl pnt, milk glass, EX 70.00
Smitty, milk glass, VG 85.00
Snowman, red hat, bl bag, milk glass, 3", NM 45.00
Star, Noma, 7", EX in orig box 48.00
Star w/face, EX pnt, milk glass 32.00
Teddy bear, red pnt, milk glass, EX 65.00
Tom the Piper's Son, mc pnt, EX 245.00
Woman in shoe, mc pnt, milk glass, NM 80.00
World globe, EX pnt, milk glass 95.00
Zeppelin, EX pnt, milk glass 65.00

Candy Containers

Banjo, Dresden, 3-D, silver/gold/red/brn, 3½x1½", EX 175.00
Barrel, Dresden, 3-D, tan & brn, 2¼", EX 165.00
Boot, gold paper, tinsel strings, 8x5½", VG 95.00
Candle, pressed paper, red w/wick & ribbon, 5½", EX 35.00
Cornucopia, crepe paper, die-cut decor, EX 88.00
Donkey, compo, detailed, head removes, Germany, 5¼" 250.00
Drum, Dresden, vertical gold strips, silver star, 2½x3" 80.00
Elf, spun glass, Dresden horn, on compo snowball, Germany, 6" ..95.00
House, glass, red brick, gr roof, 3", NM 85.00
House w/cotton Santa on cotton roof, mk Japan 90.00
Irish heart, Dresden, gr w/opal stone, 3" 125.00
Jockey cap, Dresden, blk brim, mk MIG, 1¾x4x2½" 145.00
Santa, cb, flocked, cone shape, cotton beard, W Germany, 10" 48.00
Santa, compo & cloth, bl robe, Germany, 21", VG 1,600.00
Santa, compo & fabric, fur beard, Germany, 8", EX 650.00
Santa, HP bsk face, glass eyes, Germany, 14", EX 600.00
Santa, net bag w/celluloid face, compo hands & boots, 9", EX ...185.00
Santa, papier-mache, red coat, bl pants, 4", EX 650.00
Santa, pressed cb, chimes in hat, W Germany, 6½" 95.00
Santa in chimney, papier-mache/cb/cloth, Germany, 9", VG 325.00
Santa in snow scene, tin litho, old, 4" 135.00
Santa in wagon pulled by deer, plastic, 4x8", EX 85.00
Santa on deer, compo, metal horns, Dresden trim, Germany 635.00
Slipper, Dresden, pk crepe w/gold, 8" 245.00
Snow White & 7 Dwarfs, cb, Germany, 8-pc set 465.00
Snowball, celluloid, 2" 35.00
Snowman, compo, 7" 75.00
Snowman, soft plush, top hat, bl scarf, W Germany, 7¾" 48.00
Star medallion, Dresden, cb w/glitter, 3" 115.00
Tree, cone shape, paper litho, 9½", VG 130.00
Wreath, Dresden, 4¼" 145.00

Ornaments

Angel, diecut, on tinsel cross, 4½", VG 45.00
Angel, Dresden, tree top, 7", VG 125.00
Angel, mold blown, on tinsel-covered cross, 5", VG 45.00
Angel, mold blown, pk & yel frost, 3" 65.00
Angel, molded glass, raised wings, stars on skirt, 2¾", M 65.00
Angel blowing lg horn, diecut, EX color, 4½x3", EX 65.00
Angel head in daisy, mold blown, 2-sided, early, 2", M 95.00
Angel on swing, diecut, advertising, 6¼x4½", EX 85.00
Angel praying, blown glass, molded wings, 3", G 110.00
Ballerina, mold blown, gold hair, pk blouse/shoes, Italy, 6" 105.00
Basket, Dresden, tan, 2" 115.00
Bear, mold blown, gold w/blk features, 2½", EX 115.00
Bear w/stick, mold blown, silver/red/blk, gold hat, 3½", EX 165.00
Beetle, mold blown, pk w/gr wings, 3" 150.00
Berry, mold blown, pearly bl, 2¼", EX 25.00
Bird, mold blown, spun glass tail, EX pnt, early, 3½" 55.00

Bird, mold blown, spun glass tail, in glass cage, 4", VG 85.00
Bird, mold blown, spun glass tail, unsilvered, 4½x6½", EX 65.00
Bird on branch relief on ball, mold blown, 2¼", M 65.00
Bird w/crest, spun glass tail, 8½" L, VG 45.00
Birds in nest, mold blown, spun glass tails, tinsel hanger, EX 80.00
Boy w/accordion, mold blown, 2¾", VG 45.00
Boy's head, mold blown, 2½", M 85.00
Car, mold blown, pearly wht/red/gold/bl/pk, 2¼x2¾", EX 135.00
Cat in shoe, mold blown, 3½" L, VG 135.00
Cat w/banjo, mold blown, yel hat & fiddle, 3½" 80.00
Cat washing face relief on ball, mold blown, 1¼", EX 90.00
Clown, mold blown, mc pnt, 5", EX 95.00
Clown face in oval indent, mold blown, 2¾" dia, VG 95.00
Cockatoo, mold blown, spun glass tail, EX pnt, 3¾x5¾" 45.00
Dog w/horn, mold blown, pearly bl/blk/red, 1920s, 3¼", NM 115.00
Drum, mold blown, silver/gr/gold/red, 2¼", VG 45.00
Dublin Pipe, mold blown, silk cord hanger, 5", VG 45.00
Dwarf, mold blown, gr pnt, 3½" 65.00
Elephant, mold blown, pearly wht/red/blk, 3¼x3", EX 145.00
Elf in window, mold blown, worn pnt, 2½", VG 85.00
Elk, Dresden, tan & brn, 3" 225.00
Face in pear, mold blown, pearly silver/pk/blk, 2¼", G 65.00
Father Christmas, cotton, gold Dresden belt, die-cut face, 5" 235.00
Father Christmas w/2 children, diecut, toys on bk, 4x2" 65.00
Fish, mold blown, pearly yel w/pk details, 5" 115.00
Flapper, mold blown, pearly wht, yel hair, 3", EX 85.00
Flower, mold blown, mc pnt, unsilvered, 3" 65.00
Fox, Dresden, brn & tan, 2½" 325.00
Frog climbing mushroom, mold blown, mc pnt, 4½" 165.00
Girl in flower, mold blown, flesh w/gold, 3¼", EX 110.00
Girl on ball, chenille body, paper face, 3½x2¼", EX 95.00
Girl on bicycle, Dresden, gr & red w/gold bike, 5x5" 195.00
Girl w/draped robe, mold blown, 3½", M 60.00
Girl's head, diecut, 2-sided, tinsel rings, 6", G 35.00
Girl's head, mold blown, mc pnt, ca 1910, 2¾", G 95.00
Guard tower, Dresden, 1900s, 2¾", EX 425.00
Gun, mold blown, wire wrapped, 5½" L, G 125.00
Harp, mold blown, w/Santa diecut on stem in center, 3¾", VG ...85.00
Hedgehog, mold blown, pearly wht w/blk details, rare, 5" 365.00
House, mold blown, 2x2¼", NM 45.00
Indian head, mold blown, mc pnt, 2½", EX 65.00
Joey clown head, mold blown, 2¼", VG 25.00
Joey Lewis, mold blown, mc pnt, 6" 285.00
Kittens in basket, mold blown, pearly wht, pk basket, 3" ...90.00
Kugel, ball, amber, emb brass hanger, 5" 85.00
Kugel, ball, bl, w/orig MIG label, rpr brass hanger, 5¾" ...275.00
Kugel, ball, cobalt, baroque cap, 2½" 110.00
Kugel, ball, cobalt, ribbed, common hanger, 1⅝" 250.00
Kugel, ball, cobalt, swirl leaf-end brass hanger, 4" 165.00
Kugel, ball, cobalt, 8-petal hanger, 1½" 110.00
Kugel, ball, gold, mercury lined, orig hanger, 8" 165.00
Kugel, ball, gr, brass hanger, Made in France, 7½" 475.00
Kugel, ball, lt gr, brass hanger, 3¼" 150.00
Kugel, ball, med gr, 2½" 110.00
Kugel, ball, red, baroque hanger, 2" 185.00
Kugel, ball, red, brass hanger, 4¼" 450.00
Kugel, ball, red, brass hanger, 7" 600.00
Kugel, ball, red, brass hanger, 9½", pr 850.00
Kugel, ball, red, brass hanger mk Austria, worn, 10" 220.00
Kugel, ball, red/silver/wht stripes, brass cap, 1890s, 2¾" 350.00
Kugel, ball, smoky bl, emb brass cap, French, 2½" 145.00
Kugel, grapes, bl, 6", EX 450.00
Kugel, grapes, cobalt, brass hanger, 4" 350.00
Kugel, grapes, lt gr, brass hanger, 3¼" 450.00

Kugel, grapes, silver, emb brass hanger, 7" 350.00
Kugel, grapes, silver w/gr, 8-petal cap, ca 1890, 4" 250.00
Kugel, pear, emerald gr, baroque brass hanger, 3¾" 395.00
Kugel, pear, silver, brass hanger, 9½" 395.00
Kugel, teardrop, silver, baroque hanger, 2¼" 185.00
Kugel, teardrop, silver, baroque hanger, 3½" 225.00
Lighthouse, mold blown, red & silver, 3", VG 65.00
Lobster, Dresden, orange & beige, 4" 325.00
Lyre shape w/die-cut Santa, 3¾", NM 45.00
Mountain climber, mold blown, flesh face, mc clothes, 5" 65.00
Owl, Dresden, gold w/brn details, 5", VG 245.00
Peach w/2 leaves, mold blown, lt wear, 2¼x2¾" 45.00
Peacock, mold blown, mc pnt, 3½", EX 95.00
Pickle, mold blown, 3¼", VG 85.00
Pig, Dresden, fat/sitting, flesh color, rare, 3¼" 275.00
Pine cone, mold blown, gr, 3" 45.00
Policeman, mold blown, pearly wht/blk/red/bl, 4½", G 145.00
Pug dog, mold blown, pearly wht w/blk, 1910s, 3" 165.00
Purse, Dresden, red, 1½", EX 165.00
Radio Monkey, molded, 4¼", VG 170.00
Rose w/leaf, mold blown, pk shaded w/gr leaf, 3¼", EX 60.00
Santa, compo face, cotton beard, bl suit, Japan, 4½", EX 65.00
Santa, mold blown, flesh face, gold tree, chenille legs, 5½" 265.00
Santa, scrap, on mold-blown swan, 7", EX 115.00
Santa airship, papier-mache & felt, Germany, 6", VG 150.00
Santa head & tree on ball, mold blown, worn silvering, 3", G 65.00
Santa house, celluloid, children at window, 3½", EX 145.00
Santa w/lantern, celluloid, mc, early, 5", EX 85.00
Santa w/pack on bk, mold blown, red pnt, 2", VG 25.00
Santa w/tree, mold blown, 2¾", G 45.00
Skeezix, mold blown, pearly wht/pk/gr, 4" 165.00
Snowman on ball, pearly wht/red/blk, 3¾", NM 150.00
Spaniel, sitting, mold blown, 3", VG 85.00
Squirrel, mold blown, pearly wht w/red nut, 3" 75.00
Star, tree top, molded, 7¼", VG 65.00
Sun face, tree top, mold blown, Germany, 8¾", MIB 145.00
Swan, mold blown, red pnt, 5", VG 95.00
Thumbelina on rose, mold blown, milk glass, EX 145.00
Truck, molded, worn silvering, 2x2½", G 95.00
Vase, Dresden, w/2 paper flowers, 1890s, 4" 145.00
Victorian girls w/doll & parasol, diecut, 7¾x4", EX 65.00
Walnut, mold blown, orange, unsilvered, 2½" 48.00
Watermelon, mold blown, silver/red/gr, 5", EX 150.00
Windmill, mold blown, 2½", M 165.00
Witch w/cat, mold blown, wht w/pk, unsilvered, 1910s, 4" 185.00

Miscellaneous

Noma Bubble Lites, ca 1940s, working, $55.00 per set.

Candle holder, angel, tin, pnt wear, 1¾" 75.00
Candle holder, tin, 4 outstretched arms, red pnt, 7¼" 75.00
Candles, wreath form, red & gr pnt, electric, 11", VG, pr 135.00
Cow, Putz, brn, 2¾x3¾", EX 45.00
Deer, compo, leather harness, Germany, 1920s, 4", EX 125.00
Father Christmas, compo & cloth, fur beard, Germany, 10", EX ...550.00
Father Christmas, spun glass, die-cut torso, Austria, 5½" 95.00
Fence, goose feather, gr w/red berries, 10½" sq, EX 325.00
Fence, plastic, w/gate, 1950s, EX in box 45.00
Fence, wood, red & gr pickets, red gate, 18" sq, EX 175.00
Fence, wood, red/gr pnt, folding type, 2½x18x24", EX 125.00
Fireplace, cb, Shanta/chimney, light makes fire, Noma, 40", M ...165.00
Garland, mc blown glass beads, 1900s, 132", EX 90.00
Light, Expanded Dmn, amber, Brooks, 4" 105.00
Light, Expanded Dmn, amber, 3⅜" 95.00
Light, Expanded Dmn, bl-violet (rare color), folded rim 145.00
Light, Expanded Dmn, clear, folded rim, 2⅞" 40.00
Light, Expanded Dmn, cobalt, 3½" 85.00
Light, Expanded Dmn, cranberry, flared, 4½" 165.00
Light, Expanded Dmn, gr, Brooks, 4" 105.00
Light, Expanded Dmn, sapphire bl, folded rim, 3" 95.00
Light, swirl rib, aqua, folded rim, Stiegel type 175.00
Lights, bubble, Noma, EX 45.00
Lights, Disney's Silly Symphony, Noma, EX 350.00
Lights, Mickey Mouse, full string, Noma, Disney, 1938, MIB ...245.00
Lights, Noma, Mazda, string of 15, EX 35.00
Lights, Popeye, full string, Mazda, 1930s, MIB 295.00
Mask, Santa, pnt wire & horsehair, 8", EX 135.00
Mold, aluminum, Santa, Hello Kiddies, 12" 30.00
Net bag, red, 1880s, 5", EX 45.00
Night light, Santa, plastic, hole in bk for bulb, 17", EX 45.00
Plaque, Father Christmas, pnt plaster, electric, 24", EX 350.00
Plaque, Santa, pnt chalkware, minor scuffing, 22", EX 175.00
Reflectors, foil, various colors, MIG, 1900s, EX in box 45.00
Roly poly, Santa, papier-mache, Schoenhut, 10½", EX 350.00
Santa, Belsnickel, brn robe w/gold (rare color), 5½" 650.00
Santa, Belsnickel, mustard robe, 11" 850.00
Santa, Belsnickel, turq robe, heavy, 4" 550.00
Santa, Belsnickel, wht robe, 10½", EX 600.00
Santa, cb standup, Germany, 16", VG 165.00
Santa, celluloid face, compo boots, cotton cloth, 6", EX 110.00
Santa, compo & felt, heavy, Japan, older type, 6" 110.00
Santa, compo head, fur beard, wood hands, Germany, 5" 245.00
Santa, pnt compo, fur beard, feather tree, Germany, 9½", EX ...650.00
Santa, pnt compo walker, wood legs/lead ft, Germany, 9", EX ...650.00
Santa on house, bsk, red suit, Japan, 2½", EX 60.00
Santa on reindeer, bsk, Japan, 3", EX 45.00
Santa on skis, compo & wood, bag on bk, Germany, 3¾" 135.00
Santa w/feather tree, bsk, red robe, Germany, 3" 135.00
Sheep, papier-mache, wooden legs, Germany, 2x2¾", VG 45.00
Sheep, woolly, Germany, 3¼", EX 65.00
Sleigh, compo & cloth Santa w/reindeer, Germany, 27", EX ...2,300.00
Tree, feather; gr, candle holders, rnd German base, 23" 250.00
Tree, feather; gr w/frosted tips, berries, German base, 55" 550.00
Tree, feather; gr w/red berries, candle holders, Germany, 18" ...235.00
Tree, feather; wht, gold base, Made in Western Germany, 35" ...230.00
Tree, feather; wreath stencil on wht base, Germany, 51" 250.00
Tree stand, Santa form, cast cement, EX orig pnt, 11x11" 250.00
Tree stand, tin, gr w/manger litho, 1920s, 15" dia, EX 150.00
Tree stand, tin litho, Santa scenes, 14", VG 150.00

Chrysanthemum Sprig, Blue

This is the blue opaque version of Northwood's popular pattern,

Chrysanthemum Sprig. It was made at the turn of the century and is today very rare, as its values indicate. Prices are influenced by the amount of gold remaining on the raised designs. Our advisors for this category are Betty and Clarence Maier; they're listed in the Directory under Pennsylvania.

Bowl, berry; sm	300.00
Bowl, master fruit; 10½" W	550.00
Butter dish	850.00
Compote, jelly	475.00
Condiment tray, rare, VG gold	750.00
Creamer	385.00
Cruet	775.00

Fruit bowl, 10½", $550.00.

Pitcher, water	900.00
Shakers, pr	450.00
Spooner	250.00
Sugar bowl, w/lid	450.00
Toothpick holder	450.00
Tumbler	200.00

Circus Collectibles

The 1890s — the Golden Age of the circus. Barnum and Bailey's parades transformed mundane city streets into an exotic never-never land inhabited by trumpeting elephants with jeweled gold headgear strutting by to the strains of the calliope that issued from a fine red- and gilt-painted wagon extravagantly decorated with carved wooden animals of every description. It was an exciting experience. Is it any wonder that collectors today treasure the mementos of that golden era? See also Posters.

Key:
B&B — Barnum & Bailey   RB — Ringling Bros.

Broadside, NY Circus, acrobats/chariots/etc, 1870, 26" L	135.00
Cabinet photo, Ferris wheel, Chicago, 4¼x6¼", EX	28.00
Harness, red/bl/yel feathers, bells & mirrors, EX	450.00
Magazine, B&B, 1943, EX	15.00
Magazine/program, RB B&B, w/postcards, 1973, EX	12.00
Overalls, RB B&B, EX	45.00
Pennant, cloth, RB B&B, 1940s, VG	20.00
Poster, Adam Forepaugh Circus, blk/wht, early, 27x10½"	35.00
Program, B&B, Columbus pageant, many illus, 1893, EX	110.00
Program magazine, RB B&B, 1952, EX	15.00
Ticket, RB, 1956, M	4.00

Clambroth

Clambroth is a term that refers to a type of glass popular in the Victorian period. It was semi-opaque and gray-white in color, said to resemble the broth of the clam. See also Sandwich.

Candlestick, sq base, fluted std, petal socket, 8¾"	95.00
Cruet, lt bl cuttings in paneled body, step-cut lip, 7"	700.00
Epergne, 1-lily, ftd/ruffled bowl: 6¼x4½"	125.00
Pitcher, appl hdl, 10½"	70.00
Spill holder, ltly sanded, Dmn Quilt, 3 bull's-eye dmns, 4½"	175.00
Toothpick holder, Button Arches	20.00
Toothpick holder, floral at rim, Sandwich, 2"	95.00

Clarice Cliff

Between 1928 and 1935 in Burslem, England, as the director and part owner of Wilkinson and Newport Pottery Companies, Clarice Cliff and her 'paintresses' created a body of hand-painted pottery whose influence is felt to the present time.

The name for the oevre was Bizarre Ware, and the predominant sensibility, style, and appearance was Deco. Almost all pieces are signed and include the pattern names. There were over 160 patterns and more than 400 shapes, all of which are illustrated in *A Bizarre Affair — the Life and Work of Clarice Cliff*, published by Harry N. Abrams, Inc., written by Len Griffen and our advisors, Susan and Louis Meisel, whose address is listed in the Directory under New York.

Clarice Cliff died in 1972, shortly after the Victoria and Albert Museum showed her work in retrospect, and collectors (primarily in England) began seeking and admiring her work. In September of 1982, the Metropolitan Museum of Art in New York acquired and placed on view a selection of six pieces.

Note: Non-hand-painted work (transfer printed) was produced after World War II and into the 1950s. Some of the most common names are 'Tonquin' and 'Charlotte.' These items, while attractive and enjoyable to own, have no value in the collector market.

Latona floral on Lotus Jug, 12", $5,000.00; Latona tree pattern on Isis Jug, 9½", $3,500.00; Football pattern on Lotus Jug, 12", $4,500.00; Geometrics on Lotus Jug, 12", $4,500.00; Pebbles pattern on Lotus Jug, 12", $4,500.00.

Bowl, Original Bizarre, Geometric, 3¾x8"	400.00
Demitasse set, orange w/gr & blk angle hdls, 7" pot+14 pcs	3,000.00
Isis jug, Nasturtium, 10x7½"	1,300.00
Isis jug, Summerhouse, 10"	3,000.00
Isis vase, Melon, 9½"	2,600.00

Pitcher, My Garden, blk w/purple hdl, rpr chip, 7½" 375.00
Plate, Blue Chintz, 9" 475.00
Plate, Melon, Fantasque, minor wear, 9" 600.00
Sugar sifter, Nasturtium, Bonjour, flat-sided oval, 5x1¾" 200.00
Vase, Baluster, Geometric, #14D, 9x4½" 1,300.00
Vase, Nasturtium, 8x4" 650.00
Vase, Original Bizarre, mc triangles, minor wear, 9x4¾" 1,500.00

Cleminson

A hobby turned to enterprise, Cleminson is one of several California potteries whose clever hand-decorated wares are attracting the attention of today's collectors. The Cleminsons started their business at their El Monte home in 1941 and were so successful that eventually they expanded to a modern plant that employed more than 150 workers. They produced not only dinnerware and kitchen items such as cookie jars, canisters, and accessories, but novelty wall vases, small trays, plaques, etc., as well. Though nearly always marked, Cleminson wares are easy to spot as you become familiar with their distinctive glaze colors. Their grayed-down blue and green, berry red, and dusty pink say 'Cleminson' as clearly as their trademark. Unable to compete with foreign imports, the pottery closed in 1963. Our advisor for this category is Jack Chipman, author of *The Collector's Encyclopedia of California Pottery*; he is listed in the Directory under California.

Butter dish, Distlefink 25.00
Cookie jar, 'The Way to a Man's Heart' on heart form, mk 95.00
Cookie jar, potbellied stove 95.00
Cookie jar, 6-sided shape, tulip finial 95.00
Cup & saucer, jumbo sz 30.00
Cup & saucer, There's Something About a Soldier 28.00
Egg cup, lady figural, early 25.00
Mug, Morning After, w/lid 20.00
Pie bird, mc on wht, Betty Cleminson's initials in mold, 4½" 22.00
Plate, crowing rooster, yel-striped rim, 9½" 15.00
Plate, fruit cluster, hanging, 4" 10.00
Spoon rest, cherries 15.00
Spoon rest, floral, 3-lobed, 8½" 15.00
Wall pocket, chef's head, stamped mk, 7¼" 50.00

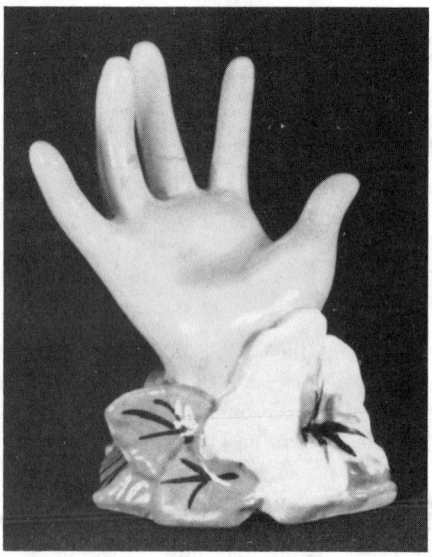

Ring holder: Hand, $45.00.

Clewell

Charles Walter Clewell was a metal worker who perfected the technique of plating an entire ceramic vessel with a thin layer of copper or bronze treated with an oxidizing agent to produce a natural deterioration of the surface. Through trial and error, he was able to control the degree of patina achieved. In the early stages, the metal darkened and, if allowed to develop further, formed a natural turquoise-blue or green corrosion. He worked alone in his small Akron, Ohio, studio from about 1906, buying undecorated pottery from several Ohio firms, among them Weller, Owens, and Cambridge. His work is usually marked. Clewell died in 1965, having never revealed his secret process to others.

Bowl, riveted, high-glaze int, L in oval on front, 4" 85.00
Mug, orig patina, 4½" 125.00
Vase, copper & bl-gr bronze, #470, 6½", NM 395.00
Vase, dk bronze to bright gr patina, #470, 6", NM 260.00
Vase, dk gr/rusty brn, ovoid, #334-24, 5" 230.00
Vase, geometrics, minor cracks in copper, 9" 250.00
Vase, gr patina, 12x9" 600.00

Vase, green patina, chalice form, 7", $600.00.

Vase, gr patina on copper, trumpet form, 8" 245.00
Vase, gr tones, oxidized, horizontal ribs, hdls, rstr, 18" 950.00
Vase, gr w/EX allover patina, Weller blank, 3½" 255.00
Vase, gr/bl/rust patina, tapering from wide shoulder, 12" 475.00
Vase, Nouveau floral, 7" 495.00

Clews

Brothers Ralph and James Clews were potters who operated in Cobridge in the Staffordshire district from 1817 to 1835. They are best known for their blue and white transfer-printed earthenwares, which included American Views, Moral Maxims, Picturesque Views, and English Views. A series called *Three Tours of Dr. Syntax* contained thirty-one different scenes with each piece bearing a descriptive title. Two other popular series were *Don Quixote* with twenty-one prints and *Pictures of Sir David Wilkie* with seven. Both printed and impressed marks were used, often incorporating the pattern name as well as the pottery. See also Staffordshire, Historical. Our advisor for this category is Richard Marden; he is listed in the Directory under New Hampshire.

Bowl, Water Girl, dk bl transfer, 3¾" 110.00

Cup & saucer, floral, dk bl transfer, bl rim, Warranted 185.00
Cup & saucer, Water Girl, dk bl transfer 200.00
Cup plate, Dr Syntax Bound to a Tree by Highwayman 325.00
Cup plate, Mosaic Tracery, dk bl transfer, ca 1825, 3½", M 135.00
Plate, castle scene, foliage & scroll border series, 8½" 110.00
Plate, Don Quixote, gr transfer, Brameld, rare, 10" 150.00
Plate, Don Quixote & Sancho Panza, dk bl transfer, 6⅝" 145.00
Plate, Don Quixote & Shepherdesses, dk bl transfer, 10" 200.00
Plate, Don Quixote Curious Impertinent, dk bl transfer, 5¼" 165.00
Plate, Don Quixote Knighthood Con'fered, dk bl transfer, 10" ..200.00
Plate, Dr Syntax Presenting...Offering, dk bl transfer, 6½" 160.00
Plate, Meeting of Sancho & Dapple, dk bl transfer, 9" 195.00
Plate, Sancho, Priest & Barber, dk bl transfer, 7⅝" 175.00
Plate, Sancho Panza's Debate w/Teresa, dk bl transfer, 9" 185.00
Teapot, floral, dk bl transfer, sm rpr 275.00
Teapot, Water Girl, dk bl transfer, prof rpr 250.00

Clifton

Clifton Art Pottery of Clifton, New Jersey, was organized ca 1903. Until 1911 when they turned to the production of wall and floor tile, they made artware of several varieties. The founders were Fred Tschirner and William A. Long. Long had developed the method for underglaze slip painting that had been used at the Lonhuda Pottery in Steubenville, Ohio, in the 1890s. Crystal Patina, the first artware made by the small company, utilized a fine white body and flowing, blended colors, the earliest a green crystalline. Indian Ware, copied from the pottery of the American Indians, was usually decorated in black geometric designs on red clay. (On the occasions when white was used in addition to the black, the ware was often not as well executed; so even though two-color decoration is very rare, it is normally not as desirable to the collector.) Robin's Egg Blue, pale blue on the white body, and Tirrube, a slip-decorated matt ware, were also produced.

Humidor, Indian Ware, geometric, blk/terra cotta 75.00

Indian Ware vase, dark brown and beige on brick red, marked Clifton, #241, 10½x12", $300.00.

Lamp, Crystal Patina base, copper/abalone shell Valk shade ...4,000.00
Teapot, Crystal Patina, gr, #271-36, unmk 95.00
Teapot, imp motif on yel lustre, gold trim, 7½" 55.00
Vase, Indian Ware, brn/blk on rust, #233, Homolobi, 8x12" 325.00

Vase, Indian Ware, geometrics, red/blk, cylinder neck, 8" 325.00
Vase, Indian Ware, w/hdl, sgn/#246, 4x7½" 175.00
Vase, Tirrube, stork & foliage, #257, 12x7" 325.00
Wall pocket, gr matt, hdls, 7½x5" 68.00

Clocks

In the early days of our country's history, clock makers were influenced by styles imported from Europe and Germany. They copied their cabinets and reconstructed their movements. But needed materials were in short supply; modifications had to be made. Of necessity was born mainspring motive power and spring clocks. Wooden movements were made on a mass-production basis as early as 1808. Before the middle of the century, metal movements had been developed.

Today's collectors prefer clocks from the 18th and 19th centuries with pendulum-regulated movements. Bracket clocks made during this period utilized the shorter pendulum improvised in 1658 by Fromentiel, a prominent English clock maker. These smaller square-face clocks usually were made with a dome top fitted with a handle or a decorative finial. The case was usually walnut or ebony and was sometimes decorated with pierced brass mountings. Brackets were often mounted on the wall to accommodate the clock, hence the name. The banjo clock was patented in 1802 by Simon Willard. It derived its descriptive name from its banjo-like shape. A similar but more elaborate style was called the lyre clock.

Prices have been stable for several years. Unless noted otherwise, values are given for clocks in mint, original condition. Clocks that have been altered, damaged, or have had parts replaced are worth considerably less.

Our advisor is Bruce A. Austin; he is listed in the Directory under New York. Our novelty clock advisors are DLK Nostalgia and Collectibles; their address is given under Pennsylvania.

Note: Numbers within the line descriptions indicate movements: 1 — 8-day time and strike with pendulum; 2 — 30-hour time and strike with pendulum.

Key:
br — brass	reg — regulator
dl — dial	rswd — rosewood
esc — escapement	T — time only
mcr — mercury	wt — weight
mvt — movement	vnr — veneer
pnd — pendulum	2nds — seconds

Victorian gingerbread clock, advertising Dickey's Indian Blood and Liver Pills, with thermometer (broken), 27", VG, $625.00.

Banjo Clocks

David Wms, Fed mahog w/rvpt, 1820s, 34", EX 1,980.00
E Howard, walnut, rvpt base panel, 29" 1,250.00
E Ingraham, Nile, walnut, 1, str side arms, finial, 34" 275.00
Gilbert, print of ship in bottom, eagle finial, 2, 1930, 24" 75.00
MA, br eagle, mahog/2 (rpl) rvpt, iron dl, 1830, 40" 650.00
S Willard, eagle finial, X-band mahog, 2 rvpt, 34", EX 500.00
Waterbury, gilt-faced mahog, Naval rvpt, 1/wts, 44", VG 850.00

Beehive Clocks

Ansonia, wood case, porc dl, 1, 9½x6" 130.00
Brewster-Ingraham, mahog vnr, cut glass, zinc dl, 1, 19", EX 400.00
Fr, wood case, porc dl, key wound, T, 6" 110.00
JC Brown, rswd vnr/ripple mouldings, 1, zinc dl, 19", EX 800.00
New Haven, wood case, label: Austin, 1, 11x9" 130.00
Terry-Andrews, rswd vnr, mirror, paper label, lyre mvt, 19" 300.00

Calendar Clocks

Burwell-Carter, perpetual, zinc dl, blk/gold rvpt, 24", EX 1,600.00
Gilbert, Longbranch, cvd/trn walnut, silver decor, 1, 27" 850.00
Ithaca, #6 wall library model, walnut, 1, 28", EX 800.00

Calendar clock by Seth Thomas, Fashion #3, walnut, 8-day time and strike, replaced finials, repainted dials, 33", $1,600.00.

S Thomas, Fashion #3, walnut, trn finials, 1, 33", EX 1,600.00
S Thomas, Fashion #6, walnut, 3 finials, 1, rfn, 34" 1,550.00
S Thomas, Office #1, rswd/2 dl, 1/T, wts, 41", EX 1,200.00

Carriage Clocks

Fr, beveled glass, wht porc dl, 1, rpl hands/etc, 6" 100.00
Fr, Bigelow/Kennard dl, 1, beveled glass, 7", EX 350.00
Fr, rope columns/Corinthian capitals, rtcl application, 8" 1,150.00

Fr, wht porc dl, 1, Wanamaker mvt, 6", EX 125.00
H&H Fr, br w/wht enamel face, key, 4⅜" 375.00
Waterbury, Midge, gun-metal color, bevel glass, porc dl, 3½" 60.00

Cottage Clocks

Daniel Pratt & Son, mahog vnr, decal tablet, 11", EX 75.00
H Sperry, grpt, rvpt, sgn zinc dl, 2, rpl pnd, 12" 300.00
Ingraham, rswd vnr, rvpt, paper-on-zinc dl, 2, 13" 160.00
JC Brown, rswd, 1, rfn dl, 15" 400.00
Jerome, rswd vnr, pnt zinc dl, 1/fusee, rfn/rpt, 14" 230.00
New England, Cigar Box, rvpt, pnt zinc dl, 2+alarm, 11", EX 475.00
S Thomas, rswd, mirror, pnt zinc dl, 2/alarm, 9", EX 175.00
SB Terry, zinc dl, 30-hr Time Ladder mvt/alarm/pnd bob, 11" ...650.00
Unmk, walnut, br mts & rpl eagle finial, 1, 1890s, 20" 100.00

Crystal Regulators

Fr, br, bevel glass, porc dl w/florals, mcr pnd, 11" 325.00
Fr, 8 beveled glass panels, mcr pnd, 1, 14", EX 650.00
Germany, Fr, br/bevel glass case, 400-day w/pnd, 11", EX 375.00
Seth Thomas, elliptic front, br w/Corinthian capitals, 9" 350.00
Waterbury, gr onyx top/base, porc dl, 11", NM 385.00
Wm Gilbert, br, bevel glass, porc dl, visible esc, 10", EX 120.00
Wm Gilbert, br/br-plated, bevel glass, porc dl, pnd, 10" 150.00

Novelty

Ansonia, pewter dog by doghouse, bee mvt 55.00
Art Deco Oriental scene, 1920s-30s, NM 155.00
Barbie, wind-up, NM 125.00
Batman, talking, battery-op, 1974, NM 35.00
Germany, birdcage w/rhinestones, on stand 40.00
Germany, owl w/blinking eyes, 2/T w/wt & pnd, 1930s, 8" 195.00
Lux, spinning wheel, alarm, MIB 165.00
Lux, tape measure, EX 25.00
New Haven, cupid in wreath on top, porc dl 95.00
Regent, clock on top of elephant 250.00
Regent, man rides St Bernard w/Victory on his collar 105.00
United, F Roosevelt steers ship, Man of Hour, electric 80.00
United, fireplace, log lights up, electric 17.50
United, Joe Lewis, electric, 12x8", EX 350.00
United, Lincoln/Roosevelt/WA, man steers ship, electric 55.00
United, Will Rogers, animated minutemen, spring wound 35.00
Waterbury, bird in nest over tree house, gr/gold/red pnt 50.00
Waterbury, bird of prey on top of gold metal case, mc dial 40.00
Waterbury, Commerce, copper case w/lady, anvil, plow, wheat 65.00
Waterbury, dog looks out of his house, sunflower atop 70.00

Ogee Clocks

C Jerome, rvpt scene, 2, wts, br works 150.00
E Terry, mahog vnr, EX rvpt, 2, wood dl, 23", EX 200.00
Geo Marsh, rvpt horses & buggies/church/bridge, 2 ....200.00
Hiram Welton, mahog vnr, EX rvpt, 2/Terry's alarm, 20", G 475.00
S Thomas, Plymouth Hollow, rvpt A Jackson, 2, rpl paper, dl 125.00
Waterbury, rswd vnr, floral rvpt, 2, pnt zinc dl, 19", EX 400.00

Pendulette Clocks by Lux or Keebler

Bird's Nest, spread-wing bird on top, #220, 6½x3½" 40.00
Bird's Nest, top bird faces right, #219, 7x5½" 25.00
Bluebird, pressed wood, #300, 6x3½" 75.00

Bobbing Bird, brn wood, no bird on top, #208, 7x4" 40.00
Bobbing Bird, top bird faces left, #328, 7x4½" 25.00
Bobbing Bird, top bird faces right, #211, 7x4" 40.00
Bobbing Bird Dove, plastic, #314, 10x6" 45.00
Bobbing Bird Dove, pressed wood, #314, 10x6" 70.00
Bulldog, 2 kittens on swing, #209, 7x4" 110.00
Cat, moving eyes & tail, #325, 7½x4½" 150.00
Checkered Sides, gr, #210, 5½x2¾" 90.00
Dixie Boy, #304, 1933, EX 775.00
Dog House, scotty dog's head moves, #333, 4½x7" 350.00
Dutch Cottage, 8-day, rare gr roof, #495, lg 65.00
Lovebird, #240, 6x4" 125.00
Petunia, bee swings on pnd bob, gr stem, #322, 7x34" 40.00
Playful Scotty, center scotty's head moves, #355, 4x5¾" 190.00
Reindeer, pressed wood, #302, 1940s, 6x3½" 75.00
Seven Dwarfs, dwarf on pnd swings, #225, 5½x4" 400.00
Swinging Bird, crossed logs, #206, 6x4" 25.00

Regulators

Ansonia, oak, long drop, 1, 31", NM 425.00
Jugans, walnut, 2 urns/eagle/EX trn/3 drops, 1, G orig, 38" 250.00
Kroeber, Vienna #51, 1, porc dl/2nds, 1880s, 44", EX 450.00
S Thomas, rswd vnr, pnt zinc dl w/2nds, 1, rfn dl, 42", NM 1,500.00
S Thomas, rswd vnr, pnt zinc dl w/2nds, 2, re-vnr/rpl, 36" 400.00
Vienna, Howard, reissue of #0010, exact copy, 31", MIB 1,200.00

Regulator by Water-
bury, oak, 8-day time
and strike, EX and orig-
inal, 32", $400.00.

Waltham, oak, 1/T, rpl brd/dial/wt, rfn case, 1900s, 34" 450.00
Waterbury, Schoolhouse, oak, 1, 1900, 32" 400.00

Shelf Clocks

Ansonia, King, walnut, cast decor, 1/NP pnd, 3 finials, 24" 250.00
Atkins, rswd vnr, 2 blk/gold tablets, 1, pnt zinc dl, 17" 350.00
E Downes, mahog w/ornate cvg, scenic rvpt, 2, iron wts, 33" 700.00
E Terry & Sons, pillar/scroll, br finials, 2, rfn, 31" 1,500.00

EN Welch, Cabinet L model, golden oak, 1, rfn, 13" 150.00
EN Welch, Maine, paper dl, 1, rfn case, rpl pnd bob, 24" 750.00
EN Welch, NY, Spanish-Am war commemorative, 1, 25" 400.00
Forestville, Gothic/4-column rswd vnr, cut tablet, 20" 800.00
Fr Empire, ebonized, 4 columns, br ornaments, 1, 27" 850.00
Fr Empire, 4 columns, w/br & inlay, rpl suspension, 26" 750.00
Geo Davis, marble w/malachite panels, 1, 12", VG 125.00
Germany, mahog, silvered dl, 1, 3-train mvt w/chimes, 12" 250.00
Gilbert, Occidental, walnut w/mirror, cast figures, 24", EX 450.00
Ingraham, Dewey, 1, pnt dl (rpl), rfn case, 23" 300.00
Ingraham, Ionic, walnut vnr, rnd w/sq base, rpl mvt, 15" 125.00
Ingraham, McKinley, 1, paper dl, rfn case/dl, 23" 350.00
Ingraham, Nat'l, capitol dome in crest, rpl tablet, rfn, 22" 300.00
Ingraham, Nat'l, wheat sheath/scythe in crest, rpl dl, 22" 300.00
JC Brown, rswd vnr w/pnt decor, rvpt w/Brown, 2, 15", EX 700.00
Jerome, rswd vnr, gutta percha dl surround/ebony trim, 16" 250.00
Ridgeway, mahog w/beveled glass, 3-train mvt w/chimes, 21" 300.00
S Thomas, mahog, gilt dl, 3-train mvt w/chimes, 19", EX 900.00
S Thomas, mahog w/silvered dl, 1, 3-train mvt w/chimes, 14" 275.00
S Thomas, oak vnr, flat top over arch, 1, enamel dl, 1870, 16" 300.00
S Thomas, rswd vnr, rnded top, pnt zinc dl, rpl block, 15" 2.50
S Thomas, rswd vnr w/patriotic rvpt, 2/alarm, 1860, 15" 250.00
Swinger, classical lady supports 8-day mvt, remake, 27" 475.00

Ship Clocks

Chelsea, Bakelite, 1940s, pc out of bk edge, 6½" dia 90.00
Chelsea, br, 1/T w/2nds, 1900, 7" dia, NM 250.00
S Thomas, br, silvered dl, 30-hr lever mvt, 7" dia, EX 225.00
S Thomas, NP br, br dl, 2nds, 2, bell strike, 7", EX 150.00
S Thomas, outside bell, silvered dl, 2nds, 2, 11", EX 350.00
Waterbury, heavy cast bronzed br, jewel lever mvt, 1930, 9" 300.00

Statue Clocks

A Boyer on porc dl, bronze lady ea side, marble base, 15x20" .1,600.00
Angel 16" H atop gr marble base w/4 fancy legs, 26x12" 425.00
China, Fr, couple atop, rococo, 1, thread suspension, 16" 600.00
Diana/Endymion by dl set in stump, bronze/gilt, 27" 3,200.00
Fr, cast/gilt wht metal w/ornate scrolls & man, 15", VG 160.00

Gilt bronze and marble case
with Cupid and Psyche, early
1900s, 20", $1,700.00.

Hammond, Admiral Dewey standing, Maine on bottom 60.00
Lady/2 children by palm tree, gilt bronze, Rococo case, 20" 1,000.00

Riderless stallion surmount, rectangular marble case, 1870s **300.00**
Wagner/Beethoven, Am Works, music box, angels, lady w/harp .**160.00**
Waterbury, cupid on br clock case, paper dl, T & strike **45.00**
Waterbury, cupid on sailing ship, Pat Sept 22, 1883 ....**27.50**

Steeple Clocks

Ansonia, mahog vnr, decor tablet, 1, rpl hands/rpr, 20" **225.00**
Brewster-Ingraham, C Kirk CI bk, 'lyre' gong base, 20", EX **400.00**
Brewster-Ingraham, zebrawood/mahog, 2, rfn, 18" **175.00**
EN Welch, rswd vnr, rvpt floral, zinc dl, 2/alarm, 15", EX **250.00**
Unmk, 2/T, 1880s, rpl hands, 13½" **125.00**
Waterbury, Washington Rock rvpt, 2, 1870s, 20", EX **100.00**

Tall Case Clocks

Abner Rogers, birch, arched hood, 1, br/iron mvt, 91" **2,800.00**
Cherry Empire, bonnet w/4 free-standing columns, trn ft, 95" ..**1,000.00**
Cherry w/flame-grain mahog, Empire, rstr bonnet top, 99" **1,100.00**
Colonial, mahog w/fluted columns, Gothic crest, 1930s, 79" ..**1,100.00**
Daniel Porter, Fed cherry w/inlay, moon dl w/maps, 91", EX ..**9,350.00**
F Wingate Augusta, maple Fed, rpl fretwork, 1, br mvt **7,000.00**
Fr Provincial, floral-pnt case, br mvt, 1850s, 94" **2,000.00**
Frederick Wingate, Fed pnt bird's-eye maple/mahog vnr, 90" .**4,500.00**
G Sunderland, ebonized cvd oak Jacobean style, 1800, 89" **1,000.00**
H Webster, Fed cherry, 2nds/calendar, 1 w/wts, rpt/rstr, 89" ...**2,750.00**
R Whiting, figured maple w/inlay, swan's neck bonnet, 82" **1,600.00**
Rogers & Son, cherry, br mvt, 1, simple case, 89" **2,000.00**
S Hoadley, scroll top w/spires, Masonic dl, ca 1830s **3,850.00**
S Hoadley, wood works, bracket base w/cutouts, red pnt **1,400.00**
W Fritz Porsmouth, cherry inlay, balls/spires in crest, 91" **13,000.00**

Miscellaneous

China, Ansonia, 1, Royal Bonn case, 11", NM **325.00**
China, Bigelow/Kennard, bl w/bronze ft, 1, VG dl, 12" **450.00**
China, Fr, bl w/gilt, lg scrolls form base, 1, 14", EX **350.00**
China, Fr, florals on ivory, 2 (no pnd), VG dl, 10x10" **150.00**
China, Silvani (dl), ornate, 1, thread suspension, 12", EX **450.00**
Crystal ball watch, Swiss, dl mk Tiffany, 2, 3½" **625.00**
Desk, Chelsea, br w/porc dl, 1/lever mvt, 5", VG **125.00**
Desk, S Thomas, brass, eng silvered dl, 1/lever mvt, 6", EX **80.00**
Iron front w/gold/MOP, 1, paper on zinc dl, 1860s, 15" **250.00**
Iron front w/MOP inserts & floral decor, 1, 1870s, rfn, 18" **400.00**
Morbier, LeRoy, emb case, fancy pressed br pnd, rpl, 56" **375.00**
Waterbury, Art Deco wht metal case w/3 lights, 30-hr, 15" **210.00**

Cloisonne

Cloisonne is a method of decorating metal with enameling. Fine metal wires are soldered onto the metal body following the lines of a predetermined design. The resulting channels are filled in with enamels of various colors, and the item is fired. The final step is a smoothing process that assures even exposure of the wire pattern. The art is predominately Oriental and has been practiced continuously, except during war years, since the 16th century. The most excellent examples date from 1865 until the turn of the century. The early 20th century export variety is usually lightweight and the workmanship inferior. Modern wares are of good quality and are produced in Taiwan as well as China.

Several variations of the basic art include plique-a-jour, achieved by removing the metal body after firing, leaving only the transparent enamel work; foil cloisonne, using transparent or semitranslucent enameling over a layer of embossed silver covering the metal body of the vessel; wireless cloisonne, made by removing the wire dividers prior to firing; and cloisonne executed on ceramic, wood, or lacquer rather than metal. Our advisor for this category is Donald Penrose; he is listed in the Directory under Ohio.

Bowl, teal w/plique-a-jour flowers, silver rim, 1900, 8" **2,500.00**
Buddha, bronze w/floral-enamel robes, 23" **2,100.00**
Charger, bird/flowers, mc on turq, yel border, 12" **395.00**
Jar, dragon on cream, 3-ftd, Japan, 1890s, 4½", EX **335.00**
Jar, flowers/butterflies on lt gr, red lid, squat, 4½" dia **350.00**
Jar, wisteria, purple on cobalt, hdls, Japan, 4" **150.00**
Plate, lg crane center, dragonfly/bamboo border, Japan, 12" **300.00**
Plate, mum/butterfly on blk, seashell/birds in border, 12" **300.00**
Plate, peacock in fir tree w/prunus blossoms & peonies, 11" **200.00**
Plate, stylized palmette design border, peonies on bl, 12" **225.00**
Plate, 2 herons fly over mtn lake, Japan, 12" **275.00**
Plate, 2 men practice martial arts by river, Japan, 12" **225.00**
Temple bell, 1700s, 10" **250.00**
Tray, crane scene, pattern border, rectangular, 1850s, 12" **385.00**
Vase, bamboo & bird on red, silver rim & ft, mk, 5", pr **95.00**

Vase, cranes on dark blue, Japanese, 25", $2,300.00.

Vase, dragons & phoenix birds in panels, 1900s, 12" **495.00**
Vase, floral on ivory, silver wire & chrome rim/ft, sgn, 6", pr **125.00**
Vase, irises, bl/purple on yel, Japan, early, 5" **275.00**
Vase, lg rose/thorny stem on peach, sgn Kumeno Taitaro, 5" **275.00**
Vase, mc floral on bl, 11" **225.00**
Vase, plique-a-jour, mums/dahlias on gr, Japan, 5½x5" **450.00**
Vase, roses/palm trees/birds on hammered red, 9½" **225.00**
Vase, samurai & geisha on blk, Japan, 7", pr **350.00**
Vase, trumpet vines on bl-gr, silver cloisons, sgn Tada, 10" **275.00**
Vase, wisteria, wht/bl on lt pk, Japan, 10", pr **400.00**
Vase, 3 lg goldfish/seaweeds on bl, sgn Kumeno Taitaro, 7" **650.00**

Clothing and Accessories

'Second-hand' or 'vintage'? It's all a matter of opinion. But these days it's considered good taste (downright fashionable) to wear clothing from Victorian to styles from the sixties. Jackets with padded shoulders from the thirties are 'trendy.' Jewelry from the Art Deco era is just as beautiful and often less expensive than current copies. But why settle for new when the genuine article can be bought for the same price with exquisite lace that no reproduction can rival! When once the 'style' of the day was so strictly obeyed, today, in New York and the larger cities of California and Texas in particular, nothing well-designed and constructed is 'out of style.' And though costumes by such designers as Chanel, Fortuny, and Lanvin may bring four-figure prices at fine auction houses, as a general rule, prices are very modest considering the wonderful fabrics one may find in vintage clothing, many of which are no longer available. Cashmere coats, elegant furs, and sequined or beaded gowns can be bought for only a small fraction of today's retail. Though some are strictly collectors, many do buy their clothes to wear. Care must be given to alterations, and gentle cleaning methods employed to avoid damage that would detract from their value. Our advisor for this category is Ruth Osborne; she is listed in the Directory under Ohio.

Key:
cap/s — cap sleeves	n/s — no sleeves
embr — embroidery	plt — pleated
hs — hand sewn	s/p — shoulder pads
lgth — length	s/s — short sleeves
l/s — long sleeves	/s — sleeves
ms — machine sewn	

Bathing suit, blk knit, w/matching shoes, Victorian, EX 55.00
Bed jacket, rayon, lace trim, 1940s 15.00
Bloomers, blk, long, 1880s, EX 24.00
Blouse, beaded georgette, beige, l/s, 1920s, EX 45.00
Blouse, blk satin, l/s, ca 1900, EX 45.00
Blouse, gauze, blk w/wht accent trim, l/s, 1880s, EX 35.00
Blouse, navy satin shirtwaist w/beads & lace, EX 35.00
Blouse, openwork eyelet (lined), peplum style, s/s, 1880s 50.00
Bonnet, child's, calico, 1890s, EX 25.00
Bonnet, child's, orig rose trim, Civil War era, EX 65.00
Bush jacket, wht cotton twill, bellows pockets, 1940s, M 20.00
Camisole, lace inserts, EX 25.00
Cape, bl feathers, long, 1920s, EX 250.00
Cape, bl feathers, short, 1920s, EX 65.00
Cape, blk w/velvet & beaded collar, 1890s, EX 75.00
Cape, jet blk, JL White San Francisco, 1880s, EX 185.00
Cape, paisley w/gathered collar, full lgth, 1875, EX 175.00
Chemise, plts, lace panels, ms, EX details, 28" 32.50

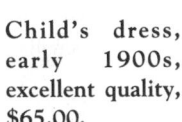
Child's dress, early 1900s, excellent quality, $65.00.

Coat, baby's, corduroy, shawl at top, 32", EX 45.00
Coat, blk silk/mc brocade, fur collar, velvet lined, 1920s 110.00
Coat, child's, brn wool w/squirrel collar, EX 45.00
Coat, evening; blk velvet, 1930s 95.00
Coat, man's top coat, blk cashmere, 1940s, EX 90.00
Coat, morning; blk wool, single-breasted, soutache trim, EX 40.00
Coat, satin, beaded/tassels, lined, long, 1880s, EX 175.00
Coat, turq velvet, silk lining, 1930s, EX 135.00
Dress, baby's, voile w/much lace, wide lace collar, EX 22.50
Dress, batiste, high neck, many lace inserts, embr, 1900s 95.00
Dress, bl/blk stripes, smocked, l/s, draped bustle, EX 235.00
Dress, blk & pk calico, l/s, 1880s, VG 50.00
Dress, blk brocade, lace & pleats, l/s, 1800s, 2-pc, EX 75.00
Dress, blk crepe, gored skirt, s/s, 1940s, EX 25.00
Dress, chintz, rhinestone trim, s/s, 1950s, M 30.00
Dress, christening; embr/cutwork, lace inserts, long, EX 75.00
Dress, christening; wht cotton w/lace & inserts, long, EX 75.00
Dress, cocktail; blk wool, 1-shoulder, Christian Dior, EX 65.00
Dress, cocktail; brn silk taffeta, Valerie Sologne, EX 75.00
Dress, cotton print, lace trim, l/s, 1920s, 2-pc, EX 40.00
Dress, evening; beaded/sequined blk flapper style, 1920s 250.00
Dress, evening; blk chiffon & satin, mc beads & jets, EX 125.00
Dress, evening; blk French lace tent style w/beige slip, EX 50.00
Dress, evening; blk net w/blk jets & sequins, flapper style 250.00
Dress, evening; blk velvet, gold stripe flared skirt, 1950s 37.50
Dress, evening; brn georgette w/sequins & bugle beads, s/s, EX 250.00
Dress, evening; chiffon, l/s underblouse, lace trim, 1880s, EX 200.00
Dress, evening; chiffon w/beads, n/s, flapper style, +slip 195.00
Dress, evening; embr flowers on pk silk bustier/jacket, EX 65.00
Dress, evening; floral beaded strap, Roman drape style, EX 60.00
Dress, evening; gr chiffon over satin, full skirt, s/s, EX 55.00
Dress, evening; gray silk w/cut steel beads, s/s, 1920s, EX 65.00
Dress, evening; navy w/many rhinestones, velvet collar, EX 50.00
Dress, evening; net over satin, tiered flapper style, 1920s 100.00
Dress, evening; orange georgette, beaded flapper style, EX 300.00
Dress, evening; pk w/gold threadwork, s/s, 1950s, EX 40.00
Dress, evening; red taffeta, strapless, short, NM 40.00
Dress, evening; silk velvet, bias/V-neck, bat/s, 1930s, EX 45.00
Dress, evening; silk w/lace/beads, dropped full/s, 1900s 200.00
Dress, evening; wht net w/bl bugle beads, embr lace, s/s, EX 95.00
Dress, evening; wht satin, Jean Harlow style, 1935, EX 90.00
Dress, ivory linen, net top, rhinestone trim, s/s, EX 32.50
Dress, organdy print, Civil War era, EX detail, VG 250.00
Dress, organdy w/embr bodice & skirt, net insert, l/s, 1900 ....75.00
Dress, plt, l/s, bustle, ca 1880s, EX 225.00
Dress, tea; plt silk, n/s, Venetian glass buttons, Fortuny 1,350.00
Dress, wedding; ecru net w/much embr, 1930s, EX 150.00
Dress, wedding; Fr silk Edwardian style, lace/tucks, 1900s 275.00
Dress, wedding; satin w/lace, seed pearls, long train, '50s, NM 500.00
Dress, wedding; silk, much lace/tucks, Fr, 1900s, 2-pc 275.00
Dress, wedding; wht lawn, l/s, full skirt, cotton slip, 1900s 215.00
Dress, wht batiste w/lace inserts, l/s, 1900s, EX 150.00
Dress, wht lawn w/embr bodice/skirt, sailor collar, 1900s 150.00
Dress, wht w/Fr lace inserts, tucks w/embr, Victorian, EX 135.00
Fur cape, maribou & ostrich leather, 1890s, +matching muff 145.00
Fur coat, blk moutton, full lgth, 1930s, EX 125.00
Fur coat, blk seal w/wide brn mink collar, 42", EX 275.00
Fur coat, brn mink, wide shawl collar to hem, cuffs, EX 950.00
Fur coat, Persian lamb, blk w/brn mink collar, 36", EX 265.00
Fur coat, Persian lamb, silk lining, designer label, EX 165.00
Fur coat, raccoon, long, EX 400.00
Fur coat, red fox, long, Victorian, EX 350.00
Fur hat, brn beaver, cloche style, EX 25.00
Fur hat, leopard, lady's pillbox, EX 150.00

Fur jacket, blk rabbit, wide collar, slash pockets, M 200.00
Fur jacket, coyote, EX 400.00
Fur jacket, sheared raccoon, 26", EX 75.00
Fur muff, fake leopard, 1940s, EX 25.00
Fur stole, brn striped mink, narrow shoulder style, 18" 35.00
Fur top hat, man's, beaver, 1870s, EX 85.00

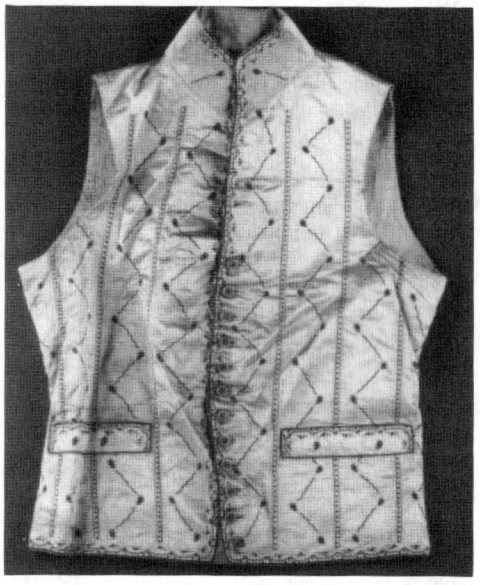

Gentleman's dress waistcoat, silk and metallic threads on silk with spangles, 1790s, VG, $600.00.

Hat, lady's, blk velvet, ca 1915, EX 27.50
Hat, lady's, Juliet style w/rhinestones & sequins, EX 30.00
Hat, lady's, red velvet, satin & braid trim, flapper style 35.00
Hat, lady's, velvet w/feathers, flapper style, 1920s, EX 75.00
Hat, lady's, wine velvet w/fuchsia feathers, EX 40.00
Hat, lady's riding; straw, rpl ribbon, ca 1760s, EX 135.00
Hat, man's, Panama style, 1930s, MIB 65.00
Hat, man's, straw, wht & gray, NM band, 1950s 30.00
Jacket, bl velvet, details on l/s, 1880s, EX 150.00
Jacket, blk wool w/blk beads, l/s, EX 35.00
Jacket, smoking; gray & blk plaid taffeta w/bronze lining, EX 65.00
Jacket, velvet w/jet beads, s/s, 1900s 115.00
Jeans, denim Levis, bell-bottom legs, 1970s, M 30.00
Jumpsuit, fuchsia satin w/mc beads, strapless, EX 50.00
Knickers, lady's, cotton tweed, +s/s jacket, 1920s, EX 35.00
Knickers, wht linen, for golfing, EX 35.00
Long underwear, Basset-Walker, NM 12.50
Mittens, bl/wht homespun, early 95.00
Nightgown, crochet trim, ca 1900, EX 75.00
Nightgown, homespun linen, 1840s, EX 145.00
Nightgown, peach, rayon, bias cut, long 40.00
Nightgown, peach satin, floral embr, knee length 25.00
Parasol, blk w/long blk fringe, cvd wood folding hdl 35.00
Petticoat, blk sateen, tucked flounce, long, M 45.00
Petticoat, ecru & wht, ms w/smocking & lace, 38" 45.00
Petticoat, quilted, changeable taffeta, 1850s, EX 75.00
Petticoat, wht cotton w/much lace & embr, EX 35.00
Robe, baby's, dimity w/lace trim, long, ca 1900 ....24.00
Serape, mc woven wool, Southwestern, '20s, 58x88"+fringe, NM .110.00
Shawl, blk crepe w/orange floral embr, 62x62", NM 250.00
Shawl, Merino wool, long fringe, 1870s, 60x72", EX 150.00
Shawl, rose/pk silk w/lt rose/lav fringe, Deco, 67x71" 65.00
Shawl, wht silk w/leaf pattern, long fringe, NM 50.00
Shawl, wool challis, paisley border, 1870s, 64x61"+fringe 225.00
Shirt, man's, brn silk, collarless, ca 1880, EX 35.00

Shoes, baby's, blk leather, 4-botton, EX, pr 65.00
Shoes, child's, blk oxfords, Red Goose, EX, pr 27.50
Shoes, child's, blk oxfords, Scaperoos, pr 35.00
Shoes, child's, blk pumps, Poll Parrot, EX 18.00
Shoes, child's, blk T-straps, Lady Frances, pr 32.00
Shoes, lady's, blk rubber boots, Chatham, pr 16.50
Shoes, lady's, grey suede pumps, Charm Step, NM, pr 27.50
Shoes, lady's, high-top, blk, ca 1900, pr 75.00
Shoes, lady's, high-top, brn suede, ca 1900, EX, pr 75.00
Shoes, lady's, high-top, wht kid, Fr heel, M, pr 85.00
Shoes, lady's, red patent leather, velvet bows, 1940s, EX, pr 28.00
Shoes, lady's, red pumps, 1940s, pr 32.50
Shoes, man's, brn, spectator toes, pr 55.00
Shoes, man's, spats, EX, pr 15.00
Shorts, man's, cotton, drawstring style, 1940s, EX 18.00
Skirt, bl w/front lace, long train, ca 1880s, EX 75.00
Skirt, blk, long, ca 1880s, EX 50.00
Skirt, blk silk shantung petal w/'U' bk, EX 70.00
Skirt, circle; appl poodle & embr, 1950s, NM 25.00
Skirt, circle; Pendleton, red wool, 1950s, EX 22.50
Skirt, circle; 3 appl poodles w/rhinestone eyes, 1950s, EX 55.00
Skirt, gr satin, quilted lining, lace trim, 1880s, EX 55.00
Skirt, wht w/Fr lace inserts, Victorian, EX 60.00
Slip, blk silk, bone bodice, Victorian 95.00
Slip, peach rayon, NM 10.00
Slip, wht cotton w/scalloped trim, ca 1900, EX 45.00
Stockings, Amish, hand knit, blk, 1920s, 14", pr 75.00
Stockings, child's, blk, Yorktown Hosiery, NM, pr 7.50
Stockings, lady's, brn cotton, Anna, NM, pr 6.50
Stockings, lady's, brn silk & cotton, Paramount, NM, pr 7.50
Suit, boy's, Lord Fauntleroy, velvet w/silk shirt 70.00
Suit, lady's traveling; satin, button-up, l/s jacket, 1870s 250.00
Suit, man's, dbl-breasted, 1900s, 3-pc, EX 95.00
Suit, man's, rayon, pleated/cuffed trousers, 1950s, EX 30.00
Sunsuit, child's, cotton, 1930s, EX 10.00
Sweater, wht wool, heavily beaded yoke & sleeves, NM 45.00
Teddy, champagne silk & georgette w/lace, EX 35.00
Teddy, rayon, lacy trim, EX 40.00
Tunic, blk georgette w/mc sequins & bugle beads, EX 225.00
Tuxedo, blk silk w/satin details, +dress shirt, EX 85.00
Tuxedo, blk wool, onyx studs, w/vest, 1930s, EX 45.00
Vest, silk, draped bottom, beaded, 1920s, EX 35.00
Waist, blk silk, quilted, 1940s, EX 32.00
Waist, voile, lace/embr collar & cuffs, l/s, EX 35.00

Cluthra

The name Cluthra is derived from the Scottish word 'clutha,' meaning cloudy. Glassware by this name was first produced by J. Couper and Sons, England. Frederick Carder developed Cluthra while at the Steuben Glass Works, and similar types of glassware were also made by Durand and Kimball. It is found in both solid and shaded colors and is characterized by a spotty appearance resulting from small air pockets trapped between its two layers. See also Steuben.

Chalice, gr/wht, sgn Stanhope, 10½" 165.00
Finger bowl, pk, hexagonal, +underplate 500.00
Vase, mauve/wht, classic form, #K-1710-4-Dec-100, 4½" 300.00
Vase, orange/gray, polished pontil, Kimball, #1910-6, 7x5" 625.00
Vase, pk/gray/wht, sgn Kimball, 6x3½" 295.00
Vase, rose/pk/clear, flared cylinder, 14½" 400.00
Vase, wht, sgn K for Kimball/#1968-6, 6" 200.00
Vase, yel, wht int, bulbous, sgn Kimball, 7" 250.00

Coalport

In 1745 in Caughley, England, Squire Brown began a modest business fashioning crude pots and jugs from clay mined in his own fields. Tom Turner, a young potter who had apprenticed his trade at Worcester, was hired in 1772 to plan and oversee the construction of a 'proper' factory. Three years later he bought the business, which he named Caughley Coalport Porcelain Manufactory. Though the dinnerware he produced was meant to be only everyday china, the hand-painted florals, birds, and landscapes used to decorate the ware were done in exquisite detail and in a wide range of colors. In 1780 Turner introduced the Willow pattern which he produced using a newly perfected method of transfer printing. (Wares from the period between 1775 and 1799 are termed 'Caughley' or 'Salopian'; see section on Caughley.) John Rose purchased the Caughley factory from Thomas Turner in 1799, adding that holding to his own pottery which he had built two years before in Coalport. (It is from this point in the pottery's history that the wares are termed 'Coalport.') The porcelain produced there before 1814 was unmarked with very few exceptions. After 1820 some examples were marked with a '2' with an oversize top loop. The term 'Coalbrookdale' refers to a fine type of porcelain decorated in floral bas relief, similar to the work of Dresden.

After 1835 highly decorated ware with rich ground colors imitated the work of Sevres and Chelsea, even going so far as to copy their marks. From about 1895 until the 1920s, the mark in use was 'Coalport' over a crown with 'England, A.D. 1750' indicating the date claimed as the founding, not the date of manufacture. From the 1920s until 1945, 'Made in England' over a crown and 'Coalport' below was used. Later, the mark was 'Coalport' over a smaller crown with 'Made in England' in a curve below. In 1926 the Coalport Company moved to Shelton in Staffordshire and today belongs to a group headed by the Wedgwood Company. See also Indian Tree.

Fruit cooler, 'Warwick Vase' form, applied grapevines, hand-painted flowers and fruit, gilt trim, ca 1825, 12½", $1,000.00.

Cup & saucer, allover gold decor on yel, miniature 100.00
Dish, Japan-style vase/flowers, shell shape w/hdl, 1815, 9" 125.00
Figurine, Bridesmaid, bl crinoline dress, 20th C, 8" 75.00
Plate, Banks of Dee, musical symbols, 1820s, 8" 200.00

Plate, floral reserve center on lt bl w/emb gold, 1900, 10½" 45.00
Teapot, flowers on 'marble,' dog spout, bird hdl, rpr, 8" 150.00
Teapot, Willow Ware, fluted/rectangular, CB Dale mk, 10" W ..185.00
Vase, ovals w/flowers on apple gr, scroll hdls, 14", pr 450.00
Vase, shaped floral reserves, ftd gourd form w/lid, 12", pr 600.00
Vase, turq/wht beads & gilt on pk, gold scroll hdls, 7½" 700.00

Cobalt Glass

Cobalt glass is characterized by its deep transparent blue color obtained by mixing cobalt oxide and alumina to the batch. It may be found in free-blown, mold-blown, and pressed glassware. See also Blown Glass.

Bottle, scent; cut decor, Germany, 6" 125.00
Bowl, HP florals, bird perched in center, gold trim, 9x10¼" 350.00
Champagne, fancy crystal stem 22.00
Jigger, 7 panels & 7 arches, 2½" 55.00
Lightning rod ornament, silvered int, teardrop shape, 5" 35.00
Match striker, mother cat & kitten, mk, 3¾x3¾" 100.00
Pitcher, gold panels & enameled scrolls, 2x1½" 55.00
Salt cellar, blown, wide ft, 2¼x2¾" 200.00
Tumble-up, floral etched through o/l, 7½" 70.00
Tumbler, blown, 3⅝" 37.50
Vase, HP floral, ruffled rim, 5" 38.00
Vase, HP florals w/gold, 4-ftd, flattened oval, 3¼" 88.00
Vase, 2 dbl spiral bands, ruffled/flared mouth, 9½x5½" 95.00

Coca-Cola

J.S. Pemberton, creator of Coca-Cola, originated his world-famous drink in 1886. From its inception the Coca-Cola Company began an incredible advertising campaign which has proven to be one of the most successful promotions in history. The quantity and diversity of advertising material put out by Coca-Cola in the last one hundred years is literally mind-boggling. From the beginning, the company has projected an image of wholesomeness and Americana. Beautiful women in Victorian costumes, teenagers and schoolchildren, blue- and white-collar workers, the men and women of the Armed Forces (even Santa Claus) have appeared in advertisements with a Coke in their hands. Some of the earliest collectibles include trays, syrup dispensers, gum jars, pocket mirrors, and calendars. Many of these items fetch prices in the thousands of dollars. Later examples include radios, signs, lighters, thermometers, playing cards, clocks, and toys — particularly toy trucks.

In 1970 the Coca-Cola Company initialed a multimillion-dollar 'image-refurbishing campaign,' which introduced the new 'Dynamic Countour' logo, a twisting white ribbon under the Coca-Cola and Coke trademarks. The new logo often serves as a cut-off point to the purist collector. Newer and very ardent collectors, however, relish the myriad of items marketed since that date, as they often cannot afford the high prices that the vintage pieces command. For more information we recommend *Petretti's Coca-Cola Collectibles Price Guide*; you may order a copy from Nostalgia Publications, Inc., whose address is listed in under Auction Houses in the Directory.

Note: Trays must be in excellent or better condition to warrant prices listed. Our advisor for this category is Gael deCourtivron; he is listed in the directory under Florida. For further information call the Cocaholics Hotline: 813-355-COLA.

Key: tm — trademark

Reproductions and Fantasies

Beware of reproductions! Prices are given for the genuine original articles, but the symbol (+) at the end of some of the following lines indicate items that have been reproduced. Watch for frauds: genuinely old celluloid items ranging from combs, mirrors, knives and forks to doorknobs that have been recently etched with a new double-lined trademark. Still another area of concern deals with reproduction and fantasy items. A fantasy item is a novelty made to appear authentic with inscriptions such as 'Tiffany Studios,' 'Trans Pan Expo,' 'World's Fair,' etc. In reality, these items never existed as originals. For instance, don't be fooled by a Coca-Cola cash register; no originals are known to exist! Large mirrors for bars are being reproduced and are often selling for $10.00 to $50.00.

Of the hundreds of reproductions (designated 'R' in the following examples) and fantasies (designated 'F') on the market today, these are the most deceiving.

Belt buckle, no originals thought to exist (F), up to 5.00
Bottle, dk amber, w/arrows, heavy, narrow spout (R) 10.00
Bottle carrier, wood, yel w/red logo, holds 6 bottles (R) 10.00
Clock, mantel; brass, battery-op, Ridgway Anniv, '80, 6x9" (R) .100.00
Clock, 1981, Ridgway, dome, electric (R) 100.00
Cooler, Glascock Jr, made by Coca-Cola USA (R) 200.00
Doorknob, glass w/etched tm (F) 3.00
Knife, bottle shape, 1970s, many variations, (F) 5.00
Knife, fork, or spoon w/celluloid hdl, newly etched tm (F) 5.00
Knife, pocket; yel & red, 1933 World's Fair (F) 2.00
Letter opener, stamped metal, Coca-Cola 5¢ (F) 3.00
Sign, cb, lady w/fur, dtd 1911, 9x11" (F) 3.00
Soda fountain glass holder, word 'Drink' not on orig (R) 5.00
Thermometer, bottle figural, DONASCO, 17" (R) 5.00
Trade card, copy of 1905 'Bathtub' foldout, emb 1978 (R) 3.00
Vanity pc (mirror/brush/etc), celluloid, newly etched tm (F) 5.00
Watch, pocket; often old watch w/new face (R) 10.00

The following items have also been reproduced and are among the most deceptive of all:

Pocket mirrors from 1905, 1906, 1908, 1909, 1910, 1911, 1916, and 1920.
Trays from 1899, 1910, 1913, 1914, 1917, 1920, 1923, 1925, 1926, 1934, and 1937.
Tip trays from 1907, 1909, 1910, 1913, 1914, 1917, and 1920.
Knives: many versions of the German brass model.
Cartons: wood versions, yellow with logo.

These items are currently being marketed:
    Brass button, Taiwan, 18", (R)
    Brass thermometer, bottle shape, Taiwan, 24"
    Cast iron toys (none ever made)
    Cast iron door pull, bottle shape, made to look old
    Poster, Yes Girl (R)
    Button sign, has 1 round hole while original has 4 slots, most have
        bottle logo, 12", 16", 20" (R)
    Bullet trash receptacles (old cans with decals)
    Paperweight, rectangular, with Pepsin Gum insert
    1949 cooler radio (new)
    Straw holders (no originals exist)
    Countless trays — most unauthorized (must read 'American Art
        works; Coshocton, OH.')

Centennial Items

1986 was the year for the Coca-Cola Company to celebrate her 100th birthday; and amidst all the fanfare came many new collectible items, all sporting the 100th anniversary logo. These items are destined to

become an important part of the total Coca-Cola Collectible spectrum. The following pieces are among the most popular centennial items.

Bottle, gold dipped, in velvet sleeve, 6½-oz 50.00
Bottle, Hutch, amber, Root Co, ½-oz, 3 in case 175.00
Bottle, International, set of 9 in plexiglas case 250.00
Bottle, leaded crystal, 100th logo, 6½-oz, MIB 110.00
Medallion, bronze, w/box, 3" dia 50.00
Pin set, wood fr, 101 pins 300.00
Scarf, silk, 30x30" 35.00
Thermometer, glass cover, 14" dia, M 22.00

Coca-Cola Originals

Art plate, 1908-12, topless lady, Western CC, w/fr, 10" dia 850.00
Ashtray, 1950s, ceramic, w/bottle lighter, NM 85.00
Ashtray, 1950s, ruby glass, card suit shapes, 4 in box 325.00
Bank, 1950s, tin, vending machine form, 4", NM 100.00
Bank, 1960s, tin, can form, EX 6.00
Blotter, 1935, A Home Run, 8x3½", NM 40.00
Booklet, 1951, Easy Hospitality, NM 5.00
Bookmark, 1904, Hilda Clark, fading, 6x2", VG 200.00
Bookmark, 1904, Hilda Clark, 6x2", NM 485.00

Bottle carrier, aluminum, 1951, 7x8", $25.00.

Bottle, amber, Huntsville, str sides, EX 45.00
Bottle, display; 1923, w/cap, NM 350.00
Bottle, display; 1953, soft plastic, 2 halves, w/cap, 20", NM 525.00
Bottle, seltzer; Billings MT, EX 200.00
Bottle, seltzer; bl, M 90.00
Bottle, seltzer; Mt Lassen, red label, unmk top, NM 125.00
Bottle, str sides, Indiana PA, lt amber, NM 40.00
Bottle, syrup; 1900s, glass label, NM 450.00
Bottle, syrup; 1920s, clear, NM 325.00
Bottle, 1951, for toy cooler, 3½", M 15.00
Bottle, 1974, 75th Anniversary, Chattanooga, NM 10.00
Bottle protector, 1942, paper, So Easy To Serve, M 2.00
Calendar, 1905, Lillian Nordica, full pad, 15¼x7¼", EX 3,000.00
Calendar, 1915, Elaine w/glass, full pad, NM 1,800.00
Calendar, 1918, June Caprice, full pad, 9x5", EX 250.00
Calendar, 1919, Marion Davis w/glass, EX 1,000.00

Calendar, 1925, girl w/fur, NM 500.00
Calendar, 1928, girl in gold dress & fur stole, EX 500.00
Calendar, 1933, Rockwell Village Blacksmith, 34x19", EX 375.00
Calendar, 1934, Rockwell Southern couple, 25x12", NM 350.00
Calendar, 1938, lady in wht w/bottle, EX 175.00
Calendar, 1939, brunette w/bottle, full pad, fr, EX 300.00
Calendar, 1949, lady in billed cap, complete, 22x13", EX 135.00
Calendar, 1972, cloth, lady w/fan, M 10.00
Calendar holder, 1976, tin, 9x12", EX 45.00
Calendar top, 1921, lady w/glass, fr, 27x11", EX 450.00
Calendar top, 1927, lady w/glass, matted in fr, EX 245.00
Calendar top, 1929, flapper w/glass, fr, 20x13", EX 350.00
Cap, soda jerk; 1920s, cloth, NM 16.00
Carafe & 4 etched glasses, new, M 40.00
Carrier, 1930s, cb, Good Houskeeping seal, 13x7", NM 65.00
Carrier, 1930s, cb, 6-bottle, EX 30.00
Carrier, 1939, cb, red/wht, Pet, 7½", NM 40.00
Carrier, 1940s, wood, red/wht, For the Home, 6-bottle, EX 40.00
Carrier, 1950s, metal, 6-bottle, wire hdl w/wood grip, EX 35.00
Case, shipping; 1918, wood, 48-bottle, EX 125.00
Chair, 1960, emb metal (beware of decals), folding, M 125.00
Change receiver, 1907, glass, 8" dia, EX 750.00
Clock, desk; 1910, leather case, bottle form, 8x3", EX 750.00
Clock, desk; 1980s, wooden, 4½x5", M 35.00
Clock, schoolhouse; pendulum, new, 41", M 125.00
Clock, 1896-1899, Baird, 15-day movement, NM 5,000.00
Clock, 1940s, maroon/red, 18", EX 125.00
Clock, 1942, neon w/metal fr, bottle, 16" sq, M (+) 650.00
Clock, 1950s, in glass dome, 9x6", NM 625.00
Clock, 1950s, metal/glass, fishtail, Pam, 15" sq, NM 125.00
Clock, 1950s, metal/glass, lights up, gr/wht/red, 15" dia, NM 350.00
Clock, 1950s, silver/red (variation of 1940s model), 18", EX 125.00
Clock, 1959, brass, fishtail, light-up, 12" dia, NM 175.00
Clock, 1980, Sessions, new issue, NM 300.00
Coaster, 1950s, aluminum, EX 3.50
Coin purse, 1910, leather w/hinged fr, VG 55.00
Coin-op machine, CC Shooting Gallery, floor model, '85, EX ..1,250.00
Coin-op machine, CC Shooting Gallery, Frantx Mfg, '86, EX .1,250.00
Cooler, 1939, salesman's sample, NM 2,600.00
Cuff links, 1950s, sterling, pr 65.00
Dictionary, 1925, Webster's Little Gem, EX 35.00
Diecut, 1908, cb, cherub w/tray, easel bk, 14¾", NM 2,300.00
Diecut, 1950s, metal, 6-pack, red/wht/brn, 11½x12", NM 425.00
Diecut, 1963, cb, Jennifer O'Neil, For Extra..., life sz, NM 175.00
Dispenser, 1940s, 22x15", EX 300.00
Dispenser, 1950s, metal, CC/Lyon's Root Beer, 15x11x14", EX .400.00
Fan, 1911, cb, Oriental lady in garden, EX 125.00
Handkerchief, 1953, Kit Carson, 22x20", NM 60.00
Holder, car window; 1940s, cb, NM 30.00
Kite, 1930s, paper, American Flyer, EX 250.00
Knife, switchblade; 1930s, Remington, lt wear, EX 200.00
Knife, 1910, Try a Bottle, EX 175.00
Lamp, bottle form, pnt milk glass, 20", EX 3,300.00
Lighter, 1960s, can form w/dmn, EX 12.00
Map, 1940s, heavy paper, sent to schools, 30x36", M 40.00
Match striker, 1938-39, porc, Canadian, 4x4", EX 225.00
Match striker, 1938-39, porc, Canadian, 4x4", VG 100.00
Matchbook holder, 1907, brn cover, M 185.00
Menu, 1903, Hilda Clark, 6⅛x4⅛", NM 500.00
Mirror, 1977, Candler/Pemberton, ltd ed, 36x26", M 300.00
Music box, 1950s, cooler form, EX orig 150.00
Necktie, 1950, Sprite Boy, NM 65.00
Needle case, 1924, cb, mc, 2x3", NM 60.00
Opener, 1900-20, CI, block print, NM 85.00

Opener, 1920s-30s, saber form, EX 100.00
Opener, 1930s, skate key, EX 30.00
Opener/ice pick, 1940s, wood hdl, EX (+) 10.00
Pen, 1950s, red, M 25.00
Pencil holder, china, 75th anniversary (of NY), 7", M 100.00
Pencil holder, 1960s, bsk, wht/red, 7½x4", EX 225.00
Pencil sharpener, 1950s, rectangular, EX 3.00
Plaque, 1984, Sprite Boy, Springtime in Atlanta, 8x8", M 25.00
Plate, sandwich; 1930, bottle & glass, EM Knowles, 7¼" 225.00
Plate, 1980, Senior Bowl, smoked glass, oval, 8½", EX 20.00
Playing cards, 1928, lady w/bottle & straw on gr, MIB 325.00
Playing cards, 1943, Army Nurse, complete, +box 75.00
Playing cards, 1958, Welcome Friend, ice man, complete, +box ..65.00
Playing cards, 1963, Things Go Better, tree planting, MIB 30.00
Pocket mirror, 1908, celluloid, lady w/glass, 1¾x2¾", EX 650.00
Pocket mirror, 1910, H King, JB Caroll, oval, NM (+) 225.00
Pocket mirror, 1911, H King, Whitehead-Hoag, oval, NM (+) ..225.00
Pocket mirror, 1916, Elaine, Whitehead-Hoag, NM (+) 275.00
Postcard, 1902, bottling plant photo, EX 65.00
Postcard, 1910, folding type, EX 250.00
Postcard, 1911, duster girl, 5½x3½", NM 500.00
Poster, 1940s, cb, Entertain Your Thirst, fr, 36x20", M 425.00
Push bar, 1950s, porc, red/yel/wht, 31½x3", NM 150.00
Radio, 1930s, Crosley, bottle figural, 30", NM 2,500.00
Radio, 1950s, cooler form, plastic crystal type, complete, EX 225.00
Radio, 1963, vending machine form, 7½x3½", NM 100.00
Radio, 1970s, can figural, NM 15.00
Score pad, 1940s, full color, 7½x4", NM 9.00
Score pad, 1940s, girl w/bottle, EX 4.00

**Sign, cardboard, in original Coca-Cola frame, 27x56",
$525.00.**

Sign, 1907, self-fr tin, Relieves Fatigue, 27x18½", EX (+) 5,000.00
Sign, 1910, paper, Gibson girl, 30x20", NM 3,200.00
Sign, 1914, tin, Betty, 41x31", EX 3,500.00
Sign, 1923, porc, bottle, yel or gray, 18" dia, EX 175.00
Sign, 1926, girl holds forth bottle, 8½x11", NM 1,000.00
Sign, 1927, tin, 2-sided arrow, 7¾x30", EX 475.00
Sign, 1930s, flange, bottle, Ice Cold, 18x20", EX 250.00
Sign, 1931, cb, Tingling..., girl w/glass, 20x36", VG 280.00
Sign, 1932, cb, 3-D hotdog, 10x20", M 250.00
Sign, 1932, glass, stand-up fan style, 24", M 2,000.00
Sign, 1936, cb, Chinese girl on bench, 14½x22", NM 650.00
Sign, 1936, tin, 5¢ Ice Cold, 19x54", NM 375.00
Sign, 1940s, plywood, arrow on triangle, 23x28", NM 600.00
Sign, 1940s, porc wraparound, red/wht, 16x43", M 195.00
Sign, 1940s, tin, Betty w/bottle, 4-color, 20x28", NM 425.00
Sign, 1941, wood & masonite, silhouette girl, 14x36", EX 250.00
Sign, 1942, cb, service girl, fr, 16x27", EX 525.00
Sign, 1943, cb case insert, Eddie Fisher, 12x20", NM 150.00
Sign, 1944, cb, cheerleader, gold fr, 16x27", NM 525.00

Sign, 1946, cb, skater girl, Right Off the Ice, 27x16", NM 225.00
Sign, 1947, cb, nurse w/tray, gold fr, 16x27", NM 525.00
Sign, 1947, porc, Sold Here Ice Cold, 12x29", VG 150.00
Sign, 1947, tin, bottle, wood fr, 36x18", VG 250.00
Sign, 1949, cb, Serve Coke at Home, fr, 16x27", EX 325.00
Sign, 1950, cb, girl by refrigerator, fr, 16x27", VG 240.00
Sign, 1950, glass & plastic, Please Pay Cashier, 12x20", NM 500.00
Sign, 1950s, cb, girl w/bottle, Enjoy Food, 12x15", NM 175.00
Sign, 1950s, cb, Home Refreshment, 20x36", EX 275.00
Sign, 1950s, celluloid, bottle, 9" dia, NM 125.00
Sign, 1950s, plastic, Sno-ee Frozen Drink, 18x18", EX 40.00
Sign, 1950s, tin, bottle, 72", NM 325.00
Sign, 1954, cb, So Delicious, 20x36", EX 225.00
Sign, 1959, tin, Enjoy King Size, fishtail, 20x28", NM 145.00
Sign, 1960, glass front, light-up, starburst, NM 325.00
Sign, 1963, tin, fishtail, 22x28", NM 100.00
Sign, 1975, cb, After the Theater..., 24x18", M 20.00
Sign, 1985, celluloid, gr/red/wht/blk, 4½x9", NM 15.00
Telephone, bottle form, M 15.00
Telephone, Olympic Cube, NM 35.00
Thermometer, 1905, wood, lt wear, 15x4", EX 250.00
Thermometer, 1915, wood, not faded, 21x5", EX 275.00
Thermometer, 1930s, tin, bottle form, 1923 tm/Pat '27, 17", NM ..225.00
Thermometer, 1936, tin, gold bottle in red oval, 16x7", EX 100.00
Thermometer, 1939, porc, silhouette girl, 18", EX 325.00
Thermometer, 1939, tin, silhouette girl, 16x6½", EX 100.00
Thermometer, 1941, tin, twin bottles, 16x7", EX 150.00
Thermometer, 1944, masonite, 17x7", NM 190.00
Thermometer, 1950s, glass front, gold bottle on gr, 12" dia, NM ..245.00
Thermometer, 1950s, glass front, Sign of Good..., 12" dia, EX ...100.00
Thermometer, 1950s, tin, bottle shape, 16x5", NM 75.00
Thermometer, 1950s, tin, button at top, 9x3", NM 90.00
Thermometer, 1955, tin, flat, 16", EX 90.00
Thermometer, 1956, gold bottle, 7½x2¼", NM 20.00
Thermometer, 1960s, glass front, Enjoy..., 12", NM 100.00
Thermometer, 1970s, plastic, 5" sq, NM 10.00
Tip tray, 1900, Hilda Clark, 6" dia, EX 2,000.00
Tip tray, 1903, Hilda Clark, 4", EX 950.00
Tip tray, 1907, Relieves Fatigue, 4½x6", EX 425.00
Tip tray, 1914, Betty, oval, 4½x6", NM 275.00
Tip tray, 1916, Elaine w/Coke, 8½x19", NM 250.00
Tongs, ice; 1920s, 3-digit phone number, NM 275.00
Toy car, 1960s, tin friction, Ford Sedan, Japan, EX 125.00
Toy car, 1960s, tin friction, Ford Sedan, Japan, MIB 250.00
Toy robot, can form, transformer, Japan, 5", M 95.00
Toy stove, 1930s, electric, NM 2,000.00
Toy train, 1950, tin wind-up, 6-pc, 14", EX 350.00
Toy truck, 1928, Metalcraft, metal wheels, 11", complete, NM .525.00
Toy truck, 1940s, Marx, Sprite Boy stake truck, red & yel, VG ..225.00
Toy truck, 1940s, Smith-Miller, wood & metal, EX 750.00
Toy truck, 1950s, Buddy L, Pause That Refreshes, yel, EX 220.00
Toy truck, 1950s, San Truck, Japan, 8", NM 475.00
Toy truck, 1950s, Volkswagon, Japan, EX 175.00
Toy truck, 1960s, Matchbox, even load, 2", NMIB 85.00
Toy truck, 1970s, Big Wheel, battery op, 10", NMIB 95.00
Toy truck, 1974, Buddy L, red & wht, NMIB 75.00
Tray, TV; 1956, assorted foods & CC, 13½x18¼", NM 10.00
Tray, TV; 1958, picnic basket, 13½x18¼", NM 25.00
Tray, 1897, Victorian lady, 9¼" dia, EX 8,500.00
Tray, 1903, Hilda Clark, oval, 18½x15", EX 5,000.00
Tray, 1907, Relieves Fatigue, 13¼x10½", EX 1,750.00
Tray, 1909, St Louis Fair girl, oval, 16½x13½", NM 1,800.00
Tray, 1913, Delicious & Refreshing, 15¼x12½", EX (+) 500.00
Tray, 1914, Betty, oval, 15¼x12½", EX (+) 500.00

Tray, 1905, Lillian Nordica with glass, 10½x13", NM, $2,500.00 up to $4,500.00.

Tray, 1914, Betty, 10½x13¼", EX (+) 425.00
Tray, 1916, Elaine, 19x8½", EX (+) 225.00
Tray, 1920, garden girl, oval, 16½x13¾", EX 600.00
Tray, 1921, autumn girl, 10½x13¼", EX 575.00
Tray, 1922, summer girl, 10½x13¼", NM 750.00
Tray, 1923, flapper girl, 10½x13¼", NM (+) 375.00
Tray, 1924, smiling girl, 10½x13¼", EX 525.00
Tray, 1925, girl w/fur, 10½x13¼", EX (+) 350.00
Tray, 1926, sports couple, 10½x13¼" (reissued '74), EX (+) 450.00
Tray, 1927, bobbed-hair girl, 10½x13¼", NM 500.00
Tray, 1927, curb-side service, 10½x13¼", EX 450.00
Tray, 1927, curb-side survice, 10½x13¼", M 800.00
Tray, 1928, soda fountain clerk, 10½x13¼", NM 750.00
Tray, 1929, girl in swimsuit w/glass, 10½x13¼", NM 425.00
Tray, 1930, bathing beauty, 10½x13¼", EX 250.00
Tray, 1930, girl w/phone, 10½x13¼", NM 425.00
Tray, 1931, Rockwell boy w/sandwich & dog, 10½x13¼", EX ...575.00
Tray, 1932, girl on bench, 10½x13¼", NM 600.00
Tray, 1933, Frances Dee, 10½x13¼", EX 350.00
Tray, 1933, Frances Dee, 10½x13¼", NM 575.00
Tray, 1934, Weismuller & O'Sullivan, 10½x13¼", EX (+) 600.00
Tray, 1935, Madge Evans, 10½x13¼", NM 475.00
Tray, 1936, hostess, lady in long gown, 10½x13¼", EX 185.00
Tray, 1937, running girl, 10½x13¼", NM (+) 450.00
Tray, 1938, girl in afternoon, 10½x13¼", NM 200.00
Tray, 1939, springboard girl, 10½x13¼", EX 175.00
Tray, 1940, ice skater, 10½x13¼", NM 325.00
Tray, 1940, sailor girl, 10½x13¼", EX 175.00
Tray, 1942, 2 girls & car, 10½x13¼", EX 165.00
Tray, 1942, 2 girls & car, 10½x13¼", M 350.00
Tray, 1950s, girl w/wind in hair, 10½x13¼", NM 90.00
Tray, 1955, menu girl, 10½x13¼", EX 35.00
Tray, 1955, menu girl, 10½x13¼", NM 50.00
Tray, 1957, umbrella girl, Canadian, 10½x13¼", EX 175.00
Tray, 1961, pansy garden, 10½x13¼", M 20.00
Trolly card, 1918, WWI rationing info, 11x20½", NM 750.00
Trolly card, 1923, flapper girl, 11x20½" 1,550.00
Trolly card, 1927, Mizen art, 11x20½", NM 950.00
Tumbler, ca 1912, flared sides, M 450.00
Tumbler, 1923-27, modified flare 85.00

Tumbler, 1930s, pewter, NM 325.00
Wallet, 1920s, leather, brn, shows 1915 bottle, 4x8½", NM 65.00
Watch fob, 1912, celluloid, lady at fence w/bottle, 1½", NM ..1,000.00
Watch fob, 1915, swastika, bk: Drink CC..., 1½x1¼", EX 150.00
Whistle, 1930s, tin, Pure Sunlight, EX pnt 100.00
Wrapper, 1913-16, CC Pepsin Gum, EX 300.00

Vendors

Though interest in Coca-Cola machines of the 1949 – 1959 era rose dramatically over the last few years, values currently seem to have leveled off and actually dropped 15% to 20%. The major manufacturers of these curved-top, 5¢ and 10¢ machines were Vendo (V), Vendorlator (VMC), Cavalier (C or CS), and Jacobs. In the following listings, 'EX' values are for machines in clean, original condition.

Cavalier, model #CS72, EX orig 900.00
Cavalier, model #CS72, M rstr 2,500.00
Cavalier, model #C27, EX orig 1,400.00
Cavalier, model #C27, M rstr 3,000.00
Cavalier, model #C51, EX orig 650.00
Cavalier, model #C51, M rstr 2,000.00
Jacobs, model #26, EX orig 1,500.00
Jacobs, model #26, M rstr 3,000.00
Vendo, model #23, EX orig 650.00
Vendo, model #23, M rstr 1,750.00
Vendo, model #39, EX orig 850.00
Vendo, model #39, M rstr 2,000.00
Vendo, model #44, EX orig 2,000.00
Vendo, model #44, M rstr 3,500.00
Vendo, model #56, EX orig 1,200.00
Vendo, model #56, M rstr 3,000.00
Vendo, model #80, EX orig 650.00
Vendo, model #80, M rstr 1,500.00
Vendo, model #81, EX orig 1,200.00
Vendo, model #81, M rstr 3,000.00
Vendorlator, model #27, EX orig 1,500.00
Vendorlator, model #27, M rstr (on stand) 2,500.00
Vendorlator, model #27A, EX orig 800.00
Vendorlator, model #27A, M rstr 2,000.00
Vendorlator, model #33, EX orig 800.00
Vendorlator, model #33, M rstr 2,000.00
Vendorlator, model #44, EX orig 1,800.00
Vendorlator, model #44, M rstr 3,200.00
Vendorlator, model #72, EX orig 750.00
Vendorlator, model #72, M rstr 2,500.00

Coffee Grinders

The serious collector of kitchenwares and country store items rank coffee mills high on the list of desirable examples. A trend is developing toward preferring items whose manufacturers are easily identifiable. Names to look for include Adams, Arcade, Baldwin Bros., Daisy, Elgin National, Elma, Enterprise, Lane Bros., Parker, Regal, and Sun Mfg. Co.; there are many others. Any of these marks found on coffee mills represent companies who were in business at or before the turn of the century.

Side mills usually have a brass tag located on the tin hopper. If the hopper was made of cast iron, the name was usually cast into the metal. Some of the less expensive versions had no identification. Decals were often used on the front of lap mills and table styles, though sometimes you will find these decals on the inside of the drawer. Because decals are prone to flake off and fade, and since they are often destroyed when the mill is being refinished, lap and table mills are the most difficult

types to attribute to a specific manufacturer. Canister mills had names and patent dates molded into the cast iron housing or on the canister itself. Commercial mills used in country and general stores were made of cast iron. Important information such as manufacture and patent dates was usually cast into the wheels, housing, or base of the mill. Such identification contributes considerably toward value.

Good examples of early coffee mills are rapidly becoming difficult to find. Beware of the many imported imposters that are on the market today.

Key: adj — adjustment

A Kendrick & Sons No 1, lap, CI w/brass hopper, CI drw 95.00
Adams Patented, lap, pewter hopper, wood box, porc knob 125.00
Arcade, Crystal No 44, CI w/glass hopper, Arcade lid & cup 80.00
Arcade, Favorite No 7, side, CI, grind adj front, CI lid 65.00
Arcade, Imperial, lap, CI closed hopper, wood box, EX 95.00
Arcade, Imperial No 200, lap, CI hopper w/eagle, Pat 88, 89 .....125.00
Arcade, IXL, table, ornate CI hopper, hdl on side, 1-lb, EX 160.00
Arcade, lap, fancy CI top & hopper, wood box, EX 95.00
Arcade, Sunbeam, CI w/glass hopper, orig lid & cup, EX 95.00
Arcade No 147, lap, fancy CI closed hopper, wood box, EX 85.00
Arcade No 4, canister, CI w/glass hopper, orig Arcade lid 80.00
Arcade No 40, canister, CI/glass 85.00
Arcade No 5, side, CI, Pat June '94 ....65.00
Blksmith made, funnel shape, 1-hdl, open hopper, wall mt 185.00
Caravan, canister, CI works, tin hopper, ca 1910, VG 65.00
Coffee Bean Roaster, tin hopper, CI trivet, wood hdl 155.00
Common unmk, lap, open CI hopper, orig drw, wood box, VG 70.00
Common unmk, table, orig drw, screw cap on top, VG 75.00
Crescent, table, wood, top-fill, cylinder, 13" 225.00
DeVe, Holland Made, lap, copper-plated hopper, decals 55.00
Elgin Nat'l, floor, silver hopper, 24" wheels 1,100.00
Elgin Nat'l No 40, counter, CI, red pnt, 2 wheels, orig, VG 495.00
Elgin Nat'l No 48, CI w/eagle, orig lily decal, 2-wheel 525.00
Elma, counter, CI, closed hopper, 10" single wheel, 17" 125.00
Enterprise, counter, CI, CI drw, closed hopper, Pat 1873, VG ...185.00
Enterprise, Pioneer, floor, CI, Pat 1873, 34" wheels, 65", VG .1,500.00
Enterprise, table clamp-on, CI w/CI cup, blk w/gold decal 65.00
Enterprise No 1, counter, open hopper, hdl, Pat 1873, 11", VG .185.00
Enterprise No 3, counter, CI w/wood drw, orig decals/pnt 495.00
Enterprise No 7, counter, CI, w/eagle, orig pnt, 17" wheel 675.00
Euclid No 4, counter, aluminum hopper, 10" wheels, VG 395.00
Grand Union Tea, canister, red pnt, orig writing, Pat 1910 ....85.00
Grand Union Tea, table, CI sq base, rnd hopper, mfg Griswold .235.00
J Fisher, dvtl mahog, pewter hopper, handmade 155.00
J Fisher Warranted, lap, dvtl walnut, pewter hopper, unique 155.00
K&M, lap, maple, aluminum closed hopper, clips on drw side 55.00
Landers, Frary & Clark, canister, CI & tin, Pat 1905, VG 70.00
Landers, Frary & Clark, Regal No 44, canister, CI/tin, orig 85.00
Landers, Frary & Clark, table, CI, Pat Feb 14, 1905, VG 70.00
Landers, Frary & Clark No 20, blk, 10" wheels 525.00
Landers, Frary & Clark No 50, counter, CI, 12" wheels, EX+ 550.00
Lap, CI, brn pnt, octagon base & hopper, cup in base, 4x4x4" 95.00
Lightning, canister, CI works, tin hopper, 1-lb, EX 75.00
Logan & Strobridge, Franco-American, lap, ornate CI hopper 90.00
Nat'l, coffee & spice counter, CI, 12" wheels, 25", VG 475.00
Nat'l, coffee & spice counter, CI, 17" wheels, 28", VG 525.00
Nat'l No 5, CI body & drw, 12" wheels, VG 425.00
Nat'l Specialty No 0, table clamp-on, CI, covered hopper 85.00
New Home, table, CI top, enclosed hopper, wood box, 1-lb, EX+ ..80.00
New Model, lap, CI w/CI drw, bottom opens all 4 sides 75.00
Parker, Charles; table, tall/thin, CI & tin top, hdl on top 95.00
Parker, side, Pat 1876, CI, on orig brd, grind adj front 65.00
Parker (Chas) No 5005, counter, CI, 12½" wheels, 17", EX 575.00

Parker No 2, counter, CI w/orig decals, 9" wheels, EX 475.00
Parker No 49, side, tin hopper w/brass eagle, tin lid 65.00
Parker No 5000, counter, CI, Pat 1897, 12" wheels, 17", VG 475.00
Parker No 555, Challenge Fast Grind, table, 1-lb, orig, EX 85.00
Peugot Freres, lap, wood box, tin-covered hopper, Fr 45.00
Primitive, lap, dvtl, red buttermilk pnt, orig drw, pewter 165.00
Primitive, lap, dvtl walnut, wrought iron, brass hopper 165.00
PSW&Co No 6, side, orig CI lid, EX 65.00
Queen, miniature, CI hopper & drw front, wood box, decal 80.00
Royal, side, CI w/CI cup, open hopper, Pat Apr 15, 1890, VG 65.00
RR Kreiterr, Lewisberry, York Co PA, dvtl, pewter hopper 165.00
Russell & Erwin, Dmn Mill, lap, CI 90.00
Russell & Erwin Mfg Co, lap, top adj, CI hopper, wood box 80.00
Russell & Erwin Mfg Co No 1008, CI hopper, wood box 90.00
Russell & Erwin Mfg Co No 60, britannia hopper, wood box 90.00
School Bell, canister, similar to Golden Rule, CI & wood 355.00
Simmons Hardware Co, Delmar Coffee, table, CI cover 285.00
Star, counter, tin drw, blk, 1-wheel, sm, VG 295.00
Star No 7, counter, CI, w/pan, 2-wheel, VG 450.00
Sun Mfg No 1080, Challenge Fast Grind, Columbus OH, table ...80.00
Sun No 1050 Improved, lap, wood, tin hopper 85.00
Swift, drug mill, CI, open hopper, Pat June 30, 1874 ....495.00
Swift No 13, counter, orig tin drw, red pnt, 12" wheels, 19" 425.00
Swift No 15, counter, orig decals/pnt, Pat 1875, 19" wheels 875.00
Turkish, brass cylinder, seal of sultan, folding hdl, old 65.00
Turkish, primitive, table, lg sq box on 28" brd, ornate, old 160.00
W Cross & Sons, lap, CI w/orig CI drw, brass hopper & pull 85.00
Walton, Bronson, canister, tin & CI, Pat 1911 ....80.00
Walton, Clevis, canister, orig cup, Pat 7/0/1901, orig, EX 75.00
Wilson, Increase, side, CI & tin 60.00
Wrights Hdwe Co, Brighton, table, 1-lb, 8" 80.00
WW Weaver Warranted, dvtl walnut, pewter hopper, ca 1830 ..195.00
Xray, canister, CI works, tin hopper w/glass, EX 75.00

Coin-Operated Machines

Coin-operated machines may be the fastest-growing area of collector interest in today's market. Many machines are bought, restored, and used for home entertainment. Older examples from the turn of the century and those with especially elaborate decoration and innovative accessories are most desirable, often bringing prices in excess of $7,000.00.

Vending machines sold a product or a service. They were already in common usage by 1900 selling gum, cigars, matches, and a host of other commodities. Peanut and gumball machines are especially popular today. The most valuable are those with their original finish and decals. Older machines made of cast iron are especially desirable, while those with plastic globes have little or no collector value. When buying unrestored peanut machines, beware of salt damage.

The coin-operated phonograph of the early 1900s paved the way for the jukeboxes of the twenties. Seeburg was first on the market with an automatic 8-tune phonograph. By the 1930s, Wurlitzer was the top name in the industry with dealerships all over the country. As a result of the growing ranks of competitors, the forties produced the most beautiful machines made. Wurlitzers from this era are probably the most popularly sought-after models on the market today. The model 1015 of 1946 is considered the all-time classic, and often brings prices in excess of $7,000.

Coin-Op Newsletter; Jukebox Collectors' Newsletter; Chicagoland Antique Advertising, Slot Machine, and Jukebox Gazette; and *Classic Amusements Magazine* are all excellent publications for those interested in coin-operated machines; see the Clubs, Newsletters, and Catalogs section of the Directory for publishing information.

Jackie and Ken Durham are our advisors (for all but Jukeboxes);

they are listed in the Directory under the District of Columbia. Our advisor for Jukeboxes is Norman Nelson; he is listed in the Directory under Ohio.

Arcade Machines

Wizard 1¢ Fortune Teller, aluminum and wood, 19x14", $1,200.00.

Bally Goofy, pinball game, 1943, EX orig 325.00
Big Game Hunter 1¢ Target Shoot, oak case, 1925, VG 495.00
Caille Atlas Lifter, ca 1910, EX orig 1,950.00
Caille Auto Mutoscope, 1905, EX orig 1,800.00
Caille Cailoscope 1¢ Peep Show, rstr 1,950.00
Caille Electric Wave, ca 1905, EX orig 3,200.00
Caille Mickey Finn Strength Tester, rstr 4,500.00
Caille Olympia Puncher, ca 1905, VG orig 1,800.00
Caille Tower Lifter, 1905, EX orig 1,800.00
Challenger Duck Shoot, ca 1940, NM orig 250.00
CTC Sales 1¢ G-Man Gripper Strength Tester, VG 195.00
Cupid's Post Office, ca 1935, EX orig 1,000.00
Exhibit Supply Grandfather's Clock, ca 1925, VG orig 1,250.00
Exhibit Supply Merchant Man, ca 1942, NM 1,200.00
Exhibit Supply Mystic Eve Fortune Teller, ca 1935, NM 500.00
Exhibit Supply Mystic Mirror, EX orig 1,500.00
Exhibit Supply Radio Love Message, ca 1930, NM 475.00
Gottleib Bank-A-Ball, pinball game, 1950s, EX orig 425.00
Groetchen Pike's Peak, skill game, 1940, EX rstr 450.00
Medina Spirometer, EX orig 1,500.00
Mills Illusion, viewer machine, ca 1900, NM 3,750.00
Mills Lion Lung Tester, ca 1905, EX 4,200.00
Mills Wizard Fortune Teller, ca 1920, EX orig 425.00
Nat'l Advanced 1¢ Duck Shoot, w/vendor, 1940s, VG 215.00
Old Witch 5¢ Fortune Teller, aluminum case, 1922, VG 280.00
Rockola, World Series, pinball game 1,200.00
Seeburg Chicken Sam, ca 1932, EX 1,200.00
Stephens Babe Ruth Baseball, 1935, EX orig 450.00

Jukeboxes

AMI #200, 1957, NM 900.00

AMI Model A, EX orig 3,200.00
AMI Streamliner, 1938, EX orig 2,800.00
Capehart Orchestrope #28-F, 1928, rstr 4,250.00
Mills Throne of Music, EX orig 1,500.00
Packard Manhattan, 1945, EX orig 2,200.00
Rockola, counter top, 1939, EX 2,800.00
Rockola #1422, 1946, EX orig 1,650.00
Rockola #1428, EX 3,000.00
Rockola #1434, EX+ 1,200.00
Rockola #456, 1974, NM 550.00
Rockola Fireball #1436, 1952, VG 600.00
Rockola Monarch, 1938, EX orig 850.00
Seeburg #100C, 1950, EX orig 850.00
Seeburg #220, EX 1,400.00
Seeburg Gem, 1938 ....1,650.00
Seeburg HF-100R, M 2,200.00
Seeburg KD-200, EX 1,750.00
Seeburg R, EX 2,400.00
Seeburg Symphonola Regal, 1935, NM 1,250.00
Wurlitzer #1015, 1946, EX orig 7,500.00
Wurlitzer #1050, 1972, NM 4,500.00
Wurlitzer #1100, 1948, EX 4,500.00
Wurlitzer #2304, EX orig 1,000.00
Wurlitzer #24, VG orig 1,800.00
Wurlitzer #316 Simplex, 1936, NM 2,100.00
Wurlitzer #42, 1942, VG 4,000.00
Wurlitzer #500, 1938, EX orig 2,000.00
Wurlitzer #51, counter top, 1937, NM 1,800.00
Wurlitzer #700, 1940, EX orig 2,800.00
Wurlitzer #750, 1941, EX orig 6,000.00
Wurlitzer #750-E, 1940, EX orig 5,750.00
Wurlitzer Ambassador, 1949, EX orig 2,500.00

Slot Machines

Bally Draw Bell, console model, 1946, EX orig 1,500.00
Bally Hold & Draw, EX 600.00
Bally 5¢/25¢ Dbl Bell, EX orig 3,200.00
Berger American Beauty, floor model, 1901, VG ...12,000.00
Buckley Track Odds, EX orig 2,200.00
Caille Ben Hur, counter top, 1908, EX 4,750.00
Caille Console Bell, 1937, EX orig 1,200.00
Caille Detroit, floor model, 1898, EX 7,500.00
Caille Dough Boy Bell, 1935, NM 1,500.00
Caille Jumbo Success, EX orig 1,750.00
Caille Superior Jackpot Bell, 1928, EX orig 1,600.00
Caille 5¢ Bullfrog, floor model, 1903, EX orig 2,200.00
Domino, counter top, 1927, EX 3,500.00
Exhibit Supply Races, console model, 1937, VG 500.00
Fey Silver Cup, counter top, 1910, EX orig 12,000.00
Fields Five Jacks 1,100.00
Groetchen Columbia Bell, 1936, VG 800.00
Groetchen Corona Blue Bell, 1950, EX orig 650.00
Jennings Electro Bell, w/vendor, 1930, EX orig 1,800.00
Jennings Improved Century Bell, 1933, EX rstr 1,750.00
Jennings Lucky Chief Bell, 1945, EX 1,700.00
Jennings Master Chief, 1940, EX orig 1,500.00
Jennings Pace Front, EX orig 1,500.00
Jennings Silver Moon Chief, 1941, NM rstr 1,500.00
Jennings Sportsman Golf Ball, w/vendor, 1937, EX orig 4,500.00
Jennings Sun Chief, 1949, EX orig 1,700.00
Jennings Today Bell, w/vendor, 1926, EX orig 1,500.00
Jennings 25¢ Standard Chief, rstr 1,800.00
Jennings 5¢ Duchess, rstr 1,750.00

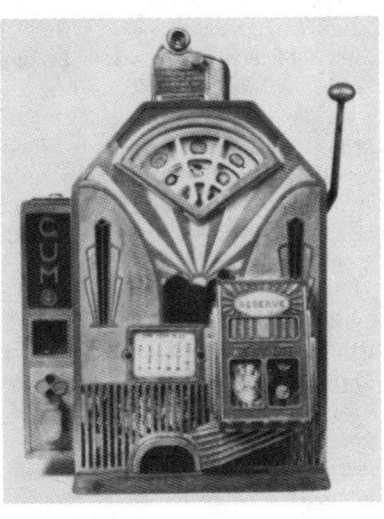

Jennings 1¢ Little Duke single jackpot with gum vendor, oak case, 1933, 20x14x10", EX, $2,500.00.

Jennings 5¢ Victory Chief, ca 1941, NM rstr 1,650.00
Keeney Track Time, console model, 1937, NM 1,500.00
Maley Investor, counter top, ca 1895, EX orig 2,000.00
Mills Castle Blue Front, 1937, rstr 1,750.00
Mills Castle Front, 1930s, EX orig 1,650.00
Mills Chrome Bell Diamond Front, 1939, VG 1,600.00
Mills Club Royale, console, 1945, EX orig 1,500.00
Mills Elf, EX orig 3,250.00
Mills Horsehead Bonus, late 1930s, EX orig 2,500.00
Mills Liberty Bell, 1909, EX orig 5,000.00
Mills Owl Jr, counter top, 1899, EX 3,000.00
Mills QT, side vendor, minor pnt loss, early, VG ...1,200.00
Mills QT Firebird, 1934, EX orig 1,600.00
Mills Silent Golden Bell, Roman head, 1932, EX orig 2,250.00
Mills 25¢ Extra Bell (Aikens) front, EX orig 2,500.00
Mills 25¢ Futurity, EX orig 2,500.00
Mills 5¢ Black Cherry, 1931, EX orig 1,600.00
Mills 5¢ Bursting Cherry, 1937, EX orig 1,800.00
Mills 5¢ Dewey, quarter-sawn oak, anchor motif, rstr 7,800.00
Mills 5¢ Hi-Top, EX orig 1,950.00
Mills 5¢ Mystery Bell Castle Front, VG front panel, EX 1,500.00
Mills 5¢ War Eagle, NM orig 2,200.00
Pace Bantam, 1938, EX orig 1,400.00
Pace Comet, w/vendor, 1932, EX orig 1,400.00
Pace Deluxe Cherry Bell, 1945, EX orig 1,400.00
Pace Kitty, 1937, EX orig 2,200.00
Rockola Imp, 1932, VG 1,500.00
Rockola 5¢ War Eagle, NM 2,000.00
Superior Golden Bell, 1934, EX orig 2,200.00
Watling Blue Seal, EX orig 1,300.00
Watling Brownie, counter top, 1900, NM 3,200.00
Watling Brownie Jackpot, counter top, 1929, EX orig 2,800.00
Watling Jackpot, floor model, 1904, VG 6,000.00
Watling Lincoln Deluxe Bell, 1926, EX orig 1,800.00
Watling Treasury Bell, 1936, EX orig 3,500.00
Watling 10¢ Rol-A-Top, NM orig pnt, +reel strips/award card ..3,500.00

Trade Stimulators

Ad-Lee 1¢ Try It, dice machine, 1927, VG 325.00
Buckley Horses, 4-reel, 1937, EX orig 450.00
Buckley Pilgrim, 5-reel, 1934, EX orig 400.00
Caille 1¢ Baseball, 1-reel, 1911, EX orig 3,500.00
Caille 1¢ Jr Bell, 1929, EX orig 585.00
Caille 1¢ Puritan Bell, CI, EX orig 800.00
Caille 1¢ Reliance, 5-reel, 1904, EX orig 1,800.00

Canda Jumbo Success, 5-reel, ca 1899, EX orig 1,400.00
Churchill Downs 1¢, coin drop, EX orig 625.00
Daval Ace, 5-reel, ca 1940, EX orig 145.00
Daval Clearing House, 3-reel, 1936, VG 350.00
Daval Comet, 3-reel, w/cigarette vendor, 1950s, EX 200.00
Daval Free Play, 1946, NM 300.00
Daval Head or Tails, 3-reel, 1940, orig pnt, EX 425.00
Daval 1¢ Penny Pack, w/cigarette vendor, 1936, rpt, EX 400.00
Decatur 1¢ Fairest Wheel #2, ca 1900, EX orig 950.00
Exhibit Supply Horseshoes, 1935, EX orig 275.00
Fey 1¢ On the Level, 1907, EX orig 2,500.00
Field Blackjack 21, 1931, EX orig 350.00
Gottlieb 1¢ Indian Dice, 1937, EX orig 625.00
Griswold Wheel of Fortune, 1893, EX 750.00
Groetchen 1¢ Gold Rush, 2-reel, 1934, EX orig 500.00
Groetchen 1¢ Highstakes, 5-reel, 1936, EX orig 450.00
Groetchen 1¢ Mercury, 3-reel, counter top, 1939, EX orig 175.00
Groetchen 1¢ Wings, cigarette packs in window, 1941, VG 150.00
Groetchen 5¢ Dixie Dominoes, 5-reel, 1937, EX orig 450.00
Groetchen 5¢ Klix, 5-reel, ca 1941, EX orig 175.00
Jennings Grand Stand, EX 400.00
Jennings Target Practice, Indian casting, EX orig 475.00
Jennings 1¢ Favorite, coin drop, 1926, EX 1,400.00
Jennings 5¢ Good Luck, wood case, electric console, EX 1,000.00
Keeney Steeplechase, ca 1935, EX orig 385.00
Keeney's Scramball 3¢ Marble Game, wood case, 1936, EX 190.00
Midwest Puritan Baby, 3-reel, 1928, EX orig 400.00
Mills Little Perfection, cards, EX orig 750.00
Mills Monte Carlo, ca 1900, EX orig 3,500.00
Mills Pilot, 1-reel, 1906, EX orig 3,500.00
Mills Success, 5-reel, 1901, EX orig 3,500.00
Mills Wild Deuces, 5-reel, 1938, all orig, EX 550.00
Mills 1¢ New Target Practice, 1925, EX orig 450.00
Mills 36 Lucky Spot, dice machine, 1926, EX orig 650.00
Pace New Deal, 5-reel, 1935, EX orig 400.00
Pierce Whirlwind, 3-reel, 1933, EX orig 900.00
Rockola 1¢ Horse Race, w/gumball vendor, EX 1,000.00
Rockola 1¢/5¢ Hold & Draw, 5-reel, 1934, EX orig 400.00
Whitney Seven Grand, ca 1939, EX orig 385.00

Sittman and Pitt 5¢ card machine, cast iron, with original marque and award cards, 12x13x9", EX, $2,500.00.

Vendors

Ace #43, smoked globe, M decal, unused 725.00
Ad-Lee 5¢ E-Z, gum, decal on globe, Pat 1908, 16", VG 500.00
Adams Tutti Frutti, gum, ca 1900, EX orig 750.00
Advance #11 Big Mouth, peanuts, 1920s, rstr 200.00
Advance Climax-10 1¢, gum, orig red pnt, Pat 1909, EX 1,375.00
Advance 1¢ D, football globe, EX 175.00
Atlas Bantam 5¢, rstr 65.00
Automatic 1¢ Prize King, gum, ca 1940, 13¾", VG 55.00
Baby Grand Golden Oak, gum, rstr 65.00
Caille Fortune, gum, ca 1928, NM 700.00
Caille Teddy Bear, gum, ca 1910, VG orig 1,250.00
Chicklets-Baker's Chocolates, red porc, wall hanging, EX 475.00
Chiclets, porc, EX 525.00
Columbus #14, gum, aluminum, EX 285.00
Columbus #21, ca 1920, EX orig 350.00
Columbus A 1¢, peanuts, w/tray, EX 275.00
Columbus M, hexagonal globe, EX 225.00
Columbus Triple, gum, NM 800.00
Crown Perfume 1¢, clockwork, Pat 1892, NM 2,400.00
Derby, Cones, marque, rpl decal, NM 1,500.00
Dixie Cups, rstr 295.00
Elde 25¢ Dial-a-Smoke, cigarettes, wall mt, 1950, EX 150.00
Eveready 1¢, 1937, EX 50.00

E-Z Gum Ball, cast iron and glass with original decals, 16", EX, $600.00.

Ford, gum, 1950, EX 55.00
Ford 1¢, gum, 1920s, EX orig 75.00
Groetchen Baby 1¢, gum, cast panel, 1932, 18", VG 275.00
Hershey's, chocolate bar, 1930s, EX 185.00
Lawrence 1¢/5¢, nuts, ca 1940, 19x8½x8", G 130.00
Life Savers, revolving 5-column, 1920s, G 75.00
Log Cabin, gum, EX 250.00
Lucky 15¢ Horoscope, cards, 16", VG 25.00
Mansfield 5¢ Automatic Clerk, gum, 1901, EX orig 600.00
Master 1¢/5¢ No 2, gum, wht porc, Pat 1924, G 150.00
Mayo Cut Plug, cut plug vendor, bevelled mirror, EX 550.00
Michigan 1¢, coin drop, gum, orig red finish, ca 1905, G 120.00
Miller's 1¢ Gold Seal, candy, Pat 1916, 9", G 255.00
Mills 1¢, perfume, orig bottles, rstr 3,950.00
Northwestern, peanuts, frosted globe, rstr 175.00
Northwestern #33, peanuts, CI & porc, EX 175.00

Northwestern #33 Jr, gum, 1933, EX orig 175.00
Northwestern Yankee, match dispenser, 1909, EX 800.00
Northwestern 1¢ Tab, gum, Pat 1954, 19", G 50.00
Penny King, 4 in 1, early version, EX orig 825.00
Popperette 10¢, popcorn, EX orig 2,000.00
Postage Stamps 5¢/8¢, 13¾", G 50.00
Premier, cards, 1950, EX 200.00
Pulver, clown figure, red case, printing on sides, EX 550.00
Pulver, clown figure, yel case, EX 700.00
Pulver, policeman figure, gum, red porc, 1931, 21", EX 700.00
Pulver 1¢ Kola-Pepsin, gum, red porc, case only, 1910s, G 1,500.00
Pulver 1¢ To Choose, gum, porc, Yel Kid, EX 300.00
Rex Silent Salesman, gum, VG orig 1,100.00
Select-o-Vend, 8-column, VG 80.00
Selmor 1¢, peanuts, CI, EX orig 225.00
Star, gum, ca 1935, EX orig 95.00
Stollwork Bros, porc sides, EX 995.00
Toy-N-Joy, EX orig 25.00
Universal Bluebird Products 1¢, gum, 11½", G 100.00
Victor Baby Grand, gum, decal, oak case, 1954, NM 60.00
Victor Topper Deluxe, gum, NM 85.00
Victory Uncle Sam, stamps, counter top, 1940s, EX 100.00
White Happy Jap, gum, 1902, NM 1,500.00
Zeno 1¢, gum, tin & iron on oak base, 16", VG 1,155.00
Zeno 1¢, gum, wooden, 1st coin return, 1895, old rstr 875.00

Miscellaneous

Decatur Ferris Wheel, gambling, EX orig 950.00
Jennings 1¢ lollipop scale, EX orig 650.00
Watling Scale, 1¢ weight/5¢ fortune, EX 300.00

Comic Books

For almost sixty years, the American public has been thrilled by the monthly adventures of everyone's favorite comic book heroes such as Superman, Captain Marvel, and Spiderman. Each 10¢ comic book issue, featuring a new saga of adventure and mystery, were usually met with excitement and anticipation by the youngsters who eagerly purchased them from their neighborhood candy store or newsstand. Unfortunately, the vast majority of these comic books were eventually discarded in favor of other worldly pursuits. Due to this fact, most comic books from the '30s and '40s did not survive, making them a very scarce and desirable collectible in today's world.

First editions in high-grade condition may bring prices as high as $500 or more. Marvel Comics #1, published in October 1939, has sold for the astounding price of $35,000. Rarity, age, and quality of artwork are prime factors in determining comic book values. Condition is also very important. A good copy of Showcase #4 (the first appearance of the silver-age Flash) might sell for around $350, but a copy of the same book would sell for $7,000 in NM condition. Some of the better comic books are evaluated below, but many are worth much less. Refer to a good comic book price guide, if you decide to buy or sell to any great extent.

Adventures of Mighty Mouse, #2, St John Publishing, 1952, EX ..35.00
All-Star Western, #8, Nat'l Periodical, NM 5.00
Batman, #18, DC Comics, EX 300.00
Blackstone the Magician, #3, Marvel, VG 27.50
Bugs Bunny Beach Party, #32, Dell Giant, M 17.50
Bugs Bunny's Great Adventure, 4-Color #88, Dell, VG 25.00
Buster Bear, #8, Quality Comics, NM 7.50
Challengers of the Unknown, #32, DC Comics, VG 10.00
Charlie Chan, #2, Dell, NM 8.50

Cinderella Love, #11, St John Publishing, EX 12.00
Comedy Comics, #33, Timely Comics, EX 15.00
Dear Lonely Heart, #4, Artful, EX 8.50
Dick Tracy, #4, lg feature, Dell, EX 150.00
Fallen Angels, #4, Marvel, M 1.50
Geronimo, #2, Avon, EX 17.50
Grandma Duck's Farm Friends, 4-Color #1279, Disney, Dell, NM .12.50
Hollywood Secrets, #5, Quality Comics, NM 35.00
Incredible Hulk & Wolverine, #1, Marvel, M 12.50
Johnny Jason, 4-Color #1302, Dell, M 10.00
Josie & the Pussycats, #46, Archie, NM 3.50
Katzenjammer Kids, #5, King, NM 25.00
King Louie & Mowgli, #1, Gold Key, EX 6.50
Little Lotta, #10, Harvey Hits, EX 17.50
Little Sad Sack, #2, Harvey, NM 3.50
Mickey Mouse, #2, David McKay, EX 245.00
Mighty Mouse in Outer Space, #43, Dell Giant, EX 50.00
Monsters Unleashed, #9, Marvel, EX 2.00
New Terrytoons, #10, Dell, M 7.50
Our Gang Comics, #2, Ace Magazines, NM 375.00
Outlaws of the West, #14, Charlton, EX 7.50
Patty Powers, #7, Atlas Comics, EX 7.50
Petticoat Junction, #4, Dell, EX 8.00
Pixie & Dixie & Mr Jinx, 4-Color #1112, Dell, NM 27.50
Rat Patrol, #4, photo cover, Dell, EX 7.00
Richie Rich Billions, #7, Harvey, NM 2.50
Rootie Kazootie, 4-Color #459, Dell, M...........................38.00
Slash Maraud, #4, DC Comics, M 2.50
Star Spangled War Stories, #32, Nat'l Periodical, VG 12.00

Strange Tales #101, EX, $165.00.

Stumbo the Giant, #63, Harvey, M.................................26.00
Super Funnies, #3, Superior Comics, NM 16.00
Tarzan's Jungle World, #25, Dell Giant, NM 98.00
Tempus Fugitive, #3, DC Comics, M 5.00
Terry & the Pirates, 4-Color #44, Dell, EX 88.00
Tiny Tots Comics, #1, Dell, EX 95.00
Transformers, #1, Marvel, M 6.00
Treasury of Comics, #5, St John, NM 42.50
United States Marines, #5, Toby Press, EX 7.50
Wild Boy of the Congo, #11, Approved Comics, EX 12.50

Compacts

The use of cosmetics before WWI was looked upon with disdain. After the war, women became liberated, entered the work force and started to use cosmetics. The compact, a portable container for cosmetics, became a necessity. The basic compact contains a mirror and a powder puff.

Vintage compacts were fashioned in a myriad of shapes, styles, materials, and motifs. They were made of precious metals, fabrics, plastics, and in almost any other conceivable medium imaginable. Commemorative, premium, patriotic, figural, Art Deco, plastic and gadgetry compacts are just a few of the most sought-after types available today. Those that are combined with other accessories (music/compact, watch/compact, cane/compact) are also very much in demand. Vintage compacts are especially desirable collectibles since the workmanship, design techniques, and materials used in their execution would be very expensive and virtually impossible to duplicate today.

Our advisor, Roselyn Gerson, has written a highly informative book, *Ladies' Compacts of the 19th and 20th Centuries;* she is listed in the Directory under New York. See Clubs and Newsletters for information concerning compact collectors' club and their periodical publication, *The Powder Puff.*

Antique gold filigree set w/gr stones, w/tassel & chain 225.00
Armed Forces copper cap mtd on lid, gold-tone metal, rnd 70.00
Blk enamel, vanity, gilt Scottie on lid, inside mirror lifts 65.00
Blk/gold keyboard lid, compact/music box, slide-out lipstick 135.00
Damascene, blk matt w/gilt Egyptian inlay, sq 85.00
Enameled gold-tone heart shape, lock motif 85.00
Evans, petit point gold-tone mesh, mirror, lid compartments 115.00
FJCo, compact/bracelet, antique gold-tone w/filigree lid 225.00
Girey Kamra-Pak, confetti plastic, vanity type, compartments 65.00
Illinois Watch Case Co, compact/watch, gold-tone, sq 115.00
Marhill MOP, oblong carryall, pnt peacock/glitter on lid 175.00
Mini, fan shape, MOP w/rhinestones 50.00
Rex 5th Ave, mc striped taffeta, vanity pocket w/mirror 85.00
Ronson, compact/lighter/cigarette case, brn/wht marbleized 135.00
Sterling, mirror form w/bloodstone cabochon, lipstick in hdl 225.00
Tiffany, sterling silver antique finish, envelope shape 275.00
Trio-ette, rose cameo molded plastic, lipstick in hdl 90.00
Volupte, gold-tone praying hands shape, manicured nails 110.00
Whiting-Davis, mc enamel mesh vanity, jewel thumbpc, fringe .300.00
Whiting-Davis, silvered mesh vanity, sapphire thumbpc, fringe .400.00

Consolidated Lamp and Glass

The Consolidated Lamp and Glass Company of Coraopolis, Pennsylvania, was incorporated in 1894. For many years their primary business was the manufacture of lighting glass such as oil lamps and shades for both gas and electric lighting. The popular 'Cosmos' line of lamps and tableware was produced from 1894 to 1915. (See also Cosmos.) In 1926 Consolidated introduced their Martele line, a type of 'sculptured' ware closely resembling Lalique glassware of France. (Compare Consolidated's 'Lovebirds' vase with the Lalique 'Perruches' vase.) It is this line of vases, lamps, and tableware which is often mistaken for a very similar type of glassware produced by the Phoenix Glass Company, located nearby in Monaca, Pennsylvania. For example, the so-called Phoenix 'Grasshopper' vases are actually Consolidated's 'Katydid' vases.

Items in the Martele line were produced in blue, pink, green, crystal, white, or custard glass decorated with various fired-on color treatments or a satin finish. For the most part, their colors were distinctively different from those used by Phoenix. Although not foolproof, one of the ways of distinguishing Consolidated's wares from those of Phoenix is that most of the time Consolidated applied color to the raised portion of the design, leaving the background plain, while Phoenix usually applied color to the background, leaving the raised surfaces undecorated. This is particularly true of those pieces

in white or custard glass.

Consolidated closed its doors for good in 1964. Subsequently a few of the molds passed into the hands of other glass companies that later reproduced certain patterns; one such reissue is the 'Chickadee' vase, found in avocado green, satin-finish custard, or milk glass.

Bird of Paradise, plate, yel wash on crystal, 8¼" 45.00
Bittersweet, lamp, ruby stain on crystal 155.00
Catalonian, creamer & sugar bowl, honey wash 25.00
Catalonian, flower bowl, honey wash 225.00
Catalonian, snack plate, gr, pear shape, 9" 20.00
Catalonian, sugar bowl, amethyst wash, hdl 25.00
Catalonian, sundae, honey wash, 4½" 20.00
Catalonian, tumbler, amethyst, flat, 4" 15.00
Catalonian, vase, gr, rosejar shape, 8" 75.00
Catalonian, vase, triangle, ruby, 10" 110.00
Cherub, lamp, baby face, satin crystal, electrified, 23" 800.00
Chickadee, vase, brn wash on crystal 115.00
Chrysanthemum, vase, 3-color on satin custard, 12" 225.00
Cockatoo, candlestick, yel wash on crystal 125.00
Cockatoo, vase, straw opal, ormolu mts 400.00
Con-Cora, cracker jar, violets on milk glass, 6½" 80.00
Dancing Girl, vase, 3-color on satin custard, 12" 425.00
Dancing Girl w/Pan, lamp, gold highlights over red wash 475.00

Dancing Nymphs, plate, green crystal, 8½", $120.00.

Dancing Nymph, plate, gr frost, 8¼" 120.00
Dancing Nymph, plate, pk frost, 10" 155.00
Dogwood, vase, gold on gloss milk glass 150.00
Dragonfly, vase, satin milk glass w/aqua, 6" 90.00
Five Fruits, goblet, yel wash 30.00
Five Fruits, plate, brn wash, 12" 90.00
Hummingbird, powder jar, purple wash, 5" 100.00
Hummingbird, puff box, brn wash, 7" 95.00
Hummingbird & Orchid, candlestick, purple wash, 8" 120.00
Iris, jug, gr cased over milk glass 275.00
Iris, plate, gr wash, 6" 35.00
Katydid, vase, gr wash on crystal, fan shape 160.00
Katydid, vase, purple wash on crystal, cylindrical 140.00
Line 700, vase, red, 10" 400.00
Line 700, vase, red, 7" 245.00
Line 700, vase, reverse ruby stain on crystal, 6½" 170.00
Lovebirds, banana boat, purple wash on crystal 300.00
Lovebirds, powder jar, yel wash on crystal 75.00
Lovebirds, puff box, pk, 5" 140.00
Lovebirds, vase, gold on straw opal 390.00

Ruba Rombic, bottle, cologne; smoky topaz 250.00
Ruba Rombic, plate, jade, 8" 85.00
Ruba Rombic, tumbler, lav, 8-oz 60.00
Ruba Rombic, vase, sunshine, 6½" 225.00
Sea Gulls, vase, gold highlights on milk glass 265.00
Sea Gulls, vase, orange highlights on custard satin 275.00
Sea Gulls, vase, tan & lt bl on custard satin, 11x10x6" 275.00
Sea Gulls, vase, yel cased 365.00

Cookbooks

Cookbooks from the 19th century, though often hard to find, are a delight to today's collectors both for their quaint formats and printing methods as well as for their outmoded, often humorous views on nutrition. Recipes required a 'pinch' of salt, butter 'the size of an egg' or a 'walnut,' or a 'handful' of flour. Collectors sometimes specialize in cookbooks issued as advertising premiums. Especially desirable are the figurals that were shaped like a jar, a slice of bread, or some other form relative to the product. Others with unique features such as illustrations by well-known artists or references to famous people or places are priced in accordance. Cookbooks written earlier than 1874 are the most valuable and when found command prices as high as $200; figurals usually sell in the $10 to $15 range. For further information we recommend *A Guide to Collecting Cookbooks* by Col. Bob Allen and *Price Guide to Cookbooks and Recipe Leaflets* by Linda Dickinson. Our advisor for this category is Charlotte Safir; she is listed in the Directory under New York.

Key:
CB — Cookbook   dj — dust jacket

Am Women's CB, indexed, Butterick, 1939, EX 20.00
Am Women's CB, 1947, VG 10.00
Art of S Am Cookery, M Waldo, 1st edition, 1961, M 10.00
Bon Appetit Summer/Winter CB, w/dust jacket, 1980, 256-pg 10.00
Borden's Eagle Brand Book of Recipes, 1920s, 32-pg, VG 12.00
Calendar of Dinners, Story of Crisco, 1925 ....15.00
Carolina Cuisine Encore, w/dust jacket, 1981, 321-pg, EX 7.50
Ceresota CB, NW Consolidated Milling Co, ca 1880s, 42-pg, G .28.00
Clabber Girl Baking Book, Hulman & Co, 1932, 19-pg, EX 10.00
Dainty Home Lunches, C Schmidt & Sons Brewing, Phila, 1913 ...7.50
Davis' OK CB, Davis Baking Powder, 1904, 64-pg, EX 16.00
Household Searchlight Recipe Book, Household Magazine, '43, EX .10.00
Joy of Cooking, 1947 edition, EX 25.00
Majestic Recipes, Dorothy A Louden, 1931, 40-pg, EX 8.00
McCormick Irish Country Cook, dust jacket, 1988, 150-pg 6.00
Metropolitan CB, Metropolitan Life Insurance, 1922, EX 6.00
Modern Priscilla CB, 1st edition, 1924, VG 12.00
Peanuts Lunch Bag CB, Scholastic Book Service, 1970, NM 5.00
President Carter's Family Favorites, dust jacket, 1977, 244-pg ...10.00
Reliable Recipes, Calumet Baking Powder, ca 1922, 80-pg, EX ...9.00
Sunset Bread, dust jacket, 1st edition, 1963, NM 5.00
Thousand Ways To Please a Husband, 1917, EX 30.00
Trader Vic's Bartender's Guide, 1972, EX 12.50
Universal CB, Landers, Frary & Clark, ca 1925, EX 12.50
Walter Baker Best Chocolate & Cocoa Recipes, 1931, EX 20.00
What Shall I Cook Today?, Lever Bros, 1930s, 48-pg, EX 3.50
500 Tasty Sandwiches, Culinary Arts Institute, 1941, 48-pg, NM ..5.00

Cookie Cutters

Early hand-fashioned cookie cutters have recently been commanding stiff prices at country auctions, and the ranks of interested collectors are growing steadily. Especially valuable are the figural cutters, and the more complicated the design, the higher the price. A follow-up of the carved wooden cookie boards, the first cutters were probably made by itinerant tinkers from leftover or recycled pieces of tin. Though most of the 18th-century examples are now in museums or collections, it is still possible to find some good cutters from the late 1800s when changes in the manufacture of tin resulted in a thinner, less expensive material. The width of the cutting strip is often a good indicator of age; the wider the strip, the older the cutter. While the very early cutters were 1" to 1½" deep, by the twenties and thirties, many were less than ½" deep. Crude, spotty soldering indicates an older cutter, while a thin line of solder usually tends to suggest a much later manufacture. The shape of the backplate is another clue. Later cutters will have oval, round, or rectangular backs, while on the earlier type the back was cut to follow the lines of the design. Cookie cutters usually vary from 2" to 4" in size, but gingerbread men were often made as tall as 12". Birds, fish, hearts, and tulips are common; simple versions can be purchased for as little as $12.00 to $15.00. The larger figurals, especially those with more imaginative details, often bring $75.00 and up. The cookie cutters listed here are tin and handmade unless noted otherwise.

Dog, 4½" 20.00
Dutchman, 5" 110.00
Elephant walking, handmade, tin, 1880s, 5½x8" 60.00
Goat, EX detail, 4¾" 80.00
Horse, 5" 50.00
Horse & rider, primitive, rpr/dents, 9" 180.00
Horse running, EX detail, 4¾" 80.00
Husky dog, tin, strap hdl, ca 1850, 3x14" 28.00
Lady w/bustle, 5" 110.00
Man, simple form, sq bk, 8" 40.00
Man (& lady), EX detail, 5½", pr 160.00
Noah's Ark, MIB 50.00
Rnd w/dome top, tin, no air hole, strap hdl, 3" 7.50
Squirrel, lg crimped-edge tail, lt rust, 5½" 100.00
Star, tin, strap hdl, crude, 5" 15.00
Turkey, EX detail, minor dents, 5" 235.00
Whale, 3¾" 20.00
6 deep scallops, tin w/strap hdl, 2¼x1½" dia 10.00

Cookie Jars

The appeal of the cookie jar is universal; folks of all ages, both male and female, love to collect 'em! The early thirties' heavy stoneware jars of a rather nondescript nature quickly gave way to figurals of every type imaginable. Those from the mid to late thirties were often decorated over the glaze with 'cold paint,' but by the early forties underglaze decorating resulted in cheerful, bright, permanent colors and cookie jars that still have a new look fifty years later.

Unmarked jars, unless properly identified and rare, bring the lowest prices, while cookie jars trimmed in gold are usually highly valued. The examples listed below were made by companies other than those found elsewhere in this book; see also specific manufacturers.

Our advisors for this catgory are Fred and Joyce Roerig, authors of *The Collector's Encyclopedia of Cookie Jars*; they are listed in the Directory under South Carolina. For further study we also recommend *An Illustrated Guide to Cookie Jars* by Ermagene Westfall.

Alice in Wonderland, Japan 125.00
Alice in Wonderland, looking-glass lid, unmk Walt Disney 600.00
Aunt Jemima, soft plastic, EX 285.00
Bambi, Walt Disney, California Originals 450.00
Barefoot Boy, Gem Refractories 350.00
Bartender, Pan American Art 165.00

Bear on Blocks, Marsh 95.00
Beaver, #2625, California Originals 50.00
Betty Boop, full figure, c 1985 King Features Syndicate 750.00
Big Bird, California Originals, Muppets Inc 976 ....125.00
Blackboard Hobo, USA, American Bisque 225.00
Butler, Twin Winton 75.00
Candy Shack, Twin Winton 25.00
Casper the Ghost, American Bisque, minimum value 800.00
Cat in Basket, unmk Japan 15.00
Chef, tray lid, American Bisque 350.00
Churn Boy, unmk Regal China 200.00
Cinderella, JC Napco 1957 K2292 ....200.00
Clown w/Stripes on Collar, USA, APCO 25.00
Coffeepot, Treasure Craft 22.00
Collegiate Owl, American Bisque 60.00
Cookie, Pearl China, gold wear 425.00
Cookie Barrel, USA, American Bisque 15.00
Cookie Chef, Henderson KY, Muppets 50.00
Cookie Monster, glass, c Muppets 50.00
Cookie Truck, yel lid, American Bisque 55.00
Cookies & Milk, USA 740, American Bisque 90.00
Cookieville, Treasure Craft 30.00
Cop, USA, American Bisque 105.00
Cow in Overalls, USA, APCO 50.00
Cow over Moon, yel, Doranne of California 195.00
Dancing Pig, unmk American Bisque 100.00
Davy Crockett, Ransburg 125.00
Davy Crockett, Sierra Vista, minimum value 800.00
Davy Crockett, Translucent Vitrified China, c C Miller 550.00
Davy Crockett in Woods, American Bisque, minimum value 800.00
Donald Duck, sitting, American Bisque 275.00
Dumbo/Pluto Turnabout, Walt Disney 150.00
Dutch Boy, Robinson Ransbottom 125.00
Eeyore, Walt Disney, California Originals 375.00
Elephant, #15 USA, Doranne of California 38.00
Elephant, Sierra Vista of California 70.00
Elephant w/Baseball Cap, American Bisque 85.00
Elf, Twin Winton 50.00
Elf Bakery, Twin Winton 45.00
Elsie, unmk Pottery Guild 300.00
Ernie, c Muppets Inc 1973, California Originals 50.00
Famous Amos, Treasure Craft, Made in USA 60.00
Feed Bag, USA, American Bisque 35.00
Fishing Hippo, Japan 28.00
Frago Mint Truck, Made in Italy...Marshall Field & Co 80.00
Franciscan Nun, unmk Hondo Ceramics 175.00
French Poodle, American Bisque 95.00
Friar Tuck, Twin Winton 35.00
Frog w/Bow Tie, #2645 USA, California Originals 40.00
Frosty the Snowman, Robinson Ransbottom 450.00
Glass Bowl Santa, Treasure Craft, Made in USA 150.00
Goldilocks, Regal China 350.00
Gorilla w/Lady in Hand, Omnibus 1987 ....150.00
Happy Bull, Twin Winton 55.00
Helmet, unmk 55.00
Hen, CJ #100, Doranne of California 48.00
Hen w/Basket of Eggs, Doranne of California 65.00
Herman & Catnip, American Bisque 3,000.00
Hi Diddle Diddle, gold trim, Robinson Ransbottom 225.00
Hobo, Treasure Craft 55.00
Holstein Cow, c Otagiri 65.00
Howdy Doody, Vandor 275.00
Howdy Doody Bumper Car 225.00
Jocko the Monkey, Robinson Ransbottom 275.00

Jonah on the Whale (also known as Pinocchio) 800.00
Jukebox, Disco, Vandor 100.00
Katrina, Treasure Craft, rare 750.00
Kitchen Witch, unmk, lg 70.00
Lighthouse, Treasure Craft 49.00
Lion, Twin Winton 45.00
Little Audrey, USA, American Bisque, minimum value 3,500.00
Little Girl, Cardinal USA #301 ....80.00
Little Girl Lamb, USA, American Bisque 80.00
Love Me Dog, Maurice of Calif USA 32.00
Ludwig Von Drake, felt tongue, M 1,050.00
Magic Bunny, USA, American Bisque 80.00
Mammy, bl, Mosaic Tile, 1944, NM 595.00
Mammy, F&F, 12" 350.00
Mammy, Nat'l Silver, EX 250.00
Mammy, Pearl China, minor wear 825.00
Mickey Mouse, leather ears, Disney 425.00
Mickey Mouse Car, Walt Disney 350.00
Milk Can, bell in lid, USA, American Bisque 50.00
Modern Rooster, USA, American Bisque 38.00
Mohawk Indian, American Bisque, minimum value 1,800.00
Monk, 'Thou Shalt not Steal!' on robe, unmk 45.00
Monk, Treasure Craft 55.00
Mrs Potts, Treasure Craft 60.00
Noah's Ark, Twin Winton 38.00
Oriental Lady, rare gr, Regal China 575.00
Paddington Bear, Paddington by Toscany, c Eden 1987 ....45.00

Peek-a-Boo, Regal China, $1,100.00.

Peter Pumpkin Eater, Vellona Star Design Pat 165.00
Pickup Truck, red, Treasure Craft, MIB 550.00
Picnic Basket, tray lid, USA, American Bisque 165.00
Pig w/Straw Hat, USA, American Bisque 85.00
Pinocchio, Walt Disney, minimum value 400.00
Pirate on Chest, Pat Pending, Starnes of Calif 250.00
Poodle at Counter, Twin Winton 65.00
Popeye, American Bisque 950.00
Quaker Oats, Regal 125.00
Rabbit in Hat, DeForest of Calif, c USA 32.00
Raggedy Andy, Maddux of Calif USA #2108 ....80.00
Raggedy Andy, Twin Winton 85.00
Raggedy Ann, unmk Japan 40.00
Ranger Bear, red collar & cuffs, Twin Winton 80.00

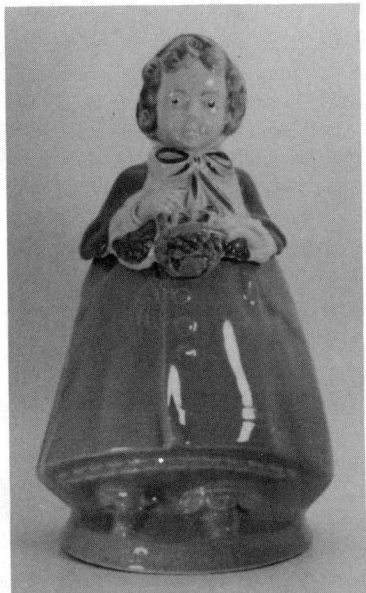

Red Riding Hood, Pottery Guild, $125.00.

Ricky Raccoon, Made in Taiwan, c 1981 Hallmark Cards Inc 70.00
Rocking Horse, Regal China 200.00
Rocking Horse, Treasure Craft 35.00
Rooster, Gilner, G-22 ....45.00
Rooster, heavy gold trim, unmk American Bisque 130.00
Rooster, Sierra Vista 55.00
Rubbles House, American Bisque 900.00
Sack of Cookies, USA, American Bisque 45.00
Sailor Elephant, Twin Winton 45.00
Sailor Elephant, USA, American Bisque 85.00
Sailor Monkey, Japan 18.00
Santa, California Originals 225.00
Scarecrow, Royal Sealy, Japan 28.00
Schoolhouse, bell in lid, USA, American Bisque 35.00
Seal on Igloo, USA, American Bisque 225.00
Sears Little Black Girl 625.00
Sheriff Pig, yel hat, gold trim, Robinson Ransbottom 170.00
Snoopy, Holiday Designs 50.00
Snow White, Walt Disney, Enesco label, minimum value 700.00
Snowman & Glass, Treasure Craft 150.00
Spaceship, Napco 75.00
Spool of Thread, thimble finial, USA, American Bisque 95.00
Sprout, Pillsbury, Made in Taiwan, c 1988 ....45.00
Squirrel, Twin Winton 40.00
Superman, California Originals 400.00
Taxi, yel checker 125.00
Teddy Bear, Treasure Craft 45.00
Telephone, Cardinal USA #311 ....50.00
Tenderheart Bear, American Greetings 60.00
Tepee, Twin Winton 150.00
Thumper, Walt Disney 150.00
Toothache Dog, American Bisque 695.00
Tortoise & Hare, 803 USA, American Bisque, minimum value .200.00
Train, Sierra Vista, California 65.00
Umbrella Kids, American Bisque 275.00
Uncle Mistletoe, Peter Pan Co, EX 450.00
Watermelon Mammy, Pearl China, rare, minimum value 3,000.00
WC Fields, Cumberland Ware 500.00
Wilma on Telephone, American Bisque 1,100.00
Windmill, FAPCo 25.00
Winnie the Pooh, California Originals 125.00
Woody Woodpecker, Walter Lantz Prod Inc 980 USA 750.00

Woody Woodpecker Head, Taiwan, MIB 650.00
Yarn Doll, unmk American Bisque 75.00
Yogi Bear, cold pnt or felt tongue, American Bisque, ea 375.00

Cooper, Susie

A 20th-century ceramic designer whose works are now attracting the attention of collectors, Susie Cooper was first affiliated with the A.E. Gray Pottery in Henley, England in 1922 where she designed in lustres and painted items with her own ideas as well. (Examples of Gray's lustreware is rare and costly.) By 1930 she and her brother-in-law, Jack Beeson, had established a family business. Her pottery soon became a success, and she was subsequently offered space at Crown Works, Burslem. In 1940 she received the honorary title of Royal Designer for Industry, the only such distinction ever awarded by the Royal Society of Arts solely for pottery design. Miss Cooper received the Order of the British Empire in the New Year's Honors List of 1979. She was the chief designer for the Wedgwood group from 1966 until she resigned in 1972. Since 1980 she has worked on a free-lance basis.

Bowl, bouillon; red/brn lines, 2" H, +underplate 35.00
Bowl, Cubist pattern, Gray's Period, 8" dia 350.00
Bowl, gr/blk w/sgraffito design, oval, 8½" 85.00
Bowl, pk matt w/blk, tubeline, 6½" H 400.00
Coffee set, orange & gray bands, Gray's Period, 8" pot 450.00
Coffee set, red-brn w/sgraffito, Faenza Kestral, 7¾" pot 350.00
Cup & saucer, 'Golfer,' man w/golf club, 2½" H 150.00
Cup & saucer, Cubist style, Gray's Period, 5¾" dia 150.00
Cup & saucer, Ferndown, 2½" 40.00
Cup & saucer, gold-banded lily, Doric shape, 2¼" H 40.00
Cup & saucer, Wild Strawberry 15.00
Plate, dinner; Wild Strawberry 15.00
Plate, gray/brn/bl-wash bands, 8" dia 20.00
Plate, luncheon; Wild Strawberry 10.00
Plate, turq sgraffito pineapple, 9" 60.00
Platter, Dresden Spray, gr-wash border, oval, 14" 85.00
Punch bowl, Wedding Ring, gray/brn/turq-wash bands, 12½" 250.00
Sweet dish, Dresden Spray, yel-wash border, 2-part, 11½" 45.00
Tea set, brn stripes, turq wash, Rex shape, 4½" pot 200.00
Tureen, sauce; brn-wash bands, w/lid, 4" H 75.00
Vase, aerographed brn/gr/yel, 7½" 225.00
Vase, pk, appl buttons at sides, 7½" 450.00

Coors

The firm that became known as Coors Porcelain Company in 1920 was founded in 1908 by John J. Herold, originally of the Roseville Pottery in Zanesville, Ohio. Though still in business today, they are best known for their artware vases and Rosebud dinnerware produced before 1939.

Coors vases produced before the late thirties were made in a matt finish; by the later years of the decade, high-gloss glazes were also being used. Nearly fifty shapes were in production, and some of the more common forms were made in three sizes. Typical colors in matt are white, orange, blue, green, yellow, and tan. Yellow, blue, maroon, pink, and green are found in high gloss. All vases are marked with a triangular arrangement of the words 'Coors Colorado Pottery' enclosing the word 'Golden.' You may find vases (usually 6" to 6½") marked with the Colorado State Fair stamp and dated 1939. For such a vase, add $10.00 to the suggested values given below.

Our Rosebud advisor is Jo Ellen Winther. Advice for miscellaneous listings was provided by Jim and Carol Carlton; all are listed in the Directory under Colorado.

Apple baker, Rosebud, 4¾" dia 25.00
Ashtray, Rosebud, rare, 3½" 125.00
Baker, Rosebud, 4¾" dia 20.00
Baking pan, Rosebud, rectangular, 2x12x8" 30.00
Bowl, fruit; Rosebud, 5" 8.00
Bowl, mixing; Rosebud, hdld, 3½-cup 25.00
Bowl, pudding; Rosebud, 2-pt, sm 20.00
Casserole, Dutch; Rosebud, 3½-cup 40.00

Rosebud, service casserole, 3½-pint, with underplate, $45.00.

Casserole, Rosebud, w/lid, 14-cup 45.00
Cup, custard; Rosebud, 4" 8.00
Egg cup, Rosebud, 6-oz 25.00
Planter, orange matt, 3-legged, 8¾" 25.00
Plate, Rosebud, 7¼" 7.50
Plate, Rosebud, 9" 15.00
Platter, Rosebud, 12x9" 15.00
Shakers, Rosebud, str sides, 4½", pr 18.00
Teapot, Rosebud, 2-cup 85.00
Tumbler, Rosebud, ftd, no hdl, 12-oz 75.00
Underplate, Rosebud, 7" 8.00
Vase, yel, imp design, 5½" 30.00
Water server, Rosebud, corked stopper, 6-cup 65.00

Miscellaneous

Ashtray, 'Beer, Butter, Malted Milk,' rnd, flat 65.00
Ashtray, ivory, common 3.00
Bank, clown, hanging 100.00
Bank, clown, sitting 100.00
Base, cvd leaves & berries, bulbous, 6½" 35.00
Bowl vase, scroll hdls extend above wide collar neck, 7¼" 75.00
Coffee maker, porc, 4-part 75.00
Crock, malted milk; porc, w/lid 100.00
Figurine, Monks, laughing/crying, pr 500.00
Lamp, cvd leaves & berries, bulbous, 7", +shade 150.00
Mug, w/Colorado State Fair, 1934 ....75.00
Mug, w/lion decal 18.00
Shaker, bottle form 15.00
Shaker, keg form 15.00
Statue, buffalo 500.00
Vase, bulbous urn form w/hdls, 7½" 45.00
Vase, bulbous urn form w/hdls, 8½" 65.00
Vase, bulbous w/collar neck, rope hdls, 9½" 60.00
Vase, Empire State Bldg, sq w/stepped buttresses, 9" 75.00
Vase, ftd bowl form w/akimbo rim-to-shoulder hdls, #7, 6½" 40.00

Vase, ftd bowl form w/akimbo rim-to-shoulder hdls, #7, 8" 75.00
Vase, horizontal ribbing, molded ring hdls, 5" 40.00
Vase, orange w/ivory int, 8½x6" 65.00
Vase, ½-circle rim-to-base hdls, Deco shape, 5¼" 25.00
Vase, ½-circle rim-to-base hdls, Deco shape, 6¼" 35.00
Vase, ½-circle rim-to-base hdls, Deco shape, 8¼" 75.00

Copper

Hand-crafted copper was made in America from early in the 18th century until about 1850 with the center of its production in Pennsylvania. Examples have been found signed by such notable coppersmiths as Kidd, Buchanan, Babb, Bently, and Harbeson. Of the many utilitarian items made, teakettles are the most desirable. Early examples from the 18th century were made with a dovetailed joint which was hammered and smoothed to a uniform thickness. Pots from the 19th century were seamed. Coffeepots were made in many shapes and sizes and along with mugs, kettles, warming pans, and measures are easiest to find. Stills ranging in sizes of up to fifty-gallon are popular with collectors today.

Our advisor, Mary Frank Gaston, has compiled a lovely book, *Antique Brass and Copper*, with many full-color photos and current market values; you will find her address in the Directory under Texas.

Architectural panel, beetle in relief, 1900s, 10x10x2½" 125.00
Dipper, hammered w/wrought iron hdl, 1850s, 25" L 125.00

Food mold, English, 7½", $250.00.

Kettle, dvtl, wrought iron hdl, dents/rpr, 20x29" 325.00
Measure, haystack, dvtl, Dring & Face London, Gallon, 11" 125.00
Measure, haystack, dvtl, hdl sgn Sykes, 8", EX 225.00
Measure, haystack, dvtl, mk Pint, battered, 5" 75.00
Mold, Turk's head, EX detail, dvtl, dents, 10" dia 125.00
Pan, dvtl, wrought copper side hdls, 7x11½" dia 95.00
Pan, tinned int, dvtl, 3½x6½"+arched 1-pc hammered hdl 85.00
Peat bucket, dvtl, ca 1840, EX 150.00
Saucepan, dvtl, 5", 6¾" hdl 85.00
Scoop, trn wood hdl, well made, soldered rpr, 15" 75.00
Teakettle, dvtl, brass hdl w/indistinct stamped mk, 7", EX 250.00
Teakettle, dvtl, gooseneck, acorn finial, brass trim, 11" 150.00
Teakettle, dvtl, gooseneck, copper finial, hdl detail, 10" 95.00
Teakettle, dvtl, gooseneck spout w/flap, swivel hdl, 9" 100.00

Teakettle, dvtl, iron legs, side spout w/flap, trn hdl, 7" **100.00**
Teakettle, gooseneck, brass trim, stamped mk, 6", EX **55.00**

Copper Lustre

Copper lustre is a term referring to a type of pottery made in Staffordshire after the turn of the 19th century. It is finished in a metallic rusty-brown glaze resembling true copper. Pitchers are found in abundance, ranging from simple styles with dull bands of color to those with fancy handles and bands of embossed, polychromed flowers. Bowls are common; goblets, mugs, teapots, and sugar bowls much less so. It's easy to find but not in good condition. Pieces with hand-painted decoration and those with historical transfers are the most valuable. Our advisor for this category is Richard Marden; he is listed in the Directory under New Hampshire.

Candlestick, cherub on scroll support, Czech, late, 6", pr **25.00**
Coffeepot, ribbed & beaded, Georgian style, 10½" **375.00**
Compote, mc flower garland, ped ft, 3¼x4¼" **65.00**
Creamer, wht vintage band, purple resist floral band, 4" **45.00**
Figurine, whippet, seated, free-standing front legs, 7½", pr **360.00**
Flowerpot, gray band w/emb birds, lion head/ring hdls, 6" **200.00**
Mug, Hope, mc transfer, ca 1800, 3⅛" **75.00**
Pitcher, allegorical scenic mc panels, 4⅝" **75.00**
Pitcher, amber band, 1840, 6" **45.00**
Pitcher, bl band w/emb floral, mask spout, 5¼" **85.00**
Pitcher, emb patterns/HP florals, 8⅜x4¼" **135.00**
Pitcher, floral, orange/pk lustre on bl band, 5¾" **75.00**
Pitcher, florals on bl band, hairlines in hdl, 9½" **150.00**
Pitcher, grapes in high relief, 5¼" **45.00**
Pitcher, London scenes, 7½" **75.00**

Pitcher, stags in relief, 7¾", $140.00.

Pitcher, wide bl band, 5½" **45.00**
Teapot, floral spray, bl trim, faceted sides, 7", NM **125.00**
Tumbler, wht band w/mc florals, wear, 2⅝" **65.00**

Coralene Glass

Coralene is a unique type of art glass easily recognized by the tiny grains of glass that form its decoration. Lacy allover patterns of seaweed, geometrics, and florals were used, as well as solid forms such as fish, plants, and single blossoms. It was made by several glasshouses both here and abroad. Values are based to a considerable extent on the amount of beading that remains. Our advisors for this category are Betty and Clarence Maier; they are listed in the Directory under Pennsylvania.

Pitcher, wht w/flying bird & leafy branch, mk Pat, 7" **200.00**
Punch cup, pk Dmn Quilt MOP w/beaded motif, 2⅜x3" **495.00**
Rose bowl, pk w/yel seaweed, 5-crimp, amber ft, 3x4½" **375.00**
Tumbler, pk shaded, Dmn Quilt MOP, floral/bugs motif, 4x2½" ..**495.00**
Tumbler, rose Dmn Quilt MOP w/yel beaded motif, 4" **395.00**
Vase, dk bl w/allover yel motif, ftd, 8" **325.00**

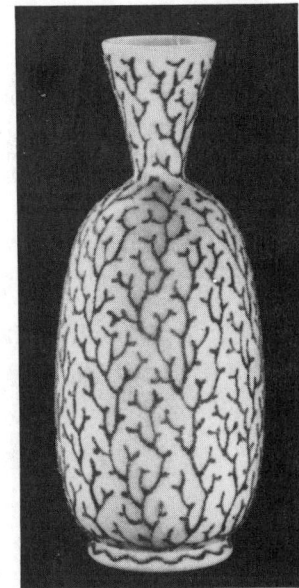

Vase, orange seaweed on pale yellow, 9", $350.00.

Vase, pk, Dmn Quilt w/allover yel seaweed motif, sq rim, 12" **900.00**
Vase, pk Dmn Quilt MOP, wheat motif in yel, 11" **1,070.00**
Vase, pk Snowflake MOP w/star motif, 4⅝x3⅜" **450.00**
Vase, pk/gr stripes, coral branch motif in yel, 8x4½" **475.00**

Coralene, Oriental

Ceramics decorated in the same manner as coralene glass were produced in Japan, during the early 1900s. Many items are marked 'Patent Pending' or with a specific patent date.

Biscuit jar, foliage/floral on bl, SP lid **365.00**
Box, floral lid, scalloped sides, gold trim, 2x4" **75.00**
Plate, florals, pk on gr bsk, much gold, 7¾" **85.00**
Plate, poppy, pk on gr w/gold beaded rim, mk Pat, 7¾" **100.00**
Vase, nasturtiums, pk on brn, cylindrical, sm hdls, 8¼" **410.00**
Vase, water lily, lav/pk on bl/pk mottle w/gold, hdls, 4" **250.00**

Cordey

The Cordey China Company was founded in 1942 in Trenton, New Jersey, by Boleslaw Cybis. The operation was small with less than a dozen workers. They produced figurines, vases, lamps, and similar wares, much of which was marketed through gift shops both nationwide and abroad. Though the earlier wares were made of plaster, Cybis soon developed his own formula for a porcelain composition which he called 'Papka.' Cordey figurines and busts were characterized by old-world charm, Rococo scrolls, delicate floral appliques, ruffles, and real lace which was dipped in liquified clay to add dimension to the work.

Although on rare occasions some items were not numbered or signed, the 'basic' figure was cast both with numbers and the Cordey signature. The molded pieces were then individually decorated and each marked with its own impressed identification number as well as a mark to indicate the artist-decorator. Their numbering system began with 200 and in later years progressed into the 8000s. As can best be established, Cordey continued production until sometime in the mid-1950s. Boleslaw Cybis died in 1957; his wife died in 1958.

Key: ff — full figure

Ashtray, #6046 ....18.00
Bird, #2037, blk & gray w/red breast, perched on stump, 8½" 110.00
Bird, #6004R, bl/wht, on tree stump, 10" 110.00
Bottle, scent; #7026, shades of bl, iris-form stopper, 8" 95.00
Box, #6029, oval 45.00
Box, trinket; #7038, roses & mixed florals, ftd 55.00
Bust, #5012, lady w/ringlets, ivory w/gold flowers, 5¾" 50.00
Bust, #5014, Junior Prom, ringlets, 7" 60.00
Bust, #5051, Old Colony, lady w/flower basket, 10" 95.00
Clock, #909, bird on roses at top, scrolled, 14½", EX 155.00
Clock, mantel; #914, rococo, Lanshire Electric, 9½" 165.00

Elizabeth, #5029, high ruffled collar, 7½", $80.00.

Lady, #300, ff, ruffles, pantaloons, holds flowers, 15½" 85.00
Lady, #3158, gold headband, much lace, 13¼" 195.00
Lady, #5054, flowers in hair, bustle, skirt forms base, 9¼" 75.00
Lady, #5061, Madame Dubarry, rare, 14", NM 215.00
Lady, #5066, Carmen, ff, lav dress, long coat, high hat, 14" 155.00
Lady, #5084, Madame, upswept hair, scrolled base, 11¾" 100.00
Lady, #5089, ringlets, lace, big bustle, 10¾" 150.00
Lamp, #155, little girl figural 95.00
Lamp, #304/#305, Grape Harvesters, 16½", pr 225.00
Lamp, #5024, scrolled base 145.00
Lamp, #5041/#5084, dbl figure (man & lady), pr 250.00
Lamp, Chinese Goddess, 12" figure on wooden base, 26" 185.00
Lamp, Madame Dubarry bust, gold lace, rococo base, 18" 265.00
Man, #303, plumed hat, ff, 16" 225.00
Man, #4153, ff, much lace, 14" 185.00
Man & lady, #302/#303, ff, 16", pr 315.00
Man & lady, #4005/#4006, ff, pr 300.00
Man & lady, Yorkshire, #4047/#4048, pr 190.00
Neopolitan Boy w/basket of breadsticks, #5045, 9½" 95.00
Pheasant, #343, vibrant mc, very early, scarce, 17" 325.00
Plaque, #902, lady's face, ringlets, 10" 235.00
Tray, card; #8047, cherub w/pk roses & leaves, 8" 80.00
Vase, #7061, birds on leaf, roses appl ea side, 8¾" 150.00
Vase, #7094, Orientals in relief, appl flowers, 8" 160.00
Wall sconce, #7028, cherubs & flowers, pr 195.00
Wall shelf, #7028, Art Nouveau nude w/cornucopia, 8x6½" 100.00

Yorkshire Girl, #5047, ff, grapes in dress folds, 10" 95.00

Corkscrews

The history of the corkscrew dates back to the mid-1600s, when wine makers concluded that the best-aged wine was that stored in smaller containers, either stoneware or glass. Since plugs left unsealed were often damaged by rodents, corks were cut off flush with the bottle top and sealed with wax or a metal cover. Removing the cork cleanly with none left to grasp became a problem. The task was found to be relatively simple using the worm on the end of a flintlock gun rod. So the corkscrew evolved. Endless patents have been issued for mechanized models. Handles range from carved wood, ivory, and bone to porcelain and repousse silver. Exotic materials such as agate, mother-of-pearl, and gold plate were also used on occasion. Celluloid lady's legs are popular. Our advisor for this category is Roger Baker; he is listed in the Directory under California.

Abyssinian type w/threaded tube, dbl hdls 78.00
Brubaker, T-shaped, twisted wire shaft, wood hdl, 4¼" 15.00
Carter's Ink, folding, Pat 1894 ....12.50
England, ebonized wood hdl, thick disk, 1880s, EX 25.00
England, pearl hdls, scent & medicine bottle puller, 3½" 60.00
England, picnic type, steel screw, ca 1800, EX 150.00
England, polished steel peg & worm, ca 1810, 4½" 130.00
England, steel w/gold finish, cube-shaped ends, 3" 130.00
England, Sulgrave Manor, 2-finger style, bronze, EX 30.00
England, swivel-over collar, bronze finish on steel, VG 42.50
England, 4-finger pull, w/button, ca 1895 ....27.50
France, wood hdl, metal ends, dimpled shaft, ca 1875, EX 30.00
France, wood dbl hdl, cvd portrait in rnd fr, NM 40.00
Germany, legs figural (gr stripes), ca 1910, EX 300.00
Germany, spring over shaft, ca 1895, VG 22.50
Germany, spring-release helix worm, steel cage, 1880s 45.00
Germany, swivel-over collar style, rubber ring on fr, 1950s 25.00

Happy Face, ca 1935, 10", $75.00.

Italy, bar man figural, dbl-lever style, 10½" 48.00
Italy, swivel-over collar type, NP brass, VG 25.00
John Watts Sheffield England, NP w/center worm, ca 1909 ....37.50
London Rack, rack & pinion actions, unmk English, 1800s 150.00
Magic Lever Cork Drawer, Pat Appl For, ca 1925, VG 45.00
Man w/straw hat figural, modern dbl-lever type, 8½" 20.00
Old Snifter, Senator Volstead, brass, fixed hat, w/opener 200.00
Old Snifter, Senator Volstead, thermoplastic w/mc pnt 225.00

Perpetual, dbl-threaded shaft, automatic reverse, unmk **75.00**
Plastic duplex (dbl worm), picnic type, modern **5.00**
Rosewood hdl, gilted shaft & worm, modern **12.00**
Staghorn hdl, mk sterling cap, 7½" **65.00**
Unmk, dbl loop of wire finger hold, helical wire screw, 3" **3.00**
US, brass band on boar's tooth hdl, 6", EX **85.00**
US, H&B Mfg Co, rosewood hdl, w/brush & ivory plug, 1880s **52.50**
US, Hollwig 1891 Pat, Pabst Milwaukee advertising, EX **130.00**
US, NP steel worm, cap lifter & ice breaker, NM **37.50**
US, roundlet style, bullet shape, EX **50.00**
US, staghorn hdl, sterling silver cap, late 1800s, 8½" **80.00**
US, Williamson 1897 Pat Bullet, copper finish, early **80.00**
US, Woodward Tool Pat Aug 24, 1875, 10 tools in 1, EX **30.00**
US Clough 1910 Pat, Hennessy advertising on wood sleeve **32.00**
US 1895 Pat, pocket type, sterling sleeve, EX **30.00**
Weir's Pat 12804 25, Sept 1884, VG bronze finish **125.00**

Cosmos

Cosmos, sometimes called Stemless Daisy, is a patterned glass tableware produced from 1894 through 1915 by Consolidated Lamp and Glass Company. Relief-molded flowers on a finely crosscut background were painted in soft colors of pink, blue, and yellow. Though nearly all were made of milk glass, a few items may be found in clear glass with the designs painted on. In addition to the tableware, lamps were also made.

Bottle, cologne; orig stopper, rare **150.00**
Butter dish **235.00**
Condiment set, 3-pc in fr **350.00**
Creamer **150.00**

Spooner, $125.00.

Lamp, banquet; kerosene, 24" **475.00**
Lamp, banquet; slender base, rnd globe, all orig, 16" **525.00**
Lamp, mini; 7" **325.00**
Lamp, 10" **400.00**
Pickle castor, dbl, mk SP fr **500.00**
Pickle castor, single, ftd SP fr **350.00**
Pitcher, milk; 5" **170.00**
Pitcher, syrup; 6" **200.00**
Pitcher, water **250.00**
Shakers, tall, orig lids, pr **100.00**
Spooner **125.00**
Sugar bowl, open **150.00**
Sugar bowl, w/lid **185.00**

Tumbler, 3¾" **65.00**

Cottageware

You'll find a varied assortment of novelty dinnerware items, all styled as cozy little English cottages or huts with cone-shaped roofs; some may have a waterwheel or a windmill. Marks will vary. English-made Price Brothers or Beswick pieces are valued in the same range as those marked Occupied Japan, while items marked simply Japan are considered slightly less pricey. Our advisor for this category is Grace Klender; she is listed in the Directory under Ohio.

Butter dish, England **45.00**
Butter pat, emb cottage, rectangular, Occupied Japan **17.50**
Chocolate pot, English **135.00**
Cookie jar, pk/brn/gr, sq, Japan, 8½x5½" **65.00**
Cookie or biscuit jar, Occupied Japan **85.00**
Creamer, windmill, Occupied Japan, 2⅝" **15.00**
Creamer & sugar bowl, England, 2½", 4½" **45.00**
Cup & saucer, English, 2½", 4½" **45.00**
Dish w/cover, Occupied Japan, sm **35.00**
Egg cup, 1¾" **15.00**
Mug, Price Bros **50.00**
Pitcher, water; English **150.00**
Platter, oval, 11¾x7½" **45.00**
Shakers, windmill, Occupied Japan, pr **20.00**
Sugar bowl, windmill, w/lid, Occupied Japan, 3⅞" **25.00**
Sugar box, for cubes, English, 5¾" long **45.00**
Teapot, English or Occupied Japan, 6½" **50.00**
Tumbler, Occupied Japan, 3½", set of 6 ....**60.00**

Coverlets

The Jacquard attachment for hand looms represented a culmination of weaving developments made in France. Introduced to America by the early 1820s, it gave professional weavers the ability to easily create complex patterns with curved lines. Those who could afford the new loom adaptation could now use hole-punched pasteboard cards to weave floral patterns that before could only be achieved with intense labor on a draw-loom.

Before the Jacquard mechanism, most weavers made their coverlets in geometric patterns. Use of indigo-blue and brightly colored wools often livened the twills and overshot patterns available to the small-loom home weaver. Those who had larger multiple-harness looms could produced warm double-woven, twill-block, or summer-and-winter designs.

While the new floral and pictorial patterns' popularity had displaced the geometrics in urban areas, the mid-Atlantic, and the Midwest by the 1840s, even factory production of the Jacquard coverlets was disrupted by cotton and wool shortages during the Civil War. A revived production in the 1870s saw a style change to a center-medallion motif, but a new fad for white 'Marseilles' spreads soon halted sales of Jacquard-woven coverlets. Production of Jacquard carpets continued to the turn of the century.

Rural and frontier weavers continued to make geometric-design coverlets through the 19th century, and local craft revivals have continued the tradition through this century. All-cotton overshots were factory produced in Kentucky from the 1940s, and factories and professional weavers made cotton-and-wool overshots during the past decade.

Many Jacquard-woven coverlets have dates and names of places and people (often the intended owner — not the weaver) woven into corners or borders.

In the listings that follow, examples are blue and white unless noted otherwise.

Jacquard

Christian/heathen borders, peacocks feeding young, EX 495.00
Floral, corners dtd 1862, maroon/gr/wht, 2-pc single, 76x90" 450.00
Floral, eagle borders, sgn corners/dtd 1833, 2-pc dbl, EX 495.00
Floral, eagle/chickens border, bl-blk/wht, sgn/1834, 73x85" 1,500.00
Floral, eagle/tree border, Liberty corners, sgn/1840, 2-pc 650.00
Floral, Hempfield RR border, 3-color, 2-pc, very worn/rpr 850.00
Floral, house borders, MA Myers Pat/1853, 3-color, wear 375.00
Floral, vintage borders, sgn Ardner 1852, 4-color, 2-pc, VG 500.00
Floral, 2-pc dbl, 72x85", NM 250.00
Floral medallion, corners: Smith/1870, 3-color, lt wear 400.00
Floral stripes, Lorenz/1845, 4-color, 2-pc single, 80x88" 950.00
Florals on stripes, bird border, GH Basil/1844, 4-color 750.00
Miniature, floral, sgn Seibert, 5-color, fringe, 39x45" 925.00
Roses/stars, pots of roses border, eagle corners, sgn, VG 650.00
Snowflake & pine tree, dbl weave, 2-pc, resewn/wear/patched ...160.00
Starflowers, eagle/tree borders, sgn/1836, red/wht, VG 450.00
Starflowers, vintage border, dtd 1859, 4-color, 2-pc, EX 450.00
Urns of fruit/flowers, peacocks feeding young, 4-color, EX 550.00
4 rose medallions, house borders, sgn/1851, 4-color, VG 395.00

Overshot

Bars w/circle devices at intersections, 3-color, 72x78", VG 295.00
Checks/sqs, geometric bands form stars at junctions, 4-color 225.00
Navy lines w/devices at X-points form 4-leaf clover on wht 150.00
Optic sqs, bl/wht, 2-pc, 61x68" 125.00
Optical pattern, red/navy/natural, 2-pc dbl weave, VG 175.00
Optical pattern, 2-pc, wear/stains, 74x99" 150.00
Wide lt & dk bands w/intervals of 2 uprights or quatrafoil 125.00
X w/o's in angles on 3-bar lt band, +dk bands, 4-color, VG 175.00

Cowan

Guy Cowan opened a small pottery near Cleveland, Ohio ca 1909, where he made tile and artware on a small scale from the natural red clay available there. He developed distinctive glazes — necessary, he felt, to cover the dark red body. After the war and a temporary halt in production, Cowan moved his pottery to Rocky River, where he made a commercial line of artware utilizing a highly fired white porcelain. Although he acquiesced to the necessity of mass-production, every effort was made to insure a product of highest quality. Fine artists, among them Waylande Gregory, Margaret Postgate, and Viktor Schreckengost, designed pieces which were often produced in limited editions, some of which sell today for prices in the thousands. Most of the ware was marked 'Cowan' or 'Lakewood Ware,' not to be confused with the name of the 1927 mass-produced line called 'Lakeware.' Falling under the crunch of the Great Depression, the pottery closed in 1931. Our advisor for this category is Mark Bassett; he is listed in the Directory under Iowa.

Bowl, April Gr & Special Ivory, scalloped, 8" 45.00
Bowl, Copper Lustre, 5½x9" 75.00
Candelabra, triple; Turq, pr 135.00
Candlestick, Radiant design, Blk, scalloped, pr 65.00
Candlestick, sea horse design, Special Ivory, pr 40.00
Comport, sea horse design, oval, Special Ivory, 3¼x6½" 30.00
Console set, Etruscan design, Oriental Red, 3-pc 200.00
Console set, Lilac Gray & Persian Bl, 3-pc 95.00

Decanters, King and Queen from Alice, Through the Looking-Glass, designed by Gregory, Oriental Red, 12", $1,200.00 for the pair.

Figurine, Spanish Dancer (lady), Ivory, 8" 275.00
Flower figure, Deco draped lady, Ivory, W Sinz, 6" 95.00
Flower figure, Scarf Dancer, Turq, 6" 300.00
Lamp base, artichoke or pine cone design, Azure 275.00
Lamp base, candlestick shape, Marigold, 12½" 80.00
Paperweight, elephant, Arabian Night, M Postgate 295.00
Plate, Danse Moderne design, Egyptian Bl & Blk 2,860.00
Punch bowl, Jazz, Egyptian Bl & Blk, 8" 20,000.00
Sculpture, Congo Head, Blk & Bronze, Gregory, ltd ed, 15" ...1,750.00
Sculpture, Madonna, Terra Cotta, M Postgate, ltd ed 2,500.00
Tea cup on tray, Federal design, Orchid, hexagonal 40.00
Vase, bud; sea horse design, Special Ivory, 7" 40.00
Vase, Delphinium bl lustre, appl moths on shoulder, 12" 375.00
Vase, fan; October, 4" 85.00
Vase, fluted, Fir Gr, 12" 190.00
Vase, Larkspur Bl, 4-ftd, 5" 45.00
Vase, Larkspur flambe over Opal, 6" 150.00
Vase, Plum, ribbed, 5" 85.00
Vase, Terra Cotta, Blk lid & base, bulbous, 8x6", pr 500.00
Vase, Turq, 12" 105.00

Cracker Jack

Kids have been buying Cracker Jack since it was first introduced in the 1890s. By 1912 it was packaged with a free toy inside. Before the first kernel was crunched, eager fingers had retrieved the surprise from the depth of the box — actually no easy task, considering the care required to keep the contents so swiftly displaced from spilling over the side! Though a little older, perhaps, many of those same kids still are looking — just as eagerly — for the Cracker Jack prizes. Point of sale, company collectibles, and the prizes as well have over the years reflected America's changing culture. Grocer sales and incentives from around the turn of the century — paper dolls, postcards and song books — were often marked Rueckheim Brothers (the inventors of Cracker Jack) or Reliable Confections. The first loose-packed prizes were toys made of wood, clay, tin, metal, and lithographed paper. Plastic toys were introduced in 1946. Paper wrapped for safety purposes in 1948, subjects echo the 'hype' of the day — Yo-Yos, tops, whistles, and sports cards in the simple, peaceful days of our country; propaganda and war toys in the forties; games in the fifties; and space toys in the sixties. Few of the estimated 15 billion prizes were marked. Advertising items from Angelus Marshmallow and Checkers Confections (cousins of the Cracker Jack family) are also collectible. When no condition is indicated, the items listed below are assumed to be in excellent condition.

'CJ' indicates that the item is marked. Note: An often-asked question concerns the tin Toonerville Trolley marked 'CJ.' No data has been found in the factory archives to authenticate this item; it is assumed that the 'CJ' merely refers to its size. Our advisor for this category is Wes Johnson; he is listed in the Directory under Kentucky.

Cast Metal Prizes

Badge, shield, CJ Jr Detective, silver, 1931, 1¼" **35.00**
Badge, 6-point star, mk CJ Police, silver, 1931, 1¼" **35.00**
Button, stud bk, Me for Cracker Jack, boy & dog **26.00**
Button, stud bk, Xd bats & ball, CJ pitcher/etc series, 1928 ....**78.00**
Chair, T (Tootsie), 3 different sectional pcs, pnt, mini, ea **12.00**
Dollhouse items: lantern, mug, candlestick, etc; no mk, ea **6.50**
Horse & wagon, CJ, 3-D, silver or gold, early, 2½", ea **250.00**
Pistol, soft lead, inked, CJ on barrel, early, rare, 2⅛" **180.00**
Ring, alphabet letter setting (series), unmk, ea **3.00**
Rocking horse, no rider, 3-D, inked, early, 1⅛" **9.00**
Rocking horse w/boy, 3-D, inked, early, 1½" **29.00**

Sign, point of sale, bathing beauty, 5-color die-cut litho on cardboard, marked Cracker Jack, early, 22x17", $300.00.

Spinner, early pkg in center, 'More You Eat...,' CJ, rare **295.00**
TootsieToy series: boats, cars, animals; '31, ¾"-1½", ea **7.00**

Dealer Incentives

Blotter, CJ question mk box, yel, 7¾x3¾" **225.00**
Cart w/2 movable wheels, wood dowel tongue, CJ **49.00**
Corkscrew/opener, metal plated, CJ/Angelus, 3" **75.00**
Corkscrew/opener, metal plated, CJ/Angelus, 3¾" tube case **75.00**
Jigsaw puzzle, CJ or Checkers, 1 of 4, 7x10", in envelope **35.00**
Magic puzzle, metal, CJ/Angelus, 1 of 15, '34, ea in envelope **14.00**
Mask, Halloween; paper, CJ, 10" or 12", ea **18.00**
Match holder, hinged, eng gold-tone case, CJ, 2½x1⅞" **650.00**
Palm puzzle, mirror bk, CJ, mk Germany/RWB, 1910-14, 1½" ...**110.00**

Pencil top clip, metal/celluloid, oval boy & dog logo **210.00**
Pencil top clip, metal/celluloid, tube shape w/package **190.00**
Postcard, bear, 1 of 16, CJ, 1907, ea **25.00**
Tablet, school; CJ, 1929, 8x10" **195.00**
Thimble, aluminum, CJ Co/Angelus, red pnt, rare, ea **165.00**

Packaging

Box, popcorn; red scroll border, CJ, ca 1920 ....**85.00**
Box, popcorn; store display, CJ, 1923, no contents **65.00**
Canister, tin, CJ Candy Corn Crisp, 10-oz **75.00**
Canister, tin, CJ Coconut Corn Crisp, 1-lb **55.00**
Canister, tin, CJ Coconut Corn Crisp, 10-oz **65.00**
CJ Commemorative canister, mc scene, 1990s, ea **9.00**
CJ Commemorative canisters, wht w/red scroll, 1980s, ea **6.50**
Crate, shipping; wood, CJ, Reuckheim Bros Eck, 1902-22, lg **175.00**

Paper Prizes

Baseball CJ score counter, 3⅜" L **145.00**
Book, Animals (or Birds), to color, Makatoy, 1949, mini **35.00**
Book, Bess & Bill on CJ Hill, series of 12, 1937, mini **85.00**
Book, Birds We Know, CJ, 1928, mini **65.00**
Book, drawing w/tracing paper, CJ, 1920s, mini **110.00**
Book, Twigg & Sprigg, CJ, 1930, mini **85.00**
Booklet, stickers/wise cracks/riddles, Borden, CJ, 1965 on **1.00**
Decal, cartoon or nursery rhyme figure, 1947-49, CJ **7.00**
Disguise, ears, red (punch out from carrier), 1950, pr **20.00**
Disguise, glasses, hinged, cellophane lenses, CJ, 1933 ....**145.00**
Disguise, glasses, hinged, w/eyeballs, 1933 ....**6.00**
Disguise, mustache, blk/brn, in carrier, CJ, 1949 ....**45.00**
Fortune Teller, boy/dog on film in envelope, CJ, '20s, 1¾x2½" **62.00**
Fortune wheel, 2-pc litho, turn for fortune, CJ, 1¾" **68.00**
Game, Midget Auto Race, wheel spins, CJ, 1949, 3⅜" H **45.00**
Game spinner, ...baseball at home, rectangle, CJ, 2¾" W **125.00**
Game spinner, ...baseball at home, unmk, 1946, 1½" dia **40.00**
Hat, fold out, More You Eat/More You Want, CJ, early **75.00**
Hat, Indian headdress, CJ, early 1930s, 2½" **110.00**
Hat, Indian headdress, CJ, 1950s, 5⅜" **275.00**
Magic game book, erasable slate, series of 13, 1946, ea **27.00**
Movie, boy at blkboard, turn wheel: draws/erases, CJ, '31, 2" **185.00**
Movie, Goofy Zoo, turn wheel(s): change animals, 1939 ....**12.00**
Movie, pull tab for 2nd picture, series, CJ, 1943, 1¼", ea **82.00**
Movie, pull tab for 2nd picture, yel, early, 3", in envelope **125.00**
Palm puzzle, ball(s) roll into holes, plastic dome, from 1966 ....**1.00**
Riddle card, 2 series of 20, in package/from factory, CJ, ea **7.00**
Sand picture, sand pours for action, series of 14, 1967, ea **9.00**
Top, golf game, wood stick center, CJ, 1933 ....**47.00**
Transfer, iron on, sport figure or patriotic, CJ, 1939, ea **26.00**
Whistle, pressed paper, series of 10, 1948-49, CJ, 1¼x2", ea **34.00**
Whistle, Razz Zooka, C Carey Cloud design, CJ, 1949 ....**32.00**

Plastic Prizes

Animals, standup, letter on bk, series of 26, Nosco, 1953, ea **3.50**
Animals, standup on base, assorted, Nosco or CJ, 1947 on, ea **1.50**
Badge, pin-bk, celluloid, pretty lady, CJ label, 1¼" **65.00**
Baseball players, 3-D, bl or gray team, 1958, 1½", ea **7.00**
Disk, emb comic character, series of 12, 1954, 1½" dia **9.00**
Disk, emb fish plaque, oval, series of 10, 1956, ea **6.00**
Dog, 3-D, hollow base, series of 10, CJCO, 1954, ea **4.50**
Figure, circus; stands on base, 1 of 12, Nosco, 1951-54 ....**1.75**
Figure on rocking base, semi-flat, 1 of 9, Cloud design, '56 ....**3.00**
Fob, alphabet letter w/loop on top, 1 of 26, 1954, 1½" **2.25**

Magnifying glass, many designs/shapes, from 1961, ea **1.00**
Pinball game, lever shoots ball/score in holes, 1964 to recent **2.00**
Signs, road; Stop, Caution, etc, yel, series of 10, 1954-60, ea **3.00**
Spinner, varied colors, 10 designs, from 1948, ea **1.50**
Toys, take apart/assemble, variety, from '62, assembled, ea **1.00**
Toys, take apart/assemble, variety, from '62, unassembled, ea **2.25**
Whistle, tube w/animals on top, CJ, 1 of 6, 1950-53, 1⅜" **6.50**

Premiums

Bat, baseball; wood, Hillerich & Bradsby, CJ, full sz **125.00**
Book, pocket; jester on cover, CJ **62.00**
Book, pocket; riddle/sailor boy/dog on cover, RWB, CJ **35.00**
Harmonica, full scale, emb CJ, early, 5⅛" **385.00**
Mirror, oval, Angelus (redhead or blond) on box **89.00**
Pen, ink; w/nib, tin litho bbl, CJ **650.00**
Recipe book, Angelus, 1930s **22.00**
Wings, air corps type, silver or blk, stud-bk, CJ, '30s, 3", ea **75.00**

Tin Prizes

Badge, emb/plated CJ officer, 2⅜" or 1⅝", early, ea **110.00**
Badge, litho, red/wht/bl, boy/dog, CJ, 1920s, 1¼" dia **150.00**
Bank, 3-D book form, red/gr/or blk, CJ Bank, early, 2" **95.00**
Boy & dog, diecut, complete w/bend-over tab, CJ **110.00**
Boy & dog, diecut, w/o tab at top **85.00**
Boy & dog, stand-up litho rectangle, ca 1916, lg or sm, ea **145.00**
Brooch or pin, various design on card, CJ/logo, early, ea **125.00**
Cash register, litho, More You Eat, CJ, early, 1⅞" **275.00**
Clicker, 'Noisy CJ Snapper,' pear shape, aluminum, 1949 ....**32.00**
Doll dishes, tin plated, CJ, '31, 1¾", 1⅞", & 2⅛" dia, ea **35.00**
Fortune Wheel, 2-pc litho, CJ, 1939-41, 1¾" **55.00**
Helicopter, yel propeller, wood stick, unmk, 1937, 2⅝" **18.00**
Horse & wagon, litho diecut, CJ & Angelus, 2⅛" **65.00**
Horse & wagon, litho diecut, gray/red mks, CJ, 1914-23, 3⅛" **395.00**
Model T Ford, License: NY 1915 #999, blk/wht, CJ, rare, 2" **410.00**
Oval standup, Am flag, 1 of 4, unmk, 1936-46 ....**37.00**
Oval standup, comic character, 1 of 10, CJ, 1936-46 ....**125.00**
Pocket watch, silver or gold, CJ as numerals, 1931, 1½" **65.00**
Sled, tin plated, CJ, 1931, 2" L **39.00**
Small box shape: electric alarm clock litho, unmk, 1⅛" **75.00**
Small box shape: electric stove litho, unmk, 1⅛" **90.00**
Small box shape: garage litho, unmk, 1⅛" **85.00**
Small box shape: radio litho, bl, unmk, 1⅛" **80.00**
Soldier, litho, die-cut standup, officer/private/etc, unmk, ea **17.00**
Tall box shape: Frozen Foods locker freezer, '47, unmk, 1¾" **65.00**
Tall box shape: grandfather clock, unmk, 1947, 1¾" **55.00**
Tall box shape: radio, Tune in w/CJ, brn/yel, 1939, 1¾" **115.00**
Tall box shape: Refrigerator Car, CJ 2006, 1947, 1¾" L **155.00**
Train, engine & tender, litho, CJ Line/512 ....**125.00**
Train, litho coach only, red, unmk, 1941 ....**22.00**
Train, litho engine only, red, 1941, unmk **17.00**
Tray, emb, litho w/early pkg, smaller version **115.00**
Tray, emb, litho w/early pkg, 2¼x1¾" **95.00**
Wagon shape: Caterpillar tractor, unmk, 1931, 1¾" L **29.00**
Wagon shape: CJ Shows, yel circus wagon, series of 5, ea **135.00**
Wagon shape: Playtime Trailer (auto trailer), unmk, 1947 ....**40.00**
Wagon shape: tank, orange/red/gr camouflage, unmk **65.00**
Wagon shape: Tank Corps No 57, gr & blk, 1941 ....**30.00**
Wheelbarrow, tin plated, bk leg in place, CJ, 1931, 2½" L **40.00**

Miscellaneous

Ad, comic book, CJ, ea **9.00**
Ad, Saturday Evening Post, mc, CJ, 1919, 11x14" **18.00**

Hat, ball park vendor cap, CJ, 1930s **30.00**
Lunch box, tin, 2 hdls, CJ, 1980s, 4½x5x6" **25.00**
Lunch box, emb tin, CJ, 1970s, 4x7x9" **30.00**
Medal, CJ salesman award, brass, 1939, scarce **125.00**
Sign, bathing beauty, 5-color cb, CJ, early, 17x22" **300.00**
Sign, boy or girl w/box of CJ, 5-color cb, early, 17x22", ea **300.00**
Sign, Jack & Bingo, die-cut litho, easel standup, CJ, early **285.00**
Sign, Santa & prizes, mc cb, Angelus, early, lg **200.00**
Sign, Santa & prizes, mc cb, Checkers, early, lg **1,000.00**
Sign, Santa & prizes, mc cb, CJ, early, lg **250.00**
Sign, Santa & prizes, standing on early CJ pkg, mc cb, rare **345.00**

Cranberry

Cranberry glass is named for its resemblance to the color of cranberry juice. It was made by many companies both here and abroad, becoming popular in America soon after the Civil War. It was made in free-blown ware as well as mold-blown. Today cranberry glass is being reproduced, and it is sometimes difficult to distinguish the old from the new. Ask a reputable dealer if you are unsure. See also Cruets; Salts; Sugar Shakers; Syrups.

Biscuit barrel, Invt T'print, HP florals w/gold, SP lid, 6½" **375.00**
Bobeches, Dmn Quilt, 3¾" dia, pr **110.00**
Bottle, scent; 8 flattened ovals/panels, faceted stopper, 8" **145.00**
Bowl, appl fans & berry prunts, berry pontil, ftd, 5½x6" **275.00**
Bowl vase, silver foil, 3 clear ft, berry pontil, 3¾x4" **165.00**
Box, HP florals & scrolls, hinged lid, 3¼x3½" dia **175.00**
Box, HP florals w/gold, lift-off lid, 2½x5" **175.00**
Box, HP village scene & flowers, hinged lid, 3¾x4½" **275.00**
Creamer, fluted, appl clear hdl, 5x2¾" **65.00**
Cruet, HP florals w/gold, 8½", +6 sm mugs+8½" tray **425.00**
Cruet, liqueur; swirl, clear rigaree, pewter mts, 8¾" **195.00**
Decanter, wine; appl rope hdl, clear bubble stopper, 8¼" **165.00**
Jug, claret; encased in Fr pewter, hinged pewter top, 8⅜" **210.00**
Mug, gold flowers w/bl & wht trim, clear hdl, 3" **75.00**
Pitcher, HP grapes & triangles, ruffled, 10", +6 4" tumblers **450.00**
Pitcher, Invt T'print, bulbous, clear hdl, 7⅞" **145.00**
Pitcher, lacy gold flowers & foliage allover, 4½x2¾" **135.00**
Pitcher, tankard; Optic, clear hdl, 11½x5" **198.00**
Ring tree, saucer w/mc florals, clear ring stick **195.00**
Rose bowl, appl clear swags/berries/ft, egg shape, 4¾" **265.00**
Salt cellar, cut decor, 4 emb ribs, ftd, 1¾x2¼" **65.00**
Tumble-up, Optic, corseted bottle+tumbler, 8⅜x3⅞" **175.00**
Vase, acorn shape, clear petal ft, 3x2¼", pr **118.00**
Vase, appl clear flower/leaf/wishbone ft, 9x4" **195.00**
Vase, appl clear flowers & ft, tricorner top, 5x3⅞" **175.00**
Vase, clear rigaree at top collar, 4¼x4⅜" **60.00**
Vase, cornucopia shape, clear ft, 10x4" **88.00**
Vase, Fleurette emb, ground pontil, 4¾x3¾", pr **175.00**
Vase, gold daffodils & buds, 7¾x3" **65.00**
Vase, gold daisies & scrolls, 5¼x2⅛" **55.00**
Vase, HP floral, 9¼x3½", pr **235.00**
Vase, HP floral & heron, appl clear rim, 10¾x3½" **325.00**
Vase, HP floral w/gold trim, 6 amber jewels, 5¾x4½" **275.00**
Vase, lg clear leaves droop from rim, body w/emb ribs, 8" **95.00**
Vase, rosette emb, clear ft & trim, 10¼x4½" **145.00**
Vase, sanded wht Greek Key band/scallops, ormolu ft, 6", pr **275.00**
Whimsey, Honeycomb, tumbler reshaped as a hat, 1½" **95.00**

Creamware

Creamware was a type of earthenware developed by Wedgwood in the 1760s and produced by many other Staffordshire potteries, including Leeds. Since it could be potted cheaply and was light in weight, it became popular abroad as well as in England, due to the lower freight charges involved in its export. It was revived at Leeds in the late 19th century, and the type most often reproduced was heavily reticulated or molded in high relief. These later wares are easily distinguished from the originals since they are thicker and tend to craze heavily. See also Leeds.

Basket, open weave, oval/dmn in bottom, mk Neale, 10" L, VG ..270.00
Coffeepot, bl sprigs/striping, dome lid, ftd, 11", EX 250.00
Dish, mc floral swags/name/1807, wear/chips, 5½" 165.00
Egg cup, rtcl, incised decor on base, ftd, 2¾", EX 525.00
Fruit basket, rtcl shaped oblong form, rstr, 10", +tray 495.00
Invalid feeder, dog head/shell hdls, minor wear, 8" L 600.00
Mug, Malster doth crave (motto), 5", EX 350.00
Pepper pot, dome top, ftd, 4½" 90.00
Pitcher, lg monogram, Liverpool type, 1800s, 11", EX 365.00
Plate, mc rose, 8" 85.00
Plate, red/gr floral, red striped rim w/foliage, 7" 140.00
Plate, rose/vine border in blk, mk Turner, 7¾" 280.00
Plate, rtcl basketweave border, 8½" 100.00
Plate, rtcl floral border, feather-edged rim, Leeds, 8", EX 140.00
Plate, 3-color lg rose/multiflora, red rim stripe, 8¼" 110.00
Plate, 5-color urn/flowers, scalloped floral border, 7", EX 300.00
Sauce boat, duck form, England, 1780s, 6" L, EX 165.00
Soup plate, ship w/British flag, florals on rim, 10", VG 330.00
Tureen, molded hdls, simple design, New Castle, 12" L, EX 200.00

Crown Milano

Crown Milano was introduced in 1884 by the Mt. Washington Glass Company. When the company merged with Pairpoint in 1894, it continued to be one of their bestsellers. It is an opaque, highly decorated ware with gold or colored enamels in intricate designs on pale backgrounds. Many pieces were marked 'CM' with a crown. Since it is nearly always found in a satin finish, in the listings that follow, satin is assumed unless glossy is indicated. Our advisors for this category are Betty and Clarence Maier; they are listed in the Directory under Pennsylvania.

Biscuit jar, bamboo, gold/brn on pnt Burmese, SP mts, 6" 1,150.00
Biscuit jar, floral jewels/much gold, turtle on lid, 5½" dia 650.00
Biscuit jar, gold scrolls & florals on pnt Burmese Hobnail 900.00
Bowl, apple blossoms, gold on yel/peach; sgn SP fr, 11" H 660.00
Bowl vase, pansies/scrolls, gold leaf/berry hdls, 10" dia 400.00
Box, collars & cuffs, poppies on top, bl bow appl to front 650.00
Box, dresser; floral sprigs in dk bl scroll sections, 7" dia 450.00
Box, mc floral on wht quartered by dk bl scrolls, 8" dia 785.00
Bride's bowl, floral/gold scrolls on pnt Burmese, 2¾x10" 875.00
Creamer & sugar bowl, pansies, mc on yel to wht, 3½", 4" 1,200.00
Cup, handleless; gold flowers, 2", +4¾" saucer 800.00
Dresser jar, multiflora scrolls, hdls, lid, 4½x4½" 1,000.00
Ewer, petit point, mc/yel on wht, rope hdl, ovoid body, 13" 1,950.00
Ewer, wht floral w/gold leaves & vines on yel, bulbous, 12" 1,400.00
Jar, floral, mc on floral ground, rnd; hdld/ftd SP fr, 11" 1,300.00
Jardiniere, oak laves/acorns on scrolls, label, 6x10" 700.00
Pitcher, red-jeweled holly berries, gr/brn leaves, 9x7" 3,000.00
Rose jar, florals w/in scrollwork, steeple stopper, 12x7" 3,200.00
Rose jar, rose, 8-rib bulbous body, bulbous rim, unmk, 8½" 495.00
Saucer, thistles, elaborate decor, 1x4½" 150.00
Sweetmeat, flowers/jewels, bl & wht decor w/gold 875.00
Sweetmeat, jeweled starfish/emb stars, SP floral lid etc, 4" 1,000.00
Sweetmeat, multifloral/gold, melon rib, metal lid, 5" dia 750.00
Tumbler, gold flower garlands & bows, glossy, 3¾x2¾" 550.00

Vase, bats in flight, allover gold scrolls, label, 13" 3,500.00
Vase, cactus flowers, squat w/stick neck, label, 9" 900.00
Vase, daisies, gold/bl on wht w/pk, bottle form, 10", pr 1,870.00
Vase, ferns pnt over griffin medallions, dbl gourd, unmk, 6" 825.00
Vase, floral, allover gold, 2 entwined hdls, mk, 8" 1,200.00
Vase, floral on wht w/pk, rose/gold shoulder band, 9x6" 1,785.00

Vase, gold, green and brown winged dragons on shaded yellow, no mark, 10½", $2,500.00.

Vase, gold jeweled floral, bulbous w/swollen stick neck, 12" ...1,900.00
Vase, gold roses, spider web in bkground, stick neck, 12" 950.00
Vase, gold/jeweled roses on peach leaves on wht waffle, 6" 900.00
Vase, ivy, red/brn/gr/gold on creamy ground w/scrolls, 8x7" 725.00
Vase, lotus blossoms/gilt/tan shadow leaves, 11x9" 1,400.00
Vase, orchids, gold-lined pk/lav on yel, hdls, 5½x5½" 1,700.00
Vase, pansies, dome lid, 7½x6½" 1,500.00
Vase, pastel pansies, 4-point floriform lip, lobed base, 9" 1,200.00
Vase, roses on ribbing, shouldered w/bulbous top, 8½" 1,100.00
Vase, snow geese, gold moon/stars/scrolls, prof rpr hdl, 15" 3,500.00
Vase, thistles/mc leaves, dbl bulbed w/stick neck, 14" 1,200.00
Vase, Venetial scene, bk: shrine/boats, dolphin hdls, 16" 3,000.00
Vase, 2 Guba ducks, gold scrolls/florals, gold hdls, 11x5" 2,500.00

Cruets

Cruets, containers made to hold oil or vinegar, are usually bulbous with tall, narrow throats and a stopper. During and for several years after the 19th century, they were produced in abundance in virtually every type of glassware available. Those listed below are assumed to be with stopper and mint unless noted otherwise.

Aladdin, cut, irregular cut neck, faceted stopper 115.00
Alaska, bl opal, HP florals 360.00
Arcadia, cut, triple-notched hdl, faceted stopper, 7" 95.00
Arched Ovals, gr 125.00
Banded Portland 75.00
Beaded Grape, gr, 7" 160.00
Beaded Loop 45.00
Beaded Oval in Sand, gr, matching stopper 250.00
Berkshire, cut, faceted stopper, 8-oz 85.00

Bl w/gold birds, twisted dbl hdl, faceted clear stopper, 8" 250.00
Blazing Cornucopia, purple stained w/gold 70.00
Broken Column 85.00
Broken Column, ruby stained 250.00
Bulbous Base Optic, cranberry, cut faceted stopper 235.00
Burmese, melon ribbed, Mt WA, 6½" 1,065.00
Button Arches 55.00
Button Arches, ruby stained & frosted band, orig stopper 295.00
Cactus, chocolate, orig chocolate stopper, Fenton, 7" 165.00
Cathedral, amber 135.00
Celtic #429, faceted stopper, 6½" 185.00
Champion, amber stained 150.00
Coinspot, amber opal, orig amber opal stopper, Phoenix, rare 435.00
Cone, bl satin, opaque faceted stopper, 6" 300.00
Cone, pk o/l, faceted stopper 300.00
Cranberry, berries, 3-petal top, clear stopper, 7½" 250.00
Cranberry, gold scrolls/baskets, clear ft/hdl/stopper, 12" 235.00
Croesus, gr w/gold, lg 335.00
Cuba, flashed fans & strawberry dmns, faceted stopper, 8-oz 75.00
Cut Log, lg 60.00
Daisy & Button w/Crossbars, amber 135.00
Dakota (Baby T'print), etched 100.00
Dbl Circle, gr 165.00
Delaware 125.00
Delaware Rose, EX gold, rare 550.00
Dmn Quilted, amber, HP wht irises w/gold trim, 8" 130.00
Dmn Quilted, cranberry, clear faceted stopper, 6¾" 235.00
Dmn Quilted, reverse amberina 435.00
Empress, gr w/gold, original stopper 315.00
End of day, 3-color, clear hdl, faceted stopper, 7" 215.00
Esther, emerald gr, matching stopper, lg 325.00
Fancy Loop, Heisey 75.00
Feather, emerald gr 400.00
Forget-Me-Not, butterscotch, rare 295.00
Forget-Me-Not, pk, Challinor 160.00
Galloway 48.00
Harvard, intaglio cuttings, 9" 70.00
Herringbone, wht opal 125.00

Illinois 75.00
Inverted Fern, cranberry, faceted stopper 380.00
Invt T'print, amber, tricorn top 150.00
Invt T'print, rubena, funnel shape 250.00
Iowa 45.00
Iris w/Meander, amber opal, clear stopper, very rare 600.00
Iris w/Meander, vaseline opal 395.00
Jewel & Flower, bl opal 800.00
Kalana Poppy, faceted stopper, Dorflinger, 8-oz 170.00
Kentucky 50.00
King George, cut, tall notched neck, notched/pointed stopper ...110.00
Lacy Daisy 50.00
Log & Star, amber, sm 75.00
Louis XV, emerald gr, EX gold 275.00
Manhattan 50.00
Mary Gregory-type boy (fishing) on clear, 5½" 275.00
Medallion Sprig, amethyst, orig amethyst stopper 350.00
Mikado, cut, faceted stopper, 6" 85.00
Millard, ruby flashed & clear, pressed stopper 250.00
Missouri, emerald gr 350.00
Nestor, purple 200.00
Netted Oak, milk glass w/pk & gr leaves, matching stopper 155.00
Oregon, cut, tricorn spout, faceted stopper, 8-oz 85.00
Paneled Daisy & Button 45.00
Paneled Thistle 75.00
Peacock Feather 50.00
Pressed Swirl, amber, str sides 95.00
Radiant Daisy, frosted w/amber stain 300.00
Reverse Swirl, cranberry opal, orig stopper 800.00
Rib Optic, cranberry opal, faceted rpl stopper 130.00
Ribbed Pillar, pk/wht satin spatter, ribbed satin stopper 335.00
Richmond, ruby stained, pointed/faceted stopper 185.00
Riverside's Ranson, vaseline 235.00
Stars & Bars, amber 95.00
Swag w/Brackets, bl opal, orig stopper 600.00
Swirl, cranberry, clear drop stopper, 7¾" 220.00
Thousand Eye, amber, 3-knob 165.00
Tokyo, bl opal, orig stopper 400.00
Tokyo, bl opal, rpl stopper 250.00
Truncated Cube, ruby flashed & clear, pressed cube stopper 225.00
Vaseline w/opal stripes, clear pressed faceted stopper, 6" 275.00
Venetian Dmn, cranberry, clear faceted stopper, 7" 275.00
Verre de soie, Hawkes eng, fancy hollow stopper, Steuben, 7" ...600.00
Waffle & Finecut (Orion), amber, str sided 110.00
Waverly, tricorn spout, faceted stopper, 8-oz 100.00
Wild Bouquet, clear opal 235.00
Windows, cranberry opal, oval, scarce, 6½" 600.00
X-Ray, gr w/gold, orig stopper 235.00
Zipper Dmn, clear hdl, faceted stopper 55.00

Cup Plates, Glass

Before the middle 1850s, it was socially acceptable to pour hot tea into a deep saucer to cool. The tea was sipped from the saucer rather than the cup, which frequently was handleless and too hot to hold. The cup plate served as a coaster for the cup. It is generally agreed that the first examples of pressed glass cup plates were made about 1826 at the Boston and Sandwich Glass Co. in Sandwich, Cape Cod, Massachusetts. Other glassworks in three major areas (New England, Philadelphia, and the Midwest, especially Pittsburgh) quickly followed suit.

Antique glass cup plates range in size from 2⅝" up to 4¼" in diameter. The earliest plates had simple designs inspired by cut glass patterns, but by 1829 they had become more complex. The span from then

Diamond Quilted rainbow Mother of Pearl, old, 7", $2,750.00.

Hobb's Hobnail, vaseline opal, rare 400.00
Hobnail, cranberry, clear hdl, clear faceted stopper, 8" 375.00
Hobnail, rubena verde, Hobbs & Brockunier 575.00

until about 1845 is known as the 'Lacy Period,' when cup plate designs and pressing techniques were at their peak. To cover pressing imperfections, the backgrounds of the plates were often covered with fine stippling which endowed them with a glittering brilliance called 'laciness.' They were made in a multitude of designs — some purely decorative, others commemorative. Subjects include the American eagle, hearts, sunbursts, log cabins, ships, George Washington, the political candidates Clay and Harrison, plows, beehives, etc. Of all the patterns, the round George Washington plate is the rarest and most valuable — only three are known to exist today.

Authenticity is most important. Collectors must be aware that contemporary plates which have no antique counterparts and fakes modeled after antique patterns have had wide distribution. Condition is also important, though it is the exceptional plate that does not have some rim roughness. More important considerations are scarcity of design and color.

Our advisor for this category is John Bilane; he is listed in the Directory under New Jersey. The book *American Glass* by George and Helen McKearin has a section on glass cup plates. A more definitive book is *American Glass Cup Plates* by Ruth Webb Lee and James H. Rose. Numbers in the listings that follow (computer sorted) refer to the latter. When no condition is indicated, the examples listed below are assumed to have only minor rim roughness as is normal. See also Staffordshire; Pairpoint.

R-102, scarce, G 42.00
R-105, scarce, G 36.00
R-124A, VG 38.00
R-13C, G 30.00
R-130, rare, VG 210.00
R-133, rare, G 65.00
R-136A, rare, VG 75.00
R-147A, scarce, VG 40.00
R-149, VG 33.00
R-150, VG 35.00
R-154B, VG 33.00
R-156A, scarce, VG 50.00
R-165, G 28.00
R-166B, rare, EX 85.00
R-173, VG 32.00
R-203, rare, G 38.00
R-208, scarce, VG 52.00
R-214, rare, VG 170.00
R-216, VG 65.00
R-216C, scarce, G 77.00
R-217A, G 48.00
R-22, VG 28.00
R-242A, VG 34.00
R-243, VG 35.00
R-245, G 26.00
R-246, VG 36.00
R-255, VG 20.00
R-257, VG 29.00
R-258, VG 30.00
R-260, scarce, VG 60.00
R-262, G 20.00
R-269, VG 30.00
R-269A, VG 31.00
R-269C, G 25.00
R-27, G 25.00
R-271A, VG 30.00
R-272, VG 30.00
R-278, VG 34.00
R-28, G 19.00

R-292, VG 27.00
R-301V, 4" variant, EX 14.00
R-313, VG 21.00
R-323, VG 20.00
R-332, G 18.00
R-334A, bl opal, scarce, VG 55.00
R-339, VG 19.00
R-340, G 15.00
R-341, VG 20.00
R-343B, VG 32.00
R-365, G 12.50
R-37, VG 41.00
R-379, VG 12.00
R-389, G 14.00
R-39, G 23.00
R-393, G 10.00
R-396, VG 13.00
R-402, VG 14.00
R-403, VG 12.00
R-416, VG 12.00
R-43, scarce, VG 42.00
R-439C, scarce, G 26.00
R-44, very G 70.00
R-440, VG 34.00
R-447A, VG 26.00
R-449, scarce, G 45.00
R-45, scarce, EX 72.00
R-455, scarce, VG 34.00
R-456, scarce, G 21.00
R-459Q, G 15.00
R-465F, G 15.00
R-465J, bl opal shoulder & cavetto, scarce, VG 55.00
R-465N, G 16.00
R-47, VG 30.00
R-48, VG 30.00
R-49, VG 30.00
R-500, rare, G 46.00
R-501, G 11.00
R-531, VG 21.00
R-54, scarce, G 42.00
R-56, scarce, G 42.00
R-562A, very rare, G 250.00
R-564, VG 30.00
R-565B, VG 30.00
R-57, scarce, G 42.00
R-570, rare, G 81.00
R-575, scarce, G 53.00
R-590, G 28.00
R-593, scarce, VG 51.00
R-596, VG 45.00
R-605A, scarce, G 90.00
R-610A, VG 34.00
R-610D, G 35.00
R-619, VG 42.00
R-619A, G 35.00
R-619B, rare, G 94.00
R-62A, scarce, G 42.00
R-628, scarce, G 53.00
R-632A, G 38.00
R-636, VG 45.00
R-637, very rare, VG 275.00
R-643, G 18.00
R-65, scarce, VG 51.00
R-661, G 18.00

R-665A, VG	40.00
R-666, VG	35.00
R-666A, scarce, G	40.00
R-670, scarce, G	42.00
R-670A, VG	40.00
R-675B, G	35.00
R-677A, bl, rare, VG	345.00
R-679, VG	30.00
R-680, VG	30.00
R-680B, VG	31.00
R-693, scarce, G	70.00
R-78, scarce, VG	60.00
R-79, G	32.00
R-853, lt amber, EX	25.00
R-95, opal opaque, VG	140.00
R-95, VG	36.00
R-98, rare, EX	80.00

Currier & Ives by Royal

During the 1950s dinnerware decorated with blue transfer-printed scenes taken from prints by Currier and Ives was manufactured by Royal China and given as premiums through A&P stores. In addition to the dinnerware, a line of Fire-King baking pans and accessories was also available, as were vinyl placemats and various sizes of glass tumblers. Today it is readily available at reasonable prices, and it has become a very popular collectible at malls and flea markets around the country. Our advisors for this category are Treva and Jack Hamlin; they are listed in the Directory under Ohio.

Ashtray	10.00
Bowl, cereal; tab hdl, rare, 6⅜"	25.00
Bowl, cereal; 6⅜"	7.00
Bowl, fruit; 5½"	3.00
Bowl, lug soup; deep, tab hdl, 2¾x4¾"	20.00
Bowl, soup; flat, 8½"	7.50
Bowl, vegetable; 10"	20.00
Bowl, 9"	18.00
Butter dish, ¼-lb	25.00
Calendar plate, ca 1970s-85, ea	12.00
Candle lamp & globe, rare, tall, 3¾" base	30.00

Casserole, $60.00.

Casserole, tab hdls, w/lid, old	100.00
Creamer	5.00
Cup & saucer	4.00
Gravy boat, w/ladle & underplate	35.00
Gravy boat (w/o ladle & underplate)	13.00
Gravy ladle	10.00
Mug, soup (or coffee); mk, 2¾x3¾"	18.00

Pie plate (6 decals made)	15.00
Plate, 10½"	4.00
Plate, 6"	2.50
Plate, 7⅜"	7.00
Plate, 9"	10.00
Platter, oval, 13"	22.00
Platter, rnd, mk, rare, 13" dia	40.00
Platter, rnd, mk, 11" dia	20.00
Platter, tab hdls, 10½"	15.00
Shakers, pr	15.00
Sugar bowl, w/lid	12.00
Teapot	75.00
Tumbler, juice	10.00
Tumbler, milk glass	7.00
Tumbler, old fashioned, 3¼"	10.00
Tumbler, 13-oz, 5½"	12.00
Tumbler, 9-oz, 4¾"	12.00
Underplate, tab hdls, sm (for gravy boat)	12.00

Custard

As early as the 1880s, custard glass was produced in England. Migrating glassmakers brought the formula for the creamy ivory ware to America. One of them was Harry Northwood, who in 1898 founded his company in Indiana, Pennsylvania, and introduced the glassware to the American market. Soon other companies were producing custard, among them Heisey, Tarentum, Fenton, and McKee. Not only dinnerware patterns but souvenir items were made. Today custard is the most expensive of the colored pressed glassware patterns. The formula for producing the luminous glass contains uranium salts which imparts the cream color to the batch and causes it to glow when it is examined under a black light.

Argonaut Shell, bowl, master berry; gold & decor, 10½" L	265.00
Argonaut Shell, bowl, sauce; ftd, gold & decor	65.00

Argonaut Shell, butter dish, gold and decoration, $375.00.

Argonaut Shell, butter dish, gold & decor	375.00
Argonaut Shell, butter dish, no gold	275.00
Argonaut Shell, compote, jelly; gold & decor, scarce	145.00
Argonaut Shell, creamer, gold & decor	135.00
Argonaut Shell, creamer, no gold	110.00
Argonaut Shell, cruet, gold & decor	700.00
Argonaut Shell, pitcher, water; gold & decor	435.00
Argonaut Shell, spooner, gold & decor	135.00
Argonaut Shell, sugar bowl, w/lid, gold & decor	200.00
Argonaut Shell, tumbler, gold & decor	110.00
Bead Swag, bowl, sauce; floral & gold	50.00
Bead Swag, goblet, floral & gold	65.00

Bead Swag, tray, pickle; floral & gold, rare 260.00
Bead Swag, wine, floral & gold 60.00
Beaded Circle, bowl, master berry; floral & gold 245.00
Beaded Circle, butter dish, floral & gold 450.00
Beaded Circle, creamer, floral & gold 180.00
Beaded Circle, cruet, floral & gold, rare 1,175.00
Beaded Circle, pitcher, water; floral & gold 675.00
Beaded Circle, shakers, floral & gold, pr 800.00
Beaded Circle, spooner, floral & gold 175.00
Beaded Circle, sugar bowl, w/lid, floral & gold 275.00
Beaded Circle, tumbler, floral & gold, very rare 100.00
Cane Insert, berry set, 7-pc 450.00
Cane Insert, table set, 4-pc 450.00
Cherry & Scales, bowl, master berry; nutmeg stain 130.00
Cherry & Scales, butter dish, nutmeg stain 225.00
Cherry & Scales, creamer, nutmeg stain 115.00
Cherry & Scales, pitcher, water; nutmeg stain, scarce 325.00
Cherry & Scales, spooner, nutmeg stain, scarce 110.00
Cherry & Scales, sugar bowl, w/lid, nutmeg stain, scarce 125.00
Cherry & Scales, tumbler, nutmeg stain, scarce 50.00
Chrysanthemum Sprig, bowl, master berry; gold & decor 275.00
Chrysanthemum Sprig, bowl, master berry; no gold 175.00
Chrysanthemum Sprig, bowl, sauce; ftd, gold & decor 50.00
Chrysanthemum Sprig, butter dish, gold & decor 300.00
Chrysanthemum Sprig, celery vase, gold & decor, rare 375.00
Chrysanthemum Sprig, compote, jelly; gold & decor 135.00
Chrysanthemum Sprig, compote, jelly; no decor 95.00
Chrysanthemum Sprig, creamer, gold & decor 125.00
Chrysanthemum Sprig, cruet, gold & decor, 6¾" 350.00
Chrysanthemum Sprig, pitcher, water; gold & decor 465.00
Chrysanthemum Sprig, shakers, gold & decor, pr 300.00
Chrysanthemum Sprig, spooner, gold & decor 130.00
Chrysanthemum Sprig, spooner, no gold 75.00
Chrysanthemum Sprig, toothpick holder, gold & decor 300.00
Chrysanthemum Sprig, toothpick holder, no decor 165.00
Chrysanthemum Sprig, tumbler, gold & decor 55.00
Dandelion, mug, nutmeg stain 165.00
Delaware, bowl, sauce; pk stain 65.00
Delaware, creamer, breakfast; pk stain 70.00
Delaware, tray, pin; gr stain 75.00
Delaware, tumbler, pk stain 55.00
Diamond w/Peg, bowl, master berry; roses & gold 215.00
Diamond w/Peg, bowl, sauce; roses & gold 40.00
Diamond w/Peg, butter dish, roses & gold 235.00
Diamond w/Peg, creamer, ind; no decor 30.00
Diamond w/Peg, creamer, ind; souvenir 45.00
Diamond w/Peg, creamer, roses & gold 75.00
Diamond w/Peg, mug, souvenir 50.00
Diamond w/Peg, napkin ring, roses & gold, rare 150.00
Diamond w/Peg, pitcher, roses & gold, 5½" 260.00
Diamond w/Peg, shakers, souvenir, pr 175.00
Diamond w/Peg, sugar bowl, w/lid, roses & gold 160.00
Diamond w/Peg, toothpick holder, roses & gold 150.00
Diamond w/Peg, tumbler, roses & gold 60.00
Diamond w/Peg, water set, souvenir, 7-pc 650.00
Diamond w/Peg, wine, roses & gold 55.00
Diamond w/Peg, wine, souvenir 40.00
Everglades, bowl, master berry; gold & decor 215.00
Everglades, bowl, sauce; gold & decor 60.00
Everglades, butter dish, gold & decor 395.00
Everglades, creamer, gold & decor 155.00
Everglades, shakers, gold & decor, pr 375.00
Everglades, spooner, gold & decor 160.00
Everglades, sugar bowl, w/lid, gold & decor 235.00

Everglades, tumbler, gold & decor 100.00
Fan, bowl, master berry; good gold 135.00
Fan, bowl, sauce; good gold 55.00
Fan, butter dish, good gold 225.00
Fan, creamer, good gold 110.00
Fan, ice cream set, good gold, 7-pc 500.00
Fan, pitcher, water; good gold 275.00
Fan, spooner, good gold 100.00
Fan, sugar bowl, w/lid, good gold 150.00
Fan, tumbler, good gold 75.00
Fan, water set, good gold, 7-pc 700.00
Fine Cut & Roses, rose bowl, fancy int, nutmeg stain 100.00
Fine Cut & Roses, rose bowl, plain int 85.00
Geneva, bowl, master berry; floral decor, ftd, oval, 9" L 90.00
Geneva, bowl, master berry; floral decor, rnd, 9" 120.00
Geneva, bowl, sauce; floral decor, oval 45.00
Geneva, bowl, sauce; floral decor, rnd 45.00
Geneva, butter dish, floral decor 225.00
Geneva, butter dish, no decor 135.00
Geneva, compote, jelly; floral decor 95.00
Geneva, creamer, floral decor 100.00
Geneva, cruet, floral decor 465.00
Geneva, pitcher, water; floral decor 250.00
Geneva, shakers, floral decor, pr 280.00
Geneva, spooner, floral decor 100.00
Geneva, sugar bowl, open, floral decor 85.00
Geneva, sugar bowl, w/lid, floral decor 150.00
Geneva, syrup, floral decor 475.00
Geneva, toothpick holder, floral w/M gold 375.00
Geneva, tumbler, floral decor 50.00
Georgia Gem, bowl, master berry; good gold 135.00
Georgia Gem, bowl, master berry; gr opaque 115.00
Georgia Gem, butter dish, good gold 190.00
Georgia Gem, celery vase, good gold 145.00
Georgia Gem, creamer, good gold 100.00
Georgia Gem, creamer, no gold 60.00
Georgia Gem, mug, good gold 45.00
Georgia Gem, powder jar, w/lid, good gold 80.00
Georgia Gem, shakers, good gold, pr 160.00
Georgia Gem, spooner, souvenir 55.00
Georgia Gem, sugar bowl, w/lid, no gold 95.00
Grape (& Cable), bottle, scent; orig stopper, nutmeg stain 600.00
Grape (& Cable), bowl, master berry; nutmeg stain, ftd, 11" 375.00
Grape (& Cable), bowl, nutmeg stain, 7½" 60.00
Grape (& Cable), bowl, sauce; nutmeg stain, ftd 50.00
Grape (& Cable), butter dish, nutmeg stain 275.00
Grape (& Cable), compote, jelly; open, nutmeg stain 145.00
Grape (& Cable), compote, nutmeg stain, 4½x8" 300.00
Grape (& Cable), cracker jar, nutmeg stain 800.00
Grape (& Cable), creamer, breakfast; nutmeg stain 80.00
Grape (& Cable), humidor, bl stain, rare 950.00
Grape (& Cable), humidor, nutmeg stain, rare 900.00
Grape (& Cable), nappy, nutmeg stain, rare 60.00
Grape (& Cable), pitcher, water; nutmeg stain 400.00
Grape (& Cable), plate, nutmeg stain, 7" 50.00
Grape (& Cable), plate, nutmeg stain, 8" 65.00
Grape (& Cable), powder jar, nutmeg stain 350.00
Grape (& Cable), punch bowl, w/base, nutmeg stain 1,750.00
Grape (& Cable), spooner, nutmeg stain 145.00
Grape (& Cable), sugar bowl, breakfast; open, nutmeg stain 75.00
Grape (& Cable), sugar bowl, w/lid, nutmeg stain 195.00
Grape (& Cable), tray, dresser; nutmeg stain, scarce, lg ...350.00
Grape (& Cable), tray, pin; nutmeg stain 135.00
Grape (& Cable), tumbler, nutmeg stain 75.00

Grape & Gothic Arches, bowl, master berry; pearl w/gold 200.00
Grape & Gothic Arches, bowl, sauce; pearl w/gold, rare 80.00
Grape & Gothic Arches, butter dish, pearl w/gold 235.00
Grape & Gothic Arches, creamer, pearl w/gold, rare 100.00
Grape & Gothic Arches, favor vase, nutmeg stain 80.00
Grape & Gothic Arches, goblet, pearl w/gold 75.00
Grape & Gothic Arches, pitcher, water; pearl w/gold 300.00
Grape & Gothic Arches, spooner, pearl w/gold 85.00
Grape & Gothic Arches, sugar bowl, w/lid, pearl w/gold 135.00
Grape & Gothic Arches, tumbler, pearl w/gold 65.00
Grape Arbor, vase, hat form 90.00
Heart w/T'print, creamer 85.00
Heart w/T'print, lamp, good pnt, scarce, 8" 435.00
Heart w/T'print, sugar bowl, ind 80.00
Honeycomb, wine 65.00
Horse Medallion, bowl, gr stain, 7" 80.00

Inverted Fan and Feather, master berry bowl, gold and decoration, $250.00.

Intaglio, bowl, sauce; gold & decor 50.00
Intaglio, butter dish, gold & decor, scarce 300.00
Intaglio, compote, jelly; gold & decor 125.00
Intaglio, creamer, gold & decor 125.00
Intaglio, cruet, gold & decor 475.00
Intaglio, pitcher, water; gold & decor 395.00
Intaglio, shakers, gold & decor, pr 235.00
Intaglio, spooner, gold & decor 125.00
Intaglio, sugar bowl, w/lid, gold & decor 165.00
Intaglio, tumbler, gold & decor 75.00
Inverted Fan & Feather, bowl, master berry; gold & decor 250.00
Inverted Fan & Feather, bowl, sauce; gold & decor 65.00
Inverted Fan & Feather, butter dish, gold & decor 350.00
Inverted Fan & Feather, compote, jelly; gold & decor, rare 500.00
Inverted Fan & Feather, creamer, gold & decor 150.00
Inverted Fan & Feather, cruet, gold & decor, scarce, 6½" 1,100.00
Inverted Fan & Feather, pitcher, water; gold & decor 600.00
Inverted Fan & Feather, punch cup, gold & decor 250.00
Inverted Fan & Feather, shakers, gold & decor, pr 600.00
Inverted Fan & Feather, spooner, gold & decor 145.00
Inverted Fan & Feather, sugar bowl, w/lid, gold & decor 225.00
Inverted Fan & Feather, tumbler, gold & decor 95.00
Jackson, bowl, master berry; good gold, ftd 135.00
Jackson, bowl, sauce; good gold 45.00
Jackson, creamer, good gold 85.00
Jackson, pitcher, water; good gold 250.00
Jackson, pitcher, water; no decor 175.00
Jackson, shakers, good gold, pr 195.00
Jackson, tumbler, good gold 50.00

Louis XV, berry set, w/nutmeg, 7-pc 375.00
Louis XV, bowl, master berry; good gold 165.00
Louis XV, bowl, sauce; good gold, ftd 47.00
Louis XV, butter dish, good gold 200.00
Louis XV, creamer, good gold 80.00
Louis XV, cruet, good gold 365.00
Louis XV, pitcher, water; good gold 225.00
Louis XV, spooner, good gold 80.00
Louis XV, sugar bowl, w/lid, good gold 150.00
Louis XV, tumbler, good gold 65.00
Maple Leaf, bowl, master berry; gold & decor, scarce 335.00
Maple Leaf, bowl, sauce; gold & decor, scarce 95.00
Maple Leaf, butter dish, gold & decor 350.00
Maple Leaf, compote, jelly; gold & decor, rare 455.00
Maple Leaf, creamer, gold & decor 150.00
Maple Leaf, cruet, gold & decor, rare 3,000.00
Maple Leaf, pitcher, water; gold & decor 400.00
Maple Leaf, shakers, gold & decor, very rare, pr 800.00
Maple Leaf, spooner, gold & decor 155.00
Maple Leaf, sugar bowl, w/lid, gold & decor 230.00
Maple Leaf, tumbler, gold & decor 95.00
Panelled Poppy, lamp shade, nutmeg stain, scarce 800.00
Peacock & Urn, bowl, ice cream; nutmeg stain, sm 80.00
Peacock & Urn, bowl, ice cream; nutmeg stain, 10" 350.00
Punty Band, shakers, pr 175.00
Punty Band, spooner, floral decor 100.00
Punty Band, tumbler, floral decor, souvenir 65.00
Ribbed Drape, bowl, sauce; roses & gold 40.00
Ribbed Drape, butter dish, scalloped, roses & gold 375.00
Ribbed Drape, compote, jelly; roses & gold, rare 200.00
Ribbed Drape, creamer, roses & gold, scarce 180.00
Ribbed Drape, cruet, roses & gold, rare 650.00
Ribbed Drape, pitcher, water; roses & gold, rare 365.00
Ribbed Drape, shakers, roses & gold, rare, pr 360.00
Ribbed Drape, spooner, roses & gold 180.00
Ribbed Drape, toothpick holder, roses & gold 475.00
Ribbed Drape, tumbler, roses & gold 65.00
Ribbed Thumbprint, wine, floral decor 80.00
Ring Band, bowl, master berry; roses & gold 150.00
Ring Band, bowl, sauce; roses & gold 45.00
Ring Band, butter dish, roses & gold 250.00
Ring Band, compote, jelly; roses & gold, scarce 195.00
Ring Band, creamer, roses & gold 115.00
Ring Band, cruet, roses & gold 450.00
Ring Band, pitcher, roses & gold, 7½" 335.00
Ring Band, shakers, roses & gold, pr 155.00
Ring Band, spooner, roses & gold 110.00
Ring Band, syrup, roses & gold 465.00
Ring Band, toothpick holder, roses & gold 135.00
Ring Band, tray, condiment; roses & gold 200.00
Singing Birds, mug, nutmeg stain 75.00
Tarentum's Victoria, bowl, master berry; gold & decor 200.00
Tarentum's Victoria, butter dish, gold & decor, rare 300.00
Tarentum's Victoria, celery vase, gold & decor, rare 275.00
Tarentum's Victoria, creamer, gold & decor, scarce 135.00
Tarentum's Victoria, pitcher, water; gold & decor, rare 375.00
Tarentum's Victoria, spooner, gold & decor 135.00
Tarentum's Victoria, sugar bowl, w/lid, gold & decor 160.00
Tarentum's Victoria, tumbler, gold & decor 70.00
Vermont, butter dish, bl decor 195.00
Vermont, toothpick holder, bl decor 155.00
Vermont, vase, floral decor, jeweled 95.00
Wide Band, bell, roses 195.00
Wild Bouquet, butter dish, gold & decor, rare 700.00

Wild Bouquet, creamer, no gold 145.00
Wild Bouquet, cruet, no decor, w/clear stopper 995.00
Wild Bouquet, sauce, gold & decor 60.00
Wild Bouquet, spooner, gold & decor 160.00
Wild Bouquet, tumbler, no decor 95.00
Winged Scroll, bowl, master berry; gold & decor, 11" L 175.00
Winged Scroll, bowl, sauce; good gold 45.00
Winged Scroll, butter dish, good gold 200.00
Winged Scroll, butter dish, no decor 150.00
Winged Scroll, celery vase, good gold, rare 400.00
Winged Scroll, cigarette jar, scarce 195.00
Winged Scroll, compote, ruffled, rare, 6¾x10¾" 495.00
Winged Scroll, cruet, good gold, clear stopper 375.00
Winged Scroll, hair receiver, good gold 135.00
Winged Scroll, pitcher, water; bulbous, good gold 350.00
Winged Scroll, shakers, bulbous, good gold, rare, pr 400.00
Winged Scroll, shakers, str sides, good gold, pr 195.00
Winged Scroll, sugar bowl, w/lid, good gold 150.00
Winged Scroll, syrup, good gold 395.00
Winged Scroll, tumbler, good gold 75.00

Cut Glass

The earliest documented evidence of commercial glass cutting in the United States was in 1810; the producers were Bakewell and Page of Pittsburgh. These first efforts resulted in simple patterns with only a moderate amount of cutting. By the middle of the century, glass cutters began experimenting with a thicker glass which enabled them to use deeper cuttings, though patterns remained much the same. This period is usually referred to as Rich Cut. Using three types of wheels — a flat edge, a mitered edge, and a convex edge — facets, miters, and depressions were combined to produce various designs. In the late 1870s, a curved miter was developed which greatly expanded design potential. Patterns became more elaborate, often covering the entire surface. The Brilliant Period of cut glass covered a span from about 1880 until 1915. Because of the pressure necessary to achieve the deeply cut patterns, only glass containing a high grade of metal could withstand the process. For this reason and the amount of handwork involved, cut glass has always been expensive.

Bowls cut with pinwheels may be either foreign or of a newer vintage, beware! Identifiable patterns and signed pieces that are well cut and in excellent condition bring the higher prices on today's market.

Key:
dmn — diamonds   X-cut — cross-cut
strw — strawberry   X-hatch — crosshatch

Basket, Russian w/hobstars & deep mitres w/X-cut dmns, 21" .6,100.00

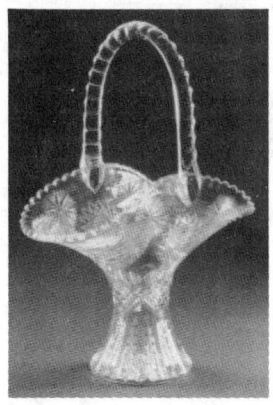

Basket, cut with zipper, hobstars and strawberry diamonds, 20", $1,700.00.

Bonbon, hobstars & fans, leaf shape, 8¾" 125.00
Bottle, hobstars in bulbous base, lapidary cut stopper, 9¾" 175.00
Bottle, scent; oval-cut, silver/glass lid w/portrait, 7x1" 220.00
Bowl, Ambrosia, 9" 295.00
Bowl, Arcadia, low, 10" 400.00
Bowl, Cetus, very rare pattern, 4x9" 3,300.00
Bowl, Comet, Hoare, 4x9¼" 825.00
Bowl, deeply cut hobstars, 4-sided, blown-out, 9" 400.00
Bowl, Expanding Star, heavy, low, 10" 475.00
Bowl, hobstar buttons & channel cuts, silver rim, 8½", pr 1,500.00
Bowl, hobstars/canes/strw dmns, 32-point hobstar ped, 8x10" .1,900.00
Bowl, hobstars/strw dmns/mitres, 4x9½x7" 325.00
Bowl, hobstars/X-cut dmns/fans, Libbey, 2x9" 150.00
Bowl, hobstars/X-cut dmns/strw dmns, 8" 200.00
Bowl, intaglio stained daisies, 3" rolled rim, Hoare, 11" 195.00
Bowl, Jubilee, vesicas & hobstars, 9" 525.00
Bowl, Marcella, 4-sided, 11½" 1,750.00
Bowl, Rex, 8¼" 1,000.00
Bowl, Russian, 2-hdld, low, 8" 500.00
Bowl, strw dmns & fans, 8" 110.00
Bowl, Trellis, sgn Eggington, 3x9¼" 1,600.00
Bowl, Wedgemere, sloped-in sides, 8" 650.00
Bowl, whirlwind, pinwheel ft, 5" 120.00
Box, hobstars cut w/rays, hinged lid, 5" dia 200.00
Box, Russian, hobstar base, hinged lid, 7" dia 600.00
Butter tub & underplate, hobstars/strw dmns, 4¾", 6¾" 525.00
Candle holder, flashed hobstars/fans/X-cut dmns, 9¼", pr 550.00
Candlestick, St Louis Dmn, teardrop stem, rayed base, 12", pr ...450.00
Carafe, hobstars/notched prisms/strw dmns/fans, pr 400.00
Celery bowl, sunburst w/stars at corners, 1920s, 4¾x12" 150.00
Celery tray, Harvard w/starred buttons, canoe shape, 13½" 275.00
Celery tray, hobstars forming blown-out ends, 10¾x4¾" 180.00
Celery tray, hobstars/canes/X-cut dmns, 11½x4¾" 100.00
Cider jug, Hindoo, Hoare, 6½" 650.00
Cider jug, Russian w/starred buttons, cut hdl, 6¾" 325.00
Compote, Comet, Hoare, 12" 675.00
Compote, Creswick, Eggington, 5" 225.00
Compote, Marseilles, rayed ped, Eggington, 11¾" 300.00
Compote, starred sqs/dbl-cut mitres/strw dmns, 7¼x10" 1,000.00
Compote, teardrop in notched stem, hobstars on ft, 7¾" 150.00
Cordial, Monarch, Hoare, 3¼", set of 3 ....120.00

Creamer and sugar bowl, $145.00.

Creamer & sugar bowl, hobstars & fans, 4", 6" dia, pr 120.00
Decanter, Harvard, step-cut neck, hobstar base, 15½" 475.00
Decanter, hobstar/fan, honeycomb neck/hdl, silver stopper, 12" ...400.00
Decanter, hobstars & bull's eyes, cut stopper, 15" 800.00
Decanter, hobstars/beads/fans, fluted neck, cut hdl, 12" 400.00
Decanter, hobstars/fans/strw dmns, cut hdl & stopper, 11" 300.00
Decanter, Middlesex, spout at collar, notched hdl, 10" 300.00
Decanter, Wheeler, St Louis Dmn hdl, 15" 250.00
Flask, lay-down, Harvard, Gorham sterling lid 325.00

Flower center, etched/wheel-cut motif, 12" 495.00
Flower center, hobstar/fan/fine cut/cane, 9x15" 1,500.00
Humidor, sunburst motif, high dome stopper, weighs 6 lbs 1,000.00
Ice bucket, Russian, 5½" 350.00
Ice cream set, Aberdeen, Jewel Glass, 12 pcs on 15¼" tray 6,800.00
Ice cream tray, Atlantic, deep cutting, 17½x10" 500.00
Ice tub, hobstars/strw dmns/fans, hobstar on base, hdls 200.00
Jam jar, X-hatched sqs w/fans, w/hdl, rayed lid, 5" 200.00
Jar, hobstars/strw dmns/bull's eyes, sterling lid, 5½" 125.00
Ladle, Harvard on glass hdl, silver bowl by JD Bergen 425.00
Lamp, blossom & cane-cut dome shade, prisms, 23x12" 1,500.00
Lamp, boudoir; geometrics, mushroom shade, 14½" 700.00
Loving cup, chair bottoms/X-hatching/fans/zippers/etc, 5½" ...1,400.00
Mayonnaise bowl, Marquis, Eggington, +6½" underplate 425.00
Nut dish, pinwheels & stars, 5" 45.00
Perfume, gr to clear, leaves, sterling repousse stopper, 5" 400.00
Perfume, Russian w/cut buttons, hinged sterling lid, 3½" 225.00
Perfume, X-hatched sqs & vesicas, sterling lid, 5" 200.00
Pitcher, Alhambra, triple-notched hdl, 10¾" 1,250.00
Pitcher, Alhambra, 11½", +6 4" tumblers 1,600.00
Pitcher, bull's eyes/sqs of X-hatching/prisms, 10½" 225.00
Pitcher, champagne; Harvard w/strw dmns, cut hdls, 12" 300.00
Pitcher, champagne; Russian, rayed base, t'print hdl, 11½" 425.00
Pitcher, Comet, bbl shape, sgn Hoare, 5½" 1,300.00
Pitcher, Cut Log, ruby stained, water sz 225.00
Pitcher, drape pattern, St Louis Dmn hdl, hobstar base, 7¾" 300.00
Pitcher, Hindoo, 3¾" 175.00
Pitcher, hobstar panels alternate w/flutes, cut hdl, 7½" 250.00
Pitcher, hobstars & notched prisms, t'print hdl, 7" 250.00
Pitcher, hobstars/fans/clear panels, intaglio flowers, 10" 500.00
Pitcher, hobstars/X-hatching, triple notch hdl, 10½" 300.00
Pitcher, Lotus, t'print hdl, Eggington, 7¼x7½" 650.00
Pitcher, pinwheels & strw dmns, 10" 100.00
Pitcher, X-cut dmns/fans, St Louis Dmn hdl, heavy, 7½" 220.00
Plate, intaglio panels of fruit & X-cut dmns, 10" 275.00
Punch bowl, Harvard allover, ped ft, 11x14" 900.00
Punch bowl, hobstars/canes/strw dmns, heavy, 6x12" 550.00
Punch bowl, Marquis, Eggington, 2-pc, 8½x12" 1,400.00
Punch bowl, star cuttings, 11½", on matching base 800.00
Rose bowl, X-hatching/hobstars/fans, 4½x5" 175.00
Rum jug, butterflies & flowers, notched hdls, 7½" 650.00
Salad tray or bowl, Bristol Rose, wood polished, 2½x8x12" 550.00
Shakers, pinwheels, sterling lids, pr 30.00
Sherbet, Creswick, ftd, Eggington, 4 for 180.00
Sherry glass, hobstars/strw dmns/fans/stars, 6½", 4 for 200.00
Spoon rest, Monarch, flat, Hoare 75.00
Spooner, hobstars & notched prisms, 5" 325.00
String holder, fans/X-hatching, sterling lid, 3½x3½" 425.00
Tankard, Drape, triple-notched hdl, Strauss, 13" 575.00
Tazza vase, Alhambra, ft rpr, 10¼" 800.00
Teapot, eng flowers & wheat, sgn Clark 700.00
Toothpick holder, sunburst & dmns, 1920s, 2" 50.00
Toothpick holder, X-hatching & fans, 2½" 55.00
Tray, Daisy Blossom, fully cut, 14½" dia 500.00
Tray, hobstars & pinwheels, 12" dia 325.00
Tray, Wheat w/Russian between, oval, 10¾x6" 725.00
Tumbler, hobstars/fans/strw dmns, 3¾" 25.00
Vase, fluted panels/notched prisms, corset shape, 12" 1,050.00
Vase, Harvard w/starred buttons, faceted stem, 11½" 175.00
Vase, hobstars/strw dmns/fans, hobstar base, bulbous, 20" 1,300.00
Vase, hobstars/strw dmns/fans, slim neck w/prisms, 12" 800.00
Vase, hobstars/X-cut dmns/beaded panels, Hoare, 12" 350.00
Vase, hobstars/X-cut dmns/snowflakes, hobstar base, 14" 550.00
Vase, pinwheel/stars/fans, ped w/rayed base, trumpet, 12" 140.00

Vase, hobstars, strawberry diamonds and notching, scalloped hobstar base, 15", $550.00.

Vase, ruby etched w/brilliant-cut panel, 10¾" 100.00
Vase, split vesicas/X-cut dmns/canes, Russian top, Hoare, 18" ...700.00
Whiskey jug, Puritan, Libbey, 8½" 500.00
Wine bottle, Tasso, 12¾" 500.00

Cut Overlay Glass

Glassware with one or more overlying colors through which a design
has been cut is called 'Cut Overlay.' It was made both here and abroad.

Bottle, scent; wht to cranberry w/florals, 3" 150.00
Compote, cobalt to clear, wild geese/turkey/etc, 11x9" 325.00
Goblet, rose to wht, Xs/t'prints, 6" 275.00
Jar, wht over red to clear, crisscross/star cuts, 5x6" 175.00
Pitcher, red to clear, X-hatch/fan, bulbous, 7", NM 1,300.00
Vase, amethyst to clear, dmn points & fans, raised base, 7½" 150.00
Vase, wht on gr, portrait/floral medallions, gilt, 12", pr 1,200.00

Cut Velvet

Cut Velvet glassware was made during the late 1800s. It is characterized by the effect achieved through the execution of relief-molded
patterns, often ribbing or diamond quilting, which allows its white
inner casing to show through the outer layer.

Celery vase, Dmn Quilt, dk bl, box-pleated top, Mt WA, 6½" ...725.00
Cruet, Dmn Quilt, bl, clear faceted stopper, 7" 475.00
Cruet, Dmn Quilt, yel, satin faceted stopper, 7" 575.00
Rose bowl, Dmn Quilt, bl, 4-crimp, 3½x3½" 165.00
Rose bowl, Dmn Quilt, dk pk, 4-crimp top, 4x3" 165.00
Rose bowl, Dmn Quilt, lav, 4-crimp, 3½x3⅝" 175.00
Rose bowl, Dmn Quilt, pk, 6-crimp, 3¾x3⅜" 165.00
Sugar sifter, Dmn Quilt, bl 395.00
Vase, Dmn Quilt, bl, bulbous w/long neck, att Mt WA, 8¾" 335.00
Vase, Dmn Quilt, bl, sq top, 6⅛x3¼" 175.00
Vase, Dmn Quilt, deep orange, ruffled, 6" 350.00
Vase, Dmn Quilt, gr, ftd/ruffled, 9½" 225.00
Vase, Dmn Quilt, lt gold, long pumpkin stem neck, 13½" 475.00
Vase, Ribbed, pk, bottle form, 8¾" 160.00

Cybis

Boleslaw Cybis was a graduate of the Academy of Fine Arts in

Warsaw, Poland, and was well recognized as a fine artist by the time he was commissioned by his government to paint murals in the Polish Pavillion's Hall of Honor at the 1939 World's Fair. Finding themselves stranded in America at the outbreak of WWII, the Cybises founded an artists' studio, first in Astoria, New York, and later in Trenton, New Jersey, where they made fine figurines and plaques with exacting artistry and craftsmanship entailing extensive handwork. The studio still operates today producing exquisite porcelains on a limited edition basis.

Alice in Wonderland **725.00**
American Wild Turkey **1,750.00**
Appaloosa colt, dtd 1972 ....**300.00**
Bathsheba **2,000.00**
Bear, 1968 ....**365.00**
Blue Headed Vireo, building nest, 1960 ....**1,000.00**
Buffalo, 1968 ....**155.00**
Bunny Pat-a-Cake, 1977 ....**100.00**
Carousel Goat **1,500.00**
Colts, Darby & Joan (2 figures on base) **385.00**
Country Fair, 1972 ....**175.00**
Deer Mouse in clover, dtd 1970 ....**135.00**
Dore, 1985 ....**800.00**
Dormouse, Maxine **185.00**
Easter Egg Hunt, 1972 ....**175.00**
Elizabeth Ann, 1976 ....**245.00**
Eskimo Child, bust, 1972 ....**325.00**
Eskimo Mother **2,200.00**
Felicity Flower Basket, 1976 ....**325.00**
George Washington Bust, 1975 ....**300.00**
Hansel & Gretel, pr **850.00**
Heidi, wht, 1962 ....**400.00**
Jessica **395.00**
Kitten, Tabitha or Topaz **115.00**
Lady Godiva **2,500.00**
Lady Macbeth **875.00**
Little Miss Muffet, 1980 ....**325.00**
Majesty Flower Basket, 1976 ....**365.00**
Male Jogger, 14½" **450.00**
Maxine Dormouse, 1978 ....**195.00**
Narcissus **500.00**
Navity Angel, color **475.00**
Navity Lamb, wht **95.00**
Pandora Blue, 1967 ....**250.00**
Pegasus **3,200.00**
Pinto Colt, on stand, dtd 1971 ....**295.00**
Pollyanna, seated on chair, dtd 1971 ....**395.00**
Queen Esther, 1974 ....**1,500.00**
Rebecca, 1964 ....**295.00**
Sabbath Morning, 1972 ....**175.00**
Seashore, 1972 ....**175.00**
Stallion, 1968 ....**725.00**
Thoroughbred **1,225.00**
Thumbelina, 1957 ....**450.00**
Unicorn **1,250.00**
Vanessa **385.00**
Wendy w/flowers, 1975 ....**300.00**
Winter **175.00**
Wood Duck, 1968 ....**675.00**
Yankee Doodle Dandy **295.00**

Czechoslovakian Collectibles

Czechoslovakia came into being as a country in 1918. Located in the heart of Europe, it was a land with the natural resources necessary to support a glass industry that dates back to the mid-14th century. This ware has recently captured the attention of today's collectors, and for good reason. There are beautiful vases — cased, ruffled, applied with rigaree or silver overlay — fine enough to rival those of the best glasshouses. Czechoslovakian art glass baskets are quite as attractive as Victorian America's, and the elegant cut glass perfumes made in colors as well as crystal are unrivaled. There are also pressed glass perfumes, molded in lovely Deco shapes, of various types of art glass. Some are overlaid with gold filigree set with 'jewels.' Jewelry, lamps, porcelains, and fine art pottery are also included in the field.

More than thirty-five marks have been recorded, including those in the mold, ink stamped, acid etched, or on a small metal nameplate. The newer marks are incised, stamped 'Royal Dux made in Czechoslovakia' (see Royal Dux), or printed on a paper label which reads 'Bohemian Glass made in Czechoslovakia.' (Communist controlled from 1948, Czechoslovakia once again was made a free country. Today it no longer exists; since 1993 it has been divided to form the world's two newest countries, the Czechoslovakian Republic and the Slovak Republic.) For a more thorough study of the subject, we recommend you refer to the book *Made in Czechoslovakia* by Ruth A. Forsythe; she is listed in the Directory under Ohio. Another fine book is *Czechoslovakian Glass & Collectibles* by Dale and Diane Barta. In the listings that follow, when one dimension is given, it refers to height; decoration is enamel unless noted otherwise. See also Erphila.

Candy Baskets

Bl w/blk ruffled rim, clear hdl, 6½" **88.00**
Blk w/silver mica, bl int, blk hdl, 8" **95.00**
Gr varicolored stripes, lt gr hdl, flared rim, 8" **85.00**
Gr w/dk gr stripes, plain gr hdl, 8" **110.00**
Hobnail, red w/blk rim, plain crystal hdl, 6½" **115.00**
Lav/pk/wht mottle w/emb raindrops, cobalt hdl, 6½x3⅞" ...**75.00**
Mc mottle, crystal flat-top hdl, slender/incurvate, 8½" **85.00**
Red & yel mottle, twisted crystal thorn hdl, 7" **130.00**
Red w/appl jet rim & hdl, ruffled, 6½" **75.00**
Streaky bl/yel/& blk in red, clear hdl, 9½" **100.00**

Cased Art Glass

Bowl, blk w/orange int, ped ft, 6¼" **90.00**
Bowl, mc mottle, 6-sided, ftd, 6" **85.00**
Bowl, 3-color mottle, ftd, 4½" **55.00**
Candlestick, dk mottle, lg rnd base, 8½" **75.00**
Candy dish, mc mottle, blk 4-ftd ped base, 8" **125.00**
Cuspidor, mc mottle, wht int, lady's, 4" **155.00**
Decanter, tomato red w/silver bird on branch, 12" **100.00**
Jar, pk spatter, wht int, blk appl ft, knob finial, 7¼" **45.00**
Lamp globe, mc mottle, ball form, 5½" **90.00**
Pitcher, orange w/cobalt rim & hdl, tricorner top, 5" **70.00**
Pitcher, red & bl mottle, cobalt hdl, 9" **115.00**
Pitcher, red w/appl jet hdl, flared cylinder, 10⅛" **165.00**
Puff box, red w/blk & wht enameling, 3½" **90.00**
Vase, autumn colors, slim form, 4 clear ft, 11½" **75.00**
Vase, bl w/blk rim, slim form w/ruffled top, 8¼" **80.00**
Vase, bl w/pk int, ruffled rim, 6¾" **90.00**
Vase, bl/yel/wht mottle w/blk rim, fan form, 8¼" **135.00**
Vase, bud; orange w/enamel decor, 8" **70.00**
Vase, mc exotic bird on blk w/silver rim, classic form, 7¼" ...**140.00**
Vase, mc mottle, appl lg cobalt hdls, ruffled, 4⅝" **90.00**
Vase, mc mottle, bl appl hdls, 8⅜" **95.00**
Vase, mc mottle, waisted form, 6" **45.00**
Vase, mc mottle base w/cobalt top, 7" **65.00**

Vase, orange, appl blk serpentine decor, 8" 85.00
Vase, orange mottle, cobalt hdls, flared/ftd cylinder, 8½" 85.00
Vase, orange w/appl cobalt base & side decor, 5½" 85.00
Vase, orange w/appl flowers, ruffled top, 7½" 90.00
Vase, orange/yel mottle, dk brn base, slim form, 11¼" 90.00
Vase, pk w/wht o/l diagonal stripes, ruffled, ftd, 8½" 115.00
Vase, red, blk rim, 3 blk angle hdls, 4" 125.00
Vase, red mottled w/jet rim, appl serpentine decor, 8" 95.00
Vase, red w/mc mottle top, appl serpentine decor, 4¼" 90.00
Vase, tomato red w/silver lady decor, 4¾" 45.00
Vase, turq w/brn mottle, ftd, tall flared neck, 6" 57.50
Vase, variegated colors, appl blk 3-ftd ped ft, 7½" 80.00
Vase, variegated colors, bulbous, long neck, 4½" 60.00
Vase, variegated w/mc loops, sgn, 7x5" 75.00
Vase, wht w/gr adventurine, bulbous, 4½" 85.00
Vase, wht w/varicolored base, lt gr int, ruffled rim, 8" 65.00
Vase, yel w/appl cobalt decor & ft, 4¾" 75.00
Vase, yel w/mc clown, appl blk rim, classic form, 6¼" 60.00
Vase, yel w/silver exotic bird, slim form, 10" 90.00
Vase, yel-orange w/silver decor, clear base, 10" 60.00

Cut Glass Perfume Bottles

Amber, overall cuttings, amber intaglio-cut stopper, 5¾" 130.00
Blk opaque, overall cuttings, matching stopper, 5½" 135.00
Clear, bl figural nude applicator, 5¼" 2,200.00
Crystal, clear cut base, prism-cut drop stopper, 4⅞" 110.00
Crystal, clear cuttings, red cut flower stopper, 4¼" 180.00
Crystal, clear/frosted, clear tree design stopper, 4¾" 135.00
Crystal, clear/frosted cuttings, lt bl drop stopper, 5½" 135.00
Crystal, overall cuttings, prism-cut stopper, 7" 95.00
Crystal, wide base, amethyst intaglio-cut stopper, 4¾" 145.00
Gr, dmn cuttings, gr dmn-cut drop stopper, 6" 155.00
Gr, overall cuttings, ball form, gr intaglio-cut stopper, 6½" 155.00

Lamps

Goebel girl in glass flower dress, 10¼" 625.00
Light bulb cover, gr flowers w/red bead centers, 5½" 90.00
Mc glass fruit, pagoda-shaped metal base, 13", M 275.00
Mc mottled globe, kneeling bearded man metal base, 20½" 155.00
Mc mottled shade, emb leaves on metal base, electric, 17" 165.00
Perfume, amethyst, crisscross base decor, electric, 4" 135.00
Rust satin base & shade, HP windmill scenes, electric, 9" 235.00
Student, acid-cut shade, slim brass std, 21" 425.00

Mold Blown and Pressed Bottles

Bl pnt w/blk enameling, atomizer, 6¼" 65.00

Perfume bottle, intaglio floral stopper, embossed florals on base, 8", $185.00.

Blk & orange cased mottle, blk base, atomizer, 5½" 155.00
Blk opaque, crystal drop stopper in metal screw-on lid, 1¾" 95.00
Clear & frosted w/gold trim, atomizer, 4¾" 65.00
Cobalt w/wht enameling & gold, atomizer, 4½" 85.00
Cobalt w/wht enameling & gold, jeweled neck/top, sm chain, 3" ..165.00
Cranberry w/gold band & HP decor, atomizer, 7¼" 100.00
Orange cased w/gold trim, atomizer, 3" 70.00
Red pnt w/mc florals, red glass-topped stopper, 3½" 65.00
Satin frost w/HP florals, clear amber base, atomizer, 5½" 90.00

Opaque, Crystal, Colored Transparent Glass

Bowl, wht satin w/maroon rim, ruffled, ped ft, 6" 75.00
Figurine, conductor, 9" 240.00
Figurine, nurse, 8" 200.00
Honey pot, dk bl irid w/HP decor, 5" 75.00
Puff box, orange w/gold & HP floral, clear finial, 3¾" 50.00

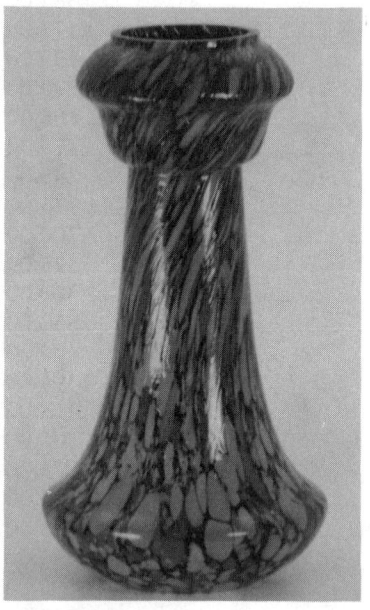

Vase, green, lime, orange and blue spots, 8", $50.00.

Vase, bl-gr satin w/HP bird on branch, ftd, 8¼" 145.00
Vase, bud; gr thorn top, cobalt base, 11" 145.00
Vase, clear w/variegated bl scallops, bulbous, 8½" 175.00
Vase, crystal, intaglio cuttings, ball form, 5" 75.00
Vase, crystal w/alternating frosted panels, 10" 235.00
Vase, dk amethyst w/gold decor, 8½" 80.00
Vase, frosted, emb running horses, ball form, 7" 82.50
Vase, lt gr w/pleated top, mottled o/l base, 6½" 40.00
Vase, lt gr w/red & brn o/l, sm ft, 7" 135.00
Vase, ruby w/gold & HP floral decor, bulbous, 9" 90.00

Pottery, Porcelain, Semi-Porcelain

Basket, mc florals on orange shaded, blk ruffled rim, 5½" 40.00
Basket, pearlescent wht w/emb braid hdl/rim/base, 4¼" 35.00
Basket, tomato red w/blk & wht scroll band, 4¼" 50.00
Candlestick, orange w/blk & wht bands, scalloped base, 10" 60.00
Cup & saucer, yel-orange lustre, bl lustre int, blk hdl 15.00
Mug, coffee; mc Deco florals on yel w/blk rim & hdl, 4½" 45.00
Pitcher, dk bl/orchid/cream/orange flame design, 4" 140.00
Pitcher, HP church scene, orange top/gr base, ornate hdl, 8" 50.00
Pitcher, mc Deco florals on cream, blk rim & hdl, 5¾" 55.00
Pitcher, milk; wht pearl lustre, curled shell form, 5¼" 70.00

Pitcher, ram form, blk & red on cream, horn hdl, 8¼" 175.00
Pitcher, red w/red & wht flower medallions, blk hdl, 8¼" 75.00

Salt box, blue on white, wood lid, $85.00.

Shakers, red & blk bands on cream, 3", pr 7.50
Sugar bowl, wht pearl lustre, shell form, 4-ftd, 2¼" 50.00
Toothpick holder, elephant form, wht w/gr howdah, 3½" 40.00
Vase, beige w/red lineation, blk base/reserve, angle hdls, 8" 60.00
Vase, bl irid w/blk rim, wht int, slim form, 9¼" 40.00
Vase, bl lustre w/rainbow oil spots, blk hdls/trim, 5⅜" 18.00
Vase, blk & orange mottle w/lustre, blk decor, hdls, 10¼" 100.00
Vase, blk & white silhouette cameo on red, blk rim, 5¼" 65.00
Vase, floral on blk & wht stripes, sm neck, flared rim, 4½" 40.00
Vase, maroon/blk/wht mottle w/blk 4-corner rim, ftd, 8¼" 40.00
Vase, mc florals on brn shaded, angle hdls, 7" 50.00
Vase, mc flower garland on orange, fan form, low hdls, 5¾" 30.00
Vase, orange to lt & dk purple sawtooth design, blk rim, 7" 125.00
Vase, Peasant Art flower & fruit motif, 8" 95.00
Vase, pk & bl florals on wht w/blk lineation & rim, 6½" 35.00
Vase, red w/mc Deco floral reserve, blk & wht scrolls, 5" 45.00
Vase, yel/orange/blk wedge design, orange/blk base, 7¾" 90.00
Wall pocket, majolica, blk, yel & purple, Eichwald, 7½" 85.00

D'Argental

D'Argental cameo glass was produced in France from the 1870s until about 1920 in the Art Nouveau style. Browns and tans were favored colors used to complement florals and scenic designs developed through acid cuttings. Our advisor for this category is Don Williams; he is listed in the Directory under Missouri.

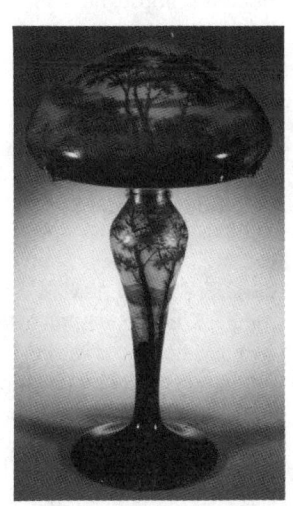

Lamp, wooded lake scene on 12" shade and base, red on yellow frost, 24", $15,000.00.

Key:
fp — fire polished

Cameo

Box, leafy boughs, red/purple on gray opal, domical, 4" H 1,750.00
Lamp, long stylized leaves on 11" dome shade/vase std, 20" ..11,500.00
Vase, apple blossoms, wine on lt gr, baluster, 6", pr 1,200.00
Vase, berried branches, bl-gray on turq, 7" 600.00
Vase, bird pecking gourd/wheat stalks, long stick neck, 17" 2,000.00
Vase, bud; floral, brn on gray/amber mottle, 7½" 650.00
Vase, bud; rose buds, olive/dusty rose on lime, 10½" 1,100.00
Vase, castle/trees, wine on yel, ovoid, 13¾" 1,300.00
Vase, cottage/castle/mtn, brn on orange, 7" 875.00
Vase, foxglove, purple on frost, slender, 9¼" 1,150.00
Vase, jack-in-pulpit; floral, red/wine on yel, 14x6" 1,750.00
Vase, lg trees/sailboats/mtns, partial fp, ovoid, 13½" 2,500.00
Vase, maple leaves/pods, cranberry/blk on red/yel, 12" 1,500.00
Vase, marsh scene, rust/brn on gray, swollen baluster, 8" 700.00
Vase, mulberry branches, wine on lt bl, ovoid, 8" 700.00
Vase, orchids, wine on yel, elongated ftd teardrop, 14" 1,300.00
Vase, pine boughs/cones, brn/olive on lt salmon, 13x5" 1,300.00
Vase, pinwheel/flame band, red on lime, bottle form, 12" 495.00
Vase, trees/river, dk gr on salmon, ovoid, 14" 1,300.00
Vase, trees/river, gr/brn on opal, bottle form, 7" 875.00
Vase, 5-petal floral, brn on yel, 9½x6" 650.00

Daum Nancy

Daum was an important producer of French cameo glass, operating from the late 1800s until after the turn of the century. They used various techniques — acid cutting, wheel engraving, and handwork — to create beautiful scenic designs and nature subjects in the Art Nouveau manner. Virtually all examples are signed. Our advisor for this category is Don Williams; he is listed in the Directory under Missouri.

Vase, lake and trees, red on yellow-mottled gray, 19", $4,500.00; Vase, pine forest and mountains, emerald green on gray streaked with yellow and orange, 15", $3,500.00.

Cameo

Bottle, aquatic plants/dragonfly (cut/appl body), 4x3" 1,200.00
Bottle, flowers cut/pnt on yel to puce, shouldered, 4½" 1,000.00
Bottle, winter scene w/windmills cut/pnt on bl, 3" 1,400.00
Bowl, bird/mtns cut/blk-pnt on opal, hdls/lid, 2¼" 1,870.00
Bowl, blackberries cut on yel/red mottle, 3½" H 1,200.00
Bowl, floral cut/pnt on opal/wine mottle, shaped rim, 8" 1,760.00
Bowl, poppies cut/pnt on yellow mottle, w/gilt, 2" 1,200.00
Bowl, winter scene cut/pnt on gray/orange/yel, 2" 1,500.00
Bowl vase, violets cut/pnt on wht to violet, oval, 4¾" 2,420.00
Box, trees/river in Autumn cut/pnt on opal, 4" dia 4,400.00
Box, winter scene w/windmills cut/pnt on lt bl, 4" dia 4,500.00
Creamer, florals, cut/pnt/gilt on frost, 2⅝x2⅜" 1,200.00
Creamer, pine tree/mtns/bridge, cut/pnt/gilt on gr, 2¾" 1,395.00
Lamp, blackberries on 8" stepped dome shade/slim std, 15" 7,500.00
Lamp, floral bell shade; C-scroll iron ft w/coils, 13" 3,300.00
Lamp, snowy trees cut/pnt on orange to yel shade/std, 15" 10,000.00
Lamp, trees/rain storm cut/pnt on 7" shade/base, 14" 18,000.00
Lamp, Winter forest cut/pnt on 6" shade/base, 12½" 11,000.00
Lamp, Winter scene/windmills cut/pnt on 5½" shade/base 8,000.00
Salt, snow scene cut/pnt on ovoid cylinder, 2" L 900.00
Tumbler, mistletoe, gr/wht on clear, gilt rim, 5" 280.00
Tumbler, mistletoe on lt bl, wht pnt berries w/gold, 4¾" 280.00
Vase, bee/orchids cut/pnt on yel, ftd U-form, 4" 3,850.00
Vase, bees/orchids/webs cut/pnt on amber/brn, slim, 28" 8,000.00
Vase, berries/branches cut/pnt on yel/purple, 4¾" 1,430.00
Vase, berries/branches orange/gr on orange/yel, dbl o/l, 9" 4,400.00
Vase, birch trees cut/pnt on shaded yel, uneven top, 7" 2,500.00
Vase, bluebells cut/pnt on bl/gr, 4-sided, 3¾" 1,300.00
Vase, buds cvd/pnt on rust, free-form overhanging top, 4x5" ..1,200.00
Vase, delicate floral, cut/pnt on yel-streaked gr & bl, 5" 1,000.00
Vase, delicate floral cut/pnt on clear to pk, gilt, 5" 550.00
Vase, floral, cut/pnt on gold/purple mottle, 7½" 1,250.00
Vase, floral, rust on yel, bun ft, 24x4" 2,000.00
Vase, fuchsia cut/pnt on frost to violet, shouldered, 9" 3,000.00
Vase, fuchsia cut/pnt on wht/violet, cylindrical, 5" 2,500.00
Vase, girl/pine trees cut/pnt on opal, ftd, 6¾" 3,850.00
Vase, leaves/fronds on hammered yel to bl, slim, 7" 1,900.00
Vase, lion, bk: fleur-de-lis, gr/gold/rust, 10x5" 900.00
Vase, morning-glories cut/pnt on yel/gr, wide top, 4¾" 1,650.00
Vase, mushrooms cut/pnt on rose/yel mottle, lg hdls, 7" 9,000.00
Vase, oak leaves, naturalistic mc, appl foil-bkd acorns, 6" 6,500.00
Vase, orchids cut/pnt, orange/yel on gr to wht, 23x4" 3,300.00
Vase, poppies, gr/red on red mottle, dbl o/l, ftd, 11" 8,250.00
Vase, poppies, red/gr on martele opal, dbl o/l, 7½x7" 7,500.00
Vase, poppies cut/pnt on yel/orange, bulbous, 3½" 1,500.00
Vase, poppies cut/pnt on yel/orange, ftd, 6" 3,000.00
Vase, rain storm/blown trees cut/pnt on frost, slim, 2¼" 1,540.00
Vase, spider webs/orchids cut/pnt on gr/bl, 4¾" 2,200.00
Vase, summer scenic cut/pnt on bl mottle, ftd ovoid, 6" 2,000.00
Vase, sunflowers on martele ground, dbl o/l, 7½x5½" 6,000.00
Vase, tobacco flowers, orange on hammered rust to brn, 24" ...2,600.00
Vase, trees & boats scenic, brns/oranges, 6" 1,250.00
Vase, trees/lake, wine on gray/yel, slim/ftd, 19" 4,500.00
Vase, vintage cut/pnt on yel/bl mottle, 2 appl snails, 10" 16,500.00
Vase, violets cut/pnt on wht/purple, gilt on ft, 10" 7,000.00
Vase, wildflowers cut/pnt on pk/gr, gilt, long neck, 3" 1,100.00
Vase, windmills/sailboats cut/pnt on wht, ftd ovoid, 4" 750.00

Miscellaneous

Bottle, scent; acid-etched berries on smoke, 6½" 880.00
Bowl, clear w/gr/bl-blk striations & wht mottling, 8" 770.00

Bowl, etched horizontal ribs on yel, cone form, 6" H 875.00
Bowl, lt peach, swirl hdls, oval, 4½" H 110.00
Ewer, Dutch seascape/landscape pnt in gray on bl irid, 8" 2,600.00
Jar, frosted w/int mc splotches, thick walled, sq, 4" 385.00
Lamp, turq/bl mottle 12" dome shade/vase std, rpl hdw, 23" ...1,100.00
Lamp, 3 martele ball shades, iron base w/leafy stems, 24" 7,500.00
Salt, Dutch scene, blk on wht/gray, hdld bucket, 1¼" 900.00
Vase, bl/gr/wine mottle, 3-sided w/buttresses, slim, 25" 825.00
Vase, blown-out teardrops, mottled colors on frost, 12" 1,400.00
Vase, clear w/rust & brn mottle, metallic flecks, hdls, 7x8" 550.00
Vase, clear with appl red lines, blk bands, ftd, 9½" 1,200.00
Vase, etched chevrons on azure bl, slim baluster, 15" 1,100.00
Vase, etched oval panels on gray, flaring top, 8" 990.00
Vase, etched panels/narrow smooth ribs on gray, bulbous, 15" ..1,650.00
Vase, etched ray-&-dot motif on dk gray, baluster, 10" 825.00
Vase, etched ribs beneath sqs, lt yel, ftd U-form, 4½" 500.00
Vase, etched rings on amber texture, spherical, 7" 770.00
Vase, etched sq-petal floral on gray-bl, spherical, 5½" 825.00
Vase, etched vertical ribbing, pk flecked, 13x5½" 1,650.00
Vase, floral, mc on mottle, tapered cylinder, 12½" 1,100.00
Vase, inlaid berries, orange/gr on yel-brn mottle, ftd, 9" 5,000.00

Vase, leaves and berries acid etched on clear with gold spangles, 8½", $1,500.00.

Vase, rust mottle, blown into iron Majorelle scroll fr, 15" 2,860.00

Davenport

W. Davenport and Company were Staffordshire potters operating in that area from 1793 to 1887, producing earthenware, creamware, porcelain, and ironstone. Many different stamps, all with 'Davenport,' were used to mark the various types of ware. See also Mulberry; Flow Blue.

Bowl, soup; sm bl flowers, yel/brn wheat, shell rim, early 700.00
Compote, landscapes, multifoil rim, 1880, 9½", pr 250.00
Creamer, floral, red w/bl/gr/blk, gold band, shell mold, 5½" 65.00
Cup & saucer, Adam's Rose-type floral, EX 225.00
Plate, creamware, rtcl rim, lav foliage on orange band, 8" 110.00
Plate, irises, purple/bl w/red buds, scalloped, 10", NM 210.00
Plate, mc florals: center & edge, blk rim stripe, early, 8½" 750.00
Plate, red/bl floral, gr/blk leaves, floral border, 9" 210.00

Plate, blue turkey transfer and molded shell rim, marked, 7", NM, $625.00.

Plate, rtcl border, red flowers/bands, Yel Flax, rpr, 7½"	300.00
Plate, sm bl flowers w/yel sprigs, shell rim, early, 8"	425.00
Plate, turkey transfer, bl shell rim, 7", NM	625.00
Soup plate, pearlware, 3-color house, gr feather edge, 8"	425.00

David Winter Cottages

This line of miniature cottages representing distinctive British architecture is designed by artist/sculpture David Winter and sold through fine giftstores everywhere. Popular since the 1980s, those that have been discontinued are finding their way to the secondary market, where they are commanding high prices.

Alms House	600.00
Ann Hathaway, tiny	1,200.00
Blacksmith's Cottage	600.00
Castle Keep	1,850.00
Cornish Cottage	1,500.00
Cotton Mill	765.00
Ebenezer Counting House	185.00
Grange	1,500.00
Hay Barn	350.00
Hermit's Humble Home	295.00
House of Master Mason	335.00
Little Forge	2,000.00
Little Mill, orig	2,545.00
Miner's Cottage	265.00
Moorland Cottage	295.00
Quayside	2,000.00
Robin Hood's Hideaway	500.00
Sabrina's Cottage	2,500.00
Shakespeare's Birthplace, lg	2,000.00
Spinner's Cottage	90.00
Squire's Hall	130.00
Suffolk House	100.00
Tudor Manor House	200.00
Tythe Barn, door on	2,200.00

Davis, Lowell

Figurines, plates, bells, and ornaments painted by Lowell Davis and produced by Border Fine Arts, Schmid Sculptured Porcelain, cap-

ture the heritage of rural America.

Lowell Davis, known better as Mr. Lowell to his farm animals, is described by many as 'just a country farmer from Missouri' fulfilling his dreams of preserving rural America as he knew it in the 1930s. Mr. Lowell rebuilt Red Oak II, a 1930 village, from actual buildings he spent hours in as a child. You can visit this unique town refurbished with antiques and 'supplies' in Grandpa's General Store in Carthage, Missouri.

A Secondary Market Price Guide is published by Rosie Wells Enterprises for his collectibles. She is listed in the Directory under Clubs, Newsletters, and Catalogs. Items below are assumed to be in mint condition with box.

Blossom, #225-032, retired, 6"	1,400.00
Blossom RFD Bell, 225-040, retired, 4¾"	500.00
Brer Rabbit, #225-252, Uncle Remus Series, retired, 4¼"	1,600.00
Bride, The; #20993, 1st club pc	300.00
Cackleberries, #892-051, 1st renewal pc	95.00
Country Crook, #225-280, retired, 1¾"	385.00
Critics, The; #223-600, ltd edition of 1200, retired, 6¼"	1,385.00
Forbidden Fruit, #225-022, retired, porc bar, 2"	200.00
Home from Market, #223-601, ltd ed of 1200, retired, 4½"	1,200.00
Ignorance Is Bliss, #225-031, retired, 6"	1,185.00
Plum Tuckered Out, #225-201, ltd edition of 2500, retired, 4"	675.00
Prairie Chorus, #225-333, retired, 4½"	1,300.00
Punkin Seeds, #25501, retired, 6½"	1,600.00
Surprise in Cellar, #225-200, ltd edition of 2500, retired, 3½"	965.00
Up To No Good, #225-218, retired, 6¼"	885.00
83 Country Christmas, #223-550, Hooker/Mail Box, ltd ed	750.00

De Vez

De Vez was a type of acid-cut French cameo glass produced by Cristallerie de Pantin in Paris around the turn of the century. Our advisor for this category is Don Williams; he is listed in the Directory under Missouri.

Cameo

Atomizer, sailboats/rowboat on lake, dk gr & orange, mk, 12"	875.00
Bucket, fisherman scene, bl/gr on cased bl, hdls, 3¾"	875.00
Vase, lake w/fisherman fr w/lg branches, baluster, 11"	1,700.00
Vase, maid sits on stone/views ruin across lake, 7"	1,400.00
Vase, sailboats, amethyst on frost, ftd heart form, 4"	600.00
Vase, seaside village/sailboat, brn/navy/rust on gray, 9"	875.00
Vase, trees/lakes/mtns, gr/wine on yel, ftd, 9"	600.00
Vase, wisteria at riverbank/mtns, dbl o/l, wide mouth, 14"	1,045.00

De Vilbiss

Perfume bottles, atomizers, and dresser accessories marketed by the De Vilbiss Company are appreciated by collectors today for the various types of lovely glassware used in their manufacture, as well as for their pleasing shapes. Various companies provided the glass, while De Vilbiss made only the metal tops. They marketed their merchandise not only here but in Paris, England, Canada, and Havana as well. Their marks were acid stamped, ink stamped, in gold script, molded in, or on paper labels. One is no more significant than another. For more information we recommend *Bedroom and Bathroom Glassware of the Depression Years* by Margaret and Kenn Whitmyer; their address is listed in the Directory under Ohio. Our advisor for this category is Randy Monsen; he is listed in the Directory under Virginia.

Atomizer, bl, pineapple form, gilded bottom	85.00
Atomizer, bl w/3 gold flamingos, 5"	50.00

Atomizer, blk Deco decor on pk opaque, mesh cord & bulb **185.00**
Atomizer, blk w/crystal stem & ft, 4¼" **50.00**
Atomizer, clear/wht cased, HP pk florals w/gold, complete, 8" ...**155.00**
Atomizer, cranberry stain, gold decor, mesh bulb & cord, 7" **95.00**
Atomizer, gold Aurene w/rare traces of pk, Steuben, 6" **450.00**
Atomizer, gold decor on smoked glass, orig label **75.00**
Atomizer, lt gr, Opalescent Windows, 5" **85.00**
Atomizer, pk satin w/gold stars, W Germany, 4" **55.00**
Atomizer, silver crackle, w/label **45.00**
Atomizer, tangerine, orig cord & bulb, 6⅜" **90.00**
Atomizer, wht cased satin w/gold & red holly **50.00**

Atomizer, silver and gold-bronze streaks on smoke gray, ca 1960s, 4", $45.00.

Bottle, allover blk/gold abstract enameling, glass dauber, 7" **255.00**
Bottle, blk w/chrome neck **45.00**
Bottle, cut crystal, metal stopper, glass dauber, 6½" **175.00**
Ginger jar, Chinese red w/gold floral **95.00**
Lamp, perfume; exotic bird on glass insert, sq, 8½" **175.00**
Lamp, perfume; nude figure on glass insert, rnd, 7" **250.00**
Vanity set, orange enamel w/blk & gold decor, 3-pc **165.00**

Decanters

Ceramic whiskey decanters were brought into prominence in 1955 by the James Beam Distilling Company. Few other companies besides Beam produced these decanters during the next ten years or so; however, other companies did eventually follow suit. At its peak in 1975, at least twenty prominent companies and several on a lesser scale made these decanters. Beam stopped making decanters in mid-1992. Now only a couple of companies are still producing these collectibles.

Liquor dealers have told collectors for years that ceramic decanters are not as valuable, and in some cases worthless, if emptied, or if the federal tax stamp has been broken. Nothing is further from the truth. Following are but a few of many reasons you should consider emptying ceramic decanters:

If the thin glaze on the inside ever cracks (and it does in a small percentage of decanters), the contents will push through to the outside. It is then referred to as a 'leaker' and worth a fraction of its original value.

2) A large number of decanters left full in one area of your house poses a fire hazard.

3) A burglar, after stealing jewelry and electronics, may make off with some of your decanters just to enjoy the contents. If they are empty, chances are they will not be bothered.

4) It is illegal in most states for collectors to sell a full decanter without a liquor license.

Unlike years ago, few collectors now collect all types of decanters. Most now specialize. For example, they may collect trains, cars, owls,

Indians, clowns, or any number of different things that have been depicted on or as a decanter. They are finding exceptional quality available at reasonable prices, especially when compared with many other types of collectibles.

We have tried to list those brands that are the most popular with collectors. Likewise, individual decanters listed are the ones (or representative of the ones) most commonly found. The following listing is but a small fraction of the thousands of decanters that have been produced.

These decanters come from all over the world. While Jim Beam owned its own china factory in the U.S., some of the others have been imported from Mexico, Taiwan, Japan, and elsewhere. They vary in size from miniatures (approximately 2-oz.) to gallons. Values range from a few dollars to more than $3,000 per decanter.

Most collectors and dealers define a 'mint' decanter as one with no chips, no cracks, and label intact. A missing federal tax stamp or lack of contents have no bearing on value. All values are given for 'mint' decanters. A 'mini' behind a listing indicates a miniature. All others are fifth or 750 ml unless noted otherwise. Our advisor for this category is Roy Willis; he is listed in the Directory under Kentucky.

Aesthetic Specialties (ASI)

Chevrolet, 1914, blk **60.00**
Golf, Bing Crosby 38th **18.00**

Kentucky Derby, 1979, $25.00.

Oldsmobile, 1910, blk or cream **75.00**

Anniversary (Marita)

Christmas Greeting **12.00**
Happy Anniversary **18.00**
John Lennon **25.00**

Beam

Centennial Series, Antioch **6.00**
Centennial Series, Civil War North **18.00**
Centennial Series, Civil War South **35.00**
Centennial Series, Key West **6.00**
Centennial Series, Reno **6.00**
Centennial Series, San Diego **5.00**
Executive Series, 1955 Royal Porcelain **250.00**
Executive Series, 1956 Gold Round **85.00**
Executive Series, 1957 Royal Di Monte **60.00**
Executive Series, 1958 Grey Cherub **175.00**
Executive Series, 1959 Tavern Scene **45.00**
Organization Series, Bartender's Guild **6.00**
Organization Series, CPO Open Mess **10.00**
Organization Series, Ducks Unlimited #3, 40th **45.00**
Organization Series, Ducks Unlimited #4, Mallard Head **40.00**

Organization Series, Ducks Unlimited #5, Canvasback 40.00
Organization Series, Ducks Unlimited #6, Bluewing Teals 35.00
Organization Series, Elks Nat'l Foundation 10.00
Organization Series, Legion Music 12.00
Organization Series, Marine Corps Emblem 45.00
Organization Series, Shrine, El Kahir Temple 15.00
Organization Series, Shrine, Moila w/Camel 15.00
Organization Series, Telephone #3, cradle 25.00
Organization Series, Telephone #5, pay phone 45.00
Organization Series, Telephone #6, battery 35.00
Organization Series, Telephone #7, 100-digit 65.00
Wheel Series, Army Jeep 40.00
Wheel Series, Chevy Camaro, 1969, convertible pacecar 75.00
Wheel Series, Chevy Corvette, 1953, wht 140.00
Wheel Series, Chevy Corvette, 1957, blk 75.00
Wheel Series, Chevy Corvette, 1963, red or silver 60.00
Wheel Series, Chevy Corvette, 1978, blk 150.00
Wheel Series, Chevy Corvette, 1986, yel pacecar 90.00
Wheel Series, Chevy Hot Rod, 1957, yel 85.00
Wheel Series, Duesenberg, 1935, convertible 175.00
Wheel Series, Fire Chief's Car, 1928 ....125.00
Wheel Series, Fire Chief's Car, 1934 ....65.00
Wheel Series, Fire Engine, Ford, 1930 ....135.00
Wheel Series, Fire Engine, Mississippi Valley Pumper 125.00
Wheel Series, Ford, Mustang, 1964, wht or red 65.00
Wheel Series, Ford, Thunderbird, 1956, gray, gr, or yel 75.00
Wheel Series, Ford, 1903 Model-A, red or blk 45.00
Wheel Series, Ford, 1913 Model-A, blk or gr 50.00
Wheel Series, Ford, 1928 Model-A 75.00
Wheel Series, Ford, 1929 Pheaton 65.00
Wheel Series, Jewel Tea Wagon 75.00
Wheel Series, Oldsmobile, 1904 ....40.00
Wheel Series, Police Car, 1929 ....95.00
Wheel Series, Police Paddy Wagon 140.00
Wheel Series, Police Tow Truck 55.00
Wheel Series, Race Car, Unser Olsonite Eagle 70.00
Wheel Series, Stutz Bearcat, gray or yel 60.00
Wheel Series, Thomas Flyer, bl or cream 75.00
Wheel Series, Trains, Locomotive, General 90.00
Wheel Series, Trains, Locomotive, Grant 70.00
Wheel Series, Trains, Locomotive, JB Turner 140.00

Brooks

Animal Series, Brahma Bull 12.00
Animal Series, Deer, Wht Tail 20.00
Animal Series, Elk 20.00
Automotive & Transportation Series, Cable Car, brn, gray, gr 7.00
Automotive & Transportation Series, Duesenberg 20.00
Automotive & Transportation Series, Racer, AB Dick #2 ....65.00
Automotive & Transportation Series, Racer, Gould #1 ....65.00
Automotive & Transportation Series, Racer, Norton #3 ....65.00
Bird Series, Macaw 55.00
Bird Series, Virginia Cardinal 15.00
Clown Series, #1 Smiley 30.00
Clown Series, #2 Cowboy 30.00
Clown Series, #3 Pagliacci 20.00
Indian Series, Kachina #4, Maiden, 1975 ....25.00
Indian Series, Kachina #5, Long Hair, 1976 ....35.00
Indian Series, Kachina #6, Buffalo Dancer, 1977 ....35.00
Institutional Series, Am Legion Convention, 1973, Houston 40.00
Institutional Series, FOE Eagle, 1981 ....35.00
Institutional Series, Golden Pharoah 25.00
Institutional Series, Shrine, King Tut Guard 20.00

People Series, Iowa Farmer 55.00
People Series, Stan Laurel or Oliver Hardy, ea 25.00
Sports Series, Basketball Players 15.00
Sports Series, Casey at the Bat 35.00
Sports Series, Football Player 12.00

Cyrus Noble

Carousel Animals, 4 different, ea 35.00
Deer, Wht Tail 75.00
Gold Miner 300.00
Gole Miner, mini 20.00
Sea Turtle 45.00
Violinist 40.00
Violinist, mini 25.00

Double Springs

Cord, 1937 ....20.00
Duesenberg, 1931 ....20.00
Kar-Kare #11, Cale Yarborough 30.00
Peasant, Boy or Girl, ea 5.00

Famous Firsts

Coffee Mill 40.00
Coffee Mill, mini 15.00
Corvette Convertible, 1953 ....75.00
Roulette Wheel 25.00
Spirit of St Louis 175.00
Spirit of St Louis, midi 100.00
Spirit of St Louis, mini 60.00

Grenadier

Frosty the Snowman 30.00
Horse, Arabian 22.00
Horse, Thoroughbred 30.00
Mr Spock, bust 40.00
Teddy Roosevelt, on horsebk 30.00
Texas Ranger, on horsebk 40.00

Hoffman

Car Series, Race Car, AJ Foyt #2 ....110.00
Car Series, Race Car, Johncock #20 ....70.00
Mr Lucky Series, Mr Lucky 30.00
Mr Lucky Series, Mr Lucky, mini 10.00
Mr Lucky Series, Mr Mailman 40.00
Mr Lucky Series, Mr Mailman, mini 15.00
Mr Lucky Series, Mr Pilot, mini 25.00
Sports Series, Big Red Machine 50.00
Wildlife Series, Bear & Cub Fishing 65.00
Wildlife Series, Doe & Fawn 30.00
Wildlife Series, Lynx & Rabbit 65.00
Wildlife Series, Mountain Goat & Puma 75.00

Jack Daniels

Belle of Lincoln 25.00
Maxwell House 35.00

Kontinental

Innkeeper 25.00

Stephen Foster 30.00

Lionstone

Automotive & Transportation Series, Johnny Lightning #1 ....85.00
Automotive & Transportation Series, Olsonite Eagle #6 ....85.00
Bicentennial Series, Molly Pitcher 25.00
Bicentennial Series, Valley Forge 18.00
Bird Series, Doves of Peace 40.00
Bird Series, Pheasant, 1977 ....50.00
Old West Series, Barber 50.00
Old West Series, Country Doctor 15.00
Old West Series, Custer's Last Stand, 4-pc set 375.00
Old West Series, Judge Roy Bean 30.00
Old West Series, Photographer 40.00
Old West Series, Photographer, mini 12.00
Sports Series, Basketball Players 40.00
Sports Series, Fisherman 35.00
Sports Series, Golfer 40.00
Sports Series, Hunter 40.00

McCormick

Automobile & Transportation, 1937 Packard, blk or cream 50.00
Bicentennial Series, Spirit of '76 ....55.00
Entertainer Series, Elvis #1, '77 ....80.00
Entertainer Series, Elvis #1, '77, mini 40.00
Entertainer Series, Elvis #2, '55 ....60.00
Entertainer Series, Elvis #2, '55, mini 40.00
Entertainer Series, Elvis #3, '68 ....65.00
Entertainer Series, Elvis #3, '68, mini 40.00
Entertainer Series, Hank Williams, Sr 85.00
Great American Series, Abe Lincoln 40.00
Great American Series, Bat Masterson 30.00
Great American Series, Billy the Kid 35.00
Great American Series, Thomas Edison 30.00
Shrine Series, Imperial Council 35.00
Shrine Series, Noble 25.00

Michter

Fleetwood Packard 25.00
King Tut 25.00
King Tut, mini 15.00
King Tut, 1.75 liter 65.00

Mount Hope

American Legion Seaman 20.00
Fireman #1, PA Volunteer 85.00
Fireman #2, PA Volunteer, holding child 95.00

Old Bardstown

Georgia Bulldog 125.00
Georgia Bulldog, 1.75 liter 250.00
Horse, Citation 200.00
Razorback 25.00

Old Commonwealth

Coal Miner #1, w/shovel 90.00
Coal Miner #1, w/shovel, mini 25.00
Coal Miner #2, w/pick 45.00

Coal Miner #2, w/pick, mini 25.00
Firefighter, Modern Hero #1 ....45.00
Firefighter, Modern Hero #1, mini 15.00
Golden Retriever 35.00
Irish, Sports of Ireland 25.00
Irish, Symbols of Ireland 25.00
Octoberfest 45.00

Old Fitzgerald

Irish, Blarney Bottle 20.00
Irish, Counties 18.00
Irish, Patriots 25.00
Irish, Wish 20.00

Old Mr. Boston

Dan Patch 20.00
Miss Madison Hydroplane 25.00
Nathan Hale 10.00

Pacesetter

Tractor, Green Machine 75.00
Tractor, John Deere 150.00
Truck, Coca-Cola 175.00

Ski Country

Bird Series, Cedar Waxwings 70.00
Bird Series, Cedar Waxwings, mini 25.00
Bird Series, Dove 75.00
Bird Series, Dove, mini 35.00
Bird Series, Duck, Ducks Unlimited Pintail 110.00
Bird Series, Duck, Ducks Unlimited Pintail, mini 35.00
Bird Series, Duck, Ducks Unlimited Pintail, ½-gal 250.00
Bird Series, Duck, Wood, 1974 ....250.00
Bird Series, Duck, Wood, 1974, mini 150.00
Bird Series, Gyrafalcon 70.00
Bird Series, Gyrafalcon, mini 30.00
Bird Series, Kestrel, wall plaque 70.00
Bird Series, Kestrel, wall plaque, mini 30.00
Bird Series, Owl, Great Gray 75.00
Bird Series, Owl, Great Gray, mini 30.00
Circus Series, Tiger on Ball 45.00
Circus Series, Tiger on Ball, mini 30.00
Circus Series, Tom Thumb 30.00
Circus Series, Tom Thumb, mini 15.00
Indian Series, Buffalo Dancer 175.00
Indian Series, Buffalo Dancer, mini 40.00
Indian Series, Eagle Dancer 225.00
Indian Series, Eagle Dancer, mini 35.00
Indian Series, North American, set of 6 ....225.00
Indian Series, North American, set of 6, mini 150.00
Wildlife Grand Slam Series, Dall Sheep 175.00
Wildlife Grand Slam Series, Desert Sheep 100.00
Wildlife Grand Slam Series, Mountain Sheep 70.00
Wildlife Grand Slam Series, Stone Sheep 75.00
Wildlife Series, Deer, Wht Tail 150.00
Wildlife Series, Deer, Wht Tail, mini 50.00
Wildlife Series, Fox Family 70.00
Wildlife Series, Fox Family, mini 25.00
Wildlife Series, Mountain Goat 100.00
Wildlife Series, Mountain Goat, mini 45.00

Wildlife Series, Mountain Goat, 1-gal 850.00

Wild Turkey

Series I, #1, 1971 ....250.00
Series I, #2 ....150.00
Series I, #3 ....70.00
Series I, #4 ....70.00
Series I, #5 ....35.00
Series I, #6 ....25.00
Series I, #7 ....20.00
Series I, #8 ....40.00
Series II (Lore Series), #1 ....25.00
Series II (Lore Series), #2 ....25.00
Series II (Lore Series), #3 ....38.00
Series II (Lore Series), #4 ....45.00

Decoys

American colonists learned the craft of decoy-making from the Indians who used them to lure birds out of the sky as an important food source. Early models were carved from wood such as pine, cedar, balsa, etc., and a few were made of canvas or papier-mache. There are two basic types of decoys: water floaters and shorebirds (also called 'stick-ups'). Within each type are many different species, ducks being the most plentiful since they migrated along all four of America's great waterways. Market hunting became big business around 1880, resulting in large-scale commercial production of decoys which continued until about 1910 when such hunting was outlawed by the Migratory Bird Treaty.

Today decoys are one of the most collectible types of American folk art. The most valuable are those carved by such artists as Laing, Crowell, Ward, and Wheeler, to name only a few. Each area, such as Massachusetts, Connecticut, Maine, the Illinois River, and the Delaware River, produces decoys with distinctive regional characteristics. Examples of commercial decoys produced by well-known factories — among them Mason, Stevens, and Dodge — are also prized by collectors. Though mass-produced, these nevertheless required a certain amount of hand carving and decorating. Well-carved examples, especially those of rare species, are appreciating rapidly, and those with original paint are more desirable. Writer Carl F. Luckey has compiled a fully illustrated identification and value guide, *Collecting Antique Bird Decoys*; you will find his address in the Directory under Alabama. *The Collector's Guide to Decoys* by Sharon and Bob Huxford contains hundreds of photos (many in color) and gives values realized at auction during the past two years, available from your local bookstore or Collector Books. In the listings that follow, all decoys are solid-bodied unless noted hollow.

Key:
OP — original paint   RP — repaint
ORP — old repaint   WOP — worn original paint
OWP — original working paint   WRP — working repaint

American Merganser pr, Fred Dobbins, NM OP, EX 150.00
American Merganser pr, Mason Factory, crazed OP, EX 900.00
Black Duck, Bill Cranmer, content/standing, NM OP, rare 750.00
Black Duck, Bob Brown, hollow, contemporary, M 150.00
Black Duck, Cal Thomas, glass eyes, OP, 1950s, 17" 50.00
Black Duck, Charles Birch, hollow, OP w/touchup, EX 675.00
Black Duck, Elmer Crowell, trn head, EX rpt, sm split 400.00
Black Duck, James Holly, in-use ORP, nailed crack, chip 350.00
Black Duck, John English, hollow, WRP, hollow, early, chips ...900.00
Black Duck, Joseph Lincoln, WRP, flaking, eye missing 375.00

Black Duck, Wildfowler, balsa body, NM OP, oversz 145.00
Black Duck, Wm Bedell, overpnt removed, some OP, '30s, VG .200.00
Black Duck pr, Mason's Standard Grade, EX OP, rpr 350.00
Black Duck pr, Walter Oller, hollow, contemporary, M 250.00
Bluebill Drake, Ira Hudson, WOP, rough bill, oversz, VG 200.00
Bluebill Drake, Nathan Cobb, inlet head, ca 1880, rare, VG ..4,500.00
Bluebill Drake, Orel LaBoeuf, low head, M 1,500.00
Bluebill Drake, Robert Elliston, WOP, loose head, near EX 1,100.00
Bluebill Drake, Wilbur Simpson, WOP, underside crack 250.00
Bluebill Hen, Frank Coombs, high head, EX OP, sm chips, EX ..425.00
Bluebill pr, John McGloughlin, balsa bodies, ORP, dents 500.00
Bluewinged Teal Drake, Mason's Premier Grade, NM OP 4,250.00
Bluewinged Teal Drake, Xavier Bourg, EX OP, sm chip 275.00

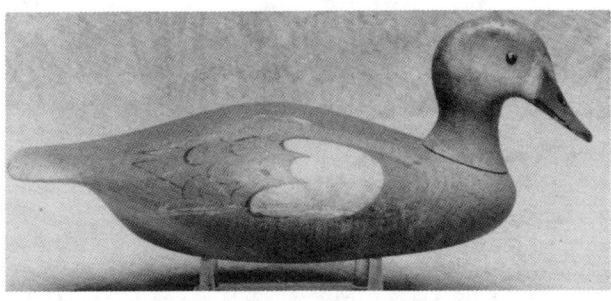

Bluewinged Teal Drake, original paint with minor wear, ca 1880s, hairline and small dents, rare, $2,800.00.

Bluewinged Teal Hen, Ken Anger, OP w/touchup, rpr seam 300.00
Bluewinged Teal Hen, Mason's Std, glass eyes, NM OP 1,000.00
Bluewinged Teal pr, Wildfowler, NM OP, structurally EX 500.00
Bluewinged Teal pr, Wildfowler Quogue LI brand, NM 400.00
Brant, Capt Bill Carmen, slightly trn head, ORP, sm, EX 550.00
Brant, Mason's Challenge Grade, EX OP, base crack 2,750.00
Brant, Percy Gant, NM OP, hairline in neck 475.00
Brant, Wildfowler, sgn C Birdsal, NM OP, EX 170.00
Bufflead pr, Ben Schmidt, WRP, 1940s, sm cracks/chips 350.00
Bufflehead Drake, Mason's Challenge Grade, rstr pnt & eyes 200.00
Bufflehead pr, Roswell Bliss, NM OP, structurally EX 525.00
Canada Goose, Chip Alsop, hollow, EX 250.00
Canada Goose, Elmer Crowell, EX orig, mini 1,000.00
Canada Goose, folding sheet metal stick-up, blk/wht pnt, 23" 65.00
Canada Goose, Mason's Premier Grade, OP, heavy wear 800.00
Canada Goose, Paul Gibson, lt wear on OP, dents/crack 275.00
Canada Goose, Thomas Chaido, relief cvd wings, NM OP 425.00
Canvasback Drake, C Klopping, glass eyes, WOP, cracks, 14" .550.00
Canvasback Drake, Mason's Premier Grade, OP, average wear ..500.00
Canvasback Drake, Mason's Premier/Seneca Lake, G OP 550.00
Canvasback Drake, NM OP, sm dents, eye missing 100.00
Canvasback Drake, Sam Barnes, OWP, neck crack, EX 800.00
Canvasback Drake, Steve Dilks, RP, average wear 90.00
Canvasback Drake, Stevens Co, ORP, sm age line in neck 550.00
Canvasback Drake, Stevens Co, ORP, 1880s, sm chips 750.00
Crow, Wildfowler, NM OP, sm dents in body, rare 350.00
Dove pr, Danny Brannock, tack eyes, nail bills, EX 275.00
Dowicher, Wm Bowman, ORP, reattached head, chip 700.00
Fish, att Oscar Peterson, wood/tin w/mc pnt, 5" L 600.00
Golden Plover, Frank Finney, NM OP, lightly shot 250.00
Goldeneye Drake, Mason's Premier, early head, NM OP 5,600.00
Goldeneye Hen, Reagon Danos, NM OP, sgn, structurally EX ...100.00
Goose, Mason's Premier Grade, OP w/some rpt 2,200.00
Greenwinged Teal Hen, Hurley Conklin, hollow, WOP, EX 475.00
Mallard Drake, Harry Canfield, ORP, minor age lines 110.00

Mallard Drake, John R Wells, EX comb pnt w/touchups **1,200.00**
Mallard Drake, Peterson Factory, OP, average wear, 1880s **245.00**
Mallard Drake, Wildfowler, balsa body, WOP, rprs, oversz **150.00**
Mallard Drake, Wm Gibian, strong OP, sgn, structurally EX **300.00**
Mallard Hen, Cecil Anger, hollow, WOP, reglued bill **150.00**
Mallard Hen, Elmer Crowell, badly WOP, hit by shot **325.00**
Mallard Hen, Mason's Challenge Grade, WOP, rstr chip **950.00**
Mallard Hen, St Clair Flats, glass eyes, WRP, 18" **65.00**
Merganser Drake, Mason's Challenge Grade, EX OP, lt wear .**4,500.00**
Merganser Hen, Mason's Std Grade, glass eyes, OP, lt wear **1,200.00**
Old Squaw, Steven Badlam, tack eyes, ORP, rare, VG **4,000.00**
Peep, Obediah Verity, cork body, cvd eyes, NM OP, 1870s **2,450.00**
Pintail Drake, Charles Althoff, hollow, WOP, sm neck cracks ...**750.00**
Pintail Drake, Charles Birch, lt wear on OP, EX **2,750.00**
Pintail Drake, Jim Pierce, NM OP, structurally EX **150.00**
Pintail Drake, Mason's Premier Grade, snaky head, NM OP **850.00**
Pintail Drake, Ward Bros, balsa body/trn head, WOP, 1948 ...**1,050.00**
Primitive, hollow, glass eyes, RP, neck cracks, 17" **35.00**
Rail, Gus Wilson, raised wing tips, WOP, pegged bill, dents **600.00**
Redbreasted Drake, Pratt Mfg, G OP, ca 1925 ....**450.00**
Redbreasted Merganser Drake, L Barkelow, EX OP, rpr, 1880s ...**1,250.00**
Redhead Drake, T Chambers, hollow, WOP, hairline, EX **925.00**
Ruddy Duck, Geo Adams, age splits, rare, ORP, EX **1,800.00**
Ruddy Duck pr, Roy Bull, EX OP, artist brand **190.00**
Widgeon Drake, Miles Hancock, EX OP, bill crack, rare **1,000.00**
Wood Duck Hen, Wildfowler Quige LI stamp, NM OP, dents ...**525.00**
Yellowlegs, Chief Cuffee, relief cvd wings, WOP, EX **350.00**
Yellowlegs, Elisha Burr, WOP, ca 1910, age lines **900.00**

Dedham Pottery

Originally founded in Chelsea, Massachusetts, as the Chelsea Keramic Works, the name was changed to Dedham Pottery in 1895 after the firm relocated in Dedham, near Boston, Massachusetts. The move was effected to make use of the native clay deemed more suitable for the production of the popular dinnerware designed by Hugh Robertson, founder of the company. The ware utilized a gray stoneware body with a crackle glaze and simple cobalt border designs of flowers, birds, and animals. Decorations were brushed on by hand using an ancient Chinese method which suspended the cobalt within the overall glaze. There were thirteen standard patterns, among them Magnolia, Iris, Butterfly, Duck, Polar Bear, and the Rabbit, the latter of which was chosen to represent the company on their logo. On the very early pieces the rabbits face left; decorators soon found the reverse position easier to paint, and the rabbits were turned to the right. In addition to the standard patterns, other designs were produced for special orders. These and artist-signed pieces are highly valued by collectors today.

Though their primary product was the blue-printed crackle-glazed dinnerware, two types of artware were also produced: crackle glaze and flambe. Their notable volcanic ware was a type of the latter. The mark is incised and often accompanies the cipher of Hugh Robertson. The firm was operated by succeeding generations of the Robertson family until it closed in 1943. Our advisor for this category is Dale MacLean; he is listed in the Directory under Massachusetts. See also Chelsea Keramic Art Works.

Vase, Dragon's Blood, striated/irid, experimental, 10", NM **1,750.00**
Vase, gr & red drip over oatmeal, HR, mfg flaw, 5x4½" **1,000.00**
Vase, gr mottle w/bl traces on wht stoneware, HCR, 5½" **330.00**
Vase, gr/bl-flecked brn gloss, experimental, 8½" **825.00**
Vase, irid gr-gray mottle drip over red, HR, 8x2¾" **850.00**
Vase, irises, wht/dk bl on lt bl crackle, Robertson, 7" **2,000.00**
Vase, sang de boeuf, swollen base, HR, 5¾x3" **900.00**

Vase, sang de boeuf flambe glaze, initialed H (Hugh Robertson), 8x5", $,1900.00.

Vase, tan semimatte, swollen cylinder, experimental, 11", NM ..**275.00**
Vase, thick gr drip over gray, mfg flaw, HR, 5x6" **600.00**
Vase, volcanic turq/brn/blk/tan, bulbous, HR, DD58S, 7" **1,100.00**

Dinnerware

Bouillon cup & saucer, Iris, stamped registered **365.00**
Bouillon cup & saucer, Rabbit, stamped **350.00**
Bowl, Grape, stamped, DP on base, 6" **475.00**
Bowl, Lotus, emb flutes, bl decor, 5½" **450.00**
Bowl, Rabbit (clockwise/2-ear), #3, stamped, 3x7" **225.00**
Bowl, Scotty dog (central medallion), stamped, 5" **1,400.00**
Bowl, soup; Pond Lily, 8½" **250.00**
Bowl, Turtle, ink mk, 2x4½" **325.00**
Bowl, whipped cream; Iris, flat border, stamped, 2½x7" **200.00**
Bowl, whipped cream; Rabbit (clockwise/2-ear), 2½x7" **175.00**
Butter pat, Pansy, stamped, 3½" **250.00**
Butter pat, Wild Rose, registered, 3½" **250.00**
Celery tray/bacon dish, Azalea, imp/stamped, 10" L **400.00**
Chamberstick, Rabbit, stamped **525.00**
Charger, Elephant, imp/stamped, 12" **1,550.00**
Charger, Turtle, imp/stamped, 12" **2,500.00**
Chocolate pot, Rabbit (clockwise/2-ear), stamped, rstr, 9" **500.00**
Coaster, Grape, 3" dia **365.00**
Creamer, Azalea, stamped, 2¼x5½" **275.00**
Creamer, Rabbit, stamped **275.00**
Cup & saucer, demitasse; Azalea **365.00**
Cup & saucer, demitasse; Rabbit **275.00**
Cup & saucer, Magnolia, stamped, cup: 4¾" **150.00**
Egg cup, Polar Bear, early **625.00**
Mug, Rabbit, imp/stamped, 6" **330.00**
Mug, Rabbit (base band, narrow top band), tankard form, NM ..**350.00**
Mug, Rabbit (clockwise/2-ear), mk, 5¾x5" **350.00**
Pitcher, Night & Morning, #10/Majolica type, 5x5½" **475.00**
Pitcher, Turtle, stamped, 6½" **3,575.00**
Plate, Azalea, 7½" **235.00**
Plate, Bending Poppy, dk bl, 1 imp rabbit, 8½" **700.00**
Plate, Birds in Potted Orange Tree, imp, 10" **700.00**
Plate, Cat, stamped, 9" **3,500.00**
Plate, Clover, stamped, 10" **825.00**
Plate, Dolphin, mk, 8½" **850.00**
Plate, Dolphin, shaped/scalloped rim, mk, 8¾" **1,500.00**
Plate, Dolphin, stamped, 1 imp rabbit **975.00**
Plate, Double Turtle & Clover, mk, 10" **3,300.00**

Plate, Dolphin and Mask, CPUS clover mark, 10", $2,400.00.

Plate, Duck, registered, 10", NM 425.00
Plate, Duck, stamped O Rebus, 8½" 365.00
Plate, Duck (emb), stamped 325.00
Plate, Elephant (12+baby), 12" 875.00
Plate, farm landscape, mk, 8½" 650.00
Plate, Flying Serpent, imp/stamped, minor bubble bursts, 8½" ..4,200.00
Plate, Grape, mk, 10" 245.00
Plate, Grouse, stamped, 8½" 2,750.00
Plate, Horse Chestnut, 10" 275.00
Plate, Iris, imp, 8½" 250.00
Plate, Iris, imp/stamped, 10" 275.00
Plate, Iris, imp/stamped, 6" 195.00
Plate, Iris, registered, 8½" 245.00
Plate, lg poppy in center, pods in border, 10" 900.00
Plate, Magnolia, imp/stamped, 8½" 220.00
Plate, Moth, imp/stamped, 10" 850.00
Plate, Moth, mk, 8½" 600.00
Plate, Moth, stamped, 6" 485.00
Plate, Mushroom, mk, 8½" 750.00
Plate, Polar Bear, mk, 10" 850.00
Plate, Pomegranate, imp, 10" 2,500.00
Plate, Poppy, glaze bubbles, mk, 8½" 700.00
Plate, Tapestry Lion, mk, 8½" 1,400.00
Plate, Turkey, stamped, 10" 375.00
Plate, Turkey, stamped, 8½" 300.00
Platter, Crab, imp/stamped, 18" L 3,600.00
Shakers, Rabbit, 2½", pr 350.00
Tea tile, Rabbit, stamped, 6" dia 200.00
Teacup & saucer, Rabbit, stamped registered 210.00
Teacup & saucer, 4 O'clock; Rabbit 285.00
Tile, Rabbit, 5½" 250.00
Tray, Rabbit (clockwise/2-ear), stamped, 13" dia 700.00

Degenhart

The Crystal Art Glass factory in Cambridge, Ohio, opened in 1947 under the private ownership of John and Elizabeth Degenhart. John had previously worked for the Cambridge Glass Company and was well known for his superior paperweights. After his death in 1964, Elizabeth took over management of the factory, hiring several workers from the defunct Cambridge Company, including Zack Boyd. Boyd was responsible for many unique colors, some of which were named for him. From 1964 to 1974, more than twenty-seven different molds were created, most of them resulting from Elizabeth Degenhart's work and creativity, and over 145 official colors were developed. Elizabeth died in 1978, requesting that the ten molds she had built while operating the

factory were to be turned over to the Degenhart Museum. The remaining molds were to be held by the Island Mould and Machine Company, who (complying with her request) removed the familiar 'D in heart' trademark. The factory was eventually bought by Zack's son, Bernard Boyd. He also acquired the remaining Degenhart molds, to which he added his own logo.

In general, slags, jades, and opaques should be valued 15% to 20% higher than crystals in color.

Toothpick holders: Forget-Me-Not, Baby Pink Slag, $30.00; Beaded Oval, Amber, $15.00; Daisy and Button, Sapphire, $15.00.

Beaded Oval Toothpick, Bittersweet, 1976 ....35.00
Beaded Oval Toothpick, Fawn 22.50
Beaded Oval Toothpick, Lavender Blue 25.00
Bicentennial Bell, Amberina 15.00
Bicentennial Bell, Blue Fire 10.00
Bicentennial Bell, Caramel 25.00
Bicentennial Bell, Cobalt 17.50
Bicentennial Bell, Crown Tuscan 15.00
Bicentennial Bell, Vaseline 10.00
Bird Salt w/Cherry, Cobalt 20.00
Bird Salt w/Cherry, Daffodil 20.00
Bird Salt w/Cherry, Lemon Opal 25.00
Bird Salt w/Cherry, Orchid 20.00
Bird Salt w/Cherry, Spring Green 20.00
Bow Slipper, Blue Marble Slag 25.00
Bow Slipper, Mint Green Opal 17.50
Candy Dish, Cobalt, unmk 22.50
Candy Dish, Holly Green 22.50
Chick, Heliotrope, unmk, 2" 50.00
Chick Salt, Custard, unmk, 2" 25.00
Chick Salt, Lemon Custard, 2" 60.00
Colonial Drape Toothpick, Amethyst 17.50
Colonial Drape Toothpick, Milk Blue 25.00
Colonial Drape Toothpick, Sapphire 17.50
Daisy & Button Toothpick, Amethyst 15.00
Daisy & Button Toothpick, Cobalt Carnival, hand stamped 35.00
Daisy & Button Toothpick, Light Amberina 27.50
Daisy & Button Wine, Crown Tuscan, unmk 25.00
Forget-Me-Not Toothpick, Amberina 25.00
Forget-Me-Not Toothpick, Dark Chocolate Creme 25.00
Forget-Me-Not Toothpick, Jade 25.00
Forget-Me-Not Toothpick, Milk Blue 20.00
Forget-Me-Not Toothpick, Tomato 35.00
Hand, Amethyst 10.00
Hand, Crown Tuscan 18.00
Hand, Crystal 6.00
Heart & Lyre Cup Plate, Cobalt, unmk 15.00

Heart & Lyre Cup Plate, Pink, unmk	12.00
Heart Box, Baby Green	30.00
Heart Box, Baby Pink	30.00
Heart Box, Caramel Custard Slag	40.00
Heart Box, Frosty Jade	35.00
Heart Box, Lavender & Green Slag	35.00
Heart Box, Milk Blue	25.00
Heart Box, Persimmon	17.50
Heart Box, Vaseline	22.50
Heart Toothpick, Daffodil	25.00
Heart Toothpick, Gray Tomato	25.00
Heart Toothpick, Heatherbloom	25.00
Heart Toothpick, Opalescent	20.00
Hen Covered Dish, Baby Blue, 3"	35.00
Hen Covered Dish, Brown Sparrow Slag, 3"	30.00
Hen Covered Dish, Sapphire, 3"	20.00
Hobo Shoe, Blue & White Slag	25.00
Hobo Shoe, Crown Tuscan	20.00
Kat Slipper, Caramel, light	27.50
Kat Slipper, Ivorene	27.50
Kat Slipper, Jade Green	27.50
Kat Slipper, Lemon Custard, unmk	30.00
Kat Slipper, Milk Blue	25.00
Kat Slipper, Mint Green Opal	35.00
Kat Slipper, Vaseline	18.00
Lamb Covered Dish, Taffeta, 5"	70.00
Owl, Amberina	50.00
Owl, Baby Green	45.00
Owl, Bluebell	30.00
Owl, Cobalt	35.00
Owl, Cobalt Carnival	125.00
Owl, Crown Tuscan	35.00
Owl, Fog Opaque	50.00
Owl, Heatherbloom	75.00
Owl, Mint Green	30.00
Owl, Mulberry	45.00
Owl, Pigeon Blood	50.00
Owl, Red Carnival	150.00
Owl, Rose Marie	30.00
Owl, Sahara Sand	50.00
Owl, Toffee	55.00
Owl, Vaseline	30.00
Pooch, Buttercup Slag	40.00
Pooch, Daffodil	20.00
Pooch, Fantastic	35.00
Pooch, Green Opal Slag	25.00
Pooch, Gun-Metal Blue	25.00
Pooch, Red	30.00
Pooch, Tomato	37.50
Pottie Salt, Amethyst	10.00
Pottie Salt, Crown Tuscan	17.50
Pottie Salt, Henry's Blue	20.00
Pottie Salt, Honey	10.00
Pottie Salt, Nile Green	17.50
Priscilla, Bernard Boyd's Ebony	150.00
Priscilla, Daffodil	90.00
Priscilla, Jade Green	100.00
Priscilla, Periwinkle	85.00
Robin Covered Dish, Crown Tuscan, hand stamped, 5"	75.00
Seal of Ohio Cup Plate, Apple Green	10.00
Seal of Ohio Cup Plate, Opalescent	12.50
Texas Boot, Amethyst	16.00
Texas Boot, Sapphire	16.00
Turkey Covered Dish, Crown Tuscan, 5"	75.00

Delatte

Delatte was a manufacturer of French cameo glass. Founded in 1921, their style reflected the influence of the Art Deco era with strong color contrasts and bold design. Our advisor for this category is Don Williams; he is listed in the Directory under Missouri.

Cameo

Vase, berry branches, magenta on gr/wht, flared ovoid, 6"	**385.00**
Vase, morning-glories, brn on gray/yel, spherical, 7¾"	**500.00**
Vase, roses, red on gray/orange mottle, spherical, 8"	**990.00**
Vase, trumpet blossoms, red/wine on gray mottle, 16x6"	**935.00**
Vase, Venetian cityscape, rose on pk/wht, frost hdls, 6x7"	**1,200.00**
Vase, 4 dancers cvd/pnt, blk on orange, gilt, ovoid, 12"	**2,300.00**

Delft

Old Delftware, made as early as the 16th century, was originally a low-fired earthenware coated in a thin opaque tin glaze with painted-on blue or polychrome designs. It was not until the last half of the 19th century, however, that the ware became commonly referred to as Delft, acquiring the name from the Dutch village that had become the major center of its production. English, German, and French potters also produced Delft, though with noticeable differences both in shape and decorative theme.

In the early part of the 18th century, the German potter, Bottger, developed a formula for porcelain; in England, Wedgwood began producing creamware — both of which were much more durable. Unable to compete, one by one the Delft potteries failed. Soon only one remained. In 1876, De Porcelyne Fles reintroduced Delftware on a hard white body with blue and white decorative themes reflecting the Dutch countryside, windmills by the sea, and Dutch children. This manufacturer is the most well known of several operating today. Their products are now produced under the Royal Delft label. Examples listed here are blue on white unless noted otherwise. (See also specific manufacturers.)

Bowl, bird on floral branch, floral int, yel rim, 1740s, 12" **265.00**

Vases with lids, Chinaman reserved on trellis diaper ground, Dutch, mid-1700s, 15", EX, $1,800.00 for the pair.

Bowl, Holland, mc stylized florals, 3½x7½", EX 625.00
Charger, Dutch, basket of flowers, 5-color, 14" 985.00
Charger, English, feathers in center, florals, 1740, 12" 275.00
Charger, Lambeth, floral, yel/lav/gr, 13½", NM 900.00
Clock, modeled as a tall case, nautical scenes, 18" 650.00
Drug jar, English, 'S Caryophil,' birds/fruits, ftd, 8", EX 600.00
Inkwell, mc flowers on wht, 4x4x2" 245.00
Plaque, man's portrait, after Hals, Thooft & Labouchere, 22" 350.00
Plate, Bristol, peacock/trees, 4-color, 1740, 8", EX 1,400.00
Plate, Dutch, 2 inscribed hearts, floral rim, 9" 220.00
Plate, English, feathers/florals, 1700s, 9" 300.00
Plate, floral, late 1700s, 9" 180.00
Plate, Holland, Oriental landscape, floral rim, 1700s, 9" 275.00
Soup, fisherman, pine cone/foliage border, 8¾" 365.00
Tea caddy, emb figures, sq w/canted corners, edge chips, 5" 225.00
Tile, att Bristol, sheep scene in manganese, 1760, 5" 325.00
Tile, Dutch, parrot perched on swing, 15x10" 175.00
Tile, 2 geese/mtns emb, mc, mk Delft, #5, 9x5" 70.00
Vase, English, floral, lobed ovoid, 1750s, 8½" 400.00

Denver

As early as 1893, Frederick J. White and his son Francis were operating a pottery in Denver, Colorado. They used locally dug clay to produce utilitarian ware, but by 1909 their output began to include pottery of a more artistic nature as well, and at this point the company began using the name 'Denver Art Pottery.' Several lines were produced, among them slip-decorated ware, swirled pieces similar to Niloak's Mission Ware, and a style they called 'Gray Ware.' Though not everything was marked, some pieces carry an impressed or incised 'Denver' with White's initial contained in the 'D' or a 2-line arrangement, 'White Denver.' The business continued until the younger White retired in the 1950s.

Vase, pine cones on white matt, signed Royse, 3¾", $275.00.

Bowl, brn gloss, hdls at top, mk W Denver, 1917, 3½x8" 80.00
Bowl, gnarled trees, dk bl on bl, Denver White, 6" 475.00
Vase, tree, wht on bl, Denver White, 7" 475.00

Depression Glass

Depression Glass is defined by Gene Florence, author of several best-selling books on the subject, as 'the inexpensive glassware made primarily during the Depression era in the colors of amber, green, pink, blue, red, yellow, white, and crystal.' This glass was mass produced, sold through five-and-dime stores and mail-order catalogs, and given away as premiums with gas and food products.

The listings in this book are far from being complete. If you want a more thorough presentation of this fascinating glassware, we recommend *The Collector's Encyclopedia of Depression Glass, Pocket Guide to Depression Glass, Elegant Glassware of the Depression Era,* and *Very Rare Glassware of the Depression Years* by Gene Florence, whose address is listed in the Directory under Kentucky.

Adam, ashtray, pk 25.00
Adam, bowl, cereal; gr, 5¾" 35.00
Adam, bowl, dessert; pk, 4¾" 12.50
Adam, bowl, gr, open, 9" 37.50
Adam, bowl, gr, w/lid, 9" 77.50
Adam, butter dish, w/lid, pk 65.00
Adam, butter dish bottom, gr 60.00
Adam, cake plate, gr, footed, 10" 20.00
Adam, candy jar, pk, w/lid 67.50
Adam, coaster, gr, 3¼" 15.00
Adam, creamer, pk 15.00
Adam, cup, yel 85.00
Adam, lamp, gr 250.00
Adam, pitcher, pk, rnd base, 32-oz 45.00
Adam, pitcher, pk, 32-oz, 8" 32.50
Adam, plate, grill; gr, 9" 15.00
Adam, plate, salad; pk, rnd 50.00
Adam, platter, pk, 11¾" 16.50
Adam, relish dish, gr, divided, 8" 18.00
Adam, shakers, gr, ftd, 4", pr 87.50
Adam, sherbet, gr, 3" 33.00
Adam, sugar bowl, gr 33.00
Adam, tumbler, gr, 4½" 20.00
Adam, tumbler, iced tea; pk, 5½" 50.00
Adam, vase, gr, 7½" 42.50
American Pioneer, bowl, amber, hdls, 5" 40.50
American Pioneer, bowl, console; gr, 10¾" 55.00
American Pioneer, bowl, gr, w/lid, 8¾" 105.00
American Pioneer, bowl, pk, hdls, 9" 17.50
American Pioneer, candy jar, pk, w/lid, 1½-lb 80.00
American Pioneer, cheese/cracker set, pk 45.00
American Pioneer, chop plate, monax, 9" 10.00
American Pioneer, coaster, gr, 3½" 25.00
American Pioneer, creamer, gr, 2¾" 19.00
American Pioneer, cup, amber 18.00
American Pioneer, dresser set, pk, w/tray 300.00
American Pioneer, goblet, cocktail; gr, 3½-oz, 4" 35.00
American Pioneer, goblet, water; pk, 8-oz, 6" 32.50
American Pioneer, goblet, wine; pk, 3-oz, 4" 32.50
American Pioneer, ice bucket, gr, 6" 50.00
American Pioneer, pilsner, gr, 11-oz, 5¾" 90.00
American Pioneer, pitcher, amber, w/lid, 5" 250.00
American Pioneer, pitcher, amber, w/lid, 7" 300.00
American Pioneer, plate, amber, hdls, 11½" 42.00
American Pioneer, plate, amber, hdls, 6" 34.50
American Pioneer, plate, pk, 6" 11.50
American Pioneer, plate, salad; monax, 8" 7.00
American Pioneer, server, monax, 15½" 175.00
American Pioneer, sherbet, gr, 4¾" 17.00
American Pioneer, sherbet, pk, 4¾" 30.00
American Pioneer, sugar bowl, amber, 3½" 52.50
American Pioneer, sugar bowl, gr, 2¾" 20.00
American Pioneer, tumbler, gr, 8-oz 30.00

American Pioneer, tumbler, juice; pk, 5-oz 23.00
American Pioneer, vase, gr, rnd, 9" 185.00
American Pioneer, whiskey, pk, 2-oz, 2¼" 40.00
American Sweetheart, bowl, berry; cremax, rnd, 9" 50.00
American Sweetheart, bowl, berry; pk, flat, 3¾" 30.00
American Sweetheart, bowl, cereal; pk, 6" 11.50
American Sweetheart, bowl, cream soup; monax, 4½" 95.00
American Sweetheart, bowl, soup; monax, flat, 9½" 65.00
American Sweetheart, creamer, bl, ftd 95.00
American Sweetheart, creamer, pk, ftd 9.50
American Sweetheart, cup, pk 13.50

American Sweetheart, lamp, floor; cremax, brass base, $650.00.

American Sweetheart, plate, salad; bl, 8" 65.00
American Sweetheart, plate, salver; red, 12" 225.00
American Sweetheart, sherbet, pk, ftd, 3¾" 15.00
American Sweetheart, tidbit, red, 3-tier, 15½" 450.00
American Sweetheart, tumbler, pk, 5-oz, 3½" 55.00
Anniversary, bowl, berry; pk, 4⅞" 6.00
Anniversary, bowl, soup; crystal, 7⅜" 6.00
Anniversary, butter dish, pk, w/lid 47.50
Anniversary, candy jar, crystal, w/lid 17.50
Anniversary, comport, iridescent, 3-ftd, open 4.50
Anniversary, cup, pk 9.00
Anniversary, plate, sandwich server; iridescent, 12½" 7.50
Anniversary, plate, sherbet; iridescent, 6¼" 1.50
Anniversary, sugar bowl, crystal 2.00
Anniversary, vase, wall pinup; pk 22.50
Aunt Polly, bowl, berry; bl, 4¾" 12.00
Aunt Polly, bowl, berry; gr, 7⅞" 16.00
Aunt Polly, bowl, pickle; bl, hdls, oval, 7¼" 30.00
Aunt Polly, butter dish, gr, w/lid 210.00
Aunt Polly, candy, gr, hdls 57.50
Aunt Polly, pitcher, bl, 48-oz, 8" 150.00
Aunt Polly, plate, luncheon; bl, 8" 16.00
Aunt Polly, shakers, bl, pr 185.00
Aunt Polly, tumbler, bl, 8-oz, 3⅝" 22.50
Aurora, bowl, cereal; gr, 5⅜" 7.00
Aurora, bowl, pk, 4½" 25.00
Aurora, creamer, pk, 4½" 15.00
Aurora, cup, cobalt 9.50
Aurora, saucer, gr 2.50

Aurora, tumbler, cobalt, 10-oz, 4¾" 16.00
Avocado, bowl, pk, hdls, 5¼" 23.00
Avocado, bowl, pk, 9½" 80.00
Avocado, bowl, relish; pk, ftd, 6" 20.00
Avocado, bowl, salad; gr, 7½" 45.00
Avocado, cake plate, gr, hdls, 10¼" 45.00
Avocado, cup, gr, ftd, 2 styles 28.00
Avocado, pitcher, pk, 64-oz 625.00
Avocado, tumbler, pk 125.00
Beaded Block, bowl, bl, fluted, rnd, 7½" 22.00
Beaded Block, bowl, jelly; amber, hdls, 5" 7.00
Beaded Block, bowl, lily; red, 4½" 100.00
Beaded Block, creamer, bl 25.00
Beaded Block, jelly, pk, stemmed, flared top, 4½" 10.00
Beaded Block, plate, bl, rnd, 8¾" 18.00
Beaded Block, vase, crystal, 6" 11.00
Block Optic, bowl, berry; gr, lg, 8½" 24.00
Block Optic, bowl, cereal; pk, 5¼" 20.00
Block Optic, bowl, gr, 4¼" 6.50
Block Optic, candy jar, pk, w/lid, 6¼" 100.00
Block Optic, goblet, wine; pk, 4½" 28.00
Block Optic, mug, gr 30.00
Block Optic, pitcher, pk, bulbous, 54-oz, 7⅝" 60.00
Block Optic, plate, grill; yel, 9" 35.00
Block Optic, plate, luncheon; yel, 8" 4.00
Block Optic, saucer, gr, w/cup ring, 6⅛" 8.00
Block Optic, sherbet, yel, 5½-oz, 3¼" 8.00
Block Optic, tumbler, gr, ftd, 10-oz, 6" 22.00
Block Optic, tumbler, pk, flat, 12-oz, 4⅞" 20.00
Block Optic, whiskey, pk, 1-oz, 1⅝" 35.00
Bowknot, bowl, berry; gr, 4½" 12.00
Bowknot, bowl, cereal; gr, 5½" 15.00
Bowknot, plate, salad; gr, 7" 9.00
Bowknot, sherbet, gr, low ftd 12.00
Bowknot, tumbler, gr, ftd, 10-oz, 5" 15.00
Bowknot, tumbler, gr, 10-oz, 5" 15.00
Bubble, bowl, fruit; bl, 4½" 9.00
Bubble, bowl, soup; crystal, flat, 7¾" 6.00
Bubble, cup, crystal or bl 3.00
Bubble, cup, pk 75.00
Bubble, saucer, gr or red 3.00
Bubble, saucer, pk 25.00
Bubble, stem, cocktail; gr, 3½" 3.50
Bubble, stem, goblet; red, 9½" 11.50
Bubble, stem, juice; red, 5½" 11.00
Bubble, stem, sherbet; crystal, 4½" 4.00
Bubble, sugar bowl, bl 17.50
Bubble, tumbler, lemonade; crystal, 16-oz, 5⅞" 9.00
Cameo, bowl, berry; gr, lg, 8¼" 30.00
Cameo, bowl, cereal; pk, 5½" 50.00
Cameo, bowl, vegetable; yel, oval, 10" 35.00
Cameo, cake plate, gr, 3 legs, 10" 17.50
Cameo, comport, mayonnaise; pk, 5" 175.00
Cameo, cookie jar, gr, w/lid 45.00
Cameo, goblet, water; pk, 6" 155.00
Cameo, jam jar, crystal, w/lid, 2" 150.00
Cameo, pitcher, water; crystal, 56-oz, 8½" 450.00
Cameo, plate, dinner; gr, 9½" 15.00
Cameo, plate, dinner; pk, 9½" 60.00
Cameo, plate, salad; crystal, 7" 3.00
Cameo, saucer, gr, w/cup ring 145.00
Cameo, sherbet, pk, blown, 3⅛" 60.00
Cameo, tumbler, juice; gr, 5-oz, 3¾" 24.50
Cameo, vase, gr, 8" 25.00

Cherry Blossom, bowl, berry; gr, 4¾" 14.50
Cherry Blossom, bowl, fruit; gr, ftd, 10½" 65.00
Cherry Blossom, butter dish, pk, w/lid 60.00
Cherry Blossom, cake plate, pk, ftd, 10¼" 24.00
Cherry Blossom, pitcher, jadite, 36-oz, 6¾" 300.00
Cherry Blossom, plate, dinner; gr, 9" 20.00
Cherry Blossom, saucer, delphite 4.00
Cherry Blossom, sugar bowl, delphite 16.00
Cherry Blossom, tray, sandwich; pk, 10½" 15.00
Cherry Blossom, tumbler, gr, flat, floral at top, 12-oz, 5" 60.00
Cherry Blossom, tumbler, gr, flat, floral at top, 4-oz, 3½" 24.00
Cherryberry, bowl, gr, 6¼" 42.50
Cherryberry, bowl, salad; crystal, 6½" 15.00
Cherryberry, comport, iridescent, 5¾" 15.00
Cherryberry, olive dish, crystal, 1-hdl, 5" 7.50
Cherryberry, plate, salad; pk, 7½" 12.00
Cherryberry, sugar bowl, pk, open, sm 15.00
Cherryberry, tumbler, iridescent, 9-oz, 3⅝" 16.00
Chinex Classic, bowl, brownstone, 11" 16.00
Chinex Classic, bowl, cereal; castle decal, 5¾" 14.00
Chinex Classic, bowl, soup; decor, 7¾" 16.00
Chinex Classic, plate, dinner; castle decal, 9¾" 15.00
Chinex Classic, saucer, decor 4.00
Chinex Classic, sugar bowl, castle decal, open 15.00
Christmas Candy, bowl, vegetable; teal, 9½" 85.00
Christmas Candy, creamer, crystal 8.00
Christmas Candy, plate, bread & butter; teal, 6" 9.00
Christmas Candy, saucer, crystal 1.50
Christmas Candy, sugar bowl, teal 17.50
Circle, bowl, gr or pk, 4½" 8.00
Circle, decanter, pk or gr, hdls 35.00
Circle, goblet, water; pk or gr, 8-oz 9.00
Circle, saucer, pk or gr, w/cup ring 1.50
Circle, tumbler, tea; pk or gr, 10-oz, 5" 16.00
Cloverleaf, bowl, dessert; yel, 4" 22.00
Cloverleaf, creamer, gr, ftd, 3⅝" 8.50
Cloverleaf, shakers, yel, pr 95.00
Cloverleaf, sherbet, blk, ftd, 3" 17.50
Cloverleaf, tumbler, pk, flat, flared, 10-oz, 3¾" 17.00
Colonial, bowl, berry; pk, 3¾" 40.00
Colonial, bowl, vegetable; gr, oval, 10" 28.00
Colonial, butter dish, crystal, w/lid 35.00
Colonial, cheese dish, gr 150.00
Colonial, goblet, cordial; crystal, 1-oz, 3¾" 17.00
Colonial, goblet, water; gr, 8½-oz, 5¾" 28.00
Colonial, pitcher, gr, 68-oz, 7¾" 60.00
Colonial, plate, dinner; gr, 10" 55.00
Colonial, platter, crystal, oval, 12" 14.00
Colonial, shakers, gr, pr 120.00
Colonial, spoon holder or celery, pk 110.00
Colonial, sugar bowl, gr, 5" 12.00
Colonial, tumbler, lemonade; gr, 15-oz 65.00
Colonial, tumbler, Royal Ruby, ftd, 10-oz, 5¼" 150.00
Colonial, tumbler, water; Royal Ruby, 9-oz, 4" 95.00
Colonial, whiskey, gr, 1½-oz, 2½" 12.00
Colonial Block, bowl, pk or gr, 4" 6.00
Colonial Block, butter dish, pk or gr 40.00
Colonial Block, butter tub, pk or gr 35.00
Colonial Block, candy jar, pk or gr, w/lid 32.50
Colonial Block, creamer, wht 6.00
Colonial Block, sugar bowl, pk or gr 9.50
Colonial Fluted, bowl, berry; gr, 4" 4.50
Colonial Fluted, bowl, salad; gr, 6½" 17.50
Colonial Fluted, cup, gr 4.00

Colonial Fluted, plate, luncheon; gr, 8" 4.00
Colonial Fluted, saucer, gr 1.50
Columbia, bowl, cereal; crystal, 5" 13.50
Columbia, bowl, crystal, ruffled edge, 10½" 17.00
Columbia, bowl, salad; crystal, 8½" 14.00
Columbia, butter dish, ruby flashed, w/lid 17.50
Columbia, plate, bread & butter; pk, 6" 10.00
Columbia, plate, chop; crystal, 11" 8.00
Columbia, plate, snack; crystal 35.00
Columbia, tumbler, juice; crystal, 4-oz, 2⅞" 16.00
Coronation, bowl, berry; Royal Ruby, 4¼" 6.00
Coronation, bowl, Royal Ruby, 8" 15.00
Coronation, sherbet, gr 50.00
Coronation, tumbler, pk, ftd, 10-oz, 5" 18.00
Coverleaf, sugar bowl, gr, ftd, 3⅝" 8.50
Cremax, bowl, cereal; 5¾" 3.00
Cremax, cup, demitasse; decor 20.00
Cremax, plate, dinner; decor, 9¾" 8.50
Cremax, saucer, demitasse; cremax 4.00
Cube, bowl, pk, 4½" H 6.50
Cube, bowl, salad; gr, 6½" 12.00
Cube, butter dish, gr or pk, w/lid 50.00
Cube, creamer, amber or wht, 2⅝" 3.00

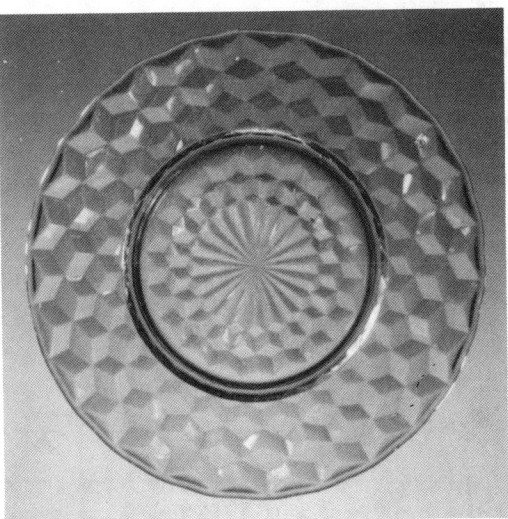

Cube, plate, luncheon; green, 8", $7.00.

Daisy, bowl, cream soup; red or amber, 4½" 12.00
Daisy, bowl, vegetable; gr, oval, 10" 9.00
Daisy, creamer, gr, ftd 4.50
Daisy, plate, sherbet; crystal or gr, 6" 1.50
Daisy, platter, red or amber, 10¾" 14.00
Daisy, saucer, crystal or gr 1.50
Daisy, tumbler, crystal or gr, ftd, 12-oz 18.50
Diamond Quilted, bowl, bl or blk, crimped edge, 7" 14.00
Diamond Quilted, bowl, cream soup; bl or blk, 4¾" 16.00
Diamond Quilted, bowl, 1 hdl, pk or gr, 5½" 6.00
Diamond Quilted, candy jar, pk or gr, w/lid, ftd 55.00
Diamond Quilted, creamer, bl or blk 15.00
Diamond Quilted, goblet, champagne; pk or gr, 9-oz, 6" 9.00
Diamond Quilted, goblet, cordial; pk or gr, 1-oz 9.00
Diamond Quilted, pitcher, pk or gr, 64-oz 42.50
Diamond Quilted, plate, luncheon; pk or gr, 8" 5.00
Diamond Quilted, punch bowl, pk or gr, w/stand 375.00
Diamond Quilted, sandwich server, pk or gr, center hdl 22.00

Diamond Quilted, tumbler, pk or gr, ftd, 12-oz 14.00
Diamond Quilted, tumbler, water; pk or gr, 9-oz 8.00
Diana, ashtray, pk, 3½" 3.00
Diana, bowl, amber, scalloped edge, 12" 15.00
Diana, bowl, cereal; pk, 5" 8.00
Diana, bowl, console fruit; pk, 11" 32.50
Diana, plate, bread & butter; amber, 6" 1.50
Diana, platter, pk, oval, 12" 25.00
Diana, sugar bowl, crystal, open 2.50
Diana, tumbler, pk, 9-oz, 4⅛" 40.00
Dogwood, bowl, cereal; gr or pk, 5½" 20.00
Dogwood, bowl, fruit; pk, 10¼" 275.00
Dogwood, cake plate, monax or cremax, heavy solid ft, 13" 150.00
Dogwood, pitcher, pk, decor, 80-oz, 8" 145.00
Dogwood, plate, grill; gr or pk, 10½" 18.00
Dogwood, saucer, monax or cremax 15.00
Dogwood, tumbler, pk, decor, 10-oz, 4" 32.50
Dogwood, tumbler, pk, molded band 14.00
Doric, bowl, cereal; pk, 5½" 40.00
Doric, bowl, cream soup; gr, 5" 300.00
Doric, butter dish, gr, w/lid 75.00
Doric, cake plate, pk or gr, ftd, 10" 20.00
Doric, candy dish, pk, 3-part 5.00
Doric, pitcher, gr, ftd, 48-oz, 7½" 750.00
Doric, plate, dinner; gr, 9" 14.00
Doric, platter, pk, oval, 12" 18.00
Doric, relish tray, gr, 4x8" 14.00
Doric, shakers, gr, pr 30.00
Doric, tumbler, gr, ftd, 10-oz, 4" 75.00
Doric & Pansy, bowl, berry; gr or teal, lg, 8" 67.50
Doric & Pansy, butter dish, gr or teal, w/lid 450.00
Doric & Pansy, creamer, pk or crystal 65.00

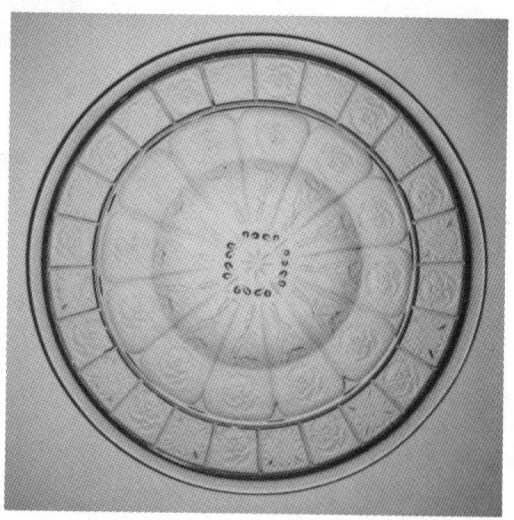

Doric & Pansy, plate, dinner; teal, 9", $25.00.

Doric & Pansy, plate, sherbet; pk or crystal, 6" 7.00
Doric & Pansy, shakers, gr or teal, pr 350.00
Doric & Pansy, tumbler, gr or teal, 9-oz, 4½" 65.00
English Hobnail, ashtray, turq, several shapes 29.00
English Hobnail, bowl, cobalt, hdls, ftd 8" 95.00
English Hobnail, bowl, cream soup; cobalt 14.00
English Hobnail, bowl, relish; amber, oval, 9" 18.00
English Hobnail, candy dish, cobalt, w/lid, ftd 70.00
English Hobnail, candy dish, pk or gr, cone shaped, ½-lb 47.50

English Hobnail, celery dish, pk or gr, 12" 25.00
English Hobnail, cologne bottle, amber 30.00
English Hobnail, creamer, turq, ftd or flat 22.00
English Hobnail, decanter, amber, w/stopper, 20-oz 98.00
English Hobnail, goblet, claret; cobalt, 5-oz 20.00
English Hobnail, goblet, cocktail; pk or gr, 3-oz 17.00
English Hobnail, grapefruit, turq, flange rim, 6½" 16.00
English Hobnail, lamp shade, crystal, 17" dia 125.00
English Hobnail, pitcher, pk or gr, 60-oz 210.00
English Hobnail, plate, dinner; amber, 10" 22.00
English Hobnail, plate, pie; pk or gr, 7¼" 5.00
English Hobnail, salt cellar, amber, w/place card holder, ftd 22.00
English Hobnail, shakers, turq, rnd or sq bases, pr 77.50
English Hobnail, sherbet, cobalt 28.00
English Hobnail, tumbler, iced tea; turq, 10-oz, 4" 16.00
English Hobnail, vase, cobalt 135.00
English Hobnail, whiskey, pk or gr, 1½-oz & 3-oz 24.00
Fire-King Oven Glass, baker, bl, rnd, 1-qt 6.00
Fire-King Oven Glass, baker, ind; ivory, 6-oz 2.50
Fire-King Oven Glass, bowl, measuring; bl, 16-oz 22.50
Fire-King Oven Glass, cake pan, ivory, 9" 12.50
Fire-King Oven Glass, cup, measuring; bl, 1 spout, 8-oz 16.00
Fire-King Oven Glass, custard cup or baker, ivory, 5-oz 2.50
Fire-King Oven Glass, pie plate, bl, 8⅜" 7.00
Fire-King Oven Glass, roaster, bl, 10⅜" 65.00
Fire-King Oven Glass, utility bowl, bl, 1-qt, 6⅞" 10.00
Fire-King Philbe, bowl, cereal; bl, 5½" 45.00
Fire-King Philbe, bowl, salad; pk or gr, 7¼" 45.00
Fire-King Philbe, bowl, vegetable; bl, oval 10" 95.00
Fire-King Philbe, cookie jar, pk or gr, w/lid 750.00
Fire-King Philbe, tumbler, juice; pk or gr, ftd, 3½" 150.00
Fire-King Turquoise Blue, ashtray, 4⅝" 8.00
Fire-King Turquoise Blue, bowl, vegetable; 8" 14.00
Fire-King Turquoise Blue, creamer 5.00
Fire-King Turquoise Blue, cup 4.00
Fire-King Turquoise Blue, mug, 8-oz 10.00
Fire-King Turquoise Blue, plate, w/cup indent, 9" 6.00
Fire-King Turquoise Blue, saucer 1.00
Fire-King Turquoise Blue, sugar bowl 5.00
Floragold, ashtray/coaster, iridescent, 4" 5.00
Floragold, bowl, cereal; iridescent, rnd, 5½" 30.00
Floragold, bowl, iridescent, ruffled, 9½" 7.50
Floragold, bowl, salad; iridescent, deep, 9½" 35.00
Floragold, butter dish, iridescent, w/lid, oblong, ¼-lb 22.50
Floragold, creamer, iridescent 8.50
Floragold, plate/tray, iridescent, 13½" 17.50
Floragold, platter, iridescent, 11¼" 17.50
Floragold, saucer, iridescent, 5¼" 10.00
Floragold, tumbler, iridescent, ftd, 10-oz or 11-oz 17.50
Floral, bowl, salad; pk, 7½" 15.00
Floral, butter dish, gr, w/lid 80.00
Floral, plate, dinner; gr, 9" 16.00
Floral, shakers, pk, flat, 6" 42.50
Floral, tumbler, water; pk, ftd, 7-oz, 4¾" 16.00
Floral & Diamond Band, bowl, berry; pk, lg 11.00
Floral & Diamond Band, bowl, nappy; pk or gr, hdls, 5¾" 9.00
Floral & Diamond Band, butter dish, iridescent, w/lid 250.00
Floral & Diamond Band, creamer, gr, 4¾" 17.00
Floral & Diamond Band, plate, luncheon; gr, 8" 30.00
Floral & Diamond Band, tumbler, iced tea; pk, 5" 30.00
Floral & Diamond Band, tumbler, water; gr, 4" 22.00
Florentine No 1, bowl, berry; gr, 5" 10.00
Florentine No 1, bowl, cereal; pk, 6" 18.00
Florentine No 1, bowl, vegetable; yel, w/lid, oval, 9½" 55.00

Florentine No 1, creamer, crystal or gr 8.50
Florentine No 1, pitcher, gr, 36-oz, 6½" 37.50
Florentine No 1, plate, dinner; yel, 10" 19.00
Florentine No 1, sugar bowl, yel or pk 11.00
Florentine No 1, tumbler, crystal or gr, ftd, 4-oz, 3¼" 12.00
Florentine No 1, tumbler, iced tea; gr, ftd, 12-oz, 5¼" 25.00
Florentine No 2, bowl, cereal; crystal or gr, 6" 24.00
Florentine No 2, bowl, cream soup; yel, 4¾" 18.00
Florentine No 2, bowl, crystal or gr, flat, 9" 22.50
Florentine No 2, butter dish, yel, w/lid 135.00
Florentine No 2, comport, gr, ruffled, 3½" 20.00
Florentine No 2, custard cup, yel 72.50
Florentine No 2, pitcher, gr, cone ftd, 28-oz, 7½" 28.00
Florentine No 2, shakers, gr, pr 40.00
Florentine No 2, tumbler, water; gr, 9-oz, 4" 11.00
Florentine No 2, tumbler, yel, ftd, 9-oz, 4½" 30.00
Flower Garden w/Butterflies, bowl, console; blk, w/base, 8½" 150.00
Flower Garden w/Butterflies, candlesticks, pk, 4", pr 50.00
Flower Garden w/Butterflies, candy dish, pk, w/lid, 7½" 125.00
Flower Garden w/Butterflies, comport, bl or yel, 3" 25.00
Flower Garden w/Butterflies, creamer, pk, gr or bl-gr 65.00
Flower Garden w/Butterflies, cup, pk, gr or bl-gr 60.00
Flower Garden w/Butterflies, plate, bl or yel, 10" 42.50
Flower Garden w/Butterflies, saucer, pk, gr or bl-gr 25.00
Flower Garden w/Butterflies, tumbler, amber, 7½-oz 125.00
Flower Garden w/Butterflies, vase, bl or yel, 10½" 175.00
Forest Green, ashtray, sq, 3½" 3.50
Forest Green, bowl, soup; 6" 14.00
Forest Green, bowl, vegetable; oval, 8½" 25.00
Forest Green, creamer, flat 5.50
Forest Green, pitcher, rnd, 86-oz 25.00
Forest Green, platter, rectangular, 11" 25.00
Forest Green, punch bowl 20.00
Forest Green, punch bowl stand 20.00
Forest Green, punch cup, rnd 2.00
Forest Green, sherbet, flat 6.00
Forest Green, stem, cocktail; 3½-oz 7.00
Forest Green, stem, goblet; 9½-oz 11.00
Forest Green, tumbler, iced tea; 13-oz 7.00
Forest Green, tumbler, 14-oz, 5" 7.00
Fortune, bowl, berry; pk or crystal, 4" 3.50
Fortune, bowl, pk or crystal, hdls, 4½" 4.00
Fortune, bowl, salad or berry; pk or crystal, 7¾" 11.00
Fortune, candy dish, pk or crystal, flat, w/lid 22.50
Fortune, plate, luncheon; pk or crystal, 8" 8.00
Fortune, saucer, pk or crystal 2.50
Fortune, tumbler, juice; pk or crystal, 5-oz, 3½" 6.00
Fruits, bowl, berry; gr, 8" 50.00
Fruits, cup, pk 7.00
Fruits, tumbler, gr, combination of fruits, 4" 20.00
Fruits, tumbler, juice; gr, 3½" 20.00
Georgian, bowl, berry; gr, lg, 7½" 55.00
Georgian, bowl, cereal; gr, 5¾" 20.00
Georgian, bowl, vegetable; gr, oval, 9" 55.00
Georgian, butter dish, gr, w/lid 72.50
Georgian, hot plate, crystal, 5" center design 40.00
Georgian, plate, dinner; gr, 9¼" 24.00
Georgian, saucer, gr 3.50
Georgian, sugar, gr, ftd, 4" 9.50
Georgian, tumbler, gr, flat, 12-oz, 5¼" 97.50
Harp, cake stand, crystal, 9" 22.50
Harp, coaster, crystal 4.50
Harp, plate, crystal, 7" 10.00
Harp, saucer, crystal 5.00

Harp, vase, crystal, 7½" 17.50
Heritage, bowl, fruit; crystal, 10½" 12.50
Heritage, cup, crystal 6.00
Heritage, plate, luncheon; 8" 8.50
Heritage, sugar bowl, crystal, ftd, open 17.50
Hex Optic, bowl, berry; pk or gr, 4¼" 5.00
Hex Optic, bowl, mixing; pk or gr, 8¼" 15.00
Hex Optic, butter dish, pk or gr, w/lid, rectangular, 1-lb 67.50
Hex Optic, creamer, pk or gr 5.00
Hex Optic, pitcher, pk or gr, sunflower motif, 32-oz, 5" 20.00
Hex Optic, plate, luncheon; pk or gr, 8" 5.00
Hex Optic, platter, pk or gr, 11" 11.00
Hex Optic, refrigerator stack set, pk or gr, 3-pc 45.00
Hex Optic, shakers, pk or gr, pr 25.00
Hex Optic, sherbet, pk or gr, ftd, 5-oz 4.00
Hex Optic, whiskey, pk or gr, 1-oz, 2" 7.00
Holiday, bowl, berry; pk, 5⅛" 10.00
Holiday, bowl, soup; pk, 7¾" 40.00
Holiday, butter dish, pk, w/lid 35.00
Holiday, cake plate, pk, 3-ftd, 10½" 80.00
Holiday, pitcher, milk; iridescent, 16-oz, 4¾" 20.00

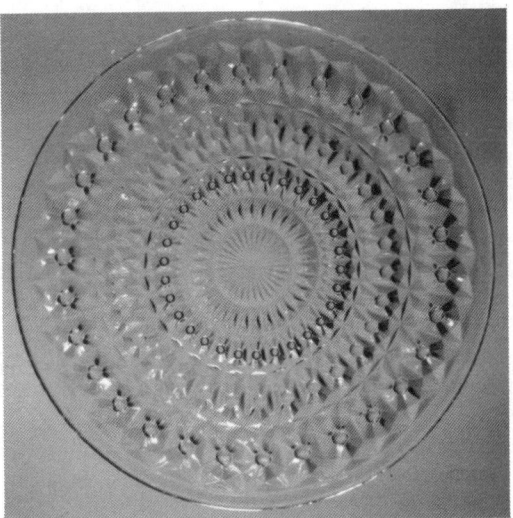

Holiday, plate, dinner; pink, 9" $14.00.

Holiday, plate, sherbet; pk, 6" 4.00
Holiday, saucer, pk 4.00
Holiday, sugar lid, pk 13.50
Holiday, tumbler, crystal, ftd, 5¼-oz, 4¼" 7.50
Holiday, tumbler, pk, ftd, 5-oz, 4" 35.00
Homespun, bowl, cereal; pk or crystal, 5" 17.50
Homespun, bowl, pk, closed hdls, 4½" 9.50
Homespun, butter dish, pk, w/lid 55.00
Homespun, creamer, pk, ftd 10.00
Homespun, plate, dinner; pk or crystal, 9¼" 14.00
Homespun, platter, pk, closed hdls, 13" 14.00
Homespun, saucer, pk or crystal 3.00
Homespun, sugar bowl, pk or crystal, ftd 8.00
Homespun, tumbler, iced tea; pk or crystal, 13-oz, 5¼" 25.00
Homespun, tumbler, pk or crystal, str, 9-oz, 3⅞" 15.00
Indiana Custard, bowl, berry; ivory, 5½" 7.50
Indiana Custard, bowl, soup; ivory, flat, 7½" 28.00
Indiana Custard, creamer, ivory 14.00
Indiana Custard, cup, ivory 35.00
Indiana Custard, plate, bread & butter; ivory, 5¾" 6.00

Indiana Custard, plate, dinner; ivory, 9¾" 20.00
Indiana Custard, plate, luncheon; ivory, 8⅞" 11.00
Indiana Custard, platter, ivory, 11½" 28.00
Indiana Custard, sherbet, ivory 82.50
Iris, bowl, berry; crystal, beaded edge, 4½" 35.00
Iris, bowl, cereal; crystal, 5" 95.00
Iris, bowl, salad; pk, ruffled, 9½" 50.00
Iris, butter dish, iridescent, w/lid 40.00
Iris, candlesticks, crystal, pr 35.00
Iris, candy jar, crystal, w/lid 95.00
Iris, creamer, iridescent, ftd 10.00
Iris, cup, demitasse; ruby 100.00
Iris, pitcher, crystal, ftd, 9½" 35.00
Iris, plate, dinner; crystal, 9" 47.50
Iris, plate, dinner; irid, 9" 35.00
Iris, plate, luncheon; crystal, 8" 60.00
Iris, saucer, crystal 9.00
Iris, saucer, demitasse; amethyst 125.00
Iris, sherbet, crystal, ftd, 2½" 20.00
Iris, sugar bowl, pk or gr 75.00
Iris, vase, pk or gr, 9" 95.00
Jubilee, bowl, fruit; yel, hdls, 9" 100.00
Jubilee, bowl, pk, 3-ftd, 8" 225.00
Jubilee, candlesticks, yel, pr 145.00
Jubilee, creamer, pk 30.00
Jubilee, goblet, water; pk, 10-oz, 6" 60.00
Jubilee, plate, luncheon; yel, 8¾" 15.00
Jubilee, plate, sandwich; pk, 13½" 75.00
Jubilee, sherbet or champagne, yel, 7-oz, 5½" 45.00
Jubilee, tray, sandwich; pk, center hdl, 11" 175.00
Lace Edge, bowl, cereal; pk, 6⅜" 15.00
Lace Edge, bowl, crystal, 8¼" 10.00
Lace Edge, candy jar, pk, ribbed, w/lid 40.00
Lace Edge, comport, pk, ftd, w/lid, 7" 40.00
Lace Edge, comport, pk, 7" 20.00
Lace Edge, cookie jar, pk, w/lid 55.00
Lace Edge, creamer, pk 19.00
Lace Edge, cup, pk 20.00
Lace Edge, flower bowl, pk w/crystal frog 20.00
Lace Edge, plate, dinner; pk, 10½" 24.00
Lace Edge, plate, pk, solid lace, 13" 25.00
Lace Edge, platter, pk, 5-compartment, 12¾" 24.00
Lace Edge, saucer, pk 9.00
Lace Edge, sugar bowl, pk 19.00
Lace Edge, tumbler, pk, ftd, 10½-oz, 5" 60.00
Laced Edge, bowl, fruit; bl or gr, 4½" 25.00
Laced Edge, bowl, soup; bl or gr, 7" 60.00
Laced Edge, bowl, vegetable; bl or gr, 9" 95.00
Laced Edge, creamer, bl or gr 35.00
Laced Edge, cup, bl or gr 30.00
Laced Edge, plate, dinner; bl or gr, 10" 65.00
Laced Edge, platter, bl or gr, 13" 125.00
Laced Edge, saucer, bl or gr 14.00
Laced Edge, tumbler, bl or gr, 9-oz 50.00
Lake Cameo, bowl, cereal; wht w/bl decor, 6" 20.00
Lake Cameo, cup, wht w/bl decor, regular 25.00
Lake Cameo, plate, dinner; wht w/bl decor, 9¼" 25.00
Lake Cameo, plate, salad; wht w/bl decor, 7¼" 16.00
Lake Cameo, shakers, wht w/bl decor, pr 35.00
Lake Cameo, sugar bowl, wht w/bl decor, ftd 25.00
Laurel, bowl, berry; opal or gr, 5" 6.00
Laurel, bowl, bl, 11" 50.00
Laurel, cheese dish, ivory, w/lid 55.00
Laurel, creamer, opal or gr, short 8.00

Laurel, plate, grill; opal or gr, 9⅛" 10.00
Laurel, plate, sherbet; bl, 6" 8.00
Laurel, saucer, bl 6.00
Laurel, shakers, opal or gr, pr 55.00
Laurel, sugar bowl, bl, tall 25.00
Laurel, tumbler, ivory, flat, 12-oz, 5" 40.00
Lincoln Inn, bonbon, cobalt or red, hdld, sq 14.00
Lincoln Inn, bowl, cereal; cobalt or red, 6" 12.00
Lincoln Inn, bowl, fruit; pk, 5" 8.00
Lincoln Inn, candy dish, blk, ftd, oval 12.00
Lincoln Inn, creamer, amethyst 14.00
Lincoln Inn, cup, gr 8.00
Lincoln Inn, goblet, water; cobalt or red 23.00
Lincoln Inn, plate, crystal, 8" 7.00
Lincoln Inn, plate, jade (opaque), 12" 15.00
Lincoln Inn, shakers, cobalt bl or red, pr 195.00
Lincoln Inn, sugar bowl, amber 13.00
Lincoln Inn, tumbler, cobalt or red, ftd, 9-oz 25.00
Lorain, bowl, salad; crystal or gr, 7¼" 35.00
Lorain, bowl, vegetable; yel, oval, 9¾" 45.00
Lorain, creamer, yel, ftd 19.00
Lorain, cup, crystal or gr 9.00
Lorain, plate, dinner; gr, 10¼" 35.00
Lorain, plate, salad; yel, 7¾" 14.00
Lorain, relish, crystal or gr, 4-compartment, 8" 16.00
Lorain, sherbet, yel, ftd 27.00
Lorain, tumbler, yel, ftd, 9-oz, 4¾" 26.00
Madrid, bowl, sauce; pk, 5" 6.00
Madrid, bowl, vegetable; bl, oval, 10" 35.00
Madrid, butter dish, gr, w/lid 75.00
Madrid, cake plate, amber, rnd, 11½" 14.00
Madrid, candlesticks, amber, 2¼", pr 20.00
Madrid, creamer, gr, ftd 10.00
Madrid, hot dish coaster, amber or gr 35.00
Madrid, jam dish, bl, 7" 30.00
Madrid, pitcher, amber, 80-oz, 8½" 60.00
Madrid, pitcher, gr, 80-oz, 8½" 200.00
Madrid, plate, dinner; bl, 10½" 65.00
Madrid, shakers, gr, ftd, 3½", pr 77.50
Madrid, sugar bowl, bl 14.00
Madrid, tumbler, 2 styles, gr, 12-oz, 5½" 28.00
Manhattan, bowl, berry; pk or crystal, hdls, 5⅜" 15.00
Manhattan, bowl, salad; crystal, 9" 18.00
Manhattan, candlesticks, crystal, 4½" sq, pr 12.00
Manhattan, coaster, crystal, 3½" 12.00
Manhattan, cup, crystal 16.00
Manhattan, cup, pk 130.00
Manhattan, plate, salad; crystal, 8½" 12.00
Manhattan, tumbler, gr or iridized, ftd, 10-oz 10.00
Manhattan, wine, crystal, 3½" 5.00

Mayfair Federal, plate, dinner; amber, 9½", $12.00.

Mayfair Federal, bowl, cereal; gr, 6" **19.00**
Mayfair Federal, bowl, cream soup; amber or gr, 5" **16.00**
Mayfair Federal, creamer, amber, ftd **12.00**
Mayfair Federal, plate, salad; crystal, 6¾" **4.00**
Mayfair Federal, tumbler, amber, 9-oz, 4½" **20.00**
Mayfair/Open Rose, bowl, bl, low/flat, 11¾" **60.00**
Mayfair/Open Rose, bowl, cream soup; pk, 5" **38.00**
Mayfair/Open Rose, bowl, vegetable; gr or yel, w/lid **1,200.00**
Mayfair/Open Rose, bowl, vegetable; gr or yel, 7" **110.00**
Mayfair/Open Rose, cake plate, bl, ftd, 12" **55.00**
Mayfair/Open Rose, cake plate, gr, ftd, 10" **90.00**
Mayfair/Open Rose, celery dish, pk, divided, 10" **175.00**
Mayfair/Open Rose, cookie jar, pk, w/lid **45.00**
Mayfair/Open Rose, cup, bl **40.00**
Mayfair/Open Rose, goblet, wine; gr, 3-oz, 4½" **375.00**
Mayfair/Open Rose, pitcher, gr or yel, 80-oz, 8½" **475.00**
Mayfair/Open Rose, plate, luncheon; pk, 8½" **20.00**
Mayfair/Open Rose, saucer, pk, w/cup ring **27.50**
Mayfair/Open Rose, shakers, bl, flat, pr **265.00**
Mayfair/Open Rose, sherbet, bl, ftd, 4¾" **65.00**
Mayfair/Open Rose, tumbler, pk, ftd, 10-oz, 5¼" **32.50**
Miss America, bowl, berry; gr, 4½" **10.00**
Miss America, cake plate, crystal, ftd, 12" **22.50**
Miss America, candy jar, pk, w/lid, 11½" **125.00**
Miss America, celery dish, pk, oblong, 10½" **25.00**
Miss America, comport, crystal, 5" **12.00**
Miss America, goblet, water; crystal, 10-oz, 5½" **20.00**
Miss America, goblet, wine; pk, 3-oz, 3¾" **60.00**
Miss America, pitcher, crystal, w/ice lip, 65-oz, 8½" **65.00**
Miss America, plate, dinner; ice bl, 10¼" **80.00**
Miss America, plate, sherbet; ice bl, 5¾" **35.00**
Miss America, relish, crystal, rnd, divided, 11¾" **20.00**
Miss America, shakers, pk, pr **50.00**
Miss America, sherbet, ice bl **35.00**
Miss America, tumbler, iced tea; crystal, 14-oz, 5¾" **24.00**
Miss America, tumbler, juice; pk, 5-oz, 4" **40.00**
Moderntone, bowl, berry; amethyst, lg, 8¾" **35.00**
Moderntone, bowl, cream soup; amethyst, 4¾" **15.00**
Moderntone, bowl, cream soup; cobalt, ruffled, 5" **40.00**
Moderntone, butter dish, cobalt, w/metal lid **95.00**
Moderntone, cheese dish, cobalt, w/metal lid, 7" **400.00**
Moderntone, creamer, amethyst **8.00**
Moderntone, plate, dinner; cobalt, 8⅞" **14.00**
Moderntone, plate, salad; cobalt, 6¾" **9.00**
Moderntone, platter, amethyst, oval, 12" **35.00**
Moderntone, saucer, amethyst **3.00**
Moderntone, sugar bowl, cobalt **9.00**
Moderntone, tumbler, amethyst, 5-oz **25.00**
Moderntone, tumbler, cobalt, 12-oz **85.00**
Moderntone, tumbler, whiskey; pk or gr, 1½" **12.50**
Moondrops, bowl, casserole; crystal, w/lid, 9¾" **95.00**
Moondrops, bowl, celery; cobalt or red, boat-shaped, 11" ...**30.00**
Moondrops, bowl, pickle; dk gr, 7½" **12.00**
Moondrops, bowl, soup; cobalt or red, 6¾" **70.00**
Moondrops, bowl, vegetable; pk, oval, 9¾" **22.00**
Moondrops, candlesticks, blk, metal stem, 8½", pr **27.50**
Moondrops, candlesticks, jadite, ruffled, 5", pr **19.00**
Moondrops, candy dish, gr, ruffled, 8" **18.00**
Moondrops, comport, smoke, 4" **15.00**
Moondrops, creamer, cobalt or red, 3¾" **15.00**
Deondrops, decanter, cobalt or red, rocket, 10¼" **400.00**
Moondrops, goblet, cobalt or red, 5-oz, 4¾" **22.50**
Moondrops, goblet, cordial; amethyst, ¾-oz, 2⅞" **25.00**
Moondrops, goblet, water; ice bl, metal stem, 9-oz, 6¼" ...**15.00**

Moondrops, goblet, wine; pk, metal stem, 3-oz, 5⅛" **10.00**
Moondrops, gravy boat, cobalt or red **115.00**
Moondrops, mug, smoke, 12-oz, 5⅛" **22.00**
Moondrops, pitcher, cobalt or red, sm, 22-oz, 6⅞" **150.00**
Moondrops, plate, cobalt or red, 5⅞" **9.00**
Moondrops, plate, dinner; cobalt or red, 9½" **22.00**
Moondrops, plate, salad; jadite, 7⅛" **9.00**
Moondrops, platter, cobalt or red, oval, 12" **30.00**
Moondrops, saucer, amber **4.50**
Moondrops, sherbet, cobalt or red, 4½" **25.00**
Moondrops, sugar bowl, blk, 4" **10.00**
Moondrops, tumbler, cobalt or red, 7-oz, 4⅜" **15.00**
Moondrops, tumbler, juice; pk, ftd, 3-oz, 3¼" **10.00**
Moondrops, tumbler, shot; cobalt or red, 2-oz, 2¾" **15.00**
Moondrops, vase, all colors, flat, ruffled top, 7¾" **55.00**
Moonstone, bowl, dessert; opal, crimped, 5½" **8.00**
Moonstone, bowl, opal, cloverleaf shape **12.00**
Moonstone, bowl, opal, crimped, 9½" **17.50**
Moonstone, candle holders, opal, pr **15.00**
Moonstone, creamer, opal **7.00**
Moonstone, cup, opal **7.00**
Moonstone, plate, sandwich; opal, 10" **20.00**
Moonstone, plate, sherbet; opal, 6¼" **5.00**
Moonstone, sugar bowl, opal, ftd **7.00**
Moroccan Amethyst, bowl, fruit; octagonal, 4¾" **6.00**
Moroccan Amethyst, bowl, rectangular w/metal hdl, 7¾" ...**14.00**
Moroccan Amethyst, candy, w/lid, short or tall **27.50**
Moroccan Amethyst, cup **5.00**
Moroccan Amethyst, goblet, sherbet; 7½-oz, 4¼" **7.00**
Moroccan Amethyst, goblet, wine; 4½-oz, 4" **9.00**
Moroccan Amethyst, plate, dinner; 9¾" **7.50**
Moroccan Amethyst, plate, salad; 7¼" **6.00**
Moroccan Amethyst, saucer **1.00**
Moroccan Amethyst, tumbler, juice; 4-oz, 2½" **7.50**
Moroccan Amethyst, tumbler, water; 9-oz **10.00**
Mt Pleasant, bowl, fruit; pk or gr, ftd, sq, 4" **12.00**
Mt Pleasant, cake plate, blk, amethyst or cobalt, 10½" **35.00**
Mt Pleasant, candlesticks, single, pk or gr, pr **17.50**
Mt Pleasant, creamer, blk, amethyst or cobalt **17.00**
Mt Pleasant, cup, pk or gr **8.50**
Mt Pleasant, mayonnaise, pk or gr, 3-ftd, 5½" **15.00**
Mt Pleasant, plate, grill; blk, amethyst or cobalt, 9" **10.00**
Mt Pleasant, saucer, blk, amethyst or cobalt **4.00**
Mt Pleasant, sugar bowl, all colors **17.00**
Mt Pleasant, tumbler, blk, amethyst or cobalt, ftd **18.00**
New Century, bowl, berry; gr or crystal, 4½" **11.00**
New Century, bowl, casserole; gr or crystal, w/lid, 9" **50.00**
New Century, bowl, cream soup; gr or crystal, 4¾" **15.00**
New Century, cup, pk, cobalt or amethyst **18.00**
New Century, decanter, gr or crystal, w/stopper **45.00**
New Century, goblet, cocktail; gr or crystal, 3¼" **20.00**
New Century, pitcher, gr or crystal, 80-oz, 8" **35.00**
New Century, plate, breakfast; gr or crystal, 7⅛" **7.00**
New Century, plate, dinner; gr or crystal, 10" **14.00**
New Century, plate, salad; gr or crystal, 8½" **8.00**
New Century, saucer, pk, cobalt or amethyst **6.00**
New Century, shakers, gr or crystal, pr **32.50**
New Century, sugar bowl, gr or crystal **6.00**
New Century, tumbler, all colors, ftd, 12-oz, 5¼" **20.00**
New Century, tumbler, pk, cobalt or amethyst, 5-oz, 3½" ...**11.00**
Newport, bowl, berry; amethyst, lg, 8¼" **28.00**
Newport, bowl, berry; cobalt, 4¾" **13.00**
Newport, bowl, cereal; amethyst, 5¼" **25.00**
Newport, creamer, cobalt **13.00**

Newport, plate, luncheon; cobalt or amethyst, 8⅞" 10.00
Newport, plate, sandwich; cobalt, 11½" 30.00
Newport, shakers, amethyst, pr 37.50
Newport, sugar bowl, cobalt 13.00
Newport, tumbler, amethyst, 9-oz, 4½" 28.00
No 610 Pyramid, bowl, berry; yel, 4¾" 30.00
No 610 Pyramid, bowl, master berry; crystal, 8½" 14.00
No 610 Pyramid, bowl, pickle; pk, 9½" 28.00
No 610 Pyramid, ice tub, yel 185.00
No 610 Pyramid, sugar bowl, crystal 15.00
No 610 Pyramid, tumbler, gr, ftd, 11-oz 50.00
No 612 Horseshoe, bowl, salad; gr, 7½" 17.50
No 612 Horseshoe, bowl, vegetable; yel, 8½" 25.00
No 612 Horseshoe, butter dish, gr, w/lid 600.00
No 612 Horseshoe, cup, yel 10.00

No 612 Horseshoe, plate, luncheon; yellow, 9⅜", $12.00.

No 612 Horseshoe, plate, sherbet; gr, 6" 4.00
No 612 Horseshoe, platter, yel, oval, 10¾" 22.00
No 612 Horseshoe, sugar bowl, yel, open 13.00
No 612 Horseshoe, tumbler, gr, ftd, 12-oz 100.00
No 616 Vernon, creamer, gr, ftd 22.00
No 616 Vernon, cup, crystal 7.00
No 616 Vernon, plate, luncheon; yel, 8" 8.00
No 616 Vernon, saucer, gr 5.00
No 616 Vernon, tumbler, crystal, ftd, 5" 13.00
No 618 Pineapple & Floral, bowl, berry; amber, 4¾" 15.00
No 618 Pineapple & Floral, bowl, salad; amber or red, 7" 9.00
No 618 Pineapple & Floral, cup, amber or red 8.00
No 618 Pineapple & Floral, plate, salad; all colors, 8⅜" 7.00
No 618 Pineapple & Floral, plate, sandwich; crystal, 11½" 14.00
No 618 Pineapple & Floral, saucer, all colors 4.00
No 618 Pineapple & Floral, tumbler, crystal, 12-oz, 5" 37.50
Nora Bird, candlesticks, pk or gr, pr 65.00
Normandie, bowl, berry; pk, 5" 6.00
Normandie, bowl, vegetable; pk, oval, 10" 30.00
Normandie, creamer, iridescent or amber, ftd 7.00
Normandie, cup, pk 7.50
Normandie, pitcher, amber, 80-oz, 8" 65.00
Normandie, plate, grill; amber, 11" 13.00
Normandie, plate, luncheon; 9¼" 12.00
Normandie, plate, salad; iridescent, 7¾" 50.00
Normandie, shakers, pk, pr 65.00
Normandie, sugar bowl, iridescent 5.50
Normandie, tumbler, juice; pk, 5-oz, 4" 40.00
Old Cafe, bowl, cereal; Royal Ruby, 5½" 9.00
Old Cafe, bowl, crystal or pk, closed hdls, 9" 8.50
Old Cafe, pitcher, crystal or pk, 36-oz, 6" 60.00
Old Cafe, plate, dinner; crystal or pk, 10" 25.00
Old Cafe, saucer, crystal or pk 2.00

Old Cafe, tumbler, juice; Royal Ruby, 3" 7.50
Old Cafe, vase, Royal Ruby, 7¼" 15.00
Old English, bowl, flat, all colors, 9½" 30.00
Old English, candlesticks, all colors, 4", pr 30.00
Old English, candy jar, all colors, w/lid 47.50
Old English, egg cup, crystal 7.50
Old English, fruit stand, all colors, ftd, 11" 37.50
Old English, goblet, all colors, 8-oz, 5¾" 27.50
Old English, pitcher, all colors 60.00
Old English, sugar bowl, all colors 18.00
Old English, tumbler, all colors, ftd, 5½" 30.00
Old English, vase, all colors, ftd, 12" 50.00
Ovide, bowl, berry; wht w/decor, 4¾" 6.00
Ovide, bowl, cereal; wht w/decor, 5½" 12.00
Ovide, candy dish, gr, w/lid 20.00
Ovide, creamer, Art Deco 75.00
Ovide, platter, wht w/decor, 11" 20.00
Ovide, saucer, gr 2.00
Ovide, shakers, blk, pr 25.00
Ovide, sugar bowl, blk, open 6.00
Ovide, tumbler, Art Deco 75.00
Oyster & Pearl, bowl, pk, hdl, 5½" 6.50
Oyster & Pearl, bowl, pk, heart-shaped, hdl, 5¼" 6.50
Oyster & Pearl, plate, sandwich; crystal, 13½" 15.00
Oyster & Pearl, relish dish, pk, oblong, 10¼" 8.50
Parrot, bowl, soup; gr, 7" 35.00
Parrot, bowl, vegetable; amber, oval, 10" 55.00
Parrot, butter dish, amber, w/lid 1,100.00
Parrot, creamer, gr, ftd 32.50
Parrot, hot plate, gr, 5" 650.00
Parrot, jam dish, amber, 7" 27.50
Parrot, plate, grill; amber, sq, 10½" 22.00
Parrot, plate, grill; gr, rnd, 10½" 25.00
Parrot, plate, salad; gr, 7½" 28.00
Parrot, shakers, gr, pr 200.00
Parrot, sherbet, bl, ftd cone 100.00
Parrot, sugar bowl, amber 32.00
Parrot, tumbler, gr, 10-oz, 4¼" 100.00
Patrician, bowl, berry; pk, lg, 8½" 22.00
Patrician, bowl, cream soup; amber or crystal, 4¾" 14.00
Patrician, cookie jar, gr, w/lid 400.00
Patrician, jam dish, amber, crystal or pk 25.00
Patrician, pitcher, gr, molded hdl, 75-oz, 8" 100.00
Patrician, plate, luncheon; amber or crystal, 9" 10.00
Patrician, plate, sherbet; pk, 6" 6.50
Patrician, platter, gr, oval, 11½" 20.00
Patrician, saucer, all colors 7.50
Patrician, tumbler, gr, ftd, 8-oz, 5¼" 45.00
Patrician, tumbler, pk, 9-oz, 4¼" 19.00
Patrick, bowl, console; yel, 11" 75.00
Patrick, bowl, fruit; yel, hdls, 9" 40.00
Patrick, cheese & cracker set, yel 85.00
Patrick, goblet, juice; yel, 6-oz, 4¾" 27.50
Patrick, mayonnaise, pk, 3-pc 185.00
Patrick, plate, luncheon; yel, 8" 25.00
Patrick, plate, salad; yel, 7½" 18.00
Patrick, sugar bowl, yel 35.00
Patrick, tray, yel, center hdl, 11" 50.00
Petalware, bowl, cereal; monax plain, 5¾" 5.00
Petalware, creamer, cobalt, ftd 45.00
Petalware, plate, dinner; pk, 9" 7.50
Petalware, plate, salad; crystal, 8" 1.75
Petalware, plate, salver; cremax, 11¾" 15.00
Petalware, saucer, fired-on decor 2.50

Petalware, sherbet, cobalt, low ftd, 4½"	30.00
Primo, bowl, yel or gr, 4½"	8.50
Primo, cake plate, yel or gr, 3-ftd, 10"	18.00
Primo, creamer, yel or gr	9.00
Primo, plate, dinner; yel or gr, 10"	14.00
Primo, sugar bowl, yel or gr	9.00
Primo, tumbler, yel or gr, 9-oz, 5¾"	15.00
Princess, bowl, cereal; gr, 5"	25.00
Princess, bowl, vegetable; pk, oval, 10"	20.00
Princess, bowl, yel, hat shaped, 9½"	100.00
Princess, butter dish, pk or gr, w/lid	85.00
Princess, cake stand, pk, 10"	25.00
Princess, cookie jar, bl, w/lid	600.00
Princess, cookie jar, pk, w/lid	50.00
Princess, cup, gr	10.00
Princess, pitcher, pk, 37-oz, 6"	48.00
Princess, plate, dinner; gr, 9½"	22.00
Princess, plate, grill; pk, closed hdls, 10½"	8.00
Princess, plate, grill; yel, 9½"	5.00
Princess, plate, sherbet; bl, 5½"	100.00
Princess, platter, pk or gr, closed hdls, 12"	20.00
Princess, relish, yel, plain, 7½"	130.00
Princess, spice shakers, gr, 5½" pr	37.50
Princess, tumbler, iced tea; gr, 13-oz, 5¼"	32.00
Princess, tumbler, juice; yel, 5-oz, 3"	24.00
Queen Mary, ashtray, pk, oval, 2x3¾"	4.00
Queen Mary, bowl, berry; crystal, 4½"	3.00
Queen Mary, bowl, berry; pk, 5"	5.00
Queen Mary, bowl, cereal; pk, 6"	20.00
Queen Mary, butter dish/preserve, pk, w/lid	95.00
Queen Mary, celery/pickle dish, pk, 5x10"	19.50
Queen Mary, cigarette jar, pk, oval, 2x3"	6.00
Queen Mary, comport, crystal, 5¾"	6.00
Queen Mary, creamer, pk, ftd	17.50
Queen Mary, plate, dinner; pk, 9¾"	35.00
Queen Mary, relish tray, crystal, 3-compartment, 12"	10.00
Queen Mary, sugar bowl, pk, ftd	17.50
Queen Mary, tumbler, juice; pk, 5-oz, 3½"	8.50
Queen Mary, tumbler, water; pk, 9-oz, 4"	8.50
Raindrops, bowl, berry; gr, 7½"	35.00
Raindrops, bowl, fruit; gr, 4½"	4.50
Raindrops, cup, gr	5.00
Raindrops, shakers, gr, pr	250.00
Raindrops, sherbet, gr	6.00
Raindrops, tumbler, gr, 4-oz, 3"	4.00
Raindrops, tumbler, gr, 9½-oz, 4⅛"	8.50
Raindrops, whiskey, gr, 1-oz, 1⅞"	6.00
Ribbon, bowl, berry; gr, 4"	9.00
Ribbon, creamer, gr, ftd	12.00
Ribbon, goblet, crystal, 9-oz, 7¼"	7.00
Ribbon, plate, sherbet; gr, 6¼"	2.00
Ribbon, saucer, gr	2.00
Ribbon, sugar bowl, gr, ftd	10.00
Ring, bowl, berry; crystal, lg, 8"	6.50
Ring, bowl, soup; gr or w/decor, 7"	12.00
Ring, creamer, gr or w/decor, ftd	5.00
Ring, cup, bl	27.50
Ring, goblet, cocktail; crystal, 3½-oz, 3¾"	10.00
Ring, ice bucket, gr or w/decor	20.00
Ring, pitcher, pk, 80-oz, 8½"	27.50
Ring, sandwich server, crystal, center hdl	15.00
Ring, sherbet, gr or w/decor, ftd, 4¾"	8.50
Ring, sugar bowl, crystal, ftd	4.00
Ring, tumbler, juice; gr or w/decor, ftd, 3½"	7.00

Rock Crystal, bowl, celery; crystal, oblong, 12"	22.50
Rock Crystal, bowl, crystal, scalloped edge, 4"	10.00
Rock Crystal, bowl, finger; red, 5", w/7" plate	55.00
Rock Crystal, bowl, salad; red, scalloped edge, 7"	60.00
Rock Crystal, butter dish, crystal, w/lid	300.00
Rock Crystal, cake stand, red, ftd, 2¾x11"	95.00
Rock Crystal, candelabra, cobalt, 2-light, pr	185.00
Rock Crystal, comport, gr, 7"	40.00
Rock Crystal, creamer, frosted pk, ftd, 9-oz	28.00
Rock Crystal, parfait, red, low ftd, 3½-oz	65.00
Rock Crystal, plate, bread & butter; gr, scalloped edge, 6"	8.50

Rock Crystal, plate, crystal, scalloped edge, 10½", $15.00.

Rock Crystal, saucer, red	17.50
Rock Crystal, tumbler, old fashioned; crystal, 5-oz	15.00
Rock Crystal, vase, red, ftd, 11"	150.00
Rose Cameo, bowl, berry; gr, 4½"	7.50
Rose Cameo, bowl, cereal; gr, 5"	12.00
Rose Cameo, tumbler, gr, ftd, 2 styles, 5"	15.00
Rosemary, bowl, berry; pk, 5"	9.00
Rosemary, bowl, cream soup; amber, 5"	14.00
Rosemary, plate, dinner; gr	12.00
Rosemary, plate, salad; amber, 6¾"	5.00
Rosemary, platter, pk, oval, 12"	25.00
Rosemary, saucer, amber	3.00
Rosemary, sugar bowl, gr, ftd	11.00
Rosemary, tumbler, pk, 9-oz, 4¼"	40.00
Roulette, bowl, fruit; pk or gr, 9"	12.50
Roulette, cup, pk or gr, ftd	5.00
Roulette, plate, luncheon; pk or gr, 8½"	5.00
Roulette, saucer, crystal	1.25
Roulette, sherbet, pk or gr	5.00
Roulette, tumbler, iced tea; pk or gr, 12-oz, 5⅛"	22.00
Roulette, tumbler, water; crystal, 9-oz, 4⅛"	12.00
Round Robin, bowl, berry; iridescent, 4"	4.25
Round Robin, creamer, iridescent, ftd	6.00
Round Robin, plate, luncheon; gr or iridescent, 8"	3.00
Round Robin, saucer, gr or iridescent	1.50
Round Robin, sugar bowl, gr or iridescent	5.50
Roxana, bowl, cereal; yel, 6"	12.00
Roxana, bowl, wht, 4½x2⅜"	12.00
Roxana, plate, yel, 5½"	5.00

Roxana, sherbet, yel, ftd 8.00
Royal Lace, bowl, berry; pk, rnd, 10" 22.00
Royal Lace, bowl, cream soup; crystal, 4¾" 9.50
Royal Lace, butter dish, pk, w/lid 135.00
Royal Lace, butter dish bottom, bl 320.00
Royal Lace, cookie jar, gr, w/lid 65.00
Royal Lace, cup, pk 11.00
Royal Lace, plate, grill; pk, 9" 14.00
Royal Lace, plate, luncheon; bl, 8½" 35.00
Royal Lace, shakers, bl, pr 225.00
Royal Lace, sherbet, amethyst, w/metal holder 35.00
Royal Lace, sugar bowl, crystal 14.00
Royal Lace, tumbler, gr, 10-oz, 4⅞" 25.00
Royal Lace, tumbler, pk, 5-oz, 3½" 22.00
Royal Ruby, bonbon, 6½" 8.00
Royal Ruby, bowl, cereal; 5½" 12.00
Royal Ruby, bowl, closed hdls, 9" 12.50
Royal Ruby, cup, rnd 4.50
Royal Ruby, goblet, ball stem 9.00
Royal Ruby, plate, dinner; rnd, 9⅛" 9.00
Royal Ruby, saucer, rnd 2.50
Royal Ruby, tray, 6x4½" 10.00
Royal Ruby, vase, 9" 15.00
S Pattern, bowl, cereal; crystal, 5½" 3.50
S Pattern, cake plate, amber, heavy, 13" 63.50
S Pattern, creamer, amber w/trim, thick or thin 6.00
S Pattern, cup, amber w/trim, thick or thin 4.00
S Pattern, pitcher, crystal, 80-oz 45.00
S Pattern, plate, dinner; crystal w/trim, 9¼" 6.50
S Pattern, plate, luncheon; red, 8¼" 40.00
S Pattern, sherbet, crystal, low ftd 4.50
S Pattern, tumbler, gr or pk, 9-oz, 4" 50.00
Sandwich (Indiana), basket, amber or crystal, 10" 30.00
Sandwich (Indiana), bowl, console; amber or crystal, 9" ...15.00
Sandwich (Indiana), butter dish, teal bl, w/dome lid 150.00
Sandwich (Indiana), cup, red 25.00
Sandwich (Indiana), mayonnaise, amber or crystal, ftd ..12.50
Sandwich (Indiana), pitcher, red, 68-oz 125.00

**Sandwich (Indiana), plate, sherbet; teal blue, 6",
$6.00.**

Sandwich (Indiana), shakers, amber or crystal, pr 15.00
Sandwich (Indiana), sugar bowl, red, lg 40.00
Sandwich (Indiana), wine, amber or crystal, 4-oz, 3" 5.50

Sharon, bowl, berry; amber, 5" 7.50
Sharon, bowl, cream soup; pk, 5" 36.00
Sharon, bowl, vegetable; gr, oval, 9½" 22.00
Sharon, cake plate, amber, ftd, 11½" 20.00
Sharon, candy jar, pk, w/lid 45.00
Sharon, cup, gr 15.00
Sharon, plate, bread & butter; pk, 6" 5.00
Sharon, plate, dinner; amber, 9½" 10.00
Sharon, sherbet, gr, ftd 27.50
Sharon, sugar bowl, gr 11.00
Sharon, tumbler, amber, ftd, 15-oz, 6½" 95.00
Sharon, tumbler, gr, thick, 9-oz, 4⅛" 55.00
Ships, cocktail mixer w/stirrer, bl w/wht decor 22.50
Ships, pitcher, bl w/wht decor, w/lip, 82-oz 45.00
Ships, plate, bread & butter; bl w/wht decor, 5⅞" 17.50
Ships, saucer, bl w/wht decor 14.00
Ships, tumbler, shot; bl w/wht decor, 2-oz, 2¼" 105.00
Ships, tumbler, str water; bl w/wht decor, 9-oz, 3¾" 12.00
Sierra, bowl, berry; gr, lg, 8½" 25.00
Sierra, creamer, gr 18.00
Sierra, pitcher, pk, 32-oz, 6½" 65.00
Sierra, serving tray, pk, hdls, 10¼" 12.50
Sierra, sugar bowl, gr 20.00
Sierra, tumbler, gr, ftd, 9-oz, 4½" 60.00
Spiral, bowl, mixing; gr, 7" 8.00
Spiral, cup, gr 4.50
Spiral, ice/butter tub, gr 25.00
Spiral, plate, sherbet; gr 1.50
Spiral, sugar, gr, flat or ftd 7.00
Spiral, tumbler, juice; 5-oz, 3" 4.00
Starlight, bowl, salad; crystal or wht, 11½" 16.00
Starlight, cereal, pk, closed hdls, 5½" 8.00
Starlight, creamer, crystal or wht, oval 4.50
Starlight, relish dish, crystal or wht 12.00
Starlight, sugar bowl, crystal or wht, oval 4.00
Strawberry, bowl, berry; gr or pk, 4" 8.00
Strawberry, bowl, salad; crystal, deep, 6½" 13.00
Strawberry, butter dish, pk or gr, w/lid 140.00
Strawberry, comport, crystal or iridescent, 5¾" 12.00
Strawberry, olive dish, pk or gr, 1-hdl, 5" 12.00
Strawberry, plate, sherbet; pk or gr, 6" 6.50
Strawberry, sugar bowl, pk or gr, lg 30.00
Strawberry, tumbler, crystal or iridescent, 8-oz, 3⅝" 17.50
Sunflower, cake plate, pk or gr, 3-leg, 10" 14.00
Sunflower, creamer, delphite 75.00
Sunflower, cup, pk 9.00
Sunflower, saucer, gr 8.00
Sunflower, trivet, gr, turned-up edge, 3-ftd, 7" 285.00
Swirl, bowl, cereal; delphite, 5¼" 11.00
Swirl, bowl, console; pk, ftd, 10½" 17.50
Swirl, bowl, salad; ultramarine, rimmed, 9" 22.50
Swirl, candy dish, pk, w/lid 85.00
Swirl, candy dish, ultramarine, 3-ftd, open 15.00
Swirl, plate, dinner; pk or delphite, 9¼" 12.00
Swirl, plate, sherbet, pk, 6½" 3.50
Swirl, saucer, pk 2.50
Swirl, shakers, ultramarine, pr 37.50
Swirl, sugar bowl, delphite, ftd 9.00
Swirl, vase, pk, ftd, ruffled, 6½" 14.50
Tea Room, bowl, banana split; pk, flat, 7½" 77.50
Tea Room, bowl, finger; gr 45.00
Tea Room, bowl, vegetable; pk, oval, 9½" 55.00
Tea Room, creamer, pk or gr, 3¼" 22.50
Tea Room, cup, pk or gr 45.00

Tea Room, goblet, gr, 9-oz	67.50
Tea Room, parfait, pk	60.00
Tea Room, saucer, pk or gr	25.00
Tea Room, shakers, gr, pr	50.00
Tea Room, tray, gr, center hdl	175.00
Tea Room, tumbler, pk, ftd, 11-oz	35.00
Tea Room, vase, pk, str or ruffled edge, 11"	80.00
Thistle, bowl, cereal; gr, 5½"	20.00
Thistle, cup, gr, thin	22.00
Thistle, saucer, pk or gr	8.50
Thumbprint, bowl, berry; gr, 4¾"	3.00
Thumbprint, bowl, cereal; gr	4.50
Thumbprint, plate, sherbet; gr, 6"	2.00
Thumbprint, sherbet, gr	5.00
Thumbprint, tumbler, gr, 12-oz, 5½"	5.00
Twisted Optic, bowl, cereal; bl, 4¾"	15.00
Twisted Optic, bowl, salad; canary yel, 7"	12.00
Twisted Optic, saucer, bl	2.25
Twisted Optic, tumbler, pk, 12-oz, 5¼"	7.50
US Swirl, bowl, berry; gr, 4⅜"	5.00
US Swirl, bowl, pk or gr, oval, 8¼"	22.50
US Swirl, butter dish, pk, w/lid	67.50
US Swirl, creamer, pk	14.00
US Swirl, plate, salad; pk, 7⅞"	6.00
US Swirl, sherbet, pk, 3¼"	4.50
US Swirl, tumbler, pk, 8-oz, 3⅝"	8.00
Victory, bonbon, bl or blk, 7"	18.00
Victory, bowl, amber, pk or gr, rolled edge, 11"	25.00
Victory, cup, bl or blk	28.00
Victory, plate, bread & butter; bl or blk, 6"	12.00
Victory, saucer, amber, pk or gr	3.00
Victory, sugar bowl, bl or blk	40.00
Vitrock, bowl, fruit; wht, 6"	5.00
Vitrock, creamer, oval	4.00
Vitrock, cup, wht	3.00
Vitrock, plate, soup; wht, 9"	10.00
Vitrock, platter, wht, 11½"	24.00
Vitrock, saucer, wht	1.50
Waterford, bowl, berry; pk, 4¾"	12.00
Waterford, cup, pk	12.00
Waterford, pitcher, juice; crystal, tilted, 42-oz	20.00
Waterford, saucer, crystal	2.00
Waterford, sugar bowl, pk	8.50
Waterford, tumbler, pk, ftd, 10-oz, 4⅞"	16.00
Windsor, bowl, berry; gr, lg, 8½"	14.00
Windsor, bowl, pk, pointed edge, 5"	15.00
Windsor, creamer, bl	40.00
Windsor, pitcher, red, 52-oz, 6¾"	400.00
Windsor, plate, salad; pk, 7"	13.00
Windsor, platter, crystal, oval, 11½"	5.00
Windsor, powder jar, yel	150.00
Windsor, shakers, gr, pr	45.00
Windsor, sherbet, pk, ftd	9.00
Windsor, tumbler, bl, 5-oz, 3¼"	55.00
Windsor, tumbler, red, 9-oz, 4"	50.00

Derby

William Duesbury operated in Derby, England, from about 1755 purchasing a second establishment, The Chelsea Works, in 1769. During this period fine porcelains were produced which so impressed the King that in 1773 he issued the company the Crown Derby patent. In

1810, several years after Duesbury's death, the factory was bought by Robert Bloor. The quality of the ware suffered under the new management, and the main Derby pottery closed in 1848. Within a short time, the work was revived by a dedicated number of former employees who established their own works on King Street in Derby.

The earliest-known Derby mark was the crown over a script 'D'; however, this mark is rarely found today. Soon after 1782, that mark was augmented with a device of crossed batons and six dots, usually applied in underglaze blue. During the Bloor period, the crown was centered within a ring containing the words 'Bloor' above and 'Derby' below the crown, or with a red printed stamp — the crowned Gothic 'D.' The King Street plant produced figurines that may be distinguished from their earlier counterparts by the presence of an 'S' and 'H' on either side of the crown and crossed batons.

In 1876 a new pottery was constructed in Derby, and the owners revived the earlier company's former standard of excellence. The Queen bestowed the firm the title Royal Crown Derby in 1890; it still operates under that name today. See also Royal Crown Derby.

Candlestick, allegoricals of Liberty & Matrimony, 11", VG	3,400.00
Coffeepot, rose/multifloral, 1760s, 9½", EX	1,400.00
Figurine, allegorical groups: Air & Earth, 8", EX, pr	2,090.00
Figurine, King Richard III, boldly striding, red mk, 11"	500.00
Figurine, pointer by stump, natural colors, 1795, 6" L	825.00
Figurine, Ranelagh Dancers, 1765, 11½", VG, pr	2,500.00
Figurine, Venus/Cupid on dolphin, 1765, rpr, 10", VG	1,100.00
Figurine, 3 Graces Distressing Cupid, bsk, 1790, 13", VG	2,200.00

Garniture, titled scenes, restored snake handles, hairline, center vase, 7½"; smaller pair, 6½", VG, $1,750.00 for the set.

Garniture, titled scenes, snake hdls, 7½" vase+2 sm vases	1,800.00
Potpourri, appl & HP floral, gilt, 1760s, 11", VG	550.00
Potpourri, flower-filled comport form, masks, 7", VG	1,100.00

Desert Sands

As early as the 1850s, the Evans family living in the Ozark Mountains of Missouri produced domestic clay products. Their small pot shop was passed on from one generation to the next. In the 1920s it was moved to North Las Vegas, Nevada, where the name Desert Sands was adopted. Succeeding generations of the family continued to relocate, taking the business with them. From 1937 to 1962 it operated in Boulder City, Nevada; then it was moved to Barstow where it remained until it closed in the late 1970s.

Desert Sands pottery is similar to Mission Ware by Niloak. Various mineral oxides were blended to mimic the naturally occuring sand formations of the American West. A high-gloss glaze was applied to add intensity to the colorful striations that characterize the ware. Not all examples are marked, making it sometimes difficult to attribute. Marked items carry an ink stamp with the Desert Sands designation. Paper labels were also used.

Bowl, swirled colors, 4"	**9.00**
Bowl, w/lid, swirled colors, 4"	**35.00**
Butter dish	**35.00**

Candle holder, 3", $15.00.

Shakers, swirled colors, pr	**25.00**
Tumbler, swirled colors, 3½"	**10.00**
Vase, swirled colors, 3½"	**15.00**

Documents

Although the word 'document' is defined in the general sense as 'anything printed or written, etc., relied upon to record or prove something. . .,' in the collectibles market, the term is more diversified with broadsides, billheads, checks, invoices, letters and letterheads, land grants, receipts, and waybills some of the most sought after. Some documents in demand are those related to a specific subject such as advertising, mining, railroads, military, politics, banking, slavery, nautical, or legal (deeds, mortgages, etc.). Other collectors look for examples representing a specific period of time such as colonial documents, Revolutionary, or Civil War documents, early western documents or those from a specific region, state, or city.

Aside from supply and demand, there are five major factors which determine the collector-value of a document. These are:

1) Age — Documents from the eastern half of the country can be found that date back to the 1700s or earlier. Most documents sought by collectors usually date from 1700 to 1900. Those with 20th-century dates are still abundant and not in demand unless of special significance or beauty.

2) Region of origin — Depending on age, documents from rural and less-populated areas are harder to find than those from major cities and heavily populated states. The colonization of the West and Mid-West did not begin until after 1850, so while an 1870s billhead from New York or Chicago is common, one from Albuquerque or Phoenix is not, since most of the Southwest was still unsettled.

3) Attractiveness — Some documents are plain and unadorned, but collectors prefer colorful, profusely illustrated pieces. Additional artwork and engravings add to the value.

4) Historical content — Unusual or interesting content, such as a letter written by a Civil War soldier giving an eye-witness account of the Battle of Gettysburg or a western territorial billhead listing numerous animal hides purchased from a trapper, will sell for more than one with mundane information.

5) Condition — Through neglect or environmental conditions, over many decades paper articles can become stained, torn, or deteriorated. Heavily damaged or stained documents are generally avoided altogether while those with minor problems are more acceptable, although their value will decrease anywhere from 20% to 50% depending upon the extent of damage. Avoid attempting to repair tears with scotch tape — sell 'as is' so that the collector can take proper steps toward restoration.

Foreign documents are plentiful; though some are very attractive, resale may be difficult. The listings that follow are generalized; prices are variable depending entirely upon the five points noted above. Values here are based upon examples with no major damage. For more information we recommend *Owning Western History* by our advisor Warren Anderson. His address and ordering information may be found in the Directory under Utah.

Key: illus — illustrated   vgn — vignette

Appointment, NH, Infantry Orderly Sergeant, 1836, 8x8"	**22.50**
Bank draft, CO, Bank of Ouray, Chief Ouray vgn, 1904, 4x9"	**25.00**
Bill, costs of schooner/wharfage/supplies/etc, 1863, 9x14"	**7.50**
Bill, Savannah, rpr of compass, masthead letterhead, 1862	**7.50**
Bill of lading, Quartermaster's Dept, preprinted, 1870s, 8x14"	**30.00**
Billhead, Fort Scot Foundry & Machine Works, 1883, 7x8"	**15.00**
Billhead, WI, CP&J Lauson Gasoline Engines, photo vgn, 1904	**15.00**
Bounty certificate, MT Territory, skins turned in, 1887, 7x8"	**20.00**
Certificate, PA, schooling funds from PA treasurer, 1852	**18.50**
Certificate, UT Territory, ore samples tested, 1879, 8x10"	**30.00**
Certificate of Discharge, CT Union soldier, 1862, EX	**6.50**
Check, Nevada County Bank, Nevada City CA, 1915, EX	**35.00**
Check, NM Territory, Silver City, 2nd Nat'l Bank, 1876	**35.00**
Check, NV, Palmer & Day Bankers, blk on wht, 1867	**30.00**
Civil War store currency, Robert Gerrish Store, ME, 1863	**8.00**
Commission, NH Infantry officer, sgn I Hill/J Whipple, 1838	**25.00**
Confirmation, MD, religious nature, preprinted, 1875, 4x7"	**20.00**
Court martial, Blk man to be hanged for attempted rape, 1860s	**6.50**
Deed, AZ Territory, Bl Dick Mine, handwritten, 1888	**20.00**
Deed, CO, sale of CO Girl lode, preprinted, 1899, 11x17"	**30.00**
Discharge, handwritten, sgn B Warner, 1780, EX	**125.00**
Discharge, 58th MA Volunteers, eagle illus, 1863	**21.00**
Discharge certificate, Portsmigh NY, handwritten, 1813	**24.00**
Envelope, Mail Via Airship Hindenburg sticker, 1937, EX	**35.00**
Folder, Louisiana lottery, 1879, 4-pg	**30.00**
Grocery bill, Star Sherman, sgn, 1771-1781, EX	**295.00**
Invitation, Stamford CT, to opera, 1861, EX	**50.00**
Invoice, Civil War, supplies transport & delivery, 8x10"	**10.00**
Land sale, handwritten on vellum, dtd 1650, 4½x19" L	**45.00**
Ledger page, doctor's notes on bleeding patient, 1770s, 7x12"	**22.50**
Legal matter, OK, illegal timber cutting charges, 1909, 2-pg	**20.00**
Letter, Camp Baker, MT Territory, business, 1875, 1-pg	**35.00**
Letter, CO, re: lien on Snow Fort lode, vgn, 1891, 5x7"	**25.00**
Letter, CO, seeking job as blksmith, 1898, 1-pg, 8x10"	**25.00**
Letter, construction of Nat'l Cemetery at Nashville, 1868	**12.50**
Letter, Foley's Camp, Rainy River, states arrival, 1897, 1-pg	**10.00**
Letter, Harrison's Landing, soldier to parents, war news, 4-pg	**35.00**
Letter, ID, requesting liquor on credit, 1889, 2-pg	**35.00**
Letter, LA, soldier's life in camp/etc, 1862, 4-pg	**20.00**
Letter, Lynchburg VA, food concerns/Yankee raid, 1864, 2-pg	**22.00**
Letter, MO, battle of Prairie Grove, w/envelope, 1863	**22.50**

Letter, NC, wife writes of child's death, 1863, 8-pg **60.00**
Letter, NY, mining deal, sgn Willard Teller, 1874, 6x9", 4-pg **50.00**
Letter, to Civil War soldier, McClellan supporter, 1864 ....**15.00**
Letter, USS Clyde off Suwanee River, war news, 1864, 3-pg **35.00**
Letter, VA, convalescent camp description, 1864, 10-pg **35.00**
Letterhead, AZ Territory, JH Greer Drugs, Tombstone, 1882 ......**35.00**
List, stores received by TX from IL, military, 1865, VG **10.00**
Muster roll, Blk Infantry, names/rank, X mks for names, 1864 ......**22.50**
Notice, WA, quartz location for Edith lode, 1896, 8x10" **15.00**
Order, Abington VA, for cornmeal to TN regiment, 1864 ....**18.50**
Orders, Plymouth MA Headquarters, call-up of men, 1812, 3-pg .**24.00**
Pamphlet, slave trade report to Congress, 1864, 159-pg **15.00**
Pay voucher, Fort Lewis CO, payment due listed, 1883, 8x11" **40.00**
Payroll, S KS Ry of TX, report of earnings/workers, 1893 ....**25.00**
Policy, New Haven CT, City Fire Ins Co, 1860, 4-pg **5.00**
Receipt, Boston, 8 pounds cash, dtd 1717 ....**18.50**
Receipt, Boston/Gloucester Steamboats, cargo, 1880, 4x8" **5.00**
Receipt, CA, lamp oil purchase, handwritten, 1851, 4x8" **30.00**
Receipt, CA, Wells Fargo, Chinese writing on bk, 1881, 4x7" **30.00**
Receipt, CA, Wells Fargo, shipping of package, 1873, 5x11" **45.00**
Receipt, gun locks purchased, Feb 1777, scarce **65.00**
Receipt, OR, Oregon Stage Co, shoeing horses, printed, 3x8" **35.00**
Receipt, Ottawa KS, care of cattle, sgn, 1890s **10.00**
Report, from Post-Master Gen of US, 1814-16, set of 4 ....**30.00**
Report, US coast/geodetic survey, pub in WA, 1887, 45 maps **25.00**
Script, $20 note, Manual Labor Banking House Phila, 1838 ....**85.00**
Treasury loan certificate, MA Bay, snake vgn, dtd 1777, 8x10" .**125.00**
Voucher, Civil War pay, NY Infantry, 10-days leave/pay, 1863 ......**6.00**
Writ, CT, order to surrender 90 acres of land, 1717, 7x10" **17.50**

Dollhouses and Furnishings

Dollhouses were introduced commercially in this country late in the 1700s by Dutch craftsmen who settled in the East. By the mid-1800s, they had become meticulously detailed, divided into separate rooms, and lavishly furnished to reflect the opulence of the day. Originally intended for the amusement of adults of the household, by the late 1800s their status had changed to that of a child's toy. Though many early dollhouses were lovingly hand-fashioned for a special little girl, those made commercially by such companies as Bliss and Schoenhut are highly valued.

Furniture and furnishings in the Biedermeier style featuring stenciled Victorian decorations often sell for several hundred dollars each. Other early pieces made of pewter, porcelain, or papier-mache are also quite valuable. Certainly less expensive but very collectible, nonetheless, is the quality, hallmarked plastic furniture produced during the forties by Renwal and Acme, and the 1960s Petite Princess line produced by Ideal. In the listings that follow, dollhouses are litho paper on wood, unless otherwise noted. When no manufacturer or country of origin is noted, examples are German, turn of the century. Our advisor for this category is Barbara Rosen; she is listed in the Directory under New Jersey. See also Miniatures.

Furniture

Bed, canopy, wooden, EX **12.00**
Bed, princess style, Petite Princess, MIB **30.00**
Bed, TootsieToy, EX **12.50**
Bed, walnut, 4-poster canopy, +wardrobe **145.00**
Chairs, TootsieToy, host+2 side, EX **35.00**
Commode, pnt tin, front opens, Rock-Graner, 1850, 2½" **215.00**
Desk, French style, gold japanning, Biedermeier, 5x4¾" **185.00**
Dining room, Petite Princess Fantasy, 1960s, MIB **80.00**

Family room, Petite Princess Royal Fantasy, 1960s, MIB **70.00**
Grand piano, TootsieToy, top/keyboard cover lifts, +stool **25.00**
Highchair, CI, bl pnt, Kilgore, 3½" **65.00**

Kitchen set: refrigerator, stove, cabinet, sink, table, two chairs, and stepladder, TootsieToy, MIB, $325.00.

Kitchen set, TootsieToy, wht, refrigerator/stove+7 pcs, MIB **325.00**
Lawn swing, Kilgore **25.00**
Living room suite, TootsieToy, 7-pc, in orig box **375.00**
Picnic set, champagne glass/bottle/food/basket/blanket, MIB **125.00**
Radio, TootsieToy, red w/gold int, in box, 1x1¼" **55.00**
Refrigerator, Petite Princess **78.00**
Sink, TootsieToy, ped ft, EX **25.00**
Table, drop-leaf, red-pnt tin w/florals, Stevens-Brn, 3" **110.00**
Table, TootsieToy, rnd style, EX **22.50**
Tea cart, Petite Princess Fantasy, 1950s, MIB **11.00**

Houses

Bliss, folding, 2-story, paper on wood, 1920, 10x8x4", EX **700.00**
Bliss, gabled, 2-story, 5 windows, paper on wood, 1910, 19" **1,600.00**
Bliss, Victorian, paper on wood, turret, 1901, 30", EX **11,500.00**
Bliss, 2-story, steepled roof, paper on wood, 9x6x3", VG **900.00**
Bliss (att), 2-story, paper on wood, 1890s, 18x10x9" **1,000.00**
Bliss copy, 2-story, paper on wood, 1974, 19x19x10", EX **500.00**
Bliss type, stable, 2 stalls, paper on wood, 11x10x6", EX **1,000.00**
Cass, bungalo, pnt wood, gabled, porch, 1912, 10x11x9", EX **500.00**
Continental, 2-story/4-room, paper on wood, 1890s, 24", VG ...**2,500.00**
European, paper/pnt on wood, 2-story/4-room, 24x22x11", EX ..**700.00**
France, stable, 2-story, pnt wood, fretwork, 1885, 15", VG **250.00**
Germany, cottage, 1-room, pnt wood, some furnishings, 14" **700.00**
Germany, 2-story, elevator, paper/wood, red roof, 1890s, 20", G ..**800.00**
Germany, 2-story/2-room, paper/wood w/metal, 1890s, 17", G ...**550.00**
Handmade, NY bungalow, 2-story/7-room, '20s, 22x26x23", EX ..**300.00**
New England, country, 2-story/4-room, wood, 1880s, 27", EX **750.00**
Schoenhut, bungalow, emb cb/pnt wood, litho int, 15x19x16" ..**515.00**
Schoenhut, bungalow, pnt wood, paper int, 17x19x25", EX ...**1,700.00**
Schoenhut, emb cb/wood, 2-story/2-room, 12x14x12", EX **515.00**
Schoenhut, RR station, pnt wood, ca 1925, 10x17x13", EX **300.00**
Schoenhut, Tudor style, 2-story/4-room, 1930s, 18", VG **300.00**
Stable, pnt wood, 2 doors in loft, 28 figures, 22x10x30", EX ...**2,950.00**
Victorian, paper on wood, clapboard, dormers, 16x13x9" **285.00**

Dolls

Collecting dolls of any sort is one of the most rewarding hobbies in the United States. The rewards are in the fun, the search, and the finds — plus there is a built-in factor of investment. No hobby, be it dolls, glass, or anything else, should be based completely on investment; but any collector should ask: 'Can I get my money back out of this item if I should ever have to sell it?' Many times we buy on impulse rather than with logic, which is understandable, but by asking this question we can save ourselves a lot of 'buyer's remorse' which we have all experienced at one time or another.

Since we want to learn to invest our money wisely while we are having fun, we must become aware of defects which may devaluate a doll. In bisque, watch for eye chips, hairline cracks and chips, or breaks on any part of the head. Composition should be clean, not crazed or cracked. Vinyl and plastic should be clean with no pen or crayon marks. Though a quality replacement wig is acceptable for bisque dolls, composition and hard plastics should have their originals in uncut condition. Original clothing is a must except in bisque dolls, since it is unusual to find one in its original costume.

A price guide is only that — a guide. It suggests the average price for each doll. Bargains can be found for less-than-suggested values, and 'unplayed-with' dolls in their original boxes may cost more. Dealers must become aware of condition so that they do not overpay and therefore overprice their dolls — a common occurrence across the country. Quantity does not replace quality, as most find out in time. A faster turnover of sales with a smaller margin of profit is far better than being stuck with an item that does not sell because it is overpriced. It is important to remember that prices are based on condition and rarity. When no condition is noted, dolls are assumed to be in excellent condition with the exceptions of Armand Marseille, Madame Alexander, and Effanbee dolls, which are priced in mint condition. In relation to bisque dolls, excellent means having no cracks, chips, or hairlines, being nicely dressed, shoed, wigged, and ready to to be placed into a collection. For a more thorough study of the subject, we recommend you refer to the many lovely doll books written by authority Patricia Smith, available at your favorite bookstore or public library.

Key:
bjtd — ball-jointed	o/m — open mouth
blb — bent limb body	p/e — pierced ears
bsk — bisque	pnt — painted
c/m — closed mouth	pwt — paperweight eyes
hh — human hair	RpC — replaced clothes
hp — hard plastic	ShHd — shoulder head
jtd — jointed	ShPl — shoulder plate
MIG — Made In Germany	SkHd — socket head
NC — no clothes	str — straight
o/c — open closed	trn — turned
OC — original clothes	

Armand Marseille

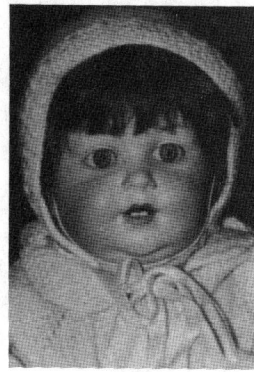

Armand Marseille, Betsy Baby, mold #329, socket head, 5-piece baby body, sleep eyes, open mouth with two teeth, marked G.B. for George Borgfelt, 1922, 13", $350.00.

Alma, ShHd, 12"	195.00
Alma, ShHd, 15"	250.00
Alma, ShHd, 26"	565.00

AM, baby, flange neck, 1907, 16"	625.00
AM, Darling Baby, 1906, 12"	325.00
AM, Floradora, ShHd, 20"	350.00
AM, Floradora, ShHd, 23"	465.00
AM, Floradora, SkHd, 12"	185.00
AM, Floradora, SkHd, 15"	300.00
AM, Floradora, SkHd, 17"	285.00
AM, Floradora, SkHd, 27"	775.00
AM, Floradora 1374, ShHd, fur eyebrows, 21"	450.00
AM, Floradora 3748, ShHd, 21"	400.00
AM, Indian, SkHd, o/c, 1890s, 8"	450.00
AM, Kiddiejoy, ShHd, cloth body, c/m, girl, 20"	1,750.00
AM, Kiddiejoy, ShHd, 9"	225.00
AM, lady, SkHd, c/m, mk MH (Max Handwerck), 1913, 10"	1,000.00
AM, My Dearie, SkHd, 1908, 14"	235.00
AM, My Playmate (body), closed dome & c/m, 18"	1,600.00
AM, Rosebud, ShHd, 1902, 15"	300.00
AM, Roseland, 1910, 18"	450.00
AM, ShHd, boy, 14"	385.00
AM, SkHd, c/m, 14"	850.00
AM, SkHd, CM Bergmann, 24"	565.00
AM, SkHd, o/c eyes, 7"	125.00
AM, SkHd, o/m, blk, 12"	475.00
AM, SkHd, 16"	275.00
AM, SkHd, 17"	295.00
AM, SkHd, 26"	600.00
AM, SkHd, 8"	165.00
AM, Sunshine, ShHd, 1910, 24"	550.00
AM, trn ShHd, talks, 16"	500.00
AM 1894, ShPl, 26"	600.00
AM 1894, SkHd, blk, 12"	475.00
AM 1894, SkHd, wht, 12"	225.00
AM 1894, SkHd, wht, 16½"	325.00
AM 1894, SkHd, 14"	250.00
AM 200, SkHd, googly eyes, 11½"	2,600.00
AM 210, SkHd, googly eyes, 6"	1,600.00
AM 231, Fany, baby, c/m, 1913, 25"	9,800.00
AM 248, mk GB (Geo Borgfeldt), o/m, 1912, 10"	350.00
AM 250, mk GB (Geo Borgfeldt), SkHd, c/m, molded hair, 10½"	375.00
AM 252, SkHd, googly eyes, 10"	900.00
AM 252, SkHd, googly eyes, 1915, 9½"	800.00
AM 253, SkHd, googly eyes, 1915, 16"	2,800.00
AM 253, SkHd, googly eyes, 6½"	750.00
AM 253, SkHd, googly eyes, 8"	900.00
AM 254, SkHd, googly eyes, molded hair, 8"	950.00
AM 255, SkHd, intaglio eyes, 7½"	425.00
AM 257, baby, SkHd, 1914, 22"	550.00
AM 300n, adult, SkHd, 15½"	1,200.00
AM 315, Queen Louise, SkHd, 27"	850.00
AM 320, SkHd, c/m, googly eyes, 6½"	650.00
AM 3200, ShHd, some trn, 15"	250.00
AM 3200, ShHd, some trn, 1898, 14"	250.00
AM 3200, ShHd, some trn, 1898, 16"	265.00
AM 3200, ShHd, some trn, 22"	450.00
AM 3200, ShHd, some trn, 26"	600.00
AM 323, SkHd, googly eyes, 11"	1,200.00
AM 323, SkHd, googly eyes, 7½"	750.00
AM 324, googly eyes, 7"	465.00
AM 327, SkHd, baby, fur hair, 1914, 12"	300.00
AM 327, SkHd, 1914, 12"	250.00
AM 327, SkHd, 1914, 20"	965.00
AM 328, baby, SkHd, closed dome, 1922, 14"	365.00
AM 329, girl, SkHd, 9"	250.00
AM 341, My Dream Baby, flange, c/m, wht, 8"	250.00

AM 341, My Dream Baby, flange, c/m, 15" 525.00
AM 341, My Dream Baby, flange, c/m, 18" 675.00
AM 341, My Dream Baby, flange, c/m, 1924, 7" 185.00
AM 341, My Dream Baby, flange, c/m, 21" 700.00
AM 341, My Dream Baby, SkHd, c/m, 16" 600.00
AM 347, SkHd, 1909, 16" 475.00
AM 3500, ShHd, 17" 425.00
AM 351, My Dream Baby, flange, o/m, wht, 22" 850.00
AM 351, My Dream Baby, flange, o/m, 26" 965.00
AM 351, My Dream Baby, flange, o/m, 6" 145.00
AM 351, Wee One, rubber body, 1922, 7" 165.00
AM 352, Baby Love, flange, 1914, 19" 625.00
AM 3524, Baby Gloria, flange neck, 18" 1,100.00
AM 362, Teenie Weenie, baby, closed dome, wht, 15" 400.00
AM 370, fur eyebrows, 22½" 400.00
AM 370, 12" 175.00
AM 370, 15" 265.00
AM 370, 16½" 300.00
AM 370, 19½" 350.00
AM 370n, 12" 195.00
AM 372, Kiddiejoy, ShHd, molded hair, 1926, 9" 350.00
AM 375, Kiddiejoy, girl, SkHd, c/m, molded hair, 20" 2,600.00
AM 390, My Dearie, SkHd, 1908-22, 18½" 425.00
AM 390, My Dearie, 23" 485.00
AM 390, o/m, 7½" 150.00
AM 390, pnt bsk, 9" 145.00
AM 390, walks, 22" 625.00
AM 390, 16" 350.00
AM 390, 18" 400.00
AM 390, 21" 450.00
AM 390, 22" 485.00
AM 390, 24" 525.00
AM 390, 9½" 225.00
AM 390n, Louisa, 1915, 27" 625.00
AM 390n, Patrice, 18" 650.00
AM 390n, 1915, 11" 275.00
AM 395, Heidi, SkHd, 1920, 9" 225.00
AM 402, SkHd, pnt bsk, 14" 285.00
AM 450, SkHd, c/m, provincial attire, 19" 1,600.00
AM 500, Infant Berry, molded hair, 1908, 10" 500.00
AM 500, Infant Berry, molded hair, 1908, 5" 250.00
AM 500, Infant Berry, molded hair, 1908, 8" 300.00
AM 550, SkHd, c/m, 16" 2,800.00
AM 560a, Dorothy, 1912, 15" 475.00
AM 590, Hoopla Girl, o/c eyes & mouth, 16" 1,800.00
AM 600, SkHd, flange, c/m, 1910, 10" 1,300.00
AM 800, Baby Sunshine, 'Mama' talker in head, 1925, 16" 2,100.00
AM 917, Mobi, baby, Germany, Skhd, 1921, 16" 525.00
AM 95, trn ShHd, 20" 425.00
AM 966, baby, SkHd, flirty eyes, 14" 450.00
AM 970, Ladie Marie, Otto Gans, 1916, 20" 650.00
AM 975, Sadie, baby, Otto Gans, 1914, 17" 525.00
AM 975, Sadie, baby, SkHd, 1914, 24" 700.00
AM 975, Sadie, baby, SkHd, 1914, 9" 200.00
AM 980, baby, SkHd, 14" 350.00
AM 985, baby, SkHd, 13½" 400.00
AM 990, Happy Tot, baby, SkHd, 13" 400.00
AM 990, Happy Tot, baby, SkHd, 1910, 16" 450.00
AM 990, Happy Tot, baby, SkHd, 1910, 21" 675.00
AM 990, Happy Tot, baby, SkHd, 8" 185.00
AM 991, Kiddiejoy, baby, SkHd, 14" 400.00
AM 992, baby, SkHd, 1914, 22" 750.00
AM 995, baby, SkHd, 12" 300.00
AM 996, baby, SkHd, 15" 425.00

AM 997, Kiddiejoy, baby, SkHd, 14" 400.00
Columbia, ShHd, 1904, 24" 550.00
Lily, ShHd, 1913, 17" 350.00
Mabel, ShHd, 1898, 15" 250.00
Mabel, ShHd, 1898, 17" 300.00
Queen Louise, SkHd, 1910, 22" 450.00
Queen Louise, 100, Germany, SkHd, 1910, 12" 250.00
Queen Louise, 100, SkHd, 1910, 18½" 425.00
Wonderful Alice, SkHd, fur eyebrows, 26" 750.00

Automaton

Bimbo, 5 monkeys, 8-track tape selections, glass front, 32" 950.00
Blk dancer on box, gessoed head, clockwork, Pat 1873, 10", G ..500.00
Blk warrior on camel's bk, Mandaville, 1870s 4,500.00
FG (att), c/m, p/e, hh, OC, Fr, plays banjo/turns head, 16" 4,700.00
Girl, ShHd, brn set eyes, stands on box, sgn Jumeau, 20" 4,500.00
Lambert, lady w/basket & dog, bsk head, pwt, c/m, 19", G 5,000.00
McIntyre, magician, nodding bsk head, OC, 16", EX 3,700.00
Schoenau & Hoffmeister, mother & child in cradle, 1890s, 12" .2,800.00
Spain, gypsy girl, bsk head, p/e, stationary eyes, OC, 20" 4,500.00
6 dancing couples, bsk heads, Germany, OC, 12", EX 3,500.00

Barbie Dolls and Related Dolls

Though the face has changed three times since 1959, Barbie is still as popular today as she was when she was first introduced. Named after the young daughter of the first owner of the Mattel Company, the original Barbie had a white iris but no eye color. These dolls are nearly impossible to find, but there is a myriad of her successors and related collectibles just waiting to be found. When no condition is indicated, the dolls listed below are assumed to be in mint condition (without original box) unless otherwise specified. For further information we recommend *The World of Barbie Dolls* and *The Wonder of Barbie, 1976 – 1986* by Paris, Susan, and Carol Manos; and *The Collectors Encyclopedia of Barbie Dolls and Collectibles* by Sibyl DeWein and Joan Ashabraner. *Barbie Fashion, Vol I, 1959 – 1967*, by Sarah Sink Eames, gives a complete history of the wardrobes of Barbie, her friends, and her family. Many of Patricia Smith's books contain chapters on Barbies as well as other dolls by Mattel.

Feelin' Groovy Barbie, includes several accessories, minimum value, $250.00.

Allen, 1963, standard doll, 12", MIB 150.00
Barbie, 1958-59, #1, doll only, M, minimum value 1,500.00
Barbie, 1958-59, #1, holes in ft w/metal cylinders, MIB 2,500.00
Barbie, 1960, #2, no holes in feet, MIB 850.00
Barbie, 1960, #3, curved brows, mk body 300.00

Barbie, 1961, #4, vinyl plastic, tan skin, MIB 265.00
Barbie, 1963, Fashion Queen, 3 wigs 200.00
Barbie, 1965, Color 'n Curl, 2 heads & accessories 450.00
Barbie, 1968, Spanish Talking 200.00
Barbie, 1969, Twist 'n Turn 90.00
Barbie, 1971, Growing Pretty Hair, bendable knees 250.00
Barbie, 1972, Ward Anniversary 200.00
Barbie, 1973, Quick Curl 95.00
Barbie, 1974, Newport 45.00
Barbie, 1974, Sweet Sixteen 85.00
Barbie, 1975, Deluxe Quick Curl 45.00
Barbie, 1975, Gold Medal Skater 50.00
Barbie, 1978, Super Size 95.00
Barbie, 1979, Pretty Changes 45.00
Barbie, 1981, Royal, Parisian 50.00
Barbie, 1981, Western 30.00
Barbie, 1982, Scottish 150.00
Casey, 1975, 11½" 145.00
Christie, 1968, Black, 11½" 95.00
Christie, 1973, Malibu 35.00
Dana, MIB 45.00
Dana, 1987, Rocker 20.00
Diva, 1986, Rocker 20.00
Donny Osmond, MIB 45.00
Francie, 1966, Black, 11½" 400.00
Francie, 1966, 11½" 90.00
Francie, 1972, Busy Hands 60.00
Ginger, Growing Up 25.00
Julia, Talking, 11½" 225.00
Kelley, 1973, Quick Curl 75.00
Kelly, Yellowstone 95.00
Ken, Busy 45.00
Ken, flocked hair 125.00
Ken, molded hair, non-bending knees 125.00
Ken, Talking 150.00
Kitty O'Neill, 1978, 11½" 25.00
Midge, 1965, bendable legs 85.00
Miko, Tropical, MIB 15.00
PJ, 1969, Talking, MIB 95.00
Skooter, 1963, freckles 65.00
Stacey, Talking 150.00
Steffie, Busy, MIB 175.00
Todd, 1970, MIB 125.00
Tressie, basic doll, MIB 55.00
Truly Scrumptious, 11½", MIB 250.00
Tutti, 1965, 6" 65.00
Twiggy, 1978, twist waist, bendable knees 165.00

Barbie Gifts Sets and Related Accessories

When no condition is indicated, the items listed below are assumed to be mint and in the original box.

Airplane, M 525.00
Clock, M 45.00
Clothes, Barbie, Knitting Pretty, MIB 135.00
Clothes, Barbie, Tennis Anyone, MIB 85.00
Clothes, Barbie Cotton Casual, MIB 90.00
Clothes, Barbie in Hawaii, MIB 125.00
Clothes, Barbie Student Teacher, MIB 285.00
Clothes, Campus Sweetheart, 1964, M 80.00
Clothes, Casey Goes Casual, MIB 675.00
Clothes, Darcy Autumn Days, MIB 22.00
Clothes, Darcy Jean Scene, MIB 22.50

Clothes, Drum Majorette, 1963, M 85.00
Clothes, Easter Parade, 1958 , MIB..400.00
Clothes, Enchanted Evening, pk gown, 1958, MIB 165.00
Clothes, Pepper Bed Time, MIB 17.50
Clothes, Stacey Night Lightning, MIB 800.00
Clothes, Tammy Puddle Jumper, MIB 35.00
Clothes, Tammy Skate Date, MIB 35.00
Clothes, Tressie Campus Casual, MIB 25.00

Barbie and Ken Dune Buggy by Irwin, very hard to find, MIB, $150.00.

Dune buggy, M 85.00
Family house, M 75.00
Horse, Dancer, brn, M 125.00
Roadster car, M 275.00
Wardrobe, M 48.00

Belton

Concave head, 2 or 3 hole, EX bsk, o/c or c/m w/wig, 10" 1,600.00
Concave head, 2 or 3 hole, EX bsk, o/c or c/m w/wig, 13" 2,200.00
Concave head, 2 or 3 hole, EX bsk, o/c or c/m w/wig, 15" 2,500.00
Concave head, 2 or 3 hole, EX bsk, o/c or c/m w/wig, 16" 2,600.00
Concave head, 2 or 3 hole, EX bsk, o/c or c/m w/wig, 17" 2,700.00
Concave head, 2 or 3 hole, EX bsk, o/c or c/m w/wig, 20" 3,200.00
Concave head, 2 or 3 hole, EX bsk, o/c or c/m w/wig, 22" 3,300.00
Concave head, 2 or 3 hole, EX bsk, o/c or c/m w/wig, 23" 3,500.00
Concave head, 2 or 3 hole, EX bsk, o/c or c/m w/wig, 26" 3,800.00
Concave head, 2 or 3 hole, EX bsk, o/c or c/m w/wig, 8" 975.00

Bru

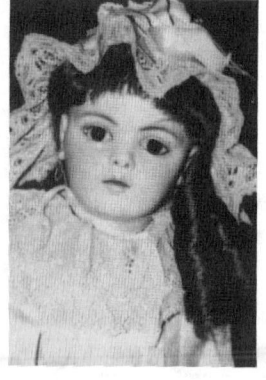

Bru, open/closed mouth, pierced ears, kid over wood body with bisque lower arms and wood lower legs, marked Bru Jne-5 and No. 5, all original, 17", $22,500.00.

Closed mouth, all kid body, bsk lower arms, Bru, 13" 9,350.00
Closed mouth, all kid body, bsk lower arms; Bru, 16" 9,600.00
Closed mouth, all kid body, bsk lower arms; Bru, 18" 14,000.00

Closed mouth, all kid body, bsk lower arms; Bru, 21" 20,000.00
Closed mouth, all kid body, bsk lower arms; Bru, 26" 26,000.00
Closed mouth, kid/wood body, bsk lower arms; Bru Jne, 12" .20,000.00
Closed mouth, kid/wood body, bsk lower arms; Bru Jne, 14" .18,000.00
Closed mouth, kid/wood body, bsk lower arms; Bru Jne, 16" .20,000.00
Closed mouth, kid/wood body, bsk lower arms; Bru Jne, 20" .24,000.00
Closed mouth, kid/wood body, bsk lower arms; Bru Jne, 25" .30,000.00
Closed mouth, kid/wood body, bsk lower arms; Bru Jne, 28" .36,000.00
Closed mouth, kid/wood body, bsk lower arms; Bru Jne, 32" .42,000.00
Closed mouth, mk Bru, circle dot, 16" 23,000.00
Closed mouth, mk Bru, circle dot, 19" 25,000.00
Closed mouth, mk Bru, circle dot, 23" 29,000.00
Closed mouth, mk Bru, circle dot, 26" 34,000.00
Open mouth, compo walker's body, throws kisses, 18" 5,600.00
Open mouth, compo walker's body, throws kisses, 22" 6,400.00
Open mouth, compo walker's body, throws kisses, 26" 7,300.00
Open mouth, nursing (Bebe), high color, late SFBJ, 12" 1,900.00
Open mouth, nursing (Bebe), high color, late SFBJ, 15" 2,800.00
Open mouth, nursing (Bebe), high color, late SFBJ, 18" 3,400.00
Open mouth, nursing Bru (Bebe), early, EX bsk, 12" 5,600.00
Open mouth, nursing Bru (Bebe), early, EX bsk, 15" 7,800.00
Open mouth, nursing Bru (Bebe), early, EX bsk, 18" 9,700.00
Open mouth, socket head, compo body; Bru, R, 14", EX bsk ..4,800.00
Open mouth, socket head, compo body; Bru, R, 17", EX bsk ..6,000.00
Open mouth, socket head, compo body; Bru, R, 22", EX bsk ..8,200.00
Open mouth, socket head, compo body; Bru, R, 25", EX bsk ..8,200.00
Open mouth, socket head, compo body; Bru, R, 28", EX bsk ..9,000.00

China, Unmarked

Adelina Patti, center part, curls at temples, 1860s, 14" 300.00
Adelina Patti, center part, curls at temples, 1860s, 18" 425.00
Adelina Patti, center part, curls at temples, 1860s, 22" 565.00
Biedermeier or Bald Head, takes wig, RpC, 14" 975.00
Biedermeier or Bald Head, takes wig, RpC, 20" 1,500.00
Brown Eyes (pnt), any hairstyle or date, 16", minimum value 950.00
Brown Eyes (pnt), any hairstyle or date, 20", minimum value .1,400.00
Common Hairdo, blond or blk hair, RpC, after 1905, 12" 150.00
Common Hairdo, blond or blk hair, RpC, after 1905, 23" 300.00
Common Hairdo, blond or blk hair, RpC, after 1905, 8" 85.00
Covered Wagon Style, sausage curls, RpC, 1840s-70s, 12" 425.00
Covered Wagon Style, sausage curls, RpC, 1840s-70s, 24" 850.00
Curly Top, loose ringlet curls, RpC, 1845-60s, 16" 625.00
Curly Top, loose ringlet curls, RpC, 1845-60s, 20" 750.00
Dolly Madison, modeled ribbon & bow, RpC, 1870-80s, 14" 275.00
Dolly Madison, modeled ribbon & bow, RpC, 1870-80s, 18" 485.00
Dolly Madison, modeled ribbon & bow, RpC, 1870-80s, 21" 550.00
Fashion, ball head, kid body, unmk Heubach, RpC, 14" 1,900.00
Flat Top, blk hair, mid-part/short curls, RpC, ca 1860, 17" 285.00
Flat Top, blk hair, mid-part/short curls, RpC, ca 1860, 20" 325.00
Glass Eyes, various hairstyles, RpC, 1840s-70s, 14" 2,000.00
Glass Eyes, various hairstyles, RpC, 1840s-70s, 22" 3,000.00
Japanese, blk or blond hair, mk or unmk, RpC, 1910-20s, 14" 165.00
Japanese, blk or blond hair, mk or unmk, RpC, 1910-20s, 17" 225.00
Man or Boy, glass eyes, side part, RpC, 14" 1,600.00
Man or Boy, pnt eyes, side part, RpC, 14", EX 1,200.00
Man or Boy, pnt eyes, side part, RpC, 16" 1,400.00
Man or Boy, pnt eyes, side part, RpC, 21½" 3,400.00
Peg Wood Body, early hairdo, 16", EX 3,800.00
Pet Name, molded shirtwaist w/name on front, RpC, 1905, 19" ...350.00
Pet Name, molded shirtwaist w/name on front, RpC, 1905, 8" ...125.00
Pierced Ears, various hairstyles, RpC, 14" 800.00
Pierced Ears, various hairstyles, RpC, 18" 1,300.00
Snood/Combs, any appl hair decor, RpC, 14" 600.00

Snood/Combs, any appl hair decor, RpC, 17" 850.00
Spill Curls, w/or w/out head band, RpC, 14" 450.00
Spill Curls, w/or w/out head band, RpC, 22" 775.00
Wood Body, articulated/slim hips, RpC, 1840s-50s, 12" 1,500.00
Wood Body, articulated/slim hips, RpC, 1840s-50s, 17" 4,600.00
Wood Body, jtd hips, covered-wagon hairdo, 1840s-50s, 12" 950.00
Wood Body, jtd hips, covered-wagon hairdo, 1840s-50s, 15" ..1,900.00

Cloth

Art Fabric, Geo & Martha Washington, 1901, cut, pr 450.00
Beecher, stuffed stockinette, pnt eyes, wool hair, 15", EX 3,000.00
Bing Art, pnt hair, cloth or felt, 10", EX 625.00
Bruckner (for Horsman), mask face, 1901 on shoulder, 12", EX ...325.00
Chase baby, stockinette, molded/pnt hair, 1900s, 15½", EX 650.00
Columbian, pnt features, stitched fingers/toes, 16", EX 4,000.00
Comic Character, 15", NM 500.00
Drayton, Chocolate Drop, printed, yarn hair, 1923, 12" 465.00
Drayton, Dolly Dingle, printed face, Averill, 1923, 12" 450.00
Homemade, embr features, primitive, 16", NM 265.00
Horsman, Babyland, oil-pnt features, 14", EX 900.00
Horsman, Babyland, printed face, 18", EX 600.00
Horsman, Peek-A-Boo, printed features, 1913-15, EX 350.00
Mammy, pnt or sewn features, 1910-20s, 15", NM 365.00
Printed, boy or girl, ca 1903, cut, 6" 95.00
Rollinson, molded hair or wig, pnt features, 21", NM 1,200.00
Sheppard, Philadelphia Baby, stockinette, 21", NM 3,600.00
Wellington, stockinette, oil-pnt features, 1883, 22", G 3,700.00

Effanbee

Bernard Fleischaker and Hugo Baum became business partners in 1910, and after two difficult years of finding toys to buy and a retail market to sell them in, they decided to manufacture dolls of their own. Their lovely dolls were a decided success largely because of their dedication to their work and the mutual trust and respect they held for each other. This is reflected in the Effanbee trademark — Eff stands for Fleischaker and bee for Baum. The company still exists today.

Alyssia, hp, vinyl head, walker, 1958, OC, 20" 285.00
American Child, Barbara Lou, compo, pnt or o/c eyes, 21" 1,100.00
American Child, boy, compo, pnt or o/c eyes, c/m, 15" 1,200.00
American Child, compo, pnt or o/c eyes, c/m, 18-19" 1,400.00
Ann Shirley, compo, mk w/name, OC, 15" 250.00
Baby Cuddleup, vinyl-coated cloth body/vinyl, 1953, OC, 20" 60.00
Babyette, cloth/compo, sleeping, OC, 12" 300.00
Babykin, compo, 1940, OC, 12" 185.00
Betty Brite, compo, fur wig, o/c eyes, mk w/name, OC, 16" 250.00
Bicentennial Boy or Girl, OC, 11", NM, ea 145.00
Brother, compo/cloth, pnt eyes, yarn hair, OC, 12" 165.00
Button Nose, compo, OC, 9" 175.00
Carolina, made for Smithsonian, 1980, OC, 12", M 65.00
Charlie McCarthy, compo/cloth, OC, 19" 325.00
Compo, pnt or o/c eyes, molded hair, OC, 1930s, 15", NM 200.00
Compo, pnt or o/c eyes, molded hair, OC, 1930s, 9", NM 165.00
Gumdrop, plastic/vinyl, 1962 on, OC, 16" 45.00
Historical, compo, all orig, 14", NM 600.00
Honey, compo, OC, 14" 285.00
Honey Walker, hp, c/m, o/c eyes, saran wig, OC, 19" 325.00
Little Bo Peep, compo, pnt eyes, fully jtd, OC, 9" 250.00
Little Girl, ShHd, compo/cloth, pnt eyes/hair, c/m, OC, 14" 165.00
Little Lady, compo/cloth, pnt eyes, 1944, OC, 27" 600.00
Lovums, o/c mouth smiling, molded hair, OC, 22" 350.00
Mae Starr, compo/cloth, o/m w/tongue & 2 teeth, OC, 30" 450.00

Marionnette, compo/wood, OC, 14" 145.00
Mary Ann, compo/cloth, o/m smiling, mk w/name, OC, 18" 350.00
Mickey, compo/cloth, flirty eyes, 1946, OC, 18" 325.00

Effanbee 'Mimi' from the Petite Filles Collection, 1980, marked 1966 on head, original clothes, 11", $85.00.

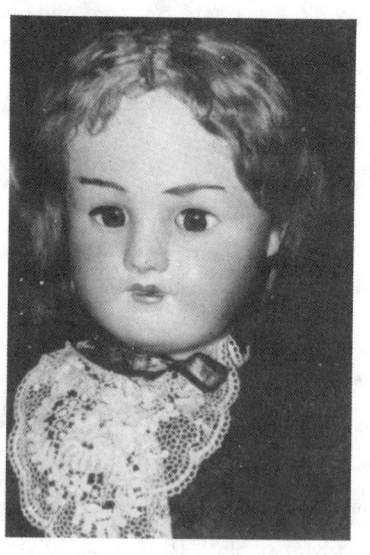

Handwerck, Heinrich; socket head on fully jointed composition body, sleep eyes, open mouth, fur eyebrows, 32", $1,400.00.

Patricia, compo, OC, 14" 385.00
Patsy, compo, pnt eyes/hair, OC, 14" 350.00
Patsy Ann, compo, tin o/c eyes, RpC, 19" 465.00
Patsy Babyette, compo, OC, 9" 185.00
Patsy Joan, compo, o/c eyes, molded hair, OC, 16" 450.00
Patsy Joan, compo, OC, 16" 450.00
Precious Baby, Limited Edition Club, 1975, M 550.00
Prince Charming, hp, OC, 16" 450.00
Rosemary, compo/cloth, o/c eyes, orig wig, OC, 25" 400.00
Suzette, compo, pnt eyes, OC as Geo Washington, 12" 265.00
Sweetie Pie, compo/cloth, RpC, 14" 65.00
WC Fields, compo/cloth, OC, 22" 695.00

Half Dolls

Half dolls, lovely porcelain figures awaiting attachment to secure bases, were never meant to be objects of play. Most of these lovely ladies were firmly sewn into pincushion bases that were beautifully decorated and served as the skirt of their gown. Other skirts were actually covers for items on milady's dressing table. Some were used for parasol or brush handles or for tops to candy containers or perfume bottles. Most popular from 1900 to about 1930, they will most often be found marked with the country of their origin — Bavaria, Germany, France, and Japan. You may also find some fine quality pieces marked Goebel, Dressel and Kester, and Heubach.

For further information we recommend *The Collector's Encyclopedia of Half Dolls* by Frieda Marion and Norma Werner, available at your local bookstore or from Collector Books.

Germany, arms & hands attached, common type, 3", up from 30.00
Germany, arms & hands attached, common type, 5", up from 40.00
Germany, arms & hands attached, common type, 8", up from 55.00
Germany, arms & hands completely away, 12", up from 900.00
Germany, arms & hands completely away, 3", up from 125.00
Germany, arms & hands completely away, 5", up from 250.00
Germany, arms & hands completely away, 8", up from 425.00
Germany, arms extended, hands attached, 3", up from 65.00
Germany, arms extended, hands attached, 5", up from 75.00
Germany, arms extended, hands attached, 8", up from 95.00
Japan mk, 3", up from 20.00
Japan mk, 5", up from 30.00
Japan mk, 8", up from 50.00

Handwerck

#0 1/2, ShHd, o/c eyes, o/m, rpl wig, RpC, 16" 485.00

#1079, SkHd (by Simon & Halbig), o/m, RpC, 20" 565.00
#109, brn o/c eyes, o/m w/4 teeth, long wig, RpC, 17" 550.00
#109-11, SkHd, o/c eyes, o/m, RpC, 19" 565.00
#109-7 1/2, SkHd, compo, jtd, o/c eyes, o/m, p/e, RpC, 17" 575.00
#79/10, SkHd, compo, jtd, o/c eyes, o/m, p/e, RpC, 18" 565.00
Germany, SkHd, compo, fully jtd, o/c eyes, o/m, RpC, 14" 600.00
Germany, SkHd, compo, jtd, molded brows, o/m, p/e, RpC, 39" ...2,400.00
Germany, SkHd, compo, jtd, o/c eyes, o/m, p/e, RpC, 17½" 525.00
Germany...Simon Halbig, SkHd, o/c eyes, o/m, p/e, RpC, 18" 450.00
HcH/12/0/H, ShHd, o/m w/4 teeth, orig caracul wig, 14" 250.00
HCH2H, ShHd, lg protruding ears, MIG, RpC, 23" 550.00
Max Handwerck, SkHd, compo, jtd, o/c eyes, p/m, RpC, 24" 625.00
ShHd, kid body, bsk forearms, o/c eyes, lg ears, RpC, 15" 450.00
Trn ShHd, full c/m, set eyes, unpierced ears, RpC, 15" 1,200.00

Heubach

#119, character, molded braids, intaglio eyes, RpC, 16" 5,400.00
#2, pnt eyes, o/c/mouth, nude, 12" 975.00
#22-126, ShHd, jtd body, molded bonnet, o/c/m, RpC, 8" 1,200.00
#3/3420, SkHd, glass eyes, c/m, OC, 12" 950.00
#4, SkHd, compo, fully jtd, intaglio eyes, RpC, 15" 1,600.00
#57/1, Indian, bsk head, OC, 13" 4,600.00
#6 1/2, SkHd, 5-pc body, o/c eyes, teeth, RpC, 19" 1,600.00
#64/5, ShHd, jtd body, bsk forearms, o/m, RpC, 19" 650.00
#8429, SkHd, glass eyes, c/m, RpC, 15" 5,400.00
#91/Germany, o/c mouth w/2 rows pnt teeth, RpC, 8" 650.00
Baby, intaglio eyes, c/m, RpC, 8½" 800.00
Baby, SkHd, glass eyes, open crown/wig, RpC, 7½" 800.00
Coquette, tilted bsk ShHd, kid body, molded ribbon, RpC, 12" .975.00
Pk lustre, china, all orig, 18½" 2,800.00
SkHd, molded bonnet, holes at sides for ribbon, RpC, 9" 1,200.00

Heubach-Koppelsdorf

#1092/0, ShHd, kid body, bsk arms, rpl wig, OC, 20" 425.00
#200.12/0, SkHd, 5-pc compo body, o/c eyes, teeth, 10½" 325.00
#242-14, baby, pnt bsk head, 5-pc bent-leg body, RpC, 11" 265.00
#250, SkHd, wide-spread fingers, ca 1900, RpC, 24" 500.00
#250 3/0, SkHd, jtd compo, o/c eyes, 4 teeth, RpC, 16" 200.00
#250 4/0, SkHd, o/c eyes, o/m, RpC, 16" 200.00
#275, ShHd, kid body, compo arms, o/c eyes, o/m, RpC, 15" 285.00
#275 9/0, bsk ShHd, c/m, RpC, 15" 195.00
#275-18, bsk ShHd, o/m w/teeth, RpC, 14" 185.00

#277, SkHd, papier-mache/compo, stick legs, set eyes, RpC, 12" ..**475.00**
#300 2/0, brn o/c eyes, o/m w/teeth, rpt limbs, wig, 14" **245.00**
#320-6, baby, RpC, 19½" **450.00**
#321, SkHd, o/c eyes, o/m w/2 teeth, OC, 14" **385.00**
Made for Welsch Co, ShHd, kid w/bsk arms, set eyes, RpC, 25" ...**425.00**

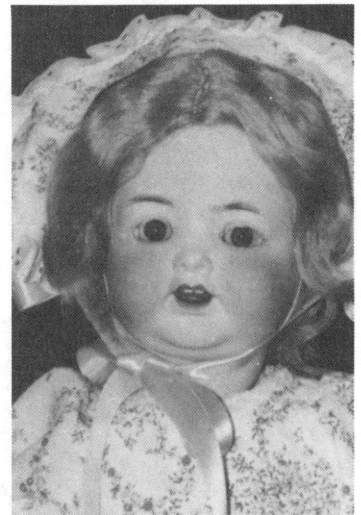

Heubach, Ernst; socket head on 5-piece toddler body, sleep eyes, open mouth with teeth and 'tremble' tongue, marked Heubach Koppelsdorf/342-d, 18", $550.00.

Ideal

April Showers, battery operated, 1968, 14", M **30.00**
Baby Snooks, wire & compo, 12", M **365.00**
Betty Big Girl, plastic/vinyl, 1968, 30", M **300.00**
Bonnie Braids, hp/vinyl, 1951, 12", EX **45.00**
Compo, child, cloth body, str legs, 14", NM **125.00**
Compo, child, o/c eyes, o/m, OC, 14", M **175.00**
Cricket, Black, OC, M **85.00**
Crissy, Look-a-Round, OC, 18", M **60.00**
Daddy's Girl, OC, 42", M **850.00**
Dew Drop, vinyl/cloth, o/c eyes, rooted hair, OC, 24" **65.00**
King Little, compo/wood, 1940, OC, 14" **300.00**
Miss Curity, hp, OC, 14" **350.00**
Pebbles, plastic/vinyl, all orig, 1963, 8" **18.00**
Soldier, WWI doughboy, compo, RpC, 12" **130.00**
Suzy Playpal, vinyl, 1960-61, OC, 24" **175.00**
Tiffany Taylor, head swivels to change hair color, 1973, M **80.00**

Jumeau

Emile Jumeau took over his father's doll company sometime in the 1870s. He brought many new innovations and ideas to the business. One fascination Jumeau had concerned dolls' eyes and led to the patents for eyelids that dropped over the eye itself; a second type allowed the doll to 'sleep.' Jumeau's distaste for German dolls is apparent in the booklets that were packaged with his dolls. These booklets referred to the German dolls as cheap and ugly and as having 'stupid' faces. In reality, these less-expensive dolls were the downfall of the French doll manufacturers, and in 1899 the Jumeau company had to combine with several others in an effort to save the French doll industry from the German competition.

Bsk SkHd, blond mohair, w/bottle/dog/music box, 18", VG **4,800.00**
Closed mouth, mk EJ (incised) Jumeau, rpr ft, 24" **8,700.00**
Closed mouth, mk EJ (incised) Jumeau, 10" **5,500.00**
Closed mouth, mk EJ (incised) Jumeau, 14" **5,900.00**
Closed mouth, mk EJ (incised) Jumeau, 16" **6,400.00**

Closed mouth, mk EJ (incised) Jumeau, 19" **6,800.00**
Closed mouth, mk EJ (incised) Jumeau, 21" **7,400.00**
Closed mouth, mk Tete Jumeau, 10" **3,700.00**
Closed mouth, mk Tete Jumeau, 14" **3,400.00**
Closed mouth, mk Tete Jumeau, 16" **4,000.00**
Closed mouth, mk Tete Jumeau, 19" **4,400.00**
Closed mouth, mk Tete Jumeau, 21" **4,800.00**
Closed mouth, mk Tete Jumeau, 23" **5,300.00**
Closed mouth, mk Tete Jumeau, 25" **5,700.00**
Closed mouth, mk Tete Jumeau, 28" **6,500.00**
Closed mouth, mk Tete Jumeau, 30" **7,200.00**
Depose/Tete Jumeau, swivel head, p/e, long curls, 18" **6,300.00**
Depose/Tete Jumeau, swivel head, p/e, long curls, 28" **9,200.00**
E 6 J/Jumeau, swivel head, inset eyes, kid body, 16" **6,400.00**
E 6 J/Jumeau, swivel head, inset eyes, kid body, 20" **7,000.00**
EJ/Depose Brevete, swivel head, inset eyes, 'mama/papa,' 16" ..**5,800.00**

Jumeau, inked 'M' over '7,' paperweight eyes, mohair wig, closed mouth, papier-mache and ball-jointed body, 18", $5,200.00.

Jumeau 1907, SkHd, appl ears, o/m, 18" **2,400.00**
Jumeau 1907, swivel head, o/m, o/c eyes, p/e, 18" **2,400.00**
Jumeau 1907, swivel head, o/m, o/c eyes, p/e, 23" **2,800.00**
Jumeau 1909, swivel head, o/m, inset eyes, p/e, 21" **2,800.00**
Long face, c/m, 21" **23,000.00**
Long face, c/m, 30" **26,000.00**
Mechanical/musical, c/m, p/e, pwt, hh, 12" on 4" box **4,200.00**
Open mouth, mk Tete Jumeau, 10" **1,400.00**
Open mouth, mk Tete Jumeau, 14" **1,800.00**
Open mouth, mk Tete Jumeau, 16" **2,300.00**
Open mouth, mk Tete Jumeau, 19" **2,500.00**
Open mouth, mk Tete Jumeau, 21" **3,000.00**
Open mouth, mk Tete Jumeau, 23" **3,300.00**
Open mouth, mk Tete Jumeau, 25" **3,600.00**
Open mouth, mk Tete Jumeau, 28" **3,900.00**
Open mouth, mk Tete Jumeau, 30" **4,200.00**
Open mouth, mk 1907 Jumeau, 14" **1,400.00**
Open mouth, mk 1907 Jumeau, 17" **2,200.00**
Open mouth, mk 1907 Jumeau, 20" **2,600.00**
Open mouth, mk 1907 Jumeau, 25" **3,300.00**
Open mouth, mk 1907 Jumeau, 28" **3,500.00**
Open mouth, mk 1907 Jumeau, 32" **3,600.00**

Phonograph in body, o/m, 20" **3,400.00**
Phonograph in body, o/m, 25" **4,800.00**
Portrait Jumeau, c/m, 16" **6,000.00**
Portrait Jumeau, c/m, 20" **7,700.00**

Kammer and Reinhardt

#100, baby, pnt hair & eyes, o/c mouth, 15" **800.00**
#100/5, SkHD, bent leg, pnt eyes & hair, 20" **1,600.00**
#101, boy or girl w/glass eyes, 12" **2,000.00**
#101, boy or girl w/glass eyes, 16" **5,000.00**
#101, boy or girl w/glass eyes, 20" **7,000.00**
#101, boy or girl w/glass eyes, 9" **2,200.00**
#101, boy or girl w/pnt eyes, 12" **1,800.00**
#101, boy or girl w/pnt eyes, 16" **2,900.00**
#101, boy or girl w/pnt eyes, 20" **3,600.00**
#101, boy or girl w/pnt eyes, 9" **1,500.00**
#109, rare, w/glass eyes, 15" **17,000.00**
#109, rare, w/glass eyes, 18" **26,000.00**
#109, rare, w/pnt eyes, 15" **14,000.00**
#109, rare, w/pnt eyes, 18" **22,000.00**
#112, rare, w/glass eyes, 15" **17,000.00**
#112, rare, w/glass eyes, 18" **20,000.00**
#112, rare, w/pnt eyes, 15" **10,000.00**
#112, rare, w/pnt eyes, 18" **17,000.00**
#114, rare, w/glass eyes, 15" **6,300.00**
#114, rare, w/glass eyes, 18" **7,200.00**
#114, rare, w/pnt eyes, 11" **3,200.00**
#114, rare, w/pnt eyes, 15" **3,700.00**
#114, rare, w/pnt eyes, 18" **5,500.00**
#115 or #115a, c/m, 15" **3,400.00**
#115 or #115a, c/m, 18" **4,600.00**
#115 or #115a, c/m, 22" **5,200.00**
#115 or #115a, o/m, 15" **1,600.00**
#115 or #115a, o/m, 18" **2,600.00**
#115 or #115a, o/m, 22" **2,500.00**
#116 or #116a, c/m, 15" **2,500.00**
#116 or #116a, c/m, 18" **3,300.00**
#116 or #116a, c/m, 22" **4,200.00**
#116 or #116a, o/m, 15" **1,600.00**
#116 or #116a, o/m, 18" **2,000.00**
#116 or #116a, o/m, 22" **2,400.00**
#117, c/m, 18" **4,600.00**
#117, c/m, 24" **6,400.00**
#117, c/m, 30" **7,400.00**
#117a, c/m, 18" **4,900.00**
#117a, c/m, 24" **7,500.00**
#117a, c/m, 30" **9,000.00**
#126, brn o/c eyes, o/m w/teeth, 5-pc body, RpC, 17" **800.00**
#126, sleeping/flirty glass eyes, o/m, silent, 28" **2,000.00**
#126, toddler, sleeping/flirty eyes, o/m, 13½" **650.00**
Buster Brown, SkHd, pnt eyes, c/m, K*R, 1900s, 23", w/Tige .**5,400.00**
Dolly face, o/m, mold #400-403-109, etc, 16" **600.00**
Dolly face, o/m, mold #400-403-109, etc, 20" **725.00**
Dolly face, o/m, mold #400-403-109, etc, 24" **850.00**
Dolly face, o/m, mold #400-403-109, etc, 28" **1,000.00**
Dolly face, o/m, mold #400-403-109, etc, 38" **2,500.00**
Dolly face, o/m, mold #400-403-109, etc, 40" **2,700.00**

Kestner

Johannes D. Kestner made buttons at a lathe in a Waltershausen factory in the early 1800s. When this line of work failed, he used the same lathe to turn doll bodies. Thus, the Kestner company began. It was one of the few German manufacturers to make the complete doll. By 1860 with the purchase of a porcelain factory, Kestner made doll heads of china and bisque as well as wax, worked-in-leather, celluloid, and cardboard. In 1895 the Kestner trademark of a crown with streamers was registered in the U.S. and a year later in Germany. Kestner felt the mark was appropriate, since he referred to himself as the 'king of German dollmakers.'

Kestner lady with bisque head, open/close eyes, open mouth with teeth, bisque shoulders and arms, 23", $725.00; Bisque head, open/close eyes, open mouth with four teeth, ball-jointed body, marked K 1/2 Made in 14 1/2 146, $625.00.

A, ShHd, o/m, MIG/Kestner, 19" **525.00**
A/5, ShHd, o/c mouth, 23" **2,600.00**
B/164-4, SkHd, googly eyes, 'watermelon smile,' RpC, 15" **3,800.00**
B/6, ShHd, kid w/bsk ½-arms, o/m w/teeth, o/c eyes, 19" **525.00**
B/6, SkHd, jtd compo, o/m w/2 teeth, set eyes, 22" **600.00**
Bergmann, SkHd, made for CM Bergmann, o/m, JDK/CM, 14" .**295.00**
Bergmann, SkHd, made for CM Bergmann, o/m, JDK/CM, 17" .**475.00**
Bergmann, SkHd, made for CM Bergmann, o/m, JDK/CM, 20" .**575.00**
Century Doll Co, flanged closed dome, c/m, 15" **650.00**
C13/129, bsk SkHd, o/m, 4 teeth, o/c eyes, RpC, 22", G **625.00**
D/8, SkHd & ShHd, kid w/bsk ½-arms, c/m, 15" **1,400.00**
E/9, ShHd, o/m, MIG, 26" **950.00**
E/9, SkHd, o/m, 1892, 26" **950.00**
Excelsior Germany, SkHd, compo, o/m w/4 teeth, OC, 32" **1,400.00**
G/11, Hilda, SkHd, o/c eyes, o/m w/2 teeth, 1920s, 15" **3,500.00**
G/11, SkHd, brn, o/m, 16" **3,500.00**
G/8, trn ShHd, o/m, MI/JDK, 19" **725.00**
Grace Putnam, bsk, 1-pc, pnt eyes, 10/10/COPR, 6" **650.00**
Grace Putnam, bsk, 1-pc body & head, 1/COPR, 1923, 6" **650.00**
Grace Putnam, Bye-Lo baby, 1360/30/COPR, RpC, 11" **750.00**
Grace Putnam, Bye-Lo baby, 6 12/COPR, 1927, 16" **800.00**
Grace Putnam, Bye-Lo baby, 6 12/COPR, 1927, 5" **650.00**
H 1/2, ShHd, o/m, 23" **650.00**
H/12, SkHd, o/c mouth, JDK, 1892, 23" **2,800.00**

Handwerck, SkHd, made for Handwerck, o/m, JDK/H/12, 23" ...550.00
Handwerck, SkHd, made for Handwerck, o/m, JDK/H/12, 27" ...750.00
Hilda, toddler, jtd body, o/m, o/c eyes, 1914, rstr, 15" 3,800.00
I/13, SkHd, o/m, JDK, 1892, 16" 475.00
I/13, SkHd, o/m, JDK, 1892, 26" 700.00
J/13, SkHd, o/m, 1896, 27" 750.00
JDK, bsk head, c/m, glass eyes, appl ears, OC, 20", EX 3,200.00
JDK, bsk head, o/c eyes, o/m w/teeth, pnt hair, 15½" 475.00
JDK, bsk head on celluloid, R Gummi Co, turtle mk, 18" 650.00
JDK 12, SkHd, o/m, pwt, bent limbs, RpC, 15", VG 400.00
JDK 12, SkHd, o/m w/2 teeth, o/c eyes, orig wig, RpC, 16" 850.00
JDK 241, SkHd, jtd compo, o/m w/4 teeth, RpC, 21½", EX 5,400.00
K/12, ShHd, made for Century, o/c mouth, molded hair, 21" ..2,200.00
Kewpie, bsk, Rose O'Neill/10 945G, 1913, 8" 350.00
KK/14 1/2d, o/m, 1896, 26" 800.00
L 1/2/15 1/2, SkHd, c/m, 14" 1,800.00
L/15, SkHd, bsk ShPl, c/m, 21" 2,200.00
L/15, SkHd, c/m, 21" 2,300.00
L/3, ShHd, o/c mouth w/molded teeth, 23" 2,800.00
N/17, SkHd, o/m, 1892, 17" 475.00
ShHd, o/c eyes, o/m, kid body & legs, bsk arms, 19", EX 400.00
SkHd, Oriental, o/m, JDK/Kestner, 14" 4,600.00
SkHd, pnt eyes, JDK/3 4/0, 8" 500.00
Trn ShHd, Kidoline w/bsk ½-arms, o/c eyes, G/MIG, 16" 450.00
10, SkHd, bsk ShPl, c/m, 21" 2,400.00
10, SkHd, o/c mouth w/2 teeth, JDK/MIG, 12" 450.00
10/G, SkHd, c/m, JDK, 1912, 12" 600.00
1070, SkHd, o/m, G11/237 15/JDK Jr 1914 HILDA/GES, 16" ..3,600.00
11, SkHd, o/c mouth, pnt eyes to side, JDK/MIG, 11" 600.00
12, SkHd, 5-pc baby, o/m/2 teeth, o/c eyes, JDK/MIG, 15" 650.00
13, SkHd, o/m, JDK/MIG, 18" 575.00
143, ShHd, jtd compo, o/c eyes, o/m, mohair wig, 14", EX 850.00
143, ShHd, kid w/bsk ½-arms, o/m, 17" 1,200.00
143, ShHd, kid w/bsk ½-arms, o/m/teeth, 12" 850.00
145, ShHd, kid w/bsk ½-arms, o/c mouth, 15" 2,200.00
145, SkHd, c/m, MI/O/G/18, 14" 1,500.00
145, SkHd, c/m, 143/4/0/JDK, 11" 700.00
146, SkHd, swivel, on ShPl, o/m, JDK, 18" 650.00
147, trn ShHd, o/m, JDK, 25" 950.00
148, ShHd, kid w/bsk ½-arms, o/m, 7 1/2, 18" 600.00
148, ShHd, kid w/bsk ½-arms, o/m, 7 1/2, 21" 725.00
150.1, bsk, Kestner seal on body, 8" 350.00
151, SkHd, 5-pc baby, o/m/teeth, intaglio eyes, MIG/5, 12" 425.00
151, SkHd, 5-pc baby, o/m/teeth, intaglio eyes, MIG/5, 16" 575.00
151, SkHd, 5-pc baby, o/m/teeth, intaglio eyes, MIG/5, 20" 675.00
152, character baby, compo, o/c eyes, o/m w/tongue, 11½" 300.00
152, SkHd, made for Wolf, o/m, LW & CO 12, 1916, 20" 750.00
154, SkHd/ShHd, kid w/bsk ½-arms, o/m/teeth, DEP, 14" 450.00
154, SkHd/ShHd, kid w/bsk ½-arms, o/m/teeth, DEP, 17" 600.00
154, SkHd/ShHd, kid w/bsk ½-arms, o/m/teeth, DEP, 20" 800.00
154, SkHd/ShHd, kid w/bsk ½-arms, o/m/teeth, DEP, 26" 1,000.00
16, SkHd, o/m, JDK/MIG, 21" 625.00
16/GES#1, ShHd, o/c mouth, molded boy's hair, 16" 2,600.00
167, SkHd, jtd compo, o/m, p/e, F 1/2/MI6 1/2/G, 16" 500.00
167, SkHd, jtd compo, o/m, p/e, F 1/2/MI6 1/2/G, 20" 600.00
168, SkHd, o/m, MID/G7, 26" 850.00
169, SkHd, jtd compo, c/m, o/c eyes, B 1/2/BI6 1/2G, 16" 2,400.00
169, SkHd, jtd compo, c/m, o/c eyes, B 1/2/BI6 1/2G, 18" 2,800.00
171, SkHd, jtd compo, o/m, o/c eyes, 'Daisy,' F/M110, 15" 465.00
171, SkHd, jtd compo, o/m, o/c eyes, 'Daisy,' F/M110, 18" 625.00
171, SkHd, jtd compo, o/m, o/c eyes, 'Daisy,' F/M110, 22" 750.00
171, SkHd, jtd compo, o/m, o/c eyes, 'Daisy,' F/M110, 32" 1,500.00
180 12/Ox/Crown seal, SkHd, o/m, 16" 465.00
201, ShHd, celluloid on kid, o/m, set eyes/lashes, JDK, 19" 650.00

211, SkHd, 5-pc baby, o/c mouth, o/c eyes, MI10/G/JDK, 12" 550.00
211, SkHd, 5-pc baby, o/c mouth, o/c eyes, MI10/G/JDK, 15" ...725.00
215, SkHd, jtd compo, fur eyebrows, o/m, MI9/GJDK, 21" 800.00
217A/Kestner, bsk, c/m smile, googly pnt eyes, 12" 2,400.00
221/GES/GESCH, SkHd, c/m smile, googly eyes, G/JDK, 21" ..8,200.00
235, toddler, kid body, 16" 725.00
241, character, SkHd, o/c eyes, JDK, OC, 22" 5,600.00
245, SkHd, 5-pc baby, G/MIG/11/JDK Jr/1914 Hilda, 14" 3,300.00
245, SkHd, 5-pc baby, G/MIG/11/JDK Jr/1914 Hilda, 17" 3,600.00
257, SkHd, 5-pc baby, o/m, G/JDK, 10" 450.00
257, SkHd, 5-pc baby, o/m, G/JDK, 16" 675.00
257, SkHd, 5-pc baby, o/m, G/JDK, 20" 850.00
257, SkHd, 5-pc baby, o/m, G/JDK, 24" 1,400.00
26, K&Co/JDK/MIG/81, 16" 465.00
260, flirty-eyed toddler, OC, 16" 1,500.00
270, SkHd, o/m, made for Carl Trautman, CP/39, 38" 2,400.00
639, trn ShHd, closed dome, c/m, G/6, 18" 1,400.00
7 1/2/B, ShHd, kid w/bsk ½-arms, o/m w/teeth, o/c eyes, 14" 425.00

Lenci

Eleanora Scavani, separated from her husband who was in the service of Italy during WWI, found herself painfully alone after the death of her baby. With her brother as her partner, this talented artist began designing lovely felt-covered dolls with beautiful hand-painted features. These dolls became her children, and she regarded them as a tribute to her lost daughter.

Following the war, her husband returned and joined the firm as a partner. The Lenci firm (a name he used as a term of endearment for his wife) soon became well-known in the doll-making industry. Great care was taken in every detail. Characteristics of Lenci dolls include seamless, steam-molded felt heads, quality clothing, childishly plump bodies, and painted eyes that glance to the side. Fine mohair wigs were used, and the middle and fourth fingers were sewn together. Look for the factory stamp on the foot, though paper labels were also used. Dolls under 10" are known as mascots and usually sell for $125.00 to $150.00. The Lenci factory continues today, producing dolls of the same high quality.

**Lenci, all felt, painted eyes, 18",
$1,200.00.**

Boy, bl eyes, o/c m, all orig, 9" 300.00
Child, brn pnt eyes, brn mohair wig, OC, 12" 600.00
Child, lg pnt eyes, mohair wig, bow in hair, all orig, 15" 900.00
Child, pouty, blond mohair wig, all orig, 21" 1,400.00
Girl, all felt, pnt features, all orig, 21" 2,000.00
Girl, all orig w/hat & shawl, pre-WWII, 11" 450.00
Girl, brn eyes, tightly curled mohair wig, all orig, 17" 1,400.00
Girl, dbl-breasted coat, orig hat, 14", EX 600.00

Girl, lt bl pnt eyes, blond hair, OC, 14" 825.00
Girl, pnt features, brn mohair wig, 1920s, OC, 9", M 300.00
Girl toddler, red wig, OC, 17" 975.00
Lady, braided wig, organdy dress, red leather boots, OC, 24" ..2,000.00
Lady, OC w/hat & coat, 14" 800.00
Portrait child, mohair wig w/braids, all orig, ca 1935, 18" 1,900.00
Southern, brn eyes, brn mohair wig, all orig, 14" 825.00
Spanish lady, all felt, blk floss hair, all orig, 27½" 2,600.00

Madame Alexander

Beatrice Alexander founded the Alexander Doll company in 1923 using a lovely doll that was designed after her daughter Mildred. With the help of her three sisters, the company prospered; and by the late 1950s there were three factories with over six hundred employees making Madame Alexander dolls. The company still produces these lovely dolls today.

Am Women's Volunteer Service, compo, Wendy Ann, '42, 14" ..800.00
Anastasia, Portrette Series, Cissette, 10" 60.00
Angel Baby, hp, Wendy Ann, 1955, 8" 950.00
Annie Laurie, compo, Wendy Ann, 1937, 14" 750.00
Aunt Agatha, hp, Wendy Ann, 1957, 8" 1,350.00
Baby Betty, compo, 1935-36, 10-12", ea 300.00
Baby Genius, cloth, 1930s, 11" 650.00
Ballerina, bend-knee walker, Golden Yellow, 1954-60, 8" 500.00
Ballerina, compo, Wendy Ann, 1936-38, 11" 275.00
Bonnie Toddler, cloth/hp head/vinyl limbs, 1950-51, 18" 100.00
Brenda Starr, beach outfit, 1964, 12" 250.00
Bride, hp, Cissette, 1957-73, 10" 300.00
Bride, hp, Lissy, 1956-59, 12" 285.00
Bride, hp, Margaret, 1950, 17" 675.00
Bride, plastic/vinyl, Mary Ann, 1973-76, 14" 70.00
Bridesmaid, compo, Wendy Ann, 1939-44, 15" 375.00
Bridesmaid, hp, Cissette, 1957-63, 10" 500.00
Bridesmaid, hp, Maggie, 1952, 18" 650.00
Bunny, plastic/vinyl, 1962 only, 18" 275.00
Butch McGuffey, compo/cloth, 1940-41, 22" 265.00
Canada, hp, bend knee, Wendy Ann, 1968-72, 8" 125.00
Careen, compo, Wendy Ann, 1937-38, 17" 675.00
Carmen, compo, Tiny Betty, 1938-43, 7" 225.00
Charity, hp, Americana Series, Wendy Ann, 1961 only, 8" 2,300.00
Cherub, vinyl, 1960-61, 12" 85.00
Cinderella, compo, Little Betty, 1936-41, 9" 245.00
Cinderella, hp, Margaret, 1950-51, 18" 700.00
Cissette, hp, formal, 1957-63, 20" 300.00
Civil War, hp, Glamour Girls Series, Margaret, 1953, 18" 1,200.00
Cleopatra, Portraits of History Series, 1980-85, 12" 60.00
Clover Kid, compo, Tiny Betty, 1935-36, 7" 245.00
Cookie, compo/cloth, 1938-40, 19" 465.00
Cornelia, Portrait Series, Jacqueline, 1974, 21" 375.00
Country Cousins, cloth, 1940s, 10" 300.00
Cowgirl, hp, bend knee, Wendy Ann, 1967-79, 8" 525.00
Cry Dolly, vinyl, 12-pc layette, 1953, 14" 165.00
Cynthia, hp, Black Margaret, 1952 only, 15" 800.00
Czechoslovakia, compo, Tiny Betty, 1935-37, 7" 165.00
Daffy Down Dilley, str legs, Wendy Ann, 1986 only, 8" 55.00
David Copperfield, compo, Tiny Betty, 1936-38, 7" 250.00
Dearest Baby, vinyl, 1962-64, 12" 135.00
Denmark, hp, Cissette, 1962-63, 10" 1,100.00
Ding Dong Dell, compo, Tiny Betty, 1937-42, 7" 200.00
Dionne Quint, cloth, 1935-36, 15" 650.00
Dionne Quint, compo, toddler, molded hair/pnt eyes, 1935-39, 8" .150.00
Dionne Quint, compo, toddler, wig, sleep eyes, 1937-38, 11" 300.00

Dionne Quint, compo, toddler, 1938-39, 20" 600.00
Dolly Dryper, vinyl, 7-pc layette, 1952 only, 11" 95.00
Dr Defoe, compo, 1937-39, 16" 1,100.00
Drum Majorette, hp, Wendy Ann, 1955 only, 7½" 750.00
Dutch, hp, bend knee, 1965-72, 8" 55.00
Dutch Boy, hp, bend-knee walker, Wendy Ann, 1964, 8" 200.00
Easter Doll, hp, Wendy Ann, 1968, 8" 1,200.00
Edith w/Golden Hair, cloth, 1940s, 18" 600.00
Egypt, str leg, Wendy Ann, 1986-89, 8" 65.00
Elise, hp/vinyl, jtd ankles & knees, street clothes, 18" 165.00
Emily, cloth/felt, 1930s 600.00
Eskimo, hp, bend knee, Wendy Ann, 1967-69, 8" 450.00
Evangeline, cloth, 1930s, 18" 700.00
Fairy Princess, compo, Tiny Betty, 1940-43, 7" 225.00
Fairy Princess, compo, Wendy Ann, 1939, 1944-46, 21" 900.00
Fairy Queen, hp, Margaret, 1949-50, 18" 825.00
Finnish, compo, Tiny Betty, 1935-37, 7" 225.00
First Communion, hp, Wendy Ann, 1957 only, 8" 850.00
Five Little Peppers, compo, 1936, 13", ea 500.00
Flora McFlimsey, compo, Princess Elizabeth, 1938-44, 15" 400.00
French, compo, Little Betty, 1937-41, 9" 225.00
French, hp, str leg, mk Alex, 1973-75, 8" 55.00
Funny, cloth, 1963/77, 18" 65.00
Gainsborough, hp, vinyl arms, Jacqueline, #2184, 1968, 21" 700.00
Garden Party, hp, Margaret, 1953 only, 18" 1,200.00
German, hp, bend knee, Wendy Ann, 1966-72, 8" 125.00
German, wht face, 1986, 8" 65.00
Gibson Girl, eyeshadow, Cissette, 1962, 10" 950.00
Girl on Flying Trapeze, cloth, pk tutu, 1951 only, 40" 750.00
Godey, compo, Wendy Ann, 1945-47, 21" 1,900.00
Godey, hp, vinyl arms, Jacqueline, #2172, 1967, 21" 600.00
Godey Bride, hp, Margaret, 1950, 14" 850.00
Goldilocks, compo, Tiny Betty, 1938-42, 8" 245.00
Good Little Girl, cloth, 1966 only, 16" 110.00
Grave Alice, cloth, 1930s, 18" 650.00
Gretel, compo, Little Betty, 1938-40, 9" 245.00
Gretel, hp, wht face, str leg, mk Alexander, 1986, 8" 50.00
Groom, hp, Wendy Ann, 1961-63, 8" 350.00
Heidi, compo, Tiny Betty, 1938-39, 7" 245.00
Highland Fling, hp, Wendy Ann, 1955 only, 8" 775.00
Hyacinth, vinyl, toddler, 1953 only, 9" 165.00
Ibiza, Wendy Ann, 1989 only, 8" 65.00
India, hp, Cissette, 1962-63, 10" 1,800.00
Indian Boy, hp, bend knee, Wendy Ann, 1966 only, 8" 385.00
Italy, hp, str leg, mk Alex, 1973-75, 8" 55.00
Jack & Jill, compo, Tiny Betty, 1938-43, 7" 200.00
Jacqueline, hp/vinyl, 1961-62, 21" 675.00
Jeannie Walker, compo, 1940s, 14" 475.00
Jenny Lind, hp, vinyl arms, Jacqueline, 1969, #2191, 21" 1,600.00
John Power's Models, hp, Maggie & Margaret, 1952, 14", ea ..1,000.00
Juliet, compo, Wendy Ann, 1937-40, 18" 1,150.00
June Wedding, hp, Wendy Ann, 1956, 8" 375.00
Karen Ballernia, compo, Margaret, 1947-49, 15" 675.00
Kathleen Toddler, rigid vinyl, 1959 only, 12" 165.00
Kelly, hp, Lissy, 1959 only, 12" 425.00
Kitty Baby, compo, 1941-42, 21" 165.00
Lady Bird, Storybook Series, Maggie, 1988-89, 8" 55.00
Laurie, hp, bend knee, Little Men, Wendy Ann, 1966-72, 8" 125.00
Letty Bridesmaid, compo, Tiny Betty, 1938-40, 8" 225.00
Lissy Bridesmaid, hp, jtd knees & elbows, 1956-57, 12" 400.00
Little Audrey, vinyl, 1954 only 200.00
Little Granny, plastic/vinyl, Mary Ann, 1966, 14" 200.00
Little Minister, hp, Wendy Ann, 1957 only, 8" 1,700.00
Little Victoria, Wendy Ann, 1953-54 only, 7½" 1,100.00

Little Women, cloth, 1930-36, 16", ea	650.00
Littlest Kitten, vinyl, play attire, 8"	175.00
Lovey Dove, vinyl, c/m, rooted hair, 1958-59, 19"	150.00
Lucy Bride, compo, Wendy Ann, 1942-44, 21"	1,600.00
Madelaine, compo, Wendy Ann, 1940-42, 14"	500.00
Maggie Mixup, hp/vinyl, Elise body, 1960 only, 16½"	325.00
Maid of Honor, compo, Wendy Ann, 1940-44, 18"	675.00
Mary Muslin, cloth, pansy eyes, 1951 only, 19"	365.00
Mary Sunshine, plastic/vinyl, Caroline, 1961, 15"	365.00
Marybel, rigid vinyl, 1959-65, 16"	235.00
Melanie, compo, Wendy Ann, 1945-47, 21"	1,900.00
Melanie, hp, Wendy Ann, 1955-56, 8"	1,350.00
Mimi, multi-jtd body, skirt & sweater, 30"	450.00
Miss Muffett, hp, bend knee, Wendy Ann, 1965-72, 8"	125.00
Mommy & Me, compo, Margaret, 1948-49, 14"	800.00
Morocco, hp, bend knee, Wendy Ann, 1968-70, 8"	425.00
Muffin, cloth, 1966 only, 19"	125.00
Nancy Ann, hp, 1950 only, 17"	925.00
Netherland Boy, hp, str leg, Wendy Ann, 1974-75, 8"	55.00
Nina Ballerina, hp, Margaret, 1949-50, 14"	500.00
Old Fashioned Girl, compo, Betty, 1945-47, 13"	345.00
Pamela, hp, Lissy, takes wigs, 1962-63 only, 12"	500.00
Peasant, compo, Tiny Betty, 1936-37, 7"	200.00
Peter Pan, hp, Wendy Ann, 1953-54, 8"	1,100.00
Pip, cloth, Dickens character, early 1930s	600.00
Pocahontas, hp, bend knee, Wendy Ann, 1967-70, 8"	425.00
Polly, plastic/vinyl, 1965 only, 17"	250.00
Poodles, standing or sitting, 1940s, 14-17", ea	225.00
Prince Charles, hp, Wendy Ann, 1957 only, 8"	600.00
Princess Elizabeth, compo, 1937-41, 14"	425.00
Priscilla, cloth, mid-1930s, 18"	650.00
Queen, hp, Margaret, wht gown, velvet cape, 1953 only, 18"	1,100.00
Queen, vinyl, Elise head, gold gown, 18"	1,000.00
Queen Alexandrine, compo, Wendy Ann, 1939-41, 21"	1,800.00
Rebecca, compo, Wendy Ann, 1940-41, 21"	1,400.00
Red Riding Hood, compo, Tiny Betty, 1936-42, 7"	225.00
Renoir Child, plastic/vinyl, Nancy Drew, 1967 only, 12"	150.00
Romance, compo, Wendy Ann, 1945-46, 21"	1,900.00
Rosamund Bridesmaid, hp, Margaret, 1951 only, 15"	600.00
Royal Wedding, compo, Wendy Ann, 1939 only, 21"	1,900.00
Rusty, cloth/vinyl, 1967-68 only, 20"	300.00
Sailorette, hp, Portrette Series, Cissette, 1988 only, 10"	60.00

Scarlett O'Hara, compo, Tiny Betty, 1937-42, 7"	325.00
Scarlett O'Hara, hp, Maggie, 1950s, 14"	950.00
Scarlett O'Hara, hp/vinyl, Jacqueline, 1962, #2152, 21"	1,000.00
Sitting Pretty, foam body, 1965 only, 18"	385.00
Sleeping Beauty, hp, Cissette, bl clothes, 1959 only, 10"	425.00
Smarty, plastic/vinyl, 1962-63, 12"	285.00
Soldier, compo, Wendy Ann, 1943-44, 14"	675.00
South American, compo, Tiny Betty, 1938-43, 7"	200.00
Spanish Girl, hp, bend-knee walker, Wendy Ann, 1962-65, 8"	200.00
Suellen, compo, Wendy Ann, 1937-38, 14"	950.00
Sweet Baby, cloth/latex, 1948 only, 18½"	250.00
Swiss, compo, Tiny Betty, 1936, 7"	265.00
Three Little Pigs & Wolf, compo, 1938-93, ea	650.00
Tiny Tim, compo, Tiny Betty, 1934-37, 7"	235.00
Tommy Bangs, hp, Maggie, 1952 only	800.00
Turkey, hp, bend knee, Wendy Ann, 1968-72, 8"	125.00
Victoria, compo, Flavia, 1945-46, 21"	1,900.00
Vietnam, hp, Wendy Ann, 1968-69, 8"	375.00
WAAC, compo, Wendy Ann, 1943-44, 14"	675.00
Wendy Ann, compo, pnt eyes, 1936-40, 8"	400.00
Wendy Bride, hp, Margaret, 1951, 23"	650.00
Yugoslavia, str leg, mk Alex, 1973-75, 8"	55.00

Papier-Mache

All pnt, molded bust, jtd shoulders/hips, 1890s, 6½", EX	65.00
Blk molded hair, cloth body/leather arms, pnt eyes, RpC, 32"	2,200.00
Blond molded hair ShHd, cloth body, pnt eyes, 1880s, 20"	400.00
Blond molded hair w/bl ribbon, compo limbs, 1880s, RpC, 15"	600.00
French ShHd, leather arms, inset eyes, wig, RpC, 1830s, 30"	3,600.00
German ShHd, pnt eyes, jtd shoulders/hips, RpC, 10½"	95.00
Greiner, molded hair, glass eyes, rpt, 1858, RpC, 29"	1,500.00
Lacquer head, cloth body/wooden limbs, 1840s, RpC, 14"	800.00
Molded band in hair, c/m, glass eyes, rpt, RpC, 27"	1,600.00
Molded clown face, cloth body, OC (felt), 13½", NM	225.00
Molded features, cloth body, pin-jtd limbs, pnt eyes, 10"	165.00
Motschmann type, wood & twill body, glass eyes, nude, 26"	1,600.00
Puppet, bellows in stomach operates mouth, glass eyes, 12"	225.00
Santa, molded-pressed cb, EX pnt, ca 1920, 9½"	165.00
ShHd, pnt hair & eyes, leather body, rpl arms, RpC, 12", EX	265.00

Parian

Blond molded hair, pnt eyes, Germany, RpC, 14"	285.00
Boy, side-part molded hair, glass eyes, RpC, 17"	1,200.00
Countess Dagmar ShPl, cloth body, leather hands, RpC, 17"	575.00
Dolly Madison, molded upper/lower lids, RpC, 24½"	1,400.00
Dresden, wispy molded curls & flowers, cloth body, RpC, 19"	1,600.00
Eugenie braids, lustre plumes & snood, bl pnt eyes, 12"	800.00
Man, molded blond hair, cloth body, OC, 18"	650.00
Mechanical walker, p/e, decor shoulder front, RpC, 12½"	595.00
Molded band across hair, pnt eyes, p/e, RpC, 17½"	1,200.00
Molded curls w/appl decor in hair & on shoulders, p/e, 19"	1,600.00
Molded ringlets & neck ribbon, pnt eyes, exposed p/e, 18"	1,400.00
PF mk, lady, kid body, stitched toes, pwt, RpC, 19"	1,400.00
Pouty boy, pnt eyes, rpl wig, RpC, 15", EX	900.00

Schoenhut

Albert Schoenhut left Germany in 1866 to go to Pennsylvania to work as a repairman for toy pianos. He eventually applied his skills to wooden toys and later designed an all-wood doll which he patented on January 17, 1911. These uniquely jointed dolls were painted with enamels and came with a metal stand. Some of the later dolls had

Madame Alexander 'Spectator Sports' Wendy, 1960s, M, $325.00.

stuffed bodies, voice boxes, and hollow heads; some were made with heads of imitation bisque. These innovations influenced the development of the popular Bye-Lo Baby which was introduced in 1924. Due to the changing economy and fierce competition, the company closed in the mid-1930s.

Baby head, pnt hair & eyes, bent limbs, 16" 700.00
Character girl, cvd hair w/bow, intaglio eyes, jtd, OC, 14" 2,400.00
Dolly face, o/m, pnt eyes, spring jtd, wig, RpC, 17", EX 625.00
Girl, bl pnt eyes, long curled wig, all orig, 22", M 875.00
Girl, cvd hair w/comb mks, intaglio brn eyes, RpC, 19" 2,600.00
Girl, sleep decal eyes, o/m, molded metal teeth, RpC, 18" 1,500.00
Sailor boy, spring jtd, OC, 15", EX 650.00
Walker, pnt decal dyes, c/ or o/c mouth, OC, 17" 1,000.00
Wood, brush-stroke hair, pnt eyes, c/m, RpC, 14" 600.00
Wood, cvd hair w/head band, pnt eyes, c/m, RpC, 17" 2,000.00

SFBJ

By 1895, Germany was producing dolls of good quality at much lower prices than the French dollmakers because of lower wages in German factories. This was a serious threat to the French companies; in a supreme effort to save the doll industry, several leading French manufacturers united to form one large company in the hope they could combine their strengths to save the French market. Bru, Raberry and Delphieu, Pintel and Godshaux, Fleischman and Bodel, and Jumeau united to form the company today known as SFBJ. Their dolls did well while Germany was otherwise occupied with WWII, but after the war German doll production proved to be too strongly competitive, and SFBJ closed in 1958.

Bebe Parisiana, bsk head, c/m, inset eyes, 1902, 16" 2,800.00
Celestine, bsk SkHd on papier-mache, o/m, inset eyes, 18" 950.00
SkHd, jtd papier-mache/wood body, o/m, o/c eyes, 30" 2,700.00
Tete Jumeau, p/e, o/m, o/c eyes/lashes, 18" 1,400.00
Tete Jumeau, p/e, o/m w/teeth, o/c eyes, jtd wrists, 22" 1,900.00
15, o/c eyes, o/m w/teeth, wood/compo body, RpC, 15", EX 1,650.00
20, molded/pnt shoes & eyes, 5-pc body, Paris/12, 10" 350.00
203, 1900 bsk head on compo, o/c mouth, inset eyes, 20" 2,800.00
215, bsk swivel on compo, c/m, inset eyes, 15" 2,000.00
223, bsk, closed dome, o/m w/8 teeth, molded hair, 17" 2,000.00
227, brn swivel closed dome head, animal skin wig, 15" 2,400.00
227, brn swivel closed dome head, animal skin wig, 18" 2,000.00
227, closed dome, o/m, inset eyes, pnt hair, 15" 1,800.00
228, toddler, papier-mache body, c/m, inset eyes, 16" 2,000.00
229, compo w/swivel head, o/c mouth, inset eyes, 18" 3,500.00
229, wood walker, o/c mouth, inset eyes, 18" 3,600.00
230, compo walker, p/e, o/m, inset eyes, 16" 1,500.00
230, SkHd, p/e, o/m, o/c eyes, 23" 2,400.00
235, closed dome, molded hair, o/c mouth & eyes, 16" 2,300.00
235, closed dome, molded hair, o/c mouth & eyes, 8" 750.00
236, laughing Jumeau, o/m, o/c eyes, dbl chin, 12" 1,600.00
236, laughing Jumeau, o/m, o/c eyes, dbl chin, 20" 2,400.00
236, laughing Jumeau, o/m, o/c eyes, dbl chin, 22" 2,500.00
238, compo w/swivel head, o/m, inset eyes, Paris 6, 15" 3,000.00
239, Poulbot, c/m, street urchin, red wig, 14" 16,000.00
239, Poulbot, c/m, street urchin, red wig, 17" 19,000.00
245, boy, o/c mouth, lg glass eyes, googly, pnt shoes, 12" 2,800.00
245, boy, o/c mouth, lg glass eyes, googly, pnt shoes, 8" 1,000.00
247, toddler, o/c mouth/2 inset teeth, 16" 2,600.00
247, toddler, o/c mouth/2 inset teeth, 20" 2,900.00
247, toddler, o/c mouth/2 inset teeth, 24" 3,400.00
247, Twirp, SkHd, o/c mouth & eyes/2 teeth, 21" 2,800.00
251, toddler, 25" 2,900.00

251, 1099 character baby, o/c mouth, eyes, hair lashes, 16" 1,700.00
251, 1099 character baby, o/c mouth, eyes, hair lashes, 18" 2,000.00
252, pouty, c/m, inset eyes, papier-mache body, 11" 4,500.00
252, pouty, c/m, inset eyes, papier-mache body, 18" 6,200.00
252, pouty, c/m, inset eyes, papier-mache body, 22" 7,900.00
257, 1900 toddler, o/c mouth, inset eyes, 16" 2,500.00
266, character, bsk head, closed dome, o/c mouth, 20" 3,800.00
301, bsk SkHd on compo, o/m, inset eyes, 16" 725.00
301, bsk SkHd on compo, o/m, inset eyes, 22" 1,200.00
301, bsk SkHd on compo, o/m, inset eyes, 24" 1,100.00
301, bsk SkHd on compo, o/m, inset eyes, 28" 1,250.00
301, bsk SkHd on compo, o/m, inset eyes, 30" 2,000.00
60, French WWI nurse, 5-pc body, SFBJ/13/0, 8½" 400.00
60, kiss-blower, cryer/walker, 22" 2,200.00
60, o/m w/teeth, o/c eyes, jtd body & wrists, 25½" 950.00
60, SkHd, compo w/str legs, o/m, curved arms, 15" 650.00
60, SkHd, papier-mache/compo, plunger cryer, o/m, 1-pc, 11" ...450.00

Shirley Temple

Bsk, Japan, 7½" 265.00
Bsk head/compo body, 9", Japan, OC, 1936 ....400.00
Compo, 11", cowboy outfit, orig pin, EX 825.00
Compo, 11", Stand Up & Cheer, 1934, OC 700.00
Compo, 13", mk #1/13 on head & bk, 1934, OC 650.00
Compo, 13", o/m, o/c eyes, jtd shoulders/hips, 1936, OC 650.00
Compo, 13", tagged bl/wht dress w/pin, 1930s, all orig 650.00
Compo, 15", flirty eyes, cotton dress, all orig, 1934 ....675.00
Compo, 16", o/c eyes, o/m, handmade clothes, 1936, EX 675.00
Compo, 16", orig trench coat, ca 1934-35 ....685.00
Compo, 16", red dotted dress, velvet coat/hat, all orig 675.00
Compo, 18", Hawaiian, body mk Shirley Temple, Ideal, all orig ...850.00
Compo, 18", o/c eyes, o/m, jtd, mohair wig, Ideal, '30s, VG 685.00
Compo, 18", Wee Willie Winkie, OC, 1937 ....975.00
Compo, 20", designed by Mollye, all orig, 1933 ....750.00
Compo, 20", organdy dress, all orig, 1935 ....750.00
Compo, 20", tagged clothes, all orig, orig box 1,200.00
Compo, 22", teeth, orig bl dress w/daisies, Ideal, 1934, NM 925.00
Compo, 25", red cotton dress, OC, 1935 ....1,000.00
Compo, 27", flirty eyes, orig, EX 1,100.00
Compo, 30", unmk, M 450.00
Vinyl, 12", Captain January, 1958 ....200.00
Vinyl, 12", gr/wht dress, slip, complete, Ideal, 1957, MIB 200.00
Vinyl, 12", Heidi, Ideal, 1982, MIB 200.00
Vinyl, 12", velveteen dress, rpl shoes, 1959 ....165.00
Vinyl, 15", Cinderella, all orig, 1961 ....300.00
Vinyl, 15", flirty eyes, orig clothes, 1952, M 265.00
Vinyl, 15", Heidi, all orig, 1960, M 265.00
Vinyl, 15", Heidi outfit, w/pin & tag, 1957 ....300.00
Vinyl, 15", Little Red Riding, all orig, 1950s 265.00
Vinyl, 16", Rebecca, Ideal, 1972 ....200.00
Vinyl, 16", Stand Up & Cheer, 1973, MIB 200.00
Vinyl, 17", Heidi outfit, w/pin, MIB 400.00
Vinyl, 19", flirty eyes, all orig, 1957 ....450.00
Vinyl, 35", RpC, 1960 ....1,500.00
Vinyl, 36", pk pleated dress, EX 1,800.00
Vinyl, 8", Stowaway, Ideal, 1982 ....45.00

Simon and Halbig

Simon and Halbig was a large German doll firm that operated from ca 1870 until the 1930s. They were a popular supplier of bisque heads to French dollmakers of the 1870s and '80s. This company made dolls for such famous companies as Gimbel Bros., Jumeau, Kammer and

Reinhardt, as well as many others. Halbig became the sole owner of the company in 1895 but did not register 'S&H' as his trademark until ten years later.

Simon and Halbig, sleep eyes, open mouth, composition body, #1078 S & H 15, 15", $650.00 (as is, $165.00).

AW, SkHd, o/m, SH/13, 21" 675.00
Baby Blanche, SkHd, o/m baby, S&H, 16" 800.00
Baby Blanche, SkHd, o/m baby, S&H, 21" 950.00
CM Bergmann, SkHd, o/m, Simon & Halbig, 3 1/2, 18" 575.00
CM Bergmann, SkHd, o/m, 1895, Halbig/S&H5, 30" 1,300.00
CM Bergmann, SkHd, o/m, 1897, S&H6, 12" 350.00
CM Bergmann, SkHd, o/m w/teeth, Simon & Halbig, RpC, 32" ...1,400.00
Elenore, SkHd, o/m, CMB/Simon & Halbig, 18" 600.00
G68, SkHd, flirty eyes, 1908, S&H/K*R, 16" 550.00
Handwerck, SkHd, o/c eyes, o/m w/teeth, p/e, RpC, 38", EX ..1,250.00
Handwerck, SkHd, o/m, G/Halbig, 4, 26" 850.00
Handwerck, SkHd, o/m, o/c eyes, rpt jtd body, RpC, 33" 285.00
Handwerck, SkHd, o/m, S&H, 30" 650.00
Handwerck, SkHd, o/m, 1893, 16" 450.00
Handwerck, SkHd, o/m, 1895, G/S&H/1, 16" 450.00
Handwerck, SkHd, o/m w/teeth, Simon & Halbig, rpl wig, 32" ..1,045.00
S&H3, all bsk, c/m, inset eyes, molded-on shoes, 6" 285.00
10, SkHd, o/m, G/Halbig/S&H, 16" 475.00
10, SkHd, o/m, G/Halbig/S&H, 19" 575.00
10, SkHd, o/m, G/Halbig/S&H, 22" 675.00
10 1/2, SkHd, o/m, flirty o/c eyes, S&H, 18" 625.00
100, SkHd, o/m, Simon & Halbig/S&C/G, 15" 475.00
100, SkHd, o/m, Simon & Halbig/S&C/G, 22" 675.00
101, SkHd, c/m, Simon & Halbig/K*R, 16" 4,800.00
1039, SkHd, flirty bl eyes, jtd walking body, p/e, wig, 22" 575.00
1039, SkHd, o/m w/teeth, p/e, jtd arms/wrists, hh, 22" 725.00
1078, SkHd, o/m, pwt, p/e, S&H, RpC, 18½" 800.00
109, SkHd, o/m, 1895, Handwerck/G/Halbig, 23" 675.00
114, SkHd, c/m, glass eyes, Simon & Halbig K*R/L, 14" 6,300.00
114, SkHd, c/m, glass eyes, Simon Halbig K*R/L, 20" 7,900.00
114, SkHd, c/m, Simon & Halbig K*R/L, 9" 1,200.00
115, SkHd, c/m, 1912, K*R/Simon & Halbig, 16" 3,400.00
115a, SkHd, c/m pouty, K*R/Simon & Halbig, 15" 3,400.00
1159, SkHd, adult, 1905, G/Simon & Halbig/S&H7, 14" 1,200.00
1159, SkHd, adult, 1905, G/Simon & Halbig/S&H7, 18" 1,800.00
1159, SkHd, adult, 1905, G/Simon & Halbig/S&H7, 24" 2,700.00
1159, SkHd, swivel on ShPl, wood w/kid fashion, o/m, 19" 2,000.00

116a, SkHd, c/m, K*R/Simon & Halbig, 17" 3,200.00
116a-38, SkHd, 2 teeth, tongue, K*R/Simon & Halbig, 17" ...2,000.00
1160, Louisa May Alcott, bsk head, cloth body, 7", EX 115.00
117, SkHd, c/m, 1919, Simon & Halbig/K*R, 16" 4,000.00
117, SkHd, c/m, 1919, Simon & Halbig/K*R, 20" 4,700.00
117a, SkHd, c/m, K*R/Simon & Halbig, 16" 4,400.00
117a, SkHd, c/m, K*R/Simon & Halbig, 20" 5,000.00
117n, SkHd, o/m, Simon & Halbig/K*R, 20" 2,000.00
119, SkHd, o/m, 13/Handwerck 5/Halbig, 16" 575.00
121, SkHd, o/c mouth/teeth, flirty o/c eyes, 1920, K*R, 16" ...1,400.00
121, SkHd, o/c toddler, 16" 1,200.00
121, SkHd, o/m, 1920, K*R/Simon & Halbig, 14" 1,000.00
121, SkHd, o/m, 1920, K*R/Simon & Halbig, 19" 1,500.00
122, SkHd, 1920, K*R/Simon & Halbig, 14" 850.00
1249 Santa, bsk head, jtd compo, o/c eyes, o/m, p/e, 20" ...1,400.00
126, SkHd, o/c mouth, SH, 23" 950.00
126, SkHd, o/m, Simon & Halbig/K*R, 14" 500.00
126, SkHd, o/m, Simon & Halbig/K*R, 19" 800.00
126/36, SkHd, o/m, pwt, Simon & Halbig/K*R, 17" 800.00
127, SkHd, o/m, K*R/Simon & Halbig, 18" 675.00
128, SkHd, o/m, K*R/Simon & Halbig, 14" 800.00
128, SkHd, o/m, K*R/Simon & Halbig, 19" 1,300.00
1296, SkHd, 1911, FS&Co/Simon & Halbig, 14" 475.00
1329, SkHd, o/m, olive, G/Simon & Halbig/SH, 14" 2,200.00
151, SkHd, o/c mouth, pnt eyes, S&H/1, 16" 6,500.00
156, SkHd, 1925, S&H, 18" 625.00
156, SkHd, 1925, S&H, 22" 725.00
159, SkHd, o/m, Simon & Halbig, 16" 550.00
179, SkHd, o/m, Simon & Halbig S11H DEP, 20" 700.00
1848, SkHd, o/m, Jutta Simon & Halbig, 16" 650.00
191, SkHd, o/m, Bergmann/CB, 18" 625.00
1923, SkHd, o/m, SH Sp 53/4/G, 14" 500.00
1923, SkHd, o/m, SH Sp 53/4/G, 21" 700.00
1923, SkHd, o/m, SH Sp 53/4/G, 26" 950.00
246, SkHd, o/m, 1900, K*R/Simon & Halbig, 18" 650.00
282, SkHd, o/m, SH, 14" 500.00
282, SkHd, o/m, SH, 18" 650.00
282, SkHd, o/m, SH, 22" 725.00
383, SkHd, flapper body, SH, 14" 1,200.00
402, SkHd, o/m, K*R SH, 16" 625.00
403, SkHd, o/c mouth, K*R, Simon & Halbig, 20" 2,800.00
403, SkHd, o/m, pwt, papier-mache body, RpC, 18½" 585.00
403, SkHd, o/m, walker, K*R SH, 21" 1,400.00
409, SkHd, o/m, S&H, 24" 685.00
409, SkHd, o/m, S&H, 26" 850.00
409, SkHd, o/m, S&H, 30" 1,400.00
48m SkHd, o/m, 1905, Simon & Halbig/K*R, 27" 1,000.00
50, SkHd, c/m, Simon & Halbig, 16" 1,800.00
50, SkHd, c/m, 1900, K*R/Simon & Halbig, 14" 500.00
53, SkHd, c/m, brn bsk, Simon & Halbig/K*R, 16" 1,800.00
530, SkHd, o/m, G/Simon & Halbig, 21" 675.00
540, SkHd, o/m, G/Halbig/S&H, 16" 750.00
540, SkHd, swivel on bsk ShPl, o/m, S&H, G, 16" 750.00
55, SkHd, o/m, flirty eyes, p/e, Simon & Halbig/K*R, 23" 575.00
550, SkHd, o/m, Simon & Halbig/S&H, 16" 525.00
570, SkHd, o/m, Halbig S&H/G, 18" 700.00
570, SkHd, o/m, walking, head turns, G/Halbig S&H, 18" 750.00
576, SkHd, o/m, Simon & Halbig, 16" 575.00
612, SkHd, o/m, MIG/S&H/CM Bergmann, 16" 550.00
670, SkHd, o/m, Simon & Halbig, 16" 575.00
70, SkHd, o/m, 1896, Halbig/K*R, 26" 850.00
70, SkHd, o/m w/teeth, Simon & Halbig/K*R, 28" 1,200.00
719, SkHd, bjtd, o/m, S12H/Dep, rpl wig, RpC, 20", EX 2,400.00
719, SkHd, c/m, S&H DEP, 16" 1,800.00

719, SkHd, swivel, ShPl, c/m, S&H, DEP, 20" 2,800.00
739, SkHd, c/m, brn, S 5 H DEP, 14" 1,800.00
739, SkHd, c/m, brn, S 5 H DEP, 18" 2,400.00
759, SkHd, o/m, brn, S 10 H DEP, 20" 900.00
769, SkHd, c/m, S&H DEP, 17" 2,300.00
905, SkHd, swivel on ShPl, c/m, SH, 21" 3,300.00
908, SkHd, swivel on ShPl, c/m, SH, 16" 2,600.00
929, SkHd, c/m, S&H, DEP, 20" 2,400.00
929, SkHd, c/m, S&H, DEP, 25" 3,200.00
939, SkHd, c/m, S 11H DEP, 17" 2,600.00
939, SkHd, c/m, S 11H DEP, 23" 3,000.00
939, SkHd, o/c eyes, o/m, S16H, 30" 3,600.00
940, SkHd, closed dome, o/c mouth, S 2 H, 26" 3,600.00
940, SkHd, swivel on ShPl, o/c mouth, S 2 H, 14" 2,000.00
945, SkHd, c/m, S 2 H DEP, 16" 2,000.00
949, ShHd, o/c eyes, o/m, S 10 H, bride clothes, 19½" 900.00
99, SkHd, o/m, 1899, 11 1/2 Handwerck/Halbig, 16" 525.00

Steiner

Jules Nicholas Steiner established one of the earliest French doll manufactories in 1855. Having been a clockmaker, he began with mechanical dolls and his patents grew to include walking and talking dolls. In 1880 he registered a patent for a doll with moving eyes. This doll could be put to sleep by turning a rod that operated a wire attached to its eyes. Though these new innovations brought much acclaim to the Steiner company, it closed around 1910 because it could not compete with the less-expensive German dolls that were flooding the market at that time.

A Series child, c/m, o/c eyes, jtd, cb pate, RpC, 16" 5,000.00
A Series child, c/m, o/c eyes, jtd, cb pate, RpC, 28" 6,800.00
A Series child, o/m, o/c eyes, jtd, cb pate, RpC, 16" 2,400.00
Bourgoin, c/m, jtd body, pwt, 1870s, RpC, 25" 8,000.00
C Ceries, jtd body, bl eyes, c/m, p/e, RpC, 16" 5,200.00
C Series w/wire eyes, RpC, 16" 5,400.00
Le Parisien, Blk, c/m, brn glass eyes, 1900, Oc, 13" 4,000.00
Le Parisien, papier-mache/wood jtd body, c/m, p/e, RpC, 14" .4,000.00
Mechanical, key wound, o/m w/teeth, RpC, 18" 1,800.00
Motchmann style, bsk, no damage, RpC, 18" 5,400.00
Pk wash over eyes, jtd body, RpC, 14" 1,200.00
Unmk, early wht bsk, rnd face, jtd, o/m w/teeth, RpC, 14" 4,200.00
Wire eyes, c/m, jtd body, RpC, 20" 4,600.00
Wire eyes, jtc compo w/str wrists, c/m, RpC, 25" 7,600.00

Vogue

Compo, o/c eyes, mohair wig, all orig, w/tag, 14" 345.00
Ginny, vinyl, Black, all orig, 8" 95.00
Ginny, vinyl, International, 1977, M 50.00
Hug a Bye Baby, OC, 1975, 16" 40.00
Jill, OC, 1957, 10" 145.00
Miss Ginny, 1974, OC, 15" 65.00
Precious Baby, vinyl, o/c eyes, rooted hair, 1975, OC, 12" 45.00
Wee Imp, red wig, OC, 8" 400.00

Wax, Poured Wax

English, leather arms, cloth body, glass eyes, 1830s, 25" 1,800.00
English baby, rooted hair, RpC, 15" 1,200.00
French fashion type, glass eyes, p/e, RpC, 18½" 950.00
Over compo, bl o/c eyes, c/m, p/e, blond wig, RpC, 17", VG 265.00
Over compo, ShHd, cloth body, kid hands, RpC, 33", VG 1,200.00
Over papier-mache, cloth body, glass eyes, 1880s, RpC, 17" 500.00

Over papier-mache, cloth body, glass set eyes, 1880s, 20" 700.00
Over papier-mache, cloth body, wood limbs, pnt eyes, 9" 185.00
Pompadour, over papier-mache, glass eyes, wig, 23" 600.00
Poured, trn ShHd, cloth body, glass eyes, 1870s, RpC, 18" 675.00
Pumpkin head, molded hair, o/c eyes, compo limbs, RpC, 17" ...600.00
Pumpkin head w/snood, wax over wood limbs, 1850s, RpC, 26" ..1,800.00
Trn ShHd, glass eyes, glued-on hair, cloth body/wax limbs, 20" .650.00

Miscellaneous

Borgfeldt #329, bsk head, o/c eyes, o/m, blond wig, RpC, 15" 300.00
Gesso over wood, glass eyes, pnt torso, English, RpC, 12" 1,300.00

Door Knockers

Door knockers, those charming precursors of the door bell, come in an intriguing array of shapes and styles. The very rare ones come from England. Cast iron examples made in this country were often produced in forms similar to the more familiar doorstop figures.

Basket of ivy, red & gr pnt, #123 ....95.00
Beaded flowers, EX mc pnt 95.00
Bear & tree, brass, Warwychi, 6½" 67.00
Butterfly, gold pnt 100.00
Eagle, CI, EX detail, 8" 145.00
Falstaff, brass 45.00
French basket, pnt CI, EX 125.00
Gargoyle, cherubs & shield on bronze, no striker, 12" 235.00
George Washington, pnt CI, EX 145.00
Girl knocking at door, pnt CI, EX 225.00
Hand w/ball at finger tips, brass, 1870s, 5" L 85.00
Lady's hand holds ball, CI, w/strike plate, 6½" 150.00
Lion's head, CI, worn gold pnt, 4¼x6½x1½" 85.00
Mexican on burrow, brass 45.00
Parrot, metal, mc pnt, NM 100.00
Parrot in flight, pnt CI, EX 110.00
Parrot on floral branch, mc pnt, EX 50.00
Parrot w/long curved tail, mc pnt 85.00

Doorstops

Although introduced in England in the mid-1800s, cast iron doorstops were not made to any great extent in this country until after the Civil War. Once called 'door porters,' their function was to keep doors open to provide better ventilation. They have been produced in many shapes and sizes, both dimensional and flat backed, and in the past few years have become a popular, yet affordable collectible. While cast iron examples are the most common, brass, wood, and chalk were also used. An average price is in the $40 to $50 range, though some are valued at more than $200. Doorstops retained their usefulness and appeal well into the thirties.

The prices below reflect market values in the East where doorstops are now at a premium. For other areas of the country, it may be necessary to adjust prices down about 25%. In the listings below, items are assumed flat backed unless noted full figured and cast iron unless noted otherwise. For further information we recommend *Doorstops, Identification and Values*, by Jeanne Bertoia.

Key: ff – full figured

Art Deco Dancer, worn mc rpt, 11⅛" 145.00
Aunt Jemima, arms akimbo, ff, 13¼x8", G 150.00

Bird w/Curved Beak, mk KS, 8x6", EX 200.00
Boston Bulldog, stands/looks right, CI w/VG blk & wht, 11" 100.00

Bobby Blake, by Hubley, very worn paint, 9½", $300.00.

Campbell Kid, standing girl, worn orig mc pnt, 9½" 300.00
Cape Cod Fisherman, 1928, orig mc pnt, 5⅝", VG 35.00
Carpenter, in orange shirt, ff, VG pnt, 5½x2¾" 175.00
Cat, Hunchbk; ff, blk pnt, 10⅝x7½", EX 140.00
Cat, Seated; ff, old blk pnt, heavy, 6¾" 85.00
Cat Licking Paw, c 1926 Waverly Studio, mc rpt, 7¾" 175.00
Cat w/Handle, ff, VG pnt, very heavy, 15½x3¼" 275.00
Chase Deco Cat, bronze & copper, wedge, 8½x4½", VG 150.00
Cockatoo, orig pnt, 7¾", VG 80.00
Comical Dog, Greenblatt #17, 1927, 10x4¾", EX 400.00
Cosmos, Hubley #182, 9x7¼", EX 140.00
Cottage, AA Richardson #19, EX pnt, 5⅛x8" 200.00
Covered Wagon, Hubley, orig mc pnt, w/paper label, 6½" L 95.00
Crazy Cat, Nat'l Foundry, ff, yel/red/blk pnt, 7x3¾", EX 325.00
Dog, Modernistic; Hubley, ff, 11x5½", VG 55.00
Dog, Seated; Greenblatt, 1927, aluminum rpt w/red, 9½" 35.00
Dog in Doghouse, G silver pnt, 6x4⅛" 75.00
Drum Major, ff, bl variation, 13½x6½", EX 300.00
Eagle w/Spread Wings, ff, mk BS Co, old gold pnt, 7" 55.00
Elephant, Hubley, ff, orig red pnt, 8¼x12", EX 125.00
Fireplace, orig mc pnt, 4⅜", VG 55.00
Flower Basket, Creation Co #163, 1930, EX pnt, 9x5⅜" 125.00
Galleon in Full Sail, old mc pnt, 5" 45.00
Geisha, seated w/instrument, Hubley, ff, EX pnt, 7x6" 225.00
Girl w/Full Dress, wedge, VG pnt, 8½x6" 225.00
Gnome Smoking Pipe, ff, 6½x10", EX 350.00
Good Night Elf, B&H, Good Night in raised letters, 8x4", EX ...375.00
Goose w/Spread Wings, ff, lt worn blk pnt, 7" 15.00
Half Gnome, Dick Bros Inc, 1930, 10¾x5½" 225.00
Horse, Nat'l Foundry #12, VG pnt, 8x10" 175.00
Lilies, orig wht/gr/yel/blk pnt, 10½", VG 140.00
Lion, mk CPR 1930 161, G beige & brn pnt, 7⅜x7¼" 75.00
Lobster, EX pnt, 12½x6½" 400.00
London & Royal Mail Coach, mk AAW, orig mc pnt, 7" 30.00
Lyre, Hubley, EX pnt, 10x6" 175.00
Man in Tuxedo, old mc pnt, 7½" 175.00
Monkey on Barrel, Taylor Cook #3, 1930, worn pnt, 8⅜x4⅞" ...325.00
Mrs Slope, comic mother w/Punch & Judy babies, brass, 11" 125.00
Narcissus, Hubley #266, 7¼x6¾", EX 125.00
Nautical Anchor, B&H, 11x5¼", EX 185.00
Oriental Man, ff, EX orig pnt, 9x7¼" 275.00
Pansy Bowl, Hubley #256, 7x6½", EX 165.00
Parrot, mk 1289, w/rubber knobs, 8x3⅞", EX 300.00
Parrot in Ring, unmk B&H, G pnt, 8x7" 75.00

Parrot on Perch, bright colors, 14" 175.00
Patrol, Grenier Studios, ff, old mc pnt, 8½", VG 175.00
Peacock w/Fan-Spread Tail, old mc pnt, 6⅛" 175.00
Pekingese, ff w/concave bk, old pnt, 5½x4¼", EX 175.00
Penguin in Top Hat, ff, CI w/orig pnt, 10" 325.00
Penguin in Top Hat, Hubley, ff, 10½x3¾", VG 200.00
Petunias & Asters, Hubley #470, 9½x6½", EX 400.00
Pheasant, ff, realistic, 10x14", VG 165.00
Pilgrim Ship, B&H, 8¾x6", EX 175.00
Pirate, ff, old mc pnt, 7", G 35.00
Pirate on Treasure Chest, ff, old silver pnt, 6", G 55.00
Pointing Setter, Hubley, 4¾x10¼", VG 165.00
Poppies & Cornflowers, Hubley #265, 7¼x6½", EX 150.00
Pot of Tulips, ribbed pot, EX orig pnt, 8" 125.00
Pup, Porcelainized; ff, 6x5", EX 125.00
Reading Girls, EX pk & bl pnt, 5x8⅝" 650.00
Rebecca at the Well, mc pnt, 10x14⅜", VG 265.00
Russian Wolfhound, ff, orig pnt, 10x15¾", VG 150.00
Sailboat, mk Made in USA, ff, orig mc pnt, 5¾", VG 105.00
Sailor, ff, orig pnt, 8½", VG 145.00
Scottish Terrier, orig mc pnt, 5½", G 55.00
Spaniel, bronze, silhouette w/relief, gr patina, 11x17" 150.00
St George & Dragon, bronze pnt, 6⅜" 25.00
Stagecoach, Hubley #376, EX pnt, 11¼x5⅞" 175.00
Stork, Hubley, ff, 12¼x7", VG 450.00
Sunbonnet Baby, old worn mc pnt, 6¼" 145.00
Tiger Lilies, Hubley #472, 10½x6", EX 225.00
Vase of Flowers, B&H, w/orig rubber knobs, 11¾x6", EX 275.00
Whippet, ff, VG pnt, 8½x9" 350.00
Windmill, mk N512, EX pnt, 9½x7" 375.00
Yawning Child, kneeling, mk M-L COOP-NYC, ff, 9x5", NM ..425.00
2 Men in Livery, Fish, orig pnt, 12", EX 900.00
3 Dogs, begging, worn orig mc pnt, 4⅝" 155.00

Dorflinger

C. Dorflinger was born in Alsace, France, and came to this country when he was ten years old. When still very young, he obtained a job in a glass factory in New Jersey. As a young man, he started his own glassworks in Brooklyn, New York, opening new factories as profits permitted. During that time he made cut glass articles for many famous people including President and Mrs. Lincoln, for whom he produced a complete service of tableware with the United States Coat of Arms. In 1863 he sold the New York factories because of ill health and moved to his farm near White Mills, Pennsylvania. His health returned, and he started a plant near his home. It was there that he did much of his best work, making use of only the very finest materials. Christian died in 1915, and the plant was closed in 1921 by consent of the family.

Dorflinger glass is rare and often hard to identify. Very few pieces were marked — many only carried a small paper label which was quickly discarded.

Humdior, Middlesex, cut lid, 9" 900.00
Pitcher, champagne; X-cut sqs & fans, 11¼" 350.00
Pitcher, X-cut dmns/strawberry dmns/fans, 7¼" 275.00
Vase, cranberry cut to clear, relief dmns, att, 10" 300.00
Vase, cut/eng, frosted floral, tumbler shape, att, 8" 120.00
Vase, Kalana Narcisci, 14½" 295.00
Vase, Kalana Pansy, ruffled, wide rim, 5x8" 145.00
Wine, Kalana Lily, 5" 90.00

Dragon Ware

Dragon Ware is fairly accessible and is still being made today. The 'new' Dragon Ware is distinguishable by the lack of detail in the dragon. In the older pieces, much care is given to the slipwork dragon's eyes, scales, and wings. In the new ware, the dragon is 'flat' and lacks detail.

Colors are 'primary,' referring to background color, not the color of the dragon. The primary color of a 'new' piece has more shine than the older ware. Old colors are vibrant but for the most part not shiny (except for the lustre colors). 'New' colors include green, lavender, yellow, pink, blue, pearlized, and orange as well as the classic blue/black. Old colors include orange, green, yellow, blue, pearlized, and blue/black. In addition to lustre finishes, you will find some background colors that are applied unevenly (and without shine), producing a 'cloud' effect behind the dragon.

Many Dragon Ware cups have lithophanes in the bottoms, often the face of a geisha girl. Nude lithophanes are more scarce but can sometimes be found in cups and saki cups. New pieces may also have lithophanes, but they are lacking in detail and tend to be flat.

Our advisor for this category is Suzi Hibbard; she is listed in the Directory under California.

Box, cigarette; +2 ashtrays	30.00
Box, egg form, ftd, mk Saji, 3"	30.00
Box, ruffled lid w/gold trim, 6½x5"	45.00
Castor set, 6-pc on 10" tray	125.00
Cup & saucer, bl, child's	12.50
Cup & saucer, demitasse; bl, no lithophane	15.00
Cup & saucer, geisha lithophane	25.00
Cup & saucer, gr, no lithophane	17.50
Cup & saucer, nude lithophane	30.00
Cup & saucer & pie plate, Bl Cloud, lithophane	40.00
Incense burner, 3"	15.00
Nappy, brn, sq, mk MIJ, 6"	25.00
Nappy, wht beads, brn rim, mk MIJ, 5"	25.00
Pitcher, mini, 1¾"	10.00
Plate, mk Japan, 10"	40.00
Plate, wht beads & lav rim, 6"	20.00
Plate, wht beads & lav rim, 8"	25.00
Saki set, +6 cups w/lithophanes	35.00
Saki set, +6 cups w/nude lithophanes	45.00
Snack set, 8½" L	45.00
Spoon holder, demitasse; bl	35.00
Tea set, Bl Cloud, lithophanes, Kutani, 21-pc	325.00
Tea set, child's, 5-pc, pot+cr/sug+cup & saucer	40.00
Tea set, gold dragons on cobalt, sgn Shofar on pot, 15-pc	425.00
Tea set, lithophane, 15-pc	150.00
Tea set, no lithophane, 15-pc	110.00
Teapot, gold hdl, 7"	45.00
Vase, ftd, integral hdls, sm neck w/ruffled rim, Nippon, 7"	200.00
Vase, gold trim, 6"	85.00
Vase, orange, 8"	60.00
Vase, orange lustre, hdls, 9"	95.00
Vase, pearlized, 6"	45.00
Vase, slender form, 6"	50.00
Vase, 3"	15.00
Vase, 4½", pr	40.00
Vase, 6"	45.00
Whistling cup & saucer, orange, mk MIJ	25.00

Dresden

The term Dresden is used today to indicate the porcelains that were produced in Meissen and Dresden, Germany, from the very early 18th century well into the next. John Bottger, a young alchemist, discovered the formula for the first true porcelain in 1708 while being held a virtual prisoner at the palace in Dresden because of the King's determination to produce a superior ware. Two years later a factory was erected in nearby Meissen with Bottger as director. There fine tableware, elaborate centerpieces, and exquisite figurines with applied details were produced. In 1731, to distinguish their product from the wares of such potters as Sevres, Worcester, Chelsea, and Derby, the Meissen company adopted their famous crossed swords trademark. During the next century, several potteries were producing porcelain in the 'Meissen style' in Dresden itself. Their wares were often marked with imitations of Meissen's crossed swords.

The Carl Theime factory produced dinnerware as well as decorative pieces in the Meissen style from 1872 until 1972. Openwork pieces were their specialty. Their mark was an intertwined 'SP' with the word Dresden below. Other companies followed suit and in 1883 began using the crown mark along with the Dresden indication. Several variations of this mark were employed over the years. Many of these companies produced Meissen-type wares well into the 20th century.

Our advisor for this category is Donald Penrose; he is listed in the Directory under Ohio. See also Meissen; Pottschappel.

Basket, rtcl, appl flowers, 4 baroque ft, floral hdl, 5x7"	150.00
Bowl, HP/appl flowers, sgn Frulauf, boat form w/4 sq ft, 17"	350.00
Ewer, floral sprays, gold latticework/scrolls, 8½"	275.00
Figurine, boy w/instrument, girl in lace dress, lamb, 7x9"	550.00
Figurine, girl in flower-trimmed lace dress, yel hat, 8"	350.00
Figurine, Gypsy seated, goat w/front ft in her lap, 11x8"	450.00
Figurine, ladies seated, 1 w/book, 2nd w/flowers, 12x10"	950.00
Figurine, lady in chair w/vase of flowers, dog at ft, 8x8"	325.00
Figurine, lady in yel bonnet & red dress, 8"	350.00
Figurine, lady on couch w/music, man w/violin, 10½x10"	850.00
Figurine, man in floral coat (& lady) on goat, 8x10", pr	1,650.00
Figurine, man in red & lady in lace dress dance, MZ, 5x6"	250.00
Figurine, man w/violin stands, 2nd sits, lady at piano, 10"	975.00
Figurine, monkey band, 8-pc, 6½"	1,200.00
Figurine, musicians w/lute & bagpipes, barmaid dances, 12"	1,250.00
Figurine, 2 ladies dressed in lace & man having tea, 8x12"	950.00
Figurine, 3 girls, arms raised, dance in circle, WR, 6½x9"	295.00

Plaque, brother and sister lost in forest, signed, framed, 6x4", $1,600.00.

Plaque, Fidelite, ¾-length portrait, sgn Wagner, 7x5"	2,500.00
Plaque, girl clutches boy's arm, lost in forest, sgn, 6x4"	1,600.00
Plaque, girl leans against sq column, sgn Wagner, 6x4"	1,400.00

Plaque, Magdalene, after Battoni, Buckner label, 7x5" 900.00
Plaque, Ruth w/sheaves of wheat, fr, 6x4" 525.00
Plaque, young mother holds sleeping baby, sgn Miller, 7x5" ...1,000.00
Urn, floral basket on bl, band of gold rings w/flowers, 21" 1,250.00
Urn, 2 panels of lovers on red w/florals, R Kelmn, 12x6½" 850.00
Vase, floral sprays on emerald, baluster, 14" 550.00
Wall pocket, HP floral & appl Cupid, 7x9", pr 495.00

Dresser Accessories

Dresser sets, ring trees, figural or satin pincushions, manicure sets — all those lovely items that graced milady's dressing table — were at the same time decorative as well as functional. Today they appeal to collectors for many reasons. The Victorian era is well represented by repousse silver-backed mirrors and brushes and pincushions that were used to display ornamental pins for the hair, hats, and scarves. The hair receiver — similar to a powder jar but with an opening in the lid — was used to hold the lovely strands of hair retrieved from the comb or brush. These were wound around the finger and tucked in the opening to be used later for hair jewelry and pictures, many of which survive to the present day. (See Hair Weaving.)

Celluloid dresser sets were popular during the late 1800s and early 1900s. Some included manicure tools, pill boxes, and buttonhooks, as well as the basic items. Because celluloid tends to break rather easily, a whole set may be hard to find today. (See also Plastics.) With the current interest in anything Art Deco, sets from the thirties and forties are especially collectible. These may be made of crystal, Bakelite, or silver, and the original boxes just as lavishly appointed as their contents.

Box, lav glass, swirled egg form, hinged lid, 7¼x4" 175.00
Box, patch; yel enamel courting scene, Cartier 185.00
Box, sapphire bl glass w/HP florals, hinged lid, 2¾x4¾" 195.00
Box, sterling/tortoise shell, Mappin & Webb, 1926, 5½x3½" 350.00

Dresser set, amber mother-of-pearl plastic, six pieces on 7x9½" tray, $60.00.

Hair receiver, SP w/emb decor, gilt int, Wilcox 25.00
Hairpin holder, Mauchlineware, cylindrical 28.00
Nail file, Nouveau lady w/flowing hair, mk Sterling, 7½" 65.00
Set, brn mottled celluloid, beveled mirror, 10-pc 50.00
Set, cut crystal, 2 colognes+powder jar+hair receiver, 1920s 395.00
Set, floral china, 2 scent cruets+2 boxes+pin tray+12" tray 225.00
Set, French ivory celluloid, 9-pc (includes clock) 85.00
Set, gold-tone metal w/HP floral medallion, 1930s, 9-pc, MIB ...225.00
Set, hand mirror & 2 brushes, German silver filigree 125.00
Set, milk glass, HP/emb florals, flower stoppers, 4-pc+tray 95.00
Set, sterling, cut glass jar, Levitt & Gold, 1920s, 11-pc 575.00
Tray, glass, cut & eng butterflies/lilies/birds, 4-ftd, '10s 195.00

Dryden

James Dryden founded Dryden Pottery in July, 1946, in Ellsworth,

Kansas. For ten years Dryden produced pottery from clay dug from the hills of Ellsworth County. Pieces were cast in molds and then glazed using processes Dryden learned while studying ceramics at the University of Kansas. Glazes were produced from volcanic ash, and recipes for them were a guarded secret. James Dryden is still numbered among the few potters who possessed the secret of decorative glazing with just one firing. Ellsworth Dryden was shipped to over six hundred retail outlets in forty different states. In the 1950s Dryden sold some pottery to Van Briggle to offset losses in counter sales. When I-70 opened taking tourist traffic away from Dryden's plant, James Dryden moved to Hot Springs, Arkansas, in 1956. Since the late 1960s, most of the pottery has been wheel thrown.

It is easy to recognize those pieces produced in Kansas, because they were made with a dark tan clay. Arkansas pottery pieces are pure white. Almost all of the pottery is marked with the Dryden signature. Kansas pieces may also show a mold number and a paper label. Of special interest to collectors are those pieces in animal shapes (elephants, panthers, and donkeys, for instance) and those sold as souvenirs (i.e., the K.U. jug).

Our advisor for this category is Ralph Winslow; he is listed in the Directory under Kansas.

Boot, Ellsworth 1867-1947, #47, 4½" 16.00
Boot, Loveland Colo, gr, #90, 4½" 16.00
Bowl, blk, #44, 14" 22.00
Bowl, yel, #40, 6½" 13.50
Candle holder, brn, Ark, #L01-74 ....8.00
Creamer, yel, #7H, 3" 9.00
Creamer & sugar bowl, #108, 3" 25.00
Creamer & sugar bowl, gr, #900, 3½" 20.00
Elephant, blk, 11" 50.00
Ewer, commemorative, #715 ....47.50
Jardiniere, aqua, Ark, 11" 45.00
Jug, #102, 5" 15.00
Jug, maroon, KU, mini 25.00
Mug, barrel, blk, #8, 3½" 12.00
Mug, face, Ark, L01-77, 3¾" 15.00
Pitcher, aqua, #180, 4" 16.00
Pitcher, bl, #98, 5½" 13.00
Pitcher, bl, Lawrence Kans, #12, 3½" 20.00
Pitcher, Canistota SD, #50, 6½" 18.00
Pitcher, Carry Nation, maroon, #H-1, mini, 3½" 18.00
Pitcher, gr, #101 ....28.00
Pitcher, maroon, #192, 6" 15.00
Pitcher, syrup; Lindsborg Kans, #94, 6" 25.00
Pitcher, Valley Forge, #950, 4" 17.00
Pitcher, water; blk, #49, 11" 35.00
Planter, rooster, maroon, #Y 22.00
Shakers, mustard, #70, 4", pr 16.00
Shakers, Wichita KS, #73, 4", pr 18.00
Tray, leaf, Brookville Hotel, #110, 4" 18.00
Tray, mustard, #7B, 2" 10.00
Tray, yel, #7A, 5" 12.50
Tumbler, blk, #4, 6" 10.00
Vase, aqua, #190, 6½" 18.00
Vase, bl, #95, pr, 7" 30.00
Vase, brn, sq, #18, 3¼" 15.00
Vase, bulbous, #106, 3½" 15.00
Vase, Bull Shoals Dam, A3, sq 47.50
Vase, deer, pk, #7X, 8½" 22.00
Vase, donkey, brn, #21, 4½" 17.50
Vase, elephant, #313, 3" 16.50
Vase, fish, yel, #7M, 4" 16.00
Vase, ivy leaves, bl, #955, 5½" 19.00

Vase, leaf, yel, Bridal Cave, #7K 14.00
Vase, leaves, gr, 5" 23.00
Vase, maroon, sq, #17, 4" 16.00
Vase, mustard, #6A, 6" 16.00
Vase, sq, #16, 5", pr 29.00
Vase, yel, bulbous, #105, 4½" 16.00
Wall pocket, leaf, #887, 6" 25.00

Duncan and Miller

The firm that became known as the Duncan and Miller Glass Company in 1900 was organized in 1874 in Pittsburgh, Pennsylvania, and was a partnership between George Duncan, his sons Harry and James, and his son-in-law Augustus Heisey. John Ernest Miller was hired as their designer. He is credited with creating the most famous of all Duncan's glassware lines, Three Face. (See Pattern Glass.) The George Duncan and Sons Glass Company, as it was titled, was only one of eighteen companies that merged in 1891 with U.S. Glass. Soon after the Pittsburgh factory burned in 1892, the association was dissolved, and Heisey left the firm to set up his own factory in Newark, Ohio. Duncan built his new plant in Washington, Pennsylvania, where he continued to make pressed glassware in such notable patterns as Bagware, Amberette, Duncan Flute, Button Arches, and Zippered Slash. The firm was eventually sold to U.S. Glass in Tiffin, Ohio, and unofficially closed in August 1955.

In addition to the early pressed dinnerware patterns, today's Duncan and Miller collectors enjoy searching for opalescent vases in many patterns and colors, frosted 'Satin Tone' glassware, acid-etched designs, and lovely stemware such as the Rock Crystal cuttings. Milk glass was made in limited quantity and is considered a good investment. Ruby glass, Ebony (a lovely opaque black glass popular during the twenties and thirties), and, of course, the glass animal and bird figurines are all highly valued examples of the art of Duncan and Miller.

Expect to pay at least 25% more than values listed for 'color' for ruby and cobalt and as much as 50% more in the Georgian, Pall Mall, and Sandwich lines. Pink, green, or amber Sandwich is worth approximately 30% more than the same items in crystal. Milk glass examples of American Way are valued up to 30% higher than color, 50% higher in Pall Mall. Add approximately 40% to listed prices for opalescent items. Etchings, cuttings, and other decorations will increase values by about 50%. For further study we recommend *The Encyclopedia of Duncan Glass* by Gail Krause; she is listed in the Directory under Pennsylvania. Another book of great interest is *Glass Animals and Figural Flower Frogs of the Depression Era* by Lee Garmon and Dick Spencer; they are both listed under Illinois. See also Glass Animals.

Astaire, crystal; cocktail 7.00
Canterbury, bl opal; relish, 3-part, 9" 32.00
Canterbury, crystal; bowl, oval, 9" 18.00
Canterbury, crystal; cigarette box, silver lid 45.00
Canterbury, crystal; clover tray, 4-part 18.00
Canterbury, crystal; cocktail 8.00
Canterbury, crystal; compote, high ft 22.00
Canterbury, crystal; gardenia bowl, 7½" 15.00
Canterbury, crystal; ice cream/sherbet 6.00
Canterbury, crystal; relish, 2-part, silver o/l 24.00
Canterbury, crystal; relish, 2-part, 7" 12.00
Canterbury, crystal; relish, 3-part 15.00
Canterbury, crystal; relish, 3-part, gold o/l 20.00
Canterbury, crystal; sandwich/cake plate, hdls, 10½" 30.00
Canterbury, crystal; wine 14.00
Caribbean, bl; champagne 45.00
Caribbean, bl; creamer 35.00

Caribbean, bl; goblet, water 40.00
Caribbean, bl; mustard 75.00
Caribbean, bl; nappy, hdl, 10" 75.00
Caribbean, bl; nappy, hdl, 5" 35.00
Caribbean, bl; olive dish, oval, hdls 35.00
Caribbean, bl; pitcher, milk 350.00
Caribbean, bl; shakers, 3", pr 85.00
Caribbean, bl; syrup, 8" 250.00
Caribbean, crystal; ashtray 9.00
Early American, crystal; goblet, water; Hilton 15.00
First Love, crystal; candlestick, 2-light, #41, 5" 40.00
First Love, crystal; candy dish, ftd 75.00
First Love, crystal; candy dish, 3-part 65.00
First Love, crystal; champagne 20.00
First Love, crystal; creamer & sugar bowl 35.00
First Love, crystal; goblet, water 24.00
First Love, crystal; plate, sandwich; hdls, #115, 11" 35.00
First Love, crystal; relish, 2-part, #115, 8" 25.00
First Love, crystal; relish, 2-part, 6" 23.00
First Love, crystal; relish, 3-part, 9" 35.00
First Love, crystal; vase, bud; #5069, 9" 45.00
First Love, crystal; vase, cornucopia; #117, 8" 85.00
First Love, crystal; vase, crimped top, #115, 5" 45.00
Georgian, amber; sugar bowl 10.00
Hobnail, bl opal; hat, 4" 45.00
Hobnail, crystal; bowl, flared, 12" 25.00
Hobnail, crystal; candlestick 12.00
Hobnail, crystal; champagne 8.00
Hobnail, crystal; cocktail 8.00
Hobnail, crystal; compote 24.00
Hobnail, crystal; creamer & sugar bowl, +tray 20.00
Hobnail, crystal; goblet, water 10.00
Hobnail, crystal; nappy, shallow, 6" 8.00
Hobnail, crystal; sherbet 8.00
Hobnail, crystal; top hat, 4" 25.00
Hobnail, pk opal; hat, 4" 45.00
Language of Flowers, crystal; compote, cheese 18.50
Language of Flowers, crystal; mayonnaise set, 3-pc 27.00
Language of Flowers, crystal; relish, 2-part 35.00
Mardi Gras, crystal; punch cup 10.00
Nautilus, crystal; bonbon, frosted anchor center hdl, 6½" 47.00
Nautilus, lt bl frost; marmalade, sterling lid & spoon 110.00
Nautilus, lt bl; plate, hdls, 6" 30.00
Pall Mall, red; swan, 7" 70.00
Plaza, amber; finger bowl 12.00
Plaza, crystal; cocktail 10.00
Radiance, lt bl; cup & saucer 25.00
Radiance, lt bl; pitcher, ice lip 125.00
Radiance, lt bl; plate, 8⅝" 20.00
Radiance, lt bl; sugar bowl 20.00
Remembrance, crystal; champagne, #5115 ....16.00
Remembrance, crystal; tumbler, iced tea; #5115 ....20.00
Sandwich, crystal; ashtray, sq, ind 8.00
Sandwich, crystal; bonbon, heart shape, hdls 20.00
Sandwich, crystal; bowl, crimped, 11½" 50.00
Sandwich, crystal; bowl, fruit salad; 6" 25.00
Sandwich, crystal; bowl, nut; 3¼" 14.00
Sandwich, crystal; box, trinket; 3¾x5" 75.00
Sandwich, crystal; butter dish, ¼-lb 40.00
Sandwich, crystal; cake salver, plain ped, 13" 75.00
Sandwich, crystal; candlestick, 1-light, 4", pr 27.00
Sandwich, crystal; champagne, 5-oz, 5¼" 14.00
Sandwich, crystal; coaster 10.00
Sandwich, crystal; cocktail, 3-oz 12.00

Sandwich, crystal; compote, cheese 22.00
Sandwich, crystal; compote, 6" 20.00
Sandwich, crystal; creamer, lg 18.00
Sandwich, crystal; creamer, 5-oz 10.00
Sandwich, crystal; cup & saucer 12.00
Sandwich, crystal; goblet, water 15.00
Sandwich, crystal; goblet, 9-oz, 6" 9.00
Sandwich, crystal; jelly dish 10.00
Sandwich, crystal; mayonnaise set, 3-pc 35.00
Sandwich, crystal; pickle dish, oval, 7" 20.00
Sandwich, crystal; plate, bread & butter 4.00
Sandwich, crystal; plate, dinner 60.00
Sandwich, crystal; plate, luncheon; 8" 8.00
Sandwich, crystal; plate, service; 13" 50.00
Sandwich, crystal; relish tray, 3-part, 10½" L 35.00
Sandwich, crystal; seafood cocktail 14.00
Sandwich, crystal; sherbet/champagne, tall 12.00
Sandwich, crystal; tray, deviled eggs 70.00
Sandwich, crystal; tumbler, juice; ftd 12.00
Sandwich, crystal; wine, ftd, 3-oz, 4¼" 16.00
Spiral Flutes, amber; bowl, flat rim, 7" 8.00
Spiral Flutes, crystal; goblet 7.00
Spiral Flutes, crystal; tumbler, juice; ftd 6.00
Spiral Flutes, gr; bowl, almond; ftd 18.00
Spiral Flutes, gr; champagne 9.00
Spiral Flutes, gr; compote, tall 22.00
Spiral Flutes, gr; goblet, 6¼" 16.00
Sylvan, crystal; relish, 3-part, cobalt hdl 40.00
Sylvan, crystal; swan, 7" 30.00
Tear Drop, crystal; ashtray, ind 3.00
Tear Drop, crystal; bowl, divided, hdls, 6" 15.00
Tear Drop, crystal; bowl, 4-part, 12" 60.00
Tear Drop, crystal; candlestick, #301, 4", pr 30.00
Tear Drop, crystal; champagne 9.00
Tear Drop, crystal; coaster 8.00
Tear Drop, crystal; compote, cheese 14.00
Tear Drop, crystal; creamer, 6-oz 6.00
Tear Drop, crystal; creamer & sugar bowl 12.50
Tear Drop, crystal; creamer & sugar bowl, +tray 18.00
Tear Drop, crystal; cup & saucer 8.00
Tear Drop, crystal; plate, hdls, 8" 15.00
Tear Drop, crystal; plate, w/ring, 6" 15.00
Tear Drop, crystal; plate, 10½" 50.00
Tear Drop, crystal; plate, 8" 5.00
Tear Drop, crystal; relish, 3-part 14.00
Tear Drop, crystal; relish, 5-part, 12¼" 30.00
Tear Drop, crystal; sherbet 8.00
Tear Drop, crystal; sweetmeat 18.50
Tear Drop, crystal; tumbler, iced tea; flat 15.00
Tear Drop, crystal; tumbler, juice; flat 8.00
Tear Drop, crystal; tumbler, juice; ftd 9.00
Terrace, cobalt; plate, hdls, 5" 35.00

Durand

Durand Art Glass was a division of Vineland Glass Works in Vineland, New Jersey. Created in 1924, it was geared specifically toward the manufacture of fine handcrafted artware. Iridescent, opalescent, and cased glass was used to create such patterns as King Tut, reminiscent of Tiffany and Steuben. Production halted in 1931 after the death of Victor Durand. Very few examples are signed, and unmarked pieces are often mistaken for Steuben or Quezal. Unmarked items are often hard to sell, sometimes bringing only about half the price of a

similar but signed piece. Our advisor for this category is Mike Roscoe; he is listed in the Directory under Michigan.

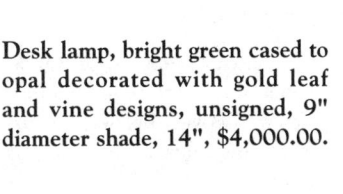

Bowl, cobalt w/wht rim, ftd, 3" 190.00
Compote, pulled feathers, wht on cobalt, yel base/stem, 6" 750.00

Desk lamp, bright green cased to opal decorated with gold leaf and vine designs, unsigned, 9" diameter shade, 14", $4,000.00.

Lamp base, bl irid w/gold threads, metal mts, 25" to finial 770.00
Torchere, Moorish Crackle, amber trumpet vase/metal ft, 16" ...465.00
Vase, bl bands w/bubbles alternate w/clear bubbly ribs, 12" 1,700.00
Vase, bl irid, ovoid w/stepped top, sgn/#1978, 7½" 880.00
Vase, bl irid w/ridged texture, 6½" 600.00
Vase, bl lustre on amber, bulbous, 10" 700.00
Vase, bl/purple/gr irid, squat body/bulb neck, #1977-8, 8" 465.00
Vase, cobalt panels separated by clear icicle panels, 10" 650.00
Vase, feathers, bl/wht/gold, allover threading, #2011, 12" 700.00
Vase, feathers, clear/emerald, cut-to-clear florals, 8½" 600.00
Vase, feathers, gr/wht on irid crackle, 8¾x4½" 965.00
Vase, hearts/vines, gold on cobalt irid, ovoid, 9" 1,200.00
Vase, hearts/vines, gr/orange irid, cone w/flared rim, 6" 625.00
Vase, hearts/vines, orange w/gr, #1710-8, lg 895.00
Vase, hearts/vines, silver-bl on cobalt irid, 10" 1,450.00
Vase, hearts/vines, wht on dk bl irid, #1710-4, 4" 990.00
Vase, King Tut, bl irid over gr, baluster, 10" 700.00
Vase, King Tut, dk bl/purple irid w/wht & gold swirls, 7" 935.00
Vase, King Tut, gold on cased pk, gold int rim, sgn, 7" 875.00
Vase, Moorish Crackle, bl/opal over orange irid, #1709, 9" 1,200.00
Vase, orange irid crackle w/in metal 4-arm mt w/cast lilacs 350.00
Vase, red/wht over amber, crackled/irid, 8½" 450.00
Vase, rows of pulled waves, opal/bl, baluster form, att, 6" 770.00
Vase, Royal Purple, 16-rib, bulbous w/trumpet neck, 9x9" 330.00

Easter

Eggs, bunnies, chicks, and baskets have all become basic elements of Easter celebrations, and the older, more interesting examples are being collected, often for nostalgic reasons, and displayed during the holidays to make the festivities brighter.

For further information, we recommend A *Guide to Easter Collectibles, Identifications and Values* by Juanita Burnett.

Candy container, bunnies playing, tin litho, oval, 1943, 7½" 40.00
Candy container, egg, pressed cb, Mary/lamb/bunny litho, 3¾" 36.00
Candy container, egg w/rabbit head, papier-mache, Germany, 5" ...150.00

Candy container, Keystone Cop on chick, compo, Germany, 5", EX ..185.00
Candy container, Peter Rabbit, porc, EX pnt, Germany, 3½" 85.00
Candy container, rabbit, compo, wht, Germany, 4", EX 85.00
Candy container, rabbit & basket, porc, Germany, 3", EX 85.00
Decoration, bunny, bsk, Japan, 3¾" 45.00
Decoration, bunny w/basket, clothes, bsk, Japan, 5" 55.00
Decoration, duck, celluloid, mc, 3", EX 60.00
Decoration, rabbit, papier-mache, pnt features, 11" 50.00
Decoration, rabbit in bonnet, celluloid, 4" 58.00
Decoration, rabbit in shoe, compo, EX pnt, 5½" 145.00

Elfinware

Made in Germany from about 1920 until the 1940s, these miniature vases, boxes, salt cellars, and miscellaneous novelty items are characterized by the tiny applied flowers that often cover their entire surface. Pieces with animals and birds are the most valuable, followed by the more interesting examples such as diminutive grand pianos, candle holders, etc. See also Salts, Open.

Baby's shoe, 3" 35.00
Basket, loop hdl, sm 35.00
Basket, 2 hdls, 2½x2½" 38.00

Basket, 3x5", $100.00.

Bottle, cologne; appl roses, gr lustre, 8½" 65.00
Box, appl flowers, oval, brass hinge, 4x3" 75.00
Candlestick, sm ring hdl, 2½" 50.00
Figurine, pig, 1⅞x1¾" 70.00
Inkwell, 3x3¾" 55.00
Place card holder, appl roses on fan shape, Germany 25.00
Shoe, Dutch; 4" L 75.00
Swan, 2¼" 55.00
Teapot, appl forget-me-nots & roses, 2½" 55.00
Vase/toothpick holder, allover florals, cylindrical, 2¾" 40.00
Watering can, sm 45.00

English Relief-Moulded Jugs

Early relief-moulded pitchers (ca 1830s-1840s) were made in two-piece molds into which sheets of clay were pressed. The relief decoration was deep and well defined, usually of animal or human subjects. Most of these pitchers were designed with a flaring lip and substantial footing. Gradually styles changed, and by the 1860s the rim had become flatter and the foot less pronounced. The relief decoration was not as deep, and foliage became a common design. By the turn of the

century, many other types of pitchers had been introduced, and the market for these early styles began to wane.

Watch for recent reproductions; these usually have been made by the slip-casting method. Unlike relief-moulded ware which is relatively smooth inside, slip-cast pitchers will have interior indentations that follow the irregularities of the relief decoration.

Our advisor for this category is Kathy Hughes; she is listed in the Directory under North Carolina.

Apostles, tan, unmk Meigh, Mar 17, 1842, 11" 550.00
Argos, gr, Brownfield, Apr 29, 1864, 8" 150.00
Ariadne, Samuel Alcock & Co, ca 1850, 9" 450.00
Barley, gr, Dudson, Apr 25, 1861, 8" 175.00
Beaded Medallions, parian, unmk, 19th C, 7" 125.00
Calla Lily & Wire, wht, unmk, 7", EX 150.00
Cattails on bl-gray, 1800s, 9" 175.00
Chrysanthemum, gr & wht, Ridgeway, 19th C, 9¼" 275.00
Four Seasons, Chas Meigh & Son, Reg Aug 25, 1852, 7" 350.00
Goddess w/7 Cherubs, wht, Copeland & Garrett, 19th C, 9" 200.00
Gothic Floral, bl/brn/wht, Beech & Hancock, July 14, 1862, 8" .200.00
Hampton, brn & wht, Brownfield, June 12, 1868, 8½" 235.00
Musical instruments, WT Copeland, ca 1855, 10" 400.00
Naomi, parian, Alcock, April 27, 1847, 6½" 250.00
Rose, parian, unmk, 19th C, 6½" 130.00
Sleeping Beauty, teal & wht, Dudson, 19th C, 5¼" 185.00
Tam O' Shanter, Ridgway, Oct 1, 1835 ....250.00
Two Drivers, Minton, ca 1850, 8¼" 500.00

Epergnes

Popular during the Victorian era, epergnes were fancy centerpieces often consisting of several tiers of vases (called lilies), candle holders, or dishes, or a combination of components. They were made in all types of art glass, and some were set in ornate plated frames.

Amethyst frost to clear, 1-lily, bronze-finish ft, 16x10" 350.00
Bl opal, 8¾x6" vase in center bowl 125.00
Bl overshot, 1-lily; floral emb SP ft, 15¼x11" 325.00
Clear opal w/cranberry rim, 3-lily, ruffled bowl, 15" 495.00
Clear w/amethyst ruffled rims, 1-lily, +10" bowl on metal ft 395.00
Cranberry, clear rigaree, 3-tier, 19x8" 400.00
Cranberry w/clear rigaree, 3 lilies+vase; cattail/mirror ft 565.00
Cranberry w/serpentine trim, 1-lily, 15x11½" 325.00
Crystal overshot w/cranberry edge, 1-lily in 10" bowl 300.00
Dmn Quilt, pk to bl, 1-lily, +sm bowl in leafy ormolu fr, 15" 325.00
Dmn Quilt, opal w/cranberry ruffled rims, 3-lily, 20" 500.00
Lt gr opal stripes, appl gr edge, 4 EX lg lilies, 20" 750.00
Orange-to-vaseline overshot, 1-lily, +ruffled bowl, 15x10" 395.00
Rose o/l w/HP florals, 1-lily, clear ruffle, ormolu fr, 11½" 225.00
Rubena, 1-lily, brass ft, 14¼x10½" 295.00

Erickson

Carl Erickson of Bremen, Ohio, produced hand-formed glassware from 1943 until 1960 in artistic shapes, no two of which were identical. One of the characteristics of his work was the air bubbles that were captured within the glass. Though most examples are clear, colored items were also made. Rather than to risk compromising his high standards by selling the factory, when Erickson retired, the plant was dismantled and sold.

Bottle, caramel cased, clear bubble stopper, sgn, 9" 275.00
Bowl, amber over crystal, paperweight, 8" 58.00

Bowl, smoke, controlled bubbles, paperweight, 13½" **95.00**
Candlestick, gr, controlled bubbles, paperweight, tall, pr **125.00**

Cocktail pitcher, green body with crystal paperweight base, 12", with stirrer, $325.00.

Compote, smoke, clear paperweight base, 9¾x7¼" **250.00**
Cruet, crystal, ground stopper, 9½" **60.00**
Decanter, cranberry, w/stopper, unsgn **95.00**
Pitcher, green to clear, 9½", +pr 4" old-fashioned tumblers **155.00**
Vase, dk gr, hourglass shape, controlled bubbles, 10" **125.00**
Vase, dk gr cased w/clear base, controlled bubbles, 7¼" **100.00**
Vase, gray, controlled bubble base, fan form, unsgn **125.00**
Vase, smoke, clear paperweight base w/bubbles, 6½" **40.00**

Erphila

Ebeling and Ruess, an importing company in Philadelphia, began operations in 1886. The acronym 'Erphila' was frequently substituted for the manufacturer's mark on the imported items. It appears that the Erphila mark was used through the late 1930s and then again after WW II on products from U.S. Zone Germany as well as from other areas. The company imported from factories such as Fustenberg, W. Goebel, Villeroy and Boch, Heinrich, Keramos, and Schumann, to name a few. Figurines, art pottery, and some utilitarian items can be found bearing the Erphila mark. Examples are hard to find. Early German marks (those prior to 1900) often contain the word 'Fayence.' After the turn of the century, a rectangular mark in green ink was used. Following WWI, porcelain items were imported from Czechoslovakia. These sometimes carried gold and silver labels. A small variety of marks were used in the 1920s and '30s, but they all contained the name 'Erphila.' Sticker labels were also used. 'Bavaria,' 'Black Forest,' and 'Italy' are sometimes found in combination with 'Erphila.'

Ebeling and Ruess continue the importing business, but it appears that since the 1940s they are also using an 'E' and 'R' on a bell-shaped mark. Because this mark does not contain the name 'Erphila,' we do not consider it to be such. We assume that they stopped using this name sometime in the 1950s.

Bookend, Dutch boy, mc, Czech **95.00**
Bookend, pouter pigeon, wht, Czech, pr **45.00**
Cake plate, mc roses, Czech, 11½" **35.00**
Candlestick, blk desert scene on sand, Czech, 3½", pr **115.00**
Candlestick, ewer on ped, flowers, Czech, 3½", pr **125.00**
Candlestick, wht/orange flowers, Czech, 5", pr **68.00**
Cracker jar, red poppies, Czech, 7½" **60.00**
Creamer, gr & wht, dog hdl, MIG **65.00**
Creamer, lady, wht & orange, Czech **115.00**

Creamer, mc floral on wht, Chelsea pattern, mk, 4¾" **40.00**
Creamer, mc/emb floral top, cream base & hdl, gold rim, 2¾" **35.00**
Creamer, orange flowers, Czech, 4½" **38.00**
Cup & saucer, mc w/gold stars, Czech, set of 8 ....**81.00**
Dish, blk/red/wht, Czech, w/lid, 5" **35.00**
Dish, Cherry Chintz, hdl, pierced, Cambridge, MIG **75.00**
Dresser doll, Madame Pompadour, yel dress, MIG, 5" **105.00**
Dresser doll, Nancy Pert, orange/blk dress, mask, Czech, 5" **185.00**
Dresser jar, gr & wht, Art Deco, MIG, 5¾", pr **65.00**
Figurine, Airdale dog, wht/blk/brn, MIG **15.00**
Figurine, beagle dog, mk Germany, 9" **48.00**
Figurine, Bull Terrier dog, blk & wht, MIG, 7" L **83.00**
Figurine, cat, wht w/gold ball, MIG, 12" L **120.00**
Figurine, chickens, mc, MIG, 4¾", pr **38.00**
Figurine, dog, blk/wht, hunting pose, MIG, 10" L **45.00**
Figurine, fighting cock, wht/mc, 6½x7", pr **90.00**
Figurine, little girl in parade hat, w/accordion, 6½" **45.00**
Figurine, spaniel, sitting, brn/wht, MIG, 6" **45.00**
Figurine, 2 pheasants on oval base, MIG, 5½" **40.00**
Juicer, orange shape w/hdl, 2-pc, Czech **70.00**
Leaf dish, wht, Czech **20.00**
Mug, Toby, bl coat, rust hat, Sam Weller, MIG **99.00**
Pitcher, men in cavalier costume on brn, 9", +3 mugs **210.00**
Pitcher, red/wht/blk rings, 9", +3 mugs **150.00**
Planter, Oxford pattern, flowers, Czech **45.00**
Planter/vase, mc fruit on cobalt w/purple rim, mk, 4⅝" **25.00**
Plate, grapes, majolica, MIG, 7¾" **65.00**
Plate, orange flower w/gr foliage, orange rim, mk, 6½" **35.00**
Shakers, flowers, Czech, pr+tray **25.00**
Spoon holder, Cherry Chintz, Czech, 4½" **20.00**
Teapot, dog begging, +matching cow creamer **75.00**
Teapot, rabbit form, brn, MIG, 8½" **80.00**
Vase, all wht ridged cylinder w/curved-up ped ft, 7½" **45.00**
Vase, blk silhouette on sand, Czech, 9½" **100.00**
Vase, orange w/gr mottled top & base, bl rim, 3-hdl, 7⅛" **170.00**
Vase, tan w/blk Bo Peep, mk, 10" **125.00**

Eskimo Artifacts

While ivory carvings made from walrus tusks or whale teeth have been the most emphasized articles of Eskimo art, basketry and wood-working are other areas in which these Alaskan Indians excel. Their designs are effected through the application of simple yet dramatic lines and almost stark decorative devices. Though not pursued to the extent of American Indian art, the unique work of this northern tribe is beginning to attract the serious attention of today's collectors.

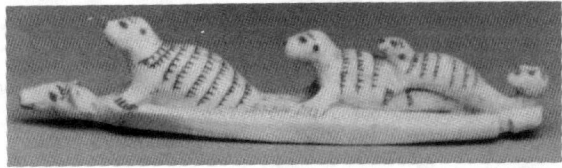

Bag fastener, carved ivory with baleen inset and brown pigment in engraving, 6" long, $2,400.00.

Basket, baleen, cone-shape finial, woven-in ivory disk, 3¾" **935.00**
Basket, geometrics, 1-rod coil, wear/losses, 3½x7" **150.00**
Basket, pnt horses, 1-rod coil, willow/conifer root, 3x4" **250.00**
Bowl, pnt wood, bird/fish in blk, red rim, 2x6" **495.00**
Breast yoke, wooden, for seal drag lines, 1800s, 24" **25.00**

Cribbage brd, eng ivory, village scene/seals/etc, 16" 550.00
Cribbage brd, eng walrus tusk, red/blk playing cards, 17" 300.00
Cvg, hunter w/bear, dk gray, Davidie Eroli, 10" 425.00
Cvg, seated billiken, inlaid baleen detail, 4", EX 250.00
Cvg, whalebone vertebra w/effigy face 200.00
Doll, cvd dk stone head, ethnic cloth costume, seated: 9½" 275.00
Effigy, Punuk figure, fossilized walrus ivory, ca 1400, 3" 275.00
Harpoon, ivory, 2 barbs, 2⅛" 35.00
Hook, grappling; ivory toggle on leather line, worn, 9" 200.00
Lance guard, ivory, cvd as polar bear, w/inlay, 3½" 1,700.00
Mask, wht facial area, bone teeth, wear/crack, 11" 500.00
Pipe, ivory, inset bear figural bowl, eng scenes/etc, 15" 2,850.00
Pipe, 1-pc ivory w/7 rows of rtcl animals/boats/etc, 10" 2,600.00
Tusk, eng bear hunts/mythical Worm-man, 17" 770.00

Fairings

Fairings, small chinaware figural groups that portray amusing (if not risque) scenes of courting couples, marital woes, and family feuds, were popular purchases and prizes at 19th-century English fairs. From 1840 through the 1850s, their bases were embossed with marks that identified the manufacturer as well as the artist who applied the polychrome enameling. From 1860 until 1870, they were no longer marked and became smaller in size. During the 1870s they retained their smaller size but once again were marked in relief, indicating manufacturer and artisan. Through the 1880s all marks were omitted, but the bases were much more shallow than those from the 1860s. About 1890 the Staffordshire potters sold the molds to German manufacturers who marked their product with the name of their country until about 1900. Examples from this period are most commonly encountered. Fairings made in Germany in the early 20th century often have two holes in their bases.

Generally, the more complex groups and those that are marked bring the higher prices. Earlier examples from the sixties and seventies are of better quality. Similar items such as small boxes and match holders with much the same type of theme and figural decoration are also listed here.

Box, child in wash bowl, 'Paddling His Own Canoe,' 4", $250.00.

Bank, pk cottage w/Present from Scarborough in gold, 4" W 150.00
Box, baby holding gold rattle, unmk German bsk, 4½" 195.00
Box, baby in cradle, unmk German bsk, 2¾x4½" 165.00
Box, cameo on front, musical instruments on lid, 3¾" 95.00

Box, cat w/frog, English, 3" 90.00
Box, child in bed w/kitten, 4¼" 120.00
Box, child on bed pulls on pajama bottoms, Elbogen mk, 4" 120.00
Box, child on sideboard taking grapes, 1880s 250.00
Box, girl w/puppy, Elbogen mk, 4½" 100.00
Box, 3 children play on oval lid, Staffordshire, 4⅝" 200.00
Cat stands on gr base, 2½x3" 130.00
Christ child w/lamb, EX colors, NM 75.00
Five O'Clock Tea, kittens/saucers of milk, Elbogen style, 6" 30.00
Girl coming out of basket, 4¾" 125.00
Girl peeking through bushes at rabbit 80.00
I Am Off w/Him, lady w/dog & basket 175.00
I Am Starting for a Long Journey, man w/satchel & book 175.00
Last in Bed to Put Out the Light 145.00
Merry Widow, lady cat w/roses at ft 250.00
O Do Leave Me a Drop, 2 cats at bowl 175.00
Tug of War, girl & dog by fence tugging at doll, 2¾x5¼" 185.00
Uncle Sam figure on sm dish, Germany 200.00
Welsh Tea Party, mk Germany 275.00
Who Said Rats?, cat in draped bed, mice on table 165.00
Will We Sleep First or How?, 5¼x4" 195.00

Fans

The Japanese are said to have invented the fan. From there it went to China, and Portuguese traders took the idea to Europe. Though usually considered milady's accessory, even the gentlemen in 17th-century England carried fans! More fashionable than practical, some were of feathers and lovely hand-painted silks with carved ivory or tortoise sticks. Some French fans had peepholes. There are mourning fans, calendar fans, and advertising fans.

Fine antique fans (pre-1900) of ivory or mother-of-pearl have recently escalated in value. Those from before 1800 often sell for upwards of $1,000.00. Examples with mother-of-pearl sticks are most desirable; least desirable are those with sticks of celluloid. Our advisor for this category is Vicki Flanigan; she is listed in the Directory under Virginia.

Carved mother-of-pearl sticks, paper-over-vellum leaf, hand-painted scene of nymphs and butterflies, signed Ch. LaBarre, VG, $800.00.

American fan factory, wood w/linen 300.00
Blk net, silver sequins, tortoise shell sticks, 6x7", EX 200.00
Brussels lace on blk gauze, cvd abalone/MOP sticks, 11", EX 400.00
Celluloid Brise, HP flowers, 8" 50.00
Ivory, cvd w/Oriental figures/monogram, in fr, 13" L, EX 450.00
Ivory, detailed scene HP ea side, Continental, sgn, 7", EX 400.00
Lace on silk, MOP sticks, Tiffany & Co, 9½", +case 425.00
Paper, HP women & stag, rtcl ivory sticks, Italian, 20" 550.00

Paper, Nouveau print 50.00
Paper on vellum, HP cherubs, cvd MOP sticks, Fr, sgn, EX 800.00
Paper w/HP architectural scenes, ivory sticks, Fr, 1750, 21" 800.00
Silver filigree w/enamel chinoiserie, silver sticks, China 900.00
Tortoise shell, rtcl/cvd, Chinese Export, in lacquer box 425.00
Tortoise shell w/gilt-lacquered scholars & landscape, 8" 350.00
Wood, lace w/HP women, 13" 200.00

Farm Collectibles

Country living in the 19th century entailed plowing, planting, harvesting, gathering eggs, milking, making soap from lard rendered on butchering day, and numerous other tasks performed with primitive tools of which we in the 20th century have had little first-hand knowledge. Our advisor for this category is Lar Hothem; his address is listed in the Directory under Ohio. See also Cast Iron; Woodenware; Wrought Iron.

Barn vent, pine w/pnt traces, 9-point star in triangle, 42" 700.00
Corn husker, NP steel, mk Clark Universal Pat Pend, 5¼" 22.50
Corn sheller, CI, F&F Co Springfield OH, Patd 7-6-69, EX 750.00

Curry and tail comb for horses, $15.00.

Hogstretcher, hewn oak, EX 25.00
Hook, cotton bale; wrought iron, w/chain, 1700s 22.00
Horse's sweat scraper, hickory, slightly curved, 16" 35.00
Implement seat, Derring, CI 70.00
Implement seat, Whiting, EX 70.00
Knife, chopping; hammered/shaped iron blade, single tang, EX 20.00
Magazine, Rockford Farmer's Monthly, 1888, EX 40.00
Manual, John Deere Model A tractor, EX 45.00
Measure, grain; bentwood, assembled set of 5, 6" to 14", EX 175.00
Measure, grain; bentwood, tin bands, EB Frye brand, 8x15" 65.00
Measure, grain; gray pnt, nesting, set of 4: 8¾" to 15" 160.00
Scales, butter-weighing; 2 trn pans on twine ropes 65.00
Scooter plow, 1-bottom, to use w/mule, 1800s, EX 55.00
Shovel, grain; hewn/cvd wood, open D hdl, 1890s, 36x11" 85.00
Shovel, grain; wood, edge damage, 48" 85.00
Thermometer, dairy; floating type, EX 9.00
Wagon jack, oak, arm clamps down to lock, 1850s, EX 95.00
Yoke, maiden's shoulder, hewn, knob ends, 36" L, EX 65.00

Fenton

Frank and John Fenton were brothers who founded the Fenton Art Glass Company in 1906 in Martin's Ferry, Ohio. The venture, at first only a decorating shop, began operations in July of 1905 using blanks purchased from other companies. This operation soon proved unsatisfactory, and by 1907 they had constructed their own glass factory in Williamstown, West Virginia. John left the company in 1909 and organized his own firm in Millersburg, Ohio.

The Fenton Company produced over 130 patterns of carnival glass. They also made custard, chocolate, opalescent, and stretch glass. This company has always been noted for its various colors of glass and has continually changed its production to stay attune with current tastes in decorating. In 1925 they produced a line of 'handmade' items that incorporated the techniques of threading and mosaic work. Because the process proved to be unprofitable, the line was discontinued by 1927. Even their glassware made in the past twenty-five years is already regarded as collectible. Various paper labels have been used since the 1920s; only since 1970 has the logo been stamped into the glass.

For information concerning Fenton Art Glass Collectors of America, Inc., see the Clubs, Newsletters, and Catalogs section of the Directory. See also Carnival Glass; Custard Glass; Stretch Glass.

Amber Crest/Gold Crest, plate, 6½" 15.00
Amber Crest/Gold Crest, plate, 8½" 30.00
Amber Crest/Gold Crest, tidbit, 3-tier, #680 ....90.00
Amber Crest/Gold Crest, vase, dbl-crimped, #192, 5" 30.00
Apple Blossom, compote, low, ftd, #7228 ....48.00
Aqua Crest, bowl, #7224, 10" 65.00
Aqua Crest, candlestick, #1523, 5", pr 55.00
Aqua Crest, plate, 12" 35.00
Aqua Crest, vase, #37, mini 57.00
Aqua Crest, vase, bowl form, #201 ....35.00
Aqua Crest, vase, triangle, #1923, 6½" 40.00
Aqua Crest, vase, tulip; crimped, #203, 5" 35.00
Basketweave, basket, Persian Bl opal, open edge, #8330, 7" 25.00
Basketweave, bowl, rosalene, #8222 ....38.00
Beaded Melon, bottle, scent; gr o/l, 3¼" 55.00
Beaded Melon, jug, gold o/l, hdl, 6" 55.00
Beaded Melon, vase, gr o/l, #2711, mini 27.50
Beaded Melon, vase, gr o/l, dbl-crimped, 5" 58.00
Beaded Melon, vase, rose o/l, #711, 8" 48.00
Beaded Melon/Peach Crest, bowl, #711, 7" 56.00
Beaded Melon/Peach Crest, vase, #711, 5" 48.00
Big Cookies, basket, ruby, wicker hdl, #1681, 10½" 120.00
Black Crest, bonbon, hdld, #7333 ....45.00
Black Rose, hurricane lamp, #7398 ....120.00
Block & Star, bowl, nappy, turq pastel, #5635 ....22.00
Blue Opal, atomizer perfume bottle, #1424 ....36.00
Blue Opal, plate, leaf form, #175, 8" 40.00
Blue Overlay, basket, #1924, 7" 65.00
Blue Overlay, basket, hat form, #1925, 5" 48.00
Blue Overlay, bowl, 7" 24.00
Blue Ridge, fairy light, 3-pc, #2604 ....58.00
Blue Ridge, pitcher 85.00
Boggy Bayou, vase, amethyst opal, 12" 80.00
Bubble Optic, vase, honey amber, 8½" 62.50

Burmese, jack-in-the-pulpit vase, decorated and signed by Louise Piper, 10", $190.00.

Burmese, basket, HP roses, #7437 ....95.00
Burmese, rose bowl, HP roses, #7424 ....60.00
Butterfly, bonbon, custard satin, #8230 ....20.00
Butterfly, bonbon, plum opal, 3-toed 50.00
Butterfly, bonbon, rosalene, #8230 ....50.00
Butterfly & Berry, basket, amethyst, #9234 ....22.00
Butterfly & Berry, basket, topaz opal, hat form, #9134 ....38.00
Butterfly & Berry, fantail bowl, topaz opal, #8428 ....38.00
Chinese Yellow, bowl, cupped, #846, on ebony base, 6" H 150.00
Chinese Yellow, bowl, mixing; ca 1933 ....32.00
Coin Dot, basket, bl opal, 4½" 50.00
Coin Dot, bowl, bl opal, #1424, 10" 85.00
Coin Dot, bowl, cranberry opal, #1522, 10" 90.00
Coin Dot, bowl, cranberry opal, #203, 6" 65.00
Coin Dot, bowl, gr opal, #203, 6" 65.00
Coin Dot, bowl, honeysuckle opal, #203, 1948-49, 6" 55.00
Coin Dot, bowl, topaz opal, #203, 6" 58.00
Coin Dot, creamer, Persian Bl opal, #1461 ....30.00
Coin Dot, creamer & sugar bowl, bl opal 80.00
Coin Dot, cruet, French opal, #208, 7" 80.00
Coin Dot, pitcher, water; cranberry opal, #1353, 9½" 165.00
Coin Dot, vase, bl opal, dbl-crimped, #1450, 5" 70.00
Coin Dot, vase, cranberry opal, #1441 ....95.00
Coin Dot, vase, cranberry opal, #1457, 7½" 105.00
Coin Dot, vase, cranberry opal, #189, 10" 135.00
Coin Dot, vase, cranberry opal, #194, 8½" 110.00
Coin Dot, vase, cranberry opal, dbl-crimped, #1450, 5" 78.00
Coin Dot, vase, cranberry opal, dbl-crimped, #203, 4x4¾" ...50.00
Coin Dot, vase, topaz opal, #1440 ....78.00
Coin Dot, vase, tulip; lime opal, 10½" 135.00
Coin Dot, vase, tulip; Persian Bl opal, #1353, 10" 38.00
Daisy & Button, bonbon, milk glass, 5½" 12.00
Daisy & Button, boot, bl satin, #1990 ....16.00
Daisy & Button, bottle, scent; French opal 22.50
Daisy & Button, bowl, crystal, #1921 ....18.00
Daisy & Button, slipper, pk opal, #1995 ....10.00
Daisy & Button, vanity set, rose, #1900, 4-pc 160.00
Daisy & Fern, pitcher, water; cranberry opal 250.00
Dancing Ladies, vase, ruby, scalloped rim, #901 ....295.00
Diamond Lace, candlestick, French opal, pr 40.00
Diamond Lace, console set, bl opal, #4804, 3-pc 90.00
Diamond Optic, basket, ruby, 7" 65.00
Diamond Optic, jug, ruby o/l, #192, 1942-48, 6" 45.00
Diamond Optic, jug, ruby o/l, hdld, #192, 8" 75.00
Diamond Optic, vase, ruby o/l, dbl-crimped, #192, 4¼" 24.00
Diamond Optic, vase, swung; lt gr opal, 12" 45.00
Dogwood, vase, burmese, dbl-crimped, #7457, 5½" 85.00
Dolphin, bowl, jade gr, hdls, #1504A 30.00
Dolphin, candlestick, ruby, #1623, 3½" 25.00
Dolphin, vase, pk, cut decor, fan form, 6" 65.00
Dot Optic, finger bowl, bl opal, #1424 ....35.00
Dot Optic, ivy bowl, emerald gr, ftd, #1021 ....45.00
Dot Optic, lamp, hurricane; bl opal, #170 ....90.00
Dot Optic, pitcher, gr opal, #1352, 9" 145.00
Dot Optic, sugar shaker, bl opal, #2993, 4½" 90.00
Ebony, bowl, cupped, #607, ca 1925, 8" 50.00
Emerald Crest, bowl, heart shape 45.00
Emerald Crest, creamer, #680, 3¼" 30.00
Emerald Crest, creamer, #7261 ....27.50
Emerald Crest, saucer 18.00
Empress, vase, Peking Bl, #8252 ....78.00
Fern Optic, fairy lamp, Persian Bl opal, #1803, 3-pc 85.00
Flame, candlestick, #549, ca 1924-26, 8", pr 165.00
Flame, candlestick, hexagonal, #449, 8¾", pr 145.00

Georgian, sherbet, rose, high ft, #1611, 6-oz 18.00
Gold Crest, bowl, 10" 35.00
Green Opal, basket, #6137, ca 1960, 7" 60.00
Green Overlay, vase, tulip; #194, 8" 60.00
Hobnail, ashtray, French opal, fan form, 5½" 37.50
Hobnail, ashtray, French opal, 5¼" 24.00
Hobnail, banana boat, pk opal, #3720, 12" 38.00
Hobnail, basket, cranberry opal, #3834, sm 75.00
Hobnail, basket, cranberry opal, #3835, 5½" 75.00
Hobnail, basket, French opal, 4" 40.00
Hobnail, basket, gr opal, #3834, 7½" 95.00
Hobnail, basket, milk glass, oval, #3839, 12" 54.00
Hobnail, basket, topaz, 4" 65.00
Hobnail, bell, Colonial Bl, #3667 ....12.00
Hobnail, berry dish, rose pastel, sq, #3928 ....18.00
Hobnail, bonbon, bl opal, triangle, #3926, 6" 16.00
Hobnail, bonbon, plum opal, #3926, 5½" 30.00
Hobnail, bonbon, topaz opal, sq, #389, 6" 20.00
Hobnail, bowl, bl opal, oval, #389, 7" 38.00
Hobnail, bowl, bl opal, 10" 65.00
Hobnail, bowl, cranberry opal, dbl-crimped, #3924, 11" 90.00
Hobnail, bowl, milk glass, #3635, 3-toed 18.00
Hobnail, bowl, plum opal, #3294, 9" 145.00
Hobnail, bowl, topaz opal, dbl-crimped, #3927, 7" 50.00
Hobnail, cake plate, milk glass, #3913 ....35.00
Hobnail, cake plate, topaz opal, ftd, 13" 145.00
Hobnail, candle bowl, plum opal, ftd, #3771 ....85.00
Hobnail, candlestick, cranberry opal, #3870, pr 135.00
Hobnail, candlestick, milk glass, #3674, 6", pr 28.00
Hobnail, candlestick, topaz opal, squat 30.00
Hobnail, compote, Colonial Bl, #3628, 6" 18.00
Hobnail, compote, gr opal, #3728 ....48.00
Hobnail, compote, gr opal, ftd, w/lid, #3887 ....68.00
Hobnail, compote, plum opal, ftd, w/lid, #3887 ....120.00
Hobnail, compote, plum opal, low, #3727, 8" 90.00
Hobnail, compote, topaz opal, ftd, w/lid, #3887 ....85.00
Hobnail, cornucopia candlestick, bl opal, #3874 ....32.00
Hobnail, cornucopia candlestick, French opal, #3874 ....18.00
Hobnail, cornucopia candlestick, topaz opal, #3874 ....38.00
Hobnail, creamer & sugar bowl, bl opal, 3" 45.00
Hobnail, creamer & sugar bowl, milk glass, #3900 ....24.00
Hobnail, creamer & sugar bowl, topaz opal, #3900, ind 36.00
Hobnail, cruet, bl opal, 4" 35.00
Hobnail, cruet, cranberry opal, #3863 ....90.00
Hobnail, cruet, pk opal, #3863 ....38.00
Hobnail, epergne, milk glass, #3902, 2-pc 42.00
Hobnail, epergne, pk opal, #3701, 10" 150.00
Hobnail, epergne, topaz opal, #3701, 10", 4-pc 150.00
Hobnail, fairy lamp, Colonial Gr, 2-pc, #3068 ....12.00
Hobnail, fairy lamp, Colonial Orange, #3608 ....12.00
Hobnail, goblet, wine; French opal 20.00
Hobnail, hurricane lamp, peachblow, #3998 ....110.00
Hobnail, ivy bowl, milk glass, #3757 ....20.00
Hobnail, jam set, milk glass, #3903, 3-pc 20.00
Hobnail, jardiniere, milk glass, #3994, 4½" 9.00
Hobnail, jug, cranberry opal, #3964, 4½" 85.00
Hobnail, jug, cranberry opal, #3965, 5½" 110.00
Hobnail, jug, milk glass, squat, #3967, 80-oz 75.00
Hobnail, jug, topaz opal, #3762, 4½" 58.00
Hobnail, mustard, bl opal, #3889, 3-pc 30.00
Hobnail, nut bowl, milk glass, 2-hdld, #3729 ....20.00
Hobnail, nut dish, milk glass, ftd, #3629 ....10.00
Hobnail, pitcher, cranberry opal, sq top, #389, 5½" 80.00
Hobnail, pitcher, milk glass, #3762, 12-oz 18.00

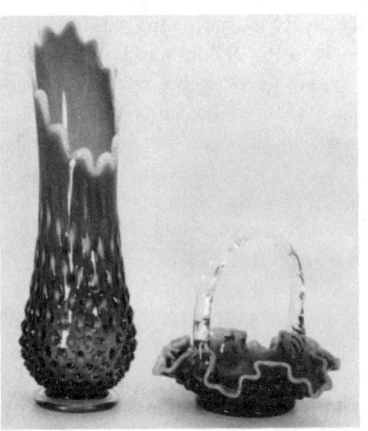

Hobnail in plum opal: Vase, unmarked, 11½", $135.00; Basket, marked in oval, #3735, 6", $60.00.

Hobnail, pitcher, plum opal, ice lip, #3664, 70-oz 165.00
Hobnail, pitcher, topaz opal, #285, 5½" 38.00
Hobnail, pitcher vase, #3670 ....44.00
Hobnail, relish, milk glass, heart shape, #3733 ....22.00
Hobnail, shakers, cranberry opal, #3806, pr 75.00
Hobnail, shakers, French opal, ftd, pr 70.00
Hobnail, syrup, cranberry opal, #3964, 5½" 85.00
Hobnail, top hat, bl opal, 3" 25.00
Hobnail, tumbler, cranberry opal, #389, 12-oz 38.00
Hobnail, tumbler, French opal, 15-oz 18.00
Hobnail, vase, bl opal, fan form, 3¾" 24.00
Hobnail, vase, bl opal, ftd fan form, 6" 35.00
Hobnail, vase, bud; topaz opal, #3756, 8" 20.00
Hobnail, vase, Colonial Bl, dbl-crimped, #3853, 3" 14.00
Hobnail, vase, Colonial Gr, #3850, 5½" 30.00
Hobnail, vase, cranberry opal, dbl-crimped, #3850, 5" 80.00
Hobnail, vase, cranberry opal, dbl-crimped, #3854, 4½" 40.00
Hobnail, vase, cranberry opal, fan form, mini 55.00
Hobnail, vase, cranberry opal, wide, #3859, 8½" 165.00
Hobnail, vase, cranberry opal, 8" 110.00
Hobnail, vase, French opal, fan form, #389, 8¼" 30.00
Hobnail, vase, handkerchief; plum opal, #3750, 6" 75.00
Hobnail, vase, lime gr opal, tricornered, #389, 4" 40.00
Hobnail, vase, swung; gr opal, #3758, med 48.00
Hobnail, vase, swung; plum opal, #3758, med, old 75.00
Hobnail, vase, topaz opal, fan form, 8¼" 65.00
Hobnail, violet bowl, milk glass, #3754 ....20.00
Hobnail, wine, French opal, #3843, sm 20.00
Ivory Crest, cornucopia candlestick, #1522, pr 50.00
Ivory Crest, vase, #186, 8" 38.00
Ivory Crest, vase, #1923, 7½" 38.00
Ivory Crest, vase, sq top, #201, 5" 45.00
Jade Green, candle holder, 1½", pr 20.00
Jade Green, ice bucket, #1616, 6½" 55.00
Jade Green, sugar bowl, #1500 ....17.50
Jade Green, vase, fan form, #551, 8½" 28.00
Leaf & Orange Tree, bowl, custard satin, 3-toed, #8223 ....24.00
Leaf & Orange Tree, bowl, rosalene, 3-toed, #8223 ....65.00
Lilac Cased, jug, #6068, ca 1955-56, 6½" 55.00
Lilac Cased, shell bowl, cased, #9020, 10" 110.00
Lilac Cased, vase, fan form, #857, 8" 130.00
Lily of the Valley, vase, bud; bl opal, #8458, 9½" 20.00
Lincoln Inn, goblet, water; red 30.00
Lincoln Inn, plate, ruby, 6" 28.00
Lincoln Inn, sherbet, cobalt, 4¾" 25.00
Lincoln Inn, sherbet, ruby 25.00
Mandarin Red, vase, crimped, #847, 6½" 75.00
Maple Leaf, bowl, burmese, #7422, 8" 85.00

Melon Rib, vase, bl satin, #7451, 6" 16.00
Melon Rib, vase, rose satin, #7451, 6" 35.00
Melon Rib/Gold Crest, candlestick, 5", pr 30.00
Ming Rose, bowl, deep, 3-toed, 7" 30.00
Ming Rose, bowl, 3-ftd, #249, 9" 50.00
Ming Rose, cornucopia centerpc, +2 candlesticks 125.00
Moonstone, candlestick, ebony base, #346, 8" 70.00
Moonstone, vase, on 5-leg ebony base, #612, 6½" 150.00
Peach Crest, bowl, dbl-crimped, #7224, 10" 68.00
Peach Crest, bowl, dbl-crimped, 7½" 35.00
Peach Crest, candlestick, #1523, 5", pr 75.00
Peach Crest, shell bowl, #9020, 10" 72.00
Peach Crest, vase, crimped, #187, 6" 30.00
Peach Crest, vase, dbl-crimped, #7254, 4½" 32.00
Peach Crest, vase, triangular, #187, 1940-43, 5" 55.00
Peach Crest, vase, tulip; #7250, 8½" 65.00
Pekin Blue, bowl, oval, #1663, 12½" 80.00
Periwinkle Blue, bowl, crimped, ca 1935, 8½" 60.00
Persian Medallion, compote, bl satin, #8234 ....24.00
Persian Medallion, compote, custard satin, #8234 ....18.00
Persian Medallion, fairy lamp, custard satin, 3-pc 32.00
Pineapple, bowl, console; wht satin, #2000A, 12½" 45.00
Plymouth, champagne, crystal, tall 17.50
Plymouth, champagne, ruby 22.00
Plymouth, highball, amber, #1620, 8-oz 25.00
Plymouth, shot glass, ruby 15.00
Polka Dot, butter dish, cranberry opal, milk glass base 120.00
Polka Dot, rose bowl, cranberry opal, 5" 120.00
Polka Dot, sugar shaker, cranberry opal, #2293, 4½" 65.00
Polka Dot, vase, tulip; cranberry opal, #2250, 8" 145.00
Priscilla, bowl, emerald gr, cupped, #1890, 1952-52, 9" 32.00
Reverse Melon, vase, amethyst, 7" 22.00
Rib Optic, finger lamp, ruby o/l, appl amber hdl 95.00
Rosalene, swan, open, #5127 ....34.00
Rosalene, vase, bud 27.00
Rose Crest, basket, 10" 90.00
Rose Crest, plate, 12" 37.00
Rose Crest, vase, #192, 6½" 20.00
Rose Crest, vase, #4517, 6½" 24.00
Rose Crest, vase, dbl-crimped, #1924, 3½" 20.00
Rose Crest, vase, dbl-crimped, #36, 4½" 16.00
Rose Crest, vase, triangle, #36, 4½" 16.00
Rose Overlay, bottle, vanity; no stopper, #192 ....15.00
Rose Overlay, candy dish, w/lid, #711 ....35.00
Rose Overlay, pitcher, #192, 5½" 42.50
Rose Pattern, bowl, Colonial Bl, #9225, 9½" 35.00
Rose Pattern, candy dish, Colonial Bl, ftd, w/lid, #9284 ....30.00
Rose Pattern, candy dish, Colonial Orange, ftd, w/lid, #9284 ....28.00
Royal Blue, ashtray, 3-ftd, #848, 4" 22.00
Ruby, plate, sq form, hdls, #1639, 12" 65.00
Ruby Overlay, basket, 5" 75.00
San Toy, cornucopia centerpc, rose, #950, 11" 85.00
San Toy, vase, etched, #898, 11½" 60.00
Scroll, vase, rose satin, #9155, 8" 65.00
Scroll & Eye, compote, rose pastel, #9021 ....30.00
September Morn, flower frog, blk opaque 185.00
September Morn, flower frog, crystal 95.00
September Morn, flower frog, lt gr, blk base 140.00
Sheffield, vase, wht stretch, unusual shape, 7¼" 125.00
Silver Crest, bonbon, ruffled, metal center hdl, 8" 30.00
Silver Crest, bowl, #7321, 11½" 40.00
Silver Crest, bowl, ftd, #7425, 7½" 18.00
Silver Crest, bowl, 3¾x7" 10.00
Silver Crest, cake plate, ftd, #7213 ....38.00

Silver Crest, cake plate, ped ft, low, 13" **40.00**
Silver Crest, candlestick, #7474, 6", pr **50.00**
Silver Crest, compote, 6x8" **18.00**
Silver Crest, dish, heart shape w/hdl **20.00**
Silver Crest, mayonnaise bowl & underplate, #7203 ....**28.00**
Silver Crest, pitcher, #7467, 70-oz **125.00**
Silver Crest, plate, 6" **15.00**
Silver Crest, sandwich server, hdls **25.00**
Silver Crest, tidbit tray, 2-tier, lg **55.00**
Silver Crest, vase, dbl-crimped, #1924, 4½" **28.00**
Silver Crest, vase, violet decor, #186, 8" **55.00**
Silvertone, bowl, amber, flared, #1002, 9" **35.00**
Snow Crest, bowl, ruby, heart shape **35.00**
Snow Crest, top hat, emerald gr, 5" **100.00**
Spanish Lace, syrup, cranberry opal **98.00**
Spanish Lace/Silver Crest, cake plate, ftd, #3510 ....**45.00**
Spiral, vase, cranberry opal, #3253, ca 1955-59, 6½" **50.00**
Spiral, vase, gr opal, #186, 8" **48.00**
Spiral Optic, pitcher, water; bl opal, #1424 ....**95.00**
Strawberry, basket, Provincial Bl opal, ftd, #9537, 7" **22.00**
Stretch, candy dish, aquamarine, #531 ....**45.00**
Stretch, tray, bl, center hdl, 11" **45.00**
Swan, bowl, amber, oval, 6", 11½" **95.00**
Swan, novelty, wht satin, #4, 4" **30.00**
Swirled Feather, fairy lamp, cranberry opal, #2090 ....**180.00**
Threaded Diamond Optic, basket, rosalene, 3-toed, #8435 ....**70.00**
Thumbprint, compote, Colonial Amber, #4429, 6" **14.00**
Thumbprint, compote, Colonial Bl, #4425, lg **20.00**
Thumbprint, compote, gr opal w/cobalt crest, #4425, 6" **48.00**
Thumbprint, goblet, Colonial Amber, #4445, 10-oz **8.00**
Thumbprint, vase, handkerchief; Colonial Orange, #4454, 8" **14.00**
Vasa Murrhina, basket, gr aventurine w/bl, #6458, 11" **100.00**
Vasa Murrhina, creamer, gr/bl, #6464, tall **78.00**
Vasa Murrhina, pitcher, Autumn Orange, sm **66.00**
Vasa Murrhina, vase, bl/gr/wht, #6454, 4" **55.00**
Vasa Murrhina, vase, gr/bl, dbl-crimped, #6456, 8" **78.00**
Vasa Murrhina, vase, rose/gr aventurine, #6454 ....**60.00**
Velvatone, bonbon, #846, 5" **65.00**
Velvatone, vase, etched, triangular, #1934, 5" **65.00**
Venetian Red, candlestick, #449, 8¾", pr **175.00**
Violets in Snow, compote, 7" **35.00**
Water Lily, bonbon, Pekin Bl, oval, #597 ....**35.00**
Water Lily, candy dish, rosalene, ftd, w/lid, #8480 ....**85.00**
Water Lily, pitcher, custard satin, #8464, 30-oz **35.00**
Water Lily, rose bowl, custard satin, #8429 ....**20.00**
Water Lily & Cattails, bowl, amethyst opal, 10" **78.00**
Wistaria, basket, crystal satin, #1684 ....**75.00**
Wistaria, vase, etched, #184, 11½" **75.00**

Fiesta

Fiesta is a line of dinnerware produced by the Homer Laughlin China Company of Newell, West Virginia, from 1936 until 1973. It was made in eleven different solid colors with over fifty pieces in the assortment. The pattern was developed by Frederick Rhead, an English Stoke-on-Trent potter who was an important contributor to the art-pottery movement in this country during the early part of the century. The design was carried out through the use of a simple band-of-rings device near the rim. Fiesta Red, a strong red-orange glaze color, was made with depleted uranium oxide. It was more expensive to produce than the other colors and sold at higher prices. Today's collectors still pay premium prices for Fiesta Red pieces. During the fifties the color assortment was gray, rose, chartreuse, and dark green. These colors are

relatively harder to find and along with Fiesta Red and medium green (new in 1959) command the higher prices.

Fiesta Kitchen Kraft was introduced in 1939; it consisted of seventeen pieces of kitchenware such as pie plates, refrigerator sets, mixing bowls, and covered jars in four popular Fiesta colors.

As a final attempt to adapt production to modern-day techniques and methods, Fiesta was restyled in 1969. Of the original colors, only Fiesta Red remained. This line, called Fiesta Ironstone, was discontinued in 1973.

Two types of marks were used: an ink stamp on machine-jiggered pieces and an indented mark molded into the hollowware pieces.

In 1986 HLC reintroduced a line of Fiesta dinnerware in five colors: black, white, pink, apricot, and cobalt (darker and denser than the original shade). Since then yellow, turquoise, and seafoam green have been added. Collectors have found that the new line poses no theat to their investments.

In the listings below, 'original colors' indicates only four of the original six — ivory, light green, turquoise, and yellow (or those remaining after specific original colors have been priced). Red and cobalt values are listed separately. For more information we recommend *The Collector's Encyclopedia of Fiesta, Harlequin, and Riviera* by Sharon and Bob Huxford, available at your local bookstore or from Collector Books.

Dinnerware

Ashtray, '50s colors **55.00**
Ashtray, orig colors **37.50**
Ashtray, red or cobalt **45.00**
Bowl, covered onion soup; cobalt & ivory **345.00**
Bowl, covered onion soup; red **365.00**
Bowl, covered onion soup; turq **1,500.00**
Bowl, covered onion soup; yel or lt gr **300.00**
Bowl, cream soup; '50s colors **47.50**
Bowl, cream soup; med gr **1,600.00**
Bowl, cream soup; orig colors **32.50**
Bowl, cream soup; red or cobalt **42.50**
Bowl, dessert; '50s colors, 6" **40.00**
Bowl, dessert; med gr, 6" **235.00**
Bowl, dessert; orig colors, 6" **28.00**
Bowl, dessert; red or cobalt, 6" **38.00**
Bowl, fruit; '50s colors, 4¾" **25.00**
Bowl, fruit; '50s colors, 5½" **28.50**
Bowl, fruit; med gr, 4¾" **260.00**
Bowl, fruit; med gr, 5½" **60.00**
Bowl, fruit; orig colors, 11¾" **120.00**
Bowl, fruit; orig colors, 4¾" **22.00**
Bowl, fruit; orig colors, 5½" **20.00**
Bowl, fruit; red or cobalt, 11¾" **160.00**
Bowl, fruit; red or cobalt, 4¾" **25.00**
Bowl, fruit; red or cobalt, 5½" **25.00**
Bowl, ftd salad; orig colors **190.00**
Bowl, ftd salad; red or cobalt **230.00**
Bowl, ind salad; med gr, 7½" **72.00**
Bowl, ind salad; red, turq, & yel, 7½" **55.00**
Bowl, nappy; '50s colors, 8½" **42.50**
Bowl, nappy; med gr, 8½" **70.00**
Bowl, nappy; orig colors, 8½" **28.00**
Bowl, nappy; orig colors, 9½" **35.00**
Bowl, nappy; red or cobalt, 8½" **38.00**
Bowl, nappy; red or cobalt, 9½" **45.00**
Bowl, Tom & Jerry; ivory w/gold letters **190.00**
Bowl, unlisted; red, cobalt, or ivory **230.00**
Bowl, unlisted; yel **65.00**
Candle holder, bulb; orig colors, pr **58.00**

Candle holder, bulb; red or cobalt, pr 75.00
Candle holder, tripod; orig colors, pr 265.00
Candle holder, tripod; red, cobalt, or ivory, pr 325.00

Carafe, original colors, $135.00.

Carafe, red or cobalt 170.00
Casserole, '50s colors 185.00
Casserole, French; standard colors other than yel 450.00
Casserole, French; yel 195.00
Casserole, med gr 310.00
Casserole, orig colors 90.00
Casserole, red or cobalt 130.00
Coffeepot, '50s colors 185.00
Coffeepot, demi; orig colors 155.00
Coffeepot, demi; red, cobalt, or ivory 200.00
Coffeepot, orig colors 110.00
Coffeepot, red or cobalt 130.00
Compote, orig colors, 12" 90.00
Compote, red or cobalt, 12" 115.00
Compote, sweets; orig colors 40.00
Compote, sweets; red or cobalt 50.00
Creamer, '50s colors 22.50
Creamer, ind; red 125.00
Creamer, ind; turq 195.00
Creamer, ind; yel 48.00
Creamer, med gr 42.00
Creamer, orig colors 15.50
Creamer, red or cobalt 18.50
Creamer, stick hdld, orig colors 25.00
Creamer, stick hdld, red or cobalt 32.00
Cup, demi; '50s colors 180.00
Cup, demi; orig colors 40.00
Cup, demi; red or cobalt 45.00
Egg cup, '50s colors 95.00
Egg cup, orig colors 35.50
Egg cup, red, cobalt, or ivory 47.50
Lid, for mixing bowl #1-#3, any color 375.00
Lid, for mixing bowl #4, any color 400.00
Marmalade, orig colors 125.00
Marmalade, red or cobalt 160.00
Mixing bowl, #1, orig colors 70.00
Mixing bowl, #1, red, cobalt, or ivory 100.00
Mixing bowl, #2, orig colors 48.00
Mixing bowl, #2, red or cobalt 58.00
Mixing bowl, #3, orig colors 52.00
Mixing bowl, #3, red or cobalt 62.00
Mixing bowl, #4, orig colors 58.00
Mixing bowl, #4, red or cobalt 65.00
Mixing bowl, #5, orig colors 63.50

Mixing bowl, #5, red or cobalt 70.00
Mixing bowl, #6, orig colors 83.50
Mixing bowl, #6, red, cobalt, or ivory 95.00
Mixing bowl, #7, orig colors 140.00
Mixing bowl, #7, red, cobalt, or ivory 170.00
Mug, Tom & Jerry, '50s colors 65.00
Mug, Tom & Jerry; ivory w/gold letters 55.00
Mug, Tom & Jerry; orig colors 42.00
Mug, Tom & Jerry; red or cobalt 58.00
Mustard, orig colors 105.00
Mustard, red or cobalt 140.00
Pitcher, disk juice; gray 1,100.00
Pitcher, disk juice; red 210.00
Pitcher, disk juice; yel 35.00
Pitcher, disk water; '50s colors 165.00
Pitcher, disk water; med gr 495.00
Pitcher, disk water; orig colors 72.50
Pitcher, disk water; red or cobalt 105.00
Pitcher, ice; orig colors 70.00
Pitcher, ice; red or cobalt 90.00
Pitcher, jug, 2-pt; '50s colors 85.00
Pitcher, jug, 2-pt; orig colors 45.00
Pitcher, jug, 2-pt; red, cobalt, or ivory 60.00
Plate, '50s colors, 10" 38.50
Plate, '50s colors, 6" 6.50
Plate, '50s colors, 7" 10.00
Plate, '50s colors, 9" 16.00
Plate, cake; lt gr or yel 435.00
Plate, cake; red or cobalt 500.00
Plate, calendar; 1954 or 1955, 10" 32.50
Plate, calendar; 1955, 9" 37.50
Plate, chop; '50s colors, 13" 46.00
Plate, chop; '50s colors, 15" 55.00
Plate, chop; med gr, 13" 75.00
Plate, chop; orig colors, 13" 25.00
Plate, chop; orig colors, 15" 27.50
Plate, chop; red or cobalt, 13" 30.00
Plate, chop; red or cobalt, 15" 37.50
Plate, compartment; '50s colors, 10½" 40.00
Plate, compartment; orig colors, 10½" 24.00
Plate, compartment; orig colors, 12" 32.00
Plate, compartment; red or cobalt, 10½" 28.50
Plate, compartment; red or cobalt, 12" 40.00
Plate, deep; '50s colors 42.00
Plate, deep; med gr 70.00
Plate, deep; orig colors 27.50
Plate, deep; red or cobalt 38.50
Plate, med gr, 10" 70.00
Plate, med gr, 6" 12.00
Plate, med gr, 7" 18.00
Plate, med gr, 9" 36.00
Plate, orig colors, 10" 25.00
Plate, orig colors, 6" 4.00
Plate, orig colors, 7" 6.50
Plate, orig colors, 9" 8.00
Plate, red or cobalt, 10" 32.00
Plate, red or cobalt, 6" 6.00
Plate, red or cobalt, 7" 8.50
Plate, red or cobalt, 9" 15.00
Platter, '50s colors 37.50
Platter, med gr 72.50
Platter, orig colors 22.50
Platter, red or cobalt 32.00
Sauce boat, '50s colors 45.00

Sauce boat, med gr 80.00
Sauce boat, orig colors 32.50
Sauce boat, red or cobalt 45.00
Saucer, '50s colors 5.00
Saucer, demi; '50s colors 47.50
Saucer, demi; orig colors 12.00
Saucer, demi; red or cobalt 12.50
Saucer, med gr 8.00
Saucer, orig colors 3.00
Saucer, red or cobalt 4.00
Shakers, '50s colors, pr 32.00
Shakers, med gr, pr 62.50
Shakers, orig colors, pr 16.50
Shakers, red or cobalt, pr 24.00
Sugar bowl, ind; turq 210.00
Sugar bowl, ind; yel 72.50
Sugar bowl, w/lid, '50s colors, 3¼x3½" 42.00
Sugar bowl, w/lid, med gr, 3¼x3½" 68.00
Sugar bowl, w/lid, orig colors, 3¼x3½" 25.00
Sugar bowl, w/lid, red or cobalt, 3¼x3½" 34.00
Syrup, orig colors 185.00
Syrup, red or cobalt 210.00
Teacup, '50s colors 30.00
Teacup, med gr 35.00
Teacup, orig colors 22.50
Teacup, red or cobalt 26.00
Teapot, lg; orig colors 95.00
Teapot, lg; red or cobalt 115.00
Teapot, med; '50s colors 175.00
Teapot, med; med gr 375.00
Teapot, med; orig colors 85.00
Teapot, med; red or cobalt 110.00
Tray, figure-8; cobalt 50.00
Tray, figure-8; turq 165.00
Tray, figure-8; yel 190.00
Tray, relish; mixed colors, no red 152.50
Tray, utility; orig colors 25.00
Tray, utility; red or cobalt 30.00
Tumbler, juice; chartreuse, Harlequin yel or dk gr 275.00
Tumbler, juice; orig colors 22.00
Tumbler, juice; red or cobalt 30.00
Tumbler, juice; rose 34.00
Tumbler, water; orig colors 40.00
Tumbler, water; red or cobalt 47.50
Vase, bud; orig colors 44.00
Vase, bud; red or cobalt 60.00
Vase, orig colors, 10" 400.00
Vase, orig colors, 12" 465.00
Vase, orig colors, 8" 300.00
Vase, red or cobalt, 10" 465.00
Vase, red or cobalt, 12" 585.00
Vase, red or cobalt, 8" 375.00

Kitchen Kraft

Bowl, mixing; lt gr or yel, 10" 63.50
Bowl, mixing; lt gr or yel, 6" 38.00
Bowl, mixing; lt gr or yel, 8" 52.00
Bowl, mixing; red or cobalt, 10" 73.50
Bowl, mixing; red or cobalt, 6" 43.00
Bowl, mixing; red or cobalt, 8" 62.00
Cake plate, lt gr or yel 37.50
Cake plate, red or cobalt 42.00
Cake server, lt gr or yel 63.50

Cake server, red or cobalt 73.50
Casserole, ind; lt gr or yel 110.00
Casserole, ind; red or cobalt 122.50
Casserole, lt gr or yel, 7½" 62.00
Casserole, lt gr or yel, 8½" 66.50
Casserole, red or cobalt, 7½" 72.50
Casserole, red or cobalt, 8½" 76.50
Covered jar, lg; lt gr or yel 185.00
Covered jar, lg; red or cobalt 205.00
Covered jar, med; lt gr or yel 165.00
Covered jar, med; red or cobalt 185.00
Covered jar, sm; lt gr or yel 180.00
Covered jar, sm; red or cobalt 200.00
Covered jug, lt gr or yel 150.00
Covered jug, red or cobalt 176.50
Fork, lt gr or yel 62.00
Fork, red or cobalt 66.50
Metal frame for platter 20.00
Pie plate, lt gr or yel, 10" 35.00
Pie plate, lt gr or yel, 9" 30.00
Pie plate, red or cobalt, 10" 40.00
Pie plate, red or cobalt, 9" 35.00
Shakers, lt gr or yel, pr 65.00
Shakers, red or cobalt, pr 75.00
Spoon, lt gr or yel 65.00
Spoon, red or cobalt 70.00
Stacking refrigerator lid, lt gr or yel 42.00
Stacking refrigerator lid, red or cobalt 48.00
Stacking refrigerator unit, lt gr or yel 27.50
Stacking refrigerator unit, red or cobalt 32.00

Finch, Kay

Kay Finch and her husband, Braden, operated a small pottery in Corona Del Mar, California, from 1939 to 1963. The company remained small, employing from twenty to sixty local residents who Kay trained in all but the most requiring tasks, which she herself performed. The company produced animal and bird figurines, most notably dogs, Kay's favorites. Figures of 'Godey'-type couples were also made, as were tableware (consisting of breakfast sets) and other artware. Most pieces were marked. Our advisor for this category is Jack Chipman, author of *The Collector's Encyclopedia of California Pottery*; he is listed in the Directory under California.

Cookie jar, Cookie Pup, 12¾" 200.00
Cookie jar, Cookie Puss, 11¾" 200.00
Figurine, Ambrosia, cat, 11" 200.00
Figurine, bunny, stands upright, 8½" 95.00
Figurine, Chinese boy & girl, 7½" 65.00
Figurine, duck, 4", pr 70.00
Figurine, elephant, 5" 75.00
Figurine, Hoot, owl, 9" 95.00
Figurine, Jezebel, cat sleeping, 5x7" 125.00
Figurine, Pete, penguin, 7½" 80.00
Figurine, pig, floral decor, 10x16" 250.00
Figurine, rooster, 8" 50.00
Figurine, Scandie, boy & girl, 5½", pr 55.00
Figurine, squirrel, sm 45.00
Figurine, Tootsie, owl, sm 35.00
Figurine, Winkie, winking pig, daisy decor, 4" 45.00
Figurine, Yorkshire puppy, 6" 95.00
Shakers, turkey, pr 25.00

Findlay Onyx and Floradine

Findlay, Ohio, was the location of the Dalzell, Gilmore, and Leighton Glass Company, one of at least sixteen companies that flourished there between 1886 and 1901. Their most famous ware, Onyx, is very rare. It was produced for only a short time beginning in 1889 due to the heavy losses incurred in the manufacturing process.

Onyx is layered glass, usually found in creamy white with a dainty floral pattern accented with metallic lustre that has been trapped between the two layers. Other colors found on rare occasions include a light amber (with either no lustre or with gilt flowers), light amethyst (or lavender), and rose. Although old tradepaper articles indicate the company originally intended to produce the line in three distinct colors, long-time Onyx collectors report that aside from the white, production was very limited. Other colors of Onyx are very rare, and the few examples that are found tend to support the theory that production of colored Onyx ware remained for the most part in the experimental stage. Even three-layered items have been found (they are extremely rare) decorated with three-color flowers. As a rule of thumb, using white Onyx prices as a basis for evaluation, expect to pay two to five times more for colored examples.

Floradine is a separate line that was made with the Onyx molds. A single-layer rose satin glassware with white opal flowers, it is usually priced in the general range of colored Onyx.

Chipping around the rims is very common, and price is determined to a great extent by condition. Our advisors for this category are Betty and Clarence Maier; they are listed in the Directory under Pennsylvania.

Floradine

Bowl, fluted, squat bulbous base, 4"	775.00
Box, dresser; 5½" dia	1,600.00
Creamer, bulbous, fluted neck, 4⅝"	1,150.00
Sugar bowl, bulbous, w/lid, 5½"	1,200.00
Sugar shaker	2,000.00
Syrup pitcher	2,500.00

Floradine toothpick holder, 2½", M, $800.00; Mustard pot, 3¾", M, $1,050.00.

Tumbler, slightly bulbous, 3⅝"	700.00
Vase, fluted cylinder neck, bulbous body, 6½"	900.00

Onyx

Bottle, tumble-up; wht w/silver decor, no tumbler, 8¾"	500.00
Bowl, master berry; wht w/silver decor, 8"	400.00
Bowl, wht w/purple decor, fluted rim, squat body, 4"	1,000.00
Box, wht w/silver decor, 5½" dia	750.00
Butter dish, wht w/silver decor	1,250.00
Celery vase, wht w/silver decor, 6½", EX	425.00
Creamer, wht w/silver decor	350.00
Jam jar, wht w/silver decor	500.00
Mustard pot, wht w/lt orange decor, rare, 3½"	1,500.00
Pitcher, wht w/silver decor, 8"	1,200.00
Spooner, wht w/silver decor, 4¼"	325.00
Sugar shaker, wht w/silver trim, NP top, 5½x3"	500.00
Tumbler, wht w/silver decor, bbl shape, 3¾x2⅞"	375.00

Fire Marks

During the early 18th century, insurance companies used fire marks — signs of insurance — to indicate to the volunteer firefighters which homes were covered by their company. Handsome rewards were promised to the brigade that successfully extinguished the blaze, so competition was fierce between rivals and sometimes resulted in an altercation at the scene to settle the matter of which brigade would be the one to fight the fire! Fire marks were originally made of cast iron or lead; later examples were sometimes tin or zinc. They were used abroad as well as in this country, and those from England tended to be much more elaborate. When municipal fire departments were organized in the mid-to late 1860s, volunteer departments and fire marks became obsolete.

Two fire marks, cast iron with polychrome paint, Fire Department Insurance, 11½" long, $375.00; City Insurance Co., Cin., 12½" long, $650.00.

FA, CI, emb hose & FA, 11½x7¾", EX	85.00
Gr tree, CI w/hollow bk, 12x8¼", EX	100.00
Hartford Fire Ins...1810, tin	22.50
Insured Mutual Hartford, brass	50.00
Invicta, lead, rearing horse, 8¾x6½"	150.00
Liverpool & London & Globe, tin	20.00
London Assurance Inc-AD 1720, tin	40.00
Reliance Insurance Co 1817, compo, oval	40.00
Royal Exchange Assurance, lead, mtd on wood panel	50.00
Steam pumper & UF on oval, pitted/rpt, 9x12"	130.00
Sun Ins Office, lead, sun w/16 rays, 7x7"	150.00
Sun London 1710, tin, 7" dia	20.00

Firefighting Collectibles

Firefighting antiques from the 19th century reflect the feeling of pride the men had in their companies and in their role as volunteer firefighters. Fancy dress uniforms and helmets, silver trumpets full of flowers recall the charisma of the 'Laddies' on parade. Leather buckets, bed keys, muffin bells, rattles, torches, lanterns, and riveted leather hose all serve as reminders of that era long past.

In the 1860s the old volunteer units begrudgingly gave way to the 'paid municipal firefighter.' The politically astute and sometimes physically aggressive volunteer organizations many times went down hard and maintained group integrity many years after paid forces were in place.

With the inception of 'disciplined' paid forces, the ascention to more sophisticated fire alarms and fire supression equipment was accelerated. Hand and horse-drawn equipment predominated until about WWI when apparatus motorization really took hold and for the most part was the dominating factor by 1920. Suspicious of the new machines, many northern fire departments kept horse-drawn sleighs in reserve well into the late 1920s.

Today there is a large, active group of collectors for fire department antiques (items over 100 years old) and an even larger group seeking related collectibles (those less than 100 years old). Note: In the extinguishers listed below, the term 'apparatus type' refers to that which is carried on or by fire apparatus; 'building type' are those found hanging on walls of buildings. Our advisors for this category are H. Thomas and Patricia Laun; they are listed in the Directory under New York.

Key: s+a — soda & acid

Alarm box, ADT, CI, institutional style 65.00
Alarm box, Auto Call, CI, industrial style 35.00
Alarm box, CI, w/key guard, case only, 12" 200.00
Alarm box, Gamewell, CI, industrial door, key guard, complete .180.00
Alarm box, Holtzer Cabot, CI & brass, institutional style 75.00
Alarm box, Star Electric, Binghamton NY, CI, complete 385.00
Alarm box, Utica FA & Tel Co, CI, full sz, complete 385.00
Axe, Viking style, 19½" L head, EX 475.00
Badge, brass, Volunteer Fireman's Assoc NY City 227, EX 50.00
Badge, complimentary, Eureka Fire Hose, metal, 1930s, 1¼"....20.00
Badge, gold-tone metal, LI City FD Exempt 42, eagle atop, EX 95.00
Badge, Hackettstown...1906, brass link w/cello inserts, 2x4" 38.00
Badge, Newburyport -8- Fire Dept #141, shield shape, worn 60.00
Badge, Union Hose #3 on 5-pointed star, NP, VG 75.00
Badge, Watertown FD #1, 5-pointed star, NP, EX 80.00
Badge, West Parke/Stowe Twp, SP brass, 1930s, 1¾", EX 25.00
Bed key, CI, 1800s, VG 200.00
Bell, apparatus, after market style, 12", NM 435.00
Bell, apparatus, chrome/brass, complete, 14" 495.00
Bell, apparatus, chrome/brass, Seagrave, w/bracket, 12" 535.00
Bell, apparatus, NP, 10" dia, EX 325.00
Bell, brass, muffin type w/trn wood hdl, 5⅜" dia, VG 325.00
Bell, brass, muffin type w/wood hdl, 5½" dia, NM 625.00
Belt, parade; canvas w/lg brass buckle, NM 100.00
Belt, parade; leather, Constitution 2 on keeper, EX 170.00
Book, As You Pass By, 1952, 260-pg, EX 35.00
Book, Foot Prints of Assurance, EX 45.00
Book, History of Am Steam...Engine, King, 1896, 150-pg, EX ...160.00
Box, ballot; walnut (worn), wooden blk & wht balls 120.00

Bucket, painted leather, dated 1807, inscribed 'NJT Ropes,' minor paint loss, 12", $3,000.00; Helmet, painted leather, dated 1852, Cairns & Bros. makers, lion holder, minor paint loss, 9½", $900.00.

Bucket, feed; pnt canvas, RFD pnt on front, EX 150.00
Bucket, leather, hand stitched, orig pnt banner: name/'06, EX ...650.00
Bucket, leather, hand stitched, rpt eagle w/banner, VG 275.00
Bucket, leather, rpt hook & ladder scene, EX 155.00
Cap, uniform; bl w/silver FD buttons, no badge, dress type 35.00
Chest, tool; wood w/pnt decor, Waltham WFA, 16x36x17", EX ..400.00
Cuff links, Firehouse Mfg Co NY, brass, pr 20.00
Extinguisher, Alfite-Speedex 5, Am LaFrance, CO2, EX in box ..35.00
Extinguisher, Badgers, pnt label, pony sz 65.00
Extinguisher, Eastern...Portland ME, copper, bldg type, s+a 35.00
Extinguisher, Instantaneous Detroit, dry chemicals, EX 25.00
Extinguisher, Liberty, dry chemicals, tube form, 22", EX 50.00
Extinguisher, Monarch Fire Killer, GS&AJ Howe Co, EX 60.00
Extinguisher, Northern Minneapolis, dry chemicals, EX 50.00
Extinguisher, Phoenix Dry Powder, tube form, 22", EX 40.00
Extinguisher, Protection Sure Death to Fire, dry chemicals, EX ...65.00
Extinguisher, Richmond Chemical, tube shape, EX 30.00
Extinguisher, Texaco, brass 37.50
Extinguisher, volunteer; Dietz, vaporizing liquid, EX 45.00
Figure, Dalmation, ceramic, lt age crazing, 11" 225.00
Frontpc, leather, NP Banks Hose 2 WFD, 8" 130.00
Frontpc, NP brass, Shiffler-7-S, 8", EX 150.00
Game, Fire Alarm Game, Parker Bros, 1899, NM 2,750.00
Gauge, Am Fire Extinguisher, NP brass, 6" 30.00
Globe, alarm pole; red glass, EX 180.00
Gong, brass bell & nut, 8" CI pull-chain mechanism 65.00
Gong, Gamewell, turtle type w/6" steel bell, EX 75.00
Gong, Gamewell Bliss, chrome, steel bell, chain wind, 10" 125.00
Grenade, Harden's, quilted, aqua 65.00
Grenade, Harden's, quilted, cobalt 170.00
Grenade, Harden's Hand Grenade Fire Extinguisher, bl 170.00
Grenade, Harkness, sapphire bl w/blk streaks, 6", EX 450.00

Grenade: Harden's Hand Fire Extinguisher - Star, turquoise, full, M, $60.00; Hayward Hand Grenade Fire Extinguisher No. 407, Broadway, New York, Design H Patd, clear, tooled lip, sealed, M, $140.00.

Grenade, Hayward's Hand Fire Grenade, lt honey amber, 6" 225.00
Grenade, Hayward's...Pat Aug 8 1871, cobalt 200.00
Grenade, Hayward's...Pat Aug 8 1871, forest gr 280.00
Grenade, Hayward's...Pat Aug 8 1871, gr, EX 180.00
Grenade, HSN, yel-amber, emb dmns, complete, 7¼" 195.00
Grenade, Pyrene, 1-qt vaporizing liquid, w/bracket 35.00
Hat, parade; stovepipe style, cb w/NM pnt 1,500.00
Helmet, aluminum w/high eagle, Asst Chief NFD, EX 180.00
Helmet, aluminum w/low leather front, Cairns, EX 75.00

Helmet, aluminum w/low leather front, Riverton Fire Dept, EX ..80.00
Helmet, Austrian, brass comb, Xd axes at front, EX 170.00
Helmet, fiberglass w/leather front, EX 60.00
Helmet, leather, high eagle, Cairns, Prov Veteran Assoc, VG ...275.00
Helmet, leather, high eagle, lacks frontpc, VG 125.00
Helmet, leather, high eagle w/frontpc, Cairns, EX 275.00
Helmet, leather, high eagle w/frontpc, 4-comb, 1840s, EX 500.00
Helmet, leather New Yorker w/Burke shield, FDNY frontpc, G .135.00
Hoister, hose; Hayward & Bresnans' Pat Oct 19, 1866, EX 45.00
Hose clamp, Akron, cast aluminum 65.00
Hose clamp, Am LaFrance, CI 95.00
Hose clamp, Pirsch, wood & CI 235.00
Hydrant, CI, red/blk/silver pnt, 33" 110.00
Hydrant, wooden, gold leaf, mini, 5" 40.00
Indian tank, brass, bk-pack style, complete, EX 65.00
Lantern, Bridgeport Brass Co, hand type, 1870s-80s, EX 425.00
Lantern, Dietz Fire King, NP brass, NM 250.00
Lantern, Dietz Fire King, Seagrave, slide-off cage, complete 450.00
Lantern, Dietz King, Am LaFrance, brass/NP, 15", EX 250.00
Lantern, Dietz King, Seagrave Co, NP, bl over clear globe, NM ...950.00
Lantern, Dietz King Fire Dept, brass, red globe, EX 220.00
Lantern, Dietz Queen Fire Dept, NP brass, hand sz 625.00
Lantern, FD Dewey & Son Boston, NP, hand type w/red globe ..175.00
Lantern globe, for Dietz King, cobalt 45.00
Lantern globe, for Dietz King, forest gr 55.00
Lantern globe, for Dietz King, red (or bl or gr) over clear 350.00
Ledger marker, Guardian Assurance Co...1821, 12¼", EX 60.00
Medal, Medal of Honor City of Plainfield, 1908, EX 150.00
Nozzle, Akron, brass, w/Am LaFrance mk control valve, 13½" ..135.00
Nozzle, Akron Model 15 Phomaire, 1½", 12½" H 45.00
Nozzle, brass & chrome w/leather grips, no shut-off, 20½" 90.00
Nozzle, Callaghan, brass, shut-off, 2½" base, 1⅛" tip, G 235.00
Nozzle, Powhatan, brass, booster sz 37.50
Nozzle, standpipe, brass, no shut off, 1½" 10.00
Permit, FD of NY Bureau of Fire Prevention, 1914, 16x10" 25.00
Photo, Pacific Engine #14-New London CT members, 1898, 12x14" .50.00
Pin-bk, Clifton Heights PA firehouse dedication, '08, 1¾" 20.00
Plaque, builder's, Amoskeag Manchester NY, 1866, EX 475.00
Plaque, builder's, brass, Standard Fire Dept, 5¼x7" 25.00
Plaque, builder's, NP brass, Built by RS Nichols...VT 400.00
Plate, Farmington Hook & Ladder #1, Royal Ironstone, dinner sz ..40.00
Rack, Gamewell, rectifier/charger control base, 2-circuit, 78" 600.00
Rattle, dbl reed, walnut wood, 10½" 150.00
Record book, NYC, 1949 ....20.00
Ribbon, Houtzpale PA convention, 1897, EX 15.00
Ribbon, Marshal BFRA, Jan 1898, EX 15.00
Slide, kerchief; brass shield form, 2" L, EX 50.00
Spotlight, Atwood, Amesbury Mass, brass, carbide, 22" 220.00
Statuary, firefighter, SP pot metal, Braxmar, 17½" 1,800.00
Tapper, NP, umbrella shape, 6" bell w/acorn finial, EX 295.00
Telephone, Gamewell, portable unit, VG 90.00
Torch, apparatus, brass, mtd on wood base, 1850s, 9", EX 180.00
Torch, engineer's, NP w/brass cap, 7", EX 30.00
Torch, parade; brass, on swivel, no burner, 8", VG 40.00
Torch, parade; NP brass, w/gimball, 7" dia 80.00
Torch, parade; wooden w/mounting pole, gold pnt, 8½" 55.00
Trumpet, brass, working, w/tassel & cord, 16" 400.00
Trumpet, NP/brass, working, 17", EX 425.00
Trumpet, pewter, Woodbury Pewters, eagle & shield, 19", EX ...150.00
Trumpet, presentation, SP w/eng steamer, 1892, 21", NM 1,300.00
Trumpet, presentation grade, SP, floral eng, dtd 1910, M 1,000.00
Watch fob, Guest, 1922 convention, SP brass, 1½x1½" 18.00
Wrench, Boston Coupling Co, combination spanner, 9½", EX 10.00
Wristwatch, Waltham, NYFD Chief on face, leather band, '15 ..250.00

Fireplace Implements

In the colonial days of our country, fireplaces provided heat in the winter and were used year round to cook food in the kitchen. The implements that were a necessary part of these functions were varied and have become treasured collectibles, many put to new use in modern homes as decorative accessories. Gypsy pots may hold magazines; copper and brass kettles, newly polished and gleaming, contain dried flowers or green plants. Firebacks, highly ornamental iron panels that once reflected heat and protected masonry walls, are now sometimes used as wall decorations.

By Victorian times the cookstove had replaced the kitchen fireplace, and many of these early utensils were already obsolete; but as a source of heat and comfort, the fireplace continued to be used for several more decades. See also Wrought Iron.

Andirons, brass, ball finials, arched spur legs, early, 18" 500.00
Andirons, brass, ball finials, arched spur legs, early 16" 350.00
Andirons, brass, ball finials, sgn Molineaux, 1810, 15" 1,300.00
Andirons, brass, lg acorn finials, arched spur legs, 1800 ....700.00
Andirons, brass, pagoda finial, arched spur legs, 15" 200.00
Andirons, brass, Queen Anne, ball top, snake ft, 24" 1,250.00
Andirons, CI, baseball players, EX detail, 20", pr 1,500.00
Andirons, CI, comical Blk man (& lady), hands on knees, 16" ...250.00
Andirons, CI, Geo Washington standing on tall base, 20" 220.00
Andirons, CI, Hessian soldiers, rpr/heat damage, 20" 225.00
Andirons, wrought iron, twist detail/gooseneck finial, 1900 ....90.00
Bellows, turtle-bk; leather w/floral, very worn, 18" 95.00
Bellows, turtle-bk; mc cornucopia on yel, worn leather, 18" 100.00

Cast iron fireback, Medusa's head relief, cast with maker's mark, attributed to Elihu Vedder, 1884, 66" total width (rare cast in three parts), $4,000.00.

Coal bucket, brass, emb florals & fruit, England, 1850s, VG 200.00
Crane, wrought iron, Y-form, folds in center, 52" L 85.00
Crane, wrought iron, 1700s, 22x20¼", EX 140.00
Fender, wire grill w/steel ft & rim, serpentine, 41" 275.00
Fender, wrought iron, simple detail, 13x70" 125.00
Firebk, CI, shaped top, allegorical scene relief, 1770s, 27" 385.00
Pan, hot coal carrier; sheet iron, wrought hdw, wood hdl 225.00
Shovel, wrought iron w/brass urn finial, early, 19" 95.00
Tongs, ember; CI, star/hearts/dmns/ovals cast in ends, 13½" 85.00

Trivet, folding, brass, 7½x24" L 575.00

Fischer

Ignaz and Emil Fischer were art pottery designers and producers from Hungary. Ignaz Fischer founded a workshop in Budapest, Hungary, in 1866. He had previously worked for M.F. Fischer, owner of the famous Herend factory, also in Hungary. His first products included domestic tableware and decorative items that utilized a cream-colored clay; styles were copied from the Herend factory. His ware is recognized by the pale yellow, soft-lead glaze, usually decorated with painted ethnic Hungarian designs.

Emil Fischer took the business over from his father around 1890. The workshop was closed in 1908 and reopened for only a short time. Production from this period was influenced by the high-style designs of the Zsolnay factory in Pecs, Hungary. Unable to compete, they turned to the manufacture of building materials. Marks (incised and painted): Fischer J. Budapest; initials: F.E. under a crown.

Bowl, centerpc; butterfly figural, rtcl, dbl mk, 11x10" 255.00
Charger, mc florals, gold trim, 13" 335.00
Pitcher, fantasy form w/Oriental graphics on tan, #815, 12" 250.00
Pitcher, mc floral, rtcl rim, 12" 275.00
Pitcher, rtcl, dolphin hdl, early, 11" 495.00

Pitcher, reticulated outer wall, shield-shaped reserve with birds and flowers, dolphin handle, very early, 11", $450.00.

Plate, Chantilly Fruit, 7½" 88.00
Urn, floral, rtcl rim, w/lid, 12" 335.00
Vase, mc on cream, areas of dbl-wall rtcl, mk, 15" 335.00

Fisher, Harrison

Harrison Fisher (1875-1934), noted illustrator and creator of the Fisher Girl, was the son of landscape artist, Hugh Antoine Fisher. His career began in his teens in San Francisco where he did artwork for the Hearst papers. Later in New York his drawings of beautiful American women attracted much attention and graced the covers of the most popular magazines of the day such as *Puck, Ladies' Home Journal, Saturday Evening Post,* and *Cosmopolitan.* He also illustrated novels, and his art books were treasured. His drawings appeared on thousands of postcards and posters. His creation of the Fisher Girl and his panel of six scenes of the *Greatest Moments in a Woman's Life* made him the most sought-after and well-paid illustrator of his day.

Book, A Girl's Life & Other Pictures, 1913, EX 395.00
Book, American Beauties, Bobbs Merril, 1st ed, 1909, EX 195.00
Book, American Belles, 11", EX 250.00
Book, Book of Sweethearts, Groset Dunlap, color plates, 1908 .....85.00
Book, Dream of Fair Women, color plates, 1907 ....155.00
Book, Fair Americans, 1911, EX 185.00
Book, Love Finds Way, Ford, Fisher illus, 1904 ....25.00
Book, Maidens Fair, 1912, EX 285.00
Book, The Harrison Fisher Book, 1907, EX 195.00
Bookplate, American Beauties, 1909, 11x8½" 65.00
Candy tin, Dancing Girl, Tindeco, 2½x7" dia 40.00
Candy tin, Snowbird, Tindeco, 1⅜x4" 40.00
Magazine cover, Ladies' Home Journal, ea 22.00
Magazine cover, Saturday Evening Post, ea 18.00
Postcard, Autumn's Beauty, lady artist, Reinthal-Newman, EX 20.00
Postcard, Greatest Moments, set of 6 in orig matting & fr 95.00
Print, All Mine, girl w/puppy, fr 35.00
Print, American Belles, 1911 ....285.00
Print, Danger, ca 1908, old fr 85.00
Print, Dumb Luck, matted print, 6½x10½", fr: 11x15" 25.00
Prints, orig, old & unmatted, 11x14", ea 35.00
Tea container, Coquette masquerade girl, Tindeco, 6½" 45.00

Fishing Collectibles

Collecting old fishing tackle is becoming more popular every year. Though at first most interest was geared toward old lures and some reels, rods, advertising, and miscellaneous items are quickly gaining ground. Values are given for examples in excellent or better condition and should be used only as a guide. For more information contact our advisor Randy Hilst, an appraiser and collector whose address and phone number are listed in the Directory under Illinois.

Catalog, Creek Chub 1947 ....50.00
Catalog, Heddon, 1949 ....55.00
Catalog, Paw Paw, 1949 ....30.00
Counter display, Pflueger, cb, 1930s 75.00
Lure, Creek Chub #100 Wiggler, glass eyes, wood 30.00
Lure, Creek Chub Baby Pikie, glass eyes, wood 10.00
Lure, Creek Chub Baby Wiggle Fish, glass eyes, wood 25.00
Lure, Creek Chub Beetle, bead eyes, wood 65.00
Lure, Creek Chub Crawdad, bead eyes, wood 12.00
Lure, Creek Chub Deluxe Wag-tail Chub, glass eyes, wood 30.00
Lure, Creek Chub Ding Bat, glass eyes, wood 20.00
Lure, Creek Chub Flip Flap, glass eyes, wood 30.00
Lure, Creek Chub Gar Minnow, glass eyes, wood 125.00
Lure, Creek Chub Injured Minnow, glass eyes, wood 10.00
Lure, Creek Chub Lucky Mouse, bead eyes, wood 65.00
Lure, Creek Chub Midget Dinger, glass eyes, wood 25.00
Lure, Creek Chub Midget Plunker, glass eyes, wood 10.00
Lure, Creek Chub Pop-N-Dunk, glass eyes, wood 25.00
Lure, Creek Chub Sarasota, glass eyes, wood 100.00
Lure, Creek Chub Surfster, glass eyes, wood 30.00
Lure, Creek Chub Tiny Tim, pnt eyes, wood 10.00
Lure, Creek Chub Wee Bug, glass eyes, wood 70.00
Lure, Creek Chub Wiggle Fish, glass eyes, wood 35.00
Lure, Heddon #00 Minnow, glass eyes, wood 90.00
Lure, Heddon #120 Torpedo, glass eyes, wood 70.00
Lure, Heddon #210 Surface Lure, glass eyes, wood 30.00
Lure, Heddon #300 Surface Minnow, glass eyes, wood 100.00
Lure, Heddon #700 Musky Minnow, glass eyes, wood 400.00
Lure, Heddon Baby Crab Wiggler, glass eyes, wood 30.00
Lure, Heddon Baby Tadpolly, glass eyes, wood 50.00

Lure, Heddon Basser, glass eyes, wood 30.00
Lure, Heddon Game Fisher, no eyes, wood 20.00
Lure, Heddon Hi-Tail, pnt eyes, plastic 8.00
Lure, Heddon Little Joe, glass eyes, wood 70.00
Lure, Heddon Lucky 13, glass eyes, wood 20.00
Lure, Heddon Vamp, glass eyes, wood 15.00
Lure, Heddon Weedless Widow, no eyes, wood 25.00
Lure, Heddon 5-Hook Underwater Minnow, glass eyes, wood 70.00

Lure, Heddon Walton Feathertail, glass eyes, wood, $60.00.

Lure, South Bend Babe Oreno, glass eyes, wood 8.00
Lure, South Bend Bass Oreno, glass eyes, wood 8.00
Lure, South Bend Mouse Oreno, tack eyes, wood 40.00
Lure, South Bend Panetalla Minnow, glass eyes, wood 70.00
Lure, South Bend Pike Oreno, tack eyes, wood 12.00
Lure, South Bend Plunk Oreno, glass eyes, wood 30.00
Lure, South Bend Two-Oreno, tack eyes, wood 15.00
Lure, South Bend Woodpecker, no eyes, wood 30.00
Reel, Pflueger Supreme, level wind 25.00
Reel, Pflueger Rocket, level wind 25.00
Rod, Winchester, metal, 9 ft 65.00

Flags of the United States

The brevity and imprecise language of the first Flag Act of 1777 allowed great artistic license for our early flag makers. As a result, vast and varied interpretations were produced until 1912 when stringent design standards were established for the new 48-star flag. Early patterns ranging from random 'scatter' arrangements to elaborate wreaths, 'Great Stars,' and other geometric variants all coexisted with traditional row formations.

The concept of combining all of the stars of the union into a single 'Great Star' configuration became popular in the early 19th century. It would remain a national favorite for more than fifty years until its gradual disappearance in the post-Civil War years.

Home-stitched 'scatter' or random star patterns continued to be produced throughout our early history until the advent of mass-produced sewn flags in the late 19th century. While most of these patterns are chance arrangements absent of any formal design organization, some examples may display an ambiguous combination of planned and random patterning.

Variants of wreath patterns beginning with the early single-wreaths eventually evolved into elegant double- and triple-wreaths of 37, 38, and 39 stars by the time of the Centennial celebration. This period is considered by many flag aficionados to be the apex of American flag design, but it was short-lived. By the mid-1880s nearly all of the late version 38-star unions were conservatively configured in quiescence or row formations. Since then, the design of all succeeding generations of American flags has been similarly influenced.

While the transfer of historical information in any transaction should always be addressed, most vintage flags in today's marketplace are of the 'generic' variety, devoid of any special pedigree or proven history. Nevertheless, these cherished artifacts continue to be avidly collected on the basis of age, scarcity, configuration, craftsmanship, and aesthetic merit.

Pre-Civil War flags of 33 stars or less are very scarce and usually surface as 'big ticket' items. In those relatively uncharted waters, the terms of any given transaction are always subject to the give-and-take of the negotiating process itself. There has also been a surging interest in Civil War-era flags of 34 and 35 stars as more Americans begin to focus on that epic period of U.S. history. That in combination with the demands of a large and well-entrenched fraternity of Civil War collectors has dramatically stimulated pricing into what is now clearly a seller's market.

Since 36-star flags are more likely to be post-Civil War flags, they, along with 37-star flags, have less broad-based appeal. Nevertheless, both vintages can fetch very respectable prices. Flags of 38 stars and the unofficial vintages of 39, 40, and 42 stars provide a popular, moderately priced marketplace for journeyman flag buffs and collectors of Americana, while the elusive 43-star flag is sought by nearly everyone. Flags of 44, 45, and 46 stars are usually production line items. Nevertheless, they are not without collecting merit and are often available at comparatively modest prices. Ordinary 48-star flags flood the flea markets and are of little interest to most collectors, but the scarcer 49-star flag can generate occasional attention. 13-star flags, produced over a period of 200 years, surface in all forms and must be judged on a case-by-case basis. Many flag buffs favor flag sizes that are manageable for wall display, and most will make allowances for normal wear and tear. With rare exception, modern-day repros of historical flags have little or no collector appeal.

The dollar value of a flag is by no means based on age alone. The wide price swings in the listings that follow are the result of a variety of special considerations and features. Mass-printed flags, for instance, are generally not the equal of handcrafted flags, nor do unions with conventional rows of stars compare to the remarkable 'Great Star' and wreath patterns of the past. In fact, almost any special feature that stands out as unusual or distinctive is a potential asset. Imprinted flags and inscribed flags; 8-pointed stars, gold stars, and added stars; extra stripes, missing stripes, tri-color stripes, and war stripes are all part of the pricing equation. And while political and military flags may rank above all others in terms of prestige and price, any flag with a significant and well-documented historical connection has 'star' potential (pardon the pun). Our advisor for this category is Robert Banks; he is listed in the Directory under Maryland.

13 stars, (4-5-4), sea captains, ca 1860s, 74x140" 280.00
13 stars, Betsy Ross flag, by grandaughter, 1903, 8x12" 500.00
13 stars, Civil War boat ensign, USS Wabash, 44x64" 1,200.00
13 stars, fraternal, sewn muslin, ca 1870s, 97x136" 135.00
13 stars, in semi-wreath, hand sewn, 1870s, 54x102" 180.00
13 stars, printed, w/advertisement, 1880s, 4x7" 40.00
13 stars, US Navy boat ensign, dtd Sept 1904, 44x78" 75.00
13 stars, 3-2 pattern, machine sewn, 1880s, 24x48" 90.00
13 stars, 3rd MD pattern, hand sewn, 1840s, 32x45" 575.00
16 stars, naval ensign, hand sewn, CW era, 44x60" 600.00
19 stars, 16 orig+3, sewn scrap fabric, 39x66" 960.00
20 stars, hand embr into Great Star, rare, 24x32" 1,050.00
23 stars, Civil War related, home-sewn muslin, 48x96" 200.00
25 stars, stenciled burlap on 24" wood tripod pole, 5x7" 220.00
26 stars, Great Star, embr on sewn silk, 30x43" 630.00

29 stars, entirely hand sewn, poor condition, 43x68" **410.00**
30 stars, gold stars/fringe, silk, delicate, 52x68" **425.00**
31 stars, Great Star, Lincoln related, printed, 11x14" **185.00**
31 stars, Great Star, 14 stripes, hand sewn, 39x69" **600.00**
32 stars, dbl wreath of inset stars, hand sewn, 36x48" **535.00**
33 stars, hand-/machine-sewn wool bunting, 66x92" **475.00**
33 stars, wreath w/10 stripes, hand sewn, 77x127" **450.00**
34 stars, dbl-wreath pattern, hand-sewn bunting, 24x36" **560.00**
34 stars, dbl-wreath pattern, printed silk, 18x28" **180.00**
34 stars, Great Star, mixed fabrics, sewn, 91x154" **670.00**
34 stars, printed, added Garfield campaign legend, 24x48" **325.00**
34 stars form shield, all hand sewn, worn, 51x66" **600.00**
34 stars in pentagonal clusters, hand sewn, 63x95" **620.00**
35 stars, hand/machine sewn, 96x180" **510.00**
35 stars, recruiting flag, sewn bunting, 50x116" **585.00**
36 stars, Civil War, 8-pointed sewn wreath, 78x90" **720.00**
36 stars, sailing ship's, inscr & dtd, 75x142" **235.00**
36 stars, 11 tricolor stripes, hand sewn, 51x99" **230.00**
37 stars, printed silk, 32x40" **40.00**
37 stars, row pattern, stitched bunting, 30x48" **180.00**
37 stars, wreath pattern, hand-sewn cotton, 72x106" **290.00**
37 stars, 6-pointed, hand-/machine-stitched cotton, 60x84" **375.00**
38 stars, Blaine campaign, printed cotton, 17x27" **340.00**
38 stars, Centennial 1886, printed cotton, 15x24" **70.00**
38 stars, dbl-wreath pattern, sewn muslin, 87x128" **190.00**
38 stars, from 1884 ocean liner, hand sewn, 68x108" **320.00**
38 stars, GAR, Lewis Post 347, machine sewn, 53x107" **95.00**
38 stars, Great Star, printed silk, gold fringe, 12x17" **65.00**
38 stars, printed glazed muslin pattern variation, 30x48" **50.00**
38 stars, triple-wreath pattern, sewn bunting, 76x136" **240.00**
38 stars, Union on red war stripe, homemade, 44x84" **75.00**
38 stars, 1776-1876 pattern, printed linen, 27½x46" **330.00**
39 stars, clamp-dye printed wool bunting, 56x117" **95.00**
39 stars, originally 34 Great Star, sewn, 69x129" **360.00**
39 stars, row pattern variation, printed silk, 12x24" **45.00**
39 stars, scatter pattern, hand sewn, 78x120" **170.00**
39 stars, triple wreath, hand-sewn bunting, 60x108" **250.00**
39 stars (6-5 pattern), printed gauze bunting, 19x34" **32.00**
40 stars, unofficial, hand/machine sewn, 61x115" **90.00**
40 stars, wreath-in-box pattern, hand sewn, 43x82" **140.00**
41 star printed flags (17), uncut muslin, rare, 24x263" **300.00**
42 stars, minor pattern variation, sewn bunting, 96x138" **68.00**
42 stars, printed cotton, unhemmed, 18x24" **22.00**
42 stars, Union scatter pattern, hand sewn, 48x72" **134.00**
43 stars, machine-sewn bunting, extremely rare, 29x70" **425.00**
43 stars (1 side only), 98989 pattern, homemade, 38x48" **175.00**
44 stars, hand-sewn bunting, 70x144", EX **85.00**
44 stars, machine-sewn cotton bunting, 53x82" **45.00**
45 stars, machine-sewn cotton bunting, 80x108" **24.00**
45 stars, modified 38-star, hand sewn, 120x192" **110.00**
45 stars, triple-wreath GAR flag, printed muslin, 11x16" **40.00**
45 stars, Union, hand-sewn wool bunting, 92x135" **30.00**
45 stars, Union Jack, machine-sewn bunting, 50x76" **37.00**
46 stars, machine-sewn wool bunting, 72x138" **35.00**
46 stars, printed silk, in baton-type carrying tube, 12x17" **17.00**
46 stars, random pattern, machine sewn, 40x100" **55.00**
47 stars, unofficial, sewn bunting, 108x137" **170.00**
48 stars, machine-sewn cotton bunting, 60x96" **12.00**
48 stars, modified 44-star flag, hand sewn, 60x90" **60.00**
48 stars, naturalization, sewn names, 1914, 14x24" **75.00**
48 stars, sewn to form 'USA,' unauthorized WWI, 45x69" **175.00**
48 stars, staggered rows (early), printed muslin, 13x23" **10.00**
48 stars, Whipple Peace Flag, printed silk, 14x24" **220.00**
48 stars, WWII liberation, from Liege, homemade, 68x93" **95.00**

48 stars, 10-9 pattern, printed bunting, rare, 39x61" **55.00**
49 stars, embr w/sewn stripes, gold fringe, 48x72" **45.00**
49 stars, machine-sewn cotton bunting, 36x60" **20.00**
49 stars, 3 uncut flags, printed cotton sheet, 37x36" **18.00**
50 stars, Carter campaign, printed plastic, 12x18" **15.00**
50 stars, flew over the capitol memento, new, 60x96" **20.00**
52 stars, Spanish Am war era, home sewn, rare, 44x84" **215.00**
56 stars, printed crepe paper, Oriental, 1920s, 9x9" **18.00**

Florence Ceramics

Figurines marked 'Florence Ceramics' were produced in the forties and fifties in Pasadena, California. The quality of the ware and the attention given to detail are prompting a growing interest among today's collectors. The names of these lovely ladies, gents, and figural groups are nearly always incised into their bases. The company name is ink-stamped. Because this is a relatively new area of collecting and the rarity of many items has yet to be determined, examples are evaluated by size and the intricacy of design. Our advisor for this category is Jack Chipman, author of *The Collector's Encyclopedia of California Pottery*; he is listed in the Directory under California.

Girl (name unknown), full-length gold-trimmed lacy pantaloons under flaring skirt, marked, 7¾", $125.00.

Amber, mint gr, w/parasol, 10" **200.00**
Ava, holds flowers, 11" **125.00**
Camille, 8¼" **125.00**
Delia, 8" **85.00**
Diana, covered powder box **125.00**
Edward, seated on chair **125.00**
Elaine, 6" **45.00**
Elizabeth, seated on settee, dk gr gown, 8x7" **200.00**
Irene, 6" **45.00**
June, planter **40.00**
Kay, planter, 6" **60.00**
Louis XVI **150.00**
Marilyn, lav, w/hat box, 8¼" **160.00**
Martin, rose waistcoat, top hat, 10½" **185.00**
Matilda, 8½" **90.00**
Melanie, planter **65.00**
Musette, 8½" **135.00**
Patsy, planter, 6" **65.00**
Pinky & Blue Boy, 12", pr **595.00**

Rebecca, seated, 7½" **95.00**
Rhett, 9" **100.00**
Sarah, 8" **95.00**
Scarlett, gold trim, 9" **100.00**
Sue **60.00**
Vivian, w/parasol, purple shaded, 9½" **150.00**
Wendy, planter, 6" **40.00**

Flow Blue

Flow Blue ware was produced by many Staffordshire potters; among the most familiar were Meigh, Podmore and Walker, Samuel Alcock, Ridgway, John Wedge Wood (who often signed his work Wedgewood), and Davenport. It was popular from about 1825 through 1860 and again from 1880 until the turn of the century. The name describes the blurred or flowing affect of the cobalt decoration, achieved through the introduction of a chemical vapor into the kiln. The body of the ware is ironstone, and Oriental motifs were favored. Later issues were on a lighter body and often decorated with gilt.

Our advisor Mary Frank Gaston has compiled a lovely book, *The Collector's Encyclopedia of Flow Blue China*, with full-color illustrations and current market values; you will find her address in the Directory under Texas.

Abbey, bowl, G Jones, ca 1900, 5x9" **185.00**
Abbey, plate, G Jones, 9½" **65.00**
Acantha, plate, Meakin, 10" **58.00**
Alaska, butter pat, Grindley **35.00**
Alaska, egg cup, Grindley **60.00**
Alaska, platter, Grindley, 14" **150.00**
Alaska, soup, rimmed, Grindley, 9" **55.00**
Alaska, soup plate, Grindley, 9¾" **75.00**
Albany, butter dish, Grindley **235.00**
Albany, cup & saucer, Grindley **65.00**
Albany, plate, Johnson Bros, 7½" **30.00**
Albany, platter, Grindley, 11¾" **125.00**
Aldine, bone dish, Grindley **35.00**
Alexandria, plate, Hancock & Sons, ca 1910, 9½" **65.00**
Alice, platter, med **80.00**
Alton, bowl, 10" **85.00**
Alton, creamer, Grindley, 3½" **80.00**
Alton, plate, Grindley, 9⅞" **95.00**
Amoy, bowl, vegetable; Davenport, 8½" L **265.00**
Amoy, cup & saucer, handleless; Davenport **135.00**
Amoy, plate, Davenport, 7¼" **90.00**
Amoy, plate, Davenport, 8¾" **100.00**
Amoy, plate, Davenport, 9¼" **110.00**
Amoy, sauce bowl, Davenport **75.00**
Arcadia, plate, Wilkinson, 10" **95.00**
Argyle, bowl, vegetable; w/lid, EX gold trim, Grindley ...**245.00**
Argyle, cup & saucer, Grindley **50.00**
Argyle, gravy tray, Wood & Sons **65.00**
Argyle, platter, Grindley, 15" **225.00**
Argyle, platter, Grindley, 17" **245.00**
Argyle, sauce dish, Grindley **30.00**
Ashburton, bowl, vegetable; w/lid, Grindley **275.00**
Ashburton, gravy boat, Grindley **95.00**
Astoria, pitcher, New Wharf Pottery, 6¾" **225.00**
Astoria, plate, New Wharf Pottery, ca 1891, 9" **75.00**
Astral, plate, Grindley, 9⅞" **85.00**
Astral, platter, Grindley, 14" **185.00**
Atlanta, plate, Wedgwood, 9" **80.00**
Bell, plate, Meakin, 8⅞" **65.00**

Belmont, bone dish, Meakin, 6x4½" **50.00**
Belmont, butter pat, Meakin **35.00**
Belmont, plate, Meakin, 6⅝" **35.00**
Belmont, platter, 13" **120.00**
Bentick, plate, Cauldon, 6⅝" **42.00**
Beryl, plate, Wedgwood, 7½" **60.00**
Bleeding Heart, sauce ladle **275.00**
Blue Rose, plate, bread & butter; Grindley **35.00**
Bouquet, bowl, vegetable; w/lid **155.00**
Brunswick, saucer, Wood & Son **12.50**
Burleigh, soup plate, Burgess & Leigh **85.00**
Cabul, plate, Challinor, 7⅜" **85.00**
Cambridge, bowl, vegetable; New Wharf Pottery **120.00**
Candia, chocolate pot **475.00**
Candia, pitcher, melon ribs, Cauldon, cream sz **165.00**
Candia, plate, Cauldon, 7" **50.00**
Candia, soup plate, Cauldon, 10⅛" **100.00**
Canton, cup & saucer, Edwards, EX **135.00**
Canton, plate, Maddocks, 7" **120.00**
Carlton, bowl, vegetable; rose finial, Alcock **425.00**
Carlton, gravy boat, w/underplate, Alcock **135.00**
Cashmere, cup & saucer, handleless; Ridgway & Morley ...**135.00**
Cashmere, plate, Ridgway & Morley, 10⅝" **135.00**
Cashmere, plate, 8" **120.00**
Cashmere, sugar bowl, w/lid **365.00**
Celeste, plate, 10½" **120.00**
Celtic, plate, 9" **78.00**
Chain of States, cup & saucer **95.00**
Chapoo, plate, 9⅜" **135.00**
Chapoo, teapot, Wedge Wood, 9x10" **600.00**
Chatsworth, toothbrush holder **75.00**
Chen-Si, plate, Meir, 1935, 8¾" **80.00**
Chinese, bowl, vegetable; lg **85.00**
Chinese, cup & saucer, Dimmock **145.00**
Chusan, cup, hot toddy; Morley **75.00**
Chusan, drainer, Wedgwood, 12¼" **450.00**
Chusan, pitcher, Wedgwood, 7½" **335.00**
Chusan, plate, Ashworth, 9¼" **135.00**
Chusan, soup tureen, Podmore Walker **400.00**
Clayton, bowl, vegetable; w/lid, Johnson Bros **225.00**
Clayton, cup & saucer, Johnson Bros **60.00**
Clayton, plate, Johnson Bros, 8" **38.00**
Clayton, plate, Johnson Bros, 9" **48.00**
Clayton, soup plate, Johnson Bros, 9" **40.00**
Clover, bowl, vegetable; oval, w/lid, Grindley, 11" **255.00**
Clover, plate, Grindley, 5¾" **32.50**
Coburg, creamer, Edwards **185.00**
Coburg, plate, Edwards, 10¼" **150.00**
Colonial, plate, Meakin, 6⅞" **50.00**
Conway, bowl, vegetable; rnd, New Wharf Pottery, 9" ...**70.00**
Conway, cup & saucer, New Wharf Pottery **70.00**
Corinthian, toothbrush holder, Wedgwood **78.00**
Countess, gravy boat **65.00**
Country Scenes, plate, 6⅞" **50.00**
Dahlia, bowl, Upper Hanley, 10" **120.00**
Dahlia, cup & saucer, lustre trim, Upper Hanley **95.00**
Dainty, egg cup, Maddocks **100.00**
Daisy, cup, demitasse; Burgess & Leigh **55.00**
Delph, bowl, Wood & Sons, 10½" **90.00**
Derby, gravy boat, Grindley **60.00**
Devon, creamer, Meakin **200.00**
Devon, gravy boat, Meakin **120.00**
Devon, relish, Meakin **45.00**
Devon, sugar bowl, Meakin **165.00**

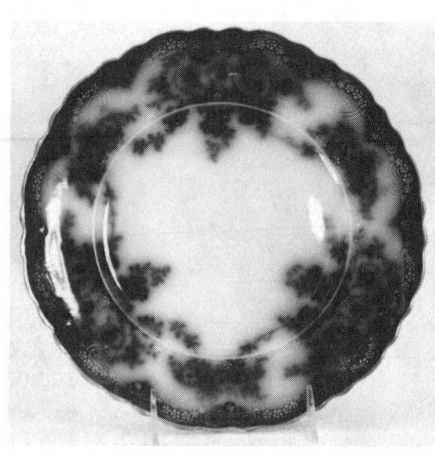

Devon plate, 9¾",
$70.00.

Dorothy, plate, Johnson Bros, 9" 45.00
Douglas, bowl, vegetable; w/lid, Furnival & Sons 75.00
Dover, plate, Grindley, 13" 68.00
Duchess, bowl, w/lid, Grindley, 5½x11" 165.00
Dundee, sauce dish, Ridgway 32.00
Excelsior, cup plate, Fell 100.00
Excelsior, plate, Fell, 9" 80.00
Fairy Villas, butter pat, Adams 30.00
Fairy Villas, coffeecup & saucer, Adams 120.00
Fairy Villas, plate, Adams, 10¼" 95.00
Fairy Villas, soup plate, Adams 65.00
Floral, gravy boat, scalloped, Johnson Bros, 8¼" 75.00
Floral, ladle 195.00
Floral, pitcher, water 495.00
Florence, bone dish, Wood & Son 35.00
Florida, bowl, vegetable; oval, Grindley, 7" 75.00
Florida, gravy boat, Johnson Bros 80.00
Florida, plate, Johnson Bros, 8⅞" 65.00
Florida, platter, Grindley, 16x11" 250.00
Formosa, bowl, vegetable; oval, Mayer, 13" 175.00
Formosa, cup & saucer, Ridgways 135.00
Formosa, saucer, Mayer 85.00
Gem, bowl, vegetable; w/lid, Maddocks 195.00
Gem, butter pat, Maddocks 25.00
Gem, egg cup, Maddocks 45.00
Gem, gravy boat, Maddocks 75.00
Georgia, bowl, berry; Johnson Bros, sm 32.00
Georgia, plate, Johnson Bros, 10" 55.00
Gipsy, plate, Grimwades, 7⅞" 65.00
Gipsy, platter, Grimwades, 12" 135.00
Gironde, bone dish, Grindley 45.00
Gironde, butter pat, Grindley 35.00
Gironde, cup & saucer, Grindley 85.00
Glenmore, bowl, vegetable; oval, w/lid, Grindley 165.00
Glenmore, platter, Grindley, 12" 85.00
Glentine, cup & saucer, Grindley 55.00
Glentine, soup plate, Grindley, 7¾" 40.00
Glenwood, bowl, vegetable; w/lid, Johnson Bros 200.00
Glenwood, plate, Johnson Bros, 9" 50.00
Gothic, gravy boat 155.00
Gothic, plate, 8½" 120.00
Grace, butter pat, Grindley 32.00
Grace, platter, Grindley, 21" 350.00
Grenada, cup & saucer, Alcock 75.00
Grenada, gravy boat, Alcock 100.00
Greville, platter, Bishop & Stonier, 18½" 300.00
Haddon, plate, Grindley, 9⅞" 90.00
Haddon, platter, Grindley, 14" 175.00

Hamilton, pitcher, Maddocks, 6½" 225.00
Harvest, pitcher, milk; Hancock & Sons, 5½" 195.00
Hindustan, cup plate, Maddocks 100.00
Hindustan, saucer, Maddocks 50.00
Hindustan, soup plate, flanged rim, Maddocks 80.00
Holland, platter, Johnson Bros, 12x9" 120.00
Holland, platter, Johnson Bros, 14" 150.00
Hong Kong, pitcher, water; Meigh 365.00
Hong Kong, plate, Meigh, 10½" 125.00
Hong Kong, platter, Meigh, 8½x6¼" 200.00
Indian, creamer 475.00
Indian, cup & saucer, handleless; Pratt 140.00
Indian, cup plate, Pratt 100.00
Indian, plate, Pratt, 7¼" 75.00
Indian Jar, creamer, Ford & Sons 175.00
Indian Jar, plate, 9½" 95.00
Indian Jar, platter, 22" 1,175.00
Indian Jar, teapot, Furnival 425.00
Janette, butter pat, Grindley 45.00
Janette, soup plate, Grindley, 9¼" 85.00
Japan, platter, Fell, 15" 325.00
Japan, soup plate, Rathbone, 10¼" 80.00
Jardiniere, plate, Utzchneider, 7¼" 50.00
Jenny Lind, bowl, vegetable; Wilkinson, 7½" 230.00
Jewel, creamer 175.00
Jewel, gravy boat, Johnson Bros 75.00
Kaolin, plate, Podmore Walker, 7½" 50.00
Keele, plate, gold trim, Grindley, 6¾" 20.00
Kenworth, bowl, oval, Johnson Bros, 8¾" 75.00
Kenworth, bowl, vegetable; oval, Johnson Bros, 9" 65.00
Keswick, bowl, vegetable; oval, Wood & Sons 125.00
Keswick, gravy boat 70.00
Kyber, bowl, vegetable; hdls, w/lid, Adams, 10½" 275.00
Kyber, plate, Adams, 10" 110.00
Kyber, plate, Adams, 7" 60.00
La Belle, bonbon, Wheeling, 7½" 55.00
La Belle, bowl, berry; Wheeling 55.00
La Belle, bowl, scalloped, Wheeling, 9" 115.00
La Belle, bowl, vegetable; rectangular 165.00
La Belle, celery dish, Wheeling, 13x6¼" 225.00
La Belle, charger, Wheeling, 11⅜" 145.00
La Belle, pitcher, Wheeling, 6½" 375.00
La Belle, plate, Wheeling, 5⅞" 45.00
La Belle, plate, Wheeling, 9" 60.00
La Belle, platter, Wheeling, 12" 150.00
La Francais, bowl, 8½" 22.00
La Francais, cup & saucer 17.50
Lahore, plate, Phillips & Son, 7½" 55.00
Lahore, plate, Phillips & Son, 8½" 115.00
Lancaster, gravy boat, New Wharf Pottery 70.00
Lancaster, plate, New Wharf Pottery, 9" 55.00
Leicester, plate, 9" 85.00
Linda, bowl, Maddocks & Son, 9" 195.00
Linda, plate, Maddocks & Son, 9" 40.00
Lonsdale, plate, Ford, 9⅞" 90.00
Lonsdale, platter, Ford, 1898-1939, 10" 110.00
Lorne, gravy boat, Grindley 85.00
Lorne, plate, Grindley, 9" 65.00
Lotus, gravy boat, Grindley 98.00
Lotus, plate, Grindley, 9" 40.00
Lotus, platter, Grindley, ca 1910, 16¼" 225.00
Lucania, plate, Clarke, 9" 48.00
Lusitania, bowl, Wood & Sons, 9⅝" 95.00
Luzerne, plate, Mercer, 7⅞" 45.00

Luzerne, plate, Mercer, 9" 65.00
Luzerne, soup bowl, Mercer 75.00
Lyndhurst, plate, Grindley, 10" 78.00
Madras, bowl, vegetable; w/lid, Doulton 245.00
Madras, gravy boat, Doulton 125.00
Madras, plate, Doulton, 5¾" 35.00
Madras, plate, Doulton, 9½" 110.00
Madras, sauce dish, Doulton 30.00
Mandarin, pitcher, water; Pountney 400.00
Mandarin, plate, Pountney, 10¼" 85.00
Mandarin, plate, Pountney, 7¼" 55.00
Mandarin, plate, Pountney, 9¼" 70.00
Manhattan, butter pat, Alcock 42.00
Manhattan, cup & saucer, Alcock 65.00
Manhattan, plate, Alcock, 9⅞" 80.00
Manilla, creamer, Podmore Walker 295.00
Manilla, plate, Podmore Walker, 7⅝" 80.00
Manilla, teapot, Podmore Walker 650.00
Marechal Niel, bowl, vegetable; w/lid, Grindley 225.00
Marechal Niel, cup & saucer, Grindley 55.00
Marechal Niel, sauce tureen, w/ladle, Grindley 300.00
Marguerite, bone dish, Grindley 40.00
Marguerite, cup & saucer, Grindley 80.00
Marguerite, soup plate, Grindley 40.00
Marie, bowl, vegetable; oval, w/lid, Grindley, 11x8" 250.00
Martha, bone dish, Grindley 40.00
Meissen, sauce tureen, Minton 300.00
Melbourne, bowl, vegetable; oval, Grindley, 9" 75.00
Melbourne, bowl, vegetable; w/lid, Grindley 275.00
Melbourne, cup & saucer, Grindley 65.00
Melbourne, plate, Grindley, 10" 65.00
Melbourne, plate, Grindley, 9" 55.00
Melbourne, platter, Grindley, 14¼x11" 185.00
Mongolia, platter, Johnson Bros, 11" 200.00
Mongolia, platter, Johnson Bros, 12½" 225.00
Montana, platter, Johnson Bros, 14" 185.00
Muriel, creamer, Upper Hanley 125.00
Naida, butter pat 45.00
Nancy, plate, Grimwades, 9½" 85.00
Nankin, platter, Doulton, 13½x10¾" 175.00
Navy, cup & saucer, Till 55.00
Navy, relish, Till, 8¾" 65.00
Non Pareil, bone dish, Burgess & Leigh 65.00
Non Pareil, bowl, cereal; Burgess & Leigh 70.00
Non Pareil, bowl, vegetable; w/lid 375.00
Non Pareil, butter dish, Burgess & Leigh 425.00
Non Pareil, butter pat 55.00
Non Pareil, plate, Burgess & Leigh, 6¾" 48.00
Non Pareil, plate, Burgess & Leigh, 8½" 85.00
Non Pareil, plate, 9¾" 105.00
Non Pareil, platter, 15½" 375.00
Non Pareil, soup tureen, Burgess & Leigh, 14" 1,250.00
Normandy, bowl, vegetable; w/lid, Johnson Bros 275.00
Normandy, butter pat, Johnson Bros 30.00
Normandy, cup & saucer, Johnson Bros 75.00
Normandy, plate, Johnson Bros, 10" 65.00
Normandy, plate, Johnson Bros, 6¼" 35.00
Olympia, bowl, vegetable; Grindley, lg 80.00
Oregon, cup & saucer, handleless; Mayer 90.00
Oregon, plate, Johnson Bros, 7" 48.00
Oregon, plate, Johnson Bros, 9" 60.00
Oregon, plate, Mayer, 9⅝" 125.00
Oriental, bowl, Ridgways, 6½" 65.00
Oriental, bowl, vegetable; oval, ftd, Ridgways, 11x8¾" 300.00

Oriental, pitcher, Ridgways, 5" 145.00
Oriental, plate, Ridgways, 8" 65.00
Oriental, platter, Ridgways, 12¾" 250.00
Oriental, platter, Ridgways, 9⅛" 150.00
Oriental, saucer, Alcock 50.00
Osborne, butter pat, Grindley 40.00
Osborne, tureen, gravy; w/attached underplate, Ridgways 100.00
Oxford, bowl, vegetable; oval, Johnson Bros, 9" 65.00
Oxford, butter dish, Johnson Bros, 3-pc 165.00
Oxford, creamer 105.00
Oxford, cup & saucer, Johnson Bros 75.00
Oxford, gravy boat, Johnson Bros 55.00
Oxford, plate, Johnson Bros, 9" 50.00
Oxford, platter, Ford & Sons, 15½x12" 275.00
Oxford, platter, Johnson Bros, 11½" 125.00
Oxford, sugar bowl, w/lid, Johnson Bros 110.00
Paisley, soup plate, Mercer, 8⅞" 80.00
Peach Royal, butter pat 30.00
Peach Royal, pitcher 95.00
Peach Royal, plate, 10" 55.00
Pekin, plate, Johnson Bros, 9" 80.00
Pelew, butter dish, Challinor 375.00
Percy, plate, Morley, 9½" 90.00
Persian Moss, bowl, 8¾" 80.00
Persian Moss, plate, 8" 50.00
Plymouth, plate, New Wharf Pottery, 8¾" 70.00
Princeton, bowl, berry; Johnson Bros, sm 45.00
Princeton, cup & saucer, Johnson Bros 65.00
Renown, bowl, vegetable; rnd, w/lid, Staffordshire 135.00
Rhine, cup plate 85.00
Rhone, bowl, vegetable; Furnival 165.00
Richmond, butter dish, Johnson Bros 300.00
Richmond, butter pat 30.00
Richmond, cup & saucer, Johnson Bros 65.00
Rosette, plate, Burgess & Leigh, 9" 35.00
Roseville, butter pat, Maddocks 45.00
Royal Blue, cup & saucer, Burgess Campbell 75.00
Sabraon, creamer 215.00
Sabraon, platter, 18" 595.00
Savoy, bowl, vegetable; w/lid 170.00
Savoy, creamer 175.00
Savoy, pitcher, Ford, ca 1900, 5" 95.00
Scinde, cup & saucer, Alcock 120.00
Scinde, plate, Alcock, 7¼" 100.00
Scinde, platter, Alcock, 13" 395.00
Scinde, platter, Alcock, 16" 750.00
Sefton, gravy boat 65.00
Seville, bowl, vegetable; w/lid, Wood & Sons 320.00
Seville, cereal bowl, Wood & Sons 65.00
Seville, plate, Wood & Sons, 6⅞" 55.00
Shanghae, bowl, vegetable; w/lid, Furnival 625.00
Shanghae, platter, Furnival, 13x10" 300.00
Shanghae, teapot, Furnival 585.00
Shanghai, bowl, cereal; Grindley 48.00
Shanghai, cup & saucer, Grindley 70.00
Shanghai, platter, Grindley, 14" 275.00
Shell, gravy boat, Challinor 175.00
Shell, plate, Challinor, 9½" 95.00
Siam, plate, 10" 50.00
Siam, plate, 9" 40.00
Stafford, bowl, Meakin, 5" 25.00
Stafford, creamer, Meakin 45.00
Temple, cup & saucer, handleless; Podmore Walker 135.00
Temple, plate, Podmore Walker, 9" 90.00

Togo, gravy boat, Winkle **75.00**
Togo, platter, 10" **135.00**
Tonquin, cup & saucer, handleless; Heath, ca 1850 ....**135.00**
Tonquin, platter, Heath, 15" **500.00**
Tonquin, soup plate, Adams & Sons **175.00**
Touraine, bowl, berry; Stanley, 5" **45.00**
Touraine, bowl, oval, Stanley, 9" **120.00**
Touraine, bowl, vegetable; Stanley, 10½" **140.00**
Touraine, cup & saucer, Stanley **75.00**

Touraine milk pitcher, Stanley, $325.00.

Touraine, plate, Alcock, 6⅝" **55.00**
Touraine, plate, Alcock, 8⅝" **65.00**
Touraine, plate, Stanley, 8¾" **65.00**
Touraine, platter, Alcock, 12" **135.00**
Touraine, platter, Stanley, 12½" **155.00**
Touraine, sugar bowl, open **85.00**
Tray, teapot **695.00**
Tyne, pitcher, Ford & Sons, 5" **175.00**
Venice, bowl, berry; Johnson Bros **45.00**
Venice, butter pat, Johnson Bros **45.00**
Verona, bowl, vegetable; w/lid, Ford & Sons, lg **245.00**
Verona, butter pat, Burgess & Leigh **30.00**
Verona, pitcher, Wood & Son, 2-qt **435.00**
Verona, platter, Ford & Sons, 13½" **275.00**
Verona, soup plate, Burgess & Leigh, 8⅞" **45.00**
Victoria, bowl, Wood & Son, 10" **90.00**
Waldorf, bowl, vegetable; rnd, New Wharf Pottery **120.00**
Waldorf, plate, New Wharf Pottery, 6" **45.00**
Waldorf, platter, New Wharf Pottery, 11" **200.00**
Warwick, saucer, Johnson Bros **25.00**
Watteau, compote, Doulton, 10¼" **375.00**
Watteau, pitcher, Doulton, 6½" **150.00**
Watteau, sauce tureen, w/underplate, Doulton **155.00**
Waverly, bowl, vegetable; w/lid, Maddocks **145.00**
Waverly, creamer, Maddocks **145.00**
Waverly, pitcher, Maddocks, 6½" **225.00**
Waverly, plate, Maddocks, 6¼" **45.00**
Weir, platter, Ford & Sons, 12x9" **140.00**
Weir, soup tureen, w/lid, Ford & Sons **400.00**
Wentworth, gravy boat, w/undertray, Meakin **55.00**
Wentworth, soup plate, Meakin **65.00**
Whampoa, milk jug, Dillwyn, ca 1811-20 ....**625.00**
Whampoa, pitcher, 1-qt **495.00**
Willow, creamer **110.00**
Windsor, bowl, vegetable; w/lid, Tunstall **135.00**
Windsor, butter dish, Edwards & Sons, 3-pc **225.00**

Windsor, platter, Tunstall, 14½" **220.00**
Windsor, platter, 18" **250.00**
Windsor Scroll, creamer **295.00**
Yedo, plate, Ashworth, 9¼" **75.00**
Yedo, soup plate, Ashworth, 10" **110.00**
Yedo, tureen stand, Ashworth, 15" **300.00**

Flue Covers

When spring housecleaning started and the heating stove was taken down for the warm weather season, the unsightly hole where the stovepipe joined the chimney was hidden with an attractive flue cover. They were made with a colorful litho print behind glass with a chain for hanging. Although scarce today, some scenes were actually reverse painted on the glass itself. The most popular motifs were florals, children, animals, and lovely ladies. Occasionally flue covers were made in sets of three — one served a functional purpose, while the others were added to provide a more attractive wall arrangement. They range in size from 7" to 14", but 9" is the average. Our advisor for this category is Cara J. Washburn; her address is in the Directory under Wisconsin.

Blond (in bl dress), shoulder up, bl-gr bkground, 4" **75.00**
Brunette (in red dress), wht wicker fr, 14" **75.00**
Girl (in wht dress) w/St Bernard, 7½" **65.00**
Greek scenic, couple in foreground, 8½" **25.00**
Mother & baby, brn-tone photo, 7" **25.00**
Steamship, rvpt, brn & gold border, G **22.00**
Victorian girl (in wht dress) w/dog, 8" **40.00**

Folk Art

That the creative energies of the mind ever spark innovations in functional utilitarian channels as well as toward playful frivolity is well documented in the study of American folk art. While the average early settler rarely had free time to pursue art for its own sake, his creative energy exemplified itself in fashioning useful objects carved or otherwise ornamented beyond the scope of pure practicality. After the advent of the Industrial Revolution, the pace of everyday living became more leisurely, and country folk found they had extra time. Not accustomed to sitting idle, many turned to carving, painting, or weaving. Whirligigs, imaginative toys for the children, and whimsies of all types resulted. Though often rather crude, this type of early art represents a segment of our heritage and as such has become valued by collectors.

Values given for drawings, paintings, and theorems are 'in frame' unless noted otherwise. See also Baskets; Decoys; Frakturs; Samplers; Trade Signs; Weathervanes; Wood Carvings.

Birdhouse, tin w/cone-shaped roof, metal perch, brn pnt, 7x6½" .**60.00**
Birdhouse, wooden, church w/steeple, dtd 1887 on door, 12" **85.00**
Birdhouse, wooden cabin, chimney & porch, 10x13x11" **135.00**
Birdhouse, wooden hexagon shape, old mc pnt, 18x18", EX **185.00**
Calligraphy, lg deer/bird, sgn, tears, 26x33" **300.00**
Calligraphy, lilies, 33x25" **145.00**
Calligraphy, Napoleon crossing Alps, stains, 23x22" **250.00**
Charcoal drawing, Harrison's Tomb, sgn, 15x18" **290.00**
Cvg, mama/baby bears w/in fr, all 1 pc, 1930s, 13x12½" **325.00**
Cvg, owl, gray sandstone, sgn E Reed, 7" **200.00**
Deer head, cement w/glass eyes, real antlers, 20th C, 23" **225.00**
Drawing, pen/ink on paper, 2 puppies, stains, 16x19" **100.00**
Drawing, pencil on paper, animals/couple, primitive, 26x30" **225.00**
Figure, lumberjack, pnt wood, woven stovepipe hat, 1930s, 12" .**135.00**
Holder, ice fishing line; cvd fish form, attached reel, 16" L **65.00**
Hose caddy, sheet metal Blk man w/silk screening, +hose, 30" ...**150.00**

Paper cutout, 8-lobe snowflake, laid paper, stains, 17x17" **300.00**
Shaving stand, shell work mirror fr/std/sq base, 51x16" **2,500.00**
Theorem on paper, compote of fruit, mica flecks, 20x22" **600.00**
Theorem on paper, fruit, lt stain, 10x12" **450.00**
Theorem on paper, fruit/flowers in basket, EX color, 18x21" **800.00**
Theorem on velvet, basket of fruit, 5-color, 10x12" **1,600.00**
Whirligig, bearded farmer chopping log, pnt wood, 16x42", EX . **255.00**
Whirligig, biplane, wood/tin/4-color pnt, 21" **350.00**
Whirligig, Ferris wheel, wood/metal/pnt, rpl, 31" **600.00**
Whirligig, fish w/propeller in mouth, pnt wood, 1900s, 4x16" **225.00**
Whirligig, Jiggs sawing wood, pnt wood, 1930s, 14x18" **175.00**
Whirligig, man fishing in boat, tin/wood/wire, 1930s, 13", EX ... **145.00**
Whirligig, windmill w/windows & door, pnt wood, '30s, 26", EX ... **185.00**
Yard ornament, cvd wood, Popeye w/box camera, 1930s, 20" **65.00**

Fostoria

The Fostoria Glass Company was built in 1887 at Fostoria, Ohio, but by 1891 it had moved to Moundsville, West Virginia. During the next two decades, they produced many lines of pressed patterned tableware and lamps. Their most famous pattern, American, was introduced in 1915 and was produced continuously until 1986 in well over two hundred different pieces. From 1920 to 1925, top artists designed tablewares in colored glass — canary (vaseline), amber, blue, orchid, green, and ebony — in pressed patterns as well as etched designs. By the late thirties, Fostoria was recognized as the largest producer of handmade glassware in the world. The company ceased operations in Moundsville in 1986.

Many items from both the American and Coin Glass lines are currently being reproduced by Lancaster Colony. In some cases the new glass is superior in quality to the old. Since the 1950s, Indiana Glass has produced a pattern called 'Whitehall' that looks very much like Fostoria's American with slight variations. Because Indiana's is not handmade glass, the lines of the 'cube' pattern and the edges of the items are sharp and untapered in comparison to the fire-polished originals. Three-footed pieces lack the 'toe' and instead have a peg-like foot, and the rays on the bottoms of the American examples are narrower than on the Whitehall counterparts. The Home Interiors Company currently offer several pieces of American look-alikes which were not even produced in the United States. Be sure of your dealer and study the books suggested below to become more familiar with the original line.

Coin Glass reproductions are flooding the market. Among items you may encounter are an 8" round bowl, 9" oval bowl, 8¼" wedding bowl, 4½" candlesticks, urn with lid, 6¼" candy jar with lid, footed comport, sugar and creamer; there could possibly be others. Colors in production are crystal, green, blue, and red. The red color is very good, but the blue is not the original color, nor is the emerald green. Buyer beware!

We are assisted in our listings by the Fostoria Glass Society of America, Inc., whose mailing address may be found in the Directory under Clubs, Newsletters, and Catalogs. For further information see *Elegant Glassware of the Depression Era* by Gene Florence and *Fostoria, the Popular Years, Third Edition Price Guide,* by Jo Ann Schliesman. *Glass Animals and Figural Flower Frogs of the Depression Era* by Lee Garmon and Dick Spencer offers an in-depth look at that particular aspect of Fostoria's production. See also Glass Animals. Their addresses are listed in the Directory under Illinois. Items with (+) at the end of the lines are currently being reproduced; prices are for original issues.

American, appetizer set, 7-pc **285.00**
American, basket, reed hdl **125.00**
American, bonbon, 3-toed, 8" **22.50**
American, bowl, cream soup; 5" **55.00**
American, bowl, fruit; ftd, 16" **165.00**

American, bowl, shrimp; 12¼" **325.00**
American, butter dish, w/lid, rnd **175.00**
American, candlestick, 6", pr **75.00**
American, cheese & cracker **62.50**
American, cookie jar, w/lid, 8⅞" **395.00**
American, decanter, w/stopper, 24-oz, 9¼" **95.00**
American, goblet, dessert; hex ft **11.00**
American, ice bucket, metal hdl **75.00**
American, lemon dish, w/lid, 5½" **45.00**
American, milk glass; vase, bud; #2056, flared/ftd, 8½" ... **40.00**
American, pitcher, ½-gal, 8" **90.00**
American, plate, torte; 18" **125.00**
American, relish, 4-part, 9" **65.00**
American, sugar bowl, w/lid, hdld, 5¼" **25.00**
American, tumbler, iced tea; flared, 12-oz, 5¼" ... **18.50**
American, vase, flared, 10" **95.00**
American Beauty, plate, #2337/550, 8" **7.00**
American Beauty, tumbler, juice; #6007/88, ftd, 4⅜" ... **7.00**
American Lady, crystal; goblet, cocktail; 3½-oz, 4" ... **14.00**
American Lady, crystal; goblet, 10-oz, 6⅛" **15.00**
Anniversary, goblet, #6055, w/gold decor, 10-oz, 6⅛" ... **12.50**
Anniversary, plate, #2337, w/gold decor, 8" **6.50**
Anniversary, tumbler, iced tea; #6055, ftd, 4⅞" ... **9.50**
April Love, plate, #2337/549, 7" **5.00**
April Love, tumbler, iced tea; #6068/63, ftd **15.00**
Arlington, banana stand, #2694, 13" **55.00**
Arlington, milk glass; banana stand, #2694, 13" ... **55.00**
Arlington, milk glass; bowl, #2694, lace, 11½" **32.50**
Arlington, milk glass; comport, #2694, w/lid, flared, 11½" ... **35.00**
Arlington, milk glass; salver, #2694, 13½" **32.50**
Aurora, goblet, sherbet; #6092/11, 7-oz, 5½" **10.00**
Aurora, plate, #2337/550, 8" **6.50**
Autumn, plate, #2337, 8" **5.00**
Autumn, tumbler, juice; #6068, ftd, 5-oz, 4½" **6.00**
Avalon, goblet, parfait; #6049, 6¾-oz, 6" **9.50**
Avalon, plate, #2337, 8" **5.00**
Ballet, goblet, oyster cocktail; #6036, 4-oz, 3¾" ... **12.50**
Ballet, plate, #2337, 8" **8.00**
Ballet, tumbler, juice; #6037, 5-oz, 4⅝" **10.00**
Baroque, bl; candlestick, 5¼", pr **60.00**
Baroque, bl; jelly, w/lid, 7½" **85.00**
Baroque, bl; relish, 3-part, 10" **45.00**
Baroque, bl; tumbler, flat, 9-oz, 4¼" **45.00**
Baroque, crystal; bowl, serving; hdld, 8½" **20.00**
Baroque, crystal; tidbit, flat, 3-toed, 8¼" **15.00**
Baroque, topaz; bowl, flared, 12" **35.00**
Baroque, topaz; goblet, 9-oz, 6¾" **30.00**
Baroque, topaz; plate, cracker; 11" **27.50**
Beacon, goblet, cocktail; #6017, 3½-oz, 4⅞" **8.50**
Beacon, goblet, sherbet; #6017, high, 6-oz, 5½" ... **7.50**
Beacon, tumbler, iced tea; #6017, ftd, 12-oz, 6" ... **12.50**
Beloved, goblet, sherbet; #6089/11, 7-oz, 5¼" **10.00**
Beloved, plate, #2337/550, 8" **8.50**
Betsy Ross, milk glass; basket, #2620, 11½" **35.00**
Betsy Ross, milk glass; bowl, #2620, cupped, 8½" ... **25.00**
Betsy Ross, milk glass; goblet, #2620, 9-oz, 6" ... **15.00**
Betsy Ross, milk glass; sugar bowl, #2620, ftd, 3¾" ... **12.50**
Betsy Ross, milk glass; tumbler, iced tea; #2620, 5¼" ... **15.00**
Bouquet, bowl, #2630, flared, 12" **42.50**
Bouquet, bowl, cereal; #2630, 6" **15.00**
Bouquet, bowl, salad; #2630, 10½" **42.50**
Bouquet, candy jar, #2630, w/lid, 7" **47.50**
Bouquet, creamer, #2630, ftd, 4¼" **15.00**
Bouquet, goblet, cordial; #6033, 1-oz, 3⅝" **24.50**

Bouquet, goblet, parfait; #6033, 6-oz, 5⅝" 17.00
Bouquet, plate, #2630, 7" 8.00
Bouquet, plate, cracker; #2630, 10¾" 27.50
Bouquet, relish, #2630, 3-part, 11⅛" 37.50
Bouquet, tidbit, #2630, 3-toed, 8⅛" 25.00
Bouquet, tray, muffin; #2630, hdld, 9½" 32.50
Bouquet, vase, #2470, ftd, 10" 85.00
Bracelet, goblet, cocktail; #6051, 3¼-oz, 3⅞" 7.50
Bracelet, goblet, sherbet; #6051, 6½-oz, 6¼" 10.00
Bracelet, tumbler, juice; #6051, ftd, 5-oz, 4" 7.50
Bridal Belle, goblet, #6072, platinum decor, 6⅜" 18.00
Bridal Belle, plate, #2337, platinum decor, 8" 12.00
Bridal Wreath, bowl, salad; #2630, 10½" 25.00
Bridal Wreath, creamer, #2639, ftd, 4¼" 12.00
Bridal Wreath, cup, #2630, ftd, 6-oz 11.00
Bridal Wreath, pitcher, jug; #6011, 53-oz, 8⅞" 125.00
Bridal Wreath, plate, #2337, 8" 8.50
Bridal Wreath, tray, lunch; #2630, center hdl, 11¼" 32.50
Bridal Wreath, tumbler, juice; #6049, 5¾-oz, 4⅞" 11.50
Brighton, goblet, #6023, 9-oz, 6⅜" 12.00
Brighton, tumbler, water; #6023, ftd, 9-oz, 5⅛" 10.00
Bristol, goblet, cocktail; #6093/21, 40-oz, 4⅜" 6.00
Bristol, goblet, sherbet, #6093/11, 7-oz, 5½" 5.00
Bristol, tumbler, iced tea; #6093/63, ftd, 12-oz, 5" 9.50
Burgandy, goblet, sherbet; #6092/11, 7-oz, 7" 8.50
Burgandy, plate, #2337/549, 7" 5.00
Buttercup, bowl, #2364, flared, 12" 45.00
Buttercup, bowl, fruit; #2364, 13" 47.50
Buttercup, candlestick, #2594, 5½", pr 45.00
Buttercup, goblet, oyster cocktail; #6030, 4-oz, 3¾" 17.50
Buttercup, plate, #2337, 7" 12.00
Buttercup, plate, cracker; # 2364, 11¼" 35.00
Buttercup, relish, #2364, 3-part, 10" 37.50
Buttercup, saucer, #2350 ....6.50
Buttercup, tumbler, #6030, ftd, 12-oz, 6" 25.00
Camellia, bonbon, #2630, 3-toed, 7¼" 22.50
Camellia, bowl, cereal; #2630, 6" 15.00
Camellia, creamer, #2639, ftd, 4¼" 12.50
Camellia, goblet, sherbet; #6036, high, 6-oz, 4¾" 15.00
Camellia, ice bucket, #2630, 4⅞" 52.50
Camellia, plate, dinner; #2630, 10½" 35.00
Camellia, saucer, #2630 ....4.00
Camellia, tidbit, #2630, 3-toed, 8⅛" 22.50
Camellia, tray, snack; #2630, 10½" 25.00
Camellia, vase, #2630, hdl, 7½" 45.00
Camellia, vase, #2657, ftd, 10" 65.00
Capri, goblet, sherbet; #6045, 9-oz, 3¾" 5.00
Capri, tumbler, iced tea; #6045, ftd, 16-oz, 6⅛" 8.00
Carousel, cocktail, #6080/20, 4-oz, 4⅜" 10.00
Carousel, plate, #2337/550, 8" 8.00
Carousel, tumbler, iced tea; #6080/63, ftd, 13½-oz, 5½" 13.00
Catalina, bowl, dessert/finger; 2¼" 3.00
Celeste, goblet, sherbet; 7¼-oz, 5" 5.00
Century, ashtray, 2¾" 11.50
Century, bowl, cereal; 6" 18.00
Century, bowl, salad; 8½" 42.50
Century, bowl, utility; oval, 10" 37.50
Century, butter dish, oblong, 7½" 42.50
Century, condiment set, 3-pc 115.00
Century, creamer, 4¼" 9.50
Century, goblet, cocktail; 3½-oz, 4⅛" 20.00
Century, party plate set, 2-pc 36.50
Century, plate, cracker; 11" 27.00
Century, plate, dinner; 9" 20.00

Century, plate, torte; 16" 37.50
Century, plate, 6" 10.00
Century, preserve, ftd, w/lid, 6" 35.00
Century, salver, cake; ftd, 12¼" 45.00
Century, sugar bowl, ftd, 4" 9.50
Century, tray, lunch; hdld, 11¼" 25.00
Century, vase, hdld, 7½" 55.00
Chalice, crystal; goblet, cordial; 1-oz, 2½" 8.00
Chalice, crystal; goblet, 11-oz, 5⅜" 5.00
Chateau, goblet, sherbet; #6087/11 ....4.00
Chateau, goblet, wine/cocktail; #6087/27, 3¼-oz, 5¼" 5.00
Chateau, tumbler, iced tea; #6087/63, ftd, 11-oz, 6⅜" 5.00
Chatham, goblet, oyster-cocktail; #6036, 4-oz, 3¾" 6.50
Chatham, plate, #2337, 8" 7.50
Chatham, tumbler, juice; ftd, 5-oz, 4⅝" 6.50
Chintz, bowl, nappy; #2496, hdld, 3-corner, 4⅝" 12.50
Chintz, bowl, serving; #2496, hdld, 8½" 25.00
Chintz, comport, #2496, 4¾" 35.00
Chintz, cup, #2496, ftd 18.50
Chintz, goblet, #6026, 9-oz, 7⅝" 26.00
Chintz, goblet, cocktail; #6026, 4-oz, 5" 26.50
Chintz, jelly, #2496, w/lid, 7½" 95.00
Chintz, plate, torte; #2496, 16" 55.00
Chintz, relish, #2496, 3-part, 10" 39.50
Chintz, saucer, #2496 ....6.00
Chintz, tray, #2375, center hdl, 11" 39.50
Chintz, tumbler, #6026, ftd, 13-oz, 6" 24.00
Christiana, goblet, #6030, low, 10-oz, 7⅞" 18.00
Christiana, plate, #2337, 7" 8.00
Christiana, tumbler, iced tea; #6030, ftd, 12-oz, 6" 20.00
Circlet, goblet, oyster cocktail; #6055, 4¾-oz, 4" 10.00
Circlet, plate, canape; #2666, 7⅜" 9.00
Circlet, plate, snack; #2666, 10" 15.00
Circlet, sugar bowl, #2666, 2⅝" 8.00
Circlet, tumbler, juice; #6055, ftd, 5½-oz, 4⅞" 9.00
Classic, colors; goblet, cocktail; 3½-oz, 6⅜" 12.00
Classic, crystal; goblet, 10-oz, 6⅜" 8.00
Classic, crystal; tumbler, ftd, 13-oz, 5⅜" 12.00

Coin Glass bowl #189, ruby, 9½" long, $55.00.

Coin, crystal; bowl, oval, #115, 9" 30.00
Coin, crystal; candlestick, #316, 4½", pr 40.00
Coin, crystal; creamer & sugar bowl, #680/#673, w/lid 35.00
Coin, crystal; plate, #550 ....22.00
Coin, crystal; punch bowl, w/base 465.00
Coin, crystal; tumbler, #73, 4¼" 30.00
Coin, crystal; vase, bud; #799, 8" 20.00
Coin, crystal; wedding bowl, #162, w/lid 65.00
Coin, emerald gr; cake stand, rare 450.00
Coin, emerald gr; candlestick, #316, 4½", pr 125.00
Coin, emerald gr; olive dish, hdls 32.00

Coin, emerald gr; pitcher, #453, 1-qt 225.00
Coin, emerald gr; shakers, pr 120.00
Coin, emerald gr; wedding bowl, #162, w/lid 155.00
Coin, olive gr or amber; ashtray, #124, 10" 40.00
Coin, olive gr or amber; ashtray, 4-coin, #114, 7½" 35.00
Coin, olive gr or amber; bowl, rnd, #179, 8" 75.00
Coin, olive gr or amber; cake stand, #630 ....65.00
Coin, olive gr or amber; candlestick, #316, 4½", pr 45.00
Coin, olive gr or amber; candy jar, #347, w/lid 35.00
Coin, olive gr or amber; cigarette urn, #381, w/lid 25.00
Coin, olive gr or amber; creamer, #680, 3½" 15.00
Coin, olive gr or amber; jelly dish, #448, 3¾" 20.00
Coin, olive gr or amber; lamp, coach; #320 ....200.00
Coin, olive gr or amber; lamp base, patio; #459 ....90.00
Coin, olive gr or amber; olive dish 15.00
Coin, olive gr or amber; pitcher, #453, 1-qt 65.00
Coin, olive gr or amber; shakers, pr 35.00
Coin, olive gr or amber; vase, bud; #799, 8" 25.00
Coin, olive gr or amber; wine, #26 ....45.00
Coin, red or bl; ashtray, #124 ....50.00
Coin, red or bl; ashtray, 1-coin, #123 ....30.00
Coin, red or bl; bowl, oval, #189, 9" 55.00
Coin, red or bl; cake stand, rare 235.00
Coin, red or bl; candlesticks, #316, 4½", pr (+) 65.00
Coin, red or bl; candy box, #354, w/lid 75.00
Coin, red or bl; candy jar, w/lid, #1372/347, 6¼" (+) 70.00
Coin, red or bl; cigarette urn, #381 ....70.00
Coin, red or bl; compote, ftd, #121, w/lid 195.00
Coin, red or bl; finger lamp 155.00
Coin, red or bl; goblet, tall, 6⅝" 99.00
Coin, red or bl; shakers, pr 50.00
Coin, red or bl; sherbet 55.00
Coin, red or bl; vase, bud; #799, 8" 55.00
Colonial Dame, colors; tumbler, ftd, 12-oz, 6" 12.00
Colonial Dame, crystal; goblet, sherbet; 6½-oz, 6⅜" 8.00
Colony, ashtray, rnd, 4½" 12.00
Colony, bowl, centerpiece; 13" 35.00
Colony, bowl, cream soup; 5" 40.00
Colony, bowl, flared, 11" 35.00
Colony, bowl, salad; 7¾" 25.00
Colony, bowl, vegetable; oval, 10½" 45.00
Colony, candlestick, 3", pr 30.00
Colony, comport, #2412, w/lid, low, 6⅜" 47.50
Colony, goblet, sherbet; 5-oz, 3⅝" 9.00
Colony, goblet, wine; 3¼-oz, 4⅛" 25.00
Colony, pitcher, ice jug; 2-qt, 7¾" 110.00
Colony, plate, torte; 15" 40.00
Colony, plate, 7" 8.00
Colony, relish, pickle; 8" 14.00
Colony, saucer 4.00
Colony, sugar bowl, ftd, 3⅜" 7.00
Colony, tumbler, flat, 9-oz, 3⅞" 17.50
Colony, tumbler, ftd, 12-oz, 5⅝" 18.00
Colony, vase, bud; flared or ftd, 6" 18.00
Contour, bowl, #2638, deep, 7" 12.50
Contour, bowl, #2639, oblong, 10½" 15.00
Contour, butter dish, #2666, w/lid, oblong, 7" 12.50
Contour, goblet, #6060, 10½-oz, 5⅞" 20.00
Contour, pitcher, #2666, qt, 6⅞" 35.00
Contour, plate, serving; #2666, 14" 17.50
Contour, relish, celery; #2666, 9" 12.00
Contour, saucer, #2666 ....3.00
Contour, sugar bowl, #2666, 2⅝" 7.00
Contour, tumbler, juice; ftd, 5½-oz, 4½" 16.00

Coronet, bonbon, 3-toed, 7¼" 6.00
Coronet, bowl, crimped, 11½" 15.00
Coronet, bowl, serving; hdld, 8½" 12.50
Coronet, bowl, whipped cream; 5" 7.50
Coronet, candlestick, 4", pr 15.00
Coronet, plate, torte; 14" 18.50
Coronet, relish, pickle; 8¾" 10.00
Coronet, sugar bowl, ftd, 3½" 5.00
Crest, goblet, sherbet; #6061, 7½-oz, 4" 6.00
Crest, plate, #2337, 7" 7.00
Crest, tumbler, iced tea; #6061, ftd, 12-oz, 6" 8.00
Cynthia, candlestick, #2560, duo, 5⅛", pr 32.00
Cynthia, creamer, #2560, ftd, 7-oz, 4⅛" 14.50
Cynthia, cup, #2560, 5½-oz 12.50
Cynthia, pitcher, jug; #6011, ftd, 53-oz, 8⅞" 95.00
Cynthia, plate, #2337, 8" 8.00
Cynthia, relish, pickle; #2650, 8¾" 15.00
Devon, goblet, #6089/2, 11½-oz, 6¼" 9.50
Devon, goblet, brandy; #6089/31, 1½-oz, 4" 15.00
Diadem, goblet, cordial; 1¼-oz, 3" 10.00
Diadem, tumbler, iced tea; ftd, 13-oz, 6⅜" 6.00
Diamond, milk glass; candy dish, #2711, w/lid, ftd, 5¾" ...34.50
Dolly Madison, goblet, #6023, 9-oz, 6⅜" 17.50
Dolly Madison, goblet, cocktail; #6023, 3¾-oz, 4⅜" 12.00
Dolly Madison, tumbler, juice; #6023, ftd, 5-oz, 4½" 12.00
Duchess, goblet, sherbet; #6068, 6½-oz, 4⅝" 5.00
Duchess, plate, #2337, 8" 5.00
Duchess, tumbler, iced tea; #6068, ftd, 13-oz, 5⅞" 5.00
Ebony, bowl, salad; #2666, 11" 25.00
Ebony, candlestick, #2545, flame, 2", pr 25.00
Ebony, cigarette box, #2592, w/lid, 6" 25.00
Ebony, vase, #2567, ftd, 7½" 17.50
Embassy, goblet, cordial; #6083/29, 1¼-oz, 3¼" 10.00
Embassy, goblet, sherbet; #6083/11, 7¾-oz, 4¾" 4.00
Embassy, tumbler, iced tea; #6083/63, ftd, 14-oz, 6¼" 6.00
Empress, goblet, cordial; 1-oz, 3⅜" 10.00
Empress, goblet, sherbet; #6079/11, 6½-oz, 5" 5.00
Empress, tumbler, iced tea; #6079/63, 13½-oz, 6¼" 9.00
Enchantment, goblet, #6074/2, 9½-oz, 6¼" 8.00
Enchantment, goblet, cordial; #6074/29, 1-oz, 3¼" 12.50
Encore, goblet, sherbet; #6077/11, 7-oz, 4¼" 4.00
Encore, plate, #2337/550, 8" 5.00
Encore, tumbler, iced tea; #6077/63, 13-oz, 5⅝" 6.00
Engagement, plate, #2337/549, 7" 6.00
Engagement, tumbler, iced tea; #6092/63, ftd, 14-oz, 6⅜" ...15.00
Envoy, goblet, oyster cocktail; 4-oz, 3" 4.50
Envoy, goblet, 10-oz, 5¼" 6.00
Envoy, tumbler, ftd, 12-oz, 5½" 6.50
Evening Star, goblet, cordial; #6087/29, 3½" 11.50
Evening Star, plate, 2337/550, 8" 4.50
Fairmont, bowl, dessert; #2718/421, 5" 3.00
Fairmont, goblet, sherbet; 6-oz, 4⅜" 3.00
Fantasy, goblet, #6086/2, 10-oz, 6¾" 8.50
Fantasy, goblet, cordial; #6086/29, 1¼-oz, 3¼" 15.00
Fantasy, plate; #2337/550, 8" 6.00
Fantasy, tumbler, juice; #6086/88, ftd, 5½-oz, 4½" 8.00
Fascination, goblet, cordial; #6080/29, 1-oz, 3½" 12.50
Fascination, tumbler, juice; #6080/63, ftd, 5-oz, 4¼" 6.50
Frisco, milk glass; toothpick holder, #1229, 2¼" 15.00
Frisco, milk glass; vase, swung; #1229, 10" 35.00
Gadroon, goblet, cocktail; #6030, 3½-oz, 5¼" 11.50
Gadroon, plate, #2337, 8" 8.00
Gadroon, tumbler, iced tea; #6030, ftd, 12-oz, 6" 14.50
Garland, goblet, sherbet; #6077/11, 7-oz, 4¼" 5.00

Garland, plate, #2337/549, 7" 4.00
Garland, tumbler, iced tea; #6077/63, 13-oz, 5⅝" 8.00
Gold Coin, cigarette box, #1372/374, w/lid 40.00
Gold Coin, jelly, #1372/448 ....17.50
Gold Coin, sugar bowl, #1372/673, w/lid, 5⅜" 32.50
Golden Flair, plate, #2337/550, 8" 5.00
Golden Flair, tumbler, juice; #6087/63, 11-oz, 6⅜" 7.00
Golden Grail, goblet, cordial; #6083/29, 1¼-oz, 3¼" 15.00
Golden Grail, plate, #2337/550, 8" 6.00
Golden Grail, tumbler, juice; #6083/88, ftd, 5½-oz, 4¾" 7.00
Golden Lace, plate, #2337/550, 8" 14.00
Golden Lace, tumbler, juice; #6085/88, ftd, 5½" 15.00
Golden Love, goblet, #6074/2, 9½-oz, 6¼" 10.00
Golden Love, tumbler, iced tea; #6074/63, 13-oz, 6⅜" ...10.00
Gossamer, bonbon, #2666/136, 6⅞" 12.00
Gossamer, plate, torte; #2364/567, 14" 25.00
Gossamer, relish, #2364/622, 3-part, 10" 19.50
Gossamer, sugar bowl, #2666/679, 2⅝" 8.50
Heather, bowl, #2630, flared, 12" 45.00
Heather, bowl, salad; #2630, 10½" 42.50
Heather, bowl, vegetable; #2630, oval, 9½" 40.00
Heather, candy dish, #2530, w/lid, 7" 57.50
Heather, creamer, #2630, ftd, 4¼" 18.50
Heather, goblet, #6037, 9-oz, 7⅞" 26.50
Heather, goblet, parfait; #6037, 6-oz, 6⅛" 32.50
Heather, pitcher vase, #2728/807, 9" 75.00
Heather, plate, cracker; #2630, 10¾" 37.50
Heather, plate, crescent salad; #2630, 7" 35.00
Heather, relish, pickle; #2630, 8¾" 25.00
Heather, salver, #2630, 12¼" 47.50
Heather, sugar bowl, #2630, 4" 17.50
Heather, tray, muffin; #2630, hdld, 9½" 32.50
Heather, tumbler, #6037, ftd, 12-oz, 6⅛" 26.50
Heirloom, basket, #2720/126, 12" 37.50
Heirloom, bowl, #2727/155, sq, 6" 27.50
Heirloom, bowl, #2729/540, oval, 10" 37.50
Heirloom, epergne, #1515/364, lg 125.00
Heirloom, flower float, #2183/415, 10" 35.00
Heraldry, bowl, #2364, flared, 12" 35.00
Heraldry, candlestick, #6023, duo, 5½", pr 37.00
Heraldry, creamer, #2666, 3½" 8.50
Heraldry, goblet, sherbet; #6012, low, 5½-oz, 4" 10.00
Heraldry, goblet, wine; #6012, 3-oz, 5¼" 18.50
Heraldry, pitcher, #2666, qt, 6⅞" 55.00
Heraldry, relish, #2364, 2-part, 8¼" 18.50
Heraldry, sugar bowl, #2666, 2⅝" 8.50
Heraldry, tumbler, iced tea; #6012, ftd, 13-oz 16.00
Holiday, cocktail mixer, 20-oz 16.50
Holiday, decanter, w/stopper, 24-oz, 10¼" 16.50
Holiday, tumbler, whiskey; 1½-oz, 2⅛" 3.50
Holly, bowl, #2364, flared, 12" 35.00
Holly, goblet, cordial; #6030, 1-oz, 3⅞" 42.50
Holly, goblet, oyster cocktail; #6030, 4-oz, 3¾" 16.50
Holly, saucer, #2350 ....6.50
Holly, sugar bowl, #2666, ind 16.50
Holly, tumbler, juice; #6030, ftd, 5-oz, 4⅝" 15.00
Homespun, tumbler, water; #4183/64, 11½-oz, 4¾" 4.00
Horizon, bowl, fruit; #2650 ....4.00
Horizon, bowl, server; 4-part, 11½" 21.50
Horizon, cup, #2650, 8½-oz 6.00
Horizon, plate, torte; #2650, 14" 12.50
Horizon, tumbler, juice/cocktail; #5650, 3⅜" 3.50
Ingrid, goblet, claret/wine; #6052, 4¼-oz, 4⅜" 10.00
Ingrid, goblet, sherbet; #6052, 6½-oz, 4⅜" 7.00

Ingrid, relish, #2364, 2-part, 8¼" 16.50
Ingrid, tumbler, iced tea; #6052, ftd, 13-oz, 9⅛" 9.00
Juliet, goblet, sherbet; #6085/11, 6-oz, 5¼" 8.00
Juliet, tumbler, juice; #6085/63, ftd, 11¾-oz, 6¼" 8.00
Karnak, tumbler, cooler; #4161, 21-oz, 6¾" 5.00
Karnak, tumbler, juice; #4161, 6-oz, 3¾" 3.00
Kent, goblet, cocktail; #6079, 3½-oz, 3⅞" 6.00
Kent, tumbler, iced tea; #6079, ftd, 13½-oz, 6¼" 6.50
Kimberly, creamer, #2574/681, ftd, 7-oz, 4" 7.50
Kimberly, goblet, sherbet; #6071, 7-oz, 4¾" 11.50
Kimberly, plate, torte; #2574/567, 14" 15.00
Kimberly, tumbler, juice; #6071, ftd, 5¼-oz, 4½" 8.00
Lacy Leaf, bonbon, #2630, 3-toed, 7¼" 22.50
Lacy Leaf, bowl, nappy; #2630, hdld, 4½" 11.50
Lacy Leaf, candlestick, #2630, duo, 7", pr 45.00
Lacy Leaf, creamer, #2630, 4¼" 12.50
Lacy Leaf, plate, torte; #2630, 14" 37.50
Lacy Leaf, relish, pickle; #2630, 8¾" 18.50
Lacy Leaf, sugar bowl, #2630, 4" 12.50
Lacy Leaf, tray, lunch; #2630, center hdl, 11¼" 27.50
Laurel, goblet, oyster cocktail; #6017, 4-oz, 3⅝" 12.00
Laurel, plate, #2337, 8" 8.00
Lido, bowl, #2496, flared, 12" 26.50
Lido, bowl, nappy; #2496, hdld, 5" 10.00
Lido, candlestick, #2496, duo, 4½", pr 25.00
Lido, comport, #2496, 5½" 18.50
Lido, creamer, #2496, ind 14.50
Lido, goblet, #6017, 9-oz, 7⅜" 18.50
Lido, jelly, #2496, w/lid, 7½" 49.50
Lido, pitcher, jug; #6011, ftd, 53-oz, 8⅞" 135.00
Lido, plate, #2496, 7" 6.50
Lido, relish, pickle; #2496, 8" 17.50
Lido, saucer, #2496 ....5.00
Lido, sugar bowl, #2496, 3½" 12.50
Lyric, colors; goblet, cordial; 1-oz, 2½" 12.50
Lyric, crystal; goblet, 11-oz, 5⅛" 5.00
Lyric, crystal; tumbler, iced tea; ftd, 12-oz, 6" 8.00
Mademoiselle, goblet, parfait; #6033, 6-oz, 5⅝" 10.00
Mademoiselle, goblet, sherbet; #6033, 6-oz, 4" 7.50
Mademoiselle, tumbler, #6033, ftd, 13-oz, 5⅞" 9.00
Marilyn, goblet, cordial; #6055, 1¼-oz, 3¼" 12.50
Marilyn, goblet, oyster cocktail; #6055, 4¾-oz, 4" 8.00
Marilyn, tumbler, juice; #6055, ftd, 5½-oz, 4⅞" 8.00
Marquis, goblet, cocktail; #6045, 1½-oz, 3" 6.00
Marquis, plate, #2337, 8" 5.00
Mayflower, bowl, #2560, flared, 12" 35.00
Mayflower, bowl, salad; #2560, 10" 32.50
Mayflower, candlestick, #2560, duo, 5⅛", pr 50.00
Mayflower, goblet, #6020, 9-oz, 7¼" 19.50
Mayflower, goblet, oyster cocktail; #6020, 4-oz, 3¾" 16.50
Mayflower, plate, cake; #2560, hdld, 10½" 32.50
Mayflower, relish, celery; #2560, 11" 25.00
Mayflower, tray, muffin; #2560, hdld, 8¼" 27.50
Mayflower, tumbler, #6020, ftd, 9-oz, 5¾" 16.00
Meadow Rose, bonbon, #2496, 3-toed, 7⅜" 27.50
Meadow Rose, candlestick, #2496, duo, 4½", pr 45.00
Meadow Rose, candlestick, #2496, trindle, 6", pr 90.00
Meadow Rose, cheese & cracker, #2496 ....75.00
Meadow Rose, creamer, #2496, ftd, 7½-oz, 3¾" 18.50
Meadow Rose, goblet, saucer champagne; #6016, 6-oz, 5⅝" ...25.00
Meadow Rose, ice bucket, #2496 ....110.00
Meadow Rose, jelly, #2496, w/lid, 7½" 110.00
Meadow Rose, plate, cracker; #2496, 11" 45.00
Meadow Rose, plate, torte; #2496, 16" 60.00

Meadow Rose, relish, #2496, 3-part, 10" **45.00**
Meadow Rose, tray, lunch; #2375, center hdl, 11" **45.00**
Meadow Rose, tumbler, #6016, ftd, 5-oz, 4⅝" **24.00**
Melody, plate, #2337/550, 8" **7.00**
Melody, tumbler, juice; #6072/88, ftd, 5¼-oz 4⅞" **7.00**
Milkweed, bowl, #2630, flared, 12" **38.50**
Milkweed, creamer, #2630, ftd, 4¼" **12.50**
Milkweed, nappy, #2630, hdld, 4½" **11.50**
Milkweed, plate, cake; #2630, hdld **24.00**
Milkweed, sugar bowl, #2630, ind **12.50**
Minuet, bowl, #2574, flared, 12" **17.50**
Minuet, creamer, #2574, 7-oz, 4" **11.50**
Minuet, goblet, oyster cocktail; #6025, 4-oz, 3½" **11.50**
Minuet, plate, #2574, 8" **8.50**
Minuet, plate, torte; #2574, 14" **22.50**
Minuet, tumbler, juice; #6025, ftd, 5-oz, 4¼" **8.50**
Monroe, milk glass; bowl, banana; #2678, 10¾" **55.00**
Monroe, milk glass; bowl, fruit; #2678, ftd, 10" **55.00**
Moon Ring, goblet, cordial; #6052, 1¼-oz, 3⅛" **9.00**
Moon Ring, tumbler, iced tea; #6052, ftd, 13-oz **8.00**
Moon Ring, tumbler, old-fashioned; #4132, 7½-oz, 3⅛" **6.00**
Moonbeam, goblet, cordial; #6072, 1-oz, 3⅛" **12.50**
Moonbeam, plate, #2337, 8" **5.00**
Moonbeam, sugar bowl, #2574/679, ftd, 3¾" **8.00**
Moonglow, goblet, #6085/2, 8¾-oz, 6½" **9.00**
Moonglow, plate, #2337/550, 8" **5.00**
Moonglow, tumbler, iced tea; #6085/63, ftd, 11¾-oz, 6¼" **10.00**
Mount Vernon, goblet, oyster cocktail; #6031, 4-oz, 3⅝" **9.00**
Mount Vernon, plate, #2337, 8" **11.00**
Mount Vernon, tumbler, iced tea; #6031, ftd, 12-oz, 5⅞" **11.50**
Mulberry, goblet, oyster cocktail; #6026, 4-oz, 3⅝" **15.00**
Mulberry, plate, #2337, 8" **11.50**
Mulberry, tumbler, iced tea; #6026, ftd, 13-oz, 6" **18.00**

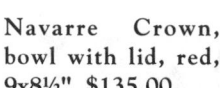

Navarre Crown, bowl with lid, red, 9x8½", $135.00.

Navarre, candlestick, #2496, trindle, 6", pr **90.00**
Navarre, cheese & cracker, #2496 ....**75.00**
Navarre, goblet, cocktail; #6016, 3½-oz, 5¼" **25.00**
Navarre, plate, cracker; #2496, 11" **45.00**
Navarre, relish, #2496, 3-part, 10" **42.50**
Navarre, saucer, #2440 ....**7.00**
Navarre, tumbler, #6016, ftd, 10-oz, 5⅜" **20.00**
Nordic, goblet, cordial; #6077, 1-oz, 3" **9.50**
Nordic, tumbler, juice; #6077, ftd, 13-oz, 5⅝" **6.00**
Nosegay, bowl, #2666, oval, 8¼" **18.50**
Nosegay, goblet, #6051, 10½-oz, 6¼" **11.00**
Nosegay, goblet, cordial; #6051, 1¼" **15.00**
Nosegay, plate, torte; #2364, 14" **17.50**

Nosegay, sugar bowl, #2666, 2⅝" **8.50**
Nosegay, tumbler, juice; #6051, ftd, 5-oz, 4" **8.50**
Orleans, plate, #2337/550, 8" **7.50**
Orleans, tumbler, juice; #6089/88, 5-oz, 4¾" **7.00**
Overture, goblet, #6086/2, 11¾-oz, 6⅜" **10.00**
Overture, plate, #2337/549, 8" **6.50**
Overture, tumbler, iced tea; #6086/63, ftd, 13-oz, 6¼" **10.00**
Petite, goblet, #6085/2, 8¾-oz, 6½" **10.00**
Petite, plate, #2337/549, 7" **3.50**
Petite, tumbler, juice; #6085/88, ftd, 5½-oz, 4½" **6.50**
Pine, bowl, salad; #2666 ....**22.50**
Pine, butter dish, #2666, w/lid, oblong, 7" **32.50**
Pine, goblet, sherbet; #6052, 6½-oz, 4⅜" **12.50**
Pine, plate, serving; #2666, 14" **35.00**
Pine, saucer, #2666 ....**3.50**
Pine, tumbler, juice; #6052, 5½ oz, 4⅞" **12.50**
Plume, creamer, #2666, 3½" **7.50**
Plume, goblet, oyster cocktail; #6051, 4½-oz, 3¾" **7.50**
Plume, plate, #2337, 8" **6.00**
Plume, plate, serving; #2666, 14" **15.00**
Plume, relish, #2666, 3-part, 10¾" **24.50**
Plume, sugar bowl, #2666, 2⅝" **7.50**
Plume, tumbler, juice; #6051, ftd, 5-oz, 4" **6.00**
Prelude, goblet, sherbet; #6071, 7-oz, 4¾" **4.50**
Prelude, tumbler, iced tea; #6071, ftd, 13-oz, 6" **7.00**
Priscilla, goblet, #6092/2, 10½-oz, 7" **8.00**
Priscilla, plate, #2337/550, 8" **6.00**
Priscilla, tumbler, juice; #6092/88, 5½-oz, 4¾" **6.00**
Puritan, goblet, cordial; 1¼-oz, 3" **10.00**
Puritan, tumbler, juice; 5-oz, 4½" **4.50**
Raleigh, bowl, fruit; #2574, 13" **17.50**
Raleigh, creamer, #2574, ftd, 7-oz, 4" **5.00**
Raleigh, relish, pickle; #2574, 3-part, 8" **9.50**
Raleigh, sugar bowl, #2574, ftd, 3¾" **5.00**
Randolph, milk glass; bowl, #2675, w/lid, ftd, 10" **50.00**
Randolph, milk glass; nappy, #2675, 6" **17.50**
Randolph, milk glass; preserve, #2675, w/lid, ftd, 5⅝" **32.50**
Randolph, milk glass; sugar bowl, #2675, w/lid, ftd, 5¾" **21.00**
Reflection, bowl, salad; #2364, 9" **15.00**
Reflection, creamer, #2666, 3½" **6.50**
Reflection, goblet, claret/wine; #6033, 4-oz, 4¾" **9.50**
Reflection, goblet, parfait; #6033, 6-oz, 5⅝" **9.50**
Reflection, sugar bowl, #2666, 2⅝" **6.50**
Regal, goblet, #6061, 11-oz, 5⅛" **6.50**
Regal, goblet, cordial; 1-oz, 2½" **9.50**
Regal, plate, #2337, 7" **3.50**
Revere, goblet, #6023, 9-oz, 6⅜" **12.50**
Revere, goblet, cordial; #6023, 1-oz, 3⅜" **15.00**
Revere, plate, #2337, 7" **5.00**
Rhapsody, goblet, cocktail; 3½-oz, 3⅞" **6.50**
Rhapsody, goblet, 10-oz, 6⅛" **8.00**
Ringlet, goblet, claret/wine; 4-oz, 4½" **9.50**
Ringlet, goblet, sherbet; 6½-oz, 4⅜" **5.00**
Ringlet, tumbler, juice; ftd, 5-oz, 4" **5.00**
Romance, bowl, salad; #2364, 10½" **42.50**
Romance, candlestick, #2594, trindle, 8", pr **95.00**
Romance, goblet, cocktail; #6017, 3½-oz, 4⅞" **25.00**
Romance, goblet, saucer champagne; #6017, 6-oz, 5½" **19.50**
Romance, plate, #2337, 6" **12.00**
Romance, relish, #2364, 3-part, 10" **37.50**
Romance, saucer, #2350 ....**8.00**
Romance, tumbler, #6017, ftd, 9-oz, 5½" **23.50**
Rondo, goblet, sherbet; #6045, 9-oz, 3¾" **6.00**
Rondo, plate, #2337, 8" **5.50**

Rondo, tumbler, juice, #6045, ftd, 7¼-oz, 4⅝" **6.00**
Rose, goblet, claret/wine; #6036, 3¼-oz, 4¾" **32.50**
Rose, plate, serving; #2666, 14" **40.00**
Rose, relish, celery; #2666, 9" **38.50**
Seascape, bowl, shallow, 11½" **39.50**
Seascape, candle holder, 4½" **15.00**
Shirley, bowl, #2545, flared, 12" **39.50**
Shirley, cheese & cracker, #2496 ....**45.00**
Shirley, goblet, saucer champagne; #6017, 6-oz, 5½" **18.00**
Shirley, tumbler, #6017, ftd, 9-oz, 5½" **16.50**
Silver Flutes, goblet, cocktail; 4-oz, 5" **11.50**
Silver Flutes, tumbler, ftd, 12-oz, 6⅛" **11.50**
Skyflower, bonbon, #2666, 6⅞" **13.50**
Skyflower, cup, #2666, 8-oz **11.50**
Skyflower, shakers, #2364, 3¼", pr **22.50**
Sonata, bowl, flared, 12" **15.00**
Sonata, plate, sandwich; 11" **12.50**
Sonata, shakers, 2⅝", pr **17.50**
Spinet, goblet, #6033, 10-oz, 6¼" **12.50**
Spinet, tumbler, juice; #6033, 5-oz, 4½" **8.00**
Spray, bowl, #2666, low, 8¼" **35.00**
Spray, plate, serving; #2666, 14" **35.00**
Spray, sugar bowl, #2666, 2⅝" **12.00**
Spring, goblet, #6060, 10½-oz, 5⅞" **7.50**
Spring, plate, #2337, 8" **4.50**
Sprite, bowl, #2630, ftd, flared, 10¾" **30.00**
Sprite, goblet, sherbet; #6033, low, 6-oz, 4" **10.00**
Sprite, shakers, #2630, 3¼" **32.50**
Star Song, goblet, #6083/2, 11¾-oz, 6¼" **10.00**
Star Song, goblet, cordial; #6083/29, 1¼-oz, 3¼" **15.00**
Stardust, creamer, #2666/681, 3½" **10.00**
Stardust, goblet, cocktail/wine; #6068, 4¼-oz, 4½" **9.00**
Stardust, relish, #2364/620, 2-part, 8¼" **15.00**
Starflower, bowl, #2630, flared, 12" **42.50**
Starflower, bowl, serving; #2630, hdld, 4½" **15.00**
Starflower, goblet, sherbet/champagne; #6049, 5¼" **15.00**
Starflower, pitcher, ice; #2630, 3-pt, 7⅛" **175.00**
Starflower, plate, torte; #2630, 14" **37.50**
Starflower, tidbit, #2630, 3-toed, 8⅛" **22.50**
Starflower, tumbler, iced tea; #6049, 15¼-oz, 6¼" **16.00**
Suffolk, goblet, #6025, 10-oz, 5½" **11.50**
Suffolk, plate, #2337, 8" **8.00**
Suffolk, tumbler, iced tea; #6025, 12-oz, 5⅝" **11.50**
Sunglow, plate, #2337/550, 8" **5.00**
Sunglow, tumbler, iced tea; #6085/63, ftd, 11¾-oz, 6¼" **8.00**
Sylvan, goblet, cordial; #6060, 1-oz, 2⅞" **42.50**
Sylvan, plate, canape; #2666, 7⅜" **12.50**
Sylvan, relish, #2666, 3-part, 10¾" **22.50**
Thistle, bonbon, #2666, 6⅞" **15.00**
Thistle, cup, #2666, 8-oz **14.50**
Thistle, plate, snack; #2666, 10" **15.00**
Thistle, shakers, #2666, 3¼", pr **27.50**
Thistle, vase, #2470, ftd, 10" **70.00**
Victoria, plate, #2337, narrow rib, 7" **5.00**
Victoria, tumbler, iced tea; ftd, 13-oz, 5⅞" **10.00**
Wedding Ring, goblet, claret/wine; #6051, 4-oz, 4½" **17.50**
Wedding Ring, sugar bowl, #2666, 2⅝" **6.50**
Wedding Ring, tumbler, juice; #6051, 5-oz, 4" **10.00**
Willow, cup, #2574 ....**12.50**
Willow, goblet, oyster cocktail; #6023, 4-oz, 3⅝" **10.00**
Willow, relish, celery; #2574, 10½" **25.00**
Willow, tumbler, #6023, ftd, 12-oz, 5¾" **14.50**
Willowmere, bonbon, #2560, 3-toed, 7¼" **25.00**
Willowmere, goblet, wine; #6024, 3½-oz, 5⅜" **35.00**

Willowmere, plate, #2560, 9" **38.50**
Willowmere, sugar bowl, #2560, ftd, 3½" **15.00**
Winburn, milk glass, jelly, #1704, oblong, 4" **15.00**
Winburn, milk glass; cracker jar, #1704, w/lid, 8¾" **57.50**
Winburn, milk glass; nappy, #1704, 3-corner **10.00**
Winburn, milk glass; sugar bowl, #1704, w/lid, 6⅞" **12.50**

Frakturs

Fraktur is a German style of black letter text type. To collectors, the fraktur is a type of hand-lettered document used by the people of German descent who settled in the areas of Pennsylvania, New Jersey, Maryland, Virginia, North and South Carolina, Ohio, Kentucky, and Ontario. These documents recorded births and baptisms and were used as bookplates and as certificates of honor. They were elaborately decorated with colorful folk-art borders of hearts, birds, angels, and flowers. Examples by recognized artists and those with an unusual decorative motif bring prices well into the thousands of dollars. Frakturs made in the late 1700s after the invention of the printing press provided the writer with a prepared text that he needed only to fill in at his own discretion. The next step in the evolution of machine-printed frakturs combined woodblock-printed decorations along with the text which the 'artist' sometimes enhanced with color. By the mid-1800s, even the coloring was done by machine. The vorschrift was a handwritten example prepared by a fraktur teacher to demonstrate his skill in lettering and decorating. These are often considered to be the finest of frakturs. Those dated before 1820 are most valuable.

The practice of fraktur art began to diminish after 1830 but hung on even to the early years of this century among the Pennsylvania Germans ingrained with such customs. Our advisor for this category is Frederick S. Weiser; he is listed in the Directory under Pennsylvania.

Key:
brd — board   p/i — pen and ink
lp — laid paper   wc — watercolored
pr — printed   wp — wove paper

Birth Record

Birth certificate, six 4-color tulips, red and green border, by Abraham Levan, Northhampton Co., Pennsylvania, 1804, 14x17", $1,650.00.

I/wc/wp, floral (primitive), 1840, 10x9", EX+ **425.00**
P/i/wc, births/deaths 1780-1829, sgn, Creswell, 20x12", G **1,700.00**

P/i/wc/lp, birds/hearts/etc, 4-color, 1816, 15x15", EX+ **1,700.00**
P/i/wc/lp, heart w/1809, tulips etc, EX color, 11x13" **1,150.00**
P/i/wc/wp, angels/cherubs/etc, 1833, 17x21", VG **700.00**
P/i/wc/wp, flowers/vines/name/1815, stains/fading, 15x11" **2,100.00**
P/i/wc/wp, lg letters, 1773, Berks Co, 12x10", VG **375.00**
Pr/p/i/wc/lp, lg parrots flank heart, 1896, rpr, 16x19", VG **1,350.00**
Pr/wc/lp, 3 hearts/birds/flowers, 1805, sgn FB, 16x18", EX **425.00**

Miscellaneous

P/i/wc, bookplate, tulip/1785, 4-color, damage, 7½x5" **250.00**
P/i/wc, prs birds/tulips/heart/inscription/sgn, 12x15", VG **250.00**
P/i/wc/lp, bookplate, bird/inscription/1834, 10x6", VG **195.00**
P/i/wc/lp, pr of birds/name/1806, minor stains, 7x9" **500.00**
P/i/wc/wp, 2 birds on branch/lg flowers, 4-color, 10x10", NM ..**4,550.00**
Wc on lined paper, 2 birds/tulip tree, 6x8", EX **850.00**

Frames

Styles in picture frames have changed with the fashion of the day, but those that especially interest today's collectors are the deep shadow boxes made of fine woods such as walnut or cherry, those with Art Nouveau influence, and the oak frames decorated with molded gesso and gilt from the Victorian era. Our advisor for this category is Michael Hinton; he is listed in the Directory under Pennsylvania.

Bird's-eye veneer ogee, gilt liner, 33x27" **160.00**
Brass, filigree, stand-up type, Victorian, 5½x8" **45.00**
Brass, florals/leaves, oval, French, 1860s, 6x4½", EX **50.00**
Brass, oval, convex glass, 14x20", EX **50.00**
Chas II, giltwood, rtcl acanthus, shield, 1670s, 26x24" **770.00**
Cherry, worn, 2" W, 19x16" **80.00**
CI w/gilt, rtcl leaves, metal bk, desk type, 11½x8¼" **65.00**
Laminated mahog/pine, shaped perimiter w/appl bosses, 9x13" **35.00**
Mahogany veneer fr, 2⅛" W, 16x18" **40.00**
Silver, branch/bird, eng/repousse, shaped top, English, 9" **800.00**
Walnut, worn, 3" W, 13x11", pr **40.00**
Walnut Victorian crisscross, cvd leaves at corners, 22x18" **150.00**

Frances Ware

Frances Ware, produced in the 1880s by Hobbs, Brockunier and Company of Wheeling, West Virginia, is either clear or frosted with amber-stained rim bands. The most often found pattern is Hobnail, but Swirl was also made.

Hobnail, clear; bowl, 7½" **65.00**
Hobnail, clear; butter dish **95.00**
Hobnail, clear; creamer **60.00**
Hobnail, clear; finger bowl, 4" **35.00**
Hobnail, clear; pitcher, 8½" **125.00**
Hobnail, clear; spooner **40.00**
Hobnail, frosted; bowl, ftd, berry pontil, 6x10" **150.00**
Hobnail, frosted; bowl, oblong, 8" **70.00**
Hobnail, frosted; bowl, 2½x5½" **40.00**
Hobnail, frosted; bowl, 4½" **30.00**
Hobnail, frosted; bowl, 8" **75.00**
Hobnail, frosted; bowl, 9" **85.00**
Hobnail, frosted; butter dish **120.00**
Hobnail, frosted; celery vase **75.00**
Hobnail, frosted; creamer **75.00**
Hobnail, frosted; finger bowl, 4" **35.00**
Hobnail, frosted; marmalade **125.00**

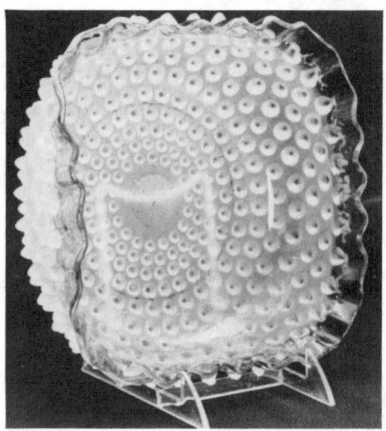

Frosted Hobnail bowl, 7½" square, $70.00.

Hobnail, frosted; pitcher, milk **150.00**
Hobnail, frosted; pitcher, water; sq top **175.00**
Hobnail, frosted; plate, sq, 5¾" **25.00**
Hobnail, frosted; sauce dish, sq, 4" **28.00**
Hobnail, frosted; shakers, pr **75.00**
Hobnail, frosted; spooner **70.00**
Hobnail, frosted; sugar bowl, w/lid **80.00**
Hobnail, frosted; syrup, pewter lid **165.00**
Hobnail, frosted; toothpick holder **60.00**
Hobnail, frosted; tray, cloverleaf, 12" **125.00**
Hobnail, frosted; tray, oblong, 14" **150.00**
Hobnail, frosted; tumbler, water **45.00**
Swirl, clear; shakers, pr **55.00**
Swirl, clear; syrup **90.00**
Swirl, frosted; bowl, 3¾" H **40.00**
Swirl, frosted; cruet **175.00**
Swirl, frosted; cruet, orig stopper, miniature **260.00**
Swirl, frosted; mustard jar **140.00**
Swirl, frosted; shakers, pr **75.00**
Swirl, frosted; sugar shaker, orig lid **125.00**
Swirl, frosted; syrup, Pat dtd **145.00**
Swirl, frosted; toothpick holder **110.00**
Swirl, frosted; tumbler **35.00**

Franciscan

Franciscan is a trade name used by Gladding McBean and Co., founded in northern California in 1875. In 1923 they purchased the Tropico plant in Glendale where they produced sewer pipe, gardenware, and tile. By 1934 the first of their dinnerware lines, El Patio, was produced. It was a plain design made in bright, attractive colors. El Patio Nouveau followed in 1935, glazed in two colors — one tone on the inside, a contrasting hue on the outside. Coronado, a favorite of today's collectors, was introduced in 1936. It was styled with a wide, swirled border and was made in pastels in both a satin and glossy finish. Before 1940 fifteen patterns had been produced. The first hand-decorated lines were introduced in 1937, the ever-popular Apple pattern in 1940, Desert Rose in 1941, and Ivy in 1948. Many other hand-decorated and decaled patterns were produced there from 1934 until 1984.

Dinnerware marks before 1940 include 'GMcB' in an oval, 'F' within a square, or 'Franciscan' with 'Pottery' underneath (which was later changed to 'Ware.') A circular arrangement of 'Franciscan' with 'Made in California USA' in the center was used from 1940 until 1949. At least forty marks were used before 1975; several more were introduced after that. At one time, paper labels were used.

The company merged with Lock Joint Pipe Company in 1963, becoming part of the Interpace Corporation. In July of 1979 Franciscan was purchased by Wedgwood Limited of England, and the Glendale plant closed in October, 1984.

Authority Delleen Enge has compiled an informative book, *Franciscan Ware*, with current values. You will find her address in the Directory under California. Our advisor for this category is Jack Chipman, author of *The Collector's Encyclopedia of California Pottery*; he is listed in the Directory under California. (See also Gladding McBean.)

Coronado

Bowl, cereal	12.00
Bowl, cream soup	15.00
Bowl, vegetable; serving, oval	20.00
Bowl, vegetable; serving, rnd	15.00
Candlesticks, pr	28.00
Casserole, w/lid	28.00
Cigarette box	40.00
Coffeepot, demitasse	50.00
Creamer & sugar bowl, w/lid	30.00
Cup & saucer	12.00
Cup & saucer, demitasse	22.00
Gravy boat, w/attached plate	28.00
Nut cup, ftd	16.00
Plate, chop; 12"	25.00
Plate, chop; 14"	35.00
Plate, 6½"	8.00
Plate, 7½"	10.00
Plate, 8½"	12.00
Platter, 11½"	25.00
Platter, 15½"	35.00
Saucer, cream soup	6.50
Shakers, pr	15.00
Sherbet	10.00
Teapot	40.00

El Patio

Bowl, cereal	12.00
Bowl, fruit	12.00
Bowl, salad; 3-qt	25.00
Bowl, vegetable; oval	30.00
Butter dish	35.00
Creamer	10.00
Cup	10.00
Cup, jumbo	18.00
Gravy boat, w/attached underplate	27.00
Plate, bread & butter	7.00
Plate, 10½"	15.00
Plate, 8½"	12.00
Saucer	4.00
Saucer, jumbo	8.00
Sherbet	10.00
Sugar bowl, w/lid	18.00
Teapot, w/lid, 6-cup	45.00

Franciscan Fine China

The main line of fine china was called Masterpiece. There were at least four marks used during its production from 1941 to 1977. Almost every piece is clearly marked. This china is true porcelain, the body having been fired at a very high temperature. Many years of research and experimentation went into this china before it was marketed. Production was temporarily suspended during the war years. More than 170 patterns and many varying shapes were produced. All are valued about the same with the exception of the Renaissance group, which is 25% higher.

Bowl, vegetable; serving, oval	50.00
Cup	20.00
Plate, bread & butter	18.00
Plate, dinner	30.00
Plate, salad	25.00
Saucer	12.00

Hand-Painted Embossed Earthenware

Values listed here apply to the following: Apple, Desert Rose, Ivy, Meadow Rose, Forget-Me-Not, October, Strawberry, Fresh Fruit, and other hand-painted patterns.

Apple, salt shaker and pepper mill, 6", $85.00 for the pair.

Ashtray, ind	12.00
Bowl, batter	50.00
Bowl, lug hdl, sm	18.00
Bowl, soup; flat	18.00
Bowl, vegetable; sm	15.00
Bowl, vegetable; w/lid	50.00
Bowl, 7½"	30.00
Bowl, 8¼"	40.00
Casserole, stick hdls, 12-oz	35.00
Coaster, 3¾"	15.00
Coffeepot	85.00
Compote, lg	40.00
Creamer, lg	15.00
Cup & saucer, demitasse; ea	25.00
Cup & saucer, jumbo	35.00
Egg cup	18.00
Goblet	27.00
Mug, lg	22.00
Pickle dish, 10¼"	35.00
Pitcher, water	65.00
Pitcher, 1-pt	30.00
Plate, chop; 14"	60.00
Plate, grill; 10¾"	38.00
Plate, 10½"	25.00
Plate, 6½"	10.00
Plate, 8½"	18.00
Plate, 9½"	20.00
Platter, 12½"	35.00
Platter, 19½"	110.00
Relish, 3-part, 11"	45.00
Shakers, Rosebud, pr	25.00
Shakers, tall, pr	35.00
Sugar bowl, open, sm	30.00
Sugar bowl, w/lid, lg	35.00

Tray, 3-tier **40.00**
Tumbler, 5⅛" **22.00**

Frankart

During the 1920s, Frankart, Inc. of New York City produced a line of accessories that included figural nude lamps, bookends, ashtrays, etc. These white metal composition items were offered in several finishes including verde green, jap black, and gun-metal gray. The company also produced a line of caricatured animals, but the stylized nude figurals have proven to be the most collectible today. With few exceptions, all pieces were marked 'Frankart, Inc.' with a patent number or 'pat. appl. for.' All pieces listed are in very good original condition unless otherwise indicated. Our advisor for this category is Walter Glenn; he is listed in the Directory under Georgia.

Ashtray, dachshund (stylized) spans 4½" sq tray, 5" **185.00**
Ashtray, nude emerging from leaves holds tray aloft, 25" **725.00**
Ashtray, nude holds 6" pottery ash bowl overhead, 13" **365.00**
Ashtray, nude kneels on cushion, holds 3" pottery tray, 6" **285.00**
Ashtray, nude stands/leans against circle, tray at ft, 7" **365.00**
Ashtray, satyr strides/holds 3" ceramic tray, 8" **310.00**
Bookends, female head, modernistic style, 6", pr **270.00**
Bookends, nude fan dancer holds books, 10", pr **390.00**
Bookends, nude sits atop human skull, 8", pr **325.00**
Bookends, nude stands w/arms bk to support books, 7½", pr **285.00**
Bookends, penguin mother & 2 chicks (stylized), 5", pr **170.00**
Clock, nude stands ea side of sqd glass clock, 10½" **1,100.00**
Flower frog, nude stands in flared 15" dia bowl, 13" **375.00**
Incense burner, female head blows smoke through mouth, 5½" .**285.00**
Lamp, elephant on ball (stylized), parchment shade, 14½" **275.00**
Lamp, nude as butterfly w/frosted glass wings, 10¼" **1,250.00**
Lamp, nude dances/embraces 11" crackle glass cylinder, 12½" ...**650.00**
Lamp, nude stands ea side of 8" crackle globe, 9" **650.00**
Lamp, 2 nudes kneel bk to bk, 8" crackle globe between, 9" **585.00**
Mirror, nude stands/holds 7" dia mirror aloft, 11" **475.00**

Frankoma

The Frank Pottery, founded in Oklahoma in 1933 by John Frank, became known as Frankoma in 1934. The company produced decorative figurals, vases, and such, marking their ware from 1936-38 with a pacing leopard 'Frankoma' mark. These pieces are highly sought. The entire operation was destroyed by fire in 1938, and new molds were cast — some from surviving pieces — and a similar line of production was pursued. The body of the ware was changed in 1954 from a honey tan (called 'Ada clay,' referring to the name of the town near the area where it was dug) to the to a red brick clay (known as Sapula), and this, along with the color of the glazes (over forty have been used), helps determine the period of production. A Southwestern theme has always been favored in design as well as in color selection.

In 1965, they began to produce a limited-edition series of Christmas plates, followed by a bottle vase series in 1969. Considered very collectible are their political mugs, bicentennial plates, Teenagers of the Bible plates, and the Wildfire series. Their ceramic Christmas cards are also very popular items with today's collectors.

Frankoma celebrated their 50th Anniversary in 1983. On September 26 of that same year, Frankoma was again destroyed by fire. Because of a fire-proof wall, master molds of all 1983 production items were saved, allowing plans for rebuilding to begin immediately.

Frankoma filed for Chapter 11 in April, 1990, and eventually sold to a Maryland investor in February of 1991, thereby ending the family-ownership era.

For a more thorough study of the subject, we recommend that you refer to *Frankoma Treasures* by Phyllis and Tom Bess, our advisors; you will find their address in the Directory under Oklahoma.

Ashtray, cocker spaniel, Ada clay, #460 ....**60.00**
Ashtray, Wht Sand, Ada clay, #469, 3½x4½" **15.00**
Ashtray set, #459, 1942, 6-pc **50.00**
Bookend, Bucking Bronco, Prairie Gr, #423, pr **250.00**
Bookend, Charger Horse, Blk Onyx, #420, pr **195.00**
Bookend, Irish Setter, blk, Ada clay, pr **165.00**
Bookend, Mountain Girl, #425, 5¾", pr **200.00**
Bookend, Ocelot, Ada clay, #422, 1934-38, 7¼", ea **200.00**
Bookend, Sea Horse, pacing leopard mk, pr **600.00**
Bowl, Carved Cactus, #207, 1949-50, 10" **60.00**
Candelabrum, #306, 11¾" **65.00**
Candle holder, Dusty Rose, #307, 3", pr **75.00**
Candle holder, Oral Roberts **12.00**
Canteen, Thunderbird, Ada clay, #59, 6½" **35.00**
Christmas card, 1950-51, ea **75.00**
Christmas card, 1955-56, ea **75.00**
Christmas card, 1958 ....**60.00**
Christmas card, 1973-74, ea **45.00**
Christmas card, 1975, bird in hand, Grace Lee, rare **115.00**
Christmas plate, 1968 ....**65.00**
Cornucopia, Ada clay, #56, 1942-49, 7" **35.00**
Creamer, Guernsey, #93-A, 3½" **25.00**
Creamer & sugar bowl, ringed, leopard mk **100.00**
Donkey mug, 1975, Autumn Yel **35.00**
Donkey mug, 1980, Terra Cotta **25.00**
Elephant mug, 1968, Wht Sand **100.00**
Elephant mug, 1970, bl **65.00**

Figurine, Rodeo Cowboy, 7¾", $400.00.

Flower bowl, blk, low, #238, 8" dia **25.00**
Flower holder, Boot, stars on sides, Ada clay, #507, 3½" **12.00**
Flower holder, Boots on Thong, #507-S, mini, 3½" **25.00**
Flower holder, Duck, #184, 3¾" **150.00**
Flower holder, Fish, #185, 2⅝" **150.00**
Honey jar, Beehive, Ada clay, #803, 12-oz **25.00**
Jug, Ada Clay, #86, w/stopper, ½-gal **45.00**
Jug, Uncle Slug, #10, 2¼" **20.00**
Lamp base, Dreamer Girl, Blk Onyx, #427, pr **235.00**
Lamp base, from Wagon Wheel sugar bowl **50.00**
Marionette head, rare **125.00**
Mask, Comedy & Tragedy, brn, pr **48.00**
Mug, Red Bud **12.00**
Pitcher, batter; #87, 4½" **35.00**

Pitcher, jug form, #554, 1942, 2¾" 20.00
Pitcher, Prairie Gr, Ada clay, #80, 2-qt 35.00
Pitcher, Snail, Old Gold, mini 15.00
Planter, Madonna of Grace, #231-B, 6" 75.00
Planter, Oblong Cactus, Ada clay, #206, 1949-52, 10½" 35.00
Plaque, Indian Head, pacing leopard mk, mini 45.00
Plaque, Oriental Man, Osage Brn, pacing leopard mk, #134 ....150.00
Plaque, Will Rogers, borderless, mk Frankoma St Clair Homer 58.00
Plate, Peter the Fisherman, 1977 ....25.00
Plate, Wagon Wheel, #94G, 7" 3.50
Plate, Wht-Tail Deer, 1973 ....85.00
Plate, Will Rogers Centennial 15.00
Pot, Prairie Gr, silver floral o/l, Ada clay, 3½x6" 300.00
Sculpture, Afro Man, Blk Onyx, Ada clay 75.00
Sculpture, Circus Horse, Cherokee Red, #138, 4½" 150.00
Sculpture, Circus Horse, Desert Gold, red clay 75.00
Sculpture, Coyote Pup, #105 ....350.00
Sculpture, English Setter, #141, 5¼" 125.00
Sculpture, Fan Dancer, Ada clay, #113 ....250.00
Sculpture, Fan Dancer, red clay, Prairie Gr, #113 ....175.00
Sculpture, Flower Girl, #700, 1942-52, 5½" 75.00
Sculpture, Gardener Boy, Prairie Gr 100.00
Sculpture, Gardener Girl, Prairie Gr, #701 ....100.00
Sculpture, Indian Bowl Maker, Ada clay, #123, 6" 90.00
Sculpture, Indian Chief, Ada clay, 8" 90.00
Sculpture, Indian Maiden, Osage Brn, Ada clay, #132 ....50.00
Sculpture, Indian Maiden, Wht Sand, #101, 13" 45.00
Sculpture, Indian Maiden & Chief, Blk Onyx, red clay, pr 85.00
Sculpture, Medicine Man, #115 ....125.00
Sculpture, Prancing Colt, #117, 8" 585.00
Sculpture, Puma, blk onyx, 1 sitting/1 lying, red clay, pr 45.00
Sculpture, Rearing Clydesdale, mk Frank Potters, #107 ....350.00
Sculpture, Swan, Peacock Bl, mini 40.00
Sculpture, Walking Elephant, #169, 1¾" 90.00
Shakers, Dutch Shoe, Terra Cotta Rose, #915-H, 4", pr 35.00

Swan (open tail), Ada clay, rose glaze,
1953, 12", $150.00.

Sign, Pacing Leopard, 8⅝" L 450.00
Teapot, Aztec, gr 20.00
Trivet, American Eagle, #AETR, 1976-78 ....15.00
Trivet, Lazybones, Prairie Gr, #4-TR 50.00
Tumbler, Bamboo, #T-2, 1962-76, 14-oz 15.00
Vase, #505, 1950-51, 2¾" 20.00
Vase, blk ft, #55, 4" 25.00
Vase, bud; snail decor, early, 6" 15.00
Vase, collector; V-1, Prairie Gr, 1969, 15" 100.00
Vase, collector; V-12, 1980 ....40.00

Vase, collector; V-14, any color, not #d 35.00
Vase, collector; V-14, Flame, bottle form, #d, w/stand 85.00
Vase, collector; V-3, red & blk, 1971, 12" 85.00
Vase, collector; V-4, blk & Terra Cotta, 1972 ....80.00
Vase, collector; V-5, Flame Red, 1973, 13" 80.00
Vase, collector; V-8, Freedom Red & wht, 1976 ....70.00
Vase, Dusty Rose, Ada clay, #501, ca 1942 ....50.00
Vase, leaf hdls, early glaze, Ada clay, #71, 10" 75.00
Vase, Ram's Head, #38, 6" 45.00
Vase, Ring, #500, mini, 2¾" 25.00
Vase, stepped hdls, Ada clay, 7" 65.00
Vase, Western theme w/cactus, pillow form, #4, 7½" 40.00
Wall pocket, Acorn, #190, 6" 15.00
Wall pocket, Leaf, #197, 8½" 45.00
Wall pocket, Phoebe, Desert Gold, Ada clay, #730 ....100.00

Fraternal Organizations

Fraternal memorabilia is a vast and varied field. Emblems representing the various organizations have been used to decorate cups, shaving mugs, plates, and glassware. Medals, swords, documents, and other ceremonial paraphernalia from the 1800s and early 1900s are especially prized. Our advisor for Odd Fellows is Greg Spiess; he is listed in the Directory under Illinois. Mike Roscoe, our Masonic advisor is listed under Michigan.

Masons

Apron, wht satin w/bl ribbon & HP decor, NM 60.00
Champagne, Syria Shrine 1911 ....65.00
Goblet, man w/camera, dtd 1911 ....75.00
Light fixture, 'G' emblem 85.00
Loving cup, 1905 ....95.00
Ribbon, conclave; 1890s, 10 for 50.00
Sampler, 1850s, lg, EX 150.00
Shaving mug, bl symbols, name, gold trim 95.00
Spoon, SP, Masonic Temple, Chicago 38.00
Sword & scabbard, Knight's Templar, M 145.00

Odd Fellows

Banner & staff, w/emblems 50.00
Belt buckle, w/3 links 25.00
Box, ballot; w/link symbols 100.00
Gavel, cvd wood w/symbols, ca 1900, 11½" L, EX 145.00
Helmet, ceremonial, cloth-covered w/brass spike, EX 20.00
Mention, convention; ca 1910 ....25.00
Staff, ceremonial, cvd walnut, owl perched on ball top, 1800s ...240.00

Shrine

Cane, Smile w/Nile, Seattle 1936 ....65.00
Tumbler, Grasshopper, June 12, 1901 ....110.00
Tumbler, Steering over Hot Sands to Dallas, June 1898 ....110.00

Miscellaneous

Scottish Rites, reunion medal, 1910 ....10.00
Woodsmen of the World, wooden lodge axe, WOW, 35" 55.00

Fruit Jars

As early as 1829, canning jars were being manufactured for use in the home preservation of foodstuffs. For the past twenty-five years, they have been sought as popular collectibles. At the last estimate, over four thousand fruit jars and variations were known to exist. Some are very rare, perhaps one-of-a-kind examples known to have survived to the present day. Among the most valuable are the black glass jars, the amber Van Vliet, and the cobalt Millville. These often bring prices in excess of $3,000.00 when they can be found. Aside from condition, values are based on age, rarity, color, and special features. Our advisor for this category is John Hathaway; he is listed in the Directory under Maine.

Acme Seal (script), regular mouth, clear, pt 145.00
AGBMCo, aqua, wax sealer, qt 35.00
AGWL Pitts, PA (base), aqua, ½-gal 55.00
American (NAGCo) Porcelain Lined, aqua, midget 148.00
American (NAGCo) Porcelain Lined, aqua, qt 23.00
Atlas E-Z Seal, amber, sm lip flake, qt 35.00
Atlas E-Z Seal, gr, bell shape, pt 20.00
Atlas E-Z Seal, gr, qt 18.00
Atlas Junior Mason, clear, ⅔-pt 9.00
Atlas Mason Patent, apple gr, qt 18.00
Atlas Strong Shoulder Mason, cornflower bl, ½-gal 23.00
Atlas Strong Shoulder Mason, gr, qt 22.00
Ball (underlined) Half Pint, base: Made in USA, clear, ½-pt 23.00
Ball (underlined) Mason, lt olive gr, ½-gal 220.00
Ball Home Canning (Wm C Hannah jar), teal bl, qt 125.00
Ball Mason, reverse: fighting bear & bull, clear, pt 23.00
Bamberger's Always the Busy Store Newark, aqua, qt 98.00
Beaver (beaver), aqua, qt 35.00
Bloeser Jar, aqua, qt 248.00
Burlington BGCO R'D 1876, clear, ½-gal 48.00
C Ihmsen & Son Pittsburgh PA (base), sky bl, scratches, qt 98.00
Canadian King (in shield) Wide Mouth Adjustable, clear, qt 23.00
Champion Pat Aug 31 1869, aqua, qt 190.00
Crystal Jar, clear, midget 60.00
Cunningham & Co Pittsburgh PA (base), aqua, wax sealer, qt 33.00
Dallas (incised on shoulder), brn stoneware, qt 43.00
DGCo (lg intertwined monogram), aqua, ½-gal 48.00
Doolittle Patented Dec 3 1904 (lid), clear, qt 23.00
Easy Trade VJC Co Mark Vacuum Jar, aqua, qt 23.00
Eclipse, aqua, qt 98.00
Eureka Pat'd Dec 27th 1864, aqua, qt 68.00
FCGCo (base), aqua, qt 23.00
Flaccus Bros Steer Head Fruit Jar, clear, no stopper, pt 48.00
Fruit Keeper, GCCo, aqua, pt 48.00
Gem (Block G), aqua, midget 35.00
Glassboro Trade Mark Improved, aqua, pt 33.00
Glassboro Trade Mark Improved, aqua, qt 18.00

Glassboro Trade 1 Mark Improved, aqua, ½-gal 18.00
Hamilton, clear, qt 83.00
Hero Improved, aqua, qt 22.00
HW Pettit Westville NJ, cornflower bl, aqua lid, pt 38.00
Ideal Imperial, aqua, qt 23.00
Improved Crown, med yel-gr, clear lid, qt 33.00
Johnson & Johnson New Brunswick NJ USA, amber, qt 22.00
Kerr Self Sealing Mason, amber, qt 18.00
King (on banner crown & flags), clear, ½-pt 38.00
Klines Patent Oct 27 63 (on blown stopper), aqua, qt 123.00
KYGW (base), aqua, wax sealer, qt 23.00
Magic (star) Fruit Jar, amber, qt 800.00
Mason Jar of 1858 TM (in circle & sq), aqua, ½-gal 88.00
Mason's (lg keystone) Improved, aqua, midget 38.00
Mason's BCCo Improved, aqua, qt 58.00
Mason's Improved, reverse: hourglass, aqua, midget 75.00
Mason's Improved (cross), aqua, midget 25.00
Mason's Patent Nov 30th 1858, apple gr, ½-gal 58.00
Mason's Patent Nov 30th 1858, reverse: CFJ, aqua, qt 35.00
Mason's Patent Nov 30th 58, aqua, midget 58.00
Mothers Jap TM PE Tongue & Bros Inc Phila PA, aqua, pt 38.00
New Paragon, aqua, qt 125.00
Pat July 11 1893 VJC Co (base), lt aqua, qt 13.00
Pat'd Sept 20th 1898 (on lid), clear, ¼-pt 14.00
Peoria Pottery (incised on base), brn stoneware, qt 28.00
Perfection, aqua, qt 43.00
Royal, blk, qt 4,000.00
Simplex (in dmn), clear, orig contents & label, ½-pt 20.00
SKO Queen Trademark, clear, ½-pt 12.00
Star (below stippled star), lt aqua, qt 48.00
Stevens Tin top Patd July 27, 1875, aqua, wax sealer, qt 73.00
The Automatic Sealer, aqua, qt 140.00
Trade Mark Lightning (base) Putnam, aqua, 1½-pt 38.00
Trade Mark Mason's CFJ Improved, aqua, midget 20.00
Trade Mark the Dandy, amber, ½-gal 158.00
UGCo (on heel), aqua, qt 30.00
Victory 1 (circled by patent dates), aqua, qt 48.00
W&J Fleet (sun) Liverpool, lt gr, no stopper, qt 23.00
Winslow Jar, aqua, qt 48.00
Wm Frank & Sons Pitts (base), aqua, wax sealer, qt 28.00
Woodbury Improved WGW, aqua, ½-gal 33.00
Woodbury WW, aqua, qt 43.00
Yoeman's Fruit Bottle, aqua, pt 48.00

Fry

Henry Fry established his glassworks in 1901 in Rochester, Pennsylvania. There, until 1933 when it was sold to the Libbey Company, he produced glassware of the finest quality. In the early years they produced beautiful cut glass; when it began to wane in popularity, Fry turned to the manufacture of occasional pieces and oven glassware. He is perhaps most famous for the opalescent pearl glass called 'Foval.' It was sometimes made with blue or jade green trim in combination. Because it was in production for only a short time in 1926 and 1927, it is hard to find.

Collectors of Depression-era glassware look for the opalescent reamers and opaque green kitchenware made during the early thirties.

For further study we recommend *The Collector's Encyclopedia of Fry Glassware* by the Fry Glass Society. Our advisor for this category is Ron Damaska; he is listed in the Directory under Pennsylvania. See also Kitchen Collectibles, Glassware.

Basket, Foval, jade gr w/festooning, 12" 525.00

Globe, yellow-amber, ground lip, glass lid, metal closure, ½-gallon, M, $95.00.

Bowl, fruit; Foval, jade stem & edge of rolled rim, 10" 225.00
Cake pan, pearl ovenware, 8" sq 20.00
Cake plate, Sunnybrook pattern, emerald gr 35.00
Candlesticks, Foval, bl threading/base/bobeche, 12", pr 365.00
Casserole, pearl ovenware, flower etching, metal holder 30.00
Compote, royal bl, polished pontil, 4x6" 145.00
Creamer & sugar bowl, Foval w/Delft bl hdls & festooning 150.00
Cruet, Foval, pearl w/Delft bl stopper, 9" 135.00
Cruet, HP florals on pk crackle, orig stopper 115.00

Cup and saucer in opal glass with wheel etching, $95.00.

Cup & saucer, Foval, pearl w/floral cutting, #2000 ....95.00
Cup & saucer, HP flowers & blk band on rose 30.00
Finger bowl, Rose etching, +matching underplate 35.00
Grill plate, amber, 3-compartment 25.00
Measure, pearl ovenware, 3-spout 45.00
Nappy, Wilhelm cutting, hdls 235.00
Percolator, Foval, glass insert 375.00
Pitcher, Foval w/jade hdl, lid w/jade finial 210.00
Pitcher, tankard, Carnation cutting 250.00
Plate, Foval, jade gr rim, 8½", set of 8 ....350.00
Reamer, emerald, ruffled 180.00
Roaster, pearl ovenware, w/lid, 14" 70.00
Vase, Foval, royal bl base, trumpet form, 10" 280.00
Vase, Foval w/3 jade gr ball ft, flared rim, 5" 225.00
Vase, Geneva, chalice form, 10" 200.00
Vase, Ivy cutting, slim form, 10" 225.00
Vase, jack-in-pulpit; Foval, Delft bl trim, 10½" 225.00
Vase, jack-in-pulpit; Foval, jade gr trim, 10½x3½" 225.00

Fulper

The Fulper Pottery was founded in 1899, after nearly a century of producing utilitarian stoneware under various titles and managements. Not until 1909 did Fulper venture into the art pottery field. Vasekraft, their first art line, utilized the same heavy clay body used for their utility ware. Although shapes were unadorned and simple, the glazes they developed were used with such flair and imagination (alone and in unexpected combined harmony) that each piece was truly a work of art. Graceful Oriental shapes were produced to complement the important 'famille rose' glaze developed by W.H. Fulper, Jr. Other shapes and glazes were developed in line with the Arts and Crafts movement of the same period.

During WWI, doll's heads and Kewpies were made to meet the demand for hard-to-find imports. Figural perfume lamps and powder boxes were made both in bisque and glazed ware. Examples prized most highly by collectors today are those made before a devastating fire destroyed the plant in 1929, resulting in an operations takeover by Martin Stangl later that same year.

Several marks were used: a vertical 'Fulper' in a line reserve, a horizontal mark, a Vasekraft paper label, 'Rafco,' 'Prang,' and 'Flemington.'

Fulper values are to a major degree determined by the desirability of the glazes and forms. And, of course, larger examples command higher prices as well. Lamps with colored glass inserts are rare and highly prized. Our advisor for this category is Douglass White; he is listed in the Directory under Florida.

Bookends, Rameses, gr, pr 650.00
Bowl, bl-gr, 3 twisted bands form ft & hdl, 5x8" 300.00
Bowl, blk drip over gr, 9" 120.00
Bowl, brn/gun-metal gray drip matt, glossy int, 3½x10" 325.00
Bowl, celadon gr w/gr crystalline, stepped sides, 2¾x11½" 300.00
Bowl, console; yel w/blk streaks, 12" 195.00
Bowl, effigy; brn crystalline w/gold, flambe int, 8x10" 650.00
Bowl, famille rose, 4-ftd ped base, 3x7" 250.00
Bowl, gr shaded crystalline, 12" 250.00
Bowl, gr/blk steaky int, matt gr at base ext, 1¾x8" 85.00
Bowl, gray drip over gr, 3½x13" 275.00
Candle holder, moss gr, 3 glass pcs in helmet-form top, 11" 990.00
Candlestick, yel-tan w/gun-metal bl drip, 10" 150.00
Chamberstick, bl-gray, hooded style, 7" 135.00
Compote, bl crystalline, 11x7" 595.00
Decanter, whiskey; sea gr, pinched, musical 100.00
Figurine, cat, tiger's eye brn, ivory, bl flambe, 5¾x9¼" 550.00
Flower frog, duck 90.00
Flower frog, leprechaun 160.00
Humidor, cafe-au-lait & gun-metal glaze, unmk, 6" 325.00
Lamp, cinnamon brn crystalline, factory made, 8x7" 250.00
Lamp, lt/dk bl slag inserts in 9½" cone shade, mk, 17" 3,300.00
Lamp base, bl flambe w/bl starburst crystals, brass ft, 10" 450.00
Lamp base, gr mottle, 9½x6¾" 120.00
Lamp base, leopard skin, gr crystalline, pinched bottle, 7" 295.00
Pitcher, gr/turq flambe on dk matt rose, 4" 85.00
Rose bowl, bl flambe gloss over bl matt w/speckles, 2½x9" 250.00
Vase, bl matt w/bl-gr glossy drip, glaze bubbles, 7" 170.00
Vase, brn w/gr streaks, bulbous, 7½x6½" 400.00
Vase, brn/yel/gr runs, ftd sphere w/4 spool-like necks, 8" 700.00
Vase, bud; bl & brn flambe on bl speckled, 5½", pr 275.00
Vase, bud; bl w/dk bl & brn specks, flambe drip, 6" 110.00
Vase, cafe au lait, #195, 4½" 275.00
Vase, caramel flambe over beige, waisted, 7" 225.00
Vase, celedon gr w/gold crystalline, 4-hdl, 7" 250.00
Vase, celedon gr w/gold crystalline at rim, 5½x5½" 250.00
Vase, cornucopia; mirror bl/gun-metal drip over bl/brn, 8x8" 300.00

Vase, cucumber green crystalline, #490, #1,700.00.

Vase, dk bl over famille rose, waisted form, 5½" **250.00**
Vase, dk bl-gr drips on brn, urn form, sm hdls, #4018, 7" **170.00**
Vase, famille rose drip over gray matt, simple form, 12x9" **200.00**
Vase, famille rose w/purple flambe drip, gr top, 10" **220.00**
Vase, gold crystalline over brn, ogee sides, 7" **300.00**
Vase, gold micro crystalline & celedon gr flambe, 3½" **125.00**
Vase, gr crystalline, 3 rim hdls, 7" **220.00**
Vase, gr over purple, hdls, sgn, 5" **200.00**
Vase, gr streaks over mustard, 4½x7" **130.00**
Vase, gr/brn flambe w/pk drip, ½" neck band, 6-side bulb, 8" **325.00**
Vase, gr/gun-metal blk, mottled/bubbled, akimbo hdls, 18" **600.00**
Vase, gr/turq crystalline, 10" **395.00**
Vase, gray/bl drip on caramel, Greek form on sq base, 7" **175.00**
Vase, gun-metal blk/brn/dk bl, can neck, Chinese hdls, 9x9" ..**1,300.00**
Vase, gun-metal blk/copperdust flambe, elongated, 13x7½" **1,600.00**
Vase, gun-metal crystalline over tiger-eye, neck band, 10x8" ..**1,500.00**
Vase, gun-metal/copperdust, angle shoulder, hand thrown, 10" .**900.00**
Vase, ivory/crystalline bl/gun-metal, 3 horn-like hdls, 7" **600.00**
Vase, leopard skin, #659, 9" **725.00**
Vase, lt bl w/bl crystalline & flambe, mk Flemington, 4" **75.00**
Vase, moss on celadon crystalline, 2-hdl, ftd ovoid, 12" **880.00**
Vase, moss to gr to mustard, hdls extend above rim, 11x9" **1,300.00**
Vase, rose drip over gray, bulbous, 12" **550.00**
Vase, rust mottle drip on taupe, 3 rtcl shoulder hdls, 6½" **300.00**
Vase, rust w/brn-gray to yel flambe drip, concave sides, 8" **225.00**
Vase, turq crystalline, 7" **225.00**
Wall pocket, brn, Greek Key cvd band at top, rnd bottom, 8½" .**275.00**

Furniture

From the cabinetmaker's shop of the early 1800s with apprentices and journeymen who learned every phase of the craft at the side of the master carpenter, the trade had evolved by the mid-century to one with steam-powered saws and turning lathes and workers who specialized in only one operation. By 1870 the Industrial Revolution was in progress, and large factories in the East and Midwest turned out increasingly elaborate styles, ornately machine carved and heavily inlaid. Rococo, Egyptian, and Renaissance Revival furniture adapted well to factory production. Eastlake offered a welcome respite from Victorian frumpery and a return to quality handcrafting. All of these styles remained popular until the turn of the century.

As early as 1880, factories began using oak; early mail-order catalogs offered oak furniture, simply styled and lighter in weight, since long-distance shipping was often a factor. Mission, or Craftsman, a style introduced around 1890, was simple to the extreme. Stickley and Hubbard were two of its leading designers. Other popular Victorian styles were Colonial Revival, Cottage, Bentwood, and Windsor. Prices are as variable as the styles.

It is very important to realize that the combination of recent economic conditions along with a scarcity of comprehensive examples in the auction marketplace in certain furniture categories could be confusing. Because of this, items that have sold at auction for at least 25% lower than their normal market values will be designated with an (*).

Our advisor for this category is Suzy McLennan Anderson, ISA, of Heritage Antiques, whose address is listed in the Directory under New Jersey. To learn more about furniture, we recommend *The Collector's Encyclopedia of American Furniture* by Robert and Harriet Swedberg.

Note: When only one dimension is given for blanket chests, dry sinks, tables, settees, and sofas, it is length.

Key:
Am — American   Geo — Georgian
brd — board   grpt — grainpainted

Chpndl — Chippendale   hdbd — headboard
Co — Country   hdw — hardware
cvd — carved   Hplwht — Hepplewhite
cvg — carving   mar — marriage
c&b — claw and ball   NE — New England
do — door   QA — Queen Anne
drw — drawer   trn — turning
Emp — Empire   Vict — Victorian
Fed — Federal   W/M — William and Mary
Fr — French   : — over (example: 1 do:2 drw —
ftbd — footboard   1 door over 2 drawers)
G — good

Armoire

Chifforobe, oak, mirror:4 drw on right, left is wardrobe **375.00**
Oak, 2 mirrored do, appl cvg, 1-drw, 1880, rfn, 48x72" **1,500.00**
Walnut Vict, 2 mirrored do, cvd crown, 1-drw, rfn, 45x78" **2,450.00**
Wardrobe, oak, 2 blind do, panelled sides, 1925, rfn **395.00**
Wardrobe, walnut Vict, urn/spire finials, cvgs, 104x90" **4,000.00**

Bed

Walnut and burled walnut veneer Victorian bed, ca 1875, 95" high, $2,000.00.

Brass Louis XVI style, floral crest etc, bevel glass panel **650.00**
Child's trundle, short trn posts, rope rails, 12x39x57" **165.00**
Limbert, #471, wide & slim slats, EX orig, branded, 50x54" **2,000.00**
Majorelle, mahog, inlaid wisteria/morning-glories, 62x48" **6,000.00**
Murphy, oak, lg mirror front, elaborately cvd sides/crest **1,000.00**
Murphy, oak, sm mirror atop, 3-panel front, press cvg **950.00**
Rope, bird's-eye maple w/cannonballs, EX trn, 45x35" W **800.00**
Rope, Cherry Co PA, trn posts w/acorn finials, cut-out hdbd **900.00**
Rope, hired man's, poplar w/orig bl-gr pnt, mattress: 49x69" **425.00**
Rope, pine/poplar, cherry stain, cannonball finials, 52x70" **450.00**
Rope, poplar Co w/rpt, trn posts/high ft, simple hdbd **225.00**
Rope, trundle, poplar w/old red, ball finials, 18x45x63" **325.00**
Tester, cherry/maple, shaped hdbd, 1840, rfn, ¾-sz **1,500.00**
Tester, maple, shaped hdbd, trn posts, 1830, 56" **2,800.00**

Bench

Limbert, drop-arm settle, 11 staggered slats, brand, 68" **600.00**
Mammy's, spindle bk, simple trn, rockers, guard, rpt, 35" **300.00**
Poplar w/worn bluish pnt, primitive, 51" **170.00**
Settle, Co w/brn grpt over wht, ½-spindle bk/trn legs, 81" **700.00**
Settle, dbl arrow bk, rpt w/grapes, 46" L **700.00**
Settle, decor Emp, orig florals on wht, scroll seat, 73" **2,000.00**

Settle, plank seat, simple trn, rfn, 84" 400.00
Walnut W/M style, needlepoint uphl, 1880s, 49" 1,000.00
Water, pine, 1-brd ends w/cut-out ft, shaped sides, 37x36" 525.00
Water, pine w/worn yel rpt, warped/water damage, 35x45" 450.00
Water, 3-shelf, dk pnt, shaped sides, 44x36x11" 200.00
Window, walnut Italian neoclassic style, 29x36" 440.00

Blanket Chest

Pine, dvtl, trn ft, base/lid moldings, 35", VG * 175.00
Pine, shoe ft, canted sides, dvtl w/appl moldings, 43", EX 150.00
Pine/poplar w/red grpt, trn ft, base molding, dvtl, 35" 800.00
Pine/poplar w/red pnt, trn ft, dvtl, till w/lid, 38", EX * 275.00
Pine/poplar w/rpt decor, paneled, trn ft, till w/lid, 45" 275.00
Poplar PA, red/brn finish, paneled, trn ft, 50", EX 325.00
Poplar w/bl pnt, initials/florals/etc, molding, 35", EX 1,200.00
Poplar w/brn grpt over wht, dvtl, till, 43", EX 350.00
Poplar w/brn grpt over yel, dvtl, initial/1885, 41", NM 1,100.00
Poplar w/worn rpt over red, trn ft, dvtl case, till, 37" 325.00
Poplar/butternut w/old red, trn tapered ft, till lid, 35" 450.00
Soap Hollow PA, red-brn grpt, dk gr ft/etc, att Stahl, 43" 3,300.00
Tulips (7) pnt on gr, lift lid, bracket ft, PA, 1750s, 50"* 1,700.00

Bookcase

Limbert, spade cutouts/open top half, label, 47x17x11" 1,900.00
Mahog Geo III, broken arch ped:glaze do:drop lid:4 drw, 88" 4,950.00
Mahog w/inlay Fed style, 2 glazed do/flip-up desk, 1800s 1,050.00
Mahog w/lnlay Fed style, tambour, flip-up top in base 1,200.00
Oak, sectional, 4-unit, 1920s, rstr/rfn 500.00
Secretary, cherry/mahog flame vnr Emp, acanthus legs, 81" 1,000.00

Bureau, See Chest

Cabinet

China, oak, curved glass front, mirror, many press-cvgs, lg 1,250.00
China, oak, curved glass front/sides, press-cvd trim/ft, lg 1,500.00
China, oak, curved glass front/sides, press-cvd trim/ft, sm 1,000.00
China, oak, glass front/sides, no decor, cvd ft, narrow 500.00
China, oak w/appl cvg & claw ft, curved glass sides, 68x48" 1,200.00
Curio, Eastlake, glazed do ea side cabinet do, 1880, 48x36" 550.00
Majorelle, glazed do, sm birch tree-inlay do, 68x28" 7,700.00

Candlestand

Birch Co, rfn w/remains of bl, 8-sided 14" top, att Dunlap 1,300.00

Mahogany Federal candlestand, stringing outlines the edge, refinished 19" octagonal top, 29", $1,800.00.

Cherry Co, tripod base/snake ft, 1-brd 14" shaped top, rfn 800.00
Cherry Co Chpndl, tripod on trn column, sq 15" galleried top * 625.00
Cherry Fed, vasiform std, shaped 25x17" top, tripod, 1820s * 275.00
Hardwood w/red varnish, tripod base w/'boot' ft, late 535.00
Mahog Co English Chpndl, tripod/snake ft, 20" tilt top, EX 375.00
Walnut Fed, birdcage, 3 cabriole legs, 19" tilt top * 325.00
Walnut Fed, ring-trn std, 15x18" ribbed top, 1820s * 375.00
Walnut w/bird's-eye Co Chpndl, rpl 19" tilt top & birdcage 750.00
Wood w/iron socket atop adjustable ratchet, rpl/wear, 32" 285.00

Chair

Arm, brn pnt w/crest decor, Hitchcock type, rush seat, EX 175.00
Arm, mahog English Regency, tapestry uphl, rprs/crack, 34" 250.00
Arm, oak, bk: rope cvgs/rtcl vines/cane insert, 1880s, 58" 200.00
Arm, oak, seat & arm supports in U-form, cvd/rtcl bk splat 650.00
Arm, rosewood Am Rococo, pierced/cvd crest, medallion bk 525.00
Arm, walnut QA, shepherd's crook arms, c/b ft, 39" 550.00
Arm, walnut W/M style, high sq bk, scroll arms, 1880s, 49" 800.00
Arm, walnut/inlay Dutch Baroque, rtcl/shaped splat/apron 2,400.00

Bannister-back side chair, old black paint with gold striping, ca late 18th century or early 19th century, replaced rush seat, New England, $825.00.

Bannister-bk side, hardwood w/old finish, rpl rush seat, 40" 450.00
Bannister-bk side, maple w/some curl, EX detail/trn, EX 595.00
Co Captain's, red rpt, 30" 95.00
Desk, oak Mission style, swivel base, rstr/frn 325.00
Ladderbk arm, att Nutting, 5 shaped slats, EX trn, 50", EX 350.00
Ladderbk arm, scalloped top slat+3, trn legs/posts, 47", VG 400.00
Ladderbk arm Co, 4 arched splats, new seat, rfn/rpr, 45" 75.00
Ladderbk arm rocker, 4-slat bk, pnt layers, splint seat 275.00
Limbert, #521, adjustable-bk, panel under arms w/3 cutouts 6,000.00
Mahog-fr Chpndl, shell-cvd knees, trifid ft, 1880 ....600.00
Rocker, Limbert #848, low bk, brand, reuphl/rfn, 32x24" 800.00
Rocker, oak, press-cvd trim, trn spindles/legs, saddle seat 375.00
Rocker, oak, shaped crest/bk splat, trn spindles/posts/legs 250.00
Rocker, worn red/blk grpt w/mc floral, arrow ½-spindles 100.00
Side, birch Co Chpndl w/some curl, pierced splat, VG 350.00
Side, cherry Co Chpndl, rtcl splat, slip seat, rpr 200.00
Side, Co QA Hudson River Valley, trn posts/legs, vase splat 1,125.00
Side, curly maple etc Co Sheraton, VG rush seat, trim loss 100.00
Side, Hitchcock-type Sheraton, grpt/oval scenes, EX detail 700.00
Side, mahog Chpndl, drape/shell crest rail, tassel splat, NY 2,100.00

Side, mahog Co Chpndl, ornate rtcl spat, damage/needs uphl **350.00**
Side, mahog Phila Sheraton style, draped/pierced bk **200.00**
Side, mahog/burl walnut Vict Renaissance Revival, cvgs **250.00**
Side, rosewood Am Rococo, cvd fruit/foliate crest **225.00**
Side, walnut Geo I, serpentine seat rail, shaped splat, pr **1,000.00**
Side, walnut Geo I, sq bk, cabriole legs/pad ft, rstr, pr **2,500.00**
Windsor, bamboo side, step-down crest, breaks/rprs, pr **550.00**
Windsor, bow-bk arm, rfn w/traces of gray pnt, o/w orig **1,500.00**
Windsor, bow-bk arm, saddle seat, rpl spindle/rfn/rpr **550.00**
Windsor, bow-bk arm, 7-spindle, saddle seat, rfn, EX **800.00**
Windsor, bow-bk side, 7-spindle, rpt w/striping, saddle seat **350.00**
Windsor, bow-bk side, 7-spindle, saddle seat, blk pnt, VG * **325.00**
Windsor, bow-bk side, 9-spindle, saddle seat, bamboo trn, rfn **900.00**
Windsor, cage-like bk, bamboo trn, shaped seat, rpr/rfn, VG **300.00**
Windsor, cage-like bk w/2 medallions, shaped seat, rfn **250.00**
Windsor, continuous arm, saddle seat, cleaned to old blk, VG ...**750.00**
Windsor, continuous arm, 9-spindle, blk pnt, breaks/rprs **700.00**
Windsor, continuous arm, 9-spindle, edge beading, EX orig **3,500.00**
Windsor, continuous arm, 9-spindle, EX trn, VG blk pnt, EX .**2,900.00**
Windsor, fan-bk arm, EX detail, knuckle arms, curved crest ...**5,700.00**
Windsor, fan-bk arm, saddle seat, considerable rstr **275.00**
Windsor, fan-bk side, bulbous trn, saddle seat, rstr/rfn **300.00**
Windsor, fan-bk side, bulbous trn, yoke crest, pnt, EX **675.00**
Windsor, sack-bk, brn pnt, 1780s, wear/pnt loss **1,400.00**
Windsor, spindle-bk, bamboo trn, rfn, 34½" **200.00**
Windsor, Wallace Nutting #415, minor rprs, 45", pr **2,500.00**
Wing, birch-fr Hplwht, bow-front seat, scrolled arms, 47" **3,100.00**
Wing, mahog-fr Chpndl, reuphl/rpr, 44" **1,100.00**
Wing, walnut w/needlepoint uphl Geo I, pointed ft, 49" **4,400.00**

Chair Set

Arrow-bk side, striping/floral, sgn Wonder, EX color, 6 for **1,650.00**
Balloon-bk, grpt w/stenciled floral, plank seat, 6 for * **570.00**
Balloon-bk, mc floral on red/blk grpt, 35", EX, 6 for **1,100.00**
Co QA, vase splat, shaped yoke, trn legs, rpl rush, 3+host **4,000.00**
Gray w/stenciled & freehand decor, ½-spindle bk, 6 for **1,500.00**
Half-spindle, mc rpt/stencil on red, rprs, 6 for **870.00**
Ladderbk side, 4-slat bk, acorn finials, bl traces, 4 for **650.00**
Mahog Hplwht, 3 fluted bk slats, uphl seat, att MA, 4 for **2,700.00**
Mahog QA style, Centennial, slip seat, 6 for **1,800.00**
Oak, press-cvd bk w/central splat, saddle seat, 4 for **600.00**
Oak, press-cvd crest/cane seat, spindles, 4 for **600.00**
Oak, press-cvd crest/slat, saddle seat, 4 for **650.00**
Red/blk grpt w/tulips & yel striping, plank seat, 6 for **540.00**
Shaped crest rail, hourglass splat, plank seat, PA, 4 for **200.00**

Chest

Birch Co Hplwht, 4-drw, cut-out ft, scrolled apron, 37x38" ...**1,200.00**
Birch/pine Co Sheraton w/red grpt, 2-drw lift-off top, 44" **900.00**
Cherry Co Chpndl, 4-drw w/refaced fronts, rpl top/ft, 35x39" **700.00**
Cherry Emp w/curly maple vnr, paw ft, 3 bowed+1 drw, EX **1,100.00**
Cherry Hplwht, cut-out ft, scrolled apron, rprs, 42x43" **1,500.00**
Cherry Hplwht w/inlay, drw ea side fluted stile:3, 44" **2,700.00**
Cherry Sheraton, herringbone banding, orig hdw, 40x40" **2,600.00**
Cherry/curly maple vnr Co Sheraton, 4-drw, rpl/rfn, 39x40" **850.00**
Cherry/walnut Co Sheraton, trn ft, panel ends, 44x39" **500.00**
Curly maple Chpndl, EX striped figure, 2 drw:4, 48x40" **7,750.00**
Curly maple Co Sheraton, 4-drw/edge beading, rpl/rfn, 48x40" .**950.00**
Curly maple Sheraton, trn ft, crest w/breadbrd ends, 44x43" ...**2,700.00**
Hardwood/poplar Co Emp w/orig red flame-grpt facade, 52x39" ..**400.00**
Limbert, #477, 2 short drw:2, EX finish, mk, 36x40" **1,100.00**
Limbert, #484, 5-drw, lg oval pulls, EX finish, mk, 45x34" **1,600.00**

Mahogany Federal bow-front bureau, original brasses, replaced foot, old refinish, ca 1800, 33" wide, $2,750.00.

Mahog Fed, bow-front, cock beaded, inlaid apron, 36x42" **1,450.00**
Mahog Geo III, 4-drw, rstr, 33x32" **1,200.00**
Mahog Late Empire, 5-drw, jelly roll ft, 48" **250.00**
Maple Co Chpndl, 6 overlapping drw, rpl ft/hdw, 59x20" **1,600.00**
Maple Emp w/some curl, 1 deep drw:3, half pilasters, EX **500.00**
Maple/pine Chpndl, 6 grad overlap drw, dvtl, 52x40", EX **5,200.00**
Mule, pine w/pnt & wash traces, scrolled base, 41x40", EX **1,450.00**
Mule, pine w/red rpt & blk grpt, cut-out ft, drw, 31x41" **650.00**
Mule, pine/poplar w/flame grpt, 2 dvtl drw, hinged lid, 36" **800.00**
Mule, red-wash pine, trn ft, paneled, drw, rpl molding, 42" **385.00**
On fr, cherry, fan inlay in drw corners/apron, 50x21" **13,300.00**
On fr, walnut QA, shell-cvd cabriole legs, 9-drw, mar, 65" **4,100.00**
Sugar, cherry Co Emp, trn legs, drw, rstr, 38x24" **1,600.00**
Tulipwood/inlay Louis XV style, shaped, marble top, 47" W ...**6,300.00**
Vnr Louis XV style, inlay panel/ormolu, marble top, 1910 ......**1,800.00**
Walnut Chpndl, fluted quarter columns/edge beading, rpl/rfn ..**1,700.00**
Walnut Co Fed, reeded columns, 2 short drw:4, 43x43", EX * ...**800.00**
Walnut Co Sheraton, 4-drw, trn legs, rpl eagle pulls, 43x38" **900.00**
Walnut Fed w/5 figured vnr drws, bow-front, 48x40" **1,000.00**
Walnut Hplwht, 4-drw, band inlay, Fr ft, water stain, 41x38" .**1,650.00**
Walnut PA Chpndl, 3 drw:5, dvtl case, rpl hdw, 64x40" **4,850.00**

Commode, see Chest

Cupboard

Corner, Cherry Co, 2-pc, 9-pane do:2 panel do, 84x42" **2,300.00**
Corner, cherry/poplar Co, 1-pc, 2 8-pane do:2, 84x49" **4,100.00**
Corner, pine Co w/gr pnt, raised panel do, molding, 100x52" .**1,000.00**
Corner, poplar Co, 1-pc, panel do top/bottom, losses, 79x41" .**1,500.00**
Corner, poplar w/brn regrpt PA, arched-top 12-pane do, 86" ..**2,450.00**
Folk art chip cvg/appl moldings, bl pnt w/red trim, 57x32" **1,100.00**
Hanging, pine Co w/rpt, panel do, int shelves, 40x23" **225.00**
Hanging, pine/primitive, cut-out wooden fastener, 24x15" **250.00**
Hanging, poplar w/orig red, brd/batten do, 2 int drw, 37" **1,125.00**
Jelly, butternut w/rpt, dentil molding, high cut-out ft, 59" **900.00**
Jelly, pine Co w/bl-gr rpt over red, brd/batten do, 54x38" **600.00**
Jelly, poplar w/red rpt, simple cut-out ft, panel do, 40" **485.00**
Jelly, red-stain poplar, 2 drw:2 panel do, rpl latch, 54x42" **700.00**
Jelly, walnut w/rosewood ink grpt, EX scalloped base, 56x43" .**1,000.00**
Oak, 2 etched glass do:step-bk w/porc top:tilt-out bins **750.00**
Pewter, hardwood w/worn pnt layers, open, primitive, 74x40" ..**1,300.00**

Pewter, pine w/red pnt, 1-pc, flush panel do, 78x49", VG 725.00
Pie safe, pine, G bl-gr pnt, 3 punched panels ea do, 3 ea end ..1,100.00
Pie safe, poplar w/rpt, 3 punched panels in ea do, 60x44" 350.00
Pie safe, poplar w/rpt grpt, 12 star/circle tin panels, EX 450.00
Pine Co, 1-pc step-bk, 4 shelves:2 drw:2 raised panel do 1,225.00
Pine w/brn-yel grpt, 2-pc step-bk, 4 panel do, 78x36" 900.00
Pine/poplar PA, red pnt/rpt trim, step-bk, 2-pc, 84" 4,250.00
Poplar cleaned to old bl-gray & yel pnt, 2-pc, rstr, 83" 800.00
Poplar Co, cleaned to old red, 1-pc, 2 6-pane do:2, 78x46" ...1,650.00
Poplar Co Emp w/red traces, trn pilasters, 2 6-pane do, 86" 2,600.00
Poplar Co w/rpt, simple ft, 2 paneled do, 78x40", EX 110.00

Desk

Birch Chpndl, slant lid, bandy legs, c/b ft, 45x42", EX 2,650.00

Birch, cherry, and mahogany veneer slant lid desk, ca 1810, minor repair and imperfections, 40" wide, $1,200.00.

Cherry Chpndl, slant lid, 4-drw, cvd fan, rpl/rfn, 43x41" 2,200.00
Fruitwood Dutch slant-front w/extensive marquetry, 42x38" ..6,300.00
Kittinger, mahog w/tooled leather top, dbl ped, 60" 450.00
Lady's, oak, drop front, curved legs, very simple, sm 450.00
Lifetime, #8569, oak, drop front, gallery top, 3-drw, mk 935.00
Mahog, partner's; Geo III style, leather top, 60" 2,400.00
Mahog Chpndl, slant lid, fitted int, rpl hdw/ft, 44x36" 2,900.00
Mahog Chpndl, slant lid, 4-drw, dvtl/beaded, cvd fan, 42x40" ..7,750.00
Oak, C-roll top, 1 ped w/3 drw, 1 drw over kneehole, sm 900.00
Oak, drop front:3 drw by 5-shelf bookcase, sm mirror atop 950.00
Oak, drop front:3 drw/bookcase, ldgl panel, lg mirror, cvgs 1,250.00
Oak, partner's, 3 drw ea ped, simple style 485.00
Oak, S-roll top, fitted int, 4 drw ea ped, 60" 1,200.00
Oak Jacobean style, lions/florals appl on drw, rope trn 525.00
Oak w/geometric inlay, slant lid, 2 short+2 L drw, 37x29" 1,200.00
Plantation, pine w/red traces, 2-panel do:drw:tall trn legs 600.00
Teak Traditional-style dbl-ped, 8-drw, glass top, 66" 500.00
Walnut Co, slant top, folk-art inlay, cut-out ft, 1815, 39" 4,300.00
Walnut Hplwht w/figured vnr drw fronts, inlay, 43x43", EX ...3,500.00

Dresser

Oak, lg oval mirror in lyre fr, base w/2 drw:1 ....400.00
Oak, lg swivel mirror in lyre fr, serpentine front, 3-drw 650.00
Vict, mirror:marble top:3 drw, candle shelves:sm drw, 92x51" ..1,400.00

Dressing Table

Deco, kidney shape, 3-drw, 3-way mirror 500.00
QA walnut, molded top, shaped apron, pad ft, 1740, rfn, 32" 7,500.00
Sheraton, scrolled splash, 3-drw, trn legs, old pnt, rstr 850.00

Dry Sink

Pine, cut-out ft, 2 raised panel do, sm drw to side, 45" 875.00

Dry sink, pine with red and green paint, 1800s, 36x27", $1,000.00.

Pine/poplar, cut-out ft, 2 panel do, galleried well, 46" 450.00
Poplar PA w/red vinegar grpt on yel w/sunbursts etc, 42" 11,500.00
Poplar w/several pnt layers, scrolled base, 40", EX 575.00

Highboy

Cherry QA flat top w/2 cvd fans, scalloped apron, 1750, 74" ..18,000.00
Curly maple Co QA, flat top, scrolled apron, rpl, 67x36" 2,900.00
Tiger maple QA, flat top, NE, 1740s, 72x39" 13,000.00

Lowboy

Figured maple QA, heart-pierced apron, Spanish ft, 29x40 .....6,000.00
Mahog QA, cvd shell in shaped apron, 3-drw, much rstr 2,800.00
Walnut/maple QA, trn drops/cvd fan, 4-drw, early brasses 11,500.00

Secretary

Mahog Fed w/flame vnr, trn pilasters, 2 do w/arch panes, 61" 2,600.00
Mahog/satinwood NE, 2-do, outfitted int, 1790 ....8,000.00
Maple w/red grpt:gr, pigeonhole top/case w/drw:fr base 1,700.00
Walnut Vict, burl cylinder lid, EX cvd crest/columns, 110" 2,500.00

Settee

Mahog Geo III style, eagle's heads, c/b ft, fret-cvd rail 1,300.00
Sheraton w/wht rpt & stenciling, EX detail, rush seat, 37" 2,300.00

Shelf

Hardwood, floor-standing, 3-tier, rfn, 38x39" 350.00
Mahog, 5 step-bk shelves, highly scrolled ends, rpr, 38x25" 425.00
Pine w/old bl, sq nails, wide shelf+2 in box-like bracket 375.00
Poplar, primitive, hanging, 10x21x6" 145.00

Sideboard

Cherry w/mahog vnr & inlay KY Hplwht style, 39x35" 2,750.00
Limbert, #1320, 2 drw:1+2 panel do, plate rack, mk, 45", EX ...1,300.00
Mahog Emp w/figured vnr, cvd paw ft, half columns, 42x56" ..1,000.00
Mahog Fed w/inlay, shaped facade, sq tapered legs, 66" 1,650.00
Mahog Hplwht, band/bellfower/fan inlay, serpentine, 74" 7,000.00
Mahog Hplwht style, figured vnr/inlay, 1932 repro, 72" 850.00
Mahog Hplwht style w/inlay, 1910 repro, 64", EX 200.00
Mahog vnr Fed, rnded do ea side step-bk do, 68", EX 8,000.00
Mahog w/figured vnr English Regency, cvd fans, 74", EX 1,550.00
Oak, free-standing column ea side of mirror, press-cvd trim 700.00

Sofa

Mahog Emp/Vict transitional, floral cvg: crest/apron, 92" * 450.00
Mahog fr Co Chpndl camel-bk, serpentine seat fr, rprs, 83" 3,100.00
Mahog-fr Fed, serpentine crest rail w/eagle inlay, sq legs 1,600.00
Mahog-fr Fed, trn/reeded legs & arm posts, needs uphl, 74" 1,300.00
Mahog-fr Fed, 8-leg, shaped arm posts, rstr, 74" 950.00
Mahog/maple vnr fr, classical, 80" L 1,800.00
Recaimer, curly maple lyre-fr Emp, cane seat/bk, 87", VG 1,200.00
Recaimer, mahog Emp, brass paw ft/castors, 69" 950.00

Stand

Birch Co, tripod base w/flaring legs, chip cvg, 14" top 175.00
Birch Co, 2-drw, rpl 2-brd 17x22" top, rpl glass pull 300.00
Birch/pine Co Hplwht, 1-drw, 1-brd 13x14" top is VG 225.00
Cherry, 2-drw, appl edging, trn legs, 1-brd 17x22" top 375.00
Cherry Co, 3 dvtl cock-beaded drw, 1-brd 10x22" (VG) top 495.00
Cherry Co Hplwht, dvtl drw, scalloped apron, rpl 19" top 450.00
Cherry Co Hplwht, rpl drw w/walnut front, rpl 18x20" top 200.00
Cherry Co w/bird's-eye drw front, 7½" drop leaves, trn legs * 500.00
Cherry Emp w/mahog flame grpt, trn legs, 2 drw w/rnd fronts 300.00
Cherry Hplwht, 2 drw w/cock beading, 1-brd 17x18" top, rfn 475.00
Cherry/curly maple vnr Co, 2-drw, 1-brd 19" top, lacy hdw 375.00
Crock, pine, A-fr, scalloped, 3-tier, 35x29" 295.00
Curly maple Co, mahog vnr trim, dvtl drw w/ogee front, VG 370.00
Curly maple Co, 2 rnd-front drw, trn legs, base shelf, 22" 775.00
Curly maple Co Sheraton, cock-beaded drw, reed molding, 19" ...700.00
Curly maple Sheraton, 2 dvtl drw, 1-brd 18x21" top 1,600.00
Curly maple/cherry Co, 3 dvtl drw, rpl 10" drop leaf, 22" 725.00
Mahog vnr Sheraton, rope-cvd legs/cock-bead drw, 16x19" top ..575.00
Pine Hplwht style, widely splayed legs, rpl 1-brd 17" sq top 100.00
Pine w/red rpt, trn splay legs, 2-brd 20x20" top 450.00
Pine/poplar Co, X-member base, str column, 13x13" top, 28" 150.00
Walnut, trn legs, dvtl drw w/mahog vnr, 10" drop leaves 350.00
Walnut Co, drw w/cvd sunburst & corner motif, trn legs, EX 850.00
Walnut Co, 2-brd 20" dia top, spool-trn column, tripod ft 185.00
Walnut Co Hplwht w/simple inlay, dvtl drw, rpl 18x20" top 400.00
Walnut/cherry Co Sheraton, 2-drw, trn legs, much rstr 275.00

Stool

Footstool, curly maple, EX detail, scalloped apron, 13" 525.00
Footstool, Geo II oak, sq uphl top, cabriole legs/pad ft 650.00
Footstool, mahog w/needlepoint uphl, lyre-style fr, 14" L 150.00
Footstool, pine w/chip-cvd drw/edges/legs, rpt, 19" L, EX 350.00
Footstool, primitive pine, late, age cracks, 24" L 85.00
Footstool, walnut Continental Rococo, cabriole legs, 23" L 440.00
Oak Co w/red pnt, pencil post legs, splint seat (VG), 20" 65.00
Organ, oak, rnd top adjusts, fluted/trn legs & column 175.00

Table

Breakfast, cherry Fed drop leaf, drw, spiral legs, 39x45" * 300.00
Breakfast, mahog Regency, brass paw ft/casters, 43"+2 leaves 985.00
Card, cherry Hplwht w/inlay, demilune, rpr vnr, 16x34" 350.00
Card, cherry/curly maple Co Hplwht, line inlay, rfn, 19x38" ..1,500.00
Card, mahog Emp style, flip top, 1-ped, leaf cvg, paw ft 400.00
Card, mahog Fed, serpentine flip top, sq legs, 1790, 18x36" * 375.00
Card, mahog Sheraton w/inlay, bird's-eye vnr, serpentine 2,300.00
Card, mahog w/inlay Hplwht, flip top, Baltimore, 1790 ....2,800.00
Card, maple Fed, curly apron, rope-trn legs, serpentine 775.00
Center, mahog Louis XVI, brass-bound frieze, 40" dia 770.00
Curly maple Emp, tripod base/sabre legs, 17x19" tilt top 450.00

Dining, mahog QA, rectangular top w/drop leaves, open: 48" 600.00
Dining, oak, lg ped w/c&b ft having some cvg 1,200.00
Dining, oak, ped w/4 cut-out scroll legs, rnd 650.00
Dining, oak, ped w/4 paw ft, little cvg, rnd 950.00
Dining, oak, 5 legs w/ball & flute cvg, rnd 650.00
Drop leaf, birch Co, drw, trn legs, rnd 10" leaves, rfn 450.00
Drop leaf, cherry Co QA, butterfly supports, 34" 2,200.00
Drop leaf, cherry/walnut Co, 1-brd 13" leaves, rpl top 375.00
Drop leaf, figured walnut English QA, 1-drw, 16" leaves 550.00
Drop leaf, hardwood/pine Co, rpl trn legs/22" leaves 275.00
Drop leaf, mahog English Chpndl, 22x42" leaves, EX 600.00
Drop leaf, mahog Fed, reeded splay legs, shaped 15" leaves 1,800.00
Drop leaf, mahog Fed, 6-leg, 22" leaves, 48", EX 1,000.00
Drop leaf, walnut Co Sheraton, swing legs, 20x42" leaves 475.00
Harvest, birch/pine Co Sheraton, 1-brd top, 11" drop leaves ..1,000.00
Hutch, pine Co, 1-brd ends, bj ft, 4-brd 39x42" top 1,250.00
Hutch, pine Co w/worn rpt, rpl 3-brd breadbrd top, 58x32" 1,650.00
Hutch, pine/poplar Co, seat w/lift lid, 40x66" top, 1900s 450.00
Hutch, walnut Co, 1-brd ends, cut-out ft, 2-brd 36x65" top 1,450.00
Library, ebonized Vict, top w/cvd fans, ring trn, 32" L * 200.00
Library, Limbert #1132, lift-top blind drw, brand, 48" 1,500.00
Library, mahog/inlay, 4-leg base revolves, 6-side case, 31" 450.00
Library, oak, oval top, simple apron, 2-ped base, scroll ft 400.00
Limbert, #153, turtle top, end panels w/sq cutouts, mk, EX 1,750.00
Limbert, #153, turtle top, 2 cutouts ea side, mk, rstr, 38" 1,600.00

Mahogany and mahogany veneer work table, ivory escutcheons, ca 1820, New England, $800.00.

Mahog Chpndl, pad ft, trn column, 25" dia tilt top, 27" H * 450.00
Mahog Chpndl, tripod legs, c/b ft, rpl 35" dia tilt top 1,500.00
Mahog Geo III, tilt top, c/b ft (rstr), 22" dia 5,500.00
Mahog Hplwht, spider legs, rpl 1-brd 20" dia tilt top 300.00
Mahog/vnr Duncan Phyfe style, cvd legs/ped, open:150" 1,850.00
Majorelle, 2 inlaid tiers, bronze floral hdls, 32x36x23" 8,800.00
Pembroke, cherry Chpndl, X-stretcher, rpl 32" top, 10" leaves ..1,950.00
Pembroke, cherry Co Hplwht, rpl 8" leaves, 18x30" top 500.00
Pembroke, cherry Co Hplwht, 2-brd 19x42" top, 13" leaves 500.00
Pembroke, cherry Fed, sq tapered legs, open: 31x30" 500.00
Pembroke, mahog Chpndl, c/b ft, rpl 15x41" top 1,000.00
Pembroke, mahog Chpndl, cut-out X-stretcher & spandrels .12,000.00
Pembroke, mahog Geo III, frieze drw/sham drw, 34" 550.00
Pine Co w/red-pnt base, 1-brd 14x24" top w/rnd corners 350.00
Sawbuck, pine, sq nails, 3-brd 32x96" VG top 1,100.00
Sawbuck, pine/hardwood, 1-brd 25x90" breadbrd top, EX 1,000.00
Settle, pine/poplar, bj ends, 1826, 72" 3,000.00
Settle, pine/poplar, 1-drw, bj ends, orig pnt, 1860, 48" 2,700.00
Side, Dutch, allover inlay, cabriole legs/pad ft, 30x35" 2,800.00

Tavern, birch Co Hplwht, rpl 2-brd 30" L pine top, drw, EX **350.00**
Tavern, maple Co QA, trn legs, rpl 19x26" oval top, VG **1,175.00**
Tavern, maple/pine Co QA, trn legs, 1-brd 20x30" oval top ...**1,800.00**
Work, poplar w/red traces, trestle base, drw, 45" L, VG **600.00**
Work, walnut Co Hplwht, 2 nailed drw, 29x48" 3-brd rpl top **550.00**
Writing, burl walnut W/M, spiral legs, end drws, rstr **2,900.00**

Washstand

Cherry Co Sheraton, base drw, cutout w/ironstone bowl, 17" W ..**175.00**
Cherry Co Sheraton, bowl cutout, bottom shelf, trn legs, sm **175.00**
Cherry Co Sheraton, high scalloped crest, base drw, 20" W **525.00**
Corner, curly maple Hplwht, curved front, 2 cutouts/drw **3,200.00**

Mahogany Classical Revival washstand, cast brass claw and ball feet, ca 1815, Boston, Massachusetts, 28x18", $3,600.00.

Oak, sm mirror in lyre fr/towel bar, 1 drw:2+do, lg **400.00**
Pine Sheraton, orig pnt decor, gallery/base drw/bowl cutout **200.00**
Pine w/rpt, bowl cutout, eared gallery, base drw, 17" W **200.00**
Poplar w/red flame grpt, base drw, shaped gallery, 21" W **250.00**

Miscellaneous

Bin, red-stained poplar, trn ft, till, slant lid, 34x37" **400.00**
Cellarette on stand, mahog Geo III, hexagonal case, 31x18" ..**3,850.00**
China closet, mahog Hplwht style w/inlay, 20th C, 81", EX **350.00**
Coat rack, oak, sq upright w/iron hooks, X base **150.00**
Credenza, walnut Italian Renaissance, paneled case, 37x27" ..**3,000.00**
Day bed, beechwood Louis XV style, 33x84" **600.00**
Floor screen, giltwood Louis XVI style, neoclassic, 4-panel **1,650.00**
Hall seat, oak, ornate crest/apron, lg shaped mirror, paw ft **1,500.00**
Hall seat, oak, press-cvd crest:lg mirror, curved arms **850.00**
Hall seat, oak, simple rnd mirror, side/bk slats, very plain **800.00**
Hall seat, rnd mirror:open lyre bk, curved arms/legs, sm **900.00**
Ice box, oak, sm panel do:lg, 4-panel sides, tall **450.00**
Ice box, oak, 4-do, lg **500.00**
Kas, pine Co w/orig red pnt, breaks down into pcs, 77x64" * ..**3,500.00**
Kas, walnut Co, raised panel do w/cvd fans, rnf, 84x54" **5,000.00**
Library steps, mahog English Vict, uphl seat, 1860s **1,400.00**
Parlor suite, steer horn, 3 chairs+2 ottomans+rnd table * **2,700.00**
Pole screen, rosewood English Vict, trn std on tripod base **350.00**

Galena

Potteries located in the Galena, Illinois, area were generally plain utility wares with lead glaze and often found in a pumpkin color with some slip decoration or splashes of other colors. These potteries thrived from the early 1830s until sometime around 1860. In the listings that follow, all items are made of red clay unless noted otherwise. These are prices realized at the same auction house from which we obtained our entries for the last edition; note that even taking into consideration that the condition of these items is not as good as those we listed last year, in comparison the values are much lower.

Crock, dk gr-orange, tooled lines/#3, ovoid, 13", NM **65.00**
Crock, gr w/orange spots, #2 on lip, rim hairline, 9¾" **50.00**
Flowerpot, hanging, unglazed, appl stars, attached saucer, EX **55.00**
Jar, gr w/orange spots, #5, ovoid, 14x12", EX **70.00**
Jar, gr-orange glaze, edge chips, 8", VG **100.00**
Jar, gr-orange w/brn sponging, flared lip, chips, 8¾", VG **85.00**
Jar, preserving; gr w/orange spots, 10", VG **110.00**
Jar, preserving; gr-amber w/gr spots & brn flecks, 8", VG **65.00**
Jug, gr gloss w/orange spots, ovoid, chips/hairlines, 11" **200.00**

Galle

Emile Galle was one of the most important producers of cameo glass in France. His firm, founded in Nancy in 1874, produced beautiful cameo in the Art Nouveau style during the 1890s using a variety of techniques. He also produced glassware with enameled decoration as well as some fine pottery — animal figurines, table services, vases, and other objects d' art. In the mid-1880s, he became interested in the various colors and textures of natural woods and, as a result, began to create furniture which he used as yet another medium for expression of his artistic talent. Marquetry was the primary method Galle used in decorating his furniture, preferring landscapes, Nouveau floral and fruit arrangements, butterflies, squirrels, and other forms from nature. It is for his furniture and his cameo glass that he is best known today. All Galle is signed.

In the listings below, 'fp' indicates items that have been fire polished. Our advisor for this category is Don Williams; he is listed in the Directory under Missouri.

Cameo

Creamer, berries, red/gold frost, frosted hdl, 3¼x2¼" **1,500.00**
Decanter, wheat, gr/brn on wht, fp, 5¼" **900.00**
Lamp, dragonflies, dbl o/l, on 5" dome shade/baluster std **7,500.00**
Lamp, 2 floral bell shades, iron vine std w/leaf base, 21" **10,000.00**
Lamp base, clematis vines, dbl o/l, bulbous, 9½" **2,200.00**
Night light, bleeding hearts, metal mt w/3 putti as ft, 4¾" **2,860.00**
Night light, roses/day lilies, red/yel, lid w/rose finial, 5" **2,640.00**
Sconce, poppies, tan on cream, convex shield shape, 10", pr ..**7,500.00**
Tumbler, thistles cut/pnt on irregular ribbed form, 2½" **550.00**
Vase, anemones on sea gr, dbl o/l, ovoid, 6" **1,430.00**
Vase, anemones/lg leaves, dbl o/l, bulbous, 11½" **4,000.00**
Vase, buttercups, amber on pk tint, ovoid w/ped ft, 7" **2,000.00**
Vase, cherry blossoms on bl frost, triple o/l, 7x5" **2,500.00**
Vase, columbines/foliage, bl/gr on frost, 3½" **950.00**
Vase, dragonfly/lily buds, bl/wine on wht, bottle form, 7" **3,000.00**
Vase, ferns, rust/gr on lt gr to pk, fp, bottle form, 7" **900.00**
Vase, floral, maroon on orange, wide base/bottle neck, 4" **800.00**
Vase, floral, orange & gold on orange/pk/wht, ovoid, 15" **3,500.00**
Vase, floral, purple on pk to purple, bottle form, 6" **600.00**
Vase, flowers/seed pods, gr/olive-amber on gr/wht, 8x7" **990.00**
Vase, freesia stalks, amber/wine on wht/orange, fp, 11" **2,400.00**
Vase, fuchsia, purple/brn on yel & wht, ovoid, 15¾" **4,500.00**
Vase, fuchsia buds, brn on yel, spool neck on ovoid, 7" **650.00**
Vase, ginko/ferns, brn/lav on pk/gr, boat form, 5½x8" **1,300.00**
Vase, leaves, purple on lt pk, tapered cylinder, 18" **1,975.00**

Vase, leaves and berries, orange and black on vivid yellow, deeply carved, 15", $5,000.00. (Both sides shown.)

Vase, leaves/berries, lt/dk gr on pk & wht, bottle neck, 12" 1,200.00
Vase, leaves/berries, lt/dk wine on mustard, spool neck, 5" 650.00
Vase, lg trees before lake, EX cvg, bulbous, 17" 25,300.00
Vase, lilies/leaves, dbl o/l, spherical, 6" 1,500.00
Vase, mold-blown apple blossoms, dbl o/l, 14" 12,100.00
Vase, mold-blown clematis, dk bl/lav, dbl o/l, ovoid, 6" 7,700.00
Vase, mold-blown clematis, plum/bl on peach, dbl o/l, 6½" 7,700.00
Vase, mold-blown grapes, red on yel, fp, flask form, 11" 15,000.00
Vase, mold-blown mtn laurel, dbl o/l, 11½x5" 9,350.00
Vase, mtns/lake, sapphire/purple on frost, dbl o/l, 5x5" 1,500.00
Vase, orchids cut/pnt on pk-swirled gr, appl hdls, 9½" 8,800.00
Vase, pods/leaves, gr on wht frost, widens at base, 18" 2,200.00
Vase, poppies, orange on gr, compressed sphere, fp, 4" 825.00
Vase, trees/lake, purple/bl on yel, dbl o/l, 2-peak rim, 8" 3,500.00
Vase, trees/mtns, triple o/l, bulbous w/long neck, 8½" 1,300.00
Vase, wildflowers, lav on peach, pear form w/flared rim, 6" 900.00
Vase, 11 sailing ships, bl/yel/amethyst on wht/amber, 5" 1,650.00

Enameled Glass

Bottle, pilgrims/forest, mc on clear, flattened/shaped, 9" 4,950.00
Dish, grasshopper/plant, mc/gilt on bl, 2-fold rim, 10" 1,050.00
Tumbler, rooster/teacher/chick/inscriptions, mc on clear, 4½" 750.00
Tumbler, dragonfly/wildflowers, mc/gilt, sgn, 4½" 500.00
Vase, ferns/florals, pk/yel/wht on amber, hdls, 5" 900.00
Vase, wildflowers, mc/gold on gray, cylinder w/wide ft, 11" 1,000.00

Marqueterie-Sur-Verre

Bowl, water lilies, foil inclusions, cvd ext, 4½x7½" 12,000.00
Box, dogwood branches inlay, sliding lid, 10" L 7,500.00
Vase, crocus flower/bud on streaky pk/yel/etc, 9" 15,000.00

Marquetry, Wood

Box, dogwood branches, sliding lid, 10" L 1,400.00
Music stand, rectangle top above open shelf, 35" 3,500.00
Table, mtns/rowboat, trestle ft, nesting set of 4 ....7,500.00
Table, 2-tier, Antarctic penguins, 29x28x19" 3,000.00
Table, 2-tier, clematis/butterfly, 30x23x16" 3,000.00
Table, 2-tier, cvd/scrolling legs, 35x35x26" 3,500.00
Table, 2-tier, woodland/florals, 31x31x23" 3,500.00
Tray, seascape w/ships, galley forms hdls, 24" 1,800.00

Pottery

Charger, Rococo border w/shells, rtcl, lion crest, 29" 1,750.00

Flagon, portrait of man, lid w/3-D cherries, rope hdl, 13" 1,000.00
Owl, mottled tan/brn, gr glass eyes, self base, 14" 3,300.00
Plate, surrealistic mc motif, scalloped, 1 side folded up 700.00
Rabbit, allover florals, glass eyes, rstr ear, 8x7" 1,700.00
Vase, bamboo w/gilt irises, sm gr stalk vase beside, 9" 2,600.00
Wall brackets, scenic, wide Rococo borders, rpr, 18", pr 3,300.00

Wall vase, modeled as a lady's hat with insects, caterpillar, ribbons, and blossoms, 12", $1,500.00.

Gambling Memorabilia

Gambling memorabilia from the infamous casinos of the West and items that were once used on the 'Floating Palace' riverboats are especially sought after by today's collectors.

Ashtray, brass w/enameled spade in center, 5x6½", NM 120.00
Book, How It's Done Cards & Coins, cheating methods, 60-pg, M ..50.00
Book, KC Card Co Blue Book No 436, illus, 68-pg, NM 125.00
Book, Pinochle Primer, Lewis Levy, 1912, 55-pg, EX 45.00
Book, Racket Squat 1952 Comic #2, mc cover, NM 50.00
Buck (designates dealer), Bakelite, 'Jackpot,' etc, 1930s 165.00
Card press, petit-point flower cvg, MOP inlay, EX 400.00
Card trimmer, shears style, unmk, ca 1910, 12¾x6½" 990.00
Chip box, wood w/4 brass inlaid cards on lid, 1930s, 8x9¾" 100.00
Chips, Bakelite, in wooden rack w/leather cover, EX 75.00
Chips, Bakelite, set of 90 in mahog box 80.00
Chips, ivory w/fancy numeral cvgs, set of 5 ....210.00
Chips, ivory w/flower cvg, set of 5, NM 110.00
Cuff links, sterling, 4 suit signs, 1920s, M 50.00
Dagger, fits in vest, Will & Fink, San Francisco, 6½", G 450.00
Dice, celluloid, ea w/different number (1-5), set of 5 ....260.00
Dice drop, felt-lined mahog, early, 7½x8x10", VG 175.00
Faro case keeper, rosewood, Mason & Co, NJ, 1890s, 11x12" 650.00
Faro layout board, wood/cloth, Mason, Denver, '50s, 18x41" ..1,000.00
Game box, metal & MOP inlay, ca 1850, 7x10½", NM 550.00
Game box, MOP & metal inlay on mahog, 1800s, 8x13", EX 600.00
Knife, 4 suit signs inlaid in celluloid hdl, 2-blade, 1940 ....50.00
Magazine, Poker Chips, 1896, 60-pg, rare, NM 300.00
Roulette watch, 17 jewels, outer wheel spins freely, M 245.00
Roulette watch, 17 jewels, suits on dial, Old England, EX 100.00
Roulette wheel, ornate, chrome, 1950, mini, 5½" 50.00
Sign, 'Betting or Gambling...Prohibited,' metal, early, 9x12" 75.00
Wheel of chance, mc pnt, 22½" 225.00

Game Calls

Those interested in hunting and fishing collectibles are beginning to take notice of the finer specimens of game calls available on today's market. Our advisor for this category is Randy Hilst; he is listed in the Directory under Illinois.

Crow call, Ditto, wood bbl, metal stopper 75.00
Crow call, Kankakee, wood 35.00
Crow call, Perdew, wood 125.00
Crow call, Sears, wood 20.00

Set of three duck calls by E.S. Stofer, Kansas City, MO, ca 1930s through '40s, reeds and wedges missing on two, all marked Bean Lake, E. Stofer, Duck Call, $25.00 to $50.00 each.

Duck call, Aubrey Headden, wood 50.00
Duck call, Broadbill, wood bbl, metal band 25.00
Duck call, Ditto, wood bbl, metal stopper 75.00
Duck call, Greenhead, wood bbl, plastic adjustable stopper 25.00
Duck call, Ludwig, all metal 500.00
Duck call, Perdew, cvd ducks, wood 2,000.00
Duck call, PS Olt, mod D-2, keyhole stopper, hard rubber 15.00
Duck call, PS Olt, mod J-15, hard rubber 25.00
Duck call, Tom Sonderman, contemporary, mini 50.00
Goose call, Herters, wood bbl, plastic stopper 15.00
Goose call, PS Olt, A-50, plastic, all wht 100.00
Goose call, Tom Sonderman, contemporary, mini 50.00
Predator call, Mallardtone, wood 15.00
Predator call, PS Olt, plastic 15.00

Gameboards

Gameboards, the handmade ones from the 18th and 19th century, are collected more for their folk art quality than their relation to games. Excellent examples of these handcrafted 'playthings' sell well into the thousands of dollars; even the simple designs are often expensive. If you are interested in this field, you must study it carefully. The market is always full of 'new' examples. Well-established dealers are often your best sources; they are essential if you do not have the expertise to judge the age of the boards yourself.

Checkers, gr & blk pnt, New England 135.00
Checkers, gr/blk sqs w/yel #s on natural/blk, edged, 31x19" 350.00
Checkers, inlaid, simple style, 14x14" 85.00
Checkers, maple w/brn-stained sqs, 2nd game on bk, 29x19" 325.00
Checkers, mustard/blk w/red trim, star ea end, 17x25", EX 500.00
Checkers, pine w/gr pnt, blk/gray/wht sqs, edge molding, 15" 250.00
Checkers, pine w/red & blk sqs, wear/age cracks, 13x13" 175.00

Checkers, pine w/worn 3-color pnt, insect damage, 19x19" 300.00
Checkers, rvpt glass, mc/gold, reeded fr, 21x21" 275.00
Checkers, walnut w/figured wood veneer, folding, 13x16", VG 45.00
Checkers, walnut w/rosewood & ebony inlay, wear, 15x15" 160.00

Gilt and polychrome gameboard, 1890s, minor paint loss, ca 1890s, 20x20", $2,400.00.

Games and Puzzles

Game collectors are finding it more difficult to find their treasures at shows and flea markets. Most of the action these days seems to be through specialty dealers and auctions. The appreciation of the art on the boards and boxes continues to grow. You see many of the early games proudly displayed as art, and they should be. The period from the 1850s to 1910 continues to draw the most interest. Many of the games of that period were executed by well-known artists and illustrators. The quality of their lithography cannot be matched today. The historical value of games made before 1850 has caused interest in this period to increase. While they may not have the graphic quality of the later period, their insights into the social and moral character of the early 19th century are interesting.

Twentieth-century games invoke a nostalgic feeling among collectors who recall looking forward to a game under the Christmas tree each year. They search for examples that bring back those Christmas morning memories. While the quality of their lithography is certainly less than the early games, the introduction of personalities from the comic strips, radio and later TV created new interest. Every child wanted a game that featured their favorite character. Monopoly, probably the most famous game ever produced, was introduced during the Great Depression. This year a Charles B. Darrow version (he later sold his game to Parker Bros.) of Monopoly, circa 1934, went for $2,400.00.

The auction market for games continues to expand. Prices remained strong for the year. Of the games sold at auction, 63% went well above estimates, 16% were sold within the estimate range, and 21% sold below estimate.

'Jigsaw' puzzles have been around almost as long as games. The first examples were handcrafted from wood, and they are extremely difficult to find. Most of the early examples featured moral subjects just as the board games did. By the 1890s jigsaw puzzles had become a major form of home entertainment. In the Depression years jigsaw puzzles were set up on card tables in almost every home. The early wood examples are the most valuable.

Cube puzzles, or blocks, were often made by the same companies as the board games. Again, early examples display the finest quality of lithography. While all subjects are collectible, some (such as Santa blocks) often command prices higher than games from the same period.

Antique American Games by Lee Dennis provides an excellent overview of games from 1840-1940. *The Games People Played* (*Collectors Showcase*, January/February) by Earnie and Ida Long is an excellent review of 19th-century games and historical material on games in general. See also Personalities.

Games

Across the Continent, NM	85.00
Alfred Hitchcock's Why, EX	75.00
Annie Oakley, w/bull's eye, NM	45.00
Atomic Submarine, Hasbro, 1950s, M in worn box	75.00
Babes in Toyland, Parker Bros, 1961, G	25.00
Baby Smurf, Milton Bradley, G	7.00
Batman Puzzle Game, Milton Bradley, 1966, VG	25.00
Battleship, Milton Bradley, 1971, NM	35.00
Beverly Hillbillies, card game, 1960s, NM in EX box	10.00
Black Beauty, Transogram, 1950s, NM	12.00
Bobbsey Twins on the Farm, Milton Bradley, 1957, NMIB	12.50
Bomb the Navy, WWII era, EX in orig 6½" sq box	25.00
Car 54, board game, 1951, M in EX box	260.00
Casey Jones, Screen Gem, 1959, NM	35.00
Cat & Mouse, Parker Bros, 1964, VG	25.00
Chiromagica Games, McLoughlin, walnut case, EX lithos	412.50
Chute-5, Milton Bradley, 1973, M	25.00
Crazy Clock, Ideal, M	65.00
Crosswalk, Strategy House, 1971, VG	20.00
Darts, Major League Baseball, metal board game, 1950s	35.00
Diver Dan Tug-O-War, Milton Bradley, 1961, EX in box	25.00
Dollar a Second, NM	145.00
Down You Go, NM	100.00
Dr Kildare Medical Game for the Young, Ideal, 1962, MIB	20.00
Electric Football, NM	55.00
Fish Pond, McLoughlin, 1890, EX	125.00
Game of Detective, board game, Bliss, 1889, EX	2,970.00
Game of Fox Hunting, board game, Spear, 1930s, EX	330.00
Game of Politics, board game, no map, Parker, EX	30.00
Game of Pussy & Three Mice, McLoughlin, 1890, EX	600.00
Game of the Christmas Jewel, McLoughlin, 1899, EX	850.00
Gee Whiz, tin horse race, Wolverine, EX	100.00
Get Smart/Don Adams Time Bomb Game, NM	38.00
GI Joe Marine Paratroop, board game, Hasbro, 1965, EX	65.00
Goosey Gruesome Gander, board game, McLoughlin, 1890, EX	550.00
Great Am War Game, Hunter, 1899, VG	1,100.00
Gruesome Mansion, pinball, Stevens, 1965, M on card	45.00
Hands Up Harry, board game, Topper, 1963, EX	75.00
Hangman, Vincent Price, Milton Bradley, 1976, NM	20.00
Hit the Beach, Milton Bradley, c 1965, EX in torn box	25.00
Honeymooners, MIB	125.00
Horse Race Wheel, 1930s, NM	225.00
Horseshoes, rubber (steel reinforced), indoor play, 1910, VG	40.00
Hullabaloo Electric Teen Game, Remco, 1965, M	85.00
I Vant to Bite Your Finger/The Dracula Game, EX	20.00
Jack & the Bean Stalk, McLoughlin, 1898, EX	990.00
Jolly Game of Snap, Palmer Cox Brownies on cards, Parker, EX	100.00
Keeping Up w/the Joneses, board game, 1921, EX	55.00
Land of the Lost, Sid & Marty Krofft, M	25.00
Lay's Lunar Landing Game, 1969, unused	50.00
Lindy the New Flying Game, card game, 1927, EX in orig box	32.00
Lost in Space, board game, Milton Bradley, 1965, EX	75.00
Lost in the Woods, board game, McLoughlin, 1895, EX	1,200.00
Man from UNCLE, card game, 1960s, NM	14.00
Man from UNCLE, Ideal, 1965, M, sealed	70.00
Mansion of Happiness, Ives, 1864 reissue of 1843 orig, EX	330.00

Meet the Presidents, Selchow, 1950, NM	25.00
Milton the Monster, Milton Bradley, 1966, EX	55.00
Monopoly, board game, Darrow, 1934, NM in EX box	4,400.00
Mouse Trap, Ideal, 1963, EX in box	125.00
Mystic Skull, Ideal, 1964, EX	55.00
Nat'l Game of Am Eagle, Ives, 1844, EX	5,390.00
New Game Piggies, Selchow & Richter, 1894, EX	600.00
Nutty Mad, pinball game, Marx, 1963, M	65.00
Peanuts, 1st game, NM	225.00
Polly Put the Kettle On, 1923, NM	40.00
Presto Magic Show, Pressman, 1975, NM	40.00
Score Four, Lakeside, 1971, G	10.00
Silly Safari, Topper, 1963, EX in box	150.00
Silly Sidney, board game, Transogram, 1963, EX	60.00
Skunk, Shafer, 1953, VG	20.00
Snagglepuss, board game, Transogram, 1962, EX	55.00
Sorry, Parker Bros, 1950, G	15.00
Spiro T Agnew's American History Challenge, M	35.00

Stars and Stripes, or Red, White, and Blue, McLoughlin Bros., ca 1900, 16½x18", $900.00.

Starflight, board game, Wilder, St Louis, 1931, EX	770.00
Sunny Andy Hoop-O-Loop, tin litho, dtd 1925	65.00
Superboy, board game, Hasbro, 1965, EX	85.00
Table Croquet, Bradley, 1890, no directions	75.00
Table Skittles, wood board game, Shakman, EX	25.00
Thunderball, Milton Bradley, 1965, M, sealed	65.00
Tiddly Winks, Parker Bros, 1930s, EX in orig box	50.00
Truth or Consequences, NM	135.00
Wacky Races, Milton Bradley, 1968, EX	65.00
Waltons, 1974, NM	7.50

Yankee Doodle, Parker Bros., 1895, wooden box, 21½x14", EX, $650.00.

Waterloo, board game, Parker Bros, 1895, EX 550.00
What's My Line, NM 125.00
Where's the Beef, Wendy's, Milton Bradley, 1984, MIB 25.00
Wide World & Journey Round It, Parker Bros, 1896, VG 525.00
Winnie the Poo, Parker Brothers, 1979, G 20.00
Wizard of Oz, Cadaco, 1974, MIB 15.00
World's Fair Game, board game, Parker Bros, 1892, EX 1,500.00
Yankee Doodle, 1893, EX 125.00
Yankee Peddler, card game, McLoughlin, 1850, EX in G box .1,320.00
You Don't Say, Milton Bradley, 1963, VG 25.00

Puzzles

Banana Splits, fr tray, Whitman, 1969, NM 40.00
Beverly Hillbillies, Granny & Ellymay, Jamar, 1963, M 35.00
Boy & fishbowl, wooden, Bessie Wilcox Smith, EX 45.00
Christmas Goose, McLoughlin, 1898, EX 935.00
Flipper, fr tray, Whitman, #4526, 1965, M 20.00
Hoppity Hooper, fr tray, Whitman, 1966, M 55.00
Huckleberry Hound, jr jigsaw, Whitman, 1962, EX 25.00
King Leonardo & His Short Subjects, Jamar, 1962, MIB 65.00
Little King, mc, 1933, 25x18", EX 60.00
Man from UNCLE, Jaymar, 1965, M 35.00

Milton Bradley framed model ship puzzle, late 1800s, wooden box, 16¾x23¾", $335.00.

Mork & Mindy, jigsaw, Milton Bradley, MIB 10.00
Road Runner w/WE Coyote, Whitman, 1971, M 7.50
Space Battle, 500-pc, Kenner, EX 10.00
Space Kidettes, jigsaw, Whitman, 1968 ....30.00
Stingray, fr tray, Whitman, 1966 ....50.00
Superman vs Brainstorm, jigsaw, Whitman, 1966, EX 30.00
Wacky Races, Hanna Barbera, 1970, NMIB 10.00
We Are Not Alone, Milton, 1977, 100-pc, NM 6.00
We Want Cantor, shows Eddie Cantor in many roles, 1933, EX ..45.00
3-masted ship, M Bradley, +wooden box w/litho top, 1800s 330.00

G. A. R. Memorabilia

'The Grand Army of the Republic' was first conceived by Chaplain W.J. Rutledge and Major B.J. Stephenson early in 1864 when they were tent-mates during our own Civil War. These men vowed to each other that if they were spared they would establish an organization that would preserve friendships and memories formed during this time. Shortly after the war ended, Rutledge and Stephenson made their desires a reality.

The first National Convention of the Grand Army of the Republic was held in Indianapolis, Indiana, on November 20, 1866. The purpose of the organization was to provide aid and assistance to the widows and orphans of the fallen Union dead and to care for the hospitalized veterans as needed. The last comrade of the G.A.R. died in 1949.

Many items are surfacing from the early encampments which were held on both state and national levels, resulting in a wide variety of souvenir items having been made. Our advisor for this category is Richard Haussmann; he is listed in the Directory under Illinois.

Pocket flask, label under glass, clear glass with diamond pattern, 29th National Encampment, 1895, Louisville, KY, IW Harper's, 6", EX, $550.00.

Badge, encampment souvenir, various, ea, from 25.00 up to 40.00
Badge, KY 22nd Nat'l Encampment...OH 1888, w/ribbon 17.50
Badge, 1st issue, shield shape 55.00
Badge, 2nd issue, wings up 40.00
Badge, 3rd issue, wings str 35.00
Book, Grand Army Blue Book, 1899 ....35.00
Book, History of the Easel-Shaped Monument..., Dux, 1893 ....50.00
Book, Proceeding of Encampment 1909, gold-emb cover, 217-pg ...20.00
Book, ritual; Phila PA, hardcover, 1898, 32-pg, 5x7", EX 15.00
Book: History of the GAR, Beath 45.00
Canteen, souvenir, GAR logo in brass, orig strap & stopper 75.00
Form, questions sent by post historian to escaped POW, 11x16" 5.00
Insignia, slough hat, brass wreath on bl wool 12.50
Lapel stud, member, logo in center 8.00
Medal, Maltese Cross drop, w/ribbon, dtd 1896 ....15.00
Medal, Woman's Relief Corps, bronze Maltese Cross, 1890s 10.00
Pamphlet, memorial services held May 29, 1880, 6x9", 44-pg 10.00
Pin-bk, Veteran's Medal in center, flags, celluloid, 1¾" 10.00
Postcard, monument to Jennie Wade w/picture insert 4.00
Tableware, SP, GAR mk, ea pc 8.00
Watch fob, metal, We Drank from the Same Canteen 1861-65 ...**75.00**

Gas Globes and Panels

Gas globes and panels, once a common sight, have vanished from the countryside but are being sought by collectors as a unique form of advertising memorabilia. Early globes from the 1920s (some date back to as early as 1912), now referred to as 'one-piece globes,' were made of molded milk glass and were globular in shape. The gas company name was etched or painted on the glass. Few of these were ever produced, and this type is valued very highly by collectors today.

A new type of pump was introduced in the early 1930s; the old 'visible' pumps were replaced by 'electric' models. Globes were changing at the same time. By the mid-thirties a five-piece globe consisting of a pair of inserts, two retaining rings, and a metal body was being produced in both 15" and 16½" sizes. Collectors prefer to call globes that are not one-piece or plastic 'three-piece glass' (Type 2) or 'metal body, glass inserts' (Type 3). Though metal-body globes (Type 3) were popular in the 1930s, they were common in the 1920s, and some were actually made as early as 1915. Though rare in numbers, their use spans many years. In the 1930s, Type 2 and Type 3 globes became the replacements of the one-piece globe. The most recently manufactured gas globes are made with a plastic body that contains two 13½" glass lenses. These were common in the fifties but were actually used as early as 1932.

Note: Standard Crowns with raised letters are one-piece globes that were made in the 1920s; those made in the 1950s (no raised letters), though one-piece, are not regarded as such by today's collectors. Both variations are listed below. Our advisor for this category is Scott Benjamin; he is listed in the Directory under California.

Type 1, Plastic Body, Glass Inserts (Inserts 13½") 1931-1950s

Ashland Diesel	175.00
Champlin	175.00
D-X Marine, rare	450.00
DX Ethyl	175.00
DX Lubricating Gasoline, tan body	175.00
Falcon	400.00
Frontier Gas, Rarin' To Go, w/horse	250.00
Marathon, no runner	150.00
Marine, sea horse, EX color	325.00
Never Nox Ethyl	225.00
Shamrock, oval body	175.00
Shamrock, w/clover, rnd	150.00
Spur, oval body	175.00
Texaco Sky Chief	175.00
Viking, pictures Viking ship	325.00
Wood River	135.00
66 Flite Fuel, Phillips, shield shape, all plastic	250.00

Type 2, Glass Frame, Glass Inserts (Inserts 13½") 1926-1940s

American	350.00
Atlantic Hi-Arc, glass gill body	375.00
Coltex Service Gasoline, unused	350.00
Derby	375.00
Esso	325.00
Frontier Gas, Double Refined	350.00
Gulf	350.00
Guyler Brand, milk glass, EX	650.00
Indian Gas, Red Dot	500.00
Koolmotor, clover shape	650.00
Mobil Gas	375.00
Pure	350.00
Shell, milk glass, clam shape	400.00
Sinclair Dino, milk glass, EX	300.00
Sinclair Pennant	550.00
Skelly Anomarx w/Ethyl	375.00
Skelly Powermax	350.00
Standard Crown, bl	500.00
Standard Crown, gr or orange, ea	600.00
Standard Crown, wht, red, or gold, ea	350.00
Texaco Diesel Chief	500.00
Texaco Ethyl	750.00
Texaco Star, blk outline on 'T'	375.00
Trophy, Our Premium Gasoline	400.00
White Flash, gill body	375.00
White Rose, boy, glass body	850.00
WNAX, w/radio station pictured	750.00

Type 3, Metal Frame, Glass Inserts (Inserts 15" or 16½") 1915-1930s

Ashland, white with red, green, yellow, and gold printing, ca 1930s, $350.00.

Atlantic Ethyl, 16½"	350.00
Atlantic White Flash, 16½"	350.00
Blue Sunoco, 15"	400.00
Cities Services Oils, 15" metal fr, 1929	350.00
Crown, crown figural, 16½", EX	800.00
Essolene, 16½"	425.00
General Ethyl, 15" metal fr, complete	700.00
Happy Gas, metal band, 16½"	500.00
Mobil Gas, winged horse, 15" or 16½" metal fr, NM	500.00
Mobilfuel Diesel, lg horse, high profile, metal band	550.00
Pure, porc body, 15"	500.00
Purol Gasoline, w/arrow, porc body	750.00
Purol Pep, porc body	550.00
Red Crown Ethyl	500.00
Richfield, w/eagle	500.00
Rocor, w/eagle, metal fr	550.00
Signal, old stoplight, 15", VG	2,200.00
Socony, milk glass inserts	750.00
Sunland Ethyl, 15"	500.00
Texaco Leaded, glass panels, in fr, pr	2,500.00
Tidex, 16½"	425.00
Tydol, cast faces, 15"	650.00
Tydol, 16½"	450.00
White Star, 15" metal fr, complete	750.00

Type 4, One-Piece Glass Globes, No Inserts, Co. Name Etched, Raised or Enameled – 1912-1931

Atlantic, chimney cap	2,400.00
Champlin Gasoline	1,300.00
Diamond	700.00
Dixie, etched, 1-pc	1,200.00
Gasoline, emb on dk gr ground, 14", NM	700.00
Iowa Gas	1,300.00
Mobil Oil Gargoyle, emb, red & blk details, 12", EX	1,400.00
Musgo	3,000.00
Pierce Pennant, etched	1,900.00
Red Crown, rnd, etched	2,600.00
Republic, 3-sided, 1-pc	950.00
Shell, rnd, etched	650.00
Sinclair, etched, milk glass	850.00
Sinclair Aircraft, etched	2,700.00
Sinclair Aircraft, pnt	2,200.00
Sinclair H-C, pnt	750.00

Skelly	650.00
Standard Red Crown Ethyl, emb letters	850.00
Super Shell, clam shape	900.00
Super Shell, rnd, etched	2,000.00
Texaco, milk glass, emb letters, brass collar	800.00
Texaco Ethyl	1,200.00
That Good Gulf..., emb, orange & blk letters, EX	800.00
White Eagle, eagle shape, blunt nose	1,000.00
White Rose, boy pictured, pnt	1,900.00

Gaudy Dutch

Inspired by Oriental Imari wares, Gaudy Dutch was made in England from 1800 to 1820. It was hand decorated on a soft-paste body with rich underglaze blues accented in orange, red, pink, green, and yellow. It differs from Gaudy Welsh in that there is no lustre (except on Water Lily). There are seventeen patterns, some of which are: War Bonnet, Grape, Dahlia, Oyster, Urn, Butterfly, Carnation, Single Rose, Double Rose, and Water Lily. For further information we recommend *The Collector's Encyclopedia of Gaudy Dutch & Welsh* by John Shuman, available from Collector Books.

Butterfly, coffeepot, 11", M	4,000.00
Butterfly, cup & saucer, butterfly in center, M	950.00
Butterfly, cup & saucer, butterfly on side, M	750.00
Butterfly, pitcher, milk; 4", M	825.00
Butterfly, plate, 6¾", M	575.00
Butterfly, plate, 9¾", M	1,500.00
Butterfly, waste bowl, M	1,350.00
Carnation, creamer, 4", M	800.00
Carnation, deep plate, 10", M	750.00
Carnation, plate, 8", M	600.00
Carnation, soup plate, 8½", M	700.00

**Creamers, Urn, base rim rough, very rare, 4½",
$800.00; Sunflower, 4½", M, $775.00.**

Carnation, sugar bowl, M	800.00
Dahlia, plate, 8", M	800.00
Dahlia, sugar bowl, M	900.00
Dahlia, tea bowl & saucer, M	750.00
Double Rose, cup & saucer, NM	565.00
Double Rose, cup plate, M	700.00
Double Rose, plate, toddy; rare, 4½", M	750.00
Double Rose, plate, 8¾", M	650.00
Double Rose, sugar bowl, M	800.00
Dove, creamer, helmet shape, rare, M	1,275.00
Dove, creamer, M	700.00

Dove, cup & saucer, bl band, M	550.00
Dove, plate, 9¾", M	800.00
Dove, teapot, M	1,000.00
Dove, waste bowl, M	700.00
Grape, creamer, M	695.00
Grape, cup & saucer, M	475.00
Grape, plate, toddy; 4½"	375.00
Grape, plate, 6", M	285.00
Grape, plate, 7", M	400.00
Grape, plate, 9¾", M	600.00
Grape, teapot, M	700.00
Leaf, sugar bowl, w/lid, M	1,000.00
Leaf, tea bowl & saucer, M	800.00
Oyster, plate, orange, 9¾", M	1,300.00
Oyster, plate, 6⅜", M	400.00
Oyster, sugar bowl, w/lid, orange, M	1,225.00
Oyster, waste bowl, 6¼", M	1,100.00
Primrose, plate, mk Riley, 8¾", M	550.00
Primrose, sugar bowl, M	900.00
Primrose, waste bowl, M	750.00
Single Rose, creamer, M	875.00
Single Rose, cup & saucer, NM	475.00
Single Rose, plate, bud dot w/single line, Riley, 9¾", M	1,125.00
Single Rose, plate, 5¼", M	375.00
Single Rose, plate, 6½", M	450.00
Single Rose, plate, 9½", M	550.00
Single Rose, tea bowl & saucer, M	300.00
Single Rose, teapot, M	1,500.00
Strawflower, plate, Riley, 10", M	1,900.00
Strawflower, plate, 8½", M	825.00
Strawflower, soup plate, M	800.00
Sunflower, creamer, M	450.00
Sunflower, plate, 8¼", M	600.00
Sunflower, sugar bowl, w/lid, rare, EX	550.00
Sunflower, tea bowl & saucer, M	800.00
Urn, cup plate, M	425.00
Urn, soup plate, 9", M	500.00
Urn, teapot, M	600.00
War Bonnet, creamer, M	600.00
War Bonnet, cup plate, M	650.00
War Bonnet, plate, 6⅜", M	575.00
War Bonnet, soup plate, M	700.00
War Bonnet, toddy plate, 5¼", NM	485.00
Zinnia, deep plate, 9¾", M	1,125.00
Zinnia, plate, 6⅜", M	600.00

Gaudy Ironstone

Gaudy Ironstone was produced in the mid-1800s in Staffordshire, England. Some of the ware was decorated in much the same colors and designs as Gaudy Welsh, while other pieces were painted in pink, orange, and red with black and light blue accents. Lustre was used on some designs, but omitted on others. The heavy ironstone body is its most distinguishing feature.

Key:
pc — polychrome   ug bl — underglaze blue

Cup & saucer, florals/foliage in red & gr	100.00
Cup & saucer, strawberries, 3-color, VG	80.00
Marble, floral, red/blk on wht, 1¾"	1,425.00
Pitcher, snake hdl, Allerton, 4¾"	55.00
Plate, blackberries/leaves in yel & orange, E Walley, 8½"	100.00

Plate, floral in red/gr, flowing bl border, mk Ironstone, 9½" 170.00
Plate, Morning-Glory, flowing bl+4 colors, crazed, 8½" 75.00
Plate, Morning-Glory, ug bl/red, 2-tone gr pnt, 9½" 125.00

Platter, orange blossoms, Japanese Imari-type border, 17", $600.00.

Plate, Strawberry, gold lustre, mk, 10", NM 325.00
Platter, orange blossoms, Japanese Imari border, 17" L 600.00
Platter, 4-color floral rim, Allerton, minor chips, 14" 25.00
Teapot, vintage, paneled, sq-top hdl, gooseneck, 9", NM 325.00
Waste bowl, Strawberry, stains/edge chips, 5½" 150.00

Gaudy Welsh

Gaudy Welsh was an inexpensive hand-decorated ware made in both England and Wales from 1820 until 1860. It is characterized by its colors — principally underglaze blue, orange-rust, and copper lustre — and by its uninhibited patterns. Accent colors may be yellow and green. (Pink lustre may be present, since lustre applied to the white areas appears pink. A copper tone develops from painting lustre onto the dark colors.) The body of the ware may be heavy ironstone, creamware, earthenware, or porcelain; even style and shapes vary considerably. Patterns, while usually floral, are also sometimes geometric and may have trees and birds. Beware! The Wagon Wheel pattern has been reproduced. For further information we recommend *The Collector's Encyclopedia of Gaudy Dutch and Welsh* by John Shuman, available from Collector Books.

Butterfly, bowl, scalloped, 3x5½" 100.00
Butterfly, coffeepot, dome lid, ftd, prof rpr, 9¾" 325.00
Butterfly, creamer, rectangular, hairline, 6½" L 120.00
Butterfly, cup & saucer, EX 100.00
Butterfly, plate, eagle mk, minor wear, 10½" 120.00
Butterfly, plate, eagle mk, 9", NM 110.00
Butterfly, plate, scalloped, eagle mk, 8", EX 70.00
Butterfly, waste bowl, scalloped, ftd, 3x5½" 140.00
Carnation, cup & saucer, M 90.00
Columbine, plate, 8¼", M 95.00
Cornflower, teapot, M 175.00
Daisy & Chain, sugar bowl, w/lid, M 150.00
Feather, cup & saucer, M 50.00
Feather, plate, 8", M 65.00
Flower Basket, bowl, 10½", M 200.00
Flower Basket, creamer, M 110.00
Flower Basket, mug, M 150.00
Flower Basket, plate, 9", M 150.00
Glamorgan, pitcher, 4¾", M 75.00
Grape, child's mug, 1¾", NM 100.00
Grape, child's mug, 2¼", NM 65.00
Grape, creamer, molded rim band, mask spout, worn, 4½" 160.00

Grape, creamer, scroll hdl, emb base, hairline/wear, 4½" 100.00
Grape, cup & saucer, pk/copper rim band, rosette mk, NM 270.00
Grape, cup plate, 3½" 100.00
Grape, ewer, scroll hdls, 4½" 170.00
Grape, pitcher, emb scrolls/foliage, leaf/rosette hdl, 6½" 165.00
Grape, plate, sq, 8½" 110.00
Grape, shaving mug, 3⅜", EX 90.00
Grape, teapot, ftd oval w/scroll hdl, 7x11½", EX 475.00
Mask Spout, creamer, 2½", M 75.00
Morning-Glory, plate, 9", M 135.00
Morning-Glory, teapot, 5½", M 225.00
Oyster, bowl, 8", M 150.00
Oyster, child's tea set, 3-pc, M 225.00
Oyster, creamer, lg, M 125.00
Oyster, cup & saucer, M 80.00
Oyster, pitcher, 4½", M 100.00
Oyster, plate, 9½", M 140.00

Grape, plate, 7¼", $125.00.

Seeing Eye, cup & saucer, M 125.00
Strawberry, 4", M 150.00
Sunflower, pitcher, snake hdl, 5", M 200.00
Tulip, condiment set, M 100.00
Tulip, dish, serving; 9", M 50.00
Tulip, plate, 7¾", M 75.00
Tulip, waste bowl, 6⅜", M 110.00
Unidentified pattern, salt dip, floral, scalloped, ftd, EX 425.00
Urn, tureen, ftd, 9½", M 275.00
Wagon Wheel, bowl, 7½", M 75.00
Wagon Wheel, creamer, ftd, 3½", M 170.00
Wagon Wheel, mug, leaf hdl, 3", NM 90.00
Wagon Wheel, plate, 7½", M 90.00
Wagon Wheel, platter, M 140.00
Wildflowers, cup & saucer, cobalt bl, M 60.00

Geisha Girl

Geisha Girl Porcelain was one of several key Japanese china production efforts aimed at the booming export markets of the U.S., Canada, England, and other parts of Europe. The wares feature colorful, kimono-clad Japanese ladies in scenes of everyday Japanese life, surrounded by exquisite flora, fauna, and mountain ranges. Nonetheless, the forms in which the wares were produced reflected the late 19th- and early 20th-century Western dining and decorating preferences: tea and coffee services, vases, dresser sets, children's items, planters, etc.

Over a hundred manufacturers were involved in Geisha Girl production. This accounts for the several hundred different patterns, well over a dozen border colors and styles, and several methods of design execution. Geisha Girl Porcelain was produced in wholly hand-painted versions and those that were hand painted over stenciled outlines. Be wary of Geisha ware executed with decals. Very few decaled examples came out of Japan. Rather, most were Czechoslovakian attempts to hone in on the market. Czech pieces have stamped marks in broad, pseudo-Oriental characters. Items with portraits of Oriental ladies in the bottom of tea or sake cups are *not* Geisha Girl Porcelain, unless the outside surface of the wares are decorated as described above. These lovely faces are formed by varying the thickness of the porcelain body and are called lithophanes.

The height of Geisha Girl production was between 1910 and the mid-1930s. Some post-WWII production has been found marked Occupied Japan. The ware continued in minimal production through the 1980s, but point of origin for the reproductions is Hong Kong. Modern productions are discerned by the pure whiteness of the porcelain; even, unemotional borders; lack of background washes and gold enameling; and overall sparseness of detail.

For further information we recommend *The Collector's Encyclopedia of Geisha Girl Porcelain* by Elyce Litts, available at your local bookstore, from Collector Books, or directly from the author. She is listed in the Directory under New Jersey.

Key:
#2 — Torii	#68 — SGK China, Occupied Japan
#4 — T in Cherry Blossom	J #1 — Yachi
#11 — diaper mk	J #6 — Tashiro
#12 — Royal Kaga	J #16 — Kutani
#16 — SNB	J #19 — Ozan
#19 — Japan	J #36 — Made by Kato
#20 — Made in Japan	J #46 — Yasutera
#35 — Plum Blossom	
#42 — Vantine	

Ashtray, Temple A, heart form, red w/gold, #2 ....35.00
Biscuit jar, Flower Gathering B, red w/gold, 6½" 55.00
Bowl, berry; Chinese Coin, Washday reserve 15.00
Bowl, Feather Fan, pierced hdls, #12, 8" 45.00
Bowl, master nut; Basket A, 9-lobed, 3-ftd, dk apple gr, 6" 35.00
Bowl, rice; Samurai Dance, red-orange w/gold 18.00
Box, dresser; Garden Bench B, cobalt w/gold, 6" dia 40.00
Box, Samisen Practice, decal, beige w/gold, #68, 6x4x2" 32.00
Chocolate pot, Battledore, ewer form, yel-gr, 9" 85.00
Chocolate pot, River's Edge, red w/gold, J#16 ....95.00
Cookie jar, Meeting B, cobalt & red w/gold 75.00
Creamer, Long-Stemmed Peony, slender, fluted, bl w/gold, #20 ...15.00
Cup, bouillon; Thousand Geisha, cobalt w/gold, J#42, w/lid 50.00
Cup & saucer, cocoa; Child wearing E-Boshi, red-orange, #2 ....15.00
Cup & saucer, demi; Bamboo Trellis, red-orange w/gold buds 12.00
Cup & saucer, demi; Plum Blossom Branch, red-orange w/gold 20.00
Cup & saucer, Mother & Son C, red, J#6, child sz 15.00
Cup & saucer, tea; Bird Cage, red-orange, int floral fr 15.00
Cup & saucer, tea; Duck Watching B, bl-gr w/wht, #6 ....12.00
Cup & saucer, tea; Pointing J, bl w/gold 25.00
Dish, Slowpoke, pattern in reserve, ftd, red w/gold, 8" 55.00
Egg cup, dbl, Temple B, red w/gold 28.00
Hair receiver, Fan Silhouette of Hoo Bird, cobalt w/gold 38.00
Jar, condensed milk; Geisha in Sampan C, cobalt w/gold, J#36 ..120.00
Jar, powder; Pug, brick red, 4¼" 35.00
Mustard jar, Gardening, bl-gr w/red hdls & finial 27.00
Pitcher, Garden Bench A, mint gr w/int gold lacing, 3½" 25.00
Plate, Battledore, swirl fluted, scalloped rim, yel-gr, 6" 14.00
Plate, Ikebana in Rickshaw, swirl fluted, cobalt w/gold, 8½" 35.00
Plate, lemon; Art Show, red w/gold, 5¾" 15.00
Plate, Visitor to the Court, bl w/gold, #19, 7¼" 22.00
Platter, cake; Parasol Modern, bl, #20 ....35.00

Pot, demi; Fan D, pattern in reserve 85.00
Spooner, Vantine's Blue, upright, scalloped edge, #42 ....40.00
Sugar shaker, Boat Festival, lt cobalt bl, #4 ....45.00
Teapot, Boy w/Scythe, cobalt w/gold, #20 ....35.00

Toothpick holder, Garden Bench H, five reserves on backdrop of phoenix and flowers, gold trim and coralene beading, cobalt blue border, Made in Japan by Kato, $45.00.

German Porcelain

Unless otherwise noted, the porcelain listed in this section is marked simply 'Germany.' Products of other German manufactures are listed in specific categories. See also Bisque; Pink Pigs; Elfinware.

Bisque bear, jointed shoulders and legs, 3¼", $400.00.

Bowl, florals, gold trim, rtcl lattice, ftd, crown mk, 9" 350.00
Bowl, violets/emb foliage, scrolled edge, CT, 13" L 85.00
Box, googly-eyed dog figural, red w/blk trim, bl eyes, 6x4" 70.00
Box, jewel; Victorian couple transfer on lt pk, Kalk Co 115.00
Box, powder; floral spray on wht, mk H under crown, 2½" L 80.00
Box, village landscape reserve, semicircular, 5" W 200.00
Candlestick, cherub std, floral-appl base, 1890s, 9", EX, pr 400.00
Chocolate pot, lovers in garden, Kauffmann, gold trim, 9½" 150.00
Dish, dancing figures/musicians, shaped gilt border, mk, 7½" ..2,090.00
Dresser bottle, gr leaves/pk flowers allover, 12", pr, +bowl 125.00
Figurine, monkey musicians, 1700s attire, 6", set of 8, EX 2,400.00
Figurine, Victorian lady standing w/basket in hand, 11" 135.00
Figurine, wht bear atop upright opera glasses, 3" 68.00
Figurine, young lovers, gr/rust shades w/gold, 13" 275.00
Figurine, 6 figures celebrate wine harvest, beehive mk, 12" 1,000.00
Plaque, child's head emb on dull gold, bl rim, 11", pr 500.00
Plaque, Der Ersten Rosen, seated maid, after Bernard, 7x5" 2,300.00

Plaque, lady holds mandolin, trees/fields, fr, 7x5" 900.00
Plate, floral center, gold/dk gr emb edge, hdls, CT, 12" 95.00
Plate, hummingbird & flowers on bl lustre, 10" 45.00
Toby jug, shepherd w/staff, wht/peach/blk, #5335, 5" 75.00
Vase, parakeets on flower, mk Elvira, 8x4¼" 100.00

Gladding McBean and Company

This company was established in 1875 in Lincoln, California. They first produced only clay drainage pipes, but in 1883 architectural terra cotta was introduced, which has been used extensively in the United States as well as abroad. Sometime later a line of garden pottery was added. They soon became the leading producers of tile in the country. In 1923 they purchased the Tropico Pottery in Glendale, California, where in addition to tile they also produced huge garden vases. Their line was expanded in 1934 to included artware and dinnerware.

At least fifteen lines of art pottery were developed between 1934 and 1942. For a short time they stamped their wares with the Tropico Pottery mark, but the majority was signed 'GMcB' in an oval. Later the mark was changed to 'Franciscan' with several variations. After 1937 'Catalina Pottery' was used on some lines. (All items marked 'Catalina Pottery' were made in Glendale.) For further information we recommend *The Collector's Encyclopedia of California Pottery* by our advisor for this category, Jack Chipman. He is listed in the Directory under California.

Bowl, Capistrano Art Ware, mauve satin, rectangular, 11¾x8" 25.00
Candle holder, Tropico Art Ware, wht 18.00
Coffeepot, demitasse; Ruby Art Ware 75.00
Compote, Avalon Art Ware, turq & ivory, 8" 20.00
Cup & saucer, Ruby Art Ware 30.00
Flowerpot, Tropico Art Ware, bl, 6" 15.00
Pitcher, Tropico Art Ware, bl, 5¾" 18.00
Vase, Bamboo, ivory/gr, cylindrical, 8" 48.00
Vase, Catalina Art Ware, coral satin, ribbed, 7¾" 35.00
Vase, Coronado Art Ware, satin ivory, bulbous base, 8½" 30.00
Vase, Encanto Art Ware, flambe, bulbous, 6½" 35.00
Vase, lady's head, cupped hands form opening, 7" 25.00
Vase, Ox Blood Art Ware, 11" 200.00

Glass Animals and Figurines

These beautiful glass sculptures have been produced by many major companies in America; in fact, some are still being made today. Heisey, Fostoria, Duncan and Miller, Imperial, Paden City, Tiffin and Cambridge made the vast majority, but there were many others involved on a lesser scale. Some, but not all, marked their animals.

As many of the glass companies went out of business, molds were often sold to others still active who used them to reproduce their own line of animals. While some are easy to recognize, others can be very confusing. For example, Summit Art Glass now owns Cambridge's 6½", 8½", and 10" swan molds. We recommend *Glass Animals of the Depression Era* by Lee Garmon and Dick Spencer, if you're thinking of starting a collection or wanting to identify and evaluate the glass animals you already have. Both are our advisors for this category and are listed in the Directory under Illinois.

Cambridge

Blue jay, flower holder 125.00
Blue jay, peg base 125.00
Buddha, amber, 5½" 225.00
Eagle, bookend, ea 80.00

Heron, lg, 12" 125.00
Heron, sm, 9" 75.00
Lion, bookend, ea 110.00
Pouter pigeon, bookend, ea 60.00
Scottie, bookend, pr 150.00
Scottie, frosted, ea 75.00
Sea gull, flower frog 50.00
Swan, candlestick, milk glass, 4½", ea 175.00
Swan, carmen, 6½" 200.00
Swan, carmen, 8½" 250.00
Swan, Crown Tuscan, 3½" 40.00
Swan, Crown Tuscan, 8½" 95.00
Swan, ebony, 10½" 250.00
Swan, ebony, 12½" 300.00
Swan, ebony, 3½" 60.00
Swan, ebony, 6½" 100.00
Swan, ebony, 8½" 125.00
Swan, emerald, 3½" 35.00
Swan, emerald, 6½" 85.00
Swan, emerald, 8½" 125.00
Swan, milk glass, 3½" 60.00
Swan, milk glass, 6½" 125.00
Swan, milk glass, 8½" 275.00
Turkey, bl, w/lid 550.00
Turkey, gr, w/lid 450.00
Turkey, pk, w/lid 400.00

Duncan and Miller

Bird of paradise 700.00
Donkey, cart & peon 475.00
Dove, head down 175.00
Duck, ashtray, 7" 70.00
Goose, fat, 6x6" 275.00
Heron, 7" 110.00
Mallard duck, cigarette box, #30, w/lid, 3½x4½" 45.00
Ruffled grouse, very rare 1,750.00
Swan, ashtray, crystal w/bl neck, 4" 35.00
Swan, bl opal, W&F, spread wings, 10x12½" 245.00
Swan, candle holder, red w/crystal neck, 7", ea 70.00
Swan, gr opal, W&F, spread wings, 10x12½" 225.00
Swan, open, 7" 45.00
Swan, solid, 3" 20.00
Swan, solid, 5" 30.00
Swan, solid, 7" 75.00
Swan, wht milk glass w/red neck, 10½" 450.00
Swordfish 300.00
Swordfish, bl opal, rare 500.00
Sylvan swan, bl or pk, 6½" 125.00
Sylvan swan, vaseline opal, 6½" 185.00

Fenton

Alley cat, Kelly gr irid, 11" 60.00
Alley cat, red slag, 11" 65.00
Bear, blk, sitting 16.00
Bear, carnival, sitting 20.00
Bear, wht, sitting 16.00
Bear, wht irid, sitting 15.00
Boy, blk, praying 12.00
Bunny, lt bl 16.00
Bunny, pale yel 16.00
Elephant, flower bowl, teal bl, 6½x9" 375.00

Elephant, whiskey bottle, 8" 300.00
Fish, paperweight, red carnival, ltd ed 55.00
Fish, vase, milk glass w/blk tail & eyes, 7" 425.00
Girl, jade gr, praying 10.00
Happiness Bird, red, 6½" 28.00

Fostoria

Chanticleer, 10¾" 200.00
Chinese lotus, Silver Mist, 10¼" 225.00
Colts, sitting 35.00
Colts, standing, bl 40.00
Deer, sitting or standing 40.00
Deer, sitting or standing, bl 40.00
Deer, sitting or standing, milk glass 55.00
Deer, sitting or standing, Silver Mist 40.00
Duck, mama 25.00
Duck w/3 ducklings, amber, set 50.00
Duckling, head bk (+) 20.00
Duckling, head down (+) 15.00
Duckling, walking (+) 15.00
Eagle, bookend, 7½", ea 90.00
Elephant, bookend, 6½", ea 65.00
Fish, horizontal, rare 125.00
Fish, vertical 95.00
Frog 35.00
Horse, bookend, 7¾", ea 45.00
Madonna, Silver Mist, orig issue, 10" (+) 50.00
Madonna, Silver Mist, w/base, orig issue, 11¾" (+) 80.00
Madonna, 10" (+) 60.00
Mermaid, 11½" 115.00
Owl, bookend, ebony, ea 225.00
Owl, bookend, 7½", ea 165.00
Pelican, pk 55.00
Penguin, topaz, 4⅝" 125.00
Polar bear, frosted 60.00
Polar bear, topaz, 4⅝" 125.00
Rooster, Chanticleer, ebony, 10¾" 500.00
Sea horse, bookend, 8", ea 115.00
Seal 60.00
Seal, frosted 45.00
Squirrel 25.00
Squirrel, amber 35.00
Squirrel, frosted 25.00
St Francis, Silver Mist, orig issue, 13½" (+) 325.00
Whale 20.00

Heisey

Heisey 'Balking Colt,' 3½x3½",
$185.00.

Airdale 450.00
Angelfish 120.00
Asiatic pheasant 300.00
Bull, sgn 1,300.00
Chick, head down 65.00
Chick, head up 65.00
Clydesdale 375.00
Colt, kicking 185.00
Colt, kicking, amber 600.00
Colt, kicking, cobalt 950.00
Colt, rearing 195.00
Colt, rearing, amber 600.00
Colt, rearing, cobalt 950.00
Colt, standing 90.00
Colt, standing, amber 550.00
Colt, standing, cobalt 900.00
Cygnet, baby swan, 2½" 185.00
Dolphin, candlestick, #110, pr 240.00
Dolphin, candlestick, Moongleam, #110, pr 500.00
Dolphin, stick lamp base 250.00
Donkey 250.00
Duck, ashtray 75.00
Duck, ashtray, Flamingo 140.00
Duck, ashtray, Marigold 195.00
Duck, flower block 110.00
Duck, flower block, Hawthorne 200.00
Elephant, amber, lg 1,850.00
Elephant, amber, med 1,850.00
Elephant, amber, sm 1,600.00
Elephant, lg 350.00
Elephant, med 375.00
Elephant, sm 195.00
Fish, bookend, ea 125.00
Fish, bowl, 9½" 425.00
Fish, candlestick, 5", ea 140.00
Fish, match holder 120.00
Fish, tropical 1,400.00
Flying mare 2,200.00
Flying mare, amber 3,000.00
Frog, cheese plate, Flamingo, #1210 ....125.00
Frog, cheese plate, Marigold 285.00
Frog, cheese plate, Moongleam 240.00
Gazelle 1,500.00
Giraffe, head bk 185.00
Giraffe, head to side 185.00
Goose, wings down 425.00
Goose, wings half 95.00
Goose, wings up 100.00
Hen 360.00
Horse head, bookend, ea 120.00
Horse head, cigarette box, #1489, 4½x4" 55.00
Horse head, cocktail shaker 85.00
Irish setter, ashtray 30.00
Irish setter, ashtray, Flamingo 45.00
Irish setter, ashtray, Moongleam 55.00
Kingfisher, flower block, Flamingo 150.00
Kingfisher, flower block, Hawthorne 200.00
Kingfisher, flower block, Moongleam 175.00
Mallard, wings down 275.00
Mallard, wings half 175.00
Mallard, wings up 130.00
Piglet, sitting 75.00
Piglet, standing 75.00
Plug horse 110.00

Plug horse, amber 600.00
Plug horse, cobalt 1,000.00
Pouter pigeon 600.00
Rabbit, paperweight 135.00
Ringneck pheasant, 11¾" 125.00
Rooster, amber, 5⅜" 2,500.00
Rooster, fighting, 8" 160.00
Rooster, vase, 6½" 85.00
Rooster, 5⅜" 350.00
Rooster head, cocktail 50.00
Rooster head, cocktail shaker, 1-qt 65.00
Scotty 95.00
Sea horse, cocktail 140.00
Show horse 1,250.00
Sow 500.00
Sparrow 80.00
Swan, ind nut, #1503 ....18.00
Swan, master nut, #1503 ....45.00
Swan, pitcher 700.00
Swan, 7" 700.00
Wood duck 550.00

Imperial

Angelfish, red, 6⅝" 300.00
Asiatic pheasant, amber 325.00
Champ terrier, caramel slag, 5¾" 95.00
Chick, head down, milk glass 10.00
Chick, head up, milk glass 10.00
Clydesdale, amber 325.00
Clydesdale, salmon 325.00
Clydesdale, Verde Gr 150.00
Colt, balking, aqua, dtd 1979 ....70.00
Colt, balking, Ultra Bl 45.00
Colt, kicking, Ultra Bl 50.00
Colt, standing, caramel slag 45.00
Colt, standing, milk glass 75.00
Cygnet, blk, 2½" 55.00
Cygnet, Horizon Bl 25.00
Dog, Airedale, caramel slag 95.00
Dog, Airedale, Ultra Bl 65.00
Dog, Airedale, Ultra Bl satin 80.00
Donkey, caramel slag 55.00
Donkey, Meadow Gr Carnival 95.00
Duck, sitting, Nut Brn, 4" 105.00
Duck, standing, Sunshine Yel, 2⅝" 20.00
Elephant, caramel slag, med 55.00
Elephant, Meadow Gr Carnival, #674, med 95.00
Elephant, pk satin, sm 70.00
Filly, head bkward, Verde Gr 145.00
Filly, head forward, satin 75.00
Fish, candlestick, Sunshine Yel, 5", ea 40.00
Fish, match holder, Sunshine Yel satin, 3" 20.00
Gazelle, Ultra Bl 125.00
Horse head, bookend, pk, rare, ea 300.00
Mallard, wings down, caramel slag 190.00
Mallard, wings down, lt bl satin 22.50
Mallard, wings half, caramel slag 35.00
Mallard, wings half, lt bl satin 22.50
Mallard, wings up, caramel slag 35.00
Mallard, wings up, lt bl satin 22.50
Owl, Hootless; caramel slag 45.00
Piglet, sitting 45.00
Piglet, standing, ruby, hole between legs 95.00

Piglet, standing, Ultra Bl 45.00
Plug horse, pk, HCA, 1978 ....40.00
Rabbit, paperweight, milk glass, 2¾" 25.00
Rooster, amber 425.00
Rooster, fighting, pk 175.00
Scottie, milk glass, 3½" 45.00
Sow, amber 400.00
Swan, nut dish, dtd 35.00
Tiger, paperweight, blk 65.00
Tiger, paperweight, jade gr, 8" L 85.00
Wood duck, caramel slag 45.00
Wood duck, Sunshine Yel satin 45.00
Wood duck, Ultra Bl satin 45.00
Wood duckling, floating, Sunshine Yel satin 15.00
Wood duckling, standing, Sunshine Yel 15.00
Wood duckling, standing, Sunshine Yel satin 15.00

L.E. Smith

Camel, recumbent, 4½x6" 50.00
Cock, Fighting; amberina, 9" 40.00
Goose Girl, orig, 6" 20.00
Horse, bookend, rearing, amber, ea 38.00
Horse, bookend, rearing, blk, ea 55.00
Horse, bookend, rearing, cobalt, ea 40.00
Horse, bookend, rearing, crystal, ea 20.00
Horse, bookend, rearing, emerald, ea 40.00
Horse, bookend, rearing, Ritz Bl, ea 38.00
Horse, bookend, rearing, ruby, ea 40.00
Horse, recumbent, gr, 9" L 110.00
King fish, aquarium, gr, 7¼x15" 265.00
Queen fish, aquarium, 7x15" 200.00
Rooster, butterscotch slag, ltd ed, #208 ....85.00
Scottie, crystal, lg, 5" 30.00
Sparrow, head down, 3½" 12.50
Swan, blk amethyst, w/silver trim, lg 30.00
Swan, milk glass, lg 45.00

New Martinsville

Bear, baby, head trn or str, 3" 50.00
Bear, mama 195.00
Bear, papa 225.00
Chick, frosted, 1" 20.00
Crow, cocktail 15.00
Duck, dk teal, Viking's Epic Line, 9" 30.00
Duck, fighting, head up or down, Viking's Epic Line 35.00
Duck, orange, Viking's Epic Line 40.00
Duck, standing, Viking's Epic Line 35.00
Elephant, bookend, 5½", ea 75.00
Gazelle, leaping, frosted base, 8¼" 65.00
German shepherd, 5" 65.00
Hen, 5" 65.00
Horse, head up, 8" 95.00
Nautilus shell, bookend, 6", ea 35.00
Piglet, standing 125.00
Porpoise on wave, orig 450.00
Rooster, lg 85.00
Seal, candlestick, lg, pr 150.00
Seal w/ball, bookends, 7", pr 130.00
Seal w/ball, candle holder, 4½", ea 65.00
Squirrel, on base, 5½" 60.00
Starfish, 7¾" 75.00
Tiger, head down, frosted, 7¼" 195.00

Tiger, head up, 6½" 185.00
Wolfhound, 7" 85.00
Woodsman, sq base, 7⅜" 95.00

Paden City

American eagle head, bookends, 7½", pr 275.00
Bird, lt bl, 5" 110.00
Bunny, cotton-ball dispenser, ears bk, bl frosted 90.00
Bunny, cotton-ball dispenser, ears bk, crystal frosted 60.00
Bunny, cotton-ball dispenser, ears bk, milk glass 95.00
Bunny, cotton-ball dispenser, ears bk, pk frosted 70.00
Bunny, cotton-ball dispenser, ears up, pk frosted 150.00
Dragon swan, 9¾" L 215.00
Goose, lt bl, 5" 115.00
Horse, rearing, 10" 170.00
Pheasant, Chinese; crystal, 13¾" 85.00
Pheasant, Chinese; med bl, 13¾" 150.00
Pheasant, head trn, lt bl, 12" L 175.00
Pony, crystal, 12" 90.00
Pouter pigeon, bookend, 6¼", ea 75.00
Rooster, Barnyard; 8¾" 85.00
Rooster, Chanticleer; 9¼" 175.00
Rooster, Elegant; lt bl, 11" 225.00
Rooster, frosted 65.00
Rooster, head down, 8¾" 75.00
Squirrel on curved log, 5½" 65.00

Viking

Angelfish, amber, 6½" 65.00
Bird, orange, 9½" 20.00
Bird, ruby, 12" 30.00
Dog, orange, 8" 45.00
Duck, red, 9" 45.00
Egret, dk med bl, 12" 45.00
Horse, amber, 11½" 85.00
Rooster, Epic; avocado, 9½" 45.00
Wise Old Owl on log, amber, 5" 18.00

Westmoreland

Bird in flight, Amber Marigold, wings out, 5" W 25.00
Bulldog, Blk Mist, pnt collar, rhinestone eyes, 2½" 30.00
Butterfly, Bl Mist, 2½" 25.00
Porky Pig, milk glass, hollow, 3" L 15.00
Pouter pigeon, Pk Mist, 1" 25.00
Pouter pigeon, 1" 20.00
Robin, 3¼" L 20.00
Starfish, candle holder, almond, 5", pr 28.00
Turtle, paperweight, Gr Mist, no holes, 4" L 22.00

Glass Knives

Glass knives were manufactured from about 1920 to 1950, with distribution at its greatest in the late thirties and early forties. Colors generally followed Depression Glass dinnerware: crystal, light blue, light green, pink (originally called rose), and more rarely amber, forest green, and white (opal). Many glass knives were hand painted in fruit or flower designs. Knife blades were ground to a sharp edge. Today knives are usually found with blades nicked through years of use or bumping in silverware drawers or reground, which is acceptable to collectors as long as the original knife shape is maintained.

Many glass knives were engraved for gift-giving, personalized with the recipient's name and occasionally with a greeting. Originally presented in boxes, most glass knives were accompanied by a paper flyer extolling the virtues of the knife and describing its care.

Boxes printed with World's Fair logos are fun to find, though not rare. Butter knives, which are smaller than other glass knives, typically were made in Czechoslovakia and sometimes match the handle patterns of glass salad sets. Knife lengths often vary slightly, because the knives were snapped off the molded glass during manufacture.

Our advisor for this category is Adrienne Escoe; she is listed in the Directory under California. For information concerning the Glass Knife Collectors Club, see the Clubs, Newsletters, and Catalogs section of the Directory.

Values reflect knives with minor blade roughness or resharpening.

Aer-Flo (Grid), crystal, 7½" 25.00
Aer-Flo (Grid), forest gr, 7½" 200.00
Aer-Flo (Grid), gr, 7½" 30.00
BK, crystal, HP flowers, 9¼" 25.00
Block, pk, Atlantic City eng, 8¼" 25.00

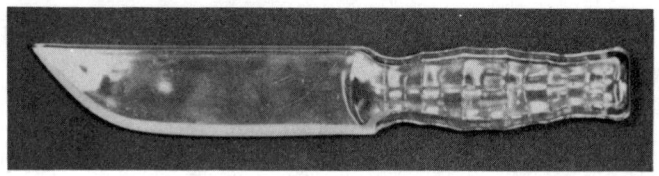

Block, vaseline, rare color, $65.00.

Butter, crystal/amber, 5½" 23.00
Butter, gr/crystal, 6¼" 25.00
Candlewick, crystal, 8½" 325.00
Cryst-o-lite, crystal, 3 pinwheels, 8½" 8.00
Dagger, crystal, 9¼" 75.00
Dur-x 3 leaf, crystal, 9¼" 12.00
Dur-x 5 leaf, bl, 9¼", +box 20.00
JCW, crystal, 9¼" 25.00
Plain hdl, gr, 9" 30.00
Plain hdl, lt pk, 9" 22.00
Rose Spray, crystal, 8½", +Christmas box 30.00
Rose Spray, gr, 8½" 65.00
Steel-ite, crystal, 8½" 24.00
Steel-ite, pk, 8½" 65.00
Stonex, amber, 8½" 110.00
Stonex, crystal, 8½" 40.00
Stonex, opal, 8½" 135.00
Thumbguard, HP flowers, 9¼" 25.00
Vitex (3 Star), bl, 9¼" 17.00
Vitex (3 Star), crystal, 8½" 10.00

Glidden

Genius designer Glidden Parker established Glidden Pottery in 1940 in Alfred, New York, having been schooled at the unrivaled New York State College of Ceramics at Alfred University. Glidden pottery is characterized by a fine stoneware body, innovative forms, outstanding hand-milled glazes, and hand decoration which make the pieces individual works of art. Production consisted of casual dinnerware, artware, and accessories that were distributed internationally.

In 1949 Glidden Pottery became the second ceramic plant in the country to utilize the revolutionary Ram pressing machine. This allowed for increased production and for the most part eliminated the previously used slip-casting method. However, Glidden stoneware continued to reflect the same superb quality of craftsmanship until the factory closed in 1957. Although the majority of form and decorative patterns were Mr. Parker's personal designs, Fong Chow and Sergio Dello Strologo also designed award-winning lines.

Glidden will be found marked on the unglazed underside with a signature that is hand incised, mold impressed, or ink stamped. Interest in this unique stoneware is growing as collectors discover that it embodies the very finest of Mid-Century High Style. Our advisor is David Pierce; he is listed in the Directory under Ohio.

Ashtray, Alfred Stoneware, #821, 6¾x6" 20.00
Ashtray, Fish (Fred Press), #275 ....15.00
Ashtray, Safex, dbl, sq 15.00
Ashtray, Sandstone, #272-U, 10" 45.00
Bowl, cobalt, #15, 4x7x5¼" 25.00
Bowl, Plaid, #27, 1¼x5¾x5¾" 15.00
Bowl, salad; Alfred Stoneware, #823, 6x12¼" 40.00
Bowl, salad; Turq Matrix, #14, 4½x8x7" 15.00
Bowl, serving; Sage & Sand, #622, 7½" 12.00
Bowl, soup; Feather, #270, 6" 10.00
Candle bench, Afrikans, 3¾x2x8¾" 35.00
Casserole, Pear, #165, 8½x5½" 30.00
Casserole, Turq Matrix, #167, 4¼x5¼" 10.00
Casserole, Will o' the Wisp, #165, 8½x5½" 24.00
Creamer & sugar bowl, Flourish, #144, #143 ....55.00
Cup & saucer, Feather, #441-A, #442 ....15.00
Cup & saucer, Flourish, #141, #142 ....20.00
Cup & saucer, Yellowstone, #441-A, #442 ....12.00
Pitcher, Glidden Bl, #616, 2-qt 75.00
Pitcher, Yellowstone, #615, 1-qt 35.00
Plate, canape; Canape Capers Circus series, #35, 5½", 8 for 175.00
Plate, canape; Weathervane, #35, 5½" 30.00
Teapot, Flourish, #140, 5¼x9x4¼" 45.00
Tray, serving; Flourish, #32, 9x6¾" 35.00
Tumbler, Flourish, #1127, 5½" 20.00
Vase, cobalt, pillow form, #87, 2¾x7½x4¼" 25.00
Vase, Early Pk, #40, 5x9½x6" 40.00
Vase, Early Pk, #480, 12x3½x3¼" 45.00
Vase, Flourish, #5 ....40.00
Vase, Gulfstream Bl, #4020, 5x4" 125.00

Goebel

F.W. Goebel founded the Hummelwork Porcelain Manufactory in 1871, located in Rodental, West Germany. They produced porcelain figurines, plates, and novelties, the most famous of which are the Hummel figurines (these are listed in a separate section). There were many other series produced by Goebel — Disney characters, birds, animals, Art Deco figurines, and the Friar Tuck Monks that are especially popular. Our advisors for this category are Gale and Wayne Bailey; they are listed in the Directory under Georgia.

Cardinal Tuck (Red Monk)

Egg timer, single; E104, 3-line mk 150.00
Jug, S141-2/0, stylized bee mk, 2½" 75.00
Jug, S141/0, stylized bee mk, 4" 100.00
Jug, S141/1, stylized bee mk, 4" 125.00
Shakers, P176A & B, w/Bible, stylized bee mk, pr 100.00

Friar Tuck (Brown Monk)

Ashtray, RF142, toes, stylized bee mk 50.00
Ashtray, ZF43/II, stylized bee mk 40.00
Ashtray, ZF43/0, stylized bee mk 50.00
Bank, SD29, stylized bee mk 50.00
Bookend, XS184/B, sitting, stylized bee mk, ea 75.00
Calendar holder, KF55, toes, stylized bee mk 50.00
Cigarette holder, RX104/A, toes, stylized bee mk 75.00
Cigarette holder, RX110, stylized bee mk 75.00
Creamer, S135, bl eyes, full bee mk, 1" 50.00
Decanter, KL92, stylized bee mk 75.00
Decanter, KL92, toes, full bee mk 100.00
Decanter, KL95, 3-line mk 50.00
Egg cup, E95A, stylized bee mk 20.00
Egg cup tray, E95/B, stylized bee mk 50.00
Egg timer, dbl; E96, stylized bee mk 50.00
Egg timer, single; E104, 3-line mk 50.00
Flask, KL97, stylized bee mk 60.00
Honey pot, H9, open bk, toes, stylized bee mk 75.00
Jug, S141-2/0, full bee mk, 2½" 25.00
Jug, S141/0, full bee mk, 4" 30.00
Liquor tot, KL94, stylized bee mk, 1¾" 15.00
Match box holder, RX111, toes, stylized bee mk 50.00
Match holder & striker, RX104/B, full bee mk 50.00
Match holder & striker, RX104/B, stylized bee mk 40.00
Mug, beer; T74/0, stylized bee mk, 4" 30.00
Mustard pot, S183, stylized bee mk, 3¾" 20.00
Mustard pot, S183, toes, full bee mk, 3¾" 40.00
Napkin ring, X98, stylized bee mk 50.00
Shakers, #176/A, red Bible, stylized bee mk, pr 50.00
Shakers, P153/0, toes, 2⅜" 35.00
Sugar bowl, M43/B, toes, stylized bee mk 30.00
Sugar bowl, Z37, toes, full bee mk, 4½" 35.00
Tray, T69, stylized bee mk 50.00

Miscellaneous

Ashtray, RF104, boy fishing, bee mk, 2¾" 40.00
Bookends, XS662/0 A&B, boy & girl, dbl crown mk, 5⅛", pr 85.00
Bottle, clown w/mandolin, wht w/red details, crown mk 75.00
Bottle, covered wagon form w/dog finial, bl & tan, crown mk 75.00
Bottle, liquor; KL24A, boy kissing girl, crown mk, 6½" 100.00
Creamer, S487, elephant, dbl crown mk, orange, 6¼" 75.00
Figurine, elf, crawling, looking at fly on bk, full bee mk, 4" 85.00
Figurine, elf, on bk, knees up, fly on nose, full bee mk, 4" 85.00
Figurine, FF320, nurse, 1971, 8" 55.00

Figurines, Pinky and Blue Boy, ca 1966, 10", $135.00 for the pair.

Figurine, FX17, dwarf on pig, full bee mk 75.00
Figurine, GF136, Lipizzaner horse & rider, 3-line mk 100.00
Figurine, GF45, couple kissing, full bee mk, 2¾" 40.00
Figurine, GM1/OA, rider on horse, wht, crown & bee mk, 3½" ...75.00
Figurine, HF6, St Francis w/4 birds, crown mk, 9¾" 75.00
Figurine, peacock, yel/gr/tan feathers on blk, 1984, 16" L 90.00
Match holder, S34, blackbird, crown & bee mk, 3" 75.00
Pipe holder, RT97, dog form, incised crown mk, 3⅜" 75.00
Pitcher, bear's head form, brn, full bee mk, EX 38.00
Pitcher, dog figural, dbl crown mk, 4½" 75.00
Planter, egg-shape receptacle, 3 girls stand beside, crown mk 85.00
Pretzel holder, KP15/0, boy figural, bee mk, 5¼" 50.00
Wall pocket, TB08, Philip Morris, dbl crown mk, 6" 75.00
Wall vase, VP82, umbrella, crown & bee mk, 7¼" 75.00

Goldscheider

The Goldscheider family operated a pottery in Vienna for many generations before seeking refuge in the United States following Hitler's invasion of their country. They settled in Trenton, New Jersey, in the early 1940s where they established a new corporation and began producing objects of art and tableware items. In 1946 Marcel Goldscheider established a pottery in Staffordshire where he manufactured bone china figures, earthenware, etc., marked with a stamp of his signature. Larger artist-signed examples from either location are very valuable.

Bust, lady in bl shawl, hands Xd over chest, Austria, 11" 135.00
Bust, Mongol, sgn Liedhoff 150.00

Dancer in a top hat, hand decorated by Lorenzl, #5523/15/7, 12", $1,150.00.

Figurine, April Showers, #275F 100.00
Figurine, butterfly girl sits, wings as skirt, Lorenzl, 10" 1,500.00
Figurine, Cinderella, high gloss, mk, 1940s, 12" 175.00
Figurine, dancer, knee raised, fans out skirt, Sarin, 16" 1,100.00
Figurine, German shepherd, recumbent, 17" L 250.00
Figurine, German shepherd, seated, 7½" 100.00
Figurine, girl w/guitar, leans bk, hand on hip, Sakon, 17" 2,200.00
Figurine, lady w/fan (torso), USA Everlast mk, 6½" 75.00
Figurine, Madonna, #781-8, 9" 55.00
Figurine, Madonna, artist sgn, 1920s, 10" 500.00
Figurine, Pierrot kisses mandolin player, artist sgn, 18" 1,750.00
Figurine, Siamese cat, 6¾x4½" 125.00
Figurine, skater holds out skirt of purple dress, Dakan, 11" 500.00
Figurine, Yankee Doodle Dandy, 7" 100.00
Figurine, 3 sailor girls step in unison, '25, 16", EX 7,700.00
Mask, Deco-style face, terra cotta, 9½x6¼" 350.00

Gonder

Lawton Gonder grew up with clay in his hands and fire in his eyes.

Gonder's interest in ceramics was greatly influenced by his parents who worked for Weller and a close family friend and noted ceramic authority, John Herold. In his early teens Gonder launched his ceramic career at the Ohio Pottery Company while working for Herold. He later gained valuable experience at American Encaustic Tile Company, Cherry Art Tile, and the Florence Pottery. Gonder was plant manager at the Florence Pottery until fire destroyed the facility in late 1941.

After years of solid production and management experience, Lawton Gonder established the Gonder Ceramic Art Company, formerly the Peters and Reed plant, in South Zanesville, Ohio. Gonder Ceramic Arts produced quality art pottery with beautiful contemporary designs which included human and animal figures and a complete line of Oriental pottery. Accentuating the beautiful shapes were unique and innovative glazes developed by Gonder such as flambe (flame red with streaks of yellow), 24k gold crackle, antique gold, and Chinese crackle.

All Gonder is marked with the company name and mold number. They include 'Gonder U.S.A' in block letters, 'Gonder' in script, 'Gonder Original' in script, and 'Gonder Ceramic Art' in block letters. Paper labels were also used. Some of the early Gonder molds closely resemble RumRill designs that had been manufactured at the Florence Pottery. Because some RumRill pieces are found with similar (if not identical) shapes, matching mold numbers, and Gonder glazes, it is speculated that some RumRill was produced at the Gonder plant. In 1946 Gonder started another company which he named Elgee (chosen for his initials LG) where he manufactured lamp bases until a fire in 1954 resulted in his shifting lamp production to the main plant. Operations ceased in 1957. Our advisors for this category are Marilyn and John McCormick; they are listed in the Directory under Kansas.

Bowl, lime gr w/wht drip, sq, #733, 2¾x6½x6½" 5.00
Bowl, Ming Bl, hexagonal, #742, 5x8½" 20.00
Bowl, oblong, flower design, J-71, 4½x12" 27.00
Cookie jar, yel, brn drip, plain lid, P-24, 8½x8" 18.00
Deer head, yel/brn, #518, 9¼" 20.00

Figure of two prancing deers, green, #690, 6½x10", $22.00.

Jug, water; wht w/purple drip, hdls, E-48, 6½" 9.00
Planter, nude frolicking w/deer, #593, 9½x14" 65.00
Planter, Pegasus, #553, 6½x8" 45.00
Planter, swan, #802, 10x6" 15.00
Vase, Chinese, dbl hdls, H-56, 8" 9.00
Vase, cornucopia; 2 rings, #308, 6" 8.00
Vase, fan form, K-15, 11½x10½" 18.00
Vase, horn shaped, H-14, 9" 13.00
Vase, horn shaped w/lg ft, H-84, 8" 18.00
Vase, lime gr w/wht drip, cylindrical, #711, 8½x5" 12.00
Vase, poinsettia design, H-79, 8" 15.00

Vase, spittoon; gr w/brn drip, #559, 8x7½" 30.00
Vase, sq base & top, bulbous, E-71/#771, 6½" 9.00
Vase, sq w/indented sides, #384, 5x5" 15.00
Vase, 3 hdls per side, H-75, 9" 14.00

Goofus Glass

Goofus was an inexpensive type of lustre-painted pressed glassware made by many companies during the first two decades of the 20th century. Bowls and trays are most common, and red and gold combinations are found more often than blues and greens.

Bonbon, strawberry & flower pod, dome ft, orig pnt, 4" dia 42.50
Bowl, berry; Bird & Strawberry, +4 ind bowls 145.00
Bowl, dahlia, scalloped, gold, ornate, 10x4" 50.00
Bowl, field flowers, crimpled & ruffled rim, orig pnt, 3½x8" 45.00
Bowl, Grape & Cable, red/gold on clear, 10", NM 24.00
Bowl, Grape & Lattice, minor rstr, 2x6½" 42.50
Bowl, grapes on amethyst, scalloped, sq, orig pnt, 10", EX 75.00
Bowl, Wheel & Block, red/gold on opal, scalloped/crimped, 9" 35.00
Cake plate, acorn & leaf, amethyst, 12" 20.00
Cake plate, Rose in Snow, 11" 18.00
Candy dish, Grape & Cable, rpt, 5¼x2" 27.50
Lamp, fairy; roses, flash-fired gr, 3 holes for smoke, 7" 35.00
Lamp, Nosegay, oil-burning, #2, EX orig pnt 155.00
Lamp, oil; cabbage rose, milk glass, mini, 9" 58.00
Pin tray, basketweave, red rose on gold, orig pnt, 4½" L 27.50
Plate, grapes in center, fancy gold rim, orig pnt, 8½" 45.00
Plate, holly, opal w/orig pnt, 10½", NM 48.00
Plate, monk drinking, rose edge, orig pnt, rare, 7", EX 35.00
Shakers, poppy, EX orig pnt, 3", pr 35.00
Tumbler, grapes, gold on crackle, orig pnt, 4", NM 48.00

Vase, Lovebirds, original paint, 10", $65.00.

Vase, dogwood blossoms, gold on milk glass, 5" 18.00
Vase, dogwood blossoms, baluster, orig pnt, 15" 50.00
Vase, dogwood blossoms & hearts, 6-sided, EX orig pnt, 15" 42.50
Vase, mixed fruit, rpt gold on clear, 10" 37.50
Vase, peacock in a tree, red/gr/gold, M orig pnt, 15" 100.00
Vase, rose, red on gold crackle, rpt, 14" 55.00
Vase, Statue of Liberty & Am Eagle, no pnt, 1880-1920, 12⅜" 90.00
Water bottle, grapes on crackle, no pnt, 7½" 35.00

Goss and Crested China

William Henry Goss received his early education at the Govern-

ment School of Design and as a result of his merit was introduced to Alderman William Copeland, who owned a large pottery firm. Under the influence of Copeland, Goss quickly learned the trade and soon became their chief designer. Little is known about this brief association, and in 1858 Goss left to begin his own business. After a short-lived partnership with a Mr. Peake, Goss opened a pottery on John Street, Stoke-on-Trent, but by 1870 he had moved to his business to a location near London Road. This pottery became the famous Falcon Works. Their mark was a spread-wing falcon centering a narrow, horizontal bar with 'W.H. Goss' printed below.

Many of the early pieces made by Goss were left unmarked and are difficult to discern from products made by the Copeland factory, but after he had been in business for about fifteen years, all of his wares were marked. Today unmarked items do not command the prices of the later marked wares.

Adulphus William Henry Goss joined his father's firm in the 1880s. He introduced cheaper lines, though the more expensive lines continued in production. Shortly after his father's death in 1906, Adulphus retired and left the business to his two younger brothers. The business suffered from problems created by a war economy, and in 1936 Goss assets were held by Cauldron Potteries Ltd. These were eventually taken over by the Coalport Group, who retained the right to use the Goss trademark. Messrs. Ridgeway Potteries bought all the assets in 1954 as well as the right to use the Goss trademark and name. Now it remains to be seen if Goss ware will ever be produced again. Our advisor for this category is Patrick Herley; he is listed in the Directory under New York.

Basket, fish 25.00
Beer barrel 10.00
Beer bowl, dragon 18.00
Beer bowl, Lorre 18.00
Bottle, Waterlooville, Army Water 27.50
Bowl, Acanthus Rose 40.00
Bowl, Christ Church Ancient 8.00
Bucket, milk; Swiss 12.00
Bucket, Norwegian 20.00
Carafe, Goodwin Sands 8.50
Creamer, Yarmouth, sm 10.00
Cup & saucer, flags decor (war allies) 35.00
Ewer, Arundel 15.00
Ewer, Doncaster 15.00
Ewer, Folkestone 12.00
Ewer, Hertford 12.50
Ewer, Japan, 3½" 20.00
Ewer, Shrewsbury, 4" 18.00
First & Last House 115.00
Flask, Caerleon Tear 12.00
Jug, Dorchester 12.00
Jug, Kendall, Assyrian Armor 21.50
Jug, Reading 10.00
Jug, Scarborough 13.00
Jug, St George 15.00
Look Out House 110.00
Manx Cottage 85.00
Milk can, Welsh, w/lid 15.00
Mortar, Hythe Gromwellian 12.00
Nogen, Irish, wood 18.50
Pipkin, Southampton, sm 8.00
Pitcher, Cambridge 18.00
Pitcher, Devon Oak, sm 10.00
Pitcher, Leiston 5.00
Rufus Stone 18.00
Sabot, Dutch 35.00

Tobacco jar, terra cotta, 5½", EX	45.00
Tyg, 1-hdl	8.50
Tyg, 2-hdl	9.50
Urn, Doncaster	9.50
Urn, Laxey, Hunting	22.50
Urn, Minster	15.00
Urn, Nottingham	13.00
Vase, bud; sm	10.00
Vase, Glastonbury	10.00
Vase, Southwold, 6"	30.00
Yorick's Skull, sm	65.00

Gouda

Since the 18th century the main center of the pottery industry in Holland was in Gouda. One of its earliest industries, the manufacture of clay pipes, continues to the present day. The artware so easily recognized by collectors today was first produced about 1885. It was decorated in the Art Nouveau manner. Stylized florals, birds, and geometrics were favored motifs; only rarely is the scene naturalistic. The Nouveau influence was strong until about 1915. Art Deco was attempted but with less success. Though most of the ware is finished in a matt glaze, glossy pieces in both pastels and dark colors are found on occasion and command higher prices. Decoration on the glossy ware is usually very well executed. Most of the workshops failed during the Depression, though earthenware is still being made in Gouda and carries the Gouda mark. Until very recently Regina was still making a limited amount of the old Gouda-style pottery in a matt finish. Watch for the Gouda name, which is usually a part of the backstamp of the various manufacturers.

Biscuit jar, florals, mc on blk, SP mts, 5"	145.00
Bowl, florals, mc, mk Pelta, hdls, 9"	95.00
Candlestick, Nouveau motif, mc on wht, mk Regina, 4½", pr	95.00
Candlestick, wide flaring base, #921, sgn, 7", pr	265.00
Creamer, Verona	50.00
Lantern candle holder, pierced design, rim hdl, 9½"	350.00
Planter, Dutch shoe	70.00
Plaque, village/harbor, artist sgn/house mk, 1910, 12x16"	770.00
Tray, floral, mc w/gold trim, 11" dia	110.00

Vase, birds and flowers, glossy glaze, marked AB #1203, 8½", $550.00.

Vase, birds of paradise/foliage, integral hdls, Zuid, 17"	700.00
Vase, flowers & S-scrolls on umber, neck hdls, Ivora, 17"	1,100.00
Vase, lg stylized orchids, sgn AR, house mk,17"	650.00
Vase, mc Art Deco sunburst, Arnhem, 2½"	45.00

Vase, Nouveau motif w/irises, bl/gold on gr, 13"	330.00
Vase, realistic floral on wht, mk NP S8, facing pr, 16"	1,300.00
Wall pocket, mc motif, 7"	50.00

Graniteware

Graniteware, made of a variety of metals with enamel coatings, derives its name from its appearance. The speckled, swirled, or mottled effect of the vari-colored enamels may look like granite — but there the resemblance stops. It wasn't especially durable! Expect at least minor chipping if you plan to collect.

Graniteware was featured in 1876 at Phily's Expo. It was mass-produced in quantity, and enough of it has survived to make at least the common items easily affordable. Color, shape, and size are important considerations in evaluating an item; cobalt blue and white, green and white, brown and white, and old red and white swirled items are unusual, thus more expensive. Pieces of heavier weight, seam constructed, riveted, and those with wooden handles and tin lids are usually older.

For further study we recommend *The Collector's Encyclopedia of Graniteware, Colors, Shapes, and Values*, Books I and II, by our advisor, Helen Greguire. Both are available from the author. For information on how to order, see her listing in the Directory under New York. For the address of the National Graniteware Society, see the section on Clubs, Newsletters, and Catalogs.

Biscuit sheet, bl & wht lg swirl, 11x8½", NM	975.00
Bowl, fruit; solid bl w/fancy cutouts, 9" dia, VG	110.00
Bowl, waste; brn & wht relish, pewter trim, ring hdls, squat	350.00
Bread pan, bl & wht fine mottle w/blk trim, oval, NM	155.00
Bucket, berry; robin's egg bl, NM	95.00
Bucket, lunch; rnd, gray, EX	50.00
Bucket, slop; wht w/grapes & leaves, wood-wrapped hdl, NM	175.00
Butter dish, gray med mottle, seamless, spun knob, sm, NM	425.00
Can, Boston cream; cobalt & wht lg swirl, w/tin lid, NM	395.00
Can, milk; gr & wht lg swirl, bl trim, Emerald Ware, NM	385.00
Candle holder, brn mottle, EX	30.00
Candlestick, wht to dk maroon w/gold trim, #449-16, VG, ea	135.00
Chamber pot, bl swirl, EX	155.00
Churn, wht, cobalt trim/letters, floor-model dasher type, VG	1,295.00
Coffee biggin, bl & wht lg mottle 'snow on mtn,' tall, 4-pc	395.00
Coffee biggin, bl & wht lg swirl, aluminum spreader, 4-pc, M	385.00
Coffee biggin, gray med mottle, tin biggin, 4-pc, M	225.00
Coffee biggin, red & wht med mottle, 4-pc, NM	565.00
Coffee biggin, solid yel w/blk trim, Bakelite knob, 5-pc, M	195.00
Coffee biggin, wht w/bl trim, hdld, squat, 4-pc, M	135.00
Coffee boiler, bl swirl, EX	225.00
Coffee boiler, gr & wht lg swirl, Emerald Ware, NM	400.00
Coffee boiler, red-brn & wht med mottle, Garnet Ware, NM	295.00
Coffee flask, brn & wht fine mottle, metal top, Onyx Ware, NM	385.00
Coffee flask, gray med mottle, rnd, seamless, 5", M	425.00
Coffee flask, solid bl, metal top, 4½x3½", NM	385.00
Coffee urn, gray med mottle, riveted hdl, brass spigot, NM	245.00
Coffeepot, bl & wht lg swirl, loop finial, VG	210.00
Coffeepot, bl solid, lg, EX	65.00
Coffeepot, dk gr & wht lg swirl, Chrysolite, NM	350.00
Coffeepot, gr & wht lg swirl, Emerald Ware, VG	395.00
Coffeepot, gray, tin lid, 8", VG	45.00
Coffeepot, gray lg mottle, pewter trim, copper bottom, M	275.00
Coffeepot, lav & wht med swirl, Purity Ware, NM	795.00
Coffeepot, robin's egg bl, wooden hdl, EX	100.00
Coffeepot, shaded sea gr to moss gr, Shamrock Ware, M	225.00
Coffeepot, wht w/bachelor buttons, pewter trim, hinged, M	225.00

Colander, bl swirl, NM 85.00
Colander, cobalt & wht lg swirl, blk trim, deep, ftd, M 275.00
Colander, robin's egg bl, EX 55.00

Cream can, gray mottle, 5", M, $195.00.

Creamer, gray lg mottle, pewter trim, M 325.00
Cup, muffin; gray med mottle, Agate Nickel Steel, ind, VG 45.00
Cuspidor, lt bl & wht lg swirl, blk trim, seamless, M 365.00
Dinner carrier, stacking; bl & wht lg mottle, Paragon, NM 450.00
Dipper, cocoa; shaded bl w/blk trim, Bluebelle Ware, VG 265.00
Dipper, suds; gray med mottle, seamless, hdl, VG 65.00
Dish, pudding; cobalt & wht lg swirl, wht int, oblong, NM 185.00
Dish, pudding; yel & wht lg swirl, blk trim, 1920s, oval, M 165.00
Dish pan, gray, lg 35.00
Double boiler, bl & wht lg mottle 'snow on mtn,' blk trim, M 165.00
Dough riser, gray, EX 135.00
Dust pan, lt gray med mottle, rivet hdl, ridged bottom, VG 195.00
Egg cup, dbl; wht w/wild rose, dk brn trim, center hdl, NM 225.00
Egg plate, shirred; bl & wht med mottle, cobalt trim, oval, VG .135.00
Egg poacher, blk & wht lg mottle, Buffalo Steam, 5-cup, NM 295.00
Food warmer, end-of-day lg swirl, ftd, hdls, w/lid, NM 425.00
Fry pan, dk gray-lav & wht lg swirl on CI, Lava Ware, NM 185.00
Fry pan, red w/blk trim, wht int, child's, M 95.00
Funnel, gr & wht lg mottle, bl trim, squat, Emerald Ware, NM ...395.00
Funnel, gray, lg, EX 60.00
Funnel, gray, 4", EX 40.00
Grater, gray med mottle, flat, Ideal, NM 495.00
Grater, revolving, wht w/bl windmill, Alice Duplex, VG 150.00
Honeypot, cobalt & wht lg swirl, squat, M 395.00
Kettle, gray, 15", EX 45.00
Kettle, preserving; bl & wht lg mottle, blk trim & hdl, NM 175.00
Ladle, soup; brn & wht, blk trim & hdl, Onyx Ware, NM 30.00
Ladle, soup; cream & gr, M 20.00
Ladle, soup; gray med mottle, blk wood trn hdl, NM 95.00
Ladle rack, teal bl w/gold edge, +3 utensils 95.00
Match holder, dbl pocket, solid lt gray on CI, M 495.00
Measure, bl & wht lg swirl, seamless, Lava Ware, NM 435.00
Measure, solid bl w/floral decor, cobalt trim & hdl, VG 75.00
Mold, rabbit, solid wht, fluted, NM 245.00
Mold, Turk's head, bl & wht chicken wire, EX 70.00
Muffin tin, cobalt swirl in & out, 8-cup, EX 325.00
Muffin tin, gray, 8-cup, EX 50.00
Mug, cobalt & wht lg swirl w/blk trim, flared base, baby sz, M ...235.00
Mug, dk gr & wht lg swirl w/blk trim, Chrysolite, NM 115.00
Mug, soup; cobalt & wht lg swirl, blk trim, w/lid, 1960s, M 75.00
Oyster patty, gray med mottle, 3-shell ft, VG 235.00

Pail, chamber; bl & wht lg swirl w/lid, Columbian Ware, NM ...250.00
Pail, water; gray, EX 25.00
Pan, baking; bl & wht chicken wire, sq, Paragon Ware, VG 115.00
Pan, cornstick; solid red, cream int, mk #273 Griswold, M 345.00
Pan, lady finger; cobalt & lg swirl, M 1,200.00
Pan, lady finger; gray, EX 295.00
Pan, sauce; brn & wht lg swirl, blk trim & hdl, w/lip, VG 115.00
Pan, tart; bl & wht fine mottle, wht int, M 65.00
Pie plate, gr & wht lg swirl, blk trim, Emerald Ware, VG 60.00
Pitcher, end-of-day confetti, salesman's sample, NM 235.00
Pitcher, gray, water sz, EX 75.00
Pitcher, milk; bl & wht fine mottle, blk trim & hdl, M 175.00
Pitcher, molasses; wht & bl checks, Elite, VG 245.00
Plate, dessert; aqua-gr & wht lg swirl, cobalt trim, VG 110.00
Plate, luncheon; brn & wht lg swirl, blk trim, 6", NM 115.00
Platter, bl & wht lg swirl, wht int, oval, M 250.00
Potty, cobalt & wht lg swirl, blk trim, child sz, NM 125.00
Roaster, bl & wht lg swirl, perforated ft, 2-pc, M 295.00
Roaster, brn swirl, w/insert, EX 185.00
Roaster, lt gray mottled, rnd 100.00
Roaster, robin's egg blue, Lisk, w/insert, med sz, EX 90.00
Rolling pin, wht w/gray screw-on hdls, CI base, M 875.00
Salt box, bl solid 110.00
Salt box, red & wht feather, red & gold trim, w/lid, NM 425.00
Salt box, wht & lt bl chicken wire, VG 225.00
Saucer, wht w/dk gr trim, Savory Ware, M 25.00
Scoop, grocer's; gray, EX 85.00
Scoop, spice; gray med mottle, pieced bk, rivet hdl, ca 1912 ......265.00
Skimmer, bl & wht fine mottle, perforated, flat, NM 65.00
Skimmer, blk & wht med mottle, perforated, flat, VG 85.00
Soup plate, cobalt & wht lg swirl, EX 140.00
Soup tureen, gray med mottle, blk wood hdl inserts, oval, VG ...325.00
Spatula, gray med mottle, brick-red hdl, NM 95.00
Spatula, wht & lt bl chicken wire, perforated, VG 135.00
Spittoon, bl swirl, EX 155.00
Spoon, cake; brn & wht med mottle, slotted, Onyx Ware, EX 75.00
Spoon, ice cream; gray & wht fine mottle, wood hdl, EX 135.00
Strainer, gravy; gray mottle, perforated insert, ftd, EX 145.00
Sugar bowl, solid lt bl, squat, Meinecke, NM 165.00
Syrup, solid gray, NM 145.00
Tea steeper, gray mottle, NM 95.00
Teakettle, gr & wht lg swirl, blk trim, wood knob, squat, M 375.00
Teakettle, gray med mottle, Granite Iron Ware, 1-qt, NM 325.00
Teapot, bl & wht fine mottle, lid w/glass insert, NM 250.00
Teapot, end-of-day med mottle, Royal Granite Steel Ware, VG ...365.00
Teapot, gray, gooseneck style, EX 90.00
Teapot, gray lg mottle, labeled Cream City Gray Ware, M 225.00

Teapot, pewter mounts on white body with heron and rushes, 11", $295.00.

Teapot, reddish-brn & wht fine mottle, pewter & brass trim, M ...**285.00**
Teapot, solid cobalt, gooseneck, EX **65.00**
Teapot, solid cobalt, shaped thumb rest, NM **165.00**
Toothbrush holder, wht & lg bl lg mottle, w/perforated lid, VG ..**65.00**
Tray, gray med mottle, oval, NM **145.00**
Tray, lt bl & wht lg swirl, wht int, rnd, NM **155.00**
Trivet, wht w/flying ducks, rnd, 3 molded ft, hdl, M **75.00**
Utensil rack, cream w/red decor, w/3 orig utensils, VG **325.00**
Wash basin, lav-bl & wht lg swirl, lg, VG **95.00**
Washboard, charcoal gray & wht med mottle, Pearl Enamel, NM .**155.00**

Green Opaque

Introduced in 1887 by the New England Glass Company, this ware is very scarce due to the fact that it was produced for less than one year. It is characterized by its soft green color and a wavy band of gold reserving a mottled blue metallic stain. It is usually found in satin; examples with a shiny finish are extremely rare.

Bowl, everted rim, shallow, 7" **750.00**
Bowl, scalloped gold in EX mottled border, 4" **600.00**
Bowl vase, NM gold & mottling, 3x4¼" **850.00**
Cruet, tricorn, 6" **1,150.00**
Shakers, squat, 2¾", pr **475.00**
Spooner, 3¾" **850.00**
Tumbler, lemonade; w/hdl, 5" **900.00**
Tumbler, 3¼" **725.00**
Tumbler, Optic Ribs, fine mottling, gold border **650.00**
Vase, flared, M gold & mottling, 6" **900.00**

Greenaway, Kate

Kate Greenaway was an English artist who lived from 1846 to 1901. She gained worldwide fame as an illustrator of children's books, drawing children clothed in the styles worn by proper English and American boys and girls of the very early 1800s. Her book, *Under the Willow Tree*, published in 1878, was the first of many. Her sketches appeared in leading magazines, and her greeting cards were in great demand. Manufacturers of china, pottery, and metal products copied her characters to decorate children's dishes, tiles, and salt and pepper shakers as well as many other items. See also Almanacs; Napkin Rings.

Salt and pepper shakers, no mark, 4¾", $135.00 for the pair.

Almanac, Greenaway illus, 1892, EX **85.00**
Almanac, London, Rutledge, 1888, VG **75.00**

Book, B'day Book for Children, London/NY, 1880, 1st ed, VG ..**145.00**
Book, Calendar of Seasons, London, Marcus Ward, 1881, EX **100.00**
Book, Pictures...Presented to Ruskin, London 1921, jacket, EX ..**315.00**
Butter pat, children playing **40.00**
Cup & saucer, pk lustre trim **125.00**
Figurine, girl sits in wicker basket, English, 6x6", NM **90.00**
Figurine, seated girl tugs on lg hat, bsk, sm **55.00**
Match safe, SP, emb children, sm **50.00**
Napkin ring, girl & boy w/pail, inscr Jack & Jill, Tufts **450.00**
Napkin ring, girl on stomach, ring on bk, Wilcox **300.00**
Napkin ring, girl w/rifle on sq ftd base **325.00**
Pitcher, milk; figural girl, head is lid, bsk, 6½" **165.00**
Plate, children at play, fruit, birds & flowers, 9" **100.00**
Plate, girl in lg hat, Staffordshire, 7" **85.00**
Stickpin holder, figural girl, Meriden SP, 4" **125.00**

Greentown Glass

Greentown glass is a term referring to the product of the Indiana Tumbler and Goblet Company of Greentown, Indiana, ca 1894 to 1903. Their earlier pressed glass patterns were #11, a pseudo-cut glass design; #137, Pleat Band; and #200, Austrian. Another line, Dewey, was designed in 1898. Many lovely colors were produced in addition to crystal. Jacob Rosenthal, who was later affiliated with Fenton, developed his famous chocolate glass in 1900. The rich, shaded opaque brown glass was an overnight success. Two new patterns, Leaf Bracket and Cactus, were designed to display the glass to its best advantage, but previously existing molds were also used. In only three years Rosenthal developed yet another important color formula, golden agate. The Holly Amber pattern was designed especially for its production. The Dolphin covered dish with a fish finial is perhaps the most common and easily recognized piece ever produced. Other animal dishes were also made; all are highly collectible. There have been many repros — not all are marked!

Our advisors for this category are Jerry and Sandy Garrett; they are listed in the Directory under Indiana. See the Pattern Glass section for clear pressed glass, only colored items are listed here.

Animal dish, bird w/berry, chocolate (+) **850.00**
Animal dish, bird w/berry, Nile gr **1,800.00**
Animal dish, bird w/berry, teal bl **275.00**
Animal dish, cat on hamper, canary, low **600.00**
Animal dish, cat on hamper, chocolate, low **600.00**
Animal dish, cat on hamper, emerald gr, tall, 4½" (+) **275.00**
Animal dish, cat on hamper, teal bl, tall, 4½" **275.00**
Animal dish, cat on hamper, wht opaque, tall, 4½" **450.00**
Animal dish, dolphin, beaded, amber **550.00**
Animal dish, dolphin, beaded, cobalt **600.00**
Animal dish, dolphin, beaded, golden agate **850.00**
Animal dish, dolphin, sawtooth, amber (+) **625.00**
Animal dish, dolphin, sawtooth, canary **600.00**
Animal dish, dolphin, smooth, chocolate **400.00**
Animal dish, fighting cocks, amber **850.00**
Animal dish, fighting cocks, cobalt **950.00**
Animal dish, fighting cocks, wht opaque **1,250.00**
Animal dish, hen on nest, canary **350.00**
Animal dish, hen on nest, chocolate **700.00**
Animal dish, hen on nest, cobalt **425.00**
Animal dish, hen on nest, golden agate **1,500.00**
Animal dish, rabbit, cobalt **425.00**
Animal dish, rabbit, teal bl **175.00**
Animal dish, rabbit, wht opaque (+) **160.00**
Austrian, bowl, canary, 8" **225.00**

Austrian, butter dish, canary 375.00
Austrian, cordial, emerald gr 235.00
Austrian, creamer, chocolate, child's 250.00
Austrian, creamer, cobalt, child's 250.00
Austrian, nappy, chocolate, w/lid 265.00
Austrian, rose bowl, canary, sm 190.00
Austrian, sugar bowl, chocolate, w/lid, 2½" dia 175.00
Austrian, tumbler, amber 250.00
Austrian, vase, Nile gr, 6" 375.00
Beehive, tumbler, chocolate 500.00
Brazen Shield, cake stand, bl, 9⅜" 225.00
Brazen Shield, creamer, bl 100.00
Brazen Shield, sugar bowl, bl, w/lid 175.00
Cactus, bowl, chocolate, 5¼" 115.00
Cactus, cheese dish, chocolate, ped ft 700.00
Cactus, creamer, chocolate 170.00
Cactus, plate, chocolate, 7¼" 115.00

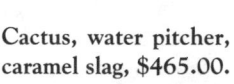
Cactus, water pitcher,
caramel slag, $465.00.

Cord Drapery, bowl, amber, 8" 145.00
Cord Drapery, butter dish, cobalt, 4¾" 300.00
Cord Drapery, creamer, emerald gr, 4¼" 165.00
Cord Drapery, syrup, chocolate 210.00
Cupid, butter dish, Nile gr 450.00
Cupid, creamer, chocolate 350.00
Cupid, sugar bowl, wht opaque 115.00
Dewey, bowl, chocolate, 8" 275.00
Dewey, bowl, emerald gr, 8" 80.00
Dewey, butter dish, cobalt, 4" 200.00
Dewey, cruet, chocolate, w/stopper 1,500.00
Dewey, parfait, canary, open 80.00
Dewey, sugar bowl, cobalt, w/lid, 2½" 160.00
Diamond Prisms, tumbler, chocolate 600.00
Early Diamond, bowl, cobalt, rectangular, 8x5" 150.00
Early Diamond, tumbler, chocolate 175.00
Fleur-de-Lis, celery holder, chocolate, 5¾" 325.00
Fleur-de-Lis, pitcher, chocolate 1,000.00
Fleur-de-Lis, tumbler, chocolate 140.00
Greentown Daisy, butter dish, frosted emerald gr 115.00
Greentown Daisy, creamer, chocolate 195.00
Greentown Daisy, mustard, chocolate, w/lid 190.00
Herringbone Buttress, bowl, emerald gr, 6¼" 225.00
Herringbone Buttress, cordial, amber, 3" 365.00
Herringbone Buttress, cordial, olive gr, 3⅜" 175.00
Herringbone Buttress, vase, emerald gr, 8" 235.00
Holly, spooner, rose agate 9,000.00
Holly, toothpick holder, wht agate 3,500.00
Holly Amber, bowl, oval 450.00
Holly Amber, butter dish 1,800.00

Holly Amber, compote, jelly; w/lid, 4½" 1,300.00
Holly Amber, compote, w/lid, 7¼" 1,700.00
Holly Amber, creamer, beaded rim, 4½" 750.00
Holly Amber, pitcher 2,950.00
Holly Amber, sugar bowl, plain rim, ped ft, w/lid 2,750.00
Holly Amber, tumbler (+) 550.00
Leaf Bracket, butter dish, cobalt 1,200.00
Leaf Bracket, plate, chocolate, 7½" 115.00
Leaf Bracket, sauce, wht opaque 125.00
Mug, indoor drinking scene, chocolate, 8½" 550.00
Mug, indoor drinking scene, Nile gr, 5" 150.00
Mug, Pepperbox, chocolate 325.00
Mug, Serenade, amber, 4¾" 115.00
Mug, Serenade, cobalt, 4¾" 350.00
Novelty, buffalo, wht opaque, dtd 1901 ....400.00
Novelty, Connecticut Skillet, Nile gr 500.00
Novelty, corn vase, amber, 4⅝" 175.00
Novelty, Dewey bust, teal bl, w/base 185.00
Novelty, hairbrush, chocolate 1,000.00
Novelty, Indian head, emerald gr, w/lid 600.00
Novelty, wheelbarrow, Nile gr (+) 290.00
Pattern #11, bowl, gr, rectangular, 8x6½" 80.00
Pattern #11, vase, emerald gr, 8" 75.00
Pitcher, heron, chocolate 575.00
Pitcher, Paneled, chocolate 575.00
Pitcher, squirrel, chocolate 500.00
Pleat Band, compote, chocolate, plain stem, smooth rim, 4¼" ...165.00
Pleat Band, cordial, canary 200.00
Pleat Band, shaker, teal bl 65.00
Pleat Band, wine, canary 150.00
Scalloped Flange, tumbler, chocolate 150.00
Scalloped Flange, vase, chocolate 85.00
Shuttle, butter dish, chocolate 950.00
Shuttle, creamer, chocolate 550.00
Shuttle, creamer, chocolate, tankard form 90.00
Shuttle, goblet, chocolate 800.00
Shuttle, nappy, chocolate 185.00
Shuttle, shaker, chocolate 325.00
Teardrop & Tassel, bowl, Nile gr, 8¼" 400.00
Teardrop & Tassel, creamer, amber 195.00
Teardrop & Tassel, pickle dish, teal bl 140.00
Teardrop & Tassel, sugar bowl, wht opaque, w/lid 100.00
Toothpick holder, dog head, amber frost 300.00
Toothpick holder, dog head, bl frost 325.00
Toothpick holder, picture fr, amber 250.00
Toothpick holder, sheaf of wheat, Nile gr 325.00
Toothpick holder, witch's head, Nile gr (+) 165.00
Tumbler, Panelled, chocolate 475.00
Tumbler, Sawtooth, chocolate 100.00

Grueby

William Henry Grueby joined the firm of the Low Art Tile Works at the age of fifteen and in 1894, after several years of experience in the production of architectural tiles, founded his own plant, the Grueby Faience Company in Boston, Massachusetts. Grueby began experimenting with the idea of producing art pottery and had soon perfected a fine glaze (soft and without gloss) in shades of blue, gray, yellow, brown, and his most successful, cucumber green. In 1900 his exhibit at the Paris Exposition Universelle won three gold medals.

Grueby pottery was hand thrown and hand decorated in the Arts and Crafts style. Vertically thrust stylized leaves and flowers in relief were the most common decorative devices. Tiles continued to be an important product, unique (due to the matt glaze decoration) as well as durable. Grueby tiles were often a full inch thick. Obviously incompatible with the Art Nouveau style, the artware was discontinued soon after 1910. The ware is marked in one of several ways: 'Grueby Pottery, Boston, USA'; 'Grueby, Boston, Mass.'; or 'Grueby Faience.' The artware is often artist signed. Our advisor for this category is David Rago; he is listed in the Directory under New Jersey.

Candlestick, dk gr, leaves, invt trumpet w/bulb top, 9" 500.00
Lamp, gr, leaves, rnd w/can neck, ldgl 14" panel shade, 15" ...2,000.00
Lamp base/vase, bl/bsk, groups of 5-petal flowers, 14x8" 2,500.00
Paperweight, brn, scarab form, 4" 330.00
Plaque, bl w/child swathed in wht robes, sgn PS, 12" dia 220.00
Tile, gr w/yel tulip & 4 leaves, 6" 770.00
Tile, 3-color, 2 trees/hills, sgn MCM, 6" 850.00
Tile, 6-color, Baker's Chocolate Cocoa lady, AF, 6", EX 365.00

Vase, 6-sided with leaves in green, 8x5", $1,500.00; Vase, 'watermelon,' leaves and buds under leathery green, 13x8", $3,500.00; Tile, candle holder in green, yellow, and black, 6x6", $800.00.

Vase, curdled gr, 7 tooled/appl leaves, #39, sgn, 8x7" 2,900.00
Vase, dk gr, leaves on bulbous base, 5-panel can neck, 7x4" 700.00
Vase, dk gr, tapered cylinder, 4½" 275.00
Vase, dk gr, tooled/appl leaves, sgn MS, ovoid, #16, 9" 1,500.00
Vase, dk gr showing wht on high points of leaves/buds, 12x8" ...3,500.00
Vase, elephant skin gr, tooled/appl leaves, sgn WP, 3x5" 900.00
Vase, gr, cut-bk leaves, tiny neck, rstr rim, rnd, 4x4" 325.00
Vase, gr, heavy walled/hand thrown, bulbous base, 13" 1,300.00
Vase, gr, leaves on bulbous base, trefoils at rim, SP, 13" 2,500.00
Vase, gr, leaves w/curled edges, tooled/appl, 7½x5", EX 800.00
Vase, gr, lg leaves alternate w/buds, incurvate, 11" 4,000.00
Vase, gr, oval leaves on bulbous bottom, long neck, 7" 1,000.00
Vase, gr, overlapping leaves on bulb base, #182, rstr, 10" 900.00
Vase, gr, overlapping vertical leaves, #140, rstr, 9x5" 1,200.00
Vase, gr w/yel buds at rim, top-to-base leaves, sgn WP, 12" 3,750.00
Vase, gr w/yel buds & leaves, squat, sgn Post, 4½x5" 3,250.00
Vase, lav, modeled leaves & buds, hand thrown, WP, 6x9" 3,000.00
Vase, med gr crackle matt, gourd shape, 7" 1,395.00
Vase, mustard yel texture, incurvate ovoid, kiln chips, 9" 875.00
Vase, yel, lt vertical ribbing, tiny rpr, 3x4" 280.00
Vase, yel crackle top/bsk bottom, spherical, 3¾x4" 375.00
Vase, 2 rows tooled/appl leaves on bulb base, Post, 20" 9,000.00
Vsae, gr, cvd oval leaves, silver palm leaf collar, WP, 8x8" 2,500.00

Gustavsberg

Gustavsberg Pottery, founded near Stockholm, Sweden, in the late 1700s, manufactured faience, creamware, and porcelain in the English taste until the end of the 19th century. During this century the factory

has produced some inventive modernistic designs, often signed by their artists. Wilhelm Kage (1889-1960) is best remembered for Argenta, a stoneware body decorated in silver overlay, introduced in the 1930s. Usually a mottled green, Argenta can also be found in cobalt blue and white. Other lines included Cintra (an execptionally translucent porcelain), Farsta (copper-glazed ware), and Farstarust (iron oxide geometric overlay). Designer Stig Lindberg's work, which dates from the 1940s through the early 1970s, includes slab-built figures and a full range of tableware. Some pieces of Gustavsberg are dated.

Figure, horse, stylized, sgn Stig L, 8" 350.00
Pin tray, silver o/l ocean liner on bl, 7x3" 95.00
Plate, lav floral transfer, 10" 35.00
Toothpick holder, silver o/l icicle on gr 45.00
Vase, bl/brn, teardrop form on tall can ft, mk Farsta, 7½" 225.00
Vase, floral vine, dk bl on lt bl, Ekberg, 1922, 8½" 395.00
Vase, silver o/l fish on gr, cylindrical, 6x2" 225.00
Vase, silver o/l mermaid on gr, triangular, 10" 750.00

Gutta Percha

Gutta percha is the plastic substance from the latex of several types of Malaysian trees. It resembles rubber but contains more resin. A patent for the use of this material in manufacturing an early type of plastic was issued in the 1850s, and it was used extensively for daguerreotype cases and picture frames. Numbers in the following listings refer to *American Miniature Case Art* by Rinhart, an excellent reference that is now out of print. When found, copies of this book usually sell for $100.00 to $150.00.

Box, Austrian man's portrait bevel-set on lid, sgn, 2½" dia 95.00
Box, collar; wheat/smithy tools/etc, Scovill Mfg, 1877, 5x5" 35.00
Box, stamp; president photo front, calendar bk, 1893, 1½" 55.00
Button, Victorian, 1" dia, 7 for 38.00

Case, Monitor and Fort, 3¾x3¼", EX, $95.00.

Case, Apple Picker, Rinhart #22, 6th plate, sm chip, EX 37.50
Case, Beehive w/Grain Border, Rinhart #20, 9th plate, VG 20.00
Case, Blind Beggar, Rinhart #27, 9th plate, VG 27.50
Case, Chess Players, Rinhart #41, 9th plate, VG 30.00
Case, Columbine floral pattern, Pat 1857 ....75.00
Case, Country Life, farm scene, Rinhart #15, half plate, VG 140.00
Case, Faithful Hound, Rinhart #40, 6th plate, NM 90.00
Case, floral emb, Littlefield & Parsons, dtd 1857, 1¾x2", M 75.00

Case, Fruited Bough, oval, 9th plate, VG 25.00
Case, geometric decor, 16th plate, EX 20.00
Case, goblet w/flowers, Wadham's, Rinhart #142, 9th plate, EX ..40.00
Case, Mary & Her Lamb, Rinhart #26, 9th plate, EX 40.00
Case, Meditating Monk, Rinhart ##9, 16th plate, VG 40.00
Case, Profile of a Patriarch, Rinhart #38, 6th plate, EX 60.00
Case, Seated Liberty, Rinhart #11, 6th plate, rpr, VG 20.00
Case, Wreath Theme, octagonal, Rinhart #159, 6th plate, VG 20.00
Mirror, hand; emb dragon amid florals on bk, ca 1870, 9" L 35.00

Hair Weaving

A rather unusual craft became popular during the mid-1800s. Human hair was used to make jewelry (rings, bracelets, lockets, etc.) by braiding and interlacing fine strands of hair into hollow forms with pearls and beads added for effect. Hair wreaths were also made, often using hair from deceased family members as well as the living. They were displayed in deep satin-lined frames along with mementoes of the weaver or her departed kin. The fad was abandoned before the turn of the century. Our advisor for this category is Steve DeGenaro; he is listed in the Directory under Ohio. See also Mourning Collectibles.

Bar pin, gold mt w/central ball of coiled hair 75.00
Bracelet, tube type w/gold clasp, 1800s, EX 175.00
Brooch, gold/blk enamel, woven garden scene, sm heart drop 250.00
Brooch, In Memory Of, blk enamel on gold, glass over hair 200.00
Pendant, cross form, lg 250.00
Ring, hair woven to resemble belt w/gold buckle 50.00

Hall

The Hall China Company of East Liverpool, Ohio, was established in 1903. Their earliest product was whiteware toilet seats, mugs, jugs, etc. By 1920 their restaurant-type dinnerware and cookingware had become so successful that Hall was assured of a solid future. They continue today to be one of the country's largest manufacturers of this type of product.

Hall introduced the first of their famous teapots in 1920; new shapes and colors were added each year until about 1948, making them the largest teapot manufacturer in the world. These and the dinnerware lines of the thirties through the fifties have become popular collectibles. For more thorough study of the subject, we recommend *The Collector's Encyclopedia of Hall China* by Margaret and Kenn Whitmyer; their address may be found in the Directory under Ohio.

Blue Bouquet, bean pot, New England, #4 ....125.00
Blue Bouquet, bowl, cereal; 6" 9.00
Blue Bouquet, bowl, Radiance, 6" 15.00
Blue Bouquet, bowl, salad; 9" 15.00
Blue Bouquet, bowl, Thick Rim, 6" 9.00
Blue Bouquet, bowl, vegetable; rnd, 9¼" 20.00
Blue Bouquet, cake plate 18.00
Blue Bouquet, casserole, Radiance 25.00
Blue Bouquet, coffeepot, Five Band 45.00
Blue Bouquet, drip jar, Thick Rim 20.00
Blue Bouquet, gravy boat 18.00
Blue Bouquet, pie baker 22.00
Blue Bouquet, plate, 6" 4.00
Blue Bouquet, platter, oval, 11¼" 18.00
Blue Bouquet, pretzel jar 125.00
Blue Bouquet, saucer 2.00
Blue Bouquet, shaker, hdld, ea 10.00

Blue Bouquet, soup tureen 175.00
Cameo Rose, bowl, cream soup; 5" 20.00
Cameo Rose, platter, oval, 15½" 18.00
Cameo Rose, tidbit tray, 3-tier 45.00
Caprice, ashtray 10.00
Caprice, gravy boat 15.00
Caprice, vinegar bottle 20.00
Coffeepot, Queen, red 75.00
Cookie jar, Five Band, ivory 25.00
Cookie jar, Sundial, red 115.00
Crocus, ball jug, #3 ....45.00
Crocus, bowl, cereal; 6" 12.00
Crocus, bowl, oval 18.00
Crocus, bowl, salad; 9" 18.00
Crocus, bowl, vegetable; rnd, 9¼" 18.00
Crocus, cake plate 25.00
Crocus, casserole, Radiance 25.00
Crocus, coffeepot, drip; Jordan 225.00
Crocus, creamer, Art Deco 20.00
Crocus, cup, St Denis 40.00
Crocus, custard 10.00
Crocus, mug, flagon style 75.00
Crocus, plate, 7¼" 5.00
Crocus, platter, oval, 11¼" 18.00
Crocus, saucer, St Denis 5.00
Crocus, shaker, hdld, ea 10.00
Crocus, soap dispenser 35.00
Crocus, sugar bowl, w/lid, Meltdown 45.00
Crocus, teapot, Aladdin 200.00
Crocus, water bottle, Zephy 325.00

**Fantasy batter pitcher, rare, 10½",
$250.00.**

Frost Flowers, candlestick, 4½" 15.00
Frost Flowers, vase 20.00
Hallcraft, Arizona, bowl, cereal; 6" 5.00
Hallcraft, Arizona, butter dish 30.00
Hallcraft, Arizona, vinegar bottle 20.00
Hallcraft, Bouquet, bowl, celery; oval 20.00
Hallcraft, Bouquet, egg cup 15.00
Hallcraft, Bouquet, ladle 10.00
Hallcraft, Buckingham, platter, 17" 20.00
Hallcraft, Buckingham, vase 20.00
Hallcraft, Fantasy, bowl, celery; oval 10.00
Hallcraft, Fantasy, candlestick, 8" 15.00
Hallcraft, Fantasy, platter, 17" 18.00
Hallcraft, Fern, bowl, vegetable; Eva Zeisel 15.00
Hallcraft, Fern, butter dish, Eva Zeisel 25.00
Hallcraft, Fern, plate, Eva Zeisel, 10¼" 6.00
Hallcraft, Fern, plate, Eva Zeisel, 8" 4.00
Hallcraft, Fern, platter, Eva Zeisel, 13¾" 15.00

Hallcraft, Fern, platter, Eva Zeisel, 15" 18.00
Hallcraft, Holiday, cookie jar 60.00
Hallcraft, Holiday, jug, 3-qt 18.00
Hallcraft, Mulberry, creamer 7.00
Harlequin, butter dish 35.00
Harlequin, teapot, Thorley 65.00
Heather Rose, bowl, salad; 9" 10.00
Heather Rose, pickle dish, 9" 12.00
Heather Rose, sugar bowl, w/lid 10.00
Heather Rose, teapot, London 30.00
Medallion, reamer, Lettuce 350.00
Mums, bowl, fruit; 5½" 5.00
Mums, bowl, salad; 9" 15.00
Mums, casserole, Medallion 35.00
Mums, coffeepot, Terrace 40.00
Mums, cup 8.00
Mums, custard 8.00
Mums, drip jar, w/lid, Medallion 20.00
Mums, jug, Simplicity 85.00
Mums, pie baker 20.00
Mums, platter, oval, 11¼" 15.00
Mums, saucer 2.00
Mums, sugar bowl, w/lid, Art Deco 20.00
Mums, teapot, New York 65.00
Orange Poppy, ball jug, #3 ....35.00
Orange Poppy, bowl, Radiance, 6" 10.00
Orange Poppy, bowl, salad 15.00
Orange Poppy, bowl, vegetable; rnd, 9¼" 25.00
Orange Poppy, bread box 35.00
Orange Poppy, cake safe 25.00
Orange Poppy, canister, Radiance 125.00
Orange Poppy, casserole, oval, 11¾" 70.00
Orange Poppy, coffeepot, Great American 45.00
Orange Poppy, custard 5.00
Orange Poppy, jug, Radiance, #4 ....35.00
Orange Poppy, match safe 20.00
Orange Poppy, pie baker 25.00
Orange Poppy, platter, oval, 11¼" 18.00
Orange Poppy, pretzel jar 80.00
Orange Poppy, saucer 2.00
Orange Poppy, sifter 40.00
Orange Poppy, spoon 65.00
Orange Poppy, tray, oval 20.00
Orange Poppy, wastebasket 35.00
Pastel Morning-Glory, ball jug, #3 ....35.00
Pastel Morning-Glory, bowl, fruit; 5½" 5.00
Pastel Morning-Glory, cake plate 18.00
Pastel Morning-Glory, casserole, Medallion 30.00
Pastel Morning-Glory, creamer, Art Deco 15.00
Pastel Morning-Glory, cup 8.00
Pastel Morning-Glory, jug, Donut 95.00
Pastel Morning-Glory, plate, 6" 4.00
Pastel Morning-Glory, platter, 11¼" 15.00
Pastel Morning-Glory, saucer 1.00
Pastel Morning-Glory, stack set, Radiance 50.00
Primrose, bowl, fruit; 5¼" 4.00
Primrose, platter, oval, 13¼" 12.00
Radiance, stack set, cobalt 50.00
Red Poppy, ball jug, #3 ....35.00
Red Poppy, bowl, oval, 10¼" 20.00
Red Poppy, bowl, Radiance, 6" 10.00
Red Poppy, bowl, salad; 9" 15.00
Red Poppy, cake safe 35.00
Red Poppy, canister, metal, 1-gal 20.00

Red Poppy, canister set, rnd, 5-pc 35.00
Red Poppy, casserole, Radiance 20.00
Red Poppy, creamer, Daniel 10.00
Red Poppy, cup 9.00
Red Poppy, custard 8.00
Red Poppy, hot pad 10.00
Red Poppy, jug, Radiance, #5 ....15.00
Red Poppy, mixer cover 18.00
Red Poppy, pie baker 20.00
Red Poppy, plate, 6" 3.00
Red Poppy, platter, oval, 11¼" 17.00
Red Poppy, saucer 1.00
Red Poppy, shaker, hdld, ea 8.00
Red Poppy, silverware box, wooden 40.00
Red Poppy, soap dispenser 30.00
Red Poppy, teapot, New York 55.00
Red Poppy, tray, rnd 20.00
Red Poppy, tumbler, clear 18.00
Red Poppy, waste can, rnd 33.00
Red Poppy, waxed paper dispenser 24.00
Sears' Arlington, pickle dish, 9" 5.00
Sears' Arlington, platter, oval, 15½" 15.00
Serenade, bowl, fruit; 5½" 4.00
Serenade, bowl, salad; 9" 12.00
Serenade, creamer, Art Deco 10.00
Serenade, platter, 13¼" 12.00
Silhouette, bowl, fruit; 5½" 5.00
Silhouette, bowl, Radiance, 9" 15.00
Silhouette, bowl, vegetable; rnd, 9¼" 25.00
Silhouette, canister set, metal, 4-pc 50.00
Silhouette, creamer, Modern 15.00
Silhouette, gravy boat 20.00
Silhouette, kitchen utensil, wooden hdl, ea 12.00
Silhouette, mug, beverage; 35.00
Silhouette, platter, oval, 11¼" 15.00
Silhouette, shakers, Five Band, ea 10.00
Silhouette, soap dispenser 40.00
Silhouette, tumbler, crystal, 10-oz 18.00
Springtime, cake plate 12.00
Springtime, gravy boat 18.00
Springtime, plate, 8¼" 4.00
Springtime, saucer 1.00
Teapot, Airflow, cobalt w/gold trim, 6-cup 45.00
Teapot, Airflow, daffodil, 6-cup 35.00
Teapot, Airflow, red, 6-cup 85.00
Teapot, Airflow, warm yel w/gold trim, 6-cup 35.00
Teapot, Aladdin, metal clad, 6-cup 85.00
Teapot, Aladdin, red, w/oval infuser, 6-cup 125.00
Teapot, Aladdin, Red Poppy, w/oval infuser, 6-cup 110.00
Teapot, Albany, mahog w/gold trim, 6-cup 65.00
Teapot, Apple, blk w/gold trim & rhinestones, 6-cup 250.00
Teapot, Automobile, blk 550.00
Teapot, Automobile, red 650.00
Teapot, Basket, emerald gr w/platinum trim, 6-cup 150.00
Teapot, Basketball, red, 6-cup 500.00
Teapot, Benjamin, yel, 6-cup 85.00
Teapot, Boston, bl, gold label, 6-cup 35.00
Teapot, Boston, Orange Poppy, 6-cup 165.00
Teapot, Bow Knot, pk, 6-cup 45.00
Teapot, Carraway, bl, short spout, 6-cup 65.00
Teapot, Carraway, lettuce gr, 6-cup 65.00
Teapot, Damascus, bl, 6-cup 150.00
Teapot, Football, maroon, 6-cup 600.00
Teapot, French, canary, flower decor, 12-cup 45.00

Teapot, French, canary, flower decor, 4-cup 25.00
Teapot, French, chartreuse, flower decor, 2-cup 35.00
Teapot, French, Delft bl, flower decor, 2-cup 35.00
Teapot, French, emerald gr, flower decor, 4-cup 45.00
Teapot, French, turq bl, flower decor, 2-cup 35.00
Teapot, French, turq bl, gold label, 6-cup 45.00
Teapot, Globe, canary w/gold trim, no drip, 6-cup 50.00
Teapot, Grape, ivory w/gold trim, 6-cup 65.00
Teapot, Grape, ivory w/rhinestones, 6-cup 125.00
Teapot, Hollywood, maroon, gold label, 6-cup 35.00
Teapot, Hollywood, red, 8-cup 150.00
Teapot, Kansas, ivory w/gold trim, 6-cup 225.00
Teapot, Los Angeles, emerald gr w/gold trim, 8-cup 40.00
Teapot, Los Angeles, pk, 6-cup 40.00
Teapot, Los Angeles, red, 4-cup 150.00
Teapot, McCormick, brn w/gold trim, 6-cup 65.00
Teapot, McCormick, gr & wht w/silver trim, 6-cup 65.00
Teapot, McCormick, maroon, w/infusor, 6-cup 20.00
Teapot, Melody, cobalt, 6-cup 175.00
Teapot, Melody, cobalt w/gold trim, 6-cup 175.00
Teapot, Melody, red, 6-cup 175.00
Teapot, Moderne, marine, 6-cup 50.00
Teapot, Musical, bl, 6-cup 175.00
Teapot, Nautilus, canary w/gold trim, 6-cup 175.00
Teapot, Nautilus, maroon w/gold trim, 6-cup 150.00
Teapot, New York, red, 6-cup 125.00
Teapot, New York, warm yel w/gold trim, 12-cup 55.00
Teapot, Philadelphia, Delft bl w/gold trim, 10-cup 65.00
Teapot, Philadelphia, red, 6-cup 150.00
Teapot, Regal, apple gr, 6-cup 125.00
Teapot, Star, delphinium, 6-cup 95.00
Teapot, Star, ivory, 6-cup 75.00
Teapot, Streamline, red, 6-cup 85.00
Teapot, Tip-Pot, daffodil, 6-cup 90.00
Teapot, Twinspout, maroon, 6-cup 60.00
Teapot, Windshield, blk w/gold trim, 6-cup 125.00
Teapot, Windshield, cobalt w/gold trim, 6-cup 125.00
Teapot, Windshield, delphinium w/gold trim, 6-cup 95.00
Teapot, World's Fair, gold trim, 6-cup 550.00
Tulip, bowl, fruit; 5½" 5.00
Tulip, casserole, Radiance 30.00
Tulip, coffeepot, Perk 10.00
Tulip, drip jar, w/lid, Thick Rim 20.00
Tulip, gravy boat 18.00
Tulip, shaker, hdld, ea 10.00
Tulip, sugar bowl, w/lid, Modern 15.00
Wildfire, bowl, rnd, 9¼" 20.00
Wildfire, bowl, Thick Rim, 7½" 15.00
Wildfire, cake plate 15.00
Wildfire, platter, 13¼" 18.00
Wildfire, teapot, Boston 110.00
Yellow Rose, bowl, fruit; 5½" 3.00
Yellow Rose, bowl, vegetable; rnd, 9¼" 15.00
Yellow Rose, casserole, Radiance 20.00
Yellow Rose, drip jar, w/lid, Radiance 15.00
Yellow Rose, shaker, hdld, ea 10.00
Yellow Rose, sugar bowl, w/lid, Norse 15.00

Hallmark

Hallmark introduced a line of artplas (molded plastic) ornaments in 1973 that have quickly become popular with collectors. They also have produced miniature ornaments since 1988, which are very collectible, as well as limited edition ornaments produced for members of the Hallmark Keepsake Ornament Collectors' Club.

'Merry Miniatures' is a line of artplas 'Table Trimmers' made in 1973 which have become quite collectible as well, and collectors are avidly searching for these tiny figures in closets, children's toy boxes, and at flea markets.

The magazine, *The Ornament Collector*, edited by Rosie Wells, our advisor for this category, is available if you want more information on ornament collecting. Rosie also publishes a yearly official Secondary Market Price Guide on Hallmark Ornaments, Merry Miniatures, Stocking Hangers, Lapel Pins, Cookie Cutters, etc. Her address is listed in the Directory under Clubs, Newsletters, and Catalogs and again under Illinois. Values are for ornaments in mint condition and with their original boxes, while Merry Miniatures are assumed to be mint.

Merry Miniatures

1974, angel holding star, XPF 506, 3" 350.00
1974, child in bunny suit, EPF 193, rare 300.00
1974, Santa standing on peppermint candy, XPF 486 ....325.00
1974, turkey on grass, TPF 13, 2" 300.00
1976, Betsey Clark, XPF 151, 2⅞" 270.00
1982, girl witch w/frog on hat, HHA 3456, rare 300.00
1982, Pilgrim mouse on orange leaf, THA 3433 ....150.00

Ornaments

1976, Tree Treats - Santa, QX 177-1, dough look 200.00
1978, Carrousel, QX 146-3, 1st in series 375.00
1978, Holly & Poinsettia Ball, QX 147-6 ....95.00
1979, Here Comes Santa, QX 155-9, 1st in series, motorcar 495.00
1980, Frosty Friends, QX 137-4, 1st in series, A Cool Yule 550.00
1981, Rocking Horse, QX422-2, 1st in series 550.00
1982, Tin Locomotive, QX 460-3, 1st in series 550.00
1984, Nostalgic Houses, QX 448-1, 1st in series, Victorian 155.00
1988, Miniature, Hold On Tight, QXC 570-4, Club renewal gift .60.00
1991, Miniature, Tiny Tea Party, QXM 582-7, 6-pc set 130.00
1991, Starship Enterprise, QLX 719-9, Star Trek Commemorative ...250.00
1991, Winnie-the-Pooh - Tigger, QX 560-9 ....85.00
1991, 1957 Corvette, QX 431-9, 1st in series 100.00
1992, Cheerful Santa, QX 515-4, Black Santa 40.00
1992, Christmas Treasures, Club members, ltd ed of 15,500 ....45.00
1992, Mary's Angel - Lily, QX 427-4, 5th in series 40.00
1992, Tobin Fraley Carousel Horse, QX 489-1, 1st in series 85.00

Halloween

The origin of Halloween can be traced back to the ancient practices of the Druids of Great Britain who began their New Year on the 1st of November. The Druids were pagans, and their New Year's celebrations involved pagan rites and superstitions. They believed that as the old year came to an end the devil would gather up all the demons and evil in the world and take them back to Hell with him. Witches were women who had sold their souls to the devil and with their black cat in attendance flew up through their chimneys on brooms. When the Roman Catholic Church came into power in 700 A.D., they changed the holiday into a religious event called 'All Saints Day,' or 'Allhallows.' The evening before, October 31, became 'Allhallow's Eve' or 'Halloween.' Today Halloween is strictly a fun time, and Halloween items are fun to collect. Pumpkin-head candy containers of papier-mache or pressed cardboard, noisemakers, postcards with black cats and witches, costumes, and decorations are only a sampling of the variety available. See also Candy Containers.

Butterick pattern, devil's costume, 1923 ....55.00
Candy container, blk cat, papier-mache, head lid, Germany 180.00
Candy container, blk cat jack-o'-lantern, Germany, 3½" 125.00
Candy container, clown head, spring nose, compo, Germany, 4" ...110.00
Candy container, jack-o'-lantern, compo, Germany, 2¼" 125.00
Candy container, pumpkin, papier-mache, cone shape, '50s, 6" ...27.50
Candy container, pumpkin man, compo, 6" 170.00
Candy container, witch, papier-mache, cone shape, '50s, 7½" ...110.00
Candy container, witch on pumpkin, papier-mache, 5" 95.00
Clacker, 2 wood balls strike tin witch, cats hdl 45.00
Costume, Darth Vader, Ben Cooper 65.00
Costume, polished cotton, wht skeleton on blk, 1900s, +mask 60.00
Decoration, blk cat musician, diecut, emb cb, HE Luhrs 45.00
Decoration, cat in moon, pressed cb, 10", EX 48.00
Decoration, devil, diecut, Germany, 15" 125.00
Decoration, Dracula, pressed cb, Japan, 1950s 48.00
Decoration, owl, diecut, emb cb, HE Luhrs, 22" 45.00
Decoration, pumpkin, diecut, emb cb, HE Luhrs, 13" 35.00
Decoration, pumpkin-head woman, diecut, Germany, 16" 65.00
Decoration, skeleton, diecut, emb cb, Luhrs, 1940s, life sz 40.00
Decoration, witch, diecut, Germany, 2" 65.00
Fan, cat face, paper w/crepe paper trim, 12½" 70.00
Horn, gr cucumber, wood mouthpc, working, 7½" 145.00
Horn, wood w/orange/blk/gold pnt, Czechoslovakia, 5½" 60.00

Jack-o'-lantern, pressed cardboard, 5½", $65.00; Witch, molded plastic body, 5", $15.00.

Jack-o'-lantern, eye & mouth tissue intact, 7" 125.00
Jack-o'-lantern, tin, opens for candle, Germany, 1900s, 7½" 650.00
Lantern, cat's face, papier-mache, Germany, 6", EX 145.00
Lantern, devil, papier-mache, orig face, 3½", EX 485.00
Noisemaker, Blk man w/guitar on paddle shape, EX 70.00
Noisemaker, clowns playing drums, litho on tin, USA 25.00
Noisemaker, wooden horn, Czechoslovakia, EX 38.00
Nut cup, jack-o'-lantern, papier-mache 70.00
Pin-bk, smiling ghost, orange & blk, 1950s, ¾", EX 35.00
Rattle, devil, tissue w/wood hdl, Germany, 2½" dia, EX 90.00
Rattle, tin cylinder w/wood hdl 40.00
Skeleton, compo body, spring arms & legs, Occupied Japan, 5" 95.00
Skeleton, compo w/spring limbs, Germany, 5" 48.00
Skull, porc, movable jaw 145.00
Tambourine, dancers around pumpkin face, tin, 6½" 65.00

Hampshire

The Hampshire Pottery Company was established in 1871 in Keene, New Hampshire, by James Scollay Taft. Their earliest products were redware and stoneware utility items such as jugs, churns, crocks,

and flowerpots. In 1878 they produced majolica ware which met with such success that they began to experiment with the idea of manufacturing art pottery. By 1883 they had developed a Royal Worcester type of finish which they applied to vases, tea sets, powder boxes, and cookie jars. It was also utilized for souvenir items that were decorated with transfer designs prepared from photographic plates.

Cadmon Robertson, brother-in-law of Taft, joined the company in 1904 and was responsible for developing their famous matt glazes. Colors included shades of green, brown, red, and blue. Early examples were of earthenware, but eventually the body was changed to semiporcelain. Some of his designs were marked with an M in a circle as a tribute to his wife, Emoretta. Robertson died in 1914, leaving a void impossible to fill. Taft sold the business in 1916 to George Morton, who continued to use the matt glazes that Robertson had developed. After a temporary halt in production during WWI, Morton returned to Keene and reequipped the factory with the machinery needed to manufacture hotel china and floor tile. Because of the expense involved in transporting coal to fire the kilns, Morton found he could not compete with potteries of Ohio and New Jersey who were able to utilize locally available natural gas. He was forced to close the plant in 1923.

Bowl, gr matt, artichoke form, mfg flaw, 2x4" 100.00
Bowl, leaf cvg, gr matt, #133/M in circle, 3x6" 100.00
Candle holder, gr matt, hdl, #29, 6½" 175.00
Candle holders, gr matt, hooded, 7", pr 225.00

Lamp, matt green with incised key device, 10", $450.00; Vase, dark brown flower on yellow gloss, 15", NM, $250.00.

Lamp base, appl florals on cobalt, 12" 595.00
Pitcher, gr matt, 9½" 225.00
Vase, dk/lt bl feathered matt, #142, M in O mk, 7" 95.00
Vase, gr matt, circle mk, 9" 200.00
Vase, high glaze blk rim w/wht Ms on bsk, dtd 1914, 3" 195.00
Vase, slate bl w/veining over pk shoulder & top, #1813, 7" 300.00
Vase, thick bl/gr, ftd Aladdin's lamp style, 6x8" 150.00
Vase, 5 repeats of cvd verticals, peacock bl w/veining, 12" 550.00

Handel

Philip Handel was best known for the art glass lamps he produced at the turn of the century. His work is similar to the Tiffany lamps of the same era. Handel made gas and electric lamps with both leaded glass and reverse-painted shades. Chipped ice shades with a texture similar to overshot glass were also produced. Shades signed by artists such as Bailey, Palme, and Parlow are highly valued.

China and glassware decorated by Handel are rare and command high prices on today's market. Teroma is a term used to describe glassware decorated on the exterior with paint that has a sandy finish. Many of Handel's chinaware blanks were supplied by Limoges. Our advisor for this category is Daniel Batchelor; he is listed in the Directory under New York.

Lamps

Chipped, lightly sanded 16" glass shade with tulips against foliage in vivid colors, bronzed base has cloth label, 24", $8,500.00.

Base only, tree trunk form, #5339, no finial, 23" 935.00
Boudoir, rvpt landscape shade; copper-finish foliate base 1,200.00
Boudoir, rvpt 3½" sqd scenic shade #2906; columnar std 800.00
Boudoir, rvpt 7" seascape shade; ribbled/floral gr-brn std 1,650.00
Boudoir, Teroma 7" poppy sgn/#7069 dome shade; 6-rib std ...2,800.00
Boudoir, Teroma 8" trees/mtns scallop-edge shade; std w/tag ..2,300.00
Bridge, sm 4-panel shade; angled harp on 4-leg sgn std, 56" 875.00
Chandelier, ldgl 15" conical shade w/mc fruits on apron 4,950.00
Chandelier, ldgl 24" cone shade w/flowers, orig hdw 2,800.00
Desk, oblong gr-pnt floral-band shade; arched arm, #6367 ......1,500.00
Desk, paneled yel/red cylinder shade; bronze base, tag, 17" 825.00
Desk, rvpt 8" cylinder scenic shade #6768G (EX); std adjusts 880.00
Floor, ldgl pond lily shade; angle-arm 3-ftd std, tag, 59" 1,650.00
Floor, Teroma 10" roses dome shade; in harp std, 56" 2,850.00
Piano, ldgl 10" cylinder brickwork shade; geometrics on base 600.00
Shade, ldgl dome w/bent panels & floral border, crown top 650.00
Slag cylinder shade; curved-arm std adjusts, 14" 800.00
Table, acid-etched band on brn dome shade; same on std 1,500.00
Table, bent glass/rtcl metal-banded 20" dia shade; 26", EX 2,500.00
Table, bent 13½" 6-side shade w/rtcl tree o/l; emb std 950.00
Table, bent 18½" shade w/rtcl pine cone o/l; sgn std 3,900.00
Table, bent-panel 18" shade w/metal brickwork o/l, 22" 2,200.00
Table, copper-plate tulip o/l on sgn slag glass shade; 13x8" 1,100.00
Table, etched/pnt 13" shade w/gold flowers; #584 std 1,200.00
Table, ldgl 14" sqd A&C shade w/filigree o/l; mk std, 23" 2,200.00
Table, pnt 18" floral/stripe exotic bird shade; Nouveau std ...13,500.00
Table, rvpt 14" #7983 shade w/floral border; coppered std 1,300.00
Table, rvpt 18" #6930 shade w/parrots in blk band; unmk std .3,200.00
Table, rvpt 18" chipped ice/sandy daffodil shade sgn Palme ..10,000.00
Table, rvpt 18" goldenrod/butterfly/clouds shade sgn Runge ...7,000.00
Table, rvpt 18" macaws/palms sgn/#6874 shade; bronze std ..18,700.00
Table, rvpt 18" spring tree sgn/#d shade; 24" 5,500.00
Table, rvpt 18" wild rose/butterflies shade; 3-scroll std 17,600.00
Table, Teroma 10" wild rose shade; tree trunk std, 15" 4,400.00
Table, Teroma 11" snake/sunburst #2186 shade; bronzed std ..2,100.00

Table, Teroma 18" birds/floral sgn/#7036 shade; 6-side std ...17,500.00
Table, Teroma 18" cascading daisies shade; 3-leg urn std 16,500.00
Table, Teroma 18" parrots/peonies #7023 shade; pnt vase std .17,500.00
Table, Teroma 20" bent-panel leafy-o/l shade; tree std, EX 1,950.00

Miscellaneous

Candlestick, Teroma, Dutch cove, sgn Gubisch, #4214, 9", pr ..1,850.00
Humidor, chipped ice w/moss gr enamel, metal mouth, 7¾" 750.00
Humidor, opalware, pnt gr w/3 dogs, sgn Kelsey, 8x8" 950.00
Tazza, opalware, pnt yel w/gold trim & violets, 9x6" 800.00
Vase, opalware, pnt lt gr w/floral ea side, #223/172, 12" 550.00
Vase, Teroma, autumn scene, concave sides, #4219, 11" 1,900.00
Vase, Teroma, frosted/acid etched on clear, 8x4" 625.00
Vase, Teroma, summer mtn scene, #4210, 8" 3,000.00
Vase, Teroma, tree scene w/birds, #4216, 11x4½" 2,250.00
Vase, Teroma, trees/sun, sgn Borggi, #4222, 8x3" 1,500.00

Harker

The Harker Pottery was established in East Liverpool, Ohio, in 1840. Their earliest products were yellow ware and Rockingham produced from local clay. After 1900 whiteware was made from imported materials. The plant eventually grew to be a large manufacturer of dinnerware and kitchenware, employing as many as three hundred people. It closed in 1972 after it was purchased by the Jeannette Glass Company. Perhaps their best-known lines were their Cameo wares, decorated with white silhouettes in a cameo effect on contrasting solid colors. Floral silhouettes are standard, but other designs were also used. Blue and pink are the most often found background hues; a few pieces are found in yellow. For further information we recommend *The Collector's Guide to Harker Pottery* by Neva Colbert.

Bean pot, Amethyst 6.00
Bowl, batter; Colonial Lady 40.00
Bowl, cereal; Colonial Lady, tab hdls 5.00
Bowl, Modern Tulip, 6" 5.00
Bowl, soup; White Rose 10.00
Bowl, vegetable; Cameo Rose, 9" 8.00
Cake plate, Pastel Tulip 18.00
Cake set, Chesterton, teal gr, 10-pc 25.00
Creamer & sugar bowl, Cameo Rose 12.50
Cup & saucer, Cameo Rose 5.00
Custard, Amethyst 5.00
Fork, spoon & lifter, Amy 50.00
Gravy boat, Pastel Tulip 12.00
Jar, Modern Tulip, oval, w/lid 30.00
Jug, Cameo Rose 20.00
Lifter, Rose II 15.00
Pie plate, Deco Dahlia, 9" 10.00
Pie plate, Petit Point 15.00
Pie plate, White Rose 15.00
Plate, Cameo, 6" 3.00
Plate, Cameo Rose, 9" 3.50
Plate, Modern Tulip, 6" 2.00
Plate, Modern Tulip, 9" 4.50
Plate, Petit Point, 8" 10.00
Plate, utility; Deco Dahlia, 12" 15.00
Plate, White Rose, 10" 10.00
Platter, Apple & Pear, 13" 12.00
Platter, Cameo Rose, 14" 10.00
Rolling pin, Amy 75.00
Rolling pin, Cameo Rose, bl & wht 95.00

Spoon, Modern Tulip 12.00
Tea tile, White Rose 25.00

Harlequin

Harlequin dinnerware, produced by the Homer Laughlin China Company of Newell, West Virginia, was introduced in 1938. It was a lightweight ware made in maroon, mauve blue, and spruce green, as well as all the Fiesta colors except ivory (see Fiesta). It was marketed exclusively by the Woolworth stores, who considered it to be their all-time bestseller. For this reason they contracted with Homer Laughlin to reissue Harlequin to commemorate their 100th anniversary in 1979. Although three of the original glazes were used in the reissue, the few serving pieces that were made were restyled, and collectors found the new line to be no threat to their investments.

The Harlequin animals, including a fish, lamb, cat, penguin, duck, and donkey, were made during the early 1940s, also for the dime-store trade. Today these are very desirable to collectors of Homer Laughlin china.

In the listings that follow, use the values designated 'high' for all colors other than turquoise and yellow. For medium green, double the 'high' values on all items other than flat items and small bowls. *The Collector's Encyclopedia of Fiesta* by Sharon and Bob Huxford contains a more thorough study of this subject. It is available from Collector Books or your local library.

Animals, mavericks, gold trim 32.00
Animals, non-standard colors 158.00
Animals, standard colors 75.00
Ashtray, basketweave, high 50.00
Ashtray, basketweave, low 30.00
Ashtray, regular, high 42.50
Ashtray, regular, low 32.00
Bowl, '36s oatmeal; high 17.00
Bowl, '36s oatmeal; low 11.50
Bowl, '36s; high 26.50
Bowl, '36s; low 17.00
Bowl, cream soup; high 20.00
Bowl, cream soup; low 16.00
Bowl, fruit; high, 5½" 9.00
Bowl, fruit; low, 5½" 6.00
Bowl, ind salad; high 26.50
Bowl, ind salad; low 17.00
Bowl, mixing; Kitchen Kraft, mauve bl, 8" 110.00
Bowl, mixing; Kitchen Kraft, red or spruce gr, 6" ...72.00
Bowl, mixing; Kitchen Kraft, yel, 10" 110.00
Bowl, nappy; high, 9" 26.50
Bowl, nappy; low, 9" 16.50
Bowl, oval baker, high 25.00
Bowl, oval baker, low 18.00
Butter dish, high, ½-lb 90.00
Butter dish, low, ½-lb 75.00
Candle holder, high, pr 195.00
Candle holder, low, pr 162.00
Casserole, w/lid, high 95.00
Casserole, w/lid, low 58.00
Creamer, high lip, any color 72.00
Creamer, ind; high 17.00
Creamer, ind; low 12.50
Creamer, novelty, high 23.00
Creamer, novelty, low 16.00
Creamer, regular, high 13.50
Creamer, regular, low 8.00
Cup, demitasse; high 46.00

Cup, demitasse; low 27.50
Cup, lg, any color 92.00
Cup, tea; high 9.50
Cup, tea; low 7.50
Egg cup, dbl, high 20.00
Egg cup, dbl, low 14.00
Egg cup, single, high 21.00
Egg cup, single, low 16.50
Gravy boat, high 23.00
Gravy boat, low 16.00

Marmalade, any color, $125.00.

Nut dish, basketweave, orig color 8.00
Perfume bottle, any color 68.00
Pitcher, service water; high 55.00
Pitcher, service water; low 37.50
Pitcher, 22-oz jug, high 46.00
Pitcher, 22-oz jug, low 26.00
Plate, deep; high 20.00
Plate, deep; low 15.00
Plate, high, 10" 24.00
Plate, high, 6" 4.50
Plate, high, 7" 6.50
Plate, high, 9" 12.00
Plate, low, 10" 14.00
Plate, low, 6" 3.50
Plate, low, 7" 4.50
Plate, low, 9" 7.00
Platter, high, 11" 17.50
Platter, high, 13" 25.00
Platter, low, 11" 12.00
Platter, low, 13" 16.50
Saucer, demitasse; high 13.50
Saucer, demitasse; low 7.00
Saucer, high 3.50
Saucer, low 2.00
Saucer/ashtray, high 47.00
Saucer/ashtray, ivory 65.00
Saucer/ashtray, low 42.50
Shakers, high, pr 16.50
Shakers, low, pr 13.00
Sugar bowl, w/lid, high 17.00
Sugar bowl, w/lid, low 12.00
Syrup, any color 200.00
Teapot, high 88.00
Teapot, low 58.00
Tray, relish; mixed colors 200.00
Tumbler, high 40.00

Tumbler, low 30.00

Hatpin Holders

Most hatpin holders were made from 1860 to 1920 to coincide with the period during which hatpins were popularly in vogue. The taller types were required to house the long hatpins necessary to secure the large hats that were in style from 1890 to 1914. They were usually porcelain, either decorated by hand or by transfer with florals or scenics, although some were clever figurals. Glass examples are rare, and those of slag or Carnival Glass are especially valuable.

If you are interested in collecting or dealing in hatpins or hatpin holders, you will find that authority Lillian Baker has several fine books available on the subject, including her most recent publication, *Hatpins and Hatpin Holders,* complete with beautiful color illustrations and current market values. She is listed in the Directory under California. For information concerning the International Club for Collectors of Hatpins and Hatpin Holders, see the Clubs, Newsletters, and Catalogs section of the Directory. Our advisor for this category is Robert Larsen; he is listed in the Directory under Nebraska.

Adams jasperware, white on blue, ca 1991-1914, 4", NM, $150.00.

Bavaria, china, silver floral, 4¾" 110.00
Carnival glass, Grape & Cable, marigold, Northwood, 7" 235.00
China, dbl-face, lady 1 side, man on other, unmk 265.00
China, HP florals on corset shape, sterling rim, ca 1875 ....245.00
China, hunchbk man w/staff figural, base flake, 5½" 125.00
Chocolate glass, emb florals, ftd, ca 1905, 7⅞x2⅝" 385.00
Flow Blue, sgn Shung, Wood & Sons, #d, 5" 165.00
Goss, City of York crest, souvenir, 3½" 90.00
Jasperware, bl w/wht Grecian figures 135.00
Limoges, floral, attached trinket box, w/lid, 4½" 300.00
Limoges, Nouveau lady & peacock decal, 3⅝" 195.00
Nippon, lg wht storks around base, turq bl body, gold top 135.00
Pickard, HP Nouveau motif w/gold top, 4¾" 185.00
Pottery, brn shaded, GH Richards, London, ca 1890 ....110.00
Rosenthal, gr china w/much silver o/l 235.00
Royal Bayreuth, Corinthian, bl mk, 4¾", 4" saucer 385.00
Royal Bayreuth, crocus figural, bl mk, 4¾" 400.00
Royal Doulton, hunt scene, ca 1920s, 4¾" 185.00
Royal Doulton, Ophelia in lav/pk on cream, 5x3½" 255.00
RS Prussia, roses on lustre, scalloped base, mk, 4¾" 285.00
Schafer & Vater, bear & tower figural, 4¾x3½" 190.00
Schafer & Vater, bsk, rtcl top, wall hanging, 6¾" 275.00

Hatpins

A hatpin was used to securely fasten a hat to the hair and head of the wearer. Hatpins, measuring from 4" to 12" in length, were worn from approximately 1850 to 1920. During the Art Deco period, hatpins became ornaments rather than the decorative functional jewels that they had been. The hatpin period reached its zenith in 1913 just prior to WWI, which brought about a radical change in women's headdress and fashion. About that time, women began to scorn the bonnet and adopt 'the hat' as a symbol of their equality. The hatpin was made of every natural and manufactured element in a myriad of designs that challenge the imagination. They were contrived to serve every fashion need and complement the milliner's art. Collectors often concentrate on a specific type: hand-painted porcelains, sterling silver, commemoratives, sporting activities, Carnival Glass, Art Nouveau and/or Art Deco designs, Victorian Gothics with mounted stones, exquisite rhinestones, engraved and brass-mounted escutcheon heads, gold and gems, or simply primitive types made in the Victorian parlor. Some collectors prefer the long pin-shanks while others select only those on tremblants or nodder-type pin-shanks.

If you are interested in collecting or dealing in hatpins, see the information in the Hatpin Holders introduction concerning reference books and a national collectors' club. For further study we recommend *The Collector's Encyclopedia of Hatpins and Hatpin Holders,* available at your local bookstore or from Collector Books. Our advisor for this category is Robert Larsen; he is listed in the Directory under Nebraska.

Amethyst stone set in gilt-over-brass mt, ¾" on 8" pin 85.00
Blk jet stone on 1¼" domed top, twist-wire caging 65.00
Brass, mythological head & ¾" faceted citrine, 7¾" 110.00
Brass (oxidized), Nouveau style w/amethyst brilliant, 9½" 110.00
Brass heart-shape fr w/many brilliants, 1905, 1¾" top 70.00
Garnet, cabachon, 1" on 5½" gilt pin 100.00
Horn, butterfly form w/mc rhinestones, 3⅜" on 9½" pin 85.00
Ivory, elephant on ball cvg, 1½" on 8½" pin 120.00
Mercury glass, crimped tubular finding, Bohemia, 1900s, 2¼" 80.00
Mosaic, in brass button-sleeve mt w/gold trim, 1" on 8" pin 65.00
Plique-a-jour, bezel-set opal, Nouveau, 1¼x1½" on 7½" pin 500.00
Porc, courting couple medallion w/gold o/l, 1890s, 1¾" 155.00
Porc, transfer & gold o/l, ball form, 1895, 1¼" on 8½" pin 115.00
Rhinestones, prong set, on domed 1¼" brass filigree top 85.00
Satsuma, HP birds & leaf, 1½" on 10½" steel pin 175.00
Satsuma, robins on mc flowers, metallic cup mt, 1½" 165.00
Silver alloy (oxidized), w/faceted amethyst glass, 1900s, 7½" 75.00
Silver foil glass, peacock eye ea side, ¾" on 8¼" pin 75.00
Sterling, etch/eng head w/florals, 1870s, 1¼" on 9" pin 65.00
Sterling, Gibson girl w/repousse, ca 1900, 1¼" on pin 75.00
Sterling, Nouveau lady w/repousse, Am, 1905, 1" on 8¾" pin 110.00
Vanity, brass, ornate filigree, w/puff & mirror intact 850.00
Vanity, red stone on brass mt, 2x1½" on 11½" pin 700.00

Haviland

The Haviland China Company was organized in 1840 by David Haviland, a New York china importer. His search for a pure white, nonporous porcelain led him to Limoges, France, where natural deposits of suitable clay had already attracted numerous china manufacturers. The fine china he produced there was translucent and meticulously decorated, with each piece fired in an individual sagger.

It has been estimated that as many as 60,000 chinaware patterns were designed, each piece marked with one of several company backstamps. 'H. & Co.' was used until 1890 when a law was enacted making it necessary to include the country of origin. Various marks have been used since that time including 'Haviland, France'; 'Haviland & Co. Limoges'; and 'Decorated by Haviland & Co.' Various associations with family members over the years have resulted in changes in management as well as company name. In 1892 Theodore Haviland left the firm to start his own business. Some of his ware was marked 'Mont Mery.' Later logos included a horseshoe, a shield, and various uses of his initials and name. In 1941 this branch moved to the United States. Wares produced here are marked 'Theodore Haviland, N.Y.' or 'Made In America.'

Though it is their dinnerware lines for which they are most famous, during the 1880s and 1890s they also made exquisite art pottery using a technique of underglaze slip decoration called Barbotine, which had been invented by Ernest Chaplet. In 1885 Haviland bought the formula and hired Chaplet to oversee its production. The technique involved mixing heavy white clay slip with pigments to produce a compound of the same consistency as oil paints. The finished product actually resembled oil paintings of the period, the texture achieved through the application of the heavy medium to the clay body in much the same manner as an artist would apply paint to his canvas. Primarily the body used with this method was a low-fired faience, though they also produced stoneware. Numbers in the listings below refer to pattern books by Arlene Schleiger.

Biscuit jar, Moss Rose, 7x5" 150.00
Bowl, vegetable; Moss Rose, w/lid 45.00
Butter pat, florals, Nenuphar form, 1876-89, 3" sq 20.00
Butter pat, Ranson 15.00
Butter tub, floral swags, 3½", +6½" plate 85.00
Cake plate, gold trim on wht, gold hdls, 10" 40.00
Cake plate, Her Majesty, Satsuma form, 8½x12" 90.00
Cake set, birds/pk flowers, platter, 16", +10 9" plates 350.00
Cheese dish, floral, dome lid, Marseillo mold 245.00

Chocolate set, hand-painted roses (not factory applied), 10" pot, six cups, $400.00.

Chocolate pot, carnations, dbl mk, 12", +6 c/s+tray 2,000.00
Chocolate pot, mc florals, Epi Haut form, 1876-89, 7¼" 85.00
Coffeepot, floral sprays, Pompador, 1888-96, 8½" 175.00
Coffeepot, Moss Rose 45.00
Compote, center medallion, ormolu mts, 1893-1930, 7x5½" 125.00
Creamer & sugar bowl, Autumn Leaf, w/lid 125.00
Creamer & sugar bowl, wht w/gold band, 1850s-65 ....150.00
Cup & saucer, Arbor 38.00
Cup & saucer, bouillon; Silver Anniversary 26.00
Cup & saucer, demi; bird & flowers, gold trim, 1876-1930 ....55.00
Cup & saucer, Ganga 30.00
Cup & saucer, orchids & dragonflies, salesman's sample, mk 100.00

Cup & saucer, Silver Anniversary 38.00
Ewer, rose & daisies HP over relief, 1865-75, 8" 165.00
Gravy boat, Autumn Leaf 38.00
Gravy boat, Gotham 40.00
Pin tray, lg roses, 6" L 35.00
Pitcher, butterflies/floral on wht, mk H&C, 9" 100.00
Pitcher, milk; Norma, Ranson form, 1893-1930, 7" 145.00
Pitcher, pottery, fruit/vines, cvd/pnt gold & gr on brn, 6" 350.00
Plate, Arbor, 7½" 25.00
Plate, Autumn Leaf, 9½" 16.50
Plate, Baltimore Rose, Ranson form, 1893-1930, 8½" 60.00
Plate, deer couple ornate border 95.00
Plate, Greenaway-style figures, Tresse mold, 1876-80, 9½" 175.00
Plate, oyster; pastel flowers, 9" 85.00
Plate, oyster; shell design, HP in factory, 1876-80, 9" 110.00
Platter, Autumn Leaf, 12" 60.00
Platter, Moss Rose, 12¾" 45.00
Platter, Ranson, 23" 195.00
Platter, Silver Anniversary, 14" 90.00
Sardine box, HP, fish form hdl, 1888-96, 1¼x4½" 100.00
Soup plate, Eden, mk Theo, 7½" 15.00
Sugar bowl, Mignonette 50.00
Sugar bowl, rose finial, 1876-89, 7" 70.00
Teapot, tea rose sprays on bl, 4", +2" creamer 95.00
Tray, relish; Princess 25.00
Tureen, soup; Blackberry 150.00
Vase, mums, fuchsia/purple on wht, 3-hdl, sgn de Feure, 8" 500.00
Vase, pottery, ladies/garden cvg, Arts & Crafts, mk, 16" 2,500.00
Vase, Terra Cotta, sculpted florals, 12", pr 1,200.00

Hawkes

Thomas Hawkes established his factory in Corning, New York, in 1880. He developed many beautiful patterns of cut glass, two of which were awarded the Grand Prize at the Paris Exposition in 1889. By the end of the century, his company was renowned for the finest in cut glass production. The company logo was a trefoil form enclosing a hawk in each of the two bottom lobes with a fleur-de-lis in the center. Most items were signed except very early designs.

Basket, hobstar chain, notched hdl, ruffled flared top, 9" 1,295.00
Bonbon, hobstars & X-cut split vesicas on corners, 7" 175.00
Bowl, Brunswick, heavy, 4½x10¼" 775.00
Bowl, hobstars, heavy blank, 3½x8" 200.00
Bowl, Lorraine, scalloped ft w/hobstar, 6½x9" 1,000.00
Bowl, Lucerne, heavy blank, low, 9" 250.00
Bowl, Triple Mitre Trellis, 2½x9" 1,650.00
Butter tub, hobstars/fans, hdls, sgn, 5x6" 350.00
Candlestick, hobstars/clear panels, 3" bubble in stem, 9", pr 650.00
Candy jar, Revere, w/lid, 10½" 300.00
Casserole, Russian, sqd trefoil base & lid, ped ft, 6x8" 1,400.00
Cider jug, Brunswick, 6½" 500.00
Cider jug, hobstars, cut hdl, 6½" 375.00
Cider jug, Teutonic, hand cut in St Louis Dmn, 6¼" 350.00
Claret jug, Kings variant w/hobstars, bulbous, 11½" 850.00
Comport, twisted stem cut w/t'print, 7¼" 175.00
Decanter, faceted stopper, bulbous w/cylinder neck, 10" 130.00
Flower bowl, floral/leaves cutting, sgn, 9" 200.00
Nappy, Jupiter, 5" 80.00
Nut bowl, hobstars w/lapidary knob ped ft, 4½" 325.00
Oil bottle, Middlesex variation, w/stopper, 9½" 90.00
Pitcher, floral eng, sterling base, sgn, 10x6" 275.00
Pitcher, Florence, honeycomb neck, hobstars, bulbous, 6½" 285.00

Plate, Marquis, hobstars, 10"	300.00
Powder jar, Gravic Iris, cut lid/base, 7½" dia	500.00
Puff box, hobstars/X-cut dmns/notched prisms, 5½" dia	325.00
Punch bowl, Albion, hobstars/stars/fans/mitres, 7¼x15"	1,600.00
Punch bowl, Queens, hobstars/bull's eyes, 2-part, 10½"	2,200.00
Rose bowl, Brunswick, hobstar in base, 7" H	1,000.00
Tray, strawberries, Gravic, 7"	600.00
Tumbler, hobstar/fan/strawberry dmn, pr	60.00
Vase, Brunswick, cylindrical, 11¾"	300.00
Vase, Brunswick, hobstar base, trumpet shape, 12"	300.00
Vase, Brunswick, hobstar ped, 16"	350.00
Vase, Dmn Point, cut rays & hobstars, 10x3⅝"	245.00
Vase, intaglio fish/crab, hammered metal top/S-hdls, 16"	700.00

Head Vases

Vases modeled as heads of lovely ladies, delightful children, clowns, Madonnas — even some animals — were once popular as flower containers. Today they represent a growing area of collector interest. Most of them were imported from Japan, although some American potteries produced a few as well.

For more information we recommend *Head Vases, Identification and Values*, by Kathleen Cole.

Baby w/blanket about head & shoulders, Samson Import, 7½"	25.00
Baby w/bow in hair, ruffled collar, Inarco, 5½"	25.00
Child at prayers, Inarco, 5"	20.00
Clown, clown w/pointed hat, ruffled collar, Inarco, 7"	20.00
Clown w/gr hat & red hair, ruffled collar, Napcoware, 6"	20.00
Deco lady in wide-brim hat, cream, unmk, 9¼"	75.00
Geisha girl, ornate hair ornamentation, Lee Wards, 5"	25.00
Girl graduate, scroll in hand, Napco, 6"	25.00
Girl in braids & scarf, Inarco, 7"	30.00
Girl w/braids, lg bow in hair, unmk, 5¾"	25.00
Girl w/flip-style hairdo, pearl necklace, Parma, 5½"	20.00
Girl w/ponytail at side, pearl earrings, Inarco, 7½"	37.50
Girl w/scarf & umbrella, unmk, 5"	25.00
Girl w/tam, 1 pearl earring, gold pin, Inarco, 5½"	20.00
Girl w/telephone in hand, Nancy Pew label, 6"	25.00

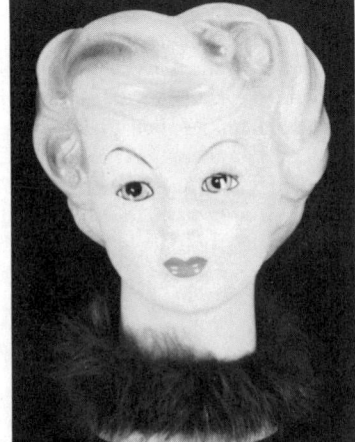

Lady with fur collar, paper Enesco label, 6", $25.00.

Indian Chief, full headdress, unmk, 8"	25.00
Lady, wht w/gold details, mk Glamour Girl, 6½"	17.50
Lady in turban-style hat, pearl necklace, Napco, 5½"	20.00
Lady in wide-brim hat, pearl jewelry, hand up, Japan, 4½"	20.00

Lady w/bonnet, bow at chin, pearl necklace, Brinn's, 7"	35.00
Lady w/bow on hat, pearl jewelry, ruffled dress, Atlas, 6"	25.00
Lady w/closed fan, pearl earings, Inarco, 6"	30.00
Lady w/flower in hair, pearl jewelry, hand to face, unmk, 7"	32.50
Lady w/flower on hat, hands to face, Lefton's, 6"	32.50
Lady w/frosted hair, pearl jewelry, leaf pin, Napcoware, 9"	50.00
Lady w/hat, pearl jewelry, hand to face, Inarco, 8½"	75.00
Lady w/hat, pearl jewelry, hands folded, Rubens, 5¾"	25.00
Lady w/lacy hat, pearl jewelry, hand to face, Napco, 5½"	25.00
Lady w/lg bow at side of hat, gold jewelry, unmk, 4"	20.00
Lady w/long curls, Relpo, #K1335, 8"	35.00
Lady w/pearl earrings, daisies at neck, Napcoware, 5"	20.00
Lady w/scarf over blond hair, unmk, 3"	15.00
Lady w/side-swept hairdo, pearl jewelry, Parma, 8½"	40.00
Lady w/wide-brim hat, ruffled collar, Thames, 5½"	20.00
Mary & Christ Child, Napcoware label, 6½"	25.00
Nun w/prayer book, Inarco, 6"	25.00
Oriental lady w/open fan, no mk, 4¾"	20.00
Teen girl w/'Love' on necklace, pearl earrings, Brinn's, 7½"	32.50
Teen girl w/windblown hair, turtleneck sweater, Inarco, 5"	25.00
Uncle Sam, overall gr, unmk, 6½"	25.00
Woman w/feather in hat, pearl jewelry, Inarco, 5½"	25.00

Heisey

A.H. Heisey began his long career at the King Glass Company of Pittsburgh. He later joined the Ripley Glass Company which soon became Geo. Duncan and Sons. After Duncan's death, Heisey became half-owner in partnership with his brother-in-law, James Duncan. In 1895 he built his own factory in Newark, Ohio, initiating production in 1896 and continuing until Christmas of 1957. At that time Imperial Glass Corporation bought some of the molds. After 1968 they removed the old 'Diamond H' from any they put into use. In 1985 HCA purchased all of Imperial's Heisey molds with the exception of the Old Williamsburg line.

During their highly successful period of production, Heisey made fine handcrafted tableware with simple, yet graceful designs. Early pieces were not marked. After November 1901 the glassware was marked either with the 'Diamond H' or a paper label. Blown ware is often marked on the stem, never on the bowl or foot. For information concerning Heisey Collectors of America, see the Clubs, Newsletters, and Catalogs section of the Directory. See also Glass Animals.

Chintz, crystal; bowl, preserve; hdld, ftd, 5½"	15.00
Chintz, crystal; creamer, 3-ftd	20.00
Chintz, crystal; ice bucket, ftd	75.00
Chintz, crystal; plate, dinner; sq, 10½"	40.00
Chintz, crystal; stem, claret; #3389, 4-oz	20.00
Chintz, crystal; stem, water; #3389, 9-oz	15.00
Chintz, crystal; tumbler, soda; #3389, 8-oz	12.00
Chintz, sahara; bowl, pickle & olive; 2-part, 13"	35.00
Chintz, sahara; plate, luncheon; sq, 8"	22.00
Chintz, sahara; stem, oyster cocktail; #3389, 4-oz	20.00
Chintz, sahara; stem, wine; #3389, 2½-oz	45.00
Chintz, sahara; tray, celery; 10"	27.50
Chintz, sahara; tumbler, juice; #3389, 5-oz	22.00
Crystolite, ashtray, w/book match holder, 5"	25.00
Crystolite, bonbon, hdld, 7½"	15.00
Crystolite, bottle, syrup; w/drip-cut top	85.00
Crystolite, bowl, preserve; hdld, 6"	13.00
Crystolite, candlestick, 2-light	25.00
Crystolite, candy box, w/lid, 7"	55.00
Crystolite, cheese, ftd, 5½"	20.00

Crystolite, cigarette holder, oval 17.50
Crystolite, cup, punch or custard 7.00
Crystolite, mayonnaise, hdld, oval, 6" 26.00
Crystolite, plate, dinner; 10½" 60.00
Crystolite, stem, water; #1503, pressed, 10-oz 480.00
Crystolite, tray, relish; 3-part, 12" 25.00
Crystolite, tumbler, #5005, pressed, 10-oz 70.00
Crystolite, vase, 12" 225.00

Elect Landon plate, $150.00.

Empress, alexandrite; ashtray 210.00
Empress, alexandrite; bowl, cream soup; w/sq liner 165.00
Empress, alexandrite; bowl, mint; dolphin ft 6" 165.00
Empress, alexandrite; creamer, ind 210.00
Empress, alexandrite; plate, bouillon liner 20.00
Empress, alexandrite; plate, 7" 40.00
Empress, cobalt; bowl, floral; dolphin ft, 11" 400.00
Empress, cobalt; bowl, nappy; dolphin ft, 7½" 275.00
Empress, cobalt; bowl, nasturtium; dolphin ft, 7½" 325.00
Empress, cobalt; candlestick, dolphin ft, 6" 250.00
Empress, cobalt; plate, sq, 7" 55.00
Empress, cobalt; plate, sq, 8" 70.00
Empress, flamingo; cup, after dinner 40.00
Empress, flamingo; plate, 10½" 100.00
Empress, flamingo; stem, sherbet; 4-oz 22.00
Empress, flamingo; tumbler, dolphin ft, 8-oz 125.00
Empress, moongleam; bowl, vegetable; oval, 10" 55.00
Empress, moongleam; comport, oval, 7" 75.00
Empress, moongleam; cup, after dinner 40.00
Empress, moongleam; cup, punch or custard; 4-oz 30.00
Empress, moongleam; mustard, w/lid 75.00
Empress, moongleam; stem, oyster cocktail; 2½-oz 30.00
Empress, moongleam; tray, sandwich; center hdl, 12" 65.00
Empress, moongleam; tumbler, ground bottom, 8-oz 39.50
Empress, sahara; bowl, jelly; hdld, ftd, 6" 23.00
Empress, sahara; bowl, jelly; w/lid, hdld, ftd 145.00
Empress, sahara; candy, dolphin ftd, w/lid, 6" 150.00
Empress, sahara; ice tub, w/metal hdls 100.00
Empress, sahara; plate, sq, 6" 13.00
Empress, sahara; saucer, after dinner 10.00
Empress, sahara; tray, relish; 3-part, 10" 30.00
Empress, sahara; vase, flared, 8" 90.00
Greek Key, bowl, jelly; w/lid, hdld, ftd 145.00
Greek Key, candy dish, w/lid, 2-lb 195.00

Greek Key, coaster 12.00
Greek Key, ice tub, tab hdld, lg 90.00
Greek Key, jar, horseradish; w/lid, sm 65.00
Greek Key, pitcher, 3-pt 125.00
Greek Key, plate, orange bowl liner; 16" 65.00
Greek Key, plate, 8" 20.00
Greek Key, sherbet, cupped rim, ftd, 4½-oz 12.50
Greek Key, stem, burgundy; 3½-oz 110.00
Greek Key, tray, French roll; 12½" 100.00
Greek Key, tumbler, str sides, 10-oz 37.00
Greek Key, water bottle 170.00
Ipswich, alexandrite; stem, goblet; 10-oz 750.00
Ipswich, cobalt; bowl, floral; ftd, 11" 250.00
Ipswich, cobalt; candlestick, 1-light, 6" 350.00
Ipswich, gr; oil bottle, w/# 86 stopper, ftd, 2-oz 200.00
Ipswich, gr; pitcher, ½-gal 750.00
Ipswich, pk; candy jar, w/lid, ½-lb 225.00
Ipswich, pk; tumbler, cupped rim, 10-oz 40.00
Ipswich, sahara; sugar bowl 37.50
Lariat, ashtray, 4" 10.00
Lariat, bowl, punch; 7-qt 110.00
Lariat, candlestick, 2-light 25.00
Lariat, cheese dish, w/lid, 8" 50.00
Lariat, plate, deviled egg; 13" 150.00
Lariat, sugar bowl 15.00
Lariat, tumbler, juice; ftd, 5-oz 15.00
Lodestar, dawn; candy jar, w/lid, 5" 135.00
Lodestar, dawn; celery, 10" 60.00
Lodestar, dawn; relish, 3-part, 7½" 55.00
Lodestar, dawn; sauce dish, #1626, 4½" 35.00
Lodestar, dawn; tumbler, juice; 6-oz 35.00
Lodestar, dawn; vase, #1626, crimped, 8" 175.00
Minuet, bowl, mint; ftd, 6" 15.00
Minuet, candlestick, #112, 1-light 25.00
Minuet, creamer, dolphin ft 40.00
Minuet, cup 35.00
Minuet, pitcher, #4164, 73-oz 225.00
Minuet, plate, service; 10½" 50.00
Minuet, stem, claret; #5010, 4-oz 30.00
Minuet, stem, sherbet; #5010, 6-oz 12.00
Minuet, tray, social hour; 15" 60.00
Minuet, tumbler, juice; #5010, 5-oz 30.00
Minuet, vase, urn; #5012, 7½" 75.00
Octagon, crystal; cup, #1231 ....5.00
Octagon, crystal; plate, muffin; #1229, sides up, 12" 20.00
Octagon, dawn; tray, #500, 4-part, 12" 300.00
Octagon, flamingo; bowl, jelly; #1229, 5½" 12.00
Octagon, flamingo; frozen dessert dish, #500 ....15.00
Octagon, flamingo; platter, oval, 12¾" 25.00
Octagon, hawthorne; cheesh dish, #1229, hdld, 6" 15.00
Octagon, hawthorne; plate, sandwich; #1229, 10" 35.00
Octagon, moongleam; bowl, soup; flat, 9" 27.50
Octagon, moongleam; plate, 6" 10.00
Octagon, moongleam; tray, celery; 9" 15.00
Octagon, sahara; bowl, grapefruit; 6½" 22.00
Octagon, sahara; mayonnaise, #1229, ftd, 5½" 30.00
Octagon, sahara; saucer, after dinner 6.00
Old Colony etch, crystal; bowl, dessert; hdld, 10" 30.00
Old Colony etch, crystal; bowl, jelly; hdld, ftd, 6" 15.00
Old Colony etch, crystal; cup, after dinner 12.00
Old Colony etch, crystal; plate, rnd, 4½" 3.00
Old Colony etch, crystal; plate, sandwich; hdld, sq, 13" ...35.00
Old Colony etch, crystal; stem, cocktail; #3390, 3-oz 7.00
Old Colony etch, crystal; stem, wine; #3380, 2½-oz 18.00

Old Colony etch, crystal; sugar bowl, dolphin ft 17.50
Old Colony etch, crystal; tumbler, #3380, ftd, 5-oz 7.00
Old Colony etch, crystal; vase, ftd, 9" 75.00
Old Colony etch, flamingo; bowl, mint; dolphin ft, 6" 22.00
Old Colony etch, flamingo; bowl, pickle & olive; 2-part, 13" 20.00
Old Colony etch, flamingo; cup 26.00
Old Colony etch, flamingo; mayonnaise, dolphin ft, 5½" 55.00
Old Colony etch, flamingo; platter, oval, 14" 35.00
Old Colony etch, flamingo; stem, claret; #3390, 4-oz 22.50
Old Colony etch, flamingo; stem, parfait; #3380, 5-oz 15.00
Old Colony etch, flamingo; tray, sandwich; center hdl, 12" 65.00
Old Colony etch, flamingo; tumbler, iced tea; #3380, 12-oz 25.00
Old Colony etch, marigold; comport, #3368, ftd, 7" 95.00
Old Colony etch, marigold; stem, cordial; #3380, 1-oz 375.00
Old Colony etch, marigold; stem, soda; #3380, tall 32.50
Old Colony etch, moongleam; bowl, salad; hdld, sq, 10" 65.00
Old Colony etch, moongleam; creamer, dolphin ft 50.00
Old Colony etch, moongleam; grapefruit, #3380, ftd 20.00
Old Colony etch, moongleam; pitcher, dolphin ft, 3-pt 210.00
Old Colony etch, moongleam; plate, rnd, 12" 75.00
Old Colony etch, moongleam; stem, cordial; #3380, 1-oz 155.00
Old Colony etch, moongleam; stem, soda; #3380, tall, 10-oz 25.00
Old Colony etch, moongleam; stem, water; #3390, tall, 11-oz 32.00
Old Colony etch, moongleam; tumbler, bar; #3380, ftd, 1-oz 52.50
Old Colony etch, moongleam; tumbler, soda; #3390, ftd, 8-oz 30.00
Old Colony etch, sahara; comport, #3368, ftd, 7" 62.50
Old Colony etch, sahara; plate, rnd, 8" 22.00
Old Colony etch, sahara; shakers, pr 110.00
Old Colony etch, sahara; stem, sherbet; #3380, 6-oz 13.00
Old Colony etch, sahara; stem, sherbet; #3390, 6-oz 25.00
Old Colony etch, sahara; tray, celery; 13" 26.00
Old Colony etch, sahara; tumbler, #3399, ftd, 2-oz 22.50
Orchid, ashtray, 3" 27.50
Orchid, bottle, French dressing; 8-oz 165.00
Orchid, bowl, floral; 11" 55.00
Orchid, bowl, gardenia; 10" 70.00
Orchid, bowl, jelly; Waverly, ftd, 6½" 40.00
Orchid, bowl, mint; Queen Ann, ftd, 5½" 35.00
Orchid, bowl, relish; rnd, 4-part, 9" 65.00
Orchid, butter dish, Cabochon, w/lid, ¼-lb 300.00
Orchid, butter dish, Waverly, w/lid, 6" 165.00
Orchid, candlestick, Cascade, 3-light 75.00
Orchid, candlestick, Flame, 2-light 135.00
Orchid, cheese & cracker, 14" 130.00
Orchid, cigarette holder, w/lid 125.00
Orchid, comport, Waverly, ftd, low, 6" 45.00
Orchid, cup, Waverly or Queen Ann 37.50
Orchid, marmalade, w/lid 200.00
Orchid, mustard, Queen Ann, w/lid 135.00
Orchid, plate, dinner, 10½" 130.00
Orchid, plate, torte; Waverly, 14" 45.00
Orchid, shakers, pr 60.00
Orchid, stem, sherry; #5022 or #5025, 2-oz 110.00
Orchid, sugar bowl, ftd 25.00
Orchid, tray, celery; 12" 45.00
Orchid, tumbler, juice; #5022 or #5025, 5-oz 50.00
Plantation, bowl, gardenia, 9½" 85.00
Plantation, butter dish, w/lid, oblong, ¼-lb 85.00
Plantation, candlestick, 1-light 75.00
Plantation, candy box, w/lid, ftd, 5" 115.00
Plantation, creamer, ftd 25.00
Plantation, plate, buffet, 18" 55.00
Plantation, plate, coupe; rare 225.00
Plantation, stem, claret; pressed, 4½-oz 30.00

Plantation, tumbler, iced tea; blown, ftd, 12-oz 45.00
Plantation, tumbler, juice; pressed, ftd, 5-oz 35.00
Plantation, vase, flared, ftd, 9" 65.00
Pleat & Panel, crystal; bowl, chow chow; 4" 5.00
Pleat & Panel, crystal; marmalade, 4¾" 10.00
Pleat & Panel, crystal; plate, luncheon; 8" 5.00
Pleat & Panel, crystal; stem, low ft, 7½-oz 10.00
Pleat & Panel, flamingo; bowl, grapefruit/cereal; 6½" 12.50
Pleat & Panel, flamingo; plate, dinner; 10¾" 40.00
Pleat & Panel, flamingo; sugar bowl, hotel, w/lid 25.00
Pleat & Panel, flamingo; vase, 8" 50.00
Pleat & Panel, moongleam; bowl, vegetable; oval, 9" 35.00
Pleat & Panel, moongleam; plate, bread; 7" 10.00
Pleat & Panel, moongleam; stem, saucer champagne; 5-oz 12.00
Pleat & Panel, moongleam; tumbler, ground bottom, 8-oz 15.00

Prince of Wales Plumes, butter dish, $125.00.

Provincial, crystal; ashtray, sq, 3" 12.50
Provincial, crystal; bowl, relish; 4-part, 10" 40.00
Provincial, crystal; candlestick, 3-light 50.00
Provincial, crystal; stem, wine; 3½-oz 20.00
Provincial, crystal; vase, violet; 3½" 20.00
Provincial, limelight; bonbon, uptrn sides, hdld, 7" 37.50
Provincial, limelight; plate, luncheon; 8" 50.00
Provincial, limelight; sugar bowl, ftd 95.00
Provincial, limelight; tumbler, iced tea; ftd, 12-oz 75.00
Ridgeleigh, ashtray, sq, 6" 20.00
Ridgeleigh, bowl, centerpiece; 8" 22.00
Ridgeleigh, bowl, fruit; flared, 12" 35.00
Ridgeleigh, bowl, lemon; w/lid, 5" 35.00
Ridgeleigh, cheese dish, hdld, 6" 11.00
Ridgeleigh, creamer 20.00
Ridgeleigh, plate, salver, 14" 40.00
Ridgeleigh, plate, scalloped, 6" 5.00
Ridgeleigh, stem, sherbet; pressed 12.00
Ridgeleigh, tumbler, juice; blown, 5-oz 24.00
Ridgeleigh, tumbler, soda; pressed, ftd, 12-oz 30.00
Ridgeleigh, vase, 8" 55.00
Rose, ashtray, 3" 37.50
Rose, bowl, lily; Queen Ann, 7" 50.00
Rose, bowl, mint; ftd, 5½" 35.00
Rose, candy dish, w/bow knot lid, low, 6" 165.00
Rose, celery tray, Waverly, 12" 55.00
Rose, compote, Waverly, low, ftd, 6½" 60.00
Rose, mayonnaise, Waverly, hdld, 5½" 55.00
Rose, plate, salad; Waverly, 8" 30.00

Rose, plate, sandwich; Waverly, 11" 50.00
Rose, stem, claret; #5072, 4-oz 110.00
Rose, stem, sherbet; #5072, 6-oz 27.50
Rose, tumbler, juice; #5072, ftd, 5-oz 45.00
Rose, vase, urn; ftd, sq, 8" 110.00
Saturn, crystal; bowl, baked apple 7.00
Saturn, crystal; creamer 15.00
Saturn, crystal; plate, luncheon; 8" 7.00
Saturn, crystal; sugar bowl 12.50
Saturn, zircon/limelight; bowl, whipped cream 150.00
Saturn, zircon/limelight; pitcher, juice 300.00
Saturn, zircon/limelight; stem, parfait; 5-oz 110.00
Saturn, zircon/limelight; tumbler, old-fashioned; 7-oz 10.00
Saturn, zircon/limelight; vase, violet 85.00
Twist, crystal; baker, oval, 9" 10.00
Twist, crystal; celery, 13" 12.00
Twist, crystal; grapefruit, ftd 10.00
Twist, crystal; plate, relish; 3-part, 13" 10.00
Twist, gr; candlestick, 1-light, 2" 25.00
Twist, gr; mayonnaise 45.00
Twist, gr; stem, sherbet; 5-oz 18.00
Twist, marigold/sahara; comport, tall, 7" 150.00
Twist, marigold/sahara; plate, sandwich; hdld, 12" 55.00
Twist, marigold/sahara; sugar bowl, ftd 60.00
Twist, marigold/sahara; tumbler, iced tea; ftd, 12-oz 50.00
Twist, pk; bowl, floral; 9" 30.00
Twist, pk; ice tub 65.00
Twist, pk; stem, wine; 2½-oz 30.00
Twist, pk; tumbler, soda; ftd, 6-oz 13.00
Waldorf Astoria, toothpick holder, w/allover silver o/l 95.00
Waverly, bowl, salad; 7" 17.00
Waverly, bowl, vegetable; 9" 20.00
Waverly, cheese dish, ftd, 5½" 20.00
Waverly, cigarette holder 50.00
Waverly, creamer, ftd 20.00
Waverly, cup 12.00
Waverly, plate, sandwich; 11" 18.00
Waverly, tray, celery; 12" 13.00
Waverly, tumbler, juice; blown, ftd, 5-oz 20.00
Waverly, vase, ftd, 7" 25.00

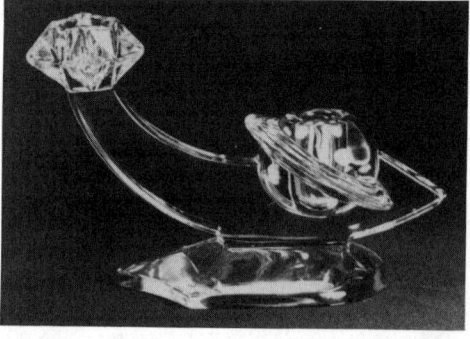

World, candle holder, 6", $325.00 each.

Yeoman, crystal; ashtray, hdld (bow tie), 4" 10.00
Yeoman, crystal; cruet, oil; 4-oz 25.00
Yeoman, crystal; plate, soup; 8" 9.00
Yeoman, crystal; stem, sherbet; 4½-oz 3.00
Yeoman, crystal; tray, relish; 3-part, 13" 20.00
Yeoman, gr; bowl, vegetable; 6" 16.00
Yeoman, gr; plate, relish; 4-part, 11" 32.00
Yeoman, gr; tumbler, soda; 4½" 15.00
Yeoman, hawthorne; bowl, baker; 9" 55.00

Yeoman, hawthorne; saucer 10.00
Yeoman, marigold; creamer 28.00
Yeoman, marigold; sugar bowl, w/lid 40.00
Yeoman, pk; bowl, banana split; ftd 23.00
Yeoman, pk; parfait, 5-oz 15.00
Yeoman, pk; tumbler, 8-oz 12.00
Yeoman, sahara; bowl, lemon; oval, 5" 15.00
Yeoman, sahara; plate, 6" 8.00

Heubach

Gebruder Heubach is a German porcelain company that has been in operation since the 1800s, producing quality figurines and novelty items. They are perhaps most famous for their doll heads and piano babies, most of which are marked with the circular rising sun device containing an 'H' superimposed over a 'C.' Our advisor for this category is Grace Ochsner; she is listed in the Directory under Illinois.

Baby in gown sits, reaches for toes, 8" 325.00
Baby in wht gown crawls, 4" L 175.00
Batter & pitcher, solid-color jerseys, mk, 9", pr 1,000.00
Blond holds hem of long pleated pk dress out at sides, 6" 345.00
Boy (or girl) beside lg turkey, bl, gold trim, #3318, 5", pr 495.00
Boy (or girl) pushes wheelbarrow, #990, 8", pr 495.00
Boy in man's top hat & coat leans on umbrella, 13" 495.00
Boy stands on 1 ft, turns both pockets wrong side out, 9¾" 450.00
Boy w/fish baskets, on base, 7" 225.00
Dancing girl, bl pleated dress, roses on base, 12" 425.00
Dog smoking pipe, polka-dot scarf around head, 6¼x8½" 450.00
Dutch boy, seated, basket on bk, mk, 7¾" 325.00
Dutch boy, seated, eyes right, 4" 250.00
Dutch boy & girl w/fruit baskets & straw hats, 10½", pr 395.00
Dutch girl seated, basket on bk, mk, 5" 250.00
Girl in long fur-trimmed red coat, cat peers from muff, 16" 750.00
Girl sitting, bl dress, wht cap, #3218, 5" 250.00
Guarding angel & cherub, gold etch, #2832, 9" 375.00
Lady sits & holds egg to side, gr dress, #5655, 4" 135.00
Lady w/bl scarf stands on base, #9031, 8", pr 375.00
Pup crouches over bowl, pipe in mouth, jaw tied w/cloth, 3" 425.00
Rooster & egg, bsk, #8160, 5½" 125.00
Vase, lady's profile w/in Nouveau floral reserve on bl, 4½" 125.00
Vase, landscape scene, ca 1900, 5¾" 135.00

Hickman, Royal Arden

Born in Willamette, Oregon, Royal A. Hickman was a genius in all aspects of design interpretation. Mr. Hickman's expertise can be seen in the designs of the lovely Heisey figurines, Kosta crystal, Bruce Fox aluminum, Three Crowns aluminum, Vernon Kilns, and Royal Haeger Pottery (as well as handcrafted silver, furniture, and paintings).

Because Mr. Hickman moved around during much of his lifetime, his influence has been felt in all forms of the media. Designs from his independent companies include 'Royal Hickman Pottery and Lamps' (sold through Ceramic Arts Inc., of Chattanooga, Tennessee), 'Royal Hickman's Paris Ware,' 'Royal Hickman — Florida,' and 'California Designed by Royal Hickman.' The following listings will give examples of pieces bearing the various trademarks. Our advisors for this category are Lee Garmon and Doris Frizzell; both are listed in the Directory under Illinois. See also Royal Haegar; Vernon Kilns, Melinda pattern.

Bruce Fox Aluminum

Banana leaf, sgn Royal Hickman-RH 6, 22½" L 20.00

Candle snuffer, sterling, sgn Royal Hickman, 12" 35.00
Dish, lobster, lg 40.00
Dish, 3-point leaf, sgn Royal Hickman, 15½" L 20.00
Leaf tray, 14" 25.00
Oak leaf, 2 acorns, 14½" L 20.00
Platter, fish, EX detail, sgn Royal Hickman-RH 3, 13x9" 50.00

California, Designed by Royal Hickman

Bowl, red w/blk highlights, #607, 9½" 15.00
Figurine, deer, apple gr w/wht spots, appl eyes, 15" 25.00
Figurine, giraffe & young, pk w/blk spots & base, 11x7" 35.00
Punch bowl, Tom & Jerry, w/8 mugs 300.00
Swan, red w/blk highlights, #643, 17" 40.00

Miscellaneous Signatures

Sea horse vase, sgn Royal Hickman USA, #468, 8" 25.00
Vase, fish figurine, 'petty crystal glaze,' #467 ....25.00
Vase, lg heart, sgn Royal Hickman, Italy, #3774 ....35.00
Vase, rooster figurine, 'petty crystal glaze,' #565 ....95.00

Royal Hickman — Florida

Vase, free-form, #578, 14" 40.00
Vase, horse's head, gray w/wht mane, 13¾" 75.00
Vase, pouter pigeon, blk cascade, #599, 8½" 40.00
Vase, swan, head down, blk cascade, #624-R, 14" 60.00

Royal Hickman — Guadal La Jara, Mexico

Vase, 3 dolphin figurines, 13" 95.00

Higgins

Contemporary glass artists Frances and Michael Higgins have been designing high-quality glassware since the late 1940s. Their designs are often created by fusing layers of glass together, though sometimes colored ground glass is used to 'paint' the decoration onto the surface. Molds are used, and through a process called 'slumping,' the glass is fired to a very high temperature, causing it to soften and take on the predetermined shape. Their work is ultramodern and is more readily found in metropolitan areas.

The earliest mark was an embossed device collector's refer to as the Higgin's 'man' — an H formed with a cup-like top and bottom superimposed over a vertical line. Later production pieces such as the piece shown are always signed with 'Higgins' etched in gold on the surface. We were assisted in our research by Dennis Hopp; he is listed in our Directory under Illinois. Our advisor for this category is Judy Potter; she is listed in the Directory under Iowa.

**Plate, astors, green with gold trim, 12",
$90.00.**

Ashtray, bl/lav/lime sqs in clear, gold tracing, 7x10" 65.00
Ashtray, gray w/appl pocket watches in yel/orange, 7x5" 400.00
Ashtray, lt gr w/lg stylized yel/gr/gilt flower, sq, 5x5" 40.00

Ashtray, Peacock, stylized feathers, gold tracing, 10x14" 125.00
Bowl, Sprite, radiating line-&-dot devices, gold traced, 12" 85.00
Charger, lime blobs w/coral-like branches on clear, 14" 145.00
Plate, Sprite, radiating line-&-dot devices, gold traced, 12" 85.00
Posey pocket, Roman Stripes, bl/lime, 2 fused planes, 10x7" 200.00
Tray, lav irid w/long triangles in bl & gr, 10x10" 130.00
Vase, Drop Out, elongated inverted hat form, ca 1970s, 3½" 65.00

Historical Glass

Glassware commemorating particularly significant historical events became popular in the late 1800s. Bread trays were the most common form, but plates, mugs, pitchers, and other items were also pressed in clear as well as colored glass. It was sold in vast amounts at the 1876 Philadelphia Centennial Exposition by various manufacturers who exhibited their wares on the grounds. It remained popular well into the 20th century.

In the listings that follow, L numbers refer to a book by Lindsey, a standard guide used by many collectors. Our advisor for this category is Darlene Yohe; she is listed in the Directory under Arkansas. See also Bread Plates; Pattern Glass.

Bottle, Columbus, milk glass, w/stopper 600.00
Bottle, Granger, L-266 ....110.00
Bottle, Grant's Tomb, milk glass, no stopper 250.00
Bottle, Statue of Liberty, milk glass, rpr stopper 500.00
Butter dish, Garfield Drape 85.00
Celery, Independence Hall 65.00
Covered dish, Battleship Oregon, milk glass, L-469, 6½" L, EX 75.00
Covered dish, Remember the Maine, gr, L-465 ....115.00
Cup, Harrison & Morton 165.00
Cup, Harrison & Morton, bl 235.00
Flask, Blaine & Logan, oval, 6¾" 550.00
Flask, Cleveland & Stevenson side-by-side jugate, 7" 50.00
Flask, Grover Cleveland, etched, flat-side rectangle, 7" 475.00
Flask, McKinley & Hobart, Distilled Protection, 7" 475.00
Goblet, Pittsburgh Centennial 95.00
Goblet, Shield, 1876 Centennial 50.00
Jar, Statue of Liberty, L-530 ....55.00
Lamp, Emblem, L-62 ....195.00
Match holder, T Roosevelt, etched, top hat form 90.00
Mug, Bumper to the Flag, sabers & 35-star flag 235.00
Mug, Garfield Assassination, 2¼" 65.00
Mug, Knights of Labor, L-513 ....50.00
Mug, Martyr's 65.00
Mug, striped shields w/3 stars front & bk, std 1776-1876 ....110.00
Paperweight, Washington, L-257 ....135.00
Pickle dish, E Pluribus Unum 45.00
Pickle dish, Emblem, L-58 ....45.00
Pitcher, Dewey, L-400 ....65.00
Plaque, Lincoln Logs, milk glass w/brn flashing, L-287, 7" 225.00
Plate, Bryan, flag/eagle/star border, milk glass, L-359 ....85.00
Plate, Columbia Shield, sapphire bl 225.00
Plate, Columbus, milk glass, 9½" 65.00
Plate, Dewey, clear/frost, sm 15.00
Plate, For President Winfield S Hancock, 8" 110.00
Plate, Harrison/Ft Meigs, amber 75.00
Plate, McKinley 35.00
Plate, Pope Leo, milk glass, L-240 ....40.00
Plate, Queen Victoria, L-435, 5¼" 25.00
Plate, St Louis Expo 1904 ....15.00
Plate, Texian Campaign, lt bl, 9½" 195.00
Plate, We Mourn Our Nation's Loss, Garfield, w/gold, 11" 55.00

Shot glass, Bryan & McKinley, 1896, NM 130.00
Spooner, Log Cabin, L-184 ....115.00
Tumbler, Admiral Dewey, etched, L-396 ....48.00
Tumbler, America, L-48 ....25.00
Wine, Washington Centennial 65.00

Homer Laughlin

The Homer Laughlin China Company of Newell, West Virginia, was founded in 1871. The superior dinnerware they displayed at the Centennial Exposition in Philadelphia in 1876 won the highest award of excellence. From that time to the present, they have continued to produce quality dinnerware and kitchenware, many lines of which are becoming very popular collectibles. Most of the dinnerware is marked with the name of the pattern and occasionally with the shape name as well. The 'HLC' trademark is usually followed by a number series, the first two digits of which indicate the year of its manufacture. See also Fiesta; Harlequin; Riviera.

Amberstone, ashtray, rare 20.00
Amberstone, bowl, jumbo salad 32.00
Amberstone, butter dish 35.00
Amberstone, creamer 7.50
Amberstone, pie plate 28.00
Amberstone, platter, rnd 16.00
Amberstone, shakers, pr 13.00
Americana, bowl, coupe soup 7.00
Americana, creamer 12.00
Americana, plate, sq, 8" 12.00
Americana, plate, 10" 20.00
Americana, plate, 6" 4.00
Americana, platter, 13" 20.00
Casualstone, bowl, jumbo salad; 10" 14.00
Casualstone, bowl, soup/cereal 4.50
Casualstone, pitcher, disk type 20.00
Casualstone, platter, oval, 13" 10.00
Casualstone, shakers, pr 7.50
Casualstone, tea server 17.00
Conchita, Hacienda or Mexicana, bowl, vegetable; 8½" 17.00
Conchita, Hacienda or Mexicana, butter dish, rnd 125.00
Conchita, Hacienda or Mexicana, egg cup, rolled edge 26.00
Conchita, Hacienda or Mexicana, plate, 9" 11.00
Conchita, Hacienda or Mexicana, platter, sq well, 11½" 16.50
Conchita, Hacienda or Mexicana, tumbler, fired-on design, 6-oz ...9.00
Conchita or Mexicana, batter jug, w/lid, Kitchen Kraft 125.00
Conchita or Mexicana, fork, Kitchen Kraft 40.00
Conchita or Mexicana, jar, w/lid, Kitchen Kraft, lg 110.00

Dreamland, handled vase, $200.00.

Dogwood, bowl, mixing; Kitchen Kraft, 10½" 25.00
Dogwood, cup & saucer 7.00
Dogwood, sugar bowl, w/lid 12.00
Embossed Line, batter pitcher, no decals 15.00
Embossed Line, bowl, mixing; no decals, 8½" 11.00
Embossed Line, casserole, w/decals, 6" 12.50
Epicure, bowl, nappy, 8¾" 12.00
Epicure, creamer 8.00
Epicure, gravy bowl 14.00
Epicure, plate, 8" 9.00
Epicure, platter, lg 14.00
Epicure, shakers, pr 12.00
Harmony, bowl, fruit; 5½" 4.50
Harmony, cake server, Kitchen Kraft 26.00
Harmony, fork, Kitchen Kraft 35.00
Harmony, plate, 9" 6.00

**Historical American, teapot, mulberry transfer, 8",
$60.00.**

Jubilee, coffeepot 28.00
Jubilee, cup & saucer, AD 12.00
Jubilee, plate, 7" 3.00
Jubilee, sauce boat 10.00
Oven-Serve, bowl, mixing; 8" 20.00
Oven-Serve, cake plate 15.00
Oven-Serve, stacking refrigerator lid 22.00
Pastel Nautilus, bowl, flat soup (deep plate) 9.00
Pastel Nautilus, bowl, soup/cereal; tab hdls 10.00
Pastel Nautilus, plate, 8" 6.00
Pastel Nautilus, platter, 13" 12.00
Priscilla, bowl, mixing; Kitchen Kraft, 6" 18.00
Priscilla, creamer 10.00
Priscilla, plate, 9" 7.00
Priscilla, platter, tab hdls, Kitchen Kraft 18.00
Rhythm, bowl, cereal/chowder; ftd 7.00
Rhythm, plate, snack 15.00
Rhythm, platter, 13½" 15.00
Rhythm, sauce boat (other than cobalt) 12.00
Rhythm, spoon rest, red 9.00
Serenade, bowl, fruit 6.00
Serenade, bowl, nappy, 9" 9.00
Serenade, plate, deep 16.00
Serenade, plate, 9" 7.00
Serenade, shakers, pr 10.00
Serenade, teacup & saucer 9.00

Tango, creamer 7.00
Tango, plate, 9" 8.00
Tango, platter, 11¾" 10.00
Tango, shakers, pr 12.00
Tango, sugar bowl, w/lid 8.00
Virginia Rose, bowl, vegetable; 8½" 12.00
Virginia Rose, pitcher, milk; 5" 25.00
Virginia Rose, plate, deep; no flange 10.00
Wells Art Glaze, bowl, fruit; 5" 4.50
Wells Art Glaze, cream soup stand 6.00
Wells Art Glaze, cup & saucer, AD 15.00
Wells Art Glaze, plate, 9" 7.50
Wells Art Glaze, platter, oval, 15½" 14.00

Hull

The A.E. Hull Pottery was formed in 1905 in Zanesville, Ohio, and in the early years produced stoneware specialities. They expanded in 1907, adding a second plant and employing over two hundred workers. By 1920 they were manufacturing a full line of stoneware, art pottery with both airbrushed and blended glazes, florist pots, and gardenware. They also produced toilet ware and kitchen items with a white semiporcelain body. Although these continued to be staple products, after the stock market crash of 1929, emphasis was shifted to tile production. By the mid-thirties interest in art pottery production was growing and over the next fifteen years, several lines of matt pastel floral-decorated patterns were designed, consisting of vases, planters, baskets, ewers, and bowls in various sizes.

The Red Riding Hood cookie jar, patented in 1943, proved so successful that a whole line of figural kitchenware and novelty items was added. They continued to be produced well into the fifties. (See also Little Red Riding Hood.) Through the forties their floral artware lines flooded the market, due to the restriction of foreign imports. Although best known for their pastel matt-glazed ware, some of the lines were high gloss. Rosella, glossy coral on a pink clay body, was produced for a short time only; Magnolia, although offered in a matt glaze, was produced in gloss as well.

The plant was destroyed in 1950 by a flood which resulted in a devastating fire when the floodwater caused the kilns to explode. The company rebuilt and equipped their new factory with the most modern machinery. It was soon apparent that the matt glaze could not be duplicated through the more modern processes, however, and soon attention was concentrated on high-gloss artware lines such as Parchment and Pine, and Ebb Tide. Figural planters and novelties, piggy banks, and dinnerware were produced in abundance in the late fifties and sixties. By the mid-seventies dinnerware and florist ware were the mainstay of their business. The firm discontinued operations in 1985.

Our advisor, Brenda Roberts, has compiled a lovely book, *The Collector's Encyclopedia of Hull Pottery*, with full-color photos and current values which has been recently reprinted. You will find her address in the Directory under Missouri.

Advertising plaque, AE Hull Pottery Co Pottery, 1938, 5x11" ..2,500.00
Bank, Corky Pig, Tawny Ridge, 5" 25.00
Bank, pig, brn, #196, 6" 20.00
Bank, pig, emb floral, cold pnt, 14" 95.00
Blossom Flite, ewer, pink/bl, pk int, rope hdl, T-13, 13½" 135.00
Blossom Flite, honey pot, pk w/bl highlights, T-1, 6" 60.00
Bow Knot, cornucopia, dbl, bl/gr, B-13-13" 210.00
Bow Knot, ewer, pk/bl, B-15-13½" 850.00
Butterfly, cornucopia, cream, B-12, 10½" 65.00
Butterfly, lavabo, cream/bl, B-24/B-25, +orig hanger, 16" 155.00
Calla Lily, candle holder, pk/bl, unmk, 2¼" 65.00

Calla Lily, cornucopia, #570/33-8" 80.00
Calla Lily, ewer, pk/bl, #505-10" 275.00
Camellia, basket, bl/pk, #142-6¼" 265.00
Camellia, candle holder, bird form, #117-6½" 110.00
Camellia, vase, bl/pk, bulbous, #123-6½" 80.00
Camellia, vase, cream, #143-8½" 115.00
Camellia, wall pocket, bl/pk, #125-8½" 235.00
Cereal Ware, canister, Conventional Rose, 8½" 70.00
Cereal Ware, canister, Flying Blue Bird, 8½" 80.00
Cereal Ware, jar, spice; Blue Star & Lattice, 4¾" 50.00
Continental, ewer, bl stripes, #56, 12½" 155.00
Continental, vase, gr stripes, #53, 8½" 40.00
Cook 'N Serve Ware, casserole, Fr hdld, #28, 8" 60.00
Cook 'N Serve Ware, creamer, #25, 3½" 14.00
Cook 'N Serve Ware, skillet tray, #27, 9¼x15½" 65.00
Country Squire, cup, gr agate, 3¼" 3.00
Country Squire, plate, gr agate, 10½" 7.00
Country Squire, soup & sandwich set (mug & tray), gr agate 22.00
Crestone, coffee server, turq w/wht foam, 11" 55.00
Crestone, sugar bowl, turq w/wht foam, w/lid, 4¼" 20.00
Debonair, casserole, pk & lav w/blk band, w/lid, #0-17, 8½" 55.00
Debonair, cookie jar, yel, #0-8, 8¾" 65.00
Dogwood, bowl, console; cream, #511-11½" 265.00
Dogwood, ewer, cream, #519-13½" 800.00
Dogwood, vase, pk/bl, #502-6½" 150.00
Dogwood, vase, turq/cream, #509-6½" 85.00
Early Art, Alpine tankard, H in circle, 9½" 235.00
Early Art, flowerpot, unmk, 4" 30.00
Early Art, matt; vase, stoneware, H in circle, 8" 70.00
Early Banded Utility, bowl, stoneware, H in circle, 9" ..32.50
Early Banded Utility, pitcher, yellow ware, H in circle, 4¾" 25.00
Early Utility, bowl, banded semiporc, Hull Ware, A-1-7½" 30.00
Early Utility, bowl, brn & bl bands on tan, E-I-10" 35.00
Early Utility, pie plate, banded semiporc, unmk, 9" 25.00
Early Utility, pitcher, banded semiporc, unmk, 6¼" 50.00
Early Utility, pitcher, pk & bl bands on tan, E-7" 50.00
Early Utility, teapot, stoneware, H in circle, 6¼" 85.00
Ebb Tide, creamer, shell form, E-15, 4" 35.00
Ebb Tide, ewer, shell form, E-10, 14" 200.00
Ebb Tide, teapot, shell form, E-14, 6½" 165.00
Fantasy, cherub planter, #90, 7¼x9" 60.00
Fiesta, cornucopia, #49, 8½" 55.00
Fiesta, jardiniere, #43, 6" 35.00
Floral, bowl, salad; yel daisies, brn band at rim, #49, 10" 55.00
Gold-Medal Flowerware, bucket jardiniere, #94B, 6" ...25.00
Gold-Medal Flowerware, vase, #102, 11½" 30.00
Heritage, cookie jar, 'Cookies' on milk can form, #0-18-9½" 60.00
Imperial, chicadee planter, Golden Mist, F-473, 6" 12.50
Imperial, gurgling fish ewer, Golden Mist, F-482, 11" ..85.00
Imperial, jardiniere, thunderbird decor, 4" 10.00
Imperial, Madonna, F-7, 1974, 7" 30.00
Imperial, vase, Mirror Black, 9" 18.00
Iris, ewer, ornate rim, pk/bl, #401-13½" 465.00
Iris, rose bowl, peach, #412-7" 135.00
Iris, vase, petal top, #407-8½" 120.00
Magnolia, cornucopia, cream/pk, #19-8½" 85.00
Magnolia, vase, yel/dusty rose, #20-15" 350.00
Marcrest, pitcher, rings emb on bulbous body, 7½" 37.50
Mardi Gras/Granada, basket, cream #32-8" 140.00
Mardi Gras/Granada, candle holder, cream, unmk, 3¼" 30.00
Mardi Gras/Granada, matt; vase, cream, #216-9" 48.00
Mirror Almond, bowl, divided; almond w/caramel trim, 11" 20.00
Mirror Almond, mug, almond w/caramel rim, 3¼" 3.00
Mirror Almond, plate, almond w/caramel rim, 10" 7.00

Mirror Brown, bowl, mixing; brn w/ivory foam, unmk, 9" 6.00
Mirror Brown, canister, brn w/ivory foam, rnd, 6"-9", set of 4 ....200.00
Mirror Brown, casserole, duck-form lid, brn w/ivory foam, 8" 32.00
Mirror Brown, coffee mug, brn w/ivory foam, 3½" 3.00
Mirror Brown, gingerbread boy coaster/spoon rest, 5" 6.00
Mirror Brown, gingerbread man server, 10" 30.00
Mirror Brown, jug/creamer, brn w/ivory foam, 4¾" 8.00
Mirror Brown, pitcher, brn w/ivory foam, ice lip, 7½" 22.50
Mirror Brown, plate, brn w/ivory foam, 10½" 5.00
Mirror Brown, server, 1-hdl, brn w/ivory foam, 11½" 18.50
New Magnolia, ewer, bl floral on cream, H-19-13½" 250.00
New Magnolia, vase, bl floral on cream, H-5-6½" 35.00
Novelty, bandana duck planter, dk gr/wine, #75, 7" 55.00
Novelty, candle holder, lustre ware, unmk, 3" 65.00
Novelty, casserole, French hdl, ind, 5" 18.00
Novelty, crazy horse planter, #959, 1938, 5" 35.00
Novelty, dachshund planter, 14" 120.00

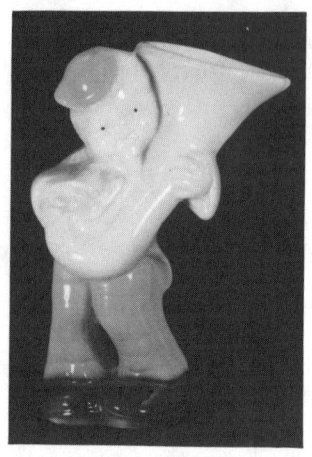

Novelty figurine, boy with tuba, 6½", $70.00.

Novelty, girl w/basket, wht matt, #954, 8" 40.00
Novelty, jardiniere, Crab Apple, semiporc, unmk, 4" 85.00
Novelty, parrot w/cart planter, #60, 6" 40.00
Novelty, rabbit, #968, 6" 25.00
Novelty, rabbit planter, mk #952 USA & sample seal, 4½" 40.00
Novelty, ribbon wall pocket, #71, 1951, 6" 40.00
Novelty, swan planter, #80, 6" 40.00
Novelty, tea bell, Sun-Glow, rope hdl, unmk, 6¼" 85.00
Novelty, unicorn vase, #99, 11½" 65.00
Novelty, vase, lustre ware, unmk, 10" 95.00
Novelty, window box, dk gr/wine, unmk, 11" 17.50
Nuline Bak-Serve, mug, coffee; Fish Scale; C-25, 3½" 30.00
Nuline Bak-Serve, pitcher, Dmn Quilt, ice lip, B-29, 8½" 85.00
Nuline Bak-Serve, teapot, Dmn Quilt, B-5, 5½" 85.00
Orchid, jardiniere, #310-9½" 300.00
Orchid, vase, bud; #306-6¾" 110.00
Parchment & Pine, basket, S-8, 16½" 160.00
Parchment & Pine, candle holder, S-10, 5" 25.00
Parchment & Pine, instant coffee server, S-15, 8" 110.00
Parchment & Pine, teapot, S-11, 6" 85.00
Plaidware, creamer, #67, USA, 3" 40.00
Plaidware, shaker, #364, 3¼" 25.00
Poppy, basket, pk/bl, #501-12" 950.00
Poppy, ewer, bl/pk, #610-13½" 850.00
Poppy, wall pocket, cream/pk, #609-9" 285.00
Rosella, lamp, dimpled body, unmk, 1946, 10¾" 600.00
Rosella, lamp, L-3, 1946, 11" 300.00
Rosella, vase, dimpled, R-7-6½" 100.00
Serenade, candle holder, Shell Pk, S-16, 6½", pr 50.00

Serenade, ewer, yel, S-2, 6½" 65.00
Serenade, vase, yel, S-12, 14" 100.00
Sun Valley Pastel, flower dish, #152, 13" 25.00
Sun Valley Pastel, window box, #153, 12½" 30.00
Sun-Glow, bowl, mixing; yel, #50, 7½" 27.50
Sun-Glow, shaker, pk, #54, 2¾", pr 12.50
Sun-Glow, wall pocket, cup & saucer form, #80, 6¼" 50.00
Tangerine, bean pot, w/warmer, 9" 35.00
Tangerine, leaf dish, 12" 30.00
Tangerine, teapot, 6½" 25.00
Thistle, vase, pk & gr on bl, #51-6½" 75.00
Tile, HP florals on gr satin, 4¼x4¼" 20.00
Tile, mottled gr & aqua wash, ink stamp, 4¼" sq 17.50
Tile, sailboat, matt bls, raised mk, 2¾x6" 50.00
Tile, stylized leaves, gr on yel, raised mk, 2¾x6" 50.00
Tokay, consolette, #14, 15¾" 135.00
Tokay, leaf dish, #19, 14" 40.00
Tropicana, flower bowl, Caribbean figure on wht, T-51, 15½" ...265.00
Tropicana, planter vase, Caribbean figure on wht, T-57, 14½" ..290.00
Tulip, ewer, mc flowers on cream/bl, #109-33-13" 325.00
Tulip, jardiniere, mc tulips on bl, #117-30-5" 75.00
Tulip, jardiniere, tulips on pk/bl, #115-33-7" 225.00
Tuscany, ewer, #13, 12" 180.00
Water Lily, lamp, unmk, 1949, 7½" 150.00
Wild Flower, ewer, cream/pk, #55-13½" 425.00
Wild Flower, teapot, cream/pk, #72-8" 375.00
Woodland, glossy; ewer, W-3, 5½" 50.00
Woodland, glossy; vase, W-1, 5½" 40.00
Woodland, matt; ewer, yel/gr, W-6, 6½" 85.00
Woodland, matt; flowerpot, attached saucer, W-11, 5¾" 135.00

Hummel

Hummel figurines were created through the artistry of Berta Hummel, a Franciscan nun called Sister M. Innocentia. The first figures were made about 1935 by Franz Goebel of Goebel Art Inc., Rodental, West Germany. Plates, plaques, and candy dishes are also produced and the older, discontinued editions are highly sought collectibles. Generally speaking, an issue can be dated by the trademark. The first Hummels from 1934-1950 were either incised or stamped with the 'Crown WG' mark. The 'full bee in V' mark was employed with minor variations until 1959. At that time the bee was stylized and represented by a solid disk with angled symmetrical wings completely contained within the confines of the 'V.' The three-line mark, 1964-1972, utilized the stylized bee and included a three-line arrangement, 'c by W. Goebel, W. Germany.' Another change in 1970 saw the 'stylized bee in V' suspended between the vertical bars of the 'b' and 'l' of a printed 'Goebel, West Germany.' Collectors refer to this mark as the 'last bee' or 'Goebel bee.' The current mark in use since 1979 omits the 'bee in V.' For a more thorough study of the subject, we recommend *Hummel Figurines and Plates, A Collector's Identification and Value Guide,* by Carl Luckey, available through your local book dealer. Idiosyncrasies in the numerical order of the following listings are due to computer sorting. See also Limited Edition Plates.

Key:
ce — closed edition   GB — Goebel bee
CM — crown mark   SB — stylized bee
FB — full bee   LB — last bee

#III/110, Let's Sing, candy box, GB, 5¼" 165.00
#III/39/0, Joyous News, candle holder, CM, 2x2½" 125.00
#III/53, Joyful, candy box, CM, 6½" 550.00

#III/57, Chick Girl, candy box, CM, 5¼" 550.00
#III/58, Playmates, candy box, CM, 6¼" 550.00
#III/69, Happy Pastime, candy box, 3-line mk, 6" ...150.00
#1, Puppy Love, CM, 5" 475.00
#1, Puppy Love, SB, 5" 250.00
#101, To Market, table lamp, SB, 7½" 650.00
#106, Merry Wanderer, plaque w/wood fr, CM, 6x6" 5,500.00
#109/II, Happy Traveler, SB, 8" 350.00
#109/0, Happy Traveler, FB, 5" 275.00
#11/0, Merry Wanderer, 3-line mk, 5" 160.00
#11/2/0, Merry Wanderer, LB, 4" 120.00
#110/0, Let's Sing, 3-line mk, 3⅞" 140.00
#11/ 3/0, Wayside Harmony, CM, 4" 350.00
#111/I, Wayside Harmony, FB, 5" 300.00
#112/3/0, Just Resting, 3-line mk, 4" 120.00
#113, Heavenly Song, candle holder, FB, 3½x4¾" 5,000.00
#114, Let's Sing, ashtray, FB, 3½x6¼" 550.00
#118, Little Thrifty, bank, LB, 5" 140.00
#119, Postman, CM, 5½" 500.00
#12/I, Chimney Sweep, SB, 5½" 135.00
#12/2/0, Chimney Sweep, 3-line mk, 4" 75.00
#123, Max & Moritz, FB, 5½" 265.00
#124/I, Hello, 3-line mk, 7" 175.00
#124/0, Hello, SB, 6" 135.00
#125, Vacation Time, plaque, LB, 4x4¼" 180.00
#126, Retreat to Safety, plaque, CM, 5x5" 525.00
#127, Doctor, FB, 4¾x5¼" 250.00
#128, Baker, SB, 4¾x5" 125.00
#129, Band Leader, 3-line mk, 5" 175.00
#13/0, Meditation, 3-line mk, 6" 200.00
#13/2/0, Meditation, FB, 4¼" 200.00
#130, Duet, LB, 5½" 200.00
#131, Street Singer, CM, 4¾" 600.00
#132, Star Gazer, FB, 4¾" 265.00
#133, Mother's Helper, SB, 5" 160.00
#134, Quartet, plaque, 3-line mk, 6x6" 250.00
#135, Soloist, LB, 5" 120.00
#136/I, Friends, CM, 5" 500.00
#136/V, Friends, FB, 11" 1,250.00
#137B, Child in Bed (looking right), SB, 2¾x2¾" 60.00
#139, Flitting Butterfly, plaque, LB, 2½x2½" 60.00
#14/A&B, Book Worm, bookends, FB, 5½", pr 575.00
#140, The Mail Is Here, plaque, LB, 4¼x6¼" 240.00
#15/I, Year Ye Hear Ye, SB, 6" 200.00
#16/I, Little Hiker, FB, 5½" 320.00
#17/0, Congratulations, CM, 5½" 375.00
#18, Christ Child, LB, 2x6" 100.00
#2/0, Little Fiddler, LB, 6" 175.00
#20, Prayer Before Battle, CM, 4" 475.00
#21/I, Heavenly Angel, FB, 7" 300.00
#21/0, Heavenly Angel, SB, 4" 100.00
#23/I, Adoration, SB, 6¾" 300.00
#23/III, Adoration, CM, 9" 1,300.00
#24/I, Lullaby, candle holder, 3-line mk, 3¼x5" 140.00
#25, Angelic Sleep, candle holder, FB, 3½x5" 225.00
#29/0, Guardian Angel, font, SB, 6x2½" 880.00
#3/I, Book Worm, FB, 5½" 500.00
#32/I, Little Gabriel, SB, 6" 2,500.00
#32/0, Little Gabriel, 3-line mk, 5" 125.00
#33, Joyful, ashtray, CM, 3½x6" 375.00
#34, Singing Lesson, ashtray, SB, 3½x6¼" 150.00
#35/0, Good Shepherd, font, FB, 2½x4¾" 60.00
#37, Herald Angels, candle holder, FB, 2¾x4" 235.00
#4, Little Fiddler, SB, 5" 135.00

#42/0, Good Shepherd, SB, 6¼x6½" 200.00
#43, March Winds, FB, 5" 180.00
#44, Culprits, table lamp, CM, 9½" 600.00
#44/B, Out of Danger, table lamp, SB, 12" 325.00
#45/I, Madonna w/Halo, wht, SB, 12" 95.00
#47/0, Goose Girl, LB, 5" 195.00
#47/3/0, Goose Girl, FB, 4" 200.00
#48/0, Madonna, plaque, 3-line mk, 3¼x4¼" 90.00
#49/I, To Market, FB, 6" 750.00
#49/3/0, To Market, 3-line mk, 4" 150.00
#5, Strolling Along, 3-line mk, 4¾" 125.00
#50/0, Volunteers, SB, 5½" 230.00
#50/2/0, Volunteers, FB, 5" 285.00
#51/I, Village Boy, CM, 7¼" 1,100.00
#51/3/0, Village Boy, SB, 4" 140.00
#52/0, Going to Grandma's, 3-line mk, 5" 180.00
#54, Silent Night, candle holder, 3-line mk, 4¾x5½" 225.00
#55, Saint George, FB, 6¾" 360.00
#56/A, Culprits, SB, 6" 220.00
#56/B, Out of Danger, 3-line mk, 6" 245.00
#57/0, Chick Girl, LB, 3½" 150.00
#58/0, Playmates, 3-line mk, 4" 145.00
#59, Skier, LB, 5¼" 195.00
#6/I, Sensitive Hunter, CM, 5½" 200.00
#6/I, Sensitive Hunter, SB, 5½" 175.00
#62, Happy Pastime, ashtray, FB, 3½x6¼" 200.00
#63, Singing Lesson, CM, 3" 325.00
#64, Shepherd's Boy, 3-line mk, 5½" 200.00
#65/I, Farewell, 3-line mk, 5" 225.00
#66, Farm Boy, FB, 5" 275.00
#67, Doll Mother, LB, 4¾" 170.00
#68/2/0, Lost Sheep, FB, 4½" 175.00
#69, Happy Pastime, SB, 3½" 120.00
#7/II, Merry Wanderer, LB, 9½" 1,000.00
#7/0, Merry Wanderer, 3-line mk, 6" 170.00
#70, Holy Child, LB, 7" 140.00
#71, Stormy Weather, CM, 6¼" 900.00
#72, Spring Cheer, SB, 5" 110.00
#73, Little Helper, 3-line mk, 4" 100.00
#74, Little Gardener, LB, 4" 100.00
#75, White Angel, font, CM, 1¾x3½" 150.00
#78/III, Infant of Krumbad (Blessed Child), SB, 5" 55.00
#79, Globe Trotter, CM, 5" 550.00
#8, Book Worm, SB, 4" 165.00
#80, Little Scholar, FB, 5½" 250.00
#81/0, School Girl, 3-line mk, 5" 155.00
#81/2/0, School Girl, SB, 4" 125.00
#82/II, School Boy, CM, 7½" 1,000.00
#82/2/0, School Boy, LB, 4" 125.00
#83, Angel Serenade, w/lamb, FB, 5" 400.00
#84/V, Worship, 3-line mk, 13" 1,200.00
#84/0, Worship, SB, 5" 145.00
#85/0, Serenade, LB, 5" 120.00
#88, Heavenly Protection, CM, 9¼" 1,300.00
#89/I, Little Cellist, FB, 6" 265.00
#9, Begging His Share, SB, 5½" 250.00
#91 A&B, Angels at Prayer, font, SB, 2x5", pr 75.00
#92, Merry Wanderer, plaque, 3-line mk, 4½x5" 125.00
#93, Little Fiddler, plaque, LB, 4½x5" 120.00
#94 3/0, Surprise, CM, 4" 380.00
#94/I, Surprise, FB, 5½" 300.00
#95, Brother, SB, 5¾" 175.00
#96, Little Shopper, 3-line mk, 5" 170.00
#97, Trumpet Boy, LB, 4¾" 115.00

#95, Brother, full bee, 5½", $215.00.

#98/0, Sister, SB, 5½" 175.00
#99, Eventide, FB, 4¼x5" 360.00

Hutschenreuther

The Porcelain Factory C.M. Hutschenreuther operated in Bavaria from 1814 to 1969. After the death of the elder Hutschenreuther in 1845, his son Lorenz took over operations, continuing there until 1857 when he left to establish his own company in the nearby city of Selb. The original manufactory became a joint stock company in 1904, absorbing several other potteries. In 1969 both Hutschenreuther firms merged, and that company still operates in Selb. They have distributing centers in both France and the United States. Our advisor for this category is Jack Gunsaulus; he is listed in the Directory under Michigan.

Bowl, floral/gold decor on swirled quatrefoil, Le Roy, 10" 175.00
Bud vase, girl in bonnet playing w/stick & hoop aside, 5½" 80.00
Cake stand, Bl Onion, 3-tier 185.00
Celery, floral w/gold, Selb Bavaria, 12" 23.00
Figurine, American Eagle, sgn K Tutter, 15" 695.00
Figurine, cat, recumbent, wht w/gr eyes, 7" 165.00
Figurine, Colonial courting couple, 1930, 6½", pr 495.00
Figurine, dancer in lt bl tunic, sgn K Tutter, 12¼" 375.00
Figurine, Faust, 7" 350.00
Figurine, girl in full skirt curtsies, sgn K Tutter, 7" 155.00
Figurine, girl running w/dog, sgn Tutter, 6½" 135.00
Figurine, Naughty Nelly, bsk, sgn, ca 1886, 9½" 395.00
Figurine, nude child w/flowers, feeds fawn, Tutter, 4½" 125.00
Figurine, tiger pr, fine details, mk, 1920s, 9½" L 750.00
Figurine, 2 cockatoos on ball, wht/gold/yel, 11½" 295.00
Plate, garlands in center & on bl rim, 10", set of 12 ....525.00
Plate, Raphael's Madonna Della Sedia, gilt wood fr, 9½" 225.00
Tray, gold florals & hdls, swirled quatrefoil shape, 10"................175.00

Imari

Imari is a generic term which covers a broad family of wares. It was made in more than a dozen Japanese villages, but the name is that of the port from whence it was shipped to Europe. There are several types of Imari. The most common features a design with panels of birds, florals, or people surrounding a central basket of flowers. The colors used in this type are underglaze blue with overglaze red, gold, and green enamels. The Chinese also made Imari wares which differ from the Japanese type in several ways — the absence of spur marks, a thinner-type body, and a more consistent control of the blue. Imari-type wares were copied on the continent by Meissen and by English potters, among them Worcester, Derby, and Bow.

Biscuit jar, florals, barrel form, 1800s, 6" 200.00
Bottle vase, flowers/dragons/bldgs, 1850s, 12", EX 300.00
Bowl, floral in bl/gr/gold, 1800s, 12½" 900.00
Bowl, flowers/geometrics, 1900s, 10" 225.00
Bowl, priest & dog around floral center, 1850s, 7½" 300.00
Charger, bouquet in center, paneled border, 1890s, 19" 350.00
Charger, floral w/wht rim reserves, 25" 900.00
Charger, flower urns/foliage/diapering, Mason's, 13¾" 185.00
Plate, floral medallion, cobalt rim w/fan panels, late, 12" 90.00
Plate, mc florals, shaped rim, 12" 150.00
Plate, 16-petal mum form w/brocade design, late, 8" 75.00
Punch bowl, phoenix birds, vines/flowers, 1800s, 15" 3,600.00
Vase, birds in costumes, ladies, wood base, 1890s, 25" 935.00
Vase, birds/flowers reserve on dk bl w/gold motif, sgn, 12" 375.00

Imperial Glass Company

The Imperial Glass Company was organized in 1901 in Bellaire, Ohio, and started manufacturing glassware in 1904. Their early products were jelly glasses, hotel tumblers, etc., but by 1910 they were making a name for themselves by pressing quantities of Carnival Glass, the iridescent glassware that was popular during that time. In 1914 NuCut was introduced to imitate cut glass. The line was so popular that it was made in crystal and colors and was reintroduced as Collector's Crystal in the 1950s. From 1916 to 1920 they used the lustre process to make a line called Imperial Jewels, now referred to as stretch glass. Free-Hand ware, art glass made entirely by hand using no molds, was made from 1922 to 1928.

The company entered bankruptcy in 1931 but was able to continue operations and reorganize as the Imperial Glass Corporation. In 1936 Imperial introduced the Candlewick line, for which it is best known. In the late thirties the Vintage Grape Milk Glass line was added, and in 1951 a major ad campaign was launched, making Imperial one of the leading milk glass manufacturers.

In 1940 Imperial bought the molds and assets of the Central Glass Works of Wheeling, West Virginia; in 1958 they acquired the molds of the Heisey Company, and in 1960, the molds of the Cambridge Glass Company of Cambridge, Ohio. Imperial used these molds, and after 1951 they marked their glassware with an 'I' superimposed over the 'G' trademark. The company became a subsidiary of Lenox in 1973; subsequently an 'L' was added to the 'IG' mark. In 1981 Lenox sold Imperial to Arthur Lorch, a private investor (who modified the L by adding a line at the top angled to the left). He in turn sold the company to Robert F. Stahl, Jr., in 1982. Mr. Stahl filed for Chapter 11 to reorganize, but in mid-1984 liquidation was ordered, and all assets were sold. The few items that had been made in '84 were marked with an 'N' superimposed over the 'I' for 'New Imperial.' See also Candlewick; Carnival Glass; Stretch Glass.

Ashtray, Cape Cod, #150/134/1, 4" 8.00
Ashtray, purple slag satin 17.00
Basket, Daisy, milk glass, Doeskin 25.00
Basket, Monticello, crystal irid 25.00
Bowl, baked apple; Tradition, bl 12.00
Bowl, Cape Cod, ftd, 10" 75.00
Bowl, swan, milk glass, Doeskin, 8" 35.00
Box, flat iron, purple slag, w/lid 100.00
Butter dish, Cape Cod, #160/144, 5" 35.00
Cake plate, Cape Cod, #160/220, 4-ftd, sq 90.00
Cake plate, Collector's Crystal, ftd 25.00
Claret, Cape Cod 9.00
Cordial, Cape Cod, #1602 ....10.00
Cruet, Cape Cod, #160/70, w/stopper 30.00

Cup & saucer, Cape Cod 10.00
Decanter, Cape Cod, #160/212, 24-oz 58.00
Decanter, Collector's Crystal, gold trim 45.00
Egg cup, Cape Cod, #160/225 ....27.50
Goblet, Cape Cod, #1602, 9-oz 9.00
Lighter, Cape Cod, purple slag 25.00
Mug, Dumbo, gr, 1974 ....50.00
Mug, Storybook, jade slag, gloss 30.00
Mustard, Cape Cod, #160/156, w/lid & spoon 25.00
Nappy, Antique Bl, 5" 18.00
Old-fashioned, Cape Cod, #160, 7-oz 8.00
Parfait, Cape Cod, #1602 ....12.00
Pepper mill, Cape Cod 20.00
Pitcher, Cape Cod, #160/19, ice lip, 40-oz 85.00
Pitcher, milk; Cape Cod, #160/240, 16-oz 49.00
Pitcher, Tradition, ice lip, 54-oz 45.00
Plate, Cape Cod, #160/1D, 6¼" 6.00
Plate, Cape Cod, #160/10D, 10" 33.00
Plate, Cape Cod, hdls, 11½" 28.00
Plate, Coin, 1971 Kennedy Series 25.00
Platter, Cape Cod, 12" 70.00
Punch set, #500, 15-pc 125.00
Relish, Cape Cod, oval, plain rim, 9½" 30.00
Server, Cape Cod, #160/93, ftd, 12" 78.00
Shakers, Cape Cod, #160/116, pr 15.00
Shakers, Stamm House, Dewdrop opal, pr 30.00
Sherbet, Cape Cod, #160, low 6.00
Sherbet, Cape Cod, #1602, tall 8.50
Sherbet, Mt Vernon, low 7.00
Sherbet, Star Holly, milk glass 10.00
Sherbet, Tradition, yel 12.00
Spider, hdl, Cape Cod, #160/180, 4½" 18.00
Stein, Cape Cod, milk glass, Doeskin 35.00
Tray, Cape Cod, #160/26 ....30.00
Tray, pastry; Cape Cod, amber, 11" 75.00
Tumbler, Cape Cod, #160, 10-oz, 5" 12.00
Tumbler, Cape Cod, #160, 12-oz, 5¼" 10.00
Tumbler, juice; Cape Cod, #160 ....5.00
Tumbler, juice; Cape Cod, #1602, amber 12.00
Tumbler, On-the-Rocks, Bambu, gold trim, 14-oz 10.00
Vase, Free-Hand, gold lustre, cone form w/flared rim, 6½" 100.00
Vase, Free-Hand, heart leaves, gr irid on wht, 7¼" 395.00
Vase, Free-Hand, hearts/vines, wht on cobalt, orange int, 11" ...550.00
Vase, Free-Hand, leaves/vines, gr/opal, orange int, rnd, 6" 400.00
Vase, Mt Vernon, pk, sq 10.00
Whiskey, Cape Cod, #160, flat, 2½-oz 15.00
Wine, Cape Cod, #1602, 3-oz 6.00
Wine, Mt Vernon 8.00

Cathay Crystal

In 1943 Imperial commissioned artist-designer, Virginia B. Evans, to design a line of Chinese-inspired giftware. Representative of China's history, this line consisted of thirty-one designs which were produced in a satin/frosted combination. Except for items too small to accomodate it, each piece bears the script signature of its designer. The line was lavishly introduced at the National China and Glass Show in Pittsburgh in 1949. Items were presented in boxes lined with green suede and lettered in gold, each piece having its own number. But as was often true for unusual art glass lines, Cathay Crystal did not meet sales expectations, and the line was manufactured for only two years. For a short time and in limited amounts, some designs were produced in color but the Evans name was removed from the molds.

#5001, pagoda 550.00
#5002, Shang candy jar 250.00
#5004, Yan & Yin ashtray 175.00
#5006, butterfly ashtray 25.00
#5007, plum blossom ashtray 25.00
#5008, peach blossom mint or nut set 20.00
#5009, dragon candle holder, pr 400.00
#5010, junk flower bowl 250.00
#5011, Wu Ling ashtray 125.00
#5012, Ku ribbon vase 750.00
#5013, pillow candle base 50.00
#5014, bamboo urn 400.00
#5016, Fu wedding vase 200.00
#5017, egrette 300.00
#5018, pillow cigarette set, 3-pc 550.00

Cathay Crystal, fan sweetmeat box, #5022, $225.00.

#5019, Ming jar 80.00
#5020, Shen console set 300.00
#5024, scolding bird 200.00
#5026, phoenix bowl 175.00
#5029, empress book stop, pr 250.00
#5030, Lu-Tunb book holder, pr 350.00
#5033/34, candle servants, pr 350.00
#5038, Celestial centerpc 350.00
#5085, Pavillion tray 350.00

Imperial Porcelain

The Blue Ridge Mountain Boys were created by cartoonist Paul Webb and translated into three-dimension by the Imperial Porcelain Corporation of Zanesville, Ohio, in 1947. These figurines decorated ashtrays, vases, mugs, bowls, pitchers, planters, and other items. The Mountain Boys series were numbered 92 through 108, each with a different and amusing portrayal of mountain life. Imperial also produced American Folklore miniatures, twenty-three tiny animals one inch or less in size, and the Al Capp Dogpatch series. Because of financial difficulties, the company closed in 1960.

American Folklore Miniatures

Cat, 1½" 40.00
Cow, 1¾" 35.00
Hound dogs 35.00
Plaque, store ad, Am Folklore Porcelain Miniatures, 4½" 400.00
Sow 30.00

Blue Ridge Mountain Boys by Paul Webb

Ashtray, #101, man w/jug & snake 75.00
Ashtray, #103, hillbilly & skunk 75.00
Ashtray, #105, baby, hound dog, & frog 110.00
Ashtray, #106, Barrel of Wishes, w/hound 75.00
Ashtray, #92, 2 men by tree stump, for pipes 125.00
Box, cigarette; #98, dog atop, baby at door, sq 115.00
Dealer's sign, Handcrafted Paul Webb Mtn Boys, rare, 9" 650.00
Decanter, #100, outhouse, man, & bird 75.00
Decanter, #104, Ma leaning over stump, w/baby & skunk 95.00
Decanter, man, jug, snake, & tree stump, Hispch Inc, 1946 ...75.00
Figurine, #101, man leans against tree trunk, 5" 90.00
Figurine, man on hands & knees, 3" 95.00
Figurine, man sitting, 3½" 95.00
Figurine, man sitting w/chicken on knee, 3" 95.00
Jug, #101, Willie & snake 75.00
Mug, #94, Bearing Down, 6" 95.00
Mug, #94, dbl baby hdl, 4¼" 95.00
Mug, #94, ma hdl, 4¼" 95.00
Mug, #94, man w/bl pants hdl, 4¼" 95.00
Mug, #94, man w/yel beard & red pants hdl, 4¼" 95.00
Mug, #99, Target Practice, boy on goat, farmer, 5¾" 95.00
Pitcher, lemonade 200.00
Planter, #100, outhouse, man, & bird 75.00
Planter, #105, man w/chicken on knee, washtub 110.00
Planter, #110, man, w/jug & snake, 4½" 65.00
Planter, #81, man drinking from jug, sitting by washtub ...75.00
Shakers, Ma & Old Doc, pr 95.00

Miscellaneous

Items in this section that are designated 'IP' are miscellaneous novelties made by Imperial Porcelain; the remainder are of interest to Paul Webb collectors, though made by an unknown manufacturer. Prints on calendars and playing cards are signed 'Paul Webb.'

Calendar, 1954, 12 sgn scenes, Brown & Bigelow, complete 48.00
Figurine, cat in high-heeled shoe, 5½" L 40.00
Hot pad, Dutch boy w/tulips, rnd, IP 30.00
Ink blotters, sgn scenes, ea 8.00
Mug, #29, man hdl, sgn Paul Webb, 4¾" 45.00
Planter, #106, dog sitting by tub, IP 75.00
Playing cards, ad: Rafe Oiling Gun, Brown & Bigelow, MIB 45.00
Shakers, pigs, 5", pr 95.00
Shakers, standing pigs, IP, 8", pr 95.00

Indian Tree

Indian Tree is a popular dinnerware pattern produced by various potteries since the early 1800s. Although backgrounds and borders vary, the Oriental theme is carried out with the gnarled, brown branch of a pink-blossomed tree. Among the manufacturers' marks, you may find represented such notable firms as Coalport, S. Hancock and Sons, Soho Pottery, and John Maddock and Sons.

Bowl, soup; Johnson Bros 12.00
Bowl, soup; shallow, Spode-Copeland 15.00
Bowl, vegetable; oval, Maddux, 9" 22.50
Bowl, vegetable; w/lid, English 75.00
Creamer & sugar bowl, Johnson Bros 30.00
Cup & saucer, AD; Minton 25.00
Gravy tureen, w/lid & ladle, English 85.00

Plate, dinner; Johnson Bros, 10" 12.00
Plate, Maddock, 9⅝" 10.00
Platter, Johnson Bros, 16" 35.00
Relish, 2-part, 6" 35.00

Inkwells and Inkstands

Receptacles for various writing fluids have been used since ancient times. Through the years they have been made from countless materials — glass, metal, porcelain, pottery, wood, and even papier-mache. During the 18th century, gold or silver inkstands were presented to royalty; the well-known silver inkstand by Philip Syng, Jr. was used for the signing of the Declaration of Independence, and impressive brass inkstands with wells and a pounce pot (sander) were proud possessions of men of letters. When literacy vastly increased in the 19th century, the dip pen replaced the quill pen; inkwells and inkstands were widely used and produced in a broad range of sizes in functional and decorative forms from ornate Victorian to flowing Art Nouveau and stylized Art Deco designs. However, the acceptance of the ballpoint pen literally put inkstands and inkwells 'out of business.' But their historical significance and intriguing diversity of form and styling fascinate today's collectors.

Alabaster, lathe-trn, glass liner, 3-hole, 1850s, 2x3" dia 85.00
Blk glass sq base w/cut sides, clear well, Mt WA, 2½x2½" 210.00
Blown, olive-amber, pyramidal, sm lip flake, 2⅜" 95.00
Brass, 2 repousse pots, latticework, scroll ft, Germany, 12" 120.00
Brass, 2 wells w/cut glass lids, pen holder, w/dip pen 135.00
Brass w/gold edge, hinged lid, Bradley & Hubbard, 5x4¾" 110.00
Bronze, well ea side Nouveau lady's head, rtcl swirls, 12" L 990.00
B3m, olive-amber, GII-18, sm flake on top lip, 2x2¾" 150.00
B3m, olive-gr, GII-18, 1⅞" 150.00
Clear glass, cylindrical, disk base, Davis Patent...1893 ....20.00
Copper, brn patina w/much silverwork, curled ft, Heintz 195.00
Copper, Greek Key, brn patina w/silver o/l, Heintz 195.00
Cut glass, Cane, eng Gorham lid 170.00
Cut glass, pyramid w/star-cut base, SP lid, 2¾x3x3" 265.00
Gilt bronze, 3 female busts on paw ft support well, 5" 250.00
Gilt bronze bell shape on marble base, ribbon finial, 6" 200.00
Gr irid glass free-form w/chick figural brass lid, 2¾" 265.00
Iron, w/pen rack & candle socket, pitted, 7½" 200.00

Metal 3-legged bird figural, red glass well, 4", $275.00.

Nailsea glass, bl w/wht loopings, hinged lid, 3½" dia 650.00
Silver, detailed camel, hump is lid, FH Clark, 1904, 8" L 1,900.00
Silver, scrolled form, taperstick, 2-well, Jos Angell, 1830 ....1,500.00
Stoneware w/Albany slip, paneled base, rnd, 2½" 45.00
Use Congress Record Ink, 2 snail bottles in iron stand, 5¼" 175.00

Insulators

The telegraph was invented in 1844. The devices developed to hold the electrical transmission wires to the poles were called insulators. The telephone, invented in 1876, intensified their usefullness; by the turn of the century, thousands of varieties were being produced in pottery, wood, and glass of various colors. Even though it has been rumored that red glass insulators exist, none have ever been authenticated. Many insulators are embossed with patent dates.

Of the more than 3,000 types known to exist, today's collectors evaluate their worth by age and rarity of color. Aqua and green are the most common colors in glass, dark brown the most common in ceramic. Threadless insulators (for example, CD #701.1) made between 1850 and 1870 bring prices well into the hundreds, if in mint condition.

In the listings that follow, the CD numbers are from an identification system developed in the late 1960s by N.R. Woodward.

Those seeking additional information about insulators are encouraged to contact Line Jewels, NIA#255 (whose address may be found in the Directory under Clubs, Newsletters, and Catalogs) or attend a club-endorsed show. (For information see Directory under Florida for Len Linscott).

Key:
* — Canadian   SDP — sharp drip points
CB — corrugated base   RB — rough base
CD — Consolidated Design   RDP — round drip points
SB — smooth base

CD 100.5, Pyrex, SB, clear 75.00
CD 1001, Cutter, SB, emerald gr 100.00
CD 102, Westinghouse No 3, SB, lt gr 250.00
CD 103, Brookfield, SB, aqua 5.00
CD 107, Armstrong No 9, SB, clear 1.00
CD 110, Brookfield, SB, aqua 100.00
CD 114, Hemingray, SDP, gr-aqua 3.00
CD 118, no name, SB, carnival 200.00
CD 120, CEW, SB, bl 125.00
CD 127, WU, SB, bl-aqua 150.00
CD 135, Chicago Insulator Co, SB, bl 50.00
CD 137, Hemingray, SB, clear 1.00
CD 142, Hemingray, RDP, carnival 15.00
CD 144*, no name, horizontal ridges, SB, gr 75.00
CD 145, KCGW, SB, gr 15.00
CD 150, Barclay, SDP, aqua 1,200.00
CD 158.1, Chester, inner skirt emb, SB, aqua 1,250.00
CD 163, Armstrong, SB, clear 1.00
CD 166, California, SB, sage gr 5.00
CD 169, Whitall Tatum No 4, SB, ice bl 3.00
CD 170, no name, SB, gr-aqua 10.00
CD 175, Hemingray-25, SB, clear 10.00
CD 180, Liquid Insulator, SB, lt aqua 1,000.00
CD 182, Dry Spot No 10, SB, straw 750.00
CD 188, Brookfield, SB, emerald gr 30.00
CD 197, Whitall Tatum No 15, SB, clear 3.00
CD 206, no name, SDP, straw 250.00
CD 210, Postal, SB, emerald gr 10.00
CD 214, Whitall Tatum 512, SB, lt aqua 2.00
CD 220, Hemingray-680, CB, clear 5.00
CD 226.3, Brookfield, SB, emerald gr 700.00
CD 229.6, no emb, SB, bl opal 800.00
CD 232, Hemingray, CB, honey-amber 150.00
CD 236, Brookfield, SB, dk aqua 150.00
CD 241, Locke, SB, aqua 1,300.00

CD 245, Th-9200, SB, lt bl 75.00
CD 248/311, Pyrex, SB, straw 30.00
CD 252, ESS, SB, aqua 100.00
CD 253, Knowles, SB, bl 40.00
CD 256, Manhattan, SB, yel-gr 50.00
CD 262, Columbia, SB, gr 100.00
CD 267.2, NFGM, SB, lt gr 75.00
CD 283, Converse, SDP, lt aqua 40.00
CD 288, Mershon, SB, aqua 40.00
CD 294, NEGM, SB, aqua 40.00
CD 300, Brookfield, SB, gr 50.00
CD 304/310, Hemingray, SDP, Hemingray Bl 50.00
CD 306, Lynchburg, RDP, aqua 250.00
CD 327, Pyrex, SB, gr 20.00
CD 701.1, no emb, SB, lime gr 1,000.00
CD 701.6, no emb, SB, olive-blk glass 200.00
CD 723.3, no emb, SB, aqua 150.00
CD 726*, no emb, SB, lt bl-aqua 20.00
CD 729, Mulford & Biddle, SB, bl 600.00
CD 734*, McMicking, SB, bl-aqua 50.00
CD 740*, no name, SB, aqua 100.00

Irons

There is a fascination in pressing irons that transcends time. As relics of a period in history, irons are a link between today and the past. Holding an iron that has survived for centuries is like shaking hands with antiquity. The weight of an iron and the feel of fine-grained metal in a pleasing design are some of the qualities that appeal to collectors everywhere.

A collection of irons can be as personal as the individual who assembles it. Usually a beginner will start with attractive specimens. Soon an educational process begins — he or she is introduced to terms like goffers, mangles, and fluters and becomes familiar with unusual shapes and materials. Some irons are made of brass, wood, or glass. There are flower irons, glove irons, hat irons, and 'fire-breathing' irons.

Some collectors specialize and concentrate their collections on one particular type — little irons (with a sole length of 4" or under), fuel irons, and charcoal irons. Others only want irons from a particular country. They may also collect iron heating devices and clothes sprinkler bottles. But most collections are diversified; the finest emphasize quality, condition, and scarcity.

In the listings that follow, prices are given for examples in very good to excellent condition. Damage, repairs, excessive wear, rust, and missing parts can dramatically reduce value. Our advisor for this category is the Iron Lady (Carol and Jimmy Walker), whose address is listed in the Directory under Texas. SASE please.

Combination sadiron and fluter, wire latch, $150.00.

Box, Belgian, w/brass trivet & slug 700.00
Box, English, AK & Son, side hinge w/slug 150.00
Box, Portuguese, brass, D uprights, w/slug 225.00
Charcoal, French, handmade Brittany 600.00
Charcoal, German, w/ball latch 50.00
Charcoal, Hungarian, brass 435.00
Charcoal, Indonesian, brass 275.00
Detachable hdl, Enterprise, w/wire rest 65.00
Detachable hdl, Sensible, Pat May 5, 08 ....55.00
Detachable hdl, Universal Thermo-Cell 100.00
Detachable slant hdl 140.00
Egg iron, hand held 90.00
Egg iron, on metal tripod stand 275.00
Egg iron, set of 5, w/bracket 625.00
Egg iron, w/wooden stand 150.00
Flower, all brass, w/cutter 195.00
Fluter, machine, Peerless 225.00
Fluter, machine; Crown, w/4" rollers 225.00
Fluter, rolling, Clark closed hdl 200.00
Fluter, rolling, Clark open hdl 200.00
Heater, Canada, Coleman No 4, blk 95.00
Heater, clay-lined tin bucket 140.00
Heater, gas, for 2 irons 120.00
Heater, pyramid, for 3 irons 180.00
Leaf, brass & iron, w/cutter 185.00
Little, curled hdl, open curls 50.00
Little, Dolly Dover 40.00
Little, rope hdl 20.00
Little, Sensible #6 ....130.00
Little, The Pearl 135.00
Little, Wapak #1 ....45.00
Polisher, Gleason's Pat Jan 22, 1870 ....135.00
Polisher, New England Butt Co 115.00
Polisher, NRS & Co, Groton, NY #80 ....50.00
Primitive, curled toe 80.00
Primitive, slave iron 140.00
Primitive, twisted hdl 85.00
Sadiron, Belgian, w/question mk upright 175.00
Sadiron, Enterprise, sq bk, ventilated hdl 50.00
Sadiron, French, open hdl 125.00
Sadiron, Hewitt, flip-over type 150.00
Sadiron, Hood's, soapstone, Pat Jan 15, 1867 ....220.00
Sleeve, Grand Union Tea Co 45.00
Sleeve, Ober Pat'd May 28, 95 ....80.00
Sleeve, Sweeney Pat Nov 17, 98 ....125.00
Sleeve, Wapak 75.00
Tailor's, ACW Williams Co, 24-lb 40.00
Tailor's, French, single post 50.00
Tailor's, French, single post, detachable hdl 170.00
Tailor's, Sensible, detachable hdl, 20-lb 220.00

Ironstone

During the last quarter of the 18th century, English potters began experimenting with a new type of body that contained calcinated flint and a higher china clay content, intent on producing a fine durable whiteware — heavy, yet with a texture that would resemble porcelain. To remove the last trace of yellow, a minute amount of cobalt was added, often resulting in a bluish-white tone. Wm and John Turner of Caughley, and Josiah Spode II were the first to manufacture the ware successfully. Others, such as Davenport, Hicks and Meigh, and Ralph and Josiah Wedgwood, followed with their own versions. The latter coined the name 'Pearl' to refer to his product and incorporated the

term into his trademark. In 1813 a 14-year patent was issued to Charles James Mason, who called his ware Patented Ironstone. Francis Morley G.L. Asworth, T.J. Mayer, and other Staffordshire potters continued to produce ironstone until the end of the century. While some of these patterns are simple to the extreme, many are decorated with in-mold designs of fruit, grain, and foliage on ribbed or scalloped shapes. In the 1830s transfer-printed designs in blue, mulberry, pink, green, and black became popular; and polychrome versions of Oriental wares were manufactured to compete with the Chinese trade. (See also Mason's Ironstone.) Our advice for this category comes from Home Place Antiques, whose address is listed in the Directory under Illinois.

Vegetable dish with lid, Ceres, Elsmore and Forster, 11" long, $120.00.

Bowl, soup; Corn & Oats, Wedgwood, 9⅞" 25.00
Bowl, soup; Flora, Wedgwood & Co, 9½" 25.00
Bowl, soup; Mocha, T&R Boote, 8⅝" 25.00
Bowl, soup; Wheat, unmk, 8¾" 25.00
Bowl, vegetable; Potomac/Blackberry, w/lid 125.00
Bowl, vegetable; President, oval, w/lid 150.00
Bowl, vegetable; Star Flower, JW Pankhurst & Co, w/lid 125.00
Bowl, waste; Lily of the Valley, Anthony Shaw, 4¾" dia 75.00
Chamber pot, Corn & Oats, Wedgwood, w/lid 175.00
Chamber pot, Panelled Thistle, Bridgwood & Clarke 125.00
Coffeepot, Lily, Burgess 195.00
Compote, New York, rnd, 9½" dia 190.00
Creamer & sugar bowl, Victor, Jones 250.00
Cup, handleless; Wheat, unmk 45.00
Cup & saucer, demitasse; Western 50.00
Cup & saucer, handleless; Lily, unmk, EX 45.00
Cup & saucer, handleless; Niagara, Paris 45.00
Dish, honey; Gothic, Royal Ironstone China, 4¼", EX 25.00
Dish, sauce; Corn & Oats, Davenport, 4½", EX 25.00
Gravy boat, Ceres, Elsmore & Forster, EX 55.00
Gravy boat, President, Edwards 60.00
Gravy boat, Sydenham 85.00
Pitcher, milk; Ceres, Goddard & Co, 8¾" 145.00
Pitcher, milk; Olympic, Elsmore & Forster, 9⅜" 90.00
Pitcher, milk; Royal, J Edwards, 8⅝" 75.00
Pitcher, milk; Scrolled Bubble, Pankhurst, 9¾" 145.00
Pitcher, President, table sz 150.00
Pitcher, Victor, Jones, ca 1865, 10" 165.00
Plate, Athenia, Adams, 8⅞" 25.00
Plate, Ceres, Turner & Goddard, 10" 25.00
Plate, cookie; Cherry Scroll, T&R Boote, EX 50.00
Plate, Prairie Flower, Powell & Bishop, 10" 30.00
Plate, Sharon Arch, Wedgwood, 10⅝" 28.00
Plate, Victor, F Jones, 7" 25.00
Plate, Western Shape, Hope & Carter, mini, 4⅞" 15.00

Platter, Columbia, Clementson, 12½x10" 45.00
Platter, Sharon Arch, Wedgwood, 16½" 47.50
Platter, Wheat, T&G Meakin, 18½", EX 50.00
Punch bowl, Scrolled Bubble, Pankhurst, w/hdls, 10¼" dia 275.00
Sugar bowl, Tuscan, Edwards, w/lid, 8" 75.00
Sugar bowl, Walled Octagon, Furnival, EX 75.00
Teapot, Full Ribbed, unmk, mini, 5¾" 165.00
Teapot, Sevres, unmk, mini, 5¼" 80.00
Tureen, sauce; Columbia, w/lid, underplate, & ladle 225.00
Tureen, sauce; Sydenham, T&R Boote 125.00
Wash bowl, Hyacinth, unmk, 13" 110.00
Wash bowl & pitcher, President, Edwards, EX 275.00
Wash bowl & pitcher, Scalloped Decagon, Davenport, EX 250.00
Wash bowl & pitcher, Sydenham, T&R Boote 275.00
Wash pitcher, Fig, Davenport, 11" 145.00
Wash pitcher, Forget Me Not, Rathbone & Co, 12" 125.00
Wash pitcher, Wheat & Blackberry, Meakin, 11¾" 125.00
Waste bowl, Tuscan, unmk, 5¼" dia 75.00

Ivory

Technically, true ivory is the substance composing the tusk of the elephant; the finest type comes from Africa. However, tusks and teeth of other animals — the walrus, the hippopotamus, and the sperm whale, for instance — are similar in composition and appearance and have also been used for carving. The Chinese have used this substance for centuries, preferring it over bone because of the natural oil contained in its pores, which not only renders it easier to carve but also imparts a soft sheen to the finished product. Aged ivory usually takes on a soft caramel patina, but unscrupulous dealers sometimes treat new ivory to a tea bath to 'antique' it! A bill passed in 1978 reinforced a ban on the importation of whale and walrus ivory. All examples listed here are Oriental in origin unless noted otherwise.

Apple, figural landscape cvg w/in, 6¾" 235.00
Beaker, cvd tusk segment, 4-season allegorical, 5", VG 775.00
Beauty, elaborate coiffure, 9" 125.00
Bijin (2) w/fans before ancient pine, dk stain, EX cvg, 9" 700.00
Birds (2) on flowering branches, minor damage, 8" 750.00
Box, monks/elephant on sides, scholar sits atop, 7" 2,100.00
Box, mums/puppies, puppy finial, sgn Mochida, oval, 5" 1,300.00
Boy eating & carrying grapes, 1900, 3¾" 150.00
Bust of a king, wood base, age cracks, 4" 200.00

Carved Japanese box, cats in reserves on background of grotesque masks, mask as finial, 4" long, $1,600.00.

Cane hdl, cvg of 3 overlapping dogs, 5" L 150.00
Chinese zodiac animals, 1900, w/stand, 5" 1,100.00
Crab, movable eyes, 6" L 250.00
Dignitary holds cards in both hands, 8½" 150.00

Dr's model, nude lady, wood base, 7" L 225.00
Eagle w/spread wings, w/stand, 20th C, 4" 70.00
Emperor (& empress), amber color, sgn in MOP, 7", pr 550.00
Fisherman w/pole, fish & basket, 5" 125.00
Fishermen w/catch & net on bk, child ea side, 1900s, 9" 600.00
Foo dog, openwork cvg, relief-cvd plinth, 12", pr 850.00
Geishas (2) standing, etched color, 20th C, 4" 175.00
God w/3 heads riding wild boar, EX detail, glued rpr, 11" 1,000.00
Grasshopper & bugs on bok choi, 1900s, cloth stand, 4" L 300.00
Horse & 4 figures on ft in landscape, 1900, 11" 775.00
Immortal/attendants on mtn, lg dragon below, intricate, 12" 500.00
Immortals (3) on pine branch, 9" L 145.00
Jar, entwined w/lg ferocious serpent, man aside, 12" 600.00
Kwannon holds lotus flower, inscribed, 9" 125.00
Kwannon on lg lotus blossom above roaring dragon, 24" 2,300.00
Lady bleeding old man's ear, 6¾" 275.00
Li Ti Gui (Immortal), 12" 375.00
Lohan, seated, w/dbl-gourd bottle, gilt highlights, 5¾" 145.00
Man on elephant's bk, w/attendants, 20th C, 4" 200.00
Monkey, dressed, holds parasol, +sm monkeys & mice, sgn, 6" ..225.00
Quan Yin, standing, w/stand, 1900, 12" 300.00
Quan Yin seated on lotus throne holding gourd bottle, 5" 125.00
Quan Yin w/plum branch, 7" 275.00
Seated man w/scroll, on wood stand, age cracks, 7½" 600.00
Tiger, climbing cvd wood base, 8" L 450.00
Vase, rtcl dragons, 2 bands of palmettes/lappets, 11", EX 400.00
Woman clutches basket of flowers to breast, sgn, 12" 350.00

European

Archer & child, ivory stand, 1800s, 4½" 400.00
Boy playing instrument, 1800s, w/stand, 7" 500.00
Boy stands w/book & bottle, 1800s, 5" 200.00
Bust of Mozart, on ivory stand, 1900, 5¾" 375.00
Candle screen, stag/doe/fawn in forest, cvd std, 16" 1,750.00
Cane hdl, figural couple, shells/scrolls, 1800s, 11" 800.00
Cavalier standing, 1800s, w/stand, 13" 900.00
Cavalier standing, 1900, 7" 425.00
Cupid, 1890s, w/stand, 7" 450.00
Demon w/ball, 1900, 5" 300.00
Duke of Wellington, glass/brass shadow stand, 1800s, 12" 650.00
Maid stands w/fan, ivory base, 1900, 6" 400.00
Man standing, rearing horse, 1900, 4¼" 750.00
Nude & putti, floral-cvd base 1800s, 5" 1,100.00
Nude seated on stylized lion, ivory stand, 1800s, 5" 1,200.00
Nude w/grape leaves about loins holds goblet, 1800s, 12" 1,200.00
Peg-leg beggar, 1900s, w/stand, 5¾" 250.00
Plaque, Apollo faced w/metamorphosis of Daphne, 17x13" 4,000.00
Plaque, battle scene, 1800s, 3x9" 1,700.00
Plaque, Edward III/Countess of Salisbury's wedding, 5x8" 2,300.00
Rape of Proserpine by Pluto, dolphin/shell at ft, 1800s, 17" ..16,000.00
Sea goddess standing on dolphin, holding shell, 1800s, 12" 1,400.00
Spoon, rtcl stags in landscape hdl, 1890s, 6" 100.00
St Anthony holding child, w/stand, 1800s, 7" 800.00

Jack-in-the-Pulpit Vases

Popular novelties at the turn of the century, jack-in-the-pulpit vases were made in every type of art glass produced. Some were simple, others elaborately appliqued and enameled. They were shaped to resemble the lily for which they were named.

Cranberry shaded, wht int, 3-dimple base, 7" 250.00

Maroon & wht spatter, vaseline opal appl top, 11x6"	95.00
Mc spatter w/mica, fluted edge, 7⅛x4¾"	80.00
Peachblow to wht, European, 13"	220.00
Pk opal to vaseline, 11¼x4⅞"	135.00
Rose to apricot MOP satin, Moire, star base, 9x4"	385.00
Wht w/apple gr int, crystal leaf ft, 7x5¾"	95.00
Wht w/gr shaded int, 8⅛x5¼"	85.00
Wht w/pk int, ruffled top, 6⅝x6½"	110.00

Japanese Lustreware

Imported from Japan during the 1920s, novelty tableware items, vases ashtrays, etc. — often in blue, tan, and mother-of-pearl lustre glazes — were sold through five-and-dime stores or given as premiums for selling magazine subscriptions. The Occupied Japan Club is listed in the Directory under Clubs, Newletters, and Catalogs.

Ashtray, conch shell form, caramel, pk int	12.50
Bowl, console; bl w/wht flowers, rolled rim, 9", +frog	15.00
Condiment set, Deco florals w/aqua trim, 4-pc	15.00
Creamer, caramel top & base, mc flowers	12.50
Shakers, goose w/hat holds 2 'chick' shakers on oval tray	15.00
Sugar shaker, caramel top & base, mc flowers	12.50
Tea set, bluebird & plum blossoms, partial set, 8-pc	35.00

Jewelry

Jewelry as objects of adornment has always been regarded with special affection. Whether it be a trinket or a costly ornament of gold, silver, or enameled work, jewelry has personal significance to the wearer. The art of the jeweler is valued as is any art object, and the names of Lalique or Faberge on collectible pieces bring prices demanded by the signed works of Picasso. Once the province of kings and noblemen, jewelry now is a legacy of all strata of society. The creativity reflected in the jeweler's art has resulted in a myriad of decorative adornments for men and women, and the modern usage of 'lesser' gems and base metals has elevated the value and increased the demand for artistic merit, so that now it is considered by collectors to be on a par with intrinsic value. Luxuriously appointed pieces of Victorian splendor and Edwardian grandeur now compete with the unique, imaginative renditions of jewelry produced in the exciting Art Nouveau period as well as the adventurous translation of jewelry executed in man-made materials versus natural elements. Today prices for gems and gemstones crafted into antique and collectible jewelry are based on artistic merit, personal appeal, pure sentimentality, and intrinsic value. Note: Diamond prices vary greatly depending on color, clarity, etc. Values given here are for diamond jewelry with a standard commercial grade of diamonds that are most likely to be encountered.

Our advisor for this category is Rebecca Dodds; her address may be found in the Directory under Florida. If you are interested in collecting or dealing in jewelry, you will find that authority Lillian Baker has several fine books available on the subject — *100 Years of Collectible Jewelry: 1850-1950; Art Nouveau and Art Deco Jewelry;* and *Fifty Years of Collectible Fashion Jewelry: 1925-1975.* These books are complete with beautiful full-color illustrations and current market values. Mrs. Baker is listed in the Directory under California. See also Plastics.

Key:

A/C	— Arts and Crafts	gf	— gold filled
AD	— Art Deco	grad	— graduated
AN	— Art Nouveau	gp	— gold plated
cab	— cabochon	gw	— gold washed
cl	— clear	k	— karat

comp	— complementary	m/c	— mine cut
ct	— carat	plat	— platinum
dmn	— diamond	r/c	— rose cut
dwt	— penny weight	r/stn	— rhinestone
Euro	— European cut	rdm	— rhodium
fl	— filigree	stn	— stone
g'el-plt	— gold electroplate	tw	— total weight
g-stn	— gemstone	wg	— white gold
g-t	— gold toned	yg	— yellow gold

Bar pin, platinum filigree with two European cut diamonds (2.50 and .65 carats), two small diamonds (.30 carat), two oval-cut sapphires (1.0 and 1.5 carats), eight small oval sapphires, and ten small marquise sapphires (1.20 carat), $7,000.00; Italian cameo brooch, gold mount with synthetic ruby cabachon, three garnets, and twenty small synthetic rubies, in original fitted rosewood box, $2,600.00.

Barrette, S Kramer, sterling free-form w/squiggle & glass eye	850.00
Bracelet, bangle; 14k rose & y/g, repousse, hinged, wide	675.00
Bracelet, bangle; 15k, eng, 5 turq cabs 7mmx9mm, hinged	775.00
Bracelet, charm; 14k yg w/4 gold coins in 14k bezels	335.00
Bracelet, cuff; Ed Wiener, 14k burnished/polished free-form	550.00
Bracelet, cuff; Wm Spratling, sterling, rtcl edge, X-bands	220.00
Bracelet, G Jensen, pansies w/moonstones+bl stns in bead fr	650.00
Bracelet, G Jensen, silver, lg beads alternate w/buds, A/C	275.00
Bracelet, gf w/locket-like medallion w/lady's profile, AN	65.00
Bracelet, plat, ribbon form w/120 sm dmns & 4 lg sapphires	3,000.00
Bracelet, 14k, 3-strand 6mm pearls, dmn separators/in clasp	800.00
Bracelet, 14k, 4-strand, hammered nugget-like links	225.00
Bracelet, 14k (unmk), A/C, hammered rectangles/stacked balls	275.00
Bracelet, 14k w/9 garnets 5mm, .50 to .60ct ea	300.00
Bracelet, 14k wg fl w/.8 dmn+2 sm sq emeralds, 1920s	375.00
Bracelet, 18k yg, Lover's Knot w/3 .5 dmns	350.00
Brooch, Fred Davis, silver leaves+13 amethyst quartz berries	220.00
Brooch, gf, lg faux amethyst, Victorian	100.00
Brooch, Kalo, sterling, leaf-bud fr, lg gr agate, 2"	400.00
Brooch, Kalo, sterling ball & scroll mt, Jasper disk, 2¼"	100.00
Brooch, Macchiarini, mixed metals, silver line & wave, 4"	160.00
Brooch, Macchiarini, silver/copper/ebony/ivory, banjo, 1950	600.00
Brooch, Mary Gage, silver, 4 lily pads around amber g-stn	325.00
Brooch, plat, Euro .40ct dmn in bar+40 sm dmns/8 sapphires	1,350.00

Bracelet, large prong-set rhinestones, marked
Eisenburg Originals, $85.00.

Brooch, S Kramer, sterling, agate cab on sq mtd atop oval 450.00
Brooch, S Kramer, sterling, leaf w/appl edging & gr stn, 2½" 325.00
Brooch, 14k yg, crescent w/17 grad 3-4½mm pearls, 2½" L 250.00
Buckle, Wm Hutton, sterling curvilinear form w/2 opals, 3" 275.00
Earrings, yg, ea w/7 opals in rosette setting 100.00
Earrings, 14k, flower form, screw bks 110.00
Earrings, 14k yg w/8 rnd garnets, Germany, 1850s, 2½" L 550.00
Locket, g/f, emb/eng florals, red center stone, 2 seed pearls 500.00
Necklace, baroque pearls, pendant: plat-set 7.5 opal+sm dmns ..600.00
Necklace, cultured pearls, grad, w/g fl clasp, 18" 250.00
Necklace, Kalo, sterling, link-joined cherries/leaves, 15" 325.00
Necklace, pearls, 2-strand, 144 grad from 7mm to 7.6mm 550.00
Necklace, pearls, 8mm, 1-strand, 16" 375.00
Pendant, Kalo, sterling, simple shield shape w/amethyst cab 650.00
Pendant, Lobel, sterling figure-8 w/glass ball in coil, 2½" 180.00
Pendant, 14k wg mt, lg amethyst+3 sm dmns, wg chain 115.00
Pendant, 14k yg mt, ⅓ct emerald+ ⅝" L pearl 175.00
Pin, bar; 14k wg, 7 sapphires (2.25+.45 faux)+12 dmn tw .48 ct .550.00
Pin, Ed Wiener, sterling/copper mobile w/appl animal, 2½" 300.00
Pin, G Jensen, sterling, rtcl disk w/bird & foliage, 1½" 250.00
Pin, G Jensen, sterling, 4 gr cabs on emb wreath, #4B, 1¾" 415.00
Pin, Kalo, sterling w/lg pk blister pearl & o/l, 2¼" L 190.00
Ring, Euro yel dmn 1.74ct+.70 w/in fr of 20 sm dmns tw 3ct ..2,200.00
Ring, Kalo, 14k, appl curvilinear floral, dk bl oval stn 600.00
Ring, plat, 3 .30 Euro dmns+6 sapphires, 1" mt 1,075.00
Ring, plat, 3 Euro dmn (.60ct+2 at .25), fl set w/sm dmns 1,500.00
Ring, plat, 3 Euro dmn (1ct & 2 at .50) 1,400.00
Ring, wg, Euro dmn .56ct+7 sq-cut faux sapphires 350.00
Ring, 10% iridium plat, 1.15 dmn+24 (tw .26ct) 2,500.00
Ring, 10k gold w/oval onyx 65.00
Ring, 10k wg, engr crystal w/sm dmn 95.00
Ring, 14k, blk/red coral w/2 dmn tw .02ct 225.00
Ring, 14k, Euro dmn 1.12ct 1,700.00
Ring, 14k, 2 3mm amethysts+3 sm amethysts, 8 dmns tw .08ct .185.00
Ring, 14k, 3 cultured 4mm pearls+2 m/c dmns tw .60ct 375.00
Ring, 14k, 3 rectangle bl topaz 4x6mm+4 rnd dmns tw .04ct 175.00
Ring, 14k fl, 3 sq cut sapphires 4x4mm 300.00
Ring, 14k wg filigree w/3 (tw .15ct) dms 225.00
Ring, 14k yg, 2 .8 dmns+.20 center ruby+2 .10 rubies, 1900s 335.00
Ring, 14k yg figural butterfly, 4 opals/20 dmns in wings 325.00
Ring, 14k yg w/5 grad marquise bl topaz, filigree mt 85.00
Ring, 15k, Euro dmns, 2 at .25 ea, +15 at .02ct ea 400.00
Ring, 15k rose gold/silver, 5 Euro dmn (3 brn)+8 sm, tw 1.36ct ...600.00
Ring, 18k, bl topaz 8x10mm+2 rnd dmns .015ct ea 150.00
Ring, 18k, m/c dmn 1.18ct, Tiffany-style mt 1,500.00
Ring, 18k, oval amethyst 11x15.6mm 300.00
Ring, 18k, oval gr jade 7.3x4mm cab+24 single-cut dmns 400.00
Ring, 18k, oval 1.8ct ruby+4 baguette/94 rnd dms tw 4.5ct 3,600.00
Ring, 18k wg, sapphire .40ct+30 dmns tw .50ct 650.00

Ring, 18k wg, 3 Euro dmn: 1.03, .50, .47ct 2,250.00
Ring, 18k y/wg, 5 Euro dmn (2 yel/2 brn/1 pk-brn)+24 tw .90 ...1,225.00
Ring, 18k yg lacy rope mt w/pearl w/18 rubies 335.00
Stickpin, 14k yg w/.4 dmn 95.00
Watch chain, 14k, braided 175.00
Watch chain, 14k, links w/dmn-shape ends 300.00

Costume Jewelry

Bracelet, Schiaparelli, 6 oval rainbow stns, silver finish 195.00
Bracelet, Sorrento, 5 tiger eye sections w/guard chain, 7" 40.00
Brooch, Trifari, maple leaf, gp openwork w/gray r'stns, 2¼" 35.00
Earrings, Carnegie, 7 vari-sz faux sapphire bevel-set cabs 90.00
Earrings, Haskell, prong-set clear/red stns, w/red drops 100.00
Earrings, Hobe, Victorian-look w/garnet-like stns, 2", pr 85.00
Earrings, KJL, faux coral sqs around seed pearl-fr 'emerald' 120.00
Earrings, Mosell, HP g'el-plt shell design 30.00
Earrings, Schiaparelli, pk r'stns/'pearl' w/lg r'stn center 45.00
Earrings, Trifari, sm g-t mts w/gr cabs & pave-set r'stns 80.00
Fur clip, Eisenberg, g'el-plt leaf w/lg pk stns+sm crystals 120.00
Fur clip, Eisenberg Orig, mask face, gilt silver w/faux stns 200.00
Fur clip, Trifari, fuchsia spray, enameled, w/pave r'stns 90.00
Necklace, Haskell, baroque pearls, 17", +matching earrings 125.00
Necklace, Haskell, gold-finish mesh chain w/2" butterfly, 19" 95.00
Necklace, Haskell, lg pearl & plastic crystals, 16½" 95.00
Necklace, Margot de Taxco, gr links w/2¾" mc fish pendant, 20" ..175.00
Pin, Accessocraft, lion head, ring in mouth, g'el-plt 75.00
Pin, Boucher, Blkamoor bust, enamel on g-t w/faux g-stns 85.00
Pin, C Ruopoli, sterling, stylized butterfly, 2" 195.00
Pin, Cini, Virgo w/Cupid, 2" 65.00
Pin, Coro, sterling, rnd/spoked w/wht stns at ends, 2½" 35.00
Pin, Coro, sterling, 5 twisted flowers, 3½", pr 75.00
Pin, Dewees, gw bow & foliage, wht stns, 2" 45.00
Pin, HAR, female w/crystal ball, g-t w/sm faux stn accents 100.00
Pin, HAR, half-figure Turk w/crystal ball, g-t w/faux stns 120.00
Pin, Hobe, sterling, leaf & flower design, 16½", +bracelet 135.00
Pin, Hobe, 4-petal floral, wht pearl & yel stns, 2½" 110.00
Pin, Jomaz, blk/wht enamel, wht stns, gold finish, 2½" 95.00
Pin, Jomaz, Buddha, bl/gr enamel, gr/wht stns, 1¾" 75.00
Pin, Lang, sterling ballerina 28.00
Pin, McClelland Barclay, grapes & vine, 2½" 150.00
Pin, Napier, sterling, geometric design, clip type, 1¼" 40.00
Pin, Norseland by Coro, pheasant on log & foliage, 1½x2½" 75.00
Pin, Otis, bow w/wht stns, 1⅝" 35.00
Pin, Pennino, sterling, fuchsia w/wht stns, 2¼" 195.00
Pin, Robert Orig, Maltese cross w/blk & smoke stns, 2½" 150.00
Pin, Rosenstein, sterling-mtd rose of rose quartz & jade 130.00
Pin, Rosenstein, wht stns, pearl center, gold finish, 1⅜" 65.00
Pin, Salvador, Blk warrior w/shield & arrow, lg 38.00
Pin, Trifari, arrow through ring, gw silver/faux g'stns 100.00
Pin, Trifari, elephant, gw sterling w/crystal saddle banket 90.00
Pin, Weiss, g'el-plt heart set w/tiny faux rubies 35.00
Pin, Weiss, trembling butterfly, blk stns, 2" 120.00

Judaica

The items listed below are representative of objects used in both
the secular and religious life of the Jewish people. They are evident of a
culture where silversmiths, painters, engravers, writers, and metal workers were highly gifted and skilled in their art. Most of the treasures
shown in recently displayed exhibits of Judaica were confiscated by the
Germans during the late 1930s up to 1945; by then, eight Jewish syna-
gogues and fifty warehouses had been filled with Hitler's plunder.

Candle holder, brass, tombstone shape, inscr, 1900s, 4¼" 250.00
Circumcision dish, Continental silver, repousse, 1900s, 8" 500.00
Circumcision knife, Am silver mt, dbl-edged, 1900s, 6½" 650.00
Ethrog container, German silver, Georgian style, 4½" 1,250.00
Ethrog container, Israeli silver gilt, oviform, 1940s, 8" 650.00
Hanukkah lamp, Bezalel brass, 2 lions, 1920s, 9" 1,000.00
Hanukkah lamp, Polish brass, foliate bkplate, 1800s, 6½" 400.00
Hanukkah lamp, Polish brass, stepped base, 1800s, 15½" 600.00
Hanukkah lamp, Polish SP, canopy form, 1900s, 12¾" 385.00
Hanukkah lamp, Russian brass, crouching lions, 1900s, 7" 500.00
Kiddush beaker, Polish silver, eng Safed style, 1890s, 2½" 850.00
Kiddush goblet, Bezalel silver, etch/3 stones, 1920s, 6" 660.00
Mezuzah case, Continental brass, rectangular, 1600s, 6¾" 250.00
Passover cloth, Palestinian silk, printed views, '20s, 18x23" 200.00
Passover dish, Continental pewter, eng scene, 1800s, 12" 400.00
Passover plate, German silver, Seder scene, 1920s, 12¾" 500.00
Passover plate, Palestinian earthenware, etch/pnt, '20s, 12" 250.00

Polish silver Mezuzah case, L-shape with rampant lion and Hebrew inscription, 4", $1,650.00.

Purim dish, Hungarian pnt porc, 1900s, 12¼" 850.00
Sabbath candelabrum, Bezalel silver, 1900s, 6" 800.00
Sabbath knife, German silver w/MOP inlay, 1920s, 4½" 350.00
Sabbath sconce, Dutch brass, rampant lions, 1900s, 12½" 1,000.00
Scribe's box, Palestinian olive wood, porc int, 1900s, 10" 250.00
Spice container, Continental silver, fish form, 1800s, 9" 300.00
Spice container, Iraqui silver, fruit form, 1600s, 6¾" 1,300.00
Spice container, Polish silver, fruit form, 1890s, 8½" 500.00
Spice container, Russian silver filigree, urn, 1850s, 4¼" 360.00
Spice tower, Continental silver, cylindrical, 1920s, 9" 150.00
Spice tower, German silver, 2-tier, gallery, 1790s, 6½" 1,750.00
Spice tower, German silver, 2-tier, pennants, 1800s, 12" 1,350.00

Jugtown

The Jugtown Pottery was started about 1920 by Juliana and Jacques Busbee in Moore County, North Carolina. Ben Owen, a young descendant of a Staffordshire potter, was hired in 1923. He was the master potter, while the Busbees experimented with perfecting glazes and supervising design and modeling. Preferred shapes were those reminiscent of traditional country wares and classic Oriental forms. Glazes were various: natural-clay oranges, buffs, 'tobacco-spit' brown, mirror black, white, 'frog-skin' green, a lovely turquoise called Chinese blue, and the traditional cobalt-decorated salt glaze. The pottery gained national recognition, and as a result of their success, several other local potteries were established. Jugtown is still in operation; however, they no longer use their original glaze colors which are now so collectible.

Bowl, redware w/orange glaze, open hdls, lt wear, 12" 35.00
Deep plate, redware w/orange glaze, lt wear, 9½" 25.00

Inkwell/vase, Chinese bl 120.00
Jug, bl, att, 4¼" 70.00
Pitcher, gr w/bl, bulbous w/pinched spout, 5½" 55.00
Plate, orange, 6" 30.00
Plate, redware, mk, 10½" 25.00
Vase, Chinese bl, red splashes, ovoid, 4½" 195.00
Vase, Chinese red/gr drip glaze, 5" 240.00
Vase, Chinese wht drip, 3¾" 89.00
Vase, cobalt, bulbous w/rim-to-width hdls, mk, 8" 195.00
Vase, tobacco-spit brn, jug form, 4½" 50.00

K. P. M. Porcelain

Under the tutelage of Frederick the Great, King of Prussia, porcelain manufacture was instituted in Berlin in 1751 by William K. Wegeley. In jealous competition with Meissen, hard-paste porcelain was produced (dinnerware, figurines, vases, etc.), some of which were undecorated while other pieces were hand painted in Watteau scenes, landscapes, or florals. It soon became evident that the factory was unable to offer serious competition. The King withdrew his support, and the factory failed in 1757. In 1761 Johann Ernst Gotzkowsky bought the rights and attempted a similar operation which soon failed due to financial difficulties. Still determined to gain the same recognition enjoyed by Meissen, the King bought the plant in 1763 and ruled the operation with an iron hand, often assuring his success by taking advantage of his position. The King died in 1786, but production has continued, and quality tableware and decorative porcelains are still being made on a commercial basis. Earliest marks were simply 'G' or 'W,' followed by the sceptre mark. After 1830 'K.P.M.' with an orb or eagle was adopted. Our advisor for this category is Don Williams; he is listed in the Directory under Missouri.

Bowl, HP roses & gold scrolls, 3-section, mk, 5x11½" 145.00
Clock, Rococo form, cherub sits on side, shaped stand, 21" 1,200.00

Ewer, continuous scene with figures, orb and sceptre mark, 1800s, 20", $1,650.00.

Figurine, boy holding tricon hat, girl in bonnet, late, 14" 250.00
Figurine, boy w/fur hat & ax, girl w/goat, late, 7" 80.00
Figurine, lady w/flowers at fountain, sceptre mk, 9" 625.00
Lamp base, wht, ftd urn form w/floriform hdls, 28½" 900.00
Plaque, Beggars, 2 barefoot girls, sgn Griener, 13x8" 11,000.00
Plaque, cockatoo lands on maid's arm, 10x7", gesso fr 4,750.00

Plaque, Giovantine, lady w/flower in hair, sgn Wagner, 6x4" .1,000.00
Plaque, girl seen in light of her candle, Knoeller, 10x8" 5,000.00
Plaque, Gitane, portrait, sgn Wagner, on ftd bronze box, 6" L ...1,100.00
Plaque, lady w/loose gown about her, sgn Wagner, oval, 5" 1,000.00
Plaque, Psyche seated on rock, sgn Brown, 9x7" 4,000.00
Plaque, seminude, sgn Kunemuller, leaf-emb gold fr, 19x20" ..4,400.00
Plaque, wht mtn against dk bl, sgn Schmuz-Baudiss, 11x8½" 660.00
Plaque, young boy, 1890s, 5½x4" 495.00
Plaque, young man dressed as a cavalier w/lace collar, 10x8" ..4,000.00
Plaque, 3 religious figures w/Baby Jesus, 12x17" 3,000.00

Kayserzinn Pewter

J.P. Kayser Sohn produced pewter decorated with relief-molded Art Nouveau motifs in Germany during the late 1800s and into the 20th century. Examples are marked with 'Kayserzinn' and the mold number within an elongated oval reserve. Items with dimensional animals, insects, birds, etc., are valued much higher than bowls, plates, and trays with simple embossed florals, which are usually priced at $100.00 to about $200.00, depending on size.

Platter with domed lid, #4413, etched 'J.A.,' 8x21", $400.00.

Beaker, poppies, #436, 4½" 125.00
Bowl, appl floral, hdls, #4227, 13½" 95.00
Bowl, cartouches, scroll legs, hdld, 16½" 375.00
Bowl, flowers & leaves, hdls, #4322, 13" 145.00
Candelabra, 5-light, 4-sided std, #4485/#4486, 19", pr 5,500.00
Flagon, acorns & leaves, squirrel finial, 13" 450.00
Ice bucket, emb foliage, cylindrical, #4860, 8" 200.00
Pitcher, satyr's face/iris mold, #4061, 12½" 375.00

Keen Kutter

Keen Kutter was a brand name of E.C. Simmons Hardware, used from about 1870 until the mid-1930s. In 1923 Winchester merged with Simmons but continued to produce Keen Kutter marked knives and tools. The merger dissolved, and in 1940 the Simmons Company was purchased by Shapleigh Hardware. Older items are very collectible. For further study we recommend *Keen Kutter*, an illustrated price guide by Jerry and Elaine Heuring, available at your favorite bookstore or public library. Our advisor for this category is Jim Calison; he is listed in the Directory under New York.

Auger bits, KS-9, in orig box 100.00
Axe, Michigan pattern, orig mkd hdl, M 50.00
Box, wood w/stenciled: Hand Tempered Axes, w/logo 15.00
Brace, K-18, 8" sweep 30.00
Broad axe, KK written out, no logo 100.00

Broad axe, lg KK logo 125.00
Calendar, 1944, girl w/doll 75.00
Can opener 28.00
Chisel, socket corner; ¾" or ⅞", EX 30.00
Drawknife, KLP, 8" blade w/offset hdls 55.00
Fan, hand-held, girl w/dog, bk: Wm Clingingsmith Hdw ad 45.00
File, mill bastard; dbl or single cut, ea 12.00
Fork, barn or ensilage, 4-tine 35.00
Garden trowel, K-2, socket pattern w/bent neck 15.00
Gauge, marking; K-45, metal bar marking & mortise, dbl-ended ..65.00
Gauge, marking; wood 25.00
Gauge, marking; wood w/brass inserts 40.00
Gauge, screw pitch; ea leaf samped showing pitch 85.00
Grinder, food; K-22, Simmons, orig box & cookbook 35.00
Grinder, meat; K-112, sliding base & thumbscrew, lg 35.00
Hair clippers, S-521-AK, in orig box 30.00
Hammer, claw; 4¼" 25.00
Hammer, Shapleigh ball pein; szs 6-oz to 16-oz, ea 40.00
Hatchet, broad or bench; 3" or 4", ea 30.00
Hatchet, broad or bench; 5" or 6" 55.00
Knife, pruning; KS-105, cocobolo hdl, extra heavy, 4⅜" 35.00
Knife, switchblade; US Pat 1909 & 1910 ....225.00
Level, K-624, CI, 24" 200.00
Level, K-69, CI, 9" 100.00
Level, KK-13, not adjustable, brass top plate, 12" or 18" 45.00
Level, KK-2, adjustable, brass plate, 28" or 30" 30.00
Lock, signal; Simmons, keyhole cover on front, bk: Santa Fe 350.00
Match holder, CI, lg lettering 110.00
Pinchers, carpenter's; any style 18.00
Plane, bull-nose rabbet; K-75, not adjustable, 4" 125.00
Plane, cabinet scraper; KK-79 or K-79 ....65.00
Plane, circular; KK-115, cuts concave or convex 200.00
Plane, iron block; K-9½, in orig box, 6" 75.00
Plane, iron; K-6 fore, smooth bottom 65.00
Plane, iron; K-8 jointer, smooth bottom 75.00
Plane, iron; KK-6, KK written on lever cap 65.00
Plane, K-35, hdl, wood bottom, 9" 45.00
Plane, K-76, tongue & groove, swing fence 115.00
Plane, KK-212, scraper & chamfer 120.00
Plane, KK-4½, smooth iron plane, 10", 2⅜" cutter 75.00
Pliers, combination; K-180 or K-160 ....20.00
Pocketknife, #882 ....47.50
Pocketknife, 3-blade, red & cream 45.00
Razor, corn; blk rubber hdl mk Germany, w/box 45.00
Razor hone, M in worn box 50.00
Router, K-171, Pat 110-29-01 ....120.00
Saw, flooring; adjustable 65.00
Saw, hand; K-88, 26" 55.00
Scissors, 8" 20.00
Scratch awl, plastic hdl 20.00
Square, K-10, long tongue, 8" 45.00
Square, tri-; CI hdl, 10" blade 30.00

Trunk lock, $50.00.

Tobacco cutter, base mk EC Simmons St Louis USA 250.00
Tool box, leather w/stamped logo, decals w/in, EX 300.00
Wagon, KK Jet, red, 34" L 200.00
Wrench, alligator; adjustable, Pat 5-26-03 ....125.00
Wrench, pipe; Shapleigh, 8", 10", or 18", ea 20.00

Kelva

Kelva was a trademark of the C.F. Monroe Company of Meriden, Connecticut; it was produced for only a few years after the turn of the century. It is distinguished from the Wave Crest and Nakara lines by its unique Batik-like background, probably achieved through the use of a cloth or sponge to apply the color. Large florals are hand painted on the opaque milk glass; and ormolu and brass mounts were used for the boxes, vases, and trays. Most pieces are signed. Our advisors for this category are Dolli and Wilfred Cohen; they are listed in the Directory under California.

Box, blown-out rose on lid, hexagonal, 2½" dia 550.00
Box, Crown mold w/scenic panels, ormolu ft, 6½" dia 1,200.00
Box, floral, pk on gr mottle, mirror in lid, 4½" 495.00
Box, hibiscus, pk on gr mottle, mk, 3½x7¾" dia 650.00
Box, metal openwork w/florals & beading on glass lid, 3x3" 425.00
Box, top w/pk HP orchids & brass band, hinged, 5" dia 425.00
Ferner, floral on pk, ogee sides, 7½" dia 550.00
Napkin ring, floral on waisted hexagonal form, rare 495.00
Shakers, floral on moss gr, 3", pr 350.00
Tray, floral on gr, unemb bowl form, ormolu bail, 3" dia 175.00
Vase, floral, pk & wht on gr mottle, ormolu top & hdls, 14½" ...850.00
Vase, floral on rose, trumpet form w/4 ormolu ft, 6x2" 450.00
Whisk broom holder, floral on red, ornate ormolu bkplate 950.00

Kenton Hills

Kenton Hills Porcelain was established in 1940 in Erlanger, Kentucky, by Harold Bopp, former Rookwood superintendent, and David Seyler, noted artist and sculptor. Native clay was used; glazes were very similar to Rookwood's of the same period. The work was of high quality, but because of the restrictions imposed on needed material due to the onset of the war, the operation failed in 1942. Much of the ware is artist signed and marked with the Kenton Hill name or cipher and shape number.

Vase, bl gloss, HB mk, #111, 6" 180.00
Vase, dk gr tiger-eye glaze, tiny rim, 8½" 450.00
Vase, leaves/flowers, peach & bl, Wm Hentschel, 12" 450.00

Kentucky Derby Glasses

Since the 1940s souvenir glasses have commemorated the famous Kentucky Derby; recently these have become popular collectibles, especially among race fans. Among the most valuable is the plastic Beetleware tumbler from the forties, the shorter version made in 1945, and the 1950 tumbler which is now valued at around $175.00. On the Gold Cup glass from 1952, current winners are shown along with those from the previous year. There were two from 1958; one was the Gold Bar tumbler, and the other was called the Iron Liege. Both were simply leftover '57 glasses with the 1958 winners added at the top.

1940s, aluminum 165.00
1940s, plastic Beetleware 300.00
1945, short 400.00

1945, tall 175.00
1948 ....65.00

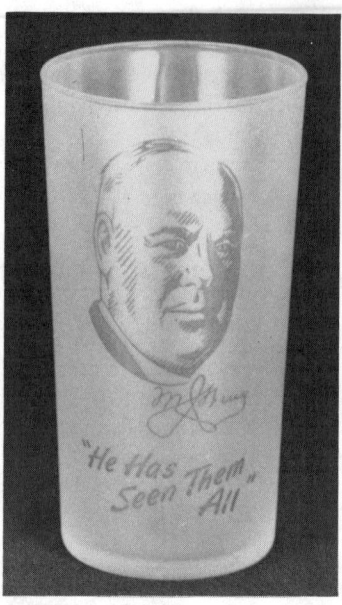

1949, He Has Seen Them All, $65.00.

1950 ....175.00
1951 ....150.00
1952, Gold Cup 65.00
1953 ....50.00
1954 ....45.00
1955 ....40.00
1956 ....40.00
1957 ....35.00
1958, Gold Bar 45.00
1958, Iron Liege 45.00
1959 ....30.00
1960 ....30.00
1961 ....25.00
1962-65, ea 22.00
1966 ....18.00
1967-68, ea 16.00
1969 ....15.00
1970-72, ea 12.00
1973 ....10.00
1974 ....8.00
1975 ....7.00
1976 ....6.00
1977-80, ea 5.00
1981-82, ea 4.00
1983-88, ea 3.00
1989-93, ea 2.00

Kew Blas

Kew Blas was a trade name used by the Union Glass Company of Summerville, Massachusetts, for their iridescent, lustered art glass produced from 1893 until about 1920. The glass was made in imitation of Tiffany and achieved notable success. Some items were decorated with pulled leaf and feather designs, while others had a monochrome lustre surface. The mark was an engraved 'Kew Blas' in an arching arrangement.

Decanter, gold, ribbed/pnt stopper, 14½" 525.00
Finger bowl, gold, ribbed, 5", +6½" underplate 475.00

Rose bowl, loops/circles on wht, gold int, 3¼x5" 1,250.00
Vase, feathers, gr on wht, gold int, 5½x6" 1,200.00
Vase, feathers, gr/gold on amber over opal, gold throat, 4" 770.00
Vase, feathers, gr/gold on opal, gold int, ftd, 8x3½" 1,100.00
Vase, feathers, gr/gold on opal, ruffled cylinder, 4½" 400.00
Vase, hooked waves, gr/gold on amber, baluster, 7¾" 600.00
Vase, pulled waves, emerald on amber, cylindrical, 8" 525.00
Vase, swirls/pulled medial band, gr/gold on opal, 10" 465.00

King's Rose

King's Rose is a soft-paste ware that was made in Staffordshire, England, from about 1820 to 1830. It is closely related to Gaudy Dutch in body type as well as the colors used in its decoration. The pattern consists of a full-blown, orange-red rose with green, pink, and yellow leaves and accents. When the rose is in pink, the ware is often referred to as Queen's Rose. Our advisor for this category is Richard Marden; he is listed in the Directory under New Hampshire.

Bowl, Queen's, floral band, rose in center, 2½x5", NM 200.00
Cake plate, Queen's, floral rim band, rose in center, 10" 130.00
Creamer, diapered, early prof rpr, mk W&B 135.00
Creamer, Queen's, helmet shape, 3½" 270.00
Cup & saucer, Queen's, miniature, 1⅝", 4¼", NM 110.00
Cup & saucer, Queen's, swirl mold, saucer w/bl dot border 225.00
Cup & saucer, Queen's, 4-color, reserves in border 190.00
Cup & saucer, 3-color, pk/red rim bands, EX 180.00
Cup & saucer, 4-color, vine/rose rim, EX 150.00
Plate, Queen's, 4-color, reserved/brn-swag border, 6½" 210.00
Plate, Queen's, 4-color, vine border, scalloped, 8" 180.00

Plates, solid border, 9¾", set of 4, EX, $500.00.

Plate, solid band, 4½", M 115.00
Plate, toddy; Queen's, scalloped, 5½" 110.00
Plate, toddy; Queen's, 4-color, vine border, 5" 130.00
Teapot, vine border, flakes, mk W&B, 11½" 225.00

Kitchen Collectibles

During the last half of the 1850s, mass-produced kitchen gadgets were patented at an astonishing rate. Most were ingeniously efficient. Apple peelers, egg beaters, cherry pitters, food choppers, and such were only the most common of hundreds of kitchen tools well designed to perform only specific tasks. Today all are very collectible. Our advisor for Cast Iron Bakers and Kettles is Denise Harned, who is the author of *Griswold Cast Collectibles*. She is listed in the Directory under Connecticut. We also recommend *Kitchen Glassware of the Depression Years* by Gene Florence and *Kitchen Antiques, 1790-1940*, by Kathryn McNerney. See also Appliances; Molds; Primitives; Reamers; Tinware; Wooden Ware.

Ashtray, Griswold #00, sm emblem, unused 70.00

Ashtray, Wagner, rnd 45.00
Bundt pan, Griswold #935, rare, 4½x9½" 400.00

Bridge pan, no mark, 8¼x10", $125.00.

Cake griddle, Mrs Sheffield's, Pat 1880 ....125.00
Cake mold, rabbit, Griswold 275.00
Cornstick pan, Griswold #273, 13" 115.00
Cornstick pan, unmk, 5 ears, scarce 50.00
Cornstick pan, unmk, 7 alternating ears 40.00
Cornstick pan, unmk, 7 ears in same direction 45.00
Doughnut mold, Ace 55.00
Dutch oven, Griswold #9, Erie, 4¼x9¾" 165.00
Grid iron/broiler, Griswold, Erie, 10½" dia 150.00
Griddle, Griswold #18, 10x16¾" 55.00
Griddle, unmk, open hdls, str sides, 18x8" 15.00
Kettle, Griswold #3, 4½x8" 100.00
Meatloaf pan, Griswold #877, 2¾x10⅛x5½" 85.00
Mold, Griswold, lamb form 175.00
Mold, Griswold, rabbit form 275.00
Mold, Griswold, Santa form 525.00
Muffin pan, Filley #10, flat, rnd 225.00
Muffin pan, Filley #12, golf ball shape, EX 225.00
Muffin pan, Filley #6, oval 225.00
Muffin pan, R&E Pat 1856, 11-cup 195.00
Popover pan, Griswold #10, 11 popovers, 7⅝" L 75.00
Roaster, Griswold #7, oval, w/trivet 150.00
Roll pan, Griswold #950, 12 rolls, 12⅞" 85.00
Saucepan, Griswold, lg emblem, 2-qt 55.00
Skillet, bacon & egg; Wagner...Pat Pending, 9¼" sq, EX 45.00
Skillet, cornbread; Corn Bread Skillet Made in USA, 9" 18.00
Skillet, egg; Griswold #53, sq 38.00
Skillet, Good Health Skillet #3, 6½", EX 15.00
Skillet, Griswold #11, lg emblem, smoke ring 150.00
Skillet, Griswold #12, lg emblem, smoke ring 150.00
Skillet, Griswold #13, lg emblem, no smoke ring 150.00
Skillet, Griswold #14, lg emblem, smoke ring 120.00
Skillet, Griswold #2, sm emblem, no smoke ring 65.00
Skillet, Griswold #8, Erie, lg emblem, smoke ring 60.00
Skillet, Sperry #8, Pat 1887 ....65.00
Skillet, Wagner #3 ....30.00
Skillet lid, Griswold #4 ....35.00
Teakettle, Wagner #0, child's 275.00
Waffle iron, Alfred Anderson & Co, heart shape, 2 pans, EX 75.00
Waffle iron, Griswold, rare, mini 350.00
Waffle iron, Griswold #19, heart & star 165.00
Waffle iron, Griswold #8, wire hdld, w/base 85.00
Waffle iron, Wagner, mini 185.00
Wheat & cornstick pan, SR&Co 95.00

Glassware

Baker, sapphire bl, Fire-King, rnd or sq, 1-pt 4.50

Batter bowl, Mayfair bl, Anchor Hocking 135.00
Batter bowl, yel opaque, Anchor Hocking 72.50
Batter jug, cobalt, Paden City 42.50
Batter jug, forest gr, New Martinsville 60.00
Batter jug, gr, Jenkins 275.00
Batter jug, red, w/liner 135.00
Beater bowl, gr, Jeannette 18.00
Bottle, oil & vinegar; clear, sterling top, Fostoria 20.00
Bottle, oil & vinegar; gr, Hawkes 70.00
Bottle, oil & vinegar; pk, Paden City 48.00
Bowl, amber, McKee, 7⅜" 27.50
Bowl, amber, US Glass, 9" 32.50
Bowl, Delphite bl, horizontal ribs, Jeannette, 5½" 27.50
Bowl, Delphite bl, w/metal beater, Jeannette 48.00
Bowl, Dots, custard, scalloped, McKee, 9" 27.50
Bowl, Fruits, wht opaque, Fire-King, 8½" 9.00
Bowl, Hex Optic, pk, 9" 20.00
Bowl, Jadite, horizontal ribs, Jeannette, 5½" 12.00

Bowls, mixing; Jennyware, sapphire blue, Jeannette Glass Co., 3-piece set, $115.00.

Bowl, Jennyware, pk, Jeannette, 10½" 32.50
Bowl, mixing; gr, paneled, Hocking, 11½" 18.00
Bowl, mixing; gr, w/spout 22.00
Bowl, mixing; pk, Hazel Atlas, 11⅝" 18.00
Bowl, pk, concentric rings, slick hdl, 9" 20.00
Bowl, sapphire bl, Fire-King, 10⅛" 14.00
Bowl, Swedish Modern, turq bl, Fire-King, 3-qt 17.50
Bowl, Tulips, wht opaque, Fire-King, 9½" 13.50
Bowl, vegetable; wht opal, 2-part, Fry, 9¾" 27.50
Bowl, Vitrock w/red trim, Hocking, 10" 17.50
Butter box, pk, emb 'B,' Jeannette, 2-lb 115.00
Butter dish, amber, Federal, 1-lb 27.50
Butter dish, amber, Federal, ¼-lb 22.50
Butter dish, Block Optic, gr, Hocking 37.50
Butter dish, cobalt, Hazel Atlas 155.00
Butter dish, Crisscross, gr or pk, Hazel Atlas, 1-lb 32.00
Butter dish, Delphite bl, emb Butter on lid, Jeannette ...185.00
Butter dish, Delphite bl, McKee 185.00
Butter dish, Hex Optic, gr, Jeannette 70.00
Butter dish, Jadite, Jeannette 32.50
Butter dish, Jennyware, ultramarine, Jeannette 115.00
Butter dish, pk, bow finial 55.00
Butter dish, pk, Federal, ¼-lb 25.00
Butter dish, red w/crystal top 100.00
Canister, caramel, McKee, 40-oz 78.00
Canister, Chalaine bl, screw-on lid 325.00
Canister, clear & frosted diagonal ribs, Owens-Illinois, 40-oz ...13.50
Canister, clear ribbed globe form, blk metal lid, 128-oz ...32.50
Canister, coffee; Chalaine bl, press-on lid 325.00
Canister, coffee; Coffee emb on clear, lg 16.00
Canister, Delphite bl, sq, Jeannette, 29-oz, 5" 115.00
Canister, forest gr, ovoid, Owens-Illinois, lg 60.00
Canister, gr tavern scene silhouette on clear, lg 24.00
Canister, Jadite, sq, Jeannette, 48-oz, 5½" 37.50

Canister, Vitrock, sq w/emb ribs, glass lid, Hocking, lg ...80.00
Canister, yel opaque, Hocking, 40-oz 60.00
Canister, Zipper, gr, globe shape, lg 165.00
Casserole, sapphire bl, Fire-King, 10-oz 10.00
Coaster, Jennyware, ultramarine, Jeannette 5.50
Cocktail shaker, amber 40.00
Cocktail shaker, red, barbell form 80.00
Cruet, amber, Faberware 17.50
Cruet, gr, Hazel Atlas 30.00
Cruet, gr, US Glass 37.50
Custard cup, Skokie gr, McKee 4.00
Decanter, red, w/matching shot glass stopper 90.00
Dripolator, clear emb ribs, Silex, 2-cup 22.00
Drippings jar, Jadite, no lettering, Jeannette 20.00
Egg cup, amber, Paden City 9.00
Egg cup, Chalaine bl 16.00
Egg cup, Skokie gr, McKee 10.00
Egg cup, yel, Hazel Atlas 4.00
Funnel, canning; gr 32.50
Funnel, clear, Tufglas 80.00
Funnel, clear, 11" 17.50
Ice bucket, gr, McKee 22.50
Ice bucket, jade gr, Fenton 37.50
Ice bucket, red, Hocking 32.00
Ice bucket, Zig-Zag, gr 24.00
Jar, pretzel; pk, Hocking 52.50
Ladle, amber, triangular bowl 7.50
Ladle, bl, wedge-shaped hdl 10.00
Ladle, blk, rnd bottom 30.00
Ladle, clear w/red hdl 40.00
Ladle, cobalt, flat bottom 27.50
Ladle, flashed or amber, flat bottom 9.00
Ladle, wht opaque 27.50
Measure, bl, 3-spout, Fire-King, 1-cup 17.50
Measure, caramel, 2-spout, McKee 550.00
Measure, clear w/red letters, 2-spout, Pyrex 22.50
Measure, cobalt, w/reamer top, Hazel Atlas, 2-cup ...225.00
Measure, Dmn Check, wht opaque, McKee, 2-cup 24.00
Measure, fired-on gr, 2-cup 10.00
Measure, Jadite, Jeannette, ¼-cup 45.00
Measure, milk glass, mc floral decal, Mckee, 2-cup ...20.00
Measure, pk, Jeannette, 1-cup 37.50
Measure, wht opaque w/floral decal, McKee, 2-cup ...22.50
Measure, yel opaque, no hdl, McKee, 4-cup 275.00
Measure pitcher, bl, 2-spout, Fire-King, 1-cup 22.00
Measure pitcher, Chalaine bl, 4-cup 185.00
Measure pitcher, custard, McKee, 4-cup 27.50
Measure pitcher, Delphite bl, McKee, 4-cup 475.00
Measure pitcher, gr, 36-oz 115.00
Meatloaf dish, wht opal, rectangular, w/lid, Fry, 9" ...45.00
Milk bottle cap, gr, Hocking 4.00
Mug, Adam's Rib, pk 15.00
Mug, amber, clear appl hdl 22.50
Mug, forest gr, ringed base, Cambridge 42.50
Mug, gr clambroth 27.50
Mug, peacock bl 27.50
Mug, red, New Martinsville 22.50
Mug, root beer; dk amber 37.50
Mug, root beer; gr 27.50
Mug, yel, Hazel Atlas 32.00
Napkin holder, forest gr, Fan Fold 100.00
Napkin holder, gr clambroth, Serv-All 140.00
Napkin holder, wht opaque, Nar-O-Fold 32.50
Pie plate, Jadite, juice-saver style, Fire-King, 10⅜" ...65.00

Pitcher, gr, ribbed base, Hocking, 60-oz 15.00
Pitcher, Jennyware, pk, Jeannette, 36-oz 65.00
Pitcher, milk; pk, Hazel Atlas 17.50
Pitcher, Skokie gr, McKee, 4-cup 27.50
Plate, snack; royal bl, Fry, 6x9", +cup 55.00
Platter, fish; wht opal, eng decor, Fry, 17" 45.00
Refrigerator dish, amber, 4½" dia 7.00
Refrigerator dish, clear, Fry, 4½x8" 27.50
Refrigerator dish, cobalt, flat knob, Hazel Atlas, 5¾" dia 55.00
Refrigerator dish, cobalt, stacking, Hazel Atlas, 4½x5", ea 42.50
Refrigerator dish, Crisscross, pk, w/lid, 5½" dia 90.00
Refrigerator dish, Dots on wht, 5x8" 12.00
Refrigerator dish, gr, emb leaves on clear lid, US Glass, 5x5" 7.50
Refrigerator dish, gr clambroth, oval, Hocking, 8" 32.00
Refrigerator dish, Jadite, Jeannette, 4x4" 12.00
Refrigerator dish, Jennyware, pk, Jeannette, 4½" sq 20.00
Refrigerator dish, pk, indented hdls, Hocking, 4x4" 12.00
Refrigerator dish, Seville yel, 7¼" sq 32.50
Refrigerator dish, ultramarine, Jeannette, 4x8" 27.50
Refrigerator dish, Vitrock, Hocking, 8x8" 27.50
Refrigerator dish, yel opaque, McKee, 7¼" sq 32.50
Relish, divided, Pyrex, Corning 12.50
Roaster, wht opal, domed lid, Fry, 7½x14x10" 135.00
Rolling pin, amethyst, blown 90.00
Rolling pin, blk 325.00
Rolling pin, forest gr, blown 135.00
Rolling pin, Jadite 300.00
Rolling pin, milk glass, mk Imperial Mfg 1921 ....75.00
Rolling pin, olive gr w/wht flecks, blown, 15" 140.00
Rolling pin, pk, screw-on wooden hdls 350.00
Rolling pin, wht clambroth, wooden hdls 95.00
Salad fork & spoon, canary yel 65.00
Salad fork & spoon, clear w/blk hdls 60.00
Salad fork & spoon, clear w/lg bl pointed hdls 55.00
Salad fork & spoon, clear w/red teardrop hdls 55.00
Salt box, peacock bl 135.00
Salt box, Zipper, gr, w/metal lid 135.00
Shakers, blk, ribbed, Hocking, pr 38.00
Shakers, blk w/EX lettering, McKee, sq, pr 28.00
Shakers, fired-on yel, Hocking, pr 17.50
Shakers, gr, emb Flour, Hocking 37.50
Shakers, gr, orig labels, Hocking, pr 22.00
Shakers, gr dots on wht opaque, Roman Arch shape, pr 22.00
Shakers, John Alden & Priscilla decals on clear, red top, pr 18.00
Shakers, milk glass, orig metal lid, McKee, lg, pr 22.50
Shakers, yel opaque, Hocking, pr 22.00
Skillet, Jadite, 2-spout, Fire-King 27.50
Spoon, yel, salad sz 32.00
Sugar shaker, amber, waisted shape, metal top, Paden City 135.00
Sugar shaker, custard, Roman Arch shape, McKee 15.00
Sugar shaker, fired-on red, metal lid 17.50
Sugar shaker, gr clambroth 27.50
Sugar shaker, Hex Optic, gr, metal lid 95.00
Sugar shaker, red, Hawkes 325.00
Syrup, amber, Paden City #198, 8-oz 45.00
Syrup, amber to yel shaded, glass lid 42.50
Syrup, metal lid, US Glass, mini 55.00
Syrup, gr, Hazel Atlas 22.50
Syrup, pk, metal hinged top, Hazel Atlas, tall 42.50
Syrup, pk, New Martinsville 37.50
Teakettle, Glasbake 18.00
Teapot, floral cutting, mk Corning Pyrex in lid 55.00
Tray, amber, oval, Fry 45.00
Tumbler, Crisscross, 9-oz 16.00

Tumbler, gr, Hazel Atlas 8.00
Tumbler, Jadite, Jeannette, 12-oz 12.00
Tumbler, Jennyware, ultramarine, 8-oz 37.50
Tumbler, pk, imprinted Mission Juice 22.50
Water bottle, cobalt, 64-oz, 10" 57.50
Water bottle, Crisscross, gr, 32-oz 95.00
Water bottle, forest gr, emb penguin 14.00
Water bottle, forest gr, w/top, Hocking 27.50
Water bottle, gr, canteen shape, Hocking 32.00
Water dispenser, custard, McKee 115.00
Water dispenser, milk glass, McKee 95.00
Whipper, milk glass, Androck 16.00

Miscellaneous

Apple peeler, Goodell Co Antrim NH, CI, emb Wht Mtn 46.00
Apple peeler, Goodell...Pat 1898, CI, turntable, EX 80.00
Apple peeler, Hudson, 3-gear, dtd 1882 ....85.00
Apple peeler, Lockey & Howland, CI, clamp-on style, Pat 1858 ..85.00
Apple peeler, Reading PA 1878, CI, turntable, EX 85.00
Apple peeler, Thompson, New England Butt Co, CI, Pat 1877 ..145.00
Apple peeler, unmk CI, 2-gear, clamp-on style, dtd 1872 ....85.00
Bread maker, Universal, tin & CI, clamps on, Pat 1904, EX 65.00
Butter scales, Dazey, red & wht, 1920s, EX 65.00
Cabbage cutter, wooden, EX 40.00
Cake mold, tin, center tube, fluted & scalloped sides, 2x8" 8.00
Cake pan, tin, center tube, 12-sided, 3x9", EX 8.00
Cake pan, tin, spring release, Kreamer #10, 10", EX 9.00
Can opener, Dazey, electric 25.00
Can opener, Dazey, wall mt, EX 15.00
Can opener, Peerless Pat Feb 11 90, CI & steel, 6¼" L 9.50
Can opener, Sure-Cut Pat 7-19-04, steel, wooden hdl, 9" L 7.50
Can opener, Vaughan's Easy Cutter, steel w/wooden hdl, 1900s 5.00
Cherry seeder, Enterprise 50.00
Cherry seeder, Home, CI, dtd 1917 ....48.00
Cherry seeder, Mt Joye, New Standard, #75, EX orig 55.00
Cherry seeder, New Standard Carrousel 110.00
Cherry seeder, New Standard Wobbly Wheel 95.00
Cherry seeder, Rollman Mfg, EX 45.00

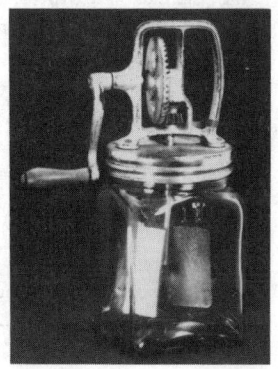

Churn, #102, no mark, 1-qt., $275.00.

Churn, Anchor Hocking, 2-qt 85.00
Churn, Dazey, #10, both pcs mkd, 1-qt, EX 1,200.00
Churn, Dazey, #20, 2-qt 155.00
Churn, Dazey, #30, 3-qt 105.00
Churn, Dazey, #40, Pat dtd, 1-gal 75.00
Churn, Dazey, #80, 2-gal 80.00
Cleaver, meat; Foster Bros, heavy steel w/wooden hdl, 15" 15.00
Clothes sprinkler, Chinaman, Sprinkle Plenty 32.00
Clothes sprinkler, Chinaman, wht 22.00

Clothes sprinkler, iron shape, ivy on sides 43.00
Cookie cutter, Rumford, tube hdl, 4x2" 15.00
Cookie cutters, 3-in-1 nested, Calumet, 1930s 12.50
Cutter, biscuit; gr plastic, Bonny Ware, 1930s, 2¼" 5.00
Cutter, boiled egg; metal scissors shape, France, 1850s, 3x4" 7.50
Egg beater, Dover, #300, 16½" L, EX 375.00
Egg beater, Dover, hotel, 1915, 12½", EX 35.00
Egg beater, Handy Andy Auto Cream, EX 50.00
Egg beater, Improved Keystone, EX 165.00
Egg beater, Ladd Beater #0, oval metal hdl, dtd Oct 10, 1921 ...12.00
Egg beater, Merry Whirl, Pat 1915, 12", EX 30.00
Egg beater, Peerless #2, iron hdl, tin beaters 32.00
Egg beater, Silver, CI top, glass bottom 200.00
Egg beater, Taplin's Dover Pattern Improved, CI/tin, 1903, EX ...35.00
Egg beater, 1898 Perfection, 2 propeller blades 55.00
Egg beater/whipper, A&J Full Vision Beater Set, metal, 7" 24.00
Egg beater/whipper, tin & wire, coiled & str, 1880s, 7½" 10.00
Egg beater/whipper, 20th Century, metal, push-down type, 11" ...32.00
Egg separator, T&S Flour 12.50
Food chopper, rounded wrought iron blade, chestnut hdl, 5" 95.00
Food chopper, sheet steel, wooden hdl, 5x5½" 10.00
Food chopper, sqd steel blade mk Brades Cast Steel, trn hdl 75.00
Food chopper, wide crescent blade, wood hdl, pitted, 8¾" 135.00
Food grinder, American #20, CI, table-top type, EX 10.00
Food grinder, Griswold #1, CI, EX 25.00
Food grinder, Pomeroy's #10, CI, table-top type, EX 12.50
Food grinder, Puritan #10, CI, table-top type, EX 10.00
Fork, tinned steel, 2-tine, 11¼" 5.00
Grater, all brass, initialed/mk, 12½x4½" 165.00
Grater, Climax, tin w/CI fr, rotary type, hand crank, 10" 32.00
Grater, nutmeg; Edgar, CI, bar-closed ends 95.00
Grater, nutmeg; Edgar, CI, open ends 95.00
Grater, nutmeg; rnd, crank style, lg blk knob 110.00
Grater, nutmeg; rnd disk, wire hdl, 1886 ....200.00
Ice crusher, Big Squeeze WDCo Pat Pending, cast aluminum 17.50
Ice crusher, Dazey, chrome & blk, standing style 20.00
Juicer, Dazey, wall mt, EX 30.00
Knife, carving; Putnam Cutlery...USA, bone hdl, 14", EX 8.00
Knife, paring; handmade, oak hdl, cooper rivets, crude, 6¾" 4.00
Mayonnaise mixer, Universal, rare 400.00
Milk bottle cap pick/lifter, Glidden Jap-O-Lac, Pat 1-26-12 ....5.00
Noodle cutter, CI w/5 different cutters, ca 1930, EX 50.00
Pan, angel food cake; tin, 4x10" 5.00
Pan, bread finger; Wagner #3, aluminum, 15" 55.00
Pan, muffin; Wagner #468B, 11" 45.00
Pie crimper, all wood, well-shaped hdl, 7" 175.00
Pie crimper, cvd bone, X-hatching, EX detail, 6" 120.00
Pot scrubber, chain, hdls, 11" L, EX 40.00
Potato masher, trn tiger-striped maple hdl, 1850s, 12½" 85.00
Potato masher, wooden, early shape, trn hdl, pestle end, 11" 12.50
Raisin seeder, Blk Lightning, CI, clamp-on style 75.00
Raisin seeder, Crown, CI 75.00
Raisin seeder, Enterprise, CI, lg 50.00
Rolling pin, porc, Kelvinator advertising 100.00
Rolling pin, porc, yel 100.00
Rolling pin, springerle, EX hand cvg, 20 blocks, EX 250.00
Scoop, tin, appl strap hdl, worn red pnt, 4" 7.50
Scoop, tin, hollow hdl, 14x6¼", EX 15.00
Scoop, tin, soldered construction, appl strap hdl, 3x3", EX 9.00
Scoop, Wagner #00C, aluminum, w/emb advertising, 10" 45.00
Scoop, Wagner #1, aluminum, w/emb advertising 35.00
Sieve, tin, flat-bottom pan type, flared rim, 10" 12.50
Sifter, Blood's, wooden, Pat Sept 17, 1861 ....295.00
Sifter, Bromwell's Measuring...Guaranteed, tin w/red knob 7.50

Sifter, Lee's Favorite Flour..., tin, crank hdl, 6x5", EX 25.00
Sifter, rotary type w/metal hdl & gr wood knob, 1-cup, EX 8.00
Sifter, wood w/leather paddles, EX 350.00
Sifter, wooden w/bootjack ends, ca 1864, EX 235.00
Skillet, tin, mk Cold Handle 25.00
Skillet, Wearever #2510, aluminum, gr wood hdl, EX 10.00
Skimmer, pierced sheet iron, 13" L 10.00
Spoon, slotted, Rumford 12.00
Spoon, steel, pierced hole in hdl, 15½" 4.00
Spoon, tinned steel, pierced hole in hdl, 17¼" 6.00
Steak cuber, Cube Steak Machine Co, gr enamel, 1930s 250.00
Tenderizer, meat; CI head w/grid & ice shaver, wood hdl, 10" 12.50
Timer, Tillie the Time, CI pilgrim form, NM in orig box 25.00
Wrench, fruit jar; Yo-Ho Monticello IA, wire w/rubber grips 7.50

Knives

Knife collecting as a hobby began in earnest during the 1960s when government regulations required for the first time that knife companies mark their product with the country of origin. The few collectors and dealers cognizant of this change at once began stockpiling the older knives made before this law was enacted. Another impetus to the growing interest in this area came with the Gun Control Act of 1968, which severely restricted gun trading. Frustrated gun dealers transferred their attention to knives. Today there are collectors clubs in many of the states.

The most sought-after pocketknives are those made before WWII. However, Case, Schrade, and Primble knives of a more recent manufacture are also collected. Most collectors prefer knives 'as found.' Do not attempt to clean, sharpen, or in any way 'improve' on an old knife.

The prices quoted here are for knives in mint condition (except for those in the Miscellaneous section). If a knife has been used, sharpened, or blemished in any way, its value decreases. The newer the knife, the greater the reduction in value. For further information refer to *The Standard Knife Collector's Guide* by Ron Stewart and Roy Ritchie and *Sargent's American Premium Guide to Knives and Razors, Identification and Values*, 3rd Edition by Jim Sargent. Our advisor for this category is Charles D. Stapp; he is listed in the Directory under Indiana.

Key:

bd — blade   p/b — push button
Cut — Cutlery

Case, B100, Xmas tree hdl, 1-bd, Tested XX, 1920-40, 3½" 250.00
Case, H2210, mottled hdl, 2-bd, Tested XX, 1920-40, 3⅜" 500.00
Case, Muskrat, bone hdl, 2-bd, USA, 1965-69, 3⅞" 50.00
Case, Muskrat, gr bone hdl, 2-bd, Tested XX, 1920-40, 3⅞" 800.00
Case, M100, bl celluloid hdl, 1-bd, XX, 1920-40, 3¼" 160.00
Case, M1218K, metal hdl, 1-bd, Tested XX, 1920-40, 3" 135.00
Case, P137, pakkawood hdl, 1-bd, 3½" 25.00
Case, RM224½, Xmas tree hdl, 2-bd, Tested XX, 3" 300.00
Case, R1212½, candy stripe hdl, 1-bd, Tested XX, 1920-40, 4" ..700.00
Case, S2LP, sterling silver hdl, 2-bd, XX, 2¼" 125.00
Case, W1216, wire hdl, 1-bd, Tested XX, 1920-40, 3⅛" 150.00
Case, 11031SH, walnut hdl, 1-bd, Tested XX, 1920-40, 3" 135.00
Case, 1116SP, bud walnut hdl, 1-bd, 10 Dot, 1970, 3½" 35.00
Case, 1139, banana, walnut hdl, 1-bd, Tested XX, 1920s, 4¼" ...185.00
Case, 2109, gunstock, bone hdl, 1-bd, Tested XX, 1920s, 3¼" ...260.00
Case, 2136B, slick blk hdl, 1-bd, XX, 1940-55, 4⅛" 150.00
Case, 2137, blk compo hdl, 1-bd, 10 Dot, 1970, 3⅝" 35.00
Case, 2138, blk compo hdl, 1-bd, 10 Dot, 1970, 5⅝" 25.00
Case, 22001R, slick blk hdl, 2-bd, Tested XX, 1920-40, 2⅝" 110.00

Case, 2217, slick blk hdl, 2-bd, XX, 1940-64, 4" 235.00
Case, 2220, slick blk hdl, 2-bd, 10 Dot, 1970, 2¾" 45.00
Case, 31024, yel compo hdl, 1-bd, Tested XX, 1920-40, 3" ...125.00
Case, 31048, yel compo hdl, 1-bd, XX, 1940-64, 4⅛" 40.00
Case, 31213, yel hdl, 1-bd, Tested XX, 5⅜" 500.00
Case, 3201, yel hdl, 2-bd, Case Bradford, 2⅝" 110.00
Case, 32024½, yel compo hdl, 2-bd, USA, 1965-69, 3" 35.00
Case, 3220, yel compo hdl, 2-bd, USA, 1965-69, 2¾" 45.00
Case, 4200SS, melon tester, wht hdl, 2-bd, USA 1965-69, 5½" ...150.00
Case, 43046, humpbk, compo hdl, 3-bd, Tested XX, 3⅝" 400.00
Case, 4318HP, wht compo hdl, 3-bd, XX, 3½" 75.00
Case, 5110½L, stag hdl, 1-bd, Tested XX, 1920-40, 3⅜" 450.00
Case, 5200LP, stag hdl, 2-bd, Tested XX, 1920-40, 4" 600.00
Case, 5220, peanut, stag hdl, 2-bd, Tested XX, 1920-40, 2¾" 250.00
Case, 61011, Hawkbill, bone stag hdl, 1-bd, USA, 1965-69 ....110.00
Case, 61011, Hawkbill, gr bone hdl, 1-bd, XX, 1940-50, 4" 150.00
Case, 6103B&G, bone hdl, 1-bd, Tested XX, 1920-40, 3¼" 200.00
Case, 6111½L, red bone hdl, 1-bd, XX, 1940-50 ....200.00
Case, 6116SH, gr bone hdl, 1-bd, Tested XX, 1920-40, 3⅜" 200.00
Case, 6143, Daddy Barlow, bone hdl, 1-bd, USA 1965-69, 5" 40.00
Case, 6143, jigged bone hdl, 1-bd, Dots, 5" 175.00

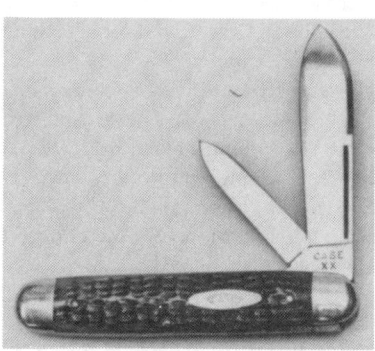

Case, #6294, L.P. green bone handle, XX, 1940-55, 2-blade, M, $350.00.

Case, 62009, bone stag hdl, 2-bd, 10 Dot, 1970, 3¾" 35.00
Case, 62009, delrin hdl, 2-bd, 10 Dot, 1970, 3¾" 30.00
Case, 62009½, gr bone hdl, 2-bd, Tested XX, 1920s, 3¼" 200.00
Case, 62009½, red bone hdl, 2-bd, XX, 1940-64, 3¼" 55.00
Case, 6202½, delrin hdl, 2-bd, 10 Dot, 1970, 3⅜" 25.00
Case, 62024, gr bone hdl, 2-bd, Tested XX, 1920-40, 3" 150.00
Case, 6205RAZ, rough blk hdl, 2-bd, XX, 1940-50, 3¾" 250.00
Case, 6207, Rogers bone hdl, 2-bd, XX, 1940-64, 3½" 250.00
Case, 6217, wood hdl, 2-bd, USA, 1965-69, 4" 45.00
Case, 6220, peanut, red bone hdl, 2-bd, XX, 1940-64, 2¾" 100.00
Case, 63052, Congress, gr bone hdl, 3-bd, Tested XX, 3½" 750.00
Case, 6308, red bone hdl, 3-bd, XX, 1940-64, 3¼" 90.00
Case, 6445R, utility, gr bone hdl, Tested XX, 1920-40, 3¾" 225.00
Case, 7129½, tortoise shell hdl, 1-bd, Tested XX, 1920-40 ....225.00
Case, 8206, pearl hdl, 2-bd, Tested XX, 1920-40, 2⅝" 200.00
Case, 9201, cracked ice hdl, 2-bd, XX, 1940-64, 2⅝" 35.00
Case, 92100, faux pearl hdl, 2-bd, Tested XX, 1920-40, 4⅝" 800.00
Case, 93042, whittler, faux pearl hdl, 3-bd, Tested XX 400.00
Case, 9327SHSP, cracked ice hdl, 3-bd, XX, 1940-64, 2¾" 50.00
Queen, 139, Barlow, brn bone hdl, 2-bd, 3½" 40.00
Queen, 14, peanut, winterbottom bone hdl, 2-bd, 2¾" 25.00
Queen, 15, Congress, Rogers bone hdl, 2-bd, 3½" 40.00
Queen, 19, fisherman's, Rogers bone hdl, 2-bd, 5" 80.00
Queen, 2175, whittler, Rogers bone hdl, 3-bd, 3½" 35.00
Queen, 22, Barlow, brn bone hdl, 2-bd, 3½" 45.00
Queen, 24, trapper, steel hdl, 2-bd 35.00
Queen, 29, jack, winterbottom bone hdl, 2-bd, 4½" 75.00
Queen, 3, winterbottom bone hdl, 2-bd, 3¼" 25.00

Queen, 33, Congress, Rogers bone hdl, 4-bd, 3½" 120.00
Queen, 36, lockback, winterbottom bone hdl, 1-bd, 4½" 60.00
Queen, 38, swell-center jumbo, jigged bone hdl, 1-bd, 5¼" 200.00
Queen, 4, sleeveboard, smoke pearl hdl, 2-bd, 3⅜" 75.00
Queen, 42, yel scale hdl, 2-bd, 2¾" 22.00
Queen, 49, stockman's, winterbottom bone hdl, 3-bd, 4¼" 40.00
Queen, 5, Rogers bone hdl, 2-bd, Crown & Dots, 2½" 38.00
Queen, 5, Senator, winterbottom bone hdl, 2-bd, 2½" 20.00
Queen, 52, moose, winterbottom bone hdl, 2-bd 40.00
Queen, 54, pearl hdl, 3-bd 30.00
Queen, 57, smoked pearl hdl, 3-bd, 3⅜" 75.00
Queen, 59, smoked pearl hdl, 2-bd, 2¾" 40.00
Queen, 6120, jack, stag hdl, 2-bd, 4½" 35.00
Queen, 6140, swell center, bone hdl, 2-bd, 3½" 30.00
Queen, 8150, hunter's, stag hdl, 2-bd, 5¼" 50.00
Queen, 8420, mini-trapper, stag hdl, 2-bd 35.00
Queen, 8460, toothpick, gr bone hdl, 1-bd 50.00
Queen, 9, stockman's, winterbottom bone hdl, 3-bd, 4" 35.00
Queen Stainless, 35, rough blk hdl, 3-bd, 2⅝" 30.00
Queen Steel, 48, whittler's, winterbottom bone hdl, 3-bd, 3½" 45.00
Queen Steel, 55, pen, gr Rogers bone hdl, 2-bd, 3¼" 30.00
Queen Steel, 61, stockman's, winterbottom bone hdl, 3-bd, 3⅝" .50.00
Queen Steel, 66, muskrat, winterbottom bone hdl, 2-bd 125.00
Remington, RB041, brn bone hdl, 2-bd, 3⅜" 90.00
Remington, RB44W, Barlow, wht hdl, 2-bd, 3⅜" 150.00
Remington, RH73, jack, brn bone hdl, 2-bd, 3⅛" 130.00
Remington, R1225, jack, wht compo hdl, 2-bd, 4½" 275.00
Remington, R1243, Barlow, bone hdl, 1-bd 350.00
Remington, R125, pyremite hdl, 3-bd, 3½" 140.00
Remington, R1379, metal hdl, 2-bd 250.00
Remington, R1437, lockback, ivory hdl, 1-bd 140.00
Remington, R1535, florist's, imitation ivory hdl, 1-bd, 3¾" 100.00
Remington, R165, jack, yel scale hdl, 2-bd, 3½" 125.00
Remington, R1653, peanut, brn bone hdl, 2-bd, 2⅞" 125.00
Remington, R1803, jack teardrop, bone hdl, 2-bd 100.00
Remington, R3059, stockman's, metal hdl, 3-bd, 4" 250.00
Remington, R31, redwood hdl, 2-bd, 3⅜" 90.00
Remington, R333, brn bone hdl, 2-bd, 3¾" 200.00
Remington, R365, gold swirl pyremite hdl, 2-bd, 3¾" 175.00
Remington, R552, blk hdl, 2-bd, 3¼" 120.00
Remington, R645, switchbd, candy-stripe hdl, 1-bd, 4" 500.00
Remington, R653, bow tie, bone hdl, 1-bd, 3⅞" 400.00
Remington, R693, gunstock, bone hdl, 2-bd, 4" 150.00
Remington, R698, hawkbill, cocobolo hdl, 1 bd, 4" 90.00
Remington, R73, Lobster, bone hdl, 3-bd 140.00
Remington, R953, toothpick, brn hdl, 1-bd, 5" 225.00
Remington, R995, jack, bl & wht compo hdl, 2-bd, 3¼" 125.00
Winchester, 1938, brn bone hdl, 1-bd, 3⅜" 125.00
Winchester, 2309, Senator, pearl hdl, 2-bd, 3" 120.00
Winchester, 2330, pen, pearl hdl, 2-bd, 3¼" 125.00
Winchester, 2380, doctor's, pearl hdl, 3¼" 400.00
Winchester, 2608, stabber, cocobolo hdl, 2-bd, 3⅝" 125.00
Winchester, 2613, sleeveboard, ebony hdl, 2-bd, 3⅜" 110.00
Winchester, 2640, Coke bottle, ebony hdl, 2-bd, 3¾" 250.00

Miscellaneous

A Saldana, plexiglas hdl, 8" fixed bd, +leather sheath 20.00
Bowie, walnut grips, S-shaped steel hand guard, 15½", EX 2,500.00
Bowie, wrought iron 8⅝" bd w/brass strip, wood hdl, EX 1,100.00
Butcher, Shapleigh, hickory hdl, 8½", EX 15.00
Confederate fighting, brass hilt & hdw, 25½" L, EX 1,250.00
Confederate handmade Bowie, bone hdl, 8½" clip point bd 300.00
Deer hoof hdl, brass band attachment, iron bd, 1800s, 10½" 30.00

Gambler's Bowie, Alexander Sheffield on bd, ivory hdl, 16" **450.00**
Ka-Bar, leather hdl, aluminum butt, 5" bd, +sheath **30.00**
Noramea 1863 New Caledonia on 7¾" bd, stag hdl, +sheath **225.00**
Puma #6377 White Hunter, stag hdl, fixed 6⅛" bd, EX **95.00**
Survival, V-44, brass hilt horn hdl, Collins scabbard, EX **125.00**
Trench, AC US Model 1917-18, M in EX scabbard **225.00**

Kosta

Kosta glassware has been made in Sweden since 1742. Today they are one of that country's leading producers of quality art glass. Two of their most important designers were Elis Bergh (1929-1950) and Vicke Lindstrand, artistic director from 1950 to 1973. Lindstrand brought to the company knowledge of important techniques such as Graal, fine figural engraving, Ariel, etc. He influenced new artists to experiment with these techniques and inspired them to create new and innovative designs. Today's collectors are most interested in pieces made during the 1950s and '60s. Our advisor for this category is Abby Malowanczyk; she is listed in the Directory under Texas.

Bowl, gr cased, acid cut-bk fish, sgn Warff, 5x6" **800.00**
Vase, bl/emerald int striations in clear, sgn LH, #1590, 8" **200.00**
Vase, bubble trap design, clear-cased bl, LH, #1336, 12½" **200.00**
Vase, clear lined w/emerald gr, paperweight base, sgn, 8½" **250.00**
Vase, clear w/gr seaweed inclusions, 2 fish, LG, #349, 10" **300.00**
Vase, eng deer, lg orange spot on side, Lindstrand, 7" **200.00**
Vase, orange/wht flecked, knopped stem, Vallien, #943, 7" **330.00**

Kutani

Kutani, named for the Japanese village where it originated, was first produced in the 17th century. The early ware, Ko Kutani, was made for only about thirty years. Several types were produced before 1800, but these are rarely encountered. In the 19th century kilns located in several different villages began to copy the old Kutani wares. This later, more familiar type has large areas of red with gold designs on a white ground decorated with warriors, birds, and flowers in controlled colors of red, gold, and black.

Bowl, exotic bird and peony branches, the underside with trailing stems and flowers, 1800s, 14½", $1,750.00.

Compote, figures & florals, 1890s, 5½x8" **165.00**
Cup, gods of good fortune, calligraphy inscription, 2", pr **125.00**
Figure, seated nobleman, gilt detailing, 1800s, 12" **985.00**
Jar, floral landscape, w/lid, 4", pr **90.00**
Plate, karako/birds/flowers in rust red, 1880s, 8½" **80.00**
Vase, brocade dragon & phoenix panels, 1870s, 9½" **440.00**
Vase, figures & flowers, on stand, 3½" **95.00**
Vase, figures/scenes in rnd reserves, egg form, 5", pr **385.00**

Vase, 100 Lohan design on rust red, cylindrical, 12" **150.00**
Vase, 2 ladies/outdoor scene in oval panel, flask form, 5" **135.00**

L. E. Smith

Perhaps best known for their line of black glass vases and novelty items, this 20th-century American glass company located in Mt. Pleasant, Pennsylvania, also made several patterns of colored Depression-type dinnerware as well as some glass animals. They reproduced the Moon and Star pattern during the 1960s which proved so successful that they continue to make a few pieces yet today, though the colors now in production (crystal, pink, cobalt, and teal green) are of no interest to collectors.

Ashtray, elephant form, blk, #2 ....**32.50**
Bean pot, blk w/silver decor, lid dbls as center-hdld tray **45.00**
Bowl, blk, ftd, #515, 7" **19.00**
Butter dish, Moon & Star, amber, ¼-lb **15.00**
Cake plate, Do-Si-Do, blk, hdls, 9½" **20.00**
Cheese dish, Moon & Star, lg domed lid, gr **30.00**
Cookie jar, amber **55.00**
Cordial tray, blk, #381 ....**10.00**
Creamer & sugar bowl, Moon & Star, red **25.00**
Dispenser, water; cobalt **375.00**
Flowerpot, blk, ca 1930, 3" **12.00**
Pitcher, water; Moon & Star, amberina **50.00**
Plate, Mt Pleasant, blk, 3-ftd **20.00**
Punch bowl, pres-cut flowers, sawtooth/fan border, 17" **75.00**
Saucer, Mt Pleasant, blk, 6½" **5.00**
Syrup pitcher, Moon & Star, chrome lid, red **28.00**
Vase, blk, #102-4, 6½" **10.00**
Vase, blk, #1900, 7¼" **19.00**
Vase, blk, #49, 6" **12.00**
Vase, blk, for Woolworth, #433/4-C **14.00**
Vase, blk, urn form, late 1920s, 7¾" **22.00**
Vase, dancing girls, blk, #433, 7" **19.00**

Labels

Before the advent of the cardboard box, wooden crates were used for transporting products. Paper labels were attached to the crates to identify the contents and the packer. These labels often had colorful lithographed illustrations covering a broad range of subjects. Eventually the cardboard box replaced the crate, and the artwork was imprinted directly onto the carton. Today these paper labels are becoming collectible — primarily for the art, but also for their advertising appeal. Our advisor for this category is Cerebro; their address is listed in the Directory under Pennsylvania.

Apple, America's Delight, orchards & mtns, Seattle, 9x11" **3.00**
Apple, Antler, 12-point buck, 9x10½" **45.00**
Apple, Appleton, Nouveau lady w/roses, 10½x9" **5.00**
Apple, Boy Blue, boy w/horn, Okanogan, 9x11" **2.00**
Apple, Chief Seattle, Indian bust in sunburst, 10½x9" **5.00**
Apple, James Parks, setter dog in forest, 10½x9" **4.00**
Apple, Mariposa, butterfly & flowers, 9x10½" **35.00**
Asparagus, Caligras, man & horse-drawn wagon **2.00**
Asparagus, Kingfish, crowned fish leaps out of water **2.00**
Cigar, Alvara, 6x8" **2.00**
Cigar, American Citizen, Geo Washington, shield, lg **1.00**
Cigar, First Cabinet, 5 men at table, 1920s, 7x8½" **10.00**
Cigar, Kelene's Buzzer, lg bee, 1920s, 4½x4½" **3.00**

Cigar, Las Gentes, 3 ladies, 4½x4½" **2.00**
Cigar, Lord Badge, man on horse, 1900s, 4½x4½" **12.00**
Cigar, Memory, man sits before fireplace, 1910, 6x10" **15.00**
Cigar, Quail, 1920s, 4½x4½" **5.00**
Cigar, Sir Loraine, knight in alcove, 1911, 6¼x8¼" **9.00**
Cigar, Surveyor, man & horse before mansion, 1920s, 6½x8½" **9.50**
Cigar, White Cat, cat atop cigar, 1930s, 7x9" **3.00**
Cigar box, Allen's RJ Perfecto, photo litho, 8½x6¾" **1.50**
Cigar box, Blue Bird, bird on branch, c 1917, 4⅜" sq **5.50**
Cigar box, Dreamlets, lady sitting in window, 5½x5¼" **3.50**
Cigar box, Irish Singer, Dennis O'Sullivan, 8½x6½" **12.50**
Cigar box, La Carito, ladies w/bl flowers, 4¼" sq **3.50**
Cigar box, La Sultana, eagle & coin cartouch, 8½x6½" **4.00**
Cigarette, John, Blk man in top hat, 2x3¼" **2.75**
Citrus, Blue Heron, bird & cattails, FL, 9" sq **2.00**
Citrus, Florigold Groves, Indian profile, FL, 9x9" **1.00**
Citrus, Jolly Roger, pirate & ship, FL, 9x9" **2.00**
Citrus, Tru-Type, Indian smokes pipe, FL, 9x9" **10.00**
Cranberry, Arrow, Indians shooting buffalo, 10x7" **10.00**
Cranberry, Holiday Brand, child w/toys under Xmas tree, 7x10" ..**22.00**
Grapefruit, Arizona Star, grove & mtns, Sacramento **5.00**
Grapefruit, Collegiate, ½-fruit on plate, Claremont **4.00**
Grapefruit, Desert Bloom, mtns/yucca on bl, Redlands, 10x11" **3.00**
Lemon, Arab, on horsebk in desert, San Dimas, 12½x8¾" **14.00**
Lemon, Bridal Veil, falls in Yosemite, Santa Paula, 12½x8¾" **5.00**
Lemon, Fontana Girl, girl drinks lemonade, 1918, 8¾x12½" **50.00**
Lemon, Galleon, galleon in high seas, Oxnard, 12½x8¾" **5.00**
Lemon, Lemonade, 3 lg lemons & orchards, Ivanhoe, 12½x9" **1.00**
Lettuce, Green Head, gr duck's head **1.00**
Orange, Annie Laurie, girl in plaid, Strathmore, 10x11" **3.00**

**Orange, Cal-oro, Santa Ana, California, color-
ful butterfly, 10x11", $75.00.**

Orange, Carefree, laughing blond on bl, Redlands, 10x11" **2.00**
Orange, Magnolia, lg flowers on bl, Porterville, 10x11" **10.00**
Orange, Memory, silhouette of girl & roses in fr, 10x11" **8.00**
Orange, Sun Idol, lg orange w/in sun rays, Ivanhoe, 10x11" **3.00**
Pear, Big Game, football player & stadium, 1930, 7½x11" **9.50**
Pear, Denison's Crest, stylized lettering, Wenatchee, 8x11" **2.00**
Pear, Duckwall, Wood Duck by brick wall, 10¾x7¼" **2.00**
Pear, Gold Wing, gold-winged pears on blk, 8x11" **5.00**
Pear, Old Orchard, 2 little girls, gilt trim, 10¾x7¼" **2.00**
Tobacco, Black Oak, Hoen litho, 6¼x12⅜", M **30.00**
Tobacco, Just the Thing, Maclin-Zimmer, Hoen litho, 6x12½", M ...**35.00**
Tobacco, Victory Brand, Hoen litho, 6½x13", M **45.00**

Vegetable, Forty-Second St, bands & dancers etc, 6½x5" **2.00**
Vegetable, Gay Johnny, barefoot boy in cowboy hat, 6½x5" **3.00**
Yam, Mary Agnes, blond girl in pigtails, 9x9" **2.00**
Yam, Sho-Am-Sweet, Blk chef, 7x4" **1.50**

Labino

Dominick Labino was a glass blower who until mid-1985 worked in his studio in Ohio, blowing and sculpting various items which he signed and dated. A ceramic engineer by trade, he was instrumental in developing the heat-resistant tiles used in space flights. His glassmaking shows his versatility in the art. While some of his designs are free-form and futuristic, others are reminiscent of the products of older glasshouses. Because of problems with his health, Mr. Labino became unable to blow glass himself; he died January, 10, 1987. Work coming from his studio since mid-1985 has been signed 'Labino Studios, Baker,' indicating ware made by his protege, E. Baker O'Brien. In addition to her own compositions, she continues to use many of the colors developed by Labino.

Bottle, amber w/3 lg blobs of swirled purple/bl, 1968, 5" **900.00**
Bowl, ruby w/gr swirls, 4 appl blobs, 1970, 3x6" **800.00**
Goblet, amber, int-twist air-trap stem, 1971, 6¾" **300.00**
Paperweight, yel w/int olive gr calla lilies, 1967, 2¾" **400.00**
Red Earth, sphere, copper smelts w/silver smelts base, 9" **4,500.00**
Sculpture, Emergence, 4 pk layers+internal bubble, 1972, 11" ..**4,700.00**
Sculpture, Sea Kingdom, 1973, 7" **2,400.00**
Vase, avocado gr w/bubbles, ovoid w/tiny opening, 1968, 4" **400.00**
Vase, dk amber w/gray pulled leafy stems, ovoid, 1982, 5" **850.00**
Vase, gold ruby, ridged/pinched free-form, sgn/1973, 7" **900.00**
Vase, gr irid w/2 opal bosses, pear form, 1968, 7½" **550.00**
Vase, Harlequin, yel/red/bl stripes, 1975, 6" **1,320.00**
Vase, irid amber, 4 appl/tooled blobs, bottle form, '69, 6" **525.00**
Vase, ruby shading to gr, bottle form, 1971, 13" **800.00**
Vase, yel/bl, free-form w/twisted cylinder neck, 1965, 6¾" **700.00**

Lace, Linens, and Needlework

It has been recorded that lace was found in the tombs of ancient Egypt. Lace has always been a symbol of wealth and fashion. Italian laces are regarded as the finest ever produced, but the differences between them and the laces of France are nearly indistinguishable. Needlework was revived during the 18th century and became the favorite of feminine pastimes. Examples of many forms (tatting, embroidery, needlepoint, and crochet, for instance) are available today, and, though fragile in appearance, have withstood the ravages of time with remarkable durability.

Key:
embr — embroidered   ms — machine sewn
hs — hand sewn

Bedspread, chenille, peacocks in center **125.00**
Bedspread, crochet, popcorn & hexagons, 90x100" **250.00**
Bedspread, crochet, popcorn stitch, twin sz, pr **395.00**
Bedspread, crochet, 66 floral sqs, 70x101", EX **155.00**
Bedspread, silk-like damask, pnt cherubs/urns/etc, dbl sz **235.00**
Blanket, wool, ivory w/bl 'chenille' embr, 1-pc, early, 90" **475.00**
Bolster cover, wht linen, gold embr, cut-out & scalloped hem **65.00**
Centerpc, Battenburg, dmn shape, 15x25½" **100.00**
Centerpc, gold w/gr embr flowers, 3" lace border, 14x16" **40.00**
Coverlet, linsey woolsey, red/wht sqs, floral quilting, sgn **600.00**

Crib cover, crochet, flowers & animals, 44x66" 185.00
Doily, crochet, Bread, 4½x11" 25.00
Doily, crochet, cat w/arched back, 8½x10" 35.00
Doily, crochet, Cupid center, 11½" sq 45.00
Doily, crochet, God Bless America, 15x16" 55.00
Doily, crochet, medallion, scalloped edge, 12½" 25.00
Doily, crochet, wht w/red border, 8x8½" 18.50
Doily, ms, wht cotton, lacy flowers, 10x14" 15.00
Dresser scarf, linen, embr flowers & bows ea end, 38x12" 25.00
Dresser scarf, linen, hemstitched edge, 2 corners w/embr 25.00
Fabric, homespun navy bl/wht, 15x51" 65.00
Mattress cover, bl/wht cotton checks, ms, tape closure 150.00
Needlepoint panel, intricate floral on blk, 20th C, 29x29" 210.00

Needlework picture depicting Rebecca at the well, wool on linen, original frame, signed and dated 1770, 11x15", $3,200.00.

Needlework, lady/dog in wool, HP on paper face/hands, 15x14" ..200.00
Piano shawl, silk, embr, long fringe 85.00
Pillowcase, cotton, embr birds & flowers 25.00
Pillowcase, drawnwork florals, 16x13", pr 35.00
Pillowcase, wht linen w/wht crocheted edge, pr 25.00
Place mat, yel w/cream border, hemstitching at edge, 8 for 65.00
Place mat & napkin, ecru cutwork, extra lg, 8 sets 200.00
Runner, Battenburg lace, scalloped border, 12x37" 135.00
Runner, Battenburg lace flowers, 13x38" 130.00
Runner, filet lace, cherubs in center, 18x42" 145.00
Sham, red flower/leaf embr, 27½x25½", pr 95.00
Sheet, homespun, 2-pc, hs, ink sgn, sm rprs, 66x98" 55.00
Sheet, homespun, 2-pc, hs seams/hems, ink sgn, 64x92" 55.00
Sheet, homespun cotton, hs, 2-pc, 77x78" 65.00
Tablecloth, Battenburg, 68" dia 350.00
Tablecloth, Battenburg lace inserts, 110", +12 napkins 350.00
Tablecloth, damask, monograms, Victorian, 88x106" 150.00
Tablecloth, damask, 66x84" 95.00
Tablecloth, European linen, drawnwork, 52" 95.00
Tablecloth, homespun bl/wht plaid, hs, 2-pc, 60x76" 165.00
Tablecloth, homespun cotton bl/wht plaid, hs, 58x72", VG 90.00
Tablecloth, homespun cotton/linen, dmn motif, 2-pc, 58x72" 65.00
Tablecloth, homespun linen, wht-on-wht pattern, 38x71", EX 85.00
Tablecloth, homespun linen gold/wht check, unhemmed, 39x55" ..125.00
Tablecloth, linen, embr mums allover, 31x33", EX 85.00
Tablecloth, Madeira embr cutwork, 106", +12 napkins 195.00
Tablecloth, Madeira lace, 72" dia 135.00
Tablecloth, Pointe Venice lace, 138", +12 napkins 525.00
Tablepc, crochet, Masonic symbols in center, 16x26" 85.00
Tea cloth, drawnwork int w/8" crochet edge 135.00
Tea cozy, Battenburg, flower center, 10x13½" 85.00
Throw, homespun wool, natural w/bl chenille, 64x94", VG 145.00

Towel, guest; hopsacking, appliqued vase/embr flowers 25.00
Towel, homespun, overshot bands, embr initials, 17x61" 25.00
Towel, show; X-stitch flowers/animals/birds/name/1847, 8x18" .165.00

Lacy Glassware

Lacy glass became popular in the late 1820s after the development of the pressing machine. It was decorated with allover patterns — hearts, lyres, sheaves of wheat, etc. — and backgrounds were completely stippled. The designs were intricate and delicate, hence the term 'lacy.' Although Sandwich produced this type of glassware in abundance, it was also made by other eastern glassworks as well as in the midwest. By 1840 its popularity on the wane and a depressed economy forcing manufacturers to seek less expensive modes of production, lacy glass began to be phased out in favor of pressed pattern glass.

Our advisor for this category is Richard Marden; he is listed in the Directory under New Hampshire. Reference numbers correspond with *Sandwich Glass* by Ruth Webb Lee. When no condition is indicated, the items listed below are assumed to be without obvious damage; minor roughness is normal.

Bowl, beehive, octagonal, sm chips, 10" 75.00
Bowl, Hairpin, L-92, Midwestern, minor roughness, 2x7½" 55.00
Bowl, Star Medallion, L-87, 6" 55.00
Creamer, Sweetheart, 4½" 75.00
Dish, L-103, Midwestern, 4x6" L 70.00
Dish, L-103, rim chips, 5x7" L 250.00
Plate, scrolls between bar terminals in rnd rim, 8" 30.00
Tea plate, Harp, L-111, lt cornflower gr, 4½" 120.00
Tea plate, Heart variant, L-107, opal, 6" 190.00
Tie back, opal, pewter posts, chips, 4½", pr 50.00
Window pane, L-161, att Pittsburgh, minor chips, 5x7" 750.00

Lalique

Beginning his lengthy career as a designer and maker of fine jewelry, Rene Lalique at first only dabbled in glass, making small panels of pate-de-verre (paste-on-paste) and cire perdue (wax casting) to use in his jewelry. He also made small flacons of gold and silver with his glass inlays, which attracted the attention of M.F. Coty, who commissioned Lalique to design bottles for his perfume company. The success of this venture resulted in the opening of his own glassworks at Combs-la-Ville in 1909. In 1921 a larger factory was established at Wingen-sur-Moder in Alsace-Lorraine. By the thirties Lalique was world renown as the most important designer of his time.

Lalique glass is lead based, either mold blown or pressed. Favored motifs during the Art Nouveau period were dancing nymphs, fish, dragonflies, and foliage. Characteristically the glass is crystal in combination with acid-etched relief. Later some items were made in as many as ten colors (red, amber, and green among them) and were occasionally accented with enameling. These colored pieces, especially those in black, are highly prized by advanced collectors.

During the twenties and thirties, Lalique designed several vases and bowls reminiscent of American Indian art. He also developed a line in the Art Deco style decorated with stylized birds, florals, and geometrics. In addition to vases, clocks, automobile mascots, stemware, and bottles, many other useful objects were produced. Most items made before his death in 1945 were marked 'R. Lalique'; later the 'R' was deleted even though some of the original molds were still used. Numbers found on the bases of some pieces are catalog numbers. Beware of fraudulent pieces that have began to surface in increasing numbers. Our advisor for this category is John Danis; he is listed in the Directory under Illinois.

Key:
cl/fr — clear and frosted   RL — signed R. Lalique
L — signed Lalique   RLF — signed R. Lalique, France

Ashtray, gargoyle form, fr, script mk, 5¾" 165.00
Atomizer, Le Parisien, line of women, amber wash, RL, 6" 700.00
Atomizer, 4 niches, ea w/nude, cylindrical, RL/MIF, 5" 550.00
Bottle, Enfants, Bacchanalian parade, brn-wash fr, LF, 3¾" 800.00
Bottle, scent; Coeur Joie, Nia Ricci, heart form, 5", MIB 500.00
Bottle, scent; Cyclamen, for Coty, blk stain, LF, 5½", MIB 1,900.00
Bottle, scent; Emiliane, flowers, disk form, RL, 7" 450.00
Bottle, scent; Guerlain Masques, face ea corner, 4", +case 550.00
Bottle, scent; Imprudence, for Worth, RL, 3", MIB 800.00
Bottle, scent; Je Reviens, bl ribs, bl stopper, RL, 5" 250.00
Bottle, scent; La Phalene, butterfly, amber, RLF, 3", MIB 1,200.00
Bottle, scent; La Violette, for Dabilla, bl flowers, RLF, 3¼" 700.00
Bottle, scent; Le Baiser du Faune, 2 nudes, RL, 6", MIB 1,500.00
Bottle, scent; Le Jade, gr opal, LF, MIB 2,000.00
Bottle, scent; Marquita, overlapping leaves, fr, RL, 3½" 700.00
Bottle, scent; Morabito, turtles, amber, RLF, 5" 1,800.00
Bottle, scent; Mystere, for D'orsay, lizards, blk, RLF, MIB 1,100.00
Bottle, scent; sq w/ropes & knots, RLF, 3½" 450.00
Bottle, scent; Styx, for Coty, stopper as 4 bees, LF, 4½" 900.00
Bowl, Calypso, 5 mermaids, opal, RLF, 11¾", MIB 7,150.00
Bowl, Coquilles, opal scallops, RLF, 5" 500.00
Bowl, Gui #2, mistletoe/opal berries, RLF, 8" 770.00
Bowl, Martigues, fish (3 forming ft), opal, RL, 15" 1,800.00
Bowl, Perruches, parakeets frieze, opal, RLF, 9" 3,500.00
Bowl, Tournon, high-relief flowerheads, cl/fr, RLF, 12" 1,100.00
Bowl, Volubilis, morning-glories, amber, 3-ftd, RLF, 9" 880.00
Bowl vase, Dahlias, blk centers/amber wash, RL, 5" H 1,850.00
Box, Amour Assis, seated putto surmount, RL, 5¾" 2,000.00
Box, D Orsay, florals, fr, imp mk, 4" dia 250.00
Box, Louveciennes, 2 figures/petals, gray wash, RL, rnd, 2" 3,300.00
Box, St-Nectaire, ferns, gray-gr wash, 6-sided, RLF, 3½" 875.00
Box, 3 Dahlias, opal lid, leather-covered base, RL, 8" dia 825.00
Box, 4 Papillons, on sectioned lid, gr wash, Depose, 3" dia 935.00
Brooch, bird ea side wreath w/glass cabochon, bl wash, L, 4" ..2,200.00
Brooch, Faune, gr frost, satyr's head, L, 1¾" 2,800.00
Brooch, Lezards, 3 lizards, cl/fr, RL, 1¾" dia 1,100.00
Brooch, Trois Anges, 2 angels, cobalt, metal mts, LF, 1¼" 2,200.00
Candlestick, bird pr in wreath as std, hex ft, LF, 6½", pr 600.00
Chandelier, Cannele, Blk-eyed Susans, brn-wash fr, RL, 12" ..1,700.00
Charger, Martigues, fish, yel opal, RL, 14" 5,500.00
Charger, swirling dots, opal, RLF, 11¼" dia 550.00
Clock, Inseparables, lovebirds ea side, sq, opal, RL, 4½" 3,850.00
Clock, Roitelets, wreath of wrens around rnd dial, RLF, 8" 2,750.00
Clock, 5 Hirondelles, flying birds, bl wash, sq, RL, 6" 4,950.00
Collector plate, 1965-76, complete set, M in boxes 2,500.00
Mascot, Tete d'Aigle, eagle, cl/fr, RLF, 4½" 850.00
Mascot, Tete de Paon, peacock head, RLF, 7" 3,300.00
Mascot, Victorie, lady's head w/streaming hair, fr, 6" 75.00
Mascot, Vitesse, nude in forward thrust, opal, RL, 7" 12,000.00
Necklace, Grosses Graines, 8 bl 1" berry beads 3,000.00
Paperweight, Archer, kneeling archer intaglio disk, RL, 4¾" 990.00
Pendant, Floret, nude in bower, fr, RL Floret Paris, 1⅜" 275.00
Pendant, Grenouilles, bl, open rectangle, L, 2" 1,700.00
Pendant, Guepes, stylized wasps, dk plum, L, 2⅜" 1,900.00
Pendant, Poissons, fish, blk, irregular form, 1⅝" 1,900.00
Plate, abstract sheaves of wheat, brn wash, RLF, 7", pr 495.00
Plate, Sirenes, 5 mermaids, opal/cl, RLF, 15" 4,950.00
Sconce, Champs-Elysees, overlapping leaves, LF, 12" 550.00
Statue, Ailes Croisees, sparrow, fr, RLF, 4½" 275.00
Statue, Moyenne Voilee, draped maid w/goblet, RL, 5½", MIB ..2,000.00

Statue, Suzanne, head right, w/drapery, amber opal, RL, 9" ..13,000.00
Tray, Medicis, nudes/garlands, fr w/lt bl wash, RLF, 6" 650.00
Tumbler, Setubal, leaves/berries, RL, set of 6, +18" tray 770.00
Vase, Acanthes, leafage, cased opal yel, spherical, L, 11" 6,000.00
Vase, Albert, falcon head hdls, gray, U-form, RLF, 7" 2,400.00
Vase, Archers, nude males/birds, gray wash, #893, RLF, 11" ...3,300.00
Vase, Borromee, peacock heads, bl wash, ovoid, RLF, 9" 3,300.00
Vase, Breese, Deco cocks, amber, yel wash, bulb, RLF, 4½" 2,300.00
Vase, Ceylon, lovebird prs, bl wash, #905, RLF, 9½" 2,800.00

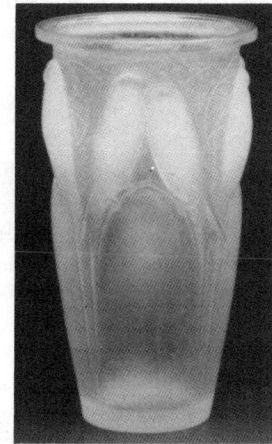

Vase, Ceylon, lovebirds, fiery opal, signed R Lalique France #905 9½", $2,500.00.

Vase, Chamarande, flower-cluster hdls, cl/fr gray, RLF, 8" 3,300.00
Vase, Coqs et Plumes, roosters, rust wash, RLF, 6x4" 1,000.00
Vase, Danaides, daughters of Danaus w/pitchers, opal, 7" 4,000.00
Vase, Davos, allover bubble pattern, amber, LF, 11½", NM 3,300.00
Vase, Formose, bands of fish, opal w/bl wash, rnd, RLF, 7" 2,500.00
Vase, Gui, mistletoe/berries, cl/fr, RL, eng France, 7" 525.00
Vase, Ibis, among rushes, bl wash, flared cylinder, RL, 9½" 1,300.00
Vase, Lievres, ferns/rabbit band, fr w/gray, bulbous, RL, 6" 1,300.00
Vase, Meduse, fern fronds, opal, RL, 6x5" 900.00
Vase, Mimosa, leaves, gray wash, cylindrical, RL, 6½" 1,400.00
Vase, Nimroud, blk-enamel triangles, str sides, RLF/970, 8" .10,450.00
Vase, Nivernais, 3 tiers of raised disks, gray, RLF, 7x7" 1,750.00
Vase, Oursin, sea urchin form, cl w/bl wash, rnd, RLF, 7½" 935.00
Vase, Ronces, thorny branches, opal w/gray wash, RLF, 9" 1,900.00
Vase, Violettes, fr/cl, tumbler form w/funnel top, RLF, 7" 750.00

Lamps

The earliest lamps were simple dish containers with a wick that hung over the edge or was supported by a channel or tube. Grease and oil from animal or vegetable sources were the first fuels used. Ancient pottery lamps, crusie, and Betty lamps are examples of these early types. In 1784, Swiss inventor Ami Argand introduced the first major improvement in lamps. His lamp featured a tubular wick and a glass chimney. During the first half of the 19th century, whale oil, burning fluid (a highly explosive mixture of turpentine and alcohol), and lard were the most common fuels used in North America. Many lamps were patented for specific use with these fuels.

Kerosene was the first major breakthrough in lighting fuels. It was demonstrated by Canadian geologist Dr. Abraham Gesner in 1846. The discovery and drilling of petroleum in the late 1850s provided an abundant and inexpensive supply of kerosene. It became the main source of light for homes during the balance of the 19th century and for remote locations until the 1950s.

Although Thomas A. Edison invented the electric lamp in 1879, it was not until two or three decades later that electric lamps replaced kerosene household lamps. Millions of kerosene lamps were made for every purpose and pocketbook. They ranged in size from tiny night or miniature lamps to tall stand or piano lamps. Hanging varieties for homes commonly had one or two fonts (oil containers), but chandeliers for churches and public buildings often had six or more. Wall or bracket lamps usually had silvered reflectors. Student lamps, parlor lamps (now called Gone-with-the-Wind lamps), and patterned glass lamps were designed to complement the popular furnishing trends of the day. The Angle Lamp Company of New York City developed a unique type of kerosene lamp that was a vast improvement over those already on the market; they were sold from about 1889 until 1929 and were expensive for their time. From about 1910, Aladdin lamps with a mantle became the mainstay of rural America, providing light that compared favorably with the electric light bulb. Gaslight, introduced in the early 19th century, was used mainly in homes of the wealthy and public places until the early 20th century. Most fixtures were wall or ceiling mounted, although some table models were also used.

Few of the ordinary early electric lamps have survived. Many lamp manufacturers made the same or similar styles for either kerosene or electricity, sometimes for gas. Top-of-the-line lamps were made by Pairpoint, Phoenix, Tiffany, Bradley and Hubbard, and Handel. (See also these specific sections.)

Currently values of peg lamps are up by about 30% to 40%, and pattern glass lamps in some of the standard lines have jumped from 25% to 100%. When buying lamps that have been converted to electricity, inspect them very carefully for any damage that may have resulted from the alterations; such damage is very common, and when it does occur, the lamp's value may be lessened by as much as 50%.

For those seeking additional information on Aladdin Lamps, we recommend *Aladdin — The Magic Name in Lamps*; *Aladdin Electric Lamps*; and *A Collector's Manual and Price Guide*, all written by our advisor for Aladdins, J. W. Courter; he is listed in the Directory under Illinois. Mr. Courter has also published a book called *Angle Lamps, Collector's Manual and Price Guide*. Another of our lamp advisors is Ruth Osborne; she is listed under Ohio. See also specific manufacturers.

Key:
ac — acorn burner	nb — nutmeg burner
hb — hornet burner	Vb — P&A Victor burner

Aladdin Lamps, Electric

Bed, #2027-SS, whip-o-lite shade, EX	32.00
Bed, #653-SS, whip-o-lite pleated shade, NM	165.00
Bedroom, M-70, metal & ceramic, M	20.00
Bedroom, P-51, ceramic, M	20.00
Bedroom, P-56, ceramic, NM	28.00
Boudoir, G-1, marble-like, 1933, EX	75.00
Boudoir, G-15, floral base, crystal, M	80.00
Boudoir, G-22, alacite, NM	65.00
Boudoir, G-23, glass, 1934, NM	55.00
Boudoir, G-30, alacite, NM	48.00
Boudoir, G-49, alacite, EX	30.00
Boudoir, G-92, moonstone, 1937, M	50.00
Bridge, #2079, walnut, NM	235.00
Bridge, #2093, M	200.00
Bridge, #7072, swing arm, reflector, EX	175.00
Bridge, #96, reflector, NM	145.00
Contemporary, M-367, iron base, spun glass shade, M	25.00
Contemporary, M-463, ivory ceramic, iron base, M	30.00
Figural, G-U, lady, moonstone, EX	1,000.00
Figural, M-123, lady, metal, NM	115.00
Floor, #1005, MOP glass bowl, w/night light, EX	325.00
Floor, #3349, standard type A, EX	110.00
Floor, #3451, standard type B, M	125.00
Floor, #3606, reflector, candle arms, M	200.00
Floor, #3690, reflector, candle arms, NM	165.00
Floor, #3767, flourescent, 2 15" tubes, NM	165.00
Floor, #4572, torchier, NM	215.00
Lounge, #1062, candle arms, M	150.00
Lounge, J-135, NM	115.00
Pinup, G-352, Panel & Scroll, alacite, M	50.00
Pinup, P-57, Gun 'n Holster, ceramic, NM	95.00
Table, #785, lg vase, gr, M	150.00
Table, E-200, Vogue Pedestal, gr, EX	250.00
Table, G-154, crystal, M	60.00
Table, G-179, opalique, M	100.00
Table, G-212, alacite, tall harp, light in base, M	60.00
Table, G-233, alacite, EX	70.00
Table, G-263-A, alacite, light in base, M	40.00
Table, G-62, NM	90.00
Table, G-7, marble-like glass, NM	215.00
Table, G-85, EX	125.00
Table, M-279, metal, NM	37.50
Table, M-3, metal, NM	55.00
Table, P-425, ceramic, M	30.00
Table, P-470, ceramic, M	30.00
Table, W-346, oak, NM	37.50
Table, W-503, wood & ceramic, M	40.00
Touch, MT-509, ceramic, M	250.00
TV, #384, shell, ceramic, M	40.00
TV, M-367, blk iron base, w/shade, M	20.00
Urn, G-213-A, closed urn, alacite, EX	150.00
Urn, G-379, tall ribbed urn w/top, alacite, M	90.00

Aladdin Lamps, Kerosene

Aladdinette, candle lamp, glass chimney, NM	110.00
Caboose Model C, B-400, aluminum font, NM	80.00
Floor Model B, #1258, bronze, EX	100.00
Floor Model B, B-284, silver & gold, NM	110.00
Hanging, #6, w/#215 shade, no chimney tube, EX	200.00
Hanging Model C, aluminum hanger/font, paper shade, NM	45.00
Model #12 Crystal Vase, #1240, variegated verde, NM	120.00
Model #12 Florentine Vase, #1220, gr moonstone, 8½", EX	1,250.00
Table, #12, str side, bronze or nickel, EX	60.00
Table, #2, plain ft, polished brass or nickel, NM	385.00
Table, Practicus, polished brass, NM	300.00
Table, Super Aladdin, Bakelite, wooden stem, Australia, M	120.00
Table Model A, #99, Venetian, clear, NM	200.00
Table Model B, B-100, Corinthian, clear, NM	80.00
Table Model B, B-130, Orientale, ivory, NM	150.00
Table Model B, B-39, Washington Drape, clear, EX	75.00
Table Model B, B-50, Washington Drape, clear, M	90.00
Table Model B, B-91, Quilt, wht/rose moonstone, EX	240.00
Wall bracket, #6, complete, EX	100.00

Angle Lamps

Barn lantern, #115, tin, blued, NM	1,000.00
Hanging, Grape, #205, nickel, EX	695.00
Hanging Fleur-de-lis, #382, antique copper, EX	625.00
Hanging Flower Garden, #MW5982, nickel, M	750.00
Table, Classic, #1, antique gold, M	2,150.00
Wall, Pinwheel, #153, polished brass, NM	325.00
Wall, plain can, #183, antique brass, EX	155.00

Chandeliers

Brass, 6 scrolling arms w/electric candles, 23" dia 400.00
Brass, 8-lite (4 gas/4 electric), 4 ribbed opal shades, 47" 1,200.00
Cut crystal, 35-lite, faceted bead drapes, Rococo, 50" 1,000.00
Gilt metal, 6-lite, Renaissance style, 34" 2,000.00
O/l (bl cut to clear), 6-arm, gilt bronze mts, 1800s 3,200.00
Wrought iron, 4 sockets on 12" ring, pitted 275.00

Decorated Kerosene Lamps

Blue cut to white cut to clear font, brass stem, marble foot, cut and frosted Oregon-style shade, 22", $650.00; Cranberry cut to clear on Baroque-style milk glass stem and foot, fancy cut and frosted Oregon-style shade, 20", EX, $1,400.00.

Bl cut to wht to clear, cylindrical font, wht base, 9½" 550.00
Clear font w/pk & wht loops, bl clambroth stem/ft, 8" 700.00
Dk bl cut to clear w/paw prints, brass/marble base, 11" 1,000.00
Gr font/fluted shade w/HP florals, brass ft, complete, 13½" 350.00
Mauve swirl MOP, orig clambroth ball shade, 20¾x6½" 850.00
Wht cut to clear pear font, emb stem, marble ft, 9" 250.00
Wht cut to clear stem/font, marble base, 14", EX 300.00
Wht cut to clear w/circles, marble base, 9" 250.00
Wht cut to cranberry pear font, blk glass stem/ft, 18" 550.00
Wht cut to gr w/florals, oval windows, wht base, 10" 375.00

Fairy Lamps

Arboresque, cranberry frost w/wht opaque, 3¾x2⅞" 110.00
Baccarat, sapphire pinwheel-emb shade/base, Clarke cup, NM ..275.00
Bl Dmn Quilt MOP, mk Clarke base, pyramid sz, 3⅝x2⅞" 145.00
Bl satin, wht opaque edge w/crimped top, 6¼x4" 165.00
Burmese, butterfly/leaves, Clarke Burmese shade cup, 6" 1,400.00
Burmese, clear mk Clarke base, unsgn Webb, 4x2¾" 175.00
Burmese, ribbon edge base, Clarke cup, 5½x4½" 450.00
Burmese, Webb, clear Clarke base, pyramid sz, 3¾x2⅞" 250.00
Burmese, 4 shades/3 vases on tall std on mirror, Webb, 17" 3,500.00
Citron verre moire, lg crimped bowl, Clarke cup, 5¾" 845.00
Cranberry, appl clear petals on shade, 5-side ruffled base 525.00
Cranberry frost w/wht opaque spatter, clear Clarke base, 3½" 125.00
Cranberry swirl overshot, clear Clarke base, 3⅜x2⅞" 110.00
Cranberry verre moire, frosted cranberry cup, 4¼x3⅝" 225.00
Cranberry w/silver mica, emb swirls, clear Clarke base, 3½" 165.00
Cranberry w/wht opaque spatter, mk Clarke base, 3½" 125.00
Crown figural, cobalt overshot, clear Clarke base, 4½x3" 175.00
Lemon, ruffled rim, matching ruffled rim base 225.00
Nailsea, rose/wht, ruffled bowl base, Clarke cup, 5", EX 375.00
Owl face on ea of 3 sides, bsk w/4-color pnt, glass eyes, 4" 350.00
Owl head figural, frosted opal, Clarke base, 4⅜" 150.00

Owl head figural, gr frost, clear Clarke base, 4¼x2⅞" 175.00
Pk Dmn Quilt MOP, clear Clarke base, pyramid sz, 3½" 145.00
Pk opal emb to simulate threading, tall shade, 8", EX 425.00
Pk shaded satin, brass trim, colored jewels, 5¾" 395.00
Pk Swirl MOP, ruffled shade & base, 5" 525.00
Rose Dmn Quilt MOP, clear Clarke base, 3½x3" 145.00
Sapphire bl emb floral panels, mk Bayel, 4½" 225.00
Spatter dome top/cup/ruffled base, crystal shell ft, 5x4" 395.00
Teal & wht swirl o/l, emb swirls, Clarke base, 4⅞x4" 195.00
Wht opaque w/emb decor, clear mk Clarke base, 5¼x4" 95.00
Yel emb swirl cased overshot, clear Clarke base, 3½x2⅛" 100.00
Yel opaque w/wht spatter, mk Clarke base, 3½x2⅞" 165.00
Yel satin, emb ribs, clear Clarke base, 3½x2⅞" 125.00

Gone-with-the-Wind and Banquet Lamps

Clear cut font; onyx/brass base, cloisonne std, 27" 625.00
Clear satin w/emb roses, electrified, 24" 650.00
Cranberry cut to clear font; ornate figural brass base, 26" 600.00
Florals emb on golden amber; marble stem, 26½x6¼" 650.00
HP opal ball shade; gilt metal/brass/onyx stand, 31" 275.00
Red satin w/emb baby faces, 24", EX 700.00
Red satin w/emb thistles, ball shade, ovoid font, 24", EX 350.00
Vaseline w/opal daisies: 9" shade/font; brass/pottery ft 850.00
Wht cut to clear font w/gilt; brass stem, marble ft, 30" 250.00
Wht w/emb cherub heads w/in scrolls; brass base, 25" 300.00
Windmills & sailboats, bl on wht; metal base, Parker, 29" 995.00
Yel pastel w/lg pk flowers, squatty; brass base, 20x8" 450.00

Hanging Lamps

Blown, copper wheel eng, emb tin 'crown,' 25" 750.00
Blown, cut vintage, folded rims on globe/bell, Austria, 27" 350.00
Blown w/geometric cut motif, smoke bell, appl printie, 19" 325.00
Cranberry Invt T'print, complete, 9x6" dia 295.00
Frosted cut to clear, clear smoke bell, folded rims, 22" 450.00
Hall, cranberry swirl, prisms, gilt metal/brass font, 14" 650.00

Lanterns

Barn, mortised pine sq fr w/4 glasses, rpl hdl/glass, 18" 500.00
Hall, bronze Louis XVI style, scrolled candle arms, 39x17" 2,475.00
Post-top, tin, wrought iron brackets, mk NY USA, 38", pr 450.00
Tin w/brass fittings, blown globe, att NE Glass, rpr, 12½" 215.00
Tin w/pressed paneled cylinder insert, 10x2½", VG 175.00
Tin w/simple punching, semicircular, glass front, 12" 125.00

Lard Oil/Grease Lamps

Betty, iron, bird finial on font lid, 6", +hanger 175.00
Betty, iron, brass nameplate: Gluck-Auf, hanger, 3⅝" 145.00
Betty, iron, stylized hen finial on swivel lid, 4"+hanger 115.00
Betty, tin, on stand w/crimped edge, rust/damage, mk JD, 11" 250.00
Betty, wrought iron, chicken finial, heart atop arm, 7" 375.00
Betty, wrought iron, latch-type font lid, wire hanger, 5" 100.00
Crusie, dbl, sheet iron, cut-out finials, mk S, 9" 100.00
Crusie, dbl, wrought iron, twisted hanger, 6" 100.00
Gimbal, brass font, heavy iron hanger, #2, 13" (w/hanger) 150.00
Pottery, bright gr glaze, lg hdl, European, 9½" 110.00
Pottery, unglazed, saucer base, hdl, 5½", EX 625.00
Rush, wrought, w/counterbalance, rpl burl base, 12½" 150.00
Rush, wrought iron, primitive, rpl wood base, 9" 100.00

Wrought iron, lg rnd pan w/spout, twisted hanger, 9" 105.00

Miniature Lamps, Kerosene

Artichoke, milk glass w/pk & gr pnt, nb, 7¾" 250.00
Beaded Drape, bl satin frost, complete, 9x4¼" 350.00
Bl cased satin, pansy-emb rnd shade, melon rib base, nb, 7" 525.00
Bl MOP Dmn Quilt, ruffled top/peg-type font, brass base, 11" ..2,200.00
Brady's Night Lamp, pk cased satin, nb, 7½", EX 325.00
Bulldog, milk glass, base is head, pnt nearly gone, hb, 8" 2,000.00
Coreopsis, all orig, 7" 325.00
Cranberry opal snowflake w/allover silver filigree, nb, 7" 1,900.00
Cranberry w/beaded swirls, squat shouldered base, hb, 8" 250.00
Defender, bl opaque, scroll-emb ball shade & base, 8½" 185.00
Drape, cranberry w/amber scallops, orig burner, 6¼" 315.00
Firefly, font & burner for bracket lamp 125.00
Gr Raindrop MOP, ball shade/wide base, ac, 8", NM 700.00
Gr w/faint swirl, simple form, S-468, 7¾" 200.00
Hexagons emb on red satin, petal shade, all orig 250.00
Little Buttercup, purple 85.00
Lt bl shade/font w/lg emb dmns, on plated iron base, 13" 400.00
Milk glass, panels w/HP florals, cone shade/dome base, 7" 325.00
Milk glass, pk & yel pnt, emb mums & swirls, hb, 8¾", NM 275.00
Milk glass w/emb shells on bottle-shape top & base, hb, 10" 250.00
Milk glass w/pansies on rnd shade/ftd squat base, nb, 9" 150.00
Millefiori, umbrella shade, rnded base, 7" 850.00
Owl, bl opaque, shade is head, nb, 8" 2,650.00
Owl, milk glass w/pnt features, top is head, 7½", NM 1,050.00
Pk cased, ogee panels w/emb scrolls, hb, S-374, 8½", NM 400.00
Pk MOP Dmn Quilt, ruffled top, appl frosted ft, fb, 9" 1,250.00
Rainbow spatter w/mica, clear hdl, finger lamp, 5½" 195.00
Rayo, brass, mk Little Jewel, 7½" 100.00
Red satin, scroll-emb rnd top & sqd base, nb, 8", EX 300.00
Santa Claus, milk glass, red coat & blk boots, nb, 9½" 1,800.00
Spanish Lace, bl opal, nb, 7", EX 900.00
Spatter, red & wht w/emb swirls, rnd top/base, clear ft, 8" 1,600.00
Twinkle, bl, collared ball shade, squat base, ac, 7", EX 135.00
Yel cased w/fired-on gold floral, ball shade/wide base, 8½" 900.00

Pattern Glass Lamps

Apollo, amber, nb, 9" 95.00
Banded Portland, flat 48.00
Cable, marble base, 8¾" 115.00
Cable w/Ring, orig burner 195.00
Cathedral, bl, 12¾" 195.00
Chapman, milk glass font, Atterbury base, dtd 1868, 10" 130.00
Columbian Coin, frosted coins, 12" 185.00
Coolidge Drape, #2 sewing lamp sz 325.00
Corn, finger lamp 45.00
Excelsior, hand lamp 100.00
Eyewinker, orig burner, 9½" 130.00
Findlay Sweetheart, gr font 250.00
Heart w/T'print, finger lamp 65.00
Heart w/T'print, 8" 115.00
Hobstar & Fine Cut, SP fittings, dome shade, 15x6" 495.00
Honeycomb, marble base 45.00
Horn of Plenty, flint, orig burner 225.00
Iowa 125.00
Janice, ftd finger lamp, 5½", EX 45.00
O'Hara Dmn 50.00
Peacock Feather, ftd finger lamp 65.00
Prince Edward 100.00
Prince Edward, pk cased, 4 medallions, all orig, 16½" 955.00

Princess Feather, cobalt, #2 sewing lamp sz 295.00
Princess Feather, finger lamp, 5" 57.50
Princess Feather, flint, 8" 70.00
Princess Feather, gr, med sz 250.00
Queen Heart, gr, stem lamp, #2, 10" 150.00
Reverse Torpedo, 9" 150.00

Santa in chimney, U.S. Glass, 10", $2,500.00.

Sheldon Swirl, 7" 195.00
Shield & Stars, 7" 80.00
Snowflake, cranberry opal, 4" sq font, stand lamp, 8" 475.00
Thousand Eye, amber base, frosted font 250.00
Three Face, ftd, 8" 175.00
Torpedo, ftd, 8½" 125.00
Torpedo, stack shade, CI base 68.00
Triple Flute & Bar, milk glass base, EX gold 125.00

Peg Lamps

Bl Dmn Quilt MOP, bulbous/ruffled shade, brass base, 11½" ..1,025.00
Blown, burning fluid burner w/'rabbit ear' tubes, 6" 250.00
Cranberry (patterned) font, old brass candlestick, 13½" 125.00
Cranberry font, ornate figural brass candle holder, 16" 225.00
Lime gr irid, orig burner, brass holder, 10x3½" 125.00
Lime gr w/gold & eng flowers, candlestick base, 14x5½" 325.00
Pk cased, emb dmns, brass std w/sq base, complete, 14½" 700.00
Pressed, panels/t'prints, pewter collar, 4½" 135.00
Swirled pattern glass, NP collar, brass base, 4" 135.00
Swirled yel satin shade/font, brass fittings, 16", pr 1,195.00

Reverse-Painted Lamps

Jefferson 15" rvpt/int-pnt forest & stream shade; dore base 1,100.00
Jefferson 16" 'marble' shade w/floral band; marble-pnt std 1,210.00

Jefferson 18" jeweled moth shade; signed 2-socket #2606 standard with coppertone patina, 24", $2,000.00.

Jefferson 16" cottage scene dome shade; baluster std **1,500.00**
Jefferson 16" poppies/grasses #2351 dome shade; trumpet std ..**1,200.00**
Jefferson 16" sunset/trees dome shade (VG); 2-light std **1,100.00**
Jefferson 18" Blk-Eyed Susan border shade; gold/blk std, 23" ..**1,750.00**
Jefferson 18" moth/flower cluster dome shade; 8-panel std **2,100.00**
Moe Bridges 15" sunset/waterfront shade; blk 2-socket std **1,400.00**
Moe Bridges 18" summer dome shade; coppered metal std **2,500.00**
Phoenix 19" river/boats/house etc dome shade; emb std **1,450.00**
Pittsburgh, 18" stormy ocean unmk shade; leaf-cast std, 22" ...**1,430.00**
Pittsburgh 17" textured snow scene dome shade; rstr std **935.00**
Pittsburgh 18" campfire/tent dome shade; hdld bronze std **1,500.00**
Unmk 10" tree scene dome shade; gr patina on sq-ftd std, 14" ...**880.00**
Unmk 17" lake scene/bridge/road shade; base w/metal frwork **375.00**
Unmk 8" birch tree shade; cast metal foliate base, 14" **495.00**

Student Lamps, Kerosene

Brass w/pk cased 7" ribbed shade, tank sgn Kleeman, 20" **600.00**
Dbl, brass, Cleveland Safety...Nov 18th 1871, EX **950.00**
Dbl, burners mk Stern Bros, B&H under ft, rpl shades, 21" **1,000.00**
Manhattan, brass, gr ribbed 7" dia shade, electrified, 22" **350.00**
Manhattan, SP brass, 7" rpl gr-pnt milk glass shade, 25" **250.00**
Yel cased shade, weighted std adjusts, balance font, 22" **300.00**

Whale Oil/Burning Fluid Lamps

Blown pear font, sq base w/multi-stacked cone std, 11", pr **280.00**
Blown w/sm rnd fonts on lg hollow stem, 10", EX, pr **650.00**
Blown/panel-cut cylinder font, pressed sq ft/stem, 9", EX **125.00**
Flint, hex base, heart/sawtooth/bull's-eye font, 9½", NM **125.00**
Flint, hex base, sawtooth/Pillar & T'print font, 10", NM **150.00**
Flint, hex base/stem, heart/sawtooth/t'print font, 11", EX **150.00**
Flint, sq base, Bigler font, brass collar, 11", VG, pr **275.00**
Pressed, onion font, short stem w/hdls, Ripley & Co, 5½" **125.00**
Pressed loop pattern, std w/wafers, sq base, 10", EX **150.00**
Ripley marriage, clambroth/bl w/wht base, mk, rpr, 12", EX **750.00**
Sparking, loop pattern, appl hdl, pewter collar/burner, 3" **150.00**

Miscellaneous

Camphene, pewter, 2-tube, short ped, saucer base, 1830s, 7" **350.00**
Candle lamp, mercury twist stem, aqua shade, 18", pr **325.00**
Lace maker's, cranberry overshot, brass base, 17x8" **395.00**
Lecturer's, bell in base, tin w/blk pnt, gold striping, 10" **250.00**
Miner's, brass, cast/wrought iron hanger, St Louis Pat '77 ....**125.00**
Miner's safety, Kohler, EX **75.00**
Petticoat, free-blown, wide folded ft, crimped hdl, 9½" **770.00**
Skater's, tin, lt aqua globe, 6½" **100.00**

Lang, Anton

Anton Lang was a German studio potter and an actor in the cast of the Oberammergau Passion Plays early in the 20th century. Because he played the role of Christ three times, his pottery was purchased by tourists overseas and brought back to the U.S. in suitcases, which accounts for the prevalence of smaller examples today. During 1923 when the play was being threatened with extinction due to Germany's postwar Depression, Anton Lang and the other 'Passion Players' toured the U.S. performing scenes from the play and selling their crafts. Lang would occasionally throw pottery when the cast passed through a pottery center such as Cincinnati, where Rookwood was located. His pottery, marked with his name in script, is fairly scarce and highly valued for its artistic quality. Postcards, programs, and photographs depicting Lang are also collectible.

Bowl, maroon w/mint gr crystalline flambe, 6½" **100.00**
Figure, goat, Deco style, wht translucent, handmade, 5" **150.00**
Flowerpot, aqua irid, mini, 2" **50.00**
Flowerpot, aqua irid, short hairline, mini, 2" **20.00**
Photograph, Lang as Christ w/Mary, sgn, dtd 1929, 8x10" **50.00**
Pitcher, cobalt irid, HP Deco flowers & dots, yel int, 5" **150.00**
Postcard, German, depicting Lang in formal dress **30.00**
Postcard, German, depicting Lang in role of Christ **20.00**
Vase, bl matt w/maroon & silver highlights, urn form, 3" **100.00**
Vase, brn glossy, squeeze-bag edelweiss, Oberammergau, 4" **150.00**
Vase, HP stripes in color on overall milky ground, mini, 2" **45.00**

Le Verre Francais

Le Verre Francais was produced during the 1920s by Schneider at Epinay-sur-Seine in France. It was a commercial art glass in the cameo style composed of layered glass with the designs engraved by acid. Favored motifs were stylized leaves and flowers or geometric patterns. It was marked with the name in script or with an inlaid filigrane. Our advisor for this category is Don Williams; he is listed in the Directory under Missouri.

Cameo

Compote, Chinese lanterns, wine on yel-streaked gray, 11" **1,700.00**
Ewer, orchids, orange/wine on yel/bl, bun ft, 13" **950.00**
Pitcher, butterflies on bl/yel, appl blk snake hdl, 13", NM **1,400.00**
Vase, arcs/lines, brn/dk bl on yel mottle, Charder, rnd, 7" **725.00**
Vase, bellflowers, brn on mottled ground, ftd U-form, 12x9" ..**1,400.00**
Vase, bellflowers, brn/orange on shaded yel, Charder, 19" **1,400.00**
Vase, circles on vines, orange/gr/tan, bun ft, 20x6" **1,500.00**
Vase, dahlias, lav/wine on gray/pk mottle, ftd U-form, 8¾" **660.00**
Vase, dandelion puffs, orange/bl mottle on mc mottle, 14x9" .**1,700.00**
Vase, floral, deeply etched on apricot-amber, 11" **1,000.00**
Vase, floral, orange/red on wht, blk ft, goblet form, 18" **2,200.00**
Vase, florals/ropes, rust/gold on frost, ftd, Charder, 10" **1,000.00**
Vase, fuchsia, orange/cobalt on gray mottle, slim/ftd, 18" **1,350.00**

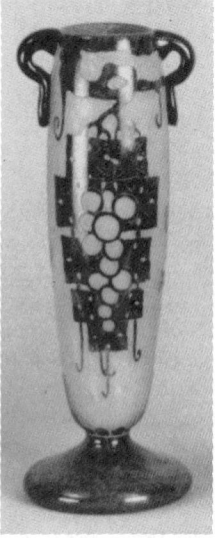

Vase, grapes and vines, orange and brown on gray and yellow mottle, signed Charder, 15", $1,500.00.

Vase, hollyhocks, lav/bl on wht, cushion ft, 9½" **875.00**
Vase, irises, rust/wine on yel/gray mottle, ftd ovoid, 18" **1,850.00**
Vase, leafy upright floral, wine on hot pk, long neck, 32" **2,850.00**
Vase, lg beetles, brns on orange/gray mottle, bun ft, 16" **2,400.00**

Vase, lg leaves/berry clusters, rust/wine on yel, rnd, 10" **1,100.00**
Vase, lotus flowers, red/bl mottle on yel/rust, 10" **1,100.00**
Vase, mums, rust/gr/wine mottle on gray/wht, Charder, 12½" .**1,300.00**
Vase, palm trees, navy on yel/gray mottle, Charder, 15½" **2,750.00**
Vase, palm trees, yel/rust on gr-mottled gray, Charder, 19" **2,850.00**
Vase, poppies, purple/red on yel, ovoid w/cushion ft, 12" **1,250.00**
Vase, poppies/buds, red/purple on yel, ovoid, 14" **1,000.00**
Vase, repeating flowers/leaves, brn/rust on yel, sphere, 11" **1,100.00**
Vase, school of fish/water plants, gr/brn, Charder, 12x9" **2,750.00**
Vase, seed pods, bulbous w/bun ft, Charder, 12½" **1,050.00**
Vase, shoulder-to-base garlands, wine on pk, Charder, 15" ...**1,400.00**
Vase, spikey forms, brn on gray/yel, mosaic-cut ft, 11" **500.00**
Vase, vines/fruit, brn on yel/orange, hdls, Ovington, 11½" **1,100.00**

Leeds, Leeds Type

The Leeds Pottery was established in 1758 in Yorkshire and under varied management produced fine creamware, often highly reticulated and transfer printed, shiny black-glazed Jackfield wares, polychromed pearlware, and figurines similar to those made in the Staffordshire area. Little of the early ware was marked; after 1775 the impressed 'Leeds Pottery' mark was used. From 1781 to 1820, the name 'Hartley Greens & Co.' was added. The pottery closed in 1898.

Today the term 'Leeds' has become generic and is used to encompass all polychromed pearlware and creamware, wherever its origin. Thus, similar wares of other potters (Wood for instance) is often incorrectly called 'Leeds.' Unless a piece is marked or can be definitely attributed to Leeds by confirming the pattern to be authentic, 'Leeds-Type' would be a more accurate nomenclature.

Key:
cw — creamware   sp — soft paste
pw — pearlware   ug — underglaze

Cup & saucer, rose in orange/bl, yel/bl flowers, blk bands, NM ..**350.00**
Loving cup, pw, name/toast/1797, ribbing, leaf hdls, 6", NM ..**1,350.00**
Plate, cw, rtcl scalloped rim, Delft-style floral, mk, 11" **825.00**
Plate, cw, swag-emb/rtcl rim, mk, stains, 8¾" **250.00**
Plate, pw, 4-color eagle, scalloped, 8" **900.00**
Plate, rose in orange/bl, yel/bl flowers, blk band, 5½" **210.00**
Tea caddy, pw, floral, 5-color, no lid, 4⅝", NM **325.00**
Tea caddy, yel floral, ug bl/gr leaves, blk stripes, mk, 6" **1,125.00**
Teapot, cw, house scene, blk transfer+3 colors, 4½x8", VG **365.00**
Teapot, Prince Wm V portrait, 1787, 4½", VG **550.00**
Toddy plate, pw, gr feather edge, 4-color eagle, 5" **500.00**

Lefton China

In 1940 the Lefton China Co. was founded by George Zoltan Lefton, a native of Hungary, who in the 1930s was in the designing and manufacturing of sportswear. His hobby of collecting fine porcelains led him to the creation of his own ceramic business. Today the company is a leading producer of ceramic giftware, and the products are found in gift shops throughout the world.

Important to collectors are Lefton trademarks which aid in the dating of pieces. Most Lefton items are identified by a fired-on trademark or a paper label found on the bottom of each piece. These marks are found in both single color and multicolored styles. Usually, any number found below the marks are the item identification numbers and if preceded by letters will, in fact, be the factory identification numbers. Older and discontinued items such as a vase formed as hands, parakeets, Little Adorables (Limited Edition), flamingo with baby, cherubs on

trees, Huckleberry Finn and dog set, Holy Family, Napoleon, and swan candy dishes are eagerly sought after by collectors. As with any antique or collectible, the prices vary, depending upon location, condition, and availability. Our advisor for this category is Loretta DeLozier; she is listed in the Directory under Iowa.

Basket, #2910, sm **27.50**
Bell, pk, #90460, 2¾" **7.50**
Birdbath dish, wht, #6077N, 4" **30.00**
Bone dish, #3708 ....**12.50**
Candy dish, #651R **12.00**
Creamer, #KW2564 ....**15.00**
Cup & saucer, bl & gr, #1350 ....**15.00**
Picture frame, 2½x4" **12.00**
Planter, Lord's Prayer, #5356 ....**10.00**
Snack set, cups & plates, 4-pc **45.00**
Tea set, fruit design, yel & bl, #SL2613 ....**150.00**
Tray, serving; 2-tier, #20124 ....**32.50**
Vase, cornucopia **17.50**
Vase, hands figural, 4 roses at base, 6½" **45.00**
Vase, Hobnail, wht, #1189, 7" **35.00**
Vase, lav, #2942, 7" **22.00**
Vase, pk, #1030, 4" **25.00**
Vase, scalloped rim, #1183 ....**25.00**
Vase, swirl, 11" **8.00**
Vase, wht, #827, 4" **25.00**

Legras

Legras and Cie was founded in St. Denis, France, in 1864. Production continued until the 1930s. In addition to their enameled wares, they made cameo art glass decorated with outdoor scenes and florals executed by acid cuttings through two to six layers of glass. Their work is signed 'Legras' in relief. Our advisor for this category is Don Williams; he is listed in the Directory under Missouri.

Cameo

Bud vase, trees, cut/pnt on lt bl/yel, bulbous rim/base, 7" **400.00**
Vase, autumn scene cut/pnt on gray/bl, waisted, 4½" **385.00**
Vase, berried stems, cut/pnt on fiery amber, sqd rim, 6½" **765.00**
Vase, berry branches on streaky gray/rust, stick neck, 24" **1,650.00**
Vase, bird on brn/wht/clear mottle, 16" **1,000.00**
Vase, daisies in band w/brn stain on brn/wht mottle, 8x5½" **595.00**
Vase, Deco floral, br on turq, elongated U-form/bun ft, 13" **990.00**
Vase, figures/trees, sqd cylinder, 7½x2¼" **325.00**

Vase, forest landcape, green on gray with lime and orange, 7½", $1,200.00; Vase, large leaves and flowers, olive green on gray with lime and orange, 5¾", $850.00.

Vase, foxglove, rust/wine on pk, ftd ovoid, 11½" **825.00**
Vase, grapevines, wine on orange mottle, flat rim/ftd, 16" **1,300.00**
Vase, leaves cut/pnt on crystal, swollen cylinder, 12" **500.00**

Vase, leaves/burrs/flowers, gr on gray etc, ovoid, 6" 850.00
Vase, sailboat, cut/pnt, baluster, 12½" 1,250.00
Vase, sea grasses/shells cut/pnt on cased beige, 7x5" 700.00
Vase, summer scene cut/pnt on pk/gr, shaped rim, 7x5" 465.00
Vase, trees cut/pnt in summer colors, pnt signature, 14" 1,500.00
Vase, 2 peasants under leafy branches, rust on gr, 8" 1,500.00

Miscellaneous

Bowl, HP gold foliage on etched olive gr, 14" 800.00
Vase, etched leafy branches w/gilt on moss, ovoid, 8" 465.00
Vase, HP rust/blk tiger lilies on etched surface, ovoid, 12" 825.00
Vase, HP snow scene, orange sunset, sqd/ribbed, slim, 12" 550.00
Vase, HP violets in gr & purple, ftd baluster, 3¾" 110.00
Vase, HP winter scene, rare lady figure, coral to yel, 16" 895.00
Vase, man in winter landscape HP in orange, slim/ftd, 14" 825.00

Lenox

Walter Scott Lenox, former art director at Ott and Brewer, and Jonathan Coxon founded The Ceramic Art Company of Trenton, New Jersey, in 1889. By 1906 Cox had left the company, and to reflect the change in ownership, the name was changed to Lenox Inc. Until 1930 when the production of American-made Belleek came to an end, they continued to produce the same type of high-quality ornamental wares that Lenox and Coxon had learned to master while in the employ of Ott and Brewer. Their superior dinnerware made the company famous, and since 1917 Lenox has been chosen the official White House China. Our advisor for this category is Mary Frank Gaston; she is listed in the Directory under Texas. See also Ceramic Art Company.

Bookend, stylized Trojan horse bust, wht, sgn ABCO '37, 7" 250.00
Bouillon cup & saucer, Empress 45.00
Bouillon cup & saucer, Ming 45.00
Bowl, fruit; Blue Tree, sm 35.00
Bowl, fruit; Empress, sm 30.00
Bowl, salad/cereal; Springdale 35.00
Bowl, vegetable; Kingsley, oval 135.00
Bowl, vegetable; Lenox Rose, 9½" L 95.00
Bowl, vegetable; Wyndcrest, oval 75.00
Box, floral relief, wht on pk, gr mk, 2½x5" 65.00
Bust of female, cascading hair, wht, gr mk, 8½" 275.00
Cake plate, Lenox Rose, low ped 135.00
Cake plate, Ming, hdls 110.00
Chocolate pot, Autumn 225.00
Compote, Lenox Rose, 4x9" 135.00
Creamer, Kingsley 85.00
Creamer, Ming 60.00
Cup, demitasse; wht, sterling holder, gr mk 25.00
Cup & saucer, Amethyst 10.00
Cup & saucer, Autumn 48.00
Cup & saucer, Biltmore 40.00
Cup & saucer, Blue Ridge 40.00
Cup & saucer, Brookdale, old style 40.00
Cup & saucer, demitasse; Lenox Rose 38.00
Cup & saucer, demitasse; Ming 38.00
Cup & saucer, demitasse; Trent 45.00
Cup & saucer, Fairfield 35.00
Cup & saucer, Flirtation 40.00
Cup & saucer, Lenox Rose 35.00
Cup & saucer, Olympia Gold 30.00
Cup & saucer, Rhodora 35.00
Cup & saucer, Sachet 35.00

Cup & saucer, Springdale 40.00
Cup & saucer, Weatherly 35.00
Gravy boat, Kingsley 150.00
Pitcher, cherries on gr/bl belleek, 6½x7" 175.00
Pitcher, toby; Wm Penn, Indian hdl 190.00
Plate, bread & butter; Fairfield 18.00
Plate, bread & butter; Flirtation 20.00
Plate, bread & butter; Wheat 20.00
Plate, dinner; Amethyst 38.00
Plate, dinner; Autumn 50.00
Plate, dinner; Blue Ridge 38.00
Plate, dinner; Brookdale 35.00
Plate, dinner; Country Garden 35.00
Plate, dinner; Empress 35.00
Plate, dinner; Fairfield 30.00
Plate, dinner; Lenox Rose 30.00
Plate, dinner; Meadow Song 38.00
Plate, dinner; Repertoire 38.00
Plate, dinner; Weatherly 30.00
Plate, dinner; Wheat 30.00
Plate, salad; Autumn 25.00
Plate, salad; Flirtation 25.00
Platter, Empress, 19" 150.00
Platter, Kingsley, 14" 145.00
Platter, Kingsley, 17" 175.00
Platter, Lenox Rose, 13" 150.00
Platter, Wyndcrest, lg 135.00
Soup bowl, Kingsley, rimmed 50.00
Soup bowl, Lenox Rose, rimmed, 9" 45.00
Sugar bowl, Kingsley 95.00
Swan, wht, gr mk, 4x5" 30.00
Teapot, Lenox Rose 225.00
Vase, belleek, peacocks on bl, sgn Hipple, on base, 12" 600.00

Letter Openers

Made in a wide variety of materials and designs, letter openers make for an interesting collection that is easy to display and easy on the budget as well. Our advisor for this category is Ron Damaska; he is listed in the Directory under Pennsylvania.

Bone, scrimshaw leaves, red/blk stain, cut-out hearts, 5¼" 78.00
Brass, Nat'l Foundry, St Louis 17.50
Brass, nude man in bbl, advertising 25.00
Celluloid, Railway Express Agency on hdl, 9", EX 5.00
Fuller Brush Man, clear 5.00
Ivory, dagger shape, ebony & abalone hdl, old 65.00
Ivory, hdl cvd as lady's leg w/high-heeled shoe 175.00
Ivory, opener/page-turner, tooled silver monogram, 17" 200.00
Ivory, w/stanhope 60.00
Keen Kutter, pen in hdl 30.00
Keen Kutter, w/knife blade in hdl 20.00
Metal, Gulf Oil 10.00
Needham Oil, Mass, gr plastic 5.00
SP, Reed & Barton, cherubs on grape arbor hdl, ornate 35.00
Sterling, Nouveau flowers 40.00
Whalebone, sword form, 4¼", EX 25.00

Libbey

The New England Glass Company was established in 1818 in Boston, Massachusetts. In 1892 it became known as the Libbey Glass

Company. At Chicago's Columbian Expo in 1893, Libbey set up a ten-pot furnace and made glass souvenirs. The display brought them worldwide fame. Between 1878 and 1918 Libbey made exquisite cut and faceted glass, considered today to be the best from the brilliant period. The company is credited for several innovations — the Owens bottle machine that made mass-production possible and the Westlake machine which turned out both electric light bulbs and tumblers automatically. They developed a machine to polish the rims of their tumblers in such a way that chipping was unlikely to occur. Their glassware carried the patented Safedge guarantee. Libbey also made glassware in numerous colors, among them cobalt, ruby, pink, green, and amber. In 1935 it was bought by Owens-Illinois and remains a division of that company. See also Amberina and other specific types.

Bottle, scent; amberina, sgn 800.00
Bottle, water; cut, Imperial, sgn 230.00

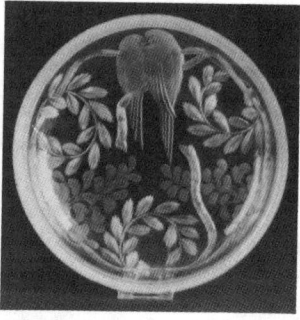

Bowl, lovebirds and wisteria cuttings, 8" diameter, $400.00.

Bowl, cut, Eulalia, sq, 11" 300.00
Bowl, cut, Kimberly, 10" 350.00
Bowl, cut, Stratford, 10" 550.00
Bowl, cut, strawberry/dmn rim band, rayed bottom, 6" 60.00
Bowl, striped lav opal, scalloped, att Nash, 11", +pr sticks 1,200.00
Box, powder; cut, Florence, 6" dia 550.00
Candle holder, dk pk w/opal stripes, clear base, bowl form 250.00
Candlestick, air-twist stem, sgn, 8" 200.00
Candlestick, opal camel stem, sgn 300.00
Champagne, opal squirrel stem, 5½" 95.00
Comport, cut, Marcella, ped ft, notched std, sgn, 10½x7½" 350.00
Comport, intaglio fuchsia, sgn, 5½" 125.00
Compote, amberina, sgn, 5" dia 700.00
Cup & saucer, vaseline, World's 1893 Expo 175.00
Goblet, controlled bubble stem, etched bowl, sgn, 5" 70.00
Goblet, cut, Cornucopia, 7" 50.00
Ice cream tray, Empress, 10½x17½" 600.00
Maize, celery vase, gold husks on custard, 6½" 165.00

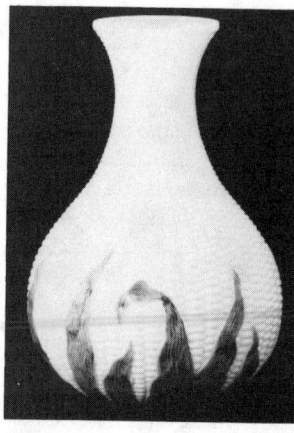

Maize, vase, 8", $375.00.

Maize, celery vase, gr husks on custard 180.00
Maize, pickle castor, gr husks on custard, SP fr 500.00
Maize, pitcher, bl husks on clear w/amber irid, clear hdl, 9" 585.00
Maize, pitcher, gr husks on custard, strap hdl, 8½x5½" 485.00
Maize, shakers, gold-edged bl husks on custard, pr 250.00
Maize, sugar shaker, gold-edged yel husks on custard, 6" 235.00
Maize, syrup, gr husks on custard, scarce, 6" 350.00
Maize, toothpick holder, gold-edged gr husks on custard 400.00
Maize, tumbler, bl husks on irid 235.00
Pitcher, cut, buzz star & fan, ray base, thumb-cut hdl, 8" 250.00
Pitcher, cut, Dmn & Fine Cut, scalloped top, sgn, 8x5½" 295.00
Pitcher, Hobstar & Pineapple, cut scalloped top, sgn, 8x5¼" 295.00
Pitcher, milk; gr threading, sgn, 1930s 200.00
Plate, cut, Ellsmere, sabre mk, 6¾" 150.00
Plate, cut, X-cut dmns at rim, rayed center, label, 12" 300.00
Plate, etched poinsettias, sgn, 7" 200.00
Punch bowl, cut, Spillane, 2-pc, sgn 3,500.00
Sherbet, etched w/fruit, sgn 215.00
Sherbet, opal rabbit stem 95.00
Tray, ice cream; cut, hobstar chain around hobstar, fan hdls 500.00
Tray, ice cream; cut, Wedgemere, 8½x3½" 300.00
Tumbler, amberina, sgn 200.00
Vase, amberina, swirled flower-form top, EX color, sgn, 8" 1,400.00
Vase, cut, hobstars/beading/X-hatching, sgn, 14½" 450.00
Vase, cut, Star & Feather, sgn, 16" 1,200.00
Vase, cut/eng, Cherry Blossom, trumpet form, knob stem, 12" ...150.00
Vase, etched roses, flared, sgn, 6" 550.00
Vase, intaglio cut, Dianthus, 12" 300.00
Wine, opal cat stem, 7" 95.00
Wine, opal polar bear stem, 5½" 125.00
Wine, opal squirrel stem 95.00

Lightning Rod Balls

Used as ornaments on lightning rods, the vast majority of these balls were made of glass, but ceramic examples can be found as well. Their average diameter is 4½" but can vary from 3½" up to 5½". Only a few of the many available pattern-and-color combinations are listed here. The most common measure 4½" and are found in sun-colored amethyst and milk glass. Our advisor is Mike Bruner, who is currently working on a book on this subject. Anyone interested in receiving a hobby-related newsletter may write to him for more information; he is listed in the Directory under Michigan.

Amethyst, sun-colored, plain, rnd 8.00
Bl opaque, Hawkeye 25.00
Bl opaque, Mast 30.00
Bl opaque, Moon & Star 25.00
Bl opaque, Nat'l 23.00
Bl opaque, 8-sided 15.00
Cobalt, Nat'l 55.00
Milk glass, Hawkeye 18.00
Milk glass, plain, rnd 7.50
Wht swirl 30.00

Limited Edition Plates

Currently values of some limited edition plates have risen dramatically while others have drastically fallen. Prices charged by plate dealers in the secondary market vary greatly; we have tried to suggest an average.

Bing and Grondahl

1895, Behind the Frozen Window 6,250.00

1896, New Moon 1,850.00
1897, Christmas Meal of Sparrows 1,100.00
1898, Roses & Star 685.00
1899, Crows Enjoying Christmas 1,500.00
1900, Church Bells Chiming 1,125.00
1901, 3 Wise Men 425.00
1902, Gothic Church Interior 365.00
1903, Expectant Children 370.00
1904, View of Copenhagen From Fredericksberg Hill ...155.00
1905, Anxiety of the Coming Christmas Night 155.00
1906, Sleighing to Church 92.00
1907, Little Match Girl 105.00
1908, St Petri Church 65.00
1909, Yule Tree 95.00
1910, Old Organist 85.00
1911, Angels & Shepherds 77.00
1912, Going to Church 85.00
1913, Bringing Home the Tree 87.00
1914, Amalienborg Castle 77.00
1915, Dog on Chain Outside Window 125.00
1916, Prayer of the Sparrows 72.50
1917, Christmas Boat 72.50
1918, Fishing Boat 72.50
1919, Outside the Lighted Window 67.50
1920, Hare in the Snow 72.50
1921, Pigeons 65.00
1922, Star of Bethlehem 62.50
1923, Hermitage 60.00
1924, Lighthouse 70.00
1925, Child's Christmas 70.00
1926, Churchgoers 70.00
1927, Skating Couple 95.00
1928, Eskimos 60.00
1929, Fox Outside Farm 65.00
1930, Tree in Town Hall Square 80.00
1931, Christmas Train 80.00
1932, Lifeboat at Work 72.50
1933, Korsor-Nyborg Ferry 68.00
1934, Church Bell in Tower 65.00
1935, Lillebelt Bridge 68.00
1936, Royal Guard 75.00
1937, Arrival of Christmas Guests 80.00
1938, Lighting the Candles 150.00
1939, Old Lock-Eye, The Sandman 150.00
1940, Delivering Christmas Letters 150.00
1941, Horses Enjoying Meal 225.00
1942, Danish Farm on Christmas Night 185.00
1943, Ribe Cathedral 175.00
1944, Sorgenfri Castle 95.00
1945, Old Water Mill 115.00
1946, Commemoration Cross 75.00
1947, Dybbol Mill 95.00
1948, Watchman 75.00
1949, Landsoldaten 75.00
1950, Kronborg Castle at Elsinore 105.00
1951, Jens Bang 90.00
1952, Old Copenhagen Canals & Thorsvaldsen Museum ...85.00
1953, Royal Boat 85.00
1954, Snowman 85.00
1955, Kaulundborg Church 85.00
1956, Christmas in Copenhagen 135.00
1957, Christmas Candles 145.00
1958, Santa Claus 95.00
1959, Christmas Eve 115.00

1960, Village Church 145.00
1961, Winter Harmony 98.00
1962, Winter Night 60.00
1963, Christmas Elf 80.00
1964, Fir Tree & Hare 39.00
1965, Bringing Home the Tree 42.00
1966, Home for Christmas 35.00
1967, Sharing the Joy 35.00
1968, Christmas in Church 32.00
1969, Arrival of Guests 24.00
1970, Pheasants in Snow 22.00
1971, Christmas at Home 19.00
1972, Christmas in Greenland 19.00
1973, Country Christmas 22.00
1974, Christmas in the Village 19.00
1975, The Old Water Mill 19.00
1976, Christmas Welcome 19.00
1977, Copenhagen Christmas 19.00
1978, A Christmas Tale 19.00
1979, White Christmas 21.00
1980, Christmas in the Woods 21.00
1981, Christmas Peace 24.00
1982, The Christmas Tree 37.00

M. I. Hummel

1971, Heavenly Angel 525.00
1972, Hear Ye, Hear Ye 50.00
1973, Globe Trotter 95.00
1974, Goose Girl 50.00
1975, Ride Into Christmas 50.00
1976, Apple Tree Girl 50.00
1977, Apple Tree Boy 60.00
1978, Happy Pastime 45.00
1979, Singing Lesson 30.00
1980, School Girl 40.00

Royal Copenhagen

1908, Madonna & Child 2,900.00
1909, Danish Landscape 160.00
1910, Magi 135.00
1911, Danish Landscape 160.00
1912, Christmas Tree 160.00
1913, Frederik Church Spire 145.00
1914, Holy Spirit Church 160.00
1915, Danish Landscape 165.00
1916, Shepherd at Christmas 100.00
1917, Our Savior Church 90.00
1918, Sheep & Shepherds 90.00
1919, In the Park 90.00
1920, Mary & Child Jesus 90.00
1921, Aabenraa Marketplace 85.00
1922, 3 Singing Angels 75.00
1923, Danish Landscape 75.00
1924, Sailing Ship 100.00
1925, Christianshavn Street Scene 85.00
1926, Christianshavn Canal 85.00
1927, Ship's Boy at Tiller 155.00
1928, Vicar's Family 87.00
1929, Grundtvig Church 87.00
1930, Fishing Boats 115.00
1931, Mother & Child 115.00
1932, Frederiksberg Gardens 110.00

1933, Ferry & Great Belt 150.00
1934, Hermitage Castle 150.00
1935, Kronborg Castle 215.00
1936, Roskilde Cathedral 185.00
1937, Main Street of Copenhagen 230.00
1938, Round Church of Osterlars 290.00
1939, Greenland Pack Ice 375.00
1940, Good Shepherd 375.00
1941, Danish Village Church 345.00
1942, Bell Tower 375.00
1943, Flight Into Egypt 525.00
1944, Danish Village Scene 290.00
1945, Peaceful Scene 475.00
1946, Zealand Village Church 175.00
1947, Good Shepherd 245.00
1948, Nodebo Church 215.00
1949, Our Lady's Cathedral 235.00
1950, Boeslunde Church 235.00
1951, Christmas Angel 365.00
1952, Christmas in Forest 135.00
1953, Frederiksberg Castle 135.00
1954, Amalienborg Palace 135.00
1955, Fano Girl 195.00
1956, Rosenborg Castle 185.00
1957, Good Shepherd 105.00
1958, Sunshine Over Greenland 145.00
1959, Christmas Night 115.00
1960, Stag 145.00
1961, Training Ship 155.00
1962, Little Mermaid 205.00
1963, Hojsager Mill 85.00
1964, Fetching the Tree 65.00
1965, Little Skaters 70.00
1966, Blackbird 38.00
1967, Royal Oak 40.00
1968, Last Umiak 39.00
1969, Old Farmyard 39.00
1970, Christmas Rose & Cat 39.00
1971, Hare in Winter 24.00
1972, In the Desert 24.00
1973, Train Home Bound 24.00
1974, Winter Twilight 28.00
1975, Queen's Palace 24.00
1976, Danish Watermill 29.00
1977, Immervad Bridge 24.00
1978, Greenland Scenery 29.00
1979, Choosing Tree 45.00
1980, Bringing Home Tree 37.50
1981, Admiring Tree 39.00
1982, Waiting for Christmas 45.00

Limoges

From the mid-18th century, Limoges was the center of the porcelain industry of France, where at one time more than forty companies utilized the local kaolin to make a superior quality china, much of which was exported to the United States. Various marks were used; some included the name of the American export company (rather than the manufacturer) and 'Limoges.' After 1891 'France' was added. Pieces signed by factory artists are more valuable than those decorated outside the factory by amateurs. For a more thorough study of the subject, we recommend you refer to *The Collector's Encyclopedia of Limoges Porcelain* by our advisor, Mary Frank Gaston, who is listed in the Directory under Texas. Her book has beautiful color illustrations and current market values.

Plate, flower basket, signed Du Val, Borgfeldt, 11½", $350.00.

Biscuit jar, floral, coral/yel on wht w/gold, 7½" 175.00
Butter tub, florals w/wide gold border, +undertray 195.00
Charger, lg bldg/trees/sm figure of boy, sgn Bauney, 12" 175.00
Charger, Sarah Bernhardt portrait, T&V, 16" 130.00
Chocolate pot, roses & much gold, artist sgn, +5 c/s 225.00
Chocolate pot, sweetheart roses & gold, mk, +5 c/s 185.00
Dish, 3-lobe, sm flowers on wht to salmon, ornate hdl, 12" 195.00
Dresser set, floral, pk on bl to yel shaded, 7-pc 395.00
Dresser set, lav floral w/gold, 10-pc 595.00
Ewer, mums/gold seed pods & stems, mum neck band, 11" 265.00
Mug, corn, sgn, T&V 60.00
Pitcher, cider; cherries on pastel, sgn Goodrick, 5½x6½" 165.00
Plaque, cupid offers fruit to lady, sgn Rip, easel bk, 5x4" 800.00
Plaque, girl knits/old man watches, sgn Schumacher, 10x7" 1,300.00
Plaque, lady in feathered hat, sgn A Dussou, 1863, 15" 450.00
Plaque, lady in plumed hat by pond, sgn, ornate fr, 15" 2,100.00
Plaque, Le Bon Vin, cavalier w/wine glass, sgn Bruin, 6x5" 800.00
Plaque, lovers on steps, sgn Augustin, fr, 5½x3½" 600.00
Plaque, Venus & cherubs reclining above waves, 1800s, 12x16" ..440.00
Plate, game fish, 1870s, set of 6, ea w/different fish 260.00
Plate, lady w/lute transfer, gold border, unmk, 13", pr 395.00
Plate, lg yel rose, gold rococo border, sgn, unmk, 13" 225.00
Plate, man & lady, rococo border, facing pr, 12" 450.00
Plate, mc roses on pastel ground, sgn, gold rim, 12¾", pr 495.00
Plate, snow/windmill/trees, gold rococo rim, unmk, 11", pr 325.00
Plate, wild game, Roman gold border, Coronet, 8⅜", pr 245.00
Potpourri, florals, gold trim, sgn R Delinieres e cie, 9" 195.00
Tazza, geisha w/chrysanthemum, sgn Garnet, 7" 700.00
Tray, fish/gulls, gilt border, 24", +sauce boat & 12 plates 1,400.00
Vase, elegant lady w/walking stick, trees, stem ft, 8" 625.00
Vase, flamingo, WG Limoges, 1890-1910, 11" 135.00
Vase, fruit/flowers/butterfly on lt bl, rope hdl/finial, 11" 165.00
Vase, lady seated in landscape, bottle form w/ormolu ft, 6" 550.00
Vase, lady's portrait in landscape, pear form, 4¾" 325.00
Vase, standing maid/lg poppies, sgn, ftd pear form, 7½" 700.00
Vase, 2 dandies/2 ladies in reserve on red, ormolu ft, 9" 400.00

Lithophanes

Lithophanes are porcelain panels with relief designs of varying degrees of thickness and density. Transmitted light brings out the pattern in graduated shading, lighter where the procelain is thin and darker in the heavy areas. They were cast from wax models prepared by artists and depict views of life from the 1800s, religious themes, or scenes of historical significance. First made in Berlin about 1803, they were used as lampshade panels, window plaques, or candle shields. Later steins, mugs, and cups were made with lithophanes in their bases. Japanese wares were sometimes made with dragons or geisha lithophanes. See also Dragon Ware; Steins.

Cup & saucer, pk w/moriage dragon, lady in bottom of cup	45.00
Lamp, open-top 13" dome shade w/3 panels, genre scenes	765.00
Panel, draped lady in flower garden, #1308, 4x5"	135.00
Panel, Emperor & Empress, MOP inlay fr on stand, 1850s	2,400.00
Panel, Maguerite praying among ruins, 9x7", bronze stand	900.00
Shade, 6 trapezoid scenic panels, sgn, 6x12"	750.00
Stein, 2 girls read letter (in base), tavern scene ext, 10"	200.00

Little Red Riding Hood

Though usually thought of as a product of the Hull Pottery Company, research has shown that a major part of this line was actually made by Regal China. The idea for this popular line of novelties and kitchenware items was developed and patented by Hull, but records show that to a large extent Hull sent their whiteware to Regal to be decorated. Little Red Riding Hood was produced from 1943 until 1957. Values have risen sharply over the past several months. For further information we recommend *Collecting Hull Pottery's Red Riding Hood* by Mark Supnick. Watch for the announcement of another book on this subject by Joyce and Fred Roerig, authors of *The Collector's Encyclopedia of Cookie Jars*.

Butter dish	350.00
Canister, salt	1,100.00
Canister, spice	650.00
Cookie canister	2,500.00
Creamer, tab hdl	225.00
Creamer & sugar bowl, head pour, w/lid	700.00
Creamer & sugar bowl, side spout	300.00
Jar, cracker; skirt held wide, 8½"	550.00
Match holder, wall hanging	800.00
Mug, decor	2,000.00
Mug, wht, no decor, minimum value	1,000.00
Pitcher, milk; ruffled skirt, w/apron, rare, 8½"	3,000.00
Pitcher, milk; standing, 8"	250.00
Planter, standing, wall hanging	475.00
Shakers, standing, rare, 4½", pr	850.00
Shakers, standing, 3¼", pr	50.00
Shakers, standing, 5¼", pr	150.00
Sugar bowl, crawling	225.00
Teapot	350.00

Liverpool

In the late 1700s Liverpool potters produced a creamy ivory ware, sometimes called Queen's Ware, which they decorated by means of the newly perfected transfer print. Made specifically for the American market, patriotic inscriptions, political portraits, or other States themes were applied in black with colors sometimes added by hand. (Obviously their loyalty to the crown did not inhibit the progress of business!) Before it lost favor in about 1825, other English potters made a similar product. Today Liverpool is a generic term used to refer to all ware of this type. Our advisor for this category is Richard Marden; he is listed in the Directory under New Hampshire.

Jug, Am ship, bk: WA Gone/Am in Tears, eagle, mc, rstr, 11"	1,750.00
Jug, Arms of Stearns, bk: allegorical/eagle, yel/gr, 9", EX	1,800.00
Jug, Autumn/Rustic Amusement, 7½", VG	220.00
Jug, Ben Franklin, bk: WA etc, inscription/1818, 9½", EX	4,600.00

Jug, James Madison, blk transfer portrait, rstr	5,500.00
Jug, Masonic symbols/ship, blk, heavy rstr, 8"	350.00
Jug, Masonic transfers, 11", NM	1,500.00
Jug, Monument to WA/13 states, bk: ship, gilt, 9", NM	2,300.00
Jug, Napoleon in cage on dory cartoon, rust transfer, 8"	1,200.00
Jug, political cartoon w/men & cow, bk: Am ship, gilt, 8"	8,500.00
Jug, ship Carpenter, bk: WA under spout/eagle, mc, 11", EX	1,875.00
Jug, ship MAC, bk: WA under spout, wreath, mc, 9", EX	1,650.00
Jug, ship Russell w/Am flag, Peace/Plenty..., mc, 9¾", EX	2,850.00
Jug, ship w/Am flag, bk: eagle/16 states, mc, 8", NM	3,500.00
Jug, ship w/Am flag, bk: Farmers' Arms/names, mc, 8½", EX	1,800.00
Jug, Success to Am Whose Militia/ship/eagle, mc, 9", VG	700.00
Jug, US Ship & figure of Hope, mc transfer, rpr, 8"	1,400.00
Jug, WA, bk: Peace..., Man w/o Example, gilt, 11", EX	2,200.00
Jug, WA in Glory, bk: Cordwainers, blk, 9", NM	1,100.00
Mug, ship w/Am flag, mc, 5¾", EX	1,100.00

Lladro

Lladro porcelains are currently being produced in Labernes Blanques, Spain. Their retired and limited edition figurines are popular collectibles on the secondary market.

Hissing goose, 6" long, $95.00.

Apple Seller, Goyescas	540.00
Back to School, #5702	300.00
Ballerina, #4855	250.00
Ballerina seated, 5"	60.00
Boy & girl hold puppy in winter wind, 13"	375.00
Boy & girl on seesaw, 9"	150.00
Boy seated on tree stump reading book, 1975, 8"	130.00
Boy w/goat, #4506	285.00
Boy yawning, #4870, MIB	50.00
Can I Play	275.00
Champion, Goyescas	1,080.00
Cinderella, 11"	65.00
Clown, prone, #4618	295.00
Clown w/alarm clock, #5056	635.00
Comforting News, Goyescas	720.00
Dancer, lady holds skirt of gown wide, 12"	85.00
Debutantes, #5486	525.00
Dutch girl sits w/doll & basket of fruit, 9"	175.00
Flower Song	400.00
Fox, lying down, 7" L	85.00
Garden Classic	235.00
Garden Song	225.00
Geisha, Oriental Spring, #4988	215.00

Girl asleep in rocker holding doll, 4½"	120.00
Girl in lg hat, right hand as though waving, 14"	85.00
Girl w/basket of flowers, 6½"	80.00
Girl w/turkey, #4569	400.00
Golfer, male, #4824	255.00
Harlequin & Columbine, 9x15"	155.00
I Love You Truly, #1528	450.00
Just a Little Kiss, #5701	275.00
Lady holds pekingese & parasol, 15"	105.00
Little Gardener, #1283	535.00
Little Pals	2,150.00
Little Traveler	975.00
Love in Bloom, #5292	295.00
Lovers from Verona, #1250	1,100.00
Madonna bust, 9"	85.00
Matrimony, #1404	400.00
Miss Valencia w/oranges, #1422	255.00
My Buddy	350.00
Nativity scene, B-18 J, 8½x5½"	150.00
Nesting Doves, Goyescas	480.00
Opening Night, #5498	195.00
Picture Perfect, #7612	435.00
Playful Romp, #5594	195.00
Profit, Goyescas	480.00
Ride in the Country, #5354	295.00
Rosalinda, #4836	355.00
School Days	350.00
Shepherdess w/goats, holding lamb, #1001	525.00
Spanish Dancer, #5390	195.00
Spring Bouquet	525.00
Summer Stroll	165.00
Touch of Class, #5377	600.00
Valencia Girl, #1304	450.00
Valencian Dreams, #1525	255.00
Veterinarian, #4825	375.00
Voyage of Columbus	875.00
Woman arranges flowers in vase, 8"	70.00
Woman holds child by donkey, 10"	150.00
Young lady w/parasol in right hand, sm dog at ft, 14"	80.00

Locke Art

Joseph Locke already had proven himself many times over as a master glass maker, working in leading English glasshouses for more than seventeen years. He came to America where he joined the New England Glass Company. There he invented processes for the manufacture of several types of art glass — amberina, peachblow, pomona, and agata among them. In 1898 he established the Locke Art Glassware Co. in Mt. Oliver, Pittsburgh, Pennsylvania. Locke Art Glass was executed using an acid-etching process by which the most delicate designs were produced on crystal blanks. Most examples are signed simply 'Locke Art,' often placed unobtrusively near a leaf or a stem. Other items are signed 'Jo Locke,' some are dated, and some are unsigned. Most of the work was done by hand. The business continued into the 1920s. For further study we recommend *American Art Glass* by Shuman, available at your local bookstore.

Pitcher, Grape & Line, tankard form, elaborate hdl, 9"	600.00
Sugar bowl, Poppy	85.00
Tumbler, Brer Rabbit & Brer Fox scene, sgn, 5⅜"	450.00
Tumbler, cherry w/vertical lines, sgn, 4¼"	95.00

Cherry dish with concave foot to hold pits, Pansy pattern, 2¾", $200.00.

Locks

The earliest type of lock in recorded history was the wooden cross bar used by ancient Egyptians and their contemporaries. The early Romans are credited with making the first key-operated mechanical lock. The ward lock was invented during the Middle Ages by the Etruscans of Northern Italy; the lever tumbler and combination locks followed at various stages of history with varying degrees of effectiveness. In the 18th century the first precision lock was constructed. It was a device that utilized a lever-tumbler mechanism. Two of the best-known of the early 19th-century American lock manufacturers are Yale and Sargent, and today's collectors value Winchester and Keen Kutter locks very highly. Factors to consider are rarity, condition, and construction. Brass and bronze locks are generally priced higher than those of steel or iron. Our advisor for this section is Joe Tanner; he is listed in the Directory under Washington.

Key:
bbl — barrel   st — stamped

Brass Lever Tumbler

Ames Sword Co, Perfection stamped on shackle, 2¾"	60.00
Bingham's Best Brand, BBB emb on front, 3¼"	150.00
Cleveland 4 Way, Cleveland 4 Way emb on front, 3⅝"	90.00
Crusader, shield, swords emb on body, 2¾"	45.00
Eagle Lock Co, word Eagle emb on front, scrolled, 3"	60.00
Jackson's, stamped Jackson's on front, 2½"	20.00
Keen Kutter, shape of KK emblem, KK emb on front, 4¾"	125.00
Mercury, Mercury emb on body, 2¾"	75.00
Motor, Motor emb on body, 3¼"	35.00
Our Very Best, OVB emb on body, 2⅞"	150.00
Roeyonoc, Roeyonoc stamped on body, 3¼"	30.00
Romer & Co, Romer & Co stamped on dust cover, 3"	55.00
Ruby, Ruby emb in scroll on front, 2¾"	20.00
Safe, Safe emb in scroll on front, 2⅜"	20.00
Siberian, Siberian emb on shackle, 2½"	110.00
Sphinx, sphinx & pharaoh head emb on front, 2¾"	35.00
W Bohannan & Co, SW emb in scroll on front, 2⅜"	30.00
Winchester, Winchester emb on front, 3"	160.00

Combinations

Chicago Combination Lock Co, stamped on front, brass, 2¾"	60.00
Corbin Sesamee 4-Dial Brass Lock, stamped Sesamee, 2¾"	12.00
Edwards Mfg Co No-Key, stamped on lock, brass, 2¾"	60.00
Junkunc Bros Mfrs, all stamped on bk, brass, 1⅞"	25.00
Karco stamped on body, 2½"	50.00
Number or letter disk type (4 disks), brass, 2¾"	130.00

Sq lock case of steel, stamped Pat Germany, 4-wheel, 3¼" 110.00
Sutton Lock Co stamped on body, 3" 200.00
Your Own stamped on body, 3⅞" 325.00

Eight-Lever Type

Armory, brass, Armory 8-Lever stamped on front 25.00
Electric, steel, Electric stamped on front 25.00
Goliath, steel, Goliath 8-Lever stamped on front 20.00
Miller, steel, Miller 8-Lever stamped on front 18.00
Samson, brass, 8-Lever stamped on front 18.00

Iron Lever Tumbler

Bull, word Bull emb on front, 2⅝" 30.00
Bulldog, word Bulldog & face of dog emb on front, 2¾" 30.00
Dan Patch, Dan Patch emb on front, horseshoe on bk, 2¾" 130.00
Dragon, word Dragon & dragon emb on front, 2⅞" 25.00
Eagle, word Eagle emb on body, 4⅜" 40.00
Indian Head, Indian head emb on front, 3" 90.00
Jupiter, word Jupiter/star & moon emb on front, 3¼" 18.00
Karo, word Karo emb on front, CI, 3⅛" 25.00
King Korn, words King Korn emb on body, 2⅞" 40.00
Nineteen O Three, 1903 emb on front, iron, 3⅞" 90.00
Red Chief, words Red Chief emb on body, 3¾" 80.00
Rugby, football emb on body, 3" 20.00
Unique, word Unique emb on front, 3¼" 120.00
Yale & Towne, lion face emb on front, shackle mk Y&T, 3" 110.00

Lever Push Key

Champion, emb Champion 6-Lever, brass push-key type, 2¼" 25.00
Climax, emb Climax 6-Lever, iron push-key type, 2¼" 35.00
Columbia, emb Columbia 6-Lever, brass push-key type, 2¼" 35.00
Dash, emb Dash 6-Lever, iron push-key type, 2¼" 25.00
Excelsior, emb Excelsior 6-Lever, brass push-key type, 2¼" 25.00
Harvard, emb Harvard 4-Lever, brass push-key type, 2" 50.00
IXL, emb IXL on body, 2¼" 75.00
Keystone, emb Keystone 6-Lever, brass push-key type, 2¼" 40.00
McIntosh, emb McIntosh on body, 2¼" 90.00
SB Co, emb SB Co on body, 3¼" 60.00
Smith & Egge Mfg Co, Smith & Egge stamped on front, 3" 75.00
Ten Star, emb Ten Star 6-Lever, 2¼" 45.00

Logo — Special Made

Brass pancake push key emb US Internal Revenue, 2¼" 185.00
Heart-shape brass lever type emb Shults Co, bbl key, 2¾" 55.00
Heart-shape brass lever type st Board Education, bbl key, 3½" 60.00
Sq brass pin-tumbler case st Regd US Mail, int counter, 2¾" 140.00
Sq Yale-type brass pin tumbler, emb w/Texaco & star, 3" 25.00
Sq Yale-type brass pin tumbler, st Shell Oil Co on body, 3⅛" 20.00
Sq Yale-type brass pin tumbler, st US/A/tree/Forest Svc, 2⅞" 125.00

Pin-Tumbler Type

Corbin, brass, Corbin in oval stamped on body, 3⅝" 25.00
Eagle, brass, Eagle stamped on body, 2⅞" 20.00
Fulton, emb Fulton on body, 2⅝" 30.00
Hope, brass, emb Hope on body, 2½" 16.00
Il-A-Noy, emb Il-A-Noy on body, 2½" 40.00
Pearl, brass, emb Pearl on body, 2⅛" 16.00
Sargent, brass, emb Sargent on body, 3" 15.00

Segal, iron, emb Segal on shackle, 3¾" 40.00
Shapleigh, emb Shapleigh on body, 2⅝" 40.00
Yale, brass, emb Yale on body, Made in England on shackle, 3" ..40.00
Yale, brass, emb Yale on body, Yale & Towne on shackle, 2⅝" 25.00

Scandinavian (Jail House) Type

JHW Climax Co, iron, 2⅞" 50.00
Star, emb line on bottom, iron, 3¾" 100.00
Star, iron, 2½" 70.00
99 Miller, emb 99, brass, 1¾" 80.00
999 Miller, emb 999, brass, 2½" 70.00

Six-Lever Type

Eagle, brass, Eagle Six Lever stamped on body 15.00
Edwards, iron, Edwards stamped on body 15.00
Safe, brass, Safe stamped on body 18.00
Yale, brass, Yale emb on front 12.00

Story and Commemorative

AYPEX Seattle (Alaska Yukon Pacific Expo), emb tin/iron, 3" .225.00
Canteen, US emb on lock, lock: canteen shape, 2" 500.00
CI, emb ornate scroll motif throughout body of lock, 3½" 170.00
CI, emb skull/X-bones w/florals, NH Co on bk, 3¼" 200.00
CQD/sinking ship Titanic & SOS waves emb on brass, 2¾" 120.00
Eagle/stars/shield & stars, emb CI, Eagle Liberty, 2½" 300.00
Mail Pouch, emb on lock, lock in shape of a mail pouch, 3⅛" 225.00
1901 Pan Am Expo, brass, emb w/buffalo, 2⅝" 175.00

Warded Type

Army, iron pancake ward key, emb letters, 2½" 35.00
Globe, iron sq lock case, emb US on bk, 2⅜" 20.00
Hex, iron, sq lock case, emb US on bk, 2⅛" 95.00
Navy, iron pancake ward key, bk: scrolled emb letters, 2½" 35.00
Red Cross, brass sq case, emb letters, 2" 10.00
Rex, steel case, emb letters, 2⅝" 18.00
Safe, brass sq case, emb letters, 1⅞" 8.00
Safety First, brass pancake type, emb letters, 2¾" 15.00
Secure, iron pancake type, emb letters, 2⅝" 20.00
Sprocket, brass oval shape, emb letters, 2⅛" 50.00
Try Me, iron pancake type, emb letters, 2½" 25.00
Winchester, brass sq case, stamped letters, 2¾" 125.00

Wrought Iron Lever Type (Smokehouse Type)

DM&Co, bbl key, 4¼" 35.00

**D M & Co., $35.00; MW & Co., $35.00;
English, VG, $35.00.**

MW&Co, bbl key, 2⅝" 10.00
MW&Co, flat key, 3½" 20.00
S&Co, bbl key, 3" 8.00

Loetz

The Loetz Glassworks was established in Klostermule, Austria, in 1840. After Loetz's death the firm was purchased by his grandson, Johann Loetz Witwe. Until WWII the operation continued to produce fine artware, some of which made in the early 1900s bears a striking resemblance to Tiffany's with whom Loetz was associated at one time. In addition to the iridescent Tiffany-style glass, he also produced threaded glass and some cameo. Our advisor for this category is Don Williams; he is listed in the Directory under Missouri.

Key:
att — attributed   o/l — overlay

Bottle, scent; bl/gold irid mottle, silver rim/stopper, 6½" 550.00
Bowl, cameo floral, brn/gr, 3 dk ball ft, flared rim, 4x6" 700.00
Bowl, emerald gr aventurine w/silver-bl swirls, 4x9" 2,000.00
Inkwell, amber irid w/gr/bl/rose waves etc, metal lid, 3x5¾" 550.00
Inkwell, amber irid w/gr/bl/rose waves etc, glass lid, 3x5¾" 900.00
Inkwell, gr irid w/drapes, brass lid w/figural bird 450.00
Sweetmeat jar, gr irid w/irregular threading, SP trim, 4½" 295.00

Vases, applied iridescent leaves around iridescent yellow trumpet form, 12", $1,800.00; Oil spots on amber iridescent shaped cylinder form with pinched shoulders, 10", $1,800.00.

Vase, amber irid w/silver waves, appl coiled snake, 5x8" 2,200.00
Vase, amber over clear, irid amber/bl spots, long neck, 8" 1,500.00
Vase, amber wavy irid bottle form, hdld floral metal mt, 8" 1,500.00
Vase, amethyst w/irid spots, lobed/cupped neck, 11x4" 400.00
Vase, bl oil spots on gold to rose, gr/gold highlights, 7" 950.00
Vase, bl/gold irid, gold floral & trailings, unmk, 9" 895.00
Vase, bl/gold/pk spots, in Nouveau pewter hdld holder, 10" 1,500.00
Vase, cameo butterflies/leaves, dk gr on yel, 14" 2,300.00
Vase, clear irid w/vertical amber zigzag trailings, 12x4" 1,950.00
Vase, cobalt w/pulled metallic ribbons, 3-fold rim, 4x6" 1,400.00
Vase, damascene purple/bl/gr on gold, waisted/ruffled, 3½" 210.00
Vase, emerald w/crackled irid, tricon/folded rim, 13" 385.00
Vase, feathers/hooks in gold/bl on dk red, dimpled, 5" 550.00
Vase, floriform; 2 lg leaves curve out from stem, 10" 1,300.00
Vase, gold, brn int, bulbous w/several protrusions, 7" 325.00
Vase, gold mottle on amber, ftd slim form, 12" 330.00
Vase, gold w/amber spots, dimpled ovoid, 6" 440.00
Vase, gold-amber w/gr band looping down to form 4 legs, 6" 465.00
Vase, gold-lined thistles on clear satin w/pk spots, 13" 2,200.00
Vase, gr irid/purple trails, in 3-leg bronze/onyx base, 12" 600.00
Vase, gr oil spots & gold irid on opal, bulbous, 6" 550.00
Vase, gr w/bl/purple/yel oil spots, crimped fan form, 10x9" 135.00
Vase, gr/bl/silver w/pk highlights, allover oil spots, 5x6" 325.00

Vase, gr/gold w/pk highlights, appl rope forms loops/ft, 6" 800.00
Vase, lime w/silver-bl & amber spots, gourd form, 8¾" 700.00
Vase, lt bl/gold waves on dk purple irid, trumpet neck, 12" 1,100.00
Vase, orange w/int silver-bl & gr irid waves, ovoid, 6" 3,500.00
Vase, Papillion, bl w/purple irid, 4 pinched-in sides, 3" 550.00
Vase, pastel irid mottle w/oil spots, shouldered, 5x4" 1,750.00
Vase, platinum w/texture, bl/gold highlights, dbl gourd, 5" 110.00
Vase, pulled/trailed gr irid on dk bl, cylindrical, 10" 700.00
Vase, red spots w/platinum, 5 prunts, free-form top, 10½" 1,500.00
Vase, silver o/l foliage, clear w/gold irid, shouldered, 7½" 2,200.00
Vase, silver o/l iris on platinum to bl oil spots, 4" 475.00
Vase, silver o/l lily of valley on bl irid, convcave/slim, 5" 935.00
Vase, silver o/l Nouveau scrolls on mottled gold, 2¾" 465.00
Vase, silver o/l scrolls on oil-spotted salmon pk, 5" 800.00
Vase, waves in orange/bl on gold/bl oil spots, 6" 1,400.00
Vase, zippers swirl down body, gold/gr/bl irid, 9" 3,250.00
Vase, 1 side w/silver o/l, red/silver/amber mottle, 4x6" 1,980.00
Vase, 3 lg pulled feathers, red/brn/irid spots on opal, 8½" 1,650.00

Lomonosov Porcelain

Founded in Leningrad in 1744, the Lomonosov porcelain factory produced exquisite porcelain miniatures for the Czar and other Russian nobility. One of the first factories of its kind, Lomonosov pieces consisted largely of vases and delicate sculptures. In the 1800s Lomonosov became closely involved with the Russian Academy of Fine Arts, a connection which has continued to this day as the company continues to supply the world with these fine artistic treasures. In 1992 the backstamp was changed to read 'Made in Russia,' instead of 'Made in USSR.'

Figurine, Afghan hound, #3548, sm 29.50
Figurine, bear, recumbent, #6570 ....20.00
Figurine, bear, standing, #6502 ....14.00
Figurine, cat, #6564 ....40.00
Figurine, doe, #6546 ....90.00
Figurine, ermine, standing, #6432 ....24.00
Figurine, foal, brn, #6497 ....28.00
Figurine, gazelle, #6530 ....10.00
Figurine, Great Dane, #6467 ....28.50
Figurine, Kazarka, #2157 ....28.50
Figurine, Nosey Bear, #2351 ....23.00
Figurine, panda, #6531, sm 16.00
Figurine, rabbit, gray, mini, #9428 ....12.50
Figurine, raccoon, sitting, #6503 ....15.50
Figurine, raccoon, standing, #6502 ....15.50
Figurine, snowbird, #6558 ....12.00
Figurine, spaniel, #6500 ....21.50
Figurine, squirrel, #7404, mini 4.00
Figurine, tiger cub, #6480 ....28.50
Figurine, Yakut woman w/fish, #6195 ....62.00
Figurine, young elk, #6111 ....81.50

Longwy

The Longwy workshops were founded in 1798 and continue today to produce pottery in the north of France near the Luxembourg-Belgian border under the name 'Societe des Faienceries de Lonswy et Senelle.' The ware for which they are best known was produced during the Art Deco period, decorated in bold colors and designs. Earlier wares made during the first quarter of the 19th century reflected the popularity of Oriental art, cloisonne enamels in particular. The designs were executed by impressing the pattern into the moist clay and filling in the depressions with enamels. Examples are marked 'Longwy,' either impressed or painted under glaze. Our advisor for this category is Wayne Kielsmeier; he is listed in the Directory under Arizona.

Bonbonniere, cream & turq w/gold dots, hexagon, lid, 5" 325.00
Bowl, cubist vine, mc on wht, bl ext, Primavera, 15" 500.00
Box, cvd/mc florals on crazed pk, Bon Marche, 5½" dia 335.00
Box, floral, cvd/pnt, mc on wht & pk crackle, 6-sided, 7" 375.00
Charger, native rides 1 of 2 elephants, 15" 2,000.00
Charger, still life, Primavera, sgn Olesiwieg, 15" 330.00
Charger, stork/flowers on bl & gr, sgn R Rizzi, 15" 600.00
Dutch shoe, rich color, 6", pr 120.00
Platter, early enameled style (cloisonne look), 11½x8½" 155.00
Vase, disk form, aqua w/cvd blk central mask, Primavera, 11" 385.00
Vase, disk form, cream crackle, stylized gr lady's face, 12" 300.00
Vase, floral band/stripes on cream crackle, bell form, 13" 1,100.00
Vase, nudes & vegetation, gourd form, Primavera, 11½" 2,600.00
Vase, shaped floral band at width of bell form, #5134, 13" 1,100.00
Vase, 8-side bell form w/low floral & fruit band, 13" 900.00

Lonsanti

Mary Louise McLaughlin, who had previously experimented in trying to reproduce Haviland faience in the 1870s and 'American faience' (a method of inlaying color by painting the inside of the mold before the vessel was cast) in the mid-1890s, developed a type of hard-paste porcelain in which the glaze and the body fused together in a single firing. Her efforts met with success in 1900, and she immediately concentrated on glazing and decorating techniques. The ware she perfected was called Lonsanti, most of which was decorated with Nouveau florals, either carved or modeled. By 1906 she had abandoned her efforts. Examples are marked with several ciphers, one resembling a butterfly, another with the letters MCL superimposed each upon the other, and L McL in a linear arrangement. Other items were marked Lonsanti, sometimes in the Oriental manner.

Plaque, profile of lady, ML McLaughlin, #406, oval, 3¼" 425.00
Vase, flowing gr/blk/red over wht, ML McLaughlin, 3" 1,400.00
Vase, pansy cvg, bl on dk brn, sgn MCL, 6x5", NM 3,250.00

Lotus Ware

Isaac Knowles and Issac Harvey operated a pottery in East Liverpool, Ohio, in 1853 where they produced both yellow ware and Rockingham. In 1870 Knowles brought Harvey's interests and took as partners John Taylor and Homer Knowles. Their principal product was ironstone china, but Knowles was confident that American potters could produce as fine a ware as the Europeans. To prove his point, he hired Joshua Poole, an artist from the Belleek Works in Ireland. Poole quickly perfected a Belleek-type china, but fire destroyed this portion of the company. Before it could function again, their hotel china business had grown to the point that it required their full attention in order to meet market demands. By 1891 they were able to try again. They developed a bone china, as fine and thin as before, which they called Lotus. Henry Schmidt from the Meissen factory in Germany decorated the ware, often with lacy filigree applications or hand-formed leaves and flowers to which he added further decoration with liquid slip applied by means of a squeeze bag. Due to high production costs resulting from so much of the fragile ware being damaged in firing and because of changes in tastes and styles of decoration, the Lotus Ware line was dropped in 1896. Some of the early ware was marked 'KT&K China'; later marks have a star and a crescent with 'Lotus Ware' added.

For further study, we recommend *American Belleek* by our advisor, Mary Frank Gaston; she is listed in the Directory under Texas.

Vases, leaves and fishscales on white, 15", $450.00; Etruscan style, with transfer on green with gilt, the foot blue and light green, 15", $1,900.00.

Dish, figural lounging lady w/lg feather fan, gilt, 6" 750.00
Dish, wht scallop shell form, coral branch ft, 8" 150.00
Jar, flowering branch, gilt on wht w/molded flutes, 6¾" 250.00
Jardiniere, branch hdls, undulating rim, gold trim, 7x11" 950.00
Pitcher, wht w/emb leaves, bulbous/squat, 5" 135.00
Potpourri, wht, allover rtcl scrollwork, melon ribbed, 7" 1,200.00
Teapot, lt peach w/gilt spout & hdls, 4½", +sug/cr, ea 4" 200.00
Teapot, wht w/fishnet, 4", +sug/cr, ea 3½" 300.00
Vase, Etruscan style, portrait front/bk, ornate hdls, 15" 1,900.00
Vase, wht w/emb leaves & fishscales, above-rim hdls, 15" 450.00
Vase, yel lily form w/mounded leafy base, gilt, 8" 200.00
Vase, 2 rtcl medallions on yel w/gold branches, fluted, 6" 300.00

Lu Ray Pastels

Lu Ray Pastels dinnerware was introduced in the early 1940s by Taylor, Smith, and Taylor of East Liverpool, Ohio. It was offered in assorted colors of Persian Cream, Sharon Pink, Surf Green, Windsor Blue, and Gray in complete place settings as well as many service pieces. It was a successful line in its day and is once again finding favor with collectors of American dinnerware.

Demitasse set (straight sides): Pot, $150.00; Sugar bowl and creamer, $80.00; Cup and saucer, $25.00.

Bowl, cream soup 24.00
Bowl, fruit; 5½" 4.50
Bowl, mixing; lg 45.00
Bowl, salad; lg 35.00
Bowl, soup; 8" 10.00
Bowl, tab hdl, 6" 10.00
Bowl, vegetable; oval 12.50
Bowl, vegetable; 9" 10.00
Bowl, 36s 25.00

Butter dish, w/lid, ¼-lb 25.00
Casserole, w/lid 60.00
Coffeepot, demi; ovoid; w/lid 95.00
Coffeepot, demi; str sides, w/lid 150.00
Creamer 5.00
Creamer, demi; ovoid 22.00
Creamer, demi; str sides 40.00
Cup & saucer 7.50
Cup & saucer, demi 16.00
Cup & saucer, demi; str sides 25.00
Egg cup 12.00
Egg cup, Chatham Gray, rare color 15.00
Epergne 75.00
Muffin cover, w/8" underplate 80.00
Nut dish 22.50
Pitcher, bulbous w/flat bottom 40.00
Pitcher, ftd 45.00
Pitcher, juice; ovoid 110.00
Pitcher, syrup 40.00
Plate, cake 25.00
Plate, Chatham Gray, rare color, 7" 6.00
Plate, chop; 14" 18.00
Plate, divided 25.00
Plate, grill 15.00
Plate, serving; tab hdl 25.00
Plate, very rare, 8" 15.00
Plate, 10" 10.00
Plate, 6" 2.00
Plate, 7" 5.00
Plate, 9" 6.00
Platter, #1040, 9½" 8.00
Platter, oval, 11½" 10.00
Platter, oval, 12" 9.00
Platter, oval, 13" 10.00
Relish, 4-part 60.00
Sauce boat, fast-stand 17.50
Sauce pitcher 18.00
Saucer, cream soup 12.50
Shakers, pr 8.50
Sugar bowl, demi; ovoid, w/lid 24.00
Sugar bowl, demi; str sides, w/lid 40.00
Sugar bowl, w/lid 9.00
Teapot, w/lid, curved spout 40.00
Teapot, w/lid, flat-top spout 45.00
Tidbit, 2-tier 18.00
Tray, pickle 15.00
Tumbler, juice 22.50
Tumbler, water 37.50
Vase, bud; 2 styles, ea 150.00

Lunch Boxes

Early 20th-century tobacco companies such as Union Leader, Tiger, and Dixie sold their products in square, steel containers with flat, metal carrying handles. These were specifically engineered to be used as lunch boxes when they became empty. (See Advertising, specific companies.) By 1930 oval lunch pails with colorful lithographed decorations on tin were being manufactured to appeal directly to children. These were made by Ohio Art, Decoware, and a few other companies. In 1950 Aladdin Industries produced the first 'real' character lunch box — a Hopalong Cassidy decal-decorated steel container now considered the beginning of the kids' lunch box industry. In 1953 the other big lunch box manufacturer, American Thermos (later King

Seely Thermos Company) brought out its 'blockbuster' Roy Rogers box, the first fully lithographed steel lunch box and matching bottle. Other companies (ADCO Liberty; Landers, Frary & Clark; Ardee Industries; Okay Industries; Universal; Tindco; Cheinco) also produced character pails. Today's collectors often tend to specialize in those boxes dealing with a particular subject. Western, space, TV series, Disney movies, and cartoon characters are the most popular. There are well over five hundred different lunch boxes available to the astute collector. These publications are of interest to lunch box collectors: a bimonthly newsletter, *The Pailentologist's Retort*, P.O. Box 3255, Burbank, CA 91508; *The Illustrated Encyclopedia of Metal Lunch Boxes* by Allen Woodall and Sean Brickell; and A *Pictorial Price Guide to Lunch Boxes and Thermoses* by Larry Aikins. Our advisor for this category is Allan Smith; he is listed in the Directory under Texas.

In the following listings, lunch boxes are metal unless noted vinyl, and values include thermoses only when they are mentioned within the descriptions.

Chow Wagon, Roy Rogers and Dale Evans, EX, $180.00.

A-Team, w/thermos, 1985, M 35.00
Archies, 1960s, VG 45.00
Batman, 1960s, EX 135.00
Battle of the Planets, 1979, M 45.00
Beany & Cecil, tan vinyl, 1963, NM 465.00
Betsy Clark, yel, w/thermos, 1976, M 40.00
Beverly Hillbillies, w/thermos, EX 180.00
Bozo, dome top, w/thermos, 1964, M 485.00
Buccaneer, dome top, w/thermos, 1957, NM 500.00
Campus Queen, w/thermos, 1967, M 95.00
Captain Kangaroo, w/thermos, 1964, M 850.00
Casper, vinyl, NM 650.00
Charlie's Angels, 1970s, VG 25.00
Chuck Wagon, dome top, 1958, NM 375.00
Disco Fever, 1980, M 45.00

Disney School Bus, yellow, 1960, EX, $35.00.

Dynomutt, NM 45.00
Emergency, dome top, NM 110.00
Fall Guy, 1980s, EX 17.50
Firehouse, dome top, labels, w/thermos, 1959, NM 475.00
Flag-o-Rama, w/thermos, 1954, NM 850.00
Flying Nun, w/thermos, 1968, M 310.00
Fox & Hound, 1981, EX 20.00
Gene Autry, w/thermos, 1954, M 800.00
GI Joe, w/thermos, 1982, M 27.50
Globetrotters, dome top, w/thermos, 1959, EX 300.00
Guns of Will Sonnet, w/thermos, 1968, NM 285.00
Gunsmoke, 1972, NM 120.00
Happy Days, 1977, M 50.00
Harlem Globetrotters, w/thermos, 1971, EX 75.00
Hogan's Heroes, dome top, NM 315.00
Hopalong Cassidy, w/thermos, 1954, M 385.00
Junior Miss, w/thermos, 1970, M 110.00
King Kong, w/thermos, 1977, NM 60.00
Knight Rider, 1984, NM 25.00
Linus the Lionhearted, vinyl, w/thermos, 1965, rare, M 750.00
Monkee's, vinyl, w/thermos, EX 275.00
Muppets, w/thermos, 1979, M 15.00
Rambo, w/thermos, 1985, M 15.00
Road Runner, 1970s, EX 45.00
Robin Hood, w/thermos, 1965, M 350.00
Roy Rogers Chow Wagon, dome top, labels, thermos, 1958, M .395.00
Roy Rogers Dbl-R Bar Ranch, bl fr, 1950s, EX 150.00
Secret of Nimh, w/thermos, 1982, M 32.50
Soupy Sales, vinyl, 1965, M 800.00
Speed Buggy, 1974, NM 32.00
Superman, 1954, M 1,200.00
Superman Movie, 1970s, M 40.00
Tammy, vinyl, NM 195.00
Tom Corbett Space Cadet, red, w/thermos, 1952, NM 270.00
Waltons, 1973, M 100.00
Welcome Back Kotter, EX 45.00
Wild Bill Hickok, Aladdin, 1950s, VG 85.00
Woody Woodpecker, w/thermos, 1971, M 230.00
Yosemite Sam, vinyl, w/thermos, 1971, M 525.00

Lutz

From 1869 to 1888, Nicholas Lutz worked for the Boston and Sandwich Glass Company where he produced the threaded and striped art glass that was popular during that era. His works were not marked; since many other glassmakers of the day made similar wares, the term Lutz has come to refer not only to his original works but to any of this type.

Wafer tray, clear with blue and white latticinio, 2½" diameter, $300.00; Bud vase, white latticinio stripes in clear, 4¾", $175.00.

Cup & saucer, bl/opal latticinio swirls 75.00
Decanter, ruby, eng floral, bulbous w/wht neck 500.00
Pen, cobalt body, paperweight end, 5-pc, 6" 295.00
Tumbler, lemonade; etched/clear, pk-threaded bottom half 100.00
Vase, pk/wht spiral latticinio, scalloped rim, 13" 875.00
Whiskey, appl cranberry threading/etched lilies, att, 3⅜" 80.00
Wine, wht/bl/clear swirl, att 135.00

Maddux of California

One of the California-made ceramics now so popular with collectors, Maddux was founded in the late 1930s and during the years that followed produced novelty items, TV lamps, figurines, planters, and tableware accessories. Our advisor for this category is Doris Frizzel; she is listed in the Directory under Illinois.

Planter, rearing horse, 10x7½", $22.00.

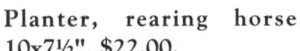

#1019, swan console bowl (set), porc wht, 11½" 20.00
#1047, Contempo bowl (set), wht satin, 16½" 15.00
#2108, cookie jar, Raggedy Andy 200.00
#2113, cookie jar, Humpty Dumpty 200.00
#3017, Seashell bowl, wht, 13" 15.00
#808, TV lamp, shell, Pearltone, 13" 20.00
#839, TV lamp, mallard, flying, natural colors 30.00
#841, TV lamp, head of Christ, 3-D planter 25.00
#859, TV lamp, Toro (bull), walnut, ft on mound, 11½" 15.00
#887, TV lamp, Persian Glory (horse head), 11½" 15.00
#894, TV lamp, Toro (bull), walnut, charging, 11½" 15.00
#896, TV lamp, basset hound, 12½" 35.00
#923, swan, blk matt, 10½", pr 25.00
#925 & #926, horse, rearing or charging, pr 20.00
#969, Early Birds, blk matt, tangerine, 14½", pr 25.00

Magazines

Magazines are collected for their cover prints and for the information pertaining to defunct companies and their products that can be gleaned from the old advertisements. In the listings that follow, items are assumed to be in very good condition unless noted otherwise. See also Movie Memorabilia; Parrish, Maxfield.

Key:
  M — mint condition, in original wrapper
  EX — excellent condition, spine intact, edges of pages clean and
    straight
  VG — very good condition, the average as-found condition

American Cookery, 1943, May - June, G 2.00
Avenger, 1941, May, pulp type, EX 28.00
Child Life, 1935, Dec, VG 4.00
Collier's, 1905, Sept 9, bear & buzzard, FX Lyendecker illus 20.00
Collier's, 1910, Feb 26, royal Fr lady & boy, FX Lyendecker 25.00
Collier's, 1915, Dec 11, street toyseller/kids, JC Lyendecker 25.00
Cosmopolitan, 1893, Columbian Expo cover, EX 35.00
Country Gentleman, 1917, Nov 3, Rockwell's Capt Kidd 55.00
Country Gentleman, 1918, Apr 6, Rockwell's Stageplay 45.00
Country Gentleman, 1921, Apr 23, Rockwell's man & lantern 40.00
Country Gentleman, 1928, Dec, Santa cover by Sundblom, VG 8.00
Esquire, 1936, June, full-pg pinup 25.00
Esquire, 1944, Jan, 12 full-pg Vargas calendar illus 75.00
Etude, 1909, VG 4.00
Fashion Book Pictorial Review, 1916, 15 colored pgs 15.00
Home Needlework, 1903, July, 'how to' text, 6½x9½" 20.00
Ladies' Home Journal, 1902, Aug, EX 12.50
Ladies' Home Journal, 1911, Apr 1, pigeons, Phillips' illus 14.00
Ladies' Home Journal, 1912, July, Parrish's Under the Roses 35.00
Life, 1937, Feb 22, Trotsky exile in Mexico article, EX 4.00
Life, 1938, Aug 22, Astaire & Rogers cover, EX 20.00
Life, 1938, Dec 5, showgirls of yesteryear cover, EX 5.00
Life, 1938, Feb 7, Gary Cooper cover 25.00
Life, 1938, May 23, Errol Flynn cover, EX 30.00
Life, 1939, Dec 11, Betty Grable cover 18.00
Life, 1939, Sept, Benito Mussolini cover, EX 40.00
Life, 1942, Nov, war cover, EX 4.00
Life, 1945, Dec 17, Emperor addresses Japanese diet, EX 3.00
Life, 1945, Oct 8, Tokyo Express to Hiroshima, EX 5.00
Life, 1947, Feb 17, Army in Arctic article, EX 4.00
Life, 1949, Joe DiMaggio cover, EX 40.00
Life, 1950, June 12, Hopalong Cassidy cover, EX 25.00
Life, 1953, May 23, Monroe & Russel cover 29.00
Life, 1957, Nov 18, Seer of Space, Wernher von Braun 10.00
Life, 1957, Oct 21, Russia's Satellite 8.00
Life, 1959, June 15, New US Advances in March to Space 8.00
Life, 1959, Nov, Jackie Gleason cover 5.00
Life, 1959, Sept 21, 7 Brave Women Behind the Astronauts 8.00
Life, 1961, Aug 18, Mantle & Maris cover, EX 50.00
Life, 1962, Apr 13, Burton & Taylor cover, VG 10.00
Life, 1965, Mickey Mantle cover, EX 23.00
Life, 1972, Nov 3, Joe Namath cover, VG 5.00
Literary Digest, 1919, Feb 9, Rockwell's Oh Boy, NM 30.00
Literary Digest, 1920, Aug 14, Rockwell cover 30.00
Literary Digest, 1931, Feb 14, color ads 5.00
Live, 1943, Roy Rogers cover 28.00
Look, 1968, Jan 9, J Lennon on cover, Beatles pull-out 15.00
Musical Observer, 1920, Caruso cover, EX 30.00
Newsweek, 1945, Apr 23, FDR cover, reduced Armed Forces sz ...35.00
People Today, 1955, Anita Ekberg cover, EX 20.00
People Today, 1955, Mansfield cover, pocket sz 25.00
Peterson's Ladies' National, 1886, Jan, VG- 4.00
Playboy, 1954, Aug 175.00
Playboy, 1955, July 75.00
Playboy, 1958, May, Tina Louise article 35.00
Playboy, 1966, Jan, Grace Kelly interview 30.00
Playboy, 1970, Jan, Raquel Welch interview 15.00
Playboy, 1976, Jan, Elton John interview 12.00
Playboy, 1983, Kim Bassinger cover & 8 pgs 35.00
Roaring Twenties, 1955, pictorial history 7.00
Saturday Evening Post, 1909, Dec 4, man w/gifts, JC Lyendecker ...15.00
Saturday Evening Post, 1909, Mar 6, Roosevelt, JC Lyendecker ...10.00
Saturday Evening Post, 1914, Nov 28, boy/lady, JC Lyendecker ...16.00
Saturday Evening Post, 1916, July 1, JC Lyendecker 13.00

Saturday Evening Post, 1921, Mar 26, baby, JC Lyendecker 12.00
Saturday Evening Post, 1926, Jan 23, hobo, JC Lyendecker 15.00
Saturday Evening Post, 1927, Jan 8, Rockwell's tearful boy 45.00
Saturday Evening Post, 1928, Sept 22, Rockwell's Serenader 32.00
Saturday Evening Post, 1930, Apr 12, Rockwell's girl artist 30.00
Saturday Evening Post, 1930, May 24, Rockwell's Gary Cooper ...50.00
Saturday Evening Post, 1930, Nov 22, doctor, JC Lyendecker 16.00
Saturday Evening Post, 1937, Jan 2, new baby, JC Lyendecker 12.00
Saturday Evening Post, 1939, Dec 16, Rockwell's Santa 55.00
Saturday Evening Post, 1949, July 9, NM 18.00
Saturday Evening Post, 1954, Apr 17, Rockwell's choirboy, ...16.00
Saturday Evening Post, 1961, Apr 1, Rockwell's Do Unto Others ..10.00
Saturday Evening Post, 1963, Dec 14, Rockwell's JF Kennedy 9.00
Saturday Evening Post, 1965, Nov 20, Hell's Angels cover 8.00
Sport, 1950, Musial cover, EX 30.00
Sport, 1964, Cassius Clay cover, EX 35.00
Sports Illustrated, 1956, Apr 9, baseball issue, NM 18.00
Sports Illustrated, 1956, Sept 24, football special, NM 10.00
Sports Illustrated, 1957, July 1, yachting flags, NM 6.00
Sports Illustrated, 1958, Sept 29, world series, NM 6.00
Sports Illustrated, 1965, Cassius Clay cover, EX 30.00
Sports Illustrated, 1967, Roberto Clemente cover, EX 25.00
Sports Illustrated, 1969, Dec 1, college basketball, NM 8.00
Sports Illustrated, 1970, Dec 14, football, NM 4.00
Tempo, 1958, Jayne Mansfield cover, EX 25.00
Time, 1931, Charlie Chaplin cover, EX 75.00
Time, 1942, Mussolini cover, EX 25.00
Time, 1952, Lucille Ball cover, EX 30.00
TV Guide, 1953, 1st Fall preview, EX 50.00
Vogue, 1928, Meserole cover, EX 42.00
Wisdom, 1958, Ernest Hemingway cover, EX 35.00
Woman's Day, 1943, July, eagle & flag cover 4.00
Woman's Day, 1956, May, President Eisenhower & family cover ...5.00
Woman's Home Companion, 1911, Greenaway article, EX 30.00
Yank Magazine, 1942, Aug 5, Japanese destroyer sinking cover 4.00
Yank Magazine, 1944, Nov 12, GIs in S France, pinup, EX 4.00

Majolica

Majolica is a type of heavy earthenware, design-molded and decorated in vivid colors with either a lead or tin type of glaze. It reached its height of popularity in the Victorian era; examples from this period are found in only the lead glazes. Nearly every potter of note, both here and abroad, produced large majolica jardinieres, umbrella stands, pitchers with animal themes, leaf shapes, vegetable forms, and nearly any other design from nature that came to mind. Few, however, marked their ware. Among those who did were Minton, Wedgwood, and George Jones in England; Griffin, Smith and Hill (Etruscan) in Phoenixville, Pennsylvania; and Chesapeake Pottery (Avalon and Clifton) in Baltimore.

For further information we recommend *The Collector's Encyclopedia of Majolica* by Mariann Katz-Marks (see Directory, Pennsylvania). Our advisor for this category is Hardy Hudson; he is listed in the Directory under Florida.

Basket, Morning-Glory, oval, twig hdl, Holdcroft, 6½x8½" 565.00
Basket, Wild Rose on turq basketweave, dbl hdl, 8½x9" 500.00
Bowl, centerpc; wicker rim, florals/ribbons, Wedgwood, 12" ..2,500.00
Bowl, Chrysanthemum, oval, scalloped rim, Wedgwood, 13" L ..600.00
Bowl, emb gr leaf on wht, gr rim, 1880s, 2¼x10" 150.00
Bowl, Fan & Prunus, abstract pattern, Wedgwood, 6½" 200.00
Bowl, florals on basketweave, ftd, 1880s, 2½x10" 235.00
Bowl, pk prunus & turq basketweave, 6-sided, 15" L 335.00

Bowl, Pond Lily, gr & brn, ftd, Holdcroft, 8" 250.00
Bowl, shell form on sm shell ft, bl int, Holdcroft, 9" 250.00
Bowl, strawberries/blossoms/leaves on wht, Wedgwood, 8" 200.00
Bowl, Water Lily, center flower hdl, 6-lobed, Minton, 9" 475.00
Butter dish, Bamboo, Etruscan 350.00
Cake stand, Fan, 3 fans on basketweave, low ft, 9" 250.00
Cake stand, Maple, Etruscan, Griffin-Smith-Hill, 9" 295.00
Cheese keeper, heron & lilies in bamboo fr, Wedgwood, 11" ..2,000.00
Compote, Crane & Heron, water lily mold, Am, 7x10" 425.00
Compote, Leaf & Basketweave, Etruscan, 8½x5½" 365.00
Creamer, Corn, Etruscan, rare 225.00
Creamer & sugar bowl, cottage figural, 4", 3", pr 400.00
Cup & saucer, Bamboo, Etruscan 300.00
Cup & saucer, Bamboo & Basketweave, 6" dia 250.00
Cup & saucer, Bamboo & Floral 175.00
Cup & saucer, Pineapple, lav int, 7" 225.00
Cup & saucer, Rose & Rope 275.00
Cuspidor, Floral & Basketweave, 7" 200.00
Cuspidor, Shell & Seaweed, waisted, Etruscan, 7" 1,000.00
Cuspidor, Sunflower, lav int, waisted form, Etruscan, 7" 600.00
Dessert set, Pond Lily, Etruscan, Griffin-Smith-Hill, 8-pc 475.00
Game dish, animals, gr/brn, rabbit finial, Wedgwood, 7" 1,200.00
Garden seat, lg rtcl Os at mid-point, leaves/ferns, 20", EX 2,000.00
Garden seat, lg storks, S Fielding & Co, 20", EX 2,500.00
Humidor, Blk boy w/melon slice on trunk, Austria, 6" L 300.00
Humidor, pipe finial, Germany 110.00
Inkwell, twin birds, head lifts for well, Minton, 9" 900.00
Jardiniere, conch shell w/Chinese creatures, Portuguese, 6½" 220.00
Jardiniere, grotesque heads on cobalt, lav int, 8" 350.00
Match holder, drummer figural, Holdcroft, 3" 325.00
Mug, Raspberry & Floral, 3½", NM 150.00
Mustache cup, Shell & Seaweed, Etruscan, 8" 350.00
Mustache cup, Water Lily, rare 400.00
Mustache cup & saucer, Bamboo & Fern, lav int, Wardle, 7" 400.00
Oyster plate, bl center well amid 5 mottled shells, 9" 425.00
Oyster plate, deep cobalt mottling, Minton, 10" 350.00
Oyster plate, dolphins among 5 striped shells, Wedgwood, 9" 500.00
Oyster plate, wave divided by seaweed, mc on wht, 9¼" 350.00
Oyster plate, 6 bl/pk/blk shells on med bl, 9" 300.00
Oyster plate, 6 sunflower indents, lav center well, 10" 300.00
Pitcher, Bamboo & Basket, 5¾" 100.00
Pitcher, banded fence w/birds, 4¾" 145.00
Pitcher, baseball & soccer players, mc, Etruscan, 7¾" 2,500.00
Pitcher, bird & nest on branch, trunk base, 1880s, 9½" 335.00
Pitcher, Butterfly & Bamboo, lav int, 3" 150.00
Pitcher, coral & shells, Etruscan, Griffin-Smith-Hill, 3½" 225.00
Pitcher, Corn, Etruscan, Griffin-Smith-Hill, 6" 365.00
Pitcher, Dogwood on Bark, taupe branch hdl, oval, 8" 195.00
Pitcher, Edward & Alexandra Commemorative, 5½" 265.00
Pitcher, English Rose on cobalt, gr & yel base, 6" 165.00
Pitcher, fish/marine life/birds, Geo Jones, 1875, 9" 1,500.00
Pitcher, Floral & Anchor 110.00
Pitcher, Floral & Drapery, England, ca 1889-1890, 6" 195.00
Pitcher, florals on cobalt, brn hdl, lav int, 8" 275.00
Pitcher, florals w/yel bands, rectangular top, rpr, 5¾" 85.00
Pitcher, Grapes, branch hdl, Copeland, flake, 7¼" 350.00
Pitcher, honey; bear figural, bl int, spoon hdl, Holdcroft, 9" 500.00
Pitcher, Hummingbird & Fan, gargoyle hdl, English, 5½" 200.00
Pitcher, Ivy on Tree Bark, gr & brn, Brownfield, 8" 150.00
Pitcher, monkey figural, mc w/lav int, 9" 400.00
Pitcher, owl figural, England, 1880, 10½" 45000
Pitcher, raspberries/flowers on basketweave, 6¼" 100.00
Pitcher, roses on dmn patterns, shell spout, 6⅛" 100.00
Pitcher, Sheaves of Wheat on bl-gr, lav int, 6", NM 95.00

Pitcher, shell figural, Fielding, 8" 400.00
Pitcher, Stork in Marsh, eel figural hdl, 9½" 400.00
Planter, Cattail on lav, bl int, w/underdish, Minton, 6" 800.00
Planter, Daisy & Banana Leaf, lav int, Geo Jones, 10" 750.00
Planter, Egyptian figures at 4 corners on cobalt, G Jones, 7" 750.00
Planter, Floral & Fern w/grotesque heads, unmk, 7" 350.00
Planter, Picket Fence & Raspberry, lav int, 8" 400.00
Plate, Basketweave & Wild Rose, Etruscan, 7" dia 125.00
Plate, begonia leaf form, brn & gr, 8½" 85.00
Plate, Blackberry on brn basketweave, unmk, ca 1880, 8½" 140.00
Plate, Bow on basketweave, gr on turq, 6" 95.00
Plate, classical figures, Corn pattern edge, Etruscan, 8" 125.00
Plate, Cosmos, Etruscan, Griffin-Smith-Hill, 11¼" 225.00
Plate, Crane, rtcl rim w/simulated basketweave, Wedgwood, 9" ..275.00
Plate, Fish & Daisy, cobalt ground, Holdcroft, 9" 175.00
Plate, Morning-Glory on med bl, lobed rim, 9" 175.00
Plate, mottled mc splotches w/yel bamboo rim, Etruscan, 8" 175.00
Plate, Pond Lily, undulating rim, 9" 175.00
Plate, Running Stag & Dog, emb florals & picket fence, 8" 150.00
Plate, Water Lily, gr, Minton, 9" 125.00
Platter, Barrel Staves & Floral, dmn shape w/hdls, 10" 165.00
Platter, Begonia Leaf, brn/gr/wht/tan, 13" 175.00
Platter, cherries & butterflies on turq, Germany, 11" 90.00
Platter, dog/doghouse/bowl on cream, 11" dia, EX 150.00
Platter, geometric stripes, daisy hdls, 6-sided, 13" L 150.00
Platter, Grapevine w/cobalt center, 13" 225.00
Platter, rose on basketweave, cobalt rim, branch hdls, 13" 200.00
Platter, shellfish on bl basketweave, Wedgwood, 23" 1,200.00
Platter, swimming seals, seal figural hdls, Wedgwood, 17" 1,200.00
Platter, wht lilacs on turq, str sides/lobed ends, 13" 200.00
Relish, dogwood blossoms on 3 (leaf) lobes, Geo Jones, 12" 600.00
Relish tray, Onion & Pickle on cobalt, Wedgwood, 8" 300.00
Salt cellar, child w/wicker basket figural, Wedgwood, 5" 300.00

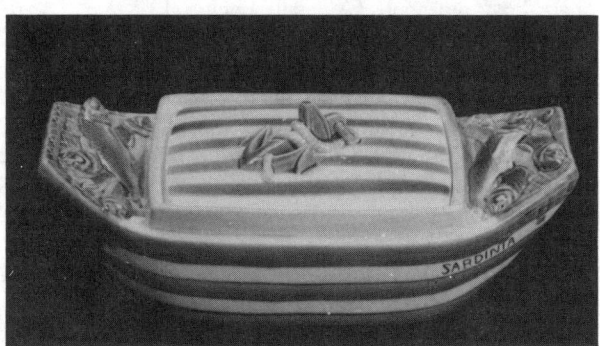

Sardine box, Wedgwood, ca 1882, $1,000.00.

Sardine box, fish finial, plain base, Etruscan, 6" sq 800.00
Sardine box, Pond Lily, fish finial, Holdcroft, 8" 600.00
Sardine box, shell motif, gr/brn/wht, shell finial, 7" W 700.00
Shakers, Coral, Etruscan, 4", pr 525.00
Spoon, Strawberry, Holdcroft, 5" 250.00
Spoon holder, Fan on brn, gr at base, 5" 110.00
Spoon warmer, conch shell form, Minton dtd 1837, 4¾", EX 770.00
Strawberry dish, bird & 2 nests at side, G Jones, 11" 1,500.00
Strawberry dish, blossoms, attached center cup, Jones, 10" 625.00
Strawberry dish, floral, 2 flower-form cups, G Jones, 10" 800.00
Sugar bowl, Fan & Scroll, w/insect, flower form lid, 5½" 300.00
Sugar bowl, Floral, Basketweave & Barrel Stave, 5" 200.00
Sugar shaker, roses on cobalt, basketweave base 165.00

Sweetmeat, sailor boy w/lg shell figural, Minton, 6" 750.00
Syrup, floral frieze, ftd, pewter lid, Wedgwood, 7½" 575.00

Tea set, Pineapple, 10 pieces, $1,700.00.

Tea set, Robin Red Breast, child's, mini, 3-pc 300.00
Teapot, Chinaman figural, Minton, 6" 1,200.00
Teapot, Chinaman on coconut figural, Holdcroft, 7" 700.00
Teapot, ferns/butterflies/beetles/cattails, pewter top, 7" 500.00
Teapot, floral w/basketweave, metal lid, 4½" 250.00
Teapot, monkey figural, Minton, 7" 1,200.00
Teapot, Sunflower & Classical Urn, Samuel Lear, 6" 350.00
Toothpick holder, chick beside open egg figural, 4" 200.00
Tray, bread; Corn, gr/yel/brn on basketweave, 13" 445.00
Tray, bread; Pineapple, yel & brn w/cobalt center, Wardle, 13" . 265.00
Tray, Palm & Grape Leaf, gr/lav/brn, Geo Jones, 8" 285.00
Tumbler, wishbones at rim, circles at base, Etruscan, 4" 225.00
Vase, bird on branch of stump figural, 7" 250.00
Vase, hand holds pineapple, EX details, English, 13" 650.00
Vase, harp figural, lav/brn/wht/gr, 6" 175.00
Vase, iris form, molded base, dbl openwork hdls, unmk, 6" 85.00
Vase, putti/sea horses, dragon head hdls, brass base, 12" 300.00
Vase, putto w/nautilus shell figural, Geo Jones, 6", pr 1,000.00
Vase, ram's head relief, unmk Thomas Shirley, 1850s, 6" 500.00
Wine caddy, Bacchus & grapes, holders ea side, G Jones, 13" . 3,000.00
Wine cooler, Bacchus scene on wht, bl int, Wedgwood, 10" ... 1,200.00

Malachite Glass

Malachite is a type of art glass that exhibits strata-like layerings in shades of green, similar to the mineral in its natural form. Some examples have an acid-etched mark of Moser/Carlsbad, usually on the base. However, it should be noted that in the past fifteen years there have been reproductions from Czechoslovakia with a paper label. Our advisor for this category is Donald Penrose; he is listed in the Directory under Ohio.

Bowl, gold floral/scrolls, ribbed, 4 gold ft, Moser, 11" L 425.00
Box, Oriental lady's portrait 85.00
Dresser set: box, bottle, atomizer, emb roses, Czech 500.00
Vase, molded nudes & grapes, att Moser, 9½" 175.00

Mantel Lustres

Mantel lustres are decorative vases or candle holders made from all types of glass, often highly decorated, and usually hung with one or more rows of prisms. In the listings that follow, values are given for a pair.

Bl opaque, gold decor, prisms, 14" 400.00
Cranberry w/HP floral, scalloped, long prisms 14" 550.00
Cut glass, gilt bronze, Regency style, 10" 750.00
Gr to wht opaque, 8 crystal prisms, appl snake at stem, 11¼" 265.00
Pk bristol w/HP florals & gold, cased, prisms, 12" 350.00
Pk o/l, scroll panels/flowers, w/gilt, long prisms, 14" 450.00
Wht cut to clear w/panels, mc flowers, prisms, 13" 400.00
Wht cut to gr w/mc flowers, prisms, Bohemian, 1800s, 12" 850.00

Pink overlay with enameled flowers and gilt, 14", $450.00.

Maps and Atlases

Maps are highly collectible, not only for historical value but also for their sometimes elaborate artwork, legendary information, or data that since they were printed has been proven erroneous. There are many types of maps including geographical, military, celestial, road, and railroad. The most valuable are those made before the mid-1800s.

Key:
hc — hand colored   p — publisher

Atlases

Compendious Geographical Dictionary, hc, Peacock, 1795, VG .. 165.00
Johnson's New Illus Family...World, Johnson/Ward, 1863, EX ... 550.00
LA, hc, RR lines (some MS shown), Milton Bradley, 1886, 19x26" .. 15.00
Mitchell's School Atlas Ed of 1858, Cowperthwait, VG 175.00
MO, color litho, hc border, St Louis insert, ca 1885, 19x26" 14.00
Modern Atlas on New Plan, Woodbridge, 1824, EX 325.00
Physical Geography, hc, CS Cartee, Boston, 1856, 11x13" 35.00
SC, hc, steamboat routes, Cowperthwait, 1850, 12x15" 35.00
School Atlas to Adams' Geography, 1818, VG 95.00
School Atlas Cummings' Ancient Modern Geography, 1823, EX . 325.00
Woodbridge's School Atlas, 1835, Beach & Beckwith, EX 245.00

Maps

AL, from Dept of Int, Bien, 1979, 27x36", EX 30.00
Am Nova Descriptio Impensis Anae Seile, 2nd ed, 1663, 13x16" .. 400.00
Am Sive Novi Orbis, Nova Descriptio, Ortelius, 14x19", EX . 1,400.00
Antietam, topographical, Act of Congress, 1864, 9x11" 12.50

AZ, Post Office Dept issue, mail routes, 1924, 32x40", EX 18.50
Baltimore, hc, city streets, 1855, 15x17" 18.50
Carte Reduite Des Costes...LA, hc, Bellin, 1764, 22x23", EX 475.00
Cincinnati, hc, EX tissue-type paper, Colton, 1855, 7x12" 15.00
Columbia River, foldouts, RT Lincoln, 1882, 26-pg text 12.50
Ft Smith AR to Rio Grande, pub Jefferson Davis, 1853, 21x48" ..65.00
ID Territory, topographical, Dept of Interior, 1879, 27x36" 35.00
KY, hc, Carey, 1814, 10x18", EX 300.00
KY & TN, hc, flowered borders, Mitchell, 1878, 12½x15" 18.50
LA, color litho, river/towns/RRs/etc, Bien, 1879, 27x36" 35.00
LA, hc, roads & important towns, Colton, 1855, 15x17" 25.00
LA & MS, hc, Tanner, 1825, 22x27", EX 450.00
Mexico, Regia et..., hc, Braun-Hogenberg, 1590, 14x21" 325.00
MO River system, Beckwith, pub J Davis, 1955, 24x32" 22.50
MO Territory Formerly LA, hc, Carey, 1814, 12x14" 350.00
MS, hc, fancy border, Colton, 1855, 15x17", EX 25.00
MS, shows 12 RRs/depots/etc, dtd 1892, 20x27" 15.00
MS River, from OH river to New Orleans, 1877, 9x11" 10.00
NB, hc, reservations/forts mkd, 1844, 18x24", EX 20.00
New Map of NA Dedicated to...Duke, Wells, 1700, 15x20" 350.00
NM Territory, Indian camps on CO river, 1860s, 24x33" 24.00
NY, complete state w/Niagara Falls insets, Colton, 1855, 15x17" .20.00
NY Counties, hydrographic, N Currier, ca 1850, 8x21" 35.00
Philadelphia, hc, fancy borders, Mitchell, 1873, 15x22" 18.50
Rocky Mtns, Lewis & Clark Pass, J Davis, 1853, 26x36" 45.00
San Francisco to Los Angeles, topographical, 1854, 30x36" 37.50
St Louis MO, hc on tissue-type paper, Colton, 1855, 7x12", M 12.50
TX, Brownsville inset, 46 RR lines shown, 1895, 20x27" 20.00
TX, hc, Indian territories color insert, Mitchell, 1852, 9x11" 22.50
Typus Oribs Terrarum, hc, Ortelius, 1587, rpr, 13x19", G 1,200.00
United States, Pony Express routes, hc, Lloyd, 1870s, 17x28" 35.00
Vicksburg, battle defenses, topographical, 1864, 9x11" 15.00

Marblehead

What began as therapy for patients in a sanitarium in Marblehead, Massachusetts, has become recognized as an important part of the Arts and Crafts movement in America. Results of the early experiments under the guidance of Arthur E. Baggs in 1904 met with such success that by 1908 the pottery had been converted to a solely commercial venture. Simple vase shapes were often incised with stylized animal and floral motifs or sailing ships. Some were decorated in low relief; many were plain. Simple matt glazes in soft yellow, gray, wisteria, rose, tobacco brown, and their most popular, Marblehead blue, were used alone or in combination. The Marblehead logo is distinctive — a boat with full sail and the letters 'M' and 'P.' The pottery closed in 1936.

Bowl, bl, incurvate, initialed 2½x6" 150.00
Bowl, dk bl, str sides, lid w/lg knob, 4x7" 750.00
Bowl, gray, 7" 95.00
Bowl vase, bl, tapered cylinder, flared rim, 5x7" 300.00
Bowl vase, whiplash cvg, gr on bl speckle, A Tutt, 3½x4½" 800.00
Candlestick, pk semigloss, curled hdls, 3" 50.00
Candlesticks, bl, 3", pr 265.00
Hanging basket, dk bl, lt bl int, rim hdls, pointed bottom 150.00
Hanging basket, gr gloss, ribbed w/crimped top, label, 6x6" 100.00
Mug, bl w/blk rim band, 4" 240.00
Plaque, lg trees, 4-color, earth tones, 9¾", in fr 2,400.00
Plaque, trees, brns on gr, A Dow's style, 1907, fr, 6" sq 2,100.00
Tile, flower basket, 5-color, mk, fr, 6" 475.00
Tile, rooster, brn/cream on brn- & bl-flecked gray, 5" dia 100.00
Tile, sailing ship, bl & wht 375.00
Tile, sailing ship, 3-color, 18 sails, mk & label, fr, 6" 395.00

Tile, stalks of flowers, 5-color, 6", in oak fr 500.00
Vase, band of flying geese, gray tones, artist sgn, 9x7" 4,000.00
Vase, berry/leaf band near top, gr/red on bl, ovoid, 5½" 750.00

Vase, berried pods, 4-color on yellow, 5", NM, $1,200.00; Pitcher, incised and painted stylized trees, brown on light green, signed Baggs, 8x7", $1,900.00.

Vase, bl, bulbous, 5" 325.00
Vase, bl, ovoid w/flared rim, 5¼" 425.00
Vase, bl, ruffled fan form, paper label, 6x7" 475.00
Vase, bl, slightly concave cylinder, 6" 375.00
Vase, bl w/lt bl int, flared, 3½" 300.00
Vase, bud; gray, 7" 275.00
Vase, cvd leaves, mustard, turq int, fluted, ribbed, 6" 700.00
Vase, floral, 5-color, 6" 2,300.00
Vase, gr, 3¾" 225.00
Vase, gr/brn, waisted cylinder, 7" 350.00
Vase, gr/pk semigloss, ovoid, 4" 180.00
Vase, gr/yel semigloss, 5" 250.00
Vase, line/sq cvg, gr on bl speckle, ship mk, cylinder, 6" 850.00
Vase, long-stem flowers, bl/brn on gray, rstr, 10x5" 1,800.00
Vase, pk, 2" 145.00
Vase, purple, 5" 300.00
Vase, row of irises, bl on gray speckle, H Tutt, squat, 3½" 1,000.00
Vase, stylized trees, 3-color, ovoid, H Tutt, 7" 1,100.00
Vase, 5 grapevine medallions, 3-color, Al Hennessey, 3½x4" .1,100.00
Vase, 5 repeating cvd trees on beige, tumbler form, 4" 495.00

Marbles

Marbles have been popular with children since the mid-1800s. They've been made in many types from a variety of materials. Among some of the first glass items to be produced, the earliest marbles were made from a solid glass rod broken into sections of the proper length which were placed in a tray of sand and charcoal and returned to the fire. As they were reheated, the trays were constantly agitated until the marbles were completely round. Other marbles were made of china, pottery, steel, and natural stones.

Below is a listing of the various types, along with a brief description of each. When size is not otherwise indicated, prices are listed for mint condition marbles of average size, ½" to 1".

Agates: stone marbles of many different colors — bands of color alternating with white usually encircle the marble; most are translucent.

Ballot Box: handmade (with pontils), opaque white or black, used in lodge elections.

Bloodstone: green chalcedony with red spots, a type of quartz.

China: with or without glaze, in a variety of hand-painted designs — parallel bands or bull's-eye designs most common.

Clambroth: opaque glass with outer evenly spaced swirls of one or alternating colors.

Clay: one of the most common older types; some are painted while others are not.

Comic Strip: a series of twelve machine-made marbles with faces of comic strip characters, Peltier Glass Factory, Illinois.

Crockery: sometimes referred to as Benningtons; most are either blue or brown, although some are speckled. The clay is shaped into a sphere, then coated with glaze and fired.

End of the Day: single-pontil glass marbles — the colored part often appears as a multicolored blob or mushroom cloud.

Goldstone: clear glass completely filled with copper flakes that have turned gold-colored from the heat of the manufacturing process.

Indian Swirls: usually black glass with a colored swirl appearing on the outside next to the surface, often irregular.

Latticinio Core Swirls: double-pontil marble with an inner area with net-like effects of swirls coming up around the center.

Lutz Type: glass with colored or clear bands alternating with bands which contain copper flecks.

Micas: clear or colored glass with mica flecks which reflect as silver dots when marble is turned. Red is rare.

Onionskin: spiral type which are solidly colored instead of having individual ribbons or threads, multicolored.

Peppermint Swirls: made of white opaque glass with alternating blue and red outer swirls.

Ribbon Core Swirls: double-pontil marble — center shaped like a ribbon with swirls that come up around the middle.

Rose Quartz: stone marble, usually pink in color, often with fractures inside and on outer surface.

Solid Core Swirls: double-pontil marble — middle is solid with swirls coming up around the core.

Steelies: hollow steel spheres marked with a cross where the steel was bent together to form the ball.

Sulfides: generally made of clear glass with figures inside. Rarer types have colored figures or colored glass.

Tiger Eye: stone marble of golden quartz with inclusions of asbestos, dark brown with gold highlights.

Vaseline: machine-made of yellowish-green glass with small bubbles.

For a more thorough study of the subject, we recommend *Antique and Collectible Marbles, Third Edition*, an identification and value guide by Everett Grist; his address is in the Directory under Illinois.

Agate, contemporary, carnelian, 1¾"	175.00
Banded Opaque, gr & wht, 2"	875.00
Banded Opaque, red & wht, 1¾"	775.00
Banded Opaque, red & wht, ¾"	75.00
Banded Transparent Swirl, bl, ¾"	50.00
Banded Transparent Swirl, lt gr, 1¾"	400.00
Bennington, bl, 1¾"	20.00
Bennington, bl, ¾"	1.00
Bennington, brn, 1¾"	15.00
Bennington, fancy, 1¾"	35.00
Bennington, fancy, ¾"	5.00
China, decorated, glazed, apple, 1¾"	450.00
China, decorated, glazed, rose, 1¾"	800.00
China, decorated, glazed, wht w/geometrics, 1¾"	45.00
China, decorated, unglazed, geometrics & flowers, ¾"	350.00
Clambroth, opaque, bl & wht, 1¾"	1,600.00
Clambroth, opaque, bl & wht, ¾"	150.00
Clambroth Swirl, red/wht, Germany, 1900, ⅞"	275.00
Clear Swirl Lutz-type, clear w/wht & gold swirls, 1¾"	750.00
Clear Swirl Lutz-type, clear w/wht & gold swirls, ¾"	100.00

Cloud, w/mica, red & wht, 1¼"	450.00
Comic, Cotes Bakery, advertising	250.00
Comic, Kayo, rare	150.00
Comic, Little Orphan Annie	80.00
Comic, Moon Mullins	100.00
Comic, set of 12	1,250.00
Comic, Skeezix	80.00
Cork Screw, machine-made	3.00
End of Day, bl & wht, 1¾"	400.00
Goldstone, ¾"	35.00
Indian Swirl, 1¾"	1,500.00
Indian Swirl Lutz-type, gold flakes, ¾"	400.00
Line Crockery, clay, 1¾"	45.00
Mica, bl, ¾"	25.00
Mica, gr, 1¾"	400.00
Onionskin, w/mica, 1¾"	800.00
Onionskin, w/mica, ¾"	85.00
Onionskin, 16-lobe, unusual, 1¾"	800.00
Onionskin, ¾"	50.00
Onionskin, 4-lobe, 1¼"	700.00

Onionskins with mica, ¾", $75.00; 1¾", $500.00.

Opaque Swirl, gr, ¾"	35.00
Opaque Swirl Lutz-type, bl, yel, gr, or vaseline, ¾"	325.00
Peppermint Swirl, opaque, red, wht, & bl, 1¾"	750.00
Peppermint Swirl, opaque, red, wht, & bl, ¾"	90.00
Pottery, 1¾"	35.00
Ribbon Core Lutz-type, red, 1¾"	1,200.00
Slag, machine-made, sm	1.00
Slag, machine-made, 1½"	85.00
Solid Opaque, gr, 1¾"	600.00
Solid Opaque, ¾"	75.00
Sulfide, American bison, 1¾"	200.00
Sulfide, angel w/wreath or w/short wings, 1¾", ea	400.00
Sulfide, baby in basket, 1¾"	400.00
Sulfide, bear, standing, 1¾"	200.00
Sulfide, bear, 1¾"	125.00
Sulfide, bird, 1¾"	150.00
Sulfide, boar, 1⅞", VG	160.00
Sulfide, cat, 1¾"	125.00
Sulfide, child, crawling, 1¾"	600.00
Sulfide, child & dog, 1¾"	700.00
Sulfide, child in long dress, 1¾"	375.00
Sulfide, child sitting, 1¾"	375.00
Sulfide, child w/hammer, 1¾"	600.00
Sulfide, clown in peaked cap, 1¾"	450.00
Sulfide, dog, begging, 1¾"	125.00
Sulfide, dog, recumbent, 1⅝", EX	170.00
Sulfide, dog, sitting, 1½", EX	150.00
Sulfide, dog, 1¾"	125.00
Sulfide, dog w/open mouth, 1¾"	175.00
Sulfide, elephant, 1¾"	200.00

Sulfide, fish, 1¾", EX 160.00
Sulfide, goat, 1¾" 150.00
Sulfide, horse, 1¾" 150.00
Sulfide, lion, 1¾" 200.00
Sulfide, Little Boy Blue, 1¾" 500.00
Sulfide, numeral 7, 1¾" 375.00
Sulfide, papoose, 1¾" 500.00
Sulfide, pig, 1¾" 125.00
Sulfide, President Garfield, 1¾" 700.00
Sulfide, razor-bk hog, 1½", VG 130.00
Sulfide, rooster, 1¾" 150.00
Sulfide, Santa Claus, 1¾" 500.00
Sulfide, sheep, dk amber, 1¾" 1,800.00
Sulfide, sheep, 1¾" 125.00
Sulfide, squirrel, standing, 1¾", EX 170.00

Marine Collectibles

See also Steamship Collectibles; Telescopes; Scrimshaw; Tools.

Quadrant, ebony and brass, incised holly
wood scale, ivory nameplate, no case,
$650.00.

Awl, sailmaker's, w/whalebone hdl, 4" 40.00
Barometer, Chas C Hutchinson Boston, aneroid, brass, 5" dia ...150.00
Barometer, US Navy BuShips, phenolic, 6½" dia 80.00
Bell, brass, 7x7"+bracket, EX 90.00
Bell, CI, 6½x7¾"+bracket 42.50
Bell, City of Ripon, brass w/ropework pull, 12" dia 200.00
Binnacle, brass dome top w/compass & burner, 9½" 210.00
Binnacle, brass w/6 glass panels, 14", EX 300.00
Binnacle, copper & teakwood, early, EX 1,200.00
Binnacle, wood base, 1890s, EX 2,400.00
Binnacle, wooden w/Ritchie Boston liquid compass, 10x10x10" ..170.00
Binoculars, ivory covered, 3½" W, EX in leather case 65.00
Binoculars, Superior Glasses Day or Night, brass/leather, EX 75.00
Cannon, ship's, 48" Lyle gun, EX 1,900.00
Clinometer, US Navy, Bakelite, 1942, 7¼x12" 60.00
Diver's helmet, brass, EX 1,800.00
Fid, ebony, cvd w/clenched fist termination, 5½", EX 60.00
Fid, whalebone, 11" 80.00
Flare gun, Mark IV, Parachute & Signal Flares, G 95.00

Gauge, pressure; Sydney Smith & Sons...England, 11" dia, EX 50.00
Harpoon, wrought iron, sgn twice, ca 1850 ....365.00
Horn, fog; hand pumped, brass pnt, 24", EX 150.00
Horn, wooden, hand cranked, 14½x22", EX 130.00
Knife, bone hdl w/brass fittings, 13½" 75.00
Lamp, binnacle; brass, missing burner, 8", EX 25.00
Lamp, running; brass, no burner, 13", EX 275.00
Lamp, Viking, copper w/clear ribbed lens, 23", EX 125.00
Lantern, brass, Kilborn Sauer Co Fairfield Conn USA, 10" 120.00
Lantern, Dietz US Brass Tubular, brass, 11"+hdl, EX 30.00
Lantern, starboard; Griffith...Birmingham, brass & copper, 18" 95.00
Light, anchor; brass & copper, electrified, 20" 100.00
Light, brass & copper, w/red lens, 11", VG 100.00
Light, Henschel Corp Amesbury MA, brass w/wood float, 17" L 55.00
Light, porthole, brass, 15" dia 45.00
Log, Lionel Corp Taffrail, w/idler & spinner, 3-pc set 80.00
Octant, Bywater Dawson & Co Liverpool, brass & ivory, EX 150.00
Octant, ebony w/ivory scales, brass fittings, E&GW Blunt NY ..475.00
Octant, eng brass swing arm, ebony w/ivory scales, 1700s, 18" ...600.00
Octant, S Braley, cased ebony w/ivory & brass, 18", VG 800.00
Rattle, battle; wooden w/dbl reed & weighted end, 8", EX 45.00
Scope, USN BuShips Telescopic Alidade, working, 13¼" 50.00
Sextant, Northern Hull, brass w/silver scales, EX in case 450.00
Sundial, solid brass w/paper compass rose, 2" dia, VG 120.00
Telegraph, ship's, brass, Chadburn, EX 1,200.00
Telephone, Loudaphone-Clifford Sutton & Snell..., 10x14" 100.00
Timer, sand type, ca 1700s, 7¾" 175.00
Trumpet, Walton Bros NY, solid brass, 10", EX 160.00
Vent, brass w/3 2" slats, 8x12", EX 25.00
Wheel, mahog w/brass hub & banding, 48", EX 250.00
Wheel, solid bronze w/6 wooden hdls, 24" dia, EX 150.00
Wheel, wooden w/brass hub & wood inlays at rim, 36", EX 300.00
Wheel, wooden w/iron hub & brass band, 48" dia, EX 275.00
Wheel, wooden w/nickel & brass hub, 18", EX 75.00

Martin Bros.

The Martin Bros. were studio potters who worked from 1873 until
1914, first at Fulham and later at London and Southall. There were
four brothers, each of whom excelled in their particular area. Robert,
known as Wallace, was an experienced stonecarver. He modeled a
series of grotesque bird and animal figural caricatures. Walter was the
potter, responsible for throwing the larger vases on the wheel, firing the
kiln, and mixing the clay. Edwin, an artist of stature, preferred more
naturalistic forms of decoration. His work was often incised or had
relief designs of seaweed, florals, fish, and birds. The fourth brother,
Charles, was their business manager. Their work was incised with their
names, place of production, and letters and numbers indicating month
and year.

Bird, curving beak, stern gaze, 8½" 3,200.00
Bird jar, eyes closed/smiling, brn/tan/dk bl, 1892, 11", NM 6,250.00
Clock case, Gothic style w/bizarre creature over dial, 11" 4,400.00
Dead parakeet, unglazed bsk, Sic Transit... on base, 12" 3,300.00
Jug, comic birds/grasses cvd on brn-glaze stoneware, 9" 770.00
Jug, smiling face ea side, brn w/wht & brn slips, 7", EX 1,100.00
Jug, smiling face ea side, cream/brn, 1902, 6½ 3,850.00
Jug, smiling face ea side, upright spout on brn, 1892, 8" 1,200.00
Jug, smiling face ea side on wht w/bl & gr, 1890, 8½" 5,500.00
Lovebirds, he w/arm about mate, mc on salt glaze, 8¾" 7,700.00
Spoon warmer, creature w/open mouth, lg ears/ft, 5½" 4,650.00
Spoon warmer, cylinder modeled as cockerel head, comb as hdl ...800.00
Vase, comic fish, emb/cvd on stoneware, mc on bl, 8" 550.00

Vase, coral-like branches in sgraffito on brn, hdls, 9x4" 1,100.00
Vase, emb & cvd allover swirls, blk/brn, 10x6½" 1,100.00
Vase, sea creatures, cvd/pnt, bls & brns on shaded brn, 4" 800.00
Vase, tiger lilies/dragonfies cvg, tan/cream, 1903, 9½" 550.00
Vase, 1 side w/smiling moon face, bkground of scallops, 8" 2,200.00
Wally Bird, owl-like, feathers suggest attire, 1901, 12" 6,600.00

Mary Gregory

Mary Gregory glass, for reasons that remain obscure, is the name-sake of a Boston and Sandwich Glass Company employee who worked for the company for only two years in the mid-1800s. Although no evidence actually exists to indicate that glass of this type was even produced there, the fine colored or crystal ware decorated with figures of children in white enamel is commonly referred to as Mary Gregory. The glass, in fact, originated in Europe and was imported into this country where it was copied by several eastern glasshouses. It was popular from the mid-1800s until the turn of the century. It is generally accepted that examples with all-white figures were made in the U.S.A., while gold-trimmed items and those with children having tinted faces or a small amount of color on their clothing are European. Though amethyst is rare, examples in cranberry command the higher prices. Blue ranks next; and green, amber, and clear items are worth the least. Watch for new glass decorated with screen-printed children and a minimum of hand painting. The screen effect is easily detected with a magnifying glass.

Atomizer, cranberry, boy & girl, complete, 5x2¼" 235.00
Bottle, scent; bl opaque, girl in foliage w/gold, 5¼" 175.00
Bottle, scent; sapphire bl, girl in garden, 9½" 355.00
Box, amber, girl, ormolu ft, hinged lid, 4½x4" 365.00
Box, blk, lady in long dress, pk accents, 5¾" dia 275.00
Box, lime gr, boy w/fishing pole on tree limb, hinged, 3x5" 245.00
Box, sapphire bl, girl in garden, 5½x4½" 300.00
Cruet, amber, boy, optic pattern, amber bubble stopper, 9¼" 250.00
Cruet, cranberry, girl w/balloon by fence, 7½x3⅜" 350.00
Cup, bl, girl w/butterfly, clear hdl, 3¼" 75.00
Cup, cranberry, girl, 3½" 90.00
Lamp, table; blk, girl riding butterfly, metal base, 31" 495.00
Liqueur set, amber, girl & boy, 8⅝" cruet+4 mugs on tray 550.00
Mug, amber, boy & girl, bbl shape, 4", facing pr 165.00
Pitcher, med gr, sailor boy w/anchor, faint ribs, 6⅜" 165.00
Pitcher, olive-amber, girl & foliage, optic, amber hdl, 11" 350.00
Pitcher, tankard; sapphire bl, boy, Optic, 3¾x2⅛" 195.00
Plate, blk amethyst, boy w/rake & dog, 8½" 195.00
Tray, dresser; lime gr, boy & girl, 10½x7⅞" 245.00
Tray, lime gr, boy, emb border, oval, 10½x7⅜" 195.00
Tumbler, amber, boy, Optic, 3¾x2¾" 45.00
Tumbler, gr, girl hanging up wash, 4x2⅞" 45.00
Tumbler, sapphire bl, girl, bbl shape, 4⅛x2½" 55.00
Vase, amber, boy, cut scalloped top, snail hdls, 7½" 165.00
Vase, amber, girl in forest, floral band at shoulder, 6" 215.00
Vase, amber, girl w/balloon, cupped 6-peak rim, ftd, 3¾" 225.00
Vase, amber, girl w/balloon, Optic, 10¼x3⅞" 225.00
Vase, amethyst, girl ties bonnet/boy at mirror, ftd, 16x5" 995.00
Vase, apple gr opaque, boy w/flowers, ruffled, 11x4½" 225.00
Vase, bl-gray, girl feeding birds, sq shape, 7½x2½" 195.00
Vase, cobalt, lady/fence, petaled cup top, ftd, 13½", pr 575.00
Vase, cranberry, boy in country scene, Invt T'print, 10½" 395.00
Vase, cranberry, girl w/hat, clear ped ft, 4x2" 145.00
Vase, emerald gr, girl w/bell, appl shell trim, 11½x5" 225.00
Vase, gr, lily of the valley & daisies, 7½", pr 145.00
Vase, lime gr, boy & girl, shell trim, 8½", pr 325.00

Vases, green with gold trim, facing pair, 4½", $325.00.

Vase, sapphire bl, boy, bulbous, 3¾x2⅜" 100.00
Vase, sapphire bl, boy & girl, 5⅞", facing pr 325.00

Mason's Ironstone

In 1813 Charles J. Mason was granted a patent for a process said to 'improve the quality of English porcelain.' The new type of ware was in fact ironstone which Mason decorated with colorful florals and scenics, some of which reflected the Oriental taste. Although his business failed for a short time in the late 1840s, Mason re-established himself and continued to produce dinnerware, tea services, and ornamental pieces until about 1852 at which time the pottery was sold to Francis Morley. Ten years later, Geo. L. and Taylor Ashworth became owners. Both Morley and the Ashworths not only used Mason's molds and patterns but often his mark as well. Because the quality and the workmanship of the later wares do not compare with Mason's earlier product, collectors should take care to distinguish one from the other. Consult a good book on marks to be sure. Our advisor for this category is Susan Hirshman; she is listed in the Directory under Oregon.

Coffeepot, Fruits 80.00
Cream soup & saucer, Vista 25.00
Creamer, Vista, lg 28.00
Egg cup, Vista, bl 12.00
Gravy boat, Fruits 35.00
Gravy boat, Vista, bl, w/underliner 65.00
Jug, milk; Watteau, 5½" 35.00
Pitcher, Fruits, milk sz 40.00
Pitcher, Gaudy Welsh style w/snake hdl, 5⅜" 225.00
Platter, Fruits, 15" 60.00
Teapot, Fruits 75.00
Tray, Vista, bl, 12½x6½" 45.00
Tureen, Vista, w/underliner & ladle 395.00

Massier

Clement Massier was a French artist-potter who in 1881 established a workshop at Golfe Juan, France, where he experimented with metallic lustre glazes. (One of his pupils was Jacques Sicardo, who brought the knowledge he had gained through his association with Massier to the Weller Pottery Company in Zanesville, Ohio.) The lustre lines developed by Massier incorporated nature themes with allover decorations of foliage or flowers on shapes modeled in the Art Nouveau style. The ware was usually incised with the Massier name, his initials, or the location of the pottery. Massier died in 1917.

Pitcher, mask under spout, figural maid handle, iridescent maroon with foliate designs overall, signed Delphine, Massier, Vallaruis, AM, 10", EX, $1,100.00.

Ewer, nude hdl, foliage on purple lustre, 24" 3,000.00
Jardiniere, emb nude, undulating waves at rim, irid, 9x8" 4,000.00
Plate, scenic, irid, sgn R, 14" 825.00
Vase, floral, maroon on gray mottled irid, 5¾" 225.00
Vase, irid, gold seaweed/5 gr carp, unusual form, rstr, 15" 1,300.00

Match Holders

Before the invention of the safety match in 1855, matches were kept in matchboxes and carried in pocket-size match safes, because they ignited so easily. John Walker, an English chemist, invented the match more than one hundred years ago, quite by accident. Walker was working with a mixture of potash and antimony, hoping to make a combustible that could be used to fire guns. The mixture adhered to the end of the wooden stick he had used for stirring. As he tried to remove it by scraping the stick on the stone floor, it burst into flames. The invention of the match was only a step away! From that time to the present, match holders have been made in amusing figural forms as well as simple utilitarian styles and in a wide range of materials. Both table-top and wall-hanging models were made — all designed to keep matches conveniently at hand. Our advisor for this category is Ron Damaska; he is listed in the Directory under Pennsylvania. See also Advertising.

Brass, man swinging on fence, desk type, lg 250.00
Brass, work-type sled carries 2 sap buckets 150.00
Bsk, boy w/butterfly net 45.00
Bsk, monkey in bow tie, hat at ft, striker on head, Germany 150.00
China, nude holding robe away from body 125.00
China, pug dog w/pack on bk 95.00
China, saucer type, box holder, Mayer 25.00
CI, Bacchus head, open pocket w/grapes & leaves, wall mt 85.00
CI, high-top shoe on base 45.00
CI, urn form w/hdls on sq saucer base, 3" 65.00
CI, 2-compartment, rtcl bkplate, 7" 65.00
Glass, hand holding match container, amber 75.00
Milk glass, Indian 68.00
Parian, 2 owls on fallen tree, English, 8" 175.00
Pressed wood, Scottie figural front, wall-hanging 25.00
Redware, acorns/leaves around pocket in wht/gr, 7" dia 150.00
Satsuma, dog beside basket on tray 85.00

Match Safes

Match safes, aptly-named cases used to carry matches in the days before cigarette lighters, were used during the last half of the 19th cen-tury until about 1920. Some incorporated added features (hidden compartments, cigar cutters, etc.), some were figural, and others were used by retail companies as advertising giveaways. They were made from every type of material, but silverplated styles abound. Our advisor for this category is Ron Damaska; he is listed in the Directory under Pennsylvania. See also Advertising.

Bakelite, rider emb on blk horseshoe figural, 1½x1⅞" 95.00
Brass, pig figural, 1x2" 145.00
Celluloid, domino figural, 1⅛x1⅞" 95.00
CI, advertising, DM&Co New Haven, self-closing, ca 1864 ....125.00
Foiled brass, fine emb vines, NM 25.00
German silver, modeled as an oval pinwheel 35.00
Gutta percha, Arm & Hammer logo, bk: plain, M 40.00
Gutta percha, book shape, Fr, EX 75.00
Gutta percha, simple, M 30.00
Nickel/brass w/celluloid wraparound, Exide Batteries, M 35.00
NP brass, jockey on horse emb on horseshoe shape, 1¾x2" 145.00
NP metal, pocket watch figural, 2½x2" 195.00

Pan American, flags and eagle on leather over metal, 1901, 3", $35.00.

Silveroin, Nouveau whiplashes/flowers, shaped 60.00
SP, Anheuser-Busch 100.00
SP, brite-cut sprig on plain rnd-top rectangle case 35.00
SP, Nouveau floral emb, EX 65.00
SP, scrolls & fleur-de-lis emb over digonal lines, oval 40.00
Sterling, Grecian lady & flowers emb 85.00
Sterling, lions' heads & scrolls emb 90.00
Sterling, monogram in rnd reserve on stippling, London mk 70.00
Sterling, Nouveau roses emb 70.00
Sterling, plain, w/monogram, 2½" 75.00
Sterling, repousse, Kirk, 1⅝x½" 85.00
Sterling, scrolls emb ea side wide band w/brite-cut florals 75.00
Sterling, scrolls on sq w/rnded corners, Birmingham, 1911 ....75.00
Sterling, sea nymph emb 85.00
Sterling, shells emb, mk Whiting Mfg Co 65.00
Tin, Sunny Brook Whiskey, bk: plain, M 27.50
Wht metal, emb Nouveau foliage w/sq center scene 65.00

McCoy

The third generation McCoy potter in the Roseville, Ohio, area was Nelson, who with the aid of his father, J.W., established the Nelson McCoy Sanitary Stoneware Company in 1910. They manufactured churns, jars, jugs, poultry fountains, and foot warmers. By 1925 they had expanded their wares to include majolica jardinieres and pedestals, umbrella stands and cuspidors, and an embossed line of vases and small jardinieres in a blended brown and green matt glaze. From the late twenties through the mid-forties, a utilitarian stoneware was produced, some of which was glazed in the soft blue and white so popular with collectors today. They also used a dark brown mahogany color and a medium to dark green, both in a high gloss. In 1933, the firm became known as the Nelson McCoy Pottery Company. They expanded their facilities in 1940 and began to make the novelty artware, cookie jars, and dinnerware that today are synonomous with 'McCoy.' More than two hundred cookie jars of every theme and description were produced.

Stimulated by the high prices commanded by desirable cookie jars, a broad spectrum of 'new' cookie jars are flooding the marketplace in three categories: 1) Manufacturers have expanded their lines with exciting new designs to attract the collector market. 2) Limited editions and artist-designed jars have proliferated. 3) Reproductions, signed and unsigned, have pervaded the market, creating uncertainty among new collectors and inexperienced dealers.

More than a dozen different marks have been used by the company; nearly all incorporate the name 'McCoy,' although some of the older items were marked 'NM USA.' For further information consult *The Collector's Encyclopedia of McCoy Pottery* by Sharon and Bob Huxford, available at your local bookstore or public library.

Alert! It should be noted that the original Nelson McCoy Pottery has closed its doors. Now an entrepreneur has emerged and has adopted the McCoy Pottery name and mark. This company is reproducing old McCoy designs as well as some classic designs of other defunct American potteries. Their wares are signed 'McCoy' with a mark which very closely approximates the old McCoy mark.

Our McCoy cookie jar advisor is Judy Posner; she is listed in the Directory under Pennsylvania.

Cookie Jars

Animal Crackers 95.00
Apollo Age, minimum value 500.00
Apple, 1950-64 ....50.00
Apple on Basketweave 45.00
Astronauts 400.00
Bananas 85.00
Barnum's Animals 325.00
Baseball Boy 175.00
Bear, cookie in vest, no 'Cookies' 55.00
Betsy Baker 200.00
Black Kettle, w/immovable bail, HP flowers 25.00
Black Vase, w/flowers on lid 165.00
Bobby Baker 65.00
Bugs Bunny, cylinder 185.00
Caboose 165.00
Cat on Coal Scuttle 150.00
Chairman of the Board, minimum value 400.00
Chef 125.00
Chiffoniere, Early American Chest 75.00
Chinese Lantern 55.00
Chipmunk 95.00
Christmas Tree, minimum value 550.00
Circus Horse 175.00
Clown Bust 85.00
Clown in Barrel 120.00
Clyde Dog 150.00
Coalby Cat 350.00
Coffee Grinder 35.00
Coffee Mug 30.00
Colonial Fireplace 85.00
Cookie Barrel 25.00
Cookie Boy 150.00
Cookie Cabin 95.00

Cookie Jug, dbl loop 30.00
Cookie Jug, single loop, 2-tone gr rope 22.00
Cookie Jug, w/cork stopper, brn & wht 22.00
Cookie Log 35.00
Cookie Safe 65.00
Cookstove 40.00
Corn 120.00
Covered Wagon 90.00
Cylinder, w/red flowers 25.00
Dalmations in Rocking Chair 325.00
Dog on Basketweave 50.00
Drum 60.00
Duck on Basketweave 50.00
Dutch Boy 45.00
Dutch Girl, boy on reverse, rare 125.00
Dutch Treat Barn 55.00
Elephant 150.00
Elephant w/Split Trunk, rare, minimum value 350.00
Engine, blk 140.00
Flowerpot, plastic flower on top, minimum value 500.00
Football Boy 175.00
Forbidden Fruit 65.00
Freddy Gleep 500.00
Friendship 160.00
Frontier Family 45.00
Fruit in Bushel Basket 75.00
Gingerbread Boy 75.00
Globe 225.00
Grandfather Clock 85.00
Granny 85.00
Granny, gold trim 125.00

Hamm's Bear, $185.00.

Happy Face 50.00
Hen on Nest 85.00
Hillbilly Bear, rare, minimum value 900.00
Hobby Horse 120.00
Honey Bear 75.00
Indian 325.00
Jack-O'-Lantern, minimum value 500.00
Kangaroo, bl 300.00
Kettle, jumbo sz 35.00
Kissing Penguins 75.00

Kitten on Basketweave 85.00
Kittens (2) on Low Basket, minimum value 600.00
Kittens on Ball of Yarn 100.00
Kookie Kettle, blk 30.00
Lamb on Basketweave 50.00
Leprechaun, minimum value 1,200.00
Liberty Bell 40.00
Little Clown 65.00
Lollipop 65.00
Mac Dog 80.00
Mammy, Cookies on base 225.00
Mammy w/Cauliflower, minimum value 1,100.00
Modern 35.00
Monk 40.00
Mother Goose 120.00
Mr & Mrs Owl 95.00
Nursery, decal of Humpty Dumpty 85.00
Oaken Bucket 25.00
Old Churn 35.00
Pears on Basketweave 45.00
Pelican 140.00
Pepper, yel 25.00
Picnic Basket 65.00
Pineapple 60.00
Pineapple, Modern 45.00
Pirates Chest 65.00
Popeye Cylinder 185.00
Potbelly Stove, blk 35.00
Puppy, w/sign 85.00
Quaker Oats, minimum value 500.00
Red Barn, cow in door, rare, minimum value 300.00
Rooster, wht, 1970-1974 ....55.00
Rooster, 1955-1957 ....95.00
Round w/HP Leaves 45.00
Sad Clown 65.00
Snoopy on Doghouse 225.00
Snow Bear 65.00
Stagecoach, minimum value 1,000.00
Strawberry, 1955-57 ....35.00
Strawberry, 1971-75 ....30.00
Teapot, 1971 ....40.00
Tepee, str top 325.00
Tilt Pitcher, blk w/roses 26.00
Tomato 30.00
Touring Car 100.00
Tudor Cookie House 110.00
Tulip on Flowerpot 150.00
Turkey, gr, rare color 200.00
Upside Down Bear, panda 55.00
WC Fields 170.00
Wedding Jar 85.00
Windmill 100.00
Wishing Well 40.00
Woodsy Owl 225.00
Wren House 125.00
Yosemite Sam, cylinder 185.00

Miscellaneous

Bookend, horse rearing, wht, mk #4, 1941-43 ....15.00
Bookend, swallow emb, mk #7, 1956, pr 55.00
Bowl, salad; El Rancho 135.00
Cache pot, dbl; flower form, mk #7, 1955 ....10.00
Coffee server, El Rancho, w/warmer, unmk 135.00

Creamer, dog form, bl, mk #4, 1940s 30.00
Dripolator, 6-sided shape, mk #7, 1943 ....22.50
Figurine, panther, blk, no mk, 1950s 25.00
Mug, coffee; El Rancho 22.50
Pitcher, cloverleaves emb, mk #7, 1948 ....20.00
Pitcher/vase, parrot form, mk #7, 1952 ....45.00
Planter, anvil form w/appl hammer & chain, mk #7, 1953 ....10.00
Planter, baby crib form, 1954 ....10.00
Planter, basket form, gr basketweave, mk #7, 1957 ....25.00
Planter, Dutch shoe, mk #4, 1947 ....12.50
Planter, pointer hunting dog form, mk #7, 1953 ....10.00
Shakers, cucumber & mango forms, 1954, pr 25.00
Sombrero serve-all, El Rancho 300.00
Soup tureen, El Rancho, 5-qt 165.00
Spoon rest, penguin form, mk #7, 1953 ....40.00
Sprinkler, turtle form, gr, mk #7, 1950 ....30.00
Sugar bowl, Grecian, w/lid, mk #7, 1958 ....15.00
Teapot, Sunburst Gold, mk #4, 1957 ....40.00
Vase, butterflies emb, pk, 1940, 8" 15.00
Vase, wheat emb in panel, 6-sided, hdls, mk #7, 1953 .....12.50
Wall pocket, lily form, mk #8, 1948 ....30.00
Wall pocket, lovebirds, mk #7, 1953 ....35.00

Fawn vase, circa 1954, $28.00.

McCoy, J. W.

The J.W. McCoy Pottery Company was incorporated in 1899. It operated under that name in Roseville, Ohio, until 1911 when McCoy entered into a partnership with George Brush, forming the Brush-McCoy Company. During the early years, McCoy produced kitchenware, majolica jardinieres and pedestals, umbrella stands, and cuspidors. By 1903 they had begun to experiment in the field of art pottery and, though never involved to the extent of some of their contemporaries, nevertheless produced several art lines of merit. Their first line was Mt. Pelee, examples of which are very rare today. Two types of glazes were used, matt green and an iridescent charcoal gray. Though the line was primarily mold formed, some pieces evidence the fact that while the clay remained wet and pliable it was pulled and pinched with the fingers to form crests and peaks in a style not unlike George Ohr.

The company rebuilt in 1904 after being destroyed by fire, and other artware was designed. Loy-Nel Art and Renaissance were standard brown lines, hand decorated under the glaze with colored slip. Shapes and artwork were usually simple but effective. Olympia and Rosewood were relief-molded brown-glaze lines decorated in natural colors with wreaths of leaves and berries or simple floral sprays. Although much of this ware was not marked, you will find examples with the die-stamped 'Loy-Nel Art, McCoy' or an incised line identification.

Loy-Nel-Art vase, 11", $250.00.

Loy-Nel-Art, bowl, mk, 1905, 2" 80.00
Loy-Nel-Art, jardiniere, mk, 1905, 6" 185.00
Loy-Nel-Art, spittoon, mk, 1905, 4½" 145.00
Loy-Nel-Art, vase, waisted, unmk, 1905, 8" 135.00
Olympia, mug, 1905 ....135.00
Olympia, pretzel bowl, unmk, 1905 ....325.00
Olympia, vase, 1905, 8½" 185.00
Rosewood, vase, 1905, 5" 145.00

McKee

McKee Glass was founded in 1853 in Pittsburgh, Pennsylvania. Among their early products were tablewares of both the flint and non-flint varieties. In 1888 the company relocated to avail themselves of a source of natural gas, thereby founding the town of Jeannette, Pennsylvania. One of their most famous colored dinnerware lines, Rock Crystal, was manufactured in the 1920s. During the thirties and forties, colored opaque dinnerware and kitchenware, Sunkist reamers, and 'bottoms up' cocktail tumblers were produced as well as a line of black glass vases, bowls, and novelty items. All are popular items with today's collectors. The company was purchased in 1916 by Jeannette Glass, under which name it continues to operate. See also Animal Dishes with Covers; Depression Glass; Kitchen Collectibles; Reamers.

Bowl, beater; w/spout, 5½" 30.00
Bowl, drippings; Red Ships, 8-oz 32.50
Bowl, mixing; Red Ships, 6" 9.00
Bowl, mixing; Red Ships, 9" 16.00
Bowl, Red Ships, 9" 25.00
Butter dish, Red Ships 40.00
Canister, Red Ships, 24-oz 28.00
Canister, Red Ships, 46-oz 32.00
Centerpiece, Honeycomb, pk, ftd 40.00
Decanter, Seville yel, pinched sides 95.00
Mug, jadite, 'Bottoms Down' 150.00
Mug, Seville yel, 'Bottoms Down' 150.00
Mug, Tom & Jerry; custard 12.00
Refrigerator dish, Blk Ships, 4x5" 20.00
Refrigerator dish, Red Ships, 4x5" 12.00
Refrigerator dish, Red Ships, 5x8" 25.00
Rolling pin, Chalaine bl 900.00
Rolling pin, crystal w/screw-on cobalt hdls 200.00
Rolling pin, jadite 325.00
Rolling pin, Seville yel 250.00
Shakers, Puritan, pr 60.00

Shakers, Red Ships, blk plastic tops, pr 30.00
Stein, Serenade (Troubador), bl opaque, 4¾" 65.00
Tray, milk glass, fleur-de-lis shape, 4½x6" 22.00
Tumbler, custard 10.00
Tumbler, Red Ships 15.00
Vase, blk, classic form, wht opaque hdls, 12" 200.00

Medical Collectibles

The field of medical-related items encompasses a wide area from the primitive bleeding bowl to the X-ray machines of the early 1900s. Other closely related collectibles include apothecary and dental items. Many tools that were originally intended for the pharmacist found their way to the doctor's office, and dentists often used surgical tools when no suitable dental instrument was available. A trend in the late 1700s toward self-medication brought a whole new wave of home-care manuals and 'patent' medical machines for home use. Commonly referred to as 'quack' medical gimmicks, these machines were usually ineffective and occasionally dangerous. Our advisor for this category is Jim Calison; he is listed in the Directory under New York.

Amputation knife, Liston type, blk hdl, John Wood, 14" 200.00
Apothecary chest, pine, 4-drw, scalloped crest, 8x18" 395.00
Bottle, display; ftd cylinder, ground glass lid, 21", pr 375.00
Bunsen burner, dental, CI base, brass head/stem/hose lead 16.00
Cabinet, Humphrey's...Household Name, sloping face, 11x11" ..250.00
Dose glass, cobalt, emb WR Warner & Co Phila, 1⅝" 20.00
Ear scoop, silver, 1804 hallmk, ebony hdl 275.00
Ear trumpet, aluminum, segmented/collapsible, 11" L 300.00
Ear trumpet, brass, ca 1880, 3½" 325.00
Ear trumpet, tortoise shell 400.00
Eyecup, clear, 8-panel bowl & stem, no mk, 2⅞" 4.00
Eyecup, cobalt, emb Wyeth on 2 sides, 2-panel, 1¾", NM 12.00
Eyecup, sapphire bl, str-side bowl w/tall sides, 2⅝" 35.00
Gold hammer/punch, dental, SS White Pat 03, 6¾" 35.00
Hot water bottle, aluminum, Worcester, Pat 1915, 7½" 15.00
Pap boat, porc teapot shape, Made in Japan 5.00
Quack device, Magneto Electric...for Nervous & ...Diseases, 8" .210.00
Quack device, Marvel #A-1, ultraviolet, Eastern Lab, 1924 ....20.00
Quack device, Voltamp Battery #6 Majestic, Chas Lenz, VG 45.00
Saw, surgeon's, brass, Pilling Phila, 11½" 150.00
Spoon, glass, emb Phillip's Milk of Magnesia, 4" 18.00
Steam bath, copper w/brass hdls, riveted, 2¾x5" dia 22.00
Syringe & needle, Carpule, all metal, open bbl, saddle type 20.00
Thermometer, Deco style in case w/1939 certificate 25.00
Tongue scraper, tortoise shell & ivory, ca 1840s 175.00

Meissen

The Royal Saxon Porcelain Works was established in 1710 in Meissen, Saxony. Under the direction of Johann Freidrick Bottger, who in 1708 had developed the formula for the first true porcelain body, fine ceramic figurines with exquisite detail and tableware of the highest quality were produced. Although every effort was made to insure the secrecy of Bottger's discovery, others soon began to copy his ware; and in 1731 Meissen adopted the famous crossed swords trademark to identify their own work. The term 'Dresden ware' is often used to refer to Meissen porcelain, since Bottger's discovery and first potting efforts were in nearby Dresden. See also Onion Pattern.

Bowl, rtcl woven sides w/2 shaped floral panels, 1880s, 10" 935.00
Charger, wht w/emb gold foliage, Xd swords, 11" 300.00

Clock, Zeus surmount, base w/2 figures, eagle by dial, 28" 5,000.00
Compote, floral/bead-emb center, emb floral edge, gilt, 12" 550.00
Compote, rtcl woven border w/5 fruit medallions, 1880s, 7" 875.00

Ewer, allegorical of 'Wind,' 24", $3,000.00.

Figurine, Cherub, Coup Sur Coup, Xd swords, 5¾" 650.00
Figurine, Cherub, Un Me Suffit, Xd swords, 5¾" 600.00
Figurine, cherub tailor cuts cloth, Xd swords, 5" 250.00
Figurine, child w/horse toy, newspaper hat dtd 1905, 6½" 650.00
Figurine, cupid blacksmith works on heart at anvil, 7½" 850.00
Figurine, cupid holds heart, quiver on bk, 8½" 1,000.00
Figurine, falconer on plinth, Xd swords, 8" 250.00
Figurine, flower girl seated on oval scrollwork base, 4½" 250.00
Figurine, huntsman on horsebk+4 dogs, Xd swords, 15x16" 2,500.00
Figurine, lady sits at table listing her goods, rpr, 7" 1,200.00
Figurine, man (& lady) stands, holds sheet music, 14", pr 3,600.00
Figurine, man & lady attend gent, dog at ft, 1880, 8", EX 1,400.00
Figurine, seated girl & cat, 1800s, 5" 875.00
Figurine, shepherdess & sheep, 1775, rpr/rstr, 9½", EX 2,700.00
Figurine, Venus in bird-drawn chariot, putto aside, 7", EX 600.00
Figurine, young god riding eagle on plinth, Xd swords, 12" 700.00
Orchestra, 12 monkey musicians, Xd swords, 1800s, 6", set 6,000.00
Plate, botanical, rtcl basketweave rim, 1800s, 9½", pr 385.00
Stein, HP porc, harbor scene, inlay lid, 1800s, mk, ¼-liter 3,080.00
Tray, floral sprays, pk border w/floral reserves, sq, 16" 850.00
Tray, modeled as mermaid emerging from ocean wave, 8½" L 450.00
Vase, cobalt urn form w/gold ft etc, snake hdls, 11", pr 1,600.00
Vase, florals on cobalt, swan-head hdls, urn form, 20" 1,300.00
Vase, lovers reserve on cobalt, snake hdls, rtcl lid, 12" 1,000.00
Vase, 2 cherubs, wht on cobalt, dbl gourd, cork stopper, 6" 850.00

Mercury Glass

Mercury glass was popular during the 1850s and enjoyed a short revival at the turn of the century. It was made with two thin layers, either blown with a double wall or joined in sections with the space between the walls of the vessel filled with a mixture of tin, lead, bismuth, and mercury. The opening was sealed to prevent air from dulling the bright color. Though most examples are silver, blue and gold can be found on occasion. Remember that the value of this type of glass hinges greatly upon condition of the mercury lining. In the listings that follow, all examples are silver unless noted another color.

Bottle, etched vintage on amber-flashed neck, 7" 200.00
Bowl, 3 clear appl ft, 4x9½" 95.00

Candlestick, child's, pr 100.00
Compote, wht florals, cylinder stem, 6" 70.00
Drw pull, 1¼" dia, set of 6 ....60.00
Mug, clear hdl, 3" 30.00
Rolling pin 90.00
Tie backs, copper wheel eng vintage, 2½", pr 30.00
Toothpick holder 35.00
Vase, enameled birds, 7½" 55.00
Vase, eng bows/grapevines/etc, flared, high knob std, 9" 45.00
Vase, 4½", pr 40.00
Wig stand, sphere on ped ft, 10" 165.00
Witch ball, w/stand, 18" overall 185.00

Merrimac

Founded in 1897 in Newburyport, Massachusetts, the Merrimac Pottery Company primarily produced tile and gardenware. In 1901, however, they introduced a line of artware that is now attracting the interest of collectors. Marked examples carry an impressed die-stamp or a paper label, each with the firm name and the outline of a sturgeon, the Indian word for which was Merrimac.

Vase, bl matt on red, oval, mfg glaze flaws, 3¾" 165.00
Vase, gr matt, appl upright leaves, 4½x4½" 450.00
Vase, gr matt, elongated ovoid, die mk, 11x5", NM 500.00
Vase, yel-gr w/bl-gr striations, 8½" 440.00

Metlox

The Metlox Manufacturing Company was founded in 1927 in Manhattan Beach, California. Before 1934 when they began producing the ceramic housewares for which they have become famous, they made ceramic and neon outdoor advertising signs. The company went out of business in 1989.

Well-known sculptor Carl Romanelli designed artware in the late 1930s and early 1940s (and again briefly in the 1950s). His work is especially sought after today. For further information we recommend *The Collector's Encyclopedia of California Pottery* by our advisor, Jack Chipman; he is listed in the Directory under California.

Antique Grape, bowl, cereal; 7½" 6.00
Antique Grape, creamer 10.00
Antique Grape, cup & saucer 7.00
Antique Grape, pitcher, 1-qt 15.00
Antique Grape, plate, 10½" 8.50
Antique Grape, plate, 6¼" 4.00
Antique Grape, plate, 7½" 6.00
Antique Grape, saucer 2.00
Antique Grape, shakers, pr 10.00
Antique Grape, soup plate, 8½" 7.00
California Ivy, bowl, cereal; 7" 8.50

California Ivy, divided vegetable bowl, $20.00.

California Ivy, bowl, fruit; 5" 65.00
California Ivy, bowl, salad; 7" 12.00
California Ivy, bowl, vegetable; sq, 9" 15.00
California Ivy, bowl, vegetable; 9" 22.00
California Ivy, bowl, 6" 6.50
California Ivy, casserole, w/lid, 9½" 35.00
California Ivy, creamer 6.00
California Ivy, cup, demitasse 15.00
California Ivy, cup & saucer 8.00
California Ivy, gravy boat 22.00
California Ivy, gravy liner 12.00
California Ivy, plate, 10" 10.00
California Ivy, plate, 6" 4.00
California Ivy, plate, 8" 4.50
California Ivy, plate, 9¼" 10.00
California Ivy, platter, 13" 22.00
California Ivy, sherbet 8.00
California Ivy, soup plate, 8½" 8.50
California Ivy, sugar bowl, w/lid 10.00
California Ivy, tumbler, 5½" 18.00
Happy Time, plate, 7½" 7.00
Happy Time, teapot, sm 50.00
Homestead Provincial, ashtray 12.00
Homestead Provincial, bowl, salad; 11" 22.00
Homestead Provincial, bowl, vegetable; divided, stick hdl 22.00
Homestead Provincial, bowl, 10" 20.00
Homestead Provincial, bowl, 6" 6.00
Homestead Provincial, bowl, 8" 12.00
Homestead Provincial, bread tray 25.00
Homestead Provincial, casserole, w/lid, 10" 35.00
Homestead Provincial, coffeepot 37.50
Homestead Provincial, creamer & sugar bowl, w/lid 18.00
Homestead Provincial, cruets (oil & vinegar), pr 40.00
Homestead Provincial, cup & saucer 10.00
Homestead Provincial, gravy boat 17.50
Homestead Provincial, plate, 10" 8.00
Homestead Provincial, plate, 6½" 6.00
Homestead Provincial, platter, 13" 20.00
Homestead Provincial, relish, divided 22.00
Homestead Provincial, soup plate, 8½" 8.50
Homestead Provincial, teapot 30.00
Homestead Provincial, wall pocket vase 42.00
La Mancha, plate, 8½" 6.00
Luau, bowl, berry; sm 4.00
Luau, bowl, soup 8.00
Luau, bowl, vegetable; rnd, 8½" 18.00
Luau, bowl, vegetable; w/lid 35.00
Luau, butter dish 20.00
Luau, coffeepot 45.00
Luau, creamer & sugar bowl 15.00
Luau, cup & saucer 8.00
Luau, gravy boat, w/ladle 20.00
Luau, plate, dinner 10.00
Luau, plate, 7½" 8.00
Navajo, bowl, deep, 13" 45.00
Navajo, butter dish 35.00
Navajo, compote, divided 15.00
Navajo, cruet 12.00
Navajo, server, divided, 16¾" 22.00
Navajo, teapot 50.00
Provincial Fruit, bowl, deep, 7" 7.00
Provincial Fruit, bowl, tab hdls, 5" 6.00
Provincial Fruit, bowl, 10" 18.00
Provincial Fruit, bowl, 6" 6.00

Provincial Fruit, butter dish 25.00
Provincial Fruit, coffeepot 45.00
Provincial Fruit, creamer 7.00
Provincial Fruit, cup 7.00
Provincial Fruit, plate, soup; 8½" 8.00
Provincial Fruit, plate, 10½" 12.00
Provincial Fruit, plate, 6½" 6.50
Provincial Fruit, plate, 7¾" 8.00
Provincial Fruit, platter, 14" 20.00
Red Rooster Provincial, bowl, hdls, 7" 18.00
Red Rooster Provincial, bowl, soup; 8½" 8.00
Red Rooster Provincial, bowl, 10" 22.00
Red Rooster Provincial, bowl, 6" 6.00
Red Rooster Provincial, butter dish 30.00
Red Rooster Provincial, coffeepot 40.00
Red Rooster Provincial, creamer 8.50
Red Rooster Provincial, cup & saucer 8.00
Red Rooster Provincial, jug, 1½-pt 22.00
Red Rooster Provincial, plate, 10" 10.00
Red Rooster Provincial, plate, 6½" 5.00
Red Rooster Provincial, plate, 7½" 6.50
Red Rooster Provincial, platter, 11x8" 12.00
Red Rooster Provincial, porringer, 5" dia 6.00
Red Rooster Provincial, shakers, hdl, pr 12.00
Red Rooster Provincial, sugar bowl, w/lid 12.00
Sculptured Daisy, bowl, deep, 7" 8.00
Sculptured Daisy, bowl, vegetable; tab hdl, 8" 20.00
Sculptured Daisy, cup & saucer 7.50
Sculptured Daisy, gravy boat 25.00
Sculptured Daisy, pitcher, 7" 40.00
Sculptured Daisy, plate, dinner; 10½" 8.50
Sculptured Daisy, plate, 6" 6.00
Sculptured Daisy, plate, 7½" 7.50
Sculptured Daisy, platter, 14" 25.00
Sculptured Daisy, teapot 40.00
Sculptured Grape, creamer & sugar bowl, w/lid 18.00
Sculptured Grape, relish, 2-part 20.00
Sculptured Zinnia, teapot 40.00
Tropicana, bowl, 5½" 8.00
Tropicana, creamer & sugar bowl 20.00
Tropicana, cup & saucer 10.00
Tropicana, gravy boat, w/underplate 25.00
Tropicana, pitcher, water; sm 25.00
Tropicana, plate, dinner 10.00
Tropicana, platter, 13" 25.00

Cookie Jars

Barrel of Apples 50.00
Basket of Fruit 50.00
Bear, bl coat 55.00
Bear, roller skates 60.00
Bear, sombrero 60.00
Bear, sweater & cookie 50.00
Beau Bear 40.00
Black Topsy Girl, bl skirt, red belt 195.00
Clown 85.00
Cow, crier in lid 195.00
Drum, bsk, mk 30.00
Dutch Boy 80.00
Fido 65.00
Frog 68.00
Humpty Dumpty 70.00
Lamb's Head 70.00

Mammy w/Mixing Bowl, bl dots 200.00
Mammy w/Mixing Bowl, red spots 200.00
Owl, gr 70.00
Puddles Duck 65.00
Raccoon 135.00
Rose 120.00
Uncle Sam Bear 250.00

Romanelli Artware

Figurine, Indian brave, 9" 145.00
Figurine, rooster, satin wht, 8¼" 65.00
Figurine, 2 birds on branch, satin bl, #1826 ....45.00
Miniature, donkey, brn, 3" 35.00
Miniature, monkey on all 4s, turq/brn, 4½" 75.00
Vase, angel fish form, 8½" 75.00
Vase, sea horse, satin bl, #1809, 9¼" 125.00
Vase, Taurus, Zodiac, 8" 95.00

Mettlach

In 1836, Nicholas Villeroy and Eugene Francis Boch, both of whom were already involved in the potting industry, formed a partnership and established a stoneware factory in an old restored abbey in Mettlach, Germany. Decorative stoneware with in-mold relief was their specialty, steins in particular. Through constant experimentation, they developed innovative methods of decoration. One process, called chromolith, involved inlaying colorful mosaic designs into the body of the ware. Later underglaze printing from copper plates was used. Their stoneware was of high quality, and their steins won many medals at the St. Louis Expo and early world's fairs. Most examples are marked with an incised castle and the name 'Mettlach.' The numbering system indicates size, date, stock number, and decorator. Production was halted by a fire in 1921; the factory was not rebuilt. Our advisor for this category is Ron Fox; he is listed in the Directory under New York.

Key:
L — liter   PUG — print under glaze
POG — print over glaze   tl — thumb lift

#1028, stein, relief: harvest on trunk body, 2.3-L, EX 200.00
#1028, stein, relief: harvest scene, face inlay lid, ½-L 150.00
#1028, stein, relief: harvest scene on trunk body, 4-L, NM 245.00
#1044, plaque, PUG: Marienburg castle, 17" 640.00
#1044/128, plaque, PUG: Nurnberg Schloss, 12" 200.00
#1044/171, plaque, PUG: deer grazing, 17½", NM 230.00
#1044/196, plaque, PUG: Coblenz (river junction), 14" 275.00
#1044/263, plaque, PUG: Lohengrin opera scene, 17", NM 715.00
#1044/355, plaque, PUG/transfer: Oriental lady, 14", NM 175.00
#1044/5159, plaque, HP Delft: seaside w/lighthouse, 17½" 300.00
#1044/5218, plaque, HP Delft: portrait, sgn N Rembrandt, 24" ..795.00
#1044/527, plaque, PUG: Wirtschraft Zur Treib..., 12" 280.00
#1154, stein, etched: hunt scenes, dog inlay lid, Warth, 1-L 800.00
#1221, stein, mosaic: floral, no lid, 1½-L 250.00
#1224, stein, etched/glazed: floral, rpl lid, ½-L 290.00
#1370, stein, relief: knight w/woman, inlay lid, ½-L, EX 200.00
#1526, stein, HP: fraternal crest, pewter lid, ½-L 785.00
#1526, stein, POG: Heidelberg, flat metal lid, ½-L 145.00
#1526, stein, transfer/HP: Baker's Dozen, flat lid, ½-L 175.00
#1526, stein, transfer/HP: Elbschloss Marzenbier, ½-L, NM 350.00
#1526/1098, stein, PUG: Uncle Sam/German troops, ½-L, NM ..280.00
#1526/1101, stein, PUG: barmaid, relief pewter lid, ½-L 250.00
#1526/1279, stein, PUG: Dutch children/rabbits, rpr, ½-L 160.00

#1526/1919, stein, PUG: students, crest relief lid, ½-L 260.00
#1526/592, stein, PUG: man & lady, hairline, ½-L 100.00
#1675, stein, etched: Heidelberg castle, inlay lid, ½-L 580.00
#171, stein, relief: people in panel, rosebud lid, 3.2-L, EX 365.00
#1849, vase, etched: lady & florals, rpr, 12" 198.00
#1909-1021, stein, PUG: dancers, barmaid lid, dwarf tl, ½-L 300.00
#1909/1042, stein, PUG: couple w/key, Schlitt, ½-L 395.00
#1909/1073, stein, PUG: hunter in forest, eagle tl, ½-L 360.00
#1909/673, stein, PUG: dwarfs, pewter lid, ½-L, NM 200.00
#1909/715, stein, PUG: Kauffungen/Hildebrand/etc, ½-L 250.00
#1909/727, stein, PUG: dwarfs bowling, relief lid, ½-L 350.00
#1909/979, stein, Athletic School E Africa, stain, ½-L 525.00
#1909/993, stein, PUG: musicians, Schlitt, ½-L 325.00
#1932, stein, etched: cavaliers toasting, Warth, 1932, ½-L 525.00
#1968, stein, etched: lovers, anchor inlay lid, ½-L, NM 525.00
#1977, stein, PUG/etched: George Ehret, inlay lid, ½-L 300.00
#2018, stein, pug dog character, ½-L 990.00
#2044, stein, etched: drinking scene, inlay lid, ½-L 800.00
#2050, stein, etched: wedding, slipper on lid, ½-L 1,815.00
#2065, stein, etched: man & barmaid, jewels, Schlitt, 2.4-L ...1,200.00
#2077, stein, relief: 3 panels, rpr inlay lid, .3-L 75.00

#2909, vase, etched Nouveau flowers, 17", $1,700.00.

#2090, stein, etched: man at table, dtd 1898 lid, ½-L 525.00
#2090, stein, etched: man at table, rpr lid, .3-L, EX 285.00
#2093, stein, etched: suits of cards, lid rpr, ½-L, VG 350.00
#2100, stein, etched: warriors, Schlitt, rpl lid, .3-L, EX 250.00
#2133, stein, etched: dwarf in trees, Schlitt, ½-L 2,500.00
#2140, stein, PUG: Harvard baseball & rugby, ½-L 1,385.00
#2140/952, stein, PUG: man on bicycle, Am tl, ½-L 635.00
#2149, plaque, etched/glazed: Papageno, 16½" 1,795.00
#2177/959, stein, PUG: drunken night, Schlitt, ¼-L, EX 100.00
#2177/960, stein, PUG: jester, Munich child tl, Schlitt, ¼-L 200.00
#2182, stein, relief: bowling scene, inlay lid, ½-L 230.00
#2192, stein, etched: Etruscan scene, jester tl, ½-L 925.00
#2210, stein, relief: bowling, pipe/radish inlay lid, 3¼-L 415.00
#2232, stein, relief: birds, inlay lid, hairline, .3-L 140.00
#2268/1047, humidor, PUG: dwarfs, sgn GK, hairline, 7" 330.00
#2327/1200, beaker, PUG: Stuttgart, sm chip, ¼-L 95.00
#2364, stein, relief: women, face spout, inlay lid, 3½-L 600.00
#2368/1091, beaker, PUG: cavalier, ¼-L, EX 140.00
#2368/1095, beaker, PUG: cavaliers, rim fracture, ¼-L 70.00
#2382, stein, etched: Thirsty Rider, watchman tl, Schlitt, ½-L ..830.00
#2384/1075, stein, firefighting scene, rpr/chip, 2¼-L 565.00

#2394, stein, etched: Siegfried w/sword, inlay lid, ½-L 745.00
#2402, stein, etched: Lohengrin scene, horn inlay lid, ½-L 900.00
#2530, stein, cameo: boar hunt, sgn Stahl, ½-L 695.00
#2580, stein, etched: DeKannenburg, inlay lid, Schlitt, ½-L 935.00
#2581, stein, etched: 3 girls singing, musical tl, ½-L 600.00
#2583, stein, etched: Egyptian scene, Quidenus, flaw, 1-L ...1,200.00
#2619/6075, vase, PUG: castle, sm rpr, 7½" 330.00
#2692, etched/glazed: drinking scene, inlay lid, rpr, 3-L 695.00
#2717, stein, etched/POG: target girl, jester tl, 1-L 4,730.00
#2745, stein, etched: man w/pipe, inlay lid, 1-L 750.00
#2755, stein, cameo/etched: people at tables, ¼-L, EX 525.00
#2765, stein, etched: knight on wht horse, tower lid, ½-L 2,530.00
#2776, stein, etched: wine cellar keeper, rpr, ½-L, VG 315.00
#2780, stein, etched: lovers in archway, inlay lid, 1-L 750.00
#2789/6134, stein, Rookwood type: man smoking, ½-L 475.00
#2829, stein, etched/glazed: Rodenstein, castle lid, ½-L 2,300.00
#2871, stein, etched: Cornell campus, owl tl, 1-L 925.00
#2882, ashtray, etched, match holder in center, 6", NM 230.00
#2922, stein, etched: campfire scene, inlay lid, ¼-L 435.00
#2958, stein, etched: bowling boy, inlay lid, 2.8-L, EX 500.00
#3002, stein, etched: people, rare tl, Ringer, ½-L, EX 290.00
#3003, stein, etched: man w/paper, att Ringer, ½-L 400.00
#3078/437, stein, transfer/HP: Q Bavaria series, ½-L 415.00
#3096, plate, Art Nouveau decor, 8½" 155.00
#3099, stein, etched: Diogenes, Socrates inlay lid, rpr, 3-L 1,385.00
#3156, stein, etched: Chicago scenes, rpr, ½-L, EX 3,000.00
#3162, plaque, etched: cavaliers toasting, 17" 1,025.00
#3321, creamer, etched: Art Nouveau decor, 4½" 98.00
#3337, humidor, etched: Nouveau decor, sm chip, 8¼" 395.00
#3349, stein, etched: indoor scene, Munich child lid, ½-L, EX ..400.00
#3454, vase, etched: flower pattern w/gold, 1920, 4" 150.00
#3465, humidor, etched: floral w/gold, dtd 1920, 7" 350.00

#1577, Flagon, sgraffito tavern scene, 20", $1,000.00.

Microscopes

The microscope has taken on many forms during its 250-year evolutionary period. The current collectors' market primarily includes examples from England, those surplused from institutions, and continental beginner and intermediate forms which sold through Sears Roebuck & Company and other retailers of technical instruments. Earlier examples have brass main tubes which are unpainted. Later, more common examples are all black with brass or silver knobs and horseshoe-

shaped bases. Early and more complex forms are the most valuable; these always had hardwood cases to house the delicate instrument and its accessories. Instruments were never polished during use, and those that have been polished to use as decorator pieces are of little interest to most avid collectors. Our advisor for this category is Dale Beeks; he is listed in the Directory under Idaho.

Acme, brass & iron, 14" case, EX 350.00
Bausch & Lomb, all brass, horseshoe base, 1897, 14", EX 350.00
Bausch & Lomb, blk, horseshoe base, 1915, EX 95.00
Bausch & Lomb, blk base, brass tube, 1897, 14", EX 275.00
Bausch & Lomb, brass, tripod base, 1876, 16", EX, +case 375.00
Bausch & Lomb, brass, tripod base, 1885, 16", EX, +case 350.00
Bulloch, Chicago, brass, complex, Y base, 1880, 15", +case 950.00
English, professional, brass, 1876, 18", +case/accessories 775.00
English, student, brass, ca 1870, 12", +case/accessories 265.00
French, drum or furnace form, 5", EX, +case 55.00
French, student, ca 1910, 9", G, +case 65.00
German, student, rnd base, ca 1860, G, +case 125.00
Grunow, New Haven, iron & brass, 15", EX, +case 950.00
Grunow, New York, iron & brass, 15", EX, + case 725.00
Gundlach, brass, Y base, 1879, 14", EX 325.00
Gundlach Manhattan, student, all brass, 11", EX 165.00
Hand-held, simple form, 1890, 3", G 45.00
McAllister, brass, chain-drive focus, 14", G, +case 325.00
McIntosh Battery & Optical, brass & iron, 12", G 325.00
Queen, brass & iron, Y base, 14", G, +case 325.00
Spencer Lens Co, brass, horseshoe base, 13", EX 155.00
Stamp magnifier, brass, 3-leg, 1½", G 40.00
Tighe, brass, 12", EX, +case 325.00
Tolles, Boston, brass, Y base, ca 1880, 16", G, +case 625.00
Watson, English binocular form, 1880, 18", EX, +case 375.00
Zentmeyer, brass, complex, dbl pillar, tripod base, 18", G 1,250.00

Midwestern Glass

As early as 1814, blown glass was made in Ohio. By 1835 glasshouses in Michigan were producing similar pattern-molded types that have long been highly regarded by collectors. During the latter part of the 19th century, all six of the states of the Northwest Territory were mass-producing the pressed glass tableware patterns that were then in vogue. Various types of art glass were produced in the area until after the turn of the century. Items listed here are attributed to the Midwest by certain physical characteristics known to be indigenous to that part of the country. Our advisor for this category is Mark Vuono; he is listed in the Directory under Connecticut. See also Findlay Onyx; Greentown Glass; Libbey; Zanesville Glass.

Bottle, amber, globular, shallow broken surface blister, 11" 325.00
Bottle, amber, globular, 8" 225.00
Bottle, aqua, club shape, 9" 85.00
Bottle, aqua, vertical ribs, flattened, 7" 100.00
Bottle, chestnut; citron, lt wear, lip slightly ground, 5" 155.00
Bottle, chestnut; 18 swirl ribs, 6" 135.00
Bottle, cologne; yel-gr, 14-rib, push-up base, cylinder, 3½" 165.00
Bottle, lt gr, club shape, 8" 275.00
Bottle, nursing; lt gr, 16-dmn, 7" 210.00
Pocket flask, gold-amber, 24 vertical ribs, sheared lip, 4¾" 150.00

Militaria

Because of the wide and varied scope of items available to collectors of militaria, most tend to concentrate mainly on the area or areas that interest them most or that they can afford to buy. Some items represent a major investment and because of their value have been reproduced. Extreme caution should be used when purchasing Nazi items. Every badge, medal, cap, uniform, dagger, and sword that Nazi Germany issued is being reproduced today. Some repros are crude and easily identified as fakes, while others are very well done and difficult to recognize as reproductions. Purchases from WWII veterans are usually your safest buys. Reputable dealers or collectors will normally offer a money-back guarantee on Nazi items purchased from them. There are a number of excellent Third Reich reference books available in bookstores at very reasonable prices. Study them to avoid losing a much larger sum spent on a reproduction. Our advisor for this category is Ron Willis; he is listed in the Directory under Oklahoma.

Imperial German

Badge, Kriegerkameradschaf Hassia, EX w/2 streamers 22.50
Buckle, Army, brass w/brass center, crown & motto 27.50
Cocard, helmet; Kurassiere, early pattern, 67mm, EX 30.00
Collartabs, red w/doubletrees, gilt w/blk border, EX 15.00
Grenade, WWI, wire hdl, steel head, EX 145.00
Helmet, Kurassiere, all brass, 1-pc construction, EX 285.00
Helmet, WWI, Army, M-16, camo steel, w/liner, EX 130.00
Leggings, WWI, mtn troop, padded, w/buckles, 1911, EX 32.50
Medal, House Order of Hohenzollern, Inhaber eagle, silver 300.00
Medal, Iron Cross, 1st Class, domed, screwbk, w/case 150.00
Medal, Konniggratz Cross, 1866, EX 37.50
Medal, non-combattant campaign, steel, 1870 ....32.00
Medal, non-combattant Honor Cross (no swords), 1914-18, EX ..12.50
Medal, Wurttemburg Bravery & Loyalty, silver, Wilhelm II 38.00
Medal, WWI Service, Fur Tapferdeit und Treue, EX 38.00
Medal, WWI Veteran, Kyffhauferbund, oval, EX 12.00
Patch, WWI, medic's specialty, yel embr on navy cloth, EX 15.00
Stein, crockery, Naval, dtd 1908, 1-liter, EX 900.00
Stick pin, Honor Cross, w/swords, 1914-18, EX 12.50
Tunic, M-16, field gray, hidden buttons, slash pockets, EX 90.00
Watch fob, Iron Cross commemorative, wht metal, 1914-15 ....24.00

Third Reich

Armband, NSDAP Party assistant, red w/swastika in wht circle ...22.50
Badge, arm; Army Jager, machine embr oak leaves on gr 12.00
Badge, cap; Kriegsmarine Submarine, cat, wht metal, EX 120.00
Badge, cap; Kriegsmarine Submarine, U-255, fox's head, brass ...100.00
Badge, cap; Kriegsmarine Submarine, U-49, elephant, brass 100.00
Badge, DLV, embr gray/wht/red winged prop & swastika on wht .12.50
Badge, DRL Sports, bronze, cut-out design, 1937 pattern 32.00
Badge, Luftwaffe wireless operator/air gunner, cotton embr 25.00
Badge, NS Fraunschaft staff, type 3, enamel on wht metal 12.50
Badge, Wehrmacht driver's proficiency, gold, M in envelope 40.00
Badge, wound; blk, hollow stamped-out type, EX 20.00
Badge, wound; WWII, solid silver, hallmk, EX 30.00
Bayonet, K-98, wood grips, +blk leather frog w/grip strap 50.00
Bayonet, parade; Army, long pattern, Eickhorn, 14½" 55.00
Bayonet, parade; Army, short pattern, 12½", +pnt scabbard 40.00
Book, DAF membership; red cr w/emb DAF gear/swastika, EX 10.00
Bottle, water; nurse's, felt cover, leather strap, EX 17.50
Bread bag, Wehrmacht, gray canvas, minor wear 27.50
Buckle, Army, parade style, aluminum, 2-pc, EX 22.50
Buckle, DAF officer, rolled aluminum rim, swastika center 44.00
Buckle, Hitler Youth, pot metal, gray finish, 1940s 17.50
Buckle, Kriegsmarine officer, gold-washed aluminum, EX 50.00
Buckle, Reichsbahn officer, gold-washed base metal, EX 32.00
Chevron, Kriegsmarine leading seaman, dbl gold Vs on bl 7.50

Chevron, Luftwaffe Gefretter, singletrees V on bl-gray 5.00
Cigarettes, 10 in orig unopened box w/eagle/swastika stamp 12.00
Collar tab, Luftwaffe Generaloberst, gold eagle/swastika, pr 750.00
Collar tab, RAD emblem, gray & wht on blk, pr 12.00
Document, WWII, Service Cross 2nd Class, dtd 1943 ....32.00
Fork, mess; RAD, aluminum, emb letters, M 7.50
Gaiters, WWII, Wehrmacht, tan canvas w/leather straps, M 22.50
Insignia, Luftwaffe, breast eagle, gray on gr herringbone 20.00
Insignia, Luftwaffe exercise shirt, blk bevo type on wht 12.50
Insignia, Luftwaffe officer, shirt eagle, wht on bl 12.00
Insignia, SA officer, field cap eagle, aluminum wire 22.50
Insignia, SS officer, cap eagle & totenkopft, silver 98.00
Knife, paratrooper gravity; take-down type, EX 125.00
Lamp, field; civilian, blk case, clear lens, w/button loop 12.50
Lighter, cigarette; Wehrmacht, aluminum, tube shape 15.00
Matchbox holder, emb soldier w/helmet on tin, 1½x2¼" 16.50
Medal, Commemorative of 1 Oktober 1938, w/ribbon 30.00
Medal, Fire Brigade Cross 2nd Class, enamel on wht metal 90.00
Medal, West Wall, ca 1940, M in orig paper packet 22.50
Medal, WWII, Iron Cross 2nd Class, hallmk, w/ribbon 38.00
Medal, WWII, Iron Cross 2nd Class, NM in issue packet 55.00
Medal, WWII, Merit Cross 2nd Class, no swords, w/ribbon 18.00
Medal, WWII, Russian Front, complete w/ribbon 18.00
Medal, WWII, Social Welfare, w/ribbon, EX 45.00
Medal, WWII, War Merit, w/orig ribbon, dtd 1939, NM 17.50
Mess kit, SS, early pattern, blk pnt, unmk, EX 42.50
Newspaper file photo, Grenadier platoon leader, 1943, 5x7" 10.00
Overalls, flight; Luftwaffe, summer weight tan, EX 150.00
Overcoat, WWII, RAD, brn wool w/dk brn collar, collar tabs 100.00
Pack, assault; WWII Wehrmacht, olive drab canvas, complete 38.00
Pants, WWII, Luftwaffe paratrooper, tropical, +cloth belt 300.00
Photo, Waffen SS, tanks & infantry on open ground, 5x7" 7.50
Photo postcard, Waffen SS, troops building bridge, M 10.00
Plaque, eagle & soldier's profile, bronze on wood, ca 1935 ....145.00
Portapee, K-98 dress bayonet; yel crown, wht stem, EX 12.50
Pouch, K-98 ammo, blk leather, 3-pocket, M 10.00
Rucksack, mtn troop, olive drab canvas, 3-pocket, EX 48.00
Shoulderboards, Allgemeine SS, blk/aluminum cord on blk, pr ...100.00
Shoulderboards, Fire Police Wachimeister, silver on red, pr 12.00
Shoulderboards, Luftwaffe Generaloberst, silver & gold cord, pr .255.00
Shoulderboards, RAD Obertgruppfuhrer, blk & silver on brn, pr ..24.00
Shoulderboards, Waffen SS Panzer, pk on blk wool, EX 45.00
Shoulderboards, Waffen SS Signals, yel on gray wool, pr 42.50
Sight cover, for field gun, canvas, artillery mks, dtd 1936 ....12.50
Sleeve shield, Waffen SS, 1st Ukrine, yel/bl/wht on wool 55.00
Sling, K-98 rifle, EX 20.00
Spoon, DAF mess, stainless steel w/emb swastika 12.50
Stickpin, Kyffhauserbund, w/swastika, EX 22.00
Tunic, Hitler Youth, 4-pocket jacket w/faux leather buttons 60.00
Wall hanging, swastika, aluminum foil/paper, 5x5", EX 6.00

Japanese

Armband, Civil Defense commander's, EX 18.00
Badge, Patriotic Ladies' Assoc, regular membership, M in case 12.00
Badge, Reserve, gilt star, anchor/Xd swords, lg, EX 20.00
Bayonet, Ariska, str crossguard, wood hdl, +scabbard 30.00
Dagger, officer's, gilt wash, sharkskin hdl, +scabbard, EX 95.00
Foot locker, Army officer's, wood w/leather straps, EX 92.50
Goggles, WWII, pilot's, fur & khaki cloth w/tinted lenses 37.50
Helmet, Army, model 1920, star on front, w/canvas liner, EX 72.50
Helmet, Tanker, complete w/liner & strap, mk, EX 245.00
Lapel rosette, Order of Golden Kite 4.50
Medal, China Incident, 1931-34, NM 55.00

Medal, Order of Golden Kite 7th Class, M in worn case 160.00
Medal, Order of Rising Sun 8th Class, no ribbon 32.00
Medal, Order of Sacred Treasure 6th Class, EX in case 175.00
Medal, Red Cross Special Membership, w/rosette, M in case 25.00
Medal, Taisho Enthronement, M 45.00
Medal, WWI Victory, EX in box 125.00
Medal, 1894-95 War, EX 85.00
Medal, 1904-05 War w/Russia, w/ribbon, NM 24.00
Saddlebag, brn leather, EX 75.00
Tunic, Army, tropical, 1942, EX 38.00
Wings, WWII, Army Air Corps, aluminum wire/gilt on bl 27.50

United States

Badge, Korean War, Infantry Combat, 1 star, clutch-bk, unmk 12.00
Banner, Son in Service, red/wht/bl cloth, 5½x9", EX 7.50
Banner, WWII, Let's Go Americans/Uncle Sam on cloth, 7" 37.50
Bayonet, Revolutionary War, 18¼", EX 42.50
Bayonet, WWI, Model 1917, long type, Remington, EX 50.00
Belt, pre-WWII, Army officer, brn leather, open brass buckle 42.50
Belt, WWII, Browning Automatic rifle ammo, w/first aid pouch ..15.00
Book, Scott's Infantry Tactics, Army, 1842, EX 48.00
Book, WWII, Strength for Service to God & Country, EX 7.50
Bugle, WWI, single twist, Besson, Paris, w/cord, EX 65.00
Button, 1855 New England Guard, cuff sz, EX 8.50
Canteen, WWII, Army, w/cup & cover, all w/issue dates 12.00
Cap, overseas; WWII, Naval officer's, gray cotton, NM 25.00
Cigarettes, WWII, full pack w/red case & matches, unopened 10.00

Civil War drum, eagle and sunburst with ribbon painted 'Reg' and 'Infantry,' 16½" heads, 11½" high (cut down from original height of about 20"), $350.00.

Coat, trench; Army officer, model 1942, olive drab, EX 32.50
Collar disk, WWI, Infantry, Xd rifles, EX 10.00
Collar disk, WWI, Medical, bronze screw-bk, EX 6.00
Compass, WWI, brass case w/US emb on cover, Whittnauer 15.00
Dog tag, WWI, Army sergeant, EX 10.00
Flare gun, Spanish-Am War, brass fr, steel bbl, 1898, EX 55.00
Flask, whiskey; Civil War officer, pewter cup bottom, 1861 ....42.50
Gloves, flying; Vietnam War, Air Force, gr leather, EX 12.00
Hat, visor; Vietnam War, Marine officer, dress bl, M 75.00
Haversack, WWII, tan canvas, w/web shoulder strap 12.00
Helmet, Vietnam War, jet pilot's, complete, NM 185.00
Helmet, WWII, complete w/liner & strap, EX 65.00
Helmet cover, WWII, desert camo, NM 6.00
Insignia, hat; 1870-1898 Infantry, Xd muskets, EX 12.50
Jacket, fatigue; Korean War, Marine Corps, 2-flap pockets 15.00
Kit, mess; WWII, GI, stainless steel, dtd 1942, EX 8.00
Kit, shaving; WWII; olive drab, w/metal mirror/blades/razor 15.00
Knife, utility; Army, w/4 attachments, Camillus, 1979 ....12.00
Knife, WWII, Navy Mark II, Camillus NY, +scabbard, EX 32.00
Leggings, WWII, Army, gr canvas, quartermaster stamps 7.50
Manual, WWII, Marine Corps, Fighting on Guadalcanal, 69-pg ..12.00

Medal, Dept of Defense Distinguished Service, gilt/enamel 75.00
Medal, pre-WWII, Navy Good Conduct, wrap brooch, w/ribbon .32.00
Medal, Spanish Am War Veteran, fob-type drop, w/ribbon, 1924 ..10.00
Medal, Spanish Am War Veteran's Reunion, bronze, 1937, EX ...12.50
Medal, WWI, NY State Victory, state seal, bl/gray ribbon 15.00
Medal, WWI, Town Service, eagle/state seal, w/ribbon, NM 17.50
Medal, WWII, Air Force commendation, w/ribbon 14.00
Medal, WWII, Air Medal, w/ribbon, M in orig bl case 32.00
Medal, WWII, Asiatic Pacific Campaign, w/ribbon 17.50
Medal, WWII, Marine Corps, Maltese Cross, sterling 15.00
Overalls, WWII, Army tanker, 1-pc, herringbone, EX 37.50
Pants, combat; WWII, Marine Corps, gr herringbone, EX 24.00
Pillow cover, WWII, Army, For Freedom & Security, M 5.00
Pin, WWI, US Navy civilian service, celluloid, 1¼x1" 3.00
Ring, WWI Veteran, red/wht/bl enameling, 1918 at top 20.00
Sabre, 1902 officer, etched blade, Peterson, +scabbard 88.00
Shoes, WWII, Marine, brn dress low-tops, pr 22.50
Shoulderpatch, WWII, 10th Mtn Division, machine embr 7.00
Shoulderpatch, WWII, 442nd Regimental Combat Team, embr ..17.50
Shoulderpatch, WWII, 9th Air Force, embr on bl wool, M 12.00
Suit, WWII, aviator flying, complete w/belt, EX 75.00
Suspenders, M-1910, tan web w/brass fittings, EX 12.00
Tunic, WWII, Army Air Corps officer, khaki, all insignia, EX 42.00
Tunic, WWII, Navy pilot's, dress gr, w/bullion wing, EX 50.00
Uniform, WWII, Navy CPO torpedo man, 4-pc set, EX 48.00
Uniform, WWII, Red Cross Nurse, gray w/wht collar/cuffs, EX 45.00
Vest, hand grenade; WWI, 11 pockets, dtd 1918, EX 27.50
Wing, WWII, Navy Aircrew, pin-bk, mk sterling 25.00
Wings, WWII, Senior Pilot, embr cloth on wool, pr 22.00
Yearbook, 5th Infantry Division, hardcover, dtd 1941, EX 37.50

Miscellaneous

China, medal, Commemorative Opposing Am in Assisting Korea ..145.00
Czechoslovakia, Commemorative Cross for Volunteers, 1918 ......32.00
E Germany, medal, Faithful Fulfillment of Duty 1st Class 12.50
Finland, medal, Order of Cross of Liberty, w/swords, 1939 ....85.00
France, medal, Croix de Guerre, Foreign Legion type 22.50
Greece, medal, Military Merit 4th Class 22.00
Iraq, hat, Republican Guard, EX 75.00
Iraq, license plate, Army 10.00
Kenya, medal, 1963 Campaign, scarce, EX 42.50
Mexico, medal, Service in Far East, EX 50.00
Netherlands, medal, Expedition Cross W Africa 1912-14, EX 85.00
Philippines, shoulder tab, Scout Ranger, M 4.00
Poland, medal, Merit for Safeguarding Public Order, M 22.50
Serbia, medal, Balkan War, 1912, EX 25.00
Serbia, medal, 1914-18 War, EX 32.00
Soviet Union, medal, Defense of Leningrad, EX 24.00
Soviet Union, medal, 25th Anniversary of WWII 17.50

Milk Glass

Milk glass is the current collector's name for milk-white opaque glass. The early glassmaker's term was Opal Ware. Originally attempted in England in the 18th century with the intention of imitating china, milk glass was not commercially successful until the mid-1800s. Pieces produced in the U.S.A., England, and France during the 1870-1900 period are highly prized for their intricate detail and fiery, opalescent edges.

Our advisor for this category is Rod Dockery; he is listed in the Directory under Texas. Several standard collectors' books have been referenced in our listings: Belknap (B), Ferson (F), Garrison (G), Lindsey (L), Millard (M), and Warman (W). See also Animal Dishes with Covers; Bread Plates; Historical Glass; Westmoreland.

Bottle, scent; Jenny Lind 75.00
Bowl, Daisy, pnt, F-165 ....80.00
Bowl, Flared Lattice, ftd, Fenton, #9023 ....25.00
Bowl, Grape, Imperial, w/lid, G-59, 11½" 30.00
Bowl, shallow, Fenton, #3622 ....40.00
Bowl, Waffle, B-110A 30.00
Butter dish, Rose, Imperial, G-161 ....35.00
Butter dish, Tree of Life & Daisy, rare 105.00
Butter dish, Versailles w/rose decor, +cr & sug w/lid ..95.00
Cake stand, Grape, ftd, Imperial, G-375, 10" 40.00
Candle holder, Crucifix, Imperial, G-119, 9½" 80.00
Candle holder, Daisy & Button, ftd, 2½", pr 15.00
Candle holder, Hobnail, Fenton, #3670, pr 18.00
Candy container, elk's tooth, w/screw-on lid, 3" ...125.00
Compote, Atlas, scalloped rim, B-103 ....95.00
Covered dish, Baby Moses on cattail base, unmk, B-160, 6¼" 200.00
Covered dish, Battleship Maine, L-466, EX orig gilt, 8" L 75.00
Covered dish, Battleship Oregon, att Flaccus, 6⅜" L 60.00
Covered dish, Battleship Wheeling, F-39 ....65.00
Covered dish, Uncle Sam on battleship base, F-552 ....55.00
Covered dish, Watch Cover, Imperial, G-260 ....35.00
Covered dish, Wooley Lamb on Bo Peep base, F-35 ....265.00
Creamer, Coreopsis 95.00
Creamer, Paneled Wheat, F-255 ....47.00
Creamer & sugar bowl, Blackberry, F-250/F-251 ....100.00
Creamer & sugar bowl, Dahlia, w/lid, M-152b 55.00
Cruet, Hobnail, Fenton, #3767, 7-oz 28.00
Dresser set, Hobnail, Imperial, G-741, 3-pc set 90.00
Epergne, Diamond Lace, Fenton, #4801, 10", 4-pc 58.00
Fern bowl, fern fronds on sides, chain rim, oval, 10x8" 35.00
Flower bowl, Swan Song, Macbeth-Evans, 2¾x4½" L 12.00
Jug, Fenton, #6066, 6" 20.00
Mustard, Bull's Head, F-53, dtd, no ladle 95.00
Pitcher, Coreopsis, EX decor 150.00

Pitcher, owl figure, Challinor and Taylor, F-587, $195.00.

Pitcher, Windmill, Imperial, G-741, 3-pt 30.00
Plate, Anchor & Yacht, B-13a 30.00
Plate, Ancient Castle, B-12e, 7" 40.00
Plate, Arch Border, M-1b, 6" 15.00
Plate, California Bear, orig gold, F-543 ....105.00
Plate, Chrysanthemum, orig pnt, B-14e, 6½" 25.00
Plate, Easter Chicks, F-492 ....35.00
Plate, Easter Ducks, F592 ....35.00
Plate, Heart Border, B-13e 15.00
Plate, Leaf, Fenton, #5108, 11" 22.00
Plate, Niagara Falls, B-4e 30.00
Plate, Pinwheel Border, B-18, 10½" 50.00
Plate, Triangular Leaf & Chain, M-10a 17.00
Plate, Triple Forget-Me-Not, SS St Louis, B-21c ...35.00

Plate, Woof Woof, B-13f 50.00
Platter, Retriever, B-53 ....95.00
Sugar bowl, Beehive, sgn Vallerysthal, M-134a 75.00
Syrup, Alba, F-139 ....60.00
Tile, Owl, fire-pnt front, 5⅞" 55.00
Tray, Barred Scrolls, shaped, 10x7" 15.00
Tray, Beaded Wheel, W-112b 15.00
Tray, buffalo heads ea end, mk M, 12x8" 35.00
Tray, dresser; floral hdls, 9" 22.00
Tray, Five Loops, butterfly shape, #72 on bottom, 6x5" 12.50
Tray, Pointed Rib, shaped, McKee, 6½" L 18.00
Urn, w/lid, M-148, 8" 24.00
Vase, Loganberry, Imperial, G-356 ....32.00
Wine, Feather 25.00

Millefiori

Millefiori was a type of art glass produced during the late 1800s. Literally, the term means 'thousand flowers,' an accurate description of its appearance. Canes, fused bundles of multicolored glass threads such as are often used in paperweights, were cut into small cross sections, arranged in the desired pattern, refired, and shaped into articles such as cruets, lamps, and novelty items. It is still being produced, and many examples found on the market today are of fairly recent manufacture. See also Paperweights.

Bottle, rose cut o/l w/millefiori base & stopper, 6⅞x2¾" 995.00
Coffeepot, cobalt bkground, bl hdl/spout, 5¾" 225.00
Cup & saucer, bl bkground, 1½x2½" 85.00
Syrup pitcher, frosted hdl, shell thumb lift, SP top 200.00
Vase, mc, gr hdls, 3" 55.00

Tumbler, 4", $95.00.

Miniatures

There is some confusion as to what should be included in a listing of miniature collectibles. Some feel the only true miniature is the salesman's sample; other collectors consider certain small-scale children's toys to be appropriately referred to as miniatures, while yet others believe a miniature to be any small-scale item that gives evidence to the craftsmanship of its creator. For salesman's samples, see specific category; other types are listed below. See also Dollhouses and Furnishings; Children's Things.

Ranking at the top of today's leading collectibles, scaled 1:12" miniatures represent the work of hundreds of artisans who supply local shops with highly prized one-of-a-kind articles and specialties, all scaled one inch to the foot. Many leading producers and distributors of collectibles have entered the field as well. Clubs for miniature enthusiasts have sprung up throughout the United States, Canada, and abroad.

Blanket box, painted green over red, signed Cornell, 1809, wood and paint loss, 13", $2,600.00.

Andirons, wrought iron, penny ft, ring top, tooling, 8" 500.00
Bed warmer, copper, brass ferrule, trn wood hdl, 9" 175.00
Bed warmer, copper, brass ferrule, trn wood hdl, 9", EX 100.00
Bellows, cvd pine, 4-color pnt decor, 5" L 135.00
Blanket chest, pine w/gr rpt, dvtl, sq nails, 9" L 150.00
Box, dome top, relief cvg, wire nails, 3" L 25.00
Box, pine w/orig mc pnt, houses/trees, tin hasp, 4" L, NM 175.00
Bucket, staved, brass band, label: Our Own, mk Murdock, 5" 175.00
Catcher's mitt & mask, leather/wire/cloth, mitt: 5" dia, EX 2,200.00
Chair, side; pine w/simple inlay, 4 shaped bk slats, 6" 50.00
Chest, Empire, pine w/curly maple grpt, 5-drw, 10x9", EX 300.00
Chest, jigsaw work, lectern-like top, birch, 11" 70.00
Chest, mahog Sheraton, trn ft, reeded corners, 4-drw, 15" 600.00
Chest, poplar w/oak veneer bow-front, 4-drw/dvtl, 13x11" 300.00
Churn, wooden dasher, ca 1900, 3" 18.00
Clock, tall case; mahog veneer, cats inlay, Cave Felem, 14" 100.00
Clock, wag-on-wall, brass gears, wood plates/case, 7" 475.00
Cupbrd, jelly; poplar, scalloped base, dbl-door, 18x14" 325.00
Desk, pine/mahog, slant front, 3-drw, rprs, 11x10" 375.00
Footstool, pine w/orig red pnt, sq nails, mortised, 9" L 375.00
Jar, stoneware, appl open hdls, sm chips, 4¼" 25.00
Rocker, curved seat apron, trn legs, vase splat, rpt, 9" 165.00
Sleigh, poplar w/pnt stripes/floral, steel runners, 14", EX 525.00
Spinning wheel, ivory, 3¾" 75.00
Spinning wheel, working model, sgn Pearson, 18" 65.00
Table, pine w/star inlay, tripod base, 7" octagon top, 5½" 80.00
Trunk, leather bound w/brass tacks, Nath'l March, 9" L, EX 200.00

Minton

Thomas Minton established his firm in 1793 at Stoke on Trent and within a few years began producing earthenware with blue-printed patterns similar to the ware he had learned to decorate while employed by the Caughley Porcelain Factory. The Willow pattern was one of his most popular. Neither this nor the porcelain made from 1798 to 1805 was marked (except for an occasional number series), making identification often impossible.

After 1805 until about 1816, fine tea services, beehive-shaped honey pots, trays, etc., were hand decorated with florals, landscapes, Imari-type designs, and neoclassic devices. These were often marked with crossed 'L's. It was Minton that invented the acid gold process of decorating, which is now used by a number of different companies.

From 1816 until 1823, no porcelain was made. Through the twenties and thirties, the ornamental wares with colorful decoration of applied fruits and florals and figurines in both bisque and enamel were usually left unmarked. As a result, they have been erroneously attributed to other potters. Some of the ware that was marked bears a deliberate imitation of Meissen's crossed swords. From the late twenties through the forties, Minton made a molded stoneware line (mugs, jugs, teapots, etc.) with florals or figures in high relief. These were marked with an embossed scroll with an 'M' in the bottom curve. Fine parian ware was made in the late 1840s, and in the fifties Minton perfected and produced a line of quality majolica for which they gained widespread recognition. Leadership of the firm was assumed by Minton's son Herbert sometime around the middle of the 19th century. Working hand in hand with Leon Arnoux, who was both a chemist and an artist, he managed to secure the company's financial future through constant, successful experimentation with both materials and decorating methods. During the Victorian era, M.L. Solon decorated pieces in the pate-sur-pate style, often signing his work; these examples are considered to be the finest of their type. After 1862 all wares were marked 'Minton' or 'Mintons,' with an impressed year cipher.

Many collectors today reassemble the lovely dinnerware patterns that have been made by Minton. Perhaps one of their most popular lines was Minton Rose. The company itself once counted forty-seven versions of this pattern being made by other potteries around the world. In addition to less expensive copies, elaborate hand-enameled pieces were also made by Aynsley, Crown Staffordshire, and Paragon China.

Dinnerware values given in the following listings are for items that were produced from 1870-1950. Current production pieces bring lower prices on the resale market. Our advisor for this category is Glenn Roe (Old China Patterns Ltd.); he is listed in the Directory under New York. See also Majolica; Pate-Sur-Pate.

Bouillon cup & saucer, #B898 ....95.00
Bouillon cup & saucer, Cockatrice, pk 95.00
Bowl, soup; #B898, rimmed 65.00
Bowl, vegetable; Kent, oval 125.00
Cake plate, Kent 75.00
Cup & saucer, Adam, #H2581 ....90.00
Cup & saucer, Adam, #S703 (new) 57.50
Cup & saucer, Ashton 50.00
Cup & saucer, Belbrachen, #S696 ....57.50
Cup & saucer, Chinese Tree, #2067 ....90.00
Cup & saucer, Gold Laurentian 65.00
Cup & saucer, Gold Pandora, #H2530 ....57.50
Cup & saucer, Kent 65.00
Cup & saucer, Porcelain Ball, w/acid gold, #H5161 ....480.00
Figurine, Education of Dog, kneeling child/dog, wht, 10" 600.00
Plate, bread; Ardmore 25.00
Plate, dinner; Adam, #H2581 ....88.00
Plate, dinner; Adam, #S703 (new) 56.50
Plate, dinner; Ardmore 55.00
Plate, dinner; Ashton 45.00
Plate, dinner; Belbrachen, #S696 ....56.50
Plate, dinner; Chinese Tree, #2067 ....88.00
Plate, dinner; Gold Laurentian 65.00
Plate, dinner; Gold Pandora; #H2530 ....56.50
Plate, dinner; Kent 55.00
Plate, dinner; Monarch, gold trim, #S729 ....37.50
Plate, dinner; Monarch, plain, #B1468 ....35.00
Plate, dinner; Monarch, platinum trim, #S728 ....37.50
Plate, dinner; Porcelain Ball, acid gold trim, #5161 ....472.50
Plate, dinner; Stanwood, #B1113 (old) 69.50
Plate, dinner; Stanwood, no # (new) 53.50
Plate, dinner; Washington, #S160 ....173.50

Plate, dinner; Windsor, bl, #K396 ....**56.50**
Plate, lady's portrait, artist sgn, gold scrolls, mk, 9½" **650.00**
Plate, salad; Ardmore **40.00**
Plate, salad; Pk Cockatrice **75.00**
Platter, Ashton, 14" **125.00**
Platter, Kent, 14" **175.00**
Urn, sailboat band on bl w/gilt, sgn JE Dean, hdls, 6", pr **900.00**
Vase, pate-sur-pate, 4-color, figure w/lamp, Solon, 8x6" **2,100.00**
Vase, pond lilies/cattails on yel, gilt ring 'hdls,' 11" **1,400.00**

Mirrors

The first mirrors were made in England in the 13th century of very thin glass backed with lead. Reverse-painted glass mirrors were made in this country as early as the late 1700s and remained popular throughout the next century. The simple hand-painted panel was separated from the mirrored section by a narrow slat, and the frame was either the dark-finished Federal style or the more elegant, often-gilded Sheraton.

Mirrors changed with the style of other furnishings; but whatever type you purchase, as long as the glass sections remain solid, even broken or flaking mirrors are more valued than replaced glass. Careful resilvering is acceptable if excessive deterioration has taken place. Our advisor for this category is Michael Hinton; he is listed in the Directory under Pennsylvania.

Key:
Emp — Empire   QA — Queen Anne
Fed — Federal

Burl veneer-on-pine line-inlay scroll, rpl glass, 22x13" **245.00**
Chpndl mahog scroll, gilt/mahog molded liner, 36x16" **550.00**
Chpndl mahog scroll, regilded eagle, rpl glass, 28x15", EX **425.00**
Chpndl mahog scroll, 18x11", EX **400.00**
Chpndl mahog veneer-on-pine scroll, molded fr, rpr, 37x19" **850.00**
Chpndl mahog veneer-on-pine scroll, molded fr, 42x23", EX .**1,500.00**
Chpndl mahog-on-pine scroll, rpl ear, age crack, 36x19" **675.00**
Chpndl mahog-on-pine scroll, rprs/rpl blocks, 45x22" **900.00**

Chippendale mahogany and parcel-gilt scroll-cut looking glass, England, ca 1780, 36", $1,500.00.

Chpndl molded walnut scroll, rpl mirror/ear rpr, 21x13" **400.00**
Chpndl-style mahog veneer scroll, gilt phoenix, rprs, 43x23" **950.00**
Chpndl-style mahog veneer scroll, gilt phoenix/liner, 29x18" **525.00**
Co Emp, 2-part, half-trn w/corner blocks, rvpt house, 22x13" **450.00**
Continental giltwood, urn/swag crest, 1780s, regilt, 23x11" **495.00**
Courting, pine fr w/rvpt inserts (VG/rpl), shaped top, 17" **850.00**

Emp, trn half columns, corner blocks/rosettes, rpt, 33x23" **150.00**
Emp 2-part, blk/gold rpt fr, rvpt fruit, 20x11", EX **325.00**
Fed 2-part, mahog veneer/curly maple, rvpt house, 31x17" **550.00**
Folding, cherry w/line inlay, 2-part oval case, 4x7" **65.00**
French giltwood, flamingo/urn crest, egg/dart fr, 60x32" **1,200.00**
Geo II style, parcel gilt, scroll crest/portrait mask, 77" **5,000.00**
Girandole, giltwood, animal/foliage crest, rstr, 40" **2,900.00**
Girandole, giltwood, eagle atop, lion head in pendant, 44" **3,250.00**
Louis XVI style giltwood, floral-filled basket atop, 54" **850.00**
Mahog Fed, gilt pediment w/urn & florals, 63x24" **3,900.00**
Mahog veneer 2-part, beveled fr, rvpt house/rpr, 22x12" **175.00**
Mahog w/fruit & rose crest, molded, 39x31" **190.00**
Pine w/orig red & yel grpt, beveled, 17x12" **300.00**
Pine w/red traces, 2-part architectural fr, VG rvpt, 17x11" **75.00**
Plateau, SP, vintage border, oval, 21" L **135.00**
QA mahog, 2-part, fret-cvd crest, str molded sides, 47" **1,050.00**
QA walnut veneer-on-pine, cut-out crest w/birds, 30" **750.00**
Regency giltwood, convex, eagle surmount, 42", 25" dia **600.00**
Regency giltwood, mirrored fr, scroll/leaf corners, 43x36" **2,000.00**
Shaving, mahog veneer Sheraton, line inlay, bow case, 19x19" .**175.00**
Shaving, mahog w/figured veneer, Empire, trn posts w/finials **400.00**
Victorian, 4-part, oak & molded gilt, beveled glass, 30x30" **225.00**
2-Part pine w/red pnt, fluted fr, EX rvpt, 19x13" **650.00**

Mocha

Mocha Ware is utilitarian pottery made principally in England (and to a lesser extent in France) between 1780 and 1840 on the then prevalent creamware and pearlware bodies. Initially only those pieces decorated in the seaweed pattern were called 'Mocha,' while geometrically decorated pieces were referred to as 'Banded Creamware.' Other types of decorations were called 'Dipped Ware.' During the last thirty to forty years, the term 'Mocha' has been applied to the entire realm of 'Industrialized Slipware' — pottery decorated by the turner on his lathe using coggle wheels and slip cups.

Mocha was made in numerous patterns — Tree, Seaweed or Dandelion, Rope (also called Worm or Loop), Cat's-eye, Tobacco Leaf, Lollypop or Balloon, Marbled, Marbled and Combed, Twig, Geometric or Checkered, Banded, and slip decorations of rings, dots, flags, tulips, wavy lines, etc. It came into its own as a collectible in the latter half of the 1940s and has become increasingly popular as more and more people are exposed to the rich colorings and artistic appeal of its varied forms of abstract decoration.

The collector should take care not to confuse the early pearlware and creamware Mocha with the later kitchen yellow ware, graniteware, and ironstone sporting mocha-type decoration that was produced in America by such potters as J. Vodrey, George S. Harker, Edwin Bennett, and John Bell. This type was also produced in Scotland and Wales and was marketed well into the 20th century.

Bowl, cat's eye, wht/brn/bl on orange, blk stripes, 5", VG **200.00**
Bowl, cat's eye band, blk stripes/bl bands, 2½x4½", NM **475.00**
Bowl, earthworm in lt bl/blk, tooled orange rim, 4x8½", EX **600.00**
Bowl, seaweed, blk rim band, 2¼x4½" **230.00**
Creamer, brn/lt bl stripes, emb gr band/leaf hdl, 3½", VG **175.00**
Creamer, seaweed, leaf hdl, prof rpr, miniature, 2" **250.00**
Cup & saucer, seaweed on gray/brn, ribbed rim, NM **900.00**
Cup & saucer, seaweed on lt brn, miniature, 2", 3¼" dia **700.00**
Measure, seaweed, gray/bl bands, emb rim, Imperial, pt **130.00**
Mug, cat's eye/seaweed, emb rim/leaf hdl, 4" dia, EX **850.00**
Mug, earthworm, yel/brn bands, blk stripes, leaf hdl, 3½", NM ..**350.00**
Mug, geometrics/stripes, 5-color, emb leaf hdl, 6", EX **700.00**
Mug, seaweed on orange band, gr emb rim, brn stripes, 5" **350.00**

Mug, wide brn band w/bl stripe top & bottom, leaf hdl, 5" 125.00
Mug, wide brn/orange marbleized band, ribbed hdl, 2¾", NM 55.00
Mug, wide 6-color marbleized band, leaf hdl, 4½", EX 675.00
Pepper castor, emb bl/wht stripes on wht, 4⅝", EX 80.00
Pepper pot, seaweed, ribbed shoulder, ftd, dome top, 4" 725.00
Pitcher, earthworm, emb band, 4-color bands, leaf hdl, 8" 900.00
Pitcher, earthworm, emb spout/band/leaf hdl, 6¾", EX 500.00
Pitcher, earthworm on wide band, leaf hdl, 5-color, 7", EX 925.00
Pitcher, emb gr bands, 3-color stripes, leaf hdl, 4¾", EX 325.00
Pitcher, geometrics/stripes, 5-color, emb leaf hdl, 7½", EX 1,450.00
Pitcher, seaweed on orange, blk stripes, bbl shape, 6", VG 300.00
Salt cellar, earthworm on tan band, ftd, 2x3", EX 300.00
Salt cellar, seaweed, gray band/blk stripes, rim chips, 3" 200.00
Sugar bowl, marbleizing, 3-color, stains, miniature, 2⅜", EX 425.00
Sugar bowl, seaweed on lt brn, w/lid, miniature, 2½" 850.00
Tea caddy, geometrics, 3-color, rpr lid, 5", EX 525.00
Teapot, seaweed on lt brn, leaf hdl, str spout, 4½", NM 925.00
Waste bowl, cat's eye, brn/wht on orange band, 3x5½", EX 105.00
Waste bowl, earthworm, blk/wht on bl, wear/hairlines, 2¾x5" ...175.00
Waste bowl, seaweed, blk on ochre, bl stripes, 3x5" 450.00

Molds

Food molds have become a popular collectible — not only for their value as antiques, but because they also revive childhood memories of elaborate ice cream Santas with candy trim or barley sugar figurals adorning a Christmas tree. Ice cream molds were made of pewter and came in a wide variety of shapes and styles. Chocolate molds were made in fewer shapes but were more detailed. They were usually made of tin, copper, and occasionally of pewter. Hard candy molds were usually metal, although primitive maple sugar molds (usually simple hearts, rabbits, and other animals) were carved from wood. (Unless otherwise indicated, those in our listings are cast aluminum or stainless steel.) Cake molds were made of cast iron or cast aluminum and were most common in the shape of a lamb, a rabbit, or Santa Claus. Our advisors for this category are Dale and Jean Van Kuren; they are listed in the Directory under New York.

Chocolate Molds

Bear, standing, 5" 150.00
Boy in hat on bicycle, EX details, half of 2-part mold, 8¾" 375.00
Boys w/heart mouths (3 rows of 3), tin plated, 17x8½" 40.00
Bride or groom, 10", ea 140.00
Bride or groom, 7½", ea 95.00
Bulldog, 5" 75.00
Chick w/hat, 5½" 40.00
Dog w/hat, 6½" 95.00
Duck, 4½" 30.00
Easter egg, Randle & Smith, 6½" 70.00
Elephant, standing, lg 65.00
Fish, full body, sits upright, 9" 125.00
Girls (3), folding, US Patent Pending, 9½" 45.00
Hen, setting, lg 75.00
Hen on nest, 5" 48.00
Indian, 5¼" 78.00
Kewpie, 10" 125.00
Lamb, tin, 11" 95.00
Rabbit in suit, 6" 40.00
Rabbit on hind legs, 11½" 95.00
Rabbit on hind legs, 16" 325.00
Rabbit on lg egg, 8½" 68.00
Rabbit on toadstool, 12½" 235.00

Rabbit pulling cart, 7½" 38.00
Rabbit smoking pipe, 7" 65.00
Rabbits (4 in row, seated), tin plated, folding, 9½" 45.00
Rabbits holding lg egg, 9" 78.00
Rooster, 3-part, USA, 5½x6½" 75.00
Rooster, 4 in a row 75.00
Rooster, 5" 40.00
Santa, 4" 95.00
Santa (4 in row), Made in Germany, 8" 55.00
Scottie dog, 4½" 48.00
Scottish girl in kilt, 10" 140.00
Sheep, 4½" 68.00

Soldier, 5½", $50.00.

Squirrel, tin, 9½" 85.00
Squirrel, 4½" 42.00
Teddy bear, 11½" 395.00
Train, 3x6" 85.00

Hard Candy Molds

Battleship in waves, TM-256, groove for stick, 2½x1¼" 55.00
Elephant, TM-138, groove for stick, 1¾x1¼" 60.00
Hand, TM-31, groove for stick, 1¾x1¼" 42.50
Lion, 3-part, TM-40, groove for stick, 4x5" 115.00
Locomotive, 3-part, TM-14, groove for stick, 3½x6" 125.00
Mouse, TM-37, groove for stick, 2¼x1¼" 90.00
Rabbits, baby in cart, T-41, groove for stick, 4½x3½" 100.00
Steamboat w/paddle wheel, groove for stick, 1¼x2¼" 88.00
Teddy bear, walnut, rectangular, 2-part, makes 6, 1½x12" 130.00

Ice Cream Molds

Apple, E-239 ....22.50
Asparagus bunch, #333, 3" 35.00
Auto, E-1080, 3" 65.00
Basket, 3-part, oval, E-305 ....35.00
Beehive, dome style, #302, 3" 40.00
Bell, #605 ....32.00
Bonnet w/face, E-968 ....125.00
Calla lily, 3-part, #210 ....35.00
Carnation w/stem, E-361, ...35.00
Chick in egg, vertical, #600, 4" 35.00
Christmas wreath w/bow, E&Co, 5¾" 65.00
Cucumber, E-226 ....25.00
Cupid sits on rose, full figure, E-959 ....55.00
Dahlia, #299, 3" 18.00

Eagle, E&Co #655 ....150.00
Easter egg, E-906 ....22.50
Engagement ring, #376 ....30.00
Football, E-1159 ....25.00
Gourd, 4" 18.00
Grape cluster, E-278 ....20.00
Log, E-987 ....25.00
Masonic emblem, Shrine, #1081 ....35.00
Orange, #307, 3" 25.00
Peach, E-233 ....25.00
Peach half w/stone, #160 ....25.00
Petunia, 3" 22.00
Pumpkin, #600, pewter 28.00
Pumpkin, E-309 ....25.00
Santa Claus, E-991 ....48.00
Spade playing card, 4" 60.00
Strawberry, E-1021 ....30.00
Tomato, #208, 3" 40.00
Wedding bell w/cupid, E-1019 ....40.00

Maple Sugar Molds

Heart, wood, iron hinge, pouring hole at top, 1890s, 5" 85.00
Heart & clover, primitive, 5x17½" 50.00
Heart w/face, hand-cvd wood, in orig tin case, 1800s, 5½" 425.00
Openwork on rnd fluted cups, CI, 1840s, 12 in 11x16" fr 110.00
Strawberry, deeply cvd pine, rectangle, 1830s, 1¾x5½x9" 165.00
6 cutouts, birds/fish/etc, 1-pc, 16x3" 155.00

Miscellaneous

Aluminum, lamb, 12" 35.00
Aluminum, Santa Claus, 12" 45.00
Cast iron, bird on branch, oval, 5" 75.00
Cast iron, 3 elephants, 2-pc, 6¾" L 75.00
Cloverleaf, for doughnuts, Pat The Ace Co 115.00
Copper, Turk's head, decorative detail, dvtl, dents, 10" 135.00
Tin, fish shape, 2½x10½x7½", EX 65.00
Tin, fruit in relief, Kreamer, 4½x8½x6½" 65.00
Wood w/cvd floral, high tin sides, curved heart form, 7" 275.00

Monot and Stumpf

The firm of Monot and Stumpf was organized in 1868, the merger of the E.S. Monot and F. Stumpf glassworks. It was located in Pantin, France. They produced fine art glass of various types until ca 1892, when the company reorganized and became known as the Cristallerie de Pantin.

Oil lamp, amber-pk opal swirl shade/font, marble std, 19" 325.00
Salt cellar, clear opal w/gold lustre int, 1¼x2½" 65.00
Salt cellar, lav-pk opal, gold lustre int, fluted, 1⅝" 75.00
Salt cellar, pk opal stripes, gold lustre int, Pantin, 1¼x2" 65.00
Shade, pk irid, lt gold lustre int, 4¾x7⅞" 175.00
Shade, pk opal, swirled ribs, ruffled/flared, 6½x8½" 225.00
Vase, pk opal to clear w/gold irid, HP florals, hdls, 10¾" 165.00

Mont Joye

Mont Joye was a type of acid-cut French cameo glass produced by Cristallerie de Pantin in Paris around the turn of the century. It is accented by enamels. Our advisor for this category is Don Williams; he is listed in the Directory under Missouri.

Bud vase, poppies, blk/gold on textured gr, 6" 200.00
Dish, floral/buds, gold/wht/yel on gray texture, 4-lobe, 6" 400.00
Rose bowl, violets, HP on clear/frosted, 4½x4" 400.00
Vase, floral, bl & mauve on purple, 7½" 850.00
Vase, floral, gold w/wht opal jewels on dk gr, 27" 1,200.00
Vase, floral w/gilt, sq, sgn, 6" 425.00
Vase, orchid, wht on red w/gold scrolls, 11" 285.00
Vase, poppies, gilt/lav on translucent clear, flat rim, 16" 600.00
Vase, poppies/leaves, gold-traced on textured amethyst, 8" 425.00
Vase, thistles/scrolls on ice gr to opaque, shouldered, 12" 1,200.00

Moorcroft

William Moorcroft began to work for MacIntyre Potteries in 1897. At first he was the chief designer but very soon took over their newly created Art Pottery department. His first important design was the Aurelian Ware, part transfer and part handpainted. Very shortly thereafter, around the turn of the century, he developed his famous Florian Ware with heavy slip, done in mostly blue and white. Since the early 1900s, there has been a sucession of designs, most of them very characteristic of the company. Moorcroft left MacIntyre in 1913 and went out on his own. He had already well established his name, having won prizes and gold medals at the St. Louis World's Fair as well as in Paris. In 1929 Queen Mary, who had been collecting his pottery, made him 'Potter to the Queen,' and the pottery was so stamped up until 1949. William Moorcroft died in 1945, and his son Walter ran the company until recent years. The factory is still in existence. They now produce different designs but continue to use the characteristic slipwork.

Moorcroft pottery was sold abroad in Canada, the United States, Australia, and Europe as well as in specialty areas such as the island of Bermuda.

Moorcroft went through a 'Japanese' stage in the early teens with his lovely lustre glazes, Oriental shapes, and decorations. During the mid-teens he began to produce his most popular Pomegranate Ware, as well as Wisteria (often called 'Fruit'). Around that time he also designed the popular Pansy line as well as Leaves and Grapes. Soon he introduced a beautiful landscape series called variously Hazeldine, Moonlit Blue, Eventide, and Dawn. These wonderful designs along with Claremont (Mushrooms) seem to be the most sought after by collectors today. It would be possible to add many other designs to this list.

During the 1920s and '30s, Moorcroft became very interested in highly fired Flambe (red) glazes. These could only be achieved through a very difficult procedure which he himself perfected in secret. He later passed the knowledge on to his son.

Dating of this pottery is done both by knowledge of the designs and shapes as well as by the signatures and marks on the bottom of each piece; an experienced person can usually narrow it down to a short time frame. Advisors for this category are Wilfred and Dolli Cohen; they are listed in the Directory under California.

Ashtray, hibiscus, red on bl, 3½x6¼" 68.00
Bowl, grapes & leaves around border on gr, 1945, 12" 440.00
Bowl, hibiscus, coral on gr, sgn, 6" 245.00
Bowl, Moonlit Bl Landscape, ca 1925, 10½" 1,850.00
Jar, pomegranates on bl/brn mottle, hdls/lid, #102, 7" 1,300.00
Plate, Claremont, toadstools on bl-gr, 7" 600.00
Vase, anemones, bls/reds/purple on bl to gr, 6" 750.00
Vase, anemones on bl, Royal Warrant label, 5" ...200.00
Vase, Claremont, toadstools, sgn/label, ca 1925, 13" 3,000.00
Vase, cornflowers, red/brn/gr, ftd trumpet form, 9x6" 2,250.00
Vase, Moonlit Bl Landscape, 5" 1,300.00
Vase, orchids, 4-color on yel & dk bl, rnd, 9" ...1,500.00
Vase, pomegranates, red/bl on brn, 7" 500.00

Vase, pomegranates, reds/gr/bl on dk bl/gr, hdls, 6" 1,300.00
Vase, wisteria, yel/bl/pk on tan to bl gloss, 21x4½" 425.00

Vase, Claremont, red and yellow toadstools on blue-green mottled ground, large blue script signature, 1928, 12x10½", $4,500.00.

Morgantown Glass

Incorporated in 1899, the Morgantown Glass Works experienced many name changes over the years. Today 'Morgantown Glass' is a generic term used to indicate all glass produced there. Purchased by Fostoria in 1965, the factory was permanently closed in 1971. Our advisor for this category is Jerry Gallagher, longtime researcher of the company and author of *A Collector's Handbook of Old Morgantown Glass, 1899-1971*. He is listed in the Directory under Minnesota. See Clubs, Newsletters, and Catalogs for information concerning Morgantown Collectors of America (a research society founded by Mr. Gallagher) and *The Morgantown Newscaster*, a quarterly M.A.C. journal with research updates and reports of current trends.

Meadow Green cased Alabaster #37 Barry jug with green foot, $585.00; matching Barry 13-oz. tumbler, $95.00.

Figurals

Chanticleer, cobalt w/crystal; stem, cocktail; 4-oz 65.00
Chanticleer, crystal; stem, cocktail; 4-oz 22.00
Chanticleer, pastel w/crystal; stem, cocktail; 4-oz 35.00
Chanticleer, ruby w/crystal; stem, cocktail; 4-oz 45.00
Jockey, crystal w/amber; stem, champagne; 6-oz 65.00
Jockey, crystal; stem, champagne; 6-oz 40.00
Mai Tai, crystal w/amber; stem, cocktail; Peacock Optic, 5-oz 58.00
Mai Tai, crystal w/amber; stem, sherbet; shallow, 10-oz 52.00
Old Crow, crystal; stem, cocktail; 6⅛", 5½-oz 70.00
Owl, ruby; tumbler, highball; 15-oz, rare 75.00

Summer Cornucopia, crystal; stem, champagne; 7-oz 115.00
Summer Cornucopia, crystal; stem, cordial; 1½-oz 175.00
Summer Cornucopia, crystal; stem, goblet; 9-oz 150.00
Top Hat, crystal w/Knickerbocker cutting; cocktail, 4½-oz 48.00
Top Hat, pastel w/crystal; stem, cocktail; 4½-oz 52.00
19th Hole, cobalt; stem, low ball; disk ft, 14-oz 55.00
19th Hole, crystal; stem, low ball; disk ft, 14-oz 42.00
19th Hole, wht opaque/gr; stem, low ball; disk ft, 14-oz 65.00

Adam Etch, crystal; stem, champagne; #7589 Laurette, 9-oz 27.50
Adam Etch, crystal; stem, goblet; #7589 Laurette, 5½-oz 25.00
Adonis etch, crystal; jug, Wide Optic, #37 Barry, 48-oz 215.00
Adonis etch, crystal; stem, goblet; #7604½ Heirloom, 9-oz 42.00
Adonis etch, crystal/gr; stem, goblet; #7606½ Athena, 9-oz 95.00
Adonis etch, gr; stem, parfait; #7604½ Heirloom, 5-oz 52.00
Adonis etch, rose; stem, goblet; #7604½ Heirloom, 9-oz 58.00
Adonis etch, topaz; stem, goblet; #7604½ Heirloom, 9-oz 58.00
Am Beauty etch, crystal; jug, no lid, #19 Flemish, 34-oz 235.00
Am Beauty etch, crystal; jug, w/lid, #2 Arcadia, 54-oz 295.00
Am Beauty etch, crystal; stem, goblet; #7695 Trumpet, 10-oz 55.00
Am Beauty etch, rose; jug, no lid, #39 Milton, 54-oz 335.00
Am Beauty etch, rose; stem, goblet; #7565 Astrid, 10-oz 60.00
Am Beauty etch, rose-amber; jug, w/lid, #39 Milton, 54-oz 335.00
Aquaria etch, crystal/gr; champagne, #7634 Oceana, 6-oz 87.50
Art Moderne, cobalt w/crystal; stem, candlestick; #7640½, pr ...335.00
Art Moderne, cobalt w/crystal; stem, cordial; #7640, 1½-oz 145.00
Art Moderne, cobalt w/crystal; stem, goblet; #7640, 9-oz 95.00
Art Moderne, crystal w/blk; stem, goblet; #7640, 9-oz 100.00
Art Moderne, crystal w/frost; stem, icer; DC Thorpe, 2-pc 245.00
Art Moderne, crystal w/pastel; stem, goblet; #7640, 9-oz 58.00
Baden etch, blk filament; stem, goblet; #7606½ Athena, 9-oz 95.00
Barry #37, crystal w/rose; jug, Palm Optic, 48-oz 325.00
Barry #37, Meadow gr cased Alabaster/gr; jug, ftd, 48-oz 585.00
Barry #37, Meadow gr/jade gr; jug, 48-oz 495.00
Barry #37AN, gr cased Alabaster/gr; tumbler, ftd, 13-oz 95.00
Biscayne etch, crystal w/gold; bar tumbler, #9715, 2½-oz 68.00
Biscayne etch, crystal w/gold; goblet; #7587 Kingsley, 9-oz 57.50
Bramble Rose etch, crystal; stem, champagne; #7577, 5½-oz 65.00
Bramble Rose etch, crystal; stem, goblet; #7577 Venus, 9-oz 57.50
Bramble Rose etch, rose; plate, luncheon; #1500, 8½" 32.00
Carlton, platinum Marco; bowl, flared, #4355 Janice, 13" 215.00
Carlton, platinum Marco; stem, goblet; #7653 Cantata, 9-oz 75.00
Carlton, topaz Madrid/crystal; stem, goblet; #7665, 9-oz 65.00
Carlton etch, crystal; stem, goblet; #7668 Galaxy, 10-oz 32.50
Carlton etch, crystal/blk; stem, goblet; #7606½, 9-oz 87.50
Cathay etch, crystal; stem, champagne; #771 Callahan, 5½-oz 50.00
Cathay etch, crystal; stem, cordial; #7711 Callahan, 1½-oz 75.00
Cathay etch, crystal; stem, goblet; #7711 Callahan, 9-oz 65.00
Corinth etch, crystal w/gold; stem, goblet; #7654 Lorna, 9-oz 58.00
Corinth etch, crystal w/gold; stem, wine; #7654 Lorna, 3-oz 68.00
Crinkle, amberina; tumbler, water; flat, #1962, 10-oz 68.00
Crinkle, amethyst; tankard, lemonade; #1962, 64-oz, 9" 75.00
Crinkle, amethyst; tumbler, iced tea; ftd, #1962, 13-oz 27.50
Crinkle, crystal; pitcher, juice; #1962, 34-oz, 6½" 48.00
Crinkle, gr; Ockner jug, #1962, 54-oz 68.00
Crinkle, gr; tumbler, iced tea; ftd, #1962, 13-oz 24.00
Crinkle, lt bl/frost; tumbler, flat, #1962, 64-oz 38.00
Crinkle, peacock bl; Ockner jug, #1962, 54-oz 95.00
Crinkle, peacock bl; tumbler, highball; flat, #1962, 12-oz 25.00
Crinkle, pk frost; Ockner jug, #1962, 54-oz 165.00
Crinkle, pk; sherbet, ftd, #1962, 6-oz 20.00
Crinkle, ruby; Ockner jug, #1962, 54-oz 135.00
Crinkle, ruby; tumbler, zombie; flat, #1962, 20-oz 38.00

El Mexicano, Hyacinth; Ockner jug, 54-oz 350.00
El Mexicano, ice; candle holder/vase, bulbous base, 4", pr 280.00
El Mexicano, Ice; sherbet, ftd, 7-oz 25.00
El Mexicano, Rose Quartz; bowl, salad; 10" 275.00
El Mexicano, Rose Quartz; decanter, liquor; w/stopper 385.00
El Mexicano, Rose Quartz; ice tub 295.00
El Mexicano, Rose Quartz; Ockner jug, 54-oz 325.00
El Mexicano, Rose Quartz; sherbet, ftd, 7-oz 52.00
El Mexicano, Rose Quartz; tumbler, iced tea; ftd, 13-oz 68.00
El Mexicano, Seaweed & Ice; bowl, salad; 10", minimum value ...210.00
El Mexicano, Seaweed & Ice; Del Rey jug, 50-oz, minimum 255.00
El Mexicano, Seaweed; relish, 3-part 100.00
El Mexicano, Seeweed; decanter, liquor; w/stopper 225.00
Elizabeth, azure; stem, goblet; #7630 Ballerina, 9-oz 80.00
Elizabeth, azure; stem, goblet; #7664 Queen Anne, 9-oz 100.00
Elizabeth, crystal; stem, wine; #7630 Ballerina, 2¾-oz 60.00
Fairwin, bl filament; stem, goblet; #7673 Lexington, 9-oz 110.00
Faun etch, crystal/blk; stem, champagne; #7640, 5½-oz 160.00
Faun etch, crystal/blk; stem, goblet; #7640 Art Moderne, 9-oz ...185.00
Fernlee, crystal/blk; stem, goblet; #7640 Art Moderne, 9-oz 125.00
Florence etch, crystal; stem, cocktail; #300 Touraine, 3-oz 45.00
Florence etch, crystal; stem, goblet; #300 Touraine, 9-oz 42.50
Floret etch, crystal; stem, goblet; #7684 Yale, 9-oz 85.00
Floret etch, crystal; stem, icer; w/insert, unknown # 65.00
Fontinelle, blk filament; stem, candlestick, low, #7620, pr 225.00
Fontinelle, blk filament; stem, goblet; #7620 Fontanne, 9-oz 145.00
Fontinelle, gr/crystal; stem, goblet; #7620 Fontanne, 9-oz 150.00
Frostie (Carlton) decor, crystal; punch bowl, #21, 12" 450.00

Golden Iris (light amber) #23 Margaret guest set, pulled pouring lip, $235.00.

Golf Ball, cobalt/crystal; candlestick; 2 styles, 4", pr 185.00
Golf Ball, cobalt/crystal; candy dish, flat, #1212 Michael, 7" 285.00
Golf Ball, cobalt/crystal; stem, champagne; 5½-oz 45.00
Golf Ball, cobalt/crystal; stem, goblet; 9-oz 55.00
Golf Ball, crystal; pilsner, 10-oz, 9", rare 145.00
Golf Ball, pastel/crystal; stem, goblet; from $48.00 up to 60.00
Golf Ball, rose/gr; candy dish, flat, #2938 Helga, 5" 650.00
Golf Ball, ruby/crystal; candy dish, #7858 Leora, 5½" 360.00
Golf Ball, ruby/crystal; candy dish, #9074 Maureen, 4½" 350.00
Golf Ball, ruby/crystal; candy dish, flat, #1212 Michael, 7" 260.00
Golf Ball, ruby/crystal; candy dish, flat, #2938 Helga, 5" 245.00
Golf Ball, ruby/crystal; compote, #643 Celeste 350.00
Golf Ball, ruby/crystal; stem, goblet; 9-oz 42.00
Golf Ball, Stiegel/crystal; candy dish, LeRoy decor, #2938, 5" 285.00
Guest set, azure; Festoon Optic, #25 Trudy, 2-pc 75.00
Guest set, azure; Peacock Optic; #24 Maria, 4-pc, rare 450.00
Guest set, bl opaque; #25 Trudy, bottle only 12.00
Guest set, bl opaque; Hollyhock decor, #23 Margaret 145.00
Guest set, Golden Iris; hdld, pulled spout, #23 Margaret 235.00
Guest set, gr opaque; #25 Trudy, 2-pc 75.00
Guest set, rose; Palm Optic, #25 Trudy, 2-pc 58.00

Guest set, yel opaque bottle/blk tumbler, #25 Trudy 195.00
Hollywood, blk band; tumbler, highball; flat, #8701, 12-oz 34.00
Hollywood, red band; jug, cocktail; #548 Fairbanks, 36-oz 225.00
Labelle etch, crystal/blk; stem, champagne; #7640 Art Moderne ..65.00
LeMons, cobalt/gold; stem, goblet; #7640 Art Moderne, 9-oz 195.00
LeMons, cobalt/platinum; stem, goblet; #7640, 9-oz 135.00
Mayfair etch, crystal; stem, champagne; #7668 Galaxy, 6-oz 27.00
Mayfair etch, crystal; stem, goblet; #7668 Galaxy, 10-oz 36.00
Melon, alabaster w/cobalt; beverage set, #20069, 7-pc 650.00
Mikado etch, crystal; stem, champagne; #7711 Callahan, 6-oz 37.50
Mikado etch, crystal; stem, goblet; #7711 Callahan, 10-oz 48.50
Monroe #7690, amber/crystal; stem, cordial; 1½-oz 110.00
Monroe #7690, amber/crystal; stem, goblet; 10-oz 88.00
Monroe #7690, amethyst/crystal; stem, cordial; 1½-oz 135.00
Monroe #7690, amethyst/crystal; stem, goblet; 10-oz 110.00
Monroe #7690, cobalt or ruby/crystal; stem, champagne; 6-oz 72.50
Monroe #7690, cobalt or ruby/crystal; stem, goblet; 9-oz 87.50
Morgantown Sq, crystal; stem, champagne; #77942, 5½-oz 130.00
Morgantown Sq, crystal; stem, goblet; flared, #77942, 10-oz 195.00
Morgantown Sq, DC Thorpe decor, stem, champagne; 5-oz 185.00
Morgantown Sq, DC Thorpe decor, stem, claret; 4½-oz 245.00
Nantucket etch, crystal; stem, goblet, Queen Anne, 10-oz 95.00
Nantucket etch, crystal/gr; stem, goblet; #7654 Lorna, 9-oz 75.00
Nasreen, crystal/blk; tumbler, #9074 Belton, 9-oz 58.00
Nasreen etch, blk filament; stem, sherbet; #7606½, 5½-oz 70.00
Nasreen etch, topaz/crystal; stem, claret; #7665 Laura, 5-oz 95.00
Old Bristol, cobalt w/opal disk-node; candlestick, 4", pr 310.00
Old Bristol, cobalt w/opal rim; plate, unknown #, 7½" 85.00
Old English #7678, cobalt/crystal; stem, champagne; 6½-oz 47.50
Old English #7678, cobalt/crystal; stem, goblet; 10-oz 58.00
Old English #7678, ruby/crystal; stem, goblet; 10-oz 55.00
Old English #7678, Stiegel gr/crystal; stem, goblet; 10-oz 45.00
Palm Optic, alexandrite; stem, iced tea; #7667, 12-oz 165.00
Palm Optic, azure; ice bucket, SP metal rim/bail 285.00
Palm Optic, azure; salver, unknown #, 7" 120.00
Palm Optic, azure; stem, champagne; #7536 Alycia, 9-oz 45.00
Palm Optic, azure; stem, goblet; #7536 Alycia, 5½-oz 50.00
Palm Optic, crystal; stem, goblet; #7577 Venus, 9-oz 35.00
Palm Optic, crystal/rose; jug, #37 Barry, 48-oz 260.00
Palm Optic, gr; stem, goblet; #7577 Venus, 9-oz 45.00
Palm Optic, rose; stem, goblet; #7577 Venus, 9-oz 38.00
Palm Optic, rose/gr; stem, goblet; #7614 Hampton, 9-oz 87.50
Palm Optic, rose/gr; stem, goblet; #7646 Sophisticate, 9-oz 90.00
Palm Optic, rose/gr; stem, wine; #7614 Hampton, 3-oz 95.00
Palm Optic, topaz; stem, goblet; #7577 Venus, 9-oz 35.00
Paragon #77943½, crystal/blk; stem, goblet; 9-oz 135.00
Paragon #77943½, crystal/blk; stem, sherbet; 5½-oz 80.00
Peacock Optic, gr or rose; stem, goblet; #7638 Avalon, 9-oz 37.50
Peacock Optic, gr; decanter, crystal stopper, #10½ Lynwood 345.00
Peacock Optic, gr; tumbler, bar; flat, #9051, 1½-oz 85.00
Picardy etch, crystal; stem, champagne; #7646, 5½-oz 35.00
Picardy etch, crystal; stem, goblet; #7646 Sophisticate, 9-oz 45.00
Pineapple Optic, amber; stem, goblet; #7544½ Vernon, 9-oz 45.00
Pineapple Optic, gr; stem, champagne; #7644½ Vernon, 5½-oz ...37.50
Pineapple Optic, gr; stem, goblet; #7644½ Vernon, 9-oz 50.00
Priscilla, w/blk filament; stem, champagne; #7620, 6-oz 85.00
Priscilla, w/blk filament; stem, goblet; #7620 Fontanne, 9-oz 110.00
Pygon #77942, crystal/blk; stem, sherbet; 5-oz 65.00
Pygon #77942, crystal/frost; stem, champagne; Thorpe, 5½-oz ...135.00
Pygon #77942, crystal/frost; stem, wine; sgn Thorpe, 3½-oz 150.00
Pygon #77942, frost; wine, Thorpe HP bird decor, 3½-oz 150.00
Richmond, crystal; stem, goblet; #7570 Horizon, 10-oz 27.00
Richmond, crystal; stem, goblet; #7589 Laurette, 9-oz 32.00
Rosalie etch, crystal; jug, w/lid, #22 Kismet, 54-oz 350.00

Rosalie etch, topaz/crystal; stem, goblet; #7662 Majesty, 10-oz **95.00**
Saranac etch, crystal; stem, champagne; #7690 Monroe, 5½-oz **48.00**
Saranac etch, crystal; stem, goblet; #7690 Monroe, 10-oz **68.00**
Sea Gulls enamel decor, jug, #545 Pickford, 60-oz **395.00**
Sea Gulls enamel decor, tumbler, ftd, #9093, 12-oz **75.00**
Sear's Lace Bouquet, crystal; stem, champagne; #7668, 6-oz **38.00**
Sear's Lace Bouquet, crystal; stem, goblet; #7668, 10-oz **47.50**
Sonoma etch, crystal; stem, champagne; #7659 Cynthia, 6-oz **55.00**
Sonoma etch, crystal; stem, goblet; #7659 Cynthia, 10-oz **65.00**
Sonoma etch, topaz; stem, champagne; #7659 Cynthia, 6-oz **65.00**
Sonoma etch, topaz; stem, goblet; #7659 Cynthia, 10-oz **78.00**
Superba, blk/filament; stem, champagne; #7664, 6½-oz **130.00**
Superba, blk/filament; stem, goblet; #7664 Queen Anne, 10-oz ..**195.00**
Superba, crystal/blk; stem, champagne; #7654½, 6½-oz **130.00**
Superba, crystal/blk; stem, goblet; #7654½, 10-oz **180.00**
Tinker Bell, azure; tumbler, ftd, #9069, 12-oz **65.00**
Tinker Bell, crystal; guest set, #24 Maria, 4-pc, very rare **650.00**
Tinker Bell, crystal; stem, goblet; #7631 Jewel, 10-oz **35.00**
Tinker Bell, gr; vase, bud; ftd, #53 Serenade, 10" **310.00**
Versailles, crystal; stem, champagne; #7688 Jamestown, 6-oz **39.00**
Versailles, crystal; stem, champagne; #7711 Callahan, 6-oz **38.00**
Versailles, crystal; stem, goblet; #7688 Jamestown, 9-oz **47.50**
Versailles, crystal; stem, goblet; #7711 Callahan, 10-oz **48.00**
Victoria, crystal; stem, champagne; #300 Touraine, 5-oz **32.50**
Victoria, crystal; stem, goblet; #300 Touraine, 5-oz **32.50**
Victoria w/cutting, blk; stem, champagne; #7640, 5½-oz **87.50**
Victoria w/cutting, blk; stem, goblet; #7640, 9-oz **42.50**
Virginia, crystal; stem, champagne; #7587 Hanover, 6-oz **24.00**
Virginia, crystal; stem, champagne; #7711 Callahan, 6-oz **38.00**
Virginia, crystal; stem, goblet; #7587 Hanover, 9-oz **24.00**
Virginia, crystal; stem, goblet; #7711 Callahan, 10-oz **48.00**
Virginia etch, amber, stem, goblet; #7614 Hampton, 9-oz **50.00**
Virginia etch, amber; stem, champagne; #7614 Hampton, 5½-oz .**40.00**
Yale #7684, cobalt or ruby; stem, champagne; 5½-oz **80.00**
Yale #7684, cobalt or ruby; stem, goblet; 9-oz **97.50**
Yale #7684, crystal; 20% less than prices above
Yale #7684, Stiegel gr; 10% less than prices above

Silk-Screen Color Printing on Crystal

Manchester Pheasant, champagne, #7664 Queen Anne, 6½-oz ...**148.00**
Manchester Pheasant, goblet, #7664 Queen Anne, 10-oz **210.00**
Manchester Pheasant, sherbet, #7664 Queen Anne, 6½-oz **130.00**
Queen Louise, rose; stem, champagne; #7614 Hampton, 6-oz **140.00**
Queen Louise, rose; stem, goblet; #7614 Hampton, 9-oz **175.00**
Queen Louise, rose; stem, sherbet; #7614 Hampton, 6-oz **115.00**

Sunrise Medallion Etch

#37 Barry, azure; jug, ftd, 48-oz **585.00**
#37 Barry, crystal; jug, ftd, 48-oz **425.00**
#45 Catherine, azure; vase, bud; ftd, 10" **275.00**
#45 Catherine, gr or rose; vase, bud; ftd, 10" **265.00**
#53 Serenade, azure; vase, bud; bulbous/ftd, 10" **365.00**
#53 Serenade, rose; vase, bud; bulbous/ftd, 10" **350.00**
#7630 Ballerina, azure; stem, champagne; 6-oz **75.00**
#7630 Ballerina, azure; stem, goblet; 9-oz **75.00**
#7630 Ballerina, crystal; 30% less than azure prices above
#7630 Ballerina, gr; 20% less than azure prices above
#7630 Ballerina, rose; 10% less than azure prices above
#7630 Ballerina, topaz; 10% less than azure prices above
#7654½ Legacy, crystal/moonstone; stem, champagne; 6-oz **135.00**
#7654½ Legacy, crystal/moonstone; stem, cocktail; 3-oz **130.00**
#7654½ Legacy, crystal/moonstone; stem, goblet; 9-oz **185.00**

#7664 Queen Anne, azure; stem, champagne; 6½-oz **68.00**
#7664 Queen Anne, azure; stem, cocktail; 3½-oz **60.00**
#7664 Queen Anne, azure; stem, cordial; 1½-oz **250.00**
#7664 Queen Anne, azure; stem, goblet; 10-oz **85.00**
#7664 Queen Anne, azure; stem, wine; 2¾-oz **95.00**
#7664 Queen Anne, crystal; stem, goblet; 10-oz **75.00**

Moriage

The term 'moriage' refers to certain Japanese wares decorated with applied slipwork designs. There are several methods used to achieve the characteristic relief effect. The decorative devices may be designed separately and applied to the vessel, piped on in narrow ribbons of clay (slip-trailed), or built up by brushing on successive layers of liquified slip. See also Dragon Ware; Nippon.

Vase, pastel moriage florals over shadow flowers and leaves, 4½", $235.00.

Ashtray, floral, 4¾" **50.00**
Chocolate pat, floral reserves, 9½" **235.00**
Cup & saucer, floral reserves, lav/rose/pk w/gold, mk **60.00**
Ewer, allover Nouveau florals, sqd hdl, bulbous bottom, 14" **400.00**
Humidor, EX slipwork, 7" **200.00**
Planter, allover florals, lg looping hdls, 8" L **235.00**
Sugar shaker, roses on gr, bbl form **95.00**
Vase, mc floral panels, 3-hdl, 5½x7" **240.00**

Mortars and Pestles

Mortars are bowl-shaped vessels used for centuries for the purpose of grinding drugs to a powder or grain into meal. The masher or grinding device is called a pestle.

Blown, heavy, ground pontil, 5x7" **50.00**
Brass, goblet shape, 6½", w/pestle **175.00**
Brass, 3½", w/pestle **85.00**
Brass, 5¾", w/pestle **100.00**
Burl, EX figure, minor age cracks, 6", w/chestnut pestle **200.00**
Burl, rfn, 7" **225.00**
Burl, tall/narrow/trn, dtd 1805, worm holes, 7", w/pestle **275.00**
Cast iron, emb 'icicles,' att S Jersey, 7", w/pestle **85.00**
Cast iron, 7x7" dia, w/pestle **75.00**
Miniature, lignum vitae, trn, worn, 3¼" **470.00**
Wood, maple, flowerpot shape **110.00**
Wood, trn, dk gr rpt, age cracks, 6½", w/pestle **90.00**

Mortens Studio

Oscar Mortens was already established as a fine sculptural artist when he left his native Sweden to take up residency in Arizona. During the 1940s he developed a line of detailed animal figures which were distributed through the Mortens Studios, a firm he co-founded with Gunnar Thelin. Thelin hired and trained artists to produce Mortens' line, which he called Royal Designs. More than two hundred dogs were modeled and over one hundred horses. Cats and wild animals such as elephants, panthers, deer, and elk were made, but on a much smaller scale. Bookends with sculptured dog heads were shown in their catalogs, and collectors report finding wall plaques on rare occasions. The material they used was a plaster-type composition with wires embedded to support the weight. Examples were marked 'Copyright by the Mortens Studio' either in ink or decal. Watch for flaking, cracks, and separations. Crazing seems to be present in some degree in many examples. When no condition is indicated, the items listed below are assumed to be in near-mint condition, allowing for minor crazing.

Afghan, standing, 7x7" 90.00
Beagle, recumbent 48.00
Beagle, standing, 4½x4½" 60.00
Beagle, standing, 6x6" 75.00
Boxer, recumbent, 8" L 60.00
Boxer, standing, tan w/blk, 5½x5½" 70.00
Bulldog, standing, 5x6½" 85.00
Chihuahua, sitting, 3½x3" 75.00
Chihuahua, standing, 4½" L 90.00
Cocker Spaniel, recumbent, tan/rust w/blk, 3x5¾" 55.00
Cocker Spaniel, standing 52.50
Collie, seated, 6" 90.00
Dalmation, standing, 5½x7" 80.00
Doberman, sitting, 6½x6" 90.00
Doberman, standing, 7½x8" 90.00
English Spaniel, standing, ivory w/blk, 5½x6½" 80.00
German Shepherd pup, sitting, 3½x3½" 40.00
Great Dane, sitting, 7½x6½" 80.00
Horse, brn w/wht blaze, tail & stockings, running, 9" L 120.00
Lion, recumbent, 4x6" 135.00
Lynx 175.00
Pekingese, standing, 3½x4½" 80.00

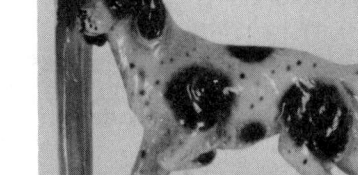

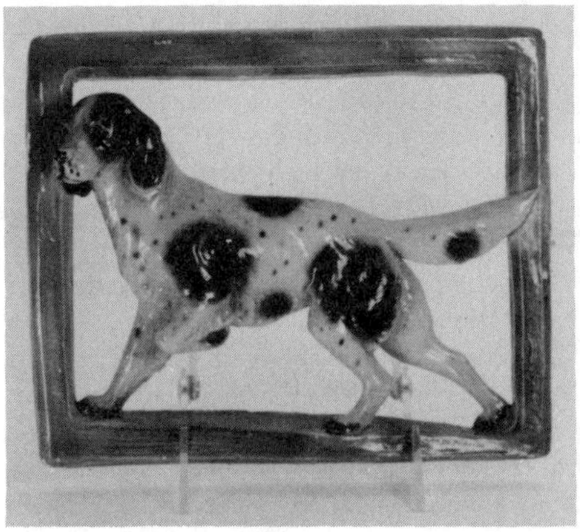

Plaque, English Setter, #9507, $160.00.

Pomeranian, standing, 4½" 70.00
Pug pup, recumbent, 2½x4" 45.00
Scottish Terrier, sitting, blk/charcoal, 4½x6" 75.00
Siamese, seated, 5" 68.00
Wire-Haired Terrier, begging, 4" 58.00

Morton Pottery

Six potteries operated in Morton, Illinois, at various times from 1877 to 1976. Each traced its origin to six brothers who immigrated to America to avoid military service in Germany. The Rapp brothers established their first pottery near clay deposits on the south side of town where they made field tile and bricks. Within a few years they branched out to include utility wares such as jugs, bowls, jars, pitchers, etc. During the ninety-nine years of pottery operations in Morton, the original factory was expanded by some of the sons and nephews of the Rapps. Other family members started their own potteries where artware, gift-store items, and special-order goods were produced. The Cliftwood Art Pottery and the Morton Pottery Company had showrooms in Chicago and New York City during the 1930s. All of Morton's potteries were relatively short-lived operations with the Morton Pottery Company being the last to shut down on September 8, 1976. For a more thorough study of the subject, we recommend *Morton's Potteries: 99 Years* by Doris and Burdell Hall; their address can be found in the Directory under Illinois.

Morton Pottery Works — Morton Earthenware Co. (1877-1917)

Bed pan, brn Rockingham, shovel shape, 18x12" 45.00
Bed pan, yellow ware, shovel shape, 18x12" 60.00
Bowl, mixing; brn Rockingham, 4½", 5½", 6", set of 3 ....135.00
Coffeepot, brn Rockingham, ind, ¾-pt 25.00
Milk boiler, brn Rockingham, bulbous, 2½-pt 50.00
Milk jug, brn Rockingham, 2¾-pt 75.00
Milk jug, brn Rockingham, 6-pt 100.00
Pie baker, yellow ware, 10" 85.00
Pie baker, yellow ware, 7" 70.00
Pie baker, yellow ware, 8" 75.00
Pie baker, yellow ware, 9" 80.00
Spittoon, brn Rockingham, 15" 70.00
Teapot, brn Rockingham, ind, 1½-cup 25.00
Teapot, brn Rockingham, ind, 2½-cup 30.00
Teapot, Rebecca at the Well, brn Rockingham, 2½-pt 60.00
Teapot, Rebecca at the Well, brn Rockingham, 8½-pt 130.00

Cliftwood Art Potteries, Inc. (1920-1940)

Bowl, console; tree trunk, brn drip, 3¾x7½x6¼" 30.00
Candlestick, tree trunk, brn drip, 3x3x2", pr 36.00
Card holder, elephant w/side boxes, brn drip, 4x6" 69.00
Chocolate set, tree trunk, brn drip, pitcher+6 mugs 175.00
Figurine, bear, natural colors, mini, rare, 3½x5½" 70.00
Figurine, cat, reclining, bl/gray drip, 6¼" 35.00
Figurine, cat, reclining, brn drip, 8½" 45.00
Figurine, cat, reclining, cobalt, 4½" 25.00
Figurine, elephant, natural colors, rare, mini, 3½x5½" 75.00
Figurine, German shepherd, recumbent, brn drip, 11" 150.00
Figurine, German shepherd, recumbent, jade gr, 8" 75.00
Figurine, German shepherd, recumbent, wht matt, 5" 50.00
Figurine, lion, natural colors, rare, mini, 3½x5½" 85.00
Figurine, lioness, natural colors, rare, mini, 3½x5½" 80.00
Flower frog, tree trunk, brn drip, 3¾" 18.00
Lamp, jade gr, spherical, 7x24" 38.00
Wine, bl mulberry drip, swirl decor 12.00
Wine jug, bl mulberry drip, swirl decor, bulbous 48.00

Midwest Potteries, Inc. (1940-1944)

Bust, Art Deco lady, wht/platinum, 8½" 75.00

Figurine, ducks, wht, 3 in row: 3x6½" 10.00
Figurine, Oriental boy & girl shelf sitters, blk/wht/gold 22.00
Figurine, pigeon, yel/gr drip, 6" 18.00
Planter, broken egg, gold, tripod base, 6" 15.00
Planter, dog w/bow tie, wht, 4x5" 8.00
Planter, elephant, yel/bl drip, 4x6" 10.00
Planter, fox, yel matt, 4x3" 8.00
Planter, lion, yel, 3½x5½" 12.00
Planter, lioness, gr, 3½x5½" 10.00
Planter, rabbit, wht w/pk ears, 4x6" 16.00
Plaque, Elizabethan Friar, head sculpture, gr 20.00
Plaque, Sad Monk, head sculpture, yel 20.00
Plaque, Winking Gigolo, head sculpture, bl 20.00
Vase, bud; hand form, Faun matt, 5¾" 14.00
Vase, bud; hand form, gr, 4¾" 12.00
Vase, bud; wht matt, hand form, 6¾" 16.00

Morton Pottery Company (1922-1976)

Amish pantry ware, baking nappy set, canary yel, 6-pc 70.00
Amish pantry ware, cereal jar, gr, 3-qt 30.00
Amish pantry ware, jar, gr, w/lid, 5-qt 40.00
Amish pantry ware, jug, water; Pilgrim Bl, 3-pt 35.00
Amish pantry ware, milk jug, Pilgrim Bl, 3-pt 25.00
Amish pantry ware, refrigerator bowls, canary yel, 3 stacking 100.00
Basket, hanging; emb bird decor, unglazed, 7½" 25.00
Figurine, boy praying, bl sleepers (or girl in pk), 3½" 7.50
Figurine, seeing-eye dog, blk, 6" 16.00
Stein, beer; emb German dancers, yel/wht spray, 10" 30.00
Tray, dresser; lady's pk collar w/HP brooch 12.00
Tray, dresser; man's wht collar w/blk bow tie (+ in Japan) 14.00
Vase, bamboo w/emb heron decor, wht, 14½" 35.00
Wall pocket, birdhouse, wht w/mc bird 15.00
Wall pocket, lovebirds on nest, mc 18.00
Wall pocket, rooster, mc 20.00
Wall pocket, scoop, wht w/HP flowers 12.00
Wall pocket, teapot, wht w/HP cherries 14.00
Wall pocket, teapot, wht w/HP cherries, as bracket lamp 28.00
Wall pocket, violin, wht w/HP forget-me-nots 16.00

American Art Potteries (1947-1961)

American Art Potteries, rooster and hen planters, 9" and 7½", $35.00.

Bottle, crown, gray/pk spray, 2x6x4" 15.00
Figurine, elephant, gray/wht spray, 6" 20.00

Figurine, hen & rooster, mauve/wht spray, 4½" 18.00
Figurine, hog, wht/gray spots spray, 5½" 35.00
Figurine, quail, mc spray, 9" 30.00
Lamp, Art Deco, dk gr, rectangular, 6x14x8" 30.00
Lamp, Driftwood, brn spray on gr, 12" 22.00
Planter/vase, baby bottle, pk or bl, 5" 12.00
Planter/vase, baby diaper w/safety pin, pk or bl, 2x4" 10.00
Planter/vase, conch shell, bl/wht spray, 6" 14.00
Planter/vase, cowboy boot, yel/gray spray, 5" 12.00
Planter/vase, duck, dk gr/yel spray, paper label, 5½" 10.00
Planter/vase, Grecian urn, brn/gr spray, mini, 3½" 5.00
Planter/vase, teddy bear on 3 blocks (ABC), wht w/HP decor 15.00

Mosaic Tile Co.

The Mosaic Tile Company was organized in 1894 in Zanesville, Ohio, by Herman Mueller and Karl Langenbeck, both of whom had years of previous experience in the industry. They developed a faster, less-costly method of potting decorative tile, utilizing paper patterns rather than copper molds. By 1901 the company had grown and expanded with offices in many major cities. Faience tile was introduced in 1918, greatly increasing their volume of sales. They also made novelty ashtrays, figural boxes, bookends, etc., though not to any large extent. Until they closed during the 1960s, Mosaic used various marks that included the company name or their initials — 'MT' superimposed over 'Co.' in a circle.

Cookie jar, Mammy, unmk 300.00
Figurine, bear, blk semigloss, 6x9" 135.00
Figurine, German shepherd, recumbent, tan, 10" L 125.00
Paperweight, Lincoln 25.00
Tile, Mickey Mouse, standing, 4¼x4¼" 30.00
Tile, Teddy Roosevelt, mc transfer, 4¼" sq 125.00

Moser

Ludwig Moser began his career as a struggling glass artist, catering to the rich who visited the famous Austrian health spas. His talent and popularity grew and in 1857 the first of his three studios opened in Karlsbad, Czechoslovakia. The styles developed there were entirely his own; no copies of other artists have ever been found. Some of his original designs include grapes with trailing vines, acorns and oak leaves, and richly enameled, deeply cut or carved floral pieces. Sometimes jewels were applied to the glass as well. Moser's animal scenes reflect his careful attention to detail. Famed for his birds in flight, he also designed stalking tigers — even elephants — all created in fine enameling.

Moser died in 1916, but the business was contined by his two sons who had been personally and carefully trained by their father. The Moser company bought the Meyr's Neffe Glassworks in 1922 and continued to produce quality glassware.

When identifying Moser, look for great clarity in the glass, perfect coloration, finely applied enameling (often covered with thin gold leaf), well-polished pontils, and deeply carved, continuous engravings. Our advisor for this category is Don Williams; he is listed in the Directory under Missouri. Items described below are enameled unless noted otherwise.

Bottle, scent; amethyst to clear, floral intaglio, sgn, 7¾" 850.00
Bottle, scent; cranberry, cut panels w/gold leaves, 4¾" 300.00
Bowl, amberina, yel lace int/ext, 3-ftd, shaped rim, 6" 385.00
Bowl, amethyst, mc & gold vines/bugs, appl bows/knots, 10" ..1,600.00
Bowl, cut o/l, emerald gr on wht, 3 medallions, 1 w/girl, 3x4½" .600.00
Bowl, Prussian bl w/roses, ribbed, 3 clear dolphin ft, 5x9" 900.00

Bowl, rubena verde, daisies/gold bees, dmn shape/ftd, 5" L 450.00
Box, amber, rabbit w/gold, hinged, 2½x7½" dia 565.00
Box, purple, lace w/gold, 3½x5½" 350.00
Champagne, gold vintage w/appl pods, stick stem, 6", 4 for 180.00
Cordial, cobalt w/gold, paneled bowl 75.00
Cornucopia, aqua w/allover gold vines etc, ftd, w/lid, 9" 925.00
Cup, gr, gold florals, 3-hdl, 6" 300.00
Decanter, cherry cluster in red/gr, 13", +6 6¾" cordials 700.00
Decanter, gr, heavy gold vintage, ribbed, clear stopper, 18" 600.00
Decanter, pk w/HP flowers, 9", +heart-form tray/2 tumblers ...1,800.00
Goblet, amethyst, florals/gold scrolls, gold twist stem, 5" 65.00
Goblet, gr, mc/gilt colonial man's portrait/vintage, 11" 750.00
Jar, ruby, thick faceted sides, Hoffmann design, w/lid, 5½" 770.00
Pitcher, med gr, elaborate vintage decor, ped ft, 12x5" 800.00
Salt cellar, allover decor w/roses-etched oval panels, 1½" 250.00
Tankard, lg peacock/elaborate gold & silver decor, 15" 875.00
Tumble-up, cranberry, mc/gilt daisies, gold coin in pontil 570.00
Tumbler, cranberry, gold leaves, raised acorns 400.00
Tumbler, emerald gr, allover mc stylized leaves, 5" 125.00
Tumbler, lt gr w/gold textured clover, 5", set of 4 ....140.00
Vase, amber, etched/gilt female warrior shoulder band, 14" 495.00
Vase, amethyst, deeply etched foliate band, cylindrical, 5" 650.00
Vase, cameo sea horses cut bk on topaz, cylindrical, 10" 700.00
Vase, dk emerald, gold frieze of women warriors, 6¾x3" 245.00
Vase, gr, mc figures, gold-traced garden, ruffled, 6" 195.00
Vase, lt to dk gr, eng tulips, bulbous/4-sided, 6" 250.00
Vase, orange to salmon, gold Moorish-style enameling, 12" 500.00

Vase, pink with exotic water birds, intaglio clouds and irises, gold trim, signed Moser Karlsbad, 14", $1,600.00.

Vase, red, leaves/acorns/beetles, long neck w/hdls, ftd, 7" 900.00
Vase, ruby, children in gold, triangular baluster, 12" 250.00

Moss Rose

Moss Rose was a favorite dinnerware pattern of many Staffordshire and American potters from the mid-1800s. In America the Wheeling Pottery of West Virginia produced the ware in large quantities, and it became one of their bestsellers, remaining popular well into the nineties. See also Haviland.

Cup & saucer, Meakin 25.00
Gravy boat, Meakin 35.00
Gravy tureen, w/underplate, Haviland 105.00
Mug, unmk, 3" 10.00

Plate, unmk, 10" 15.00
Plate, unmk, 7½" 9.00
Platter, rectangular, Meakin, 14x10" 30.00
Sugar bowl, akimbo hdls, Meakin, w/lid 50.00
Tea set, American, 14-pc 125.00
Tea set, Japan, 16-pc+lids 60.00
Toothbrush holder, scalloped top, Meakin, 5x2¾" 65.00
Tray, tiered, unmk 20.00

Coffeepot, dolphin handle, 7", $65.00.

Mother-of-Pearl Glass

Mother-of-Pearl glass was a type of mold-blown satin art glass popular during the last half of the 19th century. A patent for its manufacture was issued in 1886 to Frederick S. Shirley, and one of the companies who produced it was the Mt. Washington Glass Company of New Bedford, Massachusetts. Another was the English firm of Stevens and Williams. Its delicate patterns were developed by blowing the gather into a mold with inside projections that left an intaglio design on the surface of the glass, then sealing the first layer with a second, trapping air in the recesses. Most common are the Diamond Quilted, Raindrop, and Herringbone patterns. It was made in several soft colors, the most rare and valuable is rainbow — a blend of rose, light blue, yellow, and white. Occasionally it may be decorated with coralene, enameling, or gilt. Our advisors for this category are Betty and Clarence Maier; they are listed in the Directory under Pennsylvania.

Basket, Herringbone, bl shaded, ruffled fan form, 9¼x8¼" 625.00
Basket, Herringbone, pk, sm ft, appl frost hdl, 6½x3¾" 265.00
Bottle, scent; Peacock Eye, wht, SP lid, spherical, 3¾" 635.00
Bowl, Dmn Quilt, apple gr, frosted ft, flower pontil, 5" 595.00
Bowl, Dmn Quilt, bl, bird & flowers, brass fr, 9x7½" 995.00
Bowl, Dmn Quilt, bl, 3 branch ft extend to 9-lobe rim, 5x7" 425.00
Bowl, Dmn Quilt, chartreuse, 3 frosted ft, 3x9½" 450.00
Bowl, Dmn Quilt, pk shaded, frosted base, Webb, 4x10" 765.00
Bowl, Herringbone, red to bone, incurvate 6-crimp top, 4x5" 300.00
Bowl, Ribbon, pk shaded, incurvate/tightly crimped, 4½" 295.00
Bowl, Swirl, gold to aqua, ruffled, Stevens & Wms, 7⅜" 895.00
Bowl, Swirl, rainbow w/gold, clear ft, tricorner, 5¼x7¼" 750.00
Creamer, Dmn Quilt, bl shaded, bulbous w/can neck, Webb, 5" ...350.00
Creamer, Raindrop, bl, bulbous, rnd mouth, reeded hdl, 4½" 225.00
Creamer, Raindrop, butterscotch, frosted reed hdl, 5x4½" 325.00
Ewer, Dmn Quilt, bl, scalloped, thorny camphor hdl, 7½" 495.00
Ewer, Herringbone, rainbow, 3-lobe lip, thorn hdl, 11" 2,675.00
Lamp, Dmn Quilt, bl, melon-ribbed base, brass font, 14½" 1,140.00

Lamp, Swirl, brn, brass ft & mts, 21" 995.00
Mug, Dmn Quilt, pk shaded, flowers, frosted hdl, 3½" 285.00
Mustard, Ribbon, Am Beauty Rose, SP top, 3⅜x1¾" 225.00

Pitcher, Herringbone, pink, hexagonal top, 8½", $1,295.00.

Pitcher, Dmn Quilt, bl shaded, heart-form rim, thorn hdl, 9" 595.00
Pitcher, Dmn Quilt, peach shaded, 7", +6 3⅝" tumblers 1,285.00
Pitcher, Dmn Quilt, pk, ruffled, frosted hdl, 9x5½" 545.00
Pitcher, Raindrop, gold shaded, bulbous, 5⅝x3¼" 295.00
Plate, Drape, bl shaded, mk Patent, 7" 195.00
Rose bowl, Concentric Circles, rainbow, Patent, 2⅜x4⅜" 850.00
Rose bowl, Dmn Quilt, brn to gold, 2½x2½" 275.00
Rose bowl, Herringbone, bl, 6-crimp, 3½x3½" 145.00
Rose bowl, Herringbone, pk shaded, 4-crimp top, 3⅜x3⅛" 185.00
Rose bowl, Herringbone, red shaded, 8-crimp, 3½x3½" 195.00
Rose bowl, Ribbon, bl, frosted wafer ft, 2¼x3" 195.00
Rose bowl, Ribbon, rose red, 11-crimp top, 3x3¾" 245.00
Rose bowl, Rivulet, chartreuse gr, frosted ft, 8-crimp, 3x4" 295.00
Rose bowl, Rivulet, pk shaded, 8-crimp, 2¾x4¼" 225.00
Sugar shaker, Raindrop, rose shaded, ovoid, Mt WA 850.00
Sweetmeat, Dmn Quilt, pk, stationary hdl, not hinged, 7½" 500.00
Tumbler, Herringbone, rose shaded, 3⅝" 185.00
Tumbler, Raindrop, pk, HP floral & butterfly, 3¾" 265.00
Tumbler, Raindrop, pk shaded, 3⅞x2⅞" 225.00
Vase, bud; Dmn Quilt, bl, card plate in ornate brass fr, 10" 650.00
Vase, Dmn Quilt, lav-pk, melon ribbed, 8¾x5½" 495.00
Vase, Dmn Quilt, pk, ruffled, 10¾" 325.00
Vase, Dmn Quilt, pk, wht int, 10¼x5¼", pr 550.00
Vase, Dmn Quilt, rainbow, bottle form, 5⅝x3" 495.00
Vase, Dmn Quilt, rainbow, bulbous w/shaped stick neck, 6x3" ..500.00
Vase, Dmn Quilt, rainbow, 5x2⅞" 450.00
Vase, Dmn Quilt, yel, ruffled rim, 6¼x4" 165.00
Vase, Federzeichnung, Octopus, brn w/EX gold, mk, 7x7¼" 1,995.00
Vase, Federzeichnung, Octopus, brn w/pk int, lobed lip, 6" 2,100.00
Vase, Flower & Acorn, chartreuse gr, 3-petal top, 4¼x5" 425.00
Vase, Herringbone, bl, frosted ft/hdls, 9¾x4½", pr 750.00
Vase, Herringbone, peach shaded, frosted ribbon at neck, 6¼" ..195.00
Vase, Loop & Teardrop, bl, ruffled rim, 11½" 350.00
Vase, modified Moire, ecru, amber frost rigaree at neck, 5¼" 225.00
Vase, Moire, rose, 17x8" 1,750.00
Vase, Peacock Eye, yel, red threaded feathers, bl int, 5x5" 1,500.00
Vase, Ribbon, bl, petal top, waisted bulbous form, 4⅝" 425.00
Vase, Ribbon, bl, 3-crimp, frosted wafer ft, 3x2⅝" 195.00
Vase, Ribbon, chartreuse gr, 6⅝x4¾" 325.00
Vase, Ribbon, wht w/gold bows & medallions, 6½x3" 850.00
Vase, Ripple, apricot, ruffled/lobed, 6x2½", pr 450.00
Vase, Rivulet, bl, frosted ruffle, 6½x3" 195.00
Vase, Swirl, gr to rose, 5⅛x5" 895.00
Vase, Swirl, orange shaded, str sides widen at base, 11x5" 265.00
Vase, Swirl, pk shaded, 4-section bulbous form, 6¼x3" 500.00

Vase, Swirl, reverse amberina, bulbous, att Stevens & Wms, 9" .650.00
Vase, Swirl, rust/amber, stick neck, Stevens & Wms, 15" 750.00

Mourning Collectibles

During the 18th and early 19th centuries, ladies made needlework pictures, samplers, paintings on ivory plaques, watercolor drawings, etc., to commemorate the death of a loved one. Elements contained in nearly all examples are the tomb, mourners, a weeping willow tree, and data relating to the deceased. Often plaits of hair were included. Today these are recognized and valued as a valid form of folk art. Our advisor for this category is Steve DeGenaro; he is listed in the Directory under Ohio. See also Hair Weaving.

Coffin, child's, brass hdls, top lifts, 1880s, EX 90.00
Coffin, mahog, oval face plate, adult sz, VG 225.00
Coffin (body casket), wicker, wood hdls, ca 1900-20, EX 395.00
Needlework, tomb/willow/lady, paper label, 1820s, 14x12" 660.00
Photo, baby, In Memoriam, oval fr, convex glass, 20x13" 45.00
Pin, gutta percha, sickle & wheat design, Victorian 15.00

Movie Memorabilia

Movie memorabilia covers a broad range of collectibles from books and magazines dealing with the industry in general to the various promotional materials which were distributed to arouse interest in a particular film. Many collectors specialize in a specific area — posters, pressbooks, stills, lobby cards, or souvenir programs (also referred to as premiere booklets). In the listings below, a one-sheet poster measures approximately 27" x 41", three-sheet: 41" x 81", and six-sheet: 81" x 81". See also Autographs; Cartoon Art; Paper Dolls; Personalities.

Book, Day w/Our Gang, EL Packer, Whitman Pub Co, 1929, EX ...25.00
Book, Judy Garland, Anne Edwards, Simon & Schuster, 1974 .....15.00
Book, Romeo & Juliet picture edition, 1936, EX 35.00
Book, Sunshine & Shadows, Mary Pickford, Doubleday, 1979 .....12.00
Booth, ticket; wood, glass panels, worn gold pnt, 90", EX 1,300.00
Card, insert; Country Girl, Crosby/Kelly/Holden, 1954 ....25.00
Jigsaw puzzle, Alien 40.00
Jigsaw puzzle, Man from Uncle, w/box 40.00
Lobby card, Affair in Trinidad, Hayworth/Ford, 1952 ....35.00
Lobby card, Alvarez Kelly, title card, Columbia, 1966 ....5.00
Lobby card, Batman, 1966, orig 40.00
Lobby card, Bullet Is Waiting, scene card, 1954 ....4.00

Lobby card, *Casablanca*, Warner Brothers, 1942, 11x14", $2,500.00.

Lobby card, Fist of Fury, Bruce Lee, British, 8x10", 8 for 75.00
Lobby card, Flame & Flesh, Lana Turner, 1954, set of 8 ....66.00
Lobby card, Gidget Goes Hawaiian, title card, Columbia, 1961 .....9.00
Lobby card, Hang 'Em High, Eastwood, 11x14", set of 7 ....40.00
Lobby card, Hideous Sun Demon, scene card, 1959 ....10.00
Lobby card, House of Usher, scene card, 1960 ....8.00
Lobby card, King Creole, Elvis, 1958, 11x14" 35.00
Lobby card, Live & Let Die, James Bond, 11x14", set of 8 ....175.00
Lobby card, Lover Come Back, Lucille Ball, 1952, 11x14" 20.00
Lobby card, My Pal Trigger, Trigger, scene card, 1948 ....10.00
Lobby card, Pressure Point, Bobby Darin 3.00
Lobby card, Second Chorus, Fred Astaire, Paramount, 1940 ....45.00
Lobby card, Smokey & Bandit, Reynolds, 11x14", set of 4 ....4.00
Lobby card, Sylvia, Geo Maharis, scene card, 1965 ....5.00
Lobby card, To Trap a Spy, Man from Uncle, 11x14", set of 4 .....25.00
Lobby card, World of Suzie Wong, Wm Holden, 11x14" 3.00
Magazine, Film Comment, Mar - Apr 1979, Movie Palace issue ...10.00
Magazine, Film Comment, May - June 1978, Times Sq centerfold .5.00
Magazine, Hollywood Studio, Sept 1971 ....3.00
Magazine, Horror of Party Beach, 1964, story in photos 25.00
Magazine, Mentor, July 1921 ....10.00
Magazine, Modern Screen, Claudette Colbert cover, 1940, EX 25.00
Magazine, Modern Screen, Garland/Rooney cover, 1940 ....34.00
Magazine, Modern Screen, Kim Novak cover, Mar 1957 ....12.00
Magazine, Modern Screen, Loretta Young cover, 1948 ....15.00
Magazine, Modern Screen, T Curtis & J Leigh cover, 1956 ....12.00
Magazine, Motion Picture, Debbie Reynolds cover, Aug 1957 .....12.00
Magazine, Motion Picture, Liz Taylor cover, 1956, EX 12.00
Magazine, Movie Classics, Dec 1973, Betty Grable cover 7.00
Magazine, Movie Classics, June 1973, 1st issue 10.00
Magazine, Movie Life, July 1956, Tab Hunter & Natalie Wood ...14.00
Magazine, Movie Life, Lauren Bacall cover, 1946, EX 15.00
Magazine, Movieland, Martin & Lewis story, EX 10.00
Magazine, Photoplay, Deborah Kerr cover, Mar 1958, EX 12.50
Magazine, Photoplay, Greer Garson cover, 1945 ....15.00
Magazine, Photoplay, Liz Taylor cover, June 1958, VG 12.00
Magazine, Photoplay, Natalie Wood cover, July 1958, EX 15.00
Magazine, Photoplay Annual, many stars on cover, 1957, 96-pg ..18.00
Magazine, Screen Album, Doris Day cover, 1957-58 portraits 12.00
Magazine, Screen Stories, behind-the-scenes stories, 1958 ....12.00
Magazine, Screen Story, June 1960, Sandra Dee cover 5.00
Magazine, Sight & Sound, Apr - June 1954, Garbo cover 5.00
Magazine, Silver Screen, Bette Davis cover, 1942 ....25.00
Magazine ad, Strawberry Blonde, James Cagney, blk/wht, 1-pg 5.00
Paint book, Deanna Durbin, #3479, 1940, EX 35.00
Paper-bk, Contemporary Cinema, P Huston/Penguin, 1963, EX ..20.00
Paper-bk, Gone w/the Wind, movie edition, Macmillan, 1940 ....30.00
Paper-bk, James Dean Story, Martinetti/Pinnacle Books, 1975 ....40.00
Paper-bk, Jean Harlow Story, Pascal/Popular Library, 1964 ....35.00
Photo, Clark Gable in tuxedo dancing, 1930s 25.00
Poster, Boy Did I Get a Wrong Number, 1966, 1-sheet, EX 12.00
Poster, Boy's Night Out, Novak/Garner, 1-sheet, VG 12.00
Poster, Coney Island, Grable/Montgomery/Romero, '43, 41x27" ...1,050.00
Poster, Curse of the Werewolf, ½-sheet 50.00
Poster, From Russia w/Love, James Bond, German, 23x33" 70.00
Poster, Funny Face, Hepburn/Astaire, 1957, 1-sheet 40.00
Poster, Gidget Goes Hawaiian, 1961, 1-sheet, VG 15.00
Poster, Good Morning Vietnam, Robin Williams, Japan, 20x28" ...12.00
Poster, Gracie Allen Murder Case, portrait, 1939, 41x27", NM ..950.00
Poster, insert; X Man w/X-Ray Eyes 75.00
Poster, Long Ships, 1964, 1-sheet, EX 12.00
Poster, Men in Wht, Gable/Loy, 1934, 36x14", NM 825.00
Poster, Midnight Cowboy, X-rated version 150.00
Poster, Moonraker, James Bond, German, 21x41" 70.00

Poster, On the Beach, Peck/Gardner, 1959, 1-sheet, VG 18.00
Poster, Paris Blues, Newman/Woodward, 1961, 1-sheet, G 35.00
Poster, Phila Story, Grant/Hepburn/Stewart, '40, 36x14", NM ..3,520.00
Poster, Rambo 1st Blood Part 2, Stallone, 27x41" 12.00
Poster, Reflections in a Golden Eye, 1967, 1-sheet, VG 32.00
Poster, Revenge of Pink Panther, 27x41" 12.00
Poster, Riders of Destiny, John Wayne, 1934, 41x27", NM 3,300.00

Poster, *Stowaway,* **Shirley Temple, Robert Young, and Alice Fay, creases, 21x27", $495.00.**

Poster, She Married Her Boss, C Colbert, 1935, 41x27", NM ...3,300.00
Poster, Sheena, Tanya Roberts, 14x36" 35.00
Poster, Shock Treatment, Bacall, 1962, 27x41" 25.00
Poster, Some Kind of Wonderful, Lea Thompson, 27x41" 25.00
Poster, The Fleet's In, Clara Bow, Paramount, 1928, 41x27" ..2,200.00
Poster, Under the Yoke, Theda Bara, 1918, 41x27", EX 825.00
Poster, Wolf Man, C Raines/L Chaney, 41, 41x27", NM 17,600.00
Pressbook, Anniversary, Bette Davis 10.00
Pressbook, Boy Did I Get a Wrong Number, Elke Sommer 12.00
Pressbook, Disney's Son of Flubber, F MacMurray 15.00
Pressbook, Double Dynamite, Marx/Russell/Sinatra, 1952 ....20.00
Pressbook, Eddie Macon's Run, Douglas, 18 photos 12.00
Pressbook, French Connection, Hackman 10.00
Pressbook, In Harm's Way, John Wayne, 1965 ....45.00
Pressbook, Night of the Quarter Moon, Julie London 10.00
Pressbook, Wild One, Brando, 1953 ....20.00
Presskit, Psycho II, A Perkins, 17 photos 17.00
Program, Judy Garland, RKO Palace, 1951 ....35.00
Program, Way Down East, 3-color tinting, 1920, 16-pc, VG 75.00
Program, 10 Commandments (silent version), 1923, 17-pg, VG ..75.00
Promo stand, Texas Chainsaw Massacre, 60" 100.00
Sheet music, April Love, Pat Boone/Shirley Jones 6.50
Sheet music, I've Heard That Song Before, Harry James 10.00
Sheet music, Long Ago, Rita Hayworth on cover 10.00
Sheet music, Love in Bloom, Bing Crosby 7.00
Sheet music, Mutual Admiration Society, Ethel Merman 6.00
Sofa, red nylon lips (Marilyn's), after Dali, 1934, EX 2,300.00
Song book, Shall We Dance, Astaire/Rogers, 1937 ....20.00
Still, Mississippi, Bennett/Crosby, 1935 ....14.00
Window card, West Point Story, Cagney, 1950 ....40.00

Mt. Washington

The Mt. Washington Glass Works was founded in 1837 in South Boston, Massachusetts, but moved to New Bedford in 1869 after purchasing the facilities of the New Bedford Glass Company. Frederick S. Shirley became associated with the firm in 1874. Two years later the company reorganized and became known as the Mt. Washington Glass Company. In 1894 it merged with the Pairpoint Manufacturing Company, a small Brittania works nearby, but continued to conduct business under its own title until after the turn of the century. The combined plants were equipped with the most modern and varied machinery available and boasted a working force with experience and expertise rival to none in the art of blowing and cutting glass. In addition to their fine cut glass, they are recognized as the first American company to make cameo glass, an effect they achieved through acid-cutting methods. In 1885 Shirley was issued a patent to make Burmese, pale yellow glassware tinged with a delicate pink blush. Another patent issued in 1886 allowed them the rights to produce Rose Amber, or amberina, a transparent ware shading from ruby to amber. Pearl Satin Ware and Peachblow, so named for its resemblance to a rosy peach skin, were patented the same year. One of their most famous lines, Crown Milano, was introduced in 1893. It was an opal glass either free-blown or pattern molded, tinted a delicate color and decorated with enameling and gilt. Royal Flemish was patented in 1894 and is considered the rarest of the Mt. Washington art glass lines. It was decorated with raised, gold-enameled lines dividing the surface of the ware in much the same way as lead lines divide a stained glass window. The sections were filled in with one or several transparent colors and further decorated in gold enamel with florals, foliage, beading, and medallions.

Our advisors for this category are Betty and Clarence Maier; they are listed in the Directory under Pennsylvania. See also Amberina, Cranberry; Salt Shakers; Burmese; Crown Milano; Royal Flemish; etc.

Biscuit jar, gilt scrolls at shoulder, wildflowers, 6" 600.00
Biscuit jar, mums on lt to dk gr w/gold, 16-panel, PMC, 6" 500.00
Biscuit jar, pansies in scroll reserve, squat form, 6" 500.00
Bowl, cameo ribbons & flowers, sq crimped rim, 10" 750.00
Bowl, Napoli, pond lilies on gr, 10", SP pond lily sgn base 2,200.00
Box, jewel; blown-out lid/base edge, HP roses, gilt, 5x7x7" 1,250.00
Box, jewel; monk HP on opal, sgn Schindler, SP mts, 3x5" 550.00
Box, monk drinking wine on gr shaded, SP trim, 3¼x5¼" 550.00
Bride's basket, cameo griffins etc, wht/rose; berries on fr 825.00
Creamer, pansies, emb ribs, Fig pattern, silver mts, 3½" 350.00
Ewer, Albertine, florals/gold shadow scrolls, rope hdl, 12" 1,450.00
Flower frog, mushroom shape, HP berries on bl shaded, 3x5" 195.00
Lamp, cameo-cut cameo/ribbons, pk/wht, on shade/base, 21" .11,500.00
Mustard, HP florals on lustreless wht, SP top & hdl, 3½" 245.00
Rose bowl, asters, bl/wht on brn to clear frost, scalloped, lg 1,275.00
Shakers, stand-up egg shape, 1 w/rooster, 2nd w/hen, pr 400.00
Vase, iris w/leaves & open bud on clear, 12" 650.00
Vase, Lava, blk w/mc abstracts, flared lip, loop hdls, 9" 2,100.00
Vase, Napoli, frog in bulrushes, 8-rib, bulbous base, 9" 975.00
Vase, Napoli, gold apple blossoms, grasshoppers, 23" 965.00

Mulberry China

Mulberry china was made by many of the Staffordshire area potters from about 1830 until the 1850s. It is a transfer-printed earthenware or ironstone named for the color of its decorations, a purplish-brown resembling the juice of the mulberry. Some pieces may have faded out over the years and today look almost gray with only a hint of purple. (Transfer printing was done in many colors; technically only those in the mauve tones are 'mulberry'; color variations have little effect on value.) Some of the patterns (Corean, Jeddo, Pelew, and Formosa, for instance) were also produced in Flow Blue ware. Others seem to have been used exclusively with the mulberry color. Our advisor for this category is Mary Frank Gaston; she is listed in the Directory under Texas.

Athens, bowl, vegetable; nut finial 375.00

Pagoda, gravy boat, 5", $125.00.

Athens, cup & saucer, handleless 60.00
Athens, cup plate, Adams 55.00
Athens, gravy boat, Meigh 75.00
Athens, plate, 10" 40.00
Athens, plate, 6¼" 20.00
Avon, teapot, lg 350.00
Beauties of China, platter, 10x7¾" 165.00
Beauties of China, sauce bowl, w/lid, Mellor & Venables 150.00
Bochara, platter, 14" 95.00
Bochara, soup, shallow, John Edwards, 8½" 45.00
Bochara, wash bowl, 14" 100.00
Bryonia, sauce dish, 5" 10.00
Bryonia, tureen, soup; rnd w/lid 95.00
Calcutta, plate, 8½" 50.00
Calcutta, teapot 325.00
Chusan, plate, Podmore Walker, 8¼" 25.00
Corea, plate, 12-sided Clementson, 9½" 60.00
Corea, sugar bowl, Clementson 175.00
Corean, cup, handleless 40.00
Corean, platter, 8-sided, Clementson, 16x12" 180.00
Corean, sugar bowl, lion hdls 130.00
Corean, waste bowl, Podmore Walker, lg 75.00
Cyprus, platter, 15½" 195.00
Cyprus, teapot, Davenport 350.00
Cyprus, tureen, vegetable; w/lid 175.00
Delhi, relish dish, 5½x8½" 65.00
Delhi, soap box, w/lid 125.00
Dora, plate, luncheon 55.00
Flora, soap dish, Walker, 3-pc 150.00
Foliage, cup & saucer, handleless; Walley 65.00
Foliage, plate, 9" 24.00
Heath's Flower, soup plate, 10½" 65.00
Hyson, sugar bowl 150.00
Jeddo, bowl, vegetable; Adams & Sons, 8" 125.00
Jeddo, bowl, vegetable; w/lid, Adams & Sons 210.00
Jeddo, chamber pot, Adams, w/lid, NM 255.00
Jeddo, pitcher, milk; 1-pt 90.00
Jeddo, plate, Adams & Sons, 7½" 35.00
Jeddo, plate, 10" 52.00
Jeddo, plate, 8½" 60.00
Jeddo, teapot, Adams & Sons 375.00
Lawrence, creamer, 6" 115.00
Lozere, cup & saucer, handleless 45.00
Medina, cup & saucer 55.00
Nankin, creamer, Davenport 135.00
Neva, plate, Challinor, 9" 60.00
Neva, plate, 10⅞" 65.00
Neva, plate, 8½" 50.00

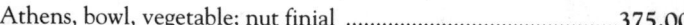

Neva, teapot, Challinor 250.00
Pelew, plate, 8" 40.00
Pelew, teapot 325.00
Pelew, tureen, sauce; w/lid, prof rpr 265.00
Pelew, waste bowl 95.00
Peruvian, platter, Wedgwood, 9½x7" 75.00
Rhone Scenery, coffeepot, Podmore Walker 375.00
Rhone Scenery, creamer, hexagonal, Mayer, 5" 110.00
Rhone Scenery, plate, 7" 30.00
Rhone Scenery, platter, 13½" 100.00
Rhone Scenery, tureen, sauce; w/underplate 225.00
Rose, cup & saucer, handleless 55.00
Rose, platter, 14x11" 165.00
Scinde, platter, Podmore Walker, 15½" 175.00
Shannon, plate, 8" 20.00
Susa, cup plate 55.00
Temple, plate, Podmore Walker, 8¾" 45.00
Temple, tea tile, Podmore Walker 75.00
Tonquin, cup & saucer 80.00
Tonquin, plate, 6" 33.00
Tonquin, plate, 8¼" 40.00
Tonquin, sugar bowl, w/lid, Heath 165.00
Vincennes, platter, 15½" 175.00
Washington Vase, creamer 175.00
Washington Vase, pitcher, milk; 7½" 295.00
Washington Vase, plate, 7¾" 45.00
Washington Vase, plate, 8¾" 55.00
Washington Vase, platter, 16" 195.00
Washington Vase, teapot 325.00
Wreath, cup & saucer, handleless 55.00

Muller Freres

Henri Muller established a factory in 1900 at Croismare, France. He produced fine cameo art glass decorated with florals, birds, and insects in the Art Nouveau style. The work was accomplished by acid engraving and hand finishing. Usual marks were 'Muller,' 'Muller Croismare,' or 'Croismare, Nancy.' In 1910 Henri and his brother Deseri formed a glassworks at Luneville. The cameo art glass made there was nearly all produced by acid cuttings of up to four layers with motifs similar to those favored at Croismare. A good range of colors was used, and some later pieces were gold flecked. Handles and decorative devices were sometimes applied by hand. In addition to the cameo glass, they also produced an acid-finished glass of bold mottled colors in the Deco style. Examples were signed 'Muller Freres' or 'Luneville.' Our advisor for this category is Don Williams; he is listed in the Directory under Missouri.

Key: fp — fire polished

Cameo

Lamp, floral on baluster base/10" dome shade, dbl o/l, 19" 8,800.00
Lamp base, lg roses, wine/red on gray/yel mottle, 13x9" 2,500.00
Vase, anemones, bl/gray on mottled yel, ovoid, 12" 1,750.00
Vase, bluebells, bl/gr on pastel mottle, flared rim, 13" 1,800.00
Vase, carnations, wine cut to rose on mottled gray, 12x5" 1,750.00
Vase, clematis, red/wine on yel-streaked gray, ovoid, 6" 1,100.00
Vase, Dutch couple/boats/trees, hdld flask form, 8¾" 2,500.00
Vase, floral, orange on lt yel, slim baluster, 16" 1,000.00
Vase, hibiscus, purple on bl/purple-streaked gray, fp, 6½" 900.00
Vase, lady in forest, wine/gr/red on yel, shaped top, 12x6" 1,600.00
Vase, leafy vines, brn on rust, teardrop form, 15" 750.00
Vase, lg pine trees fr foggy mtn scene w/waterfall, 16" 4,500.00

Vase, lg trees before mtns, peach/olive/wine on gray, 10" 2,500.00
Vase, lotus, pk on gray, fp, slim w/bulbous top, 10" 5,500.00
Vase, maple leave/2 appl bugs, brn/yel on gr/orange, 5x5" 1,800.00
Vase, mtns/lg trees, dbl o/l, orange/brn on yel, 7½x6" 1,600.00
Vase, mums, rust/brn on cream frost, 6½x4¾" 1,750.00
Vase, pine cones/bee on shaded yel, 4½x3" 450.00
Vase, poppies, dk bl on yel frost, fp blossoms, 6x5" 1,540.00
Vase, poppies, red/blk on cream, dbl o/l, ftd ovoid, 5½" 1,200.00
Vase, roses/leaves allover, bl/wht/wine/amber o/l, 13x10" 3,000.00
Vase, stylized floral/arches, brn on rust, ovoid, 12" 700.00
Vase, tiger lilies, lilac/pk opaque on gr texture, ftd, 13" 1,800.00
Vase, trees/lake, wine on gray w/orange streaks, ovoid, 7" 1,650.00
Vase, vines/grapes, orange/red/yel/brn on streaky mc, 10" 2,200.00

Miscellaneous

Chandelier, mottled bowl+3 lilies; iron mt w/leafy vines 880.00
Lamp, rtcl iron stork w/blown-in mc glass, marble base, 15" ...8,250.00
Vase, berries/leaves pnt on shaded yel/gr/purple, 13" 1,750.00
Vase, bl mottle w/foil inclusions, ftd ovoid, 16" 935.00
Vase, bl/wine mottle w/foil-inclusion drips, ovoid, 8" 440.00
Vase, stylized leaves emb on frost, dbl gourd form, 9" 825.00

Muncie

Muncie Pottery, established in Muncie, Indiana, by Charles O. Grafton, was produced from 1922 until about 1935. It is made of a heavier clay than most of its contemporaries; the styles are sturdy and simple. Early glazes were bright and colorful. In fact, Muncie was advertised as the 'rainbow pottery.' Later most of the ware was finished in a matt glaze. The more collectible examples are those modeled after Consolidated Glass vases — sculptured with lovebirds, grasshoppers, and goldfish. Their line of Art Deco-style vases bears a remarkable resemblance to the company's Ruba Rombic line. Vases, candlesticks, bookends, ashtrays, bowls, lamp bases, and luncheon sets were made. A line of garden pottery was manufactured for a short time. Items were frequently impressed with MUNCIE in block letters. Letters such as A, K, E, or D and the numbers 1, 2, 3, 4, or 5 often found scratched into the base are finishers' marks.

Juice pitcher, orange peel glaze, $85.00; Vases, 4", bittersweet glaze, $37.50 for the pair.

Chamberstick, matt bl/cream, 4" 65.00
Sugar bowl, Ruba Rombic shape 95.00
Vase, bl matt, ruffled top, hdls, 6" 45.00
Vase, gr drip over burnt orange, 9x7" 75.00
Vase, navy gloss, stick form, 8" 65.00
Vase, pale pk/gr/cream matt, corset shape, 12" 125.00
Vase, Ruba Rombic fan shape, matt gr/lav, 8" 165.00

Vase, Ruba Rombic star, gr gloss, 4" 85.00
Vase, wht drip/pk matt, ruffled top, 4" 35.00
Wall pocket, blk drip/peachskin, emb, rectangle, 9" 95.00

Musical Instruments

The field of automatic musical instruments covers many different categories ranging from tiny dolls and trinkets concealing musical movements to huge organs and orchestrions which weigh many tons. Music boxes, first made in the late 18th century by Swiss watchmakers, were produced in both disk and cylinder models. The latter type employs a cylinder studded with tiny projections. As the cylinder turns, these projections lift the tuned teeth in the 'music comb,' and the melody results. The value of the instrument depends upon the length of the cylinder and the quality of workmanship, though other factors must also be considered. Those in ornate cabinets or with extra features such as bells, mechanical birds, etc., often sell for much more. Units built into matching tables sell for about twice the amount they would bring otherwise. While small and medium size units are still being made today, most of the larger ones date from the 19th century. Disk-type music boxes utilize interchangeable steel disks with projecting studs, which by means of an intervening 'star wheel' cause a music comb to play. There are many different variations and mechanisms. Most were made in Germany, but some were produced in the United States. Among the most popular makes are Polyphon, Symphonion, and Regina. The latter was made in Rahway, New Jersey, from about 1894 through 1917.

Player pianos were made in a wide variety of styles. Early varieties consisted of a mechanism which pushed up to a piano and played on the keyboard by means of felt-tipped fingers. These use sixty-five note rolls. Later models have the playing mechanisms built in. At first these also used sixty-five note rolls, but those produced from about 1908 until 1940 use eighty-eight note rolls.

Coin-operated electric pianos are deluxe versions of player pianos. These incorporate expression mechanisms so that by using special-made rolls they can play the hand-recorded rolls of famous pianists. Popular makes include Ampico, Duo-Art, and Welte. Roll-operated organs were made in many forms, ranging from table-top models to large foot-pumped versions. Of the latter the Aeolian Orchestrelle is considered to be one of the best.

Unless noted, prices given are for instruments in fine condition, playing properly, with cabinets or cases in well-preserved or refinished condition. In all instances, unrestored instruments sell for much less, as do pieces with broken parts, damaged cases, and the like. On the other hand, particularly superb examples in especially ornate case designs and pieces which have been particularly well restored often will command more.

Our advisor for mechanical instruments is Martin Roenigk; he is listed in the Directory under Connecticut. Fred Oster advises us on non-mechanical instruments; he is listed in the Directory under Pennsylvania.

Key:
c — cylinder   d — disk

Mechanical

Box, JB Heller, 4 changeable c, MOP inlay, rstr 3,500.00
Box, Mermod Freres, 6 bells, EX 3,000.00
Box, Mira, 18½" dbl c, matching base cabinet, rstr 6,850.00
Box, Paillard, 3 interchangeable c, EX 6,500.00
Box, Polyphon, 19⅝" c, rstr 6,000.00
Box, Regina, 15½" dbl c, mahog, w/lg storage base, rstr 4,500.00
Box, Regina, 20½" d, upright mahog case, NM orig 11,000.00
Box, Regina #50, serpentine mahog case, rstr 4,850.00

Box, Regina #9, 15½" c, EX orig 4,500.00
Box, Stella, 17¼" d, w/storage base, EX 6,200.00
Box, Symphonion, 11⅝" d, clock in top, dbl comb, M 5,000.00
Box, Symphonion, 13⅝" d, dbl comb, coin-op floor model 6,000.00
Box, Symphonium, 25¼" d, ornate cabinet 7,500.00
Nickelodeon, Link R, flute pipes, art glass, 1916, EX 7,900.00
Nickelodeon, Seeburg E, EX orig 6,500.00
Nickelodeon, Seeburg K, w/pipes, EX orig 7,500.00
Nickelodeon, Seeburg L, EX orig 5,000.00
Nickelodeon, Seeburg L, rstr 7,500.00
Nickelodeon, Wurlitzer A, w/bells & roll changer 14,000.00
Nickelodeon, Wurlitzer A, w/pipes, EX orig 11,000.00
Nickelodeon, Wurlitzer IXB, w/bells & roll changer 12,500.00
Orchestrion, Link AX, EX 15,000.00
Orchestrion, Link AX, rstr 20,000.00
Orchestrion, Seeburg G, EX orig 40,000.00
Orchestrion, Seeburg KT Special, EX orig 18,000.00
Organ, band; Wurlitzer #150, EX orig 39,000.00
Organ, monkey; Molinari 6,000.00
Organ, player; Wilcox-White, NM 2,000.00
Organ, pump; Wilcox-White, walnut, 1886 ....1,800.00
Organ, theatre; Wurlitzer, 150 pipes & duplex mechanism ...22,000.00
Organette, Celestina, boudoir stand type, EX 850.00
Piano, grand; Apollo Ampico, w/art case, 74", EX 22,000.00
Piano, grand; Chickering Ampico, 77", EX orig 8,000.00
Piano, grand; Fisher Ampico, w/Queen Anne case, EX 7,000.00
Piano, grand; Fisher Ampico, w/Queen Anne case, rstr 12,000.00
Piano, grand; Knabe Ampico, 68", EX 13,500.00
Piano, grand; Reproduco, w/organ & chimes, rstr 7,000.00
Piano, grand; Steinway Duo-Art, 1928, 74", rstr 18,000.00
Piano, grand; Stroud Duo-Art, ca 1933, 64", EX orig 3,800.00
Reproduco, w/organ & chimes 9,000.00

Pump organ, Estey Organ Co., Victorian, 77", $1,000.00.

Non-Mechanical

Accordion, Empress, Germany, ca 1890, sm, EX 75.00
Accordion, 10-key, Monarch, 1880s, in damaged box 110.00
Cornet, Conn, modified shepherd's crook, USN, 1917, EX 75.00
Guitar, Gibson L-5, pearl inlaid fretboard, NM, +lined case 925.00
Guitar, steel; Ediphone, Electro, wood & Bakelite 325.00
Guitar, steel; Rickenbacher, electro nickel/chrome, 1940s, EX ..375.00
Harmonica, Hohner Blues Harp, EX 12.00
Harpsichord, Chickering & Sons, bird's-eye mahog, '08, EX ...10,000.00

Piano, grand; Ivers & Pond, 1897, 72" **10,000.00**
Piano, Steinway & Sons, ebonized, model B, 1911, 43x84" **2,750.00**
Saxophone, Beuscher, B-flat tenor, #88511, EX, +worn case **80.00**
Violin, CH Hacket, 2-pc flamed maple bk & sides, ca 1906, EX .**125.00**
Violin, Laurent Storoni Fecit Cremona, 2-pc maple bk, EX **95.00**
Violin, Vittorio Bellarose Napoli 1939 label, 14" **300.00**

Mustache Cups

Mustache cups were popular items during the late Victorian period, designed specifically for the man with the mustache! They were made in silverplate as well as china and ironstone. Decorations ranged from simple transfers to elaborately applied and gilded florals. To properly position the 'mustache bar,' special cups were designed for the 'lefties.' These are the rare ones!

Floral, bl on wht w/gold trim, Germany **60.00**
Floral w/ruffled rim & base, gold hdl, ca 1908 ....**65.00**
Knights & angels, gold trim, Royal Bavaria, w/saucer **60.00**
Lady w/flowers transfer, lg **35.00**
Oriental motif, HP, 2¾x3", +5½" saucer **55.00**
Pk lustre w/floral band, Germany, 4½" **40.00**
SP, floral eng, Barbour, EX **75.00**

Nailsea

Nailsea is a term referring to clear or colored glass decorated in contrasting spatters, swirls, or loops. These are usually white but may also be pink or blue. It was first produced in Nailsea, England, during the late 1700s but was made in other parts of Britain and Scotland as well. During the mid-1800s a similar type of glass was produced in this country. Originally used for decorative novelties only, by that time tumblers and other practical items were being made from Nailsea-type glass. See also Lamps.

Flask, clear with white and cranberry overlay loopings, applied hobnails on shoulders, tooled lip, 7", $150.00.

Bottle, wht loopings, sheared mouth, pontil scar, 8½" **135.00**
Flask, cranberry & wht loopings, folded-over lip, 1870s, 7¾" **176.00**
Flask, pk loopings on wht opaque, sheared mouth, 7¼" **155.00**
Flask, wht loopings on clear, sheared lip, 8" **100.00**
Flask, wht w/bl & pk looping, 6" **75.00**
Mug, clear w/wht loopings, appl hdl, 5½" **150.00**
Pipe, wht w/pk loopings, 2-pc, 20" **375.00**

Pipe, wht w/red loopings, 13½" **280.00**
Pitcher, cranberry & wht loopings, appl hdl/ft, 9½" **4,070.00**
Pitcher, yel/orange loops on wht w/gray streaks, 7¾" **200.00**
Powder horn, bl & wht loopings, tooled lip, 1850s, 11" **88.00**
Rolling pin, ruby/clear loopings, 1883 coin inside, 16½" **385.00**

Nakara

Nakara was a line of decorated opaque milk glass produced by the C.F. Monroe Company of Meriden, Connecticut, for a few years after the turn of the century. It differs from their Wave Crest line in several ways. The shapes were simpler; pastel colors were deeper and covered more of the surface; more beading was present; flowers were larger; and large transfer prints of figures, Victorian ladies, cherubs, etc., were used. Ormolu and brass collars and mounts complemented these opulent pieces. Most items were signed; however, this is not important since the ware was never reproduced. Our advisors for this category are Dolli and Wilfred R. Cohen; their address is listed in the Directory under California.

Ashtray, florals on bl, octagonal bowl form, 3 rests **250.00**
Box, angels w/harp on top, sgn, 3¾" dia **400.00**
Box, Bishop's Hat, floral on bl, ormolu ft, 4¼" dia **450.00**
Box, Bishop's Hat, portrait transfer, 4½" **550.00**
Box, Collars & Cuffs, lady's portrait, beading, unemb **1,450.00**
Box, Crown Mold, panels w/sailing scenes, ftd, 6½" dia **1,295.00**
Box, Crown Mold, 6 roses on top, mirror inside, 5½x6" **1,100.00**
Box, emb scrolls, lav violets on apricot, sqd, 4x9" **1,585.00**
Box, floral, wht on dk bl & tan, hexagonal, 4" dia **385.00**
Box, floral on moss gr, mirror in lid, 4½" **475.00**
Box, floral panels w/beading, octagonal, 6" dia **575.00**
Box, Greenaway-style figures on bl, mirror in lid, 6" **1,050.00**
Box, Greenaway-style girls at tea on bl, 3x4½x4½" **600.00**
Box, lady's portrait on emb scrolls, pk/peach, 5½x8" dia **1,350.00**
Box, ring; lady's portrait in wht on rose, unemb, 2x2¼" **595.00**
Box, trinket; clover, pk on lt bl & cream **175.00**
Box, 2 cherubs, 6" **625.00**
Box, 2 cherubs sculpt statue on pnt Burmese, 3½x8½" **1,250.00**
Box, 2 ladies in garden w/flowers & birds on olive, 8½" L **1,350.00**
Card holder, emb scrolls w/flowers **375.00**
Cracker jar, emb scroll panels, floral/Crackers on red **750.00**
Dresser jar, 3 Victorian ladies on bl, 4½" dia **550.00**
Ferner, emb scrolls, wht daisies on pk, ormolu ft/rim **525.00**
Hair receiver, children at tea/wht beads on lt bl, dmn shape **485.00**
Humidor, owl on tree transfer, 5½x4" **1,200.00**
Humidor, Tobacco, frog reading newspaper, metal lid, 6¾" **875.00**
Match holder, tiny beaded flowers on gr, ormolu rim, 2" dia **325.00**
Pin tray, floral on octagonal bowl form, ormolu rim **175.00**
Plaque, Queen Louise in wht reserve on bl, ormolu mt **1,850.00**
Tray, bonbon; scrolls/beads, pk & wht on bl, ormolu collar **420.00**
Umbrella stand, emb scrolls/flowers, Indian portrait, 20½" **2,750.00**

Napkin Rings

Napkin rings became popular during the late 1800s. They were made from various materials. Among the most popular and collectible today are the large group of varied silverplated figurals made by American manufacturers. Recently the larger figurals in excellent condition have appreciated considerably. Only those with a blackened finish, corrosion, or broken and/or missing parts have maintained their earlier price levels. When no condition is indicated, the items listed below are assumed to be all original and in very good to excellent condition.

A timely warning: inexperienced buyers should be aware of excellent reproductions on the market, especially the wheeled pieces. However, these do not have the fine detail and patina of the originals and tend to have a more consistent, soft pewter-like finish. These are appearing at the large, quality shows at top prices, being shown along with authentic antique merchandise. Beware!

Key:
gw — gold washed   SH&M — Simpson, Hall, &
R&B — Reed & Barton   Miller

Barrel ring held by Xd branches & leaf 65.00
Bear reaches for bee on ring, tiered oval base, R&B #475 ....250.00
Bear stands, paws on ring, scalloped base, Middletown #68 ......265.00
Beaver sits on leaves & branches, Toronto #110 ....125.00
Bird, fledgling atop nest, mouth open for feeding 75.00
Bird on branch, open wings, oval base, Meriden #291 ....90.00
Bird w/long tail on leaf, ring attached to wings 95.00

Boy stealing eggs from nest on base, Meriden #269, 2¼", $395.00.

Boy dressed for winter w/book under arm stands by ring 235.00
Boy in harness pulls ring on wheels 350.00
Boy rolls ring, lady watches, oblong base, Tufts #1597 ....395.00
Boy Scout salutes & stands beside ring 245.00
Boys kick on ea side of filigree ring, Meriden #332 ....195.00
Bulldog sits chained to doghouse, sq base, SH&M #207 ....315.00
Cat, angry expression, ornately etched ring 210.00
Cat about to pounce, fly on ring, rnd base 175.00
Cat atop ring arches bk at dog, rnd base, Rogers #296 ....250.00
Cat pushing ring w/paw, no base 85.00
Chair of tree limbs holds ring, rstr 125.00
Cherries & leaves on side of ring, leafy base, Standard #732 ......125.00
Cherub atop ring holds reins on robin 215.00
Cherub in soldier hat w/sword sits on alligator 315.00
Cherub on ring holds dog on leash, Tufts #1543 ....265.00
Cherub pushes sq ring on rectangular base, JW Tufts 250.00
Cherub sits on leaves attached to ring 115.00
Cherub sits on shell alongside of ring, Aurora #8 ....115.00
Cherub stands on rnd base, holds ring over head 125.00
Cherub w/spear rides back of fish, Meriden #157 ....250.00
Chick on wishbone, rococo base, elevated ring, NM 65.00
Chick stands behind ring, oval ball-ftd base, Meriden #222 ......150.00
Children jesters sit/hold ring, R&B #1326 ....195.00
Cockatoo rests on curved log base 75.00
Cow stands beside ring, rnd rstr base 225.00
Crane stands on leafy rnd base 120.00
Crocodile crawls w/ring on bk, unmk 150.00
Cupid on ornate base, bird supports ring, Wilcox #8263 ....215.00
Cupid pulls bbl-shaped ring on branches 125.00
Cupid w/bow sits on stool, rug-like base, R&B #1501 ....400.00
Doe on circular base w/ring at side, Toronto #1106 ....195.00
Dog on haunches tries to catch bird atop ring, Aurora #27 ......225.00
Dog rests paw on girl w/stick, Babcock #208 ....225.00

Dog sits on raised base, bbl-shaped ring, Tufts #1531 ....125.00
Dog w/ring hdl in mouth, circular base, SH&M #014 ....195.00
Dolphin w/ring on bk, Aurora #32, EX 265.00
Eagle holds shield, sits on rectangular base 115.00
Fan forms base for 2 butterflies holding ring 95.00
Fox w/ring on bk, rectangular base, Derby #304 ....205.00
Foxes on ea side of ring, no base 100.00
Frog w/glass eyes on sm leaf, fly on hammered ring 300.00
Girl w/bonnet holds ring, octagonal base, SH&M 175.00
Goat harnessed to sled-like fr holding ring 75.00
Goat on rectangular base beside ring, Knickerbocker #181 ......165.00
Goat pulling ring on wheels, Meriden #212 ....315.00
Greenaway boy holds ring in hand, oval base, Racine #182 ......185.00
Greenaway boy on bicycle before ring, sq base, Adelphi 450.00
Greenaway boy on toy horse holds stick & reins, Derby #378 ....205.00
Greenaway boy sits sleeping before ring, Pairpoint 245.00
Greenaway boy w/cookie, dog begs, rectangular base, Rogers 315.00
Greenaway girl leads goat w/rein, Meriden #0236 ....295.00
Greenaway girl on bench beside ring, rectangular base, Derby ...265.00
Greenaway girl w/muff on sled, bk to ring, Meriden-Britania 295.00
Greenaway girl w/pigtails holds ring, no base, Rogers #280 .....295.00
Horse w/ring on bk, sq ball-ftd base 165.00
Horseshoe on ring, w/emb horse's head & Good Luck, SH&M 95.00
Hummingbird perched on stem, lg leaf base, Toronto #1142 ......135.00
Jack & Jill climbing hill-shaped ring, Tufts #1667 ....450.00
Jester before ring points & holds torch, Meriden #0258 ....250.00
King Neptune kneels on oval base, ring on head 165.00
Leaves & logs ea side of bbl-form ring, R&B #625, EX 95.00
Lion rests paws on ring, ftd rectangular base, Meriden #153 ....255.00
Lotus bud & leaf base w/stem hold ring, Meriden 85.00
Miner w/pick leans against triangular ring 135.00
Monkey playing saxaphone attached to ring 250.00
Owl on sq base w/leaves, sm owls on ring, SH&M #204 ....300.00
Owl sits on ring, log base, Rogers #248 ....125.00
Parakeet on branch, leafy base, Toronto #1108 ....100.00
Parrot w/glass eyes on loop hdl by ring, #4338 ....195.00
Peacock atop ring, tail down bk, Meriden #234 ....225.00
Pear/leaves hang from ring, leaf base, Middletown #140 ....115.00
Rat on haunches by patterned ring, oblong base, Tufts #1619 ...150.00
Rifles, 2 Xd sets, filigree ring between, Meriden #335 ....175.00
Ring on sled, Wilcox #01532 ....195.00
Rip Van Winkle stands on rocky base, ring on shoulder, EX 625.00
Rooster on shovel, flat base, Meriden #181 ....215.00
Roses & leaves on oval ring, Rogers #4 ....50.00
Sailor w/anchor beside ring, R&B #1346 ....300.00
Sheep on raised patterned base, Barbour #15 ....195.00
Sphinx holds up ring w/bud vase atop, Aurora #45 ....175.00
Squirrel climbs tree, ring atop, rnd base, R&B #1150 ....145.00
Stag w/ring on bk, rectangular base, Meriden #204 ....250.00
Stork w/ring on bk, octagonal base, SH&M 245.00
Sunflower base, octagonal, Meriden #37 ....75.00
Swan rests before ring, oval ball-ftd base, R Smith #312 ......225.00
Swords crossed on triangular ring, Meriden #642 ....75.00
Tennis racquet & ball support ring, EX 165.00
Turtle on circular base supports ring, Meriden-Britania #193 ...195.00
Wheelbarrow holds ring, flat shield-type base, Tufts #1537 .....145.00
Wolf baying at moon, fancy free-form Barbour base w/ball ft 250.00
3-leaf clover supports ring, Pairpoint #6 ....65.00

Nash

A. Douglas Nash founded the Corona Art Glass Company in Long Island, New York. He produced tableware, vases, flasks, etc. using delicate artistic shapes and forms. After 1933 he worked for the Libbey Glass Company.

Bowl, Chintz, chartreuse/clear/wine, #501D, 12" 300.00
Candlestick, chartreuse/clear/maroon top, aqua base, 12" 325.00
Candlestick, gold w/pk & gr highlights, sgn/#651, 4" 110.00
Plate, Chintz, gr & crystal stripes w/bl web motif, 8½" 70.00
Vase, Chintz, bl/gr w/silvery stripes, ped ft, 9½" 500.00
Vase, Chintz, trumpet form w/crystal ball stem, 12" 350.00
Vase, gold w/emb leaves, appl base, #B32, 12x4½" 950.00
Wine, Cintra-type bl & gr vertical stripes, conical, 7", pr 435.00

Natzler, Gertrude and Otto

The Natzler's came to the United States from Vienna in the late 1930s. They settled in Los Angeles where they continued their work in ceramics, for which they were already internationally recognized. Gertrude created the forms; Otto formulated a variety of interesting glazes, among them volcanic, crystalline, and lustre. Our advisor for this category is Abby Malowanczyk; she is listed in the Directory under Texas.

Bowl, dk bl speckled gloss, L716, sgn w/label, 3½" H 880.00
Bowl, dk gr/brn crystalline, 2x5" 650.00
Bowl, gray gloss, conical w/1" base, 5", NM 260.00
Bowl, indigo bl flambe, 3" 750.00
Bowl, mc 'floral' & pebbly int decor, ftd, 1¾x9½" 800.00
Bowl, mc cratered glaze, ftd, 4x5½" 1,500.00
Bowl, textured gold/ochre flambe, 3" 750.00
Bowl, volcanic yel-gr, shallow, sgn/label, 7½" 2,200.00
Dish, bl to lav beige toward center, brn rim, shallow, 6" 330.00
Dish, blk metallic, oval, 2x5" 550.00
Vase, orange, tapered bulb w/narrow neck, 23" 5,000.00
Vase, red textured, str sides w/can neck, 9" 1,500.00

Vase, streaky orange, 23", $5,000; Vase, textured red, 9", $1,500.00.

New Hall

The New Hall Company was established in the early 1780s in the Shelton district of England. In the early years they produced hardpaste dinnerware typically decorated with simple floral sprays, often assigning a number rather than a name to their patterns. By 1812 a bone china body was favored and styles were revised to suit the fashion. Decorations became more elaborate. Much of the ware was unmarked and is often attributed to Worcester. Occasionally a piece was marked 'New Hall' within a double circle. Production ceased by 1835.

Bowl, shell in yel/red, 4-color foliage, 5" 55.00
Cup & saucer, pk/red carnations, bl/yel/gr floral, brn rim 75.00
Cup & saucer, shell in yel/blk, 4-color floral, orange rim 150.00
Plate, shell pattern, 4-color floral, yel rim, 8" 190.00
Tea bowl & saucer, shell in yel/blk, 4-color floral, bl rim 145.00
Teapot, floral sprigs, bl/pk border, fluted, 1790s 400.00
Teapot+stand, pk/bl floral sprigs, rose scrolls, 6-sided, 7" 400.00

New Martinsville

The New Martinsville Glass Company took its name from the town in West Virginia where it began operations in 1901. In the beginning years, pressed tablewares were made in crystal as well as colored and opalescent glass. Considered an innovator, the company was known for their imaginative applications of the medium in creating lamps made entirely of glass, vanity sets, figural decanters, and models of animals and birds. In 1944 the company was purchased by Viking Glass, who continued to use many of the old molds, the animals molds included. They marked their wares 'Viking' or 'Rainbow Art.' Viking recently ceased operations and has been purchased by Kenneth Dalzell, President of the Fostoria Company. They too are making the bird and animal models. Although at first they were not marked, future productions are to be marked with an acid stamp. Dalzell/Viking animals are in the $50.00 to $60.00 range. Values for cobalt and red items are two to three times higher than for the same item in clear. See also Depression Glass; Glass Animals.

Bonbon, Janice, rolled-up hdls 15.00
Bonbon, Meadow Wreath etch, hdls, 6" 14.00
Bookend, hunter, pr 150.00
Bowl, Birds & Flowers, hdls, 10½" 45.00
Bowl, crystal w/2 cobalt swan hdls, oval, 13" 110.00
Bowl, Janice, etched, dolphin ftd, 11" 35.00
Bowl, Prelude, shallow, 11½" 42.50
Cake salver, Florette 25.00
Cake stand, Prelude, ftd, 11" 45.00
Candlestick, #415, pr 40.00
Candlestick, dbl, #4536, pr 30.00
Candlestick, dbl, Prelude, pr 50.00
Candlestick, Florentine etch, pr 46.00
Cocktail, Prelude 14.00
Cocktail, ruby, platinum bands, #125 ....7.00
Compote, Radiance, red, oval, metal ped, 9" 35.00
Console set, Prelude, 12" ruffled bowl+2 8" candlesticks 60.00
Cordial, Georgian, ruby 12.00
Cordial, Prelude 20.00
Creamer & sugar bowl, Prelude 30.00
Cup & saucer, Prelude 15.00
Decanter, Michael, gr, +2 shots 35.00
Goblet, Georgian, ruby, 5⅝" 14.00
Goblet, water; Prelude 15.00
Nut bowl, Florentine etch, center hdl, #4429, 11" 19.00
Old-fashioned, Hostmaster, cobalt 8.00
Pitcher, Oscar, amber 20.00
Plate, Florentine etch, #29, 13¾" 46.00
Server, Prelude, center hdl, 10½" 65.00
Server, Princess, center hdl 22.00
Sherbet, Georgian, ruby 9.00
Sherbet, Mt Vernon, amber, ftd, 4" 4.00
Sherbet, Prelude, tall 14.00

Swan, Janice, 12" 35.00
Tumbler, Hostmaster, ruby, 4¼" 11.00
Tumbler, juice; Floral etch, ftd 65.00
Tumbler, juice; Mt Vernon, amber, 3½" 5.00
Tumbler, juice; Prelude, ftd 14.00
Tumbler, Oscar, amber w/platinum trim 6.50
Tumbler, water; Prelude, ftd 15.00
Wine, Hostmaster, ruby, 4x2½" 11.00
Wine, Mt Vernon, amber, ftd, 5" 6.00
Wine, Prelude 15.00

Newcomb

The Newcomb College of New Orleans, Louisiana, established a pottery in 1895 to provide the students with first-hand experience in the fields of art and ceramics. Using locally dug clays — red and buff in the early years, white-burning by the turn of the century — potters were employed to throw the ware which the ladies of the college decorated. Until about 1910 a glossy glaze was used on ware decorated by slip painting or incising. After that a matt glaze was favored. Soft blues and greens were used almost exclusively, and decorative themes were chosen to reflect the beauty of the South. 1930 marked the end of the matt-glaze period and the art-pottery era.

Various marks used by the pottery include an 'N' within a 'C,' sometimes with 'HB' added to indicate a 'hand-built' piece. The potter often incised his initials into the ware, and the artists were encouraged to sign their work. Among the most well-known artists were Sadie Irvine, Henrietta Bailey, and Fannie Simpson.

Newcomb pottery is evaluated to a large extent by two factors: design and condition. In the following listings, items are assumed matt unless noted otherwise. Our advisor for this category is Dave Rago; he is listed in the Directory under New Jersey.

Vase, carved iris, blue and green on dark blue, Sadie Irvine, 12x5½", $4,000.00; Jar, florals, blue and green on blue, H. Bailey, 5x6", $2,200.00.

Bowl, floral band, pk/gr on gr-bl, hairlines, 5" dia 500.00
Bowl, pk/bl matt, thrown by Meyer, 4x8" 375.00
Bowl, 2-tone bl, 3 closed gr rim hdls, Chalaron, 4x5" 600.00
Bowl vase, floral/vine band at top on bl-gr, sgn AM, 4x7" 1,300.00
Bowl vase, flowers/leaves below ea of 4 rim hdls, SI, 5x6" 500.00
Candlestick, Arts & Crafts cvd motif on lav-bl, Simpson, 8" 750.00
Jar, cvd pansies in bl & wht, high gloss, Roman, w/lid, 8" 9,000.00
Jar, floral, bl/gr on bl, H Bailey, w/lid, 6x5" 2,200.00
Match holder, blossoms in yel/wht, Sadie Irvine, 2½x3¼" 650.00
Match holder, moon & moss landscape, pk/bl, 2x3" 700.00
Mug, fuchsia, gr on lt glossy ground, SB Levy, mfg flaw, 4" 1,600.00

Plaque, tall pine tree, bl/gr, H Bailey, label, fr, 9x5" 4,250.00
Pot, long-stem seed pods, high gloss, A Duggan, 1902, 11" 2,860.00
Tea tile, nasturtiums, high gloss, D Roman, 5¾" dia 1,400.00
Trivet, holly rim, glossy/3-color, M LeBlanc, 6" dia 1,100.00
Vase, allover cvd 3-color jonquils on bl, 1910, 8x6" 6,000.00
Vase, berries, gr/red on bl to wine to red, S Irvine, 6" 1,300.00
Vase, berry clusters on bl, S Irvine, ovoid, mfg flaw, 4½" 850.00
Vase, bl volcanic drip, Sara Levy, bulbous, hdls, 9" dia 800.00
Vase, cvd floral band in bl/yel, minor rim rpr, 4x4" 900.00
Vase, cvd gardenia band, wht & yel w/gr foliage, Irvine, 7x6" 950.00
Vase, cvd magnolia, Harriet Jour, 11x7" 3,600.00
Vase, cvd pine cones, pk/bl, 11x6" 3,600.00
Vase, daffodils on bl, EX color/art, S Irving, slim, 11" 2,300.00
Vase, floral, bl/wht on bl, H Bailey, 1926, rim rpr, 11x5¼" 1,500.00
Vase, floral, pk/gr on bl-gr, Sadie Irvine, 8x3½" 1,500.00
Vase, floral, S Irvine, squat w/wide mouth, 4" 465.00
Vase, floral band at bulbous base on med bl, HB, 6x4" 1,200.00
Vase, iris, bl/gr cvd on dk bl, S Irvine, 12x5½" 4,000.00
Vase, lg roses, wht on bl-gr, AF Mason, 8x6" 1,900.00
Vase, lg wht/yel poppies on bl-gr, Littlejohn, 6x5" 1,600.00
Vase, long-stem seed pods, glossy, AI Duggan, 1902, 11" 2,860.00
Vase, lt bl speckled drip on raspberry, mk, JM, 8½x5" 800.00
Vase, medial daffodil band on dk bl, ovoid, HB, 7x5" 1,200.00
Vase, moon/moss/oaks, EX art, AF Simpson, 6" 1,300.00
Vase, moon/moss/trees, A Simpson, str sided, 7x4" 2,000.00
Vase, scenic w/lg yel flowers on bl, Irvine, base chip, 12" 2,400.00
Vase, tall narcissus on med bl, HB, waisted cylinder, 11" 1,700.00
Vase, trees (deep cvg), bl on lt bl, Irvine, 6x4" 1,650.00
Vase, vintage, dk/lt bl on pale bl gloss, SB Levy, hdls, 9" 8,000.00
Vase, 2-tone bl, 3 gr hdls, Chalaron, 4x5" 600.00

Newspapers

In addition to historic content, there are other factors that can add or take away from the value of an old newspaper. These factors are: whether or not the account is a 'first report' (the first time that the news appeared — a 'later-report' is a subsequent reporting); location of articles on the event (those with front-page articles are more highly valued); displayability (size of headlines, presence of photos or graphics to illustrate the event, etc.); whether the paper is from a small or large town; a daily or weekly; and charisma of the paper or event. Prices listed here are for a typical mid-sized town paper with front-page coverage and medium-size headlines.

Papers that do not cover a specific event are called 'atmosphere' newspapers. While these are not as valuable, they offer interesting insight into a particular era through ads for runaway slaves, ships' schedules, jobs wanted, etc. Many have interesting articles on topics such as mermaids, hangings, sea voyages, and a host of other topics.

For a more complete price guide and information on how to determine values as well as how to grade historic newspapers, detect reprints, where to buy and sell originals, and much more, the Newspaper Collectors Society of America offers a *Free Mini-Course About Historic Newspapers*. To obtain your copy of the 32-page primer and extensive price guide, send $2.00 to NCSA, Box 19134-S, Lansing, MI 48901. From it you will learn, for instance, how to recognize the original April 15, 1865, *New York Herald* version of the report of Lincoln's assassination from among the thousands of reprints which abound today. This booklet could save collectors from making bad investments and prevent dealers from losing their honest reputation. Our advisor for this category is Rick Brown; his name, address, and phone number are listed in the Directory under Michigan.

Key:

lr — letter   pub — publisher

1784-1799, Atmosphere papers 30.00
1800-1820, Atmosphere papers 8.00
1821-1859, Atmosphere papers 6.00
1861, Civil War opens, first Confederate reports 250.00
1861, Civil War opens, first Union reports 125.00
1861, Civil War opens, later Confederate reports 150.00
1861, Civil War opens, later Union reports 40.00
1861-1865, Atmosphere papers, Confederate 125.00
1861-1865, Atmosphere papers, Union 8.00
1861-1865, Major battles of Civil War, Confederate titles 250.00
1861-1865, Major battles of Civil War, first Union reports 75.00
1861-1865, Major battles of Civil War, later Union reports 35.00
1862, Emancipation Proclamation 135.00
1863, Battle of Gettysburg, first Union reports 125.00
1863, Battle of Gettysburg, later Union reports 60.00
1863, Gettysburg address 200.00
1865, Capture & death of J Wilkes Booth 115.00
1865, End of Civil War, first Union reports 125.00
1865, End of Civil War, later Union reports 60.00
1865, Fall of Richmond 175.00
1865, Harper's Weekly, Apr 29 edition 350.00
1865, Leslie's Illustrated Newspaper, Apr 29 edition 400.00
1865, Lincoln assassination, NY Herald, Apr 15 ....900.00
1865, Lincoln assassination, other titles, first reports 200.00
1865, Lincoln assassination, other titles, funeral reports 85.00
1866-1900, Atmosphere papers 4.00
1871, Chicago fire, Chicago paper, first reports 75.00
1871, Chicago fire, later reports 35.00
1876, Custer's Last Stand, first reports 200.00
1876, Custer's Last Stand, later reports 75.00
1881, Billy the Kid killed 200.00
1881, Garfield assassinated 75.00
1881, Gunfight at OK Corral 250.00
1882, Jesse James killed, first reports 225.00
1882, Jesse James killed, later reports 75.00
1892, Lizzie Borden crime & trial 40.00
1898, Sinking of Maine 40.00
1898, Spanish American War begins 20.00
1898, Spanish American War ends 30.00
1900-1945, Atmosphere papers 3.00
1901, McKinley assassinated 65.00
1903, Wright Brother's flight 250.00
1906, San Francisco earthquake, other titles 30.00
1906, San Francisco earthquake, San Francisco paper ...500.00
1912, Sinking of Titanic, first reports 350.00
1912, Sinking of Titanic, later reports 75.00
1914, WWI begins 25.00
1915, Lusitania sunk, first reports 125.00
1917, US declares war 30.00
1918, Armistice 40.00
1927, Babe Ruth hits 60th home run 75.00
1927, Lindbergh in Paris, first reports 75.00
1927, Lindbergh in Paris, later reports 30.00
1929, St Valentine's Day Massacre 135.00
1929, Stock Market crash 100.00
1931, Jack 'Legs' Diamond killed 28.00
1932, Lindbergh baby found dead 65.00
1933, Machine Gun Kelley captured 30.00
1934, Baby Face Nelson killed 35.00
1934, Bonnie & Clyde killed 135.00
1934, Dillinger killed 100.00
1934, Pretty Boy Floyd killed 30.00
1935, Will Rogers & Wiley Post in plane crash 35.00
1937, Hindenbergh explodes, first reports 65.00
1937, Hindenbergh explodes, later reports 35.00
1939-1945, Major battles in the war 25.00
1941, Pearl Harber attacked, Honolulu Star-Bulletin (+) 850.00
1941, Pearl Harbor attacked, Dec 8 issues, first reports 30.00
1941, Pearl Harbor attacked, other titles w/lg headlines 35.00
1944, D-Day 30.00
1945, FDR dies 20.00
1945, First atomic bomb dropped 30.00
1945, VE-Day or VJ-Day 30.00
1948, Dewey Defeats Truman, Chicago Daily Tribune 900.00
1950, US enters Korean War 20.00
1957, Soviets launch Sputnik 10.00
1958, Alaska joins Union 15.00
1959, Hawaii joins Union 15.00
1962, Death of Marilyn Monroe 30.00
1962, John Glenn orbits Earth 18.00
1963, JFK assassination, Nov 22, Dallas title 75.00
1963, JFK assassination, Nov 22 or 23, other titles 25.00
1968, Bobby Kennedy assassination 15.00
1968, Martin Luther King assassination 22.00
1969, Moon landing 18.00
1974, Nixon resigns 15.00
1977, Death of Elvis, Memphis paper 30.00
1986, Challenger explodes 6.00

Nicodemus

Chester Nicodemus moved from Dayton, Ohio, to Columbus in 1930 and started teaching at the Columbus Art School. During this time he made vases and commissioned sculptures, water fountains, and limestone and wood carvings. In 1941 Chester left the field of teaching to pursue pottery making full time, using local red clay containing a large amount of iron. Known for its durability, he called the ware Ferrostone. He made teapots and other utility wares, but these goods lost favor, so he started producing animal and bird sculptures, nativity sets, and Christmas ornaments, some bearing Chester's and Florine's names as personalized cards for his customers and friends. Chester died in 1990.

His glaze colors were turquoise or aqua, ivory, green mottle, (pink) pussy willow, and golden yellow. The glaze was applied so that the color of the warm red clay would show through, adding an extra dimension to each piece. Examples are usually marked with his name incised in the clay, but paper labels were also used. Our advisor for this category is James Riebel; he is listed in the Directory under Ohio.

Ashtray, fraternity 25.00
Bookend, camel, pr 400.00
Bookend, dryad (kneeling nude), pr 250.00
Cat, reclining, limestone, 6x15" 4,500.00
Christmas card 100.00
Christmas decoration 40.00
Coffeepot, ind 100.00
Figurine, bull, 7" 200.00
Figurine, cat, 3" 85.00
Figurine, Madonna of the Flowers 150.00
Figurine, robin, 4½" 150.00
Figurine, St Francis 300.00
Nativity set, 9-pc 500.00
Pitcher, bl, 3" 20.00
Pitcher, mustard, sm 35.00
Pottery festival ornament, 1986-87, ea 50.00
Sculpture, Elongation 1936 ....8,000.00
Vase, hdls, 4" 125.00
Vase, w/fish & sea horse 400.00

Wall pocket, dbl, corn 350.00
Water fountain, boy w/frog, 21" 3,500.00

Niloak

During the late 1800s, there were many small utilitarian potteries in Benton, Arkansas. By 1900 only the Hyten Brothers Pottery remained. Charles Hyten, a second generation potter, took control of the family business around 1902. Shortly thereafter, he renamed it the Eagle Pottery Company. In 1909 Hyten and former Rookwood potter Arthur Dovey began experimentation on a new swirl pottery. Dovey previously worked for the Ouachita Pottery Company of Hot Springs and produced a swirl pottery there as early as 1906. In March 1910, the Eagle Pottery Company introduced Niloak, kaolin spelled backwards. During 1911 Benton businessmen formed the Niloak Pottery corporation. Niloak, connected to the Arts and Crafts Movement and known as 'mission' ware, had a national representative in New York by 1913. Niloak's production centered on art pottery characterized by accidental, swirling patterns of natural and artificially colored clays. Many companies through the years have produced swirl pottery, yet none achieved the technical and aesthetic qualities of Niloak. Hyten received a patent in 1928 for the swirl technique. Although most examples have an interior glaze, some early pieces have an exterior glaze as well; these are extremely rare. Swirl/Mission Ware production continued steadily until the Depression when hard times and sagging sales caused Hyten to produce more traditional wares. In 1931 Niloak introduced Hywood Art Pottery, a glazed ware (sometimes similar in shape to Weller's Nile) of mostly hand-thrown vases. Soon thereafter Niloak introduced castware as its primary production and renamed the line Hywood by Niloak. Throughout its existence, the company produced utilitarian items as well as artware. In 1934 Hyten's company found itself facing bankruptcy. Hardy L. Winburn, along with other Little Rock businessmen, raised the necessary capital and were able to provide the kind of leadership needed to make the business profitable once again. Both lines (Eagle and Hywood) were renamed 'Niloak' in 1937 to capitalize on this well-known name. The pottery continued in production until 1947 when it was converted to the Winburn Tile Company, which exists to this day in Little Rock. Be careful not to confuse the swirl production of the Evans Pottery of Missouri with Niloak. The significant difference is the dark brown matt interior glaze of Evans pottery.

Our co-advisors for this category are Lila and Fred Shrader (see the Directory under California) and David Edwin Gifford (see Arkansas), author of *The Collector's Encyclopedia of Niloak*.

Mission Ware

Ashtray, 1½x5½" 145.00
Ashtray/match holder, 2½x5" 135.00
Bowl, flared, 1x3¼" 50.00
Bowl, mixing bowl style, 5x11½" 385.00
Bowl, rose bowl style, 5½x7" 185.00
Bowl, str sides, 2x10" 165.00
Box, w/lid, 4x5½" 150.00
Box, w/lid, 6½" dia 270.00
Candlestick, cupped base, 7" 150.00
Candlestick, flared base, 9½" 185.00
Chamberstick, hdl, cupped base, 5½" 175.00
Compote, w/lid, 6½x5½" 375.00
Creamer, 4½" 60.00
Humidor, w/lid, 5½x5" 325.00
Jardiniere, 12x11" 490.00
Lamp base, orig fittings, 9½" 300.00

Mission Ware tumble-up, 9", $500.00.

Mug, bbl shape, 5" 150.00
Mug, flared base, 4½" 135.00
Pitcher, bulbous, 8½" 275.00
Pitcher, lemonade; 7½" 275.00
Punch cup, 2½" 65.00
Tumbler, cone shape, 4½" 50.00
Tumbler, shot glass, 2" 50.00
Vase, bulbous, 3½" 65.00
Vase, fan form, 7" 125.00
Vase, glaze w/in & w/o, 7" 300.00
Vase, pear shape, 6½" 135.00
Vase, slim neck, broad sloping shoulders, 11" 300.00
Vase, unique 'bull's-eye' effect, 7½" 125.00
Wall pocket, 6½" 195.00

Miscellaneous

Ashtray, duck form, 4½" L 15.00
Ashtray, open-mouth frog form, 3½" 21.00
Ashtray, U of AR metal logo, 3½" sq 65.00
Basket, bouquet pattern, high gloss, 6½" 35.00
Bookends, rooster, matt, 9", pr 85.00
Bowl, conch shape, matt, 8½" 35.00
Bowl, scalloped, matt, 5½x4" 28.00
Cookie jar, matt, w/lid & tab hdls 75.00
Creamer, cow, high gloss, 4½" 55.00
Creamer & sugar bowl, matt, w/lid 35.00
Cup & saucer, demitasse; high gloss 28.00
Ewer, 7½" 18.00
Figurine, dog, 4½" 20.00
Figurine, Scottie, 4" 30.00
Figurine, Trojan horse, stylized, 9" 75.00
Jug, high gloss, remnants of orig syrup label, 7" 38.00
Jug, water; flat ball shape, matt, w/stopper, 8" 95.00
Mug, bouquet pattern, high gloss, 7" 12.00
Pitcher, high gloss, w/lid, 7" 45.00
Pitcher, petal shape, high gloss, 8" 35.00
Planter, clown, 7½" 25.00
Planter, frog, matt, 5½" 30.00
Planter, parrot, HP details 35.00
Planter, pouter pigeon w/spread wings, matt, 9" 85.00
Planter, wishing well, matt, 8" 35.00
Shakers, w/'S' & 'P' hdls, matt, 3", pr 25.00
Teapot, ball shape, matt 50.00
Toothpick holder, ball shape, matt, 1½" 25.00
Vase, bud; matt, 7" 25.00
Vase, cylindrical w/narrow vertical fluting, glossy, 8" 25.00
Vase, wing-like hdls, matt, 7½" 32.00
Wall pocket, cup & saucer design in 'bouquet' decor 35.00

Nippon

Nippon generally refers to Japanese wares made during the period from 1891 to 1921, although the Nippon mark was also used to a limited extent on later wares (accompanied by 'Japan'). Nippon, meaning Japan, identified the country of origin to comply with American importation restrictions. After 1921, 'Japan' was the acceptable alternative. The term does not imply a specific type of product and may be found on items other than porcelains. For further information we recommend *The Collector's Encyclopedia of Nippon Porcelain* by our advisor, Joan Van Patten; you will find her address in the Directory under New York. In the following listings, items are assumed hand painted unless noted otherwise. Numbers included in the descriptions refer to these specific marks:

Key:
#1 — China E-OH	#5 — Rising Sun
#2 — M in Wreath	#6 — Royal Kinran
#3 — Cherry Blossom	#7 — Maple Leaf
#4 — Double T Diamond in Circle	#8 — Royal Nippon, Nishiki
	#9 — Royal Moriye Nippon

Ashtray, Am Indian portrait, red geometric rim, #2, 5½" 255.00
Ashtray, kingfisher figure perched on rim, #2, 6½" 675.00
Ashtray, seal figure at side of 'pool' tray, #2, 3½x7" 575.00
Ashtray/matchbox holder, dog in relief, #2, 4½x5¼" 525.00
Basket vase, yel florals, integral hdls, gr #2, 6x7¼" 215.00
Bowl, Egyptian portrait reserve, blk/red rim, hdls, #2, 6½" 200.00
Bowl, fruit; Doll Face pattern, child's, Morimura, 5¼" 75.00
Bowl, fruit; man on camel scene, gold hdls, gr #2, 12" 350.00
Bowl, river scenic int, folded rim, cut-out hdls, #2, 8½" 90.00
Box, trinket; floral medallion, heart shaped, bl #7, 4" 100.00
Cake plate, gold o/l on wht, RC mk, 10½"+6 5¾" plates 275.00
Candlestick, portrait w/gold, slim, #7, 9" 285.00
Candlestick, river scene, earth tones, gr #2, 6¼" 135.00

Chocolate pot, moriage egrets, $225.00.

Celery dish, celery stalk, gold hdls, #2, 13½", +6 salts 150.00
Chocolate pot, iris on brn shaded, bl #7, 10" 300.00
Chocolate pot, roses reserve, cobalt w/much gold, #7, 10¼" 375.00
Chocolate set, roses on wht w/gold, RE mk, 9½" pot+4 c/s 475.00
Cigarette box, allover florals, gr #2, 4½" L 225.00
Cigarette box, man on camel scene, gr #2, 4½" L 285.00
Coffee set, AD; wht w/much gold o/l, #7, 9" pot+4 c/s 475.00
Compote, woodland scene, scalloped, ftd, gr #2, 3½x6½" 200.00
Compote, 3 griffin supports on triangular base, #2, 5x8" 425.00
Condensed milk holder, gold o/l on wht, RC mk, 6", +tray 115.00
Cookie jar, lg roses on cream w/cobalt & gold, #2, 7½" 425.00

Cracker jar, hunt scene, ornate hdls & finial, bl #7, 5x9½" 385.00
Creamer & sugar bowl, scenic w/Wedgwood trim, #2, 5" 235.00
Desk set, floral, gr #2, 3 pcs on 8½x5¾" tray 550.00
Egg cup, Doll Face pattern, Morimura sticker, 3½" 75.00
Ewer, portrait banded reserve, cobalt w/gold, #7, 6½" 425.00
Ferner, Egyptian decor, molded head hdls, gr #2, 8½" 275.00
Ferner, silhouette figures, 6-sided, #2, 6¾" 160.00
Ferner, tree & river scene, 4 columns, #2, 5" 265.00
Ferner, Wedgwood, cream on bl, 8-sided, #2, 7" 400.00
Flask, powder; floral, gold top, Noritake/Nippon mk, 5" 150.00
Ginger jar, exotic bird reserve, Nippon mk, 7½" 300.00
Humidor, Am Indian on horse in relief, brn tones, #2, 6½" 1,100.00
Humidor, Arab on camel relief, mk, rare, 7½" 950.00
Humidor, bird in relief, #2, 7½" 1,300.00
Humidor, cobalt w/heavy floral gold o/l, #7, 7½" 685.00
Humidor, devil & cards, gr #2, 6" 625.00
Humidor, English hunt scene, bl #2, 7¼" 675.00
Humidor, lions in relief, earth tones, #2, 7¼" 825.00
Humidor, ostriches in desert scene, sq, gr #2, 6½" 485.00
Humidor, owl on branch, 6-sided, gr #2, 6¾" 450.00
Humidor, owls in relief, gr #2, 7¼" 925.00
Humidor, river & bridge scenic, gr #2, 7" 485.00
Humidor, river scenic reserve, Deco florals, gr #2, 6½" 400.00
Humidor, sampan scene, earth tones, bl #7, 6¾" 350.00
Humidor, tiger in relief, earth tones, #2, 7" 1,100.00
Incense burner, geisha figural, Nippon mk, 5" 235.00
Light, owl figural, gr #2, 6¼" 1,450.00
Matchbox holder, sampan scene, hanging, #2, 4½" L 125.00
Mug, Egyptian figures on brn, gr #2, 5" 250.00
Mug, man on camel scene, moriage trim, gr #2, 4¾" 235.00
Mug, moriage dragon on brn mottle, gr #2, 5½" 175.00
Mustache cup, river scene w/gold, #2 ....185.00
Nut dish, Am Indian in canoe, 6-sided, hdls, #2, 5½" 150.00
Pitcher, floral band, cobalt w/heavy gold o/l, bl #7, 7½" 465.00

Pitcher, gold-traced orchids and basketweave motif, gold handle, blue maple leaf mark, 7", $275.00.

Pitcher, lemonade; roses on cream, Torii mk, 6", +6 cups 225.00
Pitcher, mtn & river scene on cobalt w/gold, #7, 6¾" 250.00
Plaque, Am Indian w/horse at sunset, gr #2, 10" 450.00
Plaque, dog portrait reserve, wide floral rim, #7, 7¾" 425.00
Plaque, Doll Face pattern, #5, 6⅛" 75.00
Plaque, Egyptian figure, geometric border, #2, 6" 185.00
Plaque, fish on shelf, gr #2, 12" dia 350.00
Plaque, flower bouquet, gold rim, gr #2, 10" dia 235.00
Plaque, fruit still life, rectangular, gr #2, 10¼" W 575.00
Plaque, Indian stands w/bow & game bird relief, 10½" 825.00
Plaque, lady's portrait reserve, ornate gold rim, #2, 10" 385.00
Plaque, lions relief, mk, 10½" 650.00
Plaque, pastoral scene w/moriage florals at side, #2, 7¾" 185.00
Plaque, river scene, wide gr border, gr #2, 11" dia 350.00
Plaque, sampan scene, gr #2, 10½" 200.00

Plaque, windmill scene, earth tones, gr #2, 9" 215.00
Plaque, 3 horses in relief on scenic ground, #2, 10" 1,050.00
Platter, pheasants reserve, ornate gold rim, hdls, #2, 17" 725.00
Potpourri jar, Wedgwood, cream on bl, gr #2, 5½" 375.00
Smoke set, horse reserve, gr #2, 3-pc set, on 7¾" tray 775.00
Stein, man on camel scene, gold hdl, gr #2, 7" 475.00
Sugar shaker, floral w/gold, hdl, gr #2, 3½" 85.00
Tankard, moriage florals, gold hdl, slim, bl #7, 14¼" 575.00
Tankard, ostrich reserve, cobalt w/gold o/l, #2, 10¼" 575.00
Tea tile, windmill scene, 8-sided, #2, 5½" 65.00
Tray, portrait & floral reserves on wht w/gold o/l, #7, 12" 285.00
Urn, portrait reserve, gold ft & hdls, #7, 9½" 550.00
Urn, portrait reserve, red & wht bands w/gold, #7, 12" 1,100.00
Urn, river scenic band, cobalt w/gold, tree crest mk, 13¾" 1,000.00
Urn, river scenic reserve, ornate gold hdls, #2, 15" 575.00
Vase, Am Indian in canoe, hdls, gr #2, 7" 300.00
Vase, Am Indian in canoe, sm angle hdls, bl #7, 12½" 475.00
Vase, Am Indian scenic, classic form, ring hdls, #2, 14" 675.00
Vase, bird on moriage branch, hdls, bl #7, 9¼" 350.00
Vase, bridge & river tapestry, bl #7, 6" 525.00
Vase, cobalt w/much gold o/l, angle hdls, #7, 12½" 575.00
Vase, dog scenic reserve, much gold, ring hdls, #2, 15" 775.00
Vase, elephant in relief, 3-leg, angle hdls, #2, 8" 850.00
Vase, floral on gr, gold trim, uptrn hdls, #2, 9½" 335.00
Vase, floral reserve, cobalt w/much gold, ring hdls, #7, 7½" 255.00
Vase, floral reserve w/moriage trim, bl #7, 6½" 250.00
Vase, florals, 3-ftd, 3 angle hdls w/rings, gr #2, 11½" 250.00
Vase, house & river scenic reserve, cobalt w/gold, #2, 12" 385.00
Vase, house on hill sponge tapestry, gold tub hdls, #7, 8½" 375.00
Vase, knights riding scene, 4 sm angle hdls, #2, 13" 375.00
Vase, man on camel scene, angle hdls, gr #2, 6" 160.00
Vase, man on camel scene, angle hdls, gr #2, 9" 250.00
Vase, man on camel scene, ornate gold integral hdls, #7, 8" 425.00
Vase, moriage birds, bulbous, hdls, Oriental China mk, 9¼" 400.00
Vase, moriage birds, cylindrical, hdls, #7, 9x9" 475.00
Vase, moriage butterflies w/jewels, hdls, #7, 9" 350.00
Vase, moriage owl, ruffled rim, hdls, bl #7, 8½" 400.00
Vase, moriage trees, house winter scene in relief, #2, 6" 500.00
Vase, moriage trees, low hdls, bl #7, 7" 400.00
Vase, ostrich reserve, cobalt w/gold, hdls, #2, 13" 500.00
Vase, pastoral scenic w/Wedgwood trim, ring hdls, #2, 11" 425.00
Vase, people in wide band on mottle, angled hdls, #2, 8¼" 350.00
Vase, river scenic, much gold o/l, long hdls, #2, 7½" 275.00
Vase, rose tapestry, bottle shape, #7, 8½" 575.00
Vase, roses in relief on mottled ground, hdls, #7, 8½" 500.00
Vase, swan reserve on cobalt w/gold, bulbous, #7, 9½" 575.00
Vase, swan scene, uptrn hdls, bl #2, 6" 150.00
Vase, Wedgwood, cream on bl, angle hdls, gr #2, 7½" 450.00
Vase, winter scene, gold o/l, ftd/hdls, bl #2, 8½" 225.00
Whiskey jug, pine cones on wht, angle hdl, #2, 7½" 425.00
Wine jug, Am Indian in canoe scene, gr #2, 8¾" 625.00
Wine jug, roses w/moriage bird & trim, #7, 8" 625.00
Wine jug, woodland scene, bl #7, 9½" 750.00

Nodders

So called because of the nodding action of their heads and hands, nodders originated in China where they were used in temple rituals to represent deity. Early in the 18th century, the idea was adopted by Meissen and by French manufacturers who produced not only china nodders but bisque as well. Most nodders are individual; couples are unusual. The idea remained popular until the end of the 19th century and was used during the Victorian era by toy manufacturers.

Bill, Germany 100.00
Blk man (& lady), pnt wood/papier-mache, Humphreys, 6", pr ..350.00
Cat, chalk w/worn pnt, extensive rpr, 7" L 200.00
Chicken driving pk car, celluloid 98.00
Clown, bsk, Lennile China, Japan, 1950s, 5¾" 45.00
Max, Germany 100.00
Mickey Mouse, Disney Productions, Disneyland 125.00
Oriental girl w/book, pottery, 6" 135.00
Oriental man w/open fan behind head, bsk, Victorian, lg 265.00
Parrot on perch beside ashtray, metal 120.00
Rabbit pushing baby buggy, celluloid 85.00
Rachel, Germany 100.00
Skeezix, Germany 100.00
Woodpecker picks up matches, w/striker, 3¾x4½" 100.00

Noritake

The Noritake Company was first registered in 1904 as Nippon Gomei Kaisha. In 1917 the name became Nippon Toki Kabushiki Toki. The 'M' in wreath mark is that of the Morimura Brothers, distributors with offices in New York. It was used until 1941. The tree crest mark is the crest of the Morimura family.

The Noritake Company has produced fine porcelain dinnerware sets and occasional pieces decorated in the delicate manner for which the Japanese are noted. Their Azalea pattern was produced exclusively for the Larkin Company, who gave the lovely ware away as premiums to club members and their home agents. From 1916 through the thirties, Larkin distributed fine china which was decorated in pink Azaleas on white with gold tracing along edges and handles. Early in the thirties, six pieces of crystal hand painted with the same design were offered: candle holders, a compote, a tray with handles, a scalloped fruit bowl, a cheese and cracker set, and a cake plate. All in all, seventy different pieces of Azalea were produced. Some, such as the fifteen-piece child's set, bulbous vase, china ashtray, and the pancake jug, are quite rare. One of the earliest marks was the Noritake M in wreath with variations. Later the ware was marked 'Noritake, Azalea, Hand Painted, Japan.' Authority Joan Van Patten has compiled a lovely book, *The Collector's Encyclopedia of Noritake*, with many full-color photos and current prices; her address is in the Directory under New York. Our advisor for Azalea is Alton Parker; he is listed in the Directory under Florida. In the following listings, examples are hand painted unless noted otherwise. Numbers refer to these specific marks:

Key:
#1 — Komaru   #3 — N in Wreath
#2 — M in Wreath

Azalea

Basket, mint; Dolly Varden, #193 ....195.00
Bonbon, #184, 6¼" 50.00
Bowl, #12, 10" 42.50
Bowl, deep, #310 ....68.00
Bowl, fruit; shell form, #188, 7¾" 385.00
Bowl, oatmeal; #55, 5½" 28.00
Bowl, vegetable; divided, #439, 9½" 295.00
Bowl, vegetable; oval, #101, 10½" 60.00
Bowl, vegetable; oval, #172, 9¼" 58.00
Butter chip, #312, 3¼" 145.00
Butter tub, w/insert, #54 ....48.00
Cake plate, #10, 9¾" 40.00
Candy bowl, #185 ....195.00
Candy jar, #313 ....695.00
Casserole, gold finial, w/lid, #372 ....540.00

Casserole, w/lid, #16 ....125.00
Celery/roll tray, #99, 12" 55.00

Azalea celery tray, #444, $330.00.

Cheese/butter dish, #314 ....135.00
Child's set, #253, 15-pc 2,500.00
Coffeepot, AD; #182 ....595.00
Compote, #170 ....98.00
Condiment set, #14, 5-pc 65.00
Creamer & sugar bowl, #122 ....158.00
Creamer & sugar bowl, #449, ind 395.00
Creamer & sugar bowl, #7 ....45.00
Creamer & sugar bowl, AD; open, #123 ....140.00
Creamer & sugar bowl, gold finial, #401 ....155.00
Cruet, #190 ....195.00
Cup & saucer, #2 ....17.50
Cup & saucer, AD; #183 ....150.00
Cup & saucer, bouillon; #124, 3½" 24.50
Egg cup, #120 ....60.00
Gravy boat, #40 ....48.00
Jam jar set, #125, 3-pc 155.00
Match/toothpick holder, #192 ....130.00
Mayonnaise set, scalloped, #453, 3-pc 495.00
Mustard jar, #191 ....60.00
Pickle/lemon set, #121 ....24.50
Pitcher, milk jug; #100, 1-qt 195.00
Plate, #4, 7½" 10.00
Plate, bread & butter; #8, 6½" 10.00
Plate, breakfast; #98, 8½" 24.00
Plate, cream soup; #363 ....175.00
Plate, dinner; #13, 9¾" 28.00
Plate, grill; 3-compartment, #338, 10¼" 165.00
Plate, scalloped sq, salesman's sample 950.00
Plate, soup; #19, 7⅛" 25.00
Plate, sq, #315, 7⅝" 85.00
Platter, #17, 14" 60.00
Platter, #186, 16" 475.00
Platter, #56, 12" 58.00
Platter, cold meat; #311, 10¼" 215.00
Refreshment set, #39, 2-pc 48.00
Relish, #194, 7⅛" 85.00
Relish, loop hdl, 2-part, #450 ....425.00
Relish, oval, #18, 8½" 20.00
Relish, 2-part, #171 ....58.00
Relish, 4-part, #119, rare, 10" 150.00
Saucer, fruit; #9, 5¼" 10.00
Shakers, #126, ind, pr 27.50
Shakers, bell form, #11, pr 30.00
Shakers, bulbous, #89, pr 30.00
Spoon holder, #189, 8" 115.00
Spoon holder, #339, 2-pc 35.00
Syrup, #97, w/underplate 135.00

Tea set, child sz, 15-pc 2,500.00
Tea tile, #169, 6" 48.50
Teapot, #15 ....110.00
Teapot, gold finial, #400 ....495.00
Toothpick holder, #192 ....130.00
Vase, bulbous, #452 ....1,150.00
Vase, fan form, ftd, #187 ....185.00
Whipped cream set, #3, 3-pc 38.50

Ashtray, Deco lady w/floral skirt, orange lustre rim, #2, 4¼" 125.00
Ashtray, dog scene, 3 rests, #2, 4¼" 70.00
Ashtray, Indian portrait, 3 rests, #2, 5½" 130.00
Ashtray, lady figural, skirt forms bowl, gr #2, 5½" 265.00
Basket, Tree in the Meadow 75.00
Basket vase, heavy gold o/l, #1, 8¾" 185.00
Bowl, floral, bl lustre rim w/gold, hdls, gr #2, 10½" 55.00
Bowl, floral w/gold o/l, orange lustre rim, #3, 9½" 45.00
Bowl, floral w/much gold, 4-lobed, #1, 6" W 35.00
Bowl, mc roses on tan, red rim, 6-lobed, red #2, 5" 35.00
Bowl, river scene, gold trim, hdls, gr #2, 5½" L 40.00
Bowl, river scene w/orange & bl lustre, hdls, #2, 7" 40.00
Bowl, salad; yel w/vegetables on wht int, scalloped, #2, 10" 70.00
Box, cigarette; cupid reserve on wht w/gold, red #2, 6" L 125.00
Box, clown figural, gr #2, 5½" 275.00
Box, elephant w/howdah figural, red #2, 6½" 255.00
Box, powder; bl lustre w/cat finial, gr #2, 4¼" 175.00
Box, puff; lady figural, base forms skirt, #2, 6½" 275.00
Box, trinket; lady w/whippet on lid, gr #2, 3" 60.00
Cake plate, Tree in the Meadow 30.00
Candlestick, bird on branch, geometrics at base, #2, 8¼", pr 175.00
Candy dish, Deco lady on red lid, blk base, #2, 6½" 215.00
Candy dish, river scene, ruffled rim, center hdl, #2, 7½" 30.00
Celery tray, florals & birds on wht, gold rim, #2, 11" 40.00
Celery tray, leaf form, cream w/red veins, #2, 12½" 40.00
Chamberstick, river & tree scene, earth tones, #2, 1¾", pr 80.00
Cheese dish, floral band on wht, slant top, #2, 4x8x6" 85.00
Chocolate pot, gold o/l on wht, gr #2, 9" 65.00
Cigarette holder, floral on cream, bird finial, #2, 5" 105.00
Coffeepot, Tree in the Meadow 275.00
Compote, mc florals, bl lustre rim, gold lustre hdls, #2, 8½" 60.00
Condiment set, floral on yel, #2, 3-pc on tray, 5½" W 90.00
Creamer, floral & orange lustre, ewer form, red #2, 5¾" 30.00
Cup, punch; scenic w/gold rim & ft, cream int, #2, 2¾" 35.00
Demitasse set, fruit basket reserve, lustre/wht, #1, 16-pc 250.00
Egg cup, river scene, earth tones, gr #2, 3½" 25.00
Ferner, blk berries/red leaves, triangular, #2, 6" W 95.00
Humidor, stork along river scene, gr #2, 6½" 300.00
Lemon dish, lemon at center, orange lustre, hdl, #2, 5¾" 30.00
Napkin ring, Deco lady, #2, 2¼" W, 2 in box 140.00
Nappy, floral, gold scalloped rim, hdl, #2, 6½" 35.00
Night light, Egyptian & owl figural, #2, 13" 925.00
Night light, lady figural, orange lustre dress, #2, 9¾" 985.00
Plaque, elk in relief, earth tones, gr #2, 10½" 500.00
Plaque, silhouette-style figure on couch, gr #2, 8½" 235.00
Potpourri jar, florals on bl, bud finial, gr #2, 6½" 75.00
Sauce dish, flower form, petal underplate, #2, 5", +ladle 70.00
Shaving mug, river scene, earth tones, gr #2, 3¾" 95.00
Smoke set, butterflies on gray, red #2, 3-pc on 7½" tray 400.00
Smoke set, florals on red w/blk, #2, 2-pc on 7" tray 150.00
Spooner, river scene, angle hdls, red #2, 8" 40.00
Sugar bowl, river & bridge scene, angle hdls, #2, 3½" 20.00
Sugar shaker, floral band, shouldered, gold top, #2, 6½" 30.00
Syrup, river scene, earth tones, gr #2, 4¼" 60.00

Tea tile, river scene, canted corners, #2, 5" 40.00
Tray, Deco fruit border, gold hdls, red #2, 11" 90.00
Tray, scenic reserves, gold borders, canted corners, #1, 13" 65.00
Urn, river/tree scene, cobalt w/gold, #1, 8¾" 235.00
Vase, exotic bird on branch, blk rim w/gold, #2, 10" 60.00
Vase, floral w/gold, cylindrical, sm hdls, #2, 11¼" 140.00
Vase, florals on wht, gold ring hdls, classic form, #2, 8½" 120.00
Vase, man on camel scene w/gold, squat, #1, 2½" 110.00
Vase, peacock feathers on tan, slim, ruffled top, #1, 8" 110.00
Vase, river & bridge scenic band on gr, hdls, #1, 9¼" 325.00
Vase, Tree in the Meadow, fan form 75.00
Vase, tulip figural, lav & gr, red #2, 5½" 175.00
Vase, wide floral border on gr, fan form, red #2, 6½" 110.00
Wall pocket, floral on lustre, appl bird at rim, #2, 8¼" 190.00
Wall pocket, swan scenic band, orange lustre, #2, 8" 85.00

North Dakota School of Mines

The School of Mines of the University of North Dakota was established in 1890, but due to a lack of funding it was not until 1898 that Earle J. Babcock was appointed as Director, and efforts were made to produce ware from the native clay he had discovered several years earlier. The first pieces were made by firms in the east from the clay Babcock sent them. Some of the ware was decorated by the manufacturer; some was shipped back to North Dakota to be decorated by native artists. By 1909 students at the University of North Dakota were producing utilitarian items such as tile, brick, shingles, etc., in conjunction with a ceramic course offered through the Chemistry Department. By 1910 a ceramic department had been established, supervised by Margaret Kelly Cable. Under her leadership, fine artware was produced. Native flowers, grains, buffalo, cowboys, and other subjects indigenous to the state were incorporated into the decorations. Some pieces have an Art Nouveau — Art Deco style easily attributed to her association with Frederick H. Rhead with whom she studied in 1911. During the twenties the pottery was marketed on a limited scale through gift and jewelry stores in the state. From 1927 until 1949 when Miss Cable announced her retirement, a more widespread distribution was maintained with sales branching out into other states. The ware was marked in cobalt with the official seal — 'Made at School of Mines, N.D. Clay, University of North Dakota, Grand Forks, N.D.' in a circle. Very early ware was sometimes marked 'U.N.D.' in cobalt by hand.

Bowl, brn high glaze, Julia Mattson, 5½" 135.00
Bowl, brn matt, Julia Mattson, 4½" 95.00
Bowl, floral, beige on gray-bl, Arneson, 7x5", NM 175.00
Bowl, Indian decor, artist sgn, 4½x5½" 395.00
Coaster, fawn outlined in buff clay on lt bl, 3½" dia 95.00
Jar, Indians riding/shooting arrows, brn on brn, w/lid, 7x6" 375.00
Pitcher, florals, Huck, 6" 195.00
Plate, American Indian, stylized, mk JCH, 1933, 9" 245.00
Vase, aqua, 3 deep vertical ribs, Julia Mattson, 9½" 165.00

Vase, carved flowers on turquoise gloss, signed Ruth Allen, 7½", $675.00.

Vase, cobalt, Julia Mattson, 7" 150.00
Vase, cvd leaves, Mattson, 3" 350.00
Vase, cvd wheat on cream w/orange & brn specks, Huck, 10" 750.00
Vase, dk bl leaves in relief at top on bl, F Huckfield, 4x4" 425.00
Vase, dk brn-gr matt, M Cable, #117, 5x7" 250.00
Vase, floral vines/butterflies, M Seim, dtd '53, 8½" 525.00
Vase, glossy teal, pear shape, 4¼x5" 225.00
Vase, gr matt, incised curvilinear design, Huck, 4" 135.00
Vase, incised stylized wheat, Mattson, UND mk, 6" 450.00
Vase, Indian motif, Bentonite glaze, sgn Stallman/1942, 8x4" 650.00
Vase, Indian motif, blk/dk red, Bentonite clay, Mattson, 4" 425.00
Vase, Indian motif cvd on gr/brn matt, M Heith, 4x5" 325.00
Vase, matt gr, sgn Huck, 3½" 125.00
Vase, turq to aqua flambe, sgn Fretz, 5¼x4" 165.00
Vase, wheat stacks, wht/bl gloss on brn clay, Huck, #164, 5" 375.00

North State

In 1924 the North State Pottery of Sanford, North Carolina, began small-scale production, founded by Mrs. Rebecca Copper with the help of her husband. Using locally dug clay, the pottery flourished and became well known for lovely shapes and beautiful glazes. They were in business for thirty-five years. Most of their ware was sold in gift and craft shops throughout North Carolina.

Ashtray, burnt orange/gr, imp mk, 1¾" H, NM 25.00
Ewer, gr, 5¼" 25.00
Jug vase, Chinese red, sm 335.00
Pitcher, copper lustre, slender form, 6½" 25.00
Pitcher, red over gr, tall 58.00
Sugar bowl, yel, imp 1920s-30s mk, 3" 30.00
Vase, beige, fan form, 3¾" 25.00

Vases, ocean green drip glaze, 5½", $32.50; 6", $45.00; 4", $28.00.

Northwood

The Northwood Company was founded in 1896 in Indiana, Pennsylvania, by Harry Northwood, whose father, John, was the art director for Stevens and Williams, an English glassworks. Northwood joined the National Glass Company in 1899 but in 1901 again became an independent contractor and formed the Harry Northwood Glass Company of Wheeling, West Virginia. He marketed his first carnival glass in 1908, and it became his most popular product. His company was also famous for its custard, goofus, and pressed glass. Northwood died in 1923, and the company closed. See also Carnival; Custard; Goofus; Opalescent; Pattern Glass.

Bowl, berry; Leaf Mold, red spatter on canary satin, ind 60.00
Bowl, master berry; Leaf Umbrella, cranberry, 7¾" 165.00
Bowl, Plum & Cherry, color/crystal, decor, 9" 80.00
Butter dish, Pods & Posies, gr w/gold 125.00
Butter dish, Royal Ivy, rubena frost 185.00
Butter dish, Royal Oak, frosted 60.00
Butter dish, Royal Oak, rubena frost 225.00
Celery vase, Leaf Mold, cranberry 135.00
Celery vase, Ribbed Pillar, cased spatter 95.00
Creamer, Leaf Medallion, gr 75.00
Cruet, Fluted Scroll, bl opal 125.00
Cruet, Leaf Medallion, amethyst w/gold 600.00
Cruet, Leaf Medallion, gr 450.00
Cruet, Royal Ivy, cased spatter, orig stopper 400.00
Cruet, Royal Ivy, rubena, faceted stopper, 6¾x3¼" 300.00
Nappy, Sunflower, gr 40.00
Pitcher, water; Cherry & Cable, +6 tumblers 325.00
Pitcher, water; Grape & Leaf, wht w/pk & gr, +4 tumblers 215.00
Pitcher, water; Leaf Mold, cased spatter, +6 tumblers 865.00
Pitcher, water; Peach, gr w/gold, +6 tumblers 350.00
Pitcher, water; Royal Ivy, cased spatter 350.00
Pitcher, water; Royal Ivy, clear/frosted 125.00
Pitcher, water; Royal Ivy, rubena frost 300.00
Pitcher, water; Royal Oak, rubena 275.00

Plate and cup, Chinese Coral, #722, rare, $95.00.

Rose bowl, Leaf Mold, cased spatter 195.00
Rose bowl, pull-up, gr/yel on wht, 3 thorny ft, 3x3" 265.00
Rose bowl, Royal Ivy, rubena 80.00
Salt shaker, Leaf Umbrella, rose agate 80.00
Sauce bowl, Ribbed Spiral, cased spatter 35.00
Shaker, Leaf Mold, red spatter on canary satin 80.00
Shaker, Royal Ivy, rubena 95.00
Shakers, Panelled Sprig, amethyst, pr 60.00
Shakers, Royal Ivy, rubena frost, pr 160.00
Shakers, Royal Oak, rubena, pr 140.00
Shakers, Royal Oak, rubena frost, pr 150.00
Spooner, Leaf Medallion, gr 85.00
Spooner, Leaf Umbrella, cased spatter 165.00
Spooner, Leaf Umbrella, rose agate 88.00
Spooner, Peach, gr w/gold 95.00
Spooner, Royal Oak, rubena 60.00
Sugar bowl, Leaf Medallion, amethyst 160.00
Sugar bowl, Leaf Umbrella, cranberry, w/lid 275.00
Sugar shaker, Leaf Mold, bl satin 245.00
Sugar shaker, Leaf Mold, cased spatter 165.00
Sugar shaker, Leaf Umbrella, cased spatter 185.00
Sugar shaker, Royal Ivy, rubena, orig top 135.00
Syrup, Grape & Leaf, wht opaque 115.00
Syrup, Royal Ivy, rubena, orig top 255.00

Toothpick holder, Leaf Mold, clear cased spatter 245.00
Toothpick holder, Leaf Umbrella, clear cased spatter 350.00
Toothpick holder, Royal Ivy, clear cased spatter 170.00
Toothpick holder, Royal Ivy, rubena frost 165.00
Toothpick holder, Royal Oak, rubena 250.00
Tumbler, Memphis, gr w/gold, 6 for 175.00
Tumbler, Oriental Poppy, gr w/M gold 60.00
Tumbler, Pods & Posies, gr w/M gold 80.00
Tumbler, Royal Ivy, rubena, 4x2⅝" 50.00
Tumbler, Teardrop & Flowers, bl w/gold 50.00
Vase, pull-up, pk on yel, 3-petal top, 3¼x3¾" 325.00
Vase, pull-up, red/gold vertical pattern, waisted neck, 9" 325.00
Vase, pull-up, rust/yel on wht, scalloped top, 4¼x4½" 695.00
Vase, pull-up feathers, mauve on beige, bl int, 5x2⅞" 750.00
Whiskey set, Grape & Cable, gold trim, decanter+5 shots 225.00

Nutcrackers

The nutcracker, though a strictly functional tool, is a good example of one to which man has applied ingenuity, imagination, and engineering skills. Though all were designed to accomplish the same end, hundreds of types exist in almost every material sturdy enough to withstand sufficient pressure to crack the nut. Figurals are popular collectibles, as are those with unusual design and construction. Patented examples are also desirable. Our advisor for this category is Earl MacSorley; he is listed in the Directory under Connecticut. For more information, we recommend *Ornamental and Figural Nutcrackers* by Judith A. Rittenhouse.

Alligator, brass, 2-part, mtd to base, 1800s, 7½" 90.00
Alligator, CI w/EX detail, 1880s 90.00
Alligator, pnt aluminum, John Wright, 1960s 40.00
Alto Knack, screw-down type 45.00
Big Ben, brass, English, 1900s 60.00
Bird, wooden screw-type, English, 1850s-80s, 6⅝" 100.00
Cook Muffler Co ad, CI w/NP, hand held, 4½" 10.00
Dog, bronzed CI, oblong stepped base, Althoff & Co 100.00
Dog, cast brass w/EX hair detail, brass base, 11" L 80.00
Dog, CI, tail hdl, rectangular base, 13" 45.00
Dog, striding, copper plated, ca 1900, 5¾x11¼" 125.00
Dragon, CI w/old gold pnt, English, 1900-10, 5½x14" 300.00
Dragon, gold-pnt CI, 2 parts bolted together, 13" L 175.00
Eagle head, CI, spring lever, wood base, 7" L 100.00
Elephant, CI w/red & blk pnt, trunk is lever, 10x5" 125.00
Hamilton, CI, table-top vise type, early 1900s 45.00
Harold Lloyd, pnt CI, NM 375.00
Home, CI, screws to table, long lever, 1800s 40.00
Horse, standing, brass, Miami Beach Fla, Pat Pending, 4¾x8" 60.00
Lady's legs, CI w/flesh-color pnt, 1940s, 7" 30.00
Lady's legs, cvd wood, 1800s 40.00
Legs w/high heels, chromium plated, Am, 1940-50s, 7⅛" 40.00
Man in red coat, pnt CI, wooden base, Am, Pat 1870, 9¼" 400.00
Perfection, CI w/NP, vise type, Pat 1889 ....40.00
Pliers, eng steel, crossover type, pointed hdls, 5½" 10.00
Uneek, CI cup & hammer 49.00

Occupied Japan

Items marked 'Occupied Japan' have become popular collectibles in the last few years. They were produced during the period from the end of WWII until April 18, 1952, when the occupation ended. By no means was all of the ware exported during that time marked 'Occupied Japan'; some was marked 'Japan' or 'Made In Japan.' It is thought that because of the natural resentment felt by the Japanese toward the occupation, only a fraction of these wares carried the 'Occupied' mark. Even though you may find identical 'Japan'-marked items, because of its limited use, only those with the 'Occupied Japan' mark are being collected to any great extent. Values vary considerably based on the quality of workmanship. Generally, bisque figures command much higher prices than porcelain, since on the whole they are of a finer quality.

For those wanting more information, we recommend *The Collector's Encyclopedia of Occupied Japan Collectibles* by Gene Florence; he is listed in the Directory under Kentucky. Our advisor for this category is Florence Archambault; she is listed under Rhode Island. She represents the Occupied Japan Club, whose mailing address may be found in the Directory under Clubs, Newsletters, and Catalogs. All items in the descriptions that follow are assumed ceramic unless noted otherwise.

Ashtray, metal, horse head w/in horseshoe form, 5" 7.50
Ashtray, Wedgwood type, 2½" 8.00
Atomizer, pk glass, flattened inv't V-form w/stepped sides 25.00
Binoculars, Prismex coated lens, 8x30, Field 850, #2013, w/case ..75.00
Bottle, scent; pressed glass, plume-mold stopper, sm 25.00
Bowl, salad; wood, 10" 20.00
Box, bsk, emb lady in swing on lid, 7½" 50.00
Box, Wedgwood type, wht on bl, rectangular, 3" L 17.50
Bracelet, faux pearls, 3-row, strung on stiff wire 20.00
Candle holder, figure between cups w/scroll stems, 4", pr 55.00
Child's set, Blue Willow, 2-place set, 9-pc 100.00
Child's set, Disney character, 2-place, 9-pc 100.00
Child's set, florals, 2-place, 9-pc 45.00
Child's set, lustre w/flowers, 4-place, 13-pc 75.00
Christmas item, blown glass bell ornament, 12 in box mk MIOJ ..35.00
Christmas item, nativity figures, 2½", 7-pc set 75.00
Christmas item, Santa by wht planter, 5½x6" 25.00
Christmas item, Santa w/pipe-cleaner body, 4" 20.00
Christmas item, snowbaby-like skier, 3½" 30.00
Cigarette lighter, metal, camera figural 35.00
Cigarette lighter, metal, Indian head form 22.50
Cigarette lighter, metal, modeled as a gun, 2½" 22.50
Cigarette lighter, metal, urn style, 3¼" 10.00
Clicker, metal, chicken, 1½" 6.00
Covered dish, chicken on nest, 2-pc, Maruhon Ware, 6" 50.00
Creamer, lustre w/flowers, 1½" 7.50
Creamer, windmill form, 3" 10.00
Creamer & sugar bowl, metal w/look of silver, 2" 30.00
Crumb butler, metal, 5x6" 10.00
Cup, elephant w/flag, red hdl, 1¾" 10.00
Cup & saucer, Blue Willow, Maruta China 20.00
Cup & saucer, demitasse; gr/wht, modeled as leaves, Merit 20.00
Cup & saucer, floral sprigs on wht, Merit 15.00
Cup & saucer, Oriental lady, HP, red mk 20.00
Dinnerware, floral w/gold, bowl, 5¾" 6.00
Dinnerware, floral w/gold, creamer 13.50
Dinnerware, floral w/gold, cup & saucer 12.50
Dinnerware, floral w/gold, gravy boat 16.00
Dinnerware, floral w/gold, plate, 10" 13.50
Dinnerware, floral w/gold, sugar bowl w/lid 18.00
Dinnerware set, complete, serves 8 ....285.00
Dinnerware set, complete, w/gravy boat+sm platter, serves 6 .....235.00
Dinnerware set, complete, w/many serving pcs, serves 12 ....425.00
Doll, celluloid, go-go dancer w/feathers & jewelry, 13" 45.00
Doll, celluloid, jtd arms/legs, molded pk hooded sleeper, 6" 25.00
Doll, celluloid, jtd shoulders, nude, 4¾" 20.00
Dolls, celluloid, 2 babies in red basket, 4½x3" 50.00
Duck, celluloid, 4½" 20.00

Fan, paper, 8" spine 15.00
Figurine, angel embracing lg gr lily vase, bsk, Paulux, 7½" 50.00
Figurine, ballerina in 2-tiered net skirt, 5¾" 40.00
Figurine, Blk fiddler, 6" 40.00
Figurine, Blk musician, 2¾" 20.00
Figurine, boy in gr coat playing cello, brn mk, 5" 12.50
Figurine, boy in short red pants w/parrot, red mk, 5" 12.50
Figurine, boy in yel/red holds hat to side, red mk, 5" 12.50
Figurine, Chinese couple, red mk, 5" 22.50
Figurine, couple at piano, 4" 22.50
Figurine, cow family, 3-pc, largest: 2¾x4" 20.00
Figurine, cupid by lg open flower on stem, bsk, 4" 30.00
Figurine, cupid stands in front of sled, bsk, MIOJ, 5" 35.00
Figurine, cupid w/in crescent moon, 3½" 8.00
Figurine, dancing couple, blk mk, 4½" 20.00
Figurine, dog by lamp, 2" 4.00
Figurine, Elsie the Cow, seated, 3½" 20.00
Figurine, Eskimo, 3" 15.00
Figurine, fancy attire, bsk, Royal Sealy, 9", pr 130.00
Figurine, girl in wht w/basket, Florence-look, 7" 35.00

Figurine, girl with book, 6", $35.00.

Figurine, Hummel-type boy & girl w/umbrella, 6" 40.00
Figurine, Hummel-type boy w/begging dog, 5" 30.00
Figurine, Hummel-type boy w/broken sprinkler, 4½" 35.00
Figurine, Indian woman, red mk, 6" 35.00
Figurine, lady, 12" 75.00
Figurine, lady w/fan, ruffled tiers, bsk, red mk, 10½" 75.00
Figurine, man in elegant attire w/violin, bsk, 9" 60.00
Figurine, monkeys, Speak, See, Hear No Evil 15.00
Figurine, Oriental, bsk, MIOJ, 6", pr 50.00
Figurine, Oriental, seated playing w/rabbits, mk Ardalt, 4" 25.00
Figurine, Oriental, 8", pr 65.00
Figurine, Oriental w/mandolin, 10" 50.00
Figurine, peacock on floral branch, 7" 27.50
Figurine, plumed hat, on sq base, bsk, MIOJ, 9¾", pr 140.00
Figurine, puppies in basket, 2½" 15.00
Figurine, seated Colonial, bsk, Andrea, 7", pr 175.00
Figurine, shepherd w/lamb on shoulder, 13½", pr 175.00
Figurine, squirrel, 1 upright, 1 crouching, 4½x5" 20.00
Figurine w/ash receiver, donkey pulling barrel w/wood lid 7.50
Furniture, bench, 1¾" 5.00
Furniture, chair w/tiny appl flowers, 3" 8.50
Furniture, couch w/tiny appl flowers, 3" 10.00
Furniture, piano, 1¾" 7.50
Furniture, refrigerator, Philco, 2½" 15.00

Hanging planter, parrot/flowers on doughnut form, Maruhon **65.00**
Jar, powder; bl w/wht floral reserve, oval, 2½" **10.00**
Lamp base, dbl pr, Colonials, bsk, 11", pr **150.00**
Lamp base, dbl pr, wht w/gold & flowers, scroll base, 11", pr **100.00**
Lamp base, lady's head, Cordey look, 10" **55.00**
Linen, damask tablecloth, 48x52", +12" napkins, paper label **100.00**
Match holder, brn w/sm yel flowers, wall mt, 6" **37.50**
Mug, bbl form w/grapes & vines **15.00**
Mug, cannibal figure hdl, 4¼" **35.00**
Planter, w/figures of man, lady & 2 rabbits, Paulux, 5x7" **150.00**
Plaque, Colonial couple, gold trim, bsk, Paulux, 6½x6" **45.00**
Plaque, Dutch boy figural, chalkware, Yomake, 7½" **22.50**
Plate, portrait of lady, Andrea, SGK China, 6" **20.00**
Plate, rtcl edge, lg flower in center, Rosetti, 8" **22.50**
Platter, Blue Willow, 6" **35.00**
Relish tray, lacquerware, red w/gold trim, Bafuri, 15" L **60.00**
Salt box, gr lines/sm florals on wht, wood lid, wall mt, mk **50.00**
Scarf, silk w/flowers, Barr & Beard Inc, 48x19" **50.00**
Shakers, baseball players, comical, pr **25.00**
Shakers, cottage & lighthouse, single base, pr **30.00**
Shakers, glass w/metal lids on metal tray **20.00**
Snack plate, leaf shape w/lg wht HP flowers, Shofu, 9" **10.00**
Stein, emb drinking scene, bl on wht w/orange bands, 6¾" **20.00**

Tea set, modeled as grape clusters, 3-piece, $50.00.

Tea set, toby figurals, 3-pc **90.00**
Teapot, tomato form, Maruhon, 4½" **50.00**
Teapot, tomato form, 2x4" **25.00**
Toy, Horse & Cart, Trade Mark Modern Toys, MIB **100.00**
Toy, Lucky Sledge, boy on sled, Kenkosha Toys, MIB **75.00**
Tray, metal, leaf form, mk Economy, 5" **5.00**
Umbrella, paper, 18" **27.50**
Vase, brn w/pk rose, hdls, 4¼" **7.50**
Vase, on common base w/ballerina figure, 8" **60.00**
Vase, swan form, mc, 5" **12.50**
Wall plaque, flying duck, EX quality, 6½" **25.00**
Water lily, celluloid, in orig box **10.00**

Ohr, George

George Ohr established his pottery around 1893 in Biloxi, Mississippi. The unusual style of the ware he produced and his flamboyant personality earned him the dubious title of 'the mad potter of Biloxi.' Though acclaimed by some of the critics of his day to be perhaps the most accomplished thrower in the history of the industry, others overlooked the eggshell-thin walls of his vessels, each a different shape and contortion, and saw only that their 'tortured' appearance contradicted their own sedate preferences.

Ohr worked alone. His work was typically pinched and pulled, pleated, crumpled, dented, and folded. Lizards and worms were often applied to the ware, each with detailed, expressive features. He was well recognized, however, for his glazes, especially those with a metallic patina. The ware was marked with his name, alone or with 'Biloxi' added. Ohr died in 1918. Our advisor for this category is Fer-Duc, Inc.; the address is listed in the Directory under New York.

Bowl, gr speckled w/orange int, pinched/4-lobe, 2x3¾"" **900.00**
Bowl, gun metal, brn/gr specked int, ftd/incurvate, 4½x5" **450.00**
Bowl, yel w/brn specks, collapsed, long dimple, 2½x4" **700.00**
House, gr triangular form on textured brn rectangle, 6" L **465.00**
Mug, brn drip over ochre, C-hdl, can neck, 4x4¾" **750.00**
Mug, brn speckled, incised 'Boss,' pleated sides, rstr, 3½" **325.00**
Mug, speckled brn-gr, appl snake, asymmetrical hdls, 5x6" **3,000.00**
Pitcher, blistered gun metal, formed from bowl shape, 3x5" **1,900.00**
Pitcher, brn w/gun-metal drip, bulbous, appl hdl, 5x7" **900.00**
Pitcher, dk scroddled bsk, contrived from bowl form, 3x4" **2,800.00**
Pitcher, gr/bl/pk/brn mottle, brn int, can neck, ftd, 6" **1,400.00**
Pitcher, gr/brn daubs on clear, 2 spouts/hdls, U-form, 4x6" **1,400.00**
Pitcher, gr/pk/gun-metal mottle, cut-out hdl, rstr, 3x6" **1,300.00**
Pitcher, gun metal, brn-gr int, long cut-out hdl, 3½x4" **1,500.00**
Pitcher, gun metal, cylindrical w/slight mid-buldge, 5½" **400.00**
Pitcher, lg brn dots under gr & clear, concave form, 3½" **900.00**
Pitcher, purple w/bl-gr, blk int, 7-shape hdl, folds, 3" **1,700.00**
Pitcher, purple w/bright bl sponged bands, orange int, 7x5" **1,850.00**

Teapot, applied snake spout and handle, applied snake at shoulder, blue and pink dappled glaze, impressed twice, 4½", $4,200.00.

Vase, bl w/gray sponging, deep twist at top, 5x3½" **2,600.00**
Vase, brn iron-oxide bsk, bulbous w/pleated neck, 4x3" **500.00**
Vase, brn specks in clear glaze, in-body twist, 2½x4" **900.00**
Vase, brn-gr, twist above wider bottom, 4x3" **1,100.00**
Vase, brn/gr irid mottle, bottle form w/flared neck, 11x4" **4,250.00**
Vase, brn/tan swirl w/yellowish-clear gloss, spherical, 3" **325.00**
Vase, cobalt, short base, crimped collar, 7½" **1,900.00**
Vase, dk bl/gray/brn sponged on tan, bottle w/wide top, 8" **1,600.00**
Vase, gr metallic mottle, crimped/dimpled top, 5" **1,210.00**
Vase, gr to blk gloss, bulbous w/crimped stovepipe top, 5" **1,000.00**
Vase, gr w/dk specks, folded/pinched body, disk ft, 3" **500.00**
Vase, gun-metal mottle on mustard/gr, dents/crimped, 7x7" ...**3,300.00**
Vase, leathery red/gr on dk gr mottle, neck twist, 7x4" **2,700.00**
Vase, lt gr speckled, neck twist over flat shoulder, 5x3" **1,100.00**
Vase, purple, deep twist above angled shoulder, 3½x4" **1,600.00**
Vase, purple & gr w/metallic drips, folded neck, rstr, 8x4" **5,250.00**
Vase, rust/gr speckle, incurvate folded rim, rnd, 4½" **825.00**
Vase, tan, in-base twist/folded rim, 3½x3¾" **1,300.00**
Vase, tortoise shell mottle, crimped rim forms star, 4x5" **825.00**

Vase, yel to bl flambe, gr int, low angular width, 3x5" 700.00

Old Ivory

Old Ivory dinnerware was produced during the late 1800s by Herman Ohme of Lower Salzbrunn in Selesia. The patterns are referred to by the numbers stamped on the bottom of many items. (Though not every piece is numbered, the vast majority bears the tiny blue fleur-de-lis/crown mark with Selesia or Germany beneath. Handwritten numbers signify something other than pattern.) Patterns #16 and #84 are the easiest to find and come in a wide variety of table items. Values are about the same for both patterns. Other floral designs include pink, yellow, and orange roses; holly; and lavender flowers — all on the same soft ivory background. The ware was not widely distributed; its two main distribution points were in Maine and, to a lesser extent, Chicago. Our prices are intended to represent a nationwide average, though you may have to pay a little more in some areas. Novice collectors should be aware of copy-cat versions from the turn of the century that are much heavier and of a coarser material. They are marked 'Old Ivory' without the blue trademark. They are not included in this listing.

Bowl, #118, brn/cream roses, 9" 115.00
Bowl, #16 or #84, 5⅝" 20.00
Bowl, #200, 9" 125.00
Bowl, #32, 9½" 120.00
Bowl, #75, 9½" 115.00
Bowl, oyster; #16 or #84 ....175.00
Bowl, vegetable; #15, deep, 10" dia 125.00
Butter dish, #16, w/insert, rare 625.00
Cake plate, #15, w/hdls, 10¾" 150.00
Cake plate, #16 or #84, 10¼" 150.00
Cake plate, #7, 9½" 125.00

Charger, no pattern number, rare, 13", $325.00.

Charger, #16 or #84, 13" dia 325.00
Chocolate pot, #11 ....450.00
Chocolate set, #28, 9-pc 650.00
Cracker jar or biscuit jar, #16 or #84 ....350.00
Creamer, #22, Holly 165.00
Creamer & sugar bowl, #16 or #84 ....165.00
Cup & saucer, #33 ....65.00
Cup & saucer, chocolate; #33 ....65.00
Cup & saucer, tea; #11 ....60.00
Cup & saucer, tea; #16 or #84 ....60.00
Gravy boat, #16 or #84, attached underplate 650.00
Jam jar, #200 ....295.00
Mayonnaise, #16 or #84, w/underplate 285.00
Mayonnaise, #38, w/underplate 175.00
Muffineer, #16 or #84 ....350.00

Mustard pot, #16 or #84, w/lid & hdls, 3½", +spoon 275.00
Mustard pot, #17, no spoon 435.00
Nappy, #73, hdl extends from rim to center, 6" 75.00
Plate, #11, rare, 9½" 165.00
Plate, #15, 6" 22.50
Plate, #15, 7⅜" 50.00
Plate, #16 or #84, 6" 25.00
Plate, #16 or #84, 7⅝" 35.00
Plate, #16 or #84, 8¼" 55.00
Platter, #15, hdls, 11½" 210.00
Saucer, #16 or #84, 5½" 10.00
Saucer, #40, 6" 10.00
Shakers, #16 or #84, pr 125.00
Shakers, #40, pr 125.00
Shaving mug, #15, pierced shelf for soap 425.00
Soup tureen, #16 or #84, oval 695.00
Spoon holder, no pattern #, wine florals, hdl 195.00
Tea tile, #16 or #84 ....225.00
Teapot, #200, 7½" 350.00
Tray, #16 or #84, rectangular, scalloped rim, 12x7" 165.00
Tray, bread; #73, lg open brn roses, 12" L 115.00
Tray, bun; #200 ....135.00
Tray, celery; #200, 11½" 100.00
Tray, dresser; #14, #16, or #84, 12" L 115.00
Tray, dresser; #28, worn gold, 12" 175.00
Tray, relish; #200, hdls, 5½" 95.00
Waste bowl, #16 or #84 ....150.00

Old MacDonald's Farm by Regal

Located in Antioch, Illinois, the Regal China Company has been in business since 1938. Products of interest to collectors are James Beam Decanters, cookie jars, salt and pepper shakers and similar novelty items. The Old MacDonald's Farm series listed below is becoming especially collectible. Our advisor for this category is Joyce Roerig, author of *The Collector's Encyclopedia of Cookie Jars*; she is listed in the Directory under South Carolina.

Spice jar, $125.00 each.

Butter dish, cow's head 235.00
Canister, Cookies, lg 350.00
Canister, flour, cereal, coffee, or cookie; med, ea 235.00
Canister, pretzels, peanuts, pocpcorn, chips, tidbits; lg, ea 350.00
Canister, salt, sugar, or tea, med, ea 235.00
Canister, soap, lg 350.00
Cookie jar, barn 275.00
Creamer, rooster 110.00
Grease jar, pig 185.00

Jar, spice; sm 125.00
Pitcher, milk 395.00
Shakers, boy & girl, pr 80.00
Shakers, churn, pr 80.00
Shakers, feed sacks w/sheep, pr 165.00
Sugar bowl, hen 125.00
Teapot, duck's head 275.00

Old Paris

Old Paris porcelains were made from the mid-18th century until about 1900. Seldom marked, the term refers to the area of manufacture rather than a specific company. In general, the ware was of high quality; characterized by classic shapes, colorful decoration, and gold application.

Bough pot, floriform in cobalt & gilt, 1840s, 6" 450.00
Bowl, fruit finial, scroll hdls, 1850, 13" L 190.00
Bowl, roses band in center, gold lattice rim & base, 10" 250.00
Box, lady's head form, mc, 3¾" 150.00
Compote, cobalt/yel/gold decor, rtcl, branch hdls, 15" 425.00
Compote, kneeling lady supports openweave bowl, gilt, 14" ...1,400.00
Cup & saucer, demi; continuous hunt scene w/gilt, 1800s 100.00

Garniture vases, applied gold vines and bisque birds, hand-painted flowers, 1850s, $1,400.00 for the pair.

Jar, apothecary; gilt stencil/leafage, 1830s, 12", pr 750.00
Jar, seated maid w/ribbed urn sits on lid, mask hdls, 14" 1,400.00
Plate, exotic birds, bl/gold rim w/reserve, titled, 10", pr 900.00
Teapot, Oriental lady, bird spout, 7", +male as tea caddy 1,400.00
Tete a tete, floral on bl, gilt, pot+cr/sug+tray+2 c/s 365.00
Tray, floral, gold scroll hdls extend to form rim, 11" 220.00
Vase, doves/garlands, leaf mouth, appl leaves ea side, 17" 300.00
Vase, figural reserves on gr & gilt, shell rim, S-hdl, 14" 800.00
Vase, floral reserve on wht w/gold, leaf appl ea side, 15" 175.00
Vase, lady in garden, appl leafy vines tie at neck, 18", pr 1,200.00

Old Sleepy Eye

Old Sleepy Eye was a Sioux Indian chief who was born in Minnesota in 1780. His name was used for the name of a town as well as a flour mill. The Sleepy Eye Milling Company of Sleepy Eye, Minnesota, contracted the Weir Pottery Company of Monmouth, Illinois, to make steins, vases, salt crocks, and butter tubs which the company gave away to their customers in each bag of their flour. A bust profile of the old Indian and his name decorated each piece of the blue and gray stoneware. In addition to these four items, the Minnesota Stoneware Company of Red Wing made a mug with a verse which is very scarce today.

In 1906 Weir Pottery merged with six others to form the Western Stoneware Company in Monmouth. They produced a line of blue and white ware using a lighter body, but these pieces were never given as flour premiums. This line consisted of pitchers (five sizes), steins, mugs, sugar bowls, vases, trivets, and mustache cups. These pieces turn up only rarely in other colors and are highly sought by advanced collectors.

Advertising items such as trade cards, pillow tops, thermometers, paperweights, letter openers, postcards, cookbooks, and thimbles are considered very valuable.

The original ware was made sporadically until 1937. Brown steins and mugs were produced in 1952.

Barrel, flour; orig paper label, 1920s 935.00
Barrel, grapevine-effect banding 1,500.00
Butter crock, Flemish 625.00
Calendar, 1904 ....375.00
Cookbook, EX 185.00
Cookbook, Indian on cover, Sleepy Eye Milling Co, 4¾x4" 70.00
Cookbook, loaf of bread shape, NM 310.00
Coupon, for ordering cookbook 60.00
Dough scraper, tin/wood, To Be Sure, EX 435.00
Fan, Indian chief, die-cut cb, 1900 ....220.00
Flour sack, cloth, mc Indian, red letters 345.00
Flour sack, paper, Indian in blk, blk lettering, NM 125.00
Ink blotter 125.00
Label, barrel end; mc Indian, 16", NM 160.00
Label, egg crate; mc Indian, 1930s, 9x11" 32.00
Letter opener, bronze 1,050.00
Match holder, pnt 1,875.00
Match holder, wht 1,050.00
Milk carton 22.50
Mirror, advertising, 1935 ....45.00
Mug, bl & wht, 4¼" 220.00
Mug, verse, Red Wing, EX 1,625.00
Paperweight, bronzed company trademk 560.00
Pillow cover, Sleepy Eye & tribe meet President Monroe 750.00
Pillow cover, trademk center w/various scenes, 22", NM 750.00
Pitcher, #1, 4" 185.00
Pitcher, #2 ....250.00
Pitcher, #3, rare 315.00
Pitcher, #3, w/bl rim 1,375.00
Pitcher, #4 ....400.00
Pitcher, #5 ....435.00
Pitcher, bl on cream, 8", M 345.00
Pitcher, bl & gray, 5" 235.00
Pitcher, gold & brn, 1981 ....160.00
Pitcher, standing Indian, good color, #5 size 1,560.00
Postcard, colorful trademk, 1904 Expo Winner 185.00
Postcard, monument 50.00
Ruler, wooden 500.00
Salt crock, Flemish, 4x6½" 560.00
Sign, self-fr tin, Old Sleepy Eye Flour, 20x24" 2,500.00
Sign, tin, Sleepy Eye Flour & Cereal Products 4,375.00
Spoon, demitasse; emb roses in bowl, Unity SP 105.00
Spoon, Indian-head hdl 125.00
Stein, bl & wht, 7¾" 625.00
Stein, brn, 1952, 22-oz 435.00
Stein, brn & wht 1,125.00
Stein, brn & yel, Western Stoneware 1,125.00
Stein, cobalt 1,000.00
Stein, Flemish 595.00
Stein, ltd edition, 1979-84, ea 125.00
Sugar bowl, bl & wht, 3" 750.00

Tumbler, etched, 1979 commemorative	32.00
Vase, bl & wht, good color, 9"	530.00
Vase, brn on yel, rare color	1,000.00
Vase, Indian & cattails, Flemish, 8½"	470.00
Watch fob, Sleepy Eye Mills, Indian, M	62.50

O'Neill, Rose

Rose O'Neill's Kewpies were introduced in 1909 when they were used to conclude a story in the December issue of *Ladies' Home Journal*. They were an immediate success, and soon Kewpie dolls were being produced worldwide. German manufacturers were among the earliest and also used the Kewpie motif to decorate chinaware as well as other items. The Kewpie is still popular today and can be found on products ranging from Christmas cards and cake ornaments to fabrics and wallpaper.

In the following listings, 'sgn' indicates that the item is signed Rose O'Neill. Unsigned items are of little interest to collectors. Items marked 'Germany' are sometimes reproductions.

Bell, brass, 3"	95.00
Bell, sterling, mk O'Neill, 2¾"	95.00
Book, Biography of a Boy, O'Neill illus, 1910, EX	35.00
Book, Garda, O'Neill illus, 1st ed, 1929, EX	50.00
Book, The Kewpies Book, 1983, M	20.00
Booklet, Jell-O recipes, O'Neill illus, 1915, EX	25.00
Christmas plate, Kewpies, 1973, M	25.00

Creamer, green Jasper with pink Kewpies and flowers, signed, Germany, 2½", $295.00.

Creamer, Kewpies, china, c Rose O'Neill Wilson, 3¾"	145.00
Cup, Kewpies on milk glass	30.00
Cup & saucer, Kewpie, Royal Rudolstadt	225.00
Doll, talcum powder; Kewpie, sgn Rose O'Neill, 7", EX	135.00
Kewpie, Blk, Strombecker, 11", MIB	50.00
Kewpie, bsk, Blk Hottentot, sgn, 5"	475.00
Kewpie, bsk, Blunderboo, on stomach, sgn, 4"	450.00
Kewpie, bsk, Confederate Soldier, sgn, 4½"	500.00
Kewpie, bsk, frozen arms, #103, Japan, 3", VG	20.00
Kewpie, bsk, Governor, sgn, 4"	450.00
Kewpie, bsk, holding butterfly, sgn, 4"	475.00
Kewpie, bsk, holding pen, sgn, 3"	385.00
Kewpie, bsk, Huggers, molded hair, Made in Japan, 3¾"	60.00
Kewpie, bsk, Huggers, Shackman, 3¼", EX	30.00
Kewpie, bsk, in basket w/flowers, sgn, 3½"	600.00
Kewpie, bsk, jtd arms & shoulders, sgn, 12"	1,500.00

Kewpie, bsk, jtd hips & shoulders, sgn, 4"	465.00
Kewpie, bsk, jtd shoulders, bl wings, eyes to side, sgn, 1½"	95.00
Kewpie, bsk, jtd shoulders, bl wings, eyes to side, sgn, 12"	1,400.00
Kewpie, bsk, jtd shoulders, bl wings, eyes to side, sgn, 2½"	125.00
Kewpie, bsk, jtd shoulders, bl wings, eyes to side, sgn, 6"	195.00
Kewpie, bsk, jtd shoulders, bl wings, eyes to side, sgn, 7"	250.00
Kewpie, bsk, ring of bsk roses on head, mk La Mott, 9"	250.00
Kewpie, bsk, Soldier, sgn, 4½"	525.00
Kewpie, bsk, w/broom, sgn, 4"	450.00
Kewpie, bsk, w/drawstring bag, sgn, 4½"	600.00
Kewpie, bsk, w/outhouse, sgn, 2½"	1,100.00
Kewpie, Buttonhole	165.00
Kewpie, celluloid, jtd shoulders, w/sticker, 16"	600.00
Kewpie, celluloid, jtd shoulders, w/sticker, 5"	95.00
Kewpie, celluloid, w/sticker, 2"	45.00
Kewpie, celluloid, w/sticker, 5"	85.00
Kewpie, chalk, on ped, starfish hands, movable arms, 13"	65.00
Kewpie, chalk, Thinker, 6½"	25.00
Kewpie, cloth, mask face, Kreuger, 12", M	185.00
Kewpie, cloth, mask face, Kreuger, 12", VG	90.00
Kewpie, compo, jtd shoulders, 24", NM	400.00
Kewpie, Jesco, 8", MIB	20.00
Kewpie, shoulder head, cloth body, sgn, 7"	600.00
Kewpie, vinyl face, sitting, Knickerbocker tag, VG	25.00
Kewpie Doodle Dog, bsk, sgn, 1½"	675.00
Perfume bottle, Kewpie, sgn, 3½", minimum value	475.00
Pincushion, Kewpie, bsk, sgn, 2½"	300.00
Puzzle, jigsaw, Kewpies, Hallmark, 500-pc, M	35.00
Sheet music, Songs of Safety, O'Neill illus, 1937	25.00
Soap, Kewpie figural, MIB	135.00
Spoon, SP, Kewpie hdl	98.00
Toothpick holder, Borgfeldt	100.00

Onion Pattern

The familiar pattern known to collectors as Onion acquired its name through a case of mistaken identity. Designed in the early 1700s by Johann Haroldt of the Meissen factory in Germany, the pattern was a mixture of earlier Oriental designs. One of its components was a stylized peach, which was mistaken for an onion; as a result, the pattern became known by that name. Usually found in blue, an occasional piece may also be found in pink and red. The pattern is commonly associated with Meissen, but it has been reproduced by many others including Villeroy and Boch and Royal Copenhagen.

Blue Danube is a modern line of Onion-patterned dinnerware produced in Japan and distributed by Lipper International of Wallingford, Connecticut. One-hundred twenty-five items are available in porcelain; it is sold in most large stores with china departments.

Compote, reticulated bowl, Meissen, 8½x9½", $325.00.

Basket, rtcl, shallow, Meissen, 1890s, 7", pr 300.00
Bouillon cup & saucer, Meissen 45.00
Bowl, scalloped, w/dome lid, Xd swords, 6x5" 400.00
Butter pat, Meissen 25.00
Cake plate, 10" dia 150.00
Canister, Zucker, stenciled, ped base 65.00
Cheese grater 250.00
Coffeepot, graniteware 50.00
Coffeepot, Meissen, 10" 175.00
Compote, twisted knopped stem, Meissen, 9x9" 375.00
Creamer, Meissen, 3½" 50.00
Cup & saucer 25.00
Cup & saucer, Meissen 35.00
Dish, leaf shape, w/hdls, Xd swords, 3½" 75.00
Egg whipper 145.00
Funnel, loop hdl, unmk Germany 95.00
Masher, lg 165.00
Masher, sm 135.00
Meat tenderizer, Germany 145.00
Pestle 145.00
Platter, bl feather edge, octagonal, 15½" 75.00
Rolling pin, heavy porc, unmk Germany, 18" 270.00
Salt box, rnd, wood lid, wall mt, Made in Japan, 7" 95.00
Sauce boat, w/attached undertray, Xd swords, 3½x5x8" ...190.00
Spatula 165.00
Spoon, 10" 85.00
Teapot, gilt trim, mk Meissen, 1890s, +creamer & sugar bowl ...365.00
Tureen, shell hdls, dome lid, 1900, 10½" H 650.00
Vase, ftd, Xd swords, 5" 125.00

Opalescent Glass

First made in England in 1870, opalescent glass became popular in America around the turn of the century. Its name comes from the milky-white opalescent trim that defines the lines of the pattern. It was produced in table sets, novelties, toothpick holders, vases, and lamps.

Acorn Burrs (& Bark), bowl, sauce; bl 40.00
Alaska, banana boat, vaseline 260.00
Alaska, butter dish, vaseline 375.00
Alaska, creamer, bl 75.00
Alaska, creamer, emerald 70.00
Alaska, creamer, vaseline 65.00
Alaska, cruet, emerald 270.00
Alaska, pitcher, water; bl 385.00
Alaska, pitcher, water; vaseline 370.00

Alaska pitcher in blue, plain, 7½", $385.00 (decorated, $425.00).

Alaska, shakers, bl, pr 100.00
Alaska, shakers, vaseline, pr 90.00
Alaska, spooner, bl 75.00
Alaska, spooner, vaseline 65.00
Alaska, sugar bowl, bl, w/lid 160.00
Alaska, sugar bowl, vaseline, w/lid 135.00
Alaska, tray, bl 180.00
Alaska, tumbler, vaseline 65.00
Arabian Nights, pitcher, water; bl 275.00
Arabian Nights, pitcher, water; vaseline 265.00
Arabian Nights, pitcher, water; wht 210.00
Arabian Nights, tumbler, cranberry 100.00
Argonaut Shell, butter dish, bl 295.00
Argonaut Shell, compote, jelly; vaseline 85.00
Argonaut Shell, spooner, bl 190.00
Argonaut Shell, sugar bowl, bl, w/lid 225.00
Argonaut Shell, tumbler, vaseline 125.00
Beaded Ovals in Sand, butter dish, bl 270.00
Beaded Ovals in Sand, creamer, gr 70.00
Beads & Bark, vase, gr, ftd 55.00
Beatty Rib, creamer, ind; wht 25.00
Beatty Rib, sugar bowl, bl 125.00
Beatty Swirl, butter dish, bl 160.00
Beatty Swirl, mug, bl 50.00
Beatty Swirl, pitcher, water; vaseline 170.00
Beatty Swirl, tray, water; bl 80.00
Beatty Swirl, tumbler, vaseline 45.00
Blown Drape, tumbler, gr 40.00
Boggy Bayou, vase, amethyst 45.00
Bubble Lattice, butter dish, gr 85.00
Bubble Lattice, cruet, vaseline 160.00
Bubble Lattice, finger bowl, gr 30.00
Bubble Lattice, spooner, bl 50.00
Bubble Lattice, sugar bowl, wht 65.00
Bubble Lattice, toothpick holder, gr 240.00
Bubble Lattice, tumbler, cranberry 95.00
Buttons & Braids, bowl, wht 35.00
Buttons & Braids, pitcher, water; gr 145.00
Buttons & Braids, tumbler, bl 40.00
Buttons & Braids, tumbler, cranberry 85.00
Christmas Pearls, shakers, gr, pr 90.00
Christmas Snowflake, tumbler, cranberry 100.00
Chrysanthemum Base Swirl, bowl, sauce; wht 25.00
Chrysanthemum Base Swirl, butter dish, bl 300.00
Chrysanthemum Base Swirl, straw holder, bl 450.00
Chrysanthemum Base Swirl, sugar shaker, bl 190.00
Chrysanthemum Base Swirl, tumbler, bl 80.00
Circle Scroll, compote, jelly; bl 145.00
Circle Scroll, spooner, gr 130.00
Circle Scroll, sugar bowl, gr 210.00
Circle Scroll, tumbler, bl 90.00
Coin Spot, bowl, master berry; cranberry 60.00
Coin Spot, celery vase, gr 110.00
Coin Spot, compote, bl 50.00
Coin Spot, pitcher, water; gr 130.00
Coin Spot, pitcher, water; rubena 170.00
Coin Spot, pitcher, water; wht 90.00
Coin Spot, sugar shaker, gr 95.00
Coin Spot, tumble-up, cranberry 260.00
Coin Spot, tumbler, bl 40.00
Criss Cross, pitcher, water; cranberry, Consolidated 900.00
Criss Cross, sauce, wht, Consolidated 45.00
Daisy & Fern, bottle, scent; cranberry 240.00
Daisy & Fern, creamer, cranberry 395.00

Daisy & Fern, mustard pot, bl 85.00
Daisy & Fern, pitcher, water; bl 275.00
Daisy & Fern, pitcher, water; wht 185.00
Daisy & Fern, sugar bowl, bl 95.00
Daisy & Fern, tumbler, gr 50.00
Daisy & Fern, vase, cranberry 175.00
Diamond Spearhead, celery vase, wht 90.00
Diamond Spearhead, compote, gr, tall 125.00
Diamond Spearhead, compote, jelly; vaseline 100.00
Diamond Spearhead, creamer, bl 90.00
Diamond Spearhead, cup & saucer, vaseline 80.00
Diamond Spearhead, mug, cobalt 70.00
Diamond Spearhead, pitcher, water; bl or vaseline 320.00
Diamond Spearhead, pitcher, water; wht 275.00
Diamond Spearhead, spooner, gr 100.00
Diamond Spearhead, sugar bowl, bl 140.00
Dolly Madison, creamer, gr 90.00
Dolly Madison, spooner, bl 70.00
Dolly Madison, spooner, wht 55.00
Dolly Madison, sugar bowl, bl, w/lid 125.00
Dolly Madison, tumbler, gr 80.00
Double Greek Key, butter dish, wht 210.00
Double Greek Key, celery vase, bl 120.00
Double Greek Key, creamer, bl 70.00
Double Greek Key, shakers, wht, pr 150.00
Double Greek Key, spooner, bl 75.00
Double Greek Key, sugar bowl, bl, w/lid 155.00
Double Greek Key, tumbler, bl 65.00
Drapery, creamer, bl 65.00
Drapery, pitcher, water; bl 175.00
Everglades, bowl, sauce; bl, oval 40.00
Everglades, butter dish, bl 230.00
Everglades, butter dish, vaseline 280.00
Everglades, compote, jelly; gr 125.00
Everglades, compote, jelly; vaseline 115.00
Everglades, creamer, bl 125.00
Everglades, pitcher, water; vaseline 375.00
Everglades, shakers, vaseline, pr 220.00
Everglades, sugar bowl, bl 135.00
Everglades, tumbler, bl 70.00
Fan, butter dish, gr 350.00
Fan, gravy boat, wht 35.00
Fern, finger bowl, bl 55.00
Fern, mustard pot, bl 130.00
Fern, pitcher, bl 225.00
Fern, shakers, wht, pr 90.00
Fern, toothpick holder, cranberry, rare 450.00
Fern, tumbler, cranberry 90.00
Fern, tumbler, wht 30.00
Flora, butter dish, wht 160.00
Flora, compote, jelly; vaseline 115.00
Flora, creamer, vaseline 80.00
Flora, cruet, bl 650.00
Flora, pitcher, water; bl 475.00
Flora, shakers, vaseline, pr 320.00
Flora, shakers, wht, pr 250.00
Flora, spooner, vaseline 90.00
Flora, sugar bowl, bl, w/lid 120.00
Flora, toothpick holder, vaseline 310.00
Flora, toothpick holder, wht 240.00
Flora, tumbler, bl 75.00
Fluted Scrolls, butter dish, bl 160.00
Fluted Scrolls, cruet, bl 180.00
Fluted Scrolls, pitcher, water; bl 200.00

Fluted Scrolls, pitcher, water; vaseline 195.00
Fluted Scrolls, puff box, vaseline 50.00
Frosted-Leaf & Basketweave, butter dish, vaseline 240.00
Frosted-Leaf & Basketweave, creamer, vaseline or canary 125.00
Frosted-Leaf & Basketweave, spooner, bl 130.00
Frosted-Leaf & Basketweave, sugar bowl, bl 170.00
Gonterman Swirl, butter dish, amber 325.00
Gonterman Swirl, celery vase, bl or amber 185.00
Gonterman Swirl, creamer, bl 80.00
Gonterman Swirl, cruet, bl 300.00
Hobnail, butter dish, bl 250.00
Hobnail, butter dish, cranberry 290.00
Hobnail, creamer, vaseline 95.00
Hobnail, finger bowl, cranberry 90.00
Hobnail, syrup, rubena 325.00
Hobnail, tray, water; bl 160.00
Hobnail, tumbler, cranberry 85.00
Honeycomb, cracker jar, bl 265.00
Honeycomb, pitcher, amber 350.00
Honeycomb & Clover, bowl, master berry; bl 60.00
Honeycomb & Clover, bowl, novelty, wht 26.00
Honeycomb & Clover, butter dish, bl 325.00
Honeycomb & Clover, tumbler, gr 75.00
Idyll, butter dish, gr 365.00
Idyll, creamer, gr 85.00
Idyll, spooner, bl 130.00
Idyll, sugar bowl, gr 160.00
Idyll, toothpick holder, bl 350.00
Idyll, tumbler, bl 80.00
Intaglio, bowl, novelty, bl 45.00
Intaglio, butter dish, bl 450.00
Intaglio, compote, jelly; wht 30.00
Intaglio, creamer, bl 60.00
Intaglio, cruet, vaseline 285.00

Intaglio pitcher in blue, 8", $145.00.

Intaglio, shakers, bl, pr 85.00
Intaglio, spooner, wht 35.00
Intaglio, sugar bowl, wht 85.00
Intaglio, tumbler, wht 50.00
Inverted Fan & Feather, creamer, bl 140.00
Inverted Fan & Feather, shakers, bl, pr 250.00
Inverted Fan & Feather, tumbler, bl 85.00
Iris w/Meander, bowl, master berry; gr 80.00
Iris w/Meander, butter dish, bl 275.00
Iris w/Meander, compote, jelly; bl or vaseline 45.00
Iris w/Meander, creamer, bl or vaseline 75.00
Iris w/Meander, pickle dish, wht 50.00
Iris w/Meander, pitcher, water; bl 375.00

Iris w/Meander, pitcher, water; gr	350.00
Iris w/Meander, spooner, bl	75.00
Iris w/Meander, sugar bowl, gr, w/lid	125.00
Iris w/Meander, toothpick holder, wht	45.00
Iris w/Meander, tumbler, gr	70.00
Iris w/Meander, tumbler, wht	55.00
Iris w/Meander, vase, vaseline	60.00
Jackson, candy dish, vaseline	40.00
Jackson, creamer, bl	75.00
Jackson, pitcher, water; bl	450.00
Jackson, spooner, vaseline	60.00
Jackson, sugar bowl, bl	115.00
Jackson, sugar bowl, vaseline	110.00
Jackson, tumbler	60.00
Jewel & Flower, bowl, novelty, bl	35.00
Jewel & Flower, butter dish, bl	350.00
Jewel & Flower, creamer, wht	55.00
Jewel & Flower, cruet, vaseline	585.00
Jewel & Flower, pitcher, water; bl	650.00
Jewel & Flower, pitcher, water; vaseline	450.00
Jewel & Flower, spooner, bl	95.00
Jewel & Flower, tumbler, vaseline	70.00
Jeweled Heart, bowl, sauce; wht	25.00
Jeweled Heart, butter dish, bl	300.00
Jeweled Heart, compote, gr	120.00
Jeweled Heart, plate, bl, sm	40.00
Jeweled Heart, sugar bowl, gr, w/lid	155.00
Jeweled Heart, tumbler, gr	55.00
Lords & Ladies, butter dish, bl	85.00
Lords & Ladies, creamer, bl	55.00
Lustre Flute, bowl, sauce; bl	25.00
Lustre Flute, butter dish, bl	285.00
Lustre Flute, pitcher, bl	325.00
Lustre Flute, spooner, bl	90.00
Lustre Flute, tumbler, wht	40.00
Over-All Hob, creamer, bl	50.00
Over-All Hob, pitcher, water; vaseline	175.00
Palm Beach, pitcher, water; vaseline	350.00
Palm Beach, spooner, vaseline	125.00
Palm Beach, sugar bowl, bl	120.00
Palm Beach, tumbler, bl	85.00
Palm Beach, wine, vaseline, rare	350.00
Paneled Holly, bowl, master berry; bl	85.00
Paneled Holly, butter dish, bl	300.00
Paneled Holly, shakers, bl, pr	105.00
Paneled Holly, spooner, wht	60.00
Paneled Holly, sugar bowl, bl	225.00
Paneled Holly, tumbler, wht	45.00
Paneled Sprig, cruet, wht	115.00
Paneled Sprig, toothpick holder, wht	70.00
Poinsettia, bowl, fruit; bl	70.00
Poinsettia, pitcher, water; bl, either shape	275.00
Poinsettia, sugar shaker, gr	200.00
Poinsettia, syrup, cranberry	350.00
Poinsettia, tumbler, bl	55.00
Princess Diana, butter dish, bl	90.00
Princess Diana, compote, bl, metal base	120.00
Princess Diana, pitcher, water; vaseline	90.00
Regal, butter dish, bl	245.00
Regal, celery vase, gr	140.00
Regal, pitcher, gr	285.00
Regal, sugar bowl, bl	150.00
Reverse Swirl, bottle, water; bl	140.00
Reverse Swirl, butter dish, vaseline	165.00

Reverse Swirl, cruet, cranberry	450.00
Reverse Swirl, custard cup, bl	45.00
Reverse Swirl, lamp, cranberry, mini	290.00
Reverse Swirl, pitcher, water; bl	195.00
Reverse Swirl, sugar shaker, vaseline	135.00
Reverse Swirl, tumbler, wht	26.00
Ribbed Spiral, creamer, vaseline	55.00
Ribbed Spiral, pitcher, water; bl	480.00
Ribbed Spiral, shakers, bl, pr	195.00
Ribbed Spiral, toothpick holder, bl	160.00
Ribbed Spiral, vase, vaseline, lg	35.00
Ruffles & Rings, bowl, nut; gr	42.00
Ruffles & Rings, rose bowl, bl	45.00
Scroll w/Acanthus, bowl, master berry; bl	40.00
Scroll w/Acanthus, butter dish, bl	350.00
Scroll w/Acanthus, compote, jelly; gr	40.00
Scroll w/Acanthus, pitcher, water; gr	360.00
Scroll w/Acanthus, shakers, gr, pr	80.00
Scroll w/Acanthus, sugar bowl, gr	135.00
Scroll w/Acanthus, toothpick holder, bl	200.00
Scroll w/Acanthus, tumbler, gr or vaseline	70.00
Seaweed, butter dish, cranberry	350.00
Seaweed, pitcher, water; bl	310.00
Seaweed, syrup, wht	115.00
Shell, Beaded; sugar bowl, bl	185.00
Shell, Beaded; toothpick holder, gr	500.00
Shell, Beaded; tumbler, gr	85.00
Spanish Lace, bottle, scent; bl	175.00
Spanish Lace, bride's basket, cranberry, 2 sizes	160.00
Spanish Lace, creamer, bl	80.00
Spanish Lace, cruet, bl	230.00
Spanish Lace, jug, liqueur; cranberry	750.00
Spanish Lace, rose bowl, vaseline	45.00
Spanish Lace, sugar shaker, cranberry	180.00
Spanish Lace, tumbler, vaseline	60.00
Stars & Stripes, pitcher, water; cranberry	975.00
Stars & Stripes, tumbler, wht	60.00
Stripe, pitcher, bl	250.00
Stripe, shakers, vaseline, pr	95.00
Stripe, tumbler, bl	45.00
Sunburst on Shield, bowl, master berry; bl	60.00
Sunburst on Shield, cruet, bl, rare	255.00
Sunburst on Shield, pitcher, water; bl	500.00
Sunburst on Shield, spooner, bl	125.00
Sunburst on Shield, sugar bowl, vaseline	175.00
Sunburst on Shield, tumbler, bl	100.00
Swag w/Brackets, bowl, novelty, vaseline	40.00
Swag w/Brackets, bowl, sauce; gr	26.00
Swag w/Brackets, butter dish, bl	250.00
Swag w/Brackets, compote, jelly; bl	48.00
Swag w/Brackets, creamer, bl	75.00
Swag w/Brackets, creamer, vaseline	70.00
Swag w/Brackets, shakers, vaseline, pr	175.00
Swag w/Brackets, spooner, bl	125.00
Swag w/Brackets, toothpick holder, gr	270.00
Swag w/Brackets, tumbler, gr	50.00
Swirl, pitcher, water; bl	125.00
Swirl, pitcher, water; cranberry	595.00
Swirl, sugar bowl, bl, w/lid	85.00
Swirl, toothpick holder, gr	100.00
Tokyo, compote, jelly; bl	40.00
Tokyo, plate, wht	30.00
Tokyo, sugar bowl, bl	110.00
Tokyo, vase, gr	45.00

Water Lily & Cattails, bowl, master berry; bl 55.00
Water Lily & Cattails, relish, gr, hdls 75.00
Water Lily & Cattails, spooner, amethyst 65.00
Water Lily & Cattails, sugar bowl, gr 140.00
Wild Bouquet, butter dish, bl 450.00
Wild Bouquet, compote, jelly, gr 100.00
Wild Bouquet, compote, jelly; bl 125.00
Wild Bouquet, creamer, gr 70.00
Wild Bouquet, shakers, bl, pr 90.00
Wild Bouquet, toothpick holder, gr 250.00
Wild Bouquet, tumbler, bl 100.00
Wild Bouquet, tumbler, wht 22.00
Windows (Swirled), celery vase, bl 75.00
Windows (Swirled), mustard, cranberry 100.00
Windows (Swirled), pitcher, water; cranberry 695.00
Windows (Swirled), plate, cranberry, either sz 200.00
Windows (Swirled), toothpick holder, bl 275.00
Wreath & Shell, bowl, master berry; bl 85.00
Wreath & Shell, bowl, novelty, vaseline 50.00
Wreath & Shell, butter dish, bl 225.00
Wreath & Shell, celery vase, bl 165.00
Wreath & Shell, pitcher, water; wht 170.00
Wreath & Shell, rose bowl, bl 80.00
Wreath & Shell, sugar bowl, cranberry, w/lid 130.00

Opaline

A type of semi-opaque opal glass, opaline was made in white as well as pastel shades and is often enameled. It is similar in appearance to English bristol glass, though its enamel or gilt decorative devices tend to exhibit a French influence.

Basket, gr w/gold & jewels, high loop hdl, 8" 95.00
Bottle, scent; bl, gold-tone metal base & hdl, 9½" 300.00
Jar, powder; bl w/cameo portraits & gold trim, 4" 135.00
Ring tree, bl w/gold & wht trim, 2½" dia 45.00
Vase, bl w/HP floral, narrow flared rim, 4¼" 45.00
Vase, lt bl, gold trim, 6½" 40.00

Orientalia

The art of the Orient is an area of collecting currently enjoying strong collector interest, not only in those examples that are truly 'antique' but in the 20th-century items as well. Because of the many aspects involved in a study of Orientalia, we can only try through brief comments to acquaint the reader with some of the more readily available examples. We suggest you refer to specialized reference sources for more detailed information. Our advisor for this category is Clarence Bodine; he is listed in the Directory under Pennsylvania. See also Canton; Champleve; Cloisonne; Coralene, Oriental; Dragon Ware; Geisha Girl; Imari; Ivory; Kutani; Moriage; Nippon; Noritake; Peking Cameo Glass; Rose Medallion; Satsuma; Soapstone; Thousand Faces.

Key:
Ch — Chinese	FV — Famille Verte
ctp — contemporary	E — export
cvg — carving	hdwd — hardwood
do — door	Jp — Japan
drw — drawer	Ko — Korean
Dy — Dynasty	lcq — lacquer
FJ — Famille Juane	rswd — rosewood
FN — Famille Noire	tkwd — teakwood
FR — Famille Rose	

Blanc de Chine

Blanc de Chine figures, female deity standing beside a deer, restoration, damage, 16", $1,500.00.

Figure, lady/servant have tea w/foreigner, sm animals, 6" 1,600.00
Figure, Quan Yin, seated by table, holding scroll, rstr, 9" 1,400.00
Figure, Quan Yin, seated on rocks, 6" 385.00
Figurine, lion, ferocious, rectangular base, 7½", pr 325.00
Teapot, molded as a laughing Buddha, Qianlong period, 6" 400.00

Blue and White Porcelain

Bottle, sprinkler; 4 stylized lotus blossoms, Kangxi, 10" 850.00
Bowl, E, willow & peonies, octagonal, 1700s, 15", VG 400.00
Bowl, landscape panels, archaic-style mk, 1600s, 6½" 365.00
Charger, dragons/foliage, brn-wash rim, Kangxi, 15" 1,650.00
Dish, fan form, seaside landscape, 1890s, 9½" L 200.00
Garden seat, rtcl bl ground w/wht florals, hexagonal, 19" 385.00
Jar, floral sprays, globular, Choson Dy, 1800s, 3½" 550.00
Jar, florals, hardstone-mtd wood cover, 1800, 2¾" 250.00
Jar, lotus flowers, onion finial, 12x10" 185.00
Jar, 4 mum medallions between scrolls, 1700s, 7", NM 1,300.00
Teabowl, scenic, Kangxi period, 2½" H 200.00
Tray, E, pagodas in landscape, 17x20" 375.00
Vase, allover prunus blossoms, bottle form, Korea, 12" 330.00
Vase, cranes in relief on bl cloud ground, cylindrical, 12" 375.00

Bronze

Basin, silver floral vine inlay, rectangular, 1800s, 6x9" 300.00
Bowl, Jp, loop hdls, short ft, 1800s, 12½" 625.00
Cache pot, Ch, bird/floral decor, paw ft, 1800s, 20x18" 500.00
Censer, floral relief on body/lid/swing hdl, seal mk, 9x8" 400.00
Dagger, archaic, early rpr, 20" 225.00
Figure, bird on bamboo stalk, 1900s, 13" 275.00
Figure, Ko, seated Buddha, 1900s, 16" 325.00
Figure, prancing horse, 3" L 150.00
Figure, seated dignitary in dragon robe, gilt traces, 16" 4,000.00
Incense burner, 2 lizards & pagoda on marble/onyx base, 6" 800.00
Jar, bird/urn on squat body, eagle atop, 3-leg, 1800s, 14" 600.00
Jar, foo dog figural, 1800s, 11" 675.00
Jardiniere, emb birds/waves, lion's head hdls, 1890s, 2½x9" 100.00
Jardiniere, emb dragon, 1800s, 8x12½" 275.00
Lamp, Jp, dragon relief, 1800s, electrified, 29" 200.00
Okimono, fish form, EX detail, 4½" 385.00
Pedestal, clouds, curved legs, bats on base, 1800s, 23" 325.00
Pedestal, cvd/emb dragon & flowers, 30" 350.00
Vase, appl dragon, ovoid w/short curved ft, 1800s, 11", pr 300.00
Vase, concave cylinder, long hdls w/short upright bars, 15" 365.00
Vase, inlaid silver/copper/shakudo wisteria, sgn, 1890s, 9" 1,000.00

Celadon

Celadon, introduced during the Ching Dynasty, is a green-glazed ware developed in an attempt to imitate the color of jade. Designs are often incised or painted on over glaze in heavy enamel applications.

Bowl, bulb; cvd lattice/florals, 3-ftd, Ming Dy, 12" 110.00
Vase, blk florals at neck, baluster, Korean, 14th C, 11" 1,000.00
Vase, key fret bands, diapering, Ch'ien Lung Dy, 16" 600.00
Vase, red/bl flowers, cvd frets/waves, mock ring hdls, 11" 440.00

Furniture

Armchair; Ch, tkwd, dragon arms/bk support, cvd legs 350.00

Armchair, back carved as an eagle and monkey flanked by two large dragons, $850.00.

Armchair, Ch, tkwd, floral crest rail, splat: urn of flowers, 36" ...350.00
Cabinet, Ch E, lcq, pagoda top, doors, several drw, 23" 985.00
Floor screen, Ch, 6-panel, pnt floral/cvd apron, 58x111" 550.00
Stand, Ch, 2-tier, rtcl trim, MOP inlay, marble top, 32" 375.00
Stand, Ch rswd/marble, rtcl apron/dragon cvd shelf, 22" dia 700.00
Table, Ch, 4 ferocious dragon legs, rnd w/center ped, 59" 2,500.00
Table, lamp; Ch, tkwd/marble, mask-head legs, claw/ball ft 500.00
Tabouret, Ch, tkwd, rtcl floral apron, 17" marble top, 23" 250.00

Hardstones

Amethyst, vase, cvd peonies/buds, peony cover, 11x9" 450.00
Amethyst, vase, tree trunk w/branch & flower cvg, 3¾" 220.00
Coral, pk; lady in flowing kimono w/flower basket, 2" 90.00
Coral, red; Hotei, standing Buddha w/flowers in hand, 1¾" 150.00
Gr hardstone, 2-hdl cup, raised bosses, jade finial, 5x7" 225.00
Jade, dk gr w/tan flecks; magpie on floral branch, 7x4" 275.00
Jade, gray-gr; Quan Yin w/lotus blossoms, 9¾", +teak stand 450.00
Jade, Honan; group of 2 foo lions, 5½" L 110.00
Jade, lt gr; lady holds bamboo rod, 8½x4½" 425.00
Jade, med gr w/gray; phoenix on floral branch+sm bird, 8" 325.00
Jade, med gr; vase, floral panels/loose ring hdls, lid, 6" 250.00
Jade, med gr; vase, florals, foo dog/ring hdls, lid, 8½" 350.00
Jade, nephrite; sq w/brn & gr foo lion, Ming Dy, 1½" 150.00
Jade, wht/blk; relief: Immortal, animals/attendant, 10" L 400.00
Jadeite, apple gr; trumpeting elephant figure, 3½" L 110.00
Jadeite, gr; brooch, floral cvg, w/silver gilt, 1¾" 55.00
Jadeite, gr; pendant, monkey/peach branch cvg, 2½" L 165.00
Jar, gr quartz, floral band, amethyst/gr floral lid, 5½" 100.00
Malachite, rabbit, ears laid bk, scratching, 2x3" 180.00
Quartz, gr; jar, floral band, amethyst/gr floral lid, 5½" 100.00
Rock crystal, Shou Lao w/spotted deer at ft, 7½" 495.00
Rose quartz, court lady stands by prunus tree, 5½" 225.00
Tiger eye, bl; reclining water buffalo, 4¾" 235.00

Lacquer

Lacquerware is found in several colors, but the one most likely to be encountered is cinnabar. It is often intricately carved, sometimes involving hundreds of layers built one at a time on a metal or wooden base. Later pieces remain red, while older examples tend to darken.

Birdcage, bamboo, domed form, 2 porc feeders, 28x15" dia 1,100.00
Box, figural motif, cinnabar, 1920s, 5" dia 50.00
Box, metalwork, lid w/figures in boat & pavilion, 4" 275.00
Box, mtn scene w/3 figures, cinnabar, mk China, 6" L 35.00
Box, passion flowers in gold & silver, 3" dia 250.00
Box, rats/grapevines cvd on top, blk, oval, 9" L 150.00
Box, rnd scene of shodana & kakemono, takamakie on brn, 6" ..1,750.00
Box, scrolling leafy vines, gilt on blk, 1800s, 11½" dia 700.00
Cabinet, relief peonies, shell inlay, much gold, 20x20" 450.00
Chest, storage; phoenix birds, red/gilt/silver, 27x39" 770.00
Chest of drws, softwood, 7-drw, red, 1800s, 29" 385.00
Figure, Guardian, gold lcq on wood, 1700s, 12", pr 600.00
Sewing stand, dragons/figures/genre scenes, gold/red, 20x25" ..1,500.00
Stand, crane/peonies, cabriole legs, lower shelf, cinnabar 300.00
Tray, figures/bldg/landscape, floral borders, 19x25" 325.00

Netsukes

A netsuke is a miniature Japanese carving made with two holes called the Himitoshi, either channeled or within the carved design. As kimonos (the outer garment of the time) had no pockets, the Japanese man hung his pipe, tobacco pouch, or other daily necessities from his waist sash. The most highly valued accessory was a nest of little drawers called an Inro, in which they carried snuff or sometimes opium. The netsuke was the toggle that secured them. Although most are of ivory, others were made of bone, wood, metal, porcelain, or semiprecious stones. Some were inlaid or lacquered. They are found in many forms—figurals the most common, mythological beasts the most desirable. They range in size from 1" up to 3", which was the maximum size allowed by law. Many netsukes represented the owner's profession, religion, or hobbies. Scenes from the daily life of Japan at that time were often depicted in the tiny carvings. The more detailed the carving, the greater the value.

Careful study is required to recognize the quality of the netsuke. Many have been made in Hong Kong in recent years; and even though some are very well carved, these are considered copies and avoided by the serious collector. There are many books that will help you learn to recognize quality netsukes, and most reputable dealers are glad to assist you. Use your magnifying glass to check for repairs. In the listings that follow, netsukes are ivory unless noted otherwise; 'stained' indicates a color wash.

Actor (movable head) sits at mirror/applies makeup, Ryomin 250.00
Badger w/erect tail, sgn Tomonobu 125.00

Netsuke: Depicting a fox dressed in monk's robe, 1800s, 4", $1,000.00; Depicting a stylized Western figure in a cloak, $100.00.

Badgers (2) eating mound of fruit & leaves, 1700s 225.00
Ball, rtcl openwork rats w/inlaid eyes, stained, 1890s 365.00
Bat, compactly cvd, wings held above its head, 1800s 275.00
Boat carrying 9 figures, sgn Tomochika, 1800s 225.00
Boy beating lg drum 225.00
Boy holds lg darum doll, 1800s 350.00
Dragon w/inlaid eyes coils about pearl, sgn Shuzan, 1890s 365.00
Ferocious oni w/drumsticks, wood, horns missing, 1800s 600.00
Fishermen in tug-of-war w/octopus, sgn Tomomitsu 450.00
Frog climbs up side of squash, sgn & set w/MOP seal plaque 600.00
Frog climbs upon seated monk, 1800s 350.00
Frogs (2) perched on lily pad, 1800s 325.00
Fukurokuiu neck wrestles w/tortoise, sgn Kazuno, 1½" 175.00
Group: dog/blind man/geisha/oni/porter/nobleman, Masatoshi ..275.00
Guardian lion, tightly coiled, sgn Masanao 300.00
Hotei dancing, holds fan, 1890s, 2¾" 150.00
Kaminari (Horned Thunder God) on drum, Shu Lo Chai, 1½" 80.00
Karako (3) play w/shishi costume & drum, 1850s 275.00
Karako perched on Hotei's treasure sack, 1800s 300.00
Karako rides on bk of nursemaid, sgn Tomomitsu, 1800s 285.00
Karako seated in lg basket holds another on his knees, 1890s 250.00
Laundress, mallet in hand, child by her side, 1⅝" 85.00
Lion perched on lg ball, staghorn 175.00
Man, seated, lg tortoise on head, uptrn bowl at ft, 1½" 125.00
Man strings bow, monkey in armor w/bird, Rakumin, 1850s 725.00
Man w/bowl, cabbage on bk, boy aside, Shomitsu, 1 ½ 80.00
Man w/lg ears & floppy cap atop lg fish, bone, 1890s 375.00
Mask of okame, sgn Gyojumin 325.00
Monkey climbing on sleeping boy 350.00
Monkey on rockery w/lg flower, 1800s 125.00
Monkey pries open shell, sgn Saimei 110.00
Monkey w/monkey mask & drum plays w/2 sm monkeys, 1890s ..650.00
Octopus w/tentacles about monkey w/lg shell, sgn Shoichi 600.00
Oni, seated, pulls on ropes of basket, sgn Yoshiyuki, 1800s 525.00
Oni mask adorns front of purse, 1800s 300.00
Oni wrestles w/skeleton, wood/ivory inlay/mc, sgn Shunsai 750.00
Rat atop pile of Dikoku's hammer, hat & basket, 1800s 375.00
Sarumawashi entertainer w/monkey on shoulder 350.00
Scholar reads while riding giant carp, sgn Seishi, 1800s 165.00
Sennin & dragon cvd on biscuit form, sgn Moritoshi+kakihan ..350.00
Shishi (cross-eyed) w/loose ball in mouth, curled into ball 200.00
Shishi w/brocade ball cvd on disk, sgn Taketoshi, 1800s 150.00
Sq form w/cvg of long-nosed man w/beard, sgn Shohosai 250.00
To Bo Saku, peach in 1 hand, staff in other, Wong Ye, 2" 105.00
Water buffalo w/EX detail, recumbent, School of Tomatada ...1,100.00
Woman w/child on bk & elder examine kettle, Gyokkosai 250.00

Ojimes

Copper doughnut form w/colored & gilt butterfly band, 1800s ...250.00
Iron, silver & gold dragon enveloped in clouds, 1850s 135.00
Iron w/brass inlay leaves & vines, Koyoto, 1800s 125.00
Ivory, cvd man w/basket emerging from rocky crevice, 1870s 200.00
Ivory, monkey & octopus wrestle, sgn Ikkosai, 1890s 635.00
Ivory, monkey swinging on vine, inlaid eyes, EX work, 1890s 400.00
Silver, conch shell form, 1800s 300.00
Silver, rtcl floral band, 1800s 125.00
Silver metal w/emb goose in flight, sgn 100.00

Porcelain

Chinese export ware was designed to appeal to Western tastes and was often made to order. During the 18th century, vast amounts were shipped to Europe and on westward. Much of this fine porcelain consisted of dinnerware lines that were given specific pattern names. Rose Mandarin, Fitzhugh, Armorial, Rose Medallion, and Canton are but a few of the more familiar.

Bottle, wht, everted rim, Choson Dy, 9", VG 220.00
Bowl, FR, floral, diapering, lozenge form, 1850s, 10" L 550.00
Bowl, Rose Canton, butterflies/mums, shallow, 9½" 200.00
Charger, E, Rose Canton, Arabic date/inscriptions, 16" 2,100.00
Charger, FV, sages drink tea while in boat, 14" 365.00
Dish, FV, butterflies/birds/prunus, mks, rstr, 10½", pr 1,200.00
Figurine, hawk perched on rock base, Hirado, 6x9" 335.00
Fishbowl, FV, paneled decor on brn, 1800s, 14" 525.00
Fishbowl, goldfish on bl, invt bell form, teak base, 16" H 900.00
Mug, figures/flowers, pear form, 1700s, 6" 475.00
Plate, E, armorial, eng Honourable E India Co, rstr, 10" 550.00
Plate, E, eagle center, gilt 'FS,' star/scallop border, 10" 120.00
Plate, E, Imari pattern, 1700s, 9", set of 4 ....600.00
Platter, Bl Fitzhugh, 13" 300.00
Platter, E, Pompadour, 2 cartouches w/eagles, 2 w/fish, 11" 700.00
Platter, Gr Fitzhugh, w/rtcl liner, imperfections, 18" 1,100.00
Platter, Nanking, 1800s, 18" 650.00
Punch bowl, E, genre scene/gilt, int decor, 1780s, 13" 2,800.00
Punch bowl, E, genre scenes, mask medallion w/in, 12", EX ...1,200.00
Punch bowl, E, Masonic, personalized w/name, rstr, 11" 3,200.00
Saucer, E, eagle w/shield & monogram, 3-color/gilt, 5½" 450.00
Tea bowl & saucer, E, armorial: Industria, spearhead band 525.00
Tea caddy, brn/gold floral sprays, floral finial, 1700s 200.00
Teapot, E, overall foliage in orange & gilt, 1800s, 8" 825.00

Temple jars, decorated with phoenix, peonies and vines in Famille Verte colors, 20", $325.00.

Tray, E, eagle/cherub w/trumpet, bl/gilt on wht, 4¾" L 225.00
Vase, figural cartouches on bl, gilt bugs/flowers, mk, 9" 200.00
Vase, FR, figural design, trumpet form, 1700s, 8" 250.00
Vase, FR, landscape panels on bl, Ju Ren Tan Zhi mk, 16" 495.00
Vase, FR, 3 bird medallions on yel w/florets, mk, 1800s, 14" ...1,100.00
Vase, gourds/leaves, blk on gr w/manganese, 1800s, 11", pr 275.00
Vase, iron rust glaze, mei ping form, 1700s, 3" 125.00
Vase, yel crackle, squat teardrop form, 1700s, 3" 120.00

Pottery

Basin, aqua-gr spatter, Jp, 19" 125.00
Bowl, bl w/red streaks, Jun-type, studio inscription, 9" 225.00
Brush pot, emb hawthorn, Yi Hsing, 5" 50.00
Funerary figure, terra cotta w/irid gr mottle, Sung Dy, 11" 175.00
Jar, storage; emb dragon & clouds, gr w/bl, 1800s, 31" 200.00
Rain barrel, terra cotta w/wht bamboo, tooled, 25x37", EX 275.00
Sake bottle, stoneware, snake in relief, mk Mune, 1920s, 6" 85.00
Tilework Bodhisattva in in arched alcove, yel/gr, Ming Dy, 16" ...650.00

Vase, cranes under willow tree, Kyoto Yaki, sgn, 1800s, 7" 100.00
Vase, gr, waisted neck, Han Dy, 5", EX 600.00
Vase, gr, 4" 65.00
Vase, molded taotieh masks/figural frieze on gr, Han Dy, 12" 650.00
Vase, teadust glaze, gu form, 8½" 165.00

Sumida bowl with ten characters around rim, 8" long, $350.00.

Rugs

The 'Oriental' or Eastern rug market has enjoyed a renewal of interest in recent years as collectors have become aware of the fact that some of the semiantique rugs (those sixty to one hundred years old) may be had at a price within the range of the average buyer.

Key:
comp — complementary   mdl — medallion
dmn — diamond   s/a — semiantique
gb — guard borde

Agra, gr w/pastel geometrics, wide tan border, 168x122" 850.00
Anatolian prayer, wine, mihrab spandrels, 1900s, 53x72", VG ...365.00
Baktiara, mc vasiform floral on dk bl, band border, 240x71" ...3,000.00
Chinese, bl w/tan/ivory/bl mdl, band gb, 116x76" 975.00
Hamadan, herati-decor red field w/ivory mdl, 1950s, 60x41" 385.00
Hamadan, red w/mdl, bl gb, 72x36" 600.00
Heriz, ivory w/mc geometrics, red spandrels & gb, 102x73" 575.00
Karadja, 3 4-color mdls on navy, 1950s, 72x56", EX 1,700.00
Kirman, ivory w/mc floral sprays, bl floral gb, 265x156" 2,700.00
Kirman, lg concentric navy/ivory oval mdl, 1800s, 146x92" ...3,300.00
Kirman, mdl on wine w/foliate motifs, multiple gb, 73x54" 2,200.00
Kirman, wine w/mc floral mdl & spandrels, 216x135" 3,100.00
Kurd, sq grid of 6-color palmettes, red Xs border, 78x51" 1,100.00
Kurd bagface, navy w/red & bl flowerheads, floral gb, 32x30" 400.00
Maslinghan, bl w/red lightning mdl, rosette/leaf gb, 72x50" ...1,100.00
Mishkin, ivory animal fields/border, 3 mdls, 152x114" 475.00
NW Persian, rose w/allover trees & vines, 1950s, 116x88" 1,750.00
Oushak, red w/floral sprays, gr floral gb, worn, 275x114" 3,800.00
Persia, dk bl w/florals, red meander gb, 1920s, 58x32" 1,500.00
Senna Kilum, lt bl w/5-color repeating pattern, 64x50" 750.00
Tabriz, brn w/ivory mdl, mc vines, vine gb, 1900, 63x44" 2,200.00
Turkish, 3 brn/ivory/bl geometric mdls on bl, 115x75" 1,300.00

Snuff Bottles

The Chinese were introduced to snuff in the 17th century, and their carved and painted snuff bottles typify their exquisite taste and workmanship. These small bottles, seldom measuring over 2½", were made of amber, jade, ivory, and cinnabar; tiny spoons were often attached to their stoppers. By the 18th century, some were being made of porcelain, others were of glass with delicate designs tediously reverse painted with minuscule brushes sometimes containing a single hair. Copper and brass were used but to no great extent.

Agate, red mineral stone stopper, 2" 60.00
Amber, lion's head/mock ring hdls, aventurine stopper, 2½" 220.00
Amber w/cvd peonies, birds & flowers, 4-character base mk 440.00
Amethyst, rose & peach cvg, jadeite stopper, 1⅞" 200.00
Bl quartz, bird/branch cvg, pear form, sodalite stopper, 2" 135.00
Canton enamel, exotic birds, greenstone stopper, 2¾" 250.00
Caramel agate, octagonal, agate stopper, 2⅝" 385.00
Chacedony agate, cloudy inclusions, greenstone stopper, 2" 300.00
Gilt metal, ivory figural panel w/mc stain & turq, 4" 50.00
Hornbill, cvd figural scenes, w/chain & hardwood stand, 8" 900.00
Ivory, cvd as man riding on elephant, 3" 185.00
Ivory, dbl, cvd as 2 women, heads are stoppers, 3¼" 275.00
Ivory, sunken cvg of sages in pine forest, mk, 1890s, 3" 110.00
Nephrite jade, eggplant form, coral stopper, 3" 300.00
Overlay glass, cormorants & lotus, jadeite stopper, 3" 440.00
Overlay glass, horses/willow tree, coral stopper, 3" 275.00
Puddingstone agate, rectangular, malachite stopper, 2½" 220.00
Rhodonite, figural cvg, matching stopper, 2½" 100.00
Rvpt, figures/boats/3 geese, quartz stopper, 2½" 250.00
Rvpt, insects & flowers on amber, 3½" 180.00
Rvpt, landscape, green glass stopper, 2½" 110.00
Rvpt, rooster/hens under wisteria, sgn, quartz stopper, 2¾" 200.00
Rvpt rock crystal, landscape/inscription, 1800s, 2¼" 1,100.00
Tigereye, fan-tail fish, bk: foo lion, 3" 90.00

Textiles

Bedspread, pheasants/birds/flowers embr on silk, 92x75" 875.00
Coat, silk, embr peonies/butterflies, ¾-length 175.00
Hanging, dragon in clouds, silk embr on cotton, 35x57", VG 150.00
Jacket, silk brocade, embr flowers & bats 85.00
Panel, unicorn/lions/etc emb in silk on linen, 1800s, 24x96" ..1,400.00
Robe, dragons/symbols/etc embr in gold on bl, 1800s, EX" 450.00
Robe, gold dragons on bl silk, horse hoof cuffs, 1800s 1,400.00

Woodblock Prints, Japanese

Actor, from Modern Heroes series, Yoshitoshi, 14x9" 300.00
Beijin w/samisen & koto, Eizan, oban tate-e 525.00

Portrait of the actor Morita Kanya as Genta Kagesuye, by Natori, oban tate-e, with original folder and titleslip, $440.00.

Couple in Kendo training room, Toyokuni III, diptych **225.00**
Dancers entertain Prince Genji, Toyokuni III, triptych **350.00**
Ladies, Mt Fuji in background, Chikanobu, triptych **300.00**
Lady in checked kimono under willow, Shunsen, oban tate-e **145.00**
Lady in floral kimono behind screen, Kunisada, oban tate-e **110.00**
Little Temple Gate, Hiroshi Yoshida, oban tate-e **325.00**
Mtn path, Hiroshi Yoshida, oban yoko-e **275.00**
Night battle scene, Kuniyoshi, oban triptych **385.00**
Night Scene of Street Stall, Taketi Asano, oban yoko-e **50.00**
Nobleman & servant, Mt Fuji behind, Kuniyoshi, oban tate-e **275.00**
Pine tree overhanging a lake, Kuniyoshi, oban tate-e **100.00**
Warrior in dragon-decorated robe, Kunichika, oban tate-e **110.00**
2 figures by footbridge, Toyokuni III, oban diptych **250.00**
3 actors in cherry blossom landscape, Toyokuni III, triptych **335.00**
4 figures in rain shower, Toyokuni III, oban tate-e **220.00**

Miscellaneous

Bowl, ruby red glass, flared, Pekin, 6½" **1,000.00**
Bowl, wht glass, sq trumpet form, Peking, 1800s, 6½" **220.00**
Coffeepot, EX, silver w/repousse prunus, Kanji mk, 15", VG **660.00**
Cvg, bamboo, Buddha's hand fruit, 1800s, 15" **650.00**
Figure, man, natural burl growth w/cvd head, losses, 12" **250.00**
Mask, tegnu, lcq on papier-mache, 10" **475.00**
Okimono, ivory, farmer w/basket & squirrels, rpr, 7¾" **700.00**
Okimono, ivory, hunter w/gun carries birds, sgn Kogetsu, 5" **495.00**
Okimono, ivory, rat catcher w/cage, rat on knee, 2½", EX **165.00**
Okimono, wood, Daruma w/inlaid eyes, 2½" **125.00**
Scroll painting, god of Longevity/3 boys on silk, Isshu **165.00**
Scroll painting, mtn landscape, ink on silk, 16x44" **135.00**
Sculpture, gilt wood, Buddha sits on cushion, 1900s, 25" **150.00**
Stirrups, Ch, iron w/silver inlay brocade, curved, 1800s **425.00**
Vase, red-amber glass, octagonal, Peking, mk, 1700s, 5½" **2,200.00**

Orrefors

Orrefors Glassworks was founded in 1898 in the Swedish province of Smaaland. Utilizing the expertise of designers such as Simon Gate, Edward Hald, Vicke Lindstrand, and Edwin Ohrstrom, it produced art glass of the highest quality. Various techniques were used in achieving the decoration. Some were wheel engraved; others were blown through a unique process that formed controlled bubbles or air pockets resulting in unusual patterns and shapes. Our advisor for this category is Abby Malowanczyk; she is listed in the Directory under Texas.

Bowl, Ariel, aquamarine w/red waves, Ohrstrom, '51, #1244E, 4" ..**700.00**
Bowl, eng nude, 6-sided, sgn Palmquist, #3076, 1x7" **150.00**
Bowl, opalescent, PM309015, 2x8" **90.00**
Decanter, eng lady's body, face on stopper, Gordon, #2037 ....**110.00**
Decanter, eng sailor looking out to sea, Landberg, 1940s **225.00**
Decanter, etched nudes etc, dbl hdls, #119/20 Gate, 9" **1,100.00**
Sculpture, concave rings on clear block, Palmquist, 10x8x2" **300.00**
Vase, bl/gr fishnet cased in clear, Palmquist, #411, 8½" **275.00**
Vase, clear w/int yel & bl swirls, Alberius, 1973, 11" **935.00**
Vase, eng lady/gazelle on topaz, Lindstrand, #1349, 8¾" **250.00**
Vase, eng male diver, blk base, #1343AB, Lindstrand, 11" **1,400.00**
Vase, eng nude w/grapes+butterflies, Landberg, #3167, 8" **200.00**
Vase, eng sailing ship on wavy clear, Lindstrand, #1462, 10" **275.00**
Vase, eng: Thunderstorm, cobalt-cased clear, #291, Hald, 5" ..**1,500.00**
Vase, Graal, fish/seaweed, E Hald, bulbous, #474B, 5" **500.00**
Vase, Kraka, bl/yel in clear, bubbles, Palmquist, #411, 9¾" **660.00**
Vase, Kraka, crystal to bl, bubbles, Palmquist, 13½" **850.00**

Ott and Brewer

The partnership of Ott and Brewer began in 1865 in Trenton, New Jersey. By 1876 they were making decorated graniteware, parian, and 'ivory porcelain' — similar to Irish belleek though not as fine and of different composition. In 1883, however, experiments toward that end had reached a successful conclusion, and a true belleek body was introduced. It came to be regarded as the finest china ever produced by an American firm. The ware was decorated by various means such as hand painting, transfer printing, gilding, and lustre glazing. The company closed in 1893, one of many that failed during that depression. In the listings below, the ware is belleek unless noted otherwise. Our advisor for this category is Mary Frank Gaston; she is listed in the Directory under Texas.

Basket, floral, appl blossoms on cactus hdl, 7½x9" **1,000.00**
Bowl, gold florals & leaves, scalloped, 2 mks, 2x4¾" **195.00**
Bowl, gold paste florals, ruffled rim, sm **125.00**
Creamer, gold florals, branch hdl, 4" **200.00**
Cup & saucer, gold paste florals **220.00**
Pin tray, gold decor, fluted rim **150.00**
Pitcher, gold thistles, emb body w/much gold, 8" **100.00**
Salt cellar, mc leaves & cattails, 3-ftd, ind **140.00**
Sugar bowl, Tridacna, gold paste florals, unmk, 4" **275.00**
Teapot, florals, bark at top, branch hdl, 8½" **725.00**

Vase, gold-paste floral and leaf designs on matt finish, 6½", $500.00.

Overbeck

The Overbeck Studio was established in 1911 in Cambridge City, Indiana, by four Overbeck sisters. It survived until the last sister died in 1955. Early wares were often decorated with carved designs of stylized animals, birds, or florals with the designs colored to contrast with the background. Others had tooled designs filled in with various colors for a mosaic effect. After 1937 Mary Frances, the last remaining sister, favored handmade figurines with somewhat bizarre features in fanciful combinations of color. Overbeck ware is signed 'OBK,' frequently with the designer's and potter's initials under the stylized 'OBK.' Our advisor for this category is Wayne Kielsmeier; he is listed in the Directory under Arizona.

Bowl, purple w/yel int, 3x7", +3-color flower-form frog **400.00**
Figurine, dog, standing, 3½x4½" **425.00**
Figurine, man, standing, 5" **295.00**
Figurine, squirrel w/nut, floral base, 2½" **195.00**

Tumbler, grasshopper band, gr on yel, sgn E F, 4x3", 4 for **1,400.00**
Vase, lg parrots, repeating design, sgn E H, 13x6" **8,500.00**
Vase, 3 cvd panels: leaves/berries, bl on olive, E H, 5x6" **1,500.00**

Overshot

Overshot glass is characterized by the beaded or craggy appearance of its surface. Earlier ware was irregularly textured, while 20th-century examples tend to be more uniform.

Bowl, bl shaded, ruffled, in ormolu fr w/hanging rings, 7½" **195.00**
Decanter, cranberry, clear hdl, ice bladder, 11¾" **325.00**
Lamp, lace-maker's; cranberry, brass base, 17x8" **395.00**

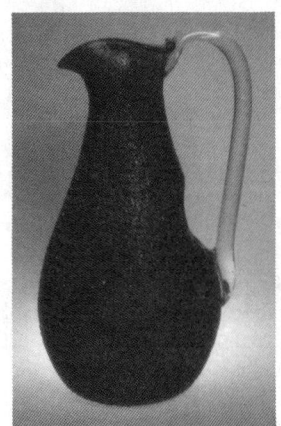

Champagne pitcher in cranberry with ice bladder, ca 1800s, attributed to Sandwich, 11", $135.00.

Pitcher, cranberry, clear hdl & wafer ft, 9⅜x5⅛" **265.00**
Pitcher, cranberry, clear rope hdl, w/ice bladder, 9¾x4½" **295.00**
Pitcher, cranberry, swirled ribs, clear reed hdl, 9" **195.00**
Pitcher, tankard, cranberry, clear hdl, 9¼x4½" **165.00**
Pitcher, tankard, cranberry, hinged metal lid, 9x4" **175.00**
Shade, bl to clear, ruffled, 5¼x7½" **185.00**

Owens Pottery

J.B. Owens founded his company in Zanesville, Ohio, in 1891 and, until 1907 when the company decided to exert most of its energies in the area of tile production, made several quality lines of art pottery. His first line, Utopian, was a standard brown ware with underglaze slip decoration of nature studies, animals, and portraits. A similar line, Lotus, utilized lighter background colors. Henri Deux, introduced in 1900, featured incised Art Nouveau forms inlaid with color. (Be aware that the Brush McCoy Pottery acquired many of Owens' molds and reproduced a line similar to Henri Deux, which they called Navarre.) Other important lines were Opalesce, Rustic, Feroza, Cyrano, and Mission, examples of which are rare today.

The factory burned in 1928, and the company closed shortly thereafter. Values vary according to the quality of the artwork and subject matter. Examples signed by the artist bring higher prices than those that are not signed.

Aborigine, vase, 4" **150.00**
Henri Deux, vase, lady's profile, #1307, 8" **350.00**
Lotus, vase, floral, wht on pk shaded, 10½" **350.00**
Lotus, vase, lg peonies, C Chilcote, #1243, 10x5" **550.00**
Matt Gr, jardiniere, 9" **250.00**
Matt Utopian, vase, clover, short/sm neck, #1067, 15" **350.00**
Plaque, ducks by pond, 3-color, matt glaze, 12x9" **700.00**

Utopian, ewer, yel roses, sgn Fanny Bell, 6" **210.00**
Utopian, mug, raspberries, sgn TS, 6" **150.00**
Utopian, tankard, wheat, str sides, 12" **250.00**
Utopian, vase, florals, sgn JJ Herold, 13" **350.00**
Utopian, vase, leaves in orange/gr, #1067, 15", NM **200.00**
Utopian, vase, spaniel w/collar, incurvate, sm neck, 16" **1,200.00**

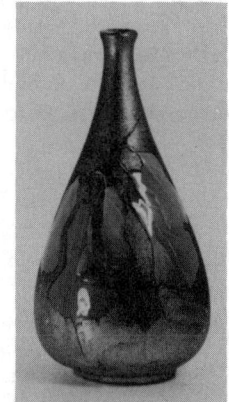

Vase, Opalesce, gold, orange and green leaves on copper ground, #817, 8", $750.00.

Pacific Clay Products

The Pacific Clay Products Company got its start in the 1920s as a consolidation of several smaller southern California potteries. The main Los Angeles plant had been founded in 1890 to make kitchen stoneware, ollas, and similar items. Terra cotta and brick were later produced.

In 1932 Hostess Ware, a vividly colored line of dinnerware, was introduced to compete with Bauer's Ring Ware. Coralitos, a lighter-weight, pastel-hued dinnerware line was first marketed in 1937, and a similar but less expensive line called Arcadia soon followed. Artware including vases, figurines, candlesticks, etc., was produced from 1932 to 1942, at which time the company went into war-related work and pottery manufacture ceased. A limited amount of hand-decorated dinnerware was also made. For further information we recommend *The Collectors Encyclopedia of California Pottery* by our advisor, Jack Chipman; he is listed in the Directory under California.

Bowl, Ring-style, 8½" **22.00**
Carafe, Ring-style, w/lid **30.00**
Chop plate, Ring-style, 12" **30.00**
Coffee cup, Ring-style, lg **20.00**
Coffeepot, demitasse; Ring-style, wht **95.00**
Cup & saucer, demitasse; Ring-style **25.00**
Figurine, nude holds feather, 15½" **125.00**
Figurine, pan, seated/playing pipes, very rare **300.00**
Figurine, Spanish dancers, Valencia Oranges, rare **200.00**
Pitcher, syrup; Ring-style **36.00**
Relish tray, Ring-style, 4-part, wood hdl **50.00**
Shakers, Ring-style, dk bl, pr **10.00**
Sugar bowl, demitasse; Ring-style, yel **12.00**
Teapot, Ring-style, dk bl, squat, sm **55.00**
Teapot, Ring-style, turq, ftd, lg **95.00**
Tumbler, Ring-style **15.00**
Vase, Art Deco, bl, 7" **45.00**
Vase, gr, #417, 4" **15.00**
Vase, gr, slender, 8" **35.00**

Paden City

The Paden City Glass Company began operations in 1916 in

Paden City, West Virginia. The company's early lines consisted largely of the usual pressed tablewares, but by the 1920s production had expanded to include colored wares in translucent as well as opaque glass in a variety of patterns and styles. The company maintained its high standards of handmade perfection until 1949, when under new management much of the work formerly done by hand was replaced by automation. The Paden City Glass Company closed in 1951; its earlier wares, the colored patterns in particular, are becoming very collectible.

Paden City Glass is not always easily recognized by collectors or dealers, as it was almost never marked. It is believed this was so the glass could be sold to decorating companies. The company assigned both line numbers and names to many of its blanks or sets of glassware. Colors were sometimes given more than one name, and etchings were named as well. All this makes identification of items offered for sale through mail order difficult, and labels prepared by dealers are often confusing.

A review of literature available on Paden City reveals the following names for the company's plate etchings: Ardith; California Poppy; Cupid; Delilah Bird (Peacock Reverse); Eden Rose; Frost; Gazebo; Gothic Garden; Lela Bird; Nora Bird; Orchid (three variations); Peacock and Rose (Peacock and Wild Rose); Samarkand; Trumpet Flower; Utopia. Names given to cuttings made on Paden City blanks are Yorktown and Lazy Daisy. It is not clear whether the names originated with Paden City or with secondary decorating companies.

Our advisors for this category are George and Mary Hurney; they are listed in the Directory under Illinois. (Note: their interest is only in Paden City glassware, not the pottery.) See also Glass Animals.

This list gives company line numbers with corresponding line names:

#69, #69½ — Georgian	#411 — Mrs B
#191 — Party	#412 — Crow's Foot Square
#210 — Regina	#890 — Crow's Foot Round
#215 — Hotcha	#895 — Lucy
#220 — Largo	#991 — Penny
#221 — Maya	#994 — Popeye and Olive
#300 — Wotta	#1503 — Trance

And, finally, a listing of colors with alternate names or descriptive phrases:

Amber — (dull)	Mulberry — amethyst
Cheriglo — (delicate) pink	Opal — opaque white
Cobalt Blue — Royal Blue	Primrose — (amber with reddish
Crystal — (clear, no tint)	tint)
Dark Green — forest green	Red — ruby
Dark Amber — (honey color)	Rose — (dark pink)
Light Blue — Copen, Neptune	Yellow — (pale, soft)

Bowl, Blk Forest, pk, hdls, 9" 60.00
Bowl, console; Cupid, gr 90.00
Bowl, cream soup; Crow's Foot, amber 10.00
Bowl, cream soup; Crow's Foot, ruby 14.00
Bowl, Crow's Foot, amber, sq, 4¼" 8.00
Bowl, Crow's Foot, amber, 11" 25.00
Bowl, Crow's Foot, ruby, 5" 25.00
Bowl, Crow's Foot, ruby, 9½" 75.00
Bowl, Crow's Foot, 11" 25.00
Bowl, fruit; Cupid, gr or pk, 10¼" 100.00
Bowl, fruit; Peacock Reverse, cobalt w/ebony ft, 4½x9½" 95.00
Bowl, Orchid, red, ftd, 10" 90.00
Bowl, Orchid, sq, 11" 75.00
Bowl, vegetable; Crow's Foot, ruby, oval 28.00
Cake plate, Ardith, ftd, 10" 65.00
Cake plate, Crow's Foot, ruby, ftd 80.00
Cake plate, Gothic Garden, yel, hdls, 10" 40.00

Cake plate, Peacock & Wild Rose, pk, ftd, 10" 45.00
Candle holders, Crow's Foot, bl, 5¾", pr 140.00
Candle holders, Cupid, gr, pr 135.00

Candle holders, Gadroon, blue, 5½", $110.00 for the pair.

Candle holders, Maya, lt bl, pr 70.00
Candlestick, Lela Bird, pk, rolled edge, Archaic shape, 5" 60.00
Candlestick, Mrs B, lt bl, low, flat, pr 25.00
Candlestick, Peacock & Wild Rose, gr, 5", pr 100.00
Candlestick, Peacock Reverse, gr, Mrs B shape, 3⅜" 60.00
Candy dish, Crow's Foot, ruby, w/lid 50.00
Cheese & cracker, Maya, lt bl 60.00
Cocktail shaker, Party Line, ruby 20.00
Compote, Ardith, topaz, 6¼" 80.00
Compote, Crow's Foot, red, rnd, ftd, 10" 70.00
Compote, Cupid, pk or gr, 6¼" 65.00
Compote, Gothic Garden, yel, Mrs B shape, 3¼" 40.00
Compote, Lela Bird, pk, Archaic shape, high std, 6" 95.00
Compote, Orchid, yel, flared, sq, 6¼" 60.00
Console set, Blk Forest, blk, Van De Man, #531, 3-pc 225.00
Creamer, Crow's Foot, ruby 25.00
Creamer, Orchid, gr 25.00
Creamer, Penny Line, ruby 12.00
Creamer & sugar bowl, Peacock Reverse, pk 135.00
Cup, Peacock Reverse, red 65.00
Cup & saucer, Blk Forest, blk 80.00
Cup & saucer, Crow's Foot, ruby 10.00
Cup & saucer, Penny Line, ruby 10.00
Goblet, cordial; Peacock & Wild Rose 15.00
Goblet, cordial; Penny Line, gr 18.00
Goblet, water; Penny Line, gr 12.00
Goblet, water; Penny Line, ruby 19.00
Goblet, wine; Futura, ruby 9.00
Ice bucket, Cupid, pk or gr, 6" 125.00
Ice bucket, Lela Bird, gr 115.00
Ice bucket, Peacock & Wild Rose, pk 130.00
Mayonnaise, Blk Forest, blk, +ladle & liner 150.00
Mayonnaise, Blk Forest, gr, w/ladle 95.00
Mayonnaise, Vermillion, w/underplate 25.00
Pitcher, Peacock & Wild Rose, cobalt, 5" 100.00
Plate, Crow's Foot, amber, 6" 3.00
Plate, Crow's Foot, amber, 8½" 7.00
Plate, Crow's Foot, red, luncheon sz 16.50
Plate, Eden Rose, hdls, Trance shape, 7¼" 20.00
Plate, Eden Rose, Hotcha shape, 7¼" 20.00
Plate, Gothic Garden, hdls, 10" 45.00
Plate, Nora Bird, pk or gr, 8" 20.00
Plate, Sasha Bird, yel, sq, hdls, 9" 125.00
Sandwich server, Orchid, cobalt, center hdl 65.00

Saucer, Peacock Reverse, cobalt **15.00**
Sugar bowl, Crow's Foot, oval, 11" **15.00**
Sugar bowl, Cupid, pk or gr, ftd, 4¼" **75.00**
Top hat, Eden Rose, 3¼" **40.00**
Tumbler, Crow's Foot, red **90.00**
Tumbler, juice; Popeye & Olive, red, flat, 5-oz **12.00**
Tumbler, Nora Bird, pk or gr, ftd, 4¾" **50.00**
Vase, Lela Bird, ebony, elliptical, 5" **95.00**
Vase, Lela Bird, gr, Regina shape, rare, 10" **250.00**
Vase, Orchid, red, 8½" **110.00**
Vase, Utopia, blk amethyst, panelled, 10½" **175.00**

Paintings on Ivory

Miniature works of art executed on ivory from the 1800s are assessed by the finesse of the artist, as are any fine paintings. Signed examples and portraits with an identifiable subject are usually preferred.

Child w/apple, sgn Dupre, ivory/tortoise fr, 1¾x1½" **250.00**
Dignitary in official robe, brass Louis XVI fr, 4x3" **500.00**
Gentleman, 1880s, oval, 2½" **175.00**
Geo (& Martha) Washington, oval w/in ivory fr, 5½x4½", pr ...**350.00**
Husband & wife in outdoor setting, sgn Rift/1893, 4" dia **425.00**
Lady, sgn Fuger (German), 1800s, 3x2⅜" **175.00**
Lady in elegant attire, style of Le Brun, sgn Leroy, 5x4" **550.00**
Lady in hat, sgn, oval ornate gilt fr, 3x4" **190.00**
Lady in lace shawl, 1880s, 3x2¼" **150.00**
Lady in lg hat, after Vigee Le Brun, filigree fr, oval, 3x2½" ...**450.00**
Lady in red gown, sgn MV, silver fr mtd as pin, 1800s **150.00**
Lady leans against horse, sgn, brass Empire-style fr, 3" **475.00**
Lovers in dragon-drawn chariot, sgn Dugor, 1800s, 2¾" **150.00**
Madame Elizabeth, sgn Rene, ivory/tortoise shell fr, 1¾x1½" ...**250.00**

Monsieur and Madame Jean Hoofer, signed Rouchier, 3½", $400.00 for the pair.

Napoleon (& Josephine), sgn Berton, 1½", fr as 1 ....**300.00**
Napoleon in military uniform, brass easel fr, 3x2½" **375.00**
Spinne, scantily clad lady in spider web, brass fr, 3½x4¾" ...**880.00**

Pairpoint

The Pairpoint Manufacturing Company was built in 1880 in New Bedford, Massachusetts. It was primarily a metalworks whose chief product was coffin fittings. Next door, the Mt. Washington Glassworks made quality glasswares of many varieties. (See Mt. Washington for more information concerning their artware lines.) By 1894 it became apparent to both companies that a merger would be to their best interest.

From the late 1890s until the 1930s, lamps and lamp accessories were an important part of Pairpoint's production. There were three main types of shades, all of which were blown: puffy — blown-out reverse-painted shades (usually floral designs); ribbed — also reverse painted; and scenic — reverse painted with scenes of land or seascapes (usually executed on smooth surfaces, although ribbed scenics may be found occasionally). Cut glass lamps and those with metal overlay panels were also made. Scenic shades were sometimes artist signed. Every shade was stamped on the lower inside or outside edge with 1) The Pairpoint Corp., 2) Patent Pending, 3) Patented July 9, 1907, or 4) Patent Applied For. Bases were made of bronze, copper, brass, silver, or wood and are always signed.

Because they produced only fancy, handmade artware, the company's sales lagged seriously during the Depression; as time and tastes changed, their style of product was less in demand. As a result, they never fully recovered; consequently part of the buildings and equipment was sold in 1938. The company reorganized in 1939 under the direction of Robert Gundersen and again specialized in quality hand-blown glassware. Isaac Babbit regained possession of the silver departments, and together they established Gundersen Glassworks Inc. After WWII, because of a sharp decline in sales, it again became necessary to reorganize. The Gundersen-Pairpoint Glassworks was formed, and the old line of cut, engraved artware was reintroduced. The company moved to East Wareham, Massachusetts, in 1957. But business continued to suffer, and the firm closed only one year later. In 1970, however, new facilities were constructed in Sagamore under the direction of Robert Bryden, sales manager for the company since the 1950s.

In 1974 the company began to produce lead glass cup plates which were made on commission as fund-raisers for various churches and organizations. These are signed with a 'P' in diamond and are becoming quite collectible. Our advisor for Pairpoint lamps is Daniel Batchelor; he is listed in the Directory under New York. See also Napkin Rings.

Key: pwt — paperweight

Glass

Atomizer, pastel flowers on white, replaced bulb, 6", $295.00.

Biscuit jar, blown-out base band, asters on pnt Burmese, 7" ...**450.00**
Biscuit jar, emb floral base, mc mums on coral, 7" dia **425.00**
Biscuit jar, poppies on dk brn & gold; mk SP fr, 7x7½" **450.00**
Bowl, alexandrite, ltd ed from 1970s, 3¾x5" **50.00**
Bowl, cranberry swan w/clear neck & head, 12x13" **330.00**
Box, gold floral on opal, quatrafoil oval, #9524, 7" L **465.00**

Box, jewel; bl opal top w/6 floral medallions, 4-ftd SP base 325.00
Candlestick, eng grapes, 10½", pr 250.00
Compote, blk w/clear bubble knob stem, 8x8" 250.00
Compote, cobalt, SP base w/gold wash, 9" 195.00
Tazza, canary w/floral cutting, clear bubble stem, 7" 350.00
Vase, wheel-cut trumpet form on sgn ormolu base, 15", pr 600.00

Lamps

Base, glass w/HP sea birds/ocean waves, mc, sgn, rstr, 25" 700.00
Candle, puffy 4½" pansy shade; mahog goblet-form std, NM 525.00
Chandelier, puffy, butterflies/pk & yel flowers, sgn, 14" 3,300.00
Pnt 18" New Bedford harbor Exeter shade; bottle form std 3,950.00

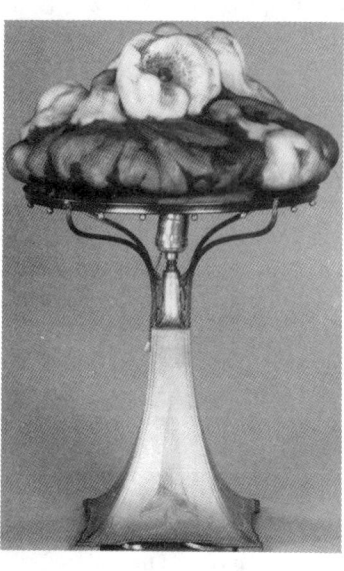

Puffy 12" shade with four large poppy blossoms on green, engraved leaves on pewter-finish base, 22", $9,000.00.

Puffy 12" daisies/scrolls Torino sqd shade; sqd floral std 13,200.00
Puffy 12" poppy shade; bulbous vase std w/eng scrolls 15,500.00
Puffy 14" butterfly/roses shaped-edge shade; std w/roses 6,325.00
Puffy 14" floral/scroll Ravenna shade (EX); floral-appl std 8,000.00
Puffy 14" hummingbirds/roses Devonshire shade; #3088 std .12,000.00
Puffy 14" hummingbirds/roses Stratford shade; B3014 std 9,900.00
Puffy 16" butterflies/roses Albemarl shade; B3000 std 11,000.00
Puffy 16" hummingbirds/roses Devonshire sgn shade; urn std ..6,875.00
Puffy 5" mums/roses Concord sgn shade; sgn std 2,600.00
Puffy 8" roses/butterfly shade w/closed top; #3047 std 4,400.00
Rvpt 15" city/fishermen sgn Palme cone shade; 3-strap std 1,500.00
Rvpt 16" unsgn cone shade w/florals at bottom; C3017 std 1,800.00
Rvpt 17" sailing ship Exeter shade w/sea horses; D3054 std 7,700.00
Rvpt 18" parrots/jungle Carlisle shade; std w/3 strap legs 6,000.00
Rvpt 18" peacocks/wall/roses shade; std w/3 scroll legs 9,300.00
Rvpt 18" Persian Many Blossom sgn Berkeley shade; urn std ..2,300.00
Rvpt 20" scenic border Ambero shade; bronzed std, 25" 1,540.00
Rvpt 8" chipped ice water lily shade; glass std 2,400.00
Rvpt 9" seascape Carlisle shade sgn Frek; vasiform std, 15" 1,600.00

Pairpoint Limoges

Limoges china blanks were imported from France in strict accordance with Pairpoint specifications. They were decorated by Pairpoint in designs that ranged from simple to elaborate florals and scenics. These are easily identified. Look for the Pairpoint name over a crown with the Limoges name below. You may also find similar ware marked 'Pairpoint Minton.'

Box, jewel; roses, pk/wht on gr, kidney shape, 7½" L 195.00
Ewer, mums on wine, gilt emb scrolls at base, 16" 1,000.00
Gravy boat, Dresden mc floral, ornate hdl, +undertray 175.00
Jewel casket, Delft, florals/scrolls/windmills/boats, 8" L 550.00
Tea caddy, peonies, pk on brn/gr, 4x3½" 185.00
Vase, mums, pk/red on gr, 8½" 200.00
Vase, spider mums, pk & red w/gr, sgn/#d, 8½" 195.00

Paper Dolls

No one knows quite how or when paper dolls originated. One belief is that they began in Europe as 'pantins' (jumping jacks) and were frequently worn as part of the costume. By the late 1790s they were being mass-produced. During the 19th century most paper dolls portrayed famous dancers and opera stars such as Fanny Elssler and Jenny Lind. In the late 1800s the Raphael Tuck Publishers of England produced many series of beautiful paper dolls; retail companies used them as advertisements to further the sale of their products. Around the turn of the century, many popular women's magazines began featuring a page of paper dolls.

Most familiar to today's collectors are the books with dolls on cardboard covers and clothes on the inside pages. These made their appearance in the late 1920s and early thirties. The most collectible (and the most valuable) are those representing celebrities, movie stars, and comic-strip characters of the thirties and forties.

Authority Mary Young has compiled an informative book, *Collector's Guide to Paper Dolls*, with current prices; her address is in the Directory under Ohio. When no condition is indicated, the dolls listed below are assumed to be in mint, uncut, original condition. Cut sets will be worth about half price if all dolls and outfits are included and pieces are in very good condition. If dolls were produced in die-cut form, these prices reflect such a set in mint condition with all costumes and accessories.

Celebrity paper dolls: Rock Hudson, Jane Powell, M, $60.00 each.

Angela Cartwright, 5 dolls, Transogram, 1960, complete 85.00
Ann Blythe, Merrill, #2550-25, 1952, NM 75.00
Annette Funicello, Whitman, 1958, EX 30.00
Ava Gardner, Whitman, #119215, 1949, 1952, EX 65.00
Baby Peggy, uncut magazine sheet, color 12.50
Babyland, Merrill, #3642, 1955, NM 60.00
Barbie & Skipper, Whitman, #1957, 1964, M 18.00
Barbie Boutique, Whitman #1954, 1973, VG 11.00
Belle of the Ball Paper Dolls, Saalfield, #2702, 1948, EX 32.00

Betsy McCall, Whitman, #4744, 1971, EX 12.00

Beverly Hillbillies, Whitman, #1955, 1964, EX 30.00

Black Lydia, uncut, 1970s, NM 7.50

Bob Hope & Dorothy Lamour, Whitman, #976, 1942, NM 200.00

Bride & Groom, Merrill #3443, 1949, M 70.00

Buffy Paper Dolls, Whitman, #1955, 1968, EX 18.00

Charming Paper Dolls, Saalfield, #1357, ca 1960, VG+ 8.00

Cinderella Steps Out, Lowe, #1242, EX 20.00

Claudette Colbert, Saalfield, #2451, 1943, EX 180.00

Connie Francis, Whitman, #1956, 1963, VG+ 44.00

Cowgirl Jill & Cowboy Joe, Merrill, #3459, VG 27.00

Cyd Charisse, Whitman, #2084, 1956, EX 57.00

Daisy & Donald Duck, uncut, 1970s, NM 6.50

Deanna Durbin, Merrill, #3480, 1940, VG 180.00

Debbie Reynolds, Whitman, cut, 1955, EX 25.00

Diana Lynn, Saalfield, #157910, 1953, EX 58.00

Dick the Sailor, Samuel Lowe, #L1074, ca 1942, EX 33.00

Dina Shore, cut, folders 35.00

Dodie from My Three Sons TV Series, Artcraft, #5115, '71, VG ..20.00

Donna Reed, Saalfield/Artcraft, #5197, 1960, VG 45.00

Doris Day, Whitman, #210325, 1952, EX 58.00

Dorothy Provine, Whitman, #1964, 1962, VG+ 44.00

Double Wedding, Merrill, #3472, 1939, NM 93.00

Down on the Farm, Lowe, #1056, 1940s, EX 27.00

Dr Kildare & Nurse Susan, Lowe, #2740, 1960s, NM 34.00

Drum Major & Majorette, Merrill, #3415, 1941, EX 55.00

Elizabeth Taylor, Whitman, #973-10, 1950s, VG 63.00

Esther Williams, Merrill, #1563, 1950, M 83.00

Eve Arden, Saalfield, #158510, 1953, EX 54.00

Family Affair, Whitman, #4767, 1968, M 30.00

Family Princess, Merrill, #1548, 1958, EX 57.00

Fire Fighters in Action, Saalfield, 1938, M 50.00

Flying Nun, Artcraft, #4417, 1968, 1969, EX 23.00

Frontier Fort, Merrill, #257225, 1952, EX 17.00

Gigi Perreau, Saalfield, #2605, 1951, NM 48.00

Girl Friend - Boy Friend, Saalfield, #1605, 1955, M 20.00

Girl Pilots of the Ferry Command, Merrill, #4852, 1943, VG 78.00

Girls in Uniform, #L1048, 1942, VG 55.00

Gone with the Wind, Merrill, #3404, 1940, NM 350.00

Good Neighbor, Saalfield, #2487, 1944, M 28.00

Gordon MacRae & Shirley Jones, Whitman, VG 25.00

Grace Kelly, Whitman, #2069, 1956, EX 58.00

Harry the Soldier, Samuel, Lowe, #L1074, 1941, EX 33.00

Hee Haw, Artcraft, #5139, 1971, VG 20.00

Heidi & Peter, Saalfield, #1355, ca 1970, EX 12.00

Here Comes the Bride, Whitman, #118915, 1952, NM 28.00

High School Girls, Merrill, #1551, 1948, M 65.00

Hollywood Fashions, Saalfield, #1535, 1949, VG 25.00

Jane Russell, Saalfield, #2611, 1955, M 75.00

Janet Leigh, Abbott, #1805, 1958, VG 48.00

Jaunty Juniors, #903, 1946, M 28.00

June Allyson, Whitman, folder, 1956, EX 45.00

Karen Goes to College, Merrill, #1564, 1955, EX 27.00

Kitty Goes to Kindergarten, Merrill, #1548, 1956, VG 27.00

Lennon Sisters, partially cut, complete in orig folder, VG 17.50

Liberty Belles, Merrill, #3477, 1943, M 60.00

Linda (Mousketeer), ballerina, EX 20.00

Little Ballerina, Merrill, #154215, 1953, NM 55.00

Lucille Ball, Saalfield, #2475, 1944, M 95.00

Martha Hyer, Saalfield, #4423, 1958, M 47.00

Mary Martin, Saalfield, #2427, 1942, EX+ 180.00

Mary Poppins, Whitman, #1977, 1973, VG 20.00

Our Nurse Nancy, uncut, Whitman, 1943, EX in box 48.00

Paper Doll Family & Their House, cut, #2094, 39-pc 60.00

Pert & Pretty, Merrill, #1552, 1948, M 55.00

Peter Pan & Wendy (B Bronson/M Brian), uncut magazine sheet ..12.50

Pig Tails, Merrill, #344410, 1949, M 47.00

Pink Wedding, Merrill, #1559, 1952, M 65.00

Pollykins Pudge, by Barbara Hale, uncut magazine sheet 12.50

Prince Valiant & Princess Aleta, Saalfield, 1954, M 65.00

Raggedy Ann & Andy, Saalfield, #2719, 1953 ....35.00

Roy Rogers & Dale Evans, #995, 1948, EX 60.00

Shirley Temple, uncut, 18", NM 95.00

Uncle Sam's Little Helpers, cut, #1430, 1943, 64-pc in book 35.00

Paperweights

All paperweights listed here are made totally of glass (including the lampwork flowers, fish, birds, snakes, lizards, and millefiori rods). The only elements that are not glass are the clay sulfides encased within some of the Baccarat and St. Louis weights. Today, antique weights (1845 to ca 1870s) and those made by contemporary artists attract the most attention and are the most expensive. Lower-priced 'gift' weights come from American glasshouses and studios, China, Murano, Italy, and Scotland. But because of the expenses involved in their manufacture (fuel, material, and labor), even they are not cheap. There is an international association of paperweight collectors with many state and regional chapters. (For information see Clubs, Newsletters, and Catalogs in the Directory.) Many books are currently available on the subject of paperweights. For the beginner we recommend *All About Paperweights* by L.H. Selmen.

Probably inspired by the work of Pierre Bigaglia (Venice), the French factories of Baccarat, Clichy, and St. Louis turned their attention to paperweight-making in the 1840s. They first made millefiori paperweights, the technique a revival of methods used in Alexandria, Damascus, Rome, and Byzantium before the time of Christ. (This art form had faded out but had been revived in 16th-century Venice.) The French Classic period was 1845 to 1860; English and American (Sandwich and New England) glasshouses followed their lead about ten years later. Gradually, as the paperweight's popularity declined, production began to wane; Clichy closed in the 1880s. Baccarat made weights as late as 1910; in the '20s and '30s, a worker by the name of Dupont revived the art. Then in the 1950s St. Louis and Baccarat sparked a renewal of interest in weight-making that is still going strong today. Some of the most desirable weights from American artists were made by the Banfords, Randall Grubb, Rick Ayotte, Chris Buzzini, Ken Rosenfeld, Gordon Smith, Paul Stankard, Charles Kaziun (d), Del (d), Debbie Tarsitano, and the Trabuccos. From Scotland, Paul Ysart (d) was also well known.

Note: Prices do not reflect the usual 10% buyer's fee charged by most auction houses. Furthermore, there are many factors which determine value, particularly of antique weights. Auction-realized prices of contemporary weights are usually other than issue price; 'list price' may be for weights issued earlier and reduced for clearance or influenced by market demand and other factors. The dimension given at the end of the description is diameter.

Key:

A — antique	latt — latticinio
cl — clear	mill — milleflori
con — concentric	o/l — overlay
fct — faceted	pm — pastry mold
gar — garland	pwt — paperweight
grd — ground	sil — silhouette
jsp — jasper	

Ayotte, Rick

Christmas poinsettia bouquet on cl grd, 1991, 3¼" 600.00
Illusion: hummingbird/flowers, window+bk cut, '92, 4" 1,200.00
Lav/rust/yel mums+3 buds, ltd ed, 1991, 3¾" 900.00
Poppy bouquet on cl grd, 1992, 3¾" 850.00
Red salamander on sand, lily/rocks/mushrooms/etc, '91, 3½" ..1,200.00
Rose, pk petals w/dk pk center, gr leaves/stem, fct, '92, 2" 250.00
Sea gull on piling on cobalt grd, 1980, ltd ed, 2¾" 300.00

Baccarat, Antique

Butterfly over dbl clematis & bud, star base, 3" 12,500.00
Close pack mil, complex canes, 3¼" 1,100.00
Close pack mushroom w/torsade, star base, 3" 1,800.00
Gar pansy, cl star base, 2¾" 2,000.00
Scramble w/variations of mc latt twists, 2½" 450.00
Spaced mill on muslin, moth cane+dog/goat/deer sil, 2" 750.00

Sulfide of Robert E. Lee, 1955, 3", $350.00.

Sulfide of Napoleon, cl grd, 1¾" 750.00
4 flower bouquet w/pansy/rose/clematis/wallflower, fct, 3¾" 18,000.00

Baccarat, Modern

Butterfly, flower & bud on bl grd, 3⅛" 525.00
Dupont type, circles around complex cane set-up, 1930s 400.00
Dupont type, interlaced trefoil gar, 1930s 400.00
Snake, 1979, 3⅛" 575.00
Sulfide of Harry Truman, o/l, 1973, 3" 300.00
Sulfide of Teddy Roosevelt, fct o/l, 1967, 3¼" 350.00

Banford, Bob

2 flowers+buds+4 pears+4 cherries, star-cut base, '92, 3⅝" 2,000.00
3 pansies+2 buds tied w/wht ribbon, dmn-cut base, '92, 3¼" 800.00
3 pears on branch, red/wht bl torsade, star-cut base, '92, 3" 750.00

Banford, Bobby

Buckeye compound, sm yel flowers, seeds on bottom, '91, 3¼" ...600.00
Pk flower w/6 buds, leaves, & knotweeds, 1992, 3⅛" 600.00

Violets, 3 flowers+3 buds, star-cut base, 1992, 3" 450.00
6 pk & wht Hawthorn blossoms & buds, 1992, 3⅛" 550.00

Banford, Ray

3 pk roses+3 buds, gr leaves/stems, ftc, 3" 800.00
5 purple iris in fancy/cut yel & wht o/l, 1992, 3¼" 1,400.00
5 ruby red roses on latt grd & torsade, 1992, 3⅛" 800.00

Buzzini, Chris

Coronilla varia (crown vetch), pk/wht, w/root system, 1991 ......475.00
Epiphytiv orchid blossoms/buds/leaves/etc, ltd ed 40, 1992 ....600.00
Mitre-cut w/wyethias & pk wildflowers, 1992, ltd ed 25, 3⅜" ...1,100.00
Yel China rose+2 buds & 2 purple asters+bud, 1991, 3" 550.00

Caithness

Aspiration, modern wht flower w/flame center, amber grd, '92 ..195.00
Contour, design suggests name, ltd ed 750, 1992 ....175.00
Dragonfly & snail w/flowers & simulated water, ltd ed, 1992 .....675.00
Faceted raspberry w/3 berries/etc on amber grd, ltd ed, 1992 ......675.00
Luckenbooth, hearts/mill cane gar on pk swirls 135.00
Paintbox, primary colors, cranberry bubble, ltd 150.00

Clichy, Antique

Gar of intertwined loops on gr grd, 3¼" 2,000.00
Pk & wht swirl w/complex center cane, 2⅞" 1,500.00
Spaced mil, pk/gr Clichy rose w/in 17 mc complex canes, 2¼" ...575.00

Donofrio, Jim

Blk raspberries w/leaves on branch, 1992, 3½" 750.00
Frog on lily pads w/lily over transparent gr water, '92, 3⅝" 1,000.00
South West series, Indian pot+corn+peppers+garlic, '92, 3⅝" ...900.00
South West series, 2 pots+jade flower+leprechaun, '92, 3⅝" ...1,000.00

Grubb, Randy

Compound gr grapes on cl grd, 3¼" 375.00
Plum blossoms+wht flowers w/yel stamens on branch 425.00
Purple dahlia on cl grd, 1987, 3" 250.00
Sprigs of knotweed+4 bl blossoms & 4 red flowers on cl 400.00
15 plum blossoms+buds & leaves, dbl o/l, flute-cut, 3¼" 800.00
2 dahlias (1 red/1 lav)+2 violets & yel floral spray, 3¼" 400.00

Kaziun, Charles

Bl/wht morning-glory+bud on 2-leaf stem on amethyst grd, 2" ...875.00
Mini bl/gold/wht pansy w/bud/gold foil bee on purple, 2⅛" 950.00
Pk crimp rose w/yel & wht o/l, 2⅜" 1,600.00

Lundberg Studios

Lundberg, S; Daisy Cluster, 3 levels of daisies 325.00
Lundberg, S; red hibiscus on cl grd, 1991, 3¼" 250.00
Lundberg, S; Underwater Seascape, ltd ed, 4½" 750.00
Lundberg, S; Underwater Seascape, 3" 270.00
Lundberg, S; voilet chrysanthemum on cl grd, 1991, 3¼" 300.00
Salazar, D; Am Dream, red flower+2 wht buds on bl, '92, 3⅝" ...600.00
Salazar, D; butterfly over clematis 250.00
Salazar, D; single angel fish, ltd ed, 1992, 3¼" 240.00

Manson, William

Lizard & flowers, 1991, 3½" 600.00
Pansy over wht swirl grd, 1992, 3" 300.00
Snake & flowers, 1991, 3½" 600.00
3-color crown w/complex top cane, 1992, 2¾" 300.00
5-petal pk & wht flower over wht latt, 1992, 3" 300.00

New England Glass

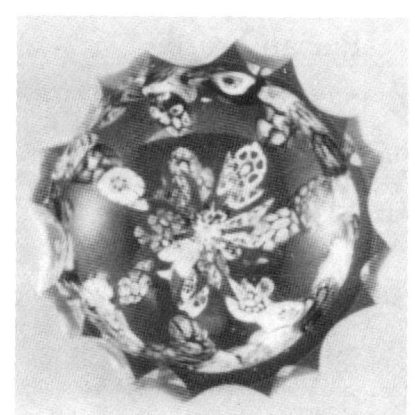

New England faceted
weight, patterned pinwheel
of multicolored canes on
clear, facets and top star,
3", EX, $350.00.

Crown, 2⅛" 950.00
Gar posy on latt, 2¼" 850.00
Scramble, complete cane w/3 rabbit sil, partial w/2, 2½" 225.00
Spaced con on latt basket, 2½" 350.00
5 apples+4 cherries & leaves on wht latt cushion, 3¼" 950.00

Parabelle

Close con mill, central Clichy rose on gr, '92, 3" 225.00
Con mill w/central pk Clichy rose on moss grd, '92, 2¼" 300.00
Mill heart+matching gar on muslin grd, ltd ed 185.00
Parabelle, mill circles w/sil on muslin grd, 1986, 3¼" 170.00
Spaced con w/7 Clichy roses, pk stardust grd, 1992, 2⅞" 600.00

Perthshire

Aquarium, fct, 1981, 3½" 400.00
Bouquet, fct bl & wht o/l, 1982, 2¾" 450.00
Crown, twist ribbons & filigree alternate, 1990 ed, mini 245.00
Gar flower on gr grd, 1982, 2½" 250.00
Nosegay on pk & chartreuse latt, 1977, 2¼" 225.00
Pansy w/in gar of dk bl/wht mill on upset muslin, fct, 1971 ....250.00
Patterned mill w/horse sil, 1982, 2½" 175.00
Strawberries/leaves+1 open & 3 closed buds, fct, 1986, 2½" 400.00
Turtle dove, fct, Christmas 1991, 3" 350.00

Rosenfeld, Ken

Cluster of red blossoms+3 buds, brn branches, 3" 375.00
Daffodils on bl grd, 3¼" 500.00
Fall Bouquet: 3 red zinnias/yel flower+7 mc buds, '91, 3½" 600.00
Fiesta: 4 ears of corn+16 red peppers, corn stalks, '91, 3½" 400.00
Marine Life: crab & starfish on water's floor, '92, 3¼" 600.00
Marine Life: lobster, 1992 ....600.00
Pk thistles w/realistic foliage, 3½" 600.00
Pumpkin Patch, 3" 350.00
Raspberries, 3½" 400.00
Stylized roses, clematis, bellflowers w/buds on cl grd 400.00

Thistles on cl grd, 1992, 3¼" 600.00
Tomatoes on vine w/leaves, 1992, 3½" 400.00
2 orange zinnias+2 buds, 2 yel flowers+bud on bl grd, '91, 3" 400.00
2 red roses+bud w/gr leaves on bl grd, 1991 ....375.00
3 bl+2 pk flowers w/buds on gr/wht honeycomb canes, 3½" 600.00
3 orange CA poppies w/2 buds, gr leaves/stems, 1991, 3½" 375.00
8 flowers in 4 colors+9 in purple on earth grd, 1991, 3½" 600.00

Smith, Gordon

Ocean Interior: Tomato Clown fish pr, cobalt grd, '92, 3¼" 800.00
Ocean Interior: 2 Skunk Anemone fish+anemones/coral, 3½" 800.00
Paphiopedilum Rothchildianum orchids+bud+foliage, '92, 3¼" 700.00
3 dogwood flowers w/twisted leaves, 1992 ....750.00
3 pk peach blossoms+2 buds, 1992, 3" 750.00
5 raspberries+blossom & bud on stems, 1992, 3" 800.00
5 strawberries w/buds on bl grd, 1992 ....800.00

St. Louis, Antique

Crown, 10 red/gr twist ribbons alternate w/latt twists, 2½" 3,500.00
Scramble, muslin grd, 1 6-petal red-center wht flower, 2¾" 425.00
Sulfide of Napoleon, 24-point star in base, att, 2¾" 675.00
Upright bouquet, fct, w/torsade, 2¾" 3,500.00
Upright bouquet on gr leaves, honeycomb ftc, 2" 650.00
4-cane nosegay+5 leaves, top fct+7 sm+6 lg on side, 2½" 650.00

St. Louis, Modern

Bl flowers on latt, 1987, 2¾" 550.00
Flower on orange grd, 1973, 3" 350.00
Kaleidoscope, yel, 1984, 3" 550.00
Lilies of the valley on ruby red grd, 1982, 3¼" 450.00
Mini apple w/2 gr leaves on lt bl grd, top fct, 1992, 2½" 250.00
Scattered mill, wht carpet grd, 1982, 3" 575.00
2 yel Clichy-type roses+bud & leaves in opaque bl, 1976 ....375.00

Stankard, Paul

Braided bouquet w/6 mixed flowers+sm yel blossoms, 1982 .....2,750.00
Mini yel meadow & wreath on gr grd, 1973, 2⅜" 500.00
Triple meadow wreath, 1976 ....1,500.00
2 pk tea roses w/3 buds, 1982, ltd ed 50, 3" 1,900.00

Tarsitano, Debbie

Fall daisy garden on cl grd, compound, 3½" 1,000.00
12 pk buds & wht flower sprigs tied w/bow, bl grd, 2¾" 550.00
5 pk flowers on gr-leaf brn stem in hdld vase on bl grd, 3" 650.00

Tarsitano, Delmo

Spider on natural grd, 3¼" 1,200.00
Strawberry & blossom w/leaves, 2¾" 350.00
2 peaches on branch w/6 leaves, 3" 800.00

Trabucco, Jon and David

Flowers & buds on bl, 1988, 3" 300.00
Pk rose w/pk buds & 6 sm bl buds, 1992, 3" 300.00
3 red raspberries w/pk flowers & buds, 1992, 3½" 400.00
8 blueberries w/pk flowers & buds, 1992, 3½" 400.00

Trabucco, Victor

Camellias, frosted/cvd sides, 1992, 3" 700.00
Morning-glory bouquet on cl grd, 1992, 3¼" 600.00
Pk rose+bud, buttercup+bud & 2 morning-glories in cl, 14" 950.00

Whittemore, Francis D.

Calla lilies on bl grd, 1970s, 2½" 350.00
Milleville-type yel-crimp rose, ped, 2½" H 400.00

Ysart, Paul

Butterfly in mill/red aventurine on dk amethyst, sgn, 3" 650.00
Dragonfly in gold/red aventurine & wht latt on cobalt, 3¼" 650.00
Pk flower on lt bl mottled grd, 2¼" 600.00
2 orange ducks on pond w/flower & gravel, fct, blk ft, 3½" 900.00

Miscellaneous Antique

Bacchus, con mill, sil of lady+4 rows of serrated canes, 3½" 900.00
Bohemian scatter on muslin w/monkey & dog sil, 3" 1,200.00
Boston & Sandwich, magnum poinsettia, 3½" 950.00
Gillinder, att; glass, sleeping child w/toy in base, 4½" 150.00
Pinchbeck fct, allegorical scene, 2¼" 950.00

Miscellaneous Modern

Bagwell, Don; 2 fish swim w/in ocean's environment, 3¾" 90.00
Ward, Mayauel; cube form w/multiflora, half blk, 2½" 450.00
Ward, Mayauel; 2 pk blooms+4 buds w/3 rocks on sand, 2¼" 240.00

Papier-Mache

The art of papier-mache was mainly European. It originated in Paris around the middle of the 18th century and became popular in America during Victorian times. Small items such as boxes, trays, inkwells, frames, etc., as well as extensive ceiling moldings and larger articles of furniture were made. The process involved building layer upon layer of paper soaked in glue, then coaxed into shape over a wood or wire form. When dry it was painted or decorated with gilt or inlays. Inexpensive 20th-century 'notions' were machine processed and mold pressed. See also Christmas; Candy Containers.

Tea tray, castle and figures in landscape, 1840s, 32" long, $3,000.00.

Box, blk w/MOP inlay roses, gold scrolls, 4 vials w/in, 4" 325.00
Box, powder; mock tortoise shell, HP florals, Victorian 80.00
Chicken, mc pnt, wood base, 3⅝", EX 75.00
Horn, monkey w/organ decor, wood mouthpc, Germany, 1915 ....10.00
Mannequin, bust of lady, French, mk Roland, 15" 800.00
Snuff box, comic hand-colored print on lid, 2", EX 45.00
Tray, floral in mc/gilt on blk lacquer w/nacre inlay, 29" L 450.00
Tray, florals, scalloped, Jennens & Bettridge, 31", +stand 1,400.00
Tray, HP floral, MOP inserts, serpentine, Victorian, 32" L 600.00

Parian Ware

Parian is hard-paste unglazed porcelain made to resemble marble. First made in the mid-1800s by Staffordshire potters, it was soon after produced in the United States by the U.S. Pottery at Bennington, Vermont. Busts and statuary were favored, but plaques, vases, mugs, and pitchers were also made.

Bust, Abraham Lincoln, rnd base, English, 1860, 16" 275.00
Bust, Schiller, Germany, 9½" 175.00
Bust, Shakespeare, on rnd ped base, Wedgwood, 13" 990.00
Bust, Shakespeare, R Monti SC, Copeland, dtd, 1860, 13" 700.00
Bust, Sir Walter Scott, England, 1860, firing lines, 15" 500.00
Bust, Stephenson, rnd ped base, 1858, Wedgwood, 14", EX 700.00
Cup & saucer, emb lotus flowers, hdl, mk, EX lg 40.00
Figurine, Bather Surprised, Royal Worcester, rstr, 26" 385.00
Figurine, Clorinda dressed in armor, Minton, 1864, 14" 400.00
Figurine, Dorothea seated on rock, Minton, 14", EX 350.00
Figurine, John A Andrews, bk: verse, Milmore SC, 21", EX 1,200.00
Figurine, Maidenhood, titled, Copeland, 22", EX 250.00
Figurine, Young Columbus, seated on post, titled, 16", EX 495.00
Group, owls on branch, titled Matchmaking, 1871 mk, 7" 245.00
Pitcher, Geo WA in relief, angle hdl, scalloped rim, 10" 935.00
Pitcher, hanging game, 9¾" 85.00
Pitcher, vines/leaves, wht on lav, mask spout, Alcock, 10" 275.00

Parrish, Maxfield

Maxfield Parrish was a painter and illustrator who began his career in the last decade of the 19th century. His work remained prominent until the early 1940s. His most famous painting, *Daybreak*, was published in print form and sold nearly two thousand copies between 1910 and 1930. All prices are for framed prints except for those from the 1960s.

Ad, Magic Circle, Fisk Tires, blk/wht, 1900, matted, 8x5½" 60.00
Ad, Pictorial Review, Jell-O, 1924, EX 45.00
Ad, Polly Put the Kettle On, Jell-O, 6x8" 90.00
Book, Arabian Nights, Scribner's, 1909, EX 195.00
Book, Children's Book, Scudder, 1901, EX 65.00
Book, Dream Days, Grahame, Dodd, Mead & Co, 1898, EX 135.00
Book, Garden Years, Carryl, 1st ed, 1904, EX 95.00
Book, Golden Age of the Poster, Dover, 1971, EX 15.00
Book, Golden Treasury of Songs & Lyrics, Palgrave, 1911, NM ...150.00
Book, Knave of Hearts, Saunders, hard-bk, 1925, EX 950.00
Book, Mother Goose in Prose, Baum, 3rd edition, 1905, NM 715.00
Book, Poems of Childhood, Field, Scribner's, 1904, EX 120.00
Calendar, Golden Hours, 1929, complete, sm 195.00
Calendar, Solitude, 1932, complete, sm 175.00
Calendar, Sunrise, 1927, complete, sm, EX 195.00
Calendar, Sunrise, 1933, complete, NM 750.00
Calendar, Venetian Lamplighter, 1924, complete, sm 200.00
Calendar, Venetian Lamplighter, 1924, pad missing, sm, VG 125.00

Calendar, Waterfall, 1931, full pad, sm, EX 200.00
Calendar print, Evening, Brown & Bigelow, 1959, med 95.00
Calendar print, Sheltering Oaks, Brown & Bigelow, 1978, lg 110.00
Calendar print, Silent Night, Brown & Bigelow, 1966, med 135.00
Calendar print, Sunlight, Brown & Bigelow, 1978, med 140.00
Calendar print, Twilight #1, Brown & Bigelow, 1937, extra lg ..200.00
Calendar print, Twilight #3, Brown & Bigelow, 1967, lg 160.00
Calendar print, Winter Twilight, Brown & Bigelow, 1973, sm 90.00
Christmas card, Christmas Eve, 1971 ....20.00
Christmas card, Christmas Morn, 1968 ....20.00

Dreaming, Reinthal and Newman, original frame, 18x30", $850.00.

Frontispiece, Collier's, Circe's Palace, Jan 1908, 9¼x11½" 55.00
Frontispiece, Collier's, History of Prince Codadad..., 9x11" 55.00
Magazine, Illustrated London News, 2 illus, Dec 1922 ....95.00
Magazine cover, Century, Aug 1917 ....70.00
Magazine cover, Life, Chef Sampling Soup, Sept 1923 ....88.00
Magazine cover, Progressive Farmer, June 1952 ....35.00
Magazine cover, Scribner's, Errant Pan, Aug 1910, 5½x7" 70.00
Magazine cover, Scribner's, girl by pool w/book, Aug 1899 ....120.00
Magazine cover, Scribner's, shepherd w/purple robe, Dec 1899 ....98.00
Poster, bicyclist, Columbia Bicycles, 1896, 28x44" 2,000.00
Poster, Peter Pumpkin Eater, Ferry Seeds, 1918, 19x19" 995.00
Print, Air Castles, EX fr, 11x15" 195.00
Print, An Ancient Tree, Brown & Bigelow, 1952, 10x10" 150.00
Print, An Ancient Tree, matted in fr, 1952, 5½x7½" 75.00
Print, Cadmus Sowing the Dragon's Teeth, 9½x12" 145.00
Print, Canyon, 1924, 12x15" 195.00
Print, Cleopatra, House of Art, 1917, 15x16" 600.00
Print, Daybreak, dtd 1935, orig fr, 23½x19" 225.00
Print, Daybreak, House of Art, orig Nouveau fr, 18x30" 400.00
Print, Daybreak, 1922, 10½x18" 155.00
Print, Daybreak, 6x10" 95.00
Print, Daybreak #1, Brown & Bigelow, 1951, 10x10" 140.00
Print, Enchanted Prince, Brown & Bigelow, 7⅜x6⅞" 70.00
Print, Errant Pan, Scribner's, 1910, 9x11" 125.00
Print, Evening Shadows #1, Brown & Bigelow, 1940, 10x10" 235.00
Print, Florentine Fete, 7x11" 125.00
Print, Garden of Allah, 30x15", EX 345.00
Print, Garden of Allah, 8¼x4¼" 90.00
Print, Garden of Allah, 9x18" 165.00
Print, Garden of Opportunity, triptych, 1925, 24x25" 400.00
Print, Glen, Brown & Bigelow, 1938, 10x10" 175.00
Print, Hilltop, 1927, 12x20" 450.00
Print, Lantern Bearers, Brown & Bigelow, blk/wht, 10x12" 140.00
Print, Lantern Bearers, Brown & Bigelow, 8½x7" 18.00
Print, Lute Players, EX fr, 6x10" 200.00
Print, Lute Players, House of Art, M fr, 18x30", EX 750.00
Print, Morning, 1926, 12x15" 215.00
Print, Morning Light, Brown & Bigelow, 1957, 8½x11" 95.00
Print, Peaceful Valley #2, Brown & Bigelow, 1955, 5x6" 60.00
Print, Perfect Day, 1943, new fr, 5½x7" 50.00

Print, Prince, Brown & Bigelow, 16x14", M 240.00
Print, Quiet Solitude, Brown & Bigelow, 16x19" 125.00
Print, Romance, 14x23" 700.00
Print, Royal Gorge, 1925, old gold fr, 17½x14½", EX 250.00
Print, Rubiayat, Reinthal & Newman, 4½x15" 235.00
Print, Sheltering Oaks, Brown & Bigelow, 16x19" 150.00
Print, Silent Night (Twilight Time 1960), 1966, 5½x7½" 62.50
Print, Spirit of Transportation, 1923, 16x20" 550.00
Print, Thy Templed Hills, 1936, 18½x13" 250.00
Print, Twilight, Brown & Bigelow, 16x19", 1961 ....175.00
Print, Under Summer Skies, Brown & Bigelow, 1959, 16x19" ...175.00
Print, Where the Dinkey Bird Is Singing, 11x15" 225.00
Print, White Birch, 5x6" 68.00
Print, Wild Geese, 1924, 12x15" 195.00

Pattern Glass

Pattern Glass was the first mass-produced fancy tableware in America and was much prized by our ancestors. From the 1840s to the Civil War, it contained a high lead content and is known as 'flint glass.' It is exceptionally clear and resonant. Later glass was made with soda lime and is known as non-flint. By the 1890s pattern glass was produced in great volume in thousands of patterns, and colored glass came into vogue. Today the highest prices are often paid for these later patterns flashed with rose, amber, canary, and vaseline, stained ruby, or made in colors of cobalt, green, yellow, amethyst, etc. Demand for pattern glass declined by 1915, and glass fanciers were collecting it by 1930. No other field of antiques offers more diversity in patterns, prices, or pieces than this unique and historical glass that represents the Victorian era in America.

Our advisor for this category is Darlene Yohe; she is listed in the Directory under Arkansas. For a more thorough study on the subject, we recommend *The Collector's Encyclopedia of Pattern Glass* by Mollie Helen McCain, available from Collector Books. See also Bread Plates; Cruets; Historical Glass; Salt and Pepper Shakers; Salts, Open; Sugar Shakers; Syrups; specific manufacturers such as Northwood.

Note: Values are given for open sugar bowls and compotes unless noted 'w/lid.'

Actress, bowl, ftd, 6" 42.50
Actress, compote, high std, 10" 95.00
Actress, creamer 75.00
Actress, pitcher, water; 9" 250.00
Actress, shakers, orig tops, pr 90.00
Admiral Dewey, see Dewey; See Also Greentown, Dewey
Alabama, butter dish, ruby stained 145.00
Alabama, creamer, ruby stained 55.00
Alabama, shakers, pr 60.00
Alabama, sugar bowl, w/lid 45.00
Alabama, toothpick holder, ruby stained 135.00
Almond Thumbprint, butter dish, flint 75.00
Almond Thumbprint, goblet, non-flint 15.00
Almond Thumbprint, tumbler, flint 45.00
Amazon, bowl, scalloped, 8" 24.00
Amazon, egg cup 12.50
Amazon, shakers, etched, pr 48.00
Amberette, see Klondike
Anthemion, marmalade 40.00
Anthemion, plate, 10" 50.00
Apollo, celery vase, flint 60.00
Apollo, compote, w/lid, 8¾x4¾" 50.00
Apollo, spooner 38.00
Apollo, tumbler 25.00

Arched Ovals, bowl, w/lid, 7" 38.00
Arched Ovals, shakers, gr, pr 48.00
Arched Ovals, tumbler, ruby stained 28.00
Argus, bottle, bitters 65.00
Argus, celery vase, plain base 85.00
Argus, goblet 38.00
Argus, sugar bowl, w/lid 60.00
Argus, wine 48.00
Art, butter dish, ruby stained 90.00
Art, celery vase 45.00
Art, creamer, regular 48.00

Art

Ashburton, carafe 165.00
Ashburton, decanter, canary yel, flint, orig stopper ...950.00
Ashburton, tumbler, lemonade 60.00
Ashburton, wine, cut decor 68.00
Atlas, butter dish 47.50
Atlas, cordial 40.00
Atlas, jelly compote, ruby stained, w/lid, 5" 60.00
Atlas, tumbler 32.00
Aurora, butter dish, ruby stained 87.50
Aurora, celery vase 32.50
Aurora, pitcher, water 45.00
Aurora, waste bowl 30.00
Austrian, bowl, 8" 50.00
Austrian, cordial, amber 148.00
Austrian, goblet 38.00
Austrian, punch cup 20.00
Austrian, spooner 38.00
Austrian, tumbler 24.00
Baby Thumbprint, see Dakota
Balder, see Pennsylvania
Baltimore Pear, cake stand, high std 50.00
Baltimore Pear, goblet 35.00
Baltimore Pear, pitcher, water 98.00
Banded Portland, candlestick, pr 85.00
Banded Portland, compote, high std, w/lid, 7" 98.00
Banded Portland, goblet 38.00
Banded Portland, ring holder 70.00
Bar & Diamond, compote, high std, 6" 28.00
Bar & Diamond, sugar bowl, w/lid 55.00
Bar & Diamond, tumbler 22.50
Barberry, bowl, oval, 7" 22.50
Barberry, celery vase 37.50
Barberry, pitcher, water 80.00
Barberry, tumbler, ftd 22.50
Barley, bowl, oval, 10" 15.00
Barley, compote, high std, w/lid, 6" 48.00
Barley, platter, 13" 28.00
Barred Forget-Me-Not, goblet 40.00

Barred Forget-Me-Not, sugar bowl, w/lid 40.00
Barrel Huber, see Huber
Basket Weave, bowl, amber 22.50
Basket Weave, egg cup, apple gr 28.00
Basket Weave, mug, 3" 20.00
Basket Weave, wine, vaseline 32.00
Beaded Acorn Medallion, pitcher, water 145.00
Beaded Acorn Medallion, sugar bowl, w/lid 42.50
Beaded Band, butter dish 37.50
Beaded Band, creamer 32.00
Beaded Band, spooner 25.00
Beaded Grape, bowl, gr, sq, 5½" 22.50
Beaded Grape, butter dish, sq 62.50
Beaded Grape, sauce dish, hdls 15.00
Beaded Grape, sugar bowl, w/lid 70.00
Beaded Grape Medallion, cake stand 135.00
Beaded Grape Medallion, goblet, buttermilk 32.00
Beaded Grape Medallion, honey dish, 3½" 12.00
Beaded Medallion, butter dish 42.50
Beaded Medallion, compote, low std, w/lid, 8¼" ...88.00
Beaded Medallion, egg cup 24.00
Beaded Mirror, see Beaded Medallion
Beaded Swirl, cake stand, gr 40.00
Beaded Swirl, compote, high std 32.00
Beaded Swirl, pitcher, water; gr 60.00
Beaded Tulip, creamer 88.00
Beaded Tulip, pitcher, water 70.00
Beaded Tulip, tray, water 50.00
Bearded Head, see Viking
Bellflower, bowl, scalloped, 8" 75.00
Bellflower, bowl, single vine, 6" 70.00
Bellflower, champagne, single vine, knob stem 100.00
Bellflower, cordial, single vine, bbl shape 120.00
Bellflower, decanter, bar-top; dbl vine, 1-pt 235.00
Bellflower, pitcher, water; dbl vine 345.00
Bellflower, sugar bowl, dbl vine, w/lid 98.00
Bent Buckle, see New Hampshire
Bigler, celery vase 90.00
Bigler, decanter, bar lip, 1-pt 60.00
Bird & Fern, see Hummingbird
Bird & Strawberry, bowl, 5½" 32.00
Bird & Strawberry, compote, high std, w/color stains ...195.00
Bird & Strawberry, creamer 55.00
Bird & Strawberry, goblet, w/color stains 285.00
Bird & Strawberry, plate, 12" 120.00
Bird & Strawberry, tumbler 50.00
Bird & Strawberry, wine 65.00
Bleeding Heart, cake stand, 10" 88.00
Bleeding Heart, creamer, molded hdl 27.50
Bleeding Heart, spooner 25.00
Bleeding Heart, wine, knob stem 165.00
Block & Fan, bowl, flat, 4" 15.00
Block & Fan, carafe, ruby stained 95.00
Block & Fan, creamer, regular 27.50
Block & Fan, goblet 50.00
Block & Fan, ice tub, ruby stained 48.00
Block & Fan, pickle dish 18.00
Block & Fan, tumbler, ruby stained 42.50
Blue Jay, see Cardinal Bird
Bohemian, butter dish, gr w/gold 125.00
Bohemian, mug, rose stained w/gold 80.00
Bouquet, pitcher, water 45.00
Bouquet, sugar bowl, w/lid 32.00
Bow Tie, bowl, flat, 6¾" 42.50

Bow Tie, goblet 62.50
Bow Tie, pitcher, water 55.00
Bow Tie, sugar bowl 37.50
Branched Tree, pitcher, water 75.00
Broken Column, banana stand 115.00
Broken Column, biscuit jar, ruby stained 155.00
Broken Column, champagne 95.00
Broken Column, compote, high std, 8" 78.00
Broken Column, decanter 90.00
Broken Column, tumbler 45.00
Buckle, bowl, flint 8" 55.00
Buckle, compote, high std, w/lid, non-flint, 6" 42.50
Buckle, goblet, flint 40.00
Buckle, salt cellar, flat, flint 32.00
Buckle, wine, non-flint 32.50
Buckle w/Star, bowl, oval, 10" 20.00
Buckle w/Star, cake stand, 9" 38.00
Buckle w/Star, pitcher, water 75.00
Buckle w/Star, sugar bowl 27.50
Bull's Eye, castor bottle 37.50
Bull's Eye, goblet 65.00
Bull's Eye, sugar bowl, w/lid 125.00
Bull's Eye, whiskey 68.00
Bull's Eye & Daisy, shaker 20.00
Bull's Eye & Daisy, spooner 18.00
Bull's Eye & Daisy, tumbler, emerald gr 15.00
Bull's Eye & Fan, bowl, berry; 8" 15.00
Bull's Eye & Fan, goblet, gr 47.50
Bull's Eye & Fan, relish, bl stained 32.00
Bull's Eye & Fan, tumbler, pk stained 67.50
Bull's Eye Band, see Reverse Torpedo
Bull's Eye in Heart, see Heart w/Thumbprint
Bull's Eye w/Diamond Point, bottle, scent 88.00
Bull's Eye w/Diamond Point, celery vase 150.00
Bull's Eye w/Diamond Point, tumbler, water 110.00
Bull's Eye w/Fleur-de-Lis, butter dish 100.00
Bull's Eye w/Fleur-de-Lis, creamer 65.00
Bull's Eye w/Fleur-de-Lis, goblet 80.00
Butterfly, pitcher, water 95.00
Button Arches, creamer 22.50
Button Arches, pitcher, milk; ruby stained 105.00
Button Arches, punch cup 12.50
Button Arches, sugar bowl, ruby stained 80.00
Button Panel, pitcher, water 48.00
Cabbage Rose, basket, 12" 120.00
Cabbage Rose, champagne 45.00
Cabbage Rose, tumbler 37.50
Cabbage Rose, wine 40.00
Cable, bowl, 9" 65.00
Cable, cake stand, 9" 95.00
Cable, creamer, rare 370.00
Cable, plate, 6" 75.00
California, see Beaded Grape
Canadian, butter dish 88.00
Canadian, compote, low std, 6" 55.00
Canadian, goblet 55.00
Canadian, pitcher, milk 95.00
Canadian, spooner 42.50
Cane, creamer, bl 45.00
Cane, spooner, apple gr 37.50
Cane, tray, water; bl 55.00
Cardinal Bird, butter dish 85.00
Cardinal Bird, cake stand 70.00
Cardinal Bird, sugar bowl, w/lid 60.00

Carnation, pitcher, water; ruby stained w/gold 265.00
Cathedral, bowl, berry; vaseline 40.00
Cathedral, compote, low std, 7" 24.00
Cathedral, goblet, amethyst 75.00
Cathedral, relish tray, fish shape, vaseline 50.00
Centennial, see Liberty Bell
Chain, bread plate 30.00
Chain, goblet 24.00
Chain, sugar bowl, w/lid 35.00
Chain & Shield, goblet 27.50
Chain & Shield, pitcher, water 55.00
Chain w/Diamonds, see Washington Centennial
Chain w/Star, bread plate, hdls, 11" 32.50
Chain w/Star, compote, 6½x8" 27.50
Chain w/Star, relish 12.50
Chandelier, banana stand 95.00
Chandelier, creamer 32.00
Chandelier, finger bowl, etched 42.50
Chandelier, pitcher, water 120.00

Checkerboard

Checkerboard, celery vase, ftd, 6½" 17.50
Checkerboard, compote, 8" 27.50
Checkerboard, punch cup 8.00
Cherry & Cable, pitcher, water 82.00
Classic, bowl, hexagonal, open log ft, 8" 115.00
Classic, compote, open log ft, 7¾" 165.00
Classic, pitcher, water; 9½" 345.00
Classic Medallion, marmalade, w/lid 125.00
Classic Medallion, sauce, ftd 10.00
Coin, see US Coin
Colorado, banana stand, bl 40.00
Colorado, cake stand 65.00
Colorado, calling card tray 27.50
Colorado, punch bowl 90.00
Colorado, spooner, gr 55.00
Colorado, sugar bowl, gr, w/lid 78.00
Colorado, tumbler 20.00
Colorado, wine, gr 40.00
Columbian Coin, butter dish, frosted coins 175.00
Columbian Coin, butter dish, gold coins 165.00
Columbian Coin, compote, w/lid, frosted coins, 8" 165.00
Columbian Coin, spooner, gold coins 45.00
Columbian Coin, syrup, frosted coins 185.00
Comet, butter dish 185.00
Comet, pitcher, water 525.00
Compact, see Snail
Connecticut, pitcher, water 50.00
Connecticut, tumbler, lemonade; hdl 20.00
Cord & Tassel, compote, low, 8" 27.50
Cord & Tassel, egg cup 38.00

Cord & Tassel, sugar bowl 55.00
Cord Drapery, butter dish, gr 170.00
Cord Drapery, compote, w/lid, 9" 68.00
Cord Drapery, sugar bowl, gr, w/lid 175.00
Cordova, cake stand 42.50
Cordova, tumbler 17.50
Cottage, butter dish 40.00
Cottage, champagne 70.00
Cottage, plate, 10" 45.00
Cottage, tumbler 20.00
Croesus, bowl, purple, 8" 95.00
Croesus, condiment tray 30.00
Croesus, creamer, purple w/gold, regular 140.00
Croesus, pitcher, water; gr 195.00
Croesus, sauce dish, ftd, amethyst 40.00
Croesus, tumbler, gr w/gold 57.50
Crow's Foot, see Yale
Crown Jewels, see Chandelier
Cryptic, see Zippered Block
Crystal Wedding, compote, 10½" 70.00

Crystal Wedding

Crystal Wedding, goblet 45.00
Crystal Wedding, pitcher, water; ruby stained, sq 235.00
Crystal Wedding, vase, twisted, ftd 27.50
Cube w/Fan, see Pineapple & Fan
Cupid & Venus, bread plate, vaseline, 10½" dia 145.00
Cupid & Venus, champagne 75.00
Cupid & Venus, pitcher, milk 68.00
Cupid & Venus, sugar bowl, w/lid 68.00
Cupid & Venus, wine 90.00
Currant, relish 14.00
Currant, wine 35.00
Currier & Ives, cup & saucer 42.50
Currier & Ives, plate, 10" 18.00
Currier & Ives, tumbler, ftd 45.00
Currier & Ives, wine 16.00
Curtain, bowl, 7½" 22.50
Curtain, butter dish 58.00
Curtain, creamer 30.00
Curtain, sugar bowl, w/lid 38.00
Curtain Tie-Back, creamer 35.00
Curtain Tie-Back, relish 12.50
Cut Log, cake stand, 10" 65.00
Cut Log, jelly dish, w/lid 55.00
Cut Log, relish, boat shape, 9¼" 27.50
Cut Log, tumbler 47.50
Dahlia, cordial, amber 50.00
Dahlia, creamer 24.00
Dahlia, pitcher, water; vaseline 90.00

Dahlia, platter, vaseline 58.00
Dahlia, wine 22.50
Daisy & Button, butter pat, vaseline 38.00
Daisy & Button, celery vase 32.00
Daisy & Button, celery vase, amber 42.50
Daisy & Button, goblet, bl 40.00
Daisy & Button, plate, amber, leaf shape, 5" 22.50
Daisy & Button w/Crossbar, cake stand, bl 90.00
Daisy & Button w/Crossbar, goblet 27.50
Daisy & Button w/Crossbar, pitcher, water; amber 65.00
Daisy & Button w/Crossbar, sugar bowl, bl, w/lid 62.50
Daisy & Button w/Thumbprint Panels, cake stand, 9½" ...52.50
Daisy & Button w/Thumbprint Panels, tumbler, bl panels ...40.00
Daisy & Button w/V Ornament, butter dish, bl 110.00
Daisy & Button w/V Ornament, mug 25.00
Daisy & Button w/V Ornament, tumbler, amber 30.00
Dakota, cake cover, etched, 8" 285.00
Dakota, compote, 9x8" 58.00
Dakota, goblet, ruby stained 75.00
Dakota, pitcher, water; etched 95.00
Dakota, tumbler, etched 30.00
Dart, creamer 34.00
Dart, jelly compote 18.00
Dart, tumbler 18.00
Deer & Dog, butter dish, dog finial 145.00
Deer & Dog, marmalade, w/lid 85.00
Deer & Pine Tree, bowl, 5x8" 25.00
Deer & Pine Tree, bread tray, 8x13" 90.00
Deer & Pine Tree, cake stand, bl 115.00
Delaware, banana bowl 40.00
Delaware, creamer, gr w/gold 60.00
Delaware, finger bowl, rose w/gold 70.00
Delaware, punch cup, rose w/gold 37.50
Dew & Raindrop, bud vase, 6" 25.00
Dew & Raindrop, pitcher, water 48.00
Dewdrop, egg cup, dbl 24.00
Dewdrop, mug 28.00
Dewdrop, relish 15.00
Dewdrop w/Star, butter dish 60.00
Dewdrop w/Star, plate, 5" 12.50
Dewey, mug, amber 50.00
Dewey, see also Greentown, Dewey
Dewey, tumbler 48.00
Diagonal Band, cake stand 37.50
Diagonal Band, pitcher, water 42.50
Diagonal Band, wine 25.00
Diamond Band w/Fan, butter dish 42.00
Diamond Band w/Fan, plate, 8" 12.50
Diamond Cut w/Leaf, butter dish 22.50
Diamond Cut w/Leaf, creamer 24.00
Diamond Horseshoe, see Aurora
Diamond Medallion, see Grand
Diamond Point, bottle, bar; flint 60.00
Diamond Point, pitcher, water; non-flint 90.00
Diamond Point, pitcher, water; tankard form, flint, qt ...175.00
Diamond Point, wine, flint 65.00
Diamond Quilted, bowl, 6" 14.00
Diamond Quilted, champagne, turq 32.00
Diamond Quilted, creamer, amber 38.00
Diamond Quilted, pitcher, water; amber 45.00
Diamond Quilted, relish, amber, leaf shape 15.00
Diamond Quilted, salt cellar, vaseline 18.00
Diamond Thumbprint, champagne 300.00
Diamond Thumbprint, cordial, 4" 315.00

Diamond Thumbprint, decanter, orig stopper, 1-qt 235.00
Diamond Thumbprint, tumbler, bar 135.00
Dinner Bell, see Cottage
Doric, see Feather
Double Leaf & Dart, see Leaf & Dart
Drapery, butter dish 40.00
Drapery, egg cup 24.00
Drapery, sugar bowl, w/lid 45.00
Egg in Sand, bread tray 35.00
Egg in Sand, pitcher, water; amber 75.00
Egg in Sand, relish 12.50
Egyptian, creamer 50.00
Egyptian, goblet 45.00
Egyptian, relish, 5½x8½" 21.00
Elephant, see Jumbo
Emerald Green Herringbone, see Florida
Empress, butter dish 57.50
Empress, sugar bowl 37.50
Empress, tumbler, gr w/gold 50.00
English Hobnail Cross, see Klondike
Esther, butter dish, ruby stained 125.00
Esther, cracker jar, ruby stained 200.00
Esther, ice cream tray, gr w/gold 150.00
Esther, pitcher, water; gr 150.00
Esther, sugar bowl, w/lid 45.00
Esther, tumbler, gr 47.50
Etched Dakota, see Dakota
Eureka, cordial 40.00
Eureka, salt cellar, ftd 37.50
Eureka, wine 32.00
Excelsior, bottle, bar; 1-pt 50.00
Excelsior, champagne, flint 65.00
Excelsior, creamer, molded hdl 85.00
Excelsior, salt cellar, master 28.00
Eyewinker, bowl, 6½" 27.50
Eyewinker, butter dish 65.00
Eyewinker, creamer, mini 55.00
Eyewinker, pitcher, water 95.00
Fairfax Strawberry, see Strawberry
Feather, bowl, 7" 25.00
Feather, cake plate 55.00
Feather, pitcher, water 40.00
Feather, tumbler, water 45.00
Festoon, creamer 38.00
Festoon, relish dish, 9x5½" 36.00
Festoon, tumbler 65.00
Fine Cut, ice cream tray, amber, lion's head hdls 47.50
Fine Cut, plate, amber, 10" 22.50
Fine Cut & Block, cruet, bl blocks, faceted stopper, 5½" ...78.00
Fine Cut & Block, goblet, pk blocks 48.00
Fine Cut & Diamond, see Grand
Fine Cut & Feather, see Feather
Fine Cut & Panel, bowl, oval, 8" 17.50
Fine Cut & Panel, butter dish, bl 75.00
Fine Cut & Panel, tumbler, vaseline 37.50
Fine Rib, champagne, flint 80.00
Fine Rib, honey dish, 3½" 20.00
Fine Rib, spoon holder 55.00
Fine Rib, wine, flint 45.00
Fingerprint, see Almond Thumbprint
Fishscale, creamer 25.00
Flamingo, goblet 40.00
Flamingo Habitat, champagne 42.00
Flamingo Habitat, tumbler 32.00

Florida, butter dish, emerald gr 78.00
Florida, goblet 22.50
Florida, relish, 6" 12.00
Florida, wine, gr 48.00
Flower Pot, butter dish 48.00
Flower Pot, creamer, vaseline 88.00
Flower Pot, spooner, vaseline 48.00
Flute, bottle, bar; flint, 1-qt 75.00
Flute, claret 25.00
Frosted Circle, punch cup 18.00
Frosted Circle, syrup; spring lid 100.00
Frosted Circle, wine 42.00
Frosted Leaf, goblet 120.00
Frosted Leaf, tumbler, ftd 100.00
Frosted Leaf, wine, flint 175.00
Frosted Lion, see Lion
Frosted Ribbon, see Ribbon
Frosted Roman Key, butter dish 50.00
Frosted Roman Key, champagne 75.00
Frosted Roman Key, goblet 45.00
Frosted Stork, compote, 8" 52.50
Frosted Stork, platter, oval, 11½" 75.00
Frosted Stork, sauce bowl 28.00

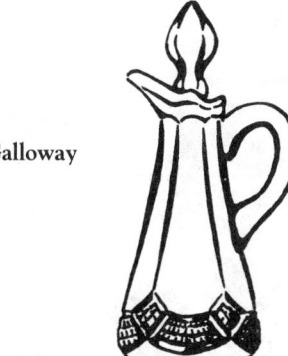

Galloway

Galloway, butter dish, clear w/gold 60.00
Galloway, egg cup, clear w/gold 32.00
Galloway, pitcher, milk; clear w/gold 60.00
Galloway, spooner, rose stained 78.00
Garfield Drape, creamer 40.00
Garfield Drape, pitcher, milk 60.00
Garfield Drape, pitcher, water 85.00
Gem, see Nailhead
Georgia, decanter 75.00
Georgia, mug 30.00
Good Luck, see Horseshoe
Gothic, goblet 55.00
Gothic, wine, 3¾" 125.00
Grand, butter dish 37.50
Grand, pitcher, water 42.50
Grand, sugar bowl, w/lid 38.00
Grape & Festoon w/Shield, goblet, w/Am shield 45.00
Grape & Festoon w/Shield, pitcher, water 72.50
Grape & Festoon w/Stippled Leaf, plate, 6" 20.00
Grape & Festoon w/Stippled Leaf, sugar bowl, w/lid 60.00
Grasshopper, butter dish, amber 98.00
Grasshopper, salt cellar 48.00
Grasshopper, sugar bowl, w/insect, w/lid 75.00
Greek Key, goblet, buttermilk 48.00
Greek Key, pitcher, tankard, 1½-qt 245.00

Greek Key, tumbler 78.00
Guardian Angel, see Cupid & Venus
Hairpin, champagne 82.50
Hairpin, goblet 42.50
Halley's Comet, celery vase 32.00
Halley's Comet, creamer 40.00
Halley's Comet, tumbler 34.00
Hamilton, butter dish 70.00
Hamilton, goblet 40.00
Hamilton, spooner 35.00
Hamilton w/Leaf, butter dish, frosted leaf 88.00
Hamilton w/Leaf, goblet, frosted leaf 55.00
Hamilton w/Leaf, whiskey, hdl, clear leaf 95.00
Hand, creamer 42.50
Hand, goblet 48.00
Hand, wine 60.00
Hartley, creamer, vaseline 42.50
Hawaiian Lei, cake stand, 9¼" 30.00
Hawaiian Lei, cup & saucer 40.00
Heart w/Thumbprint, bowl, 9" 38.00
Heart w/Thumbprint, goblet, gr w/gold 85.00
Heart w/Thumbprint, plate, 6" 24.00
Heart w/Thumbprint, wine, gr w/gold 140.00
Hearts & Spades, see Medallion
Heavy Panelled Fine Cut, salt cellar, ind 12.50
Heavy Panelled Fine Cut, tumbler, water 15.00
Herringbone, jelly compote, gr 42.50
Herringbone Band, see Ripple
Herringbone Buttress, see Greentown, Herringbone Buttress
Hickman, butter dish, gr 68.00
Hickman, cake stand 30.00
Hickman, goblet 42.00

Hidalgo

Hidalgo, creamer 40.00
Hidalgo, sugar bowl, w/lid 42.50
Hidalgo, waste bowl 27.50
Hinoto, egg cup 38.00
Hinoto, tumbler, ftd 40.00
Hinoto, wine 65.00
Holly, cake stand, 11" 125.00
Holly, goblet 95.00
Holly, tumbler 65.00
Holly Amber, see Greentown, Holly Amber
Honeycomb, cake stand, non-flint, 10½" 32.00
Honeycomb, egg cup, non-flint 12.50
Honeycomb, honey dish, w/lid, non-flint 24.00
Honeycomb, pitcher, water; flint 90.00
Honeycomb, whiskey, hdl, flint 132.00
Hops & Barley, see Wheat & Barley
Horn of Plenty, bowl, flint, 8½" 135.00

Horn of Plenty, cake stand, flint 345.00
Horn of Plenty, decanter, flint, 1-qt 175.00
Horn of Plenty, mug, appl hdl, flint, sm 135.00
Horseshoe, butter dish 95.00
Horseshoe, finger bowl 75.00
Horseshoe, pitcher, milk 115.00
Horseshoe, wine 150.00
Huber, celery vase 38.00
Huber, champagne, flint 32.00
Hummingbird, celery vase, amber 72.50
Hummingbird, pitcher, milk 50.00
Hummingbird, pitcher, water; bl 140.00
Idaho, see Snail
Illinois, basket, appl hdl, 7" 105.00
Illinois, pitcher, milk; rnd, SP trim 180.00
Illinois, plate, sq, 7" 32.00
Inverted Fern, compote, 8" 60.00
Inverted Fern, goblet 24.00
Invincible, sugar bowl, w/lid 55.00
Iowa, creamer 30.00
Iowa, pitcher, water 48.00
Iris Column, see Broken Column
Iris w/Meander, see Opalescent Glass
Ivy in Snow, creamer 18.00
Ivy in Snow, mug, ruby stained 48.00
Ivy in Snow, relish 20.00
Jacob's Ladder, butter dish, Maltese Cross finial 60.00
Jacob's Ladder, cake stand, 12" 55.00
Jacob's Ladder, spooner 32.00
Jersey Swirl, butter dish, bl 68.00
Jersey Swirl, salt cellar, bl, ind 22.00
Jersey Swirl, wine 20.00
Jewel Band, bread platter 42.50
Jewel Band, goblet 36.00
Jewel Band, pitcher, milk 45.00
Jewel w/Dewdrop, cake stand, 7" 50.00
Jewel w/Dewdrop, mug 15.00
Jewel w/Dewdrop, wine, ruby stained w/gold 100.00
Jewel w/Festoon, creamer 25.00
Jewel w/Festoon, sugar bowl, w/lid 35.00
Jewel w/Moondrop, mug 48.00
Jewel w/Moondrop, pitcher, water 65.00
Jewel w/Moondrop, tumbler 42.50
Jewelled Moon & Star, carafe 45.00
Jewelled Moon & Star, goblet 45.00
Jewelled Moon & Star, wine 25.00
Job's Tears, see Art
Jumbo, butter dish, oval 550.00
Jumbo, goblet 725.00
Jumbo, pitcher, elephant in base 700.00
Kentucky, nappy, emerald gr 12.50
Kentucky, pitcher, water 55.00
Kentucky, punch cup 10.00
Kentucky, sauce bowl, ftd 8.00
King's Crown, banana stand, ruby stained 125.00
King's Crown, cordial 40.00
King's Crown, creamer, clear w/gold, ind 30.00
King's Crown, custard cup 17.50
King's Crown, goblet 37.50
King's Crown, mustard jar, ruby stained 75.00
King's Crown, pitcher, water; bulbous 100.00
King's Crown, sugar bowl, w/lid 80.00
King's Crown, wine, ruby stained 38.00
Klondike, butter pat, amber stained 35.00

Klondike, goblet, frosted, amber stained 230.00
Klondike, shakers, frosted, amber stained, orig top, pr 120.00
Klondike, sugar bowl, frosted, amber stained 180.00
La Clede, see Hickman
Lace, see DraperyLady Hamilton, egg cup, saucer base 24.00
Lady Hamilton, sauce dish, flat, 4" 6.00
Lawrence, see Bull's Eye
Leaf, see Maple Leaf
Leaf & Dart, butter dish, ped base 95.00
Leaf & Dart, egg cup 22.50
Leaf & Dart, sugar bowl, w/lid 45.00
Leaf Bracket, see Greentown, Leaf Bracket
Leaf Medallion, see Northwood Leaf Medallion
Liberty Bell, creamer, appl hdl 125.00
Liberty Bell, goblet 55.00
Liberty Bell, spooner, mini 300.00
Lily of the Valley, egg cup 45.00
Lily of the Valley, goblet, buttermilk 35.00
Lily of the Valley, sugar bowl, 3-ftd 25.00
Lincoln Drape, goblet 88.00
Lincoln Drape, sugar bowl, w/lid 120.00
Lincoln Drape w/Tassel, salt cellar, master 120.00
Lion, bowl, oval, frosted, 8" 75.00
Lion, champagne, frosted 165.00
Lion, egg cup, frosted 65.00
Lion, pitcher, milk 325.00
Log Cabin, butter dish 300.00
Log Cabin, creamer 125.00
Long Spear, see Grasshopper
Loop, compote, w/lid, flint, 9x7" 80.00
Loop, cordial, non-flint, 2¾" 32.50
Loop, wine, flint 32.00
Loop & Dart, butter dish 48.00
Loop & Dart, pitcher, water 78.00
Loop & Dart w/Round Ornament, creamer 38.00
Loop & Dart w/Round Ornament, goblet 32.00
Loop w/Stippled Panels, see Texas
Magnet & Grape, champagne, clear leaf 42.50
Magnet & Grape, champagne, frosted leaf, flint 125.00
Magnet & Grape, pitcher, water; frosted leaf, flint 345.00
Maine, butter dish 60.00
Maine, pitcher, water 100.00
Manhattan, carafe, water; pk stained 72.50
Manhattan, creamer 50.00
Manhattan, punch cup 15.00
Maple Leaf, compote, vaseline, log ft, 7" 105.00
Maple Leaf, plate, bl, 9" 38.00
Maryland, goblet 35.00
Maryland, relish, ruby stained 50.00
Maryland, tumbler 32.00
Mascotte, butter pat 17.50
Mascotte, shaker, etched 25.00
Mascotte, tumbler 22.00
Massachusetts, basket, appl hdl, 4½" 45.00
Massachusetts, pitcher, water 75.00
Massachusetts, punch cup 14.00
Medallion, cake stand, amber 48.00
Medallion, sugar bowl, amber, w/lid 45.00
Medallion, wine 22.00
Melrose, pitcher, milk 48.00
Melrose, plate, 8" 12.00
Michigan, butter dish, yel stained, HP florals 180.00
Michigan, carafe, water 135.00
Michigan, creamer, 4" 32.00

Michigan, relish 22.50
Minerva, butter dish 95.00
Minerva, creamer 55.00
Minerva, honey dish 20.00
Minnesota, carafe 40.00
Minnesota, relish 22.00
Minnesota, tumbler, water 20.00
Minor Block, see Mascotte
Mirror, see Galloway
Missouri, butter dish 42.00
Missouri, butter dish, gr 58.00
Missouri, tumbler, gr 40.00
Moon & Star, bowl, berry; 8¼" 32.00
Moon & Star, butter dish 68.00
Moon & Star, creamer 50.00
Moon & Star, pitcher, water 175.00
Morning Glory, champagne, flint 385.00
Morning Glory, egg cup, Sandwich 95.00
Nail, decanter 35.00
Nail, pitcher, water 80.00
Nailhead, compote, w/lid, 13x8½" 98.00
Nailhead, relish 10.00

Nailhead

Nailhead, spooner 20.00
Nestor, sauce dish, gr w/HP decor 38.00
Nestor, tumbler, gr 32.00
New England Pineapple, goblet, flint 70.00
New England Pineapple, sauce dish 18.00
New Hampshire, sugar bowl, rose stained, 3" 27.50
New Hampshire, tumbler, clear w/gold 22.00
New Hampshire, vase, clear w/gold 24.00
New Jersey, carafe, water 80.00
New Jersey, goblet 37.50
Notched Rib, see Broken Column
O'Hara Diamond, creamer, ruby stained 55.00
O'Hara Diamond, goblet 22.50
O'Hara Diamond, sugar shaker 55.00
O'Hara Diamond, tumbler, ruby stained 45.00
Oaken Bucket, see Wooden Pail
One Hundred & One, butter dish 65.00
One Hundred & One, goblet 50.00
One Hundred & One, relish 18.00
One-O-One, see One Hundred & One
Opposing Pyramids, pitcher, water 50.00
Oregon #1, bread plate 32.00
Oregon #1, cake stand 32.00
Oregon #1, jelly compote 25.00
Oregon #1, tumbler, water 28.00
Orion, see Cathedral

Ostrich Looking at Moon, goblet 125.00
Palmette, cake stand 70.00
Palmette, cup plate 45.00
Panelled Daisy, bowl, oval, 5x7" 15.00
Panelled Daisy, butter dish 65.00
Panelled Daisy, goblet 27.50
Panelled Dewdrop, celery vase 40.00
Panelled Dewdrop, goblet 27.50
Panelled Forget-Me-Not, butter dish 42.50
Panelled Forget-Me-Not, marmalade 50.00
Panelled Forget-Me-Not, relish, hdls 22.50
Panelled Herringbone, see Florida
Panelled Nightshade, goblet, bl 68.00
Panelled Nightshade, wine 22.00
Panelled Star & Button, goblet 25.00
Panelled Star & Button, salt cellar, master 15.00
Panelled Thistle, basket, sm 60.00
Panelled Thistle, celery tray 17.50
Panelled Thistle, plate, 10" 30.00
Panelled Thistle, sugar bowl, w/lid 42.50
Pavonia, butter dish, ruby stained 120.00
Pavonia, creamer, etched 45.00
Pavonia, pitcher, lemonade; ruby stained 135.00
Pavonia, salt cellar, ind 15.00
Peerless, see Lady Hamilton
Pennsylvania, butter dish, clear w/gold 60.00
Pennsylvania, creamer, emerald gr 48.00
Pennsylvania, pitcher, water; clear w/gold 55.00
Pennsylvania, tumbler, water; clear w/gold 25.00
Pillow Encircled, pitcher, water; tankard form ..48.00
Pillow Encircled, sauce dish 12.00
Pineapple & Fan, pitcher, water 78.00
Pineapple & Fan, vase, trumpet form, 10" 32.00

Pineapple & Fan

Pineapple Stem, see Pavonia
Pioneer, see Westward Ho
Pleat & Panel, cake stand, sq, 10" 65.00
Pleat & Panel, goblet 30.00
Plume, bowl, w/lid, 8" 48.00
Plume, butter dish 45.00
Plume, creamer, ruby stained 65.00
Polar Bear, goblet 110.00
Polar Bear, pitcher, water; frosted 275.00
Polar Bear, tray, water; frosted, 16" 215.00
Popcorn, butter dish 50.00
Popcorn, cake stand, 11" 55.00
Popcorn, wine 32.00
Portland, basket, clear w/gold 80.00
Portland, goblet, clear w/gold 32.50
Portland, pitcher, water; str sides, clear w/gold ..60.00

Portland, spooner, pk stained 75.00
Portland, toothpick holder 24.00
Powder & Shot, butter dish 88.00
Powder & Shot, honey dish, flint 60.00
Powder & Shot, salt cellar; master; flint 40.00
Prayer Rug, see Horseshoe
Pressed Leaf, pitcher, water 105.00
Pressed Leaf, sugar bowl, w/lid 40.00
Primrose, cake plate, amber, 9" 35.00
Primrose, pickle dish 20.00
Primrose, sugar bowl, w/lid 45.00
Princess Feather, bowl, oval, 6x9" 30.00
Princess Feather, creamer 50.00
Princess Feather, goblet 42.50
Priscilla, butter dish 115.00
Priscilla, creamer 42.00
Priscilla, mug 17.50
Prism, goblet 35.00
Prism, tumbler, buttermilk 38.00
Psyche & Cupid, pitcher, water 80.00
Psyche & Cupid, sugar bowl, w/lid 45.00
Pygmy, see Torpedo
Racing Deer, pitcher, water 175.00
Recessed Pillared Red Top, see Nail
Red Block, butter dish 100.00
Red Block, decanter, 12" 165.00
Red Block, rose bowl 65.00
Red Block, sugar bowl, w/lid 80.00
Red Top, see Button Arches
Reverse Torpedo, banana stand, 9¾" 95.00
Reverse Torpedo, honey dish, sq 135.00
Reverse Torpedo, relish, oval, ruby stained, 9" ..38.00
Ribbed Ivy, champagne 235.00
Ribbed Ivy, egg cup 32.00
Ribbed Ivy, goblet 45.00
Ribbed Palm, butter dish 95.00
Ribbed Palm, honey dish 15.00
Ribbed Palm, pitcher, water; appl hdl, 9" 265.00
Ribbon, butter dish 75.00
Ribbon, compote, w/lid, 8" 92.50
Ribbon, creamer 37.50
Ribbon, goblet 35.00
Ribbon, pomade jar, w/lid 38.00
Ribbon Candy, goblet 35.00
Ribbon Candy, pitcher, milk 40.00
Ribbon Candy, plate, 11" 42.00
Ripple, goblet 20.00
Ripple, spooner 20.00
Ripple Band, see Ripple
Rising Sun, butter dish, clear w/gr 88.00
Rising Sun, goblet, clear w/gold 27.50
Rising Sun, tumbler, clear w/red 27.50
Rochelle, see Princess Feather
Roman Rosette, bread plate, ruby stained 75.00
Roman Rosette, compote, w/lid, 5" 60.00
Roman Rosette, tumbler, lemonade 34.00
Roman Rosette, wine, ruby stained 68.00
Rose in Snow, bottle, cologne; orig stopper 95.00
Rose in Snow, bowl, canary, ftd, 7" 40.00
Rose in Snow, cake plate, amber, hdld, 10" 50.00
Rose in Snow, goblet, bl 47.50
Rose in Snow, relish, dbl 95.00
Rose in Snow, tumbler, bar 65.00
Rose Sprig, cake stand, amber, sq, 10" 85.00

Rose Sprig, goblet 32.50
Rose Sprig, goblet, amber 45.00
Rose Sprig, tumbler, appl hdl 50.00
Rosette, butter dish 45.00
Rosette, goblet 37.50
Rosette, waste bowl 27.50
Rosette, wine 25.00
Royal Ivy, see Northwood, Royal Ivy
Royal Oak, see Northwood, Royal Oak
Ruby Thumbprint, see King's Crown
S-Repeat, butter dish, apple gr 130.00
S-Repeat, shakers, pr 37.50
Sandwich Star, compote, low std, 8½" 60.00
Sandwich Star, decanter, bar lip, 1-pt 65.00
Sandwich Star, spill holder 60.00
Sawtooth, butter dish, non-flint 42.50
Sawtooth, champagne, knob stem, flint 60.00
Sawtooth, creamer, flint 85.00
Sawtooth, decanter, flint, orig stopper, 14" 155.00
Sawtooth, wine, flint 38.00
Sawtooth Band, see Amazon
Scalloped Daisy Red Top, see Button Arches
Scroll w/Flowers, cordial 40.00
Scroll w/Flowers, mustard jar 45.00
Scroll w/Flowers, spooner 25.00
Sedan, see Panelled Star & Button
Seneca Loop, see Loop
Sequoia, see Heavy Panelled Fine Cut
Shell & Jewel, cake stand, 5x10" 45.00
Shell & Jewel, creamer 35.00
Shell & Jewel, pitcher, water; bl 85.00
Shell & Jewel, tumbler, bl 40.00
Shell & Tassel, bowl, vaseline, oval, 9" 180.00
Shell & Tassel, butter dish, dog finial 115.00
Shell & Tassel, goblet, knob stem 65.00
Shell & Tassel, ice cream tray 65.00
Sheraton, butter dish 42.50
Sheraton, goblet, bl 40.00
Sheraton, pitcher, water 48.00
Shoshone, butter dish, clear w/gold 65.00
Shoshone, compote, jelly 18.00
Shoshone, plate, gr, 7½" 40.00
Shoshone, tumbler, ruby stained 32.50
Shoshone, wine 45.00
Shrine, mug 20.00
Shrine, pickle dish 18.00
Shrine, sugar bowl, w/lid 50.00
Shuttle, champagne 40.00
Shuttle, punch cup 15.00
Shuttle, spooner, scalloped rim 35.00
Shuttle, tumbler 55.00
Six Panel Fine Cut, pitcher, water; amber bars 90.00
Skilton, butter dish, ruby stained 100.00
Skilton, compote, 7" 27.50
Skilton, goblet 35.00
Skilton, tumbler, ruby stained 42.50
Snail, butter dish, ruby stained 150.00
Snail, cheese dish 110.00
Snail, compote, high std, 6" 48.00
Snail, goblet, ruby stained 90.00
Snail, sugar bowl, w/lid, ruby stained, regular 95.00
Snail, tumbler, ruby stained 215.00
Spades, see Medallion
Spirea Band, cake stand, bl, 10½" 85.00

Spirea Band, creamer, amber 37.50
Spirea Band, goblet 22.50
Spirea Band, spooner, vaseline 32.50
Spirea Band, wine, amber 32.00
Spirea Band, wine, bl 32.00
Sprig, butter dish 60.00
Sprig, goblet 30.00
Sprig, pitcher, water 55.00
Sprig, sugar bowl, w/lid 45.00
Star Rosetted, butter dish 45.00
Star Rosetted, goblet 32.00
Star Rosetted, sugar bowl 15.00
Stars & Stripes, creamer 22.00
Stars & Stripes, shaker 17.50
States, butter dish 68.00
States, creamer, oval, ind 20.00
States, goblet, clear w/gold 38.00
States, shakers, clear w/gold, pr 38.00
States, tumbler, clear w/gold 25.00
Stedman, champagne 38.00
Stedman, spooner 15.00
Stedman, wine 48.00
Stippled Chain, egg cup 28.00
Stippled Chain, goblet 22.50
Stippled Double Loop, butter dish 45.00
Stippled Double Loop, tumbler 25.00
Stippled Forget-Me-Not, cup & saucer 40.00
Stippled Forget-Me-Not, tumbler 32.00

Stippled Grape & Festoon

Stippled Grape & Festoon, celery vase 40.00
Stippled Grape & Festoon, compote, low std, 8" 40.00
Stippled Ivy, egg cup 25.00
Stippled Ivy, sauce dish, flat 12.00
Stippled Ivy, sugar bowl, w/lid 38.00
Stippled Panelled Flower, see Maine
Strawberry, goblet, 6" 18.00
Strawberry, pitcher, water; bulbous 120.00
Strawberry, spooner 35.00
Strawberry & Currant, mug 36.00
Strawberry & Currant, pitcher, milk 42.00
Strigil, celery 25.00
Strigil, plate, 11" 24.00
Sunk Honeycomb, cheese dish, ruby stained 175.00
Sunk Honeycomb, cup & saucer, ruby stained 32.00
Sunk Honeycomb, tumbler, eng 25.00
Sunken Primrose, see Florida
Swan, compote, swan finial, 8" 195.00
Swan, creamer, amber 60.00
Swan, goblet, canary yel 75.00
Tarentum's Thumbprint, pitcher, water; etched 45.00

Teardrop & Diamond Block, see Art
Teardrop & Tassel, creamer 40.00
Teardrop & Tassel, goblet 145.00
Teardrop & Tassel, sauce dish 13.00
Teardrop & Tassel, see also Greentown, Teardrop & Tassel
Teardrop & Tassel, tumbler 37.50
Tennessee, butter dish 50.00
Tennessee, celery vase 35.00
Tennessee, pitcher, milk 50.00
Texas, butter dish, clear w/gold 75.00
Texas, creamer, clear w/gold, ind 22.00
Texas, goblet, ruby stained 90.00
Texas, pickle dish, clear w/gold, 8½" 32.00
Theatrical, see Actress
Thousand Eye, butter dish, apple gr 65.00
Thousand Eye, celery vase, bl, 7" 55.00
Thousand Eye, creamer, vaseline, 4" 35.00
Thousand Eye, egg cup, amber 60.00
Thousand Eye, mug, apple gr, 3½" 30.00
Thousand Eye, mug, 3½" 18.00
Thousand Eye, plate, vaseline, 10" 35.00
Thousand Eye, platter, 11x8" 35.00
Three Face, biscuit jar 900.00
Three Face, butter dish 145.00
Three Face, celery vase 125.00
Three Face, champagne, saucer type 150.00
Three Face, claret 125.00
Three Face, compote, 7½x6" 75.00
Three Face, creamer 125.00
Three Face, marmalade jar 225.00
Three Face, pitcher, water 325.00
Three Face, spooner 80.00
Three Face, sugar bowl, w/lid 120.00
Three Face, wine 175.00
Three Panel, celery vase, amber, ruffled top 50.00
Three Panel, creamer, bl 50.00
Three Panel, tumbler, vaseline 30.00
Thumbprint, see Argus
Thumbprint Band, see Dakota
Thunderbird, see Hummingbird
Torpedo, butter dish 90.00
Torpedo, cup & saucer 60.00
Tree of Life, see Portland
Tree of Life w/Hand, butter dish 130.00
Tree of Life w/Hand, creamer, hand & ball hdl 67.50
Triple Triangle, butter dish 60.00
Triple Triangle, wine, ruby stained 48.00
Truncated Cube, decanter, 12" 60.00
Truncated Cube, pitcher, water; tankard form 55.00
Tulip w/Sawtooth, creamer, flint 85.00
Tulip w/Sawtooth, tumbler, bar; flint 88.00
Tulip w/Sawtooth, wine, non-flint 20.00
Two Panel, butter dish, vaseline 60.00
Two Panel, goblet, amber 30.00
Two Panel, salt cellar, amber, master 24.00
Two Panel, tumbler, vaseline 45.00
US Coin, bowl, frosted, 6" 225.00
US Coin, bowl, frosted, 8" 380.00
US Coin, bowl, preserve; oval, frosted, 5x8" 385.00
US Coin, butter dish 400.00
US Coin, butter dish, frosted 425.00
US Coin, cake stand, 10" 350.00
US Coin, celery tray 185.00
US Coin, compote, w/lid, high std, frosted, 8" 450.00

US Coin, creamer, frosted 595.00
US Coin, epergne 625.00
US Coin, mug, frosted 350.00
US Coin, tumbler 145.00
US Coin, tumbler, frosted 225.00
US Coin, wine 235.00
US Coin, wine, frosted 450.00
Utah, creamer 30.00
Utah, tumbler 17.50
Valencia Waffle, cake stand, amber 75.00
Valencia Waffle, pitcher, water 44.00
Valencia Waffle, sauce bowl, ftd 15.00
Vermont, basket, gr w/gold 42.50
Vermont, goblet, clear w/gold 38.00
Vermont, spooner, gr w/gold 70.00
Vermont, tumbler, gr w/gold 40.00
Viking, celery vase 40.00
Viking, cup, ftd 32.50
Viking, relish 22.00

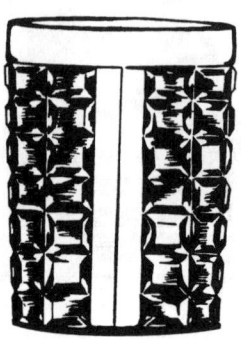

Waffle

Waffle, champagne 150.00
Waffle, creamer, ftd 125.00
Waffle, sugar bowl, w/lid 98.00
Waffle & Thumbprint, bowl, flint, 7¼" 38.00
Waffle & Thumbprint, goblet, flint 65.00
Waffle & Thumbprint, spill holder 110.00
Waffle & Thumbprint, whiskey 90.00
Waffle & Thumbprint, whiskey, hdld, 3" 285.00
Washington, champagne 120.00
Washington, cordial 145.00
Washington, tumbler 88.00
Washington, tumbler, ale 115.00
Washington Centennial, butter dish, ftd 95.00
Washington Centennial, champagne 72.50
Washington Centennial, goblet 55.00
Washington Centennial, pitcher, milk 110.00
Wedding Bells, goblet 45.00
Wedding Bells, spooner 38.00
Wedding Bells, wine 25.00
Wedding Ring, goblet 45.00
Wedding Ring, pitcher, milk 90.00
Wedding Ring, syrup 97.50
Westward Ho, butter dish 185.00
Westward Ho, creamer 88.00
Westward Ho, goblet 75.00
Westward Ho, wine 190.00
Wheat & Barley, butter dish, w/lid 40.00
Wheat & Barley, cake stand, bl, 8" 42.50
Wheat & Barley, mug, amber 35.00
Wheat & Barley, shakers, pr 37.50
Wheat Sheaf, pitcher, water 65.00

Wildflower, bowl, sq, 8" 17.50
Wildflower, creamer, amber 32.00
Wildflower, goblet, apple gr 37.50
Wildflower, tumbler, vaseline 32.00
Willow Oak, bowl, 7" 15.00
Willow Oak, creamer, bl 48.00
Willow Oak, mug 30.00
Willow Oak, sugar bowl, amber, w/lid 65.00
Willow Oak, waste bowl, canary 38.00
Windflower, butter dish 52.50
Windflower, creamer 35.00
Windflower, sauce dish 12.50
Windflower, tumbler, bar 38.00
Wisconsin, creamer 50.00
Wisconsin, goblet 50.00
Wisconsin, spooner 32.00
Wooden Pail, butter dish, amber 82.50
Wooden Pail, creamer 32.00
Wooden Pail, pitcher, water 60.00
Wooden Pail, tumbler, bar; amethyst 38.00
Wyoming, cake plate 50.00
Wyoming, creamer 48.00
X-Ray, bowl, berry; beaded rim, 8" 27.50
X-Ray, pitcher, water; emerald gr, 9½" 75.00
X-Ray, rose bowl, emerald gr w/gold 70.00
Yale, celery vase, emerald gr 48.00
Yale, goblet 35.00
Yale, spooner 25.00
Zipper, cheese dish 50.00
Zipper, goblet 35.00
Zipper, pitcher, water 45.00
Zippered Block, carafe 40.00
Zippered Block, creamer, ruby stained 85.00
Zippered Block, sugar bowl, ruby stained, w/lid 115.00
Zippered Block, tumbler 35.00

Paul Revere Pottery

The Saturday Evening Girls were a social group of young Boston ladies who met to pursue various activities, among them pottery making. Their first kiln was bought in 1906, and within a few years it became necessary to move to a larger location. Because their new quarters were near the historical Old North Church, they chose the name Paul Revere Pottery. With very little training, the girls produced only simple ware. Until 1915 the pottery operated at a deficit; then a new building with four kilns was constructed on Nottingham Road. Vases, miniature jugs, children's tea sets, tiles, dinnerware, and lamps were produced, usually in soft matt glazes often decorated with incised, hand-painted designs from nature. Occasional examples in a dark high gloss may also be found.

Several marks were used: 'P.R.P.'; 'S.E.G.'; or the circular device, 'Boston, Paul Revere Pottery' with the horse and rider.

The pottery continued to operate, and even though their product sold well, the high production costs of the handmade ware caused the pottery to fail in 1946.

Bookends, scenic on front slope of rectangular block, 5" L, pr 825.00
Bowl, groups of camels in band, SEG/sgn/1909, 2½x5" 1,100.00
Bowl, nasturtium band, 3-color on gr, SEG/SG, 8½" 935.00
Bowl, tree/mtn band on ivory, SEG/sgn/3-4-14, 3x9" 750.00
Bowl, tulip band on yel, PRP/11-26, 4x5½" 350.00
Bowl, 5 groups of 3 chickens in band, SEG/IG/1910, 1½x6" 550.00
Candlestick, bl gloss, PRP label, 7", pr 120.00
Creamer, band w/rabbits & Slow But Sure, SEG/AG/1917, 4½" ..475.00

Cup & saucer, wht lotus on bl, SEG/AM/9-12 ....150.00
Desk set, leaf band, 5-color on royal bl, SEG/AM/17, 6-pc 1,100.00
Dish, cat's; mouse heads on bl, SEG/DC/1913, 6" dia 500.00
Jar, moth band on wht, sgn Galner/Goldstein, 1911, 4½" 1,500.00
Mustard pot, tree band on yel, SEG/sgn/7-16, 2½" 650.00
Pitcher, chickens in band on yel, SEG/JT/MD, 9-19, 4½" 275.00
Pitcher, wild rose sgraffito band on bl/gray, SEG/MF/19, 4½" 350.00
Plate, Arts & Crafts-style tree scene, SEG/SG/11-15, 12" 1,100.00
Plate, band of pigs, HOS monogram, SEG/RB/dtd, 8½" 2,000.00
Plate, landscape on mc, SEG/SG/1912, 8" 600.00
Plate, wht lotus on bl, SEG/EG/4-2-13, 6" 100.00
Set: cup/bowl/plate, name/chick on navy, 1928 ....495.00
Trivet, trees, SEG/SG/2-14, 5½" dia 150.00
Tumbler, tree band, brn on gr, SEG/sgn/12-15, 4" 400.00
Vase, bl gloss, SEG/AG, 12-16/ 10" 250.00

Vase, yellow and white daffodils with green grasses on light blue band over slate blue, SEG/JMD/9-20, small drill hole has been repaired, 11", $1,200.00.

Vase, bl/gr/blk/wht drip over gr, hdld ovoid, PRP, 7" 275.00
Vase, crocus border, blk-lined wht on bl, SEG/SG/14, 8" 875.00
Vase, floral band & wht top border on yel, SEG/7-26, 9" 650.00
Vase, flying sea gulls in band, SEG/EB/1926, 9x5" 850.00
Vase, Greek Key band on mustard gloss, SEG/CL/3-15, 4" 275.00
Vase, landscape band on gr, SEG/SG/1-14, cylindrical, 8" 1,600.00
Vase, tree cluster band, 5-color on bl, SEG/FM/4-19, 10" 825.00
Vase, tree/daffodil band on yel, SEG/FL/3-15, 4", NM 300.00

Pauline Pottery

Pauline Pottery was made from 1883 to 1888 in Chicago, Illinois, from clay imported from the Ohio area. Its founder was Mrs. Pauline Jacobus, who had learned the trade at the Rookwood Pottery. Mrs. Jacobus moved to Edgerton, Wisconsin, to be near a source of suitable clay, thus eliminating shipping expenses. Until 1905 she produced high-quality wares, able to imitate with ease designs and styles of such masters as Wedgwood and Meissen. Her products were sold through leading department stores, and the names of some of these firms may appear on the ware. Not all were marked; unless signed by a noted local artist, positive identification is often impossible. Marked examples carry a variety of stamps and signatures: 'Trade Mark' with a crown, 'Pauline Pottery,' and 'Edgerton Art Pottery' are but a few.

Jug, bamboo reeds, gold on cobalt, 2-spout, 9x9" 185.00
Teapot, floral, gold trim, EX 275.00

Tray, berries & vines, gold traced, EX art, 10", M 600.00
Vase, ivory w/bl & gold arabesque motif, 5" 300.00

Peachblow

Peachblow, made to imitate the colors of the Chinese Peachbloom porcelain, was made by several glasshouses in the late 1800s. Among them were New England Glass; Mt. Washington; Webb; and Hobbs, Brockunier, and Company. Its pink shading was achieved through action of the heat on the gold content of the glass. While New England's peachblow shades from deep crimson to white, Mt. Washington's tends to shade from pink to blue-gray. Although usually glossy, a satin (or acid) finish was also produced, and many pieces were enameled and gilded. In the 1950s Gundersen-Pairpoint Glassworks initiated the reproduction of Mt. Washington peachblow, using an exact duplication of the original formula. Though of recent manufacture, this glass is very collectible. In the listings that follow, the finish is glossy unless noted acid. Our advisors for this category are Betty and Clarence Maier; they are listed in the Directory under Pennsylvania.

Candlestick, Morning Glory, Gundersen, 8", pr 1,450.00
Celery vase, Hobnail, Sandwich, 7x4" 165.00
Celery vase, NE Glass, 6½" 725.00
Compote, Morning-Glory, Gundersen, 4½x10" 965.00
Creamer & sugar bowl (open), Wheeling, 3" 1,000.00

Cruet, rare shape, applied amber handle, 6½", $1,300.00.

Cup & saucer, acid, appl wht reeded hdl, Gundersen, 2¼", 5" ...265.00
Jar, acid, gold prunus/butterfly, cylindrical, Webb, 5" 695.00
Mustard, gold prunus, 2½" 395.00
Pitcher, acid, cased, 4-lobe lip, Wheeling, 5" 935.00
Pitcher, tankard; amber hdl, Wheeling, 9" 1,750.00
Pitcher, tankard; wht hdl, NE Glass, 9x5" 1,750.00
Punch cup, NE Glass, 2⅝x2⅝" 425.00
Rose bowl, NE Glass, 4x4" 475.00
Spooner, acid, crimped top, paper label, NE Glass, 4½x3¼" ...1,200.00
Sugar shaker, orig metal top, Wheeling, 5¾" 1,200.00
Tumbler, acid, Mt WA, 3¾" 1,000.00
Tumbler, NE Glass, 3¾x2½" 325.00
Tumbler, Wheeling, 3⅞x2¾" 325.00
Vase, acid, dbl gourd form, Wheeling, 7½" 1,450.00
Vase, acid, gourd form, Mt WA, 7" 2,250.00
Vase, acid, ruffled cornucopia form, Gundersen 535.00
Vase, acid, stick neck, Wheeling, 11" 1,700.00
Vase, acid, Wheeling, 13" 975.00

Vase, amber rigaree collar, stick neck, Wheeling, 8" 1,250.00
Vase, appl crystal branch ft & florals, lg appl berry, 12" 650.00
Vase, baluster w/slender shaped neck, Wheeling, 8" 350.00
Vase, bulbous w/sqd rim, Wheeling, 7" 1,150.00
Vase, florals w/gold, ruffled rim, Webb, 5⅜" 300.00
Vase, gold dragonflies etc, bronzed neck hdls, Webb, 8x5" 395.00
Vase, gold floral & dragonfly, Webb, 7x5¾" 550.00
Vase, gold prunus & bee, Webb, 10⅝x4⅜" 450.00
Vase, gold/silver floral/bee, cup rim/long neck, Webb, 10" 475.00
Vase, lily; acid, Gundersen, 9" 400.00
Vase, lily; acid, Mt WA, 6¼" 2,750.00
Vase, lily; acid, NE Glass; in SP bird on branch fr, 5½" 675.00
Vase, lily; trefoil rim, NE Glass, 10" 950.00
Vase, mat-su-noke decor, thorny base, Webb, 4¾" 365.00
Vase, Morgan; acid, 7¾", in glass griffin holder 1,400.00
Vase, Morgan; , 8", in plastic griffin holder, Wheeling 850.00
Vase, pk band at shoulder, Gundersen, 6½x2½" 150.00
Vase, ruffled, pinched-in sides, NE Glass, 4½x5" 1,375.00
Vase, Stevens & Williams, 13¼x6" 735.00
Vase, stick neck, Wheeling, 11" 850.00
Vase, stick neck, Wheeling, 8¼x3⅜" 750.00

Pearlware

Developed by Wedgwood in the late 1770s primarily for their dinnerware lines, pearlware was soon being made by many other Staffordshire potteries as well. Much of it made for export to America. It is characterized by its blue-white body, similar in appearance to true porcelain. During the first decade of the 1800s, pearlware with chinoiserie decorations and hand-painted flowers became popular.

Bank, house w/chimney, EX details, 4", EX 450.00
Bowl, bl floral/foliage, bl-design scalloped rim, 3x6½" 175.00
Coffeepot, bl foliate swags/band, sprigs on spout/hdl, 5½" 1,225.00
Cup & saucer, bl floral/scalloped rim, swirl mold 130.00
Cup & saucer, bl foliage, floret swag, wide rim band, EX 130.00
Cup & saucer, bl sunflower-type floral/foliate rim 175.00
Cup & saucer, chinoiserie in bl, bl geometric rim band, EX 125.00
Cup & saucer, floral, dk bl/gr/orange/yel, bl stripe, EX 250.00
Cup & saucer, red flowers w/pk buds, pk sprigs, red rims 95.00
Cup & saucer, simple yel flower w/gr leaves, wide bl band 75.00
Cup plate, floral, molded bl edge w/'scales,' rosette mk 475.00
Figurine, girl sits on high cushion w/emb motif, 4½", EX 200.00
Figurine, man, brn/yel sponging, brn hat, gr base, 3", EX 150.00
Figurine, woman in chair w/cat, 4-color, sm flakes, 3" 200.00
Marriage cup, floral swags/darts in bl/orange, hdls, 4" 500.00
Pitcher, Dandies (HP/emb figures), 1820s, 5" 225.00
Pitcher, florals, dk on lt bl, yel rim band, sm rpr, 6" 600.00

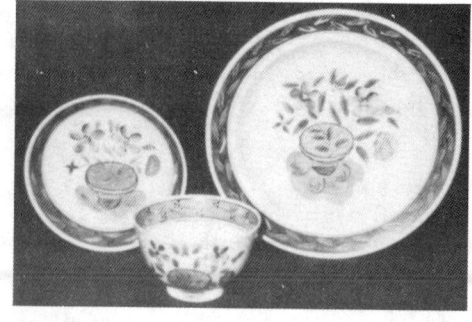

Plate, 8¼", cup and saucer, 6-color flowers, NM, $250.00 for the 3-piece service.

Plate, eagle, bl transfer/shell rim, octagonal, 5½", NM 475.00
Plate, floral, yel/orange/bl/gr/brn, bl shell rim, 8" 400.00
Plate, lady by lg urn w/floral garland, blk transfer, 4½" 175.00
Plate, Not More Than Others..., bl transfer/shell rim, 5½" 250.00
Plate, peafowl, 3-color, brn/gr branch, mc floral band, 6½" 800.00
Plate, pineapple in yel/bl/gr, bl/brn foliage at rim, 7½" 925.00
Plate, pot of flowers, gr leaves on brn band, #8, 8½", NM 140.00
Plate, rosette center in yel/blk, blk-dotted yel band, 8½" 150.00
Plate, Who Saw Me Mt the Rocking Horse..., bl transfer, 6" 195.00
Platter, Am eagle w/shield, 4-color, dk bl rim, 11" 475.00
Sugar bowl, chinoiserie, bl transfer, dbl hdls, 4", NM 500.00
Sugar bowl, red bands/florals, bk initials EM, 2¾" 150.00
Teapot, bl swags w/gr foliage & orange dots, str spout, 4" 950.00
Teapot, chinoiserie, bl transfer, floral finial, rpr, 4¾" 600.00
Teapot, yel shoulder band, bl-design band below, 3¾" 550.00

Peking Cameo Glass

The first glasshouse was established in Peking in 1680. It produced glassware made in imitation of porcelain, a more desirable medium to the Chinese. By 1725 multilayered carving that resulted in a cameo effect lead to the manufacture of a wider range of shapes and colors. The factory was closed from 1736 to 1795, but glass made in Po-shan and shipped to Peking for finishing continued to be called Peking glass. Only the cameo-type glassware is listed here. Our advisor for this category is Donald Penrose; he is listed in the Directory under Ohio. See also Orientalia.

Bowl, hibiscus flowers, bl on wht, 2x7" 195.00
Vase, birds/flowering prunus, lt turq on wht, 1800s, 8", pr 1,500.00
Vase, crane on limb of pine tree, gr on wht, 12" 350.00
Vase, cranes/peonies, gr on wht, Ching Dynasty, 14" 950.00
Vase, ducks & lotus flower, red on wht, bulbous, 8½", pr 600.00
Vase, flying crane, 2 under pine/bamboo, gr on wht, 12" 350.00
Vase, monkey in pine tree, red on wht, 9¼" 360.00
Vase, peony flowers, red on wht, gourd shape, 10", pr 715.00
Vase, rams in landscape, lappet bands, cobalt/wht, 1800, 9" ...1,750.00
Vase, 3 Friends, dragons on neck, red on snowflake cvgs, 8" ...2,500.00

Peloton

Peloton glass was first made by Wilhelm Kralik in Bohemia in 1880. This unusual art glass was produced by rolling colored threads onto the transparent or opaque glass gather as it was removed from the furnace. Usually more than one color of threading was used, and some items were further decorated with enameling. It was made with both shiny and acid finishes.

Rose bowl, lav-pk, mc strings, wishbone ft, 2¾x2½" 225.00
Rose bowl, wht, mc strings, 6-crimp, 2½x2½" 245.00
Vase, lav to wht, mc strings, ribbed, crimped, 6x4½" 450.00
Vase, wht, mc strings, bulbous w/3-fold top, 4x5" 350.00
Vase, wht, mc strings, emb ribs, tricorn top, 7x5¾" 350.00
Vase, wht, pastel strings, ribbed, 5 wishbone ft, 6½x4" 450.00
Vase, wht cased, mc strings, emb ribs, tricorn top, 3¾x4¾" 350.00

Pennsbury

Established in the 1950s in Morrisville, Pennsylvania, by Henry Below, the Pennsbury Pottery produced dinnerware and novelty items, much of which was sold in gift shops along the Pennsylvania Turnpike.

Henry and his wife, Lee, worked for years at the Stangl Pottery before striking out on their own. Lee and her daughter were the artists responsible for many of the early pieces, the bird figures among them. Pennsbury pottery was hand painted, some in blue on white, some in multicolor on caramel. Pennsylvania Dutch motifs, Amish couples, and barbershop singers were among their most popular decorative themes. Sgraffito, or hand incising, was used extensively. The company marked their wares 'Pennsbury Pottery' or 'Pennsbury Pottery, Morrisville, PA.'

In October of 1969, the company closed. Contents of the pottery were sold in December of the following year; in April of 1971, the buildings burned to the ground. Items marked Pennsbury Glenview or Stumar Pottery (or these marks in combination) were made by Glenview after 1969. Pieces manufactured after 1976 were made by the Pennington Pottery. Several of the old molds still exist, and the original Pennsbury Caramel process is still being used on novelty items, some of which are produced by Lewis Brothers, New Jersey. Production of Pennsbury dinnerware was not resumed after the closing. Our advisor for this category is Shirley Graff; she is listed in the Directory under Ohio. Note: prices may be higher in some areas of the country — particularly on the East Coast, the southern states, and Texas.

Ashtray, Don't Be So Doppich, 5" 20.00
Ashtray, Doylestown Trust 25.00
Ashtray, Outen the Light 20.00
Ashtray, Such Schmootzers 18.00
Ashtray, What Giffs 18.00
Ashtray, 2 Amish people 18.00
Bird, hummingbird, 4" 145.00
Bird, nuthatch, 3½" 80.00
Bird, wren, 3" 100.00
Bowl, divided vegetable; Red Rooster 29.00
Bowl, Fidelity Mutual, gray, 7" 40.00
Bowl, pretzel; Barbershop Quartet, 8x11" 65.00
Bowl, pretzel; Gay Nineties 85.00
Candlestick, hummingbird on flower, 5", pr 145.00
Casserole, Hex, w/lid, 9" 85.00
Coaster, Horowitz 15.00
Coaster, Olson 15.00
Coaster, Shultz 15.00
Creamer, Amish lady's head, 2" 13.00
Creamer, Red Rooster, 2" 15.00
Cruet, Amish head, pr 100.00
Cruet, Gay Nineties, pr 150.00
Cup & saucer, Blk Rooster 25.00
Cup & saucer, Red Rooster 20.00
Desk basket, Eagle 25.00
Mug, beer; Amish couple 30.00
Mug, beer; Eagle, 5" 20.00
Mug, beer; Here's Looking at You 25.00
Mug, beer; Swallow the Insult, 5" 45.00
Mug, beer; Sweet Adeline 30.00
Pitcher, Amish lady, mini 15.00
Pitcher, Amish man at fence, 2" 20.00
Pitcher, Eagle, 6¼" 29.00
Pitcher, Folkart, 1-pt, 5" 25.00
Pitcher, Red Rooster, 4" 18.00
Plaque, Amish couple 25.00
Plaque, Central Pacific RR, CP Huntington 45.00
Plaque, What Giffs, 4" dia 32.00
Plate, Angel, Stumar 30.00
Plate, Blk Rooster, 10" 22.00
Plate, Hex, 10" 20.00
Plate, Hex, 8" 18.00
Plate, Red Rooster, in factory fr, 11" 45.00

Pretzel bowl, Gay Nineties, 8x12", $85.00.

Plate, Red Rooster, 10" 18.00
Shakers, Amish head, pr 55.00
Sugar bowl, Hex 20.00
Tureen, soup; Blk Rooster, w/ladle & stand, minimum value 150.00
Wall pocket, sailboat, 6½x6½" 45.00

Pens and Pencils

The first metallic writing pen was patented in 1809, and soon machine-produced pens with steel nibs gradually began replacing the quill. The first fountain pen was invented in 1830, but due to the fact that a suitable metal for the tips had not yet been developed, they were not manufactured commercially until the 1880s. The first successful commercial producers were Waterman in 1884 and Parker with the Lucky Curve in 1888.

The self-filling pen of 1890 featured the soft, interior sack which filled with ink as the metal bar on the outside of the pen was raised and lowered. Variations of the pumping mechanism were tried until 1932 when Parker introduced the Vacumatic, a sackless pen with an internal pump. Our advisors for this category are Judy and Cliff Lawrence; they are listed in the Directory under Florida. For those seeking additional information, a magazine is published monthly by the Pen Fancier's Club, whose address can be found in the Directory under Clubs, Newsletters, and Catalogs. In the listings that follow, all pens are lever-filled unless otherwise noted.

Key:
AF — aeromatic filler
    button filler
CF — cartridge filler
CPT — chrome-plated trim
ED — eyedropper filler
GFT — gold-filled trim
GPM — gold-plated metal
GPT — gold-plated trim
HR — hard rubber
NPT — nickel-plated trim
PF — plunger filler
TD — touchdown filler
VF — vacumatic filler

Ballpoint Pens

Everhard Faber, 1946, brn/GF cap, EX 65.00
Eversharp, CA, 1946, bl/GF cap, M 95.00
Eversharp, CA, 1947, GFM, EX 125.00
Eversharp, Skyline, CA, 1944, maroon w/striped cap, EX 50.00
Eversharp, Skyline, CA, 1948, brn/gold striped cap, M 50.00
Reynold's, Internat'l, 1945, aluminum, GF clip, EX 125.00
Sheaffer, Stratowriter, 1946, GFM, M 95.00

Fountain Pens

Chilton, 1939, jade gr marble, GFM trim, TD, G 149.00
Conklin, Endura, 1930, gold/blk marble, GFM trim, lady's, EX 89.00
Eversharp, Executive Skyline, 1942, GFM trim, EX 395.00

Eversharp, Gold Seal Personal Point, 1932, GFM trim, EX 995.00
Eversharp, 64, 1944, blk w/14k gold cap & trim, LF, EX 325.00
Mont Blanc, Masterpiece, 1950, 14k gold, twist filler, EX 2,000.00
Mont Blanc, Masterpiece 12, 1960, blk, GFM trim, G 200.00
Mont Blanc, No 32, '62, charcoal w/GFM trim, twist filler, EX ..150.00
Parker, Bl Dmn Heirloom 51, blk, 14k cap & trim, VF, EX 800.00
Parker, Bl Dmn Vacumatic, 1945, bl stripes/GFM trim, VF, EX ...85.00
Parker, Challenger, 1939, silver pearl, NPT, BF, G 45.00
Parker, Duofold Jr, 1925, jade gr marble, GFM trim, BF, G 120.00
Parker, Duofold Jr, 1925, red, GFM trim, BF, EX 150.00
Parker, Duofold Sr, 1925, red, GFM trim, BF, G 295.00
Parker, Duofold Sr, 1930, blk, GFM trim, EX 295.00
Parker, Lady Duofold, 1929, jade gr, GFM trim, BF, EX 145.00
Parker, Lady Duofold, 1929, lapis bl, GFM trim, BF, EX 185.00
Parker, Super 21, 1960, turq w/chrome cap, AF, EX 32.00
Parker, 21 Deluxe, 1956, blk w/chrome cap, GFM trim, M 35.00
Parker, 51, 1947, brn, Lustraloy cap, CPT, VF, EX 55.00
Parker, 51, 1949, gr, Lustraloy cap, CPT, AF, EX 52.00
Parker, 51, 1951, gray, Lustraloy cap, CPT, AF, M 85.00
Parker, 51 Signet, 1958, GFM & trim, AF, demi-sz, G 99.00
Parker, 61, 1960, blk, Lustraloy cap, CPT, EX 69.00
Parker, 61, 1960, gray, Lustraloy cap, CPT, EX 69.00
Parker, 75, 1965, sterling, GFM trim, AF, EX 145.00
Parker, 75, 1975, sterling, GFM trim, med nib, AF, M 135.00
Sheaffer, Crest Triumph 1750, '45, blk, GFM cap/trim, PF, EX ..140.00
Sheaffer, Lifetime, 1924, jade gr marble, GFM trim, lady's, EX ..650.00
Sheaffer, Lifetime, 1932, blk, GFM trim, EX 325.00
Sheaffer, Lifetime, 1938, ebonized pearl, GFM trim, EX 395.00
Sheaffer, Lifetime, 1939, blk, GFM trim, EX 295.00
Sheaffer, Lifetime Triumph, 1945, gold pearl stripes, PF, EX 250.00
Sheaffer, Lifetime Triumph 5000, 1942, blk, gold cap, PF, EX ...399.00
Sheaffer, PFM IV Snorkel, 1959, blk, chrome/gold cap, TD, EX ...225.00
Sheaffer, Triumph Sentinel Snorkel, 1953, maroon, EX 69.00
Sheaffer, Wht Dot Triumph TM, 1950, blk, TD, EX 49.00
Sheaffer, 350, 1934, silver pearl stripes, NPT, PF, EX 49.00
Swan, Self Filler, 1925, blk chased HR, NPT, EX 89.00
Swan, 1923, GFM & trim, EX 350.00
Swan, 1923, sterling, sterling trim, EX 350.00
Wahl-Oxford, 1932, blk, GFM trim, NM 75.00
Waterman, Ideal 0552, 1928, GFM filigree, EX 695.00
Waterman, Ideal 0555, 1925, GFM & trim, G 650.00
Waterman, Ideal 12, 1899, red mottled HR, NPT, ED, EX 295.00
Waterman, Ideal 552½ V, 1924, solid 14k gold, EX 450.00
Waterman, 100 Yr Supersz, 1942, blk, GFM trim, EX 750.00
Waterman, 100 Yr Taperite, 1946, 14k gold, EX 1,200.00

Mechanical Pencils

Conklin, 1930, blk, GFM trim, crescent above clip, G 65.00
Eversharp, 5th Ave Repeater, 1945, GFM top & trim, EX 39.00
Parker, Challenger, 1940, silver pearl, NPT, EX 22.00
Parker, Duofold, 1930, Moderne pearl & blk, GFM trim, EX 95.00
Parker, Duofold, 1933, burgundy & blk, GFM trim, EX 105.00
Parker, Duofold Jr, 1926, jade gr marble, GFM trim, EX 99.00
Parker, Duofold Sr, 1930, jade gr, GFM trim, EX 225.00
Parker, Duofold Sr, 1930, jade gr, GFM trim, G 175.00
Parker, Duofold Sr Big Bro, 1928, blk, G 175.00
Parker, Flighter, 1972, stainless steel, CPT, EX 35.00
Parker, Vacumatic, 1935, pearl, NPT, EX 59.00
Parker, 1934, Moderne gr & pearl, GFM trim, EX 65.00
Parker, 51, 1945, blk w/GFM top & trim, EX 79.00
Parker, 51, 1950, brn, Lustraloy cap, CPT, G 35.00
Sheaffer, Jr, 1934, silver pearl/red streaked marble, NPT, EX 29.00
Sheaffer, Tuckaway, 1946, golden stripes, GFM trim, EX 32.00

Sheaffer, Tuckaway, 1948, maroon, GFM trim, EX 20.00
Sheaffer, Wht Dot, 1953, gray, chrome/gold-banded top, M 22.00
Sheaffer, Wht Dot PFM III, 1959, gray w/GFM trim, M 40.00
Sheaffer, 1932, red-streaked pearl marble, GFM trim, EX 49.00
Sheaffer, 1938, ebonized pearl, GFM trim, EX 99.00
Sheaffer, 1945, blk w/GFM top & trim, EX 39.00
Sheaffer, 1953, gr, GFM trim, M 18.00
Sheaffer, 500, 1946, brn w/GFM trim, EX 29.00
Wahl-Eversharp, Big Boy, 1929, woodgrain HR, GFM trim, EX 165.00
Wahl-Eversharp, 1936, gold & red marble, GFM trim, G 29.00
Waterman, Corinth, 1949, blk w/chrome top, GFM trim, M 39.00
Waterman, Repeater, 1949, gray w/gold-tone top, CPT, EX 20.00
Waterman, Stateleigh Repeater, 1949, blk w/GFM top, M 60.00

Sets

Conklin, 1926, GFM & trim, M 225.00
Eversharp, Gold Seal Doric, 1940, burgundy marble, EX 995.00
Eversharp, 1961, gr, CPT, AF, alloy nib, EX 49.00

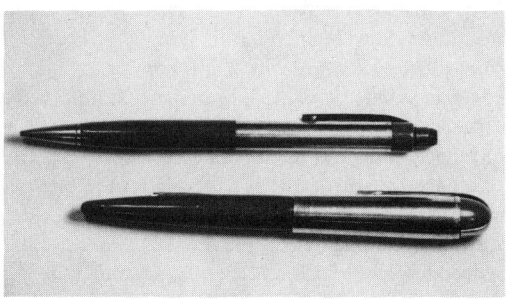

Everlast Skyline Presentation set in gray with gold-filled cap, M, $135.00.

Mont Blanc, 242 Repeater, 1952, gold pearl marble, EX 600.00
Parker, Bl Dmn Maxima, 1940, emerald pearl stripes, VG, EX ...795.00
Parker, Major Vacumatic, '38, pearl stripes, GFM trim, VF, EX ..295.00
Parker, 61 Presidential, 1950, solid 14k gold, EX 2,000.00
Sheaffer, Lifetime 2000, 1945, blk w/gold trim, M 300.00
Sheaffer, PFM Autograph Snorkel, '59, blk, gold bands, TD, M ..300.00
Sheaffer, Triumph Masterpiece, 1942, 14k gold, EX 2,000.00
Sheaffer, Triumph Masterpiece, 1946, 14k gold, M 2,500.00
Waterman, Ideal 0552, 1938, GFM filigree & trim, EX 800.00
Waterman, Ideal 452, 1926, sterling filigree, EX 800.00
Waterman, Patrician, 1932, nacre w/wht GFM trim, MIB 2,500.00

Personalities, Fact and Fiction

One of the largest and most popular areas of collecting today, if tradepaper ads and articles be any indication, is character-related memorabilia. Everyone has favorites, whether they be comic-strip personalities or true-life heroes. The earliest comic strip dealt with the adventures of the Yellow Kid, the smiling, bald-headed Oriental boy always in a nightshirt. He was introduced in 1895, a product of the imagination of Richard Fenton Outcault. Today, though very hard to come by, items relating to the Yellow Kid bring premium prices.

In 1902 Buster Brown and Tige, his dog and constant companion (more of Outcault's progenies), made it big in the comics as well as in the world of advertising. Shoe stores appealed to the younger set through merchandising displays that featured them both. Today items from their earlier years are very collectible.

Though her 1923 introduction was unobtrusively made through only one newspaper, New York's *Daily News*, Little Orphan Annie, the vacant-eyed redhead in the inevitable red dress, was quickly adopted by hordes of readers nationwide, and before the demise of her creator, Harold Gray, in 1968, she had starred in her own radio show. She made two feature films, and in 1977 'Annie' was launched on Broadway.

Other early comic figures were Moon Mullins, created in 1923 by Frank Willard; Buck Rogers by Philip Nowlan in 1928; and Betty Boop, the round-faced, innocent-eyed, chubby-cheeked Boop-Boop-a-Doop girl of the early 1930s. Bimbo was her dog and KoKo her clown friend.

Popeye made his debut in 1929 as the spinach-eating sailor with the spindly-limbed girlfriend, Olive Oyl, in the comic strip *Thimble Theatre*, created by Elzie Segar. He became a film star in 1933 and had his own radio show that during 1936 played three times a week on CBS. He obligingly modeled for scores of toys, dolls, and figurines, and especially those from the thirties are very collectible.

Tarzan, created around 1930 by Edgar Rice Burroughs, and Captain Midnight, by Robert Burtt and Willfred G. Moore, are popular heroes with today's collectors. During the days of radio, Sky King of the Flying Crown Ranch (also created by Burtt and Moore) thrilled boys and girls of the mid-1940s. Hopalong Cassidy, Red Rider, Tom Mix, and the Lone Ranger were only a few of the other 'good guys' always on the side of law and order.

But of all the fictional heroes and comic characters collected today, probably the best loved and most well known is Mickey Mouse. Created in the late 1920s by Walt Disney, Micky (as his name was first spelled) became an instant success with his film debut, Steamboat Willie. His popularity was parlayed through wind-up toys, watches, figurines, cookie jars, puppets, clothing, and numerous other products. Items from the 1930s are usually copyrighted 'Walt Disney Enterprises'; thereafter 'Walt Disney Productions' was used.

For those interested in Disneyana, we recommend *Stern's Guide to Disney Collectibles*; *Character Toys and Collectibles* (there are two volumes); and *The Collector's Encyclopedia of Disneyana*. All are available from Collector Books. Our advisors for this category are Cathy and Norm Vigue; they are listed in the Directory under Massachusetts. See also Autographs; Banks; Big Little Books; Cartoon Books; Children's Books; Comic Books; Cookie Jars; Dolls; Lunch Boxes; Movie Memorabilia; Paper Dolls; Pin-Back Buttons; Posters; Rock 'N Roll Memorabilia; Toys.

Alan Ladd, cap pistol, Schmidt, 1955, 10" L, M 100.00
Alfred E Neuman, bust, ceramic, 1960s premium, NM 185.00
Alice in Wonderland, record player, 45 rpm, 1940s, EX 225.00
Alvin, Soaky, lt pnt wear, EX 12.00
Amos (of Amos & Andy), sparkler toy, push lever, glass eyes 400.00
Andy Panda, doll, stuffed cloth, Mego, 1975, MIB 22.50
Andy Panda, shaker, ceramic, HP, 1958, 4" 40.00
Baby Huey, puppet, Gund, 1950s, MIB 45.00
Bambi, wristwatch, Ingersoll, 1949, EX 85.00
Barney Google, fr-tray puzzle, 1950s, NM 11.00
Barney Google, sheet music, 1923, EX 25.00
Batman, color book, 1966, M 22.00
Batman, eyeglasses case, NM 25.00
Batman, flashlight, figural, Larami, 1978, NM 25.00
Batman, fr-tray puzzle, Whitman, 1967, EX 10.00
Batman, girl's dress, 1960s, 6", EX 85.00
Batman, night light, figural, 1960s, EX 70.00
Batman, parachute, w/5" figure, 1966, M on card 55.00
Batman, periscope, Bar-Zim, 1966, VG 42.50
Batman, pool float, inflatable, 1967, M 140.00
Batman, shooting arcade, AHI, 1970s, 7", MIB 125.00
Batman & Robin, pin-bk, Crimefighter, 1966, 3", M in pkg 15.00
Beany & Cecil, tote bag, red, M 30.00
Beatles, see Rock 'n Roll Memorabilia

Beaver Cleaver, Big Book To Color, Saalfield, 1958, NM 35.00
Beetle Bailey, mug, ceramic, M 32.00
Ben Casey, nodder, 1950s, 7", M 95.00
Ben Casey, notebook, Hasbro, M 12.00

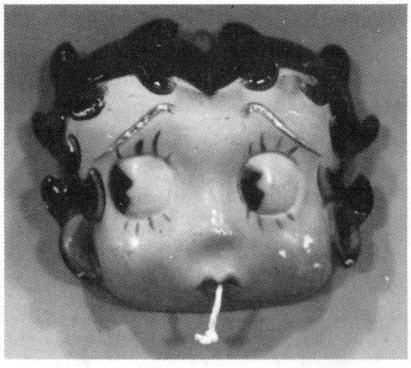

Betty Boop string holder, chalkware, ca 1930s, 10" wide, $135.00.

Betty Boop, figure, celluloid, plays violin, 1930s 125.00
Betty Boop, handkerchief, 1930s, 9" 35.00
Betty Boop, pocket watch, Ingraham, 1934, EX 255.00
Betty Boop, string holder, chalk, 10" 135.00
Betty Boop, wall pocket, ceramic, 6" 125.00
Betty Boop & Bimbo, bridge score pad, 1930s 45.00
Beverly Hillbillies, color book, 1963, M 40.00
Bewitched, story book, photo cover, 1965, EX 12.50
Bionic Woman, model kit, Bionic Repair, sealed contents 15.00
Blondie & Dagwood, fr-tray puzzle, 1950s, NM, pr 22.00
Bonanza, Little Joe doll, Am Character, NM 45.00
Bozo the Clown, color book, 1966, M 10.00
Bozo the Clown, room decal, 1950s, M 10.00
Buck Rogers, board game, 1970s, M in EX box 15.00
Buck Rogers, Galactic playset, 1979, MIB 30.00
Buck Rogers, pin, 25th Century, bright colors, EX 52.00
Buck Rogers, walkie talkies, Remco, 1950s, EX in orig box 125.00
Bugs Bunny, book, Treasure Hunt Golden Story, 1949, NM 30.00
Bugs Bunny, camera, 1976, MIB 35.00
Bugs Bunny, rub-off pictures, Whitman, 1954, NM in box 60.00
Bugs Bunny, wristwatch, EX 115.00
Bugs Bunny & Porky Pig, paint book, 1944, unused 100.00
Bugs Bunny & Tweety, bookends, 1950s, pr 10.00
Bullwinkle, bank, Pat Ward, 1972, EX 35.00
Bullwinkle, dbl boomerang, 1969, 9", M in pkg 18.00
Bullwinkle, game, Electric Quiz, 1971, M on card 20.00
Bullwinkle, game, Supermarket, 1976, M 10.00
Bullwinkle, pillow, inflatable, NM 14.50
Bullwinkle, plane, friction toy, 1970s, EX 12.00
Bullwinkle, Soaky, 1960s, 10½", EX 30.00
Bullwinkle & Rocky, pencil case, vinyl, 1962, MIB 38.00
Bullwinkle & Rocky, signal light, Madison, 1970s, M on card 28.00
Buster Brown, wristwatch, EX 150.00
Captain America, color book, 1966, M 10.00
Captain Gallant, color book, photo cover, 1956, M 25.00
Captain Kangaroo, Halloween costume, 1950s, EX in box 65.00
Captain Kangaroo, magic slate, NM 15.00
Captain Marvel, game, Shazam, Fawcett, 1944, M in envelope 40.00
Captain Marvel, puzzle, 1950s, EX in 9x13" box 65.00
Captain Midnight, manual, 1947, M 125.00
Captain Midnight, ring, Mystic Eye Detector, NM 120.00
Casper the Ghost, color book, 1966, M 18.00
Casper the Ghost, figure, ceramic, 1980s, NM 18.50
Casper the Ghost, figure, Sutton, NM 30.00

Charlie Chaplin, ashtray, ceramic figural, 1960s, M 60.00
Charlie Chaplin, backwards watch, Bradley, MIB 85.00
Charlie Chaplin, color book, Saalfield, 1941, uncolored 75.00
Charlie Chaplin, music box, ceramic, 1973, M 40.00
Charlie McCarthy, paint book, Whitman, 1939, uncolored 45.00
Charlie the Tuna, bank, ceramic, Star Kist, 1988, MIB 25.00
Cheyenne, board game, 1950s, M in VG box 30.00
Cheyenne, Pistol, Peacemaker, plastic, 1960s, EX, pr 40.00
CHIPS, Colorforms, MIB 12.00
CHIPS, emergency medical kit, Empire, MIB 20.00
Chitty Chitty Bang Bang, color book, unused 20.00
Cinderella, Soaky, 1960s, 11", EX 15.00
Cisco Kid, scarf slide, M 30.00
Crusader Rabbit, fr-tray puzzle, M 33.00
Daffy Duck, liquor decanter, Italy, 1970s, EX 20.00
Dagwood, figure, Syrocco, 1944, EX 36.00
Dale Evans, jewelry set, M on card 10.00
Dale Evans, wristwatch, EX 85.00
Daniel Boone, canoe, inflatable, 1965, M in pkg 12.00
Davy Crockett, clock, wall type, w/pendulum, MIB 150.00
Davy Crockett, game, To the Rescue, Disney, 1956, EX 48.00
Davy Crockett, gun, Auto Magic Picture, Disney, MIB 135.00
Davy Crockett, puzzle, Disney, 1955, EX in box 30.00
Dennis the Menace, doll, 1950s, 15", M in cartoon illus box 235.00
Dennis the Menace, figure, rubber, 1959, 8", EX 28.00
Dennis the Menace, Margaret hand puppet, EX 20.00
Dennis the Menace, valentines, 1960s, 14 different in pkg 23.00
Deputy Dawg, figure, Dakin, MIB 40.00
Dick Tracy, color book, Saalfield, 1946, EX 40.00
Dick Tracy, decoder, red, M 40.00
Dick Tracy, detective set, colorful graphics, 1930s, EX 60.00
Dick Tracy, game, cards, 1934, EX 45.00
Dick Tracy, puzzle, Man Hunt, 1962, EX in G box 24.00
Dick Tracy, ring, enameled hat, M 150.00
Dizzy Dean, pin, membership, M 18.00
Doc Savage, pin, membership, NM 150.00

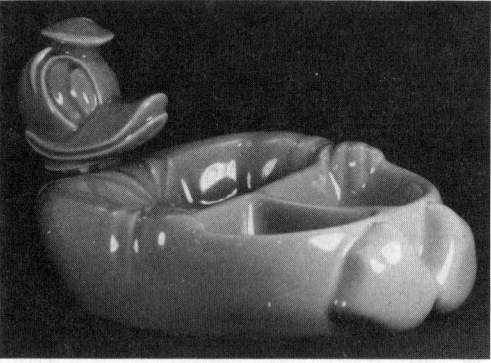

Donald Duck hot water dish, pottery, Walt Disney Enterprises, ca 1940s, $130.00.

Donald Duck, orange juice can, red, 4½", EX 15.00
Donald Duck, wristwatch, US Time, 1955, MIB 195.00
Doris Day, color book, Whitman, EX 35.00
Dr Doolittle, bendable figure, Mattel, 1967, 6", M in box 45.00
Dr Doolittle, medical playset, MIB 35.00
Dr Doolittle, talking hand puppet, Mattel, 1967, MIB 85.00
Dr Kildare, notebook, hard plastic, Hasbro, 1965, M 20.00
Dukes of Hazzard, General Lee Charger car, MPC, lg, NM 35.00
Elmer Fudd, figure, ceramic, 1940s, 6½", NM 95.00
Elmer Fudd, nodder, 1950s, 7", M 165.00

Elvis Presley, see Rock 'n Roll Memorabilia
Evel Knievel, dragster, gyro powered, NM in box **25.00**
Evel Knievel, game, Stunt, Ideal, EX **15.00**
Family Affair, color book, Whitman, 1970, M **15.00**
Family Affair, puzzle, 1970, MIB **23.00**
Ferdinand the Bull, figure, bsk, 3", M **38.00**
Flash Gordon, slide puzzle, Roalex, 1954, M on card **25.00**
Flintstones, Bamm Bamm bubble pipe, 1963, M on card **22.00**
Flintstones, Bamm Bamm Soaky, 1960s, 9", EX **25.00**
Flintstones, Barney Rubble color book, 1964, M **35.00**
Flintstones, Barney Rubble doll, Knickerbocker, 1962, MIB **120.00**
Flintstones, Barney Rubble figure, diecast, 1977, M **20.00**
Flintstones, Barney Rubble Soaky, EX **20.00**
Flintstones, Fred hobby horse, 1961, EX **75.00**
Flintstones, game, Circus, Kohner, 1960s, VG **85.00**
Flintstones, game, Cut Ups, Hanna Barbera, 1962, EX **30.00**
Flintstones, game, Mitt Full, Whitman, 1962, EX **60.00**
Flintstones, game, Stone Age, Hanna Barbera, 1961, EX **30.00**
Flintstones, Pebbles & Bamm Bamm punch-out book, 1974, M ...**10.00**
Flintstones, Pebbles hand puppet, 1956s, M **25.00**
Flintstones, throw pillow, 1960s, 12", M, set of 4 ....**65.00**
Flipper, Stitch-A-Story, 1955, M **18.00**
Flying Nun, doll, Hasbro, 1967, 4", MIB **40.00**
Flying Nun, marble maze, Hasbro, rare, NM in box **35.00**
Fonzie, model kit, motorcycle, 1970s, EX **25.00**
Frankenstein Jr, fr-tray puzzle, 1969, lt wear **26.00**
Funny Face, mug, F&F, 1969-74, NM **9.50**
Gene Autry, book, stencil, photo cover, 1950s, 6x10", EX **75.00**
Gene Autry, cowboy boot label, 1950s, NM **8.00**
Gene Autry, galoshes, metal buckles, MIB **150.00**
Gene Autry, guitar, Emenee Professional, MIB **75.00**
Gene Autry, marionette, 1940s, 18", M in EX box **350.00**
Gene Autry, wristwatch, leather band, 1950s, EX in box **285.00**
Gentle Ben, swamp buggy, Remco, MIB **250.00**
George of the Jungle, board game, 1968, EX **165.00**
Get Smart, color book, 1965, M **46.00**
Get Smart, fr-tray puzzle, Would You Believe, 1966, NM **40.00**
Get Smart, gum card wrapper, 1966 ....**35.00**
GI Joe, wristwatch, 1966, MIB **75.00**
Goofy, wristwatch, gold edition Pedre **300.00**
Great Grape Ape, Halloween costume, 1976, M **18.00**
Great Grape Ape, paint-a-picture set, 1975, MIB **18.50**
Great Grape Ape, picture making kit, Hanna Barbera, 1976, M ..**12.50**
Green Hornet, charm bracelet, Greenway, 1966, M on card **70.00**
Green Hornet, color book, Kato's Revenge, 1966, M **18.00**
Green Hornet, fr-tray puzzle, Whitman, 1960s, set of 4, MIB **145.00**
Green Hornet, game, Quick Switch, complete, EX **150.00**
Green Hornet, magic rub-offs, 1966, EX **98.00**
Green Hornet, Punch-O-Ball, M on card **145.00**
Green Hornet, record, theme, Coronet, EX **38.00**
Green Hornet, wrist radio, M in EX box **300.00**
Green Lantern, character glass **35.00**
Hecter Heathcote, Wonder Book, 1950, EX **10.00**
Helen Trent, badge, M **95.00**
Herman & Katnip, puzzle, 1960, EX in box **16.50**
Hogan's Heroes, model kit, jeep, sealed **90.00**
Hopalong Cassidy, badge, Savings Club, 1950s, M **18.00**
Hopalong Cassidy, bank, plastic bust figural, NM **33.00**
Hopalong Cassidy, brooch, lady's pistol, EX **110.00**
Hopalong Cassidy, compass, hat ring, premium, NM **155.00**
Hopalong Cassidy, jacket, blk denim, Bluebell, NM **245.00**
Hopalong Cassidy, knife w/scabbard, sm, M **35.00**
Hopalong Cassidy, sweater, gr & wht, M **150.00**
Hopalong Cassidy, TV chair **250.00**

Hopalong Cassidy, wristwatch, plastic, US Time, 1950, NM **75.00**
Howdy Doody, cookbook, Welch's Grape Juice, 1952, EX **25.00**
Howdy Doody, disguise kit, Poll Parrot premium, unpunched, M ...**45.00**
Howdy Doody, flip badge, HD for President, 1950s **20.00**
Howdy Doody, fruit bag, plastic, Kagran, 1950s, M **7.50**
Howdy Doody, Prize Doodle list, 1954-55 ....**10.00**
Howdy Doody, ring, flasher, Poll Parrot premium, 1950s, EX **88.00**
Howdy Doody, Time Teacher, cb clock w/plastic hands, '50s, EX ..**28.00**
Howdy Doody, TV Guide, on cover, Nov 1951, EX **38.00**
Howdy Doody, wallpaper strip, Bob Smith **55.00**

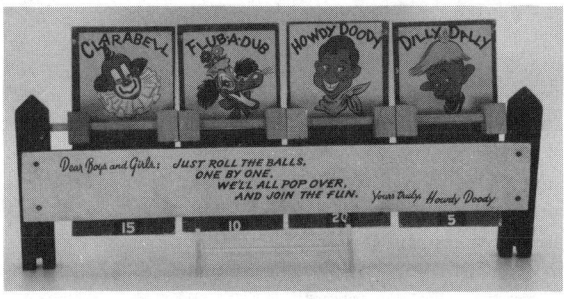

Howdy Doody's Own Game, 12½" long, $65.00.

Huckleberry Hound, game, Bumps, complete, EX **45.00**
Huckleberry Hound, game, Juggle Roll, 1960, EX **50.00**
Huckleberry Hound, game, Tiddlewinks, Hanna Barbera, '59, EX ...**30.00**
Huckleberry Hound, game, Western, 1959, EX **20.00**
Huckleberry Hound, Halloween mask, 1960, M **6.00**
Inspector Gadget, doll, 1983, MIB **88.00**
J Fred Muggs, mobile, cb, 1950s, EX **75.00**
Jack Armstrong, ring, Egyptian whistle, radio premium, NM **75.00**
Jackie Gleason, swizzle stick, emb figure, 1960s, 6" **85.00**
James Bond, album, Thunderball soundtrack **15.00**
James Bond, banner, cloth w/wooden dowels, 1960s, 16x26" **145.00**
James Bond, exploding coin, M on card **30.00**
James Bond, model kit, Moonraker spaceship, 1979, M **35.00**
James Bond, notebook, loose-leaf, 1960s, M **45.00**
James Bond, puzzle, Goldfinger, 1965, MIB **52.00**
Jetsons, fr-tray puzzle, 1962, EX **45.00**
Jetsons, game, Fun Pad, EX (no spinner) **40.00**
Jetsons, game, Space Ball pinball, 1962, M in box **165.00**
Joan Palooka, hand puppet, NM in VG box **50.00**
Joe Carioca, wristwatch, Ingersoll, 1953, MIB **350.00**
John Wayne, belt buckle, brass, w/portrait from True Grit, M **45.00**
Johnny Ringo, hand puppet, 1950s, 16", MIB **245.00**
Johnny West, doll, Marx, M in worn box **35.00**
Kaptain Kool & the Kongs, fr-tray puzzle, M **12.50**
Land of the Giants, color book, M **56.00**
Lariat Sam, Colorforms set, 1962, MIB **25.00**
Lassie, fr-tray puzzle, 1966, set of 4, M in EX box **22.00**
Lassie, hassock, cloth & vinyl, child's, EX **40.00**
Laverne & Shirley, pendant, tiger claw, 1973, M on card **10.00**
Little Audrey, balloons on illus card, 1950s, M **12.50**
Little Henry, doll, rubber, squeaker, 8", EX **65.00**
Little Orphan Annie, decoder, Whirlomatic, 1942, rare, M **65.00**
Little Orphan Annie, jtd figure, celluloid, Japan, 1930s, 7" **250.00**
Little Orphan Annie, jtd figure, wooden, 1930s, 5" **95.00**
Little Orphan Annie, nodder, bsk, German, 3½" **95.00**
Little Orphan Annie, paint box, Milton Bradley, lg, EX **115.00**
Little Orphan Annie, ring, Mystic Eye, M **120.00**
Little Orphan Annie, sport watch, 1930s, NM **200.00**
Little Orphan Annie, tea set, lustreware, 1930s, 5-pc **110.00**

Lone Ranger, badge, Safety Club, Bond Bread premium 35.00
Lone Ranger, bullet pencil, red, 1940s, EX 65.00
Lone Ranger, Deputy kit, Cheerios, 1980, M 15.00
Lone Ranger, dexterity puzzle set, 1940s, NM in box 185.00
Lone Ranger, Frontier Town, partly punched, +mailer 40.00
Lone Ranger, hairbrush, wooden hdl, 1939, EX in box 95.00
Lone Ranger, mechanical pencil, Merita Bread premium, EX 125.00
Lone Ranger, pastry tin, Clayton Moore picture, NM 25.00
Lone Ranger, pedometer, M in mailer 35.00
Lone Ranger, pencil sharpener, bullet form, Merita Bread, NM ...50.00
Lone Ranger, pocketknife, EX 15.00
Lone Ranger, ring, Atomic Bomb, Kix premium, EX 80.00
Lone Ranger, ring, flashlight, EX 80.00
Lone Ranger, ring, Nat'l Defender, EX 120.00
Lone Ranger, ring, saddle, w/film strip, premium, NM 135.00
Lone Ranger, ring, Weather, w/indicator paper 85.00
Lone Ranger, ring, 6-Shooter, 1930s premium, EX 90.00
Lone Ranger, silver bullet, secret compartment, 45-caliber 45.00
Lone Ranger, toothbrush holder, figural, 1938, NM 60.00
Lone Ranger, water pistol, 1970s, M on card 35.00
Lone Ranger, wrist compass, EX 85.00
Lone Ranger, wristwatch, Ingersoll, ca 1955, EX 150.00
Lone Ranger & Tonto, bookends, pr 125.00
Lost in Space, board game, M in NM box 65.00
Lost in Space, robot, NM in EX box 450.00
Ludwig Von Drake, squeeze toy, rubber, Dell, M 32.00
Magilla Gorilla, bank, plastic book form, Ideal, M in pkg 40.00
Magilla Gorilla, bend & flex figure, Ideal, MIB 88.00
Magilla Gorilla, slide puzzle, Roalex, 1964, M on card 35.00
Man from UNCLE, car, missile-firing, Husky, 1966, NM 65.00
Man from UNCLE, puzzle, Impossible Escape, 1965, EX 45.00
Man from UNCLE, record album, photo cover, 1965, EX 18.50
Mary Poppins, Big Golden book, 1964, NM 9.00
Mary Poppins, color book, 1973, M 13.50
Mat Mason, space shelter pack, Mattel, 1969, M on card 70.00
Maverick, cap gun, M on card 175.00
Mickey & Minnie Mouse, figure, pnt celluloid, Japan, 5", pr 600.00
Mickey Mouse, ballpoint pen, 1950s, EX 50.00
Mickey Mouse, cereal bowl, Beetleware, WDE, 1938, M 17.50
Mickey Mouse, charm, celluloid figural, EX 12.00
Mickey Mouse, doll, Dean's Rag Book, 5-finger, 8", EX 500.00

Mickey Mouse, Dixon's map, 1930s, matted and framed, $265.00.

Mickey Mouse, dominoes, WDE, 1938, boxed set, NM 60.00
Mickey Mouse, figure, bsk, playing horn, 1930s, 4½", EX 85.00
Mickey Mouse, fountain pen, Inkograph, 1936, 5½", EX 150.00
Mickey Mouse, game, Pin the Tail on Mickey, WDE, EX 110.00

Mickey Mouse, greeting card, Hall Bros, 1930s, EX 38.00
Mickey Mouse, handkerchief, Walt Disney, ca 1936, 8½", NM ..28.00
Mickey Mouse, mask & vest, Cooper, 1960, M in pkg 12.50
Mickey Mouse, paint set, Stardust, 1950s, M 18.50
Mickey Mouse, pocket watch, Ingersoll, 1934, MIB 750.00
Mickey Mouse, pocket watch, Ingersoll, 1934, NM 300.00
Mickey Mouse, pop-up book, Bl Ribbon, W Disney, 1933, EX ...250.00
Mickey Mouse, pop-up book, Ye Olden Days, 1934, EX 250.00
Mickey Mouse, radiator ornament, early, 5¾", NM 1,500.00
Mickey Mouse, roller coaster, battery operated, 1970s 25.00
Mickey Mouse, target game, Marx Bros, brd/gun/darts, box 275.00
Mickey Mouse, toy chest, 1930s, EX 165.00
Mickey Mouse, watering can, tin, Ohio Art, 7", M 110.00
Mickey Mouse, wristwatch, Ingersoll, 1933, EX in VG box 300.00
Mickey Mouse, wristwatch, Ingersoll, 1947, EX 75.00
Mickey Mouse, wristwatch, Ingersoll, 1947, MIB 275.00
Mickey Mouse, wristwatch, Kelton, 1946, VG 70.00
Mickey Mouse & Clarabelle Cow, alphabet bowl, 8", EX 200.00
Mighty Hercules, sticker book, 1963, M 55.00
Mighty Mouse, figure, Dakin, 1970s, MIB 235.00
Monkees, Davy Jones finger puppet, M in shipping box 35.00
Moon Mullins, figure, jtd wood, 1930s, 6", EX 80.00
Mork & Mindy, card game, Milton Bradley, 1978, M 8.00
Mork & Mindy, Colorforms magic set, NM in box 33.00
Mother Goose, drinking straws, 1950s, MIB 15.00
Mr Magoo, Big Top Birthday Bash, premium, M in mailer 28.00
Mummy, glow-in-dark model, Aurora, 1964, EX 48.00
Mummy, Halloween costume, Ben Cooper, 1960s, NM 85.00
Munsters, Herman talking doll, w/legs, NM 225.00
Munsters, Herman talking puppet, NM 150.00
Munsters, Lily doll, Remco, M 225.00
Munsters, TV Guide, Herman & Lily on cover, 1965, EX 25.00
Mush Mouse, pull toy w/vinyl figure, Ideal, 1960s, EX 85.00
My Favorite Martian, record, 45 rpm, M in pkg 28.00
Nanny & Professor, Colorforms, NM in EX box 35.00
Olive Oil, marionette, vinyl head, cloth body, 1962, 12", EX 65.00
Oscar the Grouch, talking alarm clock, Bradley, NMIB 25.00
Our Gang, Spanky calendar, full color, 1943, lg, EX 60.00
Peanuts, board game, Selchow & Richter, 1959, NM in box 45.00
Peanuts, Charlie Brown nodder, ceramic, Japan, '60s, 4½", NM ...30.00
Peanuts, Lucy's doctor booth friction toy, 1975, MIB 20.00
Peanuts, Snoopy bank, ceramic baseball player, 1971, M 20.00
Peanuts, Snoopy nodder, ceramic Santa, 1960s, M 18.50
Peanuts, Snoopy on apple bank, ceramic, Japan, 1950s 25.00
Peanuts, wastebasket, mc illus, 1970s, M 20.00
Penelope Pitstop, jewelry set, M on card 15.00
Pete's Dragon, color book, 1971, M 9.50
Peter Potamus, bank, Soaky type, plastic, 1960s, 10" 30.00
Peter Potamus, fr-tray puzzle, Hanna Barbera, 1965, sm 20.00
Pink Panther, Christmas plate, Royal Orleans, 1984, MIB 38.00
Pink Panther, puzzle, 1978, EX in box 9.00
Pinky Lee, paint set, photo cover, 1955, lg, M 68.00
Pinocchio, clock, Bayard, 1964, EX 50.00
Pinocchio, figure, latex, Seiberling, EX 48.00
Pinocchio, thermometer, Bakelite figural, Disney, 1939, M 85.00
Planet of Apes, Ape Phones, 1974, M on NM card 18.00
Planet of Apes, Galen Halloween costume, 1974, EX in box 18.50
Planet of Apes, periscope, 1960s, 19", EX 45.00
Pluto, doll, Sun Rubber, NM in box 55.00
Pluto, Soaky, EX 20.00
Popeye, book, Sticker Fun, 1969, M 20.00
Popeye, clock, animated Sweet Pea, Smiths, 1968, NM 200.00
Popeye, doll, cloth, 1930s, 17", VG 98.00
Popeye, game, ring toss, Transogram, 1957, M in worn box 35.00

Popeye, Getar, Mattel, NM in box 58.00
Popeye, pencil case, 1936, EX 25.00
Popeye, postcard, 1973, M, set of 12 ....12.00
Popeye, push puppet, Kohner, EX 13.00

Popeye pop-up book, *Popeye with the Hag of the Seven Seas,* very rare, NM, $150.00.

Popeye, Stick-A-Story, 1966, M in pkg 25.00
Popeye, talking hand puppet, Mattel, 1960s, 11", NM in box 165.00
Popeye & His Friends, color book, 1958, unused 30.00
Popeye & Sweet Pea, Colorforms, 1970s, NM in box 25.00
Porky Pig, bank, bsk, HP, 1930s, 5", EX 225.00
Purple People Eater, hat, 1958, M on illus card 48.00
Raggedy Ann & Andy, bank, ceramic, Merril Bobbs, 1971, M 32.00
Range Rider, color book, Mahoney photo cover, 1956, M 34.00
Red Ryder, gloves, NM, pr 25.00
Red Ryder, handbook #1, Daisy, NM 35.00
Red Ryder, pin, Victory Patrol, NM 125.00
Restless Gun, color book, Payne cover, 1958, M 40.00
Ricochet Rabbit, push puppet, Hanna Barbera, EX 24.00
Rifleman, fr-tray puzzle, Whitman, 1960s, EX 40.00
Rin-Tin-Tin, patches, Nabisco, unused set of 5 different, M 45.00
Road Runner, board game, 1960s, M in EX box 35.00
Road Runner, figure, Dakin, 1968, 9", EX 17.50
Robin Hood, vest & pouch set, Coleco, 1959, NM in box 29.00
Rocky, mug, ceramic, 1960s, 3", M 75.00
Roger Wilco, ring, metal base, NM 150.00
Rootie Kazootie, fr-tray puzzle, EX 26.00
Roy Rogers, fountain pen, M in orig box 165.00
Roy Rogers, hat, Quick Shooter, Ideal, 1950s, NM in EX box 185.00
Roy Rogers, lantern, Double-R, EX 75.00
Roy Rogers, photo, 1950s movie giveaway, 7x5" 8.00
Roy Rogers, place setting, china, 4-pc 170.00
Roy Rogers, Rider Coat, denim, NM 225.00
Roy Rogers, ring, magnifying 75.00
Roy Rogers, sign, Dbl R Bar Ranch, 24x24", M 125.00
Roy Rogers, Sugar Crisp 3-D card, for 3-D glasses, EX 28.00
Roy Rogers, wristwatch, Ingraham, 1951, MIB 150.00
Roy Rogers' dog Bullet, figure, Hartland, '50s, sm, EX in box 95.00
Ruff & Reddy, draw & color set, 1959, MIB 40.00
Ruff & Reddy, Golden Book, Hanna Barbera, 1959 ....6.50
Scooby Doo, game, Hanna Barbera, 1973, complete, EX 18.50
Scooby Doo, lamp, plastic figural, M 50.00
Scooby Doo, story book, 1975 ....5.00
Secret Agent, cap pistol, M in NM box 80.00
Secret Sam, attache case, complete w/papers & bullets, NM 65.00
Secret Squirrel, trapeze toy, EX 28.50
Sergeant Preston, premium card set (36), 1950, NM in mailer ...100.00
Shadow, color book, 1974, M 10.00
Shari Lewis, game, Shari-Land, 1958, EX in box 40.00
Shirley Temple, book, Little Colonel, Saalfield, EX 38.00
Shirley Temple, book, This Is My Crayon Book, Saalfield, 1935 ..40.00
Shirley Temple, coloring set, Saalfied, 1930s, EX in box 95.00

Shirley Temple, creamer, cobalt glass, M 35.00
Shirley Temple, figural soap, Kirk Guild, 1930s, MIB 145.00
Shirley Temple, mug, cobalt glass 35.00
Shirley Temple, pitcher, cobalt glass, 1930s, 5", NM 40.00
Shirley Temple, playing cards, ST plays drum, MIB 65.00
Shirley Temple, salt figure, 1930s, 4", EX 65.00
Shirley Temple, scrapbook, Saalfield, ca 1937, 15x11", EX 18.00
Shirley Temple, sheet music, Stowaway, EX 8.00
Shirley Temple, writing tablet, Western, 1935, M 40.00
Shirley Temple/Heidi, pocket mirror, 1937, NM 35.00
Skippy, pin-bk button, EX 15.00
Skippy, toothbrush holder, bsk, EX 85.00
Sky King, ring, Magni-Glo, M 85.00
Sky King, ring, Tele-blinker, M 125.00
Sky King, ring, TV, M 100.00
Sleeping Beauty, punch-out book, Disney, 1959, unpunched 30.00
Smilin' Jack, book, 10¢ Fast Action, EX 30.00
Smokey Bear, stuffed doll, 1985, 18", EX 25.00
Snow White, wristwatch, w/porc statue, US Time, 1958, MIB ..100.00
Space Mouse, doll, cloth, Dakin, 1960s, 7", EX 70.00
Spider-Man, bend & flex figure, Mego, M on card 40.00
Spike & Tyke, color book, 1957, M 20.00
Star Trek, doll, Captain Kirk, Knickerbocker, 1979, 12", MIB 25.00
Star Trek, figurine paint set, 1979, EX on card 11.00
Star Trek, Mr Spock Halloween costume, Collegeville, '67, M ..155.00
Star Trek, poster book, Giant, EX 10.00
Star Trek, poster book, Voyage 15, 1978, NM 11.50
Superman, book, From '30s to '70s, no dust jacket 5.00
Superman, color book, Whitman, 1965, M 30.00
Superman, contact paper, M 30.00
Superman, hand puppet, Ideal, 1955, M in pkg 100.00
Superman, play set, cb figures, Ideal, NM 25.00
Superman, ring, Jet Airplane, M 200.00
Superman, ring, Nestles 50.00
Superman, wristwatch, bl band, EX on M band 250.00
Superman, wristwatch, New Haven, 1948, EX 115.00
Superman, wristwatch, Timex, 1976, MIB 55.00
Sylvester the Cat, sheet music, 1955, EX 15.00
Tarzan, color book, Tarzan To Color, Saalfield, 1933, unused 250.00
Tarzan, color book, 1953, uncolored 30.00
Tarzan, popsicle coin, EX 8.00
Terry & Pirates, board game, 1937, NM in EX box 125.00
Terry & Pirates, puzzle, 1940s, EX 65.00
That Girl, color book, Marlo Thomas photo cover, M 33.00
Tom & Jerry, game, 1977, EX 6.00
Tom & Jerry, hooked rug, 1960, NM 75.00
Tom Mix, blueprint, EX 35.00
Tom Mix, booklet, Ralston, 1935, M 35.00
Tom Mix, branding iron, M 85.00
Tom Mix, ceiling light, M 195.00
Tom Mix, compass & magnifier, brass, NM 60.00
Tom Mix, cowboy boots, in orig box 350.00
Tom Mix, flashlight, M 125.00
Tom Mix, fob, Gold Ore, EX 75.00
Tom Mix, ID bracelet, 1947 premium, NM 40.00
Tom Mix, lucky spinner, NM 50.00
Tom Mix, makeup kit, w/mailer, 2nd version 145.00
Tom Mix, marbles, Ralston, M in mesh bag 40.00
Tom Mix, pocketknife, EX 75.00
Tom Mix, ring, Magnet, M 75.00
Tom Mix, ring, Mystery Picture, radio premium, M 200.00
Tom Mix, ring, Signature, M 250.00
Tom Mix, ring, Siren, VG 50.00
Tom Mix, ring, sliding whistle, EX 85.00

Tom Mix, ring, Straight Shooters, M 85.00
Tom Mix, ring, Tiger Eye, M w/mailer 325.00
Tom Mix, rocket parachute, NM in box 175.00
Tom Mix, signal arrowhead, Lucite, MIB 80.00
Tom Mix, telescope, Golden Bullet, 1949 premium, NM 88.00
Tom Mix, wristwatch, 50th Anniversary, M 225.00
Tony the Tiger, bank, ceramic figural, 1960s, 12", EX 40.00
Top Cat, board game, EX 100.00
Tweety, doll, Dakin, 1969, 7½", NM 20.00
Underdog, Halloween costume, 1974, M 15.00
Wagon Train, color book, photo cover, 1959, M 20.00
Wagon Train, fr-tray puzzle, sealed 30.00
Wile E Coyote, bank, ceramic, lt bl, 1970, 10", EX 45.00
Winnie the Pooh, lamp, ceramic, 1950s, EX 50.00
Wizard of Id, puzzle, 1971, boxed 8.00
Wolfman, Halloween costume, Ben Cooper, 1960s, EX 85.00
Wonder Woman, power shield, Funstuff, M in pkg 15.00
Wonder Woman, roller skates, Larami, 1977, NM in box 20.00
Woody Woodpecker, bank, figural, Imple, 1970s, EX 28.00
Woody Woodpecker, fr-tray puzzle, 1962, M 18.50
Woody Woodpecker, game, color factory, Whitman, 1972, M 42.00
Woody Woodpecker, game, Travel w/W Woodpecker, '56, NM ...48.00
Woody Woodpecker, juggle puzzles, 1950s, NM 68.00
Woody Woodpecker, slippers, figural head, 1959, M 23.00
Woody Woodpecker, Soaky, EX 20.00
Woody Woodpecker & Friends, paper doll book, M 45.00
Wyatt Earp, jigsaw puzzle, Bell Toy, photo cover box, 1958 ....30.00
Wyatt Earp, puzzle bell toy, boxed 28.00
Yogi Bear, candle, figural, M 15.00
Yogi Bear, card game, Hanna Barbera, 1959, MIB 11.00
Yogi Bear, cup, figural, EX 4.00
Yogi Bear, doll, Stuff 'N Lace, 1959, M 18.00
Yogi Bear, game, Go Fly a Kite, Hanna Barbera, 1961, EX 60.00
Yogi Bear, lamp, ceramic figural, Hanna Barbera, MIB 30.00
Yogi Bear, swim ring, inflatable, 1959, MIB 35.00
Yogi Bear, toy, vinyl, squeaker, Sanitoy, 1979, 12", EX 25.00
Yogi Bear & Boo Boo, coat rack, 1979, EX 60.00
Zorro, board game, Parker Bros, 1966, sealed 85.00
Zorro, fr-tray puzzle, 1965, NM 25.00
Zorro, pillowcase, Disney, 1958, M in sealed pkg 40.00
Zorro, View-Master set (3 reels, booklet, envelope), 1958, NM ...40.00
Zorro, wristwatch, w/hat in box, M 275.00
3 Little Pigs, wristwatch, Ingersoll, 1934, EX in G box 250.00
3 Stooges, punch-out book, unpunched, 1962, M 150.00

Peters and Reed

John Peters and Adam Reed founded their pottery in Zanesville, Ohio, just before the turn of the century, using the local red clay to produce a variety of wares. Moss Aztec, introduced about 1912, has an unglazed exterior with designs molded in high relief and the recesses highlighted with a green wash. Only the interior is glazed to hold water. Pereco (named for Peters, Reed and Company) is glazed in semi-matt blue, maroon, or cream. Orange was also used very early, but such examples are rare. Shapes are simple with in-mold decoration sometimes borrowed from the Moss Aztec line. Wilse Blue is a line of high-gloss medium blue with dark specks on simple shapes. Landsun, characterized by its soft matt multicolor or blue and gray combinations, is decorated either by dripping or by hand brushing in an effect sometimes called Flame or Herringbone. Chromal, in much the same colors as Landsun, may be decorated with a realistic scenic, or the swirling application of colors may merely suggest one. (Brush-McCoy made a very similar line called Chromart. Neither will be marked, and due to the lack of documented background material available, it may be impossible make a positive identification. Collectors nearly always attribute this type of decoration to Peters and Reed.) Shadow Ware is a glossy, multicolor drip over a harmonious base color. When the base is black, the effect is often iridescent.

Perhaps the most familiar line is the brown high-glaze artware with the 'sprigged'-type designs. Although research has uncovered no positive proof, it is generally accepted as having been made by Peters and Reed. It is interesting to note that many of the artistic shapes in this line are recognizable as those made by Weller, Roseville, and other Zanesville area companies. Other lines include Mirror Black, Persian, and an unidentified line which collectors call Mottled Colors. In this high-gloss line, the red clay body often shows through the splashed-on multicolors.

In 1922 the company became known as the Zane Pottery. Peters and Reed retired, and Harry McClelland became president. Charles Chilcote designed new lines, and production of many of the old lines continued. The body of the ware after 1922 was light in color. Marks include the impressed logo or ink stamp 'Zaneware' in a rectangle.

Bowl, Landsun, bl, 10" 80.00
Bowl, Mirror Ware, gr drip glaze on blk irid, 2½x7" 45.00
Hanging basket, Moss Aztec, basketweave mold, 5x6" 60.00
Jug, Brn Ware, cavalier, sprigged floral, 6" 90.00

Tankard, Brown Ware, 15", $250.00.

Jug, Brn Ware, cherries on 3 sides, swirl mold, 9" 125.00
Vase, Brn Ware, floral garlands, 5¾" 40.00
Vase, Brn Ware, floral wreath, rim-to-shoulder hdls, 11" 125.00
Vase, Brn Ware, florals on 3 sides, tiny rim, 3-ftd, 4½" 55.00
Vase, Brn Ware, swags on doughnut form w/hdls & ft, 11" 175.00
Vase, Chromal, trees & bridge, 9½" 395.00
Vase, Landsun, gr/brn/bl, 10" 75.00
Vase, Landsun, 3-color brush strokes, trumpet form, 4" 50.00
Vase, Marbleized, swirled colors, 12" 150.00
Vase, Moss Aztec, daisies, 8" 70.00
Vase, Moss Aztec, floral, 10" 85.00
Vase, Moss Aztec, leaves & vines, #172, 8" 70.00
Vase, Moss Aztec, pansy, 6" 42.00
Vase, Shadow Ware, drip glaze, bulbous shoulder, #781, 10" ...95.00
Vase, Wilse Blue, waisted cylinder, 7" 42.00
Wall pocket, Egyptian, 9" 125.00
Wall pocket, Moss Aztec, grapes & leaves, 8x3½" 75.00
Window box, Moss Aztec, Grecian figures, 13" L 175.00

Pewabic

The Pewabic Pottery was formally established in Detroit, Michigan, in 1907 by Mary Chase Perry Stratton and Horace James Caulkins. The two had worked together since 1903, firing their ware in a small kiln designed by Caulkins especially for use by the dental trade. Always a small operation which relied upon basic equipment and the skill of the workers, they took pride in being commissioned for several important architectural tile installations.

Some of the early artware was glazed a simple matt green; occasionally other colors were added, sometimes in combination, one over the other in a drip effect. Later Stratton developed a lustrous crystalline glaze. The body of the ware was highly fired and extremely hard. Shapes were basic, and decorative modeling, if used at all, was in low relief. Mary Stratton kept the pottery open until her death in 1961. In 1968 it was purchased and reopened by Michigan State University.

Several marks were used over the years: a triangle with 'Revelation Pottery' (for a short time only); 'Pewabic' with five maple leaves; and the impressed circle mark.

Bowl, bl irid, 4x9" 400.00
Bowl, gr-gray w/irid bl & maroon streaks, wht clay, 5" 200.00
Bowl, metallic ext, gr int w/pk highlights, 3x8" 500.00
Figurine, turtle, burgundy to gray-gr irid, unmk, 6x10", EX 450.00
Lamp, ochre, bulbous, in twisted iron mt w/scroll ft, 29" 2,000.00
Plate, rabbit/tree rim, bl lines on ivory, sgn Perry, 10" 1,100.00
Tile, geometrics in opposing corners, copper fr, 6½" 200.00
Tile, scarab, 3" sq 110.00
Trivet, mc inlaid triangles w/central star, hexagonal, 10" 400.00
Vase, bl drip on dk bsq, imp mk, 3x2½" 350.00
Vase, bl/purple/gr irid drip, bulbous, imp mk, 6½x4" 650.00
Vase, burgundy/gr drip on blk matt, long neck, label, 8x5" 1,400.00
Vase, burgundy/gr irid, bulbous base, imp mk, 5x4" 500.00

Vase, grayed-down turquoise with iridescence, 4x5", $650.00.

Vase, burgundy/gr irid, wide flat shoulder, label, 7x4" 650.00
Vase, cobalt matt, squat w/flat shoulder, incised mk, 4x5" 425.00
Vase, copper irid drip on cobalt, label, rstr rim, 9x7" 1,100.00
Vase, dk bl irid, flaring sides w/bulbous base, 13½x7" 2,300.00
Vase, dk gun-metal purple, sphere w/short neck, imp mk, 6" 900.00
Vase, irid w/bl drippings, 2½", NM 250.00
Vase, irid w/pk & gr highlights, 11", EX 900.00
Vase, lt pk metallic w/orange highlights, gourd form, 5" 800.00
Vase, pk-bronze w/copper highlights, gourd form, 5x4" 800.00
Vase, pk/gold irid w/aquamarine drip, 6" 550.00
Vase, yel/tan over brn, gourd form w/can neck, 8" 1,100.00

Pewter

Pewter is a metal alloy of tin, copper, very small parts of bismuth and/or antimony, and sometimes lead. Very little American pewter contained lead, however, because much of the ware was designed to be used as tableware, and makers were aware that the use of lead could result in poisoning. (Pieces that do contain lead are usually darker in color and heavier than those that have no lead.) Most of the fine examples of American pewter date from 1700 to the 1840s. Many pieces were melted down and recast into bullets during the American Revolution in 1775; this accounts to some extent why examples from this period are quite difficult to find. The pieces that did survive may include buttons, buckles, and writing equipment as well as the tableware we generally think of.

After the Revolution makers began using antimony as the major alloy with the tin in an effort to regain the popularity of pewter, which glassware and china was beginning to replace in the home. The resulting product, known as britannia, had a lustrous silver-like appearance and was far more durable. While closely related, britannia is a collectible in its own right and should not be confused with pewter.

Key: tm — touchmark

Basin, Continental, angel tm, initials on rim, 3x13", EX 145.00
Basin, Continental, angel tm, 2½x11", NM 210.00
Basin, Nathaniel Austin, lt eagle tm, wear/rpr, 2x8½" 135.00
Basin, Samuel Hamlin tm, wear/scratches/rpr, 2x5¾" 250.00
Basin, Townsend & Compton tm, minor wear, 3x11" 300.00
Bowl, S Duncomb London tm, wear/pitting, 1¼x13" 150.00
Candlestick, Flagg & Homan, 7½", pr 420.00
Candlestick, unmk, 11½", pr 240.00
Candlestick, unmk Am, 8", pr 375.00
Candlestick, w/push-up, minor battering, 8¾", pr 200.00
Chalice, communion; unmk, late, 9" 65.00
Chalice, unmk, dk patina, 6½" 110.00
Chalice, unmk Am, minor battering/old soldered rpr, 7" 50.00
Charger, Continental, angel tm, wide flat rim, polished, 15" 215.00
Charger, European, faint tm, wear/scratches, 13" 185.00
Charger, London tm (indistinct), wear/dents, 13½" 150.00
Charger, Love tm, wear/pitting, 1½x11" 300.00
Charger, S Danforth, lt tm, wear/pitting, 13" 325.00
Charger, S Ellis, crowned rose tm, pitting/corrosion, 17" 300.00
Charger, unmk, wear/scratches, 13½" 175.00
Cup, unmk Am, cast ear hdl, dents/rim split, 3" 55.00
Desk set, rectangular w/well & sander, ftd, soldered, 6" L 190.00
Flagon, I Trask tm, 10½", EX 400.00
Funnel, unmk European, slightly crooked/dents, 6" 95.00
Goblet, communion; unmk Boardman, soldered rpr, 7" 75.00
Inkwell, unmk, wide flat base, no insert, hinge rpr, 7" dia 65.00
Inkwell, wide flat base, ceramic insert, 6" dia 165.00
Inkwell, wide flat base, hinged lid, VG ceramic insert, 8" 190.00
Lamp, angel tm, wick pick on chain, 11" 115.00
Lamp, spout; unmk, resoldered lid hinge, 11" 220.00
Lamp, unmk, whale oil burner, lg base, 6¾" 175.00
Measure, English, bellied, some rpr, assembled set of 6 ....300.00
Measure, English, II tm, bellied tankard form, ear hdl, 8" 250.00
Measure, English, side-spout tankard form, pub eng, dents, 6" 100.00
Measure, Townsend & Compton, w/tm, tankard form, rpr, 6" 115.00
Measure, unmk, tankard form w/side spout, pub/crown mks, 5" ..125.00
Measure, unmk English, bellied, cleaned/dented/rpr, qt, 6" 100.00
Measure, unmk English, bellied, set of 6, qt to ¼-gill 600.00
Muffineer, 7½" 200.00
Pitcher, Boardman, lion tm, hinged lid, cleaned, 8", EX 400.00
Pitcher, F Porter, Westbrook, 6¾" 400.00
Pitcher, R Dunham, hinged lid, 8" 550.00
Plate, Ashbil Griswold, eagle tm, wear/scratches, 8" 130.00
Plate, Continental, dragon tm, minor wear, 8½" 85.00

Plate, Continental, mermaid tm, eng rims/1763, 9½", EX 125.00
Plate, J Danforth, eagle tm, minor wear, 8" 285.00
Plate, Joseph Danforth, rampant lion tm, wear/scratches, 7½" ...275.00
Plate, Love tm, dents/wear/scratches, 9" 200.00
Plate, Nathaniel Austin, eagle tm, wear/scratches, 8" 225.00
Plate, Roswell Gleason, minor wear, 9" 200.00
Plate, S Kilbourne, eagle tm, minor wear, 7¾" 155.00
Plate, Samuel Danforth, eagle tm, wear/soldered center, 8" 95.00
Plate, Smith & Feltman Albany, 10" 110.00
Plate, Thos Danforth Boardman, eagle tm, minor wear, 7¾" 275.00
Plate, toddy; unmk, wear/scratches/dent, 5" 80.00
Plate, Townsend & Compton tm, wear/pitting, 8" 75.00
Plate, unmk Continental, rim eng Keilig 1818, scratches, 9" 150.00
Plate, Wm Danforth, eagle tm, wear/scratches, 8" 225.00
Plate, Wm Will, eagle tm, sm hole rpr, 8" 650.00
Platter, English, faint tm, wear/scratches, 18" L 245.00
Platter, Made in London, eng monogram w/griffin, 14", EX 250.00
Porringer, eagle tm, att S Hamlin Sr, flower hdl, wear, 5½" 400.00
Porringer, Hamlin, eagle tm, Old English hdl, dents/rpr, 4" 350.00
Porringer, IG on bk of crown hdl, 4¾" 175.00
Porringer, tm for Gleason or Lee, cast heart hdl, 3⅜" dia 175.00
Porringer, tm for Lee or Lewis, cast hdl, 2¼" dia 150.00
Porringer, unmk Am, crown hdl, 4⅜" 160.00
Porringer, unmk Am, heart & crescent hdl, dents, 3¼" 225.00
Porringer, unmk Am, very minor breaks in flower hdl, 5½" 225.00
Punch bowl, John Foster tm inside, ftd, eng w/1757, 6x10" 500.00
Salt cellar, X mk, pitted sm soldered holes, 2½", pr 90.00
Soup plate, Boardman & Co NY, eagle tm, minor wear, 9½" 300.00
Soup plate, Continental, angel tm, 8" 100.00
Soup plate, G Richardson #A Warranted, sm eagle tm, 9½", EX....375.00
Tall pot, Cincinnati Britannia Co #1, 9½" 135.00
Tall pot, F Porter tm, str sides w/waisted neck & ft, 12" 350.00
Tall pot, G Richardson, dents/rpr to lid hinge, 10½" 300.00
Tall pot, Homan & Co on bottom, cast floral finial, 10" 150.00
Tall pot, J Danforth #3 tm, lt battering/sm hole in hdl, 10" 250.00
Tall pot, JH Palethorp tm, ftd pear form, wood finial, 10" 250.00
Tall pot, Rosewell Gleason tm, ribbed ftd ogee, 13" 300.00
Tall pot, Sellew & Co, 11½" 325.00
Tall pot, unmk, str sides/simple tooling, wood finial, 11" 165.00
Tall pot, unmk Am, bulbous w/tall neck & base, 11", EX 185.00
Tall pot, unmk Am, some battering/EX rpr, 11" 185.00
Tankard, IH London, hinged lid resoldered, 8" 150.00
Tankard, unmk, hinged lid, 6" 150.00
Teapot, Boardman NY, eagle tm, 7" 400.00
Teapot, C Parker #14, squat ftd pear form, rpr/dents, 8" 140.00
Teapot, F Porter Westbrook tm, bulb body, 8¾", EX 170.00
Teapot, G Richardson #A Warranted, sm eagle tm, 7¾" 250.00
Teapot, G Richardson Warranted tm, 8½" 175.00
Teapot, Grenfell, griffin tm, pear form, rpl wood hdl, 5½" 200.00
Teapot, unmk, squat pear form, rpr, 7" 375.00
Teapot, unmk Am, onion body, gooseneck, peaked lid, 8", EX ..155.00

Phoenix Bird

Blue and white Phoenix Bird china has been produced by various Japanese potteries from the early 1900s. With slight variations the design features the Japanese bird of paradise and scroll-like vines of Kara-Kusa, or Chinese grass. Although some of their earlier ware is unmarked, the majority is marked in some fashion. More than one hundred different stamps have been reported. 'Made in Japan' is the one most often found with Morimura's wreath or crossed stems (both having the letter 'M' within) coming in second. The cloverleaf with 'Japan' below very often indicates an item having a high-quality transfer print

design. Newer items, if marked at all, carry a paper label. Compared to the older ware, the coloring of the new is whiter and the blue more harsh; the design is sparse with more ground area showing. Although collectors buy even 'new' pieces, the older is of course more highly prized and valued. For further information we recommend *Phoenix Bird Chinaware, Books I — IV*, written and privately published by our advisor, Joan Collett Oates; her address is in the Directory under Michigan. Join Phoenix Bird Collectors of America (PBCA) and receive the *Discoveries* newsletter, an informative publication that will further your appreciation of this chinaware.

Bowl, cereal; 6" 15.00
Butter pat, old 12.00
Butter tub & drain, hdls, 2¾x5" 65.00
Candy/nut tub, hdls, 2" 25.00
Casserole, rnd, w/lid 135.00
Chamberstick, scalloped ring hdl, no mk, 2x5" 135.00
Chocolate pot 150.00
Condensed milk container, #2, w/underplate 125.00
Creamer, #6, bell form 20.00
Creamer & sugar bowl, #20, w/lid 45.00
Cup, bouillon; inside border, w/hdls & underplate 35.00
Cup & saucer, demitasse; Occupied Japan 22.00
Custard cup, inside border 15.00
Egg cup, dbl, 3¼" 16.50
Egg cup, single, 2¼" 12.00
Ladle, gravy; 6" 45.00
Plate, dinner; 9¾" 48.00
Plate, HP, scalloped rim, 7¼" 35.00
Plate, transfer print, plain rim, 7¼" 9.00
Plate, 6" 6.00
Plate, 8" 18.00
Platter, 10" 35.00
Platter, 12" 50.00
Platter, 17" 145.00
Shakers, #2, 2", pr 30.00
Shakers, 6-sided, pr 25.00
Sugar bowl, #10, w/lid, Nippon 22.00
Tea set, #6, child's, 3-pc 115.00
Tureen, vegetable; oval, w/lid 135.00

Phoenix Glass

Founded in 1880 in Monaca, Pennsylvania, the Phoenix Glass Company became one of the country's foremost manufacturers of lighting glass by the early 1900s. They also produced a wide variety of utilitarian and decorative glassware, including art glass by Joseph Webb, colored cut glass, Gone-with-the-Wind style oil lamps, hotel and bar ware, and pharmaceutical glassware. Today, however, collectors are primarily interested in the 'Sculptured Artware' produced in the 1930s and 1940s. These beautiful pressed and mold-blown pieces are most often found in white milk glass or crystal with various color treatments or a satin finish.

Phoenix did not mark their 'Sculptured Artware' line on the glass; instead, a silver and black or gold and black foil label in the shape of the mythical phoenix bird was used.

Quite often glassware made by the Consolidated Lamp and Glass Company of nearby Coraopolis, Pennsylvania, is mistaken for Phoenix's 'Sculptured Artware.' Though the style of the glass is very similar, one distinguishing characteristic is that perhaps 80% of the time Phoenix applied color to the background leaving the raised design plain in contrast, while Consolidated generally applied color to the raised design and left the background plain. Also, for the most part, the patterns and colors used by Phoenix were distinctively different from those used by Consolidated. The glassware of both firms is of equal quality and comparable value.

In 1970 Phoenix Glass became a division of Anchor Hocking which in turn was acquired by the Newell Group in 1987. Phoenix has the distinction of being one of the oldest, continuously operating glass factories in the United States. For more information, see the section on Consolidated Glass.

Key: MG — milk glass

Wild Geese, white on blue, 9½", $200.00.

Ashtray, slate gray bkground on MG, MOP flowers, 3" L **40.00**
Bowl, Diving Girl, lav bkground, frosted pattern, oblong **245.00**
Bowl, Lacy Dew Drop, pk on MG, 8" sq **40.00**
Bowl, Tiger Lily, wht bkground, crystal satin pattern, 11½" **235.00**
Box, powder; Hummingbirds, bl **100.00**
Candlestick, Sawtooth, dk bl on MG, pr **135.00**
Candlestick, Strawberry, bl on MG, 4", pr **135.00**
Comport, Moon & Star, pearl lustre on MG, 8" dia **45.00**
Goblet, Blackberry, caramel lustre on MG, 7-oz **25.00**
Mold, Jell-O; Queen Anne, crystal, star-shape **4.00**
Platter, Jonquil, lt bl bkground on crystal frost, 14" dia **265.00**
Platter, Jonquil, yel over crystal, frosted pattern, 14" **265.00**
Sugar bowl, Lacy Dewdrop, bl wash, w/lid **60.00**
Vase, Aster, tan on MG, MOP pattern, 7" **80.00**
Vase, Bachelor Button, gr bkground on satin MG, 7" **165.00**
Vase, Bachelor Button, pearl wht, 7" **200.00**
Vase, Bicentennial, crystal w/red, wht & bl pattern **50.00**
Vase, Bluebell, pk on MG, MOP pattern, 7" **82.50**
Vase, Bluebell, rose bkground on MG, MOP pattern, 7" **125.00**
Vase, Cosmos, aqua bkground, wht flowers on crystal, 7½" **150.00**
Vase, Cosmos, tan bkground on MG, MOP pattern, 7½" **175.00**
Vase, Daisy, bl bkground on MG, MG pattern, 9x9" **235.00**
Vase, Dancing Girl, bl bkground on MG, MG pattern, 12" **485.00**
Vase, Fern, bl on crystal, crystal pattern, 7" **80.00**
Vase, Freesia, cedar rose bkground on crystal, 8" **165.00**
Vase, Freesia, wine bkground on MG, 8" **150.00**
Vase, Jewel, gr on MG, MG pattern, 5" **100.00**
Vase, Lily, aqua on crystal, frosted pattern, tri-crimp, 8" **250.00**
Vase, Madonna, brn bkground, 10" **265.00**
Vase, Madonna, tan on MG, MOP pattern, 10" **200.00**
Vase, Philodendron, amber, 11" **45.00**
Vase, Philodendron, burgundy on MG, MOP pattern, 11" **175.00**

Vase, Pine Cones, no cones, aqua on crystal frost, 6½" **235.00**
Vase, Primrose, gr on MG, MG pattern, 8¾" **350.00**
Vase, Thistle, bl on MG, MOP pattern, 18" **425.00**
Vase, Wild Geese, bl-gray bkground on satin MG, 8" **195.00**
Vase, Wild Geese, pearlized wht on wht **175.00**
Vase, Wild Geese, wht on tan, 11x9" **215.00**
Vase, Wild Rose, wht on lt bl, 10½" **165.00**
Vase, Wild Rose, wine on MG, MOP pattern, 10½" **235.00**
Vase, Zodiac, med bl on MG, frosted pattern, 10" **495.00**

Phonographs

The phonograph, invented by Thomas Edison in 1877, was the first practical instrument for recording and reproducing sound. Sound wave vibrations were recorded on a tinfoil-covered cylinder and played back with a needle that ran along the grooves made from the recording, thus reproducing the sound. Other companies further improved Edison's invention: Victor, Edison, Columbia, Zonophone, Vitaphone, and others. Wooden-horn phonographs with outside horns are the most valuable. Spring models were produced until 1929 (and later); after 1929 most were electric (though some electric motor models were produced as early as 1910). Our advisor for this category is J.R. Wilkins; he is listed in the Directory under Texas. Unless another condition is noted, prices are for complete, original phonographs in at least fine to excellent condition. Note: Edison coin-operated cylinder players start at $7,000.00 and may go up to $20,000.00 each.

Key:
mg — morning-glory   rpd — reproducer
NP — nickel plated

Berliner, C rpd, side brake, early funnel horn, VG **3,500.00**
Bing Pignyphone, w/orig box **225.00**
Birch, wind-up, plays 78s, in case **150.00**
Busy Bee Grand, red mg horn **350.00**
Columbia, disk, oak cabinet, shutter door, volume control **250.00**
Columbia, disk player, oak case, front mt, 24" horn **600.00**
Columbia A, orig blk Bakelite rpd & recorder, NY, EX **1,000.00**
Columbia A Graphophone, unique fluted 10" horn, 1897 ....**350.00**
Columbia AA Graphophone, cylinder type, EX decal, blk horn....**450.00**
Columbia AB Graphophone, cylinder player, orig 5" mandrel ...**1,200.00**
Columbia AB McDonald Graphophone, oak case, key wind **850.00**
Columbia AJ, disk player, oak case, top wind, Columbia rpd ..**1,000.00**
Columbia AQ, open works, EX pnt on horn **350.00**
Columbia AT Graphophone, decal/chrome, 14" brass bell horn ...**375.00**
Columbia AZ Graphophone, cylinder player, NM decal **450.00**
Columbia B, M finish & decal, EX nickel **400.00**
Columbia B Eagle Graphophone, cylinder type, oak dome top ...**400.00**
Columbia BF Graphophone, EX **600.00**
Columbia BG Sovereign Graphophone, 2" mandrel, 14" horn ...**800.00**
Columbia BK Graphophone, cylinder player, rstr **425.00**
Columbia BO, Exposition decal, nickel horn, VG **950.00**
Columbia BQ, Rex model, rear mt cylinder, oak case, mg horn .**925.00**
Columbia CI, electric, EX orig finish, EX **650.00**
Columbia Eagle, EX orig **400.00**
Columbia N, orig blk Bakelite rpd, rstr **950.00**
Columbia Q, cased model w/nickeled mechanism, EX **350.00**
Columbia Q, open works, key wind, 14" aluminum horn **250.00**
Columbia S, coin-operated, orig horn, EX **2,800.00**
Edison A-100, upright w/open shelf, disk player **300.00**
Edison Amberola 75, mahog floor model w/drws for cylinders **450.00**
Edison B-80, table top, internal horn, disk player **350.00**
Edison C-150 Sheridan, mahog floor model w/wire rack **200.00**

Edison C-250, mahog upright, dmn disk, complete, NM 350.00
Edison C-250, oak upright, dmn disk, complete, NM 450.00
Edison Chippendale, disk player, oak case, EX orig 400.00
Edison Concert A, banner type, 43" brass horn, NM 2,400.00
Edison Fireside, C rpd, 2/4-min, lg mg horn 500.00
Edison Fireside, H rpd, 2/4-min, Fireside horn 625.00
Edison Fireside A, K rpd, rstr 550.00
Edison Gem A, EX orig 500.00
Edison Gem B, C rpd, EX decal, EX orig 500.00
Edison Gem C, EX orig 550.00
Edison Gem D, maroon, EX orig 1,000.00
Edison Home, banner decal, old crane & mg horn 600.00
Edison Home, C rpd, crane & mg horn 600.00
Edison Home, C rpd, lg red mg horn 600.00
Edison Home, C rpd, script decal, 14" brass bell horn 500.00
Edison Home, H rpd, 2/4-min, script decal, metal cygnet horn ..750.00
Edison Opera Schoolhouse, L rpd, #11 cygnet horn, rstr 4,500.00
Edison Standard, C rpd, banner decal, sm horn 450.00
Edison Standard, C rpd, box style, oak case, 14" brass bell horn .450.00
Edison Standard, C rpd, mg horn & crane 450.00
Edison Standard, C rpd, script logo, sm horn 450.00
Edison Standard, old-style rpd, oak box type, 14" bell horn 450.00
Edison Standard A, suitcase model, automatic rpd, 4-clip, EX ...600.00
Edison Triumph A, EX decal & orig finish, repeat attachment ..750.00
General Electric Electronic Toys, red pnt metal, 1930s, EX 185.00
Kameraphone, box camera style, w/speaker & rpd 210.00
Midnophone, disk player, outside horn, EX 265.00
Puck, lyre base, open works, emb lav mg horn 450.00
Puck, lyre base, open works, nickel bell horn, EX 400.00
Standard, open works w/¾" center post, orig horn, VG 500.00
Standard A, disk player w/½" spindle, red mg horn, EX 550.00
Standard X, front mt w/blk & gold horn, EX 400.00
Thornward, Montgomery Ward, cylinder type, 14" horn, 1903 ..700.00
Vanophone, orig rpd, steel disk player, internal horn 150.00
Vcitor VI, EX orig 3,500.00
Victor E, front mt, EX orig 900.00
Victor E, rear mt horn 1,000.00
Victor I, EX orig 850.00
Victor I, Exhibition rpd, oak case, rear mt w/mg horn 900.00
Victor I, Exhibition rpd, rear mt w/16" brass bell horn 900.00
Victor II, Exhibition rpd, oak case, 18" brass bell horn 1,200.00
Victor II, wood horn, EX orig 1,950.00
Victor III, EX orig 1,500.00
Victor III, wood horn, EX orig 2,250.00
Victor IV, EX orig 1,800.00
Victor IV, table top, oak case, internal horn 150.00
Victor IV, wood horn, EX orig 2,550.00
Victor M Monarch, Exhibition rpd, w/brush, 30" brass horn 825.00
Victor O, Exhibition rpd, oak case, peach 8-petal horn 950.00
Victor Orthophonic Credenza X, 15½" 900.00
Victor Talking Machine VV-XI, oak floor model, EX 300.00
Victor V, oak disk player, 24" brass bell horn, EX 2,200.00
Victor V, wood horn, EX orig 2,950.00
Victor VI, wood horn, EX orig 4,250.00
Victor XV, EX orig 3,500.00
Victrola VV-XI, mahog upright, #2 rpd, EX 300.00
Victrola VV-XVI, mahog cabinet, L-shaped doors, EX 500.00

Photographica

Photographic collectibles include not only the cameras and equipment used to 'freeze' special moments in time but also the photographic images produced by a great variety of processes that have evolved since the daguerrean era of the mid-1800s. Among the earliest daguerrean cameras was the sliding box-on-a-box camera. It was focused by sliding one box in and out of the other, thus adjusting the distance of the lens to the ground glass. This was replaced on later models with leather bellows. These were the forerunners of the multilens cameras developed in the late 1870s which were capable of recording many small portraits on a single plate. Double-lens cameras produced stereo images which, when viewed through a device called a stereoscope, achieved a 3-dimensional effect. In 1888 George Eastmann introduced his box camera, the first to utilize roll film. This greatly simplified the process, making it possible for the amateur to enjoy photography as a hobby. Detective cameras, those disguised as books, handbags, etc., are among the most sought after by today's collectors.

Many processes have been used to produce photographic images: daguerreotypes — the most-valued examples being the full-plate which measures 6½" x 8½"; ambrotypes, produced by an early wet-plate process whereby a faint negative image on glass is seen as positive when held against a dark background; and tintypes, contemporaries of ambrotypes but produced on japanned iron and not as easily damaged. Other collectible images include carte de visites, known as CDVs, which are 2¼" x 4" portraits printed on paper and produced in quantity. The CDV fad of the 1800s enticed the famous and the unknown alike to pose for these cards which were circulated among the public to the extent that they became known as 'publics.' When the popularity of CDVs began to wane, a new fascination developed for the cabinet photo, a larger version measuring about 4½" x 6½". Note: A common portrait CDV is worth only about 50¢ unless it carries a revenue stamp on the back; those that do are valued at about $1.00 each.

Stereo cards, photos viewed through a device called a stereoscope, are another popular collectible. The glass stereo plates of the mid-1800s and photo prints produced in the darkroom are among the most valuable. In evaluating stereo views, the subject, date, and condition are all-important. Some views were printed over a thirty- to forty-year period; 'first generation' prices are far higher than later copies. Right now, quality stereo views are at a premium.

For the most part, good quality images have either maintained or increased in value. Poor quality examples (regardless of rarity) are not selling well. Interest in cameras and stereo equipment is down, and dealers report that often average-priced items that were moving well are often completely overlooked. Though rare items always have a market, collectors seem to be buying only if they are bargain priced.

Our advisor for this category is John Hess; he is listed in the Directory under Massachusetts. For more information on the market values of collectible photographs, we recommend *Huxford's Fine Art Value Guide*, available at your local bookstore or from Collector Books. See also Gutta Percha.

Key: CW — Civil War

Albumens

African tribesman, woven cap w/shell tassels, 1869, EX 40.00
Brigadier Gen JA Haskin & Staff, Gardner, 12x17", EX 600.00
Colonel Dickinson & Major Ludlow, Fairfax, 1863, EX 700.00
Corcoran's Art Building WA from SW, Gardner, 13x19" 600.00
Gen McClellan's Headquarter Guard, 1862, Gardner/Brady, 7x9" ...300.00
Incidents of War, Stone Church, Centreville, Gardner, 7x9" 300.00
Jubilee Statue, Bombay of Queen Victoria, 12x10", EX 12.50
Lincoln, Abraham; inscribed mt: c J Holyland, 8x6" image 200.00
Lincoln 1864 campaign portrait in oval, Hacker, EX 25.00
Man in chair reading book, Gardner, 18x15", EX 200.00
Mayors of the Olden Time, Gardner, orig mt, 17x13" 400.00
Musician w/sm over-the-shoulder horn, 1860s, 8x10" 12.50
Railroad yard switch of steam locomotive, Phila, 1885, 7x9" 30.00

Storefront w/horse-drawn hearse & coach in front, 1890s, 8x10" ..**95.00**
4-horse-drawn steam fire pumper w/hose carriage, 1880s, 10x13" ...**50.00**

Walpi Village, signed Hillers Photo in the negative, mounted on board, 9½x12¾", $475.00.

Ambrotypes

Whole plate, soldier, lt color/gilt, ruby glass, 7½x7" **320.00**
Whole plate, 2 men face Niagara Falls, ruby glass image **250.00**
4th plate, Artillery militiaman, bayonetted flintlock, +case **120.00**
6th plate, Lincoln & Hamlin, +patriotic leather case **7,500.00**
6th plate, postmortem of baby on her side, +case **25.00**
6th plate, soldier w/rifle & bayonet, +gutta percha case **450.00**

6th Plate, main street view, Cincinnati, OH, known to be the earliest identifiable location in Cincinnati on glass, ca 1851, EX, $2,000.00.

9th plate, Edward Everett, 1860 Candidate for VP under J Bell ...**110.00**
9th plate, harness & tack maker seated at wooden vise, VG **40.00**
9th plate, man plays violin, music in lap, 1850s, EX, +case **36.00**
9th plate, NY soldier w/M1840 sword, NY on buckle, EX, +case ..**125.00**
9th plate, painting of wht-haired baby, EX, +case **12.50**

Cabinet Photos

Actor, 10-yr-old boy w/hat & cane, drama company ad **9.00**
Benjamin & Mrs Harrison, 1888, pr **15.00**
Blk man in formal clothes, Kimball, Boston, 1880s, EX **5.00**
Chang-Yu-Sing Chinese Giant, 8-ft, 26-stone, Bogardus, rare **22.50**
Gen Ulysses S Grant memorial, birth/death dates/etc **12.00**
Gen Willis Carver (midget) between parents, Eisenmann, EX **12.00**

General Tom Thumb & Wife, Bogardus, dtd 1881, EX **10.00**
Girl in coat & hat on wagon pulled by boy in knickers **12.00**
Girl in wht dress w/china doll, full view of doll, EX **10.00**
Highland Cliffs Lighthouse, Provincetown MA, WM Smith, EX ...**10.00**
Little Thunder US Indian Police, native clothes/saber, EX **90.00**
Man w/high-wheeled bicycle, knee pants, Lynn MA **35.00**
McKinley portrait, 'Late President McKinley' on bottom, VG **10.00**
Mt Vernon, East View, LC Dillon, WA DC, EX **9.50**
Police Sergeant, full-length, full insignia, 1890s, EX **22.00**
S Pasadena ostrich farm, outside view, story on bk, EX **15.00**
Sailor, USS Lancaster on headband, full-length, 1880s, EX **12.50**
Sioux Chief, maiden, & couple, Barry, set of 3 ....**250.00**
Sioux Chief Rain-in-the-Face, Barry, EX **550.00**
Sioux Indian lady, ½-view, necklace & earings, Zimmerman **40.00**
Sitting Bull, portraits, house, family, Barry, set of 4 ....**300.00**
Street car conductor in full uniform, BF Bogden, EX **10.00**
3 brothers (12 to 14 yrs old) in nickers & sm sister w/doll **10.00**

Cameras

Canon III, 2-pc finder selector lever, Serenar lens, NM **160.00**
Canonflex, single lens reflex, 1959-60, EX **125.00**
Conley Junior, folding roll film, 1917-22, EX **20.00**
Coronet Polo, leather-covered metal box, France, EX **12.50**
Eastman Kodak #4, string-set box, factory loaded, 1890-97 ....**350.00**
Eastman Kodak Coquette, bl, w/lipstick holder/compact, 1930s ...**625.00**
Eastman Kodak Rainbow Hawk-Eye #2, folding style, 1930s, EX **35.00**
Graflex No 0 Graphic, fixed-focus lens, 1909-03, EX **200.00**
Junior Reflex, single lens reflex box type, 1911, EX **50.00**
Kodak #3-A, folding pocket type, ballbearing shutter, EX **15.00**
Kodak Baby Brownie Special, EX **7.50**
London Stereoscopic, twin lens artist hand type, 1889, EX **300.00**
Minolta Memo, 35mm viewfinder, helical lever focus, 1949, M .**120.00**
Minolta Nifca-Sport, folding plate, ca 1930, EX **225.00**
Olympus Chrome Six V, no rangefinder, lever advance, 1955, M ..**85.00**
Pentacon FB, built-in exposure meter, Steinheil lens, 1959, EX ...**45.00**
Rochester Carlton, wood, dbl extension view, 1893-1903, EX ...**175.00**
Stereocrafters Videon II, 33mm cassettes, 1950s, EX **95.00**
Universal Falcon Junior, Bakelite, folding vest pocket, NM **15.00**
Wirgin Edixa Electronica, fully automatic, 1962, M **215.00**
Wunsche Elite, stereo magazine, leather-covered body, 1900s **375.00**
Zeiss Ikon Contaflex II, 1954-58, M **65.00**

Carte De Visites

Admiral Farragut, ⅓-view, Joseph Ward, Boston, EX **15.00**
Arab lady breast feeding her child, Hammerschmidt, EX **35.00**
Assassin's Vision, Lincoln & Booth cartoon, Hacker, 1865 ....**28.00**
Commodore Nutt & Miss Warren, midgets, E Anthony, EX **10.00**
Gen Chas F Smith, full view, civilian clothes, Anthony/Brady **12.00**
Gen Lyon, full length, w/hat & sword, Anthony **17.50**
General HW Benham leaning on cavalry saber, Fredricks, 1861 ..**35.00**
Jefferson Davis as woman, cartoon, Emerson, 1865 ....**24.00**
Jefferson Davis in His Camp, cartoon, Hacker, 1865 ....**24.00**
John Wilkes Booth, seated, holds cane, EX **35.00**
Lincoln, Abraham; seated, Brady, 1864, EX **350.00**
Lincoln & family, Robert in uniform, EX **6.00**
Little Hill Winnebago Chief, standing, Whitney, MN **30.00**
Michelangelo, from painting by Gendreau, EX **9.00**
Militia bandsman w/flute, fringed epaulets, M1851 shako, EX **16.00**
Minne-Ha-Ha falls & bridge, Whitney's Gallery, St Paul MN, EX ...**7.50**
Palace in Stockholm Sweden from Across River, 1865, EX **7.50**
Pickett's Charge, Battle of Gettysburg, taken from painting **6.50**
Postmortem, sm boy in suit on sofa **28.00**

Postmortem, sm girl w/ribbon in long curly hair **22.00**
Principal Landing & Road to Yorktown, river scene, Brady, VG ..**25.00**
Sailing-clipper ship, beached scene, masts off **12.50**
St John's Church interior, FB Coggeshal, Lowell, 1865, EX **7.50**
Twin girls, identical clothes, about 5 yrs old **12.00**
Union Infantryman w/bayonetted musket across chest, EX **30.00**
Union officer in frockcoat, 2nd lieutenant shoulder straps **15.00**
Union officer stands, McDowell-type kepi on table, Brady, EX **20.00**
Waino & Plutano, weight 45 lbs, age 50 to 60, Eisenmann, EX **20.00**
Wilhelm I, seated in uniform w/21 medals on chest, VG **9.00**
Wm A Wheeler, Vice Pres of US from 1861-63, EX **9.00**
Wm H Seward, unusual side profile, Brady, EX **10.00**
Younger gang composite, 6 sm photos (all postmortem), EX ...**1,300.00**
7 Generals of Army of Potomac, EX **12.00**
7th NY Infantry State Militia camp scene, men at stove, 1861 .....**32.50**

Daguerreotypes

Half plate, firehouse, men & firewagon, Newport RI, EX **4,000.00**
Half plate, Geo Caleb Bingham painting: Jolly Flat Boat Men ...**140.00**
Half plate, lady in fancy dress in Victorian chair, EX, +case **85.00**
Half plate, man w/kinky hair/beard, waist-up view, EX, +case **75.00**
4th plate, couple holding hands while seated, VG, +case **35.00**
4th plate, Mexican War officer, close-up, +gutta percha case **750.00**
6th plate, dog on wooden step, +leather case **480.00**
6th plate, girl seated w/red-tinted flowers, MA&S Root NY **75.00**
6th plate, lady in blk lace-trimmed dress, CM Ising...Phila **18.50**
6th plate, lady w/child & china doll, +gutta percha case **110.00**
6th plate, Lodge fellow w/sash, cockade w/tassels, 1850s **125.00**
6th plate, man w/mourning book, dtd 1851 ....**150.00**
6th plate, men in fancy clothes, Brady, EX, +case **50.00**
6th plate, mother & 2 daughters, +floral leather case **250.00**
6th plate, pipe fitter/machinist w/threading device, +case **425.00**
6th plate, sm girl sitting/reading book, Bogardus NY, +case **20.00**
9th plate, man w/concertina, in gutta percha case, EX **75.00**

Photos

Bromide, textile mill women w/yarn spindles, leather aprons **14.00**
Glossy, US Frigate Constitution after 1917 rstr, 8x10" **12.50**

Photograph, sepia silver print, 'Last of His People,' by Karl Moon, copyright 1914, 6x9", $825.00.

Sepia gravure, Talullah Bankhead, by DeMeyer, early, 4x7" **48.00**
Sepia tone, Blk man in fine clothes, 4x6" **7.50**
Sepia tone, Charles Chaplin (sgn), very early, 4x6", EX **375.00**
Sepia tone, farmer & 2 boys w/horses at plow, ca 1900, 9x7" **10.00**
Sepia tone, Lillian Gish, 1922, 7x9", EX **60.00**
Sepia tone, monoplane w/Union Oil logo on side, 1920s, 3x4½" ...**3.50**
Sepia tone, NY Union Sq traffic scene, 1901, 9x7½", EX **150.00**
Sepia tone, Ronald Colman, by James Abbe, 7x9", EX **60.00**
Sepia-tone salt print, Blk laborers of NY tunnel, 1900, EX **65.00**

Shaker people, horses, buggy & barn, early, 6x8" **65.00**
Silverprint, Hindenburg Explosion, Internat'l News, 1937 ....**280.00**
Silverprint, Lily Dache modeling, by N Muray, 8x10" **550.00**
Silverprint, 3 fishermen on Colu River (OR), Gifford, 8x5" **75.00**
Yosemite, Pierce Arrow touring car before redwood, 1915, 7x5" ..**12.00**

Stereoscopic Views

Birthplace in 1809 of A Lincoln, Hodgensville KY, Keystone **8.50**
Blk men & women picking cotton, Savanna GA, VG **12.50**
Boston, street view in Union Sq, Barnum, 1859, EX **48.00**
Chicago, harbor scene, EX detail, I Crater, 1859, NM **45.00**
Civil War dead soldier, Anthony, 1865, EX **35.00**
Civil War scenes, Gardner, 1860s, set of 9 ....**320.00**
Couple in love before mirror, Kilburn, EX **15.00**
Eskimos w/Summer Tents, Keystone, EX **5.50**
Grand Hotel San Francisco..., w/streetcar & carriages, Taber ...**22.50**
Great Fountain from Machinery Hall, Columbian Expo, Kilburn ...**16.00**
Hydraulic Mining Gold Run CPRR, JJ Reiley, VG **35.00**
Indian War Blk cavalry soldiers on horsebk **15.00**
Libby Prison, soldiers in front, barred windows, Anthony **21.50**
Lincoln funeral procession on Broadway NY, ca 1865, VG **90.00**
McKinley & Hobart 1896 jugate, Littleton, VG **10.00**
Our Father Which Art in Heaven, mother & daughter, EX **12.50**
Pickers on ladders in orange grove, Riverside CA, EX **10.00**
Piute Indians, 4 w/children, Lawrence & Housewoth, CA, 1865 ...**35.00**
President McKinley at council table, Strohmeyer & Wyman, 1900 .....**6.50**
President McKinley at desk in Wht House, Strohmeyer & Wyman ..**7.50**
President Roosevelt & Envoys of Mikado & Czar on Mayflower **7.50**
Russian Hill San Francisco CA, view of bay, Kilburn, 1870s **10.00**
Russo-Japanese War, Russian fleet in Port Arthur Harbor **5.00**
Spanish-Am soldiers on horsebk at Ft Tampa **6.00**
Spanish-Am War, Insurgent House of Congress on Fire, 1899 ....**5.00**
Swiss Village, Paris Expo, blk/wht, 1900, EX **15.00**
Telegraph Hill San Francisco, panoramic view, Kilburn, 1870s **20.00**
Tell Me Dat You Lub Me, Blk man w/banjo, EX **12.50**
Tomb w/stone rolled away, Underwood & Underwood, 1901, EX ..**4.00**

Tintypes

Half-plate, frontiersman aiming Allen & Wheelock rifle, EX **70.00**
4th plate, bugler seated w/bugle in lap, frock coat, EX **130.00**
4th plate, man drives horse in 2-wheeled racing sulky, EX **30.00**
4th plate, Pioneer Corps soldier, patriotic bkdrop, VG **50.00**
4th plate, Union soldier w/bayonetted M1858 Enfield rifle **95.00**
6th plate, Canadian or English soldier w/Snyder-Enfield rifle **40.00**
6th plate, fireman w/Liberty Hose helmet beside him, 1870s, VG.....**36.00**
6th plate, Indian Wars soldier in kepi, full-length, EX **25.00**
6th plate, miners in lg boots, striped shirts, 1860s **75.00**
6th plate, soldier & cannon, tents & horses beyond, EX **420.00**
6th plate, Zouave w/red-tinted fez holds bayonet, EX, +case **170.00**
6th plate, 3 sailors from Frigate Minnesota, VG, +case **40.00**
6th plate, 4 soldiers w/triple-button coats, 1870s, EX **30.00**

Viewers and Slides

Brewster, walnut, scalloped mirror flap, EX in fitted box **285.00**
Graphoscope, for stereo/cabinet card photos, 1870s, EX **225.00**
Graphoscope, mono viewer, self-contained in box, 2x9½x5½" ..**185.00**
Keystone Telebinocular, collapsible, book-form box, EX **75.00**
Magic lantern, tin w/brass plaque, wood hdl, AT Thompson **95.00**
Stereopticon, lacquered, bird/flower decor, brass clasp, EX **165.00**
Stereopticon, Victor #2, Pat 1913, +78 slides **115.00**
Stereoscope, aluminum hood, Underwood/Underwood, Pat 1901 ....**45.00**

Zeotrope, see movies through slots, 9½" dia, EX **500.00**

Miscellaneous

Album, gold emb florals on cover, brass latch, +48 CDVs, EX **50.00**
Album, leather, 4 wht porc knobs ea side, gold edges, 48-pg **50.00**
Album, leather w/heavy clasp, CDVs & cabinet photos, 1870s **40.00**
Catalog, Eastman Kodak, Kodaks & Supplies, 1924, 64-pg **32.00**
Display pc, Kodak Instamatic #104 camera, w/flash, 22x21" **60.00**
Lens, Burke & James, color filter, NM in orig case **5.00**
Magazine, Kodakery, Eastman Kodak Co, July 1927, 32-pg, EX **5.00**
Stanhope, binoculars, bone, Statue of Liberty view **50.00**
Stanhope, cross, bone, WWI, troups in trenches, ca 1914, EX **50.00**
Stanhope, inkwell, ivory, chalet form, German views **50.00**
Stanhope, pen, rhinestones, Lord's Prayer **45.00**
Stanhope, pipe, cvd wood, 6 Port Erin views, 1" L, EX **50.00**
Stanhope, scent bottle, brass, w/neck chain, 6 views, EX **155.00**

Pickard

Founded in 1893 in Edgerton, Illinois, the Pickard China Company was originally a decorating studio, importing china blanks from European manufacturers. Some of these early pieces bear the name of those companies as well as Pickard's. Trained artists decorated the wares with hand-painted studies of fruit, florals, birds, and scenics and often signed their work. In 1915 Pickard introduced a line of 23k gold over a dainty floral-etched ground design. In the 1930s they began to experiment with the idea of making their own ware and by 1938 had succeeded in developing a formula for fine translucent china. Since 1976 they have issued an annual limited edition Christmas plate. They are now located in Antioch, Illinois.

The company has used various marks. The earliest (1893-1894) was a double-circle mark, 'Edgerton Hand Painted' with 'Pickard' in the center. Variations of the double-circle mark (with 'Hand Painted China' replacing the Edgerton designation) were employed until 1915, each differing enough that collectors can usually pinpoint the date of manufacture within five years. Later marks included the crown mark, 'Pickard' on a gold maple leaf, and the current mark, the lion and shield. Work signed by Challinor, Marker, and Yeschek is especially valued by today's collectors. Our advisor for this category is Milt Steinfeld; he is listed in the Directory under New Jersey.

Bowl, berries & flowers, sgn MP, scalloped gold rim, 9" **150.00**
Bowl, carnations & butterfly, gold hdls, 7" **125.00**
Bowl, fruit, sgn J Nessy, clover shape, much gold, 9¼" **250.00**
Bowl, hazelnuts, much gold on rolled rim, 4-ftd **100.00**
Bowl, Modern Conventional, Hessler, 4¾x9½", EX **285.00**
Bowl, poppies w/in & w/out, sgn LOH, much gold, 3x9¼" **200.00**
Bowl, red poppies, artist sgn, 3-hdld, 8" **200.00**
Bowl, violets, scalloped gold rim, 3 gold hdls, 6" **130.00**
Cake plate, Deserted Garden, much gold, 12½" **200.00**
Cake plate, oranges, sgn Schoner, gold scalloped rim, 11¾" **225.00**
Chamberstick, roses & ribbons, sgn Reury, much gold **250.00**
Chocolate set, Deserted Garden, sgn Vokral, 3-pc+tray **425.00**
Compote, lemon trees/florals, sgn, 1910-12 mk, 2½x7" **185.00**
Creamer, Aura Argenta Linear, 1898-1904, 3¾x3" **65.00**
Creamer & sugar bowl, gold floral on cream, boat form, 1905 ....**195.00**
Creamer & sugar bowl, stylized berries, sgn Tolly, w/lid **175.00**
Cup & saucer, poppies & daisies, sgn Faladik, much gold, pr **130.00**
Flask, gold-traced ears of corn on burgundy, 10¾" **550.00**
Hatpin holder, yel flowers, sgn Beutlich, gold top, 5" **250.00**
Mug, canal scene & church on lustre, sgn Comyn, 5" **900.00**
Pitcher, lemonade; currants, sgn Reau, much gold, 6¾" **250.00**

Pitcher, Deserted Garden, signed Challinor, 5½", $495.00.

Pitcher, milk; violets, sgn Kriesche, gold rim, 5" **110.00**
Pitcher, water; poppies, sgn Kiefer, much gold, 11" **450.00**
Plate, berries/blooms, sgn Challinor, ornate gold rim, 8⅝" **100.00**
Plate, garden & flower scene, Challinor, heavy gold rim, 10¾" ..**150.00**
Platter, plums, sgn Gibson, gold molded rim, 12¼" **200.00**
Shakers, poppies & daisies, sgn Osborne, much gold, pr **105.00**
Syrup, lilies & leaves, sgn Yeschek, much gold, +underplate **250.00**
Tankard, mums on orange, sgn Reau, gold rim & hdl, 16" **550.00**
Vase, daisies & carnations, Challinor, trumpet form, 10½" **425.00**
Vase, mc floral w/gold on blk, sgn Gifford, 1895-98 mk, 7⅝" **325.00**
Vase, mc roses, Bavaria blank, ca 1920, 10" **275.00**
Vase, mtn landscape, sgn Marker, gold rim & hdls, 10" **550.00**
Vase, roses, sgn Podlaha, gold rim, 12½" **600.00**
Vase, roses/riverbanks medial band, gilt decor, Marken, 12" **300.00**
Vase, wht roses, sgn Mullen, gilt rim/base, slim form, 16" **750.00**
Whiskey jug, ears of corn, sgn Gifford, gold hdl/stopper, 6" **325.00**

Pickle Castors

Pickle castors, which were both functional and decorative, became popular after the Civil War, reaching their peak about 1885. By 1900 they had virtually disappeared from factory catalogs. Numerous styles were available. They consisted of a decorated, silverplated frame that held either a fancy clear pressed-glass insert or one of decorated colored art glass — the latter being popular in the more affluent Victorian households and more desirable with collectors today.

In the listings below, the description prior to the semicolon refers to the jar (insert), and the remainder of the line describes the frame. When no condition is indicated, the silverplate is assumed to be in very good to excellent condition; glass jars are assumed near-mint.

Key:
rsl — resilvered   3-D — three-dimensional

Barley; orig SP fr, +tongs **95.00**
Block, clear; rstr Homan SP fr, fancy bail **165.00**
Burmese shaded; Rogers-Smith fr w/2 Greenaway boys, +fork **700.00**
Chry'mum Base Reverse Swirl, bl opal; fr: 3-D elephant heads ...**425.00**
Cone, cranberry, Consolidated; ornate SP fr on ped base **395.00**
Coreopsis, mc florals on wht satin; SP fr & tongs **375.00**
Cranberry, clear rigaree, scalloped; ornate SP fr **395.00**
Cranberry, Paneled Sprig w/decor; rsl Rogers ftd fr, +tongs **595.00**
Cranberry, ribbed; Wilcox fr: Greenaway girl skipping rope **350.00**
Crown Milano, acorns/leaves w/gold; Pairpoint std w/gargoyle....**1,100.00**
Cupid & Venus; orig SP fr & tongs **245.00**
Daisy & Button, amber; ornate SP fr w/scrolled ft, +tongs **195.00**
Daisy & Button canoe, amber; Homan wheeled fr w/owls, +fork **850.00**
Daisy & Button vaseline; SH&M fr, floral rim, +tongs **300.00**
Daisy & Button w/V Bar ornament, amber; plain SP fr **225.00**
Daisy & Fern, cranberry opal; orig SP fr, +tongs **395.00**
Dmn Point, clear; plain rsl fr, +tongs **125.00**
Fine Cut & Panel, sapphire bl; rsl SP fr, 11", +tongs **225.00**

Frosted, emb birds/insects; Reed & Barton dbl-hdl fr, +fork 325.00
Frosted Pumpkin w/bird finial; Wilcox fr w/3-D leaf, +fork 450.00
Frosted Stork; orig Meriden fr, +tongs 200.00
Frosted w/wood texture & flowers; Poole fr, +tongs 350.00
Heart Arches, florals on wht satin; orig fr & lid 350.00
Herringbone MOP, bl; Aurora SP fr 550.00
Hobnail, amber; Racine fr w/floral emb lid, +fork 425.00
Hobnail, raspberry/wht opal; fancy Derby fr, figural lid 550.00
Honeycomb, bl opal, Beatty; ftd Forbes fr 325.00
Invt T'print, apricot w/HP daisies, Mt WA; sgn Pairpoint fr 550.00
Invt T'print, cranberry, gold butterfly etc; Meriden fr 500.00
Invt T'print, cranberry; Cromwell fr, 4 3-D ladies, claw tongs 425.00
Invt T'print, cranberry; ornate rstr ftd fr, bud finial, +fork 575.00
Invt T'print, sapphire bl, flowers/leaves; orig ftd fr 395.00
Invt T'print w/swirls, rubena w/coralene roses; ornate fr, +tongs 800.00
Mc spatter (cased); ornate Wilcox ftd fr 395.00
Optic Panel, cranberry w/peonies & gold; Wilcox fr, +tongs 325.00
Optic Rib, cranberry w/florals; orig SP fr, +tongs 295.00
Purple slag, waffle/panel mold; birds/fountain emb fr 300.00
Royal Ivy, rubena frost; chased fr, +tongs 425.00
Shell & Seaweed, pk; Meriden fr, hdl: cherubs cutouts, tongs 500.00
Swirl, clear; low ftd Meriden fr w/hdls, no tongs 110.00

Pie Birds

A pie bird (also known as a pie vent or pie funnel) is placed in the middle of a pie to serve the dual purpose of supporting the pastry (to prevent sogginess) and to act as a vent that allows the steam to escape, thus avoiding runover. They are open-bottomed, hollow, and glazed inside and out. They are designed with a top vent, and most have two arches around the base. The steam enters the pie bird via the arches and exits through the top vent. In Victorian times pie funnels were first used in deep-dish meat pies. Bird-shaped vents were made as early as 1910 in England and from 1930 until the '60s in America. Later, figural pie vents were made in England. In the past two years, over 100 new U.S.-made pie vents have flooded the collectibles market, only one of which was made by a commercial pottery. Incense burners, one-hole pepper shakers, and a dated brass toy bird whistle should not be mistaken for pie vents.

Our advisors for this category are Alan Pedel (representing the English market; see England in the Directory) and Lillian Cole (listed under New Jersey).

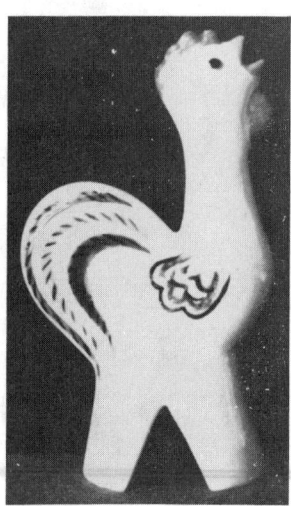

Rooster, multicolor detailing on white, ceramic, 5", $35.00.

Bennie the Baker, Cardinal China 68.00
Bl salt glazed, mk Rowe Pottery 10.00

Blackbird, mk Scotland 25.00
Blackbird, on log, England 30.00
Blackbird, yel beak, rnd tummy 15.00
Canary, yel w/pk lips 18.00
Chess pc 15.00
Dragon, mc pnt 40.00
Elephant, mk Cleverly 60.00
Granny Pie Baker 40.00
Pie funnel, mk Nutbrn 23.00
Pillsbury Chick, pk or bl base 18.00
Rooster, Bl Willow 18.00
Rooster, Cleminson 22.00
Song Bird, bl or pk 20.00
Witch, 1-color 40.00

Pierce, Howard

Howard Pierce opened a studio in Claremont, California, in the mid-1940s where he produced small ceramic models of birds and animals, figurines, and vases, making his molds and decorating his ware with no outside help except for his wife and more recently his daughter. He is best known for his skill at sculpting his models, which he decorates entirely with the airbrush. Early items were incised 'Howard Pierce, Claremont, California' or stamped 'Howard Pierce Porcelain.' Not all of his ware is marked, however, and some pieces carry only his initials. For more information we recommend *The Collector's Encyclopedia of California Pottery* by Jack Chipman, whose address may be found in the Directory under California.

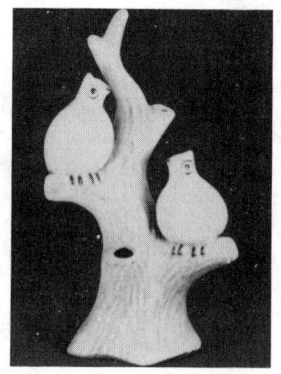

Quail pair perched in tree, light gray with black wash, 9", ca 1970s, $40.00.

Dealer sign, recent 35.00
Figurine, bear, brn, 1950s, 5¼" 30.00
Figurine, cat, seated, sandstone, 14" 50.00
Figurine, eagle, blk, 1960s 35.00
Figurine, goose, wht, 1950s-60s, pr 35.00
Figurine, hippo, 'volcanic' brn glaze, recent, 6" 22.00
Figurine, monkey, seated, stylized, gray, rare, 9½" 65.00
Figurine, rooster & hen, brn & wht, 1950s, 9¼", 7¼", pr 45.00
Figurine, squirrel, gray, 4" 12.00
Figurine, turtle, speckled brn on wht, 1950s, 5" 25.00
Flower frog, quail w/2 young, 6½" 35.00
Planter, deer in central opening, gr gloss, rectangular, 8" 62.50
Vase, Deco girl w/in circular cutout, creche style, gr, sq 45.00
Vase, fish insert, creche style, gr, 8" 35.00

Pigeon Blood

Pigeon blood glass, produced in the late 1800s, may be distinguished from other dark red glass by its distinctive orange tint.

Biscuit jar, Torquay, $475.00.

Cookie jar, Florette, SP hdl/rim/lid 200.00
Creamer, Venecia, w/enamel decor 160.00
Hand cooler, cut panels, 2-compartment, silver mts, 5" L 135.00
Pitcher, clear appl hdl, 7" 200.00
Rose bowl, HP floral w/gilt, 5" dia 65.00
Shakers, Flower Band, pr 160.00
Shakers, Torquay, orig metal tops, pr 150.00
Syrup pitcher, Torquay 275.00
Tumbler, HP floral, int ribs 60.00
Wine, 6" 40.00

Pilkington

Founded in 1892 in Manchester, England, the Pilkington Pottery experimented in wonderful lustre glazes that were so successful that when they were diplayed at exhibition in 1904, they were met with critical acclaim. They soon attracted some of the best ceramic technicians and designers of the day who decorated the lustre ground with flowers, animals, and trees; some pieces were more elaborate with scenes of sailing ships and knights on horseback. Each artist signed his work with his personal monogram. Most pieces were dated and carried the company mark as well. After 1913 the company became known as Royal Lancastrian.

Their Lapis Ware line was introduced in the late 1920s, featuring intermingling tones of color under a matt glaze. Some pieces were very simply decorated while others were painted with designs of stylized leafage, scrolls, swirls, and stripes. The line continued into the thirties. Other pieces of this period were molded and carved with animals, leaves, etc., some of which were reminescent of their earlier wares.

The company closed in 1938 but reopened in 1948. During this period, their mark was a simple P within the outline of a petaled flower shape. Our advisor for this category is David Erhard; he is listed in the Directory under California.

Bowl, Lapis, William S Mycock, geometric design 200.00
Bowl, matt gr 95.00
Candle holder, matt gr 75.00
Vase, Gwladys M Rodgers, simple form, subtle design 135.00
Vase, Lapis, GM Rodgers, bold design, sm 150.00
Vase, Lapis, Gwladys M Rodgers, bulbous, bold design 185.00
Vase, Lapis, Richard Joyce, dbl gourd shape, bold design 350.00
Vase, lustre ware, birds decor, Walter Crane, 8" 750.00
Vase, lustre ware, dragon decor, Mycock, 7" 450.00
Vase, lustre ware, fish decor, R Joyce, 8" 500.00
Vase, matt gr, rnded shoulder, flared neck, emb decor 225.00

Pillin

Polia Pillin was born in Poland in 1909; many of her family were

artisians and craftsmen. Except for a few weeks of formal instruction at the Hull House in Chicago, Pillin is self-taught in the arts. Her work has been shown in many exhibits, and she has received awards from the Los Angeles County Art Institute, Syracuse Museum, Los Angeles County Fair, and the California State Fair. First interested in oils and watercolors, she has carried the same Byzantine quality over to her pottery. All of her work is signed 'Pillin' or 'W&P Pillin,' both with the loop of the P extended in an arc over the remaining letters of her name.

Bowl, bust portraits & birds on bl, 5½x10½" 375.00
Bowl, bust portraits on blk, 6½x5½" 350.00
Bowl, punch; mc yel, rare, 16" 1,500.00
Bowl, red abstract, 3¾x5½" 175.00
Charcoal, Southwest scene, fr, 19x12" 475.00
Lamp base, 12 figurals, rare, 14" 1,500.00
Painting, abstract, paper, fr, 15x11" 750.00
Pendant, horse on bl, 2" 55.00
Plaque, farm scene, 12x12" 900.00
Plaque, HP scene, 11x10" 950.00
Plate, children w/balloons on yel, 7½" 100.00
Plate, frolicking horses on gr, 7½" 110.00
Plate, ochre tones, 9" sq 250.00
Vase, Bentonite, abstract, 6" 250.00
Vase, Bentonite, fish decor, 4" 425.00
Vase, birds on gr w/pastels, 5¼" 150.00
Vase, birds on yel, 1½" 50.00
Vase, bust portraits on blk, bulbous, 9½" 395.00
Vase, bust portraits on gr, bulbous, 8½" 325.00
Vase, figural, blk, 11" 900.00
Vase, fish, pk & gr, squat, 2" 75.00
Vase, gr/pastel, bottle form, 11½" 140.00
Vase, horses on pastels, 5¾" 195.00
Vase, nudes on red, 12x6", NM 1,250.00
Vase, 3 nudes on bl, 9¼" 425.00
Vase, 3 nudes on pastels, 4½" 195.00

Pin-Back Buttons

Most of the advertising buttons made until the 1920s were top-quality, full-color, celluloid-covered buttons termed 'cellos.' Many were issued in sets on related topics featuring historical people and events, animals, birds, and other themes. Several cigarette, gum, and candy companies used buttons as inserts in their products. Usually the name of the company or product was printed on a paper placed in the back of the button and held securely by the pin. Most of the back papers are still in place today, aiding in the identification of the button. Beginning in the 1920s, a large number of buttons were lithographed (printed on metal); these buttons are referred to as 'lithos.' Nearly all advertising buttons are collected today with perhaps these exceptions: common buttons picturing flags of various nations, general labor union buttons denoting the payment of dues, and similar buttons with clever sayings.

Following is a listing of some of the most popular non-political buttons. Values reflect buttons which have designs centered, colors aligned, no fading or yellowing, no spots or stains, and no cracks, splits, or dents. See also Personalities; Political.

Archie Bunker for President, 1972, M 3.50
Back to School Days at Penney's, children, 1950s, EX 12.00
Ceresota, Best Flour on Earth, no illus 8.00
Chapman Dancing, Oakland CA, man w/mustache, EX 10.00
Cygnet, lady w/3-wheel bicycle, ¾" 45.00
Dad's Root Beer on rectangle, Good Co above, 2½" 7.50
Deering Harvester, NM 65.00

Elk's Carnival Fulton NY...1914, elk picture on clock, EX 22.00
G Man, in lg star, Sun Spot, 1¼" 12.00
Gold Dust Washing Powder, boys in tub, VG 18.00
Grate Lakes Exposition, Federal Day, 1937, NM 5.00
I'm a Buick Man, 1½" 7.50
Jackie Cooper, NM 5.00
Liberty Bell, Panama Pacific Expo, 1915, EX 12.00
Maine Centennial, 1920, NM 5.00
Opening Day State Fair of TX 1932, EX 20.00
Peter's Shells, NM 45.00
Remember Pearl Harbor, red/wht/bl, 3¼" 20.00
Rockne of Notre Dame, w/photo, 1¾" 45.00
Rumford Baking Powder, can illus, 1" 8.00
Sampeck Triple Service Suit, Charlie Chaplin portrait 75.00
Taxi Cab Driver's Union, 1954 ....2.50
Tim McCoy's Vigilantes, EX 45.00
Try a Canada Dry Tahitian Treat, hula girl 10.00
UPS Since 1907, 1¼" 7.00

Pink Lustre Ware

Pink lustre was produced by nearly every potter in the Stafford-shire district in the 18th and 19th centuries. The application of gold lustre on white or light-colored backgrounds produced pinks, while the same over dark colors developed copper. The wares ranged from hand-painted plaques to transfer-printed dinnerware. Design features in the phrase immediately following the item (i.e. cup, plate, etc.) are in pink lustre unless specifically described within the line.

Creamer, foliage band, Oriental genre transfer w/mc, 3½" 170.00
Cup & saucer, bands/foliage, transfer girl/bird, mc floral 40.00
Cup & saucer, florals/bands, emb florals/scrolls, gr leaves 50.00
Cup & saucer, foliage/band, yel/red sunbursts etc, mk Wood 110.00
Cup & saucer, house pattern, hairline in saucer 50.00
Cup & saucer, rim stripe/rosette band, red/gr floral 60.00
Cup & saucer, wide band, purple transfer Victoria & Albert 110.00
Cup & saucer, wide band w/4-color floral, NM 180.00
Mug, child's, vines/leaves, red/gr strawberries, 2⅜" 95.00
Pitcher, grapevine border, horses/cows, 1830, 5½" 200.00
Pitcher, resist strawberries/vintage, 5⅝", EX 75.00
Plate, banded dmn-emb rim, King's Rose-type flower, 7½" 65.00
Plate, banded rim, Duke of Wellington 131 Guns transfer, 9½" .235.00
Plate, banded rim w/emb floral, transfer of children 60.00
Plate, leaves/band, band of 3-color flowers, 7½" 45.00
Plate, red Adam's Rose-type flowers, pk lustre leaves, 8" 90.00
Plate, swags alternate w/red swags & gr leaves, 7¾" 35.00
Plate, 4-color floral border, pk lustre leaves/rim, 7½" 50.00

Pink Paw Bears

These charming figural pieces are very similar to the Pink Pigs described in the following category. They were made in Germany dur-ing the same time frame. The cabbage green is identical; the bears themselves are whitish-gray with pink foot pads. You'll find some that are unmarked while others are marked 'Germany' or 'Made in Ger-many.' In theory, the unmarked bears are the oldest, made prior to 1890 when the McKinley Tariff Act required imports to be marked with the country of origin. Those marked 'Made in' were probably produced after the revision of the Act in 1914.

1 by graphophone 120.00
1 by honey pot 120.00

1 by top hat 110.00
1 in roadster (car identical to pk pig car) 145.00
1 on binoculars 125.00
1 peeking out of basket 115.00
1 peering in hand mirror 135.00
1 sitting in wicker chair 150.00
2 by bean pot 120.00
2 in purse 135.00
2 in roadster 150.00
2 on pin dish 120.00
2 peering in floor mirror 150.00
2 sitting by mushroom 125.00
3 on pin dish 130.00

Pink Pigs

Pink Pigs on cabbage green were made in Germany around the turn of the century. They were sold as souvenirs in train depots, amuse-ment parks, and gift shops. 'Action pigs' (those involved in some amus-ing activity) are the most valuable, and prices increase with the number of pigs. Though a similar type of figurine was made in white bisque, most serious collectors prefer only the pink ones. They are marked in two ways: 'Germany' in incised letters, and a black ink stamp 'Made in Germany' in a circle.

1 beside gr drum, wall-mt match holder 60.00
1 beside stump, camera around neck, toothpick holder 120.00
1 coming out of cup 65.00
1 coming out of suitcase 85.00
1 coming through gr fence, post at sides, open for flowers 95.00
1 driving touring car 125.00
1 in case looking through binoculars 115.00
1 in gr Dutch shoe 50.00
1 in gr suitcase bank, head 1 side, bk other, gold trim 75.00
1 in Japanese submarine, Japan imp on both sides 125.00
1 in jaws of trap, rare, unmk, 5" L 110.00
1 in money sack bank 85.00
1 in roadster 125.00
1 lg pig sitting behind 3" trough 75.00
1 napping on side, Schlite Patent, 5" L 98.00
1 on binoculars, gold trim 100.00
1 on gr trinket dish, leg caught in lobster claw 65.00
1 on horseshoe-shaped dish w/raised 4-leaf clover 75.00
1 on keg playing piano 125.00
1 on shoulder of gr ink bottle 75.00
1 plays accordion on side of tray, wht bear ea side 125.00
1 pushing head through wooden gate 75.00
1 putting letter in mail box 75.00
1 reclining on horseshoe ashtray 70.00
1 riding train, 4½" 145.00
1 sits, holds orange Boston Baked Beans pot match holder 65.00
1 sits by high-top boot 70.00
1 sitting in bathtub 95.00
1 sitting on log, mk Germany 80.00
1 standing in gr tub 95.00
1 w/attached toothpick holder 65.00
1 w/front ft in 3-part dish containing 3 dice, 1 ft on dice 75.00
1 w/tennis racket stands beside vase, Lawn Tennis, 3¾" 95.00
1 wearing chef's costume holds frypan, w/basket 95.00
2, mother & baby in bl blanket in tub, rabbit on board atop 85.00
2, mother in tub gives baby a bottle, lamb looks on, 4x3½" 85.00
2, 1 at telephone booth, 1 inside, 4½" 80.00
2 at confession, 4½" 90.00

2 behind trough, unmk	65.00
2 by eggshell	80.00
2 by lg gr telephone	80.00
2 dancing in top hat, tux & cane	110.00
2 holding hands in roadster, 4½" L	145.00
2 in basket, Merry Squeelers, 3½x3"	90.00
2 in bed, Good Night on footboard, 4x3x2½"	145.00
2 in carriage	95.00
2 in love sit on lg log, 2 openings on tree stump, 7" L	75.00
2 in open trunk, 3¾"	95.00
2 in purse	75.00
2 on basket, head raising lid, plaque on front	80.00
2 on binoculars, gold trim	125.00
2 on cotton bale, 1 peers from hole, 1 over top	95.00
2 on gr tray	50.00
2 on seesaw on top of pouch bank	75.00
2 on top hat	95.00
2 on tray hugging, 3x4½"	65.00
3, 1 on lg slipper playing banjo, 2 dancing on side	145.00
3, 2 sit in front of coal bucket, 3rd inside	110.00
3 at trough, 4½" L	98.00
3 dressed up on edge of dish	80.00
3 sm pigs behind oval trough, mk, 2¾x2½x1¾"	90.00
3 w/baby carriage, father & 2 babies, Wheeling His Own	95.00
3 w/carriage, mother & 2 babies, Germany	95.00

Pisgah Forest

The Pisgah Forest Pottery was established in 1920 near Mount Pisgah in Arden, North Carolina, by Walter B. Stephen, who had worked in previous years at other locations in the state — Nonconnah and Skyland (the latter from 1913 until 1916). Stephen, who was born in the mountain region near Asheville, was known for his work in the Southern tradition. He produced skillfully executed wares exhibiting an amazing variety of techniques. He operated his business with only two helpers. Recognized today as his most outstanding accomplishment, his Cameo line was decorated by hand in the pate-sur-pate style (similar to Wedgwood Jasper) in such designs as Fiddler and Dog, Spinning Wheel, Covered Wagon, Buffalo Hunt, Mountain Cabin, Square Dancers, Indian Campfire, and Plowman. Stephen is known for other types of wares as well. His crystalline glaze is highly regarded by today's collectors.

At least nine different stamps mark his wares, several of which contain the outline of the potter at the wheel and 'Pisgah Forest.' Cameo is sometimes marked with a circle containing the line name and 'Long Pine, Arden, NC.' Two other marks may be more difficult to recognize: 1) a circle containing the outline of a pine tree, 'N.C.' to the left of the trunk and 'Pine Tree' on the other side; and 2) the letter 'P' with short uprights in the middle of the top and lower curves. Stephen died in 1961, but the work was continued by his associates. Our advisor for this category is R.J. Sayers; he is listed in the Directory under North Carolina.

Beaker, turq/pk, 1936, 6"	50.00
Creamer, Cameo, house w/man & dog, wht/gr, sgn Stephen, 3"	100.00
Mug, Cameo, potter at wheel	110.00
Pitcher, forest gr w/pk int, hand thrown, 6½"	85.00
Vase, aqua, Stephens, 1937, 10x6"	100.00
Vase, bl/gr crystalline, kiln blister, 5"	100.00
Vase, bl/wht crystalline, 1949, concave cylinder, 5"	200.00
Vase, Cameo, Indian chasing buffalo, bsk on gr, 8x5"	300.00
Vase, Cameo, wagons/oxen, wht/gr band on turq, 1929, 12x7"	600.00
Vase, Cameo wagons/oxen, wht/bl on gr crystalline, WBS, 8"	400.00
Vase, gr/red gloss, emb mk, 1928, 11", NM	200.00
Vase, mauve to turq, sgn, 5"	55.00

Vase, ivory crystalline, pink interior, 5", $150.00.

Vase, purple crackle, Forest, 3"	65.00
Vase, red drip on gray, rare colors, 7"	150.00
Vase, turq, pk int, hdls, 6"	100.00
Vase, turq, pk int, 6¾"	75.00
Vase, turq, 4"	55.00
Vase, turq crackle, pk int, 1934, 3½"	65.00
Vase, wht crystalline, 6½"	150.00

Pittsburgh Glass

As early as 1797, utility window glass and hollowware were being produced in the Pittsburgh area. Coal had been found in abundance, and it was there that it was first used instead of wood to fuel the glass furnaces. Because of this as many as 150 glass companies operated there at one time. However, most failed due to the economically disastrous effects of the War of 1812. By the mid-1850s those that remained were producing a wide range of flint glass items including pattern-molded and free-blown glass, cut and engraved wares, and pressed tableware patterns. Our advisor for this category is Mark Vuono; he is listed in the Directory under Connecticut.

Bottle, appl cobalt bl rings, 12½"	700.00
Candlestick, petal top, hex stem, pewter inserts, 10", pr	420.00

Celery vase, allover printies, ca 1850s, 9", $300.00.

Compote, cut ovals/circles, panel-cut stem, appl ft, 8x9"	165.00
Compote, cut strawberry/dmn/fans, knop stem, 6x8", NM	300.00
Compote, folded rim, baluster stem, wide ft, 6½x8", NM	175.00
Decanter, pillar mold, appl collar/lip, 12"	135.00
Lamp, flattened rnd font, appl ft/stem, 6"	90.00
Lamp, whale oil burner, wide appl ft, pewter collar, 6"	130.00
Pitcher, cut rings/ribs/strawberry dmns, appl hdl, 5", NM	200.00

Salt cellar, sapphire bl, drawn ped ft, rolled lip, att, 3" **160.00**
Tumbler, cobalt, 8-panel, minor roughness on base, 4" **115.00**
Tumbler, sapphire bl, 6-panel, 4", NM **105.00**
Tumbler, sapphire bl, 8-panel, 4" **125.00**
Vase, cut strawberry/dmns/foliage fans, ball stem, 9" **425.00**
Vase, orange cased in clear, wht int, clear ft/hdls, 7" **550.00**
Vase, pillar mold, wide ft, baluster stem, 9" **85.00**

Plastics

The term 'collectible plastics' is defined as those types produced between 1868 (when synthetic plastics were invented) and the period immediately following WWII. There are several, and we shall mention each one and attempt briefly to acquaint you with their characteristics:

1) Pyroxylin (Celluloid, Loalin, French Ivory, Pyralin). Chemical name: cellulose nitrate. Earliest form, invented in 1868 by John Wesley Hyatt; highly flammable; yellows with age; much used in toiletry articles. Fairly lightweight, many articles of pyroxylin were made by heating and molding thin sheets.

2) Cellulose Acetate (Tenite, Similoid). Made in attempt to produce a product similar to cellulose nitrate but without the flammability. Had limited use in the costume jewelry trade; most often encountered as car knobs and handles of the thirties and forties. Surfaces tend to crack with age and exposure to light. Always molded, never cast. Colors varied; imitation horn and marble were most popular.

3) Casein Plastics (Ameroid, Galalith, Dorcasine, Casolith). Invented in 1904 using milk proteins. Use limited to buttons and buckles due to warping and lengthy curing time. Made in a wide range of colors; very easy to laminate or to carve from stock rods or sheets, but never molded.

4) Phenol Formaldehyde (Bakelite, Catalin, Marblette, Agatine, Gemstone, Durite, Durez, Prystal). Invented by L.H. Baekland in 1908 and used extensively in the thirties. There are two major types: cast and molded. Molded types include Durez and Bakelite, dark-toned, wood flour-filled plastics that were used extensively for early telephones (still used when non-conductivity of heat and electricity is vital). The most popular name in cast phenolics was Catalin, trade name of the American Catalin Corporation of New York. Made in a wide range of colors; widely used for costume jewelry, cutlery handles, decorative boxes, lamps, desk sets, etc. Heavyweight material with a slightly 'greasy' feel; very hard but can be carved with files, grinding tools, and abrasive cutters. Buffs to high, durable polish. Cast phenolics were used primarily from 1930 to around 1950 when they proved too labor-intensive to be economical.

5) Urea Formaldehyde (Beetleware, Plaskon, Duroware, Hemocoware, Uralite). Invented around 1929, this was lighter in color than phenol formaldehyde, thus, used for injection-molded products in pastel colors. Lightweight, not strong; shiny rather than glossy. It cannot be carved and was used mainly for cheap radio and clock cases, never for jewelry.

The period between the two World Wars produced acrylic resins such as Lucite and vinyl. Polystryene made its appearance then, and furfural-phenols were in use in industrial applications. Though a great future was predicted for ethyl cellulose, by the late thirties it was still in the experimental phase. For most purposes the field of decorative plastics from the first half of the century can be narrowed down to the five major types listed above. Of these, cellulose acetate is rarely encountered. Casein is limited to button and belt buckle manufacture; urea is easily identifiable as a cheap, brittle material. Pyroxylin is the celluloid of which so many vanity sets were made. Molded phenolics such as Bakelite were dark in color and used for utilitarian objects; cast phenolics such as Catalin were used most notably for jewelry (please don't call it Bakelite), cutlery handles, desk sets, and novelties.

Dealers and collectors should be aware of '70s reproduction Marblette animal napkin rings (they have no eye rods and no age patina)

and molded acrylic bracelets in imitation of carved Catalin ones (look for a seam line or lack of definition in carved areas). As prices rise copies become more common. 1986 saw the mass-production of inlaid polka-dot bracelets using old-stock findings but without the precision fit (or patina) of the originals.

In 1988 and continuing to the present, a large number of 'collage' pieces appeared in vintage clothing and antique stores on the West and East Coasts. These are over-sized, glued-together assemblages of old Catalin stock parts including buttons with the shanks filed off, poker chips, etc. made into brooches or pendants, sometimes hung on necklaces of re-strung Catalin beads. They can be recognized by their aesthetically jumbled, 'put-together' look. Although some may claim they are old, they are not.

Our advisor for this category is Catherine Yronwode, who also publishes an informative newsletter, *The Collectible Plastics*; she is listed in the Directory under California. Our thanks to Benjamin Rose for help with radio prices.

Bakelite

Cigarette box, half-cylinder, rotates open, dk brn **40.00**
Clock, electric, alarm, Deco design, blk or dk brn **65.00**
Clock, mantel, wind-up alarm, Deco design, dk brn **60.00**
Inkwell, streamlined, blk, w/lid **25.00**
Penholder, streamlined, blk **22.50**
Radio, Majestic #55, dk brn, 1939 ....**250.00**
Radio, Silvertone Compact, Sears, dk brn, 1936-1937 ....**250.00**
Radio, Stewart Warner Varsity College, dk brn, 1938-1939 ....**250.00**
Roulette wheel, dk brn, 1930s **80.00**
Roulette wheel, mc Catalin chips, wood rack, w/box, 1930s **200.00**
Watch, lady's handbag; Westclox, blk, 2¾" dia **70.00**

Catalin

Catalin salt and pepper shakers, stepped design, 3½", $25.00 for the pair.

Ashtray, marbleized lt gr, sq, 4½" **30.00**
Barometer, Taylor, amber & dk gr, rectangular, 4" **40.00**
Blotter, Carvacraft, Great Britain, amber/blk **45.00**
Bottle opener, chrome plate, red, gr, or amber hdl **10.00**
Bracelet, bangle; apple-juice clear, figural bk-cvg **175.00**
Bracelet, bangle; apple-juice clear, floral bk-cvg **150.00**
Bracelet, bangle; apple-juice clear, geometric bk-cvg **130.00**
Bracelet, bangle; deep cvg, w/rhinestones **80.00**
Bracelet, bangle; elaborate floral cvg, narrow **40.00**
Bracelet, bangle; elaborate floral cvg, wide **65.00**
Bracelet, bangle; lt geometric cvg, narrow **28.00**
Bracelet, bangle; lt geometric cvg, wide **45.00**

Bracelet, bangle; novelty, mc, figural or animal cvg 250.00
Bracelet, bangle; scratch cvd, narrow 18.00
Bracelet, bangle; scratch cvd, w/rhinestones 25.00
Bracelet, bangle; scratch cvd, wide 25.00
Bracelet, bangle; stylized floral cvg, narrow 28.00
Bracelet, bangle; stylized floral cvg, wide 45.00
Bracelet, bangle; uncvd, narrow 6.00
Bracelet, bangle; uncvd, wide 10.00
Bracelet, bangle; 12 inlaid polka dots, wide 180.00
Bracelet, bangle; 2-color stripes 70.00
Bracelet, bangle; 3-color stripes 90.00
Bracelet, bangle; 4-color (or more) stripes 125.00
Bracelet, bangle; 6 inlaid polka dots, narrow 180.00
Bracelet, cellulose acetate chain, 7 cvd figural charms 250.00
Bracelet, clamper; figural, animal, or novelty applique 225.00
Bracelet, clamper; inlaid geometric designs 150.00
Bracelet, clamper; stylized floral cvg 52.00
Bracelet, clamper; w/inlaid rhinestones 40.00
Bracelet, curved/flat links, deeply cvd 60.00
Bracelet, curved/flat links, uncvd 45.00
Bracelet, stretch; orig elastic, Catalin & metal 48.00
Bracelet, stretch; orig elastic, deeply cvd 60.00
Bracelet, stretch; orig elastic, mc, uncvd 50.00
Buckle, latch type, mc, novelty or figural applique 40.00
Buckle, latch type, mc, stylized floral or geometric, cvd 40.00
Buckle, latch type, mc, uncvd 25.00
Buckle, latch type, 1-color, novelty or figural applique 25.00
Buckle, latch type, 1-color, stylized floral or geometric 10.00
Buckle, latch type, 1-color, uncvd 5.00
Buckle, latch type, 1-color w/rhinestones, Deco 25.00
Buckle, slide type, mc, stylized floral or geometric, cvd 35.00
Buckle, slide type, mc, uncvd 12.50
Buckle, slide type, 1-color, stylized floral or geometric, cvd 8.00
Buckle, slide type, 1-color, uncvd 4.00
Butter mold, gr/amber/brn, floral cvg, 2½" 32.00
Buttons, card of 6, red or blk laminated, 1½" rod 18.00
Buttons, card of 6, scotty, fruit, or cvd floral figural 28.00
Buttons, card of 6, uncvd octagonal, amber, 1" dia 10.00
Cake breaker, CJ Schneider, red, gr, or amber hdl 4.00
Carving set, knife, fork, steel 30.00
Carving set, 3-pc w/wood wall rack 40.00
Checkers, red & blk, full set, in box 32.00
Cheese slicer, scotty hdl, wood & chrome base 15.00
Chess set, hand cvd, red & blk, leather box 250.00
Chopsticks, ivory, pr 3.00
Cigarette box, chrome inserts, cylindrical, 4½" 40.00
Cigarette box, lt gr, wood bottom, rectangular, 5½x3¾" 30.00
Cigarette holder, imitation amber, sterling tip, orig case 25.00
Cigarette holder, long, mc or w/rhinestones 25.00
Cigarette lighter, Arco-Lite devil's head, red or blk 175.00
Cigarette lighter, mc stripes or inlay 45.00
Clock, New Haven, wind-up alarm, amber, Deco, 3⅝" 52.00
Clock, Sessions, electric alarm, scalloped case, 4¼" dia 52.00
Clock, Seth Thomas, wind-up alarm, maroon case, 3½" 42.00
Clock, Westclox, Moonbeam, electric flashing light alarm 60.00
Clothesline, Jigger, red anchors, 10 pins, metal box 10.00
Cocktail recipes, Ben Hur, mtd on drunk, red w/blk base 45.00
Cocktail recipes, Ben Hur, mtd on fighting roosters 45.00
Cork, Ben Hur, w/red fighting roosters, blk base 20.00
Corkscrew, chrome, red, gr, or amber hdl 12.50
Corn holder, Kob Knobs, diamond shape or lathe trn, 8 +box 40.00
Crib toy, Tykie Toy, boy, girl, clown, kitten, etc, ea 100.00
Crib toy, Tykie Toy, clown, loalin head/Catalin body 60.00
Crib toy, Tykie Toy, elephant, laolin head/Catalin body 60.00

Crib toy, Tykie Toy, 11 mc spools on string, 1940s 50.00
Crib toy, Tykie Toy, 12-1½" rings on 2⅞" ring, 1940s 50.00
Crib toy, Tykie Toy catalog, 1946 ....25.00
Crib toy, Tykie Toy Tales (book about these toys), 1946 ....35.00
Dice, ivory or red, 2½", pr 15.00
Dice, ivory or red, ¾", pr 2.00
Dice cage, metal/red Catalin, blk Lucite base, w/dice 75.00
Dice cup, leather or cork lined 30.00
Dominoes, ivory or blk, full set, w/wood box 30.00
Dominoes, red or gr, full set, w/wood box 40.00
Drawer pull, 1-color, w/pnt inlay stripe 2.00
Drawer pull, 2-color, octagon, w/inlaid dot 3.00
Dress clip, mc inlaid Deco design 20.00
Dress clip, novelty, figural, animal, or vegetable 50.00
Dress clip, scratch cvd 14.00
Dress clip, stylized floral cvg 20.00
Dress clip, 1-color, w/rhinestones, Deco design 20.00
Earrings, lg drop style, pr 10.00
Earrings, novelty, figural, animal, or vegetable, pr 35.00
Earrings, stylized floral cvg, pr 15.00
Earrings, uncvd disks, pr 6.00
Egg beater, red, gr, or amber hdl 16.00
Flatware, chrome plate, 1-color hdl 1.50
Flatware, chrome plate, 3-pc matched place setting 6.00
Flatware, stainless, 1-color hdl 2.00
Flatware, stainless, 1-color hdl, leatherette box, 36-pc 180.00
Flatware, stainless, 1-color hdl, 3-pc matched place setting 7.50
Flatware, stainless, 2-color hdl 3.50
Flatware, stainless, 2-color hdl, wood box, 36-pc 225.00
Flatware, stainless, 2-color hdl, 3-pc matched place setting 12.00
Gavel, lathe turned, ivory 18.00
Gavel, lathe turned, red, blk, & ivory 25.00
Gavel, lathe turned, red, w/presentation box, dtd 1946 ....28.00
Ice cream scoop, stainless, red hdl 19.00
Inkwell, Carvacraft Great Britain, amber, dbl well 90.00
Inkwell, Carvacraft Great Britain, amber, single well 70.00
Knife, cvd red, gr, or amber hdl 6.00
Lamp base, brass & amber, Deco design, 10" 30.00
Lamp base, red, amber, & blk, Deco design, 8" 44.00
Letter opener, blk & amber stripes, Deco design 20.00
Letter opener, chrome/Catalin, Deco design 14.00
Letter opener, marbleized gr, dagger shape 20.00
Mah-Jong set, tiles, rails, 6-color, complete, w/box 45.00
Memo pad, Carvacraft Great Britain, amber 45.00
Nail brush, Ducky, duck shape, translucent eye rod 32.00
Nail brush, marbleized lt gr, 2½x1½" 8.00
Nail brush, Masso, amber octagon, 2" dia 8.00
Nail brush, turtle shape, dark amber, 3½" 16.00
Napkin ring, amber, red, or gr, 2" dia band 8.00
Napkin ring, animal or bird, no inlaid eye or ball on head 25.00
Napkin ring, elephant w/ball on head 35.00
Napkin ring, lathe turned, amber, red, or gr, 1¾" dia 8.00
Napkin ring, Mickey Mouse or Donald Duck shape w/decal 58.00
Napkin ring, rabbit w/inlaid eye rod 35.00
Napkin ring, rocking horse or camel w/inlaid eye rod 66.00
Napkin ring, scotty, w/inlaid eye rod 38.00
Napkin ring set, 6-colors, 2" band, orig box 40.00
Necklace, cellulose acetate chain, animal figurals 250.00
Necklace, cellulose acetate chain, Deco dangling pcs 175.00
Necklace, cvd red & amber beads, 18" 65.00
Necklace, uncvd gr beads, 20" 40.00
Ozone generator, Air-Clear, dk amber, streamlined case 70.00
Pencil sharpener, Disney character decal, silhouette shape 38.00
Pencil sharpener, gun, tank, or plane shape w/decal 30.00

Pencil sharpener, orange, no decal, ¾x1" 8.00
Pencil sharpener, red, Mickey Mouse decal, ¾x1" 30.00
Pencil sharpener, scotty, red, cvd details, blk base 30.00
Pencil sharpener, scotty, yel, silhouette shape 20.00
Pencil sharpener, Trylon & Perisphere, 1939 World's Fair 50.00
Penholder, amber & blk striped, Deco design 35.00
Penholder, marbleized amber, Deco design 25.00
Penholder, scotty, red w/blk base 45.00
Picture frame, amber & red Deco design, 6x7" 45.00
Picture frame, red, gr, or amber, sq, 6" 35.00
Pin, animal, resin wash w/glass eye, lg 110.00
Pin, animal, resin wash w/glass eye, sm 75.00
Pin, animal or vegetable, inlaid or appl in several colors, lg 170.00
Pin, animal or vegetable, inlaid or appl in several colors, sm 95.00
Pin, animal or vegetable, 1-color, lg 80.00
Pin, animal or vegetable, 1-color, sm 60.00
Pin, mc Deco design, lg 60.00
Pin, mc Deco design, sm 40.00
Pin, novelty or patriotic figural, resin wash/inlay/appl, lg 185.00
Pin, novelty or patriotic figural, resin wash/inlay/appl, sm 120.00
Pin, novelty or patriotic figural, 1-color, lg 95.00
Pin, novelty or patriotic figural, 1-color, sm 65.00
Pin, stylized floral cvg, lg 40.00
Pin, stylized floral cvg, sm 32.00
Pin, w/danglers, animal or vegetable, resin wash/inlay/appl 195.00
Pin, w/danglers, animal or vegetable, 1-color 100.00
Pin, w/danglers, geometric form, mc 60.00
Pin, w/danglers, geometric form, 1-color 45.00
Pin, w/danglers, novelty or patriotic, resin wash/inlay/appl 210.00
Pin, w/danglers, novelty or patriotic, 1-color 110.00
Pipe, amber & gr, bowl lined w/clay 28.00
Pitcher, glass, red, gr, or amber hdl, syrup size 18.00
Pocket watch, Debonaire, yel Deco case, 1⅞" dia 60.00
Poker chip rack, cylindrical, w/50 chips, 2½" 85.00
Poker chip rack, rectangular, w/200 chips, 4" 120.00
Powder box, amber & blk fluted cylinder, 2½" 45.00
Powder box, amber & gr fluted cylinder, 4" 56.00
Radio, AMC 'Peaktop,' amber, maroon trim 2,500.00
Radio, Emerson Cathedral (AU190), amber 1,200.00
Radio, Emerson Cathedral (AU190), bright red, very rare 13,000.00
Radio, Emerson Cathedral (AU190), gr marbled 2,200.00
Radio, Emerson College model, amber or gr, 1938 ....950.00
Radio, Emerson College model, red, 1938 ....1,200.00
Radio, Fada Streamliner, amber, amber knobs/bezel, 1941 ......950.00
Radio, Fada Streamliner, amber, red knobs/bezel, 1941 ....1,100.00
Radio, Fada Streamliner, red, amber knobs/bezel, 1941, rare ...9,800.00
Radio, Kadette Klockette, amber, gr, or maroon, 1937 ....1,200.00
Radio, Kadette Klockette, red, 1937 ....1,500.00
Ring, inlaid Deco stripe design, 2-color 45.00
Ring, stylized floral cvg, 1-color 35.00
Ring, uncvd, 1-color 15.00
Ring, uncvd, 2-color 25.00
Ring case, hinged-lid style, amber or maroon 100.00
Ring case, open-top style, amber, red, or blk, Deco design 85.00
Safety razor, Schick Injector, amber hdl 12.00
Safety razor, Schick Injector, extra blades, orig box, 1939 ....40.00
Salad servers, Chase chrome, ivory, blk, or brn, pr 30.00
Salad servers, chrome, red, gr, or amber hdls, pr 12.00
Shakers, ball shape or half-cylinder shape, 1½", pr 25.00
Shakers, glass, in 3⅛" Catalin holder, pr 19.00
Shakers, mushroom shape, amber & ivory, 1⅞", pr 25.00
Shakers, Washington Monument, 3¼", pr 25.00
Shaving brush, red, gr, or amber 18.00
Shaving brush, red, gr, or amber, w/holder 30.00

Spatula, stainless, red, gr, or amber hdl 4.50
Spoon, iced tea, chrome, w/Catalin knob, 6-pc set 18.00
Spoon, slotted, stainless, red, gr, or amber hdl 4.50
Steering knob, chrome clamp 18.00
Stirrer, iced tea; Chase, chrome ball/mint leaf, 6-pc set 26.00
Stirrer, iced tea; shovel blade, Catalin hdl, 6-pc set 36.00
Strainer, red, gr, or amber hdl, 2¾" dia 4.00
Strainer, red, gr, or amber hdl, 5" dia 6.00
Swizzle stick, baseball-bat shape, amber or red 4.00
Swizzle stick holder, amber or red, Rheingold Lager decal 70.00
Thermometer, BT Co, amber & blk, 2¾" dia 38.00
Thermometer, Taylor, amber & dk gr, rectangular, 4" 45.00
Writing set, blk, amber, or gr marble, Deco, 5-pc, orig box 150.00

Celluloid

Bracelet, imitation tortoise w/inlaid rhinestones 40.00
Bracelet, snake w/inlaid rhinestones 48.00
Bridge marker, pnt ivoroid animal or figure, France 20.00
Bridge pencil holder, animal, pearlescent ivory on blk 60.00
Buttons, ivoroid or pearlescent, ¾" dia, card of 6 ....8.00
Carving set, ivoroid, knife/fork/steel, eng blade 30.00
Clock, Greek temple facade, wind-up alarm, ivoroid 45.00
Dresser set, amberoid & gr marbleized, 7-pc 70.00
Dresser set, ivoroid, 10-pc, w/9" bevel glass mirror 100.00
Dresser set, ivory pearlescent or amberoid, 5-pc 50.00
Flatware, gr pearl on blk hdl, 3-pc set 9.00
Flatware, ivoroid hdl, table knife, fork, or spoon, ea 1.00
Hair receiver, ivoroid, pearlescent or amberoid, w/2-part lid 10.00
Manicure set, ivoroid, pearlescent or amberoid, 10-pc, +case 30.00
Manicure set, ivoroid, 18-pc, roll-up leather case 25.00
Manicure set, 4 mini-tools in coral-color tube, Germany 22.00
Manicure set, 4 mini-tools in tube holder w/pnt florals 35.00
Mirror, dresser; ivoroid, cut-out hdl, bevel glass, 8" 18.00
Mirror, dresser; ivoroid, oval bevel glass, 13" 28.00
Mirror, dresser; pearlescent or amberoid, bevel glass, 12" 20.00
Picture frame, easel bk, ivoroid, 2" dia 12.00
Powder box, ivoroid, pearlescent or amberoid 10.00
Shaving stand, ivoroid, 5-pc, w/razor 75.00

Lucite

Bottle, perfume; w/atomizer, rose inclusion 10.00
Bracelet, stretch, orig elastic, clear, bk-cvd 25.00
Picture frame, Deco, clear, sq, 6" 14.00

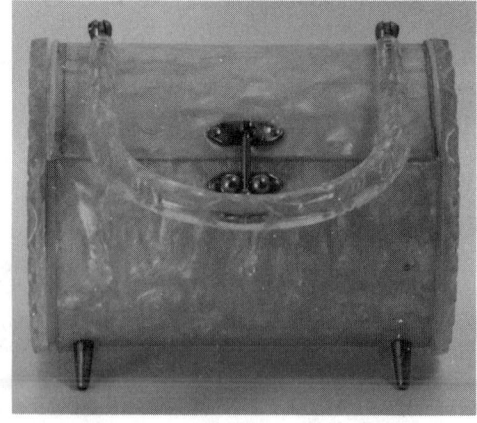

**Purse, ivory mother-of-pearl with crystal sides
and handle, 6½" long, $45.00.**

Purse, box style, clear, pearl, ivory, or tortoise 45.00
Shakers, translucent red, 4", pr 12.00

Playing Cards

Playing cards can be an enjoyable way to trace the course of history. Knowledge of the art, literature, and politics of an era can be gleaned from a study of its playing cards. When royalty lost favor with the people, Kings and Queens were replaced by common people. During the periods of war, generals, officers, and soldiers were favored. In the United States, early examples had portraits of Washington and Adams as opposed to Kings, Indian chiefs instead of Jacks, and goddesses for Queens.

Tarot cards were used in Europe during the 1300s as a game of chance, but in the 18th century they were used to predict the future and were regarded with great reverence.

The backs of cards were of no particular consequence until the 1890s. The marble design used by the French during the late 1800s and the colored wood-cut patterns of the Italians in the 19th century are among the first attempts at decoration. Later the English used cards printed with portraits of royalty. Eventually cards were decorated with a broad range of subjects from reproductions of fine art to advertising.

Although playing cards are becoming popular collectibles, prices are still relatively low. Complete decks of cards printed earlier than the first postage stamp can still be purchased for less than $100. Our advice for this category comes from the American Antique Deck Collectors Club, 52 Plus Joker; see Directory under Clubs, Newsletters, and Catalogs.

Key:
C — complete   OB — original box
cts — courts   std — standard
hc — hand colored   sz — size
J — joker   XC — extra card

Advertising

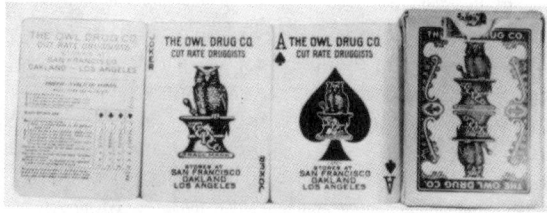

The Owl Drug Co., 54 cards, ca 1900-1908, very rare, NM in box, $210.00.

Anheuser-Busch Spanish Am War #2, 1900, 51+XC, NMIB 370.00
Arrow Beer, gold & brn bks, 52+J, EX in box 34.00
Black Velvet Blended Canadian Whiskey, 52+2J, MIB 23.00
Budweiser's Greatest Triumph, wide, dbl deck, M in tin 25.00
Cambridge University, wide, Goodall, 52+J, NMIB 32.00
Chicago Cubs, history since 1876, picture cards, 1984, MIB 17.00
Florsheim, red/blk/gold circles around logo, 52+J, VG in box 4.00
Gerber, Gerber doll w/cereal bks, 1950s, MIB, sealed 20.00
Gold Medal Flour, wide, colorful bks, 52+J+XC, EX in box 35.00
Harlem Globetrotters, 50th yr, dbl deck, ea: MIB 15.00
Hunter Baltimore Rye, wide, Dougherty, 1900, 52, EX in box 44.00
Illinois Athletic Club, wide, patterned bk, 52+2J, MIB 6.00
Jack Daniel's, wide, non-standard, MIB, sealed 7.00
Kansas Expansion Flour, logo bks, 1930s, 52+J+XC, EX in box ...33.00
Kelly Springfield, wide, Lotta Miles, 1915, 52+XC, NMIB 68.00

Laugh-In, jokes on cts & pips, 1969, 52+2J, MIB 40.00
Lewandos Cleaners, reversible logo bks, 52, EX in torn box 9.00
Links, wide, golfer bks, 1930s, MIB, sealed 28.00
Marlboro, wide, Wild West, recent issue, dbl deck, M, sealed 5.00
Michelin, wide, tire men bks, 1920s, 52+J+XC, EX in box 52.00
Minneapolis Athletic Club, logo bks, 52+2XC, MIB 7.00
Old English Pipe Tobacco, wide, 1905, 52+J, VG in poor box 30.00
Playboy, wide, Bicycle-type bk w/bunny inserts, MIB, sealed 8.00
President Suspenders, special cts, ca 1905, 52, VG in box 140.00
Sigma Phi Epsilon, fraternity shield bks, 1932, 52+J+2XC, MIB ..88.00
Time Magazine, oversz, 1962, 52, NMIB 50.00
Union-Made Cigars, wide, label bk, 1900s, 52+XC, G 160.00
Van Camp's, wide, Hier ist es!, 1911, 52+J, VG in box 73.00
Walk-Over Shoes, wide, gr & gold bks, 1900s, 52, VG in box 12.00
Western Printing, plant on bks, 52+special J, VG in box 15.00

Modern Decks

Aquarius, astrological sign on bks, 52+J+XC, MIB 3.00
Cardinal/Blue Jay, dbl deck, Nat'l Wildlife Federal, M, sealed 7.00
Comme Ci Comme Ca, Vargas pinup faces, 104+2J+2XC, MIB ..275.00
Elvgren, seated lady, ad at bottom, 52+J, NM in torn box 20.00
Esquire, Vargas bks, std faces, 52, VG, no box 28.00
Florentine, risque cts/aces, Philibert, '55, 52+2J+2XC, MIB 125.00
Grand Prix, wide, Lirola designs, Grimaud, '73, 52+2J+XC, MIB ...13.00
In the Mtns, Maxfield Parrish, ltd ed of 1000, MIB, sealed 50.00
Kennedy, family member cts, 1963, 52+J+XC, MIB 18.00
Les Quatre Saisons, Picart Le Doux, 1964, 52+XC, M, no box 28.00
Marilyn Monroe, nude photo bks, 52+2J, G in torn box 17.00
Michelangelo, photo bks, Grimaud, MIB 7.00
Party Pack, naughty cartoons, 1953, oversz, 52+J, NMIB 20.00
Politicards, spades are Nixon Administration, 1971, MIB 11.00
Romance Espanol, Tejada, 1953, 52+2J+XC, M, no box 8.00
Shakespeare, wide, character cts, Waddington, 52+2J+book, MIB..17.00
Survival, wide, survival tips, Environs, 1974, 52, M, no box 9.00
Tee-Up, cartoon bks, Creative Cards, 1963, 52+2J, MIB 13.00

Older Decks, Narrow, Odd Sizes or Shapes

Bid-Rite, pattern bks, 1932, 104+2XC, VG+ in boxes 33.00
Buster Brown, USPC, 1906, 53C, mini, EX in torn box 55.00
Columbia #133, enameled aluminum, Nat'l, 1895, NMIB 28.00
Culbertson's Own, instructions ea card, Russell, '32, 52, EX 23.00
Culbertson's Own, red bks, Russell, 1932, 52+XC, EX in box 28.00
Debutante, Congress #606, 1923 tax stamp, MIB, sealed 35.00
Dionne Quintuplets, portrait bks, 1936, 52+J+XC, MIB 68.00
Fan-C-Pack-Past-L-Eze, 1935, 52+J+XC, EX-, no box 28.00
Fauntleroy #329, USPC, 1932, 52+J+2XC, mini, EX in torn box ...6.00
Globe, circular, IW Richardson, 1880s, 52+J, G in box 85.00
Grimaud, plain bl bks, Skat type, Fr, 1900, 32C, EX in box 21.00
King Geo Silver Jubilee, Geo bust, 1935, MIB 44.00
Rondo, circular, watch gear bks, Waddington, 52+J, MIB 7.00
Santa-Christmas scenes, Merrimack, 52+2J, mini, NMIB..............9.00
Summer, gold edges, Gibson-Diana Brand, 52+J, EX in box 23.00
Victory, non-std cts, VE Day 1945, 52+J, G, no box 28.00
Whist #454, gold edges, Am Bank Note, 1910, 52+J, NM, no box...22.00

Older Decks, Wide

Aircraft Spotters II, 3 views of aircraft ea card, 1943, MIB 41.00
Bismarck #904, bl bks, pinochle, Standard, 48C, MIB 25.00
Can-Can, bl w/gold, Philibert, 1956, 52+XC, M in vinyl case 58.00
Cyclist #1, USPC-Bicycle #808, 1898, 52, G, no box 28.00
Dragon bks, USPC #500, 1907, 60C+J, VG in broken box 34.00

Dutch girl bks, Standard, 1895, 52+J, VG in snap-case box **47.00**
El Dorado, gold & pk bks, Nat'l Cards, 1885, 52+J+XC, EX **225.00**
Empire #97, Dougherty, 52+J+2XC, EX in torn box **55.00**
Fast Mail #44, train bks, Standard, 1900, 52+J, G in torn box **15.00**
Hold-to-light risque scenes, Transparent, 1860, 52, G **385.00**
Lady w/lg hat bks, Cany by NYCC, 1910, 52+J, VG, no box **19.00**
Military Fortune Tellers, 1918, non-std cts & aces, NMIB **40.00**
Mogul-Lady Brand #2002, Belgium, Biermans, 52+J+XC, MIB **22.00**
Nat'l-Rambler #23, bl w/gold edges, 52+J+XC, VG in torn box ...**20.00**
Nile Fortune, fortunes in margins, 52+Life card, VG in box **11.00**
Nunes #22, Portugal, European-type cts, 1925, 40C, NMIB **25.00**
Priscilla, USPC-Congress #606, 1900, 52, VG- in damaged box ..**20.00**
Shakespeare, Dondorff #192, 1900, 52+J+info card, NMIB **237.00**
Squeezers, angel bks, NY Card Co, 52, EX in torn box **18.00**
Steamboat #222, N Am Card Co, 1891, 52+J, EX in box **406.00**
Vital Question, gold edges, Kalamazoo, 52+J, NM, no box **33.00**
Willis & Co, reversible cts, England, 1880s, 32", EX, no box **22.00**

Souvenir and Expositions

California, poinsettias & mission bell, 52+J, EX in box **22.00**
California, wide, seal w/poppies, 1898, 52+bear J+XC, MIB **52.00**
Century of Progress, scenic, Electrolite, '34, 52+J, MIB **22.00**
Circus #47, wide, pk & gr bks, USPC, 1896, 52 in worn box **455.00**
Columbian Expo, colorful bks, 1893, 52+Special J, EX+ in box ...**85.00**
Columbian Expo, Winters Art, 1892, 52+special J, VG, no box ..**75.00**
Florida E Coast, photo bks, 1915, 52+J, VG in ½-box **11.00**
Indians of SW, F Harvey, linen finish, 52+J+map, EX in box ...**205.00**
Maine, State House bks, 1900, 52+scenic J, G in ½-box **33.00**
Nat'l Parks, 52 photos of 6 parks, 52+2 special J, MIB **11.00**
New Orleans & Gulf, magnolias/plantation, 1900, 52, EX in box....**135.00**
New Zealand #2, Scott, 52+'Tiki' J+XC, MIB **10.00**
Niagara Falls, 4 corner indices, 1901, 52+J+XC, NMIB **44.00**
Pan-Am Expo, wide, 52 scenes, 1901, 52+special J, NMIB **55.00**
Panama, Chagres River bks, 1910, 52+scenic J+map, MIB **75.00**
Panama, Royal Palm Tree bks, USPC, '08, 52+J+XC+map, MIB **55.00**
Panama, ship in canal bks, 1925, 52+J+map, EX in G box **22.00**
Queen Victoria, 60 Yrs Reign, DeLaRue, 1897, 52, EX, no box ...**85.00**
Reno, night photo bks, 52 scenes, 1950s, 52+2J, NM **22.00**
Rhode Island, State Capitol bk, USPC, 1910, 52, EX in box **50.00**
Scotland, narrow scenic, 52 blk/wht views, 52+J, MIB **30.00**
St Louis World's Fair, seal bks, 52 photos, 52+J+XC, G, no box ..**36.00**
Stage #65, red & gold bks, star on ea ct, 52+J, EX in box **110.00**
Texas Centennial, 100th Anniversary, 1936, 52+J+XC, MIB **27.00**
Treasure Island, photo bks, 1920s tax stamp, MIB **17.00**
Vermont, State Capitol bks, 1910, 52+scenic J+XC, VG in box ..**28.00**
Washington DC, Goddess of Justice bk, 1925, 52+J+2XC, MIB ..**45.00**
Wht Mtns, Old Man of Mtns bks, 1910, 52+J, VG in box **23.00**
Yellowstone, orange w/blk border, 52+special J+XC, MIB **33.00**

Transformations

Kinney Brothers, pips & cts transformed, 52+J, G, no box **250.00**
Murphy Varnish, cartoons on pips, ca 1883, 52+J, G, no box .**1,530.00**
Vanity Fair, pips/aces transform, 1895, 52+devil J, EX in box **380.00**
Ye Witches #62, USPC, 1896, 52+J, G in damaged box **55.00**

Transportation: Airline, Steamship, Railroad

Air India, Maharajas on bks, dbl deck, 1974, M, sealed **35.00**
Air India, reversed First Class in red, 52+J, MIB **30.00**
Air New Zealand, 747 photo bks, miniature, 52, MIB **7.00**
Alaska, Fly w/a Happy Face, Hoyle, MIB, sealed **12.00**
Amtrack, logo w/bl border, 1975, 52+2J, NMIB **4.00**

Auto-Train, logo w/purple border, 1972, 52+J, MIB **4.00**
C&O, Chessie & Peake, dbl deck, 104, G **9.00**
Canadian Nat'l, lady bks, 52 photos, 52+J, NM in torn box **42.00**
Cathay Pacific, silver logo on bl, 52+J, MIB **9.00**
CB&Q, Observers viewing train bks, 1956, 52+2J, MIB **29.00**
CB&Q, Passing Zephyrs, 1951, 52, G, no box **5.00**
Cunard, wide, gold/bl bks, older DeLaRue, 52+J, VG in box **46.00**
Czechoslovak, Fly OK, Fly CSA bks, 52+J, MIB **17.00**
Flying Tigers, World's Leading...Airline, MIB, sealed **8.00**
Great Northern, wide scenic, 52 photos, linen, 52+XC, MIB **385.00**
Gulf Air, bl & beige bks, plastic, 52+2 Viking J, NMIB **12.00**
Iberia, red & butterscotch logo, oversz, MIB **10.00**
IL Central, Panama Ltd, 52, VG in box **22.00**
Korean Air, 747 in air photo bks, MIB, sealed **14.00**
Lufthansa, logo on orange, special cts, 52+2J, MIB **7.00**
Malaysia, wide, mc painting, 52+3 special Js, MIB **22.00**
Milwaukee RR, Hiawatha, Nothing Faster..., 52+J+2XC, G, OB ..**18.00**
Milwaukee RR, 1 track, scenic, ca 1916, 52+J+XC, VG in box **40.00**
Nickel Plate, logo bk, dbl deck, 1950s, 104+4J, MIB **12.00**
Northwest Orient, translations, 52+2J+booklet, MIB **7.00**
Northwestern, bathing beauty bks, Carfax, MIB, sealed **33.00**
P&O, sea horse bk, DeLaRue, 52+J, MIB **22.00**
Puerto Rico, reversible logo bk, ca 1925, 52+J+2XC, MIB **79.00**
Qantas, triangles w/bl Roo, 1985, MIB **10.00**
Rock Island, wide, reversible logo, 1910, 52C, G, no box **30.00**
Santa Fe, train in mtns, ca 1952, 52+J, NMIB **20.00**
Singapore Air, wide, mc pattern on bl, MIB, sealed **8.00**
South Shore Line, gr dmn, reversible logo, 1930s, MIB, sealed ..**166.00**
Southern Pacific, wide, Daylight scenic, 52+J+XC, MIB **25.00**
Tap-Air Portugal, wide, gr bks w/repeat logo, 52+2J, MIB **17.00**
Worldways Canada, wide, logo aces, 52+2J, MIB **18.00**

Political

The most valuable political items are those from any period which relate to a political figure whose term was especially significant or marked by an important event or one whose personality was particularly colorful. Posters, ribbons, badges, photographs, and pin-back buttons are a few examples of the items popular with collectors of political memorabilia.

Political campaign pin-back buttons were first mass-produced and widely distributed in 1896 for the president-to-be William McKinley and for the first of three unsuccessful attempts by William Jennings Bryan. Pin-back buttons have been used during each presidential campaign ever since and are collected by many people. The most scarce are those used in the presidential campaigns of James Davis in 1924 and James Cox in 1920. Our advisor for this category is Paul J. Longo; he is listed in the Directory under Massachusetts. See also Autographs; Broadsides; Historical Glass; Watch Fobs.

Poster, W.J. Bryan, 1900, minor restoration, 26x32", $2,800.00.

Ashtray, Nixon, ceramic, 8-sided 22.00
Badge, Blaine, silk w/image on glass, fringed, 1884 ....500.00
Badge, Nixon Inaugural, Hostess, bl ribbon 20.00
Badge, WM J Bryan, w/photo & ribbon, EX 75.00
Ballot, Nat'l Republican Ticket, Grant/Colfax, 1868, 4x12" 50.00
Bandana, flag on silk, 19x19" 285.00
Bandana, Garfield/Arthur jugate on red, 20" 130.00
Bandana, Hancock/English, 20" 325.00
Bandana, Win w/Ike, portrait in corner on red, 26" 45.00
Book, campaign; Life Explanations...JC Fremont, 1856 ....40.00
Book, Kennedys, An American Drama, Collier/Horowitz, '84, VG ..10.00
Book, Portrait: Emergence of JF Kennedy, J Lowe, 1961, VG 10.00
Booklet, Democratic Nat'l Convention, 1940, w/8 tickets 75.00
Bottle opener, Carter, smiling face w/hdl 20.00
Brooch, Lincoln, callotype, albumen photo under glass 650.00
Button, clothing; Grant, metal 45.00
Card, Wallace for Governor, early 20.00
Cigar cutter, T Roosevelt, orig card, 1912 ....100.00
Compact, Kefauver for President, portrait on lid 100.00
Cup plate, Bust of WH Harrison, Sandwich, NM 65.00
Doll, MacArthur, w/orig Man of Hour tag 275.00
Engraving, Taft/Sherman & Cabinet, w/portraits, 1909 ....95.00
Flag, Stephen Douglas, portrait, 1860 ....6,000.00
Flag/banner, Cleveland, vertical, 24" 200.00
Fob, Carter Inaugural, 1977, in orig box 20.00
General order #1, Truman, inaugural parade order etc, EX 125.00
Guide, voting; Blaine/Logan jugate, EX 40.00
Key holder, Truman, leather 50.00
Knife, pen; Woodrow Wilson, emb metal 85.00
Label, James G Blaine 5¢ Cigars, about 10x9" 125.00
License plate, Al Smith for President, red/wht, 12" 50.00
License plate, I Like Ike, bl/red on yel, 10" L 35.00
License plate, Nixon/Agnew, blk/wht, 12" L 20.00
License plate attachment, donkey silhouette atop Roosevelt 85.00
Match safe, Grover Cleveland, figural head, hinged lid 225.00
Match safe, Wilson, celluloid insert on metal, EX 85.00
Medal, Gerald R Ford, Vice President of US, silver, 1973 ....65.00
Medal, Harrison inauguration, brass, 1889, 1" 25.00
Mug, Mamie Eisenhower's face form, ivory w/brn hdl 40.00
Mug, Nixon/Agnew, plastic, ftd 30.00
Nail, Blaine/Logan, metal 50.00
Napkin, Give JFK a Republican Congress, paper 15.00
Necktie, Goldwater/Percy jugate, red/wht/bl 75.00
Paperweight, Grant, articulated figure w/in, anti-Grant 1,500.00
Paperweight, McKinley, full-face, glass 50.00
Pennant, FD Roosevelt Inauguration, 1941, bl/red/wht felt 30.00
Pennant, President Truman, w/portrait, bl/wht felt 65.00
Pin, Cleveland, tin litho, pop-up portrait, NM 185.00
Pin, Grant, cardboard photo on eagle & flag shape, EX 275.00
Pin, Grant ferro, lg 195.00
Pin, Grant/Colfax ferro jugate, bl paper-inset border 250.00
Pin, Horatio Seymour ferro, star shape, 1868 ....300.00
Pin, LaFollette/Wheeler jugate, brass, 1924, 1", EX 12.00
Pin-bk, Al Smith for President, bl on wht, 7" 200.00
Pin-bk, Atkinson for Governor (OK 1962), NM 3.00
Pin-bk, Dewey, elephant figural, celluloid, ¾" dia 18.00
Pin-bk, Eugene V Debs, Socialist, ⅞" 150.00
Pin-bk, FDR, Gallant Leader 10.00
Pin-bk, For President Willkie, portrait, EX 10.00
Pin-bk, Gen MacArthur, Bakelite, +leather strap/brass shield 50.00
Pin-bk, George Wallace for President, EX 3.00
Pin-bk, Henry Wallace, for Vice President, Iowa's Choice, ⅞" 150.00
Pin-bk, Hughes w/flag shield, ½", EX 10.00
Pin-bk, I Like Ike, red/wht/bl, ⅞" 2.00

Pin-bk, Ike & Dick Junior Club, EX 40.00
Pin-bk, Kennedy, w/portrait, ⅞" 4.00
Pin-bk, Nixon, For Vice President, 1952, ⅞" 75.00
Pin-bk, Nixon for President, w/portrait, 1960, ⅞" 10.00
Pin-bk, Please Vote Dry for Me 15.00
Pin-bk, Roosevelt for Humanity, EX 10.00
Pin-bk, Roosevelt/Fairbanks w/flag, ¾" 24.00
Pin-bk, T Roosevelt, bunting down side, 1898 NY campaign, ⅞" .65.00
Pin-bk, Teapot Dome Scandal, Communist, ⅞", EX 225.00
Pin-bk, Wendell L Willkie, For President, red/wht/bl, 1¼" 12.00
Pin-bk, Wilson, Peace, Prosperity, celluloid, 1912, ⅞" 12.00
Pin-bk, Wilson, Safety First 20.00
Pin-bk, Wings for America, Willkie, plane, EX 4.00
Pin-bk, WJ Bryan w/flag motif border, celluloid, ⅞" 12.00
Plaque, McKinley profile cutout of emb tin 65.00
Plate, ABC, tin w/Grant emb in center, 5" 200.00
Plate, T Roosevelt, bk: speech quote, bl transfer, Wedgwood 110.00
Plate, T Roosevelt, from 1905 Lewis & Clark Expo, R&M 135.00
Pocket mirror, FD Roosevelt, portrait in oval reserve 70.00
Pocket mirror, Pershing & other WWI leaders, oval 75.00
Postcard, flasher type, T Roosevelt changes to Wht House 25.00
Postcard, leather, States' Rights Democrats 200.00
Postcard, Taft, w/brooch attached 50.00
Poster, Kennedy, Leadership for the 60s, 21" 75.00
Poster, Kennedy/Johnson jugate, red/wht/bl, 21" 150.00
Program, FD Roosevelt/John Garner inaugural, Mar '33, 64-pg 50.00
Ribbon, Blaine/Logan, 1884 ....75.00
Ribbon, Clay, 1844, NM 200.00
Ribbon, Garfield/Arthur, pictures Garfield, 1880, VG 125.00
Ribbon, Hancock/English jugate, red/wht/bl, 1880, sm 225.00
Ribbon, Jackson, Benevolent Society, EX 500.00
Ribbon, Lincoln, Brady portrait design, EX 2,900.00
Ribbon, McKinley/Roosevelt, Full Dinner Bucket, red w/gold 150.00
Ribbon, Republican Club, Manheim Township, 1904, w/fringe .150.00
Ribbon, T Roosevelt, Welcome...Candidate, 1900, wine 225.00
Shaving mug, T Roosevelt/Grant/Lincoln portraits, ceramic 250.00
Sheet music, Harding's the Man for Me, custom fr 75.00
Sheet music, Roosevelt March, in fr 65.00
Sheet music, Row Row Row w/Roosevelt, w/portrait 50.00
Sheet music, 1900 Campaign March, w/4 portraits 60.00
Snuff box, Zachary Taylor, papier-mache w/portrait 1,800.00
Spoon, McKinley as hdl finial, Wht House in bowl, M 50.00
Spoon, T Roosevelt on horsebk as hdl, sterling 150.00
Stereo card, street banners: Hayes/Wheeler jugate 40.00
Stud, McKinley sits on struggling WJ Bryan, brass, 1896 ....350.00
Stud, T Roosevelt 1904 Rough Rider Brigade 35.00
Stud, Taft across center, celluloid, bl/wht stripes, ½" 15.00
Sweater guard, Hoover, head on 1 end, banner on other 85.00
Thimble, Nixon for Senator, wht 30.00
Ticket stub, Republican Nat'l Convention, 1916 ....25.00
Tip tray, World's Fair 1904, 4 portraits, EX 100.00
Toby mug, McKinley, no name on bottom, lg 400.00
Token, Garfield, brass, assassination on reverse, 1880, NM 15.00
Token, Henry Clay, 1844, EX 20.00
Token, James Buchanan, brass, 1856, EX 35.00
Token, McClellan, copper, Civil War era, EX 35.00
Torch, Grant (vertical) on glass sides, 15" 650.00
Trivet, Cleveland, bronze, bust profile in horseshoe 135.00

Pomona

Pomona glass was patented in 1885 by the New England Glass Works. Its characteristics are an etched background of crystal lead glass often decorated with simple designs painted with metallic stains of amber or blue. The etching was first achieved by hand cutting through an acid resist. This method, called first grind, resulted in an uneven feather-like frost effect. Later, to cut production costs, the hand-cut process was discontinued in favor of an acid bath which effected an even frosting. This method is called second grind. Our advisors for this category are Betty and Clarence Maier; they are listed in the Directory under Pennsylvania.

Bowl, 1st grind, rare, 3x4" 275.00
Butter dish, 1st grind, acanthus leaves on lid, 4x8" 540.00
Carafe, 1st grind, ruffled, amber stain, 6½", +tumbler 335.00
Celery vase, 1st grind, cornflowers, ruffled, appl base, 6¼" 370.00

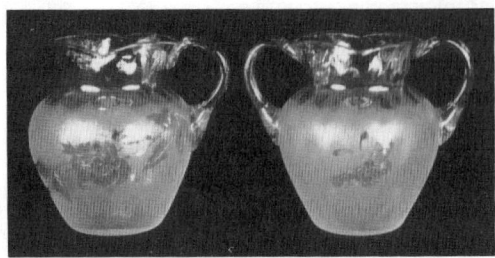

Creamer and sugar bowl, second grind, butterfly and pansy pattern, gold and blue staining, $600.00.

Creamer, 2nd grind, amber stain, mini 250.00
Creamer, 2nd grind, bl cornflowers, appl crimped base, 3x6" 225.00
Creamer, 2nd grind, bl cornflowers, ruffled top, 3x6" 225.00
Creamer & sugar bowl, 1st grind, ruffled, amber stain 585.00
Creamer & sugar bowl, 1st grind, wishbone ft, crimped, 4" 675.00
Cruet, 2nd grind, no decor, 7" 365.00
Finger bowl, 1st grind, ruffled, 1¾x5½" 220.00
Finger bowl, 2nd grind, bl cornflowers, amber stain 55.00
Pitcher, tankard, 1st grind, scalloped, 9", +6 punch cups 1,045.00
Pitcher, 1st grind, acanthus leaves, long neck, 8¾" 450.00
Pitcher, 2nd grind, Dmn Quilt, jug style, 6½", +4 tumblers 1,125.00
Punch cup, 1st grind, EX bl & amber stain, 2¾x2⅝" 195.00
Toothpick holder, 1st grind, appl rigaree at waist, 2½" 325.00
Tumbler, 2nd grind, bl cornflowers, amber stain, 3⅞" 150.00
Tumbler, 2nd grind, blueberries, EX staining, 3¾x2¾" 175.00
Tumbler, 2nd grind, pansies/butterfly on Dmn Quilt, 3¾" 175.00
Vase, lily; 2nd grind, Invt T'print, amber stain, 16" 650.00

Postcards

Postcards are distinguished from almost any other collectible due to the fact that nearly any topic can be found represented on cards! For this reason, postcard collecting is considered the 'all-encompassing hobby'! A German by the name of Emmanuel Herrman is credited for inventing the postcard, first printed in Austria in 1869. They were eagerly accepted by the Continentals and the English alike, who saw them as a more economical way to send written messages.

The first to be printed in the United States were on U.S. government postals. The Columbian Exposition of 1892-1893 served as the spark that ignited the postcard phenomenon. Souvenir cards by the thousands were sent to folks back home — expo scenes, transportation themes, animals, birds, and advertising messages became popular. There were patriotic themes, Black themes, and cards for every occasion and holiday. Scenics, cards with small-town railroad depots, and views of U.S. towns (especially photos) are very much sought after.

Some of the earliest postcard publishers were Raphael Tuck, Nister, and Gabriel. Early 20th-century illustrators such as Frances Brundage, Rose O'Neill, and Ellen Clapsaddle designed cards that are especially popular today.

Although the postcard rage waned at the onset of WWI, they rank today among the most sought-after paper collectibles, second only to stamps.

Even though postcards may be sixty to ninety years old, they must be in excellent condition. As a worth-accessing factor, condition is second only to subject matter. When no condition is indicated, the items listed below are assumed to be in excellent condition, whether used or unused. Our advisor for this category is Mrs. Sally Carver; she is listed in the Directory under Massachusetts.

Key:
p/ — publisher   s/ — signed

Advertising, Silver Slipper Saloon, Las Vegas, 1950s, unused 6.50
Animals, cat hanging socks on line, p/Nister, EX 12.50
Animals, Zebra, p/Tuck, EX 20.00
Bien, Julius; Child's Journal, 1907, 6-card set 75.00
Bien, Julius; Santa portrait, German pipe, color, EX 10.00
Black theme, man has drunk from ink bottle, 1906, unused 27.50
Black theme, man strapped in chair/tooth being pulled, 1910 ......22.50
Black theme, smiling boy picks cotton, mc, 1950, NM 4.00
Brundage, I'm Real Glad, well-dressed girl, Tuck #6373, VG 25.00
Buster Brown & His Bubble, RF Outcault, 1903, NM 17.50
Christmas, Santa in red robe w/angel & boy, p/PFB, EX 35.00
Christy, University Girl Series, VG 17.50
Clapsaddle, Best Christmas Wishes, Santa w/holly, VG 12.50
Clapsaddle, Halloween mechanical, girl moves arm, #1236, VG ..65.00
Clapsaddle, kaleidoscope, Joyful Easter, p/Internat'l, VG 28.00
Clapsaddle, St Valentine Greeting, boy & 2 girls, VG 10.00
Comic, You Needn't Cover It Up..., man w/Ford, 1910, EX 20.00
Dwig, We're Having Ticklish Weather, lady/feather, Tuck, VG ..17.50
Dwig, What's the Use Worrying..., p/Gross, VG 12.50
Fantasy, oversz mosquito in garden, pnt, 1920, M 6.50
Fisher, Harrison; Dreaming of You, lady asleep, VG 17.50
Golliwog, drives w/doll in roadster, p/London, VG 30.00
Halloween, Josephine Is You a Witch-Cat?, p/Tuck, EX 15.00
Hamburg-Amerika Line, SS Amerika view, color, 1906, EX 25.00
Hold-to-light, Mississippi River Steamer, p/Cupples, VG 30.00
Hold-to-light, Old South Church, Boston, p/Koehler 30.00
Hold-to-light, St Louis Expo, silver series, 1904, EX 15.00
Hold-to-light/cutout, Festund Manur Vor Dem Fall, #58, EX 28.00
Hold-to-light/cutout, valentine, cupid holding doves, EX 37.50
Jewish, Belief Me, man smoking, ca 1906, unused 25.00
Landsdorf, Miss Illinois, lady w/mini train, emb, VG 22.50
Leap Year, Tis Sweet To Think Tis Nine-Teen Twelve, 1911, M ...10.00
Leather, I Can't Bear To Leave, bear, 1907 ....15.00
Leather, lady golfer, Schlesinger Bros, blk/wht, 1911 ....10.00
Leather, 2 teddy bears, flag background, ca 1906, rare 35.00
Linen, I Wondered Where My Wife..., parachuting GI/clothes 6.00
Linen pinup, Orchids to You, p/Postage Stamp, 1940s, EX 10.00
Mechanical, man's arm hits lady's bkside, 1940s, EX 17.50
Morman, Brigham Young & wives, #d/identified, 1905, EX 6.00
Panama Pacific Expo, Ghirardelli's Milk Chocolate, sepia, EX 6.00
Payne, Harry; Bound for Shore, #100, early, scarce 30.00
Photo, Chinese restaurant interior, NY, 1950, NM 3.00
Photo, City Hall Eugene OR, Air Force recruiting, 1948, EX 8.00
Photo, Curley (Gen Custer's scout), pnt face/feathers, pre-1910 ....50.00
Photo, fire scene in Bangor ME, sepia, 1911, EX 11.00
Photo, General Pidsulski of Polish Legion, 1914, EX 4.50
Photo, Joliet IL high school, blk/wht, 1923, VG 5.00

Photo, Kharabransk, Siberia, main street, 1919, EX 60.00
Photo, risque lady, 1930s, EX 17.50
Photo, Texas Hotel, FT Worth TX, 1953, EX 3.50
Photo, WWI Am Army of Occupation Band giving concert, 1919 ...4.00
Photo, 30 WWI German soldiers at ease, ca 1918, EX 4.00
Political, Ike & Nixon, In God We Trust, p/Don Bartels, EX 15.00
Political, Martyred Presidents, c/Sheahan, 1908, VG 12.00
Political, Pres-Elect Reagan & Nancy greet Sinatra, mc, M 5.00
Puzzle, Can You Mount the Jockeys?, horses/jockeys, blk/wht 6.00
Railroad, map of US w/Santa Fe routes, linen, WWII, M 6.50
Rotograph, NY Stock Exchange, blk/wht, 1904, unused, M 5.00
Royalty, Call of the Flag Series #8862, p/Tuck, EX 15.00
Royalty, Czar & family aboard ship, p/Rotary, VG 20.00
Russell, Roping a Wolf, VG 24.00
Silk, Clan Cameron, crest/plaids/dragons, p/Sharpe, VG 22.50
Thanksgiving, A Joyful..., turkey & pumpkins, mc, 1910, NM 5.00
Thanksgiving Greetings, Uncle Sam/turkey, mc, emb, 1911, EX ..17.50
Tournament of Roses Parade, Moby Dick Float, 1950s 4.00
Tuck, cutout/paper doll, Little Geisha, #3394, EX 100.00
Tuck, Yel Thunder, Indian chiefs, silverette, #6593, EX 25.00
Wain, Louis; Blind Man's Bluff, 6 cats, EX 40.00
Wain, Louis; Dancer's Mascot, cat dancing, VG 35.00
Washington taking oath of office, WA birthday series #1, 1909 .....7.50
Winsch, To My Sweetheart, lady in silk oval center, EX 30.00
Woven silk, bombs on church, WWI Flame series, p/Duffrene 35.00

Posters

Advertising posters by such French artists as Cheret and Toulouse-Lautrec were used as early as the mid-1800s. Color lithography spurred their popularity. Circus posters by the Strobridge Lithograph Co. are considered to be the finest in their field, though Gibson and Co. Litho, Erie Litho, and Enquirer Job Printing Co. printed fine examples as well. Posters by noted artists such as Mucha, Parrish, and Hohlwein bring high prices. Other considerations are good color, interesting subject matter and, of course, condition. The WWII posters listed below are among the more expensive examples; 80% of those on the market bring less than $50.00. See also Movie Memorabilia; Political Entourage; Rockwell, Norman.

Key:
B&B — Barnum and Bailey   RB — Ringling Bros.

Advertising

Bodega Wine & Liquor, Indian princess, 20x15", VG 50.00
CJ Fell & Bro Spices, ca 1857, 16x18½", EX 425.00

Alphonse Mucha, Biscuits Lefevre, Utile/Gaufrette Vanille, 24x17½", EX, $9,000.00.

Dr Clark's Life Balsam, lady in yel, 9x13", VG 425.00
E Dupont & Co, hunters & pups, 32x25", VG 220.00
Great Interstate Fair, T NJ, Donaldson, 1896, 38x40", VG 525.00
His Lordship, story to appear in newspaper, LJ Rhead, 47x28" 220.00
Ingersol Watch Co, boy w/'His First Watch,' 19x11", VG 80.00
King's Quick Rising Flower, woman at stove, 1885, 26x21", EX ...500.00
Lighthouse Footwear, reptile shoe, Warhol, 1979, 45x30", M 100.00
Martine's Patent Kerosene Burner, Avens, fr, 15x12", G 200.00
Merrimack Brand Feeds, Indian, 23x13", EX 40.00
Phoenix White Lead, factory scene, 1900s, 22x34", EX 450.00
Prince Albert Tobacco, Chief Lean Wolf, 26x20", EX 425.00
Resolute Fire Insurance, Indian & sailor, 23x18", EX 700.00
Triumph Cycles, lady & bike, Misti, 1907, 46x30", VG 700.00
Willimantic Thread, girl w/dog, 20x24", EX 250.00

Circus

B&B, clown acts, German, Strobridge, 1989, 1-sheet, EX 350.00
B&B, French, monkeys/ponies, 1898, 30x40", EX 650.00
B&B, smiling clown, 106x80", EX 660.00
B&B Rare Zoological Features, 1909, 37x27", EX 800.00
Bentley's Old-Fashioned Country Circus, Donaldson, 27x38" 400.00
Buffalo Bill, portrait, vignettes surround, 1888, 25x18" 850.00
Cole Bros, Quarter Million Pounds of Elephants, 28x41" 165.00
RB B&B, Colleano, high-wire act, Strobridge, 79x42", EX 500.00
RB Circus Sideshow, Erie, 17x26", EX 450.00
RB World's Greatest Shows, clowns/riders, Courier, 3-sheet 450.00
Sells Brothers, Romeski Troup, Strobridge, full-sheet, EX 320.00
Tom Mix, Menagerie of Wild Beasts, 1934, 42x28", EX 275.00

Theatrical

And a Nightingale Sang, lady, Demoney/Stahl, 1989, 46x30", M ...45.00
Billy the Kid, saloon scene, US Litho, 1907, 27½x20", VG 170.00
Blue Jeans, dramatic scenes, unknown artist, 29x43" 165.00
Cyrk, contortionist, Czevniawkei, sm rpr, 36x29", EX 150.00
Folies Bergere, linen bk, Jules Cheret, 49x34" 500.00
Going Some, cowboys/college boys, Metropolitan, 26x19", VG ...100.00
In Old Kentucky, horse scene, 27x37", G 300.00
Karmi Swallows Loaded Gun Barrel, Nat'l Litho, 1914, 42x28" 265.00
La Nuit de la Dentelle, lady in red, Muller, 1949, 24x16" 165.00
La Nuit des Cabaret, dancers at Moulin Rouge, 1949, 23x16" 180.00
Nuit de la Rose a Bagatelle, dancer, Fumerton, 1949, 23x15" 165.00
Tile Club in Idle Hours, canal boat/train, Forbes, 22x28", VG ...275.00
Uncle Dave Holcomb, family/graphophone, 1909, 26x19", VG 465.00
Yankee Doodle Detective, Russell & Morgan, 1909, 26x19", VG ...80.00

Travel

Catania, snowflake/seashell, Lalia, 39x26", NM 185.00
Cie Gle Transatlantique, French, no date, 40x25", EX 200.00
Cie Gle Transatlantique, P Colin, 1937, 40x25" 325.00
Come to Britain for Motoring, countryside, Hepple, 30x20" 210.00
Firenze, Florence's Duomo, 1930s, sm rpr, 41x24" 185.00
Lufthansa, logo on dk bl, Abeking, 40x25" 185.00
Napoli, painting-style study of Naples, 1930s, 39x26", NM 215.00
Normandy, Fr Nat'l RR, countryside, Dufy, 1952, 39x24", NM ...130.00
Polka Wystawa, Polish tour ad, Gronowski, 39x27" 195.00
Polska, natives dressed for winter in mtns, Jarocki, 39x27" 165.00

War

$1 in War Stamps...Will Build Mystery Ship..., WWII, 20x26" ...17.50
Assurance for Young Men of the Navy, WWII, 32x24" 88.00

Buy a Share in America, Billings, WWII, 40x28" 90.00
Buy Liberty Bond & Wear This Button, WWII, 30x20" 95.00
Buy War Bonds, Doing All You Can...?, Sloan, WWII, 28x22" ..90.00
Buy War Bonds, statue w/town beyond, sgn JA, WWII, 22x28" ..12.00
Careless Word...Another Cross, Atherton, 1943, 27x22" 100.00
Carless Word...Needless Sinking, Fischer, 1942, 27x22" 100.00

Come On, by Walter Whitehead, 1918, WWI, 20x30", VG, $100.00.

Doctors Are Scarce...First Aid & Home Nursing, WWII, 22x28" 15.00
Everyone Should Do His Bit, scout, Low, WWI, 29x19", EX 200.00
Fight, HC Christy, WWI, 30x20" 165.00
Greatest Mother in the World, Foringer, WWI, 42x27" 55.00
Guerre, orphans lay flowers on grave, Forester, 1914, 47x32" 265.00
Help, hands hold barbed wire, Yugoslav Relief, WWII, 17x22" ...17.50
I Need Your Skill in War Job, Flagg, 1943, 28x22" 80.00
Journee de Poilu, children solicit, Poulbot, WWI, 47x33" 265.00
Know Your Navy..., battleships, WWII recruiting, 14x19", EX 17.50
Let Em Have It, sailors loading charges, WWII, 14x19", EX 17.50
Liberty Bonds, red handprint, JA St John, WWI, 20x30", EX 95.00
Liberty Loans, young family, AE Orr, 1918, 20x30", EX 65.00
Liberty ship in yard, Allied flags, WWII, 17x22", EX 17.50
Oh Les Aura!, charging French soldier, Fairve, WWI, 45x32" ...365.00
Saving Stamps, Joan of Arc, Haskell Coffin, WWI, 30x40", EX ...85.00
Seeds of Victory Insure Fruits of Peace, Flagg, 1918, 34x22" 120.00
They Shall Not Perish, Volk, 1918, 40x38" 100.00
War Bonds, Squander Bug, Seuss, WWII, 11x46", EX 85.00
Xmas Overseas..., Santa w/helmet on, Graves, WWII, 21x27" 12.50

Pot Lids

Pot lids were pottery covers for containers that were used for hair dressing, potted meats, etc. The most desirable were decorated with colorful transfer prints under the glaze in a variety of themes, animal and scenic. The first and probably the largest company to manufacture these lids was F & R Pratt of Fenton, Staffordshire, established in the early 1800s. The name or initials of Jesse Austin, their designer, may sometimes be found on exceptional designs. Although few pot lids were made after the 1880s, the firm continued into the 20th century.

American pot lids are very rare. Most have been dug up by collectors searching through sites of early gold rush mining towns in California. Minor rim chips are expected and normally do not detract from listed values.

American

Dr EJ Coxe's Extract of Copaiva..., blk transfer, 3¼", EX 200.00
Genuine Beef Marrow...X Bazin..., blk transfer, 3¼" 350.00

Holloway's Ointment, brn transfer, rough spot, 3⅛" 50.00
HP Wakelee Druggist Burdells Tooth Powder, blk/yel/gold, 3" ..475.00
Liston's Extract of Beef, Chicago IL, blk transfer, 2" 150.00
Premium Almond Cream Jules Hauel..., red transfer, 3⅜" 170.00
Rose Vegetable Tooth Paste...Hauel..., red transfer, 2¾" 475.00

World's Fair Premium Perfumery, Jules Hauel, Wholesale Perfumer, Philadelphia, black transfer with light green band, very rare, two small chips, one large chip on outer rim, $60.00.

World's Fair Premium...Jules Hauel..., blk transfer, 2⅝" 1,000.00
World's Fair...Tooth Paste, blk transfer, Hauel Perfumer, 3" 300.00
Wright's Gold Medal...Shaving Compound, blk transfer, 4¼" ...600.00

English

Cherry Tooth Paste...John Gosnell..., blk transfer, 1¼" 140.00
Enthusiast, man fishing from pail, Pratt 120.00
Fall of Sabastopol, mc transfer, Pratt 60.00
Landing the Fair, Pratt, ca 1850 ....57.50
Snow Drift, dog & sheep, mc transfer, sm chip, 5⅜" 80.00
Square in Strasburg, mc transfer, Pratt 125.00
Village Wedding, mc transfer, Pratt, 4", G 85.00
Winchester Cathedral, blk/wht, 3½" 7.50
Wolf & Lamb, Pratt, 4¼" dia, M w/EX base 120.00
Woods Areca Nut Tooth Paste, blk transfer, 1860-80, 2⅝" 30.00

Potschappel

In the town of Potschappel in 1872, Carl Thieme began a porcelain factory called the Saxonian Porcelain Factory. His work was of excellent quality and consisted of figures, vases, urns, lamp bases, birds, bowls, and animals, the work being similar to Dresden-Meissen and Sitzendorf. After WWII the company was incorporated and became Saxonian Porcelain Factory Dresden. There are four or five marks assigned to his work. Our advisor for this category is Donald Penrose; he is listed in the Directory under Ohio.

Figurine, Colonial man (& woman) holds rose, 21", pr 1,350.00
Figurine, he (& she) w/flower basket, Greek Key band, 9", pr 695.00
Figurine, pug dogs, tan & wht, male & female, 7x7", pr 570.00
Urn, appl florals, silver reserve, mask/scroll hdls, 14" 300.00
Vase, figures in garden reserve, floral panels, 1880s, 12" 450.00

Powder Horns and Shot Flasks

Though powder horns had already been in use for hundreds of years, collectors usually focus on those made after the expansion of the United States westward in the very early 1800s. While some are basic and very simple, others were scrimshawed and highly polished. Especially nice carvings can quickly escalate the value of a horn that has survived intact to as high as $400.00. Those with detailed maps, historical scenes, etc., bring even higher prices.

Metal flasks were introduced in the 1830s; by the middle of the century they were produced in quantity and at prices low enough that they became a viable alternative to the powder horn. Today's collector regards the smaller flasks as the more desirable and valuable, and those made for specific companies bring premium prices.

Flask, copper, Colt's Navy, Dixon...Sheffield, Model 1851 ....**495.00**
Flask, copper, eagle on branch above slain eagle, Paris, 6½" **325.00**
Flask, copper, emb shells, spring at top, 1850s, 1-lb **37.50**
Flask, copper, hanging game, orig cord/tassels, 8½", NM **195.00**
Flask, copper, lilies/rifles/horn/etc, violin shape, 9½x5" **175.00**
Flask, copper, lioness attacking horse, French, lt wear **350.00**
Flask, copper, Peace, circular star pattern, Ames 1837, EX **275.00**
Flask, copper (heavy), eagle/bugle/US, NY 1833, 9½" **375.00**
Flask, copper/brass, emb shell, eng Pike/1887, rpr, 7" **60.00**
Flask, pistol; copper, compartments, Dixon & Sons, 3" **250.00**
Flask, tin, John Hall & Sons, EX **100.00**

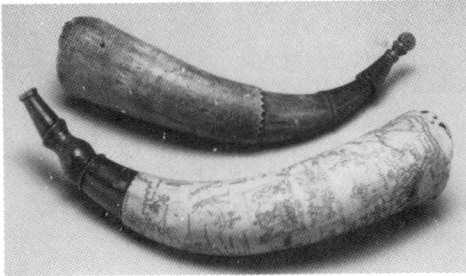

Engraved powder horns: Hunting scene and British coat-of-arms, 11½", $2,500.00; British arms above cannons, flags, drum, and a New York banner, map of towns and forts, 12½", $5,200.00.

Horn, battle flags/drum/cannon/deer/etc eng, 11", EX **850.00**
Horn, British arms/cannons/map eng, 1765, 12½" **5,000.00**
Horn, foliage/fob/birds eng, dtd 1847, 14", VG **150.00**
Horn, hunting scene by city eng, coat-of-arms, 12" **2,400.00**
Horn, Indian brave/1849 eng, flat plug, 12½", EX **250.00**
Horn, scrimshaw band of Xs at plug, 1812 period, 7", EX **35.00**
Horn, stag horn, eng lady & man, wheel lock, 8¼", G **950.00**
Horn, tepees & X-hatched eng, brass stud, 19½", VG **250.00**
Horn, wooden matchlock, iron hardware, 9", VG **450.00**
Horn, 1" raised panel w/ring on lg end, wood plug, 1800s, 8" **35.00**

Pratt

Prattware is a type of relief-molded earthenware with polychrome decoration. Scenic motifs with figures were popular; sometimes captions were added. Jugs are most common, but teapots, tableware, even figurines were made. The term 'Pratt' refers to Wm. Pratt of Lane Delph, who is credited with making the first of this type, though similar wares were made later by other Staffordshire potters.

Bottle, relish; triangular w/titled scenes, 8", EX, pr **425.00**
Cow creamer w/milkmaid, yel/blk sponged, tier base, 5", EX **440.00**
Creamer, children/dog emb in hearts, emb floral rim, 4¾" **550.00**
Figurine, lion, brn/ochre w/blk eyes, 1815-1820, 7" L, EX **800.00**
Figurine, 4 Seasons (2 are EX/1 rstr), 9", set of 4 ....**3,500.00**
Mug, emb sides: man in brn hat/shirt, leaf hdl, 3½" **550.00**
Pitcher, hounds/deer/boar emb in band, hound hdl, 6", NM **725.00**

Pitcher, house shape w/thatched roof & vines, 6½", VG **225.00**
Plate, Blk man, My Bible..., mc floral relief, 6" **675.00**
Plate, But Thou Art Dear (verse), couple, bl transfer, 7" **180.00**
Plate, butterfly/floral transfer, emb floral border, 5½" **190.00**
Plate, castle transfer, emb floral border, scalloped, 8" **180.00**
Plate, floral wreath transfer, My Heart Is Fix'd, 6½", EX **110.00**
Plate, Franklin's Proverb: Keep They Shop..., octagonal, 5" **150.00**
Plate, Franklin's Proverb: Silks & Satins..., 8-sided, 5" **180.00**
Plate, Grecian woman, fruit basket on head; man w/torch, 7½" .**200.00**
Plate, Justice/Father Time/Lion & Lamb/Upon My Honor, 7" **95.00**
Plate, King Geo IV portrait relief, mc, 8½", NM **525.00**
Plate, rose, red w/gr leaves, emb rosette border, 7", NM **320.00**
Plate, Who'll Treat Me...My Daughter, brn transfer, 7", NM **135.00**

Pratt-type pitcher, 8", EX, $375.00.

Salt cellar, rtcl w/emb gr acanthus, bl/yel beaded base, VG **425.00**
Sugar bowl, reserves w/eagle & shield, lady/cherub, 6", EX **250.00**
Sugar bowl, 4 floral reserves, ribbing/basketweave, 6", EX **750.00**

Precious Moments™

Known as 'America's Hummels,' Precious Moments™ are a line of well-known collectibles created by Samuel J. Butcher and produced by Enesco Inc. These pieces have endeared themselves to many, because of the inspirational messages they portray. To date over 300,000 club members have joined the National Club.

The collection is approximately twelve years old and is produced in bisque porcelain in the Orient. Each piece is produced with a different mark each year. This mark, not the date, is usually the link to the value of the piece. Most mold changes result in increased values, and when a piece is retired or suspended, its price increases as well. As an example, 'God Loveth a Cheerful Giver' retailed for $9.50 in 1980; it was retired in 1981 and has a secondary market price now of $650.00. The majority of the collection has increased in value from its original retail.

Rosie Wells Enterprises Inc., our advisor for this category, has published the Precious Moments™ collector magazine, *Precious Collectibles*®, as well as a secondary market price guide. She has hosted International Conventions for Precious Moments™ collectors since 1983. Her address is in the Directory under Clubs, Newsletters, and Catalogs. Items listed below are assumed to be in mint condition with the original box.

Bride'n Groom Dolls, Tammy/Cubby, E-7267G/E7267G, no mk ..**1,000.00**
Come Let Us Adore Him, E-2800, no mk **210.00**
Fishing for Friends, BC-861, Birthday Club pc, Dove mk **150.00**
God Loveth a Cheerful Giver, E-1378, retired, no mk **850.00**

Hello, Lord, It's Me Again, PM-811, Club pc, Triangle mk **450.00**
I'll Play My Drum for Him, E-2357, plate, 1983, no mk **85.00**
I'll Play My Drum for Him, E-2359, ornament, '82, Hourglass mk ...**100.00**
Jesus Loves Me, #104531, Easter Seals, Cedar Tree mk, 9" **1,750.00**
Let Heaven & Nature Sing, E-2346, suspended, Hourglass mk ..**140.00**
Let the Heavens Rejoice, E-5629, ornament, dtd 1981, no mk ..**240.00**
Lord Bless You & Keep You, The; E-3114, no mk **100.00**
Love One Another, E-1376, no mk **130.00**
Make a Joyful Noise, E-1374G, no mk **125.00**
Peace on Earth, #523062, ball ornament, '89, Bow 'n Arrow mk ...**80.00**
Reindeer, #102466, ornament, Birthday series, Olive Branch mk ..**190.00**
Thee I Love, E-3116, no mk **125.00**
Voice of Spring, The; #12068, ltd ed, Cross mk **325.00**

Primitives

Like the mouse that ate the grindstone, so has collectible interest in primitives increased, a little bit at a time, until demand is taking bites instead of nibbles into their availability. Although the term 'primitives' once referred to those survival essentials contrived by our American settlers, it has recently been expanded to include objects needed or desired by succeeding generations — items representing the cabin-n'-cornpatch existence as well as examples of life on larger farms and in towns. Through popular usage, it also respectfully covers what are actually 'country collectibles.'

From the 1600s into the late 1800s, factories employed carvers, blacksmiths, and other artisans whose handwork contributed to turning out quality items. When buying, 'touchmarks,' a company's name and/or location and maker's or owner's initials, are exciting discoveries.

Primitives are uniquely individual. Following identical forms, results often show typically personal ideas. Using this as a guide (combined with circumstances of age, condition, desire to own, etc.) should lead to a reasonably accurate evaluation. For items not listed, consult comparable examples. Authority Kathryn McNerney has compiled several lovely books on primitives and related topics: *Primitives, Our American Heritage; Collectible Blue and White Stoneware;* and *Antique Tools, Our American Heritage.* You will find her address in the Directory under Florida. See also Butter Molds and Stamps; Boxes; Copper; Farm Collectibles; Fireplace Implements; Kitchen Collectibles; Molds; Tinware; Weaving; Woodenware; and Wrought Iron.

Candle mold, 24-tube, tin in wooden frame with old red paint, labeled J. Walker, 11x13x7", $1,200.00.

Bed key, wooden T-shape, early 1800s, 15x18" **60.00**
Bed warmer, brass, hinged top, 1790-1810, 11x42", EX **265.00**
Bed warmer, brass, punched/eng floral, rpr/damage, 44" **200.00**
Box, Conestoga; pine w/bl rpt, decorative iron hdw, 19", EX ..**1,000.00**
Candle mold, 1-tube, tin, 17¼", EX **200.00**
Candle mold, 12-tube, pewter in pine fr, 16x16x16" **825.00**
Candle mold, 12-tube, tin, widely spaced, ear hdls, 11½" **250.00**
Candle mold, 12-tube, tin w/gray-pnt pine fr, 21x20x6", EX **900.00**

Candle mold, 12-tube (2 rows of 6), tin, 11" **130.00**
Candle mold, 12-tube (3 rows of 4), tin, battered hdl, 11" **110.00**
Candle mold, 21-tube, tin, circular arrangement, 12½", EX **450.00**
Candle mold, 24-tube, pewter in pine fr, ca 1800, EX **1,800.00**
Candle mold, 24-tube, tin, label: JEM 1877, 9½", EX **450.00**
Candle mold, 24-tube (3 rows of 8), tin, w/hdl, 10" **250.00**
Candle mold, 3-tube, tin, 10½" **110.00**
Candle mold, 36-tube, tin, 2 rows of 18, 12x24" **400.00**
Candle mold, 4-tube, tin, somewhat battered, 10" **55.00**
Candle mold, 48-tube (6 rows of 8), tin, dbl hdl, 10½", EX **545.00**
Candle mold, 6-tube, tin, 10" **115.00**
Candle mold, 72-tube, tin, hdls missing, 11" H **400.00**
Candle mold filler, tin w/wood hdl, pitted, 18" **210.00**
Carpet beater, Goodenough's Improved, wood, paper label, 41" ...**110.00**
Cheese ladder, maple, mortised & pinned, old, 31x11", EX **110.00**
Churn, coopered oak staves w/iron bands, dasher type, mk #3 ...**265.00**
Churn, Mammoth, 2-gal **175.00**
Churn, pine, dasher type, 5 bentwood bands **325.00**
Churn, syllabub; lid & dasher, dtd Sept 14, 1875 ....**125.00**
Churn, syllabub; tin, 2 side hdls, table model, 1840s, 8" **90.00**
Churn, tin, lap type w/CI gears **115.00**
Churn, tin, wooden dasher, side hdl, funnel top lid **275.00**
Clock jack, tin w/brass trim, emb tag: Show Bros, 14" **135.00**
Cranberry scoop, tin, sm hinged lid, some resoldering, 7x14" **25.00**
Crane, hardwood, rpl wall bracket, 50" L **450.00**
Crane, wooden, minor damage/rpr, 94" L **425.00**
Doll, simple relief cvg, arms missing, 10" **100.00**
Dough box, rpt pine, splay base, canted sides, 3-brd 48" top ...**1,100.00**
Dough scraper, wrought iron, early **50.00**
Dough scraper, wrought iron, flat, short hdl **95.00**
Dough scraper, wrought iron, hoe shape, short rnd hdl **75.00**
Driving whip, trn curly maple w/bone ends & horsehair, 26" **90.00**
Ember tongs, wrought iron, 14" L **125.00**
Foot warmer, CI, ftd, ornate style, hinged lid, bail hdl **350.00**
Foot warmer, oak w/cvd bird/deer/heart panels, dtd 1871, 9" **445.00**
Foot warmer, punched tin in mortised cherry fr w/trn posts **250.00**
Foot warmer, punched tin in mortised fr w/trn posts, red pnt **325.00**
Foot warmer, wood, holes in dmn design, iron charcoal pan **325.00**
Foot warmer, wood & dk punched tin, rnd, w/charcoal pan **395.00**
Hearth bread pan, open/half-rnd, Pat Feb 14 1893, pr **35.00**
Hot coals carrier, pierced brass, iron hdl, 20" **70.00**
Hourglass, blown glass in trn pine fr, minor damage, 6" **325.00**
Kraut cutter, walnut, lollipop hdl, 8x23" **85.00**
Ladle, heavy tin w/holes, wrought iron hdl **75.00**
Lamp cleaner, twisted wire **22.50**
Lighting device, wrought, 2 sockets on ratchet, adjusts, 25" **325.00**
Meat fork, 2-tine, wrought iron **75.00**
Mold, bronze, for casting pewter spoons, 2-part, 8" **250.00**
Peel, bread; wrought iron, curved hdl, 1700s, 8x46" **115.00**
Peel, muffin; wrought iron, 5¼" dia, 16" L **85.00**
Pie lifter, wrought iron, U-shape w/long hdl **185.00**
Rack, candle-drying; trn posts, gr pnt/blk stripes, 27", EX **275.00**
Rack, candle-drying; 8 removable disks w/wire hooks, 32" dia **575.00**
Rack, clothes drying; wooden, EX patina, 10x8x11" **85.00**
Rack, drying; pine, shoe ft, 3 mortised/pinned bars, 50x25" **175.00**
Rack, drying; pine w/gray pnt, lg shoe ft, 3 bars, 41x42" **175.00**
Rack, herb-drying; wood/wire, folding, att Shakers **90.00**
Rack, meat; cvd pine w/5 wrought iron hooks **210.00**
Rack, utensil; yel-rpt pine, scalloped edge, 9-hook, 10x43" **250.00**
Roaster, fowl; brass/wrought iron w/4 hooks on revolving arm ...**150.00**
Roaster, tin hemispherical hoppers w/long wrought hdls, 28" **175.00**
Sock stretcher, wire, dbl, child sz, 12" **20.00**
Sock stretcher, wooden, w/rnd holes, pr **30.00**
Spatula w/holes, wrought iron, long hdl **95.00**

Spoon, cvd cow horn, rattail end, 8" L 30.00
Stone fruit, EX orig pnt decor, 4 pcs 180.00
Sugar devil, CI w/wood hdl, 16" 120.00
Sugar nippers, wrought steel, EX detail, 8" 200.00
Tinder box, dk trn wood, side hdl, w/striker/snuffer/flint 425.00
Tinder box, w/candle socket, tin hdl, 1800s, +contents 350.00
Vegetable washing cage, all wood, 17x24" 110.00
Wagon seat, Conestoga; red rpt, shoe ft, cut-out ends, 31" 575.00
Washboard, handmade, early, lg, EX 95.00
Washboard, roller type, wooden, early, EX 68.00
Wig stand, slender trn mahog support, 9½" 85.00

Prints

The term 'print' may be defined today as almost any image printed on paper by any available method. Examples of collectible old 'prints' are Norman Rockwell magazine covers and Maxfield Parrish posters and calendars. 'Original print' refers to one achieved through the efforts of the artist or under his direct supervision. A 'reproduction' is a print produced by an accomplished print maker who reproduces another artist's print or original work. Thorough study is required on the part of the collector to recognize and appreciate the many variable factors to be considered in evaluating a print. Prices vary from one area of the country to another and are dependent upon new findings regarding the scarcity or abundance of prints as such information may arise. Although each collector of old prints may have their own varying criteria by which to judge condition, for those who deal only rarely in this area or newer collectors, a few guidelines may prove helpful. Staining, though unquestionably detrimental, is nearly always present in some degree and should be weighed against the rarity of the print. Professional cleaning should improve its appearance and at the same time help preserve it. Avoid tears that affect the image; minor margin tears are another matter, especially if the print is a rare one. Moderate 'foxing' (brown spots caused by mold or the fermentation of the rag content of old paper) and light stains from the old frames are not serious unless present in excess. Margin trimming was a common practice; but look for at least ½" to 1½" margins, depending on print size.

For further study see *Huxford's Fine Art Value Guide*, available from your local bookstore or Collector Books. When no condition is indicated, the items listed below are assumed to be in very good to excellent condition. See also Parrish, Maxfield.

Audubon, John J.

Audubon is the best known of American and European wildlife artists. His first series of prints, 'Birds of America,' was produced by Robert Havell of London. They were printed on Whitman watermarked paper bearing dates of 1826 to 1838. The Octavo Edition of the same series was printed in seven editions, the first by J.T. Bowen under Audubon's direction. There were seven volumes of text and prints, each 10" x 7", the first five bearing the J.J. Audubon and J.B. Chevalier mark, the last two, J.J. Audubon. They were produced from 1840 through 1844. The second and other editions were printed up to 1871. The Bien Edition prints were full size, made under the direction of Audubon's sons in the late 1850s. Due to the onset of the Civil War, only 105 plates were finished. These are considered to be the most valuable of the reprints of the 'Birds of America Series.'

In 1971 the complete set was reprinted by Johnson Reprint Corp. of New York and Theaturm Orbis Terrarum of Amsterdam. Examples of the latter bear the watermark G. Schut and Zonen. In 1985 a second reprint was done by Abbeville Press for the National Audubon Society.

Although Audubon is best known for his portrayal of birds, one of his less-familiar series, 'Vivaparous Quadrupeds of North America,' por-

trayed various species of animals. Assembled in corroboration with John Bachman from 1839 until 1851, these prints are 28" x 22" in size. Several octavo editions were published in the 1850s.

American Sparrow Hawk, #142, Havell, 38x25" 3,500.00
Barn Swallow, #173, Havell, 38x25" 2,200.00
Barred Owl, #46, Havell, ca 1828, 39x27" 5,500.00
Brown Pelican, #421, Havell, 26x37" 18,000.00
Canvas-Bk Duck...View of Baltimore, #301, 25x38" 20,000.00
Chestnut-Crowned Titmouse, #353, Havell, 1836/37, 21x15" ..2,100.00
Common Crossbill, #198, Havell, 38x26" 3,000.00
Ground Dove, #182, Havell, 26x37" 3,500.00
Ivory-Billed Woodpecker, #66, ca 1829, 39x26" 12,000.00
Mallard Duck, #221, Havell, ca 1831, 25x38" 30,000.00
Mocking Bird, Havell, 38x25" 14,000.00

Owls of North America, Snowy Owl, Amsterdam Edition, #25, Plate CXXI, 40x26", $2,500.00.

Pigeon Hawk, #92, 1830, 38x25" 2,000.00
Prairie Starling, #420, Havell, 38x25" 1,900.00
Roscoe's Yellow Throat, 1827, 37x26" 1,900.00
Roseate Spoonbill, #321, Havell, 1836, 25x38" 25,000.00
Snow Owl, #121, Havell, ca 1833, 38x25" 25,000.00
Tree Sparrow, #188, Havell, 38x26" 3,000.00
Velvet Duck, #247, Havell, ca 1835, 21x30" 1,650.00
Velvet Duck, #247, Havell, ca 1835, 25x37" 2,800.00
Yellow-Breasted Chat, #244, chromo, Bien, ca 1860 ....800.00
Yellow-Crowned Warbler, #153, Havell, 38x25" 2,000.00

Currier and Ives

Nathaniel Currier was in business by himself until the late 1850s when he formed a partnership with James Merrit Ives. Currier is given credit for being the first to use the medium to portray newsworthy subjects, and the Currier and Ives views of 19th-century American culture are familiar to us all. In the following listings, 'C' numbers correspond with a standard reference book by Cunningham. Values are given for prints in very good condition; all are colored unless indicated black and white. Unless noted 'NC' (Nathaniel Currier), all prints are published by Currier and Ives.

Alexander (spirited wht horse), undtd, C-73, sm folio 175.00
Am Country Life, Summer's Evening; NC, 1885, C-124, lg 2,800.00
Am Farm Scenes, No 2; NC, 1853, C-135, lg folio 3,000.00
Am Farm Yard, Evening; FF Palmer, 1857, C-138, lg folio 2,500.00

Am Field Sports, Flush'd; after Tait, 1857, C-149, lg folio **3,000.00**
Am Forest Game, FF Palmer, 1866, C-156, lg folio **900.00**
Am Homestead, Winter (sleigh scene); 1868, C-172, sm folio ...**750.00**
Am Mountain Scenery (deer scene), 1868, C-172, sm folio **450.00**
Assassination of President Lincoln, 1865, C-291, sm folio **150.00**
Autumn (girl's head, fruit in hair), 1871, C-312, sm folio **75.00**
Battle of Antietam, MD...1862; undtd, C-384, sm folio **195.00**
Battle of Bunker's Hill...1775; NC, undtd, C-388, sm folio **235.00**
Battle of Corinth, MS...1862; undtd, C-401, sm folio **195.00**
Battle of Gettysburg, PA...1863, undtd, C-407, sm folio **235.00**
Battle of Mexico (battle scene), NC, 1847, C-411, sm folio **135.00**
Bear Hunting, Close Quarters; undtd, C-447, sm folio **750.00**
Beautiful Persian (girl in oval), undtd, C-457, sm folio **75.00**
Bombardment of Fort Pulaski..., 1862, C-595, sm folio **275.00**
Boss of the Road, Thos Worth on stone, undtd, C-615, sm folio ...**225.00**
Boyne Water, This Obelisk...; undtd, C-642, sm folio **85.00**
Brave Wife (McClellan w/wife & son), undtd, C-651, sm folio ..**100.00**
Bride (¾-length), NC, 1847, C-661, sm folio **125.00**
Brook Trout, Just Caught; undtd, C-705, med folio **650.00**
Burning Glass (boy & girl under tree), 1860, C-737, med folio ..**175.00**
Burning of Chicago (bird's-eye view), 1871, C-738, sm folio **450.00**
Burning of Steamship Austria...1858, undtd, C-748, sm folio **250.00**
By the Seashore, after JP Rossiter, 1868, C-760, med folio **325.00**
Catterskill Falls (falls in center), undtd, C-858, sm folio **250.00**
Caught on the Fly, T Worth on stone, 1879, C-864, sm folio **300.00**
Cause & Effect/A Natural Result, 1887, C-866, sm folio **225.00**
Cedars of Lebanon (foreign view), undtd, C-872, sm folio **50.00**
Celebrated Horse Dexter..., 1865, C-883, lg folio **2,000.00**
Central Park, The Drive (NY view); 1862, C-951, med folio ..**2,200.00**
Champion Stallion George Wilkes..., 1888, C-976, lg folio **1,800.00**
Chicago in Flames...Randolph St Bridge, C-1027, sm folio **600.00**
Chicky's Dinner (3 chicks/lobster), undtd, C-1029, sm folio **150.00**
Choice Bouquet (flower basket), 1874, C-1041, sm folio **125.00**
Clipper Ship Dreadnought..., NC, 1856, C-1144, lg folio **3,500.00**
Clipper Ship in Hurricane, 1855, C-1154, med folio **2,000.00**
Clipper Yacht America of NY, NC, C-1176, sm folio **700.00**
Come into the Garden, Maude... (cat); C-1217, sm folio **125.00**
Coming Home w/a Family (cat/kittens), C-1220, sm folio **150.00**
Crack Team at...Gait, Worth on stone, 1869, C-1282, lg folio ..**1,700.00**
Dartmouth College, Ami B Young, ca 1834, C-1446, sm folio ..**2,500.00**
Dearest Spot on Earth to Me (comic), 1878, C-1470, sm folio ...**275.00**
Death of Gen Z Taylor 12th President..., 1850, C-1485, sm folio .**95.00**
Death of Harrison April 4...1841, NC, 1841, C-1487, sm folio **95.00**
Death Shot (buck), undtd, C-1523, sm folio **195.00**
El Capitan from Mariposa Trail, undtd, C-1681, sm folio **650.00**
Elephant & His Keepers, Cameron on stone, C-1687, med folio...**300.00**
English Winter Scene (churchgoers), undtd, C-1745, sm folio ...**600.00**
Enoch Arden the Lonely Isle, 1869, C-1749, lg folio **300.00**
Fannie (lady w/fan), undtd, C-1866, sm folio **75.00**
First Lesson (terrier/pups/rat), NC, undtd, C-1973, lg folio **475.00**
Fording the River, FF Palmer, undtd, C-2081, med folio **500.00**
Forest Scene, Summer (deer); undtd, C-2086, sm folio **225.00**
Fourth of July..., L Maurer on stone, 1858, C-2102, lg folio **950.00**
Frontier Lake (tree-lined lake), undtd, C-2153, sm folio **250.00**
Fruit & Flowers, NC, 1848, C-2163, sm folio **150.00**
Fruits of the Season (mixed fruit), 1870, C-2198, sm folio **150.00**
Garden, Orchard & Vine; FF Palmer, 1867, C-2221, med folio .**700.00**
General US Grant, President of US; undtd, C-2317, sm folio **125.00**
Geo Washington, 1st President...; NC, undtd, C-2353, sm folio ...**150.00**
Gertrude (in bridal gown), NC, 1846, C-2362, sm folio **95.00**
Getting a Hoist...Case of Heaves; Worth, 1875, C-2365, sm **225.00**
Going to Pasture, Early Morning; undtd, C-2403, sm folio **200.00**
Grazing Farm (rural scene), 1867, C-2563, lg folio **1,200.00**
Great Fire at Boston (waterfront), 1872, C-2614, sm folio **325.00**

Great Victory in Shenendoah Valley VA, C-2653, sm folio **200.00**
Great West (mtn & train), 1870, C-2658, sm folio **1,100.00**
Happy Family (3 puppies), NC, undtd, C-2708, sm folio **125.00**
Harvest (men cut wheat), NC, 1849, C-2741, sm folio **250.00**
Helen (red dress), NC, 1855, C-2777, sm folio **85.00**
Hiawatha's Wooing (scene from poem), 1860, C-2809, lg folio .**550.00**
High Bridge at Harlem NY, NC, 1849, C-2810, sm folio **550.00**
Home from Brook, Lucky Fisherman; 1867, C-2856, lg folio ...**2,300.00**
Home of Florence Nightengale, undtd, C-2864, med folio **275.00**
Home Sweet Home (motto/flowers/etc), 1874, C-2878, sm folio ..**200.00**
Hues of Autumn on Racquet River, undtd, C-2982, sm folio **300.00**
Hundred Leaf Rose (6 roses/5 buds), 1870, C-2988, sm folio **125.00**
Ice-Boat Race on Hudson, undtd, C-3021, sm folio **2,800.00**
In Springtime (children w/flowers), undtd, C-3074, sm folio **150.00**
Inviting Dish (peaches/grapes/etc), 1870, C-3124, sm folio **125.00**
James Buchanan 15th President...; NC, C-3151, sm folio **175.00**
James K Polk, 11th President...; NC, C-3162, sm folio **130.00**
John (full-length/seated), NC, 1845, C-3250, sm folio **175.00**
Julia (full-length, wht dress), NC, 1845, C-3305, sm folio **85.00**
Kitties Among the Roses (2 kittens), 1873, C-3352, sm folio **150.00**
Knitting Lesson (lady & girl), undtd, C-3363, med folio **350.00**
Lady Thorn & Mtn Boy...Great Match..., 1867, C-3394, lg **1,725.00**
Lake George NY (2 deer at water), undtd, C-3407, sm folio **250.00**
Lake in the Woods (deer near lake), undtd, C-3409, sm folio **225.00**
Life & Age of Man...(baby/old man), undtd, C-3498, sm folio ...**225.00**
Life in Woods, Returning to Camp; 1860, C-3513, lg folio **3,500.00**
Life of a Fireman, The Fire; NC, 1854, C-3515, lg folio **3,000.00**
Life of Hunter...Tartar, after Tait, 1861, C-3521, lg folio **6,000.00**
Life of Sportsman...in Woods, 1872, C-3523, sm folio **450.00**
Little Fairy (full-length), undtd, C-3616, sm folio **85.00**
Little Red Riding Hood (girl w/dog), undtd, C-3696, sm folio ...**150.00**
Looking Down Yo-Semite (landscape), undtd, C-3767, sm folio ...**375.00**
Loss of Steamboat Swallow, NC, 1845, C-3779, sm folio **425.00**
Love Is Lightest (lady w/scale), NC, 1847, C-3796, sm folio **150.00**
Lover's Adieu (young couple), NC, 1852, C-3807, sm folio **100.00**
Low Water in Mississippi, FF Palmer, 1868, C-3824, lg folio ..**4,800.00**
Lucy (seated), NC, Sarony on stone, undtd, C-3835, sm folio **95.00**
Maiden's Rock, Mississippi River; undtd, C-3891, sm folio **500.00**
Mambrino Sire...Messenger, after Stubb, C-3951, sm folio **350.00**
Man Who Kept Bridge, Worth on stone, 1881, C-3964, sm folio **200.00**
Maple Sugaring, Early Spring...; 1872, C-3975, sm folio **1,250.00**
Mary (full-length), NC, 1845, C-4036, sm folio **95.00**
Midnight Race on Mississippi, Palmer, 1860, C-4116, lg folio **5,000.00**
Minute Men of Revolution, 1876, C-4144, sm folio **250.00**
Moosehead Lake (moose in center), undtd, C-4186, sm folio **250.00**
Morning of Life (child in boat), undtd, C-4198, sm folio **100.00**

Morning in the Woods,
F.F. Palmer, Del.; N.C.,
large folio, $2,100.00.

Mother & Child (doing ABCs), NC, 1846, C-4228, sm folio **95.00**
Mother's Dream (mother & child), undtd, C-4233, med folio **125.00**
Mother's Wing, FF Palmer, 1866, C-4239, med folio **200.00**
Mtn Spring, W Point...; Palmer, 1862, C-4245, med folio **800.00**

My Dear Little Pet (girl w/kitten), 1877, C-4289, sm folio **95.00**

My Little Wht Kitties...Dominoes, undtd, C-4336, sm folio **135.00**

My Pony & Dog (wht pony in stable), undtd, C-4350, sm folio .**135.00**

My Three Wht Kitties...ABCs, undtd, C-4357, sm folio **135.00**

Narrows from Staten Island, undtd, C-4380, sm folio **375.00**

Niagara Falls from Goat Island, undtd, C-4458, med folio **350.00**

Night After the Battle (war scene), 1862, C-4470, sm folio **125.00**

Night by the Campfire (men & dogs), 1861, C-4472, med folio **550.00**

Nip & Tuck!, Thos Worth on stone, 1878, C-4481, sm folio **275.00**

Noah's Ark, NC, Sarony on stone, undtd, C-4494, sm folio **295.00**

Nosegay (flowers in vase), undtd, C-4510, sm folio **125.00**

O'Sullivan's Cascade...Killarney, undtd, C-4633, sm folio **100.00**

Old Farm House (winter scene), 1872, C-4557, sm folio **1,300.00**

Old Oaken Bucket (man drinking), 1872, C-4577, sm folio **225.00**

On a Point (dogs in field), Palmer, 1855, C-4592, med folio **600.00**

Our Pasture (sheep), NC, undtd, C-4650, sm folio **150.00**

Pacing Wonder Sleepy Tom..., 1879, C-4687, sm folio **350.00**

Papa's Darlings (girl & boy), 1877, C-3697, sm folio **85.00**

Parting Hour (couple by tree), undtd, C-4713, sm folio **95.00**

Pasture in Summer, Drinking Trough; 1867, C-4721, lg folio **975.00**

Peace Be to This House (motto), 1872, C-4734, sm folio **150.00**

Perry's Victory on Lake Erie, NC, Sarony, C-4754, sm folio **650.00**

Playful Family (puppies), undtd, C-4797, sm folio **125.00**

Pond in the Woods (duck family), undtd, C-4832, med folio **300.00**

Prairie Hens (birds in tall grass), undtd, C-4860, sm folio **350.00**

Puzzled Fox (puzzle print), 1872, C-4984, sm folio **300.00**

Quail Shooting, NC, Palmer on stone, 1852, C-4989, lg folio ...**3,250.00**

Queen of Love & Beauty, 1870, C-5003, sm folio **75.00**

Queen Victoria (equestrian), NC, 1848, C-5022, sm folio **75.00**

Rabbit Catching, Trap Sprung; undtd, C-5034, sm folio **725.00**

Rafting on St Lawrence, undtd, C-5051, med folio **425.00**

Raspberries (on plate), 1870, C-5065, sm folio **135.00**

Ready for Trot, Bring Up...; Worth, 1877, C-5084, lg folio **1,700.00**

Rebecca (full-length), NC, 1846, C-5087, sm folio **85.00**

Rising Family (snipes), after Tait, 1857, C-5151, lg folio **5,000.00**

Rival Roses (red & wht roses), 1873, C-5154, sm folio **95.00**

Rubber (couple playing cards), undtd, C-5246, sm folio **250.00**

Rural Lake, after FF Palmer, undtd, C-5261, med folio **325.00**

Safe Sailing (children in boat on land), C-5292, sm folio **175.00**

Scene on Susquehanna (sheep/village), C-5415, sm folio **300.00**

Scenery of Upper MS Indian Village, C-5422, sm folio **350.00**

See-Saw (4 children), undtd, C-5457, med folio **300.00**

Shade & Tomb of Napoleon (puzzle print), C-5473, sm folio **95.00**

Silver Cascade, Wht Mtns; undtd, C-5521, sm folio **300.00**

Sleigh Race (2 sleighs/4 horses), undtd, C-5558, sm folio **2,500.00**

Soldier's Adieu (soldier/lady), NC, 1847, C-5593, sm folio **125.00**

Southern Beauty (lady), undtd, C-5630, sm folio **75.00**

Spaniel (dog by stream), NC, 1842, C-5637, sm folio **250.00**

Spirit of the Union (Washington/etc), 1860, C-5655, sm folio ..**185.00**

Split Rock, St John River; NC, undtd, C-5663, sm folio **275.00**

Spring (brunette lady), undtd, C-5674, sm folio **75.00**

Spring (horse scene), NC, undtd, C-5672, sm folio **225.00**

Squirrel Shooting (hunt scene), C-5681, sm folio **500.00**

Stag at Bay, after Landseer, undtd, C-5687, sm folio **150.00**

Straw-Yard Winter (animals), undtd, C-5837, med folio **1,200.00**

Summer Afternoon (cattle in stream), C-5852, sm folio **175.00**

Summer Evening (man drives cattle), undtd, C-5853, sm folio ..**175.00**

Summer Gift (peaches & pears), 1870, C-5860, sm folio **125.00**

Summer Night (couple near lake), undtd, C-5871, sm folio **175.00**

Sunnyside on Hudson (home of W Irving), C-5893, sm folio **200.00**

Surrender of Cornwallis..., NC, 1845, C-5904, sm folio **275.00**

Sylvan Lake (man fishing), undtd, C-5940, sm folio **200.00**

Taking Comfort, FF Palmer, 1866, C-5958, med folio **275.00**

Thatched Cottage (rural scene), undtd, C-6002, sm folio **175.00**

Three Little Wht Kitties Fishing, 1871, C-6043, sm folio **150.00**

Three Sisters (embracing youngest), 1871, C-6045, sm folio **100.00**

Trial of Patience (boy & grandmother), C-6146, med folio **400.00**

Tribute of Autumn (apples/grapes), 1870, C-6149, sm folio **200.00**

Trotters on Snow, J Cameron on stone, C-6167, sm folio **1,200.00**

Trotting...Swill Against Swell, Worth, 1873, C-6195, sm folio ..**375.00**

Trout Pool (fishing scene), undtd, C-6229, sm folio **950.00**

Two Little Fraid Cats (kittens & mouse), C-6263, sm folio **150.00**

Uncle Tom & Little Eva, NC, undtd, C-6280, sm folio **150.00**

Under the Rose (girl w/bouquet), 1872, C-6283, sm folio **125.00**

US Frigate Constitution (ship to right), NC, C-6304, sm folio ..**600.00**

US Frigate Independence, 64 Guns; NC, 1841, C-6307, sm folio...**500.00**

US Ship of the Line in a Gale, NC, 1847, C-6332, sm folio **500.00**

Valley Falls VA (fisherman), undtd, C-6355, sm folio **250.00**

Vase of Flowers, undtd, C-6363, sm folio **125.00**

View of Baltimore, von Baltimor; NC, 1848, C-6389, sm folio **600.00**

View on Delaware, Water Gap..., 1860, C-6440, lg folio **1,200.00**

View on Hudson, Crow's Nest; undtd, C-6447, sm folio **275.00**

View on Rondout, FF Palmer, undtd, C-6451, med folio **250.00**

Virginia Home in Olden Time, 1872, C-6474, sm folio **300.00**

Washington at Prayer (in tent), NC, undtd, C-6517, sm folio **125.00**

Washington Columns, Yo-Semite Valley; C-6520, sm folio **350.00**

Washington Crossing Delaware..., Hewitt, C-6521, sm folio **300.00**

Washington Taking Command,, NC, 1848, C-6546, sm folio **200.00**

Watchers (boy & dog), undtd, C-6561, sm folio **100.00**

Welcome (motto & flowers), 1873, C-6604, sm folio **175.00**

Whale Fishery 'Laying On,' NC, 1852, C-6626, sm folio **1,500.00**

Why Don't He Come: First at Rendezvous; C-6653, sm folio **125.00**

Wild Duck Shooting, On the Wing; 1870, C-6671, sm folio **600.00**

Wild Turkey Shooting (hunt scene), 1871, C-6677, sm folio **750.00**

William Tell...Son's Head, undtd, C-6712, sm folio **95.00**

Windsor Castle & Park, undtd, C-6720, med folio **200.00**

Winter Evening (skating scene), NC, C-6734, med folio **1,800.00**

Winter Sports, Pickerel Fishing; 1872, C-6747, sm folio **1,400.00**

Woodcock (pr), 1871, C-6770, sm folio **300.00**

Wooding Up on Mississippi, Palmer, 1863, C-6776, lg folio ...**9,600.00**

Wounded Bittern (attacked by dog), undtd, C-6784, sm folio **100.00**

Yacht Henrietta 205 Tons (ship to right), C-6802, sm folio **400.00**

Young Brood (children w/ducks), 1870, C-6840, sm folio **150.00**

Young Housekeepers (couple), NC, undtd, C-6856, sm folio **95.00**

Z Taylor, 12th President...; NC, 1849, C-6879, sm folio **150.00**

Erte (Romain de Tirtoff)

Autumn Song, 20s Remembered Suite, 1977, 17x14" **525.00**

Bath of the Marquise, Chicago Serigraphics, no fr, 19x13" **875.00**

Devotion, Chalk & Vermilion Fine Arts, 36x27" **2,000.00**

Les Poupees Russes, Chicago Serigraphics, no fr, 25x18" **825.00**

Queen of Sheba, Chicago Serigraphics, no fr, 25x18" **875.00**

Vintage, Chicago Serigraphics, no fr, 1980, 26x18" **1,750.00**

Wings of Victory, Circle Fine Art, 1978, 27x19" **2,200.00**

Fox, R. Atkinson

A Canadian who worked as an artist in the 1880s, R. Atkinson Fox moved to New York about ten years later, where his original oils were widely sold at auction and through exhibitions. Today he is best known, however, for his prints, published by as many as twenty print-makers. More than thirty examples of his work appeared on Brown and Bigelow calendars, and it was used in many other forms of advertising as well. Though he was an accomplished artist able to interpret any subject well, he is today best known for his landscapes. Fox died in 1935. Our advisor for Fox prints is Pat Gibson whose address is listed in the Directory under California.

At the Pool, cows, #579, 7½x10" 175.00
Dawn, #1, orig fr, 18x10" 88.00
Departure of Columbus, #544, 8½x12" 380.00
English Garden, garden w/brn stone path, #57, 14x20" 75.00
Faithful & True, old couple, #533, 7½x5½" 245.00
Garden of Love, fountain, #42, orig fr, 10x15" 75.00
Girl of Golden West, sgn Geo White (pseudonym), 6x8" 85.00
Good Shepherd, #29, 14x20" 145.00
Guardian of the Valley, mountains, puzzle, #591 ......95.00
Land of Dreams, #14, 10x8" 65.00
Monarchs, The; lions, #442, 6x8" 225.00
Mount Hood, pastel colors, #136, 8½x11" 65.00
Mountain Lake, #301, 8x11" 70.00
October Days, birch trees & flowers, #44, 6x8" 65.00
Old Faithful, sheep & dog, #620, 13x8" 150.00
Playmates, boy & girl at beach, DeForest (pseudonym), 6x8" 75.00
Ready for All Comers, horse's head, #428, 14x11" 250.00
Repairing of All Kinds, blksmith, #640, 13x10" 375.00
Sentinels of the Pass, pseudonym used, 6x8" 45.00
Silent Rockies, bears, #318, 7x9" 180.00
Silvery Divide, pseudonym used, 6x8" 50.00
Spirit of Youth, sgn, #4, orig fr, 18x10" 88.00
Sunset Dreams, sgn, #23, orig fr, 18x10" 98.00
Trusty Guardian, collie dog & lamb, #11, 11x14" 175.00
Untitled, landscape in nearly all grs, #180, 10x14" 78.00
White Feather, Indian maiden, #309, 15x11" 250.00

Gutmann, Bessie Pease

Delicately tinted prints of appealing children sometimes accompanied by their pets, sometimes asleep, often captured at some childhood activity are typical of the work of Gutmann; she painted lovely ladies as well and was a successful illustrator of children's books. Her career spanned the earlier decades of this century. Our advisor for this category is Earl MacSorley; he is listed in the Directory under Connecticut.

Awakening (originally Angel's Kin), #664 ....75.00
Buddies, child w/puppy on bench, #779, 17½x13½" 525.00
Butterfly, #632 ....125.00
Chuckles, #216, 1937, 11x14" 60.00
Chums, #665, 14x21" 200.00
Double Blessing, #232, sepia, 1915, 15x10½" 235.00
Friendly Enemies, #215, girl in pk w/kitten & puppy, 11x14" 50.00
Home Builders, #655, 14x21" 125.00
In Disgrace, #792, 1935, 14x21" 125.00
In Port of Dreams, #214, 11x14" 75.00
Love's Blossom, #223, 1927, 13½x10½" 60.00
Miss Flirt, #217, 11x14" 60.00
On Dreamland's Border, #692, 1921, 14x16½" 100.00
On the Up & Up, toddler on stairs, #796, 1945, 14x21" 75.00
Sunbeam, #730, all orig 175.00
Tasting, child w/cup, #21, sepia, 1909, 11½x8½" 100.00
Television, girl w/open book, #821, ca 1949, 14x21" 75.00
To Love & Cherish, #615, 1911 ....175.00
Tommy, #788, sepia, 14x21", EX 100.00

Homer, Winslow

Baggage Train, sgn, 1863, 13x19" 800.00
College Life in New England, sgn, 1857, 15x21" 105.00
Fly Fishing, 1889, 17x23" 8,000.00
Gloucester Harbor, on newsprint, 1973 ....175.00
Mending the Tears, 1888, 22x27" 9,900.00
Our Women of the War, on newsprint, 1862 ....150.00

Ship Building, Gloucester Harbor, on newsprint, 9x13" 225.00
Snap the Whip, on newsprint, 1873 ....600.00

Icart, Louis

Louis Icart was a Parisian artist who immortalized the women of France through his etchings, which were widely produced in the 1920s. During the thirties and forties, his popularity waned, and etchings from this period are harder to find. He also produced a few lithographs and about four hundred oils. Most etchings made after 1925 have Icart's embossed 'windmill' seal at the lower left. Be skeptical of watercolors and sketches that look similar in subject to one of the etchings. Prices appear to be stabilizing, as the art market adjusts to American recession and Japanese lethargy. Our Icart advisor is William Holland; he is listed in the Directory under Pennsylvania.

Arrival, 1941, 17x12" 935.00
Basket of Apples, 1928, offset print, 18x14" 220.00
Bubbles, 1930, oval, 17x12" 7,000.00
Chilly One, 1924, 17x11" 2,200.00
Coursing II, 1929, 15x25" 4,000.00
Desire, 1926, 14x19" 1,600.00
Dressing, 1926, 18½x14" 1,800.00
Fair Model, 1937, 18½x11" 3,300.00
Farewell, 1927, 14x18" 1,500.00
Faust, 1928, A-427/500, 20½x13" 1,650.00
Fishbowl, 1925, 17½x11½" 1,600.00
Hydrangeas, 1929, 16x20" 2,200.00
Joan of Arc, 1929, 19x15½" 1,500.00
Kittens, 1925, A-041/500, 14x18¾" 1,800.00
Lacquered Screen, 1922, foxing throughout, 14x8" 1,100.00
Lassitude, 1923, 49/50, 9x11¾" 1,400.00
Leda & Swan, 1934, 20x31" 10,000.00
Lemon Tree, 17x11½" 1,800.00
Louise, 1927, 20x13" 1,980.00
Lovers, 1930, 21x14" 1,950.00

Love's Blossom, 1937, laid down and glued, light stains, minor foxing, 17½x25", $8,000.00.

Masks, 1926, A-11, 19x15" 1,500.00
Meditation, 1928, 11¾x16½" 2,400.00
Memories, 1931, 15x18" 4,800.00
Minuet, 1929, 20x13½" 1,500.00
Mockery, 1928, 16x18" 1,750.00
Muff, 1914, 20x11" 2,000.00
New Hat, 1924, 8x11" 1,000.00
On the Beach, 1925, 10½x15½" 1,500.00
Orchids, 1937, 27x18" 4,800.00
Peacock, 1925, 19x15" 2,200.00
Poem, 1928, #186, 18x22" 2,200.00
Puppies, 1925, inscribed Petits Chiens EA, 17x21" 1,800.00
Red Cage, 1925, 14½x19" 1,650.00
Seville, 1928, 20x13" 1,400.00
Smoke, 1926, A-219/500, 14x19½" 2,200.00

Solitare, 1926, 14x18" **1,500.00**
Speed, 1927, 14¾x25" **4,000.00**
Speed II, 1933, 15x25" **4,500.00**
Swing, 1928, E-34/500, 18¾x13" **6,600.00**
Tennis, 1928, 18½x13½" **2,200.00**
Tosca, 1928, mk E/308, 21x13" **2,200.00**
Unmasked, 1933, foxing throughout, 12x8" **1,100.00**
White Underwear, 1925, #6/363, 14½x19" **2,100.00**
Wisteria, 1940, 17½x21" **2,800.00**
Youth, 1930, A/358, 24x15½" **5,500.00**
Zest, 1928, 19x15" **2,900.00**

Kellogg

Cares of a Family, girl w/chicks, sm folio **85.00**
Don't Say Nay, couple in garden, sm folio **65.00**
Double Fishing, boys tease old man, sm folio **150.00**
Duck Shooting, sm folio **385.00**
Fishing, wht kitten w/paw in goldfish bowl, sm folio **135.00**
Prodigal Son Returned to His Father, sm folio **65.00**
Repose, man & children herd cattle, sm folio **100.00**
Swing, lady in swing, pk dress w/gold sash, sm folio **95.00**
Tree of Life, quotes, sm folio **65.00**

Kurz and Allison

Louis Kurz founded the Chicago Lithograph Company in 1833. Among his most notable works were a series of thirty-six Civil War scenes and one hundred illustrations of Chicago architecture. His company was destroyed in the Great Fire of 1871, and in 1880 Kurz formed a partnership with Alexander Allison, an engraver. Until both retired in 1903, they produced hundreds of lithographs in color as well as black and white.

Battle of Bull Run...1861, McDowell vs Beauregard, lg folio **395.00**
Battle of Cedar Creek, Sheridan vs Early, lg folio **275.00**
Benjamin Franklin Opening the Lodge, lg folio **215.00**
Declaration of Independence, after Trumbull painting, lg folio ..**200.00**
Fall of Petersburg VA, Grant vs Lee, lg folio **250.00**
Flags of the Union, Kugler (artist), lg folio **175.00**
Gen James Garfield & Family, lg folio **95.00**
Gen Wm McKinley, bust view, lg folio **90.00**
Storming Stony Point, med folio **50.00**
Washington Entering Trenton...to Inauguration, med folio **85.00**

McKenney and Hall

Mar Ko Mete, Menominee Chief, Greenough, 1838, 14x20" **120.00**
Monkaushka, Sioux Chief, Biddle, 1837, 14x20" **300.00**
Pashenine, Chippewa Chief, Rice & Clark, 1842, 14x20" **200.00**
Pashepahaw (Stabber), Sioux & Fox Chief, Greenough, 14x20" ...**190.00**
Selocta, Creek Chief, Greenough, 1838, 14x20" **300.00**
Sha Ha Ka, Mandan Chief, Bowen, 1841, 24x20" **200.00**
Timpooche Barnard, Uchee Chief, Greenough, 1838, 14x20" ...**325.00**
Waapashaw, Sioux Chief, Biddle, 1836, 14x20" **200.00**

Mucha, Alphonse

Mucha became famous for his beautiful Art Nouveau lithographs-featuring Sarah Berhardt and Job cigarette papers, which he issued in the 1890s. Born in Prague in 1860, he studied there as well as in Paris and for a time taught at the New York School of Applied Design for women before returning to Prague.

Bieres de La Meuse, 1897, 58x38", EX **3,850.00**
Dame aux Camelias, 1896, 81x28" **10,450.00**
Flirt Biscuits, Lefevre Utile, 1895, 24x11" **2,860.00**
L'Amethyste, 1900, 39x14" **4,600.00**
L'Emeraude, 1900, 38x14" **5,000.00**
Leslie Carter, 1908, 81x31" **5,720.00**
Marovian's Teachers' Choir, canvas-bk, 1911, 42x32", EX **3,850.00**
Monaco/Monte-Carlo, 1897, 44x30" **1,760.00**
Redhead Among Flowers, on velvet, Haines/Stroud, 25x25" ..**3,000.00**
Repos de la Nuit, 1899, 40x14½" **3,300.00**
Reverie, 1896, 25x19" **7,000.00**

Tete Byzantine Brunette, 16x14", $3,300.00.

Rose, les Fleurs; 1898, 42x18" **7,000.00**

Nutting, Wallace

Born in 1862, Nutting pursued many careers. His hand-tinted photographs of landscapes and interior scenes are prized by collectors today. He was also a writer, minister, farmer, and a furniture maker, designing reproductions of early American pieces. Collectors of his prints should be aware of rosy-hued, inconsistently bright or dark examples — especially large prints of *An Elaborate Dinner* and *A Chair for John;* these have been reproduced. Prices for large interior prints have recently been on the increase. Those with animals have risen at least 50% in the past few years, and prints with men are commanding extremely high prices. Those with babies and/or adolescent children bring very high prices as well. Our advisor for this category is Milt Steinfeld; he is listed in the Directory under New Jersey.

All Smiles, lady looks in mirror, 7½x9¼" **250.00**
At the Side Door **550.00**
Birch Grove, trees on hill by lake, 4½x6¼" **125.00**
Birch Paradise **45.00**
Equinox Pond **50.00**
Feminine Finery, lady examines bonnet, 7¼x9½" **275.00**
Floral Arrangement, rare **1,000.00**
Forest Window, path along river, mahog fr, 4½x6½" **125.00**
Garden Steps **60.00**
Indian Maidens **575.00**
LaJolla **300.00**
Little Dutch Cove, homes along bay, 7¼x9½" **400.00**
Old Parlor Idyl, couple beside fireplace, 7½x9½" **595.00**
On the Shores of the Zuyder Zee, 18 people & auto **2,700.00**
Parson's Gate **200.00**
Preparing for Thanksgiving, couple at fireplace, 7½x9½" **400.00**
Primrose Cottage, roses on thatched cottage, 7¼x9½" **150.00**

Sea Cap'n's Daughter, girl in wht, 9½x6" 500.00
Under the Blossoms, sheep scene, 7½x9½" 265.00

Untitled, path through apple orchard, $75.00.

Warm Spring Day 250.00
Warner House, mansion in summer, 7½x9½" 400.00
Wavering Footsteps, tottering child, 7½x9½" 600.00
Windsor Maid 210.00
Winter Welcome Home, men/children/horse, rare 1,500.00

Picasso

La Suite Vollard: Model Nu et Sculptures, sgn, 1933, 15x12" ...8,250.00
Les Mains Liees, II; litho, sgn/#d, 1952, 18½x24¼" 2,200.00
Nature Morte, Compotier; drypoint, sgn, 1909, 5¾x4⅜" 9,350.00
Tete d'Homme, on laid paper, sgn, 1912, fr, 5⅛x4⅜" 16,500.00
Toros en Vallauris, sgn/#d, 1960, fr, 25x20¾" 2,200.00

Prang, Louis

Battle of Antietam, lg folio 150.00
Battle of Kenesaw Mountain, lg folio 150.00
Battle of Manila, 1896, lg folio 135.00
Battle of Shiloh, lg folio 150.00
Capture of New Orleans, naval scene, med-lg folio 400.00
Sheridan's Final Charge at Winchester, lg folio 150.00

Warhol, Andy

Marilyn, silkscreen on wove paper, sgn in pencil on bk, 6x6" 3,575.00
Mick Jagger, silkscreen on D'Arches paper, 1975, 44x29" 5,000.00
Self portrait, silkscreen, blk on silver, sgn, 22x21" 1,540.00

Yard Longs

Values for yard-longs are given for examples in very good to excellent condition, full length, nicely framed, and with the original glass. To learn more about this popular area of collector interest, we recommend *Those Wonderful Yard-Long Prints and More*, and *More Wonderful Yard-Long Prints* by our advisors W.D. and M.J. Keagy and C.G. and J.M. Rhoden. They are listed in the Directory under Indiana and Illinois respectively. A word of caution: watch for reproductions; know your dealer.

American Girl, Pabst Extract, calendar on bk, 1912 ....225.00
Assorted Fruit, Jos Hoover, c 1897 ....150.00
At the North Pole, Jos Hoover & Son, 1904 ....250.00
Bridal Favors, Mary E Hart 150.00
Butterfly Time, Maud Humphrey, c 1903 ....250.00
Girl w/Laughing Eyes, F Carlyle, c 1910 ....190.00
Home Sweet Home, Paul DeLongpre, 1901 ....150.00

Mixed Flowers, S Clarkson, c 1892 ....130.00
Pabst Extract Indian calendar, Hiawatha's Wooing on bk, 1906.....300.00
Pompeian Beauty, Forbes, calendar on bk 250.00
Roses & Lilacs, vertical 125.00
Selz Good Shoes, lady in blk holding rose, 1918 ....250.00
Study of Roses, Paul DeLongpre, c 1895 ....150.00
Yard of Cherries, Guy Bedford, c 1906 ....150.00
Yard of Dogs, c 1903 ....175.00
Yard of Kittens, CL Van Vredenburgh 150.00
Yard of Youth, FL Martini 200.00

Purinton

Founded in 1936 in Wellsville, Ohio, Purinton Pottery relocated in 1941 in Shippenville, Pennsylvania, and began producing hand-painted wares that are today attracting the interest of collectors of 'country-type' dinnerware. Using bold brush strokes of vivid color, simple yet attractive patterns such as Apple, Fruits, Tea Rose, and Pennsylvania Dutch were manufactured in tableware sets and accessory pieces.

Canister, coffee; Chartreuse 35.00
Canister, Heather Plaid, pr 70.00
Canisters, Apple, 4-pc set 150.00

Casserole, various hand-painted fruit on lid $45.00.

Chop plate, Chartreuse 18.00
Coffeepot, Apple, 8-cup 30.00
Cookie jar, Apple 50.00
Cookie jar, Intaglio 65.00
Creamer, Apple 10.00
Creamer & sugar bowl, Apple & Pear, w/lid 25.00
Creamer & sugar bowl, Maywood 35.00
Cup & saucer, Maywood 20.00
Drip jar, Apple, w/lid 20.00
Jug, Kent; Apple, 1-pt 15.00
Pitcher, Apple & Pear, lg 40.00
Plate, Maywood, 7" 10.00
Plate, Maywood, 9¾" 17.50
Platter, Normandy Plaid 15.00
Range set, Ivy, 3-pc 40.00
Relish, Intaglio, 3-part, center hdl 25.00
Server, Intaglio, rectangular, 11" 25.00
Shakers, Apple, jug, pr 15.00
Shakers, Apple, range sz, pr 20.00
Shakers, Maywood, jug form, pr 25.00
Shakers, Normandy Plaid, pr 12.50
Sugar bowl, Apple, w/lid 10.00
Teapot, Apple, 2-cup 15.00

Purses

Beaded purses and bags represent an area of collecting interest that is very popular today. Purses from the early 1800s are often decorated with small, brightly colored glass beads. Cut steel beads were popular in the 1840s and remained stylish until about 1930. Mesh purses are also popular. In the 1820s mesh was woven. Chain-link mesh came into usage in the 1890s, followed by the enamel mesh bags carried by the flappers in the 1920s. Purses are divided into several categories by (a) construction techniques — whether beaded, embroidered, or a type of needlework; (b) material — fabric or metal; and (c) design and style. Condition is very important. Watch for dry, brittle leather or fragile material. For those interested in learning more, we recommend *Antique Purses, A History, Identification, and Value Guide, Second Edition,* by Richard Holiner; *More Beautiful Purses,* and *Combs and Purses,* both by Evelyn Haertigi of Carmel, California. Our advisor for this category is Veronica Trainer; she is listed in the Directory under Ohio.

Beaded, amber, dbl beaded fringe, lg, EX 165.00
Beaded, floral tapestry, orante fr, chain hdl, 9x12" 315.00
Beaded, gilt clasp & fr w/'jade' & 'ruby' florals, tasseled 370.00
Beaded, gold metal, mesh drawstring, Whiting & Davis, EX 70.00
Beaded, gold/silver/bl florals on pearl wht, Fr, 10x5"+fringe 200.00
Beaded, mc Deco florals, chain hdl, 6x11" 275.00
Chatelaine, SP, bows & stripes design, chain hdl, 4½x3" 175.00
Lucite, Tyrolean, 1950s, NM 90.00
Lucite w/rhinestones, clutch style, 1950s, EX 40.00

Mandalian Mfg. Co., mesh bags, left to right: $175.00; $200.00; $200.00.

Mesh, blk/pk enamel on wht, Whiting & Davis, 6½x3" 175.00
Mesh, German silver, 5x7" 110.00
Mesh, silver, heavy fr, link chain & strap, EX 90.00
Metal, silver openwork, gold trim, Vanglo, 6¼x4½", EX 45.00
Petit point, mc flowers & scrolls, mc on tan, gilt fr, lg 135.00
Plastic, snakeskin-look, Roban by Feiner, NY-Miami, 3½x9" 125.00
Plastic, wht marble, Hillary, NM 45.00
Plastic coffin style, blk flowers under clear dome, 3x5x7" 250.00
Rhinestones, hand set, Czechoslovakia, sm 75.00
Tapestry (floral), gold chain & clasp, Fr, EX 50.00
Velvet, blk w/ornate brocade design, chain hdl, India, 7x4" 30.00
Velvet, SP repousse fr, chain hdl w/medallion clip, NM 125.00

Quezal

The Quezal Art Glass and Decorating Company of Brooklyn, New York, was founded in 1901 by Martin Bach. A former Tiffany employee, Bach's glass closely resembled that of his former employer. Most pieces were signed 'Quezal,' a name taken from a Central American bird. After Bach's death in 1920, his son-in-law, Conrad Vohlsing, continued to produce a Quezal-type glass in Elmhurst, New York, which he marked 'Lustre Art Glass.' Examples listed here are signed unless noted otherwise.

Bowl, gold, flat ft, wide flaring rim, 4½x10½" 200.00
Chandelier, 6 ribbed gold/opal shades, floral-emb fixture 1,200.00
Lamp, desk; amber irid bell shade; gooseneck std/rtcl base 550.00
Lamp, pulled feather shades; 4-arm bronze unmk base, 17x12" ..1,100.00
Shade, damascene on gr, wht int, dbl-waisted dome, 12" dia ..1,800.00
Shade, feathers on amber irid, wht int, 8x10" 770.00
Shade, gold irid, ribbed, bell form, sgn, 6", pr 440.00
Shade, lily; gr feathers, 4", set of 4 ....800.00
Vase, bl irid, waisted neck, 6x4" 550.00
Vase, bud; feathers, gr on amber irid, wht int, flared, 6" 880.00

Vase, cream iridescent with trailing gold vines and green flowers, all above a pulled feather motif, 12½", $3,250.00.

Vase, dbl hooked/pulled feathers, gr/gold on opal/amber, 4½" ...1,300.00
Vase, feathers, gr/gold on opal, lily form, #206, 7" 1,050.00
Vase, feathers, orange on gold, gr rickrack motif, 5x6½" 2,000.00
Vase, feathers at bulbous base, gold/gr on wht, 4" 2,300.00
Vase, feathers/lines, gr/gold on wht, flared/ruffled, 5" 900.00
Vase, feathers/spider web, gold on opal, bottle form, 10" 1,300.00
Vase, floriform; feathers, gr/gold on opal, gold int, 6" 770.00
Vase, gold w/purple to pk highlights, threaded at waist, 4" 180.00
Vase, hooked swirls, irid bl/orange/gold on opal, ovoid, 6½" 875.00
Vase, jack-in-pulpit; feathers in gr/wht, gold throat, 8" 1,200.00
Vase, loops/trails, wht/yel on bl irid, segmented/ftd, 10" 800.00
Vase, swirled trailings, olive on amber irid, unmk, 7" 550.00
Vase, swirls, wht/gold on bl, 4-bulb slim ftd form, 12" 1,000.00

Quilts

Quilts, while made of necessity, nevertheless represent an art form which expresses the character and the personality of the designer. During the 17th and 18th centuries, quilts were considered a necessary part of a bride's hope chest; the traditional number required to be properly endowed for marriage was a 'baker's dozen'! Quilts were used not only for bed coverings but for curtains, extra insulation, and mattresses as well. The early quilts were made from pieces salvaged from cloth items that had outlived their original usefulness and from bits left over from sewing projects. Regardless of shape, these scraps were fitted together following no organized lines. The resulting hodge-podge design was called a crazy quilt.

In 1793 Eli Whitney developed the cotton gin; as a result, textile production in America became industrialized. Soon inexpensive fabrics were readily available, and ladies were able to choose from colorful prints and solids to add contrast to their work. Both pieced and appliqued work became popular. Pieced quilts were considered utilitarian, while appliqued work was shown with pride of accomplishment at the fair. Today many collectors prize pieced quilts and their intricate geometric patterns above all other types. Many of these designs were given names: Daisy and Oak Leaf, Grandmother's Flower Garden, Log Cabin, and Ocean Wave are only a few. Appliqued quilts involved stitching one piece — carefully cut into a specific form such as a leaf, a flower, or a stylized device — onto either a large one-piece ground fabric or an individual block. Often the background fabric was quilted in a decorative pattern.

Amish women scorned printed calicos as 'worldly' and instead used colorful blocks set with black fabrics to produce a stunning pieced effect. During the Victorian era, the crazy quilt was revived, but the ladies of the 1870s used plush velvets, brocades, silks, and linen patches and embroidered along the seams with feather or chain stitches.

Another type of quilting, highly prized and rare today, is trapunto. These quilts were made by first stitching the outline of the design onto a solid sheet of fabric which was backed with a second having a much looser weave. White was often favored, but color was sometimes used for accent. The design (grapes, flowers, leaves, etc.) was padded through openings made by separating the loose weave of the underneath fabric; a backing was added and the three layers quilted as one.

Besides condition, value is judged on intricacy of pattern, color effect, and craftsmanship. In the listings that follow, examples rated excellent have minor defects. Values given here are auction results; retail may be somewhat higher.

Pieced and appliqued quilt in the Mariner's Compass pattern, late 1800s, minor discoloration, 78x83", $1,250.00.

Key:
dmn — diamond   ms — machine sewn
embr — embroidered   X — cross
hs — hand sewn

Amish

Carolina Lily Flower Basket, 1930s, 88x90" 1,650.00
Crib, Star, dk colors, bl border/binding, EX work, 34x44" 375.00
Lg center sq w/4 rows of 3 'dbl Xs,' pastels, 45x61", EX 275.00
Orange, bk: gray, well quilted, Holty family, IN, 70x84" 135.00
Sunshine & Shade, purple/gr/red/pk/blk, 20th C, 80x86" 250.00
Weathervane, blk/dk & lt bl/lav, 1940s, 80x102", EX 300.00
9-Patch, dk colors, fan-stitched border, 1930s, 72x80" 650.00

Appliqued

Animals & cherries, crib sz 145.00

Arrowheads & sqs, red/wht/bl, cotton, 1790s, lg, EX 295.00
Butterfly, yel on wht, fine quilting, 1930s, 70x88", EX 225.00
Circles of flowers joined by leaves, 1930s, 68x86", EX 225.00
Floral branches/sunbursts/vine border, EX quilting, VG 600.00
Floral medallions, 4 rows of 3, calicos, cut down/rpr 425.00
Floral pinwheels (4), vining border, calicos, EX 550.00
Flower Basket, blk & wht/lav/peach/yel/gr, 66x80", NM 350.00
Pinwheel in red & gr, minor stains, crib sz, 41x41" 460.00
Sunbonnet Lady w/Parasol, mc solids/prints, 1930s, 86x68" 235.00
Sunbonnet Sue, ltweight, 1940s, full sz, EX 225.00
Tulip, gr/yel/red/bl on wht w/pk blocks, 1930s, 68x82" 500.00
Tulips in 3-line gridwork, meandering border, EX hs, VG 400.00
4 repeats: mum-like flowerhead ea point of X (stems), EX 450.00

Mennonite

Compass stars in grid, modern, Ohio, 86x104" 145.00
Single Star, mc solids on wht, some bleeding, crib sz, 36x36" 300.00
Star of Bethlehem, vivid colors, sm stars in corners, 1890s 3,300.00
Starflowers, colorful prints, modern, Iowa, 86x102" 160.00
Sunshine & Shadow, mc solids/calico, bar pattern bk, 82x86" ...550.00

Pieced

Album, mc prints/bl grid, sgn/inscribed, 1847, post cutouts 350.00
Album, Xs on lt ground, ea intersection sgn/dtd 1846, VG 400.00
Altar Steps, mc wool, Turkey Tracks stitching, lg, EX 285.00
Baby Aster, mc prints, wht cotton corners, 1920s, 67x69", EX ...295.00
Baskets, 6 rows of 7, calicos, homespun bk, 81x78" 450.00
Bear's Paws, autumn colors, EX hs, lg, unused 400.00
Bow Tie, bl/blk/pk/wht, 1920s, full sz, EX 235.00
Bow Tie, wine/dk bl, hand-carded cotton, 1900s, 64x82", EX 375.00
Broken Pinwheel, mc prints, tiny stitching, 1920s, 72x86" 425.00
Building Blocks, mc on wht, 1930s, 64x80", EX 325.00
Cactus Basket, bl/pk/yel on wht, 1930s, 64x82", EX 450.00
Carpenter's Wheel, mc prints, pk & yel sashing/border, 68x78" .350.00
Checked sqs, 3 rows of 3, +4 trapunto medallions, lt stain 700.00
Churn Dash, bl/blk/red, red sashing, ms, 1890s, 68x80" 600.00
Crazy, wools, feather stitching, ca 1885, 68x70", VG 285.00
Crazy Star, cotton prints/wht, yel border, 1930s, 70x84", NM ...350.00
Crib, stamp-sz sqs of pastel prints, zigzag border, 45x37" 395.00
Double Pyramid, red on wht, red border, ca 1910, 70x72", EX ...595.00
Double Wedding Ring, bright colors on wht, full sz, NM 300.00
Double Wedding Ring, gr & wht, scalloped, 1930s, 72x80" 465.00
Double Wedding Ring, lav/yel, EX quilting, 1930s, lg, EX 325.00
Double Wedding Ring, ltweight, 1930s, full sz, EX 450.00
Double wedding Ring, mc prints, scalloped edge, 1930s, 77x86" 500.00
Dresden, dk bl/rose/red/yel prints on wht, 1920s, 72x84" 300.00
Dresden Plate, mc cotton prints/plain, scalloped edge, 72x81" ...275.00
Dresden Plate, mc on wht, 1930s, wear on binding, 70x90" 395.00
Dresden Plate, mc prints on muslin, scalloped, 72x88", M 465.00
Drunkard's Path, reds, early, full sz, EX 495.00
Drunkard's Path, rose print on wht, rebound, lt wear, 74x88" 265.00
Drunkard's Path, turkey red/wht, EX quilting, 1900s, 66x88" 350.00
Ducks in Pond, bl & wht, full sz, EX 495.00
Fan, mc prints & unbleached muslin, 1930s, crib sz, 46x66" 135.00
Flower Garden, mc prints, scalloped edge, 1930s, 70x72", EX 350.00
Irish Chain Variation, yel prints/blk, 1930s, 65x76", EX 495.00
LeMoyne Star, dk mc prints w/pk border, 1880s, 68x78", EX 500.00
LeMoyne Star Variation, calicos/wht, 1880s, 84x78", EX 435.00
Lightening, wine/dk bl/blk/red, EX quilting, 1880s, 74x88" 450.00
Little Stars, blk/wine/bl/mc prints on wht, 1930s, 66x82", NM ..265.00
Log Cabin, bl & mc prints, 1930s, EX quilting, lg, EX 395.00
Log Cabin, mc prints of 1880s to 1920s era, 72x78", NM 600.00

Log Cabin, mc prints/red sqs & octagons, fragile, 80x89" 350.00
Log Cabin, red/wht/bl, 1900s, crib sz 195.00
Log Cabin, wool & silk, old pressed method, lg, EX 475.00
Log Cabin-Courthouse Steps Variation, calico, 1900s, 80x65" ...495.00
Lone Star, goldenrod/olive gr on red & gr, fragile/faded 2,200.00
Lone Star, lt to dk purple shades, lt wear, lg 500.00
Lone Star, muted prints, dbl triangle border, 1900s, lg, EX 450.00
Lone Star, yel/mauve/bl, 1880s, 68x72", EX 325.00
Maple Leaf, gr/gold/brn, ca 1900, lg 275.00
Mill Wheel, lt purple/gingham/calicos, 1910s, 76x86, EX 250.00
Missouri Star, mc prints/gold on wht, 1930s, 74x88", EX 265.00
Monkey Wrench, bl calico/wht, muslin bk, hs, 70x78", EX 325.00
Monkey Wrench, homespun bk, corners cut for posts, VG 250.00
Ocean Waves, mc on pk ground, ca 1900, lg, EX 450.00
Ocean Waves, mc prints/feedsacks/wht, 1930s, full sz, EX 465.00
Ohio Star, bls, ltweight, full sz, EX 450.00
Pickle Dish, mc, ca 1900, lg, EX 325.00
Pieced Basket, mc calico/wht, shell quilting, 1880s, 76x80", M ..465.00
Pinwheel, mixed prints on wht, full sz, EX 215.00
Pinwheel, 4-color w/lav dbl border, 1930s, 70x84", EX 350.00
Seven Sisters, mc prints, yel/orange sashing, 1930s, 76x94" 450.00
Single Irish Chain, orange on muslin, ltweight, 70x75", EX 275.00
Star, corners w/star, pk/wht calico, wear, 20x30" 375.00
Steeple Chase, indigo bl on muslin, red binding, 1880s, 62x76" ...575.00
Steps Around the World, red/blk/bl, 1880s, 66x78", EX 525.00
Sunbonnet Girl, prints & pk strips, 1930s, 76x94", EX 395.00
Sunshine & Shadow, mc prints & solids, 1930s, 89x99", NM 695.00
Texas Star, mc prints/yel/bl, hs, 1930s, 76x98", NM 595.00
Tree of Life, mc prints on wht w/rose blocks, 1880s, 72x72" 695.00
Tulip Basket, mc prints on wht w/lav blocks, 1930s, 72x82" 465.00
Tumbling Blocks, mc prints, 62x65" 595.00
Tumbling Blocks, mc silks, crib sz, 36x47", VG 395.00
Turkey Track, wine/gold tracks on wht, 1880s, 72x82", NM 695.00
Variable Star, pk & bl w/red & wht, EX quilting, 70x84", EX 495.00
Wagon Wheel, mc prints on tan, 1920s, 70x80", NM 500.00
Wild Goose Chase, cream/bl/burgundy, full sz, EX 495.00
Windmill Blade, 4-color on muslin w/peach edge, '30s, 70x76" ..395.00
Windmill Variant, bl/red/orange/gr/wht, EX hs, 70x90", EX 495.00
1-Patch, brn/turq/red, rose sateen border/bk, heavy, lg, EX 495.00
1-Patch, prints & solids, EX quilting, crib sz, 34x42", NM 250.00
4-Patch, pk/wht calico alternating w/brn sqs, ms binding 400.00
9-Patch, dk bls, EX quilting, navy/maroon border, 1950s, lg 350.00
9-Patch, lav/pk/bl/wht prints, 1920s, 78x95", EX 350.00

Quimper

Quimper is a type of pottery produced in Quimper, France. A tin enamel-glazed earthenware pottery with hand-painted decoration, it was first produced in the 1600s by the Bousquet and Caussy Factories. Little of this early ware was marked. By the late 1700s three factories were operating in the area, all manufacturing the same type of pottery. The Grande Maison de HB, a company formed as a result of a marriage joining the Hubaudiere and Bousquet families, was a major producer of Quimper pottery. They marked their wares with various forms of the 'HB' logo; of the pottery they produced, collectors value examples marked with the 'HB' within a triangle most highly.

Francois Eloury established another pottery in Quimper in the late 1700s. Under the direction of Charles Porquier, the ware was marked simply 'P.' Adolph Porquier replaced Charles in the 1850s, marking the ware produced during that period with an 'AP' logo. 'PB' (for Porquier-Beau) was used ca 1875 until 1900.

Jule HenRiot began operations in 1886, using molds he had purchased from Porquier. His mark was 'HR,' and until the 20th century

he was in competition with The Grande Maison de HB. In 1926 he began to mark his wares 'HenRiot Quimper.' In 1968 the two factories merged. They are still in operation under the name Les Faenceries de Quimper. The factory sold in the fall of 1983 to Sarah and Paul Janssens from the United States, making it the first time the owners were not French. For those interested in learning more about Quimper, we recommend *Quimper Pottery: A French Folk Art Faience* by Sandra V. Bondhus, our advisor for this category, whose address can be found in the Directory under Connecticut.

Basket, biniou player, lady spinning flax, HBQ, 6¼" 300.00
Bell, dinner; lg bl stylized rose & red buds, unmk, 4" 25.00
Bell, man on rock/strutting rooster, HBQ, 1904, 3½x3" 175.00
Bowl, Breton lady, scalloped rim, HRQ, 4x12" 300.00
Bowl, Panier aux Fleurs (flower basket), HBQ, 3¼x9½", EX 50.00
Box, bonboniere; boys & toy boat, PB, 19th C, 2½x4½" sq 975.00
Box, Breton musicians, decor riche, shield shape, HRQ, 7x7" 575.00
Box, powder; lady seated on rock, floral sides, HQF, 3½" 170.00
Cake plate, man w/walking stick, flat, hdls, unmk, 12" 160.00
Candlestick, man & lady, croisille panels, HRQ, 8½", pr 275.00
Chamberstick, man on rock w/pipe, canted corners, HBQ 200.00
Clock, Breton musicians, inverted heart form, HB, 1800s, 7" ..1,900.00
Compote, Breton lady & soldier, ped ft, HB, 5½x10¼" 350.00
Cup, dejeuner; man & lady, HB, 1880s, +9¼" oval plate 195.00
Cup & saucer, Breton lady/floral garland, trefoil shape, AP 130.00
Cup & saucer, Breton man & lady in panels, hexagonal, HRQ ..125.00
Figurine, St Marie w/Christ Child, ca 1875-1904, 13" 250.00
Inkwell, man & lady, heart form, HRQ, NM 230.00
Jardiniere, swan figual, medallion on breast, HRQ, 6½x8" 245.00

Odetta art pottery, Box: 8-pointed star design with Art Deco portrait, 6" diameter, $300.00; Vase: stoneware gray-blue glaze with three black sgraffito portrait repetitions, 7", $300.00.

Pitcher, Breton lady, florals at sides, HQF, 6" 95.00
Pitcher, Lys pattern (fleur-de-lis), HB, 3" 110.00
Pitcher, man w/pipe, 4-lobed, HBQ, 5" 95.00
Plate, armorial design, Crest of Brittany, HB, 19th C, 9⅛" 300.00
Plate, Billiard au Touliguen (title), couple, Malicorne, 9½" 300.00
Plate, Bleuets pattern (bl floral), scalloped, unmk, 9" 50.00
Plate, Breton lady w/basket, Brittany crest, PB, 19th C, 9¼" ...1,000.00
Plate, exotic bird on branch, mc, HQ, rstr, 8" 25.00
Plate, man w/walking stick & knapsack, PB, 19th C, 9½" 925.00
Plate, mc floral pattern, mc banded rim, 1860-80, 9½" 125.00
Plate, Panier aux Fleurs pattern, mc, HBQ, 9" 225.00
Platter, Bleuets pattern (bl floral), HBQ, 11x8¼" 130.00
Platter, Breton fisherman & lady at well, unmk, 1800s, 19½" ...1,000.00
Platter, Breton wedding scene w/9 people, HBQ, 17½x13" 1,200.00
Platter, fish; Breton couple & florals, HQ, 21x9¼" 550.00
Snuff bottle, crowing rooster, book form, late 1800s, 3" 185.00

Sweetmeat, birch/spruce/pine on lt bl, Botanical, PB, 6x6½" **725.00**
Teacup & saucer, man w/walking stick & pipe, HBQ, 2½" **55.00**
Teapot, man & lady, dolphin hdl & spout, HRQ, 7½x10¼" **375.00**
Teapot, peasant lady w/distaff, HRQ, 5¼" **275.00**
Tray, floral w/emb flower center, 6-lobed, PB, 19th C, 18" **2,450.00**
Tureen, mc floral, child's, HBQ, 5¼x8" **75.00**
Vase, Breton couple, fan form, HB, 1800s, 6x10½", NM **400.00**
Vase, Breton man & lady, fleur-de-lis form, HB, 7x6½" **500.00**
Vase, bud; Breton lady, horn shape, HBQ, 9½" **110.00**
Vase, cornucopia; man w/walking stick & pipe, HB, 4½" **75.00**
Vase, man w/walking stick, fleur-de-lis form, HR, rstr, 8x7" **375.00**
Wall pocket, Breton lady, cornucopia form, HQF, 10¾" **135.00**
Wall pocket, dbl, man & lady, cornucopia form, HBQ, 6" **100.00**

Radford

Pottery associated with Albert Radford (1882-1904) can be categorized by three periods of production. Pottery produced in Tiffin, Ohio, (1896-1899) consists of high-quality jasperware with applied Wedgwood-like cameos; this ware is often impressed 'Radford Jasper' in small block letters. At Zanesville, Ohio, Radford jasperware was marked only with an incised, two-digit shape number, and the cameos were not applied but rather formed within the mold and filled with a white slip. Zanesville Radford ware was produced for only a few months before the Radford pottery was acquired by the Arc-en-Ciel company in 1903. Production in Zanesville was handled by Radford's father, Edward (1840-1910), who remained in Zanesville after Albert moved to Clarksburg, West Virginia, where the Radford Pottery Co. was completed shortly before Albert's death in 1904. Jasperware was not produced in Clarksburg, and the molds appear to have been left in Zanesville, where some were subsequently used by the Arc-en-Ciel pottery. The Clarksburg, West Virginia, pottery produced a standard glaze, slip-decorated ware, Ruko (often signed by Albert Haubrich, Alice Bloomer, and other artists) and Radura, a semimatt green glaze developed by Albert Radford's son, Edward. The Clarksburg plant closed in 1912. Our advisor for this category is James L. Murphy; he is listed in the Directory under Ohio.

Bowl, muses, vintage, bl, fluted rim, imp mk **295.00**
Candlestick, Ruko, floral, brn streaked, imp mk, 6" **125.00**
Ewer, grapes/blkberries, lt bl, face on hdl, #17, 9" **285.00**
Jardiniere, Radura, papyrus leaves, matt pea gr, imp mk, 10" **150.00**
Pitcher, lady at censer, bl-gr, imp Radford Jasper, 6" **270.00**
Tankard, vintage, lt bl, #28, 12" **200.00**
Vase, bust of Gladstone, lt bl, twisted, #56, 5" **150.00**
Vase, cherubs w/instruments, tan, brn bark, #14, 8" **150.00**
Vase, lady w/dog, bk: Roman kneels, bark trim, #18, 7" **275.00**
Vase, Radura, matt gr, 4-hdl, imp mk, 9" **225.00**
Vase, Thera, gr bsk w/pk floral, 8", NM **160.00**

Radios

Vintage radios are becoming very collectible. There were thousands of styles and types produced, the most popular of which today are the breadboard and the cathedral. Consoles are usually considered less saleable, since their size makes them hard to display and store. For those wishing to learn more about antique radios, we recommend *The Collector's Guide to Antique Radios* by Sue and Marty Bunis, available from your local bookstore or Collector Books.

Key:
tbl/m — table model   phono — phonograph

Addison 5F, Catalin, 1940, $1,000.00.

Adler #325, wood, stretcher base, console, 1930, NM **135.00**
Admiral #4P28, turq, thumbwheel knob, transistor, 1957, EX **35.00**
Admiral #5R11, plastic, checked grill, tbl/m, 1949, NM **30.00**
Admiral #9E15, wood, fold-down phono door, console, 1949 ....**75.00**
Air Castle #5036, wood, lift top, phono, tbl/m, '49, NM **28.00**
Air Castle G-722, wood, phono drw, console, '48, EX **70.00**
Air King, A-604, wood, slanted dial, louvers, 1950, M **30.00**
Air-Way G, wood, 3-dial, 5-tube, tbl/m, 1923, EX **175.00**
Airline #5D8-1, plastic, louvers, hdls, tbl/m, EX **35.00**
Airline #62-553, wood, Deco cutouts on grill, tbl/m, EX **75.00**
Apex #60, walnut, petal cuts on grill, console, 1928, NM **110.00**
Arvin #402, walnut metal, midget tbl/m, 1939, EX **65.00**
Arvin #746P, plastic, metal lattice grill, portable, '53, EX **60.00**
Atwater Kent #535, wood, cloth grill w/bars, console, '36, EX ...**115.00**
Atwater Kent #60, window dial w/escutcheon, console, '29, EX ...**125.00**
Atwater Kent #84D, Cathedral, wood, Gothic cutouts, '31, NM ..**350.00**
Automatic #458, wood, tapered cylinder, tbl/m, 1939, EX **75.00**
Automatic #720, wood, crisscross grill, tbl/m, 1947, NM **42.50**
Belmont #8A59, wood, phono in drw, console, 1946, NM **70.00**
Bendix #526C, gr & blk Catalin, tbl/m, 1946, EX **500.00**
Bendix #55P3, walnut plastic, rear handhold, tbl/m, '49, EX **40.00**
Bremer-Tully #7-71, wood, highboy, cutouts, console, 1928, EX ...**150.00**
Brunswick #11, wood, shouldered case, upright tbl/m, 1931, NM ..**150.00**
Capeheart #115P2, wood, lift top/woven grill, console, '49, EX **225.00**
Channel Master #6518, plastic, transistor, portable, '60, M **50.00**
Clarion C103, plastic, cloth grill, tbl/m, 1946, EX **35.00**
Cleartone #82, wood, drop front, 5 tubes, console, 1925, NM **150.00**
Continental TR-300, transistor, portable, 1960, M **25.00**
Coronado #675, Tombstone, airplane dial, 1934, EX **75.00**
Crosley #11, plastic, wraparound louvers, tbl/m, EX **35.00**
Crosley #59 Show Boy, Cathedral, ornate case, 1931, NM **225.00**
Crosley #6H2, Tombstone, wood, cloth grill, 1933, NM **100.00**
Crosley E15TN, plastic, perforated grill, tbl/m, 1953, EX **65.00**
Deforest D-6, wood, rectangular, battery, tbl/m, 1922, NM **1,100.00**
Detrola #383, cloth covered, sq dial, portable, 1941, NM **30.00**
Dumont RA-354 Beachcomber, leather case, portable, 1957, EX .**30.00**
Echophone #6, Cathedral, wood, lyre cut-out grill, EX **155.00**
Emerson #368, walnut, upper dial, console, 1940, EX **110.00**
Emerson #713, wood, sunburst front, rayed grill, tbl/m, NM **65.00**
Emerson CV-289, wood, lift top, phono, tbl/m, 1939, M **35.00**
Eveready #32, wood, ornate panel w/window, console, 1929, EX....**155.00**
Fada #602, wood, lower grill, phono, tbl/m, 1947, EX **22.50**
Fada PL50, wood, sq dial, lift top, phono, tbl/m, '39, NM **30.00**
Federal #144, wood, lowboy, 5 tubes/battery, console, EX **350.00**
Firestone #4-A-89, plastic, half-moon dial, tbl/m, '50, NM **30.00**

General Electric #113, plastic, half-moon dial, tbl/m, EX **30.00**
General Electric #507, plastic, alarm clock, tbl/m, '50, EX **40.00**
General Electric K-43, Cathedral, wood, low case, 1933, NM **165.00**
General Electric M-81, Tombstone, wood, 5 knobs, 1934, EX ...**145.00**
Globe #456, leatherette, battery, portable, 1948, EX **15.00**
Hallicrafters #5R61, ivory plastic, checked grill, tbl/m, EX **30.00**
Howard #20, Cathedral, wood, center window dial, 7 tubes, EX ...**250.00**
Knight #5H-570, plastic, rnd dial, tbl/m, 1951, NM **25.00**
Majestic #167, Tombstone, wood, rnd dial, cloth grill, '39, M **95.00**
Majestic #5M1, plastic, rnd dial w/eagle, portable, 1955, NM **35.00**
Motorola #5H12, plastic, rnd dial, 2 knobs, tbl/m, 1952, M **30.00**
Motorola #66T1, transistor, lg hdl, portable, 1958, NM **28.00**
Olympic #7-925, wood, pull-out phono drw, console, 1948, NM .**65.00**
Philco #37-34, Cathedral, rnd dial, 5 tubes, console, '37, EX **80.00**
Philco #40-124, wood, Deco cutouts on grill, tbl/m, 1940, M **50.00**
Philco #42-340, 2-tone wood, 4 knobs, tbl/m, 1942, NM **48.00**
Philco #50-526 Transitone, maroon plastic, tbl/m, 1950, EX **35.00**
Philco PT-61 Transitone, 2-tone wood, Deco, tbl/m, 1940, NM ..**50.00**

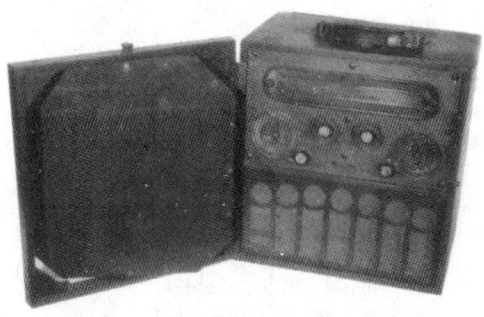

Radiola 26, portable, walnut case, 1925, $350.00.

Raytheon T-100-5, ivory/gray plastic, transistor, portable, EX **75.00**
RCA #45X1, brn plastic, front dial, tbl/m, 1940, NM **42.50**
RCA #6K2, wood, cloth grill, 6 tubes, console, EX **100.00**
RCA #8-X-541, maroon plastic w/brass strip, tbl/m, 1949, NM **35.00**
RCA C1E, plastic, rnd dial, clock, tbl/m, 1959, NM **17.50**
RCA Radiola II, mahog, 2-dial panel, portable, 1923, EX **250.00**
RCA Radiola #33, metal, Deco style, console, 1929, NM **200.00**
Regal #271, plastic, half-moon dial, tbl/m, 1953, EX **22.50**
Sentinel #168BT, walnut, slide-rule dial, battery, tbl/m, NM **38.00**
Sentinel #344, plastic, half-moon dial, tbl/m, 1953, NM **45.00**
Silvertone #1905, Tombstone, wood, 9 tubes, EX **100.00**
Silvertone #1954, Tombstone, wood, rnd dial, cloth grill, EX **70.00**
Silvertone #220, plastic, checkered grill, portable, '50, NM **32.00**
Silvertone #6002, metal, louvers, midget tbl/m, 1946, EX **60.00**
Silvertone #8020, plastic w/metal grill, tbl/m, 1948, NM **35.00**
Sonora PL-29 Playboy, cloth cover, sq case, portable, 1939, NM **35.00**
Sparton #401 Junior, wood, upright tbl/m, 1930, EX **195.00**
Sparton #53, wood, rnd dial, 5 tubes, tbl/m, EX **60.00**
Steelman #450, plastic, rnd dial, alarm clock, tbl/m, 1952, M **25.00**
Steelman #517, suitcase-style, phono, tbl/m, 1952, M **20.00**
Stewart-Warner #9000B, wood, slant dial, tbl/m, 1947, EX **35.00**
Stromberg-Carlson #1400, plastic, raised top, tbl/m, '49, M **48.00**
Stromberg-Carlson #255L, wood, tuning eye, 13-tube console, EX..**165.00**
Stromberg-Carlson #50M, wood, lowboy, cloth grill, console, M .**140.00**
Temple G-515, wood, slant dial, cloth grill, tbl/m, '47, EX **30.00**
Trav-ler, #131, walnut, cloth grill, 11 tubes, console, NM **135.00**
Trav-ler #5010, wood, front dial, cloth grill, tbl/m, NM **35.00**
Truetone D2483, plastic, slide rule dial, tbl/m, 1954, EX **30.00**
Truetone D3490, plastic, battery, portable, 1955, NM **30.00**

Universal #72A6, Tombstone, wood, rnd dial, battery, EX **65.00**
Western Electric #4B, wood, rectangular, tbl/m, 1923, EX **385.00**
Westinghouse H-169, wood, pull-out phono, console, EX **100.00**
Westinghouse H-312P4, plastic, slide-rule dial, portable, M **35.00**
Westinghouse H-486T5, ivory plastic, clock face, tbl/m, NM **27.50**
Westinghouse WR-21, wood, cloth grill, 5 tubes, tbl/m, M **62.50**
Wurlitzer Lyric M-4-L, wood, wraparound louvers, tbl/m, EX **50.00**
Zenith #40-A, wood, ornate cvg, console, 1929, NM **575.00**
Zenith #5-G-40 Transoceanic, leatherette, portable, 1950, NM ...**75.00**
Zenith #5-R-236W, bone wht, storage, chair-side, 1937, NM **115.00**
Zenith #5-S-137 Zephyr, Tombstone, wood, blk dial, 1936, EX ...**155.00**
Zenith #6-D-219Y, ebony, Deco style, tbl/m, 1937, EX **55.00**
Zenith #6-D-520W, plastic, blk dial, 6 tubes, tbl/m, NM **40.00**
Zenith #7-S-547, wood, blk dial, castors, chair-side, EX **135.00**
Zenith B-600 Transoceanic, leatherette, portable, EX **65.00**
Zenith Royal #1000, fold-down front, transistor, portable, M **135.00**
Zephyr #41X6, walnut w/inlay, 5 tubes, tbl/m, 1937, EX **45.00**

Novelty

Archer Radar Patrol, for bike, Hong Kong, 3x4¾", NM **15.00**
California Raisin Man, posable arms, CalRab, 1988, M **32.50**
Dice, red/wht plastic, Sanyo RP 1711, 3¼" sq, NM **17.50**
Football helmet, Radio Shack Sales, Tandy, Korea, 5⅛" **15.00**
Garfield, plastic, United Features Syndicate, 3¾x4", EX **25.00**
Grand piano, 10 keys, Newtone LT-291, Hong Kong, EX **18.00**
Hand grenade, metal base & trigger (lighter), Japan, 5", EX **35.00**
Helping Hand, nose volume control, Hong Kong, 6½", M **40.00**
McDonald's french fries, plastic, Hong Kong, 6x4½", EX **15.00**
Melody coins, bank/coin-op radio, wood/metal, Japan, 4x6¼", M ...**20.00**
Mercedez Benz sedan, plastic, Hong Kong, 8½" L, NM **28.00**
Mobil Premier Poly car battery, Hong Kong, 3⅞x4x4", EX **15.00**
Monkey head, button eyes, Internat'l, Hong Kong, NM **20.00**
Overland Stage Express, plastic/brass, Japan, 7¼" L, NM **45.00**
Snoopy on doghouse, plastic, United Features Syndicate, M **42.50**
Telephone, candlestick, blk plastic, Tandy, 9x4", NM **27.50**
Telephone, crank style, wood/brass plate, Japan, 11¾x9", EX **22.50**
Tombstone radio, JVC JR12D, Japan, 5½x4¼", EX **30.00**
Union automatic pistol, 2 transistors, Hong Kong, 5x7", NM **88.00**
Wurlitzer 1015 juke box, Beetland, 1986, 7¼", MIB **60.00**

Railroadiana

Collecting railroad-related memorabilia has become one of America's most popular hobbies. The range of collectible items available is almost endless, considering the fact that more than 175 different railroad lines are represented. Some collectors prefer to specialize in only one, while others attempt to collect at least one item from every railway line known to have existed. For the advanced collector, there is the challenge of locating rarities from short-lived railroads; for the novice, there are abundant keys, buttons, passes, and playing cards. Among the most popular specializations are dining-car collectibles — flatware, glassware, dinnerware, etc., in a wide variety of patterns and styles.

For a more thorough study, we recommend *Railroad Collectibles, Third Revised Edition*, by Stanley L. Baker, available at your local library or bookstore. Because prices are so volatile, the best pricing sources are often monthly or quarterly 'For Sale' lists. Two you may find helpful may be ordered from Golden Spike, P.O. Box 422, Williamsville, NY 14221, and Grandpa's Depot and Caboose, P.O. Box 480030, Denver, CO 80248-0030. Our advice for the dinnerware section comes from Shrader's Antiques (see Directory, California), while Grandpa's Depot (see Colorado) advises us for the remainder.

Key:

BL — bottom logo   SL — side logo
BS — bottom stamped   SM — side marked
NBS — no bottom stamp   TL — top logo
R&B — Reed and Barton   TM — top marked

Dinnerware

Ashtray, C&O, Chessie, 3¾" dia 65.00
Ashtray, C&O, Geo Washington, 3¾" dia 85.00
Ashtray, C&O, Geo Washington, 7x3" 95.00
Ashtray, GN, Mountains & Flowers, BS, 4" sq 95.00
Ashtray, MP, cobalt, 5x4½" 85.00
Bowl, baker; ACL, Flora of the South, oval, BS, 4x6" 110.00
Bowl, baker; B&O, Derby, oval, BS, 4x6" 38.00
Bowl, baker; WP, Feather River, oval, 4½x6" 145.00
Bowl, berry; ACL, Flora of the South, BS 75.00
Bowl, berry; CRI&P, Golden Rocket, NBS 135.00
Bowl, berry; NYNH&H, Platinum Blue, BS 70.00
Bowl, berry; PRR, Purple Laurel, BS 45.00
Bowl, berry; SP, Prairie Mountain Wildflowers 65.00
Bowl, bouillon; CMStP&P, Traveler, NBS, w/lid 95.00
Bowl, cereal; ATSF, Adobe, TL 40.00
Bowl, cereal; B&O, Capitol, NBS 45.00
Bowl, cereal; CB&Q, Violets & Daisies, NBS 22.00
Bowl, cereal; CMStP&P, Traveler, NBS 45.00
Bowl, cereal; Pullman, Indian Tree, TM 95.00
Bowl, cereal; UP, Desert Flower, BS 45.00
Bowl, salad; ATSF, Mimbreno, BS, 9" 285.00
Bowl, salad; MP, Eagle, BS, 8" 420.00
Bowl, salad; SL&SF, Denmark, NBS, 8¼" 95.00
Bowl, soup; B&O, Centenary, BS, 9" 165.00
Bowl, soup; CMStP&P, Galatea, NBS, 9½" 90.00
Bowl, soup; MStP&SSM, Logan, NBS, 9" 85.00
Bowl, soup; Pullman, Indian Tree, TM, 9" 255.00
Bowl, soup; SP, Harriman Blue, BS, 9" 55.00
Bowl, soup; UP, Desert Flower, BS, 9" 55.00
Bowl, soup; UP, Harriman Blue, TM, 9" 85.00
Bowl, vegetable; B&O, Centenary, oval, BS, 4x5½" 110.00
Bowl, vegetable; SP, Sunset, oval, BS, 4x5½" 110.00
Bowl, vegetable; UP, Harriman Blue, oval, 4½x6" 50.00
Butter pat, ATSF, Black Chain, NBS 40.00
Butter pat, B&O, Capitol, NBS 95.00
Butter pat, B&O, Centenary, Shenango, BS 32.00
Butter pat, CMStP&P, Galatea, NBS 110.00
Butter pat, CMStP&P, Peacock, NBS 85.00
Butter pat, CRI&P, LaSalle, NBS 125.00
Butter pat, FEC, Mistic, NBS 38.00
Butter pat, GN, Empire, NBS 110.00
Butter pat, NYNH&H, Platinum Blue, BS 100.00
Butter pat, PRR, Purple Laurel, BS 48.00
Butter pat, Pullman, Calumet 175.00
Butter pat, SP, Prairie Mountain Wildflowers, NBS 95.00
Butter pat, UP, Portland Rose, NBS 195.00
Chocolate pot, B&O, Centenary, BS 275.00
Compote, ACL, Flora of the South, ped ft, BS 325.00
Compote, C&NW, Depot Ornaments, ped ft, NBS 175.00
Compote, NYC, DeWitt Clinton, ped ft, BS 235.00
Creamer, ATSF, California Poppy, hdl, NBS, 3" 150.00
Creamer, ATSF, Mimbreno, hdl, BS, 3¼" 195.00
Creamer, BR&P, Ontario, no hdl, NBS, 3" 250.00
Creamer, FEC, Sea Horse, no hdl, NBS, 3¼" 30.00
Creamer, Fred Harvey, Trend, no hdl, 3¼" 35.00

Creamer, Pullman, Indian Tree, hdl, NBS, 3½" 95.00
Creamer, SP, Sunset, hdl, BS, 3¾" 165.00
Cup & saucer, B&O, Centenary, BS 100.00
Cup & saucer, C&O, Chessie, NBS 110.00
Cup & saucer, CN, Continental, BS 45.00
Cup & saucer, demitasse; B&O, Centenary, BS 65.00
Cup & saucer, demitasse; CMStP&P, Traveler, NBS 95.00
Cup & saucer, demitasse; CN, Queen Elizabeth, NBS 75.00
Cup & saucer, demitasse; D&RGW, Prospector, NBS 150.00
Cup & saucer, demitasse; NYC, Platinum Blue, BS 365.00
Cup & saucer, Fred Harvey, cactus logo, NBS 75.00
Cup & saucer, GN, Mountains & Flowers, NBS 95.00
Cup & saucer, Kansas City System, Flying Crow, NBS 450.00
Cup & saucer, N&W, Coach & Four, NBS 125.00
Cup & saucer, SL&SF, Denmark, NBS 55.00
Cup & saucer, UP, Desert Flower, BS 110.00
Egg cup, dbl; FEC, Mistic, lg 35.00
Egg cup, dbl; GN, Oriental, NBS, lg 82.00
Egg cup, dbl; MKT, Katy Ornaments, NBS, lg 85.00
Egg cup, GTW, City of Grand Rapids, NBS, sm 250.00
Egg cup, WP, Feather River, NBS, sm 250.00
Gravy boat, B&O, Capitol, NBS 165.00
Gravy boat, C&O, Geo Washington, NBS 75.00
Gravy boat, NYC, DeWitt Clinton, NBS 65.00
Gravy boat, UP, Blue & Gold, NBS 30.00
Gravy boat, WP, Feather River, NBS 285.00
Hot food cover, ATSF, Mimbreno, BS 250.00
Hot food cover, CMStP&P, Galatea, NBS 175.00
Mustard pot, ATSF, Black Chain, NBS, w/lid, 3" 55.00
Mustard pot, C&NW, Flambeau, NBS, w/lid, 3" 52.00
Mustard pot, C&O, Staffordshire, BS, w/lid, 3" 185.00
Mustard pot, N&W, Coach & Four, NBS, w/lid, 3" 150.00
Mustard pot, SAL, Seaboard, NBS, w/lid, 3¼" 325.00
Pitcher, ATSF, Griffon, NBS, 7" 125.00
Pitcher, CP, Bows & Leaves, BS, 6½" 75.00
Pitcher, GM&O, Rose, NBS, 5¾" 275.00
Plate, Alaska, McKinley, NBS, 5½" 285.00
Plate, ATSF, Adobe, TL, 9½" 75.00
Plate, ATSF, Bleeding Blue, TL, 9" 225.00
Plate, B&O, Centenary, BS, 9" 88.00

Plate, Chessie, CB & Q, 9¾", $150.00.
(Beware of reproductions.)

Plate, CN, Continental, BS, 9" 42.00
Plate, CRI&P, Golden Rocket, NBS, 6" 160.00

Plate, D&RGW, Prospector, NBS, 9" 100.00
Plate, Fred Harvey, Webster, NBS, 8½" 60.00
Plate, GN, Oriental, NBS, 9½" 85.00
Plate, NYC, Mercury, BS, 10" 110.00
Plate, PRR, Gotham, BS, 10½" 88.00
Plate, PRR, Mountain Laurel, BS, 9½" 55.00
Plate, SP, Prairie Mountain Wildflowers, BS, 6½" 45.00
Plate, UP, Challenger, NBS, 6½" 42.00
Plate, UP, Portland Rose, BS, 8½" 250.00
Plate, WP, Feather River, NBS, 6½" 65.00
Plate, WP, Feather River, NBS, 9¾" 250.00
Platter, Alaska RR, McKinley, NBS, 7x5½" 375.00
Platter, ATSF, Adobe, NBS, 7x5½" 60.00
Platter, Erie, Gould, NBS, 9x6" 110.00
Platter, FEC, Starucca, NBS, 9x6" 85.00
Platter, Flora of the South, BS, 7" sq 175.00
Platter, GN, Hill, NBS, 9x6" 175.00
Platter, GN, Mountains & Flowers, BS, 9x7" 55.00
Platter, N&W, Cavalier, NBS, 14x10" 85.00
Platter, NP, Yellowstone, NBS, 7½x6" 65.00
Platter, NYNH&H, Old Saybrook, NBS, 9x6" 75.00
Platter, PRR, Broadway, NBS, 8½x6" 45.00
Platter, Reading, Stotesbury, BS, 8½x6½" 135.00
Platter, SAL, Miami, NBS, 12½x8½" 325.00
Platter, SP, Prairie Mountain Wildflowers, BS, 9½x7½" 95.00
Platter, UP, Columbine, NBS, 8¼x6" 145.00
Platter, UP, Winged Streamliner, NBS, 8x5½" 45.00
Platter, WP, Feather River, NBS, 9x6½" 85.00
Relish, ATSF, Mimbreno, BS, 9½x4¼" 165.00
Relish, B&O, Centenary, NBS, 12x6" 175.00
Relish, C&O, Train Ferry, NBS, 9½x4½" 45.00
Relish, CB&Q, Aristocrat, NBS, 9½x4½" 190.00
Relish, L&N, Green Leaf, NBS, 7½x4" 32.00
Relish, NP, Monad, NBS, 7½x4" 185.00
Relish, SR, Piedmont, BS, 7½x4" 18.00
Sherbet, ATSF, Mimbreno, ped ft 65.00
Sherbet, B&O, Derby, ped ft, BS 95.00
Teapot, ATSF, California Poppy, NBS 110.00
Teapot, ATSF, Griffon, NBS 350.00
Teapot, Pullman, Verde Green, SL 225.00
Toothpick holder, SL&SF, Denmark, NBS, 2" 32.00

Glassware

Ashtray, Erie in bl/wht w/in dmn logo, 3½" 15.00
Ashtray, L&N, red center logo, 6-sided, 4½", EX 15.00
Ashtray, NP, red/blk Monad center on clear, sq, EX 15.00
Ashtray, NP, red/blk Monad w/Yellowstone Park Line, 4½" 20.00
Ashtray, SF, wht center logo on clear, oval, 5¼" L 17.50
Ashtray, SP&S, red center oval on clear, 4" dia 20.00
Bottle, milk; Mopac, buzz saw logo, qt 55.00
Bottle, milk; MP, buzz saw logo, ½-pt 25.00
Cordial, NP, etched Yellowstone Park logo, 3¾" 50.00
Cordial, NYC, oval logo 24.00
Highball, Southern Ry, gr & wht diesel, gold rim, 3¼" 8.00
Roly poly, EL, dtd 1969, 2¾" 7.50
Roly poly, PRR, Keystone logo & train 10.00
Shot glass, UP, frosted shield & wht stripe, 2½" 10.00
Shot glass, UP, name in wht, 2½" 13.00
Tumbler, Erie, red #, logo, dtd 1969, water sz 17.50
Tumbler, Frisco, bl bearskin, 6-oz 8.00
Tumbler, PRR, Tuscan red/wht train & buildings, 4⅜" 8.50
Tumbler, SR, diesel engine & Southern Serves South, 3½" 12.50
Tumbler, UP, shield logo, ped ft, 5½" 12.50

Tumbler, UP, shield logo, str sides, 4½" 9.00
Whiskey, Pullman, logo inside bottom 27.50
Wine, IC, frosted dmn logo, stemmed 16.50
Wine, SF, Santa Fe in script, 4½" 24.00

Lamps

Berth, Pullman, aluminum, milk glass shade, 1950s, EX 50.00
Caboose, SPCo, wall type, worn silver pnt, pitting, 16", G 20.00
Crossing, RACo, wht metal, orig blk pnt, 4½", VG 35.00
Depot, RI, CI, desk top, fancy base, brass tab at top, VG 150.00
Hand, ICRR, Adlake #31-B, battery op, yel pnt, EX 17.50
Highway, KCPSCo on lid, 8-day type, sq base, red globe, VG 15.00
Inspector's, Dietz Ideal, clear Vesta 4½" globe, VG 65.00
Inspector's, SP, Dietz Acme, glass reflector, sm dents, VG 40.00
Marker, B&O, Handlan, 1 red/3 aqua lenses, VG, pr 150.00
Marker, NYC East, Dressel, 2 clear lenses, electric, EX 115.00
Semaphore, GN, Adlake, oil, w/fuel pot, clear lens 132.50
Switch, Adlake, oil, red/wht lenses, complete, EX 185.00

Lanterns

Before 1920 kerosene brakemen's lanterns were made with tall globes, usually 5⅜" tall. These are the most desirable and are usually found at the top of the price scale. Short globes from 1921 through 1940 normally measure 3½" in height, except for those manufactured by Dietz, which are 4" tall. (Soon thereafter, battery brakemen's lanterns came into widespread useage; these are not popular with collectors and are generally not railroad marked.)

All should be marked with the name or initials of the railroad. Look on the top, the top apron, or the bell base (if it has one). Globes may be found in these colors (listed in order of popularity): clear, red, amber, aqua, cobalt, and two-color.

B&O, Dressel, clear Corning 3¼" globe, Pat 1939, EX 60.00
BR, Handlan 1928P, red unmk 3¼" globe, Badger burner, VG 60.00
C&S, Adlake Kero, unmk red 3¼" globe, Pat 1923, EX 75.00
C&WI, Adlake Kero, clear unmk 3¼" globe, 1947, VG 60.00
D&HCo, Dressel 1913P, clear Corning 5⅜" globe, EX 60.00
L&N, Adlake Kero, unmk short clear globe, NM 60.00

Nickel-plated presentation lantern, '3rd Asst Engineer BFD' etched on clear fixed globe, marked J.E. Ambroll Mfg., ca 1870, 13½", $2,400.00.

N&S, Keystone Casey, unmk 5⅜" globe, Pat 1903, EX 150.00
N&W, Armspear, clear unmk 5⅜" globe, Handlan burner, 1913 ...150.00
NYNH&H, Adlake Reliable, clear mk 5⅜" globe, Pat 1913 ....150.00
StL&SF, Adlake #250 Kero, dome top, clear globe, Pat 1923 ....60.00

Linens

Apron, cook's, UP, Overland logo, metal grommets, 34x36", EX ...20.00

Bib, CA Zephyr, blocks & train on yel plastic, EX 10.00
Blanket, Canadian Nat'l, maple leaf logo, Pendleton wool, EX 70.00
Blanket, NP, cross stitch on cinnamon, lg, G 250.00
Blanket, PRR, gray w/appl Keystone logo, minor fading, EX 155.00
Headrest cover, RI, Golden State Route/oranges on tan, EX 17.50
Headrest cover, SF, cross logo, bl on brn, EX 15.00
Napkin, Amtrak, stamped letters, 17x18", EX 5.00
Napkin, Burlington Route, center logo, wht on wht, 20" sq 7.50
Napkin, D&RG, Greek Key design on tan, 20" sq, EX 10.00
Napkin, GN, old logo, wht on wht, 19x22", VG 8.00
Napkin, Milwaukee, center logo, wht on wht, 18" sq, EX 8.50
Napkin, NP, Yellowstone Monad logo, wht on wht, EX 15.00
Napkin, Rio Grande, speed letters, plum on tan, EX 10.00
Napkin, WAB, interwoven flag logo, 22x20", EX 14.00
Pants, cook's, Burlington Route, red logo in waist, wht, EX 7.00
Pants, waiter's, D&RG, wht w/gold stripe down legs, EX 7.50
Pillowcase, Burlington Route, brn logo on wht, EX 5.00
Pillowcase, CA Zephyr, stamped logo, VG 5.00
Sheet, UP, Overland & Pullman stamped on wht, single sz, EX ...15.00
Tablecloth, CN, maple leaf logo, wht, 44x48", EX 10.00
Tablecloth, D&RG, oak leaves/speed letters on wht, 100x62" 15.00
Tablecloth, D&RG, speed letters on wht, 36x36", NM 10.00
Tablecloth, RI, bearskin logo, wht on wht, 32x50", EX 20.00
Tablecloth, SF, script letters, wht on wht, 46x52", EX 30.00
Towel, C&O, bl center stripe on wht, EX 10.00
Towel, CM&STP, bl center stripe, 1920s, EX 14.00
Towel, Lehigh Valley, red center stripe on wht, EX 12.50
Towel, Pullman, bl stripe on wht, EX 12.00
Towel, Reading, bl center stripe on wht, EX 12.50
Towel, UP, red stripes on wht, 22x17", EX 8.00
Towel, 19 Soo Line-Soo Line 23 on bl stripes, 16x20" 15.00
Vest, bartender's, Amtrak, maroon w/mc epaulets, M 15.00

Locks

Brass switch locks (pre-1920) were made in two styles: heart-shaped and Keen Kutter style. Values for the heart-shaped locks are determined to a great extent by the railroad represented and just how its name appears on the lock. Most in demand are those with large embossed letters; if the letters are small and incised, demand is minimal. For instance, one from the Union Pacific line (even with heavy-embossed letters) may go for only $45.00, while the same from the D&RG railroad could easily sell for $250.00. Old Keen Kutter styles (brass with a 'pointy' base) from Colorado & Southern and Denver & Rio Grande could range from $600.00 to $1,200.00.

Steel switch locks (circa 1920 on) with the initials of the railroad incised in small letters — for example BN, L&H, and PRR — are usually valued at $12.00 to $15.00.

Lock, Adlake, steel, 1920-1940, common, depending on railroad, $17.00 to $35.00.

Signal, B&O, steel, sm body, early, EX 15.00
Signal, PR, ET Fraim, brass, EX 75.00
Signal, SR, Adams & Westlake, brass, heart shape, EX 75.00
Signal, UP, Eagle, brass, rnd shape, w/chain & key, NM 50.00
Switch, BN, steel, incised sm letters 15.00
Switch, D&RG, brass, heavy emb letters, heart shape 250.00
Switch, D&RG, brass, old Keen Kutter style (pointy base) 900.00
Switch, L&N, steel, sm incised letters 15.00
Switch, N&W, brass, heart shape, old chain, EX 100.00
Switch, PRR, steel, sm incised letters 15.00
Switch, UP, brass, heavy emb letters, heart shape 45.00

Silverplate

Butter pat, SF, BS, lt wear 18.00
Champagne cooler, B&O, BM, 6½x22" on 6" base, EX 275.00
Change tray, UP, BS, EX 35.00
Coffeepot, Burlington Route, SM, 14-oz 57.50
Coffeepot, Fred Harvey, Deco style, mushroom finial 70.00
Coffeepot, IC, Pompeian, SM, BS, 10-oz 250.00
Coffeepot, NC&StL, appl/emb banner logo, R&B, BS, 2-pt 200.00
Coffeepot, T&P, R&B, BS, 10-oz 175.00
Coffeepot, UP, Challenger, BS 60.00
Compote, ice cream; Pullman, ped ft, 1929 ....48.00
Corn dish, Pullman, Wallace, 8" L 100.00
Corn holder, Pullman, BS, pr 45.00
Creamer, Fred Harvey, Gorham, ⅝-pt, EX 95.00
Creamer, WAB, 1-hdl, BS, 1941, 2-oz 48.00
Crumber, GN, Hutton, w/crumb well, TM 88.00
Crumber, SP, American, BS, EX 65.00
Finger bowl, CA Zephyr, Deco style, BS, 1962 ....78.00
Finger bowl, GN, pierced side, BS, 1946 ....45.00
Fork, cocktail; D&RG, Navarre, Rogers, TM, EX 75.00
Fork, dinner; D&RG, Belmont, R&B, TM, EX 18.00
Fork, dinner; NYC, Century, Internat'l, BS 8.50
Fork, pickle; Fred Harvey, Albany 17.50
Gravy boat, C&NW, BM, 6-oz, EX 50.00
Gravy boat, UP, dtd 1954, 4-oz 65.00
Horseradish holder, CA Zephyr, Internat'l, BS, 1952, EX 155.00
Knife, dinner; Fred Harvey, Albany, BS 18.00
Knife, dinner; GN, Hutton, TM, 1950, EX 18.00
Knife, dinner; GN, intertwined logo, TM, EX 18.00
Knife, dinner; N&W, Cromwell, Internat'l, TM, EX 12.00
Knife, dinner; WAB, Ambassador, Internat'l, 1937, EX 17.50
Knife, fruit; Alaska RR, Greene-Winkler, 1917, EX 27.50
Knife, luncheon; NP, Silhouette, BM, M 18.00
Ladle, soup; D&RG, Navarre, TM, VG 175.00
Ladle, soup; Milwaukee, LaSalle, BS, 7" 98.00
Ladle, soup; SF, Cromwell, BS, 7" 78.00
Mayonnaise holder, UP, w/attached tray, 1947 ....65.00
Menu holder, UP, SM, BS, 1951, EX 85.00
Pitcher, UP, winged ball finial, BS, 64-oz, EX 18.00
Plate, Pullman, recessed center, 6" 78.00
Platter, CA Zephyr, 10", EX 120.00
Spoon, cheese; UP, R&B, BM 17.50
Spoon, demitasse; PRR, Kings, Merid-Brit, TM 32.00
Spoon, iced tea; NP, R&B, TM, BM, M 18.00
Spoon, place; SP, Westfield, Meriden, BS, 1930 ....18.00
Spoon, serving; Pullman, BS 18.00
Spoon, serving; Soo Line, Stanhope, Gorham, TM, 1900, EX 18.00
Spoon, soup; CP Hotels, Oneida, TM 10.00
Spork, ice cream; UP, Westfield, Merid-Brit, BS, EX 22.50
Steak cover, UP, 1936, 14" 100.00
Sugar bowl, ACL, SM, 10-oz, G 50.00

Sugar bowl, Atlantic Coast, w/lid, BM 50.00
Sugar tongs, IC, Dartmouth, EX 78.00
Sugar tongs, NP, Embassy, R&B, TM 98.00
Sugar tongs, UP, winged train, TM 20.00
Syrup, HNC&StL, hinged lid, R&B, SM, BS 50.00
Tablespoon, B&O, Cromwell, R&B, TM, 1912, VG 12.00
Teapot, PR, emb Keystone, SM, 10-oz 60.00
Teaspoon, CM&StP, GMCo, 1914, EX 15.00
Teaspoon, NP, Monad, R&B, TM, BS, EX 15.00
Teaspoon, Pullman, BS 15.00
Teaspoon, SF, Internat'l, lt wear 8.50
Teaspoon, SR, BS 9.50
Teaspoon, Western Union, Internat'l, TM 7.50
Teaspoon, WP, Hutton, Internat'l, BM 17.50
Toast cover & tray, NC&StL, R&B, SM, BS, EX 200.00
Toothpick holder, CStPM&O in script, ftd, R&B, BS, 3¼" 100.00
Tray, NC&StL, Gorham, BS, 12" 200.00
Tray, Pullman, Meriden, 1930s, 12x9", EX 215.00
Tray, Pullman, oval, 1933, 10" L 200.00
Tray, SF, oval, BS, TM, 12" 125.00
Tureen, soup; NC&StL, hdls, R&B, 3¾x10¾" 255.00

Wax Sealers

Adams Express, brass, toadstool hdl, EX 150.00
Adams Express Co, Loup City NB, brass, mushroom top 150.00
Am Rwy Express Agency On Hand, Omaha NB 100.00
Am Ry Express #3156 Messenger, brass/wood, ca 1920, EX 65.00
For Public Use, Arkansas, EX 60.00
KCM&B, Sullicent AL, iron bulb hdl, EX 125.00
Wells Fargo Express, Steel MO 250.00

Miscellaneous

Switch keys are brass with a hollow barrel and a round head with a hole in the center. The initials or the name of the railroad company that used it are incised on the head. Examples representing common railroads are valued at $15.00 and up, while those from the Colorado & Southern Ry are now selling for $60.00, as are some of the early predecessors.

Annual passes are skyrocketing in popularity (as opposed to trip or one-time passes, which are not very desirable in the field of pass collecting). Their values are contingent upon the specific railroad, its length of run (whether it was a short line or a major one), and their appearance. Many were tiny works of art lettered with fancy calligraphy and decorated with vignettes.

Timetables are climbing rapidly in popularity, and pins with the names of railroad companies are very good right now. On the other hand, 'Brotherhood' pins (or any item) hold little interest for collectors.

**Bell, brass, Southern Pacific Ry, 8",
$150.00.**

Airhorn, diesel; Nathan, 5-chime, wht metal, worn pnt, EX 465.00
Airhorn, diesel; Westinghouse, 1-chime, cast steel, EX 115.00
Ashtray, SR, ceramic, BS Mac Mannes, gold rim, 6½", M 37.50

Badge, breast; conductor, gold, eng name/1871, 1⅝" dia 125.00
Badge, breast; PRR Police, state seal, pie-plate style, EX 150.00
Badge, cap; FJ&G, motorman, Am Ry Supply, hallmk, EX 175.00
Badge, employee; PRR, red/bl/chrome, 1¾" dia, EX 100.00
Bell box, dvtl hardwood, orig pnt, 6½x5", EX 45.00
Book, CB&Q Freight Car Diagrams, 1956, 9½x4", EX 40.00
Booklet, PA RR, Jeffersonian All-Coach Streamliner, EX 7.50
Brake stick, N&W, brakeman's, M 30.00
Button, CStPM&O, silver, flat, lg, EX 4.00
Button, Southwestern, gold-tone, flat, Gaunt & Son, lg, EX 5.50
Calendar, MKT, 1969, on slanted 3½x6¼" wooden base, EX 10.00
Call card, Ry Express Agency, dbl-sided, cb/metal, EX 150.00
Cap, SP, brakeman, dk bl/blk, mk Forbcraft, EX 60.00
Clip, Soo Line, red-on-gold metal, 2⅝x2⅛", NM 12.50
Clip board, Cotton Belt Route, metal w/mc enameling, 6x4" 45.00
Compass, MP, coppery metal, loop for chain, 1⅛", NM 22.50
Directory, Wells Fargo Express Official, 1916, 304-pg, EX 115.00
Fire grenade, B&O, gr glass, star in circle, May 27, 1884 ....110.00
Insulator, B&O, aqua, 4x3" 10.00
Key, CM&StP, Loeffelholz, EX patina 15.00
Key, switch; common RR, brass, rnd head, hole in center 15.00
Key, switch; early/uncommon RR, brass, hollow bbl, rnd head ...60.00
Key, WAB, steel, #d, early, EX 35.00
Lapel stud, Burlington Rte, Safety First, mc enamel, M 15.00
Lighter, BN, Zippo, gr on silver-finish metal, MIB 12.00
Lucky piece, UP, aluminum, 1934, M 4.50
Menu, CA Zephyr, 1950 ....12.00
Menu, Denver Zephyr (Burlington), 1939 ....25.00
Menu, NP, 1931 ....10.00
Menu, Pullman, 1949 ....12.00
Menu, Rio Grande, 1950 ....12.00
Menu, SF, Fred Harvey, 1949 ....15.00
Menu, UP, Portland Rose, 1954 ....25.00
Oil can, Eagle, for bench use, NM 22.00
Paperweight, Chicago Union Station, glass, 1918, EX 24.00
Paperweight, Milwaukee Road, bear walking, bronze, EX 70.00
Paperweight, NYC, Hudson, cast metal, 1938, NM 285.00
Pass, annual; B&MR RR (in Nebraska), 1873 ....150.00
Pass, annual; C&NW, 1887, fancy masthead, EX 20.00
Pass, annual; C&NW, 1911, minor edge wear 10.00
Pass, annual; C&RI, 1865 ....150.00
Pass, annual; CM&StP, 1906, minor soiling 10.00
Pass, annual; CO, KS & OK, 1915 ....40.00
Pass, annual; commonly found, 1910s, up to 12.00
Pass, annual; commonly found, 1930s-40s 7.50
Pass, annual; CStPM&O, 1905, EX 10.00
Pass, annual; D&RGW, 1926 ....25.00
Pass, annual; IC, 1911, EX 10.00
Pass, annual; L&N, 1917 ....10.00
Pass, annual; Marietta & Cincinnati, 1864 ....150.00
Pass, annual; SC&P, 1889, fancy masthead, EX 18.00
Pass, annual; Tioga RR, 1864 ....150.00
Photograph, N&W, builder's specifications on bk, 12x17" 40.00
Pin, lapel; Brotherhood of RR Trainmen, 10k gold, 20-Yr 10.00
Pin, lapel; JC, Liberty w/torch, dull silver, 1¼", pr 22.50
Pin, lapel; OSL, trainman, silver color, skeleton style, old 17.50
Pin, service; Rio Grande, diesel logo, VG 35.00
Pin-bk, SP&S, red/wht logo on tin, oval, 1¼" W, EX 6.00
Playing cards, D&RGW, steam engine in gorge, 51+1, 1915, EX .27.50
Playing cards, MP, diesel train, 52, +1948 score card, MIB 22.00
Playing cards, Soo Line, Pined Shoreline, M in case 22.50
Playing cards, UP, First Snow, 1960, unopened 12.50
Punch, conductor's, worn plating, VG 20.00
Ruler, table for determining train speed, 6", leather case 20.00

Sewing kit, UP souvenir, complete, 2¾" sq (closed), NM 15.00
Sign, Market Street Ry Co, porc shield, 8x10", EX 175.00
Spittoon, Pullman, ornate, early design, NM 75.00
Spittoon, SAL, CI, early, VG 85.00
Stepbox, T&P, Morton, orig worn pnt 175.00
Stepbox, WAB, emb heavy steel, Morton, EX 250.00
Telephone, desk; Western Electric scissors type, Pat 1909, EX ...120.00
Telephone, wall; Northern Electric, wood box, brass bells, VG ..250.00
Timetable, B&Me, 1895 ....25.00
Timetable, B&O, Nov 1927, full sz, EX 7.50
Timetable, CM, 1887 ....150.00
Timetable, DL&W, 1937 ....7.50
Timetable, GN, 1902 ....12.00
Timetable, Milwaukee, 1907 ....17.00
Timetable, NYNH&H, 1899 ....40.00
Timetable, NYNH&H, 1927 ....7.50
Timetable, PRR, 1938 ....5.50
Tool check, SM&StP, brass, hexagonal 6.50
Watch fob, Canadian Nat'l Ry, brass, hinged, 2-pc 60.00
Wrench, pipe; NHRR, Stillson, 18", EX 40.00

Razors

As straight razors gain in popularity, prices increase. And with the lure of investment appreciation, the novice or the speculator sometimes find themselves making purchases that later prove to be unwise. It is important to be able to recognize the material of which the handle is made. This has a great bearing on value, and imitations abound. Learn to distinguish between celluloid and genuine ivory. Razors with plain celluloid handles are practically worthless unless the blade carries a desirable trademark. Those with decorations of scrollwork, leaves and vines, or decorative metal on each end fall into the $8 to $12 price range. Even plain ivory-handled razors are not especially valuable unless the blade is well marked and from a good manufacturer. On a more positive note, celluloid-handled razors with designs such as castles, windmills, nudes, deer, alligators, automobiles, horses, cowboys, peacocks, and various kinds of birds, etc., are very desirable (some more than others) and are usually worth from $25 to $50 to collectors. Those with a figural handle such as a fish, shotgun, eagle, or a barber pole might be worth in excess of $100 for an especially nice example. Ivory, on the other hand, is rarely found; if the carvings are well done, clean, undamaged specimens should start at about $100 and escalate according to the intricacy of the design.

Buffalo horn is sometimes mistakenly called bone. It is usually black, translucent tan, or gray. Though plain handles are worth very little, the early heat-molded examples with a motif such as mentioned above often sell for more than $100. In the same range are mother-of-pearl and stag (deer horn) handles; very elaborate designs go even higher, but watch for imitations.

There is one imitation, however, that is highly desirable. That is jigged bone made to look like stag. This material is rough textured and dyed a handsome tan or brown; usually examples with these handles sell in the $40 to $75 range. Razors with wooden handles are very rare, but even those from the 1800s are worth only about $35, since they are usually very plain. 20th-century examples are only valued at around $15. Don't be fooled by buffalo horn colored in imitation of tortoise — and you'll find celluloid imitations, too. Genuine tortoise handles are worth from $25 to $100 depending on age, condition, and workmanship. Sterling razors are valued at $75 and up, but make sure they are marked 'sterling.' Even if you were to mistake aluminum for silver, those with relief-cast designs are worth $50 to $75, but only $20 or so if the design is incised.

Corn razors were made to pare troublesome corns on the feet.

They are a bit smaller and if plain worth a little more than plain full-size razors. Fancy examples are generally not worth as much as their full-size couterparts.

The older blades are wedge-shaped (flat-sided) in cross-section; hollow-ground blades (made after 1880) are concave. Generally speaking, those etched with words are only worth a little more than a plain common blade. Try to find those with people, places, and things — the more famous, the better.

Key:
cell — celluloid   gw — gold washed
bd — blade

Bay S Hamburg...Donovan Springfield MS, hdl: red/blk 'wood' ...18.00
Blk Demon, sterling devil on cell hdl 18.00
Corn, Henkel, faux ivory cell hdl 25.00
Corn, Krusius Bros Germany, EB Extra on bd, blk hdl, box 28.00
Corn, Pauls Bros Germany, bone hdl 18.00
Corn, WH Morely & Sons Gunstock, hdl: blk compo, etch bd 32.00
Covalt & Smith...Germany, blk hdl, brass bolsters w/Dutch kids .32.00
Dbl Duck Shrimp/Bresnick NY TM Solingen Germany, cell hdl .10.00
Durham Omino, Pat USA May 07 & Foreign Co, cell hdl, case 4.00
East St Louis BS Co Germany, hdl: brn/cream, fancy bolsters 18.00
Fein Stahl Solingen, gw etch bd, wht compo hdl w/fancy inlay 24.00
Gem, Christy, Pat Dec 1925, in orig box w/instructions 12.00
Genco, hdl: fine blk/wht stripes 30.00
Genco Co Bradford PA Easy Aces, hdl: cracked ice cell, EX 33.00
Genco Heavy Geneva NY USA, blk hard rubber hdl, metal ends ..5.00
Geneva Cutlery Co Geneva NY, red/pk mottled Bakelite hdl 9.00
H Boker & Co, hdl: cream cell w/scrolls & face, etch bd 30.00
Ingersoll, str edge, w/strop, directions, M in felt case 25.00
Jackson Fremont O, hdl: orange w/cream swirl 28.00
Joseph Allen & Sons Sheffield, scrolls/geometrics, etch bd 35.00
Keen Kutter, slick blk hdl w/logo in circle, Bl Steel on bd 20.00
Kinfolks Real Red Point, red logo on wht compo hdl 33.00
King's Crown etch on bd, hdl: wht cell w/face & vines 24.00
Lion Razor Works Germany, blk hdl, bd w/etch eagle 22.00
Novelty Cutlery, Canton OH, faux buffalo horn hdl 35.00
Packare Lifetime, Bakelite hdl, EX in leather case 25.00
Schatt & Morgan Cut Co Titusville PA, slick blk hdl 35.00
T Turners Everlasting, 'Eberlast' on clear horn hdl, EX 38.00
Tula KC Seelbach Solingen, hdl: ivory cell w/checkered ends 30.00
Walter H Gable York PA...Barber Hand Made, rust/wht stripes ...16.00
Weck Bantam E Weck & Co, red marbled ivory cell hdl 9.50
WH Morley & Son, hdl: blk w/face & vines (rpr) 17.00
Wilbert Cutlery Co Chicago, hdl: brn/cream swirl 28.00
Winchester TM, hdl: blk & brn stripes, #d tang 60.00
Wostenholm Geo & Son Wtd IXL Sheffield, cell hdl w/scrolls 8.00

Reamers

Reamers have been made in hundreds of styles and colors and by as many manufacturers. Their purpose is to extract the juices from lemons, oranges, and grapefruits. The largest producer of glass reamers was McKee, who pressed their products from many types of glass — custard; delphite and Chalaine blue; opaque white; Skokie green; black; caramel and white opalescent; Seville yellow; and transparent pink, green, and clear. Among these, the black and the caramel opalescents are the most valuable.

The Fry Glass Company also made reamers that are today very collectible. The Hazel Atlas Crisscross orange reamer in pink often brings in excess of $250; the same in blue, $275. Hocking produced a light blue orange reamer and, in the same soft hue, a two-piece reamer and measuring cup combination. Both are considered rare and very valuable with currently-quoted estimates at $400 and up for the former and $800 and up for the latter. In addition to the colors mentioned, red glass examples — transparent or slag — are rare and costly.

Among the most valuable ceramic reamers are those made by American potteries. The Spongeband reamer by Red Wing is valued in excess of $500; Coorsite reamers with gold or silver trim are worth $200 and up. Figurals are popular — Mickey Mouse and John Bull may bring $300 to $400. Others range from $45 to $150. Fine china one- and two-piece reamers are also very desirable and command very respectable prices.

A word about reproductions: A series of limited edition reamers is being made by Edna Barnes of Uniontown, Ohio. These are all marked with a 'B' in a circle. Other repoductions have been made from old molds. The most important of these are: Anchor Hocking 2-piece 2-cup measure and top, Gillespie 1-cup measure with reamer top, Westmoreland N-365 with flattened handle, Westmoreland 4-cup measure embossed with orange and lemons, Duboe (hand held), Easley's diamonds 1-piece, and spiral 1-piece #202.

Our advisor for this category is Dee Long; she is listed in the Directory under Illinois. For more information concerning reamers and reproductions, contact our advisor or the National Reamer Collectors Association (see Clubs, Newsletters, and Catalogs). Be sure to include an SASE when requesting information. Reference numbers in the ceramic reamer listings correspond with *200 Years of Reamers* by Mary Walker, available at your local library or from the National Reamer Collectors Association.

Yellow reamer on matching 2-cup measure, $285.00.

Ceramic

Clown figural, gr/wht/orange/blk, Japan, C-29, 7½" 55.00
Clown figural, purple, bl & wht, C-65, 6" 50.00
Elephant figural, Japan, 2-pc, 4¼" 150.00
Leaf base, gr & tan w/orange trim, brn hdl, D-40, 4¼" 40.00
Mexican w/cactus figural, Japan 200.00
Orange form, gr leaves, Japan, L-39, 4½" 42.50
Pail w/hdl form, tan & yel, Japan, P-73, 7¾" 65.00
Pear form, wht w/gr leaves, gold trim, rare color, L-39 ....55.00
Pear form, yel & orange w/gr leaves, L-39, Japan, 4½" 50.00
Pitcher form, mc floral on beige, tan trim, T-16 ....25.00
Pitcher form, rust leaves, dk bl trim, D-55, 3½" 35.00
Pitcher form, yel lustre, L-2, 4" 32.00
Puddinhead figural, gr hat, F-32, 6¼" 135.00
Royal Rudolstadt, china, 2-pc 165.00
Saucer form, wht, France, D-85, 3¼" dia 15.00
Saucer form w/Negro head reamer, Japan, 3½" 275.00

Glass

Anchor Hocking, fired-on blk, tab hdl 12.50
Anchor Hocking, gr, pitcher form, ftd, 4-cup 35.00
Cambridge, Chalaine bl, grapefruit reamer 250.00
Cambridge, crystal, tab hdl 15.00
Clambroth, boat shape 200.00
Federal, amber, spout opposite hdl, N275 ....300.00
Federal, amber, 6-sided cone, vertical hdl 225.00
Federal, crystal, horizontal hdl 12.50
Federal, gr, ribbed, seed dam, tab hdl 16.00
Federal, pk, ribbed, loop hdl 35.00
Federal, vaseline, ruffled top 135.00
Fenton, blk, pitcher form, 2-pc 1,200.00
Fenton, elephant decor on base, 2-pc, baby's 75.00
Fleur-de-Lis, milk glass 85.00
Glasbake, crystal, McKee on hdl 125.00
Hazel Atlas, gr, pitcher form, mk A&J, 4-cup 35.00
Hazel Atlas, wht, pitcher form, red trim 30.00
Hazel Atlas, wht w/gr leaves, yel trim, tab hdl 35.00
Hazel Atlas, yel, pitcher form, 2-cup 275.00
Jeannette, dk jadite, lg 35.00
Jeannette, Hex Optic, pk, bucket form 55.00
Jeannette, lt jadite, sm 22.00
Jenkins, gr, baby's, 2-pc 175.00
Milk glass, saucer form, tab hdl, 5" 40.00
Radnt, crystal 115.00
Sunkist, butterscotch caramel 300.00
Sunkist, custard 40.00
Sunkist, gr opal 175.00
Sunkist, Skokie gr, loop hdl 55.00
US Glass, amber, horizontal ribs, slick hdl, 2-pc 300.00
US Glass, crystal, slick hdl, insert at top of cup 25.00
US Glass, lt pk, pitcher form, 2-cup 40.00
US Glass, pk, pitcher set, 3-pc 250.00
US Glass, pk, tub+reamer, wire stand 65.00
Valencia, pk 200.00
Westmoreland, amber, baby's, 2-pc 125.00
Westmoreland, gr, pitcher form, emb orange/lemon, 2-pc 140.00
Westmoreland, pk, baby's, 2-pc 150.00
Westmoreland, pk w/pnt decor, baby's, 2-pc 125.00

Records

Records of interest to collectors are often not the million-selling hits by 'superstars.' Very few records by Bing Crosby, for example, are of any more than nominal value, and those that are valuable usually don't even have his name on the label! Collectors today are most interested in records that were made in limited quantities, early works of a performer who later became famous, and those issued in special series or aimed at a limited market. Vintage records are judged desirable by their recorded content as well; those that lack the quality of music that makes a record collectible will always be 'junk' records in spite of their age, scarcity, or the obsolescence of their technology.

Records are usually graded visually rather than by audio quality, since it is seldom if ever possible to first play the records you buy at shows, by mail, at flea markets, etc. Condition is one of the most important value-assessing factors. For example, a truly mint-condition Elvis Presley 45 of Milk Cow Blues (Sun 215) has a potential value of over $1,000.00. If that same 45 had a sticker on it that was one-eighth of an inch square, it could lose up to half of that value! To be judged mint, a record and sleeve must be in original, unsealed condition. It may have been played but has no visual or audible deterioration. Excellent condition is a rating applied to a record that may show slight signs of wear and use but will have almost no audible defect. Sleeves may show marginal deterioration but no repairs, pen or pencil marks, stickers, or physical damage. A Good record has both visual and audible distractions but is still playable. Sleeves will show ring wear but will not be physically damaged, and Fair indicates a record that is both visually and audibly distracting, one that has obvious damage — no skips, but possible 'play through' scratches. It can still be usable. Sleeves will show heavy ring wear and some minor physical damage. A Poor record may or may not play. Sleeves are faded, torn, marked, or otherwise damaged beyond pleasurable viewing.

Many promo records being discarded by radio stations today are finding their way into collections. These may say 'Not for Sale,' 'Audition Copy,' 'D.J.,' etc. These radio station versions are sometimes different than commercial issues and usually more sought after than their commercial twins.

Our advisor for this category is L.R. Docks, author of *American Premium Record Guide*, which lists 60,000 records by over 7,000 artists, now in its fourth edition. He is listed in the Directory under Texas. In the listings that follow, prices are suggested for records that are in excellent condition.

Key:
Bru — Brunswick   Para — Paramount
Ch — Champion   Orch — Orchestra
Col — Columbia   Vi — Victor
Edi — Edison   Vo — Vocalion

Jelly-Roll Morton and His Red Hot Peppers, Strokin' Away, ca 1930, $75.00.

Blues, Rhythm and Blues, Rock 'N Roll, Rockabilly

Adkins, Katherine; Individual Blues, Okeh 8363, 78 rpm 40.00
Adventurers, Rock & Roll Uprising, Col 42227, 45 rpm 8.00
Allen, Milton; Just Look, Don't Touch, RCA Vi 6994, 45 rpm 10.00
Ames, Tessie; Rider Blues, Silvertone 3565, 78 rpm 45.00
Angel, Johnny; Baby I'm Confessin', Excello 2077, 45 rpm 14.00
Baker, Willie; Before She Leaves Town, DeLuxe 6023, 45 rpm 30.00
Barry, Jeff; It's Called Rock & Roll, RCA Vi 7477, 45 rpm 8.00
Bartlette, Viola; Tennessee Blues, Para 12322, 78 rpm 100.00
Bees, Toy Bell, Imperial 5314, 45 rpm 30.00
Boyd, Jimmy; Shakin' Down the Mississippi, Col 21571, 45 rpm 8.00
Carnations, Long Tall Girl, Lescay 3002, 45 rpm 16.00
Carolina Slim, Pleading Blues, Acorn 319, 78 rpm 10.00
Casanova, Tony; Boogie Woogie Feeling, Dore 535, 45 rpm 18.00
Darby, Teddy; My Loana Blues, Para 12828, 78 rpm 250.00
Davis, Genevieve; I've Got Something, Vi 20648, 78 rpm 95.00
Domino, Fats; Reeling & Rocking, Imperial 5180, 45 rpm 25.00
Erby, John; Lonesome Jimmy Blues, Col 14151-D, 78 rpm 40.00
Foster, Jim; Riverside Blues, Ch 15301, 78 rpm 200.00
Glinn, Lillian; Doggin' Me Blues, Col 14275-D, 78 rpm 45.00
Harlan, Billy; I Wanna Bop, Bru 55066, 45 rpm 18.00
Harris, Clarence; Try My Whiskey Blues, Bluebird 8138, 78 rpm .20.00

Hickey, Ersel; Hangin' Around, Epic 9263, 45 rpm 10.00
Howard, Johnny; Hastings Street Jump, DeLuxe 6044, 78 rpm 25.00
Jammin' Jim, Shake Boogie, Savoy 1106, 78 rpm 8.00
Kelly, Willie; Sad & Lonely Day, Vi 23416, 78 rpm 250.00
Little Milton, I'm a Lonely Man, Bobbin 101, 45 rpm 8.00
Lowery, Florence; Poor Girl Blues, Vo 1106, 78 rpm 85.00
Martin, Sam; Alabamy Bound, Okeh 8262, 78 rpm 65.00
Mathes, Minnie; Ball Game Blues, Vo 04431, 78 rpm 16.00
Moore, Merrill; Big Bug Boogie, Capitol 2226, 45 rpm 6.00
Nesbitt, Scottie; Sundown Blues, Bluebird 7125, 78 rpm 12.00
Orbison, Roy; Sweet & Innocent, RCA Vi 7381, 45 rpm 12.00
Orioles, Dare to Dream, Jubilee 5001, 78 rpm 14.00
Paris Brothers, This Is It, Bru 55132, 45 rpm 12.00
Pickett, Dan; Lemon Man, Gotham 516, 78 rpm 20.00
Roberts, Sally; Black Hearse Blues, Okeh 8500, 78 rpm 50.00
Slick Slavin, Speed Crazy, Imperial 5540, 45 rpm 10.00
Smith, Bessie; Down Hearted Blues, Col A-3844, 78 rpm 12.00
Smokehouse Charlie, My Texas Blues, Ch 15794, 78 rpm 125.00
Taylor, Walter; Yo-Yo Blues, Ch 15972, 78 rpm 250.00
Tolleson, Tommie; A Girl Named Sue, Kool 1005, 45 rpm 16.00
Victorians, Part Time Sweetheart, Specialty 420, 45 rpm 65.00
Wallace, Frances; Low Down Man Blues, Bru 7076, 78 rpm 90.00
Washboard Sam, Diggin' My Potatoes, Chess 1545, 45 rpm 90.00
Woody, Don; Bird Dog, Decca 30277, 45 rpm 16.00

Country and Western

Alabama Four, Looking This Way, Broadway 8209, 78 rpm 20.00
Allen Brothers, Salty Dog Blues, Col 15175-D, 78 rpm 85.00
Ashley, Clyde; Down in Arkansas, Superior 2558, 78 rpm 18.00
Baker, Buddy; Box Car Blues, Vi 21549, 78 rpm 12.00
Behrens, Jerry; Drifting Along, Okeh 45535, 78 rpm 20.00
Blanchard, Dan; The West Plains Explosion, Ch 15526, 78 rpm 8.00
Boone, Jimmy; Brakeman's Reply, Superior 2638, 78 rpm 25.00
Buckeye Boys, Duck Foot Sue, Ch 16168, 78 rpm 10.00
Card, Ken; Last Flight of Wiley Post, Ch 45148, 78 rpm 8.00
Carson, Bert; My Red Haired Lady, Superior 2520, 78 rpm 16.00
Cedar Creek Sheik, What a Pity, Bluebird 6587, 78 rpm 18.00
Cook, Joe; Sweet Little Girl in Blue, Bluebird 5135, 78 rpm 8.00
Crystal Spring Ramblers, Down in Arkansas, Vo 03856, 78 rpm 8.00
Darling, Chuck; Harmonica Rag, Bluebird 5285, 78 rpm 10.00
Davis, Jimmie; Lonely Hobo, Vi 23648, 78 rpm 100.00
Delmore Brothers, I'm Leaving You, Bluebird 5299, 78 rpm 12.00
Dixon Trio, Carolina Lullaby, Vi 23790, 78 rpm 15.00
Dudgeon, Frank; Atlanta Bound, Ch 16532, 78 rpm 65.00
Elkins, Ray; Boy's Best Friend, Ch 15831, 78 rpm 12.00
Elm City Quartet, Tree Song, Ch 16827, 78 rpm 8.00
Farley, JD; Bill Was a Texas Lad, Vi V40269, 78 rpm 30.00
Fleming & Townsend, First Time in Jail, Vi 23666, 78 rpm 40.00
Gaydon, Whit; Tennessee Coon Hunt, Vi V40315, 78 rpm 18.00
Georgia Yellow Hammers, Fourth of July, Vi 20549, 78 rpm 12.00
Grant Trio, Under the Old Umbrella, Vi 23667, 78 rpm 10.00
Greene, Amos; Memphis Yodel, Supertone 9671, 78 rpm 15.00
Hackberry Ramblers, Jolie Blonde, Bluebird 2002, 78 rpm 10.00
Hart Brothers, Miner's Prayer, Para 3162, 78 rpm 14.00
Honolulu Strollers, Don't Say No, Vi 23600, 78 rpm 35.00
Hopkins, Andy; Prison Warden's Secret, Supertone 9713, 78 rpm ...8.00
Irwin, Harvey; Sunny Tennessee, Okeh 45052, 78 rpm 12.00
Johnson Brothers, Down in Happy Valley, Vi 20661, 78 rpm 15.00
Kentucky Thorobreds, Mother's Advice, Para 3011, 78 rpm 18.00
Kincaid, Bradley; Methodist Pie, Bru 420, 78 rpm 8.00
Lawson, Jimmie; Tennessee Blues, Vi 20477, 78 rpm 14.00
Leake County Revelers, Johnson Gal, Col 15149, 78 rpm 18.00
Louisiana Lou, Sinful To Flirt, Bluebird 5424, 78 rpm 16.00

Mack, Bill; Big Bad Daddy, Imperial 8151, 78 rpm 8.00
Marlow, Andy; My Little Lady, Ch 15875, 78 rpm 20.00
Massey Family, Sweet Mama Tree Top Tall, Vo 02993, 78 rpm ...12.00
Moreland, Peg; Prisoner at the Bar, Vi 21548, 78 rpm 8.00
Morris, Zeke; Garden of Prayer, Bluebird 7362, 78 rpm 10.00
Narmour & Smith, Whistling Coon, Okeh 45263, 78 rpm 30.00
Newman, Fred; San Antonio, Para 3177, 78 rpm 15.00
Oak Mountain Four, Medley, Ch 15874, 78 rpm 8.00
Oaks, Charlie; Little Mary Phagan, Vo 5069, 78 rpm 6.00
Peterson, Walter; Over the Waves, Gennett 6102, 78 rpm 12.00
Pickard Family, Rabbit in the Pea Patch, Para 3213, 78 rpm 6.00
Quadrillers, Drunk Man Blues, Para 3008, 78 rpm 18.00
Red Headed Fiddlers, Texas Quickstep, Bru 285, 78 rpm 16.00
Ritter, Tex; Oregon Trail, Ch 45154, 78 rpm 10.00
Rodgers, Jimmie; Old Love Letters, Bluebird 6198, 78 rpm 20.00
Rogers, Roy; Colorado Sunset, Vo 04453, 78 rpm 12.00
Scottsdale String Band, Carolina Glide, Okeh 45142, 78 rpm 14.00
Shafer, Bill; Kicking Mule, Vo 5413, 78 rpm 12.00
Steen, Joe; Crazy Engineer, Vi 23634, 78 rpm 25.00
Tennessee Travelers, Forked Deer, Ch 15300, 78 rpm 35.00
Tommie & Willie, By the Old Oak Tree, Ch 16034, 78 rpm 10.00
Tuttle, Frank; Prison Fire, Velvet Tone 2148-V, 78 rpm 6.00
Vagabonds, My Pretty Quadroon, Vi 23849, 78 rpm 45.00
Vass Family, Deep Blue Sea, Decca 5432, 78 rpm 8.00
Walker's Corbin Ramblers, I Had a Dream, Vo 02719, 78 rpm 18.00
West, CA; Oh Willie Come Back, Supertone 9650, 78 rpm 7.50

Jazz, Dance Bands, Personalities

Alomo Garden Band, Spanish Mamma, Buddy 8052, 78 rpm 60.00
Ambassadors, Military Mike, Vo 15156, 78 rpm 12.00
Andrew Sisters, Just a Simple Melody, Decca 1496, 78 rpm 10.00
Austin, Gene; Dear Old Southland, Decca 1656, 78 rpm 15.00
Bailey, Mildred; Blues in My Heart, Bru 6190, 78 rpm 12.50
Banta, Frank; Wild Cherry Rag, Gennett 4735, 78 rpm 20.00
Bernard, Mike; Everybody Two-Step, Col A1266, 78 rpm 10.00
Boots & His Buddies, Rose Room, Bluebird 6063, 78 rpm 8.00
Cab Calloway & His Orchestra, Black Rythm, Bru 6141, 78 rpm ...12.00
Campus Boys, My Supressed Desire, Banner 6263, 78 rpm 6.50
Candy & Coco, China Boy, Vo 2849, 78 rpm 25.00
Choo Choo Jazzers, Snuggle Up a Bit, Ajax 17038, 78 rpm 18.00
Crosby, Bing; Lazy Day, Bru 6306, 78 rpm 12.50
Davis, Genevieve; I've Got Something, Vi 20648, 78 rpm 85.00
Dixie Washboard Band, My Own Blues, Col 14141-D, 78 rpm 35.00
Dodds & Parham, Oh Daddy, Para 12471, 78 rpm 125.00
Dubin's Dandies, Gettin' Along, Banner 0505, 78 rpm 8.00
Eddie's Hot Shots, That's a Serious Thing, Vi V-38046, 78 rpm ..45.00
Ernie Fields & His Orchestra, Lard Stomp, Vo 5073, 78 rpm 10.00
Etting, Ruth; Close Your Eyes, Bru 6657, 78 rpm 10.00
Evans, Roy; One More Time, Crown 3154, 78 rpm 8.50
Finnie, Ethel; Hula Blues, Ajax 17027, 78 rpm 25.00
Five Hot Chocolates, Baby Knows How, Radiex 952, 78 rpm 30.00
Georgians, Everybody Loves My Baby, Col 252-D, 78 rpm 8.00
Gibson, Cleo; Nothing but Blues, Okeh 8700, 78 rpm 45.00
Golden Gate Orchestra, Lucille, Edison 51388, 78 rpm 12.00
Goodner, Lillian; Ramblin' Blues, Ajax 17018, 78 rpm 25.00
Hall, Wendell; Headin' Home, Col 1028-D, 78 rpm 8.00
Handy, Katherine; Loveless Love, Para 12011, 78 rpm 50.00
Happiness Boys, If You Knew Susie, Bru 2888, 78 rpm 6.00
Harlem Trio, Clarinet Laughing Blues, Okeh 8072, 78 rpm 55.00
Harris, Marion; Charleston Charlie, Bru 2735, 78 rpm 7.50
Herwin Hot Shots, Salty Dog, Herwin 93015, 78 rpm 250.00
Hollywood Shufflers, Low Down Rhythm, Vo 15837, 78 rpm 125.00
Idaho, Bertha; Move It on Out of Here, Col 14437-D, 78 rpm 40.00

Imperial Orchestra, Sing Me a Baby Song, Bell 534, 78 rpm 8.00
Jamaica Jazzers, West Indies Blues, Okeh 40117, 78 rpm 65.00
James, Jeanette; Midnight Stomp, Para 12470, 78 rpm 175.00
Jolson, Al; Pullman Porter's Parade, Col A-1374, 78 rpm 30.00
Jungle Band, Tiger Rag, Bru 3956, 78 rpm 12.00
Kaley, Charles; Alabama Stomp, Col 910-D, 78 rpm 10.00
Kaufman, Irving; St Louis Blues, Banner 6508, 78 rpm 6.00
Kay, Dolly; Buzz Mirandy, Col A3644, 78 rpm 8.00
Kentucky Blowers, Rambling Blues, Gennett 5517, 78 rpm 12.00
Kopp, Howard; Calico Rag, Col A2241, 78 rpm 20.00
La Palina Broadcasters, Sweetness, Perfect 15203, 78 rpm 8.50
Ladd's Black Aces, Brother Low Down, Gennett 4806, 78 rpm 10.00
Langford, Frances; Moon Song, Bluebird 5016, 78 rpm 10.00
Lazy Levee Loungers, Shout Sister Shout, Col 2243-D, 78 rpm 35.00
Lewis, Alfred; Friday Moan Blues, Vo 1498, 78 rpm 60.00
Louisiana Five, Slow & Easy, Col A2949, 78 rpm 6.00
Louisiana Stompers, Hop Off, Para 12550, 78 rpm 90.00
Lumberjacks, Black Beauty, Cameo 8352, 78 rpm 7.50
Lytell, Jimmy; Old Folks Shuffle, Perfect 14749, 78 rpm 15.00
Mater, Frank; Let's Do It, Harmony, 808-H, 78 rpm 12.00
McAlpineers, One More Night, Edison 52237, 78 rpm 15.00
Metropolitan Orchestra, Creole Belles, Monarch 1023, 78 rpm ...30.00
Miami Lucky Seven, So Tired, Challenge 757, 78 rpm 12.50
Mills Brothers, Diga Diga Doo, Bru 6519, 78 rpm 15.00
Moran & Mack, Foolishments, Col 1929-D, 78 rpm 12.00
Moskowitz, Joseph; Operatic Rag, Vi 17978, 78 rpm 18.00
Nelson, Jewell; Beating Me Blues, Col 14390-D, 78 rpm 60.00
New Orleans Jazz Band, Tiger Rag, Banner 6049, 78 rpm 8.00
New Orleans Wanderers, Papa Dip, Col 735-D, 78 rpm 60.00
New Yorkers, Parkin' in the Moonlight, Bru 6164, 78 rpm 15.00
Nowlin, Sam; So What, Ch 16828, 78 rpm 75.00
Original Indiana Five, Indiana Shuffle, Banner 1931, 78 rpm 8.00
Original Memphis Five, Anything, Col 2588-D, 78 rpm 25.00
Perkins, Alberta; Levee Man, Ajax 17125, 78 rpm 30.00
Peters, Teddy; Georgia Man, Vo 1006, 78 rpm 175.00
Pierrot Syncopators, Dixie Drag, Crown 81020, 78 rpm 14.00
Preer, Evelyn; Muddy Water, Banner 1972, 78 rpm 8.00
Queen City Blowers, Stomp Off, Let's Go, Ch 15030, 78 rpm 60.00
Radiolites, Sweet Lorraine, Col 1432-D, 78 rpm 8.00
Ramblers, Lonely Eyes, Romeo 315, 78 rpm 6.00
Red Heads, Feelin' No Pain, Melotone 12443, 78 rpm 10.00
Red Onion Jazz Babies, Terrible Blues, Gennett 5607, 78 rpm ...125.00
Riffers, Rhapsody in Love, Col 14677-D, 78 rpm 35.00
Robinson, Elzadie; Barrel House Man, Para 12417, 78 rpm 100.00
Rubinoff, Dave; Fiddlin' the Fiddle, Perfect 14483, 78 rpm 10.00
Sam Lanin & His Orchestra, Mona, Banner 0601, 78 rpm 6.00
Seminole Syncopators, Blue Grass Blues, Okeh 40228, 78 rpm 90.00
Sepia Serenaders, Alligator Crawl, Bluebird 5803, 78 rpm 20.00
Silent Joe & His Boys, Cooler Hot, Ch 15051, 78 rpm 15.00
Six Black Diamonds, Long Lost Mama, Banner 1217, 78 rpm 8.00
Slim & His Hot Boys, That's a Plenty, Vi V38044, 78 rpm 70.00
Smith, Kate; Moon Song, Bru 6497, 78 rpm 12.00
Spangler, Rex; Cannon Ball Rag, Rex 5024, 78 rpm 50.00
Thomas, Hociel; I Must Have It, Buddy 8020, 78 rpm 120.00
Tucker, Sophie; Some of These Days, Col 826-D, 78 rpm 10.00
University Boys, Lovable & Sweet, Oriole 1668, 78 rpm 15.00
Vagabonds, Ukelele, Gennett 3100, 78 rpm 12.00
Walters, Eddie; It Must Be Love, Col 2232-D, 78 rpm 10.00
Watson, Al; Bay Rum Blues, Vi 21585, 78 rpm 35.00
Young, Margaret; High Brown Blues, Bru 2253, 78 rpm 7.50

Red Wing

The Red Wing Stoneware Company, founded in 1878, took its

name from its location in Red Wing, Minnesota. In 1906, the name was changed to the Red Wing Union Stoneware Company after a merger with several of the other local potteries. For the most part they produced utilitarian wares such as flowerpots, crocks, and jugs. Their early 1930s catalogs offered a line of art pottery vases in colored glazes, some of which featured handles modeled after swan's necks, snakes, or female nudes. Other examples were quite simple, often with classic styling. After the addition of their dinnerware lines in the 1935, 'Stoneware' was dropped from the name, and the company became known as Red Wing Potteries, Inc. They closed in 1967. For further study we recommend *Red Wing Stoneware, An Identification and Value Guide*, and *Red Wing Collectibles* by Dan and Gail DePasquale and Larry Peterson, available at your bookstore or from Collector Books. Our advisor for the general dinnerware lines is Doug Podpeskar; he is listed in the Directory under Minnesota. Karen Silvermintz (see Texas) submitted information for the new section on the Town and Country dinnerware.

Key:
c/s — cobalt on stoneware
MN — Minnesota
NS — North Star
RW — Red Wing
RWUS — Red Wing Union Stoneware

Commercial Art Ware and Miscellaneous

Ash receiver, elephant figural	60.00
Ashtray, mini flowerpot center, advertising	300.00
Ashtray, red wing form, emb feathers	35.00
Ashtray, 75th Anniversary, 1953	135.00
Bank, bear form, Hamm's Beer, 1960s	225.00
Figurine, lady w/tambourine, cinnamon, 10"	175.00
Mug, Hamm's Krug Club, brn	55.00
Sign, True China by Red Wing, rectangular	125.00
Toothpick holder, gopher on stump form	120.00
Trivet, yel, 1858-1958	69.00

Vase, busts of stylized humans with relief outlines, gold and caramel, M3013, 15", $350.00.

Vase, cherubs & garlands, Brushware, mk	90.00
Wall clock, Mammy	125.00

Cookie Jars

Bob White, unmk	80.00
Carousel, unmk	350.00
Crock, wht	25.00

Dutch Girl, yel w/brn trim	60.00
Friar Tuck, cream w/brn trim, mk	60.00
Friar Tuck, gr, mk	150.00
Friar Tuck, yel, unmk	60.00
Grapes	70.00
Grapes, cobalt or dk purple, ea	80.00
Jack Frost, unmk	600.00
King of Tarts, mc, mk	500.00
King of Tarts, pk w/bl & blk trim, mk	350.00
King of Tarts, wht, unmk	350.00
Peasant design, emb/pnt figures on brn	60.00
Pierre (chef), brn, unmk	60.00
Pierre (chef), gr, unmk	200.00
Pierre (chef), pk, mk	250.00
Pineapple	100.00

Dinnerware

Bob White, bowl, hdls, 9"	25.00
Bob White, bowl, vegetable; divided	25.00
Bob White, bowl, 6½"	10.00
Bob White, butter dish	75.00
Bob White, casserole, 2-qt	25.00
Bob White, cookie jar	140.00
Bob White, hors d'oeuvres bird	30.00
Bob White, mug	50.00
Bob White, pitcher, water; 60-oz	35.00
Bob White, plate, 7½"	9.00
Bob White, platter, 20"	45.00
Bob White, relish, 3-part, 12"	22.00
Bob White, shakers, bird form, pr	35.00
Bob White, water cooler, 2-gal, w/lid & stand, M	450.00
Capistrano, bowl, divided vegetable	20.00
Country Garden, bowl, vegetable; divided	20.00
Country Garden, gravy boat	22.00
Country Garden, nappy	16.00
Country Garden, plate, 10½"	15.00
Country Garden, plate, 8"	10.00
Country Garden, sauce dish	10.00
Lanterns, cup & saucer	10.00
Lotus, plate, 10½"	10.00
Lotus, plate, 6"	3.50
Lotus, plate, 7½"	6.50
Lute Song, beverage server	45.00
Lute Song, bowl, vegetable; 8"	15.00
Lute Song, bread tray, 19"	20.00
Lute Song, butter dish	20.00
Lute Song, casserole	25.00
Lute Song, creamer	10.00
Lute Song, cup & saucer	10.00
Lute Song, plate, 10"	10.00
Lute Song, plate, 7"	7.00
Lute Song, platter, 13"	20.00
Magnolia, chop plate	16.00
Magnolia, cup & saucer	8.00
Magnolia, plate, 10"	10.00
Magnolia, plate, 6"	3.50
Magnolia, saucer	2.00
Pepe, plate, 10"	10.00
Pepe, saucer	3.00
Random Harvest, celery	12.00
Random Harvest, coffeepot, tall	25.00
Random Harvest, cup & saucer	8.00
Random Harvest, plate, 10"	7.50

Random Harvest, platter, 13" 12.50
Round-Up, bowl, divided vegetable 55.00
Round-Up, cup & saucer 40.00
Round-Up, gravy boat 95.00
Round-Up, plate, 6" 16.00
Round-Up, relish, 3-part 65.00
Tampico, cup & saucer 12.00
Tampico, plate, 10½" 10.00
Tampico, sugar bowl, w/lid 15.00
Village Green, casserole stand, 10" 18.00
Village Green, casserole stand, 8" 10.00
Village Green, marmite, w/lid 15.00
Village Green, warmer 18.00
Willow Wind, tidbit tray, 3-pc 20.00

Stoneware

Bean pot, Albany slip, Boston style, NS, 1-gal 110.00
Bean pot, Albany slip, Boston style, RWUS, ½-gal 110.00
Bean pot, brn & wht, later style, bail hdl, RWUS, 1-qt 65.00
Bowl, beater; Albany Slip, RW 20.00
Bowl, Greek Key, bl & wht, 12" 145.00
Bowl, milk; bl, RW, 7" 120.00
Bowl, paneled, red & bl sponging on wht, 11" 150.00
Bowl, Red & Bl Banded, sm 35.00
Bowl, Saffron Grape, zigzags emb on rim, RWUS 115.00
Box, salt; Spongeband & Saffron, RWUS 750.00
Chamber pot, Albany slip, fancy hdl, MN 200.00
Chamber pot, bl banded on wht, MN 115.00
Chamber pot, wht, fancy hdl, RW, 7" 90.00
Churn, birch leaves/#2 on salt glaze, ear hdls, RWUS, 2-gal 225.00
Churn, bird/#5, c/s, RW, 5-gal 1,050.00
Churn, butterfly/#6, c/s, RW, 6-gal 750.00
Churn, parrot/#3, c/s, MN, molded seam, 3-gal 2,600.00
Combinette, emb floral garland, bl to wht shaded, RW 200.00
Cooler, butterfly/#6, c/s, RW, 6-gal 1,600.00
Cooler, daisy/#6, c/s, RW, 6-gal 1,500.00
Cooler, dbl leaves/#4, c/s, RW, 4-gal 1,600.00
Cooler, dbl leaves/#4, c/s, unmk, 4-gal 375.00
Cooler, flower/#6/Ice Water, c/s, RW, 6-gal 4,250.00
Cooler, 4 leaves/Ice Water/#25, c/s, RWUS, 25-gal 275.00
Crock, birch leaves/#2, c/s, MN, 2-gal 35.00
Crock, butterfly/#20, c/s, RW, 20-gal 425.00
Crock, butterfly/#6, c/s, RW, 6-gal 350.00
Crock, dbl 'P'/#4, c/s, MN, 4-gal 325.00
Crock, leaves/#25, c/s, MN, 25-gal 425.00
Crock, lily/#30/stencilling, c/s, RW, 30-gal 1,000.00
Crock, target/#2, c/s, RW, 2-gal 115.00
Crock, 2 elephant-ear leaves/#10, c/s, RWUS, 10-gal 75.00
Crock, 2 leaves/#25, cobalt on wht, RWUS, 25-gal 250.00
Cuspidor, brn & salt glaze, unsgn, toy sz 300.00
Cuspidor, molded seam, bl & wht sponging, RW, 8" dia 450.00
Flowerpot, Albany slip, geometric decor at rim, MN, 7" 250.00
Jar, butter; Albany slip, low style, RW, 5-lb 35.00
Jar, butter; Albany slip, MN, 10-lb 60.00
Jar, butter; salt glaze, RW, 10-lg 65.00
Jar, fruit; Stone Mason, c/s, RWUS, ½-gal 175.00
Jar, pantry; red wing & bl bands on wht, 5-lb 350.00
Jar, preserve; Albany slip, RW stamp on side, 1-gal 350.00
Jar, preserve; salt glaze, tall cylinder, MN 350.00
Jar, preserve/snuff; Albany slip, MN, 1-gal 55.00
Jar, wax sealer; wht, MN, 1-gal 85.00
Jug, beehive; #5 etched on Albany slip, hand-trn, RW, 5-gal 650.00
Jug, beehive; birch leaves/#5 on wht, 5-gal 425.00

Jug, beehive; birch/leaves/#3 on wht, RWUS, 3-gal 200.00
Jug, beehive; leaf/#5, c/s, RW, 5-gal 1,400.00
Jug, beehive; red wing/#5 on wht, RWUS, 5-gal 200.00
Jug, beehive; 2 elephant-ear leaves/#5, c/s, RWUS, 5-gal 550.00
Jug, common, Albany slip, ball top, NM, 1-gal 165.00
Jug, common, Albany slip, dome top, MN, 1-gal 100.00
Jug, common, dome top, MN, 1-gal 65.00
Jug, common, wht, dome top, MN, ½-gal 55.00
Jug, fancy, bl band on wht, brn ball top, MN, 1-pt 600.00
Jug, fancy, wht w/brn ball top, MN, ¼-pt 200.00
Jug, fancy, wht w/brn ball top, RW, ½-gal 165.00
Jug, fancy, wht w/brn top, RW, 2-gal 225.00
Jug, molded seam, Albany slip, bail hdl, RW, 1-gal 300.00
Jug, molded seam, Albany slip, bird mk/RW, ½-gal 135.00
Jug, molded seam, wht, bail hdl, MN, 1-qt 115.00
Jug, molded seam, wht, bail hdl, MN, ½-gal 90.00
Jug, molded seam, wht, bail hdl, RW, 1-gal 125.00
Jug, molded seam, wht, wide mouth, RW, 1-qt 40.00
Jug, shoulder; Albany slip, cone top, RW, 2-gal 475.00
Jug, shoulder; birch leaves/#5 on wht, standard top, 5-gal 115.00
Jug, shoulder; bl bands on wht, MN, 1-qt 375.00
Jug, shoulder; brn & salt glaze, ball top, RW, 1-gal 175.00
Jug, shoulder; brn & salt glaze, cone top, 2-gal 250.00
Jug, shoulder; brn & salt glaze, dome top, 2-gal 115.00
Jug, shoulder; brn & salt glaze, funnel top, MN, 1-gal 70.00
Jug, shoulder; brn & salt glaze, funnel top, MN, ½-gal 115.00
Jug, shoulder; brn & salt glaze, pear top, NS, 2-gal 300.00
Jug, shoulder; brn & salt glaze, wide mouth, NS, 1-gal 325.00
Jug, shoulder; red wing on wht, brn std top, RW, 2-gal 325.00
Jug, shoulder; red wing/#3 on wht, standard top, RWUS, 3-gal 85.00
Jug, shoulder; standard top, RW, 1-gal 32.50
Jug, shoulder; turkey eye drippings on salt glaze, NS, 2-gal 650.00
Jug, shoulder; wht, cone top, RW, ½-gal 85.00
Jug, shoulder; wht, funnel top, MN, 2-gal 65.00
Jug, shoulder; wht, standard top, MN, ½-gal 30.00
Jug, shoulder; wht, standard top, MN, 2-gal 42.50
Jug, syrup; wht, cone top, MN, 1-gal 50.00
Pan, milk; wht, MN, 7" 55.00
Pan, milk; wht, NS 75.00
Pipkin, bl & wht sponging, MN 500.00
Pipkin, wht, unsgn, 1-pt 60.00
Pitcher, Albany slip, bbl shape, RW 100.00
Pitcher, bl mottled, fancy hdl, RWUS 300.00
Pitcher, Cherryband, bl on wht, ca 1915 ....185.00
Pitcher, dk gr, emb band at top, RWUS 325.00
Pitcher, Dutch boy & girl, bl & wht, RW, 1920s, lg 635.00
Pitcher, milk; Albany slip, Russian style, ½-gal 75.00
Pitcher, mustard; Albany slip, NS 200.00
Pitcher, Spongeband & Saffron, RWUS, lg 175.00
Spittoon, Albany slip, MN, lg 450.00
Spittoon, bl bands on salt glaze, German style, MN 600.00
Spittoon, bl bands on salt glaze, German style, unsgn 375.00
Umbrella stand, bl & wht sponging 800.00
Wash bowl & pitcher, emb lily, lt bl & wht 600.00

Town and Country

A dinnerware line produced for only one year in the late 1940s, Town and Country was created by Eva Zeisel for Red Wing Potteries, Inc., of Minnesota. Zeisel was a free-lance designer whose work was already highly regarded in the ceramics field. The shapes she favored were ultra-modern, clean, and flowing. She chose simple, subdued glazes, sometimes lining the serving pieces in white. Plates and platters were designed with one side of the rim higher than the other, so that when the undersides are examined, the table ring appears off center. Bowls are free-form teardrop shapes and handles often merely extensions of the rim. The ware is not signed, but collectors recognize it by the three sagger pin marks on its glazed bottom. Though it is unusual in white, color has little or no impact on value.

Bean pot, w/lid	125.00
Bowl, fruit; free-form teardrop, either of 2 szs	12.00
Bowl, mixing; spout opposite hdl formed by rim extension	75.00
Bowl, salad; free-form teardrop, lg	75.00
Casserole, stick hdl, ind	25.00
Casserole, stick hdl, lg	45.00
Creamer & sugar bowl	45.00
Cruets, oil & vinegar, w/orig stoppers, pr	150.00
Cup & saucer	20.00
Pitcher, strap hdl follows curve of side to above rim, 2-pt	45.00
Pitcher, strap hdl follows curve of side to above rim, 3-pt	75.00
Plate, 1 side higher, rim slants, 10½"	15.00
Plate, 1 side higher, rim slants, 8"	12.00
Platter, free-from teardrop, lg	40.00
Shakers, gourd form, pr	30.00
Spoon rest/ashtray, tab hdl, w/rest, sm	12.00
Syrup pitcher, rim flange extends to pouring lip on 1 side	75.00
Teapot	150.00

Town and Country: Platter, $40.00; Plate, 6½", $5.00; Fruit bowl, $12.00, Pitcher 2-pint, $45.00.

Redware

The term redware refers to a type of simple earthenware produced by the Colonists as early as the 1600s. The red clay used in its production was abundant throughout the country, and during the 18th and 19th centuries redware was made in great quantities. Intended for utilitarian purposes such as everyday tableware or use in the dairy, redware was simple in design and decoration. Glazes of various colors were used, and a liquid clay referred to as 'slip' was sometimes applied in patterns such as zigzag lines, daisies, or stars. Plates often have a 'coggled' edge, similar to the way a pie is crimped or jagged, which is done with a special tool. In the following listings, EX (excellent condition) indicates only minor damage. Our advisor for this category is Barbara Rosen; she is listed in the Directory under New Jersey.

Bank, seated dog, brn spots, worn/flaked, 4"	85.00
Beaker, gr w/brn flecks, 3⅝"	350.00
Bowl, brn sponging, mug shape w/spout & strap hdl, 6"	100.00
Bowl, dk umber w/blk splotches, cup hdl, 4x6½", EX	185.00

Bowl, yel slip spiral stripe, dk brn band/dots, 3x8", EX	85.00
Bowl, 3-line yel slip 'commas,' coggled edge, 7", EX	140.00
Creamer, side spout, str sides, ribbed strap hdl, 4½", EX	35.00
Cup, blk splotches, sm chips/hdl hairline, 3"	300.00
Dish, yel slip free-forms, coggled edge, minor wear, 5"	325.0
Dish, 3-line yel slip 'S,' coggled, 4"	550.0
Figurine, cat, seated, hand molded/tooled, ear chipped, 6"	110.0
Flowerpot, appl saucer base, tooled/finger-crimped, 6", EX	150.0
Jar, brn speckled, ovoid, minor wear/sm flakes, 4¾"	150.0
Jar, brn splotches, mismatched lid, 8¼"	155.0
Jar, brn sponging, rim spout, lid, ovoid, #1½, 6¾", EX	200.0
Jar, brn-flecked gr-yel slip w/simple flower, ovoid, 7", VG	2,000.0
Jar, brn-gr w/brn flecks, imp: Wilcox, ovoid, 9½", EX	495.0
Jar, brn/wht swirled slip, tooled wavy band, Southern, 6x9"	215.0
Jar, brushed brn swags, tooled str/wavy lines, 7", EX	225.0
Jar, dk brn, tooled lines, pinched sides, ovoid, 5¾"	55.0
Jar, gr mottle w/orange spots, ovoid, 7½"	165.0
Jar, gr-orange spots, 3½x4½"	175.0
Jug, deep yel, pouring spout lip, 8", EX	115.0
Jug, dk brn, bottom imp NS, ovoid, ribbed strap hdl, 8", EX	95.0
Jug, dk gr w/orange spots, ovoid, minor wear/sm chips, 6"	300.0
Jug, gr speckles, ovoid, hairlines, 5½"	105.0
Loaf pan, yel slip waves & center oval, coggled edge, 14", EX	825.0
Loaf pan, 1-line yel slip waves/zigzags, prof rpr, 14"	425.0
Mold, amber, Turk's head, scalloped rim, edge chips, 10"	55.0
Mold, deep yel, Turk's head, 8", EX	65.0
Mold, dk amber w/brn, scalloped, miniature, 4½"	75.0
Pan, milk; brn flecks, minor wear, 17½"	145.0
Pan, milk; dk brn sponging, wear/sm chip, 3¾x9"	250.0
Pan, milk; int glaze, minor edge chips, 4x16"	95.0
Pie plate, #2 in yel slip, coggled edge, firing crack, 12"	300.0
Pie plate, yel slip initials, 12"	1,100.0
Pie plate, yel slip puddled in center, coggled edge, 7", EX	125.0
Pie plate, 1-line yel slip waves (4 repeats), 9", NM	350.0
Pie plate, 3-line gr/brn slip on lt slip, coggled edge, 8", EX	1,000.0
Pie plate, 3-line yel slip, X in center, coggled edge, 9", EX	450.0
Pie plate, 3-line yel slip 'wishbone' band etc, 9¾", NM	725.0
Pie plate, 3-line yel slip waves, coggled edge, 10", EX	325.0
Pie plate, 3-line yel slip waves etc, minor wear, 8"	475.0
Pie plate, 3-line yel slip waves/commas, coggled edge, 8½", EX	225.0
Pitcher, brn runs, imp tooled bands, str sides, 4½"	75.0
Pitcher, brn sponging, ribbed strap hdl, squat, 6"	175.0
Pitcher, dk brn/gr, mk Bell & Son, flake, 10"	650.0
Pitcher, dk splotches, cup shape w/side spout, rib hdl, 3"	225.0
Pitcher, mottled brn/yel slip, S Bell & Son, 9½", EX	1,100.0
Pitcher, rare bl glaze, pinched spout, strap hdl, chips, 8"	75.0
Pitcher, shiny w/dk spots, tooled lines, rpr, 9", VG	300.0
Pitcher, wht slip w/gr & brn, tooled, wear/chips, 4¾"	130.0
Pot, brn flecks w/brn drips on shoulder, tooled, 5x7"	85.0
Vase, yel slip, sgraffito leaf, hdls, att Bucks Co, 5"	235.0

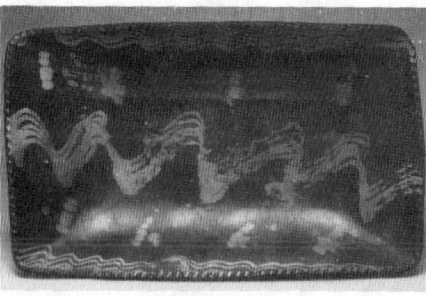

Platter, yellow slip waves and yellow and green splotches, 20" long, EX, $2,750.00.

Restraints

Since the beginning of time, many things from animals to treasures have been held in bondage by hemp, bamboo, chests, chains, shackles, and other constructed devices. Many of these devices were used to hold captives who awaited further torture, as if the restraint wasn't torturous enough. The study and collecting of restraints enables one to learn much about the advancement of civilization in the country or region from which they originated. Such devices at various times in history were made of very heavy metals — so heavy that the wearer could scarcely move about. It has only been in the last sixty years that vast improvements have been made in design and construction that afford the captive some degree of comfort. Our advisor for this category is Joseph Tanner; he is listed in the Directory under Washington.

Key:
bbl — barrel	lc — lock case
d-lb — double lock button	NST — non-swing through
K — key	ST — swing through
Kd — keyed	stp — stamped

Foreign Handcuffs

Adams, teardrop lc, bbl Kd, NST, usually not stp 170.00
Australian, Saf Lock, ST, takes pin-tumbler K in side, stp 140.00
Deutsche Polizei, ST, middle hinge, folds, takes bbl-bit K 80.00
English, Chubb, NST, hi-security 10-slider lock mechanism 275.00
English, Chubb Arrest, steel, ST, multi-bit solid K 225.00
English, Latrobe, aluminum alloy, center chain, ST, dbl-bit K ...140.00
French Lapegy, ST, aluminum alloys, takes flat bitted K 65.00
German, 3-lb steel set, 2⅝" thick, center chain, bbl K 175.00
German Clejuso, oval design, ST, dbl-cuff weight, 22-oz 100.00
German Clejuso, sq lc, adjusts/NST, d-lb on side, bbl K 100.00
German Darby, adjusts, well finished, sm 120.00
German Hamburg 8, non-adjust NST, center bar/post w/K-way ...250.00
Hiatt, English Darby, like US CW Darby, stp Hiatt & #d 65.00
Hiatt, solid state, 2 separate cuffs joined bk to bk, stp/#d 150.00
Hiatt English non-adjust screw K Karby style, uses screw K 100.00
Hiatt Figure 8, swings open to insert/withdraw wrists 125.00
Italian, stp New Police, modern Peerless type, ST, sm bbl K 35.00
Plug 8, remove plug before inserting external threaded K 200.00
Spanish, stp Alcyon/Star, modern Peerless type, flat K 65.00
Spanish, stp Alcyon/Star, modern Peerless type, ST, sm bbl K 45.00

Foreign Leg Shackles

German Clejuso, sq lc, adjusts/NST, d-bl on side, bbl K 125.00
German Clejuso Darby type, adjusts/NST/plated, uses screw K ..160.00
Hiatt English combo manacles, handcuff/leg irons w/chain 275.00
Hiatt English non-adjust screw K Darby style, uses screw K 100.00
Hiatt Plug leg irons, same K-ing as Plug-8 cuffs, w/chain 225.00

U.S. Handcuffs

American Munitions, modern/rnd, sm bbl Kd, ST bow, stp 45.00
Bean Giant, sideways figure 8, solid center lc, dbl-bit K 400.00
Bean Patrolman, kidney-bean form, d-lb on lc, NST, stp T 100.00
Bean-Cobb, sm rnd lc, removable cylinder, d-lb, NST, 1899 ....80.00
Cavenay, looks like Marlin Daley but w/screw K, NST 150.00
Civil War padlocking type, various designs w/loop for lock 150.00
Colt, modern ST bow, sm bbl Kd, stp w/Colt & co name 100.00
Flash Action Manacle, like Bean Giant w/ST, K-way center 200.00

Flexibles, steel segmented bows, NST Darby type, screw K 150.00
H&R Super, NST, shaft-hinge connector takes hollow titted K ...90.00
Harvard, takes sm bbl K, ST, stp Harvard Lock Co 65.00
Judd, NST, used rnd/internally triangular K, stp Mattatuck 100.00
Lilly Hand Iron, 2" strap iron (8" L), oval bands, NST, sq K 400.00
Marlin Daley, NST, bottle-neck form, neck stp, dbl-titted K 175.00
Mattatuck, NST, propeller-like K-way, stp Mattatuck/etc 85.00
Palmer, 2" steel bands, 2 K-ways (top & center), NST stp 300.00
Peerless, ST, takes sm bbl K, stp Mfg'ered by Peerless Co 40.00
Peerless, ST, takes sm bbl K, stp Mfg'ered by S&W Co 75.00
Phelps, NST, twist chain between cuffs, Tower Look-alike 200.00
Pratt combo, 1 cuff connnects w/nipper/claw, ST, mk Pratt 225.00
Rankin, steel NST, mk screw K 200.00
Romer, NST, takes flat K, resembles padlock, stp Romer Co 225.00
S&W 94 Maximum Security, ST, takes Ace-type K, stp S&W 80.00
Strauss, ST, takes lg solid bitted K, stp Strauss Eng Co 85.00
Tower, NST, bottom K, solid/flat fitted K goes in cuff edge 100.00
Tower bar cuffs, cuffs separate by 10-12" steel bar 120.00
Tower Dbl Lock, NST, takes bbl-bitted K, usually stp Tower 50.00
Tower Detective Pinkerton, NST, sq lc, bbl-bitted K, no stp 110.00
Tower Single Lock, NST, bbl-bit K, K-way slanted on lc, sm 70.00
Tower-Bean, NST, sm rnd lc, takes tiny bbl-bitted K, stp 75.00
Walden 'Lady Cuff,' NST, takes sm bbl K, lightweight, stp 250.00

U.S. Leg Shackles

American Munitions, as handcuffs 55.00
Civil War or prison ball & chain, padlocking or rivet type 250.00
Clog spike, 30" L opening for ankle w/padlock & 2 spikes 500.00
H&R Supers, as handcuffs 400.00
Harvard, as handcuffs 75.00
Judd, as handcuffs 135.00
Leg lock brace, metal brace, ankle to knee, lever locked 225.00
Oregon boot, break-apart shackle on above-ankle support 400.00
Palmer, as handcuffs but w/detachable chain, NST 400.00
Strauss, as handcuffs 125.00
Tower, bottom K, as handcuffs 90.00
Tower ball & chain, leg iron w/chain & 6-lb to 50-lb ball 200.00
Tower Dbl-Lock, as handcuffs 75.00
Tower Detective, as handcuffs 150.00

Various Other Restraining Devices

African slave Darby-style cuffs, heavy iron/chain, handmade 130.00
African slave Darby-style leg shackles, heavy/hand forged 160.00
African slave padlocking or riveted forged iron shackles 135.00
Darby neck collar, rnd steel loop opens w/screw K 150.00
English figure-8 nipper, claws open by lifting top lock tab 65.00
Gale finger cuff, knuckle duster, non-K, mk GFC 125.00
German nipper, twist hdl opens/closes cuff, stp Germany/etc 75.00
Jay Pee, thumb cuffs, mk solid body, bbl K 15.00
Mighty-Mite, thumb cuffs, solid body, ST, mk, bbl K 65.00
Tower Lyon, thumb cuffs, solid body, NST, dbl-bit center K 125.00

Reverse Painting on Glass

Verre eglomise is the technique of painting on the underside of glass. Dating back to the early 1700s, this art became popular in the 19th century when German immigrants chose historical figures and beautiful women as subjects for their reverse glass paintings. Advertising mirrors of this type came into vogue at the turn of the century.

Couple in Renaissance-style attire, Dieppe, 1800s, 4¾" 600.00
Cupid & Psyche, Dieppe, 1800s, 9", VG 1,000.00

Falstaff w/ewer & cup, ped base, Dieppe, 8¾", EX **1,200.00**
Figures in open-air enclosure, fr mk China, 13x15" **250.00**
Floral, on tinsel, 14x13" **150.00**
Geo WA silhouette, intricate border, fr w/gilt liner, 13x11" **250.00**
Girl in bonnet w/ostrich plume, sgn Holanderm, 12x9", EX **275.00**
Girl in hat on bl, 'I Am Promest,' 12x9" **275.00**
La Belle Polonaise, lady's portrait, some flaking, 9x12" **300.00**
Landscape/3 people in European dress, Chinese Export, 14x17" ...**875.00**
Lion, recumbent on weapons & shield, Dieppe, 7" L **875.00**
Man in wht uniform, 3-color trim, 'F Napoleon,' 15x12" **275.00**
Still life w/fruit, gilt fr, 14x16" **145.00**

Pair, in faux marble frames, 14x17", $1,800.00.

Richard

Richard, who at one time worked for Galle, made cameo art glass in France during the 1920s. His work was often multilayered and acid cut with florals and scenics in lovely colors. The ware was marked with his name in relief. Our advisor for this category is Don Williams; he is listed in the Directory under Missouri.

Cameo

Bowl, mtns/trees, brn on yel, 4½x7½" **900.00**
Cordial, floral, purple on yel/wht, silver ft, 3" **450.00**
Vase, European town, rust/red on bright pk, gourd form, 8" **1,000.00**
Vase, exotic floral, dk gr on orange to dk gr, bun ft, 15" **1,250.00**
Vase, lake/trees/church, emerald on brn mottle, slim, 22" **1,250.00**
Vase, river/trees/bldgs, bl on rust, ftd baluster, 14" **1,500.00**
Vase, river/trees/bldgs/boats, navy on yel, 14x8" **1,500.00**
Vase, 3 landscape reserves, lav/wine on gray, slim/ftd, 18" **2,500.00**

Ridgway

As early as 1792, the Ridgway brothers, Job and George, produced fine quality earthenwares in Shelton, Staffordshire, marking their products 'Ridgway, Smith, & Ridgway' and later 'Job & George Ridgway.' Around 1800 the brothers split, and each had his own firm, both in Shelton. They were joined in the business by various members of the Ridgway family, and in fact their descendants still operate there today.

The two firms created by the split were the Bell Works and the Cauldon Pottery. Bell produced stone china and earthenware decorate with blue transfer printing. Their mark was 'J. & W. Ridgway' or 'J. W.R.' (John and William) until 1848 when 'William Ridgway' wa used. The Cauldon Pottery made earthenware, stone china, and high quality porcelains fine enough to win them the distinction of bein appointed potters to the Queen. From 1830 their wares attest to th fact, bearing the Royal Arms mark with 'J.R.' within the crest. In 184 '& Co.' was added. Most examples of Ridgway's wares found today ar transfer-printed historical scenes. See also Staffordshire, Historical; an Flow Blue.

Bowl, Coaching Days, 10" **50.0**
Creamer, Coaching Days, Henry VII/Abbey of Reading **65.0**
Mug, Coaching Days, 4" **35.0**
Mug, Coaching Days, 5" **40.0**
Pitcher, Coaching Days, 5½" **60.0**
Pitcher, Coaching Days, 7½" **80.0**
Pitcher, Coaching Days, 9½", +6 4" mugs on 12½" tray **295.0**
Plate, Coaching Days, Waiting for the Stage Coach, 9" **35.0**
Plate, Coaching Days, 10" **45.0**
Tray, Coaching Days, oval, 12½" **80.0**

Riviera

Riviera was a line of dinnerware introduced by the Homer Laugh lin China Company in 1938. It was sold exclusively by the Murph Company through their nationwide chain of dime stores. Riviera wa unmarked, lightweight, and inexpensive. It was discontinued sometim prior to 1950. Colors are mauve blue, red, yellow, light green, an ivory. On rare occasions, dark blue pieces are found, but this was not standard color. For further information we recommend *The Collector Encyclopedia of Fiesta* by Sharon and Bob Huxford, available from Col lector Books.

Batter set, complete **210.0**
Batter set, ivory, w/decals **145.0**
Bowl, baker; 9" **18.0**
Bowl, cream soup; w/liner, ivory **62.0**
Bowl, fruit; 5½" **9.0**
Bowl, nappy, 9¼" **18.0**
Bowl, oatmeal; 6" **25.0**
Butter dish, cobalt, ¼-lb **200.0**
Butter dish, colors other than cobalt & turq, ¼-lb **95.0**
Butter dish, turq, ¼-lb **185.0**
Butter dish, ½-lb **85.0**
Casserole **80.0**
Creamer **8.0**
Cup & saucer, demi; ivory **50.0**
Jug, w/lid **100.0**
Pitcher, juice; mauve bl **175.0**
Pitcher, juice; yel **90.0**
Plate, deep **16.0**
Plate, 10" **30.0**
Plate, 6" **5.5**
Plate, 7" **8.0**
Plate, 9" **12.5**
Platter, cobalt, 12" **45.0**
Platter, w/closed hdls, 11¼" **17.5**
Platter, 11½" **14.0**
Sauce boat **16.5**
Saucer **3.0**
Shakers, pr **14.0**
Sugar bowl, w/lid **14.0**

Syrup, w/lid 110.00
Teacup 8.50
Teapot 100.00
Tidbit, ivory, 2-tier 70.00
Tumbler, hdld 55.00
Tumbler, juice 40.00

Robj Bottles

Robj was the name of a retail store that operated in Paris for only a few years from about 1925 to 1931. Robj solicited designs from the best French artisans of the period to produce decorative objects for the home. These objects were produced mostly in porcelain but also in glass and earthenware. The most well known are the figural bottles which were particularly popular in the United States. However, Robj also produced tea sets, perfume lamps, chess sets, ashtrays, bookends, humidors, powder jars, cigarette boxes, figurines, lamps, and milk pitchers. Robj objects tend to be whimsical, and all embody the Art Deco style. Our advice for this category comes from Randall Monsen and Rod Baer; their address is listed in the Directory under Virginia.

Bottle, clergyman 275.00
Decanter, musical, Russian man, hat is stopper, 12" 275.00
Decanter, preacher in blk robe, hands at waist, 11" 165.00

Inkwell, figural Blackamoor in gold-trimmed white turban and costume, marked, $660.00.

Inkwell, Blackamoor in gold/wht robe holds well, no lid, 6" 275.00
Inkwell, seated Indian in turban holds ink pot, 6" 660.00
Lamp, iron std: 4 posts/rnd base, emb 6" glass shade 1,500.00
Lamp base, porc, gr leaves/red berries, appl wht balls, 7" 220.00
Perfume burner, wht-robbed Oriental, X-legged on steps, 8" 550.00

Rock 'N Roll Memorabilia

Memorabilia from the early days of Rock 'n Roll recalls an era that many of us experienced firsthand; these listings are offered to demonstrate the many and various aspects of this area of collecting. Values are for mint condition examples. Some are one-of-a-kind items that have sold at specialty auctions and are included as a reference guide to demonstrate price range and rarity.

Avalon, Frankie; pillow, stuffed, 1950s, 10x10" 125.00
Beatles, blanket, cotton w/screen print, M 235.00
Beatles, calendar, 1964, EX 95.00
Beatles, dolls w/instruments, inflatable, Nems, 15", set of 4 ....165.00
Beatles, game, Flip Your Wig, 1964 ....90.00
Beatles, guitar, Four-Pop, NM 250.00
Beatles, nodders, Carmascot, orig box, NM 595.00
Beatles, Paul doll, Remco, 5", M in torn box 100.00

Beatles, 4" plastic guitar pin on original card, 1964, $45.00.

Beatles, puzzle, Yel Submarine, 19x19", M 125.00
Beatles, record album, Yesterday & Today, Apple label, VG 25.00
Beatles, Ringo poster, Avedon, sealed 75.00
Beatles, Ringo wall plaque, ceramic, NM 85.00
Beatles, T-shirt transfer (group photos), 1960s, 5-pcs 40.00
Beatles, wallet, red/wht, names on front, bk: photo, M 100.00
Bee Gees, jigsaw puzzle, 1979, in sealed box 18.50
Burns, Kookie; comb, 1959, M on card 50.00
Jackson, Michael; doll, 1984, w/stand, 12" 20.00
Kiss, backpack 50.00
Kiss, doll set, set of 4, NM in box 350.00
Kiss, dress shirt, photo tag, 1977, M 65.00
Kiss, Halloween costume, M in EX box, set of 4 ....175.00
Kiss, van model, MIB 75.00
Partridge Family, paper doll book, uncut, 1970, M 24.00
Partridge Family, photo album activity book, 1973, M 20.00
Presley, Elvis; bandana, Elvis Enterprises, 1956, EX 175.00
Presley, Elvis; book, Elvis & Me, by Priscilla, 1985, hardbk 10.00
Presley, Elvis; book, Elvis in Hollywood, Ochs & Pond, 108-pg ...30.00
Presley, Elvis; demo album, sgn/inscribed on cover, 1950s 700.00
Presley, Elvis; karati jacket, wht cotton w/embr initials 500.00
Presley, Elvis; musical decanter, McCormick, gold or platinum ..225.00
Presley, Elvis; phonograph, automatic changer, EX 900.00
Presley, Elvis; photo charm 45.00
Presley, Elvis; sgn 45 rpm Heartbreak Hotel cover, fr w/plaque ..325.00
Presley, Elvis; toy guitar, 1984 ....25.00
Presley, Elvis; 78 rpm record, Love Me Tender, RCA, M 65.00

Rockingham

In the early part of the 19th century, American potters began to favor brown- and buff-burning clays over red because of their durability. The glaze favored by many was Rockingham, which varied from a dark brown mottle to a sponged effect sometimes called tortoise shell. It consisted in part of manganese and various metallic salts and was used by many potters until well into the 20th century. Over the past two years, demand and prices have risen sharply, especially in the east. See also Bennington.

Bank, church figural, 3¾" 75.00
Bottle, pistol shape, EX detail/appl name, prof rstr, 11" 95.00
Bottle, Queen Victoria 1st, figural, 9" 125.00

Bowl, EX spotted glaze, octagonal, minor wear, 12" L 175.00
Bowl, rim flakes, 3½x12" 95.00
Bowl, shallow, 3¾x13" 60.00
Bowl, sm chips, 3¼x8½" 65.00
Bowl, wear/hairline, 4½x12½" 115.00
Bowl, 3x10" 45.00
Bowl, 5¾x12¾" 150.00
Cuspidor, vintage, brn/gr, Steeler-Taylor-Bloor, rpr, 10" 375.00

Dog, free-standing front legs, excellent detail, 12", $495.00.

Dog, seated, gr specks, 6¾", M 170.00
Dog, Staffordshire type, oblong base, 9½", EX 85.00
Flowerpot, acanthus leaves, 2-pc, hairline, 10" 65.00
Flowerpot, tulips, E Liverpool, 2-pc, 8¾", EX 165.00
Inkwell, sleeping girl, base chips, 5" L 145.00
Jar, canning; no lid, 6" 95.00
Jar, good spotted glaze, 6x5½" 65.00
Jar, molded hdls, acorn finial, cylindrical, 11" 145.00
Mold, oval, 5" L 150.00
Mold, Turk's head, some bl flecks, sm flakes, 4x10½" dia 145.00
Mold, Turk's head, 9" dia 75.00
Mug, emb rim band, 3¾" 125.00
Mug, str sides, 3½" 100.00
Pitcher, hanging fish, bulbous, w/lid, prof rpr, 9" 225.00
Pitcher, hunt scenes, minor edge chips, 7" 200.00
Pitcher, hunt scenes/vintage, sm chips, 8½" 175.00
Pitcher, lg anchor, rope rim, 10" 250.00
Pitcher, mask spout, serpent hdl, 9¾" 565.00
Pitcher, oval bust of Geo WA, bubbled glaze, 6" 45.00
Pitcher, paneled, bulbous, hairlines/sm chips, 9" 195.00
Pitcher, paneled, str sides, minor wear, 8" 225.00
Pitcher, plain, 11", EX 125.00
Pitcher, Toby form, sm glaze flakes, 9½" 75.00
Pitcher, Winter King mask under spout, 8", EX 160.00
Plate, 10½" 110.00
Soap dish, leaves, 6" L 85.00
Soap dish, oval, 4¾" 85.00
Soap dish, 4" dia 80.00
Teapot, Rebecca at the Well 155.00
Tumbler, tavern scenes, 6" 65.00

Rogers, John

John Rogers (1829-1904) was a machinist from Manchester, New Hampshire, who turned his hobby of sculpting into a financially successful venture. From the originals he meticulously fashioned of red clay, he had bronze master molds made from which plaster copies were cast. He specialized in five different categories: theatrical, Shakespeare, Civil War, everyday life, and horses. His large detailed groupings portrayed the life and times of the period between 1859 and 1892. When

no condition is indicated, examples are assumed to be in very good t excellent condition. Our advisor for this category is George Humphrey he is listed in the Directory under Maryland.

Bath 2,000.0
Bushwacker 2,000.0
Checkers Players, sm 1,500.0

Checkers Up at the Farm $450.00.

Country Post Office 750.0
Fairy's Whisper, ca 1881 ....1,400.0
Fetching the Doctor 750.0
Fighting Bob, ca 1889 ....1,100.0
First Ride 725.0
Football, inscr, 16x11" 1,000.0
Frolick at the Ol' Homestead, 1887, 22½" 800.0
Going for the Cows 450.0
Home Guard 800.0
Madam Your Mother Craves a Word 700.0
Mail Day 2,000.0
Matter of Opinion 600.0
One More Shot 550.0
Playing Doctor 700.0
Rip Van Winkle at Home, 18½" 425.0
School Days 600.0
Slave Auction 2,000.0
Speak for Yourself John 600.0
Taking the Oath & Drawing Rations, sgn, 23" 525.0
Tap on the Window 525.0
Village Schoolmaster 850.0
Washington 1,250.0
Watch for the Santa Maria 700.0
Weighing the Baby, Pat 1875, 21" 600.0
Wounded Scout, ca 1864 ....750.0

Rookwood

The Rookwood Pottery Company was established in 1879 in Cincinnati, Ohio. Its founder was Maria Longworth Nichols Storer daughter of a wealthy family who provided the backing necessary to make such an enterprise possible. Mrs. Storer hired competent cerami workers who through constant experimentation developed many line of superior art pottery. While in her employ, Laura Fry invented the airbrush-blending process for which she was issued a patent in 1884 From this, several lines were designed that utilized blended back rounds. One of their earlier lines, Standard, was a brown ware decorated with underglaze slip-painted nature studies, animals, portraits, etc. Iris and Sea Green were introduced in 1894 and Vellum, a transparent mat-glaze line, in 1904. Other lines followed: Ombroso in 1910 and Soft Porcelain in 1915. Many of the early artware lines were signed by the artist. Soon after the turn of the 20th century, Rookwood manufactured 'production' pieces that relied mainly on molded designs and forms rather than freehand decoration for their esthetic appeal. The Depression brought on financial difficulties from which the pottery never recovered. Though it continued to operate, the quality of the ware deteriorated, and the pottery was forced to close in 1967.

Unmarked Rookwood is only rarely encountered. Many marks may be found, but the most familiar is the reverse 'RP' monogram. First used in 1886, a flame point was added above it for each succeeding year until 1900. After that a Roman numeral added below indicated the year of manufacture. Impressed letters that related to the type of clay utilized for the body were also used — G for ginger, O for olive, R for red, S for sage green, W for white, and Y for yellow. Artware must be judged on an individual basis. Quality of the artwork is a prime factor to consider. Portraits, animals, and birds are worth more than florals; and pieces signed by a particularly renowned artist are highly prized. Our advice for this category comes from Fer-Duc Inc., whose address is listed in the Directory under New York.

Bisque

Ewer, honeysuckle on lt peach, S Toohey, #62, 1888, 7" 625.00
Jar, wild roses, G Young, bulbous w/can neck, 1889, 6" 600.00
Jardiniere, magnolias on lt bl, gold neck, AR Valentien, 10" ..1,900.00
Jug, water; spider/bats/moon, artist sgn, #41, 1883, 9" 650.00
Mug, cherubs emb, Cincinnati Cooperage Co in ribbon, 8" 290.00
Pilgrim flask, cvd outlines of Oriental figures etc, 8x5" 850.00
Pilgrim flask, inscribed figural cvg, Cranch, 1884, 8x5" 2,500.00
Vase, floral branch on lt bl, Shirayamadani, 1887, 22" 3,000.00
Vase, floral on peach, cvd/gilt accents, MA Daly, 1887, 11" 550.00
Vase, floral/gold bands, Daly, bottle form, #238C, 1887, 11" 950.00
Vase, sm wht flowers on lt bl, Artus Van Briggle, 1888, 5½" 800.00

Cameo

Bowl, floral, S Toohey, crimped rim, #362, 1887, 2x5" 170.00
Bowl, magnolias on lt peach, artist sgn, #305, 1886, 11" 250.00
Creamer, floral spray on peach/wht, S Toohey, #47, 1887, 2" 150.00
Cup & saucer, daisies, E Abel, #291, 1891, 2¾" 325.00
Pitcher, floral, AM Valentien, ovoid body, 1887, 6", EX 190.00
Pitcher, floral, wht/rust on peach, L Perkins, #13, 1887, 6" 400.00
Pitcher, floral on peach, A Sprague, #251, 1889, 8½" 425.00
Pitcher, mums/Oriental motif on bl, Shirayamadani, lid, 8" 2,300.00
Plate, daisies on lt peach, O Reed, scalloped, 1891, 7½" 275.00
Rose jar, roses, Artus Van Briggle, rtcl/gilt stopper, 8x6" 850.00

Iris

Bowl, cherry blossoms, L Asbury, #956, 1906, 2x5" 280.00
Vase, band of peacock feathers, C Schmidt, 1908, 10" 4,500.00
Vase, cranes/blk pine trees & bands, Shirayamadani, 12" 41,000.00
Vase, dogwood base band, L Asbury, #1278D, 1910, 10x5" 1,100.00
Vase, gaggle of geese, Olga Reed, #808, 1896, 7½" 2,600.00
Vase, goldenrod, S Sax, #808, 1901, 7" 1,500.00
Vase, iris, L Asbury, #954C, 1905, 10" 3,300.00
Vase, lg carnations, EX art, C Schmidt, 1903, 13" 11,000.00
Vase, lg dogwood bouquet, S Toohey, 1900, 12x4½" 1,700.00
Vase, lg floral/leaves, cream/bl on brn, J Jensen, 1944, 8" 850.00
Vase, lg iris/buds, EX art/design, C Schmidt, 1907, 10" 5,200.00

Vase, lg irises on blk, C Schmidt, 1903, drilled, 13" 37,000.00
Vase, lg mc pansies, E Hurley, bulbous, 1945, 4½" 900.00
Vase, lg poppies, EX art, C Schmidt, #S1750, 1903, 16x11" ...6,500.00
Vase, lg poppies/heavy slip leaves, J Zettel, 1902, 8" 1,400.00
Vase, milkweed pods on shaded tan, Rothenbusch, 1902, 8x6"..1,000.00
Vase, nasturtiums at shoulder, R Fechheimer, 1903, 6x3" 850.00
Vase, rose branch, coral on pk to lav, SE Coyne, 1906, 8x5" ..1,300.00
Vase, roses, pk on lt to dk gr, Ed Diers, #745C, 1902, 6" 650.00
Vase, roses cvd/pnt, branches to bottom, W McDonald, 10" ...1,700.00
Vase, roses on gray, S Coyne, 1904, 5½" 500.00
Vase, 2 lg fish, ET Hurley, #860, 1899, 6" 2,700.00

Jewel Porcelain

Vase, cherry blossoms/birds in sqs on pk, P Conant, 1918, 9" 1,700.00
Vase, floral wreath at shoulder, L Epply, 1919, 5½x6½" 1,000.00
Vase, gooseberry branches at top, M McDonald, 1942, 7x4" 550.00
Vase, lg parrot, Shirayamadani, 1930, 9" 2,750.00

Limoges

Ewer, spiders/webs/daisies, artist sgn, 1882, 12" 650.00
Honey jug, dragonflies/grasses/gilt, M Retting, 1882, 4" 425.00
Jug, swallows on tan/brn, W McDonald, 1883, 4½" 550.00
Pitcher, bamboo trees/clouds, blk/wht/brn/gilt, Horton, 7" 400.00
Pitcher, bats/grasses, gold accents, MP McDonald, #200, 8" 700.00
Pitcher, insects/grasses, AR Valentien, 1882, 7" 750.00
Plate, bird/grasses, artist sgn, swirl rim, 1885, 6½" 175.00

Vase, high-gloss floral, att Shirayamadani, 1925, 5", $550.00; Vase, tiger-eye background with dark birds, A.R. Valentien, 1891, 12½", $850.00; Honey jug, Limoges style, dragonflies and grasses with gold highlights, M. Rettig, 1882, 4", $425.00.

Vase, fish trapped in appl gold net, ML Nichols, 19½" 1,500.00
Vase, lg bird/several sm birds, AR Valentien, 1883, 12" 600.00
Vase, rabbit jumps fox over log, att Cranch, hdls, 1882, 11" ...1,800.00

Mat

Bowl, Arts & Crafts floral emb at rim, bl, 1928, #2151, 8" 160.00
Bowl, carnations cvd in bl/red, S Toohey, #366Z, 1904, 3x5" 550.00
Bowl, swirl cvg, bl on yel, W Hentschel, #923, 1913, 7", EX 200.00
Bowl, 4 floral panels emb on yel, #2568, 1922, 8" 70.00
Candlestick, floral emb on bl, petal cup, #1192, 1922, 7" 150.00
Lamp, nasturtiums cvg, rtcl vine base, Shirayamadani, 11" 2,800.00
Pitcher, geometrics cvd on gr, crimped 3-side top, 1907, 5" 210.00
Vase, Arts & Crafts floral cvd/emb on yel/gr, #1877, 1908, 5" ...200.00
Vase, Arts & Crafts leaves emb on pk/gr, #2379, 1917, 9" 375.00
Vase, Aztec faces on pk/gr, #2873, 1925, 4" 110.00
Vase, berries/leaves emb on bl, #6444, 1914, 6" 80.00
Vase, bud/leaf/line cvg on gr, Fechheimer, #167Z, 1904, 4" 230.00

Vase, butterfly band emb on pk, #2076, 1925, 6" 110.00
Vase, curved banding forms panels & ft, yel, #2093, 1921, 3" 80.00
Vase, floral stems emb/cvd to base, bl/brn, #2373, 1926, 7" 100.00
Vase, floral-emb mat gr/pk, Van Briggle style, 1913, 9" 750.00
Vase, floral/lines/dots emb, E Barrett, #6864, 1944, 8" 700.00
Vase, geometric floral cvg on brn, gourd form, #934, 13x9" 600.00
Vase, leaves & mistletoe emb alternate, bl, #2413, 1927, 8" 160.00
Vase, leaves sculpted/cvd, lime/gr/red, Shirayamadani, 14" 1,500.00
Vase, lg leaf emb on dk bl, #2482, 1920, 12" 210.00
Vase, long pointed leaves emb, bl, #1822, 1926, 6" 140.00
Vase, neck band cvd on gr, 3 lg hdls, #659D, 1907, 6" 250.00
Vase, poppies cvd on lt gr drip,#2862, 1925, 11" 250.00
Vase, poppy emb, red/gr, Shirayamadani, #1298, 1913, 6" 260.00
Vase, red tulips cvd on gr, R Fechheimer, #939D, 1906, 7" 550.00
Vase, sea horses/vegetation emb on bl, #2176, 1919, 9" 170.00
Vase, shoulder band w/emb triangles, lt bl, #2439, 1927, 7" 240.00
Vase, silver o/l mk Shreve at bottom, floral top, Todd, 8" 1,600.00
Vase, tiny flowers emb on bl, 5-sided, #2811, 1925, 4" 75.00

Porcelain

Box, 4 brn horses drawn on wht to lt bl, L Abel, 1946, 5x6" 230.00
Flowerpot, tulips, pk/yel on bl gloss, Shirayamadani, 1946 ....750.00
Plaque, scenic, EX color/composition, Ed Diers, 10x6" 3,000.00
Teapot, band of ships, salmon on wht, S Sax, 1912, 4x8" 375.00
Vase, abstract swirls, J Jensen, #30E, 1945, 9" 750.00
Vase, berries in heavy slip, W Rhem, #6374, 1955, 5" 220.00
Vase, berries/leaves, Barrett, w/lid, #6569, 1946, 7x7" 450.00
Vase, bluebirds/flowers on wht gloss, #6183F, 1944, 5" 350.00
Vase, daffodils, geometric bands, Shirayamadani, 1933, 8" 2,200.00
Vase, deer outlines, brn/bl/gray, Jens Jensen, 1945, 8x4" 1,300.00
Vase, floral, red/gray on wht, E Barrett, #6199F, 1946, 4x5" 350.00
Vase, honeysuckle, EX art, Shirayamadani, 1922, 13" 6,500.00
Vase, impressionistic bird on branch, ET Hurley, 1929, 10" 2,000.00
Vase, impressionistic mc floral, E Hurley, #2983, 1930, 15" 2,700.00
Vase, plums/leaves relief, brn/bl/wht, Jensen, 1944, 8x9" 1,100.00
Vase, watercolor birds/lilies, ET Hurley, #6204C, 1946, 7x7" .1,200.00
Vase, watercolor-style poppies, Shirayamadani, hdls, 10" 750.00

Sea Green

Vase, fish, MA Daly, teardrop form, 1897, 5½" 3,000.00
Vase, hyacinths cvd on dk gr, S Toohey, #614, 1900, 8" 700.00
Vase, jonquils on med ocean gr, AR Valentien, 1895, 10" 5,500.00
Vase, pansies on lt to dk gr, C Baker, #932, 1903, 8½" 2,800.00
Vase, poplar leaves, Artus Van Briggle, #743C, 1896, 7x4" 1,600.00
Vase, tulips, lt on dk gr, S Coyne, #902, 1903, 9" 5,250.00
Vase, 4 butterflies/grasses, L Asbury, ovoid w/sq base, 8" 4,000.00
Vase, 5 flying geese, hand thrown, CA Baker, 1899, 11x10" 9,000.00

Standard

Basket, wild roses, Artus Van Briggle, #45, 1888, 5" 500.00
Bowl, holly, AB Sprague/L&W, incurvate, 2x6" 175.00
Candle holder, wild roses, C Bonsall, #635, hdl, 1903, 2¾" 300.00
Chamberstick, clover, curled hdl, FV, 1901, 3" 160.00
Chocolate pot, jonquils, E Lincoln, #771, 1904, 9½" 500.00
Creamer, berries/ferns, S Markland, #543, 1893, 2½x5", NM 100.00
Cup & saucer, floral, AB Sprague, fluted edges, #414, 1889 ....190.00
Ewer, floral w/lg wraparound leaves, F Vreeland, 7" 375.00
Ewer, roses, M Perkins, #467, 1888, 9" 750.00
Ewer, turtle/goldstone effect, MA Daly, #26, 1886, 12" 1,400.00
Humidor, cigars/matches/pipes etc, Ed Diers, 1899, 6½" 1,600.00
Jug, floral, O Reed, spout to side, #694, 1893, 6½" 500.00

Jug, grapes, R Fechheimer, #767, 1898, no stopper, 6" 240.00
Loving cup, ghost/bats/inscription, HE Wilcox, rpr, 7x6" 2,300.00
Loving cup, Indian, silver o/l bands, G Young, 1898, 7" 4,750.00
Loving cup, mums, WP McDonald, #609, 1892, 8" 950.00
Mug, ears of corn, C Steinle, #587, 5½" 300.00
Mug, frightened man in tree, Shirayamadani, #587, 1891, NM ..935.00
Mug, Queen's guard, Alice in Wonderland, H Wilcox, rstr, 5" ..475.00
Pitcher, dandelions w/detailed leaves, M Nourse, 1891, 6x8" 500.00
Vase, Blk-Eyed Susans, L Van Briggle, #916E, 1903, 4" 325.00
Vase, clover, CC Lineman, #932C, 1904, 8", Xd/M 260.00
Vase, clover, ET Hurley, #352, 1897, 6" 270.00
Vase, daisies on yel to brn, L Hanscomb, 7x4½" 650.00
Vase, dragon/clouds, butterfly hdls, lid, Shiraymadani, 6" 3,250.00
Vase, floral, HR Strafer, melon ribbed, #459D, 7½x5" 800.00
Vase, Indian portrait, titled, S Laurence, 1900, 13" 5,500.00
Vase, lg all-around cvd irises, Shirayamadani, 1900, 18x10" ...7,250.00
Vase, lg full-blown roses, MA Daly, #560A, 1890, 16" 1,900.00
Vase, lg irises, EX art, AR Valentien, #139A, 1890, 20" 3,150.00
Vase, lotus, EX art, AR Valentien, long neck, 1890, 21" 3,500.00
Vase, mum bouquet in rust, Shirayamadani, 1901, 12x4¾" 1,400.00
Vase, poppies, EX art, CC Lindeman, #913D, 1907, 8" 425.00
Vase, portrait of cavalier, G Young, 1903, 8", Xd/M 1,300.00
Vase, silver o/l scrolls on leaves, L Asbury, bulbous, 5½" 4,000.00
Vase, sweet peas, CA Baker, rnd w/long neck, #352, 1895, 6" 280.00

Tiger Eye

Vase, dk birds on gr/yel, AR Valentien, #589C, 1891, 13" 850.00
Vase, lg crayfish, AR Valentien, 1894, 6" 1,900.00
Vase, 1888, daffodils, Shirayamadani, #216, 13" 1,600.00

Vellum

Plaque, Dull Day, twilight sky, Rothenbusch, 1915, 8x6" 1,500.00
Plaque, houses/woodland, F Rothenbusch, 1929, 7x11½" 4,600.00
Plaque, Morning Mist, L Epply, 1925, 8x5", orig fr 2,600.00
Plaque, Venetian harbor, C Schmidt, 1922, uncrazed, 9x7" ..12,250.00
Teapot, floral, K Hickman, bulbous, 1889, 4½" 500.00
Vase, berries/leaves, bl/wine on gray, Rothenbusch, 1931, 6" 850.00
Vase, birch trees/lake, EX art, E Hurley, #1121C, 1917, 10" ...2,700.00
Vase, bldgs/windmill in sq on purple, A Conant, '16, 9", EX 950.00
Vase, cherries, EX art, S Coyne, #1357C, 1926, 11" 900.00
Vase, cherry blossoms on pk, wht top band, Hurley, 1920, 10" ...700.00
Vase, dogwood, K Van Dorne, #942D, 1911, 6" 495.00
Vase, fish at top/seaweed, artist sgn, 14" 5,000.00
Vase, fish on peach to gr, ET Hurley, #989D, 1905, 8" 2,700.00
Vase, fish on turq, ET Hurley, minor glaze flaws, 11" 3,250.00
Vase, floral, EX art/color, K Van Horn, #907D, 1916, 12" 1,050.00
Vase, floral around shoulder, L Abel, #562, 1925, 10" 550.00
Vase, floral cvd on pastels, Shirayamadani, #2191, 1931, 5" 550.00
Vase, floral under rim, F Rothenbusch, #233, 1915, 8" 425.00
Vase, geometrics at top on lt gr w/rust, #1552D, 1911, 9" 350.00
Vase, Greek Key band cvd on gr w/pk & yel streaks, 5x9" 240.00
Vase, Greek Key band on lt gr wash over rose, 1907, 4" 300.00
Vase, harbor w/boats on gr, EX color/art, S Sax, 1904, 8" 3,250.00
Vase, landscape, incised bands, EX style/color, S Sax, 7" 1,800.00
Vase, lg trees, Ed Diers, #900D, 1923, 7" 1,700.00
Vase, lg trees/mtns, ET Hurley, #937, 1916, 10" 1,980.00
Vase, lily pond/flowers/grasses, Ed Diers, #988C, 1913, 9" 1,000.00
Vase, meadow, deep colors, L Asbury, 1923, uncrazed, 7¾" 2,000.00
Vase, mtn range/lowland lakes, Ed Diers, 1910, 10" 1,500.00
Vase, narcissus, OG Reed, #080V, 1912, 8" 550.00
Vase, peonies, pk/wht on bl shaded, MH McDonald, 1934, 8" ...600.00
Vase, poppies w/long stems that form panels, E Lincoln, 6" 500.00

Vase, river scene, ET Hurley, uncrazed, 1938, 8x3" 1,300.00
Vase, sailboat fleet, C Schmidt, gourd form, 1922, 8x4½" 1,700.00
Vase, sailboats, EX art, S Coyne, #932D, 1913, 10" 2,500.00
Vase, tree scene w/full moon, Shirayamadani, 1901, 16" 2,750.00
Vase, trees blend into top band, S Coyne, #952F, 1913, 7" 900.00
Vase, trees on pk/bl, ET Hurley, bulbous, 1941, 9¾" 3,800.00
Vase, trees/lake/birds, Shirayamadani, 1910, 8" 4,100.00
Vase, trees/lake/mtns, EX color, L Asbury, #800C, 1915, 9" ... 2,500.00
Vase, trees/lake/mtns, L Asbury, #946, 1915, 11", EX 900.00
Vase, trees/pond, CJ McLaughlin, #922, 1913, 6" 935.00
Vase, trees/pond, S Coyne, #829V, 1921, 10" 2,000.00
Vase, wide dogwood band, pk/bl on brn, sgn KJ, 1923, 7x7½" .. 1,400.00
Vase, wild roses, Ed Diers, #130, 1927, 7x7" 1,100.00
Vase, winter scene w/trees, S Coyne, #2441, 1919, 14", NM ..6,000.00
Vase, wisteria branches, EX art, ET Hurley, #977, 1927, 11" .. 1,800.00
Vase, 13 cvd flamingos on bl, EX cvg/pnt, JD Wareham, 14" ..6,000.00
Vase, 4-petal upright flowers alternate w/leaves, #2129, 9" 180.00
Vase, 9 birds/vines & trees, EX art, Shirayamadani, 13" 6,000.00

Wax Mat

Bowl, pk/gray, canoe shape, #643D, 1922, 8" L 70.00
Potpourri, pk/gray, rtcl lid over inner lid, #1322, 1920, 5" 250.00
Vase, beaded motif at top/base, pk/gray, 4-sided, #2762, 4" 50.00
Vase, dogwood, EX color, Shirayamadani, #2745, 1940, 9" 750.00
Vase, floral at top/stems to base, gr/pk, #2392, 1920, 9" 140.00
Vase, floral band at shoulder, K Jones, 1930, 6" 350.00
Vase, lg berries/leaves, EX art, J Jensen, #2885, 1930, 8" 850.00
Vase, lg floral, EX art, W Rhem, #356E, 1929, 7" 600.00
Vase, oval leaves/stylized floral at base, bl/gr, #463B, 20" 1,300.00
Vase, watercolor-style floral, EX art, J Jensen, 1931, 9" 900.00

Miscellaneous

Vase, large fish and floral, Jens Jensen, 1945, 8¾", $1,000.00.

Ashtray, 1946, rook, gr gloss, #1139, 4x8" 140.00
Bookends, 1948, owl, brn gloss, #2655, 6", Xd/M 240.00
Bookends, 1953, puppy, brn gloss, #2998, 5x5" 250.00
Bowl, 1920, stylized clover band on gr, #2162, 8" 140.00
Bowl, 1928, gr gloss w/blk int, 13", +frog w/open flowers 90.00
Bowl, 1929, bowl, lt bl crystalline, gray ext, #2258C, 7" 120.00
Bust, 1930, lady, wht mat, #2026, 8x7" 300.00
Figurine, undtd, bird, wht/gray gloss, #6981, 10" 240.00
Figurine, 1925, seated nude, wht mat, L Abel, #2628, 4x5" 350.00
Figurine, 1934, boxer dog, brn/bl gloss, L Abel, 4½" 400.00
Figurine, 1944, standing bulldog, naturalistic colors, 10" 800.00
Frieze, Arts & Crafts pastel scenic, rstr, 8-tile, ea 9" 3,250.00
Inkwell, 1922, sphinx, brn mat, #2504, no lid, 10" 450.00
Jar, 1885, insect, yel on mahog, red clay, AR Valentien, 7" 1,500.00
Jar, 1928, bl gloss, Oriental-style hexagon, dome lid, 8" 120.00

Paperweight, 1924, rook on rectangular base, lt brn, #2810 .... 400.00
Paperweight, 1935, potter at wheel, mat gr, 12-sided, 4" 150.00
Pin tray, 1946, reclining nude, wht mat, #2595, 2x4" 140.00
Pitcher, 1946, Grecians emb on bright gr gloss, #6791, 11" 80.00
Sign, advertising; 1947, dbl sided, scroll ends, #2788 .... 1,175.00
Tile, unmk, oak tree/lake cvg, 3-color mat, 18x12" 400.00
Trivet, 1937, bird on branch, yel/gr on lav, 6" dia 275.00
Vase, undtd, berries/leaves on yel gloss, Shirayamadani, 6" 100.00
Vase, 1884, leaves cvd on glossy red clay, Bookprinter, 12" 270.00
Vase, 1884, molded medallion/band on dk yel gloss, #80B, 7" 220.00
Vase, 1894, Aerial Blue, cattle, WP McDonald, #273, 5½" 4,500.00
Vase, 1911, fish on gr aventurine, S Coyne, #1658E, 9" 550.00
Vase, 1924, abstract patterns/Blk Opal glaze, S Sax, 12" 2,500.00
Vase, 1926, bl mat, hexagonal, 5" 90.00
Vase, 1932, brn/bl feathered gloss, #8303, 4" 130.00
Vase, 1932, rose drip over bl/caramel gloss, #6306, 7" 300.00
Vase, 1933, butterfat w/floral, ET Hurley, 5" 500.00
Vase, 1936, butterfat w/daffodils, MH McDonald, mk S, 7" 650.00
Vase, 1941, lg oval upright leaves, gr aventurine, #2282, 5" 160.00
Vase, 1946, butterfat w/allover circles, E Barrett, 10" 700.00
Vase, 1946, daffodils/leaves emb on bl, #6830, 7" 100.00
Vase, 1946, impalas in blk on bl w/crystals, E Barett, 12¾" 1,200.00
Vase, 1946, iris drawn/pnt on wht gloss, J Jensen, 9" 775.00
Vase, 1947, dk burgundy gloss, #778, 10", pr 400.00
Vase, 1949, emb leaves, bl gloss, #6894 9" 50.00
Vase, 1949, Mexicans/animals emb on brn gloss, #6762, 5" 80.00
Vase, 1950, clover-shaped neck, dk gray/bl/wht drip, 7" 90.00
Vase, 1952, yel gloss, sq, #6562, 2½x2" 40.00
Vase, 1953, daisies emb on gr gloss, #6434, 5" 80.00
Vase, 1953, raised vertical ½-columns, gr gloss, sq, 10" 180.00
Vase, 1955, emb cattail band, pk gloss, #2472, 5" 80.00
Vase, 1965, floral emb on gr gloss, mk Starkville MS, 9" 100.00

Rorstrand

The Rorstrand Pottery was established in Sweden in 1726 and is today Sweden's oldest existing pottery. The earliest ware, now mostly displayed in Swedish museums, was much like old Delft. Later types were hard-paste porcelains that were enameled and decorated in a peasant style. Contemporary pieces are often described as Swedish Modern. Rorstrand is also famous for their Christmas plates.

Beaker, relief-sculpted flowers, pk/gray, sgn, 4½" 325.00
Coffeepot, floral sprays emb, lav/gr, 1900s, 9" 500.00
Urn, majolica, fruit/scrolls/masks, figural hdls, 20", EX 500.00
Vase, magnolias, pk/purple on lt gr, sgn Erikson/#3161, 21" 1,200.00

Rose Mandarin

Similar in design to Rose Medallion, this Chinese Export porcelain features the pattern of a robed mandarin, often separated by florals, ladies, genre scenes, or butterflies in polychrome enamels, often having gold trim. Elaborate in decoration, this pattern was popular from the late 1700s until the early 1840s.

Bowl, vegetable; 1840, 11" L, pr 1,500.00
Brush box, 1840, 7¾" L, EX 875.00
Dish, 1840s, sq, 9", pr 1,800.00
Pilgrim flask, lizard hdl, bk: peacocks, 1840, 10", pr 3,500.00
Platter, fruit; shaped rim, 1840s, rpr, 16" L 875.00
Punch bowl, chips, 14" 975.00
Punch bowl, gilt, 19", NM 4,500.00
Punch bowl, 1840, 16" 2,750.00

Punch bowl, 1840s, hairlines, 21" 3,400.00
Shrimp dish, lobed rims w/extended ends, 1840, 11" L, pr 1,800.00
Temple jar, foo dog finial, 4 appl dog heads, 1830, 17" 2,500.00
Vase, 1860s, rpr, 9½", pr 495.00
Wash basin, 17", +water bottle, 16", both VG 1,200.00

Rose Medallion

Rose Medallion is one of the patterns of Chinese export porcelain produced before 1850 until the second decade of the 20th century. It is decorated in rose colors with panels of florals, birds, and butterflies that form reserves containing Chinese figures. Pre-1850s ware is unmarked and is characterized by quality workmanship and gold trim. From about 1850 until circa 1860, the kilns in Canton did not operate, and no Rose Medallion was made. Post-1860 examples (still unmarked) can often be recognized by the poor quality of the gold trim or its absence. In the 1890s, the ware was often marked 'China'; 'Made in China' was used from 1910 through the 1930s.

Bowl, vitreous ware, Royal Worcester blank, 1870, 12" L 1,100.00
Bowl, 1880, 16" 1,400.00
Bowl, 4 panels, 2 w/birds & flowers, 2x9½" 250.00
Canister, sqd, dome lid, 1800s, 3x5¾", set of 5, EX 2,100.00

Fruit basket, leaf handles, chips, 11" long, $450.00; Chamber pot, 7¾", EX, $350.00; Jardiniere, 10" diameter, $650.00.

Garden seat, 1800s, lt wear, 18" 2,200.00
Platter, fruit; shaped oval, 1860, gilt wear, 15" 990.00
Punch bowl, 14" 1,650.00
Tea bowl & saucer, 1880s 55.00
Umbrella stand, cylindrical, 1880s, 24", EX 850.00
Vase, foo dog hdl, 2 lizards, gilt, 1880s, 17½" 700.00
Wash basin, hairlines, 18" 700.00

Roselane

Founded in California in 1938 by William and Georgia Fields, the Roselane company at first produced only figurines for the local florists. But by the forties they offered candle holders, wall pockets, vases, and a line of modernistic animals mounted on wooden bases. In the fifties their 'Sparklers' became popular — small stylized animal and bird figures with rhinestone eyes. (Today these are worth from $4.00 to $9.00, depending on size.) The company closed in 1977. A variety of marks was used; all incorporate the Roselane name.

Dealer sign, deep aqua, glossy, 3x12½" 135.00
Dish, brn & gr, sq, #106 ....25.00
Figurine, boy w/dog, 5½" 10.00

Figurine, elephant, brn lustre, modernistic, wood base, 8" ....100.0(
Figurine, owl, sgraffito feathers on tan, 6½" ....55.0(

Rosemeade

Rosemeade was the name chosen by Wahpeton Pottery Compan of Wahpeton, North Dakota, to represent their product. The founde of the company were Laura Meade Taylor and R.J. Hughes, who orga nized the firm in 1940. It is most noted for small bird and animal figu rals, either in high gloss or a Van Briggle-like matt glaze. The ware wa marked 'Rosemeade' with an ink stamp or carried a 'Prairie Ros sticker. The pottery closed in 1961. Our advisor for this category Bryce L. Farnsworth; he is listed in the Directory under North Dakota.

Basket, pk, twist hdl, sm ....30.0(
Bell, elephant ....185.0(
Bell, flamingo ....195.0(
Bookend, buffalo, brn, pr ....650.0(

Bookend, wolfhound, gun-metal glaze, 7½", $100.00 each.

Bookend, wolfhound, wine red, ea ....139.0(
Bud vase, chartreuse, 7½" ....20.0(
Figurine, alligator ....650.0(
Figurine, buffalo, head turned, lg ....300.0(
Figurine, coyote, lg ....450.0(
Figurine, dove, lg ....550.0(
Figurine, fox, laying down, mini ....120.0(
Figurine, kangaroo, lg ....90.0(
Figurine, mountain goat, lg ....350.0(
Figurine, pheasant, lg, 14½" ....400.0(
Figurine, seals, mini, set of 3 ....40.0(
Figurines, penguins, mini, set of 3 ....40.0(
Flower frog, fish ....50.0(
Flower frog, heron ....25.0(
Lamp, TV; panther ....650.0(
Lamp, TV; pheasant, M ....550.0(
Pitcher, ball type, novelty ....24.0(
Planter, elephant, 5" ....75.0(
Planter, fox ....375.0(
Planter, squirrel on log ....25.0(
Planter, swan ....17.5(
Shakers, buffalo, pr ....75.0(
Shakers, coyote pup, pr ....185.0(
Shakers, dog head, chihauhua, pr ....250.0(
Shakers, dog head, chow chow, pr ....35.0(

Shakers, dog head, greyhound, pr 20.00
Shakers, donkey head, pr 45.00
Shakers, duckling, pr 45.00
Shakers, elephant, pr 60.00
Shakers, finch, pr 65.00
Shakers, flamingo, pr 145.00
Shakers, mallard duck (drake & hen), pr 60.00
Shakers, oxen, red, pr 65.00
Shakers, parrot, pr 80.00
Shakers, quail, pr 38.00
Shakers, rabbit, running, pr 75.00
Shakers, roadrunner, pr 210.00
Shakers, Siamese cat, pr 40.00
Shakers, sunfish, flat, pr 250.00
Spoon rest, pheasant 60.00

Rosenthal

In 1879 Phillip Rosenthal established the Rosenthal Porcelain Factory in Selb, Bavaria. Its earliest products were figurines and fine tablewares. The company has continued to operate to the present decade, manufacturing limited edition plates.

Bowl, fruit; White Velvet, SM 7.00
Bowl, vegetable; Chippendale, w/lid 100.00
Candelabra, 3-light, silver over porc, leaf mold, 12", pr 1,500.00
Figurine, angel in pk gown, sgn, 5¼" 120.00
Figurine, Borzoi, recumbent, mouth open 400.00
Figurine, Brittany Spaniel, duck in mouth, 5½x9" 295.00
Figurine, colt, tan & gray, ears forward, sgn Karner, #1528 ....125.00
Figurine, dachshund, sgn Karner, lg, 7x7" 265.00
Figurine, dachshund puppy, 3½" 200.00
Figurine, doe, wht, 2" 49.00
Figurine, fox, sgn F Diller, 12" L 375.00
Figurine, German Shepherd, recumbent, 11⅜" 495.00
Figurine, German Shepherd, sitting up, 5¾" 150.00
Figurine, German Short Hair Pointer 395.00
Figurine, nude kneeling, sgn Klimsch, hard paste, 14" 595.00
Figurine, nude standing, sgn Davmiller, hard paste, 15" 450.00
Figurine, penguin, sgn, 3½" 95.00

Figure of Pierrot, artist signed, repaired, $275.00.

Figurine, Russian Wolfhound, recumbent, sgn Valenlin, 7x15" 485.00
Figurine, squirrel holding nut, #7290, 6½x6½" 170.00
Gravy boat, Chippendale 50.00
Pendant, Libra, artist sgn 25.00
Plate, bread & butter; Chippendale 15.00
Plate, bread & butter; White Velvet 8.00
Plate, Studio Line, sgn, 8½" 28.50
Platter, White Velvet, 12" 38.00

Relish, White Velvet, oval, 9½" 19.00
Teapot, Chippendale 95.00
Vase, boy on elephant, wht w/much gold, Wiinblad, 17½" 475.00
Vase, moth on pine cone, brn & yel, 2¾x1½" 25.00

Roseville

The Roseville Pottery Company was established in 1892 by George F. Young in Roseville, Ohio. Finding their facilities inadequate, the company moved to Zanesville in 1898, erected a new building, and installed the most modern equipment available. By 1900, Young felt ready to enter into the stiffly competitive art pottery market. Roseville's first art line was called Rozane. Similar to Rookwood's Standard, Rozane featured dark blended backgrounds with slip-painted underglaze artwork of nature studies, portraits, birds, and animals. Azurean, developed in 1902, was a blue and white underglaze art line on a blue blended background. Egypto (1904) featured a matt glaze in a soft shade of old green and was modeled in low relief after examples of ancient Egyptian pottery. Mongol (1904) was a high-gloss oxblood red line after the fashion of the Chinese Sang de Boeuf. Mara (1904), an iridescent lustre line of magenta and rose with intricate patterns developed on the surface or in low relief, successfully duplicated Sicardo's work. These early lines were followed by many others of highest quality: Fudjiyama and Woodland (1905-06) reflected an Oriental theme; Crystalis (1906) was covered with beautiful frost-like crystals. Della Robbia, their most famous line (introduced in 1906), was decorated with designs ranging from florals, animals, and birds to scenes of Viking warriors and Roman gladiators. These designs were accomplished by sgraffito with slip-painted details. Very limited but of great importance to collectors today, Rozane Olympic (1905) was decorated with scenes of Greek mythology on a red ground. Pauleo (1914) was the last of the artware lines. It was varied — over two hundred glazes were recorded — and some pieces were decorated by hand, usually with florals.

During the second decade of the century until the plant closed forty years later, new lines were continually added. Some of the more popular of the middle-period lines were Donatello, 1915; Futura, 1928; Pine Cone, 1931; and Blackberry, 1933. The floral lines of the later years have become highly collectible. Pottery from every era of Roseville production — even its utility ware — attest to an unwavering dedication to quality and artistic merit.

Examples of the fine art pottery lines present the greatest challenge to evaluate. Scarcity is a prime consideration. The quality of artwork varied from one artist to another. Some pieces show fine detail and good color, and naturally this influences their values. Studies of animals and portraits bring higher prices than the floral designs. An artist's signature often increases the value of any item, especially if the artist is one who is well recognized. For further information consult *The Collector's Encyclopedia of Roseville Pottery, First and Second Series*, by Sharon and Bob Huxford, available at your local library or bookstore. Our advisors for this category are Jeanette and Marvin Stofft; they are listed in the Directory under Indiana.

Apple Blossom, basket, hanging 125.00
Apple Blossom, vase, bud; hdls, #379, 7" 40.00
Aztec, pitcher, geometric decor on bl, no mk, 5" 250.00
Azurean, vase, floral, sgn V Adams, integral hdls, 4½" 450.00
Baneda, bowl, console; foliate band on red, hdls, 13" 200.00
Baneda, candle holder, foliate band on red, 4½", pr 225.00
Bank, buffalo, no mk, 3x6" 150.00
Bank, pig, no mk, 2½x5" 115.00
Bank, Uncle Sam, no mk, 4" 115.00
Bittersweet, basket, #809, 8" 95.00
Bittersweet, vase, sm angle hdls, #972, 5" 40.00

Blackberry, bowl, console, sm hdls, 13" 225.00
Blackberry, jardiniere, 6" 275.00
Blackberry, jug, 5" 200.00
Blackberry, vase, hdls, 12½" 800.00
Blackberry, wall pocket 400.00
Bleeding Heart, basket, floral, #360, 10" 150.00
Bleeding Heart, wall pocket, floral, #1287, 8" 250.00
Bushberry, bowl, berries & leaves, #657, 3" 38.00
Bushberry, tea set, berries & leaves, #2, 3-pc 250.00
Carnelian I, bowl, console; drip glaze, 14" 75.00
Carnelian I, loving cup vase, drip glaze, 5" 45.00
Ceramic Design, jardiniere, no mk, 4" 90.00
Ceramic Design, wall pocket, Persian type, no mk 250.00
Cherry Blossom, candle holder, ring hdls, 4", pr 235.00
Cherry Blossom, lamp base 425.00
Cherry Blossom, vase, hdls, 10" 300.00
Chloron, sconce, no mk, 12½x12" 525.00
Chloron, wall pocket, boy or girl, no mk, 9½", ea 475.00
Clemana, candle holder, floral, no mk, 4½", pr 120.00
Clematis, tea set, #5, 3-pc 225.00
Clematis, vase, cornucopia; #140, 6" 35.00
Columbine, basket, integral hdl, #365, 7" 150.00
Columbine, vase, sm angle hdls, #20, 8" 60.00
Corinthian, ashtray, 2" H 65.00
Cosmos, candle holder, floral, low hdls, 2½", pr 100.00
Cosmos, vase, floral, #954, 4" 45.00
Creamware, chocolate pot, cherry & gold line decal, 10" ...265.00
Creamware, stein set, mug, floral decal, no mk, 5" 85.00
Creamware, stein set, mug, Knights of Pythias scenes, 5" ...185.00
Creamware, stein set tankard, Elk, no mk, 12" 425.00
Creamware, stein set tankard, FOE, no mk, 10½" 275.00
Cremona, bowl, sq w/canted corners, 9" 55.00
Cremona, candle holder, 4", pr 45.00
Crystalis, ewer, seal mk, 7½" 1,250.00
Crystalis, vase, orange w/crystals, ftd U-form, hdls, 8x11" ...1,500.00
Dahlrose, bowl, floral, angle hdls, oval, 10" 110.00
Dahlrose, vase, floral, slim form w/angle hdls, 10" 175.00
Decorated Utility Ware, pitcher, floral, 4" 45.00
Decorated Utility Ware, pitcher, wide orange band, 7" ...68.00
Della Robbia, pitcher, chariots/horses, 10x10", NM ...2,500.00
Della Robbia, pitcher, Roman in chariot, 8" 3,250.00
Della Robbia, teapot, Rozane Ware seal, 6" 1,150.00
Della Robbia, vase, floral, Rozane Ware seal, 8½" ...2,000.00
Della Robbia, vase, grapevines, brn/gr on celadon, 12x4½" ...2,500.00
Dogwood I, wall pocket, floral, ink stamp 150.00
Dogwood II, basket, floral, 6" 115.00
Dogwood II, jardiniere, floral, 8" 175.00
Donatello, candlestick, 8", pr 150.00
Donatello, flowerpot & saucer, impressed mk, 5" 125.00
Donatello, jardiniere & ped 450.00
Dutch, mug, Biblical scene decal on cream, no mk, 5" ...165.00
Earlham, candle holder, butresses at base, 6", pr 75.00
Early Pitcher, Bridge, no mk, 6" 125.00

Early Pitcher, Goldenrod, no mk, 9½" 125.00
Early Pitcher, Grapes, 6" 85.00
Early Pitcher, Landscape, 7½" 125.00
Egypto, compote, gr, tree shape, 9" 450.00
Egypto, lamp, oil; gr, 5" 400.00
Elsie the Cow, mug, #B1, mk Borden Co in relief 125.00
Falline, vase, long side hdls, 9" 375.00
Falline, vase, urn form, rnd hdls, 8" 250.00
Ferella, bowl, rtcl at rim & ft, 12" 325.00
Ferella, vase, brn, long side hdls, 9" 350.00
Ferella, vase, slim neck, wide angle hdls, 4" 185.00
Florane, Late Line; bowl, #61, 9" 45.00
Florane, Late Line; vase, #80, 6" 45.00
Florentine, basket, ink stamp, 8" 165.00
Florentine, umbrella stand, angle hdls 325.00
Florentine, vase, ivory, angle hdls, 9" 85.00
Forget-Me-Not, dresser set, decal on creamware, no mk ...275.00
Foxglove, conch shell, #426, 6" 65.00
Foxglove, ewer, #4, 6½" 70.00
Freesia, basket, #391, 8" 130.00
Freesia, cookie jar, #4, 10" 250.00
Freesia, flowerpot, #670, 5" 75.00
Fuchsia, bowl, floral, #346, 4" 60.00
Fuchsia, pitcher, floral, ice lip, #1322, 8" 265.00
Fudji, vase, Oriental stylized floral, no mk, 9" 1,200.00
Fudji, vase, shaped panels w/floral, rnd shoulder, 10" ...1,500.00
Fujiyama, jardiniere, butterflies, ink stamp, 9" 1,100.00
Fujiyama, vase, floral, cylindrical, ink stamp, 15" 950.00

Futura vase, 8½", $475.00.

Futura, vase, bl/gr spear clusters on ivory ball, ftd, 7½" ...550.00
Futura, vase, gr leaves on bl/ivory, hdld trophy form, 7x6" ...850.00
Futura, vase, gr shaded, long ringed neck, angle hdls, 9x5" ...650.00
Futura, vase, lt/dk bl triangle panels, 3-sided, ftd, 8x4" ...450.00
Futura, vase, urn form, stepped shoulders, 10" 775.00
Gardenia, bowl, #600, 4" 35.00
Gardenia, ewer, #616, 6" 95.00
Imperial I, basket, 13" 150.00
Imperial I, vase, triple bud; 8" 75.00
Iris, bowl base, #2117, impressed mk, 4" 47.50
Iris, ewer, floral, #926, impressed mk, 10" 175.00
Ivory II, candelabra, Velmoss II shape, #1116, 5½", pr ...125.00
Ivory II, vase, Carnelian shape, hdls, 10" 60.00
Ixia, basket, floral, #346, 10" 140.00
Ixia, bowl, floral, #326, 4" 42.50
Jonquil, basket, floral, high pointed hdl, 9" 190.00
Jonquil, vase, floral, hdls, 8" 135.00
Juvenile, bowl, oatmeal; rabbit, 5½" 75.00

Early pitcher with owl, $325.00.

Juvenile, mug, rabbit, 3" 70.00
Juvenile, pitcher, milk; chicks 65.00
Juvenile, plate, Little Bo Peep, rolled rim, 8" 115.00
La Rose, bowl, floral swags, ink stamp, 6" 50.00
La Rose, candle holder, floral, ink stamp, 4", pr 90.00
Landscape, sugar bowl, bl sailing scene, w/lid, no mk, 3½" 65.00
Laurel, vase, sm angle hdls, paper sticker, 7" 125.00
Lotus, candle holder, L-5, 2½", pr 70.00
Luffa, bowl, floral, sm angle hdls, 4" H 70.00
Luffa, vase, floral, sm angle hdls, flared ft, 13" 275.00
Lustre, candle holder, paper label, 8", pr 55.00
Lustre, vase, paper label, 10" 70.00
Magnolia, cookie jar, angle hdls, #15, 15" 250.00
Magnolia, ewer, #13, 6" 65.00
Magnolia, planter, 3389, 8" L 87.50
Mara, vase, arabesques on burgundy, convex cylinder, 8x5" 1,100.00
Matt Green, wall pocket, no mk, 15" 250.00
Mayfair, bowl, #1110, 4" 22.50
Mayfair, planter, #113, 8" 27.50
Ming Tree, candle holder, #551, pr 50.00
Ming Tree, ewer, #516, 10" 90.00
Mock Orange, bowl, #900, 4" 30.00
Mock Orange, planter, sq, tall 50.00
Moderne, lamp, #799, 9" 225.00
Mongol, vase, angle hdls at inverted cone neck, 7½" 2,100.00
Monticello, vase, integral hdls, 4" 68.00
Monticello, vase, sm ring hdl, 7" 165.00
Morning-Glory, vase, floral, urn form, angle hdls, 6" 225.00
Morning-Glory, vase, shouldered form, angle hdls, 12" 400.00
Moss, vase, hdls, #744, 6" 85.00
Mostique, bowl, geometric florals on glossy beige, 2½" H 40.00
Mostique, jardiniere, geometric floral, 10" 165.00
Olympic, vase, classical figures, ftd, ink mk, 13" 2,750.00
Orian, bowl, ftd, hdls, 6" 85.00
Orian, vase, gourd shape, hdls, 8" 120.00
Panel, vase, dbl bud; floral, ink stamp 85.00
Panel, vase, nude, fan form, ink stamp, 8" 350.00
Panel, vase, nudes, 10x4½" 550.00
Pasadena, planter, #L-17, 3½x9" 32.50
Pauleo, vase, purple/lav/pk separated glaze, flat rim, 15" 1,300.00
Pauleo, vase, spotted red/lt bl irid, label, drilled, 19" 550.00
Peony, bowl, sm angle hdls, #427, 4" 45.00
Peony, ewer, #7, 6" 60.00
Peony, wall pocket, #1293, 8" 150.00
Persian, creamer & sugar bowl, stylized florals, w/lid, no mk 135.00

Pine Cone basket, 10", $375.00.

Pine Cone, bowl, console, #323, 15" 200.00
Pine Cone, candle holder, triple; #1106, 5½" 225.00
Pine Cone, pitcher, #415, 9" 325.00
Pine Cone, umbrella stand 1,100.00

Poppy, basket, ##47, 10" 150.00
Poppy, wall pocket/candle holder, #1281, 9" 225.00
Primrose, bowl, angle hdls, 4" 65.00
Primrose, vase, angle hdls, #767, 8" 115.00
Raymor, bean pot, #195 ....40.00
Raymor, cup & saucer, #151 ....17.50
Raymor, plate, dinner; #152 ....17.50
Rosecraft, vase, bl, sm angle hdls, 6" 65.00
Rosecraft Black, vase, gourd shape w/hdls, no mk, 10" 135.00
Rosecraft Hexagon, vase, angle hdls, 6" 135.00
Rosecraft Vintage, candlestick, grapes, flared base, 8", pr 175.00
Rosecraft Vintage, vase, grapes, urn form, 10" 200.00
Rozane Light, pitcher, floral, sgn Mary Pierce, 7" 750.00
Rozane Light, vase, floral, sgn J Imlay, 14" 1,000.00
Rozane Light, vase, floral, 3-ftd, 6" 335.00
Rozane Mongol, mug, 3-hdld, seal mk, 6" 775.00

Rozane Mongol vase, excellent color and shape, seal mark, 7½", $2,100.00 at auction.

Rozane Mongol, vase, gourd shape, 8" 850.00
Rozane Royal, ewer, floral, #870-4, 11" 300.00
Rozane Royal, jug, floral, #888, 4½" 215.00
Rozane Royal, urn, floral, w/lid, #901, 7½" 500.00
Rozane Royal, vase, bud; floral, #842, 8" 135.00
Rozane Royal, vase, bud; floral, integral hdls, shape #862, 4" 135.00
Rozane Royal, vase, daffodils, EX art, Pillsbury, ovoid, 9" 550.00
Rozane Woodland, vase, poppies, rust w/gr stems, 8x5" 1,400.00
Russco, vase, bud; crystals, trumpet form w/2 low hdls, 8" 80.00
Russco, vase, sm uptrn hdls, flared rim, 6½" 55.00
Silhouette, planter, #731, 14" 55.00
Silhouette, vase, floral, #785, 8" 75.00
Silhouette, vase, nude, fan form, #783, 7" 225.00
Snowberry, ashtray 42.50
Snowberry, basket, #1BK, 8" 95.00
Sunflower, jardiniere, floral, 9" 350.00
Sunflower, vase, floral, sm hdls, 8" 450.00
Teasel, basket, floral, #349, 10" 165.00
Teasel, vase, floral, hdls, 5" 45.00
Thornapple, basket, #342, 10" 220.00
Thornapple, planter, #262, 5" 55.00
Topeo, vase, bl, urn form, 6" 120.00
Topeo, vase, red, decor at shoulder, 9½" 175.00
Tourmaline, vase, bowl form, 5" 55.00
Tuscany, bowl, console; no mk, 11" 65.00
Tuscany, flower arranger/vase, no mk, 5" 37.50
Velmoss II, vase, dbl cornucopia; floral, 8½" 75.00
Velmoss II, vase, floral, hdls, 7" 55.00
Velmoss Scroll, candlestick, floral, 9" 145.00
Velmoss Scroll, jardiniere & ped, floral, 30" 1,000.00
Water Lily, basket, #380, 8" 95.00
Water Lily, ewer, #12, 15" 250.00

Water Lily, vase, gourd shape, hdls, #73, 6"	45.00
White Rose, pitcher, #1324	95.00
White Rose, vase, cornucopia; #143, 6"	30.00
White Rose, vase, dbl cornucopia; #145, 8"	42.50
Wincraft, basket, floral, #209, 12"	95.00
Wincraft, planter, grasses, boat shape, #231, 10"	65.00
Windsor, candlestick, shoulder-to-base hdls, 4½", pr	185.00
Windsor, vase, ferns, gourd shape, hdls, 9"	325.00
Wisteria, vase, cylindrical, sm angle hdls, 10"	400.00
Wisteria, vase, gourd shape, hdls, 6"	200.00
Zephyr Lily, basket, ruffled rim, #395, 10"	150.00
Zephyr Lily, console boat, #475, 10"	85.00

Rowland and Marsellus

Though the impressive back stamp seems to suggest otherwise, Rowland and Marsellus were not Staffordshire potters but American importers who commissioned various English companies to supply them with the transfer-printed historical ware that had been a popular import item since the early 1800s. Plates (both flat and with a rolled edge), cups and saucers, pitchers, and platters were sold as souvenirs from 1890 through the 1930s. Though other importers — Bawo & Dotter, and A. C. Bosselman & Co., both of New York City — commissioned the manufacture of similar souvenir items, by far the largest volume carries the R. & M. mark, and Rowland and Marcellus has become a generic term that covers all 20th-century souvenir china of this type. Their mark may be in full or 'R. & M.' in a diamond. Though primarily made with blue transfers on white, other colors may occasionally be found as well. Our advisor for this category is David Ringering; he is listed in the Directory under Oregon.

Key:
r/e — rolled edge   v/o — view of
s/o — souvenir of

Cup & saucer, Brooklyn, s/o	65.00
Cup & saucer, Lewis & Clark Expo	120.00
Cup & saucer, Pittsburgh, s/o	65.00
Cup & saucer, Tacoma, s/o	65.00

Plate, souvenir of Memphis, rolled edge, 10", $60.00.

Plate, Albany NY, s/o, State Capitol, R&M No 54S, 9"	35.00
Plate, Altoona PA, Horseshoe Curve, fruit & flower border	50.00
Plate, Asbury Park NJ, v/o, Casino, r/e, 10"	50.00
Plate, Bangor ME, v/o, Court House, 9"	35.00
Plate, Bermuda, Alias Somers Island 1609-1909, r/e, 10"	50.00
Plate, Buffalo NY, s/o, Lafayette Sq, r/e, 10"	55.00
Plate, Cape Cod, fisherman portrait, made for EJ Jones, 9"	35.00
Plate, Chicago IL, s/o, Old Fort Dearborn, r/e, 10"	55.00
Plate, coupe; Burlington VT, s/o, Samuel De Champlain, 6"	30.00

Plate, coupe; Denver CO, s/o, 5 scenes/elk seal, 6"	30.00
Plate, coupe; Montreal, s/o, Royal Victoria College, 6"	30.00
Plate, coupe; Plymouth Rock, canopy over Plymouth Rock, 6"	30.00
Plate, coupe; Toronto, v/o, 5 scenes, Sutcliffe Emison, 6"	30.00
Plate, Dallas TX, Confederate Monument, 9"	35.00
Plate, Decator IL, s/o, An IL Cornfield, r/e, 10"	50.00
Plate, Fall River MA, s/o, Public High School, r/e, 10"	55.00
Plate, Fall River MA, v/o, City Hall, 9"	35.00
Plate, Hamilton Canada, s/o, City Hall, r/e, 10"	55.00
Plate, Home of Washington, Mt Vernon, fruit & flower border	50.00
Plate, La Crosse WI, Post Office, 9"	35.00
Plate, Lake Champlain NY, s/o, Au Sable Chasm, r/e, 10"	55.00
Plate, Nantucket MA, Old Windmill Built 1746, r/e, 10"	55.00
Plate, New London Ct, v/o, The Market Place, r/e, 10"	55.00
Plate, Newark NJ, v/o, City Hall, 9"	30.00
Plate, Niagara Falls, fruit & flower border	45.00
Plate, Provincetown MA, Pilgrim Monument, 9"	30.00
Plate, Valley Forge, Washington's Headquarters 1777-78, 9"	30.00
Plate, White House, fruit & flower border	45.00
Plate, Yale University, s/o, New Haven CT, 9"	35.00
Tumbler, Albany NY, s/o	65.00
Tumbler, Niagara Falls NY, s/o	65.00
Tumbler, Plymouth, v/o	65.00

Royal Bayreuth

Founded in 1794 in Tettau, Bavaria, the Royal Bayreuth firm originally manufactured fine dinnerwares of superior quality. Their figural items, produced before the turn of the century until the onset of WWI, are highly sought by today's collectors. Perhaps the most abundantly produced and easily recognized of these are the tomato and lobster pieces. Fruits, flowers, people, animals, birds, and vegetables shapes were also made. Aside from figural items, pitchers, toothpick holders, cups and saucers, humidors and the like were decorated in florals and scenic motifs. Some, such as the very popular Rose Tapestry line, utilized a cloth-like tapestry background. Transfer prints were used as well. Two of the most popular are Sunbonnet Babies and Nursery Rhymes (in particular, those decorated with the complete verse).

Caution: Many pieces were not marked; some were marked 'Deponiert' or 'Registered' only. While marked pieces are the most valued, unmarked items are still very worthwhile. Our advisors for this category are Larry Brenner from New Hampshire and Dee Hooks from Illinois; they are listed in the Directory under their home states.

Figurals

Ashtray, clown, red, bl mk, 4½"	425.00
Ashtray, devil, red, bl mk	335.00
Ashtray, eagle, bl mk, hdld, 5¼"	525.00
Ashtray, goose over top, bl mk	475.00
Berry set, oak leaf, pearlized, bl mk, 7-pc	600.00
Bowl, Devil & Cards, bl mk, Devil's ft over edge, 8"	3,200.00
Bowl, salad; lobster & leaf, bl mk, lg	235.00
Bowl, shell, bl mk, 8½"	325.00
Box, stamp; Devil & Cards, bl mk, 3½" L	800.00
Candlestick, basset, bl mk, 4¼"	500.00
Candlestick, clown, sitting, bl mk	2,100.00
Candlestick, clown woman, bl mk, tall	1,900.00
Candlestick, Devil & Cards, bl mk, low	350.00
Candlestick, Devil & Cards, bl mk, 8"	3,000.00
Candlestick, owl, bl mk	1,000.00
Candlestick, Santa Claus, red, bl mk	4,000.00
Candy dish, Art Nouveau, Bavaria mk, 7½"	1,800.00

Candy dish, Devil & Cards, recumbent, bl mk, 7" 500.00
Covered dish, turtle, bl mk, 5" 475.00
Covered dish, turtle, bl mk, 6" 325.00
Covered dish, turtle, bl mk, 7" 650.00
Creamer & sugar bowl, elk, bl mk 385.00
Creamer & sugar bowl, grapes, purple, bl mk 275.00
Cup & saucer, demitasse; Devil & Cards, bl mk 265.00
Cup & saucer, demitasse; orange, bl mk 280.00
Hair receiver, rose, gold, bl mk 555.00
Hatpin holder, basset, bl mk 800.00
Hatpin holder, owl, bl mk 650.00
Humidor, Arab, gray turban, bl mk 500.00
Humidor, chimpanzee, bl mk, 6½" 1,200.00
Humidor, clown, bl mk, 9" 1,700.00
Match holder, clown, bl mk, wall hanging, 5¼" 475.00
Match holder, Devil (full body) & Cards, bl mk, hanging 1,800.00
Mug, beer; Devil & Cards, bl mk 225.00
Mug, beer; elk, bl mk, 5¾" 475.00
Mug, shaving; elk, bl mk, 3½" 625.00
Mustard, pansy, bl mk, 3¼" 250.00
Mustard, shell, bl mk, w/spoon 115.00
Mustard, tomato, bl mk 70.00
Pitcher, apple, bl mk, cream sz 215.00
Pitcher, bull, blk, bl mk, cream sz 195.00
Pitcher, bull, rust, bl mk, cream sz 215.00
Pitcher, cat, blk, bl mk, cream sz 155.00
Pitcher, cat, wht, bl mk, cream sz 350.00
Pitcher, clown, yel, bl mk, milk sz 555.00
Pitcher, coachman, bl mk, cream sz 215.00
Pitcher, crow, blk, bl mk, cream sz 150.00
Pitcher, dachshund, bl mk, cream sz 255.00
Pitcher, dachshund, bl mk, milk sz 350.00
Pitcher, Devil & Cards, bl mk, cream sz 195.00
Pitcher, Devil & Cards, bl mk, milk sz, 5" 500.00
Pitcher, Devil & Cards, bl mk, water sz 500.00
Pitcher, duck, bl mk, cream sz 200.00
Pitcher, eagle, bl mk, water sz 700.00
Pitcher, eagle, blk, bl mk, cream sz 345.00
Pitcher, elk, bl mk, cream sz 155.00
Pitcher, elk, bl mk, milk sz 285.00
Pitcher, fish, open mouth, bl mk, milk sz 300.00
Pitcher, lamplighter, bl mk, cream sz 300.00
Pitcher, lemon, bl mk, cream sz 255.00
Pitcher, lemon, bl mk, water sz 875.00
Pitcher, lobster, bl mk, water sz 415.00
Pitcher, maple leaf, bl mk, 4¼" 175.00
Pitcher, melon, bl mk, cream sz 300.00
Pitcher, monk, mk Deponiert, cream sz 650.00
Pitcher, murex shell, iridized w/bl & gold trim, unmk, 4" 85.00

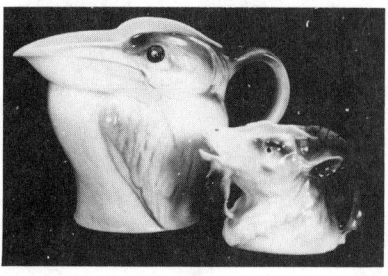

**Pitchers, Pelican, no mark, 6¼",
$895.00; Goat, black mark, 3¾",
$450.00.**

Pitcher, oak leaf, pearlized, bl mk, milk sz 625.00
Pitcher, owl, bl mk, milk sz 625.00
Pitcher, parrot, bl mk, cream sz 475.00
Pitcher, pig, red, bl mk, cream sz 700.00
Pitcher, poodle, red, bl mk, cream sz 375.00
Pitcher, Santa Claus, bl mk, (odd) milk sz, 5¼" 3,500.00
Pitcher, Santa Claus, bl mk, water sz, 6¼" 3,100.00
Pitcher, St Bernard, bl mk, cream sz 255.00
Pitcher, St Bernard, bl mk, milk sz 335.00
Pitcher, St Bernard, blk, bl mk, cream sz 295.00
Pitcher, tomato, bl mk, cream sz 65.00
Pitcher, tomato, bl mk, milk sz 100.00
Pitcher, tomato, bl mk, water sz 435.00
Pitcher, turtle, unmk, cream sz 525.00
Plate, shell, bl mk, 8" 85.00
Relish, shell, bl mk, 12" 235.00
Shakers, cherries, bl mk, pr 250.00
Shakers, coachmen, bl mk, pr 600.00
Shakers, Devil & Cards, unmk, 3", pr 450.00
Shakers, lobster & leaf, bl mk, pr 80.00
Shakers, shell, bl mk, pr 78.00
Sugar bowl, apple, yel, bl mk 150.00
Sugar bowl, Devil & Cards, bl mk, w/lid, 4" 650.00
Sugar bowl, lobster, bl mk 180.00
Sugar bowl, tomato, bl mk 98.00
Toothpick holder, bellringer, bl mk 375.00
Toothpick holder, coachman, bl mk 500.00
Toothpick holder, Devil & Cards, bl mk 350.00
Toothpick holder, elk, bl mk 190.00
Tray, dresser; elk, bl mk, 11" dia 1,900.00
Vase, Art Nouveau, bl mk, 8" 2,800.00
Vase, cavalier bust, bl mk, 4½" 525.00
Wall pocket, Santa Claus, bl mk, 5¼" 3,500.00

Nursery Rhymes

Bowl, child's feeding; Jack & Jill, bl mk 245.00
Cake plate, Ring Around Rosie, bl mk 265.00
Candlestick, Jack & Jill, bl mk, 4¼" 135.00
Candlestick, Little Boy Blue, bl mk 198.00
Dish, Little Jack Horner, bl mk, leaf form 145.00
Mug, Little Jack Horner, bl mk, 2¾" 110.00
Pin dish, Jack & the Beanstalk, bl mk 98.00
Pitcher, Jack & the Beanstalk, bl mk, milk sz 198.00
Pitcher, Little Jack Horner, bl mk, cream sz 120.00
Pitcher, Little Jack Horner, bl mk, milk sz 180.00
Pitcher, Ring Around Rosie, bl mk, cream sz 165.00
Plate, Jack & Jill w/verse, bl mk, 7½" 175.00
Plate, Little Bo Peep, bl mk, 6¼" 130.00
Plate, Little Boy Blue, bl mk, 7" 150.00
Vase, Jack & Jill, bl mk, 6" 215.00

Scenics and Action Portraits

Ashtray, goose girl, bl mk, spade shape 65.00
Ashtray, hunt scene, bl mk, scalloped 98.00
Basket, cows, bl mk, 4½" 220.00
Bell, hunt scene, bl mk 230.00
Box, pin; musicians, bl mk 98.00
Box, pin; sunset, bl mk, oval 98.00
Candle holder, stork scene, bl mk, ring hdl 198.00
Candlestick, Blk Corinthian, bl mk, 5" 140.00
Candlestick, tavern scene, bl mk 198.00
Chamberstick, musicians, bl mk, w/hood 235.00

Clock, hunt scene, bl mk 465.00
Compote, mountain sheep, bl mk 98.00
Cup & saucer, boat scene, bl mk, matt finish 200.00
Ferner, cattle, bl mk, hdls 265.00
Ferner, musicians, bl mk 145.00
Hair receiver, sheep grazing, bl mk 175.00
Humidor, castle, bl mk 365.00
Mug, beer; Arab scene, bl mk 190.00
Mug, beer; Blk Corinthian, bl mk 115.00
Nappy, courting couple, bl mk, leaf form 235.00
Pitcher, Arab scene, bl mk, pinched spout, cream sz 130.00
Pitcher, Blk Corinthian, bl mk, bulbous, 2½" 60.00
Pitcher, boat scene, bl mk, cream sz 155.00
Pitcher, Brittany Girl, bl mk, cream sz 145.00
Pitcher, hunt scene, bl mk, cream sz 110.00
Pitcher, mountain sheep, bl mk, cream sz 195.00
Pitcher, musicians, bl mk, cream sz 125.00
Pitcher, penguin scene, bl mk, cream sz 180.00
Pitcher, Red Corinthian, bl mk, milk sz, 6½" 195.00
Pitcher, Snowbabies sledding, bl mk, 3" 125.00
Pitcher, tavern scene, bl mk, cream sz, 3" 130.00
Plate, Blk Corinthian, bl mk, 8" 60.00
Plate, Brittany Girl, bl mk, 6" 98.00
Plate, Brittany Girl, bl mk, 7" 78.00
Relish, rooster & hens, bl mk, 8" 175.00
Rose bowl, sunset, bl mk, 3" 98.00
Sugar bowl, Brittany Girl, bl mk 170.00
Sugar bowl, courting couple, bl mk 400.00
Toothpick holder, girl tending geese, no mk 65.00
Toothpick holder, man fishing, bl mk, boat shape, gold rim 150.00
Tray, Blk Corinthian, bl mk 195.00
Tumbler, rooster & hens, bl mk 98.00
Vase, Andover England scene, bl mk, hdls, sm 45.00
Vase, Blk Corinthian, bl mk, 5½" 98.00
Vase, cabin by woods & lake, bl mk, 7" 395.00
Vase, castle, bl mk, ovoid, 4" 235.00
Vase, cockfight scene, bl mk, 4" 365.00
Vase, girl & turkeys, bl mk, hdls, 3" 115.00
Vase, hunt scene, bl mk, 4-hdl, 2" 98.00
Vase, musicians, bl mk, 3-ftd, 2" 125.00
Vase, musicians, bl mk, 4" 365.00
Vase, tavern scene, bl mk, 3" 122.50
Vase, turkey & cock fighting, bl mk, 5" 198.00

Sunbonnet Babies

Tray, Sunbonnet Babies, hanging out
laundry, 11" long, $695.00.

Bell, babies cleaning, bl mk, orig clapper 450.00
Bowl, cereal; babies sweeping, bl mk, 5¼" 355.00
Candlestick, babies cleaning, bl mk, shield bk 500.00

Chamberstick, babies sewing, bl mk, ring hdl 400.00
Cup & saucer, demitasse; bl mk 275.00
Ferner, babies fishing, bl mk, rnd ft, 3" 335.00
Hair receiver, babies washing, bl mk, 4-leg 425.00
Mug, babies washing, bl mk 345.00
Pitcher, babies cleaning, bl mk, cream sz, 4" 300.00
Pitcher, babies fishing, bl mk, cream sz, 4" 300.00
Pitcher, babies ironing, bl mk, cream sz, 4" 300.00
Pitcher, babies sweeping, bl mk, cream sz, 3½" 335.00
Plate, babies ironing, bl mk, 6" 65.00
Sugar bowl, babies fishing, bl mk 300.00
Sugar bowl, babies washing, bl mk, w/lid 345.00
Teapot, babies cleaning, bl mk, bulbous 450.00
Tumbler, babies cleaning, bl mk, 3½" 350.00

Tapestries

Ashtray, Japanese Chrysanthemum, bl mk, 4¾x4¾" 275.00
Ashtray, Rose Tapestry, bl mk, sq w/4 indents 300.00
Box, lady & man, bl mk, 2" sq 115.00
Box, Rose Tapestry, yel, quarter-rnd, bl mk, 1¼" H 95.00
Hatpin holder, Rose Tapestry, 3-color, bl mk, scroll base, 4¾" ...450.00
Nappy, Rose Tapestry, 3-color, bl mk, hdls, 4" 235.00
Nut dish, Rose Tapestry, bl mk 215.00
Pin dish, Rose Tapestry, 3-color, bl mk, w/lid, 3" 325.00
Pitcher, goats, pinched spout, bl mk, 4¼" 355.00
Pitcher, lady w/turkeys, bl mk, cream sz 100.00
Pitcher, mountains & river, bl mk, 5" 300.00
Pitcher, Rose Tapestry, pk, bl mk, cream sz, 2½" 210.00
Pitcher, Rose Tapestry, pk, bl mk, 5¾" 420.00
Pitcher, Rose Tapestry, 3-color, bl mk, milk sz, 4" 295.00
Planter, Rose Tapestry, 3-color, bl mk, 2¾x3¼" 280.00
Plaque, Rose Tapestry, pk, 9½" dia 345.00
Rose bowl, Rose Tapestry, 3-color, bl mk, 4" dia 360.00
Shakers, Rose Tapestry, bl mk, pr 550.00
Tray, dresser; Rose Tapestry, pk, bl mk, 7¾x11" 385.00
Tray, dresser; Rose Tapestry, 2-color, bl mk, 10" 340.00
Tray, dresser; Rose Tapestry, 3-color, bl mk, 11" 365.00
Vase, pheasant, bl mk, 8" 725.00
Vase, Rose Tapestry, 2-color, bl mk, 5" 365.00

Royal Bonn

Royal Bonn is a fine-paste porcelain, ornately decorated with
scenes, portraits, or florals. The factory was established in the mid-
1800s in Bonn, Germany; however, most pieces found today are from
the latter part of the century.

Vase, emb floral, wht on gr mottle, leaf hdls, bulbous, 13" 330.00
Vase, floral, gold on bl to pk shaded, mk, 7½x4" 75.00
Vase, floral, mc on cream, fancy gold hdls, sq ftd base, 18" 350.00
Vase, floral w/much gold, mk, 5½x6¾" 125.00
Vase, lady on lt brn/gold mottle, ornate hdls/cup top, 4½" 265.00
Vase, lady's portrait, sgn Muller, gold hdls & trim, 10¾" 450.00
Vase, orchids w/gilt on gr w/bl band, 8½" 150.00
Vase, pear shape w/2 ogre-head hdls, sgn FM, 14" 350.00
Vase, roses, mc on shaded ground, 8x3" 88.00
Vase, wht hydrangeas, lg hdls from ruffled rim to base, 14" 450.00
Vase, Worcester-style florals w/gold, hdls, ped ft, 12x6¼" 175.00

Royal Copenhagen

The Royal Copenhagen Manufactory was established in Denmark
in about 1775 by Frantz Henrich Muller. When bankruptcy threatened

in 1779, the Crown took charge. The fine dinnerware and objects of art produced after that time carry the familiar logo, the crown over three wavy lines. See also Limited Edition Plates.

Butter pat, Full Lace 25.00
Charger, blk silhouettes on ivory, HC Anderson, 13½" 75.00
Figurine, bird preening, #1041 ....35.00
Figurine, boy & girl from Netherlands on oval base, 9" 475.00
Figurine, boy on barrel, #3647 ....110.00
Figurine, boy seated on rock rolls up pants legs, 8" 185.00
Figurine, boy w/beach ball, #3542 ....230.00
Figurine, cat playing w/tail, gray tabby, 7½" 140.00
Figurine, couple kissing, Wave & Rock, sgn TL, 18" 1,100.00
Figurine, dachshund puppy, recumbent, #856 ....275.00
Figurine, dog seated, #259, 8" 250.00
Figurine, girl (& boy) kneeling, Amager, 6", pr 600.00
Figurine, girl seated, Tylland, 4" 375.00
Figurine, girl w/doll, #1938, ca 1952, 5¼" 285.00
Figurine, Kristine Svendshatter, kneeling Swiss maid, 8½" 450.00
Figurine, lady fishmonger sits behind basket of fish, 9" 265.00
Figurine, lambs, #2769 ....110.00
Figurine, little girl models new dress, 8" 140.00
Figurine, man seated wearing Tam-o'-shanter, 8" 295.00
Figurine, old lady w/prayer book, 9" 125.00
Figurine, Pan & parrot, #752 ....180.00
Figurine, Pan on column, #1020/433 ....295.00
Figurine, Pan w/frog, #1713 ....215.00
Figurine, Pan w/young kid, #498 ....245.00
Figurine, penguin, #1283, 4" 48.00
Figurine, penguin, #3003, 3" 65.00
Figurine, polar bear, #1137, lg 195.00
Figurine, polar bear, #729, 4½" L 80.00
Figurine, rabbit, #1019 ....65.00
Figurine, robin, #1235, 8" L 160.00
Figurine, robin, #2266 ....50.00
Figurine, rooster, 3½" 70.00
Figurine, seal, #1441 ....140.00
Figurine, swan, #606 ....125.00
Figurine, wire-hair terrier, #3170, 3" 45.00
Figurine, 2 ducks, mc, sgn P Cerald, 7x7" 170.00
Figurine, 2 old ladies going to market, 11½" 295.00
Plate, dinner; Full Lace, gold edge 75.00
Plate, Flora Dancia, sgn, gold rim, 5½" 450.00
Platter, Full lace, oval 285.00
Ring dish, mermaid 75.00
Tray, lg lobster in high relief, fish swimming, 11" L 175.00
Tureen, Full Lace, w/lid 495.00
Vase, bud; #1259 ....38.00

Royal Copley

Royal Copley is a decorative type of pottery made by the Spaulding China Company in Sebring, Ohio, from 1942 to 1957. They also produced two other major lines — Royal Windsor and Spaulding. Royal Copley was primarily marketed through five-and-ten cent stores; Royal Windsor and Spaulding were sold through department stores, gift shops, and jobbers. Items trimmed in gold are worth 25% to 50% more than the same item with no gold trim.

For more information we recommend *Royal Copley* and *More About Royal Copley* by Leslie and Marjorie Wolfe, edited by our advisor for this category, Joe Devine; he is listed in the Directory under Iowa. These books have been brought back by popular demand and include updated values.

Dog figure, 6", $18.00; Dog planter, $22.00.

Ashtray, bow & ribbon around edge, Lights Out, Chum, 5¾" 17.50
Bank, pig figural, saying on shirt, 7½" 35.00
Bank, rooster, slot at top of tail, paper label, 7½" 48.00
Blade bank, barber pole figural, gold trim, paper label, 6¼" 30.00
Figurine, cockatoo, full bodied, paper label, 7¼" 25.00
Figurine, kitten w/ball of yarn, paper label, 6½" 24.00
Figurine, mallard duck w/erect head, 9¼" 35.00
Figurine, sparrow, paper label, 5" 12.00
Figurine, swallow, extended wings, paper label, 7" 32.00
Figurine, swallow, full bodied, paper label, 8" 17.50
Figurine, thrush, full bodied, paper label, 6½" 14.00
Figurine, wren, paper label only, scarce, 3½" 24.00
Lamp base, cocker spaniel figural, rare, 10" 40.00
Open vase/planter, deer in relief, paper label, 7½" 18.00
Planter, barefoot boy, paper label, 7½" 13.50
Planter, big blossom, red & bl, 3" 9.00
Planter, Blackamoor, mk, 8" 26.00
Planter, cockatiel perched on kidney-shaped planter, 8½" 22.50
Planter, Copley's Big Apple, mk on bk, 5½" 10.00
Planter, dog w/raised paw, paper label, 7½" 26.00
Planter, duck & mailbox, paper label, rare, 6¾" 37.50
Planter, Dutch boy w/bucket, paper label, 6" 13.50
Planter, elephant w/ball, paper label, 6" 17.50
Planter, girl w/wheelbarrow, paper label, 7" 16.00
Planter, girl w/wide-brim hat, 7½" 25.00
Planter, hummingbird on flower, paper label, 5¼" 16.00
Planter, Indian boy w/drum, paper label, 6½" 12.50
Planter, island lady, scarce, 8" 30.00
Planter, ivy, gr on ivory, ftd, 4" 6.00
Planter, kitten & birdhouse, paper label, rare, 8" 38.00
Planter, lady w/gloves, head-to-shoulder figural, 6" 18.00
Planter, fine ribbed, flared cylinder, 3½" 7.00
Planter, pirate head, pk head covering, 8" 28.00
Planter, poodle prances before rectangular planter, 6" 18.00
Planter, ram's head figural, paper label, 6½" 18.00
Planter, running gazelles in relief, paper label, 6" 10.00
Planter, salmon (3) jumping, pk on teal waves, 6½x11½" 40.00
Planter, tanager, stamped or emb mk, 6¼" 13.50
Planter, Teddy bear, blk & wht w/pk sucker, 8" 42.50
Planter, Teddy bear w/concertina, 7½" 44.00
Planter, 3 sections, emb mk, 2½x6½" 9.00
Plaque planter, rooster in relief, mk, 6¾" 30.00
Sugar bowl, leaves form sides, yel, hdls 12.00
Vase, Blackamoor head 45.00
Vase, bud; parrot on stump figural, 5" 10.00
Vase, Carol's Corsage, yel & gr, 7" 12.00
Vase, deer head w/fawn 20.00
Vase, fish emb on cylindrical form, 7" 13.00

Vase, flower decal, pk on wht, hdls, 6¼" **9.00**
Vase, trailing leaf & vine, cylindrical, paper label, 8½" **12.50**
Window box, Harmony pattern, paper label, 4¼" **10.00**

Royal Crown Derby

In the late 1870s, a new firm, the Derby Crown Porcelain Company Ltd., began operations in Derby, England. Since 1890 when they were appointed Manufacturers of Porcelain to Her Majesty, their fine porcelain wares have been known as Royal Crown Derby. Their earliest wares were marked with a crown over 'Derby'; often a complicated dating code indicated the year of manufacture. After 1890 the 'Royal Crown Derby, England'; mark was employed; in 1921 'Made In England' was substituted in the wording. 'Bone China' was added after 1945. See also Derby.

Bowl, Imari, oval, w/lid, 11" **250.00**
Creamer, wht w/red birds in Chinese garden, fluted can form **45.00**
Cup & saucer, Imari, 1907 ....**85.00**
Ewer, florals on pk, squat form, strap hdl, 7" **250.00**
Ewer, gold florals & arabesques on Chinese red, 7½" **250.00**
Figurine, falcon on rock base, 1957, 10" **365.00**
Group, Tithe Pig, #293, rstr/chips, 6½" **1,750.00**
Pitcher, florals, mc on ivory, gold hdl, mk, 9" **395.00**

Tray, Imari pattern, 12" long, $800.00.

Vase, florals/butterflies, gold on yel, floral hdls, 9" **285.00**
Vase, foliage/swags, gilt on cobalt, dome top, lid, 1890, 11" **700.00**
Vase, Imari, hdls, ca 1887, 6" **200.00**

Royal Doulton, Doulton

The range of wares produced by the Doulton Company since its inception in 1815 has been vast and varied. The earliest wares produced in the tiny pottery in Lambeth, England, were salt-glazed pitchers, plain and fancy figural bottles — all utility-type stoneware geared to the practical needs of everyday living. The original partners, John Doulton and John Watts, saw the potential for success in the manufacture of drain and sewage pipes and during the 1840s concentrated on these highly lucrative types of commercial wares. Watts retired from the company in 1854, and Doulton began experimenting with a more decorative style of product. As time passed, many glazes and decorative effects were developed, among them Faience, Impasto, Silicon, Carrara, Marqueterie, Chine, and Rouge Flambe. Tiles and architectural terra cotta were an important part of their manufacture. Late in the 19th century at the original Lambeth location, fine artware was decorated by such notable artists as Hannah and Arthur Barlow, George Tinworth, and J.H. McLennan. Stoneware vases with incised animal drawings, gracefully shaped urns with painted scenes, and cleverly modeled figurines rivaled the best of any competitor.

In 1882 a second factory was built in Burslem which continues even yet to produce the famous figurines, character jugs, series ware, and table services so popular with collectors today. Their Kingsware line, made from 1899 to 1946, featured flasks and flagons with drinking scenes, usually on a brown-glazed ground. Some were limited editions, while others were commemorative and advertising items. The Gibson Girl series, twenty-four plates in all, was introduced in 1901. It was drawn by Charles Dana Gibson and is recognized by its blue and white borders and central illustrations, each scene depicting a humorous or poignant episode in the life of 'The Widow and Her Friends.' Dickensware, produced from 1911 through the early 1940s, featured illustrations by Charles Dickens, with many of his famous characters. The Robin Hood series was introduced in 1914; the Shakespeare series #1, portraying scenes from the Bard's plays, was made from 1914 until WWII. The Shakespeare series #2 ran from 1906 until 1974 and was decorated with featured characters. Nursery Rhymes was a series that was first produced in earthenware in 1930 and later in bone china. In 1933 a line of decorated children's ware, the Bunnykins series, was introduced; it continues to be made to the present day. About 150 'bunny' scenes have been devised, the earliest and most desirable being those signed by the artist Barbara Vernon.

Factors contributing to the value of a figurine are age, color, and detail. Those with a limited production run and those signed by the artist or marked 'Potted' (indicating a pre-1939 origin) are also more valuable. After 1920 wares were marked with a lion — with or without a crown — over a circular 'Royal Doulton.' Our advisor for this category is Nicki Budin; she is listed in the Directory under Ohio.

Animals and Birds

Cat, character **225.00**
Dog, Airedale, K5 ....**175.00**
Dog, Alsation, #1116, med **155.00**
Dog, American Foxhound, #2526 ....**265.00**
Dog, Black Labrador, #2667 ....**200.00**
Dog, Boxer, #2643, tan, med **150.00**
Dog, Bulldog, #1074, sm **155.00**
Dog, Bulldog, K1, 2¼" **125.00**
Dog, Cairn, #1035, sm **140.00**
Dog, Cocker Spaniel, #1002, lg **335.00**
Dog, Cocker Spaniel, blk & wht, #1109, med **135.00**
Dog, Cocker Spaniel, liver & wht, #1036, med **135.00**
Dog, Collie, #1058, med **225.00**
Dog, Collie, #1059, sm **250.00**
Dog, Dachshund, #1140, 4" **275.00**
Dog, Doberman Pinscher, #2645, sm **145.00**
Dog, English Setter, #1050, med **145.00**
Dog, English Setter, #2622, sm **195.00**
Dog, Fox Hound, K7, 2½" **65.00**
Dog, Fox Terrier, #1014, sm **115.00**
Dog, Irish Setter, #1056, sm **145.00**
Dog, Pekingese, #1012, sm **120.00**
Dog, Sealyham, #2508, sm **115.00**
Dog, Sheepdog & Pup, #176 ....**48.00**
Dog, St Bernard, K19, 1¾" **55.00**
Dog, Terrier, K9 ....**60.00**
Elephant, #2644, 5½" **100.00**
Hare, ears up, K39 ....**135.00**
Horse, Merely a Minor, gray, HN2531, 12" **395.00**
Horse, Merely a Minor, gray, HN2567, sm **325.00**

orse, Pride of Shires, w/foal, gray, HN2523, lg 395.00
g, recumbent, #2648, 1¾" 250.00
olar Bear, #119 ....150.00
ren, #144 ....115.00

unnykins

owl, oatmeal; father w/wheelbarrow, bunnies w/tools 65.00
owl, oatmeal; orange vendor, sgn Barbara Vernon, 1952 ....75.00
igurine, mother bunny sweeps, ca 1972 ....38.00
1ug, bunnies & ice cream vendor, 1-hdl, 1979 ....45.00
1ug, playing at cowboys & Indians, 2-hdl 45.00
late, baby's, 7 bunnies on seesaw, father nearby 35.00
late, bunnies dress before lg mirror, 6½" 35.00
late, bunnies watering flowers, sgn Barbara Vernon, 6½".............75.00
late, mother & babies at Mr Piggly's store, 1968, 8" 75.00
eacup, bunnies unravel knitted piece, ca 1976 ....50.00
umbler, mother swings baby, bk: skipping, 1950s 95.00

haracter Jugs

Trapper, D6609, 6", $110.00.

Airman, D6870, sm 70.00
Ann Boleyn, D6644, lg 130.00
Anne of Cleves, D6653, lg 130.00
Antony & Cleopatra, D6728, lg 145.00
Apothecary, D6581, mini 65.00
Aramis, D6508, mini 50.00
Ard of 'Earing, D6591, sm 795.00
Arriet, D6236, sm 95.00
Arriet, D6250, mini 85.00
Athos, D6439, lg 110.00
Auld Mac, D5823, lg 110.00
Auld Mac, D6253, mini, A 55.00
Bacchus, D6505, sm 55.00
Beefeater, D6206, GR hdl, earlier version 155.00
Beefeater, D6251, ER hdl, mini 50.00
Blacksmith, D6585, mini 65.00
Bootmaker, D6572, lg 120.00
Cap'n Cuttle, D6266, 4" 195.00
Captain Ahab, D6500, lg 120.00
Captain Ahab, D6522, mini 55.00
Captain Hook, D6597, lg 495.00
Captain Hook, D6605, mini 345.00
Cardinal, D5614, lg 155.00

Catherine Howard, D6645, lg 130.00
Catherine Parr, D6664, lg 130.00
D'Artagnan, D6764, sm 55.00
Dick Turpin, D5618, 1st version (mask up), sm 75.00
Dick Turpin, D6535, 2nd version (mask down), sm 65.00
Dick Whittington, D6375, lg 385.00
Elephant Trainer, D6841, lg 195.00
Falconer, D6547, mini 50.00
Falstaff, D6287, lg 110.00
Fortune Teller, D6503, sm 355.00
Friar Tuck, D6321, lg 445.00
Gaoler, D6577, sm 65.00
Gardener, D6630, lg 215.00
George Washington, D6825, mini 50.00
Golfer, D6623, lg 110.00
Golfer, D6756, sm 55.00
Gone Away, D6531, lg 120.00
Granny, D5521, w/tooth, lg 110.00
Granny, D6520, mini 55.00
Gulliver, D6563, sm 350.00
Gunsmith, D6580, sm OF 75.00
Henry Morgan, D6469, sm 55.00
Henry VIII, D6888, 2-hdl, ltd edition 950.00
Jayne Seymour, D6646, lg 115.00
Jester, D5556, reverse, sm 120.00
Jockey, D6625, lg 400.00
John Barleycorn, D5327, lg 165.00
John Peel, D5731, sm 80.00
Lord Mayor, D6864, lg 150.00
Lumberjack, D6613, sm 65.00
Mae West, D6688, lg 130.00
Mephistopheles, D5757, lg 1,950.00
Michael Doulton, D6808, ltd edition 75.00
Mine Host, D6488, lg 100.00
Mr Micawber, D6138, mini 55.00
Mr Pickwick, D5839, sm 75.00
Mr Pickwick, D6060, lg, A 165.00
Mr Quaker, D6738, lg 555.00
Night Watchman, D6569, lg 110.00
North American Indian, D6665, mini 50.00
Old Charley, D5527, sm 55.00
Old King Cole, D6036, lg 250.00
Old Salt, D6557, mini 50.00
Othello, D6673, lg 115.00
Paddy, D5753, lg, A 145.00
Parson Brown, D5529, sm, A 70.00
Pearly Boy, D6207, brn buttons, lg 1,995.00
Pearly King, D6760, lg 100.00
Pied Piper, D6403, lg 100.00
Poacher, D6429, lg 95.00
Poacher, D6515, mini 50.00
Punch & Judy Man, D6593, sm 375.00
Queen Victoria, D6816, lg 95.00
Regency Beau, D6559, lg 950.00
Rip Van Winkle, D6517, mini 50.00
Robin Hood, D6234, 1st version, sm 80.00
Sairey Gamp, D5528, sm 55.00
Sam Weller, D6140, mini 55.00
Samuel Johnson, D6289, lg 300.00
Sancho Panza, D6461, sm 60.00
Scaramouche, D6184, lg 95.00
Scaramouche, D6561, sm 425.00
Sherlock Holmes, D6661, lg 105.00
Sir Thomas Moore, D6792, lg 100.00

Toby Philpots, D5736, lg	155.00
Tony Weller, D5530, sm	55.00
Town Crier, D6537, sm	110.00
Trapper, D6612, sm	55.00
Ugly Duchess, D6603, sm	325.00
Uncle Tom Cobbleigh, D6337, lg	475.00
Veteran Motorist, D6633, lg	130.00
Viking, D6526, mini	125.00
Walrus & Carpenter, D6608, mini	60.00
Winston Churchill, D6172, sm	95.00
Winston Churchill, D6175, mini	65.00
Yachtsman, D6622, lg	115.00

Figurines

Twilight, #2256, 5", $175.00.

A'Courting, HN2004	395.00
Abdullah, HN2104	450.00
Adrienne, HN2152	160.00
Affection, HN2236	125.00
Ajax, HN2908	400.00
Amy, HN3326	145.00
Ann Boleyn, HN3232	450.00
Annabella, HN1871	665.00
Annette, HN1550, gr skirt	495.00
Antoinette, HN2326	150.00
Ascot, HN2356	185.00
At Ease, HN2473	195.00
Autumn Breezes, HN2147, blk & wht	295.00
Autumn Glory, HN2766	120.00
Baby Bunting, HN2108	250.00
Ballerina, HN2116	295.00
Balloon Clown, HN2894	125.00
Balloon Lady, HN2935	195.00
Barbara, HN1421	955.00
Beachcomber, HN2487, matt	200.00
Bess, HN2002	225.00
Blacksmith of Williamsburg, HN2240	185.00
Bo-Peep, HN1810	550.00
Boatman, HN2417	150.00
Bon Appetit, HN2444, matt	195.00
Breezy Day, HN3162	120.00
Bride, HN2166	195.00
Bridesmaid, HN2874	75.00
Bridget, HN2070	325.00
Captain, HN2260	250.00
Captain Cook, HN2889	295.00
Carolyn, HN2974	165.00
Carpet Seller, HN1464, hand closed	275.00
Cavalier, HN2716, 2nd version	185.00

Centurion, HN2726	175.00
Charlie Chaplin, HN2771	250.00
Charlotte, HN2421	150.00
Cherie, HN2341	100.00
China Repairer, HN2943	175.00
Christine, HN2792	275.00
Christmas Time, HN2110	350.00
Circe, HN1249	2,200.00
Clockmaker, HN2279	250.00
Clown, HN2890	225.00
Collinette, HN1999, red cloak	550.00
Cookie, HN2218	150.00
Coralie, HN2307, yel	135.00
Country Lass, HN1991	125.00
Covent Garden, HN1339	1,500.00
Cup of Tea, HN2322	165.00
Dancers of the World, Balinese Dancer, HN2808	750.00
Dancers of the World, Chinese Dancer, HN2840	750.00
Dancers of the World, Indian Temple Dancer, HN1830	1,550.00
Dancers of the World, Philippine Dancer, HN2439	850.00
Dancers of the World, Polish Dancer, HN2836	850.00
Darling, HN1985	95.00
Debutante, HN2210, bl gown, 5¼x5x7"	275.00
Deidre, HN2020	345.00
Delight, HN1772	160.00
Devotion, HN3228	145.00
Dinky Do, HN2120, red & pk	80.00
Dulcie, HN2305	175.00
Elegance, HN2264	150.00
Encore, HN2751	135.00
Favourite, HN2249	185.00
First Dance, HN2803	180.00
Flower Seller's Children, HN1342	650.00
Fortune Teller, HN2159	450.00
Francine, HN2422	95.00
Francis Duncombe, HN3009	385.00
Geisha, HN1223	950.00
Genevieve, HN1962	250.00
Giselle, HN2139	395.00
Good Day Sir, HN2896	140.00
Goody Two Shoes, HN1905	455.00
Goody Two Shoes, HN2037	125.00
Grand Manner, HN2723	175.00
Harmony, HN2824	180.00
Harvestime, HN3084	130.00
Heart to Heart, HN2276	395.00
Helmsman, HN2499	225.00
Her Ladyship, HN1977	295.00
Hilary, HN2335	155.00
Innocence, HN2842	155.00
Isadora, HN2938	150.00
Jack, HN2060	165.00
Jane, HN2806	150.00
Jane Seymour, HN3349	455.00
Jean, HN2032	295.00
Jersey Milkmaid, HN2057	195.00
Jill, HN2061	150.00
Judith, HN2089	295.00
Julia, HN2705	150.00
Karen, HN1994	465.00
Kathleen, HN2933	195.00
Kathy, HN2346, Greenaway	145.00
Lady Anne Neville, HN2006	675.00
Lady April, HN1958, red & purple	315.00

Lady Charmian, HN1949, 1st version 195.00
Lady Pamela, HN2718 ....150.00
Lady Sheffield 375.00
Laird, HN2361 ....180.00
Lambing Time, HN1890 ....195.00
Last Waltz, HN2315 ....200.00
Laurel & Hardy 450.00
Lavinia, HN1955 ....110.00
Leisure Hour, HN2055 ....375.00
Lifeboat Man, HN2764 ....180.00
Little Boy Blue, HN2062, 5½" 125.00
Lobster Man, HN2317 ....180.00
Love Letter, HN2149 ....325.00
Lucy, HN2863, Greenaway 145.00
Lunchtime, HN2485 ....155.00
Lynne, HN2329 ....160.00
Mary Countess of Howe 395.00
Mary Had a Little Lamb, HN2048, 3½" 110.00
Mary Mary, HN2044, 5" 165.00
Masque, HN2554 ....245.00
Meditation, HN2330 ....295.00
Megan, HN3306 ....115.00
Memories, HN1856 ....625.00
Midinette, HN2090 ....295.00
Moon Dancer, HN3181 ....130.00
Morning Glory, HN3093 ....95.00
Morning Ma'am, HN2895 ....130.00
My Love, HN2339 ....195.00
Nadine, HN1886, orange & red dress 925.00
Nell, HN3014, Greenaway 145.00
News Vendor, HN2891 ....175.00
Nina, HN2347 ....150.00
Officer of the Line, HN2733 ....225.00
Old Balloon Seller, HN1315, earthenware, 1933 ....250.00
Old King Cole, HN2217 ....495.00
Old Mother Hubbard, HN2314 ....335.00
Orange Lady, HN1953 ....265.00
Paisley Shawl, HN1987, 1st version 315.00
Paisley Shawl, HN1988, 2nd version 165.00
Pearly Girl, HN2769 ....165.00
Pecksniff, HN2098 ....295.00
Phyllis, HN1420 ....625.00
Poacher, HN2043 ....250.00
Polka, HN2156 ....335.00
Potter, HN1493 ....450.00
Priscilla, HN1337 ....625.00
Prized Possessions, HN2942 ....550.00
Punch & Judy Man, HN2765 ....250.00
Queen Anne, ltd edition 395.00
Queen Elizabeth II, HN3440, ltd edition 400.00
Queen Mother, HN2882 ....995.00
Rag Doll, HN2142 ....95.00
Rose, HN1368 ....95.00
Rowena, HN2077 ....600.00
Samurai Warrior, HN3402 ....455.00
Sandra, HN2275, yel 150.00
Secret Thoughts, HN2382 ....225.00
Sheikh, HN3083 ....95.00
Shore Leave, HN2254 ....195.00
Sibell, HN1695 ....595.00
Silks & Ribbons, HN2017 ....190.00
Sleeping Beauty, HN3079 ....155.00
Sophie, HN3257 ....225.00
Spring Flowers, HN1807 ....300.00

Stitch in Time, HN2352 ....200.00
Summer, HN2086 ....450.00
Sunday Best, HN2698 ....125.00
Susan, HN3962 ....210.00
Suzette, HN2026 ....295.00
Sweet & Twenty, HN1298, 1st version 275.00
Sweet Seventeen, HN2734 ....190.00
Taking Things Easy, HN2677 ....175.00
Teatime, HN2255 ....155.00
Tinsmith, HN2146 ....350.00
Tip-Toe, HN3293 ....150.00
Top o' the Hill, HN1833, 7½" 195.00
Top o' the Hill, HN1849, pk gown 195.00
Town Crier, HN2119 ....295.00
Toymaker, HN2250 ....350.00
Traveler's Tale, HN3185 ....95.00
Uriah Heep, HN3101 ....285.00
Vanity, HN2475 ....100.00
Veronica, HN1517 ....350.00
Vivienne, HN2073 ....250.00
Wardrobe Mistress, HN2145 ....495.00
Winsome, HN2220 ....155.00
Wintertime, HN3060 ....245.00
Wizard, HN2877 ....275.00
Yvonne, HN3038 ....145.00

Flambe

Buddha, standing, 5" 950.00
Confucious, #3314 ....150.00
Dog of Fo, #48 ....175.00
Duck, #395, 2½" 125.00
Duck, floating, 7¼" 400.00
Duck, sitting, mk, 3½" L 88.00
Elephant & young, #3548 ....90.00
Fox, #42, 13" L 465.00
Fox, recumbent, #32, 5" 345.00
Genie, #2999 ....150.00
Hare, #1157, 2¾" 95.00
King Penguin, #84, 6" 125.00
Monkeys, hugging pr, #486, old 325.00
Penguin on base, 9" 1,000.00
Rhino, half-seated, head up, rouge, 9x17" 875.00
Tiger, #809 ....450.00
Vase, house scene 200.00
Vase, house w/woodland scene, dtd 1947, 7" 175.00
Vase, plowing scene, globular, 1930s, 6½" 125.00
Vase, Sung, melon top w/tapered base, sgn FM, 7½" 750.00
Vase, Veined Sung, woodcut, #1603, 7" 185.00
Vase, woodcut, #1619, 11" 295.00
Vase, 1619 Country House, #31 ....200.00
Wizard, #3121 ....119.00

Series Ware

Ashtray, Gnomes, bl underglaze 125.00
Biscuit jar, Coaching Days, Royal Mail Coach, 8" 195.00
Biscuit jar, Dutch People, SP top/rim/hdl, mk, 6¼x5" 245.00
Bowl, Bobby Burns, 7½" 150.00
Candlestick, Dutch People, D1881, pr 195.00
Candlestick, Dutch People, Haystack, ca 1906 ....195.00
Coffeepot, Moorish Gate, merchants, 7x3¾" 145.00
Cup & saucer, demitasse; Dickensware, mk, 2¼" 65.00
Cup & saucer, Don Quixote 50.00

Cup & saucer, Under the Greenwood Tree, Robin Hood 70.00
Flask, Kingsware, Scotsman 250.00
Jardinere, Shakespeare, Ophelia/Hamlet, mk, 8¾x10" 300.00
Mug, Kingsware, Drink Wisely 195.00
Mug, Welsh Ladies, 3 ladies & child, mk, 1⅜x1⅜" 75.00
Pitcher, Coaching Days, innkeeper talks to driver, 6" 195.00
Pitcher, Cottage Home, ca 1910, 5" 95.00
Pitcher, Dickensware, Alfred Jingle, sq, mk, 7½" 135.00
Pitcher, Dutch People, ladies, boy on bk, mk, 2x1¾" 95.00
Pitcher, Gleaners, ca 1909, 7" 195.00
Pitcher, hot water; Shakespeare, Orlando, 7" 200.00
Pitcher, Moorish Gate, 2 Arabs by gate, mk, 4¾x4" 95.00
Pitcher, Night Watchman, 8" 105.00
Pitcher, Polar Bear, D3128 ....95.00
Pitcher, Welsh Ladies, pinched spout, 2¼" 115.00
Plate, Arabian Nights, Arrival of Unknown Princess, 10⅜" 85.00
Plate, chop; Dickensware, Tony Weller w/whip, 13½" 165.00
Plate, Coaching Days, William Ye Driver, 10" 125.00
Plate, Eglington Tournament, knights in combat, 10" 95.00
Plate, Fox Hunting, Simpson, Across the Moor, 10" 95.00
Plate, Hiawatha, Wampum Belt, 10" 95.00
Plate, Old English Sayings 55.00
Plate, Rip Van Winkle, group playing around nine pins, 10" 95.00
Plate, Town Officials, night watchman w/pike & lantern, 10" 65.00

Punch bowl, scenes of Holland within, exterior floral band, 8x14" diameter, $300.00.

Plate, Treasure Island, Long John Silver, 13½" 195.00
Sugar bowl, Fox Hunting, John Peel, hunters lead horses 75.00
Sugar bowl, Tony Weller, D6013 ....750.00
Teapot, Monks, bl & wht 150.00
Teapot, Robin Hood, Little John & Friar Tuck, 5½" 215.00
Tray, Shakespeare, Katharine, 15½" 150.00
Vase, Babes in Woods, blindman's buff, gold trim, 7½" 245.00
Vase, Babes in Woods, lady & child in snow scene, 6½" 425.00
Vase, Dickensware, Mr Micawber, hdls, 5" 95.00
Vase, Dunolly Castle, mk, 4½x2¾" 185.00
Vase, Dutch People, girl on rock, gold trim, mk, 5½" 145.00
Vase, Gleaners & Gypsies, woman w/boy, girl w/bundle, 2" 80.00
Vase, Rustic England, 2 men w/horses, sq, mk, 7¼" 85.00
Vase, Shakespeare, Ophelia in pk, hdls, 6½x4" 150.00
Vase, Welsh Ladies, ladies w/dog, mk, 2½x2¼" 95.00
Vase, Welsh Ladies, 1¾x2¼" 88.00

Stoneware

Ashtray, Courage's Ale 55.00
Beaker, hunt scene, brass rim 60.00

Creamer & sugar bowl, Slater's Patent 115.00
Humidor, cattle/children incised, H Barlow, dtd 1878, 5¾" 695.00
Humidor, frieze of farm animals, Barlow, worn SP rim, 8" 985.00
Jug, brn/gray/beige motif, sgn EM, dtd 1880, 5⅝" 120.00
Lawn fountain, pelican figural, 15" 325.00
Pilgrim flask, mc/cvd floral/pods, FA Butler, 1885, 13" 1,200.00
Pitcher, band of cvd ducks, stylized floral at neck, 9", EX 440.00
Pitcher, dog in grass, stippled ground, H Barlow, 6½" 1,100.00
Pitcher, dogs/pate-sur-pate quail, stippled, H Barlow, 9" 2,000.00
Pitcher, goats, dog tied to base of hdl, H Barlow, 9½" 1,500.00
Pitcher, pate-sur-pate birds/leaves, FE Barlow, 7" 465.00
Ring dish, owl figural, brn & tan, 4x3¼" 165.00
Tazza, leaves, bl/cvd on gr to brn, ED Lupton, 8x9", EX 900.00
Teapot, floral tapestry, mk, 5x4½" 145.00
Teapot, frieze of goats, eagle spout, Barlow, 5½" 1,500.00
Tray, koala figure at bk, leaves at rim, Lambeth, 10½x5¼" 300.00
Umbrella stand, HP decor/appl floral medallions, 1910, 24" 500.00
Vase, allover florals/gilt, Slater's Pat, 25", EX 165.00
Vase, banded Deco design, bl/purple/brn, sgn BN, 5½", pr 125.00
Vase, bead-fr ovals w/animals, stippled, H & F Barlow, 11" ...2,500.00
Vase, donkeys, sgn Hanna Barlow, 12" 950.00
Vase, floral, sgn F Roberts, Lambeth, 1885, 10½" 250.00
Vase, frieze of cattle/horses/dog, H Barlow, 14x5" 1,100.00
Vase, frieze of deer, stylized bands, hdls, H Barlow, 14" 1,750.00
Vase, frieze of kangaroos, leaf borders, H Barlow, 12", EX 985.00
Vase, frieze of lions, hunting inscription, Barlow, 7½" 1,750.00
Vase, frieze of sheep, emb foliage bands, H Barlow, 15" 3,500.00
Vase, frieze of sheep, floral borders, H Barlow, 11" 985.00
Vase, frieze w/horses, (1 w/dog & boy), Barlow, 19", NM, pr ..2,750.00
Vase, frieze w/pigs & flowers, foliage border, Barlow, 11" ...1,000.00

Toby Jugs

Cap'n Cuttle, D6266, 4½" 185.00
Cliff Cornell, bl, lg 300.00
Cliff Cornell, bl, med, 5½" 325.00
Double XX, D6088, lg 300.00
Falstaff, D6062, lg 145.00
Falstaff, D6063, sm 75.00
Fat Boy, D6264, 4½" 230.00
Happy John, D6070, sm 75.00
Honest Measure, D6108, 4½" 85.00
Huntsman, D6320, 7½" 145.00
Jolly Toby, D6109, 6½" 90.00
Old Charley, seated, sm 175.00
Sam Weller, D6265, seated, 4" 200.00
Sherlock Holmes, D6661, 8¾" 145.00
Sir Francis Drake, D6660, 9" 145.00
Sir Winston Churchill, D6172, 5½" 95.00
Squire, D6319 ....265.00

Miscellaneous

Ash bowl, Farmer John, D6007 ....110.00
Ash bowl, Parson Brown, D6008 ....110.00
Ashtray, Dick Turpin, D5601 ....110.00
Ashtray, Old Charley, D5599 ....110.00
Ashtray, Parson Brown, D5600 ....110.00
Bottle, whiskey; John Bull, 5" 75.00
Bottle, Zorro, yel 45.00
Bust, Mr Pickwick 85.00
Bust, Sam Weller, D6052 ....85.00
Cigarette lighter, Beefeater, D6233 ....145.00
Cigarette lighter, Buzz Fuzz 295.00

Cigarette lighter, Lawyer, D6498 ....**250.00**
Cigarette lighter, Mr Pickwick, D5839 ....**255.00**
Container, liquor; Falstaff, D6385 ....**110.00**
Decanter, Uncle Sam, Dewars Whiskey, eagle hdl **185.00**
Jug, Tony Weller, musical, D5888 ....**550.00**
Napkin ring, Sam Weller, DM61 ....**550.00**
Pitcher, Aubrey, Arts/Crafts floral, orange/bl on wht, 14" **600.00**
Pitcher, floral on cream, turq jewels, Burslem, #d, 5" **245.00**
Pitcher, Sporting Squire, Dewars Whiskey, 8¼" **275.00**
Teapot, Falstaff, D6854 ....**125.00**
Teapot, Old Charlie **1,650.00**
Vase, Aubrey, Arts/Crafts floral, orange/bl on wht, 6" **280.00**
Vase, floral, pk/wine on bl, gray-gr neck, sgn MB, 16", pr **880.00**
Vase, florals/gilt on cream, bulbous, Burslem, 1885, 16" **800.00**
Vase, tapestry, artist sgn, Slater's Patent, Lambeth, 11" **145.00**
Wall pocket, Old Charley **2,225.00**

Royal Dux

The Duxer Porzellan Manufactur was established by E. Eichler in 1860. Located in what is now Duchcov, Czechoslovakia, the area was known as Dux, Bohemia, until WWI. The war brought about changes in both the style of the ware as well as the mark. Prewar pieces were modeled in the Art Nouveau or Greek Classical manner and marked with 'Bohemia' and a pink triangle containing the letter 'E.' They were usually matt glazed in green, brown, and gold. Better pieces were made of porcelain, while the larger items were of pottery. After the war, the ware was marked with the small pink triangle but without the Bohemia designation; 'Made in Czechoslovakia' was added. The style became Art Deco, with cobalt blue a dominant color.

Bowl, girl kneels, pours water from jug into water lily, 9" **650.00**
Bowl, shell held aloft by maid/2 cherubs, base w/waves, 20" **1,250.00**
Bust, Vanity, lady in bonnet, sgn, Elly Strobach, mk **350.00**
Bust of maid, blond hair, bodice strewn w/orchids, 21", NM ...**2,400.00**
Bust of Roman, gold shirt w/pk floral toga on shoulder, 9" **350.00**

Cockatoos, pink triangle mark, #36, ca 1918-41, 16", $495.00 for the pair.

Centerpc, boy & girl hold basket between them, 10x13" **200.00**
Centerpc, nymph in ea of 2 lily pads, stem w/lotus, 14" **525.00**
Figurine, Art Deco-style girl, #754 ....**110.00**
Figurine, brunette dancer in pk midriff & floral skirt, 23" **1,300.00**
Figurine, clown playing accordion, mk, 12" **450.00**
Figurine, Colonial man (& lady) stand at fence, 12", pr **1,150.00**
Figurine, elephant, wht glossy, pk triangle mk **85.00**
Figurine, lady by basket, water jug in arms, triangle mk, 10" **298.00**

Figurine, lady w/flower, man w/palette & ewer, 9", pr **375.00**
Figurine, lady w/oval basket, triangle mk, 11x4⅞" **325.00**
Figurine, Nouveau lady & beige shell, triangle mk, 6¾" **195.00**
Figurine, Spanish dancer w/tambourine, 8" **275.00**
Figurine, wheat harvesters, he w/sickle, gold trim, 21", pr **850.00**
Figurine, 2 children w/basket, pk triangle mk, 8½" **395.00**
Figurine, 2 hunting dogs, 1 sniffing ground, brn/wht, 9x16" **100.00**
Mirror fr, full-length maid to side, lotus buds, 24" **1,500.00**
Vase, flower form, behind Rebecca at well w/jug, 17x9" **950.00**
Vase, fruit/floral relief, rtcl branch hdls, 15x6", pr **300.00**
Vase, girl w/flute figural, flowers in relief, 14½" **650.00**

Royal Flemish

Royal Flemish was introduced in the late 1880s and was patented in 1894 by the Mt. Washington Glass Company. Transparent glass was enameled with one or several colors and the surface divided by a network of raised lines suggesting leaded glasswork. Some pieces were further decorated with enameled florals, birds, or Roman coins. Our advisors for this category are Betty and Clarence Maier; they are listed in the Directory under Pennsylvania.

Biscuit jar, gold coins on maroon, beige & brn, 8x5½" **3,200.00**
Ginger jar, gold winged dragon, 7" **1,900.00**
Rose bowl, allover wht/bl asters on brn to clear frost, lg **1,285.00**
Sugar shaker, Queen Anne's Lace, clear satin, ovoid **825.00**
Vase, boy/griffin, bk: cherub/dragon, hdld bottle w/lid, 17" **6,500.00**
Vase, floral/heraldic symbols on clear, stick neck, 13x8" **1,400.00**
Vase, flowers/medallions, gold scrolls, stick neck, 13" **3,000.00**
Vase, griffin, bk: lion, bulbous w/can neck, 10" **1,650.00**
Vase, lg snow geese against sun, dragons on neck band, 15" ...**8,500.00**
Vase, lg sun+11 Guba ducks in flight, gold lines/stars, 7" **3,750.00**
Vase, much gold, Cupid etc on gr mottle, hdls & lid, 16" **5,500.00**
Vase, mums & wild roses w/gold, sgn, 14" **4,250.00**
Vase, peonies, gold-traced wht on yel, bl medallions, 6" **850.00**
Vase, 5 birds/emb gold stars on yel & frost, slim, 6" **1,150.00**

Royal Haeger, Haeger

In 1871, David Henry Haeger, a young son of German immigrants, purchased a brick factory at Dundee, Illinois, and began an association with the ceramic industry that his descendants have pursued to the present time. Soon their production was expanded to include drainage tile. By 1914 they had ventured into the field of commerical artware. Vases, figurines, lamp bases, and gift items in a pastel matt glaze carried the logo of the company name written over the bar of an 'H.' From 1929 to 1933, they produced a line of dinnerware in solid colors — blue, rose, green, and yellow — which they marketed through Marshall Fields. Royal Haeger, their premium line designed in 1938 by Royal Hickman, and the Flower Ware line (1954 to 1963, marked 'RG' for Royal Garden) are especially desirable with collectors today. Ware produced before the mid-thirties sometimes is found with a paper label; these are also of special interest. A stylized script mark, 'Royal Haeger' in raised lettering, was used during the thirties and forties; later a paper label in the shape of a crown was used. The Macomb plant, built in 1939, primarily made ware for the florist trade. A second plant, built there in 1969, produces lamp bases.

For those interested in learning more about the subject, we recommend *Collecting Royal Haeger* by our advisors, Lee Garmon and Doris Frizzell; both are listed in the Directory under Illinois.

Basket, Rose of Sharon, R-575, 7" **25.00**

Bowl, daisy, R-224, 12" 20.00
Box, cigarette; sm leopard, R-631, 7" L 40.00
Figurine, blk panther, tail curled, R-495, 24" L 65.00
Figurine, blk panther, tail out, R-495, 24" L 95.00
Figurine, bull, red, R-1510, 17¼" L 150.00
Figurine, hen pheasant, R-434, 15" L 30.00
Figurine, mare & foal, standing, R-451, 10" L 40.00
Figurine, matador, R-6343, 11¼" 50.00
Figurine, mountain lion, R-808, 10" 60.00
Figurine, peasant lady, R-383, 16" 50.00
Figurine, peasant man, R-382, 16" 50.00
Figurine, rooster pheasant, R-435, 12" 30.00
Figurine, Russian wolfhound, head down, R-318, 7" L 60.00
Figurine, Russian wolfhound, head up, R-319, 7" L 60.00
Figurine, Shetland pups (3), R-782 ....18.00
Flower block, nude astride fish, R-363, 10" 35.00
Flower block, nude figurine w/seal at feet, R-363, 13" 50.00
Flower block, 2 tropical fish, R-360, 11" 45.00
Flower block, 3 birds on branch, R-361, 4" 35.00
Flower block, 3 fish, noses down, R-157B, 12½" 45.00
Mug, Mexican, R-699, 4½" 8.00
Pitcher, Mexican head, R-698, 7½" 30.00
Planter, Lorelei mermaid, reclining, R-1257S, 15" L 60.00
Planter/bookend, moon fish, R-1240, 10¼" 35.00
Vase, angel, R-1141, 7" 18.00
Vase, bow, R-455, 15½" 25.00
Vase, lg sailfish, R-1168, 14½" 75.00
Vase, lily, R-446, 14" 25.00
Vase, sphere w/3 plumes, R-281, 10" 45.00
Vase, swan, neck up, cutouts around base, R-36, 16" 45.00
Vase, tall basket w/bow, R-279, 21" 65.00
Vase, triple sea gull, R-208 ....75.00

Ashtray, panther in center, 8½" diameter, $25.00.

Royal Rudolstadt

The hard-paste porcelain that has come to be known as Royal Rudolstadt was produced in Thuringia, Germany, in the early 18th century. Various names and marks have been associated with this pottery. One of the earliest was a hay fork symbol associated with Johann Frederich von Schwarzburg-Rudolstadt, one of the first founders. Variations, some that included an 'R,' were also used. In 1854 Earnst Bohne produced wares that were marked with an anchor and the letters 'EB.' Examples commonly found today were made during the late 1800s and early 20th century. These are usually marked with an 'RW' within a

shield under a crown and the words 'Crown Rudolstadt.' Items marked 'Germany' were made after 1890.

Chocolate pot, pk roses/gold trim, gr/wht flowers, 10" 275.00
Chocolate pot, roses, mc on cream w/gold, mk, 9¾x4" 88.00
Chocolate pot, roses, yel on pastel, mk, 9½x4" 88.00
Ewer, florals on cream, 9" 65.00
Ewer, fruit reserve on gr w/gilt florals, sgn, ornate, 14" 300.00
Figurine, seated lady/maid in boudoir, damage to lace, 15" 935.00
Lamp, Delft, windmill pnt on globe, 23" 700.00
Smoking set, dog after cat on fence figural, mk, 6x6½" 165.00
Teapot, roses, pk on wht w/gold, mk, ind 115.00
Vase, floral on yel, hdls, 12" 110.00

Royal Vienna

In 1719 Claude Innocentius de Paquier established a hard-paste porcelain factory in Vienna where he made highly ornamental wares similar to the type produced at Meissen. Early wares were usually unmarked. After 1744, when the factory was purchased by the Empress, the Austrian shield (often called 'beehive') was stamped on under the glaze. In the following listings, values are for hand-painted items unless noted otherwise. Decal-decorated items would be considerably lower.

Note: An influx of Japanese reproductions on the market have influenced values to decline on genuine old Royal Vienna. Buyer beware! On new items the beehive mark is over the glaze, the weight of the porcelain is heavier, and the decoration is obviously decaled. Our advisor for this category is Madeleine France; she is listed in the Directory under Florida.

Floor vase, two titled scenes signed L. Kroeller, cobalt with gilt accents and bronze satyr-mask handles, base chipped, 50", $17,600.00.

Box, portrait on cobalt w/much gold, bl mk, 2x4" dia 295.00
Candlestick, HP portraits on maroon & gold, 5½", pr 650.00
Charger, Rape of Sabines, centaur/young woman, 15" 875.00
Charger, Venus & Aeolus, nymphs/peacocks/etc, 12" 2,000.00
Cup, Hector, Paris, & Flitera on red, sgn Hept, 3", +saucer 200.00
Cup, Philippine Welser, lady on cobalt w/gold, ftd, +saucer 450.00
Demitasse pot, garden w/ladies, +sug/cr, 4 c/s, 15" tray 900.00
Demitasse pot, ladies on dk rose/heavy gold, +tray/9-pcs 550.00
Mug, Rosina, lady's portrait, sgn Gorref, 2", +bowl saucer 175.00

Plaque, lady in full gown in rose garden, Wasserrose, 7x9" 1,075.00
Plate, La Bella Temperia: lady in chair, gold/gr border, 9½" 600.00
Plate, lady on bench, 2nd w/basket, doves at ft, Wagner, 9½" 850.00
Plate, lady w/garland of grapes, mc/gilt border, 1880s, 9½" 500.00
Plate, Lecture, 2 young women read in garden, gilt fr, 10" 275.00
Plate, Marie de Medicis, jeweled/gilt border, 1800s 500.00
Plate, Odalisque: bare-breasted maid on wine, Wagner, 10" 600.00
Plate, Oleander: nymph on stone bench, sgn Wagner, 9½" ...1,500.00
Plate, Pearl, sgn Carl Larson, bl & orange rim, 1840s, 9½" 250.00
Plate, portrait w/much gold over burgundy, beehive mk, 9⅝" 155.00
Plate, quail in nature scene, gold/wine border, mk, lg 135.00
Plate, Spinne: bare-breasted lady/moth in web, A Rau, 9½" ...1,400.00
Plate, 2 ladies & courtier in garden, sgn Wagner, 8½" 595.00
Teapot, lady/cherubs in garden, allover gold, ftd, rstr, 5" 200.00
Urn, Adriane (or Naxos) on wine, mask hdls, ped ft, 18", pr ..1,200.00
Urn, classical scene on dk bl body/sq base, sgn Rericha, 24" ...4,800.00
Urn, figural reserves on wine, columnar ped, mask hdls, 18" ...1,100.00
Urn, Hector & Grazien on wine, bk: angel, sq base, 18" 1,100.00
Urn, lady/children on body & can ft, mask hdls, titled, 16" 1,600.00
Urn, lovers in reserve on bl w/gilt, hdls, late, 17" 475.00
Urn, Muses & Lorelei, bk: putti, on dk gr w/gilt, 14", pr 3,500.00
Vase, Solitude: seminude, heavy gold, Richter, hdls, 9" 2,500.00

Royal Worcester, Worcester

The Worcester Porcelain Company was deeded in 1751. During the first or Dr. Wall period (so called for one of its proprietors), porcelain with an Oriental influence was decorated in underglaze blue. Useful tablewares represented the largest portion of production, but figurines and decorative items were also made. Very little of the earliest wares were marked and can only be identified by a study of forms, glazes, and the porcelain body, which tends to transmit a greenish cast when held to light. Late in the fifties, a crescent mark was in general use, and rare examples bare a facsimile of the Meissen crossed swords. The first period ended in 1783, and the company went through several changes in ownership during the next eighty years. The years from 1783-1792 are referred to as the Flight period. Marks were a small crescent, a crown with 'Royal,' or an impressed 'Flight.' From 1792-1807 the company was known as Flight and Barr and used the trademark 'F&B' or 'B,' with or without a small cross. From 1807-1813 the company was under the Barr, Flight, and Barr management; this era is recognized as having produced porcelain with the highest quality of artistic decoration. Their mark was 'B.F.B.' From 1813-1840 many marks were used, but the most usual was 'F.B.B.' under a crown to indicate Flight, Barr, and Barr. In 1840 the firm merged with Chamberlain, and in 1852 they were succeeded by Kerr and Binns. The firm became known as Royal Worcester in 1862. Since 1930 Royal Worcester has been considered one of the leaders in the field of limited edition plates and figurines.

Basket, basketweave, beige satin w/gold, 1911 mk, 3x3¼x4½" ...115.00
Biscuit jar, flowers in relief w/gold, SP trim, 6x7" 350.00
Bowl, floral on ivory, rtcl edge, sq, 4" H 465.00
Bowl, salad; emb foliage, plated rim, 9", +pr servers 165.00
Candle snuffer, Cook, ca 1903 ....225.00
Candle snuffer, jester's head, Grainger, 1885, 3½" 700.00
Candle snuffer, Mr Caudle, ca 1898 ....225.00
Candle snuffer, owl, ca 1892 ....245.00
Candlestick, spirals/beads emb on tall std, 1884, 11", pr 550.00
Cup & saucer, dk bl rim band, gold foliage/thistle, Flight 85.00
Cup & saucer, Japan, ca 1770s, NM 425.00
Cup & saucer, roses, pk & yel on beige, 1906 mk, 2½", 5⅝" 95.00
Dish, leaf shape, wht w/bl design, Dr Wall, 10" L, NM 250.00

Ewer, floral on pk, emb bands, satyr mask, animal hdl, 17" 650.00
Ewer, zigzag mold, bulbous, Patent Metallic, 1884 mk, 13" 350.00
Figurine, Aberdeen Angus bull, Doris Linder, 10" L 425.00
Figurine, Bather Surprised, ivory/gilt, 1875, 16", EX 600.00
Figurine, Bl Angel Fish, Van Ruyckevelt, #3603, 1956, 12" 300.00
Figurine, Bob-Wht Quail, Van Ruyckevelt, wood base, 6½", EX ..275.00
Figurine, boy w/basket on shoulder, #880, 1881, 9¾", EX 275.00
Figurine, boy w/parakeet, FG Doughty, 7" 98.00
Figurine, boy/girl at fountain, #813, 1882, 7" 585.00
Figurine, Carolina Wren/Trumpet Creeper, J Alder, 1977, 11" ..220.00
Figurine, December 275.00
Figurine, First Dance 168.00
Figurine, gent stands/holds monocle, #1016, 1886, 8½" 330.00
Figurine, girl holds keg on left hip, arms akimbo, 8" 220.00
Figurine, Grandmother's Dress 195.00
Figurine, Handy Man, #2110, 1899, 7" 220.00
Figurine, Irishman, shamrocks on vest, #835, 1895, 7" 220.00
Figurine, Joy (& Sorrow), James Hadley, 9½", pr 440.00
Figurine, lady w/hand in muff, #1016, 1884, 8" 365.00
Figurine, Lissette, #3442 ....850.00
Figurine, parakeet, #2663, 7" 95.00
Figurine, Parakeet Boy 150.00
Figurine, Punch kneels (& Judy sits), F Doughty, 5½", pr 770.00
Figurine, Saturday's Child 195.00
Figurine, seated child holds urn on right, 1901, 4½" 220.00
Figurine, seated lady w/lute, Watteau, #547, 1900, 3½" 365.00
Figurine, seated male (& lady) musician, 1900s, 4", pr 325.00
Figurine, Sorrow, dead bird in hand, #58, 1893, rstr, 10" 165.00
Figurine, Thursday's Child 145.00
Figurine, Tuesday's Boy 150.00
Figurine, Water Baby, FG Doughty, #3151, 1936, 6" 525.00
Figurine, Yel Grunt, 3 in coral, Van Ruyckevelt, 1956, 6" 165.00
Figurine, Yel Hammers, 2 on leaf-covered stump, 1942, 5" 165.00
Flower holder, center pot+3 on foliate arms, #1688, 5½" 250.00
Jar, floral on cream, rtcl lid w/spire atop, gilt, 1902, 13" 700.00
Jardiniere, Hadley Ware, allover florals/molded borders, 6" 525.00
Jardiniere, swirl attached base, scroll ft/hdls, 1890, 10" 500.00
Jug, bird in mc/gilt, mask under spout, #1366, 1889, 10" 525.00
Pitcher, butterfly/foliage, coiled snake hdl, 1884, 11" 400.00
Pitcher, Malvern, city scenes, bl w/gilt, 1800s, 5½" 375.00
Pitcher, milk; yel w/gold trim, fluted lip, 6" 90.00
Pitcher, owl on branch/moon, gold snake hdl, 1885, 11" 930.00
Plaque, Delft, portrait, sgn Van der Bosch, 20" 250.00
Plate, burgundy & gold, Rococo, artist sgn, set of 6 ....1,200.00
Plate, dinner; Evesham 25.00
Plate, dinner; Lavinia 20.00
Plate, Tewkesbury village scene, Nickolls, 1953 mk, 10¾" 225.00
Plate, Victoria Jubilee 1837-1887, 10" 185.00
Sauce boat, bl transfer chinoiserie, minor wear, 7" 450.00
Sugar bowl, Canterbury 25.00
Sugar shaker, Pineapple, mk Locke, SP top, 6x2⅝" 75.00
Teapot, Canterbury 40.00
Teapot, Japan, 1770s, rstr, 6", EX 935.00
Tumbler, emb leaves/berries w/gold trim, 1934 mk, 3⅞" 65.00
Vase, birds/marsh, U-form widening at base, bamboo hdls, 8" 365.00
Vase, butterflies/floral, flask form, shaped hdls, 1884, 12" 500.00
Vase, cornucopia; flowers at neck, 3", EX 95.00
Vase, Crown Ware, paneled landscapes, gold highlights, 5" 165.00
Vase, dbl; 2 szs 'tied together' w/drape, mottled, rstr, 9" 660.00
Vase, emb Oriental scenes, branch hdls/ft, rtcl rim, 4¾" 550.00
Vase, emb storks in panels w/rtcl edging 4 sides, 1875, 6" 330.00
Vase, floral, fluted bands, lg griffin hdls, ftd, 1893, 11" 500.00
Vase, foliage, mc/gilt, cylindrical w/sm elephant hdls, 9" 220.00
Vase, fruit/florals in mc/gilt, ornate hdls, ftd, 1896, 15" 1,100.00

Vase, gold foilage on red, 2 cojoined flask forms, 1877, 6" **410.00**
Vase, mums on ivory, Persian style, rtcl lip/hdls, 11" **465.00**
Vase, nautilus shape, gilt seaweed/shells on stem/base, 9" **450.00**
Vase, peacocks in garden, sgn Lewis, ornate hdls, 6x6", EX **935.00**

Roycroft

Near the turn of the century, Elbert Hubbard established the Roycroft Printing Shop in East Aurora, New York. Named in honor of two 17th-century printer-bookbinders, the print shop was just the beginning of a community called Roycroft, which came to be known worldwide. Hubbard became a popular personality of the early 1900s, known for his talents in a variety of areas from writing and lecturing to manufacturing. The Roycroft community became a meeting place for people of various capabilities and included shops for the production of furniture, copper, leather items, and a multitude of other wares which were marked with the Roycroft symbol, an 'R' within a circle below a stylized cross. Hubbard lost his life on the Lusitania in 1915; production in the community continued until the Depression.

Interest is strong in the field of Arts and Crafts in general, and in Roycroft items in particular. Copper items are evaluated to a large extent by the condition of the original patina that remains.

Our advisor for this category is Bruce Austin; he is listed in the Directory under New York.

Book, *The Last Ride* by Robert Browning, signed by Elbert Hubbard, illuminated by Lily Elss, vellum cover with linen ties, $250.00.

Ashtray stand, #621, orig patina, worn tray, mk, 29" **500.00**
Ashtray stand, wood grain ft/tray joined by 4 straps, NM **1,000.00**
Bed, twin; #0106, MacMurdo ft, 8-slat head/ftbrd, mk, VG **2,400.00**
Bookends, #308, flat-iron trivet shape, worn patina, 5x4" **160.00**
Bookends, #312, rectangular w/owl, 4x6", EX **130.00**
Bookends, #320, rnd top w/owl, orig patina, 5x6" **200.00**
Bookends, floral, 3x3", EX **75.00**
Bookends, open fr w/canted corners & floral decor, 9x6" **90.00**
Bowl, #238, brass-washed, emb leaves, 3x4", VG **180.00**
Bowl, hammered copper, 3 ft, rolled rim, orb mk, 4x10", EX **300.00**
Box, mahog w/hammered copper hdls & hinges, orb mk, 23" L ..**475.00**
Candelabrum, #84, 3-lite, 2 slim arms & std w/2 twists, 20" **420.00**
Candle holder, #414, strap hdl from bobeche to base, 3" **170.00**
Candle holder, 6 cups on horizontal scroll-end strap, 3x15" **200.00**
Candlestick, #403, brass on copper, long 2-strap std, 8" **375.00**
Candlestick, #405, wide cupped base, dent at edge, 2x4" **140.00**
Candlestick, 3-stem w/twists & curled terminals, orb mk, 20" **350.00**
Dinner bell, hammered copper/brass, orig patina, 3" **200.00**
Humidor, #626, wood lining, orig patina, 2x9x6" **750.00**

Humidor, emb trefoils, lid w/monogram, orig patina, mk, 7" **300.00**
Lamp, hammered metal w/mica band, orb mk, 14x10" **1,700.00**
Lamp, 4 scroll-end straps on std/base, Steuben shade, #913 ....**3,500.00**
Letter holder, #714, lt wear, 4x4" **150.00**
Magazine pedestal, #080, 5-shelf, cvd orb ea side, 63", EX **4,750.00**
Paperweight, wood, rectangular, orb/X mk burned into top **235.00**
Plate, fruit; #C805, fruit border, orig patina, 10" **160.00**
Stand, Little Journeys, keyed tenons, brass tag, minor wear **440.00**
Table, #072½, 4 ogee legs, orb mk, orig finish, 30" dia **3,750.00**
Tray, #824, 8-sided, hdls, orig patina, 15", EX **375.00**
Tray, #826, 8-sided, hdls, orig patina, 10" **375.00**
Tray, card; hammered, orig patina, 8" dia **110.00**
Vase, #212, hammered cylinder, cvd long-stem floral, 11" **1,200.00**
Vase, #219A, ruffled top, orig patina, 6" **200.00**
Vase, #234, hammered, orig patina, tapered ovoid, 9" **325.00**
Vase, #244, hammered base section, cleaned, 5" **250.00**
Vase, Am Beauty, hammered brass, stick neck, 7", VG **375.00**
Vase, Am Beauty, long trumpet neck, squat riveted body, 19" ...**880.00**
Vase, Am Beauty, rivets in wide base, no patina, orb mk, 22" .**1,400.00**
Vase, att Dard Hunter, 3-stem nickel fr over glass tube, 9" **1,600.00**
Vase, hammered cylinder, flared/riveted base, EX patina, 11" .**1,500.00**
Walking stick, oak, tapering/4-sided, no strap, mk, 32" **220.00**

Rozenburg

Some of the most innovative and original Art Nouveau ceramics were created by the Rozenberg factory at The Hague in The Netherlands between 1885 and 1916. Some pieces are similar to Gouda. Rozenburg also made highly prized eggshell ware, so called because of its very thin walls; this is eagerly sought after by collectors. T.A.C. Colenbrander was their artistic leader with Samuel Schellink and J. Kok designing many of the eggshell pieces.

Key: eg — eggshell

Cup & saucer, Nouveau floral, octagonal, Van Rossum **515.00**
Jug, Nouveau butterflies/florals, sgn VW, #614, mks, 7" **500.00**
Plaque, 5 flowers on bl, cobalt rim, 1890s, rstr, 18" **550.00**
Plate, eg, mc stylized flowers on wht, octagonal, 6" **450.00**
Tile, windmill, pastoral, pictoral fr, sgn Gabriel **465.00**

Pair of vases, florals and dragons on brown, 1898, 9½", $1,300.00; Plaque, thistles in gray, rust, and brown, 1898, 11", $700.00.

Vase, butterflies/florals, mc on dk gr, rstr, 22" **1,950.00**
Vase, Nouveau florals/vines/waves, long hdls, #DW-366, 15" **900.00**
Vase, pansies, orange on bl, blk-dotted yel neck/hdls, 10" **695.00**

Rubena

Rubena glass was made by several firms in the late 1800s. It is a blown art glass that shades from clear to red. See also Art Glass Baskets; Cruets; Sugar Shakers; Salts; specific manufacturers.

Bottle, scent; allover cutting, matching cut stopper, 3¼" 110.00
Bottle, scent; SP rim, cranberry cut stopper, 3¼" 132.00
Bowl, Daisy & Scroll, 4½" 62.50
Condiment set, cut dmn pattern, 3-pc in SP fr 210.00
Decanter, bulbous, appl clear hdl, 9" 145.00
Pitcher, tankard, clear reeded hdl, 10" 200.00
Tumbler, Invt T'print, HP florals, 4⅛x2⅞" 45.00
Vase, acid-etch floral, rib int/bell-shape top, Mt WA, 6" 275.00
Vase, bud; dmn cuttings, HP florals, 6" 65.00
Vase, 4-lobed cylinder, HP/gilt decor, appl threading, 10" 225.00

Rubena Verde

Rubena Verde glass was introduced in the late 1800s by Hobbs, Brockunier and Company of Wheeling, West Virginia. Its transparent colors shade from red to green. Our advisor for this category is Mike Roscoe; he is listed in the Directory under Michigan. See also Art Glass Baskets; Cruets; Sugar Shakers; Salts.

Bowl, Honeycomb, rolled rim, ftd, 9" 98.00
Butter dish, Invt T'print, rnd verde finial 500.00
Cup, punch; Invt T'print 70.00
Pitcher, Hobnail, bulbous, Hobbs & Brockunier, 7½" 395.00
Toothpick holder, egg-shaped body w/scalloped, ruffled ped ft ...285.00
Tumbler, Hobnail 115.00
Vase, appl threading, 4" 235.00
Vase, HP pk & wht florals w/gold tracery, att Moser, 11½" 495.00
Vase, mc floral/bl ribbon, ruffled w/str ribbed sides, 11" 175.00

Ruby Glass

Produced for over one hundred years by every glasshouse of note in this country, ruby glass has been used to create decorative items such as one might find in gift shops, utilitarian bottles and kitchenware, figurines, and dinnerware lines such as were popular in the Depression era. For further information and study, we recommend *Ruby Glass of the 20th Century* by our advisor, Naomi Over; she is listed in the Directory under Colorado.

Banana boat, Moon & Star, LG Wright, 1974-81, 12" 40.00
Bank, owl figural, Anchor Hocking, 1981, 7" 250.00
Basket, scalloped rim, yel hdl on 4½" body 60.00
Bowl, cereal; Old Cafe, Anchor Hocking, 1940s, 5½" 12.00
Cake plate, Sandwich, Indiana, 1960s-70s, 13" 85.00
Candle holder, Barred Oval, Fenton, 1985-87, 6", pr 25.00
Candlestick, swan neck, Viking, 6¼" 25.00
Candy dish, Sweetheart, LG Wright, 3¾" 20.00
Console set, Tiara's Sunset Leaf, Indiana, bowl+pr 5" sticks 45.00
Creamer & sugar bowl, rnd, Anchor Hocking, 1940s 10.00
Cup, Sweetheart, Macbeth-Evans, 1930-36, rare 100.00
Cup & saucer, sq form, Anchor Hocking, 1940s 4.00
Door stop, Alley Cat, 11¼" 40.00
Figurine, bird, Swedish Glass, ca 1980, 3" 8.00
Figurine, bird, Swedish Glass, 4" 15.00
Figurine, seal, Mirror Images, Viking Glass, 4¼" 45.00
Goblet, wine; Czechoslovakia, 5-oz 20.00
Lamp, fairy; Sweetheart, LG Wright, 1974-81, 4¼" 15.00
Lamp, oil; Rose Wreath, Pittsburgh, 8¼" 750.00
Marmalade, Eyewinker, LG Wright, 1974-81, 8¾" 30.00

Mustard jar, ruby lid, crystal base, Anchor Hocking, 1940s 15.00
Nappy, Royal Ruby, Anchor Hocking, 6½" 8.00
Paperweight, apple, Viking, 3¾" 20.00
Paperweight, pear, Viking, 8½" 40.00
Pickle dish, Royal Ruby, Anchor Hocking, 7" 15.00
Pie shell, Pyrex, 9½" 50.00
Pitcher, Blenko, #3750, 16-oz 20.00
Pitcher, Blenko, #939P, ca 1952, 14" 60.00
Plate, Bubble, Anchor Hocking, 1960, 9⅜" 10.00
Plate, Oyster & Pearl, Anchor Hocking, 13½" 40.00
Plate, Royal Ruby, Anchor Hocking, 9" 8.00
Punch bowl, Rachel, Anchor Hocking, 1940s, 11", +liner 80.00
Saucer, American, Macbeth-Evans, 1930-36, scarce 25.00
Shakers, Mirror & Rose, LG Wright, 3¼", pr 20.00
Sherbet, Anchor Hocking 6.00
Sherbet, plain stem, Anchor Hocking, ca 1942 ....6.00
Snack set, Fan, Anchor Hocking, 1940s 10.00
Syrup, Moon & Star, LG Wright, 1981, 4-oz 25.00
Tray, Anchor Hocking, 14" 25.00
Tumbler, Georgian, Anchor Hocking, 1940s, 9-oz 6.00
Tumbler, Hobnail, Anchor Hocking, 1930s, 4½" 7.50
Tumbler, iced tea; Provincial, Anchor Hocking, 1963, 16-oz 15.00
Vase, Knotted Beads, slim form, 11" 65.00
Vase, Rachel, Anchor Hocking, 1940s, 10" 40.00
Vase, swan hdls, Venetian, 12" 125.00

Ruby-Stained Souvenirs

Ruby-flashed or ruby-stained glass was made through the application of a thin layer of color over clear. It was used in the manufacture of some early pressed tableware and from the Victorian era well into the 20th century for souvenir items which were often engraved on the spot with the date, location, and buyer's name.

Pitcher, Diamond Point Band, name and '1897,' $95.00; Creamer, $65.00; Sugar bowl with lid, $80.00.

Butter dish, Button Arches 80.00
Creamer, Arched Ovals, mini 25.00
Creamer, Heart Band, mini 25.00
Cup, Arched Ovals, Philadelphia 1899 ....25.00
Cup, Regland, Sleepy Eye MN, 1903, 3" 60.00
Goblet, Ruby T'print 28.00
Mug, Dmn Point Band 30.00
Mug, Heart, Eureka Springs Crescent Hotel 30.00
Spooner, Buttons & Arches 30.00
Toothpick holder, Shamrock 40.00
Toothpick holder, Witch's Kettle 15.00

Tumbler, Invt Strawberry 32.00
Tumbler, Pavonia 50.00
Tumbler, Ruby T'print, World's Fair 1893 ....35.00
Wine, Honeycomb 30.00

Rugs

Hooked rugs are treasured today for their folk-art appeal. It was a craft that was introduced to this country in about 1830 and flourished its best in the New England states. The prime consideration is not age but artistic appeal. Scenes with animals, buildings, and people; patriotic designs; or whimsical themes are preferred. Condition is, of course, also a factor. Marked examples bearing the stamps of 'Frost and Co.,' 'Abenakee,' 'C.R.,' and 'Ouia' are highly prized. Note: the rugs listed here are rag unless noted otherwise.

Bird/flowers, braid/crochet border, oval, 35x23", VG 125.00
Cat & kitten w/semicircular 'Welcome,' mc on wht, 39x24" 725.00
Comport of flowers, maker's name, 1850s, rpr, 64x35" 660.00
Concentric rectangles, mc, mtd on stretcher, 38x28" 110.00
Conestoga wagon w/6 horses, man/barn/trees, 1950s, 48x25" 265.00
Cottage in landscape, yarn/rag, 31x19" 150.00
Cottage/fence/trees/garden, EX mc, blk cloth bound, 42x27" 200.00
Deer pr (sm images) in forest landscape, EX color, 37x19" 200.00
Diagonal blk bands w/roses on mc streaky ground, 46x24" 150.00
Dog (stylized), brn/olive on bl, lt wear, 39x24" 200.00
Dog/2 fawns in stylized landscape, 41x19" 175.00

Dog, 'Old Shep,' with kitten and puppy, early 20th century, 27x34", $900.00.

Flowers/butterflies on oval, 55x39" 225.00
Folk art design: 4 animals/butterfly on gray, late, 31x24" 185.00
Geometrics, EX color, wear/rebk/rpr, 89x52" 500.00
Grenfell, dog sled/2 men in parkas, 38x25", EX 500.00
Grenfell, dog team/man running/man on sled, 39x26" 350.00
Hourglass/angel/tombstones/8-line verse, 1900s, 48x35" 2,750.00
Indian in canoe, tepees in bkground, yarn detail, 36x19" 125.00
Int scene: spinning wheel, chair, broom, faded, 40x24" 150.00
Lion peering out of jungle foliage, EX color, 22" L, EX 325.00
Lions in jungle, intricate Ebenezer Ross pattern, 64x35" 700.00
Mat, Welcome & florals on blk, semicircular, 24x18" 70.00
Seaside house/garden w/harbor & lighthouse, 50x35" 430.00
Sqs/stripes, mc, 42x23" 200.00
Striped sqs, minor wear, 58x33" 250.00
Stylized floral, meandering border, 1850s, rpr, 70x36" 880.00
Winter scene, detailed, rag/yarn, 35x24" 295.00
Winter scene w/cabin, people, chickens, horses, 35", VG 300.00

RumRill

George Rumrill designed and marketed his pottery designs from 1933 until his death in 1942. During this period of time, four different companies produced his works. Today the most popular designs a those made by the Red Wing Stoneware Company from 1933 un 1936 and Red Wing Potteries from 1936 until early 1938. Some these popular lines include Trumpet Flower, Classic, Manhattan, a Athena, the Nudes.

For a period of months in 1938, Shawnee took over the produ tion of RumRill pottery. This relationship ended abruptly and the Fl rence Pottery took over and produced his wares until the plant burn down. The final producer was Gonder. Pieces from each individual po tery are easily recognized by their designs, glazes, and/or signatures. It interesting to note that the same designs were produced by all thr companies. They may be marked RumRill or with the name of the sp cific company that made them. Our advisors for this category a Wendy and Leo Frese; they are listed in the Directory under Texas.

Candle holder, Athena, Egg Shell, #576, 9½" 175.0
Candle holder, Fluted, Dutch Bl, #454, 4½" 45.0
Candle holder, Shell, Seashell, #545, 8½" 35.0
Cornucopia, Shell, Turq, #413, 7½" 25.0

Pedestal with bowl insert, Athena, #572 and #574, 11½", $350.00; Candle holder, Athena, #576, 9½", $175.00.

Pitcher, Indian, Goldenrod, #50, 8" w/cap 40.0
Pitcher, novelty, Dutch Bl, #547, 7½" 30.0
Vase, Athena, Egg Shell, #568, 11½" 225.0
Vase, Athena, Jade, #570, 10" 300.0
Vase, Continental, Turq, #252, w/lid, 14" 85.0
Vase, Fern, Ocean Gr, #518, 7½" 20.0
Vase, Fluted, Charcoal, #320, 5½" 25.0
Vase, Grecian, Lilac, #303, 11½" 45.0
Vase, Manhattan, Marigold, #314, 6" 40.0
Vase, Swan, Egg Shell, #388, 8½" 50.0
Vase, Trumpet Flower, Egg Shell, #486, 7" 30.0

Ruskin

This English pottery operated near Birmingham from 1989 unt 1935. Its founder was W. Howson Taylor, and it was named in honor c the reknown author and critic, John Ruskin. The earliest marks wer 'Taylor' in block letters and the initials 'WHT,' the smaller W and H superimposed over the upright leg of a larger T. Later marks include the Ruskin name.

Candlestick, pk lustre, 7", pr 175.00
Jardiniere, red/wht speckles on cream, high-fired, '25, 7x8" 770.00
Vase, dots/squiggles on streaky bl, dtd 1908, 8", EX 180.0
Vase, red-brn w/cream & lt bl sprinkles, drilled, 10½" 150.0
Vase, yel irid w/grapevine at rim, baluster form, 1921, 9¾" 225.0

Russel Wright Dinnerware

Russel Wright, one of America's foremost industrial designers, also designed several lines of ceramic dinnerware, glassware, and aluminum ware that are now highly sought after collectibles. His most popular dinnerware then and with today's collectors, American Modern, was manufactured by the Steubenville Pottery Company from 1939 until 1959. It was produced in a variety of solid colors in assortments chosen to stay attune with the times. Casual (his first line sturdy enough to be guaranteed against breakage for ten years from date of purchase) is relatively easy to find today — simply because it has held up so well. During the years of its production, the Casual line was constantly being restyled, some items as many as five times. Early examples were heavily mottled, while later pieces were smoothly glazed and patterned. The ware was marked with Wright's signature and 'China by Iroquois.' It was marketed in fine department stores throughout the country. After 1950 the line was marked 'Iroquois China by Russel Wright.'

To calculate values for items in American Modern, add 100% to the suggested prices in the following listings for examples in these colors: White, Bean Brown, Cantaloupe, and Glacier Blue. In Casual, Brick Red and Aqua items go for around 200% more than any other color, while those in Avocado Yellow are priced lower than suggested values. For those wanting to learn more about the subject, we recommend *The Collectors Encyclopedia of Russel Wright Designs* by our advisor, Ann Kerr. She is listed in the Directory under Ohio. Updated values are included.

Residential: Divided vegetable bowl, $18.00; Cup and saucer, $7.00.

American Modern

Ashtray, coaster	13.00
Bowl, lug fruit	12.50
Bowl, salad	70.00
Bowl, vegetable	20.00
Butter dish	160.00
Carafe	160.00
Casserole, w/lid, 12"	45.00
Celery dish	24.00
Coffeepot, 8x8½"	140.00
Creamer	10.00
Cup & saucer	12.00
Gravy boat, 10½"	18.00
Lug soup	12.00
Mug (tumbler)	55.00

Pickle dish	15.00
Pitcher, water	85.00
Pitcher, water; w/lid	150.00
Plate, dinner; 10"	10.00
Plate, salad; 8"	10.00
Platter, 13¼"	22.50
Refrigerator jar	155.00
Salad fork & spoon	85.00
Shakers, pr	14.00
Sugar bowl, w/lid	12.00
Teapot, 6x10"	65.00
Tumbler, child's	55.00

Casual

Bowl, cereal; orig or restyled, 5", ea	7.00
Bowl, fruit; restyled, 5¾"	7.00
Bowl, soup; 11½-oz	10.00
Bowl, vegetable; 36-oz, 8⅛"	18.00
Butter dish, ½-lb	60.00
Casserole, 10"	45.00
Casserole lid, for 4-qt casserole	20.00
Coffeepot, AD; 4½"	65.00
Creamer, lg family sz	22.50
Cup & saucer, restyled	10.00
Cup & saucer, tea	12.50
Gravy bowl, 12-oz, 5¼"	10.00
Gravy stand cover, 7½"	85.00
Mug, 13-oz	65.00
Pitcher, water; restyled, 2-qt	125.00
Pitcher, water; 1½-qt, 5¼"	70.00
Plate, chop; 13⅞"	25.00
Plate, salad; 7½"	8.00
Platter, oval, 14½"	27.50
Sugar bowl, lg family sz	17.50
Sugar bowl, stacking, 4"	10.00

Glass

American Modern, bowl, dessert; Smoke	40.00
American Modern, chilling bowl	100.00
American Modern, cocktail, Chartreuse	25.00
American Modern, cocktail, Gray	30.00
American Modern, cordial, Coral	38.00
American Modern, cordial, Seafoam	38.00
American Modern, goblet, Chartreuse	35.00
American Modern, goblet, Smoke	35.00
American Modern, sherbet, Chartreuse	25.00
American Modern, sherbet, Gray	30.00
American Modern, tumbler, iced tea; Coral, 13-oz	30.00
American Modern, tumbler, pilsner; Coral	95.00
American Modern, wine, Chartreuse	25.00
American Modern, wine, Smoke, 4-oz, 3"	30.00
Eclipse, old-fashioned	15.00
Eclipse, shot glass	10.00
Flair, tumbler, iced tea; 14-oz	60.00
Flair, tumbler, juice; 6-oz	50.00
Flair, tumbler, water; 11-oz	50.00
Pinch, tumbler, iced tea; 14-oz	30.00
Pinch, tumbler, water; 11-oz	30.00
Pinch, tumbler, juice; 6-oz	30.00
Snow Glass, tumbler, iced tea; 14-oz	115.00
Snow Glass, tumbler, juice; 5-oz	115.00

Highlight

Bowl, vegetable; Citron, rnd 50.00
Bowl, vegetable; Wht, Pepper, or Blueberry, oval 60.00
Creamer, Wht, Pepper or Blueberry 30.00
Lid, for soup, Citron or Nutmeg 35.00
Plate, dinner; Citron or Nutmeg 25.00
Platter, Wht, Pepper, or Blueberry 60.00
Shakers, Citron or Nutmeg, lg or sm, pr 45.00
Sugar bowl, high gloss 30.00
Sugar bowl, Wht, Pepper, or Blueberry 35.00

Spun Aluminum

Russel Wright's aluminum ware may not have been especially well accepted in its day — it tended to damage easily and seems to have had only limited market appeal — but today's collectors feel quite differently about it, as is apparent in the suggested values noted in the following listings.

Baine Marie, server 400.00
Candelabrum, rare, 18x14" 200.00
Casserole 85.00
Cheese board 85.00
Flower ring 125.00
Gravy boat 125.00
Hot relish server 175.00
Humidor, sandwich 160.00
Ice bucket 75.00
Muffin warmer, wire insert, w/lid 100.00
Old-fashioned set, 20-pc 450.00
Pitcher, sherry 250.00
Portable bar/serving cart 2,000.00
Punch set 1,500.00
Relish rosette, sm 125.00
Serving accessory, sm 100.00
Smoking stand 650.00
Spaghetti set, 3-pc 400.00
Tea set, 4-pc 450.00
Tray, tidbit 85.00
Vase, 12" 110.00
Vase or flowerpot, sm, ea 85.00
Wastebasket 110.00

Sterling

Ashtray 75.00
Bowl, fruit; 5" 5.00
Bowl, onion soup; 10-oz 18.00
Bowl, salad; 7½" 8.00
Coffee bottle 80.00
Creamer, 1-oz 8.00
Pitcher, water; restyled 55.00
Plate, dinner; 10¼" 10.00
Plate, salad; 7½" 6.00
Platter, oval, 10½" 15.00
Sauce boat, 9-oz 16.00
Teapot, 10-oz 55.00

Miscellaneous

Bauer, ashtray, Pinch, 6½" 275.00
Bauer, flowerpot, sq, 4½" 250.00
Bauer, vase, oval, 12" 700.00

Flair, creamer 8.00
Flair, tumbler 13.00
Harker White Clover, bowl, vegetable; 7½" 18.00
Harker White Clover, casserole, clover decor, w/lid, 2-qt 45.00
Harker White Clover, plate, dinner; clover decor, 9¼" 12.50
Home Decorator, bowl, vegetable; oval, shallow 10.00
Home Decorator, cup & saucer 7.00
Ideal Ware, child's boxed set 135.00
Ideal Ware, child's serving item, ea 25.00
Ideal Ware, decanter, juice 30.00
Ideal Ware, tumbler, either sz 20.00
Knowles, cup & saucer, 7½-oz 15.00
Knowles, plate, dinner; 10¾" 12.50
Knowles, platter, oval, 13" 16.00
Knowles, teapot 100.00
Meladur, cup, 7-oz 7.00
Meladur, plate, compartmented, 9½" 8.00
Meladur, plate, dinner; 9" 5.00
Meladur, plate, service; 10" 8.00
Residential, lug soup 12.00
Residential, platter 15.00

Russian Art

Before the Revolution in 1917, many jewelers and craftsmen created exquisite marvels of their arts, distinctive in the extravagant detail of their enamel work, jeweled inlays, and use of precious metals. These treasures aptly symbolized the glitter and the romance of the glorious days under the reign of the Tsars of Imperial Russia. The most famous of these master jewelers was Carl Faberge (1852-1920), goldsmith to the Romanovs. Following the tradition of his father, he took over the Faberge workshop in 1870. Eventually Faberge employed more than 500 assistants and set up workshops in Moscow, Kiev, and London as well as in St. Petersburg. His specialties were enamel work, clockwork automated figures, carved animal and human figures of precious or semiprecious stones, cigarette cases, small boxes, scent flasks, and his best-known creations, the Imperial Easter Eggs — each of an entirely different design. By the turn of the century, his influence had spread to other countries, and his work was revered by royalty and the very wealthy. The onset of the war marked the end of the era. Very little of his work remains on the market, and items that are available are very expensive. But several of his contemporaries were goldsmiths whose work can be equally enchanting. Among them are Klingert, Ovchinnikov, Smirnov, Ruckert, Loriye, Cheryatov, Kuzmichev, Nevalainen, Adler, Sbitnev, Third Artel, Wakewa, Holmstrom, Britzin, Wigstrom, Orlov, Nichols, and Plincke. Most of them produced excellent pieces similar to those made by Faberge between 1880 and 1910.

Perhaps the most important bronze Russian artist was Eugenie Alexandrovich Lanceray (1847-87). From 1875 until 1887, he modeled many equestrian groups of falconers and soldiers ranging in height from about 20" to 30". Some of them bear the Chopin foundry mark; they are presently worth from $4,000 up. Other excellent artists were Schmidt Felling (19th Century), who specialized in mounted figures of cossacks wearing military uniforms, and Nicholas Leiberich (late 19th Century), who also specialized in equestrian groups. Most of the pieces made by the above artists were signed and had the foundry mark (Chopin, Woerfell, etc.)

Russian porcelain is another field where Imperial connections have undoubtedly added to the interest of collectors and museums worldwide. The most important factories were: Imperial Russian Porcelain, St. Petersburg (or Petrograd or Leningrad, 1744-1917); Gardner, Moscow (1765-1872); Kuznetsoff, St. Petersburg and Moscow (1800-1900); Korniloff, St. Petersburg (1800-1900); and Babunin, St. Petersburg (1800-1900).

Key: lcq — lacquered

Beaker, repousse/chased silver, gilt int, ball ft, 1761, 2½" 700.00
Cake basket, silver, Empire style, ftd, Blasball, 1834, 4" 925.00
Candlestick, caryatid figural, ormolu/malachite, 1800s, 10" 450.00
Cigarette case, silver, ribbed band, oval, ca 1890, 4" 700.00
Cigarette case, wht metal, CCCP/plane/factory emb, 4½" 1,400.00
Claret jug, cut glass w/wht metal top, mk Faberge, 9" 650.00
Easter egg, robins HP on wht opaque glass, Faberge, 1890 ....1,600.00
Figurine, peasant mother & child, porc, Gardner, 1885, 6⅝" 745.00
Figurine, poacher w/dog & game, HP porc, Popov, 1800s, 7½" ..835.00

Hot water kettle on Art Nouveau stand, K. Faberge, Moscow, 1899-1908, 12", 72 troy oz., $3,300.00.

Match holder, lcq papier-mache, peasant lady, 1800s 450.00
Napkin ring, lcq papier-mache, Kremlin view, 1890s, pr 650.00
Statuette, gilt-bronze musician, malachite base, 1800s, 5⅝" 1,485.00
Stirrup cup, silver, ram's head form, ruby eyes, 1860s, 3" 2,785.00
Tea set, repousse/chased silver, ebony hdls, 1820s, 4-pc 3,900.00

Sabino

Sabino art glass was produced by Marius-Ernest Sabino in France during the 1920s and '30s. It was made in opalescent, frosted, and colored glass and was designed to reflect the Art Deco style of that era. In 1960, using molds he modeled by hand, Sabino once again began to produce art glass using a special formula he himself developed that was characterized by a golden opalescence. Although the family continued to produce glassware for export after his death in 1971, they were never able to duplicate Sabino's formula.

Figurine, Barbarin fish 50.00
Figurine, butterfly, wings closed, sm 30.00
Figurine, cat 25.00
Figurine, chick drinking 55.00
Figurine, dove, head down or up, sm 24.00
Figurine, dragonfly 125.00
Figurine, gazelle, 4x6" 65.00
Figurine, kneeling nude surrounded by 3 doves, label, 6" 220.00
Figurine, lady & doves 325.00
Figurine, rooster, lg 465.00
Figurine, snail 27.50
Figurine, Suzanne, nude, cape in outstretched arms, 1927, 9" .3,520.00
Figurine, woodpecker 60.00
Knife rest, duck 25.00
Plate, Birth of Star, 3 nude maids drift around rim, 12" 650.00
Tray, sea urchin, lg 85.00
Tray, swallow, sm 35.00

Vase, Art Decoratifs, dancing nude on ea of 4 sides, 10" 2,750.00
Vase, bl, 6 indented panels w/molded sunflowers, 7x7" 1,300.00
Vase, Deco nudes w/hands joined encircle vase, 10" 1,875.00
Vase, emb procession of seminudes, ovoid, flared rim, 14" 2,200.00
Vase, turq, concave flower-molded sides, ca 1925, 11x6" 3,000.00
Vase, turq, 6 lg concave dahlias, ca 1930, 7½x7½" 1,650.00
Vase, 8 dancing maids in flowing gowns, ovoid, 1930s, 14" 2,750.00

Salesman's Samples and Patent Models

Salesman's samples and patent models are often mistaken for toys or homemade folk art pieces. They are instead actual working models made by very skilled craftsmen who worked as model-makers. Patent models were made until the early 1900s. After that, the patent office no longer required a model to grant a patent. The name of the inventor or the model-maker and the date it was built is sometimes noted on the patent model. Salesman's samples were occasionally made by model-makers, but often they were assembled by an employee of the company. These usually carried advertising messages to boost the sale of the product. Though they are still in use today, the most desirable examples date from the 1800s to about 1945.

Many small stoves are incorrectly termed a 'salesman's sample'; remember that no matter how detailed one may be, it must be considered a toy unless accompanied by a carrying case, the indisputable mark of a salesman's sample.

Half-poster bed, ca 1880s, 30x21" long, $800.00.

Bathtub, porc, Wilcox Plumbing, M 35.00
Bed, Art Bed Co, CI, EX 425.00
Book, Will Rogers-Ambassador of Good Will, '35, M in wrapper .25.00
Bride's basket, pk cased glass in ornate Tufts SP fr 335.00
Calendar, Marilyn Monroe, pnt-on clothes, 1955, EX 160.00
Cash drawer, RC Allen, cast aluminum 50.00
Casket, plush int, 21" L 485.00
Dexter washing machine, copper/brass on wood fr, 12", G 600.00
Furnace, Anthanor, May & Fieberger, cast aluminum, 17-pc 550.00
Furnace, Meuller, EX 325.00
Goblet, shows varied eng scripts, hollow stem, 1860s, 6½" 465.00
Kraut-washing machine, wood/iron, Pat 1888, 14x15x10", EX ...770.00
Meat grinder, clamp style, EX 25.00
Pan, Royal Granite Steelware, gray 75.00

Safe, CI w/wooden int, EX pnt, 6x6x9", EX 770.00
Street lamp 600.00
Teakettle, copper & brass 75.00
Trade stimulator, Budowil Gambling Machine, 8x15x8½", MIB ..60.00

Salt Glaze

As early as the 1600s, potters used common salt to glaze their stoneware. This was accomplished by heating the salt and introducing it into the kiln at maximum temperature. The resulting gray-white glaze was a thin, pitted surface that resembles the peel of an orange.

Cup, 10 arched flutes, HP floral, Staffordshire, 1760s, NM **3,300.00**
Dish, leaf shape, emb bird/leaves etc, 7¾" **1,500.00**
Dish, leaf shape, emb currant branches, 3 floral ft, 6" **1,400.00**
Figurine, cat seated w/tail curled around ft, 5", NM **1,500.00**
Figurine, recumbent dog, incised ribs, blk eyes, 2" L, EX **1,100.00**
Gravy boat, grape leaf mold, 1760, rstr, 5" L **330.00**
Mug, foliate hdl terminal, banding, 3⅜", NM **75.00**
Plate, emb scalloped rim, lt wear, 9½" **75.00**
Sauceboat, 4 emb/HP cows & meadow, Staffordshire, 7" **1,500.00**
Spoon tray, emb flowers/scrolls, rope border, 6", NM **1,700.00**
Spoon tray, HP flowering branch, quatraform, Staffordshire ... **3,800.00**
Sugar bowl, emb Prince-of-Wales feathers, ribbed, 3½x5" **75.00**
Sweetmeat dish, molded as 3 overlapped leaves, hdl, rpr, 5" **700.00**
Tea caddy, emb Chinaman w/bird, no lid, 4", EX **1,700.00**
Teapot, emb acanthus/bellflowers, scrolled reeded hdl, 5x7" **185.00**
Teapot, lg rose/fence/willow tree, Staffordshire, rstr, 5" **1,500.00**
Vase, floral spray, scratched in w/cobalt, 3½", EX **650.00**
Vase, sprigs/cartouches, hexagonal bottle form, 4½", EX **1,200.00**

Salt Shakers

The screw-top salt shaker was invented by John Mason in 1858. In 1871 when salt became more refined, some ceramic shakers were molded with pierced tops. 'Christmas' shakers, so called because of their December 25, 1877, patent date, were fitted with a rotary agitator designed to break up any lumps in the salt. There are four types: Christmas Barrel (rare in cranberry and amethyst), Christmas Panel (rare in colors), Christmas Pearl (opaque, pearly white with painted decor), and Octagon Waffle (clear, thick glass made in three sizes with a rotary agitator, sometimes having undated tops). The dated tops and patented agitators were produced by Dana K. Alden of Boston, who contracted with various glasshouses to make the glass bodies. The Christmas Barrel and Christmas Panel patterns were produced by Boston and Sandwich (though the Christmas Barrel was made elsewhere as well). Alden contracted with Mt. Washington to make the Christmas Pearl pattern, and Waffle Octagon was made by several glass factories, McKee and Federal among them. Both of the latter patterns were made as late as 1900. Identical shakers which have no agitator or dated top are the companion peppers; these fetch about 30% less than the salts on today's markets.

Today much of the interest in collecting is concentrated on art glass, Wave Crest, and custard glass examples. (See also specific categories.) If you would like to learn more about salt shakers, we recommend *The World of Salt Shakers, Second Edition* by Mildred and Ralph Lechner; their address may be found in the Directory under Virginia. In the following listings, prices are for single shakers unless noted 'pair.' Values are for old, original shakers. Some of these have been reproduced, and this will be noted in the description.

Alaska, clear bl to wht opal, Northwood 70.00
Amberette, amber stained, Geo Duncan & Sons 45.00

Apple Blossom, pr 85.00
Arched Ovals 35.00
Barrel, vasa murrhina, Hobbs, Brockunier, & Co 192.50
Bead & Panel, clear to wht opal, Jefferson Glass 44.00
Beaded Bottom, bl opaque, Dithridge & Co 34.00
Beaded Panel, gr opaque, Consolidated 35.00
Beaded Twist, wht opaque opalware, Gillinder & Sons 22.00
Beatty Honeycomb, bl opal 65.00
Block & Star, bl opaque, Fenton 20.00
Bow & Tassel, wht opaque opalware, Eagle Glass & Mfg 15.00
Broken Column 40.00
Bulging Fleur-de-Lis, custard opaque w/fired-on pk, Dithridge 42.50
Bulging Leaf, bl satin, pr 50.00
Bulging Lobes, opaque opalware w/HP brn decor, Fostoria 20.00
Bulging Loops, pk opaque, triple cased, Consolidated 65.00
Bulging Nine Leaf Variant, wht opaque, Dithridge & Co 27.50
Button Arches, ruby stained, pr 65.00
Chick on Ped, tan & brn shading on wht opal, CF Monroe 295.00
Christmas Barrel, amber, w/lid (dtd) & agitator, Dana K Alden 100.00
Christmas Barrel, apple gr, w/lid & agitator 110.00
Christmas Barrel, cobalt, w/lid & agitator, +pepper, pr 200.00
Christmas Barrel, cranberry, w/lid & agitator 290.00
Christmas Barrel, cranberry, w/lid & agitator, +pepper, pr 450.00
Christmas Barrel, dk amethyst, w/lid & agitator 100.00
Christmas Barrel, gr, w/lid & agitator, pr 225.00
Christmas Barrel, lt gr, w/lid & agitator, 2½" 70.00
Christmas Barrel, peacock bl, w/lid & agitator, +pepper, pr 250.00
Christmas Panel, amethyst, w/lid & agitator 225.00
Christmas Panel, cranberry, w/lid & agitator 300.00
Christmas Panel, dk amethyst, w/lid & agitator 275.00
Christmas Panel, sapphire bl, w/lid & agitator 225.00
Circled Scroll, gr, Northwood 70.00
Concave T'print, cranberry rubena, Hobbs, Brockunier, & Co ..115.00
Cone, bl opaque, Consolidated 45.00
Cordova, pr 40.00
Corn, sphere, wht opaque, Dithridge & Co 62.50
Cotton Bale, bl opaque, Consolidated 30.00
Dahlia Beaded, pigeon blood, pr 120.00
Daisy Sprig Variant, pr 40.00
Dakota (Baby T'print), ruby stained, pr 150.00
Double Deck, wht opaque, Dithridge & Co 32.50
Draped Beads, wht opaque opalware, pk & tan decor, Fostoria 17.50
Empress, gr w/gold, Riverside 68.00
Erie Twist, red to wht satinized opalware, HP florals 70.00
Eye-Winker, Dalzel, Gilmore & Leighton (+) 27.50
Fandangle, gr opaque, West Virginia 37.50
Feather, pr 50.00
Fern Leaf, wht opaque opalware w/gilt, Eagle Glass & Mfg 12.50

Fig, blue flowers on tapestry texture, Mt. Washington, 2⅝", $325.00 for the pair.

Fine Cut & Panel, amber, pr 60.00
Florida, gr, US Glass 50.00
Flower & Rib, pk cased, Consolidated 60.00
Flower Band, pigeon blood satin, Lancaster 57.50
Flower Bouquet, bl opaque, Challinor, Taylor, & Co 30.00
Flower Mold, cranberry, Beaumont 85.00
Flower Panel, gr opaque, McKee 22.50
Forget-Me-Not, pk variegated, Challinor, Taylor, & Co, tall 45.00
Fostoria's Victoria, clear & frosted thick crystal 55.00
Gaudy Rose, NM goofus pnt, Eagle Glass & Mfg 50.00
Georgian, deep royal bl, Fenton 42.00
Heron & Lighthouse, milk glass, pr 100.00
Hobnail in Square, crystal & wht opal 57.50
Holly Amber, Indiana Glass 275.00
Illinois, pr 60.00
Imperial's Grape, pigeon blood 21.00
Interlocking Ovals, bl, McKee 17.50
Iowa, clear w/gold, US Glass 37.50
Iris w/Meander, clear to wht opal at base, Jefferson Glass 72.50
Jewel & Flower, bl w/opal base, Northwood 75.00
Kentucky 50.00
King's Crown, ruby stained, pr 75.00
Lacy Scroll, yel cased, Consolidated, 2-pc metal top 120.00
Leaf & Flower, rose stained w/HP floral band, Hobb's 95.00
Leaf & Spear, wht decor, CF Monroe, pr 180.00
Leaf Berry, 4-ftd, pr 60.00
Liberty Bell, orig metal lid, Central Glass 92.50
Low Scroll, pk cased, pr 75.00
Manhattan, pr 45.00
Mellon, wht opaque satin, HP florals, Gillinder & Sons 32.50
Missouri, emerald gr, pr 95.00
Pleated Skirt, pk opaque, Challinor, Taylor, & Co 40.00
Prize 25.00
Punty Band, custard opaque, Heisey 65.00
Radiance, ruby, New Martinsville 50.00
Reverse Swirl, cranberry opal 105.00
Rib, Optic, cranberry & wht, Fenton, pr 65.00
Ribbed Pillar, burmese, Mt WA, pr 450.00
Ringed Panels, clear/pk/wht spatter, Hobbs, Brockunier, & Co 87.50
Rooster, Head, crystal, pr 200.00
Scroll in Scroll, bl opaque, Dithridge & Co 30.00
Silver Crest, wht opaque w/crystal ruffled base, Fenton 25.00
Single Dice, wht opaque, HP red/wht/florals, Locke ...122.50
Snail, ruby stained, US Glass 65.00
Spirea Band, dk amber, Central Glass 27.00
Square S, bl opaque, Challinor, Taylor, & Co, scarce 30.00
Square Twist, wht opaque, Dalzel, Gilmore & Leighton, scarce ...30.00
Sunk Daisy, ruby stained, Co-Operative Flint Glass 47.50
Swag w/Brackets, amethyst w/gold 35.00
Tapered Panel, Wave Crest opalware, transfer/HP decor 70.00
Tarentum's Atlanta 22.50
Thousand Eye, clear vaseline, scarce 35.00
Truncated Cube, ruby stained, pr 85.00
Twenty Rib, ruby, New Martinsville 52.50
Virginia, US Glass 78.00
Wild Rose w/Bow Knot, frosted crystal w/goofus decor, McKee 42.50
Tappered Block, ruby stained, Geo Duncan & Sons 42.50

Novelty

Those interested in novelty shakers will enjoy *Salt and Pepper Shakers*, an illustrated price guide by Helene Guarnaccia, and *The Collectors Encyclopedia of Salt and Pepper Shakers, Figural and Novelty* by Melva Davern. Both are available at your local library or from Collec-

tor Books. Note: 'Mini' shakers are no taller than 1½". Instead of having a cork, the user was directed to 'use tape to cover hole.'

Airflow trailer & streamline car, yel & blk, ceramic, 1950s, pr 15.00

Black boy's head, 3", and melon slice, 1½", Japan, $35.00 for the pair.

Bride & groom, ceramic bench sitters, pr 18.00
Buffalo, brn shaded, realistic, ceramic, scarce, pr 15.00
Cactus & skull, ceramic, Vandor, pr 15.00
Cat w/umbrella & sunglasses, ceramic, pr 10.00
Cow & calf, brn & wht, realistic, ceramic, Japan, pr 22.00
Hippo, mouth wide open, comic, ceramic, pr 12.00
Huggers, Blk boy hugging puppy, ceramic, Van Tellingen, pr 45.00
Huggers, bunny, ceramic, Van Tellingen, pr 22.00
Huggers, Dutch boy & girl, ceramic, Van Tellingen, pr 35.00
Huggers, love bug, red, lg, pr 110.00
Huggers, love bug, red, sm, pr 75.00
Huggers, Mary & lamb, ceramic, Van Tellingen, pr 35.00
Huggers, sailor & mermaid, ceramic, Van Tellingen, pr 100.00
Huggers, yel ducks, ceramic, Van Tellingen, pr 35.00
Octopus, bright red, ceramic, pr 10.00
Oriental good luck figure, wht, ceramic, pr 10.00
Santa & Mrs Claus, ceramic bench sitters, pr 12.00
Sausage & eggs, ceramic, pr 24.00
Siamese cats, bsk, pr 15.00
Sweethearts of All Nations series, Napco, 3½", ea pr 18.00
Winnie & Woody Woodpecker, ceramic, Napco, Japan, pr 25.00

Salts, Open

Before salt became refined, processed, and free-flowing as we know it today, it was necessary to serve it in a salt cellar. An innovation of the early 1800s, the master salt was placed by the host and passed from person to person. Smaller individual salts were a part of each place setting. A small silver spoon was used to sprinkle it onto the food. If you would like to learn more about the subject of salts, we recommend *5,000 Open Salts*, written by William Heacock and our advisor for this category, Patricia Johnson, with many full-color illustrations and current values. You will find Patricia Johnson's address in the Directory under California.

In the listings below, the numbers refer to *Open Salts* by Johnson and Heacock and *Pressed Glass Salt Dishes* by L.W. and D.B. Neal. Lines with 'repro' within the description reflect values for reproduced salts.

Key:
EPNS — electroplated nickel silver HM — hallmarked

Animals, Figurals, and Novelties

Baby buggy, HP porc, w/spoon, sgn Germany, HJ-1204, M 100.00

Bird, amethyst, Fostoria, HJ-1001, ca 1930 ....25.00
Bird & Berry, amber, bl, or vaseline, McKee, old, M 55.00
Bird & Berry, unsgn Degenhart, HJ-997 ....12.00
Bird & Berry, various colors, sgn Degenhart, HJ-998, minimum ...25.00
Cart, Thousand Eye, gr, Richards & Hartley, HJ-860, 1860 ....85.00
Condiment set, Bird & Berry, on ped, bl, 5¼", EX 450.00
Condiment set, Bird & Berry, on ped, clear, 5¼", VG 350.00
Duck, covered, bsk, Staffordshire, HJ-1008, M 65.00
Elephant, soapstone, HJ-1920, M 35.00
Shoes, Pilgrim, clear, HJ-3736, ca 1900 ....35.00
Sleigh, clear, HJ-3734, ca 1890, M 95.00
Squirrel on stump, Portland Glass, HJ-3756, 1890, master, M 65.00
Swan, blk, sgn Cambridge, HJ-395/396, M 65.00
Swan, Elfinware, Germany, HJ-1039, M 35.00
Swan pulling cart, caramel, HJ-941, repro, M 25.00

Art Glass

Bl, ruffled rigaree, SP holder, M 225.00
Cranberry, ruffled rigaree, tulip top, SP holder, M 125.00
Daum Nancy, blkbirds, sgn, M 950.00
Daum Nancy, floral, sgn/#7, M 750.00
Lobmeyer, HP women, clear ped ft, sgn, M 95.00
Millefiori, Italian, HJ-609, ca 1890, 2" dia, M 250.00
Monot-Stumpf, HJ-19-22, M 110.00
Moser, clear w/HP florals, ped ft, sgn, similar to HJ-55, M 75.00
Nakara, sgn CF Monroe, ormolu holder, HJ-49, M 300.00
Steuben, Calcite, ped ft, HJ-34, M 250.00
Steuben, threading, clear ped ft, HJ-113, M 250.00
Tiffany, witch's pot, sgn LCT, HJ-3, 1¾", M 250.00
Webb, cranberry, acorn design, HJ-84, M 1,050.00

China

Belleek, blk mk, M 65.00
Belleek, gr mk, HJ-4510-4512, M 25.00
Dbl, HP, hdl, HJ-1150, M 35.00
Dresden, HP, oval, HJ-1832, ca 1900, M 35.00
French, HP, silver garland o/l, HJ-1712 ....35.00
French, Napoleon/Desire portraits, HJ-1402/1403, 1900, M, pr .250.00
Haviland, HP pattern, HJ-1396 ....35.00
Meissen, bl design, rnd, 3-ftd, HJ-1369, ca 1880, ind, M 55.00
Meissen, trencher shape, flared ft, HJ-1812-1814, M 125.00
Nippon, celery salt, HJ-1714, M 8.00
Nippon, HP, bucket form, tab hdls, HJ-1466, M 15.00
Nippon, HP, rnd, 3-ftd, HJ-1358-1362, M 15.00
Nippon, HP floral, rnd, ped ft, HJ-1500-1501 ....20.00
Royal Bayreuth, figural, claw/radish/etc, HJ-1664-1669 ....95.00
Royal Copenhagen, tureen shape, HJ-1200, ca 1890 ....45.00

Cut Glass

Cranberry to clear, SP holder, HJ-135, M 75.00
Dbl, sgn Baccarat, w/sterling toothpick holder, ca 1850, M 125.00
Dmn Point, HJ-3101, M 10.00
Faceted, HJ-2919 ....10.00
Fan & Dmn, HJ-3146-3147, M 15.00
Hexagonal, gr, amethyst, amber, etc, HJ-344, ca 1895, M 15.00
Libbey, similar to HJ-3072, M 55.00
Oblong, scalloped & serrated, HJ-3474, master, VG 55.00
Waterford, rnd, ped ft, HJ-3722, new, 2¾" 35.00

Lacy Glass

American, non-flint, HJ-3503, ca 1920-40, VG 65.00

Avon, HJ-3506, repro, M ....5.
Lafayette Boat, sgn Pairpoint, repro, ca 1980, M ....15.
Metro Museum of Art, vaseline, bl, etc, repro, M ....15.
Neal-CT-1, wht opaque, Sandwich, very rare, NM ....650.
Neal-CT-1a, Sandwich, scarce ....150.
Neal-EE-1A, eagles on side, Sandwich, HJ-3482, VG ....175.
Neal-EE-3B, eagles on 4 corners, ftd, VG ....200.
Neal-EE-4, Sandwich ....1,300.
Neal-EE-6, Sandwich, NM ....125.
Neal-GA-5, Sandwich, scarce, NM ....110.
Neal-HN-18A, opal, ftd, HN-4460 ....275.
Neal-MV-1, aqua non-flint, Boston & Sandwich, HJ-3473, VG ..125.
Neal-MV-1a, Sandwich, very rare, NM ....125.
Neal-NE-5, gr, Sandwich, scarce ....175.
Neal-OL-15, bl opaque, Sandwich, very rare, NM ....700.
Neal-SD-14, Sandwich ....85.
Neal-SD-7, Sandwich, NM ....80.

Pottery and Faience

Chinese, oblong, HJ-1883-1888, M ....20.
Italian, dbl, w/donkey, HJ-1141, recent, M ....12.
Quimper, dbl, HJ-1132, M ....75.
Royal Doulton, sterling hallmk rim, HJ-1851, ca 1897, M ....65.
Royal Doulton, sterling hallmk rim, HJ-1870, ca 1873, M ....110.
Wedgwood, sterling hallmk rim, HJ-1850, ca 1900, M ....125.

Pressed Glass, Clear

Ada, HJ-2663, ind, M ....12.
All-Over Dmn, HJ-2651, ind, M ....10.
Apollo, HJ-3576, M ....15.
Arched Leaf, HJ-3530, M ....22.
Bagware, HJ-2795, M ....10.
Cabbage Rose, HJ-3529, M ....25.
Cabinet, HJ-2942, M ....10.
Currier & Ives, HJ-3579, M ....35.
Duncan #30, HJ-2661, M ....15.
Electric, HJ-2567, M ....12.
Empress, HJ-2938, M ....25.
Fancy Loop, Heisey, HJ-2674, M ....22.
Fostoria, #112, HJ-2748, M ....10.
Frosted Eagle, HJ-2927, master, M ....55.
Giant Sawtooth, HJ-3675, M ....12.
Grape Band, HJ-3534, M ....35.
Grasshopper, HJ-3573, master, M ....35.
Hidalgo, HJ-3663, M ....25.
Horn of Plenty, HJ-3513, M ....35.
King's Crown, HJ-2775, ind, M ....22.
Late Buckle, HJ-3622, M ....35.
Liberty Bell, HJ-2689, M ....45.
Lincoln Drape, HJ-3619, M ....45.
Morning-Glory, HJ-3385, M ....150.
Oaken Bucket, HJ-2837, M ....25.
Panel, Rib & Shell, HJ-2778, M ....12.
Pavonia, HJ-2678, M ....10.
Puritan, HJ-2804, M ....8.
Roman Key, HJ-3582, M ....35.
Sawtooth Circles, HJ-3540, M ....20.
Snail, HJ-2656, ind ....27.
Snail, master, M ....35.
Three Face, rnd dots, HJ-4430-4431, repro, M ....10.
Three Face, sq dots, old, HJ-4428, M ....55.

Pressed Glass, Colored

Empress, gr, HJ-4675, M 140.00
English, Lady Caroline, M 65.00
English, Lords & Ladies, M 55.00
English, William & Mary, HJ-568, M 55.00
Eyewinker, HJ-893, repro, M 6.00
Fostoria #95, HJ-333, M 15.00
Jersey Swirl, HJ-869, repro, M 6.00
Leaf & Rib, amber/bl/etc, HJ-435, M 22.00
Mardi Gras, ruby stained, HJ-4644, M 75.00
Moon & Star, HJ-870, repro, M 6.00
Pressed Dmn, HJ-427, M 15.00
Wreath & Shell, opal, HJ-444, M 110.00
3-Panel, HJ-544, ind, M 18.00

Silverplate

Medallion design, dbl, HJ-3847, M 175.00
Oval, ftd, cobalt liner, Sheffield, HJ-679, worn 65.00
Oval in lattice holder, James Dixon, HJ-3945, M 45.00
Overshot glass, sq holder, HJ-4215, M 95.00
Rnd, English, cobalt liner, HJ-669, ca 1950, M 20.00
Rnd, ftd, gr liner, Wallace Bros, HJ-380, M 25.00
Rnd, lion leg, paw ft, cranberry liner, HJ-321, M 65.00
Salt & pepper, English, HJ-4134, ca 1890, VG 35.00
Swan, glass body, plated neck, HJ-4295, M 35.00
Tulip on leaf, American, HJ-4155, VG 25.00

Sterling

**Albert Cole, Medallion, HJ-4208, ca 1836-1876, 2½",
$450.00 for the pair.**

American, oval, gr liner/spoon, boxed set of 2, HJ-4793, VG 250.00
Austria, Hungary, dbl, cobalt, w/mustard, HJ-751, ca 1850, M ...350.00
Dutch, 2 salts, pepper, & mustard, HJ-713, 4-pc, M 350.00
English, ped ft, Ann & Peter Bateman, HJ-3857, 1790s, pr 450.00
English Baroque, ftd oval, HJ-4165, ca 1890, M 75.00
French, dbl, cobalt bowl, HJ-761, M 140.00
French Baroque, ftd, clear liner, w/spoon, ca 1890, M 125.00
German, mk #800, garlands, cobalt liner, HJ-724, M 55.00
German, swan, glass liner, HJ-4294, ca 1900, M 75.00
German, triangular, #800, glass liner, w/spoon, HJ-3944, M 115.00
Gorham, cranberry liner, HJ-323, ca 1890, M 150.00
Gorham, medallion, HJ-3976, ca 1870, M 125.00

Lion medallions, #800 holder, HJ-682, ca 1890, M 250.00
Overlay, clear glass, Alvin, HJ-4766, 1920s, 6 in box, VG 125.00
Russian, chair, HJ-3735-3737, 3", M 450.00
Russian enamel, w/spoon, HJ-2008, ca 1970, M 75.00
Swan, glass w/sterling head & wings, HJ-4289, ca 1920, M 65.00
Tiffany, lion medallion, pepper insert, HJ-4220, ca 1970, M 250.00
Tiffany, rnd, ped ft, w/spoon, HJ-4126, ca 1890, ind 95.00
Viking ship #830, liner w/spoon, HJ-4260, recent, M 35.00

Other Types

Cloisonne, HJ-1964, early, M 45.00
Cloisonne, salt & pepper set, HJ-1995, ca 1970, M 25.00
Daum Nancy, clear, HJ-3436, new, M 35.00
Intaglio, cut & beveled, clear, HJ-3412, M 10.00
Intaglio, cut & beveled, color, HJ-220, M 18.00
Lalique, oval, HJ-4444, ca 1970, M 55.00
Purple slag, tureen shape, sgn Sowerby, HJ-385, M 65.00
Rose quartz, irregular shape, HJ-1955-1956, M 55.00
Satsuma, HJ-1903, ca 1970, set of 4, M 65.00

Samplers

    American samplers were made as early as the the colonial days; even earlier examples from 17th-century England still exist today. Changes in style and decorative motif are evident down through the years. Verses were not added until the late 17th century. By the 18th century, samplers were used not only for sewing experience but also as an educational tool. Young ladies, who often signed and dated their work, embroidered numbers and letters of the alphabet and practiced fancy stitches as well. Fruits and flowers were added for borders; birds, animals, and Adam and Eve were popular subjects. Later houses and other buildings were included. By the 19th century, the American Eagle and the little red schoolhouse had made their appearances.

Mariette Harris wrought this in the 12th year of her age, Middletown, July 1826, some discoloration, 15x18", $2,500.00.

ABCs/flowers/birds/crowns/name/1799, 15x10", VG 550.00
ABCs/house/name/1801, linen, wear/fading/rprs, 22x14", VG ...180.00
ABCs/house/trees/floral border/name/1817, EX color, 17x22" 800.00
ABCs/name/1873, homespun, faded, modern fr, 12x9" 225.00
ABCs/name/1895, bright wool on wht, 13x12" 200.00
ABCs/sm house/trees/name/verse/1822, faded/stains, 19x13" 450.00
ABCs/verse/house/2 trees/name/1820, homespun, 18x18", VG ..750.00
Adam/Eve (stylized)/many sm components/name/1845, 18x12" ...700.00
Alphanumerics, memorial verse etc & 1837 on right, 18x19" .1,250.00
Alphanumerics, wide floral border, sgn/dtd 1877, 12½x12" 245.00
Alphanumerics, 3-color on homespun w/lt bl stripe, unfr, 18" 300.00
Birds/flowers above ABCs/verse/house/name/1812, 16x12" 700.00
Cottage/dog/girl/trees/verse/name/1835, 15x15", VG 700.00
Floral border/rows of ABCs/vines/verse/name, 1833, 16" 700.00

Floral border/verse/scene in oval/name/1798, 19x20", EX **1,550.00**
Flowers/bldg/ABCs/name/1853, wool/silk, EX color, 22x23" **450.00**
Miniature, verse/name, silk on gauze, ogee fr, 8½x7½" **300.00**
Miniature, verse/name/1848, red silk on linen, new fr, 7x7" **400.00**
Pots of flowers/verse/name/1850, silk on linen, 19x15" **450.00**
Strawberry border/ABCs/name/1783, dk linen, faded, 14x14" **550.00**
Verse/birds/flowers/vines/name/1828, stains/faded, 24x23" **900.00**
Verse/dog/windmill/flowers/name, silk on wool, 15x15" **1,000.00**

Sandwich Glass

The Boston and Sandwich Glass Company was founded in 1820 by Deming Jarves in Sandwich, Massachusetts. Their first products were simple cruets, salts, half-pint jugs, and lamps. They were attributed as being one of the first to perfect a method for pressing glass, a step toward the manufacture of the 'lacy' glass which they made until about 1840. Many other types of glass were made there — cut, colored, snakeskin, hobnail, and opalescent among them. After the Civil War, profits began to dwindle due to the keen competition of the Western factories which were situated in areas rich in natural gas and easily accessible sand and coal deposits. The end came with an unreconcilable wage dispute between the workers and the company, and the factory closed in 1888. Our advisor for this category is Richard Marden; he is listed in the Directory under New Hampshire. See also Cup Plates; Salts, Open; specific types of glass.

Bird feeder, opaque bl **95.00**
Bottle, cologne; red cut to clear, 6-point lip flange, rare **790.00**
Bottle, scent; med amethyst, 8-panel, corseted, 1850s, 6" **850.00**
Bowl, b3m, folded rim, pontil scar, 1820-40, 1⅝x5⅛" **95.00**
Bowl, lacy, acanthus leaves, L-122, 9", NM **100.00**
Bowl, lacy, Daisy & Peacock Eye, L-134, dbl walled, 6", NM **100.00**
Bowl, lacy, Fleur-de-Lis & Thistle, L-120, rim roughness, 9" **450.00**
Bowl, lacy, Heart, L-106, 6½" **55.00**
Bowl, lacy, Industry, L-89, minor rim chips **115.00**
Bowl, lacy, Princess Feather, L-119, short hairlines, 10" **600.00**
Bowl, lacy, Princess Feather, L-135, under filled, 7½" **60.00**
Bowl, lacy, Rayed Peacock Eye, L-132, scalloped, 7½" **85.00**
Bowl, lacy, Tulip & Acanthus, L-131, 7½", EX **55.00**
Bowl, vegetable; lacy, Peacock Eye, L-133, chip, 7½x10" L **175.00**
Candlestick, clambroth petal socket, bl sanded column, 9" **275.00**
Candlestick, opaque bl w/clambroth dolphins, pr **1,500.00**

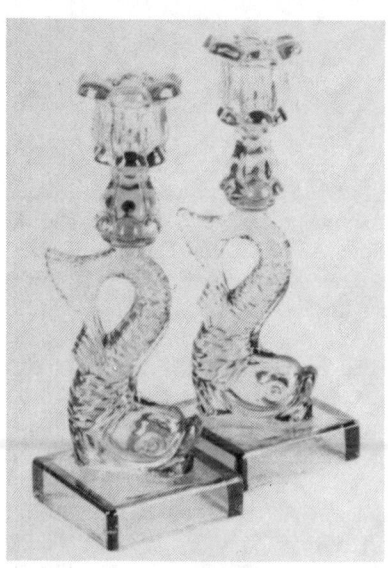

Candlesticks, dolphin base, electric peacock blue, 10½", EX, $2,900.00 for the pair.

Celery vase, Gothic Arch, Printie Panel & Loop **95.00**
Cup plate, lacy, Cornucopia, L-108, rare, 6" **275.00**
Decanter, GII-22, flared mouth, period stopper, 1-pt **140.00**
Dish, lacy, Feather & Quatrefoil, L-124, deep, 9½", NM **125.00**
Dish, lacy, L-168, w/lid, rare, 6x4x5", VG, +NM 7" undertray ..**1,000.00**
Finger bowl, ruby flashed cut to clear, 1870s **200.00**
Plate, lacy, floral, L-133, 8" **55.00**
Plate, lacy, Heart, L-106, 8" **25.00**
Plate, lacy, Oak Leaf, L-127, 6½" **25.00**
Plate, lacy, Peacock Eye & Thistle, L-114, rim chips, 8" **35.00**
Salt cellar, hexagonal, ped base, mini **195.00**
Sugar bowl, lacy, Gothic Arch, L-158, w/EX lid, 5" **100.00**
Tray, lacy, butterfly, L-95, 5x8" **55.00**
Tray, lacy, Gothic Arch, L-101, minor roughness, 5x7" **75.00**
Tray, lacy, US Constitution, L-167, rare, 7" L, VG **1,300.00**
Vase, dk amethyst, cased, triple t'print, tulip top, EX **500.00**

Sarreguemines

Sarreguemines, France, is the location of Utzschneider and Company, founded in 1770, producers of majolica, transfer-printed dinner ware, figurines, and novelties which are usually marked 'Sarreguemines.'

Chamber pot, floral, red & bl on wht **95.00**
Decanter, man astride potato figural, 9½" **120.00**

Face jugs, Night Watchman, 7½", $225.00; 5¼", $75.00.

Jug, comical man w/red nose & cheeks, 5⅜" **75.00**
Plate, hunter in landscape, blk transfer, 'worker' border, 7" **30.00**
Platter, fruit in relief, w/gold, 10" **50.00**
Tea service, floral, ornate shapes, ca 1860, 14-pc **500.00**
Vase, majolica, emb leaves/dolphin figures etc, rstr, 14" **700.00**

Satin Glass

Satin glass is simply glassware with a velvety matt finish achieved through the application of an acid bath. This procedure has been used by many companies since the 20th century, both here and abroad, on many types of colored and art glass. See also Mother-of-Pearl.

Bottle, scent; ferns, 2-color w/gold on ivory, SP lid, 4" **355.00**
Bowl, bl o/l, wht daisies/gold branches, ruffled, 5x10" **275.00**
Bowl, bl o/l w/wide ruffled brn edge, florals/dots, 5x11" **295.00**
Bride's bowl, rose to pk w/HP floral, 2½x10" **225.00**
Cookie jar, Fleurette, pk, matching lid, 6¼" **200.00**

Creamer, bl o/l, HP florals, bulbous, frosted hdl, 6x4¾" **235.00**
Creamer, Swirl, butterscotch o/l, bulbous, 5¼x4⅛" **195.00**
Creamer & sugar bowl, pk, Fleurette, SP lids, 3¾", 5½" **235.00**
Ewer, lt bl, gold foliage/pk flowers, 3-petal top, 9¾", pr **225.00**
Ewer, peach o/l, birds/roses, ribbed section, angle hdl, 13" **245.00**
Ewer, pk shaded, raspberry branch/bees, melon ribbed, 12x4½" .**225.00**
Pitcher, bl emb swirl, wht int, rnd mouth, frosted hdl, 4¾" **155.00**
Rose bowl, bl o/l, HP florals w/red jewels, frosted ft, 4½" **135.00**
Rose bowl, chartreuse gr, emb florals, 8-crimp, 3¼x3⅞" **125.00**
Rose bowl, pk shaded, emb melon ribs, 8-crimp, 3x3⅝" **75.00**
Rose bowl, Shell & Seaweed, bl, 8-crimp top, 3½x3¾" **120.00**
Rose bowl, yel shaded o/l, HP florals, 5x4¼" **125.00**
Vase, bl & pk rainbow striped o/l, hdls, 7¼x4⅝" **295.00**
Vase, bl to wht, English, 10½x5½" **265.00**
Vase, peach o/l, HP birds/flowers, ewer form, 12¾" **245.00**
Vase, peach o/l, HP florals, tricorner top, ewer form, 7⅝" **115.00**
Vase, pk, leaves/2 birds, 9½", pr **350.00**
Vase, pk o/l, HP florals, acid-cut sqs allover, 7½" **225.00**
Vase, pk o/l, HP florals, appl leaf ft, 9¼" **125.00**
Vase, pk o/l, HP florals, ruffled top, ewer form, 9" **110.00**
Vase, pk o/l, HP florals/butterfly, 4⅞x3" **60.00**
Vase, pk-cased opal, bluebird on branch, scroll hdls, 10" **350.00**

Satsuma

Satsuma is a type of fine cream crackle-glaze pottery or earthenware made in Japan as early as the 17th century. The earliest wares, made at the original kiln in the Satsuma province, were enameled with only simple florals. By the late 18th century, a floral brocade (or nishikide design) was favored, and similar wares were being made at other kilns under the direction of the Lord of Satsuma. In the early part of the 19th century, a diaper pattern was added to the florals. Gold and silver enamels were used for accents by the late years of the century. During the 1850s, as the quality of goods made for export to the western world increased and the style of decoration began to evolve toward becoming more appealing to the Westerners, human forms such as Arhats, Kannon, geisha girls, and samurai warriors were added. Today the most valuable pieces are those marked 'Kinkozan,' 'Shuzan,' 'Ryuzan,' and 'Kozan.' The genuine Satsuma 'mon' or mark is a cross within a circle — usually in gold on the body or on the lid or in red on the base of the ware. Character marks may be included.

Caution: Much of what is termed 'Satsuma' comes from the Showa Period (1926 to the present); it is not true Satsuma but a simulated type, a cheaper pottery with heavy enamel. Our advisor for this category is Donald Penrose; he is listed in the Directory under Ohio.

Bowl, birds & butterflies etc, int: figures, sgn Senzan, 5" **1,400.00**
Bowl, figural panels, brocade ground, sgn Fuzan, 1800s, 6" **275.00**
Bowl, figures & dragons, sgn floriform, 1800s, 9½" dia **875.00**
Bowl, Immortals on mtn, sgn Hododa, 9½" **825.00**
Bowl, Kwannon surrounded by Arhats, 6" **175.00**
Charger, bust-length portrait of Kannon, 12" **275.00**
Cricket cage, florals, ovoid basket form, sgn, 6" **450.00**
Cup, flower garden scene, 2-hdl, w/lid, 1840s, 8" **200.00**
Ewer, allover fan motif, w/lid, sgn Keizan, 1800s, 4½" **700.00**
Inkwell, 1000 Faces, dmn shape, sgn 4x3½" **275.00**
Koro, panels of Shaka w/Rikan & gods, shishi finial, 13" **550.00**
Koro, scenic panels on mum ground, sgn Denchu sai, 4½" **1,200.00**
Plate, dragons & lohans, sgn w/Satsuma mon, 32 scallops, 9" **600.00**
Plate, scene of ladies & children, sgn Suzan, 8¾", pr **550.00**
Tea caddy, crane & pine branch on yel **100.00**
Teabowl, mums, int: 1000 Butterflies, sgn Shizan, 3" **1,950.00**
Vase, allover Rakan, sgn Shotei, Satsuma mon & seal, 18" **1,500.00**

Vase, figural reserve on bl, dragon hdls, 1900s, 25", pr **525.00**
Vase, figural scenes, baluster, 1800s, 10", NM, pr **660.00**
Vase, figural scenes in panels, 1800s, 29", pr **6,600.00**
Vase, immortals ea side, drum neck hdls, tripod ft, sgn, 6" **950.00**
Vase, processional scene, sgn Kyoto Kinkozan, 4¾" **3,300.00**

Vase, reserves of eight immortals and samurai, signed Dai Nihon Kinkozan, 15", $9,500.00.

Vase, swirled floral & butterfly motif, sgn Yabu Meizan, 2" **1,300.00**
Vase, wisteria, ovoid, 1900, sgn, 6" **400.00**
Vase, 3 boys support vase w/lion head & loose ring hdls, 6" **185.00**
Vase, 4 maidens, 1800s, 4" **200.00**

Scales

In today's world of pre-measured and pre-packaged goods, it is difficult to imagine the days when such products as sugar, flour, soap, and candy first had to be weighed by the grocer. The variety of scales used at the turn of the century was highly diverse; at the Philadelphia Exposition in 1876, one company alone displayed over three hundred different weighing devices. Among those found today, brass, cast iron, and plastic models are the most common. Fancy postal scales in decorative wood, silver, marble, bronze, and mosaic are also to be found. Those seeking additional information concerning antique scales are encouraged to contact the International Society of Antique Scale Collectors, whose address can be found in the Directory under Clubs, Newsletters, and Catalogs.

Key:
bal — balance	lb — pound
g — gram	NP — nickel plated

Chatillon, brass, hanging, wht 13" porc pan, dtd 1884, EX **350.00**
Chatillon Balance #2, Pat Jan 26, 1892, 0-50 lb **32.00**
Enterprise/Jacob Bros, candy/kitchen, NP brass pan, 5", EX **60.00**
Eureka, CI w/red pnt, brass pan, 0-16 lb, 18", EX **350.00**
Exact Weight, candy store, w/weights **75.00**
Fairbanks, oak case, red pnt w/gold, brass pans, 12", M **330.00**
Fairbanks & Greenleaf, grain weighing, brass w/iron mts **200.00**
Fulton's Quality, CI, Pat 1869, 0-25 lbs, 18", VG **165.00**
Jacobs Bros, candy, ped ft, 3 weights, EX **98.00**
Landers, Frary & Clark, postal, up to 4 lbs, EX **40.00**
Novelty, CI, counter-top spring type, 1877, 8" **250.00**
Philadelphia Scoop & Scale Co, brass scoop **135.00**
Postal, NP brass & CI, stencil, eng eagle, 1890s **150.00**
Salter's Improved, spring bal, EX **45.00**
Sanitary Scales, wht porc, milk glass platform, 1924, 30" **230.00**
Steelyard, CI, mk from 10 lbs to 50 lbs, complete, 21½" **22.00**
Toledo, Pat 1901...1903...1914, 2 counterweights, 31" **400.00**

Toledo Confectionery, 5-lb capacity scoop, all orig 145.00
Troemner, brass/steel pan bal, w/compartment for 5 weights 135.00
Troemner, drugstore, tan marble on brass, 12½x5½x7", EX 150.00
Troemner #1, candy, wood/CI, brass bowls, 11½x20x13" 250.00
Troy, for dentists & physicians, NP, 1900s, 4" L, EX 75.00
Turnbull Family Scale, rnd brass face, 0-24 lbs, 10", EX 80.00

Schafer and Vater

Established in 1890 by Gustav Schafer and Gunther Vater in the Thuringia district of Germany, by 1913 this firm employed two hundred workers. The original factory burned in 1918, but production and export continued until WWII. Schafer & Vater produced a tremendous variety of products including (but not limited to) tea sets, dresser sets, flasks, pitchers, humidors, knickknacks, nodders, etc. Items often came in more than one size and in a variety of finishes — glazed and unglazed bisque, jasperware, and twice fired. Most items were incised with a crown over an 'R' within a nine-point star. Collectors should look for pieces with good paint, clean mold lines, and character. They might also consider narrowing their interests to a specific category or type of finish.

Bottle, baby & lady w/protruding lips, 4", EX 440.00
Bottle, baseball player, pnt bsk, 5", set of 3 ....1,045.00
Bottle, Santa w/tree & sack 350.00
Bottle, smiling pear figural, w/stopper 125.00
Box, gr/wht jasper w/bl lady medallion on lid, 2x2⅝x3½" 85.00
Box, lady & rose on lid, bl/wht jasper, 1⅞x3" dia 88.00
Box, red lobster figural, 2½x2¾x4⅝" 85.00
Box, woman & man medallions on lid, wht on gr w/gold, 3¾" L ..65.00
Bud vase, Uncle Sam seated in egg, att, 4" 195.00
Candlestick, lion, yel w/wht eyes, cubist shape, mk, 5¾" 110.00
Figurine, catcher w/mask, pnt bsk, rare, 5" 300.00
Figurine, googly-eyed boy w/dog, gold trim, mk, 3¼x3⅛" 75.00

Hatpin holders, both jasperware, either style, $275.00.

Hatpin holder, Oriental lady w/fan, lav/gr jasper w/gold, 4½" 150.00
Match holder, cat & kitten, Don't Scratch Me..., 3¾x3¾" 100.00
Mug, elk relief ea side, brn/tan, mk, 3¼" 75.00
Nodder, bug-eyed man & dog w/bee, 4½", EX 150.00
Pitcher, devil, bsk, 3½" 90.00
Pitcher, Dutch girl w/basket on bk & keys, mk, 3¾" 70.00
Pitcher, girl w/pitcher figural, mk, 4x3¾" 125.00
Sugar bowl, lady & cupid, bl/wht, jasper, mk, 3½x4½" 95.00
Vase, classical lady & birds, jasper, mk, 7⅞" 85.00
Vase, girl w/googly eyes reading book, bsk, 7" 100.00
Vase, Leda & swans, bl/wht jasper, mk, 8" 225.00

Scheier

The Scheiers began their ceramics careers in the late 1930s and soon thereafter began to teach their craft at the University of New Hampshire. After WWII they cooperated with the Puerto Rican government in establishing a native ceramic industry, an involvement which would continue to influence their designs. In the fifties they retired and moved to Mexico; they currently reside in Arizona.

Bowl, leaves (repeating/sgraffito) on tan, brn rim/int, 6" 525.00

Bowl, figures, flowers, and the sun in relief on brown bisque, glossy brown interior, incised Scheier/41, 7x8¾", $2,500.00.

Mug, sylized deer in bl, 4" 65.00
Vase, Evolution series, turq/bl, cvd masks, 10" 900.00
Vase, facial features/mother & child relief, dk gray, 12x9" 750.00
Vase, medallions w/relief figures, charcoal, ftd, 7½x7½" 500.00
Vase, sgraffito figures on dk brn, U-form, dtd 1958, 7½" 1,000.00

Schlegelmilch Porcelain

Authority Mary Frank Gaston, who is our advisor, has completed two volumes of *The Collector's Encyclopedia of R.S. Prussia* with full-color illustrations and current values. A third volume is soon to be released. Mold numbers appearing in some of the listings refer to these books. You will find Mrs. Gaston's address in the Directory under Texas.

Key:
BM — blue mark   SM — steeple mark
GM — green mark   RM — red mark

E.S. Germany

Fine chinaware marked 'E.S. Germany' or 'E.S. Prov. Saxe' was produced by E.S. Schlegelmilch at his Suhl factory in the Thuringia region of Prussia from sometime after 1861 until about 1925.

Bowl, lady w/flowers, pierced border, open hdls, mk, 11¾" 275.00
Bowl, lady w/swallows, dk bl Tiffany irid finish, mk, 10¾" 550.00
Bowl, 4 portrait medallions, Kortense, 10⅜" 395.00
Cake plate, fox hunting scene, 10" 275.00
Cake plate, Gibson girl portrait on bl, gold trim, mk, 10½" 425.00
Candlesticks, lilies, wht on gr, mk, 5", pr 60.00
Candy dish, 4 portrait medallions, Recamier, 7" 175.00

Celery, 4 portrait medallions, Hortense, 12" 295.00
Chamberstick, bl flowers, cobalt inner border, mk, 2x6" 115.00
Creamer, classic scene, maroon w/gold, ftd, mk 35.00
Cup & saucer, Queen Louise portrait reserve on red, mk 175.00
Cuspidor, floral on bl shaded, mk, 5x7¾" 900.00
Cuspidor, roses, mk 395.00
Egg dish, pastel flowers, gold ruffled rim, center hdl, mk 450.00
Pitcher, milk; flower, pk on turq, brn mk, 4½" 225.00
Pitcher, tankard; gold florals on wht w/red, Rococo, mk, 15" ..1,100.00
Plate, bird on branch, smooth rim, mk, 6" 35.00
Plate, floral w/cobalt rim, mk, 8½" 75.00
Plate, girl w/wheat & sickle, gold stencilling, mk, 10" 85.00
Plate, lady w/roses on pearl lustre w/gold, mk, 8" 200.00
Plate, mc roses on cream shaded, smooth gold rim, mk, 8½" 45.00
Plate, spotted horse, mk, 7" 85.00
Relish, poppies on cream w/gold rim, open hdls, mk, 8x3½" 50.00
Relish, windmill scene tapestry, 4-lobed form, mk, 8x6½" 90.00
Tankard, Easter lilies, cobalt trim, mk, 10½" 595.00
Toothpick holder, lady w/daisy crown, mk, 2½" 85.00
Vase, chickens & daisies, ornate/pierced gold hdls, mk, 7½" 550.00
Vase, Fall allegorical portrait on lav, gold hdls, mk, 10¼" 395.00
Vase, figures in court scene, slim, mk, 7½" 195.00
Vase, goddess of the sea, much gold, integral hdls, mk, 8" 900.00
Vase, Indian portrait reserve/florals, uptrn hdls, mk, 6" 300.00
Vase, lady w/doves, gargoyles in relief at hdls, mk, 12" 1,350.00
Vase, lady w/doves (4 portraits), 3 gold hdls at base, mk, 14" ..1,100.00
Vase, lady w/peacock, unmk, #d, 10" 225.00
Vase, lady's portrait, gold tub hdls, mk, 7½" 300.00
Vase, Madame DuBoise, ornate gold hdls, mk, 7" 250.00
Vase, woman w/letter in reserve on red w/gold, mk, 9¼" 450.00

R.S. Germany

In 1869 Reinhold Schlegelmilch began to manufacture porcelain in Suhl in the German province of Thuringia. In 1894 he established another factory in Tillowitz in upper Silesia. Both areas were rich in resources necessary for the production of hard-paste porcelain. Wares marked with the name 'Tillowitz' and the accompanying 'R.S. Germany' phrase are attributed to Reinhold. The most common mark is a wreath and star in a solid color under the glaze. Items marked 'R.S. Germany' are usually more simply decorated than R.S. Prussia. Some reflect the Art Deco trend of the 1920s. Certain hand-painted floral decorations and themes such as 'Sheepherder,' 'Man with Horses,' and 'Cottage' are especially valued by collectors — those with a high-gloss finish or on Art Deco shapes in particular. Not all hand-painted items were painted at the factory. Those with an artist's signature but no 'Hand Painted' mark indicate that the blank was decorated outside the factory.

Ashtray, poppies, mk 40.00
Basket, robin on branch on yel, center hdl, mk 200.00
Bowl, berry; roses, molded flowers at border, SM, 7½" 35.00
Bowl, lettuce; iris on pearl lustre, ruffled, mk, 9" 350.00
Bowl, roses, 4 openwork areas along rim, mk, 7" 55.00
Bowl, snowballs w/in & w/out, scalloped rim, mk 65.00
Butter dish, mc flowers w/much gold, w/liner, SM 1,100.00
Cake plate, cottage scene, sawtooth mold, RM, 10¼" 675.00
Cake plate, mixed florals w/heavy gold rim, SM, 11½" 275.00
Cake plate, Queen Louise portrait, floral mold, hdls, SM, 10" 700.00
Chocolate pot, poppies on cream shaded w/gold, mk, 9" 225.00
Chocolate pot, snowballs on cream shaded, mk 275.00
Coffeepot, floral w/gold trim, stick hdl, mk, ind, 5½" 200.00
Cup & saucer, blk swans, gold mk, lg 1,200.00
Cup & saucer, mustache; floral, mk 85.00

Hatpin holder, florals on tan, mk 60.00
Match holder, roses, pk on pearl lustre, mk 165.00
Napkin ring, floral on wht w/gold, mk 135.00
Nut dish, mixed flowers, floral mold, 3-ftd, SM, 3¼x6" 85.00
Pitcher, milk; clown figural, unmk 300.00
Pitcher, milk/lemonade; roses on cream shaded, mk, 6x9" 115.00
Plate, bird of paradise, RM, 6¼" 500.00
Plate, flamingos & roses, smooth gold rim, mk, 8" 175.00
Plate, horse chestnut, smooth rim, mk, 6½" 35.00
Plate, mill scene, sawtooth mold, RM, 10¼" 625.00
Plate, poppies on pearl lustre, scalloped, mk, 6½" 40.00
Plate, roses, wht on bl shaded, pierced hdls, mk, 10" 45.00
Plate, snowballs, 3 hdls, mk, 8" 52.50
Plate, tulips w/gold leaves, Nouveau style, mk, 10½" 60.00
Plate, village scene, brn, RM, 6¼" 275.00
Plate, woman w/wings, red irid inner border, SM, 8¼" 900.00

R.S. Germany portrait ewer, green with gold trim, 9½", $275.00.

Spooner, floral, pierced work at ftd base, angle hdls, SM, 5" 175.00
Sugar bowl, calla lilies, angle hdls, mk, 5" 50.00
Syrup, dogwood, mk underplate 150.00
Syrup, roses, much gold stencilling, mk, 3" 175.00
Toothbrush holder, violets w/gold, wing mk, 4½x3" 200.00
Toothpick holder, HP florals, gold hdls & trim, mk, 2½x3" 75.00
Toothpick holder, roses, mk 145.00
Vase, tigers on brn shaded, uptrn angle hdls, unmk, 12" 6,000.00

R.S. Poland

'R.S. Poland' is a mark attributed to Reinhold Schlegelmilch's factory in Tillowitz, Silesia. It was in use for a few years after 1945.

Creamer, violets on cream w/gold, ftd, angle hdl, mk, 4½" 85.00
Flower holder, pheasants, attached metal frog, mk, 7" 750.00
Planter, floral band w/gold, ped ft, 6¾x6½" dia 235.00
Sugar bowl, roses, ftd, angle hdls, mk, 4½" 115.00
Talcum shaker, roses on cream shaded, 3 hdls at base, mk 250.00
Tray, bird on branch, floral/geometric border, mk, 14" 115.00
Vase, brn & wht pheasants, gold rim, mk, 13" 900.00
Vase, crowned cranes, salesman's sample, 3½" 800.00
Vase, man w/cow, farm scene beyond, classic form, mk, 9" 1,100.00
Vase, roses, wht & tan on brn & gold shaded, mk, 9x4½" 150.00

R.S. Prussia

Art porcelain bearing the mark 'R.S. Prussia' was manufactured by Reinhold Schlegelmilch from the late 1870s to the early 1900s in a Germanic area known until the end of WWI as Prussia. The vast array of mold shapes in combination with a wide variety of decorations is the basis for R.S. Prussia's appeal. Themes can be categorized as figural (usually based on a famous artist's work), birds, florals, portraits, scenics, and animals.

Basket, hanging; floral, oval reserves, medallion mold, mk, 11" .275.00
Biscuit barrel, flowers reflecting in water, RM, 5½x9" 295.00
Biscuit jar, hydrangeas on gr shaded, unmk 225.00
Bowl, Autumn, floral border mold, mk, 10½" 1,300.00
Bowl, berry, roses, grape mold variation, mk, 10½" 250.00
Bowl, berry; roses, acorn mold, RM, 10½", +6 5½" bowls 525.00
Bowl, carnations on bl shaded, carnation mold, mk, 10½" 350.00
Bowl, Countess Catherine Litta, shell mold, unmk, 9" 165.00
Bowl, Easter lilies, feather mold, RM, 9¼" 250.00
Bowl, floral, emb floral rim, Tiffany finish, unmk, 10¼" 175.00
Bowl, floral, mc on aqua, ftd, unmk, 2½x7" 145.00
Bowl, floral & blkberries, carnation mold, unmk, 12" 350.00
Bowl, floral on pearl finish, Hidden Image mold, unmk, 7¾" 325.00
Bowl, floral on wht, locket mold, mk, 10" 275.00
Bowl, Gibson girl portrait, scalloped mold, mk, 11" 1,150.00
Bowl, lilies reflecting, irregular scallops, mk, 11" 325.00
Bowl, Madame Lebrun, stippled floral mold, unmk, 9¾" 900.00
Bowl, masted schooner scene, oval, RM 915.00
Bowl, mc roses, lettuce mold, RM, 10" 275.00
Bowl, ostrich, RM, 10¾" 2,825.00
Bowl, poppies, daisy mold, RM, 10¼" 215.00
Bowl, reflecting poppies & daisies, teardrop mold, mk, 11" 300.00
Bowl, roses, lettuce mold variation, mk, 9" 550.00
Bowl, roses, pastel mc on wht, berry mold, mk, 11" 275.00
Bowl, roses & garlands, ribbon & jewel mold, mk, 10½" 275.00
Bowl, roses & shadow flowers, lily mold, ftd, unmk, 10½" 350.00
Bowl, roses on bl shaded, iris mold, gold border, mk, 9½" 325.00
Bowl, roses on pastel shaded, scalloped rim, mk, 2½x9" 135.00
Bowl, roses w/much gold, sea creature mold, unmk, 11" 325.00
Bowl, swallows/shadow flowers, medallion mold, oval, hdls, 13" ...550.00
Bowl, swans & evergreens, swag & tassel mold, unmk, 10½" 495.00
Bowl, violets on wht w/gold, scalloped, 3-ftd, mk, 5¼" 135.00
Bowl, yel roses, shield mold w/gold at rim, mk, 10½" 275.00
Cake plate, barnyard scene, mold #155, glossy, mk, 9¾" 1,000.00
Cake plate, chickens/ducks/lilies, swag & tassel mold, mk, 10" ..1,010.00
Cake plate, flower basket, flower rim, plume mold, RM, 11" 275.00
Cake plate, mc florals, open hdls, RM 135.00
Cake plate, mill scene on gr, RM, 10¼" 325.00
Cake plate, pheasant & fir trees, RM, 9¾" 485.00
Cake plate, poppies on cream, leaf mold variation, mk, 10" 200.00
Cake plate, swans, icicle mold, unmk 325.00
Celery, portrait, lily mold, unmk, 12½x6" 650.00
Celery, Victorian lady (4 medallions), poppies, RM, 14" 995.00
Chocolate pot, dogwood, swirl mold, RM, +4 c/s 425.00
Chocolate pot, floral, bl on wht, RM 275.00
Chocolate pot, floral, RM, 10½" 310.00
Chocolate pot, lilacs, leaf mold, unmk 350.00
Chocolate pot, snowballs & roses, wht & pk on gr, RM, 10½" ...325.00
Chocolate pot, swans & pines, mold #521, mk, +6 c/s 2,425.00
Coffeepot, demitasse; dogwood & pine on wht, angle hdl, mk, 9" ..750.00
Coffeepot, floral, stippled mold, unmk 295.00
Cracker jar, fruit, stippled floral mold, unmk, 3½x9" 450.00
Cracker jar, lilies, wht w/gold on gr shaded, mk 175.00
Cracker jar, pastel mc flowers, scalloped base, mk, 7" 300.00

Creamer, cottage scene, RM, 3½" 175.00
Creamer, HP/emb floral, mk 55.00
Creamer, Melon Boy w/jewels, RM, 2¾" 250.00
Creamer & sugar bowl, floral, rose to wht, tulip mold, unmk 185.00
Creamer & sugar bowl, gr & gold swags, ftd, RM 175.00
Creamer & sugar bowl, hanging baskets w/gold, RM 185.00
Ferner, peonies on lustre int, crimped, porc, RM, 8¼x2¾" 265.00
Hair receiver, dogwood & pine, ftd, 4" 175.00
Muffineer, roses on cream, scalloped ft, uptrn hdls, mk 225.00
Mustard, poppies, scalloped top & ft, mk, 3" 200.00
Mustard pot, carnations, fleur-de-lis mold, RM 145.00
Mustard pot, daisies & violets, morning-glory mold, unmk 95.00
Mustard pot, floral panels much gold, hdl, RM 300.00
Pin box, bird of paradise, pillow form, mk, 3" sq 900.00
Pitcher, lemonade; floral, lily of valley mold, RM 725.00
Pitcher, lemonade; roses, carnation mold, mk, 9½" 750.00
Pitcher, poppies, gold trim, smooth base/ornate top, mk, 9½" 450.00
Pitcher, tankard; poppies, Dmn Quilt mold, unmk, 10¼" 795.00
Pitcher, tankard; reflecting lilies, icicle mold, mk, 11¾" 600.00
Pitcher, tankard; wht flowers on wht, scalloped top/ft, unmk 600.00
Plate, Dice Players, rope-edge mold, unmk, 8¾" 600.00
Plate, Man in Mountain, RM, 8½" 450.00
Plate, Melon Boys, keyhole/ribbon/jewel mold, mk, 6" 495.00
Plate, poppies, fleur-de-lis mold, mk, 8½" 175.00
Plate, Quiet Cove, medallion mold, mk, 8¾" 495.00
Plate, roses, sunflower mold, mk, 9" 300.00
Plate, roses on gr shaded, RM, 9" 215.00
Plate, swans, unmk, 7¾" 225.00

R.S. Prussia plaque, Quiet Cove, 8½", $795.00.

Relish, peacock & evergreens, icicle mold, RM, 9½x4½" 395.00
Salt cellar, master; floral, oval, RM 45.00
Shaving mug, pk/bl shadow flowers w/gold, mirror on front 185.00
Slipper, man's, dogwood blossoms on pearl lustre, unmk, 5" L 165.00
Syrup, swans & terrace on bl, mk, 5½", +underplate 400.00
Teapot, roses & lilies, lily of valley mold, mk, 7½" 375.00
Teapot, swan scenic, mold #510, 5", +cr/sug 750.00
Toothpick holder, floral, hdls, 6-ftd, RM 175.00
Toothpick holder, poppies, RM 195.00
Tray, bread; snowballs, RM, 10¾x6¾" 150.00
Tray, bun; 6 domed sections w/5 jewels in ea, unmk, 13x8½" 185.00
Tray, floral, carnation mold, open hdls, RM, 11x7½" 280.00
Tray, florals on pearl lustre, ribbon & jewel mold, mk, 12" 275.00
Tray, lilies reflecting on water, icicle mold, unmk, 11¾" 355.00
Tray, pk & wht snowballs, open hdls, oval, 9½" 55.00
Urn, cottage & mill scene, w/lid, mk 3,475.00
Vase, Melon Boys, bulbous, unmk, 6" 695.00
Vase, mill scene, salesman's sample, RM, 4½" 250.00
Vase, poppies w/gold on gr shaded, mk, 9x3¼" 225.00

Vase, 3 swans on lake, fleur-de-lis gold border, RM, 12" **495.00**

R.S. Suhl, E.S. Suhl

Porcelains marked with this designation are attributed to Reinhold Schlegelmilch's Suhl factory.

Box, floral, w/beveled mirror, mk **200.00**
Cake plate, floral, floral border, hdls, 10" **135.00**
Ewer, floral on gr, gold hdl, mk, 13¼" **325.00**
Tazza, roses w/gold stencilling, mk, 2½x4¼" **250.00**
Vase, Gibson girl portrait, gold uptrn hdls, mk, 9½" **1,100.00**
Vase, Melon Boys, flared sides, mk, 7½" **1,500.00**
Vase, night watchman on brn shaded, gold uptrn hdls, mk, 6" ...**600.00**
Wall plaque, daisies, 10½" **125.00**

R.S. Tillowitz

R.S. Tillowitz-marked porcelains are attributed to Reinhold Schlegelmilch's factory in Tillowitz, Silesia.

Bowl, pheasants, scalloped rim, open hdls, oval, mk, 10" **225.00**
Cup & saucer, demitasse; wht flowers, mk **60.00**
Gravy boat, wht flowers on cream shaded, mk **70.00**
Pitcher, lemonade; poppies, mk **125.00**
Pitcher, pk floral garland at neck on wht, mk, 8½" **65.00**
Plate, stylized butterfly border w/gold, gold hdls, mk, 7" **35.00**

Schneider

The Schneider Glass Company was founded in 1914 at Epinay-sur-seine, France. They made many types of art glass, some of which sandwiched designs between layers. Other decorative devices were applique and carved work. These were marked 'Charder' or 'Schneider.' During the twenties commercial artware was produced with Deco motifs cut by acid through two or three layers and signed 'LeVerre Francais' in script or with a section of inlaid filigrane. Our advisor for this category is Don Williams; he is listed in the Directory under Missouri. See also Le Verre Francais.

Bowl, pk/wht striations, cluthra type, appl decor, 5½x11" **1,000.00**
Compote, clear/mint gr mottle on dk amber stem/ft, 12x15" ...**2,200.00**
Compote, faux marble, pk/wine/yel, amethyst ped ft, 5x9" **400.00**
Compote, red w/purple swirls, purple base, flared rim, 10x7" **190.00**
Ewer, pk/rust-streaked gray, wine hdl w/tendril, slim, 18" **880.00**
Tazza, orange & purple stemmed base, sgn, 4½x8½" **435.00**
Torchere, mottle shade, open leaf/scroll iron base/std, 69" **1,100.00**
Vase, appl flowers w/cabachon centers on purple, 10x10" **1,650.00**
Vase, clear w/pastel streaks & bubbles, flaring rim/ft, 12" **275.00**
Vase, etched & clear rectilinears, dk purple ft, 17" **1,300.00**
Vase, etched spiral band, dk gray, ftd U-form, 12" **1,100.00**
Vase, mottled pk/wht/clear w/cluthra-like bubbles, 12" **365.00**
Vase, mottled/swirled pk/rust/orange/etc, ftd ovoid, 14" **440.00**
Vase, orange mottle to dk red & mustard streaks, sgn, 12½" ...**1,195.00**
Vase, orange mottled acorn form blown into ftd iron fr, 8" **975.00**
Vase, poppies, appl/cvd, red/blk on yel to gr, wine ft, 15" **10,450.00**
Vase, yel/clear mottle w/rust/lime gr splotches, 13x12" **875.00**

Cameo

Ewer, leaves/snails, brn/rust on citron, bun ft, 13" **1,200.00**
Pitcher, water; Deco design, lg **1,425.00**
Vase, floral, bl/brn on rust/yel, Charder, trumpet neck, 7" **400.00**

Vase, flowers, bl on orange mottle, 21x9" **1,650.00**
Vase, flowers, orange/red on bubbly, slim/ftd, 8½" **2,800.00**
Vase, geometrics, acid-cut on amethyst, ftd ovoid, 8½" **700.00**

Schoolhouse Collectibles

Schoolhouse collectibles bring to mind memories of a bygone era when the teacher rang her bell to call the youngsters to class in a one-room schoolhouse where often both the 'hickory stick' and an apple occupied a prominent position on her desk. Our advisor for this category is Kenn Norris; he is listed in the Directory under Texas.

Bell, brass w/iron clapper, 3½" **45.00**
Book, Brook's 6th Reader, 1906, EX **6.00**
Book, Dick & Jane, We Look & See, dk red cover, VG **60.00**

Book, *Fun with Dick and Jane*, copyright 1940s, Scott, Foresman & Co., VG-, $30.00.

Book, McGuffey's 5th Reader, VG **12.50**
Book, Warren's School Geography, 1860 ....**25.00**
Desk, schoolmaster's; cherry, slant top, trn legs, 33x28x22" **625.00**
Desk, schoolmaster's; walnut Co Hplwht, 2-part, drw, 45x26" ...**400.00**
Map, pull-down canvas, Universal, NY, 54x47", VG **18.00**
Paste bottle, rnd, cork top, early, EX **3.00**
Slate, oval, hickory fr, 10x7", EX **55.00**
Slate, peg-constructed fr, 9x13" **48.00**
Spelling board, wood w/movable letters, Pat 1886, EX **65.00**
Stand, flag pole; 2 for **25.00**

Schoop, Hedi

Swiss-born Hedi Schoop started her ceramics business in North Hollywood in 1940. With a talented crew of about twenty decorators, she produced figurines, figure-vases, console sets, TV lamps, and other decorative housewares — much of which was accented with gold or platinum trim. Schoop's pottery closed after a fire destroyed the building in 1958. Marks are impressed or printed. For further information we recommend *The Collector's Encyclopedia of California Pottery* by our advisor Jack Chipman; he is listed in the Directory under California.

Bowl, shell form, pk w/gold, 12" **30.00**
Candle holder, mermaid holds 2 shell holders aloft, 13½" **150.00**
Figurine, Chinese couple, blk & wht, pr **85.00**
Figurine, clown playing cello, over-glaze platinum, 12½" **75.00**
Figurine, Josephine, holds bowl at hip, 13" **65.00**
Figurine, Repose, lady sits w/bowl in lap, 1949 ....**65.00**

Figurine, Siamese dancers, male/female, 14½", 14", pr **100.00**
Flower holder/lamp base, Colbert, lady w/2 baskets, 11½" **55.00**
Tray, King of Diamonds, in-mold mk **35.00**
Vase, crowing cock figural, over-glaze gold, 12" **45.00**

Pair of dancers, white with gold trim, $125.00.

Scouting Collectibles

Scouting was founded in England in 1907 by a retired Major General, Lord Robert Baden-Powell. Its purpose is the same today as it was then — to help develop physically strong, mentally alert boys and to teach them basic fundamentals of survival and leadership. The movement soon spread to the United States, and in 1910 a Chicago publisher, William Boyce, set out to establish Scouting in America. The first World Scout Jamboree was held in 1911 in England. Baden-Powell was honored as the Chief Scout of the World. In 1926 he was awarded the Silver Buffalo Award in the United States. He was knighted in 1929 for distinguished military service and for his scouting efforts. Baden-Powell died in 1941. For more information you may contact our advisor, R.J. Sayers, author of *Guide to Scouting Collectibles,* whose address (and ordering information regarding his book) may be found in the Directory under North Carolina.

Badge, BSA, Sea Scout Apprentice, blk felt **5.50**
Bank, CI, scout w/staff & pack, slot in pack, 1930s **25.00**
Bank, CI, Scouts in Camp, 1914 era (fakes produced) **2,000.00**
Book, Air Scout Manual, HW Hunt, Barclay, 1942, Dec 1, EX **8.00**
Book, souvenir; BSA Official, 1957 Nat'l Jamboree **5.00**
Bracelet, GSA, brass links w/gr emblem, ca 1960, NM **10.00**
Bust, Baden-Powell, brass, 2" **50.00**
Calendar, 1951, Brown & Bigelow, Rockwell illus, 34x16", VG ..**20.00**
Cigarette card, Baden-Powell, Adkin & Sons **7.50**
Compass, BSA, Litenite, floating dial, glows in dark, 1918-24 .....**20.00**
Emblem, BSA, gold/bl litho, ca 1930s, ⅝" **10.00**
Flag, 1937 World Jamboree, full logo, 36x60", VG **100.00**
Lantern, BSA, Dietz, kerosene, hdl, dtd, 1930s era **27.00**
Lantern slide, Baden-Powell in full uniform, 1930 ....**30.00**
Lapel stud, bronze shield w/running scout, 1913, ¾x⅞" **80.00**
Letter opener/bookmark, BSA, brass w/gr enamel, 1930s, 3¾" **20.00**
Medal, BSA, Eagle Scout, Strange Co, type 6, 1968-71 ....**10.00**
Neckerchief, BSA, 1959 World Jamboree **22.50**
Neckerchief, BSA, 1969 Nat'l Jamboree, cotton, 1 of 4 styles **8.00**
Neckerchief, 1935-37 Jamboree, full sq, red or bl, ea **35.00**
Patch, BSA, Explorer Silver Award, wings, type 2, 1958-68 ....**30.00**
Patch, BSA, 1935 World Jamboree, felt, 3" (fakes produced) **40.00**
Patch, BSA, 1937 World Jamboree, felt, 3" (fakes produced) **35.00**
Patch, BSA, 1951 World Jamboree, leather, gr letters **85.00**
Patch, jacket; BSA, 1960 Nat'l Jamboree, 6" **13.00**
Pennant, BSA Official, Honor Patrol, bl felt **10.00**

Pin, BSA, Official Press Club, 1937-45 ....**10.00**
Pin, BSA, Rover Scout, red enamel, 1938-46 ....**50.00**
Pin-bk, I'll be a Tenderfoot...1928 BS Round Up, 1¼", EX **60.00**
Pocketknife, BSA, Camillus, 3-blade, blk plastic hdl, 1947 ....**11.00**
Pocketknife, BSA, Remington, 4-blade, bone hdl, 1928-39 ....**60.00**
Pocketknife, BSA, 4-blade, #1567, 1925 ....**100.00**
Pocketknife, Imperial, rare cream-color hdl, EX **25.00**
Postcard, Home Coming, P Baleu, mc **12.00**
Postcard, Lord Baden-Powell w/personal signature, mc **5.00**
Postcard, Scouts on parade, w/staffs & vehicles, 1920 ....**5.00**
Poster, scout kneeling for WSS program, Lyendecker, 1918 ....**75.00**
Poster, 1937-37 World Jamboree, Rockwell art, 24x42", VG **100.00**
Ring, BSA, Nat'l Staff, 10k gold, Nat'l logo **100.00**
Ring, Eagle Scout, mc enamel on sterling, 1930-50s **30.00**
Ring, rope/fretwork, sterling, 1930s, VG **20.00**
Ring, 1935-37 World Jamboree, silver, w/logo **30.00**
Sash, merit badge; w/22 sq badges, VG **90.00**
Sash, merit badge; w/25 tan crimped badges, VG **50.00**
Scarf slide, BSA, brass, Statue of Liberty/emblem, lt wear **5.00**
Signaler, BSA Official, 1950s, MIB **20.00**
Tie holder, BSA, laminated wood w/metal loops, logo **10.00**
Uniform, 2-snap collar, WWI type, 1912-17 era, w/label **55.00**
Uniform, 4 billows pocket type, w/wht label, 1920s era **40.00**
Wallet, BSA, camp craft, sewn leather, 1940s **7.00**
Watch fob, BSA Official, Scoutmaster, gr enamel **100.00**
Whistle, Be Prepared, SP brass, w/loop, 1930s, EX **35.00**
Wristwatch, BSA Official, Elgin, 1934 ....**30.00**

Scrimshaw

The most desirable examples of the art of scrimshaw can be traced back to the first half of the 19th century to the heyday of the whaling industry. Some voyages lasted for several years, and conditions on board were often dismal. Sailors filled the long hours by using the tools of their trade to engrave whale teeth and make boxes, pie crimpers (jagging wheels), etc. from the bone and teeth of captured whales. Eskimos also made scrimshaw, sometimes borrowing designs from the sailors who traded with them.

Beware of fradulent pieces; fakery is prevelant in this field. If you're in doubt, it's best to deal with reputable people who guarantee the items they sell. There are also many carved teeth that are actually made of plastic. A listing of these plastic items has been published by the Kendall Whaling Museum in Sharon, Massachusetts. Our advisor for this category is John Rinaldi; he is listed in the Directory under Maine. See also Powder Horns.

Basket, cvd circles & scallops, swing hdl, 1840s, 9x10x7", EX.....**7,500.00**
Bodkin, tortoise shell inlay, silver bands, 1850s, 4" **1,200.00**
Box, sewing; mahog, geometric whalebone inlay, 1850s, 10" L ..**3,750.00**

Busk, geometrics, eng/colored, 1850s, 11⅜" 500.00
Busk, Neptune/ships/sea horses, eng/colored ea side, 13" 700.00
Busk, panoramic ship launching scene, 1850s, 13½" 700.00
Busk, whaling scene, hearts w/portraits, city, w/blk, 14" 1,400.00
Busk, whaling scene/storm-tossed ship, eng/colored, 14" 1,750.00
Busk, whaling scenes, deep cvg, w/blk & red, 1800s, 15", EX 880.00
Club, seal-killing; primitive cvg of creature on lg end, 15" 400.00
Jagging wheel, female body w/serpent's head, 1850s, 6½" 9,000.00
Jagging wheel, female body w/3-tined fork at pelvis, 8⅝" 4,000.00
Jagging wheel, unicorn w/dbl horns, ebony inlay, 1860s, NM 10,000.00
Jagging wheel, 4-tined fork, 7-point star hub, 1850s, 7" 500.00
Letter opener, ornate horn hdl: 2 clasped hands, 1870s, 8½" 1,250.00
Ring, nude lady w/arched bk forms ring, 1850s, EX 1,100.00
Ring, sperm whale at top, 1850s, EX 700.00
Ruler, whalebone, primitive, 11¼", G 50.00
Salt cellar, delicate trn, tortoise shell base, 3¼", pr 500.00
Seam rubber, cvd ropework, 3 baleen separators, 1850s, 5" 2,600.00
Sewing basket, openwork, strap hdl, mahog base, sgn, 7" L 2,900.00
Swift, heightened w/red scribe lines, sgn, 18" 660.00
Tooth, Am ship/eagle/flags/cannons, color, 1850s, 6½" 6,500.00
Tooth, Constitution & Laws, people salute flag, 6" 600.00
Tooth, lady's portrait, color, 1850s, 8⅛" 4,000.00
Tooth, steamer, bk: Captain eagle, w/red & blk, 5" 1,400.00
Tooth, titled whaling scene, sgn P (Wm Perry), ca '20, 6½" 1,000.00
Tooth, Whaleship Young Phoenix, Le Long (living artist), 6" 600.00
Tusk, figure of Am/Diana, presentation, dtd 1854, 23" 1,500.00
Tusk, lady/stallion/flag/sailor/flowers, color, 1850s, 15" 2,500.00
Yardstick, dmn cvgs w/dk wood & baleen inlays, 1850s, 36" 600.00

Sebastians

Sebastian miniatures were first produced in 1938 by Prescott W. Baston in Marblehead, Massachusetts. Since then more than five hundred have been modeled. These figurines have been sold through gift shops all over the country, primarily in the New England states. In 1976 Baston withdrew his Sebastians from production. Under an agreement with the Lance Corporation of Hudson, Massachusetts, one hundred designs were selected to be produced by that company under Baston's supervision. Those remaining were discontinued. In the short time since then, the older figurines have become very collectible. Price is determined by two factors: 1) in production/out of production; 2) labels — color of oval label, i.e. red, blue, green, etc.; Marblehead label, a green and silver palette-shaped label used until 1977; or no label. If there is no label and the varnish coat is quite yellowed, then it is considered to be of the Marblehead era. Dates are merely copyright dates and have no particular significance in regard to value. (Signed) 'P.W. Baston' should only have impact on price when the signature is an actual autograph. Most pieces are manufactured with an imprinted 'P.W. Baston' on the base. Baston died in 1984; the miniatures are now being done by P.W. Baston, Jr.

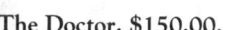
The Doctor, $150.00.

Abe Lincoln, head up 100.00
Aunt Betsy Trotwood, PP 50.00
Aunt Polly 50.00
Ben Franklin, PS 115.00
Betsy Ross, pewter 45.00
Colonial Glassblower, PS 125.00
Cow Hand 45.00
Dahl's Fisherman 125.00
Deborah Franklin 65.00
Doctor, PW 150.00
Evangeline 75.00
Family Feast 75.00
Family Sings 100.00
Gabriel 75.00
Gem Baby Land Furniture, PS 150.00
George Washington 45.00
George Washington, standing, pewter 55.00
George Washington w/cannon, pewter 65.00
Holgrave Daguerreotypist 200.00
Howard Johnson's Pieman 250.00
James Madison, pewter 45.00
John Hancock, pewter 45.00
John Smith & Pocahontas, pr 140.00
Judge Thatcher 45.00
Juliet 45.00
Katrina Van Tassel 45.00
Martha Washington 45.00
Mary Lyon, blk 175.00
Mr Obocell (advertising weight-loss product) 95.00
Mrs Cratchit, PP 50.00
Nathaniel Hawthorne 150.00
Nell & Grandfather 45.00
Old Salt 45.00
Peggotty 45.00
Perplexed Husband, Jell-O 275.00
Phoebe (House of 7 Gables) 90.00
Pilgrims 65.00
Plaque, Collector's Xmas series, 1985 ....40.00
Priscilla Alden 50.00
Romeo 45.00
Sairey Gamp 45.00
Sarah Henry 55.00
Scrooge 45.00
Self Portrait 35.00
Songs at Cratchit's 45.00
Town Crier 45.00

Sevres

Fine-quality porcelains have been made in Sevres, France, since the early 1700s. Rich ground colors were often hand painted with portraits, scenics, and florals. Some pieces were decorated with transfer prints and decalcomania; many were embellished with heavy gold. These wares are the most respected of all French porcelains. Their style and designs have been widely copied, and some of the items listed below are Sevres-type wares.

Bowl, center; lattice/scrolls, leaf/floral appl ped ft, 12" 2,400.00
Box, powder; gold stars on red, floral wreath/dots atop, 1¾" 350.00
Creamer & sugar bowl, cornflower, gold/wht, 1910, 5½"; 4¾" 300.00
Figurine, dancers, flowered attire, he in purple coat, 11" 1,650.00
Figurine, equestrian Louis XIV, bsk, ormolu base, 16" 1,200.00

Figurine, Ice Queen, 2 putti under train of gown, 1907, 13" **1,850.00**
Plate, literary scene, bk: title, bl/gold/floral rim, 9" **150.00**
Plate, nymph & 2 cherub attendants, bl border, gilt fr, 15" **1,500.00**
Plate, 3 portraits, P Bonaparte/Prince & Princess Murat, 15" ..**1,200.00**
Platter, garden w/2 ladies & gent holding birdcage, 14" L **200.00**
Urn, courting scene on bl, sgn Morin, mask hdls, 27" **300.00**
Urn, Cupid/Psyche, bk: scene, paw-ft base, no lid/hdls, 15" **450.00**

Urn, reserves with lovers in a garden on blue and gold background, signed F. Auchlet, 17", $2,700.00 for the pair.

Urn, romantic pr on bl, ormolu winged-lady hdls, sgn, 32" **1,900.00**
Urn, scenic w/people, figural ormolu hdls, Demonceaux, 22" ..**2,500.00**
Vase, floral on bl, mask/wreath hdls & mts, now lamp, 19" **1,000.00**
Vase, titled scenes on cobalt, ormolu mt, Laurence, 20", pr **1,000.00**
Vase, Venus/2 cupids on bsk, ormolu finial/hdls/base, 18" **950.00**

Sewer Tile

Whimsies, advertising novelties, and other ornamental items were sometimes made in potteries where the primary product was simply tile.

Bookends, lg owl on stacked books, sgn ETE, 5⅝", pr **425.00**
Desk set, fireplace shape, glued rpr/chips, 5x8" **90.00**
Dog, seated, EX tooling, 11" **280.00**
Dog, seated, open legs, base w/cvd names/1893, 10", EX **935.00**
Dog, seated, solid mold, simple band tooling, 7½" **145.00**
Dog, solid body, hand tooled, minor chips, 4¾" **85.00**
Dog, Staffordshire type, molded/some tooling, 12", EX **150.00**
Dog, Staffordshire type, some tooling, pnt traces, 8", EX **110.00**
Dog, Staffordshire type, tooled collar & chain, 7", EX **85.00**
Frog, simple tooled detail, minor chips, 6" **90.00**
Horse's head, sq base, Jack Fink/1861, firing cracks, 6" **225.00**
Lion, EX molding/tooling, inscribed/1889, 9½", VG **325.00**
Owl, EX tooling, sgn EJE, on stump-like base, 14" **950.00**
Shoe, lady's, 4" L **40.00**
Umbrella stand, stump form, minor chips, 23" **325.00**

Sewing Items

Sewing collectibles continue to intrigue collectors, and fine 19th-century and earlier pieces are commanding higher prices due to increased demand and scarcity. Complete needlework boxes and chatelaines in original condition are rare. But even though they may be incomplete, as long as boxes contain fittings of the period, the chains of the chatelaine are intact and contemporary with the style, the individual holders original, and matching the brooch, they should be considered prime additions to any collection. As 19th-century items become harder to find, new trends in collecting develop. Among them are needlebooks, many of which were decorated with horses, children,

beautiful ladies, etc. Some were giveaways printed with advertisements of products and businesses. Even early pins are collectible; the earliest were made in two parts with the round head attached separately. Pin disks, pin cubes, and other pin holders make interesting additions to a sewing collection as well.

Tape measures are now popular. Victorian figurals command premium prices. Early wooden examples of transferware and Tunbridge ware have gained in popularity as have figurals of vegetable ivory, celluloid, and other early plastics. From the 20th century, tatting shuttles made of plastics as well as bone, brass, sterling, and wood decorated with Art Nouveau, Deco, and more modern designs are in demand; so are darning eggs, stillettos, and thimbles. Because of the decline in the popularity of needlework after the 1920s (due to increased production of machine-made items), many novelty-type items were made in an attempt to regain consumer interest, and many collectors today find them appealing.

Watch for reproductions. Sterling thimbles are being made in Holland and in the U.S. and are available in many designs from the Victorian era. But the originals are usually plainly marked, either in the inside apex or outside on the band. Avoid testing gold and silver thimbles for content; this often destroys the inside marks. Instead, research the manufacturer's mark; this will often denote the material as well. Even though the reproductions are well finished, they do not have the manufacturers' marks. Many thimbles are being made specifically for the collectible market; reproductions of porcelain thimbles are also found. Prices should reflect the age and availability of these thimbles. Our advisor for this cateogry is Marjorie Geddes; she is listed in the Directory under Oregon.

Chatelaine, sterling chain with scissors case, strawberry emery, and needle case, London hallmarks, 1889, $395.00.

Bobbin, bone, inscribed Love the Giver **75.00**
Bobbin, wood, mother-'n-babe type, cvd window, 6¼" L **135.00**
Bobbin, wood, orig beads, 1800s, England **25.00**
Bodkin, scrimshaw whale tooth ivory, 4½", EX **200.00**
Book, Complete Book of Sewing, Talbot, 1943, EX **17.50**
Box, Lehn Ware, 4-color pnt, gilt, decoupage, dtd 1875, 12" **350.00**
Box, Mauchline Ware, Brooks thread, bird litho, EX **95.00**
Button, silver, emb Nouveau flowers, London, 1904 hallmk, ¾" ..**50.00**
Buttonhole cutter, metal, DMCo, Pat 1878, 3½" **32.00**
Clamp, quilt frame; CI, ornate screw hdl on 'C', 4" **35.00**
Clamp, sewing; bone, cvd Oriental motif, 3" **88.00**
Clamp, sewing; oak, trn, pincushion top, 9" L **150.00**
Crochet hook, bone, 5" **15.00**
Crochet hook, brass, emb florals, retractable, England **55.00**

Crochet hook, silver, hallmk	32.00
Darner, child's, blk egg, repousse sterling hdl, 4½"	75.00
Darner, dk gr blown glass, ball-shaped end, 5¼"	95.00
Darner, glove; sterling, emb leaves, chatelaine ring, 4½"	125.00
Darner, glove; sterling, repousse hdl, chatelaine loop, 4"	125.00
Darner, glove; sterling; eng center rod, 4½"	135.00
Darner, milk glass, blown, ridged hdl, 6"	95.00
Darner, pk blown glass egg, Czechoslovakia	95.00
Emery, face wrapped in turban, pnt features, 1½", EX	85.00
Emery, strawberry, embr silk, Merry Christmas on ribbon	125.00
Emery, strawberry w/sterling cap, 1½", EX	95.00
Emery, Tunbridge Ware, mosaic pattern, dbl-ended, 1850s	150.00
Gauge, hem; SP, Pat Oct 2 1894, 5½"	65.00
Gauge, hem; sterling, eng mums, Webster, 4½"	95.00
Guard, knitting; celluloid, hoof shape w/fur trim, 1850s, pr	165.00
Hem ripper, sterling hdl w/blk celluloid cover	55.00
Kit, German enamel & silver, complete	250.00
Knife, retractable, sterling, on chatelaine ring	78.00
Knitting sheath, goose-wing type, 1830s, EX	195.00
Knitting sheath, wooden, South Pennine style, 1800s, 6¾"	125.00
Measure, brass, pig, standing, EX	145.00
Measure, celluloid, Colgate's Fab, 1930s, 1⅜" dia	35.00
Measure, celluloid, Lydia Pinkham, blk/wht portrait, 1½" dia	65.00
Measure, celluloid, photolitho of Hoover dam, 1½"	20.00
Measure, celluloid, pig in boot, red & wht, EX	95.00
Measure, plastic, Hoover vacuum cleaner	45.00
Measure, vegetable ivory, Stanhope scene in hdl, bbl shape	145.00
Needle book, gr silk, flannel pgs, 2¼x1½"	37.50
Needle book, MOP cvd covers, silk w/flannel pgs, 1½x2¼"	145.00
Needle box, secret compartment, Japan, 1920s, EX	165.00
Needle case, bone, fish figural, 4"	175.00
Needle case, bone, knobs ea end, 2⅝"	27.50
Needle case, bone, parasol shape, missing stanhope	75.00
Needle case, faux tortoise shell w/brass filigree, 1800s, 5x3"	235.00
Needle case, German enamel & silver	165.00
Needle case, Mauchline Ware	125.00
Needle case, sterling, flat tubular form, chatelaine loop, 2"	95.00
Needle case, sterling, plain cylinder, 2½x⅜"	65.00
Needle case, sterling w/gold wash o/l, France, 3¼"	165.00
Needle case, trn bone, awl tip	60.00
Needle case, wood, bbl shape, advertising	95.00
Needle case, wood, cvd decor, knob ea end, 3¼"	78.00
Needle case, wood, lighthouse shape, Germany, 3"	165.00
Needle case, wood w/advertising, Germany	135.00
Needle case, wooden, rolling pin shape, 2 hdls, 3½" L	20.00
Needle threader, tin, oval, chromolitho of Gibraltar, 1x2"	17.50
Pin disk, celluloid, Nouveau lady & advertising	45.00
Pincushion, base metal, mouse figural, cushion on bk, 2"	65.00
Pincushion, metal, high-heeled shoe, sgn SCC, 4", EX	35.00
Pincushion, pewter, high-heeled shoe, velvet cushion, England	80.00
Pincushion, pnt wood, lady's shoe, florals, 7" L	45.00
Pincushion, pnt wood, lady's shoe, high top, curving heel, 6"	65.00
Pincushion, silk patchwork, stuffed disk type, Victorian, 2"	95.00
Pincushion/tape measure, dog w/glass eyes atop, Japan, 5"	25.00
Punch, cvd MOP hdl, 4½"	45.00
Punch, plain MOP hdl, 3½"	22.50
Punch, sterling, eng scrolls & flowers, 6½"	68.00
Scissors, buttonhole; 1800s	37.50
Scissors, embroidery; rooster figural, Germany, 4", EX	145.00
Scissors, embroidery; swan figural, Germany, 3½"	145.00
Scissors, Wiss 1 KS Pat 2027785, gr pnt hdls, 1936, 8", EX	10.00
Sewing basket, sweet grass, EX patina, 2x7¾"	15.00
Sewing basket, wicker, flowered cloth top, 2 hdls	24.00
Sewing bird, brass, clamp-on, dtd 1853 on wing, 5¼x4x2"	165.00

Sewing bird, brass, emb Norton's Improved, 6"	175.00
Sewing bird, gilded brass, 2 cushions, 1 on clamp, 4½"	225.00
Sewing case, sterling, bullet shape, w/reel & thimble, 1¾" L	195.00
Shuttle, tatting; bone, no cvg, old	40.00
Shuttle, tatting; celluloid, Lydia Pinkham, NM	50.00
Shuttle, tatting; German silver, eng scrolls, common	35.00
Shuttle, tatting; MOP, 2½x¾", EX	85.00
Shuttle, tatting; sterling, eng florals & scrolls	145.00
Shuttle, tatting; sterling, eng Greek Key border, 1915	135.00
Shuttle, tatting; sterling, eng initials & 1914	135.00
Shuttle, tatting; sterling, Foster & Bailey, EX	95.00
Shuttle, tatting; sterling, in orig flowered box	145.00
Shuttle, tatting; tortoise shell	195.00
Spool knave, SP, scrolled decor, all orig, English, 2½"	200.00
Thimble, brass, wide plain band, vertical ribs	12.50
Thimble, sterling, Simons, plain w/eng monogram	32.00
Thimble, sterling, 8-panel band w/3 concentric rings, unmk	25.00
Thimble case, brass, purse shape, England, 1880, 2⅛x1½"	150.00
Thimble case, MOP, egg shape, brass bound, HP ivy, 1870s	125.00
Thimble case, treenware, bbl form, pnt bridge scene, 2"	145.00
Thimble stand, metal, turtle on base, w/thread post	45.00
Thimble stand, nickeled metal, cat on rug form, 2½" base	75.00
Thread reel, MOP top, bone base, 1¼"	37.50
Threader, Lydia Pinkham, celluloid	20.00
Waxer, sterling, for chatelaine	98.00
Waxer, sterling, repousse	125.00
Waxer, Tunbridge Ware, mosaic pattern, bbl shaped, 2-pc	150.00
Winder, silk; ivory, rectangular, 2", EX	55.00
Winder, silk; MOP, cvd decor, 1½x1"	65.00
Winding clamp, grpt, 1830s, EX	195.00

Sewing Machines

The fact that Thomas Saint, an English cabinetmaker, invented the first sewing machine in 1790 was unknown until 1874 when Newton Wilson, an English sewing machine manufacturer and patentee, chanced on the drawings included in a patent specification describing methods of making boots and shoes. By the middle of the 19th century, several patents were granted to American inventors, among them Isaac M. Singer, whose machine used a treadle. These machines were ruggedly built, usually of cast iron. By the 1860s and '70s, the sewing machine had become a popular commodity, and the ironwork became more detailed and ornate.

Though rare machines are costly, many of the old oak treadle machines (especially these brands: Davis, Home, Household, National, New Home, Singer, Weed, Wheeler & Wilson, and Willcox & Gibbs) have only nominal value. Our advisors for this category are Sandra and Peter Frei; they are listed in the Directory under Massachusetts.

Child's, Automatic, CI, knob-trn wheel, early, EX	235.00
Child's, Casige, pressed steel, blk/red/gr pnt, EX	80.00
Child's, Singer Sewhandy #20, in box	98.00
Singer Featherweight #221, blk, w/case & attachments	295.00
Singer Featherweight #221-1, blk/gold, w/case & attachments	300.00
Singer Sewhandy, tan metal, 6x3¼x4½", EX	115.00

Shaker Items

The Shaker community was founded in America in 1776 at Niskeyuna, New York, by a small group of English 'Shaking Quakers.' The name referred to a group dance which was part of their religious rites. Their leader was Mother Ann Lee. By 1815 their membership had grown to more than one thousand in eighteen communities as far west as Indiana and Kentucky. But in less than a decade, their numbers began to decline until today only a handful remain. Their furniture is prized for its originality, simplicity, workmanship, and practicality. Few pieces were signed. Some were carefully finished to enhance the natural wood; a few were painted.

Although other methods were used earlier, most Shaker boxes were of oval construction with overlapping 'fingers' at the seams to prevent buckling as the wood aged. Boxes with original paint fetch triple the price of an unpainted box; number of fingers and size should also be considered.

Although the Shakers were responsible for weaving a great number of baskets, their methods are not easily distinguished from those of their outside neighbors, and it is nearly impossible without first-hand knowledge to positively attribute a specific example to their manufacture. They were involved in various commercial efforts other than woodworking — among them sheep and dairy farming, sawmilling, and pipe and brick making. They were the first to raise crops specifically for seed and to market their product commercially. They perfected a method to recycle paper and were able to produce wrinkle-free fabrics. Our advisor for this category is Nancy Winston; she is listed in the Directory under New Hampshire. Standard two-letter state abbreviations have been used throughout the following listings.

Key:
bj — bootjack
CB — Canterbury
EF — Enfield
NL — New Lebanon
PH — Pleasant Hill
ML — Mt. Lebanon
SDL — Sabbathday Lake
WV — Watervliet

Basket, blk ash, hickory hoop hdl, WV, 20x29x19" 425.00
Basket, hickory splint,, 3 runners, copper rivets, 15x13" 650.00
Basket, kittenhead; blk ash, EX patina, cvd loop hdl, 5x4" 550.00
Basket, laundry; blk ash, early pnt, hoop hdls, 14x23x19" 250.00
Basket, sewing; poplarware, velvet cushion, SDL, 3x6" 650.00
Basket, wool; blk ash, dbl hickory hdls, 10½x14½" 250.00
Basket, work; blk ash, cvd side hdls, WV, 14x24x16" 400.00
Bed, maple/poplar, trn leg, natural finish, 42x79x35" 500.00
Bed, poplar/oak, lt orig varnish, NL, 1830s, 32x79x32", pr 4,000.00
Bellows, pine, orig bl pnt & tin, worn leather, NL, 1830s, 28" ...700.00
Bench, chair-taping; maple, red pnt, iron device, 32" H 950.00
Bench, meetinghouse; pine/maple, red pnt, CB, 1840s, 32" L .9,000.00
Bench, work; pine, orig gray pnt, SDL, 1850s, 21x45x15" 600.00
Bobbin winder, maple/oak/hickory, EX patina, 1820s, 42x49" ...800.00
Bowl, chopping; maple, yel varnish, cvd/appl hdls, NL, 4x17" ...800.00
Bowl, maple, orig red pnt, 1840s, 5¼x19" 650.00
Bowl, porc, floral, Union Porc Works, ML, 3½x9½" 900.00
Box, blanket; pine, red pnt, dvtl, strap hinges, WV, 34" L 1,200.00
Box, butter; pine, lt bl pnt, dvtl, bail hdls, EF, 12x21x17" 4,900.00
Box, desk; cherry, ivory escutcheon, dvtl, 1840s, 4x12x3" 1,600.00
Box, maple/cherry, 3-finger, copper nails, oval, 1850s, 2x6" 450.00
Box, maple/pine, 3-finger, sgn EK, 2½x6" 400.00
Box, maple/pine, 3-finger, varnish, oval, 1830s, 1½x3⅝" 300.00
Box, maple/pine, 4-finger, dk varnish, 1840s, 3½x8½" 400.00
Box, maple/pine, 4-finger, orig pnt, sm rpr, 1820s, 5x15" 395.00
Box, maple/pine, 4-finger, orig yel pnt, tacks, oval, 4x10" 4,000.00
Box, maple/pine, 4-finger, red stain, SDL, 1840s, 4x10" 800.00
Box, spit; maple/pine, 3-finger, orig yel pnt, NL, 3½x10" 1,250.00
Box, spit; maple/pine, 3-finger, orig yel wash, NL, 4x12" 750.00
Box, storage; pine, orig pnt, dvtl, leather hinges, 8x15x6" 650.00
Box, storage; pine, red stain, dvtl, strap hinges, WV, 22" L 1,200.00
Box, storage; pine/maple, orig gr pnt, nailed lap, NL, 7x14" ...6,500.00
Bucket, pine, blk steel bands, birch hdl, 6½x9" 500.00
Bucket, pine, orig bl pnt, NL, 1840s, 7½x10" 2,900.00
Bucket, pine, orig mustard yel pnt, iron bail, 5½x7" dia 1,300.00
Bucket, pine, orig yel pnt, stencil: Beans, 7x10" dia 7,000.00

Candlestand, butternut/cherry, varnish, NL, 1820s, 26x17" .11,000.00
Candlestand, cherry, varnish, spider leg, NL, 1820s, 24x15" .20,000.00
Cape, gr waterproof fabric, velvet trim, child's, CB, 1860 ....350.00

Carrier, cherrywood with arched splint handle initialed P.A.S., 4-finger, Sabbath Day Lake Community, Maine, 20th century, 11", $600.00.

Carrier, butternut, dvtl, swing hdl, 1840s, 5x5½x3½" 950.00
Carrier, maple/pine, 4-finger, cvd hdl, oval, 1830s, 8x11" 1,100.00
Carrier, pine, orig yel stain, dvtl, rectangular, 11x14x10" 550.00
Chair, arm #5; tiger maple, ML, 1870s, 37" 1,600.00
Chair, convenience; maple/pine, hinged seat & door, WV, 34" .1,300.00
Chair, elder's rocker; maple, red stain, tape seat, WV, 44" 1,500.00
Chair, maple, mustard pnt, cane seat, child's, 1830s, 29½" 2,750.00
Chair, rocker #3; maple, dk stain, tape seat, ML, 1880s, 34" 700.00
Chair, rocker #3; maple, lt varnish, tape seat/bk, ML, 34" 500.00
Chair, rocker #3; maple, ML, 1880s, 33½" 450.00
Chair, rocker #3; maple, tape seat, lg mushroom hdls, ML, 33" ..600.00
Chair, rocker #3; maple, tape seat, ML, 1830s, 34" 600.00
Chair, rocker #3; maple, varnish, tape seat, ML, 1880s, 33" 350.00
Chair, rocker #4; maple, ebony finish, tape seat/bk, ML, 37½" ...650.00
Chair, rocker #4; maple, tape seat, shawl bar, ML, 33½" 600.00
Chair, rocker #5; maple, tape seat, ML, 1880s, 38" 1,000.00
Chair, rocker #6; maple, decal on slat, ML, 1880s, 41" 1,100.00
Chair, rocker #7; maple, tape seat, shawl bar, ML, 1880s, 40" ..1,100.00
Chair, rocker #7; maple, walnut stain, tape seat/bk, ML, 42" ..1,100.00
Chair, rocker #7; maple/tiger maple, tape seat, 41" 700.00
Chair, side #13; maple, early tape seat, NL, 1830s, 38" 750.00
Chair, side #3; figured maple, tape seat, WV, 38½" 1,700.00
Chair, side; cherry/birch, red stain, woven cane seat, 40" 1,100.00
Chair, side; maple, cane seat, steam-bent bk, NL, 1830s, 43" ..2,800.00
Chair, side; maple, oak splint seat, ML, 1910s, 41" 1,100.00
Chair, side; maple, splint seat, ML, 1910s, 41" 650.00
Chair, side; maple/birch, cane seat, tilters, 1820s, 38½" 1,400.00
Chair, side; maple/birch, rpl cane seat, MA, 1830, 38½" 1,900.00
Chair, side; maple/figured maple, tape seat, ML, 1830s, 42" 1,200.00
Chest, blanket; pine, dvtl drw, rstr, 1840s, 33x29x19" 5,000.00
Chest, blanket; pine, orange pnt, dvtl, NL, 1820s, 36x46x18" ...8,000.00
Chest, blanket; pine, orig pnt, CI escutcheon, SDL, 14x10x17" 900.00
Chest, pine/yel pine, 8 dvtl/nailed drws, 1850s, 65" 1,500.00
Chest, storage; pine, orig pnt, CI hdls, NL, 1860s, 13x21x13" 500.00
Cloak, red wool, CB, 1900s, 37½" L, VG 500.00
Counter, tailor's; pine, red wash traces, 6-drw, WV, 54" L 15,000.00
Cupboard, cherry, door over door, cut-out vent, NL, 76" 6,500.00
Cupboard, hanging; pine, 2 doors, 3-shelf, CB, 31x19x9" 700.00
Cupboard, herb; pine, dk red stain, 4-door, NL, 1840s, 91" 5,000.00
Cupboard, jelly; pine/chestnut, red stain, 2-door, 1850s, 47" ..1,150.00
Cupboard, pine, 2 paneled doors, NL, 1830s, 74x30x6¼" 14,500.00
Cupboard, yel pine/poplar/butternut, NL, 1840s, 73x34x16" ..8,250.00
Desk, pine, 1-drw, pegged/nailed, EF, 36x25x25" 1,050.00
Dipper, maple burl, orig bl pnt, curled hdl, NL, 7" 1,700.00
Dress, woven purple fabric w/bl lining, WV, 1840s, EX 800.00

Duster, maple, gold dyed wool, 15" 175.00
Footstool, maple, orig walnut stain, ML, 1880s, 7x12x12" 650.00
Footstool, pine, orig yel wash, nailed, 1840s, 6x12x6" 500.00
Footstool, pine w/cvd leaves, walnut stain, ML, 7½x12½" 700.00
Footstool, pine/maple, dk stain/varnish, decal, 7x12x12" 600.00
Hanger, dbl; cherry/maple, iron tacks, hanging hole, 1850s 250.00
Measure, oak/pine, iron bound, brass hdls, ME, 8x14" dia 350.00
Pill roller, walnut & brass, 2-pc, 1860s, 16x13" 300.00
Pincushion, cherry, velvet cushion, 8 spool holders, 6x6" dia 275.00
Rack, drying; pine, mortised/wedged, rpr, 1850s, 29x24" 400.00
Sack, flour; Shaker Mills New Gloucester, matted/fr, 20x14" 350.00
Sewing box, poplarware, lift lid w/pincushion, kid trim 700.00
Sewing carrier, maple/pine, 3-finger, oval, SDL, 6½x8" 500.00
Sewing carrier, walnut/pine, 4-finger, oval, 1880s, 6x7½", EX ...375.00
Sieve, pine/horsehair/string, wire-joined at lap, 1850s, 5x8" 200.00
Spinning wheel, maple/oak, red pnt, flyer adjusts, 1840s, 61" 300.00
Spinning wheel, oak/maple/ash, Alfred ME, 1840s, 35x34" 700.00
Stepladder, pine, pnt traces, mortised, NL, 1850s, 46" 400.00
Stool, maple, lt varnish, faded tape seat, 1880s, 14x13x12" 275.00
Stool, maple, orig varnish, tape seat, 17x20½x12" 400.00
Stool, 2-step; butternut, arch cutouts, 1870s, 9x10x8" 700.00
Stool, 2-step; pine, screws, 20x15x18" 375.00
Stove, CI, penny ft, lift lid, log stops, 1830s, 25x22x24" 1,000.00
Suspenders, wht cotton, MOP buttons, NL, 23½x2" 450.00
Swift, maple, orig pnt, 1870s, 26" 450.00
Table, sewing; butternut/pine, 3-drw, NL, 26x28x18" 17,000.00
Table, work; cherry/pine, red pnt, nailed, 1840s, 27x36x22" 950.00
Table, work; cherry/pine, red stain, 2-drw, 1830s, 35" L 36,000.00
Table, work; maple/birch, trn legs, EF, 1840s, 38x16x15" 3,750.00
Washstand, butternut/pine, dvtl gallery, 1-drw, 1840s, 37" 1,200.00
Washstand, pine, orig yel stain, towel bar, NL, 1830s, 52" 3,250.00

Shaving Mugs

In the 1860s it became a popular practice for every man who shaved to have his own special shaving mug. Mugs belonging to men who frequented the barber shop for their tonsorial services were often personalized with their owner's name and kept on display on the barber's shelf. Occupational shaving mugs became the high point of individualism during this period. China mugs, mostly made in France, Germany, and Austria, were imported by American barber-supply companies where artists hand painted the occupation or the fraternal or sports affiliation of its customer on the mug. Often his name was added in gold. Because of sanitary rules and restrictions imposed around 1915, these personalized mugs were eventually taken off the barbers' shelves. Today occupational shaving mugs are the most valuable. Although some are valued by the excellence of the artist, most are priced by the rarity of the subject matter.

Advertising, Use Tonique DeLuxe, gold traces, Limoges 75.00
Capitol Building, much gold, early 1900s, EX 100.00
Cherubs, gold trim, Victoria, sm, NM 50.00
Flowers & name w/much gold, T&V Limoges, NM 40.00
Fraternal, Knights of Pythias emblem, T&V Limoges, NM 75.00
Fraternal, Masonic Lodge emblem, NM gold 75.00
Fraternal, Masonic Royal Arch Keystone, T&V, EX 95.00
Fraternal, Odd Fellows emblem, EX gold, T&V Limoges 50.00
Fraternal, Odd Fellows Lodge, lg eye, CA Smith, NM 125.00
Fraternal, Patriotic Order Sons of Am, Washington/swords, EX ...115.00
Horses in field, EX details & gold, NM 100.00
Lady's portrait in reserve, lt wear 175.00
Man being groomed by woman & child, parian, 1900s, VG 150.00
Occupational, artist, brushes & palette, EX gold 200.00

Occupational, bartender, barroom scene, Germany, M 600.00
Occupational, bartender, man making toast, 1914, EX 280.00
Occupational, baseball player, ball scene, 1900s, EX gold 900.00
Occupational, baseball player, man at bat, Otto Taylor, EX 1,320.00
Occupational, billiard player at table, KT&K, 1920, EX 440.00
Occupational, blksmith, man shoeing horse, worn gold 300.00
Occupational, bricklayer, man on scaffolding, CA Smith, NM ..700.00
Occupational, carpenter, man w/tools at bench, Germany, NM ...400.00
Occupational, carpenter, men at workbench, M gold 250.00
Occupational, cattleman, bull's head, EX gold, 1900s 100.00
Occupational, cattleman, steer, worn gold, Limoges, EX 250.00
Occupational, delivery man, man w/coal cart & horses, T&V ...325.00
Occupational, dentist, set of teeth, EX gold 550.00
Occupational, doctor, horse & buggy, MIG, EX gold 250.00
Occupational, draftsman, tools w/much gold, 1900s, M 325.00
Occupational, driver, horse & wagon, mc/gold, Austria, NM 500.00
Occupational, grocer, store scene, Koken, M gold 1,300.00
Occupational, gymnast, man doing chin-up, NM gold, sm stain 800.00
Occupational, horse breeder, horse's head, T&V France, EX 125.00

Occupational, horse-drawn grocery wagon, owner's name, gold trim, Vienna Austria, minor wear, $650.00; Horse-drawn coal wagon, owner's name, gold trim, $650.00.

Occupational, house painter, can & brushes, much gold 395.00
Occupational, hunter, dog on point/birds on bk, 3", NM 200.00
Occupational, mason, tools encircled in flowers, Germany, NM ..450.00
Occupational, musician, violin & bow, much gold, Haviland 375.00
Occupational, oil driller, man by derrick/etc, much gold 575.00
Occupational, pool player, table & balls, Bavaria, NM 1,750.00
Occupational, seaman, Battleship Maine, Limoges, EX 1,500.00
Occupational, seaman, man waving flags, T&V, NM 650.00
Occupational, tailor, treadle sewing machine, worn gold, EX 400.00
Occupational, telegrapher, key/birds on branch, Austria 300.00
Occupational, trainman, train scene, WG&Co France, NM 700.00
Occupational, watchmaker, watch & chain w/gold, EX 495.00

Shawnee

The Shawnee Pottery Company operated in Zanesville, Ohio, from 1937 to 1961. They produced inexpensive novelty ware (vases, flowerpots, and figurines) as well as a very successful line of figural cookie jars, creamers, and salt and pepper shakers.

They also produced three dinnerware lines, the first of which, Valencia, was designed by Louise Bauer in 1937 for Sears & Roebuck. A starter set was given away with the purchase of one of their refrigerators. Second and most popular was the King Corn line. It was produced from 1946 to 1954, when the colors were changed to a lighter yellow for the kernels and darker green for the shucks. This variation was called Queen Corn. Their third dinnerware line, produced after 1954, was called Lobsterware. It was made in either black, brown, or gray;

lobsters were usually applied to serving pieces and accessory items.

For further study we recommend these books: *The Collector's Guide to Shawnee Pottery* by our advisors, Janice and Duane Vanderbuilt, who are listed in the Directory under Indiana; and *Collecting Shawnee Pottery, A Pictorial Reference and Price Guide*, by Mark Supnick (see Directory under Florida). Watch for a book due out in late '93 or early '94 by Jim and Bev Mangus; it will include planters and vases.

Cookie Jars

Bean Pot Snowflake, pot shape w/emb snowflakes, USA 50.00

Cookie jar, Lucky Elephant, gold trim and flowers, $350.00.

Cottage, mk USA 6, minimum value	400.00
Drum Major, mk USA 10, minimum value	150.00
Dutch Boy, cold pnt, mk USA, minimum value	50.00
Dutch Boy, dbl stripes on pants, mk USA, minimum value	125.00
Dutch Boy, patches on pants, gold trim, mk USA	225.00
Dutch Girl, gold decals, mk USA, minimum value	200.00
Dutch Girl, paint under glaze, mk USA, minimum value	75.00
Fruit Basket, mk Shawnee 84, minimum value	125.00
Hexagon Basketweave, 6-sided, w/decals & gold trim, USA	100.00
Jo Jo the Clown, gold trim, mk Shawnee 12, minimum value	300.00
Jug, bl w/cold-pnt flowers, mk USA, minimum value	75.00
Jug, gr, mk USA, minimum value	75.00
Little Chef, gr, mk USA, minimum value	75.00
Little Chef, wht w/gold trim, mk USA, minimum value	150.00
Muggsy, gr scarf, w/decals & gold, mk Pat Muggsy USA	700.00
Owl, gold trim, mk USA, minimum value	225.00
Owl, mk USA, minimum value	125.00
Pink Elephant, mk Shawnee 60, minimum value	80.00
Puss 'n Boots, tail behind ft, minimum value	150.00
Puss 'n Boots, tail over ft, decals & gold, mk, minimum value	275.00
Sailor Boy, blond hair, gold trim, mk USA, minimum value	400.00
Sitting Elephant, cold pnt, mk USA, minimum value	75.00
Sitting Elephant, decals & gold trim, mk USA, minimum value	350.00
Smiley the Pig, bl bib, mk USA, minimum value	150.00
Smiley the Pig, chrysanthemums, mk USA, minimum value	150.00
Smiley the Pig, gold w/decals, mk USA	225.00
Smiley the Pig, tulips on pants, mk USA, minimum value	150.00
Winnie the Pig, bl collar, gold trim, mk USA, minimum value	250.00
Winnie the Pig, clover bud, mk Pat Winnie USA	200.00
Winnie the Pig, red collar, gold trim, mk USA, minimum value	250.00

Corn Line

Bowl, fruit; 6"	25.00
Bowl, mixing; 5"	22.00
Bowl, mixing; 6½"	25.00
Bowl, mixing; 8"	35.00

Butter dish	45.00
Casserole, #74, lg	55.00
Casserole, ind	50.00
Casserole, 1½-qt	35.00
Cookie jar	130.00
Creamer	20.00
Creamer & sugar bowl, ind	35.00
Pitcher, lg	50.00
Plate, dinner; 10"	35.00
Platter, 12"	45.00
Saucer, #91	10.00
Shakers, 3½", pr	12.00
Shakers, 5¼", pr	20.00
Sugar bowl, w/lid	20.00
Teapot, 30-oz	65.00

Kitchenware

Coffeepot, Sunflower, marked USA, $100.00.

Fernware, batter pitcher	45.00
Fernware, matchbox, wall hanging	65.00
Fernware, salt box	50.00
Fernware, shakers, sm, pr	15.00
Fernware, teapot, lg	40.00
Snowflake, bowls, nesting set of 5	75.00
Snowflake, shakers, pr	12.00
Snowflake, teapot, ind	25.00
Valencia, candle holder, bulb	15.00
Valencia, chocolate cup & saucer	65.00
Valencia, chop plate, 15"	35.00
Valencia, egg cup	12.00
Valencia, ice pitcher	25.00
Valencia, relish tray	75.00
Valencia, sugar bowl, w/lid	20.00
Valencia, teacup & saucer	30.00
Valencia, teapot	40.00

Miscellaneous

Candle holders, cornucopia form, mk USA, pr	12.00
Figurine, deer	65.00
Figurine, Oriental boy, mk USA, #602	12.00
Figurine, Oriental girl w/parasol, gold trim, mk USA, #601	15.00
Figurine, rabbit	35.00
Figurine, raccoon	35.00
Figurine, squirrel	35.00
Pitcher, mk USA, #808	17.50

Pitcher, water; mini **7.50**
Pitcher, water; on a log, mini **12.00**
Planter, Bow Knot, mk USA **6.00**
Planter, boy w/chicken, #645 ....**20.00**
Planter, clown, mk USA, #607 ....**22.50**
Planter, cockatiel, #523 ....**7.50**
Planter, donkey w/basket, #722 ....**17.50**
Planter, fish figural, gold trim, mk USA, #717 ....**55.00**
Planter, hound & pekingese, gold trim, mk USA, #611 .....**25.00**
Planter, mouse w/cheese, mk USA, #705 ....**25.00**
Planter, rickshaw, mk USA, #539 ....**7.50**
Vase, bud; emb flowers, mk USA, #875 ....**6.00**
Vase, bud; gold trim & decals, mk Shawnee USA, #865 ....**22.00**
Vase, bud; integral hdls, mk USA, #1178 ....**14.00**
Vase, cornucopia; mini **7.50**
Vase, cornucopia; mk USA, #835 ....**7.50**
Vase, swan, mini **7.50**
Vase, swan figural, mk USA, #806 ....**18.00**

Shearwater

Since 1928, generations of the Peter, Walter, and James McConnell Anderson families have been producing figurines and artwares in their studio at Ocean Springs, Mississippi. Their work is difficult to date. Figures from the twenties and thirties won critical acclaim and have continued to be made to the present time. Early marks include a die-stamped 'Shearwater' in a dime-sized circle, a similar ink stamp, and a half-circle mark. Any older item may still be ordered in the same glazes as it was originally produced, so many pieces on the market today may be relatively new. However, the older marks are not currently in use. Retail sales are available at the pottery or by mail order. Black figures and pirates are usually valued at $35.00 – $50.00.

Bowl, metallic, 6" **25.00**
Cup & saucer, Oriental decor, gr **35.00**
Figurine, Blk man carrying bag/cane/basket, mc, mk, 4" **50.00**
Teapot, dusty gr, hand trn, appl hdl & spout, imp mk, 6" **65.00**
Vase, pelicans emb, Deco style, lav/brn flecks, 7" **495.00**
Vase, turq/bl/periwinkle flambe, die-stamp mk, thrown, 8" **150.00**

Sheet Music

Sheet music is often collected more for the colorful lithographed covers rather than for the music itself. Transportation songs, which have pictures or illustrations of trains, ships, and planes; ragtime tunes, which feature popular entertainers such as Al Jolson; or those with Disney characters are among the most valuable. Much of the sheet music on the market today is valued at under $5.00; some of the better examples are listed here. Our advisor for this category is Jeannie Peters; she is listed in the Directory under Ohio.

All Aboard for Santa Claus, Santa on train, 1939, EX **12.00**
America Forever March, ET Paull Liberty cover, 1898 ....**12.00**
Anything Goes, Cary Grant/Alexis Smith, ca 1946, EX **6.00**
Aunt Jemima, drawing cover, EX **10.00**
Blue Shadows on the Trail, cartoon cover, ca 1948, EX **15.00**
Boy Scouts on Parade, Scout cover **8.00**
Burning of Rome, volcano cover, ET Paull, EX **12.50**
California Here I Come, Al Jolson cover, 1923, EX **10.00**
Chant of the Jungle, Joan Crawford cover, ca 1929, EX **6.00**
Don't Be Like That, Helen Kane cover, EX **12.50**

Dapper Dan from Dixie Land, $12.50.

Give Me a Band & My Baby, ladies' legs dancing, 1955, M **9.00**
How Are You Green Backs?, Magnus cover of ragged bum, 1860s ...**24.00**
I Didn't Raise My Boy To Be a Solider, WWI, EX **3.00**
I Don't Believe in Rumors, Sinatra cover, 1943, VG **6.00**
If I'm Not at Roll Call Kiss Mother Goodbye for Me, WWI, EX **3.00**
In My Merry Oldsmobile, car & passengers color drawing, EX **9.00**
It's All Over Now, marching troop cover, 1918, EX **3.50**
Johnny Over the Sea, pictorial wraps, 1917, 3-pg, EX **28.00**
Just Kiss Yourself Good-Bye, comic Starmer cover, EX **12.50**
Kinda Lonesome, Dorothy Lamour cover, ca 1939, EX **20.00**
Laugh Clown Laugh, Lon Chaney as clown on cover, 1928, VG **5.00**
Louisville You, Yellen & Ager, Deco cover, EX **5.00**
Lovable & Sweet, Betty Compson cover, 1929, EX **10.00**
Ma Curly-headed Baby, plantation cover, 1897, EX **7.50**
Marine Hymn, marine w/submachine gun, WWII, EX **6.00**
Moon Is Low, Joan Crawford cover, ca 1930, VG **5.00**
Night at the Opera, Marx Bros **22.00**
No Village Like Mine, man & woman embracing, 1943, NM **7.00**
Oh Jeff! Oh Jeff! How Are You?, colored Magnus cover, 1860s **28.00**
On the Good Ship Lollipop, Shirley Temple cover, EX **15.00**
Our Hero, dedicated to Captain Charles Lindbergh **12.50**
Pretty Girl Is Like a Melody, Irving Berlin, 1919, EX **5.00**
Sailor Beware, Bing Crosby/Ethel Merman cover, ca 1935, EX **5.00**
Soldier in the Grey, printed cover, 1908, 2-pg, EX **15.00**
Teddy Bear March, piano music (no words), Teddy bear cover **10.00**
That Mysterious Rag, woman playing piano, 1911, EX **10.00**
That Night in Araby, Rudolph Valentino cover, ca 1926, EX **10.00**
Two Cigarettes in the Dark, Jimmy Dorsey cover, 1941, VG **5.00**
When Flowers Bloom on No Man's Land..., angel cover, WWI **3.50**
When I Get Back from Over There, soldier & girl cover, '18, EX ...**10.00**
4 Little Blackberries, Blk children (drawing) cover, EX **20.00**

Shelley

In 1872 Joseph Shelley became partners with James Wileman, owner of Foley China Works, thus creating Wileman & Co. in Stoke-on-Trent. Twelve years later James Wileman withdrew from the company, though the firm continued to use his name until 1925 when it became known as Shelley Potteries, Ltd. Like many successful 19th-century English potteries, this firm continued to produce useful household wares as well as dinnerware of considerable note. In 1896 the beautiful Dainty White shape was introduced, and it is regarded by many as synonymous with the name Shelley. In addition to the original Dainty 6-Flute design, other lovely shapes were produced: 12-Flute, 14-Flute, Oleander, Queen Anne, and the more modern shapes of Vogue, Regent, and Eve.

Though often overlooked, striking earthenware was produced

under the direction of Frederick Rhead and later Walter Slater and his son Eric. Many notable artists contributed their talents in designing unusual, attractive wares: Rowland Morris, Mabel Lucie Attwell (identified by her initials in the following listings), and Hilda Cowham, to name a few.

In 1966 Allied English Potteries acquired control of the Shelley Company, and by 1967 the last of the exquisite Shelley China had been produced to honor remaining overseas orders. In 1971, Allied English Potteries merged with the Doulton group. The name Shelley China, Ltd., still exists, and it has been reported that Royal Doulton has produced trial wares bearing the Shelley backstamp. Our advisors for this category are Lila and Fred Shrader; they are listed in the Directory under California.

Ashtray, Bridal Rose, 3½" dia 20.00
Ashtray, Dainty Pink, 4½" sq 25.00
Ashtray, Heraldic w/flags, 4½" sq 18.00
Ashtray, Lilac Time, 3½" dia 25.00

Blue Rock, cup and saucer, $52.50; egg cup, small, $52.00.

Bowl, cereal; Begonia, 6½" 35.00
Bowl, cereal; Blue Rock, 6½" 35.00
Bowl, cereal; Dainty Pink, 6½" 39.00
Bowl, cereal; Phlox in Regent shape, 6¾" 25.00
Bowl, cream soup; Bridal Rose, Oleander, +underplate 65.00
Bowl, cream soup; Dainty Blue, +underplate 75.00
Bowl, cream soup; Regency, +underplate 50.00
Bowl, sauce; Dainty Blue, 5½" 30.00
Bowl, sauce; Harebell, Oleander shape, 5½" 30.00
Bowl, sauce; Heavenly Blue, 6-flute 30.00
Bowl, sauce; Iris, Regent shape, 5½" 22.00
Bowl, soup; Dainty Blue, rimmed, 8" 65.00
Bowl, soup; Regency, rimmed, 8" 50.00
Bowl, soup; Wildflowers, rimmed, 8" 60.00
Bowl, vegetable; Begonia, oval, 9½" 75.00
Bowl, vegetable; Dainty Blue, oval, 9½" 85.00
Bowl, vegetable; Heavenly Blue, oval, 9½" 85.00
Bowl, vegetable; Primrose, 6-flute, oval, 9½" 85.00
Bowl, vegetable; Regency, w/lid, 11" dia 175.00
Bowl, vegetable; Swirl, Regent shape, oval, 11" 110.00
Box, Dainty Blue, w/lid, 4x5½" 110.00
Butter dish, Blue Rock, oblong, 6-flute, w/lid 95.00
Butter dish, Blue Rock, 6-flute, rnd, w/lid 125.00
Butter dish, Bridal Rose, 6-flute, rnd, w/lid 125.00
Butter dish, Hedgerow, rnd, w/lid 65.00
Butter dish, Sheraton, oblong, w/lid 60.00
Butter pat, Archway of Roses 45.00

Butter pat, Campanula, 6-flute 55.00
Butter pat, Hibiscus 45.00
Butter pat, Rosebud 45.00
Butter pat, Rosebud, 6-flute 55.00
Cake plate, Begonia, ped ft, 6-flute, 8" 165.00
Cake plate, Blue Rock, tab hdls, 6-flute, 9" sq 75.00
Cake plate, Celandine, ped ft, 6-flute, 8" 165.00
Cake plate, Heavenly Blue, ped ft, 6-flute, 8" 185.00
Cake plate, Mabel Lucie Attwell, tab hdls, 6-flute, 9" sq 150.00
Cake plate, Primrose, tab hdls, 6-flute, 9" sq 79.00
Cake plate, Rose Arches, Queen Anne shape, 9" sq 145.00
Candle holder, Festival of Empire, w/match holder 225.00
Candle holder, Indian Peony, w/metal ring 85.00
Candle holder, Jazz Circles, 9" 95.00
Candle holder, Rose-Pansy-Forget-Me-Not, w/metal insert 50.00
Candy dish, Blue Iris, 6-flute, 5" sq 28.00
Candy dish, Blue Rock, 6-flute, 5" dia 32.00
Candy dish, Bridal Rose, scroll-like shape, 7" 55.00
Candy dish, Bridal Rose, 6-flute, 5" sq 32.00
Candy dish, HP fruit on lid, 8½" 65.00
Candy dish, Old Bowl, tab hdls, w/lid, 5½" dia 65.00
Chamber set, blk matt w/mc enamel flowers, +5 sm pcs 115.00
Chamber set, Cloisonne, pitcher+bowl+4 sm pcs 145.00
Cheese dish, Bridal Rose, 6-flute, oval 185.00
Children's ware, bowl, Hilda Cowham, Pussy Cat decor, 8½" 110.00
Children's ware, bowl, Hilda Cowham, Ride a...Horse..., 6x9" 95.00
Children's ware, bowl, Jack & Jill decor 110.00
Children's ware, cup & saucer, Mabel Lucie Attwell, pixies 135.00
Children's ware, egg cup, Hilda Cowham, toy train scene 50.00
Children's ware, jug, Mabel Lucie Attwell, Fairy Folk, 3½" 90.00
Children's ware, plate, Hilda Cowham, puppy & kittens, 8" 50.00
Children's ware, plate, Mabel Lucy Attwell, Cowboy James, 7" ...95.00
Children's ware, plate, naval scene, 8" 35.00
Chocolate pot, Dainty Blue, sm 145.00
Chocolate pot, Harmony Ware, 7½" 125.00
Chocolate pot, Regency, 7½" 125.00
Cigarette holder, Dainty White 20.00
Cigarette holder, Wild Anenome, 6-flute 50.00
Coffeepot, Daffodil Time, med 160.00
Coffeepot, Dainty Blue, lg 225.00
Coffeepot, Tulips, Eve shape, lg 145.00
Coffeepot, Wisteria, Regent shape, lg 165.00
Comport, Moonlight decor, 9" 250.00
Comport, Moorcroft style, 9" 325.00
Condiment set, Dainty Blue, shakers+mustard w/lid+tray 195.00
Creamer & sugar bowl, Blue Rock, 6-flute, med 65.00
Creamer & sugar bowl, Blue Rock, 6-flute, w/lid, lg 110.00
Creamer & sugar bowl, Celandine, 6-flute, w/lid, med............85.00
Creamer & sugar bowl, Dainty White, med 45.00
Creamer & sugar bowl, Garland of Flowers, Queen Anne, w/lid ..135.00
Creamer & sugar bowl, Heavenly Blue, 6-flute, lg 75.00
Creamer & sugar bowl, Rosebud, 6-flute, med, +tray 145.00
Creamer & sugar bowl, sm Pansies, 6-flute, ind 65.00
Creamer & sugar bowl, Violets, 6-flute, med, +tray 185.00
Cup & saucer, Archway of Roses, Queen Anne shape 60.00
Cup & saucer, Begonia, 6-flute 50.00
Cup & saucer, Blue Rock, 6-flute, farmer 65.00
Cup & saucer, Bluebell Wood, 6-flute 55.00
Cup & saucer, Bridal Rose, 6-flute, mini 125.00
Cup & saucer, Campanula, 12-flute 52.00
Cup & saucer, demitasse; Bridal Rose, 6-flute 52.00
Cup & saucer, demitasse; Celandine, 12-flute 50.00
Cup & saucer, demitasse; Country Bluebell, Queen Anne shape ..55.00
Cup & saucer, demitasse; Dainty White 42.00

Cup & saucer, demitasse; Georgian 35.00
Cup & saucer; demitasse; Indian Peony, Gainsborough 45.00
Cup & saucer, demitasse; My Garden, Queen Anne shape 60.00
Cup & saucer, demitasse; Shamrock, 6-flute 52.00
Cup & saucer, DuBarry, Gainsborough shape 40.00
Cup & saucer, Eastern Star emblem, Queen Anne shape 35.00
Cup & saucer, gr dots on Dainty White 60.00
Cup & saucer, Harebell, Oleander shape 50.00
Cup & saucer, Heavenly Pink, 6-flute 55.00
Cup & saucer, heraldic design, 6-flute 45.00
Cup & saucer, Iris, 6-flute 55.00
Cup & saucer, Lakeland, Regent shape 55.00
Cup & saucer, Lily of the Valley, Mocha shape 50.00
Cup & saucer, Martian, Eve shape, gold hdl 55.00
Cup & saucer, Melody Chintz, Henley shape 52.00
Cup & saucer, Pansy, 6-flute 55.00
Cup & saucer, Primrose Chintz, Oleander shape 60.00
Cup & saucer, Rosebud, 6-flute 52.00
Cup & saucer, scenics, 6-flute 55.00
Cup & saucer, Syringa, Regent shape 52.00
Cup & saucer, Woodland Bluebells, Queen Anne shape 65.00
Egg cup, Anenome, sm 45.00
Egg cup, Blue Rock, 6-flute, lg 65.00
Egg cup, Dainty Blue, sm 50.00
Egg cup, Rose-Pansy-Forget-Me-Not, 6-flute, sm 45.00
Egg cup set, Rosebud, 4 sm cups on indented 6x6" plate 325.00
Gravy boat, Heavenly Blue, 6-flute, w/underplate 175.00
Gravy boat, Martian, Vogue shape, w/underplate 225.00
Gravy boat, Peaches & Grapes, Queen Anne shape, w/underplate ..185.00
Gravy boat, Regency, w/underplate 130.00

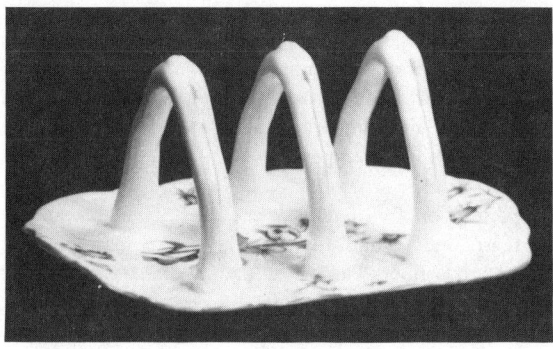

Harebell, toast rack, $65.00.

Horseradish container, Iris, 6-flute, w/underplate & lid 110.00
Horseradish container, Lilac Time, 6-flute, w/underplate & lid ...135.00
Jam container, Hibiscus, 6-flute, w/underplate & lid 110.00
Jam container, Mayfair, w/lid 65.00
Kitchen reminder, 'vegetable' people, 6x8" 95.00
Lamp base, Harmony Drip Ware, 11½" 185.00
Lamp base, Kingfisher pattern, 12" 125.00
Mug, Bridal Rose, 6-flute, 4¾" 75.00
Mug, Honeysuckle, 6-flute, 4¾" 85.00
Mug, sm Pansies, 6-flute, 3¾" 50.00
Mustard container, Harmony Ware, w/lid 65.00
Mustard container, Shamrock, 6-flute, w/underplate & lid 95.00
Mustard container, Thompkins Ltd, w/lid 75.00
Napkin ring, Celandine 55.00
Pitcher, cow figural, 6" 165.00
Pitcher, Harmony Drip Ware, 7½" 95.00
Pitcher, Lilac Time, 6-flute, 7" 110.00

Pitcher, utilitary ware, bl stripes at base, 8½" 75.00
Plate, Archway of Roses, Queen Anne shape, 8" 45.00
Plate, Bands & Shades, 9" 35.00
Plate, Blue Rock, 6-flute, 10½" 65.00
Plate, Campanula, 6-flute, 8" 42.00
Plate, Columbine, Sterling shape, 8" 15.00
Plate, Dainty Blue, 10½" 75.00
Plate, Drifting Leaves, 10" 35.00
Plate, Duchess, 6" 12.00
Plate, Forget-Me-Nots, 6-flute, 8" 45.00
Plate, Garland of Flowers, Queen Anne shape, 10¼" 75.00
Plate, Glorious Devon, 6-flute, 6" 30.00
Plate, Hibiscus, 6-flute, 8" 45.00
Plate, Horn of Flowers, Mode shape, 8½" 50.00
Plate, Indian Peony, 10½" 55.00
Plate, Maytime, Henley shape, 8" 55.00
Plate, Melody Chintz, Henley shape, 8" 55.00
Plate, Pansy Spray, 6-flute, 10½" 65.00
Plate, Primrose Chintz, Oleander shape, 8" 50.00
Plate, Rosebud, Ludlow shape, 14-flute, 8" 40.00
Plate, Wild Anenome, 6-flute, 10½" 75.00
Platter, Blue Rock, 6-flute, 16x14" 225.00
Platter, Bridal Rose, 6-flute, 14" dia 225.00
Platter, Dainty White, 12x9" 75.00
Platter, Drifting Leaves, 12x9" 85.00
Platter, Duchess, 12x10" 75.00
Platter, Garden Urn, Queen Anne shape, 12½x10" 175.00
Platter, Regency, 6-flute, 14" dia 175.00
Platter, Rose Arches, Queen Anne shape, 14x12" 210.00
Pudding mold, geometric shape, 7½" 75.00
Relish, Campanula, 6-flute, 8x5" 72.00
Relish, Primrose, 6-flute, 8x5" 75.00
Shakers, Bridal Rose, pear shape, 3½", pr 79.00
Shakers, Celandine, cylindrical, 6-flute, 3½", pr 85.00
Shakers, Regency, cylindrical, 6-flute, 3½", pr 65.00
Snack set, Dainty Blue, cup+8" sq indented plate 75.00
Snack set, Dainty White, cup+8" sq indented plate 50.00
Snack set, Primrose, 6-flute, cup+8" rnd indented plate 75.00
Tea & toast set, Begonia, 6-flute, cup+6x9" tray 65.00
Tea & toast set, Dainty Green, 6-flute, cup+6x9" tray 85.00
Tea & toast set, Wild Anenome, 6-flute, cup+5x8" tray 85.00
Teapot, Archway of Roses, Queen Anne shape shape, lg 195.00
Teapot, Begonia, 6-flute, med 210.00
Teapot, bl w/gold hdl & finial, 6-flute, med 225.00
Teapot, bl w/mc flower hdl, 6-flute, med 225.00
Teapot, Dainty White w/sm bl polka dots, sm 225.00
Teapot, Drifting Leaves, Gainsborough shape, med 145.00
Teapot, Harebell, Oleander shape, lg 185.00
Teapot, Hedgerow, Gainsborough shape, lg 160.00
Teapot, Morning Glory, 6-flute, sm 195.00
Teapot, Regency, 6-flute, lg 195.00
Toast rack, Harmony Ware 72.00
Toast rack, Primrose, lg 75.00
Tray, tea; Regency, 6-flute, 18" 375.00
Tray, triple; Rosebud, 6-flute, w/hdl, lg 175.00
Tureen, Dainty Blue, 6-flute, w/hdls & lid 385.00
Vase, blk matt w/mc enamel-like flowers, 7" 75.00
Vase, Harmony Ware, bulbous, 5½" 50.00
Vase, Moorcroft style, bulbous, 8" 475.00

Silhouettes

Silhouette portraits were made by positioning the subject between a bright light and a sheet of white drawing paper. The resulting shadow was then traced and cut out, the paper mounted over a contrasting color and framed. The hollow-cut process was simplified by an invention called the Physiognotrace, a device that allowed tracing and cutting to be done in one operation. Experienced silhouette artists could do full-length figures, scenics, ships, or trains freehand. Some of the most famous of these artists were Charles Peale Polk, Charles Wilson Peale, William Bache, Doyle, Edouart, Chamberlain, Brown, and William King. Though not often seen, some silhouettes were completely painted or executed in wax. Examples listed here are hollow-cut unless noted.

Key:
bk — backing
c/p — cut and pasted
fl — full length
p — profile
wc — watercolor

Three children with toys, cat and dog, inscribed with their names and ages, cut paper applied to a watercolor and ink background, signed Edouart, 1842, 7x14", $2,100.00.

Family, fl, 5 people, giltwood fr, 12x19" 750.00
Gent, c/p, p, emb brass fr, 4½x3¾" 100.00
Gent in frock coat, fl, c/p, ink detail, fr, 7x5", VG 150.00
Gent in tailcoat, fl, c/p, gilt fr, 6½x5¾" 250.00
Gent w/wig, frilly shirt front, p, emb Peale, fold, 8x7" 150.00
Girl, ink/wc, bl dress/wht collar, gilt brass/wood fr, 5x4½" 325.00
Girl, p, EX cutting/ink detail, cloth bk, 5x4" 275.00
Girl, p, faint mk (att Peale), pine fr, 5x4½" 150.00
Jonathan Trumbull, rvpt p, 1780, ogee bird's-eye fr, 7x8½" 280.00
Lady, p, blk cloth bk, emb Peale, dk paper, 8x6" 150.00
Lady w/elaborate coiffure, ink on paper, stains, 6x5" 120.00
Man, top hat/riding crop, fl, litho bk, identified, 17x12" 775.00
Man (& lady), p, ink detail, emb brass fr, 5x4", pr, EX 900.00
Man (& lady), p, mk 1822 Eractin Barnes, 6x5", pr 250.00
Man (& lady), p, rvpt glass/blk molded fr, 6x8", pr 395.00
Man in top hat, ink, fl, gilt detail, poor paper, 13x10" 85.00
Man w/checked pants, ink/gouache/gilt, fl, 11x9" 200.00
Man w/top hat, c/p, fl, identified, mk Clarke, 1850, 12x10" 150.00

Silver

Coin Silver

The mark 'Coin Silver' was used after the 1830s to indicate items made with 900 parts of silver to every 1000 parts of content.

C Boyce, NY; sugar bowl, fluted urn form w/dome lid, 9½" 330.00

Davis-Palmer Co, Boston; ewer, appl acanthus bands, 9" 300.00
Duhme & Co, butter knife, twisted detail, eng blade/hdl, 8" 160.00
Duhme & Co, ladle, twisted/eng hdl w/inscription, 13" 360.00
E Benjamin, New Haven CT; tongs, ca 1840 .... 50.00
J Jones, pitcher, bud finial, fluted/gadrooned body, 9", EX 880.00
Jones-Ball-Poor, entree dish, Geo III style, 63-oz 1,400.00
Jones-Ball-Poor, salver, eng, shaped edge, scroll ft, 14-oz 330.00
Newel Harding Co, Boston; tray, oak leaf border, crest, 21" ... 4,400.00
Wood & Hughes, berry spoon, medallion pattern, monogram 165.00

Flatware

Silver flatware is being collected today either to replace missing pieces of heirloom sets or, in lieu of buying new patterns, by those who admire and appreciate the style and quality of the older ware. Prices vary from dealer to dealer; some pieces are harder to find and are therefore more expensive. Items such as olive spoons, cream ladles, lemon forks, etc., once thought a necessary part of a silver service, may today be slow to sell; as a result, dealers may price them low and make up the difference on items that sell more readily. Many factors enter into evaluation. Popular patterns may be high due to demand though easily found, while scarce patterns may be passed over by collectors who find them difficult to reassemble. See also Tiffany, Silver.

Key:
FH — flat handle
HH — hollow handle
t-oz — troy ounce

Chantilly, bouillon spoon, Gorham 17.00
Chantilly, buffet fork, Gorham 45.00
Chantilly, demitasse spoon, Gorham 13.00
Chantilly, dinner fork, Gorham 32.00
Chantilly, dinner knife, Gorham 18.00
Chantilly, ice cream fork, Gorham 32.00
Chantilly, luncheon fork, Gorham 18.00
Chantilly, luncheon fork, Imperial 18.00
Chantilly, luncheon knife, Imperial 20.00
Chantilly, nut spoon, Gorham 26.00
Chantilly, tablespoon, Gorham 45.00
Chantilly, teaspoon, Gorham 13.00
Chrysanthemum, bonbon, Durgin 130.00
Chrysanthemum, lettuce fork, Durgin 230.00
Classic Rose, baby fork, Reed & Barton 12.00
Classic Rose, salad fork, Reed & Barton 20.00
Damask Rose, cold meat fork, Oneida 37.00
Damask Rose, flat butter spreader, Oneida 10.00
Damask Rose, gravy ladle, Oneida 37.00
Damask Rose, salad fork, Oneida 21.00
Damask Rose, tablespoon, Oneida 36.00
Dresden, fish slice, Whiting, 12" 295.00
Dresden, sardine fork, Whiting 65.00
El Grandee, gravy ladle, Towle 58.00
El Grandee, letter opener, Towle 28.00
El Grandee, luncheon knife, Towle 20.00
El Grandee, master butter spreader, Towle 29.00
El Grandee, salad fork, Towle 29.00
El Grandee, tablespoon, Towle 54.00
El Grandee, teaspoon, Towle 16.00
Flemish, roast carving set, Tiffany 120.00
Fleury, beef fork 40.00
Fleury, buffet fork, 10¼" 100.00
Fleury, gravy ladle 65.00
Francis I, pie server, Reed & Barton 95.00
Francis I, punch ladle, Reed & Barton 295.00

English King, Tiffany, twelve 6-piece place settings plus two tablespoons, $3,500.00.

Francis I, tablespoon, Reed & Barton 58.00
Francis I, tomato server, Reed & Barton 80.00
Frontenac, strawberry fork, Internat'l 17.00
Frontenac, teaspoon, Internat'l 16.00
Grande Baroque, bouillon spoon, Wallace 30.00
Grande Baroque, cake fork, Wallace 28.00
Grande Baroque, cheese server, HH, Wallace 30.00
Grande Baroque, cocktail fork, Wallace 26.00
Grande Baroque, cold meat fork, Wallace 70.00
Grande Baroque, cream soup, Wallace 35.00
Grande Baroque, gravy ladle, Wallace 60.00
Grande Baroque, place fork, Wallace 33.00
Grande Baroque, salad fork, Wallace 35.00
Grande Baroque, salad serving fork, Wallace 145.00
Grande Baroque, sauce ladle, Wallace 45.00
Grande Baroque, strawberry fork, Wallace 18.00
Grande Baroque, sugar spoon, Wallace 33.00
Grande Baroque, teaspoon, Wallace 16.00
Heiress, cream soup, Oneida 14.00
Heiress, iced teaspoon, Oneida 18.00
Heiress, salad fork, Oneida 18.00
Heiress, teaspoon, Oneida 12.00
Lancaster, chocolate spoon, Gorham 33.00
Lancaster, dinner knife, Gorham 45.00
Lancaster, luncheon fork, Gorham 14.00
Lancaster, pie server, Gorham 145.00
Lancaster, teaspoon, Gorham 20.00
Lotus, gravy ladle, Wallace 45.00
Lotus, luncheon knife, Wallace 18.00
Lotus, master butter spreader, Wallace 32.00
Lotus, olive fork, Wallace 17.00
Lotus, salad fork, Wallace 21.00
Lotus, sugar spoon, Wallace 19.00
Lotus, tablespoon, Wallace 39.00
Lotus, tomato server, Wallace 60.00
Louis XIV, carving fork, Towle 10.00
Louis XIV, flat butter knife, Towle 10.00
Louis XIV, salad fork, Towle 18.00
Louis XIV, sugar spoon, Towle 10.00
Love Disarmed, gravy ladle, Reed & Barton 115.00
Love Disarmed, ice cream server, Reed & Barton 55.00
Love Disarmed, tablespoon, Reed & Barton 115.00
Love Disarmed, toast server, Reed & Barton 275.00
Madeira, dinner fork, Towle 22.00

Madeira, jelly server, Towle 22.00
Madeira, luncheon knife, Towle 18.00
Madeira, master butter spreader, Towle 20.00
Madeira, salad fork, Towle 23.00
Madeira, sugar spoon, Towle 18.00
Madeira, tablespoon, Towle 35.00
Madeira, teaspoon, Towle 15.00
Mary Chilton, berry spoon, Towle 55.00
Mary Chilton, bonbon, Towle 22.50
Mary Chilton, flat butter spreader, Towle 12.00
Mary Chilton, jelly spoon, Towle 18.00
Mary Chilton, tablespoon, Towle 42.50
Meadow Rose, cold meat fork 58.00
Meadow Rose, demitasse spoon 16.00
Meadow Rose, dinner knife 28.00
Meadow Rose, salad fork 25.00
Meadow Rose, teaspoon 24.00
Mt Vernon, citrus spoon, Lunt 18.00
Mt Vernon, dinner knife, Lunt 10.00
Mt Vernon, jelly server, Lunt 18.00
Mt Vernon, luncheon fork, Lunt 14.00
Mt Vernon, teaspoon, Lunt 12.50
Repousse, bacon fork, S Kirk & Sons 65.00
Repousse, butter spreader, FH, S Kirk & Sons 20.00
Repousse, ice tongs, S Kirk & Sons 80.00
Repousse, lettuce fork, S Kirk & Sons 60.00
Repousse, pea spoon, S Kirk & Sons 92.00
Romance of Sea, cream soup, Wallace 35.00
Romance of Sea, flat butter spreader, Wallace 25.00
Romance of Sea, pickle fork, Wallace 28.00
Romance of Sea, place fork, Wallace 34.00
Rondo, cream soup, Gorham, sm 24.00
Rondo, luncheon fork, Gorham 23.00
Rondo, master butter spreader, Gorham 20.00
Rondo, sugar shell, Gorham 22.00
Rondo, teaspoon, Gorham 13.00
Rose, demitasse spoon, Stieff 14.00
Rose, lemon fork, Stieff 17.00
Rose, master butter spreader, FH 25.00
Rose, salad fork, Stieff 28.00
Rose, tablespoon, Stieff 45.00
Rose, teaspoon, Stieff 17.50
Rose Point, baby fork, Wallace 18.00
Rose Point, berry fork, Wallace 18.00
Rose Point, bonbon, Wallace 32.00
Rose Point, cocktail, Wallace 18.00
Rose Point, cream soup, Wallace 25.00
Rose Point, dinner knife, Wallace 25.00
Rose Point, lemon fork, Wallace 24.00
Rose Point, luncheon fork, Wallace 20.00
Rose Point, luncheon knife, Wallace 20.00
Rose Point, olive fork, Wallace 24.00
Rose Point, sugar spoon, Wallace 25.00
Rose Point, teaspoon, Wallace 16.00
Sir Christopher, cold meat fork 70.00
Sir Christopher, flat butter spreader 22.00
Sir Christopher, gravy ladle 60.00
Sir Christopher, iced teaspoon 28.00
Sir Christopher, luncheon fork 25.00
Spanish Lace, dinner knife, Wallace 12.00
Spanish Lace, gravy ladle, Wallace 36.00
Spanish Lace, luncheon fork, Wallace 22.00
Spanish Lace, salad fork, Wallace 18.00
Spanish Lace, sugar spoon, Wallace 18.00

Spanish Lace, tablespoon, Wallace 40.00
Spanish Lace, teaspoon, Wallace 15.00
Strasbourg, cream soup, Gorham 26.00
Strasbourg, iced teaspoon, Gorham 26.00
Strasbourg, tablespoon, Gorham 40.00
Strasbourg, teaspoon, Gorham 15.00
Waverly, demitasse spoon 8.00
Waverly, sherbet spoon 14.00
Wildflower, cream soup, Royal Crest 14.00
Wildflower, iced teaspoon, Royal Crest 22.50
Wildflower, luncheon fork, Royal Crest 18.00
Wildflower, luncheon knife, Royal Crest 12.00

Hollow Ware

Until the middle of the 19th century, the silverware produced in America was custom made on order of the buyer directly from the silversmith. With the rise of industrialization, factories sprung up that manufactured silverware for retailers who often added their trademark to the ware. Silver ore was mined in abundance, and demand spurred production. Changes in style occurred at the whim of fashion. Repousse decoration (relief work) became popular about 1885, reflecting the ostentatious preference of the Victorian era. Later in the century, Greek, Etruscan, and several classic styles found favor. Today the Art Deco styles of this century are very popular with collectors. In the listings that follow, manufacturer's name or trademark is noted first; in lieu of that information, listings are by item. Weight is given in troy ounces. See also Tiffany, Silver.

AFB, Germany; tankard, eng motif, rtcl apron, 1850s, 9" 500.00
Alvin, tray, oblong octagon, monogram, 18" 465.00
American, fruit bowl, rtcl border, sq ftd base, 1780s, 8" 200.00
Amiger, candy dish, wide floral repousse border 100.00
Bailey & Kitchen, waste bowl, leaf-eng rim/base, ftd, 6¾" 170.00
Ball-Blk & Co, compote, mythical bird detailed stem, 26-t-oz ...660.00
Benjamin Burt, tankard, flame finial, armorial, 1908, 9" 11,000.00
Cartier (retailer), tray, serpentine rim, 11" dia 250.00
Catherine Pratt, tray, rnd w/stylized paw ft, 1910, 6" 330.00
Chinese export, teapot, repousse dragon, 1880s, 14-t-oz 385.00
Continental, sugar box, bombe form, bright-cut, 9-t-oz 465.00
CR Ashbee, porringer, leaves where hdl joins body, 6" 1,300.00
Daniel Egan, Dublin; bowl, plain w/ring ft, 3½", 14-t-oz 770.00
De Matteo, sugar cube stand, blossom hdls, Jensen's style 60.00
Dominick & Haff, coffee set, eng floral/scrolls, 5-pc 1,900.00
Dominick & Haff, fruit bowl, rtcl/floral emb, ftd, 10" 220.00
Ebenezer Coker, salver, shell/scroll rim, hoof ft, rpr, 10" 465.00
Frank Smith, pitcher, ftd pear form w/repousse florals, 9" 1,000.00
French, sauce boat, mythical beast hdl, scrolls/florals, 8" 4,950.00
FW Smith Co, compote, rtcl sides, C-scroll rim, 7x10" 475.00
G Jensen, bowl, appl grapevines on base, #296E, 6" 8,800.00
G Jensen, bowl, base w/appl grapes, 4 ring/grapes hdls, 14" ...24,000.00
G Jensen, bowl, openwork ped w/leaves & berries, 8x10" 5,200.00

Georg Jensen 5-light candelabra in the Grape pattern, 10½", $11,000.00.

G Jensen, cigarette box, bud ft, foliate lid band, 9" L 4,400.00
G Jensen, cocktail shaker, stepped top/leafy finial, 13½" 2,600.00
G Jensen, coffee set, open hdls w/blossoms, 3-pc+14" tray 8,250.00
G Jensen, pitcher, water; hammered, rim extends to hdl, 11" .3,500.00
G Jensen, plate, Acorn, Rhode design, 10" 1,000.00
G Jensen, platter, Acorn, deep/circular, Rhode design, 14" 3,300.00
G Jensen, tea/coffee, Cosmos, fluted rims, by Rhode, 5-pc 7,700.00
G Jensen, tray, simple scrolls at rim, ivory hdls, 21" 6,600.00
G Townsend, Dublin; hot milk jug, rattan hdl, 1770s, 8½" 1,300.00
Geo Hanners, mug, scroll hdl, mid-band, 4¾" 5,500.00
Germany, goblet, Renaissance style, w/lid, 1800s, 11" 250.00
GJ DF in shield, bowl, boat form, rtcl foliage, '02, 30-t-oz 935.00
Goldsmiths & Silversmiths, teapot, paw ft, Regency, 6" 300.00
Gorham, cake tray, serpentine scroll border, 10½" 110.00
Gorham, candelabra, Danish Floral, 7½", pr 625.00
Gorham, comport, 4-lobed w/gallery, winged lion ft, 17-t-oz 440.00
Gorham, fruit bowl, floral/scroll repousse, 9" 120.00
Gorham, fruit bowl, rtcl, serpentine, 10½" dia 180.00
Gorham, fruit bowl, shell/scroll border, 10½" 180.00
Gorham, loving cup, shell borders/hdls, gilt int, 8½" 425.00
Gorham, mug, bbl form acid-etched Nouveau decor, 3⅝", EX ...385.00
Gorham, serving tray, Edgeworth, 12" 130.00
Gorham, tea/coffee, fluted Colonial Revival, 6-pc 2,300.00
Gorham, tray, chased/scrolled rim w/reserves, 15½" L 525.00
H Man, Germany; tankard, stippled/allover foliage, lid, 10" ...1,650.00
H&Cie, tea/coffee, octagonal forms, ca 1930, pot: 8" 1,650.00
Heer-Scofield, bowl, eng floral/scroll rim, 4 ball ft, 11" 100.00
International, bowl, Prelude, 9¾" 90.00
International, bowl, rnd on flaring ft, 9½" dia, 12-t-oz 125.00
International, tray, leaf form, 9" 150.00
J Dixon & Sons, tray, monogrammed, 26" 1,900.00
JE Caldwell, bowl, scroll-rtcl sides, lattice hdls, 14" L 300.00
Jenkins & Jenkins, tray, wavy rim w/repousse flowers, 12" 500.00
John Waite, cream jug, scroll hdl, eng initials, 1775, 2¾" 1,200.00
Joseph Lownes, teapot, pineapple finial, crest, 11" 2,300.00
JS Hunt, ewer, Cellini, presentation, 12" 1,700.00
Juhn Burt, cann, scroll hdl, baluster form, 4¼" 4,900.00
KCH, cocktail shaker, open vintage finial, 12", +12 cups 4,400.00
Kochi zo, tea set, allover repousse mums, dragon hdls, 4-pc 2,850.00
L Urouhart, Edinburgh; bowl, chased hunt scene/scrolls, 9" ...2,500.00
LeTelier, creamer, pear form w/crimped border, Phila/1770 ....2,000.00
Lincoln-Foss, pitcher, floral stem hdl/leaf spout, 10" 770.00
London, pap boat, Geo III, shell/scroll/floral border, 1790 ....230.00
M Fray, French; fluted, eng scrolls, female on hdl, 12½" 1,950.00
Mayo & Co, bowl, shaped edge w/foliage decor, 14" 360.00
Mexican, bowl, monteith; notched rim, ped ft, 1910, 6x9" 400.00
Mexican, cake stand, w/3 leaf-edged trays, folding, 71-t-oz 300.00
Mexican, platter, gadrooned serpentine rim, cast hdls, 21" 700.00
Mexico #925, sauce boat, scrolled rim, 12" L 250.00
Philadelphia, sugar urn, bright-cut festoons, 1800, 9" 825.00
Potter & Mellen, cocktail shaker+stirrer, by Miller, 9" 425.00
R Sibley, plate, cyma edge/gadrooned, eng armorial, 10" 350.00
Redlich, bowl, flared hexagonal floral-rtcl shaped rim, 12" 600.00
Redlich, tureen, boat form w/reeded scroll rim, 9", 57-t-oz 4,100.00
Reed & Barton, Francis I, compote, ftd, 8" dia, +12" tray 675.00
Reed & Barton, pitcher, octagonal w/etched foliage, 10" 875.00
Reed & Barton, tea service, Vogue, rib bands/hdls, 4-pc 6,000.00
Reed & Barton, teapot, Colonial Manor, pear form, 10" 225.00
Reed & Barton, vegetable dish, reed decor, 9" L 130.00
Robert & Wm Wilson, ewer, emb scrolls/acanthus, 16" 1,400.00
S Kirk, beaker, eng initial, molded ft/rim, 3½" 935.00
S Kirk, coffeepot, emb/eng scroll & floral cartouches, 11" 1,400.00
S Kirk & Son, candy tray, floral repousse border, 7½" 165.00
S Kirk & Son, compote, floral/grape/leaf emb border, 10" 725.00

S Kirk & Son, tea caddy, emb florals, ovoid, 1903, 4", 5-t-oz **365.00**
S Kirk & Son, tea caddy, floral repousse **400.00**
S Kirk & Son, tureen, repousse florals/pineapple finial, 11" **4,200.00**
S Kirk & Son, waste bowl, emb floral/berry, leaf ft, 16-t-oz **325.00**
S Kirk & Sons, wine coaster, Baltimore Rose, 6-t-oz **100.00**
Shreve, bowl, hammered, strapwork rim, 5", +undertray **425.00**
Shreve, dish, scalloped/floral-&-leaf chased edge, 16" L **375.00**
Simmons & Alexander, teapot, bright-cut monogram, 1800, 7"....**880.00**
Thos Swift, creamer, Geo III, invt pear w/beaded rim, 4½" **110.00**
Towle, tea/coffee, C-scroll moldings, 7-pc, 270-t-oz **4,400.00**
Tuttle, cocktail shaker, flagon form, inscr, 1942, 30-t-oz **330.00**
Wallace, fruit tray, reeded center & border, 10" dia **120.00**
Whiting, bowl, shells/foliage appl on ft, emb crabs, 9" **4,600.00**
Whiting, dish, rtcl scroll/shell rim, fluted sides, 9¾" **180.00**
Whiting, pitcher, chased rim, 1900s, 7½", 28-t-oz **440.00**
Wm Crowell, porringer, geometric pierced tab hdl, 6" **4,100.00**
Wm Fountain, bowl, molded rim/base, eng crest, 1804, 10-t-oz ..**770.00**
Wm Hollingshead, cann, acanthus-clad scroll hdl, 1770, 5" **550.00**
Wm Lawdery, jug, eng armorial, tiered finial, 1720s, 13" **21,000.00**

Silver Overlay

The silver overlay glass made during the 1800s was decorated with a cut-out pattern of sterling silver applied to the surface of the ware.

Bottle, scent; gr w/floral o/l, orig o/l stopper, 6" **995.00**
Bowl, clear w/fluted sides, lily-of-valley o/l, 12½" **140.00**
Decanter, perfume; clear, leaf/scroll o/l, monogram, 7", pr **150.00**
Decanter, perfume; emerald, leaf/scroll o/l, ball form, 4" **360.00**
Pitcher, amethyst, ribbon/garland o/l, ca 1920s, 7½" **160.00**
Pitcher, clear, geometric o/l, faceted stopper, 5½" **140.00**
Vase, gr w/floral o/l, bulbous, 10" **895.00**

Vase, green with intricate Nouveau floral overlay, marked, 12¼", **$800.00**.

Silverplate

Silverplated hollow ware is fast becoming the focus of attention for many of today's collectors. See also Pairpoint, Silverplate; Railroadiana, Silverplate.

Key: gw — gold wash

Hollow Ware

Basket, repousse florals/cherubs/etc, minor wear, 13½" **125.00**

Champagne bucket, band of roses, hdls, mk WMF, 9" **330.00**
Cocktail shaker, milk can form **40.00**
Desk set, Independence Hall Bicentennial repro, 10" L **85.00**
Hot water kettle on stand, mk PB&P Co, 1800s, no burner, 17" ..**135.00**
Hot water urn, Regency style, tapered form, 1880s, 21" **330.00**
Humidor, 2 cherubs hold match holder, Rogers & Smith **395.00**
Nut bowl, squirrel on branch as hdl, Reed & Barton **395.00**

Pitcher, hammered surface chased with foliage, applied with cast dragonflies, attributed to Reed and Barton, ca 1885, 8", **$1,800.00.**

Salver, 3 trefoil sections joined by triangle, Gallia, 11" **220.00**
Shakers, eng jug form w/hdls, pr **35.00**
Stirrup cup, fox head as base, eng horse head, 5½", 6 for **350.00**
Sugar spooner, heavy repousse, holds 12 spoons, Meriden **175.00**
Tea service, Neoclassic, eng scrolls/foliage, 5-pc **280.00**
Tea/coffee, gadrooned/shell border, Reed & Barton, 7-pc **400.00**
Teapot, Vintage pattern, tall neck, ebonized hdl, 1875, 9" **150.00**
Tray, reeded rim, hdls, 1910, 22x16" **150.00**
Tray, Rococo scroll rim, 16" dia **50.00**
Tray, scroll eng, rtcl floral rim, English, 1910, 21" L **200.00**
Trophy, figural dog & 2 6" rifles, Simpson, Hall & Miller **450.00**

Sheffield

Cake basket, swing hdl, gadroon rim, eng garland/rtcl, 18" **110.00**
Candelabra, 5 scrolled arms, fluted/acanthus base, 29" **660.00**
Candlestick, EX Rococo detail, England, 18", pr **10,000.00**
Candlestick, Geo III style, ram masks, sgn HE, 11", 4 for **4,400.00**
Coffeepot, pear shape w/pineapple finial, ebony hdl, 1800s **220.00**
Dish, repousse shells/foliage, 2-part, hdls, Walker & Hall **80.00**
Dish, serving; scalloped scroll/flower-eng lid, scroll hdls **650.00**
Goblet, Fordhan & Faulkner, 6" **45.00**
Hot water kettle, reeded, scrolled legs/paw ft, 1835, 12" **400.00**
Punch bowl, eng band w/crest & line of music, lyre hdls, 14" **300.00**
Sugar shaker, tooled floral swags, 8" **175.00**
Tea set, Regency style, mk TM, 1800s, pot: 6", 3-pc **220.00**
Vase, tapered hexagon w/dome ft, appl vintage, 28" **250.00**

Silver Resist

The process for decorating pottery with the silver-resist method involved first coating the design or that portion of the pattern that was to be left unsilvered with a water-soluble solution. The lustre was applied to the entire surface of the vessel and allowed to dry. Before the final firing, the surface was washed, removing only the silver from the coated areas. This type of ware was produced early in the 1800s by many English potteries, including Wedgwood.

Goblet, vintage decor, 4½" **95.00**

Mug, girl reading book & florals, child sz **95.00**
Pitcher, floral resist, 5⅝", EX **100.00**
Pitcher, florals, 7⅜" **465.00**
Pitcher, satyr face mold, enamel, resist w/florals, 4½" **330.00**

Sinclaire

In 1904 H.P. Sinclaire and Company was founded in Corning, New York. For the first sixteen years of production, Sinclaire used blanks from other glassworks for his cut and engraved designs. In 1920 he established his own glass-blowing factory in Bath, New York. His most popular designs utilize fruits, flowers, and other forms from nature. Most of Sinclaire's glass is unmarked; items that are carry his logo: an 'S' within a wreath with two shields.

Box, hobstars, X-hatching & notches, star bottom, oval, sgn **245.00**
Candlestick, cut & etched w/flowers on gr, 3", pr **150.00**
Candlestick, Daisy, eng ft, 9" **200.00**
Comport, eng flowers, teardrop stem, 8" **80.00**
Creamer & sugar bowl, frosted eng daisies, sgn **125.00**
Creamer & sugar bowl, Holly, 4½", 2¼x5" **700.00**
Plate, Chrysanthemum intaglio, 10¾" **200.00**
Plate, floral cutting all around, monogram in center, sgn **200.00**
Vase, Wreath & Flower, trumpet shape w/ped ft, 10" **100.00**

Sitzendorf

The Sitzendorf factory began operations in East Germany in the mid-1800s, adopting the name of the city as the name of their company. They produced fine porcelain groups, figurines, etc. in much the same style and quality as Meissen and the Dresden factories. Much of their ware was marked with a crown over the letter 'S' and a horizontal line with two slash marks. Our advisor for this category is Donald Penrose; he is listed in the Directory under Ohio.

Bowl, HP/appl florals, rtcl rim, appl cupids, 1887, 12½" **550.00**
Candelabra, 4-light, 2 children at base, Voight, 15", pr **250.00**
Candlestick, cherub w/arm about std, flower-decor base, 15" **350.00**

Figures on stands, 27", $1,500.00 for the pair.

Figurine, artist flirts w/lady, man looks at easel, 17" L **850.00**
Figurine, boy (& girl) w/basket of apples, 21", pr **2,100.00**
Figurine, boy & girl w/lambs, 10", pr **395.00**
Figurine, Dutch man (& lady) w/lamb & flower basket, 8", pr ...**550.00**

Figurine, he: flower basket on shoulder (she holds 1), 8", pr **550.00**
Figurine, male dancer w/lamb (she w/tamborine), 11x10", pr **695.00**
Figurine, Romans on balcony, cheetah-pulled chariot, 15" L ..**1,950.00**
Figurine, 2 dogs by lady on couch, man stands at end, 9x10" **850.00**
Figurine, 8 figures surround piano, scroll base, 20", NM **770.00**
Vase, appl couple w/instruments, HP florals, rtcl, 12" **295.00**

Slag Glass

Slag glass is a marbleized opaque glassware made by several companies from about 1870 until the turn of the century. It is usually found in purple or caramel (see Chocolate Glass), though other colors were also made. Pink is rare and very expensive.

Inverted Fan and Feather fruit bowl in pink, 9", $750.00.

Blue, humidor, drum shape, cap-shaped finial, 6½x5¼" **250.00**
Pink, Invt Fan & Feather, butter dish **1,000.00**
Pink, Invt Fan & Feather, compote, jelly; 5" **550.00**
Pink, Invt Fan & Feather, creamer **450.00**
Pink, Invt Fan & Feather, cruet **1,250.00**
Pink, Invt Fan & Feather, pitcher, 8" **1,450.00**
Pink, Invt Fan & Feather, punch cup **275.00**
Pink, Invt Fan & Feather, sauce dish **265.00**
Pink, Invt Fan & Feather, spooner **325.00**
Pink, Invt Fan & Feather, sugar bowl, w/lid **665.00**
Pink, Invt Fan & Feather, toothpick holder **650.00**
Pink, Invt Fan & Feather, tumbler **400.00**
Purple, Beads & Bark, vase, novelty **50.00**
Purple, cake stand, plain baluster std **100.00**
Purple, compote, Panel & Waffle mold, w/lid, 8x8" **80.00**
Purple, Fan & Leaf, tray, shield form, hdls **90.00**
Purple, Flute & Cross Bar, spill vase, Belknap 295A **48.00**
Purple, Fluted Shell, bowl, pie-crust rim, 8½" **75.00**
Purple, oil lamp, emb spears, clear font, 13" **135.00**
Purple, Oval Medallion, spooner **85.00**
Purple, plate, lattice edge, 10½" **50.00**
Purple, plate, lattice edge, 13" **85.00**
Purple, Scroll w/Acanthus, creamer & sugar bowl **90.00**
Purple, Scroll w/Acanthus, spooner **65.00**
Purple, vase, Panel & Waffle mold, ftd, scalloped, 8" **40.00**
Red, vase, mc/gold decor at top, 7" **60.00**

SMF (Schramberg/Wheelock Black Forest)

Since 1918 the Schramberger Majolica Factory in Schramberg, Wurttemberg, Germany, has produced majolica, stoneware, and porceain. Various marks were used (Schramberg, and Wheelock 'Black Forest' Hand Painted Pottery), but the common link is the SMF insignia. They produced a number of hand-painted pieces, but those of most interest to collectors are painted in gaudy colors in bizarre designs on equally bizarre shapes. As a result, it is often referred to as the 'poor man's Clarice Cliff.' Collectors will note that most pieces bear an incised mold number, a painter's number, and the SMF mark. Of special note are the pieces marked Gobelin, followed by a number (or simply G and the number). Gobelin wares have a gray background with as many as ten colors used in the design. The number denotes particular color combinations. For example, Gobelin 3 pieces will be painted in green and orange leaves and yellow eyes, along with other colors specific to that design. Expect to find Gobelin-numbered pottery in various unusual shapes. It is not uncommon to find pieces that are chipped, and a perfect piece should be valued by its owner. Our advisor for this category is Ralph Winslow; he is listed in the Directory under Kansas.

Ashtray, 4-color, G-5, Deco style, SMF Wheelock 48.00
Basket, 4-color, G-5, SMF-W, #2706 ....39.00
Biscuit plate, flowers, SMF, #2154 ....48.00
Boat, 4-color, SMF, #2390 ....45.00
Bowl, G-2, eyes, Mepoco Ware 42.00
Candle holder, flowers, SMF-W 25.00
Candle holder, G-2, SMF-W, #6932 ....39.00
Inkwell, 3-color, eyes, G-3, SMF-W 39.00
Planter, eyes, G-3, SMF-W, #3118 ....48.00
Plate/plaque, leaves, G-6, SMF-W 37.00
Tray, flowers, SMF-W, #3047 ....35.00

Vase, black and orange leaves on white, SMF, #2822, $72.00.

Vase, drip glaze, SMF, #2929, 6" 39.00
Vase, flowers, SMF, #2688, 7½" 35.00
Vase, gray, hdls, G-4, SMF-W, #2627 ....42.00
Vase, 3-color, G-1, SMF, #2984 ....45.00
Vase, 3-color, G-7, SMF-W 46.00
Vase, 3-color, G-7, SMF-W 46.00
Vase, 6-color, flowers, SMF, #2608, 8" 42.00

Smith Bros.

Alfred and Harry Smith founded their glassmaking firm in New Bedford, Massachusetts. They had been formerly associated with the Mt. Washington Glass Works, working there from 1871 to 1875 to aid in establishing a decorating department. Smith glass is valued for its excellent enameled decoration on satin or opalescent glass. Pieces were often marked with a lion in a red shield. Our advisors for this category are Betty and Clarence Maier; they are listed in the Directory under Pennsylvania.

Bowl, HP daisies, melon ribs, SP rim, sgn, 3½x10½" 395.00
Bowl, lilies/leaves, gold-traced on tan, melon ribs, 4x9" 675.00
Box, powder; gold irises w/gr accents on melon ribs, 4" dia 350.00
Cracker jar, daisies/shadow leaves, sq w/emb swirls, 7" 425.00
Cracker jar, jeweled circles/fans, melon ribs, NM 975.00
Jar, carnations/violets on glossy wht, melon ribs, 3½x6" 325.00
Mustard, butterfly, rust/bl/gr on golden tan, SP trim, 3½" 250.00
Shaker, lay-down egg, roses on gr gloss, metal lid, 1½x2¾" 85.00
Sugar shaker, daisies on tan, 25-rib, 5½" 675.00
Syrup, gold florals, orig spring lid, lion mk 225.00
Tumbler, daisies, pk on wht opaque, 4⅜x2⅛" 40.00
Vase, apple blossoms w/birds, lake in bk, fr in circle, 6" 225.00
Vase, bird on branch, gray/wht w/red berries on gray, 4¼x2" 300.00
Vase, egret scene on bl shaded, ringed, 7⅞x2½" 175.00
Vase, floral, HP w/gold on pk opaque, 4¼x2" 45.00
Vase, lily among leaves, wht/gr on pk, maroon trim, 7", pr 385.00
Vase, pansies in bl/purple, gold beaded rim, 4x4" 175.00
Vase, stork scene, yel shaded, 4¾x1⅞" 175.00
Vase, winter house scene, lt gr w/wht gold trim rings, 6" 175.00
Vase, wisteria, gold leaves/branches, dbl canteen form, 9x7" ...1,250.00

Snow Babies

During the last quarter of the 19th century, snow babies — little figurals in white snowsuits — originated in Germany. They were made of sugar candy and were often used as decorations for Christmas trees. Later on they were made of marzipan, a confection of crushed almonds, sugar, and egg whites. Eventually porcelain manufacturers began making them in bisque. They were popular until WWII. These tiny china figures range in size from just over 1" to the very rare jointed babies sometimes nearly 7" tall. Any example brings a very respectable price on the market today. Beware of reproductions. Our advisor for this category is Linda Vines; she is listed in the Directory under New Jersey.

Babies, twins joined, Germany, 2" 90.00
Babies, twins joined, Japan, 2" 35.00
Babies, 2 sliding down brick wall, Germany, 2½" 125.00

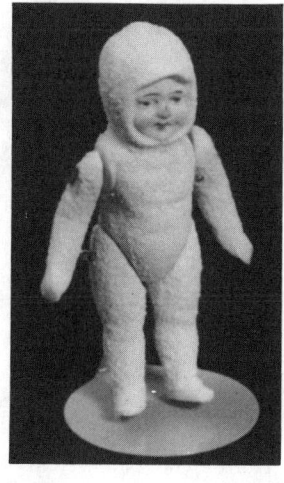

Baby, jointed arms and legs, 3½", $200.00.

Baby, googly-eyed, oversz head w/open bk, Germany, 2¾" 175.00
Baby, sitting or standing, Germany, 1" 40.00
Baby in sled pulled by huskies, Germany, 3" 150.00
Baby inside igloo, Santa on top, Germany, 2½" 150.00
Baby inside igloo, Santa on top, Japan, 2½" 65.00
Baby on red or silver airplane, Germany, 2" 125.00
Baby on snow bear, Germany, 2¾" 125.00

Baby playing musical instrument, Germany, 2" **90.00**
Baby pulling 3 penguins on sled, Germany, 2½" **150.00**
Baby w/tennis racket, Germany, 2" **90.00**
Carollers, 3 w/snow hats on snow base, lantern, Germany, 2" **90.00**
Child, girl or boy no-snow, pushing lg snowball, Germany, 2¼" ..**90.00**
Child, girl or boy skater, snow hat & sweater, Germany, 2¼" **75.00**
Child skier, red pants/wht sweater, glass beads, Germany, 2½" ...**125.00**
Child skier, snow hat & sweater, wood skis & pole, Germany, 3" ..**110.00**
Children, 3 no-snows on sled, Germany, 2½" **50.00**
Santa in boat by snow-toppped lighthouse, Germany, 3" **110.00**
Santa riding on snow bear, Germany, 2½" **200.00**
Santa riding on yel train, pixie in bk, Germany, 3" **125.00**
Santa standing w/angel, Germany, 2½" **90.00**
Snow bear between 2 red-suited babies, snow base, Germany, 2" ...**110.00**
Snow bear on hind legs, Germany, 2½" **75.00**
Snow cat, dog, or rabbit, Germany, 1", ea **50.00**
Snow mother pushing twins in red carriage-sled, Germany, 3" ...**165.00**
Snowman w/top hat & cigar, Germany, 2" **65.00**

Snuff Boxes

As early as the 17th century, the Chinese began using snuff. By the early 19th century, the practice had spread to Europe and America. It was used by both the gentlemen and the ladies alike, and expensive snuff boxes and bottles were the earmark of the genteel. Some were of silver or gold set with precious stones or pearls, while others contained music boxes. In the following listings, the dimension noted is length. See also Orientalia, Snuff Bottles.

Viennese silver-gilt and enamel with Judgement of Paris theme, 1880s, 3" long, $2,750.00.

Burl & tortoise shell, finely tooled lid, 3½" dia **125.00**
Delft, bl/wht scene, 3¾" L, NM **700.00**
German silver, blk w/gr Deco enameling, marcasite clasp, 3" **325.00**
Horn w/eng flowers/couple/inscription, oval, 3", EX **150.00**
Horn/bone, simple tooling, swivel lid over access hole, 3" **35.00**
Mahog, HP castle, Germany, 1860s, 2½x4½" **165.00**
Marbleized/gilt paper on cb, mirror, transfer rvpt, 5", EX **75.00**
Papier-mache shoe, blk lacquer w/floral, wire inlay, 5" **125.00**
Porc, HP couples dancing at ball on red, Continental, 3½" **425.00**
Silver, plain w/scalloped lid, Birmingham 1884 ....**175.00**
Silver (.900) w/mc MOP inlay garden/swans/etc, Austrian, 3" ...**850.00**
Silver (.935) ovoid set w/moss agate on top/bottom **200.00**

Sterling, incised design, NM London, 1813, ¾x1¾x3" ....**225.**

Soapstone

Soapstone is a soft talc in rock form with a smooth, greasy f from whence comes its name. In colonial times it was extracted fr out-croppings in large sections with hand saws, carted by oxen to mi and fashioned into useful domestic articles such as footwarmers, coo ing utensils, inkwells, etc. During the early 1800s, it was used to ma heating stoves and kitchen sinks. Most familiar today are the carv vases, bookends, and boxes made in China during the Victorian e Our advisor for this category is Donald Penrose; he is listed in t Directory under Ohio.

Buddha, lotus throne, flame at bk, flecked gr, 10" ....**78.**
Censer, dragon-mask/ring hdls, dragon finial, 3-leg, 8" ....**150.**

Double vase with berried branch, 6½x8½", $100.00.

Horse rearing, flying mane, red-brn, 12x9" ....**150.**
Inkwell, cvd ribbed dome, 4 corner quill holders, sq ....**165.**
Oriental girl w/basket of fish, 11" ....**55.**
Quan Yin w/vase & basket, 15", pr ....**220.**
Seal, oxen, head bent down, brn, rstr, 2½" ....**150.**
Vase, dbl; brn, joined by floral cvg, 3x6" ....**115.**

Soda Fountain Collectibles

As the neighborhood ice cream parlor becomes a thing of the pa soda fountain memorabilia from fancy backbars to ice cream advertisir is becoming a popular field of collecting. One area of interest is th glassware used to serve the more elaborate ice cream concoctions. sundae glass is familiar to us all, but there was also a 'lucky monda glass, narrow at the bottom and flaring to a top dimension equal to or scoop. There are footed banana split dishes and soda pop glasses wit the name or logo of the beverage company painted on them.

Syrup dispensers, especially those from the teens, today commar high prices. These had spherical or urn-shaped dispensers and carrie names such as Jersey Creme, Buckeye, Cherry Smash, etc.

It is estimated that ice cream dippers may be found in approx mately two hundred different styles — some bowl shaped or cylindrica some for making ice cream sandwiches, and even a very rare hear shaped dipper. (This one was used along with matching heart-shape ice cream dishes.)

Glass straw holders are very collectible. Clear is the most commo color, but they are also found in green and pink; some are made of frosted glass. Early examples were pattern molded; some had matching glass lids — these are the most desirable. Our advisors for this category are Joyce and Harold Screen; they are listed in the Directory under Maryland. See also Advertising.

Book, equipment & supply, pre-1900, per illus pg 1.00
Book, equipment & supply, 1901-19, per illus pg 75
Book, formulas & recipes, pre-1910, per pg 25
Bottle, root beer; stoneware, Cleary 30.00
Bottle, syrup; Cherry Smash, label under glass, w/cap, 11½", G ..300.00
Bottle, syrup; Hires Root Beer, label under glass, 11½", EX 500.00
Bottle, syrup; Stromeyer's...Punch, label under glass, 11½" 100.00
Bottle, syrup; vanilla, w/lid 30.00
Bottle, 7-Up, pnt glass, Bicentennial, 11" 5.00
Bottle holder, rnd bottom bottles 50.00
Bottle opener, Orange Crush 25.00
Bowl, crushed fruit; ftd, Heisey 225.00
Cone holder, glass, ind 35.00
Cone holder, glass, orig lid, 13" 365.00
Dipper, banana split; United 700.00

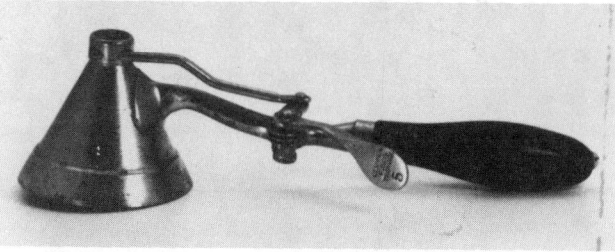

Dipper, Clipper #5, black wood handle, 9½", $325.00.

Dipper, Dover Mfg, 2-way action 115.00
Dipper, Dover Slicer 600.00
Dipper, Gilchrist #31, sz 8-30 ....35.00
Dipper, heart shaped 4,000.00
Dipper, Indestructo #4, sz 8-30 ....32.00
Dipper, New Gem, sz 8-30 ....40.00
Dipper, sandwich; Mayer, flat 175.00
Dish, banana split; gr, ftd boat type 50.00
Dispenser, blk amethyst glass base, Deco emb, 14x6x6", VG 60.00
Dispenser, Cherry Chick, emb porc potbelly, brass pump, rare ..2,000.00
Dispenser, Cherry Smash 5¢, ceramic potbelly, orig pump, EX ...1,700.00
Dispenser, Crawford's Cherry-Fizz, wht porc potbelly, w/pump ...2,800.00
Dispenser, Dr Brown's Celery, milk glass, 10½x7x7", EX 65.00
Dispenser, Dr Swett's Root Beer, ceramic, w/pump, rare 4,000.00
Dispenser, Fowler's Cherry Smash, w/orig sgn pump 800.00
Dispenser, Fowler's Root Beer, wht ceramic potbelly, orig pump ..900.00
Dispenser, Ginger-Mint Julep, bbl shape, wht, EX 700.00
Dispenser, Hires, porc, hourglass, orig pump, ca 1910, EX 600.00
Dispenser, Hires Little Boy urn, Mettlach 22,500.00
Dispenser, Hunter's, milk glass base, 9½x7½x7½", EX 65.00
Dispenser, Mission Grapefruit Juice, gr glass bowl, VG 150.00
Dispenser, Mission Orange, conical peach bowl, VG 150.00
Dispenser, Nu Grape, milk glass base, clear bowl, 11½", VG 80.00
Dispenser, Orange Crush, glass, orange figural, EX 175.00
Dispenser, Pepsi Cola, musical 295.00
Dispenser, Richardson's Root Beer, bbl form, 26", EX 270.00
Dispenser, Ward's Lemon Crush, orig ball pump 750.00
Flavor board, J Hungerford Smith, tin, ca 1900 ....400.00
Flavor board, rvpt, 1930s 75.00

Flavor bottle, complete paper label, 1-pt 25.00
Flyer, Blue Ribbon Fountain Specialties, supplies, 4-pg, EX 35.00

Footed banana split dish, $25.00.

Fountain glass, clear, ribbed, 4½", set of 6 ....22.50
Fountain glass, Cleo-Cola 30.00
Fountain glass, Green River, paneled, w/syrup line 30.00
Fountain glass, Hayner's Florida Orange emb, EX 20.00
Fountain glass, Julep 30.00
Fountain glass, Lucky Mondae 25.00
Fountain glass, Major Cola 40.00
Fountain glass, Nestles in red at top, syrup line, 6¼" 12.50
Fountain glass, Zipp's Grape-O, grape cluster 40.00
Hat, soda jerk; Orange Crush, paper, 14" L, NM 8.00
Hot water urn, Lighthouse, electric, 1915 ....100.00
Ice shaver, Lippencott 500.00
Malted milk container, Borden's, aluminum 70.00
Malted milk container, Horlick's, aluminum, 10" 70.00
Malted milk container, Thompson's, aluminum 70.00
Malted milk container, Thompson's, dome lid 200.00
Menu board, Cherry Smash, tin, rnd top w/vertical bottom 150.00
Menu board, Dr Pepper, tin, logo atop, vertical, EX 35.00
Menu board, 7-Up, chalkboard, food & bottle, vertical, NM 45.00
Mixer, Arnold, Pat Apr 15, 1919 ....90.00
Mixer, Gilchrist #22, polished 150.00
Mixer, Hamilton Beach, triple head, 3-speed, gr enamel, M 225.00
Mixer, Hamilton Beach, 2-speed, gr enamel, EX 75.00
Mixer, Hires, hand-cranked malt mixer 700.00
Mixer, Walker's Quick & Easy, hand-cranked floor model 900.00
Mug, A&W Root Beer, glass, 4" 4.00
Mug, Richardson's Root Beer emb on glass 15.00
Name plate, manufacturer's, from soda fountain, Tufts 100.00
Paperweight, Orange Crush, glass, bottle at left, 3x4" 145.00
Photo, soda fountain, ca 1890 ....40.00
Pump, Hires, slight wear on nickel 115.00
Pump, Ward's Lime Crush, EX orig 125.00
Sign, True Fruit, cb, various flavors, 9x16", ea 50.00
Soda apparatus, pk marble, w/8 dispensers, Pat 1863, EX 2,500.00
Stereoview card, Tufts Centennial SF 25.00
Straw dispenser, Hires, CI 750.00
Straw dispenser, Jewel Sanitary 250.00
Straw holder, clear, Illinois pattern, w/lid 350.00
Straw holder, gr, Illinois pattern, w/lid 500.00
Straw holder, gr, w/lid 400.00
Straw holder, horizontal, Heisey 600.00
Straw holder, Near Cut, all glass (including lid) 500.00
Straw holder, wide-ribbed glass, orig top & insert 100.00
Table, wood, glass top, +4 wire chairs 175.00
Watch fob, Ice Cream, brick color 100.00
Watch fob, Lippencott SF Co 125.00

Spangle Glass

Spangle glass, also known as Vasa Murrhina, is cased art glass characterized by the metallic flakes embedded in its top layer. It was made both abroad and in the United States during the late years of the 19th century, and it was reproduced in the 1960s by the Fenton Art Glass Company.

Vasa Murrhina was a New England distributor who sold glassware of this type manufactured by a Dr. Flower of Sandwich, Massachusetts. Flower had purchased the defunct Cape Cod Glassworks in 1885 and used the facilities to operate his own company. Since none of the ware was marked, it is very difficult to attribute specific examples to his manufacture. See also Art Glass Baskets; Fenton.

Basket, pk w/pk mica, wishbone ft, 6¼x3¾" 95.00
Bowl, red w/silver mica, mc florals, SP stand, 7x16" 450.00
Condiment set, cranberry w/mica, 3-pc in SP fr, 6" 225.00
Ewer, purple, wht int, thorn hdl, dbl gourd, att Mt WA, 8" 375.00
Pitcher, 4-color splashes in wht w/silver mica, 9" 125.00
Rose bowl, bl/wht spatter w/silver mica, 8-crimp, 3⅜x3½" 85.00
Rose bowl, pk/beige/maroon spatter w/silver mica, 3¼x3⅞" 110.00
Rose bowl, pk/wht spatter w/silver mica, 8-crimp, 3¾x3¼" 118.00
Tumbler, gr & wht spatter w/gold mica, 3¾x2½" 45.00
Tumbler, mc spatter w/silver mica, emb swirl, 3¾x2¾" 70.00
Vase, bl w/silver mica, thorn hdl, ewer form, 7½", pr 165.00
Vase, pk spatter w/silver mica, vaseline hdls, 8⅛x3" 95.00
Vase, pk w/silver mica, ruffled, clear shell trim, 9¼" 145.00
Vase, pk w/silver mica, ruffled rim, 8⅞x4" 85.00
Vase, yel w/silver mica, crystal edge, wht int, bulbous, 4" 95.00

Spatter Glass

Spatter glass, characterized by its multicolor 'spatters,' has been made from the late 19th century to the present by American glass houses as well as those abroad. Although it was once thought to have been made entirely by workers at the 'end of the day' from bits and pieces of leftover scrap, it is now known that it was a standard line of production. See also Art Glass Baskets.

Basket, pk/brn/wht o/l, clear thorn hdl, 6x4¾" 140.00
Basket, 4-color, wht int, clear thorn hdl, 8x5" 165.00
Basket, 4-color o/l, emb swirls, ruffled rim, clear hdl, 7x5" 185.00
Bowl, pk, appl vaseline flowers/3 ft, rim w/lg ruffles, 5x6" 495.00
Candlestick, mc, clear o/l, swirled w/flanged socket, 7½" 55.00
Candlestick, 6-color, 8¾x3⅞", pr 135.00
Covered dish, pk & gr, wht int, clear appl leaves, 5¾x4" 75.00
Creamer & sugar bowl, red/orange/yel, wht int, 4x6" 125.00
Decanter, mc w/thin amber casing, amber ft/stopper, 12½" 150.00
Ewer, cranberry w/clear hdl, lg 60.00
Pitcher, Invt T'print, maroon & wht, bulbous, clear hdl, 8" 110.00
Pitcher, yel & wht, gold flowers & hdl, bulbous, 2x1¼" 60.00
Pitcher, 3-color, yel int, emb swirls, 3-petal top, 5" 88.00
Tumbler, mc w/wht int, emb swirls, 4" 55.00
Vase, cranberry & wht w/clear o/l, clear hdls, 5" 125.00
Vase, mc, emb swirls, cupped goblet neck, 10" 160.00
Vase, rainbow pastel o/l, clear thorn hdls, 9" 92.50
Vase, 4-color w/wht int, ring neck, 7" 50.00

Spatterware

Spatterware is a general term referring to a type of decoration used by English potters beginning in the late 1700s. Using a brush or a stick,

brightly colored paint was dabbed onto the soft-paste earthenwa items, achieving a spattered effect which was often used as a bord Because much of this type of ware was made for export to the Unit States, some of the subjects in the central design — the schoolho and the eagle patterns, for instance — reflect American tastes. Yello green, and black spatterware is scarce and highly valued by collectors.

In the descriptions that follow, the color listed after the item in cates the color of the spatter. The central design is identified next, a the color description that follows that refers to the design.

Bowl, bl, fort, 3-color, hairline, 3x4¾" 235.0
Bowl, bl, Peacock at Fountain, w/lid, 10½" 255.0
Creamer, bl, emb leaf hdl, 3¾", NM 85.0
Creamer, bl, rose, 3-color, paneled, 5¾", EX 270.0
Creamer, rainbow, bl/gr, crazing, 4½", NM 625.0
Creamer, rainbow, pk-red/bl, stain/edge wear, 3½" 100.0
Creamer, rainbow, red/bl, hairline, 3½" 95.0
Cup plate, rainbow, bl/gr, bull's-eye center, crazed, 3½" 675.0
Cup plate, yel, rose, 3-color, crow's ft/rim flake, 4" 600.0
Mug, bl, hairline/stains, 3" 55.0

Plate, purple with dahlia in dark purple and blue, 10½", $750.00; Platter, red and green spatter with tulip in red and blue with green leaves, 13¾", $1,800.00.

Plate, bl, eagle transfer, hairline/stains, 10" 125.0
Plate, cut sponge, camellia, red/gr, 9", EX 100.0
Plate, cut sponge, rabbit transfer on border, 9½" 500.0
Plate, design spatter, gr daisies w/purple center, 8½", NM 55.0
Plate, purple/mustard/gr florets & line border, HP pansy, 7¼" 165.0
Plate, rainbow, bl/gr, gr dot center, 8", EX 300.0
Plate, rainbow, red/bl, minor stains, 8½" 100.0
Plate, rainbow, red/bl, X design in center, 6½" 325.0
Plate, rainbow, red/gr, bull's-eye center, 9½", VG 115.0
Plate, rainbow, red/purple, 13½", NM 950.0
Plate, red, floral center, bl transfer, 8" 225.0
Plate, red, peafowl, 4-color, chip/rpr, 8" 100.0
Plate, red, peafowl, 4-color, 8" 400.0
Plate, red/bl, tulip, 3-color, Cotton & Barlow, 10", NM 275.0
Plate, stick spatter rim, red stripes/mc flower, 9", EX 100.0
Plate, toddy; bl, bull's-eye center, 5¼" 115.0
Plate, toddy; bl, wigwam, 5", NM 425.0
Plate, yel, profile tulip, red/blk/gr, rpr chips, 9" 950.0
Sugar bowl, bl, Chinese at trade, mc transfer, 9¼" 115.0
Sugar bowl, bl, tulips, 4-color, chipped lid, 4¾", EX 175.0
Sugar bowl, rainbow, purple/bl, w/lid, 4½x4¼", NM 350.0
Sugar bowl, yel, thistle, red/gr, paneled, lid, rpr, 7", VG 500.0
Tea bowl, rainbow, red/yel/gr/blk, mini, 3" dia, NM 425.0
Tea bowl & saucer, bl, fort, miniature 550.0
Tea bowl & saucer, bl, peafowl, 4-color, NM 425.0
Tea bowl & saucer, bl, wigwam, NM 550.0

Tea bowl & saucer, cut sponge, flower band, gr/red, mini 65.00
Tea bowl & saucer, gr, peafowl, 3-color, rosette mk, NM 250.00
Tea bowl & saucer, gr, peafowl, 4-color, NM 450.00
Tea bowl & saucer, purple, holly berry, red/blk/gr, NM 375.00
Tea bowl & saucer, purple, rooster, 4-color, EX 650.00
Tea bowl & saucer, purple, 8-point star in bl, rosette mk 300.00
Tea bowl & saucer, rainbow, red/bl, mini 375.00
Tea bowl & saucer, rainbow, red/bl/gr, mk Adams w/heart, EX ..300.00
Tea bowl & saucer, rainbow, red/gr, mini 275.00
Tea bowl & saucer, rainbow, red/gr, saucer w/O mk 300.00
Tea bowl & saucer, red, 6-pointed star, red/gr/bl, EX 325.00
Tea bowl & saucer, red, 6-pointed star, red/gr/bl, NM 500.00
Tea bowl & saucer, stick spatter, red/gr/blk geometrics 95.00
Tea bowl & saucer, yel, thistle, red/gr, mini 950.00
Tea bowl & saucer, yel, 5-petal bl flower, VG 340.00
Teapot, bl/wht, stains/sm rim chips, 5½" 200.00

Spectacles

Collectors of Americana are beginning to appreciate the charm of antique optical items, and those involved in the related trade find them particularly fascinating. Anyone, however, cannot help but notice the evolution of technology apparent when viewing a collection of old eye ware and at the same time admire the primitive ingenuity involved in its construction. Our advisor for this category is Dale Beeks; he is listed in the Directory under Idaho.

Opera glasses, lorgnette style, florals, B Altman, EX 185.00
Spectacles, brass, sm rectangle lenses, temples w/cord holes 15.00
Spectacles, nickel silver, sm oval lenses, extending temples 40.00
Spectacles, pince-nez, gutta purcha, ca 1870s 35.00
Spectacles, pince-nez, rnd rimless lenses, brass noseguards 15.00
Spectacles, silver, sm oval lenses, mk Philad, 1840s, EX 65.00
Spectacles, 14k, sm oval lenses, in papier-mache mk case 35.00
Spectacles case, nickel-plated brass coffin shape, 1850s 20.00
Spectacles case, plain papier-mache, slip-over top, 5" L 24.00
Sunglasses, blued steel fr, temple ends w/spoons, 1890, case 40.00

Spelter

Spelter figurines are cast from commercial zinc and coated with a metallic patina. The result is a product very similar to bronze in appearance, yet much less expensive.

Bookends, Scotty heads, silvered, 20th C, 4½x5", pr 65.00
Bust, Bacchante-type lady, 11" 270.00
Figurine, dancer, scantily clad, w/tambourine, 27" 495.00
Figurine, maid kneels/feeds pigeon, after Chiparus, 22" L 585.00
Group, L'Abondance Recompense le Travail, after Brousse, 27" ..600.00
Lamp, Psyche figural, 4 leafy-stem lights, frog/snail, 36" 1,200.00
Lamp, Statue of Liberty, light on torch, 1930s, 12½" 65.00
Mantel clock, modeled as a horse w/attendent, GE, 17" 125.00
Pincushion, touring car, USA, 3x1½" 32.00
Urn, patinated floral, marble base, ormolu ft, 15", pr 250.00
Vase, flower w/emerging nude, 20" 425.00

Spode-Copeland

The Spode Works was established in 1770 and continued to operate under that title until 1843. Their earliest products were typical underglaze blue-printed patterns, though basalt was also made. After 1790 a translucent porcelain body was the basis for a line of fine enamel-decorated dinnerware. Stone china was introduced in 1805, often in patterns reflecting an Oriental influence. In 1833 Wm Taylor Copeland purchased the company, continuing business in much the same tradition. During the last half of the 19th century, Copeland produced excellent parian figures and groups with such success that many other companies attempted to reproduce his work. He employed famous painters to decorate plaques, vases, and tablewares, many examples of which were signed by the artist. Most of the Copeland wares are marked with one of several variations that incorporate the firm name. Today the company is owned by Royal Worcester, Ltd., and operates under the name of Royal Worcester Spode, Ltd. Our advisor for this category is Don Haase; he is listed in the Directory under Washington.

Bowl, cream soup; Aster 35.00
Bowl, cream soup; Gainsborough, w/underplate 35.00
Bowl, cream soup; Tower 45.00
Bowl, fruit; Billingsley Rose, sm 20.00
Bowl, vegetable; Aster, oval 65.00
Bowl, vegetable; Billingsley Rose, 9" L 65.00
Bowl, vegetable; Camilla, bl, oval, 9" 65.00
Bowl, vegetable; Florence, oval 65.00
Bowl, vegetable; Florence, sq 75.00
Bowl, vegetable; Tower, bl, w/lid, Spode, 10x8" 265.00
Bowl, vegetable; Tower, bl, w/lid, Spode, 11x9" 295.00
Butter pat, Mayflower 25.00
Butter pat, Tower, pk 25.00
Cake plate, Florence, hdls, 9" 85.00
Chop plate, Irene, 13" 225.00
Coffee urn, transfer floral/gilt, w/tray revolves+14 pcs 550.00
Coffeepot, Famille Rose, 6-cup 155.00
Coffeepot, Gainsborough, 6-cup 145.00
Coffeepot, Tower, bl, 6-cup 225.00
Creamer & sugar bowl, Aster, 8-cup 45.00
Cup & saucer, Aster 32.00
Cup & saucer, Camilla, bl 35.00
Cup & saucer, demitasse; Shanghai, bone china 45.00
Cup & saucer, Florence 29.00
Cup & saucer, Irene 70.00
Cup & saucer, Mayflower 35.00
Cup & saucer, Moss Rose 35.00
Cup & saucer, Tower, bl 45.00
Egg cup, Gainsborough 32.00
Gravy boat, Gainsborough, w/attached underplate 100.00
Gravy boat, Tower, bl, w/attached underplate 135.00
Muffin dish, Tower, pk, domed lid 125.00
Pitcher, milk; Tower, bl, 4" 85.00
Pitcher, parian, Independence, w/WA & flags, Copeland, 8" 150.00
Pitcher, tan & gr w/emb wht stripes & swags, Copeland, 7" 150.00
Pitcher, Tower, bl, bbl shape, 6" 100.00
Pitcher, Tower, pk, bbl shape, 6" 85.00
Plate, dinner; Aster 35.00
Plate, dinner; Billingsley Rose 35.00
Plate, dinner; Camella, pk 32.00
Plate, dinner; Florence 32.00
Plate, dinner; Mayflower 35.00
Plate, dinner; Moss Rose 35.00
Plate, dinner; Romney 35.00
Plate, dinner; Rosebud Chintz 35.00
Plate, dinner; Tower, bl 45.00
Plate, Imari style, Spode, 9½", set of 12 ....750.00
Plate, luncheon; Famille Rose 29.00
Plate, salad; Jewell 22.00
Plate, salad; Moss Rose 25.00

Platter, Aster, 15¼" 135.00
Platter, Florence, 17" 155.00
Platter, Gainsborough, 14" 125.00
Platter, Imari, octagonal, Copeland, 1850s, 18½" 375.00
Potpourri vase, pattern #967, paw ft, rtcl lid, 6" 875.00
Relish, Tower, pk, divided, Spode 75.00
Soup, Mayflower, rimmed, 7" 35.00
Teapot, Aster, 6-cup 135.00
Teapot, Tower, bl, 8-cup 180.00
Teapot, Tower, pk, Spode, 8-cup 155.00

Spongeware

Spongeware is a type of factory-made earthenware that was popular during the last quarter of the 19th century. It was decorated by dabbing color onto the drying ware with a sponge, leaving a splotched design at random or in simple patterns. Sometimes a solid band of color was added. The vessel was then covered with a clear glaze and fired at a high temperature. Blue on white is the most preferred combination, but green on ivory, orange on white, or those colors in combination may also occasionally be found.

Bowl, bl/tan on cream, 4x7" 60.00
Bowl, flared, glaze chip, 4½x9" 180.00
Bowl, mixing; molded arches, rim chip, 3x16" 270.00
Bowl, ribbed, 1½x4¼", NM 120.00
Bowl, rnd ft, 2x5" 130.00
Bowl, soup; brn/cream, sponging at rim, 2¼x9½", NM 38.00
Bowl, str sides, 2¼x7½" 135.00
Chamber pot, gr/yel, emb vintage band, 6½x11" 98.00
Cuspidor, bl bands rim & base, concave sides, 5x10" 75.00
Cuspidor, pattern sponging, emb basketweave 135.00
Cuspidor, wide bl bands at rim & base, concave sides, 6x12" 150.00
Custard cup, gr/cream, pattern sponging, 1¾x3½" 18.00
Mush cup, flowing bl sponging, 5x8", w/8" saucer 200.00

Pitcher, pattern sponging, barrel form, 8", $325.00.

Pitcher, bl/wht band, can top, bulbous bottom, 7", M 425.00
Pitcher, cylindrical, slightly tapered sides, 9" 250.00
Pitcher, flared rim, rim hairlines, 5½" 170.00
Pitcher, pattern sponging, bbl form, 9", EX 225.00
Pitcher, pattern sponging, emb rose on side, 9" 285.00
Plate, serving; flowing bl sponging, 10½", M 210.00
Platter, flowing bl sponging, scalloped, emb scrolls, 13", NM 140.00
Platter, flowing bl sponging, 13½", M 180.00
Shaving mug, dbl bl bands below rim & at base, rpr, 4", VG 170.00
Soap dish, mfg flaw, 3⅜x4⅝" 80.00
Toothbrush holder, flowing bl, scalloped, emb scrolls, 6" 260.00
Wash bowl & pitcher (no spout), bl/wht bands, 11", 14" dia 725.00
Wash pitcher, bl banding, 11" 195.00

Wash pitcher, wide bl base band, 12" 250.00
Waste bowl, flowing bl sponging, emb scrolls, 3x5" 75.00

Spoons

Souvenir spoons have been popular remembrances since the 1890s. The early hand-wrought examples of the silversmith's art are especially sought and appreciated for their fine craftsmanship. Commemorative, personality-related, advertising, and those with Indian busts or floral designs are only a few of the many types of collectible spoons. In the following listings, spoons are entered by city, character or occasion.

Key:
B — bowl   FF — full figure
BR — bowl reverse   GW — gold wash
emb — embossed   H — handle
eng — engraved   HR — handle reverse

Alaska scenes on H & HR; plain B 20.00
Alaska Totem Pole (words) on HR; totem pole FF H 10.00
Alberta (word) emb in H w/oil well finial; Banff (word) in B 22.50
Bermuda (word) on HR, florals on H; palms in B; Shiebler 30.00
Brooklyn Bridge emb on H; dtd Oct 18, 02 on HR 70.00
Buffalo in high relief w/daggers/rifle/rope on H; plain B 30.00
CA state seal H w/bear finial; Golden Gate emb in GW B 22.00
Cannon figural H; plain B; coffee sz 68.00
Chicago emb on H w/bird finial; Fort Dearborn in B 30.00
Chicago Fair 1891 (words) & Women's building emb in B 55.00
Crossed mining picks on H: plain B 6.50
Denver (word) eng in spade-shaped B; miner FF H 37.50
Duluth (word) eng in GW B; Indian FF H; Shepard 42.50
Eagle w/snake on cactus finial; twist H; plain B 25.00
Egyptian hieroglyphics on H; GW rnd B, foreign 42.50
Fleur-de-lis finial H; GW bowl; Gorham 25.00
Ft Sumter emb in B; male figure on H 42.50
Galveston TX (words) & sailboat in GW B; lg fish emb on H 45.00
Golden Gate Bridge in GW B; scrolled H 17.50
Hampton VA (words) eng in B; appl crab on H 22.50
Hannibal Hamlin finial H; tree & plow emb in B 40.00
Independence Hall Phila view in B; Wm Penn FF H 47.50
Indian in headdress emb on H; canoe emb in B 22.50
Jacksonville FL (words) emb in B; alligator finial H 57.50
Lake Placid NY (words) eng in heart-shaped B; cherub finial 32.00
Los Angeles & Indian head w/corn emb on H; poinsettia in B 17.50
Madeira (word) eng on H; church view emb in B 25.00
Madison WI (words) eng in GW B; 1892 on H; Pat 1889, demi 35.00
Massachusetts & state seal on H; Hoosac tunnel in B; Watson 30.00
Mt Vernon (words) on H; mansion view in B; Wallace 28.00
New Jersey state seal on H; State House view in B, Watson 27.50
New Orleans view in B; sugar cane & cotton plant FF H 75.00
New York City & Statue of Liberty on H; Brooklyn Bridge in B 25.00
Normal School Hays KS eng in B; floral emb/pnt H 45.00
Old Faithful emb in GW B; Great Falls of Yellowstone on H 35.00
Pasadena (word) in B; bear & miner on H: Eureka on HR 10.00
Peterson IA (words) on H; power plant view eng in B; demitasse 25.00
Pharoah's head finial H; pyramids in B; sm 37.5
Phoenix Capitol Building eng in GW B; filigree H: Smith 30.00
Pittsfield emb on HR; tree emb on H; Dominick & Haff 37.5
Pleasant View view emb in B; Mary Baker Eddy on H, Durgin 140.00
Rising City (words) in B; scrolled H 15.00
Salem & witch emb on H; plain B; Daniel Low, Durgin 75.00
Salt Lake City & flowers w/cutouts on H; plain B; Watson 22.5

San Diego CA (words) in B; floral H 7.00
San Francisco & bridge scene on H; plain B 17.50
Singer in lilies/Christ is Risen on H; lilies on HR; Whiting 45.00
Sonoma Mission eng in B; state seal/miner/grapes on H 15.00
St Louis Union Station scene emb in B; crown finial H 58.00
Texas (word), steer head & symbols emb on H; plain B; Watson .20.00
Tucson (word) & mule w/load on H; St Xavier in B 15.00
TX state seal finial H: Waco TX (words) in B; demitasse 20.00
Union Depot San Francisco in B; floral H 10.00
Vatican view emb in GW B; Pope Leo on H; Dominick & Haff ..37.50
Washington bust emb in H: capitol scene in B 55.00
Washington Monument w/pnt shield H; plain B 48.00
Watson HO scenes on H; Indian symbols on HR; plain B 22.50
Yellowstone Park, elk/bear on H: Old Faithful Inn in B 37.50

Sporting Goods

When sports cards became so widely collectible several years ago, other types of related memorabilia started to interest sports fans. Now, they search for baseball uniforms, autographed baseballs, game-used bats and gloves, and all sorts of ephemera. Although baseball is America's all-time favorite, other sports have their own groups of interested collectors. Our advice for this category comes from Paul Longo Americana, Box 490, Chatham Rd., South Orleans, Cape Cod, Massachusetts 2662. See also Target Balls.

Alarm clock, baseball shape, opens, Rensie, 1948, 2½", EX 110.00
Ashtray, batter in hitting stance, cast bronze, 9", EX 200.00

Babe Ruth's autographed baseball in original box, $1,500.00.

Bank, Cleveland Indians Chief Wahoo, Standford Pottery, 9" ...125.00
Baseball, sgn Ted Williams (bold), MIB 80.00
Baseball card, Nolan Ryan Rookie, #177, 1968, EX 450.00
Baseball card, Nolan Ryan Rookie, #177, 1968, M 1,400.00
Basketball, sgn by Dave Robinson 100.00
Bat, Louisville Slugger, Georgia Peach, Ty Cobb decal, 22" 900.00
Bat, Louisville Slugger, sgn by Brooks Robinson, unused, M 150.00
Book, baseball, Connie Mack, autographed, w/dust cover 95.00
Book, Baseball Personalities, illus, 1949, EX 20.00
Booklet, Batting Tips by Mantle, 1962, EX 20.00
Booklet, Ted Williams Baseball Camp Baseball Basics, 1960s 25.00
Bumper sticker, Willie Mays, Say Hey! Buy USA, NM 35.00
Clock, lady golfer figural, brass-plated pot metal, 1890s, 8" 275.00
Clock, table model, Joe Lewis 400.00
Dumbbells, wood, mk Providence RI, ca 1900, pr 50.00
Football, Otto Graham autograph 150.00
Inkwell, baseball form, wht metal, opens, 1913, EX 350.00
Jersey, Cincinnati Reds, autographed by Pete Rose, M 175.00
Jersey, Cincinnati Reds, home wht, #14 Pete Rose, game used ..2,000.00

Jersey, Cleveland Indians, Joe Carter autograph 100.00
Jersey, Detroit Tigers, gray, 1974, #6 Al Kaline, game used 1,500.00
Mascot, stuffed dog w/NY Yankee's ribbon, 1960s, EX 20.00
Nut dish, baseball shape, milk glass, 3" dia, EX 35.00
Pennant, Cleveland Indians, wht on red felt, 1946-47 ....75.00
Pennant, 1963 World Series, Dodgers vs Yankees, M 60.00
Plate, Detroit's First Baseball Park, bl/wht, Spode, 10" 465.00
Plate, Won in the Ninth, ceramic, baseball scene, 6" dia 135.00
Poster stamp book, NY Yankees, 1943, scarce, EX 100.00
Program, boxing; Ali vs Norton at Yankee Stadium, 1976, M 60.00
Program, World Series, Yankee ed, Larsen's perfect game, 1956 ...450.00
Program, Yankees vs Giants 1951 World Series, EX 125.00
Putter, sgn by Tom Watson 100.00
Statue, catcher in action, plaster, Am Mfg, 1907, 21", EX 600.00
Statue, pitcher in action, SP wht metal, Internat'l, 12" 385.00
Ticket stub, Cleveland Indians World Series, 1948 ....40.00
Yearbook, Brooklyn Dodgers Baseball's Beloved Bums, '47, EX ..150.00
Yearbook, NY Mets World Series, 45-pg, 1969, EX 100.00

St. Clair

The St. Clair Glass Company began as a small family-oriented operation in Elwood, Indiana, in 1941. Most famous for their lamps, the family made numerous small items of carnival, pink and caramel slag, and custard glass as well. Later, paperweights became popular production pieces; many command considerably high prices on today's market. Weights are stamped and usually dated, while small production pieces are often unmarked. Our advisor for this category is Bonnie Pruitt, author of the *St. Clair Glass Collector's Book*. Her listing is in the Directory under Indiana; it includes information about how to order her book.

Ash bowl, aqua flowers in paperweight base 52.00
Bell, mc florals, 4½" 42.00

Liberty bell, blue carnival, dated 1776-1976, 3", $18.00.

Paperweight, bl floral 44.00
Paperweight, JF Kennedy, sulfide, Joe St Clair 75.00
Paperweight, JFK, sulfide, etched/windowed, sgn Joe St Clair 200.00
Paperweight, mc teapot form, Joe St Clair 60.00
Ring holder, bl paperweight 30.00
Toothpick holder, Invt Fan & Feather, ice gr carnival 25.00
Toothpick holder, Invt Fan & Feather, red carnival 25.00
Toothpick holder, sq, cobalt carnival, dtd 6-26-27-71 ....25.00
Tumbler, Grape & Cable, red carnival, Joe St Clair 35.00

Staffordshire

Scores of potteries popped up in England's Staffordshire district in the early 18th century; several remain to the present time. (See also specific companies.) Figurines and groups were made in great numbers; dogs were favorite subjects. Often they were made in pairs, each a mirror image of the other. They varied in heights from 3" or 4" to the largest, measuring 16" to 18". From 1840 until about 1900, portrait figures were produced to represent specific characters, both real and fictional. As a rule these were never marked.

The Historical Ware listed here was made throughout the district; some collectors refer to it as Staffordshire Blue Ware. It was produced as early as 1820; because much was exported to America, it was very often decorated with transfers depicting scenic views of well-known American landmarks. Early examples were printed in a deep cobalt. By 1830 a softer blue was favored, and within the next decade black, pink, red, and green prints were used. Although sometimes careless about adding their trademark, many companies used their own border designs that were as individual as their names.

This ware should not be confused with the vast amounts of modern china (mostly plates) made from early in the century to the present. These souvenir or commemorative items are usually marketed through gift stores and the like. (See Rowland and Marcellus.) Our advisor for this category is Richard Marden; he is listed in the Directory under New Hampshire. See also specific manufacturers.

Key:
blk — black	l/b — light blue
gr — green	m/b — medium blue
d/b — dark blue	m-d/b — medium dark blue

Historical

Bowl, birdcage, d/b, 6¼", NM 110.00
Bowl, Boston State House, d/b, ftd, Rogers, 4½x10¼" 2,450.00
Bowl, fisherman, English estate beyond, d/b, 5½" 175.00
Bowl, floral, d/b, Am eagle & shield mk on base, 6" 155.00
Bowl, Hudson, Hudson River, sepia, Clews, 11¾" 225.00
Bowl, Little Falls NY, train & village, l/b, Ridgway, 10" 265.00
Bowl, Mt Vernon, d/b, Ridgway, rpr, 11¼" 695.00
Bowl, Osterly Park, d/b, rtcl rim, Riley, 11½" 650.00
Bowl, pudding; lion & water buffalo, d/b, Hall, 10¾", EX 950.00
Bowl, pudding; St Peter's Chapel, d/b, beaded rim, Wood, 9¾" .495.00
Bowl, serving; Euston Hall, d/b, Stevenson, mini, 5¼" 225.00
Bowl, vegetable; Boston State House, d/b, Rogers, 11½", NM 975.00
Bowl, vegetable; Catskill Mtns Hudson River, d/b, Wood, 9¾" ..1,650.00
Bowl, vegetable; Wild Rose, m/b, w/lid, 10" 275.00
Coffeepot, bird on branch, bl, 1820s, 12", EX 425.00
Compote, McDonnough's Victory/Dix Cove Africa, d/b, 10½" ..6,500.00
Creamer, Lafayette at Franklin's Tomb, d/b, Wood 795.00
Creamer, Oxford Anglican, pk 175.00
Creamer, Rural England w/village & sheep, d/b 275.00
Cup, custard; grapes, d/b 165.00
Cup, floral, d/b, 2½", pr 185.00
Cup & saucer, Am Eagle on Urn, d/b 450.00
Cup & saucer, Landing of Lafayette, Clews, sm rpr 325.00
Cup & saucer, The Woodsman, l/b 55.00
Cup & saucer, WA at Tomb w/Scroll in Hand, d/b, Wood 375.00
Cup plate, Battery, d/b, regular shell border 365.00
Cup plate, Battery, trefoil border 350.00
Cup plate, Cadmus, d/b, trefoil border, Wood 350.00
Cup plate, Constitution of US Love Joy, l/b, Wood, 4" 400.00
Cup plate, English estate, d/b, Riley, 3⅞" 145.00
Cup plate, English rural scene, d/b, 4⅜" 135.00
Cup plate, Hudson River view, blk, Adams, 3¾" 85.00
Cup plate, river scene, d/b, stains/pinpoint flakes, 4" 120.00

Cup plate, sailboat, animals in border, brn transfer, 4" 75.00
Cup plate, sailing ship, brn, 3¾" 45.00
Cup plate, Ship at Anchor, d/b, Wood's shell border, 4⅝" 425.00
Cup plate, Sower, lav, Adams, 3⅞" 125.00
Egg hoop, view of English country cottage, m-d/b, Stags, rare 225.00
Ladle, gravy tureen; Eagle Head, d/b, grapevine border 250.00
Pitcher, Boston State House, d/b, Rogers, 6½" 1,200.00
Pitcher, castle & mansion, d/b, rim flake, 5½" 195.00
Pitcher, Erie Canal Views, d/b, ewer form, Wood, 9½", NM ...1,800.00
Pitcher, Lafayette at Franklin's Tomb, d/b, Wood, 6" 800.00
Pitcher, Texian Campagne, blk, ewer form, Shaw, 11", NM ...1,700.00
Plate, Alnwick Castle, d/b, Adams, 10¼" 185.00
Plate, Am & Independence, d/b, Clews, 10½" 300.00
Plate, Am Independence, Landing of Fathers, m/b, Wood, 10" ..165.00
Plate, Am Independence, Landing of Fathers, m/b, Wood, 8¾" .150.00
Plate, Am Villa, d/b, 10" 225.00
Plate, Arms of SC, d/b, Mayer, 7¼" 450.00
Plate, B&ORR, incline, d/b, Wood, 9⅛" 700.00
Plate, B&ORR, on the level, d/b, Wood, 10" 700.00
Plate, Boston State House, d/b, Wood, 6½" 135.00
Plate, Buenos Ayres, d/b, 10", NM 185.00

Plate, Beauties of America, City Hall NY, Ridgway, 10" $385.00.

Plate, Cadmus, d/b, Wood's shell border, 10" 625.00
Plate, Canon Hall Yorkshire, d/b, Riley, 8½" 145.00
Plate, Canterbury Cathedral, d/b, Clews, 10", NM 165.00
Plate, Capitol at WA, d/b, Wood, rpr, 7½" 165.00
Plate, Cascade de Grecy Pres Chambrey, d/b, Wood, 7½" 155.00
Plate, Castle of Lavenza, d/b, Wood's Italian Scenery, 10" 185.00
Plate, Chief Justice Marshall, d/b, Enoch Wood, 8" 425.00
Plate, Christ Church Oxford, m/b, Ridgway, 9¾", NM 75.00
Plate, City Hall NY, d/b, Ridgway, 9⅞" 385.00
Plate, City Hall NY, l/b, Jackson, 10½", EX 95.00
Plate, Commodore McDonnough's Victory, d/b, Wood, 10" 450.00
Plate, Commodore McDonnough's Victory, d/b, Wood, 6½" 375.00
Plate, couple & child before building, d/b, 10¼" 175.00
Plate, deer, m-l/b, 10" 85.00
Plate, Drury Lane Theatre, d/b, Tams, 8¾" 185.00
Plate, Erie Canal at Buffalo, purple, Stevenson, 10½" 165.00
Plate, Falls of Montmorenci Near Quebec, d/b, Wood, 9" 325.00
Plate, Fort Hamilton NY, purple, Mellor-Venables, 9½" 165.00
Plate, Grand Erie Canal, DeWitt Clinton Eulogy, d/b, 10¼" 450.00
Plate, Harvard, d/b, Stevenson's oak leaf & acorn border, 10" 450.00
Plate, Harvard College, sepia, Wood's Celtic series, 10½" 145.00
Plate, Hoboken in NJ, m/b, Stubbs' eagle border, 8" 225.00
Plate, hunters & dogs, d/b, minor wear, 9" 125.00
Plate, Landing of Lafayette, d/b, Clews, 10" 325.00
Plate, Landing of Lafayette, d/b, Clews, 9" 275.00

Plate, Montreal Steamship British America, lav, Davenport, 9" ...185.00
Plate, NY, pk, Adams, 6" 60.00
Plate, NY, pk, Mellor-Venables' Arms of States, 6½" 145.00
Plate, NY City Hall, m-d/b, Stubb's rose border, rpr, 7½" 250.00
Plate, Octagon Church, Boston, m-d/b, Ridgway, 9⅞" 385.00
Plate, Pains Hill Surrey, d/b, Hall, 10" 165.00
Plate, Palestine, d/b, Stevenson, 9½" 145.00
Plate, Panoramic Scenery, d/b, Stevenson, 10¼" 165.00
Plate, Panshanger Hertfordshire, d/b, Hall, 5½" 125.00
Plate, Peace & Plenty, d/b, Clews, 10¼" 375.00
Plate, Peace & Plenty, d/b, Clews, 9" 350.00
Plate, Quadrupeds Hall, m-d/b, 8½" 175.00
Plate, R Hall's Picturesque Scenery, m/b, 10", EX 100.00
Plate, Saxam Hall, d/b, British Views, 8¼" 155.00
Plate, soup; Arms of NY, d/b, Mayer, 10" 695.00
Plate, soup; Canterbury Cathedral, d/b, Clews, 9¾" 195.00
Plate, soup; Lakes of Killarney, m/b, 10" 65.00
Plate, soup; Landing of Lafayette, d/b, Clews, 10" 325.00
Plate, soup; View Near Phila, d/b, early rpr w/rivets, 9¾" 145.00
Plate, soup; Vue du Chateau de Ermenonville, d/b, Wood, 9¼" .180.00
Plate, soup; Winter View of Pittsfield, d/b, Clews, 10½", EX 350.00
Plate, soup; Writtle Lodge Essex, d/b, Stevenson, 10¼" 175.00
Plate, soup; Yorkminster, d/b, 9¾" 325.00
Plate, Table Rock Niagara, d/b, Wood's shell border, 10" 500.00
Plate, The Lake, Regents Park, d/b, Wood, 9¾" 165.00
Plate, toddy; View Near Conway NH, dk pk, Jackson, 5", NM ..250.00
Plate, View of Liverpool, d/b, Wood's shell border, 10" 275.00
Plate, View of Swiss Chalet, d/b, Davenport, 10¼" 165.00
Plate, View of Trenton Falls, d/b, Wood, 7¾" 325.00
Plate, Villa in Regents Park, d/b, Adams, 8¾" 165.00
Plate, Villa in Regents Park, d/b, Wood, 10¼" 185.00
Plate, Vue D-une Ancienne Abbaye, d/b, Wood, 9" 180.00
Plate, Winter View of Pittsfield MA, d/b, Clews, 10½" 425.00
Platter, Baltimore, l/b, Meigh Am Cities & Scenery, 16", EX 225.00
Platter, Boughton House, Northamptonshire, d/b, Hall, 13" 475.00
Platter, Canova, purple, T Mayer, wear, 20" 225.00
Platter, Castle Garden Battery NY, d/b, Wood, 18½" 2,700.00
Platter, Hallowell, Bay of Quinte, Canada, l/b, Morley, 19" 375.00
Platter, Highlands Hudson River, d/b, Wood, 12¾" 1,850.00
Platter, hunt party outside tavern, d/b, 17", VG 250.00
Platter, Lake George State of NY, d/b, Wood, 16½" 1,950.00
Platter, Mendenhall Ferry, d/b, Stubbs, 16½", NM 1,450.00
Platter, moose, d/b, animal medallions in border, Hall, 15" 1,400.00
Platter, PA Hospital Phila, d/b, Ridgway, 18¾", NM 1,800.00
Platter, Upper Ferry Bridge...Schuylkill, d/b, Stubbs, 19" 1,850.00
Platter, WA from President's House, l/b, Meigh, 20", EX 225.00
Sauce boat, Batalha Portugal, d/b 195.00
Serving dish base, Polar Bear, Hall, NM 695.00
Sugar bowl, Lafayette at Franklin's Tomb, d/b, Wood, rpr 495.00
Sugar bowl, NY City Hall, m/b, Stubbs, sm rim chip 375.00
Sugar bowl, Oriental view, d/b 275.00
Teapot, floral w/Oriental bldgs, d/b, chips, 7" 150.00
Teapot, Lafayette at Franklin's Tomb, d/b, Wood, prof rpr 525.00
Teapot, Seat of...Gen WA, Mt Vernon, d/b, lid flake, 11½" 650.00
Tureen, sauce; Bank of Savannah Charleston..., d/b, Ridgway ..1,450.00
Tureen, sauce; dog/rabbit/bird, w/lid, Hall, fox/rooster on tray ...995.00
Wash bowl, Arms of States, l/b, Mellor-Venables, 12¼" 275.00
Wash bowl, Lafayette at Franklin's Tomb, d/b, 12" 950.00
Wash bowl & pitcher, Boston State House, d/b, Rogers, EX ...2,100.00

Miscellaneous

Coffeepot, Chinese pagoda, m-d/b, high dome, w/lid 400.00
Covered dish, hen, wht, 9½" 350.00

Cottage, gable end removes to contain the pastille cone, encrusted with garden flowers, early 1800s, 10" long, $8,000.00.

Covered dish, hen on brn basket, bsk, 6¾x6¾x5" 245.00
Covered dish, swan, wht, w/egg cups inside, 8" 495.00
Creamer, gaudy floral, w/underglaze bl, 5¾" 125.00
Cup & saucer, pansies, purple/yel, +multiflora, scalloped 45.00
Cup & saucer, strawberries around rim, blk rim stripes 65.00
Cup & saucer, sunflower band, bl rim band, Wood, eagle mk 195.00
Cup plate, Jacobean-type floral, bl transfer, 3½", NM 65.00
Cup plate, red rose/bl & yel flowers, red striping, Wood 100.00
Cup plate, ruins, floral border, red transfer, 4" 35.00
Figurine, cat, sits, wht/blk, copper lustre collar, 7", pr 400.00
Figurine, clown, mc, 4" 200.00
Figurine, cobbler & his wife, mc, lustre trim, 6¾", pr 245.00
Figurine, dog, lg/upright, w/boy on bk, minor wear, 7" 325.00
Figurine, equestrian (equestrienne), 1800s, 9½", pr 210.00
Figurine, equestrienne, mc, 3⅝" 85.00
Figurine, Franklin, titled Washington, 1850, wear, 15" 660.00
Figurine, girl & goat, mc, minor base flakes, 3" 200.00
Figurine, girl by cradle w/baby, 7" 50.00
Figurine, girl w/pitcher, 4", NM 95.00
Figurine, greyhound, gr/wht mottle, on brn/gr oval base, 8" 400.00
Figurine, lady & man in kilt flank clock face, 9½" 170.00
Figurine, lamb w/flag, sanded coat, mc, 3", NM 125.00
Figurine, lion & lamb, both recumbent, 1850s, 3¾x4¾" 200.00
Figurine, lion w/ft on ball, shaped base, facing pr, 8" 350.00
Figurine, Naval officer, arms crossed, mc, 6", NM 125.00
Figurine, poodle w/basket in mouth, wht coleslaw, 3¼", EX 130.00
Figurine, rabbit on oval grassy plinth, 1850s, 3" 275.00
Figurine, ram, sanded coat, pastel trim, 3" 165.00
Figurine, Red Riding hood by tree vase, 11" 110.00
Figurine, romantic couple beneath arch, 1800s, 8½", EX 180.00
Figurine, Tom King on horsebk, looking left 10½" 125.00
Figurine, Vavandiere on horsebk, maid by side, 12" 175.00
Figurine, whippet seated on bl pillow base, 4¾" 185.00
Figurine, Young Queen (Victoria)?, mc/gilt, 8", EX 150.00
Figurine, zebra on rocky oval base, 1870, chip/rpr, 8" 495.00
Inkwell, whippet, recumbent, tan/blk on bl base, England, 4" 150.00
Jug, Tax Collector, gold vest, bl jacket, early, 10x4½" 345.00
Mug, young woman w/yoke, blk transfer, 3" 85.00
Pitcher, Geo Peabody, brn transfer on gr, 1870s, 8", VG 110.00
Plate, chinoiserie, m/b, Davenport, 9½" 45.00
Plate, floral center, wide mc rim band, mk W & Wood, 6¾" 70.00
Plate, gaudy pk/gr flowers, gold lustre accents, mk, 8½" 120.00

Plate, pk rose w/bl buds, wide rim band, Wood, 6¾", NM 50.00
Plate, red rose/bl & yel flowers, scalloped, Wood, 7½" 75.00
Plate, sunflower, 3-color border, scalloped, mk W, 10" 195.00
Spaniel, seated, coleslaw coat, mc features/gilt, 5½", NM, pr 600.00
Spaniel, seated, copper lustre spots, 7" 175.00
Spaniel, seated, wht w/gilt/blk/red, glass eyes, 12", NM, pr 250.00
Spaniel, seated, wht w/red spots, 4½", NM 225.00
Spaniel, standing, sanded coat, flowers at ft, 4½" 85.00
Spill vase, boy/girl/goat by tree, 7½" 150.00
Spill vase, boy/maid/dog/2 sheep by tree, 9", NM 375.00
Spill vase, dog by tree, leg damaged, 6" 185.00
Spill vase, dog by tree, mc w/gilt, 6½" 225.00
Spill vase, girl & lg dog by tree, 8", VG 155.00
Spill vase, hunter & dog by tree trunk, 1840s, 13" 300.00
Spill vase, musicians/owl/squirrel/3 sheep by tree, 7", EX 475.00
Tea bowl & saucer, Oriental, red transfer, hairlines/stains 50.00
Waste bowl, gaudy rose, minor wear, 5½" 135.00

Stained Glass

There are many factors to consider in evaluating a window or panel of stained glass art. Besides the obvious factor of condition, intricacy, jeweling, beveling, and the amount of selenium (red, orange, and yellow) present should all be taken into account. Remember, repair work is itself an art and can be very expensive. Our advisor for this category is Carl Heck; he is listed in the Directory under Colorado.

Lamps

Bigelow Kennard, 18" acorn-band dome form shade; std 3,250.00
Ceiling, ribbon band on cone w/lg oval panels, mts, 27" 3,850.00
Duffner-Kimberly, 22" fishscale/water lily band shade, VG 3,000.00
Duffner-Kimberly, 26" geometric-band floral shade (EX); 33" ...3,740.00
Duffner-Kimberly, 28" cone shade w/irregular floral border 4,500.00
Duffner-Kimberly att, 22" floral irregular-border shade 6,000.00
Suess, 25" apple blossom umbrella shade; trunk std 5,500.00

Table lamp, Wilkinson, 26" shade with fan, shell, and lappet segments, overall height, 33", $3,750.00.

Wilkinson, 22" floral curved panel scallop-edge shade, 29" 5,775.00
Wilkinson, 23" Nouveau-scroll incurvate shade; baluster std ..4,100.00

Windows

Duffner-Kimberly att, trees/mtns, 50x30" 13,200.0
Fruit still life center, 24x36", pr 1,750.0
Nouveau scrolls w/jewels, beveled glue-chip border, 22x40" ...2,750.0

Stanford

The Stanford Pottery Co. was founded in 1945 in Sebring, Ohio. One of the founders was George Stanford, a former manager at Spaulding China (Royal Copley). They continued in operations until the factory was destroyed by a fire about 1961. They produced a Corn Line similar to that of the Shawnee Company, that is today becoming very collectible. Most examples are marked (either Stanford Sebring Ohio or with a paper label), so there should be no difficulty in distinguishing one from the other.

In addition to their Corn line, they produced planters and figurines, many of which were black trimmed with gold, made to be sold as pairs or sets. Wall pockets and vases were made as well. In 1949, they introduced a line called Tomatoe Ware, consisting of a cookie jar, grease jar, salt and pepper shakers, creamer and sugar bowl, mustard jar, marmalade jar, etc. These were shaped as bright red tomatoes with green leaves and stems (often used as lid finials), and were marketed under the name 'Pantry Ware.' Our advisor for this category is Jo Devine; he is listed in the Directory under Iowa.

Cookie jar, $85.00.

Corn Line, butter dish 45.0
Corn Line, cookie jar 85.0
Corn Line, creamer & sugar bowl 45.0
Corn Line, pitcher, 7½" 55.0
Corn Line, relish tray 35.0
Corn Line, shakers, pr 25.0
Corn Line, spoon rest 25.0
Corn Line, teapot 60.0
Planter, drum major or majorette, ea 15.0
Planter, Dutch boy or girl by tulip, blk w/gold trim, ea 15.0
Tomatoe Ware, cookie jar 50.0
Tomatoe Ware, creamer 25.0
Tomatoe Ware, grease jar 25.0
Tomatoe Ware, marmalade jar 25.0
Tomatoe Ware, mustard jar 25.0
Tomatoe Ware, shakers, pr 40.0
Tomatoe Ware, sugar bowl 25.0
Wall pocket, bird, bl & cobalt w/gold trim 28.0

Stangl

Stangl Pottery was one of the longest-existing potteries in the

United States, having as its beginning in 1814 the Sam Hill Pottery, becoming the Fulper Pottery which gained eminence in the field of art pottery (ca. 1860), and then coming under the aegis of Johann Martin Stangl. The German-born Stangl joined Fulped in 1910 as chemical engineer, left for a brief stint at Haeger in Dundee, Illinois, and rejoined Fulper as general manager in 1920. He became president of the firm in 1928. Although Stangl's name was on much of the ware from the late twenties onward, the company's name was not changed officially until 1955. J.M. Stangl died in 1972; the pottery continued under the ownership of Wheaton Industries until 1978, then closed. Stangl is best known for its extensive Birds of American line, styled after Audubon; its brightly colored hand-carved, hand-painted dinnerware; and its great variety of giftware, including its dry-brushed gold lines. For more information we recommend *Stangl Pottery* by Harvey Duke; for ordering information refer to the listing for Nancy and Robert Perzel, Popkorn Antiques (our advisors for this category), in our Directory under New Jersey.

Birds

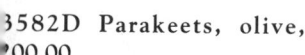
3582D Parakeets, olive,
200.00.

3250E, Drinking Duck, gold	65.00
3273, Rooster, 5¾"	400.00
3276, Bluebird	85.00
3276D, Bluebirds	160.00
3285/#3286, Rooster & Hen shakers, late, pr	100.00
3286, Hen, early, 3¼"	85.00
3400, Lovebird	55.00
3401, Wren, tan	100.00
3401, Wren, revised	50.00
3401D, Wrens, tan	150.00
3402, Oriole, 3¼"	60.00
3402D, Orioles	125.00
3402D, Orioles, old	200.00
3405, Cockatoo, 6"	55.00
3405D, Cockatoos	175.00
3405D, Cockatoos, revised	150.00
3406, Kingfisher, paper label	70.00
3408, Bird of Paradise	100.00
3443, Flying Duck, gray, 9"	265.00
3444, Cardinal, pk, revised male	75.00
3444, Cardinal, red matt, 6½"	110.00
3445, Rooster, gray	200.00
3445, Rooster, yel, 9"	150.00
3446, Hen, yel, 7"	150.00
3447, Prothonatary Warbler	70.00
3448, Bl Headed Vireo	65.00
3452, Painted Bunting, 5"	100.00

#3454, Key West Quail Dove, single wing up	275.00
#3456, Cerulean Warbler, 4½"	70.00
#3457, Pheasant, 7¼x15"	800.00
#3490D, Redstarts	175.00
#3491, Hen Pheasant	200.00
#3492, Cock Pheasant, antique gold	125.00
#3492, Cock Pheasant, 6¼x11"	200.00
#3580, Cockatoo, 8⅞"	120.00
#3581, Chickadee Group	175.00
#3583, Parula Warbler, dk bl	50.00
#3584, Cockatoo, sgn Jacob on side, 11½"	275.00
#3584, Cockatoo, 11½"	225.00
#3585, Rufous Hummingbird, 3"	55.00
#3589, Indigo Bunting	60.00
#3590, Carolina Wren	135.00
#3592, Titmouse, 2½"	50.00
#3593, Nuthatch, 2½"	50.00
#3594, Red-Faced Warbler	60.00
#3596, Gray Cardinal, 4¾"	75.00
#3597, Wilson Warbler, yel, 3½"	50.00
#3598, Kentucky Warbler, 3"	55.00
#3599D, Hummingbirds	275.00
#3626, Broadtail Hummingbird	120.00
#3627, Rivoli Hummingbird, w/pk flower	120.00
#3628, Rieffers Hummingbird	120.00
#3629, Broadtail Hummingbird, w/wht flower	120.00
#3634, Allen Hummingbird, 3½"	60.00
#3635, Goldfinch Group, 4x11½"	180.00
#3715, Bl Jay, w/peanut	550.00
#3722, European Finch	200.00
#3746, Canary, w/red flower	200.00
#3749S, Western Tanager	200.00
#3750D, Western Tanagers	250.00
#3751, Red-Headed Woodpecker, pk gloss	125.00
#3751, Red-Headed Woodpecker, red matt	150.00
#3752D, Red-Headed Woodpeckers, red matt	300.00
#3754D, Wht-Wing Grossbills, 8¾"	200.00
#37545, Crossbill (single)	400.00
#3757, Scissor-Tailed Flycatcher	500.00
#3811, Chestnut-Backed Chickadee	100.00
#3812, Chestnut-Sided Warbler	100.00
#3813, Evening Grosbeak	120.00
#3814, Blk-Throated Gr Warbler, 3⅛"	125.00
#3848, Golden-Crowned Kinglet	100.00
#3851, Red-Breasted Nuthatch	65.00
#3868, Summer Tanager	250.00
#3921, Verdin, yel-headed	400.00
#3924, Yel-Throated Warbler	150.00
#3925, Magnolia Warbler	300.00

Miscellaneous

Amberglo, bowl, 8"	20.00
Amberglo, cruet, w/stopper	20.00
Amberglo, gravy boat & undertray	20.00
Amberglo, pitcher, ½-pt	15.00
Americana, lug soup	6.00
Antique Gold, ashtray, #3904	12.00
Antique Gold, bowl, tapered, 22k gold trim, #3980	20.00
Antique Gold, candlestick, #5138, pr	25.00
Antique Gold, flower bowl, #3410-9	32.50
Antique Gold, horn of plenty, #5065	30.00
Antique Gold, vase, #5144, 4½x5"	15.00
Antique Gold, vase, bud; #3981, 6½"	15.00

Antique Gold, vase, horse head, #3611 ....265.00
Apple Tree, coaster, #3845 ....12.00
Artware, vase, tangerine, hdls, #2017 ....20.00
Aztec, candle holder, #A-4064, pr 48.00
Aztec, pitcher, Granada Gold, #A-4053 ....30.00
Bittersweet, plate, dinner 8.00
Black Gold, candle holder, #5062 ....15.00
Blue Daisy, mug, 2-cup 20.00
Blueberry, bowl, 10" 35.00
Blueberry, candle warmer 18.00
Blueberry, coffeecup 9.00
Blueberry, shakers, pr 15.00
Carribean, apple dish, single, #3785 ....12.00
Carribean, candy dish, w/lid, #3676 ....29.00
Cigarette box, hummingbird 50.00
Cigarette box, tree w/apples 40.00
Colonial, candlestick, pr 25.00
Colonial, custard cup 7.50
Colonial Silver, ashtray, #5174, 7" 12.00
Colonial Silver, bowl, oval, #5115M, 14" 30.00
Colonial Silver, flower bowl, #3410-7 ....20.00
Colonial Yellow, candle holder, #3099, 1¼x2½" 15.00
Cotton holder, rabbit form 250.00
Country Garden, bowl, divided vegetable 35.00
Country Garden, bowl, 8" 35.00
Country Garden, coaster, 6 for 60.00
Country Garden, cup & saucer 15.00
Country Garden, plate, 10" 14.00
Country Garden, plate, 8" 10.00
Country Garden, plate, 9" 12.00
Della Ware El Rosa, plate, 9¼" 12.50
Fruit, bowl, cereal; 5⅝" 10.00
Fruit, bowl, salad; 10" 30.00
Fruit, bowl, soup; 7¾" 15.00
Fruit, bowl, 8½" 22.50
Fruit, cup & saucer 12.50
Fruit, pitcher, ½-pt 15.00
Fruit, plate, 10" 15.00
Fruit, plate, 6" 6.00
Fruit, plate, 8" 12.00
Fruit, sugar bowl, w/lid 18.00
Fruit & Flowers, bowl, cereal; 6" 10.00
Fruit & Flowers, cup & saucer 15.00
Fruit & Flowers, gravy boat 18.00
Garden Flower, chop plate, 12½" 35.00
Garden Flower, pitcher, 5½" 15.00
Golden Harvest, lug soup 10.00
Golden Harvest, pitcher, lg 25.00
Golden Harvest, plate, 10" 10.00
Granada Gold, candle holder, #5062 ....15.00
Granada Gold, pear dish (single), #3553, 7¾" 15.00
Kiddieware Five Little Pigs, cup 60.00
Kiddieware Five Little Pigs, 3-part dish 100.00
Kiddieware Meal Time Special, cup 35.00
Kiddieware Meal Time Special, 3-part dish 65.00
Magnolia, butter dish 25.00
Magnolia, plate, 10" 12.00
Magnolia, plate, 6" 6.00
Miniature, ashtray, pig form, med bl, 3" 40.00
Miniature, pitcher, orange, w/label, #3053 ....15.00
Miniature, soap dish, tub form, Patrician, lt bl 20.00
Orchard Song, cup & saucer 12.00
Orchard Song, plate, 8" 10.00
Orchard Song, server, center hdl 6.00

Pebblestone, urn, #3993, 13" ....75.
Prelude, cup & saucer ....15.
Prelude, plate, 10" 12
Scroll, bowl, tangerine, #3020, 7x7½" 37
Sculptured Fruit, saucer 5
Sportsman, ashtray, pheasant, oval ....35.
Sportsman, plate, Canada goose ....45.
Star Flower, coaster, 5" ....10.
Star Flower, sugar bowl, w/lid ....15.
Stoby mug, Chief, Terra Rose bottom, gr w/wht hdl ....150.
Terra Rose, bowl, gr, 7" ....22.
Terra Rose, chop plate, yel, 12" ....22.
Terra Rose, leaf bowl, bl, #3540 ....35.
Terra Rose, pig bank, Tulip #1076 ....125.
Terra Rose, pitcher, 2-qt ....20.
Terra Rose, vase, pitcher form, #3214, 8" ....25.
Terra Rose, vase, Tulip, #3694 ....25.
Thistle, bowl, 10" ....30.
Thistle, bowl, 8" ....25.
Thistle, coaster, 5" ....10.
Thistle, cup & saucer ....10.
Thistle, plate, bread & butter ....6.
Vase, bl matt, dbl hdls, #3103 ....250.
Wig stand, blond, on sq wood base, w/label ....225.
Wig stand, brunette, on ceramic base ....200.
Wild Rose, bowl, fruit ....12.
Wild Rose, bowl, vegetable; 8" ....30.
Wild Rose, butter dish ....35.
Wild Rose, cup & saucer ....12.
Wild Rose, lug soup ....15.
Wild Rose, plate, 10" ....15.
Wild Rose, plate, 6" ....6.
Wild Rose, plate, 8" ....10.
Wild Rose, platter, 14x10½" ....30.
Wild Rose, relish tray ....18.
Wild Rose, sugar bowl ....15.

Statue of Liberty

Long before she began greeting immigrants in 1886, the Statue
Liberty was being honored by craftsmen both here and abroad. Her li
ness was etched on blades of the finest straight razors from England, ca
tured in finely detailed busts sold as souvenirs to Paris fairgoers in 18
and presented on colorfully lithographed trade cards, usually satirical,
American shoppers. Perhaps no other object has been represented
more forms or with such frequency as the universal symbol of Ameri
Liberty's keepsakes are also universally accessible. Delightful souve
models created in 1885 to raise funds for Liberty's pedestal are frequen
found at flea markets, while earlier French bronze and terra cotta Lib
ties have been auctioned for over $100,000. Some collectors hunt for
countless forms of 19th-century Liberty memorabilia, while many coll
tions were begun in anticipation of the 1986 Centennial with concent
tion on modern depictions. Our advisor for this category is Mike Broo
he is listed in the Directory under California.

Album, celluloid image front, velvet bk, 10x8", EX ....275.
Bookmark, fabric, Bartholdi Souvenir, 1886 ....25.
Bottle, Liberty Maraschino Cherries, ca 1940 ....12.
Bottle, seltzer; etched Liberty, A Doeink, Liberty NY ....35.
Cigarette photo card, Virginia Brights, 1886 ....18.
Coffeepot, enameled scene on metal, 11" ....200.
Cup, sterling, Windsor Club, 1907, 2" ....22.
Engraving, from dedication ceremony, 1883, 5½x4", EX ....110.

Hanukkah menorah, Liberty figures candle holders, M Anson ..1,800.00
Lamp base, wht metal, clock at base, ca 1885, 20", EX 300.00
Medal, Democratic Nat'l Convention, NY, 1924 ....30.00
Medal, Emma Lazarus, 'Give Me Your Tired...,' bronze, 1986 ....35.00
Medal, World Liberty Penny, July 18, 1918 ....30.00
Model, CI w/NP & silver flame, Committee model, 36", EX ..11,000.00
Model, plaster, Max Voight, Phila, 1918, 72", EX 880.00
Napkin holder, sterling 15.00
Painting, rvpt scene, 22x15", EX 100.00
Plate, glass, eng statue, heart shape 22.00
Program, souvenir; Oct 28, 1886 ....200.00
Radio speaker stand, wht metal casting, Palcone, 17", EX 175.00
Smoking stand, figural, copper-plated cast metal, EX 150.00
Spoon, figural hdl, SP, 5¾" 75.00
Statue, cast metal on marble base, June 13, 1885 ....1,000.00
Statue, cast metal on oak base, 12" 25.00

Statue, pot metal with silver finish, 9", $25.00.

Straight razor, Liberty etched blade, Sheffield, ca 1880 ....75.00
Tin can, long top, Liberty polish, 1922 ....17.00
Vase, frosted Liberty hand, Gillinder, 1876 Centennial 70.00
Watercolor, harbor scene, JW Goppard, 21x15", EX 220.00

Steamship Collectibles

For centuries, ocean-going vessels with their venturesome officers and crews were the catalyst that changed the unknown aspects of our world to the known. Changing economic conditions, unfortunately, have now placed the North American shipping industry in the same jeopardy as the American passenger train. They are becoming a memory. The surge of interest in railroad collectibles and the railroad-related steamship lines has lead collectors to examine the whole spectrum of steamship collectibles. Our advisors for this category are Lila and Fred Shrader; they are listed in the Directory under California.

Dinnerware

Ashtray, Matson w/red M on wht ground, 4½" dia 22.00
Butter pat, United Fruit Co, flag logo 25.00
Creamer, Canadian Nat'l, Maritime, 3" 38.00
Creamer, Canadian Pacific, Tremblant, 3½" 49.00
Cup & saucer, Alaska 45.00
Cup & saucer, demitasse; American Mail 65.00
Cup & saucer, Texaco 65.00
Gravy boat, Puerto Rico Line, w/attached underplate 45.00
Ice cream shell, NESS Co, New England 65.00
Plate, Pacific Coast, flag logo, 8½" 75.00

Plate, Southern Pacific, Harriman Bl, Morgan, 6½" 95.00
Plate, Swedish-Am Line, ship w/anchor border, 7½" 25.00
Plate, Western Canada SS, flag logo 22.00
Platter, Matson, floral border, 6x8" 35.00
Platter, Royal Caribbean, 8x6" 20.00
Teapot, Holland-Am, crossed flags 55.00
Toothpick, Cunard, blk & wht stripes, 1½" sq 28.00

Miscellaneous

Baggage label, Cunard 4.50
Baggage tag, Alaska, brass, w/logo 25.00
Bookmark, Alaska, celluloid, w/1925 calendar 28.00
Bookmark, Am-Hawaii Lines, bl leather, 9" 5.00
Brochure, Grace Lines, CA-Havanna-NY-S Am, fares/info, 1935 ..60.00
Brochure, Prudential Cruises, deck plans & fares, 1977 ....5.00
Clock, ship's; Chelsea, brass, 7¼" face, w/orig key 425.00
Hanger, Swedish Am Lines, wooden, eng w/ship's monogram 15.00
Hat ribbon, French Line SS Normandie, red w/gold lettering 85.00
Label, luggage; French Line, rnd, 1930s, M 15.00
Letter opener, Princess Cruises, wood, laser eng, 9", MIB 9.00
Menu, dinner; SS Constitution, 1980 ....8.00
Menu, Matson Lines SS Monterey, farewell dinner, 1960 ....10.00
Pen, Pacific & Orient SS Sea Princess, floating ship inside 4.50
Place mat, Holland American Line, SS Rotterdam, 12x18" 10.00
Postcard, Matson Line SS Lurline, blk/wht stateroom, M 15.00
Program, concert; German Atlantic Line, TS Hamburg, 1972 .....10.00
Ship model, SS Pacific Princess, wht compo, 1984, 11", MIB 20.00
Stationery, Cunard Wht Star, red lettering, +envelope 20.00
Ticket folio, Cunard Line, w/related paper items, 1928 ....38.00

Steins

Steins have been made from pottery, pewter, glass, stoneware, and porcelain, from very small up to the four-liter size. They are decorated by etching, in-mold relief, decals, and occasionally they may be hand painted. Some porcelain steins have lithophane bases. Collectors often specialize in a particular type — faience, regimental, or figural — while others limit themselves to the products of only one manufacturer. Our advisor for this category is Ron Fox; he is listed in the Directory under New York. See also Mettlach.

Key:
L — liter
lith — lithophane
tl — thumb lift

PUG — print under glaze
POG — print over glaze

Brewery, Budweiser, transfer on relief, 50th Anniversary, ½-L ...105.00
Brewery, Lowenbrau, stoneware, eng, pewter lid, 1-L, NM 230.00
Brewery, Mathasen-Brau, stoneware transfer, rpl tl, 1-L 578.00
Brewery, Schifferer Brau, stoneware, transfer, 1½-L 250.00
Character, alligator, porc, Schierholz, ½-L, NM 1,050.00
Character, artillery shell, stoneware, 1914-15, ½-L 580.00
Character, Bismark, porc, lith, ½-L 770.00
Character, Bismark, porc, Schierholz, rpr, .3-L, EX 220.00
Character, Blk man w/pipe, majolica glaze, ½-L, EX 290.00
Character, bowling pin, pottery, ½-L, EX 150.00
Character, Burgermeister, pottery, pewter lid, ½-L, NM 230.00
Character, dog in barrel, pottery, dog hdl, rpr, ½-L 198.00
Character, elephant, lid forms head, Schierholz, ½-L 715.00
Character, Fox, Schierholz, rpr rim & body, ½-L, EX 715.00
Character, Funnel Man, pottery, Hanke, ½-L, EX 185.00
Character, high-wheel bicycle, rpl lid, Schierholz, ½-L 245.00
Character, hops lady, pottery, pewter lid, ½-L, NM 230.00

Character, Indian, porc, Bohne & Sohne, ¼-L, EX 330.00
Character, jovial face, pottery, pewter lid, ½-L, NM 250.00
Character, Ludwig, stoneware, mk RH, ½-L, NM 465.00
Character, monk, porc, lith, inlaid lid, ½-L, NM 275.00
Character, monk, pottery, inlaid lid, ½-L, NM 112.00
Character, monk, pottery, ¼-L, NM 250.00
Character, monk, stoneware, Merkelbach-Wick, ½-L 245.00
Character, monkey, pottery, DRGM Diesinger, ½-L 660.00
Character, monkey, pottery, rpl tl, ½-L, EX 195.00
Character, Mozart, porc, Bohne & Sohne, 1756-91, ½-L 1,385.00
Character, Munich child, lith, Schierholz, ½-L 1,040.00
Character, Munich child, porc, lith, Martin Pauson, rpr, ½-L 300.00
Character, Munich child, pottery, chip, ½-L 150.00
Character, Munich child, pottery, Reinemann, .2-L 275.00
Character, nun, pottery, M&W, ½-L, M 175.00
Character, Nurnberg funnel, lith, Schierholz, ½-L 720.00
Character, Nurnberg Tower, pottery, #978, ½-L 330.00
Character, Nurnberg Tower, stoneware, pewter lid, ½-L, EX 200.00
Character, Oriental man, majolica glaze, rstr pnt, ½-L, NM 175.00
Character, pig w/pipe, porc, Schierholz, ½-L 200.00
Character, rabbit, Schierholz, rpr, ½-L, EX 685.00
Character, rabbit hunter, porc, ca 1920s, ½-L, NM 525.00
Character, rich man, pottery, Thewalt, ½-L, EX 350.00
Character, sleeping hunter, porc, Bauer, rpr, ½-L 1,250.00
Character, stag, porc, Schierholz, sm chip, ½-L 2,900.00
Character, suit of armor, stoneware, dragon finial, ½-L 360.00
Character, tower, pottery, rpr, ½-L 525.00
Character, woman, pottery, Merkelbach-Wick, ½-L 300.00
Character, woman's face relief, majolica glaze, ½-L, EX 290.00
Faience, florals & trees, rpl pewter lid, 1900s, 1-L, VG 225.00
Faience, plain body, pewter lid, ball tl, 1820s, 1-L, EX 230.00
Glass, blown, amber w/pewter o/l & hdl, ½-L 400.00
Glass, blown, cased mc glass w/mica, pewter lid, 1910s, ½-L 925.00
Glass, blown, cobalt, appl hdl, pewter lid, 1840s, ½-L, VG 693.00
Glass, blown, eng stag, pewter lid, .3-L, NM 175.00
Glass, blown, HP edelweiss, pewter lid, .3-L, NM 145.00
Glass, blown, HP hunting dog, metal lid, ½-L 115.00
Glass, blown, HP jovial radishes, pewter lid, ½-L 495.00
Glass, blown, HP Munich child, inlay lid, ½-L 340.00
Glass, blown, HP Munich skyline/man at table, ½-L 295.00
Glass, blown, HP Prussian eagle, pewter lid, ½-L 300.00
Glass, blown, manganese, appl hdl, pewter lid, 1860s, ½-L 600.00
Glass, blown, red stain, eng: luck/health/etc, chip, ½-L 165.00
Glass, blown, ruby, clear hdl, ruby inlay lid, .3-L, M 185.00
Glass, blown, ruby stain, inlay/eng lid, 1860s, ½-L, EX 350.00
Glass, blown/cut, prism inlay lid, horse head tl, 1-L 465.00
Glass, pressed, Lowenbrau transfer, ½-L 88.00
Glass, pressed, porc crest inlay lid, 1926 eagle tl, .3-L 155.00
Glass, pressed Saxon, beaded, HP florals/shield, ½-L 72.00
Nazi, Fiegerhorstkompanie-Prenzlau, pottery, ½-L 885.00
Nazi, KP/IR 63 Ingolstadt, pottery, ½-L 500.00
Nazi, planes in relief, stoneware, metal lid, ½-L 585.00
Nazi, 10/IR 61 Trauenstein, pottery, 1937, ½-L 165.00
Nazi, 17 EMG Komp IR 42 Hof, stoneware, ½-L 795.00
Occupational, porc, transfer: blksmith, lith, ½-L, EX 360.00
Occupational, porc, transfer: brewer, lith, ½-L 500.00
Pewter, relief: couple dancing, ½-L, VG, 6¼" 100.00
Pewter, relief: spirals & vintage, ball tl, 1½", EX 175.00
Porc, etched: tapestry, Munich child lid, HR 156, ½-L 285.00
Porc, etched: tapestry scene, HR 217, ½-L 290.00
Porc, HP: children playing, silver lid, Nymphenburg, ½-L 1,625.00
Porc, HP: floral w/gold, man tl, Rauenstein, 1½-L 270.00
Porc, HP: Onion pattern, inlay lid, Rauenstein, ½-L 465.00
Porc, HP: Onion pattern, lith in lid, ½-L 265.00

Porcelain, hand painted, Lenox, O'Hara Dial inlaid lid with eagle, 3.0L, $550.00; Pottery, etched, Gerz, inlaid lid, marked 1384, 2.0L; Student Fox, pottery, by Diesinger, 2.5L, $770.00; Bowling Pin, pottery, #1186, 1.75L, $385.00.

Porc, transfer/HP: bicycle/mtn scene, lith, ½-L, EX 600.0
Porc, transfer: couple walking, jewels, lith, rpr, ½-L 70.0
Pottery, etched/relief: people talking, JWR 905, ½-L 165.0
Pottery, etched/threading: couple w/puppies, Thewalt 601, 1-L .150.0
Pottery, etched: dwarf & cherub, Gerz 258, hairline, ½-L 200.0
Pottery, etched: dwarf on ladder, HR 416, flakes, ½-L 400.0
Pottery, etched: dwarfs drinking, Merkelbach-Wick, ½-L 300.0
Pottery, etched: fox hunt, HR 520, ½-L 400.0
Pottery, etched: hunter, deer inlay lid, Germsheid 1260, 1-L 200.0
Pottery, etched: hunter smoking, Germsheid 1256, ½-L 135.0
Pottery, etched: man bowling, Germsheid 1087A, 1-L 175.0
Pottery, etched: Masonic symbols/pyramids, ½-L 350.0
Pottery, etched: people at table/windmill, dwarf on lid, ½-L 200.0
Pottery, etched: 3 men & barrel, metal lid, Thewalt 335, ½-L ...140.0
Pottery, relief: couple dancing, cherubs, pewter lid, 2½-L 198.0
Pottery, relief: King & Queen, griffin tl, 2½-L 350.0
Pottery, relief: Nurnberg scenes, pewter lid, ½-L 165.0
Pottery, relief: people at table, HR 450, rpl lid, ½-L 140.0
Pottery, relief: 4-F athletic scene, rpr lid, 2-L, EX 245.0
Pottery, transfer/HP, bicycle scene, #599, 2-L 798.0
Pottery, transfer/HP: bowling scene, pewter lid, ½-L, NM 110.0
Pottery, transfer/HP: dragon & phoenix, ½-L 975.0
Pottery, transfer/HP: men at cards, Merkelbach-Wick, ½-L 485.0
Pottery, transfer/HP: monk & cavaliers, Merkelbach-Wick, ½-L ..485.0
Pottery, transfer: bicycle scene, hairline, ½-L 495.0
Pottery, transfer: drunken man, pewter lid, M&W, 1-L 140.0
Pottery, transfer: lawn hockey scene, pewter lid, ½-L 515.0
Regimental, III Infantry Rastatt 1894-96, porc, ½-L, EX 150.0
Regimental, Luftschiffer...1899-01, stoneware, ½-L 4,400.0
Regimental, 1 Garde Zu Foss...1900-02, porc, lith, ½-L 4,000.0
Regimental, 100 Anniv Inf Wurzburg 1803-1903, porc, ½-L 380.0
Regimental, 112 Inf Mulhausen 1911-13, porc, lith, ½-L 400.0
Regimental, 120 Inf Ulm 1903-05, porc, bird tl, lith, ½-L 450.0
Regimental, 124 Inf Weingarten 1907-09, lion tl, lith, ½-L 375.0
Regimental, 14 Dragooner Colmar 1911-14, porc, rpr, ½-L 825.0
Regimental, 14 Ulan St Avoid 1911-14, porc, lith, ½-L 695.0
Regimental, 15 Ulan Saarbug 1911-14, porc, lith, ½-L, NM 350.0
Regimental, 179 Inf Wurzen 1901-03, porc, lith, ½-L, NM 375.0
Regimental, 22 Inf Zwelbrucken 1904-06, porc, lith, ½-L 400.0
Regimental, 25 Feld Artl...1893-95, porc, lith, ½-L, NM 500.0
Regimental, 39 Feld Artl...1911-13, pottery, ½-L 495.0
Regimental, 62 Feld Artl...1909-11, porc, eagle tl, lith, ½-L 450.0
Regimental, 8 Lieb Inf Munchen 1907-09, porc, lith, ½-L 1,100.0

Stoneware, etch: men in red coats, Merkelbach, '30s, ½-L, EX **75.00**
Stoneware, etched: 4-leaf clovers, porc inlay lid, M&W, 1-L **235.00**
Stoneware, relief: musical scene, lions on side, rpr, 2-L **95.00**
Stoneware, relief: Nouveau-Deco pattern, pewter lid, ½-L **92.00**
Stoneware, relief: Whites, man & vines, SP lid, ½-L, NM **300.00**
Stoneware, transfer/HP: bowling scene, pewter lid, ½-L **145.00**
Stoneware, transfer/HP: couple toasting, M&W, ½-L **198.00**
Stoneware, transfer/HP: lady serving, pewter rpr, ½-L, EX **110.00**
Stoneware, transfer/HP: man drinking, Merkelbach, ½-L **145.00**
Stoneware, transfer/HP: shooting festival, Ringer, 1912, 1-L **700.00**
Stoneware, transfer/HP: shooting festival, Ringer, 1912, ¼-L **350.00**
Stoneware, transfer/HP: shooting festival, 1909, ¼-L **140.00**
Stoneware, transfer/photo/HP: singing mushrooms, ½-L, NM **255.00**
Stoneware, transfer/photo/HP: Wilhelm II/Franzjosef, ½-L **245.00**
Stoneware, transfer: Hofbrauhaus scene, Merkelbach-Wick, ½-L ..**370.00**
Stoneware, transfer: lady in formal attire, hairline, ½-L **95.00**
Stoneware, transfer: train car, M&W, pewter lid, ½-L **370.00**
Wood, cvd: Oriental-type pattern, ½-L, G **58.00**

Steuben

Carder Steuben glass was made by the Stueben Glass Works in
Corning, New York, while under the direction of Frederick Carder from
1903 to 1932. Perhaps the most popular types of Carder Steuben glass
are Gold Aurene which was introduced in 1904 and Blue Aurene,
introduced in 1905. Gold and Blue Aurene objects shimmer with the
lustrous beauty of their metallic iridescence. Carder also produced other
types of 'Aurenes' including Red, Green, Yellow, Brown, and Decorated, all of which are very rare. Aurene also was cased upon Calcite
glass. Some pieces had paper labels.

Other types of Carder Steuben include Cluthra, Cintra, Florentia,
Rosaline, Ivory, Ivorene, Jades, Verre de Soie; there are many more.

Frederick Carder's leadership of Steuben ended in 1932 and the
production of colored glassware soon ceased. Since 1932 the tradition
of fine Steuben art glass has been continued in crystal.

Our advisor for this category is Thomas P. Dimitroff; he is in the
Directory under New York. In the following listings, examples are
signed unless noted otherwise.

Key: ACB — acid cut back

Basket, Gold Aurene, sgn/#153, 8¾x8¼" **1,200.00**
Basket, topaz/gr, #5069 ....**550.00**
Bottle, scent; Bl Aurene, bell shape, sgn/#2871, 5⅛" **1,200.00**
Bottle, scent; Bl Aurene, teardrop stopper, slim, #1414, 6¾" **900.00**
Bottle, scent; Gold Aurene, bulbous, 4-lobed body, 4½" **475.00**
Bottle, scent; Gold Aurene, melon ribs, sgn/#2183, 6½x4" **700.00**
Bowl, ACB Chinese bronze vessels/medallions, Plum Jade, 6" ...**1,800.00**
Bowl, Amethyst Silverina, dmn air-trap motif, 12½" L **1,200.00**
Bowl, Bl Aurene, inverted rim, #2687, 3½" **550.00**
Bowl, Bl Silverene Dmn Quilt, sgn F Carder, 10" **1,300.00**
Bowl, Celeste Bl, #112 ....**550.00**
Bowl, centerpc; Bl Aurene on Calcite, #5149, 12" dia **750.00**
Bowl, Cluthra, gr to wht, squatty, #6905, 4½" H **750.00**
Bowl, Gold Aurene, incurvate rim, sgn/#2687, 2½x5" **550.00**
Bowl, Gold Aurene, stretched rim, sgn/#2608, 14½" **750.00**
Bowl, Gold Aurene on Calcite, wide flat floral-eng rim, 6" **750.00**
Bowl, Ivorene, Grotesque, 12" **650.00**
Bowl, mint; Gold Aurene, folded rim, 4-ftd, sgn/#192, 3x6" **450.00**
Bowl, Rouge Flambe w/Bl Aurene decor, 4⅜" **17,000.00**
Bud vase, Bl Aurene, slim cylinder w/disk ft, sgn/#2556, 8" **400.00**
Candlestick, Bl Aurene, shaped 2-knob std, sgn/#2956, 9¾" **750.00**
Candlestick, Bl Aurene, twist stem, sgn/#686, 10", pr **1,500.00**

Candlestick, Gold Aurene, twist stem, sgn/#686, 10", pr **900.00**
Candlestick, Gold Aurene on Calcite, wide/flat rim, 6", pr **900.00**
Cologne, Jade Gr, melon ribs, Alabaster stopper, #1455, 4½" **550.00**
Cologne, Verre de Soie, ribs, Ruby Cintra stopper, #1455, 4½" .**500.00**
Compote, amber, yel/red pear w/gr leaves on lid, SP ft, 11" **500.00**
Compote, amethyst, #2848, 10" **350.00**
Compote, Bl Aurene, sgn/#2642, 8" **1,200.00**
Compote, Bl Aurene, twist stem w/4 prunts, sgn/#2604, 7x8" .**1,500.00**
Compote, Celeste Bl o/l w/clear twist stem, #5194 ....**350.00**
Compote, Gold Aurene, flared stretched rim, sgn/#2760, 11" **750.00**
Compote, Gold Aurene, sgn/#2642, 8x6" **700.00**
Cordial set, Gold Aurene, sgn/#2025, decanter+tray+4 cordials .**3,000.00**
Cruet, Bl Aurene, teardrop stopper, sgn/#2062 ....**1,200.00**
Cruet, Gold Aurene, hdl, teardrop stopper, sgn/#2063 ....**950.00**
Cup & saucer, Rosalene, Alabaster ring hdl, 1⅞", 4¼" **300.00**
Finger bowl, Gold Aurene on Calcite, +underplate, sgn/#d **275.00**
Flower frog, Gold Aurene, sgn Aurene, F Carder, 2½" dia **325.00**
Goblet, opal, w/Cintra stem, paper label, 7" **325.00**
Goblet, Oriental Poppy, gr stem/ft, 8" **600.00**

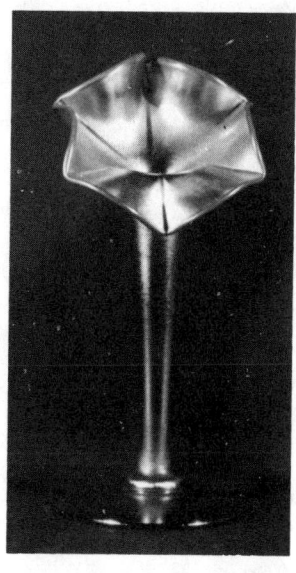

**Gold Aurene jack-in-the-pulpit
vase, signed Aurene #2699,
$1,100.00.**

Lamp, Moss Agate, plum color, all orig **4,700.00**
Lamp base, ACB mums on Gr Jade, 12"; silvered Roycroft mts ...**1,100.00**
Nut cup, Gold Aurene, Haviland mk, 1¼x3⅝" **325.00**
Pitcher, Gold Aurene, sgn/#1119, 7" **550.00**
Pitcher, Pomona Gr w/topaz hdl, ribbed, #6232, 9½" **275.00**
Plate, Gold Aurene w/pk highlights, 6" **250.00**
Rose jar, Gold Aurene, w/lid, Haviland label/#2812, 5½" **900.00**
Salt cellar, Bl Aurene, 8-rib, #564 ....**500.00**
Sherbet, Bl Aurene, sgn/#2680, +6" saucer **575.00**
Sherbet, Gold Aurene, +underplate **400.00**
Sherbet, Gold Aurene & Calcite, +underplate **275.00**
Tumbler, Gold Aurene, #2361, 6" **250.00**
Tumbler, Gold Aurene, flared top, sgn, 4⅛x3¼" **300.00**
Tumbler, gr w/allover swirl, mk, 4¼x2¾" **95.00**
Vase, ACB, Matsu Deco motif, Gr Jade/Alabaster, rnd, 8x7" ..**1,200.00**
Vase, amber, ovoid w/can neck, fleur-de-lis mk, 8" **250.00**
Vase, amber, swirled, bulbous shoulder, 7" **250.00**
Vase, amber w/gr vertical ribs, eng vintage, 12" **350.00**
Vase, amethyst, #6988 variant **300.00**
Vase, Aurene, gr decor, sgn/#584, 10" **3,000.00**
Vase, Aurene, red decor, sgn/#270, 7½" **12,000.00**
Vase, Bl Aurene, #2891 ....**1,000.00**
Vase, Bl Aurene, angular shoulder, sgn/#214, 8" **1,600.00**

Vase, Bl Aurene, decor, fan shape, sgn/#2697, 8½" 1,650.00
Vase, Bl Aurene, flared/ruffled top, sgn, sm blemish, 8" 765.00
Vase, Bl Aurene, ovoid w/flared rim, sgn/#7416, 8" 1,100.00
Vase, Bl Aurene, slim form w/flared top, 7" 550.00
Vase, Bl Aurene, 3 shoulder hdls/indents, sgn/#2767, 4" 1,200.00
Vase, Bl Aurene cut to cobalt, vintage, sgn/#2683, 10x10" 3,500.00
Vase, Bl Cintra, flared, ruffled, sgn, 8" 2,500.00
Vase, bud; verre de soie, eng florals, #451 shape, 10" 375.00
Vase, Cluthra, mottled purple shading, bulbous, 10" 1,300.00
Vase, Cluthra, rose/pk/berry mottling, triangular form, 10" 1,100.00
Vase, Cluthra amethyst w/'M' opal hdls, #2959, 10¾" 1,800.00
Vase, emerald gr, 3-prong tree trunk form, sgn, 6½" 350.00
Vase, Gold Aurene, #355, 11" 750.00
Vase, Gold Aurene, bulbous classic form, sgn/#2683, 8" 850.00
Vase, Gold Aurene, bulbous top/4-column base, sgn/#2764, 9"..1,500.00
Vase, Gold Aurene, classic mini urn, sgn/#2648, 2¾" 600.00
Vase, Gold Aurene, EX highlights, ruffled, sgn/#723, 9x9" 950.00
Vase, Gold Aurene, floriform, sgn/#3175, 10¾" 1,600.00
Vase, Gold Aurene, gr drag loop decor, sgn/#195, 8" 1,500.00
Vase, Gold Aurene, gr leaves/vines, sgn/#0297, 8½" 2,200.00
Vase, Gold Aurene, pear form, flared/ruffled, sgn/#145, 5½" 750.00
Vase, Gold Aurene, ribbed trumpet form, sgn, 5½" 495.00
Vase, Gold Aurene, 10-rib dbl-gourd trumpet form, sgn, 6" 750.00
Vase, Gold Aurene, 3 angular shoulder hdls, sgn/#2765, 10" ..1,800.00
Vase, Gold Aurene, 4-lobed bowl form, sgn/#7276, 4¾" 1,200.00
Vase, Gold Aurene, 6-sided trumpet form, sgn/#6241, 8" 900.00
Vase, Gold Aurene w/gr leafy vines & wht flowers, #506, 7" ..2,850.00
Vase, Gr Aurene, decor, sgn/#549, 5" 3,300.00
Vase, Gr Jade ribbed conical fan on Alabaster ped ft, 9" 550.00
Vase, Gr Jade/Alabaster, 2-prong, 9¼x5¼" 750.00
Vase, Gr/Gold Aurene on Alabaster, 4 feathers, #598, 7" 7,500.00
Vase, Grotesque, Bl Jade, quatrafoil/ribbed, 6x12" 2,500.00
Vase, Grotesque, gr shaded, ftd quatrafoil, ruffled rim, 9" 550.00
Vase, Ivorene, #354, 4" 350.00
Vase, Ivorene, trumpet form w/lily vase ea side, 12" 1,600.00
Vase, Ivorene, 10-rib ftd fan form, 10x11" 550.00
Vase, Ivory, 3 tapering triangles on rnd base, no mk, 9" 650.00
Vase, jack-in-the-pulpit; Gold Aurene, sgn/#2699, 6" 1,300.00
Vase, Jade Gr on Alabaster, ACB bird pattern, 9⅞" 1,500.00
Vase, Jade Gr on Alabaster, ACB dragon decor, 9½" 1,800.00
Vase, Jade Gr w/Alabaster 'M' hdls, #2939, 10¾" 1,000.00
Vase, Matsu-no-ke decor in Rosa on clear, #3331, 8" 650.00
Vase, Moss Agate, sgn, 12" 6,500.00
Vase, Pomona Gr, diagonal swirl, #6030, 7x7" 250.00
Vase, Rosaline w/Alabaster ft, 4" 450.00
Vase, Rose Quartz, acid-etched leaves, spherical, 11" 2,500.00
Vase, Roseline Jade, Alabaster ft, amethyst hdl rings, 6" 600.00

Stevengraphs

A Stevengraph is a small picture made of woven silk resembling an elaborate ribbon, created by Thomas Stevens in England in the late 1800s. They were matted and framed by Stevens, usually with his name appearing on the mat or, more commonly, the trade announcement on the back of the mat. He also produced silk postcards and bookmarks, all of which have 'Stevens' woven in silk on one of the mitered corners. Anyone wishing to learn more about Stevengraphs is encouraged to contact the Stevengraph Collectors' Association; the address can be found in the Directory under Clubs, Newsletters, and Catalogs.

Are You Ready? 135.00
Crystal Palace (inside), orig mat, G 285.00
Final Spurt, VG 185.00

First Innings, 2x6", VG, $400.00.

First Innings, G 295.00
First Touch, EX 365.00
For Life or Death, Heroism on Land (2 horses), dtd 1879 ....300.00
Good Old Days, EX 165.00
Grace Darling, EX 160.00
Meet, fr, NM 200.00
Present Time (60 Miles an Hour), EX 175.00
Struggle, EX 150.00
Wellington & Blugher, EX 165.00

Miscellaneous

Bookmark, Behold the Man, blk fr, G 50.00
Bookmark, Birthday Gift 50.00
Bookmark, Home Sweet Home 65.00
Bookmark, Love's Remembrance 75.00
Bookmark, New Year's Gift, child & dog, blk fr 60.00
Bookmark, Remember Me 65.00
Postcard, Ann Hathaway's Cottage 40.00
Postcard, Houses of Parliament 60.00
Postcard, RMS Lusitania 75.00

Stevens and Williams

Stevens and Williams glass was produced at the Brierly Hill Glass works in Stourbridge, England, for nearly a century, beginning in the 1830s. They were credited with being among the first to develop a method of manufacturing a more affordable type of cameo glass. Other lines were also made — silver deposit, alexandrite, and engraved rock crystal, to name a few. Our advisor for this category is Don Williams; he is listed in the Directory under Missouri.

Bottle, floral intaglio, mk silver top, bubble stopper, 13½" 225.00
Pitcher, swirled stripes in sapphire/wht/yel, 50-rib, 8" 475.00
Rose bowl, basketweave, pk satin o/l, pleated edge, 6x4½" 425.00
Rose bowl, citron/cranberry air-trap swirl, crimped rim, 5" 220.00
Rose bowl, gold florals on brn o/l, egg shape, 4⅞x3½" 450.00
Rose bowl, pk shaded, emb flowers, 8-crimp, 3¼x4¾" 125.00
Rose bowl, Pompeian Swirl, glossy, pleated top, 4½x6" 775.00
Shade, swirled rainbow stripes, ruffled/lobed rim, 8½" W 650.00
Vase, bl/wht/crystal stripes on satin, 3-sided, ftd, 7½" 225.00
Vase, coral o/l, appl opal frilly leaves/pointed rim, 12x5" 395.00
Vase, cream w/pk int, gr rim, appl flowers, 6x5" 395.00
Vase, cream w/pk int, lg appl 3-color leaves, ruffled, 7½" 395.00
Vase, Rock Crystal, fan form w/5-opening rim, stepped ft, 9" 495.00
Vase, turq opal, clear ft, ruffled fan form, 6¼x4" 165.00

Cameo

Mustard, floral, pk on wht satin, SP hinged top, 3¼x1⅞" 950.00

Vase, butterfly/maidenhair ferns, wht on med bl, ovoid, 4" **900.00**
Vase, dogwood branches, turq on wht, wide flask form, 8" **1,900.00**
Vase, ferns/grasses, wht on bl, ovoid, 4½" **900.00**
Vase, floral, gr on clear, dbl gourd w/star-cut base, 12" **1,425.00**
Vase, jonquil, wht on maroon shaded to orange, rnd mk, 4¼" ...**1,250.00**
Vase, nasturtiums/2 floral bands, wht/turq, dbl gourd, 12" **3,500.00**

Stickley

Among the leading proponents of the Arts and Crafts Movement, the Stickley brothers — Gustav, Leopold, Charles, Albert, and John George — were at various times and locations separately involved in designing and producing furniture as well as decorative items for the home. (See Arts and Crafts for further information.) The oldest of the five Stickley brothers was Gustav; his work is the most highly regarded of all. He developed the style of furniture referred to as Mission. It was strongly influenced by the type of furnishings found in the Spanish missions of California — utilitarian, squarely built, and simple. It was made most often of oak, and decoration was very limited or non-existent. The work of his brothers display adaptations of many of Gustav's ideas and designs. His factory, the Craftsman Shops, operated in Eastwood, New York, from the late 1890s until 1915, when he was forced out of business by larger companies who copied his work and sold it at much lower prices. Among his shopmarks are the early red decal containing a joiner's compass and the words 'Als Ik Kan,' the branded mark with very similar components and paper labels.

The firm known as Stickley Brothers was located first in Binghamton, New York, and then Grand Rapids, Michigan. Albert and John made the move to Michigan, leaving Charles in Binghamton (where he and an uncle continued the operation under a different name). After several years John George left the company to rejoin Leopold in New York. (These two later formed their own firm called L. & J.G. Stickley.) The Stickley Brothers Company under Albert's sole direction produced furniture that featured fine inlay work and decorative cutouts and leaned strongly toward a style of Arts and Crafts with an English influence. It was tagged with a paper label 'Made by Stickley Brothers, Grand Rapids' or with a brass plate or decal with the words 'Quaint Furniture,' an English term he chose to refer to his product. In addition to his furniture, he made metal furnishings as well.

The workshops of the L. & J.G. Stickley Company first operated under the name 'Onandaga Shops.' Located in Fayetteville, New York, their designs were often all but copies of Gustav's work. Their products were well made and marketed, and their business was very successful. Their decal labels contained all or a combination of the words 'Handcraft' or 'Onandaga Shops,' along with the brothers' initials and last name. The firm continues in business today. Our advisor for this category is Bruce Austin; he is listed in the Directory under New York. Note: When only one dimension is given for tables, it is length.

Gustav Stickley

Book cabinet, #93, open top over door, unmk, 40x17", EX **1,900.00**
Book rack, #74, mahog, V top shelf, hdl cutouts, decal, VG **650.00**
Book rack, #90, 4-compartment, revolving, decal, 9x12" **700.00**
Bookcase, #717, 2 8-pane doors, label, 48x56", VG **2,800.00**
Bookcase, 2 glazed doors over 2-door cabinet, 1903, 64x42" .**19,000.00**
Box, cigar; #268, hammered/riveted copper, cedar int, mk **700.00**
Cabinet, music; #70, door w/10 ldgl panels (losses), label **4,000.00**
Chafing dish, copper w/oak base, Craftsman mk, 16" base dia **400.00**
Chair, arm; #302, spring cushions/thru tenons, decal, EX **600.00**
Chair, arm; #353-A, 3-slat bk/rush seat, Ellis, decal, 41" **600.00**
Chair, ladderbk side; rush seat, arched top rail, unmk, 37" **450.00**
Chair, Morris; #332, recliner, 5-slat sides, mk, reuphl, EX **3,500.00**

Chair, Morris; #332, 5-slat sides, 4-slat bk, decal, EX **4,000.00**
Chair, Morris; #369, slant arm, 5-slat bk/sides, brand, rfn **4,650.00**
Chair, side; #270, 3-slat bk, uphl seat, 37", pr **550.00**
Chair, side; #3533, 3 bk slats, arched aprons, inset seat **200.00**
Chair, vanity; #398, H-bk, EX orig rush seat/finish, decal **475.00**
Chair, vanity; #398, H-bk, rush seat, blk lacquer, 33" **275.00**
Chair set, #306½, 3-slat bk, rfn, VG, 6 for **950.00**
Chair set, #308, H-bk, decal/brand, 40", EX, 4 for **900.00**
Chair set, #353, bk w/3 vertical slats, slip seat, 4 for **2,000.00**
Chest, #902, 2 sm drw over 4, red decal, 54x40" **3,250.00**
Chest, 6 short drw over 3, Ellis design, brand, 51x33" **3,000.00**
Desk, #709, 5-drw/recessed kneehole, decal, NM finish, 42" L ..**1,000.00**
Desk, #731, drop front, 2 short drw over 1, mk, 31" L **1,300.00**
Desk, chalet; #505, drop front, shoe ft, decal, 46x25" **1,800.00**
Dresser, #905, 2 sm drw+3, strap hdw, brand, 66x48", EX **5,500.00**
Dresser, #909, 2 short drw over 3, horseshoe mk, 40x37" **1,400.00**
Footstool, #300, leather top/sq tacks, EX orig, mk, 20" L **750.00**
Footstool, #301, mahog footrest, rpl rush/rfn, 20" W, VG **150.00**

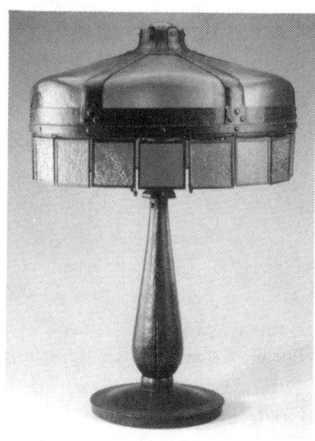

Gustav Stickley wrought iron and amber glass table lamp, 21" diameter shade, 30", $8,000.00.

Lamp, #262, 6-panel copper-fr shade, split body, unmk, 28" ...**1,300.00**
Lamp, corbelled X-ftd oak base, 22" wicker shade, brand **4,500.00**
Lamp, floor; #500, copper harp, opal bell shade, mk, 58" **2,200.00**
Lamp, rtcl copper panel/opal glass 18" shade; oak base, VG **2,300.00**
Lantern, copper cap w/heart cutouts on glass cylinder, 9x6" **1,200.00**
Magazine stand, 4-shelf, panel sides, sq posts, 45x16" **1,900.00**
Mirror, #68, 3-panel, arched crest rail, 4 hooks, 28x48" **1,600.00**
Mirror, cheval; #918, Ellis design, all orig, decal, 70" **8,500.00**
Plate rack, #801, arched top, decal, rfn, 28x48" **2,000.00**
Rocker, #323, 5-slat sides, spring cushions, decal, EX **850.00**
Rocker, child's, #343, 3-slat bk, recoated, 26", VG **400.00**
Rocker, sewing; #303, 4 bk slats, decal/label, wear **250.00**
Rocker, sewing; #307, H-bk, slip seat, unmk, 35", VG **165.00**
Screen, cutouts/leather windows, decal, 3-panel, ea 67x21" **5,000.00**
Settle, #207, 5-slat (inward slanted) sides, rfn, unmk, 72" **5,000.00**
Settle, #225, 1-plank bk, 5-slat sides, reuphl, 77" **3,500.00**
Settle, #291, sm sq spindles bk/sides, sq posts, decal, 78" **12,100.00**
Sideboard, #814, strap hdw on door ea side of 3 drw, 66" **2,600.00**
Sideboard, #815, plate rack, door ea side 2-drw center, sgn **2,000.00**
Table, #668, sq legs w/X-stretchers, unmk, rfn, 44" dia **825.00**
Table, dining; #632, 5-leg, rnd waxed top overhangs, decal ...**1,800.00**
Table, dining; #656, label, +6 leaves, 54" dia, EX **3,500.00**
Table, director's; #631, trestle ft/deep apron, brand, 72" **16,500.00**
Table, library; #614, leather top, medial shelf, 42" L **3,500.00**
Table, library; #614, 2-drw, elongated corbels, decal, EX **1,750.00**
Table, library; #651, mahog, sq legs/base shelf, label, VG **775.00**
Table, library; #655, 13-spindle sides, decal/label, VG **2,300.00**
Table, side; #477, drw ea end, mk, top: 30x18" **2,200.00**

Table, tea; #439, legs mortised through rnd top, med finish **950.00**
Table, tea; #604, arched X-stretchers, rfn 30" dia top, EX **1,600.00**
Table, tea; #604, rnd 20" recoated top, label, 26", VG **1,300.00**
Telephone stand, #605, 14" sq top w/some stains, brand, VG .**1,100.00**
Umbrella stand, #100, wide slats on iron hoops, 24x12" dia **1,500.00**
Umbrella stand, #54, sq corner posts, drip pan, label, 33" **700.00**
Wardrobe, #920 (similar), hooks/pole, decal, 70x35", VG **3,500.00**
Wastebasket, #95, wide slats on iron hoops, 14x12", EX **1,500.00**

L. & J.G. Stickley

L. &. J.G. Stickley stand, #574, factory decal, 29x18x18", $700.00.

Ashtray, #21, copper tray, Xd base, decal, 22x10" dia, VG **700.00**
Bookcase, #644, 4-shelf, orig finish/decal, 55x39" **2,750.00**
Cabinet, china; #728, 2 9-pane doors, 55x48", EX **3,750.00**
Chair, arm; #420, 4-slat bk, flat arms w/front corbels, EX **550.00**
Chair, arm; #450, 6-slat bk/sides, thru-posts in arms, mk, EX .**1,200.00**
Chair, arm; fixed bk, long paddle arms, spring seat, decal **1,400.00**
Chair, Morris; #411, 4-slat bk, flat arms over corbels, EX **700.00**
Chair, Morris; #471, 6-slat sides, 4-slat bk, mk, 41", VG **1,500.00**
Chair, Morris; #498, floor-length slats, orig finish/decal **4,500.00**
Chair, Morris; #498, 5-slat sides, decal, 42", VG **2,800.00**
Chair, open arms, concave crest rail over 2 slats, mk, 37" **220.00**
Chair, side; #820, 5-slat bk, decal, orig finish, 36" **350.00**
Chair set, 3-slat bk, wide aprons, decal, host+3 side **850.00**
Chaise, #291, 5 slats front & rear, 76" L **850.00**
Couch, #295, 4 end slats, angled headrest, unmk, 73" **350.00**
Daybed, 4 slats under head & ft rails, faceted post tops **1,000.00**
Dresser, 2 short drw over 3 grad drw, label, 48x36x22" **1,500.00**
Footstool, #391, orig hard leather top, 18x19" **500.00**
Magazine stand, #47, 3-shelf, decal, EX orig finish, 42x20" ...**1,200.00**
Settle, #223, tall-post 22-slat bk, 7 ea side, decal, 84" **11,000.00**
Settle, #262, V crest rail over 16 slats, shaped arms, decal **1,200.00**
Settle, #281, 16-slat bk/5-slat sides, decal, 76", EX **5,200.00**
Settle, open arms w/corbels, 16-slat bk, decal, 77", VG **1,850.00**
Settle, str crest rail, 15-slat bk, open arms, unmk, 74" **650.00**
Sideboard, #731, extended top, copper hdw, rfn, 72" L **3,000.00**
Stand, #22, rstr finish, decal, 29x18" dia **1,300.00**
Stand, cut corners, post legs/X-stretcher, rfn, 18x16" **525.00**
Stand, sq cut-corner 16" rnf top, X-stretcher, mk, rfn **1,600.00**
Table, #539, rnd 42" top, shaped X-stretcher, 4-leg **800.00**
Table, #577, 30" rnd top, sm rnd medial shelf, 4-leg, decal **800.00**
Table, #599, cut-out slab sides, mk, 60", VG **3,000.00**
Table, lamp; #350, 36" dia top/rnd shelf, unmk, EX **2,500.00**
Table, library; #532, 2-drw, dbl-key tenons, stains, 54" **1,600.00**
Table, library; blind drw, rpl top, unmk, 39" L **275.00**

Stickley Bros.

Bookcase, 2 8-pane doors, sq posts extend above top, 48x48" .**1,200.0**
Chest, #9011, 2 short drw over 3, 47x42", EX **2,400.0**
Footstool, branded, new uphl/finish, 15x17x12" **280.0**
Rocker, Morris; #631, Quaint, new leather, orig finish, 37" **1,200.0**
Rocker, shaped cvd bk slat, saddle seat, arched apron, 38" **400.0**
Settee+chair, child's, 11-slat bk settee: 32" L, chair: 29" **200.0**
Settle, 12-slat bk w/leather-uphl top half, unmk, 39" **350.0**
Table, #607, legs mortised through top, rfn, 29x40" dia **500.0**
Table, child's, 24" dia top, X-stretchers, 24", EX **325.0**
Table, hall; 3 sq spindles ea end, orig color/rfn, tag, 30" **1,000.0**
Table, tea; #2516, X-stretchers, orig finish, tag, 28" dia **750.0**
Wastebasket, 5 thin slats ea of 4 sides, cut-out hdls, VG **650.0**

Stiegel

Baron Henry Stiegel produced glassware in Pennsylvania as earl
as 1760. It was very similar to glass being made concurrently in Ger
many and England. Without substantiating evidence, it is impossible t
positively attribute a specific article to his manufacture. Although h
made other types of glass, today the term Stiegel generally refers to an
very early ware made in shapes and colors similar to those he is know
to have produced — especially that with etched or enameled decora
tion. It is generally conceded, however, that most glass of this type is o
European origin. Our advisor for this category is Mark Vuono; he i
listed in the Directory under Connecticut.

Bottle, pocket; amethyst, 12-dmn, minor wear/stain, 5" **3,800.0**
Bottle, purple, HP birds/heart, bk: German letters, rpr, 6" **850.0**
Flip, eng florals & baskets, sheared rim, pontil scar, 8⅜" **125.0**
Flip, eng florals/baskets, Stiegel type, 12¼" **275.0**
Tumbler, eng birds, 3⅜" **25.0**
Tumbler, pale gr, eng flower basket, 7⅞" **175.0**

Stocks and Bonds

Scripophily (scrip-awfully), the collecting of 'worthless' old stock
and bonds, gained recognition as an area of serious interest around th
mid-1970s. Today there are an estimated 5,000 collectors in the Unite
States and 15,000 worldwide. Collectors who come from numerou
business fields mainly enjoy its hobby aspect, though there are thos
who consider scripophily an investment. Some collectors like the his
torical significance that certain certificates have. Others prefer th
beauty of older stocks and bonds that were printed in various color
with fancy artwork and ornate engravings. Even autograph collector
are found in this field, on the lookout for signed certificates.

Many factors help determine the collector value: autograph value
age of the certificate, the industry represented, whether it is issued o
not, its attractiveness, condition, and collector demand. Certificate
from the mining, energy, and railroad industries are the most popula
with collectors. Other industries or special collecting fields includ
banking, automobiles, aircraft, and territorials. Serious collectors usu
ally prefer only issued certificates that date from before 1910. Unissue
certificates are usually worth one-fourth to one-eighth the value of on
that has been issued. Inexpensive issued common stocks and bond
dated between the 1940s and 1980s usually retail between $1.00 an
$10.00. Those dating between 1890 and 1930 usually sell for $10.00 t
$50.00. Those over one hundred years old retail between $25.00 an
$100.00 or more, depending on the quantity found. Autographed stock
normally sell anywhere from $100.00 to $1,000.00. A formal collectin
organization for scripophilists is known as The Bond and Share Societ
with an American chapter located in New York City.

Our advisor for this category is Warren Anderson; he is listed in the Directory under Utah. In many of the following listings, two-letter state abbreviations immediately follow company name. All are in fine condition unless noted otherwise.

Key:
cp — coupon
I/C — issued/cancelled
I/U — issued/uncancelled
U — unissued
vgn — vignette

AJ Brown Developing Corp, TX/1926, 7" oil field vgn, I/U 20.00
AR & Memphis Ry Bridge & Terminal, TN/1918, eagle vgn, I/C ..15.00
Bonanza Belt Copper, AZ Territory/1907, dog vgn, I/U 20.00

California mining stock, vignette of mining camp in mountains, 25¢ revenue stamp, 1865, uncancelled, $90.00.

Centennial-Eureka Mining, ME/1901, goddess vgn, ABNCo, I/U ...30.00
Chicago, Rock Island & TX Ry, IL/1902, train vgn, U 15.00
CO Mine Developing, CO/1880, mining scene, title banner, I/U 60.00
CO Toggery Divide Mining, NV/1919, ornate title banner, I/U ..15.00
Edna Mines, CO/1926, title on banner, I/U 10.00
Elk Auto Supply, TX/1916, stag's head in tire vgn, rare, I/U 35.00
Gibson Live Stock & Feed, IN/1920, goddess vgn, gold seal, I/U ..10.00
Gilpin-Orion Gold Mining, AZ Territory/1911, miners vgn, I/U 25.00
Goldfield Belmont Mining, NV/1905, draped nudes w/wings, I/U ...25.00
Highland Gold Mines, OR/1905, 3 vgns, I/U 25.00
Hyland Mining & Milling, CO/1904, miners vgn, I/C 30.00
IL Central RR, IL/1880s, map vgn of system, U 10.00
Ingersoll Warner Mercantile, KS/1906, Indian/train vgn, sgn, I/U 35.00
Jay Gould Mining, MT Territory/1880s, miners vgn, U 20.00
LA Consolidated Mining, NV/1919, title banner, gold border, I/U ..25.00
Leonora Mining, OK/1918-23, 3 mining vgns, I/U 20.00
Lincoln Mining, NV/1908, title banner, blk on wht, I/U 20.00
Log Cabin Mining, UT/1918, eagle on dome vgn, red stamp, I/U ...15.00
Lucky Strike Mining & Smelting, WY/1907, 2 maiden vgns, I/U 25.00
Lutcher & Moore Lumber, TX/1892, 1 lg/2 sm vgns, I/U 70.00
ME Central RR, ME/1916, oval train vgn, ABNCo, I/C 20.00
MI Central RR, MI/1909, $1000 Gold Bond, vgn, ABNCo, I/C ..30.00
MT Phonograph, MT Territory/1889, phonograph vgn, U 25.00
N Pacific Ry, WI/1954, $1000 bond, w/some coupons, I/C, 9x15" ...20.00
NY, Pittsburgh & Chicago Construction, NY/1881, train vgn, I/C ...20.00
NY Oil Development Corp, TX/1926, gusher vgn, I/U 15.00
Oil Fields Development, AZ/1918, ornate title, gold seal, I/U 15.00
Oswego Mining, SD/1906, miners vgn, gr seal, I/U 25.00
Pawhuska OK/1926, $100 city bond, sgn by mayor, I/U 10.00
Peabody Gold Mining, CO/1898, ornate title, blk on wht, I/U 30.00
Publishers Oil & Gas, AZ Territory/1904, sgn HH Tucker, I/U ...30.00
Queen Mining, CO/1880, miners at tunnel vgn, blk/wht, U 15.00

Radarsburg Gold Mining, WA/1911, miners vgn, gold seal, I/U ...20.00
Rochester Silver Corp, NV/1921, bl border on lt bl, I/U 20.00
S Park Mining & Development, UT/1917, miners vgn, I/C 20.00
Star Petroleum, TX/1902, star & cloud vgn, gold seal, I/U 20.00
Sterling Iron & Ry Co, NY/1890s, ABNCo, U 5.00
Tabor Mines & Mills, CO/1890s, eagle & scenic vgns, U 15.00
Uncle Sam Oil, AZ/1913, gusher vgn, sgn HH Tucker, I/U 25.00
Valley Oil, NM/1919, gusher & train vgns, brn border, I/U 20.00
W Shore RR, NY/1913, $1000 bond, lg vgn, ABNCo, I/C, 9x14" ...30.00
Weimar Oil, TX/1919, gusher vgn, gr border, I/U 15.00
XT Land & Cattle Co, NM Territory/1900, blk/wht on tan, U 25.00

Stoneware

There are three broad periods of time that collectors of American pottery can look to in evaluating and dating the stoneware and earthenware in their collections. Among the first permanent settlers in America were English and German potters who found a great demand for their individually turned wares. The early pottery was produced from red and yellow clays scraped from the ground at surface levels. The earthenware made in these potteries was fragile and coated with lead glazes that periodically created health problems for the people who ate or drank from it. There was little stoneware available for sale until the early 1800s, because the clays used in its production were not readily available in many areas and transportation was prohibitively expensive. The opening of the Erie Canal and improved roads brought about a dramatic increase in the accessibility of stoneware clay, and many new potteries began to open in New York and New England.

Collectors have difficulty today locating earthenware and stoneware jugs produced prior to 1840, because few have survived intact. These ovoid or pear-shaped jugs were designed to be used on a daily basis. When cracked or severely chipped, they were quickly discarded. The value of handcrafted pottery is often determined by the cobalt decoration it carries. Pieces with elaborate scenes (a chicken pecking corn, a bluebird on a branch, a stag standing near a pine tree, a sailing ship, or people) may easily bring $1,000 to $12,000 at auction.

After the Civil War there was a need and a national demand for stoneware jugs, crocks, canning jars, churns, spittoons, and a wide variety of other pottery items. The competition among the many potteries reached the point where only the largest could survive. To cut costs, most potteries did away with all but the simplest kinds of decoration on their wares. Time-consuming, brush-painted birds or flowers quickly gave way to more simply executed swirls or numbers and stenciled designs. The coming of home refrigeration and Prohibition in 1919 effectively destroyed the American stoneware industry. In the following listings, 'c/s' means 'cobalt on salt glaze'; all decoration described before this abbreviation is in cobalt. See also Bennington, Stoneware.

Bank, tiered top highlighted w/bl, ovoid, incised name, 7" 625.00
Bottle, pig form, Albany slip, 7" L, EX 295.00
Bowl, floral/#2, c/s, brn int, appl hdls, 12" 335.00
Bowl, milk; imp: Holt-Palmer, c/s, rim spout, brn int, 14" 275.00
Bowl, milk; rim design, brushed, c/s, hairline, 9" 150.00
Butter stamp, dots/lines, c/s, brn slip stamp, 4½" 1,450.00
Chicken fountain, Albany slip, Pat'd Apr 7, 1885, 7½" 75.00
Churn, deer (much detail), c/s, Wm A Lewis, 6-gal, EX 3,700.00
Churn, floral, (stylized/lg), c/s, Haxtun Ottman, 17", EX 475.00
Churn, floral/#3, c/s, stains/hairline, 15" 100.00
Churn, floral/#4, brushed, c/s, 15¾" 325.00
Churn, floral/#4, c/s, w/lid & dasher, hairline, 17" 275.00
Churn, stamped cow, c/s, Gardiner Stoneware Co, 5-gal 700.00
Cooler, emb bands, c/s, keg form, 22" 350.00
Cooler, floral, brushed, c/s, keg shape, 22" L, on stand 750.00

Cooler, floral vines (heavy), c/s, Germany, 1900s **300.00**
Crock, #2/flourish, quilled, c/s, stains/hairlines, 9" **75.00**
Crock, bird on branch, quilled, c/s, White's Utica, 11", EX **300.00**
Crock, bird on branch (looks bk), quilled, c/s, Burger, 11" **600.00**
Crock, bird w/lg tail on branch, NA White & Son, 13½" **1,250.00**
Crock, bird w/topknot looks bk, c/s, brn int, Burger, 10" **1,500.00**

**Crock, bird on branch, dark blue slip, 10½",
$350.00; Churn, large freehand flower, applied
handles, 17½", NM, $450.00.**

Crock, butter; leaves, c/s, hdls, no lid, 6x10", EX **325.00**
Crock, feather/#1, quilled, c/s, 7½" **110.00**
Crock, floral, brushed, c/s, ovoid, 13" **225.00**
Crock, floral (lg/simple), brushed, c/s, M Woodruff, 12", VG **350.00**
Crock, floral (precise), quilled, c/s, J Burger, 9" **400.00**
Crock, flower & leaf, c/s, NA White & Son Utica NY, 1-gal **225.00**
Crock, foliage, quilled, c/s, West Troy NY Pottery #3, 11" **265.00**
Crock, leaves (1 striped/1 dotted), cs/, 3-gal **265.00**
Crock, Mrs Jane Henderson...Ohio, quilled, c/s, 9x12" **325.00**
Crock, partridge in pear tree, c/s, unmk, 1870s, 6-gal **575.00**
Crock, stencil: ES&B New Brighton PA, c/s, 11", NM **70.00**
Crock, vintage (detailed), blk on salt glaze, L Lehman, 9" **485.00**
Figurine, dog, seated, bl face & ears, 7¾" **1,875.00**
Flask, salt glaze, ovoid, 8½" **120.00**
Flowerpot, floral, c/s, AK Ballard, hdls, 12" **295.00**
Inkwell, zigzags, c/s, conical, 2½" **365.00**
Jar, Albany slip w/sgraffito bird, flowers, border, 4", EX **350.00**
Jar, appl open hdls, sm chips, miniature, 4¼" **25.00**
Jar, brushwork, c/s, 7⅝" **200.00**
Jar, canning; commas, brushed, c/s, minor flakes, 8" **145.00**
Jar, canning; curliques, brushed, c/s, 9½" **175.00**
Jar, canning; floral, brushed, c/s, Lyons, 10", VG **105.00**
Jar, canning; floral, brushed, c/s, Cowden & Wilcox, hdls, 9½", EX ..**250.00**
Jar, canning; floral (primitive), brushed, c/s, 8½", EX **110.00**
Jar, canning; floral around shoulder, brushed, c/s, 8", EX **240.00**
Jar, canning; fruit-like design, brushed, c/s, 10", EX **120.00**
Jar, canning; stencil; AP Donaghho, 5⅝" **215.00**
Jar, canning; stencil/freehand: Hamilton & Jones, c/s, 10" **165.00**
Jar, canning; stripes, brushed, c/s, 8" **135.00**
Jar, canning; wavy lines, brushed, c/s, 6", EX **85.00**
Jar, canning; 4 stenciled stars, c/s, chipped lip, 6" **465.00**
Jar, floral, brushed, c/s, J Swank & Co, ovoid, 15", EX **175.00**
Jar, floral, brushed, c/s, ovoid w/hdls 11", NM **175.00**
Jar, floral, brushed, c/s, stenciled mk, 1880s, 12-gal **325.00**
Jar, floral (stylized) ea side, c/s, ovoid, hdls, 14", NM **325.00**
Jar, floral (2 w/Xd stems), brushed, c/s, ovoid, rpr, 12" **300.00**
Jar, floral band, brushed, c/s, ovoid, hairlines/chips, 15" **115.00**
Jar, floral/leafy shoulder decor, c/s, ovoid, 15" **400.00**

Jar, floral/stencil: From JE Eneix, c/s, hdls, 16", EX **650.00**
Jar, flowers allover (sm/4-petal), brushed, c/s, ovoid, 14" **400.00**
Jar, foliage (simple), brushed, c/s, ovoid, appl hdls, 8½" **145.00**
Jar, foliage/#4, c/s, John Burger, stains, 20" **350.00**
Jar, incised: Hanna & Co Snuff/#4, highlighted in c/s, 15" **300.00**
Jar, stencil/freehand: Hamilton & Jones, c/s, ovoid, 11" **275.00**
Jar, stencil/freehand: Williams & Reppert/#2/etc, c/s, EX **200.00**
Jar, stencil: From FH Behrens Grocer..., c/s, ovoid, 10" **200.00**
Jar, stencil: Hamilton & Jones, c/s, 12½", EX **125.00**
Jar, stencil: Hamilton & Jones PA, brushed swirls, c/s, 5-gal **365.00**
Jug, batter; floral, brushed, c/s, Cowden & Wilcox, 8½" **2,050.00**
Jug, bird (incised/long-tailed), c/s, ovoid, chips, 14" **900.00**
Jug, bird (looking bk/dotted), quilled, c/s, 13½" **500.00**
Jug, bird on flowering branch, quilled, c/s, W Roberts, 12" **850.00**
Jug, bird pr (dotted), quilled, c/s, Penn Yan, ovoid, 19", NM ..**2,600.00**
Jug, chicken on table, c/s, Wm Warner, rpr, 13" **700.00**
Jug, daub at hdl/imp #2, c/s, ovoid, wear/flakes, 13" **60.00**
Jug, daubs at label/hdl, c/s, Goodwin/Webster, ovoid, 17" **200.00**
Jug, floral (bold), c/s, Crowden & Wilcox, 16" **365.00**
Jug, floral (lg), quilled, c/s, NY Stoneware #3, 16", VG **275.00**
Jug, floral (lg/EX color), quilled, c/s, WH Farrar, 14" **1,300.00**
Jug, floral (lg/long stem), c/s, 15", NM **320.00**
Jug, floral sprig (cvd), name Seymour Troy, c/s, ovoid, 11" **650.00**
Jug, floral/#2, quilled, c/s, Burger & Lang, ovoid, 14½" **400.00**
Jug, floral/2 leaves/#2, c/s, N Clark & Co, ovoid, NM **465.00**
Jug, flourishes/#2, brushed, c/s, S Hart, ovoid, 13", VG **125.00**
Jug, flower (simple)/#2, quilled, c/s, ovoid, 14", EX **275.00**
Jug, flower/#2, brushed, c/s, IM Mead, ovoid, 13½", VG **300.00**
Jug, flower/daubs, c/s, PH Smith, ovoid, ear hdls, 18", EX **450.00**
Jug, foliage, quilled, c/s, JS Taft, 11", NM **165.00**
Jug, grapes & leaves, c/s, Edmonds & Co, MA, 2-gal **495.00**
Jug, imp label: C Crolius, NY, ovoid, base chips, 14" **325.00**
Jug, imp Rum/fish & berry band, gray-brn, ovoid, 9½", EX **410.00**
Jug, imp: JV Machett/hdl/lip, c/s, ribbed hdl, ovoid, 12" **350.00**
Jug, MJ Madden, quilled, c/s, 12" **150.00**
Jug, pecking chicken, c/s, West Troy, flakes, 11" **1,200.00**
Jug, rose, c/s, Haxtun & Co, 2-gal, NM **265.00**
Jug, stencil/freehand: Hamilton & Jones, c/s, 15", EX **275.00**
Jug, stencil/freehand: J Epple Groceries..., c/s, ovoid, 11" **450.00**
Jug, stencil/freehand: James Hamilton Co, c/s, ovoid, 14" **525.00**
Jug, stencil: Hamilton & Jones, c/s, sm chips, 11" **225.00**
Jug, stencil: Geo A Kelly...Druggists, c/s, TF Reppert, 12" **1,500.00**
Jug, tooled lines/lip trim/X, c/s, ovoid, 4" **150.00**
Measure, no decor, unmk, 1890s **95.00**
Pitcher, Albany slip w/sgraffito inscription, 6", EX **150.00**
Pitcher, allover tulips/etc, c/s, milk sz, VG **650.00**
Pitcher, appl hunt scenes/cvd JN Wells, 2-tone brn, 9", NM ..**1,700.00**
Pitcher, batter; foilage under spout, c/s, no lid, 9", EX **500.00**
Pitcher, brushed devices at neck/leafy spray, c/s, 11", EX **700.00**
Pitcher, daub under spout, c/s, Albany slip int, 12", VG **150.00**
Pitcher, emb roses/people on treebark, c/s, bbl form, 8" **110.00**
Pitcher, floral, brushed, c/s, base chips, 8¾" **600.00**
Pitcher, floral (lg), brushed, c/s, tooled, hairlines, 14" **1,450.00**
Pitcher, leafy twig incised ea side, c/s, ovoid, chips, 9½" **650.00**
Salt cellar, brushwork, c/s, 2½" dia **90.00**
Tenderizer, serrated surface, Pat Dec 25 1877, 10" **90.00**

Store

Perhaps more than any other yesteryear establishment, the country
store evokes the most nostalgic feelings for folks old enough to remember its charms — barrels for coffee, crackers, and big green pickles;
candy in a jar for the grocer to weigh on shiny brass scales; beheaded

chickens in the meat case outwardly devoid of nothing but feathers. Today mementos from this segment of Americana are being collected by those who 'lived it' as well as those less fortunate! Our advisor for this category is Charles Reynolds; he is listed in the Directory under Virginia. See also Advertising.

Back bar, oak & chestnut, glass front, 98x166x16", EX 1,980.00
Bill clip, CI, Indian head form, hole for hanging, 2x2¾" 85.00
Bill spike, ornate CI, hexagonal base, NM pnt, 6¾" H 12.00
Bread box, Truth Spice, Geo Washington on front & sides 195.00
Broom holder, CI, holds 24, EX 90.00
Cabinet, bolt; revolving, 6-sided, 60" H, EX 3,300.00
Case, candy display; oak & glass, 21-compartment, 30x34x9" 990.00
Case, oak w/glass sides, casters, 70x24x24", EX 1,375.00
Case, rotating, oak on 4-leg ped, 66x25x23", EX 440.00
Case, umbrella display; oak w/curved glass, 50x32", EX 1,400.00
Cheese cutter, pnt CI, Enterprise, rare, VG, 30" 330.00
Counter, mahog & oak, marble top, 14-drw, 32x74x30", EX ..2,200.00
Dispenser, ribbon; oak, holds 21 spools, 39x24" dia, EX 525.00
Dispenser, wrapping paper; CI/wood, 3 rollers/2 cutters, VG 300.00
Glove form, wht china, Pat 1922, 14¼" 95.00

Label cutter, holds three rolls of labels, 9½", $85.00.

Ledger, creditors listed w/payments in kind, 1839-68, EX 45.00
Ledger, leather binding, gold on spine, 1899, VG 15.00
Ledger, lists products, hay & services, 1851-60, 7x8", EX 35.00
Mannequin, girl, wax, period clothing, 1880s, 52", EX 1,150.00
Rack, bag; Honey Bread 165.00
Rack, broom; Blue-J, 2 full-color signs, EX 495.00
Rack, meat; CI w/oak, cowboy & steer at top, 1892, 36x60" ..2,600.00
Rack, postcard; rotates, wood finial, 44", EX 300.00
Receipt holder, desk; CI w/emb letters, Nat'l Cash Register 35.00
Seed bin, 18 glass-front drws, orig hardware, 72x24x36" 2,500.00

Stoves

The desirability of antique stoves is based on two criteria: their utility and their decorative value. It's the latter that adds an 'antique' premium to the basic functional value that could be served just as well by a modern stove. Sheer age is usually irrelevant. Decorative features that enhance desirability include fancy, embossed ornamentation, nickel-plated trim, mica windows, ceramic tiles, and (in cooking stoves) water reservoirs, and high warming closets rather than mere high shelves. The

less sheet metal and the more cast iron, the better. Look for crisp, sharp designs in preference to those made from worn or damaged and repaired foundry patterns. Stoves with a pastel porcelain finish can be very attractive; blue is a favorite, white is least desirable. Chrome trim, rather than nickel, is the mark of a stove too recent to be interesting. Among stove types, base burners with self-feeding coal magazines are the most desirable. Then come the upright, cylindrical 'oak' stoves, kitchen ranges, and wood parlors. Potbellies approach the margin of undesirability; laundries and gasoline stoves plunge through it.

In judging condition, look out for deep rust pits, warped or burnt-out parts, unsound firebricks, poorly fitting parts, poor repairs, and empty mounting holes indicating missing trim. Search meticulously for cracks in the cast iron. Our listings reflect auction prices of completely restored, safe, and functional stoves, unless indicated otherwise.

There's a thin but continuing stream of desirable antique stoves going to the high-priced Pacific Coast market. Interest in antique stoves is least in the Deep South. Demand for wood/coal stoves is strongest in areas where firewood is affordable and storage of it is practical. Demand for antique gas ranges has become strong, especially in metropolitan markets, and interest in antique electric ranges is starting to surface. The market for antique stoves is so limited and the variety so bewildering that a consensus on a going price can hardly emerge. They are only worth something to the right individual, and prices realized depend very greatly on who happens to be in the auction crowd. Even an expert's appraisal will usually miss the realized price by a substantial percent.

Base Burners

Art Amherst #15, NP trim, tiles, 11" urn, 50x25x28" 1,875.00
Burdett-Smith #44, swivel top, tiles, 38" 1,185.00
Detroit Emerald Jewel #14, mica doors, NP trim, 69", EX 3,125.00
Favorite #30, Piqua OH, ornate mica windows, 52" 2,000.00
Michigan Stove, Art Garland #400, gargoyles/NP/mica, 1889, rstr .9,800.00
Ranson Art Denmark #15, Albany NY, tiles/NP/mica, 1887, VG ..4,500.00
Thos Caffney Waverly #12, Boston MA, 40x20x22" 1,875.00
Weir Glenwood #5, NP trim, mica windows, 1909, 68" 875.00

Box Stoves

A Belanger Barge #14, scrollwork, CI, 1905, sm 187.50
BF&M Co #1, front load, early legs, 1800s 17x13x24" 125.00
E Eaton #24, Amherst NH, schoolhouse type, 24x38x16" 435.00
Shaker, 1-pc cast body, wrought latch, 1800s, 21x35x14" 345.00
Unknown, parlor type, reeded column sides, 1830s, 25x37x17" .500.00
Walker & Pratt Laconia, ornate CI, NP footrail, 1860s, 35" 125.00

Franklin Stoves

AC Barstow parlor Franklin #5, ornate CI, 1852, 35x24x38" 375.00
Acme #18 Orient 1890, 6 tiles, mica window, fancy 375.00
Atlanta Franklin #8M, CI, 2 burner, coal/wood, EX 125.00
Barstow #137 Orient 1886, CI fireplace, coal, 37"+6" urn 1,125.00
C Newcomb & Co, Worcester, fireplace, 1800s, 38x24x30" ...1,565.00
Corner-type fireplace, #214, CI, 1915, 31x24" 1,560.00
Fuller-Warren PWC #4, 7 tiles, 10" urn, 38" 315.00
Home Franklin #2, CI fireplace, dtd 1850, 31x36" 188.00
Magee Ideal #3, CI fireplace, 2 side trivets, 1892, 32x28" 250.00
Muzzy & Co Villa Franklin, fancy CI fireplace, 20x29x19" 188.00
Orr, Painter & Co Sunshine Franklin #15, 1850s, 35"+9" urn ...315.00
SH Ransom Ben Franklin Air Tight, CI fireplace, Pat 1850 ....250.00
Werhle Co Newark OH Franklin Gem #16, 1890s, 43"+urn 345.00
Wyer & Noble, CI/brass-trim fireplace, old 2,000.00

Parlor

Albany #2, CI 2-column, ornate, urn atop, 40x32" 250.00
Anthony, Davy & Co Lady Washington, CI, 1848, 26"+7" urn .280.00
B&H Radiant Handwarmer Cool Morning, Pat 1893-94, 33" 435.00
Barstow...Boston MA...NY, cottage type, 1880s, 37"+8" urn 125.00
C Williams Forest #19, CI, 1870, 27" 375.00
C&EL Granger #3, bulbous columns, emb vines, 1840, 41x27" ..1,125.00
Cooperative Cycle #12, rnd coal burner, mica door, ornate 125.00
Cooperative Cycle #23, rnd coal burner, mica door, ornate 125.00
De Soto #1, CI, Pat 1854, 42x26x21" 685.00
EG Ruggles Gr Mtn #2, willows decor, Pat 1850, 27"+7" urn 470.00
Enterprise/Burnside #20A, CI, potbelly, 48", EX 470.00
Fuller-Warren-Morrison Floral #2, CI, 1853, 45x22x27" 1,250.00

Gothic Revival 'Castle' cast iron parlor stove, G.W. Eddy Manufacturer, Troy, NY, patented 1853, 36", $1,100.00.

Johnson-Cox-Fuller Home Parlor #3, CI, Pat 1852, 25"+10" urn ...375.00
Low & Hicks #4, Revere Air-Tight, cathedral front, 29"+urn 345.00
Newberry-Filley #4, ornate CI, urn atop, 1856, 26" 375.00
Newberry-Filley Oven Parlor #7, Pat 1855, 34x22x27" 250.00
Oak Peninsular #216, rnd coal burner, 11" urn, 48x31" 435.00
Portland Radiant #22, CI, top loading, mica window 215.00
PP Stewart L'Hiver #17, NP trim, 1890s, 57"+12" finial 560.00
Pratt & Perkins Organ #2, CI, slide doors, 1852, 36x22x25" 345.00
Rathbone-Sard Floral Acorn #38, NP trim, ca 1894, 37"+urn 750.00
SH Ransom...Albany, CI, side door, Pat 1848, 31"+13" urn 280.00
Somersworth Oak #18, rnd oak/coal burner, nickel trim, 1894 ..250.00
Standard Lighting Globe Incandescent, kerosene heater, 29" 315.00
Tropic Crawford #114, rnd coal burner, nickel trim, mica 188.00
Warnick & Liebrandt Union Airtight, ornate CI, 1851, 26" 250.00
Weir Glenwood #25, oven in top, nickel trim, mica 875.00
Wood/Bishop Clarion #4, CI, mica door, w/urn, 39x29" 250.00
Wood/Bishop Eva, CI, Pat 1865, 8" urn, 29x27" 215.00
Wood/Bishop Sunrise Sunshine #23, CI, w/oven, 28" 345.00

Ranges (Gas)

Cribben-Sexton Univ, 4-burner, gr/cream, high oven, '27, VG 375.00
Detroit Jewel, 4-burner, blk/nickel, glass oven door, 1918, VG ..500.00
Magic Chef, 6-burner/2-oven, warming closet, 1932, EX 2,500.00
Weir Insulated Glenwood, 6-burner/2-oven, wht, 1931, rstr ...4,125.00

Ranges (Wood and Coal)

Cribben-Sexton Universal, bl porc, high closet/no reservoir ...2,750.00
EC Simmons, cream enamel w/gr, reservoir, warming oven 438.00
Kalamazoo, tan enamel, EX 315.00
Kalamazoo Banner, VG 875.00
Noyes/Nutter Star Kineo #8-20, CI, plain, high shelf 750.00
Portland Atlantic Grand, ornate bk shelf, 12x20x18", EX 2,125.00
Portland Queen Atlantic #8, ornate CI, NP trim, mid-1800s ..1,560.00
Quick Meal, bl graniteware, EX 3,125.00
Rugby, CI/nickel silver pnt, ornate, 6-burner, high shelf 2,000.00
Walker/Pratt Village Crawford Royal, NP trim, 1910s 750.00
Weir Glenwood E, ornate CI, ca 1890, oven: 11x20x22" 815.00
Weir Modern Glenwood E 508, NP trim, oven: 12x20x19" 875.00
Wood/Bishop Home Clarion, CI, 1907, oven: 12x19x19" 750.00
Wood/Bishop Modern Clarion #8, side shelf, 1910s 1,000.00
Wood/Bishop New Clarion #8, low closet, 1882, 32x28x46" ..1,875.00

Miscellaneous

B&M # 5 RR, depot potbelly, 1915s, 48x32x32" 375.00
Fireplace, #116, scrollwork front, 1850s, 33x25x32", EX 250.00
Fireplace w/grate, #115, scrollwork/tiles, 1850s, 33x25x32" 250.00
Griswold, space heater, sheet steel, iron base & top, 27" 110.00
Kerosene, Monitor #20, CI range, 1887, 29x23" 125.00
Laundry, common rectangular 2- or 4-hole top, any maker 32.00
Laundry, Stamford Laundry #20, 4-ring lid, 21½x21x26" 188.00
RR, Union Stove Works, NY, Station Agent, CI potbelly, 46" ..435.00
Sears & Roebuck Signal Oak #22, coal burning, 42½" 138.00

Stove Manufacturers' Toy Stoves

Buck's Jr Range, St Louis MO, new body/pnt/recast parts, 26" ...850.00
Charter Oak #503, GF Filley, St Louis MO, 14x12x25", EX ...2,050.00
Dainty, Reading Stove Works, PA, 7x13x8", VG 150.00
Great Majestic Jr, Majestic Mfg, 31x16x23", M 5,650.00
Karr, Qualified, bl porc w/nickel, Belleville IL, 1925, EX 2,500.00
Karr repro, Qualified, bl porc w/nickel, 1960s EX 2,500.00
Karr Range, Belleville IL, bl porc, old model, 21½x9x13" 3,100.00
Little Eva T Southard, NYC, 8½x14x11", G 350.00
Little Fanny, CI, minor rust, EX 300.00
Little Willie, CI, EX 75.00
Royal American, Bridgeford, Louisville KY, 14x12x20", G 950.00

Toy Manufacturers' Toy Stoves

Eagle, Hubley, Lancaster PA, nickeled, recast parts 450.00
Eclipse, CI, EX 175.00
Little Giant, unmk/unidentified, 7½x8½x11", EX orig 675.00
Novelty, Kenton Hdwe, bl pnt/nickel trim, rfn, 13x6½x8½" 600.00
Pet, The; Young Bros, Albany NY, 10½x6x8½" 165.00
Queen, The; unmk/unidentified, copper o/l, 23½", M 2,400.00
Rival, J&E Stevens, Cromwell CT, 14x9x16", M, +2 kettles ..1,350.00
Rival, J&E Stevens, Cromwell CT, 1895, 13x7½x18½", G 240.00
Triumph, Kenton Hdwe, OH, 14x8½x19", G 195.00

Stretch Glass

Stretch glass, produced from 1916 until after 1930, was made in a effort to emulate the fine art glass of Tiffany and Carder. The glassware was sprayed with a special finish while still hot, and a reheating proce caused the coating to contract, leaving a striated, crepe-like iridescence. Northwood, Imperial, Fenton, Diamond, Lancaster, and the United States Glass Company were the largest manufacturers of this type of glass. See also specific companies.

Basket, wht, 10" 90.00
Bowl, amber irid, Jeannette, 4x9½" 35.00
Bowl, bl opaque, ribbed, flared, Northwood, 3x9½" 40.00
Bowl, Dbl Scroll, amberina, fluted, Imperial 100.00
Bowl, olive; pk, frost/flower decor, gold rim, Imperial, 7" 40.00
Bowl, purple, rolled rim, collar base, Vineland, 2¼x9½" 35.00
Bowl, vaseline, Northwood, 3x13" 45.00
Candlestick, Dmn, bl, hollow, pr 45.00
Candlestick, Dmn, gr, wht enamel decor, 9", pr 65.00
Candlestick, vaseline, twist, blk edge decor, US Glass, pr 125.00

Comport, vaseline, U.S. Glass, 4½x9¾", $40.00.

Compote, gray, scalloped, Imperial, 8½" 55.00
Compote, wht, bl band, orange flowers, Lancaster, 8¾x5¼" 38.00
Guest set, bl, Fenton #401, 2-pc 40.00
Plate, bl, EX irid, Imperial, 8¾" 12.00
Sherbet, amberina, ribbed, 3½" 40.00
Sugar bowl, vaseline, ftd, Fenton #3 ...... 25.00

String Holders

Today, if you want to wrap and secure a package, you have a variety of products from which to choose: cellophane tape, staples, etc. But in the 1800s, string was about the only available binder; thus the string holder, either the hanging or counter type, was a common and practical item found in most homes and businesses. Chalkware and ceramic figurals from the 1930s and 1940s contrast with the cast and wrought iron examples from the 1800s to make for an interesting collection. Our advisor for this category is Charles Reynolds; he is listed in the Directory under Virginia.

Ball type, CI, hinged, ca 1910, EX 110.00
Barrister face atop ftd sphere, opening in mouth, pnt CI, 8" 575.00
Beehive shape, CI, dtd 1861 & 66, 5½x6½", EX 60.00
Blk porter, Fredericksburg Art Pottery, 6½", M 150.00
Chef's face, ceramic, gold trim, lg 65.00
Compote shape w/emb leaves, tall finial on lid, CI, 10" 125.00
Girl's head, ceramic 50.00
Group of 3 girls, ceramic, Japan 25.00
Lacy, CI, 2-part 42.50
Mechanical, ball runs on track, CI 365.00
Old lady in rocker, chalkware 32.00

Postem Beverages, tin, Pat 1915, 5x11½" dia, EX 55.00
Sailor, eyes to side, w/pipe, chalkware 35.00
Spanish lady, chalkware, lg, EX 85.00
SSS for the Blood, CI, orig lid, 7x5", EX 195.00
Strawberry w/face, chalkware, EX 30.00
Tabby, CI, mc pnt, 1880s, 5⅝" 900.00
Treen, EX trn/detail, lid w/hole & finial, metal cutter, 3" 185.00

Sugar Shakers

Sugar shakers (or muffineers, as they were also called) were used during the Victorian era to sprinkle sugar and spice onto breakfast muffins, toast, etc. They were made of art glass in pressed patterns and in china. See also specific types and manufacturers.

Albertine, swirl relief, gilt decor, Mt WA, 5" 365.00
Apollo, etched orig top 85.00
Argus Swirl, peachbloom 235.00
Baby T'print, amberina, lg floral, ovoid, Mt WA 500.00
Banded Portland 65.00
Beatty Rib, bl opal 250.00
Bulging Loops, bl cased 450.00
Chandelier, etched 95.00
China, floral spray, pk/wht on wht, unmk 60.00
China, roses, pk & red on cream w/gold, Nippon, 5x3" 95.00

Chrysanthemum Base Swirl, cranberry satin opalescent, 4½", $400.00.

Coin Spot, cranberry opal, wide waist 200.00
Coin Spot, rubena, HP florals, 5½x2⅝" 250.00
Coinspot MOP, apricot to wht w/HP florals, 5½" 800.00
Cranberry, molded panels, SP lid, English, 5¾x2⅜" 115.00
Cut o/l, cobalt to clear, dmn/fan motif, 5¾" 150.00
Flower & Pleat, ruby flashed, rare 395.00
Flower Mold, cranberry 400.00
Forget-Me-Not, chartreuse 135.00
Invt T'print, amber w/decor, pewter collar & lid 195.00
Jumbo & Barnum 165.00
Medallion Sprig, clear to cobalt 375.00
Netted Oak, milk glass 110.00
Optic Panel, honey amber, HP florals, orig collar & lid 150.00
Parian Swirl, wht opaque, HP roses, Northwood, EX 110.00
Raindrop MOP, rose shaded, ovoid, Mt WA 850.00
Reverse Swirl, canary yel opal 195.00
Ribbed Lattice, cranberry opal 375.00
Ring Neck, cranberry frost spatter 150.00
Strawberry, Dmn & Fan cut w/rayed base, sterling lid 165.00
Teepee 75.00
Tomato, ornate top, Mt WA 295.00

Tomato, unfired Burmese, bl dots/oak leaves, Mt WA **595.00**
Wht satin w/gr shamrocks & bl dots, Dithridge **145.00**

Sunderland Lustre

Sunderland lustre was made by various potters in the Sunderland district of England during the 18th and 19th centuries. It is characterized by a splashed-on application of the pink lustre, which results in an effect sometimes referred to as the 'cloud' pattern. Some pieces are transfer printed with scenes, ships, florals, or portraits.

Bowl, Loss of Gold Is Much/CI Bridge..., Moore, 9", EX **350.00**
Chamber pot, verse 'Marriage'/other blk transfers w/mc, EX **550.00**
Jug, puzzle; Gaudy Welsh-type floral, prof rpt, 7" **300.00**
Jug, Wasp Boarding Frodic/Constitutions..., 6", EX **1,900.00**

Plaque, Praise Ye the Lord, shell-relief rim, 8x9", NM, $200.00.

Plaque, Thou God Seest..., blk transfer, wear, 6" dia **175.00**
Vase, emb design w/pk lustre & mc, sm edge flakes, 6¾" **175.00**
Wine, wht band w/mc florals, copper lustre trim, wear, 4" **115.00**

Surveying Instruments

The practice of surveying offers a wide variety of precision instruments primarily for field use, most of which are associated with the recording of distance and angular measurements. These instruments were primarily made from brass; the larger examples were fitted with tripods and protective cases. These cases also held accessories for the instruments, and these can sometimes play a key part in their evaluation. Instruments in complete condition and showing little use will have much greater values than those that appear to have had moderate or heavy use. Instruments were never polished during use, and those that have been polished as decorator pieces are of little interest to most avid collectors. Our advisor for this category is Dale Beeks; he is listed in the Directory under Idaho.

Abney level, K&E, ca 1910, w/case **65.00**
Abney level, K&E, w/top compass, +case **175.00**
Alidade, folding sight vanes, +leather case **45.00**
Alidade, telescopic, exploration type, 10" **225.00**
Alidade, telescopic, w/post, ca 1910 ....**250.00**
Barometer, pocket-watch type, 1½" dia, +case **60.00**
Barometer, surveyor's aneroid, w/magnifier, 4" dia **175.00**
Chain, Chesterman Sheffield, 100-ft **225.00**
Chain, Chesterman Sheffield, 4-pole, 66-ft **275.00**

Chain, Grumann's patent **350.00**
Chain, Gurley, 4-pole, 66-ft **225.00**
Chain, K&E, convertible type, 50 & 100-ft **200.00**
Circumferentor, 4 vanes, ca 1810 ....**1,250.00**
Clinometer, ca 1890, +leather case **75.00**
Compass, B Pike & Son, plain **550.00**
Compass, B Platt, vernier, ca 1870 ....**450.00**
Compass, Chandlee, plain, ca 1810 ....**2,250.00**
Compass, Dirigo Eugene Sherman Seattle USA, brass, +6" box .**105.00**
Compass, France, brass housing, 5" **75.00**
Compass, geologist's, w/inclinometer needle, 4" sq **100.00**
Compass, Hand Philadelphia-Baltimore PEX, brass, no cover **45.00**
Compass, HM Poole, ca 1850 ....**520.00**
Compass, HM Poole..., brass, surveyor's, w/levels etc, boxes **465.00**
Compass, pocket type, wooden housing, 3" **55.00**
Compass, prismatic, ca 1900, +leather case **145.00**
Compass, Randolf, telescopic vernier **450.00**
Compass, S Thaxter & Son Boston, brass, 7", EX in 10" box **300.00**
Compass, Sold by Max Kuner Seattle, brass, 10½", EX, +box **200.00**
Compass, staff, folding sight vanes **95.00**
Compass, Star Boston, brass, EX in 5½" sq dvtl mahog box **30.00**
Compass, W&LE Gurley, solar, ca 1890, +case & tripod **3,500.00**
Compass, W&LE Gurley, vernier, ca 1880, 15" **450.00**
Compass, WM J Young No, railroad type **550.00**
Compass, wooden, ca 1810, 12" **750.00**
Cross staff head, simple type w/4 slits, +case **75.00**
Cross staff head, w/top-mtd compass **120.00**
Drawing instruments, K&E, w/12x8" tray in wooden case **195.00**
Drawing instruments, set in 10" leatherette roll **25.00**
Drawing instruments, 8 items, +5x8" wooden case **75.00**
Jacob's staff, oak w/steel tip, octagonal **120.00**
Level, architect's, wye, convertible, 12" **275.00**
Level, Bostrom, unused, +case & tripod **120.00**
Level, Brunson, dumpy, blk pnt **125.00**
Level, builder's, wye, 12" telescope **110.00**
Level, CG King, wye, ca 1855, 14" **450.00**
Level, farmer's drainage type, simple, 10", +box & tripod **120.00**
Level, Gurley, wye, ca 1880, 18" **350.00**
Level, Gurley #18345, wye, 22" **350.00**
Level, hand, peep, w/bubble, 6" L, +leather case **35.00**
Level, K&E, dumpy, 18" **150.00**
Level, Phelps & Gurley, wye, 24" **950.00**
Level, Spencer, London, wye, w/compass **550.00**
Level, Stackpole Bros, wye, ca 1870, 16" **425.00**
Plumb-bob, mining type w/wick & gimbals, +box **450.00**
Plumb-bob, w/internal reel **110.00**
Semi-circumferentor, Am, all brass, ca 1800 ....**1,250.00**
Semi-circumferentor, Am, wooden w/brass sights **950.00**
Theodolite, Buff & Buff, 8" horizontal circle **1,250.00**
Theodolite, English, 18th C **950.00**
Theodolite, Fauth & Co, 16" horizontal circle **3,250.00**
Theodolite, Wm Wurdemann #2 — , 12" telescope **1,250.00**
Transit, blk pnt, ca 1930 ....**225.00**
Transit, Bostrom, K&E, Leitz, builder's type, ca 1930 ....**150.00**
Transit, convertible, solar-mining, complete **1,850.00**
Transit, exploration type, ca 1890, 8" **450.00**
Transit, K&E, bent-standard design, ca 1910 ....**550.00**
Transit, lt mountain, ca 1900 ....**450.00**
Transit, mining, dbl telescope **950.00**
Transit, pocket; Brunton, Wm Ainsworth, 1893 ....**150.00**
Transit, W&LE Gurley Troy NY, ca 1860 ....**600.00**
Transit, W&LE Gurley Troy NY #1235 ....**450.00**
Transit, w/Burt solar attachment **1,200.00**
Transit, w/side-mtd solar attachment, ca 1910 ....**950.00**

transit, w/tip-mtd solar attachment, ca 1900 ....950.00
transit, Wm J Young Maker Phila 600.00
tripod, compass type, 1-pc legs 75.00
tripod, transit type, pc legs 75.00
tripod, transit type, telescopic legs 45.00
tripod, w/alidade table 150.00

Swastika Keramos

Swastika Keramos was a line of artware made by the Owens China Co. of Minerva, Ohio, circa 1902-1904. It is characterized either by a 'coralene' type of decoration (similiar to the Opalesce line made by the B. Owens Pottery Company of Zanesville) or by the application of metallic lustres, usually in simple designs. Shapes are often plain and handles squarish and rather thick, suggestive of the Arts and Crafts style.

Pitcher, silver oil-spot panels fr w/gold swastikas, 10" 300.00
Vase, coralene scrollwork, minor wear, slim, 12" 160.00
Vase, gr w/variegated gold lines, mk, 8" 175.00
Vase, red/dk gr drip on gold, slim, surface wear, 14" 120.00

Syracuse

Syracuse was a line of fine dinnerware and casual ware which was made for nearly a century by the Onondaga Pottery Company of Syracuse, New York. Early patterns were marked O.P. Company. Collectors of American dinnerware are focusing their attention on reassembling some of their many lovely patterns. In 1966 the firm became officially known as the Syracuse China Company in order to better identify with the name of their popular chinaware. Many of the patterns were marked with the shape and color names (Old Ivory, Federal, etc.), not the pattern names. By 1971 dinnerware geared for use in the home was discontinued, and the company turned to the manufacture of hotel, restaurant, and other types of commercial tableware. Our advisor for this category is Mary Delucchi; she is listed in the Directory under California.

Apple Blossom, plate, 8" 20.00
Arcadia, cream soup, w/underplate 30.00
Arcadia, creamer & sugar bowl, w/lid 65.00
Arcadia, cup & saucer 28.00
Arcadia, demitasse cup & saucer 25.00
Arcadia, gravy boat 65.00
Arcadia, plate, 7" 18.00
Arcadia, plate, 9¾" 25.00
Arcadia, platter, 14" 55.00
Arcadia, rimmed soup 25.00
Avalon, cup & saucer, gold trim 27.50
Avalon, plate, salad 18.00
Avalon, plate, 10" 25.00
Bombay, bowl, vegetable; ivory w/gold trim, w/lid 95.00
Bombay, chop plate, ivory w/gold trim 85.00
Bombay, coffeepot, ivory w/gold trim 95.00
Bombay, creamer & sugar bowl, ivory w/gold trim 65.00
Bombay, gravy boat, ivory w/gold trim 65.00
Bombay, platter, ivory w/gold trim, 14" 40.00
Bracelet, plate, 10¼" 35.00
Bracelet, platter, 12" 50.00
Briarcliff, bowl, fruit; sm 20.00
Briarcliff, cream soup 25.00
Briarcliff, cup & saucer 28.00
Briarcliff, plate, 10" 25.00
Carvel, platter, 14" 65.00
Coralbel, plate, 10¼" 30.00

Coronet, cup & saucer 30.00
Coronet, plate, salad 20.00
Gardenia, plate, dinner 25.00
Indian Tree, bowl, cereal 20.00
Jefferson, cup & saucer 30.00
Jefferson, gravy boat 65.00
Jefferson, plate, 10" 28.00
Jefferson, platter, 14" 75.00
Jefferson, rimmed soup 25.00
Lady Mary, plate, 9¾" 20.00
Lady Mary, platter, 12" 55.00
Lady Mary, platter, 8" 30.00
Lyric, bowl, vegetable; ftd 55.00
Lyric, bowl fruit; sm 20.00
Lyric, cup & saucer 30.00
Meadow Breeze, cup & saucer 38.00
Meadow Breeze, platter, 14" 125.00
Meadow Breeze, sugar bowl, w/lid 55.00
Royal Court, plate, 10¼" 50.00
Stansbury, bowl, vegetable; w/lid 125.00
Stansbury, bowl, vegetable; 10½" L 50.00
Stansbury, cream soup, w/underplate 30.00
Stansbury, gravy boat 65.00
Suzanne, bowl, dessert; 7" 18.00
Suzanne, bowl, fruit; sm 22.00
Suzanne, gravy boat 75.00
Victoria, cup & saucer 36.00

Syrups

Values are for old, original syrups. Beware of reproductions! See also various manufacturers and specific types of glass.

Amberina, Inverted Thumbprint, New England Glass, 5½", $975.00.

Arched Ovals...75.00
Artichoke, frosted, orig pewter hinged lid 165.00
Banded Portland 75.00
Broken Column 135.00
Bull's Eye, scallops, pewter lid, lg 65.00
Button Arches 95.00
Catherine Ann, milk glass, orig lid & hdl 115.00
Coin Spot, bl opal, ring neck, lid dtd 185.00
Coin Spot, gr, bulbous 135.00
Coin Spot & Swirl, bl opal 160.00
Cone, bl 165.00
Cordova 135.00
Coreopsis, EX decor 225.00
Dahlia, amber 85.00
Eyewinker 135.00

Feather, emerald gr 475.00
Fishnet & Poppies, milk glass 145.00
Flower & Pleat, clear/frosted 145.00
Gonterman Swirl, amber, pewter lid, rare 450.00
Guttate, pk cased, metal lid 295.00
Heart & T'print, 4" 95.00
Hercules Pillar, amber 185.00
Hobnail, bl, pewter lid, dtd 275.00
Jacob's Ladder, knight's head finial 145.00
Leaf Umbrella, bl cased, scarce 800.00
Leaf Umbrella, mauve cased, pewter lid, rare 850.00
Lens & Star, bellflower etch 85.00
Locket on Chain, rare 350.00
Medallion Sprig, rubena 400.00
Melligo, bl opaque 145.00
Missouri 85.00
Moon & Star, orig tin lid, rare 145.00
Priscilla 145.00
Priscilla, gr w/gold, scarce 395.00
Reverse Swirl, cranberry opal, rare 750.00
Reverse Torpedo 95.00
Ribbed Pillar, pk spatter 275.00
Ring Band, custard w/EX gold 425.00
Robin's Nest 155.00
Shoshone, yel flashed, rare 350.00
Swan 165.00
Thousand Eye, amber 145.00
Venetia, cranberry 335.00

Tamac Pottery

At the close of World War II, jobs were almost impossible to find for homecoming military men. Leonard Tate and Allen Macauley were two such men. The state of Oklahoma, at that time, was trying to encourage industry and was offering free factory sites for new businesses. As a result of economic necessity, the two young men and their wives, Marjorie Tate and Betty Macauley, moved from New Jersey to the town of Perry, Oklahoma. The two women were already acquainted and had worked together in the design department at Congoleum Nairn in New Jersey. The foursome decided to combine efforts and past experiences and thus formed 'Tamac' pottery, a conglomeration of the two last names.

The company was first organized in September 1946, in the garage of Leonard Tate's parents in Perry, Oklahoma. Although it was a twenty-four hour job, only a few pieces of pottery were produced daily. The plant expanded in 1948 with over three hundred pieces of earthenware manufactured in a single day.

The Tates and Macauleys were directly responsible for all phases of Tamac production: designing and making the molds, mixing the Oklahoma and Kansas clays, final processing and shipping. The pottery process took approximately ten days to complete. All of the phases were carried out in the Perry, Oklahoma, plant. All four took turns in the retail store and conducted tours. The business had customers from every state in the union and from several foreign countries.

Approximately seventy various pieces of Tamac pottery were produced, mainly consisting of buffet/dinnerware. Other 'specialty' pieces included candle holders, ashtrays, vases, and table centerpieces. One of their most popular sellers was the barbeque line which consisted of tray-like plates with unique coffee mugs having non-traditional handles. The barbeque sets were designed with the idea that more casual backyard dining and entertaining would be done in the postwar era.

Six colors were produced, each with a 'frosted' rim of a different color. The six colors were: Frosty Pine, Avacado, Frosty Fudge, Honey, Raspberry, and Beige. The Frosty Pine and Avacado (both with dark

green bases) are the most readily available and the most collectible. Few items, mainly 'specialty' pieces, were manufactured in Raspberry.

By 1950 the Macauleys became homesick for the East and sold their shares to the Tates. Around 1952 the Tamac business had expanded and required bank financing. Bankers didn't understand the manufacturing business and refused to give the Tates the backing they needed. Consequently the plant was sold. Although others took over the plant, they too encountered the same difficulties. The plant was permanently closed in the early 1970s.

Tamac pottery can easily be identified by its unique design and the stamp on the bottom of each piece: 'TAMAC Perry, Okla USA.' Some earlier pieces carry the etched 'TAMAC' mark.

Our advisors for this category are Bob and Dondee Klein. They are listed in the Directory under Oklahoma.

Bowl, gourd shape, 22" 20.00
Bowl, serving; 2-qt 10.00
Bowl, serving; 4-qt 15.00
Butter dish, no lid 5.00
Candle holder, dbl 12.00
Candle holder, single 8.00
Casserole, 2-qt, w/lid 25.00
Coffee cup or mug 5.00
Creamer, 8-oz 8.00
Goblet, wine; 6-oz 8.00
Pitcher, juice; 24-oz 15.00
Pitcher, 2-qt 25.00
Pitcher, 4-qt 30.00
Planter vase, w/tray & drain hole 15.00
Planter vase, 5x6" dia 10.00
Plate, barbeque; 15" 12.00
Plate, dinner; 10" 8.00
Platter, turkey, 18" 30.00
Saucer 3.00
Shakers, pr 10.00
Spoon holder 12.00
Sugar bowl, w/lid 8.00
Teapot 25.00
Toothpick holder 4.00
Tumbler, juice; 4-oz 5.00
Tumbler, 16-oz 7.00
Vase, free-form, 5½" 12.00
Violet planter, w/tray & drain hole 15.00
Wall vase, 5" 8.00

Target Balls

Prior to 1880 when the clay pigeon was invented, blown glass target balls were used extensively for shotgun competitions. Approximately 2¾" in diameter, these balls were hand blown into a three-piece mold. All have a ragged hole where the blowpipe was twisted free. Target balls date from approximately 1840 (English) to World War I, although they were most widely used in the 1870-1880 period. Common examples are unmarked except for the blower's code — dots, crude numerals, etc. Some balls are embossed in a dot or diamond pattern so they were more likely to shatter when struck by shot, and some have names and/or patent dates. When evaluating condition, bubbles and other minor manufacturing imperfections are acceptable; cracks are not. The prices below are for mint condition examples.

Bogardus' Glass Ball Pat'd April 10 1877, amber 350.00
Bogardus' Glass Ball Pat'd April 10 1877, other than amber 800.00
CTB Co (Composition Target Ball Co), blk pitch 250.00

Emb ribs, amber 150.00
English, shooter emb in 2 rnd panels, clear 300.00
English, shooter emb in 2 rnd panels, gr 300.00
English, shooter emb in 2 rnd panels, purple 300.00
For Hockey's Patent Trap, gr 500.00
Great Western Gun Works, amber 900.00
Gurd & Son, London, Ontario, amber 500.00
Ira Paine's Filled Ball Pat Oct 23 1877, amber 250.00
Ira Paine's Filled Ball Pat Oct 23 1877, other than amber 800.00
NB Glass Works Perth, other than pale gr 300.00
NB Glass Works Perth, pale gr, almost clear 200.00
Plain, amber 65.00
Plain, clear, w/mold mks 1,000.00
Plain, cobalt 150.00
Plain, purple 150.00
Unemb central band w/geometrics, med bl, 1880s, 2⅝" 75.00
WW Greener St Mary's Works Brim/68 Haymarket London 250.00

Related Memorabilia

Ball thrower, dbl; old red pnt, ME Card, Pat...78, 79, VG 900.00
Clay birds, Winchester, Pat May 29 1917, 1 flight in box 100.00
Pitch bird, blk DUVROCK 1.00
Shell, dummy, w/single window, any brand 35.00
Shell, dummy shotgun, Winchester, window w/powder, 6" 125.00
Shell set, dummy, Gamble Stores, 2 window shells, 3 cut out 125.00
Shell set, dummy, Winchester, 5 window shells 175.00
Shell set, dummy shotgun, Peters, 6 window shells+full box 175.00
Shotshell loader, rosewood/brass, Parker Bros, Pat 1884 ....50.00

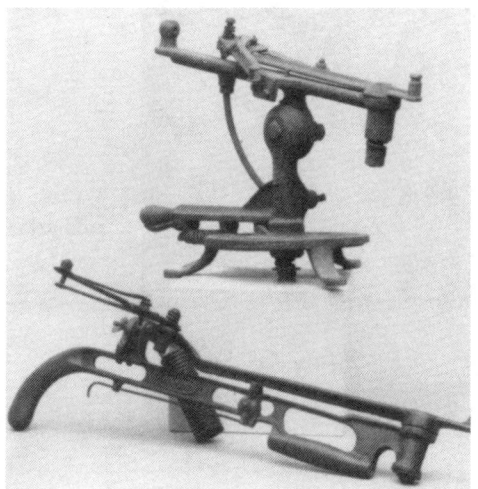

Trap throwers: The Expert, Pat 1902, Chamberlain Cartridge and Target Co., $175.00; Dupont brand, old red paint, VG, $100.00.

Target, Am sheet metal, rod ends mk Pat Feb 8 '21, set 25.00
Target, blk japanned sheet metal, Bussy Patentee, London 50.00
Target, BUST-O, blk or wht breakable wafer 20.00
Trap, DUVROCK, w/blk pitch birds 150.00
Trap, MO-SKEET-O, w/birds 150.00

Tea Caddies

Because tea was once regarded as a precious commodity, special boxes called caddies were used to store the tea leaves. They were made from various materials: porcelain, carved and inlaid woods, and metals ranging from painted tin or tole to engraved silver. Our advisor for this category is Tina Carter; she is listed in the Directory under California.

Burlwood, Regency, brass hdls/paw ft, 2 bowls w/in, 7½" 700.00
China, florals, pk on gr w/moriage decor, unmk, 5x4" 115.00
Exotic figured wood, 2-compartment, w/bowl, English, 14" 575.00
Ivory w/tortoise shell banding, MOP inlay, octagonal, rstr 450.00
Mahog Empire, brass ball ft, rectangular, 5½x4¾x4¾" 185.00
Quillwork, rvpt scene in front panel, damage/rpr, 4½" 650.00
Rosewood, tapering rectangular form, Wm IV, 1800s, 14" L 250.00
SP, people/scenes/etc repousse, 6-sided, Derby 100.00

Tortoise shell, embossed front, silver-plated feet, 9", $850.00.

Tortoise shell, dome lid, ball ft, Regency, 1830s, 6" 700.00
Tunbridge, burl inlay, ca 1810 ....195.00

Tea Leaf Ironstone

Tea Leaf Ironstone became popular in the 1880s when middle-class American housewives became bored with the plain white stone china that English potters had been exporting to this country for nearly a century. The original design has been credited to Anthony Shaw of Longport, who decorated the plain ironstone with a hand-painted copper lustre design of bands and leaves. Originally known as Lustre Band and Sprig, the pattern has since come to be known as Tea Leaf Lustre. It was produced with minor variations by many different firms both in England and the United States. By the early 1900s, it had become so commonplace that it had lost much of its appeal.

Items marked Red Cliff are reproductions made from 1950 until 1980 for this distributing and decorating company of Chicago, Illinois. Hall China provided many of the blanks.

Our advice for this category comes from Home Place Antiques, whose address is listed in the Directory under Illinois.

Bone dish, crescent shape, scalloped, Meakin 75.00
Bowl, for chamber set, Meakin, 14¾" 150.00
Bowl, soup; flanged rim, EX lustre, Meakin, 8¾" 30.00
Bowl, vegetable; Cable, w/lid, Burgess, EX 195.00
Bowl, vegetable; Fish Hook, bracket ft, w/lid, Meakin, 11x7" 165.00
Bowl, vegetable; Medallion finial, Mellor-Taylor, EX 175.00
Bowl, vegetable; Pagoda, octagonal, ribbed, Wedgwood, 11" 145.00
Butter dish, Fish Hook, w/drain, Meakin, EX 165.00
Butter dish, simple sq drain, Wedgwood, 5½" 165.00

Butter pat, rnd, Meakin 14.00
Butter pat, sq, Meakin, 2¾" 14.00
Butter pat, unmk, 3" dia 12.00
Butter pat, Wilkinson 12.00
Chamber pot, Bamboo finial on lid, unmk, EX 245.00
Coffeepot, Bamboo, Meakin, 9" 185.00
Compote, fluted, Shaw, 3½x9½" 245.00
Creamer, Bamboo, Meakin, 5¼" 150.00
Creamer, Fish Hook, Meakin, 5¼" 140.00
Cup & saucer, Chelsea type, Johnson Bros, 2⅝", 3½" 85.00
Cup & saucer, Chinese shape, Shaw 95.00
Cup & saucer, farm type, Meakin, 2¼", 3½" 75.00
Cup & saucer, handleless; Meakin, 3", 3½" 85.00
Cup & saucer, str sides, Meakin, 2¾", 3½" 75.00
Cup plate, gold lustre, Johnson Bros, 3⅜" 30.00
Cup plate, unmk, 3½" 50.00
Egg cup, unmk, rare, 3½" 350.00
Gravy boat, Fish Hook, Meakin, 2¾x8" 75.00
Ladle, sauce; unmk, M 265.00
Nappy, Chinese shape, Shaw 25.00
Nappy, Wilkinson, 4½" 22.50
Pitcher, Fish Hook, Meakin, 7" 185.00
Pitcher, J&E Mayer, stained, 7½" 85.00
Pitcher, Meakin, 6", EX 125.00
Pitcher, Meakin, 8½x7¾", EX 175.00
Plate, Cloverleaf Variant, gold lustre, child's, unmk, 4⅝" 25.00
Plate, Meakin, 8¾" 20.00
Plate, Meakin, 9¾" 30.00
Plate, Mellor-Taylor, 7⅝" 12.00
Plate, Mellor-Taylor, 9" 25.00
Plate, Red Cliff, 8¼" 8.00
Plate, Shaw, 9", EX 25.00

Plate, square, with handles, Meakin, 9",
$62.00.

Plate, Wedgwood, 9¾" 30.00
Plate, Wilkinson, 9¼" 25.00
Platter, oval, Shaw, lg 55.00
Platter, rectangular, Meakin, 10" 37.50
Platter, rectangular, Meakin, 12¾x9⅛" 50.00
Platter, rectangular, Meakin, 16x12" 50.00
Platter, ribbed, rectangular, Wedgwood, 12" 55.00
Relish tray, Bamboo, Meakin 40.00
Sauce dish, scalloped, gold lustre, Powell Bishop, 4½" sq 15.00
Shaving mug, Chinese shape, Shaw, 3¼" 175.00
Shaving mug, Meakin, 3¼" 150.00

Shaving mug, 12-sided, Shaw, extra lg 225.00
Soap dish, w/lid & liner, Meakin 195.00
Sugar bowl, bulbous, w/lid, Wilkinson 85.00
Sugar bowl, Fish Hook, w/lid, Meakin, 5½" 85.00
Sugar bowl, Lily of the Valley, w/lid, Shaw, 5½x5½" ...150.00
Sugar bowl, Pepper Leaf, w/lid, Elsmore & Forster, 7" ...140.00
Sugar bowl, Teaberry, w/lid, Clementson, EX 170.00
Teapot, Chinese shape, Shaw, 10", VG 265.00
Teapot, Fish Hook, Meakin, 8½", EX 195.00
Toothbrush holder, Meakin, 5" 165.00
Toothbrush holder, Mellor-Taylor 155.00
Waste bowl, Pepper Leaf Variant, Elsmore & Forster 95.00

Teapots

The custom of drinking tea has resulted in the production of many tea-related collectibles; the most popular is the teapot. The first teapots were manufactured in the Chinese village of Vi-Hsing during the late 16th century and were no bigger than the tiny cups previously used for tea drinking. Amazingly these same tiny teapots are still being used today.

A wide range of teapots can be found by the avid searcher; those most readily available today were produced from about 1870 to the present. Almost every pottery and porcelain manufacturer in Europe as well as in America have produced teapots. Some are purely functional, others decorative and whimsical. Refer to various manufacturers' names for further listings. Our advisor for this category is Tina Carter; she is listed in the Directory under California.

Automobile, gr glaze, no mk, 8" L 300.00

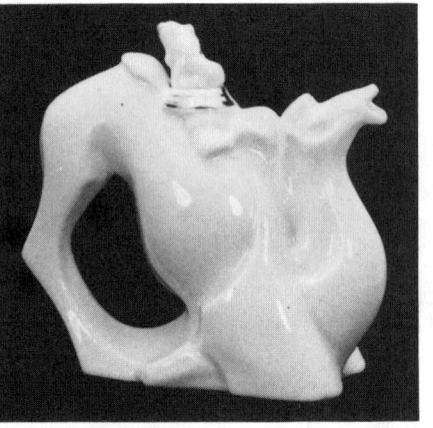

Camel, white porcelain,
unmarked, 6", $50.00.

Dbl spout, earthenware, slip decor, ca 1890 ....85.00
DM mk, Japan, coralene dragon, 6-cup 28.00
Ellgreave, Wood & Sons, England, ironstone w/floral 35.00
England, bunny, mk, ca 1950, 6-cup 45.00
England, H&K, Old English Sampler, 6-cup, EX 45.00
England, S Derbyshire, barge, brn, emb mk, lg 75.00
England, Spode's Tower, bl/wht transfer, London shape, VG ...45.00
England, Susie Cooper, horizontal lines, bulbous, mk 65.00
England, Sutherland, silver lustre, mk, 6-cup 60.00
England, SYP, Wedgwood, bone china, bl/wht/gold, ca 1905-06 ..110.00
England, Wedgwood, bl/wht jasperware, ca 1784, 2-cup 210.00
English, dmn shape, brn w/HP flowers in formal rows, #405097 ...35.00
Flow bl, man seated, legs outstretched, conical hat, 8x9" 50.00
Germany, Bonn, HP floral, mk, 4-cup 45.00
Germany, Royal Hanover, gr luster, HP, 6½" 75.00
Iced Tea dispenser, 2-pc, brn, USA 175.00
Japan, rooster w/gold specks, head creamer, neck sugar, 9" 28.00

Japan, Tea for Two, man in tux hdl, girl in gown forms pot **45.00**
Ming Tea Co, made in Japan, w/label, 1½-cup **18.00**
Monterey, made in CA, pk spatter, lg **28.00**
Pyrex mk, blown glass, etched flowers, 6-cup **45.00**
Royal Bayreuth, tomato, mk, ca 1910 ....**85.00**
Rudolph the Red Nosed Reindeer, w/creamer & sugar **75.00**
Sadler, pk w/flowers, mk, 6-cup **35.00**
Tank, gr w/silver details, Made in England, 8½" L **200.00**
US Zone, Germany, cat figural, paw spout, blk/gray/cream, 9" **45.00**
Wade, mk, HP, +matching cr/sug **55.00**
Wales CM, Charles & Diana, brn pottery, 2½" **78.00**
Walt Disney Productions, Snow White w/Dwarfs, musical **50.00**
WWII, Esc to US by Royal Navy or Allied Fleets, MIE, brn **35.00**

Teco

Teco artware was made by the American Terra Cotta and Ceramic Company, located near Chicago, Illinois. The firm was established in 1886 and until 1901 produced only brick, sewer tile, and other redware. Their early glaze was inspired by the matt green made popular by Grueby. 'Teco Green' was made for nearly ten years. It was similar to Grueby's yet with a subtle silver-gray cast. The company was one of the first in the United States to perfect a true crystalline glaze. The only decoration used was through the modeling and glazing techniques; no hand painting was attempted. Favored motifs were naturalistic leaves and flowers. The company broadened their lines to include garden pottery and faience tiles and panels. New matt glazes (browns, yellows, blue, and rose) were added to the green in 1910. By 1922 the artware lines were discontinued; the company was sold in 1930.

Values are dictated by size and shape, with architectural and organic forms being more desirable. Teco is usually marked with a vertical impressed device comprised of a large 'T' to the left of the remaining three letters.

Bowl, gr, ribbed, mk twice, 7" **200.00**
Chamberstick, gr, invt trumpet form, loop hdl, #289, 6½" **385.00**
Vase, brn, dimpled sphere w/collar, #360A, 4" **500.00**
Vase, brn, elongated 'top'-form sits in 4-prong base, 9" **2,000.00**

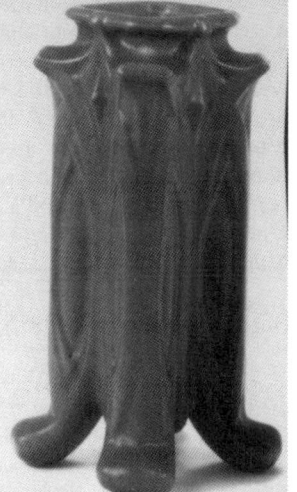

Vase, brown matt, F. Moreau design, #434, 12x7", $4,750.00.

Vase, gr, band of rings at rim, 3-line uprights, ovoid, 12" **5,500.00**
Vase, gr, bulbous, dbl mk, 5" **450.00**
Vase, gr, classic form, 15x5½" **1,000.00**
Vase, gr, dbl gourd w/4 buttresses, #287, mk, 6½x5", EX **900.00**

Vase, gr, Gates design #432, 10" **1,400.00**
Vase, gr, integral rim-to-width hdls, 5¾x8½" **1,000.00**
Vase, gr, long pointed buttress hdl ea side, #266, 12" **1,200.00**
Vase, gr, mk, 7x5" **400.00**
Vase, gr, Pompeian classic shape, #165, 8" **625.00**
Vase, gr, sm mouth, #200, 4" **345.00**
Vase, gr, 12 upright blade leaves form openwork base, 12" **6,600.00**
Vase, gr, 3 protrusions w/rtcl 'clover,' 3 ft, #115, 9" **2,000.00**
Vase, gr, 4 bars form sq 'cage' around cylinder, #265, 12" **3,300.00**
Vase, gr, 4 leaf hdls on gourd form w/petal lip, #220, 14" **3,850.00**
Vase, gr, 4 long curved hdls, low angled width, rstr, 12x5" **1,000.00**
Vase, gr, 4-lobed, sq peaked rim, #268, 11" **2,400.00**
Vase, gr shaded, broad oval body, #147, 7" **495.00**
Vase, gr w/gun metal, classic form, #64D, 11", NM **300.00**
Vase, gr w/gun metal, dbl gourd w/buttresses, #287, 7" **1,300.00**
Vase, gr w/gun metal, low shoulder, 4-lobe top, #182, 15" **2,000.00**
Vase, gr w/gun metal, 4 open rim-to-body straps, #175, 14" **2,700.00**
Vase, lt gr, concave w/4 ribbed buttress hdls, 18x11", NM **6,500.00**
Vase, lt gr w/gun metal, tulips/geometric band, Jenney, 10" **1,200.00**
Vase, ovoid, brn, 4" **325.00**
Vase, rose, WB Mudie design, #266, 11" **525.00**
Wall pocket, gr, sqd top/emb disk bottom, 6½" **385.00**

Teddy Bear Collectibles

The story of Teddy Roosevelt's encounter with the bear cub has been oft recounted with varying degrees of accuracy, so it will suffice to say that it was as a result of this incident in 1902 that the teddy bear got his name. These appealing little creatures are enjoying renewed popularity with collectors today. To one who has not yet succumbed to their obvious charms, one bear seems to look very much like another. How to tell the older ones? Look for long snouts, jointed limbs, large feet and felt paws, long curving arms, and glass or shoe-button eyes. Most old bears have a humped back and are made of mohair stuffed with straw or excelsior. Cute expressions, original clothes, a nice personality, and, of course, good condition add to their value. Some Steiff bears in mint condition may go as high as $100 per inch. These are easily recognized by the trademark button within the ear. For further information we recommend *Teddy Bears, Annalee's & Steiff Animals* by Margaret Fox Mandel, available from Collector Books. See also Toys, Steiff.

Key: jtd — jointed

Bears

Am, cotton plush, jtd limbs, glass eyes, 1940s, 23" **850.00**
Am, hump, worn rust mohair, rpl pads, glass eyes, early, 22" **875.00**
Bing, Benny, wht mohair, jtd, button eyes, 17", EX **245.00**
Bing, Buddie, tan mohair, jtd, button eyes, 1915, 12", EX **1,750.00**
Chad Valley, gold mohair, glass eyes, early, 12" **375.00**
Chad Valley, mohair, fully jtd, vest/bow tie, 1930s, 15" **315.00**
Chiltern, Chester, long gold mohair, jtd, 10" **245.00**
Chiltern, Griff, worn gold mohair, glass eyes, 1930s, 21" **395.00**
Chiltern, long gold mohair, glass eyes, embr nose, 12", VG **365.00**
Chiltern, lt gold mohair, glass eyes, felt pads, 18", EX **750.00**
Clemens, silvery mohair, hump, jtd, tag, 14", NM **265.00**
Clemens, squeaker, fully jtd, straw filled, standing, 11" **250.00**
England, growler, cotton plush, glass eyes, linen pads, 20", EX ...**450.00**
Fully jtd, gold mohair, bead eyes, leather collar, 13", VG **600.00**
Fully jtd, gold mohair, glass eyes, 1920s, 24", EX **695.00**
Fully jtd, mohair, hump, glass eyes, long nose, 20" **500.00**
Fully jtd, mohair, hump, straw filled, glass eyes, skinny, 14" **335.00**
Fully jtd, squeaker, mohair, floss nose/mouth, 1920s, 12" **465.00**

Germany, jtd, gold mohair, voice box, glass eyes, 1920s, 23" 850.00
Germany, musical, mohair, jtd, straw filled, 1920s, 24" 1,200.00
Grisly, growler, tan mohair, jtd, rpl paws, 21", EX 495.00
Growler, brn mohair, glass eyes, on wheels, 1950s, 26" 350.00
Herman, Floppy Zotty, mohair, not jtd, glass eyes, 1960, 8" 175.00
Herman, gray frosted fur, jtd, 11", EX 225.00
Herman, growler, beige mohair, jtd, 1940, 20", VG 925.00
Herman, squeaker, long mohair, not jtd, w/tag, 11" 175.00
Herman, squeaker, mohair, w/tag, 12" 165.00
Ideal, Barnaby, beige mohair, rpl eyes & pads, very early, 24" .1,550.00
Ideal, beige mohair, glass eyes, orig sailor dress, early, 29" 1,500.00
Ideal, long auburn mohair, jtd, 1950s, 23", VG 225.00
Ideal, Smokey, rubber face, tag on bk, 17", EX 125.00
Schuco, mohair, fully jtd, metal eyes, 2¾" 395.00
Schuco, Sherlock, wht long mohair, glass eyes, 26", NM 1,800.00
Schuco, short mohair, jtd, glass eyes, 1935, 18", EX 495.00
Schuco, Watson, wht mohair, jtd, glass eyes, 24", NM 1,250.00
Schuco, yes/no, gold mohair, jtd, orig ribbon, 5", EX 650.00

Steiff, fully jointed, glass eyes, embroidered nose, stitched paws, button in ear, 9", $1,500.00.

Steiff, gold mohair, hump, w/button, 14", 1935-40, NM 950.00
Steiff, growler, tan mohair, jtd, glass eyes, 1965, 15", NM 265.00
Steiff, long gold mohair, fully jtd, w/button, 1905, 13", M 965.00
Steiff, mohair, blk button eyes, floss nose, early, 24", EX 1,200.00
Steiff, mohair, squeaker, hump, w/button, 1950s, 8½", NM 625.00
Voice box, jtd, mohair, glass eyes, straw stuffed, 21", VG 450.00

Miscellaneous

Book, Mother Goose's Teddy Bears, Cavally, 1907, EX 335.00
Bottle warmer, wht, straw head, glass eyes, 12" 165.00
Puppet, teddy w/blk ears, embr nose, Chad Valley, 10" 110.00
Spoon, sterling, bear hdl, eng initials/'08, 5½" 125.00
Tea set, teddy bears play soccer, Japan, 1920s, 16-pc 575.00
Tip tray, Roosevelt bears, dress shop ad, 1906, EX 350.00
Toothpick holder, Teddy & the Bears, souvenir 85.00

Telephones

Since Alexander Graham Bell's first successful telephone communication, the phone itself has undergone a complete evolution in style as well as efficiency. Early models, especially those wall types with ornately carved oak boxes, are of special interest to collectors. Also of value are the candlestick phones from the early part of the century and any related memorabilia.

Am Electric, str shaft desk stand, 1903, 11", VG.......................150.00

Automatic Electric, str-shaft upright desk stand, 1912, NM 250.00
Automatic Electric #50, EX 65.00
Automatic Electric monophone, Bakelite, cradle type, 1920s, EX ..75.00

Candlestick telephone with attached coin-operated mechanism, Cracraft-Leigh Electric Co., M, $450.00.

Cracraft, oak, wall type, complete 225.00
Cradle style, off-wht plastic, 1930s, 6x8x5" 65.00
Eastern, tapered desk stand, ca 1900, 12x5½", EX 625.00
Ericsson, dial, 1920s 185.00
Gray #50, pay type, blk 385.00
Kellogg Silver Dollar Gray, pay station, walnut, 1904, NM 425.00
Manhattan Electric Intercom, walnut, 1899, 5¾x5x3½", EX 235.00
Monarch, upright desk stand, CI base, 1904, EX 300.00
Nat'l ship-to-ship, Blake transmitter, 1880s, EX 1,650.00
North Electric H-6, blk, 'Bogart phone,' EX 85.00
Stromberg-Carlson, clear plastic desk type, 1930s, EX 35.00
Stromberg-Carlson, Kansas City-type candlestick, 1900s, EX 425.00
Stromberg-Carlson intercom, Bakelite, blk, EX 65.00
Swedish-Am, wall type, ornate oak fiddle-bk cabinet, 1902, EX ...450.00
Table model, golden oak, metal plate: Long Distance, 40", EX....2,600.00
Trimline, rotary dial, push button, 1968, M 10.00
Viaduct Mfg, 3-box wall type, Blake transmitter, 1883, EX 1,750.00
Western Electric, candlestick desk type, NP brass 175.00
Western Electric, gr, 3-slot pay type, 1950s, NM 250.00
Western Electric, left-handed desk stand, 1920s, 12", EX 235.00
Western Electric, walnut wall type, 1880s, 13x6x4½", EX 600.00
Western Electric #102, dial, cradle style, late 1920s 135.00
Western Electric #20, upright desk stand, non-dial, EX 150.00
Western Electric #202, gold-metal cradle type, 1931, EX 175.00
Western Electric #205, blk variation, 1938, EX 115.00
Western Electric #300, red, cradle type, NM 250.00
Western Electric #354, ivory wall type, Deco style, EX 95.00
Western Electric #500, blk cradle type, EX 60.00
Western Electric AA-1, NP candlestick desk type 450.00
Western Electric Interphone, wall type, watch case receiver 85.00
Williams-Abbot, upright desk stand, 1904, 10½", EX 600.00

Blue Bell Paperweights

First issued in the early 1900s, these bell-shaped glass weights were used as giveaways and by telephone company executives to prevent stacks of papers from blowing off their desks in the days of overhead fans. Over the years they have all but vanished — some taken by retiring employees, others accidently broken. The weights came to be widely used as advertising by individual telephone companies; and as the smaller companies merged to form larger companies, more and more new weights were created. They were widely distributed with the opening of the first transcontinental telephone line in 1915. The weight embossed 'Opening of Trans-Pacific Service, Dec. 23, 1931,' in peacock blue glass is very rare, and the price is negotiable. In 1972 the st Pioneer bell paperweights were made to sell to raise funds for the arities the Pioneers support. This has continued to the present day. ese bell paperweights have also become collectible. For further study recommend *1992 Revised Edition, Blue Bell Paperweights*, by Jacque- e Linscott; she is listed in the Directory under Florida.

ll of Pennsylvania 1879-1979, dk peacock	40.00
ll System, peacock	225.00
ll System Ches & Pot Telephone Co & Assoc Cos, ice bl	450.00
eak-Up the Bell System, bl opaline swirl	50.00
ebraska Telephone Company, peacock	325.00
w York Telephone, cobalt	110.00
gion 10 Assembly, bl	100.00
uthern Bell Telephone & Telegraph Company, cobalt	175.00
e Bell Telephone System, cobalt	200.00

elated Memorabilia

lmanac, Am Telephone & Telegraph, 1938, NM	5.00
ooth, cherry wood, glass windows, brass plate, 90x36x36", EX	550.00
ooth, walnut, bevelled glass, much brass, w/sign, EX	1,800.00
oggles, safety; Bell System, NM in orig case	75.00
mp, Local & Long Distance, leaded glass, '20s, 22x20", EX	5,500.00
gn, blk w/wht letters, 2-sided, electric, 1940s, EX	150.00
earbook, Western Electric Electrical Supply, 1919, 1120-pg	50.00

Telescopes

Old telescopes are still appreciated for the quality of the workman- ip and materials that went into their production. Large telescopes ere mounted on tripod stands; spyglasses were hand held. Most were ade of brass and wood.

stronomical, B Pike & Sons...NY, leather, 1850s, 64", EX	2,000.00
stronomical, Pinkham & Smith Boston, brass, +2 eyepcs/box	1,870.00
euler London, brass, 3-draw, wood bbl, cord cover, 1800s, VG	200.00
ritish Naval, Ross, 1908, 17"	125.00
Vion, brass, NM pnt, 7-draw, 46", NM	925.00
euffel & Esser, US Navy Officer of Deck Spyglass, 1-draw, EX	200.00
nmk, brass, 2-draw, decorative, 35", EX	200.00
nmk, solid brass, 3-draw, 15", EX	80.00
nmk captain's, brass, 1-draw, 35", VG	100.00
nmk captain's, brass w/wooden bbl, 1-draw, EX	210.00
S Navy BuShips QM Spyglass 16x Mark 2, 31", EX in case	225.00
JS Navy Power 30 Pardou & Son Paris, brass, 1-draw, 32", EX	200.00
/ London Day or Night, brass w/wooden bbl, 2-draw, 36", VG	250.00

Televisions

Collectible TV's are becoming popular. Those made prior to VWII (circa 1925-1940) often sell for up to $4,000.00 and more! Jnusual wood and Bakelite sets from the '40s are worth $50.00 to 400.00; metal sets and those with square cabinets usually sell for under 100.00. Large screen TV's (over 14") are still poor sellers in most mar- ets. Color TV's with 19" or smaller tubes from 1953-54 are of value. Our advisor for this category is Harry Poster; he is listed in the Direc- ory under New Jersey.

Admiral, Bakelite console, 14" or 16"	50.00
Air King A-1000, similar to RCA 630TS, 10" table top	100.00
Andrea CO-VK12 or CO-VJ12, 12" combination, ea	50.00
Ansley #701, similar to RCA #630, 10" table top	100.00

Automatic #1649 or similar 16" set	50.00
Belmont #10DX21 or X22, pull-out tube console, ea	200.00
Bendix Model #325, 10" push-button combo	75.00
CBS-Columbia Model #205, 19" color console, ca 1954	200.00
Crosley #9-407, 1949, 12" table top	100.00
DeWald BT-100, similar to RCA 630, 10" table top	150.00
Dumont RA-101, 20" picture tube, raises automatically	100.00
Emerson Model #571, #611, or similar 10" table top	75.00
Emerson Model #621, 10" Bakelite font, 4 knobs	125.00
Fada #700, similar to RCA #630, 10" table top	150.00
General Electric, sq, 12" or larger	50.00
General Electric #800, #805, streamlined Bakelite table top	200.00
Hallicrafters T68, projection console	150.00
Motorola VK-106, console w/stepped top	150.00
Philco #48-1001 or #1002, 10" table top	125.00

1959 Philco Predicta Model 4654, 'Barber Pole,' metal housing on lami- nated base with walnut finish, work- ing, NM, $750.00.

Pilot, sq cabinet, 12" or larger	75.00
RCA metal set, ltweight 1950s portable	55.00
RCA 721-TS, mass-produced, 10" table top	125.00
Sentinel #412, 10" combination	50.00
Sparton #4920 or similar 12" console	50.00
Stromberg Carlson TV-12-M5M, Chinese combination	100.00
Transvision #10BL, built-in magnifier in cabinet, 10" kit	200.00
Westinghouse H-181, 10" table top on legs, w/doors	175.00
Westinghouse H-242, H-251 or similar set, electric magnifier	150.00
Zenith #28T960, Waldorf, porthole console	150.00
Zenith porthole combination, 1948-50	100.00

Teplitz

Teplitz, in Bohemia, was an active art pottery center at the turn of the century. The Amphora Pottery Works was only one of the firms that operated there. (See Amphora.) Art Nouveau and Art Deco styles were favored, and much of the ware was hand decorated with the pri- mary emphasis on vases and figurines. Items listed here are marked 'Teplitz' or 'Turn,' a nearby city. Our advisor for this category is Jack Gunsaulus; he is listed in the Directory under Michigan.

Bust, girl w/curly hair & hat, Nouveau style, att, 11"	295.00
Ewer, yel florals, 9½"	150.00
Figurine, Nouveau lady entwined in flower, Wahliss, 7½"	475.00
Pitcher, vintage emb, female as hdl, 11"	575.00
Vase, emb florals on gr, much gold, 12"	165.00
Vase, gold emb lion pr against bl/gr trees, RS&K, 13", pr	1,000.00
Vase, HP, farm scene, Stellmacher, 8x8"	95.00

Vase, HP bird on branch, dragon hdls, rtcl rim, squatty, 6" **400.00**
Vase, HP butterflies & mc flowers w/gold, mk, 14" **525.00**
Vase, HP grapes in purple/gilt, lg gold lizard hdls, 10" **550.00**
Vase, jeweled flowers, 3-D lady w/arms extended, RS&K, 18" ...**2,400.00**
Vase, lady's portrait on gr & gold irid, RS&K, 5¾" **395.00**
Vase, lattice neck w/appl teardrops, wide base w/3 hdls, 8" **650.00**

Vase, modernistic designs in five colors, marked Stell-macher, 10¾", $325.00.

Vase, Nouveau floral extends above rim, gr wash on tan, 15" **375.00**
Vase, Nouveau portrait, intricate execution, ovoid, 5½" **550.00**
Vase, profile: maid in gilt helmet, trees behind, RS&K, 6" **1,300.00**
Vase, rtcl overhanging floral rim, HP moth on ovoid, 7½" **800.00**
Vase, 2 cherubs apply roses/ribbons to gr basketweave, 23" **600.00**

Terra Cotta

Terra cotta is a type of earthenware or clay used for statuary, architectural facings, or domestic articles. It is unglazed, baked to durable hardness, and characterized by the color of the body which may range from brick red to buff.

Two cherubs battle over a heart, after Falconet, restoration, 16", $1,650.00.

Bust, nude female, hair to shoulder, sgn Thierry/1717, 12" **200.00**
Figurine, man brushing hair, mc pnt, 10" **250.00**
Figurine, satyr/nymph on stump, cherub below, Clodion, 21" .**4,000.00**
Figurine, 3 Graces raise pleated drape, L Faguays, 18", EX **2,200.00**

Thermometers

Though the collecting of advertising thermometers has been popular for years, only recently have decorative thermometers come into

their own as bona fide items of interest and value. Indoor and outdo decorative models have been manufactured for hundreds of years, their relative scarcity enhances their value and interest for the coll tor. Most American thermometers manufactured early in the 20th ce tury were produced by Taylor (Tycos), and today their thermomete remain the most plentiful on the market.

Decorative thermometers manufactured before 1850 are n ensconced in the permanent collections of approximately a dozen Europe museums. Because of their fragility (and relatively small size compared barometers), few devices of this era have survived in private collections.

Insofar as sheer beauty, uniqueness, and scientific accuracy, dec rative thermometers are far superior to the ordinary and inexpensi versions which carry advertising. Decorative thermometers run t gamut from plain tin household varieties to the highly ornate creatio of Tiffany and Bradley and Hubbard. They have been manufactur from nearly every conceivable material — oak, sterling, brass, and gla being the favorites — and have tested the artistry and technical ski of some of America's finest craftsmen. Ornamental models can found in free-hanging, wall-mounted, or desk/mantel versions.

Thermometer prices are based on age, ornateness, and wheth mercury or alcohol is used as the filler in the tube. Thermometers wi damaged, missing, or substitute parts bring greatly reduced prices. Pap scales indicate either replacement of a broken metal scale or a device lower quality.

Virtually all American-made thermometers available today as co lectors' items were made between 1875 and 1940. The Golden Age decoratives ended in the early 1940s as modern manufacturing pro cesses and materials robbed them of their natural distinctiveness. Eur pean thermometers, because of their scarcity and fine workmanshi have almost doubled in price over the last eighteen months.

Key:
br — brass
F & C — Fahrenheit & Celsius
F & R — Fahrenheit & Reamer
mrc — mercury
pmc — permacolor
sc — scales
stl — stainless

Adams, G; hanging, mahog/br bulb cap, lg sc, red spirit, 9x2" **225.0**
Alexandre, folding, F&R sc, mrc, 1850s **320.00**
Amadio, F, Corn Hill, desk, ivory pillar/compass, mrc, 1890, 10" ...**850.0**
Army & Navy (Westminster), travel, ivory sc, 1875, 5", +case ..**300.0**
Bargess Reversible Box, br sc, oak case, mrc, 5½" **90.00**
Bearskin Ltd, wall, metal clip, rnd mcr, 1930, 3x4" **300.0**
Blk/Starr/Frost, desk, barometer, stl, F&C, mrc, '10, 11" **1,850.0**
Bradley & Hubbard, desk, br/ornate lion, br sc/mrc, 9", VG **95.0**
Capendium, desk, handmade br/porc fr, F&C sc, rnd mrc, 4" **850.0**
Carpenter & Westley, desk, ivory w/glass dome mrc, 1880, 6" ...**675.0**
Casella London, wall, maxi/minimum, 2 units, wood, plastic sc .**260.0**
CE Lange, kitchen, The Modern Thermometer, tin, pmc **165.0**
Cheshire Silversmiths, desk, br candelabra, mrc, 1875, 10" **4,500.0**
Chester, desk, stl sc, sterling bezel, mrc, 2x6" **180.0**
Clark, desk, ivory ped, crown, mrc, 1904, 7" **295.0**
Cloister, inkwell, stl bk & base w/angels at side, 1901 ....**975.0**
Creswel, travel, ivory case/mirror, removable sc, mrc, 2½" ...**2,800.0**
CW Wilder...NH, bear & billboard br figural, mrc, 6½" **165.0**
CW Wilder...NH, desk, Deco women, br F sc, mrc, 8" **750.0**
Desk, cvd walrus tusk, 2-tier disk base, inlay sc, 1860, 9" **300.0**
Desk, picture fr w/glass, mrc, 1902, 7" **180.0**
Desk, Spirit of St Louis, dragon, F br sc/mrc, '01, 6" **1,800.0**
Diamond, wall, br F sc on wood, rare, 7½x1½" **400.0**
Dixie, W (London); desk, gilt/br, Gothic, SP sc, mrc, 8" **710.0**
Dollard London, desk, sterling, br sc, mrc, 1908, 6" **750.0**
Dring & Fage, desk, marble, ivory sc, mrc, 1880, 6" **1,350.0**

English, desk, trn ivory, glass dome, mrc, 1860, 11" 475.00
Freeborn, desk, bronze w/lead decor/br sc, mrc, 8" 130.00
G Barnes, oak fold-out box, Bakelite sc, mrc, 2½" 120.00
G Cooper, desk, bell shape w/cupola, sterling, dial, 2x3" 100.00
Gilbert & Co, travel, silver eng sc, mrc, 1850, 8" 630.00
Gloucester Scientific, stl case, glass front, pmc, 42" 1,200.00
Haris, P, & Co (Birmingham); desk, box wood, 3-tube, mrc, 12" ...410.00
Heath & Wing, figural calender, br w/porc sc, mrc, 1870 ....930.00
Hiergelsell Bros, indoor, cabinet/oak bk, bl liquid, #159 ....160.00
Hohmann Maurer Co, steel F&C sc & bk, mrc, 12" 80.00
Honeywell, desk, Bakelite bell base, dial sc, 1935, 3" dia 300.00
Waldstein, wall, br R sc on wood, mrc, 1900s, 10½" 780.00
os Somalvico, desk, figural, flared base, br sc, mrc, 10" 480.00
Nova Products, desk, rnd, glass encased, dial sc, Pat 1923 ....75.00
Orchard, iron case, br face, w/glass intact, 14" 95.00
Pairpoint, desk, sterling picture fr, mrc, 1907, 5" 220.00
Pairpoint, mantel, br, w/angel, sterling sc/mrc, 1904 ....325.00
Phila Therm Co, hygrometer, br sc, rotating bezel, 1928 ....30.00
Reau, desk, ornate blk bronze, wood F&C sc, mrc 90.00
Reau, desk, sq incline base, floral top, mrc, 1895 ....180.00
Rowley & Sons, travel, ivory sc, mrc, 1894, 4", +case 180.00
S Mitzutani, alabaster ped, candle figural atop, mrc, 15" 80.00
Short & Mason, recording drum, copper case, 1910 ....75.00
Slouche, desk, alabaster ped, paper sc inset, mrc, 8x2½" 95.00
Standard, for Fairbanks & Co, rnd, br case, 1886, 7" 90.00
Standard, hanging; rnd, br rim, -40 to 150, dial 60.00
Standard, wall, br case, dial counterbalance, 1885, 9" 210.00
Standard, wall, ivory F sc on ebony, mrc, 9" 375.00
Taylor, hanging, ornate wood bk, br sc, 10x7" 80.00
Taylor, hanging, pnt wood, red spirit, 6x24" 50.00
Taylor, lady's profile, cvd wood, emb Art Deco, 20½", EX 250.00
Taylor, wall, blk enameled case, F&R sc on stl, mrc, 12" 35.00
Taylor, wall, octagonal wood fr/metal sc, red liquid, 5" 45.00
Thermindex Switzerland, desk, Bakelite stand, F sc, 5" 530.00
Thomas Wright, desk, octagon, pot metal, F&C sc, 5x3" 190.00
Tiffany, desk, horoscope, bronze, mrc, 1907, 4x7" 120.00
Tycos, incubator hygrometer, glass reservoir, 4x4" 16.00
Tycos, maxi/minimum, japanned tin/br, mrc, T-5452, 8" 125.00
Tycos-Taylor, outdoor wall, wood fr, red liquid, 27x5" 55.00
JD Inc, wall, clip, F br sc, mrc tube, 4" 700.00
Vogue, desk, Victorian, dial, gr, 1931 ....60.00
W Pratt, desk, wood inlays, ivory sc, mrc, 1900, 6" 90.00
Wall, Fr gilt, wood fr, silver eng, F&R sc, mrc, 1776, 10x14" ..3,600.00
Warren Foundries, wall, umbrella w/dragon hdl, br sc, mrc, 12" .220.00
West, desk, Gothic design, brass, 1900, 12" 1,250.00
WG Loveday, wall, Clearside, F metallic sc, 5" dia 400.00
White & Westall, wall, wht Bakelite F sc, mrc, 7" 450.00
Whitehead & Hoag, Lambrecht's Polymeter, wall, mrc, 9" 890.00
Wise, desk, Tunbridge, twin columns, mrc, 1870, 5" 1,250.00
Zeradatha, desk, cast metal, dial w/rotate sc, 1926, 7" 75.00

1000 Faces China

So named because of its many hand-painted faces, much of this chinaware was made during the '30s through the '50s (some even earlier). Though many pieces are unmarked, others are marked 'Made in Japan.' There are two primary patterns, and variations exist. The 'Black Face' pattern is distinguishable by the range of colors used in the designs — primarily red, white, and yellow, with some green and blue — and, of course, the black hand-painted faces. The 'Gold' pattern is dominated by gold throughout the multicolored design, and the faces are done in gold. Both patterns employ colors in a similar fashion. On a dinner plate, the outer-most ring of color is usually comprised of two to

three colors with a simple design such as flowers. The next ring contains either the black or gold faces, and the inner ring is usually comprised of many colors 'shooting' out from the center circle, which may itself be a primary color (for instance, red) with a design such as a dragon or clouds painted in gold. Our advisor for this category is Suzi Hibbard; she is listed in the Directory under California.

Cup & saucer, blk faces 40.00
Cup & saucer, demitasse; gold 25.00
Cup & saucer, gold 35.00
Cup & saucer & pie plate, blk faces 50.00
Plate, blk, 10" 45.00
Plate, 6" 10.00
Shaker, gold 7.50
Shakers, pr 18.00
Snack set, 8½" L 45.00
Soup set, blk faces, 3-pc 75.00
Sweetmeat set, w/lacquer box, 12", 9-pc 125.00
Sweetmeat set, 5 pcs in 6" lacquer box 75.00
Tea set, blk faces, 15-pc, serves 6 ....150.00
Tea set, gold, 15-pc, serves 6 ....125.00
Teapot, gold, dragon spout, 7" 50.00

Tiffany

Louis Comfort Tiffany was born in 1848 to Charles Lewis and Harriet Young Tiffany of New York. By the time he was eighteen, his father's small dry goods and stationery store had grown and developed into the world-renowned Tiffany and Company. Preferring the study of art to joining his father in the family business, Louis spent the next six years under the tutelage of noted artists. He returned to America in 1870 and until 1875 painted canvases that focused on European and North African scenes. Deciding the more lucrative approach was in the application of industrial arts and crafts, he opened a decorating studio called Louis C. Tiffany and Co., Associated Artists. He began seriously experimenting with glass, and eschewing traditionally painted-on details, he instead learned to produce glass with qualities that could suggest natural textures and effects. His experiments broadened, and he soon concentrated his efforts on vases, bowls, etc. that came to be considered the highest achievements of the art. Peacock feathers, leaves and vines, flowers and abstracts were developed within the plane of the glass as it was blown. Opalescent and metallic lustres were combined with transparent color to produce stunning effects. Tiffany called his glass Favrile, meaning handmade.

In 1900 he established Tiffany Studios and turned his attention full time to producing art glass, leaded-glass lamp shades and windows, and household wares with metal components. He also designed a complete line of jewelry which was sold through his father's store. He became proficiently accomplished in silverwork and produced such articles as hand mirrors embellished with peacock feather designs set with gems and candlesticks with Favrile glass inserts.

Tiffany's work exemplified the Art Nouveau style of design and decoration, and through his own flamboyant personality and business acumen he perpetrated his tastes onto the American market to the extent that his name became a household word. Tiffany Studios continued to prosper until the second decade of this century when due to changing tastes his influence began to diminish. By the early 1930s the company had closed.

Serial numbers were assigned to much of Tiffany's work, and letter prefixes indicated the year of manufacture: A-N for 1896-1900, P-Z for 1901-1905. After that, the letter followed the numbers with A-N in use from 1906-1912; P-Z from 1913-1920. O-marked pieces were made especially for friends of relatives; X indicated pieces not made for sale.

Our listings are primarily from the auction houses in the East where Tiffany sells at a premium. Although in the past the market has been slightly uncertain due to the economy, it now has strengthened, especially for the top-quality pieces. Our advisor for Tiffany lamps is Carl Heck; he is listed in the Directory under Colorado.

Glass

Bowl, bl w/gold & pk highlights, 4x10", +frog, EX 375.00
Bowl, feathers, gold/gr on wht, gold int, 2x3" 900.00
Bowl, gold, etched vintage, 10 swirled ribs, 3x7" 650.00
Bowl, gold, intaglio leaves around wide flat rim, unmk, 10" 400.00
Bowl, gold, prunts w/in, 3x5" 280.00
Bowl, gold, 10 swirled ribs, 3x6" 550.00
Bowl, pastel gr opal irid, onionskin brim, 10" 850.00
Bowl, Wht Pastel w/gold int, 3x8" 375.00
Candlestick, wisteria pastel, sq bobeche, 3¾", pr 1,500.00
Comport, Yel Pastel, 10 opal stripes, wide/flat rim, 4x8" 440.00
Compote, bl/gr irid, stretch rim/eng flowers, 2½x8" 1,200.00
Compote, dk gold w/gr & pk highlights, wavy rim, 4x6" 400.00
Compote, floriform; gold, #1937G, 4½" 770.00
Compote, floriform; gold, goblet form w/wide rim, 5" 700.00
Compote, gold, purple/pk/bl highlights, 4x6" 375.00
Compote, gold w/bl rim on ft, intaglio vine, 9½" 1,400.00
Decanter, gold, long neck/dimpled sides, 10", +8 cordials 3,500.00
Decanter, wheel cut, rib-mold hollow hdl, silver top, 13" 425.00
Finger bowl, pk/gold/bl irid, scalloped, +underplate, 8 for 4,400.00
Goblet, Yel Pastel w/lt opal, dbl-bulb hollow stem, 8" 440.00
Jardiniere, gold, pulled hdl ea side, 2⅛" H 465.00
Parfait flute, Aqua Pastel, morning-glory form, 6" 440.00
Plate, Gr Pastel, sgn, 8½" 310.00
Plate, Gr Pastel, stretched edge, 8" 180.00
Platter, Aqua Pastel, radiating opal stripes, 11" 330.00

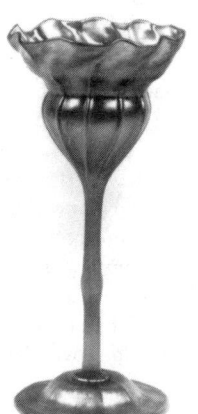

Vase, floriform; brilliant platinum, gold and blue iridescence, #2384G, 10", $1,900.00.

Vase, aquamarine & gold w/mc int criss-Xs, dbl gourd, 13" 2,850.00
Vase, bud; gold, slender trumpet form, 12" 700.00
Vase, feathers, gr/gold, trumpet form on bronze stem, #1043 ...1,100.00
Vase, feathers, gr/ivory, fluted cylinder on metal base, 12" 1,200.00
Vase, feathers, red/gold on raspberry & opal, long neck, 8" 4,950.00
Vase, feathers, wht/gr/gold on wht, gilt int, metal ft, 14" 1,200.00
Vase, feathers/chains/int zigzags, gr/brn/opal, 24-rib, 6½" 1,400.00
Vase, floriform; bl, trumpet form, 10" 935.00
Vase, floriform; bl irid, 10-rib stem, 15" 2,200.00
Vase, floriform; feathers, sm bulb w/wide-flared rim, 4½" 700.00
Vase, floriform; gold, #2185B, 11" 880.00
Vase, floriform; gold, flared, 10-rib top/dome ft, 13" 1,100.00
Vase, floriform; gold, sm bulb w/widely flared rim, 5" 650.00

Vase, floriform; gold, 10-rib body, cupped ped ft, 12" ....935.
Vase, floriform; gold/EX irid, swirled/ruffled/ribbed, 10" ....1,900.
Vase, gold, angle shoulder, lt shape to sides, #1054, 3" ....450.
Vase, gold, angle shoulder, 16-rib body, 9" ....825.
Vase, gold, angled shoulder w/swirled prunts as hdls, 6" ....1,100.
Vase, gold, flared goblet form, incurvate rim, 7" ....600.
Vase, gold, fluted trumpet on bronze base, #153, 17" ....1,500.
Vase, gold, int leaves, trumpet form; bronze leaf base, 17" ....990.
Vase, gold, sm bulb w/stretched wide-flared rim, 4½" ....550.
Vase, gold, trumpet form, in bronze artichoke holder, 14" ....990.
Vase, gold, trumpet form, knob above dome ft, 10½" ....935.
Vase, gold, trumpet form, 5" ....600.
Vase, gold, 8-rib bottle form, scalloped rim, 5¾" ....525.
Vase, gold irid w/soft pk highlights, 12x8" ....1,200.
Vase, gold w/EX irid, wide ringed top, 2 sm hdls, ftd, 9" ....950.
Vase, gold w/swirled irid, irregular gourd form, 6¾" ....765.
Vase, gr irid w/gold lines, silver o/l tulips etc, 4x4" ....1,975.
Vase, Gr Pastel w/stretched irid, 10-rib, flat rim, 6x7" ....875.
Vase, gr/purple irid, ribbed gourd form w/diagonal lip, 4" ....700.
Vase, jack-in-pulpit; gold, lustre halo edge, bulb ft, 18" ....3,200.
Vase, jack-in-pulpit; gold, stretched/ruffled, slim std, 19" ....3,300.
Vase, jack-in-pulpit; gold, wide face/slim stem/bun ft, 20" ......8,800.
Vase, leaves, gold on wht irid, wht ft, slim form, 10" ....800.
Vase, paperweight flowers on lt gr opal, wide shoulder, 9" ....11,000.
Vase, peacock feathers, mc irid, bulbous shoulder, 12" ....17,500.
Vase, Tel El Amarna, gold cuff on ribbed aqua, 9½" ....3,300.
Vase, vines/heart leaves, gr irid/gold, widens at base, 3" ....1,200.
Wine, gold w/purple to gr highlights, twisting dbl stem, 6" ....200.

Lamps

Linenfold glass and bronz table lamp, 14" shade has tw minor cracks, standard #58 $8,000.00.

Base, for floor lamp, counterbalance, #619, 52½" 1,500.0
Base, for floor lamp, counterbalance, gilded, #677, 55½" 1,650.0
Base, for floor lamp, telescoping 12-sided shaft, #578 ....825.0
Base, ribbed, cushion base w/foliage, 4-ftd, #395, 23" 2,200.0
Base, sq base w/bl-enamel border, #369, 10½" 550.0
Base, wide ftd pineapple base, std w/wrapped vines, #8619 .....4,600.0
Base, 3-arm stem w/scrolled tendrils, ftd bun base, #25875 ......5,500.0
Base, 3-arm urn form on 4 legs w/paw ft, #26870/76, 13½" 1,000.0
Bridge, damascene 10" shade in harp; std w/2 ashtrays, 57" 3,500.0
Candle, fine-rib gold melon-form shade; #154 std, 16" 1,980.0
Candle, gold ruffled shade; twist-rib flaring std, 15" 1,400.0
Candle, gold 7½" shade & twist std w/flower-form lip, 12" 1,100.0

andelier, ldgl/turtle-bk tile bowl on chains+6 lilies **22,000.00**
k, feathered 6" bell shade; 12-sided harp std, 19" **1,500.00**
k, gold bell-form shade w/in gilt bronze std w/16-rib ft **1,300.00**
k, gr damascene shade; ram-emb bronze-over-pottery base ...**3,500.00**
k, gr w/wavy gold 7" bowl shade; counterbalance #417 base....**4,600.00**
k, linenfold 12-panel 10" amber shade; inlaid #604 std **6,050.00**
k, Spanish, gilt bronze, #643, 14" **2,640.00**
k, 2 turtle-bk tiles in beaded bronze fr, harp std, EX **4,800.00**
k, 2 turtle-bk tiles in shade; forked support, #408, 14½" **4,600.00**
or, damascene 10" shade; counterbalance 4-leg #468 std **4,400.00**
or, ldgl 25" curtain-band shade; std #936, 77" **66,000.00**
or, ldlg 22" Greek Key-band shade; 6-ftd std #307, 65" **8,800.00**
or, spun bronze 10" shade; #681 counterbalance std, 57" **2,300.00**
tern, turtle-bk tile in ea of 4 sides, chain hung, 13" **8,800.00**
tern, 14" inverted dome shade hangs from 7 chains **7,700.00**
y, 10-lite, amber irid shades; base #29738, 22" **55,000.00**
y, 10-lite, gold shades; layered lily pad base #383, 21" **23,100.00**
y, 3-lite, gold shades; #319 std, 13", EX **3,300.00**
y, 7-lite, gold shades (5 w/damage); #385 std, VG **5,700.00**
ght light, feathered Arabian shade, wood base, 7½", EX **1,320.00**
dent, A&C rtcl bronze shade w/blown-in glass; #25566 .....**9,350.00**
ble, intaglio leaves on 8" gr & gold shade/vasiform std **4,400.00**
ble, ldgl 14" pomegranate-band shade; bulbous #166 base ..**7,150.00**
ble, ldgl 16" dragonfly shade; open-leaf std #586, 23" **31,000.00**
ble, ldgl 16" lotus bell-form shade; harp std #6874, 18" **24,200.00**
ble, ldgl 16" mushroom-band shade, Grueby base w/leaves ...**13,200.00**
ble, ldgl 16" peacock feather dome shade; #D795 std **24,200.00**
ble, ldgl 16" turtle-bk tile-band shade; #9535 tiled std **19,800.00**
ble, ldgl 16" 7-dragonfly shade; #258979 ball-ft std, EX **16,500.00**
ble, ldgl 18" Oriental poppy shade; #358 std, 27" **36,300.00**
ble, ldgl 18" peony shade; gr/brn patina #368 std, 27" **64,900.00**
ble, ldgl 20" acorn-band shade; simple std: gr/brn wash **9,350.00**
ble, ldgl 20" dragonfly shade; std #587 w/gilt 'tiles' **26,400.00**
ble, ldgl 20" red poppy/rtcl o/l shade (EX); #359 std **26,400.00**
ble, ldgl 22" nasturtium shade; #9933 std, 38" **38,500.00**
ble, ldgl 22" peony shade; Empire-style #550 std, 34" **11,000.00**
ble, ldgl 26" Lotus shade; slender #1695/374 std, 33" **33,000.00**
ble, linenfold 19" 24-panel gr shade; #203 std w/canister ..**10,000.00**
ble, 4 gold tulip shades (3 inverted), tendril-cast stem **8,800.00**

etal Work

Items are bronze unless noted otherwise.

otter, Zodiac, dk brn patina, #990, 5½x2" **170.00**
ookends, seated Buddha under arch, #1025, 6", pr **275.00**
ookends, Zodiac, mc astrological medallions, #1091 ....**300.00**
ox, cigar; Am Indian, gold dore, wood liner, #1196, 8" L **700.00**
ox, stamp; bronze w/irid glass 'bricks,' 2 scarabs on lid **19,800.00**
ox, Zodiac, dk brn patina, #810, 1x5" sq **350.00**
andlestick, Bamboo, brn-gr patina, 10", pr **2,200.00**
andlestick, base is cobra, #1203, 8", pr **2,600.00**
andlestick, cup in tripod support, pencil std, gilt, 17" **600.00**
andlestick, glass-lined rtcl bronze cup, 3 tall legs, 11" **1,000.00**
andlestick, irid bl ribbed cups, glass cabs on stem, 23" **5,500.00**
ard tray, nude at side, 7½" L **265.00**
hamberstick, metal mesh shade w/pnt pansy; adjustable arm ...**880.00**
lock, bl enamel panels around rnd face, #360, 5½" **1,500.00**
lock, bronze w/enamel, sq face/rnd dial, Chelsea works, 6" ...**2,750.00**
lock, Grapevine, gr/wht mottled glass, ftd rectangle, 7½" **3,300.00**
esk set, Chinese, calendar/rocker blotter/2 boxes+3 pcs **1,980.00**
esk set, Graduate, dk patina w/gr, letter rack/box+6 pcs **650.00**
esk set, Graduate, gold dore, blotter ends/inkwell+2 pcs **425.00**
esk set, Modelled, lg picture fr/sm lamp/letter rack+3 pcs **3,300.00**

Dish, enameled fleur-de-lis on wide flat rim, 4" **350.00**
Figurine, bulldog chained to post, 3½" **375.00**
Frame, bronze leaf o/l on bl mottled glass, 7½" H **1,300.00**
Frame, gilt bronze, Omnia Vincit Veritas, 12x10" **880.00**
Frame, Grapevine, gr mottled glass, 8¾" H **2,000.00**
Frame, Pine Needle, tan glass, oval reserve, 10" H **3,500.00**
Frame, Pine Needle, tan/plum mottled glass, 15" H **5,200.00**
Frame, Venetian, gilt bronze w/ermine border, 9x12" **1,300.00**
Frame, 9th Century, w/glass jewels, #1697, 8½" H **3,300.00**
Inkwell, Bookmark, gilt bronze, #1094, sq, 3" **250.00**
Inkwell, butterfly relief, domed, gold glass insert, #2155 ....**3,700.00**
Inkwell, Chinese, octagon, #1732, 3½" **400.00**
Inkwell, Zodiac, red/gr patina on dome top, #1072, 6¾" dia **300.00**
Letter opener, Zodiac, gold dore, 10" L **120.00**
Letter rack, Zodiac, gold dore, 6x9" **180.00**
Note pad holder, Zodiac, hinged top, gold dore, 4½x7½" **150.00**
Pen wipe, mosaic glass dome over orig chamois, #28137 ....**4,400.00**

Planter, bronze and turtle-back tiles, paw feet, #2092, 12" diameter, 16", $9,350.00.

Planter, Pine Cone, gr glass & copper liners, #833, 4x11" **770.00**
Smoking stand, dk gold dore, #1649, worn, 28" **275.00**
Vase, copper w/enamel magnolias, wht on turq/lav, 11", VG ..**2,600.00**

Pottery

Bowl, bronze clad w/vine & floral relief, shouldered, 3x7" **1,400.00**
Bowl vase, bl/gr/red mottled drip, #P1065, 5" **1,650.00**
Vase, brn/tan/amber speckle on wht clay, 9½" **1,975.00**
Vase, fruit on branches emb on wht bsk, gr int, 10x4½" **900.00**
Vase, leaves/buds emb on bsk, cylindrical, 8x4" **800.00**
Vase, molded as an artichoke, cream w/olive wash, 11" **1,925.00**
Vase, random drips of pk/bl/cream/wht, shouldered, 16" **2,200.00**
Vase, sm leaves at base, deep vertical ridges, wht bsk, 8" **900.00**
Vase, stems form ribs, foliage band at rim, olive/ivory, 7" **2,400.00**

Silver

Asparagus tongs, Marquine, monogram, pr, 6 troy oz **385.00**
Berry spoon, strawberry finial, intertwined hdl, shell bowl **650.00**
Bowl, clover pattern, 1905, 9" **415.00**
Bowl, geometric-rtcl rim, monogram, 9" **350.00**
Bowl, shell w/appl gilt-copper crab, 3 paw ft, 4½" **1,300.00**
Box, red/blk enamel decor, 6" L **1,700.00**
Candy compote, rose-cast border & base, 13 troy oz, pr **700.00**
Coffee set, emb ivy, pear form, 1864, w/tongs, 28 troy oz **2,600.00**
Compote, scalloped, openwork base, 33 troy oz **1,500.00**
Courting lamp, dragonfly/floral emb, scarab/corn hdl, 3" W **200.00**

Demitasse pot, paneled gourd form, 8", +cr/sug 660.00
Flask, etched knight, bk: squirrel & initials, 7⅝" 2,200.00
Goblet, ca 1865, 7 troy oz 290.00
Ladle, Colonial, monogram, 6 troy oz 300.00
Pitcher, emb lily of valley on hammered ground, ftd, 12" 8,500.00
Pitcher, ribbed hdl terminates in lg elephant head, 9½" 4,600.00
Shoe horn & buttonhook 140.00
Tazza, repousse florals, 1890s, 5", 36 troy oz 2,700.00
Tray, shell/scroll border, inscription, 31 troy oz 1,300.00
Trophy bowl, detailed horse's head hdls, eng scenes, 20" 19,000.00

Miscellaneous

Plaque, mosaic lobster on bronze disk, 7" 3,300.00
Purse, clutch; 18k yel gold mesh, 3-compartment, 7" 5,000.00
Vase, porc, water lilies emb on lt celadon, 7x3¾" 1,500.00
Window, ldgl borders, turtle-bk tile center+14 jewels, 18x14" ...3,300.00
Window, trees/mtns/23rd Psalm, arch at top, 144x48" 44,000.00

Tiffin Glass

The Tiffin Glass Company was founded in 1887 in Tiffin, Ohio, one of the many factories composing the U.S. Glass Company. Its early wares consisted of tablewares and decorative items such as lamps and globes. Among the most popular of all Tiffin products was the black satin glass produced there during the 1920s. In 1959 U.S. Glass was sold, and in 1962 the factories closed. The plant was re-opened in 1963 as the Tiffin Art Glass Company. Products from this period were tableware, hand-blown stemware, and other decorative items.

Those interested in learning more about Tiffin glass are encouraged to contact the Tiffin Glass Collectors' Club, whose address can be found in the Directory under Clubs, Newsletters, and Catalogs. See also Black Glass.

Roses, canary yellow, circa 1920s: Trinket box, coralene decoration, 7" long, $100.00; Perfume bottle with stopper, canary yellow, 7½", $185.00. (May also be found in blue and satin.)

Bowl, centerpiece; Athens-Diana, #5831 ....45.00
Bowl, centerpiece; Cherokee Rose, 13" 65.00
Bowl, Juno, Mandarin Yel, 3-toed, #348, 11" 37.00
Bowl, Tear Drop, Smoke, low, 12" 75.00
Cafe parfait, Rambler Rose, #188 Line, pk 40.00
Candlestick, Cherokee Rose, 2-light, #5902, pr 70.00
Candlestick, Roselyn, yel, blown 45.00
Celery dish, Fuchsia, beaded edge 45.00
Champagne, Carillon 10.00
Champagne, Casual 3.00
Champagne, Chardonnay 17.00
Champagne, Cherokee Rose, #17399 ....22.00
Champagne, Cherokee Rose, #17403 ....22.00
Champagne, Classic 24.00
Champagne, Classic, pk 32.00

Champagne, Eternally Yours 10
Champagne, Flanders 18
Champagne, Flying Nun 34
Champagne, Fontaine, pk 30
Champagne, Fontaine, Twilight 50
Champagne, Fuchsia 22
Champagne, Julia, amber, saucer type 25
Champagne, June Night, #17538 23
Champagne, Linda, cut 13
Champagne, Mansard 12
Champagne, Nouvelle 20
Champagne, Nymph w/Flute 40
Champagne, Palais Versailles 32
Cigarette holder, Copen Bl 65
Claret, Flanders, pk 75
Claret, Julia, amber, 6⅛" ....35.
Claret, June Night, #358 32
Cocktail, Athens-Diana ....18.
Cocktail, Cerice ....19.
Cocktail, Classic ....35.
Cocktail, Fontaine, Twilight ....44.
Cocktail, Fuchsia, #15083 ....18.
Cocktail, June Night, #17538 ....22.
Cocktail, June Night, #358 ....22.
Cocktail, oyster; Athens-Diana ....18.
Cocktail, oyster; Rambler Rose, #188 Line, pk ....30.
Cocktail, Paulina, topaz ....12.
Cocktail, Princess etch, #643 ....12.
Compote, cheese; Sylvan, gr ....15.
Compote, Fuchsia ....65.
Compote, Palais Versailles, gold trim ....100.
Cordial, Byzantine ....35.
Cordial, Cherokee Rose, #17399 ....45.
Cordial, Fuchsia ....45.
Cordial, Persian Pheasant, #17538 ....40.
Cordial, Wistaria, #17477 ....45.
Cornucopia, Copen Bl, 11½" ....175.
Cornucopia, Copen Bl, 8¼" ....75.
Cornucopia, Twilight, 11½" ....275.
Creamer, Cerice, ftd ....25.
Creamer & sugar bowl, Roselyn, yel, ftd ....45.
Cup & saucer, Athens-Diana ....22.
Cup & saucer, Roselyn, yel, blown ....18.
Cup & saucer, Sylvan, pk ....35.
Decanter, Athens-Diana, #185 ....135.
Flower arranger, Twilight, #9115/112, 5½" ....85.
Goblet, water; Arcadian, pk, #24 ....48.
Goblet, water; Beaumont ....12.
Goblet, water; Cherokee Rose, #17399 ....25.
Goblet, water; Cherokee Rose, #17403 ....20.
Goblet, water; Classic ....25.
Goblet, water; Eternally Yours ....15.
Goblet, water; Flying Nun ....34.
Goblet, water; Fontaine, pk ....40.
Goblet, water; Fuchsia, #15083 ....28.
Goblet, water; Heirloom ....10.
Goblet, water; Huntington ....15.
Goblet, water; Julia, amber ....25.
Goblet, water; June Night, #17392, gold trim ....25.
Goblet, water; June Night, #358 ....24.
Goblet, water; La Fleur, topaz, crystal stem, 8" ....32.
Goblet, water; Palais Versailles ....55.
Goblet, water; Psyche, etched bowl, gr #016-style stem .....35.
Goblet, water; Rambler Rose ....23.

Goblet, water; Rambler Rose, #188 Line, pk 45.00
Goblet, water; Renaissance, platinum trim 27.00
Goblet, water; Riveria 20.00
Goblet, water; Rose, cut 13.00
Goblet, water; Theme, cut 17.00
Goblet, water; Tiara 24.00
Grapefruit & liner, Rambler Rose, #188 Line, pk 35.00
Jug, Rambler Rose, #188 Line, pk, w/lid 195.00
Jug, Roselyn, yel 325.00
Parfait, Classic 45.00
Parfait, Fontaine, Twilight w/crystal stem 45.00
Plate, #024, pk, 10½" 15.00
Plate, Athens-Diana, 7½" 15.00
Plate, Cadena, yel, 8" 12.00
Plate, Cerice, 12" 45.00
Plate, Cherokee Rose, 8" 18.50
Plate, Empire, Twilight, 8" 17.50
Plate, Flanders, pk, 8" 20.00
Plate, Flanders, yel, 10½" 35.00
Plate, Flanders, 8" 12.00
Plate, Flying Nun, gr, 8" 14.00
Plate, Fontaine, gr, 8" 15.00
Plate, La Fleur, yel, 7½" 12.50
Plate, Old T'print, cranberry, 8" 7.00
Plate, Roselyn, yel, 8" 10.00
Plate, Wistaria, red, 8" 16.00
Relish, Rambler Rose, 3-part, rnd 17.50
Saucer champagne, Rambler Rose, #188 Line, pk 40.00
Sherbet, Camelot 7.50
Sherbet, Cordelia 5.00
Sherbet, Fontaine, Twilight 38.00
Sherbet, Fuchsia, low 16.00
Sherbet, Psyche, etched bowl, gr #016-style stem 25.00
Sherbet, Rambler Rose 20.00
Sherbet, Renaissance, platinum band 20.00
Sherry, Classic 60.00
Sherry, Persian Pheasant, wide mouth 18.00
Sugar bowl, Flying Nun, gr 65.00
Sundae, Cerice, #071 ....18.00
Sundae, Flanders 15.00
Tankard, Swedish Modern, blown, #5935, 11½" 65.00
Tumbler, iced tea; Athens-Diana, ftd 24.00
Tumbler, iced tea; Cerice, #071 ....24.00
Tumbler, iced tea; Cherokee Rose, #17403 ....24.00
Tumbler, iced tea; Flanders 26.00
Tumbler, iced tea; Flanders, pk 38.00
Tumbler, iced tea; Flanders, yel 24.00
Tumbler, iced tea; Fuchsia, ftd 30.00
Tumbler, iced tea; Georgette 24.00
Tumbler, iced tea; June Night, #17358 ....28.00
Tumbler, iced tea; Manchester 22.00
Tumbler, iced tea; Mansard, ftd 15.00
Tumbler, iced tea; Melissa 24.00
Tumbler, iced tea; Rambler Rose 23.00
Tumbler, iced tea; Rambler Rose, #188 Line, pk 45.00
Tumbler, iced tea; Tiara 24.00
Tumbler, juice; Cadena, Mandarin Yel, ftd, 5" 20.00
Tumbler, juice; Cherokee Rose, #17403, 5-oz 25.00
Tumbler, juice; Cordelia, yel, ftd 15.00
Tumbler, juice; Fontaine, gr 30.00
Tumbler, juice; Wistaria, #17394 ....25.00
Tumbler, water; Byzantine, Mandarin Yel, ftd 20.00
Vase, bud; Cerice, 10½" 45.00
Vase, bud; Cherokee Rose, sterling base, 10½" 50.00

Vase, bud; Cherokee Rose, 8" 45.00
Vase, Carnation, acid cut, #3322, 6" 34.00
Vase, Dawn, lav, #9115-113, 8½" 135.00
Vase, Princess, 4" 22.50
Vase, Swedish Modern, blown, #17350, 11½" 55.00
Vase, teal & crystal, 7¾" 95.00
Whiskey, Flanders 32.00
Wine, Athens-Diana 26.00
Wine, Cherokee Rose, #17399 ....30.00
Wine, Eternally Yours 15.00
Wine, Flanders 28.00
Wine, Flanders, pk 55.00
Wine, Flanders, yel 30.00
Wine, Jefferson 10.00
Wine, Manchester 25.00
Wine, Medici 24.00
Wine, Palais Versailles 42.00
Wine, Rambler Rose, #188 Line, pk 45.00
Wine, Riveria 24.00

Tiles

Though originally strictly functional, tiles were being produced in various colors and used as architectural highlights as early as the Ancient Roman Empire. By the 18th century, Dutch tiles were decorated with polychrome landscapes and figures. During the 19th century, there were over a hundred companies in England involved in the manufacture of tile. By the Victorian era, the use of decorative tiles had reached its peak. Special souvenir editions, campaign and portrait tiles, and Art Nouveau motifs with lovely ladies and stylized examples from nature were popular. Today all of these are very collectible. See also specific manufacturers.

Delft Company, Viking ship, 5-color, 4½", $65.00.

European, owl, moon & stars relief, 4-color, 4" 195.00
Franklin, tulips, 4-color matt, 6" 45.00
Low, floral, stylized, yel-brn, 3⅛" 28.00
Low, man w/snuff box, monogram, bl, 5" 115.00
Minton, cattle in stream, blk transfer, Wm Wise, 1879, 6" 80.00
Minton, Taming of the Shrew, 6" 55.00
Pardee, duck/frog/pond, cvd/pnt, 3-color, mk, 4⅜" 225.00
Unmk, tree scene, 5-color w/wht border, fr, 6" 195.00
Volkmar, impressionistic tree scene, grs/bl, 9", EX 350.00
Wedgwood, 1903 ....75.00

Tinware

In the American household of the 17th and 18th centuries, tinware items could be found in abundance, from food containers to foot warmers and mirror frames. Although the first settlers brought much of their tinware with them from Europe, by 1798 sheets of tin plate were being imported from England for use by the growing number of American tinsmiths. Tinwares were often decorated either by piercing or painted designs which were both freehand and stenciled. (See Toleware.) By the early 1900s, many homes had replaced their old tinware with the more attractive aluminum and graniteware.

In the 19th century, tenth wedding anniversaries were traditionally celebrated by gifts of tin. Couples gave big parties, dressed in their wedding clothes, and reaffirmed their vows before their friends and family who arrived bearing (and often wearing) tin gifts, most of which were quite humorous. Anniversary tin items may include hats, cradles, slippers and shoes, rolling pins, etc. See also Primitives and Kitchen Collectibles.

Anniversary, hat, admiral's type, w/'ostrich plume,' 6½x16" 200.00
Candle box, cylindrical, hanging, tab hangers at bk 265.00
Cheese drainer, ring ft, 5¼" dia, 5" hdl 120.00
Cheese grater, rolled edges, angled end, 13¼x5½" 30.00
Coffeepot, angular, C-hdl, curved spout, pewter finial, 10" 150.00
Coffeepot, curved side spout, trn stick hdl, str sides, 10" 145.00
Collander, pierced heart shape, circle ft, 4" H 130.00
Dinner bucket, cup cover, inside trays 42.50
Dutch oven, w/wrought iron spit, soldered rpr, 19" L 125.00
Egg coddler, dk gray, ornate base, burner 195.00
Flour sifter, dark, handmade scoop shape, rnd stick hdl 125.00
Foot warmer, drum shape, wood hdl, wire bail, 11" dia 65.00
Pastry sheet, curved bottom, dtd 1838, w/tin rolling pin 495.00

Wall sconce, oblong concave reflector, fluted drip cup, 1780s, 10", $3,000.00 for the pair.

Sconce, crimped semicircle top on tall narrow bk, 14", EX 170.00
Sconce, oval crimped-edge reflector, 14", pr 700.00
Sconce, oval sunburst bks, S-arms, crimped pans, 13", pr 1,300.00
Sconce, tall/slim simple crimped crest, 9", pr 350.00
Torch, horizontal font w/2 burners, wide reflector, 28" 185.00

Tobacciana

Tobacciana is the generally accepted term used to cover a field of collecting that includes smoking pipes, cigar molds, cigarette lighters, humidors — in short, any article having to do with the practice of using tobacco in any form. Perhaps the most valuable variety of pipes is the meerschaum, hand carved from hydrous magnesium, an opaque white-gray or cream-colored mineral of the soapstone family. (Much of this is today mined in Turkey which has the largest meerschaum deposit in the world, though there are other deposits of lesser significance around the globe.) These figural bowls often portray an elaborately carved mythological character, an animal, or a historical scene. Amber is sometimes used for the stem. Other collectible pipes are corn

cob (Missouri Meerschaum) and Indian peace pipes of clay or catlinite. (See American Indian Art.)

Chosen because it was the Indians who first introduced the white man to smoking, the cigar store Indian was a symbol used to identify tobacco stores in the 19th century. The majority of them were hand carved between 1830 and 1900 and are today recognized as some of the finest examples of early wood sculptures. When found they command very high prices. Our advisor for this category is Chuck Thompson; he is listed in the Directory under Texas. See also Advertising; Snuff Boxes.

Album, Costumes of All Nations, tobacco premium, color, EX ..250.00
Album, Geo Washington, premium, Allen & Ginter 250.00
Album, Napoleon, premium, Allen & Ginter 250.00
Album, Paris Exhibition of 1889, premium, Allen & Ginter 250.00
Bag, Genuine Durham Smoking Tobacco, cloth, paper label, EX .16.00
Book, Golden Harvest-Way of Life in...Industry, 1941, EX 800.00
Box, tobacco; Dutch brass, eng scenes/nude/etc, 6" L 675.00
Bridge pad, Chesterfield Cigarettes, lady cameos, 1930s, NM 15.00
Case, cigarette; sterling w/turq stones, 1920s 125.00
Cheroot holder, meerschaum, claw shape, amber stem, 5", +case ...300.00
Cheroot holder, meerschaum, monk's head, amber stem, 6¾" 950.00
Cheroot holder, meerschaum, nude woman, amber stem, 8" 150.00
Cigar box, Eisenlohr's Cinco Cigars, Deco, VG 15.00
Cigar holder, meerschaum, str sides, ¾x3¼," +case 35.00
Cigar holder, meerschaum, 3 bulldogs, amber mouthpc 75.00
Cigarette cards, Uniforms of Territorial Army, '50s, set of 50 ....75.00
Cigarette holder, Bakelite, Art Deco, 9" 24.00
Cigarette holder, meerschaum, dragons 35.00
Cutter, cigar; Abercrombie Royal Standard, metal/wood, EX 350.00
Cutter, cigar; Peter Schuyler, 10¢ 145.00
Cutter, cigar; Pico Grande 5¢ Cigars, dtd 1902 ....250.00
Cutter, cigar; Tom Benton Cigars, early, EX 300.00
Cutter, plug; Brighton #3, elf figural, 13" L, VG 250.00
Cutter, plug; Climax 65.00
Cutter, plug; Evans Terry, CI, counter top, 1914, NM 150.00
Cutter, plug; Griswold, CI 85.00
Cutter, plug; Lorillard's 85.00
Cutter, plug; Prize Cutter by S Lee, w/cork former 60.00
Cutter, plug; Star, Pat 1885 ....65.00
Felt, foreign flag, 4x8", M, 5 for 20.00
Figure, Indian, cvd wood, EX patina, ca 1904, 36", EX 5,000.00
Humidor, human skull form, china, brn/beige/blk, 5x5½" 145.00
Humidor, monkey w/pipe, pottery, 1910s, 6" 110.00
Humidor, Oriental man's head form, German porc, 4¾" 95.00
Humidor, stump figural, pottery, LFC, 1920, 8x7¼" 125.00
Humidor, wolf's head form, German porc, 4x3⅝" 65.00
Lighter, baseball figure, wht metal, 1913, 5" 330.00
Lighter, commode figural, chrome, 4" 20.00
Lighter, Evans, blk w/HP flowers, table model, EX 22.50
Lighter, Evans, gold-tone metal, lady's 8.00
Lighter, figural cupid stem, brass/dk copper, 8½" 85.00
Lighter, golf club head figural, chrome, 5" 25.00
Lighter, Ronson, chrome bartender at chrome/plastic bar, 7½" ..1,200.00
Lighter, table; Ronson Crown, silver 55.00
Lunch box, Geo Washington Cut Plug, EX 75.00
Machine, cigarette-making; Brown & Williams, EX 28.00
Opener, cigar box; El Verso Cigars 10.00
Pack, Half & Half Cigarettes, unopened, 1960s, NM 12.50
Pack, Lark Cigarettes, unopened, 1960s, NM 7.50
Pipe, clay, nude figural stem, 1880s, 4" L 65.00
Pipe, hag in bonnet, cvd bone/wood 130.00
Pipe, man in moon, cvd bone, EX detail 130.00
Pipe, meerschaum, animals fighting, amber stem, rpr, 20" 1,000.00
Pipe, meerschaum, cvd horse, 1900s, EX, +leather case 110.00

Pipe, meerschaum, cvd lion, 1½x4¾", NM, +case 155.00
Pipe, meerschaum, dog, 1½x3", +case 90.00
Pipe, meerschaum, lion, 1½x4¾", +case 155.00
Pipe, meerschaum, lion pr, amber stem, 8", +fitted case 250.00
Pipe, meerschaum, man's head w/glass cigarette, 1½x4" 245.00
Pipe, meerschaum, man's head w/glass cigarette, 1½x4", MIB 260.00
Pipe, meerschaum, Romeo/Juliet, amber stem/silver ferrule, 10" ...1,100.00
Plug maker, wood w/plunger, Ohio, 21" L 55.00
Pouch, Yorkshire Mixture 7, Sears, unopened, 1960, 1½-oz, NM ...5.00
Press, plug; Brown's Mule, emb metal, 1920s, 12x12" 12.50
Rack, pipe; molded compo w/baseball batter, holds 2, 6", VG 275.00
Smoking set, Bakelite/amber glass, 4-pc+tray 25.00
Smoking stand, Policeman figural, terra cotta, Germany, 9", VG ..100.00
Snuff jar, Lorillard Maccoboy, rose scented, dtd 1872, M 150.00

Snuff mull, lid inlay inscribed William Green, 1830, 2½", $200.00.

Tamper, pipe; animal's leg & hoof, cvd bone 60.00
Tamper, pipe; lady's leg, cvd ivory, 1700s 225.00
Tamper, pipe; sterling, mk Leonore Doskow, w/spoon & pick 45.00

Toby Jugs

The delightful jug known as the Toby dates back to the 18th century, when factories in England produced them for export to the American colonies. Named for the character Toby Philpots in the song *The Little Brown Jug,* the Toby was fashioned in the form of a jolly fellow, usually holding a jug of beer and a glass. The earlier examples were made with strict attention to details such as fingernails and teeth. Originally representing only a non-entity, a trend developed to portray well-known individuals such as George II, Napoleon, and Ben Franklin. Among the most-valued Tobies are those produced by Ralph Wood I in the late 1700s. By the mid-1830s Tobies were being made in America. See also Doulton, Lenox, and Occupied Japan.

Cat, in robe, Staffordshire, 1880s, rstr hat, 11" 200.00
Man w/jug, warty face, striped stockings, 6-sided base, 10" 300.00
Portobello, standing, enameled/spatter base, lid, 1840, 10" 250.00
Pratt type, red face, caryatid hdl, att Yorkshire, 1810, 8" 825.00

Toleware

The term 'toleware' originally came from a French term meaning 'sheet iron.' Today it is used to refer to paint-decorated tin items, most popular from 1800 to 1850s. The craft was very popular in Pennsylvania, Connecticut, Maine, and New York state. Early toleware has a very distinctive look. The surface is dull and unvarnished; background colors range from black to cream. Geometrics are quite common, but florals

and fruits were also popular motifs. Items made after 1850 were often stenciled, and gold trim was sometimes added.

American toleware is usually found in practical, everyday forms — trays, boxes, and coffeepots are most common — while French examples might include candlesticks, wine coolers, jardinieres, etc. Be sure to note color and design when determining date and value, but condition of the paint is the most important worth-assessing factor. Our advisors for this category are Barbara and Frank Pollack; they are listed in the Directory under Illinois. In the listings that follow, the dimension given for boxes and trays indicates length.

Bowl, floral, 3-color on dk gr, oval w/rim hdls, 13", EX 350.00
Box, deed; dome top, floral, 3-color on blk, 8¾" L, VG 200.00
Box, deed; floral, mc on dk japanning, wear/EX color, 7" 100.00
Box, deed; red w/gold & blk stencil floral, wear, 8" 150.00
Box, deed; red w/yel stripes & simple lid design, worn, 7½" 50.00
Box, spice; emb lid, blk/gold stencil, 6 containers, 9", VG 85.00
Bucket, chinoiserie, gilt/blk, helmet form, Europe, 20", VG 300.00
Can, red w/gold stencil: Coffee, minor wear, miniature, 2½" 150.00
Canister, floral, 5-color on brn, hdls, 6" 300.00
Canister, tea; swags, yel/red on brn, worn but EX color, 7" 115.00
Coffeepot, faint traces of orig decor, 11" 115.00
Coffeepot, floral (EX/lg), 5-color on dk brn, angle spout, 11" .3,100.00
Coffeepot, fruit (bold) on blk, curved spout, 11" 900.00
Coffeepot, red, minor wear, miniature, 2¾" 120.00
Creamer, floral, 3-color on worn brn, str sides, w/lid, 4" 450.00

Deed box, stylized flowers on red ground, in the Pennsylvania Dutch style, 1800s, 9½" long, NM, $1,800.00.

Match holder, simple 3-color design on brn, hanging, 7½" 295.00
Mug, red w/worn stencil: My Girl, 2" 35.00
Sugar bowl, blk w/red & yel designs, 2¾", EX 90.00
Tea caddy, blk w/yel band & 3-color decor, dents, 8" 325.00
Tea caddy, commas, 4-color on red w/wht band, worn, 4", EX ...325.00
Tea caddy, floral (stylized sunburst), 3-color on red, 4", EX 625.00
Tea caddy, floral (stylized), 3-color on red, 4", NM 1,800.00
Tea caddy, floral/swags, mc on dk brn, some flaking, 5¾" 235.00
Tea caddy, swags/foliage, red/yel on dk japanning, rpr, 4" 225.00
Teapot, floral, mc rpt on dk brn, str spout/sides, 9" 275.00
Tray, blk w/wht band & 3-color floral, EX color, wear, 9" 200.00
Tray, brn w/crystalized pnt, wht band/4-color floral, 12½" 200.00
Tray, farmers on country road on blk, gilt floral rim, 15" 375.00
Tray, wick trimmer; red rpt w/mc floral, 9" L 65.00
Tub, yel w/blk striping, ring hdls, wear, miniature, 3½" 25.00

Tools

Before the Civil War, tools for the most part were handmade. Some were primitive to the point of crudeness, while others reflected the skill of those who took pride in their trade. Increasing demand for quality tools and the dawning of the age of industrialization resulted in tools that were mass-produced. Factors important in evaluating antique tools are scarcity, usefulness, and portability. Those with a manufacturer's mark are worth more than unmarked items. When no condition is indicated, the items listed here are assumed to be in excellent condition. See also Winchester and Keen Kutter. Our advisor for this category is Jim Calison; he is listed in the Directory under New York.

Auger, dbl-twist bit secured to trn T hdl, 10½", EX 15.00
Auger bit, G&G Mfg, Coors PA, 19", VG 17.50
Axe, dbl bitted; Buhl, Detroit Michigan 25.00
Axe, off-set hdl, maker's stamp, blade: 13" W, 21" L 350.00
Axe head, mk Kelly Hand Made, VG 25.00
Brace, beam; blacksmith's 32.00
Brace, Davis Level & Tool Co 50.00
Broadax, goose-wing type w/offset hdl, Pennsylvania 450.00
Calipers, Caron, cast brass, dbl 275.00
Calipers, W Roker, 8", VG 15.00
Chisel, firmer; Charles Buck, socket type, EX 12.50
Chisel, ice fisherman's, New Haven Tool Co, long hdl 40.00
Crown molder, Thomas Napier, CI, 14x5", EX 775.00
Drawknife, Booth & Mills Phila, cvd applewood 200.00
Gauge, butt & rabbet; Stanley #93 ....35.00
Gauge, marking; maple w/oak thumbscrew, uncalibrated, 10½" 6.50
Gauge, mortising; DS English, rosewood/brass pistol grip hdl 25.00
Gauge, wheel; cooper's, Wiley's Russell Mfg, CI, 13" 35.00
Hammer, brass, sq heads w/leather faces, EX 65.00
Hammer, slate; Belden, 9" head, VG 30.00
Hatchet, hewing; D Sharp, 18", VG 20.00
Hook, reaping; sgn TS, early shape 35.00
Knife, hay; fishtail shape w/curved hdl, EX 75.00
Knife, hoof; farrier's, Burdizzo, Made in Italy, wood hdl, EX 12.50
Knife, unhairing; tanner's, curved blade, EX 55.00
Leather cutter, crescent blade, ornate cut-out wood hdl, 10" 95.00
Level, adjustable & graduating; Stanley #32, sights added 400.00
Level, Davis, Pat 1883, 3-bubble, 6" 400.00
Level, railroad track; Stanley PRR-G-1943, 62", EX 130.00
Level, Stanley, CI, Nicholson Pat style, 24" 150.00
Level, Stanley #03, mahog w/brass ends, ca 1910, EX 20.00
Level, Stanley #1194, brass bound, 28" 45.00
Level, Stanley #25, Pat 6-2-91, 6-23-96, mahog/brass, 26" 32.50
Level, Stanley #5, Pat 1906, VG 15.00
Level, Stratton Bros #10, rosewood w/brass mts, 6½", EX 425.00
Molder, Casey & Co, Auburn NY, ca 1857, 2¾" W, EX 50.00
Panel raiser, EW Carpenter, Lancaster, 3½" cut 400.00
Plane, A Model, unusual shape, 7¾" 130.00
Plane, beltmaker's, Stanley #11 ....48.00
Plane, block; Stanley #100½, EX 78.00
Plane, bull-nose; Edward Preston & Sons 55.00
Plane, chamfer; Stanley #72½, +5 cutters & bull nose 495.00
Plane, chamfer; Stanly #72 ....195.00
Plane, circular; Stanley #113, EX 100.00
Plane, dvtl; Stanley #444, NM 750.00
Plane, edge; Stanley #96, NMIB 200.00
Plane, jack; Kellogg/Baldwin, dbl blade, 16x2¾", VG 12.50
Plane, jack; Steer's Pat #305, 13⅞", VG 115.00
Plane, molding; F Nicholson, Wrentham 1,000.00
Plane, molding; J Kellogg, Amherst MA, EX 45.00

Stanley plane/cutter, #45, $185.00.

Plane, molding; T Donoho, Phila 150.0
Plane, plow; EW Carpenter's, Improved Arms, Pat, Lancaster ...900.0
Plane, plow; G Rosebloom, Cincinnati OH, wooden, 14" 45.0
Plane, reeding; Marten Doscher, late 1890s, VG 27.5
Plane, scraper; cabinetmaker's, Stanley #85 ....425.0
Plane, Stanley #101, toy sz, EX 20.0
Rabbet, carriage maker's, brass, laminated in-fill, 7½" 365.0
Rope machine, New Era, complete 145.0
Rope maker, Bendyke, Pat Nov 12, 1901, complete 130.0
Rule, aluminum zigzag type, sweetheart logo, EX 20.0
Rule, combination; Chapin-Stephens #036, VG 135.0
Rule, Lufkin, 4-fold, 24", w/compass & level 135.0
Rule, Lufkin #2072, 3-fold, w/level, 24" 155.0
Rule, Rabone #1380, 4-fold, 36" 22.5
Rule, slide; Post #1444P, 6", +case 17.5
Rule, Stanley #53½, 4-fold, EX 32.5
Rule, Stanley #94, folding, brass trimmed, EX 100.0
Rule, Thomas Foulds, 2-fold, 2-level, EX 750.0
Saw, butcher's; Livingston/Cheritree Mfg, Pat 1863, 26", EX 70.0
Saw, tenon; H Disston & Sons, 13", VG 15.0
Scorp, cherry wood, curvilinear, forged blade, 3¾" L 95.0
Screwdriver, Perfect Hdl Six-Sixty HEHOS&Co USA...22, EX ...10.0
Shears, sailmaker's, mk OAL, heavy, 16" 50.0
Smoother, Stanley #2, 1910-20, EX 135.0
Square, tailor's, AD Rude, Cleveland, Pat 1893 ....45.0
Tin snips, knuckle joint; Bartlett Mfg, Pat 1909, EX 20.0
Trammel, Stanley #1, bronze, fancy, EX 50.0
Wrench, buggy; E in circle stamp, CI, sq socket end, EX 12.0
Wrench, pipe; Stillson & Walfworth Mfg, wooden hdl, 1920s, 7" ..10.0

Toothpick Holders

Once common on every table, the toothpick holder was relegate to the china cabinet near the turn of the century. Fortunately, this cor tributed to their survival. As a result, many are available to collecto today. Because they are small and easily displayed, they are a very pop lar collectible. They come in a wide range of prices to fit every budge The rare ones have been reproduced and, unfortunately, are bein offered for sale right along with the originals. These 'repros' should b priced in the $10.00 to $30.00 range. Unless you're sure of what you' buying, choose a reputable dealer. In addition to pattern glass, you' find examples in china, bisque, art glass, and various metals. Toothpic holders in the listings that follow are glass unless noted otherwis Those that have been reproduced are designated with a (+); howeve values are for the originals. Our advisor for this category is Judy A Knauer; she is listed in the Directory under Pennsylvania.

corn, peachblow, gold trim 125.00
gata, tricorner top, NE Glass, ca 1888 ....675.00
lexandrite, bulbous, collared sq top, 3x2½" 650.00
pollo 20.00
rched Fleur-de-Lis, ruby stained 250.00
rched Ovals, ruby stained 32.50
tlas, etched decor 30.00
anded Portland, Maiden's Blush 45.00
eaded Ovals in Sand, apple gr 175.00
eatty Honeycomb, bl 45.00
rd w/Basket, amber 37.50
x-in-Box, crystal, ruby-stained top 40.00
ritannic, ruby stained 65.00
ll's Eye & Fan, gr 42.50
urmese, swirled w/pie crust rim, Mt WA, ca 1887 .....450.00
at on Pillow holds Daisy & Button bowl, amber 65.00
hampion, gr 55.00
hrysanthemum Base Swirl, clear opal 95.00
olorado, cobalt w/gold ft, 2¾" 35.00
olumbian Coin, red coins 200.00
ord & Pleat, cobalt 88.00
ordova, ruby stained 40.00
aisy & Button, vaseline, flared scalloped top 30.00
elaware, gr w/gold 90.00
amond Peg, custard w/rose decor 75.00
nn Quilt, amberina, sq rim, 2¼" 200.00
npress, gr w/gold 215.00
ncy Loop, emerald gr, Heisey 110.00
e Cut, bl, hat shape 30.00
eur-de-Lis shape 22.00
orette, gr 65.00
rget-Me-Not, turq 65.00
amed Ovals, clambroth w/gold 70.00
sco 70.00

Gatling Gun, amber, 3", $40.00.

lloway, rose stained 60.00
nterman Swirl, amber w/frosted base 225.00
ttate, pk satin 60.00
rvard, ruby stained 45.00
t w/turned-over rim, HP florals on bl Bristol 48.00
oped Barrel, custard, ca 1895 ....45.00
rseshoe & Clover, milk glass, little decor 28.00
ll, apple gr 80.00

Illinois 30.00
Invt T'print, amberina, ped ft 185.00
Iris w/Meander, lt bl 75.00
Jefferson Optic, amethyst w/decor 45.00
Jefferson Optic, gr, souvenir 35.00
Kentucky, emerald gr, sq 88.00
Lacy Medallion, gr w/gold (+) 32.00
Manhattan, clear w/gold 30.00
Masonic 75.00
Medallion Sprig, cranberry to clear, ca 1895 .....225.00
Menagerie Fish, amber 68.00
Michigan 42.50
Michigan, Maiden's Blush w/gold 175.00
National's Eureka 28.00
Nestor, bl 65.00
Owl in Tree, pottery (has been reproduced in glass) 55.00
Paddle Wheel 45.00
Palm Leaf, pk variegated to wht, Consolidated 85.00
Paneled Grape 45.00
Peek-A-Boo, amber (+) 28.00
Pineapple & Fan, emerald gr, Heisey 110.00
Priscilla, Findlay 30.00
Prize 42.50
Queen Mary, bl to wht satin, HP florals, ruffled 195.00
Queen's Necklace 60.00
Reverse Swirl, bl w/wht speckles 85.00
Reverse Swirl, vaseline opal 140.00
Ribbed Lattice, cranberry w/wide opal stripes 195.00
Ribbed Pillar, frosted cranberry spatter 60.00
Rising Sun, 3-hdld, gr trim 35.00
Scrolled Shell, milk glass w/HP decor 30.00
SP, dog & basket, Tufts 70.00
Tennessee 55.00
Texas 35.00
Trophy, emerald 20.00
Twist, bl opal 45.00
Uncle Sam's Hat, EX pnt 75.00
Vermont, clear w/gold 35.00
Vermont, gr w/gold 65.00
Wild Bouquet, custard, EX decor 850.00
Windows, cranberry opal, minor rim flake 225.00

Torquay 'Devon Motto' Ware

Torquay is a unique type of pottery made in the South Devon area of England as early as 1867. At the height of productivity, at least a dozen companies flourished there, producing simple folk pottery from the area's natural red clay. The ware was both wheel-turned and molded and decorated under the glaze with heavy slip resulting in low-relief nature subjects or simple scrollwork. Three of the best-known of these potteries were: Watcombe (1867-1962); Aller Vale (in operation from the mid-1800s, producing domestic ware and architectural products); and Longpark (1890 until 1957). Watcombe and Aller Vale merged in 1901 and operated until 1962 under the name of Royal Aller Vale and Watcombe Art Pottery.

Perhaps the most famous type of ware potted in this area was Motto Ware, so called because of the verses, proverbs, and quotations that decorated it. This was achieved by the sgraffito technique — scratching the letters through the slip to expose the red clay underneath. The most popular patterns were Cottage, Black Cockerel, Multi-Cockerel, and a scrollwork design called Scandy. Other popular decorations were Kerswell Daisy, ships, kingfishers, and many other birds on blue ground. Aller Vale ware may sometimes be found marked 'H.H.

and Company,' a firm who assumed ownership from 1897 to 1901. 'Watcombe Torquay' was an impressed mark used from 1884 to 1927.

Our advisors for this category are Jerry and Gerry Kline; they are listed in the Directory under Ohio. If you're interested in joining a Torquay club, the address of The North American Torquay Society is given under Clubs, Newsletters, and Catalogs.

Ashtray, Cottage, 'Frae Killin, A Place for Ashes,' 4½" 55.00
Ashtray, Cottage, Royal Watcombe, 'Mind the Carpet,' 4¾" 47.50
Biscuit barrel, Cottage, Watcombe, 'Do the Work...,' 6½" 185.00
Bottle, scent; Cornish Lavender, crown stopper, 3¾" 40.00
Bowl, Cottage, 'Better Wait on the Cook...,' 5¼" 85.00
Bowl, Cottage, Watcombe, 'Take a Little Cheese,' 8½" L 110.00
Bowl, Longpark, 'Giants Causeway None of Your Blarny,' 4½" 65.00
Bowl, Primrose, American, 'Some Hae Meat an...,' 8" 75.00
Butter dish, Scandy, Longpark, 'Elp Yerzel...,' 5¼" dia 90.00
Candle holder, Kingfisher, 'Sleep Falls Sweetly...,' 4" 75.00
Candlestick, Blk Cockerel, Longpark, 'Many Are Called...,' 3" 95.00
Candlestick, Blk Cockerel, Longpark, 'Night Is Long...,' 3½" 95.00
Candlestick, Scandy, Watcombe, 'To Bed To Bed...,' 4" 85.00
Chamberstick, Royal Torquay, 'Pleasant Dreams,' 5½" 125.00
Chamberstick, Scandy, Aller Vale, 'Last in Bed...,' 2" 115.00
Chamberstick, Scandy, Longpark, 'Dauntee Light Yer...,' 5" 112.50
Coffeepot, Scandy, 'Better Do One...,' 7¼x4½" 175.00
Condiment set, shakers, egg cup & mustard, 3½" 150.00
Creamer, Blk Cockerel, Longpark, 'Be Aisy w/Tha Craim,' 2½" ...48.00
Creamer, Cottage, 'First Things First,' 3½x2⅞" 38.00
Creamer, Cottage, 'Hope Well & Have Well,' 3⅛x2⅞" 35.00
Creamer, Cottage, 'Look Before You Leap,' 3x2⅜" 35.00
Creamer, Scandy, 'Fresh from the Dairy,' 3x3" 35.00
Cup & saucer, Cockerel, Longpark, 'Duee Drink a...,' 2½" 55.00
Cup & saucer, Cottage, 'There's No Wealth...,' 2½", 4¾" 40.00
Cup & saucer, Cottage, 'To Thine Own Self...,' 3", 3¼" 45.00
Cup & saucer, demitasse; Cottage, 2¼", 5" 40.00
Egg cup, Blk Cockerel, Longpark, 'Fresh Today,' 2½", +plate 42.50
Hair receiver, Scandy, Watcombe, 'Save While...,' 6½" 90.00
Humidor, Scandy, Longpark, w/motto, 5½" 175.00
Inkwell, Scandy, unmk, 'Gin a Budy Meet a Budy...,' 2" 70.00
Inkwell, Scandy, Watcombe, 'Send Us a Scrape o Yer...,' 1½" 75.00
Jam dish, Cottage, Longpark, 'Elp Yerzel...,' 5" 75.00
Jam dish, Swan, unmk Crown Dorset, 'Vor Time an Time...,' 3½" ..160.00
Jam pot, Cottage, 'More Haste Less Speed,' 3½x3½" 55.00
Jug, Cottage, 'Time & Tide...,' sq form, 3½x3¼" 55.00
Jug, Sailboat, Southenden Sea, 'Straucht Frae the Coo,' 2¾" 55.00
Match striker, Scandy, Longpark, 'A Match for Any Man,' 3½" ..98.00
Mustard, Longpark, Frae Burns Cottage, 2¼" 65.00
Pen tray, Aller Vale, 'Wa'Alus Be Main Glad...,' 9¼" 110.00
Pin tray, Cottage, 'Actions Speak...,' 5½x3¼" 48.00
Pin tray, Cottage, Watcombe, 'A Stitch in Time...,' 5" 42.00
Pin tray, Scandy, 'A Place for Pins,' 5x2½" 42.00
Pitcher, Aller Vale, 'Straight from the Cow,' 2½" 75.00
Pitcher, Aller Vale, Kerswell Daisy, 'Come Fill Me Full...,' 6" 175.00
Pitcher, Aller Vale, Kerswell Daisy, 'For Every Evil...,' 4½" 100.00
Pitcher, Blk Cockerel, Watcombe, 'Good Morning...,' 4½" 100.00
Pitcher, Cottage, Watcombe, 'Brendon Help Yourself...,' 4¼" 65.00
Pitcher, Crown Dorset (unmk), 'If You Can't Be...,' 3¾" 88.00
Pitcher, Longpark, 'Dawnter Try To Rin Bevore...,' 5" 98.00
Pitcher, sailboat scene, Longpark, 'Guid Folks...,' 5½" 75.00
Pitcher, ship scene, 'Welcome Is the Best Cheer,' 3¾x3¼" 45.00
Plate, Cottage, Babbacombe, 'Elp Yursel Tu More,' 9¾" 80.00
Plate, Cottage, Dartmouth, 'Be Like the Sundial...,' 10" 60.00
Plate, Cottage, Dartmouth, 'Us Be Always Plased...,' 10" 60.00
Plate, Cottage, Watcombe, 'A Rolling Stone...,' 5" 48.00
Plate, Cottage, Watcombe, 'A Rolling Stone...,' 6" 60.00

Plate, Cottage, Watcombe, 'Enough's As Good...,' 5" 50
Plate, Cottage, Watcombe, 'One Today Is Worth...,' 5" 55
Sugar bowl, Cottage, Watcombe, 'Time & Tide Wait...,' 3¾" 40
Sugar bowl, Longpark, 'Help Yersel Tae Sugar,' 3" 35
Sugar bowl, Scandy, Aller Vale, w/motto, 3½" 40
Teapot, Allervale, 'Shamrock Gr Oer Earth...,' 3", +cr/sug 198
Teapot, Primrose, 'Take a Cup of Tea...,' 4½" 125
Teapot, Scandy, Aller Vale, 'Droon Yer Sorrows...,' 4½" 150
Teapot, Scandy, Longpark, 'Droon Yer Sorrows...,' 5" 170
Teapot, Scandy, Longpark, 'You'll Ave a Cup a Tay...,' 5" 170

Teapot, Watcomb, 'Take a Cup of Kindness...,' 6", $145.00.

Teapot, Scandy, Watcombe, 'Elp Yerzels...,' 4" 100
Teapot stand, Blk Cockerel, Longpark, 'When You've...,' 4¼" 70
Toast rack, Forget-me-not, Watcombe, 'Help Yourself...' 130
Toilet tidy, 'See a Pin Pick It Up...,' unmk, 3½" 75
Tray, dresser; Kingfisher, Watcombe, 10½x7½" 150
Vase, Aller Vale, 'Do the Work That's Nearest...,' 3¾" 75
Vase, Colored Cockerel, Aller Vale, 'Have Courage...,' hdls, 5" .125
Vase, Scandy, 'Souvenir from...,' 2x3" 40
Vase, Scandy, Aller Vale, 'Isn't Your Life...,' hdls, 4½" 70
Vase, udder; Passion Flower, 'Guid Folks Are Scarce...,' 3½" 80
Vase, udder; unmk Royal Torquay, 'Lost Time Is Never...,' 3½" ...98

Tortoise Shell Glass

By combining several shades of glass — brown, clear, and yel — glass manufacturers of the 19th century were able to produce an glass that closely resembled the shell of the tortoise. Some of this t of glassware was manufactured in Germany. In America it was made several firms, the most prominent of which was the Boston and Sa wich Glass Works.

Reproductions abound, and items made from glass with the sa mottled colors but obvious 20th-century styling are common on tod market. These values are for old glassware.

Basket, wide hdl w/gold prunt & prunus flowers, 8" 185
Bowl, amber base/ft, 4x7¾" 125
Bowl, appl amber ft w/folded rim, 6x8½" 250
Bowl, 3-ftd, 4" 110
Cruet, clear shell hdl, 7" 150
Ice bucket, hdls, 8½x7½" 175
Pitcher, amber hdl, 8" 175
Vase, crimped rim, 9" 135

...ase, random fluted top, 10" 130.00

Toys

The prices shown in this edition review auction reports, known ...les, and sales lists. We have shown prices of toys in various conditions ...nd noted which toys sold with boxes. To get the most out of this ...uide, when you see the same toys with different prices, you must con...der those two important factors. On occasion, a toy will bring a much ...igher-than-normal price at auction. This is 'auction fever.' Sometimes ... collector simply wants to add a toy to his collection, and to him price ... not as important as availability.

Toys can be classified into at least two categories: early collectible ...ys with an established history and the newer toys. The antique toys ...e easier to evaluate. A great deal of research has been done on them, ...d much data is available. The newer toys are just beginning to be ...udied; relative information is only now being published, and the lack ... production records makes it difficult to know how many may be ...ailable. Often warehouse finds of these newer toys can change the ...arket. This has happened with battery-operated toys and to some ...tent to robots. Review past issues of this guide. You will see the ...anging trends for the newer toys. All toys become more important as ...llectibles when a fixed period of manufacture is known. When we ...ow the numbers produced and documentation of the makers is estab...hed, the prices become more predictable.

The best way to learn about toys is to attend toy shows and auc...ons. This will give you the opportunity to compare prices and condi...ons. The more collectors and dealers you meet, the more you will ...arn. There is no substitute for holding a toy in your hand and seeing ... yourself what they are. If you are going to be a serious collector, buy ... the books you can find. Read every article you see. Knowledge is ...al to building a good collection. Study all books that are available. ...ese are some of the most helpful: *American Toy Cars and Trucks* by ...lian Gottschalk; *Toy Autos, 1890-1939*, the Peter Ottenheimer Col...tion; *Collecting the Tin Toy Car, 1950-1970*, by Dale Kelley; *Arcade ...ys* by Al Aune; *The Art of the Tin Toy* by David Pressland; *Lehmann ...ys* by Cieslik; *The History of Martin Mechanical Toys* by Marchand; ...chanical Toys* by Spilhaus; *American Antique Toys* by Barenholtz, Mc...intock, and Holland; *American Clockwork Toys* by Whitton; *The ...orge Brown Sketchbook* by Edith Barenholtz; *Toy Dreams* by Kitahara; ...d *Collecting Toys* by O'Brien. *The Dictionary of Toys Sold in America, ...l. I & II*, by Earnest and Ida Long are good for identification and dat...g. The Longs are our advisors for all toys except Farm Toys, Steiff, ...y Soldiers, and Trains; they are listed in the Directory under Califor...a. In the listings that follow, toys are listed by manufacturer's name if ...ssible, otherwise by type. Condition is given when known. Measure...nts are given when appropriate and available; if only one dimension ...noted, it is the greater one — height if the toy is vertical, length if it ... horizontal. See also Children's Things; Personalities. For toy stoves, ... Stoves.

Key:
b/o — battery operated   NP — nickel plated
...td — jointed   w/up — wind-up

...st Iron

Cast iron toys were made from shortly before the Civil War until ... beginning of the 20th century. They are evaluated to a large extent ... scarcity, complexity, design, and detail. See next section for exam...s of cast iron toys listed by company name.

...to transport, pnt chips, crazed tires, 10", G 160.00

Battleship NY, worn 5-color pnt, pull toy, 20" L 1,700.00
Bulldog, pnt, 8½", G 350.00
Cart pulled by bulls, 2-wheeled, EX orig 85.00
Champion motorcycle, scuffed pnt, 7½", VG 225.00
Contractor's wagon pulled by 2 horses, worn pnt, 1892 ....1,200.00
Convertible w/rumble seat, red pnt, 10½", EX 475.00
Coupe, rpt, 5¼", G 80.00
Delivery wagon, worn pnt, 14", G 265.00
Dray w/driver, worn pnt, 1889, 19" 1,200.00
Dray w/horse & standing driver, 1892, 11½", EX 850.00
Engine #125, VG orig pnt, 1892, 19" 1,600.00
Express wagon, w/horses, pnt touchups, 17", G 500.00
Express wagon pulled by 2 horses, VG pnt, 1890s, 17½" 1,250.00
Fire captain's wagon, EX orig pnt, 1892, 12½" 1,200.00
Fire Patrol wagon, 2 horses/3 men/driver/bell, mc pnt, 20" 900.00
Fire wagon w/hose reel, pnt, 14", G 500.00
Horse cart, rpt, 10", G 95.00
Ice wagon, partial rpt, 14", G 180.00
Mack gasoline truck, rpt, rpl wheels, 7" 60.00
Model A wrecker, working winch, metal tires, worn pnt, 11" 400.00
Ox cart, worn pnt, shaft cracked, rpl figure, 13" 200.00
Popeye Spinach Wagon, HP, ca 1929, 5½", EX 600.00
Pumper, metal tires, G pnt, 5" 65.00
Pumper, partial rpt, rpr driver, 8", G 125.00
Racing sulky, VG pnt, few rust spots, 6" 90.00
Santa & His Sleigh, VG pnt, 1880s, 17" 1,850.00
Sedan, rpt, 5", G 60.00
Stake truck, chipped pnt, 4¼", G 70.00
Stroller, pnt, NP hdl bars, 4", G 85.00
Touring car, worn pnt, 7", G 220.00
Transfer wagon, rpt, 17", G 250.00

Company or Country of Manufacturer

Alps, Droopy Pete, cloth covered, b/o, 1960s, 10", MIB 95.00
Alps, Santa Claus, bell-ringing w/up, 1950s, 7", MIB 145.00
Arcade, Airplane, CI, blk & yel pnt, NM 1,850.00
Arcade, Ford Yel Cab, CI, 1933 World's Fair mk, 6¾", NM ...1,550.00
Arcade, Greyhound Bus, CI & NP, ca 1939, worn pnt, 8¾" 350.00
Arcade, Ice Truck, CI w/orig red pnt, 7" 450.00
Arcade, Mac Dump Truck, CI, EX 1,550.00
Arcade, Model-T Pickup Truck, CI, 8½", EX 950.00
Arcade, Stake Truck, pnt CI, lt rust, 7", G 175.00
Arcade, Taxi Coupe w/driver, CI, worn pnt, 1920s, 8½" 2,000.00
Arcade, Wrecker, pnt CI, broken crane, 10", G 245.00
Arcade, Yel Cab, CI, driver missing, pnt flakes, 8", VG 660.00
Auburn Rubber, Internat'l Stake Truck, 1939, 4½", EX 40.00
Auburn Rubber, Oldsmobile Six Sedan, 1939, 5¾", NM 65.00
Automatic, Auto Speedway, 2 w/up cars on track, 1930, EX 225.00
Automatic, Captain Marvel Car, tin w/up, 1947, 4", VG 40.00
Aviva, Snoopy Express, w/2 cars, MIB 22.00
Aviva, Snoopy Train Engine, tin, friction, MIB 10.00
Bandai, Excalibur Car, pnt metal, b/o, 11", NM 185.00
Bandai, GT-40 Car, tin litho, b/o, NM 175.00
Bandai, Rolls Royce Silver Cloud Car, tin, b/o, 12", G 110.00
Bandai, Rolls Royce Silver Cloud Car, tin, b/o, 12", NM 395.00
Borgfelt, Nifty Mickey Mouse Sparkler, 5", NM in torn box 770.00
Boycraft, Mack Truck, pnt steel, 1930s, 24", EX 250.00
Buddy L, Aerial Truck, steel, rpt, 34", G 200.00
Buddy L, Coupe, steel, pnt blisters, 11", G 600.00
Buddy L, Coupe, steel, worn pnt, 11", VG 725.00
Buddy L, Dump Truck, pnt steel, rubber tires, 1930s, 22", EX 220.00
Buddy L, Greyhound Bus, pnt steel w/up, b/o lights, 16", VG 400.00
CE Carter, Pangee Dancer, tin litho w/up, 10", EX 385.00

Champion, Mack Wrecker, pnt CI, orig crane, 8½", EX 715.00
Chein, Aero Swing, tin litho w/up, 10", NMIB............................300.00
Chein, Barnacle Bill walker, tin litho w/up, 6", EX 330.00
Chein, Checker Taxicab, tin litho w/up, 1922, 6", NM 525.00
Chein, Clipper Passenger Sea Plane, tin w/up, 10½", EX 300.00
Chein, Clown, hand-standing, tin w/up, 1930s, NM 175.00
Chein, Clown at Punching Bag, tin litho w/up, 8", EX 440.00
Chein, Clown in Barrel, tin w/up, pnt scuffs, 8" 175.00
Chein, Disneyland Roller Coaster, tin w/up, 9½", NMIB 495.00
Chein, Ferris Wheel, tin litho w/up, 1930s, 16½", VG 150.00
Chein, Greyhound Lines Bus, tin litho, 9", VG 210.00
Chein, Happy Hooligan Walker, tin litho w/up, 6", EX 550.00
Chein, Jr Oil Tank Truck, tin push toy, 1930s, 8½", EX 350.00
Chein, Junior Bus, tin litho w/up, 9", EX 150.00
Chein, Man on Alligator, tin litho w/up, 15", EX 220.00
Chein, Playland Whip, tin litho w/up, EX in box 330.00
Chein, Popeye Heavy Hitter, tin w/up, ca 1935, 11½", EX 1,760.00
Chein, Popeye in Barrel, tin litho w/up, 1932, 7", EX 300.00
Chein, Popeye Overhead Punching Bag, tin w/up, 9½", NMIB ..4,950.00
Chein, Popeye Upright Punching Bag, w/up, 1932, 7½", NM .1,200.00
Chein, Popeye Walker, tin litho w/up, 1932, 6½", EX 350.00
Chein, Racing Car, tin litho w/up, 9", EX 300.00
Chein, Roller Coaster, tin litho w/up, 9½", EX in box 250.00
Chein, Sedan, tin litho w/up, 1922, 6", EX 220.00
Chein, Transport Truck, sm dents, 8", VG 100.00
Chein, Yel Taxi, tin litho, turn-set front wheels, 7¾", EX 200.00
Chein (att), Doughboy Walker, tin litho w/up, 5", EX 220.00
Cohn, Fire Chief Car, tin litho w/bell, 1940s, MIB 500.00
Corgi, Chitty Chitty Bang Bang car, lg, MIB 325.00
Corgi, Chitty Chitty Bang Bang car, sm, MIB 100.00
Corgi, Circus Crane Truck, MIB 150.00
Corgi, Hardy Boys Van, lg, MIB 200.00
Corgi, Mobil Gas Tanker, MIB 250.00
Corgi, Tractor w/scoop, #74, MIB 125.00
Dinky, British 450 Sports Coupe #163, EX in box 90.00
Dinky, Cadillac El Dorado, MIB 150.00
Dinky, Jeep w/cannon, MIB 150.00
Dinky, Leyland Cement Wagon #933, EX in box 120.00
Dinky, Mersey Tunnel Police Van #225, EX in box 50.00
Dinky, Mobilgas Tanker #440, EX in box 150.00
Dinky, Nash Rambler, MIB 125.00
Dor-Mei, Godzilla Monster, 14", M 95.00
Drayton, Am Deluxe...Bus, pressed steel, 1900s, 26", VG 1,000.00
Fisher-Price, Allie Gator, pull toy, 1960, NM 20.00
Fisher-Price, Bouncy Race Car, lg plastic tires, 1960, NM 15.00
Fisher-Price, Bunny Pushing Cart, pull toy, 1936, EX 95.00
Fisher-Price, Ding Dong Ducky, pull toy, 1949, NM 55.00
Fisher-Price, Drummer Bear, pull toy, 1930s, NM 75.00
Fisher-Price, Fido Zilo, pull toy, 1955, NM 48.00
Fisher-Price, Granny Doodle, pull toy, 1930s, NM 95.00
Fisher-Price, Mickey Mouse Drummer w/cymbals, 1937, EX 450.00
Fisher-Price, Monkey on Tricycle, pull toy, 1931, NM 80.00
Fisher-Price, Popeye, pull toy, paper litho on wood, 10", VG 700.00
Germany, Bird in Cage, tin w/up, 1920s, 7¾", EX 35.00
Germany, Cock Fight, tin litho w/up, 10", EX 400.00
Germany, Duck on Trike, tin/plastic, 8½", NM 95.00
Germany, Magic Car, tin litho w/up, 1940s-50s, 6", MIB 275.00
Germany, Passenger Plane, tin w/up, 1920s, 10", EX 165.00
Germany, Peacock, tin litho w/up, 9", EX 285.00
Germany, Wishing Well, tin litho, 1920s-30s, 12", EX 850.00
Girard, Bus, tin litho w/up, lt rust, 14", G 450.00
Girard, Bus w/driver, tin litho w/up, spare tire, 14", EX 375.00
Girard, Coupe, tin w/up, b/o lights, 14", NM 695.00
Gunthermann, Bonzo Scooter, tin litho w/up, 7", VG 465.00

Hubley, Army Motor Truck, CI, 15", EX ....1,850.
Hubley, Bell Telephone Truck, pnt CI, 4", VG ....195.
Hubley, Cadillac Sedan, diecast, 1940s, rpt, 7" ....50.
Hubley, Chrysler Airflow Car, take-apart body, 4½", NM ....150.
Hubley, Fire Engine, pnt CI, crazed tires, 11½", VG ....260.

Hubley, motorcycle and sidecar with uniformed policeman driver, rubber tires, 9" long, $850.00.

Hubley, Motorcycle & Sidecar, pnt CI, rubber tires, 9", VG ....500.
Hubley, Packard Roadster, from metal kit, '30, 9½", MIB ....70.
Hubley, Racer, CI, rpt, loose wheels, 6", G ....50.
Hubley, Racer, pnt CI, rpl tires, 8", VG ....180.
Hubley, School Bus, tin litho, 3½", M in worn box ....100.
Hubley, Sedan, pnt CI, rstr, 6" ....175.
Hubley, Studebaker Car, pnt CI, rpl tires, EX ....150.
Ideal, Motorific Torture Track, 1966, MIB ....125.
Ives, Dancing Blk Man, metal/wood w/up, early, 12", VG ....2,300.
Ives, Hose Reel w/horse & driver, CI, 1880, 15" ....1,850.
Jaeger, Mixer, pnt CI, lt rust spots, 9½", VG ....275.
Japan, Action Planet Robot, tin litho w/up, 9", EX in box ....275.
Japan, Bird in Cage, metal/plastic w/up, 1950s, 7", MIB ....65.
Japan, Circus Boy on Trike, celluloid/tin w/up, 4½", EX ....95.
Japan, Clown Violinist on Stilts, tin litho w/up, 9", EX ....110.
Japan, Concrete Mixer Truck, tin litho, 7½", NM ....65.
Japan, Dancing Merry Chimp, tin, mechanical, 1960, 11", NM .250.
Japan, Donald Duck Carousel, celluloid w/up, 7", NM ....1,450.
Japan, Electromobile Electric Buick, metal, 1950s, 8", EX ....140.
Japan, Fire Dept Chief Car, tin litho, b/o lights, 9½", MIB ....95.
Japan, Ford Fairlane 500 Car, tin, 1957, 5", EX ....75.
Japan, Grandpa's New Car, tin w/up, 1950s, 6", EX ....85.
Japan, Helicopter, tin/plastic/rubber, b/o, '60s, 13½", M ....75.
Japan, Henry Riding Elephant, celluloid w/up, 6", NM ....2,650.
Japan, Highway Patrol Motorcycle, b/o, 1960s, 12", MIB ....135.
Japan, Hopping Chick, vinyl w/plush wings, w/up, 3", EX ....20.
Japan, Mama Rabbit & Baby Carriage, tin litho, b/o, 7", VG ....50.
Japan, Pan Am Strato Clipper, tin friction, 11", NM ....55.
Japan, Patrol Plane, tin, friction, 1950s, 14", MIB ....145.
Japan, Road Roller, tin, b/o, NM pnt, 1950s, 5x9", EX in box ....105.
Japan, Robot, tin w/plastic front, b/o, 12", EX in box ....375.
Japan, Romping Mechanical Puppy, tin w/up, 1950s, MIB ....95.
Japan, Rotate-O-Matic Super Astronaut, b/o, 1970s, 13", MIB ....75.
Japan, Santa Drummer, tin/cloth w/up, 11", EX ....200.
Japan, School Bus, tin friction, 1950s, 9", EX ....25.
Japan, Smokey Bear Jeep, tin litho, b/o, 10½", VG in box ....80.

pan, Space Trip, tin litho, b/o, 19", VG in box 120.00
pan, Sparkling Robot, tin litho w/up, 6", EX in box 160.00
pan, Sparky Robot, tin litho w/up, 7½", EX in box 275.00
pan, Strange Explorer, tin, b/o, 1960s, 4¼", EX in box 100.00
pan, Stunt Plane, tin/plastic, b/o, 10⅜" span, '60s, MIB 75.00
pan, Swinger Car, tin, 1960s, 10½", EX in box 25.00
pan, Swinging Baby Robot, tin litho w/up, 5", EX in box 250.00
pan, Television Spaceman, tin litho w/up, 6", EX in box 75.00
pan, Touring Car, tin litho, rubber tires, 1940s, 10", EX 80.00
pan, Trick Seal, celluloid w/up, 4½", EX 65.00
pan, 1929 Antique Sedan, tin litho/rubber, 1940s, 8", MIB 95.00
ro, Mortimer Snerd ventriloquist dummy, 32", MIB 75.00
itz, Coney Island Roller Coaster, tin litho w/up, 18", EX 660.00
nton, Contractor's Dump Wagon, pnt CI, 15", G 160.00
nton, Delivery Wagon, CI, rpt, 14¾", G 170.00
nton, Ladder Truck, CI, rpt, 8", G 70.00
nton, Pumper, pnt CI, scuffed, 6½", G 100.00
ystone, Am Railway Express, steel, rpt, 26", G 425.00
ystone, Army Truck, steel, rpt, 27", G 375.00
ystone, Bus, steel, pnt wear/rust, hinged top, 32", G 1,550.00
ystone, Packard Dump Truck, steel, rpt, 27", G 200.00
ystone, Packard Police Patrol Car, steel, rpt, 26", G 475.00
ystone, Water Tower Truck, steel, VG pnt, 32", G 475.00
ngsbury, Biplane, pressed steel, EX pnt, 15½" 465.00
hmann, Beetle #431, tin litho w/up, 4", NM 175.00
hmann, Clown & Balky Mule, tin litho w/up, 7", G 125.00
hmann, Garage, tin litho, 1 door, 3x6x3½", EX 88.00
hmann, Mikado Family #350, tin litho w/up, 7", EX 1,100.00
hmann, Naughty Boy #495, tin w/up, 5", NM 825.00
hmann, Paak-Paak, tin litho w/up, 7½", EX 440.00
hmann, Paddy & the Pig #500, tin w/up, 6", NM 1,000.00
hmann, Playing Mice #427, tin w/up, 16", EX 150.00
amann, Tut-Tut Auto & Driver, tin litho w/up, 6¾", EX ...1,760.00
hmann, Windmill Climber, pnt tin, 17", NM 90.00
dstrom, Launch, tin litho w/up, 1930s, 11¼", VG 275.00
emar, Donald Drummer, tin litho w/up, 6", G 150.00
emar, Drummer Boy, tin litho w/up, 9", VG 180.00
emar, Fred Flintstone on Dino, tin litho w/up, 1962, M 350.00
emar, Mickey Mouse Unicyclist, tin w/up, MIB 1,870.00
emar, Mickey Mouse Xylophone Player, tin w/up, 6", VG 325.00
emar, Minnie Mouse Knitting, tin litho w/up, 7", EX 385.00
emar, Pluto Walker, plush-covered w/up, 4½", EX in box 335.00
emar, Popeye in Rowboat, tin litho, remote b/o, 10", NM .5,500.00
emar, Popeye Lantern, tin litho, b/o, 7½", EX 245.00
emar, Popeye on Roller Skates, tin w/up, 6½", EX 715.00
nel, Mickey Mouse Handcar, compo figures, 7", EX in box ..2,300.00
noil, Roadster #708, vertical radiator, 1930s, M 35.00
rusan, Racer, tin w/rubber tires, 1950s, 11½", EX 275.00
rx, Airmail Passenger Biplane, tin w/up, 1940s, 13½", EX 330.00
rx, Amos 'N Andy Fresh Air Taxi, tin w/up, '30, 8", MIB ..2,750.00
rx, Andy Walker, tin litho w/up, 1930s, 11", EX 660.00
rx, Big Parade, tin litho w/up, 24", NMIB 1,875.00
rx, Blk Man Dancer, tin litho w/up, 8", EX 220.00
rx, BO Plenty Walker, tin litho w/up, 8½", EX 285.00
rx, Buck Rogers Interplanetary Rocket Cruiser, 12", MIB ..2,850.00
rx, Buck Rogers Rocket Police Patrol, w/up, 1934, 12", NM .990.00
rx, Busy Bridge, tin litho w/up, 24", EX 880.00
rx, Butter & Eggs Man Walker, tin litho w/up, 7½", EX 495.00
rx, Charleston Trio, tin w/up, 8½", VG 575.00
rx, Charlie McCarthy Walker, tin w/up, 8", EX 300.00
rx, Charlie the Drummer, tin w/up, 8", EX in box 2,400.00
rx, City Coal Dump Truck, tin litho w/up, 13", VG 225.00
rx, Climbing Tank, gold pnt w/gr wheels, rpl tracks, 9½" 100.00
rx, Coal Miners & Car, tin litho w/up, 16" track, EX 75.00

Marx, Buck Rogers Rocket Ship, original box, EX, $1,200.00.

Marx, Coast Defense, tin w/up, plane missing, 9", VG 220.00
Marx, Coo-Coo Car, tin litho w/up, 8", EX 325.00
Marx, Coupe, 2-door, steel w/up, rpt, 14", G 60.00
Marx, Cow Puncher Porky, tin w/up walker, 1949, 8", EX 400.00
Marx, Cowboy Whoopee Car, tin litho w/up, 8", EX 275.00
Marx, Dagwood the Driver, tin litho w/up, 8", EX in box 1,540.00
Marx, Dapper Dan Dancer, tin w/up, 10", EX in torn box 465.00
Marx, Deluxe Delivery Truck, tin litho, 1940s, 11", EX 85.00
Marx, Dick Tracy Squad Car #2, friction, b/o lights, 11", EX 265.00
Marx, Dippy Dumper, celluloid/tin w/up, 8½", EX 325.00
Marx, Donald Duck Duet, tin litho w/up, 1946, 10", EX 500.00
Marx, Drummer Boy, tin litho w/up, 7", NM 330.00
Marx, Electra Jet, tin/plastic, b/o, 17" wingspan, 1960s, M 145.00
Marx, Electric Robot & Son, plastic, b/o, 14½", G 300.00
Marx, Fantasy Doll House, complete/unassembled, 1971, MIB 65.00
Marx, Fireman Climbing Ladder, tin litho w/up, 22", EX 245.00
Marx, Flash Gordon Rocket Fighter #5, tin litho, 12", MIB 990.00
Marx, Funny Face Walker, tin litho w/up, 11", NMIB 660.00
Marx, Funny Fliver, tin litho w/up, 8", VG 230.00
Marx, George the Drummer Boy, tin litho w/up, 9", G 115.00
Marx, Golden Pecking Goose, tin litho w/up, 1924, 9½", NM ...275.00
Marx, Hess Semi, sliding doors on trailer, 1950s, 13", EX 35.00
Marx, Hey Hey the Chicken Snatcher, tin w/up, 9", NMIB.....2,650.00
Marx, Honeymoon Cottage Dollhouse, tin, 1949, 10x10", MIB ...75.00
Marx, Honeymoon Express, tin litho w/up, 9½", EX 235.00
Marx, Honeymoon Express, tin litho w/up, 9½", EX in box 375.00
Marx, Hoppo the Walking Monkey, tin w/up, 9½", NMIB 350.00
Marx, Joe Penner & Goo-Goo, tin litho w/up, 8", NMIB........1,760.00
Marx, Joy-Rider Jalopy, tin litho w/up, 8", EX in box 350.00
Marx, Komikal Kop Crazy Car, tin litho w/up, 7", EX 265.00
Marx, Lone Ranger, tin litho w/up, 1938, 8", VG 245.00
Marx, Lucky Stunt Flyer, tin litho w/up, 6½", EX 425.00
Marx, Main Street, tin litho w/up, 24", EX in box 330.00
Marx, Main Street, tin litho w/up, 24", NMIB 415.00
Marx, Mammy's Boy Walker, tin litho w/up, 10½", EX 550.00
Marx, Merry Makers Orchestra, tin litho w/up, 9", EX 660.00
Marx, Milk Wagon w/Horse, tin litho w/up, 1950s, 10¼", VG 150.00
Marx, Milton Berle Whoopie Car, tin litho w/up, 1950s, EX 425.00
Marx, Moon Mullins & Kayo Handcar, tin w/up, 5", EX in box ...1,760.00
Marx, Mortimer Snerd Drummer, tin w/up, 8½", EX 660.00
Marx, Mortimer Snerd Walker, tin w/up, 1939, 8½", EX 245.00
Marx, Moving Van, tin litho, friction, rust spots, 5", G 110.00
Marx, Mystery Taxi, pnt pressed steel, 1930s, NM 295.00
Marx, Old Jalopy, tin litho w/up, 1940s-50s, EX 200.00
Marx, Pinocchio Delivery Wagon, tin litho w/up, 9", EX 770.00
Marx, Pinocchio the Acrobat, tin litho w/up, 16", EX 245.00

Marx, Pinocchio the Acrobat, tin litho w/up, 16", VG in box ...**325.00**
Marx, Planet Patrol Space Tank, tin litho w/up, 10", MIB **330.00**
Marx, Policeman on Motorcycle w/Sidecar, tin w/up, 8½", EX ..**330.00**
Marx, Popeye & Olive Oyl on Roof, tin w/up, 1932, 9½", NM ..**1,500.00**
Marx, Popeye Express (still parrot), tin w/up, 1935, 8", EX **825.00**
Marx, Popeye Express Airport, tin w/up, 1935, 9½", NMIB **1,200.00**
Marx, Popeye Flyer, tin litho w/up, slight damage, 9", EX **550.00**
Marx, Popeye the Champ, tin litho w/up, 1935, 7x7", EX **7,150.00**
Marx, Popeye the Pilot, tin litho w/up, 1940, 7", NM **550.00**
Marx, Popeye the Pilot, tin litho w/up, 8½", EX **770.00**
Marx, Porky Pig walker, tin w/up, 1939, 8", EX in box **420.00**
Marx, Project Mercury Play Set, M (unopened) in EX box **475.00**
Marx, Queen of Campus, tin litho w/up, 5½", EX **195.00**
Marx, Red Cap Porter, tin litho w/up, 8", M in worn box **660.00**
Marx, Ring-A-Ling Circus, tin litho w/up, 8", EX **600.00**
Marx, Roll-Over Pluto, tin litho w/up, 8", NMIB **300.00**
Marx, Royal Line Bus, tin litho w/up, 10", EX **525.00**
Marx, Skyscraper Go-Round (plane/zeppelin), w/up, 13½", EX .**600.00**
Marx, Smitty on Scooter, tin litho w/up, rare, 8", EX **1,320.00**
Marx, Speed Boy Motorcycle Delivery Wagon, tin w/up, 10", EX ...**330.00**
Marx, Speed Delivery Boy, tin litho w/up, 9½", G **140.00**
Marx, Spick & Span, tin litho w/up, 10", NMIB **4,625.00**
Marx, Spick Drummer, tin litho w/up, 8½", EX **1,045.00**
Marx, Superman Racing Airplane, tin litho w/up, 5", NM **1,200.00**
Marx, Swing Tail Airplane, tin/plastic, '50s, 21", MIB **270.00**
Marx, Tom & Jerry on Motorcycle w/Sidecar, MIB **80.00**
Marx, Trombone Player, tin litho w/up, 5", EX **385.00**
Marx, Uncle Wiggly Crazy Car, tin litho w/up, NMIB **990.00**
Marx, US Army Bomber, tin litho, 1940s, 18" wingspan, M **450.00**
Marx, Walking Tiger, plush w/up, 1960s, 8" L, MIB **50.00**
Marx, Whoopie Car w/flappers, tin litho w/up, 7", EX in box **550.00**
Marx, Wrecker, tin litho w/up, rpl wheel, 8½", G **60.00**
Marx, WWI tank, tin litho w/up, 9", EX **245.00**
Marx, 2-car Auto Transport, tin litho, 13½", NMIB **220.00**
Metal Masters, Station Wagon, rubber tires, 1940, 8¾", VG **40.00**
Mohawk, Yel Taxi, tin litho w/up, 6¾", EX **155.00**
Nifty, Jiggs Jazz Car, tin litho w/up, 6½", NM **3,080.00**
Nyling, Michigan Shovel #2200, 1949, 31½", NM **235.00**
Occupied Japan, Dancing Couple, celluloid, 5", NM **150.00**
Pratt & Letchworth, Horse Dray, CI, 1890, 12" **950.00**
Remco, Bulldog Tank, tin litho, b/o, 22", EX in box **175.00**
Remco, Lost in Space Robot, b/o, 1968, 12", EX **200.00**
Remco, Space Model QX-2 walkie-talkies, 1950s, MIB **45.00**
Rich, Borden's Delivery Wagon, tin w/wooden horse, 20", VG ..**275.00**
Rich, Borden's Farm Products Wagon, tin/wood, 20", G **200.00**
Schuco, Bellhop Monkey, metal face, felt hands/ft, M **375.00**
Schuco, Blecky Monkey, metal face, animated tongue, 3½", M .**155.00**
Schuco, Fiddler Pig, tin w/up, 4½", VG **80.00**
Schuco, Ford Coupe 1917, tin litho w/up, MIB **165.00**
Schuco, Golliwog Bear, gold mohair, M **750.00**
Schuco, Monkey Drummer, mechanical, 4½", M **130.00**
Schuco, Monkey in Car, cloth/tin litho w/up, 6", NM **2,860.00**
Schuco, Old Timer 1902 Mercedes Simplex, w/up, 8½", MIB **160.00**
Schuco, 1913 Mercer, tin w/up, 7½", M **145.00**
Steelcraft, Army Scout Plane, steel, pnt scratches, 22", VG **500.00**
Steelcraft, Army Truck, pnt steel, 1930s, 23", EX **750.00**
Strauss, Boob McNutt Walker, tin litho w/up, 8½", VG **880.00**
Strauss, Dandy Jim Dancer, tin litho w/up, 10", EX **525.00**
Strauss, Deluxe Bus, tin w/up, worn pnt, 13", EX **415.00**
Strauss, Flapping Butterfly, tin litho w/up, 6½", EX **135.00**
Strauss, Ham & Sam at Piano, tin w/up, 1921, 5½", EX in box ..**660.00**
Strauss, Inter-State Dbl-Decker Bus, tin w/up, 10½", EX **770.00**
Strauss, Jackie Hornpipe Dancer, tin w/up, 1910, 9¼", NM **1,000.00**
Strauss, Jackie Hornpipe Dancer, tin w/up, 8½", EX **880.00**

Strauss, Jenny the Balking Mule, tin w/up, 1925, 9", VG **220**
Strauss, Jenny the Balking Mule, tin w/up, 1930s, NMIB **190**
Strauss, Knock-Out Prize Fighters, tin w/up, 5½", EX **150**
Strauss, Knock-Out Prize Fighters, tin w/up, 5½", EX in box **220**
Strauss, Open Speedster, tin litho w/up, 1922, 8½", EX **245**
Strauss, Santee Sleigh, tin litho w/up, 10", EX **1,540**
Strauss, Standard Oil Truck, tin litho w/up, 11", EX **750**
Strauss, Tombo Dancer, tin litho w/up, 9", EX **330**
Strauss, Yel-O-Taxi, tin litho w/up, 7½", EX **770**
Strauss, Yel-O-Taxi, tin litho w/up, 7½", G **275**
Structo, Racer, pressed steel, mechanical, 15", G **300**
Structo, Racer, steel w/up, rpt, 12½", G **250**
Structo, Steam Shovel, EX pnt, missing tracks, EX **115**
Structo, Truck, pnt steel, friction, b/o lights, 17", G **85**
Sturdi-Toy, Dump Truck, pnt steel, lt rust spots, 27", G **425**
Sun Rubber, Master Truck, futuristic style, 1930s, 6", EX **40**
Sun Rubber, Racer #5, lt pnt wear, 1930s, 4½", EX **35**
Sun Rubber, Teardrop Sedan, lt pnt wear, 1936, 5½" **35**
Taiwan, Piston Robot, tin/plastic, b/o, 1970s, 12", MIB **75**
Tonka, Pickup Truck, steel, 1950s, 12", M **32**
Tonka, Wrecker, pressed steel, #518, 1950s, M in 6x14" box **100**
TootsieToy, Army Truck, 1939, EX **48**
TootsieToy, Graham Sedan, 1939, VG **85**
TootsieToy, Model A Car, 1928, EX **35**
TootsieToy, Pickup Truck, Ford, open tailgate, NM **15**
TootsieToy, Pickup Truck, Ford Econoline, EX **18**
TootsieToy, Pontiac Chief, 1950, EX **25**
TootsieToy, Yel Cab, 1921, rstr **65**
Toplay, Chef on Roller Skates, tin litho w/up, 6", EX **175**
Toplay, Pango-Pango Dancer, tin litho w/up, 6", NMIB **265**
Unique Art, Artie the Clown, tin litho w/up, 8", EX in box **660**
Unique Art, Bombo, Monkey & Palm, tin w/up, '30s, 9½", EX **110**
Unique Art, Capitol Hill Racer, tin w/up, 1930s, 17½", EX **125**
Unique Art, GI Joe & Bouncing Jeep, tin w/up, 8", MIB **330**
Unique Art, GI Joe & K-9 Pups, tin litho, 1941, 9½", EX **325**
Unique Art, Hee Haw Kart, tin litho w/up, 10½", EX **135**
Unique Art, Hobo Train, tin litho w/up, 8½", EX **350**
Unique Art, Jazzbo Jim Dancer, tin w/up, 5", EX **600**
Unique Art, Jazzbo Jim Roof-top Dancer, tin w/up, 5", VG **440**
Unique Art, Kiddy Cyclist, tin litho w/up, 9", EX **165**
Unique Art, Li'l Abner Dogpatch Band, w/up, 6½", EX in box .**1,100**
Unique Art, Lincoln Tunnel, tin litho w/up, 24", EX **385**
Unique Art, Luggage Handler, tin litho w/up, 1940s, 13½", G ...**200**
Unique Art, Motorcycle & Policeman, tin litho w/up, 8½", EX **275**
Unique Art, Rodeo Joe, tin litho w/up, 7", VG **180**
Unique Art, Unique Artie, tin litho w/up, 7", EX **260**
US Zone Germany, Elephant on Scooter, tin w/up, 8½", NM **110**

W. Germany, clown band, 8½", VG, $200.00.

W Germany, Clown Tightrope Walker, celluloid, MIB 125.00
White, Dump Truck, steel, pnt loss, 27", G 300.00
Wilson, Flying Saucer, metal w/up, 1950s, MIB 200.00
Wolverine, Automatic Sand Crane #103, tin litho, '15, 15", EX ..220.00
Wolverine, Coal Loader, tin, removable crane, 1940s, 11", G 65.00
Wolverine, Merry-Go-Round, tin w/up, 12", NM in EX box 440.00
Wolverine, Skyscraper Elevator, tin litho, 1915, 24", EX 265.00
Wolverine, Sunny Andy Fun Fair, marble activated, 14", NM ...385.00
Wyandotte, ambulance, pnt steel, 11", VG 120.00
Wyandotte, Bank Truck, pressed steel, rpt, 6", G 65.00
Wyandotte, China Clipper, pressed steel, partial rpt, 9", G 90.00
Wyandotte, Coupe, pnt steel, crazed tires, 8", G 70.00
Wyandotte, Dump Truck, pnt metal, 1930s, 6", NM 200.00
Wyandotte, Dump Truck, pnt steel, 1930s, 12½", EX 275.00
Wyandotte, Gymnast, tin litho w/up, 9", G 60.00
Wyandotte, Hoky Poky, tin litho w/up, 6", EX 65.00
Wyandotte, Stake-Bed Truck, metal, 1920s, rpt, 10" 115.00

Farm Toys

Cattle truck, CI, Kenton, ca 1938, 8", NM 100.00
Cattle truck, metal, rubber tires, Kenton, 1930s, 8", EX 200.00
Combine, John Deere, CI, w/driver, Vindex, EX 1,200.00
Combine, Massey Harris Self-Propelled, metal/wood, 10", G 395.00
Hay loader, Vindex, M 525.00
Horse trailer, TootsieToy, NM 12.50
Manure spreader, McCormick-Deering, team of horses, Arcade .100.00

Oliver, corn picker, SLIK, #9828 E.I., 9½" long, $150.00.

Pickup truck, pnt metal w/wooden tires, 1940s, 9", EX 40.00
Thresher, McCormick-Deering, Arcade 400.00
Tractor, Allis Chalmers, Model AC-6, decal, Arcade, EX 195.00
Tractor, Farmall, plastic, 1940s, 8", EX 195.00
Tractor, Ford #7710 Custom, EX 65.00
Tractor, Fordson, AC Williams, EX 65.00
Tractor, Fordson, Arcade, rstr tires, 3", EX 55.00
Tractor, Fordson, Arcade, w/mower & plow, orig decal, NM 550.00
Tractor, Fordson, Gunthermann, tin w/up, 1910, +3 pcs 525.00
Tractor, Internat'l, Ertl, 8" 15.00
Tractor, Internat'l Harvester, Caterpillar, Arcade, NM 165.00
Tractor, Internat'l Harvester #1466, 1970s, MIB 200.00
Tractor, Internat'l Harvester #986 Custom RP, NM 165.00
Tractor, John Deere #50 Series, NMIB 110.00
Tractor, John Deere #5020 Custom, EX 75.00
Tractor, Massey Harris, w/driver, 7½", w/7" wagon, EX 265.00
Tractor, Minneapolis-Moline G-1000, wht wheels, MIB 475.00
Trailer, 4-wheel, Arcade, 3¼", EX 40.00
Truck, b/o, w/mooing cow, Alps, 11", NM 120.00
Truck, steel, Structo, 20", +7 plastic animals, M 100.00

Wagon, Arcade, 3½", EX 40.00
Wagon, McCormick-Deering, 2-horse, Arcade, EX 150.00

Guns

Though toy guns were patented as early as the 1850s, the cap pistol was not invented until 1870, when paper caps that were primarily developed to detonate muzzleloaders became available. Some of the earlier models were very ornate and were occasionally decorated with figural heads. Most are marked with the name of their manufacturer; Ace, Daisy, Bulldog, Victor, and Excelsior are the most common.

Avenger Tommy Gun, 30-cal, 1944, M 95.00
Benjamin Franklin Air Pistol, brass, early, EX 95.00
Buck, CI, 3¼", EX 45.00
Buddy L Machine Gun, EX 150.00

Buzz Henry, Lone Rider, 8", $50.00.

Daisy #8 Water Pistol, EX 35.00
Daisy Buck Rogers Gun, pnt steel, ca 1927, 9¾", G 150.00
Daisy Model #299 BB Gun, wood stock & grip, VG 20.00
Daisy Model #98 BB Gun, emb logo on plastic stock, scope, VG .25.00
Daisy Pop Gun, w/scope smoker, EX 55.00
Daisy Red Ryder Air Rifle, 1940s, EX in box 325.00
Daisy Superman Krypto Ray Gun, b/o, MIB 660.00
Eagle Cap Gun, Pat June 17 90, 7" 90.00
Eber Cap Pistol, tin, 4¾", EX 65.00
Hawk Cap Gun, dbl bbl, tin, takes roll, 3½", VG 35.00
Hubley Flintlock Cap Gun, over/under dbl bbl, 10", EX 75.00
Hubley Flintlock Jr Cap Pistol, 1950s, M in VG box 45.00
Hubley Jr Flintlock Pistol, EX in orig box 60.00
Hubley Ric-O-Shay Cap Pistol, EX 150.00
Hubley Scout Rifle, tan stock, EX 250.00
Hubley Texan Jr Cap Gun, 1940s, 9", w/holster 130.00
Johnny One-Shot Cap Gun, w/wrist holster, EX in box 30.00
Krest Marble Shooter, automatic style, 5¾", EX 65.00
Lone Star P-38 Cap Pistol, metal w/red plastic grips, VG 65.00
Marx G-Man Tommy Gun, EX 125.00
Marx Johnny Ringo, M 195.00
Mattel Fanner 50 Cap Gun, cylinder type, MIB 210.00
Mattel Indian Scent Rifle, MIB 195.00
Mattel Thunder Burp Gun, MIB 95.00
Mattel Winchester Cap Gun, shooting shell, EX 175.00
Nichols Mark I Cap Gun, EX 195.00
Nichols Mustang Cap Gun, EX 175.00
Nichols Paint Cartridge Loader, diecast, w/holster, 1950s 35.00
Nichols Stallion 38 Cap Gun, EX 65.00
Pilaz Pellet Shooter, mk FBI, 4", VG 35.00
Ping Pong, tin litho, Japan, 1940s-50s, EX 95.00

Pirate emb on brn marbleized plastic-hdld pistol, pr, EX 100.00
Repeater Pistol, wood & tin, clicker type, 9", VG 65.00
Star Cork Gun, tin, 4¼", VG 35.00
Topper Johnny Seven, 7 guns in 1, ca 1964, MIB 175.00
Weasel Pop Gun, cylinder type, EX 65.00
Wyandotte Pop Gun, dbl bbl, EX 55.00
Wyandotte Water Pistol, 7", EX 75.00

Pedal Cars and Ride-On Toys

Air Mail Plane, orig pnt, ca 1930s, 44", EX 765.00
Cadillac, sheet metal, orig pnt, Steelcraft, 36", EX 265.00
Cannonball Express, Garton, pnt steel, rubber tires, 39", VG 300.00
Car, Am Nat'l, pressed steel on wood fr, rpt, 50", VG 4,500.00
Car, pnt steel, head lamp, EX gr pnt, 35", G 180.00
Car, pressed steel, spoked wheels, rpt, rpl tires, 43", EX 400.00
Car, REO, pnt pressed steel, rstr, 44", EX 900.00
Car, wood/tin/steel, orig 3-color pnt, flat box style, 45" 350.00
Dr Pepper Convertible, pnt steel, 41", EX 600.00

Gendron, painted steel, folding windshield, restored, 38" long, EX, $1,500.00.

Good Humor Ice Cream Truck, orig pnt, EX 225.00
Lincoln Tandem, red & yel, b/o lights, 1930, 76", M 7,700.00
Pontiac Fire Truck, prof rstr, ca 1950, 21x40" 1,500.00
Pullman car, ride-on, Keystone, EX 200.00
Red Baron Triwinged Plane, ltd ed, 1980s, 34x48", M 750.00
Station wagon, pnt pressed steel, 44", EX 175.00
Van, pnt metal, ride-on, Dugan Bros, M 195.00
Wagon, Paris Mfg, pnt wood, iron rim wheels, 35", VG 475.00

Penny Toys

Black Man Dancer, crank in crate base, Germany, 1900s, 3" 465.00
Car, tin litho, silver wheels, MIG, 1900-17, G 160.00
Cow w/horns & bell, wheeled base, Germany, EX 200.00
Electric Omnibus, tin litho, Germany, 3¼", NM 1,400.00
Fire Truck, men/ladder/bell, tin litho w/up, MIG, 4½" 245.00
Kayak w/rower, tin litho, Chicago souvenir, 5", NM 825.00
Man in rowboat, wheeled base, Germany, EX 200.00
Monkey on climbing string, tin litho, Germany, 4" 175.00
Parrot in cage, tin litho, 3½", EX 250.00
Porter, tin litho, Germany, lt rust, 4", VG 130.00
Seesaw, couple swing in boat from A-frame, Germany, 3" 465.00

Pipsqueaks

Pipsqueak toys were popular among the Pennsylvania German. The earliest had bellows made from sheepskin. Later cloth replaced t sheepskin, and finally paper bellows were used.

Baby in cradle, wood/cb/cloth/papier-mache, 5½", EX 345.0
Bird feeds young, animated wings, papier-mache/mc, 5", EX 325.0
Black boy in striped costume, glass eyes, silent, 12" 915.0
Cat w/2 kittens, striped flocking, animated mouth, 7", VG 450.0
Chickens in cage, open door: papier-mache rooster pops up 85.0
Duck, rectangle base, papier-mache, mc pnt, silent, 3", VG 65.0
Duck on nest, papier-mache, orig pnt, rpr, silent, 5¾" 425.0
Duck w/young, mc pnt, glass eyes, 6", EX 350.0
Goose on spring legs, squeaks, glued rprs, 7" 165.0
Horse in cage, dapple gray flanel coat, glass eyes, 9", EX 475.0
Husky dog, wht w/gr pnt, rpr/touchup, silent, 7" 250.0
Jack-in-box, drunk in barrel, papier-mache, 8", VG 275.0
Parrot on stump, papier-mache, EX color, squeaks, 4" 145.0
Rabbit, haircloth, animated ears, glass eyes, silent, 9" 425.0
Rooster, papier-mache, jtd neck, cast metal legs, 7⅝", EX 400.0
Rooster, papier-mache, orig pnt, rpr, silent, 7¼" 85.0
Rooster, papier-mache, spring legs, bellows base, 7", VG 150.0
Rooster, papier-mache, spring legs, orig pnt/gilt, 8", VG 250.0
Rooster & hen in cage on wheels, squeaks, worn, 6" 65.0
Rooster in cage, faint squeak, Made in Germany, 4½" 95.0
Turkey, papier-mache, mc, silent, 3½", EX 300.0

Pull Toys

Buttercup & Spareribs on platform, tin litho, 7½", EX 770.0
Camel on platform, pnt tin, offset wheels, Am, 9", EX 2,700.0
Cow, suede on wood, moos, glass eye, rpl base, 18", VG 475.0
Derby Rider, paper litho on wood, Gibbs, 1914, 8", EX 425.0
Dog on platform, wood/papier-mache, blk/wht, 23", EX 825.0
Donkey nodder, papier-mache on wheeled base, Germany, EX ..185.0
Elephant, HP wood, on 8" platform w/wheels, 1924, EX 300.0
Felix the Cat, tinplate, minor scuffs, 7½" 715.0
Goat on platform, bell ringer, pnt tin, Am, 7¾", VG 550.0
Goat on rocker, pnt tin, Am, pnt chips, 6", VG 475.0
Goose, wood, orig worn pnt, ca 1921, 10", VG 95.0
Goose w/nodding head, tin, minor wear, 3½" 350.0
Horse, cvd wood, orig pnt, fur tail, EX details, 12" L 350.0
Horse, haircloth w/fur & horsehair, glass eyes, Germany, 30" 425.0
Horse, wood w/brn wooly coat, fur mane/tail, Germany, 11" 175.0
Horse & buggy, tin, 1900, 5", EX 225.0
Horse & cart, tin w/worn orig pnt, damage/rpr, 9½" 85.0
Horse & cart, wood w/flannel coat, fur mane, hair tail, 9" 400.0
Jockey, pnt tin/CI, bell toy, Am, early, 7½", VG 225.0
Pony Circus Wagon, paper litho on wood, Gibbs, 14", EX 1,500.0
Steamship Puritan, side wheeler, pnt CI, rocker bar, 11" 600.0
Tiger, cloth over papier-mache, glass eyes, 16", VG 100.0

Schoenhut

Acrobat Lady, bsk head, long neck, 8", VG 350.0
Acrobat Man, bsk head, 8", VG 325.0
African Native, carved ft, orig clothes, 7½", EX 1,400.0
Black Dude, 1-pc compo head, orig clothes, 8½", VG 375.0
Buffalo, pnt eyes, regular, EX 360.0
Buffalo, style 4, pnt eyes, twine tail, leather horns, 8", VG 250.0
Burro, glass eyes, leather ears, twine tail, 7", VG 400.0
Burro, pnt eyes, regular, EX 350.0

Camel, Arabian; pnt eyes, regular, EX 375.00
Camel, Bactrian; style 2, pnt eyes, cord tail, 7", EX 1,200.00
Clown, compo head, cotton clothes, reduced, VG 110.00
Clown, pnt eyes, 9", EX 130.00
Monkey, style 3, glass eyes, twine tail, 9½", G 50.00
Monkey, style 3, pnt eyes, twine tail, 9½", EX 75.00
Elephant, style 1, glass eyes, twine tail, 9", EX 110.00
Felix the Cat, decal on ft, rpl ears, 8", EX 300.00
Giraffe, pnt eyes, regular, EX 260.00
Hippo, pnt eyes, regular, VG+ 300.00
Hippo, style 3, pnt eyes, 9½", VG 310.00
Hobo, 1-pc molded compo head, 8", VG 195.00
Hoop & whip, string intact, rare, EX 185.00
Horse, pnt eyes, brush tail, dk pnt, 7", EX 150.00
Horse, pnt eyes, brush tail, wht pnt, 7", VG 150.00
Horse, style 1, glass eyes, dk pnt, w/saddle, 9½", EX ...225.00
Horse, style 1, glass eyes, leather ears, 9½", VG 140.00
Humpty Dumpty Cage Wagon, stenciled wood, rpr, 10", VG .1,050.00
Jiggs & Maggie, orig clothes, 9", 7", VG, pr 900.00
Lady Rider, bsk head, long neck, 8", VG 225.00
Leopard, glass eyes, regular, EX 550.00
Lion, reduced, VG 250.00
Lion Tamer, molded head, thumb & finger hands, 8", EX 185.00
Mary (w/o lamb), straw hat, pnt wear on face, 8", EX 700.00
Milkmaid, style 1, 2-part head, orig clothes, 8", VG ...550.00
Ostrich, pnt eyes, regular, EX 425.00
Pedestal, paper labels, minor wear, 4½", VG, pr 75.00
Polar bear, style 1, glass eyes, cord tail, 8", NM 850.00
Poodle, pnt eyes, 9½", VG 120.00
Poodle, style 3, tooled mane fur, pnt eyes, 7½", EX 150.00
Rhino, pnt eyes, regular, EX+ 450.00
Rhino, reduced, EX 350.00
Rhino, style 1, glass eyes, cord tail, rpl horn, 9", VG ...350.00
Ringmaster, bendable elbows, thumb & finger hands, 8", VG 425.00
Ringmaster, molded wooden head, pnt chips, 8", VG 140.00

Steiff

Margaret Steiff began making her felt stuffed toys in Germany in the late 1800s. The animals she made were tagged with an elephant in a circle. Her first teddy bear, made in 1903, became such a popular seller that she changed her tag to a bear. Felt stuffing was replaced with excelsior and wool; when it became available, foam was used. In addition to the tag, look for the 'Steiff' ribbon and the button inside the ear. For further information we recommend *Teddy Bears and Steiff Animals*, a full-color identification and value guide by Margaret Fox Mandel, available from Collector Books or your public library. See also Teddy Bears.

Baboon, Coco, w/button & 2 tags, 4", M 75.00
Beagle, Biggie, red collar, w/button & tags, 7", M 80.00
Bear, beige mohair/glass eyes, Replica 1930 Teddy Baby, 17" 420.00
Beaver, Nagy, swivel head, w/chest tag, 6½", M 70.00
Boar baby, velvet, w/button & tag, 3", NM 50.00
Cat, Fiffy, recumbent, w/button & tag, NM 150.00
Cat, Gussy, button, chest & stock tags, 4", M 85.00
Cat, Gussy, orig ribbon, w/button & 2 tags, 6½", M 125.00
Cat, Lixie, w/button, 4", EX 125.00
Chicken, Floppy, w/button & tags, rare, NM 150.00
Chinchilla, GoGo, draylon, swivel head, w/button, 6", M 150.00
Clown, Clownie, w/chest tag, 5", NM 100.00
Cow, Bessy, orig collar & bell, w/stock tag, 4½", NM 145.00
Cow, Bessy, w/udder & orig collar, w/chest tag, 6½", M ...165.00
Dog, Cockie, raised button/chest tag, US Zone, 10½", NM 315.00
Dog, Cockie, sitting, w/button & tag, 5½", NM 125.00
Dog, Peky, w/button & 2 tags, 3¼", M 75.00
Dog, Revu Susi, w/button & tag, 4¾", M 68.00
Dog, Sulac, dangling legs, w/button & 2 tags, 15½", NM 575.00
Dog, Terry, orig red collar, w/button & tags, 7½", M 130.00
Dog, Tessie, w/button, chest & stock tags, 4", M 75.00
Dwarf, Pucki, w/button & 2 tags, 5", NM 50.00

Schoenhut Rubber Ball Shooting Gallery, 17", VG, $500.00.

Tiger, reduced, EX 300.00
Tiger, style 1, glass eyes, jtd neck, cord tail, 7", VG 450.00
Wolf, pnt eyes, regular, NM 1,800.00
Zebra, reduced, VG 400.00
Zebra, style 1, glass eyes, cloth mane, 8½", VG 700.00

Steiff elephant, cast iron base and wheels, cord for squeaker gone, 15x19", EX, $450.00.

Finch, mohair, metal ft, w/button & tags, 5", M 200.00
Fox, Xorry, standing, w/button & chest tag, 4", M 88.00
Frog, wooly, w/button & tag, 3", NM 20.00
Giraffe, cream mohair w/orange spots, w/button & tag, 72" 1,450.00
Giraffe, velvet, closed mouth, w/button & tag, 6", M 60.00
Gnome, felt covered, ca 1910, w/sm button, 8", EX 985.00
Goat, Zicky, w/button & 2 tags, 5½", M 85.00

Hamster, wooly, w/button & tag, 2½", NM 28.00
Hedgehog, Joggi, standing, w/chest tag, 5", NM 75.00
Hippo, Mockie, wooden teeth, w/button & 2 tags, M 140.00
Kangaroo, Kangoo (no pouch), w/button & tag, 11", NM 125.00
Lamb, Lamby, w/incised button & 2 tags, 5½", M 85.00
Leopard, running, w/chest tag, 3½" H, M 88.00
Lizard, Lizzy, w/chest tag, 12" L, M 335.00
Lobster, Crabby, w/button & 2 tags, 4", M 185.00
Mickey Mouse, non-jtd, orig clothes, ca 1930, 6½", EX 995.00
Moose, Moosy, no button or tags, 5½", NM 200.00
Penguin, Peggy, swivel head, glass eyes, w/button, 12", EX 165.00
Rabbit, Lulac, w/button, 15½", NM 250.00
Rabbit, Manni, w/button, chest & stock tags, 8", M 95.00
Rabbit, Pummy, raised button & chest tag, 10", M 135.00
Raccoon, Raccy, mohair, w/button & neck tag, 4", VG 115.00
Raven, Hucky, metal ft, w/button & stock tag, 6½", NM 125.00
Rooster, mohair & felt, w/button & tag, 11", M 125.00
Rooster, wooly, plastic ft, w/button & tag, 3¼", EX 25.00
Sea gull, wooly, metal ft, 3", EX 28.00
Seal, Robby, mohair, w/neck tag, 7", M 125.00
Squirrel, Possy, mohair, glass eyes, w/button, 4", EX 70.00
Tiger cub, jtd, w/chest tag, 3¾", M 75.00
Turkey, Tucky, w/button & 2 tags, 4", M 195.00
Turtle, Slo, brn mohair, rubber shell, w/button & tag, 7", EX 77.50
Wolf, w/brass button & wht tag, 4¾", NM 55.00
Zebra, mohair, no button or tags, 8", NM 48.00

Toy Soldiers

Unique to this country are what are called 'Dimestore' soldiers; they were made by various companies from the 1930s until sometime in the 1950s. The most common are Barclay, Manoil, and Jones (hollow cast lead); Grey Iron (cast iron); and Auburn (rubber). They're about 4 to 4½" high. They were sold in Woolworth and Kresge's 5 & 10 Stores (most for just five cents), hence the name 'Dimestore.' Marx made tin soldiers for use in target gun games; these sell for about $4.00. Condition is most important as these toys were made to play with. They're most often found with much of the paint worn off. In the listings that follow, prices are for examples in excellent condition which means they show very little wear. Please remember that these pieces are only representative. There were over 600 made, plus a number of others by minor makers such as Tommy Toy and All-Nu, all of which are higher priced. Serious collectors should to refer to *Collecting Toys* (1993) or *Toy Soldiers* (1992), both by Richard O'Brien, Books Americana, Inc. Reference numbers are those used in O'Brien's books and are considered the standard for the hobby. Another very popular toy soldier has been made by Britains of England since 1893. They are smaller and more detailed than 'Dimestores,' and variants number in the thousands. O'Brien's 'Toy Soldier' book has over 200 pages devoted to Britains and other foreign makers. Our advisor for this category is Tim O'Callaghan; he is listed in the Directory under Michigan.

Auburn, A001, infantry private 12.00
Auburn, A003, bugler 15.00
Auburn, A007, Ethiopian w/rifle & shield 92.00
Auburn, A015, Red Cross nurse, wht uniform 30.00
Auburn, A019, signalman 55.00
Auburn, A027, soldier marching 15.00
Auburn, A033, tank defender 37.50
Barclay, B007, flagbearer, cast helmet 18.00
Barclay, B012, sniper kneeling & firing rifle 12.00
Barclay, B020, charging, separate tin helmet 78.00
Barclay, B029, bugler 20.00
Barclay, B041, Italian officer 140.00

Barclay, B060, sailor w/signal flags 20.0
Barclay, B087, sharpshooter standing & firing 12.5
Barclay, B093, Army motorcyclist 32.0
Barclay, B119, wounded soldier w/crutches 18.0
Barclay, B214, drummer 40.0

Britains, set #2172, French Algerian Spahis mounted with carbines in review order, ca 1950s, very rare, EX-, $1,300.00.

Grey Iron, G002, Colonial foot soldier 25.0
Grey Iron, G006, cadet 22.0
Grey Iron, G012, infantry officer 16.0
Grey Iron, G020, doughboy w/range finder 80.0
Grey Iron, G028, doughboy officer 15.0
Grey Iron, G038, cavalry officer 35.0
Grey Iron, G062, machine gunner 17.5
Grey Iron, G083, legion drummer 18.0
Grey Iron, G090, Ethiopian soldier charging 60.0
Grey Iron, G096, patient on stretcher 28.0
Grey Iron, G104, nurse & wounded soldier 210.0
Jones, J007, stretcher bearer 100.0
Jones, J015, prone, firing machine gun 100.0
Jones, J017, cook w/frying pan 60.0
Jones, J021, kneeling and holding searchlight 75.0
Jones, J027, nurse w/medical bag 80.0
Jones, J029, standing & firing rifle 90.0
Manoil, M002, flag bearer 21.0
Manoil, M012, bugler 18.0
Manoil, M026, marine, 2nd version 16.0
Manoil, M028, signalman, hollow base 40.0
Manoil, M039, machine gunner, sitting on pillows 23.0
Manoil, M048, sniper standing & firing rifle 18.0
Manoil, M058, stretcher carrier w/medical kit 19.0
Manoil, M060, aviator 20.0
Manoil, M067, soldier crouching & holding hand grenade 60.0
Manoil, M086, paymaster 150.0
Manoil, M116, radio operator standing 55.0
Manoil, M120, soldier w/barbed wire 35.0

Trains

Electric trains were produced as early as the late 19th century. Names to look for are Lionel, Ives, and American Flyer.

The following listings were prepared by our advisor, Bruce C Greenberg (see the Directory under Maryland), and are taken from h comprehensive publications on Lionel, American Flyer, and Ives train

The prices presented are the most common versions of each item. In many cases, there are several other variations often having a substantially higher value. Identification numbers given in the listings below actually appear on the item.

Key: Std Gauge — Standard Gauge

American Flyer 283, S Gauge engine w/tender, EX **65.00**
American Flyer 332DC, S Gauge engine w/tender, EX **380.00**
American Flyer 332DC, S Gauge engine w/tender, G **80.00**
American Flyer 360, 361 S Gauge diesels, EX **175.00**
American Flyer 360, 361 S Gauge diesels, G **45.00**
Ives 11, 0 Gauge steam engine w/tender, EX **250.00**
Ives 11, 0 Gauge steam engine w/tender, G **110.00**
Ives 1118, 0 Gauge Steam engine w/tender, EX **150.00**
Ives 1118, 0 Gauge steam engine w/tender, G **75.00**
Ives 1132, Wide Gauge steam engine w/tender, 1921-26, EX **900.00**
Ives 1132, Wide Gauge steam engine w/tender, 1921-26, G **450.00**
Ives 3240, 1 Gauge electric engine, 1912-20, EX **800.00**
Ives 3240, 1 Gauge electric engine, 1912-20, G **400.00**
Ives 3241, Wide Gauge electric engine, 1921-25, EX **200.00**
Ives 3241, Wide Gauge electric engine, 1921-25, G **100.00**
Ives 3243, Wide Gauge electric engine, 1921-28, EX **600.00**
Ives 3243, Wide Gauge electric engine, 1921-28, G **350.00**
Lionel 1668, 0 Gauge steam engine w/tender, 1937-41, EX **130.00**
Lionel 1668, 0 Gauge steam engine w/tender, 1937-41, G **70.00**
Lionel 2037, 0 Gauge steam engine/tender, 1954-55, 57-63, EX ..**90.00**
Lionel 2037, 0 Gauge steam engine/tender, 1954-55, 57-63, G **50.00**
Lionel 224, 0 Gauge steam engine w/tender, 1938-42, EX **100.00**
Lionel 224, 0 Gauge steam engine w/tender, 1938-42, G **80.00**
Lionel 2343, 0 Gauge diesels, 2 units, EX **500.00**
Lionel 2343, 0 Gauge diesels, 2 units, G **200.00**
Lionel 252, 0 Gauge electric engine, 1926-32, EX **150.00**
Lionel 252, 0 Gauge electric engine, 1926-32, G **100.00**
Lionel 380, Std Gauge electric engine, 1923-27, EX **400.00**
Lionel 380, Std Gauge electric engine, 1923-27, G **200.00**
Lionel 400E, Std Gauge steam engine, 1931-40, EX **2,300.00**
Lionel 400E, Std Gauge steam engine, 1931-40, G **1,200.00**
Lionel 408E, Std Gauge electric engine, 1927-36, EX **1,400.00**
Lionel 408E, Std Gauge electric engine, 1927-36, G **700.00**
Lionel 42, Std Gauge electric engine, 1913-23, rnd hood, EX **600.00**
Lionel 42, Std Gauge electric engine, 1913-23, rnd hood, G **250.00**
Lionel 50, 027 Gauge gang car, 1954-64, EX **60.00**
Lionel 50, 027 Gauge gang car, 1954-64, G **30.00**
Lionel 58, 027 Gauge rotary snowplow, 1959-61, EX **625.00**
Lionel 58, 027 Gauge rotary snowplow, 1959-61, G **275.00**
Lionel 60, 0 Gauge trolly, 1955-58, EX **125.00**
Lionel 60, 0 Gauge trolly, 1955-58, G **60.00**
Lionel 700E, 0 Gauge steam engine w/tender, 1937-42, G **2,000.00**
Lionel 726, 0 Gauge steam engine w/tender, 1946-49, EX **400.00**
Lionel 726, 0 Gauge steam engine w/tender, 1946-49, G **200.00**
Lionel 773, 0 Gauge steam engine w/tender, 1950, 64-66, EX **750.00**
Lionel 773, 0 Gauge steam engine w/tender, 1950, 64-66, G **375.00**
Lionel 8, Std Gauge electric engine, 1925-32, EX **200.00**
Lionel 8, Std Gauge electric engine, 1925-32, G **110.00**

Miscellaneous

Blocks, wood w/litho ABCs, children/pets, 5", 26 for **550.00**
Horse head silhouettes w/seat between, rockers, wood/uphl, 36" ..**425.00**
Jumping jack monkey, hand cvd/pnt, 21" L **420.00**
Noah's Ark, 133 animals/people (EX to G), pnt wood, 15" **2,000.00**
Noah's Ark, 14 animals/people, wood w/bright mc decor, 12" **425.00**
Noah's Ark, 48 animals, poplar w/paper covering, 16" L **450.00**

Rooster silhouettes w/seat between, rockers, pnt wood, 40" **700.00**
Tricycle, wood w/CI fittings, steel rims, wood spokes, 33" **575.00**

Trade Signs

Trade signs were popular during the 1800s. They were usually made in an easily recognizable shape that one could mentally associate with the particular type of business it was to represent, especially appropriate in the days when many customers could not read!

Bell, wood on iron stand, for iron foundry, 14x13", EX **345.00**
Boot, rubber w/pin-striping, Ales Goodyear Shoe Co, 36", EX ...**935.00**
Damarin Rooms & Bath, 2-sided pnt wood, weathered, 13x33" .**140.00**
Dinner fork shape, CI, for restaurant, 22" L **315.00**
Dr Daniels Stock Medicines, pnt wood, weathered, 12x29" **130.00**
Dressmaking, pnt letters on brd, alligatored surface, 6x35" **200.00**
Eddy Plows, wood, plow & portrait of Walden Eddy, 24x60", EX ..**475.00**
H Coltin Ladies' & Gentlemen's Tailor, 2-sided wood, 12x32", G ..**100.00**
Hat & glove, wrought iron/metals, EX pnt, 35x44x12", EX **2,650.00**
Horse head, cvd/laminated wood, no pnt, for stable, 30", VG **990.00**
Jewelry/Crockery/name, gold/wht pnt on sanded blk, 15x108" ...**350.00**
Key shape, Keys Made, enamel on metal, locksmith's, EX **150.00**
Lacakawanna Coal Office, pnt on wood, 1900, 18x72" **990.00**
Mortar & pestle, pnt wood, 3-D, apothecary, 30x23" dia, EX **80.00**
Mortar & pestle, zinc w/worn gilt, 3-D, apothecary, 32" **450.00**

Steamer trunk, wooden frame with pasteboard facings, 3-dimensional painted effect, wrought iron hangers and chains, 1800s, 42½x61", EX, $1,750.00.

Shotgun, wooden dbl-bbl w/ramrod, gunsmith's, 1800s, 100" .**1,000.00**
Walter F Fontaine, architect, wood, 5¾x57½", G **140.00**
Watch, wood, iron stem, gold-pnt numerals, 15" dia **885.00**
Watch, zinc, 2-sided, EX pnt, watch repairer's, 21x26", EX **1,100.00**

Tramp Art

Today considered a type of American folk art, tramp art was primarily made from the end of the Civil War until the 1930s. Often produced by tramps and hobos from wooden materials which could be scavenged (crates and cigar boxes, for instance), articles such as jewelry boxes and picture frames were usually decorated by chip carving and then stained. Some of them were painted; the best were polychromed. Our advisor for this category is Matt Lippa; he is listed in the Directory under Iowa.

Box, trinket; 2-drw, simple chip cvg, 7x2½x9" 85.00
Comb case, layered dmns & rectangular chips, 5x9x6" 130.00
Cradle, chip cvd, leaf designs, orig pnt, 1900s, doll sz, EX 50.00

Desk, painted green and decorated with silver foil and gilt labels with cupids and 'Aurora,' 20th century, 50x33x16", $2,600.00.

Frame, layered w/angle cuts, bow ties on sides, 15x13" 135.00
Mirror, hand; 5 chip-cvd layers, 1800s, 11x7x5½" 155.00
Mirror frame, simple notched bands, 12x13" 95.00
Shelf, pine, scalloped, chip cvd, appl cvd flowers, 9x16x17" 140.00
Shelves (2), chip cvd, intersecting invt V shape, 19x24x5½" 185.00

Traps

Though of interest to collectors for many years, trap collecting has gained in popularity over the past ten years in particular, causing prices to appreciate rapidly. Traps are usually marked on the pan as to manufacturer, and the condition of these trademarks are important when determining their values. Grading is as follows:

Good: one-half of pan legible.
Very Good: legible in entirety, but light.
Fine: legible in entirety, with strong lettering.
Mint: in like-new, shiny condition.

Our advisor for this category is Boyd Nedry; he is listed in the Directory under Michigan. Prices listed here are for traps in fine condition.

Acme Mouse, wood snap 18.00
Aldrich Snare, bear sz 20.00
Alexander Clutch, sz C 250.00
Alligator #2, Trappers Supply Co 125.00
Aurouze, wire live trap, mouse sz 20.00
Automatic, metal, rat 15.00
Bell Spring #1¼, single long spring 125.00
Belmont Steel, Sure Grip #2, dbl long spring 40.00
Better 3 way, auto set, mouse 5.00
Bigelow, killer 15.00

Black Cat, plastic 4-hole choker, mouse ....10.
Blake & Lamb #2½, single long spring ....15.
Blake & Lamb #44, dbl long spring ....35.
Bonafied, wood snap, mouse ....15.
Buffalo Bill, Snappy Mfg Co, wood snap, rat ....22.
Bullock, jump ....225.
Canada Trap, killer, sm ....40.
Catch Em Alive, tin, live mouse ....125.
Chasse, 3-hole choker, mouse ....25.
Cinch, The; gopher ....18.
Clincher #1, NFMS Works, long spring ....35.
Coghill, jar top, live mouse ....20.
Connibear #110 ....6.
Cooper Clutch, dbl jaw, long spring ....35.
Crago Clutch #4 ....150.
Crosby Trip Trap, mouse ....14.
Davenport Choker, full circles ....135.
Dead Easy, wood snap, rat ....10.
Dearborn #3, dbl long spring ....200.
Death Clamp, killer, 4" ....35.
Delusion, live mouse ....45.
Diamond #21½, single long spring ....20.
Diener, Geo W Mfg Co, fruit jar, mouse ....20.
Doubleshot, Victor ....18.
Easy Set, Triumph #2, dbl coil spring ....15.
Eclipse #1, dbl under spring ....35.
Economy #1, single long spring ....35.
Electrocuter, Ratchford, mouse killer ....35.
Elgin, metal, rat ....15.
End-O-Mice, throwaway, cb snap mouse ....15.
Evans, brass, mouse & fish ....200.
EZ Set, HJ Perco Co, mouse ....20.
Fenn Mk, English, killer, rabbit ....30.
Fut Set, metal, rat ....15.
Gabriel, game & fish ....235.
Gibbs Dope Trap #3 ....250.
Gibbs Gladiator, metal snap, rat ....30.
Gomber, Beaten Path, metal, rat ....20.
Half Moon, tin, mouse ....60.
Hand Forged #4, beaver ....85.
Havahart #0, mouse sz ....10.
Hawley & Norton #3, dbl long spring ....30.
Hector #1½, long spring ....15.
Herters #1, coil spring ....6.
Herters #121, dbl jaw, dbl long spring ....80.
Herters Bear Trap, 44" L ....425.
Holdfast, wood snap, rat ....12.
Hotchkiss & Sons #2, dbl long spring ....50.
Imbra, English, killer ....35.
It, tin, mouse ....40.
Jack Frost, Nev-R-Lose #1 ....25.
Jillson's, spear, mole ....130.
Juby, English, killer ....40.
Kangaroo, Triumph #3, coil spring ....12.
Ketchum Runway Trap #2 ....30.
King Bee #0, coil spring ....30.
Klincher, wood snap, mouse ....15.
Kwik Grip #1, coil spring ....12.
Lic-Lur, metal snap, rat ....15.
Louisiana Special, Victor ....15.
Lovell, 4-hole wood choker, mouse ....15.
Luth Hardware Co, wood snap, mouse ....8.
Master Grip, Triumph #34X, dbl coil spring ....150.
Mockba CCCP, Russian, wood snap, mouse ....20.

Montgomery Digger #2, coil spring 45.00
Montgomery Step In #1½, coil 8.00
Museum Special, snap type, mouse 15.00
Nash, choker, mole 8.00
Nelson Boode Trailsend #7, dbl long spring 300.00
Nesbit Pat 1887 #1, single long spring 400.00
New York, wood snap, mouse 10.00
Newhouse #0, single long spring 40.00
Newhouse #15, bear 350.00
Newhouse #3½, w/teeth, single long spring 35.00
Newhouse #5, bear 350.00
OK Rat Trap, Abington Trap Co, wood snap 22.00
Oneida Community #0, jump 10.00
Oneida Community #14, jump, w/teeth 35.00
Prott #1½, single long spring 30.00
PS&W Good Luck #1, swastika cut in pan 50.00
PS&W Victoria #1, single long spring 50.00
Pullinger's Repeating Live Mouse, wood 125.00
Quigley, wood snap, mouse 12.00
Reddick Mole, spear-type killer 12.00
Rev-O-Noc #103, dbl long spring 35.00
Rex, Lovell Co, wood snap, rat 15.00
Runway, tin, mouse 15.00
Sabo, den trap, w/setting tool 65.00
Sargent #23, dbl long spring 150.00
Sav-A-Leg #110 ....40.00
Shene #4, coil spring 125.00
Sherman, folding aluminum box, mouse 15.00
Sta-Kawt #1, single long spring 10.00
Star, metal snap, rat 80.00
Taylor Special #2, dbl long spring 20.00
Tom Cat, wood snap, mouse 15.00
Tornado, McGill Mfg Co, wood snap, rat 18.00
Trailsend #2, dbl long spring 100.00
Triumph #415X, dbl long spring 135.00
Triumph Three Jaw #1, single long spring 25.00
U-Neek, Otto Kamphe, glass, mouse 90.00
US Standard, Gibbs #3, dbl long spring 60.00
Verbail #2, chain ft snare 125.00
Victor #1, long spring 5.00
Victor #22, dbl coil spring 12.00
Victor Special #11, single long spring 30.00
Vee Stinky Fly Trap, metal 35.00
Viggington Mouse Exterminator, glass 38.00
Woods & Waters killer 12.00
World's Best Roach Trap, Memphis TN 35.00

Trivets

Although strictly a decorative item today, the original purpose of the trivet was much more practical. They were used to protect table tops from hot serving dishes, and irons heated on the kitchen range were placed on trivets during use to protect work surfaces. The first patent date was 1869; many of the earliest trivets bore portraits of famous people or patriotic designs. Florals, birds, animals, and fruit were other favored motifs. Watch for remakes of early original designs. Some of these are marked Wilton, Emig, Wright, Iron Art, and V.M. for Virginia Metalcrafters. However, many of these reproductions are becoming collectible in the '90s. Expect to pay considerably less for these than for the originals, since they are in abundance.

Brass

Cutout top, ped ft, 9½x7" dia 90.00

English, openwork, rectangular, 12x4" 75.00
English, ornate pierced work, ped ft, 1850s, 9¼x9" sq ...115.00
English, repousse w/stippled bkground, ftd, ca 1900, 7" sq ...70.00
Fox & tree design on V formation, 7¼" L 135.00
Smooth top w/fancy scalloped border, 4-ftd, 3½x8" dia 135.00

Wrought iron trivet, formed as a snake, 11", $550.00.

Cast Iron

Banded Sheath, ca 1900, toy, 5⅜x2" 40.00
Cathedral pattern, toy, 3¾x1⅝" 20.00
Cherubs, Wilton 12.00
Crown & Maltese Cross, 6⅛x4⅛" 25.00
Dmn shape w/5 in center, 4-ftd, 7x4" 40.00
Doves emb near bottom, open point contains X-bars, 11" ...45.00
Geo Washington bust in relief, long hdl, 9½" 300.00
Girl's torso as hdl, heart/circle openwork w/'W,' 9½" 30.00
God Bless Our Home around horseshoe, dtd 1892, EX 62.00
Good Luck For Us All on horseshoe, ftd, 7½x4½" 95.00
Good Luck on horseshoe, scroll hdl, 8x4⅝" 35.00
Grapes, Wilton 10.00
Horseshoe w/1884 in center, short metal hdl 58.00
Open circle contains 4 open hearts, heart at hdl end, 6" ...85.00
Order of Cincinnati pattern, 4-leg, 9⅜x5⅜" 55.00
Sunburst in point, open scrolls on str side, loop hdl, 11" ...125.00

Wrought Iron

Arrow-shaped ft, simple tooling, 9¾" L 225.00
Leafy plant device w/in open triangle, loop hdl, 11" ...280.00
Open circle w/2 'waves,' 4½" dia 145.00
Open heart shape, no hdl, 5" 145.00
Open heart shape w/loops inside by point, hdl, sgn, 7" ...250.00
Revolving, 22½x11" 125.00
V formation w/in simple strapwork triangular fr, hdl, 11" ...100.00

Trolls

The modern-day version of the troll was designed in 1952 by Helena and Marti Kuuskoski of Tampere, Finland. Those made by Dam and those marked with a horseshoe are among the most valuable, since both are made from the original Kuuskoski design. Many copies have been produced, the best of which are the Wishniks, made by the Uneeda Doll Company. These were first marketed in 1979 and are currently still available. Troll animals are scarce, and values are rising. New Dam animals are easily distinguished from the old ones, and though they are popular sellers, it's the old issues that hold their value and collectors' interest. Our advisor for this category is Roger Inouye; he is listed in the Directory under California.

Ape	75.00
Astronaut, red hair, Dam Things, 12"	125.00
Common, 10"	50.00
Common, 12"	75.00
Common, 18"	100.00
Common, 2½" to 3", minimum	15.00
Common, 5", from $20.00 up to	25.00
Common, 7", from $30 up to	40.00
Cow	65.00
Donkey	80.00
Elephant, gray w/red bell, Dam, lg	215.00
Giraffe	65.00
Gorilla	45.00
Halloween mask & costume, Wishnik, MIB	75.00
Hawaiian	15.00
Horse, Dam Things, 9"	225.00
Jolly Nessen, Denmark	50.00
Lamp, Wishnik, complete, rare, 18"	225.00
Love Bug, orig clothes, Regal, 4½"	115.00
Mr & Mrs Santa Claus	25.00
Pencil topper, Dam Things, 1965, 1½"	32.50
Porcupine	38.00
Scandia House, 1965, w/tags, 3"	38.00
Turtle	50.00
Viking, molded helmet & sword, Dam Things, 3½"	120.00

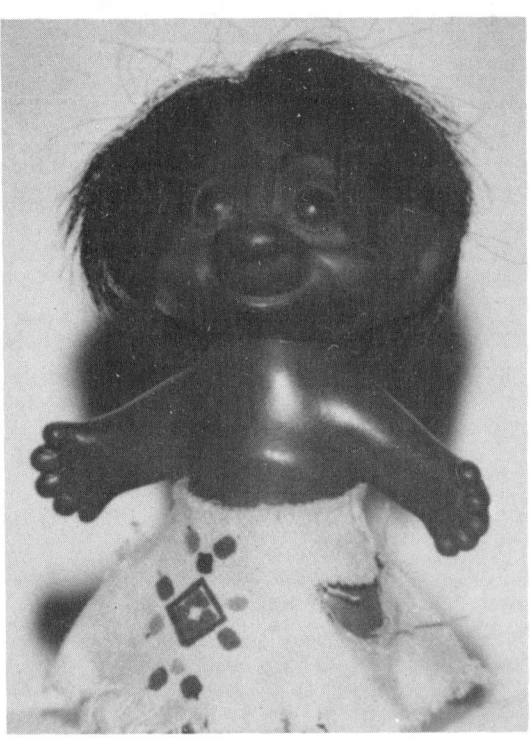

Wishnik, black with painted black eyes, rooted hair, Indian dress, 3½", $75.00.

2-headed, all orig, 1965, 3"	45.00
2-headed, 8"	175.00

Trunks

In the the days of steamboat voyages, stagecoach journeys, and railroad travel, trunks were used to transport clothing and personal belongings. Some, called 'dome top' or 'turtle backs,' were rounded on top to better accommodate milady's finery. Today some of the more interesting examples are used in various ways in home decorating. For instance, a flat-topped trunk may become a coffee table, while a smaller dome style may be 'home' for antique dolls or a teddy bear collection. In the listings that follow, the dimension given is length.

Iron-bound dome-top oak trunk, Teutonic, dated 1502 but probably early 19th century, initialed, 32x48x24", $1,200.00.

Oak, dome lid, dvtl, primitive, edge rpr, 47"	175.00
Pine w/gr pnt, dome top, iron hdw, 1800s, 40" L	500.00
Pine w/mc floral, dome top, iron bound, some rpt, 32"	190.00
Pine w/pnt, dome top, wrought iron straps, 1868, 54", EX	300.00
Pine w/red & yel grpt, dome top, dvtl, 41", VG	90.00
Pine w/worn gray pnt, dome top, iron binding, key, 33"	100.00
Pine/poplar w/red & blk grpt, dome top, 28" L	250.00

Tuthill

The Tuthill Glass Company operated in Middletown, New York, from 1902 to 1923. Collectors look for signed pieces and those with an identifiable pattern. Condition is of utmost importance, and examples with brilliant cutting and intaglio (natural flowers and fruits) combined fetch the highest prices.

Bread tray, Vintage, intaglio grapes, hobstars, 9¾x7"	750.00
Cake plate, hobstars/X-hatching/X-cut fans, low std, 10"	400.00
Comport, morning-glories, cut stem, att, 7½x6"	175.00
Plate, Wild Rose Intaglio, 8¼"	275.00
Vase, Blackberry Intaglio, 10"	200.00
Vase, flashed hobstars in ped ft, fan form, 11½"	900.00
Vase, Primrose, star-cut base, urn shape, 14"	725.00

Typewriters

The first commercially successful typewriter was the Sholes and Glidden, introduced in 1874. By 1882 other models appeared, and by the 1890s dozens were on the market. At the time of the First World War, the ranks of typewriter-makers thinned, and by the 1920s only a few survived.

Collectors informally divide typewriter history into the pioneering

od, up to about 1890; the classic period, from 1890 to 1920; and the
dern period, since 1920. There are two broad classifications of early
ewriters: (1) Keyboard machines, in which depression of a key prints
haracter and via a shift key prints up to three different characters per
. (2) Index machines, in which a chart of all the characters appears
the typewriter; the character is selected by a pointer or dial and is
ited by operation of a lever or other device. Even though index
ewriters were simpler and more primitive than keyboard machines,
y were none-the-less a later development, designed to provide a
aper alternative to the standard keyboard models that were selling
upwards of $100. Eventually second-hand keyboard typewriters sup-
d the low-price customer, and index typewriters vanished except as
s. Both classes of typewriters appeared in a great many designs.

It is difficult, if not impossible, to assign standard market prices to
ly typewriters. Unlike collectors of postage stamps, carnival glass,
., few people collect typewriters, so there is no active marketplace
m which to draw stable prices. Also, condition is a very important
tor, and typewriters can vary infinitely in condition. A third factor
consider is that an early typewriter achieves its value mainly through
skill, effort, and patience of the collector who restores it to its origi-
condition, in which case its purchase price is insignificant. Some
usual-looking early typewriters are not at all rare or valuable, while
ne very ordinary-looking ones are scarce and could be quite valuable.
general rules apply. When no condition is indicated, the items
ed below are assumed to be in excellent, unrestored condition. Our
visor for this category is Mike Brooks; he is listed in the Directory
der California.

ng #2, 1926, EX...135.00
ckensderfer #5, wood case, +manual & accessories 135.00
nkensderfer Electric, 1903 ....2,000.00
ooks...525.00
andall..1,000.00
ison, index 1,000.00
ch..700.00
ll, index 165.00
mmond Multiplex, for all languages, w/accessories, M 265.00
iver #5 Standard Visible Writer, old upright keys, M 85.00
mington Rand #5, portable, 1930s, EX in case 50.00
yal #10, 1922, EX 50.00

Smith #1 Premier, $115.00.

mith-Corona #4, portable, 1920s, EX in case 50.00
ictor, index 215.00
orld, last Pat date 1885, orig case 200.00

Uhl Pottery

Founded in Evansville, Indiana, in 1849 by German immigrants,
the Uhl Pottery was moved to Huntingburg, Indiana, in 1908 because
of the more suitable clay available there. They produced stoneware —
Acorn Ware jugs, crocks, and bowls — which were marked with the
acorn logo and 'Uhl Pottery.' They also made mugs, pitchers, and vases
in simple shapes and solid glazes marked with a circular ink stamp containing the name of the pottery and 'Huntingburg, Indiana.' The pottery closed in the mid-1940s. Those seeking additional information
about Uhl pottery are encouraged to contact the Uhl Collectors' Society, whose address is listed in the Directory under Clubs, Newsletters,
and Catalogs.

Ashtray, bl, mk, #140 ....125.00
Bowl, batter; pk, mk, 10" 90.00
Bowl, DOG, gr, #145, 7½" 70.00
Bowl, mixing; basketweave, wht, 10" 45.00
Bowl, mixing; reverse pyramid, bl, 9" 60.00
Bowl, Tulip, brn, #120, mk, 6½" 45.00
Candle holder, gr, hand-trn, w/shield 100.00
Casserole, bl, mk, #151 ....70.00
Casserole, bl, mk, #528, 5-pt 60.00
Cookie jar, globe, pk 100.00

**Cookie jar, yellow, #522, circular blue mark, M,
$75.00.**

Cookie jar, yel, mk, #522 ....75.00
Jar, Acorn Ware, 10-gal 80.00
Jar, Acorn Ware, 3-gal 50.00
Jug, Acorn Ware, wht, 5-gal 65.00
Jug, Acorn Ware, 1-gal 35.00
Jug, baseball, wht, mini 75.00
Jug, bellied, pk, #176, ½-pt 35.00
Jug, canteen, pk, ½-pt 45.00
Jug, Egyptian, bl, #125, 25-oz 65.00
Jug, Grecian, bl, #8, 2½-oz 50.00
Jug, harvest, w/air vent, wire bail 125.00
Jug, Merry Christmas, 1937, mini 225.00
Jug, shoulder; Great Smoky Mts advertising, 2-oz 175.00

Mug, bbl form, pk, mk, 3-oz 90.00
Mug, bbl form, Rhinegold advertising, 20-oz 80.00
Mug, bbl form, tan, mk, 16-oz 15.00
Mug, grape, bl, 16-oz 125.00
Pitcher, acid, brn, mk, 1-qt 45.00
Pitcher, bellied, bl/wht sponging, 1-gal 300.00
Pitcher, bl, ice restrainer, 5-pt 90.00
Pitcher, rustic bbl form, brn, 100-oz 50.00
Plate, gr, mk, 10" 40.00
Shoe, Dutch; yel, #3 ....25.00
Shoe, lady's slipper, mk, mini, pr 85.00
Vase, cut flower, pk, #113, mk 45.00
Vase, cut flower, wht, #117, mk 40.00
Vase, gr, #152, mk 50.00
Vase, tan, mk, #22, mini 50.00
Vase, yel, mk, #30, mini 85.00

Unger Brothers

The Art Nouveau silver produced by Unger Brothers, who operated in Newark, New Jersey, from the early 1880s until 1909, is fast becoming very popular with today's collectors. In addition to tableware, they also made brushes, mirrors, powder boxes, and the like for milady's dressing table as well as jewelry and small personal accessories such as match safes and flasks. They often marked their products with a circle seal containing an intertwined 'UB' and '925 fine sterling.' In addition to sterling, a very limited amount of gold was also used. Note: This company made no pewter items; Unger designs may occasionally be found in pewter, but these are copies. Items dated in the mark or signed 'Birmingham' are English (not Unger).

Ashtray, lady whose flowing hair wraps around face of man in the moon, 7" wide, $700.00.

Baby's food pusher, monogram, 4" 325.00
Bowl, repousse, w/monogram, 6½" 95.00
Box, jewelry; domed velvet lift-off top, 2½x3¾" dia 575.00
Clothes brush, heavy repousse floral, 7" 145.00
Curling iron, Love's Dream, travel stand collapses 625.00
Fork, pickle; Duvaine 55.00
Glove stretcher, 9" 235.00
Hatpin, Nouveau lady, repousse, mk/#925, 1" on 8½" pin 145.00
Letter opener, ivory blade 250.00
Pincushion, coin shape, rim holds pins, mirror bk, EX 185.00
Sewing awl, 6" 175.00
Soap dish, very ornate lid, shaped sides, 3¾x2¾x2" 575.00
Spoon, berry; Duvaine 335.00

Thimble case, walnut figural, w/chatelaine loop, 1" 255.0
Vase, for automobile, 6" 325.0

Universal

Universal Potteries Incorporated operated in Cambridge, Oh from 1934 to 1956. Many lines of dinnerware and kitchen items we produced in both earthenware and semiporcelain. In 1956 the empha was shifted to the manufacture of floor and wall tiles, and the name w changed to the Oxford Tile Company, Division of Universal Potteri The plant closed in 1976. Our advisor for this category is Ted Haun; is listed in the Directory under Indiana.

Ballerina, creamer 10.0
Ballerina, cup 5.0
Ballerina, egg cup 16.0
Ballerina, shakers, pr 12.0
Calico Fruit, bowl, w/lid, 5" 20.0
Calico Fruit, custard cup, 5-oz 3.5
Calico Fruit, plate, utility; 11½" 17.5
Calico Fruit, plate, 6" 4.0
Calico Fruit, refrigerator jug 20.0
Calico Fruit, water jug 28.0
Cattail, bowl, berry; sm 6.5
Cattail, butter dish, 1-lb 37.5
Cattail, jug, cork stopper 28.0
Cattail, pie plate 15.0
Cattail, pie server 18.0
Cattail, platter, 14¾x10½" 18.0
Cattail, shakers, pr 12.0
Cattail, soup, flat 12.5
Cattail, spoon, long 18.0
Cattail, sugar bowl, open, Sears 3.5
Cattail, teapot 25.0
Cattail, tumbler, glass, 4¾" 17.0
Cattail, tumbler, pottery 35.0
Circus, pie server 18.0

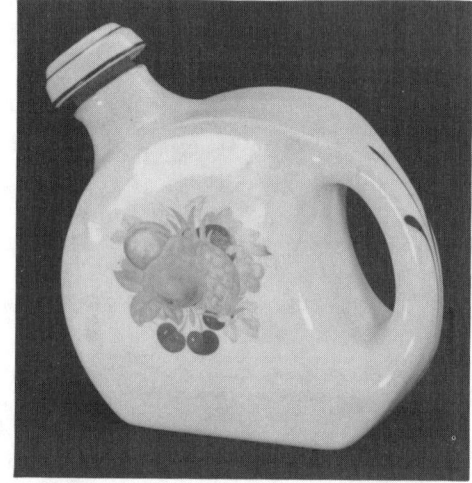

Fruit pattern water jug, $40.00.

Fruit & Flowers, tray, utility 14.0
Iris, casserole, w/lid 18.0
Iris, jug, canteen 18.0
Largo, pie baker, 10" 10.0

Largo, plate, luncheon **4.00**
Largo, shakers, pr **6.00**
Poppy, shakers, pr **12.00**
Rambler Rose, gravy boat **7.50**
Rambler Rose, pitcher, milk **17.50**
Rambler Rose, plate, dinner **2.50**
Windmill, bowl, utility; w/lid **5.50**
Woodvine, creamer & sugar bowl, w/lid **17.00**
Woodvine, cup & saucer **7.50**
Woodvine, shakers, pr **12.00**

Val St. Lambert

Since its inception in Belgium at the turn of the 19th century, the Val St. Lambert Cristalleries has been involved in the production of high quality glass, specializing in cameo. The factory is still in production. Our advisor for this category is Don Williams; he is listed in the Directory under Missouri.

Cameo

Lamp, flowers on shallow shade & candlestick base, 11" **850.00**
Tumbler, flowers, leaves & scrolls, gr on clear, unmk, 4x4½" **125.00**

Vase, cameo elderberry plants, amethyst on clear, 10", $700.00.

Vase, elderberry plants, amethyst on clear, stick neck, 10" **700.00**
Vase, flowers, gold-traced on textured emerald, 8½" **300.00**
Vase, Venetian canal scene, dbl o/l, baluster, 12" **600.00**

Valentines

Handmade Valentines date back to the mid-1700s in the United States; as time went on, increased interest resulted in other types of Valentine cards being made. Today Valentine collectors are not the only ones who buy; Valentines are often considered a desirable addition to other collections as well — Black memorabilia, advertising, transportation memorabilia, Walt Disney, cartoon and movie characters, etc. Besides examples representing these areas, 3-dimensionals and mechanical Valentines (1860s to the present) are becoming highly prized by many collectors. There are six qualifying specifications to

consider when evaluating a Valentine card: age, size, category, manufacturer, artist signature, and condition. Our advisor for this category is Katherine Kreider; she is listed in the Directory under California.

Key: HCPP — honeycomb paper puff

Airplane, 2-D, chromolitho, MIG, 1920s, 4⅜x3½x3", EX **30.00**
Airplane, 3-D, lobster on wing, MIG, 1920, 9x8", NM **125.00**
Ambassador, 3-D, train, 1960, 7x10", EX **35.00**
Angel amid flowers, 2-D, chromolitho, MIG, 1900s, 3x4x2", NM ...**25.00**
Ballerina, chromolitho, HCPP tutu, MIG, 1927, 5¼x4½", EX **30.00**
Big-eyed boy, litho, cobweb center, 1900s, EX **75.00**
Big-eyed child rides mechanical duck, 5½x7", VG **35.00**
Big-eyed children in 1920s car w/dog, 2-D, 7x8x3", VG **75.00**
Big-eyed girl in bonnet, mechanical litho, MIG, '23, 8x5", EX **45.00**
Big-eyed kids on HCPP atomizer, tab stand, '20s, 8x7½", NM ...**150.00**
Black child under sprinkling can, USA, 1940s, 5½x3½", NM **35.00**
Black harmonica player, USA, 1900s, 3¾x2¾", NM **40.00**
Brownie & Cub Scout, USA, 1960s, 6x3¼", EX **15.00**
Buster Brown, mechanical, chromolitho, MIG, 9¼x6½", NM ...**175.00**
Cagney, James; USA, 1935, 5⅞x3½", EX **45.00**
Cherub on HCPP base of 3-D windmill, chromolitho, 5½", NM ..**35.00**
Cherub w/butterfly net, 2-D, litho, MIG, 4x2½x1½", NM **55.00**
Choked to Death, dtd 1909, 7½x6", NM in orig box **175.00**
Cinderella-type coach, 3-D w/HCPP, 1900s, 11¼x13x6", VG **95.00**
Clapsaddle, cherub in cart w/hearts, 3-D, 4¼x6¼x2½", NM **75.00**
Cobweb, HP orig, 1850, 8x9", EX **250.00**
Dirigible, HCPP top, child in basket, tab stand, MIG, 4", EX **50.00**
Dopey, mechanical, Walt Disney Enterprises, 4¼x3", NM **75.00**
Drayton, Grace; 3-D, children w/pony, USA, 9⅜x7½", NM **125.00**

Dutch boy with original piece of Wrigley's gum, 6½x3½", NM, $75.00.

Elephant w/clown, USA, 1940s, 4½x3½", NM **10.00**
Geppetto on raft, mechanical, Walt Disney Productions, '39, EX ...**65.00**
Girl & boy at piano, 2-D, MIG, 3⅜x4x1", EX **45.00**
Goat & cart, girl delivers milk, tab stand, USA, 10x7", VG **35.00**
Hallmark, 3-D castle, 1958, 9x14", NM **50.00**
Halls Bros, dog w/felt ears, 1940s, 8½x6¾", VG **15.00**
Hanging, litho hearts, 4 tiers w/orig ribbon, 12", EX **75.00**
Harp, litho stands w/tab accented w/Victorian scraps, 7", EX **75.00**
HCPP, apple core w/2 litho children, USA, '20s, 10¼", NM **125.00**
HCPP basket & hearts, litho cherubs, ca 1925, 8½", EX **85.00**

Hold-to-light, 3-D children w/pk flowers, MIG, 8¼", NM 150.00
Hot air balloon, litho w/orig ribbon, MIG, 9½x4", NM 150.00
Howland, Esther; orig, 1845, EX, w/HP envelope 350.00
Kautz, artist paints portrait, mechanical, '25, 6x4½", EX 35.00
Kautz, boy in winter garb, mechanical, tab stand, 7⅜", EX 25.00
Kautz, cat, mechanical, tab stand, USA, 1925, 4½x3½", NM 35.00
Kautz, cowboy on horse, mechanical, tab stand, USA, 6¾", EX ...45.00
Loverville Telephone Card, cast metal phone, 4x3¼", EX 75.00
Manuscript type w/HP litho, 1845, 5x8", EX 100.00
Mechanical, airplane, 1940s-50s, 3¼x4½", EX 8.00
Mechanical, baseball player, USA, 1940s, 5½x3", NM 20.00
Mechanical, bear on stump, Stecher Litho, tab stand, 5", EX 25.00
Mechanical, chubby child on scales, MIG, 6¼x3¼", NM 25.00
Mechanical, cow, head & neck moves, USA, '40s, 7¼x4¾", NM ..20.00
Mechanical, girl w/slate, litho, tab stand, 1924, 6x4", EX 20.00
Mechanical, gypsy, USA, 6½x2¼", NM 15.00
Mechanical, lobster, tab stand, MIG, '27, 6¾x4½", EX 35.00
Mechanical, miner panning for gold, Canada, 5½x3", EX 15.00
Mechanical, parrot, chromolitho, tab stand, MIG, 6¾", EX 35.00
Mechanical, Russian bear & child, tab stand, MIG, 8½", EX 55.00
Native American w/orig feather, USA, 7x4", EX 35.00
Nister, boy & girl, litho, Bavaria, 1900s, 4¾x3", EX 35.00
Nister, mother & children, hanging litho, #114, 13x6½", VG 80.00
Olive Oyl & Popeye, USA, 1940s, 5¾x5", EX 45.00
Pinocchio, mechanical, Walt Disney Enterprises, 1938, 5", NM ..75.00
St Bernard dog, w/orig chain to doghouse, MIG, 10", VG 75.00
Steamship, 4-D all orig, MIG, 10½x6x3", 1900s, NM 250.00
Tuck, Artistic Series, carriage/Blk Child/3-D flowers, 7", VG 95.00
Tuck, girl w/orig ribbon in hair, Series #1557, 5x2", NM 75.00
Tuck, horse-drawn carriage, 3-D, 6½x10⅜x4½", EX 175.00
Uncle Sam, Made in USA, 1943, 5x6", VG 15.00
3-D Victorian scene in open heart, To My..., MIG, 3½", NM 75.00

Van Briggle

The Van Briggle Pottery of Colorado Springs, Colorado, was established in 1901 by Artus Van Briggle, whose early career had been shaped by such notables as Karl Langenbeck and Maria Nichols Storer. His quest for several years had been to perfect a completely flat matt glaze; and, upon accomplishing his goal, he opened his pottery. His wife, Anne, worked with him, and they, along with George Young, were responsible for the modeling of the wares. Their work typified the flow and form of the Art Nouveau movement, and the shapes they designed played as important a part in their success as their glazes. Some of their most famous pieces were Despondency, Lorelei, and Toast Cup. Increasing demand for their work soon made it necessary to add to their quarters as well as their staff. Although much of the ware was eventually made from molds, each piece was carefully trimmed and refined before the glaze was sprayed on. Their most popular colors were Persian Rose, Ming Blue, and Mustard Yellow.

Van Briggle died in 1904, but the work was continued by his wife. New facilities were built; and by 1908, in addition to their artware, tiles, gardenware, and commercial lines were added. By the twenties the emphasis had shifted from art pottery to novelties and commercial wares. As late as 1970, reproductions of some of the early designs continued to be made. Until about 1920 most pieces were marked with the date and shape number; after that the AA mark was used.

Bookends, owl w/spread wings form, bl-gr, dbl A mk, 5" 250.00
Bookends, polar bear, Persian Rose w/bl accents, 5x5½" 275.00
Bowl, floral, bl, 1916, 3x8½" 275.00
Bowl, lt to dk bl, ftd, dtd 1917, 5x10" 300.00
Bowl, spade leaf band, lt bl, #579, 1907, 8" 950.00

Chamberstick, leaf-shape hood, gr, 5½" 165.00
Figurine, donkey, dk gray, 4x3" 60.00
Figurine, elephant, raised trunk, sienna brn, 3x4" 60.00
Figurine, Indian girl w/bowl, Persian Rose, 6" 250.00

Night light, lavender with blue highlights, ca 1915, 6", $375.00.

Plaque, bust of lady w/hair blowing bk, rose w/gr-bl, 9x12" 500.00
Plate, floral, dk turq on burgundy, #17, 1908-11, 8" 450.00
Vase, bl/gr, #654, 1908-11, 4" 195.00
Vase, columbine on yel, gourd form, #188, 1903, 6" 1,000.00
Vase, crocuses, ochre, #145, 1903, 3¾x4¾" 800.00
Vase, daffodils, maroon/bl, EX mold, #738, 10" 425.00
Vase, feathered apple gr, top width, incurvate, 1905, 6x4" 500.00
Vase, feathered gr/purple, #378, 1905, 15x10" 1,350.00
Vase, flamingo, lt bl w/cobalt overspray, ca 1935, 22", pr 3,850.00
Vase, floral, red w/bl touches, 1914, 4" 125.00
Vase, gray-gr texture, bulbous, #476, 1907, 5x4" 400.00
Vase, leaves, gr mottle, thick bottle form, #202, 1903, 10" 1,700.00
Vase, leaves alternate w/3-petal flower, dk red, 1907, 9x9" 1,400.00
Vase, leaves at top, red/gr, cylindrical, 7" 140.00
Vase, leaves/berries at top, yel over gr, #502, 1907, 9" 850.00
Vase, lily pads, feathery purple, #106, 1903, rstr, 15x6" 2,700.00
Vase, Nouveau floral, dk brn, #217, 1904, hairline, 10" 500.00
Vase, peacock feathers, gr, cylindrical, 1904, 11" 1,600.00
Vase, Persian Rose, #310, ca 1920, 3¼" 65.00
Vase, plants, very stylized, gr w/blk, #721, 1908-11, 14x10" 3,000.00
Vase, pods w/long stems, gr on bl, #853, 1908-11, 8" 1,000.00
Vase, poppies at shoulder, mc w/drips, #150, 1903, 11x9" 5,000.00
Vase, rose, bulbous shoulder, #256, 1905, 10" 650.00
Vase, shield/spider/tomahawk/man, lt gr, 1902, 4x4", NM 500.00
Vase, shoulder band, lime gr, #424, 1906, 3½" 180.00
Vase, tulips, lt gr w/tan clay exposed, 1906, #450, 7" 235.00
Vase, 3 Indian faces, Persian Rose w/dk bl, Co Spgs, 11" 550.00
Vase, 4 Indian head masks around top, Persian Rose, 12x5" 325.00

Venetian Glass

Venetian glass is a thin, fragile ware usually made in colors, often with internal gold or silver flecks. It was produced on the island of

Murano, near Venice, as early as the 13th century. 20th-century glassware is always heavier and thicker than the older ware. Note: Only special 1920s pieces are commanding high prices. The '50s pieces have come down in price, because many of these companies are still in business today and are reissuing '50s designs. Ribbon glass scent bottles with flower stoppers; small leaf-shape compotes with bird head finials; figural pieces such as clowns, fish and roosters; and handkerchief vases are among 'new' items currently on the market. Most carry the Murano label.

Ashtray, clown standing, Murano, 7½" 125.00
Ashtray, swirls of gold flecks & red, Murano, 3x6" 105.00
Ashtray, wht/red/silver, cased in wht, lg 85.00
Bottle, scent; sea horse, Salviati, 12" 95.00
Candelabra, appl bl rigaree on verre-de-soie, '10s, 16", pr 750.00
Candlestick, dbl; flower center, lt yel ruffles/cups 70.00

Clowns, 11", $350.00; 9", $250.00.

Dresser set, gr/blk/copper, Murano, 5-pc 450.00
Dresser set, wht spirals, gold mica stoppers, 1925, 3-pc 395.00
Figurine, bird, gr w/gold flecks, 15" 125.00
Figurine, clown, hands out, blk shoes, many colors, label, 8" 150.00
Figurine, dog, seated, clear w/blk/wht/gold inclusions, 9" 400.00
Figurine, duck, blk w/silver flecks, sm 195.00
Figurine, lady, bl gown, lg hat, gold dusted gown/hair, 12" 225.00
Finger bowl, gold flecks, ruffled, 4¾", +7" plate 225.00
Goblet, pigeon blood w/gold flakes, HP lovers scene, 8" 225.00
Tumbler, turq/gold swirls, gold threads, berry prunts, ftd 125.00
Vase, gold & clear, Cappelin, 10" 175.00
Vase, handkerchief; latticinio, unmk, 10" 300.00
Vase, pk w/wht lattice at shoulder, rnd w/angle hdls, 10" 700.00
Vase, swirled/overlapping red Xs on clear, 11" 225.00

Venini Glass

Fine contemporary art glass signed Venini (sometimes with Murano added) has been commanding high prices in some of the Eastern auction galleries. Art Deco items and those from the fifties are the most sought after.

Ashtray, patchwork, Barovier 445.00
Bottle, ocean bl, striated texture, shouldered, #4588, 9" 400.00
Box, topaz w/orange casing, spiral pattern, 6" dia 650.00
Dish, hat shape, clear/swirling, blk rim/knob, 8" 245.00
Figurine, bird, red & gold, Barovier, 18" 225.00

Figurine, poodle, blk w/wht eyes on bl base, label, 5½" 400.00
Sculpture, fluted gr base, red/wht spirals, cone top, 11" 550.00
Sculpture, oval on 6-sided gr base, 3-color int spirals, 7" 300.00
Vase, amber, heavy clear bottom, air bubbles, cylinder, 14" 325.00
Vase, amber, ribbed, Martinuzzi, 8" 535.00
Vase, aquamarine, oval off-center opening, bimorphic, 12" 1,700.00
Vase, bl/yel/clear, Flavio Poli for Seguso, 10" 335.00
Vase, handkerchief; med bl cased, sgn, 7x7" 650.00
Vase, handkerchief; orange/lav latticinio bands, mk, 5x10" 495.00
Vase, internal wht spirals, gourd form, 1950, Murano, 8" 550.00
Vase, narrow clear stripes alternate w/bands of color, 4" 330.00

Vase, patchwork design with red, blue, green, and clear squares, slightly flattened, Fulvio Bianconi, ca 1957, 8", NM, $7,500.00.

Vase, red & gold w/flower hdls, Barovier, 12" 450.00
Vase, spiraling bl/gr stripes, cylindrical, Tapio, 14" 1,100.00
Vase, 6-color bands, flared cylinder w/irregular rim, 6" 650.00

Verlys

Verlys art glass, produced in France after 1931 by the Holophane Company of Verlys, was made in crystal with acid-finished relief work in the Art Deco style. Colored and opalescent glass was also used. In 1935 an American branch was opened in Newark, Ohio, where very similar wares were produced. French Verlys was signed with one of three mold-impressed script signatures, all containing the company name and country of origin. The American-made glassware was signed 'Verlys' only, either scratched with a diamond-tipped pen or impressed in the mold. There is very little if any difference in value between items produced in France and America. Though some seem to feel that the French should be higher priced (assuming it to be scarce), many prefer the American-made product.

In June of 1955, about sixteen Verlys molds were leased to the A.H. Heisey Company. Heisey's versions were not signed with the Verlys name; so if an item is unsigned, it is almost certainly a Heisey piece. The molds were returned to Verlys of America in July 1957. Our advisor for this category is Don Frost; he is listed in the Directory under Oregon.

Bowl, beaded bands, rectangular, 16" L 600.00
Bowl, Butterflies & Blossoms, clear w/frost, 14" 400.00
Bowl, Chrysanthem (known as Casket), opal, 6¼x10" 275.00

Bowl, Goldfish, fishtail hdls, frosted, 19" W 250.00
Bowl, Poppy, crystal etch, 3x14" 195.00
Bowl, Thistle, 8½" 68.00
Box, bouquet of coreopsis emb on lid, opal, 6¾" dia 300.00
Charger, Birds & Dragonflies, 12" 125.00
Figurine, pigeon, frosted, 4¼" 285.00

Thistle bowl, blue, 8½", $180.00.

Vase, Butterflies, 5" 225.00
Vase, Lovebirds, crystal frost, fan form, 4¾", pr 150.00
Vase, Mandarin, 9" 295.00
Vase, Mermaids & Dolphins, amber, 10½" 800.00
Vase, Mermaids & Dolphins, electric bl, 11", NM 750.00

Vernon Kilns

    Vernon Potteries Ltd. was established by Faye G. Bennison in Vernon, California, in 1931. The name was later changed to Vernon Kilns; until it closed in 1958, dinnerware and figurines were their primary products. Among its wares most sought after by collectors today are items designed by such famous artists as Rockwell Kent, Walt Disney, and Don Blanding. Our advisor for this category is Maxine Nelson; she is listed in the Directory under California.

Ashtray, Connecticut 12.50
Barkwood, bowl, divided; oval 9.00
Barkwood, creamer & sugar bowl, w/lid 10.00
Barkwood, cup & saucer 4.50
Barkwood, plate, 10" 4.50
Barkwood, plate, 6" 2.00
Barkwood, platter, 13½" 10.00
Barkwood, shakers, pr 7.00
Brown-Eyed Susan, chop plate, 12" 12.00
Brown-Eyed Susan, teapot 45.00
Delores, teapot, HP 35.00
Dreamtime, bowl, chowder 5.00
Dreamtime, plate, 6" 5.00
Dumbo, figurine, lying on ear, #40 ....75.00
Dumbo, figurine, Mr Stork 800.00
Dumbo, figurine, sitting, #41 ....150.00
Early California, chop plate, 13" 25.00
Early California, creamer 14.00
Early California, cup 15.00
Early California, lug soup 12.00

Early California, platter, 12" 18.00
Fantasia, bowl, Sprites, HP, #125, 11½" 250.00
Fantasia, figurine, baby Pegasus, #19 ....300.00
Fantasia, figurine, Centaurette, #17 ....650.00
Fantasia, figurine, elephant in pk, #25, 5" 400.00
Fantasia, shakers, Milk Weed, pr 40.00
Fantasia, shakers, mushroom, pr 110.00
Fantasia, vase, goldfish, c 1940 Walt Disney, #121 ....300.00
Frontier Days, shakers, pr 38.50
Gingham, bowl, serving; rnd, 9" 16.00
Gingham, casserole, hdls 25.00
Gingham, coffee carafe 28.00
Gingham, pitcher, ice lip, 2-qt, 11½" 45.00
Gingham, pitcher, 1-pt, 7" 18.00
Gingham, soup bowl, rimmed, 8½" 12.00

Harvest plate, 12", $30.00.

Heavenly Days, creamer 8.00
Heavenly Days, mug 10.00
Hibiscus, tureen, lg, w/lid & underplate 325.00
Homespun, bowl, mixing; 8" 25.00
Homespun, plate, bread & butter 6.00
Mayflower, plate, 10½" 15.50
Mayflower, plate, 6" 6.00
Mayflower, platter, oval, 14" 22.50
Mojave, bowl, fruit; 5½" 5.00
Mojave, creamer 9.00
Monterey, bowl, chowder 10.00
Monterey, chop plate, 12" 20.00
Monterey, cup 12.00
Monterey, plate, 7" 8.00
Monterey, plate, 9½" 12.00
Monterey, shakers, pr 12.00
Native California, chop plate, 14" 30.00
Native California, shakers, pr 16.00
Organdie, bowl, chowder, 6" 6.00
Organdie, bowl, fruit; 5½" 3.00
Organdie, bowl, serving; 9" 15.00
Organdie, chop plate, 12" 12.00
Organdie, creamer & sugar bowl, w/lid 15.00
Organdie, cup & saucer 12.50
Organdie, gravy bowl 18.00
Organdie, mug 18.00

Organdie, pitcher, iced beverage, 2-qt 35.00
Organdie, pitcher, 1-pt, 7" 12.00
Organdie, plate, 6½" 3.50
Organdie, plate, 9¾" 10.00
Organdie, platter, oval, 10" 12.00
Organdie, platter, oval, 12" 15.00
Organdie, platter, oval, 14" 20.00
Organdie, shakers, pr 12.00
Organdie, soup, flat rim, 8" 10.00
Organdie, teapot, ind 18.00
Organdie, tidbit tray, 2-tier 22.00

Our America pitcher, 2-qt., 6½", $200.00.

Plate, Arizona map, maroon 18.00
Plate, Grand Canyon, bl 15.00
Plate, New York, mc 8.00
Plate, Spartanburg, scalloped, bl/maroon 20.00
Plate, Statue of Liberty, Davidson, mc 25.00
Rippled, cup & saucer 35.00
Rippled, plate, 10½" 30.00
Rose-A-Day, casserole, w/lid 30.00
Rose-A-Day, creamer 10.00
Rose-A-Day, platter, 13½" 17.50
Salamina, chop plate, 14" 450.00
Salamina, cup & saucer 50.00
Salamina, plate, 9½" 95.00
Salamina, sugar bowl, w/lid, regular 95.00
Salamina, tumbler 100.00
Tam O'Shanter, bowl, divided, oval, 11½" 25.00
Tam O'Shanter, mug 18.00
Tam O'Shanter, pitcher, 1-qt 30.00
Tam O'Shanter, pitcher, 2-qt 45.00
Tam O'Shanter, platter, oval, 12" 16.50
Tam O'Shanter, teapot 40.00
Tam O'Shanter, tidbit tray, 3-tier, wooden hdl 37.50
Tickled Pink, bowl, divided 25.00
Tickled Pink, cup & saucer 10.00
Tickled Pink, relish tray 22.00
Tweed, plate, 10½" 10.00
Ultra California, bowl, serving; 8" 17.00
Ultra California, bowl, serving; 9" 20.00
Ultra California, creamer 10.00

Ultra California, plate, 7½" 9.00

Viennese Enameled Ware

Box, ring; couple/cherubs in landscape, lg harp atop, 6½" 700.00
Carriage, cupids/floral garlands, ormolu mts, 3¼" 1,100.00
Clock, sq base w/4 panels, standing cupid w/dial atop, 5" 475.00
Music box, piano form, portrait w/in, 6" L 1,300.00
Music box, piano form, 2 panels w/romantic scenes, 4½" 800.00
Plaque, man plays mandolin in garden, ormolu stand, 4x6" 400.00

Villeroy and Boch

The firm of Villeroy and Boch, located in Mettlach, Germany, was brought into being by the 1841 merger of three German factories — the Wallerfangen factory, founded by Nicholas Villeroy in 1787; the Mettlach factory, founded by Jean Francis Boch 1809; and Boch's father's factory in Septfontaines, established in 1767. Villeroy and Boch produced many varieties of wares, including earthenware with printed under-glaze designs which carried the well-known castle mark with the name 'Mettlach.' See also Mettlach.

Beaker, baseball pitcher, print under glaze, ¼-liter 350.00
Beaker, soccer player, print under glaze, ¼-liter 100.00
Bowl, mixing; Bl Willow pattern, stack set, 4-pc, 4x8½" 385.00
Box, salt; bl & wht 250.00
Candlestick, geometrics, red & tan on cream, 8" 200.00
Charger, Meissen castle on Elbe, 12" 200.00
Ewer, cupid figure under spout, scroll hdl, 13" 200.00
Pitcher, bowler, print under glaze, 7¼" 125.00
Pitcher, horse rider, print under glaze, 7¼" 100.00
Pitcher, 2 soccer players, print under glaze, 7¼" 195.00
Plaque, Germania w/crown, eagle & angel, sgn RF&C, 20x14" ...465.00
Plate, touring car w/passengers, 8½" 55.00

Vistosa

Vistosa was produced from about 1938 through the early forties. It was Taylor, Smith, and Taylor's answer to the very successful Fiesta line of their nearby competitor, Homer Laughlin. Vistosa was made in four solid colors: mango red, cobalt blue, light green, and deep yellow. 'Pie crust' edges and a dainty five-petal flower molded into handles and lid finials made for a very attractive yet nevertheless commercially unsuccessful product. Our advisor for this category is Ted Haun; he is listed in the Directory under Indiana.

Bowl, fruit; 5¾" 8.00
Bowl, salad; ftd 95.00
Bowl, 8½" 24.00
Chop plate, 11" 15.00
Chop plate, 13" 18.00
Chop plate, 15" 35.00
Creamer 10.00
Cup & saucer 15.00
Egg cup 22.50
Pitcher, cobalt 75.00
Pitcher, red 75.00
Plate, salad; 7" 8.00
Plate, 9" 10.00
Shakers, pr 18.00
Sugar bowl, w/lid 15.00

Teapot **95.00**

Volkmar

Charles Volkmar established a workshop in Tremont, New York, in 1882. He produced artware decorated under the glaze in the manner of the early barbotine work done at the Haviland factory in Limoges, France. He relocated in 1888 in Menlo Park, New Jersey, and together with J.T. Smith established the Menlo Park Ceramic Company for the production of art tile. The partnership was dissolved in 1893. From 1895 until 1902, Volkmar located in Corona, New York, first under the name Volkmar Ceramic Company, later as Volkmar and Cory, and for the final six years as Crown Point. During the latter period he made art tile, blue under-glaze Delft-type wares, colorful polychrome vases, etc. The Volkmar Kilns were established in 1903 in Metuchen, New Jersey, by Volkmar and his son. Wares were marked with various devices consisting of the Volkmar name, initials, or 'Crown Point Ware.'

Plaque, four cows in a spring meadow, signed and dated, 24x14", $13,200.00 at auction.

Plaque, pastoral scene w/4 cows, dtd 1877, orig fr, 24x14" **13,200.00**
Plaque, windmill scene, dished plate form, 14" **1,400.00**
Vase, lg veined rnd leaves cvd on yel-gr, rnd, 6x5½", NM **1,700.00**

Volkstadt

There were several porcelain factories in and around Volkstedt, Province of Thuringio, the original and earliest one established in 1762 by George Heinrich Macheleid. Others soon followed, producing many fine porcelain figures and groups in the Sheib-Alsbach, Potschappel, and Sitzendorf style. The 'crossed hayforks' mark was used from 1787 to 1800 by Christian Nonne; it was later modified with the addition of a crown by R. Ekhart (1906-08). An 'M' crossed by a 'V' with a crown was used from 1907-47 by Muller, who used an oval-shaped diamond with an 'M,' 'V' and a crown from 1910-1960. The Greiner Bros. mark was a double crossed 'G' and a crown, in use from 1850-1920. Our advi-

sor for this category is Donald Penrose; he is listed in the Director under Ohio.

Candlesticks, man & lady in period clothes, 1886 mk, 11", pr ...**750.00**
Figurine, artist & seated lady in lace dress w/fan, 8x9" **550.00**
Figurine, man offers flowers to girl on bench, 7x7" **450.00**
Figurine, musical trio, 2 ladies/1 man, 9½x9" **1,050.00**
Figurine, 2 girls precede bride/groom/page boy, 9x13" **1,250.00**
Plaque, gr Jasper, dancing cupids, floral fr, 11x9" **450.00**

Wade

The Wade Group of Potteries originated in 1810 with a small, single-oven pottery near Chesterton, just west of Burslem, England. This pottery, first owned by a Henry Hallen, was eventually taken over by George Wade who had opened his own pottery (also in Burslem) in 1867. Both the Hallen pottery and the original Wade pottery specialized in ceramic and pottery items for the textile industry, then booming in northern England. By the early 20th century, the two potteries were merged, taking the name of George Wade Pottery, which in 1919 became George Wade & Son Ltd.

George Wade's brother, Albert, had interests in two potteries, A.J. Wade Ltd. and Wade Heath & Co. Ltd. which manufactured decorative tiles, teapots, and other related dinnerware. In 1938 Wade Heath took over the Royal Victoria Pottery, also in Burslem, and began producing a wide range of figurines and other decorative items. In 1947 a new pottery was opened in Portadown, Northern Ireland, to produce both industrial ceramics and Irish porcelain giftware. In 1958 all the Wade potteries were amalgamated, becoming the Wade group of Potteries. The most recent addition to the group is Wade (PDM) Limited, a marketing arm for the advertising ware made by Wade Heath at the Royal Victoria Pottery. Wade (PDM) Limited was incorporated in 1969. In 1989 the Wade Group of Potteries was bought out by Beauford Engineering. With this takeover, Wade Heath and George Wade & Son Ltd. were combined to form Wade Ceramics. Wade (Ireland) Ltd. and Wade (PDM) Ltd. became subsidiaries of Wade Ceramics. In 1990 Wade (Ireland) Ltd. changed its name to Seagoe Ceramics Limited. For those interested in learning more about Wade pottery, we recommend *The World of Wade* by Ian Warner and Mike Posgay; Mr. Warner is listed in the Directory under Canada.

Addis shaving mug, various color decors **22.50**
Addis shaving mug, various single color decors **18.50**
Blow-up Disney, Bambi **120.00**
Blow-up Disney, Jock **250.00**
Blow-up Disney, Lady, 1961-65 ....**180.00**
Blow-up Disney, Si **120.00**
Blynkin, figurine, 1951, 2¼" **140.00**
British Character set, Fishmonger, 1962 ....**160.00**
British Character set, Lawyer, 1962 ....**195.00**
British Character set, Pearly King, 1962 ....**160.00**
British Character set, Pearly Queen, 1962 ....**145.00**
Flower jug, Gothic decor, 9" **80.00**
Flower jug, woodpecker hdl, 7" **180.00**
Happy Families, adults, all sets, 1978-86, ea **12.00**
Happy Families, babies, all sets, 1978-86, ea **6.00**
Man in the Boat, 1978-1984 ....**60.00**
Musical jug, Big Bad Wolf, 1935, 9½" **1,800.00**
Nod, figurine, 1951, 2½" **140.00**
Piggy Bank Family, Lady Hillary, 7" **35.00**
Piggy Bank Family, Maxwell, 6¾" **28.00**
Piggy Bank Family, Sir Nathaniel, 7¼" **44.00**
Piggy Bank Family, Woody, 5" **25.00**
Plaque, peony decor, 12½" dia **75.00**

Salt shaker, Boots and Saddle, 5¼",
$30.00.

Sea Gull Boat, 1961 ....70.00
Spirit container, Chick, 1961, 3⅜" 35.00
Spirit container, cockatoo, 1961-5" 160.00
Winkyn, figurine, 1951, 2¾" 140.00

Wallace China

Dinnerware with a Western theme produced by the Wallace China Company, who operated in Caifornia from 1931 until 1964, has become very popular. Artist Till Goodan designed three lines, Rodeo, Pioneer Trails, and Boots and Saddle, which they marketed under the package name Westward Ho. They made other dinnerware lines as well. If you'd like to learn more about this company, we recommend *The Collector's Encyclopedia of California Pottery* by Jack Chipman.

Ashtray, Christmas Greetings, rnd, stamped mk, 1950s 35.00
Ashtray, Los Angeles Biltmore Hotel commemorative, 1949 ....35.00
Ashtray, Sam Houston 80.00
Boots & Saddle, ashtray 65.00
Boots & Saddle, creamer 45.00
Boots & Saddle, salad bowl, lg 350.00
Chuck Wagon, bowl, restaurant type, 1955, 6¾" 15.00
Desert Ware, bowl, Willow pattern, restaurant type, sm 20.00
El Rancho, platter 110.00
Hibiscus, plate, dinner 12.00
Mission Palm Tree, platter, 11½" 45.00
Pioneer Trails, bowl, 3x9" dia 100.00
Pioneer Trails, creamer & sugar bowl 110.00
Pioneer Trails, platter, lg 125.00
Rodeo, ashtray 75.00
Rodeo, bowl, cereal; 5¾" 55.00
Rodeo, creamer & sugar bowl, w/lid 125.00
Rodeo, cup, 7½-oz 45.00
Rodeo, pitcher 125.00
Rodeo, plate, bread & butter; 7¼" 35.00
Rodeo, plate, dinner; 10¾" 50.00
Rodeo, saucer 20.00
Rodeo, shakers, range sz, pr 200.00
Rodeo, shakers, regular, pr 60.00

Walley

The Walley Pottery operated in West Sterling, Massachusetts,

from 1898 to 1919. Never more than a one-man operation, Walley himself handcrafted all his wares from local clay. The majority of his pottery was simple and unadorned and usually glazed in matt green. On occasion, however, you may find high- and semi-gloss green, as well as matt glazes in blue, cream, brown, and red. The rarest and most desirable examples of his work are those with applied or relief-carved decorations. Some pieces are marked 'WJW.'

Bud vase, ecru gloss, rnd w/elongated neck, 4½" 150.00
Mug, 5 cvd leaf elements, organic hdl, gr/brn, red clay, 6" 1,400.00
Vase, gr-brn flambe drip on gr gloss, cylindrical, 20x7" 2,300.00
Vase, trout emb on gr mottle, imp WJW, paper label, 12" 2,300.00

Walrath

Frederick Walrath was a studio potter who worked from around the turn of the century until his death in 1920. He was located in Rochester, New York, until 1918 when he became associated with the Newcomb Pottery in New Orleans, Louisiana.

Candlestick, bl matt, 2x5" 140.00
Chamberstick, stylized floral, brn/blk on ochre, mk, 7" 350.00
Vase, floral, pk/dk gr on apple gr, spherical, 5½x5" 2,100.00
Vase, pine cone band, ochre on gr speckled, cylindrical, 8" 1,800.00
Vase, stems & buds, dk gr on lt gr, 6" 975.00
Vase, stylized flowers, mustard/brn on gr matt, ovoid, 5" 850.00

Walter, A.

Almaric Walter was employed from 1904 through 1914 at Verreries Artistiques des Freres Daum in Nancy, France. After 1919 he opened his own business where he continued to make the same type of quality objects d'art in pate-de-verre glass as he had earlier. His pieces are signed A. Walter, Nancy H. Berge Sc.

Bird on sq base, lime/olive/blk streaks in gray, 4" 1,800.00
Box, grasshopper atop, berried sides, gr/bl/rust, rpr, 3" 2,200.00
Inkwell, lizard on shoulder, berries on lid, 4" 6,000.00
Paperweight, mouse nibbles on nut atop grassy mound, 3½" ...1,700.00
Pendant, blk/gr beetle on turq oval, 1½" 275.00
Pendant, purple flower/gr leaf on yel, 1½" dia 300.00
Pendant, scarab, brn/gr on yel mottle, 2" L, on silk cord 495.00
Plaque, Japanese maid/pine tree/pond on yel, octagonal, 9¾" .1,000.00
Sea lion, olive gr, sgn Mercier, 6½" 770.00
Tray, triangular w/bumble bee at apex, 4½" L 1,650.00

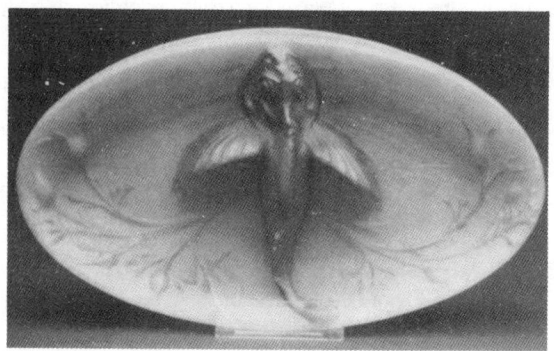

Tray in green with darker green fish, small rim hairline, 9" wide, $2,200.00.

Vase, emb florals, sgn, pillow shape, 5x7" 950.00

Warwick

The Warwick China Company operated in Wheeling, West Virginia, from 1887 until 1951. They produced both hand-painted and decaled plates, vases, teapots, coffeepots, pitchers, bowls, and jardinieres featuring lovely florals or portraits of beautiful ladies done in luscious colors. Backgrounds were usually blendings of brown and beige, but ivory was also used (and on rare occasion, pink). Various marks were employed, all of which incorporate the Warwick name. For a more thorough study of the subject, we recommend *Warwick, A to W*, a supplement to *Why Not Warwick* by our advisor, Donald C. Hoffmann; his address can be found in the Directory under Illinois.

In order to conserve space without omitting listings, we have combined descriptions of two or more items when their values were not more than $5.00 to $10.00 apart. These values are to be used as a general guide; dealer's asking prices will vary, and actual selling prices will depend on your bargaining skills as well.

Vase, A Beauty, bl (or gr or wht), floral (roses), 15" 275.00
Vase, A Beauty, brn, portrait of Madame Le Brun (adult), 15" ...300.00
Vase, Albany, brn, floral, 7" 195.00
Vase, Albany, matt tan, nut decor, 7" 200.00
Vase, Alexandria, red (or brn), floral, 12½" 285.00
Vase, Bonnie, brn, floral, 10¼" 290.00
Vase, Bonnie, wht, floral, 10¼" 320.00
Vase, Bouquet #1, brn, lady w/pearls (or roses), 11½", ea 265.00
Vase, Bouquet #1, matt, lady w/lg hat, 11½" 295.00
Vase, Bouquet #1, red, Madame Le Brun (child), 11½" 255.00
Vase, Bouquet #1, wht, birds, 11½" 285.00
Vase, Bouquet #2, brn, gypsy, 10½" 245.00
Vase, Bouquet #2, brn, lady, sgn Bonfits, 10½" 270.00
Vase, Bouquet #2, brn, lady w/bow, 10½" 255.00
Vase, Bouquet #2, brn, lady w/violets, 10½" 285.00
Vase, Bouquet #2, brn, Madame Re Camier, 10½" 270.00
Vase, Bouquet #2, brn, red-headed lady, 10½" 280.00
Vase, Bouquet #2, charcoal (or cream to tan), floral, 10½" 290.00
Vase, Bouquet #2, gr, Madame Le Brun (child), 10½" 285.00
Vase, Bouquet #2, matt tan/brn, nut decor, 10½" 255.00
Vase, Bouquet #2, pk, Hilda type, 10½" 295.00
Vase, Bouquet #2, red, floral (poinsettias), 10½" 280.00
Vase, Bouquet #2, red, Madame Le Brun (child or adult), 10½" .295.00
Vase, Bouquet #2, wht, lady w/roses (or wht flowers), 10½" 300.00
Vase, Carnation, brn, floral, 9" 125.00
Vase, Carnation, gr, floral (roses), 9" 165.00
Vase, Carnation, matt, nut decor (or pine cones), 9" 165.00
Vase, Carnation, red, Anna Potaka (or Lebrun as child), 9" 175.00
Vase, Carnation, red, floral (poinsettias), 9" 175.00
Vase, Carol, gr, roses, 8" 240.00
Vase, Carol, pk, Hilda w/boa, 8" 270.00
Vase, Chicago, brn, floral, 8" 280.00
Vase, Chicago, brn, Hilda w/flower in hair, 8" 300.00
Vase, Chrys #1, brn, Anna Potaka (or Le Brun as child), 15" 200.00
Vase, Chrys #1, brn, floral, A-26 (or A-40), 15" 185.00
Vase, Chrys #2, brn, floral, 13" 165.00
Vase, Chrys #2, brn, Madame Le Brun (adult), 13" 170.00
Vase, Clematis, matt, nut decor, 10½" 290.00
Vase, Clematis, red, Anna Potaka, 10½" 285.00
Vase, Clematis, wht, egrets, 10½" 300.00
Vase, Cloverleaf, matt, nut decor, 10½" 290.00
Vase, Clytie, red, floral (poinsettias), 6½" 300.00
Vase, Clytie, red, Madame Le Brun (adult), 6½" 315.00

Vase, Cuba, brn, Madame Le Brun (child), 7¼" 290.00
Vase, Cuba, red, floral (poinsettias), 7¼" 285.00
Vase, Dahlia, brn, Madame Le Brun (child), 8½" 280.00
Vase, Dahlia, matt, nut decor, 8½" 260.00
Vase, Dahlia, red, floral (poinsettias), 8½" 275.00
Vase, Dainty, pk, Hilda type w/flower in hair, 4½" 320.00
Vase, Den, matt gr/brn, nut decor, 6½" 285.00
Vase, Duchess, brn, floral, 8" 185.00
Vase, Duchess, wht, birds, 8" 210.00
Vase, Egyptian, brn (or charcoal), floral, 11¾" 325.00
Vase, Favorite, brn, floral, A-27, 10½" 280.00
Vase, Favorite, pk, Hilda type w/flower in hair, 10½" 310.00
Vase, Flower, brn (or matt), floral, 10" 145.00
Vase, Flower, pk, Hilda type, H-1, 12" 180.00
Vase, Flower, red, floral, 12" 165.00
Vase, Flower, yel/gr, Hilda type w/boa, K-1, 12" 200.00
Vase, Gem, brn, Madame Re Camier, 12" 230.00
Vase, Gem, red, floral, E-2, 12" 240.00
Vase, Geran, red (or gr), floral, 11" 275.00
Vase, Grecian, brn, floral, A-6, 8" 230.00
Vase, Helen, red (or brn), floral, 12" 240.00
Vase, Helene, wht, cockatiel, D-1, 12" 255.00
Vase, Hibiscus (canteen shape), brn, acorns (or floral), 11½" 300.00
Vase, Hibiscus (canteen shape), charcoal, nude, Carreno, 11½" ...345.00
Vase, Hyacinth, red, Madame Le Brun (adult), E-1, 11" 250.00
Vase, Iris, matt, nut decor, M-4, 9¾" 155.00
Vase, Lemonade, brn, fruit, A-26, 6½" 160.00
Vase, Lemonade, pk, Hilda type w/flower, 6½" 200.00
Vase, Lemonade, red (or brn), gypsy w/bow, 6½" 155.00
Vase, Lily, brn, A-64 (or A-17 w/bow), 9½" 215.00
Vase, Lily, matt, acorn decor, 9½" 255.00
Vase, Louise, brn, floral, A-27, 9½" 225.00
Vase, Magnolia, brn, floral, A-27, 10½" 235.00
Vase, Magnolia, charcoal, floral, C-6, 10½" 265.00
Vase, Magnolia, matt, nut decor, M-4, 10½" 255.00
Vase, Magnolia, pk, Hilda type w/hat, 10½" 285.00
Vase, Magnolia, red, gypsy w/earrings, E-1, 10½" 260.00
Vase, Maria, brn, floral, A-27 (or A-40), 10½" 200.00
Vase, Maria, charcoal, floral, C-6, 10½" 235.00
Vase, Maria, wht, w/birds, D-1, 10½" 250.00
Vase, Monroe, matt tan to brn, lady w/red cap, 10½" 250.00
Vase, Monroe, pk, Hilda type w/hat, H-1, 10½" 275.00
Vase, Monroe, wht, birds, D-1, 10½" 260.00
Vase, Narcis #1, brn, portrait, A-17, 8½" 230.00
Vase, Narcis #1, charcoal, nude, Carreno, C-1, 8½" 260.00
Vase, Narcis #2, charcoal, floral, C-6, 6¾" 245.00
Vase, Narcis #2, red, portrait w/Re Camier, E-1, 6¾" 255.00
Vase, Nasturium, brn, floral, A-40 ....265.00
Vase, Orchid, brn, floral, A-27, 10¼" 240.00
Vase, Orchid, red, floral, E-2, 10¼" 245.00
Vase, Oriental, brn, floral, A-21, 11" 275.00
Vase, Oriental, red, floral, #-2, 11" 295.00
Vase, Pansy, brn, floral, A-6 (or A-27), 4" 80.00
Vase, Pansy, red, floral, E-2, 4" 80.00
Vase, Parisian, brn, floral, A-27, 4" 245.00
Vase, Parisian, pk, Hilda type, H-1, 4" 285.00
Vase, Penn, charcoal, floral, C-6, 9½" 235.00
Vase, Poppy, brn (or charcoal), floral, 10½" 270.00
Vase, Poppy, wht, floral, w/roses, 10½" 285.00
Vase, President, matt, pine cones (or nut decor), 11½" 260.00
Vase, Queen, charcoal, nude, C-1, 12" 325.00
Vase, Regency, brn (or charcoal), floral, 11½" 285.00
Vase, Roberta, matt, acorns, M-4, 10" 300.00
Vase, Roman, brn, floral, A-40, 11½" 280.00

se, Rosalie, brn, floral, A-6 (or A-27), 9½" 200.00
se, Rosalie, gr, floral, w/roses, 9½" 245.00
se, Rosalie, pk, portrait, Hilda type, H-1, 9½" 265.00
se, Rosalie, wht, birds, D-1, 9½" 275.00
se, Rose, brn, floral, A-26 (or A-27), 8" 170.00
se, Rose, red, floral, E-2, 8" 185.00
se, Rose, red, portrait, Re Camier (or Anna Potaka), 8" 195.00
se, Royal #1, brn, floral, A-40, 10" 295.00
se, Royal #2, brn, floral, A-27, 10" 295.00
se, Senator #1, brn, floral, A-6, 15" 210.00
se, Senator #1, matt (or red), floral, 15" 220.00
se, Senator #2, matt, gypsy w/scarf, 13½" 245.00
se, Senator #2, matt, nut decor, 13½" 230.00
se, Thelma, brn, floral, 9¼" 235.00
se, Tobio Jug #1, brn, floral (or monk), 7¾" 150.00
se, Tobio Jug #1, gr, floral, B-30, 7¾" 165.00
se, Tobio Jug #1, pk, Hilda type, H-1, 7¾" 200.00
se, Tobio Jug #1, red, E-1, 7¾" 190.00
se, Tobio Jug #1, wht, D-1, 7¾" 185.00
se, Tobio Jug #1, wht, floral, 7¾" 220.00
se, Tobio Jug #2, brn, floral, A-6, 7" 155.00
se, Tobio Jug #2, wht, D-1, 7" 180.00
se, Verbenia #1, red, floral, 9½" 185.00
se, Verbenia #2, brn, floral, 7½" 170.00
se, Verbenia #2, charcoal, C-1, 7½" 215.00
se, Verbenia #2, gr, B-30, 7½" 225.00
se, Verbenia #2, red, portraits, 7½" 225.00

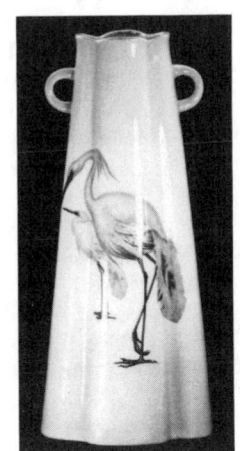

ase, Verona, storks on white ground, D-1,
¾", $230.00.

ase, Verona, brn, floral, A-6, 11¾" 160.00
ase, Verona, charcoal, nude, C-1, 11¾" 225.00
ase, Verona, wht, D-1, 11¾" 230.00
ase, Victoria, brn, floral, 8¼" 220.00
ase, Victoria, red, E-1 (or E-2), 8¼" 250.00
ase, Violet, charcoal, floral, C-6, 4" 120.00
ase, Violet, red, E-2, 4" 120.00
ase, Virginia, pk, floral (poinsettias), 10" 225.00
ase, Virginia, yel-gr, K-1, 10" 225.00
ase, Warwick, brn, A-40, 10" 245.00
ase, Warwick, matt brn, portrait, 10" 255.00
ase, Warwick, matt to pk, portrait, 10" 300.00
ase, Windsor, brn, floral (or nut decor), 9¼" 300.00
ase, Windsor, pk, portrait, 9¼" 325.00

Wash Sets

Before the days of running water, bedrooms were standardly

equipped with a wash bowl and pitcher as a matter of necessity. A 'toilet set' was comprised of the pitcher and bowl, toothbrush holder, covered commode, soap dish, shaving dish, and mug. Some sets were even more elaborate. Through everyday usage, the smaller items were often broken, and today it is unusual to find a complete set.

Porcelain sets decorated with florals, fruits, or scenics were produced abroad by Limoges in France; some were imported from Germany and England. During the last quarter of the 1800s and until after the turn of the century, American-made toilet sets were manufactured in abundance. Tin and graniteware sets were also made.

Blue Willow, Myott, 9½" pitcher+bowl+chamber pot 600.00
Empire, bl/wht mindmills, 12" pitcher+bowl+chamber pot 250.00
Festoon, med bl transfer, Wedgwood, bowl+pitcher, EX 135.00
Gertrud, semivitreous, Arts & Crafts floral, pitcher+bowl 600.00
Imari style, foliage, gilt/orange/bl, 12" pitcher+18" bowl 700.00
Mercer Pottery, Trenton NJ, wht w/gold trim, 5-pc, EX 415.00
Minton, child's, gr ivy on cream, 7" pitcher+9½" bowl 225.00
Old Paris, floral & scrollwork panels on wht, bowl+pitcher 575.00
Oriental Gardens, brn transfer, W Hall & Co, bowl+pitcher 175.00
Palestine, red transfer, English, 10½" pitcher+bowl, EX 215.00
Roses/ribbons, pk on cream, mk Trier, pitcher+bowl 150.00
Rosetti, Royal Doulton, bowl+pitcher 235.00
3 ladies by stream & trees, autumn tones, 2-pc 465.00

Watch Fobs

Watch fobs have been popular since the last quarter of the 19th century. They were often made by retail companies to feature their products. Souvenir, commemorative, and political fobs were also produced. Of special interest today are those with advertising, heavy equipment in particular. Some of the more pricey fobs are listed here, but most of those currently available were produced in such quantities that they are relatively common and should fall into a price range of from $3.00 to $10.00. Our advisor for this category is Tony George; he is listed in the Directory under Washington.

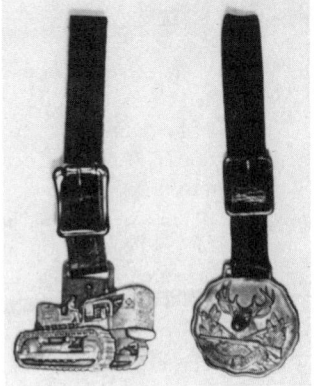

Allis Chalmers, bulldozer,
$20.00; National Sportsman,
brass, $25.00.

Alumina Soapalite, celluloid center 55.00
Am flag, full color on celluloid 22.00
Am Legion 10th Nat'l Convention, mc enamel on brass, 1923 ....12.00
Am Surety Co of NY, porc 75.00
Aultman & Taylor, rooster 65.00
Avery Co, bulldog figural 95.00
Baseball, brass 25.00
Birdsell Hullers, farming machine, EX 38.00
Boston Store Silver Jubilee, silver color metal, 1925, EX 15.00
BPOE, sterling 80.00
Bull Durham 5¢ Cigar 65.00

Bulldog 'Won't Bite' Tobacco, enameled 95.00
Cedar Rapids Crushers, enamel shield 30.00
Centenary...Am Baptist Foreign Mission Society, brass, 1914 ......12.50
Corbin Brakes, metal w/celluloid inlay, VG 15.00
Disciples of Christ Centennial, brass, Whitehead-Hoag, 1909 .....12.00
Diston Tools 55.00
Dodge Brothers, enameled 75.00
Everwear Saddlery, red dmn logo on brass, EX 45.00
Fink & Co RR Overalls, train on celluloid center, EX 80.00
Geo B Miller & Sons Products, celluloid, EX 40.00
Glad Hand Soap 65.00
Gleason's Grape & Apple Juice, grape cluster form 125.00
Harley Davidson, shield shape, worn NP 50.00
Heider Rock Island Plow Co, steam tractor 85.00
IA state seal, 14k gold plate on bronze, EX 25.00
Indian paddling canoe w/village beyond, emb brass, 1½" 25.00
Jap Rose Soap 45.00
John Deere, MOP 150.00
Leisy Brewing, enameled 95.00
Lindbergh, NY to Paris, w/compass 48.00
LJ Mueller Furnace Co, EX 22.00
Longhorn w/saddle 150.00
Manitowoc Speed Shovel, NP/enamel 28.00
Master Brewers' Assoc 25th Anniv, 1911 ....47.50
Michigan Equipment, enamel 88.00
Moline Plows 55.00
Molly Pitcher at Battle of Monmouth, brass, Whitehead & Hoag ..27.50
Nashville TN, Nat'l building shape, enameled, 1924 ....35.00
Nat'l Sportsman, NP 38.00
NE Industrial Expo, 1911 ....28.00
Newark NJ 250th Anniv, enameling, 1916 ....35.00
NY Am Legion, 1937, enameled emblem/Statue of Liberty, 1937 ..15.00
NY C Letter Carriers, celluloid 15.00
NY to Paris on wings of plane, w/compass, EX 58.00
Panama-CA Expo, sailing ship, dtd 1915, EX 35.00
Phoenix Glass, phoenix/sun/rays on SP brass shield form, NM 75.00
Plattner Implements, emb machinery 10.00
Polarine Oil 65.00
Red Dmn Overalls 75.00
Red Steer Brand, celluloid 75.00
Roosevelt Dam, silver-color metal 15.00
Santa Fe Red Cross, paper under celluloid, sq 50.00
Star Brand Shoes, St Louis 50.00
Starved Rooster, Aultman Taylor 150.00
State Farm Insurance, enamel 70.00
Studebaker, brass & enamel, leather strap 48.00
Summit of Pikes Peak, bronze, old leather strap 22.00
Taft-Sherman campaign, Our Choice..., copper, EX 65.00
TL Wolfe, wolf's head in high relief 48.00
US Steel, bk: 25 Yrs of Service, sterling, EX 40.00
Waterloo Playford Silo Co, emb silo, NP 68.00
Wear-Ever Aluminum, trademark on aluminum 15.00
WI state seal & motto on brass, EX 25.00
1893 Columbian Expo, Keystone, pocket watch shape, EX 50.00

Watch Stands

Watch stands were decorative articles designed with a hook from which to hang a watch. Some displayed the watch as the face of a grandfather clock or as part of an interior scene with figures in period costumes and contemporary furnishings. They were popular products of Staffordshire potters and silver companies as well.

Bust of lady, chalk, cloth & paper flowers in niche, 14", EX 900.0
Dbl, ornate cvg/gilt, architectural, Austrian, 1800s, 12" 800.0
Eagle w/aperature in body, giltwood, Austrian, 1800s, 11" 440.0
Father Time stands by aperature, giltwood, 1800s, 10" 450.0
Figure of a Moor, bronze, silver finish, Austrian, 6" 435.0
Mahog, scrollwork crest, bone pin door closure, 8", EX ....2,450.
Oak veneer on pine w/inlay, crest w/8 rvpt, drw, 21", VG ....400.
Oriental gong on hex base, wood, 1800s, 13" ....300.

Watches

First made in the 1500s in Germany, early watches were actua small clocks, suspended from the wrist or belt. By 1700 they h become the approximate shape and size we know today. The fi watches produced in America were made in 1810. The well-know Waltham Watch Company was established in 1850. Later Waterbu produced inexpensive watches which they sold by the thousands.

Open-face and hunting-case watches of the 1890s were solid go or gold-filled and were often elaborately decorated in several colors gold. Gold watches became a status symbol in this decade and we worn by both men and women on chains with fobs or jeweled slide Ladies sometimes fastened them to their clothing with pins often s with jewels. The chatelaine watch was worn at the waist, only one several items such as scissors, coin purses, or needle cases, ea attached by small chains.

Most turn-of-the-century watch cases were gold-filled; these a plentiful today. Sterling cases, though interest in them is on t increase, are not in great demand. Our advisor for this category is M M. Sandler (Maundy International Watches), an Antiquarian Horol gist, dealer, price consultant, and researcher for many watch referen guides and books on Horology. His firm is one of the world's large dealers in antique watches of all varieties. He is listed in the Directo under Kansas. For character-related watches, see Personalities.

Key:
adj — adjusted	k/s — key set
brg — bridge plate design	k/w — key wind
d/s — double sunk dial	l/s — lever set
fbd — finger bridge design	mvt — movement
gf — gold-filled	o/f — open face
g/j/s — gold jewel setting	p/s — pendant set
h/c — hunter case	r/g/p — rolled gold plate
HCI#P — heat, cold,	s — size
isochronism & position	s/s — single sunk dial
adjusted	s/w — stem wind
j — jewel	w/g/f — white gold-filled
k — karat	y/g/f — yellow gold-filled

Am Watch Co, 0s, 7j, #1891, 14k, h/c, Am Watch Co 350.0
Am Watch Co, 12s, 17j, #1894, 14k, o/f, Royal 275.0
Am Watch Co, 12s, 21j, #1894, 14k, h/c 425.0
Am Watch Co, 16s, 11j, #1872, p/s, silver h/c, Park Road 370.0
Am Watch Co, 16s, 15j, #1883, y/g/f, 2-tone, Railroad King 575.0
Am Watch Co, 16s, 15j, #1899, y/g/f, h/c 165.0
Am Watch Co, 16s, 16j, #1884, 5-min, coin silver, Repeater .3,650.0
Am Watch Co, 16s, 17j, #1888, Railroader, rare, NM 1,245.0
Am Watch Co, 16s, 19j, #1872, 14k, h/c, Am Watch Co 2,450.0
Am Watch Co, 16s, 21j, #1888, o/f, 14k, Riverside Maximus .1,450.0
Am Watch Co, 16s, 21j, #1899, y/g/f, l/s, o/f, Crescent St 225.0
Am Watch Co, 16s, 21j, #1908, y/g/f, o/f, Grade #645 ....165.0
Am Watch Co, 16s, 23j, #1908, o/f, 18k, Premier Maximus 7,250.0
Am Watch Co, 16s, 23j, #1908, y/g/f, o/f, adj, RR, Vanguard 250.0
Am Watch Co, 16s, 23j, #1908, y/g/f, o/f, Vanguard Up/Down ..450.0

Am Watch Co, 18s, 11j, #1857, k/w, 1st run, PS Barlett 850.00
Am Watch Co, 18s, 11j, #1857, silver h/c, k/w, DH&D 925.00
Am Watch Co, 18s, 11j, #1857, silver h/c, k/w, s/s, Ellery, EX ...275.00
Am Watch Co, 18s, 15j, #1877, k/w, RE Robbins 425.00
Am Watch Co, 18s, 17j, #1883, y/g/f, o/f, Crescent St. 150.00
Am Watch Co, 18s, 17j, #1892, HC, Canadian Pacific Railway 925.00
Am Watch Co, 18s, 17j, #1892, y/g/f, o/f, Sidereal, rare 1,650.00
Am Watch Co, 18s, 17j, 25-yr, y/g/f, o/f, s/s, PS Bartlett 140.00
Am Watch Co, 18s, 21j, #1892, y/g/f, o/f, d/s, Crescent St 325.00
Am Watch Co, 18s, 21j, #1892, y/g/f, o/f, Grade #845 ....185.00
Am Watch Co, 18s, 21j, #1892, y/g/f, o/f, PA Special 1,775.00
Am Watch Co, 18s, 7j, #1857, k/w, CT Parker, scarce 2,300.00
Am Watch Co, 6s, 7j, #1873, y/g/f, h/c, Am Watch Co 170.00
Auburndale Watch Co, 18s, 7j, k/w, l/s, Lincoln 1,095.00
Aurora Watch Co, 18s, 11j, o/f, k/w, h/c 425.00
Aurora Watch Co, 18s, 15 ruby j, k/w, h/c 975.00
Ball (Elgin), 18s, 17j, o/f, silver, Official RR Standard 525.00
Ball (Hamilton), 16s, 21j, #999, g/f, o/f, l/s 325.00
Ball (Hamilton), 16s, 23j, #998, y/g/f, o/f, Elinvar, model case ...645.00
Ball (Hamilton), 18s, 19j, #999, g/f, o/f, l/s 375.00
Ball (Hampden), 18s, 17j, o/f, adj, RR, Superior Grade 1,150.00
Ball (Illinois), 12s, 19j, w/g/f, o/f 165.00
Ball (Waltham), 16s, 17j, y/g/f, o/f, Commercial Std 165.00
Ball (Waltham), 16s, 21j, o/f, Offical Standard 325.00
Columbus, 18s, 11-15j, k/w, k/s 440.00
Columbus, 18s, 15j, o/f, l/s 175.00
Columbus, 18s, 15j, y/g/f, o/f, Jay Gould 450.00
Columbus, 18s, 21j, y/g/f, h/c, train on dial, Railway King 395.00
Columbus, 18s, 23j, 14k h/c, Columbus King 1,750.00
Columbus, 6s, 11j, 14k h/c 425.00
Cornell, 18s, 15j, s/w, JC Adams 425.00
Cornell, 18s, 15j, silver h/c, k/w, John Evans 440.00
Dudley, 12s, #1, 14k, o/f, flip-bk case, Masonic 3,250.00

European enamel portraiture painting, 18k
gold open face, 18s, ca 1890, $3,650.00.

Elgin, 10s, 18k, h/c, k/w, k/s, s/s, Gail Borden 675.00
Elgin, 12s, 15j, 14k, h/c 450.00
Elgin, 12s, 17j, 14k, h/c, GM Wheeler 495.00

Elgin, 16s, 15j, doctor's, 4th model, 14k, 2nd sweep hand 1,450.00
Elgin, 16s, 15j, 14k, h/c 575.00
Elgin, 16s, 21j, g/f, 3 fbd, grade #72-91, scarce 1,750.00
Elgin, 16s, 21j, y/g/f, g/j/s, o/f, BW Raymond 225.00
Elgin, 16s, 21j, y/g/f, g/j/s, 3 fbd 340.00
Elgin, 16s, 21j, y/g/f, o/f, l/s, RR, Father Time 250.00
Elgin, 16s, 23j, up/down indicator, BW Raymond 775.00
Elgin, 17s, 7j, k/w, orig silver case, Leader 250.00
Elgin, 18s, 11j, silver, h/c, k/w, gilded, MG Odgen 250.00
Elgin, 18s, 15j, o/f, d/s, k/w, silveroid, RR, BW Raymond 250.00
Elgin, 18s, 15j, silver h/c, PA RR on dial, Raymond k/w mvt ..1,450.00
Elgin, 18s, 15j, 14k, k/w, k/s, h/c, HL Culver 1,245.00
Elgin, 18s, 17j, silveroid, BW Raymond 230.00
Elgin, 18s, 21j, y/g/f, o/f, Father Time 300.00
Elgin, 18s, 23j, y/g/f, o/f, 5-position, RR, Veritas 375.00
Elgin, 6s, 11j, 14k, h/c 400.00
Elgin, 6s, 15j, 20-yr, y/g/f, h/c, s/s 150.00
Fredonia, 18s, 11j, y/g/f, h/c, k/w 240.00
Hamilton, #4992B, 16s, 22j, o/f, steel case 250.00
Hamilton, #910, 12s, 17j, 20-yr, y/g/f, o/f, s/s 75.00
Hamilton, #912, 12s, 17j, y/g/f, o/f, adj 85.00
Hamilton, #920, 12s, 23j, 14k, o/f 445.00
Hamilton, #922MP, 12s, 18k case, Masterpiece (sgn) 1,150.00
Hamilton, #925, 18s, 17j, y/g/f, h/c, s/s, l/s 190.00
Hamilton, #928, 18s, 15j, y/g/f, o/f, s/s 160.00
Hamilton, #933, 18s, 16j, h/c, nickel plate 1,200.00
Hamilton, #938, 18s, 17j, 10k, y/g/f, adj 495.00
Hamilton, #940, 18s, 21j, nickel plate, coin silver, o/f 260.00
Hamilton, #946, 18s, 23j, y/g/f, o/f, g/j/s, EX 585.00
Hamilton, #947, 18s, 23j, h/c, orig/sgn, EX 6,250.00
Hamilton, #950, 16s, 23j, y/g/f, o/f, l/s, sgn d/s 550.00
Hamilton, #965, 16s, 17j, 14k, p/s, h/c, brg, scarce 965.00
Hamilton, #972, 16s, 17j, y/g/f, g/j/s, o/f, d/s, l/s, adj 160.00
Hamilton, #974, 16s, 17j, 20-yr, y/g/f, o/f, s/s 125.00
Hamilton, #992, 16s, 21j, y/g/f, o/f, adj, d/s, dbl roller 265.00
Hamilton, #992B, 16s, 21j, y/g/f, o/f, l/s, Bar/Crown RR case 300.00
Hampden, 12s, 17j, w/g/f, o/f, thin model, Aviator 100.00
Hampden, 16s, 17j, o/f, adj 70.00
Hampden, 16s, 17j, y/g/f, h/c, s/w 155.00
Hampden, 16s, 21j, g/j/s, y/g/f, NP, h/c, Dueber, ¾-mvt 240.00
Hampden, 16s, 21j, o/f, adj, dbl roller, Special Railway 260.00
Hampden, 16s, 7j, gilded, nickel plate, ¾-mvt 60.00
Hampden, 18s, 15j, k/w, mk on mvt, Railway 900.00
Hampden, 18s, 15j, s/w, gilded, JC Perry 225.00
Hampden, 18s, 15j, silver, k/w, h/c, Hayward 215.00
Hampden, 18s, 15j, y/g/f, damascened, h/c, Dueber 200.00
Hampden, 18s, 21j, y/g/f, g/j/s, h/c, New Railway 280.00
Hampden, 18s, 21j, y/g/f, o/f, d/s, l/s, N Am Railway 270.00
Hampden, 18s, 23j, y/g/f, d/s, adj, New Railway 340.00
Hampden, 18s, 23j, 14k, h/c, Special Railway 875.00
Hampden, 18s, 7-11j, k/w, gilded, Springfield Mass 150.00
Howard, E; 16s, 15j, s/w, 14k h/c, Series V, L sz 1,275.00
Howard, E; 18s, 15j, h/c, silver case, k/w, Series I, N sz 1,500.00
Howard, E; 18s, 15j, h/c, 14k case, k/w, Series II, N sz 1,650.00
Howard, E; 18s, 15j, 18k h/c, k/w, Series II, N sz 2,950.00
Howard, E; 18s, 17j, 25-yr, y/g/f, o/f, orig case 350.00
Howard, E; 6s, 15j, s/w, 18k h/c, Series VI, G sz 1,375.00
Howard (Keystone), 12s, 23j, 14k, h/c, brg, Series 8 ....875.00
Howard (Keystone), 16s, 17j, y/g/f, o/f, Series #9, checkerbrd mvt..250.00
Howard (Keystone), 16s, 21j, y/g/f, o/f, RR Chronometer II 395.00
Howard (Keystone), 16s, 23j, y/g/f, o/f, Series 0, jeweled bbl 625.00
Illinois, 0s, 7j, 14k, l/s, h/c 325.00
Illinois, 12s, 17j, y/g/f, o/f, d/s dial 95.00
Illinois, 16s, 17j, silver h/c, RR King 575.00

Illinois, 16s, 17j, y/g/f, o/f, d/s, Bunn, EX 270.00
Illinois, 16s, 19j, y/g/f, o/f, d/s, 60-hr, Sangamo Special 820.00
Illinois, 16s, 21j, g/j/s, h/c, Burlington 250.00
Illinois, 16s, 21j, o/f, d/s, Santa Fe Special 325.00
Illinois, 16s, 21j, y/g/f, o/f, s/s, Bunn Special 265.00
Illinois, 16s, 23j, y/g/f, o/f, d/s, RR, Bunn Special 650.00
Illinois, 16s, 23j, y/g/f, stiff bow case, o/f, Sangamo Special 550.00
Illinois, 18s, 11j, #1, silver, k/w, Alleghany 340.00
Illinois, 18s, 11j, #3, o/f, s/w, l/s, Comet 250.00
Illinois, 18s, 11j, Forest City 195.00
Illinois, 18s, 15j, #1, adj, k/w, k/s, Stuart 1,400.00
Illinois, 18s, 15j, #1, y/g/f, k/w, h/c, gilt, Bunn 1,100.00
Illinois, 18s, 15j, k/w, k/s, gilt, Railway Regulator 950.00
Illinois, 18s, 15j, s/w, silveroid 95.00
Illinois, 18s, 17j, g/j/s, adj, B&O RR Special 1,425.00
Illinois, 18s, 17j, h/c, s/w, nickel plate, coin silver, Bunn 350.00
Illinois, 18s, 17j, o/f, d/s, adj, silveroid case, Lakeshore 325.00
Illinois, 18s, 17j, o/f, s/w, 5th pinion, Miller 275.00
Illinois, 18s, 21j, g/j/s, g/f, o/f, A Lincoln 340.00
Illinois, 18s, 21j, g/j/s, o/f, adj, B&O RR Special 1,750.00
Illinois, 18s, 21j, 14k, g/j/s, h/c, Bunn Special 1,450.00
Illinois, 18s, 23j, g/j/s, Bunn Special 570.00
Illinois, 18s, 24j, g/j/s, adj, o/f, Chesapeake & Ohio Special 3,600.00
Illinois, 18s, 24j, g/j/s, Bunn Special 675.00
Illinois, 18s, 24j, g/j/s, o/f, Ben Franklin USA 3,250.00
Illinois, 18s, 26j, 14k, Penn Special, orig case 6,750.00
Illinois, 18s, 7j, #3, Interior 220.00
Illinois, 18s, 7j, #3, silveroid, America 170.00
Illinois, 18s, 9-11j, o/f, k/w, s/s, silveroid case, Hoyt 210.00
Illinois, 8s, 13j, ¾-mvt, Rose LeLand, scarce 490.00
Ingersoll, 16s, 7j, wht base metal, Reliance 45.00
Lancaster, 18s, 7j, o/f, k/w, k/s, eng case 275.00
Marion US, 18s, h/c, k/w, k/s, ¾-plate, Asa Fuller 495.00
Marion US, 18s, 15j, nickel plate, h/c, s/w, Henry Randel 625.00
Melrose Watch Co, 18s, 7j, k/w, k/s 495.00
New York Watch Co, 18s, 7j, silver, h/c, k/w, Geo Sam Rice 375.00
New York Watch Co, 19j, low sz #, wolf's teeth wind 2,450.00
Patek Philippe, 12s, 18j, 18k, o/f 2,400.00
Patek Philippe, 16s, 20j, 18k, h/c 3,250.00
Rockford, 16s, 17j, y/g/f, h/c, brg, dbl roller 200.00
Rockford, 16s, 21j, #515, y/g/f 595.00
Rockford, 16s, 21j, g/j/s, o/f, grade #537, rare 1,550.00
Rockford, 16s, 23j, o/f, mk Doll on dial & mvt, rare 1,650.00
Rockford, 18s, 15j, o/f, k/w, silver case 175.00
Rockford, 18s, 17j, silveroid w/mc dial, fancy mvt/hands 275.00
Rockford, 18s, 17j, y/g/f, o/f, Winnebago 350.00
Rockford, 18s, 21j, o/f, King Edward 425.00
Samuel Curtiss, 18s, #1857, silver h/c, k/w 2,450.00
Seth Thomas, 18s, 17j, #2, g/j/s, adj, Henry Molineux 950.00
Seth Thomas, 18s, 17j, Edgemere 150.00
Seth Thomas, 18s, 25j, g/j/s, g/f, Maiden Lane 3,000.00
Seth Thomas, 18s, 7j, ¾-mvt, bk: eagle/Liberty model 275.00
South Bend, 12s, 21j, dbl roller, Grade #431 ....225.00
South Bend, 12s, 21j, orig o/f, d/s, Studebaker 325.00
South Bend, 18s, 21j, g/j/s, h/c, full plate, grade #328 ....675.00
South Bend, 18s, 21j, 14k, h/c 875.00
Swiss, 18s, 18k, h/c, 1-min, Repeater, High Grade 3,950.00

Waterford

The Waterford Glass Company operated in Ireland from the late 1700s until 1851 when the factory closed. One hundred years later (in 1951) another Waterford glassworks was instituted that produced glass similar to the 18th century wares — crystal glass, usually with cut decoration. Today Waterford is a generic term referring to the type of glass first produced there.

Flute, Cashel, 6" ....36.0[]
Goblet, Curragmore, 5½" ....45.0[]
Goblet, Lismore, 7⅝" ....65.0[]
Goblet, water; Ashling ....35.0[]
Sherry, Sheila ....24.0[]
Wine, Curragmore ....25.0[]
Wine, Sheila, 7⅛" ....36.0[]

Watt Pottery

The Watt Pottery Company was established in Crooksville, Ohio on July 5, 1922. From approximately 1922 until 1935, they manufactured hand-turned stone containers — jars, jugs, milk pans, preserv jars, and various sizes of mixing bowls, usually marked with a cobalt blue acorn stamp. In 1936 production of these items was discontinued and the company began to produce kitchen utility ware and ovenware such as mixing bowls, spaghetti bowls and plates, canister sets, covered casseroles, salt and pepper shakers, cookie jars, ice buckets, pitchers bean pots, and salad and dinnerware sets. Most Watt ware is individually hand-painted with bold brush strokes of red, green, or blue contrasting with the natural buff color of the glazed body. Several patterns were produced: Apple, Autumn Foliage, Cherry, Dutch Tulip, Morning-Glory, Pansy, Rooster, Tear Drop, Starflower, and Tulip, to name few. Much of the ware was made for advertising premiums and is often found stenciled with the name of the retail company.

Tragedy struck the Watt Pottery Company on October 4, 196[] when fire completely destroyed the factory and warehouse. Production never resumed, but the ware they made has withstood many years of service in American kitchens and is today highly regarded and prized by collectors. The vivid colors and folk art-like execution of each cheery pattern create a homespun ambiance that will make Watt pottery treasure for years to come.

For further study we recommend *Watt Pottery, An Identification and Price Guide*, by our advisors for this category, Sue and Dave Morris, who are listed in the Directory under Iowa. For the address of the *Watt's New* newsletter, see the section on Clubs, Newsletters, and Catalogs.

Apple, bowl, #04 ....75.0[]
Apple, bowl, cereal; #74 ....45.0[]
Apple, bowl, mixing; #7 ....45.0[]
Apple, casserole, w/lid, #96 ....145.0[]
Apple, cheese crock, w/lid, #80 ....500.0[]
Apple, creamer, #62 ....90.0[]
Apple, grease jar, w/lid, #01 ....400.0[]
Apple, ice bucket, w/lid ....250.0[]
Apple, pitcher, #16 ....110.0[]
Apple, plate, divided ....800.0[]
Apple, shakers, hourglass form, pr ....250.0[]
Apple, tumbler, #56 ....325.0[]
Autumn Foliage, bowl, mixing; #6 ....35.0[]
Autumn Foliage, pie plate, #33 ....90.0[]
Autumn Foliage, pitcher, #16 ....70.0[]
Banded, cookie jar, lt bl/wht bands, w/lid ....65.0[]
Banded, pitcher, wht bands ....45.0[]
Brn glaze, electric warmer ....125.0[]
Cherry, bowl, cereal; #23 ....45.0[]
Cherry, pitcher, #15 ....85.0[]
Dogwood, platter ....110.0[]
Dutch Tulip, bowl, mixing; #64 ....100.0[]

Dutch Tulip, casserole, w/lid, ind, #18 ....245.00
Dutch Tulip, cheese crock, w/lid, #80 ....400.00
Dutch Tulip, pitcher, #15 ....150.00
Eagle, bowl, ribbed, #8 ....125.00
Goodies jar, w/lid, #76 ....275.00
Kitch-N-Queen, bowl, mixing; #6 ....35.00
Kla-Ham'rd, pitcher, #43-14 ....55.00
Moonflower, plate, dinner; pk-on-gr starflower 110.00
Morning Glory, bowl, mixing; #7 ....80.00
Morning Glory, sugar bowl, #98 ....250.00
Rio Rose, casserole, w/lid, #3/19 ....85.00
Rio Rose, pie plate, cut leaf, #33 ....90.00
Rio Rose, pitcher, #17 ....200.00
Rio Rose, platter, #49 ....100.00
Rooster, baking dish, rectangular 800.00
Rooster, creamer, #62 ....125.00
Rooster, pitcher, #15 ....90.00
Rooster, shakers, hourglass form, pr 250.00
Silhouette, casserole, w/lid, gr-on-brn starflower 125.00
Starflower, baker, w/lid, #53 ....90.00
Starflower, bowl, mixing; #6 ....45.00
Starflower, canister; flour; w/lid, #81 ....350.00
Starflower, casserole, stick hdl, w/lid, ind, #18 ....150.00
Starflower, mug, #501 ....90.00
Starflower, shakers, bbl shape, pr 165.00

Tear Drop tea canister, #82,
250.00.

Tear Drop, bean pot, w/lid, #76 ....100.00
Tear Drop, bowl, #05 ....45.00
Tear Drop, casserole, w/lid, #67 ....165.00
Tear Drop, pitcher, #16 ....100.00
Tulip, bowl, #65 ....100.00
Tulip, casserole, w/lid, #601 ....250.00
Tulip, creamer, #62 ....125.00
Tulip, pitcher, ice lip, #17 ....300.00
White Daisy, bowl, #7 ....55.00
White Daisy, pitcher 150.00
Woodgrain, bowl, w/lid, #608W 90.00

Wave Crest

Wave Crest is a line of decorated opal ware (milk glass) patented in 1892 by the C.F. Monroe Co. of Meriden, Connecticut. They made a full line of items for every room of the house, but they are probably best known for their boxes and vases. Most items were hand painted in various levels of decoration, but more transfers were used in the later years prior to the company's demise in 1916. Floral themes are common; items with the scenics and portraits are rarer and more highly prized. Many pieces have ornately scrolled ormolu and brass handles,

feet and rims attached. Early pieces were often signed with a black mark; later a red banner mark was used, and occasionally a paper label may be found. However, the glass is quite distinctive and has not been reproduced, so even unmarked items are easy to recognize. Our advisors for this category are Dolli and Wilfred Cohen; they are listed in the Directory under California.

Ashtray, floral on scroll-emb 4½" bowl form 125.00
Biscuit jar, Swirl, HP florals in beaded reserves on pastel 550.00
Blotter, floral on scroll-emb 5" L rectangle, ormolu mts 1,000.00
Box, Baroque Shell w/purple & wht flowers, 7" 725.00
Box, blown-out florals on aqua, 4½" 495.00
Box, Christmas holly on crystal, 7" 950.00
Box, cobalt w/floral in wht reserve, ormolu ft, 6x5½" dia 750.00
Box, Collars & Cuffs, floral on wht, emb scroll mold, ftd 1,170.00
Box, cornflowers, bl on lt pk, oval, 5" 375.00
Box, dbl shell, sm flowers & beading on bl, 3½" 198.00
Box, floral & blown-out shell on lid, ormolu ft/rim, 4" dia 395.00
Box, HP floral on bl w/blown-out swirls, hinged lid, 3½" 350.00
Box, Puffy, lady in wht, overall wht beading, 6½" sq 1,600.00
Box, young man on knee proposing to girl (on lid), 5½" 650.00
Candlestick, emb scrolls w/floral sprays, ormolu top/ft, 7" 675.00
Card holder, Puffy, florals, ornate rim, 4x3x6" 385.00
Cologne, ribbon & floral, swirl-emb neck, str sides, stopper 350.00

Ewers, florals on glass inserts, elaborate ormolu tops and bases, figural handles, 12½", $895.00 for the pair.

Humidor, Egg Crate, floral/Tobacco, ormolu corner mts, 4x5" ...595.00
Inkwell, holly & berries on bl-gr, glass lid & insert 925.00
Jar, toothpowder; forget-me-nots, brass emb lid, banner mk 395.00
Photograph holder, clovers, pk on lt bl, ftd 525.00
Planters, daises & beaded brass rim, 7½" 420.00
Plaque, daisies & clover on 10" scroll-emb disk, ormolu fr 1,650.00
Shakers, Artichoke, spiked pewter lid, pr 150.00
Shakers, Creased Neck, HP floral, pr 150.00
Shakers, Tulip, HP floral, pr 125.00
Tray, floral on scroll-emb 6" bowl, metal leaf-appl rim 250.00
Tray, jewel; emb scrolls, flowers, 3½" dia 125.00
Vase, emb scrolls w/purple & pk lilacs, 9½" 550.00
Vase, floral sprays on unemb form w/bun base, 4½x4" 375.00
Vase, iris on bl, ormolu ft, hdls, collar, 9" 720.00
Vase, lg floral, unemb classic form, ornate ormolu hdls, 8" 500.00
Vase, mums, mc on lt pk, wht beaded rim, 10" 575.00
Whisk broom holder, floral cartouch on yel, ornate ormolu 895.00

Weapons

Among the varied areas of specialization within the broad category of weapons, guns are by far the most popular. Muskets are among the earliest firearms; they were large-bore shoulder arms, usually firing black powder with separate loading of powder and shot. Some ignited the charge by flintlock or caplock, while later types used a firing pin with a metallic cartridge. Side arms, referred to as such because they were worn at the side, include pistols and revolvers. Pistols range from early single-shot and multiple barrels to modern types with cartridges held in the handle. Revolvers were supplied with a cylinder that turned to feed a fresh round in front of the barrel breech. Other firearms include shotguns, which fired round or conical bullets and had a smooth inner barrel surface; and rifles, so named because the interior of the barrel contained spiral grooves (rifling) which increased accuracy. For further study we recommend *Modern Guns, Seventh Edition*, by Russell Quartermous and Steve Quartermous, available at your local bookstore. Our advisor for swords is Steve Hess; he is listed in the Directory under Florida. All other weapons are under the advisement of Steve Howard, see the Directory under California. See also Militaria.

Key:
bbl — barrel		hdw — hardware	
cal — caliber		h/s — half stock	
conv — conversion		mag — magazine	
cyl — cylinder		mod — modified	
f/l — flintlock		oct — octagon	
f/s — full stock		p/b — patch box	
ga — gauge		perc — percussion	

Carbine

Austrian perc, 70-cal rifled bore, saddle ring, 14½" bbl, VG 300.00
Budapest 95 Military, 8mm cal, bolt action, 19½" bbl, G 350.00
Burnside Civil War, 54 cal, military sights, 21" rnd bbl, G 800.00
Gallagher, 50 cal perc, military sights, 22" rnd bbl, G 500.00
Japanese Cavalry Type 44, 6.5 cal, w/bayonet, 19" bbl, EX 525.00
Joslyn, 52 cal rimfire, breech loading, 22" rnd bbl, G 550.00
Manlicher Schoenauer 1903, 6.5x54 cal, 18" bbl, VG 750.00
Manlicher 1906, 8x56 cal, steel butt w/track, 20" bbl, VG 600.00
Marlin 1936, 32 Special cal, sporting rear sights, 20" bbl, EX 450.00
Marlin 336, 44 mag cal, hooded ramp front sight, 20" bbl, EX ...200.00
Maynard, 50 cal, 20" rnd bbl octagon at breech, G 550.00
Ruger, 44 mag cal, peep rear sights, 18½" bbl, EX 300.00
Ruger No 3, 375 Winchester cal, single shot, 22" rnd bbl, NM ..350.00
Sharps & Hankins 1862 Navy, 52 cal rimfire, 24" bbl, VG 1,500.00
Sharps New Model 1863, 52 cal, front/rear sights, 22" bbl, EX ..2,200.00
Smith (Poultney & Trimble) perc, 52 cal, 21" half rnd bbl, G ...650.00
Spencer Civil War, 52 cal, no mag cutoff, 22" rnd bbl, G 200.00
Spencer Civil War, 52 cal rimfire, saddle ring, 22" bbl, G 600.00
Spencer Contract 1865, 50 cal, saddle ring, 20" bbl, VG 650.00
Underwood WWII M-1, 30M-1 cal, military sights, 18" bbl, EX ..200.00
US Springfield 1884, 45/70 cal, saddle ring bar, 22" bbl, VG ..1,200.00
Winchester Hotchkiss 2nd, 45/70 cal, bolt action, 24" bbl, G 300.00
Winchester Pre-64 94, 30/20 cal, full mag, 20" bbl, EX 200.00
Winchester 1894, 30-30 cal, w/saddle ring, 20" bbl, EX 500.00
Winchester 1894, 32 spec cal, str grip stock, 20" bbl, EX 650.00
Winchester 1894 Delux, 30/30 cal, w/saddle ring, VG 1,200.00
Winchester 1894 Eastern, 30/30 cal, rpl sight, 20" bbl, VG 300.00
Winchester 1894 Semi Deluxe, 30/30 cal, peep sight, 20" bbl, G ..1,200.00
Winchester 94 Eastern, 30/30 cal, full mag, 20" bbl, VG 225.00
Winchester 94 Proto Type, 30/30 cal, full mag, 20" bbl, M 3,000.00
Wm Palmer Civil War, 50 cal, saddle ring, 20" rnd bbl, G 1,000.00

Musket

Arabian, 55 cal, lockplate dtd 1811, brass inlay, 44" bbl, G 250.00
Belgium military f/l, 70 cal, f/s, iron hdw, 43" bbl, G 200.00

Brown Bess Revolutionary War f/l, 69 cal, f/s, 42" bbl, VG 1,800.00
Charleville Revolutionary War f/l, 69 cal, f/s, 44" bbl, VG ...1,050.00
Charleville 1777 f/l, 69 cal, breech dtd 1814, 45" bbl, VG 1,500.00
E Robinson US 1861, 58 cal, breech dtd 1864, 40" bbl, G 750.00
European f/l, 58 cal, f/s, iron hds, 37" bbl mk M Berlens, EX 300.00
European f/l, 80 cal, 2 brass bbl bands, 40½" bbl, G 750.00
Harper's Ferry 1816 perc conv, 69 cal, 21½" bbl, VG 250.00
Military f/l, 70 cal, hammer dtd 1812, f/s w/ramrod, 45" bbl, G ..350.00
New England Committee of Safety f/l, 75 cal, 45" bbl, G 950.00
Savage 1863, 58 cal, military sights, NP, f/s, 40" bbl, NM 1,500.00
Sharps New Model 1863 perc, 52 cal, f/s w/swivels, 30" bbl, G ..750.00
Tower f/l Brown Bess, 80 cal, mk hammer, f/s, 39" bbl, G 250.00
Trenton 1861 Civil War, 58 cal, 40" bbl, dtd 1864, VG 450.00
US Norfolk, 58 cal rifled bbl, f/s, 40" bbl, dtd 1863, G 600.00
US Springfield 1855, 58 cal, f/s, dtd 1857, 40" bbl, G 500.00
US Springfield 1855, 58 cal, 1860 on lock plate, 38" bbl, VG ...1,750.00
US Springfield 1861, 58 cal rifled bore, f/s, cut 39½" bbl, G 200.00
US Watertown 1863 perc, 58 cal, military f/s, 40" NP bbl, EX 750.00
US 1861 Bridesburg, cartridge conv, 58 cal, 40" bbl, VG 900.00
Winchester Low-Wall, 22 short cal, peep sight, 28" bbl, VG 600.00

Pistol

Am Arms derringer, 32 cal, 2⅝" over/under bbls, G 425.00
Belgium f/l, 60 cal rifled bores, brass hdw, 7" bbl, VG, pr 900.00
Browning Medalist Target, 22 long rifle cal, 6¾" bbl, M 600.00
Browning 1927 Semi-Auto, 32 cal, w/Nazi proofs, 4¾" bbl, EX .550.00
Colt Government Delta Elite, 10mm cal, 5" bbl, MIB 550.00
Colt 1903 Pocket, 32 ACP cal, rubber grips, 3¾" bbl, EX 300.00
Colt 1903 Pocket Auto, 38 rimless/smokeless cal, 4½" bbl, VG .375.00
Colt 1908 Pocket, 25 ACP cal, rubber grips, 2" bbl, VG 225.00
Colt 1911-A1 US Army, 45 ACP cal, plastic grips, 5" bbl, VG .300.00
Ethan Allen perc, 32 cal, under-hammer single shot, 8" bbl, G ..300.00
James Rodgers Sheffield perc knife, 32-cal, 3½" oct bbl, VG 700.00
Luger (by Erfurt), 9mm cal, wood grips, 4" bbl, dtd 1918, EX 850.00
Mauser Commercial Broom Hdl, 30 cal, 5¼" bbl, EX 2,500.00
Mauser HSC Dbl Action Pocket, 7.65mm, 32 cal, NM 450.00
Remington dbl derringer 2nd type, 41 cal, 3 over/under bbls, VG ...450.00
Remington derringer 3rd type, 41 cal, 3" over/under bbl, VG 500.00
Remington Rand Colt 1911-A1 Army, 45 cal, 5" bbl, VG 250.00
Remington UMC 1911 Army, 45 cal, walnut grips, 5" bbl, VG .550.00
Remington 1867 Navy Rolling Block, 50 cal, 7" rnd bbl, G 450.00
Remington-Elliot Derringer, 32 cal, 4-shot, 3⅜" bbls, VG 450.00
Savage 1917 Semi-Auto Pocket, 32 cal, 3¾" bbl, EX 225.00
Smith & Wesson 1913 Semi-Auto Pocket, 35 cal, 3½" bbl, VG ...350.00
Smith & Wesson 61 Pocket, 22 long rifle cal, 2" bbl, M 250.00
Spanish Star Semi-Auto Target, 22 long rifle cal, 6" bbl, EX 350.00
Stevens Offhand Target No 35, 22 long cal, 6" oct bbl, VG 175.00
Stevens 43, 22 cal, single shot, walnut grips, 6" bbl, EX 250.00
Steyr 1915 Semi-Auto, 38 auto cal, 5⅛" bbl, G 150.00
Taylor Single Shot Pocket, 32 cal rimfire, 3½" oct bbl, VG 400.00
Tower f/l, 67-69 cal, smooth bore, 9⅛" bbl, VG 500.00

Revolver

Bacon 6-Shot Pepperbox, 22 cal, 2½" fluted bbls, VG 750.00
Colt Army Special, 38 cal, walnut grips, 6" rnd bbl, EX 400.00
Colt Bisley Flat Top Target, 455 Eley cal, 7½" bbl, EX 5,000.00
Colt Blk Powder 1860 Army perc, 44 cal, 8" rnd bbl, MIB 450.00
Colt New Service Target, 44 Russian cal, 7½" bbl, G 750.00
Colt Open Top Pocket, 22 short cal, 2½" rnd bbl, G 250.00
Colt Pre-War II single action, 45 long cal, 5½" bbl, EX 3,750.00
Colt 1851 Navy perc, 36 cal, wood grips, 7⅜" bbl, G 300.00
Colt 1860 US Army, 44 cal, 8" rnd bbl, VG 1,500.00

Colt 1877 dbl action, 38 long cal, rubber grips, 4½" bbl, G 750.00
Colt 1909 Army dbl action, 45 long cal, 5½" bbl, EX 450.00
CS Shattuck Pocket, 32 cal, rubber grips, spur trigger, EX 300.00
Forehand-Wardsworth New Army, 44/40 Win cal, 6⅝" bbl, VG ..1,350.00
Mass Arms Co (Adams Pat) perc, 36 cal, 6" oct bbl, G 600.00
Remington Civil War New Model perc, 44 cal, 8" oct bbl, VG .750.00
Remington New Model Army, 44 cal, 8" oct bbl, G 750.00
Ruger New Model Blackhawk, 41 Mag cal, 6½" bbl, EX 300.00
Ruger New Model single action, 45 long Colt cal, 4¾" bbl, EX ..300.00
Ruger Single Six, 22 long rifle cal, 6½" rnd bbl, EX 225.00
Savage Civil War Navy perc, 36 cal, 6-shot, 7⅛" bbl, G 600.00
Savage Revolving Firearms Navy perc, 36 cal, 7⅛" bbl, VG ...1,750.00
Smith & Wesson #3 2nd Model, 44 cal, 8" bbl, EX 2,000.00
Smith & Wesson Schofield Army, 2nd Model, 45 cal, 7" bbl, G ..1,100.00
Smith & Wesson 1st Safety, 32 S&W center/fire cal, 3" bbl, VG ..225.00
Smith & Wesson 1950 Target, 44 special cal, 6½" bbl, NM 775.00
Smith & Wesson 27 Target, early 5-screw model, 6" bbl, EX 650.00
Star Civil War perc, 44 cal, walnut grips, 6" rnd bbl, VG 800.00
Whitney Pocket perc, 31 cal, wood grips, 5" oct bbl, EX 1,450.00

Rifle

Browning Bar, 270 Win cal, 22" bbl, +4X scope, EX 550.00
Frank Wesson Med Fr Pocket, 32 rimfire cal, 15" oct bbl, G 300.00
F Bussey Plains, 40 cal, half stock, 30" bbl, VG 675.00
Marlin 1881 Deluxe factory eng, 45/70 cal, 28" oct bbl, VG ...7,000.00
Marlin 1893 Semi-Deluxe, 32/40 cal, 24" half rnd/oct bbl, VG ..450.00
Marlin 1893 takedown, 38/55 cal, half mag, 24" rnd bbl, G 300.00
Remington 14 pump, 30 REM cal, 22" rnd bbl, G 225.00
Remington 66 bolt action, 22 cal, nylon grip, 19" bbl, EX 150.00
Remington 742 Woods Master, 30-06 cal, 22" rnd bbl, EX 400.00
Remington 8 Semi-Auto, 25 REM cal, 22" bbl, G 200.00
Savage 1899 takedown, 250/3000 cal, 22" rnd bbl, G 245.00
Savage 23 Sporter bolt action, 25/20 cal, 24½" rnd bbl, G 200.00
Savage 29-A pump, 22 long cal, 2/3 mag, 24" rnd bbl, EX 375.00
Savage 99, 308 Win cal, pistol grip stock, 24" rnd bbl, VG 300.00
Sharps New 1863 Military perc, 52 cal, 30" rnd bbl, G 750.00
Springfield 1868 Trapdoor, 45/70 cal, 32⅝" military bbl, VG 550.00
Springfield 1873 Trapdoor, 45/70 cal, 32½" bbl, G 300.00
Stevens Ideal 44, 32/40 cal, 26" rnd/oct bbl, G 300.00
Stevens 14½ Little Scout, 22 long cal, 20" rnd bbl, VG 125.00
US Eddystone 1917 Military, 30-06 cal, 26" rnd bbl, G 250.00
US Springfield (M-1 Garand), 30-06 cal, 24" rnd bbl, VG 300.00
Weatherby Delux bolt action, 270 cal, 26" rnd bbl, M 1,500.00
Whitney Armory lever action repeater, 44/40 cal, 24" bbl, G 600.00
Winchester 1886 Light Weight, 33 cal, half mag, 24" bbl, G ..1,000.00
Winchester 1894, 38/55 cal, full mag, 26" rnd bbl, VG 650.00
Winchester 1894 takedown, 30/30 cal, 26" oct bbl, G 350.00
Winchester 1902 boy's, 22 short & long cal, 8" rnd bbl, EX 150.00
Winchester 1907 self loading, 351 cal, 20" rnd bbl, G 200.00
Winchester 55 takedown, 30/30 cal, half mag, 24" rnd bbl, VG .675.00
Winchester 709 XTR Featherweight, 243 cal, 22" bbl, M 500.00

Shotgun

Ames Artillery, leather hdl, 32¼" curved blade, +scabbard 600.00
Ames Screaming Eagle 1840 officer's, 31" blade, +scabbard 600.00
Ames 1840 Wristbreaker, 36" dtd 1846 blade, + scabbard 1,000.00
Ames 1859 foot officer's, 30½" blade, VG, +scabbard 600.00
British Sea Service cutlass/bayonet, 26⅝" steel blade, EX 675.00
Browning A-5, 20-ga, mod choke, pistol grip, 28" bbl, EX 450.00
Browning A-5 Semi-Auto, 20-ga, 26" vent rib bbl, M 650.00
Browning 2000 Semi-Auto, 12-ga, 28" vent rib bbl, M 600.00
Roby 1860 Cavalry, leather hdl, 35" mk curved blade, EX 400.00

Emerson & Silver 1860 Cavalry, 34½" mk blade, EX 550.00
Francotte, 12-ga, mod/full choke, 26" fluid steel bbls, VG 1,000.00
Holland & Holland Damascus, 12-ga, 30" dbl bbls, G 1,500.00
Ithaca 100 (SKB), 20-ga, 25" improved cyl & mod bbl, NM 375.00
Iver Johnson, 16-ga, box lock action, 30" dbl bbls, VG 750.00
Iver Johnson, 410-ga, box lock action, 26" dbl bbls, EX 950.00
LC Smith Field Grade, 12-ga, 28" dbl bbls, VG 750.00
LC Smith Premiere Skeet, 12-ga, 26" dbl bbls, VG 1,000.00
LF&C 1917 US Patten,1918, NM, + canvas-covered scabbard ..400.00
Parker (V) Grade, 12-ga, 28" dbl Vulcan steel bbls, G 900.00
Parker GH Grade Damascus, 12-ga, 30" dbl bbls, EX 1,150.00
Remington 32, 12-ga, 30" vent rib over/under bbls, VG 1,150.00
Richland Arms, 20-ga, 32" dbl bbls, made in Spain, EX 400.00
USN 1917 Cutlass, steel guard, 24½" blade, +scabbard 400.00
Winchester 12, 12-ga, 30" full choke nickel/steel bbl, G 200.00
Winchester 1897 Riot, 12-ga, rubber butt plate, 20" bbl, VG 500.00
Winchester 1901 lever action, 10-ga, half mag, 30" bbl, G 250.00
Winchester 1901 lever action, 10-ga, half mag, 32" bbl, G 225.00
Winchester 20, 410-ga, full choke, 26" single bbl, EX 250.00
Winchester 37, 12-ga, full choke, 30" single bbl, VG 200.00
Winchester 42 Field Grade, 410-ga, 26" plain bbl, EX 850.00
Winchester 50, 20-ga, mod choke, 28" bbl, EX 250.00
WW Greener Damascus, 12-ga, 30" dbl bbls, VG 900.00

Sword

Ames Artillery, mk 1856 on 19" blade, emb brass pommel, EX ..900.00
Ames 1850 foot officer's, etched blade, 31", +25" scabbard 650.00
Civil War (non-regulation) officer's, 32" blade, +scabbard 750.00
Confederate, D guard, bone hdl w/iron rivets, 23" blade, G 1,150.00
European, all metal 2-handed type, 1500s, 40" blade, VG 800.00
Japanese Navy officer's, 26" slender blade, 1900s, +scabbard 500.00
Remington (Zouave) saber baoynet, brass hilt, 20" blade, EX 500.00
Star Contract of 1812-13 Cavalry, 34" blade, EX, +scabbard 500.00

Weathervanes

The earliest weathervanes were of handmade wrought iron and were generally simple angular silhouettes with a small hole suggesting an eye. Later copper, zinc, and polychromed wood with features in relief were fashioned into more realistic forms. Ships, horses, fish, Indians, roosters, and angels were popular motifs. In the 19th century, silhouettes were often made from sheet metal. Wooden figures became highly carved and were painted in vivid colors. E.G. Washburne and Company in New York was one of the most prominent manufacturers of weathervanes during the last half of the century. Two-dimensional sheet metal weathervanes are increasing in value due to the already heady prices of the full-bodied variety. Originality, strength of line, and patination help to determine value. When no condition is indicated, the items listed below are assumed to be in excellent condition.

Key:
fb — full-bodied   f/fb — flattened full-bodied

Airplane, copper, 20th C, minor dents, 25" L 775.00
Arrow, copper w/EX patina, J Howard Co, rpr, 59" L 1,100.00
Bull, copper, cast head/hollow body, EX detail, dents, 20" L 800.00
Cow, molded copper/zinc, att Cushing-Wht, rpr, 28" L 2,600.00
Cow, sheet metal, w/directionals, 16" L 550.00
Cow, tin, James, 9x15x¾", on 32" CI arrow, EX 250.00
Deer, f/fb pnt copper w/cast antlers, tooling, 29", VG 4,750.00
Gabriel w/trumpet, molded gilt copper, att Cushing-Wht, 31" ..1,700.00
Horse, Blk Hawk, molded copper, gilt traces, 1800s, 25" L 2,500.00

Horse, copper/zinc, Jewell, bullet holes/etc, 42" L **4,400.00**
Horse, prancing circus; pressed tin, 1900s, 11x15x1¼" **265.00**
Horse & jockey, molded copper w/zinc head, att Fiske, 32" **2,950.00**
Horse & rider, sheet steel silhouette, rpr/rpl/rpt, 31" L **400.00**
Horse running, zinc, 7x14", mtd on ornate CI 26" arrow **365.00**
Horse standing, copper, 10", on 22" CI arrow, EX **285.00**
Horse trotting, copper/zinc, directionals, 15x30" **2,200.00**
Hunting dog pointing, sheet iron, worn pnt, 11x20½" **125.00**
Man rolling 3 logs, sheet metal w/pnt traces, 1800s, 28x35" ...**1,100.00**
Man w/cane, lg dog, sheet iron, pitted/mc rpt, 24x25" **300.00**
Nude, molded copper, 44x60x23", EX **1,650.00**
Pig, tin, old wht pnt, 5x9" on 22" CI arrow, EX **185.00**
Rooster, copper, EX detail, 18", EX **1,750.00**
Rooster, copper w/gilt traces, 1800s, rpr, 20" **1,800.00**
Rooster, zinc, hollow mold, flat w/relief, 13¾" **130.00**
Stag, molded copper w/EX patina, Harris, 1800s, 25x31", EX .**4,675.00**
Windmill wheel, wood w/sheet metal tail, 3-color pnt, 46" **145.00**

Weaving

Early Americans used a variety of tools and a great amount of time to produce the material from which their clothing was made. Soaked and dried flax was broken on a flax brake to remove waste material. It was then tapped and stroked with a scutching knife. Hackles further removed waste and separated the short fibers from the longer ones. Unspun fibers were placed on the distaff of the spinning wheel for processing into yarn. The yarn was then wound around a reel for measuring. Three tools used for this purpose were the niddy-noddy, the reel yarn winder, and the click reel. After it was washed and dyed, the yarn was transferred to a barrel-cage or squirrel-cage swift and fed onto a bobbin winder.

Today flax wheels are more plentiful than the large wool wheels since they were small and could be more easily stored and preserved. The distaff, an often-discarded or misplaced part of the wheel, is very scarce. French spinners from the Quebec area painted their wheels. Many have been stripped and refinished by those unaware of this fact. Wheels may be very simple or have a great amount of detail, depending upon the owner's ethnic background and the maker's skill.

Oak spinning wheel, turned legs and posts, 1800s, $300.00.

Distaff, chip cvg, worn patina, 42" **85.00**
Hatchel, primitive, 2 groups spikes: 1 fine/1 coarse, 24" **45.00**
Loom basket, wide splint, minor damage, wall hanging, 13x12" .**100.00**
Loom basket, wide splint, 2-tier, yel pnt, lt wear, 17" **375.00**
Niddy noddy, cherry, trn detail, rare sm size, 9" **195.00**
Reel, dvtl pine, 4 scalloped dividers in base, trn posts, 37" **150.00**

Reel, hardwood, EX detail, tripod base, 12" **250.0**
Reel, various hardwoods w/bl pnt, rpl hdl, 26x22" **160.0**
Shuttle, maple wood, arched hdl, 3¼x4" **30.0**
Spinning wheel, EX trn, blk pnt, 35", VG **150.0**
Spinning wheel, EX trn, dbl bobbins/spinners, 46", EX **245.0**
Spinning wheel, rpl distaff, 19" wheel, 32"+distaff **325.0**
Spinning wheel, rpl distaff, 25" fr, 48", EX **300.0**
Swift, squirrel cage; adjustable top reel, 47" **105.0**
Swift, umbrella; att Shakers, wood, some damaged slats, 24" **125.0**
Tape loom, metal/leather fittings (VG), 2 heddles, 12x22" **150.0**
Tape loom, oak, primitive, 28" **45.0**
Tape loom, oak, simple w/fishtail hdl, age crack, 15" **150.0**
Tape loom, on base, various hardwoods w/dk finish, 28" **55.0**
Tape loom, poplar w/gray-bl pnt, hdl incomplete, 19" L **125.0**

Webb

Thomas Webb and Sons have been making fine art glass in Stou-bridge, England, since 1837. Besides their fine cameo glass, they have also made enameled ware and pieces heavily decorated with applie-glass ornaments. The butterfly is a motif that has been so often feature-that it tends to suggest Webb as the manufacturer. Our advisor for th-category is Don Williams; he is listed in the Directory under Missou-See also specific types of glass such as Alexandrite, Burmese, Mother-Pearl, and Peachblow.

Bottle, lay-down; gold floral/bird, mk silver lid, 5" L **250.0**
Bride's bowl, floral HP on pk shaded satin, 2½x10" **235.0**
Creamer & sugar bowl, Dmn Quilt, brn to gold, 2½", 3¾" **650.0**
Ewer, apples (yel & gr)/gold leaves on gr satin, 9x4" **425.0**
Ewer, leaves/branches, gold on gr shaded satin, 9x4" **435.0**
Rose bowl, floral emb on gr shaded satin, 4" **275.0**
Rose bowl, gold prunus/butterfly on brn satin, 2½x2½" **295.0**
Sweetmeat, Flower & Acorn, bl MOP satin, SP trim **1,100.0**
Vase, berried branches, amethyst on orange satin, ovoid, 6" **465.0**
Vase, bird, silver/wht/gold on yel satin, propeller mk, 9½" **415.0**
Vase, bird in flight w/prunus on bl shaded, 8¼" **425.0**
Vase, birds/butterfly/florals/frieze, yel on bl satin, 8x6" **425.0**
Vase, cluthra, crystal w/yel/red/bl/wht/gold mottle, 10" **330.0**
Vase, gold floral, apricot shaded, bulbous w/long neck, 11" **335.0**
Vase, gold prunus/butterfly on yel, unsgn, 6⅛x3½" **325.0**
Vase, gold prunus/butterfly on yel o/l, 3¼x4" **325.0**
Vase, pk & wht stripes, frilly top, bulbous, 8x4" **425.0**
Vase, rock crystal, cut Oriental design, Fritsche, 8x7" **3,000.0**
Vase, 14" cranberry trumpet form in clear 'caged' vase, ftd **575.0**

Cameo

Biscuit jar, floral branch, wht on red, SP mts, rnd, 7" **1,800.0**
Bottle, lay-down; floral, wht on citron, teardrop form, 3½" **750.0**
Bottle, lay-down; lilies & pads/dragonfly, wht on bl, 3" **1,000.0**
Bottle, lay-down; 2 butterflies/palms, wht on gr, 5½" **1,250.0**
Bottle, scent; appl floral plaque, waffle-cut sphere, 5" **750.0**
Bottle, scent; ferns, wht on yel, cylindrical, 3" **600.0**
Bottle, scent; floral, wht on citron, silver cap, 1¾" **550.0**
Bottle, scent; floral/butterfly, wht on red, flat lid, 5x5" **1,800.0**
Bottle, scent; floral/moth, wht on turq, sq, silver top, 6" **1,800.0**
Bottle, scent; morning-glories, wht on red, spherical, 4" **1,600.0**
Bowl, allover tapestry design, wht/bl on cobalt, 3¾x5" **6,000.0**
Bowl, flowers/butterflies, wht on citron, 3¾", +underplate **1,000.0**
Bowl, stippled w/repetitive motif, wht on raisin, 2¾x5" **7,250.0**
Inkwell, bellflowers, wht on citron, silver top, bulbous, 4" **1,700.0**
Vase, apple blossoms, wht on citron, rnd w/long neck, 6" **1,600.0**

Vase, apple blossoms, wht/lt bl on bl, sgn Woodall, 8" 23,100.00
Vase, Arabesque motif, 4-layer, bottle form, Gem, 7" 8,250.00
Vase, bee/butterfly/lg iris, red/wht on citron, 9" 3,000.00
Vase, Blk-Eyed Susan, wht on citron, cylinder neck, 9" 1,900.00
Vase, blkberries/flowers, red/wht on citron, bulbous, 2½" 800.00
Vase, butterflies/floral, wht on citron, can neck, 6" 1,500.00
Vase, butterfly/allover zinnias, wht on red, dbl gourd, 8" 2,000.00
Vase, butterfly/bee/grapevines, pk/bl on citron, 5x3½" 1,300.00
Vase, dragon cartouches, elephant head hdls, ivory, 9" 3,000.00
Vase, floral branch/butterfly, red/wht on citron, 8" 2,500.00
Vase, fuchsias, red/wht on citron, waisted neck, 5" 2,000.00
Vase, honeysuckle/3 bees, wht on citron, bottle form, Gem, 15" ..5,500.00
Vase, lg flowers, wht/purple on turq frost, gourd form, 8" 3,900.00
Vase, lg leaves/buds, wht on med bl, 5x7½" 1,450.00
Vase, lg leaves/floral, bk: insects, wht on raisin, 3" 2,500.00
Vase, lg lilies, citron on clear, U-form, 8" 500.00
Vase, lilac branches, bk: plum blossoms, wht on bl, 8" 2,000.00
Vase, lilies on honeycomb, amber on crystal, ftd, 8x8" 600.00
Vase, morning-glories/butterfly, wht on cased red, att, 2" 1,100.00
Vase, morning-glories/insects, wht on red, bottle form, 11" 1,600.00
Vase, orchids, bk: daisies, 3-color w/gilt, Barbe, 6x6" 8,250.00
Vase, passion flowers, wht/red on clear, 5x5" 1,200.00
Vase, raspberry branch, bk: moth, wht on bl, bulbous, 9½" 1,300.00
Vase, repeating Persian-style motif, wht on clear, 3½" 900.00
Vase, woven bottle neck, floral body, wht on brn, Gem, 9" 5,225.00
Vase, 3 birds on branch, simulated ivory, ovoid, 6½" 6,600.00
Vase, 4 lilies, red on crystal, flared U-form, mk, 9½" 1,900.00

Wedgwood

Josiah Wedgwood established his pottery in Burslem, England, in
'59. He produced only molded utilitarian earthenwares until 1770
hen new facilities were opened at Etruria. It was there he introduced
s famous Basalt and Jasperware. Jasperware, an unglazed fine
oneware decorated with classic figures in white relief, was usually pro-
ced in blues; but it was also made in ground colors of green, lilac, yel-
w, black, or white. Occasionally three or more colors were used in
mbination. It has been in continuous production to the present day
d is the most easily recognized of all the Wedgwood lines. Jasper-dip
a ware with a solid-color body or a white body that has been dipped
an overlay color. It was introduced in the late 1700s and is the type
ost often encountered on today's market.

Though Wedgwood's Jasperware was highly acclaimed, on a more
ctical basis his improved creamware was his greatest success. Due to
e ease with which it could be potted and because its lighter weight
nificantly reduced transportation expenses, Wedgwood was able to
er 'chinaware' at affordable prices. Queen Charlotte was so pleased
th the ware that she allowed it to be called 'Queen's Ware.' Most
amware was marked simply 'Wedgwood.' ('Wedgwood & Co.' and
edgewood' are marks of other potters.) From 1769 to 1780, Wedg-
od was in partnership with Thomas Bently; artwares of the highest
ality bear the mark indicating this partnership. Moonlight Lustre, an
over splashed-on effect of pink intermingling with gray, brown, or
low, was made from 1805 to 1815. Porcelain was made, though not
any great extent, from 1812 to 1822. Bone china was produced
ore 1822 and after 1872. These types of wares were marked 'Wedg-
od.' Stone china and Pearlware were made from about 1820 to 1875.
amples of either may be found with a mark to indicate their body
e. During the late 1800s, Wedgwood produced some fine parian and
jolica. Creamware, hand painted by Emile Lessore, was sold from
ut 1860 to 1875. From the 20th century, several lines of lustre wares
Butterfly, Dragon, and Fairyland (designed by Miss Makeig-Jones)
have attracted the collector and, as their prices suggest, are highly
ght-after and admired.

Nearly all of Wedgwood's wares are clearly marked. 'Wedgwood'
was used before 1891, after which time 'England' was added. Most examples marked 'Made In England' were made after 1905. A detailed study of
all marks is recommended for accurate dating. See also Majolica.

Key:
WW — Wedgwood   WWE — Wedgwood England

**Fairyland Lustre, Malfrey pot
shape, 9½", $4,000.00.**

Basket, Creamware, rust, raffia hdl, ca 1840 ....235.00
Basket, silver & pk lustre w/appl wht vintage, WW, 3⅜" 185.00
Biscuit jar, Jasper, dk bl, ladies/cupids, SP lid, WW, 6" 225.00
Biscuit jar, Jasper, dk bl, Muses, SP lid, ca 1860 ....300.00
Biscuit jar, Jasper, lt bl, ladies/cherubs, SP trim, WW, 6" 225.00
Biscuit jar, Jasper, yel/blk, WW, 5½" 525.00
Bowl, Bone China, Chinese boys on seesaw, att Cutts, 12" 1,200.00
Bowl, Butterfly Lustre, gold/umber, bl/gr int, WWE, 8" 500.00
Bowl, Butterfly Lustre, mk England, 3" 200.00
Bowl, Butterfly Lustre, 8-sided, #Z832, 6" 400.00
Bowl, Dragon Lustre, bl w/gold, 8½" 550.00
Bowl, Dragon Lustre, bl w/yel-gr int, octagonal, wear, 9" 465.00
Bowl, Fairyland Lustre, elves & bell branches, #Z5360, 9" 3,000.00
Bowl, Fairyland Lustre, fairy in lg hat, WW, #Z4968, 3x7" 3,000.00
Bowl, Fairyland Lustre, Leapfrogging Elves, #Z4968, 3¾" 880.00
Bowl, Hummingbird Lustre, bl w/orange int, octagonal, 8" 525.00
Bowl, Hummingbird Lustre, geese borders, WW, 4½x10" 525.00
Bowl, Jasper, lt bl, WWE, 2x4¾" 80.00
Bowl, punch; Butterfly Lustre, #Z4827, ped ft, 8" 770.00
Bowl, vegetable; Creamware, Patrician, WWE 150.00
Box, Jasper, bl, Pegasus & man, WW, 2x2⅝x3" 90.00
Box, Jasper, bl, Portland, octagonal, WWE, 1½x3" 225.00
Box, Jasper, dk bl, vintage, WWE, 3¾x4¾" 95.00
Box, Jasper, lilac, heart form, WWE, 1981 ....175.00
Box, Stoneware, olive gr, heart form, 2x3½x4½" 150.00
Brooch, Butterfly Lustre, MOP bkground, silver fr, 1923 ....300.00
Brooch, Jasper, lt bl, in sterling fr, WW, 1½" dia 235.00
Brooch, Jasper, 3-color, octagonal, sterling fr, 1¼x1½" 435.00
Bust, Basalt, bearded man, WW, 4⅜x2⅛" 385.00
Butter pat, Creamware, Eastern Flowers 48.00
Butter pat, Gr Glaze, shell shape, ca 1880 ....48.00
Candlestick, Jasper, dk bl, WW, 7" 135.00
Coffeepot, Creamware, Tea Party transfer, 1780, 12", VG 3,000.00
Compote, Jasper, terra cotta/wht, WWE, 3¾x6" 245.00
Compote, Jasper, yel, blk/grapes & leaves, 8", +underplate 825.00
Creamer, Drabware, salt-glazed Egyptian decor, WW, ca 1805 ..350.00
Creamer, Drabware, thistles etc, ca 1840, 2½x5" 165.00
Creamer, Jasper, lt bl, St Louis shape, WWE, 2¼x3½" 125.00

Cup & saucer, Caneware, blk, vintage, WW, ca 1810 ....435.00
Cup & saucer, demitasse; Basalt, WWE, ca 1958 ....55.00
Cup & saucer, handleless; Basalt, no decor, WW, 2¼x3" 50.00
Dish, Dragon Lustre on MOP, sq, #4831, 1925, 8½" 365.00
Dish, Moonlight Lustre, shell form, rim roughage, 1810, 11" 300.00
Dish, portrait of classical female, oval, Lessore, 7x9" 1,000.00
Drainer, Pearlware, HP flowers, ca 1840 ....335.00
Figurine, Basalt, cupid sits on rocks, WW, 8" 875.00
Figurine, Basalt, elephant, trunk lowered, 1916, 3½" 800.00
Figurine, Basalt, Nymph at Well, 1840s, 11" 1,050.00
Figurine, Basalt, Psyche, seated nude, WW, 8" 825.00
Figurine, Basalt, sleeping boy, rpr, WW, 7" 2,000.00
Figurine, kingfisher, basalt 750.00
Figurine, monkeys, cream, Skeaping, 1930, 7½" 785.00
Figurine, polar bear, Creamware, sgn, ca 1927, 7x4⅛x10" 800.00
Figurine, tiger w/buck, Skeaping 900.00
Flower frog, Creamware, tree trunk form, WWE, 6" dia 75.00
Humidor, Jasper, dk bl, ball finial, WW, 6" 325.00
Inkwell, Basalt, appl Rosso Antico motifs, sq base, 1700s 700.00
Inkwell, Basalt, drum form, for plume pen, unmk, 2⅛x2¾" 225.00
Jar, Jasper, lt bl, WWE, 1¾x3" dia 75.00
Jardiniere, Jasper, dk bl, WWE, 4½x5" 300.00
Jardiniere, Jasper, lt bl, WWE, 4¼x4¾" 155.00
Jardiniere, Stoneware, olive gr, flared top, WW, 7½" 435.00
Loving cup, Jasper, lt bl, 3-hdl, WWE, 4½" 170.00
Medallion, Jasper, Elizabeth & Phillip, WWE, '53, 4¼x3¼", pr 325.00
Medallion, Jasper, lt bl, Trinity Church, WWE 120.00
Mug, Basalt, acorn/oak leaf, silver rim, 1820s, 3¾" 660.00
Pitcher, Basalt, mc florals, WW, 5½" 275.00
Pitcher, Basalt, Victoria BC, WWE, 3½" 130.00
Pitcher, Bone China, purple lustre, Ferrara, WWE 130.00
Pitcher, Bramble, majolica, 6½" 425.00
Pitcher, Creamware, lt bl, fruit/flowers, WW, ca 1869, 6½" 335.00
Pitcher, Jasper, bl, bulbous, WW, ca 1850, 4½" 210.00
Pitcher, Jasper, dk bl, trefoil spout, WW, 5½" 175.00
Pitcher, tankard; Jasper, dk bl, WW, 5⅜x3⅜" 225.00
Pitcher, tankard; Jasper, dk bl, WWE, 6⅜" 250.00
Plaque, Fairyland Lustre, elves in pine tree, #Z5287, 10½x8" ..5,000.00
Plaque, Jasper, bl, Fall of Phaeton, 1977, 12x10" 1,000.00
Plaque, Jasper, bl, Sacrifice of Iphigenia, WW, fr, 3½x8" 500.00
Plaque, wht w/cobalt portrait of lady w/fan, 1877, 15" 300.00
Plate, Bone China, portrait of dog, rtcl border, 1880, 9" 250.00
Plate, Creamware, Buns Buns Buns, child/vendor, Lessore, 9" 425.00
Plate, Creamware, Knave of Hearts, WWE, ca 1905 ....150.00
Plate, Creamware, mc, Ivanhoe, WWE 160.00
Plate, Creamware, Nouveau decor, WWE, ca 1907 ....95.00
Plate, Dragon Lustre on MOP, #X4831, 1925, 9", pr 770.00
Plate, Gr Glaze, Sunflower, WW, 8⅝" 100.00
Plate, Jasper, lt bl, WWE, 9½" 75.00
Plate, Jasper, Portland bl, WWE, 10" 165.00
Plate, wedding; Jasper, 3-color, Prince of Wales, ltd ed 440.00
Platter, Creamware, red/bl florals, WWE, 12¾x10" 130.00
Potpourri, Pearlware, apple gr/rust/bl, ca 1850, 16" 2,250.00
Ring, Jasper, dk bl, cameo in sterling setting 235.00
Ring tree, Jasper, dk bl, floral border, WW, 2¾x3" 175.00
Salt cellar, Jasper, bl, Dancing Hours, 1780s, 2", EX 440.00
Salt cellar, Jasper, bl, WWE, 2x2½" 100.00
Shaker, Jasper, lt bl, lighthouse shape, WWE, 3¾" 105.00
Sugar bowl, Drabware, w/lid, WW, 1810 ....245.00
Sugar bowl, Jasper, dk bl, w/lid, WWE, 5½" dia 155.00
Sugar bowl, Stoneware, wht, Gothic, w/lid, ca 1830 ....275.00
Tea caddy, Jasper, dk bl, WWE 200.00
Tea set, Basalt, Muses/trophy medallions, WW, 3-pc 825.00
Teapot, Basalt, Capri, ca 1840, lg 545.00

Teapot, Caneware, Rosso decor, WW, ca 1805, lg 525.00
Teapot, Jasper, gr, WW, pre-1915, 4¼" 200.00
Tile, Stoneware, Eanymede & Eagle, 6x6"+fr 455.00
Toothpick holder, Jasper, dk bl, WWE, 1⅞x1¾" 140.00
Tray, Fairyland Lustre, Garden of Paradise I, #Z4968, 11" dia .2,300.00
Tray, Jasper, blk, mk, ca 1967, 5¾x3" 80.00
Tray, Jasper, lilac, dmn shape, WWE 65.00
Tray, Jasper, lt bl, Taurus, WWE 45.00
Tray, Jasper, pk, heart shape, WWE 65.00
Tray, Jasper, primrose, WWE, 3" dia 45.00
Urn, Jasper, lav, classic figures, sq base/lid/hdls, WW, 9" 1,190.00
Vase, Bone China, Imari colors, hexagonal, WW, ca 1880, 7" ...195.00
Vase, Butterfly Lustre, flame lustre inside top, WW, 8½" 385.00
Vase, Dragon Lustre, gold on lt bl mottle, WW, 8¾x6" 475.00
Vase, Fairyland Lustre, Firbolgs V, sq, #15200 (?), 7½" 1,900.00
Vase, Fairyland Lustre, Rainbow, #Z5349, w/lid, 1920, 9" 2,750.00
Vase, horizontal rings, gr matt, bulbous, Keith Murray, 6" 495.00
Vase, Jasper, blk, Geo III/Caesar commemorative, WW, 5½" 325.00
Vase, Jasper, blk, w/lid, mk, ca 1905, 11½" 1,500.00
Vase, Jasper, dk bl, WWE, 2" 125.00
Vase, Jasper, dk gr, Portland, ca 1930, 6¼" 365.00
Vase, Jasper, lt bl, cupid finial, ovoid, WW, ca 1825, 9½" 1,275.00
Wall pocket, majolica, word on edge, 12x9" 1,500.00
Wine cooler, Rosso Antico, classical figures, hdls, WW, 9" 825.00

Weil Ware

Max Weil came to the United States in the 1940s, settling in California. There he began manufacturing dinnerware, figurines, cookie jars, and wall pockets. American clays were used, and the dinnerware was all hand decorated. Weil died in 1954; the company closed two years later. The last backstamp to be used was the outline of a burro with the words 'Weil Ware — Made in California.' Many unmarked pieces found today originally carried a silver foil label; but you'll often find a four-digit handwritten number series, especially on figurines. For further study we recommend *The Collector's Encyclopedia of California Pottery* by our advisor, Jack Chipman. He is listed in the Directory under California.

Figure of a girl, 11", $35.00.

Bowl, cream soup; Rose ....6.
Bowl, divided vegetable; Rose ....12.
Bowl, salad; Rose, sm ....4.
Bowl, vegetable; Rose ....10.
Butter dish, Rose ....13.
Comport, sweets; Rose ....12.
Cup & saucer, Rose ....6.

igurine, boy w/wheelbarrow, #4005 ....22.00
igurine, Buddy, boy, 7" 15.00
igurine, girl, lifted chin, sgraffito floral on skirt, lg 32.00
igurine, girl w/bowl, 11" 25.00
Gravy boat, Rose 17.50
Plate, Rose, 10" 6.00

Weller

The Weller Pottery Company was established in Zanesville, Ohio, in 1882, the outgrowth of a small one-kiln log cabin works Sam Weller had operated in Fultonham. Through an association with Wm. Long, he entered the art pottery field in 1895, producing the Lonhuda Ware Long had perfected in Steubenville six years earlier. His famous Louwelsa line was merely a continuation of Lonhuda and was made in at least five hundred different shapes until 1924. Many fine lines of artware followed under the direction of Charles Babcock Upjohn, Art Director from 1895 to 1904: Dickens Ware (1st Line), under-glaze slip decorations on dark backgrounds; Turada, featuring applied ivory bands of delicate openwork on solid dark brown backgrounds; and Aurelian, similar to Louwelsa, but with a brushed-on rather than blended ground. One of their most famous lines was 2nd Line Dickens, introduced in 1900. Backgrounds, characteristically caramel shading to turquoise matt, were decorated by sgraffito with animals, golfers, monks, Indians, and scenes from Dickens novels. The work is often artist signed. Sicardo, 1903, was a metallic lustre line in tones of rose, blue, green, or purple with flowing Art Nouveau patterns developed within the glaze.

Frederick Hurten Rhead, who worked for Weller in 1903 to 1904, created the prestigious Jap Birdimal line decorated with geisha girls, landscapes, storks, etc., accomplished through application of heavy slip traced through the tiny nozzle of a squeeze bag. Other lines to his credit are L'Art Nouveau, produced both in high-gloss brown and matt pastels, and 3rd Line Dickens, often decorated with Cruikshank's illustrations in relief. Other early artware lines were Eocean, Floretta, Hunter, Perfecto, Dresden, Etched Matt, and Etna.

In 1920 John Lessel was hired as Art Director, and under his supervision several new lines were created. LaSa, LaMar, Marengo, and Besline attest to his expertise with metallic lustres. The last of the artware lines and one of the most sought after by collectors today is Hudson, first made during the early 1920s. Hudson, a semimatt-glazed ware, was beautifully artist decorated on shaded backgrounds with florals, animals, birds, and scenics. Notable artists often signed their work, among them Hester Pillsbury, Dorothy England Laughead, Ruth Axline, Claude Leffler, Sarah Reid McLaughlin, E.L. Pickens, and Mae Timberlake.

During the thirties Weller produced a line of gardenware and naturalistic life-sized figures of dogs, cats, swans, geese, and playful gnomes. The Depression brought a slow, steady decline in sales, and by 1948 the pottery was closed. For a more thorough study we recommend *The Collector's Encyclopedia of Weller Pottery* by Sharon and Bob Huxford, available at your local library or from Collector Books.

Arvin, vase, 4 openings on trunk form, no mk, 8½" 35.00
Atcola, planter, floral, ruffled rim, up-trn hdls, no mk, 5x9" 85.00
Ardsley, vase, bud; cattails & water lily, 7½" 45.00
Ardsley, vase, corner; iris ea corner, 3-ftd, 7" 85.00
Ardsley, wall pocket, dbl; cattails & water lily, 11½" 125.00
L'Art Nouveau, umbrella stand, floral, glossy, no mk, 26" 850.00
L'Art Nouveau, vase, ear of corn figural, 4½" 95.00
L'Art Nouveau, vase, lady, glossy, sq sides, no mk, 12½" 375.00
L'Art Nouveau, vase, Nouveau lady, slim, no mk, 17½" 500.00
L'Art Nouveau, wall pocket, floral, no mk, 6½" 165.00
Athens, vase, swags & medallions, no mk, 10" 375.00
Aurelian, ewer, cavalier, sgn Fouts, 16½" 1,050.00

Aurelian, jardiniere & ped, floral, no mk, 38" 1,500.00
Aurelian, lamp, banquet; floral, sgn Schnieder, 27" 1,150.00
Aurelian, vase, floral, H Mitchell, sm/short neck, 12" 300.00
Aurelian, vase, floral, sgn Fouts, ornate ring hdls, 18" 1,850.00
Aurelian, vase, floral, sgn RA, classic form, 13" 500.00
Aurelian, vase, floral, TJW, flared cylinder, 16" 875.00
Auroro, vase, goldfish, Hattie Mitchell, 9" 1,100.00
Baldin, vase, apples, bulbous, no mk, 5½" 150.00
Baldin, vase, apples, twig hdls, bulbous, no mk, 9½" 225.00

Barcelona vase, 14", $300.00.

Bedford Matt, umbrella stand, floral, 20" 350.00
Besline, vase, leaves/berries, orange ground, 8½", NM 260.00
Besline, vase, vintage, 11" 525.00
Blossom, wall vase, floral on brn, 7½" 60.00
Blue Drapery, candlestick, floral, no mk, 9½" 70.00
Blue Drapery, jardiniere, floral, no mk, 5½" 35.00
Blue Drapery, vase, floral, no mk, 4" 22.50
Blue Ware, comport, fruit swags on bl, 5½" 165.00
Blue Ware, jardiniere, 2 angels, no mk, 8½" 185.00
Blue Ware, vase, classical lady, 8½" 190.00
Bonito, bowl, floral on cream, sgn CF, 3½" H 75.00
Bonito, vase, daisies/banded decor, U-form, 10" 170.00
Bonito, vase, floral on cream, sgn NC, sm angle hdls, 10" 215.00
Breton, bowl, floral, gr, no mk, 4" 70.00
Breton, vase, floral, brn, no mk, 6" 35.00
Brighton, flamingo, no mk, 6" 225.00
Brighton, kingfisher, half kiln ink stamp, 9" 200.00
Brighton, parakeets on perch, 9" 875.00
Brighton, parrot on perch, 7½" 450.00
Brighton, parrot w/spread wings, hanging, no mk, 15" 800.00
Brighton, pheasant, 7x11½" 450.00
Brighton, vase, dbl bud; bird perched on limb, no mk, 12" 225.00
Burntwood, plaque, bird on branch, no mk, 12" 300.00
Burntwood, vase, bird on branch, cylindrical, no mk, 8½" 120.00
Burntwood, vase, floral on tan, brn rim & base, ftd, 6½" 125.00
Camelot, vase, geometric decor, no mk, 8" 225.00
Cameo, bowl, creamware, rtcl rim, hdls, 2½" H 35.00
Cameo Jewell, jardiniere, 7½" 175.00
Cameo Jewell, umbrella stand, gr shaded, 22" 550.00
Candis, basket, hanging, no mk, 5½" 85.00
Candis, candle holder, 1½", pr 35.00
Candis, ewer, wht, 11" 60.00
Chase, vase, fox hunt scene on bl, 6½" 185.00
Chase, vase, fox hunt scene on brn, 10½" 300.00
Chengtu, ginger jar, 12" 200.00
Chengtu, urn, 5½" 70.00
Chengtu, vase, classic form, 16" 325.00
Chengtu, vase, slim form, 8" 65.00
Claywood, mug, floral, cylindrical, 5" 85.00
Claywood, spittoon, floral, no mk, 4½" 115.00

Claywood, vase, floral on tan, brn rim & base, no mk, 3½" 65.00
Cloudburst, vase, lav/wht/rose w/lustre, 7" 220.00
Cloudburst, vase, orange bkground, 8" 170.00
Coppertone, frog, 4" 175.00
Coppertone, pitcher, fish hdl, 7½" 1,000.00
Dickens I, jardiniere, floral, 8½" 275.00
Dickens I, jug, ear of corn, 6½" 300.00
Dickens I, loving cup, floral, artist sgn, 3-hdl, 5½" 335.00
Dickens I, mug, floral, 7" 185.00
Dickens I, vase, portrait, 3-ftd, pillow form, 7" 1,950.00
Dickens II, ewer, fish, sgn EL Pickens, swirled body, 11½" 525.00
Dickens II, ewer, mermaid, no mk, 10½" 425.00
Dickens II, humidor, Irishman, sgn RD, no mk, 6½" 700.00
Dickens II, tankard, nude, sgn EL Pickens 1902, no mk, 12" ...2,500.00
Dickens II, vase, Dombey & Son, sgn Gibson, cylindrical, 10½" ...785.00
Dickens II, vase, Don Quixote & Sancho..., Pickens, 16" 1,850.00
Dickens II, vase, dragon, sgn Pickens, classic form, 15½" 800.00
Dickens II, vase, floral, incising around pattern, 9½" 350.00
Dickens II, vase, hunting dog portrait, sgn Pickens, 9" 1,200.00
Dickens II, vase, lady golfer, sgn DS, flared ft, 8" 500.00
Dickens II, vase, lady in billowy dress, Dusenbury, 12" 1,350.00
Dickens II, vase, man fishing, classic form, 15½" 1,350.00
Dickens III, creamer, Charles Dickens on disk, #0034, 4" 175.00
Dickens III, ewer, Squeers, sgn LM, 12½" 500.00
Dickens III, vase, portrait, sm angle hdls, 6" 285.00

Dickens, Second Line, vase incised with ladies in a country landscape, 18", $2,500.00.

Dresden, vase, windmill, bl on shaded bl, sgn LJB, 10½" 525.00
Dresden, vase, windmill scene, widens at base, 5" 425.00
Dunton, umbrella stand, birds on floral branches, no mk, 23" 750.00
Dupont, bowl, floral panels, Roma glaze, no mk, 3" 45.00
Dupont, vase, floral panels, cylindrical, 10" 115.00
Dynasty, vase, gr to dk bl, ring hdls, 6" 50.00
Eocean, basket, floral sprig, ruffled rim, no mk, 6½" 250.00
Eocean, Late Line; vase, bud; floral, no mk, 6½" 70.00
Eocean, Late Line; vase, floral, ring ft, 8½" 225.00
Eocean, Late Line; vase, yel roses, elongated ovoid, 8" 215.00
Eocean, vase, daffodil, initialed, 8" 260.00
Eocean, vase, floral, sgn AH, cylindrical, sm hdls, 13½" 535.00
Eocean, vase, floral, sgn LJB, classic form, 13" 550.00
Eocean, vase, floral, sgn LJB, slim neck, flared rim, 11½" 350.00
Eocean, vase, holly berries/leaves, sgn B, slim, 8" 350.00
Eocean, vase, long-stem roses, sgn JB, rnd shoulder, 10" 450.00
Eocean, vase, owl on branch w/full moon, sgn Blake, 9x4" 850.00
Eocean, vase, owl on limb, sgn EB, 10½" 1,350.00
Eocean Rose, vase, floral, sgn Leffler, elongated ovoid, 12" 240.00
Eocean Rose, vase, lg stork, sgn Chilcote, cylindrical, 10" 800.00
Etched Matt, vase, grapes among vines, slim form, 14" 365.00

Etched Matt, vase, roses w/prickly stems, classic form, 6½" 185.00
Ethel, vase, creamware, fan form, 6" 50.00
Ethel, vase, creamware, ftd, 11" 225.00
Etna, jardiniere, floral rim, 9½" 250.00
Etna, pitcher, floral on shaded bkground, die stamp, 6" 135.00
Etna, vase, floral, waisted form, 5½" 85.00
Etna, vase, lizard on shaded brn to pk, 4½" 400.00
Etna, vase, sm pk flowers, twisted hdls, sqat, 5x9" 215.00
Evergreen, bowl, console; 5" 65.00
Evergreen, candlestick, 1½", pr 32.00
Evergreen, vase, slightly waisted, 4½" 35.00
Fairfield, vase, flared cylinder, no mk, 9½" 100.00
Flask, All's Well, no mk, 4" 125.00
Flask, FOE, no mk, 5½" 100.00
Flask, Never Dry, no mk, 6" 125.00
Flask, Suffer-E-Get, no mk, 6" 125.00
Flemish, comport, floral, flower finial, 8½" 125.00
Flemish, jardiniere, floral, 8" 175.00
Flemish, tub, floral, hdls, 4" 65.00
Flemish, umbrella stand, floral panels, 21½" 365.00
Flemish, vase, floral, shape #8, 10" 150.00
Florala, candle holder, floral, 6-sided, 5", pr 55.00
Florala, wall pocket, floral, 10" 90.00
Floretta, ewer, grape cluster, simple hdl, 10½" 125.00
Floretta, vase, floral, up-trn hdls, 6½" 100.00
Floretta, vase, floral on shaded brn to pk, 19" 550.00
Floretta, vase, floral on shaded brn to tan, squat, 5½" 70.00
Forest, jardiniere & ped, woodland scene, no mk, 26" 600.00
Forest, pitcher, woodland scene, glossy, 5" 175.00
Forest, planter, woodland scene, tub hdls, 6" 120.00
Forest, vase, woodland scene, flared cylinder, no mk, 13½" 225.00
Fruitone, vase, 6-sided, 8" 135.00
Fruitone, wall pocket, 5½" 70.00
Garden Ornament, goose, 12½x13" 1,150.00
Garden Ornament, Pan w/fife, 16½" 1,100.00
Garden Ornament, rabbit, 7½x13" 650.00
Garden Ornament, squirrel, no mk, 12" 725.00
Garden Ware, Coppertone frog, no mk, 11½x15" 875.00
Glendale, vase, bird, cylindrical, no mk, 6" 235.00
Glendale, vase, bird at nest, bulbous, 9" 375.00
Glendale, vase, bird in nest, classic form, 12" 400.00
Glendale, vase, dbl bud; bird, no mk, 7" 200.00
Greenaways, jardiniere, windmill, tub hdls, 10" 450.00
Hobart, vase, dbl bud; nude amid 2 tree trunk forms, 10" 200.00
Hudson, bud vase, roses, sgn, 7" 140.00
Hudson, vase, bird on blk branch on gray gloss, 14" 1,200.00
Hudson, vase, daisies, S Timberlake, trumpet form, 9" 275.00
Hudson, vase, dogwood, Axline, loop hdls, 10x10" 600.00
Hudson, vase, fruit on branch, sgn Pillsbury, hdls, 13½" 825.00
Hudson, vase, lg iris, D England, cylindrical, 8½" 375.00
Hudson, vase, lily of valley, hdls, sgn McLaughlin, 7" 325.00
Hudson, vase, nasturtiums, EX art, Pillsbury, ovoid, 9" 300.00
Hudson, vase, nasturtiums, yel on shaded pk & gr, slim, 12" 425.00
Hudson, vase, rider in landscape, sgn Timberlake, 9" 1,300.00
Hudson, vase, sailboats/ocean, glossy, sgn Mull, 7x6" 1,200.00
Hudson, vase, 3 daisies, S McLaughlin, 11" 350.00
Hudson, vase, 4 birds, Pillsbury, ovoid, 9" 1,400.00
Hudson, wall pocket, floral branches on wht, 8" 190.00
Hudson-Perfecto, vase, iris, sgn C Leffler, 13½" 1,100.00
Hudson-Perfecto, vase, man on horse, classic form, 13" 2,800.00
Hudson-Perfecto, vase, mums, sgn Leffler, 9½" 725.00
Hudson-Perfecto, vase, pine cones, sgn Leffler, no mk, 10" 425.00
Hunter, vase, birds soaring, sgn UJ, #413, 7½" 750.00
Hunter, vase, duck, ewer form, 7" 500.00

voris, ginger jar, w/lid, 8½" 65.00
voris, pitcher, 6" 40.00
voris, powder box, w/lid, 4" 45.00
voris, vase, 3-ftd, 6" 25.00
vory, jardiniere & ped, molded in 1-pc, no mk, 26½" 800.00
vory, planter, dragonfly, sq, no mk, 4" 85.00
vory, vase, floral swags, pillow form, ftd, no mk, 5" 60.00
vory, vase, foliage panels, cylindrical, 10" 60.00
vory, wall pocket, floral, no mk, 9" 85.00
vory, window planter, floral, 6x15½" 135.00
p Birdimal, pitcher, oil; sampans, sgn HMR, 10½" 800.00
p Birdimal, trees, bl on pk shaded, flared cylinder, 14" 700.00
p Birdimal, vase, birds, twisted/ruffled form, no mk, 11" 550.00
p Birdimal, vase, geisha, EX mc on turq, Rhead, 12", NM 1,300.00
wel, vase, tapered cylinder, sm ft, 9" 275.00
enova, bowl, floral, 3½" 115.00
enova, vase, floral, squat, 5½" 250.00
yro, basket, floral, ftd, no mk, 7" 65.00
yro, planter, floral, no mk, 3½" 45.00
yro, vase, floral, circle form, 8" 80.00
nifewood, bowl, swans, glossy, no mk, 4" 115.00
nifewood, humidor, hunting dog in pointing pose, no mk, 7" ..400.00
nifewood, jar, bird on branch, w/lid, 8" 335.00
nifewood, tobacco box, foxes, 3½" 115.00
nifewood, vase, floral, glossy, 4½" 70.00
nifewood, vase, floral, 7" 115.00
nifewood, wall vase, floral on bl, 8" 135.00
Sa, bud vase, palm trees/mtns/sunset, 8" 170.00
Sa, lamp base, landscape, 12" 285.00
Sa, vase, biplane, cylindrical, 9" 1,650.00
Sa, vase, landscape, classic form, 6½" 225.00
Sa, vase, landscape, pyramid form, no mk, 6½" 185.00
Sa, vase, tree scene, ovoid, 4" 200.00
mar, vase, scenic, gourd shape, ink stamp, 14½" 500.00
mar, vase, water scenic, classic form, no mk, 11½" 300.00
mar, vase, water scenic, slim, no mk, 7½" 160.00
oanon, vase, bulbous, rnd hdls, no mk, 9" 525.00
oanon, vase, shouldered form, no mk, 6" 385.00
nhuda, ewer, floral, sgn JRS, ornate hdl, bulbous, #215, 7" 400.00
nhuda, ewer, floral, shield mk, 6" 235.00
uwelsa, Blue; vase, floral, cylindrical, 10½" 800.00
uwelsa, Blue; vase, floral, 1 integral hdl, 3" 350.00
uwelsa, candle holder, floral, sgn MH, 4½" 135.00
uwelsa, clock, floral, 10½x12½" 700.00
uwelsa, ewer, floral, #74, 6" 155.00
uwelsa, ewer, floral w/silver o/l, 9" 1,400.00
uwelsa, ewer, roses, sgn, #88, 7" 195.00
uwelsa, ewer, yel roses, sgn MS, #423, 3x4" 125.00
uwelsa, jardiniere, floral, ruffled rim, 9½" 275.00
uwelsa, jug, floral, 3" 165.00
uwelsa, mug, floral, sgn MM, 5½" 175.00
uwelsa, mug, portrait, sgn Ferrell, #432, 6½" 825.00
uwelsa, pitcher, floral, sgn MT, 5" 155.00
uwelsa, star, floral, w/lid, 2½" 235.00
uwelsa, tankard, portrait, sgn LJ Burgess, 12½" 1,600.00
uwelsa, vase, berries, 3 pointed hdls, 3 ft, #583, 7" 175.00
uwelsa, vase, cherries, artist sgn, 3 hdls/ft, 6x7" 175.00
uwelsa, vase, dog's portrait, sgn A Wilson, bulbous, 10½" ...1,350.00
uwelsa, vase, floral, integral hdls, squat, 2" 145.00
uwelsa, vase, floral, sgn D, jug form, 6½" 145.00
uwelsa, vase, floral, sgn Haubrich, hdls, 23½" 925.00
uwelsa, vase, floral, sgn MH, 3-ftd, integral hdls, 5" ...155.00
uwelsa, vase, floral, sgn MM, cylindrical, angle hdls, 11" 250.00
uwelsa, vase, floral, sgn WH, classic form, 14½" 300.00

Louwelsa, vase, grape clusters, sgn Pillsbury, 24½" 1,500.00
Louwelsa, vase, portrait, sgn TTH, pillow form, 7½" 1,300.00
Louwelsa, vase, roses, sgn K, ovoid, 9" 155.00
Lustre, candlestick, 8" 47.50
Lustre, comport, butressed ft, 7" 50.00
Lustre, vase, classic form, 9½" 42.50
Lustre, vase, integral hdls, 5" 35.00
Malverne, jardiniere & ped, floral, 34" 550.00
Malverne, vase, leaves, circle form, 8" 52.50
Malverne, wall pocket, leaves, no mk, 11" 60.00
Mammy Line, creamer, nude child forms hdl, 3½" 275.00
Mammy Line, sugar bowl, children form hdls, w/lid, 3½" 300.00
Mammy Line, syrup, Mammy figural, 6" 400.00
Marbleized, bowl, 1½x5½" 40.00
Marbleized, comport, long stem w/flared base, 8" 85.00
Marbleized, jardiniere, 10" 250.00
Marbleized, vase, bulbous, 4½" 60.00
Marbleized, vase, cylindrical, 10" 160.00
Marengo, vase, trees & landscape, 6-sided, no mk, 8" 235.00
Marvo, vase, foliage, gr, cylindrical, ink stamp, 8½" 55.00
Marvo, wall vase, foliage, no mk, 9" 115.00
Matt Floretta, tankard, apples, sgn CD, no mk, 13½" 425.00
Melrose, basket, grape cluster, twig hdl, 10" 160.00
Melrose, bowl, console; floral, ruffled rim, hdls, 5x8½" 85.00
Melrose, vase, fruit/foliage at top, hdl, 11" 140.00
Minerva, vase, flamingos, cylindrical, 8½" 425.00
Minerva, vase, forest scene, classic form, 13½" 325.00
Mirror Black, vase, bud; no mk, 5½" 37.50
Mirror Black, vase, dbl bud; 9" 65.00
Mirror Black, vase, waisted form, long hdls, no mk, 8" 70.00
Modeled Etched Matt, vase, tulip, red/gr on yel, 10", NM 200.00
Monochrome, bowl, bl, no mk, 2½x10" 42.50
Monochrome, comport, gr, 10" 65.00
Montego, vase, gr runs on brn, angle hdls, ftd, 9½" 125.00
Muskota, boy fishing, no mk, 6½" 225.00
Muskota, fence, 5" 165.00
Muskota, flower frog, geese at side, no mk, 6" 175.00
Muskota, flower frog, 2 boys, 7" 300.00
Muskota, girl kneeling, hand up to hair, no mk, 4" 225.00
Muskota, girl on stump, 8½" 250.00
Muskota, girl w/flowers & hat, no mk, 9" 325.00
Muskota, nude on rock, 8" 235.00
Noval, bowl, fruit, no mk, 3½x9½" 60.00
Noval, comport, fruit hdls, no mk, 5½" 55.00
Novelty, butterfly, bl, no mk, 2" 150.00
Novelty, dragonfly, no mk, 3¼" 150.00
Novelty, name card w/blk bird, no mk, 2x3" 90.00
Novelty, pin tray, appl flower at side, sgn DE, 2½" 90.00
Novelty, vase, St Louis World's Fair, angle hdls, no mk, 4" 115.00
Novelty, vase, St Louis 1904, no mk, 3" 175.00
Novelty, wall vase, teapot form, bl, 9" 60.00
Paragon, bowl vase, 4½" 50.00
Paragon, vase, floral, bulbous, 7½" 85.00
Parian, vase, floral, 8½" 155.00
Parian, wall pocket, floral, no mk, 10" 175.00
Pearl, basket, pearls & florals, ftd, no mk, 6½" 135.00
Pearl, candle holder, pearls & florals, 8½", pr 115.00
Pearl, vase, pearls & florals, 4 sm hdls, 9" 175.00
Pearl, wall pocket, pearls & florals, lustre, no mk, 8½" 100.00
Pearl, wall vase, pearls & florals, 8½" 150.00
Perfecto, ewer, floral, #580/2, no mk, 12" 450.00
Perfecto, vase, horse, sgn H Pillsbury, pillow form, 10½" 3,000.00
Pop-Eye Dog, blk w/cream spots, 4" 475.00
Pumila, bowl, flower form, 3½" 25.00

Pumila, plate, console, flower form, no mk, 3x12" 45.00
Ragenda, vase, drape swag, cylindrical, 12" 65.00
Ragenda, vase, drape swag, pk, 6½" 35.00
Rochell, vase, floral, sgn TF, 6" 250.00
Roma, bowl, floral, tub hdls, ftd, 3" 50.00
Roma, candlestick, triple; floral, no mk, 9" 135.00
Roma, comport, floral, 5½" 85.00
Roma, comport, medallion & floral swags, no mk, 4½x11" 115.00
Roma, jardiniere, flower basket reserves, no mk, 10½" 215.00
Roma, vase, bud; grapes, sq sides, ftd, no mk, 6½" 45.00
Rosemont, jardiniere, bird on floral branch, 7" 225.00
Rosemont, jardiniere, fruit basket reserves, no mk, 8" 165.00
Rosemont, jardiniere, long-stemmed flowers, 7" 155.00
Rosemont, vase, bird on leafy branch, 10½" 325.00
Rosemont, vase, 3 birds on branches, EX color, 10" 450.00
Sabrinian, bowl, console; shell, w/sea horse frog, 2½x9" 100.00
Sabrinian, window box, shell & sea horse, 3½x9" 135.00
Sicardo, bowl, emb floral, shaped rim, ftd, emb mk, 4x8" 550.00
Sicardo, figurine, Tambourine Boy, no mk, 9½" 3,000.00
Sicardo, lamp base, floral, 15½" 2,250.00
Sicardo, lamp base, lg blossoms, drilled, ovoid, 22" 2,850.00
Sicardo, mug, floral, mo mk, 3½" 450.00
Sicardo, vase, arabesques on wine/gr, flat shoulder, 8x7½" 1,600.00
Sicardo, vase, clover, bl-gr irid, 5" 600.00
Sicardo, vase, daisies, horn-like hdls, 9x9" 1,650.00
Sicardo, vase, daisies on irid, widening at 4-ftd base, 4" 440.00
Sicardo, vase, dandelion/flower/seeds (3 sides), ftd, 12½" 2,000.00
Sicardo, vase, floral, cylindrical, 9" 825.00
Sicardo, vase, floral, EX art, concave w/rnd shoulder, 6" 800.00
Sicardo, vase, floral, pillow form, hdls, 6½x10" 800.00
Sicardo, vase, floral, red/purple w/gold, cylinder, 8" 600.00
Sicardo, vase, floral, sqd ovoid, sgn, 5" 450.00
Sicardo, vase, floral, 4-lobed top, 5½" 350.00
Sicardo, vase, panels w/sqs & florals, 4 buttress ft, 4x4" 600.00
Sicardo, vase, plants/feathers, gr/wine, bottle form, 7½" 650.00
Sicardo, vase, snails/swirls, cylindrical, 9" 1,300.00
Sicardo, vase, stylized trees, cylindrical, 7" 660.00
Silvertone, vase, floral, experimental, no mk, 7½" 185.00
Silvertone, wall pocket, floral, 11" 165.00
Souevo, humidor, geometric decor, 6" 225.00
Souevo, vase, geometric decor, waisted, no mk, 8" 125.00
Teakwood, umbrella stand, griffins in wide band, 21" 450.00
Tivoli, vase, classic form on ftd base, no mk, 9½" 95.00
Tivoli, vase, flared cylinder, ftd, no mk, 8½" 75.00
Turada, lamp base, appl filigree, 4-ftd, 8" 750.00
Turada, mug, appl filigree, #562/7 on base, 6" 245.00
Turada, umbrella stand, appl filigree, cylindrical, 21" 700.00
Velva, bowl, floral, up-trn hdls, 9½" 60.00
Velva, vase, floral on gr, up-trn hdls, 6" 35.00
Voile, jardiniere, floral, scalloped rim, no mk, 6" 70.00
Voile, vase, floral, fan form, no mk, 8" 70.00
Wht & Decorated, vase, 2 lg birds/branches, EX art, 8" 800.00
Woodcraft, bowl, hanging fruit, no mk, 3" 60.00
Woodcraft, bowl, squirrel on branch, 3½" 115.00
Woodcraft, jardiniere, bird appl to side, 5½" 225.00
Woodcraft, lamp, owl perched on branch of stump form, 16" 850.00
Woodcraft, mug, foxes, 6" 225.00
Woodcraft, vase, bud; foliage, integral branch hdls, 8½" 45.00
Woodcraft, wall vase, fruit on branch w/4 openings, 9" 80.00
Woodcraft-Muskota, crane on fishbowl base, 11" 325.00
Woodcraft-Muskota, fisher boy on fishbowl vase, 12" 375.00
Woodrose, basket, floral, 5½" 85.00
Woodrose, jardiniere, floral, tub hdls, 7" 155.00
Zona, bowl, rabbit & bird, Juvenile line, 5½" 35.00

Zona, jardiniere, floral on basketweave, 6½" 115
Zona, pickle dish, branch hdl, 11" 55
Zona, pitcher, bird, gr, 8" 185
Zona, plate, baby's, squirrels, ABC rim, no mk, 7½" 90
Zona, platter, fruit on branch at rim, closed hdls, 12" dia 30
Zona, teapot, fruit on branch, 5" 65
Zona, umbrella stand, ladies/garlands, glossy, no mk, 20½" 475

Western Americana

The collecting of Western Americana encompasses a broad sp
trum of memorabilia and collectibles. Examples of various areas wit
the main stream would include the following fields: weapons, bott
photographs, mining/railroad artifacts, cowboy paraphernalia, farm a
ranch implements, maps, barbed wire, tokens, Indian rel
saloon/gambling items, and branding irons. Some of these areas h
their own separate listings in this book. Western Americana is not c
a collecting field but is also a collecting era with specific boundr
Depending upon which field the collector decides to specialize
prices can start at a few dollars and run into the thousands.

Our advisor for this category is Bill Mackin, author of Cowboy
Gunfighter Collectibles (order from the author); he is listed in the Di
tory under Colorado.

Belt, money; leather, lg sq buckle, bullet loops, 2½" W 395
Bit, nude lady chased silver o/l 185
Book, Wild West Dock Carver Spirit Gun of West, RW Thorp, EX ..35
Branding iron, all iron, 48" shank, lt rust 25
Buffalo skull, lg bull, no sheaths or horns, old 125
Chaps, batwing type, 10 conchos, mk Andy Card OK City, EX .600
Chaps, Miles City Saddlery, buffalo fur, EX 750
Chaps, wooly angora, mk Clark, Portland OR, 1910, EX 800
Clock, horse, bronzed pot metal, 1950 135
Coat, horse hide, McKibben Droscol & Dorsey, St Paul MN, VG ..275
Cowboy boots, lady's, mc butterflies, VG 325
Cuffs, Gopher Brand, lace & snap closure, emb florals, 6", pr 125
Gold pan, rusted through, 14" 15
Hamper, clothes; Hopalong Cassidy, 1955, M 625
Hitching post, CI, horse head, late 1800s, 10x7½x3" 150
Horse hames, wood, brass balls w/iron hdw, NM, 27", pr 50
Lamp, handmade mini saddle, WY prison 150
Long horns, mtd on brd, covered w/red cloth, 52" spread 175
Match safe, cowboy & buffalo, nickel 125
Picture, Custer's Last fight, cb, Budweiser ad, fr 95
Program, Buffalo Bill's Wild West Show, June 1908, VG 135
Quirt, woven horse hair, frills on wrist loop & shaft, VG 195
Saddle, FG Eldred, Sheridan WY, handmade, tooled leather, EX ..450
Saddle, lady's side; tooled leather, silk stitching, 1880s 325
Saddle, RT Frazier, Pueblo CO, hand tooled, sq skirts, 1900 650
Saddle pockets, leather, floral tooling, EX 135
Shirt, wool gabardine, embr, fringed 185
Spurs, Buermann, drop shank w/jingle bobs, pr 135
Spurs, Buermann cowboy style, steel, drop shank, 1¾", pr 105
Spurs, Eureaka, mail-order type, ltweight metal, pr, EX 80
Vest, bl wool, silk bk, 4-pocket, EX 30
Wanted card, Levenworth KS, picture/$100 reward, 1920s 25
Watch fob, RT Frazier Saddlery, saddle style 135
Whip, bull snake; leather wrapped, EX 90

Western Pottery Manufacturing Compar

This pottery was originally founded as the Denver China and I
tery Company; William Long was the owner. The company's as

were sold to a group who in 1905 formed the Western Pottery Manufacturing Company, located at 16th Street and Alcott in Denver, Colorado. By 1926, 186 different items were being produced, including crocks, flowerpots, kitchen items, and other stoneware. The company dissolved in 1936.

Seven various marks were used during the years, and values may be higher for items that carry a rare mark. Numbers within the descriptions refer to specific marks, see the line drawings. Prices may vary depending on demand and local. Our advisors for this category are Cathy Segelke and Pat James; they are listed in the Directory under Colorado.

Churn, #2, no lid, 5-gal, G 80.00
Crock, #2, hdl, 4-gal, M 75.00
Crock, #2, hdl, 5-gal, M 65.00

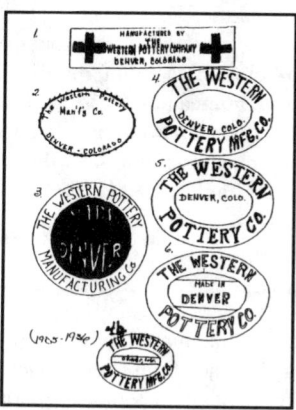

Crock, #4, bail lip, 4-gal, G 55.00
Crock, #4, hdl, no lid, 8-gal, M 90.00
Crock, #4, ice water; bl/wht sponge pnt, 3-gal, NM 30.00
Crock, #4, 2-gal, M 32.00
Crock, #4, 6-gal, EX 72.00
Crock, #4b, 20-gal, M 200.00
Crock, #4b, 22x17½", 15-gal, NM 150.00
Crock, #4b, 30-gal, NM 225.00
Crock, #5, bail lip, 1½-gal, M 45.00
Crock, #5, no lid, 6-gal, M 70.00
Crock, #6, wire hdl, 10-gal, NM 100.00
Crock, #6, 2-gal, NM 30.00
Crock, #6, 3-gal, M 40.00
Crock, #6, 4-gal, M 50.00
Crock, #6, 5-gal, NM 60.00
Crock, water; #6, brn/wht, 5-gal, NM 200.00
Pot warmer, #6, M 50.00
Jug, #6, brn/wht, 1-gal, EX 25.00
Jug, #6, brn/wht, 5-gal, M 75.00
Rabbit feeder, #1, EX 25.00
Rabbit waterer, #1, M 25.00

Westmoreland

Originally titled the Specialty Glass Company, Westmoreland began operations in East Liverpool, Ohio, producing utility items as well as tableware in milk glass and crystal. When the company moved to Grapeville, PA, in 1890, lamps, vases, covered animal dishes, and decorative plates were introduced. Prior to 1920 Westmoreland was a major manufacturer of carnival glass and soon thereafter added a line of lovely reproduction art glass items. High-quality milk glass became their speciality, accounting for about 90% of their production. Black glass was introduced in the 1940s, and later in the decade ruby-stained

pieces and items decorated in the Mary Gregory style became fashionable. By the 1960s colored glassware was being produced, examples of which are very popular with collectors today. Early pieces were marked with a paper label; by the 1960s the ware was embossed with a superimposed 'WG.' The last mark was a circle containing 'Westmoreland' around the perimeter and a large 'W' in the center. The company closed in 1985. See also Animal Dishes with Covers; Carnival Glass.

Appetizer set, Panelled Grape, milk glass, 3-pc set 65.00
Ashtray, Beaded Grape, milk glass, 5" 12.00
Banana bowl, Old Quilt, milk glass 65.00
Banana bowl, Wildflower & Lace, bl 30.00
Basket, Panelled Grape, milk glass, split hdl, oval 30.00
Basket, Panelled Grape, milk glass, 12x7¼" 85.00
Basket, Panelled Grape, red carnival, ltd ed, lg 80.00
Bowl, Beaded Grape, milk glass, sq, w/lid, ftd, 7" (+) 35.00
Bowl, fruit; Della Robbia, w/colors, ftd, 6½x11¾" 88.00
Bowl, fruit; Wildflower & Lace, 10" 22.50
Bowl, Old Quilt, milk glass, flared, rare, 13" 105.00
Bowl, Old Quilt, milk glass, shallow, ftd, 9" 55.00
Bowl, Panelled Grape, milk glass, bell shape, rare, 12½" 125.00
Bowl, Panelled Grape, milk glass, oval, 6½" 22.50
Box, cigarette; Beaded Grape, milk glass, 4x6" 37.50
Box, cigarette; Old Quilt, milk glass, rare, 5x4" 55.00
Box, puff; Beaded Grape, milk glass, HP roses & bows 32.00
Box, puff; Panelled Grape, milk glass 28.00
Butter dish, Old Quilt, milk glass, rnd, w/lid 55.00
Butter dish, Old Quilt, milk glass, ¼-lb 32.00
Canape set, Panelled Grape, milk glass, 3-pc 68.00
Candlestick, dolphin form, milk glass, pr 50.00
Candlestick, Panelled Grape, milk glass, octagonal, 4", pr 22.50
Candlestick, Spiral, purple slag, 6½" 42.50
Candy dish, Della Robbia, milk glass, scalloped, ftd 32.50
Candy dish, English Hobnail, milk glass, 3-ftd 30.00
Candy dish, Old Quilt, milk glass, w/lid, low ftd 22.50
Candy dish, Panelled Grape, milk glass, w/lid, 7" 20.00
Card receiver, hand form, milk glass, pnt roses & bows 30.00
Celery vase, Old Quilt, milk glass, 6½" 22.00
Cheese dish, Panelled Grape, milk glass, skirted 45.00
Cigar holder, clear etched, #352 ....15.00
Compote, Dolphin, pk, #1049, 6x8" 48.00
Compote, Panelled Grape, milk glass, HP roses/bows, ftd, 7" 45.00
Compote, 1861 Lincoln Drape, milk glass, ftd, w/lid 175.00
Creamer & sugar bowl, Della Robbia, milk glass 20.00
Creamer & sugar bowl, Della Robbia, w/color 35.00
Creamer & sugar bowl, Panelled Grape, milk glass, lg, pr 42.50
Creamer & sugar bowl, swan, cobalt carnival, w/lid (+) 42.50
Cup & saucer, Panelled Grape, milk glass 15.00
Goblet, Della Robbia, milk glass, plain, 6" 15.00
Goblet, Panelled Grape, milk glass, 8-oz 17.50
Goblet, Panelled Grape, 5¾" 12.50
Honey dish, Beaded Grape, milk glass, w/lid, 5" 28.00
Jardiniere, Old Quilt, milk glass, cupped, 6½" 42.50
Jardiniere, Panelled Grape, milk glass, 6" 22.50
Jelly dish, Panelled Grape, milk glass, w/lid, 4½" 18.00
Mayonnaise, Old Quilt, milk glass, bell shape, 2-pc set 32.00
Mayonnaise, Panelled Grape, milk glass, ftd 22.00
Nappy, Beaded Grape, milk glass, bell shape, 8" 20.00
Nappy, Panelled Grape, milk glass, 4½" (+) 15.00
Pickle dish, Old Quilt, milk glass, 10" 28.00
Pitcher, Old Quilt, milk glass, 1-qt 30.00
Pitcher, syrup; Old Quilt, milk glass 24.00
Planter, Panelled Grape, milk glass, 3x8½" 35.00
Planter, Panelled Grape, milk glass, 5x9" 32.00

Plate, Panelled Grape, milk glass, 10½" 40.00
Plate, Panelled Grape, milk glass, 14½" 88.00
Plate, Panelled Grape, milk glass, 6" 12.00
Plate, Panelled Grape, milk glass, 8½" 24.00
Punch bowl, Panelled Grape, milk glass, +stand/12 cups/ladle ...625.00
Sauce boat, Panelled Grape, milk glass, w/undertray 65.00
Shakers, Lotus, milk glass, pr 35.00
Shakers, Old Quilt, milk glass, pr 22.00
Shakers, Panelled Grape, milk glass, ftd, pr 15.00
Sherbet, Della Robbia, milk glass 15.00
Sherbet, Old Quilt, milk glass, low ft 22.50
Slipper, Bl Mist, HP decor 20.00
Spooner, Panelled Grape, milk glass, 6" 30.00
Sweetmeat, Old Quilt, milk glass, w/lid, ftd 25.00
Tidbit, Panelled Grape, milk glass, 2-tier 65.00
Toothpick holder, Panelled Grape, milk glass 17.50
Tumbler, Beaded Edge, milk glass, ftd 8.50
Tumbler, Old Quilt, milk glass, juice sz 22.50
Tumbler, Panelled Grape, milk glass, 12-oz 20.00
Tumbler, Panelled Grape, milk glass, 8-oz 19.00
Vase, bud; Panelled Grape, milk glass, 10" 16.00
Vase, Old Quilt, aqua ice carnival, ruffled top, ftd, 7" 38.00
Vase, Old Quilt, milk glass, fan form 22.00
Vase, Old Quilt, milk glass, ftd, str sides, 9" 48.00
Vase, Panelled Grape, milk glass, bell shape, 6" 16.00
Vase, Panelled Grape, milk glass, str sides, 9½" 22.50
Vase, Panelled Grape, milk glass, 11" 60.00
Vase, swung; Old Quilt, milk glass 35.00
Wine, Panelled Grape, milk glass, 2-oz 16.00

Wheatley, T. J.

In 1880 after a brief association with the Coultry Works, Thomas J. Wheatley opened his own studio in Cincinnati, Ohio, claiming to have been the first to discover the secret of under-glaze slip decoration on an unbaked clay vessel. He applied for and was granted a patent for his process. Demand for his ware increased to the point that several artists were hired to decorate the ware. The company incorporated in 1880 as the Cincinnati Art Pottery, but until 1882 it continued to operate under Wheatley's name. Ware from this period is marked 'T.J. Wheatley' or 'T.J.W. and Co.,' and it may be dated.

Charger, cottage/lake/mtns, Limoges style, #38, rstr, 14½" 1,300.00
Lamp base, dk gr matt, Grueby-style top-to-base leaves, 14" ...1,100.00

Vase, country scene with large tree and fence, 7½", $875.00.

Vase, curdled gr matt, 4 stem hdls w/webbed ends, 14", NM ...1,400.00
Vase, floral impasto, Limoges bkground, mfg flaw, 13x10" 325.00
Vase, florals, salmon/pk/gr on dk bl, slim, sgn, 1879, 29" 1,950.00
Vase, gr matt, leaves at base, dbl-gourd form, 13" 1,000.00
Vase, landscape, 1 ea side, Limoges style, disk form, 8x7" 1,300.00
Vase, lg flowers on smear glaze, ftd pillow form, sgn, 8x8" 325.00

Vase, ochre matt, lg ribbed rim-to-base leaves, drilled, 20" 2,100.00
Vase, silver o/l emb leaves on gr Nouveau form, 11x10" 1,500.00
Wall pocket, lg appl leaves envelop grapes, gr matt, 7x7" 800.00

Whieldon

Thomas Whieldon was regarded as the finest of the Staffordshire potters of the mid-1700s. He produced marbled and black Egyptian wares as well as tortoise shell, a mottled brown-glazed earthenware accented with touches of blue and yellow. In 1754 he became a partner of Josiah Wedgwood. Other potters produced similar wares, and today the term Whieldon is used generically.

Jug, cream; cauliflower, gr/cream, 4½", EX 990.00
Plate, brn sponging, miniature, 3", NM 300.00
Plate, tortoise shell, blk w/gr/bl/amber, octagonal, 9" 450.00
Plate, tortoise shell, 5-color, molded rim, rpr, 9" 225.00
Tea canister, cauliflower, gr/cream, 4½", VG 660.00
Teapot, appl vines/ornaments on brn mottle w/gilt, rstr, 3¾" 550.00
Teapot, cauliflower, gr/cream, base chips, 4" 935.00
Teapot, cauliflower, gr/cream, 5½", NM 4,950.00

Wicker

Wicker is the basket-like material used in many types of furniture and accessories. It may be made from bamboo cane, rattan, reed, or artificial fibers. It is airy, lightweight, and very popular in hot regions. Imported from the Orient in the 18th century, it was first manufactured in the United States in about 1850. The elaborate, closely-woven Victorian designs belong to the mid-to-late 1800s, and the simple styles with coarse reedings usually indicate a post-1900 production. Art Deco styles followed in the twenties and thirties. The most important consideration in buying wicker is condition — it can be restored, but only by a professional. Age is an important factor, but be aware that 'Victorian style' furniture is being manufactured today.

Key:
HB — Heywood Brothers   H-W — Heywood-Wakefield
WR — Wakefield Rattan Co.

Armchair, tightly woven, Deco shape, 1920s, 32" 125.00
Box, stencil: Spices, w/8 sm glass containers, 3½x10" dia 125.00
Chair, reception, heart-shaped bk, cabriole legs 225.00
Chair, side; close-woven bk w/curlicues, rnd cane seat, 43" 275.00
Cradle, swinging in harp support w/base shelf, 43x47" 325.00
Daybed, scrolled headrest, att H-W, 158" 465.00
Floor lamp, pyramidal shade, sq flaring post, 68x21", EX 875.00
Footstool, tightly woven top, dmn-patterned sides, 12x20x12" 165.00
Lamp, table; w/18" mushroom shade, 31" 215.00
Loveseat, rolled bk & armrests, caned seat, 35" 500.00
Potty chair, pine lid, EX 80.00
Rocker, cathedral bk, 1920s, child's, 24" 100.00
Rocker, flat crest rail continues to flat arms, #W59D, HB 220.00
Rocker, platform; att H-W, 48x24x30", EX 990.00
Rocker, platform; rolled serpentine fr, crown headrest, EX 350.00
Rocker, simple style, wht pnt, EX 185.00
Rocker, tightly woven, Deco style, 1930s, child's, 22" 140.00
Settee, spindle bk w/ornate curlicues, cane seat, 31x35" 425.00
Settee, tightly machine woven, no arms, cushion seat, 32x38" 265.00
Settee, tightly woven sq style w/lift seat, 29x41x18", EX 425.00
Table, tightly woven, rnd, w/2 shelves 195.00
Tray, breakfast; w/cup holder, paper rack on side, 1920s 125.00

Willets

The Willets Manufacturing Company of Trenton, New Jersey, produced a type of belleek porcelain during the late 1880s and 1890s. Examples were often marked with a coiled snake that formed a 'W' with 'Willets' below and 'Belleek' above. Not all Willet's is factory decorated. Items painted by amateurs outside the factory are worth considerably less. In the listings below, all items are belleek unless noted otherwise. For more information we recommend *American Belleek*, with full-color photos and current market values, by Mary Frank Gaston. You will find her address in the Directory under Texas.

Bowl, allover gold & bl flowers, 2¼x3¼" dia 35.00
Bowl, gold spray, pk buds, coral-shape hdls, pk mk, 2½x4½" 195.00
Bowl, roses, artist sgn, ruffled, 8¾" 295.00
Charger, mc florals w/gold, scalloped rim, 10½" 185.00
Chocolate pot, gilt decor, mk, 8½" 110.00
Cider set, fruit/foliage/flowers, 14½" tankard+6 mugs 675.00
Cup & saucer, demi; emb veining traced in gold, pk mk 60.00
Demitasse pot, gold & wht w/monogram, 1890s, +4 ftd c/s 450.00
Egg cup, petal design w/gold trim, mk, 2¾" 185.00
Pitcher, nautilus shell mold, ivory/pk/gold, coral hdl, 8" 515.00
Salt cellar, roses, ped ft, 1¼" 50.00
Tankard, pelican & trees at sunset, gilt dragon hdl, 6" 375.00
Vase, butterflies on gold lustre, tapered cylinder, 9" 155.00
Vase, sterling o/l, Deco-style hdls/neck, mk, 12¾" 350.00

Willow Ware

Willow Ware, inspired no doubt by the numerous patterns of the blue and white Nanking imports, has been popular since the late 18th century and has been made in as many variations as there were manufacturers. English transfer wares by such notable firms as Allerton and Ridgway are the most sought after and the most expensive. Japanese potters have been producing Willow-patterned dinnerware since the late 1800s, and American manufacturers have followed suit. Although blue is the color most commonly used, mauve, black, and even multicolor Willow Ware may be found. Complementary glassware, tinware, and linens have also been made. In addition to 'Allerton' and 'Ridgway,' both companies used the possessive forms of their names in marking their wares (i.e. Allerton's, Ridgway's). For further study we recommend the book *Blue Willow*, with full-color photos and current prices, by Mary Frank Gaston. You will find her address in the Directory under Texas. In the following listings, if no manufacturer is noted, the ware is unmarked.

Bowl, berry; Japan, sm 5.00
Bowl, berry; no mk, red, sm 5.00
Bowl, berry; Royal, USA, 5½" 4.50
Bowl, cereal; no mk 4.00
Bowl, Shenango, oval, 5½" 15.00
Bowl, soup; Ridgway 22.00
Bowl, soup; Royal 10.00
Bowl, vegetable; Occupied Japan, oval 35.00
Bowl, vegetable; Royal, 9" 15.00
Casserole, Gibson, England, 1912-30, w/lid 130.00
Coffeepot, Japan, electric, 8", M 100.00
Condiment & cruet set 225.00
Creamer, Barrots, Staffordshire, 1946 ....35.00
Creamer, Royal, USA 5.00
Creamer & sugar bowl, Japan, child sz 30.00
Creamer & sugar bowl, Occupied Japan, w/lid 40.00
Creamer & sugar bowl, Ridgway, w/lid 75.00

Creamer & sugar bowl, Stevenson, England, lg 35.00
Cup, Occupied Japan 10.00
Cup & saucer, Japan 15.00
Cup & saucer, Japan, child sz 12.00
Cup & saucer, no mk, pk 8.00
Cup & saucer, Royal, USA, angular hdl 7.50
Cup & saucer, Royal Venton, England 20.00

Farmer's cup and saucer, 'Take Ye a Cuppe O'Kindness for Auld Lang Syne,' 7½" diameter saucer, $67.50.

Gravy boat, Japan, w/attached tray, child sz 65.00
Lamp, ball shape, kerosene burner, no shade 25.00
Mold, pudding; Staffordshire 50.00
Mug, Japan, decal inside 15.00
Pitcher, Ashworth, scalloped top, 1880s, 8½" 150.00
Pitcher, milk; no mk 35.00
Pitcher, water; Mason's, octagonal, 11" 475.00
Plate, grill; Adams 25.00
Plate, grill; Japan 12.00
Plate, grill; Sterling, pk 10.00
Plate, Homer Laughlin, 6" 5.00
Plate, Japan, 9½" 12.00
Plate, Maastricht, 6" 10.00
Plate, Occupied Japan, 6½" 10.00
Plate, Ridgway, pk, 7¾" 10.00
Plate, Ridgway, 10½" 18.00
Plate, Ridgway, 9" 14.00
Plate, Royal, hdls, 10½" 10.00
Plate, Royal, 10" 10.00
Plate, Royal, 6" 4.00
Plate, Royal, 9" 8.00
Plate, Staffordshire, brn, 1890s, 9" 30.00
Plate, Staffordshire, brn, 8" 25.00
Platter, Japan, child sz 40.00
Platter, Japan, 12½" 25.00
Platter, Shenango, 13" 35.00
Rolling pin 25.00
Salad fork & spoon, Japan 25.00
Salt cellar, Ridgway, pk 8.00
Saucer, Occupied Japan 6.00
Shakers, Japan, pr 18.00
Sugar bowl, Japan, w/lid 25.00
Tidbit, Royal, 3-tier, pk 50.00
Toaster, electric, rare 1,250.00
Toddy plate, Staffordshire, scalloped, 4½" 40.00
Tumbler, glass, heavy bottom, 4¾" 10.00

Winchester

The Winchester Repeating Arms Company lost their important government contract after WWI and of necessity turned to the manufacture of sporting goods, hardware items, tools, etc., to augment their gun production. Between 1920 and 1931, over 7,500 different items, each marked 'Winchester Trademark U.S.A.,' were offered for sale by thousands of Winchester Hardware stores throughout the country. After 1931 the firm became Winchester-Western. See also Knives. Our advisor for this category is James Anderson; he is listed in the Directory under Minnesota.

Air rifle, #416, Made in Germany, G	100.00
Awl, scratch; w/wooden hdl, #9501, 8½", G	65.00
Bait rod, EX in orig cloth bag, VG	175.00
Bicycle	450.00
Calendar, 1912	750.00
Can opener, CI, VG	75.00
Catalog, Winchester tackle, 1922	30.00
Chisel, wood; #4707, 1"	55.00
Clock, horse/rider, 100th Anniv (1966), electric, wall type	200.00
Display case, counter top, for knives, G	300.00

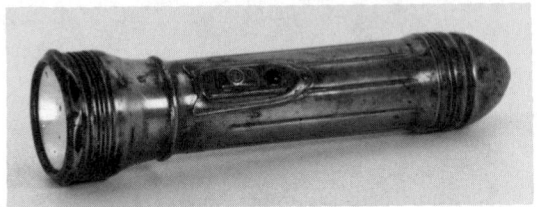

Flashlight, copper, 8", EX, $40.00.

Flashlight, blk, 3-cell, EX	40.00
Fly rod, steel, EX in orig bag	250.00
Food grinder, #12, M	75.00
Fork, spading; G	95.00
Golf club, Mashie Niblick, MJ Brady, #6633, EX	175.00
Golf putter, VG	170.00
Gun solvent, full bottle, EX	45.00
Hammer, claw type	95.00
Hand saw, 24"	90.00
Hatchet, shingling	80.00
Hockey puck	75.00
Ice skates, leather, Lake Placid, M	125.00
Lamp, miner's, mk	55.00
Level, EX wood, orig decal, #3, 28", EX	125.00
Level, metal, #3612, 12"	160.00
Lithograph, Winchester Hounds	500.00
Lure, wooden, 3-hook	400.00
Oil can, red, M	25.00
Padlock, 6-lever, w/key	75.00
Pin, employee; 45 years of service, MIB	150.00
Plane, metal, #3030, 18"	160.00
Plane, metal, #3205, 10"	145.00
Pliers, October Special, 6"	55.00
Price list, guns, 1955, NM	10.00
Price list & catalog, rifles & shotguns, 1952, 29-pg, 5x7"	12.00
Print, Stagecoach, Norman Rockwell, M	75.00
Radio, floor model	900.00
Rasp, wooden, 8", G	40.00
Rod & reel, #5565 & #2292, M	250.00
Ruler, wooden, mk Winchester Store, 12", EX	85.00
Scissors, #9059, 9"	35.00
Screwdriver, brass/wood, #7125, 11"	35.00
Spinner, #9515, EX	80.00
Square, #9650, VG	75.00
Tackle box, sm, VG	155.00
Trout fly leader, #3111, M on card	95.00

Wire cutters, 6"	75.0

Windmill Weights

Windmill weights were used to protect the windmill's plunger ro from damage during high winds by adding weight that slowed down th speed of the blades.

Bull, Fairbury (unmk), CI, mc pnt, 38-lb, 18¼x24¼x1⅛"	800.0
Eclipse Moon, B-13, CI, worn blk pnt, 27-lb, 10½x6½x3½"	185.0
Horse, bob-tailed, Dempster, CI, G wht pnt, 16⅝x17¼x¾"	265.0
Horse, CI w/tan pnt, silhouette w/some relief, 17"	260.0
Horse, Dempster #58-G, old red pnt, modern wood base, 17"	400.0
Rooster, Elgin #2, CI, worn orig pnt, 34-lb, 16½"	800.0
Rooster, Hummer, Elgin, half-sphere base, worn pnt, 14"	575.0
Spear, Challenge, no pnt, 35-lb, 24"	475.0
W shape, Althouse & Wheeler, no pnt, 22-lb, 9¼x17x3"	385.0

Wire Ware

Two thousand years B.C. wire was made by cutting sheet met into strips which were shaped with mallet and file. By the late 13 century, craftsmen in Europe had developed a method of pulling the strips through progressively smaller holes until the desired gauge w obtained. During the Industrial Revolution of the late 1800s, machi ery was developed that could produce wire cheaply and easily; and became a popular commercial commodity. It was used to produce lar items such as garden benches and fencing as well as innumerable sm pieces for use in the kitchen or on the farm. Beware of reproduction Our advisor for this category is Rosella Tinsley; she is listed in th Directory under Kansas.

Basket, dmn weave, wavy design, 2¾x11x7"	52.
Basket, fruit; heart-shaped hdls w/majolica plate, 3x8½"	95.
Basket, fruit; rnd openwork designs, ca 1900, 5x14"	85.
Basket, fruit; twisted heart design w/glass plate, 7¼"	85.
Basket, ornate twisted wire, ftd, 1850s, 5" dia	95.
Basket, potato boiling; bulbous, fixed wire hdl, 1820s, 8" dia	120.
Basket, vegetable; fine wire, bail hdl, 1870s, sm	38.
Bottle holder, circular, top hdl, ftd	32.
Bread basket, oval, fancy, end hdls	85.
Calling card receiver, ornate twisted wire holds glass plate	85.
Compote, twisted wire, looped edge, 2 loop hdls, ftd	125.
Egg cooker, 6-compartment, simple style	30.
Egg holder, 2-tier, fine wire, ftd, center hdl, 1860	110.
Letter holder, 2 rows of twisted wire coils, 13" L	30.
Napkin ring, twisted wire, fancy design, pr	100.
Pie lifter, heavy wire, spring hdl, dbl-wire sides, old	25.
Pie rack, heavy wire, for 6 pies	125.
Pot scrubber, mesh chain link, CI loop hdl, 10" L	35.
Rolling pin holder, fine twisted wire, 4 hearts, old, EX	60.
Soap dish, twisted wire edge, bow shape, 4 loop legs, old	60.
Trivet, ornately twisted wire, curved edge, ftd, 9" dia	65.
Trivet, triangular, dbl wire at sides, loop hdl, 3-ftd	35.
Trivet, twisted, spoked-wheel shape, 6¼" dia	58.
Whisk, tined loops w/twisted hdl, Germany, 8", EX	17.

Wisecarver, Rick

Rick Wisecarver is a contemporary ceramic artist from Ohio wh well known not only for his renderings of Indian portraits on brown-gl

...are reminiscent of similiar lines made by earlier Ohio potteries but for ...is figural cookie jars as well, most of which have a Black theme.

Cookie jar, Cookie Jar Mammy 185.00
Cookie jar, Cookstove Mammy 185.00
Cookie jar, Mammy w/Child 185.00
Cookie jar, Mixing Bowl Mammy 185.00
Cookie jar, Pappy Bust 125.00
Cookie jar, Quilting Mammy 120.00
Cookie jar, Young Blk Woman 185.00
Vase, Indian w/sheath of arrows, 8x8" 140.00
Vase, rainbow trout on bl, 9x7" 160.00
Vase, spaniel dog on matt, 10x7" 170.00

Witch Balls

Witch balls were a Victorian fad touted to be meritorious toward ...dding the house of evil spirits, thus warding off sickness and bad luck. ...olklore would have it that by wiping the dust and soot from the ball, ...e spirits were exorcised. It is much more probable, however, consider- ...g the fact that such beautiful art glass was used in their making, that ...e ostensive Victorians perpetrated the myth rather tongue-in-cheek ...hile enjoying them as lovely decorations for their homes.

...methyst w/wht loops, +matching 9¾" ftd stand 1,450.00
...qua, opal looping, 4¼" 125.00
...quamarine, opal ribs & loops alternate, 1860s, 3" 110.00
...ear, bl/wht/cranberry loops, 1840-80, 5½" 160.00
...obalt on cobalt stand w/clear base, S Jersey, 14½" 665.00
...ailsea, pk & wht swirl, 5¼" on wooden stand, EX 125.00
...live-amber, 4½" 100.00
...ortoise shell, lt amber w/red splotches, 1860s, 4" 110.00
...l-gr, wht opal stripes, ground mouth, Am, ca 1900, 5" 135.00

Wood Carvings

Wood sculptures represent an important section of American folk ... Wood carvings were made not only by skilled woodworkers such as ...binetmakers, carpenters, etc., but by amateur 'whittlers' as well. They ...ke the form of circus-wagon figures, carousel animals, decoys, busts, ...urines, and cigar store Indians. Oriental artists show themselves to ...ve been as proficient with the medium of wood as they were with ...ory or hardstone. See also Decoys; Tobacciana.

...ar's head, sgn E Reed, 9" 295.00
...k lady in rocker, mc pnt, 3⅜" 85.00
...st, pine, bald elderly man, wire glasses, 1900s, 7x3½x3" 85.00
...ardinal, wings spread, EX pnt, designed to hang, 1940s, 7" 65.00
...g, glass eyes, worn brn finish, edge chips, 5½" 30.00
...onkey, old gray & blk pnt, thread mane/tail, 1900s, 5" 40.00
...gurehead, lady w/wreath in hair, worn pnt, 60", EX 1,200.00
...oat w/kid attacked by 2 bears under tree, rpr/damage, 14" 325.00
...an in bib overalls w/beer, mc pnt, 1900s, 7½x3x3", EX 115.00
...easant, primitive, mc pnt w/worn fiber tail, 2½", pr 165.00
...eated woodpecker, EX pnt, wire legs, 5½x9½x2" 180.00
...ooster, long 4-feather tail, mc pnt, 20th C, 12" 320.00
...ooster, mc pnt, primitive, 1900s, 9" 75.00
...ooster, pine w/orig mc pnt, Schimmel type, 4", EX 175.00
...eep, orig wht pnt w/red & blk detail, minor wear, 2" 30.00
...elf, detailed eagle support, w/gesso & gilt, 9x11", EX 600.00
...uirrel, sitting upright w/lg pine cone, mc pnt, 6", EX 225.00
...all pocket, walnut, cut out/chip cvd, ornate crest, 26x13" 125.00

Whimsey, goblet w/in cage, gold pnt, 5½" 95.00

Woodenware

Woodenware (or treenware, as it is sometimes called) generally refers to those wooden items such as spoons, bowls, food molds, etc., that were used in the preparation of food. Common during the 18th and 19th centuries, these wares were designed from a strictly functional viewpoint and were used on a day-to-day basis. With the advent of the Industrial Revolution which brought with it new materials and prod- ucts, many of the old woodenwares were simply discarded. Today origi- nal handcrafted American woodenwares are extremely difficult to find.

Apple grinder, orig bl pnt, ca 1850 ....225.00
Biscuit board, handmade, w/large attached roller, ca 1820 ....210.00
Bowl, age crack w/laced rpr, leather thong hanger, 6x9x18" 175.00
Bowl, age cracks/worm holes, 8x15x34" 75.00
Bowl, bird's-eye maple, 13" 125.00
Bowl, bird's-eye maple, 7½" 75.00
Bowl, burl, EX figure, hollow-cvd hdls, oval, 5x14x18" 1,425.00
Bowl, burl, EX figure, minor rim crack, 3x8" 450.00
Bowl, burl, EX figure, relocated iron hdl 1 end, 7x21" 1,150.00
Bowl, burl, EX figure, trn, puttied imperfections, 8" 375.00
Bowl, burl, EX figure, well-shaped lip, 7x18x19" 2,200.00
Bowl, burl, EX figure, 5x16" 1,250.00
Bowl, burl, EX figure & detail, simple ft, rfn, 2¼x5" 400.00
Bowl, burl, EX figure/patina, hdls protrude, rpr, 8x18x25" 2,500.00
Bowl, burl, irregular oval w/short protuding end hdls, 9" 450.00
Bowl, burl, lg animal head hdls, chip cvg, sgn, 14" L 1,400.00
Bowl, burl, red ext, trn lip, separations, 5x13½" 700.00
Bowl, chopping; maple, lathe trn, early rpr, 2¼x4½" 30.00
Bowl, maple, lathe trn, orig mellow patina, 1830s, 4x15" 50.00
Bowl, maple, metal reinforcement, oblong, scrubbed, 18x41" 225.00
Bowl, some burl, age cracks, 3x7x8" 175.00
Bowl, some burl, filled age cracks, 6x13x16" 375.00
Bowl, trn, red on ext, scrubbed int, 6x20" 475.00
Box, bbl shape, mk Factory #902 1st Dist Mich, 5½" 25.00
Box, cutlery; pine, center hdl, handmade, dvtl, 1850s 175.00
Box, holly wood, EX trn/tooling, 2x2⅝" dia 175.00
Box, poplar w/orig yel & brn sponging, trn, 6" dia, NM 350.00
Box, spice; bentwood, tin bands, 8 containers w/stenciling 310.00
Bucket, pine w/tined iron bands, wire hdl, 1900s, 11" dia, EX 80.00
Bucket, staved, iron bands, gr pnt w/stencil: 1-gal oil, 8" 200.00
Bucket, staved, iron bands, rpt, bentwood hdl, 11", EX" 155.00
Bucket, sugar; fingered laps w/wrought fasteners, 10x10" 115.00
Bucket, sugar; gr rpt, wire bail hdl, 8" 185.00
Bucket, sugar; staved, copper tacks, 9½", VG 75.00
Bucket, sugar; staved, gr pnt over early bl, 10" 250.00

Burl bowl, carved with carrying han- dles, one with hole for hanging, age cracks, 8x22½", $1,600.00.

Bucket, sugar; staved, gray-bl pnt, copper tacks, 7" 275.00
Bucket, sugar; staved, old red, minor damage, 10" 275.00
Bucket, sugar; staved, varnished, wood hdl/wire bail, 6½" 165.00
Bucket, sugar; staved, Wilder & Son brand, rfn, 14½" 75.00
Butter paddle, burl, EX figure, bird's head hdl, rfn, 9" 550.00
Butter paddle, burl, EX figure, early, wear/edge damage, 8" 200.00
Butter paddle, burl, EX figure throughout, 9" 475.00
Butter paddle, burl maple, bird's head hdl, 11" 350.00
Butter paddle, curly maple, horse's head hdl, age crack, 10" 390.00
Butter paddle, curly maple, 8¾" 90.00
Butter paddle, maple w/some curl, age crack, 10" 65.00
Butter paddle, oval, hdl is rim extension, 4¾x5½" 150.00
Butter paddle, w/flower-cvd lollipop butter print hdl, 11" 475.00
Butter print wheel, florals, scrubbed, 5½" 65.00
Cabinet, spice; cherry wood, pewter labels, 1 lg/8 sm drws 245.00
Churn, handmade, box shape, orig bl pnt 325.00
Compote, burl, trn detail, worn finish, 5¾x8¾" 1,300.00
Cookie board, bird, bk: bird, primitive, 4½x6" 225.00
Cookie board, fish/birds/etc, 12 blocks, 5½x8½" 150.00
Cookie board, fruit/flowers/compote in almond reserve, 6x16" ...260.00
Cookie board, lg rooster, bk: folk art couple, 7x11", EX 375.00
Cookie board, roses/equestrian in almond shape, glued, 26" L ...1,100.00
Cookie board, running horse, bk: star, 6⅜x9" 100.00
Cookie board, ship/animals/birds/etc, 6 blocks, 3¼x3¾" 75.00
Cookie board, wolf, 2 blocks, 5x2½" 75.00
Cranberry scoop, lg hdl on front, 10½x16" 225.00
Cup, Lehnware, mc floral on bl, EX color, ftd, 3", EX 925.00
Dipper, burl, shaped curly hdl w/curved hook, 10½" 250.00
Dipper, burl, uneven edges on bowl, 12" 85.00
Dipper, simple chip cvg, cut-out hdl end, age cracks 70.00
Dough box, early red pnt, w/lid 295.00
Flour sifter, Blood's, Pat Sept 17, 1861 ....295.00
Grater, cheese; punched tin top, w/drw 195.00
Jar, trn, Pease, age cracks, w/lid, 6x5½" 195.00
Jar, trn, Pease, wire bail w/wood hdl, w/lid, 6½x7", VG 375.00
Jar, trn, wood-burned eagle/ship/bldg, 1864, no lid, 5" 435.00
Pastry roller, cvd leaf/strawberry on wheel, 5" 75.00
Peel, age cracks in 13" dia wood blade, 9" hdl 95.00
Pestle, curly maple, trn hdl, rfn, age cracks, 11" 40.00
Plate, burl, dense figure, pits/putty rpr, 8" 250.00
Plate, cherry, 1700s, 10¾x11⅛" 350.00
Pricker, biscuit; knob hdl, 1" bottom tines 75.00
Rack, pine, natural patina, 7 trn pegs, 48" L 110.00
Reamer, cherry, hand cvd, 1-pc, trn hdl, 1820s, 5¾" L 130.00
Rolling pin, dbl hdl across top 225.00
Rolling pin, maple, 22" 35.00
Salt box, barrel shape, rnd, hanging, ca 1880 ....120.00
Scoop, birch w/little curl, edge damage, 11" 155.00
Scoop, bird's-eye maple, short hdl, 4½x8" 90.00
Skimmer, cream; maple, shallow bowl shape, 1700s, 6x6¼" 95.00
Spice grinder, trn, dk grain, 9¾" 125.00
Spigot, key; #8 Palmer's Standard, butternut 18.00
Spoon, burl, EX figure/detail, glued hdl rpr, 4½" 175.00
Tub, burl, EX detail w/trn rings, S-lock on lid, 4x6" dia 525.00

Woodworking Machinery

Vintage cast iron woodworking machines are monuments to the highly skilled engineers, foundrymen, and machinists who devised them, thus making possible the mass production of items ranging from clothespins, boxes, and barrels to decorative moldings and furniture. Though attractive from a nostalgic viewpoint, many of these machines are bought by the hobbyist and professional alike, to be put into actual

use — at far less cost than new equipment. Many worth-assessing tors must be considered; but as a general rule, a machine in good co tion is worth about 65¢ a pound (excluding motors). A machine n ing a lot of restoration is not worth more than 35¢ a pound, while professionally rebuilt and with a warranty can be calculated at $1. pound. Modern, new machinery averages over $3.00 a pound. Tw the best sources of information on purchasing or selling such mach are *Vintage Machines — Searching for the Cast Iron Classics* by T Howell, and *Used Machines and Abused Buyers* by Chuck Seidel Fine Woodworking, November/December 1984. Prices quoted are machines in good condition, less motors and accessories. Our adv for this category is Mr. Dana Martin Batory; he is listed in the Direc under Ohio. No phone calls, please.

Ideal
12-Inch Jointer.

Parks 'Ideal' 12" join
ca 1925, $400.00.

American Saw Mill Machinery Company, 1890s

Band saw, Monarch Line, #X20, 16" 260
Band saw, Monarch Line, #X25, 30" built-in ball bearing motor ..770
Band saw, Monarch Line, #X9, 12" 145
Jointer, Monarch Line, #X11, ball bearing, 12" 1,040
Jointer, Monarch Line, #X11, ball bearing, 16" 1,200
Jointer, Monarch Line, ball bearing bench, 6" 190
Jointer, Monarch Line, ball bearing bench, 8" 475
Lathe, Monarch Line, manual training, 12x24" 535
Lathe, Monarch Line, 4-speed, 12x72" 500
Mortiser, Monarch Line, #X1, hollow chisel, motorized 345
Planer, Monarch Line, single surface, 24" 2,340
Planer, Monarch Line, single surface, 30" 2,600
Sander, Monarch Line, #X8, ball bearing drum & disk 560
Saw, Monarch Line, #65, tilting table variety, 18" 780
Shaper, Monarch Line, #X19, single spindle 470
Table saw, Monarch Line, #X17, ball bearing, 8" 140
Table saw, Monarch Line, #X24, tilting arbor, 16" 425
Table saw, Monarch Line, Universal, ball bearing, 14" 1,140

Blue Star Products, 1939

Band saw, #1200, 12" floor model 85
Drill press, #500, 12" bench model 30
Lathe, #1002, 72" bed, 10" swing 60
Table saw, #800, 8" 95

Boice-Crane Power Tools, 1937

Belt sander, #1136, hand stroke 125
Drill press, #1600, 15" 75
Jointer, #950, 4" 50
Lathe, #1100, gap bed 50
Spindle sander, #560 100

Crescent Machine Company, 1921

Band saw, 36" 975.00
Jointer, bench; 4" 50.00
Mortiser, hollow chisel 525.00
Shaper, single spindle 650.00
Table saw, cut off; 16" 550.00
Universal Wood-Worker #59, 5 machines in 1 ....2,050.00

Defiance Machine Works, 1910

Band saw, 28" 520.00
Lathe, #3, iron bed, 10" swing 1,365.00
Planer, 4-roll, single surface, 24" 1,300.00
Shaper, #4, dbl spindle, upright 1,430.00
Table saw, #2, hand feed, 20" 650.00
Table saw, #2, power feed, 20" 1,100.00

Fallmeyer & Livingston Company, 1927

Band saw, Union, 16" 210.00
Band saw, Union, 20" 390.00
Borer, Union, horizontal 240.00
Borer, Union, vertical 270.00
Combination, Union #128, Universal 12" saw/8" jointer 580.00
Combination, Union #86, Universal 8" saw/6" jointer 340.00
Jointer, Union, motor on arbor, 8" 370.00
Jointer, Union, 4" 190.00
Jointer, Union, 6" 190.00
Mortiser, Union, hollow chisel 275.00
Shaper, Union, dbl spindle 780.00
Shaper, Union, single spindle 335.00
Table saw, Union #12, motor on arbor, 12" 390.00
Table saw, Union #7, 7" 210.00
Table saw, Union #8, 8" 265.00

N. Goodspeed Company, 1876

Boring machine, upright 225.00
Planer, New & Improved, Pony, 24" 900.00
Swing & boring machine 200.00
Table saw, 12" 200.00

Greenlee Bros. & Company, 1925

Borer, #351, light post 130.00
Borer, #355, single spindle, vertical 520.00
Jointer, #560, 6½" bench 215.00
Mortiser, #207, hollow chisel, horizontal 1,495.00
Mortiser, #225, hollow chisel 750.00
Rip saw, #405, heavy, 36" 2,115.00
Rip saw, #426, self feed, 20" 1,380.00
Sharpening machine, #720, hollow chisel 55.00
Swing saw, #445, belt-driven, heavy, 40" 975.00
Table saw, #478, dbl arbor, 18" 1,750.00
Tenoner, #530, sash, door & cabinet, ball bearing 1,530.00

Power & Co., 1888

Mortiser & borer, #2 ....780.00
Planer & matcher (combined), #5, 24" 5,525.00
Rip saw, #2, self feed, 24" 1,040.00
Shaper, single spindle, reversible 585.00
Table saw, self feed, 14" 715.00

Ober Manufacturing Company, 1889

Rip saw, self feed, 14" 725.00
Saw, swing cutoff, 18" 275.00
Shaper, saw & jointer combination 400.00

Oliver Machinery Company, 1912

Lathe, #24, dbl end, 8-ft bed, 16" 1,175.00
Mortiser, #91, vertical hollow chisel 650.00
Saw, #97, heavy swing cutoff, 48" 1,050.00
Shaper, #483, high speed, dbl spindle 1,300.00
Table saw, #29, Patent 325.00
Table saw, #60, Universal, 16" 1,300.00

Parks Ball Bearing Machine Company, 1925

Band saw, H-62, Jewel, 22" 250.00
Band saw, H-66, Century, 30" 450.00
Planer, H-117, Endurance, 20" 950.00
Planing Mill Special, H-87, 8 machines in 1 ....1,250.00
Sanding machine, H-165, Economy, 24" 230.00
Saw, H-97, swing cutoff, Alert, 12" 225.00

P.B. Yates Machine Company, 1917

Sander, #430, flexible belt 780.00
Saw, #232, swing cutoff, 16" 260.00
Saw, #235, swing cutoff, 36" 500.00
Scroll/band saw, #50, 30" 700.00
Shaper, N-I 2,150.00
Table saw, #226, 16" 725.00

S.A. Woods Machine Company, 1876

Circular re-sawing machine, Joslin's Improved, 50" 2,275.00
Molding machine, #1, 2-roll, 12" 2,275.00
Planer, panel; Improved, 20" 520.00
Planer, Patent Improved, shop surface, 30" 1,430.00

Sprunger Power Tools, 1950s

Band saw, 14" 60.00
Jigsaw, 20" 40.00
Lathe, gap bed, 10" 50.00
Sander, 12-disk 35.00
Table saw, tilt arbor, 10¼" 75.00

World's Fairs and Expos

Since 1851 and the Crystal Palace Exhibition in London, World's Fairs and Expositions have taken place at a steady pace. Many of them commemorate historical events. The 1904 Louisiana Purchase Exposition, commonly known as the St. Louis World's Fair, celebrated the 100th anniversary of the Louisiana Purchase agreement between Thomas Jefferson and Napoleon in 1803. The 1893 Columbian Exposition, known as The Chicago World's Fair, commemorated the 400th anniversary of the discovery of America by Columbus in 1492. (Both of these fairs were held one year later than originally scheduled.) The multitude of souvenirs from these and similar events have become a growing area of interest to collectors in recent years. Many items have a 'crossover' interest into other fields: i.e., collectors of postcards and souvenir spoons eagerly search for those from various fairs and expositions.

For additional information collectors may contact World's Fairs Collectors Society (WFCS), whose address is in the Directory under Clubs, Newsletters, and Catalogs, or our advisor, D.D. Woollard, Jr. His address is listed in the Directory under Missouri.

Key:
T&P — Trylon & Perisphere   WF — World's Fair

1876 Centennial, Philadelphia

1876 Philadelphia Centennial, frosted glass lion, Gillinder, 2½", $125.00.

Charm, Liberty 1886/Liberty Bell 1776, bronze, EX 25.00
Goblet, 1776/1876 inside 5-pointed star, pressed glass, 7" 25.00
Handkerchief, Memorial Hall Art Gallery, 3-color, 18x24", EX ...45.00
Match holder, bust of Columbus, pressed glass, 4½", EX 70.00
Medal, Her Works Praise Her..., milk glass, rnd, EX+ 85.00
Mug, Liberty & the Republic, amber glass, 5" 55.00
Photo book, holds 13 images, w/map inside bk cover, 3¼x4¾" 30.00
Silk, Memorial Hall, bl, woven 75.00

1893 Columbian, Chicago

Badge, 400th Anniv Discovery of Am, brass, w/hanger 65.00
Book, Dream City, 1893, photos, 11x13", G 40.00
Book, Jackson's Famous Pictures, lithos & drawings, 18x15" 100.00
Book, Official Guide..., blk/wht photos of fair, 192-pg, EX 25.00
Book, The Vanished City, photo engravings, hard cover, EX 100.00
Coin, US Govt Treasury Building, lg, EX 20.00
Handkerchief, Am flag w/view of Expo, mc on cotton, 16x16" 40.00
Jigsaw puzzle, view of entire Expo, MIB 400.00
Match safe, silver on brass, Administration Building 48.00
Mug, busts of WA & Columbus emb on clear glass, 2¾" 45.00
Paperweight, Columbus 1492/Chicago 1893, brass w/mc enamel ..25.00
Paperweight, Machinery Hall, mc image in glass, rectangular 40.00
Pin-bk, Columbus Day Celebration, mc cello, EX 25.00
Plate, Mines & Mining Building, mc transfer on china, 8" 35.00
Playing cards, landing scene on bk, NM in tattered box 65.00
Pop gun, blk images on wood, orig cork & string, 10", EX 330.00
Press ribbon, Indiana, rare 150.00
Scarf, Compliments of ..., red embr on wht cotton, 25x28", EX ...50.00
Sheet music, World's Columbian Expo Waltz, color illus cover ...50.00
Spoon, Art Palace eng in bowl, SP, 4½", EX 20.00
Ticket, Children's Special, brn/wht, EX 27.50

1901 Pan American

Doll, celluloid Kewpie type, Pan-Am on ft, crochet clothes, 3" 50.00
Match safe, Maid of Mist, NP, Expo mk, cigar cutter bottom, G ..50.00
Medallion, buffalo head emb on brass shield shape, 1¾" 20.00
Napkin ring, buffalo emb/florals eng on aluminum, 1½" dia 20.00

Playing cards, Official...Souvenir, fair views, NM in G box 80
Press pass, yel/blk/gr cardboard, rectangular, EX 50
Ribbon, woven silk, 5x3½" in orig mat: 6x8", EX 55
Scarf, Electric Tower on pk silk, 20" sq, EX 50
Shot glass, buffalo etched on clear, When You Drink..., 2½" 30
Token, World's Greatest Wonder Niagara Falls, aluminum 7
Tray, pen; Electric Tower, Temple of Music, aluminum, 9x3" 45
Tumbler, Liberal Arts Building etched on glass, gold rim, 3½" 30

1904 St. Louis

Axe head, I'm from Missouri, mule form 70
Booklet, RI Building, mc cover, 35-pg, EX 15
Bookmark, Amorilas Water, mc, 5¾", EX 20
Charm, Heinz/St Louis '04, pickle shape, gr compo, NM 10
Flue cover, Education Building, mc paper in glass w/tin fr 40
Fob, Palace of Liberal Arts, mc cello, EX 80
Hand mirror, Mines Building view (sepia)in gold-tone fr 50
Handkerchief, St Louis 1803-1904, monument in center, 18" sq ..50
Hatchet, CI, 12½" 65
Match safe, Souvenir of..., NP brass, c IGK, EX 60
Pincushion, Souvenir of..., seashell w/cushion center, 5½" L 25
Plaque, Blks in wagon drawn by mule w/peg leg, pressed wood 95
Pocketknife, Electricity & Cascade Garden on aluminum fr, EX .50
Postcard, hold to light, Official Souvenir..., mc, unused, M 20
Postcard, woven silk, Cascade Gardens, unused, NM 250
Poster stamp, Miss Liberty, E Baumgart-Sudende, mc paper, EX ..10
Ring, Louisiana Purchase 1803-1903, Gorham Sterling, VG 75
Tray, Transportation Building, brass, 6" dia, EX 22

1905 Lewis and Clark

Handkerchief, Foreign Exhibits Building, mc embr, 14½", EX ......12.
Pin, Westward the Course of Empire..., SP brass, EX ....30.
Punch tag, cut-out star, Portland Fair 1905 in center, EX ....20.
View book, Sights & Scenes at..., 94 pgs of photos, 7x5", EX ....27.

1907 Jamestown

Badge, Landing of...May 13, 1607, gilt & enamel, w/ribbon ....20.
Handkerchief, English receiving Indians, linen, 8¼", EX ....12.
Napkin ring, 3 views on copper-plated base metal, 2" dia ....10.
Pass, employee's monthly; photograph & 18 tickets, VG ....40.
Pin, Jamestown Expo 1607-1907, sterling, oval, .48-oz, EX ....30.
Plate, bird's-eye Expo view, sites at rim, Staffordshire, 10" ....40.
Postcard, Mines & Metallurgy Palace, emb/mc, used, EX ....5.
Tray, Fort Monroe Point Comfort, copper-plated metal, 2⅞x4" ......8.

1909 Alaska Yukon Pacific

Handkerchief, bird's-eye view of Expo, mc flags, silk, 15"sq ....60.
Pass, employee's monthly; photograph & 12 tickets, EX ....60.
Plate, Oregon State Building, mc transfer on china, 8" ....85.
Postcard, Carnation Milk Modern Milkman, mc, used, EX ....20.
Scarf, Liberal Arts & other buildings, silk, 19" sq, EX ....40.
Silk, 5 views of Expo, blk print on lt brn, 18" sq, fr ....60.
Tumbler, logo & 3 Expo scenes on copper-plated metal, 3½" ....15.

1915 Panama Pacific

Badge, Good-By, Closing Day...Dec 4, 1915, mc cello, w/ribbon ..55.
Book, Art of the Expo, hard cover, Elder, 92-pg, EX ....25.
Book, calendar; celluloid cover, EX ....25.
Book, Pan-Pacific Cookbook, McLaren, hard cover, 170-pg, EX ..35.

ook, Red Book of Views, Reid, soft cover, 96-pg, M 10.00
ooklet, Map of San Francisco, Southern Pacific RR, EX 5.00
untain pen, Souvenir of..., bl/yel plastic, Blaisdell, EX 70.00

926 Sesquicentennial

ok, Flags of Am, John Wanamaker Store, 32-pg, 5½x8" 12.50
ompact, Liberty Bell inset of mc stones on brass, EX 90.00
vitation, formal opening ceremonies, heavy stock, 7½x10" 30.00
mp, Liberty Bell, glass shade w/wht metal posts, 5", EX 25.00
ailing folder, Official Souvenir, 18 color postcards, 6x4¼" 12.50
edal, Lutheran Walther League, brass, sm, EX 8.00
edallion, bust of WA, Liberty Bell, etc, brass, 1¼" dia 12.50
ncil case, Liberty Bell on leather, calendar inside, 3x8" 30.00
ogram, official daily; Ohio Day, 32-pg, 6x9", EX 10.00
apestry, patriotic images, mc woven cloth, 24x48", EX 80.00

933 Chicago

shtray, Chrysler Building emb on copper, 3x3" 7.50
shtray, Firestone, glass in mini tire fr, 5½", EX 35.00
ok, Life Giving Light, comet logo, hard cover, 174-pg, EX 10.00
ooklet, Story of Royal Scot, train info, 31-pg, EX 15.00
ookmark, Hall of Science, gold metal, M 20.00
acelet, comet logo+6 fair designs, gold-tone metal, EX 15.00
ane, 1833-1933 Century of Progress, wood w/brass tag, 36", EX ...50.00
n, Welcome..., Oriental scene, paper w/wood spokes, 10", M ...45.00
tter opener, Federal Building, blk enamel on brass, 8½", EX 10.00
agazine, Official WF Weekly, mc cover, 48-pg, EX 8.00
ap, Chicago & Century of Progress, Standard Oil, mc, EX 10.00
edal, Federal Building emb on brass, 1¼" dia, EX 12.50
ncil, mechanical; Eagle, Century of Progress, bl/silver, EX 20.00
a-bk, I Was There, comet logo, red/wht/bl, ¾" dia, EX 15.00
te, Carillon Tower, blk transfer, Pickard, 8¼" 35.00
aying cards, Belgian Village, Century of..., EX in box 35.00
ker chip, Century of Progress, bl lettering on wht compo, EX 9.00
ster, Go! Century of Progress..., blk/wht/gr/red, 13x19", VG 50.00
pe measure, Hall of Science, mc cello, EX 25.00
a strainer, Century of Progress, wht enamel/aluminum 35.00
e clip, medallion w/comet logo, metal bar type, WF mk 17.50
e, Travel Building, bl transfer on wht, 6" sq 40.00
iform, Lieutenant of Guards, gray knit, Expo buttons, EX 125.00

39 New York

nk, glass sphere w/elongated penny inside, 10" dia 135.00
ok, Dawn of a New Day, T&P on hard cover, 123-pg, EX 25.00
ok, Official Guide, 1st edition, 256-pc, 5x8", EX 22.50
mpact, fair logo & date on fabric-covered metal top, 2x1¾" 50.00
mpact, Hall of Communications, mc, complete, 2¾" sq, EX 32.50
lder, General Motors Exhibit Building, open: 18x17", EX 10.00
ailing folder, Greetings from..., T&P on front, Grinnel, EX 12.50
edallion, T&P, Inauguration of Geo WA, brass, 1¼", EX 10.00
ncil sharpener, T&P shape, orange on blk base, 4", EX 35.00
a-bk, Polish Day, red on wht cello, ⅝", EX 35.00
te, potter at wheel, Joint Exhibit of Capitol & Labor, 7" 30.00
ster, Boy Scout Camp NYWF 1939, mc, 7x10½", EX 80.00
cket, For Peace & Freedom, mc, T&P logo, 3x2¼", EX 5.00
e clip, T&P in gold/bl enameling on gold-tone metal, 2", NM .25.00
se, T&P in gold w/lettering, ruby stained, 3½x2¼" 20.00

39 San Francisco

ok, Picture...WA, Seattle & WF, aerial-view cover, 24-pg, M .15.00

Booklet, Modern Locomotives & Cars, Penn RR, 28-pg, EX 15.00
Catalog, History of Am Paintings, Trumbull, 12-pg, EX 18.00
Comb, emb brass medallion on amber plastic, in metal case, M ...30.00
Folder, SFWF, mc cover, many illus, 10-pg, M 7.50
Program, Grand...Show Takarazuka girls..., geisha cover, EX 35.00
Sticker, Oakland...Invites You, red/wht/bl, 1⅞x2½", M 4.00

1962 Seattle

Bottle opener, Space Needle shape, enamel on steel, MIB 25.00
Scarf, fair images, mc on silk, 30" sq, EX 27.50
Slide, Official Souvenir, 4 in 2x2" orig sealed pkg 3.50
Tray, Space Needle & fair scenes, mc on bl, tin, 11" dia, EX 15.00

1964 New York

Bookend, Unisphere figural, ceramic, brn/gold, 5", pr 20.00
Clip, lapel; I Have Seen...General Motors Futurama, mc tin, EX ...3.50
Flashlight, decal on gilt tin, 3¼" L, EX 15.00
Pass, employee photo ID; Allied Exhibit Service Corp, EX 7.50
Pin, Peace Through..., Unisphere, mc, 1½", in case, M 7.50
Poster, Official Postcard Sales promotional, mc, 17x18", EX 20.00

Wright, Frank Lloyd

Born in Richland Center, Wisconsin, in 1869, Wright became a pioneer in architectural expression, developing a style referred to as 'prairie.' From early in the century until he died in 1959, he designed houses with rooms that were open, rather than divided by walls in the traditional manner. They exhibited low, horizontal lines and strongly projecting eaves, and he filled them with furnishings whose radical aesthetics complemented the structures to perfection. Several of his homes have been preserved to the present day, and collectors who admire his ideas and the unique, striking look he achieved treasure the stained glass windows, furniture, chinaware, lamps, and other decorative accessories designed by Wright.

Bed, spruce, platform style, rectangular headbrd/side panels 350.00
Bookcase/room divider, 4 shelves ea side cabinet, 50x62" 2,500.00

Bolt of 'Taliesin' fabric, ca 1955, 47x214", $1,650.00.

Buffet, 2-door cabinet & 8 drws, Heritage Henredon, 66" 3,500.00
Cabinet, walnut, 2-door, Greek Key bands, ca 1945, 17x33x20" ...990.00
Ceiling panel, ldgl, allover Indian motif, 34x17" 19,800.00
Chair, lounge; horizontal bk slats, flat arms/legs, 1955 ....330.00
Chairs, decorative copper edging, rfn/reuphl, 4 side+2 arm 1,200.00
Dinnerware, mc concentric circles, Noritake, 1960s, 48-pc 8,250.00
Doors, ldgl, sq geometrics in clear, 76x24" ea panel, pr 28,600.00
Drawing, ink/gouache on brd, Oboler home/mtns, 18x30" 13,200.00
Shade, ldgl, row of sm sqs on narrow panels, Linden, 27" 3,500.00

Table, mahog, triangle inlays, angle-joined legs, +4 stools **19,800.00**
Window, ldgl, chevron section, gr/wht/amber, 33x28" **6,000.00**
Window, ldgl, X lines & simple floral, red/wht, 41x22" **4,950.00**

Wrought Iron

Until the middle of the 19th century, almost all the metal hand forged in America was made from a material called wrought iron. When wrought iron rusts it appears grainy, while the mild steel that was used later shows no grain but pits to an orange-peel surface. This is an important aid in determining the age of an ironwork piece.

Broiler, rotary, EX detail, well-shaped hdl, 20" overall **225.00**
Broiler, rotary, 13½" dia, 26" L **150.00**
Chandelier, 4-arm, twisted rod hanger, pitted, 25" **250.00**
Ember tongs, primitive, 9" **50.00**
Ember tongs, 14½" **125.00**
Fire shovel, brass urn finial, early, 19" **95.00**
Fire tools: tongs & shovel, brass hdls, 30", pr **100.00**
Fork, heart ornament in tines, 31" **275.00**
Fork, 2-tine, pierced end for hanging, early, 18" **44.00**
Garden ornament, 4 tiers of scallops, sunburst top, 30" **250.00**
Hinge, ram's horn, pitted, 10½", pr **170.00**
Jig, torpedo shape w/4 hooks, 1900s, 15" **85.00**
Kettle stand, scrolled detail, penny ft, 12" **125.00**
Lighting stand, candle arm w/wide drip pan adjusts, 58" **900.00**
Lighting stand, rush holder w/counterbalance socket, 48" **350.00**
Lighting stand, 3 ft, rnd disk base, w/Betty lamp & socket **550.00**
Lock, simple decorative detail, 10" **55.00**
Loom light, hanging, candle arm adjusts, socket broken, 33" **150.00**
Padlock, heavy, w/key & spikes to fasten to door & jamb, 9" **75.00**
Skewer holder, tooled heart-shaped finial, 5", +3 skewers **225.00**
Spatula, flared blade, rattail finial, ca 1800, 18" **90.00**
Spear, ice fishing; 4-point fork end, 20x5½x1½", EX **26.00**
Sugar nippers, 9¾" **125.00**
Taper jack, EX detail, curved legs, rust, 5½" **145.00**
Thumb latch, tulip finial, 8" **125.00**
Toaster, scrolled detail, 15" W, 28" hdl **175.00**
Toaster, scrolled/twisted detail, 17½" W, 19" hdl **275.00**
Toaster, simple twisted iron/wood hdl, rusted, 12" **105.00**
Utensil rack, 6-hook, decorative crest, pitted, 13x21" **180.00**
Utensil rack, 7-hook, EX scroll detail, 14x19" **225.00**
Wagon jack, blacksmith-made w/rivet construction **115.00**

Yellow Ware

Ranging in color from buff to deep mustard, yellow ware which almost always has a clear glaze can be slip-banded, plain, Rockingham-decorated, flint enamel-glazed, or mocha-decorated. Mocha-decorated pieces are usually the most expensive and desirable. The majority of pieces are plain and do not bear a manufacturer's mark. Yellow ware which was primarily produced in the United States, England, and Canada was popular from the mid-19th century to the early 20th century. A utilitarian ware, it was first domestically produced in New York, New Jersey, Pennsylvania, and Vermont. With more than thirty active potteries, East Liverpool, Ohio, became the center for yellow ware production. After experiencing several years of dramatic price increases, the market has begun to stabilize. For further information we recommend *Collecting Yellow Ware, An Identification and Value Guide*, written by our advisor, John Michel, and Lisa S. McAllister. Mr. Michel's address is in the Directory under New York.

Baking dish, oval w/extended lip, 12¼", NM **210.00**

Bowl, batter; brn bands, hdls, 9½", M 110
Bowl, batter; emb, wht int, mk JE Jeffords, 13", M 165
Bowl, wht band w/bl seaweed, 12", NM 385
Bowl, wht band w/gr seaweed, 10", M 315
Chamber pot, wht band w/bl seaweed, mini, 2¼", EX 190
Colander, pie plate shape, M 395
Colander, 13 wht bands, 12½", NM 625
Creamer, cow figural, chips/hairlines 1,650
Cup, measuring; spearpoints & flowers emb, 6¼", M 245
Custard cup, cone shape w/lip, 2½", M 28
Egg cup, plain, 2¾", M 225
Flask, fish form, 10½" L, NM 950
Flowerpot, wht band w/bl seaweed, 10", NM 925
Funnel, plain, 3", NM 500
Jar, canning; molded staves/bands, keg shape, 6", VG 100
Jar, canning; octagonal, 7½", M 225
Mold, cluster of roses, oval, 7½", NM 225
Mold, ear of corn, 6½x8½", M 75
Mold, heart shape, mini, 2½" L, M 225
Mold, melon shape, mk Yel Rock, Phila, mini, 2½", M 195
Mold, pineapple, oval, 8", M 200
Pepperpot, wht band w/blk seaweed, 4½", NM 575
Pitcher, seaweed, bl on wht band w/blk stripes, 8", EX 750
Plate, dinner; Westward Expansion, 13", M 175
Plate, sandwich; Westward Expansion, 9", M 145
Rolling pin, trn wood hdls, 15" 295
Syllabub or punch cup, 2¾", NM 175
Tureen, melon shape, w/lid, 11" L, NM 3,100
Vase, ribbed & flared, 1900s, 8" 60
Washboard, rare, NM 795

Zanesville Art Pottery

In 1900 the Zanesville Roofing Tile Company changed its na to the Zanesville Art Pottery Company and began the manufacture standard glaze art pottery as well as cobalt blue jardinieres. Da Schmidt (1847-1922) was president of the concern during its twe years of operation, and Albert Radford was general manager for a sh time about 1901. The plant burned in 1901, possibly due to arson, a again in 1910, but was rebuilt both times. In 1920 the plant was sold S.A. Weller and became Weller Plant No. 3. All identified pieces the company's art pottery are impressed 'La Moro' with a shape nu ber. Our advisor for this category is James L. Murphy; he is listed in Directory under Ohio.

Vase, standard glaze w hand-painted yellow iris marked La Moro, #831, 9½", $185.00.

owl, pansies, std glaze, oblate hdls, #834/5, 6x8" 130.00
owl, pansies, std glaze, oval, sgn KH, #85¾, 2x3½" 40.00
owl, red clover, std glaze, oval, sgn KH, #866/5, 7" 150.00
abinet vase, matt, bl w/wht squeezebag net, #864/4, 3" 55.00
abinet vase, pansies, std glaze, #854/4, 2" 40.00
abinet vase, pansies, std glaze, spherical, #861/5, 3" 95.00
abinet vase, roses, peach matt, sgn W Hull, #864/5, 4" 170.00
reamer, leaves, std glaze, sgn MG, #806/4, 6", EX 40.00
ug, red catchfly, std glaze, sgn KH, #882/5, 6" 145.00
ase, gr grapes, std glaze, lyre hdls, sgn MG, #847/5, 9" 175.00
ase, red clover, std glaze, #807/4, 8" 50.00
ase, red clover, std glaze, ovoid, 2-hdld, #808/4, 5" 150.00
ase, roses, matt, cylindrical, sgn MG, #811/4, 8" 190.00
ase, roses, std glaze, fluted mouth, #819/4, 11" 200.00
ase, yel iris, std glaze, urn form, #831/6, 9½" 185.00

Zanesville Glass

Glassware was produced in Zanesville, Ohio, from as early as 1815
til 1851. Two companies produced clear and colored hollowware
eces in five characteristic patterns: 1) diamond faceted, 2) broken
irls, 3) vertical swirls, 4) perpendicular fluting, 5) plain, with scal-
ped or fluted rims and strap handles. The most readily identified
oduct is perhaps the whiskey bottles made in the vertical swirl pat-
rn, often called globular swirls because of their full, round bodies.
eir necks vary in width; some have a ringed rim and some are col-
ed. They were made in several colors; amber, light green, and light
uamarine are the most common. Our advisor for this category is
ark Vuono; he is listed in the Directory under Connecticut.

ttle, club; aqua, 24-rib broken swirl, ribs are lt, 8" 250.00
ttle, globular; aqua, 24 swirled ribs, 8" 300.00
ttle, globular; citron, 24 swirled ribs, 8" 700.00
ttle, globular; gold-amber, 24-rib, lt impression, 7¾" 975.00

ttle, globular; gold-
ber, 24-rib right
irl, M, $400.00.

ttle, globular; med gold-amber, 24 swirled ribs, 8¾" 400.00
ttle, wine; lt to med bl-gr, 15 swirled ribs, 12" 450.00
tler, globular; gold-amber, 24-rib right swirl, 8" 400.00
sk, chestnut; aqua, 24 swirled ribs, minor wear, 6" 150.00
sk, chestnut; gold-amber, 24 swirled ribs, lt wear, 5" 220.00

Flask, pocket; gold-amber, 24-rib left swirl, 5" 180.00
Flask, red-amber, 24-rib, 5" 220.00

Zsolnay

Only until the past decade has the production of the Zsolnay factory become more correctly understood. In the beginning they produced only cement, industrial and kitchen ware manufacture began in
the 1850s, and in the early 1870s a line of decorative architectural and
art pottery was initiated which has continued to the present time.

The city of Pecs (pronounced Paach) is the major provincial city
of southwest Hungary close to the Yugoslav border. The old German
name for the city was Funfkirchen, meaning 'Five Churches.' (The
'five-steeple' mark became the factory's logo in 1878.)

Although most Americans only think of Zsolnay in terms of the
bizarre, reticulated examples of the 1880s and '90s and the small
'Eosine' green figures of animals and children that have been produced
since the 1920s, the factory went through all the art trends of major
international art potteries and produced various types of forms and decorations. The 'golden period,' circa 1895-1920, is when its Art Nouveau (Sezession in Austro-Hungarian terms) examples were unequaled.
Vilmos Zsolnay was a Renaissance man devoted to innovation, and his
children carried on the tradition after his death in 1900. Important
sculptors and artists of the day were employed (usually anonymously)
and married into the family, creating a dynasty.

Nearly all Zsolnay is marked, either impressed 'Zsolnay Pecs' or
with the 'five steeple' stamp. Variations and form numbers can date a
piece fairly accurately. For the most part, the earlier ethnic historial-
revival pieces do not bring the prices that the later Sezession and second Sezession (Deco) examples do. Our advisor for this category is John
Gacher; he is listed in the Directory under Rhode Island.

Bowl, cherry branches on indigo irid, E4669/1/m, 7" 600.00
Figurine, mother & child, cubistic, gr irid, 8½" 300.00
Pitcher, gourd form w/leaf spout, vine hdl, red/purple, 7" 2,000.00

Vase, after Miklos, designed
as a siren about to drop a
rock on the heads of drowning sailors, purple-green iridescence on tawny ground,
1909, 24", $4,125.00.

Vase, fully emb siren about to drop rock, drowning men, 24" 4,125.00
Vase, gr/yel irid on bl/purple/pk, simple form, 10" 210.00
Vase, lg emb leaves, gold/wine/gr on red irid, sqd/ftd, 7½" 850.00
Vase, Picasso-style female on gr irid, 6½" 295.00
Vase, 4 mice, red/mustard irid, 4-hdld dbl-gourd form, 7" 900.00

The editors and staff take this opportunity to express our sincere gratitude and appreciation to each person who has in any way contributed to the preparatic this guide. We believe the credibility of our book is greatly enhanced through their efforts. See each advisor's Directory listing for information concerning their cific areas of expertise.

You will notice that at the conclusion of some of the narratives the advisor's name is given. This is optional and up to the discretion of each individual. Sin because no name is mentioned does not indicate that we have no advisor for that subject. Our board grows with each issue and now numbers over 350; if you car correspond with any of them or anyone listed in our Directory, you must send a SASE with your letter. If you are seeking an appraisal, first ask about their fee, s; many of these people are professionals who must naturally charge for their services. Because of our huge circulation, every person who allows us to publish their n; runs the risk of their privacy being invaded by too many phone calls and letters. We are indebted to every advisor and very much regret losing any one of them. By the majority of those we lose give this reason. Please help us retain them on our board by observing the simple rules of common courtesy. For suggestions that help you evaluate your holdings, see the Introduction.

Charles and Barbara Adams
Middleboro, Massachusetts

Jay Adams
Washington Township, New Jersey

Geneva D. Addy
Winterset, Iowa

Margaret Alves
Shelton, Connecticut

James Anderson
New Brighton, Minnesota

Suzy McLennan Anderson
Holmdel, New Jersey

Tim Anderson
Provo, Utah

Warren R. Anderson
Cedar City, Utah

Dorothy Malone Anthony
Fort Scott, Kansas

John Apple
Racine, Wisconsin

Dick and Ellie Archer
St. Augustine, Florida

Una Arnbal
Ames, Iowa

Bruce Austin
Fairport, New York

Rod Baer
Vienna, Virginia

Wayne and Gale Bailey
Dacula, Georgia

Mrs. Lillian Baker, Fellow IBA, Cambridge, England
Gardena, California

Roger Baker
Woodside, California

Robert Banks
Brookeville, Maryland

Jim Barker
Hawley, Pennsylvania

Kit Barry
Brattleboro, Vermont

Henry Bartsch
Rockaway, Oregon

Mark Bassett
Nevada, Iowa

Daniel J. Batchelor
Oswego, New York

Dana Martin Batory
Crestline, Ohio

D.R. Beeks
Coeur d'Alene, Idaho

Scott Benjamin
Lancaster, California

Joanne Berman
Carmichael, California

Phyllis and Tom Bess
Tulsa, Oklahoma

Robert Bettinger
Mt. Dora, Florida

John E. Bilane
Union, New Jersey

Dale Blann
Wheatland, Indiana

Clarence H. Bodine, Jr.
New Hope, Pennsylvania

Sandra V. Bondhus
Unionville, Connecticut

Clifford Boram
Monticello, Indiana

Dick and Waunita Bosworth
Kansas City, Missouri

Jeff Bradfield
Dayton, Virginia

Tom Bradshaw
Ventura, California

Larry Brenner
Manchester, New Hampshire

William J. Brinkley
McLeansboro, Illinois

Mike Brooks
Oakland, California

Jim Broom
Effingham, Illinois

David L. Brown
Victoria, British Columbia, Canada

Rick Brown
Newspaper Collector's Society of America
Lansing, Michigan

Mike Bruner
West Bloomfield, Michigan

Nicki Budin
Worthington, Ohio

Robert C. Butz
Newbury Park, California

Jim Calison
Wallkill, New York

Carol and Jim Carlton
Englewood, Colorado

Fran Carter
Coos Bay, Oregon

Tina M. Carter
El Cajon, California

Sally S. Carver
Chestnut Hill, Massachusetts

Cerebro
Lancaster, Pennsylvania

Jackie Chamberlain
La Canada, California

Chase Collectors Society
Mesa, Arizona

Jack Chipman
Redondo Beach, California

Wilfred and Dolli Cohen
Santa Ana, California

Lillian M. Cole
Flemington, New Jersey

J.W. Courter
Simpson, Illinois

Ron Damaska
New Brighton, Pennsylvania

John Danis
Rockford, Illinois

Patricia M. Davis
Wilmington, Delaware

Gael deCourtivron
Sarasota, Florida

Steve DeGenaro
Youngstown, Ohio

Richard K. Degenhardt
Hendersonville, North Carolina

Mary Delucchi
Stockton, California

Joe Devine
Council Bluffs, Iowa

Thomas P. Dimitroff
Corning, New York

Ginny Distel
Tiffin, Ohio

DLK Nostalgia & Collectibles
Johnstown, Pennsylvania

Rod Dockery
Ft. Worth, Texas

L.R. 'Les' Docks
San Antonio, Texas

Rebecca Dodds
Ft. Lauderdale, Florida

Pat Dole
Birmingham, Alabama

Ron Donnelly
Panama City Beach, Florida

Robert A. Doyle, CAI, ISA
Fishkill, New York

Louise Dumont
Coventry, Rhode Island

Ken and Jackie Durham
Washington, DC

William Durham
Belvidere, Illinois

Rita and John Ebner
Columbus, Ohio

Bill Edwards
Madison, Indiana

J. David Ehrhard
Los Angeles, California

J.M. Ellwood
Scottsdale, Arizona

Adrienne S. Escoe
Los Alamitos, California

Bryce Farnsworth
Fargo, North Dakota

Maurice Feinblatt
Wilmette, Illinois

Joseph Ferrara
Newburgh, New York

Vicki Flanigan
Winchester, Virginia

Gene Florence
Lexington, Kentucky

Ruth Forsythe
Galena, Ohio

Daniel Fortney
Milwaukee, Wisconsin

Fostoria Glass Society of America, Inc.
Moundsville, West Virginia

Ron Fox
North Babylon, New York

Madeleine France
Ft. Lauderdale, Florida

James Fred
Cutler, Indiana

Sandra and Peter Frei
Brimfield, Massachusetts

Wendy and Leo Frese
Dallas, Texas

Terry Friend
Galax, Virginia

Doris Frizzell
Springfield, Illinois

Donald M. Frost
Roseburg, Oregon

John Gacher
Newport, Rhode Island

We wish to thank the following auction houses whose catalogs have been used as sources for pricing information. Many have granted us permission to reproduce their photographs as well.

A-1 Auction Service
P.O. Box 540672, Orlando, FL 32854; 407-341-6681. Specializing in American antique sales

America West Archives
Anderson, Warren
P.O. Box 100, Cedar City, UT 84721; 801-586-9497; quarterly 26-page illustrated catalog includes auction section of scarce and historical early western documents, letters, autographs, stock certificates, and other important ephemera. Subscription: $12 per year

Andre Ammelounx
The Stein Company
P.O. Box 136, Palatine, IL 60078; 708-991-5927 or (Fax) 708-991-5947. Specializing in steins, catalogs available

Annual Perfume Bottle Auction
Monsen & Baer
310 Maple Ave., West #270, Vienna, VA 22180; 703-938-2129

Anthony J. Nard & Co.
US Rt. 220, Milan, PA 18831; 717-888-9404 or (Fax) 717-888-7723

Arman Absentee Auctions
P.O. Box 174, Woodstock, CT 06281; 203-928-5838. Specializing in American glass, Historical Staffordshire, English soft paste, paperweights

Autographs of America
Anderson, Tim
P.O. Box 461, Provo, UT 84603. Free sample catalog of hundreds of autographs for sale

Barrett Bertoia Auctions & Appraisals
2217 Glenwood Dr., Vineland, NJ 18630; 609-692-4092. Specializing in antique toys and collectibles

Bider's
241 S. Union St., Lawrence, MA 01843; 508-388-4347 or 508-683-3944. Antiques appraised, purchased, and sold on consignment

Brian Riba Auctions Inc.
P.O. Box 53, Main St., S. Glastonbury, CT 06073; 203-633-3076

Butterfield & Butterfield
220 San Bruno Ave., San Francisco, CA 91043; 415-861-7500 or (Fax) 415-861-8951. Also located at: 7601 Sunset Blvd., Los Angeles, CA 90046; 213-850-7500 or (Fax) 213-850-5843. Fine Art Auctioneers and Appraisers since 1865

C.E. Guarino
Box 49, Denmark, ME 04022

Charles E. Kirtley
P.O. Box 2273, Elizabeth City, NC 27096; 919-335-1262. Specializing in World's Fair, Civil War, political, advertising, and other American collectibles

Cincinnati Art Gallery
635 Main St., Cincinnati, OH 45202; 513-381-2128. Specializing in American art pottery, American and European fine paintings, watercolors

Col. Doug Allard
P.O. Box 460, St. Ignatius, MT 59865

Collectors Auction Services
326 Seneca St., Oil City, PA 16301; 814-677-6070. Specializing in advertising, oil and gas, toys, rare museum and investment-quality antiques

David Rago
P.O. Box 3592, Station E, Trenton, NJ 08629; 609-397-9374
Gallery: 17 S. Main St., Lambertville, NJ 08530. Specializing in American art pottery and Arts & Crafts

Don Treadway Gallery
2128 Madison Rd., Cincinnati, OH 45208; 513-321-6742 or (Fax) 513-871-7722. Member: National Antique Dealers Association, American Art Pottery Association, International Society of Appraisers, and American Ceramic Arts Society

Doyle, Auctioneers & Appraisers
109 Osborne Hill Rd., Fishkill, NY 12524; 914-896-9492. Thousands of collectibles offered: call for free calendar of upcoming events

Dynamite Auctions
Franklin Antique Mall & Auction Gallery
1280 Franklin Ave., Franklin, PA 16323; 814-432-8577 or 814-786-9211

Du Mouchelles
409 Jefferson Ave., Detroit, MI 48226

Early Auction Co.
123 Main St., Milford, OH 45150

Garth's Auctions Inc.
2690 Stratford Rd., Box 369, Delaware, OH 43015; 614-362-4771

Glass-Works Auctions
James Hagenbuch
102 Jefferson, East Greenville, PA 18041; 215-679-5849. America's leading auction company in early American bottles and glass

Greenberg Auctions
7566 Main St., Sykesville, MD 21784. Specializing in trains: Lionel, American Flyer, Ives, Marx, Ho

Guernsey's
136 E. 73rd St., New York, NY 10021; 212-794-2280. Specializing in carousel figures

Gunther's International Auction Gallery
P.O. Box 235, 24 S. Virginia Ave., Brunswick, MD 21716; 301-834-7101 or 800-274-8779. Specializing in political, Oriental rugs, art, bronzes, antiques, the unusual

Hake's Americana & Collectibles
Specializing in character and personality collectibles along with all artifacts of popular culture for over 20 years. To receive a catalog for their next 3,000-item mail/phone bid auction, send $5 to Hake's Americana, P.O. Box 1444M, York, PA 17405

Jack Sellner
Sellner Marketing of California
P.O. Box 308, Fremont, CA 94536; 415-745-9463

James D. Julia
P.O. Box 210, Showhegan Rd., Fairfield, ME 04937

James R. Bakker Antiques, Inc.
James R. Bakker
370 Broadway, Cambridge, MA 02139; 617-864-7067. Specializing in American paintings, prints, and decorative arts

Joy Luke Fine Arts Brokers and Auctioneers
The Gallery
300 East Grove St., Bloomington, IL 61701; 309-828-5533

Ken Farmer Realty & Auction Company
1122 Norwood St., Radford, VA 24141; 703-639-0939 or (Fax) 703-639-1759

L.R. 'Les' Docks
Box 691035, San Antonio, TX 78269-1035. Providing occasional mail-order record auctions, rarely consigned; the only consignments considered are exceptionally scarce and unusual records

Litchfield, Auction Gallery
425 Bantam Rd., P.O. Box 1337, Litchfield, CT 06759; 203-567-3126 or (Fax) 203-567-3266

Lloyd Ralston Toys
447 Stratford Rd., Fairfield, CT 06432

Manion's International Auction House, Inc.
P.O. Box 12214, Kansas City, KS 66112

Maritime Auctions
R.R. 2, Box 45A, York, ME 03909; 207-363-4247

Mid-Hudson Auction Galleries
One Idlewild Ave., Cornwall-on-Hudson, NY 12520; 914-534-7828 or (Fax) 914-534-4802

Milwaukee Auction Galleries, Ltd.
4747 W. Bradley Rd., Milwaukee, WI 53223; 414-355-5054

Monsen & Baer
Monsen, Randall; and Baer, Rod
310 Maple Ave. West, Suite #115, Vienna, VA 22180; 703-938-2129. Cataloged auctions of perfume bottles. We purchase, sell, and accept consignments. Specializing in commercial, Czechoslovakian, Lalique, Baccarat, Victorian, crown top, factices, miniatures

Noel Barrett Antiques & Auctions
P.O. Box 1001, Carversville, PA 18913; 215-297-5109

Nostalgia Co.
21 S. Lake Dr., Hackensack, NJ 07601; 201-488-4536

Nostalgia Galleries
657 Meacham Ave., Elmont, NY 11003; 516-326-9595. Auctioning items from almost every area of the collectible field, catalogs available

Phillips
406 E. 79th St., New York, NY 10021

The Political Gallery
1325 W. 86th St., Indianapolis, IN 46260; 317-257-0863. Publishes quarterly catalogs

Refinders
737 Barberry Rd., Highland Park, IL 60035; 708-831-1102 or 708-831-1160. Refinders will find your wants from 1860-1960

Rex Stark Auctions
49 Wethersfield Rd., Bellingham, MA 02019

Richard A. Bourne Co., Inc.
Estate Auctioneers & Appraisers
Box 141, Hyannis Port, MA 02647; 617-775-0797

Richard Opfer Auctioneering, Inc.
1919 Greenspring Dr., Timonium, MD 21093; 301-252-5035

Roan, Inc.
Box 118, R.D. 3, Cogan Station, PA 17728

Robert W. Skinner, Inc.
Auctioneers & Appraisers
Rt. 117, Bolton, MA 01740; 617-779-5528

Soldiers Trunk
60 Craigs Rd., Windsor, CT 06095; 203-688-0580. Specializing in American & foreign military items; 4 catalog issues for $20.00.

Sotheby Parke Bernet, Inc.
980 Madison Ave., New York, NY 10021

TSACO
(The Stein Auction Company) East
Ron Fox
416 Throop St., N. Babylon, NY 11704.
Telephone and Fax:
516-669-7232

Weschler's
Adam A. Weschler & Son
905 E. St. N.W., Washington, DC 20004

Willis Henry Auctions
22 Main St., Marshfield, MA 02050

When contacting any of the buyers/sellers listed in this part of the Directory, please remember to include an SASE if you are corresponding by mail. If you cal and get their answering machine, when you leave your number so that they can return your call, tell them to call back collect. Some of these people are licensec appraisers and may charge a fee for the information they provide. Find out if this is the case before you ask their advice. We need your help. This book sells in suct great numbers that allowing their names to be published can create a potential nightmare for each advisor and contributor. Please do you part to alleviate this situa tion so that we can retain them on our board and in turn pass their experience and knowledge on to you.

Alabama

Dole, Pat
9825 Red Mill Rd.
Birmingham, 35215; 205-833-9853. Specializing in Purinton pottery

Luckey, Carl
Carl F. Luckey Communications
R.R. 4, Box 301, Lingerlost Tr., Killen, 35645. Freelance writer specializing in art, antiques, and collectibles. No telephone calls will be accepted.

Arizona

Chase Collectors Society
c/o Barry L. Van Hook
2149 Jibsail Loop, Mesa, 85202-5524; 602-838-6971. Publishes (6 issues per year) newsletter *Art Deco Reflections*; Membership: $10, newsletter sample copy: $1

Ellwood, J.M.
7077 E. Main #4, Scottsdale, 85251; 602-947-9679. Specializing in cast iron banks, toys, irons, trivets, doorstops and miscellaneous cast iron

Kielsmeier, Wayne B.
Covington Fine Arts Gallery, Inc.
4951 E. Grant, Rd. 107, Tucson, 85712; 602-326-6111. Specializing in 19th- and 20th-century American and European paintings, prints, water colors, and art pottery

Arkansas

Gifford, David Edwin
Arkansas Pottery Research
P.O. Box 7617, Little Rock, 72217; 501-664-2846. Historian/author/collector of Arkansas art pottery from 1905 to 1932. Seeking all information and company literature on the Ouachita Pottery, Niloak Pottery, and Camark Pottery companies as well as quality pieces marked Ouachita Hot Springs, Niloak Patent Pend'G, LeCamark or Hywood Art Pottery, will answer queries — LSASE please

Hall, Doris and Burdell
B&B Antiques
P.O. Box 1501, Fairfield Bay, 72088 or 210 W. Sassafras Dr., Morton, IL 61550. Authors of *Morton's Potteries: 99 Years*, Specializing in Morton pottery, American dinnerware, early American pattern glass, historical items

Musgrave, Marge
Look Nook Antiques
R.R. 3, Box 352, Mountain Home, 72653; 501-499-5283. Specializing in art glass and colored Victorian glass

Whysel, Steven
Antique & Art Galleries Ltd., Inc.
101 N. Main, Bentonville, 72712; 501-273-7770. Specializing in Art Nouveau, full line, books and art

Yohe, Darlene
Timberview Antiques
P.O. Box 343, Stuttgart, 72160; 501-673-3437. Specializing in American pattern glass, historical glass, Victorian pattern glass, carnival glass, and custard glass

California

Baker, Mrs. Lillian
15237 Chanera Ave., Gardena, 90249; 213-329-2619. Author Collector Books on antique, collectible, and high-fashion costume jewelry, hatpins and hatpin holders, miniatures

Baker, Roger
Baker's Lady Luck Emporium
Box 620417, Woodside, 94062. Specializing in Saloon — Americana advertising, gambling, bar bottles, cigar lighters, match safes, bowie knives, dirks, daggers, cowboy hats, spurs, chaps, saddles, barber items: bottles, shaving mugs, razors

Benjamin, Scott
2616 Via Madalena, Lancaster, 93535; 805-946-0075. Specializing in gasoline pump globes

Berman, Joanne
6130 Rampart Dr., Carmichael, 95608; 916-966-3490. Specializing in decorative (non-advertising) thermometers

Bradshaw, Tom
325 Carol Dr., Ventura, 93003; 805-653-2723 or 310-450-6486. Specializing in antique Bohemian glass

Brooks, Mike
7335 Skyline, Oakland, 94611; 510-339-1751. Specializing in typewriters, early televisions, Statue of Liberty

Butz, Robert C.
Collector's Wedgwood
P.O. Box 462, Newbury Park, 91319; 805-496-7805. Specializing in Wedgwood

Carter, Tina M.
882 S. Mollison, El Cajon, 92020; 619-440-5043. Specializing in teapots, tea-related items, tea tins, children's and toy tea sets, coffeepots, etc.

Chamberlain, Jackie
P.O. Box 594, La Canada, 91012-0594; 818-952-2513. Specializing in holiday collectibles, antique reference books, pewter ice cream molds, rare out-of-print books. Holiday slide program available for rent

Chipman, Jack
California Spectrum
Box 1429, Redondo Beach, 90278. Specializing in California ceramics; author of *Collector's Encyclopedia of California Pottery*, autographed copies available from author for $24.95+$3.50 postage and handling+(CA) tax of $2.35

Cohen, Wilfred and Dolli
Antiques & Art Glass
P.O. Box 27151, Santa Ana, 92799; 714-545-5673 (best to phone after 6:00 p.m. Pacific time). Specializing in Wave Crest (C.F. Monroe); Victorian Era art and pattern glass (salt shakers, toothpick holders, syrups, cruets, sugar shakers, tumblers, biscuit jars, table and pitcher sets); art and cameo glass open salts; custard and ruby stain glass; burmese, peachblow and amberina glass; pottery by Moorcroft (pre-1935 only); Buffalo (Deldare and Emerald ware); and Polia Pillin

Delucchi, Mary
Classic Tableware
P.O. Box 4265, Stockton 95204; 209-956-4645 (Shop: 1868 Country Club Blvd). Specializing in discontinued patterns: china, earthenware, crystal and silver

Ehrhard, J. David
Psycho-Ceramic Restorations
1336 Sutherland St., Los Angeles, 90026; 213-481-3956. Specializing in restoration of ceramics, collects Susie Cooper and British pottery, Mabel Lucie Attwell

Enge, Delleen
Franciscan Dinnerware Matching Service
323 E. Matilija, Ste. 112, Ojai, 93023

Escoe, Adrienne S.
Glass Knife Collectors Club
P.O. Box 342, Los Alamitos, 90720; 310-430-6479. Specializing in glass knives

Gibson, Pat
38280 Guava Dr., Newark, 94560; 510-792-0586. Specializing in R.A. Fox

Harrison, Gwynne
P.O. Box 1, Mira Loma, 91752-0001; 909-685-5434. Specializing in Autumn Leaf

Hibbard, Suzi
Wander Wares
Walnut Creek, 94596; 510-947-1076. Specializing in Dragonware, 1000 Faces china, Oriental china. Also may be reached in Boise, ID, at 208-383-4142, depending on schedule

Howard, Steve
101 1st St., Suite 404, Los Altos, 94022; 510-484-4488. Specializing in antique American firearms, bowie knives, Western Americana, old advertising and vintage gambling items

Inouye, Roger
2622 Valewood Ave., Carlsbad, 92008-7925. Specializing in Trolls

Johnson, Patricia A.
Box 1221, Torrance, 90505. Specializing in open salts

Kreider, Katherine
Kingsbury Productions
4555 N. Pershing Ave., Suite 33-138, Stockton, 95207; 209-467-8438. Specializing in Valentines

Long, Earnest and Ida
Long's Americana
P.O. Box 90, Mokelumne Hill, 95245; 209-286-1348. Specializing in children's items: toys, banks, games, etc.; publishers of *Dictionary of Toys, Vol. I & II*; *Dictionary of Still Banks*; and *Penny Lane*, a history of antique mechanical toy banks

MacKie, Jim and Linda
P.O. Box 1419, Soquel, 95073; 408-475-8049. Specializing in all advertising and (Linda's specialty) early lithography citrus and cigar labels

Maurer, Oveda L.
Oveda Maurer Antiques
34 Greenfield Ave., San Anselmo, 94960; 415-454-6439. Specializing in 18th-century and early 19th-century American furniture, lighting, pewter, and hearthware

Nelson, Maxine
873 Marigold Ct., Carlsbad, 92009. Specializing in Vernon Kilns

Pardini, Dick
3107 N. El Dorado St., Dept. SAPG, Stockton, 95204-3412; 209-466-5550 (recorder may answer). Specializing in California Perfume Company items: buyer and information center. Not interested in items that have Avon, Perfection, or Anniversary Keepsake markings. California Perfume Company offerings must be accompanied by a photo, Xerox copy, or sketching along with a condition report and, most important, price wanted. Inquiries require large SASE; not necessary if offering items for sale

Sanford, Steve and Martha
230 Harrison Ave., Campbell, 95088; 408-978-8408. Specializing in Brush McCoy

Shrader, Fred and Lila
Shrader Antiques
2025 Hwy. 199, Crescent City, 95531; 707-458-3525. Specializing in railroad, steamship an other transportation memorabilia; Shelley and select Americana

Stella's Collectibles
Memory Lanes Antique Mall
20740 S. Figueroa St, Carson, 90745; 310 316-7198

Westchester Faire Mall and Farmer's Mar ket Showcase Gallery in Los Angeles.
Second location:
PCH Mall, Long Beach
Nana's Antiques & Collectibles, Temecula. Spe cializing in quality glass and china, paperweights figurines, plates, jewelry

Yronwode, Catherine
6632 Covey Rd., Forestville, 95436; 707 887-2424. Specializing in pre-1950 col lectible plastic

Zeder, Audrey
6755 Coralite St. S., Long Beach, 9080((appointment only). Specializing in British Royal Commemorative Souvenirs (mail order catalog available). Author (Wallace Homestead) of *British Royal Commemorative*

Canada

Brown, David L.
Stevengraph Collectors Assn.
2103-2829 Arbutus Rd., Victoria, British Columbia, V8N 5X5; 604-477-9896. Specializing in Stevengraphs

Melis, Mirko
Marcelle Antiques
4589 Longmoor Rd., Mississauga, Ontario L5M 4H4; 416-820-8066. Specializing in American and European art glass, Russian works of art (enamels, porcelains, silver etc.), English and Continental glass an china, member of Antique Appraisal Asso ciation of America, Inc.

Warner, Ian
P.O. Box 93022, 499 Main St. S., Bramp ton, Ontario, L6Y 4V8; 905-453-9074 o (Fax) 905-453-2931. Specializing in Wad porcelain and Swankyswigs, author of *Th World of Wade*, Co-author: Mike Posgay

Colorado

Carlton, Carol and Jim
8115 S. Syracuse St., Englewood, 80112 303-773-8616. Specializing in Broadmoo Coors, and other Colorado pottery

Heck, Carl
Carl Heck Decorative Arts
Box 8416, Aspen, 81612; 303-925-8011. Spe cializing in original Tiffany lamps, window and chandeliers. Also reverse-painted an leaded glass table lamps, stained and bevele glass windows

Mackin, Bill
Author of *Cowboy and Gunfighter Collectibles* available from author: P.O. Box 70, Meeke 81641; 303-824-6717, clothbound: $29.95 paperback: $19.95; 1993-94 updated Pric Guide: $9.00. Specializing in old and fin spurs, guns, gun leather, cowboy gear, Western Americana (Collection in the Museum c Northwest Colorado, Craig)

Over, Naomi L.
909 Sharon Lane, Arvada, 80002; 303-24-5922. Specializing in ruby glassware

egelke, Cathy; and James, Pat
illrose, 303-847-3758. Specializing in crocks, Western Pottery Mfg. Co. (Denver, CO)

oohey, Marlena
03 S. Pratt Parkway, Longmont, 80501; 03-424-5922. Specializing in black glass

White, John 'Grandpa'
Grandpa's Depot
Denver Union Station, P.O. Box 480030, Den-er, 80248-0030; 303-892-1177 or (Fax) 303-73-5505. Specializing in railroad-related items, atalogs available

Vinther, Jo Ellen
449 W. 75th Way, Arvada, 80005; 800-872-345 or 303-421-2371. Specializing in Coors

Connecticut

Alves, Margaret
4 Oak Ave., Shelton, 06484; 1-203-924-678. Specializing in spoons: plated, ster-ng, silver, pre-1920s

ondhus, Sandra V.
ox 100, Unionville, 06085; 203-678-1808. Author of *Quimper Pottery: A French Folk rt Faience*; specializing in Quimper pottery

Harned, Denise
.O. Box 330373, Elmwood, 06133-0373. Author of *Griswold Cast Collectibles*. Special-ing in Griswold cast iron and aluminum

ilbride, Mrs. Richard J.
1 Willard Terrace, Stamford, 06903; 203-22-0568. Has available for sale: *Art Deco Chrome, The Chase Era*, and *Art Deco Chrome, Book 2, A Collector's Guide, Indus-ial Design in the Chase Era*

MacSorley, Earl
23 Indian Hill Rd., Orange, 06477; 203-37-1793 (after 7:00 p.m.). Specializing in utcrackers, Bessie Pease Gutmann prints, gural spittoons

ivera, Ted
ox 163, Torrington, 06790; 203-489-4325. pecializing in inkwells and inkstands; co-uthor of *Inkstands and Inkwells: A Collec-r's Guide*

oenigk, Martin
lechantiques
5 Barton Hill, E. Hampton, 06424; 203-267-682. Specializing in mechanical musical struments, music boxes, band organs, etc.

halberg, Bruce
lountain View Dr., Weston, 06883; 203-27-8175. Specializing in canes and walk-g sticks: novelty, carved, and Black

hompson, Roy M., Jr.
outhern Folk Pottery Collectors' Society
224 Main St., Glastonbury, 06033; 203-33-3121

an Deusen, Hobart
8 The Green, Watertown, 06795; 203-45-3456. Specializing in Canton, SASE quired when requesting information

uono, Mark
06 Mill Rd., Stamford, 06903; 203-329-744 (6-10 p.m. EST). Specializing in his-rical flasks, blown 3-mold glass, blown merican glass

Delaware

avis, Patricia M.
00 Greenhill Ave., Wilmington, 19805; 02-658-2992

District of Columbia

Chester, Joan
The Cruet Lady
4327 Nebraska Ave., NW, Washington, DC 20016; 202-363-2481. Selling limited edi-tion signed and dated reproductions of Vic-torian cruets

Durham, Ken and Jackie (By appointment)
909 26 St. N.W., Washington, DC 20037; 202-338-1342. Specializing in counter-top arcade machines, trade stimulators, and vending machines; publish *Coin-Op Newsletter*, 16-page illustrated list: $2; Send SASE for free list of books on coin-operated machines

England

Pedel, Alan
Collectibles from England
Marwood Lee, Barnstaple, Devon, EX31 4EB; 011-44-271-75166 (anytime). Special-izing in pie birds and most other collectibles

Florida

Archer, Dick and Ellie
Artiques
419 Sevilla Dr., St. Augustine, 32086; 904-797-4678. Specializing in Victorian silverplate: figu-rals, fancy hollowware, and collectibles

Bettinger, Robert
P.O. Box 333, Mt. Dora, 32757; 904-735-3575. Specializing in American art pottery

Cohen, Joel
Cohen Books & Collectibles
P.O. Box 810310, Boca Raton, 33481; 407-487-7888. Specializing in Disneyana

deCourtivron, Gael
Cocaholics
4811 Remington Dr., Sarasota, 34234; 813-351-1560. Specializing in Coca-Cola memorabilia. Cocaholics hot line: 813-355-2652 (COLA)

Dodds, Rebecca
Silver Flute
Box 39644, Ft. Lauderdale, 33339. Special-izing in jewelry

Donnelly, Ron
Saturday Heroes
Box 7047, Panama City Beach, 32413. Special-izing in Big Little Books, movie posters, premi-ums, western heroes, character collectibles, early Disney. For inquiries include SASE

France, Madeleine
P.O. Box 15555, Ft. Lauderdale, 33318; 305-584-0009. Specializing in top-quality perfume bottles: Rene Lalique, Steuben, Czechoslo-vakian, DeVilbiss, Baccarat, Commercials

Harry, Pauline
Pauline Harry Paper Collectibles
11493 Spring Hill Dr., Spring Hill, 34609; 904-686-9418. Specializing in pinups, illustrators, Rockwell, Leyendecker, etc., old magazines

Hess, Steve
Confederate Swords
P.O. Box 3476; Deland, 32723; 904-254-1809 or 904-736-1067. Specializing in Confederate swords

Hudson, Hardy
Our Antiques Market
5453 Lake Howell Rd., Winter Park, 32792; 407-657-2100 from 11:00 a.m. to 6:00 p.m. Specializing in majolica, Ameri-can art pottery

Lawrence, Judy and Cliff
1169 Overcash Dr., Dunedin, 34698; 813-734-4742. Specializing in fountain pens, dip-pers, and mechanical pencils

Linscott, Jacqueline
3557 Nicklaus Dr., Titusville, 32780. Spe-cializing in Blue Bell paperweights; author of *1992 Revised Edition, Blue Bell Paper-weights*, complete with history, illustrations, and price guide; Available from author for $12 (including postage and handling)

Linscott, Len
Line Jewels
3557 Nicklaus Dr., Titusville, 32780. Special-izing in glass insulators, and other telephone items (SASE required)

McNerny, Kathryn
118 Creek Hollow Lane, Middleburg, 32068. Author (Collector Books) on blue and white stoneware, primitives, tools

Parker, Alton B.
Box 110, 5030 W. 14 St., Bradenton, 34207; 813-756-0386. Specializing in Azalea china, Depression Glass, Roseville pottery

Supnick, Mark
8524 N.W. 2 St., Coral Springs, 33065; 305-755-3448. Author of *Collecting Hull Pottery's Little Red Riding Hood*. Specializing in Ameri-can pottery

White, Douglass
Classic Interiors & Antiques
2144 Edgewater Dr., Orlando, 32804; 407-841-6681. Specializing in Fulper, other American art pottery

Georgia

Bailey, Wayne and Gale
3152 Fence Rd., Dacula, 30211; 404-963-5736. Specializing in Goebels (Friar Tuck, Santa Claus, Toby pitchers by Goebel)

Glenn, Walter
Geode Ltd.
3393 Peachtree Rd., Atlanta, 30326; 404-261-9346. Specializing in Frankart

Joiner, John R.
245 Ashland Trail, Tyrone, 30290; 404-487-3732. Specializing in commercial avia-tion collectibles

Idaho

Beeks, D.R.
P.O. Box 2515, Coeur d'Alene 83814; 208-667-0830. Specializing in instruments of early science, technology, and medicine. Also surveying instruments, microscopes

Illinois

Ammelounx, Andre
The Stein Auction Company
P.O. Box 136, Palatine, 60078; 708-991-5927 or (Fax) 708-99-5947. Specializing in steins, catalogs available

Axley, Gilbert E.
Pleasant Hill Antique Mall
111 Post Oak Dr., Morton, 61550; 309-266-6190. Specializing in antiques and collectibles

Brinkley, Wm. J.
Brinkley Galleries
401 S. Washington Ave., McLeansboro, 62859. Specializing in Meissen, Dresden, Euro-pean porcelains, American porcelains (Cybis)

Broom, Jim
Box 65, Effingham, 62401. Specializing in opalescent pattern glassware

Childs, Charles and Peggy
Peg's Antiques & Collectibles
2800 W. Krause, Peoria 61605; 309-637-8174. Specializing in antiques and collectibles

Courter, J.W.
R.R. 1, Simpson, 62985; 618-949-3884. Specializing in Aladdin lamps; Author of *Aladdin — The Magic Name in Lamps*, soft-bound, 180 pages; and *Aladdin Electric Lamps*, hardbound, 229 pages

Danis, John
11028 Raleigh Ct., Rockford, 61111; 815-963-0757 or (Fax) 815-877-6042. Specializ-ing in R. Lalique

Feinblatt, Maurice
Wilmette Porcelain Shop
3207 Lake Ave., Wilmette, 60091; 708-251-1170. Specializing in Lladro (since 1973), finer American and European porcelain figurines, western and Art Nouveau bronze recasts

Frizzell, Doris
Doris' Dishes
5687 Oakdale Dr., Springfield, 62707; 217-529-3873. Specializing in Royal Haeger, and Depression Glass; Co-author (Collec-tor Books) of *Royal Haeger* book

Garmon, Lee
1529 Whittier St., Springfield, 62704; 217-789-9574. Specializing in Royal Haeger, Royal Hickman, glass animals; co-author (Collector Books) of *Glass Animals and Fig-ural Flower Frogs of the Depression Era*

Gilbert, Harold and Donnna
Pepper Ridge Country Antiques
240 Magnolia Ave., Forsyth, 62535; 217-877-2608. Specializing in cookie jars, string hold-ers, doorstops, milk bottles, toys, baseball cards, clothes sprinkler bottles, razor blade banks, Disney items, and Royal Copley

Griffith, Woody
Chicago, 312-348-6275. Specializing in Jewel Tea, Noritake, Hall, perfumes

Grist, Everett
3417 Dewitt, Mattoon, 61938. Specializing in marbles

Hahn, Bill and Donna
Cobweb Corner Antiques
419 W. Walnut St., Metamora, 61548; 309-367-4043. Specializing in general line

Hall, Doris and Burdell
B&B Antiques
210 W. Sassafras Dr., Morton, 61550 or P.O. Box 1501, Fairfield Bay, AR 72088. Authors of *Morton's Potteries: 99 Years*; specializing in Morton pottery, American dinnerware, early American pattern glass, historical items

Haussmann, Richard A., Past President, Aurora Historical Society
Aurora, 60507

Higgins, Joyce and Rudy
Abe's Antiques
2001 N. Wisconsin Ave., Peoria 61603; 309-682-8181. Specializing in a complete line of American antiques

Hilst, Randy
1221 Florence #4, Pekin, 61554; 309-346-2710. Specializing in old fishing tackle, duck and goose calls

Hoffmann, Pat and Don, Sr.
1291 N. Elmwood Dr., Aurora, 60506; 708-859-3435. Authors of *Warwick, A to W*, a supple-ment to *Why Not Warwick? China Collector's Guide*; specializing in Warwick china

Hopp, Dennis Carl
Chicago, 312-935-7872. Specializing in Higgins glass

The Home Place Antiques
Durham, William; Galaway, William
615 South State St. Belvidere, 61008; 815-544-0577. Specializing in Tea Leaf ironstone, and white ironstone

Hooks, Dee
Dee's China Shop
P.O. Box 142, Lawrenceville, 62439; 618-943-2741. Specializing in R.S. Prussia, Royal Bayreuth, Haviland, other fine china

Hurney, George and Mary
Glass Connection (mail-order only)
312 Babcock Dr., Palatine, 50067; 708-359-3839. Specializing in Depression Glass and Paden City Glass (not advising on pottery)

International Society of Antique Scale Collectors
Bob Stein, President
176 W. Adams, Suite 1706, Chicago, 60603; 312-263-7500

Laub, Marge and Myron
Laub's Loft
112 Commercial St., Neponset, 61345; 309-594-2025. Specializing in general line of antiques, lots of paper memorabilia

Long, Dee
112 S. Center, Lacon, 61540. Specializing in reamers

Loos, Ron
Classic Collectibles
167 Seaton Lane, Washington, 61571; 309-745-5661. Specializing in '40s and '50s collectibles

Lubliner, Larry
Refinders mail/telephone auction
737 Barberry Rd., Highland Park, 60035; 708-831-1102 or 708-831-1160. Refinders will find your wants from 1860-1960

Martha's Cobwebs
Pleasant Hill Antique Mall
3155 Pleasant Hill Rd., E. Peoria, 61611; 309-694-4040. Specializing in antiques and collectibles in general

McMorrow, Tom and Gennie
Doc's Holiday
729 W. Stratford Dr., Peoria, 61614; 309-682-6232. Specializing in pottery, Old Sleepy Eye, Fairings, and Staffordshire

Miller, Carol
218 Devron Circle, E. Peoria, 61611-1605

Miller, Larry; and Strickfaden, Dick
218 Devron Circle, E. Peoria, 61611-1605. Specializing in German and Czechoslovakian Erphila

Ochsner, Grace
Grace Ochsner Doll House
R.R. 1, Box 95, Niota, 62358; 217-755-4362. Specializing in piano babies, bisque

German dolls
Owen, Larry and Sally
Specializing in Morten Studio dogs, etc.
Pollack, Frank and Barbara (Appointment only)
1214 Green Bay Rd., Highland Park, 60035; 708-433-2213. Specializing in American country antiques and art

Randy's Ol' Time Collectibles
Hilst, Randy
1811 Broadway, Pekin, 61554; 309-347-5873. Specializing in outdoor collectibles and general line

Rastello, Lisa
Milkweed Antiques
5N531 Ancient Oak Lane, St. Charles, 60175; 708-377-4612. Specializing in Depression-era collectibles

Rhoden, Joan and Charles
Memories/Rhoden's Antiques
605 N. Main, Georgetown, 61846; 217-662-8046. Specializing in Heisey and other Elegant Glassware, general line antiques. Co-authors of *Those Wonderful Yard-Long Prints and More*, and *More Wonderful Yard-Long Prints*, illustrated value guides

Rodrick, Tammy
Stacey's Treasures
R.R. 2, Box 163, Sumner, 62466; 618-947-2240. Specializing in antiques and collectibles

Siebenthal, Sheila
Sheila's Selectables
5819 W. Colt Dr., Peoria, 61607; 309-697-4119. Specializing in antiques and collectibles

Spencer, Dick
Glass and More (Shows only)
1203 N. Yale, O'Fallon, 62269; 618-632-9067. Specializing in Cambridge, Fenton, Fostoria, Heisey, etc.

Spiess, Greg
230 E. Washington, Joliet, 60433; 815-722-5639. Specializing in Odd Fellows lodge items

Trimble, Donna
DJ's Antiques
16520 Woodfield Ct., Mackinaw 61755; 309-359-8578

Trinkets & Treasures
Box 123, Metamora, 61548; 309-367-2391. Specializing in vintage costume jewelry, Illinois and Midwestern stoneware

Van Tine, Sandra I.
Lora's Memory Lane
13133 N. Caroline St., Chillicothe, 61523; 309-579-3040. Specializing in inkwells and inkstands

Weldi-Skinner, Mary
1656 W. Farragut Ave., Chicago, 60640. Specializing in American and European art pottery, designer collectibles

Wells, Rosalie J. 'Rosie'
R.R. 1S, Canton, 61520; 1-800-445-8745. Publishes magazines and annual price guides for Precious Moments Collectibles, Hallmark Ornament Collectibles, Hallmark Merry Miniatures, Lowell Davis Collectibles, and others! She has hosted the International Convention for Precious Moments Collectors each year since 1984 and hosts the Annual Midwest Collectibles Fest. Write for free literature. She also offers a touch-tone 900 line for collectors 18 years and older to leave their Voice Ad for collectors across the USA. (1-900-740-7575) $2 per minute

Willis, Richard
Dick Willis Antiques
2006 N. Abbey Circle, Peoria, 61604; 309-674-2679

Wood, Richard and Helen
Wood's Nostalgia
804 Second St., Lacon, 61540; 309-246-8240

Woods, James and Sandra
R.R. 4, Box 22, Galesburg, 61401; 309-342-7612. Specializing in railroad and telegraph memorabilia and pressed flint glass

Wright, Vernon and Adel
Wright's Collectibles
822 N. Cortland, Peoria, 61604; 309-637-2839

Yester-Daze Glass
c/o Illinois Antique Center
100 Walnut St., Pekin, 61554; 309-347-1679. Specializing in Cambridge, Fostoria, Depression Glass and '50s glass

Indiana

Adkins, William
Twin Lakes Antiques
7208 W. St., Rd. 114, Silver Lake, 46982; 219-982-2939. Specializing in miscellaneous items.

Alexander, Charles H.
221 E. 34th St., Indianapolis, 46205; 317-924-9665. Specializing in American dinnerware, glassware, pottery

Allman, Clyde
Seymour, 812-522-6521. Specializing in tools and fishing items

Allman, Elaine
Peddlers Two
Seymour, 812-522-6521. Specializing in kitchen items, cloth, and smalls

Baker's Dozen
Baker, John G.
4172 S., Co. Rd. 1010 E., Crothersville, 47229; 812-793-2257

Blann, Dale
President of Uhl Collectors' Society
R.R. 1, Box 136, Wheatland, 47597; 812-321-4141. Contact for membership and newsletter information

Boram, Clifford
Antique Stove Information Clearinghouse
Monticello; Free consultation by phone only: 219-583-6465

Brown, Brenda
739 W. 5th St., Marion, 46953; 317-662-6126. Specializing in 1950s toys, space toys, Barbies, Pez

Brown, Tammy
R. R. 6, Box 19, N. Vernon, 47265; 812-346-3918. Specializing in general line.

Burgett, Paul
R.R. 1, Box 111, Whiteland, 46184; 317-535-8672. Specializing in good glassware

Cox, Joseph C.
Alice's Collectibles
P.O. Box 127, Deputy, 47230; 812-866-5675. Crossroads Antique Mall
311 Holiday Square, Seymour, 47274; 812-522-5675. Open 7 days a week

Dean, Ginny and Tom
G & T Antiques
50 Broadmoor Dr., Wabash, 46922; 219-563-5682. Specializing in Flemish and blue and white stoneware

Dovin, Rosemary
Ro-Mar Antiques 317-644-4094 or 317-642-5674. Specializing in flow blue

Dunn, Ruth
R. R. 1, Box 383, Kirkland, 46050; 317-758-6282. Specializing in Depression Glass, Fiesta

Edwards, Bill
620 W. 2nd, Madison, 47250. Author (Collector Books) on Carnival Glass

Evans, Fran
2005 N. Salesbury St., W. Lafayette, 47906; 317-463-6858. Specializing in art pottery, ironstone, primitives

Farrow, Charlene
6875 N. 1000 E., Seymour, 812-522-6463. Specializing in general merchandise

Fisher, Todd
Crossroads Antique Mall
311 Holiday Square, Seymour, 47274; 812-522-5675. Open 7 days a week

Fred, James A.
Antique Radio Labs
R.R. 1, Box 41, Cutler, 46920; 317-268-2214. Specializing in radios made from 1922 to 1950

Gagnon, John
P.O. Box 47003, Indianapolis, 317-887-3224. Specializing in country primitives, glassware, kitchen items

Garrett, Jerry and Sandi
Jerry's Antiques (shows only)
1807 W. Madison St., Kokomo, 46 317-457-5256. Specializing in Green glass, old postcards

Gerth, Bev
714 Wendemere Dr., Seymour, 812-1231. Specializing in Hallmark and cious Moments

Givens, Oscar
Givens Antiques
Box 76, Converse, 46919; 317-395-367 317-395-3838

Haun, Ted
2426 N. 700 East, Kokomo, 46901; 317-3640. Specializing in American pottery china, '50s items, Russel Wright designs

Heiss, Virginia
7777 N. Alton Ave., Indianapolis, 462 317-875-6797. Specializing in Mun AMACO, Brandt Steele, Marblehe Kenton Hills

Henry, Lana
5186 N. 700 W., Jasper, 47546; 812-6 9819. Specializing in primitives

Hoover, Dave
Hoover's Angling Oddities
1023 Sky View Dr., New Albany, 471 812-945-3614. Specializing in fishing gea

Hutcheson, Joyce
130 Brook Acre Lane, Indianapolis, 462 317-881-2315. Specializing in glasswa toys, advertising

Keagy, William and June
P.O. Box 106, Bloomfield, 47424; 812-3 3471. Co-authors of *Those Wonderful Ya Long Prints and More*, and *More Wonder Yard-Long Prints*, illustrated value guides

Lyons, Phyllis
7151 W. 500 S., Swayzee, 46986; 317-9 7394. Specializing in general line.

Miller, David and Sheila
Cobbly Knob Antiques
1008 Cottonwood Dr., Kokomo, 4690 317-457-8837. Specializing in general li butter molds, Hummels

Miller, Susan
606 E. Wabash Ave., Crawfordsville, 479 317-362-0352. Specializing in trolls

Moore, Doug
57 Hickory Ridge Crest, Cicero, 46034; 3 877-1741. Specializing in toys, advertising

Nunemaker, Barbara C.
B&C Antiques and Collectibles
1330 W. Lowell Rd., Columbus, 4720 812-376-7949

Old Storefront Antiques
P.O. Box 357, Dublin, 47335; 317-47 4809. Specializing in country store item tins, primitives, pharmaceuticals, advert ing, etc. Active in mail order with catalo available. Information requires LSASE

Payton, Jewell
606-787-6329. Specializing in Jewel Tea

Percell, Ron
Webb's Antiques Mall
106 E. Main St., Centerville, 47330; 31 855-5733 or 317-855-5551. Specializing i folk art and country collectibles

Prather, Jean
Prather's Antiques
604 Lafayette Ave., #1, Columbus 4220 812-372-3481. Specializing in art glas milk glass, etc.

rentice, Richard
rrowhead Farms
.R. 12, Box 143, Bedford, 47421; 812-279-
241. Specializing in R.S. Prussia, cut glass

ruitt, Bonnie
& W Bargain Barn
350 W. 700 N., Anderson, 46011; 317-754-
010. Author of *St. Clair Glass Collector's
ook*, available for $15 each from author

osena, Will
524 Wiltshire Ct, Bloomington, 47408;
12-336-7739. Specializing in pottery,
ookwood, Van Briggle, etc.

oush, James
39 W. 5th St., Marion, 46953; 317-662-
26. Specializing in art glass, toys, paintings

oush, Scott E.
iving in the Past Antiques
189 S. Morgantown Rd., Indianapolis,
6217; 317-881-7872

acco, Debra
318 M St., Bedford, 47421; 812-279-4616.
pecializing in cookie jars, Black memora-
lia, flow blue

cowden, Virgil
illiamsport, 47993; 317-762-3408 or 317-762-
78. Antiques museum, general line, tours

heets, Helen
zalia Antiques
2-522-5675. Specializing in toys

ater, Thomas D.
he Political Gallery
325 W. 86th St., Indianapolis, 46260; 317-
57-0863. Specializing in political and
orts memorabilia

app, Charles Dennis
37 Haynes Rd., Georgetown, 47122. Spe-
alizing in jack knives, hunting knives,
ilitary knives, straight and safety razors

offt, Marvin and Jeanette
arnette Antiques
ll City, 47586; 812-547-5707. Specializing in
hio art pottery, buy and sell

wayzee Antique Mall
5 N. Washington St., Swayzee, 46986;
7-922-7903

ylor, Sondra and Tom
ylor Antiques (appointment only)
3 N. Hartsville, 47244; 812-546-4066. Spe-
lizing in Heisey glass, furniture, collectibles

homas, George and Betty
homas Treasures
00 Sherman Dr., Kokomo, 46902; 317-
3-1178. Specializing in Westmoreland,
andlewick, Fiesta

anderbilt, Duane and Janice
40 W. Over Dr., Indianapolis, 46268; 317-
5-8932. Authors (Collector Books) of *Collec-
's Guide to Shawnee Pottery*

alker, Patty
44 E. Longview Ct., Columbus, 47203; 812-
6-9330. Specializing in general line

ebb's Antique Mall
er 400 Quality Dealers
0 W. Union St., Centerville, 47330

illiams, Connie
wayzee Antique Mall
11 Patricia Lane, Marion, 46952; 317-
4-1425. Specializing in paper

immer, S. Jan
wayzee Antique Mall
55 N. Willow Dr., Marion, 46952; 317-664-
24. Specializing in Lionel trains, toy guns

Wright, Patty
Swayzee Antique Mall
115 N. Washington, Swayzee, 46986; 317-
922-7903

Iowa

Addy, Geneva D.
Winterset, 50273; 515-462-3027

Arnbal, Una
Woodland Antiques
236 Trail Ridge Rd., Ames, 50010; 515-
292-1005. Specializing in china, glass,
Lomonosov figurines

Bassett, Mark
1235 Fifth St., Nevada, 50201; 515-382-
3103. Specializing in American and European art pottery; Art Deco ceramics,
including Cowan (and Cowan Artists),
Galloway, AMACO, Roseville, Weller,
Rookwood, Boch Freres, Longwy, Gouda,
Gustavsberg, Anton Lang and others

Cueno, Mable E.
Treasures of Yesteryear
534 Sailfish, Hiawatha, 52233;
319-393-5861

DeGood, Hal and Meredith
The Baggage Car
513 Elm St., W. Des Moines, 50265; 515-
225-3070. Specializing in Hallmark collectibles; publishers of Hallmark newsletter

Devine, Dennis; Norman; and Joe
D & D Antique Mall
1411 3rd St., Council Bluffs, 51503; 712-
323-5233 or 712-328-7305. Specializing in
furniture, phonographs, collectibles, general
line. Joe Devine: Royal Copley collector

Jaarsma, Ralph
De Pelikaan Antieks
812 Washington St., c/o Red Ribbon
Antique Mall, Pella, 50219. Specializing in
Dutch antiques

Lippa, Matt; and Schaaf, Elizabeth
Artisans
P.O. Box 4902, Davenport, 52808; 319-
326-0342. Specializing in folk art, quilts,
painted and folky furniture, tramp art,
whirligigs, windmill weights

Morris, Dave and Sue
P.O. Box 708, Mason City, 50401. Specializing in Watt pottery; authors of *Watt Pottery
— An Identification and Price Guide*; also
available: *Watt's News* newsletter. Subscription: $10 per year

Nichols, Harold J.
632 Agg, Ames, 50010; 515-292-9167.
Author of *McCoy Cookie Jars from the First
to the Last*. Specializing in Roseville,
Weller, McCoy

Picek, Louis
Main Street Antiques
110 W. Main St., Box 340, West Branch,
52358. Specializing in folk art, country
Americana, the unusual

Kansas

Allen, Helen
12230 W. 104th St., Overland Park, 66215.
Specializing in Depression Glass

Anthony, Dorothy Malone
World of Bells Publications
802 S. Eddy, Fort Scott, 66701; 316-223-3404.
Specializing in publishing and selling books on
all types of small bells

McCormick, John and Marilyn
P.O. Box 3174, Shawnee, 66226; 913-441-0793.
Specializing in Gonder pottery

Robison, Joleen A.
502 Lindley Dr., Lawrence, 66044. Author
(Collector Books) on advertising dolls

Sandler, M.
Maundy International
P.O. Box 13028-SA, Overland Park, 66212;
1-800-235-2866. Specializing in watches —
antique pocket and vintage wristwatches

Tinsley, Rosella
105 15th St., Osawatomie, 66064; 913-755-
3237. Specializing in primitives, kitchen,
farm, woodenware, and miscellaneous

Winslow, Ralph
9905 Lee Blvd., Leawood, 66206. Specializing in
Dryden and Shramberg pottery

Kentucky

Florence, Gene
Box 7186H, Lexington, 40522. Author
(Collector Books) on Depression Glass,
Occupied Japan

Johnson, Wes
R.F.D., Glenview, KY 40025 (Louisville suburb).
Specializing in Cracker Jack: toys, point of sale,
packages, etc.; Checkers Confection, Schoenhut
toys, Victor Toy Oats, Universal Theatre
(Chicago), old toys

Willis, Roy M.
Heartland of Kentucky Decanters and Steins
P.O. Box 428, Lebanon Jct., 40150; 502-833-
2827. Specializing in most brands of decanters,
domestic beer steins, and advertising; open
showroom. Include large self-addressed
stamped envelope with correspondence

Louisiana

Decker, Dorothy B. and Wade N.
Dottie's Antiques (shows only)
P.O. Box 1141, St. Francisville, 70775; 504-
635-3284. Specializing in Elegant and
Depression Glass

Sexton, Sarah
1131 Quail Hollow, Baton Rouge, 70810;
504-766-2214. Specializing in Shawnee,
Hull, Black memorabilia, etc.

Maine

Hathaway, John
Hathaway's Antiques
Upper Main St., Bryant Pond, 04219; 207-
665-2124. Specializing in fruit jars; mail
order a specialty

Rinaldi, John
Nautical Antiques and Related Items
Box 765, Dock Square, Kennebunkport,
04046; 207-967-3218. Specializing in nautical antiques, 19th- & 20th-century American paintings; Annual Fall catalog: $3.00

Maryland

Banks, Robert
18901 Gold Mine Court, Brookeville, 20833.
Specializing in American flags of historical
significance and exceptional design

Dennis & George Collectibles
O'Brien, Dennis; and Goehring, George
3407 Lake Montebello Dr., Baltimore,
21218; 410-889-3964. Specializing in
upright pocket tobacco tins, advertising
items, character collectibles, unusual items

Greenberg, Bruce C., Ph. D.
Greenberg Publishing Company, Inc.
7566 Main St., Sykesville, 21784. Specializing in toy trains; author and publisher of
comprehensive publications on Lionel,
American Flyer, and Ives trains

Gunther's International Auction Gallery
P.O. Box 235, 24 S. Virginia Ave.,
Brunswick, 21716; 301-834-7101 or 800-274-
8779. Specializing in political, Oriental rugs,
bronzes, art, antiques, and the unusual

Humphrey, George C.
4932 Prince George Ave., Beltsville, 20705; 301-
937-7899. Specializing in John Rogers groups

Rudisill's Alt Print Haus
Rudisill, John and Barbara
24305 Waterview Dr., Worton, 21678; 410-
778-9290. Specializing in Currier & Ives

Screen, Harold and Joyce
2804 Munster Rd., Baltimore, 21234; 410-
661-6765. Specializing in soda fountain
'tools of the trade' and paper: catalogs, *Soda
Fountain* magazine, etc.

Massachusetts

Adams, Charles and Barbara
Middleboro, 02346; 508-947-7277. Specializing in Bennington (brown only)

Carver, Mrs. Sally S.
179 South St., Chestnut Hill, 02167; 617-
469-9175. Author of *The American Postcard
Guide to Tuck*; columnist for *Hobbies*; *Collector's News*; *Postcard Collector*; *Antique
Trader Price Guide*. Specializing in all bet-
ter-quality antique pre-1930 postcards; does
not accept consignment material; SASE
required with correspondence (questions
must be specific); phone calls: M-F, 12
noon to 6 p.m. EST only

Frei, Peter and Sandra
P.O. Box 500, Brimfield, 01010; 1-800-942-
8968. Specializing in sewing machines,
adding machines, and hand-powered vacuum
cleaners; SASE required with correspondence

Hess, John A.
Fine Photographic Americana
P.O. Box 3062, Andover, 01810; 508-470-0327.
Specializing in 19th-Century photography

Longo, Paul J.
Paul Longo Americana
Box 490, Chatham Rd., South Orleans,
Cape Cod, 02662; 508-255-5482. Specializing in political pins, ribbons, banners, autographs, old stocks and bonds, baseball and
sports memorabilia of all types

MacLean, Dale
Dale's
593 High St., Dedham, 02026; 617-326-3010.
Specializing in Dedham pottery

Morin, Albert
668 Robbins Ave. #23, Dracut, 01826; 508-
454-7907. Specializing in miscellaneous
Akro Agate and Westite

Owings, K.C., Jr.
Antiques Americana
Box 19, N. Abington, 02351; 617-857-1655.
Specializing in Civil War, Revolutionary
War, autographs, documents, books, antiques

Vigue, Norm and Cathy
62 Bailey St., Stoughton, 02072; 617-344-
5441. Buying and selling TV, western, and
cartoon show collectibles

Wellman, BA
9 Cottage St., Southboro, 01772. Specializing in
Ceramic Arts Studio and Pennsbury pottery;
price guide and video-tape identification guides
available

Michigan

Brown, Rick
Newspaper Collector's Society of America
Box 19134-S, Lansing, 48901; 517-372-
8381 or (Fax) 517-485-9115. Specializing
in newspapers

Bruner, Mike
Mike's Americana
6980 Walnut Lake Rd., West Bloomfield,
48323; 313-661-2359. Specializing in lightning rod balls

Gunsaulus, Jack
Gray's Gallery/Jack's Corner Bookstore
583 W. Ann Arbor Trail, Plymouth, 48170;
313-455-2373. Specializing in porcelain,
books, jewelry, glass

Haas, Norman
264 Clizbe Rd., Quincy, 49082; 517-639-
8537. Specializing in American art pottery

Marsh, Linda K.
1229 Gould Rd., Lansing, 48917. Specializing in Degenhart glass

Nedry, Boyd W.
728 Buth Dr., Comstock Park, 49321; 616-
784-1513. Specializing in traps (including
mice, rat, and fly traps) and trap-related items

Newbound, Betty
4567 Chadsworth, Commerce, 48382.
Author (Collector Books) on Blue Ridge
dinnerware. Specializing in collectible
china and glass

Nickel, Mike
A Nickel's Worth
P.O. Box 456, Portland, 48875; 517-647-
7646. Specializing in Roseville, Weller,
Rookwood and other important American art
pottery, Venetian/Murano glass, Art Deco

O'Callaghan, Tim
46878 Betty Hill, Plymouth, 48170; 313-
459-4636. Specializing in dimestore soldiers, also Ford Motor Co., and 'Old Iron-
sides' (USS Constitution) memorabilia

Oates, Joan
685 S. Washington, Constantine, 49042;
616-435-8353. Specializing in Phoenix Bird
chinaware

Ricker, Dawn V.
39145 Marne, Sterling Heights, 48313;
313-566-0891. Schafer & Vater collector

Roscoe, Mike
Lane St. Antiques
106 S. Lane St., Blissfield, 49228; 517-486-
4243; Specializing in toys, advertising, coin-
operated machines, furniture, and miscellaneous

Minnesota

Anderson, James
Box 12704, New Brighton, 55112; 612-
484-3198. Specializing in old fishing lures
and reels, also tackle catalogs, posters, calendars, Winchester items

Gallagher, Jerry
420 1st Ave. N.W., Plainview, 55964; 507-
534-3511. Specializing in Morgantown
research; matching service for Morgantown,
Heisey, Fostoria, Cambridge, Duncan, and
Tiffin. Publisher of Morgantown 1931 Catalog Reprint, Morgantown Colors Placard,
and *The Morgantown Newscaster*, quarterly
journal of the Morgantown Collectors of
America, Inc. (subscription: $15 per year)

Harrigan, John
1900 Hennepin, Minneapolis, 55403; 612-
872-0226. Specializing in Battersea
(English enamel) boxes

Ketcham, Steve
Steve Ketcham Antiques (Shows and mail
order only)
Box 24114, Edina, 55424; 612-920-4205.
Specializing in early American bottles, Red
Wing stoneware, advertising signs; trays;
and trade cards

Podpeskar, Doug
624 Jones St., Eveleth, 55734-1631; 218-744-
4854. Specializing in Red Wing dinnerware

Schoneck, Steve
P.O. Box 56, Newport, 55055; 612-459-2980.
Specializing in American art pottery, Arts &
Crafts, Handicraft Guild of Minneapolis

Missouri

Bosworth, Dick and Waunita
Kansas City Trade Winds
7307 N.W. 75th St., Kansas City, 64152.
Specializing in American art pottery, Parrish prints, art glass

Graves, Ferne
Graves Antiques
R.R. 7, Warrensburg, 64093; 816-747-3028

Harris, Aletha
R.R. 1, Box 125, Clearmont, 4431-9801.
Specializing in Laughlin Art China, Dream-
land and similar lines by Homer Laughlin

International Rose O'Neill Club
Contact Karen Stewart
P.O. Box 668, Branson, 65616. Dues: $7
(single) or $10 (family) includes newsletter
Kewpiesta Kourier, published quarterly

Old World Antiques
1715 Summit, Kansas City, 64108
Branch Location: 4436 State Line Rd.,
Kansas City 66103. Specializing in 18th-
and 19th-century furniture, paintings,
accessories, clocks, medical and scientific
instruments, chandeliers, sconces, Sabino,
and much more

Our McCoy Matters
Lynch, Kathy
McCoy Publications, P.O. Box 14255,
Parkville, 64152; 816-587-9179. Subscrip-
tion: $24 per year (6 issues)

Roberts, Brenda
Country Side Antiques
R.R. 2, Marshall, 65340. Specializing in Hull
pottery and general line. Author of *Roberts'
Ultimate Encyclopedia of Hull Pottery*, with
companion price guide; SASE required

Smith, Pat
Independence
Author (Collector Books) of doll book series

Wiesehan, Doug
D&R Farm Antiques
4535 Hwy. H, St. Charles, 63301. Specializing in salesman's samples and patent models, antique toys, farm toys, metal farm signs

Williams, Don
P.O. Box 147, Kirksville 63501. Specializing in art glass; SASE required with all correspondence

Woollard, D.D., Jr.
11614 Old St. Charles Rd., Bridgeton, 63044;
314-739-4662. Specializing in World's Fair &
Exposition memorabilia

Nebraska

Larsen, Robert V.
3214 19th St., Columbus, 68601. Specializing in
old hatpins and hatpin holders

New Hampshire

Brenner, Larry L.
Brenner Antiques
1005 Chestnut St., Manchester, 03104;
603-625-8203. Specializing in Royal
Bayreuth

Marden, Richard G.
Box 524, Elm St., Wolfeboro, 03894;
603-569-3209

Winston, Nancy
Willow Hollow Antiques
R.F.D. 1, Box 550, Northwood, 03261; 603-
942-5739. Specializing in Shaker baskets,
primitives, country smalls, paper Americana, toys

New Jersey

Adams, Jay (Mail order only)
289 Pascack Rd., Washington Twp., 07675;
908-756-6229. Specializing in Depression-
era china and glass

Anderson, Suzy McLennan
Heritage Antiques & Appraisal Services
65 E. Main St., Holmdel, 07733; 908-946-
8801. Specializing in American furniture
and decorative accessories

Bilane, John E. (Mail order only, no shop)
2065 Morris Ave., Apt. 109, Union, 07083.
Specializing in antique glass cup plates

Cole, Lillian M., Editor of *Piebirds Unlimited* newsletter
14 Harmony School Rd., Flemington,
08822; 908-782-3198. Specializing in pie
birds, pie funnels, pie vents

Litts, Elyce
P.O. Box 394, Morris Plains, 07950; 201-361-
4087. Author (Collector Books) of *Collector's
Encyclopedia of Geisha Girl Porcelain*

Perzel, Robert and Nancy
Popkorn
4 Mine St. (near Main St.), P.O. Box 1057,
Flemington, 08822; 908-782-9631. Specializ-
ing in Stangl dinnerware, birds, and artware;
Depression Glass

Poster, Harry
Vintage TVs
Box 1883, S. Hackensack, 07606; 201-794-
9606 (before 7 p.m.); Fax: 201-794-9553 or
24 hours: 201-410-7525. Publishes *Poster's
Price Guide to Collectible Radios and Televisions*; Specializes in vintage TVs, transister
radios, 3-D stereo

Rago, David
9 S. Main St., Lambertville, 08530; 609-397-
9374. Specializing in Arts & Crafts, art pottery

Rosen, Barbara
6 Shoshone Trail, Wayne, 07470. Specializing in figural bottle openers and antique
dollhouses

Steinfeld, Milt
633 Westfield Ave., Box 457, Westfield,
07091. Specializing in collectible glass and
china, Victorian silverplate, and other
small collectibles

Vines, Linda L.
Yesterday Once More
P.O. Box 721, Upper Montclair, 07043;
201-746-5206. Specializing in Snow Babies,
all holidays (Christmas, Easter, Halloween),
dolls and toys

New Mexico

Nelson, Scott H.
Box 6081, Santa Fe, 87502. Specializing in
African art

New York

Austin, Bruce A.
40 Selborne Chase, Fairport, 14450; 716-
223-0711 (evenings); 716-475-2879 (days).
Specializing in clocks and in Arts & Crafts
furnishings and accessories

Batchelor, Daniel J.
R.R. 10, Box 1010, Oswego, 13126; 315-349-
2671. Specializing in Pairpoint, Handel,
Bradley and Hubbard lamps

Calison, Jim
Tools of Distinction
Wallkill, 12589; 914-895-8035. Speciali
ing in antique and collectible tools, buyir
and selling

Dimitroff, Thomas P.
Dimitroff's Antiques (appointment)
140 E. First St., Corning, 14830; 607-96
6745. Specializing in Steuben and cut glas

Doyle, Robert A.
Doyle Auctioneers & Appraisers
109 Osborne Hill Rd., Fishkill, 1252
Thousands of collectibles offered, call f
free calendar of upcoming auctions

Fer-Duc Inc.
Ferrara, Joseph
Box 1303, Newburgh, 12550; 914-56
5990. Specializing in American art potte
(Ohr, Rookwood, Zanesville), 19th- a
20th-century American paintings

Fox, Ron
TSACO (The Stein Auction Compan
East
416 Throop St., N. Babylon, 11704; Tel
phone and Fax: 516-669-7232. Specializi
in steins; auctions with illustrated catalo
and video tapes

Greguire, Helen
Helen's Antiques
103 Trimmer Rd., Hilton, 14468; 716-39
2704. Specializing in graniteware (any colo
Carnival Glass lamps and shades, Carniv
Glass lighting of all kinds; Author (Collect
Books) of *The Collector's Encyclopedia of Gra
iteware, Colors, Shapes & Values*, (updated v
ues) for $27.95 (including postage and ha
dling); Second book on graniteware now ava
able (same price); Also available is *Carnival
Lights*, featuring Carnival Glass, lamps, shade
etc., for $11.95+$1.50 postage and handlir
all available from author at above address

Herley, Patrick J.
P.O. Box 606, E. Setauket, 11733; 516-92
6052. Specializing in Goss china

Jordan, Ruth E.
Meridale, 13806; 607-746-2082. Special
ing in cut glass, American Brilliant period

Laun, H. Thomas and Patricia
Little Century
215 Paul Ave., Syracuse, 13206; 315-43
4156 Summer residence: Box 69-A, Ca
Vincent, 13618; 315-654-3244. Special
ing in firefighting collectibles

Meisel, Louis K. and Susan P.
Meisel Decorative Arts Gallery
133 Prince St., New York City, 10012. Sp
cializing in Clarice Cliff and 20th-centu
designs in jewelry, watches, toys, unusu
vintage bicycles, and model sailboats

Michel, John and Barbara
Americana Blue
200 E. 78th St., 18E, New York Cit
10021; 212-861-6094. Specializing in ye
low ware and cast iron

Old China Patterns Limited
P.O. Box 290, Fineview, 13640; 800-83
2446 or 315-482-3829. Fax: 800-724-55
or 315-482-5827. Specializing in disconti
ued china dinnerware, matching servi
(since 1966); charter member I.A.D.M.

Owens, Lowell
Owens' Collectibles
12 Bonnie Ave., New Hartford, 13413. Sp
cializing in beer advertising

Pisello, Faye
577 Lake St., Wilson, 14172. Specializi
in Brownies by Palmer Cox

Rifken, Blume J.
Author of *Silhouettes in America — 1790-1840 — a Collector's Guide*. Specializing in American antique silhouettes from 1790 to 1840

Safir, Charlotte F.
1349 Lexington Ave., 9-B, New York City, 10128; 212-534-7933. Specializing in cookbooks, children's books (out-of-print only)

Schleifman, Roselle
Ed's Collectibles
16 Vincent Rd., Spring Valley, 10977; 914-356-2121. Specializing in Duncan & Miller

Steinbock, Nancy
Nancy Steinbock Posters & Prints
518-438-1577. Specializing in posters: travel, war, literary, advertising

Tuggle, Robert
105 W. St., New York City, 10023; 212-595-0514. Specializing in John Bennett, Anglo-Japanese china

Van Kuren, Jean and Dale
Ruth's Antiques, Inc.
9060 Main St., Clarence, 14031; 716-632-1630. Specializing in Buffalo pottery, general line

Van Patten, Joan F.
Box 102, Rexford, 12148. Author (Collector Books) of books on Nippon and Noritake

North Carolina

Degenhardt, Richard K.
Sugar Hollow Farm
24 Cypress Point, Hendersonville, 28739; 704-696-9750. Author of *Belleek, The Complete Collectors' Guide and Illustrated Reference*. Specializing in Belleek (The only Belleek is the Irish. Established by legal action in 1929)

Hughes, Kathy (Mrs. Paul)
Tudor House Galleries
1401 E. Blvd., Charlotte, 28203; 704-377-3748. Specializing in Relief-Moulded Jugs, 18th- and 19th-century English pottery and 19th-century oil paintings

Kirtley, Charles E.
P.O. Box 2273, Elizabeth City, 27096; 919-335-1262. Specializing in monthly auctions and bid sales dealing with World's Fair, Civil War, political, advertising, and other American collectibles

Sayers, R.J.
Southeastern Antiques & Appraisals
P.O. Box 629, Brevard, 28712. Specializing in Boy Scout collectibles, Pisgah Forest pottery, primitive American furniture; Author of *Guide to Scouting Collectibles*, available from author for $19.95+$3.50 postage

North Dakota

Farnsworth, Bryce
1334 14½ St. South, Fargo, 58103; 701-237-3597. Specializing in Rosemeade pottery

Ohio

Baker, Shirley and John
Shirley's Collectibles
973 W. Twp. Rd. #118, Tiffin, 44883; 419-447-9875. Specializing in Tiffin glass

Batory, Mr. Dana Martin
402 E. Bucyrus St., Crestline, 44827. Specializing in antique woodworking machinery, old and new woodworking machinery catalogs. In order to prepare a difinitive history on American manufacturers of woodworking machinery, Dana is interested in acquiring by loan, gift, or photocopy, any and all documents, catalogs, manuals, photos, personal reminiscences, etc., pertaining to woodworking machinery and/or their manufacturers. No phone calls please.

Blair, Betty
Golden Apple Antiques
216 Bridge St., Jackson, 45640; 614-286-4817. Specializing in art pottery, Watt, cookie jars, chocolate molds, general line

Briggs, Karen S.
Toledo
Specializing in glass, china, pottery, knives

Budin, Nicki
Gourmet Antiques, Inc./Curio Cabinet
679 High St., Worthington, 43085; 614-885-1986. Specializing in Royal Doulton

China Specialties, Inc.
19238 Dorchester Circle, Strongsville, 44136; 216-238-2528. Specializing in Autumn Leaf

Cincinnati Auction Gallery
635 Main St., Cincinnati, 45202; 513-381-2128. Specializing in American art pottery (especially Rookwood), American and European fine paintings, watercolors

Collectors of Findlay Glass
P.O. Box 256, Findlay, 45840. An organization dedicated to the study and recognition of Findlay glass, newsletter *The Melting Pot*, published quarterly, convention held annually, membership: $10 per year

DeGenaro, Steve
P.O. Box 5662, Youngstown, 44505; 216-759-7151. Specializing in post-mortem photos, mourning collectibles

De Luca, Mary A.
Red Barn Antiques
5510 W. Lakeshore Dr., Port Clinton, 43452; 419-635-2045. Specializing in general line

Distel, Ginny
Distel's Antiques
4041 S.C.R. 22, Tiffin, 44883; 419-447-5832. Specializing in Tiffin glass

Ebner, Rita and John
Cracker Barrel Antiques
4540 Helen Rd., Columbus, 43232. Specializing in door knockers, cast iron bottle openers, doorstops, general line

Ferguson, Maxine
Wayside Antiques
2290 E. Pike, Zanesville, 43701. General line, furniture, dolls, pottery, glass

Forsythe, Ruth A.
Box 327, Galena, 43021. Author of *Made in Czechoslovakia*

Graff, Shirley
4515 Grafton Rd., Brunswick, 44212. Specializing in Pennsbury pottery

Guenin, Tom
Box 454, Chardon, 44024. Specializing in antique telephones and antique telephone restoration

Hermes, Dianne
5664 W. Harbor Rd., Port Clinton, 43452; Specializing in Depression Glass, general line

Hothem, Lar
Hothem House
Box 458, Lancaster, 43130. Specializing in books about Indians and artifacts

Huffman, Mary (Shows only)
3143 S. State Rd. 53, Tiffin, 44883; 419-447-5938. Specializing in glass

Kao, Fern
Lustre Pitcher Antiques
P.O. Box 312, Bowling Green, 43402; 419-352-5928. Specializing in jewelry, sewing implements, ladies' accessories

Kerr, Ann
P.O. 437, Sidney, 45365; 513-492-6369. Author (Collector Books) of *Collector's Encyclopedia of Russel Wright Designs*. Specializing in work of Wright, interested in 20th-century decorative arts

Kitchen, Lorrie
Toledo, 419-478-3815 or Tavares, FL (winter), 904-742-2638. Specializing in Depression-era glass, Hall china, Fiesta, Blue Ridge, Shawnee

Klender, James and Grace
Town & Country Antiques & Collectibles
P.O. Box 447, Pioneer, 43554; 419-737-2880. Specializing in Depression Glass, and general line

Kline, Mr. and Mrs. Jerry and Gerry
Members of North American Torquay Society and Torquay Pottery Collectors' Society
604 Orchard View Dr., Maumee, 43537; 419-893-1226. Specializing in collecting Torquay pottery

Loucks, Walter L.
The Carousel News & Trader
87 Parke Ave. W., Suite 206, Mansfield, 44902. A monthly magazine for the carousel enthusiast. Subscription: $22 per year, sample: $3

Moore, Carolyn
445 N. Prospect, Bowling Green, 43402. Specializing in primitives, yellowware, graniteware

National Cambridge Collectors Inc.
Box 416, Cambridge, 43725 Specializing in Cambridge glass

National Heisey Glass Museum
Heisey Collectors of America Inc.
6th & Church Sts., P.O. Box 4367, Newark, 43055; 614-345-2932

Nelson, Norman
449 N. Town St., Fostoria, 44830; 419-435-6446. Specializing in jukeboxes

Nicholson's
472 Lakeridge Dr., Cincinnati, 42531; 513-771-4949. Specializing in pottery, Rookwood, Weller, Owens

Osborne, Ruth
Box 85, Higginsport, 45131. Specializing in vintage clothing, lamps, jewelry

Penrose, Donald M. (Mail order only)
6351 Garber Rd., Dayton, 45415; 513-890-3728. Specializing in continental porcelains and art glass

Peters, Jeannie L.
Mt. Washington Antiques
3742 Kellogg, Cincinnati, 45226; 513-231-6584. Specializing in sheet music

Pierce, David
27544 Black Road, P.O. Box 248, Danville, 43014; 614-599-6394; Specializing in Glidden pottery

Radel, Erle and Janice
Rapids Renovations & Antiques
Grand Rapids. Specializing in furniture and fine jewelry, (collectors only) Labino art glass

Rees, Debbie
Zanesville.
Specializing in Watt, blue and white stoneware, Steiff, cookie jars, Roseville pottery

Regal Relics
P.O. Box 303, Dayton, 45401; 513-254-2937. Specializing in Elegant Glass: Cambridge, Heisey, Fostoria, and Imperial

Riebel, James; Krause, Terry
Pottery Peregrinators
Zanesville, 614-452-7687. Specializing in American art pottery, Nicodemus, and Carnival Glass

Rodgers, Joanne
Stretch Glass Society
P.O. Box 770643, Lakewood, 44107. Specializing in stretch glass

Trainer, Veronica
Bayhouse
Box 40443, Cleveland, 44140; 216-871-8584. Specializing in beaded and enamelled mesh purses

Tucker, Dan
Toledo, 419-478-3815 or Tavares, FL (winter), 904-742-2638. Specializing in Depression-era glass, Hall china, Fiesta, Blue Ridge, Shawnee

Walczak, Mary Jo
Toledo. Specializing in dolls and snow babies

Walker, Bunny
Box 502, Bucyrus, 44820; 419-562-8355. Specializing in Steiff teddy bears, penny toys, pottery

Whitmyer, Margaret and Kenn
Box 30806, Gahanna, 43230. Author (Collector Books) on children's dishes. Specializing in Depression-era collectibles

Wilkins, Juanita
The Bird of Paradise
Lima, 419-227-2163. Specializing in R.S. China, Old Ivory china, colored pattern glass, lamps, and jewelry

Young, Mary
1040 Greenridge Dr., Kettering, 45429. Author (Collector Books) of *Collector's Guide to Paper Dolls*

Oklahoma

Bess, Phyllis and Tom
Authors of *Frankoma Treasures*, 14535 E. 13th St., Tulsa, 74108; 918-437-7776. Specializing in Frankoma pottery

Klein, Bob and Dondee
1343 E. 35th Place, Tulsa, 74105; 918-747-0295. Specializing in Tamac pottery

Moore, Art and Shirley
2145 S. Norfolk Ave., Tulsa, 74114; 918-747-4164. Specializing in Lu Ray Pastels, Depression Glass

Willis, Ron L.
2110 Fox Ave., Moore, 73160. Specializing in militaria

Oregon

Bartsch, Henry
Antique Registers
2050 N. Hwy. 101, Rockaway Beach, 97136; 503-355-2932. Specializing in antique cash registers, co-author of *Antique Cash Registers 1880-1920*

Bird, Leah and Walt
Bird's Nest
503-779-9138. Specializing in half-dolls, old lace and fabric

Boline, Keith & Kevin
BCC Enterprises
7811-35th Ave. N.E., Salem, 97303; 503-393-0321. Specializing in Red Wing Stoneware, American gray graniteware, and tin lithographed advertising pot scrapers

Brady, Glen
P.O Box 3933, Central Point, 97502; 503-772-0350. Specializing in Autumn Leaf, cookie jars, Smokey Bear

Carter, Fran (Appointment only)
Box 3220, Coos Bay, 97420; 503-888-5780. Specializing in estate sales

Coe, Debbie
Coe's Mercantile
Lafayette School House Mall, 748 3rd, Lafayette; 97127; 503-640-9122. Specializing in elegant Depression Glass

Frost, Donald M.
Country Estate Antiques
690 Lower Cleveland Rapids Rd., Roseburg, 97470; 503-672-7613. Specializing in fine glass and porcelain

Geddes, Marjorie
Beaverton, 503-649-1041. Specializing in sewing items, butter pats, egg cups, miscellaneous small and elegant collectibles

Hirshman, Susan and Larry
Everyday Antiques
542 Siskiyou Blvd., Ashland, 97250; 503-482-9411. Specializing in china, glassware, kitchenware, quilts

Matthews, Skip and Kathy
Aristocratic Attic
344 S.W. 'K' St., Grants Pass, 97526; 503-474-6660. Specializing in Disneyana, cartoon TV and advertising characters, other children's items

Miller, Don and Robby
P.O. Box 508, Talent, 97504; 503-535-1231 Specializing in milk bottles, TV Siamese cat lamps, seltzer bottles, red cocktail shakers.

Morris, Thomas G.
Prize Publishers
P.O. Box 8307, Medford, 97504; 503-779-3164. Author of *The Carnival Chalk Prize*, a pictorial price guide on carnival chalkware figures with brief histories and values for each

Ringering, David
Belle Ringer Antiques
1480 Tamale Dr. SE, Salem, 97301; 503-585-8253. Specializing in Rowland & Marsellus and other souvenir/historical china w/scenes of buildings, parks, and other tourist attractions of the 1890s-1930s. Feel free to contact David if you have any questions about Rowland & Marsellus or other souvenir china. He will be happy to answer questions about souvenir china.

Pennsylvania

Atkinson, Phil and Karol
903 Apache Trail, Mercer, 16137; 412-475-2490. Specializing in antique advertising, country store collectibles

Barker, Jim
Toastermaster Antique Appliances
P.O. Box 592, Hawley, 18428; 717-253-1951. Specializing in electric toasters and appliances

Barrett, Noel
Rosebud Antiques
P.O. Box 1001, Carversville, 18913; 215-297-5109. Specializing in toys

Bodine, Clarence H., Jr., Proprietor
East/West Gallery
41B Ferry St., New Hope, 18938; 908-782-3430 (evenings). Specializing in antique Japanese woodblock prints, netsuke, inro, tsuba

Cerebro
P.O. Box 1221, Lancaster, 17603; 717-656-7875 or 800-69-LABEL. Specializing in antique advertising labels, especially cigar box labels, cigar bands, food labels, firecracker labels

Damaska, Ron
738 9th Ave., New Brighton, 15066; 412-843-1393. Specializing in Fry cut glass, match holders, oil lamps, silver; SASE required when requesting information

DLK Nostalgia & Collectibles
P.O. Box 5112, Johnstown, 15904. Specializing in corkscrews and openers, Art Deco, clocks, toys, breweriana, football cards, radios, miscellaneous

Garvin, Joann
P.O. Box 182, Beaver Falls, 15010; 412-843-3999. Specializing in Fiesta

Hagenbuch, James
Glass Work Auction
102 Jefferson, East Greenville, 18041; 215-679-5849. America's leading auction company in early American bottles and glass

Hain, Henry F., III
Antiques & Collectibles
2623 N. Second St., Harrisburg, 17110; 717-238-0534. Lists available of items for sale

Hansen, Kathy
1621 Princess Ave., Pittsburgh, 15216; 412-561-3379. Buying Phoenix glass and related items, glass company catalogs, trade journals, Monaca PA postcards

Hinton, Michael C.
Arts & Antiques
R.D. 2, Box 313, Mertztown, 19539; 215-682-7096. Specializing in painting and frame restoration. Catalog of paintings and frames available

Holland, William
William Holland Fine Arts
1708 E. Lancaster Ave., Paoli, 19301; 215-648-0369 or (Fax) 215-647-4448. Specializing in Louis Icart etchings and oils, Art Nouveau and Art Deco items; Author of *Louis Icart: The Complete Etchings*

Kamm, George
George Kamm Paperweights
24 Townsend Ct., Lancaster, 17603; 717-872-7858. Specializing in paperweights — color brochure published bimonthly. $5 annual fee (refundable)

Knauer, Judy A.
National Toothpick Holder Collectors' Society
1224 Spring Valley Lane, West Chester, 19380; 215-431-3477. Specializing in toothpick holders and Victorian glass

The Krauses
Krause, Gail
97 W. Wheeling St., Washington, 15301; 412-228-5034. Author of book on Duncan glass

Lindsay, Ralph
P.O. Box 21, New Holland, 17557. Specializing in target balls. SASE required with correspondence

Maier, Clarence and Betty
Mail order: The Burmese Cruet
Box 432, Montgomeryville, 18936; 215-855-5388. Specializing in Victorian art glass. SASE required with correspondence

Marks, Mariann Katz
P.O. Box 750, Honesdale, 18431. Author (Collector Books) of *Majolica Pottery, Second Series*. Specializing in collecting, buying, and selling American and English majolica of the Victorian period; LSASE required for mail order list. Enclose photo and price wanted with offers to sell

Oster, Frederick
Frederick W. Oster Fine Violins
1529 Pine St., Philadelphia, 19102; 215-545-1100 or (Fax) 215-735-3634. Specializing in rare and antique instruments of the violin family, as well as antique stringed and wind instruments

Posner, Judy
R.D. 1, Box 273, Effort, 18330; 717-629-6583. Specializing in figural pottery, cookie jars, salt and peppers, Black memorabilia, Disneyana

Rosso, Philip J. and Philip Jr.
Wholesale Glass Dealers
1815 Trimble Avenue, Port Vue, 15133; 412-678-7352. Specializing in Westmoreland glass

Weiser, Pastor Frederick S.
55 Kohler School Rd., New Oxford, 17350; 717-624-4106. Specializing in frakturs

Rhode Island

Dumont, Louise
579 Old Main St., Coventry, 02816; 401-828-2799. Specializing in cookie jars, Abington

Gacher, John
The Zsolnay Store
152 Spring St., Newport, 02840; 401-841-5060. Specializing in Zsolnay, Fischer, Amphora, and Austro-Hungarian art pottery

The Occupied Japan Club
c/o Florence Archambault
29 Freeborn St., Newport, 02840. Publishes bimonthly newsletter, *The Upside Down World of an O.J. Collector*. SASE required when requesting information

South Carolina

Roerig, Fred and Joyce
R.R. 2, Box 504, Walterboro, 29488; 803-538-2487. Specializing in cookie jars; authors of *Collector's Encyclopedia of Cookie Jars, an Illustrated Value Guide*, publishers of *Cookie Jarrin' with Joyce: The Cookie Jar Newsletter*

Tennessee

Hardwick, Pat
135 Collis St., Rutherford, 38369; 901-665-6754. Specializing in Depression Glass, cookie jars

Texas

Dockery, Rod
4600 Kemble St., Ft. Worth, 76103; 817-536-2168. Specializing in milk glass; SASE required with correspondence

Docks, L.R. 'Les'
Shellac Shack; Discollector
Box 691035, San Antonio, 78269-1035. Author of *American Premium Record Guide*. Specializing in vintage records

Frese, Leo and Wendy
Three Rivers Collectibles
Box 551542, Dallas, 75355; 214-341-5165. Specializing in RumRill, Red Wing pottery and stoneware, Hull

Gaston, Mary Frank
Box 342, Bryan, 77806. Author (Collector Books) on china and metals

Malowanczyk, Abby and Wlodek
Collage-20th Century Classics
3017-B Routh St., Dallas, 75201; 214-880-0020 or (Fax) 214-241-7445. Specializing in architect-designed furniture and decrative arts from the modern movement

Norris, Kenn
Schoolmaster Auctions
P.O. Box 4830, 208 Kerr St., Sanderson, 79848; 915-345-2640. Specializing in school-related items and barbed wire

Potter, Judy
Collector's Gallery/Megan's
4511 McKinney Ave., Dallas, 75206; 520-7579 or 1540 8th Ave., Marion 52302; 319-377-1206. Specializing in gins, Bellaire, Vernon Kilns

Pringle, Joyce M.
Chip & Dale Collectables
3500 S. Cooper St., Arlington, 76015. S cializing in Boyd, Summit, and Mosser g

Silvermintz, Karen
5254 Vanderbilt, Dallas, 75206; 214-8 4028. Specializing in American pott Russel Wright American dinnerware

Smith, Allan
1806 Shields Dr., Sherman, 75090; 9 893-3626. Specializing in children's lu boxes and all types of advertising, especi Coca-Cola, Dr. Pepper, Pepsi Cola, Cola, Red Goose, Buster Brown Sho character tin wind-up toys, and west stars' items

Thompson, Chuck
Chuck Thompson & Associates
P.O. Box 11652, Houston, 77293. Thor son is a collector/researcher/ writer, act with pro-Bible projects.

Tucker, Richard and Valerie
Argyle Antiques
P.O. Box 262, Argyle, 76226; 817-4(3752. Specializing in windmill weigh shooting gallery targets, figural lawn spr klers and cast iron advertising paperweig

Walker, Jimmy and Carol
The Iron Lady
501 N. 5th, Waelder, 78959; 512-665-71(Specializing in pressing irons

Wilkins, James R.
Olden Year Musical Museum
Box 180444, Arlington, 76096; 214-29 5587. Specializing in music boxes, phor graphs, grind organs, nickelodeons

Utah

Anderson, Tim
Box 461, Provo, 84603; 801-226-1787. Sp cializing in autographs; Buys single items collections — historical, movie stars, U. Presidents, sports figures, and pre-1860 cc respondence

Anderson, Warren R.
America West Archives
P.O. Box 100, Cedar City, 84721; 801-58 9497. Specializing in old stock certifica and bonds, western documents and book financial ephemera, autographs, maps, ph tos. Author of *Owning Western Histor* with over 75 photos of old documents ar recommended reference guide. Availab ($17.50 softcover or $27.50 hardbac) from author at above address

Vermont

Barry, Kit
143 Main St., Brattleboro, 05301; 802-25 3634. Author of *The Advertising Trade Car* Specializing in advertising trade cards ar ephemera in general

Virginia

Bradfield, Jeff
Jeff's Antiques
745 Hillview Dr., Dayton 22821; 703-87 9961. Also located in Rocky's Antique Mall (81), Exit 60, Weyers Cave. Specializing postcards, candy containers, sugar shakers, to pottery, furniture, lamps, and advertising items

Flanigan, Vicki
Flanigan's Antiques
P.O. Box 1662, Winchester, 22601. Specializing in antique dolls and hand fans

Friend, Terry
R.R. 4, Box 152-D, Galax, 24333; 703-236-9027 after 9:30 p.m. EST. Specializing in coffee mills; SASE required

Haigh, Richard (Mail-order & shows)
P.O. Box 29888, Richmond, 23242; 804-741-5770. Specializing in art glass (Locke Art, Steuben, Loetz, Durand, Quezal, Czechoslovakian, Hawkes, Dorflinger, Honesdale, Scandinavian)

Kenney, Ed
Audubon Prints & Books
9720 Spring Ridge Lane, Vienna, 22182; 703-759-5567. Specializing in Audubon and other natural history antique prints

Lechner, Mildred and Ralph
Box 554, Mechanicsville, 23111; 804-737-3347. Author (Collector Books) on glass salt shakers. Specializing in art and pattern glass salt shakers circa 1870-1940. Directors of Antique and Art Glass Salt Shakers Society Club, 1991-92

Monsen, Randall; and Baer, Rod
Monsen & Baer
310 Maple Ave. West, #270, Vienna, 22180; 703-938-2129. Specializing in perfume bottles, Roseville pottery, Art Deco

Reynolds, Charles
Reynolds Toys
2836 Monroe St., Falls Church, 22042; 703-533-1322. Specializing in limited edition mechanical and still banks, figural bottle openers

Tutton, John
R.R. 4, Box 929, Front Royal, 22630; 703-635-7058. Specializing in milk bottles

Washington

George, Tony
16212 Bothell Way S.E. #F215, Mill Creek, 98012; 206-483-6074. Specializing in watch fobs

Haase, Don (Mr. Spode)
D&D Antiques
P.O. Box 818, Mukilteo, 98275; 206-348-7443. Specializing in Spode china

Lozoski, Walter
910-4th Ave. N #102, Seattle, 98109; 206-285-4986. Specializing in ABC Plates and real photo postcards

Rothe, Linda
P.O. Box 27374, Seattle, 98125-1874. Specializing in Black Americana

Wheeler-Tanner Escapes
Tanner, Joseph and Pamela
3024 E. 35th Ave., Spokane, 99223; 509-448-8457. Specializing in handcuffs, leg shackles, balls and chains, restraints and padlocks of all kinds (including railroad) locking and non-locking devices

West Virginia

Fostoria Glass Society of America, Inc.
Box 826, Moundsville, 26041. Specializing in Fostoria glass

Wisconsin

Apple, John
John Apple Antiques
1720 College Ave., Racine, 53403; 414-633-3086. Specializing in brass cash registers and parts

Fortney, Daniel
Suite 713, Chalet at the River, 823 N. 2nd St., Milwaukee, 53203. Specializing in china and glass

Knapper, Mary
Phoneco, Inc.
207 E. Mill Rd., P.O. Box 70, Galesville, 54630; 608-582-4124. Specializing in telephones, antique to modern

Matzke, Gene
Gene's Badges & Emblems
2345 S. 28th St., Milwaukee, 53215; 414-383-8995. Specializing in police badges, leg irons, old police photos, fire badges (old), patches, old handcuffs, and memorabilia

Rice, Ferill J.
302 Pheasant Run, Kaukauna, 54130. Specializing in Fenton art glass

Washburn, Cara
751 E. Thomas St., Osseo 54758; 715-597-2666 (M-F). Specializing in glass (over 2,000 pieces), tools, toys, general merchandise

Clubs, Newsletters, and Catalogs

Akro Agate Collectors Club and *Clarksburg Crow* quarterly newsletter
Roger Hardy
10 Bailey St., Clarksburg, WV 26301-2524; 304-624-4523. Annual membership fee: $15

America West Archives
Anderson, Warren
P.O. Box 100, Cedar City, UT 84721; 801-586-9497; 26-page illustrated catalogs issued quarterly. Has both fixed-price and auction sections offering early western documents, letters, stock certificates, autographs, and other important ephemera. Subscription: $12 per year

American Antique Deck Collectors 52 Plus Joker Club
Clear the Decks, quarterly publication
Ray Hartz, President
P.O. Box 1002, Westerville, OH 43081; 614-891-6296. Specializing in antique playing cards

American Bell Association, Int., Inc.
c/o The Bell Tower
P.O. Box 19443, Indianapolis, IN 46219.
Dorothy Malone Anthony, Past President

American Willow Report
Lisa Kay Henze, Editor
P.O. Box 900, Oakridge, OR 97463.
Bimonthly newsletter, subscription: $15 per year; Out of country: add $5 per year

Antique & Art Glass Salt Shaker Collectors' Society (AAGSSCS)
2832 Rapidan Trail, Maitland, FL 32751

Antique & Collectors Reproduction News
Antiques Coast to Coast
c/o Lorna Bambrook
Box 71174, Des Moines, IA 50325; 515-270-8994 or (subscriptions only) 800-227-5531. Monthly newsletter, subscription: $32 per year in US; $41 in Canada.

Antique Purses Catalog: $4.00
Bayhouse
P.O. Box 40443, Bay Village, OH 44140; 216-871-8584. Includes colored photos of beaded and enameled mesh purses.

Antique Radio Club of America
81 Steeplechase Rd., Devon, PA 19333

Antique Souvenir Collectors' News
Gary Leveille, Editor
P.O. Box 562, Great Barrington, MA 01230

Antique Stove Association
Clifford Boram, Secretary
417 N. Main St., Monticello, IN 47960. Inquiries should be accompanied by SASE and marked 'Urgent' in red

Antique Wireless Association
Ormiston Rd., Breesport, NY 14816

Arkansas Pottery Collector's Society
P.O. Box 7617, Little Rock, AR 72217

Arts & Crafts Quarterly
9 S. Main St., Lambertville, NJ 08530; 609-397-9374

Avon Times (National Newsletter Club)
c/o Dwight or Vera Young
P.O. Box 9868, Dept P., Kansas City, MO 64134. Inquiries should be accompanied by LSASE

Black Memorabilia Catalog
Judy Posner
R.D. 1, Box 273 SC, Effort, PA 18330. Send $2 and LSASE

Boyd's Art Glass Collectors Guild
P.O. Box 52, Hatboro, PA 19040-0052. Books available: *Boyd's Crystal Art Glass, The Tradition Continues*, P.O. Box 127, Cambridge, OH 43725; and *Boyd's Art Glass Production 1978-1991*, P.O. Box 11806, Kansas City, MO 64138

British Royal Commemorative Souvenirs
Mail Order Catalog
Audrey Zeder
6755 Coralite St. S, Long Beach, CA 90808

Butter Pat Collectors' Notebook
c/o 5955 S.W. 179th Ave., Beaverton, OR 97007. Send LSASE for subscription information

California Perfume Company
For information contact Dick Pardini
3107 North El Dorado St., Dept. SAPG, Stockton, CA 95204-3412. Information requires LSASE; not necessary when offering items for sale

Candy Container Collectors of America
P.O. Box 1088, Washington, PA 15301

The Cane Collector's Chronicle
Linda Beeman
15 2nd St. N.E., Washington, D.C. 20002; $30 for 4 issues

The Carousel News and Trader
87 Parke Ave. W., Suite 206, Mansfield, OH 44902. A monthly magazine for the carousel enthusiast. Subscription: $22 per year, sample: $3

Central Florida Insulator Collectors
557 Nicklaus Dr., Titusville, FL 32780

Character Collectibles Catalog
Judy Posner
R.D. 1, Box 273 SC, Effort, PA 18330. Send $2 and LSASE

Chase Collectors Society
c/o Barry L. Van Hook
2149 W. Jibsail Loop, Mesa, AZ 85202-5524; 602-838-6971. Publishes newsletter *Art Deco Reflections*, Membership: $10, Sample copy of newsletter: $1

Chicagoland Antique Advertising Slot Machine & Jukebox Gazette
Ken Durham, Editor
P.O. Box 2426, Dept. S, Rockville, MD 20852. 20-page newspaper published twice a year. Subscription: 4 issues for $10; sample: $5

Classic Amusements Magazine
Jackie Durham, Agent
909 26th St. N.W., Washington, DC, 20037. Subscription (10 issues): $36 per year (payable to Jackie Durham)

Coin-Op Newsletter
Ken Durham, Publisher
909 26th St. N.W., Washington, DC 20037. Subscription (10 issues): $24, sample: $5

The Cola Clan
Alice Fisher, Treasurer
2084 Continental Drive N.E., Atlanta, GA 30345

Collectors of Findlay glass
P.O. Box 256, Findlay, OH 45840. An organization dedicated to the study and recognition of Findlay Glass, newsletter *The Melting Pot*, published quarterly, convention held annually, membership: $10 per year

The Compact Collectors
Roselyn Gerson
P.O. Box S, Lynbrook, NY 11563. Publishes *Powder Puff* newsletter, which contains articles covering all aspects of compact collecting, restoration, vintage ads, patents, history, and articles by members and prominent guest writers. A seeker and sellers column is offered free to members

Cookie Jar Catalog
Judy Posner
R.D. 1, Box 273 SC, Effort, PA 18330. Send $2 and LSASE

Cookie Jarrin' with Joyce: The Cookie Jar Newsletter
R.R. 2, Box 504, Walterboro, SC 29488

The Copley Connection: Royal Copley Collector's Newsletter
Joe Devine
1411 3rd St., Council Bluffs, IA 51503; or
Barbara Burke
4213 Sandhurst Dr., Orlando, FL 32817.
Bimonthly publication, Subscription: $10 per year

Currier & Ives Catalog
Rudisill's Alt Print Haus
P.O. Box 119, Worton, MD 21678. Please include LSASE

The Cutting Edge, quarterly publication of the Glass Knife Collectors Club
Adrienne S. Escoe, Editor
P.O. Box 342, Los Alamitos, CA 90720. Subscription: $5 per year, sample: $1

Depression Glass Daze
Teri Steel, Editor/Publisher
Box 57, Otisville, MI 48463; 313-631-4593.
The nation's market place for glass, china, and pottery

Disneyana Catalog
Judy Posner
R.D. 1, Box 273 SC, Effort, PA 18330.
Send $2 and LSASE

Docks, L.R. 'Les'
Shellac Shack
Box 691035, San Antonio, TX 78269-1035.
Send $2 for a 72-page catalog of 78s that Docks wants to buy, the prices he will pay, and shipping instructions

Doyle Auctioneers & Appraisers
Doyle, Robert A.
109 Osborne Hill Rd., Fishkill, NY 12524;
800-551-5161. Newsletter: *Auction Opportunities, Inc.* for $25 per year

Drawing Room of Newport
Gacher, John
152 Spring St., Newport, RI 02840; 401-841-5060. Book on Zsolnay available.

The Elegance of Old Ivory Newsletter
Box 1004, Wilsonville, OR 97070

Fenton Art Glass Collectors of America, Inc.
Williamstown, WV 26187

Figural Bottle Opener Collectors
c/o Craig Dinner
Box 251, Townsend, VT 05353. Please include SASE

Fostoria Glass Society of America, Inc.
P.O. Box 826, Moundsville, WV 26041

H.C. Fry Society
P.O. Box 41, Beaver, PA 15009. Founded in 1983 for the sole purpose of learning about Fry glass; Publishes quarterly newsletter *Shards*

GAR Post 20 Illinois
Richard A. Haussman, Chaplain
P.O. Box 1865, Aurora, 60507

George Kamm Paperweights
24 Townsend Court, Lancaster, PA 17603;
717-872-7858. Membership: $15 per person or $25 per couple. Publishes 5 newsletters a year; Biannual conventions to promote and study paperweights

Glass Knife Collector's Club
Adrienne S. Escoe
P.O. Box 342, Los Alamitos, CA 90720

Gonder Pottery Collectors' Newsletter
c/o John and Marilyn McCormick
P.O. Box 3174, Shawnee, KS 66226

Grandpa's Depot & Caboose
John 'Grandpa' White
Denver Union Station, P.O. Box 480030,
Denver, CO 80248-0030; 303-892-1177 or
(Fax) 303-573-5505. Publishes catalogs on railroad-related collectibles

Hake's Americana & Collectibles
Specializing in character and personality collectibles along with artifacts of popular culture for over 20 years. To receive a catalog for their next 3,000-item mail/phone bid auction, send $3 to:
Hake's Americana
P.O. Box 1444M, York, PA 17405

Heisey Collectors of America Inc.
National Heisey Glass Museum
169 W. Church St., Newark, OH 43055;
614-345-2932

Ice Screamer
c/o Ed Marks, Publisher
P.O. Box 5387, Lancaster, PA 17601. Published bimonthly, dues: $15 per year; annual convention late June

Indiana Historical Radio Society
245 N. Oakland Ave., Indianapolis, IN 46201

International Club for Collectors of Hatpins & Hatpin Holders (ICC of H&HH)
Lillian Baker, Founder
15237 Chanera Ave., Gardena, CA 90249;
213-329-2619. Monthly *Points* newsletter and *Pictorial Journal*

International Rose O'Neill Club
Contact Karen Stewart
P.O. Box 668, Branson, MO 65616 Publishes quarterly newsletter *Kewpiesta Kourier*. Dues: (includes newsletter) $7 (single) or $10 (family)

International Society of Antique Scale Collectors
Bob Stein, President
176 West Adams, Suite 1706, Chicago, IL 60603; 312-263-7500. Publishes quarterly magazine

Kitchen Antiques & Collectibles News newsletter
Dana & Darlene DeMore, Editors
4645 Laurel Ridge Dr., Harrisburg, PA 17110; 717-545-7320. Subscription (6 issues): $24 per year

The Lady's Gallery, publication of fashion, decorative arts, and collectibles
Subscription: $23.95 (U.S., 6 issues) per year;
Call 800-622-5676 for further information

The Laughlin Eagle
Joan Jasper, Publisher
Richard Racheter, Editor
1270 63rd Terrace S., St. Petersburg, FL 33705; Subscription: $14 (4 issues) per year; sample issue: $4

Line Jewels, NIA#255
Linscott, Len
3557 Nicklaus Dr., Titusville, FL 32780. Specializing in glass insulators and other telephone items. SASE required.

Mabel Lucie Attwell Catalogs
c/o Showcase Antiques
440 S. Fair Oaks Ave., Pasadena, CA 91105; 818-577-9660

Majolica Mail Order Catalog
Items from the collection of Mariann Katz Marks
P.O. Box 750, Honesdale, PA 18431. Please send LSASE for majolica listing

Marble Collectors' Society of America
P.O. Box 222, Trumbull, CT 06611
Claire Block, Secretary
Publishes *Marble Mania*, gathers and disseminates information to further the hobby of marbles and marble collecting. $12 adds your name to the contributor mailing list ($21 covers 2 years).

The Melting Pot
Published quarterly by the Collectors of Findlay glass, a non-profit organization for collectors.
Bob Sanford, President
Dues of $10 is payable to Marilyn Jackson, Treasurer, P.O. Box 256, Findlay, OH 45840

Metropolis Quarterly Catalog (comics)
7 W. 18th St., New York, NY 10011. Subscription: $4 per year

Mike's General Store
52 St. Anne's Rd., Winnepeg, Manitoba, Canada R2M 2Y3; 204-255-3464. Catalog subscription: $4 per issue or next 3 issues for $10

Morgantown Collectors of America
Jerry Gallagher
420 1st Ave. N.W., Plainview, MN 55964;
507-534-3511. *The Morgantown Newscaster*, quarterly journal of Morgantown Glass only; affiliated with no club. Subscription: $15 per year. Morgantown 1931 Catalog Reprint: $20 postpaid. Morgantown Colors Placard: $3 postpaid. SASE required for answers to queries

Mystic Lights of the Aladdin Knights bimonthly newsletter
c/o J.W. Courter
R.R. 1, Simpson, IL 62985; 618-949-3884.
Information requires LSASE

National Association of Avon Collectors
c/o Connie Clark
6100 Walnut, Dept. P, Kansas City, MO 64113. Information requires LSASE

National Association of Miniature Enthusiasts (N.A.M.E.)
Box 2621, Anaheim, CA 92804-0621; 714-871-NAME

National Autumn Leaf Collectors' Club
c/o Gwynne Harrison
P.O. Box 1, Mira Loma, CA 91752-0001;
909-685-5434

National Blue Ridge Newsletter
Norma Lilly
144 Highland Dr., Blountville, TN 37617.
Subscription: $12 per year (6 issues)

National Cambridge Collectors, Inc.
P.O. Box 416, Cambridge, OH 43725

National Graniteware Society
P.O. Box 10013, Cedar Rapids, IA 52410

National Greentown Glass Association
1807 W. Madison, Kokomo, IN 46901

National Imperial Glass Collectors' Society
P.O. Box 534, Bellaire, OH 43906. Dues $12 per year (plus $1 for each additional member in same household), quarterly newsletter, convention every June

National Insulator Association #256
3557 Nicklaus Dr., Titusville, FL 32780

National Milk Glass Collectors' Society and *Opaque News* quarterly newsletter
c/o Helen D. Storey
46 Almond Dr., Cocoa Townes, Hershey PA 17033. Please include SASE

National Reamer Association
c/o Larry Branstad
R.R. 3, Box 67, Frederic, WI 54837

National Toothpick Holder Collectors Society
c/o Joyce Ender
Box 246, Sawyer, MI 49125. Dues: $10 (single) or $15 (couple) per year (includes monthly *Toothpick Bulletin*). Annual convention held in August

National Valentine Collectors Association
Evalene Pulati
P.O. Box 1404, Santa Ana, CA 92702; 714-547-1355. Specializing in Valentines and love tokens

New England Society of Open Salt Collectors
Mimi Waible, Membership Chairman
P.O. Box 177, Sudberry, MA 01776; 508-443-3613. Dues: $5 per year

New York Decorative Ceramic Society
9 S. Main St., Lambertville, NJ 08530.
Meetings held 4-6 times a year in New York and New Jersey, at museums, galleries, and collectors' homes

Newspaper Collectors' Society of America
Rick Brown
Box 19134-S, Lansing, MI 48901; 517-372-8381 or (Fax) 517-485-9115

North American Torquay Society
Jerry and Gerry Kline, Archivists
604 Orchard View Dr., Maumee, OH 43537. Quarterly newsletter sent to members; Information and membership form requires #10 SASE

North American Trap Collectors' Association
c/o Tom Parr
P.O. Box 94, Galloway, OH 43119-0094. Dues $10.00 per year; Publishes bimonthly newsletter

The Occupied Japan Club
c/o Florence Archambault
29 Freeborn St., Newport, RI 02840. Publishes *The Upside Down World of an O.J. Collector*, a bimonthly newsletter. Information requires SASE

Old Storefront Antiques
P.O. Box 357, Dublin, IN 47335; 317-478-4809. Publishes catalogs on store items, primitives, advertising, profession-related etc. Each is available for $1.50 or all 17 for $17 postpaid. Include LSASE

Open Salt Collectors of the Atlantic Regions (O.S.C.A.R.)
Lee Anne Gommer, Secretary
56 Northview Dr., Lancaster, PA 17601
Dues: $5

Open Salt Seekers of the West, Northern California Chapter
Sarah Kawakami, Secretary
2005 Pitnam St., Antioch, CA 95409. 510-757-9603. Dues: $5 per year

Open Salt Seekers of the West, Southern California Chapter
Pat and Chris Christensen, Newsletters
1067 Salvador, Costa Mesa, CA 92626; 714-540-1225. Dues: $5

Our McCoy Matters
Kathy Lynch, Editor
McCoy Publications, P.O. Box 14255, Parkville, MO 64152; 816-587-9179. Subscription: $24 for 6 issues

Paperweight Collectors' Association, Inc
P.O. Box 1059, Easthampton, MA 01027; 413-527-2598. Membership: $15 (single), $25 (couple); bimonthly newsletter; biannual conventions. To promote and study paperweights

Pen Fancier's Club
1169 Overcash Dr., Dunedin, FL 34698. Publishes bimonthly magazine of pens and mechanical pencils. Subscription: $45 per year, sample: $6

Perfume & Scent Bottle Collectors
Jeane Parris
3022 E. Charleston Blvd., Las Vegas, NV 89104; 702-385-6059. Membership: $15 USA or $30 Foreign (includes quarterly newsletter). Information requires SASE

Phoenix Bird Collectors of America (PBCA)
685 S. Washington, Constantine, MI 49042; 616-435-8353. Membership (payable to Joan Oates): $10 per year includes newsletter, *Phoenix Bird Discoveries*, published 3 times a year

Pie Birds Unlimited Newsletter
Lillian M. Cole
4 Harmony School Rd., Flemington, NJ 08822; 908-782-3198. Specializing in pie birds, pie funnels, pie vents

The Political Gallery
Thomas D. Slater
3325 W. 86th St., Indianapolis, IN 46260; 317-257-0863. Specializing in political and sports memorabilia

Precious Collectibles magazine for Precious Moments figurine collectors, *The Ornament Collector* magazine for Hallmark ornaments and other ornaments, and the *Collectors' Bulletin* magazine for all Limited Edition collectibles
Rosie Wells Enterprises, Inc.
R. 1S, Canton, IL 61520. Write for free literature. Rosie also has informational secondary market price guides for Lowell Davis collectors, Precious Moments collectibles, Hallmark Ornaments and Hallmark Merry Miniatures. She also has a Buy-Sell-Trade Ad telephone line for collectors across the USA on over 42 collectibles, 1-900-740-7575. For additional information, call 309-668-2211

R. Lalique
John Danis
11028 Raleigh Ct., Rockford, IL 61111; 815-963-0757 or (Fax) 815-877-6042

Roseville's of the Past newsletter
Jack Bomm, Editor
P.O. Box 681117, Orlando, FL 32868-1117. $19.95 per year for 6 to 12 newsletters

Salt & Pepper Catalog
Judy Posner
R.D. 1, Box 273 SC, Effort, PA 18330. Send $2 and LSASE

Shawnee Pottery Collectors' Club
P.O. Box 713, New Smyrna Beach, FL 32170-0713. Monthly nationwide newsletter. SASE (c/o Pamela Curran) required when requesting information. Optional: $3 for sample of current newsletter

Stretch Glass Society
P.O. Box 770643, Lakewood, OH 44107. Membership: $8; quarterly newsletter, annual convention

Southern Folk Pottery Collectors Society
Roy M. Thompson, Jr., Founder
1224 Main Street, Glastonbury, CT 06033; 203-633-3121

Southern Oregon Antiques & Collectibles Club
P.O. Box 508, Talent, OR 97540; 503-535-1231 Meets 1st Wednesday of the month, promotes 2 shows a year in Medford, OR

Stevengraph Collectors' Assn.
David L. Brown
2103-2829 Arbutus Rd., Victoria, British Columbia, Canada, V8N 5X5; 604-477-9896

Surveyors Historical Society Identification Committee
D.R. Beeks
P.O. Box 2515, Coeur d'Alene, ID 83814; 208-667-0830

Susie Cooper Catalogs
J. David Ehrhard
c/o Showcase Antiques
4405 Fair Oaks Ave., Pasadena, CA 91105; 818-577-9660

Table Toppers
1340 West Irving Park Rd., P.O. Box 161, Chicago, IL 60613; 312-769-3184. Membership: $18 (single) per year, which includes *Table Topics*, a bimonthly newsletter for those interested in table-top collectibles

The Tanner Restraints Collection
3024 E. 35th, Spokane, WA 99223; 509-448-8457. 40-page catalog of magician/escape artist equipment from trick and regulation padlocks, handcuffs, leg shackles, straight jackets to picks, and pick sets. Books on all of the above and much more. Catalog: $3.00

Tea Leaf Club International
222 Powderhorn, Dr. Houghton Lake, MI 48629. Publishes *Tea Leaf Reading* newsletter for members. Membership: $20 (single) or $25 (couple) per year

Tea Talk
Tina M. Carter, teapot columnist
Diana Rosen and Lucy Roman, Editors
419 N. Larchmont Blvd., Los Angeles, CA 90004; 213-659-9650. Subscription: $17.95 per year, sample: $2

Thermometer Collectors' Club of America
Warren D. Harris, President
6130 Rampart Dr., Carmichael, CA 95608; 916-966-3490

Thimble Collectors International
6411 Montego Rd., Louisville, KY 40228
Three Rivers Depression Era Glass Society
Meetings held 1st Monday of each month in Pittsburgh, PA; for more information contact:
Al Brerman
c/o And-Tiques
1829 E. Carson St., Pittsburgh, PA 15203; 412-381-2250

Tiffin Glass Collectors
P.O. Box 554, Tiffin, OH 44883. Meetings at Seneca Cty. Museum on 2nd Tuesday of each month

Tops & Bottoms Club (Rene Lalique perfumes only)
c/o Madeleine France
P.O. Box 15555, Ft. Lauderdale, FL 33318

Toy Gun Collectors of America Newsletter
Jim Buskirk, Editor & Publisher
312 Starling Way, Anaheim, CA 92807; 714-998-9615. Published quarterly, covers both toy and BB guns. Dues: $15 per year

The Trade Card Journal
Kit Barry
143 Main St., Brattleboro, VT 05301. A quarterly publication on the social and historical use of trade cards

UHL Collectors' Society
Dale Blann, President
R.R. 1, Box 136, Wheatland, IN 47597; 812-321-4141.
Tom Eubelhor, Secretary/Treasurer
233 E. Timberlin Lane, Huntingburg, IN 47542; 812-482-9575
Tim Hodges, Newsletter
1378 W. Andrew Lane, Jasper, IN 47546; 812-482-3016. For membership and newsletter information contact any of the above

Vernon Views newsletter
P.O. Box 945, Scottsdale, AZ 85252. Published quarterly beginning with the spring issue, $10 per year

Walking Stick Notes
Cecil Curtis, Editor
4051 E. Olive Rd., Pensacola, FL 32514. Quarterly publication with limited distribution

Watt's News
c/o Susan Morris and Jan Seeck
P.O. Box 708, Mason City, IA 50401. Subscription: $10 per year

Western World (National Avon Collectors Marketplace)
c/o Floyd or Ellen Busby
P.O. Box 23785, Dept. P, Pleasant Hill, CA 94523. Information requires LSASE

The Whimsey Club
c/o Christopher Davis
522 Woodhill, Newark, NY 14513. *Whimsical Notions*, quarterly newsletter; dues: $5 per year. Annual meeting in Rochester, NY, in April during Genessee Valley Bottle Collectors' Show

World's Fair Collectors' Society, Inc.
Fair News, monthly newsletter (for members)
Michael R. Pender, Editor
P.O. Box 20806, Sarasota, FL 34238; 813-923-2590. Dues: $12 per year in U.S.A., $13 in Canada, and $20 for overseas members

The Zsolnay Store
152 Spring St., Newport, RI 02840; 401-841-5060. Zsolnay book available

Books on Antiques and Collectibles

This is only a partial listing of the books on antiques that are available from Collector Books. All books are well illustrated and contain current values. Most of the following books are available from your local book seller or antique dealer, or from your public library. If you are unable to locate certain titles in your area you may order by mail from COLLECTOR BOOKS, P.O. Box 3009, Paducah, KY 42002-3009. Customers with Visa or MasterCard may phone in orders from 8:00-4:00 CST, M-F – Toll Free 1-800-626-5420. Add $2.00 for postage for the first book ordered and $.30 for each additional book. Include item number, title and price when ordering. Allow 14 to 21 days for delivery.

BOOKS ON GLASS AND POTTERY

1810	American Art Glass, Shuman	$29.95
2016	Bedroom & Bathroom Glassware of the Depression Years	$19.95
1312	Blue & White Stoneware, McNerney	$9.95
1959	Blue Willow, 2nd Ed., Gaston	$14.95
3719	Coll. Glassware from the 40's, 50's, 60's, 2nd Ed., Florence	$19.95
3311	Collecting Yellow Ware - Id. & Value Gd., McAllister	$16.95
2352	Collector's Ency. of Akro Agate Glassware, Florence	$14.95
1373	Collector's Ency. of American Dinnerware, Cunningham	$24.95
2272	Collector's Ency. of California Pottery, Chipman	$24.95
3312	Collector's Ency. of Children's Dishes, Whitmyer	$19.95
2133	Collector's Ency. of Cookie Jars, Roerig	$24.95
3724	Collector's Ency. of Depression Glass, 11th Ed., Florence	$19.95
2209	Collector's Ency. of Fiesta, 7th Ed., Huxford	$19.95
1439	Collector's Ency. of Flow Blue China, Gaston	$19.95
1915	Collector's Ency. of Hall China, 2nd Ed., Whitmyer	$19.95
2334	Collector's Ency. of Majolica Pottery, Katz-Marks	$19.95
1358	Collector's Ency. of McCoy Pottery, Huxford	$19.95
3313	Collector's Ency. of Niloak, Gifford	$19.95
3433	Collector's Guide To Harker Pottery - U.S.A., Colbert	$17.95
1039	Collector's Ency. of Nippon Porcelain I, Van Patten	$19.95
2089	Collector's Ency. of Nippon Porcelain II, Van Patten	$24.95
1665	Collector's Ency. of Nippon Porcelain III, Van Patten	$24.95
1447	Collector's Ency. of Noritake, 1st Series, Van Patten	$19.95
1034	Collector's Ency. of Roseville Pottery, Huxford	$19.95
1035	Collector's Ency. of Roseville Pottery, 2nd Ed., Huxford	$19.95
3314	Collector's Ency. of Van Briggle Art Pottery, Sasicki	$24.95
2339	Collector's Guide to Shawnee Pottery, Vanderbilt	$19.95
1425	Cookie Jars, Westfall	$9.95
3440	Cookie Jars, Book II, Westfall	$19.95
2275	Czechoslovakian Glass & Collectibles, Barta	$16.95
3315	Elegant Glassware of the Depression Era, 5th Ed., Florence	$19.95
3318	Glass Animals of the Depression Era, Garmon & Spencer	$19.95
2024	Kitchen Glassware of the Depression Years, 4th Ed., Florence	$19.95
3322	Pocket Guide to Depression Glass, 8th Ed., Florence	$9.95
1670	Red Wing Collectibles, DePasquale	$9.95
1440	Red Wing Stoneware, DePasquale	$9.95
1958	So. Potteries Blue Ridge Dinnerware, 3rd Ed., Newbound	$14.95
3739	Standard Carnival Glass, 4th Ed., Edwards	$24.95
1848	Very Rare Glassware of the Depression Years, Florence	$24.95
2140	Very Rare Glassware of the Depression Years, Second Series	$24.95
3326	Very Rare Glassware of the Depression Era, Third Series	$24.95
3327	Watt Pottery - Identification & Value Guide, Morris	$19.95
2224	World of Salt Shakers, 2nd Ed., Lechner	$24.95

BOOKS ON DOLLS & TOYS

2079	Barbie Fashion, Vol. 1, 1959-1967, Eames	$24.95
3310	Black Dolls - 1820-1991 - Id. & Value Guide, Perkins	$17.95
1514	Character Toys & Collectibles 1st Series, Longest	$19.95
1750	Character Toys & Collectibles, 2nd Series, Longest	$19.95
1529	Collector's Ency. of Barbie Dolls, DeWein	$19.95
2338	Collector's Ency. of Disneyana, Longest & Stern	$24.95
3441	Madame Alexander Price Guide #18, Smith	$9.95
1540	Modern Toys, 1930-1980, Baker	$19.95
3442	Patricia Smith's Doll Values Antique to Modern, 9th ed	$12.95
1886	Stern's Guide to Disney	$14.95

2139	Stern's Guide to Disney, 2nd Series	$14.9
1513	Teddy Bears & Steiff Animals, Mandel	$9.9
1817	Teddy Bears & Steiff Animals, 2nd, Mandel	$19.9
2084	Teddy Bears, Annalees & Steiff Animals, 3rd, Mandel	$19.9
2028	Toys, Antique & Collectible, Longest	$14.9
1808	Wonder of Barbie, Manos	$9.9
1430	World of Barbie Dolls, Manos	$9.9

OTHER COLLECTIBLES

1457	American Oak Furniture, McNerney	$9.9
2269	Antique Brass & Copper, Gaston	$16.9
2333	Antique & Collectible Marbles, 3rd Ed., Grist,	$9.9
1712	Antique & Collectible Thimbles, Mathis	$19.9
1748	Antique Purses, Holiner	$19.9
1868	Antique Tools, Our American Heritage, McNerney	$9.9
1426	Arrowheads & Projectile Points, Hothem	$7.9
1278	Art Nouveau & Art Deco Jewelry, Baker	$9.9
1714	Black Collectibles, Gibbs	$19.9
1128	Bottle Pricing Guide, 3rd Ed., Cleveland	$7.9
1752	Christmas Ornaments, Johnston	$19.9
2132	Collector's Ency. of American Furniture, Vol. I, Swedberg	$24.9
2271	Collector's Ency. of American Furniture, Vol. II, Swedberg	$24.9
2018	Collector's Ency. of Graniteware, Greguire	$24.9
3430	Coll. Ency. of Granite Ware, Book II, Greguire	$24.9
2083	Collector's Ency. of Russel Wright Designs, Kerr	$19.9
2337	Collector's Guide to Decoys, Book II, Huxford	$16.9
2340	Collector's Guide to Easter Collectibles, Burnett	$16.9
1441	Collector's Guide to Post Cards, Wood	$9.9
2276	Decoys, Kangas	$24.9
1629	Doorstops, Id. & Values, Bertoia	$9.9
1716	Fifty Years of Fashion Jewelry, Baker	$19.9
3316	Flea Market Trader, 8th Ed., Huxford	$9.9
3317	Florence's Standard Baseball Card Price Gd., 5th Ed.	$9.9
1755	Furniture of the Depression Era, Swedberg	$19.9
3436	Grist's Big Book of Marbles, Everett Grist	$19.9
2278	Grist's Machine Made & Contemporary Marbles	$9.9
1424	Hatpins & Hatpin Holders, Baker	$9.9
3319	Huxford's Collectible Advertising - Id. & Value Gd.	$17.9
3439	Huxford's Old Book Value Guide, 5th Ed.	$19.9
1181	100 Years of Collectible Jewelry, Baker	$9.9
2023	Keen Kutter Collectibles, 2nd Ed., Heuring	$14.9
2216	Kitchen Antiques - 1790-1940, McNerney	$14.9
3320	Modern Guns - Id. & Val. Gd., 9th Ed., Quertermous	$12.9
1965	Pine Furniture, Our Am. Heritage, McNerney	$14.9
3321	Ornamental & Figural Nutcrackers, Rittenhouse	$16.9
2026	Railroad Collectibles, 4th Ed., Baker	$14.9
1632	Salt & Pepper Shakers, Guarnaccia	$9.9
1888	Salt & Pepper Shakers II, Guarnaccia	$14.9
2220	Salt & Pepper Shakers III, Guarnaccia	$14.9
3443	Salt & Pepper Shakers IV, Guarnaccia	$18.9
3737	Schroeder's Antiques Price Guide, 12th Ed.	$12.9
2096	Silverplated Flatware, 4th Ed., Hagan	$14.9
3325	Standard Knife Collector's Guide, Stewart	$12.9
2348	20th Century Fashionable Plastic Jewelry, Baker	$19.9
3444	Wanted To Buy, 4th Ed.	$9.9